## MISCELLANEOUS

Investment in U.S. Space Systems   285–286
Prioritizing projects at NASA   463–464
Biotechnical engineering   576–577

## OPERATIONS MANAGEMENT

Queueing problems   4–7, 796–850
Ordering problems (newsboy)   25–28, 604–613, 617–631, 632–639, 649, 760–763
Ordering with quantity discounts   42–46, 747–748
Manufacturing operations   71–72
Choosing an optimal diet   75–92
Product mix problems   98–107, 127–130, 168–172, 298–307
Production scheduling   108–117, 150–159, 432–437, 650
Production, inventory management   131–132, 499–501, 661–666
Scheduling workers   142–148
Aggregate planning   150–159
Gasoline, oil blending   161–166, 207–209
Logistics problems   221–222, 223–234, 241–249
Assigning workers to jobs   235–236
Assigning school buses to routes   237–240
Finding a shortest route   250–254
Equipment replacement   254–258
Airline crew scheduling   260–265
Airline flight scheduling   265–271
Aircraft maintenance   272
Global manufacturing and distribution   280–281
Motor carrier selection   282–284

Airline hub location   309–314
Locating plants and warehouses   314–325, 378–381
Cutting stock problems   327–330
Plant expansion and retooling   341–342
Telephone call processing   343, 857–858
Railway planning   411–412
Loading a gas truck   429–432
Traveling salesperson problem   454–457
Determining trade–off between profit and pollution   477–479
Airline boarding strategies   579–580
Deming's funnel experiment   667–671
Global supply chain decisions   737–738
Economic order quantity models   743–758
Ordering decisions with demand uncertainty   764–771, 773–778
Production planning in fashion industry   779–784
Reducing work in progress   793–794
Operations at banks   859–860
Scheduling multiple projects   861–862, 885–889
Project scheduling with CPM   865–885, 890–895
Forecasting problems   903–904, 910–919, 921–929, 938–941, 944–956, 964–965

## SPORTS AND GAMES

Rating NFL teams   382–386
Playing craps   708–710
NCAA basketball tournament   710–713

REVISED
3RD
EDITION

# Practical Management Science

**Wayne L. Winston**
*Kelley School of Business, Indiana University*

**S. Christian Albright**
*Kelley School of Business, Indiana University*

*With Cases by*
**Mark Broadie**
*Graduate School of Business, Columbia University*

**Lawrence L. Lapin**
*San Jose State University*

**William D. Whisler**
*California State University, Hayward*

SOUTH-WESTERN
CENGAGE Learning™

Australia • Brazil • Japan • Korea • Mexico • Singapore • Spain • United Kingdom • United States

SOUTH-WESTERN
CENGAGE Learning™

**Practical Management Science,
Revised Third Edition**

Wayne L. Winston,
S. Christian Albright

VP/Editorial Director:
Jack W. Calhoun

Editor-in-Chief:
Alex von Rosenberg

Senior Acquisitions Editor:
Charles McCormick Jr.

Senior Developmental Editor:
Laura Bofinger

Editorial Assistant:
Bryn Lathrop

Marketing Communications Manager:
Libby Shipp

Marketing Manager:
Bryant Chrzan

Content Project Manager:
Emily Nesheim

Managing Media Editor:
Matt McKinney

Senior Manufacturing Coordinator:
Diane Gibbons

Production Service:
ICC Macmillan Inc.

Art Director:
Stacy Jenkins Shirley

Cover Designer:
Lou Ann Thesing/Kathy Heming

For product information and technology assistance, contact us at **Cengage Learning Academic Resource Center, 1-800-423-0563**

For permission to use material from this text or product, submit all requests online at **www.cengage.com/permissions**
Further permissions questions can be emailed to
**permissionrequest@cengage.com**

Library of Congress Control Number: 2008926488
Student Edition PKG ISBN-13: 978-0-324-66250-4
Student Edition PKG ISBN-10: 0-324-66250-5
Student Edition ISBN-13: 978-0-324-66251-1
Student Edition ISBN-10: 0-324-66251-3
Student CD-ROM ISBN-13: 978-0-324-66252-8
Student CD-ROM ISBN-10: 0-324-66252-1
Instructor's Edition PKG ISBN-13: 978-0-324-66343-3
Instructor's Edition PKG ISBN-10: 0-324-66343-9
Instructor's Edition ISBN-13: 978-0-324-66342-6
Instructor's Edition ISBN-10: 0-324-66342-0

**South-Western Cengage Learning**
5191 Natorp Boulevard
Mason, OH 45040
USA

Cengage Learning products are represented in Canada by Nelson Education, Ltd.

For your course and learning solutions, visit
**academic.cengage.com**

Purchase any of our products at your local college store or at our preferred online store **www.ichapters.com**

Printed in the United States of America
1 2 3 4 5 6 7 12 11 10 09 08

*To Mary, my wonderful wife, best friend, and constant companion*

And to our Welsh Corgi, Bryn, who still just wants to play ball     S.C.A.

*To my wonderful family*

Vivian, Jennifer, and Gregory     W.L.W.

# About the Authors

**S. Christian Albright** got his B.S. degree in Mathematics from Stanford in 1968 and his Ph.D. degree in Operations Research from Stanford in 1972. Since then he has been teaching in the Operations & Decision Technologies Department in the Kelley School of Business at Indiana University. He has taught courses in management science, computer simulation, and statistics to all levels of business students: undergraduates, MBAs, and doctoral students. He has also taught courses on database analysis to the U.S. Army. He has published over 20 articles in leading operations research journals in the area of applied probability, and he has authored several books, including *Practical Management Science, Data Analysis and Decision Making, Data Analysis for Managers, Spreadsheet Modeling and Applications,* and *VBA for Modelers.* He jointly developed *StatTools,* a statistical add-in for Excel, with the Palisade Corporation. His current interests are in spreadsheet modeling and the development of VBA applications in Excel, as well as Web programming with Microsoft's .NET technology.

On the personal side, Chris has been married to his wonderful wife Mary for 37 years. They have one son, Sam, who is currently finishing a law degree at Penn Law School. Chris has many interests outside the academic area. They include activities with his family (especially traveling with Mary), going to cultural events at Indiana University, playing golf and tennis, running and power walking, and reading. And although he earns his livelihood from statistics and management science, his *real* passion is for playing classical music on the piano.

**Wayne L. Winston** is Professor of Operations & Decision Technologies in the Kelley School of Business at Indiana University, where he has taught since 1975. Wayne received his B.S. degree in Mathematics from MIT and his Ph.D. degree in Operations Research from Yale. He has written the successful textbooks *Operations Research: Applications and Algorithms, Mathematical Programming: Applications and Algorithms, Simulation Modeling Using @RISK, Data Analysis and Decision Making,* and *Financial Models Using Simulation and Optimization.* Wayne has published over 20 articles in leading journals and has won many teaching awards, including the schoolwide MBA award four times. He has taught classes at Microsoft, GM, Ford, Eli Lilly, Bristol-Myers Squibb, Arthur Andersen, Roche, PriceWaterhouseCoopers, and NCR. His current interest is in showing how spreadsheet models can be used to solve business problems in all disciplines, particularly in finance and marketing.

Wayne enjoys swimming and basketball, and his passion for trivia won him an appearance several years ago on the television game show *Jeopardy,* where he won two games. He is married to the lovely and talented Vivian. They have two children, Gregory and Jennifer.

# Brief Contents

Preface   xi

1 Introduction to Modeling   1

2 Introduction to Spreadsheet Modeling   23

3 Introduction to Optimization Modeling   71

4 Linear Programming Models   131

5 Network Models   221

6 Optimization Models with Integer Variables   285

7 Nonlinear Optimization Models   345

8 Evolutionary Solver: An Alternative Optimization Procedure   411

9 Multiobjective Decision Making   463

10 Decision Making Under Uncertainty   503

11 Introduction to Simulation Modeling   579

12 Simulation Models   651

13 Inventory Models   737

14 Queueing Models   793

15 Project Management   861

16 Regression and Forecasting Models   903

References   966

Index   969

# Contents

Preface   xi

CHAPTER 1   Introduction to Modeling   1

1.1   Introduction   3
1.2   A Waiting-Line Example   4
1.3   Modeling Versus Models   7
1.4   The Seven-Step Modeling Process   8
1.5   A Successful Management Science Application   14
1.6   Why Study Management Science?   17
1.7   Software Included in This Book   18
1.8   Conclusion   20

CHAPTER 2   Introduction to Spreadsheet Modeling   23

2.1   Introduction   24
2.2   Basic Spreadsheet Modeling: Concepts and Best Practices   24
2.3   Cost Projections   29
2.4   Breakeven Analysis   33
2.5   Ordering with Quantity Discounts and Demand Uncertainty   42
2.6   Estimating the Relationship Between Price and Demand   47
2.7   Decisions Involving the Time Value of Money   57
2.8   Conclusion   63
Appendix: Tips for Editing and Documenting Spreadsheets   67

CHAPTER 3   Introduction to Optimization Modeling   71

3.1   Introduction   72
3.2   Introduction to Optimization   73
3.3   A Two-Variable Model   74
3.4   Sensitivity Analysis   85
3.5   Properties of Linear Models   93
3.6   Infeasibility and Unboundedness   96

3.7   A Product Mix Model   98
3.8   A Multiperiod Production Model   108
3.9   A Comparison of Algebraic and Spreadsheet Models   118
3.10  A Decision Support System   118
3.11  Conclusion   120
Appendix: Information on Solvers   126
CASE 3.1 Shelby Shelving   127
CASE 3.2 Sonoma Valley Wines   129

CHAPTER 4   Linear Programming Models   131

4.1   Introduction   132
4.2   Advertising Models   133
4.3   Workforce Scheduling Models   142
4.4   Aggregate Planning Models   150
4.5   Blending Models   160
4.6   Production Process Models   167
4.7   Financial Models   173
4.8   Data Envelopment Analysis (DEA)   184
4.9   Conclusion   191
CASE 4.1 Amarco, Inc.   207
CASE 4.2 American Office Systems, Inc.   210
CASE 4.3 Lakefield Corporation's Oil Trading Desk   215
CASE 4.4 Foreign Currency Trading   220

CHAPTER 5   Network Models   221

5.1   Introduction   222
5.2   Transportation Models   223
5.3   Assignment Models   235
5.4   Minimum Cost Network Flow Models   241
5.5   Shortest Path Models   250
5.6   Other Network Models   260
5.7   Conclusion   273
CASE 5.1 International Textile Company, Ltd.   280

CASE 5.2 Optimized Motor Carrier Selection at Westvaco 282

# CHAPTER 6 Optimization Models with Integer Variables 285

6.1 Introduction 286
6.2 Overview of Optimization with Integer Variables 287
6.3 Capital Budgeting Models 290
6.4 Fixed-Cost Models 297
6.5 Set-Covering and Location-Assignment Models 309
6.6 Cutting Stock Models 327
6.7 Conclusion 331
CASE 6.1 Giant Motor Company 341
CASE 6.2 Selecting Telecommunication Carriers to Obtain Volume Discounts 343

# CHAPTER 7 Nonlinear Optimization Models 345

7.1 Introduction 346
7.2 Basic Ideas of Nonlinear Optimization 347
7.3 Pricing Models 351
7.4 Advertising Response and Selection Models 368
7.5 Facility Location Models 378
7.6 Models for Rating Sports Teams 382
7.7 Portfolio Optimization Models 387
7.8 Estimating the Beta of a Stock 396
7.9 Conclusion 401
CASE 7.1 GMS Stock Hedging 407
CASE 7.2 Durham Asset Management 409

# CHAPTER 8 Evolutionary Solver: An Alternative Optimization Procedure 411

8.1 Introduction 412
8.2 Introduction to Genetic Algorithms 415
8.3 Introduction to Evolutionary Solver 416
8.4 Nonlinear Pricing Models 422
8.5 Combinatorial Models 428
8.6 Fitting an S-Shaped Curve 437
8.7 Portfolio Optimization 442
8.8 Cluster Analysis 444
8.9 Discriminant Analysis 450
8.10 The Traveling Salesperson Problem 454
8.11 Conclusion 458
CASE 8.1 Assigning MBA Students to Teams 462

# CHAPTER 9 Multiobjective Decision Making 463

9.1 Introduction 464
9.2 Goal Programming 465
9.3 Pareto Optimality and Trade-Off Curves 475
9.4 The Analytic Hierarchy Process (AHP) 484
9.5 Conclusion 494
CASE 9.1 Play Time Toy Company 499

# CHAPTER 10 Decision Making Under Uncertainty 503

10.1 Introduction 505
10.2 Elements of a Decision Analysis 506
10.3 The PrecisionTree Add-In 522
10.4 Bayes' Rule 534
10.5 Multistage Decision Problems 538
10.6 Incorporating Attitudes Toward Risk 554
10.7 Conclusion 561
CASE 10.1 Jogger Shoe Company 574
CASE 10.2 Westhouser Paper Company 575
CASE 10.3 Biotechnical Engineering 576

# CHAPTER 11 Introduction to Simulation Modeling 579

11.1 Introduction 581
11.2 Real Applications of Simulation 582
11.3 Probability Distributions for Input Variables 583
11.4 Simulation with Built-In Excel Tools 603
11.5 Introduction to @RISK 615
11.6 The Effects of Input Distributions on Results 632
11.7 Conclusion 640
Appendix: Creating Histograms with Excel Tools 646
CASE 11.1 Ski Jacket Production 649
CASE 11.2 Ebony Bath Soap 650

## CHAPTER 12 Simulation Models    651

12.1   Introduction   653

12.2   Operations Models   653

12.3   Financial Models   672

12.4   Marketing Models   695

12.5   Simulating Games of Chance   708

12.6   Using TopRank with @RISK for Powerful Modeling   714

12.7   Conclusion   722

CASE 12.1 College Fund Investment   732

CASE 12.2 Bond Investment Strategy   733

CASE 12.3 Financials at Carco   734

## CHAPTER 13 Inventory Models   737

13.1   Introduction   739

13.2   Categories of Inventory Models   740

13.3   Types of Costs in Inventory Models   741

13.4   Economic Order Quantity (EOQ) Models   743

13.5   Probabilistic Inventory Models   759

13.6   Ordering Simulation Models   773

13.7   Supply Chain Models   778

13.8   Conclusion   784

CASE 13.1 Subway Token Hoarding   792

## CHAPTER 14 Queueing Models    793

14.1   Introduction   795

14.2   Elements of Queueing Models   796

14.3   The Exponential Distribution   799

14.4   Important Queueing Relationships   804

14.5   Analytical Steady-State Queueing Models   807

14.6   Approximating Short-Run Behavior Analytically   830

14.7   Queueing Simulation Models   835

14.8   Conclusion   852

CASE 14.1 Catalog Company Phone Orders   857

CASE 14.2 Pacific National Bank   859

## CHAPTER 15 Project Management   861

15.1   Introduction   863

15.2   The Basic CPM Model   865

15.3   Modeling Allocation of Resources   874

15.4   Models with Uncertain Activity Times   890

15.5   A Brief Look at Microsoft Project   896

15.6   Conclusion   898

## CHAPTER 16 Regression and Forecasting Models   903

16.1   Introduction   904

16.2   Overview of Regression Models   905

16.3   Simple Regression Models   909

16.4   Multiple Regression Models   921

16.5   Overview of Time Series Models   932

16.6   Moving Averages Models   937

16.7   Exponential Smoothing Models   942

16.8   Conclusion   958

CASE 16.1 Demand for French Bread at Howie's   964

CASE 16.2 Forecasting Overhead at Wagner Printers   964

CASE 16.3 Arrivals at the Credit Union   965

References   966

Index   969

# Preface

*Practical Management Science* provides a spreadsheet-based, example-driven approach to management science. Our initial objective in writing the book was to reverse negative attitudes about the course by making the subject relevant to students. We intended to do this by imparting valuable modeling skills that students can appreciate and take with them into their careers. We are very gratified by the success of the first two editions. The book has exceeded our initial objectives. We are especially pleased to hear about the success of the book at many other colleges and universities around the world. The acceptance and excitement that has been generated has motivated us to revise the book and make the third edition even better. By incorporating our own teaching experience and the many user comments and suggestions, we believe this third edition is a significant improvement over the first two. We hope you will agree.

When we wrote the first edition, management science courses were regarded as irrelevant or uninteresting to many business students, and the use of spreadsheets in management science was in its early stages of development. Much has changed since the first edition was published in 1996, and we believe that these changes are for the better. We have learned a lot about the best practices of spreadsheet modeling for clarity and communication. We have also developed better ways of teaching the materials, and we understand more about where students tend to have difficulty with the concepts. Finally, we have had the opportunity to teach this material at several Fortune 500 companies (including Eli Lilly, Price Waterhouse Coopers, General Motors, Tomkins, Microsoft, and Intel). These companies, through their enthusiastic support, have further enhanced the realism of the models included in this book.

The success of the book outside of the classroom justifies our approach in the third edition. Although we have retained many of the features that have made this book a bestseller, we have enhanced the coverage to make it more relevant and more accessible to students of varying backgrounds. Throughout the book, you will find many new models that are based upon real problems, and you will find a much clearer presentation of the modeling, solution, and interpretation of the examples. We have found that professionals, like students, have differing backgrounds in terms of their command of mathematics and Excel, but they both desire skills and knowledge they can immediately apply to the challenges they face in their professions. Those of you who are sympathetic to this approach will find the third edition is better suited to meet these needs.

Our objective in writing the first edition was very simple—we wanted to make management science relevant and practical to students and professionals. This book continues to distinguish itself in the market in four fundamental ways:

- **Teach by Example.** The best way to learn modeling concepts is by working through examples and solving an abundance of problems. This active learning approach is not new, but our text has more fully developed this approach than any book in the field. The feedback we have received from many of you has confirmed the success of this pedagogical approach for management science.

- **Integrate Modeling with Finance, Marketing, and Operations Management.** We integrate modeling into all functional areas of business. This is an important feature because the majority of business students major in finance and marketing. Almost all competing textbooks emphasize operations management-related examples. Although these examples are important, and many are included in the book, the application of modeling to problems in finance and marketing are too important to ignore. Throughout the book, we use real examples from all functional areas of business to illustrate the power of spreadsheet modeling to all of these areas. At Indiana University, this has led to the development of two advanced MBA electives in finance and marketing that build upon the content in this book. The inside front cover of the book illustrates the integrative applications contained in the book.

- **Teach Modeling, Not Just Models.** Poor attitudes among students in past management science courses can be attributed to the way in which they were taught: emphasis on algebraic formulations and memorization of models. Students gain more insight into the power of management science by developing skills in modeling. Throughout the book, we stress the logic associated with model development and formulation, and we discuss solutions in this context. Because real problems and real models often include limitations or alternatives, we include many "Modeling Issues" sections to discuss these important matters. Finally, we include "Modeling Problems" in most chapters to help develop these skills.

■ **Provide Numerous Problems and Cases.** Whereas all textbooks contain problem sets for students to practice, we have carefully and judiciously crafted the problems and cases contained in this book. The third edition contains many new problems and cases. Each chapter contains four types of problems: Skill-Building Problems, Skill-Extending Problems, Modeling Problems, and Cases. A new feature to this edition is that almost all of the problems following sections of chapters ask students to extend the examples in the preceding section. The end-of-chapter problems then ask students to explore new models. Selected solutions are available to students who purchase the Student Solution Files online and are denoted by the second color numbering of the problem. Solutions for all of the problems and cases are provided to adopting instructors. In addition, shell files (templates) are available for most of the problems for adopting instructors. The shell files contain the basic structure of the problem with the relevant formulas omitted. By adding or omitting hints in individual solutions, instructors can tailor these shell files to best meet the individual/specific needs of their students.

## Enhancements to the Third Edition

Our extensive teaching experience has provided more insights about the instruction of a spreadsheet-based course in management science, and we have incorporated many suggestions from users of the first two editions to improve the book. In addition, there have been several advances in spreadsheet-based technology in recent years. The software accompanying new copies of the third edition includes the most extensive and valuable suite of tools ever available in a management science textbook. Important changes to the third edition include the following:

■ **Improved Spreadsheet Readability and Documentation.** Many professionals we have taught instinctively document their spreadsheet models for the purpose of sharing them with colleagues or communicating them in presentations and reports. This is an important element of good spreadsheet modeling, and the third edition does even more to emphasize good practices.

Furthermore, grading homework assignments and exams can be a very time-consuming chore if students are permitted to construct their models in any form. Therefore, we place early and consistent emphasis on good spreadsheet habits. This should benefit both students and instructors. Although we try not to force any one approach on everyone, we do suggest some good habits that lead to better spreadsheet models.

To achieve this goal of better readability and documentation, we have reworked many examples in the chapters, and we have incorporated our new habits in the many new examples. This is especially important because this edition's most important feature continues to be the set of examples that illustrates the concepts in each chapter. For users of the first two editions, the changes will sometimes appear subtle, but they make a significant difference pedagogically.

■ **Pedagogical Enhancements.** We have borrowed the pedagogical enhancements from our *Spreadsheet Modeling and Applications* text. These include (1) "Objectives" sections following most examples that briefly describe the objectives of the example; (2) "Where Do the Numbers Come From" sections following most examples that discuss how the model inputs might be obtained in real business situations; (3) tables of key variables and constraints following most examples in the optimization chapters that form a bridge from the statement of the problem to the spreadsheet implementation; (4) "Fundamental Insight" sections that highlight important concepts; and (5) summaries of key terms at the ends of chapters. All of these enhancements make it easier for students to study the material and prepare for exams.

■ **Interpretation of Results and Sensitivity Analysis.** Some users mentioned that we often show solutions to models and then move too quickly to other models. In this edition, we spend more time discussing the solutions to models for the insights they contain. We often try to understand why a solution comes out as it does, and we spend plenty of time doing sensitivity analyses on the solutions. As we have heard from practitioners, this is often where the real benefits of management science are found. In this sense, a developed model is not an *end*; it is a *beginning* for understanding the business problem.

- **Range Names.** In the second edition, we perhaps overemphasized the use of range names. We still believe strongly that range names are an important way to document spreadsheet formulas, so we continue to use them but to a somewhat lesser extent. We also emphasize how easy it is to create range names, in many cases, by using adjacent labels.

- **New Problems.** We have added more than 100 new problems, many of which follow sections of the chapters. These problems ask students to extend the examples covered in the preceding sections in a variety of directions. These "model extension" problems are arguably as important as any other enhancement to this edition. We have always emphasized model *development,* and we continue to do so. But it is also extremely important to understand how completed models can be *extended* to answer various business questions. Students now have plenty of opportunity to extend existing models.

- **New Chapter on Project Scheduling.** The material on project scheduling included in the optimization and simulation chapters of previous editions has now been assembled into its own chapter, Chapter 15. This allows many instructors who feel strongly about this topic to cover it in a more integrated manner.

- **New Examples in Queueing.** Given the support for the Erlang loss model from the queueing chapter, we have reinstated it in the third edition. We have also added a very insightful queueing spreadsheet model that approximates transient behavior of queues. This model is not very difficult to implement in Excel, and we're surprised that it hasn't been taught more often in management science courses. This model illustrates interesting short-run behavior of queues that does not appear in the traditional steady-state analysis.

- **Combination of Regression and Forecasting Chapters.** These two topics are of obvious importance to management scientists, but we decided to combine them into a single chapter, focusing on the most essential concepts and methods. Our rationale is twofold. First, we doubt that many instructors have enough time to cover regression and forecasting in as much depth as we included in the second edition. Second, we suspect that many students have already been exposed to this material in a statistics class, so a quick refresher chapter should suffice.

- **New Chapter Opening Vignettes and Other Real Applications.** It is important for students to realize the important role management science plays in today's business world. The *Interfaces* journal chronicles the many successful applications that have saved companies millions or even billions of dollars. The third edition contains descriptions of many new *Interfaces* applications, both in the chapter opening vignettes and throughout the chapters.

## Reason for this Revised Edition

In 2007, Microsoft released its newest version of Office, Office 2007 (also called Office 12). This was not just another version with a few changes at the edges. It was a completely revamped package. Suddenly, many of the screenshots and instructions in our books were no longer correct because of the extensive user interface changes in Excel 2007. To add to the confusion, third-party developers of add-ins for Excel, particularly Palisade for our books, had to scramble to update their software for Excel 2007. We also had to scramble as the Fall semester of 2007 approached. By the time we obtained the updated software, even in beta version, it was too late to produce updates to our books by Fall 2007. Therefore, we put "changes" files on our Web site (http://www.kelley.iu.edu/albrightbooks) to help many of you to make the transition.

Of course, a more permanent solution was needed—hence, this revised edition. It is entirely geared to Excel 2007 and the updated add-ins for Excel 2007. If you have moved to Excel 2007, you should use this revised edition. If you are still using an earlier version of Excel, you should continue to use the original third edition. Almost all of the content in the two versions are identical. We changed as little as possible, mostly just the screenshots and accompanying explanations.

Two other comments are in order. First, Palisade was in the midst of an extensive rewrite of its

DecisionTools™ suite when Office 2007 came out. To get through the 2007–2008 academic year, Palisade developed a slightly revised version of its *old* DecisionTools suite (for example, version 4.5.7 of @RISK) that was compatible with Excel 2007, and we made that version available to users for the 2007–2008 year. Fortunately, their new version of the DecisionTools suite, version 5.0, is now out. Therefore, the educational version of it accompanies this book, and the screenshots and explanations are geared to it. We believe you will like its much friendlier user interface.

Second, the example files on the CD-ROM inside the revised edition have been updated slightly. They still have the same content, but they are now in Excel 2007 format (.xlsx or .xlsm). Also, although we still provide templates and finished versions of all these example files (in different folders), we have appended "Finished" to the names of all the finished files. This should avoid the confusion of having the same name for two different files that some of you have mentioned. Finally, we have included "Annotated" versions of these finished example files, plus a few "Extra" application files, to instructors. The annotated versions include our insights and suggestions for the examples. We hope these help you to teach the material even more effectively.

## Accompanying Student Resources

We continue to be very excited about offering the most comprehensive suite of software ever available with a management science textbook. The commercial value of the enclosed software exceeds $1000 if purchased directly. This software is packaged free with **NEW** copies of the third edition. It is for students only and, in contrast to the previous edition, it requires no online registration. The following software is included on the accompanying Palisade CD-ROM:

- Palisade's **DecisionTools™ Suite,** including the award-winning **@RISK, PrecisionTree, TopRank**, and **RISKOptimizer,** and Palisade's **StatTools** add-in for statistics are included in the box that is packaged with new copies of the book. This software is not available with any competing textbook and comes in an educational version that is only slightly scaled down from the expensive commercial version. (StatTools replaces Albright's StatPro add-in that came with the second edition. If you are interested, StatPro is still freely available from

http://www.kelley.iu.edu/albrightbooks, although it will not be updated for Excel 2007.) For more information about the Palisade Corporation, the DecisionTools Suite, and StatTools, visit Palisade's Web site at http://www.palisade.com.

- Also available with *new* copies of the revised third edition is a Student CD-ROM. This resource provides the Excel files for all of the examples in the book, as well as the data files required for a number of problems and cases. As in the second edition, there are two versions of the example files: a completed version and a template to get students started. To make sensitivity analysis useful and intuitive, we continue to provide Albright's **SolverTable** add-in (which is also freely available from http://www.kelley.iu.edu/albrightbooks). SolverTable provides data table-like output that is easy to interpret. Finally, the newest version of Frontline Systems' **Premium Solver™ for Education** is included for use in Chapter 8. Its Evolutionary Solver uses genetic algorithms to solve nonlinear optimization problems. For more information on Premium Solver or Frontline Systems, visit Frontline's Web site at http://www.frontsys.com. (Note that the versions of SolverTable and Premium Solver included are updates compatible with Excel 2007.)

- Additionally, a 60-day trial version of Microsoft Project 2007 is packaged with *new* copies of the revised third edition.

## Companion VBA Book

Soon after the first edition appeared, we began using Visual Basic for Applications (VBA), the programming language for Excel, in some of our management science courses. VBA allows us to develop decision support systems around the spreadsheet models. (An example appears at the end of Chapter 3.) This use of VBA has been popular with our students, and many instructors have expressed interest in learning how to do it. For additional support on this topic, a companion book, *VBA for Modelers, 2e* (ISBN 0-495-10683-6) is available. It assumes no prior experience in computer programming, but it progresses rather quickly to the development of interesting and nontrivial applications. The revised third edition of *Practical Management Science* depends in no way on this companion VBA book, but we expect that many instructors will want to incorporate some VBA into their management science courses.

## Ancillary Materials

Besides the Student CD-ROM that accompanies new copies of the third edition, the following materials are available:

- An Instructor's Resource CD (ISBN-10: 0-324-59557-3; ISBN-13: 978-0-324-59557-4) that includes PowerPoint slides, Instructor's Solutions Files, and Test Bank files is available to adopters. This useful tool reduces class preparation time, aids in assessment, and contributes to students' comprehension and retention.

- Student Solution Files (ISBN-10: 0-495-01643-8; ISBN-13: 978-0-495-01643-4) are available for purchase through the Student Resources Web page at the book support Web site. Visit academic.cengage.com/decisionsciences/ winston for more information on purchasing this valuable student resource.

If you are interested in requesting any of these supplements or *VBA for Modelers,* contact your local South-Western Sales Rep or the Academic Resource Center at 800-423-0563.

## Acknowledgments

This book has gone through several stages of reviews, and it is a much better product because of them. The majority of the reviewers' suggestions were very good ones, and we have attempted to incorporate them. We would like to extend our appreciation to:

Timothy N. Burcham, University of Tennessee at Martin
Spyros Camateros, California State University, East Bay
Michael F. Gorman, University of Dayton
Cagri Haksoz, City University of London
Levon Hayrapetyan, Houston Baptist University
Bharat K. Kaku, Georgetown University
Bingguang Li, Albany State University
Jerrold May, University of Pittsburgh
Paul T. Nkansah, Florida A&M University
Ferdinand C. Nwafor, Florida A&M University
Lynne Pastor, Carnegie Mellon University
Ronald K. Satterfield, University of South Florida
Phoebe D. Sharkey, Loyola College in Maryland
John Wang, Montclair State University
Kari Wood, Bemidji State University
Roger Woods, Michigan Tech
Zhe George Zhang, Western Washington University

We would also like to thank two special people. First, we want to thank our previous editor Curt Hinrichs. Although Curt has moved from this position and is no longer our editor, his vision for the past decade has been largely responsible for the success of the first and second editions of *Practical Management Science.* We want to wish Curt the best of luck in his new position at SAS. Second, we were lucky to move from one great editor to another in Charles McCormick Jr. Charles is a consummate professional, he is both patient and thorough, and his experience in the publishing business ensures that the tradition Curt started will be carried on.

In addition, we would like to thank Marketing Manager, Bryant Chrzan; Senior Developmental Editor, Laura Bofinger; Content Project Manager, Emily Nesheim; Art Director, Stacy Shirley; Editorial Assistant, Bryn Lathrop; and Project Manager at ICC Macmillan Inc., Leo Kelly.

We would also enjoy hearing from you—we can be reached by e-mail. And please visit either of the following Web sites for more information and occasional updates:

- http://www.kelley.iu.edu/albrightbooks
- academic.cengage.com/decisionsciences/winston

**Wayne L. Winston** (winston@indiana.edu)
**S. Christian Albright** (albright@indiana.edu)
*Bloomington, Indiana*
*January 2008*

# Introduction to Modeling

## COMPLEX ALGORITHMS AND THE "SOFT OR" APPROACH SOLVE REAL-WORLD PROBLEMS

As you embark on your study of management science, you might question the usefulness of quantitative methods to the "real world." A front-page article in the December 31, 1997 edition of *USA Today* entitled "Higher Math Delivers Formula for Success" provides some convincing evidence of the applicability of the methods you will be learning. The subheading of the article, "Businesses turn to algorithms to solve complex problems," says it all. Today's business problems tend to be very complex. In the past, many managers and executives used a "seat of the pants" approach to solve problems—that is, they used their business experience, their intuition, and some thoughtful guesswork to solve problems. But common sense and intuition go only so far in the solution of the complex problems businesses now face. This is where management science models—and the algorithms mentioned in the title of the article—are so useful. When the methods in this book are implemented in user-friendly computer software packages that are applied to complex problems, the results can be amazing. Robert Cross, whose company, DFI Aeronomics, sells algorithm-based systems to airlines, states it succinctly: "It's like taking raw information and spinning money out of it."

The methods in this book are powerful because they apply to so many problems and environments. The article mentions the following "success stories" in which management science has been applied; others will be discussed throughout this book.

- United Airlines installed one of DFI's systems, which cost between $10 million and $20 million. United expected the system to add $50 million to $100 million *annually* to its revenues.

- The Gap clothing chain uses management science to determine exactly how many employees should staff each store during the Christmas rush.

- Management science has helped medical researchers test potentially dangerous drugs on fewer people with better results.

- IBM obtained a $93 million contract to build a computer system for the U.S. Department of Energy that would do a once-impossible task: make exact real-time models of atomic blasts. It won the contract—and convinced the DOE that its system was cost-effective—only by developing management science models that would cut the processing time by half.

- Hotels, airlines, and television broadcasters all use management science to implement a method called *yield management*. In this method, different prices are charged to different customers, depending on their willingness to pay. The effect is that more customers are attracted and revenues increase.

Although most of this book describes how quantitative methods can be used to solve business problems, solutions do not always need to be quantitatively based. In a recent article, Kimbrough and Murphy (2005), two academics located in Philadelphia, describe how they were commissioned by the city to study the knowledge economy of the region and make recommendations on ways to improve its rate of growth. Unlike most of the success stories chronicled in the *Interfaces* journal (which is described on page 16), the authors state right away that they used no quantitative methods or mathematical models to develop recommendations for the city. Instead, they used a *soft OR* approach.[1] By this, they imply that they used a systematic approach to formulate and solve their client's problem, even though the approach does not employ quantitative methods.

Specifically, Kimbrough and Murphy used two interrelated approaches in their study. First, using ideas in the management science and economics literature, they developed a comprehensive framework for thinking about regional economic development. This allowed them to identify the many factors that influence a region's economic vitality or lack thereof. Second, they interviewed a wide range of people from the region, including researchers in science and technology, business people, government officials, and academics. Instead of asking these people what ought to be done, they asked them to propose ideas or policy initiatives that might improve the region's economy. As they state, "The results were gratifying. The framework we developed focuses people's thinking on problems, bottlenecks, and leverage points in the knowledge economy. Asking for specific ideas produced a rich and constructive list of more than 50 promising, realistic, and detailed policy initiatives."

However, the study went beyond brainstorming. After conducting the interviews and analyzing the responses, the authors made specific recommendations to their client on initiatives that might be implemented to improve the knowledge economy. Based on these recommendations, the board

---

[1] OR is an abbreviation for *operations research*, another term for management science. Over the years, the two terms have become practically synonymous, although some people in the field still prefer to be called management scientists, whereas others prefer to be called operations researchers.

of directors of Greater Philadelphia First adopted *Six for Success*, a strategy that commits leaders to (1) attract more research dollars and expertise; (2) implement strategies to accelerate science and technology; (3) promote an entrepreneurial climate; (4) launch a business marketing plan; (5) leverage quality-of-life infrastructure and amenities; and (6) streamline and rationalize business-oriented nonprofits. Granted, these ideas are not necessarily ground breaking, but they made sense to leaders in Philadelphia. The important point is that they were developed through a systematic approach to solving a problem—even if it wasn't the quantitative approach discussed through most of this book. ■

## 1.1 INTRODUCTION

The purpose of this book is to expose you to a variety of problems that have been solved successfully with management science methods and to give you experience in modeling these problems in the Excel spreadsheet package. The subject of management science has evolved for more than 50 years and is now a mature field within the broad category of applied mathematics. This book will emphasize both the applied and mathematical aspects of management science. Beginning in this chapter and continuing throughout the rest of the book, we discuss many successful management science applications, where teams of highly trained people have implemented solutions to the problems faced by major companies and have saved these companies millions of dollars. Many airlines and oil companies, for example, could hardly operate as they do today without the support of management science. In this book, we will lead you through the solution procedure of many interesting and realistic problems, and you will experience firsthand what is required to solve these problems successfully. Because we recognize that most of you are not highly trained in mathematics, we use Excel spreadsheets to solve problems, which makes the quantitative analysis much more understandable and intuitive.

The key to virtually every management science application is a *mathematical model*. In simple terms, a **mathematical model** is a quantitative representation, or idealization, of a real problem. This representation might be phrased in terms of mathematical expressions (equations and inequalities) or as a series of interrelated cells in a spreadsheet. We prefer the latter, especially for teaching purposes, and we concentrate primarily on spreadsheet models in this book. However, in either case, the purpose of a mathematical model is to represent the essence of a problem in a concise form. This has several advantages. First, it enables a manager to understand the problem better. In particular, the model helps to define the scope of the problem, the possible solutions, and the data requirements. Second, it allows analysts to employ a variety of the mathematical solution procedures that have been developed over the past half-century. These solution procedures are often computer intensive, but with today's cheap and abundant computing power, they are usually feasible. Finally, the modeling process itself, if done correctly, often helps to "sell" the solution to the people who must work with the system that is eventually implemented.

This chapter begins with a relatively simple example of a mathematical model. You'll then examine the difference between modeling and a collection of models and learn about a seven-step model-building process that you should follow—in essence if not in strict conformance—in all management science applications. Next, you'll learn about a successful application of management science and how the seven-step model-building process was followed. Finally, you'll see why the study of management science is valuable, not only to large corporations, but also to students like you who are about to enter the business world.

## 1.2 A WAITING-LINE EXAMPLE

As indicated earlier, a mathematical model is a set of mathematical relationships that represent, or approximate, a real situation. Models that simply describe a situation are called **descriptive models.** Other models that suggest a desirable course of action are called **optimization models.** To get started, consider the following simple example of a mathematical model. It begins as a descriptive model, but then expands to an optimization model.

Consider a convenience store with a single cash register. The manager of the store suspects that customers are waiting too long in line at the checkout register and that these excessive waiting times are hurting business. Customers who have to wait a long time might not come back, and potential customers who see a long line might not enter the store at all. Therefore, the manager builds a mathematical model to help understand the problem. The manager wants the model to reflect the current situation at the store, but it should also suggest improvements to the current situation.

### A Descriptive Model

This example is a typical waiting line, or **queueing,** problem. (Such problems are studied in detail in Chapter 14.) The manager first wants to build a model that reflects the *current* situation at the store. Later, he will alter the model to predict what might make the situation better. To describe the current situation, the manager realizes that there are two important *inputs* to the problem: (1) the arrival rate of potential customers to the store and (2) the rate at which customers can be served by the single cashier. Clearly, as the arrival rate increases and/or the service rate decreases, the waiting line will tend to increase and each customer will tend to wait longer in line. In addition, more potential customers likely will decide not to enter at all. These latter quantities (length of waiting line, time in line per customer, fraction of customers who don't enter) are commonly referred to as *outputs*. The manager believes he has some understanding of the relationship between the inputs and the outputs, but he is not at all sure of the *exact* relationship between them.

This is where a mathematical model is useful. By making several simplifying assumptions about the nature of the arrival and service process at the store (as discussed in Chapter 14), you can relate the inputs to the outputs. In some cases, when the model is sufficiently simple, you can write an *equation* for an output in terms of the inputs. For example, in one of the simplest queueing models, if $A$ is the arrival rate of customers per minute, $S$ is the service rate of customers per minute, and $W$ is the average time a typical customer waits in line (assuming that all potential customers enter the store), then the following relationship can be derived mathematically:

$$W = \frac{A}{S(S - A)} \tag{1.1}$$

This relationship is intuitive in one sense. It correctly predicts that as the service rate $S$ increases, the average waiting time $W$ decreases; as the arrival rate $A$ increases, the average waiting time $W$ increases. Also, if the arrival rate is just barely less than the service rate—that is, the difference $S - A$ is positive but very small—the average waiting time becomes quite large. [This model requires that the arrival rate be *less than* the service rate; otherwise, equation (1.1) makes no sense.]

In many other models, there is no such closed-form relationship between inputs and outputs (or if there is, it is too complex for the level of this book). Nevertheless, there may still be a mathematical procedure for calculating outputs from inputs, and it may be possible to implement this procedure in Excel. This is the case for the convenience store problem. Again, by making certain simplifying assumptions, including the assumption

Figure 1.1

Descriptive
Queueing Model for
Convenience Store

| | A | B |
|---|---|---|
| 1 | Descriptive queueing model for convenience store | |
| 2 | | |
| 3 | Inputs | |
| 4 | Arrival rate (customers per minute) | 0.5 |
| 5 | Service rate (customers per minute) | 0.4 |
| 6 | Maximum customers (before others go elsewhere) | 5 |
| 7 | | |
| 8 | Outputs | |
| 9 | Average number in line | 2.22 |
| 10 | Average time (minutes) spent in line | 6.09 |
| 11 | Percentage of potential arrivals who don't enter | 27.1% |

that potential customers will not enter if the waiting line is sufficiently long, you can develop a spreadsheet model of the situation at the store.

Before developing the spreadsheet model, however, we must determine how the manager can obtain the inputs he needs. There are actually three inputs: (1) the arrival rate $A$, (2) the service rate $S$, and (3) the number in the store, labeled $N$, that will induce future customers not to enter. The first two of these can be measured with a stopwatch. For example, the manager can instruct an employee to measure the times between customer arrivals. Let's say the employee does this for several hours, and the average time between arrivals is observed to be 2 minutes. Then the arrival rate can be estimated as $A = 1/2 = 0.5$ (1 customer every 2 minutes). Similarly, the employee can record the times it takes the cashier to serve successive customers. If the average of these times (taken over many customers) is, say, 2.5 minutes, then the service rate can be estimated as $S = 1/2.5 = 0.4$ (1 customer every 2.5 minutes). Finally, if the manager notices that potential customers tend to take their business elsewhere when 5 customers are in line, he can let $N = 5$.

These input estimates can now be entered in the spreadsheet model shown in Figure 1.1. Don't worry about the details of this spreadsheet—they are discussed in Chapter 14. The formulas built into this spreadsheet reflect an adequate approximation of the convenience store's situation. For now, the important thing is that this model allows the manager to enter any values for the inputs in cells B4 through B6 and observe the resulting outputs in cells B9 through B11. The input values in Figure 1.1 represent the store's current input values. These values indicate that slightly more than 2 customers are waiting in line on average, an average customer waits slightly more than 6 minutes in line, and about 27% of all potential customers do not enter the store at all (due to the perception that waiting times will be long).

The information in Figure 1.1 is probably not all that useful to the manager. After all, he probably already has a sense of how long waiting times are and how many customers are being lost. The power of the model is that it allows the manager to ask many what-if questions. For example, what if he could somehow speed up the cashier, say, from 2.5 minutes per customer to 1.8 minutes per customer? He might guess that because the average service time has decreased by 28%, all the outputs should also decrease by 28%. Is this the case? Evidently not, as shown in Figure 1.2. The average line length decreases to 1.41, a 36% decrease; the average waiting time decreases to 3.22, a 47% decrease; and the percentage of customers who do not enter decreases to 12.6%, a 54% decrease. To illustrate an

Figure 1.2

Queueing Model
with a Faster Service
Rate

| | A | B |
|---|---|---|
| 1 | Descriptive queueing model for convenience store | |
| 2 | | |
| 3 | Inputs | |
| 4 | Arrival rate (customers per minute) | 0.5 |
| 5 | Service rate (customers per minute) | 0.556 |
| 6 | Maximum customers (before others go elsewhere) | 5 |
| 7 | | |
| 8 | Outputs | |
| 9 | Average number in line | 1.41 |
| 10 | Average time (minutes) spent in line | 3.22 |
| 11 | Percentage of potential arrivals who don't enter | 12.6% |

**Figure 1.3**

Queueing Model
with an Even Faster
Service Rate

| | A | B |
|---|---|---|
| 1 | Descriptive queueing model for convenience store | |
| 2 | | |
| 3 | Inputs | |
| 4 | Arrival rate (customers per minute) | 0.5 |
| 5 | Service rate (customers per minute) | 0.8 |
| 6 | Maximum customers (before others go elsewhere) | 5 |
| 7 | | |
| 8 | Outputs | |
| 9 | Average number in line | 0.69 |
| 10 | Average time (minutes) spent in line | 1.42 |
| 11 | Percentage of potential arrivals who don't enter | 3.8% |

even more extreme change, suppose the manager could cut the service time in half, from 2.5 minutes to 1.25 minutes. The spreadsheet in Figure 1.3 shows that the average number in line decreases to 0.69, a 69% decrease from the original value; the average waiting time decreases to 1.42, a 77% decrease; and the percentage of customers who do not enter decreases to 3.8%, a whopping 86% decrease. The important lesson to be learned from the spreadsheet model is that as the manager increases the service rate, the output measures improve more than he might have expected.

In reality, the manager would attempt to validate the spreadsheet model before trusting its answers to these what-if questions. At the very least, the manager should examine the reasonableness of the assumptions. For example, one assumption is that the arrival rate remains *constant* for the time period under discussion. If the manager intends to use this model—with the *same* input parameters—during periods of time when the arrival rate varies a lot (such as peak lunchtime traffic followed by slack times in the early afternoon), then he is almost certainly asking for trouble. Besides determining whether the assumptions are reasonable, the manager also check the outputs predicted by the model when the *current* inputs are used. For example, Figure 1.1 predicts that the average time a customer waits in line is approximately 6 minutes. At this point, the manager could ask his employee to use a stopwatch again to time customers' waiting times. If they average close to 6 minutes, then the manager can have more confidence in the model. However, if they average much more or much less than 6 minutes, the manager probably needs to search for a new model.

## An Optimization Model

So far, the model fails to reflect any *economic* information, such as the cost of speeding up service, the cost of making customers wait in line, or the cost of losing customers. Given the spreadsheet model developed previously, however, incorporating economic information and then making rational choices is relatively straightforward. To make this example simple, assume that the manager can do one of three things: (1) leave the system as it is, (2) hire a second person to help the first cashier process customers more quickly, or (3) lease a new model of cash register that will speed up the service process significantly. The effect of (2) is to decrease the average service time from 2.5 to 1.8 minutes. The effect of (3) is to decrease the service time from 2.5 to 1.25 minutes. What should the manager do?

He needs to examine three types of costs. The first is the cost of hiring the extra person or leasing the new cash register. We assume that these costs are known. For example, the hourly wage for the extra person is $8, and the cost to lease a new cash register (converted to a per-hour rate) is $11 per hour. The second type of cost is the "cost" of making a person wait in line. Although this is not an out-of-pocket cost to the store, it does represent the cost of potential future business—a customer who has to wait a long time might not return. This cost is difficult to estimate on a per-minute or per-hour basis, but we assume it's approximately $13 per customer per hour in line.[2] Finally, there is the opportunity cost for

---

[2] Here we are charging only for time in the queue. An alternative model is to charge for time in the queue *and* for time in service.

customers who decide not to enter the store. The store loses not only their current revenue but also potential future revenue if they decide never to return. Again, this is a difficult cost to measure, but we assume it's approximately $25 per lost customer.

The next step in the modeling process is to combine these costs for each possible decision. Let's find the total cost per hour for decision (3), where the new cash register is leased. The lease cost is $11 per hour. From Figure 1.3, you see there is, on average, 0.69 customer in line at any time. Therefore, the average waiting cost per hour is 0.69($13) = $8.91. (This is because 0.69 customer-hour is spent in line each hour on average.) Finally, from Figure 1.3 you see that the average number of potential arrivals per hour is 60(1/2) = 30, and 3.8% of them do not enter. Therefore, the average cost per hour from lost customers is 0.038(30)($25) = $28.52. The combined cost for decision (3) is $11 + $8.91 + $28.52 = $48.43 per hour.

The spreadsheet model in Figure 1.4 incorporates these calculations and similar calculations for the other two decisions. As you see from row 24, the option to lease the new cash register is the clear winner from a cost standpoint. However, if the manager wants to see how sensitive these cost figures are to the rather uncertain input costs assessed for waiting time and lost customers, it's simple to enter new values in rows 10 and 11 and see how the "bottom lines" in row 24 change. This flexibility represents the power of spreadsheet models. They not only allow you to build realistic and complex models, but they also allow you to answer many what-if questions simply by changing input values.

**Figure 1.4**

Queueing Model with Alternative Decisions

| | A | B | C | D |
|---|---|---|---|---|
| 1 | Decision queueing model for convenience store | | | |
| 2 | | | | |
| 3 | Inputs | Decision 1 | Decision 2 | Decision 3 |
| 4 | Arrival rate (customers per minute) | 0.5 | 0.5 | 0.5 |
| 5 | Service rate (customers per minute) | 0.4 | 0.556 | 0.8 |
| 6 | Maximum customers (before others go elsewhere) | 5 | 5 | 5 |
| 7 | | | | |
| 8 | Cost of extra person per hour | $0 | $8 | $0 |
| 9 | Cost of leasing new cash register per hour | $0 | $0 | $11 |
| 10 | Cost per customer per hour waiting in line | $13 | $13 | $13 |
| 11 | Cost per customer who doesn't enter the store | $25 | $25 | $25 |
| 12 | | | | |
| 13 | Outputs | | | |
| 14 | Average number in line | 2.22 | 1.41 | 0.69 |
| 15 | Average time (minutes) spent in line | 6.09 | 3.22 | 1.42 |
| 16 | Percentage of potential arrivals who don't enter | 27.1% | 12.6% | 3.8% |
| 17 | | | | |
| 18 | Cost information | | | |
| 19 | Cost of extra person per hour | $0 | $8 | $0 |
| 20 | Cost of leasing new cash register per hour | $0 | $0 | $11 |
| 21 | Cost per hour of waiting time | $28.87 | $18.31 | $8.91 |
| 22 | Cost per hour of lost customers | $203.29 | $94.52 | $28.52 |
| 23 | | | | |
| 24 | Total cost per hour | $232.16 | $120.82 | $48.43 |

## 1.3 MODELING VERSUS MODELS

Management science, at least as it has been taught in many traditional courses, has evolved as a collection of mathematical models. These include various linear programming models (the transportation model, the diet model, the shortest route model, and others), inventory models, queueing models, and so on. Much time has been devoted to teaching the intricacies of these particular models. Management science *practitioners,* on the other hand, have justifiably criticized this emphasis on specific models. They argue that the majority of real-world management science problems cannot be neatly categorized as one of the handful of models typically included in a management science textbook. That is, often no "off-the-shelf" model can be used without modification to solve a company's real problem. Unfortunately, management science students have gotten the impression that all problems must be "shoe-horned" into one of the textbook models.

The good news is that this emphasis on specific models has been changing in the past decade, and our goal in this book is to continue that change. Specifically, this book stresses *modeling,* not models. The distinction between modeling and models will become clear as you proceed through the book. Learning specific models is essentially a memorization process—memorizing the details of a particular model, such as the transportation model, and possibly learning how to "trick" other problems into looking like a transportation model. **Modeling,** on the other hand, is a *process,* where you abstract the essence of a real problem into a model, spreadsheet or otherwise. Although the problems fall naturally into several categories, in modeling, you don't try to shoe-horn each problem into one of a small number of well-studied models. Instead, you treat each problem on its own merits and model it appropriately, using whatever logical, analytical, or spreadsheet skills you have at your disposal—and, of course, drawing analogies from previous models you have developed whenever relevant. This way, if you come across a problem that does not look exactly like anything you studied in your management science course, you still have the skills and flexibility to model it successfully.

This doesn't mean you won't learn some "classical" models from management science in this book; in fact, we'll discuss the transportation model in linear programming, the $M/M/1$ model in queueing, the EOQ model in inventory, and others. These are important models that should not be ignored; however, we certainly do not emphasize memorizing these specific models. They are simply a few of the many models you will learn how to develop. The real emphasis throughout is on the modeling *process*—how a real-world problem is abstracted into a spreadsheet model of that problem. We discuss this modeling process in more detail in the following section.

## 1.4 THE SEVEN-STEP MODELING PROCESS

The discussion of the queueing model in Section 1.2 presented some of the basic principles of management science modeling. This section further expands on these ideas by characterizing the modeling process as the following seven-step procedure.

### Step 1: Problem Definition

The analyst first defines the organization's problem. Defining the problem includes specifying the organization's objectives and the parts of the organization that must be studied before the problem can be solved. In the simple queueing model, the organization's problem is how to minimize the expected net cost associated with the operation of the store's cash register.

### Step 2: Data Collection

After defining the problem, the analyst collects data to estimate the value of parameters that affect the organization's problem. These estimates are used to develop a mathematical model (step 3) of the organization's problem and predict solutions (step 4). In the convenience store queueing example, the manager needs to observe the arrivals and the checkout process to estimate the arrival rate $A$ and the service rate $S$.

### Step 3: Model Development

In the third step, the analyst develops a model of the problem. In this book, we describe many methods that can be used to model systems.[3] Models such as the equation for $W$,

---

[3] All these models can generically be called **mathematical models.** However, because we implement them in spreadsheets, we generally refer to them as **spreadsheet models.**

where you use an equation to relate inputs such as $A$ and $S$ to outputs such as $W$, are called **analytical models.** Most realistic applications are so complex, however, that an analytical model does not exist or is too complex to work with. For example, if the convenience store had more than one register and customers were allowed to join any line or jump from one line to another, there would be no tractable analytical model—no equation or system of equations—that could be used to determine $W$ from knowledge of $A$, $S$, and the number of lines. When no tractable analytical model exists, you can often rely instead on a **simulation model,** which enables you to approximate the behavior of the actual system. Simulation models are covered in Chapters 11 and 12.

### Step 4: Model Verification

The analyst now tries to determine whether the model developed in the previous step is an accurate representation of reality. A first step in determining how well the model fits reality is to check whether the model is valid for the current situation. As discussed previously, to validate the equation for the waiting time $W$, the manager might observe actual customer waiting times for several hours. As you've already seen, the equation for $W$ predicts that when $A = 0.5$ and $S = 0.4$, the average customer spends 6.09 minutes in line. Now suppose the manager observes that 120 customers spend a total of 750 minutes in line. This indicates an average of $750/120 = 6.25$ minutes in line per customer. Because 6.25 is reasonably close to 6.09, the manager's observations lend credibility to the model. In contrast, if the 120 customers had spent 1,200 minutes total in line, for an average of 10 minutes per customer, this would not agree very well with the model's prediction of 6.09 minutes, and it would cast doubt on the validity of the model.

### Step 5: Optimization and Decision Making

Given a model and a set of possible decisions, the analyst must now choose the decision or strategy that best meets the organization's objectives. (We briefly discussed an optimization model for the convenience store example, and we discuss many others throughout the book.)

### Step 6: Model Communication to Management

The analyst presents the model and the recommendations from the previous step to the organization. In some situations, the analyst might present several alternatives and let the organization choose the best one.

### Step 7: Model Implementation

If the organization has accepted the validity and usefulness of the study, the analyst then helps to implement its recommendations. The implemented system must be monitored constantly (and updated dynamically as the environment changes) to ensure that the model enables the organization to meet its objectives.

### Flowchart of Procedure and Discussion of Steps

Figure 1.5 illustrates this seven-step process. As the arrows pointing down and to the left indicate, there is certainly room for feedback in the process. For example, at various steps, the analyst might realize that the current model is not capturing some key aspects of the real problem. In this case, the analyst should revise the problem definition or develop a new model.

**Figure 1.5** Flowchart for the Seven-Step Process

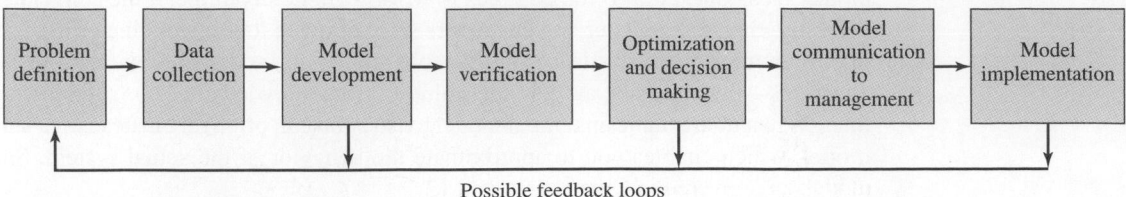

Possible feedback loops

Now that you've seen the basic outline of the seven steps and the flowchart, let's delve into the modeling proces in more detail.

### Step 1: Problem Definition

Typically, a management science model is initiated when an organization believes it has a problem. Perhaps the company is losing money, perhaps its market share is declining, perhaps its customers are waiting too long for service—any number of problems might be evident. The organization (which we refer to as the client) calls in a management scientist (the analyst) to help solve this problem.[4] In such cases, the problem has probably already been defined by the client, and the client hires the analyst to solve *this particular problem*.

As Miser (1993) and Volkema (1995) point out, however, the analyst should do some investigating before accepting the client's claim that the problem has been properly defined. Failure to do so could mean solving the wrong problem and wasting valuable time and energy.

*It's important to solve the correct problem, and defining that problem is not always easy.*

For example, Miser cites the experience of an analyst who was hired by the military to investigate overly long turnaround times between fighter planes landing and taking off again to rejoin the battle. The military (the client) was convinced that the problem was caused by inefficient ground crews—if they worked faster, turnaround times would presumably decrease. The analyst nearly accepted this statement of the problem and was about to do classical time-and-motion studies on the ground crew to pinpoint the sources of their inefficiency. However, by snooping around, he found that the problem lay elsewhere. It seems that the trucks that refueled the planes were frequently late, which in turn was due to the inefficient way they were refilled from storage tanks at another location. After this latter problem was solved—and its solution was embarrassingly simple—the turnaround times decreased to an acceptable level without any changes on the part of the ground crews. If the analyst had accepted the client's statement of the problem, the *real* problem would never have been located or solved.

The moral of this story is clear: If an analyst defines a problem incorrectly or too narrowly, the best solution to the real problem might never emerge. In his article, Volkema (1995) advocates spending as much time thinking about the problem and defining it properly as modeling and solving it. This is undoubtedly good advice, especially in real-world applications where problem boundaries are often difficult to define.

### Step 2: Data Collection

*The data collection step often takes the most time.*

This crucial step in the modeling process is often the most tedious. All organizations keep track of various data on their operations, but the data is often not in the form the analyst requires. In addition, data is often stored in different places throughout the organization and in all kinds of formats. Therefore, one of the analyst's first jobs is to gather exactly the right data and put the data into an appropriate and consistent format for use in the model. This

---

[4] Most organizations hire outside consultants, sometimes academics, to help solve problems. However, a number of large organizations employ a staff of management scientists who function as inside consultants.

typically requires asking questions of key people (such as the accountants) throughout the organization, studying existing organizational databases, and performing time-consuming observational studies of the organization's processes. In short, it typically entails a lot of legwork.

In this book, as in most management science textbooks, we shield you from this data-collection process by supplying the appropriate data to develop and solve a model. Although this makes the overall modeling process seem easier than it really is, in most class settings, having you go to companies and gather data is just not practical. (In many cases, it would not even be allowed for proprietary reasons.) Nevertheless, we provide some insights with "Where Do the Numbers Come From?" sections. If nothing else, these sections remind you that in real applications, someone has to gather the necessary inputs.

### Step 3: Model Development

*Steps 3 and 5, developing and optimizing models, are the steps emphasized most heavily in this book.*

This step, along with step 5, is where the analyst brings his or her special skills into play. After defining the client's problem and gathering the necessary data, the analyst must develop a model of the problem. Several properties are desirable for a good model. First, it should represent the client's real problem accurately. If it uses a linear (straight-line) function for costs when the real cost function is highly nonlinear (curved), the recommendations of the model could be very misleading. Similarly, if the model ignores an important constraint, such as an upper bound on capacity, its recommendations might not be possible to implement.

On the other hand, the model should be as simple as possible. Most good models (where "good" really means *useful*) capture the essence of the problem without getting bogged down in less important details. They should be *approximations* of the real world, not mirror images in every last detail. Overly complex models are often of little practical use. First, overly complex models are sometimes too difficult to solve with the solution algorithms available. Second, complex models tend to be incomprehensible to clients. If a client cannot understand a model, the chances are that the model's recommendations will never be implemented. Therefore, a good model should achieve the right balance between being too simple and too complex.

### Step 4: Model Verification

This step is particularly important in real management science applications. A client is much more likely to accept an analyst's model if the analyst can provide some type of verification. This verification can take several forms. For example, the analyst can use the model with the company's current values of the *input* parameters. If the model's outputs are then in line with the *outputs* currently observed by the client, the analyst has at least shown that the model can duplicate the current situation.

A second way to verify a model is to enter a number of sets of input parameters (even if they are not the company's current inputs) and see whether the outputs from the model are *reasonable*. One common approach is to use extreme values of the inputs to determine whether the outputs behave as they should. For example, for the convenience store queueing model, you could enter an extremely large service rate or a service rate just barely above the arrival rate in the equation for $W$. In the first case, you would expect the average waiting time to approach 0, whereas in the latter case, you would expect it to become very large. You can use equation (1.1) for $W$ to verify that this is exactly what happens. This provides another piece of evidence that the model is reasonable.

If you enter certain inputs in the model, and the model's outputs are *not* as expected, there are two possible causes. First, the model could simply be a poor approximation of the actual situation. In this case, the analyst must refine the model until it lines up more accurately with reality. Second, the model might be fine, but the analyst's intuition is not very good. That is, when asked what he or she thinks would happen if certain input values were used, the analyst might provide totally wrong predictions. In this case, the fault lies with the analyst, not the model. Sometimes, good models prove that people's ability to predict outcomes in complex environments is lacking. In such cases, the verification step becomes harder because of "political" reasons (office politics).

### Step 5: Optimization and Decision Making

After the problem has been defined, the data has been collected, and the model has been developed and verified, it's time to use the model to recommend decisions or strategies. In the majority of management science models, this requires the optimization of an objective, such as maximizing profit or minimizing cost.

The optimization phase is typically the most difficult phase from a mathematical standpoint. Indeed, much of the management science literature (mostly from academics) has focused on complex solution algorithms for various classes of models. Fortunately, this research has led to a number of solution algorithms—and computer packages that implement these algorithms—that can be used to solve real problems. The most famous of these is the simplex algorithm. This algorithm, which has been implemented by many commercial software packages (including Excel's Solver), is used on a daily basis to solve linear optimization models for many companies. (We take advantage of the simplex method in Chapters 3 through 5.)

*A heuristic is a relatively simple solution method that often provides "good" but not necessarily optimal solutions.*

Not all solution procedures find the optimal solution to a problem. Many models are either too large or too complex to be solved exactly. Therefore, many complex problems use *heuristic* methods to locate "good" solutions. A **heuristic** is a solution method that is guided by common sense, intuition, and trial and error to achieve a good, but probably not optimal, solution. Some heuristics are "quick and dirty," whereas others are sophisticated. As models become larger and more complex, good heuristics are sometimes the best that can be achieved—and frequently they are perfectly adequate.

### Step 6: Model Communication to Management

Sooner or later, an analyst must communicate a model and its recommendations to the client. To appreciate this step, you must understand the large gap that typically exists between the analyst and the managers of organizations. Managers know their business, but they often don't understand much about mathematics and mathematical models—even spreadsheet implementations of these models. The burden is therefore on the analyst to present the model in terms that nonmathematical people can understand; otherwise, a perfectly good model might never see the light of day.

The best strategy for successful presentation is to involve key people in the organization, including top executives, in the project *from the beginning*. If these people have been working with the analyst, helping to supply appropriate data and helping the analyst to understand the way the organization really works, they are much more likely to accept the eventual model. Step 6, therefore, should really occur throughout the modeling process, not just toward the end.

The analyst should also try to make the model as intuitive and user-friendly as possible. Clients appreciate menu-driven systems with plenty of graphics. They also appreciate the ability to ask what-if questions and get answers quickly in a form that is easy to understand. This is one reason for developing *spreadsheet* models. Although not all models can be developed in spreadsheets due to size and/or complexity, the spreadsheet approach in this book is an excellent choice whenever possible because most business people are comfortable with spreadsheets. Spreadsheet packages support the use of graphics, customized menus and toolbars, data tables and other tools for what-if analyses, and even macros (that can be made transparent to users) for running complex programs.

### Step 7: Model Implementation

A real management science application is not complete until it has been implemented. A successful implementation can occur only when step 6 has been accomplished. That is, the analyst must demonstrate the model to the client, and the client must be convinced that the model adds real value and can be used by the people who need to use it. For this reason, the analyst's job is not really complete until the system is up and running on a daily basis. To achieve a successful implementation, it isn't enough for management to accept the model; the people who will run it every day must also be thoroughly trained to use it. At the very least, they should understand how to enter appropriate inputs, run what-if analyses, and interpret the model's outputs correctly. If they conclude that the model is more trouble than it's worth, they might simply refuse to use it, and the whole exercise has been a waste of time. An interesting trend (as evidenced in many of the *Interfaces* articles discussed shortly) is for analysts to build a user-friendly Excel "front end" for their clients, even if the actual number crunching is performed behind the scenes in some non-Excel package. Because many employees understand at least the basics of Excel, such a user-friendly front end makes the system much more attractive for daily use.

Many successful management science applications take on a life of their own after the initial implementation. After an organization sees the benefits of a useful model—and of management science in general—it is likely to expand the model or create new models for uses beyond those originally intended. Knowing that this is often the case, the best analysts design models that can be expanded. They try to anticipate problems the organization might face besides the current problem. They also stay in contact with the organization after the initial implementation, just in case the organization needs guidance in expanding the scope of the model or in developing new models.

This discussion of the seven-step modeling process has taken an optimistic point of view by assuming that a successful study employs these seven steps, in approximately this chronological order, and that everything goes smoothly. It does not always work out this way. Numerous potential applications are never implemented even though the *technical* aspects of the models are perfectly correct. The most frequent cause is a failure to communicate. The analyst builds a complex mathematical model, but the people in the organization don't understand how it works and hence are reluctant to use it. Also, company politics can be a model's downfall, especially if the model recommends a course of action that top management simply does not want to follow—for whatever reasons.

Even for applications that are eventually implemented, the analyst doesn't always proceed through the seven steps exactly as described in this section. He or she might backtrack considerably throughout the process. For example, based on a tentative definition of the problem, a model is built and demonstrated to management. Management says that the model is impressive, but it doesn't really solve the company's problem. Therefore, the analyst goes back to step 1, redefines the problem, and builds a new model (or modifies the original model). In this way, the analyst generates several iterations of some or all the seven steps before the project is considered complete.

## The Model as a Beginning, Not an End

This book heavily emphasizes *developing* spreadsheet models, which is step 3 of the seven-step modeling process. We lead you, step-by-step, through the model development process for many examples, and we ask you to do this on your own in numerous problems. Given this emphasis, it's easy to think of the completed model as the *end* of the process— you complete the model and then go on to the next model. However, a completed model is really a *starting* point. After you have a working model of the problem, you can—and should—use it as a tool for gaining insights. For most models, many what-if questions can be asked. If the model has been developed correctly, it should be capable of answering such what-if questions fairly easily. In other words, it should be relatively easy to perform *sensitivity analysis* on the model. This is, in fact, how management science models are used in the business world. They are typically developed to solve a particular problem, but they are then used as a tool to analyze a number of variations of the basic problem.

For most of the examples in the book, we not only develop a model to obtain an "answer," but we often include a section called "Discussion of the Solution" (or a similar title) and a section called "Sensitivity Analysis." The first of these gets you to step back and look at the solution. Does it make sense? Does it provide any insights, especially surprising ones? The second section expands the model in one or more natural ways. What happens if there is more or less of some scarce resource? What happens if a new constraint is added? The point is that before moving to the next model, you should spend some time taking a close look at the model you just developed. This is not just for pedagogical purposes; it is exactly the way real management science projects proceed.

## 1.5 A SUCCESSFUL MANAGEMENT SCIENCE APPLICATION

This section discusses a successful management science application. Besides a detailed (but nonquantitative) description of the application, you'll see how it ties into the seven-step model-building process discussed in the previous section.

### GE Capital

GE Capital, a subsidiary of the General Electric Company's financial services business, provides credit card service to 50 million accounts. The average total outstanding balance exceeds $12 billion. GE Capital, led by Makuch et al. (1992), developed the PAYMENT system to reduce delinquent accounts and the cost of collecting from delinquent accounts. The following describes how the seven-step model-building process played out for GE Capital:

1. At any time, GE Capital has more than $1 billion in delinquent accounts. The company spends $100 million annually processing these accounts. Each day employees contact more than 200,000 delinquent credit card holders with letters, taped phone messages, or live phone calls. However, there was no real scientific basis for the methods used to collect on various types of accounts. For example, GE Capital had no idea whether a two-month due account should receive a taped phone message, a live phone call, some combination of these, or no contact at all. The company's goal was to reduce delinquent accounts and the cost of processing these accounts, but it was not sure how to accomplish this goal. Therefore, GE Capital's retail financial services component, together with management scientists and statisticians from GE's corporate research and development group, analyzed the problem and eventually developed a model called PAYMENT. The purpose of this model was to assign the most cost-effective collection methods to delinquent accounts.

2. The key data requirements for modeling delinquent accounts are **delinquency movement matrices** (DMMs). A DMM shows how the probability of the payment on a delinquent account depends on the collection action taken (no action, live phone call, taped message, or letter), the size of the unpaid balance, and the account's performance score. (The higher the performance score associated with a delinquent account, the more likely the account is to be collected.) For example, if a $250 account is two months delinquent, has a high performance score, and is contacted with a phone message, then certain events might occur with certain probabilities. The

events and the probabilities listed in Table 1.1 illustrate one possibility. The key is to estimate these probabilities for each possible collection action and each account type.

**Table 1.1    Sample DMM Entries**

| Event | Probability |
|---|---|
| Account completely paid off | 0.30 |
| One month is paid off | 0.40 |
| Nothing is paid off | 0.30 |

Fortunately, because GE Capital had millions of delinquent accounts, plenty of data was available to estimate the DMMs accurately. To illustrate, suppose there are 1000 two-month delinquent accounts, each with balances under $300 and a high performance score. Also, suppose that each of these is contacted with a phone message. If 300 of these accounts are completely paid off by the next month, then an estimate of the probability of an account being completely paid off by next month is 0.30 (= 300/1000). By collecting the necessary data to estimate similar probabilities for all account types and collection actions, GE Capital finally had the basis for determining which collection strategies were most cost-effective.

3.  After collecting the required data and expressing it in the form of DMMs, the company had to discover which collections worked best in which situations. Specifically, they wanted to maximize the expected delinquent accounts collected during the following six months. However, GE Capital realized that this is a *dynamic* decision problem. For example, one strategy is called **creaming.** In this strategy, most collection resources are concentrated on live phone calls to the delinquent accounts classified as most likely to pay up—the best customers. This creaming strategy is attractive because it's likely to generate short-term cash flows from these customers. However, it has two negative aspects. First, it's likely to cause a loss of goodwill among the best customers. Second, it gains nothing in the long run from the customers who are most likely to default on their payments. Therefore, the analysts developed the PAYMENT model to find the best **decision strategy,** a contingency plan for each type of customer that specifies which collection strategy to use at each stage of the account's delinquency. The constraints in the PAYMENT model ensure that available resources are not overused.

4.  A key aspect of GE Capital's problem is uncertainty. When the PAYMENT model specifies the collection method to use for a certain type of account, it implies that the probability of collecting on this account with this collection method is relatively high. However, there is still a chance that the collection method will fail. With this high degree of uncertainty, it's difficult to convince skeptics that the model will work as advertised until it has been demonstrated in an actual environment. This is exactly what GE Capital did. It piloted the PAYMENT model on a $62 million portfolio for a single department store chain. To see the real effect of PAYMENT's recommended strategies, the pilot study used manager-recommended strategies for some accounts and PAYMENT-recommended strategies for others. (They referred to this as the "champion" versus the "challenger.") The challenger (PAYMENT) strategies were the clear winners, with an average monthly improvement of $185,000 over the champion strategies during a five-month period. In addition, because the PAYMENT strategies included more "no contact" actions (don't bother the customer this month), they led to lower collection costs and greater customer goodwill. This demonstration was very convincing. In no time, other account managers wanted to take advantage of PAYMENT.

5. As described in step 3, the output from the PAYMENT model is a contingency plan. The model uses a very complex optimization scheme, along with the DMMs from step 2, to decide what collection strategy to use for each type of delinquent account at each stage (month) of its delinquency. At the end of each month, after the appropriate collection methods have been used and the results (actual payments) have been observed, the model then uses the status of each account to recommend the collection method for the next month. In this way, the model is used dynamically through time.

6. In general, the analyst demonstrates the model to the client in step 6. In this application, however, the management science team members were GE's own people—they came from GE Capital and the GE corporate research and development group. Throughout the model-building process, the team of analysts strived to understand the requirements of the collection managers and staff—the end users—and tried to involve them in shaping the final system. This early and continual involvement, plus the impressive performance of PAYMENT in the pilot study, made it easy to "sell" the model to the people who had to use it.

7. After the pilot study, PAYMENT was applied to the $4.6 billion Montgomery Ward department store portfolio with 18 million accounts. Compared to the collection results from a year earlier, PAYMENT increased collections by $1.6 million per month, or more than $19 million per year. (This is actually a conservative estimate of the benefit obtained from PAYMENT, because PAYMENT was first applied to the Montgomery Ward portfolio during the depths of a recession, when it's much more difficult to collect delinquent accounts.) Since then, PAYMENT has been applied to virtually all of GE Capital's accounts, with similar success. Overall, GE Capital estimates that PAYMENT has increased collections by $37 million per year and uses less resources than previous strategies. The model has since been expanded in several directions. For example, the original model assumed that collection resources (such as the amount available for live phone calls) were fixed. The expanded model treats these resource levels as decision variables in a more encompassing optimization model.

## A Great Source for Management Science Applications: *Interfaces*

The GE Capital application is reported in the *Interfaces* journal, which is a highly respected bimonthly journal that chronicles real applications of management science that have generated proven benefits, often in the millions or even hundreds of millions of dollars. The applications are in a wide range of industries, are global, and employ a variety of management science techniques.

Of special interest are the January-February and (since 1999) the September-October issues. Each January-February issue contains the winner and finalists for that year's Franz Edelman Award for Achievement in Operations Research and the Management Sciences. This is the profession's most honored prize for the *practice* of management science. The prize is awarded for "implemented work that has had significant, verifiable, and preferably quantifiable impact." Similarly, each September-October issue contains the winner and runners-up for that year's Daniel H. Wagner Prize for Excellence in Operations Research Practice. Each prize is named after a pioneer in the field of operations research and management science, and the winning papers honor them by documenting the practice of management science at its best. Many of the chapter openers and citations in this book are based on these winning articles, as well as on other *Interfaces* articles.

The journal is probably available from your school's library. Alternatively, you can browse the abstracts of the articles online at http://pubsonline.informs.org. You must pay a membership fee to read the entire articles, but you can log in as a guest to read the abstracts.

## 1.6  WHY STUDY MANAGEMENT SCIENCE?

After reading the previous section, you should be convinced that management science is an important area and that highly trained analysts are needed to solve the large and complex problems faced by the business world. However, unless you are one of the relatively few students who intends to become a professional management scientist, you are probably wondering why you need to study management science. This is a legitimate concern. For many years, those in the field of management science education received criticism from students and educators that management science courses were irrelevant for the majority of students who were required to take them. Looking back, it's difficult to argue with these critics. Typical management courses were centered primarily around a collection of very specific models and, worse, a collection of mind-numbing mathematical solution techniques—techniques that students were often required to implement *by hand!* (Some courses are probably still taught this way, but we hope the number is decreasing rapidly.)

Two forces have helped to change this tendency toward irrelevance. First, the many vocal critics motivated many of us to examine our course materials and teaching methods. Certain topics have been eliminated and replaced by material that is more relevant and interesting to students. The second force is the emergence of powerful computers and the accompanying easy-to-use software, especially spreadsheet software. With the availability of computers to do the number crunching, there is no need—except in advanced courses—to delve into the mathematical details of the solution techniques. We can delegate this task to machines that are far better at it than we are. We can now use the time formerly spent on such details to develop modeling skills that are valuable to a wide audience.

The intent in this book is not just to cover specific models and specific approaches to these models, but to teach a more general approach to the model-building process. The spreadsheet approach is the best way to do this because it appeals to the largest audience. We have been teaching our own courses with this spreadsheet-modeling approach for more than a decade—to a wide range of business students—and have received very few complaints about irrelevance. In fact, many students have stated that this is the most valuable business course they have taken. The following are some of the reasons for this new-found relevance:

■ The modeling approach emphasized throughout this book is an important way to think about problems in general, not just the specific problems we discuss. This approach forces you to think logically. You must discover how given data can be used (or which data are necessary), you must determine the elements of the problem that you can control (the decision variables), and you must determine how the elements of the problem are logically related. Students realize that these logical thinking skills are valuable for their careers, regardless of the specific fields they enter.

■ Management science is admittedly built around *quantitative* skills—it deals primarily with numbers and relationships between numbers. Some critics object that not everything in the real world can be reduced to numbers, but as one of our reviewers correctly points out, "a great deal that is of importance can." As you work through the many models in this book, your quantitative skills will be sharpened immensely. In a business world driven increasingly by numbers, quantitative skills are an obvious asset.

■ No matter what your spreadsheet abilities are when you enter this course, by the time you're finished, you'll be a proficient spreadsheet user. We deliberately chose the spreadsheet package Excel, which is arguably the most widely used package (other than word-processing packages) in the business world today. Many of our students state that the facility they gained in Excel was worth the price of the course. That doesn't mean this is a course in spreadsheet fundamentals and neat tricks, although you will undoubtedly pick up a few useful tricks along the way. A great spreadsheet package—and we strongly believe that Excel is the greatest spreadsheet package written to date—gives you complete control over your model. You can apply spreadsheets to an endless variety of problems. Spreadsheets give you the flexibility to work in a way that suits *your* style best, and spreadsheets present results (and often catch errors) almost immediately. As you succeed with relatively easy problems, your confidence will build, and before long, you'll be able to tackle more difficult problems successfully. In short, spreadsheets enable everyone, not just technical people, to develop and use their quantitative skills.

■ Management science modeling helps you develop your intuition, and it also indicates where intuition alone sometimes fails. When you confront a problem, you often make an educated (or maybe not so educated) guess at the solution. If the problem is sufficiently complex, as many of the problems in this book are, this guess will be frequently wide of the mark. In this sense, the study of management science can be a humbling experience—you find that your unaided intuition is often not very good. But by studying many models and examining their solutions, you can sharpen your intuition considerably. This is sometimes called the "Aha!" effect. All of a sudden, you see why a certain solution is best. The chances are that when you originally thought about the problem, you forgot to consider an important constraint or a key relationship, and this caused your poor initial guess. Presumably, the more problems you analyze, the better you become at recognizing the critical elements of new problems. Experienced management scientists tend to have excellent intuition, the ability to see through to the essence of a problem almost immediately. However, they are not born with this talent; it comes through the kind of analysis you'll be performing as you work through this book.

## 1.7 SOFTWARE INCLUDED IN THIS BOOK

Very few business problems are small enough to be solved with pencil and paper. They require powerful software. The software included in this book, together with Microsoft® Excel, provides you with a powerful software combination that you will use for this course and beyond. This software is being used—and will continue to be used—by leading companies all over the world to solve large, complex problems. The experience you obtain with this software, through working the examples and problems in this book, will give you a key competitive advantage in the marketplace.

It all begins with Excel. All the quantitative methods that we discuss are implemented in Excel. Specifically, in this edition, we use Excel 2007. Although it's impossible to forecast the state of computer software into the long-term or even medium-term future, as we are writing this book, Excel is *the* most heavily used spreadsheet package on the market, and there is every reason to believe that this state will persist for quite awhile. Most companies use Excel, most employees and most students have been trained in Excel, and Excel is a *very* powerful, flexible, and easy-to-use package.

Although Excel has a huge set of tools for performing numerical analysis, we have included several add-ins with this book (available on the CD-ROM inside this book and the package bundled with the book) that make Excel even more powerful. We discuss these briefly here and in much more depth in the specific chapters where they apply. Throughout the text, you will see icons that denote where each of these add-ins is used.

Together with Excel and the add-ins included in this book, you have a wealth of software at your disposal. The examples and step-by-step instructions throughout the book will help you to become a power user of this software. This takes plenty of practice and a willingness to experiment, but it's certainly within your grasp. When you are finished, don't be surprised if you rate improved software skills as one of the most valuable things you have learned from the book.

## PREMIUM SOLVER

Excel contains a built-in add-in called Solver that is developed by Frontline Systems. This add-in is used extensively throughout the book to find optimal solutions to spreadsheet models. The version of Solver that ships with Excel is powerful and suffices for the majority of the optimization models we discuss. However, Frontline Systems has developed several other versions of Solver for the commercial market, and one of these, called Premium Solver for Education (for Excel 2007), is included in the book. The primary advantage of Premium Solver is that it enables you to solve some problems with a kind of algorithm (called a genetic algorithm) that is different from the algorithms used by the built-in Solver. Only a small percentage of all optimization models require a genetic algorithm, but in Chapter 8 (and in a few examples in later chapters), we illustrate several very interesting models that take advantage of genetic algorithms and hence Premium Solver. These models could either not be solved with the built-in Solver, or they would require nonobvious modeling tricks to make them amenable to the built-in Solver.

## Palisade Software

The Palisade Corporation has developed several powerful add-ins for Excel that we have included in this book. These are educational versions of commercial software packages used widely in the business world.

### Decision Tools® Suite

Decision Tools is a collection of add-ins that Palisade sells separately or as a suite. All of the items in this suite are Excel add-ins—so the learning curve is not very steep. The four separate add-ins in this suite are @RISK, PrecisionTree, TopRank, and RISKOptimizer.[5] The first two are the most important for our purposes, but all are useful for certain tasks.

**@RISK** The @RISK add-in is extremely useful for the development and analysis of spreadsheet simulation models. First, it provides a number of probability functions that enable you to build uncertainty explicitly into Excel models. Then when you run a simulation, @RISK automatically keeps track of any outputs you select, displays the results in a number of tabular and graphical forms, and enables you to perform sensitivity analyses, so that you can see which inputs have the most effect on the outputs.

**PrecisionTree®** The PrecisionTree add-in is used in Chapter 10 to analyze decision problems with uncertainty. The primary tool for performing this type of analysis is a decision tree. Decision trees are inherently graphical, and they have always been difficult to implement in spreadsheets, which are based on rows and columns. However, PrecisionTree does this in a very clever and intuitive way. Equally important, after the basic decision tree has been built, PrecisionTree makes it easy to perform sensitivity analysis on the model inputs.

**TopRank®** Although we do not use the other Palisade add-ins as extensively as @RISK and PrecisionTree, they are all worth investigating. TopRank is a "what-if" add-in used for sensitivity analysis. It starts with any spreadsheet model, where several inputs are used,

---

[5] The Palisade suite has traditionally included two stand-alone programs, BestFit and RISKview. The functionality of both of these is now included in @RISK, so they are no longer included in the suite. As this book is going to press, we have been told by Palisade that two new add-ins, NeuralTools and Evolver, will be added to the suite, but we haven't seen them yet, and they won't be discussed in the book.

together with spreadsheet formulas, to produce one or more outputs. TopRank then performs sensitivity analysis to see which inputs have the largest effects on the outputs. For example, it might tell you which affects after-tax profit the most: the tax rate, the riskfree rate for investing, the inflation rate, or the price charged by a competitor. Unlike @RISK, TopRank is used when uncertainty is not *explicitly* built into a spreadsheet model. However, TopRank considers uncertainty implicitly by performing sensitivity analysis on the important model inputs.

**RISKOptimizer** RISKOptimizer combines optimization with simulation. Often, you want to use simulation to model some business problem, but you also want to optimize a summary measure, such as the mean, of an output distribution. This optimization can be performed in a trial-and-error fashion, where you try a few values of the decision variable(s) and see which provides the best solution. However, RISKOptimizer provides a more automatic (and time-intensive) optimization procedure.

### StatTools™

Palisade has also developed a statistics add-in called StatTools, which enhances the statistical capabilities of Excel. Excel's built-in statistical tools are rather limited. It has several functions, such as AVERAGE and STDEV for summarizing data, and it includes the Analysis ToolPak, an add-in that was developed by a third party. However, these tools are not sufficiently powerful or flexible for the heavy-duty statistical analysis that is sometimes required. StatTools provides a collection of tools that help fill this gap. Admittedly, this is not a statistics book, but StatTools will come in particularly handy in Chapter 16 when you study regression analysis and forecasting.

## 1.8 CONCLUSION

In this chapter, we have introduced the field of management science and the process of mathematical modeling. To provide a more concrete understanding of these concepts, we reviewed a simple queueing model and a successful management science application. We also explored a seven-step model-building process that begins with problem definition and proceeds through final implementation. Finally, we discussed why the study of management science is a valuable experience, even if you do not intend to pursue a professional career in this field.

Don't worry if you don't understand some of the terms, such as *linear programming,* that were used in this chapter. Although the seven-step process is not too difficult to comprehend, especially when discussed in the context of real applications, it typically entails some rather complex logical relationships and mathematical concepts. These ideas are presented in much greater detail in the rest of this book. Specifically, you'll learn how to build spreadsheet models in Excel, how to use them to answer what-if questions, and how to find optimal solutions with the help of a spreadsheet Solver. For practical reasons, most of your work will take place in the classroom or in front of your own PC as you work through the examples and problems. The primary emphasis of this book, therefore, is on steps 3 through 6, that is, developing the model, testing the model with different inputs, optimizing the model, and presenting (and interpreting) the results to a client—probably your instructor.

Keep in mind, however, that with real problems you must take crucial steps before and after the procedures you'll be practicing in this book. Because real problems don't come as nicely packaged as those we discuss and because the necessary data are seldom given to you on a platter, you'll have to wrestle with the problem's scope and precise data requirements when you solve problems in a real setting. (We have included "modeling problems" at the ends of most chapters. These problems are not as well structured as the "skill" problems, so the burden is on you to determine an appropriate structure and decide the necessary data.) Also, because a mathematically accurate model doesn't necessarily result in a successful implementation, your work is not finished just because the numbers check out. To gain acceptance for a model, an analyst must have the right combination of technical skills *and* people skills. Try to keep this in mind as you write up your solutions to the problems in this book. Don't just hand in a mass of numbers with little or no explanation. *Sell* your solution!

# Introduction to Spreadsheet Modeling

© Dan Burn-Forti/Photographer's Choice/Getty Images

## ANALYSIS OF HIV/AIDS

Many of management science's most successful applications are traditional functional areas of business, including operations management, logistics, finance, and marketing. Indeed, many such applications are analyzed in this book. However, another area where management science has had a strong influence over the past decade has been the analysis of the worldwide HIV/AIDS epidemic. Not only have theoretical models been developed, but even more important, they have also been *applied* to help understand the epidemic and reduce its spread. To highlight the importance of management science modeling in this area, an entire special issue (May–June 1998) of *Interfaces*, the journal that reports successful management science applications, was devoted to HIV/AIDS models. Some of the highlights are discussed here to give you an idea of what management science has to offer in this important area.

Kahn et al. (1998) provides an overview of the problem. They discuss how governments, public-health agencies, and health-care providers must determine how best to allocate scarce resources for HIV treatment and prevention among different programs and populations. They discuss in some depth how management science models have influenced, and will continue to influence, AIDS policy decisions. Other articles in the issue discuss more specific problems. Caulkins et al. (1998) analyze whether the distribution of difficult-to-reuse syringes would reduce the spread of HIV among injection drug users. Based on their model, they conclude that the extra expense of these types of syringes would not be worth the marginal benefit they might provide.

Paltiel and Freedberg (1998) investigate the costs and benefits of developing and administering treatments for cytomegalovirus (CMV), an infection to which HIV carriers are increasingly exposed. (Retinitis, CMV's most common manifestation, is associated with blindness and sometimes death.) Their model suggests that the costs compare unfavorably with alternative uses of scarce resources. Owens et al. (1998) analyze the effect of women's relapse to high-risk sexual and needle-sharing behavior on the costs and benefits of a voluntary program to screen women of childbearing age for HIV. They find, for example, that the effect of relapse to high-risk behaviors on screening program costs and benefits can be substantial, suggesting that behavioral interventions that produce sustained reductions in risk behavior, even if expensive, could be cost-saving.

The important point is that these articles (and others not mentioned here) base their results on rigorous management science models of the HIV/AIDS phenomenon. In addition, they are backed up with real data. They are not simply opinions of the authors. ■

## 2.1 INTRODUCTION

This book is all about spreadsheet modeling. By the time you are finished, you'll have seen some reasonably complex—and realistic—models. Many of you will also be transformed into Excel "power" users. However, we don't want to start too quickly or assume too much background on your part. For practice in getting up to speed with basic Excel features, we have included an Excel tutorial in the CD-ROM that accompanies this book. (See the **Excel Tutorial.docx** file.) You can work through this tutorial at your own speed and cover the topics you need help with. Even if you have used Excel extensively, give this tutorial a look. You might be surprised how some of the tips can improve your productivity.

Second, this chapter provides an introduction to Excel modeling and illustrates some interesting and relatively simple models. The chapter also covers the modeling process and includes some of the less well known, but particularly helpful, Excel tools that are available. These tools include data tables, Goal Seek, lookup tables, and auditing commands. Keep in mind, however, that our objective is not the same as that of the many "how-to" Excel books on the market. Specifically, we are not teaching Excel just for its many interesting features. Rather, we plan to *use* these features to provide insights into real business problems. In short, Excel is a problem-solving tool, not an end in itself, in this book.

## 2.2 BASIC SPREADSHEET MODELING: CONCEPTS AND BEST PRACTICES

Most mathematical models, including spreadsheet models, involve *inputs*, *decision variables*, and *outputs*. The **inputs** have given fixed values, at least for the purposes of the model. The **decision variables** are those a decision maker controls. The **outputs** are the ultimate values of interest; they are determined by the inputs and the decision variables. For example, suppose a manager must place an order for a certain seasonal product. This product will go out of date fairly soon, so this is the only order that will be made for the product. The inputs are the fixed cost of the order; the unit variable cost of each item ordered; the price charged for each item sold; the "salvage" value for each item, if any, left in inventory after the product has gone out of date; and the demand for the product. The decision variable is the number of items to order. Finally, the key output is the profit (or loss) from the

Some inputs, such as demand in this example, contain a considerable degree of uncertainty. In some cases, as in Example 2.4 later in this chapter, we model this uncertainty explicitly.

product. You can also break this output into the outputs that contribute to it: the total ordering cost, the revenue from sales, and the salvage value from leftover items. You certainly have to calculate these outputs to obtain profit.

Spreadsheet modeling is the process of entering the inputs and decision variables into a spreadsheet and then relating them appropriately, by means of formulas, to obtain the outputs. After you've done this, you can then proceed in several directions. You might want to perform a sensitivity analysis to see how one or more outputs change as selected inputs or decision variables change. You might want to find the values of the decision variable(s) that minimize or maximize a particular output, possibly subject to certain constraints. You might also want to create charts that show graphically how certain parameters of the model are related.

These operations are illustrated with several examples in this chapter. Getting all the spreadsheet logic correct and producing useful results is a big part of the battle; however, we go further by stressing good spreadsheet modeling *practices*. You probaby won't be developing spreadsheet models for your sole use; instead, you'll be sharing them with colleagues or even a boss (or an instructor). The point is that other people will probably be reading and trying to make sense out of your spreadsheet models. Therefore, you must construct your spreadsheet models with *readability* in mind. Several features that can improve readability include the following:

- A clear, logical layout to the overall model
- Separation of different parts of a model, possibly across multiple worksheets
- Clear headings for different sections of the model and for all inputs, decision variables, and outputs
- Liberal use of range names
- Liberal use of boldface, italics, larger font size, coloring, indentation, and other formatting features
- Liberal use of cell comments
- Liberal use of text boxes for assumptions and explanations

Obviously, the formulas and logic in any spreadsheet model must be correct; however, correctness will not take you very far if no one can understand what you've done. Much of the power of spreadsheets derives from their flexibility. A blank spreadsheet is like a big blank canvas waiting for you to insert useful data and formulas. Practically anything is allowed. However, you can abuse this power if you don't have an overall plan for what should go where. Plan ahead before diving in, and if your plan doesn't look good after you start filling in the spreadsheet, revise your plan.

The following example illustrates the process of building a spreadsheet model according to these guidelines. We build this model in stages. In the first stage, we build a model that is correct, but not very readable. At each subsequent stage, we modify the model to make it more readable. You do not need to go through each of these stages explicitly when you build your own models. You should strive for the final stage right away, at least after you get accustomed to the modeling process. The various stages are shown here simply for contrast.

## EXAMPLE | 2.1 ORDERING NCAA T-SHIRTS

It is March, and the annual NCAA Basketball Tournament is down to the final 4 teams. Randy Kitchell is a t-shirt vendor who plans to order t-shirts with the names of the final 4 teams from a manufacturer and then sell them to the fans. The fixed cost of any order is $750, the variable cost per t-shirt to Randy is $6, and Randy's selling price is $10. However, this price will be charged only until a week after the tournament. After that time,

Randy figures that interest in the t-shirts will be low, so he plans to sell all remaining t-shirts, if any, at $4 each. His best guess is that demand for the t-shirts during the full-price period will be 1500. He is thinking about ordering 1400 t-shirts, but he wants to build a spreadsheet model that will let him experiment with the uncertain demand and his order quantity. How should he proceed?

**Objective**   To build a spreadsheet model in a series of stages, all stages being correct but each stage being more readable and flexible than the previous stages.

## Solution

The logic behind the model is simple. If demand is greater than the order quantity, Randy will sell all the t-shirts ordered for $10 each. However, if demand is less than the order quantity, Randy will sell as many t-shirts as are demanded at the $10 price and all leftovers at the $4 price. You can implement this logic in Excel with an IF function.

A first attempt at a spreadsheet model appears in Figure 2.1. (See the file **TShirt Sales Finished.xlsx,** where we have built each stage on a separate worksheet.) You enter a possible demand in cell B3, a possible order quantity in cell B4, and then calculate the profit with the formula

**=-750-6*B4+IF(B3>B4,10*B4,10*B3+4*(B4-B3))**

This formula subtracts the fixed and variable costs and then adds the revenue according to the logic just described.

**Figure 2.1**
Base Model

| | A | B |
|---|---|---|
| 1 | NCAA t-shirt sales | |
| 2 | | |
| 3 | Demand | 1500 |
| 4 | Order | 1400 |
| 5 | Profit | 4850 |

### Excel Function: *IF*

*Excel's IF function is probably already familiar to you, but it's too important not to discuss. It has the syntax =IF(condition,resultIfTrue,resultIfFalse). The* condition *is any expression that is either true or false. The two expressions* resultIfTrue *and* resultIfFalse *can be any expressions you would enter in a cell: numbers, text, or other Excel functions (including other IF functions). Note that if either expression is text, it must be enclosed in double quotes, such as*

**=IF(Score>=90,"A","B")**

*Finally,* Condition *can be complex combinations of conditions, using the keywords AND or OR. Then the syntax is, for example,*

**=IF(AND(Score1<60,Score2<60),"Fail","Pass")**

*Never hard code numbers into Excel formulas. Use cell references instead.*

This model is entirely correct, but it isn't very readable or flexible because it breaks a rule that you should strive never to break: It *hard codes* input values into the profit formula. A spreadsheet model should *never* include input numbers in formulas. Instead, the spreadsheet model should store input values in separate cells and then include *cell references* to these inputs in its formulas. A remedy appears in Figure 2.2. Here, the inputs have been entered in the range B3:B6, and the profit formula in cell B10 has been changed to

**=-B3-B4*B9+IF(B8>B9,B5*B9,10*B8+B6*(B9-B8))**

**Figure 2.2**

Model with Input
Cells

| | A | B |
|---|---|---|
| 1 | NCAA t-shirt sales | |
| 2 | | |
| 3 | Fixed order cost | $750 |
| 4 | Variable cost | $6 |
| 5 | Selling price | $10 |
| 6 | Discount price | $4 |
| 7 | | |
| 8 | Demand | 1500 |
| 9 | Order | 1400 |
| 10 | Profit | $4,850 |

This is exactly the same formula as before, but it's now more flexible. If an input changes, the profit recalculates automatically. Most important, the inputs are no longer "buried" in the formula.[1]

Still, the profit formula is not very readable as it stands. You can make it more readable by using range names. The mechanics of range names are covered in detail later in this chapter. For now, the results of using range names for cells B3 through B6, B8, and B9 are shown in Figure 2.3. This model looks exactly like the previous model, but the formula in cell B10 is now

**=-Fixed_order_cost-Variable_cost\*Order+IF(Demand>Order, Selling_price\*Order,Selling_price\*Demand+Salvage_value\*(Order-Demand))**

This formula is admittedly more long-winded, but it's certainly easier to read.

**Figure 2.3**

Model with Range
Names in Profit
Formula

| | A | B | C | D | E | F |
|---|---|---|---|---|---|---|
| 1 | NCAA t-shirt sales | | | | | |
| 2 | | | | | | |
| 3 | Fixed order cost | $750 | | Range names used | | |
| 4 | Variable cost | $6 | | Demand | ='Model 3'!$B$8 | |
| 5 | Selling price | $10 | | Discount_price | ='Model 3'!$B$6 | |
| 6 | Discount price | $4 | | Fixed_order_cost | ='Model 3'!$B$3 | |
| 7 | | | | Order | ='Model 3'!$B$9 | |
| 8 | Demand | 1500 | | Selling_price | ='Model 3'!$B$5 | |
| 9 | Order | 1400 | | Variable_cost | ='Model 3'!$B$4 | |
| 10 | Profit | $4,850 | | | | |

Randy might like to have profit broken down into various costs and revenues (Figure 2.4), rather than one single profit cell. The formulas in cells B12, B13, B15, and B16 are straightforward, so they are not repeated here. You then accumulate these to get profit in cell B17 with the formula

**=-(B12+B13)+(B15+B16)**

**Figure 2.4**

Model with
Intermediate
Outputs

| | A | B | C | D | E | F |
|---|---|---|---|---|---|---|
| 1 | NCAA t-shirt sales | | | | | |
| 2 | | | | | | |
| 3 | Fixed order cost | $750 | | Range names used | | |
| 4 | Variable cost | $6 | | Demand | ='Model 4'!$B$8 | |
| 5 | Selling price | $10 | | Discount_price | ='Model 4'!$B$6 | |
| 6 | Discount price | $4 | | Fixed_order_cost | ='Model 4'!$B$3 | |
| 7 | | | | Order | ='Model 4'!$B$9 | |
| 8 | Demand | 1500 | | Selling_price | ='Model 4'!$B$5 | |
| 9 | Order | 1400 | | Variable_cost | ='Model 4'!$B$4 | |
| 10 | | | | | | |
| 11 | Costs | | | | | |
| 12 | Fixed cost | $750 | | | | |
| 13 | Variable costs | $8,400 | | | | |
| 14 | Revenues | | | | | |
| 15 | Full-price shirts | $14,000 | | | | |
| 16 | Discount-price shirts | $0 | | | | |
| 17 | Profit | $4,850 | | | | |

[1] Some people refer to such numbers buried in formulas as *magic numbers* because they just seem to appear out of nowhere. Avoid magic numbers!

**Figure 2.5**

Model with
Category Labels and
Color Coding

| | A | B | C | D | E | F |
|---|---|---|---|---|---|---|
| 1 | NCAA t-shirt sales | | | | | |
| 2 | | | | | | |
| 3 | **Input variables** | | | **Range names used** | | |
| 4 | Fixed order cost | $750 | | Demand | ='Model 5'!$B$10 | |
| 5 | Variable cost | $6 | | Discount_price | ='Model 5'!$B$7 | |
| 6 | Selling price | $10 | | Fixed_order_cost | ='Model 5'!$B$4 | |
| 7 | Discount price | $4 | | Order | ='Model 5'!$B$13 | |
| 8 | | | | Selling_price | ='Model 5'!$B$6 | |
| 9 | **Uncertain variable** | | | Variable_cost | ='Model 5'!$B$5 | |
| 10 | Demand | 1500 | | | | |
| 11 | | | | | | |
| 12 | **Decision variable** | | | | | |
| 13 | Order | 1400 | | | | |
| 14 | | | | | | |
| 15 | **Output variables** | | | | | |
| 16 | Costs | | | | | |
| 17 | Fixed cost | $750 | | | | |
| 18 | Variable costs | $8,400 | | | | |
| 19 | Revenues | | | | | |
| 20 | Full-price shirts | $14,000 | | | | |
| 21 | Discount-price shirts | $0 | | | | |
| 22 | Profit | $4,850 | | | | |

Of course, range names could be used for these intermediate output cells, but it's probably more work than it's worth. You must always use some judgment when deciding how many range names to use.

If Randy's assistant is presented with this model, how does she know at a glance which cells contain inputs or decision variables or outputs? Labels and/or color coding can help to distinguish these types. A blue/red/gray color-coding style has been applied in Figure 2.5, along with descriptive labels in boldface. The blue cells at the top are input cells, the red cell in the middle is a decision variable, and the gray cell at the bottom is the key output.[2] There is nothing sacred about this particular convention. Feel free to adopt your own convention and style, but be sure to use it consistently.

The model in Figure 2.5 is still not the last word on this problem. As shown in later examples, you could create data tables to see how sensitive profit is to the inputs, the demand, and the order quantity. You could also create charts to show any numerical results graphically. But this is enough for now. You can now see that the model in Figure 2.5 is much more readable and flexible than the original model in Figure 2.1. ∎

Because good spreadsheet style is so important, an appendix to this chapter is included that discusses a few tools for editing and documenting your spreadsheet models. Use these tools right away and as you progress through the book.

In the rest of this chapter, we discuss a number of interesting examples and introduce important modeling concepts (such as sensitivity analysis), important Excel features (such as data tables), and even some important business concepts (such as

---

### FUNDAMENTAL INSIGHT

#### Spreadsheet Layout and Documentation

If you want your spreadsheets to be used (and you want your stock in your company to rise), give a lot of thought to your spreadsheet layout and then document your work carefully. For layout, think about whether certain data are best oriented in rows or columns, whether your work is better placed in a single sheet or in multiple sheets, and so on. For documentation, you can use descriptive labels and headings, color coding and borders, cell comments, and text boxes to make your spreadsheets more readable. It takes time and careful planning to design and then document your spreadsheet models, but the time is well spent. And if you come back in a few days to a spreadsheet model you developed and you can't make heads or tails of it, don't be afraid to redesign your work completely—from the ground up.

---

[2] For users of the previous edition, we find it easier in Excel 2007 to color the cells rather than place colored borders around them, so we adopt this convention throughout the book. This color convention shows up clearly in the Excel files that accompany the book. However, in this two-color book (shades of gray and blue), it is difficult to "see" the color-coding scheme. We recommend that you look not only at the figures in the book, but at the actual Excel files.

net present value). To get the most from these examples, follow along at your own PC, starting with a blank spreadsheet. It's one thing to read about spreadsheet modeling; it's quite another to actually *do* it!

## 2.3 COST PROJECTIONS

In this next example, a company wants to project its costs of producing products, given that material and labor costs are likely to increase through time. We build a simple model and then use Excel's charting capabilities to obtain a graphical image of projected costs.

---

**2.2**  **PROJECTING THE COSTS OF BOOKSHELVES AT WOODWORKS**

The Woodworks Company produces a variety of custom-designed wood furniture for its customers. One favorite item is a bookshelf, made from either cherry or oak. The company knows that wood prices and labor costs are likely to increase in the future. Table 2.1 shows the number of board-feet and labor hours required for a bookshelf, the current costs per board-foot and labor hour, and the anticipated annual increases in these costs. (The top row indicates that either type of bookshelf requires 30 board-feet of wood and 16 hours of labor.) Build a spreadsheet model that enables the company to experiment with the growth rates in wood and labor costs so that a manager can see, both numerically and graphically, how the costs of the bookshelves vary in the next few years.

**Table 2.1**   **Input Data for Manufacturing a Bookshelf**

| Resource | Cherry | Oak | Labor |
|---|---|---|---|
| Required per bookshelf | 30 | 30 | 16 |
| Current unit cost | $7.30 | $4.30 | $18.50 |
| Anticipated annual cost increase | 2.4% | 1.7% | 1.5% |

**Business Objectives**[3]   To build a model that allows Woodworks to see, numerically and graphically, how its costs of manufacturing bookshelves increase in the future and to allow the company to answer what-if questions with this model.

**Excel Objectives**   To learn good spreadsheet practices, to enable copying formulas with the careful use of relative and absolute addresses, and to create line charts from multiple series of data.

### Solution

Listing the key variables in a table before developing the actual spreadsheet model is useful, so we'll continue to do this in many later examples (see Table 2.2.) This practice forces you to examine the roles of the variables—which are inputs, which are decision variables, and which are outputs. Although the variables and their roles are fairly clear for this example, later examples will require more thought.

---

[3] In later chapters, we simply list the "Objective" of each example as we did in Example 2.1 in this chapter. However, because this chapter has been written to enhance basic spreadsheet skills, we separate the business objectives from the Excel objectives.

## Table 2.2 Key Variables for the Bookshelf Manufacturing Example

| | |
|---|---|
| **Input variables** | Wood and labor requirements per bookshelf, current unit costs of wood and labor, anticipated annual increases in unit costs |
| **Output variables** | Projected unit costs of wood and labor, projected total bookshelf costs |

The reasoning behind the model is straightforward. You first project the unit costs for wood and labor into the future. Then for any year, you multiply the unit costs by the required numbers of board-feet and labor hours per bookshelf. Finally, you add the wood and labor costs to obtain the total cost of a bookshelf.

### DEVELOPING THE SPREADSHEET MODEL

The completed spreadsheet model appears in Figure 2.6 and in the file **Bookshelf Costs.xlsx.**[4] We develop it with the following steps.

**Figure 2.6**
Bookshelf Cost Model

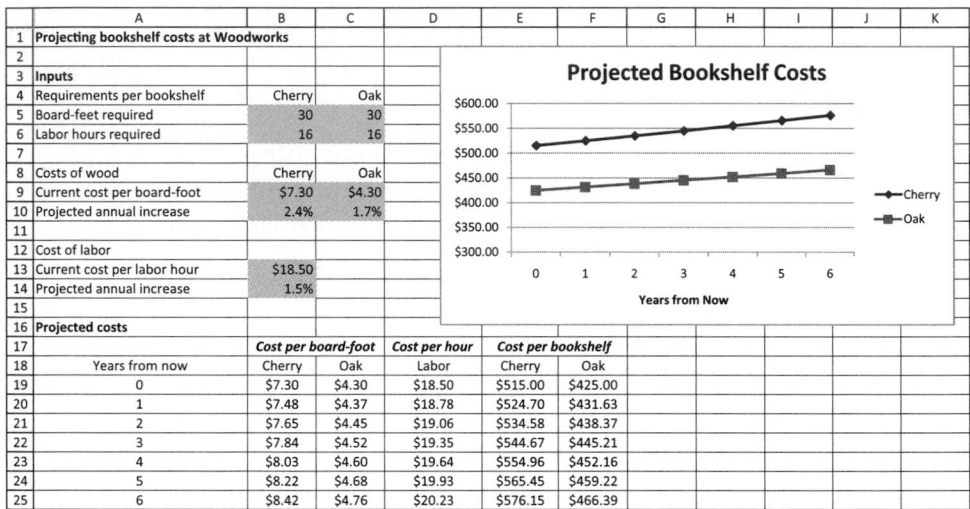

*Always enter input values in input cells and then refer to them in Excel formulas. Do not bury input values in formulas!*

**1 Inputs.** You should usually enter the inputs for a model in the upper-left corner of a worksheet as you can see in the shaded ranges in Figure 2.6, using the data from Table 2.1. We have used our standard convention of coloring inputs—the numbers from the statement of the problem—blue. You can develop your own convention, but the input cells should be distinguished in some way. Note that the inputs are grouped logically and are explained with appropriate labels. You should always document your spreadsheet model with informational labels. Also, note that by entering inputs explicitly in input cells, you can *refer* to them later with Excel formulas.

**2 Design output table.** Think ahead of time how you want to structure your outputs. We created a table where there is a row for every year in the future (year 0 corresponds to the current year), there are three columns for projected unit costs (columns B–D), and there are two columns for projected total bookshelf costs (columns E–F). The headings reflect this design. Of course, this isn't the only possible design, but it works well. The important point is that you should have *some* logical design in mind before diving in.

---

[4] The CD-ROM accompanying this book includes templates and completed files for all examples in the book, where all of the latter have "Finished" appended to their file names. However, especially in this chapter, we suggest that you start with a blank spreadsheet and follow the step-by-step instructions on your own.

**3** **Projected unit costs of wood.** The dollar values in the range B19:F25 are all calculated from Excel formulas. Although the logic in this example is straightforward, it is still important to have a strategy in mind before you enter formulas. In particular, you should design your spreadsheet so that you can enter a *single* formula and then copy it whenever possible. This saves work and avoids errors. For the costs per board-foot in columns B and C, enter the formula

**=B9**

in cell B19 and copy it to cell C19. Then enter the general formula

**=B19*(1+B$10)**

in cell B20 and copy it to the range B20:C25. We assume you know the rules for absolute and relative addresses (dollar sign for absolute, no dollar sign for relative), but it takes some planning to use these so that copying is possible. Make sure you understand why we made row 10 absolute but column B relative.

**Excel Tip:** *Relative and Absolute Addresses in Formulas*
*Relative and absolute addresses are used in Excel formulas to facilitate copying. A dollar sign next to a column or row address indicates that the address is absolute and will not change when copying. The lack of a dollar sign indicates that the address is relative and will change when copying. After you select a cell in a formula, you can press the F4 key repeatedly to cycle through the relative/absolute possibilities, for example, =B4 (both column and row relative), =$B$4 (both column and row absolute), =B$4 (column relative, row absolute), and =$B4 (column absolute, row relative).*

**4** **Projected unit labor costs.** To calculate projected hourly labor costs, enter the formula

**=B13**

in cell D19. Then enter the formula

**=D19*(1+B$14)**

in cell D20 and copy it down column D.

**5** **Projected bookshelf costs.** Each bookshelf cost is the sum of its wood and labor costs. By a careful use of absolute and relative addresses, you can enter a single formula for these costs—for all years and for both types of wood. To do this, enter the formula

**=B$5*B19+B$6*$D19**

in cell E19 and copy it to the range E19:F25. The idea here is that the units of wood and labor per bookshelf are always in rows 5 and 6, and the projected unit labor cost is always in column D, but all other references must be relative to allow copying.

**6** **Chart.** A chart is an invaluable addition to any table of data, especially in the business world, so charting in Excel is a skill worth mastering. Although not everyone agrees, the many changes Microsoft made regarding charts in Excel 2007 help you create charts more efficiently and effectively. We illustrate some of the possibilities here, but we urge you to experiment with other possibilities on your own. Start by selecting the range E18:F25—yes, including the labels in row 18. Next, click on the Line dropdown on the Insert ribbon and select the Line with Markers type. (The various options in the Charts group replace the Chart Wizard in previous versions of Excel.) You instantly get the basic line chart you want, with one series for Cherry and another for Oak. Also, when the chart is selected (has a border around it), you see three new Chart Tools ribbons: Design, Layout, and Format. The most important button on any of these ribbons is the Select Data

**Figure 2.7**

Select Data
Dialog Box

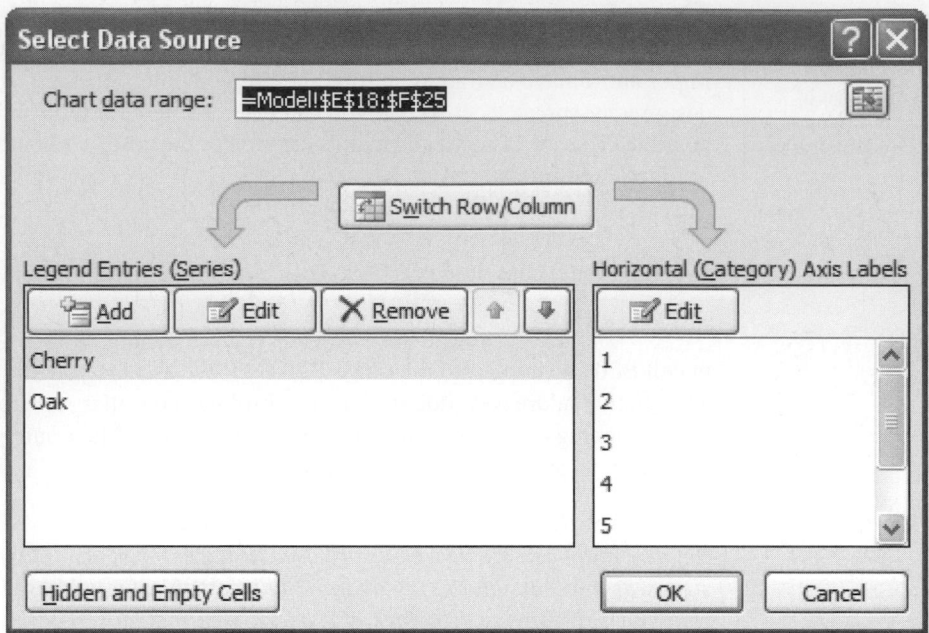

**Figure 2.8**

Dialog Box for
Changing
Horizontal
Axis Labels

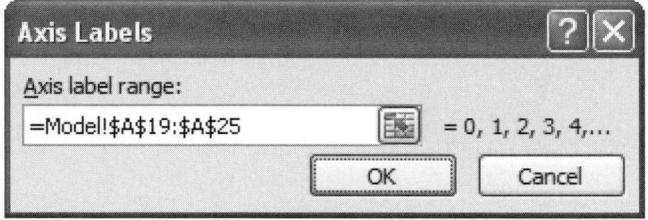

*The many chart
options are easily
accessible from the
three new Chart Tools
ribbons in Excel 2007.
Don't be afraid to
experiment with
them to produce
professional-looking
charts.*

button on the Design ribbon. It lets you choose the ranges of the data for charting in case Excel's default choices (which are based on the selected range when you create the chart) are wrong. Click on Select Data now to obtain the dialog box in Figure 2.7. On the left, you control the one or more series being charted; on the right, you control the data used for the horizontal axis. By selecting E18:F25, you have the series on the left correct, including the names of these series (Cherry and Oak), but if you didn't, you could select one of the series and click on Edit to change it. The data on the horizontal axis is currently the default 1, 2, and so on. We want it to be the data in column A. So click on the Edit button on the right and select the range A19:A25. (See Figure 2.8.) Your chart is now correctly labeled and charts the correct data. Beyond this, you can experiment with various formatting options to make the chart even better. For example, we rescaled the vertical axis to start at $300 rather than $0 (right-click on the numbers on the vertical axis and select Format Axis, or look at the many options under the Axes dropdown on the Layout ribbon), and we added a chart title at the top and a title for the horizontal axis at the bottom (see buttons on the Labels group on the Layout ribbon). You can spend a lot of time fine-tuning charts—maybe even *too* much time—but professional-looking charts are definitely appreciated.

## Using the Model for What-If Questions

The model in Figure 2.6 can now be used to answer any what-if questions. In fact, many models are built for the purpose of permitting experimentation with various scenarios. The important point is that the model has been built in such a way that a manager can enter any desired values in the input cells, and all the outputs, including the chart, update automatically. As a simple example, if the annual percentage increases for wood costs are twice as high as Woodworks anticipated, you can enter these higher values in row 10 and immediately see the effect, as shown in Figure 2.9. By comparing bookshelf costs in this scenario to those in the original scenario, the projected cost in year 6 for cherry bookshelves, for example, increases by about 6.5%, from $576.15 to $613.80.

**Figure 2.9**    Effect of Higher Increases in Wood Costs

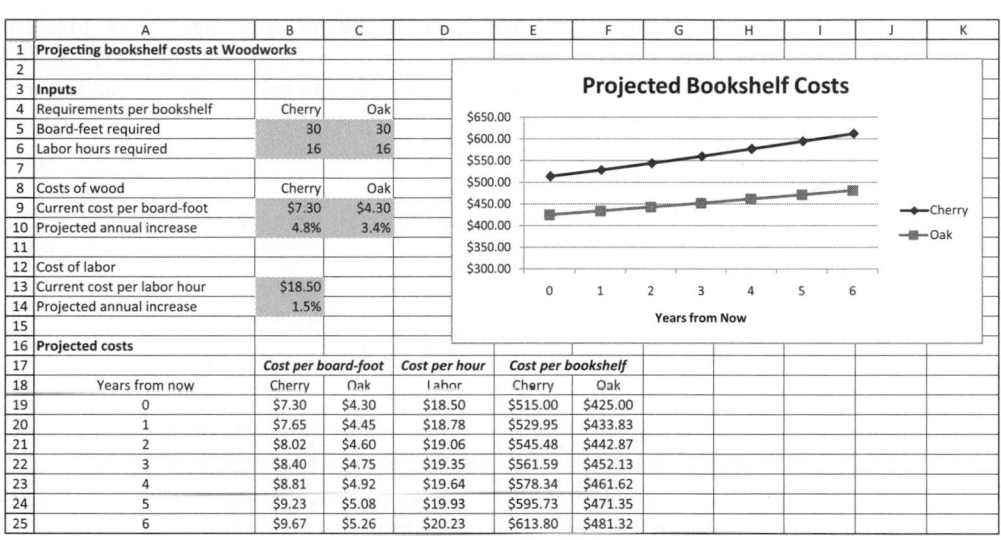

| | A | B | C | D | E | F | G | H | I | J | K |
|---|---|---|---|---|---|---|---|---|---|---|---|
| 1 | Projecting bookshelf costs at Woodworks | | | | | | | | | | |
| 2 | | | | | | | | | | | |
| 3 | Inputs | | | | | | | | | | |
| 4 | Requirements per bookshelf | Cherry | Oak | | | | | | | | |
| 5 | Board-feet required | 30 | 30 | | | | | | | | |
| 6 | Labor hours required | 16 | 16 | | | | | | | | |
| 7 | | | | | | | | | | | |
| 8 | Costs of wood | Cherry | Oak | | | | | | | | |
| 9 | Current cost per board-foot | $7.30 | $4.30 | | | | | | | | |
| 10 | Projected annual increase | 4.8% | 3.4% | | | | | | | | |
| 11 | | | | | | | | | | | |
| 12 | Cost of labor | | | | | | | | | | |
| 13 | Current cost per labor hour | $18.50 | | | | | | | | | |
| 14 | Projected annual increase | 1.5% | | | | | | | | | |
| 15 | | | | | | | | | | | |
| 16 | Projected costs | | | | | | | | | | |
| 17 | | Cost per board-foot | | Cost per hour | Cost per bookshelf | | | | | | |
| 18 | Years from now | Cherry | Oak | Labor | Cherry | Oak | | | | | |
| 19 | 0 | $7.30 | $4.30 | $18.50 | $515.00 | $425.00 | | | | | |
| 20 | 1 | $7.65 | $4.45 | $18.78 | $529.95 | $433.83 | | | | | |
| 21 | 2 | $8.02 | $4.60 | $19.06 | $545.48 | $442.87 | | | | | |
| 22 | 3 | $8.40 | $4.75 | $19.35 | $561.59 | $452.13 | | | | | |
| 23 | 4 | $8.81 | $4.92 | $19.64 | $578.34 | $461.62 | | | | | |
| 24 | 5 | $9.23 | $5.08 | $19.93 | $595.73 | $471.35 | | | | | |
| 25 | 6 | $9.67 | $5.26 | $20.23 | $613.80 | $481.32 | | | | | |

*A carefully constructed model—with no input numbers buried in formulas—allows a manager to answer many what-if questions with a few keystrokes.*

You should appreciate by now why burying input numbers inside Excel formulas is such a bad practice. For example, if you had buried the annual increases of wood costs from row 10 in the formulas in columns B and C, imagine how difficult it would be to answer the what-if question in the previous paragraph. You would first have to find and then change all the numbers in the formulas, which is a lot of work. Even worse, it's likely to lead to errors. ∎

## 2.4 BREAKEVEN ANALYSIS

Many business problems require you to find the appropriate level of some activity. This might be the level that maximizes profit (or minimizes cost), or it might be the level that allows a company to break even—no profit, no loss. We discuss a typical breakeven analysis in the following example.

EXAMPLE | **2.3 BREAKEVEN ANALYSIS AT GREAT THREADS**

The Great Threads Company sells hand-knitted sweaters. The company is planning to print a catalog of its products and undertake a direct mail campaign. The cost of printing the catalog is $20,000 plus $0.10 per catalog. The cost of mailing each catalog (including postage, order forms, and buying names from a mail-order database) is $0.15. In addition, the company plans to include direct reply envelopes in its mailings and incurs $0.20 in extra costs for each direct mail envelope used by a respondent. The average size of a customer order is $40, and the company's variable cost per order (due primarily to labor and material costs) averages about 80% of the order's value—that is, $32. The company plans to mail 100,000 catalogs. It wants to develop a spreadsheet model to answer the following questions:

1. How does a change in the response rate affect profit?

2. For what response rate does the company break even?

3. If the company estimates a response rate of 3%, should it proceed with the mailing?

4. How does the presence of uncertainty affect the usefulness of the model?

**Business Objectives**   To create a model to determine the company's profit and to see how sensitive the profit is to the response rate from the mailing.

**Excel Objectives**   To learn how to work with range names, to learn how to answer what-if questions with one-way data tables, to introduce Excel's Goal Seek tool, and to learn how to document and audit Excel models with cell comments and the auditing toolbar.

## Solution

The key variables appear in Table 2.3. Note that we have designated all variables as input variables, decision variables, or output variables. Furthermore, there is typically a key output variable, in this case, profit, that is of most concern. (In the next few chapters, we refer to it as the "target" variable.) Therefore, we distinguish this key output variable from the other output variables that we calculate along the way.

---

**Table 2.3**   **Key Variables in Great Threads Problem**

| | |
|---|---|
| **Input variables** | Various unit costs, average order size, response rate |
| **Decision variable** | Number mailed |
| **Key output variable** | Profit |
| **Other output variables** | Number of responses, revenue, and cost totals |

---

The logic for converting inputs and decision variable into outputs is straightforward. After you do this, you can investigate how the response rate affects the profit with a sensitivity analysis.

The completed spreadsheet model appears in Figure 2.10. (See the file **Breakeven Analysis.xlsx**.) First, note the clear layout of the model. The input cells are colored blue, they are separated from the outputs, headings are boldfaced, several headings are indented, numbers are formatted appropriately, and a list to the right spells out all range names we have used. (See the upcoming Excel Tip on how to create this list.) Also, following the convention we use throughout the book, the decision variable (number mailed) is colored red, and the bottom-line output (profit) is colored gray.

*Adopt some layout and formatting conventions, even if they differ from ours, to make your spreadsheets readable and easy to follow.*

**Figure 2.10**  Great Threads Model

| | A | B | C | D | E | F | G | H | I |
|---|---|---|---|---|---|---|---|---|---|
| 1 | Great Threads direct mail model | | | | | | Range names used | | |
| 2 | | | | | | | Average_order | =Model!$B$11 | |
| 3 | Catalog inputs | | | Model of responses | | | Fixed_cost_of_printing | =Model!$B$4 | |
| 4 | Fixed cost of printing | $20,000 | | Response rate | 8% | | Number_mailed | =Model!$B$8 | |
| 5 | Variable cost of printing mailing | $0.25 | | Number of responses | 8000 | | Number_of_responses | =Model!$E$5 | |
| 6 | | | | | | | Profit | =Model!$E$13 | |
| 7 | Decision variable | | | Model of revenue, costs, and profit | | | Response_rate | =Model!$E$4 | |
| 8 | Number mailed | 100000 | | Total Revenue | $320,000 | | Total_cost | =Model!$E$12 | |
| 9 | | | | Fixed cost of printing | $20,000 | | Total_Revenue | =Model!$E$8 | |
| 10 | Order inputs | | | Total variable cost of printing mailing | $25,000 | | Variable_cost_of_printing_mailing | =Model!$B$5 | |
| 11 | Average order | $40 | | Total variable cost of orders | $257,600 | | Variable_cost_per_order | =Model!$B$12 | |
| 12 | Variable cost per order | $32.20 | | Total cost | $302,600 | | | | |
| 13 | | | | Profit | $17,400 | | | | |

*We refer to this as the Create from Selection shortcut. If you like it, you can get the dialog box in Figure 2.11 even quicker: Press **Ctrl-Shift-F3**.*

**Excel Tip:** *Creating Range Names*

*To create a range name for a range of cells (which could be a single cell), highlight the cell(s), click in the Name Box just to the left of the Formula Bar, and type a range name. Alternatively, if a column of labels appears next to the cells to be range-named, you can use these labels as the range names. To do this, highlight the labels and the cells to be named (for example, A4:B5 in Figure 2.10), select the Create from Selection item on the Formulas ribbon, and make sure the appropriate box in the resulting dialog box (see Figure 2.11) is checked. The labels in our example are to the left of the cells to be named, so the Left column box should be checked. This is a very quick way to create range names, and we did it for all range names in the example. In fact, by keeping your finger on the Ctrl key, you can select multiple ranges.[5] After all your ranges are selected, you can sometimes create all your range names in one step. Note that if a label contains any "illegal" range-name characters, such as a space, the illegal characters are converted to underscores.*

**Figure 2.11**

Range Name Create Dialog Box

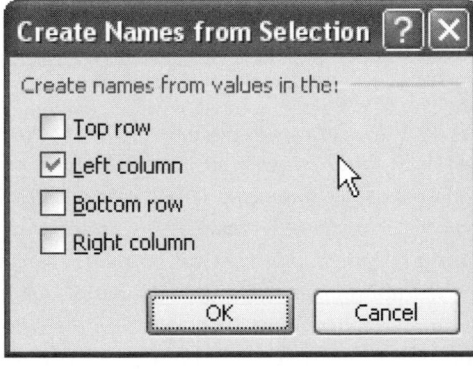

*If you like this tip, you can perform it even faster: Press the **F3** key to bring up the Paste Name dialog box.*

**Excel Tip:** *Pasting Range Names*

*Including a list of the range names in your spreadsheet is often useful. To do this, select a cell (such as cell G4 in Figure 2.10), select the Use in Formula dropdown from the Formulas ribbon, and then click on the Paste List option. You get a list of all range names and their cell addresses. However, if you change any of these range names (delete one, for example), the paste list does not update automatically; you have to create it again.*

---

[5] Many users apparently believe range names are more work than they are worth. This shortcut for creating range names remedies that problem.

## DEVELOPING THE SPREADSHEET MODEL

To create this model, proceed through the following steps.

**1** **Headings and range names.** We've named a lot of cells, more than you might want to name, but you'll see their value when you create formulas. In general, we strongly support range names, but it is possible to go overboard. You can waste a lot of time naming ranges that do not *really* need to be named. Of course, you can use the Create from Selection shortcut described previously to speed up the process.[6]

**2** **Values of input variables and the decision variable.** Enter these values and format them appropriately. As usual, we've used our blue/red/gray color-coding scheme. Note that the number mailed has been designated as a *decision* variable, not as an input variable (and it's colored red, not blue). This is because the company gets to choose the value of this variable. Finally, note that some of the values have been combined in the statement of the problem. For example, the $32.20 in cell B12 is really 80% of the $40 average order size, plus the $0.20 per return envelope. To document this process, comments appear in a few cells, as shown in Figure 2.12.

**Figure 2.12**   Cell Comments in Model

| | A | B | C | D | E | F | G | H | I |
|---|---|---|---|---|---|---|---|---|---|
| 1 | Great Threads direct mail model | | | | | | Range names used | | |
| 2 | | | | | | Trial value, will do | | | =Model!$B$11 |
| 3 | Catalog inputs | | | Model of responses | | sensitivity analysis on | printing | | =Model!$B$4 |
| 4 | Fixed cost of printing | $20,000 | Includes $0.10 for | | 8% | | Number_mailed | | =Model!$B$8 |
| 5 | Variable cost of printing mailing | $0.25 | printing and $0.15 for mailing each catalog | ponses | 8000 | | Number_of_responses | | =Model!$E$5 |
| 6 | | | | | | | Profit | | =Model!$E$13 |
| 7 | Decision variable | | | Model of revenue, costs, and profit | | | Response_rate | | =Model!$E$4 |
| 8 | Number mailed | 100000 | | Total Revenue | $320,000 | | Total_cost | | =Model!$E$12 |
| 9 | | | | Fixed cost of printing | $20,000 | | Total_Revenue | | =Model!$E$8 |
| 10 | Order inputs | | Includes 80% of the average | t of printing mailing | $25,000 | | Variable_cost_of_printing_mailing | | =Model!$B$5 |
| 11 | Average order | $40 | $40 order size, plus $0.20 per return envelope | t of orders | $257,600 | | Variable_cost_per_order | | =Model!$B$12 |
| 12 | Variable cost per order | $32.20 | | Total cost | $302,600 | | | | |
| 13 | | | | Profit | $17,400 | | | | |

**Excel Tip:** *Inserting Cell Comments*

*Inserting comments in cells is a great way to document your spreadsheet models without introducing excessive clutter. To enter a comment in a cell, right-click on the cell, select the Insert Comment item, and type your comment. This creates a little red mark in the cell, indicating a comment, and you can see the comment by resting the mouse pointer over the cell. When a cell contains a comment, you can edit or delete the comment by right-clicking on the cell and selecting the appropriate item. If you want all the cell comments to be visible (for example, in a printout as in Figure 2.12), click on the Office button, then on Excel Options, then on the Advanced link, and select the Comment & Indicator option from the Display group. Note that the Indicator Only option is the default.*

**3** **Model the responses.** We have not yet specified the response rate to the mailing, so enter *any* reasonable value, such as 8%, in the Response_rate cell. We will perform sensitivity on this value later on. Then enter the formula

**=Number_mailed*Response_rate**

in cell E5. (Are you starting to see the advantage of range names?)

---

[6] We heard of one company that does not allow any formulas in its corporate spreadsheets to include cell references; they must all reference range names. This is pretty extreme, but that company's formulas are certainly easy to read!

**4** **Model the revenue, costs, and profits.** Enter the formula

=**Number_of_responses*Average_order**

in cell E8, enter the formulas

=**Fixed_cost_of_printing**

=**Variable_cost_of_printing_mailing*Number_mailed**

and

=**Number_of_responses*Variable_cost_per_order**

in cells E9, E10, and E11, enter the formula

=**SUM(E9:E11)**

in cell E12, and enter the formula

=**Total_revenue-Total_cost**

in cell E13. These formulas should all be self-explanatory, especially because of the range names used.

## Forming a One-Way Data Table

*Data tables are also called what-if tables. They let you see what happens to selected outputs if selected inputs change.*

Now that a basic model has been created, we can answer the questions posed by the company. For question 1, we form a one-way data table to show how profit varies with the response rate as shown in Figure 2.13. Data tables are used often in this book, so make sure you understand how to create them. We walk you through the procedure once or twice, but from then on, you are on your own. First, enter a sequence of trial values of the response rate in column A, and enter a "link" to profit in cell B17 with the formula =**Profit.** This cell is shaded for emphasis, but this isn't necessary. (In general, other outputs could be part of the table, and they would be placed in columns C, D, and so on. There would be a link to each output in row 17.) Finally, highlight the entire table range, A17:B27, and select Data Table from the What-If Analysis dropdown on the Data ribbon to bring up the dialog box in Figure 2.14. Fill it in as shown to indicate that the only input, Response_rate, is listed along a column. (You can enter either a range name or a cell address in this dialog box.)

**Figure 2.13**
Data Table for Profit

| | A | B | C | D | E | F |
|---|---|---|---|---|---|---|
| 15 | Question 1 - sensitivity of profit to response rate | | | | | |
| 16 | Response rate | Profit | | | | |
| 17 | | $17,400 | | | | |
| 18 | 1% | -$37,200 | | | | |
| 19 | 2% | -$29,400 | | | | |
| 20 | 3% | -$21,600 | | | | |
| 21 | 4% | -$13,800 | | | | |
| 22 | 5% | -$6,000 | | | | |
| 23 | 6% | $1,800 | | | | |
| 24 | 7% | $9,600 | | | | |
| 25 | 8% | $17,400 | | | | |
| 26 | 9% | $25,200 | | | | |
| 27 | 10% | $33,000 | | | | |

Profit versus Response Rate

**Figure 2.14**
Data Table Dialog Box

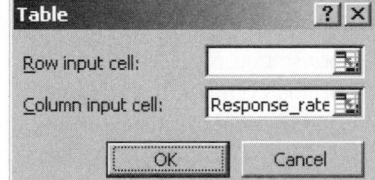

When you click on OK, Excel substitutes each response rate value in the table into the Response_rate cell, recalculates profit, and reports it in the table. For a final touch, we have created a scatter chart of the values in the data table. (To do this, highlight the A18:B27 range and select the default type of Scatter from the Insert ribbon. Then you can fix it up by adding titles, removing the legend, and so on to suit your taste.)

### Excel Tool: *One-Way Data Table*

*A one-way data table allows you to see how one or more output variables vary as a single input variable varies over a selected range of values. These input values can be arranged vertically in a column or horizontally in a row. We'll explain only the vertical arrangement because it's the most common. To create the table, enter the input values in a column range, such as A18:A27 of Figure 2.13, and enter links to one or more output cells in columns to the right and one row above the inputs, as in cell B17 of Figure 2.13. Then highlight the entire table, beginning with the upper-left blank cell (A17 in the figure), select Data Table from the What-If Analysis dropdown on the Data ribbon, and fill in the resulting dialog box as in Figure 2.14. Leave the Row Input cell blank and use the cell where the original value of the input variable lives as the Column Input cell. When you click on OK, each value in the left column of the table is substituted into the column input cell, the spreadsheet recalculates, and the resulting value of the output is placed in the table. Also, if you click anywhere in the body of the table (B18:B27 in the figure), you will see that Excel has entered the =TABLE function to remind you that a data table lives here. Note that the column input cell must be on the same worksheet as the table itself; otherwise, Excel issues an error.*

---

### FUNDAMENTAL INSIGHT

#### The Power of Data Tables

Many Excel users (most of them?) are unaware of data tables, but they shouldn't be. Data tables are among the most powerful and useful tools Excel has to offer. After you have developed a model that relates inputs to outputs, you can then build data tables in a matter of seconds to see how the outputs vary as key inputs vary over some range. Data tables are the perfect means for answering a large number of what-if questions quickly and easily.

---

As the chart indicates, profit increases in a linear manner as the response rate varies. More specifically, each percentage point increase in the response rate increases profit by $7800. Here is the reasoning. Each percentage point increase in response rate results in $100,000(0.01) = 1000$ more orders. Each order yields a revenue of $40, on average, but incurs a variable cost of $32.20. The net gain in profit is $7.80 per order, or $7800 for 1000 orders.

## USING GOAL SEEK

*The purpose of the Goal Seek tool is to solve one equation in one unknown. Here, we find the response rate that makes profit equal to 0.*

From the data table, you can see that profit changes from negative to positive when the response rate is somewhere between 5% and 6%. Question 2 asks for the exact breakeven point. This could be found by trial and error, but it's easier to use Excel's Goal Seek tool. Essentially, Goal Seek is used to solve a *single* equation in a *single* unknown. Here, the equation is Profit=0, and the unknown is the response rate. In Excel terminology, the unknown is called the **changing cell** because you can change it to make the equation true. To implement Goal Seek, select Goal Seek from the What-If Analysis dropdown on the Data ribbon and fill in the resulting dialog box as shown in Figure 2.15. (Range names or cell addresses can be used in the top and bottom boxes, but a *number* must be entered in the middle box.) After you click on OK, the Response_rate and Profit cells have values 5.77% and $0. In words, if the response rate is 5.77%, Great Threads breaks even. If the response rate is greater than 5.77%, the company makes money; if the rate is less than 5.77%, the company loses money. Of course, this assumes that the company mails 100,000 catalogs. If it sends more or fewer catalogs, the breakeven response rate will change.

**Figure 2.15**
Goal Seek Dialog
Box

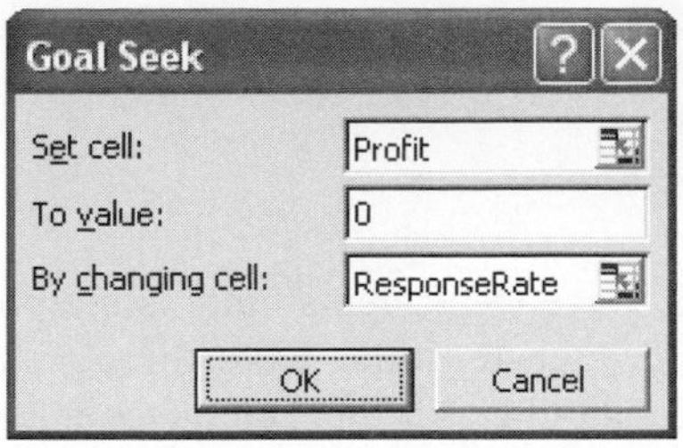

### Excel Tool: *Goal Seek*

*The purpose of the Goal Seek tool is to solve one equation in one unknown. Specifically, Goal Seek allows you to vary a single* input *cell to force a single* output *cell to a selected value. To use it, select Goal Seek from the What-If Analysis dropdown on the Data ribbon and fill in the resulting dialog box in Figure 2.15. Enter a reference to the output cell in the Set cell box, enter the numeric value you want the output cell to equal in the To value box, and enter a reference to the input cell in the By changing cell box. Note that Goal Seek sometimes stops when the Set cell is close, but not* exactly *equal to, the desired value. To improve Goal Seek's accuracy, click on the Office button, then Excel Options, and then the Formulas link. Then check the Enable iterative calculation box and reduce Maximum Change to any desired level of precision. We chose a precision level of 0.000001. For this level of precision, Goal Seek searches until profit is within 0.000001 of the desired value, $0.*

### Limitations of the Model

Question 3 asks whether the company should proceed with the mailing if the response rate is only 3%. From the data table (see Figure 2.13), the apparent answer is "no" because profit is negative. However, like many companies, we are taking a short-term view with this reasoning. We should realize that many customers who respond to direct mail will *re order* in the future. The company nets $7.80 per order. If each of the respondents ordered two more times, say, the company would earn 3000($7.80)(2) = $46,800 more than appears in the model, and profit would then be positive. The moral is that managers must look at the long-term impact of their decisions. However, if you want to incorporate the long term explicitly into the model, you must build a more complex model.

*Later chapters, especially Chapters 10 through 12, deal explicitly with uncertainty.*

Finally, question 4 asks about the impact of uncertainty in the model. Obviously, not all model inputs are known with certainty. For example, the size of an order is not always $40—it might range, say, from $10 to $100. When there is a high degree of uncertainty about model inputs, it makes little sense to talk about *the* profit level or *the* breakeven response rate. It makes more sense to talk about the *probability* that profit will have a certain value or the *probability* that the company will break even. You'll see how this can be done in the following example and in many more such examples in Chapters 10 through 12.

### Using the Formula Auditing Tool

The model in this example is fairly small and simple. Even so, we can use a little-known Excel feature to see how all the parts fit together. This is the Formula Auditing tool, which is available on the Formulas ribbon. (It was buried in a menu in previous versions of Excel, but is now much more prominent, as it should be, in Excel 2007) See Figure 2.16.

**Figure 2.16**

Formula Auditing
Toolbar

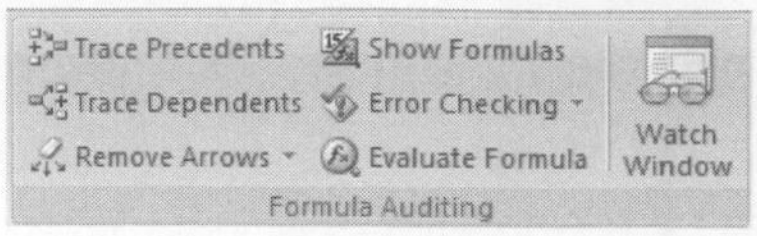

*The Formula Auditing
tool is indispensable
for untangling the logic
in a spreadsheet,
especially if someone
else developed it!*

The Trace Precedents and Trace Dependents buttons are probably the most useful buttons in this group. To see which formulas have direct links to the Number_of_responses cell, select this cell and click on the Trace Dependents button. Arrows are drawn to each cell that directly depends on the number of responses, as shown in Figure 2.17. Alternatively, to see which cells are used to create the formula in the Total_revenue cell, select this cell and click on the Trace Precedents button. Now you see that the Average_order and Number_of_responses cells are used directly to calculate revenue, as shown in Figure 2.18. Using these two buttons, you can trace your logic (or someone else's logic) as far backward or forward as you like. When you are finished, just click on the Remove Arrows button.

**Figure 2.17**

Dependents of
Number_of_
responses Cell

| | A | B | C | D | E |
|---|---|---|---|---|---|
| 1 | Great Threads direct mail model | | | | |
| 2 | | | | | |
| 3 | Catalog inputs | | | Model of responses | |
| 4 | Fixed cost of printing | $20,000 | | Response rate | 8% |
| 5 | Variable cost of printing mailing | $0.25 | | Number of responses | 8000 |
| 6 | | | | | |
| 7 | Decision variable | | | Model of revenue, costs, and profit | |
| 8 | Number mailed | 100000 | | Total Revenue | $320,000 |
| 9 | | | | Fixed cost of printing | $20,000 |
| 10 | Order inputs | | | Total variable cost of printing mailing | $25,000 |
| 11 | Average order | $40 | | Total variable cost of orders | $257,600 |
| 12 | Variable cost per order | $32.20 | | Total cost | $302,600 |
| 13 | | | | Profit | $17,400 |

**Figure 2.18**

Precedents of
Total_revenue Cell

| | A | B | C | D | E |
|---|---|---|---|---|---|
| 1 | Great Threads direct mail model | | | | |
| 2 | | | | | |
| 3 | Catalog inputs | | | Model of responses | |
| 4 | Fixed cost of printing | $20,000 | | Response rate | 8% |
| 5 | Variable cost of printing mailing | $0.25 | | Number of responses | 8000 |
| 6 | | | | | |
| 7 | Decision variable | | | Model of revenue, costs, and profit | |
| 8 | Number mailed | 100000 | | Total Revenue | $320,000 |
| 9 | | | | Fixed cost of printing | $20,000 |
| 10 | Order inputs | | | Total variable cost of printing mailing | $25,000 |
| 11 | Average order | $40 | | Total variable cost of orders | $257,600 |
| 12 | Variable cost per order | $32.20 | | Total cost | $302,600 |
| 13 | | | | Profit | $17,400 |

**Excel Tool:** *Formula Auditing Toolbar*
*The formula auditing toolbar allows you to see dependents of a selected cell (which cells have formulas that reference this cell) or precedents of a given cell (which cells are referenced in this cell's formula). In fact, you can even see dependents or precedents that reside on a different worksheet. In this case, the auditing arrows appear as dashed lines and point to a small spreadsheet icon. By double-clicking on the dashed line, you can see a list of dependents or precedents on other worksheets. These tools are especially*

*useful for understanding how someone else's spreadsheet works. Unlike in previous versions of Excel, the Formula Auditing tools in Excel 2007 are clearly visible on the Formulas ribbon.* ■

## MODELING ISSUES

*You can place charts on the same sheet as the underlying data or on separate chart sheets. The choice is a matter of personal preference.*

Is the spreadsheet layout in Figure 2.12 the best possible layout? This question is not too crucial because this model is so small. However, we have put all the inputs together (usually a good practice), and we have put all the outputs together in a logical order. You might want to put the answers to questions 1 and 2 on separate sheets, but with such a small model, it is arguably better to keep everything on a single sheet. We generally use separate sheets only when things start getting bigger and more complex.

One final issue is the placement of the chart. From the Chart Tools Design ribbon, you can click on the Move Chart button to select whether you want to place the chart on the worksheet ("floating" above the cells) or on a separate chart sheet that has no rows or columns. This choice depends on your personal preference—neither choice is necessarily better than the other—but for this small model, we favor keeping everything on a single sheet.

Finally, we could have chosen the number mailed, rather than the response rate, as the basis for a sensitivity analysis. When running a sensitivity analysis, it's typically based on an uncertain input variable, such as the response rate, or a decision variable that the decision maker controls. And, of course, there is no limit to the number of data tables you can create for a particular model. ■

## PROBLEMS

*Solutions for problems whose numbers appear within a color box can be found in the Student Solutions Files. Order your copy today at the Winston/Albright product Web site, academic.cengage.com/decisionsciences/winston.*

### Skill-Building Problems

1. In the Great Threads model, the range E9:E11 does not have a range name. Open your completed Excel file and name this range **Costs.** Then look at the formula in cell E12. It does *not* automatically use the new range name. Modify the formula so that it does. Then click on cell G4 and paste the new list of range names over the previous list.

2. The sensitivity analysis in the Great Threads example was on the response rate. Suppose now that the response rate is *known* to be 8%, and the company wants to perform a sensitivity analysis on the number mailed. After all, this is a variable under direct control of the company. Create a one-way data table and a corresponding XY chart of profit versus the number mailed, where the number mailed varies from 80,000 to 150,000 in increments of 10,000. Does it appear, from the results you see here, that there is an "optimal" number to mail, from all possible values, that will maximize profit? Write a concise memo to management about your results.

3. Continuing the previous problem, use Goal Seek for *each* value of number mailed (once for 80,000, once for 90,000, and so on). For each, find the response rate that allows the company to break even. Then chart these values, where the number mailed is on the horizontal axis, and the breakeven response rate is on the vertical axis. Explain the behavior in this chart in a brief memo to management.

### Skill-Extending Problem

4. As the Great Threads problem is now modeled, if all inputs remain fixed except for the number mailed, profit will increase indefinitely as the number mailed increases. This hardly seems realistic—the company could become infinitely rich! Discuss realistic ways to modify the model so that this unrealistic behavior is eliminated.

# 2.5 ORDERING WITH QUANTITY DISCOUNTS AND DEMAND UNCERTAINTY

In the following example, we again attempt to find the appropriate level of some activity: how much of a product to order when customer demand for the product is uncertain. Two important features of this example are the presence of quantity discounts and the explicit use of probabilities to model uncertain demand. Except for these features, the problem is very similar to the one discussed in Example 2.1.

---

**EXAMPLE** | **2.4 ORDERING WITH QUANTITY DISCOUNTS AT SAM'S BOOKSTORE**

Sam's Bookstore, with many locations across the United States, places orders for all of the latest books and then distributes them to its individual bookstores. Sam's needs a model to help it order the appropriate number of any title. For example, Sam's plans to order a popular new hardback novel, which it will sell for $30. It can purchase any number of this book from the publisher, but due to quantity discounts, the unit cost for all books it orders depends on the number ordered. Specifically, if the number ordered is less than 1000, the unit cost is $24. After each 1000, the unit cost drops: to $23 for at least 1000 copies, to $22.25 for at least 2000, to $21.75 for at least 3000, and to $21.30 (the lowest possible unit cost) for at least 4000. For example, if Sam's orders 2500 books, its total cost is $22.25(2500) = $55,625. Sam's is very uncertain about the demand for this book—it estimates that demand could be anywhere from 500 to 4500. Also, as with most hardback novels, this one will eventually come out in paperback. Therefore, if Sam's has any hardbacks left when the paperback comes out, it will put them on sale for $10, at which price, it believes all leftovers will be sold. How many copies of this hardback novel should Sam's order from the publisher?

**Business Objectives**   To create a model to determine the company's profit, given fixed values of demand and the order quantity, and then to model the demand uncertainty explicitly and to choose the expected profit maximizing ("best") order quantity.

**Excel Objectives**   To learn how to build in complex logic with IF formulas, to get online help about Excel functions with the $f_x$ button, to learn how to use lookup functions, to see how two-way data tables allow you to answer more extensive what-if questions, and to introduce Excel's SUMPRODUCT function.

## Solution

The key variables for this model appear in Table 2.4. Our primary modeling tasks are (1) to show how any combination of demand and order quantity determines the number of units sold, both at the regular price and at the leftover sale price, and (2) to calculate the total ordering cost for any order quantity. After we accomplish these tasks, we can model the uncertainty of demand explicitly and then choose the "best" order quantity.

---

**Table 2.4**   Key Variables for Sam's Bookstore Problem

| | |
|---|---|
| **Input variables** | Unit prices, table of unit costs specifying quantity discount structure |
| **Uncertain variable** | Demand |
| **Decision variable** | Order quantity |
| **Key output variable** | Profit |
| **Other output variables** | Units sold at each price, revenue, and cost totals |

---

We first develop a spreadsheet model to calculate Sam's profit for any order quantity and any possible demand. Then we perform a sensitivity analysis to see how profit depends on these two quantities. Finally, we indicate one possible method Sam's might use to choose the "best" order quantity.

## DEVELOPING THE SPREADSHEET MODEL

*Whenever the term trial value is used for an input or a decision variable, you can be fairly sure that we will follow up with a data table or (in later chapters) by running Solver to optimize.*

The profit model appears in Figure 2.19. (See the file **Quantity Discounts.xlsx**.) Note that the order quantity and demand in the Order_quantity and Demand cells are "trial" values. (Comments are in these cells as a reminder of this.) You can put any values in these cells, just to test the logic of the model. The Order_quantity cell is colored red because the company can choose its value. In contrast, the Demand cell is colored green here and in later chapters to indicate that an input value is uncertain and is being treated explicitly as such. Also, note that a table is used to indicate the quantity discounts cost structure. You can use the following steps to build the model.

**Figure 2.19** Sam's Profit Model

| | A | B | C | D | E | F | G | H | I | J | K |
|---|---|---|---|---|---|---|---|---|---|---|---|
| 1 | Ordering decision with quantity discounts | | | | | | | Range names used: | | | |
| 2 | | | | | | | | Cost | | | =Model!$B$18 |
| 3 | Inputs | | | Quantity discount structure | | | | CostLookup | | | =Model!$D$5:$E$9 |
| 4 | Unit cost - see table to right | | | At least | Unit cost | | | Demand | | | =Model!$B$12 |
| 5 | Regular price | $30 | | 0 | $24.00 | | | Leftover_price | | | =Model!$B$6 |
| 6 | Leftover price | $10 | | 1000 | $23.00 | | | Order_quantity | | | =Model!$B$9 |
| 7 | | | | 2000 | $22.25 | | | Probabilities | | | =Model!$B$35:$J$35 |
| 8 | Decision variable | | | 3000 | $21.75 | | | Profit | | | =Model!$B$19 |
| 9 | Order quantity | 2500 | | 4000 | $21.30 | | | Regular_price | | | =Model!$B$5 |
| 10 | | | | | | | | Revenue | | | =Model!$B$17 |
| 11 | Uncertain quantity | | | | | | | Units_sold_at_leftover_price | | | =Model!$B$16 |
| 12 | Demand | 2000 | | | | | | Units_sold_at_regular_price | | | =Model!$B$15 |
| 13 | | | | | | | | | | | |
| 14 | Profit model | | | | | | | | | | |
| 15 | Units sold at regular price | 2000 | | | | | | | | | |
| 16 | Units sold at leftover price | 500 | | | | | | | | | |
| 17 | Revenue | $65,000 | | | | | | | | | |
| 18 | Cost | $55,625 | | | | | | | | | |
| 19 | Profit | $9,375 | | | | | | | | | |

**1** **Inputs and range names.** Enter all inputs and name the ranges as indicated in columns H and I. Note that we used the Create from Selection shortcut to name all ranges except for CostLookup and Probabilities. For these latter two, we highlighted the ranges and entered the names in the Name Box—the "manual" method. (Why the difference? To use the Create from Selection shortcut, you must have appropriate labels in adjacent cells. Sometimes this is simply not convenient.)

**2** **Revenues.** The company can sell only what it has, and it sells any leftovers at the discounted sale price. Therefore, enter the formulas

=MIN(Order_quantity,Demand)

=IF(Order_quantity>Demand, Order_quantity-Demand,0)

and

=Units_sold_at_regular_price*Regular_price
+Units_sold_at_leftover_price*Leftover_price

in cells B15, B16, and B17. The logic in the first two of these cells is necessary to account correctly for the cases when the order quantity is greater than demand and when it's less than or equal to demand. Note that you could use the following equivalent alternative to the IF function:

=MAX(Order_quantity-Demand,0)

## Excel Tool: $f_x$ Button

*If you want to learn more about how an Excel function operates, use the $f_x$ button next to the Formula bar. This is called the Insert Function button, although some people call it the Function Wizard. If you've already entered a function, such as an IF function, in a cell and then click on the $f_x$ button, you get help on this function. If you select an empty cell and then click on the $f_x$ button, you can choose a function to get help on.*

**3** **Total ordering cost.** Depending on the order quantity, we find the appropriate unit cost from the unit cost table and multiply it by the order quantity to obtain the total ordering cost. This could be accomplished with a complex nested IF formula, but a much better way is to use the VLOOKUP function. Specifically, enter the formula

**=VLOOKUP(Order_quantity,CostLookup,2)*Order_quantity**

in cell B18. The VLOOKUP part of this formula says to compare the order quantity to the first (leftmost) column of the table in the CostLookup range and return the corresponding value in the second column (because the last argument is 2). In general, there are two important things to remember about lookup tables: (1) The leftmost column is always the column used for comparison, and (2) the entries in this column must be arranged in increasing order from top to bottom.

## Excel Function: *VLOOKUP*

*The VLOOKUP function acts like a tax table, where you look up the tax corresponding to your adjusted gross income from a table of incomes and taxes. To use it, first create a vertical lookup table, with values to use for comparison listed in the left column of the table in increasing order and corresponding output values in as many columns to the right as you like. (See the CostLookup range in Figure 2.19 for an example.) Then the VLOOKUP function typically takes three arguments: (1) the value you want to compare to the values in the left column, (2) the lookup table range, and (3) the index of the column you want the returned value to come from, where the index of the left column is 1, the index of the next column is 2, and so on. (See online help for an optional fourth argument, which is either TRUE or FALSE. The default is TRUE.) Here, "compare" means to scan down the leftmost column of the table and find the last entry less than or equal to the first argument. There is also an HLOOKUP function that works exactly the same way, except that the lookup table is arranged in rows, not columns.*

**4** **Profit.** Calculate the profit with the formula

**=Revenue-Cost**

## Two-Way Data Table

*A two-way data table allows you to see how a single output varies as two inputs vary simultaneously.*

The next step is to create a two-way data table for profit as a function of the order quantity and demand (see Figure 2.20). To create this table, first enter a link to the profit with the formula **=Profit** in cell A22, and enter possible order quantities and possible demands in column A and row 22, respectively. (We used the same values for both order quantity and demand, from 500 to 4500 in increments of 500. This is not necessary—we could let demand change in increments of 100 or even 1—but it's reasonable. Perhaps Sam's is required by the publisher to order in multiples of 500.) Then select Data Table from the What-If Analysis dropdown on the Data ribbon, and enter the Demand cell as the Row Input cell and the Order_quantity cell as the Column Input cell (see Figure 2.21).

# Figure 2.20 Profit as a Function of Order Quantity and Demand

| | A | B | C | D | E | F | G | H | I | J |
|---|---|---|---|---|---|---|---|---|---|---|
| 21 | Data table of profit as a function of order quantity (along side) and demand (along top) | | | | | | | | | |
| 22 | $9,375 | 500 | 1000 | 1500 | 2000 | 2500 | 3000 | 3500 | 4000 | 4500 |
| 23 | 500 | $3,000 | $3,000 | $3,000 | $3,000 | $3,000 | $3,000 | $3,000 | $3,000 | $3,000 |
| 24 | 1000 | -$3,000 | $7,000 | $7,000 | $7,000 | $7,000 | $7,000 | $7,000 | $7,000 | $7,000 |
| 25 | 1500 | -$9,500 | $500 | $10,500 | $10,500 | $10,500 | $10,500 | $10,500 | $10,500 | $10,500 |
| 26 | 2000 | -$14,500 | -$4,500 | $5,500 | $15,500 | $15,500 | $15,500 | $15,500 | $15,500 | $15,500 |
| 27 | 2500 | -$20,625 | -$10,625 | -$625 | $9,375 | $19,375 | $19,375 | $19,375 | $19,375 | $19,375 |
| 28 | 3000 | -$25,250 | -$15,250 | -$5,250 | $4,750 | $14,750 | $24,750 | $24,750 | $24,750 | $24,750 |
| 29 | 3500 | -$31,125 | -$21,125 | -$11,125 | -$1,125 | $8,875 | $18,875 | $28,875 | $28,875 | $28,875 |
| 30 | 4000 | -$35,200 | -$25,200 | -$15,200 | -$5,200 | $4,800 | $14,800 | $24,800 | $34,800 | $34,800 |
| 31 | 4500 | -$40,850 | -$30,850 | -$20,850 | -$10,850 | -$850 | $9,150 | $19,150 | $29,150 | $39,150 |

## Figure 2.21

Dialog Box for
Two-Way Data Table

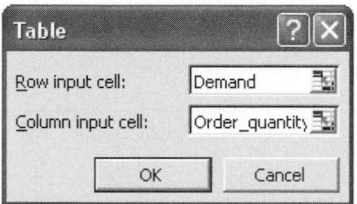

### Excel Tool: *Two-Way Data Table*

*A two-way data table allows you to see how a single* output *cell varies as you vary two* input *cells. (Unlike a one-way data table, only a* single *output cell can be chosen.) To create this type of table, enter a reference to the output cell in the top-left corner of the table, enter possible values of the two inputs below and to the right of this corner cell, and highlight the entire table. Then select Data Table from the What-If Analysis dropdown on the Data ribbon, and enter references to the cells where the original two input variables live. The Row Input cell corresponds to the values along the top row of the table, and the Column Input cell corresponds to the values along the left column of the table. When you click on OK, Excel substitutes each pair of input values into these two input cells, recalculates the spreadsheet, and enters the corresponding output value in the table. By clicking on any cell in the body of the table, you can see that Excel also enters the function =TABLE as a reminder that the cell is part of a data table.*

The resulting data table shows that profit depends heavily on both order quantity and demand and (by scanning across rows) how higher demands lead to larger profits. But which order quantity Sam's should select is still unclear. Remember that Sam's has complete control over the order quantity (it can choose the *row* of the data table), but it has no direct control over demand (it cannot choose the column).

*This is actually a preview of decision making under uncertainty. To calculate an expected profit, you multiply each profit by its probability and add the products. We cover this topic in depth in Chapter 10.*

The ordering decision depends not only on which demands are *possible,* but on which demands are *likely* to occur. The usual way to express this information is with a set of probabilities that sum to 1. Suppose Sam's estimates these as the values in row 35 of Figure 2.22. These estimates are probably based on other similar books it has sold in the past. The most likely demands are 2000 and 2500, with other values on both sides less likely. You can use these probabilities to find an *expected* profit for each order quantity. This expected profit is a weighted average of the profits in any row in the data table, using the probabilities as the weights. The easiest way to do this is to enter the formula

**=SUMPRODUCT(B23:J23,Probabilities)**

**Figure 2.22** Comparison of Expected Profits

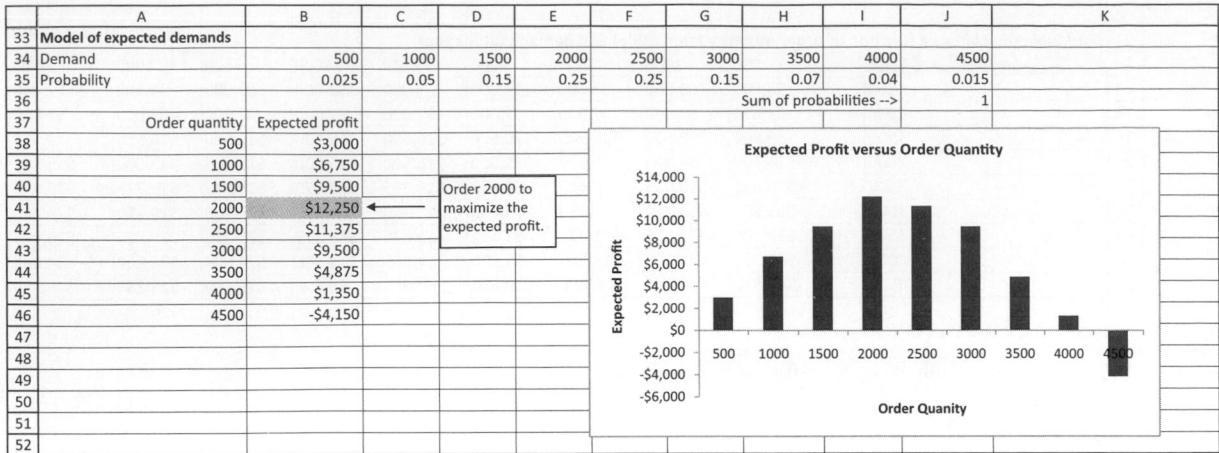

in cell B38 and copy it down to cell B46. You also create a bar chart of these expected profits, as shown in Figure 2.22. (Excel refers to these as *column charts*. The height of each bar is the expected profit for that particular order quantity.)

### Excel Function: *SUMPRODUCT*

*The SUMPRODUCT function takes two range arguments, which must be exactly the same size and shape, and it sums the products of the corresponding values in these two ranges. For example, the formula =SUMPRODUCT(A10:B11,E12:F13) is a shortcut for a formula involving the sum of 4 products: =A10\*E12+A11\*E13+B10\*F12+B11\*F13. This is an extremely useful function, especially when the ranges involved are large, and it's used repeatedly throughout this book. (Actually, the SUMPRODUCT function can have more than two range arguments, all of the same size and shape, but the most common use of SUMPRODUCT is when just two ranges are involved.)*

The largest of the expected profits, $12,250, corresponds to an order quantity of 2000, so we would recommend that Sam's order 2000 copies of the book. This does not guarantee that Sam's will make a profit of $12,250—the actual profit depends on the eventual demand—but it represents a reasonable way to proceed in the face of uncertain demand. You'll learn much more about making decisions under uncertainty and the expected value criterion in Chapter 10. ∎

# PROBLEMS

## Skill-Building Problems

**5.** The spreadsheet model for Sam's Bookstore contains a two-way data table for profit versus order quantity and demand. Experiment with Excel's chart types to create a chart that shows this information graphically in an intuitive format. (Choose the format you would choose to give a presentation to your boss.)

**6.** In some ordering problems, like the one for Sam's Bookstore, whenever demand exceeds existing inventory, the excess demand is not lost but is filled by expedited orders—at a premium cost to the company. Change Sam's model to reflect this behavior. Assume that the unit cost of expediting is $40, well above the highest "regular" unit cost.

7. In the Sam's Bookstore problem, the quantity discount structure is such that *all* the units ordered have the same unit cost. For example, if the order quantity is 2500, then each unit costs $22.25. Sometimes the quantity discount structure is such that the unit cost for the first so many items is one value, the unit cost for the next so many units is a slightly lower value, and so on. Modify the model so that Sam's pays $24 for units 1 to 1500, $23 for units 1501 to 2500, and $22 for units 2501 and above. For example, the total cost for an order quantity of 2750 is 1500(24) + 1000(23) + 250(22). (*Hint*: Use IF functions, not VLOOKUP.)

## Skill-Extending Problems

8. The current spreadsheet model essentially finds the expected profit in several steps. It first finds the profit in cell B19 for a *fixed* value of demand. Then it uses a data table to find the profit for each of several demands, and finally it uses SUMPRODUCT to find the expected profit. Modify the model so that expected profit is found directly, without a data table. To do this, change row 11 so that instead of a single demand, there is a list of possible demands, those currently in row 34. Then insert a new row below row 11 that lists the probabilities of these demands. Next, in the rows below the Profit Model label, calculate the units sold, revenue, cost, and profit for *each* demand. For example, the quantities in column C will be for the second possible demand. Finally, use SUMPRODUCT to calculate *expected* profit below the Profit row.

9. Continuing Problem 6, create a two-way data table for expected profit with order quantity along the side and unit expediting cost along the top. Allow the order quantity to vary from 500 to 4500 in increments of 500, and allow the unit expediting cost to vary from $36 to $45 in increments of $1. Each column of this table will allow you to choose a "best" order quantity for a given unit expediting cost. How does this best order quantity change as the unit expediting cost increases? Write up your results in a concise memo to management. (*Hint*: You have to modify the existing spreadsheet model so that there is a cell for expected profit that changes automatically when you change either the order quantity or the unit expediting cost. See Problem 8 for guidelines.)

# 2.6 ESTIMATING THE RELATIONSHIP BETWEEN PRICE AND DEMAND

The following example illustrates a very important modeling concept: estimating relationships between variables by **curve fitting.** You'll study this topic in much more depth in the regression discussion in Chapter 16, but we can illustrate the ideas at a relatively low level by taking advantage of some of Excel's useful features.

EXAMPLE | **2.5 ESTIMATING SENSITIVITY OF DEMAND TO PRICE AT THE LINKS COMPANY**

The Links Company sells its golf clubs at golf outlet stores throughout the United States. The company knows that demand for its clubs varies considerably with price. In fact, the price has varied over the past 12 months, and the demand at each price level has been observed. The data are in the data sheet of the file **Golf Club Demand.xlsx** (see Figure 2.23.) For example, during the past month, when the price was $390, 6800 sets of clubs were sold. (The demands in column C are in hundreds of units. The cell comment in cell C3 reminds you of this.) The company wants to estimate the relationship between demand and price and then use this estimated relationship to answer the following questions:

1. Assuming the unit cost of producing a set of clubs is $250 and the price must be a multiple of $10, what price should Links charge to maximize its profit?

2. How does the optimal price depend on the unit cost of producing a set of clubs?

3. Is the model an accurate representation of reality?

**Figure 2.23**

Demand and Price
Data for Golf Clubs

| | A | B | C |
|---|---|---|---|
| 1 | Demand for golf clubs | | |
| 2 | | | |
| 3 | Month | Price | Demand |
| 4 | 1 | 450 | 45 |
| 5 | 2 | 300 | 103 |
| 6 | 3 | 440 | 49 |
| 7 | 4 | 360 | 86 |
| 8 | 5 | 290 | 125 |
| 9 | 6 | 450 | 52 |
| 10 | 7 | 340 | 87 |
| 11 | 8 | 370 | 68 |
| 12 | 9 | 500 | 45 |
| 13 | 10 | 490 | 44 |
| 14 | 11 | 430 | 58 |
| 15 | 12 | 390 | 68 |

**Business Objectives**   To estimate the relationship between demand and price, and to use this relationship to find the optimal price to charge.

**Excel Objectives**   To illustrate Excel's trendline tool, and to illustrate conditional formatting.

## Solution

This example is divided into two parts: estimating the relationship between price and demand, and creating the profit model.

### Estimating the Relationship Between Price and Demand

A scatterplot of demand versus price appears in Figure 2.24. (This can be created in the usual way with Excel's Scatter chart.) Obviously, demand decreases as price increases, but we want to quantify this relationship. Therefore, after creating this chart, select the More Trendline Options from the Trendline dropdown on the Chart Tools Layout ribbon to bring up the dialog box in Figure 2.25. This allows you to superimpose several different curves

**Figure 2.24**

Scatterplot of
Demand Versus
Price

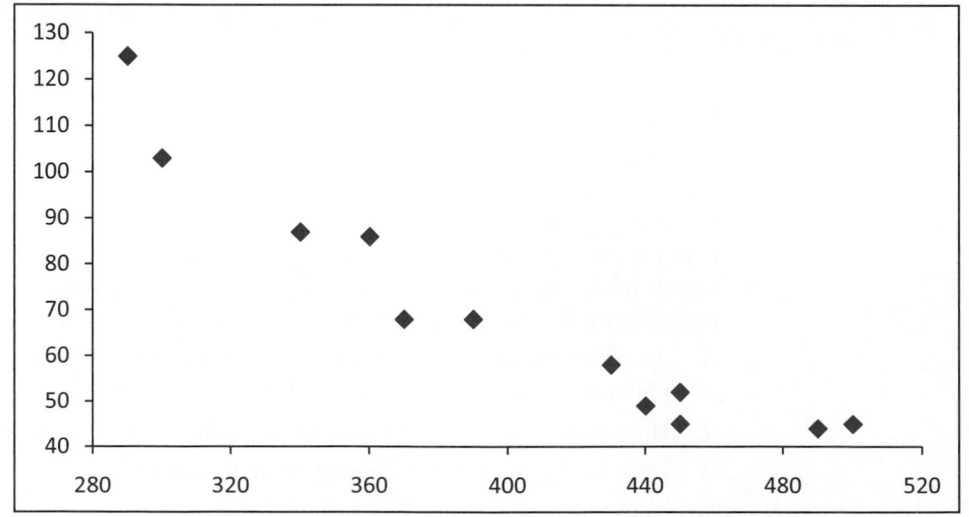

(including a straight line) onto the scatterplot. We consider three possibilities, the **linear, power,** and **exponential** curves, defined by the following general equations (where $y$ and $x$, a general output and a general input, correspond to demand and price for this example):

- Linear: $y = a + bx$
- Power: $y = ax^b$
- Exponential: $y = ae^{bx}$

Before proceeding, we need to describe some general properties of these three functions because of their widespread applicability. The linear function is the easiest. Its graph is a straight line. When $x$ changes by 1 unit, $y$ changes by $b$ units. The constant $a$ is called the intercept, and $b$ is called the slope.

The power function is a curve except in the special case where the exponent $b$ is 1. (Then it is a straight line.) The shape of this curve depends primarily on the exponent $b$. If $b > 1$, $y$ increases at an increasing rate as $x$ increases. If $0 < b < 1$, $y$ increases, but at a decreasing rate, as $x$ increases. Finally, if $b < 0$, $y$ decreases as $x$ increases. An important property of the power curve is that when $x$ changes by 1%, $y$ changes by a constant percentage, and this percentage is approximately equal to $b\%$. For example, if $y = 100x^{-2.35}$, then every 1% increase in $x$ leads to an approximate 2.35% decrease in $y$.

The exponential function also represents a curve whose shape depends primarily on the constant $b$ in the exponent. If $b > 0$, $y$ increases as $x$ increases; if $b < 0$, $y$ decreases as $x$ increases. An important property of the exponential function is that if $x$ changes by 1 unit, $y$ changes by a constant percentage, and this percentage is approximately equal to $100 \times b\%$. For example, if $y = 100e^{-0.014x}$, then whenever $x$ increases by 1 unit, $y$ decreases by approximately 1.4%. Here $e$ is the special number $2.7182\ldots$, and $e$ to any power can be calculated in Excel with the EXP function. For example, you can calculate $e^{-0.014}$ with the formula **=EXP(-0.014)**.

Returning to the example, if you superimpose any of these curves on the scatterplot of demand versus price, Excel chooses the best-fitting curve of that type. Better yet, if you

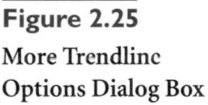

**Figure 2.25**

More Trendline Options Dialog Box

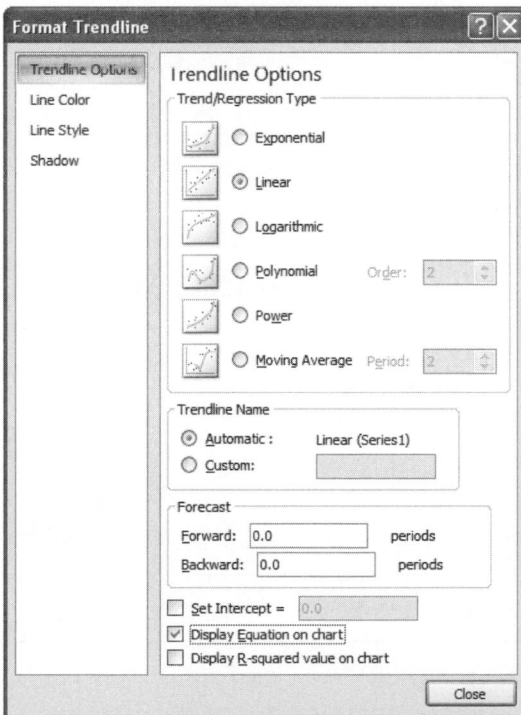

check the Display Equation on Chart option, you see the equation of this best-fitting curve. Doing this for each type of curve, we obtain the results in Figures 2.26, 2.27, and 2.28. (The equations might not appear exactly as in the figures. However, they can be resized and reformatted to appear as shown.)

**Figure 2.26**

Best-Fitting
Straight Line

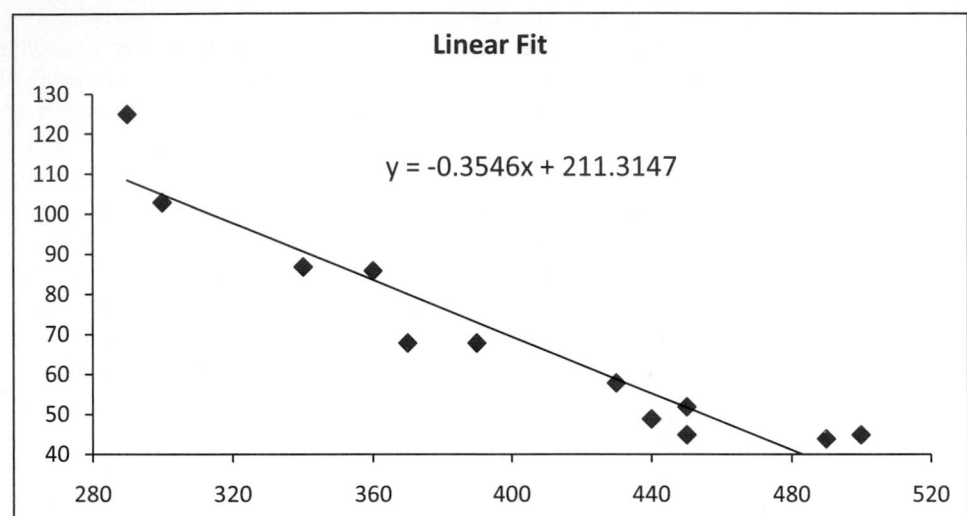

**Figure 2.27**

Best-Fitting
Power Curve

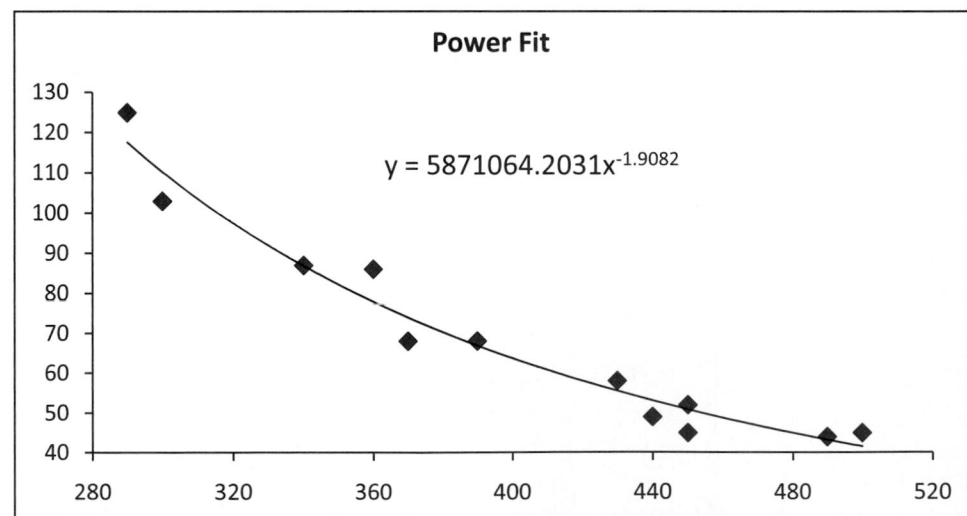

**Figure 2.28**   Best-Fitting Exponential Curve

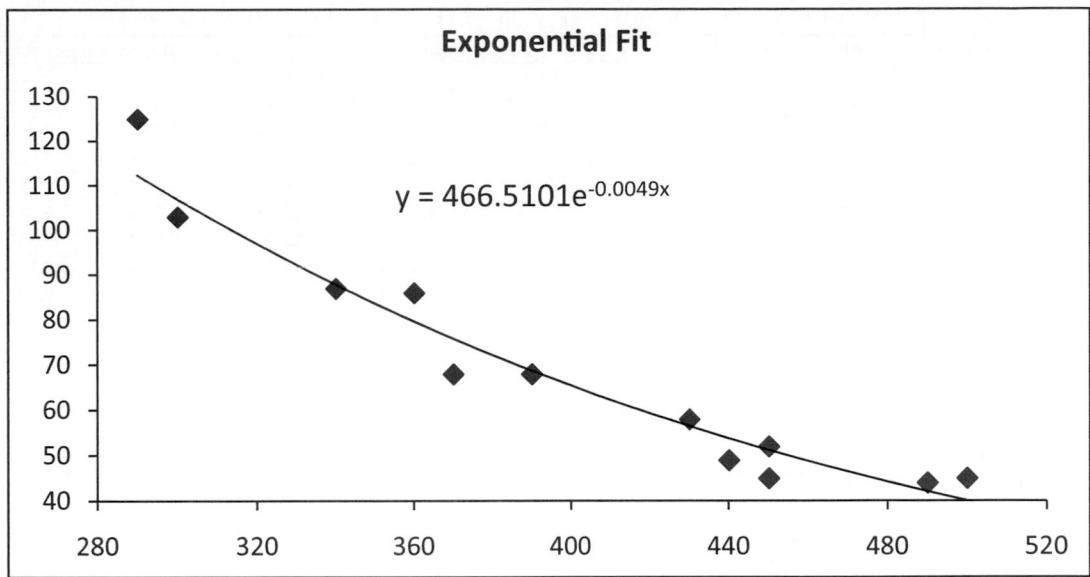

Each of these curves provides the best-fitting member of its "family" to the demand/price data, but which of these three is best overall? We can answer this question by finding the **mean absolute percentage error** (MAPE) for each of the three curves. To do so, for any price in the data set and any of the three curves, we first predict demand by substituting the given price into the equation for the curve. The predicted demand is typically not the same as the observed demand, so we calculate the absolute percentage error (APE) with the general formula:

$$APE = \frac{|\text{Observed demand} - \text{Predicted demand}|}{\text{Observed demand}} \qquad (2.1)$$

Then we average these APE values for any curve to get its MAPE. The curve with the smallest MAPE is the best fit overall.

The calculations appear in Figure 2.29. After (manually) entering the parameters of the equations from the scatterplots into column B, proceed as follows.

**1** **Predicted demands.** Substitute observed prices into the linear, power, and exponential functions to obtain the predicted demands in columns E, F, and G. Specifically, enter the formulas

=$B$19+$B$20*B4

=$B$22*B4^$B$23

and

=$B$25*EXP($B$26*B4)

in cells E19, F19, and G19, and copy them down their respective columns.

**Figure 2.29**   Finding the Best-Fitting Curve Overall

| | A | B | C | D | E | F | G | H | I | J |
|---|---|---|---|---|---|---|---|---|---|---|
| 17 | Parameters of best-fitting curves | | | | Prediction | | | Absolute percentage error | | |
| 18 | Linear | | | | Linear | Power | Exponential | Linear | Power | Exponential |
| 19 | Intercept | 211.31 | | | 51.74 | 50.80 | 51.20 | 14.98% | 12.89% | 13.78% |
| 20 | Slope | -0.3546 | | | 104.93 | 110.12 | 106.94 | 1.87% | 6.91% | 3.83% |
| 21 | Power | | | | 55.29 | 53.02 | 53.78 | 12.83% | 8.21% | 9.75% |
| 22 | Constant | 5871064 | | | 83.65 | 77.76 | 79.65 | 2.73% | 9.58% | 7.38% |
| 23 | Exponent | -1.9082 | | | 108.48 | 117.48 | 112.32 | 13.22% | 6.01% | 10.14% |
| 24 | Exponential | | | | 51.74 | 50.80 | 51.20 | 0.50% | 2.31% | 1.53% |
| 25 | Constant | 466.51 | | | 90.75 | 86.73 | 87.87 | 4.31% | 0.32% | 1.00% |
| 26 | Exponent | -0.00491 | | | 80.11 | 73.80 | 75.84 | 17.81% | 8.53% | 11.52% |
| 27 | | | | | 34.01 | 41.55 | 40.06 | 24.42% | 7.67% | 10.99% |
| 28 | | | | | 37.56 | 43.18 | 42.07 | 14.65% | 1.86% | 4.38% |
| 29 | | | | | 58.83 | 55.40 | 56.49 | 1.43% | 4.48% | 2.61% |
| 30 | | | | | 73.02 | 66.75 | 68.74 | 7.38% | 1.84% | 1.09% |
| 31 | | | | | | | | | | |
| 32 | | | | | | | MAPE | 9.68% | 5.88% | 6.50% |

**2** **Average percentage errors.** Apply equation (2.1) to calculate APEs in columns H, I, and J. Specifically, enter the general formula

**=ABS($C4-E19)/$C4**

in cell H19 and copy it to the range H19:J30. (Do you see why column C is made absolute? Remember that this is where the observed demands are stored.)

**3** **MAPE.** Average the APEs in each column with the AVERAGE function to obtain the MAPEs in row 32.

Evidently, the power curve provides the best fit, with a MAPE of 5.88%. In other words, its predictions are off, on average, by 5.88%. This power curve predicts that each 1% increase in price leads to an approximate 1.9% decrease in demand. (Economists would call this relationship elastic—demand is quite sensitive to price.)

## DEVELOPING THE PROFIT MODEL

Now we move to the profit model, using the best-fitting power curve to predict demand from price. The key variables appear in Table 2.5. Note there is now one input variable, unit variable cost, and one decision variable, unit price. (The red background for the decision variable distinguishes it as such.) The profit model is straightforward to develop using the following steps (see Figure 2.30).

**Table 2.5**   Key Variables for Golf Club Problem

| | |
|---|---|
| **Input variable** | Unit cost to produce |
| **Decision variable** | Unit price |
| **Key output variable** | Profit |
| **Other output variables** | Predicted demand, total revenue, total cost |

**Figure 2.30**

Profit Model

| | A | B | C | D | E |
|---|---|---|---|---|---|
| 1 | Profit model, using best fitting power curve for estimating demand | | | | |
| 2 | | | | | |
| 3 | Parameters of best-fitting power curve (from Estimation sheet) | | | | |
| 4 | Constant | 5871064 | | | |
| 5 | Exponent | -1.9082 | | | |
| 6 | | | | | |
| 7 | Monetary inputs | | | | |
| 8 | Unit cost to produce | $250 | | | |
| 9 | | | | | |
| 10 | Decision variable | | | | |
| 11 | Unit price (trial value) | $400 | | | |
| 12 | | | | | |
| 13 | Profit model | | | | |
| 14 | Predicted demand | 63.601 | | | |
| 15 | Total revenue | $25,441 | | | |
| 16 | Total cost | $15,900 | | | |
| 17 | Profit | $9,540 | | | |

**①** **Predicted demand.** Calculate the *predicted* demand in cell B14 with the formula

**=B4\*B11^B5**

This uses the power function we estimated earlier.

**②** **Revenue, cost, profit.** Enter the following formulas in cells B15, B16, and B17:

**=B11\*B14**

**=B8\*B14**

and

**=B15-B16**

Here we assume that the company produces exactly enough sets of clubs to meet customer demand.

**Maximizing Profit** To see which price maximizes profit, we build the data table shown in Figure 2.31. Here, the column input cell is B11 and the "linking" formula in cell B25 is **=B17**. The corresponding chart (a line chart) shows that profit first increases and then decreases. You can find the maximum profit and corresponding price in at least three ways. First, you can attempt to read them from the chart. Second, you can scan down the data table for the maximum profit, which is shown in the figure. The following Excel Tip describes a third method that uses some of Excel's more powerful features.

**Excel Tip:** *Conditional Formatting*
*We colored cell B53 in Figure 2.31 because it corresponds to the maximum profit in the column, but Excel's Conditional Formatting tool can do this for you—automatically.[7] This tool was completely revised in Excel 2007 and is not only more prominent (on the Home ribbon) but much easier to use. To color the maximum profit, select the range of profits, B26:B75, select the Conditional Formatting dropdown, then Top/Bottom Rules, and then Top 10 Items to bring up the dialog box in Figure 2.32. By asking for the top 1 item, we automatically color the maximum value in the range. You should experiment with the many other Conditional Formatting options. This is a great tool!*

[7]The value in cell B52 also appears to be the maximum, but to two decimals, it is slightly lower.

**Figure 2.31**

Profit as a
Function of Price

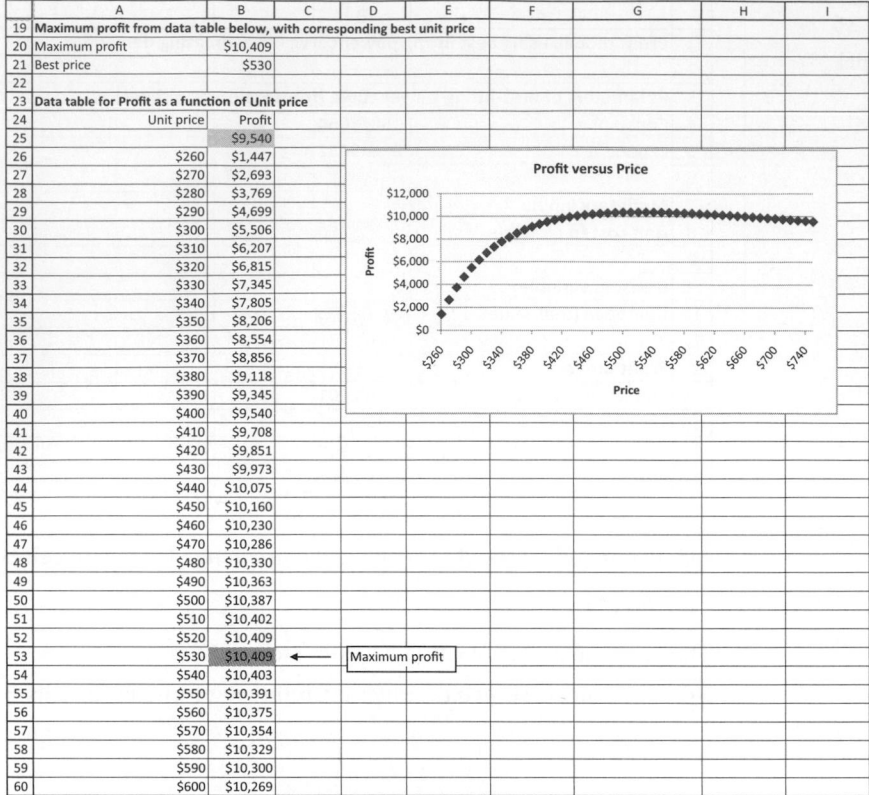

**Figure 2.32**

Conditional
Formatting
Dialog Box

What about the corresponding best price, shown in cell B21 of Figure 2.31? You could enter this manually, but wouldn't it be nice if you could get Excel to find the maximum profit in the data table, determine the price in the cell to its left, and report it in cell B21, all automatically? Just enter the formula

**=INDEX(A26:A75,MATCH(B20,B26:B75,0),1)**

in cell B21, and the best price appears. This formula uses two Excel functions, MATCH and INDEX. MATCH compares the first argument (the maximum profit in cell B20) to the range specified in the second argument (the range of profits), and returns the index of the cell where a match appears. (The third argument, 0, specifies that we want an *exact* match.) In this case, the MATCH function returns 28 because the maximum profit is in the 28th cell of the profits range. Then the INDEX function is called effectively as =INDEX(A26:A75,28,1). The first argument is the range of prices, the second is a row index, and the third is a column index. Very simply, this function says to return the value in the 28th row and first column of the prices range.

To find these functions, you can click on the $f_x$ button and examine the functions in the Lookup & Reference category. After experimenting, we found that the INDEX and

MATCH combination solves the problem. You don't have to memorize these functions, although this combination really does come in handy. Rather, you can often solve a problem by investigating some of Excel's less well-known features. You don't even need a manual—everything is in online help.

### Sensitivity to Variable Cost

We now return to question 2 in the example: How does the best price change as the unit variable cost changes? We can answer this question with a two-way data table. Remember that this is a data table with two inputs—one along the left side and the other across the top row—and a single output. The two inputs for this problem are unit variable cost and unit price, and the single output is profit. The corresponding data table is in the range A83:F168, the top part of which appears in Figure 2.33. To develop this table, enter desired inputs in column A and row 83, enter the linking formula =**B17** in cell A83 (it always goes in the top-left corner of a two-way data table), highlight the entire table, select Data Table from the What-If Analysis dropdown, and enter B8 as the Row Input cell and B11 as the Column Input cell.

**Figure 2.33**    Profit as a Function of Unit Cost and Unit Price

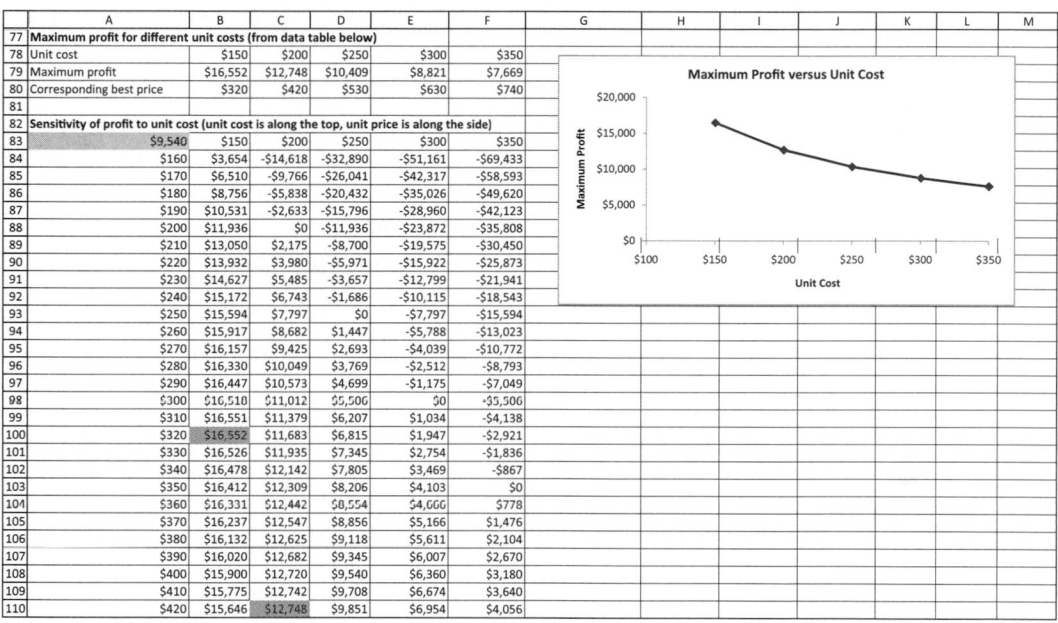

| | A | B | C | D | E | F | G | H | I | J | K | L | M |
|---|---|---|---|---|---|---|---|---|---|---|---|---|---|
| 77 | Maximum profit for different unit costs (from data table below) | | | | | | | | | | | | |
| 78 | Unit cost | $150 | $200 | $250 | $300 | $350 | | | | | | | |
| 79 | Maximum profit | $16,552 | $12,748 | $10,409 | $8,821 | $7,669 | | | | | | | |
| 80 | Corresponding best price | $320 | $420 | $530 | $630 | $740 | | | | | | | |
| 81 | | | | | | | | | | | | | |
| 82 | Sensitivity of profit to unit cost (unit cost is along the top, unit price is along the side) | | | | | | | | | | | | |
| 83 | $9,540 | $150 | $200 | $250 | $300 | $350 | | | | | | | |
| 84 | | $160 | $3,654 | -$14,618 | -$32,890 | -$51,161 | -$69,433 | | | | | | |
| 85 | | $170 | $6,510 | -$9,766 | -$26,041 | -$42,317 | -$58,593 | | | | | | |
| 86 | | $180 | $8,756 | -$5,838 | -$20,432 | -$35,026 | -$49,620 | | | | | | |
| 87 | | $190 | $10,531 | -$2,633 | -$15,796 | -$28,960 | -$42,123 | | | | | | |
| 88 | | $200 | $11,936 | $0 | -$11,936 | -$23,872 | -$35,808 | | | | | | |
| 89 | | $210 | $13,050 | $2,175 | -$8,700 | -$19,575 | -$30,450 | | | | | | |
| 90 | | $220 | $13,932 | $3,980 | -$5,971 | -$15,922 | -$25,873 | | | | | | |
| 91 | | $230 | $14,627 | $5,485 | -$3,657 | -$12,799 | -$21,941 | | | | | | |
| 92 | | $240 | $15,172 | $6,743 | -$1,686 | -$10,115 | -$18,543 | | | | | | |
| 93 | | $250 | $15,594 | $7,797 | $0 | -$7,797 | -$15,594 | | | | | | |
| 94 | | $260 | $15,917 | $8,682 | $1,447 | -$5,788 | -$13,023 | | | | | | |
| 95 | | $270 | $16,157 | $9,425 | $2,693 | -$4,039 | -$10,772 | | | | | | |
| 96 | | $280 | $16,330 | $10,049 | $3,769 | -$2,512 | -$8,793 | | | | | | |
| 97 | | $290 | $16,447 | $10,573 | $4,699 | -$1,175 | -$7,049 | | | | | | |
| 98 | | $300 | $16,518 | $11,012 | $5,506 | $0 | -$5,506 | | | | | | |
| 99 | | $310 | $16,551 | $11,379 | $6,207 | $1,034 | -$4,138 | | | | | | |
| 100 | | $320 | $16,552 | $11,683 | $6,815 | $1,947 | -$2,921 | | | | | | |
| 101 | | $330 | $16,526 | $11,935 | $7,345 | $2,754 | -$1,836 | | | | | | |
| 102 | | $340 | $16,478 | $12,142 | $7,805 | $3,469 | -$867 | | | | | | |
| 103 | | $350 | $16,412 | $12,309 | $8,206 | $4,103 | $0 | | | | | | |
| 104 | | $360 | $16,331 | $12,442 | $8,554 | $4,666 | $778 | | | | | | |
| 105 | | $370 | $16,237 | $12,547 | $8,856 | $5,166 | $1,476 | | | | | | |
| 106 | | $380 | $16,132 | $12,625 | $9,118 | $5,611 | $2,104 | | | | | | |
| 107 | | $390 | $16,020 | $12,682 | $9,345 | $6,007 | $2,670 | | | | | | |
| 108 | | $400 | $15,900 | $12,720 | $9,540 | $6,360 | $3,180 | | | | | | |
| 109 | | $410 | $15,775 | $12,742 | $9,708 | $6,674 | $3,640 | | | | | | |
| 110 | | $420 | $15,646 | $12,748 | $9,851 | $6,954 | $4,056 | | | | | | |

As before, you can scan the columns of the data table for the maximum profits and enter them (manually) in rows 79 and 80. (Alternatively, you can use the Excel features described in the previous Excel Tip to accomplish these tasks. Take a look at the finished version of the file for details. This file also explains how conditional formatting is used to color the maximum profit in each column of the table.) Then you can create a chart of maximum profit (or best price) versus unit cost. The chart in Figure 2.33 shows that the maximum profit decreases, but at a decreasing rate as the unit cost increases.

### Limitations of the Model

Question 3 asks you to step back from all these details and evaluate whether the model is realistic. First, there is no real reason to restrict golf club prices to multiples of $10. This was only required so that we could use a data table to find the profit-maximizing price. Ideally, we want to search over *all* possible prices to find the profit-maximizing price. Fortunately, Excel's built-in Solver tool enables us to accomplish this task fairly easily. The problem of finding a profit-maximizing price is an example of an **optimization model.** In optimization models, we try to maximize or minimize a specified output cell by changing the values of the decision variable cells. Chapters 3 through 9 contain a detailed discussion of optimization models.

A second possible limitation of our model is the implicit assumption that price is the *only* factor that influences demand. In reality, other factors, such as advertising, the state of the economy, competitors' prices, strength of competition, and promotional expenses, also influence demand. In Chapter 16, you'll learn how to use multiple regression to analyze the dependence of one variable on two or more other variables. This technique allows you to incorporate other factors into the model for profit.

A final limitation of the model is that demand might not *equal* sales. For example, if actual demand for golf clubs during a year is 70,000 but the company's annual capacity is only 50,000, the company would observe sales of only 50,000. This would cause it to underestimate *actual* demand, and the curve-fitting method would produce biased predictions. (Can you guess the probable effect on pricing decisions?)

As these comments indicate, most models are not perfect, but we have to start somewhere!

### Other Modeling Issues

The layout of the **Golf Club Demand.xlsx** file is fairly straightforward. However, note that instead of a single sheet, there are two sheets, partly for logical purposes and partly to reduce clutter. There is one sheet for estimation of the demand function and the various scatterplots, and there is another for the profit model.

One last issue is the placement of the data tables for the sensitivity analysis. You might be inclined to put these on a separate Sensitivity sheet. However, Excel does not allow you to build a data table on one sheet that uses a row or column input cell from *another* sheet. Therefore, you are forced to put the data tables on the same sheet as the profit model. ∎

# PROBLEMS

## Skill-Building Problems

**10.** Suppose you have an extra 6 months of data on demands and prices, in addition to the data in the example. These extra data points are (350,84), (385,72), (410,67), (400,62), (330,92), and (480,53). (The price is shown first and then the demand at that price.) After adding these points to the original data, use Excel's Trendline tool to find the best-fitting linear, power, and exponential trendlines. Finally, calculate the MAPE for each of these, based on all 18 months of data. Does the power curve still have the smallest MAPE?

**11.** Consider the power curve $y = 10000x^{-2.35}$. Calculate $y$ when $x = 5$; when $x = 10$; and when $x = 20$. For each of these values of $x$, find the percentage change in $y$ when $x$ increases by 1%. That is, find the percentage change in $y$ when $x$ increases from 5 to 5.05; when it increases from 10 to 10.1; and when it increases from 20 to 20.2. Is this percentage change constant? What number is it very close to? Write a brief memo on what you have learned about power curves from these calculations.

**12.** Consider the exponential curve $y = 1000e^{-0.014x}$. Calculate $y$ when $x = 5$; when $x = 10$; and when $x = 20$. For each of these values of $x$, find the percentage change in $y$ when $x$ increases by 1 unit. That is, find the percentage change in $y$ when $x$ increases from 5 to 6; when it increases from 10 to 11; and when it increases from 20 to 21. Is this percentage change constant? When expressed as a decimal, what number is it very close to? Write a brief memo on what you have learned about exponential curves from these calculations.

## Skill-Extending Problems

**13.** In the profit model in this section, we used the power curve to relate demand and price because it has the lowest MAPE. However, the exponential curve was not far behind. Rework the profit model using the exponential curve to relate demand to price. Write a brief memo indicating whether you get basically the same results as with the power curve or you get substantially different results.

## 2.7 DECISIONS INVOLVING THE TIME VALUE OF MONEY

In many business situations, cash flows are received at different points in time, and a company must determine a course of action that maximizes the "value" of cash flows. Here are some examples:

■ Should a company buy a more expensive machine that lasts for 10 years or a less expensive machine that lasts for 5 years?

■ What level of plant capacity is best for the next 20 years?

■ A company must market one of several midsize cars. Which car should it market?

To make decisions when cash flows are received at different points in time, the key concept is that the later a dollar is received, the less valuable the dollar is. For example, suppose you can invest money at a 10% annual interest rate. Then $1.00 received now is essentially equivalent to $1.10 a year from now. The reason is that if you have $1.00 now, you can invest it and gain $0.10 in interest in one year. If $r = 0.10$ is the interest rate (expressed as a decimal), we can write this as

$$\$1.00 \text{ now} = \$1.10 \text{ a year from now} = \$1.00(1 + r) \qquad \textbf{(2.2)}$$

Dividing both sides of equation (2.2) by $1 + r$, we can rewrite it as

$$\$1.00 \times 1/(1 + r)\text{now} = \$1.00 \text{ a year from now} \qquad \textbf{(2.3)}$$

The value $1/(1 + r)$ in equation (2.3) is called the **discount factor,** and it's always less than 1. The quantity on the left, which evaluates to $0.909 for $r = 0.10$, is called the **present value** of $1.00 received a year from now. The idea is that if you had $0.909 now, you could invest it at 10% and have it grow to $1.00 in a year.

In general, if money can be invested at annual rate $r$ compounded each year, then $1 received $t$ years from now has the same value as $1/(1 + r)^t$ dollars received today—that is, the $1 is discounted by the discount factor raised to the $t$ power. If you multiply a cash flow received $t$ years from now by $1/(1 + r)^t$ to obtain its present value, then the total of these present values over all years is called the **net present value (NPV)** of the cash flows. Basic financial theory states that projects with positive NPVs increase the value of the company, whereas projects with negative NPVs decrease the value of the company.

The rate $r$ (usually called the **discount rate**) used by major corporations generally comes from some version of the **capital asset pricing model.** Most companies use a discount rate ranging from 10% to 20%. The following example illustrates how spreadsheet models and the time value of money can be used to make complex business decisions.

> The **discount factor** is 1 divided by (1 plus the **discount rate**). To discount a cash flow that occurs $t$ years from now, multiply it by the discount factor raised to the $t$ power. The **NPV** is the sum of all discounted cash flows.

**The Time Value of Money**

Money earned in the future is less valuable than money earned today, for the simple reason that money earned today can be invested to earn interest. Similarly, costs incurred in the future are less "costly" than costs incurred today, which is why you don't simply sum up revenues and costs in a multiperiod model. You instead *discount* future revenues and costs to put them on an even ground with revenues and costs incurred today. The resulting sum of discounted cash flows is the net present value (NPV), and it forms the cornerstone of much of financial theory and applications.

EXAMPLE | **2.6 CALCULATING NPV AT ACRON**

Acron is a large drug company. At the current time, the beginning of year 0, Acron is trying to decide whether one of its new drugs, Niagra, is worth pursuing. Niagra is in the final stages of development and will be ready to enter the market in year 1. The final cost of development, to be incurred at the beginning of year 1, is $9.3 million. Acron estimates that the demand for Niagra will gradually grow and then decline over its useful lifetime of 20 years. Specifically, the company expects its gross margin (revenue minus cost) to be $1.2 million in year 1, then to increase at an annual rate of 10% through year 8, and finally to decrease at an annual rate of 5% through year 20. Acron wants to develop a spreadsheet model of its 20-year cash flows, assuming its cash flows, other than the initial development cost, are incurred at the *ends* of the respective years.[8] Using an annual discount rate of 12% for the purpose of calculating NPV, the drug company wants to answer the following questions:

1.  Is the drug worth pursuing, or should Acron abandon it now and not incur the $9.3 million development cost?

2.  How do changes in the model inputs change the answer to question 1?

3.  How realistic is the model?

**Business Objectives**    To develop a model that calculates the NPV of Acron's cash flows, to use this model to determine whether the drug should be developed further and then marketed, and to see how sensitive the answer to this question is to model parameters.

**Excel Objectives**    To illustrate efficient selection and copying of large ranges and to learn Excel's NPV function.

## Solution

The key variables in Acron's problem appear in Table 2.6. The first two rows contain the inputs stated in the problem. We have made a judgment call as to which of these are known with some certainty and which are uncertain. Although we won't do so in this chapter, a thorough study of Acron's problem would treat this uncertainty explicitly, probably with simulation. For now, we accept the values given in the statement of the problem and leave the simulation for a later chapter.

---

[8]To simplify the model, taxes are ignored.

## Table 2.6 Key Variables for Acron's Problem

| | |
|---|---|
| **Input variables** | Development cost, first year gross margin, rate of increase during early years, years of growth, rate of decrease in later years, discount rate |
| **Key output variable** | NPV |
| **Other calculated variables** | Yearly gross margins |

The model of Acron's cash flows appears in Figure 2.34. As with many financial spreadsheet models that extend over a multiyear period, we enter "typical" formulas in the first year or two and then copy this logic down to all years. (In the previous edition, we made the years go across, not down. In that case, splitting the screen is useful so that you can see the first and last years of data. Splitting the screen is explained in the following Excel Tip. The reason we modified the model to have the years go down, not across, is that it now fits easily on a screen, without needing to split the screen.)

**Figure 2.34**

Acron's Model of 20-Year NPV

| | A | B | C | D | E | F | G |
|---|---|---|---|---|---|---|---|
| 1 | Calculating NPV at Acron | | | Range names used: | | | |
| 2 | | | | Development_cost | | =Model!$B$4 | |
| 3 | Inputs | | | Discount_rate | | =Model!$B$9 | |
| 4 | Development cost | 9.3 | | Gross_margin_year_1 | | =Model!$B$5 | |
| 5 | Gross margin year 1 | 1.2 | | Gross_margin | | =Model!$B$13:$B$32 | |
| 6 | Rate of increase | 10% | | Increase_through_year | | =Model!$B$7 | |
| 7 | Increase through year | 8 | | Rate_of_decrease | | =Model!$B$8 | |
| 8 | Rate of decrease | 5% | | Rate_of_increase | | =Model!$B$6 | |
| 9 | Discount rate | 12% | | | | | |
| 10 | | | | | | | |
| 11 | Cash flows | | | | | | |
| 12 | End of year | Gross margin | | | | | |
| 13 | 1 | 1.2000 | | | | | |
| 14 | 2 | 1.3200 | | | | | |
| 15 | 3 | 1.4520 | | | | | |
| 16 | 4 | 1.5972 | | | | | |
| 17 | 5 | 1.7569 | | | | | |
| 18 | 6 | 1.9326 | | | | | |
| 19 | 7 | 2.1259 | | | | | |
| 20 | 8 | 2.3385 | | | | | |
| 21 | 9 | 2.2215 | | | | | |
| 22 | 10 | 2.1105 | | | | | |
| 23 | 11 | 2.0049 | | | | | |
| 24 | 12 | 1.9047 | | | | | |
| 25 | 13 | 1.8095 | | | | | |
| 26 | 14 | 1.7190 | | | | | |
| 27 | 15 | 1.6330 | | | | | |
| 28 | 16 | 1.5514 | | | | | |
| 29 | 17 | 1.4738 | | | | | |
| 30 | 18 | 1.4001 | | | | | |
| 31 | 19 | 1.3301 | | | | | |
| 32 | 20 | 1.2636 | | | | | |
| 33 | | | | | | | |
| 34 | NPV | 3.3003 | | | | | |

**Excel Tip:** *Splitting the Screen*
*To split the screen horizontally, drag the separator just to the right of the bottom scrollbar to the left. To split the screen vertically, drag the separator just above the right scrollbar downward. Drag either separator back to its original position to remove the split.*

## DEVELOPING THE SPREADSHEET MODEL

To create the model, complete the following steps. (See the file **Calculating NPV.xlsx**.)

**1** **Inputs and range names.** Enter the given input data in the blue cells, and name the ranges as shown. As usual, note that the range names for cells B4 through B9 can be created all at once with the Create from Selection shortcut, as can the range name for the gross margins in column B. In the latter case, highlight the whole range B12:B32 and then use the Create from Selection shortcut.

**2** **Cash flows.** Start by entering the formula

**=Gross_margin_year_1**

in cell B13 for the year 1 gross margin. Then enter the general formula

**=IF(A14<=Increase_through_year,B13\*(1+Rate_of_increase),
B13\*(1-Rate_of_decrease))**

in cell B14 and copy it down to cell B32 to calculate the other yearly gross margins. Note how this IF function checks the year index in column A to see whether sales are still increasing or have started to decrease. Of course, by using the (range-named) input cells in this formula, we can change any of these inputs in cells B6 through B8, and the calculated cells will automatically update. This is a *much* better practice than embedding the numbers in the formula itself.

**Excel Tip:** *Efficient Selection*
*An easy way to select a large range, assuming that the first and last cells of the range are visible, is to select the first cell and then, with your finger on the Shift key, select the last cell. (Don't forget that you can split the screen horizontally and/or vertically to make these first and last cells visible.) This selects the entire range and is easier than scrolling.*[9]

Use the Ctrl+Enter shortcut to enter a formula in a range all at once.

**Excel Tip:** *Efficient Copying with Ctrl+Enter*
*An easy way to enter the same formula in a range all at once is to select the range (as in the preceding Excel Tip), type the formula, and press Ctrl+Enter (both keys at once). After you get used to this shortcut, you'll use it all the time.*

**3** **Net present value.** The NPV is based on the sequence of cash flows in column B. From our general discussion of NPV, to discount everything back to the beginning of year 1, the value in cell B13 should be multiplied by $1/(1 + r)^1$, the value in cell B14 should be multiplied by $1/(1 + r)^2$, and so on, and these quantities should be summed to obtain the NPV. (Here, $r = 0.12$ is the discount rate.) Fortunately, however, Excel has a built-in NPV function to accomplish this calculation. To use it, enter the formula

**=-Development_cost+NPV(Discount_rate,Gross_margin)**

in cell B34. The NPV function takes two arguments: the discount rate and a range of cash flows. Furthermore, it assumes that the first cell in this range is the cash flow at the *end* of year 1, the second cell is the cash flow at the end of year 2, and so on. This explains why the development cost is subtracted *outside* of the NPV function—it's incurred at the *beginning* of year 1. In general, any cash flow incurred at the beginning of year 1 must be placed outside the NPV function.

To get some understanding of NPV, note that the *sum* of the cash flows in column B is slightly more than $34.14 million, but the NPV (aside from the development cost) is only about $12.60 million. This is because values further into the future are discounted so heavily. At the extreme, the $1.2636 million cash flow in year 20 is equivalent to only $1.2636[1/(1 + 0.12)^{20}] = \$0.131$ million now!

**Excel Function:** *NPV*
*The NPV function takes two arguments, the discount rate (entered as a decimal, such as 0.12 for 12%) and a stream of cash flows. These cash flows are assumed to occur in consecutive years, starting at the end of year 1. If there is an initial cash flow at the beginning of year 1, such as an initial investment, it should be entered outside the NPV function. (There is also an XNPV function that has* three *arguments: a discount rate, a series of cash flows, and a series of dates when the cash flows occur. Because these dates do not have to be equally*

The stream of cash flows in the NPV function must occur at the ends of year 1, year 2, and so on. If the timing is irregular, you must discount "manually"; the NPV function will not work properly.

---

[9]You'll find other tips like this for increasing your efficiency in the **Excel Tutorial.docx** file on the accompanying CD-ROM.

*spaced through time, this function is considerably more flexible than the NPV function. To use it, the Analysis Toolpak add-in that ships with Excel must be loaded. We do not use the XNPV function in this book, but you can learn more about it in Excel's online help.)*

### Deciding Whether to Continue with the Drug

NPV calculations are typically used to see whether a certain plan should be undertaken. If the NPV is positive, the plan is worth pursuing. If the NPV is negative, the company should look for other ways of investing its money. Figure 2.34 shows that the NPV for this drug is positive, over $3 million.[10] Therefore, if Acron is comfortable with its predictions of future cash flows, it should continue with the development and marketing of the drug. However, Acron might first want to see how sensitive the NPV is to changes in the sales predictions. After all, these predictions are intelligent guesses at best.

One possible sensitivity analysis appears in Figure 2.35. Here we build a one-way data table to see how the NPV changes when the number of years of increase (the input in cell B7) changes. Again, the important question is whether the NPV stays positive. It certainly does when the input variable is greater than its current value of 8. However, if sales start decreasing soon enough—that is, if the value in B7 is 3 or less—then the NPV turns negative. This should probably not concern Acron, because its best guess for the years of increase is considerably greater than 3.

**Figure 2.35**

Sensitivity of NPV to Years of Sales Increase

| | D | E | F |
|---|---|---|---|
| 11 | Sensitivity to years of increase (cell B7) | | |
| 12 | | 3.3003 | |
| 13 | 3 | -0.7190 | |
| 14 | 4 | 0.1374 | |
| 15 | 5 | 0.9687 | |
| 16 | 6 | 1.7739 | |
| 17 | 7 | 2.5516 | |
| 18 | 8 | 3.3003 | |
| 19 | 9 | 4.0181 | |
| 20 | 10 | 4.7027 | |

Another possibility is to see how long *and* how good the good years are. To do this, we create the two-way data table shown in Figure 2.36, where cell B6 is the row input cell and cell B7 is the column input cell. Now you can see that if sales increase through year 6, all reasonable yearly increases result in a positive NPV. However, if sales increase only through year 5, then a low enough yearly increase can produce a negative NPV. Acron might want to step back and estimate how likely these "bad" scenarios are before proceeding with the drug.

**Figure 2.36**

Sensitivity of NPV to Years of Increase and Yearly Increase

| | D | E | F | G | H | I | J |
|---|---|---|---|---|---|---|---|
| 22 | Sensitivity to rate of increase in early years (cell B6) and years of increase (cell B7) | | | | | | |
| 23 | 3.3003 | 5% | 6% | 7% | 8% | 9% | 10% |
| 24 | 3 | -1.3405 | -1.2184 | -1.0951 | -0.9708 | -0.8454 | -0.7190 |
| 25 | 4 | -0.8203 | -0.6352 | -0.4469 | -0.2554 | -0.0606 | 0.1374 |
| 26 | 5 | -0.3383 | -0.0897 | 0.1652 | 0.4265 | 0.6943 | 0.9687 |
| 27 | 6 | 0.1074 | 0.4195 | 0.7419 | 1.0750 | 1.4189 | 1.7739 |
| 28 | 7 | 0.5182 | 0.8934 | 1.2838 | 1.6899 | 2.1123 | 2.5516 |
| 29 | 8 | 0.8958 | 1.3330 | 1.7912 | 2.2711 | 2.7738 | 3.3003 |
| 30 | 9 | 1.2413 | 1.7392 | 2.2643 | 2.8182 | 3.4023 | 4.0181 |
| 31 | 10 | 1.5559 | 2.1125 | 2.7033 | 3.3306 | 3.9963 | 4.7027 |

[10]You might wonder why we didn't discount back to the beginning of the current year, year 0, instead of year 1. This is a fairly arbitrary decision on our part. To discount back to year 0, we would simply divide our NPV by 1.12. The important point, however, is that this would have no bearing on Acron's decision: A positive NPV would stay positive, and a negative NPV would stay negative.

### Limitations of the Model

Probably the major flaw in this model is that it ignores uncertainty, and future cash flows are highly uncertain, due mainly to uncertain demand for the drug. Incorporating uncertainty into this type of model is covered when we discuss simulation in Chapters 11 and 12. Aside from this uncertainty, there are almost always ways to make *any* model more realistic—at the cost of increased complexity. For example, we could model the impact of competition on Niagra's profitability. Alternatively, we could allow Acron to treat its prices as decision variables. However, this might influence the likelihood of competition entering the market, which would certainly complicate the model. The point is that this model is only a start. When millions of dollars are at stake, a more thorough analysis is certainly warranted. ■

## PROBLEMS

### Skill-Building Problems

14. Modify Acron's model so that development lasts for an extra year. Specifically, assume that development costs of $7.2 million and $2.1 million are incurred at the beginnings of years 1 and 2, and then the sales in the current model occur one year later, that is, from year 2 until year 21. Again, calculate the NPV discounted back to the beginning of year 1, and perform the same sensitivity analyses. Comment on the effects of this change in timing.

15. Modify Acron's model so that sales increase, then stay steady, and finally decrease. Specifically, assume that the gross margin is $1.2 million in year 1, then increases by 10% annually through year 6, then stays constant through year 10, and finally decreases by 5% annually through year 20. Perform a sensitivity analysis with a two-way data table to see how NPV varies with the length of the increase period (currently 6 years) and the length of the constant period (currently 4 years). Comment on whether Acron should pursue the drug, given your results.

16. Create a one-way data table in the Acron model to see how the NPV varies with discount rate, which is allowed to vary from 8% to 18% in increments of 0.5%. Explain intuitively why the results go in the direction they go—that is, the NPV decreases as the discount rate increases. Should Acron pursue the drug for all these discount rates?

### Skill-Extending Problems

17. The NPV function automatically discounts each of the cash flows and sums the discounted values. Verify that it does this correctly for Acron's model by calculating the NPV the long way. That is, discount each cash flow and then sum these discounted values. Use Excel formulas to do this, but don't use the NPV function. (*Hint:* Remember that the discounted value of $1 received $t$ years from now is $1/(1 + r)^t$ dollars today.)

18. In a situation such as Acron's, where a one-time cost is followed by a sequence of cash flows, the **internal rate of return** (IRR) is the discount rate that makes the NPV equal to 0. The idea is that if the discount rate is greater than the IRR, the company will not pursue the project; whereas if the discount rate is less than the IRR, the project is financially attractive.

   a. Use Excel's Goal Seek tool to find the IRR for the Acron model.
   b. Excel also has an IRR function. Look it up in online help to see how it works, and then use it on Acron's model. Of course, you should get the same IRR as in part **a.**
   c. Verify that the NPV is negative when the discount rate is slightly greater than the IRR, and that it's positive when the discount rate is slightly less than the IRR.

19. The XNPV function can calculate NPV for any (possibly irregular) series of cash flows. Look this function up in Excel's online help. Then use it to set up a spreadsheet model that finds the NPV of the following series: a payment of $25,000 today (assumed to be June 15, 2006), and cash inflows of $10,000 on March 1, 2007; $15,000 on September 15, 2007; $8000 on January 20, 2008; $20,000 on April 1, 2008; and $10,000 on May 15, 2008. Discount these back to "today" using a discount rate of 12%. (*Note:* To use the XNPV function, Excel's Analysis ToolPak must be added in. To ensure this, select the Tools/ Add-Ins menu item, and make sure the Analysis ToolPak is checked.)

## 2.8 CONCLUSION

The examples in this chapter provide a glimpse of things to come in later chapters. You've seen the spreadsheet modeling approach to realistic business problems, learned how to design spreadsheet models for readability, and explored some of Excel's powerful tools, particularly data tables. In addition, at least three important themes have emerged from these examples: relating inputs and decision variables to outputs by means of appropriate formulas, optimization (finding a "best" order quantity), and the role of uncertainty (uncertain response rate or demand). Although you've not yet learned the tools to explore these themes fully, these themes will occupy you for most of the rest of this book.

### Summary of Key Management Science Terms

| Term | Explanation | Page |
|---|---|---|
| Model inputs | The numeric values that are "givens" in any problem statement | 24 |
| Decision variables | The variables a decision maker has control over to effect better solutions | 24 |
| Model outputs | The numeric values that result from combinations of inputs and decision variables through the use of logical formulas | 24 |
| Net present value (NPV) | The current worth of a stream of cash flows that occur in the future | 57 |
| Discount rate | Interest rate used for discounting future cash flows to get the net present value | 57 |

### Summary of Key Excel Terms

| Term | Explanation | Excel | Page |
|---|---|---|---|
| IF function | Useful for implementing logic | =IF(*condition,resultIfTrue, resultIfFalse*) | 26 |
| Relative, absolute cell addresses | Useful for copying formulas; absolute row or column stays fixed, relative row or column "moves" | A1 (relative), $A1 or A$1 (mixed), $A$1 (absolute); press F4 to cycle through possibilities | 31 |
| Range names | Useful for making formulas more meaningful | Type name in Name box, or use Create from Selection shortcut | 35 |
| Pasting range names | Provides a list of all range names in the current workbook | Use Paste List from Use in Formula dropdown | 35 |
| Cell comments | Useful for documenting contents of the cell | Right-click on cell, select Insert Comment menu item | 36 |
| One-way data table | Shows how one or more outputs vary as a single input varies | Use Data Table from What-If Analysis dropdown | 38 |
| Goal Seek | Solves one equation in one unknown | Use Goal Seek from What-If Analysis dropdown | 38 |
| Formula auditing toolbar | Useful for checking which cells are related to other cells through formulas | Use Formula Auditing buttons on Formulas ribbon | 39 |
| $f_x$ button | Useful for getting help on Excel functions | On Formula Bar | 44 |

| Term | Explanation | Excel | Page |
|------|-------------|-------|------|
| VLOOKUP function | Useful for finding a particular value based on a comparison | =VLOOKUP(*valueToCompare, lookupTable, columnToReturn*) | 44 |
| Two-way data table | Shows how a single output varies as two inputs vary | Use Data Table from What-If Analysis dropdown | 44 |
| SUMPRODUCT function | Calculates the sum of products of values in two (or more) similar-sized ranges | =SUMPRODUCT(*range1,range2*) | 46 |
| Splitting screen | Useful for separating the screen horizontally and/or vertically | Use screen splitters at top and right of scrollbars. | 59 |
| Trendline tool | Superimposes the best-fitting line or curve of a particular type on a scatter chart | With chart selected, use Trendline dropdown from Chart Tools Layout ribbon | 48 |
| Conditional formatting | Formats cells depending on whether specified conditions hold | Use Conditional Formatting from Home ribbon | 53 |
| NPV function | Calculates NPV of a stream of cash flows at the ends of consecutive years, starting in year 1 | =NPV(*discountRate,cashFlows*) | 60 |
| Efficient selection | Useful for selecting a large rectangular range | While pressing the Shift key, click on upper-left and bottom-right cells of range. | 60 |
| Efficient copying | Shortcut for copying a formula to a range | Select the range, enter the formula, and press Ctrl+Enter. | 60 |

# PROBLEMS

## Skill-Building Problems

**20.** Julie James is opening a lemonade stand. She believes the fixed cost per week of running the stand is $50.00. Her best guess is that she can sell 300 cups per week at $0.50 per cup. The variable cost of producing a cup of lemonade is $0.20.

    **a.** Given her other assumptions, what level of sales volume will enable Julie to break even?

    **b.** Given her other assumptions, discuss how a change in sales volume affects profit.

    **c.** Given her other assumptions, discuss how a change in sales volume and variable cost jointly affect profit.

    **d.** Use Excel's formula auditing tool to show which cells in your spreadsheet affect profit directly.

**21.** You are thinking of opening a Broadway play, *I Love You, You're Mediocre, Now Get Better!* It will cost $5 million to develop the show. There are 8 shows per week, and you project the show will run for 100 weeks. It costs $1000 to open the theater each night. Tickets sell for $50.00, and you earn an average of $1.50 profit per ticket holder from concessions. The

theater holds 800, and you expect 80% of the seats to be full.

    **a.** Given your other assumptions, how many weeks will the play have to run for you to earn a 100% return on the play's development cost?

    **b.** Given your other assumptions, how does an increase in the percentage of seats full affect profit?

    **c.** Given your other assumptions, determine how a joint change in the average ticket price and number of weeks the play runs influence profit.

    **d.** Use Excel's formula auditing tool to show which cells in the spreadsheet are directly affected by the percentage of seats full.

**22.** You are thinking of opening a small copy shop. It costs $5000 to rent a copier for a year and costs $0.03 per copy to operate the copier. Other fixed costs of running the store will amount to $400 per month. You plan to charge an average of $0.10 per copy, and the store will be open 365 days per year. Each copier can make up to 100,000 copies per year.

    **a.** For 1 to 5 copiers rented and daily demands of 500, 1000, 1500, and 2000 copies per day, compute annual profit. That is, compute annual profit for *each* of these combinations of copiers rented and daily demand.

 **b.** If you rent 3 copiers, what daily demand for copies will allow you to break even?

 **c.** Graph profit as a function of the number of copiers for a daily demand of 500 copies; for a daily demand of 2000 copies. Interpret your graphs.

23. Georgia McBeal is trying to save for her retirement. She believes she can earn 10% on average each year on her retirement fund. Assume that at the beginning of each of the next 40 years, Georgia will allocate $x$ dollars to her retirement fund. If at the beginning of a year Georgia has $y$ dollars in her fund, by the end of the year, it will grow to $1.1y$ dollars. How much should Georgia allocate to her retirement fund each year to ensure that she will have $1 million at the end of 40 years? What key factors are being ignored in this analysis of the amount saved for retirement?

24. A European call option on a stock earns the owner an amount equal to the price at expiration minus the exercise price, if the price of the stock on which the call is written exceeds the exercise price. Otherwise, the call pays nothing. A European put option earns the owner an amount equal to the exercise price minus the price at expiration, if the price at expiration is less than the exercise price. Otherwise, the put pays nothing. The file **P02_24.xlsx** contains a template that computes (based on the well-known Black–Scholes formula) the price of a European call and put based on the following inputs: today's stock price, the duration of the option (in years), the option's exercise price, the risk-free rate of interest (per year), and the annual volatility in stock price. For example, a 40% volatility means approximately that the standard deviation of annual percentage changes in the stock price is 40%.

 **a.** Consider a 6-month European call option with exercise price $40. Assume a current stock price of $35, a risk-free rate of 5%, and an annual volatility of 40%. Determine the price of the call option.

 **b.** Use a data table to show how a change in volatility changes the value of the option. Give an intuitive explanation for your results.

 **c.** Use a data table to show how a change in today's stock price changes the option's value. Give an intuitive explanation for your results.

 **d.** Use a data table to show how a change in the option's duration changes the option's value. Give an intuitive explanation for your results.

25. Repeat parts **a–d** of the previous problem for a 6-month European put option with exercise price $40. Again, assume a current stock price of $35, a risk-free rate of 5%, and an annual volatility of 40%.

26. Dataware is trying to determine whether to give a $10 rebate, to cut the price $6, or to have no price change

on a software product. Currently, 40,000 units of the product are sold each week for $45. The variable cost of the product is $5. The most likely case appears to be that a $10 rebate will increase sales 30%, and half of all people will claim the rebate. For the price cut, the most likely case is that sales will increase 20%.

 **a.** Given all other assumptions, what increase in sales from the rebate would make the rebate and price cut equally desirable?

 **b.** Dataware does not really know the increase in sales that will result from a rebate or price cut. However, the company is sure that the rebate will increase sales by between 15% and 40% and that the price cut will increase sales by between 10% and 30%. Perform a sensitivity analysis that could be used to help determine Dataware's course of action.

27. The file **P02_27.xlsx** lists sales (in millions of dollars) of Dell Computer during the period 1987–1997 (where year 1 corresponds to 1987).

 **a.** Fit a power and an exponential trend curve to these data. Which fits the data better?

 **b.** Use your part **a** answer to predict 1999 sales for Dell.

 **c.** Use your part **a** answer to describe how the sales of Dell have grown from year to year.

 **d.** Go to the Web and find more recent sales data for Dell. Then repeat the preceding parts using all of the data.

28. The file **P02_28.xlsx** gives the annual sales for Microsoft (in millions of dollars) for the years 1984–1993, where 1984 = year 1.

 **a.** Fit an exponential curve to these data.

 **b.** By what percentage do you estimate that Microsoft will grow each year?

 **c.** Why can't a high rate of exponential growth continue for a long time?

 **d.** Rather than an exponential curve, what curve might better represent the growth of a new technology?

 **e.** Go to the Web and find more recent sales data for Microsoft. Then repeat the preceding parts using all the data.

29. Assume that the number of units sold of a product is given by $100 - 0.5P + 26\sqrt{A}$, where $P$ is the price (in dollars) charged for product and $A$ is the amount spent on advertising (in thousands of dollars). Each unit of the product costs $5 to produce. What combination of price and advertising will maximize profit? (*Hint*: Use a data table.)

30. You are given the data on the price of new Taurus sedans and used Taurus sedans in the file **P02_30.xlsx.** All used prices are in amounts paid in 1995. For example, a new Taurus bought in 1985 cost $11,790 and the wholesale used price of that car in 1995 was

$1700. A new Taurus bought in 1994 cost $18,680 and sold used in 1995 for $12,600.

  **a.** You want to predict the resale value (as a percentage of the original price of the vehicle) as a function of the vehicle's age. Develop an equation to do this. You should try two different curves and choose the one that fits best.

  **b.** Suppose all police cars are Ford Tauruses. If you were the business manager for the New York Police Department, what use would you make of the information from part **a**?

**31.** The yield of a chemical reaction is defined as the ratio (expressed as a percentage) of usable output to the amount of raw material input. Suppose the yield of a chemical reaction is found to depend on the length of time the process is run and the temperature at which the process is run. The yield can be expressed as follows:

$$\text{Yield} = 90.79 - 1.095x_1 - 1.045x_2 - 2.781_1^2 \\ - 2.524x_2^2 - 0.775x_1x_2$$

Here $x_1 = (\text{Temperature} - 125)/10$ and $x_2 = (\text{Time} - 300)/30$, where temperature is measured in degrees Fahrenheit, and time is measured in seconds. Find the temperature and time settings that maximize the yield of this process. (*Hint:* Use a data table.)

**32.** A bond is currently selling for $1040. It pays the amounts listed in the file **P02_32.xlsx** at the end of the next 6 years. The yield of the bond is the interest rate that would make the NPV of the bond's payments equal to the bond's price. Use Excel's Goal Seek tool to find the yield of the bond.

**33.** Assume the demand for the drug Wozac during the current year is 50,000, and assume demand will grow at 5% a year. If you build a plant that can produce $x$ units of Wozac per year, it will cost $16x$. Each unit of Wozac is sold for $3. Each unit of Wozac produced incurs a variable production cost of $0.20. It costs $0.40 per year to operate a unit of capacity. Determine how large a Wozac plant to build to maximize expected profit over the next 10 years.

**34.** Consider a project with the following cash flows: year 1, −$400; year 2, $200; year 3, $600; year 4, −$900; year 5, $1000; year 6, $250; year 7, $230. Assume a discount rate of 15% per year.

  **a.** Compute the project's NPV if cash flows occur at the ends of the respective years.

  **b.** Compute the project's NPV if cash flows occur at the beginnings of the respective years.

  **c.** Compute the project's NPV if cash flows occur at the middles of the respective years.

**35.** The payback of a project is the number of years it takes before the project's total cash flow is positive. Payback ignores the time value of money. It's interesting, however, to see how differing assumptions

on project growth impact payback. Suppose, for example, that a project requires a $300 million investment at year 0 (right now). The project yields cash flows for 10 years, and the year 1 cash flow will be between $30 million and $100 million. The annual cash flow growth will be between 5% and 25% per year. (Assume that this growth is the *same* each year.) Use a data table to see how the project payback depends on the year 1 cash flow and the cash flow growth rate.

**36.** A software company is considering translating its program into French. Each unit of the program sells for $50 and incurs a variable cost of $10 to produce. Currently, the size of the market for the product is 300,000 units per year, and the English version of the software has a 30% share of the market. The company estimates that the market size will grow by 10% a year for the next 5 years, and at 5% per year after that. It will cost the company $6 million to create a French version of the program. The translation will increase its market share to 40%. Given a 10-year planning horizon, for what discount rates is it profitable to create the French version of the software?

## Skill-Extending Problems

**37.** You are entering the widget business. It costs $500,000, payable in year 1, to develop a prototype. This cost can be depreciated on a straight-line basis during years 1–5. Each widget sells for $40 and incurs a variable cost of $20. During year 1, the market size is 100,000, and the market is growing at 10% per year. You believe you will attain a 30% market share. Profits are taxed at 40%, but there are no taxes on *negative* profits.

  **a.** Given your other assumptions, what market share is needed to ensure a total free cash flow (FCF) of $0 over years 1 to 5? (*Note:* FCF during a year equals after-tax profits plus depreciation minus fixed costs, if any.)

  **b.** Explain how an increase in market share changes profit.

  **c.** Explain how an increase in market size growth changes profit.

  **d.** Use Excel's auditing tool to show how the market growth assumption influences your spreadsheet.

**38.** Suppose you are borrowing $25,000 and making monthly payments with 1% interest. Show that the monthly payments should equal $556.11. The key relationships are that for any month $t$

(Ending month $t$ balance)
= (Ending month $t - 1$ balance)
    − ((Monthly payment) − (Month $t$ interest))

(Month $t$ interest) = (Beginning month $t$ balance) × (Monthly interest rate)

Of course, the ending month 60 balance must equal 0.

**39.** You are thinking of starting Peaco, which will produce Peakbabies, a product that competes with Ty's Beanie Babies. In year 0 (right now), you will incur costs of $4 million to build a plant. In year 1, you expect to sell 80,000 Peakbabies for a unit price of $25. The price of $25 will remain unchanged through years 1 to 5. Unit sales are expected to grow by the same percentage ($g$) each year. During years 1 to 5, Peaco incurs two types of costs: variable costs and SG&A (selling, general, and administrative) costs. Each year, variable costs equal half of revenue. During year 1, SG&A costs equal 40% of revenue. This percentage is assumed to drop 2% per year, so during year 2, SG&A costs will equal 38% of revenue, and so on. Peaco's goal is to have profits for years 0 to 5 sum to 0 (ignoring the time value of money). This will ensure that the $4 million investment in year 0 is "paid back" by the end of year 5. What annual percentage growth rate $g$ does Peaco require to "pay back" the plant cost by the end of year 5?

**40.** Suppose the demand (in thousands) for a toaster is given by $100p^{-2}$, where $p$ is the price in dollars charged for the toaster.
  **a.** If the variable cost of producing a toaster is $10, what price will maximize profit?
  **b.** The elasticity of demand is defined as the percentage change in demand created by a 1% change in price. Show that the demand for toasters appears to have constant elasticity of demand. Would this be true if the demand for toasters were linear in price?

**41.** The file **P02_41.xlsx** contains the cumulative number of bits (in trillions) of DRAM (a type of computer memory) produced and the price per bit (in thousandths of a cent).
  **a.** Fit a power curve that can be used to show how price per bit drops with increased production. This relationship is known as the learning curve.
  **b.** Suppose the cumulative number of bits doubles. Create a prediction for the price per bit. Does the change in the price per bit depend on the current price?

**42.** A large U.S. drug company, Pharmco, has 100 million yen coming due in one year. Currently the yen is worth $0.01. Because the value of the yen in U.S. dollars in one year is unknown, the value of this 100 million yen in U.S. dollars is highly uncertain. To hedge its risk, Pharmco is thinking of buying one-year put options on the yen with an exercise price of $0.008. For example, if the yen falls in value a year from now to $0.007, then the owner of the put receives $0.001. The price of such a put is $0.00007. Show how the dollar value of Pharmco's receipts and hedging expenses depends on the number of puts purchased and the final $/yen exchange rate. Assume final exchange rates between 0.006 $/yen and 0.015 $/yen are possible.

**43.** How could you determine a discount rate that makes two projects have the same NPV?

**44.** The IRR is the discount rate $r$ that makes a project have an NPV of $0. You can find IRR in Excel with the built-in IRR function, using the syntax =IRR(range of cash flows). However, it can be tricky. In fact, if the IRR is not near 10%, this function might not find an answer, and you'll get an error message. Then you must try the syntax =IRR(range of cash flows, guess), where "guess" is your best guess for the IRR. It's best to try a range of guesses (say, −90% to 100%). Find the IRR of the project described in Problem 34.

**45.** A project does not necessarily have a unique IRR. (Refer to the previous problem for more information on IRR.) Show that a project with the following cash flows has two IRRs: year 1, −$20; year 2, $82; year 3, −$60; year 4, $2. (*Note:* It can be shown that if the cash flow of a project changes sign only once, the project is guaranteed to have a unique IRR.)

**46.** How could you use Goal Seek to find a project's IRR? (Refer to Problem 44 for more information on IRR.)

# APPENDIX TIPS FOR EDITING AND DOCUMENTING SPREADSHEETS

Editing and documenting your spreadsheet models is crucial, and the following tips make these tasks much easier.

## Format Appropriately

Appropriate formatting can make a spreadsheet model much easier to read. To boldface, for example, select one or more cells and click on the **B** button on the Home ribbon (or press Ctrl+B). Similarly, to italicize, indent, increase or decrease the number of decimal places, right-justify, or perform other common formatting tasks, use the buttons on the Home ribbon.

## Use Range Names

Naming ranges takes time but makes formulas much easier to read and understand. To enter a range name, highlight any cell or range of cells and enter a name for the range in the Name box (just to the left of the Formula Bar). If you want to edit or delete range names, select Name Manager on the Formulas ribbon. Here are some other options you have from the Defined Names group on the Formulas ribbon.

- After you've named some ranges, you can get a list of them in your spreadsheet by placing the cursor at the top of the range where you want the list to be placed, selecting the Use in Formula dropdown on the Formula ribbon, and clicking on the Paste List option. Alternatively, press the F3 button.

- Suppose you have labels such as Fixed Cost, Variable Cost, Revenue, and Profit in the range A3:A6, with their values next to them in column B. If you want to name the cells in column B with the labels in column A, highlight the range A3:B6, select Create from Selection on the Formulas ribbon (or press Ctrl+Shift+F3), and make sure the Left Column box is checked. This creates the range names you want.

- If you have a formula, such as =SUM(A10:A20), and then you name the range A10:A20 Costs, say, the formula does *not* change automatically to =SUM(Costs). However, you can make it adapt to your new range name by selecting Apply Names from the Define Name dropdown on the Formulas ribbon.

- Sometimes you might want to use the *same* range name, such as Total_cost, on multiple worksheets of a workbook. For example, you might want Total_cost to refer to cell B26 in Sheet1 and to cell C59 in Sheet2. The trick is to use a *sheet* level name rather than a *workbook* level name for one or both versions of Total_cost. This is easy to do from the Name Manager. When you define the a new name, just select a sheet as the Scope of the name.

## Use Text Boxes

Text boxes are very useful for documenting your work. To enter an explanation or any other text into a text box, go to the Insert ribbon, click on the Text Box button and drag a box, and start typing. This technique is much better than typing explanations into cells because text boxes have word wrap. Therefore, text in text boxes is much easier to edit than text in cells.

## Use Cell Comments

Cell comments provide another good way to document your work. To enter a comment in a cell, select the cell and right-click. This brings up a dialog box (which is also useful for other tasks such as formatting). Click on the Insert Comment item to enter a comment. If a comment is already in the cell, this menu will contain Edit Comment and Delete Comment items. The cells with comments should have small red triangles in their corners.

## Create Useful Macros

In the previous edition, we explained how to record macros to perform useful functions and then attach them to buttons on your own customized toolbar. Unfortunately, you can no longer modify the built-in ribbons in Excel 2007, at least not easily. (You can do so with a technology called RibbonX, but this is advanced.) Nevertheless, you can still record (or write) macros to perform repetitive tasks and then run them by clicking on Macros from the Developer ribbon and selecting a desired macro. If the Developer tab isn't visible on your PC, you can make it visible by clicking on the Office button, then on Excel Options, and then checking the Show Developer tab in the Ribbon from the Popular group.

## Other Tips

Finally, we urge you once again to open the **Excel Tutorial.docx** file on the accompanying CD-ROM and work through it. The file includes a number of techniques that will make you a better and more efficient Excel user. (We recommend downloading this file to your hard drive before working with it. Some of our students have had problems working with it right off the CD-ROM.)

# Introduction to Optimization Modeling

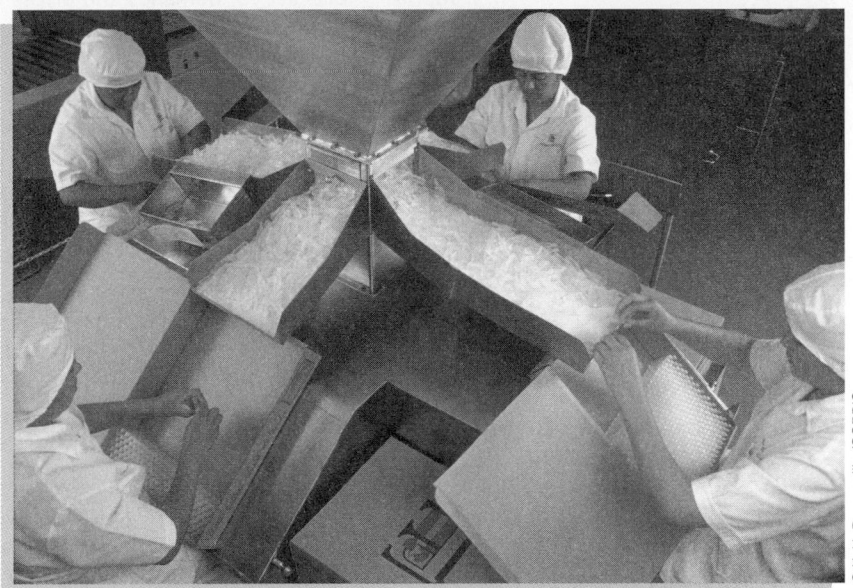

© Keith Dannemiller/CORBIS

## OPTIMIZING MANUFACTURING OPERATIONS AT GE PLASTICS

The General Electric Company (GE) is a global organization that must deliver products to its customers anywhere in the world in the right quantity, at the right time, and at a reasonable cost. One arm of GE is GE Plastics (GEP), a $5 billion business that supplies plastics and raw materials to such industries as automotive, appliance, computer, and medical equipment. (GEP has now been reorganized into GE Advanced Materials [GEAM].) As described in Tyagi et al. (2004), GEP practiced a "pole-centric" manufacturing approach, making each product in the geographic area (Americas, Europe, or Pacific) where it was to be delivered. However, it became apparent in the early 2000s that this approach was leading to higher distribution costs and mismatches in capacity as more of GEP's demand was originating in the Pacific region. Therefore, the authors of the article were asked to develop a global optimization model to aid GEP's manufacturing planning. Actually, GEP consists of seven major divisions, distinguished primarily on the capability of their products to withstand heat. The fastest growing of these divisions, the high performance polymer (HPP) division, was chosen as the pilot for the new global approach.

All GEP divisions operate as two-echelon manufacturing systems. The first echelon consists of resin plants, which convert raw material stocks into resins and ship them to the second echelon, the finishing plants. These latter plants combine the resins with additives to produce various grades of the end products. Each physical plant consists of several "plant lines" that operate independently, and each of these plant lines is capable of producing multiple products. All end products are then shipped to GE Polymerland warehouses throughout the world. GE Polymerland is a wholly owned subsidiary that acts as the commercial front for GEP. It handles all customer sales and deliveries from its network of distribution centers and warehouses in more than 20 countries. Because of its experience with customers, GE Polymerland is able to aid the GEP divisions in their planning processes by supplying forecasts of demands and prices for the various products in the various global markets. These forecasts are key inputs to the optimization model.

The optimization model itself attempts to maximize the total contribution margin over a planning horizon, where the contribution margin equals revenues minus the sum of manufacturing, material, and distribution costs. There are demand constraints, manufacturing capacity constraints, and network flow constraints (of the type that will be discussed in Chapter 5). The decision variables include (1) the amount of resin produced at each resin plant line that will be used at each finishing plant line, and (2) the amount of each end product produced at each finishing plant line that will be shipped to each geographic region. The completed model has approximately 3100 decision variables and 1100 constraints and is completely linear. It was developed and solved in Excel (using LINGO, a commercial optimization solver, not Excel's built-in Solver), and execution time is very fast—about 10 seconds.

The demand constraints are handled in an interesting way. The authors constrain manufacturing to produce *no more than* the forecasted demands, but they do not force manufacturing to meet these demands. Ideally, manufacturing would meet demands exactly. However, because of its rapid growth, capacity at HPP in 2002 appeared (at the time of the study) to be insufficient to meet the demand in 2005 and later years. The authors faced this challenge in two ways. First, in cases where demand exceeds capacity, they let their model of maximizing total contribution margin determine which demands to satisfy. The least profitable demands are simply not met. Second, the authors added a new resin plant to their model that would come online in the year 2005 and provide much needed capacity. They ran the model several times for the year 2005 (and later years), experimenting with the location of the new plant. Although some of the details are withheld in the article for confidentiality reasons, the authors indicate that senior management approved the investment of a Europe-based plant that would cost more than $200 million in plant and equipment. This plant was planned to begin operations in 2005 and ramp up to full production capacity by 2007.

The decision support system developed in the study has been a success at the HPP division since its introduction in 2002. Although the article provides no specific dollar gains from the use of the model, it is noteworthy that the other GEP divisions are adopting similar models for their production planning. ∎

## 3.1 INTRODUCTION

Spreadsheet optimization is one of the most powerful and flexible methods of quantitative analysis. The specific type of optimization discussed here is **linear programming** (LP). LP is used in all types of organizations, often on a daily basis, to solve a variety of problems, including problems in labor scheduling, inventory management, selection of advertising media, bond trading, management of cash flows, operation of an electrical utility's hydro-electric system, routing of delivery vehicles, blending in oil refineries, hospital staffing, and many others. The goal of this chapter is to introduce the basic elements of LP: the types of problems it can solve, how LP problems can be modeled in Excel, and how Excel's powerful Solver add-in can be used to find optimal solutions. Then in the next several chapters, we examine a variety of LP applications, and we will look at applications of integer and nonlinear programming, two important extensions of LP.

## 3.2 INTRODUCTION TO OPTIMIZATION

Before getting to the details of LP modeling, it's useful to discuss optimization in general. All optimization problems have several elements in common. They all have **decision variables,** the variables whose values the decision maker can choose. Either directly or indirectly, the values of these variables determine such outputs as total cost, revenue, and profit. Essentially, they are the variables an organization must know to function properly because they determine everything else. All optimization problems have an **objective function (objective,** for short) whose value is to be optimized—maximized or minimized.[1] Finally, most optimization problems have **constraints** that must be satisfied. These are usually physical, logical, or economic restrictions that depend on the nature of the problem. In searching for the values of the decision variables that optimize the objective, we must choose values that satisfy the constraints.

Excel uses its own terminology for optimization, which is also used throughout this book. Excel refers to the decision variables as the **changing cells.** These cells must contain *numbers* that are allowed to change freely; they are *not* allowed to contain formulas. Excel refers to the objective as the **target cell.** There can be only one target cell—which could contain profit, total cost, total distance traveled, or others—and it must be related through formulas to the changing cells. When the changing cells change, the target cell should change accordingly.

*Changing cells must contain numbers, not formulas.*

> The **changing cells** contain the values of the decision variables.
> The **target cell** contains the objective to be minimized or maximized.
> The **constraints** impose restrictions on the values in the changing cells.

Finally, there must be appropriate cells and cell formulas that allow us to operationalize the constraints. For example, there might be a constraint on labor: The amount of labor used cannot be more than the amount of labor available. In this case, there must be cells for each of these two quantities, and typically at least one of them (probably the amount of labor used) is related through formulas to the changing cells. Constraints can come in a variety of forms. One very common form is *nonnegativity.* Nonnegativity constraints state that changing cells must have nonnegative (zero or positive) values. Nonnegativity constraints are usually included for physical reasons. For example, it is impossible to produce a negative number of automobiles.

> Nonnegativity constraints imply that changing cells must contain nonnegative values.

*Typically, most of your effort goes into the model development step.*

Two steps are involved in solving an optimization problem. The first step is the **model development** step, in which we decide what the variables are, what the objective is, which constraints are required, and how everything fits together. If we are developing an algebraic

---

[1] Actually, some optimization models are *multiobjective* models, where we try to optimize several objectives simultaneously. These types of models are covered in Chapter 9.

model, we must derive the correct algebraic expressions. If we are developing a spreadsheet model, which is the focus of this book, we must relate all variables with appropriate cell formulas. In particular, we must ensure that our model contains formulas for relating the changing cells to the target cell and that it contains formulas for operationalizing the constraints. This model development step is where most of our effort goes.

The second step in any optimization model is to **optimize.** This means that we must systematically choose the values of the decision variables that make the objective as large (for maximization) or small (for minimization) as possible and satisfy all the constraints. Any set of values of the decision variables that satisfies all the constraints is called a **feasible solution.** The set of all feasible solutions is called the **feasible region.** In contrast, an **infeasible solution** violates at least one constraint. We must rule out infeasible solutions to get the feasible solution that provides the *best* value—minimum for a minimization problem, maximum for a maximization problem—of the objective. This solution is called the **optimal solution.**

> A **feasible solution** is a solution that satisfies all the constraints.
> The **feasible region** is the set of all feasible solutions.
> An **infeasible solution** violates at least one of the constraints.
> The **optimal solution** is the feasible solution that optimizes the objective.

*An algorithm is basically a plan of attack. It's a prescription for carrying out the steps required to achieve some goal, such as finding an optimal solution. An algorithm is typically translated into a computer program that does the work.*

Although most of our effort typically goes into the model development step, much of the published research in optimization has gone into the optimization step. Algorithms have been devised for searching through the feasible region to find the optimal solution. One such algorithm is the **simplex method,** which is an extremely efficient method for solving linear programming models. Other more complex algorithms are suitable for other types of models (those with integer decision variables and/or nonlinearities).

We do not discuss the details of these algorithms in this book. Fortunately, they have been programmed into the Solver add-in that is part of Excel. All we need to do is develop the model and then tell Solver the target cell, the changing cells, the constraints, and the type of model (linear, integer, or nonlinear). Solver then goes to work, finding the best feasible solution with the most suitable algorithm. You should appreciate that if we used a trial and error procedure, even a clever and fast one, it could take hours, weeks, or even years to complete. However, by using the appropriate algorithm, Solver typically finds the optimal solution in a matter of seconds.

There is really a *third* step in the optimization process: **sensitivity analysis.** We typically choose the most likely values of input variables, such as unit costs, forecasted demands, and resource availabilities, and then find the optimal solution for these particular input values to provide a single "answer." However, in any realistic setting, it's wishful thinking to believe that all of the input values we use are exactly correct. Therefore, it's useful—in fact, mandatory in most real studies—to follow up the optimization step with many what-if questions. What if the unit costs increased by 5%? What if forecasted demands were 10% lower? What if resource availabilities could be increased by 20%? What effects would such changes have on the optimal solution? This type of sensitivity analysis can be done informally or in a highly structured way. Sensitivity analysis is discussed a lot in later examples. Fortunately, as with the optimization step itself, good software allows us to obtain answers to a lot of what-if questions quickly and easily.

## 3.3 A TWO-VARIABLE MODEL

The first example is a very simple two-variable problem. We show how to model this problem algebraically and then how to model it in Excel. We also show how to find its optimal solution with Excel's Solver add-in. Next, because it contains only two decision variables, we show how it can be solved graphically. Although this graphical solution is not practical for most realistic problems, it provides useful insights into general optimization models. Finally, we ask a number of what-if questions about the completed model.

---

EXAMPLE | **3.1 PLANNING DESSERTS**

---

Maggie Stewart loves desserts, but due to weight and cholesterol concerns, she has decided that she must plan her desserts carefully. There are two possible desserts she is considering: snack bars and ice cream. After reading the nutrition labels on the snack bar and ice cream packages, she learns that each "serving" of snack bar weighs 37 grams and contains 120 calories and 5 grams of fat. Each serving of ice cream weighs 65 grams and contains 160 calories and 10 grams of fat. Maggie allows herself no more than 450 calories and 25 grams of fat in her daily desserts, but because she loves desserts so much, she requires at least 120 grams of dessert per day. Also, she assigns a "taste index" to each gram of each dessert, where 0 is the lowest and 100 is the highest. She assigns a taste index of 95 to ice cream and 85 to snack bars (because she prefers ice cream to snack bars). What should her daily dessert plan be to stay within her constraints and maximize the total taste index of her dessert?[2]

**Objective**  To use linear programming to find the tastiest combination of desserts that stays within Maggie's constraints.

## Solution

*Tables such as this serve as a bridge between the problem statement and the ultimate spreadsheet (or algebraic) model.*

In all optimization models, we are given a variety of numbers—the inputs—and we are asked to make some decisions that optimize an objective, while satisfying some constraints. This information is summarized in a table, as shown in Table 3.1. You should create such a table before diving into the modeling details. In particular, you always need to identify the appropriate decision variables, the appropriate objective, and the constraints, and you should always think about the relationships between them. Without a clear idea of these elements, it's almost impossible to develop a correct spreadsheet (or algebraic) model.

---

**Table 3.1**  Variables and Constraints for Dessert Model

| | |
|---|---|
| **Input variables** | Ingredients (calories, fat) per serving, serving sizes, taste indexes, maximum allowed daily ingredients, minimum required daily grams |
| **Decision variables (changing cells)** | Daily servings of each dessert consumed |
| **Objective (target cell)** | Total taste index |
| **Other calculated variables** | Daily ingredients consumed, daily grams consumed |
| **Constraints** | Daily ingredients consumed must be less than or equal to Maximum allowed |
| | Daily grams consumed must be greater than or equal to Minimum required |

---

[2] Although this diet problem might seem silly, LP has been used in a number of more important situations to recommend low-cost nutritious diets. See Lancaster (1992), for example. For a more humorous aspect of the diet problem, see Dantzig (1990).

*Be sure to decide on a convenient unit of measurement and then be consistent in its use.*

The decision variables must be the daily amounts of the desserts consumed, but why choose *servings* rather than *grams?* The answer is that it doesn't really matter. Because we know the number of grams per serving of each dessert, it is simple to convert from servings to grams or vice versa. Choosing the unit of measurement is a common problem in modeling. It usually doesn't matter which unit of measurement we select, but we should be consistent. Also, note that Maggie assigns a taste index of 85 to each gram of snack bar and 95 to each gram of ice cream. If she consumes, say, 50 grams of snack bar and 100 grams of ice cream, it seems reasonable that a measure of her total "taste satisfaction" is 50(85) + 100(95). This is how the total taste index is defined, which is the objective we attempt to maximize.

### An Algebraic Model

In the traditional algebraic solution method, we first identify the decision variables.[3] In this small problem, they are the numbers of servings of each dessert to consume daily. We label these $x_1$ and $x_2$, although any other labels would do. Next, we write expressions for the total taste index and the constraints in terms of the $x$'s. Finally, because only nonnegative amounts can be consumed, we add explicit constraints to ensure that the $x$'s are nonnegative. The resulting algebraic model is

$$\text{Maximize } 37(85)x_1 + 65(95)x_2$$

subject to

$$120x_1 + 160x_2 \le 450$$
$$5x_1 + 10x_2 \le 25$$
$$37x_1 + 65x_2 \ge 120$$
$$x_1, x_2 \ge 0$$

To understand this model, consider the objective first. Each serving of snack bar weighs 37 grams, and each of these grams contributes 85 "points" to the total taste index. If $x_1$ servings of snack bar are consumed, they contribute $37(85)x_1$ points to the total taste index. A similar statement holds for ice cream. We then sum the contributions from snack bars and ice cream to obtain the total taste index.

The constraints are similar. For example, each serving of snack bar contains 120 calories and 5 grams of fat. These explain the $120x_1$ and $5x_1$ terms in the top two constraints (the calorie and fat constraints). We add these to the similar terms for ice cream to the left-hand sides of these constraints. Then the right-hand sides of these constraints are the given maximum daily allowances. The third constraint (minimal daily requirement of calories) follows similarly. Finally, we can't consume negative amounts of either dessert, so we include nonnegativity constraints on $x_1$ and $x_2$.

*Many commercial optimization packages require, as input, an algebraic model of a problem. If you use one of these packages, you will be required to think algebraically.*

For many years, all LP problems were modeled this way because many commercial LP computer packages were written to accept LP problems in essentially this format. In the past 10 to 15 years, however, a more intuitive method of expressing LP problems has emerged that takes advantage of the power and flexibility of spreadsheets. Actually, LP problems could always be *modeled* on spreadsheets, but now with the addition of Solver add-ins, spreadsheets have the capability to *solve*—that is, optimize—LP problems as well. Specifically, Excel has a built-in Solver. (An LP add-in called What's Best! can also be used with Excel.) Excel's Solver is used for all examples in this book.

---

[3] This is not a book about algebraic models; our main focus is on *spreadsheet* modeling. However, algebraic models of the examples are presented in this chapter for comparison with spreadsheet models.

## A Graphical Solution

When there are only two decision variables in an LP model, as in the dessert model, we can solve the problem graphically. Although this solution approach is not practical in most realistic optimization models—where there are many more than two decision variables—the graphical procedure illustrated here still yields important insights.

*This graphical approach works only for problems with two decision variables.*

In general, if the two decision variables are labeled $x_1$ and $x_2$, we express the constraints and the objective in terms of $x_1$ and $x_2$; we graph the constraints to find the feasible region—the set of all pairs $(x_1, x_2)$ satisfying the constraints, where $x_1$ is on the horizontal axis and $x_2$ is on the vertical axis—and finally, we then move the objective through the feasible region until it is optimized.

To do this for the dessert problem in Example 3.1, note that the constraint on calories can be expressed as $120x_1 + 160x_2 \leq 450$. To graph this, we consider the associated equality (replacing $\leq$ with $=$) and find where the associated line crosses the axes. Specifically, when $x_1 = 0$, then $x_2 = 450/160 = 2.81$, and when $x_2 = 0$, then $x_1 = 450/120 = 3.75$. This provides the line labeled "calories constraint" in Figure 3.1. It has slope $-120/160 = -0.75$. The set of all points that satisfy the calories constraint includes the points on this line plus the points below it, as indicated by the arrow drawn from the line. We know that the feasible points are *below* the line because the point $(0, 0)$ is obviously below the line, and $(0, 0)$ clearly satisfies the calories constraint. Similarly, we can graph the fat constraint and the grams constraint, as shown in the figure. The points that satisfy all three of these constraints and are nonnegative comprise the feasible region, which is shaded in the figure.

*Recall from algebra that any line of the form $ax_1 + bx_2 + c$ has slope $-a/b$. This is because it can be put into the slope–intercept form $x_2 = c/b - (a/b)x_1$.*

**Figure 3.1**

Graphical Solution for Dessert Problem

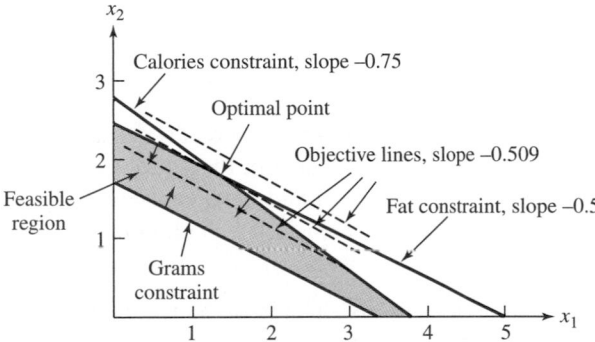

To see which feasible point maximizes the objective, we draw a sequence of lines where, for each, the objective is a constant. The typical line is of the form $37(85)x_1 + 67(95)x_2 = c$, where $c$ is a constant. Any such line has slope $-[37(85)]/[65(95)] = -0.509$, regardless of the value of $c$. This line is slightly steeper than the constraint line for fat, but it isn't as steep as the constraint line for calories. Move a line with this slope up and to the right, making $c$ larger until it just barely touches the feasible region. The last feasible point that it touches is the optimal point.

Several lines with slope $-0.509$ are shown in Figure 3.1. The one farthest up and to the right is the one with the largest total taste index. The associated optimal point is clearly the point where the calories and fat lines intersect. We will eventually find (from Solver) that this point is $(1.25, 1.875)$, but even if we didn't have the Solver add-in, we could find the coordinates of this point by solving two equations (the ones for calories and fat) in two unknowns.

Again, the graphical procedure illustrated here can be used only for the simplest of LP models, those with two decision variables. However, the type of behavior pictured in

Figure 3.1 generalizes to *all* LP models. In general, all feasible regions are (the multidimensional versions of) solid polygons. That is, they are bounded by straight lines (actually, hyperplanes) that intersect at corner points. (There are five corner points in Figure 3.1, four of which are on the axes.) When we push the objective line (again, really a hyperplane) as far as possible toward better values, the last feasible point it touches is one of the corner points. The relative slopes of the objective and constraint lines determine the actual corner point it last touches. Because there are only a finite number of corner points, we need to search only among this finite set, not the infinite number of points in the entire feasible region.[4] This insight is largely responsible for the efficiency of the simplex method for solving LP problems.

---

FUNDAMENTAL INSIGHT

### Geometry of LP Models and the Simplex Method

The feasible region in any LP model is always a multidimensional version of a polygon, and the objective is always a hyperplane, the multidimensional version of a straight line. We always want to push the objective as far as possible in the maximizing or minimizing direction until it just touches the edge of the feasible region. Because of this geometry, the optimal solution is always a corner point of the polygon. The simplex method for LP works so well because it can search through the finite number of corner points extremely efficiently and recognize when it has found the best corner point. This rather simple insight, plus its clever implementation in software packages, has saved companies many, many millions of dollars in the past 50 years.

---

### A Spreadsheet Model

There are many ways to develop an LP spreadsheet model. Everyone has his or her own preferences for arranging the data in the various cells. We do not give any exact prescriptions, but the examples should help you develop good habits. The common elements in all LP spreadsheet models are the inputs, changing cells, target cell, and constraints.

- **Inputs.** All numerical **inputs**—that is, all numeric data given in the statement of the problem—must appear somewhere in the spreadsheet. As discussed in Chapter 2, all inputs are colored blue. Most of the inputs are also placed in the upper-left section of the spreadsheet. However, we sometimes violate this latter convention when certain inputs fit more naturally somewhere else.

- **Changing cells.** Instead of using variable names, such as $x$'s, spreadsheet models use a set of designated cells for the decision variables. The values in these cells can be changed to optimize the objective. Excel calls these cells the changing cells. To designate them clearly in this book, they are colored red.

- **Target (objective) cell.** One cell, called the target cell, contains the value of the objective. Solver systematically varies the values in the changing cells to optimize the value in the target cell. In this book, the target cell is colored gray.[5]

---

[4] This is not entirely true. If the objective line is exactly parallel to one of the constraint lines, there can be multiple optimal solutions—a whole line segment of optimal solutions. Even in this case, however, at least one of the optimal solutions is a corner point.

[5] Our blue/red/gray color scheme shows up effectively on a color monitor. However, as mentioned in the previous chapter, the colors don't show up well in this two-color book. The main difference is that deep blue on the page corresponds to red in Excel, whereas light blue on the page corresponds to blue in Excel.

- **Constraints.** Excel does not show the constraints directly on the spreadsheet. Instead, constraints are specified in a Solver dialog box, discussed shortly. For example, a set of related constraints might be designated by

  **B15:D15<=B16:D16**

  This implies three separate constraints. The value in B15 must be less than or equal to the value in B16, the value in C15 must be less than or equal to the value in C16, and the value in D15 must be less than or equal to the value in D16. Range names are also assigned to the ranges that appear in the constraints. Then a typical constraint might be specified as

  **Ingredients_consumed<=Ingredients_allowed**

  This is much easier to read and understand.

- **Nonnegativity.** Normally, we want the decision variables—that is, the values in the changing cells—to be nonnegative. These constraints do not need to be written explicitly; we simply check an option in a Solver dialog box to indicate that we want nonnegative changing cells. Note, however, that if we want to constrain any *other* cells to be nonnegative, we need to specify these constraints explicitly.

### Overview of the Solution Process

As discussed previously, the complete solution of a problem involves three stages. In the model development stage, we enter all of the inputs, trial values for the changing cells, and formulas relating these in a spreadsheet. This stage is the most crucial because all the "ingredients" of the model are included and related appropriately here. In particular, the spreadsheet *must* include a formula that relates the objective to the changing cells, either directly or indirectly, so that if the values in the changing cells vary, the objective value varies accordingly. Similarly, the spreadsheet must include formulas for the various constraints (usually their left-hand sides) that are related directly or indirectly to the changing cells.

After the model is developed, we can proceed to the second stage—invoking Solver. At this point, we formally designate the objective cell, the changing cells, the constraints, and selected options, and we tell Solver to find the *optimal* solution. If the first stage has been done correctly, the second stage is usually straightforward.

The third stage is sensitivity analysis. Here we see how the optimal solution changes (if at all) as we vary the selected inputs. This often provides important insights about how the model works.

We now carry out this procedure for the dessert problem in Example 3.1.

### DEVELOPING THE SPREADSHEET MODEL

The spreadsheet model appears in Figure 3.2. (See the file **Dessert Planning.xlsx**.) To develop this model, use the following steps.

**Figure 3.2**

Spreadsheet Model
for Dessert Problem

| | A | B | C | D | E | F | G | H |
|---|---|---|---|---|---|---|---|---|
| 1 | Planning desserts | | | | | Range names used | | |
| 2 | | | | | | Grams_consumed | =Model!$B$25 | |
| 3 | Ingredients (per serving) of each dessert | | | | | Grams_required | =Model!$D$25 | |
| 4 | | Snack bar | Ice cream | | | Ingredients_allowed | =Model!$D$20:$D$21 | |
| 5 | Calories | 120 | 160 | | | Ingredients_consumed | =Model!$B$20:$B$21 | |
| 6 | Fat (grams) | 5 | 10 | | | Servings_per_day | =Model!$B$16:$C$16 | |
| 7 | | | | | | Total_taste_index | =Model!$B$27 | |
| 8 | Grams per serving | 37 | 65 | | | | | |
| 9 | | | | | | | | |
| 10 | Taste index of each dessert (on a 100-point scale, per gram) | | | | | | | |
| 11 | | Snack bar | Ice cream | | | | | |
| 12 | | 85 | 95 | | | | | |
| 13 | | | | | | | | |
| 14 | Dessert plan | | | | | | | |
| 15 | | Snack bar | Ice cream | | | | | |
| 16 | Servings per day | 1.5 | 2.0 | | | | | |
| 17 | | | | | | | | |
| 18 | Constraints on calories and fat (per day) | | | | | | | |
| 19 | | Ingredients consumed | | Ingredients allowed | | | | |
| 20 | Calories | 500 | <= | 450 | | | | |
| 21 | Fat (grams) | 27.5 | <= | 25 | | | | |
| 22 | | | | | | | | |
| 23 | Constraint on total grams of dessert per day | | | | | | | |
| 24 | | Grams consumed | | Grams required | | | | |
| 25 | | 185.5 | >= | 120 | | | | |
| 26 | | | | | | | | |
| 27 | Total taste index | 17067.5 | | | | | | |

**①** **Inputs.** Enter all the inputs from the statement of the problem in the shaded cells as shown. In later examples, there is usually a brief section called "Where Do the Numbers Come From?" For this problem, however, it's easy to get the numbers. The inputs in rows 5, 6, and 8 are printed on the packages of most foods, and the other inputs are Maggie's preferences.

**②** **Range names.** Create the range names shown in columns F and G. Enter enough range names but don't go overboard. Specifically, enter enough range names so that the setup in the Solver dialog box, to be explained shortly, is entirely in terms of range names. Of course, you can add more range names if you like. And, of course, you can use the Create from Selection shortcut discussed in the previous chapter to speed up the range-naming process.

*At this stage, trying to "outguess" the optimal solution is not necessary. Any values in the changing cells will suffice.*

**③** **Changing cells.** Enter any two values for the changing cells in the Servings_per_day range. *Any* trial values can be used initially; Solver will eventually find the *optimal* values. Note that the two values shown in Figure 3.2 cannot be optimal because they are not feasible—they contain more calories and fat than are allowed. However, you do not need to worry about satisfying constraints at this point; Solver will take care of this later on.

**④** **Ingredients consumed.** To operationalize the calorie and fat constraints, we must calculate the amounts consumed by the dessert plan. To do this, enter the formula

**=SUMPRODUCT(B5:C5,Servings_per_day)**

in cell B20 for calories and copy it to cell B21 for fat. This formula is a shortcut for the "written out" formula

**=B5\*B16+C5\*C16**

*The "linear" in linear programming is all about sums of products. Therefore, the SUMPRODUCT function is a natural and should be used whenever possible.*

As discussed in Chapter 2, the SUMPRODUCT function is very useful in spreadsheet models, especially LP models, and we see it often. Here, it multiplies the amount of calories per serving by the number of servings for each dessert and then sums these products over the two desserts. When there are only two products in the sum, as in this example, the SUMPRODUCT formula is not really simpler than the "written out" formula. However, imagine that there are 50 desserts. Then the SUMPRODUCT formula becomes *much* simpler to enter (and read). For this reason, you should use it in your own models. Note that each range in this function, B5:C5 and Servings_per_day, is a one-row, two-column range. The SUMPRODUCT function requires that the two ranges be exactly the same size and shape.

**⑤ Grams consumed.** Similarly, we must calculate the total number of grams of dessert consumed daily. To do this, enter the formula

**=SUMPRODUCT(B8:C8,Servings_per_day)**

in cell B25. Each product in this SUMPRODUCT is grams per serving multiplied by the number of servings; hence, its units are grams.

**⑥ Total taste index.** To calculate the total taste index, enter the formula

**=SUMPRODUCT(B12:C12,B8:C8,Servings_per_day)**

in cell B27. This formula shows that the SUMPRODUCT function can use three ranges (or more), provided that they are all exactly the same size and shape. Three are required here because we need to multiply taste points per gram by grams per serving by number of servings. Again, this formula is equivalent to the "written out" formula

**=B12*B8*B16+C12*C8*C16**

*Although the SUMPRODUCT function usually takes two range arguments, it can take three or more, provided they all have the same size and shape.*

### Experimenting with Possible Solutions

The next step is to specify the changing cells, the target cell, and the constraints in a Solver dialog box and then instruct Solver to find the optimal solution. Before we do this, however, try a few guesses in the changing cells. There are two reasons for doing this. First, by entering different sets of values in the changing cells, you can confirm that the formulas in the other cells are working correctly. Second, this experimentation sometimes helps you develop a better understanding of the model.

For example, Maggie prefers the taste of ice cream to snack bars, so you might guess that her dessert plan will consist of ice cream only. If so, she should consume as much ice cream as will fit into her constraints on calories and fat. You can check that this is 2.5 servings per day, as shown in Figure 3.3. With this plan, she could eat more calories, but

**Figure 3.3**
Best Plan with Ice Cream Only

| | A | B | C | D | E | F | G | H |
|---|---|---|---|---|---|---|---|---|
| 1 | Planning desserts | | | | | Range names used | | |
| 2 | | | | | | Grams_consumed | =Model!$B$25 | |
| 3 | Ingredients (per serving) of each dessert | | | | | Grams_required | =Model!$D$25 | |
| 4 | | Snack bar | Ice cream | | | Ingredients_allowed | =Model!$D$20:$D$21 | |
| 5 | Calories | 120 | 160 | | | Ingredients_consumed | =Model!$B$20:$B$21 | |
| 6 | Fat (grams) | 5 | 10 | | | Servings_per_day | =Model!$B$16:$C$16 | |
| 7 | | | | | | Total_taste_index | =Model!$B$27 | |
| 8 | Grams per serving | 37 | 65 | | | | | |
| 9 | | | | | | | | |
| 10 | Taste index of each dessert (on a 100-point scale, per gram) | | | | | | | |
| 11 | | Snack bar | Ice cream | | | | | |
| 12 | | 85 | 95 | | | | | |
| 13 | | | | | | | | |
| 14 | Dessert plan | | | | | | | |
| 15 | | Snack bar | Ice cream | | | | | |
| 16 | Servings per day | 0 | 2.5 | | | | | |
| 17 | | | | | | | | |
| 18 | Constraints on calories and fat (per day) | | | | | | | |
| 19 | | Ingredients consumed | | Ingredients allowed | | | | |
| 20 | Calories | 400 | <= | 450 | | | | |
| 21 | Fat (grams) | 25 | <= | 25 | | | | |
| 22 | | | | | | | | |
| 23 | Constraint on total grams of dessert per day | | | | | | | |
| 24 | | Grams consumed | | Grams required | | | | |
| 25 | | 162.5 | >= | 120 | | | | |
| 26 | | | | | | | | |
| 27 | Total taste index | 15437.5 | | | | | | |

she can't eat any more fat. Is this plan optimal? It turns out that it isn't, as we will see shortly, but this fact is not obvious. By the way, if Maggie decided to go entirely with snack bars and no ice cream, you can check that she could then consume 3.75 servings, which would exhaust her calorie allowance, but not her fat allowance, and would provide a total taste index of 11,793.75. Because this is well less than the total taste index for the plan with ice cream only, it certainly cannot be optimal.

You can continue to try different values in the changing cells, attempting to get as large a total taste index as possible while staying within the constraints. Even for this small model with only two changing cells, it isn't easy! You can only imagine how much more difficult it is when there are hundreds or even thousands of changing cells and many constraints. This is why software such as Excel's Solver is so helpful. It uses a quick and efficient algorithm to search through all feasible solutions and eventually find the optimal solution. Fortunately, Solver is easy to use.

## USING SOLVER

To invoke Excel's Solver, select Solver from the Data ribbon. (If there is no such item on your PC, select the Office button, then Excel Options, then Add-Ins, then Go, and make sure the Solver item is checked in the resulting list of add-ins. If there is no Solver item in the list, Solver was probably not installed when Office was installed on this PC. In this case, you must run the Office setup program to install Solver.) The dialog box in Figure 3.4 appears. It has three important sections that we must fill in: the target cell, the changing cells, and the constraints. For the dessert problem, we can fill these in by typing cell references or we can point, click, and drag the appropriate ranges in the usual way. Better yet, if there are any named ranges, we can use these range names instead of cell addresses. In fact, for reasons of readability, our convention is to make sure that *only* range names, not cell addresses, appear in this dialog box.

**Figure 3.4**

Solver Dialog Box
for Dessert Model

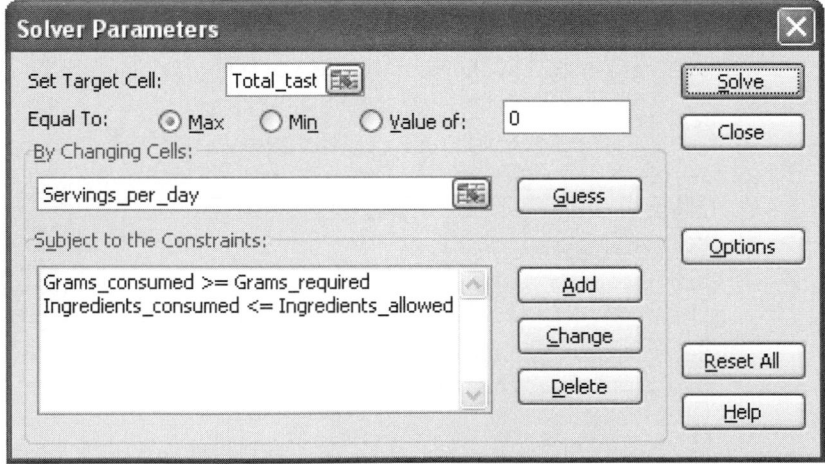

**Excel Tip:** *Range Names in Solver Dialog Box*
*The usual procedure is to use the mouse to select the relevant ranges for the Solver dialog box. Fortunately, if these ranges have already been named, the range names automatically replace the cell addresses in the dialog box.*

**1** **Objective.** Select the Total_taste_index cell as the target cell, and make sure the Max option is selected.

**2** **Changing cells.** Select the Servings_per_day range as the changing cells.

**3** **Constraints.** Click on the Add button to bring up the dialog box in Figure 3.5. Here we specify a typical constraint by entering a cell reference or range name on the left, the type of constraint from the drop-down list in the middle, and a cell reference, range name, or numeric value on the right. Use this dialog box to enter the constraint

**Ingredients_consumed<=Ingredients_allowed**

(*Note:* You can type these range names in the dialog box, or you can drag them in the usual way. If you drag them, the cell addresses eventually change to range names if range names exist.) Then click on the Add button and enter the constraint

**Grams_consumed>=Grams_required**

The first constraint says to consume no more calories and fat than are allowed. The second constraint says to consume at least as many grams as are required. Then click on OK to get back to the Solver dialog box.

**Figure 3.5**
Add Constraint
Dialog Box

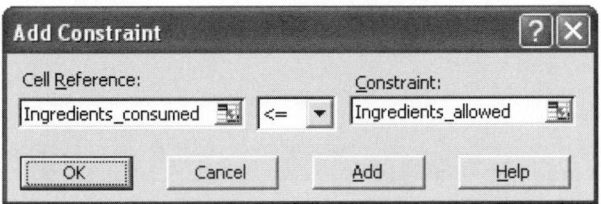

**Excel Tip:** *Inequality and Equality Labels in Spreadsheet Models*
*The <= signs in cells C20:C21 and the >= sign in cell C25 (see Figure 3.2 or Figure 3.3) are not a necessary part of the Excel model. They are entered simply as labels in the spreadsheet and do not substitute for entering the constraints in Solver's Add Constraint dialog box. However, they help to document the model, so they are included in all the examples. In fact, we plan our spreadsheet models so that the two sides of a constraint are in nearby cells, with "gutter" cells in between where we can attach a label like <=, >=, or =. This convention tends to make the resulting spreadsheet models much more readable.*

*Checking the Assume Non-Negative box ensures only that the changing cells, not any other cells, will be nonnegative.*

**4** **Nonnegativity.** Because negative quantities of dessert make no sense, we must tell Solver *explicitly* to make the changing cells nonnegative. To do this, click on the Options button in Figure 3.4 and check the Assume Non-Negative box in the resulting dialog box (see Figure 3.6.) This automatically ensures that *all* changing cells will be nonnegative.

**5** **Linear model.** Solver uses one of several algorithms to solve various types of models. The models discussed in this chapter are all *linear* models. (The properties of linear models are discussed shortly.) Linear models can be solved most efficiently by the simplex method. To instruct Solver to use this method, you must check the Assume Linear Model in the Solver options dialog box shown in Figure 3.6.

**6** **Optimize.** Click on the Solve button in the dialog box in Figure 3.4. At this point, Solver does its work by searching through a number of possible solutions until it finds the optimal solution. (You can watch the progress on the lower-left of the screen, although for small models the process is almost instantaneous.) When finished, Solver displays the message in Figure 3.7. You can then instruct it to return the values in the changing cells to their original (probably nonoptimal) values or retain the optimal values found by Solver. In most cases, you should choose the latter. For now, click on the OK button to keep the Solver solution. You should see the solution shown in Figure 3.8.

**Figure 3.6**
Solver Options
Dialog Box

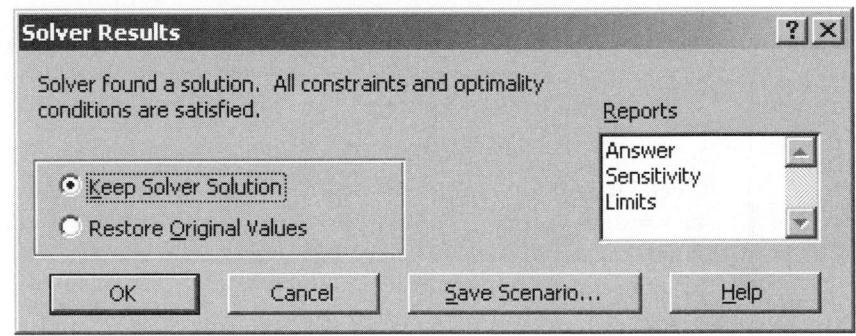

**Solver Options**

| Max Time: | 100 | seconds |
| Iterations: | 100 | |
| Precision: | 0.000001 | |
| Tolerance: | 5 | % |
| Convergence: | 0.0001 | |

OK
Cancel
Load Model...
Save Model...
Help

☑ Assume Linear Model    ☐ Use Automatic Scaling
☑ Assume Non-Negative    ☐ Show Iteration Results

Estimates
  ◉ Tangent
  ○ Quadratic

Derivatives
  ◉ Forward
  ○ Central

Search
  ◉ Newton
  ○ Conjugate

**Figure 3.7**
Solver Message That
Optimal Solution
Has Been Found

**Solver Results**

Solver found a solution. All constraints and optimality
conditions are satisfied.

Reports

◉ Keep Solver Solution
○ Restore Original Values

Answer
Sensitivity
Limits

OK    Cancel    Save Scenario...    Help

**Figure 3.8**
Optimal Solution
for Dessert Model

| | A | B | C | D | E | F | G | H |
|---|---|---|---|---|---|---|---|---|
| 1 | Planning desserts | | | | | Range names used | | |
| 2 | | | | | | Grams_consumed | =Model!$B$25 | |
| 3 | Ingredients (per serving) of each dessert | | | | | Grams_required | =Model!$D$25 | |
| 4 | | Snack bar | Ice cream | | | Ingredients_allowed | =Model!$D$20:$D$21 | |
| 5 | Calories | 120 | 160 | | | Ingredients_consumed | =Model!$B$20:$B$21 | |
| 6 | Fat (grams) | 5 | 10 | | | Servings_per_day | =Model!$B$16:$C$16 | |
| 7 | | | | | | Total_taste_index | =Model!$B$27 | |
| 8 | Grams per serving | 37 | 65 | | | | | |
| 9 | | | | | | | | |
| 10 | Taste index of each dessert (on a 100-point scale, per gram) | | | | | | | |
| 11 | | Snack bar | Ice cream | | | | | |
| 12 | | 85 | 95 | | | | | |
| 13 | | | | | | | | |
| 14 | Dessert plan | | | | | | | |
| 15 | | Snack bar | Ice cream | | | | | |
| 16 | Servings per day | 1.25 | 1.875 | | | | | |
| 17 | | | | | | | | |
| 18 | Constraints on calories and fat (per day) | | | | | | | |
| 19 | | Ingredients consumed | | Ingredients allowed | | | | |
| 20 | Calories | 450 | <= | 450 | | | | |
| 21 | Fat (grams) | 25 | <= | 25 | | | | |
| 22 | | | | | | | | |
| 23 | Constraint on total grams of dessert per day | | | | | | | |
| 24 | | Grams consumed | | Grams required | | | | |
| 25 | | 168.125 | >= | 120 | | | | |
| 26 | | | | | | | | |
| 27 | Total taste index | 15509.375 | | | | | | |

### Discussion of the Solution

This solution says that Maggie should consume 1.25 servings of snack bars and 1.875 servings of ice cream per day. This plan leaves no room for any more calories or fat, and it more than satisfies her requirement of 120 dessert grams per day. It provides a total taste index that is slightly more than the plan with ice cream only in Figure 3.3. In fact, we now know that *no* plan can provide a total taste index larger than this one—that is, without violating at least one of the constraints.

The solution in Figure 3.8 is typical of solutions to optimization models in the following sense. Of all the inequality constraints, some are satisfied exactly and others are not. In this solution, the calorie and fat constraints are met exactly, which means they are **binding.** However, the constraint on grams is **nonbinding.** The number of grams consumed is *greater than* the number required. The difference is called **slack.**[6] You can think of the binding constraints as "bottlenecks" because they prevent the objective from being improved. If it were not for constraints on calories and fat, Maggie could obtain an even higher total taste index. ∎

> An inequality constraint is **binding** if the solution makes it an equality. Otherwise, it is **nonbinding,** and the positive difference between the two sides of the constraint is called the **slack.**

## FUNDAMENTAL INSIGHT

### Binding and Nonbinding Constraints

Most optimization models contain constraints expressed as inequalities. In an optimal solution, each such constraint is either binding (holds as an equality) or nonbinding. It's extremely important to identify the binding constraints, because they are the constraints that prevent the objective from improving. A typical situation is a constraint on the availability of a resource. If such a constraint is binding, the objective would typically improve by having more of that resource. But if such a resource constraint is nonbinding, we have more of the resource than necessary.

---

## 3.4 SENSITIVITY ANALYSIS

Now that we have solved Maggie's dessert problem, it might appear that we are finished. But in real LP applications, the solution to a *single* model is hardly ever the end of the analysis. It is almost always useful to perform a sensitivity analysis to see how (or if) the optimal solution changes as we change one or more inputs. We illustrate systematic ways of doing so in this section. Actually, we discuss two approaches. The first uses an optional sensitivity report that Solver offers. The second uses an add-in called SolverTable that we developed.

---

[6] Some analysts use the term **slack** only for ≤ constraints and the term **surplus** for ≥ constraints. We refer to each of these as slack—the absolute difference between the two sides of the constraint.

## Solver's Sensitivity Report

When we run Solver, the dialog box in Figure 3.7 offers us the option to obtain a sensitivity report.[7] This report is based on a well-established theory of sensitivity analysis in optimization models, especially LP models. This theory has been developed around algebraic models that are arranged in a "standard" format. Essentially, all such algebraic models look alike, so the same type of sensitivity report applies to all of them. Specifically, they have an objective function of the form $c_1x_1 + \cdots + c_nx_n$, where $n$ is the number of decision variables, the $c$'s are constants, and the $x$'s are the decision variables; and each constraint can be put in the form $a_1x_1 + \cdots + a_nx_n \leq b$, $a_1x_1 + \cdots + a_nx_n \geq b$, or $a_1x_1 + \cdots + a_nx_n = b$, where the $a$'s and $b$ are constants. Solver's sensitivity report performs two types of sensitivity analysis: (1) on the coefficients of the objective, the $c$'s, and (2) on the right-hand sides of the constraints, the $b$'s.

To illustrate the typical analysis, look at the sensitivity report for Maggie's dessert planning model in Example 3.1. For convenience, the algebraic model is repeated here, and the spreadsheet model is shown again in Figure 3.9.

$$\text{Maximize } 37(85)x_1 + 65(95)x_2$$

subject to

$$120x_1 + 160x_2 \leq 450$$
$$5x_1 + 10x_2 \leq 25$$
$$37x_1 + 65x_2 \geq 120$$
$$x_1, x_2 \geq 0$$

**Figure 3.9**

Dessert Model with Optimal Solution

| | A | B | C | D | E | F | G | H |
|---|---|---|---|---|---|---|---|---|
| 1 | Planning desserts | | | | | Range names used | | |
| 2 | | | | | | Grams_consumed | =Model!$B$25 | |
| 3 | Ingredients (per serving) of each dessert | | | | | Grams_required | =Model!$D$25 | |
| 4 | | Snack bar | Ice cream | | | Ingredients_allowed | =Model!$D$20:$D$21 | |
| 5 | Calories | 120 | 160 | | | Ingredients_consumed | =Model!$B$20:$B$21 | |
| 6 | Fat (grams) | 5 | 10 | | | Servings_per_day | =Model!$B$16:$C$16 | |
| 7 | | | | | | Total_taste_index | =Model!$B$27 | |
| 8 | Grams per serving | 37 | 65 | | | | | |
| 9 | | | | | | | | |
| 10 | Taste index of each dessert (on a 100-point scale, per gram) | | | | | | | |
| 11 | | Snack bar | Ice cream | | | | | |
| 12 | | 85 | 95 | | | | | |
| 13 | | | | | | | | |
| 14 | Dessert plan | | | | | | | |
| 15 | | Snack bar | Ice cream | | | | | |
| 16 | Servings per day | 1.25 | 1.875 | | | | | |
| 17 | | | | | | | | |
| 18 | Constraints on calories and fat (per day) | | | | | | | |
| 19 | | Ingredients consumed | | Ingredients allowed | | | | |
| 20 | Calories | 450 | <= | 450 | | | | |
| 21 | Fat (grams) | 25 | <= | 25 | | | | |
| 22 | | | | | | | | |
| 23 | Constraint on total grams of dessert per day | | | | | | | |
| 24 | | Grams consumed | | Grams required | | | | |
| 25 | | 168.125 | >= | 120 | | | | |
| 26 | | | | | | | | |
| 27 | Total taste index | 15509.375 | | | | | | |

This time, when we run Solver, we ask for a sensitivity report in Solver's final dialog box (see Figure 3.7). This creates the sensitivity report on a new worksheet with two sections, as shown in Figure 3.10.[8] The top section is for sensitivity to changes in the

---

[7] It also offers Answer and Limits reports. We don't find these particularly useful, so they are not discussed here.
[8] If your table looks different from this one, make sure you have checked Assume Linear Model. Otherwise, Solver uses a nonlinear algorithm and produces a different type of sensitivity report. Also, we should mention that we have gotten error messages when we have tried to create these sensitivity reports in Excel 2007. Frontline Systems confirms that Microsoft "broke" these reports with Excel 2007 and that a fix is being sought.

two coefficients—37(85) = 3145 and 65(95) = 6175—of the decision variables in the objective function. Each row in this section indicates how the optimal solution changes if we change one of these coefficients. The bottom section is for the sensitivity to changes in the right-hand sides—450, 25, and 120—of the constraints. Each row of this section indicates how the optimal solution changes if we change one of these right-hand sides.

**Figure 3.10**
Solver's Sensitivity Report for Dessert Model

| | A | B | C | D | E | F | G | H |
|---|---|---|---|---|---|---|---|---|
| 6 | Adjustable Cells | | | | | | | |
| 7 | | | | Final | Reduced | Objective | Allowable | Allowable |
| 8 | | Cell | Name | Value | Cost | Coefficient | Increase | Decrease |
| 9 | | $B$16 | Servings per day Snack bar | 1.25 | 0 | 3145 | 1486.25 | 57.50 |
| 10 | | $C$16 | Servings per day Ice cream | 1.875 | 0.000 | 6175 | 115 | 1981.67 |
| 11 | | | | | | | | |
| 12 | Constraints | | | | | | | |
| 13 | | | | Final | Shadow | Constraint | Allowable | Allowable |
| 14 | | Cell | Name | Value | Price | R.H. Side | Increase | Decrease |
| 15 | | $B$20 | Calories Ingredients consumed | 450 | 1.4375 | 450 | 150 | 50 |
| 16 | | $B$21 | Fat (grams) Ingredients consumed | 25 | 594.5 | 25 | 3.125 | 6.25 |
| 17 | | $B$25 | Grams_consumed | 168.125 | 0 | 120 | 48.125 | 1E+30 |

Now let's look at the specific numbers and their interpretation. In the first row of the top section, the *allowable decrease* and *allowable increase* indicate how much the coefficient of snack bars in the objective, currently 3145, can change before the optimal dessert plan changes. If the coefficient of snack bars stays within this allowable range, the optimal dessert plan—the values in the changing cells—do not change at all. However, outside of these limits, the optimal mix between snack bars and ice cream might change.

To see what this implies, change the value in cell B12 from 85 to 84. Then the coefficient of snack bars decreases by 37, from 37(85) to 37(84). This change is within the allowable decrease of 57.5. If you rerun Solver, you'll get the *same* values in the changing cells, although the objective value will decrease. Next, change the value in cell B12 to 83. This time, the coefficient of snack bars decreases by 74 from its original value, from 37(85) to 37(83). This change is outside the allowable decrease, so the solution might change. If you rerun Solver, you will see a change—no snack bars are now in the optimal solution.

The *reduced costs* in the second column indicate, in general, how much the objective coefficient of a decision variable that is currently 0—that is, not in the optimal solution—must change before that variable becomes positive. These reduced costs are always 0 if the corresponding decision variables are already positive, as they are in the original example. However, when we change the value in cell B12 to 83, as we did previously, and rerun Solver, snack bars drop out of the optimal solution, and the new sensitivity report appears as shown in Figure 3.11. Now the reduced cost is –16.5. This implies that the coefficient of snack bars must be increased by 16.5 before snack bars enters the optimal mix.

**Figure 3.11**
Sensitivity Table for Revised Model

| | A | B | C | D | E | F | G | H |
|---|---|---|---|---|---|---|---|---|
| 6 | Adjustable Cells | | | | | | | |
| 7 | | | | Final | Reduced | Objective | Allowable | Allowable |
| 8 | | Cell | Name | Value | Cost | Coefficient | Increase | Decrease |
| 9 | | $B$16 | Servings per day Snack bar | 0 | -16.5 | 3071 | 16.5 | 1E+30 |
| 10 | | $C$16 | Servings per day Ice cream | 2.500 | 0.000 | 6175 | 1E+30 | 33.00 |
| 11 | | | | | | | | |
| 12 | Constraints | | | | | | | |
| 13 | | | | Final | Shadow | Constraint | Allowable | Allowable |
| 14 | | Cell | Name | Value | Price | R.H. Side | Increase | Decrease |
| 15 | | $B$20 | Calories Ingredients consumed | 400 | 0 | 450 | 1E+30 | 50 |
| 16 | | $B$21 | Fat (grams) Ingredients consumed | 25 | 617.5 | 25 | 3.125 | 6.54 |
| 17 | | $B$25 | Grams_consumed | 162.5 | 0 | 120 | 42.5 | 1E+30 |

> The **reduced cost** for any decision variable not currently in the optimal solution indicates how much better that coefficient must be before that variable enters at a positive level. The reduced cost for any variable already in the optimal solution is automatically 0.[9]

In the bottom section of the report in Figure 3.10, each row corresponds to a constraint. To have this part of the report make economic sense, the model should be developed so that the right-hand side of each constraint is a numeric constant, not a formula. For example, the right-hand side of the calories constraint is 450, the maximum allowable calories. Then the report indicates how much these right-hand side constants can change before the optimal solution changes. To understand this more fully, you need to understand *shadow prices*. A **shadow price** indicates the amount of change in the objective when a right-hand-side constant changes.

> **Shadow price** is an economic term that indicates the change in the optimal value of the objective function when the right-hand side of some constraint changes by a unit amount.

The shadow prices are reported for each constraint. For example, the shadow price for the calorie constraint is 1.4375. This means that if the right-hand side of the calorie constraint increases by 1 calorie, from 450 to 451, the optimal value of the objective increases by 1.4375 units. It works in the other direction as well. If the right-hand side of the calorie constraint *decreases* by 1 calorie, from 450 to 449, the optimal value of the objective decreases by 1.4375 units. However, as we continue to increase or decrease the right-hand side, this 1.4375 change in the objective does not necessarily continue indefinitely. This is where the reported allowable decrease and allowable increase are relevant. As long as the right-hand side increases or decreases within its allowable limits, the same shadow price of 1.4375 applies. Beyond these limits, however, a different shadow price probably applies.

You can prove this for yourself. First, increase the right-hand side of the calorie constraint by 150, from 450 to 600, and rerun Solver. You will see that the objective indeed increases by 1.4375(150), from 15,509.375 to 15,725. Now increase this right-hand side from 600 to 601 and rerun Solver. You will observe that the objective doesn't increase at all. This means that the shadow price beyond 600 is *less than* 1.4375; in fact, it is 0. This is typical. When a right-hand side is increased beyond its allowable increase, the new shadow price is typically less than the original shadow price (although it doesn't typically fall to 0, as in this example).

The idea is that a constraint "costs us" by keeping the objective from improving. A shadow price indicates how much we would be willing to pay (in units of the objective function) to "relax" a constraint. In this example, we would be willing to pay 1.4375 taste index units to increase the right-hand side of the calorie constraint by 1 calorie. This is because such a change would increase the objective by 1.4375 units. But beyond a certain point—150 calories in this example—further relaxation of the calorie constraint does us no good, so we are not willing to pay for any further increases.

The constraint on grams consumed is slightly different. It has a shadow price of 0. This is always true for a nonbinding constraint, and it makes sense. If you change the right-hand side of this constraint from 120 to 121, nothing happens to the optimal dessert plan or its objective value; there is just one less gram of slack in this constraint. However, the allowable increase of 48.125 indicates that something *will* change when the right-hand side reaches 168.125. At this point, the constraint becomes binding—the grams consumed

---

[9]As shown in Example 3.2, this is not quite true. If there are upper bound constraints on certain decision variables, the reduced costs for these variables have a slightly different interpretation.

### The Effect of Constraints on the Objective

If a constraint is added or an existing constraint becomes more constraining (for example, less of some resource is available), the objective can only get worse; it can never improve. The easiest way to understand this is to think of the feasible region. When a constraint is added or an existing constraint becomes more constraining, the feasible region shrinks, so some solutions that were feasible before,

maybe even the optimal solution, are no longer feasible. The opposite is true if a constraint is deleted or an existing constraint becomes less constraining. In that case, the objective can only improve; it can never get worse. Again, the idea is that when a constraint is deleted or an existing constraint becomes less constraining, the feasible region expands. In this case, all solutions that were feasible before are still feasible, and there are some additional feasible solutions to choose from.

equals the grams required—and beyond this, the optimal dessert plan starts to change. By the way, the allowable decrease for this constraint, shown as $1 + E30$, means that it is essentially infinite. We can decrease the right-hand side of this constraint below 120 as much as we like, and absolutely nothing changes in the optimal solution.

## The SolverTable Add-In

*Solver's sensitivity report is almost impossible to unravel for some models. In these cases, SolverTable is preferable because of its easily interpreted outputs.*

We can interpret Solver's sensitivity report for the dessert model in a fairly natural way because the spreadsheet model is almost a direct translation of a standard algebraic model. However, given the flexibility of spreadsheets, this is not always the case. Many perfectly good spreadsheet models—and some we have developed ourselves—are structured differently from their standard algebraic-model counterparts. In these cases, Solver's sensitivity report is arguably more confusing than useful. Therefore, we developed an Excel add-in called SolverTable. SolverTable allows you to ask sensitivity questions about *any* of the input variables, not just coefficients of the objective and right-hand sides, and it provides straightforward answers.

The SolverTable add-in is contained on the CD-ROM that comes with this book.[10] To install it, run the Setup program on the CD-ROM. You can then check that it's installed by selecting the Office button, selecting Excel Options, selecting Add-Ins, and clicking on Go. There should be a SolverTable item in the resulting list of add-ins. To actually load SolverTable into memory, check the SolverTable box in this list. To unload it from memory, uncheck the box.

The SolverTable add-in was developed to mimic Excel's built-in data table tool. Recall that data tables allow you to vary one or two inputs in a spreadsheet model and see instantaneously how selected outputs change. SolverTable is similar except that it runs Solver for every new input value (or pair of input values). SolverTable can be used in two ways:

■ **One-way table.** A one-way table means that there is a *single* input cell and *any number* of output cells. That is, there can be a single output cell or multiple output cells.

■ **Two-way table.** A two-way table means that there are *two* input cells and one or more outputs. (You might recall that an Excel two-way data table allows only *one* output. SolverTable allows more than one. It creates a separate table for each output as a function of the two inputs.)

To illustrate some of the possibilities for the dessert example, we can check how sensitive the optimal dessert plan and total taste index are to (1) changes in the number of

---

[10] SolverTable (along with any updates) is also on our Web site at http://www.kelley.iu.edu/albrightbooks under the Free Downloads link.

calories per serving of snack bars and (2) the number of daily dessert calories allowed. Then we can check how sensitive the optimal objective value is to simultaneous changes in the taste indexes of snack bars and ice cream.

We chose the input range from 60 to 140 in increments of 10 fairly arbitrarily. You can choose any desired range of input values.

Assuming that the dessert model has been developed and optimized, as shown in Figure 3.8, and that the SolverTable add-in has been loaded, the sensitivity to changes in the number of calories per serving of snack bars is shown in Figure 3.12. To obtain this output (the part in the range A30:D39), select Run SolverTable from the SolverTable dropdown on the Add-Ins ribbon, select a one-way table in the first dialog box, and fill in the second dialog box as shown in Figure 3.13. (Note that ranges can be entered as cell addresses or range names. Also, multiple ranges in the Outputs box should be separated by commas.)

**Figure 3.12**

Sensitivity to Calories per Serving of Snack Bars

| | A | B | C | D |
|---|---|---|---|---|
| 29 | Sensitivity to calories per serving of snack bars | | | |
| 30 | | $B$16 | $C$16 | $B$27 |
| 31 | 60 | 5 | 0.000 | 15725 |
| 32 | 70 | 5 | 0.000 | 15725 |
| 33 | 80 | 5 | 0.000 | 15725 |
| 34 | 90 | 5 | 0.000 | 15725 |
| 35 | 100 | 2.5 | 1.250 | 15581.25 |
| 36 | 110 | 1.667 | 1.667 | 15533.333 |
| 37 | 120 | 1.25 | 1.875 | 15509.375 |
| 38 | 130 | 1 | 2.000 | 15495 |
| 39 | 140 | 0.833 | 2.083 | 15485.417 |

**Figure 3.13**

SolverTable Dialog Box for a One-Way Table

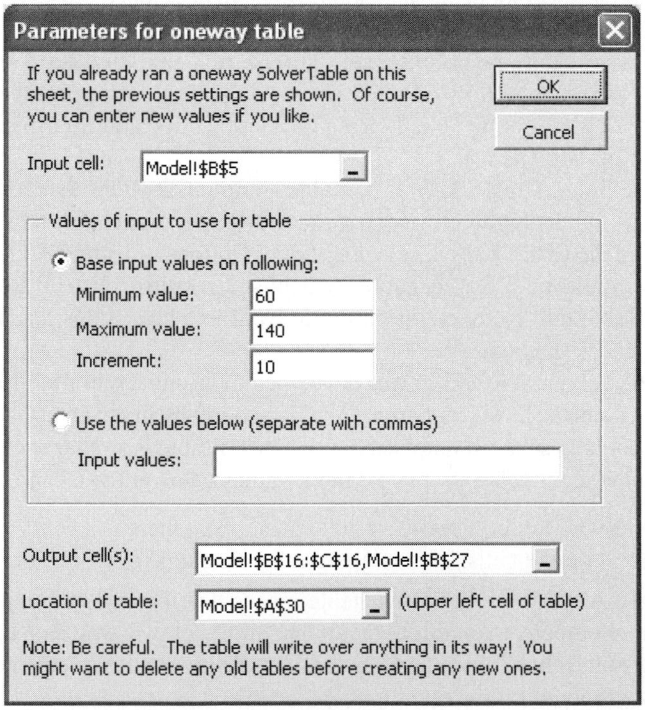

**Parameters for oneway table**

If you already ran a oneway SolverTable on this sheet, the previous settings are shown. Of course, you can enter new values if you like.

OK

Cancel

Input cell: Model!$B$5

Values of input to use for table

● Base input values on following:

Minimum value: 60

Maximum value: 140

Increment: 10

○ Use the values below (separate with commas)

Input values:

Output cell(s): Model!$B$16:$C$16,Model!$B$27

Location of table: Model!$A$30 (upper left cell of table)

Note: Be careful. The table will write over anything in its way! You might want to delete any old tables before creating any new ones.

**Excel Tip:** *Selecting Multiple Ranges*

*If you need to select multiple output ranges, the trick is to keep your finger on the Ctrl key as you drag the ranges. This automatically enters the separating comma(s) for you. The same trick works for selecting multiple changing cell ranges in Solver's dialog box.*

When you click on OK, Solver solves a separate optimization problem for each of the rows of the table and then reports the requested outputs (servings consumed and total taste index) in the table. It can take a while, depending on the speed of your computer, but everything is automatic. However, if you want to update this table—by using new calorie values in column A, for example—you must repeat the procedure. SolverTable enters comments (indicated by the small red triangles) in several cells to help you interpret the output.

The outputs in this table show that as the calories per serving of snack bars increase, the optimal dessert plan is initially to eat snack bars only, and it stays this way for a while. But beyond 90 calories per serving, the optimal plan gradually uses fewer snack bars and starts using ice cream. Beyond some point—somewhere above 140 calories per serving—the optimal plan probably uses no snack bars at all. (This point could be found with another SolverTable run, using a different input range.) Also, note that as calories per serving increase beyond 90, the optimal total taste index in column D continually decreases. This makes sense because as one ingredient increases in calories, the total calorie limit dictates that not as much dessert can be eaten, so the total taste index decreases.

The sensitivity to changes in the number of daily dessert calories allowed appears in Figure 3.14. It's formed through the same dialog box as in Figure 3.13, except that the input variable is now in cell D20, which is allowed to vary from 400 to 600 calories in increments of 25 calories. Now we see that as the total calorie allowance increases, the optimal dessert plan uses more snack bars and less ice cream, and the total taste index increases. In fact, we calculate this latter increase in column E. (We do this manually, not with SolverTable. For example, the formula in cell E44 is =D44-D43.) At least for this input range, the objective increases by the *same* amount, 35.9375, for each 25-calorie increase in the daily calorie allowance. Alternatively, the *per unit* change, 1.4375 (=35.9375/25), is the same shadow price we saw previously. In this sense, SolverTable outputs can reinforce outputs from Solver's sensitivity report.

**Figure 3.14**

Sensitivity to Daily Calorie Allowance

|    | A | B | C | D | E |
|----|---|---|---|---|---|
| 41 | Sensitivity to calories allowed | | | | |
| 42 | | $B$16 | $C$16 | $B$27 | Increase |
| 43 | 400 | 0 | 2.500 | 15437.5 | |
| 44 | 425 | 0.625 | 2.187 | 15473.4375 | 35.9375 |
| 45 | 450 | 1.25 | 1.875 | 15509.375 | 35.9375 |
| 46 | 475 | 1.875 | 1.563 | 15545.3125 | 35.9375 |
| 47 | 500 | 2.5 | 1.250 | 15581.25 | 35.9375 |
| 48 | 525 | 3.125 | 0.938 | 15617.1875 | 35.9375 |
| 49 | 550 | 3.75 | 0.625 | 15653.125 | 35.9375 |
| 50 | 575 | 4.375 | 0.312 | 15689.0625 | 35.9375 |
| 51 | 600 | 5 | 0.000 | 15725 | 35.9375 |

The final sensitivity analysis is for simultaneous changes in the taste indexes of snack bars and ice cream. This requires a two-way SolverTable. The resulting output appears in Figure 3.15 and is produced by the dialog box settings shown in Figure 3.16. Here we specify two inputs and two input ranges and we are again allowed to specify multiple output cells. An output table is generated for *each* of the output cells. For example, the top table in Figure 3.15 shows how the optimal servings of snack bars vary as the two taste index inputs vary. The results, especially in the two top tables, are probably not very surprising. When the taste index of either dessert increases, more of it is used in the optimal dessert plan.

**Figure 3.15**

Sensitivity to Taste Indexes of Both Desserts

| | G | H | I | J | K | L | M |
|---|---|---|---|---|---|---|---|
| 29 | Sensitivity to taste indexes of snack bars (along side) and ice cream (along top) | | | | | | |
| 30 | $B$16 | 70 | 75 | 80 | 85 | 90 | 95 |
| 31 | 60 | 0 | 0 | 0 | 0 | 0 | 0 |
| 32 | 65 | 1.25 | 0 | 0 | 0 | 0 | 0 |
| 33 | 70 | 1.25 | 1.25 | 0 | 0 | 0 | 0 |
| 34 | 75 | 1.25 | 1.25 | 1.25 | 1.25 | 0 | 0 |
| 35 | 80 | 1.25 | 1.25 | 1.25 | 1.25 | 1.25 | 0 |
| 36 | 85 | 1.25 | 1.25 | 1.25 | 1.25 | 1.25 | 1.25 |
| 37 | 90 | 1.25 | 1.25 | 1.25 | 1.25 | 1.25 | 1.25 |
| 38 | 95 | 3.75 | 1.25 | 1.25 | 1.25 | 1.25 | 1.25 |
| 39 | | | | | | | |
| 40 | $C$16 | 70 | 75 | 80 | 85 | 90 | 95 |
| 41 | 60 | 2.500 | 2.500 | 2.500 | 2.500 | 2.500 | 2.500 |
| 42 | 65 | 1.875 | 2.500 | 2.500 | 2.500 | 2.500 | 2.500 |
| 43 | 70 | 1.875 | 1.875 | 2.500 | 2.500 | 2.500 | 2.500 |
| 44 | 75 | 1.875 | 1.875 | 1.875 | 1.875 | 2.500 | 2.500 |
| 45 | 80 | 1.875 | 1.875 | 1.875 | 1.875 | 1.875 | 2.500 |
| 46 | 85 | 1.875 | 1.875 | 1.875 | 1.875 | 1.875 | 1.875 |
| 47 | 90 | 1.875 | 1.875 | 1.875 | 1.875 | 1.875 | 1.875 |
| 48 | 95 | 0.000 | 1.875 | 1.875 | 1.875 | 1.875 | 1.875 |
| 49 | | | | | | | |
| 50 | $B$27 | 70 | 75 | 80 | 85 | 90 | 95 |
| 51 | 60 | 11375 | 12187.5 | 13000 | 13812.5 | 14625 | 15437.5 |
| 52 | 65 | 11537.5 | 12187.5 | 13000 | 13812.5 | 14625 | 15437.5 |
| 53 | 70 | 11768.75 | 12378.12 | 13000 | 13812.5 | 14625 | 15437.5 |
| 54 | 75 | 12000 | 12609.38 | 13218.75 | 13828.12 | 14625 | 15437.5 |
| 55 | 80 | 12231.25 | 12840.63 | 13450 | 14059.38 | 14668.75 | 15437.5 |
| 56 | 85 | 12462.5 | 13071.88 | 13681.25 | 14290.63 | 14900 | 15509.37 |
| 57 | 90 | 12693.75 | 13303.13 | 13912.5 | 14521.88 | 15131.25 | 15740.63 |
| 58 | 95 | 13181.25 | 13534.38 | 14143.75 | 14753.13 | 15362.5 | 15971.88 |

**Figure 3.16**

SolverTable Dialog Box for a Two-Way Table

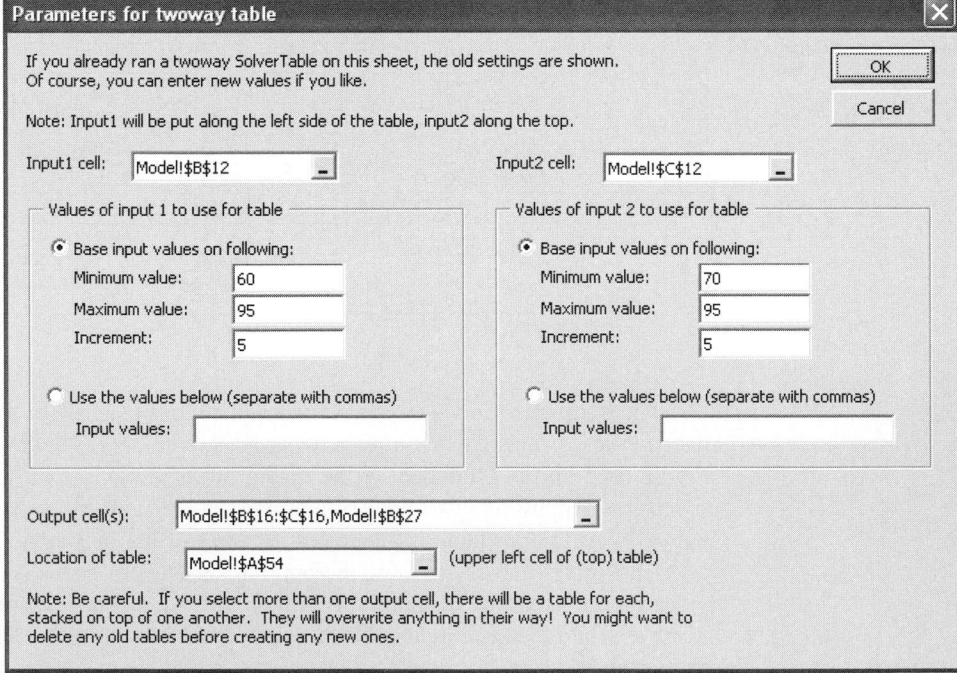

92    Chapter 3    Introduction to Optimization Modeling

We can always run a sensitivity analysis by changing inputs manually in the spreadsheet model and rerunning Solver. With SolverTable, however, we can perform a *systematic* sensitivity analysis for any selected inputs and outputs, and it keeps track of the results in a table. We will see other applications of this useful add-in later in this chapter and in subsequent chapters.

## Comparison of Solver's Sensitivity Report and SolverTable

Sensitivity analysis in optimization models is extremely important, so you need to understand the pros and cons of the two tools discussed in this section. Here are some points to keep in mind:

- Solver's sensitivity report focuses only on the coefficients of the objective and the right-hand sides of the constraints. SolverTable allows you to vary *any* of the inputs.

- Solver's sensitivity report provides very useful information through its reduced costs, shadow prices, and allowable increases and decreases. This same information can be obtained with SolverTable, but it requires a bit more work and some experimentation to find the appropriate input ranges.

- Solver's sensitivity report is based on changing only one objective coefficient or one right-hand side at a time. This one-at-a-time restriction prevents us from answering certain questions directly. SolverTable is much more flexible in this respect.

- Solver's sensitivity report is based on a well-established mathematical theory of sensitivity analysis in linear programming. If you lack this mathematical background—as many users do—the outputs can be difficult to understand, especially for somewhat "nonstandard" spreadsheet models. In contrast, SolverTable's outputs are straightforward. You can vary one or two inputs and see directly how the optimal solution changes.

- Solver's sensitivity report is not even available for integer-constrained models, and its interpretation for nonlinear models is more difficult than for linear models. SolverTable's outputs have the same interpretation for any type of optimization model.

- Solver's sensitivity report comes with Excel. SolverTable is a separate add-in that is not included with Excel—but it is included with this book and is freely available from the author's Web site at http://www.kelley.iu.edu/albrightbooks under Free Downloads.

In summary, each of these tools can be used to answer certain questions. We tend to favor SolverTable because of its flexibility, but in the optimization examples in this chapter and later chapters, both tools are used to show how they can each provide useful information.

## 3.5 PROPERTIES OF LINEAR MODELS

Linear programming is an important subset of a larger class of models called **mathematical programming models.**[11] All such models select the levels of various activities that can be performed, subject to a set of constraints, to maximize or minimize an objective such as total profit or total cost. In Maggie's dessert example, the activities are the amounts of the

[11] The word *programming* in linear programming or mathematical programming has nothing to do with computer programming. It originated with the British term *programme,* which is essentially a plan or a schedule of operations.

two desserts consumed daily, and the purpose of the model is to find the levels of these activities that maximize the total taste index subject to specified constraints.

In terms of this general setup—selecting the optimal levels of activities—LP models possess three important properties that distinguish them from general mathematical programming models: **proportionality, additivity,** and **divisibility.**

## Proportionality

Proportionality means that if the level of any activity is multiplied by a constant factor, then the contribution of this activity to the objective, or to any of the constraints in which the activity is involved, is multiplied by the same factor. For example, suppose that the consumption of snack bars is cut from its optimal value of 1.25 (refer to Figure 3.8) to 0.625—that is, it is multiplied by 0.5. Then the amounts of calories, fat, and grams contributed to the dessert plan by snack bars are all cut in half, and the total taste index contributed by snack bars is also cut in half.

Proportionality is a valid assumption in the dessert model, but it is often violated in certain types of models. For example, in various *blending* models used by petroleum companies, chemical outputs vary in a nonlinear manner as chemical inputs are varied. If a chemical input is doubled, say, the resulting chemical output is not necessarily doubled. This type of behavior violates the proportionality property and takes us into the realm of *nonlinear* optimization, which is discussed in Chapter 7.

## Additivity

The additivity property implies that the sum of the contributions from the various activities to a particular constraint equals the total contribution to that constraint. For example, if the two types of dessert contribute, respectively, 180 and 320 calories (as in Figure 3.2 shown earlier), then the total number of calories in the plan is the *sum* of these amounts, 500 calories. Similarly, the additivity property applies to the objective. That is, the value of the objective is the *sum* of the contributions from the various activities. The additivity property implies that the contribution of any decision variable to the objective or to any constraint is *independent* of the levels of the other decision variables.

## Divisibility

The divisibility property simply means that both integer and noninteger levels of the activities are allowed. In the dessert example, the optimal values in the changing cells turned out to be nonintegers: 1.25 and 1.875. Because of the divisibility property, such values are allowed in LP models. In some problems, however, they do not make physical sense. For example, if we are deciding how many refrigerators to produce, it makes no sense to make 47.53 refrigerators. If we want the levels of some activities to be integer values, there are two possible approaches: (1) We can solve the LP model without integer constraints, and if the solution turns out to have noninteger values, we can attempt to round them to integer values; or (2) we can explicitly constrain certain changing cells to contain integer values. The latter approach, however, takes us into the realm of *integer programming,* which is discussed in Chapter 6.

## Discussion of the Linear Properties

This discussion of the linear properties, especially proportionality and additivity, is a bit abstract. Recognizing whether a model satisfies proportionality and additivity is easy if the model is described algebraically. In this case, the objective must be of the form

$$a_1 x_1 + a_2 x_2 + \cdots + a_n x_n$$

where $n$ is the number of decision variables, the $a$'s are constants, and the $x$'s are decision variables. This expression is called a **linear combination** of the $x$'s. Also, each constraint must be equivalent to a form where the left-hand side is a linear combination of the $x$'s, and the right-hand side is a constant. For example, the following is a typical linear constraint:

$$3x_1 + 7x_2 - 2x_3 \leq 50$$

Recognizing proportionality and additivity—or the lack of them—in a spreadsheet model isn't so easy because the logic of the model can be embedded in a series of cell formulas. However, the ideas are the same. First, the target cell must ultimately (possibly through a series of formulas in intervening cells) be a sum of products of constants and changing cells, where a "constant" is defined by the fact that it does not depend on changing cells. Second, each side of each constraint must ultimately be either a constant or a sum of products of constants and changing cells. Sometimes it's easier to recognize when a model is *not* linear. Two particular situations that lead to nonlinear models are when (1) there are products or quotients of expressions involving changing cells and (2) there are nonlinear functions, such as squares, square roots, or logarithms, of changing cells. These are typically easy to spot, and they guarantee that the model is nonlinear.

*Real-life problems are almost never exactly linear. However, a linear approximation often yields very useful results.*

Whenever we model a real problem, we usually make some simplifying assumptions. This is certainly the case with LP models. The world is frequently *not* linear, which means that an entirely realistic model typically violates some or all of the three properties just discussed. However, numerous successful applications of LP have demonstrated the usefulness of linear models, even if they are only *approximations* of reality. If you suspect that the violations are serious enough to invalidate a linear model, then you should use an integer or nonlinear model, as discussed in Chapters 6 and 7.

In terms of Excel's Solver, if the model is linear—in particular if it satisfies the proportionality and additivity properties—then you should check the Assume Linear Model box in the Solver Options dialog box. Solver will then use the simplex method, a very efficient method for a linear model, to solve the problem. Note that you can check the Assume Linear Model box even if the divisibility property is violated—that is, for linear models with integer-constrained variables—but Solver then uses a method other than the simplex method in its solution procedure.

## Linear Models and Scaling[12]

In some cases, you are sure that a model is linear, but when you check the Assume Linear Model box and then solve, you get a Solver message that "the conditions for Assume Linear Model are not satisfied." This can indicate a logical error in your formulation, so that at least one of the proportionality or additivity conditions is not satisfied. However, it can also indicate that Solver erroneously *thinks* the linearity conditions are not satisfied, which is typically due to roundoff error in its calculations—not any error on your part. If the latter occurs and you are convinced that the model is correct, you can try *not* checking the Assume Linear Model box to see whether that works. If it doesn't work, you should consult your instructor. It's possible that the nonlinear algorithm employed by Solver when this box is not checked simply cannot find the solution to your problem. (You can also change the Precision level in Solver's Options dialog box, say, from 0.0000001 to 0.00001.)

In any case, it always helps to have a *well-scaled* model in which all of the numbers are roughly the same magnitude. If the model contains some very large numbers—100,000

---

[12] This section might seem overly technical. However, if you develop a model that you are sure is linear, and Solver then tells you it doesn't satisfy the linear conditions, you'll appreciate this section.

or more, say—and some very small numbers—0.001 or less, say—it is *poorly scaled* for the methods used by Solver, and roundoff error is far more likely to be an issue not only in Solver's test for linearity conditions but in all of its algorithms.

If you believe your model is poorly scaled, there are two possible remedies. The first is to check the Use Automatic Scaling box in the Solver Options dialog box (refer to Figure 3.6). This might help and it might not; we have had mixed success. (Frontline Systems, the company that develops Solver, reports that the only drawback to checking this box is an increase in computing time.) The second option is to redefine the units in which the various quantities are defined. For example, if we had originally defined your changing cells in the dessert model as the number of *grams* consumed, we might decide later to rescale to the number of *servings* consumed. (In fact, this is partly why we chose number of *servings* in the first place, although scaling doesn't really cause any difficulties in this small problem.)

## 3.6 INFEASIBILITY AND UNBOUNDEDNESS

Two things can go wrong when you invoke Solver. Both of these can indicate that there is a mistake in the model. Therefore, because mistakes are common in LP models, you should be aware of the error messages you can encounter.

### Infeasibility

The first problem is infeasibility. Recall that a solution is *feasible* if it satisfies all of the constraints. Among all of the feasible solutions, we are looking for the one that optimizes the objective. However, it's possible that there are no feasible solutions to the model. There are generally two reasons for this: (1) There is a mistake in the model (an input was entered incorrectly, such as a $\geq$ instead of a $\leq$), or (2) the problem has been so constrained that no solutions are left! In the former case, a careful check of the model should find the error. In the latter case, we might need to relax, or even eliminate, some of the constraints.

*A perfectly reasonable model can have no feasible solutions because of too many constraints.*

To show how an infeasible problem can occur, suppose in Maggie's dessert problem that we change the required daily grams of dessert from 120 to 200 (and leave everything else unchanged). If Solver is then used, the message in Figure 3.17 appears, indicating that Solver cannot find a feasible solution. The reason is clear: There is no way, given the constraints on daily allowances of calories and fat, that Maggie can find a dessert plan with at least 200 grams. Her only choice is to relax at least one of the constraints: increase the daily allowances of calories and/or fat, or decrease the required daily grams of dessert. In general, there is no foolproof way to find the problem when a "no feasible solution" message appears. Careful checking and rethinking are required.

**Figure 3.17**
Solver Dialog Box
Indicating No
Feasible Solution

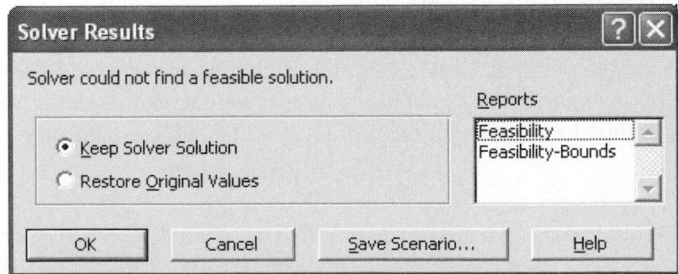

## Unboundedness

*Except in very rare situations, if Solver informs you that your model is unbounded, you have made an error.*

A second type of problem is **unboundedness.** In this case, the model has been formulated in such a way that the objective is unbounded—that is, it can be increased (or decreased for minimization problems) without bound. If this occurs, we have probably entered a wrong input or forgotten some constraints. To see how this can occur in the dessert problem, suppose that we enter daily allowance constraints on calories and fat with ≥ instead of ≤. Now there is no upper bound on how much of each dessert Maggie can consume (at least not in the model!). If we make this change in the model and then use Solver, the message in Figure 3.18 appears, stating that the target cell does not converge. In other words, the total taste index can grow without bound.

**Figure 3.18**

Solver Dialog Box Indicating an Unbounded Solution

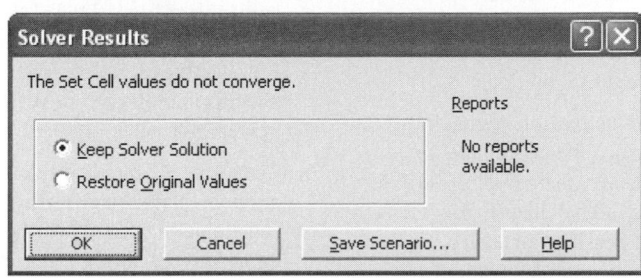

## Comparison of Infeasibility and Unboundedness

Infeasibility and unboundedness are very different in a practical sense. A reasonable model can have no feasible solutions. The marketing department might impose several constraints, the production department might add some more, the engineering department might add even more, and so on. Together, they can constrain the problem so much that no feasible solutions are left. The only way out is to relax or eliminate some of the constraints. An unboundedness problem is different. There is no way a realistic model can have an unbounded solution. If you get the message in Figure 3.18, then you must have made a mistake: You entered an input incorrectly, you omitted one or more constraints, or there is a logical error in your model.

---

## PROBLEMS

*Solutions for problems whose numbers appear within a color box can be found in the Student Solutions Files. Order your copy today at the Winston/Albright product Web site, academic.cengage.com/decisionsciences/winston.*

### Skill-Building Problems

1. Other sensitivity analyses besides those discussed could be performed on Maggie's dessert model. Use SolverTable to perform each of the following. In each case, keep track of the values in the changing cells and the target cell, and discuss your findings.
   a. Let the fat per serving of snack bars vary from 1 to 7 grams in increments of 1 gram.
   b. Let the calories per serving of ice cream vary from 140 to 200 in increments of 5.
   c. Let the total daily gram requirement vary from 100 to 200 in increments of 10.

   d. Let the calorie and fat daily allowances vary simultaneously, with the calorie allowance varying from 300 to 500 in increments of 50, and the fat allowance varying from 20 to 40 in increments of 5.

2. In Maggie's dessert problem, assume there is another possible dessert, in addition to snack bars and ice cream, that Maggie can consider: oatmeal raisin cookies. Each cookie, which is considered a "serving," weighs 43 grams, contains 140 calories, and contains 6 grams of fat. Maggie likes these cookies almost as much as ice cream, and she gives each gram a taste index of 90. Modify the spreadsheet model to include this new dessert, and use Solver to find the optimal dessert plan.

3. Continuing the previous problem, perform a sensitivity analysis on the taste index of the cookies. Let this index vary from 60 to 100 in increments of 5, and keep track of the values in the changing cells and the target cell. Discuss your findings.

4. Changing cells in the dessert model can be measured in servings or in grams. Modify the spreadsheet model so that they are measured in grams, and use Solver to find the optimal solution. Discuss how the solution to this modified model is different from the solution we found; discuss how they are the same.

5. Use the graphical solution of Maggie's dessert problem to determine all values of the right-hand side of the total daily gram requirement that make the model infeasible—that is, it has no feasible solutions.

6. There are five corner points in the feasible region for the dessert problem. We identified the coordinates of one of them: (1.25, 1.875). Identify the coordinates of the others. If we vary the taste index values in row 12 of the spreadsheet model, is it possible for each of these corner points to become an optimal solution? Why or why not?

## Skill-Extending Problems

7. The graphical solution to the dessert problem indicates that the optimal solution contains both snack bars and ice cream because the slope of the total taste index line is *between* the slopes of the two constraint lines for calories and fat. With this in mind, consider changes in the taste index of snack bars, which is currently 85. How large would this have to be for Maggie to consume all snack bars and no ice cream? How small would it have to be for Maggie to consume all ice cream and no snack bars? Answer in terms of slopes and which corner points would become optimal.

8. The SolverTable add-in can be used for less obvious sensitivity analyses. Suppose in the dessert model that you want to vary both of the calories per serving values in row 5, but you want them to stay in the same ratio, 4 to 3. You want calories per serving of snack bars to vary from 100 to 140 in increments of 5, and you want to keep track of the values in the changing cells and the target cell. Modify the model slightly so that this analysis can be performed with a *one-way* SolverTable.

9. Consider the graphical solution to the dessert problem. Now imagine that another constraint—any constraint—is added. Which of the following three things are possible: (1) feasible region shrinks; (2) feasible region stays the same; (3) feasible region expands? Which of the following three things are possible: (1) optimal value in target cell decreases; (2) optimal value in target cell stays the same; (3) optimal value in target cell increases? Explain your answers. Do they hold just for this particular model, or do they hold in general?

## 3.7 A PRODUCT MIX MODEL

The problem examined in this section is often considered the prototype LP problem. The basic *product mix* problem is to select the optimal mix of products to produce to maximize profit.

EXAMPLE | 3.2 PRODUCING FRAMES AT MONET

The Monet Company produces four types of picture frames, which we label 1, 2, 3, and 4. The four types of frames differ with respect to size, shape, and materials used. Each type requires a certain amount of skilled labor, metal, and glass, as shown in Table 3.2. This table also lists the unit selling price Monet charges for each type of frame. During the coming week, Monet can purchase up to 4000 hours of skilled labor, 6000 ounces of metal, and 10,000 ounces of glass. The unit costs are $8.00 per labor hour, $0.50 per ounce of metal, and $0.75 per ounce of glass. Also, market constraints are such that it's impossible to sell more than 1000 type 1 frames, 2000 type 2 frames, 500 type 3 frames, and 1000 type 4 frames. Monet does not want to keep any frames in inventory at the end of the week. What should the company do to maximize its profit for this week?

**Table 3.2** Data for Monet Picture Frame Example

|  | Frame 1 | Frame 2 | Frame 3 | Frame 4 |
|---|---|---|---|---|
| **Skilled labor** | 2 | 1 | 3 | 2 |
| **Metal** | 4 | 2 | 1 | 2 |
| **Glass** | 6 | 2 | 1 | 2 |
| **Selling price** | $28.50 | $12.50 | $29.25 | $21.50 |

**Objective**  To use LP to find the mix of frames to produce that maximizes profit and stays within the resource availability and maximum sales constraints.

## WHERE DO THE NUMBERS COME FROM?

Textbooks typically state a problem, including a number of input values, and proceed directly to a solution—without saying where these input values might come from. However, finding the correct input values is often the most difficult step in a real-world application. (Recall that finding the necessary data is step 2 of the overall modeling process, as discussed in Chapter 1.) There are a variety of inputs in Monet's problem, some easy to find and others more difficult. Here are some ideas on how they might be obtained:

- The unit costs in cells B4:B6 should be easy to obtain (see Figure 3.19.) These are the going rates for these resources. The $8 per hour labor rate is probably a regular-time rate. If Monet wants to consider overtime hours, then the overtime rate (and labor hour availability during overtime) is necessary, and the model needs to be modified.

- The resource usages in the range B9:E11, often called *technological coefficients,* should be available from the production department. These people know how much of each resource it takes to make the various types of frames.

- The unit selling prices in row 12 have actually been *chosen* by Monet's management, probably in response to market pressures and the company's own costs. In reality, they would be chosen based on production costs and market pressures.

- The maximum sales values in row 18 are probably forecasts from the marketing department. These people have some sense of how much they can sell, based on current outstanding orders, historical data, and the unit prices they plan to charge.

- The labor hour availability in cell D21 is probably based on the current workforce size and possibly on new workers who could be hired in the short run. The other resource availabilities in cells D22 and D23 are likely the amounts available from the regular suppliers, whereas any additional quantities require prohibitively expensive expediting costs.

## Solution

Table 3.3 lists the variables and constraints for this model. We must choose the number of frames of each type to produce, which cannot be larger than the maximum we can sell. This choice determines the amounts of resources used and all revenues and costs. We must also ensure that no more resources are used than are available.

**Table 3.3**  Variables and Constraints for Product Mix Model

| | |
|---|---|
| **Input variables** | Unit costs of resources (labor, glass, metal), resources used per frame of each type, unit selling prices of frames, maximum sales of frames, availabilities of resources |
| **Decision variables (changing cells)** | Numbers of frames of various types to produce |
| **Objective (target cell)** | Profit |
| **Other calculated variables** | Amounts of resources used, revenues, costs |
| **Constraints** | Frames produced must be less than or equal to maximum sales |
| | Amounts of resources used must be less than or equal to amounts available |

### An Algebraic Model

To model this problem algebraically, we let $x_1$, $x_2$, $x_3$, and $x_4$ represent the numbers of frames of types 1, 2, 3, and 4 to produce. Next, we write total profit and the constraints in terms of the $x$'s. Finally, because only nonnegative amounts can be produced, we add explicit constraints to ensure that the $x$'s are nonnegative. The resulting algebraic model is as follows:

$$\text{Maximize } 6x_1 + 2x_2 + 4x_3 + 3x_4 \text{ (profit objective)}$$

subject to

$$2x_1 + x_2 + 3x_3 + 2x_4 \leq 4000 \text{ (labor constraint)}$$
$$4x_1 + 2x_2 + x_3 + 2x_4 \leq 6000 \text{ (metal constraint)}$$
$$6x_1 + 2x_2 + x_3 + 2x_4 \leq 10{,}000 \text{ (glass constraint)}$$
$$x_1 \leq 1000 \text{ (frame 1 sales constraint)}$$
$$x_2 \leq 2000 \text{ (frame 2 sales constraint)}$$
$$x_3 \leq 500 \text{ (frame 3 sales constraint)}$$
$$x_4 \leq 1000 \text{ (frame 4 sales constraint)}$$
$$x_1, x_2, x_3, x_4 \geq 0 \text{ (nonnegativity constraints)}$$

To understand this model, consider the profit objective first. The profit from $x_1$ frames of type 1 is $6x_1$ because each frame contributes \$6 to profit. This \$6 is calculated as the unit selling price minus the cost of the inputs that go into a single type 1 frame:

$$\text{Unit profit for type 1 frame} = 28.50 - [2(8.00) + 4(0.50) + 6(0.75)] = \$6$$

Profits for the other three types of frames are obtained similarly. Their unit profits are \$2.00, \$4.00, and \$3.00, respectively. Then the total profit is the sum of the profits from the four products.

Next, consider the skilled labor constraint. The right-hand side, 4000, is the number of hours available. On the left-hand side, each type 1 frame uses 2 hours of labor, so $x_1$ units require $2x_1$ hours of labor. Similar statements hold for the other three products, and the total number of labor hours used is the sum over the four products. Then the constraint states that the number of hours used cannot exceed the number of hours available. The constraints for metal and glass are similar. Finally, the maximum sales constraints and the nonnegativity constraints put upper and lower limits on the quantities that can be produced.

Again, many LP software packages accept this algebraic model exactly as stated here. However, let's now turn to a spreadsheet model of Monet's problem.

*Note how the expressions in the model are sums of terms like $2x_1$. This makes the model linear and also accounts for the widespread use of the SUMPRODUCT function in spreadsheet LP models.*

## DEVELOPING THE SPREADSHEET MODEL

The spreadsheet in Figure 3.19 illustrates the solution procedure for Monet's product mix problem. (See the file **Product Mix.xlsx**.) The first stage is to develop the spreadsheet model using the following steps.

**Figure 3.19**   An Initial Solution for the Product Mix Model

| | A | B | C | D | E | F | G | H | I |
|---|---|---|---|---|---|---|---|---|---|
| 1 | Product mix model | | | | | | Range names used | | |
| 2 | | | | | | | Frames_produced | =Model!$B$16:$E$16 | |
| 3 | Input data | | | | | | Maximum_sales | =Model!$B$18:$E$18 | |
| 4 | Hourly wage rate | $8.00 | | | | | Profit | =Model!$F$32 | |
| 5 | Cost per oz of metal | $0.50 | | | | | Resources_available | =Model!$D$21:$D$23 | |
| 6 | Cost per oz of glass | $0.75 | | | | | Resources_used | =Model!$B$21:$B$23 | |
| 7 | | | | | | | | | |
| 8 | Frame type | 1 | 2 | 3 | 4 | | | | |
| 9 | Labor hours per frame | 2 | 1 | 3 | 2 | | | | |
| 10 | Metal (oz.) per frame | 4 | 2 | 1 | 2 | | | | |
| 11 | Glass (oz.) per frame | 6 | 2 | 1 | 2 | | | | |
| 12 | Unit selling price | $28.50 | $12.50 | $29.25 | $21.50 | | | | |
| 13 | | | | | | | | | |
| 14 | Production plan | | | | | | | | |
| 15 | Frame type | 1 | 2 | 3 | 4 | | | | |
| 16 | Frames produced | 500 | 800 | 400 | 1500 | | | | |
| 17 | | <= | <= | <= | <= | | | | |
| 18 | Maximum sales | 1000 | 2000 | 500 | 1000 | | | | |
| 19 | | | | | | | | | |
| 20 | Resource constraints | Resources used | | Resources available | | | | | |
| 21 | Labor hours | 6000 | <= | 4000 | | | | | |
| 22 | Metal (oz.) | 7000 | <= | 6000 | | | | | |
| 23 | Glass (oz.) | 8000 | <= | 10000 | | | | | |
| 24 | | | | | | | | | |
| 25 | Revenue, cost summary | | | | | | | | |
| 26 | Frame type | 1 | 2 | 3 | 4 | Totals | | | |
| 27 | Revenue | $14,250 | $10,000 | $11,700 | $32,250 | $68,200 | | | |
| 28 | Costs of inputs | | | | | | | | |
| 29 | Labor | $8,000 | $6,400 | $9,600 | $24,000 | $48,000 | | | |
| 30 | Metal | $1,000 | $800 | $200 | $1,500 | $3,500 | | | |
| 31 | Glass | $2,250 | $1,200 | $300 | $2,250 | $6,000 | | | |
| 32 | Profit | $3,000 | $1,600 | $1,600 | $4,500 | $10,700 | | | |

**❶ Inputs.**  Enter the various inputs in the shaded ranges. Again, remember that our convention is to color all input cells blue. Enter only *numbers,* not formulas, in input cells. They should always be numbers directly from the problem statement.

**❷ Range names.**  Name the ranges we have indicated. According to our convention, we have named enough ranges so that the Solver dialog box contains only range names, no cell addresses. Of course, you can name additional ranges if you like. (Note that we have again used the range-naming shortcut discussed in Chapter 2. That is, we have taken advantage of labels in adjacent cells, except for the Profit cell.)

**❸ Changing cells.**  Enter *any* four values in the Frames_produced range and color these cells red. This range contains the changing cells. You do *not* have to enter the values shown in Figure 3.19. Any trial values can be used initially; Solver will eventually find the *optimal* values. Note that the four values shown in Figure 3.19 cannot be optimal because they do not satisfy all of the constraints. Specifically, this plan uses more labor hours and metal than are available, and it produces more type 4 frames than can be sold. However, you do not need to worry about satisfying constraints at this point; Solver will take care of this later on.

**4** **Resources used.** Enter the formula

=SUMPRODUCT(B9:E9,Frames_produced)

in cell B21 and copy it to the rest of the Resources_used range. These formulas calculate the units of labor, metal, and glass used by the current product mix. Again, the SUMPRODUCT function proves its usefulness in LP models by instructing to multiply each value in the range B9:E9 by the corresponding value in the Frames_produced range and then sum these products.

**Excel Tip:** *Copying Formulas with Range Names*
*When you enter a range name in an Excel formula and then copy it, the range name reference acts like an absolute reference.*

**5** **Revenues, costs, and profits.** The area from row 25 down shows the summary of monetary values. Actually, all we need is the total profit in cell F32, but it's useful to calculate the revenues and costs associated with each product. To obtain the revenues, enter the formula

=B12*B16

in cell B27 and copy this to the range C27:E27. For the costs, enter the formula

=$B4*B$16*B9

in cell B29 and copy this to the range B29:E31. (Note how the mixed absolute and relative references enable copying to the entire range.) Then calculate the profit for each product by entering the formula

=B27-SUM(B29:B31)

in cell B32 and copying this to the range C32:E32. Finally, calculate the totals in columm F by summing across each row with the SUM function. (The cost sums in column F are easy to understand. For example, the $32,000 labor cost in cell F29 is the 4000 labor hours used multiplied by the unit $8 cost per labor hour.)

## Experimenting with Other Solutions

Before going any further, you might want to experiment with other values in the changing cells. For example, here is one reasonable strategy. Because frame 1 has the highest profit margin ($6) and its market constraint permits at most 1000 frames, enter 1000 in cell B16. Note that none of the resources are yet used up completely. Therefore, we can make some type 3 frames, the type with the next highest profit margin. Because the type 3 market constraint permits at most 500 frames, enter 500 in cell D16. There is still some availability of each resource. This allows us to make some type 4 frames, the type with the next largest profit margin. However, the most we can make is 250 type 4 frames, because at this point the available labor hours are completely exhausted. The resulting solution appears in Figure 3.20. Its corresponding profit is $8750.

**Figure 3.20** Another Possible Solution for the Product Mix Model

| | A | B | C | D | E | F | G | H | I |
|---|---|---|---|---|---|---|---|---|---|
| 1 | Product mix model | | | | | | Range names used | | |
| 2 | | | | | | | Frames_produced | =Model!$B$16:$E$16 | |
| 3 | Input data | | | | | | Maximum_sales | =Model!$B$18:$E$18 | |
| 4 | Hourly wage rate | $8.00 | | | | | Profit | =Model!$F$32 | |
| 5 | Cost per oz of metal | $0.50 | | | | | Resources_available | =Model!$D$21:$D$23 | |
| 6 | Cost per oz of glass | $0.75 | | | | | Resources_used | =Model!$B$21:$B$23 | |
| 7 | | | | | | | | | |
| 8 | Frame type | 1 | 2 | 3 | 4 | | | | |
| 9 | Labor hours per frame | 2 | 1 | 3 | 2 | | | | |
| 10 | Metal (oz.) per frame | 4 | 2 | 1 | 2 | | | | |
| 11 | Glass (oz.) per frame | 6 | 2 | 1 | 2 | | | | |
| 12 | Unit selling price | $28.50 | $12.50 | $29.25 | $21.50 | | | | |
| 13 | | | | | | | | | |
| 14 | Production plan | | | | | | | | |
| 15 | Frame type | 1 | 2 | 3 | 4 | | | | |
| 16 | Frames produced | 1000 | 0 | 500 | 250 | | | | |
| 17 | | <= | <= | <= | <= | | | | |
| 18 | Maximum sales | 1000 | 2000 | 500 | 1000 | | | | |
| 19 | | | | | | | | | |
| 20 | Resource constraints | Resources used | | Resources available | | | | | |
| 21 | Labor hours | 4000 | <= | 4000 | | | | | |
| 22 | Metal (oz.) | 5000 | <= | 6000 | | | | | |
| 23 | Glass (oz.) | 7000 | <= | 10000 | | | | | |
| 24 | | | | | | | | | |
| 25 | Revenue, cost summary | | | | | | | | |
| 26 | Frame type | 1 | 2 | 3 | 4 | Totals | | | |
| 27 | Revenue | $28,500 | $0 | $14,625 | $5,375 | $48,500 | | | |
| 28 | Costs of inputs | | | | | | | | |
| 29 | Labor | $16,000 | $0 | $12,000 | $4,000 | $32,000 | | | |
| 30 | Metal | $2,000 | $0 | $250 | $250 | $2,500 | | | |
| 31 | Glass | $4,500 | $0 | $375 | $375 | $5,250 | | | |
| 32 | Profit | $6,000 | $0 | $2,000 | $750 | $8,750 | | | |

*This type of "greedy" analysis—produce in the decreasing order of profit margins—is easy and intuitive. Unfortunately, as we have seen, it is not guaranteed to produce an optimal solution.*

We have now produced as much as possible of the three frame types with the three highest profit margins; however, this does not guarantee that this solution is the best possible product mix. The solution in Figure 3.20 is *not* optimal. In this small model, it's difficult to guess the optimal solution, even when using a relatively intelligent trial-and-error procedure. The problem is that a frame type with a high profit margin can use up a lot of the resources and preclude other profitable frames from being produced. Therefore, we turn to Solver to eliminate the guesswork and find the *real* optimal solution.

## USING SOLVER

To use Solver, select Solver from the Data ribbon, and fill it in as shown in Figure 3.21. (Again, note that we have named enough ranges so that only range names appear in the dialog box.) Also, click on the Options button, and check the Assume Linear Model and Assume Non-Negative boxes, as shown earlier in Figure 3.6. This is because the model is linear, and we do not want to allow negative numbers of frames to be produced.

## Figure 3.21

Solver Dialog Box for the Product Mix Model

**Solver Parameters**

Set Target Cell: Profit

Equal To: ⦿ Max ◯ Min ◯ Value of: 0

By Changing Cells:

Frames_produced

Subject to the Constraints:

Frames_produced <= Maximum_sales
Resources_used <= Resources_available

[Solve] [Close] [Guess] [Options] [Add] [Change] [Delete] [Reset All] [Help]

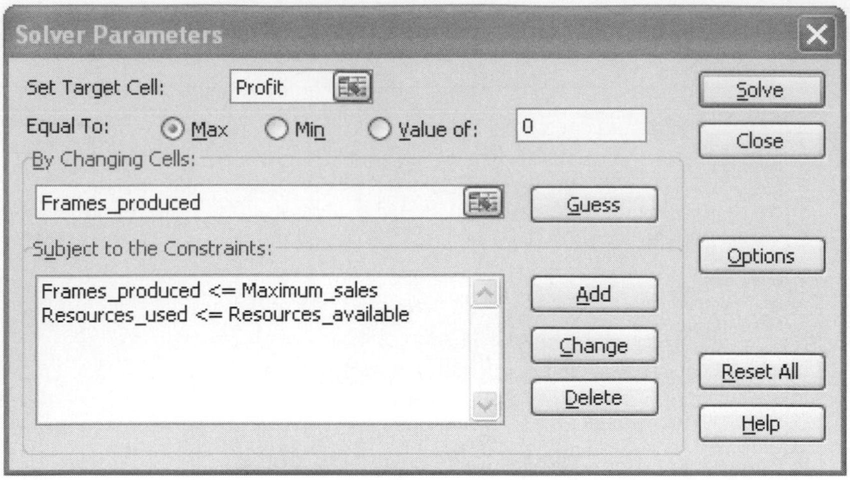

*You typically gain insights into a solution by checking which constraints are binding and which contain slack.*

## Discussion of the Solution

When you click on Solve, you get the optimal solution shown in Figure 3.22. The optimal plan is to produce 1000 type 1 frames, 800 type 2 frames, 400 type 3 frames, and no type 4 frames. This is close to the production plan from Figure 3.20, but the current plan earns $450 more profit. Also, it uses all of the available labor hours and metal, but only 8000 of the 10,000 available ounces of glass. Finally, in terms of maximum sales, the optimal plan could produce more of frame types 2, 3, and 4 (if there were more skilled labor and/or metal available). This is typical of an LP solution. Some of the constraints are met exactly—they are binding—whereas others contain a certain amount of slack. The binding constraints are the ones that prevent Monet from earning an even higher profit.

## Figure 3.22

Optimal Solution for the Product Mix Model

| | A | B | C | D | E | F | G | H | I |
|---|---|---|---|---|---|---|---|---|---|
| 1 | Product mix model | | | | | | Range names used | | |
| 2 | | | | | | | Frames_produced | =Model!$B$16:$E$16 | |
| 3 | Input data | | | | | | Maximum_sales | =Model!$B$18:$E$18 | |
| 4 | Hourly wage rate | $8.00 | | | | | Profit | =Model!$F$32 | |
| 5 | Cost per oz of metal | $0.50 | | | | | Resources_available | =Model!$D$21:$D$23 | |
| 6 | Cost per oz of glass | $0.75 | | | | | Resources_used | =Model!$B$21:$B$23 | |
| 7 | | | | | | | | | |
| 8 | Frame type | 1 | 2 | 3 | 4 | | | | |
| 9 | Labor hours per frame | 2 | 1 | 3 | 2 | | | | |
| 10 | Metal (oz.) per frame | 4 | 2 | 1 | 2 | | | | |
| 11 | Glass (oz.) per frame | 6 | 2 | 1 | 2 | | | | |
| 12 | Unit selling price | $28.50 | $12.50 | $29.25 | $21.50 | | | | |
| 13 | | | | | | | | | |
| 14 | Production plan | | | | | | | | |
| 15 | Frame type | 1 | 2 | 3 | 4 | | | | |
| 16 | Frames produced | 1000 | 800 | 400 | 0 | | | | |
| 17 | | <= | <= | <= | <= | | | | |
| 18 | Maximum sales | 1000 | 2000 | 500 | 1000 | | | | |
| 19 | | | | | | | | | |
| 20 | Resource constraints | Resources used | | Resources available | | | | | |
| 21 | Labor hours | 4000 | <= | 4000 | | | | | |
| 22 | Metal (oz.) | 6000 | <= | 6000 | | | | | |
| 23 | Glass (oz.) | 8000 | <= | 10000 | | | | | |
| 24 | | | | | | | | | |
| 25 | Revenue, cost summary | | | | | | | | |
| 26 | Frame type | 1 | 2 | 3 | 4 | Totals | | | |
| 27 | Revenue | $28,500 | $10,000 | $11,700 | $0 | $50,200 | | | |
| 28 | Costs of inputs | | | | | | | | |
| 29 | Labor | $16,000 | $6,400 | $9,600 | $0 | $32,000 | | | |
| 30 | Metal | $2,000 | $800 | $200 | $0 | $3,000 | | | |
| 31 | Glass | $4,500 | $1,200 | $300 | $0 | $6,000 | | | |
| 32 | Profit | $6,000 | $1,600 | $1,600 | $0 | $9,200 | | | |

## Sensitivity Analysis

To experiment with different inputs to this problem—the unit revenues or resource availabilities, for example—we can simply change the inputs and then rerun Solver. The second time we use Solver, we do not have to specify the target and changing cells or the constraints. Excel remembers all of these settings and saves them when we save the file.

As a simple what-if example, consider the modified model in Figure 3.23. Here the unit selling price for frame type 4 has increased from $21.50 to $26.50, and all other inputs are as before. By making type 4 frames more profitable, we might expect them to enter the optimal mix. This is exactly what happens. The new optimal plan (the one shown in the figure) discontinues production of frame types 2 and 3 and instead calls for production of 1000 type 4 frames. This solution increases the total profit to $14,000.

### Excel Tip: *Roundoff Error*
*Because of the way numbers are stored and calculated on a computer, the optimal values in the changing cells and elsewhere can contain small roundoff errors. For example, the value that really appeared in cell D16 (in Figure 3.23) was 8.731E-09, a very small number (0.000000008731). For all practical purposes, this number can be treated as 0, and we formatted it as such in the spreadsheet.*

**Figure 3.23**
Optimal Solution
for the Product Mix
Model with a
Changed Input

| | A | B | C | D | E | F | G | H | I |
|---|---|---|---|---|---|---|---|---|---|
| 1 | Product mix model | | | | | | Range names used | | |
| 2 | | | | | | | Frames_produced | =Model!$B$16:$E$16 | |
| 3 | Input data | | | | | | Maximum_sales | =Model!$B$18:$E$18 | |
| 4 | Hourly wage rate | $8.00 | | | | | Profit | =Model!$F$32 | |
| 5 | Cost per oz of metal | $0.50 | | | | | Resources_available | =Model!$D$21:$D$23 | |
| 6 | Cost per oz of glass | $0.75 | | | | | Resources_used | =Model!$B$21:$B$23 | |
| 7 | | | | | | | | | |
| 8 | Frame type | 1 | 2 | 3 | 4 | | | | |
| 9 | Labor hours per frame | 2 | 1 | 3 | 2 | | | | |
| 10 | Metal (oz.) per frame | 4 | 2 | 1 | 2 | | | | |
| 11 | Glass (oz.) per frame | 6 | 2 | 1 | 2 | | | | |
| 12 | Unit selling price | $28.50 | $12.50 | $29.25 | $26.50 | | | | |
| 13 | | | | | | | | | |
| 14 | Production plan | | | | | | | | |
| 15 | Frame type | 1 | 2 | 3 | 4 | | | | |
| 16 | Frames produced | 1000 | 0 | 0 | 1000 | | | | |
| 17 | | <= | <= | <= | <= | | | | |
| 18 | Maximum sales | 1000 | 2000 | 500 | 1000 | | | | |
| 19 | | | | | | | | | |
| 20 | Resource constraints | Resources used | | Resources available | | | | | |
| 21 | Labor hours | 4000 | <= | 4000 | | | | | |
| 22 | Metal (oz.) | 6000 | <= | 6000 | | | | | |
| 23 | Glass (oz.) | 8000 | <= | 10000 | | | | | |
| 24 | | | | | | | | | |
| 25 | Revenue, cost summary | | | | | | | | |
| 26 | Frame type | 1 | 2 | 3 | 4 | Totals | | | |
| 27 | Revenue | $28,500 | $0 | $0 | $26,500 | $55,000 | | | |
| 28 | Costs of inputs | | | | | | | | |
| 29 | Labor | $16,000 | $0 | $0 | $16,000 | $32,000 | | | |
| 30 | Metal | $2,000 | $0 | $0 | $1,000 | $3,000 | | | |
| 31 | Glass | $4,500 | $0 | $0 | $1,500 | $6,000 | | | |
| 32 | Profit | $6,000 | $0 | $0 | $8,000 | $14,000 | | | |

We can also use SolverTable to perform a more systematic sensitivity analysis on one or more input variables. One possibility appears in Figure 3.24, where the number of available labor hours varies from 2500 to 5000 in increments of 250, and the optimal product mix and profit is tracked. There are several ways to interpret the output from this sensitivity analysis. First, we can look at columns B through E to see how the product mix changes as more labor hours become available. For example, frames of type 4 are finally produced when 4500 labor hours are available, and frames of type 2 are discontinued in the final row. Second, we can see how extra labor hours add to the total profit. This is shown numerically in column G, where each value is the increase in profit from the previous row. (We created column G manually; it's not part of the SolverTable output.) Note exactly what this increased profit means. For example, when labor hours increase from 2500 to 2750, the model requires that we *pay*

$8 apiece for these extra hours (if we use them). But the *net* effect is that profit increases by $500. In other words, the labor cost increases by $2000 [=$8(250)], but this is more than offset by the increase in revenue that comes from having the extra labor hours.

**Figure 3.24**

Sensitivity of Optimal Solution to Labor Hours

| | A | B | C | D | E | F | G |
|---|---|---|---|---|---|---|---|
| 34 | Sensitivity of optimal solution to number of labor hours | | | | | | |
| 35 | | $B$16 | $C$16 | $D$16 | $E$16 | $F$32 | Increase |
| 36 | 2500 | 1000 | 500 | 0 | 0 | $7,000 | |
| 37 | 2750 | 1000 | 750 | 0 | 0 | $7,500 | $500 |
| 38 | 3000 | 1000 | 1000 | 0 | 0 | $8,000 | $500 |
| 39 | 3250 | 1000 | 950 | 100 | 0 | $8,300 | $300 |
| 40 | 3500 | 1000 | 900 | 200 | 0 | $8,600 | $300 |
| 41 | 3750 | 1000 | 850 | 300 | 0 | $8,900 | $300 |
| 42 | 4000 | 1000 | 800 | 400 | 0 | $9,200 | $300 |
| 43 | 4250 | 1000 | 750 | 500 | 0 | $9,500 | $300 |
| 44 | 4500 | 1000 | 500 | 500 | 250 | $9,750 | $250 |
| 45 | 4750 | 1000 | 250 | 500 | 500 | $10,000 | $250 |
| 46 | 5000 | 1000 | 0 | 500 | 750 | $10,250 | $250 |

As column G illustrates, obtaining those extra labor hours is worthwhile, even though we have to pay for them, because profit increases. However, the increase in profit per extra labor hour—the *shadow price* of labor hours—is not constant. It decreases as more labor hours are already owned. An extra 250 labor hours first results in $500 more profit, then $300, and then only $250. This is typical of shadow prices for scarce resources in LP models, where each extra unit of a resource is worth *at most* as much as the previous unit.

We can also chart the optimal profit values in column F (or any other quantities from a SolverTable output). The line chart in Figure 3.25 illustrates how the shadow price (slope of the line) decreases as more labor hours are already owned. (The first decrease in slope is perceptible; the second is hard to see in the chart, but it *is* there.)

Finally, we can gain additional insight from Solver's sensitivity report, shown in Figure 3.26. This report contains a twist we did not see in the diet example. Now there are two types of constraints: upper bounds on the changing cells (the maximum sales constraints)

*The reduced cost for a variable with an upper constraint can be nonzero if that variable is currently at its upper bound.*

**Figure 3.25**

Sensitivity of Optimal Profit to Labor Hours

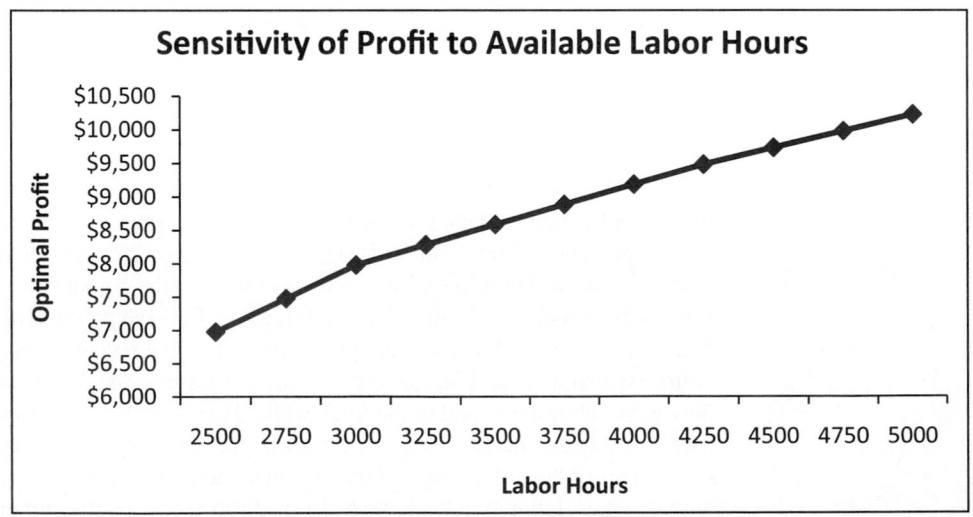

## Resource Availability and Shadow Prices

If a resource constraint is binding in the optimal solution, we are willing to pay up to some amount, the shadow price, to obtain more of the resource. This is because the objective improves by having more of the resource. However, there is typically a "decreasing marginal" effect: As we own more and more of the resource, the shadow price tends to decrease. This is usually because *other* constraints become binding, which causes extra units of this resource to be less useful (or not useful at all).

and resource availability constraints. Solver treats the upper bound constraints differently from "normal" constraints in this report. First, it doesn't include rows for the upper bound constraints in the bottom section of the report. Second, in the top part of the report, a reduced cost can be nonzero even for a variable that is positive in the solution, provided that this variable is at its upper bound. Specifically, Monet is producing as many type 1 frames, 1000, as it's allowed to produce. The reduced cost of 2 means that the profit margin on type 1 frames must *decrease* by at least $2 before the company will produce less than 1000 of these frames.

**Figure 3.26**
Solver's Sensitivity Report

| A | B | C | D | E | F | G | H |
|---|---|---|---|---|---|---|---|
| 6 | Adjustable Cells | | | | | | |
| 7 | | | Final | Reduced | Objective | Allowable | Allowable |
| 8 | Cell | Name | Value | Cost | Coefficient | Increase | Decrease |
| 9 | $B$16 | Frames produced | 1000 | 2 | 6 | 1E+30 | 2 |
| 10 | $C$16 | Frames produced | 800 | 0 | 2 | 1 | 0.25 |
| 11 | $D$16 | Frames produced | 400 | 0 | 4 | 2 | 0.5 |
| 12 | $E$16 | Frames produced | 0 | -0.20 | 3 | 0.2 | 1E+30 |
| 13 | | | | | | | |
| 14 | Constraints | | | | | | |
| 15 | | | Final | Shadow | Constraint | Allowable | Allowable |
| 16 | Cell | Name | Value | Price | R.H. Side | Increase | Decrease |
| 17 | $B$21 | Labor hours Resources used | 4000 | 1.20 | 4000 | 250 | 1000 |
| 18 | $B$22 | Metal (oz.) Resources used | 6000 | 0.40 | 6000 | 2000 | 500 |
| 19 | $B$23 | Glass (oz.) Resources used | 8000 | 0 | 10000 | 1E+30 | 2000 |

In contrast, the reduced cost of −0.2 for type 4 frames implies that the profit margin on these frames must increase by at least $0.20 before the company includes them in its optimal mix (because they are currently *not* included).[13]

Finally, there are positive shadow prices on labor hours and metal, the two resources that are being used to capacity. The company's profit would increase by $1.20 for every extra labor hour and by $0.40 for every extra ounce of metal—but only up to the allowable increases shown in the report. ∎

# MODELING ISSUES

Some students believe the maximum sales constraint should be changed to be a "greater than or equal" constraint. Their reasoning is that Monet should produce enough to satisfy forecasted demands. We ask you to explore this issue in problem 11 later in this chapter. The "correct" model depends on the company's goals. Does the company want to ensure that there are no extra frames on hand (that can't be sold), or does the company want to ensure that there are at least enough frames on hand to satisfy customer demands? ∎

---

[13] Solver formats the numbers in its sensitivity reports in a strange way. Some numbers have a lot of decimals and some have none, so you have to be careful and possibly reformat. For example, the −0.2 in cell E12 was formatted as 0 in our report.

## Skill-Building Problems

**10.** Modify Monet's product mix model so that there is no maximum sales constraint. (In the Solver dialog box, highlight the constraint and click on the Delete button.) Does this make the problem unbounded? Does it change the optimal solution at all? Explain its effect.

**11.** In the product mix model, it makes sense to change the maximum sales constraint to a "minimum sales" constraint, simply by changing the direction of the inequality. Then the input values in row 18 can be considered customer demand that must be met. Make this change and rerun Solver. What do you find? What do you find if you run Solver again, this time making the values in row 18 half their current values?

**12.** Use SolverTable to run a sensitivity analysis on the cost per ounce of metal in the product mix model. Let this unit cost vary from $0.30 to $1.30 in increments of $0.20, and keep track of the values in the changing cells and the target cell. Discuss what happens to the optimal product mix. Also, does each 20-cent increase in the cost of metal result in the *same* decrease in profit?

**13.** Create a two-way SolverTable for the product mix model, where profit is the only output and the two inputs are the hourly cost of labor and the total labor hours available. Let the hourly cost of labor vary from $6 to $10 in increments of $1, and let the total labor hours vary from 3000 to 7000 in increments of 500. Discuss the changes in profit you see as you look across the various rows of the table. Discuss the changes in profit you see as you look down the various columns of the table.

**14.** In the current solution to the product mix model, type 4 frames are not produced at all. This is due, at least in part, to the low unit selling price of type 4 frames. Use SolverTable appropriately to determine how large this unit selling price would have to be before type 4 frames would be included in the optimal product mix.

## Skill-Expanding Problems

**15.** Suppose we want to increase *all three* of the resource availabilities in the product mix model simultaneously by the same factor. We want this factor to vary from 0.8 to 2.0 in increments of 0.1. For example, if this factor is 1.0, we get the current model, whereas if the factor is 2.0, the resource availabilities become 8000, 12,000, and 20,000. Modify the spreadsheet model slightly so that this sensitivity analysis can be performed with a *one-way* SolverTable, using the factor as the single input. Keep track of the values in the changing cells and the target cell. Discuss the results.

**16.** Some analysts complain that spreadsheet models are difficult to resize. We'll let you be the judge of this. Suppose the current product mix problem is changed so that there is an extra resource, plastic, and two additional frame types, 5 and 6. What additional data are required? What modifications are necessary in the spreadsheet model (including range name changes)? Make up values for any extra required data and incorporate these into a modified spreadsheet model. (You might want to try inserting new columns in the *middle* of your range, rather than inserting them at the end. See if you can discover why the former is more efficient.) Then optimize with Solver. Do you conclude that it's easy to resize a spreadsheet model? (By the way, algebraic models are typically *much* easier to resize.)

# 3.8 A MULTIPERIOD PRODUCTION MODEL

The dessert and product mix examples illustrate typical LP models. However, LP models come in many forms. For variety, the next problem is quite different, but it can also be solved with LP. (In the next few chapters, we illustrate many other examples, linear and otherwise.) The distinguishing feature of the following problem is that it relates decisions made during several time periods. This type of problem occurs when a company must make a decision now that will have ramifications in the future. The company does not want to focus completely on the near future and forget about the long run.

EXAMPLE | **3.3 PRODUCING FOOTBALLS AT PIGSKIN**

The Pigskin Company produces footballs. Pigskin must decide how many footballs to produce each month. The company has decided to use a 6-month planning horizon. The forecasted demands for the next 6 months are 10,000, 15,000, 30,000, 35,000, 25,000, and 10,000. Pigskin wants to meet these demands on time, knowing that it currently has 5000 footballs in inventory and that it can use a given month's production to help meet the demand for that month. (For simplicity, assume that production occurs during the month, and demand occurs at the end of the month.) During each month, there is enough production capacity to produce up to 30,000 footballs, and there is enough storage capacity to store up to 10,000 footballs at the end of the month, after demand has occurred. The forecasted production costs per football for the next 6 months are $12.50, $12.55, $12.70, $12.80, $12.85, and $12.95, respectively. The holding cost per football held in inventory at the end of any month is figured at 5% of the production cost for that month. (This cost includes the cost of storage and also the cost of money tied up in inventory.) The selling price for footballs is not considered relevant to the production decision because Pigskin plans to satisfy all customer demand exactly when it occurs—at whatever the selling price is. Therefore, Pigskin wants to determine the production schedule that minimizes the total production and holding costs.

**Objective**    To use LP to find the production schedule that meets demand on time and minimizes total production costs and inventory holding costs.

## WHERE DO THE NUMBERS COME FROM?

The input values for this problem are not all easy to find. Here are some thoughts on where they might be obtained.

- The initial inventory in cell B4 (see Figure 3.27) should be available from the company's database system or from a physical count.

- The unit production costs in row 8 are probably estimated in two steps. First, the company might ask its cost accountants to estimate the current unit production cost. Then it could examine historical trends in costs to estimate inflation factors for future months.

- The holding cost percentage in cell B5 is typically difficult to determine. Depending on the type of inventory being held, this cost can include storage and handling, rent, property taxes, insurance, spoilage, and obsolescence. It can also include capital costs—the cost of money that could be used for other investments. In any case, holding costs are often expressed as percentages of the variable production costs, as we have done here.

- The demands in row 18 are probably forecasts made by the marketing department. They might be "seat-of-the-pants" forecasts, or they might be the result of a formal quantitative forecasting procedure. (Such procedures are covered in Chapter 16.) Of course, if there are already some orders on the books for future months, these are included in the demand figures.

- The production and storage capacities in rows 14 and 22 are probably supplied by the production department. They are based on the size of the workforce, the available machinery, availability of raw materials, and physical space.

## Solution

The variables and constraints for this model are listed in Table 3.4. There are two keys to relating these variables. First, the months cannot be treated independently because the ending inventory in one month is the beginning inventory for the next month. Second, to ensure that demand is satisfied on time, we must ensure that the amount on hand after production in each month is at least as large as the demand for that month.

---

**Table 3.4  Variables and Constraints for Production/Inventory Planning Model**

| | |
|---|---|
| **Input variables** | Initial inventory, unit holding cost, unit production costs, forecasted demands, production and storage capacities |
| **Decision variables (changing cells)** | Monthly production quantities |
| **Objective (target cell)** | Total cost |
| **Other calculated variables** | Units on hand after production, ending inventories, monthly production, and inventory holding costs |
| **Constraints** | Units on hand after production must be greater than or equal to demand (each month) |
| | Units produced must be less than or equal to production capacity (each month) |
| | Ending inventory must be less than or equal to storage capacity (each month) |

---

*By modifying the timing assumptions in this type of model, we can get alternative—and equally realistic—models with different solutions.*

When modeling this type of problem, we must be very specific about the *timing* of events. In fact, depending on the assumptions we make, there can be several potential models. For example, when does the demand for footballs in a given month occur: at the beginning of the month, at the end of the month, or continually throughout the month? The same question can be asked about production in a given month. The answers to these two questions indicate how much of the production in a given month can be used to help satisfy the demand in that month. Also, are the maximum storage constraint and the holding cost based on the *ending* inventory in a month, the *average* amount of inventory in a month, or the *maximum* inventory in a month? Each of these possibilities is reasonable and could be implemented.

To simplify the model, we assume that (1) all production occurs at the beginning of the month, (2) all demand occurs *after* production so that all units produced in a month can be used to satisfy that month's demand, and (3) the storage constraint and the holding cost are based on *ending* inventory in a given month. (You are asked in the problems to modify these assumptions.)

### An Algebraic Model

In the traditional algebraic model, the decision variables are the production quantities for the 6 months, labeled $P_1$ through $P_6$. It is also convenient to let $I_1$ through $I_6$ be the corresponding end-of-month inventories (after demand has occurred).[14] For example, $I_3$ is the number of footballs left over at the end of month 3. Therefore, the obvious constraints are on production and inventory storage capacities: $P_j \leq 300$ and $I_j \leq 100$ for each month $j$, $1 \leq j \leq 6$. (From here on, to minimize the number of zeros shown, we express all quantities in *hundreds* of footballs.)

In addition to these constraints, we need "balance" constraints that relate the $P$'s and $I$'s. In any month, the inventory from the previous month plus the current production equals

---

[14] This example illustrates a subtle difference between algebraic and spreadsheet models. It is often convenient in algebraic models to define "decision variables," in this case the $I$'s, that are really determined by other decision variables, in this case the $P$'s. In spreadsheet models, however, we typically define the changing cells as the smallest set of variables that really must be chosen—in this case the production quantities. Then we calculate values that are determined by these changing cells, such as the ending inventory levels, with spreadsheet formulas.

the current demand plus leftover inventory. If $D_j$ is the forecasted demand for month $j$, then the balance equation for month $j$ is

$$I_{j-1} + P_j = D_j + I_j$$

The balance equation for month 1 uses the known beginning inventory, 50, for the previous inventory (the $I_{j-1}$ term). By putting all variables ($P$'s and $I$'s) on the left and all known values on the right (a standard LP convention), we can write these balance constraints as shown in equations (3.1)

$$
\begin{aligned}
P_1 - I_1 &= 100 - 50 \\
I_1 + P_2 - I_2 &= 150 \\
I_2 + P_3 - I_3 &= 300 \\
I_3 + P_4 - I_4 &= 350 \\
I_4 + P_5 - I_5 &= 250 \\
I_5 + P_6 - I_6 &= 100
\end{aligned}
\tag{3.1}
$$

As usual, we also impose nonnegativity constraints: all $P$'s and $I$'s must be nonnegative.

What about meeting demand on time? This requires that, in each month, the inventory from the preceding month plus the current production must be at least as large as the current demand. But take a look, for example, at the balance equation for month 3. By rearranging it slightly, we can write it as

$$I_3 = I_2 + P_3 - 300$$

Now, the nonnegativity constraint on $I_3$ implies that the right side of this equation, $I_2 + P_3 - 300$, is also nonnegative. But this implies that demand in month 3 is satisfied—the beginning inventory in month 3 plus month 3 production is at least 300. Therefore, the nonnegativity constraints on the $I$'s *automatically* guarantee that all demands are satisfied on time, and no other constraints are needed. Alternatively, we could write directly that $I_2 + P_3 \geq 300$. In words, the amount on hand after production in month 3 must be at least as large as the demand in month 3. We can take advantage of this interpretation in the spreadsheet model.

Finally, the objective we want to minimize is the sum of production and holding costs, which is the sum of unit production costs multiplied by $P$'s, plus unit holding costs multiplied by $I$'s.

## DEVELOPING THE SPREADSHEET MODEL

The spreadsheet model of Pigskin's production problem is given in Figure 3.27. (See the file **Production Scheduling.xlsx**.) The main feature that distinguishes this model from the product mix model is that some of the constraints, namely, the balance equations (3.1), are built into the spreadsheet by means of formulas. This means that the only changing cells are the production quantities. The ending inventories shown in row 20 are *determined* by the production quantities and equations (3.1). The decision variables in an algebraic model (the $P$'s and $I$'s) are not *necessarily* the same as the changing cells in an equivalent spreadsheet model. (The only changing cells in the spreadsheet model correspond to the $P$'s.)

**Figure 3.27** Nonoptimal Solution to Pigskin's Production Model

| | A | B | C | D | E | F | G | H | I | J | K |
|---|---|---|---|---|---|---|---|---|---|---|---|
| 1 | Multiperiod production model | | | | | | | | Range names used | | |
| 2 | | | | | | | | | Demand | =Model!$B$18:$G$18 | |
| 3 | Input data | | | | | | | | Ending_inventory | =Model!$B$20:$G$20 | |
| 4 | Initial inventory (100s) | 50 | | | | | | | On_hand_after_production | =Model!$B$16:$G$16 | |
| 5 | Holding cost as % of prod cost | 5% | | | | | | | Production_capacity | =Model!$B$14:$G$14 | |
| 6 | | | | | | | | | Storage_capacity | =Model!$B$22:$G$22 | |
| 7 | Month | 1 | 2 | 3 | 4 | 5 | 6 | | Total_Cost | =Model!$H$28 | |
| 8 | Production cost/unit | $12.50 | $12.55 | $12.70 | $12.80 | $12.85 | $12.95 | | Units_produced | =Model!$B$12:$G$12 | |
| 9 | | | | | | | | | | | |
| 10 | Production plan (all quantities are in 100s of footballs) | | | | | | | | | | |
| 11 | Month | 1 | 2 | 3 | 4 | 5 | 6 | | | | |
| 12 | Units produced | 150 | 150 | 300 | 300 | 250 | 100 | | | | |
| 13 | | <= | <= | <= | <= | <= | <= | | | | |
| 14 | Production capacity | 300 | 300 | 300 | 300 | 300 | 300 | | | | |
| 15 | | | | | | | | | | | |
| 16 | On hand after production | 200 | 250 | 400 | 400 | 300 | 150 | | | | |
| 17 | | >= | >= | >= | >= | >= | >= | | | | |
| 18 | Demand | 100 | 150 | 300 | 350 | 250 | 100 | | | | |
| 19 | | | | | | | | | | | |
| 20 | Ending inventory | 100 | 100 | 100 | 50 | 50 | 50 | | | | |
| 21 | | <= | <= | <= | <= | <= | <= | | | | |
| 22 | Storage capacity | 100 | 100 | 100 | 100 | 100 | 100 | | | | |
| 23 | | | | | | | | | | | |
| 24 | Summary of costs (all costs are in hundreds of dollars) | | | | | | | | | | |
| 25 | Month | 1 | 2 | 3 | 4 | 5 | 6 | Totals | | | |
| 26 | Production costs | $1,875.00 | $1,882.50 | $3,810.00 | $3,840.00 | $3,212.50 | $1,295.00 | $15,915.00 | | | |
| 27 | Holding costs | $62.50 | $62.75 | $63.50 | $32.00 | $32.13 | $32.38 | $285.25 | | | |
| 28 | Totals | $1,937.50 | $1,945.25 | $3,873.50 | $3,872.00 | $3,244.63 | $1,327.38 | $16,200.25 | | | |

To develop the spreadsheet model in Figure 3.27, proceed as follows:

**1 Inputs.** Enter the inputs in the blue ranges. Again, these are all entered as *numbers* straight from the problem statement. (Unlike some spreadsheet modelers who prefer to put all inputs in the upper-left corner of the spreadsheet, we enter the inputs wherever they fit most naturally. Of course, this takes some spreadsheet planning.)

**2 Name ranges.** Name the ranges indicated. Note that all but one of these (Total_cost) can be named easily with the Create from Selection shortcut, using the labels in column A.

**3 Production quantities.** Enter *any* values in the Units_produced range as production quantities. As always, you can enter values that you believe are good, maybe even optimal. This is not crucial, however, because Solver will eventually find the *optimal* production quantities.

*In multiperiod problems, we often need one formula for the first period and a slightly different formula for all other periods.*

**4 On-hand inventory.** Enter the formula

=B4+B12

in cell B16. This calculates the first month's on-hand inventory after production (but before demand). Then enter the "typical" formula

=B20+C12

for on-hand inventory after production in month 2 in cell C16 and copy it across row 16.

**5 Ending inventories.** Enter the formula

=B16-B18

for ending inventory in cell B20 and copy it across row 20. This formula calculates ending inventory in the current month as on-hand inventory before demand minus the demand in that month.

**6** **Production and holding costs.** Enter the formula

**=B8*B12**

in cell B26 and copy it across to cell G26 to calculate the monthly production costs. Then enter the formula

**=$B$5*B8*B20**

in cell B27 and copy it across to cell G27 to calculate the monthly holding costs. Note that these are based on monthly ending inventories. Finally, calculate the cost totals in column H by summing with the SUM function.

## USING SOLVER

To use Solver, fill out the main dialog box as shown in Figure 3.28. The logic behind the constraints is straightforward. We must guarantee that (1) the production quantities do not exceed the production capacities, (2) the on-hand inventories after production are at least as large as demands, and (3) ending inventories do not exceed storage capacities. Then check the Assume Linear Model and Assume Non-Negative options, and click on Solve.

**Figure 3.28**
Solver Dialog Box for Production Model

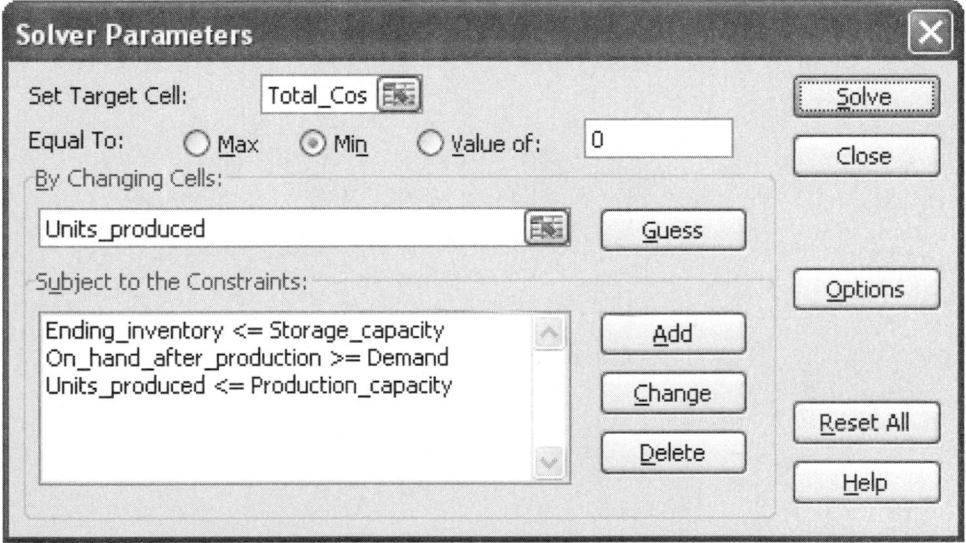

### Discussion of the Solution

The optimal solution from Solver is shown in Figure 3.29. This solution is also represented graphically in Figure 3.30. We can interpret the solution by comparing production quantities with demands. (Remember that all spreadsheet quantities are in hundreds of footballs.) In month 1, Pigskin should produce just enough to meet month 1 demand (taking into account the initial inventory of 5000). In month 2, it should produce 5000 more footballs than month 2 demand, and then in month 3, it should produce just enough to meet month 3 demand, while still carrying the extra 5000 footballs in inventory from month 2 production. In month 4, Pigskin should finally use these 5000 footballs, along with the maximum production amount, 30,000, to meet month 4 demand. Then in months 5 and 6, it should produce exactly enough to meet these months' demands. The total cost is $1,535,563, most of

**Figure 3.29**  Optimal Solution for the Production Model

| | A | B | C | D | E | F | G | H | I | J | K |
|---|---|---|---|---|---|---|---|---|---|---|---|
| 1 | **Multiperiod production model** | | | | | | | | **Range names used** | | |
| 2 | | | | | | | | | Demand | =Model!$B$18:$G$18 | |
| 3 | **Input data** | | | | | | | | Ending_inventory | =Model!$B$20:$G$20 | |
| 4 | Initial inventory (100s) | 50 | | | | | | | On_hand_after_production | =Model!$B$16:$G$16 | |
| 5 | Holding cost as % of prod cost | 5% | | | | | | | Production_capacity | =Model!$B$14:$G$14 | |
| 6 | | | | | | | | | Storage_capacity | =Model!$B$22:$G$22 | |
| 7 | Month | 1 | 2 | 3 | 4 | 5 | 6 | | Total_Cost | =Model!$H$28 | |
| 8 | Production cost/unit | $12.50 | $12.55 | $12.70 | $12.80 | $12.85 | $12.95 | | Units_produced | =Model!$B$12:$G$12 | |
| 9 | | | | | | | | | | | |
| 10 | **Production plan (all quantities are in 100s of footballs)** | | | | | | | | | | |
| 11 | Month | 1 | 2 | 3 | 4 | 5 | 6 | | | | |
| 12 | Units produced | 50 | 200 | 300 | 300 | 250 | 100 | | | | |
| 13 | | <= | <= | <= | <= | <= | <= | | | | |
| 14 | Production capacity | 300 | 300 | 300 | 300 | 300 | 300 | | | | |
| 15 | | | | | | | | | | | |
| 16 | On hand after production | 100 | 200 | 350 | 350 | 250 | 100 | | | | |
| 17 | | >= | >= | >= | >= | >= | >= | | | | |
| 18 | Demand | 100 | 150 | 300 | 350 | 250 | 100 | | | | |
| 19 | | | | | | | | | | | |
| 20 | Ending inventory | 0 | 50 | 50 | 0 | 0 | 0 | | | | |
| 21 | | <= | <= | <= | <= | <= | <= | | | | |
| 22 | Storage capacity | 100 | 100 | 100 | 100 | 100 | 100 | | | | |
| 23 | | | | | | | | | | | |
| 24 | **Summary of costs (all costs are in hundreds of dollars)** | | | | | | | | | | |
| 25 | Month | 1 | 2 | 3 | 4 | 5 | 6 | Totals | | | |
| 26 | Production costs | $625.00 | $2,510.00 | $3,810.00 | $3,840.00 | $3,212.50 | $1,295.00 | $15,292.50 | | | |
| 27 | Holding costs | $0.00 | $31.38 | $31.75 | $0.00 | $0.00 | $0.00 | $63.13 | | | |
| 28 | Totals | $625.00 | $2,541.38 | $3,841.75 | $3,840.00 | $3,212.50 | $1,295.00 | $15,355.63 | | | |

**Figure 3.30**

Graphical Representation of Optimal Production Schedule

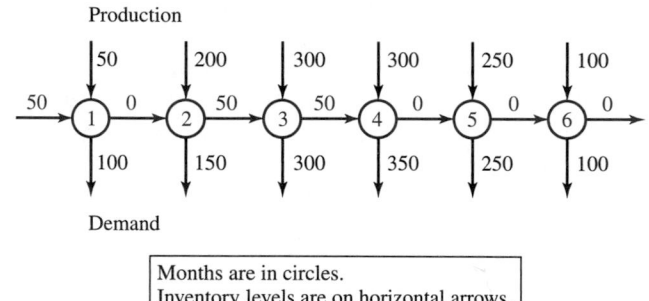

Months are in circles.
Inventory levels are on horizontal arrows.

which is production cost. (This total cost is expressed in actual dollars. The value in the spreadsheet is in hundreds of dollars.)

Could you have guessed this optimal solution? Upon reflection, it makes perfect sense. Because the monthly holding costs are large relative to the differences in monthly production costs, there is little incentive to produce footballs early to take advantage of "cheap" production months. Therefore, the Pigskin Company produces footballs each month as they are needed—when this is possible. The only exception to this rule is the 20,000 footballs produced during month 2 when only 15,000 are needed. The extra 5000 footballs produced in month 2 are needed to meet month 4 demand of 35,000, because month 3 production capacity is used entirely to meet month 3 demand. That is, month 3 capacity is not available to help meet month 4 demand, so 5000 units of month 2 capacity are used to help meet month 4 demand.

*You can often improve your intuition by trying to reason why Solver's solution is optimal.*

**FUNDAMENTAL INSIGHT**

**Multiperiod Optimization Problems and Myopic Solutions**

Many optimization problems are of a multiperiod nature, where a sequence of decisions must be made over time. When making the *first* of these decisions, the one for this week or this month, say, it's usually best to include future decisions in the model, as we have done here. If we ignore future periods and make the initial decision based only on the first period, the resulting decision is called **myopic** (short-sighted). Myopic decisions are occasionally optimal, but not very often. The idea is that if we act now in a way that looks best in the short run, it might lead us down a strategically unattractive path for the long run.

*If you want SolverTable to keep track of a quantity that is not in your model, you need to create it with an appropriate formula in a new cell.*

### Sensitivity Analysis

We can use SolverTable to perform a number of interesting sensitivity analyses. We illustrate two possibilities here. First, note that the most inventory ever carried at the end of a month is 50 (5000 footballs), although the storage capacity each month is 100. Perhaps this is because the holding cost percentage, 5%, is fairly large. Would more ending inventory be carried if this holding cost percentage were lower? Or would even less be carried if it were higher? We can check this with the SolverTable output shown in Figure 3.31. Now the single input cell is cell B5, and the *single* output we track is the maximum ending inventory ever held, which we calculate in cell B31 with the formula

**=MAX(Ending_inventory)**

As we can see, only when the holding cost percentage decreases to 1% do we hit the storage-capacity limit. (From this output, we cannot tell which month or how many months the ending inventory is at this upper limit.) On the other side, even when the holding cost percentage reaches 10%, we still continue to hold a maximum ending inventory of 50.

**Figure 3.31**
Sensitivity of Maximum Ending Inventory to Holding Cost Percentage

| | A | B | C | D |
|---|---|---|---|---|
| 30 | **Sensitivity of maximum ending inventory to holding cost percentage** | | | |
| 31 | Output formula | 50 | | |
| 32 | | | | |
| 33 | | $B$31 | | |
| 34 | 1% | 100 | | |
| 35 | 2% | 50 | | |
| 36 | 3% | 50 | | |
| 37 | 4% | 50 | | |
| 38 | 5% | 50 | | |
| 39 | 6% | 50 | | |
| 40 | 7% | 50 | | |
| 41 | 8% | 50 | | |
| 42 | 9% | 50 | | |
| 43 | 10% | 50 | | |

A second possible sensitivity analysis is suggested by the way the optimal production schedule will probably be implemented. The optimal solution to Pigskin's model specifies the production level for each of the next 6 months. In reality, however, the company will probably implement the model's recommendation only for the *first* month. Then at the beginning of the second month, it will gather new forecasts for the *next* 6 months, months 2 through 7, solve a new 6-month model, and again implement the model's recommendation for the first of these months, month 2. If the company continues in this manner, it is using a 6-month **rolling planning horizon.**

The question, then, is whether the assumed demands (really, forecasts) toward the end of the planning horizon have much effect on the optimal production quantity in month 1.

We hope not, because these forecasts could be quite inaccurate. The two-way Solver table in Figure 3.32 shows how the optimal month 1 production quantity varies with the forecasted demands in months 5 and 6. As we can see, if the forecasted months 5 and 6 demands remain fairly small, the optimal month 1 production quantity remains at 50. This is good news because it means that the optimal production quantity in month 1 is fairly insensitive to the possibly inaccurate forecasts for months 5 and 6.

**Figure 3.32**

Sensitivity of Month 1 Production to Demands in Months 5 and 6

| | A | B | C | D | E | F |
|---|---|---|---|---|---|---|
| 45 | Sensitivity of month 1 production to demands in months 5 (along side) and 6 (along top) | | | | | |
| 46 | $B$12 | 100 | 200 | 300 | | |
| 47 | 100 | 50 | 50 | 50 | | |
| 48 | 200 | 50 | 50 | 50 | | |
| 49 | 300 | 50 | 50 | 50 | | |

Solver's sensitivity report for this model appears in Figure 3.33. The bottom part of this report is fairly straightforward to interpret. The first six rows are for sensitivity to changes in the storage capacity, whereas the last six are for sensitivity to changes in the demands. (There are no rows for the production capacity constraints because these are simple upper bound constraints on the decision variables. Recall that Solver's sensitivity report handles this type of constraint differently from "normal" constraints.) In contrast, the top part of the report is very difficult to unravel because the objective coefficients of the decision variables are each based on *multiple* inputs. (Each is a combination of a unit production cost and the holding cost percentage.) Therefore, if we want to know how the solution changes if we change a single unit production cost or the holding cost percentage, this report does not answer our question, at least not easily.

**Figure 3.33**

Solver's Sensitivity Report for Production Model

| | A | B | C | D | E | F | G | H |
|---|---|---|---|---|---|---|---|---|
| 6 | | Adjustable Cells | | | | | | |
| 7 | | | | Final | Reduced | Objective | Allowable | Allowable |
| 8 | | Cell | Name | Value | Cost | Coefficient | Increase | Decrease |
| 9 | | $B$12 | Units produced | 50 | 0 | 16.3175 | 1E+30 | 0.5750 |
| 10 | | $C$12 | Units produced | 200 | 0 | 15.7425 | 0.5750 | 0.4775 |
| 11 | | $D$12 | Units produced | 300 | -0.4775 | 15.2650 | 0.4775 | 1E+30 |
| 12 | | $E$12 | Units produced | 300 | -1.0125 | 14.7300 | 1.0125 | 1E+30 |
| 13 | | $F$12 | Units produced | 250 | 0 | 14.1400 | 1.6025 | 0.5425 |
| 14 | | $G$12 | Units produced | 100 | 0 | 13.5975 | 0.5425 | 13.5975 |
| 15 | | | | | | | | |
| 16 | | Constraints | | | | | | |
| 17 | | | | Final | Shadow | Constraint | Allowable | Allowable |
| 18 | | Cell | Name | Value | Price | R.H. Side | Increase | Decrease |
| 19 | | $B$16 | On hand after production <= | 100 | 0.575 | 100 | 100 | 50 |
| 20 | | $C$16 | On hand after production <= | 200 | 0 | 150 | 50 | 1E+30 |
| 21 | | $D$16 | On hand after production <= | 350 | 0 | 300 | 50 | 1E+30 |
| 22 | | $E$16 | On hand after production <= | 350 | 1.6 | 350 | 50 | 50 |
| 23 | | $F$16 | On hand after production <= | 250 | 0.5 | 250 | 50 | 200 |
| 24 | | $G$16 | On hand after production <= | 100 | 13.6 | 100 | 100 | 100 |
| 25 | | $B$20 | Ending inventory >= | 0 | 0 | 100 | 1E+30 | 100 |
| 26 | | $C$20 | Ending inventory >= | 50 | 0 | 100 | 1E+30 | 50 |
| 27 | | $D$20 | Ending inventory >= | 50 | 0 | 100 | 1E+30 | 50 |
| 28 | | $E$20 | Ending inventory >= | 0 | 0 | 100 | 1E+30 | 100 |
| 29 | | $F$20 | Ending inventory >= | 0 | 0 | 100 | 1E+30 | 100 |
| 30 | | $G$20 | Ending inventory >= | 0 | 0 | 100 | 1E+30 | 100 |

This is one case where sensitivity analysis with SolverTable is more straightforward and intuitive. It allows us to change *any* of the model's inputs and directly see the effects on the solution.

**MODELING ISSUES**

We assume that Pigskin uses a 6-month planning horizon. Why 6 months? In many multiperiod models, a company has to make forecasts about the future, such as the level of customer demand. Therefore, the length of the planning horizon is usually the length of time for which the company can make reasonably accurate forecasts. Here, Pigskin evidently believes that it can forecast up to 6 months from now, so it uses a 6-month planning horizon. ■

**PROBLEMS**

## Skill-Building Problems

**17.** Can you guess the results of a sensitivity analysis on the initial inventory in the Pigskin model? See if your guess is correct by using SolverTable and allowing the initial inventory to vary from 0 to 100 in increments of 10. (These are in hundreds of footballs.) Keep track of the values in the changing cells and the target cell.

**18.** Modify the Pigskin model so that there are 8 months in the planning horizon. You can make up reasonable values for any extra required data. Don't forget to modify range names. Then modify the model again so that there are only 4 months in the planning horizon. Do either of these modifications change the optimal production quantity in month 1?

**19.** As indicated by the algebraic model of the Pigskin problem, there is no real need to calculate inventory on hand after production and constrain it to be greater than or equal to demand. An alternative is to calculate ending inventory directly and constrain it to be non-negative. Modify the current spreadsheet model to do this. (Delete rows 16 and 17, and calculate ending inventory appropriately. Then add an *explicit* nonnegativity constraint on ending inventory.) Is the optimal solution to this modified model the same as before? It should be.

**20.** In one modification of the Pigskin problem, the maximum storage constraint and the holding cost are based on the *average* inventory (not ending inventory) for a given month, where the average inventory is defined as the sum of beginning inventory and ending inventory, divided by 2, and beginning inventory is before production or demand. Modify the Pigskin model with this new assumption, and use Solver to find the

optimal solution. How does this change the optimal production schedule? How does it change the optimal total cost?

## Skill-Extending Problems

**21.** Modify the Pigskin spreadsheet model so that except for month 6, demand need not be met on time. The only requirement is that all demand be met eventually by the end of month 6. How does this change the optimal production schedule? How does it change the optimal total cost?

**22.** Modify the Pigskin spreadsheet model so that demand in any of the first 5 months must be met no later than a month late, whereas demand in month 6 must be met on time. For example, the demand in month 3 can be met partly in month 3 and partly in month 4. How does this change the optimal production schedule? How does it change the optimal total cost?

**23.** Modify the Pigskin spreadsheet model in the following way. Assume that the timing of demand and production are such that only 70% of the production in a given month can be used to satisfy the demand in that month. The other 30% occurs too late in that month and must be carried as inventory to help satisfy demand in later months. How does this change the optimal production schedule? How does it change the optimal total cost? Then use SolverTable to see how the optimal production schedule and optimal cost vary as the percentage of production usable for this month's demand (now 70%) is allowed to vary from 20% to 100% in increments of 10%.

## 3.9 A COMPARISON OF ALGEBRAIC AND SPREADSHEET MODELS

To this point, we have seen three algebraic optimization models and three corresponding spreadsheet models. How do they differ? If you review the first two examples in this chapter, the diet and product mix examples, we believe you will agree that (1) the algebraic models are straightforward and (2) the spreadsheet models are almost direct translations into Excel of the algebraic models. In particular, each algebraic model has a set of $x$'s that corresponds to the changing cell range in the spreadsheet model. In addition, each objective and each left-hand side of each constraint in the spreadsheet model corresponds to a linear expression involving $x$'s in the algebraic model.

However, the Pigskin production planning model is different. The spreadsheet model includes one set of changing cells, the production quantities, and everything else is related to these through spreadsheet formulas. In contrast, the algebraic model has *two* sets of variables, the $P$'s for the production quantities and the $I$'s for the ending inventories, and together these comprise the "decision variables." These two sets of variables must then be related algebraically, which is done through a series of balance equations.

This is a typical situation in algebraic models, where one set of variables (the production quantities) corresponds to the *real* decision variables; whereas other sets of variables, along with extra equations, must be introduced to get the logic straight. This extra level of abstraction makes algebraic models much more difficult for typical users to develop and comprehend, which is the primary reason this book focuses almost exclusively on spreadsheet models.

## 3.10 A DECISION SUPPORT SYSTEM

If your job is to develop an LP spreadsheet model to solve a problem such as Pigskin's production problem, then you will be considered the "expert" in LP. Many people who need to use such models, however, are *not* experts. They might understand the basic ideas behind LP and the types of problems it is intended to solve, but they probably do not understand the details. In this case, it is useful to provide these users with a **decision support system** (DSS) that can help them solve problems without having to worry about technical details.

Although we won't attempt to teach you how to build a full-scale DSS, we do show you what a typical DSS looks like and what it can do.[15] (We consider only DSSs built around spreadsheets. There are many other platforms for developing DSSs that we do not consider.) Basically, a spreadsheet-based DSS contains a spreadsheet model of a problem, such as the one in Figure 3.27. However, users probably never even see this model. Instead, they see a *front end* and a *back end*. The front end allows them to select input values for their particular problem. The user interface for this front end can include several features, such as buttons, dialog boxes, toolbars, and menus—the things you are used to seeing in Windows applications. The back end then produces a report that explains the optimal policy in nontechnical terms.

A DSS for a slight variation of the Pigskin problem is illustrated in the file **Decision Support.xlsm**. This file has three sheets. When you open the file, you see the Explanation sheet (see Figure 3.34) that contains two buttons: one for setting up the problem (getting the user's inputs) and one for solving the problem (running Solver). When you click the Set Up Problem button, you are asked for the inputs: the initial inventory, the forecasted

---

[15] If you are interested in learning more about this DSS, the accompanying CD-ROM includes notes about its development in the file Developing the Decision Support Application.docx under the Chapter 3 Example Files folder. If you are interested in learning more about spreadsheet DSSs in general, Albright has written the book *VBA for Modelers,* now in its second edition. The book contains a primer on the VBA language and presents many applications and instructions for creating DSSs with VBA.

demands for each month, and others. An example appears in Figure 3.35. These input boxes should be self-explanatory, so that all you need to do is enter the values you want to try. (To speed up the process, the inputs from the previous run are shown by default.) After you have entered all of these inputs, look at the Model sheet. This sheet contains a spreadsheet model similar to the one we saw previously in Figure 3.29, but with the inputs you just entered.

**Figure 3.34**
Explanation Sheet
for DSS

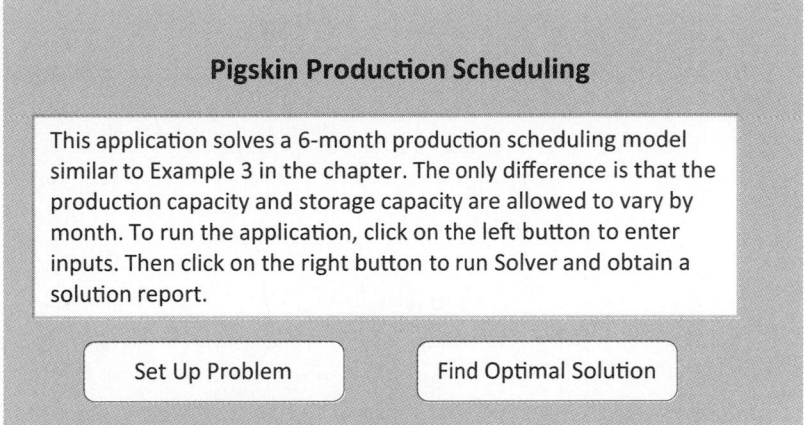

**Figure 3.35**
Input Dialog Box
for DSS

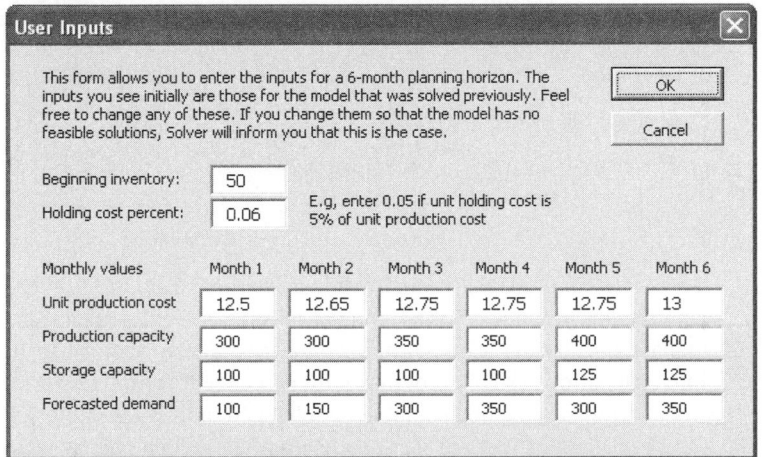

Now go back to the Explanation sheet and click the Find Optimal Solution button. This automatically sets up the Solver dialog box and runs Solver. There are two possibilities. First, it's possible that there is no feasible solution to the problem with the inputs you entered. In this case, you see a message to this effect, as shown in Figure 3.36. In most cases, however, the problem will have a feasible solution. In this case, you see the Report sheet, which summarizes the optimal solution in nontechnical terms. Part of one sample output appears in Figure 3.37.

**Figure 3.36**
No Solution Message

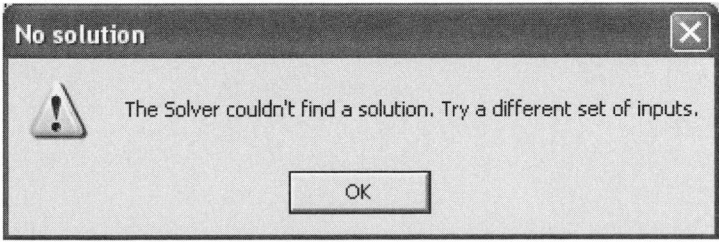

**Figure 3.37**

Report Sheet for DSS

## Monthly schedule

### Month 1

| Units | | Dollars | |
|---|---|---|---|
| Start with | 50 | | |
| Produce | 50 | Production cost | $625.00 |
| Demand is | 100 | | |
| End with | 0 | Holding cost | $0.00 |

### Month 2

| Units | | Dollars | |
|---|---|---|---|
| Start with | 0 | | |
| Produce | 150 | Production cost | $1,897.50 |
| Demand is | 150 | | |
| End with | 0 | Holding cost | $0.00 |

### Month 3

| Units | | Dollars | |
|---|---|---|---|
| Start with | 0 | | |
| Produce | 300 | Production cost | $3,825.00 |
| Demand is | 300 | | |
| End with | 0 | Holding cost | $0.00 |

After studying this report, you can then click on the Solve Another Problem button, which takes you back to the Explanation sheet so that you can solve a new problem. All of this is done automatically with Excel macros. These macros use the Microsoft Visual Basic for Applications (VBA) programming language to automate various tasks. In most professional applications, nontechnical people need only enter inputs and look at reports. Therefore, the Model sheet and VBA code are often hidden and protected from users.

## 3.11 CONCLUSION

This chapter provides a good start to LP modeling—and to optimization modeling in general. We have discussed how to develop three basic LP spreadsheet models, how to use Solver to find their optimal solutions, and how to perform sensitivity analyses with Solver's sensitivity reports or with the SolverTable add-in. We have also discussed how to recognize whether a mathematical programming model satisfies the linear assumptions. In the next few chapters, we discuss a variety of other optimization models, but the three basic steps of model development, Solver optimization, and sensitivity analysis remain the same.

# Summary of Key Management Science Terms

| Term | Explanation | Page |
|---|---|---|
| Linear programming model | An optimization model with a linear objective and linear constraints | 72 |
| Objective | The value, such as profit, to be optimized in an optimization model | 73 |
| Constraints | Conditions that must be satisfied in an optimization model | 73 |
| Nonnegativity constraints | Constraints that require the decision variables to be nonnegative, usually for physical reasons | 73 |
| Feasible solution | A solution that satisfies all the constraints | 74 |
| Feasible region | The set of all feasible solutions | 74 |
| Optimal solution | The feasible solution that has the best value of the objective | 74 |
| Simplex method | An efficient algorithm for finding the optimal solution in an LP model | 74 |
| Sensitivity analysis | Seeing how the optimal solution changes as various input values change | 74 |
| Algebraic model | A model that expresses the constraints and the objective algebraically | 76 |
| Graphical solution | A solution that shows the constraints and objective graphically so that the optimal solution can be identified; useful only when there are two decision variables | 77 |
| Spreadsheet model | A model that uses spreadsheet formulas to express the logic of the model | 78 |
| Binding constraint | A constraint that holds as an equality | 85 |
| Nonbinding constraint, slack | A constraint where there is a difference, called the slack, between the two sides of the inequality | 85 |
| Reduced cost | Amount the objective coefficient of a variable currently equal to 0 must change before it is optimal for that variable to be positive (or to decrease from its upper bound, if there is an upper bound constraint) | 88 |
| Shadow price | The change in the objective for a change in the right-hand side of a constraint; used to see how much more of a scarce resource is worth | 88 |
| Mathematical programming model | Any optimization model, whether linear, integer, or nonlinear | 93 |
| Proportionality, additivity, divisibility | Properties of optimization model that result in an LP model | 94 |
| Infeasibility | Condition where a model has no feasible solutions | 96 |
| Unboundedness | Condition where there is no limit to the objective; always a sign of an error in the model | 97 |
| Decision support system (DSS) | User-friendly system where an end user can enter inputs to a model and see outputs, but need not be concerned with technical details | 118 |

## Summary of Key Excel Terms

| Term | Explanation | Excel | Page |
|---|---|---|---|
| Changing cells | Cells that contain the values of the decision variables | Specify in Solver dialog box | 73 |
| Target cell | Cell that contains the value of the objective | Specify in Solver dialog box | 73 |
| Solver | Add-in that ships with Excel for performing optimization | Use Solver from Data ribbon | 82 |
| Solver's sensitivity report | Report available from Solver that shows sensitivity to objective coefficients and right-hand sides of constraints | Available in Solver dialog box right after Solver runs | 86 |
| SolverTable add-in | Add-in that performs sensitivity analysis to any inputs and reports results similar to an Excel data table | Use SolverTable from Add-Ins ribbon | 89 |
| Selecting multiple ranges | Useful when changing cells, e.g., are in noncontiguous ranges | Press Ctrl key, drag ranges, one after the other | 90 |

# PROBLEMS

## Skill-Building Problems

**24.** Leary Chemical manufactures three chemicals: A, B, and C. These chemicals are produced via two production processes: 1 and 2. Running process 1 for an hour costs $4 and yields 3 units of A, 1 unit of B, and 1 unit of C. Running process 2 for an hour costs $1 and yields 1 unit of A and 1 unit of B. To meet customer demands, at least 10 units of A, 5 units of B, and 3 units of C must be produced daily.
   **a.** Use Solver to determine a daily production plan that minimizes the cost of meeting Leary's daily demands.
   **b.** Confirm graphically that the daily production plan from part **a** minimizes the cost of meeting Leary's daily demands.
   **c.** Starting with the optimal solution, use SolverTable to see what happens to the decision variables and the total cost when the hourly processing cost for process 2 increases in increments of $0.50. How large must this cost increase be before the decision variables change? What happens when it continues to increase beyond this point?

**25.** Furnco manufactures desks and chairs. Each desk uses 4 units of wood, and each chair uses 3 units of wood. A desk contributes $40 to profit, and a chair contributes $25. Marketing restrictions require that the number of chairs produced be at least twice the number of desks produced. There are 20 units of wood available.
   **a.** Use Solver to maximize Furnco's profit.
   **b.** Confirm graphically that the solution in part **a** maximizes Furnco's profit.
   **c.** Starting with the optimal solution, use SolverTable to see what happens to the decision variables and the total profit when the availability of wood varies from 10 to 30 in 1-unit increments. Based on your findings, how much would Furnco be willing to pay for each extra unit of wood over its current 20 units? How much profit would Furnco lose if it lost any of its current 20 units?

**26.** A farmer in Iowa owns 45 acres of land. He is going to plant each acre with wheat or corn. Each acre planted with wheat yields $200 profit, requires 3 workers, and requires 2 tons of fertilizer; each with corn yields $300 profit, requires 2 workers, and requires 4 tons of fertilizer. The farmer has 100 workers and 120 tons of fertilizer available.
   **a.** Use Solver to help the farmer maximize the profit from his land.
   **b.** Confirm graphically that the solution from part **a** maximizes the farmer's profit from his land.
   **c.** Starting with the optimal solution, use SolverTable to see what happens to the decision variables and the total profit when the availability of fertilizer varies from 20 tons to 220 tons in 10-ton increments. When does the farmer discontinue producing wheat? When does he discontinue producing corn? How does the profit change for each 10-ton increment? Make this more obvious by creating a line chart of profit (vertical axis) versus fertilizer availability.

**27.** A customer requires during the next 4 months, respectively, 50, 65, 100, and 70 units of a commodity, and no backlogging is allowed (that is, the customer's requirements must be met on time). Production costs are $5, $8, $4, and $7 per unit during these months. The storage cost from one month to the next is $2 per unit (assessed on ending inventory). It is estimated that each unit on hand at the end of month 4 can be sold for $6.

    **a.** Determine how to minimize the net cost incurred in meeting the demands for the next 4 months.

    **b.** Starting with the optimal solution, use SolverTable to see what happens to the decision variables and the total cost when the initial inventory varies from 0 (the implied value in the problem) to 100 in 10-unit increments. How much lower would the total cost be if the company started with 10 units in inventory, rather than none? Would this same cost decrease occur for *every* 10-unit increase in initial inventory?

**28.** A company faces the following demands during the next three weeks: week 1, 20 units; week 2, 10 units; week 3, 15 units. The unit production costs during each week are as follows: week 1, $13; week 2, $14; week 3, $15. A holding cost of $2 per unit is assessed against each week's ending inventory. At the beginning of week 1, the company has 5 units on hand. In reality, not all goods produced during a month can be used to meet the current month's demand. To model this fact, assume that only half of the goods produced during a week can be used to meet the current week's demands.

    **a.** Determine how to minimize the cost of meeting the demand for the next 3 weeks.

    **b.** Revise the model so that the demands are of the form $D_t + k\Delta_t$, where $D_t$ is the original demand in month $t$, $k$ is a factor, and $\Delta_t$ is an amount of change in month $t$ demand. (The Greek symbol $\Delta$ is typically used to indicate change.) Formulate the model in such a way that you can use SolverTable to analyze changes in the amounts produced and the total cost when $k$ varies from 0 to 10 in 1-unit increments, for any fixed values of the $\Delta_t$'s. For example, try this when $\Delta_1 = 2$, $\Delta_2 = 5$, and $\Delta_3 = 3$. Describe the behavior you observe in the table. Can you find any "reasonable" $\Delta_t$'s that induce *positive* production levels in week 3?

**29.** Bloomington Brewery produces beer and ale. Beer sells for $5 per barrel, and ale sells for $2 per barrel. Producing a barrel of beer requires 5 pounds of malt and 2 pounds of hops. Producing a barrel of ale requires 2 pounds of corn and 1 pound of hops. The brewery has 60 pounds of corn and 25 pounds of hops.

    **a.** Use Solver to maximize Bloomington Brewery's revenue.

    **b.** Confirm graphically that the solution in part **a** maximizes Bloomington Brewery's revenue.

    **c.** Starting with the optimal solution, use SolverTable to either substantiate or refute the following

statements: The availability of corn can decrease by any amount (up to 60 pounds), and each unit decrease will cost Bloomington Brewery the same amount in terms of lost revenue. On the other hand, increases in the availability of corn do *not* have a constant effect on total revenue; the first few extra units have a larger effect than subsequent units.

**30.** For a telephone survey, a marketing research group needs to contact at least 150 wives, 120 husbands, 100 single adult males, and 110 single adult females. It costs $2 to make a daytime call and (because of higher labor costs) $5 to make an evening call. The file **P03_30.xlsx** lists the results that can be expected. For example, 30% of all daytime calls are answered by wives, and 15% of all evening calls are answered by single males. Because of a limited staff, at most half of all phone calls can be evening calls.

    **a.** Determine how to minimize the cost of completing the survey.

    **b.** Starting with the optimal solution, use SolverTable to investigate changes in the unit cost of either type of call. Specifically, investigate changes in the cost of a daytime call, with the cost of an evening call fixed, to see when (if ever) 50% of all calls will be evening calls. Then repeat the analysis by changing the cost of an evening call and keeping the cost of a daytime call fixed.

**31.** Woodco manufactures tables and chairs. Each table and chair must be made entirely out of oak or entirely out of pine. A total of 150 board feet of oak and 210 board feet of pine are available. A table requires either 17 board feet of oak or 30 board feet of pine, and a chair requires either 5 board feet of oak or 13 board feet of pine. Each table can be sold for $40, and each chair for $15.

    **a.** Determine how Woodco can maximize its revenue.

    **b.** Suppose you want to investigate the effects of simultaneous changes in the selling prices of the products. Specifically, you want to see what happens to the total revenue when the selling prices of oak products change by a factor $1 + k_1$, and the selling prices of pine products change by a factor $1 + k_2$. Revise your model so that you can use SolverTable to investigate changes in total revenue as $k_1$ and $k_2$ both vary from $-0.3$ to $0.3$ in increments of 0.1. Would you conclude that total revenue changes *linearly* within this range?

**32.** Alden Enterprises produces two products. Each product can be produced on either of two machines. The time (in hours) required to produce each product on each machine is listed in the file **P03_32.xlsx**. Each month, 500 hours of time are available on each machine. Each month, customers are willing to buy up to the quantities of each product at the prices also given in the file **P03_32.xlsx**. The company's goal is to maximize the revenue obtained from selling units during the next 2 months.

a. Determine how it can meet this goal. Assume that Alden will not produce any units in either month that it cannot sell in that month.

b. Suppose Alden wants to see what will happen if customer demands for each product in each month simultaneously change by a factor $1 + k$. Revise the model so that you can use SolverTable to investigate the effect of this change on total revenue as $k$ varies from $-0.3$ to $0.3$ in increments of $0.1$. Does revenue change in a linear manner over this range? Can you explain intuitively why it changes in the way it does?

33. There are three factories on the Momiss River: 1, 2, and 3. Each emits two types of pollutants, labeled $P_1$ and $P_2$, into the river. If the waste from each factory is processed, the pollution in the river can be reduced. It costs $15 to process a ton of factory 1 waste, and each ton processed reduces the amount of $P_1$ by 0.10 ton and the amount of $P_2$ by 0.45 ton. It costs $10 to process a ton of factory 2 waste, and each ton processed will reduce the amount of $P_1$ by 0.20 ton and the amount of $P_2$ by 0.25 ton. It costs $20 to process a ton of factory 3 waste, and each ton processed will reduce the amount of $P_1$ by 0.40 ton and the amount of $P_2$ by 0.30 ton. The state wants to reduce the amount of $P_1$ in the river by at least 30 tons and the amount of $P_2$ by at least 40 tons.

a. Use Solver to determine how to minimize the cost of reducing pollution by the desired amounts.

b. Are the LP assumptions (proportionality, additivity, divisibility) reasonable in this problem?

c. Suppose you want to investigate the effects of increases in the minimal reductions required by the state. Specifically, you want to see what happens to the amounts of waste processed at the three factories and the total cost if both requirements (currently 30 and 40 tons, respectively) are increased by the *same* percentage. Revise your model so that you can use SolverTable to investigate these changes when the percentage increase varies from 10% to 100% in increments of 10%. Do the amounts processed at the three factories and the total cost change in a linear manner?

## Skill-Extending Problems

34. Truckco manufactures two types of trucks, types 1 and 2. Each truck must go through the painting shop and the assembly shop. If the painting shop were completely devoted to painting type 1 trucks, 800 per day could be painted; whereas if the painting shop were completely devoted to painting type 2 trucks, 700 per day could be painted. If the assembly shop were completely devoted to assembling truck 1 engines, 1500 per day could be assembled, and if the assembly shop were completely devoted to assembling

truck 2 engines, 1200 per day could be assembled. It is possible, however, to paint *both* types of trucks in the painting shop. Similarly, it is possible to assemble both types in the assembly shop. Each type 1 truck contributes $300 to profit; each type 2 truck contributes $500. Use Solver to maximize Truckco's profit. (*Hint:* One approach, but not the only approach, is to try a graphical procedure first and then deduce the constraints from the graph.)

35. U.S. Labs manufactures mechanical heart valves from the heart valves of pigs. Different heart operations require valves of different sizes. U.S. Labs purchases pig valves from three different suppliers. The cost and size mix of the valves purchased from each supplier are given in the file **P03_35.xlsx.** Each month, U.S. Labs places an order with each supplier. At least 500 large, 300 medium, and 300 small valves must be purchased each month. Because of the limited availability of pig valves, at most 500 valves per month can be purchased from each supplier.

a. Use Solver to determine how U.S. Labs can minimize the cost of acquiring the needed valves.

b. Suppose U.S. Labs wants to investigate the effect on total cost of increasing its minimal purchase requirements each month. Specifically, it wants to see how total cost changes as the minimal purchase requirements of large, medium, and small valves all increase from their values in the problem by the *same* percentage. Revise your model so that SolverTable can be used to investigate these changes when the percentage increase varies from 2% to 20% in increments of 2%. Explain intuitively what happens when this percentage is at least 16%.

36. Sailco Corporation must determine how many sailboats to produce during each of the next 4 quarters. The demand during each of the next four quarters is as follows: first quarter, 40 sailboats; second quarter, 60 sailboats; third quarter, 75 sailboats; fourth quarter, 25 sailboats. Sailco must meet demands on time. At the beginning of the first quarter, Sailco has an inventory of 10 sailboats. At the beginning of each quarter, Sailco must decide how many sailboats to produce during that quarter. For simplicity, assume that sailboats manufactured during a quarter can be used to meet demand for that quarter. During each quarter, Sailco can produce up to 40 sailboats with regular-time labor at a total cost of $400 per sailboat. By having employees work overtime during a quarter, Sailco can produce additional sailboats with overtime labor at a total cost of $450 per sailboat. At the end of each quarter (after production has occurred and the current quarter's demand has been satisfied), a holding cost of $20 per sailboat is incurred.

a. Determine a production schedule to minimize the sum of production and inventory holding costs during the next 4 quarters.

**b.** Suppose Sailco wants to see whether any changes in the $20 holding cost per sailboat could induce the company to carry more or less inventory. Revise your model so that SolverTable can be used to investigate the effects on ending inventory during the 4-month interval of systematic changes in the unit holding cost. (Assume that even though the unit holding cost changes, it is still constant over the 4-month interval.) Are there any (nonnegative) unit holding costs that would induce Sailco to hold *more* inventory than it holds when the holding cost is $20? Are there any unit holding costs that would induce Sailco to hold less inventory than it holds when the holding cost is $20?

**37.** During the next 2 months, General Cars must meet (on time) the following demands for trucks and cars: month 1, 400 trucks and 800 cars; month 2, 300 trucks and 300 cars. During each month, at most 1000 vehicles can be produced. Each truck uses 2 tons of steel, and each car uses 1 ton of steel. During month 1, steel costs $400 per ton; during month 2, steel costs $600 per ton. At most 2500 tons of steel can be purchased each month. (Steel can be used only during the month in which it is purchased.) At the beginning of month 1, 100 trucks and 200 cars are in the inventory. At the end of each month, a holding cost of $150 per vehicle is assessed. Each car gets 20 mpg, and each truck gets 10 mpg. During each month, the vehicles produced by the company must average at least 16 mpg.
 **a.** Determine how to meet the demand and mileage requirements at minimum total cost.
 **b.** Check how sensitive the total cost is to the 16-mpg requirement by using SolverTable. Specifically, let this requirement vary from 14 mpg to 18 mpg in increments of 0.25 mpg, and write a short report of your results. In your report, explain intuitively what happens when the requirement is greater than 17 mpg.

**38.** The Deckers Clothing Company produces shirts and pants. Each shirt requires 2 square yards of cloth, and each pair of pants requires 3 square yards of cloth. During the next 2 months the following demands for shirts and pants must be met (on time): month 1, 1000 shirts and 1500 pairs of pants; month 2, 1200 shirts and 1400 pairs of pants. During each month, the following resources are available: month 1, 9000 square yards of cloth; month 2, 6000 square yards of cloth. (Cloth that is available and not used during month 1 can be used during month 2.) During each month, it costs $4 to make an article of clothing with regular-time labor and $8 with overtime labor. During each month, a total of at most 2500 articles of clothing can be produced with regular-time labor, and an unlimited number of articles of clothing can be produced with overtime labor. At the end of each month, a holding cost of $3 per article of clothing is assessed.

 **a.** Determine how to meet demands for the next 2 months (on time) at minimum cost. Assume that, at the beginning of month 1, 100 shirts and 200 pairs of pants are available.
 **b.** Use SolverTable to investigate the effect on total cost of two *simultaneous* changes. The first change is to allow the ratio of overtime to regular-time production cost (currently $8/$4 = 2) to decrease from 20% to 80% in increments of 20%, while keeping the regular-time cost at $4. The second change is to allow the production capacity *each* month (currently 2500) to decrease from 10% to 50% in increments of 10%. The idea here is that less regular-time capacity is available, but overtime is becoming relatively cheaper. Is the net effect on total cost positive or negative?

**39.** Each year, Comfy Shoes faces demands (which must be met on time) for pairs of shoes as shown in the file **P03_39.xlsx**. Employees work 3 consecutive quarters and then receive 1 quarter off. For example, a worker might work during quarters 3 and 4 of one year and quarter 1 of the next year. During a quarter in which an employee works, he or she can produce up to 500 pairs of shoes. Each worker is paid $5000 per quarter. At the end of each quarter, a holding cost of $10 per pair of shoes is assessed.
 **a.** Determine how to minimize the cost per year (labor plus holding) of meeting the demands for shoes. To simplify matters, assume that at the end of each year, the ending inventory is 0. (*Hint:* You may assume that a given worker will get the *same* quarter off during each year.)
 **b.** Suppose Comfy Shoes can pay a flat fee for a training program that will increase the productivity of all of its workers. Use SolverTable to see how much the company would be willing to pay for a training program that increases worker productivity from 500 pairs of shoes per quarter to $P$ pairs of shoes per quarter, where $P$ varies from 525 to 700 in increments of 25.

**40.** A company must meet (on time) the following demands: quarter 1, 3000 units; quarter 2, 2000 units; quarter 3, 4000 units. Each quarter, up to 2700 units can be produced with regular-time labor, at a cost of $40 per unit. During each quarter, an unlimited number of units can be produced with overtime labor, at a cost of $60 per unit. Of all units produced, 20% are unsuitable and cannot be used to meet demand. Also, at the end of each quarter, 10% of all units on hand spoil and cannot be used to meet any future demands. After each quarter's demand is satisfied and spoilage is accounted for, a cost of $15 per unit is assessed against the quarter's ending inventory.
 **a.** Determine how to minimize the total cost of meeting the demands of the next 3 quarters. Assume

that 1000 usable units are available at the beginning of quarter 1.

b. The company wants to know how much money it would be worth to decrease the percentage of unsuitable items and/or the percentage of items that spoil. Write a short report that provides relevant information. Base your report on three uses of SolverTable: (1) where the percentage of unsuitable items decreases and the percentage of items that spoil stays at 10%; (2) where the percentage of unsuitable items stays at 20% and the percentage of items that spoil decreases; and (3) where both percentages decrease. Does the sum of the separate effects on total cost from the first two tables equal the combined effect from the third table? Include an answer to this question in your report.

41. A pharmaceutical company manufactures two drugs at Los Angeles and Indianapolis. The cost of manufacturing a pound of each drug depends on the location, as indicated in the file **P03_41.xlsx**. The machine time (in hours) required to produce a pound of each drug at each city is also shown in this table. The company must produce at least 1000 pounds per week of drug 1 and at least 2000 pounds per week of drug 2. It has 500 hours per week of machine time at Indianapolis and 400 hours per week at Los Angeles.

a. Determine how the company can minimize the cost of producing the required drugs.

b. Use SolverTable to determine how much the company would be willing to pay to purchase a combination of *A* extra hours of machine time at Indianapolis and *B* extra hours of machine time at Los Angeles, where *A* and *B* can be any positive multiples of 10 up to 50.

42. A company manufactures two products on two machines. The number of hours of machine time and labor depends on the machine and product as shown in the file **P03_42.xlsx**. The cost of producing a unit of each product depends on which machine produces it. These unit costs also appear in the file **P03_42.xlsx**. There are 200 hours available on each of the two machines, and there are 400 labor hours available. This month at least 200 units of product 1 and at least 240 units of product 2 must be produced. Also, at least half of the product 1 requirement must be produced on machine 1, and at least half of the product 2 requirement must be made on machine 2.

a. Determine how the company can minimize the cost of meeting this month's requirements.

b. Use SolverTable to see how much the "at least half" requirements are costing the company. Do this by changing *both* of these requirements from "at least half " to "at least *x* percent," where *x* can be any multiple of 5% from 0% to 50%.

## APPENDIX INFORMATION ON SOLVERS

Office (or Excel) ships with a built-in version of Solver. This version and all other versions of Solver are developed by Frontline Systems, not Microsoft. When you install Office (or Excel), you have the option of installing or not installing Solver. In most cases, a "typical" install should install Solver. To check whether Solver is installed on your system, open Excel, select the Office Button, select Excel Options, select Add-Ins, and click on Go. If there is a Solver item in the list, then Solver has been installed. (To actually add it in, make sure this item is checked.) Otherwise, you need to run the Office Setup program with the Add/Remove feature to install Solver. For users of previous versions of Excel (2003 or earlier), the actual Solver add-in file is a different one in Excel 2007. In previous versions, it was Solver.xla; now it is Solver.xlam. However, the functionality hasn't changed.

The built-in version of Solver is able to solve most problems you are likely to encounter. However, it does have one important limitation you should be aware of: It allows only 200 changing cells. This might sound like plenty, but many real-world problems go well beyond 200 changing cells. If you want to solve larger problems, you need to purchase one of Frontline's commercial versions of Solver. For more information, check Frontline Systems' Web site at http://www.solver.com.

Shelby Shelving is a small company that manufactures two types of shelves for grocery stores. Model S is the standard model, and model LX is a heavy-duty model. Shelves are manufactured in three major steps: stamping, forming, and assembly. In the stamping stage, a large machine is used to stamp (i.e., cut) standard sheets of metal into appropriate sizes. In the forming stage, another machine bends the metal into shape. Assembly involves joining the parts with a combination of soldering and riveting. Shelby's stamping and forming machines work on both models of shelves. Separate assembly departments are used for the final stage of production.

The file **Shelby Shelving.xlsx** contains relevant data for Shelby (see Figure 3.38). The hours required on each machine for each unit of product are shown in the range B5:C6 of the Accounting Data sheet. For example, the production of one model S shelf requires 0.25 hour on the forming machine. Both the stamping and forming machines can operate for 800 hours each month. The model S assembly department has a monthly capacity of 1900 units. The model LX assembly department has a monthly capacity of only 1400 units. Currently Shelby is producing and selling 400 units of model S and 1400 units of model LX per month.

Model S shelves are sold for $1800, and model LX shelves are sold for $2100. Shelby's operation is fairly small in the industry, and management at Shelby believes it cannot raise prices beyond these levels because of the competition. However, the marketing department feels that Shelby can sell as much as it can produce at these prices. The costs of production are summarized in the Accounting Data sheet. As usual, values in blue borders are given, whereas other values are calculated from these.

Management at Shelby just met to discuss next month's operating plan. Although the shelves are selling well, the overall profitability of the company is a concern. The plant's engineer suggested that the current production of model S shelves be cut back. According to him, "Model S shelves are sold for $1800 per unit, but our costs are $1839. Even though we're only selling 400 units a month, we're losing money on each one. We should decrease production of model S." The controller disagreed. He said that the problem was the model S assembly department trying to absorb a large overhead with a small production volume. "The model S units are making a contribution to overhead. Even though production doesn't cover all of the fixed costs, we'd be worse off with lower production."

**Figure 3.38** Accounting Data for Shelby

| | A | B | C | D | E | F | G | H | I |
|---|---|---|---|---|---|---|---|---|---|
| 1 | Shelby Shelving Data for Current Production Schedule | | | | | | | | |
| 2 | | | | | | | | | |
| 3 | Machine requirements (hours per unit) | | | | | Given monthly overhead cost data | | | |
| 4 | | Model S | Model LX | Available | | | Fixed | Variable S | Variable LX |
| 5 | Stamping | 0.3 | 0.3 | 800 | | Stamping | $125,000 | $80 | $90 |
| 6 | Forming | 0.25 | 0.5 | 800 | | Forming | $95,000 | $120 | $170 |
| 7 | | | | | | Model S Assembly | $80,000 | $165 | $0 |
| 8 | | Model S | Model LX | | | Model LX Assembly | $85,000 | $0 | $185 |
| 9 | Current monthly production | 400 | 1400 | | | | | | |
| 10 | | | | | | Standard costs of the shelves -- *based on the current production levels* | | | |
| 11 | Hours spent in departments | | | | | | Model S | Model LX | |
| 12 | | Model S | Model LX | Totals | | Direct materials | $1,000 | $1,200 | |
| 13 | Stamping | 120 | 420 | 540 | | Direct labor: | | | |
| 14 | Forming | 100 | 700 | 800 | | Stamping | $35 | $35 | |
| 15 | | | | | | Forming | $60 | $90 | |
| 16 | Percentages of time spent in departments | | | | | Assembly | $80 | $85 | |
| 17 | | Model S | Model LX | | | Total direct labor | $175 | $210 | |
| 18 | Stamping | 22.2% | 77.8% | | | Overhead allocation | | | |
| 19 | Forming | 12.5% | 87.5% | | | Stamping | $149 | $159 | |
| 20 | | | | | | Forming | $150 | $229 | |
| 21 | Unit selling price | $1,800 | $2,100 | | | Assembly | $365 | $246 | |
| 22 | | | | | | Total overhead | $664 | $635 | |
| 23 | Assembly capacity | 1900 | 1400 | | | Total cost | $1,839 | $2,045 | |

Your job is to develop an LP model of Shelby's problem, then run Solver, and finally make a recommendation to Shelby management, with a short verbal argument supporting the engineer or the controller.

### Notes on Accounting Data Calculations

The fixed overhead is distributed using activity-based costing principles. For example, at current production levels, the forming machine spends 100 hours on model S shelves and 700 hours on model LX shelves. The forming machine is used 800 hours of the month, of which 12.5% of the time is spent on model S shelves, and 87.5% is spent on model LX shelves.

The \$95,000 of fixed overhead in the forming department is distributed as \$11,875 (= 95,000 × 0.125) to model S shelves and \$83,125 (= 95,000 × 0.875) to model LX shelves. The fixed overhead per unit of output is allocated as \$29.69 (= 11,875/400) for model S and \$59.38 (= 83,125/1400) for model LX. In the calculation of the standard overhead cost, the fixed and variable costs are added together, so that the overhead cost for the forming department allocated to a model S shelf is \$149.69 (= 29.69 + 120, shown rounded up to \$150). Similarly, the overhead cost for the forming department allocated to a model LX shelf is \$229.38 (= 59.38 + 170, shown rounded down to \$229). ∎

After graduating from business school, George Clark went to work for a Big Six accounting firm in San Francisco. Because his hobby has always been wine making, when he had the opportunity a few years later, he purchased 5 acres plus an option to buy 35 additional acres of land in Sonoma Valley in Northern California. He plans eventually to grow grapes on that land and make wine with them. George knows that this is a big undertaking and that it will require more capital than he has at the present. However, he figures that, if he persists, he will be able to leave accounting and live full-time from his winery earnings by the time he is 40.

Because wine making is capital-intensive and growing commercial-quality grapes with a full yield of 5 tons per acre takes at least 8 years, George is planning to start small. This is necessitated by both his lack of capital and his inexperience in wine making on a large scale, although he has long made wine at home. His plan is first to plant the grapes on his land to get the vines started. Then he needs to set up a small trailer where he can live on weekends while he installs the irrigation system and does the required work to the vines, such as pruning and fertilizing. To help maintain a positive cash flow during the first few years, he also plans to buy grapes from other nearby growers so he can make his own label wine. He proposes to market it through a small tasting room that he will build on his land and keep open on weekends during the spring–summer season.

To begin, George is going to use $10,000 in savings to finance the initial purchase of grapes from which he will make his first batch of wine. He is also thinking about going to the Bank of Sonoma and asking for a loan. He knows that if he goes to the bank, the loan officer will ask for a business plan; so he is trying to pull together some numbers for himself first. This way he will have a rough notion of the profitability and cash flows associated with his ideas before he develops a formal plan with a pro forma income statement and balance sheet. He has decided to make the preliminary planning horizon two years and would like to estimate the profit over that period. His most immediate task is to decide

how much of the $10,000 should be allocated to purchasing grapes for the first year and how much to purchasing grapes for the second year. In addition, each year he must decide how much he should allocate to purchasing grapes to make his favorite Petite Syrah and how much to purchasing grapes to make the more popular Sauvignon Blanc that seems to have been capturing the attention of a wider market during the past few years in California.

In the first year, each bottle of Petite Sirah requires $0.80 worth of grapes and each bottle of Sauvignon Blanc uses $0.70 worth of grapes. For the second year, the costs of the grapes per bottle are $0.75 and $0.85, respectively.

George anticipates that his Petite Sirah will sell for $8.00 a bottle in the first year and for $8.25 in the second year, whereas his Sauvignon Blanc's price remains the same in both years at $7.00 a bottle.

Besides the decisions about the amounts of grapes purchased in the 2 years, George must make estimates of the sales levels for the two wines during the 2 years. The local wine-making association has told him that marketing is the key to success in any wine business; generally, demand is directly proportional to the amount of effort spent on marketing. Thus, because George cannot afford to do any market research about sales levels due to his lack of capital, he is pondering how much money he should spend to promote each wine each year. The wine-making association has given him a rule of thumb that relates estimated demand to the amount of money spent on advertising. For instance, they estimate that, for each dollar spent in the first year promoting the Petite Sirah, a demand for 5 bottles will be created; and for each dollar spent in the second year, a demand for 6 bottles will result. Similarly, for each dollar spent on advertising for the Sauvignon Blanc in the first year, up to 8 bottles can be sold; and for each dollar spent in the second year, up to 10 bottles can be sold.

The initial funds for the advertising will come from the $10,000 savings. Assume that the cash earned from wine sales in the first year is available in the second year.

A personal concern George has is that he maintain a proper balance of wine products so that he will be well positioned to expand his marketing

[16] This case was written by William D. Whisler, California State University, Hayward.

capabilities when he moves to the winery and makes it his full-time job. Thus, in his mind, it is important to ensure that the number of bottles of Petite Sirah sold each year falls in the range between 40% and 70% of the overall number of bottles sold.

## Questions

1. George needs help to decide how many grapes to buy, how much money to spend on advertising, how many bottles of wine to sell, and how much profit he can expect to earn over the 2-year period. Develop a spreadsheet LP model to help him.

2. Solve the linear programming model formulated in Question 1.

*The following questions should be attempted only after Questions 1 and 2 have been answered correctly.*

3. After showing the business plan to the Bank of Sonoma, George learns that the loan officer is concerned about the market prices used in estimating the profits; recently it has been forecasted that Chile and Australia will be flooding the market with high-quality, low-priced white wines over the next couple of years. In particular, the loan officer estimates that the price used for the Sauvignon Blanc in the second year is highly speculative and realistically might be only half the price George calculated. Thus, the bank is nervous about lending the money because of the big effect such a decrease in price might have on estimated profits. What do you think?

4. Another comment the loan officer of the Bank of Sonoma has after reviewing the business plan is: "I see that you do have an allowance in your calculations for the carryover of inventory of unsold wine from the first year to the second year, but you do not have any cost associated with this. All companies must charge something for holding inventory, so you should redo your plans to allow for this." If the holding charges are $0.10 per bottle per year, how much, if any, does George's plan change?

5. The president of the local grape growers' association mentions to George that there is likely to be a strike soon over the unionization of the grape workers (currently they are not represented by any union). This means that the costs of the grapes might go up by anywhere from 50% to 100%. How might this affect George's plan?

6. Before taking his business plan to the bank, George had it reviewed by a colleague at the accounting firm where he works. Although his friend was excited about the plan and its prospects, he was dismayed to learn that George had not used present value in determining his profit. "George, you are an accountant and must know that money has a time value; and although you are only doing a 2-year planning problem, it still is important to calculate the present value profit." George replies, "Yes, I know all about present value. For big investments over long time periods, it is important to consider. But in this case, for a small investment and only a 2-year time period, it really doesn't matter." Who is correct, George or his colleague? Why? Use an 8% discount factor in answering this question. Does the answer change if a 6% or 10% discount rate is used? Use a spreadsheet to determine the coefficients of the objective function for the different discount rates.

7. Suppose that the Bank of Sonoma is so excited about the prospects of George's wine-growing business that they offer to lend him an extra $10,000 at their best small business rate—28% plus a 10% compensating balance.[17] Should he accept the bank's offer? Why or why not?

8. Suppose that the rule of thumb George was given by the local wine-making association is incorrect. Assume that the number of bottles of Petite Sirah sold in the first and second years is at most 4 for each dollar spent on advertising. And likewise for the Sauvignon Blanc, assume that it can be at most only 5 in years 1 and 2.

9. How much could profits be increased if George's personal concerns (that Petite Sirah sales should account for between 40% and 70% of overall sales) are ignored? ∎

[17] The compensating balance requirement means that only $9,000 of the $10,000 loan is available to George; the remaining $1,000 remains with the bank.

# Linear Programming Models

© RAMIN TALAIE/Bloomberg News/Landov

## PRODUCTION, INVENTORY, AND DISTRIBUTION AT KELLOGG

The Kellogg Company is the largest cereal producer in the world and is a leading producer of convenience foods. Its worldwide sales in 1999 were nearly $7 billion. Kellogg's first product in 1906 was Corn Flakes, and it developed a variety of ready-to-eat cereals over the years, including Raisin Bran, Rice Krispies, Corn Pops, and others. Although the company continues to develop and market new cereals, it has recently gone into convenience foods, such as Pop-Tarts and Nutri-Grain cereal bars, and has also entered the health-food market. Kellogg produces hundreds of products and sells thousands of stock-keeping units (SKUs). Managing production, inventory, and distribution of these—that is, the daily operations—in a cost-effective manner is a challenge.

By the late 1980s, Kellogg realized that the increasing scale and complexity of its operations required optimization methods to coordinate its daily operations in a centralized manner. As described in Brown et al. (2001), a team of management scientists developed an optimization software system called KPS (Kellogg Planning System). This system was originally in-tended for operational (daily and weekly) decisions, but it expanded into a system for making tactical (longer-range) decisions about issues such as plant budgets, capacity expansion, and consolidation. By the turn of the century, KPS had been in use for about a decade. Operational decisions made by KPS reduced production, inventory, and distribution costs by approximately

$4.5 million per year. Better yet, the tactical side of KPS recently suggested a consolidation of production capacity that saved the company approximately $35 to $40 million annually.

Kellogg operates 5 plants in the United States and Canada, has 7 distribution centers (DCs) in such areas as Los Angeles and Chicago, and has about 15 co-packers, companies that contract to produce or pack some of Kellogg's products. Customer demands are seen at the DCs and the plants. In the cereal business alone, Kellogg has to coordinate the packaging, inventorying, and distributing of 600 SKUs at about 27 locations with a total of about 90 productions lines and 180 packaging lines. This requires a tremendous amount of day-to-day coordination to meet customer demand at a low cost. The KPS operational system that guides operational decisions is essentially a large linear programming model that takes as its inputs the forecasted customer demands for the various products and specifies what should be produced, held, and shipped on a daily basis. The resulting model is similar to the model of football production discussed in the previous chapter, except that it's *much* larger.

Specifically, for each week of its 30-week planning horizon, the model specifies (1) how much of each product to make on each production line at each facility; (2) how much of each SKU to pack on each packaging line at each facility; (3) how much inventory of each SKU to hold at each facility; and (4) how much of each SKU to ship from each location to other locations. In addition, the model has to take constraints into account. For example, the production within a given plant in a week cannot exceed the processing line capacity in that plant. Linear programming models such as Kellogg's tend to be very large—thousands of decision variables and hundreds or thousands of constraints—but the algorithms Kellogg uses are capable of optimizing such models very quickly. Kellogg runs its KPS model each Sunday morning and uses its recommendations in the ensuing week.

The KPS system illustrates a common occurrence when companies turn to management science for help. As stated earlier, the system was originally developed for making daily operational decisions. Soon, however, the company developed a tactical version of KPS for long-range planning on the order of 12 to 24 months. The tactical model is similar to the operational model except that time periods are now months, not days or weeks, and other considerations must be handled, such as limited product shelf lives. The point is, however, that when companies such as Kellogg become comfortable with management science methods in one part of their operations, they often look for other areas to apply similar methods. As with Kellogg, such methods can save the company millions of dollars. ∎

## 4.1 INTRODUCTION

In a recent survey of Fortune 500 firms, 85% of those responding said that they used linear programming. In this chapter, we discuss some of the LP models that are most often applied to real applications. In the chapter's examples, you will discover how to build optimization models to

- purchase television ads.
- schedule postal workers.
- create an aggregate labor and production plan at a shoe company.

- create a blending plan to transform crude oils into end products.
- plan production of interdependent products at a drug company.
- choose an investment strategy at a financial investment company.
- manage a pension fund.
- determine which of several hospitals use their inputs "efficiently."

The two basic goals of this chapter are to illustrate the wide range of real applications that can take advantage of LP and to increase your facility in modeling LP problems on a spreadsheet. We present a few principles that will help you model a wide variety of problems. The best way to learn, however, is to see many examples and work through numerous problems. In short, mastering the art of LP spreadsheet modeling takes hard work and practice, which you will find plenty of in this chapter.

Before continuing, remember that all of the models in this chapter are *linear* models as described in the previous chapter. This means that the target cell is ultimately (possibly through a series of formulas in intervening cells) a sum of products of constants and changing cells, where a "constant" is defined by the fact that it does not depend on changing cells. Similarly, each side of each constraint is either a constant or a sum of products of constants and changing cells. Also, each changing cell (except in a few cases where it's specified otherwise) is allowed to contain a continuous range of values, not just integer values. These properties allow us to check the Assume Linear Model option in Solver, which in turn allows Solver to use its very efficient simplex method to find the optimal solution.[1]

## 4.2 ADVERTISING MODELS

Many companies spend enormous amounts of money to advertise their products. They want to ensure that they are spending their money wisely. Typically, they want to reach large numbers of various groups of potential customers and keep their advertising costs as low as possible. The following example illustrates a simple model—and a reasonable extension of this model—for a company that purchases television ads.

EXAMPLE | **4.1 PURCHASING TELEVISION ADS**

The General Flakes Company sells a brand of low-fat breakfast cereal that appeals to people of all age groups and both genders. The company advertises this cereal in a variety of 30-second television ads, and these ads can be placed in a variety of television shows. The ads in different shows vary by cost—some 30-second slots are much more expensive than others—and by the types of viewers they are likely to reach. The company has segmented the potential viewers into six mutually exclusive categories: males age 18 to 35, males age 36 to 55, males over 55, females age 18 to 35, females age 36 to 55, and females over 55. A rating service can supply data on the numbers of viewers in each of these categories who will watch a 30-second ad on any particular television show. Each such viewer is called an *exposure*. The company has determined the required number of exposures it wants to obtain for each group. It wants to know how many ads to place on each of several television shows to obtain these required exposures at minimum cost. The data on costs per ad, numbers of exposures per ad, and minimal required exposures are listed in Table 4.1, where numbers of exposures are expressed in millions, and costs are in thousands of dollars. What should the company do?

[1] In the special cases where we impose integer constraints on some changing cells, we can still check the Assume Linear Model box. However, Solver uses another algorithm, not the simplex method, to optimize when there are integer-constrained changing cells. This is covered in more depth in Chapter 6.

Table 4.1  Data for Advertising Problem

| Viewer Group/ TV Show | "Desperate Housewives" | "Monday Night Football" | "Malcolm in the Middle" | "Sports Center" | "The Real World" (MTV) | Lifetime Evening Movie | CNN | "Law & Order" | Minimal Required Exposures |
|---|---|---|---|---|---|---|---|---|---|
| Men 18–35 | 5 | 6 | 5 | 0.5 | 0.7 | 0.1 | 0.1 | 3 | 60 |
| Men 36–55 | 3 | 5 | 2 | 0.5 | 0.2 | 0.1 | 0.2 | 5 | 60 |
| Men over 55 | 1 | 3 | 0 | 0.3 | 0 | 0 | 0.3 | 4 | 28 |
| Women 18–35 | 6 | 1 | 4 | 0.1 | 0.9 | 0.6 | 0.1 | 3 | 60 |
| Women 36–55 | 4 | 1 | 2 | 0.1 | 0.1 | 1.3 | 0.2 | 5 | 60 |
| Women over 55 | 2 | 1 | 0 | 0 | 0 | 0.4 | 0.3 | 4 | 28 |
| Cost per Ad | 140 | 100 | 80 | 9 | 13 | 15 | 8 | 140 | |

*This list is a small subset of shows from which a company could choose, but it is a good representation of the types of shows favored by various age groups and genders.*

**Objective**    To develop an LP spreadsheet model that relates the numbers of ads on various television shows to the exposures to various viewer groups, and to use Solver to find the minimum cost advertising strategy that meets minimum exposure constraints.

## WHERE DO THE NUMBERS COME FROM?

The data for this problem would probably be straightforward to obtain, as suggested here:

- The advertising costs per ad are the going rates for 30-second slots for the various types of shows.

- The exposures per ad on the various shows are typically supplied by the media planning departments of advertising agencies. (However, see the "Modeling Issues" section at the end of this example.)

- The required numbers of exposures are probably determined internally by the company. The company's marketing department knows which population groups are its best customers and probably has some sense of the numbers of exposures the company should obtain for a general level of advertising.

## Solution

This problem is straightforward to model. As indicated in Table 4.2, we need to decide on the number of ads to place on each television show. This determines the total advertising cost, which we want to minimize, and the total number of exposures to each viewer group. The only constraint, other than nonnegativity, is that there must be at least the required number of exposures for each group.

Table 4.2    Variables and Constraints for Advertising Model

| | |
|---|---|
| **Input variables** | Cost per ad, exposures per ad, minimal required exposures |
| **Decision variables (changing cells)** | Numbers of ads to place on various types of shows |
| **Objective (target cell)** | Total advertising cost |
| **Other calculated variables** | Total exposures to each viewer group |
| **Constraints** | Actual exposures must be greater than or equal to Required exposures |

### Comparison to Product Mix Model

Before continuing, note that this model is essentially the opposite of the product mix model in the previous chapter. With that model, we tried to make the values of the decision variables (numbers of frames to produce) as large as possible to make a large profit. The

*LP models tend to fall into "types," at least from a structural point of view, even though their actual contexts might be very different. The two types mentioned here are among the most common.*

constraints on resource availability restricted us from making these values as large as we would like. In contrast, we now want to make the values of the decision variables as *small* as possible to minimize cost. This time, the constraints on required exposures prevent us from making these values as *small* as we would like. These two prototype LP models— maximizing profit subject to "less than or equal to" constraints, and minimizing cost subject to "greater than or equal to" constraints—are certainly not the only types of LP models that exist, but they are very common.

## DEVELOPING THE SPREADSHEET MODEL

The spreadsheet model for the advertising problem appears in Figure 4.1.[2] (See the file **Advertising 1.xlsx**.) The model can be created by following these steps:

**Figure 4.1**  Optimal Solution for the Advertising Model

| | A | B | C | D | E | F | G | H | I |
|---|---|---|---|---|---|---|---|---|---|
| 1 | Advertising model | | | | | | | | |
| 2 | | | | Note: All monetary values are in $1000s, and all exposures to ads are in millions of exposures. | | | | | |
| 3 | Inputs | | | | | | | | |
| 4 | Exposures to various groups per ad | | | | | | | | |
| 5 | | Desperate Housewives | MNF | Malcolm in Middle | Sports Center | The Real World | Lifetime movie | CNN | Law & Order |
| 6 | Men 18-35 | 5 | 6 | 5 | 0.5 | 0.7 | 0.1 | 0.1 | 3 |
| 7 | Men 36-55 | 3 | 5 | 2 | 0.5 | 0.2 | 0.1 | 0.2 | 5 |
| 8 | Men >55 | 1 | 3 | 0 | 0.3 | 0 | 0 | 0.3 | 4 |
| 9 | Women 18-35 | 6 | 1 | 4 | 0.1 | 0.9 | 0.6 | 0.1 | 3 |
| 10 | Women 36-55 | 4 | 1 | 2 | 0.1 | 0.1 | 1.3 | 0.2 | 5 |
| 11 | Women >55 | 2 | 1 | 0 | 0 | 0 | 0.4 | 0.3 | 4 |
| 12 | Total viewers | 21 | 17 | 13 | 1.5 | 1.9 | 2.5 | 1.2 | 24 |
| 13 | | | | | | | | | |
| 14 | Cost per ad | 140 | 100 | 80 | 9 | 13 | 15 | 8 | 140 |
| 15 | Cost per million exposures | 6.667 | 5.882 | 6.154 | 6.000 | 6.842 | 6.000 | 6.667 | 5.833 |
| 16 | | | | | | | | | |
| 17 | Advertising plan | | | | | | | | |
| 18 | | Desperate Housewives | MNF | Malcolm in Middle | Sports Center | The Real World | Lifetime movie | CNN | Law & Order |
| 19 | Number ads purchased | 0.000 | 0.000 | 8.719 | 20.625 | 0.000 | 6.875 | 0.000 | 6.313 |
| 20 | | | | | | | | | |
| 21 | Constraints on numbers of exposures | | | | | Range names used: | | | |
| 22 | | Actual exposures | | Required exposures | | Actual_exposures | =Model!$B$23:$B$28 | | |
| 23 | Men 18-35 | 73.531 | >= | 60 | | Number_ads_purchased | =Model!$B$19:$I$19 | | |
| 24 | Men 36-55 | 60.000 | >= | 60 | | Required_exposures | =Model!$D$23:$D$28 | | |
| 25 | Men >55 | 31.438 | >= | 28 | | Total_cost | =Model!$B$31 | | |
| 26 | Women 18-35 | 60.000 | >= | 60 | | | | | |
| 27 | Women 36-55 | 60.000 | >= | 60 | | | | | |
| 28 | Women >55 | 28.000 | >= | 28 | | | | | |
| 29 | | | | | | | | | |
| 30 | Objective to minimize | | | | | | | | |
| 31 | Total cost | $1,870.000 | | | | | | | |

**1** **Input values and range names.**  Enter the inputs from Table 4.1 in the shaded ranges, and name the ranges as shown.

**Excel Tip:** *Range Name Shortcut*
*We've said it before, but we'll say it again. Whenever possible, use "nice" labels such as in cells A19 and B22. Then you can take advantage of these labels, along with the Create from Selection shortcut, to name as many desired ranges as possible.*

**2** **Ads purchased.**  Enter *any* values in the Number_ads_purchased range. These are the only changing cells for this model.

---

[2] From here on, to save space we typically show only the *optimal* solution. However, remember that when you develop a spreadsheet optimization model, you can enter *any* values in the changing cells initially. Solver will eventually find the optimal solution.

**③ Exposures obtained.** The numbers of ads purchased determine the numbers of exposures to the various viewer groups. To calculate these exposures, enter the formula

**=SUMPRODUCT(B6:I6,Number_ads_purchased)**

in cell B23 and copy it down to cell B28.

**④ Total cost.** The quantities of ads purchased also determine the total cost of advertising. Calculate this cost in cell B31 with the formula

**=SUMPRODUCT(B14:I14,Number_ads_purchased)**

## USING SOLVER

The main Solver dialog box appears in Figure 4.2. After filling it out as shown and checking the usual Assume Linear Model and Assume Non-Negative options, click on the Solve button to obtain the solution shown earlier in Figure 4.1.

**Figure 4.2**

Solver Dialog
Box for the
Advertising
Model

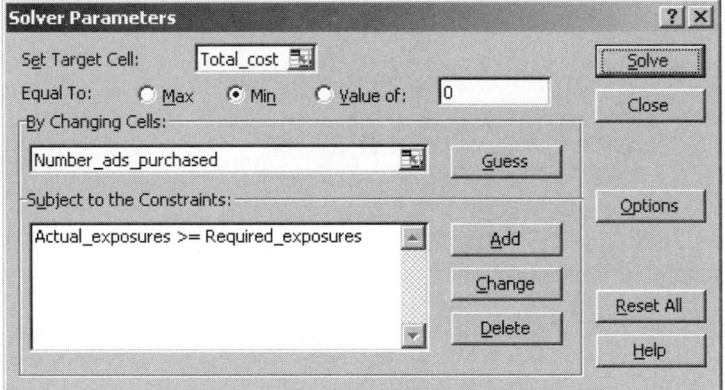

### Discussion of the Solution

The optimal solution is probably not the one you would have guessed. With a set of ads that cost very different amounts and reach very different mixes of viewers, it's difficult to guess the optimal strategy. For comparison, however, we calculated the total number of viewers from each type of ad in row 12 and divided the costs in row 14 by the numbers of viewers in row 12 to obtain the cost per million viewers in row 15. You might expect the ads with low cost per million viewers to be chosen most frequently. However, this is not necessarily the case. For example, "Monday Night Football" (MNF) has the second-lowest cost per million viewers, but the optimal solution includes no ads for this show.

### Sensitivity Analysis

Solver's sensitivity report, shown in Figure 4.3, is enlightening for this solution. Here is a sample of the information it provides.

■ The company is not currently purchasing any ads on "Desperate Housewives." The reduced cost for this show implies that the cost per ad would have to decrease by at least 10 ($10,000) before it would be optimal to purchase any ads on this show.

■ The company is currently purchasing about 20 ads on "Sports Center." The allowable increase and decrease for this show indicate how much the cost per ad would have to

**Figure 4.3**   Sensitivity Report for the Advertising Model

| | A | B | C | D | E | F | G | H |
|---|---|---|---|---|---|---|---|---|
| 6 | Adjustable Cells | | | | | | | |
| 7 | | | | Final | Reduced | Objective | Allowable | Allowable |
| 8 | | Cell | Name | Value | Cost | Coefficient | Increase | Decrease |
| 9 | | $B$19 | Number ads purchased Desperate Housewives | 0.000 | 10.000 | 140 | 1E+30 | 10 |
| 10 | | $C$19 | Number ads purchased MNF | 0.000 | 7.500 | 100 | 1E+30 | 7.5 |
| 11 | | $D$19 | Number ads purchased Malcolm in Middle | 8.719 | 0.000 | 80 | 1.744 | 29.091 |
| 12 | | $E$19 | Number ads purchased Sports Center | 20.625 | 0.000 | 9 | 0.762 | 0.451 |
| 13 | | $F$19 | Number ads purchased The Real World | 0.000 | 0.500 | 13 | 1E+30 | 0.5 |
| 14 | | $G$19 | Number ads purchased Lifetime movie | 6.875 | 0.000 | 15 | 2.286 | 1.103 |
| 15 | | $H$19 | Number ads purchased CNN | 0.000 | 2.250 | 8 | 1E+30 | 2.25 |
| 16 | | $I$19 | Number ads purchased Law & Order | 6.313 | 0.000 | 140 | 11.034 | 6.957 |
| 17 | | | | | | | | |
| 18 | Constraints | | | | | | | |
| 19 | | | | Final | Shadow | Constraint | Allowable | Allowable |
| 20 | | Cell | Name | Value | Price | R.H. Side | Increase | Decrease |
| 21 | | $B$23 | Men 18-35 Actual exposures | 73.531 | 0.000 | 60 | 13.531 | 1E+30 |
| 22 | | $B$24 | Men 36-55 Actual exposures | 60.000 | 15.000 | 60 | 44 | 5.116 |
| 23 | | $B$25 | Men >55 Actual exposures | 31.438 | 0.000 | 28 | 3.4375 | 1E+30 |
| 24 | | $B$26 | Women 18-35 Actual exposures | 60.000 | 10.000 | 60 | 11 | 14.931 |
| 25 | | $B$27 | Women 36-55 Actual exposures | 60.000 | 5.000 | 60 | 44.889 | 4.889 |
| 26 | | $B$28 | Women >55 Actual exposures | 28.000 | 2.500 | 28 | 6.286 | 7.586 |

change before the optimal number of ads on the show would change. For example, if the price per ad increased above 9 + 0.762 ($9762), the company might purchase fewer than 20 ads. How many fewer? We must rerun Solver to know.

- The constraint on exposures to men in the 36–55 age range has the largest shadow price, 15.000. If the company relaxed this constraint to require only 59 million exposures, it would save $15,000 in total advertising cost. On the other side, if the company required 61 million exposures to this group, rather than 60 million, its cost would increase by $15,000.

### A Dual-Objective Extension of the Model

*We refer to this as a dual-objective optimization model. Typically, the two objectives are pulling in different directions, as they are here.*

This advertising model can be extended in a very natural way. General Flakes really has two competing objectives: (1) obtain as many exposures as possible, and (2) keep the total advertising cost as low as possible. In the original model, we decided to minimize total cost and constrain the exposures to be at least as large as a required level. An alternative is to maximize the total number of excess exposures and put a budget constraint on total cost. Here, "excess exposures" are those above the minimal required level.

To implement this alternative, only minor modifications to the original model are necessary, as shown in Figure 4.4. (See the file **Advertising 2.xlsx**.) We can do this with the following steps:

**1 Excess exposures.** For each viewer group, calculate the number of excess exposures by entering the formula

=B23-D23

in cell F23 and copying it down. Then sum these in cell B35 with the SUM function. This cell becomes the new target cell to maximize.

**2 Budget constraint.** Calculate the total cost exactly as before, but now constrain it to be less than or equal to a given budget in cell D32.

**3 Solver dialog box.** Modify the Solver dialog box as shown in Figure 4.5.

**Figure 4.4**   Spreadsheet Model for Extension to the Advertising Problem

| | A | B | C | D | E | F | G | H | I |
|---|---|---|---|---|---|---|---|---|---|
| 1 | Two-objective advertising model | | | | | | | | |
| 2 | | | | Note: All monetary values are in $1000s, and all | | | | | |
| 3 | Inputs | | | exposures to ads are in millions of exposures. | | | | | |
| 4 | Exposures to various groups per ad | | | | | | | | |
| 5 | | Desperate Housewives | MNF | Malcolm in Middle | Sports Center | The Real World | Lifetime movie | CNN | Law & Order |
| 6 | Men 18-35 | 5 | 6 | 5 | 0.5 | 0.7 | 0.1 | 0.1 | 3 |
| 7 | Men 36-55 | 3 | 5 | 2 | 0.5 | 0.2 | 0.1 | 0.2 | 5 |
| 8 | Men >55 | 1 | 3 | 0 | 0.3 | 0 | 0 | 0.3 | 4 |
| 9 | Women 18-35 | 6 | 1 | 4 | 0.1 | 0.9 | 0.6 | 0.1 | 3 |
| 10 | Women 36-55 | 4 | 1 | 2 | 0.1 | 0.1 | 1.3 | 0.2 | 5 |
| 11 | Women >55 | 2 | 1 | 0 | 0 | 0 | 0.4 | 0.3 | 4 |
| 12 | Total viewers | 21 | 17 | 13 | 1.5 | 1.9 | 2.5 | 1.2 | 24 |
| 13 | | | | | | | | | |
| 14 | Cost per ad | 140 | 100 | 80 | 9 | 13 | 15 | 8 | 140 |
| 15 | Cost per million exposures | 6.667 | 5.882 | 6.154 | 6.000 | 6.842 | 6.000 | 6.667 | 5.833 |
| 16 | | | | | | | | | |
| 17 | Advertising plan | | | | | | | | |
| 18 | | Desperate Housewives | MNF | Malcolm in Middle | Sports Center | The Real World | Lifetime movie | CNN | Law & Order |
| 19 | Number ads purchased | 0.000 | 0.000 | 6.030 | 0.000 | 0.000 | 12.060 | 0.000 | 9.548 |
| 20 | | | | | | | | | |
| 21 | Constraints on numbers of exposures | | | | | | | Range names used: | |
| 22 | | Actual exposures | | Required exposures | | Excess exposures | | Actual_exposures | =Model!$B$23:$B$28 |
| 23 | Men 18-35 | 60.000 | >= | 60 | | 0.000 | | Budget | =Model!$D$32 |
| 24 | Men 36-55 | 61.005 | >= | 60 | | 1.005 | | Excess_exposures | =Model!$F$23:$F$28 |
| 25 | Men >55 | 38.191 | >= | 28 | | 10.191 | | Number_ads_purchased | =Model!$B$19:$I$19 |
| 26 | Women 18-35 | 60.000 | >= | 60 | | 0.000 | | Required_exposures | =Model!$D$23:$D$28 |
| 27 | Women 36-55 | 75.477 | >= | 60 | | 15.477 | | Total_cost | =Model!$B$32 |
| 28 | Women >55 | 43.015 | >= | 28 | | 15.015 | | Total_excess_exposures | =Model!$B$35 |
| 29 | | | | | | | | | |
| 30 | Budget constrain on total cost | | | | | | | | |
| 31 | | Total cost | | Budget | | | | | |
| 32 | | $2,000 | <= | $2,000 | | | | | |
| 33 | | | | | | | | | |
| 34 | Objective to maximize | | | | | | | | |
| 35 | Total excess exposures | 41.688 | | | | | | | |

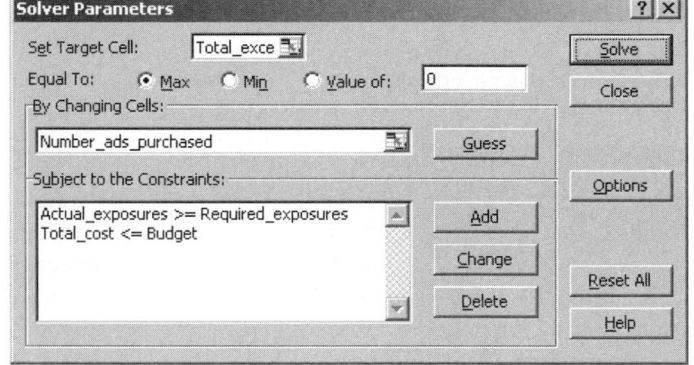

**Figure 4.5**

Modified Solver Dialog Box for Extension to the Advertising Problem

At this point, you are probably wondering where the budget of $2 million in Figure 4.4 comes from. This requires some explanation of the solution strategy in this extension of the original model. The basic assumption is that the company has two objectives: to maximize total excess exposures *and* minimize total cost. Unfortunately, it's impossible to do both because they are pulling in different directions. Whenever we have a multi objective problem such as this, we typically must use one of the objectives as the target cell and constrain the other(s). Here, we are asking how many excess exposures we can get for a given budget. There is no natural budget to use, and it makes perfect sense to ask questions such as these: How many exposures can we get for $1.9 million? How many for $2.0 million? How many for $2.1 million?

Fortunately, SolverTable is the precise tool we need to answer all of these questions in one step. We develop the model as in Figure 4.4, using *any* budget such as $2.0 million

*For two-objective models, we optimize one objective and put a constraint on the other. Then we can use SolverTable to vary the right-hand side of this constraint. The result is a trade-off curve.*

in cell D32, and use Solver in the usual way. Then we run a one-way SolverTable, allowing the budget to vary over some desired range and keeping track of selected output variables. Typical results appear in Figure 4.6, which are based on the SolverTable settings in Figure 4.7. For low budget levels, the problem is infeasible—there is no way with this budget to obtain the minimal required exposures. Above a certain budget level, the problem becomes feasible, and the optimal solutions are shown. As the budget increases, the company can clearly obtain larger numbers of excess exposures, but the optimal advertising strategy in columns B through I changes in a somewhat unpredictable way.

**Figure 4.6**   Sensitivity of Optimal Solution to the Advertising Budget

| | A | B | C | D | E | F | G | H | I | J |
|---|---|---|---|---|---|---|---|---|---|---|
| 37 | Sensitivity of optimal solution to budget | | | | | | | | | |
| 38 | | Desperate Housewives | MNF | Malcolm in Middle | Sports Center | The Real World | Lifetime movie | CNN | Law & Order | Total excess exposures |
| 39 | | $B$19 | $C$19 | $D$19 | $E$19 | $F$19 | $G$19 | $H$19 | $I$19 | $B$35 |
| 40 | 1800 | Not feasible | | | | | | | | |
| 41 | 1850 | Not feasible | | | | | | | | |
| 42 | 1900 | 0.000 | 0.000 | 8.208 | 0.000 | 0.000 | 1.887 | 0.000 | 8.679 | 23.717 |
| 43 | 1950 | 0.000 | 0.000 | 6.934 | 0.000 | 0.000 | 8.491 | 0.000 | 9.057 | 32.726 |
| 44 | 2000 | 0.000 | 0.000 | 6.030 | 0.000 | 0.000 | 12.060 | 0.000 | 9.548 | 41.688 |
| 45 | 2050 | 0.000 | 0.000 | 5.653 | 0.000 | 0.000 | 11.307 | 0.000 | 10.201 | 50.583 |
| 46 | 2100 | 0.000 | 0.000 | 5.276 | 0.000 | 0.000 | 10.553 | 0.000 | 10.854 | 59.477 |
| 47 | 2150 | 0.000 | 0.000 | 4.899 | 0.000 | 0.000 | 9.799 | 0.000 | 11.508 | 68.372 |
| 48 | 2200 | 0.000 | 0.000 | 4.523 | 0.000 | 0.000 | 9.045 | 0.000 | 12.161 | 77.266 |
| 49 | 2250 | 0.000 | 0.000 | 4.146 | 0.000 | 0.000 | 8.291 | 0.000 | 12.814 | 86.161 |
| 50 | 2300 | 0.000 | 0.000 | 3.769 | 0.000 | 0.000 | 7.538 | 0.000 | 13.467 | 95.055 |
| 51 | 2350 | 0.000 | 0.000 | 3.392 | 0.000 | 0.000 | 6.784 | 0.000 | 14.121 | 103.950 |
| 52 | 2400 | 0.000 | 0.000 | 3.015 | 0.000 | 0.000 | 6.030 | 0.000 | 14.774 | 112.844 |
| 53 | 2450 | 0.000 | 0.000 | 2.638 | 0.000 | 0.000 | 5.276 | 0.000 | 15.427 | 121.739 |
| 54 | 2500 | 0.000 | 0.000 | 2.261 | 0.000 | 0.000 | 4.523 | 0.000 | 16.080 | 130.633 |

**Figure 4.7**

SolverTable Settings for Sensitivity Analysis

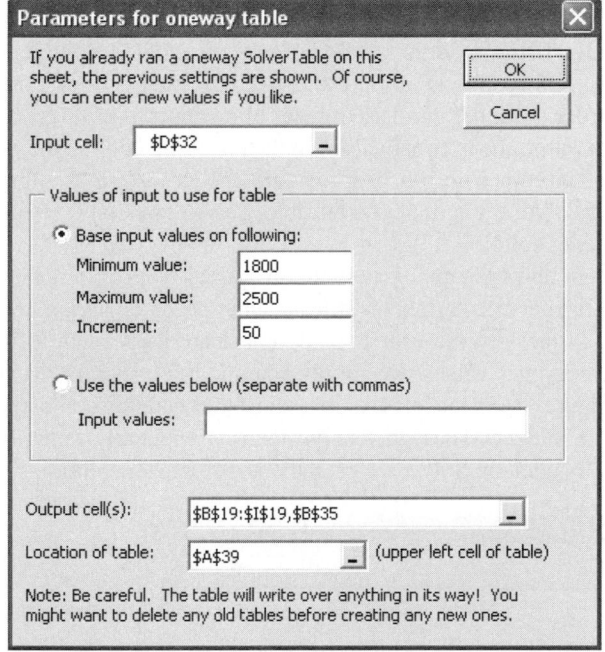

The results of this sensitivity analysis can be shown graphically in a **trade-off curve,** as in Figure 4.8. To create this, highlight the numbers in columns A and J of Figure 4.6 (from row 43 down) and insert a chart of the Scatter type with the "dots connected." This chart illustrates the rather obvious fact that when the company is allowed to spend more on advertising, it will get more total excess exposures.

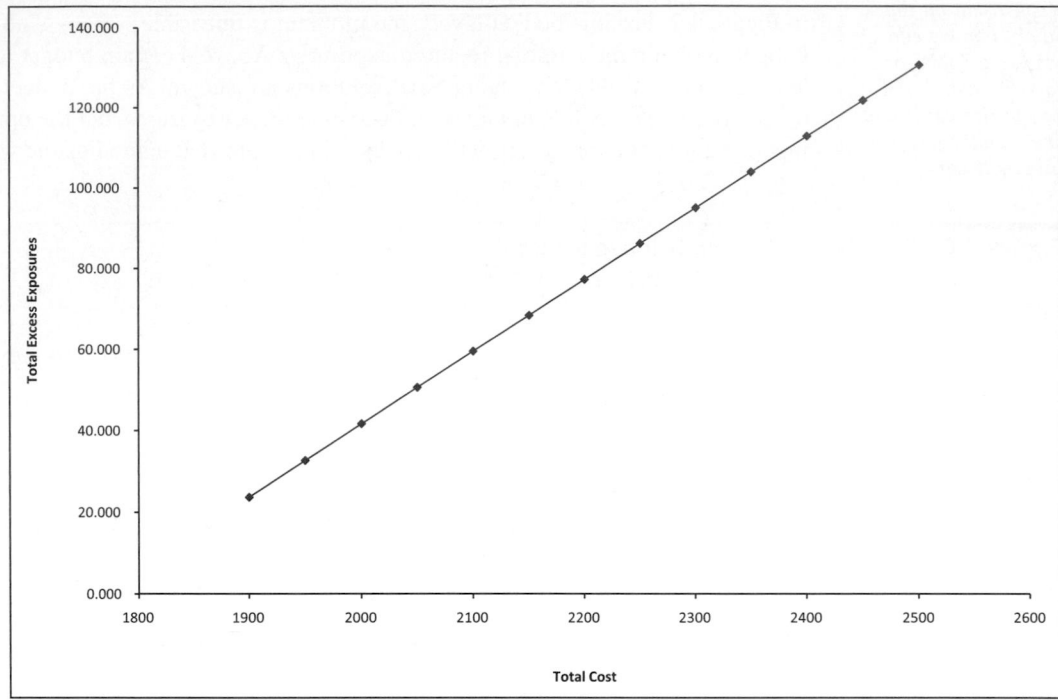

### Using Integer Constraints

The two advertising models to this point have allowed noninteger values in the changing cells. In reality, this is not allowed; the company cannot purchase, say, 6.313 ads on "Law & Order." It must purchase integer numbers of ads. Given this, your first instinct is probably to round the optimal values in the changing cells to the nearest integers to obtain the optimal integer solution. Unfortunately, this can have unpredictable results. First, the rounded solution might not be feasible. Second, even if it's feasible, it might not be the *optimal* integer solution.

*Use the int option in the Solver constraint dialog box to constrain changing cells to be integers.*

Although all of Chapter 6 is spent on special types of *integer programming models*—those with integer constraints on at least some of the changing cells—we can preview the topic here. In fact, from a user's standpoint, there isn't much to it. To force the changing cells to have integer values, we simply add another constraint in the Solver dialog box, as shown in Figure 4.9. In the left text, select the changing cell range. In the middle text box, select **int** (for integer). The right text box then automatically contains the word Integer. When we eventually click on Solve, we get the optimal integer solution shown in Figure 4.10.

**Figure 4.9**

Specifying an Integer Constraint

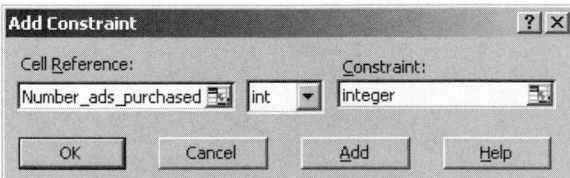

Consider the following about this integer solution:

■   The total cost in the target cell is now worse (larger) than before. This illustrates the general rule that when *any* additional constraints are imposed, including integer constraints, the objective can only get worse or remain the same; it can never get better.

# Figure 4.10 Optimal Integer Solution to the Advertising Problem

| | A | B | C | D | E | F | G | H | I |
|---|---|---|---|---|---|---|---|---|---|
| 1 | Advertising model | | | | | | | | |
| 2 | | | | Note: All monetary values are in $1000s, and all exposures to ads are in millions of exposures. | | | | | |
| 3 | Inputs | | | | | | | | |
| 4 | Exposures to various groups per ad | | | | | | | | |
| 5 | | Desperate Housewives | MNF | Malcolm in Middle | Sports Center | The Real World | Lifetime movie | CNN | Law & Order |
| 6 | Men 18-35 | 5 | 6 | 5 | 0.5 | 0.7 | 0.1 | 0.1 | 3 |
| 7 | Men 36-55 | 3 | 5 | 2 | 0.5 | 0.2 | 0.1 | 0.2 | 5 |
| 8 | Men >55 | 1 | 3 | 0 | 0.3 | 0 | 0 | 0.3 | 4 |
| 9 | Women 18-35 | 6 | 1 | 4 | 0.1 | 0.9 | 0.6 | 0.1 | 3 |
| 10 | Women 36-55 | 4 | 1 | 2 | 0.1 | 0.1 | 1.3 | 0.2 | 5 |
| 11 | Women >55 | 2 | 1 | 0 | 0 | 0 | 0.4 | 0.3 | 4 |
| 12 | Total viewers | 21 | 17 | 13 | 1.5 | 1.9 | 2.5 | 1.2 | 24 |
| 13 | | | | | | | | | |
| 14 | Cost per ad | 140 | 100 | 80 | 9 | 13 | 15 | 8 | 140 |
| 15 | Cost per million exposures | 6.667 | 5.882 | 6.154 | 6.000 | 6.842 | 6.000 | 6.667 | 5.833 |
| 16 | | | | | | | | | |
| 17 | Advertising plan | | | | | | | | |
| 18 | | Desperate Housewives | MNF | Malcolm in Middle | Sports Center | The Real World | Lifetime movie | CNN | Law & Order |
| 19 | Number ads purchased | 0 | 0 | 7 | 28 | 6 | 10 | 0 | 6 |
| 20 | | | | | | | | | |
| 21 | Constraints on numbers of exposures | | | | | | | | |
| 22 | | Actual exposures | | Required exposures | | | | | |
| 23 | Men 18-35 | 72.200 | >= | 60 | | | | | |
| 24 | Men 36-55 | 60.200 | >= | 60 | | | | | |
| 25 | Men >55 | 32.400 | >= | 28 | | | | | |
| 26 | Women 18-35 | 60.200 | >= | 60 | | | | | |
| 27 | Women 36-55 | 60.400 | >= | 60 | | | | | |
| 28 | Women >55 | 28.000 | >= | 28 | | | | | |
| 29 | | | | | | | | | |
| 30 | Objective to minimize | | | | | | | | |
| 31 | Total cost | $1,880.000 | | | | | | | |

- The optimal integer solution is *not* the rounded noninteger solution. In fact, it isn't even close. (Compare the before and after "The Real World" and "Sports Center" values, for example.) Rounding noninteger solutions sometimes works, and sometimes it doesn't. Using Solver with explicit integer constraints is always safer.

*Specifying integer constraints in the Solver dialog box is easy. Be aware, however, that Solver must typically do a lot more work to solve problems with integer constraints.*

- When there are integer constraints, Solver uses an algorithm—called *branch and bound*—that is significantly different from the simplex method. Integer-constrained models are typically *much* harder to solve than models without any integer constraints. Although this small model still solves in a fraction of a second, larger integer models can take *minutes* or even *hours* of solution time.

- If the model is linear except for the integer constraints, that is, it satisfies the proportionality and additivity assumptions of linear models, you should still check the Assume Linear Model box under Solver Options. ■

## MODELING ISSUES

The advertising model has one weakness, at least for realistic applications. Perhaps you've already spotted it: double-counting. Suppose a company runs 3 ads for the same product on a "Monday Night Football" telecast. Also, let's suppose that the rating service claims that an ad reaches, say, 6 million men age 18–35. How many *total* exposures do these 3 ads reach for this viewer group? Our model claims that it reaches 3(6) = 18 million. However, the "effective" number of exposures is probably much lower than 18, for the simple reason that the *same* men are watching all 3 ads.

*Unfortunately, many marketing models, including this one, are inherently nonlinear.*

This presents two difficulties for the modeler. First, it is probably difficult to estimate the effective number of exposures to any viewer group when an ad is run multiple times on the same show. Second, even if a company can obtain such estimates, it faces a nonlinear model, as discussed in Chapter 7. This is because the proportionality assumption of LP no longer holds. Specifically, each extra ad on a given show reaches a decreasing number of "new" exposures. (We revisit this model in Chapter 7.) ■

## PROBLEMS

*Solutions for problems whose numbers appear within a color box can be found in the Student Solutions Files. Order your copy today at the Winston/Albright product Web site, academic.cengage.com/decisionsciences/winston.*

### Skill-Building Problems

1. Suppose, as a matter of corporate policy, that General Flakes decides not to advertise on the Lifetime channel. Modify the original advertising model appropriately and find the new optimal solution. How much has it cost the company to make this policy decision?

**2.** In addition to the constraints already in the (original) advertising model, suppose General Flakes also wants to obtain at least 180 million exposures to men and at least 160 million exposures to women. Does the current optimal solution satisfy these constraints? If not, modify the model as necessary, and rerun Solver to find the new optimal solution.

3. Suppose, in addition to the shows already listed, General Flakes wants to open the possibility of purchasing ads on the "Good Morning America" show on ABC. Make up any reasonable input data you need to include this possibility in the (original) model, and find the optimal solution.

4. Suppose that General Flakes decides that it shouldn't place any more than 10 ads on any given show.

Modify the (original) advertising model appropriately to incorporate this constraint, and then reoptimize (with integer constraints on the numbers of ads). Finally, run SolverTable to see how sensitive the optimal solution is to the maximum number of ads per show allowed. You can decide on a reasonable range for the sensitivity analysis.

### Skill-Extending Problems

5. In the two-objective advertising model, we put a budget constraint on the total advertising cost and then maximized the total number of excess exposures. Do it the opposite way, reversing the roles of the two objectives. That is, model it so that you put a lower limit on the total number of excess exposures and minimize the total advertising cost. Then run a sensitivity analysis on this lower limit, and create a trade-off curve from the results of the sensitivity analysis.

6. Suppose we consider *three* objectives, not just two: the total advertising cost, the total number of excess exposures to men, and the total number of excess exposures to women. Continuing the approach suggested in the previous problem, how might you proceed? Take it as far as you can, including a sensitivity analysis and a trade-off curve.

## 4.3 WORKFORCE SCHEDULING MODELS

Many organizations must determine how to schedule employees to provide adequate service. The following example illustrates how LP can be used to schedule employees.

| EXAMPLE | 4.2 POSTAL EMPLOYEE SCHEDULING |

A post office requires different numbers of full-time employees on different days of the week. The number of full-time employees required each day is given in Table 4.3. Union rules state that each full-time employee must work five consecutive days and then receive two days off. For example, an employee who works Monday to Friday must be off on Saturday and Sunday. The post office wants to meet its daily requirements using only full-time employees. Its objective is to minimize the number of full-time employees that must be hired.

**Table 4.3    Employee Requirements for Post Office**

| Day of Week | Minimum Number of Employees Required |
|---|---|
| Monday | 17 |
| Tuesday | 13 |
| Wednesday | 15 |
| Thursday | 19 |
| Friday | 14 |
| Saturday | 16 |
| Sunday | 11 |

**Objective**    To develop an LP spreadsheet model that relates five-day shift schedules to daily numbers of employees available, and to use Solver on this model to find a schedule that uses the fewest number of employees and meets all daily workforce requirements.

## WHERE DO THE NUMBERS COME FROM?

*In real employee scheduling problems, much of the work involves forecasting and queueing analysis to obtain worker requirements. This must be done before any schedule optimizing can be accomplished.*

The only inputs we need for this problem are the minimum employee requirements in Table 4.3, but these are not necessarily easy to obtain. They would probably be obtained through a combination of two quantitative techniques discussed in later chapters: forecasting (Chapter 16) and queueing analysis (Chapter 14). The postal office would first use historical data to forecast customer and mail arrival patterns throughout a typical week. It would then use queueing analysis to translate these arrival patterns into worker requirements on a daily basis. Actually, we have kept the problem relatively simple by considering only *daily* requirements. In a realistic setting, the organization might forecast worker requirements on an hourly or even a 15-minute basis.

## Solution

The variables and constraints for this problem appear in Table 4.4. The trickiest part is identifying the appropriate decision variables. Many people think the decision variables should be the numbers of employees working on the various days of the week. Clearly, we need to know these values. However, it is not enough to specify, say, that 18 employees are working on Monday. The problem is that we don't know when these 18 employees start their five-day shifts. Without this knowledge, it is impossible to implement the five-consecutive-day, two-day-off requirement. (If you don't believe this, try developing your own model with the "wrong" decision variables. You will eventually reach a dead end.)

*The key to this model is choosing the correct changing cells.*

   The trick is to define the decision variables as the numbers of employees working each of the seven possible five-day shifts. For example, we need to know the number of employees who work Monday through Friday. By knowing the values of these decision variables, we can calculate the other output variables we need. For example, the number working on Thursday is the total of those who begin their five-day shifts on Sunday, Monday, Tuesday, Wednesday, or Thursday.

**Table 4.4    Variables and Constraints for Postal Scheduling Problem**

| | |
|---|---|
| **Input variables** | Minimum required number of workers each day |
| **Decision variables (changing cells)** | Number of employees working each of the five-day shifts (defined by their first day of work) |
| **Objective (target cell)** | Total number of employees on the payroll |
| **Other calculated variables** | Number of employees working each day |
| **Constraints** | Employees working must be greater than or equal to Employees required |

### Choosing the Changing Cells

The changing cells, which are really just the decision variables, should always be chosen so that their values determine all required outputs in the model. In other words, their values should tell the company exactly how to run its business. Sometimes the choice of changing cells is fairly obvious, but in many cases (as in this workforce scheduling model), the proper choice of changing cells takes some deeper thinking about the problem. An improper choice of changing cells typically leads to a dead end, where their values do not supply enough information to calculate required outputs or implement certain constraints.

Note that this is a "wrap-around" problem. We assume that the daily requirements in Table 4.3 and the worker schedules continue week after week. So, for example, if we find that eight employees are assigned to the Thursday–Monday shift, then these employees always wrap around from one week to the next on their five-day shift.

### DEVELOPING THE SPREADSHEET MODEL

The spreadsheet model for this problem is shown in Figure 4.11. (See the file **Worker Scheduling.xlsx**.) To form this spreadsheet, proceed as follows:

**Figure 4.11** Postal Scheduling Model with Optimal Solution

| | A | B | C | D | E | F | G | H | I | J | K |
|---|---|---|---|---|---|---|---|---|---|---|---|
| 1 | Worker scheduling model | | | | | | | | Range names used | | |
| 2 | | | | | | | | | Employees_available | =Model!$B$23:$H$23 | |
| 3 | Decision variables: number of employees starting their five-day shift on various days | | | | | | | | Employees_required | =Model!$B$25:$H$25 | |
| 4 | Mon | 6.33 | | | | | | | Employees_Starting | =Model!$B$4:$B$10 | |
| 5 | Tue | 3.33 | | | | | | | Total_employees | =Model!$B$28 | |
| 6 | Wed | 2.00 | | | | | | | | | |
| 7 | Thu | 7.33 | | | | | | | | | |
| 8 | Fri | 0.00 | | | | | | | | | |
| 9 | Sat | 3.33 | | | | | | | | | |
| 10 | Sun | 0.00 | | | | | | | | | |
| 11 | | | | | | | | | | | |
| 12 | Result of decisions: number of employees working on various days (along top) who started their shift on various days (along side) | | | | | | | | | | |
| 13 | | Mon | Tue | Wed | Thu | Fri | Sat | Sun | | | |
| 14 | Mon | 6.33 | 6.33 | 6.33 | 6.33 | 6.33 | | | | | |
| 15 | Tue | | 3.33 | 3.33 | 3.33 | 3.33 | 3.33 | | | | |
| 16 | Wed | | | 2.00 | 2.00 | 2.00 | 2.00 | 2.00 | | | |
| 17 | Thu | 7.33 | | | 7.33 | 7.33 | 7.33 | 7.33 | | | |
| 18 | Fri | 0.00 | 0.00 | | | 0.00 | 0.00 | 0.00 | | | |
| 19 | Sat | 3.33 | 3.33 | 3.33 | | | 3.33 | 3.33 | | | |
| 20 | Sun | 0.00 | 0.00 | 0.00 | 0.00 | | | 0.00 | | | |
| 21 | | | | | | | | | | | |
| 22 | Constraint on worker availabilities | | | | | | | | | | |
| 23 | Employees available | 17.00 | 13.00 | 15.00 | 19.00 | 19.00 | 16.00 | 12.67 | | | |
| 24 | | >= | >= | >= | >= | >= | >= | >= | | | |
| 25 | Employees required | 17 | 13 | 15 | 19 | 14 | 16 | 11 | | | |
| 26 | | | | | | | | | | | |
| 27 | Objective to maximize | | | | | | | | | | |
| 28 | Total employees | 22.33 | | | | | | | | | |

**1 Inputs and range names.** Enter the number of employees needed on each day of the week (from Table 4.3) in the shaded range, and create the range names shown.

**② Employees beginning each day.** Enter *any* trial values for the number of employees beginning work on each day of the week in the Employees_starting range. These beginning days determine the possible five-day shifts. For example, the employees in cell B4 work Monday through Friday.

**③ Employees on hand each day.** The key to this solution is to realize that the numbers in the Employees_starting range—the changing cells—do not represent the number of workers who will show up each day. As an example, the number in B4 who start on Monday work Monday through Friday. Therefore, enter the formula

**=$B$4**

in cell B14 and copy it across to cell F14. Proceed similarly for rows 15–20, being careful to take wrap arounds into account. For example, the workers starting on Thursday work Thursday through Sunday, plus Monday. Then calculate the total number of workers who show up on each day by entering the formula

**=SUM(B14:B20)**

in cell B23 and copying it across to cell H23.

**Excel Tip:** *Ctrl+Enter Shortcut*
*You will enter a "typical" formula into a cell and then copy it many times throughout this book. To do this efficiently, highlight the entire range, here B23:H23. Then enter the typical formula, here =SUM(B14:B20), and press Ctrl+Enter. This has the same effect as copying, but it is slightly quicker.*

**④ Total employees.** Calculate the total number of employees in cell B28 with the formula

**=SUM(Employees_starting)**

Note that there is no double counting in this sum. For example, the employees in cells B4 and B5 are *different* people.

At this point, you might want to try experimenting with the numbers in the changing cell range to see whether you can guess an optimal solution (without looking at Figure 4.11). It is not that easy! Each worker who starts on a given day works the next four days as well, so when you find a solution that meets the minimal requirements for the various days, you usually have a few more workers available on some days than are needed.

## USING SOLVER

Invoke Solver and fill out its main dialog box as shown in Figure 4.12. Also, check the Assume Linear Model and Assume Non-Negativity options in the Options dialog box.

**Figure 4.12**
Solver Dialog
Box for the
Postal Model

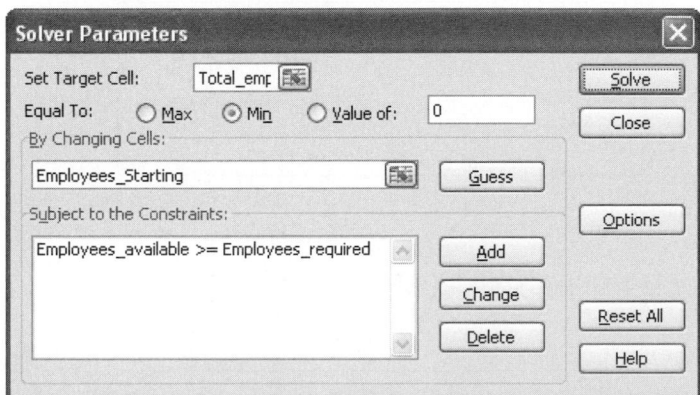

## Discussion of the Solution

The optimal solution shown in Figure 4.11 has one drawback: It requires the number of employees starting work on some days to be a fraction. Because part-time employees are not allowed, this solution is unrealistic. However, as we discussed in Example 4.1, adding integer constraints on the changing cells is simple. We need to fill in a new constraint as shown in Figure 4.13 and then reoptimize. This produces the optimal integer solution shown in Figure 4.14.

**Figure 4.13**

Solver Dialog Box with Integer Constraint

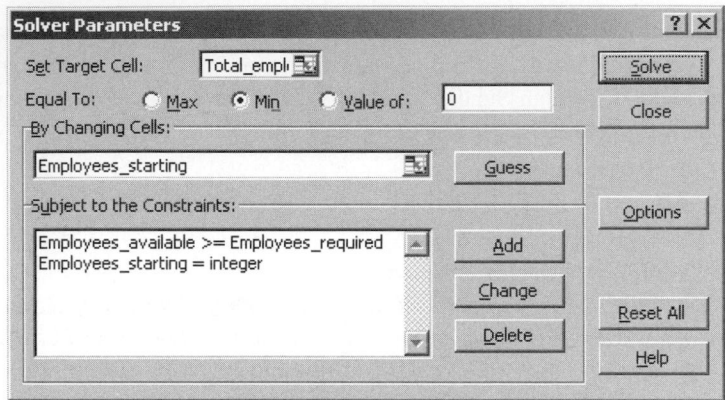

**Figure 4.14**   Optimal Integer Solution to Postal Scheduling Model

| | A | B | C | D | E | F | G | H | I | J | K |
|---|---|---|---|---|---|---|---|---|---|---|---|
| 1 | Worker scheduling model | | | | | | | | Range names used | | |
| 2 | | | | | | | | | Employees_available | =Model!$B$23:$H$23 | |
| 3 | Decision variables: number of employees starting their five-day shift on various days | | | | | | | | Employees_required | =Model!$B$25:$H$25 | |
| 4 | Mon | 6 | | | | | | | Employees_Starting | =Model!$B$4:$B$10 | |
| 5 | Tue | 6 | | | | | | | Total_employees | =Model!$B$28 | |
| 6 | Wed | 0 | | | | | | | | | |
| 7 | Thu | 7 | | | | | | | | | |
| 8 | Fri | 0 | | | | | | | | | |
| 9 | Sat | 4 | | | | | | | | | |
| 10 | Sun | 0 | | | | | | | | | |
| 11 | | | | | | | | | | | |
| 12 | Result of decisions: number of employees working on various days (along top) who started their shift on various days (along side) | | | | | | | | | | |
| 13 | | Mon | Tue | Wed | Thu | Fri | Sat | Sun | | | |
| 14 | Mon | 6 | 6 | 6 | 6 | 6 | | | | | |
| 15 | Tue | | 6 | 6 | 6 | 6 | 6 | | | | |
| 16 | Wed | | | 0 | 0 | 0 | 0 | 0 | | | |
| 17 | Thu | 7 | | | 7 | 7 | 7 | 7 | | | |
| 18 | Fri | 0 | 0 | | | 0 | 0 | 0 | | | |
| 19 | Sat | 4 | 4 | 4 | | | 4 | 4 | | | |
| 20 | Sun | 0 | 0 | 0 | 0 | | | 0 | | | |
| 21 | | | | | | | | | | | |
| 22 | Constraint on worker availabilities | | | | | | | | | | |
| 23 | Employees available | 17 | 16 | 16 | 19 | 19 | 17 | 11 | | | |
| 24 | | >= | >= | >= | >= | >= | >= | >= | | | |
| 25 | Employees required | 17 | 13 | 15 | 19 | 14 | 16 | 11 | | | |
| 26 | | | | | | | | | | | |
| 27 | Objective to maximize | | | | | | | | | | |
| 28 | Total employees | 23 | | | | | | | | | |

The changing cells in the optimal solution indicate the numbers of workers who start their five-day shifts on the various days. We can then look at the *columns* of the B14:H20 range to see which employees are working on any given day. This optimal solution is typical in scheduling problems. Due to a labor constraint—each employee must work five consecutive days and then have two days off—it is typically impossible to meet the minimum employee requirements exactly. To ensure that enough employees are available on busy days, companies often must have more than enough on hand on light days.

Another interesting aspect of this problem is that if you solve this problem on your own PC, you might get a *different* schedule that is still optimal—that is, it still uses a total of 23 employees and meets all constraints. This is a case of **multiple optimal solutions** and is not at all uncommon in LP problems. In fact, it is typically good news for a manager, who can then choose among the optimal solutions using other, possibly nonquantitative criteria.[3]

*Multiple optimal solutions have different values in the changing cells, but they all have the same objective value.*

### Technical Note: Solver Tolerance Setting

*Set Solver's Tolerance to 0 to ensure that you get the optimal integer solution. Be aware, however, that this can incur significant extra computing time for larger models.*

When there are integer constraints, you should be aware of Solver's **Tolerance** setting. As Solver searches for the best integer solution, it often finds a "good" solution fairly quickly, but it then has to spend a lot of time finding slightly better solutions (or confirming that the best solution so far is optimal). A *nonzero* tolerance setting allows it to quit early. The default tolerance setting is 0.05. This means that if Solver finds a feasible solution that is guaranteed to have an objective value no more than 5% from the optimal value, it will quit and report this "good" solution (which might even be the *optimal* solution). Therefore, if you keep this default tolerance value, your integer solutions will sometimes not be optimal, but they will be close. If you want to ensure that you get an optimal solution, you can change the Solver tolerance value to 0. (For the standard Solver that accompanies Excel, this setting is directly under the Solver Options. If you happen to use Premium Solver, you can find the setting by clicking on the Solver Options button and then on the Integer Options button.)

### Sensitivity Analysis

*To run some sensitivity analyses with SolverTable, you need to modify the original model slightly to incorporate the effect of the input being varied.*

The most obvious type of sensitivity analysis involves examining how the work schedule and the total number of employees change as the number of employees required each day changes. Suppose the number of employees needed on each day of the week increases by two, four, or six. How does this change the total number of employees needed? We can answer this by using SolverTable, but we first have to alter the model slightly, as shown in Figure 4.15. The problem is that we want to increase *each* of the daily minimal required values by the same amount. Therefore, move the original requirements up to row 12, enter a trial value for the extra number required per day in cell K12, enter the formula **=B12+$K$12** in cell B27, and then copy this formula across to cell H27. Now we can use the one-way SolverTable option, using cell K12 as the single input, letting it vary from 0 to 6 in increments of 2, and specifying the Total_employees cell as the single output cell.

The results appear in rows 34 through 37 of Figure 4.15. When the requirement increases by two each day, only two extra employees are necessary (scheduled appropriately). However, when the requirement increases by four each day, *more* than four extra employees are necessary. The same is true when the requirement increases by six each day. This might surprise you at first, but there is an intuitive explanation: Each extra worker works only five days of the week.

---

[3] It's usually difficult to tell whether there are multiple optimal solutions. We typically discover this by rerunning Solver from different starting solutions.

**Figure 4.15** Sensitivity Analysis for the Postal Model

| | A | B | C | D | E | F | G | H | I | J | K |
|---|---|---|---|---|---|---|---|---|---|---|---|
| 1 | Worker scheduling model | | | | | | | | | | |
| 2 | | | | | | | | | | | |
| 3 | Decision variables: number of employees starting their five-day shift on various days | | | | | | | | | | |
| 4 | Mon | 6 | | | | | | | | | |
| 5 | Tue | 6 | | | | | | | | | |
| 6 | Wed | 0 | | | | | | | | | |
| 7 | Thu | 7 | | | | | | | | | |
| 8 | Fri | 0 | | | | | | | | | |
| 9 | Sat | 4 | | | | | | | | | |
| 10 | Sun | 0 | | | | | | | | | |
| 11 | | | | | | | | | | | |
| 12 | Employees required (original values) | 17 | 13 | 15 | 19 | 14 | 16 | 11 | | Extra required each day | 0 |
| 13 | | | | | | | | | | | |
| 14 | Result of decisions: number of employees working on various days (along top) who started their shift on various days (along side) | | | | | | | | | | |
| 15 | | Mon | Tue | Wed | Thu | Fri | Sat | Sun | | | |
| 16 | Mon | 6 | 6 | 6 | 6 | 6 | | | | | |
| 17 | Tue | | 6 | 6 | 6 | 6 | 6 | | | | |
| 18 | Wed | | | 0 | 0 | 0 | 0 | 0 | | | |
| 19 | Thu | 7 | | | 7 | 7 | 7 | 7 | | | |
| 20 | Fri | 0 | 0 | | | 0 | 0 | 0 | | | |
| 21 | Sat | 4 | 4 | 4 | | | 4 | 4 | | | |
| 22 | Sun | 0 | 0 | 0 | 0 | | | 0 | | | |
| 23 | | | | | | | | | | | |
| 24 | Constraint on worker availabilities | | | | | | | | | | |
| 25 | Employees available | 17 | 16 | 16 | 19 | 19 | 17 | 11 | | | |
| 26 | | >= | >= | >= | >= | >= | >= | >= | | | |
| 27 | Employees required | 17 | 13 | 15 | 19 | 14 | 16 | 11 | | | |
| 28 | | | | | | | | | | | |
| 29 | Objective to maximize | | | | | | | | | | |
| 30 | Total employees | 23 | | | | | | | | | |
| 31 | | | | | | | | | | | |
| 32 | Sensitivity of total employees to extra required each day | | | | | | | | | | |
| 33 | | $B$30 | | | | | | | | | |
| 34 | 0 | 23 | | | | | | | | | |
| 35 | 2 | 25 | | | | | | | | | |
| 36 | 4 | 28 | | | | | | | | | |
| 37 | 6 | 31 | | | | | | | | | |

Note that we did not use Solver's sensitivity report here for two reasons. First, Solver does not offer a sensitivity report for models with integer constraints. Second, even if we delete the integer constraints, Solver's sensitivity report is not suited for questions about *multiple* input changes. It is used only for questions about one-at-a-time changes to inputs, such as a change to a *specific* day's worker requirement. In this sense, SolverTable is a more flexible tool. ∎

# MODELING ISSUES

1. The postal employee scheduling example is called a *static* scheduling model, because we assume that the post office faces the same situation each week. In reality, demands change over time, workers take vacations in the summer, and so on, so the post office does not face the same situation each week. *Dynamic* scheduling models are discussed in the next section.

*Heuristic solutions are often close to optimal, but they are never guaranteed to be optimal.*

2. If we wanted to develop a weekly scheduling model for a supermarket or a fast-food restaurant, the number of variables could be very large, and optimization software such as Solver could have difficulty finding an exact solution. In such cases, **heuristic** methods (essentially clever trial-and-error algorithms) can often be used to find a good solution to the problem. Love and Hoey (1990) indicate how this can be done for a particular staff-scheduling example.

3. Our model can easily be expanded to handle part-time employees, the use of overtime, and alternative objectives such as maximizing the number of weekend days off received by employees. You will have a chance to explore such extensions in the "Problems" section. ∎

## ADDITIONAL APPLICATIONS

### Scheduling Employees in Quebec's Liquor Stores

The SAQ is a public corporation of the Province of Quebec that is responsible for distributing and selling alcohol-based products through a large network of more than 400 stores and warehouses. Every week, the SAQ has to schedule more than 3000 employees. Until 2002, the scheduling of these employees was done manually, incurring an annual expense of about $1,300,000 (CAN). Gendron (2005) developed an integer programming model that is estimated to have saved the SAQ about $1,000,000 (CAN) annually. The model has to deal with complex union rules. For example, there is a rule that shifts of six hours or more can be split between two employees, but it must be coupled with another rule that forces employees to take one-hour unpaid lunch or dinner breaks. ∎

## PROBLEMS

### Skill-Building Problems

**7.** Modify the post office model so that employees are paid $10 per hour on weekdays and $15 per hour on weekends. Change the objective so that you now minimize the weekly payroll. (You can assume that each employee works eight hours per day.) Is the previous optimal solution still optimal?

**8.** How much influence can the worker requirements for one, two, or three days have on the weekly schedule in the post office example? Explore this in the following questions:
   **a.** Let Monday's requirements change from 17 to 25 in increments of 1. Use SolverTable to see how the total number of employees changes.
   **b.** Suppose the Monday and Tuesday requirements can each, independently of one another, increase from 1 to 8 in increments of 1. Use a two-way SolverTable to see how the total number of employees changes.
   **c.** Suppose the Monday, Tuesday, and Wednesday requirements each increase by the *same* amount, where this increase can be from 1 to 8 in increments of 1. Use a one-way SolverTable to investigate how the total number of employees changes.

**9.** In the post office example, suppose that each full-time employee works 8 hours per day. Thus, Monday's requirement of 17 workers can be viewed as a requirement of 8(17) = 136 hours. The post office can meet its daily labor requirements by using both full-time and part-time employees. During each week, a full-time employee works 8 hours a day for 5 consecutive days, and a part-time employee works 4 hours a day for 5 consecutive days. A full-time employee costs the

post office $15 per hour, whereas a part-time employee (with reduced fringe benefits) costs the post office only $10 per hour. Union requirements limit part-time labor to 25% of weekly labor requirements.
   **a.** Modify the model as necessary, and then use Solver to minimize the post office's weekly labor costs.
   **b.** Use SolverTable to determine how a change in the part-time labor limitation (currently 25%) influences the optimal solution.

### Skill-Extending Problems

**10.** In the post office example, suppose the employees want more flexibility in their schedules. They want to be allowed to work five consecutive days followed by two days off *or* to work three consecutive days followed by a day off, followed by two consecutive days followed by another day off. Modify the original model (with integer constraints) to allow this flexibility. Might this be a good deal for management as well as labor? Explain.

**11.** In the post office example, suppose that the post office can force employees to work one day of overtime each week on the day immediately following this five-day shift. For example, an employee whose regular shift is Monday to Friday can also be required to work on Saturday. Each employee is paid $100 a day for each of the first five days worked during a week and $124 for the overtime day (if any). Determine how the post office can minimize the cost of meeting its weekly work requirements.

**12.** Suppose the post office has 25 full-time employees and is not allowed to hire or fire any of them. Determine a schedule that maximizes the number of weekend days off received by these employees.

# 4.4 AGGREGATE PLANNING MODELS

In this section, the production planning model discussed in Example 3.3 of the previous chapter is extended to include a situation where the number of workers available influences the possible production levels. The workforce level is allowed to change each period through the hiring and firing of workers. Such models, where we determine workforce levels and production schedules for a multiperiod time horizon, are called **aggregate planning** models. There are many versions of aggregate planning models, depending on the detailed assumptions we make. The following example is a fairly simple version that you will have a chance to modify in the "Problems" section.

| EXAMPLE | 4.3 WORKER AND PRODUCTION PLANNING AT SURESTEP |
|---|---|

During the next 4 months, the SureStep Company must meet (on time) the following demands for pairs of shoes: 3000 in month 1; 5000 in month 2; 2000 in month 3; and 1000 in month 4. At the beginning of month 1, 500 pairs of shoes are on hand, and SureStep has 100 workers. A worker is paid $1500 per month. Each worker can work up to 160 hours a month before he or she receives overtime. A worker can work up to 20 hours of overtime per month and is paid $13 per hour for overtime labor. It takes 4 hours of labor and $15 of raw material to produce a pair of shoes. At the beginning of each month, workers can be hired or fired. Each hired worker costs $1600, and each fired worker costs $2000. At the end of each month, a holding cost of $3 per pair of shoes left in inventory is incurred. All of the production in a given month can be used to meet that month's demand. SureStep wants to use LP to determine its optimal production schedule and labor policy.

**Objective**   To develop an LP spreadsheet model that relates workforce and production decisions to monthly costs, and to use Solver to find the minimum cost solution that meets forecasted demands on time and stays within limits on overtime hours and production capacity.

## WHERE DO THE NUMBERS COME FROM?

This type of problem requires a number of inputs. Some, including initial inventory, holding costs, and demands, are similar to requirements for Example 3.3 in the previous chapter, so we won't discuss them again here. Others might be obtained as follows:

- The data on the current number of workers, the regular hours per worker per month, the regular hourly wage rates, and the overtime hourly rate, should be well known. The maximum number of overtime hours per worker per month is probably either the result of a policy decision by management or a clause in the workers' contracts.

- The costs for hiring and firing a worker are not trivial. The hiring cost includes training costs and the cost of decreased productivity due to the fact that a new worker must learn the job (the "learning curve" effect). The firing cost includes severance costs and costs due to loss of morale. Neither the hiring nor the firing cost would be simple to estimate accurately, but the human resources department should be able to estimate their values.

- The unit production cost is a combination of two inputs, the raw material cost per pair of shoes and the labor hours per pair of shoes. The raw material cost is the going rate from the supplier(s). The labor hours per pair of shoes represents the "production function"—the average labor required to produce a unit of the product. The operations managers should be able to supply this number.

## Solution

The variables and constraints for this aggregate planning model are listed in Table 4.5. As you can see, there are many variables to keep track of. In fact, the most difficult aspect of modeling this problem is knowing which variables the company gets to choose—the decision variables—and which variables are *determined* by these decisions. It should be clear that the company gets to choose the number of workers to hire and fire and the number of shoes to produce. Also, because management sets only an upper limit on overtime hours, it gets to decide how many overtime hours to use within this limit. But after it decides the values of these variables, everything else is determined. We show how these are determined through detailed cell formulas, but you should mentally go through the list of "Other output variables" in the table and deduce how they are determined by the decision variables. You should also recognize that the three constraints listed are the only ones required.

**Table 4.5** Variables and Constraints for the Aggregate Planning Problem

| | |
|---|---|
| **Input variables** | Initial inventory of shoes, initial number of workers, number and wage rate of regular hours, maximum number and wage rate of overtime hours, hiring and firing costs, data for unit production and holding costs, forecasted demands |
| **Decision variables (changing cells)** | Monthly values for number of workers hired and fired, number of shoes produced, and overtime hours used |
| **Objective (target cell)** | Total cost |
| **Other calculated variables** | Monthly values for workers on hand before and after hiring/firing, regular hours available, maximum overtime hours available, total production hours available, production capacity, inventory on hand after production, ending inventory, and various costs |
| **Constraints** | Overtime labor hours used must be less than or equal to Maximum overtime hours allowed<br>Production must be less than or equal to Capacity<br>Inventory on hand after production must be greater than or equal to Demand |

### DEVELOPING THE SPREADSHEET MODEL

The spreadsheet model appears in Figure 4.16. (See the file **Aggregate Planning 1.xlsx.**) It can be developed as follows:

**1** **Inputs and range names.** Enter the input data in the range B4:B14 and the Forecasted_demand range. Also, create the range names listed. (As usual, take advantage of the Create from Selection shortcut.)

**2** **Production, hiring, and firing plan.** Enter *any* trial values for the number of pairs of shoes produced each month, the overtime hours used each month, the workers hired each month, and the workers fired each month. These four ranges, in rows 18, 19, 23, and 30, comprise the changing cells.

**3** **Workers available each month.** In cell B17 enter the initial number of workers available with the formula

=B5

## Figure 4.16  SureStep Aggregate Planning Model

| | A | B | C | D | E | F | G | H | I |
|---|---|---|---|---|---|---|---|---|---|
| 1 | SureStep aggregate planning model | | | | | | | | |
| 2 | | | | | | | | | |
| 3 | Input data | | | | | | Range names used: | | |
| 4 | Initial inventory of shoes | 500 | | | | | Forecasted_demand | =Model!$B$36:$E$36 | |
| 5 | Initial number of workers | 100 | | | | | Inventory_after_production | =Model!$B$34:$E$34 | |
| 6 | Regular hours/worker/month | 160 | | | | | Maximum_overtime_labor_hours_available | =Model!$B$25:$E$25 | |
| 7 | Maximum overtime hours/worker/month | 20 | | | | | Overtime_labor_hours_used | =Model!$B$23:$E$23 | |
| 8 | Hiring cost/worker | $1,600 | | | | | Production_capacity | =Model!$B$32:$E$32 | |
| 9 | Firing cost/worker | $2,000 | | | | | Shoes_produced | =Model!$B$30:$E$30 | |
| 10 | Regular wages/worker/month | $1,500 | | | | | Total_cost | =Model!$F$46 | |
| 11 | Overtime wage rate/hour | $13 | | | | | Workers_fired | =Model!$B$19:$E$19 | |
| 12 | Labor hours/pair of shoes | 4 | | | | | Workers_hired | =Model!$B$18:$E$18 | |
| 13 | Raw material cost/pair of shoes | $15 | | | | | | | |
| 14 | Holding cost/pair of shoes in inventory/month | $3 | | | | | | | |
| 15 | | | | | | | | | |
| 16 | Worker plan | Month 1 | Month 2 | Month 3 | Month 4 | | | | |
| 17 | Workers from previous month | 100 | 94 | 93 | 50 | | | | |
| 18 | Workers hired | 0 | 0 | 0 | 0 | | | | |
| 19 | Workers fired | 6 | 1 | 43 | 0 | | | | |
| 20 | Workers available after hiring and firing | 94 | 93 | 50 | 50 | | Notes: We originally omitted integer constraints on workers | | |
| 21 | | | | | | | hired and fired, and Solver found a noninteger solution with | | |
| 22 | Regular-time hours available | 15040 | 14880 | 8000 | 8000 | | no problems. Then we added these integer constraints and | | |
| 23 | Overtime labor hours used | 0 | 80 | 0 | 0 | | Solver reported "no feasible solution." So we tried checking | | |
| 24 | | <= | <= | <= | <= | | the Automatic Scaling in Solver's Options dialog box, and | | |
| 25 | Maximum overtime labor hours available | 1880 | 1860 | 1000 | 1000 | | we got the solution shown here. | | |
| 26 | | | | | | | | | |
| 27 | Total hours for production | 15040 | 14960 | 8000 | 8000 | | | | |
| 28 | | | | | | | | | |
| 29 | Production plan | Month 1 | Month 2 | Month 3 | Month 4 | | | | |
| 30 | Shoes produced | 3760 | 3740 | 2000 | 1000 | | | | |
| 31 | | <= | <= | <= | <= | | | | |
| 32 | Production capacity | 3760 | 3740 | 2000 | 2000 | | | | |
| 33 | | | | | | | | | |
| 34 | Inventory after production | 4260 | 5000 | 2000 | 1000 | | | | |
| 35 | | >= | >= | >= | >= | | | | |
| 36 | Forecasted demand | 3000 | 5000 | 2000 | 1000 | | | | |
| 37 | Ending inventory | 1260 | 0 | 0 | 0 | | | | |
| 38 | | | | | | | | | |
| 39 | Monetary outputs | Month 1 | Month 2 | Month 3 | Month 4 | Totals | | | |
| 40 | Hiring cost | $0 | $0 | $0 | $0 | $0 | | | |
| 41 | Firing cost | $12,000 | $2,000 | $86,000 | $0 | $100,000 | | | |
| 42 | Regular-time wages | $141,000 | $139,500 | $75,000 | $75,000 | $430,500 | | | |
| 43 | Overtime wages | $0 | $1,040 | $0 | $0 | $1,040 | | | |
| 44 | Raw material cost | $56,400 | $56,100 | $30,000 | $15,000 | $157,500 | | | |
| 45 | Holding cost | $3,780 | $0 | $0 | $0 | $3,780 | | | |
| 46 | Totals | $213,180 | $198,640 | $191,000 | $90,000 | $692,820 | ◄──  Objective to minimize | | |

Because the number of workers available at the beginning of any other month (before hiring and firing) is equal to the number of workers from the previous month, enter the formula

**=B20**

in cell C17 and copy it to the range D17:E17. Then in cell B20, calculate the number of workers available in month 1 (after hiring and firing) with the formula

**=B17+B18-B19**

and copy this formula to the range C20:E20 for months 2 through 4.

❹ **Overtime capacity.** Because each available worker can work up to 20 hours of overtime in a month, enter the formula

**=$B$7*B20**

in cell B25 and copy it to the range C25:E25.

❺ **Production capacity.** Because each worker can work 160 regular-time hours per month, calculate the regular-time hours available in month 1 in cell B22 with the formula

**=$B$6*B20**

*In Example 3.3 from the previous chapter, production capacities were given inputs. Now they are based on the size of the workforce, which itself is under the decision maker's control.*

and copy it to the range C22:E22 for the other months. Then calculate the total hours available for production in cell B27 with the formula

**=SUM(B22:B23)**

and copy it to the range C27:E27 for the other months. Finally, because it takes 4 hours of labor to make a pair of shoes, calculate the production capacity in month 1 by entering the formula

**=B27/$B$12**

in cell B32 and copy it to the range C32:E32.

**6** **Inventory each month.** Calculate the inventory after production in month 1 (which is available to meet month 1 demand) by entering the formula

**=B4+B30**

in cell B34. For any other month, the inventory after production is the previous month's ending inventory plus that month's production, so enter the formula

**=B37+C30**

in cell C34 and copy it to the range D34:E34. Then calculate the month 1 ending inventory in cell B37 with the formula

**=B34-B36**

and copy it to the range C37:E37.

**7** **Monthly costs.** Calculate the various costs shown in rows 40 through 45 for month 1 by entering the formulas

**=$B$8*B18**
**=$B$9*B19**
**=$B$10*B20**
**=$B$11*B23**
**=$B$13*B30**
**=$B$14*B37**

in cells B40 through B45. Then copy the range B40:B45 to the range C40:E45 to calculate these costs for the other months.

**8** **Totals.** In row 46 and column F, use the SUM function to calculate cost totals, with the value in F46 being the overall total cost.

**Excel Tip:** *Calculating Row and Column Sums Quickly*
*A common operation in spreadsheet models is to calculate row and column sums for a rectangular range, as we did for costs in step 8. You can do this quickly by highlighting the row and column where the sums will go (remember to press the Ctrl key to highlight non-adjacent ranges) and clicking on the summation (Σ) button. (You can find this on the Home ribbon and on the Formula ribbon.) This enters all the sums automatically and even calculates the "grand sum" in the corner (cell F46 in the example) if you highlight this cell.*

 **USING SOLVER**

The Solver dialog box should be filled in as shown in Figure 4.17. Note that the changing cells include four separate named ranges. To enter these in the dialog box, drag the four ranges while keeping your finger on the Ctrl key. (Alternatively, you can drag a range, type a comma, drag a second range, type another comma, and so on.) As usual, you should also check the Assume Linear Model and Assume Non-Negative options before optimizing.

**Figure 4.17**

Solver Dialog Box
for the SureStep
Model

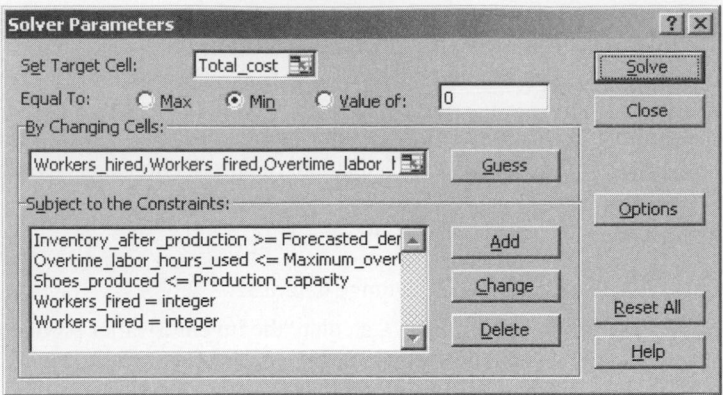

Note that we entered integer constraints on the numbers hired and fired. We could also constrain the numbers of shoes produced to be integers. However, integer constraints typically require longer solution times. Therefore, it is often best to omit such constraints, especially when the optimal values are fairly large, such as the production quantities in this model. If the solution then has noninteger values, we can usually round them to integers for a solution that is at least close to the optimal integer solution.

### Discussion of the Solution

The optimal solution was given earlier in Figure 4.16. Observe that SureStep should never hire any workers, and it should fire 6 workers in month 1, 1 worker in month 2, and 43 workers in month 3. Concerning overtime, 80 hours are used, but only in month 2. The company produces more than 3700 pairs of shoes during each of the first 2 months, 2000 pairs in month 3, and 1000 pairs in month 4. A total cost of $692,820 is incurred. The model recommends overtime hours only when regular-time production capacity is exhausted because overtime labor is more expensive.

*Because integer constraints make a model harder to solve, use them only when they are really needed.*

Again, we probably shouldn't force the number of pairs of shoes produced each month to be an integer. It makes little difference whether the company produces 3760 or 3761 pairs of shoes during a month, and forcing each month's shoe production to be an integer can greatly increase the time Solver needs to find an optimal solution. On the other hand, it is somewhat more important to ensure that the numbers of workers hired and fired each month are integers, given the small numbers of workers involved.

Finally, if we want to ensure that Solver finds the optimal solution in a problem where some or all of the changing cells must be integers, it is a good idea to go into Options (in the Solver dialog box) and set the tolerance to 0. Otherwise, Solver might stop when it finds a solution that is *close* to optimal.

### Sensitivity Analysis

There are many sensitivity analyses we could perform on this final SureStep model. One is illustrated with SolverTable, where we see how the overtime hours used and the total cost varies with the overtime wage rate.[4] The results appear in Figure 4.18. As we can see, when the wage rate is really low, considerably more overtime hours are used, whereas when the wage rate is sufficiently large, we use no overtime hours. It is not surprising that the company uses much more overtime when the overtime rate is $7 or $9 per hour. The *regular-time* wage rate is $9.375 per hour ($=1500/160$). Of course, it is not likely that the company would pay *less* per hour for overtime than for regular-time!

---

[4] As mentioned in Example 4.2, Solver's sensitivity report isn't even available here because of the integer constraints.

Figure 4.18

Sensitivity to
Overtime Wage
Rate

| | A | B | C | D | E | F |
|---|---|---|---|---|---|---|
| 48 | Sensitivity of overtime hours used and total cost to overtime wage rate | | | | | |
| 49 | | $B$23 | $C$23 | $D$23 | $E$23 | $F$46 |
| 50 | 7 | 1620 | 1660 | 0 | 0 | $684,755 |
| 51 | 9 | 80 | 1760 | 0 | 0 | $691,180 |
| 52 | 11 | 0 | 80 | 0 | 0 | $692,660 |
| 53 | 13 | 0 | 80 | 0 | 0 | $692,820 |
| 54 | 15 | 0 | 80 | 0 | 0 | $692,980 |
| 55 | 17 | 0 | 80 | 0 | 0 | $693,140 |
| 56 | 19 | 0 | 0 | 0 | 0 | $693,220 |
| 57 | 21 | 0 | 0 | 0 | 0 | $693,220 |

## The Rolling Planning Horizon Approach

In reality, an aggregate planning model is usually implemented via a rolling planning horizon. To illustrate, assume that SureStep works with a 4-month planning horizon. To implement the SureStep model in the rolling planning horizon context, we can view the "demands" as forecasts and solve a 4-month model with these forecasts. However, we implement only the month 1 production and work scheduling recommendation. Thus (assuming that the numbers of workers hired and fired in a month must be integers and that shortages are not allowed) SureStep should hire no workers, fire 6 workers, and produce 3760 pairs of shoes with regular-time labor in month 1. Next, we observe month 1's actual demand. Suppose it is 2950. Then SureStep begins month 2 with 1310 (= 4260 − 2950) pairs of shoes and 94 workers. We would now enter 1310 in cell B4 and 94 in cell B5 (refer to Figure 4.16). Then we would replace the demands in the Demand range with the updated forecasts for the *next* 4 months. Finally, we would rerun Solver and use the production levels and hiring and firing recommendations in column B as the production level and workforce policy for month 2.

## Model with Backlogging Allowed

*The term* backlogging *means that the customer's demand will be met at a later date. The term* backordering *means the same thing.*

In many situations, backlogging of demand is allowed—that is, customer demand can be met later than it occurs. To include the option of backlogging demand in the SureStep model, assume that at the end of each month a cost of $20 is incurred for each unit of demand that remains unsatisfied at the end of the month. This is easily modeled by allowing a month's ending inventory to be negative. For example, if month 1's ending inventory is –10, a shortage cost of $200 (and no holding cost) is incurred. To ensure that SureStep produces any shoes at all, we constrain month 4's ending inventory to be nonnegative. This implies that all demand is *eventually* satisfied by the end of the 4-month planning horizon. We now need to modify the monthly cost computations to incorporate costs due to shortages.

There are actually several modeling approaches to this backlogging problem. The most natural approach is shown in Figure 4.19. (See the file **Aggregate Planning 2.xlsx**.) To begin, we enter the per-unit monthly shortage cost in cell B15. (We inserted a new row for this cost input.) Note in row 38 how the ending inventory in months 1 to 3 can be positive (leftovers) or negative (shortages). We can account correctly for the resulting costs with IF functions in rows 46 and 47. For holding costs, enter the formula

**=IF(B38>0,$B$14*B38,0)**

in cell B46 and copy it across. For shortage costs, enter the formula

**=IF(B38<0,–$B$15*B38,0)**

in cell B47 and copy it across. (The minus sign makes this a *positive* cost.)

## Figure 4.19  Nonlinear SureStep Model with Backlogging Using IF Functions

| | A | B | C | D | E | F | G | H | I |
|---|---|---|---|---|---|---|---|---|---|
| 1 | SureStep aggregate planning model with backlogging: a nonsmooth model Solver might not handle correctly | | | | | | | | |
| 2 | | | | | | | | | |
| 3 | Input data | | | | | | Range names used: | | |
| 4 | Initial inventory of shoes | 500 | | | | | Forecasted_demand_4 | =Model!$E$37 | |
| 5 | Initial number of workers | 100 | | | | | Inventory_after_production_4 | =Model!$E$35 | |
| 6 | Regular hours/worker/month | 160 | | | | | Maximum_overtime_labor_hours_available | =Model!$B$26:$E$26 | |
| 7 | Maximum overtime hours/worker/month | 20 | | | | | Overtime_labor_hours_used | =Model!$B$24:$E$24 | |
| 8 | Hiring cost/worker | $1,600 | | | | | Production_capacity | =Model!$B$33:$E$33 | |
| 9 | Firing cost/worker | $2,000 | | | | | Shoes_produced | =Model!$B$31:$E$31 | |
| 10 | Regular wages/worker/month | $1,500 | | | | | Total_cost | =Model!$F$48 | |
| 11 | Overtime wage rate/hour | $13 | | | | | Workers_fired | =Model!$B$20:$E$20 | |
| 12 | Labor hours/pair of shoes | 4 | | | | | Workers_hired | =Model!$B$19:$E$19 | |
| 13 | Raw material cost/pair of shoes | $15 | | | | | | | |
| 14 | Holding cost/pair of shoes in inventory/month | $3 | | | | | | | |
| 15 | Shortage cost/pair of shoes/month | $20 | | | | | | | |
| 16 | | | | | | | | | |
| 17 | Worker plan | Month 1 | Month 2 | Month 3 | Month 4 | | | | |
| 18 | Workers from previous month | 100 | 94 | 93 | 38 | | | | |
| 19 | Workers hired | 0 | 0 | 0 | 0 | | | | |
| 20 | Workers fired | 6 | 1 | 55 | 0 | | | | |
| 21 | Workers available after hiring and firing | 94 | 93 | 38 | 38 | | | | |
| 22 | | | | | | | | | |
| 23 | Regular-time hours available | 15040 | 14880 | 6080 | 6080 | | | | |
| 24 | Overtime labor hours used | 0 | 0 | 0 | 0 | | | | |
| 25 | | <= | <= | <= | <= | | | | |
| 26 | Maximum overtime labor hours available | 1880 | 1860 | 760 | 760 | | | | |
| 27 | | | | | | | | | |
| 28 | Total hours for production | 15040 | 14880 | 6080 | 6080 | | | | |
| 29 | | | | | | | | | |
| 30 | Production plan | Month 1 | Month 2 | Month 3 | Month 4 | | | | |
| 31 | Shoes produced | 3760 | 3720 | 1520 | 1500 | | | | |
| 32 | | <= | <= | <= | <= | | | | |
| 33 | Production capacity | 3760 | 3720 | 1520 | 1520 | | | | |
| 34 | | | | | | | | | |
| 35 | Inventory after production | 4260 | 4980 | 1500 | 1000 | | | | |
| 36 | | | | | >= | | | | |
| 37 | Forecasted demand | 3000 | 5000 | 2000 | 1000 | | | | |
| 38 | Ending inventory | 1260 | -20 | -500 | 0 | | | | |
| 39 | | | | | | | | | |
| 40 | Monetary outputs | Month 1 | Month 2 | Month 3 | Month 4 | Totals | | | |
| 41 | Hiring cost | $0 | $0 | $0 | $0 | $0 | | | |
| 42 | Firing cost | $12,000 | $2,000 | $110,000 | $0 | $124,000 | | | |
| 43 | Regular-time wages | $141,000 | $139,500 | $57,000 | $57,000 | $394,500 | | | |
| 44 | Overtime wages | $0 | $0 | $0 | $0 | $0 | | | |
| 45 | Raw material cost | $56,400 | $55,800 | $22,800 | $22,500 | $157,500 | | | |
| 46 | Holding cost | $3,780 | $0 | $0 | $0 | $3,780 | | | |
| 47 | Shortage cost | $0 | $400 | $10,000 | $0 | $10,400 | | | |
| 48 | Totals | $213,180 | $197,700 | $199,800 | $79,500 | $690,180 | ← Objective to minimize | | |

Note that we use IF functions in rows 46 and 47 to capture the holding and shortage costs. These IF functions make the model nonlinear (and "nonsmooth"), and Solver can't handle these functions in a predictable manner. We just got lucky here! Try changing the unit shortage cost in cell B15 to $40 and rerun Solver. Then you won't be so lucky -- Solver will converge to a solution that is pretty far from optimal.

*IF functions involving changing cells make a model nonlinear.*

Although these formulas accurately compute holding and shortage costs, the IF functions make the target cell a *nonlinear* function of the changing cells, and we must use Solver's GRG (generalized reduced gradient) nonlinear algorithm, as indicated in Figure 4.20, where the Assume Linear Model box is *not* checked.[5] (How do we know the model is nonlinear? Although there is a mathematical reason, it is easier to try running Solver with the Assume Linear Model box checked. Solver will then *inform* you that the model is not linear.)

We ran Solver with this setup from a variety of initial solutions in the changing cells, and it always found the solution shown previously in Figure 4.19. It turns out that this is indeed the optimal solution, but we were lucky. When certain functions, including IF, MIN, MAX, and ABS, are used to relate the target cell to the changing cells, the resulting model becomes not only nonlinear but also *nonsmooth*. Essentially, nonsmooth functions have sharp edges or discontinuities. Solver's GRG nonlinear algorithm can handle *smooth* nonlinearities, as we see in Chapter 7, but it has trouble with nonsmooth functions. Sometimes it gets lucky, as it did here, and other times it finds a nonoptimal solution that is not even close to the optimal solution. For example, we changed the unit shortage cost from $20 to $40 and reran Solver. Starting from a solution where all changing cells contain 0, Solver stopped at a solution with total cost $725,360, even though the optimal solution has total cost $692,820. In other words, we weren't so lucky on this problem.

[5] GRG is a technical term for the mathematical algorithm used.

**Figure 4.20**

Setup for GRG
Nonlinear
Algorithm: Assume
Linear Model Box
Not Checked

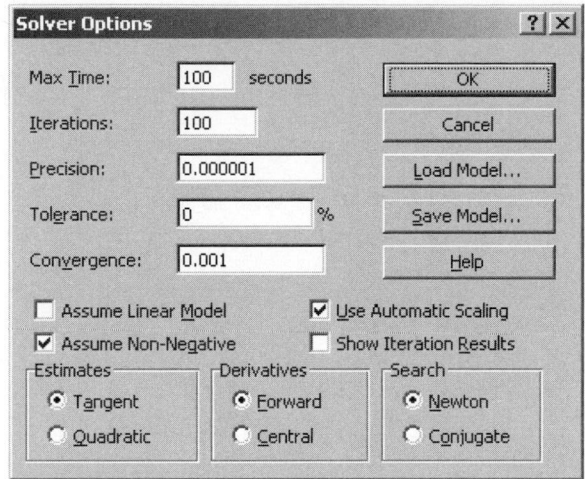

### Nonsmooth Functions and Solver

Excel's Solver, as well as most other commercial optimization software packages, has trouble with nonlinear functions that are not smooth. These nonsmooth functions typically have sharp edges or discontinuities that make them difficult to handle in optimization models, and (in Excel) they are typically implemented with functions such as IF, MAX, MIN, ABS, and a few others. There is nothing *wrong* with using such functions to implement complex logic in Excel optimization models. The only problem is that Solver cannot handle models with these functions predictably. This is not really the fault of Solver. Such problems are inherently difficult.

The moral is that you should avoid these nonsmooth functions in optimization models if at all possible. If you *do* use them, as we have done here, then you should run Solver several times, starting from different initial solutions. There is still absolutely no guarantee that you will get the optimal solution, but you will get more evidence of how Solver is progressing.

Sometimes alternatives to using IF, MIN, MAX, and ABS functions make a model linear. Unfortunately, these alternatives are often far from intuitive, as illustrated next. Alternatively, nonsmooth functions can be handled with a totally different kind of algorithm, called a **genetic algorithm,** and Frontline's[6] Premium Solver includes an Evolutionary Solver that implements a genetic algorithm. Genetic algorithms are discussed in Chapter 8.

### Linearizing the Backlogging Model

Although this nonlinear model with IF functions is "natural," the fact that it is not guaranteed to find the optimal solution is disturbing. Fortunately, we can handle shortages and maintain a *linear* formulation. The method is illustrated in Figure 4.21. (See the file **Aggregate Planning 3.xlsx**.) To develop this modified spreadsheet model, starting from the original model in the **Aggregate Planning 1.xlsx** file, follow these steps:

**1** **Enter shortage cost.** Insert a new row below row 14 and enter the shortage cost per pair of shoes per month in cell B15.

**2** **Rows for amounts held and short.** Insert 5 new rows (which will now be rows 38 through 42) between the Demand and Ending inventory rows. The range B39:E40 will be changing cells. The Leftover range in row 39 contains the amounts left in inventory (if any), whereas the Shortage range in row 40 contains the shortages (if any). Enter *any* values in these ranges.

---

[6] The educational version of Premium Solver is included with this book.

# Figure 4.21  Linear Formulation of SureStep Model with Backlogging

| | A | B | C | D | E | F | G | H | I | J | K |
|---|---|---|---|---|---|---|---|---|---|---|---|
| 1 | SureStep aggregate planning model with backlogging: a nonsmooth model Solver might not handle correctly | | | | | | | | | | |
| 2 | | | | | | | | | | | |
| 3 | Input data | | | | | | Range names used: | | | | |
| 4 | Initial inventory of shoes | 500 | | | | | Ending_inventory | =Model!$B$43:$E$43 | | | |
| 5 | Initial number of workers | 100 | | | | | Forecasted_demand_4 | =Model!$E$37 | | | |
| 6 | Regular hours/worker/month | 160 | | | | | Inventory_after_production_4 | =Model!$E$35 | | | |
| 7 | Maximum overtime hours/worker/month | 20 | | | | | Maximum_overtime_labor_hours_available | =Model!$B$26:$E$26 | | | |
| 8 | Hiring cost/worker | $1,600 | | | | | Overtime_labor_hours_used | =Model!$B$24:$E$24 | | | |
| 9 | Firing cost/worker | $2,000 | | | | | Production_capacity | =Model!$B$33:$E$33 | | | |
| 10 | Regular wages/worker/month | $1,500 | | | | | Shoes_produced | =Model!$B$31:$E$31 | | | |
| 11 | Overtime wage rate/hour | $13 | | | | | Total_cost | =Model!$F$53 | | | |
| 12 | Labor hours/pair of shoes | 4 | | | | | Units_left_over | =Model!$B$39:$E$39 | | | |
| 13 | Raw material cost/pair of shoes | $15 | | | | | Units_left_over_minus_units_short | =Model!$B$41:$E$41 | | | |
| 14 | Holding cost/pair of shoes in inventory/month | $3 | | | | | Units_short | =Model!$B$40:$E$40 | | | |
| 15 | Shortage cost/pair of shoes/month | $20 | | | | | Workers_fired | =Model!$B$20:$E$20 | | | |
| 16 | | | | | | | Workers_hired | =Model!$B$19:$E$19 | | | |
| 17 | Worker plan | Month 1 | Month 2 | Month 3 | Month 4 | | | | | | |
| 18 | Workers from previous month | 100 | 94 | 93 | 38 | | | | | | |
| 19 | Workers hired | 0 | 0 | 0 | 0 | | | | | | |
| 20 | Workers fired | 6 | 1 | 55 | 0 | | | | | | |
| 21 | Workers available after hiring and firing | 94 | 93 | 38 | 38 | | | | | | |
| 22 | | | | | | | | | | | |
| 23 | Regular-time hours available | 15040 | 14880 | 6080 | 6080 | | | | | | |
| 24 | Overtime labor hours used | 0 | 0 | 0 | 0 | | | | | | |
| 25 | | <= | <= | <= | <= | | | | | | |
| 26 | Maximum overtime labor hours available | 1880 | 1860 | 760 | 760 | | | | | | |
| 27 | | | | | | | | | | | |
| 28 | Total hours for production | 15040 | 14880 | 6080 | 6080 | | | | | | |
| 29 | | | | | | | | | | | |
| 30 | Production plan | Month 1 | Month 2 | Month 3 | Month 4 | | | | | | |
| 31 | Shoes produced | 3760 | 3720 | 1520 | 1500 | | | | | | |
| 32 | | <= | <= | <= | <= | | | | | | |
| 33 | Production capacity | 3760 | 3720 | 1520 | 1520 | | | | | | |
| 34 | | | | | | | | | | | |
| 35 | Inventory after production | 4260 | 4980 | 1500 | 1000 | | There is a somewhat unintuitive trick to making this backlogging model linear, without using any IF functions. The trick is to create new changing cells in rows 39 and 40 for the amounts leftover and short. The purpose of these is to enable simple linear formulas in rows 51 and 52 for the holding and shortage costs. However, because these are changing cells, they can freely vary. To make sure they have "sensible" values, we need to constrain them. This is done by equating rows 41 and 43. Essentially, these two rows evaluate ending inventory in two different ways: (1) as Leftover minus Shortage (row 41) and (2) as Inventory after production minus Forecasted demand (row 43). These two should be the same, so we add a constraint to force them to be equal. | | | | |
| 36 | | | | | >= | | | | | | |
| 37 | Forecasted demand | 3000 | 5000 | 2000 | 1000 | | | | | | |
| 38 | | | | | | | | | | | |
| 39 | Leftover | 1260 | 0 | 0 | 0 | | | | | | |
| 40 | Shortage | 0 | 20 | 500 | 0 | | | | | | |
| 41 | Leftover minus shortage | 1260 | -20 | -500 | 0 | | | | | | |
| 42 | | = | = | = | = | | | | | | |
| 43 | Ending inventory | 1260 | -20 | -500 | 0 | | | | | | |
| 44 | | | | | | | | | | | |
| 45 | Monetary outputs | Month 1 | Month 2 | Month 3 | Month 4 | Totals | | | | | |
| 46 | Hiring cost | $0 | $0 | $0 | $0 | $0 | | | | | |
| 47 | Firing cost | $12,000 | $2,000 | $110,000 | $0 | $124,000 | | | | | |
| 48 | Regular-time wages | $141,000 | $139,500 | $57,000 | $57,000 | $394,500 | | | | | |
| 49 | Overtime wages | $0 | $0 | $0 | $0 | $0 | | | | | |
| 50 | Raw material cost | $56,400 | $55,800 | $22,800 | $22,500 | $157,500 | | | | | |
| 51 | Holding cost | $3,780 | $0 | $0 | $0 | $3,780 | | | | | |
| 52 | Shortage cost | $0 | $400 | $10,000 | $0 | $10,400 | | | | | |
| 53 | Totals | $213,180 | $197,700 | $199,800 | $79,500 | $690,180 | ← ⟶ Objective to minimize | | | | |

**3** **Ending inventory (positive or negative).** The key observation is the following. Let $L_t$ be the amount of leftover inventory at the end of month $t$, and let $S_t$ be the amount short at the end of month $t$. Then $L_t = 0$ if $S_t \geq 0$, and $S_t = 0$ if $L_t \geq 0$. So if we allow ending inventory to be negative (meaning that there is a shortage), then for each month we have

$$I_t = L_t - S_t$$

For example, if $I_2 = 6$, then $L_2 = 6$ and $S_2 = 0$, indicating that SureStep has 6 pairs of shoes left over at the end of month 2. But if $I_2 = -3$, then $L_2 = 0$ and $S_2 = 3$, indicating that SureStep has a shortage of 3 pairs of shoes at the end of month 2. To incorporate this into the spreadsheet, enter the formula

**=B39–B40**

in cell B41 and copy it to the range C41:E41.

**④ Monthly costs.** Insert a new row (which will be row 52) below the holding cost row. Modify the holding cost for month 1 by entering the formula

**=$B$14*B39**

in cell B51. Calculate the shortage cost for month 1 in cell B52 with the formula

**=$B$15*B40**

Then copy the range B51:B52 to the range C51:E52 for the other months. Make sure the totals in row 53 and column F are updated to include the shortage costs.

## USING SOLVER FOR THE BACKLOG MODEL

The changes from the original Solver setup are as follows.

**① Extra changing cells.** Add the Leftover and Shortage ranges as changing cells. This allows Solver to adjust each month's amount leftover and amount short to be consistent with the desired ending inventory for the month.

**② Constraint on last month's inventory.** Change the constraints that were previously listed as **Inventory_after_production>=Forecasted_demand** to **Inventory_after_ production_4>=Forecasted_demand_4**. This allows months 1 through 3 to have negative ending inventory, but it ensures that all demand is met by the end of month 4.

**③ Logical constraint on ending inventory.** Add the constraint **Leftover_minus_ shortage=Ending_inventory**. If you study the model closely, you will notice that ending inventory is calculated in two different ways (in rows 41 and 43). This constraint ensures that both ways produce the same values.

**④ Optimize.** Make sure the LP algorithm is selected, and click on Solve to obtain the optimal solution shown in Figure 4.21.

Note that this solution is the same as the one in Figure 4.19 that was obtained with the "IF function" model. So this time, Solver handled the IF function correctly, but it might not always do so. Although the linearized version in Figure 4.21 admittedly involves a somewhat unintuitive trick, it does guarantee a linear model, which means that Solver will find the optimal solution. ■

## MODELING ISSUES

1. Silver et al. (1998) recommend that when demand is seasonal, the planning horizon should extend beyond the next seasonal peak.
2. Beyond a certain point, the cost of using extra hours of overtime labor increases because workers become less efficient. We haven't modeled this type of behavior, but it would make the model nonlinear. ■

## Skill-Building Problems

**13.** Extend SureStep's original no-backlogging aggregate planning model from 4 to 6 months. Try several different values for demands in months 5 and 6, and run Solver for each. Is your optimal solution for the *first* 4 months the same as the one in the book?

**14.** The current solution to SureStep's no-backlogging aggregate planning model does a lot of firing. Run a one-way SolverTable with the firing cost as the input variable and the numbers fired as the outputs. Let the firing cost increase from its current value to double that value in increments of $400. Do high firing costs eventually induce the company to fire fewer workers?

**15.** SureStep is currently getting 160 regular-time hours from each worker per month. This is actually calculated from 8 hours per day times 20 days per week. For this, they are paid $9.375 per hour (=1500/160). Suppose workers can change their contract so that they only have to work 7.5 hours per day regular-time—everything above this becomes overtime—and their regular-time wage rate increases to $10 per hour. They will still work 20 days per month. Will this change the optimal no-backlogging solution?

**16.** Suppose SureStep could begin a machinery upgrade and training program to increase its worker productivity. This program would result in the following values of labor hours per pair of shoes over the next 4 months: 4, 3.9, 3.8, and 3.8. How much would this new program be worth to SureStep, at least for this 4-month planning horizon with no backlogging? How might you evaluate the program's worth *beyond* the next 4 months?

## Skill-Extending Problems

**17.** In the current no-backlogging problem, SureStep doesn't hire any workers and uses almost no overtime.

This is evidently because of low demand. Change the demands to 6000, 8000, 5000, and 3000, and reoptimize. Is there now hiring and overtime? With this new demand pattern, explore the trade-off between hiring and overtime by running a two-way SolverTable. As inputs, use the hiring cost per worker and the maximum overtime hours allowed per worker per month, varied as you see fit. As outputs, use the total number of workers hired over the 4 months and the total number of overtime hours used over the 4 months. Write up your results in a short memo to SureStep management.

**18.** In the SureStep no-backlogging problem, change the demands so that they become 6000, 8000, 5000, 3000. Also, change the problem slightly so that newly hired workers take 6 hours to produce a pair of shoes during their first month of employment. After that, they take only 4 hours per pair of shoes. Modify the model appropriately, and use Solver to find the optimal solution.

**19.** We saw that the "natural" way to model SureStep's backlogging model, with IF functions, leads to a nonsmooth model that Solver has difficulty handling. Another version of the problem is also difficult for Solver. Suppose SureStep wants to meet all demand on time (no backlogging), but it wants to keep its employment level as constant across time as possible. To induce this, it charges a cost of $1000 each month on the absolute difference between the beginning number of workers and the number after hiring and firing—that is, the absolute difference between the values in rows 17 and 20 of the original spreadsheet model. Implement this extra cost in the model in the "natural" way, using the ABS function. Using demands of 6000, 8000, 5000, and 3000, see how well Solver does in trying to solve this nonsmooth model. Try several initial solutions, and see whether Solver gets the same optimal solution from each of them.

## 4.5 BLENDING MODELS

In many situations, various inputs must be blended together to produce desired outputs. In many of these situations, linear programming can find the optimal combination of outputs as well as the "mix" of inputs that are used to produce the desired outputs. Some examples of blending problems are given in Table 4.6.

**Table 4.6** Examples of Blending Problems

| Inputs | Outputs |
| --- | --- |
| Meat, filler, water | Different types of sausage |
| Various types of oil | Heating oil, gasolines, aviation fuels |
| Carbon, iron, molybdenum | Different types of steel |
| Different types of pulp | Different kinds of recycled paper |

The following example illustrates how to model a typical blending problem in a spreadsheet. Although this example is small relative to blending problems in real applications, it is still fairly complex. If you can guess the optimal solution, your intuition is much better than ours!

EXAMPLE | **4.4 BLENDING AT CHANDLER OIL**

Chandler Oil has 5000 barrels of crude oil 1 and 10,000 barrels of crude oil 2 available. Chandler sells gasoline and heating oil. These products are produced by blending together the two crude oils. Each barrel of crude oil 1 has a "quality level" of 10 and each barrel of crude oil 2 has a quality level of 5.[7] Gasoline must have an average quality level of at least 8, whereas heating oil must have an average quality level of at least 6. Gasoline sells for $25 per barrel, and heating oil sells for $20 per barrel. We assume that demand for heating oil and gasoline is unlimited, so that all of Chandler's production can be sold. Chandler wants to maximize its revenue from selling gasoline and heating oil.

**Objective** To develop an LP spreadsheet model that relates a detailed blending plan to relevant quantities on crude oil inputs and gasoline/heating oil outputs, and to use Solver to find the revenue-maximizing plan that meets quality constraints and stays within limits on crude oil availabilities.

### WHERE DO THE NUMBERS COME FROM?

Most of the inputs for this problem should be easy to obtain:

- The selling prices for outputs are dictated by market pressures.
- The availabilities of inputs are based on crude supplies from the suppliers.
- The quality levels of crude oils are known from chemical analysis, whereas the required quality levels for outputs are specified by Chandler, probably in response to competitive pressures.

## Solution

*In typical blending models, the correct decision variables are the amounts of each input blended into each output.*

The variables and constraints required for this blending model are listed in Table 4.7. The key to a successful model of this problem is selecting the appropriate decision variables. Many people, when asked what decision variables should be used, specify the amounts of the two crude oils used and the amounts of the two products produced. However, this is not enough! The problem is that this information doesn't tell Chandler how to *make* the outputs from the inputs. What we need instead is a blending plan: how much of each input to use in the production of a barrel of each output. After you understand that this blending plan is the basic decision, then all other output variables follow in a straightforward manner.

---

[7] To avoid getting into an overly technical discussion, we use the generic term *quality level*. In real oil blending, qualities of interest might be octane rating, viscosity, and others.

**Table 4.7** Variables and Constraints for the Blending Model

| | |
|---|---|
| **Input variables** | Unit selling prices, availabilities of inputs, quality levels of inputs, required quality levels of outputs |
| **Decision variables (changing cells)** | Barrels of each input used to produce each output |
| **Objective (target cell)** | Revenue from selling gasoline and heating oil |
| **Other calculated variables** | Barrels of inputs used, barrels of outputs produced (and sold), quality obtained, and quality required for outputs |
| **Constraints** | Barrels of inputs used must be less than or equal to Barrels available |
| | Quality of outputs obtained must be greater than or equal to Quality required |

A secondary, but very important, issue in typical blending problems is how to implement the "quality" constraints. (The constraints here are in terms of quality. In other blending problems they are often expressed in terms of percentages of some ingredient. For example, a typical quality constraint might be that some output can contain no more than 2% sulfur. Such constraints are typical of blending problems.) When we explain how to develop the spreadsheet model, we'll indicate the preferred way to implement quality constraints.

## DEVELOPING THE SPREADSHEET MODEL

The spreadsheet model for this problem appears in Figure 4.22. (See the file **Blending Oil.xlsx**.) To set it up, proceed as follows:

**Figure 4.22** Chandler Oil Blending Model

| | A | B | C | D | E | F | G | H |
|---|---|---|---|---|---|---|---|---|
| 1 | Chandler oil blending model | | | | | Range names used | | |
| 2 | | | | | | Barrels_available | =Model!$F$16:$F$17 | |
| 3 | Monetary inputs | Gasoline | Heating oil | | | Barrels_used | =Model!$D$16:$D$17 | |
| 4 | Selling price/barrel | $25.00 | $20.00 | | | Blending_plan | =Model!$B$16:$C$17 | |
| 5 | | | | | | Quality_points_obtained | =Model!$B$22:$C$22 | |
| 6 | Quality level per barrel of crudes | | | | | Quality_points_required | =Model!$B$24:$C$24 | |
| 7 | Crude oil 1 | 10 | | | | Revenue | =Model!$B$27 | |
| 8 | Crude oil 2 | 5 | | | | | | |
| 9 | | | | | | | | |
| 10 | Required quality level per barrel of product | | | | | | | |
| 11 | | Gasoline | Heating oil | | | | | |
| 12 | | 8 | 6 | | | | | |
| 13 | | | | | | | | |
| 14 | Blending plan (barrels of crudes in each product) | | | | | | | |
| 15 | | Gasoline | Heating oil | Barrels used | | Barrels available | | |
| 16 | Crude oil 1 | 3000 | 2000 | 5000 | <= | 5000 | | |
| 17 | Crude oil 2 | 2000 | 8000 | 10000 | <= | 10000 | | |
| 18 | Barrels sold | 5000 | 10000 | | | | | |
| 19 | | | | | | | | |
| 20 | Constraints on quality | | | | | | | |
| 21 | | Gasoline | Heating oil | | | | | |
| 22 | Quality points obtained | 40000 | 60000 | | | | | |
| 23 | | >= | >= | | | | | |
| 24 | Quality points required | 40000 | 60000 | | | | | |
| 25 | | | | | | | | |
| 26 | Objective to maximize | | | | | | | |
| 27 | Revenue | $325,000 | | | | | | |

**1** **Inputs and range names.** Enter the unit selling prices, quality levels for inputs, required quality levels for outputs, and availabilities of inputs in the blue ranges. Then name the ranges as indicated.

**2** **Inputs blended into each output.** As we discussed, the quantities Chandler must specify are the barrels of each input used to produce each output. Therefore, enter *any* trial values for these quantities in the Blending_plan range. For example, the value in cell B16 is the amount of crude oil 1 used to make gasoline, and the value in cell C16 is the amount of crude oil 1 used to make heating oil. The Blending_plan range contains the changing cells.

**3** **Inputs used and outputs sold.** We need to calculate the row sums (in column D) and column sums (in row 18) of the Blending_plan range. As noted in an earlier Excel tip, just highlight both the row and column where the sums will go (highlight one, then hold down the Ctrl key and highlight the other), and click on the Summation ($\Sigma$) button on the main Excel toolbar. This creates SUM formulas in the highlighted cells.

**4** **Quality achieved.** Keeping track of the quality level of gasoline and heating oil in the Quality_points_obtained range is tricky. Begin by calculating for each output the number of quality points (QP) in the inputs used to produce this output:

QP in gasoline = 10 (Oil 1 in gasoline) + 5 (Oil 2 in gasoline)
QP in heating oil = 10 (Oil 1 in heating oil) + 5 (Oil 2 in heating oil)

For the gasoline produced to have a quality level of at least 8, we must have

QP in gasoline ≥ 8 (Gasoline sold)                    **(4.1)**

For the heating oil produced to have a quality level of at least 6, we must have

QP in heating oil ≥ 6 (Heating oil sold)                    **(4.2)**

To implement inequalities (4.1) and (4.2), calculate the QP for gasoline in cell B22 with the formula

**=SUMPRODUCT(B16:B17, $B$7:$B$8)**

Then copy this formula to cell C22 to generate the QP for heating oil.

**5** **Quality required.** Calculate the required quality points for gasoline and heating oil in cells B24 and C24. Specifically, determine the required quality points for gasoline in cell B24 with the formula

**=B12*B18**

Then copy this formula to cell C24 for heating oil.

**6** **Revenue.** Calculate the total revenue in cell B27 with the formula

**=SUMPRODUCT(B4:C4,B18:C18)**

## USING SOLVER

To solve Chandler's problem with Solver, fill out the main Solver dialog box as shown in Figure 4.23. As usual, check the Assume Linear Model and Assume Non-Negative options before optimizing. We obtain the optimal solution shown in Figure 4.22.

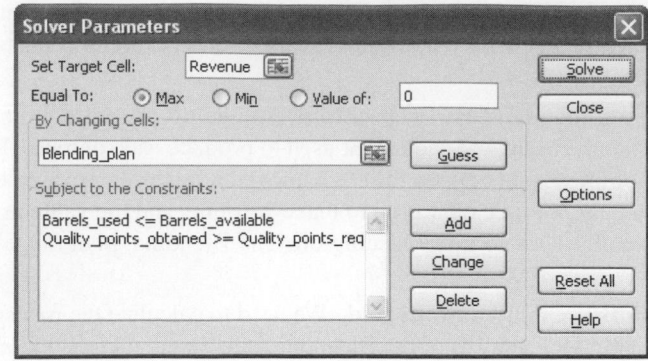

## Figure 4.23

Solver Dialog Box
for the Blending
Model

### Discussion of the Solution

The optimal solution implies that Chandler should make 5000 barrels of gasoline with 3000 barrels of crude oil 1 and 2000 barrels of crude oil 2. The company should also make 10,000 barrels of heating oil with 2000 barrels of crude oil 1 and 8000 barrels of crude oil 2. With this blend, Chandler obtains a revenue of $325,000. As stated previously, this problem is sufficiently complex to defy intuition. Clearly, gasoline is more profitable per barrel than heating oil, but given the crude availability and the quality constraints, it turns out that Chandler should sell twice as much heating oil as gasoline. This would have been very difficult to guess ahead of time.

### Sensitivity Analysis

We perform two typical sensitivity analyses on the Chandler blending model. In each, we'll see how revenue and the amounts of the outputs produced (and sold) vary. In the first analysis, we use the unit selling price of gasoline as the input and let it vary from $20 to $80 in increments of $5. The SolverTable results appear in Figure 4.24. Two things are of interest. First, as the price of gasoline increases, Chandler produces more gasoline and less heating oil, exactly as we would expect. Second, the revenue always increases, as the changes in column E indicate.

## Figure 4.24

Sensitivity to the
Selling Price of
Gasoline

| | A | B | C | D | E |
|---|---|---|---|---|---|
| 29 | Sensitivity of outputs sold and revenue to selling price of gasoline | | | | |
| 30 | | $B$18 | $C$18 | $B$27 | Increase |
| 31 | 20 | 5000 | 10000 | $300,000 | |
| 32 | 25 | 5000 | 10000 | $325,000 | $25,000 |
| 33 | 30 | 5000 | 10000 | $350,000 | $25,000 |
| 34 | 35 | 5000 | 10000 | $375,000 | $25,000 |
| 35 | 40 | 5000 | 10000 | $400,000 | $25,000 |
| 36 | 45 | 5000 | 10000 | $425,000 | $25,000 |
| 37 | 50 | 5000 | 10000 | $450,000 | $25,000 |
| 38 | 55 | 5000 | 10000 | $475,000 | $25,000 |
| 39 | 60 | 8333 | 0 | $500,000 | $25,000 |
| 40 | 65 | 8333 | 0 | $541,667 | $41,667 |
| 41 | 70 | 8333 | 0 | $583,333 | $41,667 |
| 42 | 75 | 8333 | 0 | $625,000 | $41,667 |
| 43 | 80 | 8333 | 0 | $666,667 | $41,667 |

In the second sensitivity analysis, we vary the availability of crude 1 from 2000 barrels to 20,000 barrels in increments of 1000 barrels. The resulting SolverTable output appears in Figure 4.25. These results make sense if we analyze them carefully. First, the revenue increases, but at a decreasing rate, as more crude 1 is available. This is a common occurrence in LP models. As more of a resource is made available, revenue can only increase or remain the same; however, each extra unit of the resource produces less (or at least no more) revenue than the previous unit. Second, the amount of gasoline produced increases, whereas the amount of heating oil produced decreases. The reason is that crude 1 has a higher quality than crude 2, and gasoline requires higher quality. Gasoline also sells for a higher price. Therefore, as more crude 1 is available, Chandler can produce more gasoline, receive more revenue, and still meet quality standards.

**Figure 4.25**

Sensitivity to the Availability of Crude 1

| | G | H | I | J | K | L |
|---|---|---|---|---|---|---|
| 29 | Sensitivity of outputs sold and revenue to availability of crude 1 | | | | | |
| 30 | | $B$18 | $C$18 | $B$27 | Increase | |
| 31 | 2000 | 0 | 10000 | $200,000 | | |
| 32 | 3000 | 1000 | 12000 | $265,000 | $65,000 | |
| 33 | 4000 | 3000 | 11000 | $295,000 | $30,000 | |
| 34 | 5000 | 5000 | 10000 | $325,000 | $30,000 | |
| 35 | 6000 | 7000 | 9000 | $355,000 | $30,000 | |
| 36 | 7000 | 9000 | 8000 | $385,000 | $30,000 | |
| 37 | 8000 | 11000 | 7000 | $415,000 | $30,000 | |
| 38 | 9000 | 13000 | 6000 | $445,000 | $30,000 | |
| 39 | 10000 | 15000 | 5000 | $475,000 | $30,000 | |
| 40 | 11000 | 17000 | 4000 | $505,000 | $30,000 | |
| 41 | 12000 | 19000 | 3000 | $535,000 | $30,000 | |
| 42 | 13000 | 21000 | 2000 | $565,000 | $30,000 | |
| 43 | 14000 | 23000 | 1000 | $595,000 | $30,000 | |
| 44 | 15000 | 25000 | 0 | $625,000 | $30,000 | |
| 45 | 16000 | 26000 | 0 | $650,000 | $25,000 | |
| 46 | 17000 | 27000 | 0 | $675,000 | $25,000 | |
| 47 | 18000 | 28000 | 0 | $700,000 | $25,000 | |
| 48 | 19000 | 29000 | 0 | $725,000 | $25,000 | |
| 49 | 20000 | 30000 | 0 | $750,000 | $25,000 | |

Could these sensitivity questions also be answered with Solver's sensitivity report, shown in Figure 4.26? Consider the sensitivity to the change in the price of gasoline. The first and third rows of the top table in this report are for sensitivity to the objective coefficients of decision variables involving gasoline. The problem is that when we change the price of gasoline, we automatically change *both* of these coefficients. The reason is that we sum these two decision variables to calculate the amount of gasoline sold, which we then multiply by the unit price of gasoline in the objective. However, Solver's sensitivity report is valid only for one-at-a-time coefficient changes. Therefore, it cannot answer the question posed.

**Figure 4.26**

Sensitivity Report for the Blending Model

| A | B | C | D | E | F | G | H |
|---|---|---|---|---|---|---|---|
| 6 | Adjustable Cells | | | | | | |
| 7 | | | Final | Reduced | Objective | Allowable | Allowable |
| 8 | Cell | Name | Value | Cost | Coefficient | Increase | Decrease |
| 9 | $B$16 | Crude oil 1 Gasoline | 3000 | 0 | 25 | 58.333 | 8.333 |
| 10 | $C$16 | Crude oil 1 Heating oil | 2000 | 0 | 20 | 8.333 | 58.333 |
| 11 | $B$17 | Crude oil 2 Gasoline | 2000 | 0 | 25 | 87.5 | 6.25 |
| 12 | $C$17 | Crude oil 2 Heating oil | 8000 | 0 | 20 | 6.25 | 14.583 |
| 13 | | | | | | | |
| 14 | Constraints | | | | | | |
| 15 | | | Final | Shadow | Constraint | Allowable | Allowable |
| 16 | Cell | Name | Value | Price | R.H. Side | Increase | Decrease |
| 17 | $D$16 | Crude oil 1 Barrels used | 5000 | 30 | 5000 | 10000 | 2500 |
| 18 | $D$17 | Crude oil 2 Barrels used | 10000 | 17.5 | 10000 | 10000 | 6666.667 |
| 19 | $B$22 | Quality points obtained Gasoline | 40000 | -2.5 | 0 | 5000 | 20000 |
| 20 | $C$22 | Quality points obtained Heating oil | 60000 | -2.5 | 0 | 10000 | 6666.667 |

In contrast, the first row of the bottom table in Figure 4.26 complements the SolverTable sensitivity analysis on the availability of crude 1. It shows that if the availability increases by no more than 10,000 barrels or decreases by no more than 2500 barrels, then the shadow price stays at $30 per barrel—that is, the same $30,000 increase in profit per 1000 barrels we saw in Figure 4.25. Beyond that range, the sensitivity report indicates only that the shadow price will change. The SolverTable results indicate *how* it changes. For example, when crude 1 availability increases beyond 15,000 barrels, the SolverTable results indicate that the shadow price decreases to $25 per barrel.

### A Caution About Blending Constraints

Before concluding this example, let's consider why the model is linear. The key is the implementation of the quality constraints, as shown in inequalities (4.1) and (4.2). To keep a model linear, each side of an inequality constraint must be a constant, the product of a constant and a variable, or a sum of such products. If we implement the quality constraints as in inequalities (4.1) and (4.2), we get linear constraints. However, it is arguably more natural to rewrite this type of constraint by dividing through by the amount sold. For example, the modified gasoline constraint is

$$\frac{\text{QP in gasoline}}{\text{Gasoline Sold}} \geq 8 \qquad\qquad (4.3)$$

Although this form of the constraint is perfectly valid—and is possibly more natural to many users—it suffers from two drawbacks. First, it makes the model nonlinear because the left-hand side is no longer a sum of products; it involves a quotient. We prefer linear models whenever possible. Second, suppose it turned out that Chandler's optimal solution called for *no* gasoline at all. Then we would be dividing by 0 in inequality (4.3), and this would cause an error in Excel. Because of these two drawbacks, you should clear denominators in all such blending constraints. ∎

---

### FUNDAMENTAL INSIGHT

#### Clearing Denominators

Some constraints, particularly those that arise in blending models, are most naturally expressed in terms of ratios. For example, the percentage of sulfur in a product is the ratio (amount of sulfur in product)/(total amount of product), which could then be constrained to be less than or equal to 6%, say. This is a perfectly valid way to express the constraint, but it has the undesirable property of making the model nonlinear. The fix is simple. To make the model linear, multiply through by the denominator of the ratio. This has the added benefit of ensuring that there will be no division by 0.

---

## MODELING ISSUES

In reality, a company using a blending model would run the model periodically (each day, say) and set production on the basis of the current inventory of inputs and the current forecasts of demands and prices. Then the forecasts and the input levels would be updated, and the model would be run again to determine the next day's production. ∎

### Blending at Texaco

Texaco, in DeWitt et al., (1989), uses a nonlinear programming model (OMEGA) to plan and schedule its blending applications. Texaco's model is nonlinear because blend volatilities and octanes are nonlinear functions of the amount of each input used to produce a particular gasoline.

### Blending in the Oil Industry

Many oil companies use LP to optimize their refinery operations. Magoulas and Marinos-Kouris (1988) discuss one such blending model that has been used to maximize a refinery's profit. ∎

## PROBLEMS

### Skill-Building Problems

**20.** Use SolverTable in Chandler's blending model to see whether, by increasing the selling price of gasoline, you can get an optimal solution that produces only gasoline, no heating oil. Then use SolverTable again to see whether, by increasing the selling price of heating oil, you can get an optimal solution that produces only heating oil, no gasoline.

**21.** Use SolverTable in Chandler's blending model to find the shadow price of crude oil 1—that is, the amount Chandler would be willing to spend to acquire more crude oil 1. Does this shadow price change as Chandler keeps getting more of crude oil 1? Answer the same questions for crude oil 2.

**22.** How sensitive is the optimal solution (barrels of each output sold and profit) to the required quality points? Answer this by running a two-way SolverTable with these three outputs. You can choose the values of the two inputs to vary.

**23.** In Chandler's blending model, suppose a chemical ingredient called CI is needed by both gasoline and heating oil. At least 3% of every barrel of gasoline must be CI, and at least 5% of every barrel of heating oil must be CI. Suppose that 4% of all crude oil 1 is CI, and 6% of all crude oil 2 is CI. Modify the model to incorporate the constraints on CI, and then optimize. Don't forget to clear denominators.

**24.** As we have formulated Chandler's blending model, a barrel of any input results in a barrel of output. However, in a real blending problem, there can be losses. Suppose a barrel of input results in only a fraction of a barrel of output. Specifically, each barrel of either crude oil used for gasoline results in only 0.95 barrel of gasoline, and each barrel of either crude used for heating oil results in only 0.97 barrel of heating oil. Modify the model to incorporate these losses, and reoptimize.

### Skill-Extending Problem

**25.** We warned you about clearing denominators in the quality constraints. This problem indicates what happens if you don't do so.
  **a.** Implement the quality constraints as indicated in inequality (4.3) of the text. Then run Solver with Assume Linear Model checked. What happens? What if you uncheck the Assume Linear Model option?
  **b.** Repeat part **a**, but increase the selling price of heating oil to $40 per barrel. What happens now? Does it matter whether you check or uncheck the Assume Linear Model option? Why?

## 4.6 PRODUCTION PROCESS MODELS

LP is often used to determine the optimal method of operating a production process. In particular, many oil refineries use LP to manage their production operations. The models are often characterized by the fact that some of the products produced are *inputs* to the production of other products. The following example is typical.

EXAMPLE | **4.5 DRUG PRODUCTION AT REPCO**

Repco produces three drugs, A, B, and C, and can sell these drugs in unlimited quantities at unit prices $8, $70, and $100, respectively. Producing a unit of drug A requires 1 hour of labor. Producing a unit of drug B requires 2 hours of labor and 2 units of drug A. Producing 1 unit of drug C requires 3 hours of labor and 1 unit of drug B. Any drug A that is used to produce drug B cannot be sold separately, and any drug B that is used to produce drug C cannot be sold separately. A total of 4000 hours of labor are available. Repco wants to use LP to maximize its sales revenue.

**Objective**   To develop an LP spreadsheet model that relates production decisions to amounts required for production and amounts available for selling, and to use Solver to maximize sales revenue, subject to limited labor hours.

### WHERE DO THE NUMBERS COME FROM?

The inputs for this problem should be easy to obtain:

- The company sets its selling prices, which are probably dictated by the market.

- The available labor hours are based on the size of the current workforce assigned to production of these drugs. These might be flexible quantities, depending on whether workers could be diverted from other duties to work on these drugs and whether new labor could be hired.

- The labor and drug usage inputs for producing the various drugs are probably well known, based on productivity levels and chemical requirements.

## Solution

*The decision variables should be the smallest set of variables that determines everything else. After the company decides how much of each drug to produce, there is really nothing left to decide.*

The variables and constraints required to model this problem are listed in Table 4.8. The key to the model is understanding which variables can be chosen—the decision variables— and which variables are determined by this choice. It is probably clear that Repco must decide how much of each drug to produce. However, it might not be clear why the amounts used for production of other drugs and the amounts sold are *not* decision variables. The idea is that as soon as Repco decides to produce, say, 10 units of drug B, it automatically knows that it must produce at least 20 units of drug A. In fact, it cannot decide to produce just *any* quantities of the three drugs. For example, it can't produce 10 units of drug B and only 15 units of drug A. Therefore, the drugs required for producing other drugs put automatic constraints on the production quantities. Of course, any drugs left over, that is, not used in production of other drugs, are sold.

---

**Table 4.8**   Variables and Constraints for the Production Process Model

| | |
|---|---|
| **Input variables** | Labor inputs to drug production, drugs required for production of other drugs, selling prices of drugs, labor hours available |
| **Decision variables (changing cells)** | Units of drugs to produce |
| **Objective (target cell)** | Revenue from sales |
| **Other calculated variables** | Units of drugs used to make other drugs, units of drugs left over to sell |
| **Constraints** | Drugs produced must be greater than or equal to Drugs required for production of other drugs |
| | Labor hours used must be less than or equal to Labor hours available |

## DEVELOPING THE SPREADSHEET MODEL

The key to the spreadsheet model is that everything produced is used in some way. Either it's used as an input to the production of some other drug, or it's sold. Therefore, the following "balance" equation holds for each product:

$$\text{Amount produced} = \text{Amount used to produce other drugs} + \text{Amount sold} \qquad (4.4)$$

This balance equation can be implemented in three steps:

**1** Specify the amounts produced in changing cells.

**2** Calculate the amounts used to produce other drugs based on the way the production process works.

**3** Calculate the amounts sold from equation (4.4) by subtraction. Then impose a constraint that equation (4.4) must be satisfied.

The spreadsheet model for Repco appears in Figure 4.27. (See the file **Production Process.xlsx**.) To proceed, carry out the following steps:

---

**Figure 4.27**  Repco Production Process Model

| | A | B | C | D | E | F | G | H | I | J |
|---|---|---|---|---|---|---|---|---|---|---|
| 1 | Repco production process model | | | | | Range names used: | | | | |
| 2 | | | | | | Hours_available | =Model!$D$23 | | | |
| 3 | Inputs used (along side) to make one unit of product (along top) | | | | | Hours_used | =Model!$B$23 | | | |
| 4 | | Drug A | Drug B | Drug C | | Revenue_from_sales | =Model!$B$25 | | | |
| 5 | Labor hours | 1 | 2 | 3 | | Units_produced | =Model!$B$16:$D$16 | | | |
| 6 | | | | | | Units_sold | =Model!$B$19:$D$19 | | | |
| 7 | Drug A | 0 | 2 | 0 | | Units_used_in_production | =Model!$B$18:$D$18 | | | |
| 8 | Drug B | 0 | 0 | 1 | | | | | | |
| 9 | Drug C | 0 | 0 | 0 | | | | | | |
| 10 | | | | | | | | | | |
| 11 | Unit selling prices | Drug A | Drug B | Drug C | | | | | | |
| 12 | | $8 | $70 | $100 | | | | | | |
| 13 | | | | | | | | | | |
| 14 | Production and sales plan | | | | | Units of products used (along side) to make products (along top) | | | | |
| 15 | | Drug A | Drug B | Drug C | | | Drug A | Drug B | Drug C | Total used |
| 16 | Units produced | 2000 | 1000 | 0 | | Drug A | 0 | 2000 | 0 | 2000 |
| 17 | | >= | >= | >= | | Drug B | 0 | 0 | 0 | 0 |
| 18 | Units used in production | 2000 | 0 | 0 | | Drug C | 0 | 0 | 0 | 0 |
| 19 | Units sold | 0 | 1000 | 0 | | | | | | |
| 20 | | | | | | | | | | |
| 21 | Labor hour constraint | | | | | | | | | |
| 22 | | Hours used | | Hours available | | | | | | |
| 23 | | 4000 | <= | 4000 | | | | | | |
| 24 | | | | | | | | | | |
| 25 | Revenue from sales | $70,000 | ◀— | Objective to maximize | | | | | | |

**1 Inputs and range names.** Enter the inputs in the shaded blue ranges. For example, the 2 in cell C7 indicates that 2 units of drug A are needed to produce each unit of drug B, and the 0's in this range indicate which drugs are not needed to produce other drugs. (Note, however, the 0 in cell D7, which could be misleading. Drug A is required to make drug B, and drug B is required to make drug C. Therefore, drug A is required *indirectly* to make drug C. However, this indirect effect is accounted for by the values in cells C7 and D8, so the 0 in cell D7 is appropriate.) Then create the range names indicated.

**2 Units produced.** Enter *any* trial values for the number of units produced in the Units_produced range. This range contains the only changing cells.

**3** **Units used to make other products.** In the range G16:I18, calculate the total number of units of each product that are used to produce other products. Begin by calculating the amount of A used to produce A in cell G16 with the formula

**=B7*B$16**

and copy this formula to the range G16:I18 for the other combinations of products. For example, in the solution shown, 10 units of drug B are produced, so 2000 units of drug A are required, as calculated in cell H16. Then calculate the row totals in column J with the SUM function. Then it's convenient to "transfer" these sums in column J to the B18:D18 range. There are two ways to do this, that is, to make a column into a row or vice versa. The easiest way is to copy the range J16:J18, then select cell B18, select the Edit/Paste Special menu item, and check the Transpose option. Unfortunately, this method doesn't copy formulas correctly. The second way uses Excel's TRANSPOSE function. To copy the formulas correctly, highlight the B18:D18 range, type the formula

**=TRANSPOSE(J16:J18)**

and press Ctrl+Shift+Enter (all three keys at once).

**Excel Tool:** *Paste Special Transpose*
*To copy a row range to a column range, copy the row range, select the first cell in the column range, and select Transpose from the Paste dropdown on the Home ribbon. The same method can be used to copy a column range to a row range. However, this method doesn't copy formulas correctly.*

**Excel Function:** *TRANSPOSE and Other Array Functions*
*The TRANSPOSE function is useful for linking a row to a column or vice versa. It has the syntax =TRANSPOSE(Range). To implement it, highlight the row or column range where the results will go, type the formula, and press Ctrl+Shift+Enter. This function is one of several* array *functions in Excel, which means that it fills up an entire range, not just a single cell, all at once. All array formulas require you to highlight the entire range where the results will go, type the formula, and then press Ctrl+Shift+Enter. After you do this, you will notice curly brackets around the formula in the Formula Bar. You should* not *actually type these curly brackets. They simply indicate the presence of an array function.*

**4** **Units sold.** Referring to equation (4.4), determine the units sold of each drug by subtraction. Specifically, enter the formula

**=B16-B18**

in cell B19 and copy it to the range C19:D19.

**5** **Labor hours used.** Calculate the total number of labor hours used in cell B23 with the formula

**=SUMPRODUCT(B5:D5,Units_produced)**

**6** **Total revenue.** Calculate Repco's revenue from sales in cell B25 with the formula

**=SUMPRODUCT(B12:D12,Units_sold)**

## USING SOLVER

To use Solver to maximize Repco's revenue, fill in the main Solver dialog box as shown in Figure 4.28. As usual, check the Assume Linear Model and Assume Non-Negative options before optimizing. Note that we have constrained the drugs produced to be greater than or equal to the drugs used in production of other drugs. An equivalent alternative is to constrain the units sold to be nonnegative.

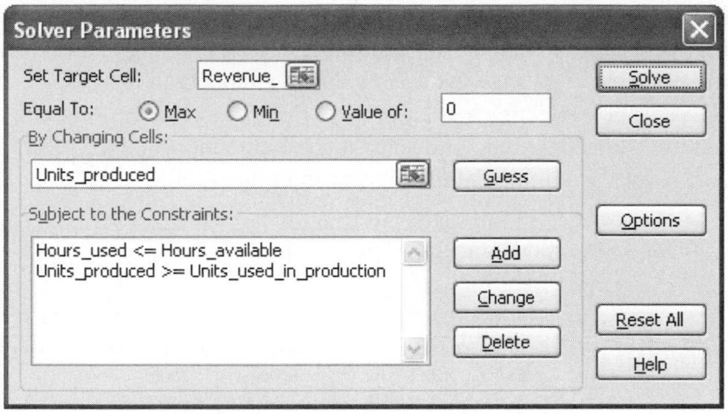

## Figure 4.28

Solver Dialog Box for Repco Model

**Solver Parameters**

Set Target Cell: `Revenue_`
Equal To: ⊙ Max ○ Min ○ Value of: `0`
By Changing Cells:
`Units_produced`
Subject to the Constraints:
```
Hours_used <= Hours_available
Units_produced >= Units_used_in_production
```
[Solve] [Close] [Guess] [Options] [Add] [Change] [Delete] [Reset All] [Help]

### Discussion of the Solution

The optimal solution in Figure 4.27 indicates that Repco obtains a revenue of $70,000 by producing 2000 units of drug A, all of which are used to produce 1000 units of drug B. All units of drug B produced are sold. Even though drug C has the highest selling price, Repco produces none of drug C, evidently because of the large labor requirement for drug C.

### Sensitivity Analysis

Drug C is not produced at all, even though its selling price is by far the highest. How high would this selling price have to be to induce Repco to produce any of drug C? We can use SolverTable to answer this, using drug C selling price as the input variable, letting it vary from $100 to $200 in increments of $10, and keeping track of the total revenue, the units produced of each drug, and the units used (row 18) of each drug. The results are shown in Figure 4.29.

**Figure 4.29** Sensitivity to Selling Price of Drug C

| | A | B | C | D | E | F | G | H |
|---|---|---|---|---|---|---|---|---|
| 28 | Sensitivity of revenue, units produced, and units used as inputs to drug C selling price | | | | | | | |
| 29 | Drug C selling price | A produced | B produced | C produced | A used | | B used | C used | Revenue |
| 30 | | $B$16 | $C$16 | $D$16 | $B$18 | | $C$18 | $D$18 | $B$25 |
| 31 | 100 | 2000.0 | 1000.0 | 0.0 | 2000.0 | | 0.0 | 0.0 | $70,000 |
| 32 | 110 | 2000.0 | 1000.0 | 0.0 | 2000.0 | | 0.0 | 0.0 | $70,000 |
| 33 | 120 | 2000.0 | 1000.0 | 0.0 | 2000.0 | | 0.0 | 0.0 | $70,000 |
| 34 | 130 | 1142.9 | 571.4 | 571.4 | 1142.9 | | 571.4 | 0.0 | $74,286 |
| 35 | 140 | 1142.9 | 571.4 | 571.4 | 1142.9 | | 571.4 | 0.0 | $80,000 |
| 36 | 150 | 1142.9 | 571.4 | 571.4 | 1142.9 | | 571.4 | 0.0 | $85,714 |
| 37 | 160 | 1142.9 | 571.4 | 571.4 | 1142.9 | | 571.4 | 0.0 | $91,429 |
| 38 | 170 | 1142.9 | 571.4 | 571.4 | 1142.9 | | 571.4 | 0.0 | $97,143 |
| 39 | 180 | 1142.9 | 571.4 | 571.4 | 1142.9 | | 571.4 | 0.0 | $102,857 |
| 40 | 190 | 1142.9 | 571.4 | 571.4 | 1142.9 | | 571.4 | 0.0 | $108,571 |
| 41 | 200 | 1142.9 | 571.4 | 571.4 | 1142.9 | | 571.4 | 0.0 | $114,286 |

As we can see, until the drug C selling price reaches $130, Repco uses the same solution as before.[8] However, when it increases to $130 and beyond, 571.4 units of drug C are produced. This in turn requires 571.4 units of drug B, which requires 1142.9 units of drug A, but only drug C is actually sold. Of course, Repco would like to produce even more of drug C (which would require more production of drugs A and B), but the labor hour constraint does not allow it. Therefore, further increases in the selling price of drug C have no effect on the solution—other than increasing revenue.

[8] If you obtain Solver's sensitivity report, you'll see that the change actually occurs when the price of drug C reaches $122.50. Our SolverTable grid of prices is too coarse to detect this exact changeover point.

Because available labor imposes an upper limit on the production of drug C even when it is very profitable, it is very profitable, it is interesting to see what happens when the selling price of drug C *and* the labor hours available both increase. Here we can use a two-way SolverTable, selecting selling price of drug C and labor hour availability as the two inputs with reasonable values, and selecting the amount produced of drug C as the single output. The results from SolverTable appear in Figure 4.30.

**Figure 4.30** Sensitivity to Price of Drug C and Labor Hour Availability

| | A | B | C | D | E | F | G | H |
|---|---|---|---|---|---|---|---|---|
| 43 | Sensitivity of amount of C produced to selling price of C (along side) and labor hour availability (along top) | | | | | | | |
| 44 | $D$16 | 4000 | 5000 | 6000 | 7000 | 8000 | 9000 | 10000 |
| 45 | 100 | 0.0 | 0.0 | 0.0 | 0.0 | 0.0 | 0.0 | 0.0 |
| 46 | 110 | 0.0 | 0.0 | 0.0 | 0.0 | 0.0 | 0.0 | 0.0 |
| 47 | 120 | 0.0 | 0.0 | 0.0 | 0.0 | 0.0 | 0.0 | 0.0 |
| 48 | 130 | 571.4 | 714.3 | 857.1 | 1000.0 | 1142.9 | 1285.7 | 1428.6 |
| 49 | 140 | 571.4 | 714.3 | 857.1 | 1000.0 | 1142.9 | 1285.7 | 1428.6 |
| 50 | 150 | 571.4 | 714.3 | 857.1 | 1000.0 | 1142.9 | 1285.7 | 1428.6 |
| 51 | 160 | 571.4 | 714.3 | 857.1 | 1000.0 | 1142.9 | 1285.7 | 1428.6 |
| 52 | 170 | 571.4 | 714.3 | 857.1 | 1000.0 | 1142.9 | 1285.7 | 1428.6 |
| 53 | 180 | 571.4 | 714.3 | 857.1 | 1000.0 | 1142.9 | 1285.7 | 1428.6 |
| 54 | 190 | 571.4 | 714.3 | 857.1 | 1000.0 | 1142.9 | 1285.7 | 1428.6 |
| 55 | 200 | 571.4 | 714.3 | 857.1 | 1000.0 | 1142.9 | 1285.7 | 1428.6 |

This table again shows that no drug C is produced, regardless of labor hour availability, until the selling price of drug C reaches $130. (Of course, the actual breakpoint is probably *between* $120 and $130. We can't tell from the grid of input values used in the table.) The effect of increases in labor hour availability is to let Repco produce more of drug C. Specifically, Repco produces as much of drug C as possible, given that 1 unit of drug B, and hence 2 units of drug A, are required for each unit of drug C.

Before leaving this example, we provide further insight into the sensitivity behavior in Figure 4.29. Specifically, why should Repco start producing drug C when its unit selling price increases to some value between $120 and $130? There is a straightforward answer to this question because the model contains a *single* resource constraint: the labor hour constraint. (The analysis would be more complicated with multiple resources.)

*As this analysis illustrates, we can sometimes—but not always—gain an intuitive understanding of the information obtained by SolverTable.*

Consider the production of 1 unit of drug B, which requires 2 labor hours plus 2 units of drug A, each of which requires 1 labor hour, for a total of 4 labor hours. It returns $70 in revenue. Therefore, revenue per labor hour when producing drug B is $17.50. To be eligible as a "winner," drug C has to beat this. Note that each unit of drug C requires 7 labor hours (3 for itself and 4 for the unit of drug B it requires). To beat the $17.50 revenue per labor hour of drug B, the unit selling price of drug C must be at least $122.50 [= 17.50(7)]. If its selling price is below this, for example, $121, Repco will sell all drug B and no drug C. If its selling price is above this, for example, $127, Repco will sell all drug C and no drug B. ∎

# PROBLEMS

## Skill-Building Problems

**26.** Run a one-way sensitivity analysis on the optimal solution to the unit selling price of drug A in the Repco problem. If this price is high enough, will Repco start selling drug A in addition to producing it? Then run a similar one-way sensitivity analysis on the optimal solution to the price of drug B. If this price gets low enough, what happens to the optimal solution?

**27.** We claimed in the Repco model that we could either constrain the units produced to be greater than or equal to the units used by production or the units sold to be nonnegative. We chose the former. Modify the model to implement the latter (deleting the former), and verify that you get the same optimal solution.

**28.** Suppose there is a fourth drug, drug D, that Repco can produce and sell. Each unit of drug D requires 4 labor hours, 1 unit of drug A, and 1 unit of drug C to produce, and it sells for $150 per unit. Modify the current model to incorporate drug D and reoptimize. If drug D isn't produced in the optimal solution, use sensitivity analysis to see how much higher its selling price would have to be before Repco would produce it. If drug D is produced in the optimal solution, use

sensitivity analysis to see how much lower its selling price would have to be before Repco would stop producing it.

### Skill-Extending Problem

**29.** In a production process model such as Repco's, certain inputs make no sense in the "usage" table (the range B7:D9 of the model). For example, suppose that, in addition to current usages, each unit of drug A requires 1 unit of drug C. Why does this result in a nonsensical problem? What happens if you run Solver on it anyway? What happens if you run Solver on it after adding a constraint that the sum of the units produced (over all three drugs) must be at least 1?

# 4.7 FINANCIAL MODELS

The majority of optimization examples described in management science textbooks are in the area of operations: scheduling, blending, logistics, aggregate planning, and others. This is probably warranted, because many of the most successful management science applications in the real world have been in these areas. However, optimization and other management science methods have also been applied successfully in a number of financial areas, and they deserve recognition. Several of these applications are discussed throughout this book. In this section, we begin the discussion with two typical applications of LP in finance. The first involves investment strategy. The second involves pension fund management.

---

**EXAMPLE** | **4.6 FINDING AN OPTIMAL INVESTMENT STRATEGY AT BARNEY-JONES**

At the present time, the beginning of year 1, the Barney-Jones Investment Corporation has $100,000 to invest for the next 4 years. There are five possible investments, labeled A–E. The timing of cash outflows and cash inflows for these investments is somewhat irregular. For example, to take part in investment A, cash must be invested at the beginning of year 1, and for every dollar invested, there are returns of $0.50 and $1.00 at the beginnings of years 2 and 3. Similar information for the other investments is as follows, where all returns are per dollar invested:

- **Investment B:** Invest at the beginning of year 2, receive returns of $0.50 and $1.00 at the beginnings of years 3 and 4.

- **Investment C:** Invest at the beginning of year 1, receive return of $1.20 at the beginning of year 2.

- **Investment D:** Invest at the beginning of year 4, receive return of $1.90 at the beginning of year 5.

- **Investment E:** Invest at the beginning of year 3, receive return of $1.50 at the beginning of year 4.

We assume that any amounts can be invested in these strategies and that the returns are the same for each dollar invested. However, to create a diversified portfolio, Barney-Jones decides to limit the amount put into any investment to $75,000. The company wants an investment strategy that maximizes the amount of cash on hand at the beginning of year 5. At the beginning of any year, it can invest only cash on hand, which includes returns from previous investments. Any cash not invested in any year can be put in a short-term money market account that earns 3% annually.

**Objective** To develop an LP spreadsheet model that relates investment decisions to total ending cash and to use Solver to find the strategy that maximizes ending cash and invests no more than a given amount in any one investment.

## WHERE DO THE NUMBERS COME FROM?

There's no mystery here. Assuming that the terms of each investment are spelled out, Barney-Jones knows exactly when money must be invested and what the amounts and timing of returns will be. Of course, this isn't the case for many real-world investments, such as money put into the stock market, where considerable uncertainty is involved. We'll illustrate one such example of investing with uncertainty when portfolio optimization is discussed in Chapter 7.

## Solution

*There are often multiple equivalent ways to state a constraint. You can choose the one that is most natural for you.*

The variables and constraints for this investment model are listed in Table 4.9. On the surface, this problem looks very straightforward. We must decide how much to invest in the available investments at the beginning of each year, and we can use only the cash available. If you try modeling this problem without our help, however, you might have some difficulty. It took us a few tries to get a "nice" model, one that is easy to read and generalizes to other similar investment problems. By the way, the second constraint in the table can be expressed in two ways. It can be expressed as shown, where the cash on hand *after* investing is nonnegative, or it can be expressed as "cash on hand at the beginning of any year must be greater than or equal to cash invested that year." These are equivalent. The one we choose is a matter of taste.

---

**Table 4.9** Variables and Constraints for Investment Model

| | |
|---|---|
| **Input variables** | Timing of investments and returns, initial cash, maximum amount allowed in any investment, money market rate on cash |
| **Decision variables (changing cells)** | Amounts to invest in investments |
| **Objective (target cell)** | Ending cash at the beginning of year 5 |
| **Other calculated variables** | Cash available at the beginning of years 2 through 4 |
| **Constraints** | Amount in any investment must be less than or equal to Maximum amount per investment |
| | Cash on hand after investing each year must be greater than or equal to 0 |

---

The spreadsheet model for this investment problem appears in Figure 4.31. (See the file **Investing.xlsx**.) To set up this spreadsheet, follow these steps:

**Figure 4.31**  Spreadsheet Model for Investment Problem

| | A | B | C | D | E | F | G | H | I | J |
|---|---|---|---|---|---|---|---|---|---|---|
| 1 | Investments with irregular timing of returns | | | | | | | Range names used | | |
| 2 | | | | | | | | Cash_after_investing | =Model!$E$32:$E$35 | |
| 3 | Inputs | | | | | | | Dollars_invested | =Model!$B$26:$F$26 | |
| 4 | Initial amount to invest | $100,000 | | | | | | Final_cash | =Model!$B$38 | |
| 5 | Maximum per investment | $75,000 | | | | | | Maximum_per_Investment | =Model!$B$28:$F$28 | |
| 6 | Interest rate on cash | 3% | | | | | | | | |
| 7 | | | | | | | | | | |
| 8 | Cash outlays on investments (all incurred at beginning of year) | | | | | | | | | |
| 9 | | Investment | | | | | | | | |
| 10 | Year | A | B | C | D | E | | | | |
| 11 | 1 | $1.00 | $0.00 | $1.00 | $0.00 | $0.00 | | | | |
| 12 | 2 | $0.00 | $1.00 | $0.00 | $0.00 | $0.00 | | | | |
| 13 | 3 | $0.00 | $0.00 | $0.00 | $0.00 | $1.00 | | | | |
| 14 | 4 | $0.00 | $0.00 | $0.00 | $1.00 | $0.00 | | | | |
| 15 | | | | | | | | | | |
| 16 | Cash returns from investments (all incurred at beginning of year) | | | | | | | | | |
| 17 | | Investment | | | | | | | | |
| 18 | Year | A | B | C | D | E | | | | |
| 19 | 1 | $0.00 | $0.00 | $0.00 | $0.00 | $0.00 | | | | |
| 20 | 2 | $0.50 | $0.00 | $1.20 | $0.00 | $0.00 | | | | |
| 21 | 3 | $1.00 | $0.50 | $0.00 | $0.00 | $0.00 | | | | |
| 22 | 4 | $0.00 | $1.00 | $0.00 | $0.00 | $1.50 | | | | |
| 23 | 5 | $0.00 | $0.00 | $0.00 | $1.90 | $0.00 | | | | |
| 24 | | | | | | | | | | |
| 25 | Investment decisions | | | | | | | | | |
| 26 | Dollars invested | $64,286 | $75,000 | $35,714 | $75,000 | $75,000 | | | | |
| 27 | | <= | <= | <= | <= | <= | | | | |
| 28 | Maximum per investment | $75,000 | $75,000 | $75,000 | $75,000 | $75,000 | | | | |
| 29 | | | | | | | | | | |
| 30 | Constraints on cash balance | | | | | | | | | |
| 31 | Year | Beginning cash | Returns from investments | Cash invested | Cash after investing | | | | | |
| 32 | 1 | $100,000 | $0 | $100,000 | $0 | >= | | 0 | | |
| 33 | 2 | $0 | $75,000 | $75,000 | -$0 | >= | | 0 | | |
| 34 | 3 | -$0 | $101,786 | $75,000 | $26,786 | >= | | 0 | | |
| 35 | 4 | $27,589 | $187,500 | $75,000 | $140,089 | >= | | 0 | | |
| 36 | 5 | $144,292 | $142,500 | | | | | | | |
| 37 | | | | | | | | | | |
| 38 | Final cash | $286,792 | ← | Objective to maximize: final cash at beginning of year 5 | | | | | | |

*The two input tables at the top of the spreadsheet allow us to use and copy the SUMPRODUCT function for cash outflows and inflows. Careful spreadsheet planning can often greatly simplify the necessary formulas.*

**❶ Inputs and range names.** As usual, enter the given inputs in the blue ranges and name the ranges indicated. Pay particular attention to the two blue tables. This is the first model we have encountered where model development is affected significantly by the way we enter the inputs, specifically, the information about the investments. We suggest separating cash outflows from cash inflows, as shown in the two ranges B11:F14 and B19:F23. The top table indicates when we invest, where a 0 indicates no possible investment, and a 1 indicates a dollar of investment. The bottom table then indicates the amounts and timing of returns per dollar invested.

**❷ Investment amounts.** Enter *any* trial values in the Dollars_invested range. This range contains the changing cells. Also put a link to the maximum investment amount per investment by entering the formula

=$B$5

in cell B28 and copying it across.

**❸ Cash balances and flows.** The key to the model is the section in rows 32 to 36. For each year, we need to calculate the beginning cash held from the previous year, the returns from investments that are due in that year, the investments made in that year, and cash balance after investments. Begin by entering the initial cash in cell B32 with the formula

=B4

Moving across, calculate the return due in year 1 in cell C32 with the formula

**=SUMPRODUCT(B19:F19,Dollars_invested)**

Admittedly, no returns come due in year 1, but this formula can be copied down column C for other years. Next, calculate the total amount invested in year 1 in cell D32 with the formula

**=SUMPRODUCT(B11:F11,Dollars_invested)**

Now find the cash balance after investing in year 1 in cell E32 with the formula

**=B32+C32-D32**

The only other required formula is for the cash available at the beginning of year 2. Because any cash not invested earns 3% interest, enter the formula

**=E32*(1+$B$6)**

in cell B33. This formula, along with those in cells C32, D32, and E32, can now be copied down. (The 0's in column G are a reminder of the nonnegativity constraint on cash after investing.)

*Always look at the Solver solution for signs of implausibility. This can often lead you to an error in your model.*

**4** **Ending cash.** The ending cash at the beginning of year 5 is the sum of the amount in the money market and any returns that come due in year 5. Calculate this sum with the formula

**=SUM(B36:C36)**

in cell B38. (*Note:* Here is the type of error to watch out for. We originally failed to calculate the return in cell C36 and mistakenly used the beginning cash in cell B36 as the target cell. We realized the error when the optimal solution called for no money in investment D, which is clearly an attractive investment. The lesson is that you can often catch errors by looking at the *plausibility* of your optimal solution.)

### Review of the Model

Take a careful look at this model and how it has been set up. There are undoubtedly many alternative ways to model this problem, but the attractive feature of the model is the way the tables of inflows and outflows in rows 11 to 14 and 19 to 23 allow us to copy formulas for returns and investment amounts in columns C and D of rows 32 to 36. In fact, this same model setup, with only minor modifications, works for *any* set of investments, regardless of the timing of investments and their returns. This is a quality you should strive for in your own spreadsheet models: generalizability.

 **USING SOLVER**

To find the optimal investment strategy, fill in the main Solver dialog box as shown in Figure 4.32, check the Assume Linear Model and Assume Non-Negative options, and optimize. Note that the explicit nonnegativity constraint in Figure 4.32 is necessary, even if the Assume Non-Negative option is checked. Again, this is because the Assume Non-Negative option covers only the changing cells. If we want other output cells to be nonnegative, we must add such constraints explicitly.

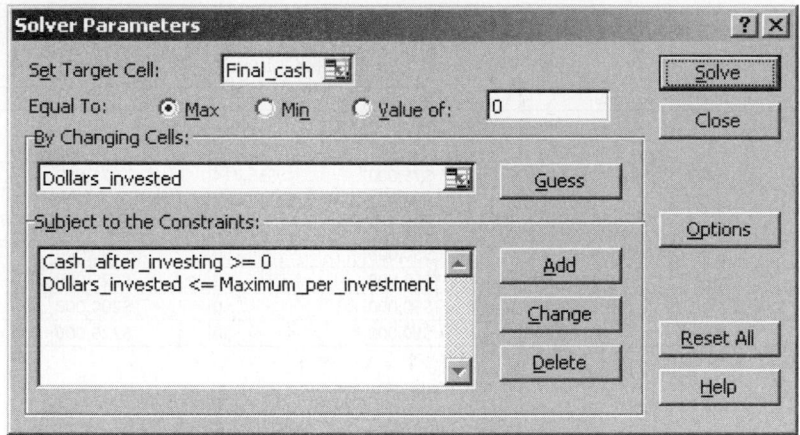

**Figure 4.32**
Solver Dialog Box
for the Investment
Model

## Discussion of the Results

The optimal solution appears in Figure 4.31. Let's follow the cash. The company spends all its cash in year 1 on the two available investments, A and C ($64,286 in A, $35,714 in C). A total of $75,000 in returns from these investments is available in year 2, and all of this is invested in investment B. (The minus signs in cells E33 and B34 are due to round-off error. The values in these cells are very small negative numbers, but they are equal to 0 for all practical purposes.) At the beginning of year 3, a total of $101,786 is available from investment A and B returns, and $75,000 of this invested in investment E. This leaves $26,786 for the money market, which grows to $27,589 at the beginning of year 4. In addition, returns totaling $187,500 from investments B and E come due in year 4. Of this total cash of $215,089, $75,000 is invested in investment D, and the rest, $140,089, is put in the money market. The return from investment D, $142,500, plus the money available from the money market, $144,292, equals the final cash in the target cell, $286,792.

## Sensitivity Analysis

*Constraints always have the potential to penalize the objective to some extent. SolverTable is a perfect tool for finding the magnitude of this penalty.*

A close look at the optimal solution in Figure 4.31 indicates that Barney-Jones is really penalizing itself by imposing a maximum of $75,000 per investment. This upper limit is forcing the company to put cash into the money market fund, despite this fund's low rate of return. Therefore, a natural sensitivity analysis is to see how the optimal solution changes as this maximum value changes. We can perform this sensitivity analysis with a one-way SolverTable, shown in Figure 4.33.[9] It uses the maximum in cell B5 as the input cell, varied from $75,000 to $225,000 in increments of $25,000, and keeps track of the optimal changing cells and target cell. As we can see, the final cash (column G) grows steadily as we allow the maximum investment amount to increase. This is because the company can take greater advantage of the attractive investments and put less in the money market.

---

[9] Because Solver's sensitivity reports do not help answer the specific sensitivity questions in this example or the next example, we discuss only the SolverTable results.

**Figure 4.33** Sensitivity of Optimal Solution to Maximum Investment Amount

|    | A | B | C | D | E | F | G |
|----|---|---|---|---|---|---|---|
| 40 | Sensitivity of optimal solution to maximum per investment | | | | | | |
| 41 | | $B$26 | $C$26 | $D$26 | $E$26 | $F$26 | $B$38 |
| 42 | 75000 | $64,286 | $75,000 | $35,714 | $75,000 | $75,000 | $285,118 |
| 43 | 100000 | $61,538 | $76,923 | $38,462 | $100,000 | $100,000 | $319,462 |
| 44 | 125000 | $100,000 | $50,000 | $0 | $125,000 | $125,000 | $352,250 |
| 45 | 150000 | $100,000 | $50,000 | $0 | $150,000 | $125,000 | $374,250 |
| 46 | 175000 | $100,000 | $50,000 | $0 | $175,000 | $125,000 | $396,250 |
| 47 | 200000 | $100,000 | $50,000 | $0 | $200,000 | $125,000 | $418,250 |
| 48 | 225000 | $100,000 | $50,000 | $0 | $225,000 | $125,000 | $440,250 |

*To perform sensitivity on an output variable not calculated explicitly in the spreadsheet model, calculate it in some unused portion of the spreadsheet before running SolverTable.*

We go one step further with the two-way SolverTable in Figure 4.34. Here both the maximum investment amount and the money market rate are allowed to vary, and the maximum amount ever put in the money market is tracked. Because this latter amount is not calculated in the spreadsheet model, we need to calculate it with the formula **=MAX(Cash_after_investing)** in cell B51 and then use it as the output cell for SolverTable. In every case, even with a large maximum investment amount and a low money market rate, the company puts *some* money in the money market. The reason is simple. Even when the maximum investment amount is $225,000, the company evidently has more cash than this to invest at some point (probably at the beginning of year 4). Therefore, the company must put some of it in the money market. ∎

**Figure 4.34** Sensitivity of Maximum in Money Market to Two Inputs

|    | A | B | C | D | E | F | G | H |
|----|---|---|---|---|---|---|---|---|
| 51 | Maximum in money market | $140,089 | ← | Extra output for use in sensitivity analysis below | | | | |
| 52 | | | | | | | | |
| 53 | Sensitivity of maximum placed in money market to interest rate on cash and maximum per investment | | | | | | | |
| 54 | $B$51 | 75000 | 100000 | 125000 | 150000 | 175000 | 200000 | 225000 |
| 55 | 0.5% | $139,420 | $126,923 | $112,500 | $87,500 | $62,500 | $37,500 | $12,500 |
| 56 | 1.0% | $139,554 | $126,923 | $112,500 | $87,500 | $62,500 | $37,500 | $12,500 |
| 57 | 1.5% | $139,688 | $126,923 | $112,500 | $87,500 | $62,500 | $37,500 | $12,500 |
| 58 | 2.0% | $139,821 | $126,923 | $112,500 | $87,500 | $62,500 | $37,500 | $12,500 |
| 59 | 2.5% | $139,955 | $126,923 | $112,500 | $87,500 | $62,500 | $37,500 | $12,500 |
| 60 | 3.0% | $140,089 | $126,923 | $112,500 | $87,500 | $62,500 | $37,500 | $12,500 |
| 61 | 3.5% | $140,223 | $126,923 | $112,500 | $87,500 | $62,500 | $37,500 | $12,500 |
| 62 | 4.0% | $140,357 | $126,923 | $112,500 | $87,500 | $62,500 | $37,500 | $12,500 |
| 63 | 4.5% | $140,491 | $126,923 | $112,500 | $87,500 | $62,500 | $37,500 | $12,500 |

The following pension fund example illustrates a common situation where fixed payments are due in the future and current funds must be allocated and invested so that their returns are sufficient to make the payments.

## EXAMPLE | 4.7 MANAGING A PENSION FUND AT ARMCO

James Judson is the financial manager in charge of the company pension fund at Armco Incorporated. James knows that the fund must be sufficient to make the payments listed in Table 4.10. Each payment must be made on the first day of each year. James is going to finance these payments by purchasing bonds. It is currently January 1, 2008, and three bonds are available for immediate purchase. The prices and coupons for the bonds are as follows. (All coupon payments are received on January 1 and arrive in time to meet cash demands for the date on which they arrive.)

- Bond 1 costs $980 and yields a $60 coupon in the years 2009 to 2012 and a $1060 payment on maturity in the year 2013.
- Bond 2 costs $970 and yields a $65 coupon in the years 2009 to 2018 and a $1065 payment on maturity in the year 2019.
- Bond 3 costs $1050 and yields a $75 coupon in the years 2009 to 2021 and a $1075 payment on maturity in the year 2022.

James must decide how much cash to allocate (from company coffers) to meet the initial $11,000 payment and buy enough bonds to make future payments. He knows that any excess cash on hand can earn an annual rate of 4% in a fixed-rate account. How should he proceed?

**Table 4.10**  **Payments for Pension Problem**

| Year | Payment | Year | Payment | Year | Payment |
|------|---------|------|---------|------|---------|
| 2008 | $11,000 | 2013 | $18,000 | 2018 | $25,000 |
| 2009 | $12,000 | 2014 | $20,000 | 2019 | $30,000 |
| 2010 | $14,000 | 2015 | $21,000 | 2020 | $31,000 |
| 2011 | $15,000 | 2016 | $22,000 | 2021 | $31,000 |
| 2012 | $16,000 | 2017 | $24,000 | 2022 | $31,000 |

**Objective**   To develop an LP spreadsheet model that relates initial allocation of money and bond purchases to future cash availabilities, and to use Solver to minimize the initialize allocation of money required to meet all future pension fund payments.

### WHERE DO THE NUMBERS COME FROM?

As in the previous financial example, the inputs are fairly easy to obtain. A pension fund has known liabilities that must be met in future years, and information on bonds and fixed-rate accounts is widely available.

## Solution

The variables and constraints required for this pension fund model are listed in Table 4.11. When modeling this problem, we'll see a new twist that involves the money James must allocate in 2008 for his funding problem. Clearly, he must decide how many bonds of each type to purchase in 2008 (note that no bonds are purchased *after* 2008), but he must also decide how much money to allocate from company coffers. This allocated money has to cover the initial pension payment in 2008 *and* the bond purchases. In addition, James wants to find the *minimum* allocation that will suffice. Therefore, this initial allocation serves two roles in the model: it's a decision variable *and* the objective  to be minimized. In terms of spreadsheet modeling, it's perfectly acceptable to make the target cell one of the changing cells, as is done here. You might not see this in many

---

### FUNDAMENTAL INSIGHT

#### The Objective as a Changing Cell

In all optimization models, the objective cell has to be a function of the changing cells, that is, the objective value should change as values in the changing cells change. It is perfectly consistent with this requirement to have the objective cell *be* one of the changing cells. This doesn't occur in very many optimization models, but it is sometimes useful, even necessary.

models—because the objective typically involves a linear combination of several decision variables—but it is occasionally the most natural way to proceed.

---

**Table 4.11**   **Variables and Constraints for Pension Model**

| | |
|---|---|
| **Input variables** | Pension payments, information on bonds, fixed interest rate on cash |
| **Decision variables** (changing cells) | Money to allocate in 2008, numbers of bonds to purchase in 2008 |
| **Objective (target cell)** | Money to allocate in 2008 (minimize) |
| **Other calculated variables** | Cash available to meet pension payments each year |
| **Constraints** | Cash available for payments must be greater than or equal to Payment amounts |

---

## DEVELOPING THE SPREADSHEET MODEL

The completed spreadsheet model is shown in Figure 4.35. (See the file **Pension Fund Management.xlsx**.) It can be created with the following steps:

---

**Figure 4.35**   Spreadsheet Model for Pension Fund Management

| | A | B | C | D | E | F | G | H | I | J | K | L | M | N | O | P |
|---|---|---|---|---|---|---|---|---|---|---|---|---|---|---|---|---|
| 1 | Pension fund management | | | | | | | | | | | | | | | |
| 2 | | | | | | | | | | | | | | | | |
| 3 | Costs (in 2008) and income (in other years) from bonds | | | | | | | | | | | | | | | |
| 4 | Year | 2008 | 2009 | 2010 | 2011 | 2012 | 2013 | 2014 | 2015 | 2016 | 2017 | 2018 | 2019 | 2020 | 2021 | 2022 |
| 5 | Bond 1 | $980 | $60 | $60 | $60 | $60 | $1,060 | | | | | | | | | |
| 6 | Bond 2 | $970 | $65 | $65 | $65 | $65 | $65 | $65 | $65 | $65 | $65 | $65 | $1,065 | | | |
| 7 | Bond 3 | $1,050 | $75 | $75 | $75 | $75 | $75 | $75 | $75 | $75 | $75 | $75 | $75 | $75 | $75 | $1,075 |
| 8 | | | | | | | | | | | | | | | | |
| 9 | Interest rate | 4% | | | | | | | | | | | | | | |
| 10 | | | | | | | | | | | | | | | | |
| 11 | Number of bonds (allowing fractional values) to purchase in 2008 | | | | | | | | | | | | | | | |
| 12 | Bond 1 | 73.69 | | | | | | | | | | | | | | |
| 13 | Bond 2 | 77.21 | | | | | | | | | | | | | | |
| 14 | Bond 3 | 28.84 | | | | | | | | | | | | | | |
| 15 | | | | | | | | | | | | | | | | |
| 16 | Money allocated | $197,768 | ← Objective to minimize, also a changing cell | | | | | | | | | | | | | |
| 17 | | | | | | | | | | | | | | | | |
| 18 | Constraints to meet payments | | | | | | | | | | | | | | | |
| 19 | Year | 2008 | 2009 | 2010 | 2011 | 2012 | 2013 | 2014 | 2015 | 2016 | 2017 | 2018 | 2019 | 2020 | 2021 | 2022 |
| 20 | Amount available | $20,376 | $21,354 | $21,332 | $19,228 | $16,000 | $85,298 | $77,171 | $66,639 | $54,646 | $41,133 | $25,000 | $84,390 | $58,728 | $31,000 | $31,000 |
| 21 | | >= | >= | >= | >= | >= | >= | >= | >= | >= | >= | >= | >= | >= | >= | >= |
| 22 | Amount required | $11,000 | $12,000 | $14,000 | $15,000 | $16,000 | $18,000 | $20,000 | $21,000 | $22,000 | $24,000 | $25,000 | $30,000 | $31,000 | $31,000 | $31,000 |
| 23 | | | | | | | | | | | | | | | | |
| 24 | Range names used: | | | | | | | | | | | | | | | |
| 25 | Amount_available | =Model!$B$20:$P$20 | | | | | | | | | | | | | | |
| 26 | Amount_required | =Model!$B$22:$P$22 | | | | | | | | | | | | | | |
| 27 | Bonds_purchased | =Model!$B$12:$B$14 | | | | | | | | | | | | | | |
| 28 | Money_allocated | =Model!$B$16 | | | | | | | | | | | | | | |

The value in cell B16 is the money allocated to make the 2008 payment and buy bonds in 2008. It is both a changing cell and the target cell to minimize.

---

**①   Inputs and range names.**   Enter the given data in the blue cells and name the ranges as indicated. Note that the bond costs in the range B5:B7 are entered as *positive* quantities. Some financial analysts might prefer that they be entered as negative numbers, indicating outflows. It doesn't really matter, however, as long as we are careful with spreadsheet formulas later on.

*Always document your spreadsheet conventions as clearly as possible.*

**②   Money allocated and bonds purchased.**   As we discussed previously, the money allocated in 2008 and the numbers of bonds purchased are both decision variables, so enter *any* values for these in the Money_allocated and Bonds_purchased ranges. Note that the color-coding convention is modified for the Money_allocated cell. Because it is both a changing cell and the target cell, we color it red but add a note to emphasize that it is the objective to maximize.

**3** **Cash available to make payments.** In 2008, the only cash available is the money initially allocated minus cash used to purchase bonds. Calculate this quantity in cell B20 with the formula

**=Money_allocated-SUMPRODUCT(Bonds_purchased,B5:B7)**

For all other years, the cash available comes from two sources: excess cash invested at the fixed interest rate the year before and payments from bonds. Calculate this quantity for 2009 in cell C20 with the formula

**=(B20-B22)*(1+$B$9)+SUMPRODUCT(Bonds_purchased,C5:C7)**

and copy it across row 20 for the other years.

As you see, this model is fairly straightforward to develop after you understand the role of the amount allocated in cell B16. However, we have often given this problem as an assignment to our students, and many fail to deal correctly with the amount allocated. (They usually forget to make it a changing cell.) So make sure you understand what we have done and why we have done it this way.

## USING SOLVER

The main Solver dialog box should be filled out as shown in Figure 4.36. As usual, the Assume Linear Model and Assume Non-Negative options should be checked before optimizing. Again, notice that the Money_allocated cell is both the target cell and one of the changing cells.

**Figure 4.36**

Solver Dialog Box for the Pension Model

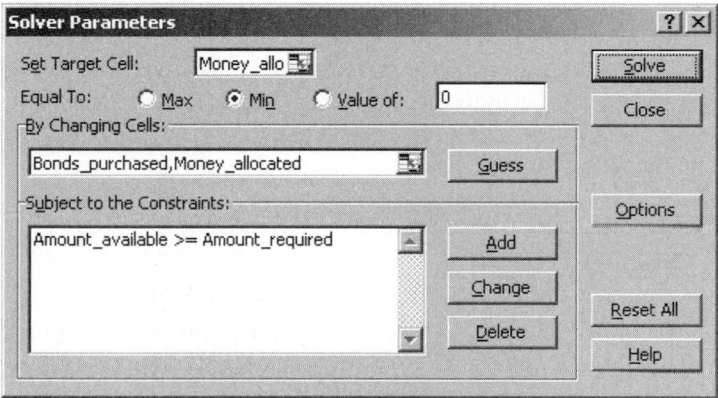

### Discussion of the Solution

The optimal solution appears in Figure 4.35. You might argue that the numbers of bonds purchased should be constrained to integer values. We tried this and the optimal solution changed very little: The optimal numbers of bonds to purchase changed to 74, 79, and 27, and the optimal money to allocate increased to $197,887. With this integer solution, shown in Figure 4.37, James sets aside $197,887 initially. Any less than this would not work—he couldn't make enough from bonds to meet future pension payments. All but $20,387 of this initial allocation (see cell B20) is spent on bonds, and of the $20,387, $11,000 is used to make the 2008 pension payment. After this, the amounts in row 20, which are always sufficient to make the payments in row 22, are composed of returns from bonds and cash with interest from the previous year. Even more so than in previous examples, there's no way to "guess" this optimal solution. The timing of bond returns and the irregular pension payments make an optimization model an absolute necessity.

**Figure 4.37**    Optimal Integer Solution for the Pension Model

| | A | B | C | D | E | F | G | H | I | J | K | L | M | N | O | P |
|---|---|---|---|---|---|---|---|---|---|---|---|---|---|---|---|---|
| 1 | Pension fund management | | | | | | | | | | | | | | | |
| 2 | | | | | | | | | | | | | | | | |
| 3 | Costs (in 2008) and income (in other years) from bonds | | | | | | | | | | | | | | | |
| 4 | Year | 2008 | 2009 | 2010 | 2011 | 2012 | 2013 | 2014 | 2015 | 2016 | 2017 | 2018 | 2019 | 2020 | 2021 | 2022 |
| 5 | Bond 1 | $980 | $60 | $60 | $60 | $60 | $1,060 | | | | | | | | | |
| 6 | Bond 2 | $970 | $65 | $65 | $65 | $65 | $65 | $65 | $65 | $65 | $65 | $65 | $1,065 | | | |
| 7 | Bond 3 | $1,050 | $75 | $75 | $75 | $75 | $75 | $75 | $75 | $75 | $75 | $75 | $75 | $75 | $75 | $1,075 |
| 8 | | | | | | | | | | | | | | | | |
| 9 | Interest rate | 4% | | | | | | | | | | | | | | |
| 10 | | | | | | | | | | | | | | | | |
| 11 | Number of bonds (allowing fractional values) to purchase in 2008 | | | | | | | | | | | | | | | |
| 12 | Bond 1 | 74.00 | | | | | | | | | | | | | | |
| 13 | Bond 2 | 79.00 | | | | | | | | | | | | | | |
| 14 | Bond 3 | 27.00 | | | | | | | | | | | | | | |
| 15 | | | | | | | | | | | | | | | | |
| 16 | Money allocated | $197,887 | ← | Objective to minimize, also a changing cell | | | | | | | | | | | | |
| 17 | | | | | | | | | | | | | | | | |
| 18 | Constraints to meet payments | | | | | | | | | | | | | | | |
| 19 | Year | 2008 | 2009 | 2010 | 2011 | 2012 | 2013 | 2014 | 2015 | 2016 | 2017 | 2018 | 2019 | 2020 | 2021 | 2022 |
| 20 | Amount available | $20,387 | $21,363 | $21,337 | $19,231 | $16,000 | $85,600 | $77,464 | $66,923 | $54,919 | $41,396 | $25,252 | $86,422 | $60,704 | $32,917 | $31,019 |
| 21 | | >= | >= | >= | >= | >= | >= | >= | >= | >= | >= | >= | >= | >= | >= | >= |
| 22 | Amount required | $11,000 | $12,000 | $14,000 | $15,000 | $16,000 | $18,000 | $20,000 | $21,000 | $22,000 | $24,000 | $25,000 | $30,000 | $31,000 | $31,000 | $31,000 |
| 23 | | | | | | | | | | | | | | | | |
| 24 | Range names used: | | | | | | | | | | | | | | | |
| 25 | Amount_available | =Model!$B$20:$P$20 | | | | | | | | | | | | | | |
| 26 | Amount_required | =Model!$B$22:$P$22 | | | | | | | | | | | | | | |
| 27 | Bonds_purchased | =Model!$B$12:$B$14 | | | | | | | | | | | | | | |
| 28 | Money_allocated | =Model!$B$16 | | | | | | | | | | | | | | |

The value in cell B16 is the money allocated to make the 2008 payment and buy bonds in 2008. It is both a changing cell and the target cell to minimize.

## Sensitivity Analysis

Because the bond information and pension payments are evidently fixed, we see only one promising direction for sensitivity analysis: on the fixed interest rate in cell B9. We tried this, allowing this rate to vary from 2% to 6% in increments of 0.5%, and we kept track of the optimal changing cells, including the target cell. The results appear in Figure 4.38. They indicate that as the interest rate increases, James can get by with fewer bonds of types 1 and 2, and he can allocate less money for the problem. The reason is that he is making more interest on excess cash.

**Figure 4.38**

Sensitivity to Fixed Interest Rate

| | A | B | C | D | E |
|---|---|---|---|---|---|
| 30 | Sensitivity to interest rate | | | | |
| 31 | | $B$12 | $B$13 | $B$14 | $B$16 |
| 32 | 2.0% | 77.12 | 78.71 | 28.84 | $202,010 |
| 33 | 2.5% | 76.24 | 78.33 | 28.84 | $200,930 |
| 34 | 3.0% | 75.37 | 77.95 | 28.84 | $199,863 |
| 35 | 3.5% | 74.53 | 77.58 | 28.84 | $198,809 |
| 36 | 4.0% | 73.69 | 77.21 | 28.84 | $197,768 |
| 37 | 4.5% | 72.88 | 76.84 | 28.84 | $196,741 |
| 38 | 5.0% | 72.09 | 76.49 | 28.84 | $195,727 |
| 39 | 5.5% | 71.30 | 76.13 | 28.84 | $194,725 |
| 40 | 6.0% | 70.54 | 75.78 | 28.84 | $193,737 |

## ADDITIONAL APPLICATIONS

### Using LP to Optimize Bond Portfolios

Many Wall Street firms buy and sell bonds. Rohn (1987) developed a bond selection model that maximizes profit from bond purchases and sales subject to constraints that minimize the firm's risk exposure. The method used to model this situation is closely related to the method used to model the Barney-Jones problem. ∎

## Skill-Building Problems

**30.** Modify the Barney-Jones investment problem so that a minimum amount must be put into any investment, although this minimum can vary by investment. For example, the minimum amount for investment A might be $0, whereas the minimum amount for investment D might be $50,000. These minimum amounts should be inputs; you can make up any values you like. Run Solver on your modified model.

**31.** In the Barney-Jones investment problem, increase the maximum amount allowed in any investment to $150,000. Then run a one-way sensitivity analysis to the money market rate on cash. Capture one output variable: the maximum amount of cash ever put in the money market. You can choose any reasonable range for varying the money market rate.

**32.** We claimed that our model for Barney-Jones is generalizable. Try generalizing it to the case where there are two more potential investments, F and G. Investment F requires a cash outlay in year 2 and returns $0.50 in *each* of the next 4 years for every dollar invested. Investment G requires a cash outlay in year 3 and returns $0.75 in each of years 5, 6, and 7 for every dollar invested. Modify the model as necessary, making the objective the final cash after year 7.

**33.** In the Barney-Jones spreadsheet model, we ran investments across columns and years down rows. Many financial analysts seem to prefer the opposite. Modify the spreadsheet model so that years go across columns and investments go down rows. Run Solver to ensure that your modified model is correct! (There are two possible ways to do this, and you can experiment to see which you prefer. First, you could basically start over on a blank worksheet. Second, you could use Excel's TRANSPOSE function.)

**34.** In the pension fund problem, suppose there's a fourth bond, bond 4. Its unit cost in 2006 is $1020, it returns coupons of $70 in years 2007 to 2010 and a payment of $1070 in 2011. Modify the model to incorporate this extra bond and reoptimize. Does the solution change— that is, should James purchase any of bond 4?

**35.** In the pension fund problem, suppose there is an upper limit of 60 on the number of bonds of any particular type that can be purchased. Modify the model to incorporate this extra constraint and then reoptimize. How much more money does James need to allocate initially?

**36.** In the pension fund problem, suppose James has been asked to see how the optimal solution will change if the required payments in years 2011 to 2020 all increase by the same percentage, where this percentage could be anywhere from 5% to 25%. Use an appropriate one-way SolverTable to help him out, and write a memo describing the results.

**37.** The pension fund model is streamlined, perhaps too much. It does all of the calculations concerning cash flows in row 20. James decides he would like to "break these out" into several rows of calculations: Beginning cash (for 2006, this is the amount allocated; for other years, it is the unused cash, plus interest, from the previous year), Amount spent on bonds (positive in 2006 only), Amount received from bonds (positive for years 2007 to 2020 only), Cash available for making pension fund payments, and (below the Amount required row) Cash left over (amount invested in the fixed interest rate). Modify the model by inserting these rows, enter the appropriate formulas, and run Solver. You should obtain the same result, but you get more detailed information.

## Skill-Extending Problems

**38.** Suppose the investments in the Barney-Jones problem sometimes require cash outlays in more than one year. For example, a $1 investment in investment B might require $0.25 to be spent in year 1 and $0.75 to be spent in year 2. Does our model easily accommodate such investments? Try it with some cash outlay data you make up, run Solver, and interpret your results.

**39.** In the pension fund problem, if the amount of money initially is *less* than the amount found by Solver, then James will not be able to meet all of the pension fund payments. Use the current model to demonstrate that this is true. To do so, enter a value less than the optimal value into cell B16. Then run Solver, but remove the Money_allocated cell as a changing cell and as the target cell. (If there is no target cell, Solver simply tries to find a solution that satisfies all of the constraints.) What do you find?

**40.** Continuing the previous problem in a slightly different direction, continue to use the Money_allocated cell as a changing cell, and add a constraint that it must be less than or equal to any value, such as $195,000, that is less than its current optimal value. With this constraint, James will again not be able to meet all of the pension fund payments. Create a new target cell to minimize the total amount of payments not met. The easiest way to do this is with IF functions. Unfortunately, this makes the model nonsmooth, and Solver might have trouble finding the optimal solution. Try it and see.

# 4.8 DATA ENVELOPMENT ANALYSIS (DEA)

The **data envelopment analysis** (DEA) method can be used to determine whether a university, hospital, restaurant, or other business is operating efficiently. Specifically, DEA can be used by inefficient organizations to benchmark efficient and "best-practice" organizations. According to Sherman and Ladino (1995):

> Many managers of service organizations would describe benchmarking and best practice analysis as basic, widely accepted concepts already used in their businesses. Closer examination indicates that the traditional techniques used to identify and promulgate best practices are not very effective, largely because the operations of these service organizations are too complex to allow them to identify best practices accurately. DEA provides an objective way to identify best practices in these service organizations and has consistently generated new insights that lead to substantial productivity gains that were not otherwise identifiable.

The following example illustrates DEA and is based on Callen (1991). See also Norton (1994).

---

## EXAMPLE | 4.8 DEA IN THE HOSPITAL INDUSTRY

Consider a group of three hospitals. To simplify matters, assume that each hospital "converts" two inputs into three different outputs. (In a real DEA, there are typically many more inputs and outputs.) The two inputs used by each hospital are

> input 1 = capital (measured by hundreds of hospital beds)
> input 2 = labor (measured by thousands of labor hours used in a month)

The outputs produced by each hospital are

output 1 = hundreds of patient-days during month for patients under age 14

output 2 = hundreds of patient-days during month for patients between 14 and 65

output 3 = hundreds of patient-days for patients over 65

The inputs and outputs for these hospitals are given in Table 4.12. Which of these three hospitals is efficient in terms of using its inputs to produce outputs?

**Table 4.12   Input and Output for the Hospital Example**

|  | Inputs | | Outputs | | |
|---|---|---|---|---|---|
|  | 1 | 2 | 1 | 2 | 3 |
| Hospital 1 | 5 | 14 | 9 | 4 | 16 |
| Hospital 2 | 8 | 15 | 5 | 7 | 10 |
| Hospital 3 | 7 | 12 | 4 | 9 | 13 |

**Objective**   To develop an LP spreadsheet model, using the DEA methodology, to determine whether each hospital is efficient in terms of using its inputs to produce its outputs.

In a general DEA analysis, the organization's inputs and outputs must first be defined. Then for each input or output, a unit of measurement must be selected. Neither of these is necessarily an easy task, because organizations such as hospitals, banks, and schools consume a variety of inputs and produce a variety of outputs that can be measured in alternative ways. However, after the list of inputs and outputs has been chosen and units of measurement have been selected, we can use accounting data to find the required data, as in Table 4.12.

## Solution

The idea is that when focusing on any particular hospital, we want to show it in the best possible light. That is, we want to *value* the inputs and outputs in such a way that this hospital looks as good as possible relative to the other hospitals. Specifically, to determine whether a hospital is efficient, we define a price per unit of each output and a cost per unit of each input. Then the efficiency of a hospital is defined to be

$$\text{Efficiency of hospital} = \frac{\text{Value of hospital's outputs}}{\text{Value of hospital's inputs}}$$

The DEA approach uses the following four ideas to determine whether a hospital is efficient.

- No hospital can be more than 100% efficient. Therefore, the efficiency of each hospital is constrained to be less than or equal to 1. To make this a *linear* constraint, we express it in this form:

   Value of hospital's outputs $\leq$ Value of hospital's inputs

- When we are trying to determine whether a hospital is efficient, it simplifies matters to scale input prices so that the value of the hospital's inputs equals 1. Any other value would suffice, but using 1 causes the efficiency of the hospital to be equal to the value of the hospital's outputs.

- If we are interested in evaluating the efficiency of a hospital, we should attempt to choose input costs and output prices that maximize this hospital's efficiency. If the hospital's efficiency equals 1, then the hospital is efficient; if the hospital's efficiency is less than 1, then the hospital is inefficient.

- All input costs and output prices must be nonnegative.

Putting these ideas together, the variables required for the DEA model are summarized in Table 4.13. Note the reference to "selected hospital." The model is actually analyzed three times, once for each hospital. So the selected hospital each time is the one currently in focus.

**Table 4.13**  Variables and Constraints for the DEA Model

| | |
|---|---|
| **Input variables** | Inputs used, outputs produced for each hospital |
| **Decision variables** (changing cells) | Unit costs of inputs, unit prices of outputs for selected hospital |
| **Objective (target cell)** | Total output value of selected hospital |
| **Other calculated variables** | Total input cost, total output value (for each hospital) |
| **Constraints** | Total input cost must be greater than or equal to Total output value (for each hospital) |
| | Total cost for selected hospital must equal 1 |

## DEVELOPING THE SPREADSHEET MODEL

Figure 4.39 contains the DEA spreadsheet model used to determine the efficiency of hospital 1. (See the file **Hospital DEA.xlsm.**) To develop this model, proceed as follows.

**Figure 4.39**   DEA Model for Hospital 1

| | A | B | C | D | E | F | G | H | I | J | K |
|---|---|---|---|---|---|---|---|---|---|---|---|
| 1 | DEA model for checking efficiency of a selected hospital | | | | | | | | | Range names used | |
| 2 | | | | | | | | | | Input_costs | =Model!$B$14:$B$16 |
| 3 | Selected hospital | 1 | | | | | | | | Output_values | =Model!$D$14:$D$16 |
| 4 | | | | | | | | | | Selected_hospital | =Model!$B$3 |
| 5 | Inputs used | Input 1 | Input 2 | | Outputs produced | Output 1 | Output 2 | Output 3 | | Selected_hospital_input_cost | =Model!$B$19 |
| 6 | Hospital 1 | 5 | 14 | | Hospital 1 | 9 | 4 | 16 | | Selected_hospital_output_value | =Model!$B$22 |
| 7 | Hospital 2 | 8 | 15 | | Hospital 2 | 5 | 7 | 10 | | Unit_costs_of_inputs | =Model!$B$10:$C$10 |
| 8 | Hospital 3 | 7 | 12 | | Hospital 3 | 4 | 9 | 13 | | Unit_prices_of_outputs | =Model!$F$10:$H$10 |
| 9 | | | | | | | | | | | |
| 10 | Unit costs of inputs | 0.000 | 0.071 | | Unit prices of outputs | 0.0857 | 0.0571 | 0.000 | | | |
| 11 | | | | | | | | | | | |
| 12 | Constraints that input costs must cover output values | | | | | | | | | | |
| 13 | Hospital | Input costs | | Output values | | | | | | | |
| 14 | 1 | 1.000 | >= | 1.000 | | | | | | | |
| 15 | 2 | 1.071 | >= | 0.829 | | | | | | | |
| 16 | 3 | 0.857 | >= | 0.857 | | | | | | | |
| 17 | | | | | | | | | | | |
| 18 | Constraint that selected hospital's input cost must equal a nominal value of 1 | | | | | | | | | | |
| 19 | Selected hospital input cost | 1.000 | = | 1 | | | | | | | |
| 20 | | | | | | | | | | | |
| 21 | Maximize selected hospital's output value (to see if it is 1, hence efficient) | | | | | | | | | | |
| 22 | Selected hospital output value | 1.000 | | | | | | | | | |

**❶ Input given data and name ranges.** Enter the input and output information for each hospital in the ranges B6:C8 and F6:H8 and name the various ranges as indicated.

**❷ Selected hospital.** Enter **1**, **2**, or **3** in cell B3, depending on which hospital you want to analyze.

**❸ Unit input costs and output prices.** Enter *any* trial values for the input costs and output prices in the Unit_costs_of_inputs and Unit_prices_of_outputs ranges.

**❹ Total input costs and output values.** In the Input_costs range, calculate the cost of the inputs used by each hospital. To do this, enter the formula

**=SUMPRODUCT(Unit_costs_of_inputs,B6:C6)**

in cell B14 for hospital 1, and copy this to the rest of the Input_costs range for the other hospitals. Similarly, calculate the output values by entering the formula

**=SUMPRODUCT(Unit_prices_of_outputs,F6:H6)**

in cell D14 and copying it to the rest of the Output_values range. Note that even though we are focusing on hospital 1's efficiency, we still calculate input costs and output values for the other hospitals so that we have something to compare hospital 1 to.

**❺ Total input cost and output value for the selected hospital.** In row 19, constrain the total input cost of the *selected* hospital to be 1 by entering the formula

**=VLOOKUP(Selected_hospital,A14:B16,2)**

in cell B19, and enter a **1** in cell D19. Similarly, enter the formula

**=VLOOKUP(Selected_hospital,A14:D16,4)**

in cell B22. (Make sure you understand how these VLOOKUP functions work.) Remember that because the selected hospital's input cost is constrained to be 1, its output value in cell B22 is automatically its efficiency.

# USING SOLVER TO DETERMINE WHETHER HOSPITAL 1 IS EFFICIENT

To determine whether hospital 1 is efficient, use Solver as follows. (When you are finished, the Solver dialog box should appear as shown in Figure 4.40.)

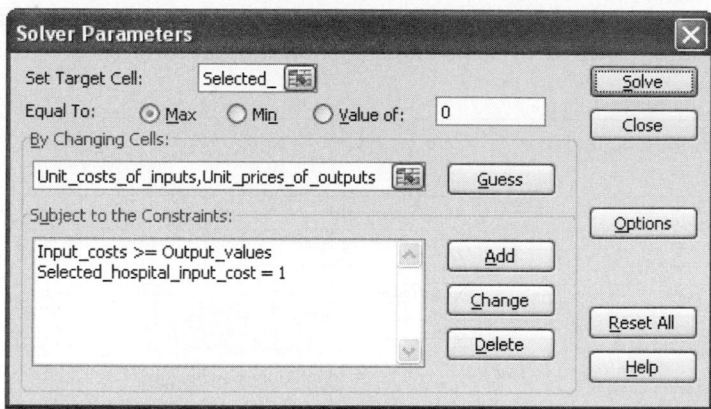

**1** **Objective.** Select cell B22 as the target cell to maximize. Because the cost of hospital 1 inputs is constrained to be 1, this causes Solver to maximize the efficiency of hospital 1.

**2** **Changing cells.** Choose the Unit_costs_of_inputs and Unit_prices_of_outputs ranges as the changing cells.

**3** **Selected hospital's input cost constraint.** Add the constraint Selected_hospital_input_cost=1. This sets the total value of hospital 1's inputs equal to 1.

**4** **Efficiency constraint.** Add the constraint Input_costs>=Output_values. This ensures that no hospital is more than 100% efficient.

**5** **Specify nonnegativity and optimize.** Under Solver Options, check the Assume Linear Model and Assume Non-Negative options and then solve to obtain the optimal solution shown in Figure 4.39.

The 1 in cell B22 of this solution means that hospital 1 *is* efficient. In words, Solver has found a set of unit costs for the inputs and the unit prices for the outputs such that the total value of hospital 1's outputs equals the total cost of its inputs.

---

**Figure 4.41** DEA Model for Hospital 2

| | A | B | C | D | E | F | G | H | I | J | K |
|---|---|---|---|---|---|---|---|---|---|---|---|
| 1 | DEA model for checking efficiency of a selected hospital | | | | | | | | | Range names used | |
| 2 | | | | | | | | | | Input_costs | =Model!$B$14:$B$16 |
| 3 | Selected hospital | 2 | | | | | | | | Output_values | =Model!$D$14:$D$16 |
| 4 | | | | | | | | | | Selected_hospital | =Model!$B$3 |
| 5 | Inputs used | Input 1 | Input 2 | | Outputs produced | Output 1 | Output 2 | Output 3 | | Selected_hospital_input_cost | =Model!$B$19 |
| 6 | Hospital 1 | 5 | 14 | | Hospital 1 | 9 | 4 | 16 | | Selected_hospital_output_value | =Model!$B$22 |
| 7 | Hospital 2 | 8 | 15 | | Hospital 2 | 5 | 7 | 10 | | Unit_costs_of_inputs | =Model!$B$10:$C$10 |
| 8 | Hospital 3 | 7 | 12 | | Hospital 3 | 4 | 9 | 13 | | Unit_prices_of_outputs | =Model!$F$10:$H$10 |
| 9 | | | | | | | | | | | |
| 10 | Unit costs of inputs | 0.000 | 0.067 | | Unit prices of outputs | 0.0800 | 0.0533 | 0.000 | | | |
| 11 | | | | | | | | | | | |
| 12 | Constraints that input costs must cover output values | | | | | | | | | | |
| 13 | Hospital | Input costs | | Output values | | | | | | | |
| 14 | 1 | 0.933 | >= | 0.933 | | | | | | | |
| 15 | 2 | 1.000 | >= | 0.773 | | | | | | | |
| 16 | 3 | 0.800 | >= | 0.800 | | | | | | | |
| 17 | | | | | | | | | | | |
| 18 | Constraint that selected hospital's input cost must equal a nominal value of 1 | | | | | | | | | | |
| 19 | Selected hospital input cost | 1.000 | = | 1 | | | | | | | |
| 20 | | | | | | | | | | | |
| 21 | Maximize selected hospital's output value (to see if it is 1, hence efficient) | | | | | | | | | | |
| 22 | Selected hospital output value | 0.773 | | | | | | | | | |

## Determining Whether Hospitals 2 and 3 Are Efficient

To determine whether hospital 2 is efficient, we simply replace the value in cell B3 by 2 and rerun Solver. The Solver settings do not need to be modified. (In fact, for your convenience, a button is included on the spreadsheet that runs a macro to run Solver.) The optimal solution appears in Figure 4.41. From the value of 0.773 in cell B22, we can see that hospital 2 is *not* efficient. Similarly, we can determine that hospital 3 *is* efficient by replacing the value in cell B3 by 3 and rerunning Solver (see Figure 4.42).

---

**Figure 4.42** DEA Model for Hospital 3

| | A | B | C | D | E | F | G | H | I | J | K |
|---|---|---|---|---|---|---|---|---|---|---|---|
| 1 | DEA model for checking efficiency of a selected hospital | | | | | | | | | Range names used | |
| 2 | | | | | | | | | | Input_costs | =Model!$B$14:$B$16 |
| 3 | Selected hospital | 3 | | | | | | | | Output_values | =Model!$D$14:$D$16 |
| 4 | | | | | | | | | | Selected_hospital | =Model!$B$3 |
| 5 | Inputs used | Input 1 | Input 2 | | Outputs produced | Output 1 | Output 2 | Output 3 | | Selected_hospital_input_cost | =Model!$B$19 |
| 6 | Hospital 1 | 5 | 14 | | Hospital 1 | 9 | 4 | 16 | | Selected_hospital_output_value | =Model!$B$22 |
| 7 | Hospital 2 | 8 | 15 | | Hospital 2 | 5 | 7 | 10 | | Unit_costs_of_inputs | =Model!$B$10:$C$10 |
| 8 | Hospital 3 | 7 | 12 | | Hospital 3 | 4 | 9 | 13 | | Unit_prices_of_outputs | =Model!$F$10:$H$10 |
| 9 | | | | | | | | | | | |
| 10 | Unit costs of inputs | 0.000 | 0.083 | | Unit prices of outputs | 0.1000 | 0.0667 | 0.000 | | | |
| 11 | | | | | | | | | | | |
| 12 | Constraints that input costs must cover output values | | | | | | | | | | |
| 13 | | Hospital | Input costs | | Output values | | | | | | |
| 14 | | 1 | 1.167 | >= | 1.167 | | | | | | |
| 15 | | 2 | 1.250 | >= | 0.967 | | | | | | |
| 16 | | 3 | 1.000 | >= | 1.000 | | | | | | |
| 17 | | | | | | | | | | | |
| 18 | Constraint that selected hospital's input cost must equal a nominal value of 1 | | | | | | | | | | |
| 19 | Selected hospital input cost | 1.000 | = | 1 | | | | | | | |
| 20 | | | | | | | | | | | |
| 21 | Maximize selected hospital's output value (to see if it is 1, hence efficient) | | | | | | | | | | |
| 22 | Selected hospital output value | 1.000 | | | | | | | | | |

In summary, we have found that hospitals 1 and 3 are efficient, but hospital 2 is inefficient.

### What Does It Mean to Be Efficient or Inefficient?

This idea of efficiency or inefficiency might still be a mystery, so let's consider it further. A hospital is efficient if the inputs and outputs can be priced in such a way that this hospital gets out all of the value that it puts in. The pricing scheme depends on the hospital. Each hospital tries to price inputs and outputs to put its operations in the best possible light. In the example, hospital 1 attaches 0 prices to input 1 (hospital beds) and output 3 (patient-days for patients over 65), and it attaches positive prices to the rest. This makes hospital 1 look efficient. Hospital 3, which is also efficient, also attaches 0 prices to input 1 and output 3, but its prices for the others are somewhat different from hospital 1's prices.

If DEA finds that a hospital is inefficient, then there is no pricing scheme where that hospital can recover its entire input costs in output values. Actually, it can be shown that if a hospital is inefficient, then a "combination" of the efficient hospitals can be found that uses no more inputs than the inefficient hospital, yet produces at least as much of each output as the inefficient hospital. In this sense, the hospital is inefficient.

To see how this combination can be found, consider the spreadsheet model in Figure 4.43. Begin by entering any positive weights in the Weights range. For any such weights (they don't even need to sum to 1), consider the combination hospital as a fraction of hospital 1 and another fraction of hospital 3. For example, with the weights shown, the combination hospital uses about 26% of the inputs and produces about 26% of the outputs of hospital 1, and it uses about 66% of the inputs and produces about 66% of the outputs of hospital 3. When they are combined in row 6 with the SUMPRODUCT function [for example, the formula in cell D6 is **=SUMPRODUCT(Weights,D4:D5)**], we find the quantities of inputs this combination hospital uses and the quantities of outputs it produces. To find weights where the combination hospital is better than hospital 2, we find any *feasible* solution to the inequalities indicated in rows 6 to 8 by using the Solver setup in Figure 4.44. (The weights in Figure 4.43 do the job.) Note that there is no objective to maximize or minimize; all we want is a solution that satisfies the constraints. Furthermore, we know there is a feasible solution because we have already identified hospital 2 as being inefficient.

**Figure 4.43**

Illustrating How Hospital 2 Is Inefficient

|  | A | B | C | D | E | F | G | H | I |
|---|---|---|---|---|---|---|---|---|---|
| 1 | Comparing combination of hospitals 1 and 3 to inefficient hospital 2 | | | | | | | | |
| 2 | | | | | | | | | |
| 3 | | Weights | | Input 1 | Input 2 | | Output 1 | Output 2 | Output 3 |
| 4 | Hospital 1 | 0.2615 | | 5 | 14 | | 9 | 4 | 16 |
| 5 | Hospital 2 | 0.6615 | | 7 | 12 | | 4 | 9 | 13 |
| 6 | Combination | | | 5.938 | 11.6 | | 5 | 7 | 12.785 |
| 7 | | | | <= | <= | | >= | >= | >= |
| 8 | Hospital 2 | | | 8 | 15 | | 5 | 7 | 10 |

**Figure 4.44**

Solver Setup for Finding an Inefficiency

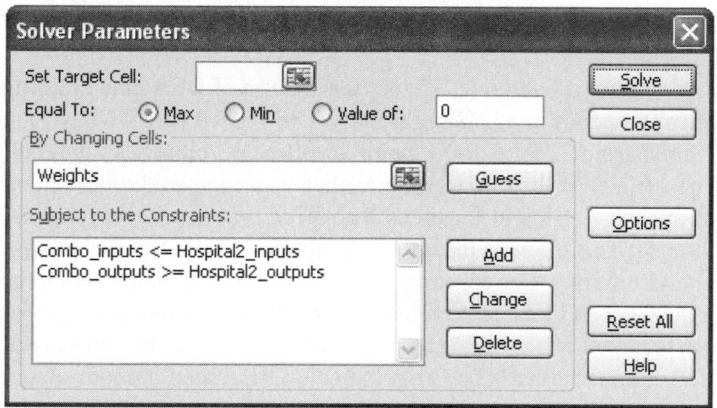

In reality, after DEA analysis identifies an organizational unit as being inefficient, this unit should consider benchmarking itself relative to the competition to see where it can make more efficient use of its inputs. ■

# MODELING ISSUES

1. The ratio (*input i* cost)/(*input j* cost) can be interpreted as the marginal rate of substitution (at the optimal solution) of input $i$ for input $j$. That is, the same level of outputs can be maintained if we decrease the use of input $i$ by a small amount $\Delta$ and increase the use of input $j$ by [(input $i$ cost)/(input $j$ cost)]$\Delta$. For example, for hospital 2, (input 2 cost/input 1 cost) = 6700. This implies that if the use of input 2 decreases by a small amount $\Delta$, hospital 2 can maintain its current output levels if the usage of input 1 increases by 6700$\Delta$.

2. The ratio *(output i* price)/(output *j* price) can be interpreted as the marginal rate of substitution (at the optimal solution) of output $i$ for output $j$. That is, the same level of input usage can be maintained if we decrease the production of output $i$ by a small amount $\Delta$ and increase the production of output $j$ by [(output $i$ price)/(output $j$ price)]$\Delta$. For example, for hospital 2, (output 2 price)/(output 1 price) = 0.67. This implies that if the use of output 2 decreases by a small amount $\Delta$, hospital 2 can maintain its current resource usage if the production of output 1 increases by 0.67$\Delta$. ■

## DEA for Evaluating School Bus Transportation

Sexton et al. (1994) used DEA to evaluate the efficiency of school bus transportation for the counties of North Carolina. For each county, they used two inputs: buses used and total operating expense. They used a single output: pupils transported per day. However, they noted a problem with "traditional" DEA. Consider two counties (county 1 and county 2) that use exactly the same inputs and produce the same outputs. Suppose that county 1 is very sparsely populated and county 2 is densely populated. Clearly, county 1 is transporting pupils more efficiently than county 2, but a DEA conducted by the method described will not show this. Realizing this, Sexton et al. developed a method to adjust the output of county 2 downward and the output of county 1 upward to compensate for this problem. The North Carolina Department of Education penalized the inefficient counties by reducing their budgetary appropriations. Since the time DEA was performed, most counties have greatly increased their efficiency.

## DEA in the Banking Industry

Sherman and Ladino (1995) discuss the use of DEA in identifying the most and least efficient branches in a banking firm with 33 branch banks. They found efficiency ratings that varied from 37% to 100%, with 23 of the 33 branches rated below 100% and 10 below 70%. Each of the inefficient branches was compared to a reference set of "best-practice" branches—efficient branches that offered the same types of services as the inefficient branch. This allowed them to make specific suggestions as to how the inefficient branches could improve. For example, they showed that branch 1 should be able to provide its current level and mix of services with 4.5 fewer customer-service personnel, 1.8 fewer sales service personnel, 0.3 fewer managers, $222,928 less in operating expenses, and 1304 fewer square feet. They also indicated the added amount of service that the inefficient branches could provide, in addition to resource savings, if these branches could become as efficient as the best-practice branches. For example, branch 1 could handle (per year) about 15,000 additional deposits, withdrawals, and checks cashed; 2000 added bank checks, bonds, and travelers' checks; and 8 additional night deposits, while reducing the resources needed if it attained the efficiency level of the best-practice branches. See the May–June 1999 issue of *Interfaces* for more applications of DEA in the banking industry. ■

# PROBLEMS

## Skill-Building Problems

**41.** The Salem Board of Education wants to evaluate the efficiency of the town's four elementary schools. The three outputs of the schools are
- output 1 = average reading score
- output 2 = average mathematics score
- output 3 = average self-esteem score

The three inputs to the schools are
- input 1 = average educational level of mothers (defined by highest grade completed: 12 = high school graduate; 16 = college graduate, and so on)

- input 2 = number of parent visits to school (per child)
- input 3 = teacher-to-student ratio

The relevant information for the four schools is given in the file **P04_41.xlsx**. Determine which (if any) schools are inefficient.

**42.** Pine Valley Bank has three branches. You have been asked to evaluate the efficiency of each. The following inputs and outputs are to be used for the study:
- input 1 = labor hours used (hundreds per month)
- input 2 = space used (in hundreds of square feet)

- input 3 = supplies used per month (in dollars)
- output 1 = loan applications per month
- output 2 = deposits processed per month (in thousands)
- output 3 = checks processed per month (in thousands)

The relevant information is given in the file **P04_42.xlsx**. Use these data to determine whether any bank branches are inefficient.

43. You have been asked to evaluate the efficiency of the Port Charles Police Department. Three precincts are to be evaluated. The inputs and outputs for each precinct are as follows:
- input 1 = number of policemen
- input 2 = number of vehicles used
- output 1 = number of patrol units responding to service requests (thousands per year)
- output 2 = number of convictions obtained each year (in hundreds)

You are given the data in the file **P04_43.xlsx**. Use this information to determine which precincts, if any, are inefficient.

44. You have been commissioned by Indiana University to evaluate the relative efficiency of four degree-granting units: Business, Education, Arts and Sciences, and Health, Physical Education, and Recreation (HPER). You are given the information in the file **P04_44.xlsx**. Use DEA to identify all inefficient units.

---

# 4.9 CONCLUSION

In this chapter, we have developed LP spreadsheet models of many diverse situations. Although there is no standard procedure that can be used to attack all problems, there are several keys to most spreadsheet optimization models:

- Determine the changing cells, the cells that contain the values of the decision variables. These cells should contain the values the decision maker has direct control over, and they should determine all other outputs, either directly or indirectly. For example, in blending models, the changing cells should contain the amount of each input used to produce each output; in employee scheduling models, the changing cells should contain the number of employees who work each possible five-day shift.

- Set up the spreadsheet so that you can easily compute what you want to maximize or minimize (usually profit or cost). For example, in the aggregate planning model, a good way to compute total cost is to compute the monthly cost of operation in each row.

- Set up the spreadsheet so that the relationships between the cells in the spreadsheet and the problem constraints are readily apparent. For example, in the post office scheduling example, it is convenient to calculate the number of employees working each day of the week near the number of employees needed for each day of the week.

- Make your spreadsheet readable. Use descriptive labels, use range names liberally, use cell comments and text boxes for explanations, and think about your model layout before you dive in. This might not be too important for small, straightforward models, but it is crucial for large, complex models. Just remember that *other* people are likely to be examining your spreadsheet models.

- LP models tend to fall into categories, but they are definitely not all alike. For example, a problem might involve a combination of the ideas discussed in the workforce scheduling, blending, and production process examples of this chapter. Each new model presents new challenges, and you must be flexible and imaginative to meet these challenges. It takes practice and perseverance.

## Summary of Key Management Science Terms

| Term | Explanation | Page |
|------|-------------|------|
| Dual-objective model | Model with two competing objectives; usual strategy is to constrain one of them and optimize the other | 137 |
| Integer constraints | Constraints that limit (some) changing cells to integer values | 140 |
| Multiple optimal solutions | Case where several solutions have the same optimal value of the objective | 147 |
| Heuristic | An "educated guess" solution, not guaranteed to be optimal but usually quick and easy to obtain | 148 |
| Nonsmooth problems | Nonlinear models with "sharp edges" or discontinuities that make them difficult to solve | 156 |
| DEA (Data Envelopment Analysis) | Method for determining whether organizational units are efficient in terms of using their inputs to produce their outputs | 184 |

## Summary of Key Excel Terms

| Term | Explanation | Excel | Page |
|------|-------------|-------|------|
| Range name shortcut | Quick way to create range names, using labels in adjacent cells | Use Create from Selection on Formulas ribbon | 135 |
| Solver integer constraints | Constraints on changing cells forcing them to be integers | Specify in Add Constraint dialog box with Solver | 140 |
| Row, column sums shortcut | Quick way of getting row and/or column sums from a table | Highlight row under table and column to right of table, click on $\Sigma$ buttom | 153 |
| Nonsmooth functions with Solver | Avoid use of functions such as IF, MIN, MAX, and ABS in Solver models; Solver can't handle them predictably. | | 156 |
| TRANSPOSE function | Useful function for transferring column range to row range, or vice versa | Highlight result range, type **=TRANSPOSE(*range*)**, press Ctrl+Shift+Enter | 170 |
| Array functions | Excel functions such as TRANSPOSE that fill a whole range at once | Highlight result range, type formula, press Ctrl+Shift+Enter | 170 |

## PROBLEMS

### Skill-Building Problems

45. During each 4-hour period, the Smalltown police force requires the following number of on-duty police officers: eight from midnight to 4 A.M.; seven from 4 A.M. to 8 A.M.; six from 8 A.M. to noon; six from noon to 4 P.M.; five from 4 P.M. to 8 P.M.; and four from 8 P.M. to midnight. Each police officer works two consecutive four-hour shifts.

a. Determine how to minimize the number of police officers needed to meet Smalltown's daily requirements.
b. Use SolverTable to see how the number of police officers changes as the number of officers needed from midnight to 4 A.M. changes.

46. A bus company believes that it will need the following numbers of bus drivers during each of the next 5 years: 60 drivers in year 1; 70 drivers in year 2;

50 drivers in year 3; 65 drivers in year 4; 75 drivers in year 5. At the beginning of each year, the bus company must decide how many drivers to hire or fire. It costs $4000 to hire a driver and $2000 to fire a driver. A driver's salary is $10,000 per year. At the beginning of year 1, the company has 50 drivers. A driver hired at the beginning of a year can be used to meet the current year's requirements and is paid full salary for the current year.

    **a.** Determine how to minimize the bus company's salary, hiring, and firing costs over the next 5 years.

    **b.** Use SolverTable to determine how the total number hired, total number fired, and total cost change as the unit hiring and firing costs *each* increase by the same percentage.

**47.** Shoemakers of America forecasts the following demand for the next 6 months: 5000 pairs in month 1; 6000 pairs in month 2; 5000 pairs in month 3; 9000 pairs in month 4; 6000 pairs in month 5; 5000 pairs in month 6. It takes a shoemaker 15 minutes to produce a pair of shoes. Each shoemaker works 150 hours per month plus up to 40 hours per month of overtime. A shoemaker is paid a regular salary of $2000 per month plus $50 per hour for overtime. At the beginning of each month, Shoemakers can either hire or fire workers. It costs the company $1500 to hire a worker and $1900 to fire a worker. The monthly holding cost per pair of shoes is 3% of the cost of producing a pair of shoes with regular-time labor. The raw materials in a pair of shoes cost $10. At the beginning of month 1, Shoemakers has 13 workers. Determine how to minimize the cost of meeting (on time) the demands of the next 6 months.

**48.** NewAge Pharmaceuticals produces the drug NasaMist from four chemicals. Today, the company must produce 1000 pounds of the drug. The three active ingredients in NasaMist are A, B, and C. By weight, at least 8% of NasaMist must consist of A, at least 4% of B, and at least 2% of C. The cost per pound of each chemical and the amount of each active ingredient in 1 pound of each chemical are given in the file **P04_48.xlsx**. At least 100 pounds of chemical 2 must be used.

    **a.** Determine the cheapest way of producing today's batch of NasaMist.

    **b.** Use SolverTable to see how much the percentage of requirement of A is really costing NewAge. Let the percentage required vary from 6% to 12%.

**49.** You have decided to enter the candy business. You are considering producing two types of candies: Slugger candy and Easy Out candy, both of which consist solely of sugar, nuts, and chocolate. At present, you have in stock 10,000 ounces of sugar, 2000 ounces of nuts, and 3000 ounces of chocolate. The mixture used to make Easy Out candy must contain at least 20%

nuts. The mixture used to make Slugger candy must contain at least 10% nuts and 10% chocolate. Each ounce of Easy Out candy can be sold for $0.50, and each ounce of Slugger candy for $0.40.

    **a.** Determine how you can maximize your revenue from candy sales.

    **b.** Use SolverTable to determine how changes in the price of Easy Out change the optimal solution.

    **c.** Use SolverTable to determine how changes in the amount of available sugar change the optimal solution.

**50.** Sunblessed Juice Company sells bags of oranges and cartons of orange juice. Sunblessed grades oranges on a scale of 1 (poor) to 10 (excellent). At present, Sunblessed has 100,000 pounds of grade 9 oranges and 120,000 pounds of grade 6 oranges on hand. The average quality of oranges sold in bags must be at least 7, and the average quality of the oranges used to produce orange juice must be at least 8. Each pound of oranges that is used for juice yields a revenue of $1.50 and incurs a variable cost (consisting of labor costs, variable overhead costs, inventory costs, and so on) of $1.05. Each pound of oranges sold in bags yields a revenue of $1.50 and incurs a variable cost of $0.70.

    **a.** Determine how Sunblessed can maximize its profit.

    **b.** Use SolverTable to determine how a change in the cost per bag of oranges changes the optimal solution.

    **c.** Use SolverTable to determine how a change in the amount of grade 9 oranges available affects the optimal solution.

    **d.** Use SolverTable to determine how a change in the required average quality required for juice changes the optimal solution.

**51.** A bank is attempting to determine where its assets should be invested during the current year. At present, $500,000 is available for investment in bonds, home loans, auto loans, and personal loans. The annual rates of return on each type of investment are known to be the following: bonds, 10%; home loans, 16%; auto loans, 13%; personal loans, 20%. To ensure that the bank's portfolio is not too risky, the bank's investment manager has placed the following three restrictions on the bank's portfolio:

    ■ The amount invested in personal loans cannot exceed the amount invested in bonds.

    ■ The amount invested in home loans cannot exceed the amount invested in auto loans.

    ■ No more than 25% of the total amount invested can be in personal loans.

Help the bank maximize the annual return on its investment portfolio.

**52.** Young MBA Erica Cudahy can invest up to $15,000 in stocks and loans. Each dollar invested in stocks yields

$0.10 profit, and each dollar invested in a loan yields $0.15 profit. At least 30% of all money invested must be in stocks, and at least $6000 must be in loans. Determine how Erica can maximize the profit earned on her investments.

**53.** Bullco blends silicon and nitrogen to produce two types of fertilizers. Fertilizer 1 must be at least 40% nitrogen and sells for $70 per pound. Fertilizer 2 must be at least 70% silicon and sells for $40 per pound. Bullco can purchase up to 8000 pounds of nitrogen at $15 per pound and up to 10,000 pounds of silicon at $10 per pound.

   **a.** Assuming that all fertilizer produced can be sold, determine how Bullco can maximize its profit.

   **b.** Use SolverTable to explore the effect on profit of changing the minimum percentage of nitrogen required in fertilizer 1.

   **c.** Suppose the availabilities of nitrogen and silicon both increase by the same percentage from their current values. Use SolverTable to explore the effect of this change on profit.

**54.** Eli Daisy uses chemicals 1 and 2 to produce two drugs. Drug 1 must be at least 70% chemical 1, and drug 2 must be at least 60% chemical 2. Up to 4000 ounces of drug 1 can be sold at $6 per ounce; up to 3000 ounces of drug 2 can be sold at $5 per ounce. Up to 4500 ounces of chemical 1 can be purchased at $6 per ounce, and up to 4000 ounces of chemical 2 can be purchased at $4 per ounce. Determine how to maximize Daisy's profit.

**55.** Hiland's TV-Radio Store must determine how many TVs and radios to keep in stock. A TV requires 10 square feet of floor space, whereas a radio requires 4 square feet; 5000 square feet of floor space is available. A TV sale results in an $80 profit, and a radio earns a profit of $20. The store stocks only TVs and radios. Marketing requirements dictate that at least 60% of all appliances in stock be radios. Finally, a TV ties up $200 in capital, and a radio $50. Hiland wants to have at most $60,000 worth of capital tied up at any time.

   **a.** Determine how to maximize Hiland's profit.

   **b.** Use SolverTable to explore how much profit the minimum percentage of radio requirement is costing Hiland's.

   **c.** Use SolverTable to explore how much profit the upper limit on capital being tied up is costing Hiland's.

**56.** Many Wall Street firms use LP models to select a desirable bond portfolio. The following is a simplified version of such a model. Solodrex is considering investing in four bonds; $1 million is available for investment. The expected annual return, the worst-case annual return on each bond, and the "duration" of each bond are given in the file **P04_56.xlsx**. (The

duration of a bond is a measure of the bond's sensitivity to interest rates.) Solodrex wants to maximize the expected return from its bond investments, subject to three constraints:

   ■ The worst-case return of the bond portfolio must be at least 8%.

   ■ The average duration of the portfolio must be at most 6. For example, a portfolio that invests $600,000 in bond 1 and $400,000 in bond 4 has an average duration of $[600,000(3) + 400,000(9)]/1,000,000 = 5.4$.

   ■ Because of diversification requirements, at most 40% of the total amount invested can be invested in a single bond.

Determine how Solodrex can maximize the expected return on its investment.

**57.** Coalco produces coal at three mines and ships it to four customers. The cost per ton of producing coal, the ash and sulfur content (per ton) of the coal, and the production capacity (in tons) for each mine are given in the file **P04_57.xlsx**. The number of tons of coal demanded by each customer and the cost (in dollars) of shipping a ton of coal from a mine to each customer are also provided in this same file. The amount of coal shipped to each customer must contain at most 6% ash and at most 3.5% sulfur. Show Coalco how to minimize the cost of meeting customer demands.

**58.** Furnco manufactures tables and chairs. A table requires 40 board feet of wood, and a chair requires 30 board feet of wood. Wood can be purchased at a cost of $1 per board foot, and 40,000 board feet of wood are available for purchase. It takes 2 hours of skilled labor to manufacture an unfinished table or an unfinished chair. Three more hours of skilled labor will turn an unfinished table into a finished table, and 2 more hours of skilled labor will turn an unfinished chair into a finished chair. A total of 6000 hours of skilled labor is available (and have already been paid for). All furniture produced can be sold at the following unit prices: an unfinished table, $70; a finished table, $140; an unfinished chair, $60; a finished chair, $110.

   **a.** Determine how to maximize Furnco's profit from manufacturing tables and chairs.

   **b.** Use a two-way SolverTable to see how the numbers of unfinished products (both chairs and tables) sold depend on the selling prices of these unfinished products. Of course, neither unfinished selling price should be as large as the corresponding finished selling price.

**59.** A company produces three products, A, B, and C, and can sell these products in unlimited quantities at the following unit prices: A, $10; B, $56; C, $100. Producing a unit of A requires 1 hour of labor; a unit of B, 2 hours of labor plus 2 units of A; and a unit of C, 3 hours of labor plus 1 unit of B. Any A that is used to produce B cannot be sold. Similarly, any B that is used to produce C cannot be sold. A total of 40 hours of labor is available. Determine how to maximize the company's revenue.

60. Abotte Products produces three products, A, B, and C. The company can sell up to 300 pounds of each product at the following prices (per pound): product A, $10; product B, $12; product C, $20. Abotte purchases raw material at $5 per pound. Each pound of raw material can be used to produce either 1 pound of A or 1 pound of B. For a cost of $3 per pound processed, product A can be converted to 0.6 pound of product B and 0.4 pound of product C. For a cost of $2 per pound processed, product B can be converted to 0.8 pound of product C. Determine how Abotte can maximize its profit.

61. Moneyco has $100,000 to invest at time 1 (the beginning of year 1). The cash flows associated with the five available investments are listed in the file **P04_61.xlsx**. For example, every dollar invested in A in year 1 yields $1.40 in year 4. In addition to these investments, Moneyco can invest as much money each year as it wants in CDs, which pay 6% interest. The company wants to maximize its available cash in year 4. Assuming it can put no more than $50,000 in any investment, develop an LP model to help Moneyco achieve its goal.

62. At the beginning of year 1, you have $10,000. Investments A and B are available; their cash flows are shown in the file **P04_62.xlsx**. Assume that any money not invested in A or B earns interest at an annual rate of 8%.
    a. Determine how to maximize your cash on hand in year 4.
    b. Use SolverTable to determine how a change in the year 3 yield for investment A changes the optimal solution to the problem.
    c. Use SolverTable to determine how a change in the yield of investment B changes the optimal solution to the problem.

63. You now have $10,000, and the following investment plans are available to you during the next three years:
    - **Investment A:** Every dollar invested now yields $0.10 a year from now and $1.30 three years from now.
    - **Investment B:** Every dollar invested now yields $0.20 a year from now and $1.10 two years from now.
    - **Investment C:** Every dollar invested a year from now yields $1.50 three years from now.

    During each year, you can place uninvested cash in money market funds that yield 6% interest per year. However, you can invest at most $5000 in any one of

plans A, B, or C. Determine how to maximize your cash on hand three years from now.

64. Sunco processes oil into aviation fuel and heating oil. It costs $65,000 to purchase each 1000 barrels of oil, which is then distilled and yields 500 barrels of aviation fuel and 500 barrels of heating oil. Output from the distillation can be sold directly or processed in the catalytic cracker. If sold after distillation without further processing, aviation fuel sells for $80,000 per 1000 barrels, and heating oil sells for $65,000 per 1000 barrels. It takes 1 hour to process 1000 barrels of aviation fuel in the catalytic cracker, and these 1000 barrels can be sold for $145,000. It takes 45 minutes to process 1000 barrels of heating oil in the cracker, and these 1000 barrels can be sold for $125,000. Each day at most 20,000 barrels of oil can be purchased, and 8 hours of cracker time are available. Determine how to maximize Sunco's profit.

65. All steel manufactured by Steelco must meet the following requirements: between 3.2% and 3.5% carbon; between 1.8% and 2.5% silicon; between 0.9% and 1.2% nickel; tensile strength of at least 45,000 pounds per square inch (psi). Steelco manufactures steel by combining two alloys. The cost and properties of each alloy are given in the file **P04_69.xlsx**. Assume that the tensile strength of a mixture of the two alloys can be determined by averaging the tensile strength of the alloys that are mixed together. For example, a 1 ton mixture that is 40% alloy 1 and 60% alloy 2 has a tensile strength of 0.4(42,000) + 0.6(50,000). Determine how to minimize the cost of producing a ton of steel.

66. Steelco manufactures two types of steel at three different steel mills. During a given month, each steel mill has 200 hours of blast furnace time available. Because of differences in the furnaces at each mill, the time and cost to produce a ton of steel differ for each mill, as listed in the file **P04_66.xlsx**. Each month, Steelco must manufacture at least 500 tons of steel 1 and 600 tons of steel 2. Determine how Steelco can minimize the cost of manufacturing the desired steel.

67. Based on Heady and Egbert (1964). Walnut Orchard has two farms that grow wheat and corn. Because of differing soil conditions, there are differences in the yields and costs of growing crops on the two farms. The yields and costs are listed in the file **P04_67.xlsx**. Each farm has 100 acres available for cultivation; 11,000 bushels of wheat and 7000 bushels of corn must be grown.
    a. Determine a planting plan that will minimize the cost of meeting these requirements.
    b. Use SolverTable to see how the total cost changes if the requirements for wheat and corn both change by the *same* percentage, where this percentage change can be as low as −50% or as high as +50%.

**68.** Candy Kane Cosmetics (CKC) produces Leslie Perfume, which requires chemicals and labor. Two production processes are available. Process 1 transforms 1 unit of labor and 2 units of chemicals into 3 ounces of perfume. Process 2 transforms 2 units of labor and 3 units of chemicals into 5 ounces of perfume. It costs CKC $3 to purchase a unit of labor and $2 to purchase a unit of chemicals. Each year up to 20,000 units of labor and 35,000 units of chemicals can be purchased. In the absence of advertising, CKC believes it can sell 1000 ounces of perfume. To stimulate demand for Leslie, CKC can hire the lovely model Jenny Nelson. Jenny is paid $100 per hour. Each hour Jenny works for the company is estimated to increase the demand for Leslie Perfume by 200 ounces. Each ounce of Leslie Perfume sells for $5. Determine how CKC can maximize its profit.

**69.** Sunco Oil has refineries in Los Angeles and Chicago. The Los Angeles refinery can refine up to 2 million barrels of oil per year, and the Chicago refinery up to 3 million. After the oil is refined, it's shipped to two distribution points, Houston and New York City. Sunco estimates that each distribution point can sell up to 5 million barrels per year. Because of differences in shipping and refining costs, the profit earned (in dollars) per million barrels of oil shipped depends on where the oil was refined and on the point of distribution. This information is listed in the file **P04_65.xlsx**. Sunco is considering expanding the capacity of each refinery. Each million barrels of annual refining capacity that is added will cost $120,000 for the Los Angeles refinery and $150,000 for the Chicago refinery. Determine how Sunco can maximize its profit (including expansion costs) over a 10-year period.

**70.** Feedco produces two types of cattle feed, both consisting totally of wheat and alfalfa. Feed 1 must contain at least 80% wheat, and feed 2 must contain at least 60% alfalfa. Feed 1 sells for $1.50 per pound, and feed 2 sells for $1.30 per pound. Feedco can purchase up to 1000 pounds of wheat at $0.50 per pound and up to 800 pounds of alfalfa at $0.40 per pound. Demand for each type of feed is unlimited. Determine how to maximize Feedco's profit.

**71.** Carrington Oil produces gas 1 and gas 2 from two types of crude oil: crude 1 and crude 2. Gas 1 is allowed to contain up to 4% impurities, and gas 2 is allowed to contain up to 3% impurities. Gas 1 sells for $72 per barrel, whereas gas 2 sells for $84 per barrel. Up to 4200 barrels of gas 1 and up to 4300 barrels of gas 2 can be sold. The cost per barrel of each crude, their availability, and the level of impurities in each crude are listed in the file **P04_71.xlsx**. Before blending the crude oil into gas, any amount of each crude can be "purified" for a cost

of $3.50 per barrel. Purification eliminates half of the impurities in the crude oil.
   **a.** Determine how to maximize profit.
   **b.** Use SolverTable to determine how an increase in the availability of crude 1 affects the optimal profit.
   **c.** Use SolverTable to determine how an increase in the availability of crude 2 affects the optimal profit.
   **d.** Use SolverTable to determine how a change in the price of gas 2 changes the optimal profit and the types of gas produced.

**72.** A company produces two products: A and B. Product A sells for $11 per unit and product B sells for $23 per unit. Producing a unit of product A requires 2 hours on assembly line 1 and 1 unit of raw material. Producing a unit of product B requires 2 units of raw material, 1 unit of A, and 2 hours on assembly line 2. On line 1, 1300 hours of time are available, and 500 hours are available on line 2. A unit of raw material can be bought (for $5 a unit) or produced (at no cost) by using 2 hours of time on line 1.
   **a.** Determine how to maximize profit.
   **b.** The company will stop buying raw material when the price of raw material exceeds what value? (Use SolverTable.)

**73.** Based on Thomas (1971). Toyco produces toys at two plants and sells in three regions. The current demands at these regions are given in the file **P04_73.xlsx**. Each plant can produce up to 2500 units. Each toy sells for $10, and the cost of producing and shipping a toy from a given plant to a region is also given in the file **P04_73.xlsx**. Toyco can advertise locally and nationally. Each $1 spent on a local ad raises sales in a region by 0.5 units, whereas each $1 spent advertising nationally increases sales in each region by 0.3 units.
   **a.** Determine how Toyco can maximize its profit.
   **b.** If sales stimulated by advertising exhibits diminishing returns, how would you change your model?

**74.** A bank needs exactly two employees working each hour from 9 A.M. to 5 P.M. Workers can work the shifts and are paid the wages listed in the file **P04_74.xlsx**. For example, a worker working 9 A.M. to 2 P.M. is paid $42.00. Find an assignment of workers that provides enough workers at minimum cost.

**75.** Based on Gatalla and Oearce (1974). Northwest Airlines has determined that it needs the number of ticket agents during each hour of the day, as listed in the file **P04_75.xlsx**. Workers work nine-hour shifts, one hour of which is for lunch. The lunch hour can be either the fourth or fifth hour of their shift. What is the minimum number of workers needed by Northwest?

**76.** A rock company uses five types of rocks to fill four orders. The phosphate content, availability of each type of rock, and the production cost per pound for each rock are listed in the file **P04_76.xlsx**, as well as the size of each order and the minimum and maximum phosphate percentage in each order. What is the cheapest way to fill the orders?

77. Autoco produces cars. Demand during each of the next 12 months is forecasted to be 945, 791, 364, 725, 268, 132, 160, 304, 989, 293, 279, and 794. Other relevant information is as follows:
   - Workers are paid $5000 per month.
   - It costs $500 to hold a car in inventory for a month. The holding cost is based on each month's ending inventory.
   - It costs $4000 to hire a worker.
   - It costs $20,000 to fire a worker.
   - Each worker can make up to 8 cars a month.
   - Workers are hired and fired at beginning of each month.
   - At the beginning of month 1 there are 500 cars in inventory and 60 workers.

   How can the company minimize the cost of meeting demand for cars on time?

78. Oilco produces gasoline from five inputs. The cost, density, viscosity, and sulfur content, and the number of barrels available of each input are listed in the file **P04_78.xlsx**. Gasoline sells for $72 per barrel. Gasoline can have a density of at most 0.98 units per barrel, a viscosity of at most 37 units per barrel, and a sulfur content of at most 3.7 units per barrel.
   a. How can Oilco maximize its profit?
   b. Describe how the optimal solution to the problem changes as the price of gasoline ranges from $65 to $80 per barrel.

79. The HiTech company produces DVD players. Estimated demand for the next 4 quarters is 5000; 10,000; 8000; and 2000. At the beginning of quarter 1, HiTech has 60 workers. It costs $2000 to hire a worker and $4000 to fire a worker. Workers are paid $10,000 per quarter plus $80 for each unit they make during overtime. A new hire can make up to 60 units per quarter during regular-time, whereas a previously hired worker can make up to 90 units per quarter. Any worker can make up to 20 units per quarter during overtime. Each DVD player is sold for $160. It costs $20 to hold a DVD player in inventory for a quarter. Assume workers are hired and fired at the beginning of each quarter and that all of a quarter's production is available to meet demand for that quarter. Initial inventory at the beginning of quarter 1 is 1000 DVD players. How can the company maximize its profit? Assume that demand is lost if insufficient stock is available. That is, there is no backlogging of demand (and there is no requirement that HiTech must satisfy all of its demand).

## Skill-Extending Problems

80. MusicTech manufactures and sells a portable music device called an mTune (similar to an iPod). At beginning of month 1, the company has $70,000 and 6 employees. Each machine the company owns has the capacity to make up to 900 mTunes per month, and each worker can make up to 600 mTunes per month. The company cannot use more labor or machine capacity than is available in any given month. Also, the company wants to have a nonnegative cash balance at all points in time. The company's costs are the following:
   - Holding cost of $2 each month per mTune in ending inventory
   - Cost in month 1 of buying machines ($3000 per machine)
   - Raw material cost of $6 per mTune
   - Monthly worker wage of $3500
   - Hiring cost of $4000 per worker
   - Firing cost of $2000 per worker

   In the absence of advertising, the monthly demands in months 1 through 6 are forecasted to be 5000, 8000, 7000, 4000, 5000, and 6000. However, MusicTech can increase demand each month by advertising. Every $10 (up to a maximum of $10,000 per month) spent on advertising during a month increases demand for that month by 1 mTune. The devices are sold for $25 each. The sequence of events in any month is that the company buys machines (month 1 only), hires and fires workers, makes the mTunes, advertises, pays all costs for the month, and collects revenues for the month. Develop a model to maximize profit (total revenue minus total costs) earned during the next 6 months.

81. Assume we want to take out a $300,000 loan on a 20-year mortgage with end-of-month payments. The annual rate of interest is 6%. Twenty years from now, we need to make a $40,000 ending balloon payment. Because we expect our income to increase, we want to structure the loan so at the beginning of each year, our monthly payments increase by 2%.
   a. Determine the amount of each year's monthly payment. You should use a lookup table to look up each year's monthly payment and to look up the year based on the month (e.g., month 13 is year 2, etc.).
   b. Suppose payment each month is to be same, and there is no balloon payment. Show that the monthly payment you can calculate from your spreadsheet matches the value given by the Excel PMT function PMT(0.06/12,240,−300000,0,0).

82. A graduated payment mortgage (GPM) enables the borrower to have lower payments earlier in the mortgage and increases payments later on. The

assumption is the borrower's income will increase over time so that it will be easier for the borrower to meet all payments. Suppose we borrow $60,000 on a 30-year monthly mortgage. We obtain a GPM where monthly payments increase 7.5% per year through year 5 and then remain constant from year 5 through year 30. For annual interest rates of 10%, 11%, 12%, 13%, and 14%, use Solver to find the amount of each year's monthly payment.

83. Suppose you are planning for retirement. At the beginning of this year and each of the next 39 years, you plan to contribute some money to your retirement fund. Each year, you plan to increase your retirement contribution by $500. When you retire in 40 years, you plan to withdraw $100,000 at the beginning of each year for the next 20 years. You assume the following about the yields of your retirement investment portfolio:

- During the first 20 years, your investments will earn 10% per year.
- During all other years, your investments will earn 5% per year.

All contributions and withdrawals occur at the beginnings of the respective years.

a. Given these assumptions, what is the least amount of money you can contribute this year and still have enough to make your retirement withdrawals?

b. How does your answer change if inflation is 2% per year and your goal is to withdraw $100,000 per year (in today's dollars) for 20 years?

84. Based on Brahms and Taylor (1999). Eli Lilly and Pfizer are going to merge. Merger negotiations must settle the following issues:

- What will the name of the merged corporation be?
- Will corporate headquarters be in Indianapolis (Lilly wants this) or New York (Pfizer wants this)?
- Which company's chairperson will be chairperson of the merged corporation?
- Which company gets to choose the CEO?
- On issue of layoffs, what percentage of each company's view will prevail?

Brahms developed a remarkably simple method for the two adversaries to settle their differences. (This same method could be used to settle differences between other adversaries, such as a husband and wife in a divorce, Arab and Israel in Middle East, and so on.) Each adversary allocates 100 points between all of the issues. These allocations are listed in the file **P04_84.xlsx**. For example, Lilly believes headquarters is worth 25 points, whereas Pfizer thinks headquarters is only worth 10 points. Layoffs may be divided (for example, Lilly might get 70% of the say in layoffs and Pfizer 30%), but on all other issues, only one company gets its way. The **adjusted winner procedure** says that the "best" way to make decisions on each issue is to:

- Give each adversary the same number of points.
- Ensure that each company prefers its allocation to the allocation of its opponent.
- Maximize the number of points received by either participant.

Such a solution is equitable (because each party receives the same number of points) and is envy-free (because neither side prefers what its opponent receives to what it receives). It can also be shown that the adjusted winner procedure yields a Pareto optimal solution. This means that no other allocation can make one player better off without making the other player worse off. Find the adjusted winner solution to the merger example. Also show that the adjusted winner solution for this example is Pareto optimal.

85. AdminaStar processes Medicare claims. At the beginning of month 1 they have a backlog of 40,000 difficult claims and 60,000 easy claims. The predicted claim volume for months 1 through 8 is listed in the file **P04_85.xlsx**. At the beginning of month 1, AdminaStar has 70 experienced claim processors. Each month it can hire up to 10 trainees. At the end of each month, 5% of experienced employees quit, and 20% of trainees are fired. Each worker is available for 160 hours per month. The number of minutes needed by each worker to process each type of claim is also listed in the file **P04_85.xlsx**. AdminaStar wants ending inventory for months 2 through 7 to be no greater than 50,000 of each type of claim. All claims must be processed by the end of month 8. What is the minimum number of trainees that need to be hired during months 1 to 8? (*Note:* Trainees must be integers. Experienced workers will probably end up being fractional, but don't worry about this.)

86. Based on Charnes and Cooper (1955). A small company is trying to determine employee salary based on following attributes: effectiveness, responsibility, initiative, experience, education, self expression, planning ability, intelligence, and the ability to get things done. Each of the company's seven executives has been rated on each of these attributes, with the ratings shown in the file **P04_86.xlsx**. The company wants to set each executive's salary by multiplying a weight for each attribute by the executive's score on each attribute. The salaries must satisfy the following constraints:

- The salary of a lower-numbered executive must be at least as large as the salary of a higher-numbered executive.
- Executive 1's salary can be at most $160,000 and executive 7's salary must be at least $40,000.
- The salaries of executives 1, 5, and 7 should match $160,000, $100,000, and $40,000, respectively, as closely as possible.
- All attribute weights must be nonnegative.

Develop a method for setting salaries. [*Hint*: For executives 1, 5, and 7, define over and under changing cells and add a constraint such as Executive 5 salary + (Amount executive 5 salary under $100,000) − (Amount executive 5 salary over $100,000) = $100,000. Then the target cell to minimize is the sum of over and under changing cells for positions 1, 5, and 7. If you did not include the over and under changing cells, why would your model fail to be linear?]

87. During the next 4 quarters, Dorian Auto must meet (on time) the following demands for cars: 4000 in quarter 1; 2000 in quarter 2; 5000 in quarter 3; 1000 in quarter 4. At the beginning of quarter 1, there are 300 autos in stock. The company has the capacity to produce at most 3000 cars per quarter. At the beginning of each quarter, the company can change production capacity. It costs $100 to increase quarterly production capacity by one unit. For example, it would cost $10,000 to increase capacity from 3000 to 3100. It also costs $50 per quarter to maintain each unit of production capacity (even if it is unused during the current quarter). The variable cost of producing a car is $2000. A holding cost of $150 per car is assessed against each quarter's ending inventory. At the end of quarter 4, plant capacity must be at least 4000 cars.
    a. Determine how to minimize the total cost incurred during the next 4 quarters.
    b. Use SolverTable to determine how much the total cost increases as the required capacity at the end of quarter 4 increases (from its current value of 4000).

88. The Internal Revenue Service (IRS) has determined that during each of the next 12 months it will need the numbers of supercomputers given in the file **P04_88.xlsx**. To meet these requirements, the IRS rents supercomputers for a period of 1, 2, or 3 months. It costs $1000 to rent a supercomputer for 1 month, $1800 for 2 months, and $2500 for 3 months. At the beginning of month 1, the IRS has no supercomputers.
    a. Determine the rental plan that meets the requirements for the next 12 months at minimum cost. You can assume that fractional rentals are allowed. Thus, if your solution says to rent 140.6 computers for one month, you can round this up to 141 or down to 140 without much effect on the total cost.
    b. Suppose the monthly requirement increases anywhere from 10% to 50% each month. (Assume that whatever the percentage increase is, it is the *same* each month.) Use SolverTable to see whether the total rental cost increases by this same percentage.

89. You own a wheat warehouse with a capacity of 20,000 bushels. At the beginning of month 1, you have 6000 bushels of wheat. Each month, wheat can be bought and sold at the prices per 1000 bushels listed in the file

**P04_89.xlsx**. The sequence of events during each month is as follows:
- You observe your initial stock of wheat.
- You can sell any amount of wheat up to your initial stock at the current month's selling price.
- You can buy as much wheat as you want, subject to the limitation of warehouse size.
    a. Determine how to maximize the profit earned over the next 10 months.
    b. Use SolverTable to determine how a change in the capacity of the warehouse affects the optimal solution.
    c. Use SolverTable to determine how simultaneous changes in the buying and selling price for month 6 affect the optimal solution.

90. You can calculate the risk index of an investment by taking the absolute values of percentage changes in the value of the investment for each year and averaging them. Suppose you are trying to determine what percentage of your money you should invest in T-bills, gold, and stocks. The file **P04_90.xlsx** lists the annual returns (percentage changes in value) for these investments for the years 1968 through 1988. Let the risk index of a portfolio be the weighted average of the risk indices of these investments, where the weights are the fractions of the portfolio assigned to the investments. Suppose that the amount of each investment must be between 20% and 50% of the total invested. You would like the risk index of your portfolio to equal 0.15, and your goal is to maximize the expected return on your portfolio. Determine the maximum expected return on your portfolio, subject to the stated constraints. Use the average return earned by each investment during the years 1968 to 1988 as your estimate of expected return.

91. Based on Magoulas and Marinos-Kouris (1988). Oilco produces two products: regular and premium gasoline. Each product contains 0.15 gram of lead per liter. The two products are produced from these six inputs: reformate, fluid catalytic cracker gasoline (FCG), isomerate (ISO), polymer (POL), Methyl Tertiary Butyl Ether (MTBE), and butane (BUT). Each input has four attributes: research octane number (RON), Reid Vapor Pressure (RVP), ASTM volatility at 70 degrees Celsius, and ASTM volatility at 130 degrees Celsius. (ASTM is the American Society for Testing and Materials.) The attributes and daily availability (in liters) of each input are listed in the file **P04_91.xlsx**. The requirements for each output are also listed in this file. The daily demand (in thousands of liters) for each product must be met, but more can be produced if desired. The RON and ASTM requirements are minimums; the RVP requirement is a maximum. Regular gasoline sells for $0.754 per liter; premium gasoline for $0.819. Before each product is ready for sale, 0.15 gram per liter of lead must be

removed. The cost of removing 0.1 gram per liter is $0.213. At most, 38% of each type of gasoline can consist of FCG. How can Oilco maximize its daily profit?

92. Capsule Drugs manufactures two drugs: 1 and 2. The drugs are produced by blending two chemicals: 1 and 2. By weight, drug 1 must contain at least 65% chemical 1, and drug 2 must contain at least 55% chemical 1. Drug 1 sells for $6 per ounce, and drug 2 sells for $4 per ounce. Chemicals 1 and 2 can be produced by one of two production processes. Running process 1 for an hour requires 7 ounces of raw material and 2 hours skilled labor, and it yields 3 ounces of each chemical. Running process 2 for an hour requires 5 ounces of raw material and 3 hours of skilled labor, and it yields 3 ounces of chemical 1 and 1 ounce of chemical 2. A total of 120 hours of skilled labor and 100 ounces of raw material are available. Determine how to maximize Capsule's sales revenues.

93. Molecular Products produces 3 chemicals: B, C, and D. The company begins by purchasing chemical A for a cost of $6 per 100 liters. For an additional cost of $3 and the use of 3 hours of skilled labor, 100 liters of A can be transformed into 40 liters of C and 60 liters of B. Chemical C can either be sold or processed further. It costs $1 and 1 hour of skilled labor to process 100 liters of C into 60 liters of D and 40 liters of B. For each chemical, the selling price per 100 liters and the maximum amount (in 100s of liters) tha can be sold are listed in the file **P04_93.xlsx**. A maximum of 200 labor hours is available. Determine how Molecular can maximize its profit.

94. Bexter Labs produces three products: A, B, and C. Bexter can sell up to 3000 units of product A, up to 2000 units of product B, and up to 2000 units of product C. Each unit of product C uses 2 units of A and 3 units of B and incurs $5 in processing costs. Products A and B are produced from either raw material 1 or raw material 2. It costs $6 to purchase and process 1 unit of raw material 1. Each processed unit of raw material 1 yields 2 units of A and 3 units of B. It costs $3 to purchase and process a unit of raw material 2. Each processed unit of raw material 2 yields 1 unit of A and 2 units of B. The unit prices for the products are A, $5; B, $4; C, $25. The quality levels of each product are: A, 8; B, 7; C, 6. The average quality level of the units sold must be at least 7. Determine how to maximize Bexter's profit.

95. Mondo Motorcycles is determining its production schedule for the next 4 quarters. Demands for motorcycles are forecasted to be 400 in quarter 1; 700 in quarter 2; 500 in quarter 3; 200 in quarter 4. Mondo incurs four types of costs, as described here:
   - It costs Mondo $800 to manufacture each motorcycle.

- At the end of each quarter, a holding cost of $100 per motorcycle left in inventory is incurred.
- When production is increased from one quarter to the next, a cost is incurred, primarily for training employees. If the increase in production is $x$ motorcycles, the cost is $700x$.
- When production is decreased from one quarter to the next, a cost is incurred, primarily for severance pay and decreased morale. If the decrease in production is $x$ motorcycles, the cost is $600x$.

All demands must be met on time, and a quarter's production can be used to meet demand for the current quarter (as well as future quarters). During the quarter immediately preceding quarter 1, 500 Mondos were produced. Assume that at the beginning of quarter 1, no Mondos are in inventory.
   a. Determine how to minimize Mondo's total cost during the next 4 quarters.
   b. Use SolverTable to determine how Mondo's optimal production schedule would be affected by a change in the cost of increasing production from one quarter to the next.
   c. Use SolverTable to determine how Mondo's optimal production schedule would be affected by a change in the cost of decreasing production from one quarter to the next.

96. Carco has a $1,500,000 advertising budget. To increase its automobile sales, the firm is considering advertising in newspapers and on television. The more Carco uses a particular medium, the less effective each additional ad is. The file **P04_96.xlsx** lists the number of new customers reached by each ad. Each newspaper ad costs $1000, and each television ad costs $10,000. At most, 30 newspaper ads and 15 television ads can be placed. How can Carco maximize the number of new customers created by advertising?

97. Broker Sonya Wong is currently trying to maximize her profit in the bond market. Four bonds are available for purchase and sale at the bid and ask prices shown in the file **P04_97.xlsx**. Sonya can buy up to 1000 units of each bond at the ask price or sell up to 1000 units of each bond at the bid price. During each of the next 3 years, the person who sells a bond will pay the owner of the bond the cash payments listed in the file **P04_97.xlsx**. Sonya's goal is to maximize her revenue from selling bonds minus her payment for buying bonds, subject to the constraint that after each year's payments are received, her current cash position (due only to cash payments from bonds and not purchases or sales of bonds) is nonnegative. Note that her current cash position can depend on past coupons and that cash accumulated at the end of each year earns 5.25% annual interest. Determine how to maximize net profit from buying and selling bonds, subject to the constraints previously described. Why do you think

we limit the number of units of each bond that can be bought or sold?

**98.** Pear produces low-budget cars. Each car is sold for $7900. The raw material in a car costs $5000. Labor time and robot time are needed to produce cars. A worker can do the needed labor on, at most, 100 cars per month; a robot can complete the needed work on, at most, 200 cars per month. Initially, Pear has 4 workers. Each worker receives a monthly salary of $6000. It costs $2500 to hire a worker and $1000 to fire a worker. Hired workers are fully productive during the month they are hired. Robots must be bought at the beginning of month 1 at a cost of $15,000 per robot. The (assumed known) demand for cars is listed in the file **P04_98.xlsx**. At the end of each month, Pear incurs a holding cost of $200 per car. How can Pear maximize the profit earned during the next 6 months?

**99.** The ZapCon Company is considering investing in three projects. If it fully invests in a project, the realized cash flows (in millions of dollars) will be as listed in the file **P04_99.xlsx**. For example, project 1 requires a cash outflow of $3 million today and returns $5.5 million 3 years from now. Today ZapCon has $2 million in cash. At each time point (0, 0.5, 1, 1.5, 2, and 2.5 years from today), the company can, if desired, borrow up to $2 million at 3.5% (per 6 months) interest. Leftover cash earns 3% (per 6 months) interest. For example, if after borrowing and investing at time 0, ZapCon has $1 million, it would receive $30,000 in interest at time 0.5 year. The company's goal is to maximize cash on hand after cash flows 3 years from now are accounted for. What investment and borrowing strategy should it use? Assume that the company can invest in a fraction of a project. For example, if it invests in 0.5 of project 3, it has, for example, cash outflows of –$1 million at times 0 and 0.5.

**100.** You are a CFA (chartered financial analyst). An overextended client has come to you because she needs help paying off her credit card bills. She owes the amounts on her credit cards listed in the file **P04_100.xlsx**. The client is willing to allocate up to $5000 per month to pay off these credit cards. All cards must be paid off within 36 months. The client's goal is to minimize the total of all her payments. To solve this problem, you must understand how interest on a loan works. To illustrate, suppose the client pays $5000 on Saks during month 1. Then her Saks balance at the beginning of month 2 is $20,000 − [$5000 − 0.005(20,000)]. This follows because she incurs 0.005(20,000) in interest charges on her Saks card during month 1. Help the client solve her problem. After you have solved this problem, give an intuitive explanation of the solution found by Solver.

**101.** Aluminaca produces 100-foot-long, 200-foot-long, and 300-foot-long ingots for customers. This week's demand for ingots is listed in the file **P04_101.xlsx**. Aluminaca has four furnaces in which ingots can be produced. During 1 week, each furnace can be operated for 50 hours. Because ingots are produced by cutting up long strips of aluminum, longer ingots take less time to produce than shorter ingots. If a furnace is devoted completely to producing one type of ingot, the number it can produce in 1 week is listed in the file **P04_101.xlsx**. For example, furnace 1 could produce 350 300-foot ingots per week. The material in an ingot costs $10 per foot. A customer who wants a 100-foot or 200-foot ingot will accept an ingot of that length or longer. How can Aluminaca minimize the material costs incurred in meeting required weekly demands?

**102.** Each day, Eastinghouse produces capacitors during three shifts: 8 A.M. to 4 P.M., 4 P.M. to 12 A.M., and 12 A.M. to 8 A.M. The hourly salary paid to the employees on each shift, the price charged for each capacitor made during each shift, and the number of defects in each capacitor produced during a given shift are listed in the file **P04_102.xlsx**. The company can employ up to 25 workers, and each worker can be assigned to one of the three shifts. A worker produces 10 capacitors during a shift, but due to machinery limitations, no more than 10 workers can be assigned to any shift. Each capacitor produced can be sold, but the average number of defects per capacitor for the day's production cannot exceed 3. Determine how Eastinghouse can maximize its daily profit.

**103.** During the next 3 months, Airco must meet (on time) the following demands for air conditioners: month 1, 300; month 2, 400; month 3, 500. Air conditioners can be produced in either New York or Los Angeles. It takes 1.5 hours of skilled labor to produce an air conditioner in Los Angeles, and it takes 2 hours in New York. It costs $400 to produce an air conditioner in Los Angeles, and it costs $350 in New York. During each month, each city has 420 hours of skilled labor available. It costs $100 to hold an air conditioner in inventory for a month. At the beginning of month 1, Airco has 200 air conditioners in stock. Determine how Airco can minimize the cost of meeting air conditioner demands for the next 3 months.

**104.** Gotham City National Bank is open Monday through Friday from 9 A.M. to 5 P.M. From past experience, the bank knows that it needs the numbers of tellers listed in the file **P04_104.xlsx**. Gotham City Bank hires two types of tellers. Full-time tellers work 9 A.M. to 5 P.M. five days a week, with one hour off each day for lunch. The bank determines when a full-time employee takes his or her lunch hour, but each teller must go between 12 P.M. and 1 P.M. or between 1 P.M. and 2 P.M. Full-time employees are paid (including fringe benefits) $8 per hour, which includes payment for lunch hour. The bank can also hire part-time tellers. Each part-time teller must work exactly three consecutive hours each day. A part-time teller is paid $5 per hour and receives no fringe benefits. To maintain adequate quality of service, the bank has decided that, at most, five part-time tellers can be hired. Determine how to meet the bank's teller requirements at minimum cost.

105. Based on Rothstein (1973). The Springfield City Police Department employs 30 police officers. Each officer works 5 days per week. The crime rate fluctuates with the day of the week, so the number of police officers required each day depends on the day of the week, as follows: Saturday, 28; Sunday, 18; Monday, 18; Tuesday, 24; Wednesday, 25; Thursday, 16; Friday, 21. The police department wants to schedule police officers to minimize the number whose days off are *not* consecutive. Determine how to accomplish this goal.

106. Based on Charnes and Cooper (1955). Alex Cornby makes his living buying and selling corn. On January 1, he has 500 tons of corn and $10,000. On the first day of each month, Alex can buy corn at the following prices per ton: January, $300; February, $350; March, $400; April, $500. On the last day of each month, Alex can sell corn at the following prices per ton: January, $250; February, $400; March, $350; April, $550. Alex stores his corn in a warehouse that can hold 1000 tons of corn. He must be able to pay cash for all corn at the time of purchase. Determine how Alex can maximize his cash on hand at the end of April.

107. City 1 produces 500 tons of waste per day, and city 2 produces 400 tons of waste per day. Waste must be incinerated at incinerator 1 or 2, and each incinerator can process up to 500 tons of waste per day. The cost to incinerate waste is $40 per ton at incinerator 1 and $30 per ton at incinerator 2. Incineration reduces each ton of waste to 0.2 ton of debris, which must be dumped at one of two landfills. Each landfill can receive at most 200 tons of debris per day. It costs $3 per mile to transport a ton of material (either debris or waste). Distances (in miles) between locations are listed in the file **P04_107.xlsx**. Determine how to minimize the total cost of disposing of the waste from both cities.

108. Based on Smith (1965). Silicon Valley Corporation (Silvco) manufactures transistors. An important aspect of the manufacture of transistors is the melting of the element germanium (a major component of a transistor) in a furnace. Unfortunately, the melting process yields germanium of highly variable quality.

Two methods can be used to melt germanium. Method 1 costs $50 per transistor, and method 2 costs $70 per transistor. The qualities of germanium obtained by methods 1 and 2 are listed in the file **P04_108.xlsx**. Silvco can refire melted germanium in an attempt to improve its quality. It costs $25 to refire the melted germanium for one transistor. The results of the refiring process are also listed in the file **P04_108.xlsx**. For example, if grade 3 germanium is refired, half of the resulting germanium will be grade 3, and the other half will be grade 4. Silvco has sufficient furnace capacity to melt or refire germanium for at most 20,000 transistors per month. Silvco's monthly demands are for 1000 grade 4 transistors, 2000 grade 3 transistors, 3000 grade 2 transistors, and 3000 grade 1 transistors. Determine how to minimize the cost of producing the needed transistors.

109. The Wild Turkey Company produces two types of turkey cutlets for sale to fast-food restaurants. Each type of cutlet consists of white meat and dark meat. Cutlet 1 sells for $4 per pound and must consist of at least 70% white meat. Cutlet 2 sells for $3 per pound and must consist of at least 60% white meat. At most, 5000 pounds of cutlet 1 and 3000 pounds of cutlet 2 can be sold. The two types of turkey used to manufacture the cutlets are purchased from the Gobble-Gobble Turkey Farm. Each type 1 turkey costs $10 and yields 5 pounds of white meat and 2 pounds of dark meat. Each type 2 turkey costs $8 and yields 3 pounds of white meat and 3 pounds of dark meat. Determine how to maximize Wild Turkey's profit.

110. The production line employees at Grummins Engine work 4 days a week, 10 hours a day. Each day of the week, the following minimum numbers of line employees are needed: Monday through Friday, 70 employees; Saturday and Sunday, 30 employees. Grummins employs 110 line employees. Determine how to maximize the number of consecutive days off received by these employees. For example, a worker who gets Sunday, Monday, and Wednesday off receives 2 consecutive days off.

111. Based on Lanzenauer et al. (1987). To process income tax forms, the IRS first sends each form through the data preparation (DP) department, where information is coded for computer entry. Then the form is sent to data entry (DE), where it is entered into the computer. During the next 3 weeks, the following quantities of forms will arrive: week 1, 40,000; week 2, 30,000; week 3, 60,000. All employees work 40 hours per week and are paid $500 per week. Data preparation of a form requires 15 minutes, and data entry of a form requires 10 minutes. Each week, an employee is assigned to either data entry or data preparation. The IRS must complete processing all forms by the end of week 5 and wants

to minimize the cost of accomplishing this goal. Assume that all workers are full-time employees and that the IRS will have the same number of employees each week. Assume that all employees are capable of performing data preparation and data entry. Determine how many workers should be working and how the workers should allocate their hours during the next 5 weeks.

112. Based on Robichek et al. (1965). The Korvair Department Store has $100,000 in available cash. At the beginning of each of the next 6 months, Korvair will receive revenues and pay bills as listed in the file **P04_112.xlsx**. It is clear that Korvair will have a short-term cash flow problem until the store receives revenues from the Christmas shopping season. To solve this problem, Korvair must borrow money. At the beginning of July, the company takes out a 6-month loan. Any money borrowed for a 6-month period must be paid back at the end of December along with 9% interest (early payback does not reduce the total interest of the loan). Korvair can also meet cash needs through month-to-month borrowing. Any money borrowed for a 1-month period incurs an interest cost of 4% per month. Determine how Korvair can minimize the cost of paying its bills on time.

113. Mackk Engine produces diesel trucks. New government emission standards have dictated that the average pollution emissions of all trucks produced in the next 3 years cannot exceed 10 grams per truck. Mackk produces 2 types of trucks. Each type 1 truck sells for $20,000, costs $15,000 to manufacture, and emits 15 grams of pollution. Each type 2 truck sells for $17,000, costs $14,000 to manufacture, and emits 5 grams of pollution. Production capacity limits total truck production during each year to at most 320 trucks. The maximum numbers of each truck type that can be sold during each of the next 3 years are listed in the file **P04_113.xlsx**. Demand can be met from previous production or the current year's production. It costs $2000 to hold 1 truck (of any type) in inventory for 1 year. Determine how Mackk can maximize its profit during the next 3 years.

114. Each hour from 10 A.M. to 7 P.M., Bank One receives checks and must process them. Its goal is to process all checks the same day they are received. The bank has 13 check processing machines, each of which can process up to 500 checks per hour. It takes one worker to operate each machine. Bank One hires both full-time and part-time workers. Full-time workers work 10 A.M. to 6 P.M., 11 A.M. to 7 P.M., or 12 P.M. to 8 P.M. and are paid $160 per day. Part-time workers work either 2 P.M. to 7 P.M. or 3 P.M. to 8 P.M. and are paid $75 per day. The numbers of checks received each hour are listed in the file **P04_114.xlsx**. In the interest of maintaining continuity, Bank One believes that it must have at least 3 full-time workers

under contract. Develop a work schedule that processes all checks by 8 P.M. and minimizes daily labor costs.

115. Owens-Wheat uses 2 production lines to produce 3 types of fiberglass mat. The demand requirements (in tons) for each of the next 4 months are shown in the file **P04_115.xlsx**. If it were dedicated entirely to the production of one product, a line 1 machine could produce either 20 tons of type 1 mat or 30 tons of type 2 mat during a month. Similarly, a line 2 machine could produce either 25 tons of type 2 mat or 28 tons of type 3 mat. It costs $5000 per month to operate a machine on line 1 and $5500 per month to operate a machine on line 2. A cost of $2000 is incurred each time a new machine is purchased, and a cost of $1000 is incurred if a machine is retired from service. At the end of each month, Owens would like to have at least 50 tons of each product in inventory. At the beginning of month 1, Owens has 5 machines on line 1 and 8 machines on line 2. Assume the per-ton cost of holding either product in inventory for 1 month is $5.
    a. Determine a minimum cost production schedule for the next 4 months.
    b. There is an important aspect of this situation that cannot be modeled by linear programming. What is it? (*Hint:* If Owens makes product 1 and product 2 on line 1 during a month, is this as efficient as making just product 1 on line 1?)

116. Rylon Corporation manufactures Brute cologne and Chanelle perfume. The raw material needed to manufacture each type of fragrance can be purchased for $60 per pound. Processing 1 pound of raw material requires 1 hour of laboratory time. Each pound of processed raw material yields 3 ounces of Regular Brute cologne and 4 ounces of Regular Chanelle perfume. Regular Brute can be sold for $140 per ounce and Regular Chanelle for $120 per ounce. Rylon also has the option of further processing Regular Brute and Regular Chanelle to produce Luxury Brute, sold at $360 per ounce, and Luxury Chanelle, sold at $280 per ounce. Each ounce of Regular Brute processed further requires an additional 3 hours of laboratory time and a $40 processing cost and yields 1 ounce of Luxury Brute. Each ounce of Regular Chanelle processed further requires an additional 2 hours of laboratory time and a $40 processing cost and yields 1 ounce of Luxury Chanelle. Each year, Rylon has 6000 hours of laboratory time available and can purchase up to 4000 pounds of raw material.
    a. Determine how Rylon can maximize its profit. Assume that the cost of the laboratory hours is a fixed cost (so that it can be ignored for this problem).
    b. Suppose that 1 pound of raw material can be used to produce either 3 ounces of Brute or 4 ounces of

Chanelle. How does your answer to part **a** change?

c. Use SolverTable to determine how a change in the price of Luxury Chanelle changes the optimal profit.

d. Use SolverTable to determine how simultaneous changes in lab time and raw material availability change the optimal profit.

e. Use SolverTable to determine how a change in the lab time required to process Luxury Brute changes the optimal profit.

117. Sunco Oil has three different processes that can be used to manufacture various types of gasoline. Each process involves blending oils in the company's catalytic cracker. Running process 1 for an hour costs $20 and requires 2 barrels of crude oil 1 and 3 barrels of crude oil 2. The output from running process 1 for an hour is 2 barrels of gas 1 and 1 barrel of gas 2. Running process 2 for an hour costs $30 and requires 1 barrel of crude 1 and 3 barrels of crude 2. The output from running process 2 for an hour is 3 barrels of gas 2. Running process 3 for an hour costs $14 and requires 2 barrels of crude 2 and 3 barrels of gas 2. The output from running process 3 for an hour is 2 barrels of gas 3. Each month, 4000 barrels of crude 1, at $45 per barrel, and 7000 barrels of crude 2, at $55 per barrel, can be purchased. All gas produced can be sold at the following per-barrel prices: gas 1, $85; gas 2, $90; gas 3, $95. Determine how to maximize Sunco's profit (revenues less costs). Assume that only 2500 hours of time on the catalytic cracker are available each month.

118. Flexco produces six products in the following manner. Each unit of raw material purchased yields 4 units of product 1, 2 units of product 2, and 1 unit of product 3. Up to 1200 units of product 1 can be sold, and up to 300 units of product 2 can be sold. Demand for products 3 and 4 is unlimited. Each unit of product 1 can be sold or processed further. Each unit of product 1 that is processed further yields 1 unit of product 4. Each unit of product 2 can be sold or processed further. Each unit of product 2 that is processed further yields 0.8 unit of product 5 and 0.3 unit of product 6.

Up to 1000 units of product 5 can be sold, and up to 800 units of product 6 can be sold. Up to 3000 units of raw material can be purchased at $6 per unit. Leftover units of products 5 and 6 must be destroyed. It costs $4 to destroy each leftover unit of product 5 and $3 to destroy each leftover unit of product 6. Ignoring raw material purchase costs, the unit price and production cost for each product are listed in the file **P04_118.xlsx**. Determine a profit-maximizing production schedule for Flexco.

119. Each week, Chemco can purchase unlimited quantities of raw material at $6 per pound. Each pound of purchased raw material can be used to produce either input 1 or input 2. Each pound of raw material can yield 2 ounces of input 1, requiring 2 hours of processing time and incurring $2 in processing costs. Each pound of raw material can yield 3 ounces of input 2, requiring 2 hours of processing time and incurring $4 in processing costs. Two production processes are available. It takes 2 hours to run process 1, requiring 2 ounces of input 1 and 1 ounce of input 2. It costs $1 to run process 1. Each time process 1 is run, 1 ounce of product A and 1 ounce of liquid waste are produced. Each time process 2 is run requires 3 hours of processing time, 2 ounces of input 2, and 1 ounce of input 1. Each process 2 run yields 1 ounce of product B and 0.8 ounce of liquid waste. Process 2 incurs $8 in costs. Chemco can dispose of liquid waste in the Port Charles River or use the waste to produce product C or product D. Government regulations limit the amount of waste Chemco is allowed to dump into the river to 1000 ounces per week.

Each ounce of product C costs $4 to produce and sells for $11. Producing 1 ounce of product C requires 1 hour of processing time, 2 ounces of input 1, and 0.8 ounce of liquid waste. Each ounce of product D costs $5 to produce and sells for $7. Producing 1 ounce of product D requires 1 hour of processing time, 2 ounces of input 2, and 1.2 ounces of liquid waste. At most, 5000 ounces of product A and 5000 ounces of product B can be sold each week, but weekly demand for products C and D is unlimited. Product A sells for $18 per ounce and product B sells for $24 per ounce. Each week, 6000 hours of processing time are available. Determine how Chemco can maximize its weekly profit.

120. Bexter Labs produces three products: A, B, and C. Bexter can sell up to 30 units of product A, up to 20 units of product B, and up to 20 units of product C. Each unit of product C uses 2 units of A and 3 units of B and incurs $5 in processing costs. Products A and B are produced from either raw material 1 or raw material 2. It costs $6 to purchase and process 1 unit of raw material 1. Each processed unit of raw material 1 yields 2 units of A and 3 units of B. It costs $3 to purchase and process a unit of raw material 2. Each processed unit of raw material 2 yields 1 unit of A and 2 units of B. The unit prices for the products are A, $5; B, $4; C, $25. The quality levels of each product are A, 8; B, 7; C, 6. The average quality level of the units sold must be at least 7. Determine how to maximize Bexter's profit.

121. Based on Franklin and Koenigsberg (1973). The city of Busville contains three school districts. The numbers of minority and nonminority students in each district are given in the file **P04_121.xlsx**. The local court has decided that each of the town's two high schools (Cooley High and Walt Whitman High)

must have approximately the same percentage of minority students (within 5%) as the entire town. The distances (in miles) between the school districts and the high schools are also given in the file **P04_121.xlsx**. Each high school must have an enrollment of 300 to 500 students. Determine an assignment of students to schools that minimizes the total distance students must travel to school.

122. Based on Carino and Lenoir (1988). Brady Corporation produces cabinets. Each week, Brady requires 90,000 cubic feet of processed lumber. The company can obtain lumber in two ways. First, it can purchase lumber from an outside supplier and then dry it at the Brady kiln. Second, Brady can chop down trees on its land, cut them into lumber at its sawmill, and then dry the lumber at its kiln. The company can purchase grade 1 or grade 2 lumber. Grade 1 lumber costs $3 per cubic foot and when dried yields 0.7 cubic foot of useful lumber. Grade 2 lumber costs $7 per cubic foot and when dried yields 0.9 cubic foot of useful lumber. It costs the company $3 to chop down a tree. After being cut and dried, a log yields 0.8 cubic feet of lumber. Brady incurs costs of $4 per cubic foot of lumber it dries. It costs $2.50 per cubic foot of logs sent through the sawmill. Each week, the sawmill can process up to 35,000 cubic feet of lumber. Each week, up to 40,000 cubic feet of grade 1 lumber and up to 60,000 cubic feet of grade 2 lumber can be purchased. Each week, 40 hours of time are available for drying lumber. The time it takes to dry 1 cubic foot of lumber is as follows: grade 1, 2 seconds; grade 2, 0.8 second; log, 1.3 seconds. Determine how Brady can minimize the weekly cost of meeting its demand for processed lumber.

123. Based on Dobson and Kalish (1988). Chandler Enterprises produces two competing products, A and B. The company wants to sell these products to two groups of customers, group 1 and group 2. The values each customer places on a unit of A and B are shown in the file **P04_123.xlsx**. Each customer will buy either product A or product B, but not both. A customer is willing to buy product A if she believes that the Premium of product A is greater than or equal to the Premium of product B and Premium of product A is greater than or equal to 0. Here, the "premium" of a product is its value minus its price. Similarly, a customer is willing to buy B if she believes the Premium of product B is greater than or equal to the Premium of product A and the Premium of product B is greater than or equal to 0. Group 1 has 1000 members, and group 2 has 1500 members. Chandler wants to set prices for each product to ensure that group 1 members purchase product A and group 2 members purchase product B. Determine how Chandler can maximize its revenue.

124. Based on Robichek et al. (1965). At the beginning of month 1, Finco has $400 in cash. At the beginning of months 1, 2, 3, and 4, Finco receives certain revenues, after which it pays bills. (See the file **P04_124.xlsx**.) Any money left over can be invested for 1 month at the interest rate of 0.1% per month; for 2 months at 0.5% per month; for 3 months at 1% per month; or for 4 months at 2% per month. Determine an investment strategy that maximizes cash on hand at the beginning of month 5.

125. During each 6-hour period of the day, the Bloomington Police Department needs at least the number of police officers shown in the file **P04_125.xlsx**. Police officers can be hired to work either 12 consecutive hours or 18 consecutive hours. Police officers are paid $4 per hour for each of the first 12 hours they work in a day and $6 per hour for each of the next 6 hours they work in a day. Determine how to minimize the cost of meeting Bloomington's daily police requirements.

126. Based on Glassey and Gupta (1978). A paper recycling plant processes box board, tissue paper, newsprint, and book paper into pulp that can be used to produce three grades of recycled paper (grades 1, 2, and 3). The prices per ton and the pulp contents of the four inputs are shown in the file **P04_126.xlsx**.

   Two methods, de-inking and asphalt dispersion, can be used to process the four inputs into pulp. It costs $20 to de-ink a ton of any input. The process of de-inking removes 10% of the input's pulp, leaving 90% of the original pulp. It costs $15 to apply asphalt dispersion to a ton of material. The asphalt dispersion process removes 20% of the input's pulp. At most, 3000 tons of input can be run through the asphalt dispersion process or the de-inking process. Grade 1 paper can be produced only with newsprint or book paper pulp; grade 2 paper only with book paper, tissue paper, or box board pulp; and grade 3 paper only with newsprint, tissue paper, or box board pulp. To meet its current demands, the company needs 500 tons of pulp for grade 1 paper, 500 tons of pulp for grade 2 paper, and 600 tons of pulp for grade 3 paper. Determine how to minimize the cost of meeting the demands for pulp.

127. At the beginning of month 1, GE Capital has 50 million accounts. Of these, 40 million are paid up (0-due), 4 million are 1 month overdue (1-due), 4 million are 2 months overdue (2-due), and 2 million are 3 months overdue (3-due). After an account is more than 3 months overdue, it's written off as a bad debt. For each overdue account, GE Capital can either phone the cardholder, send a letter, or do nothing. A letter requires an average of 0.05 hour of labor, whereas a phone call requires an average of 0.10 hour of labor. Each month 500,000 hours of labor are available. We assume that the average amount of a monthly payment is $30. Thus, if a 2-due account

remains 2-due, it means that 1 month's payment ($30) has been received, and if a 2-due account becomes 0-due, it means that 3 months' payments ($90) have been received. On the basis of thousands of accounts, DMMs (Delinquency Movement Matrices) shown in the file **P04_127.xlsx** have been estimated. For example, the top-left 0.60 entry in the first table means that 60% of all 1-due accounts that receive a letter become 0-due by the next month. The 0.10 and 0.30 values in this same row mean that 10% of all 1-due accounts remain 1-due after receiving a letter, and 30% of all 1-due accounts become 2-due after receiving a letter. Your goal is to determine how to allocate your workforce over the next 4 months to maximize the expected collection revenue received during that time. (*Note:* 0-due accounts are never contacted, which accounts for the lack of 0-due rows in the first two tables.)

128. It is February 15, 2006. Three bonds, as listed in the file **P04_128.xlsx**, are for sale. Each bond has a face value of $100. Every 6 months, starting 6 months from the current date and ending at the expiration date, each bond pays 0.5*(coupon rate)*(Face value). At the expiration date the face value is paid. For example, the second bond pays
- $2.75 on 8/15/06
- $102.75 on 2/15/07

Given the current price structure, the question is whether there is a way to make an infinite amount of money. To answer this, we look for an arbitrage. An arbitrage exists if there is a combination of bond sales and purchases today that yields
- a positive cash flow today
- nonnegative cash flows at all future dates

If such a strategy exists, then it is possible to make an infinite amount of money. For example, if buying 10 units of bond 1 today and selling 5 units of bond 2 today yielded, say, $1 today and nothing at all future dates, then we could make $k$ by purchasing 10$k$ units of bond 1 today and selling 5$k$ units of bond 2 today. We could also cover all payments at future dates from money received on those dates. Clearly, we expect that bond prices at any point in time will be set so that no arbitrage opportunities exist.

a. Show that an arbitrage opportunity exists for the bonds in the file **P04_128.xlsx**. (*Hint:* Set up an LP that maximizes today's cash flow subject to constraints that cash flow at each future date is nonnegative. You should get a "no convergence" message from Solver.)

b. Usually bonds are bought at an ask price and sold at a bid price. Consider the same three bonds as before and suppose the ask and bid prices are as listed in the same file. Show that these bond prices admit no arbitrage opportunities.

## Modeling Problems

129. You have been assigned to develop a model that can be used to schedule employees at a local fast-food restaurant. Assume that computer technology has advanced to the point where very large problems can be solved on a PC at the restaurant.
   a. What data would you collect as inputs to your model?
   b. Describe in words several appropriate objective functions for your model.
   c. Describe in words the constraints needed for your model.

130. You have been assigned to develop a model that can be used to schedule the nurses working in a maternity ward.
   a. What data would you collect as inputs to your model?
   b. Describe in words several appropriate objective functions for your model.
   c. Describe in words the constraints needed for your model.

131. Keefer Paper produces recycled paper from paper purchased from local offices and universities. The company sells three grades of paper: high-brightness paper, medium-brightness paper, and low-brightness paper. The high-brightness paper must have a brightness level of at least 90, the medium-brightness paper must have a brightness level of between 80 and 90, and the low-brightness paper must have a brightness level no greater than 80. Discuss how Keefer might use a blending model to maximize its profit.

132. In this chapter, we give you the cost of producing a product and other inputs that are used in the analysis. Do you think most companies find it easy to determine the cost of producing a product? What difficulties might arise?

133. Discuss how the aggregate planning model could be extended to handle a company that produces several products on several types of machines. What information would you need to model this type of problem?

134. A large CPA firm currently has 100 junior staff members and 20 partners. In the long run—say, 20 years from now—the firm would like to consist of 130 junior staff members and 20 partners. During a given year, 10% of all partners and 30% of all junior staff members leave the firm. The firm can control the number of hires each year and the fraction of junior employees who are promoted to partner each year. Can you develop a personnel strategy that would meet the CPA firm's goals?

Saudi Arabia is a kingdom in the Middle East with an area of 865,000 square miles, occupying about four-fifths of the Arabian Peninsula. With a population of about 10 million, this Muslim and Arab state is generally recognized as being formed in 1927 when Ibn Sa'ud united the country and was acknowledged as the sovereign independent ruler. Summer heat is intense in the interior, reaching 124°F, but it is dry and tolerable in contrast to coastal regions and some highlands, which have high humidity during the summer. Winters (December through February) are cool, with the coldest weather occurring at high altitudes and in the far north. A minimum temperature recorded at at-Turayf in 1950 was 10°F, and it was accompanied by several inches of snow and an inch of ice on ponds. Average winter temperatures are 74°F at Jidda and 58°F at Riyadh (the capital city), which has an annual precipitation of 2.5 to 3 inches.

After oil was discovered in Bahrain in 1932, many companies turned to Saudi Arabia and started exploring. Thus, in 1937, the American Arabian Oil Company, Inc. (AMARCO), was formed as a joint venture between Standard Oil Company of California (SOCAL) and the Government of Saudi Arabia to explore, produce, and market any petroleum found in the country. The year before, a geologist from SOCAL had discovered a small quantity of oil in the Eastern Province at Dammam Dome, on which the oil company town of Dhahran is now built. It was just beginning to be developed when another discovery was made—of what was to prove to be the largest oil field in the world. Called the Ghamar field, it would start Saudi Arabia on the road to becoming a highly developed country in just a generation. Located about 50 miles inland from the western shores of the Persian Gulf, the Ghamar field is a structural accumulation along 140 miles of a north–south anticline. The productive area covers approximately 900 square miles, and the vertical oil column is about 1,300 feet. It is generally considered to have recoverable reserves of about 75 billion barrels of oil. Total proven reserves in Saudi Arabia are estimated at more than 500 billion barrels, enough for more than a hundred years of production.

Since 1950, Saudi Arabia has experienced greater and more rapid changes than it had in the several preceding centuries. For example, during this time, as skilled nationals became available, more and more of the exploration, drilling, refining, and other production activities came under the control of the country. SOCAL was left primarily with the marketing and transportation functions outside the country.

During the 1960s, AMARCO increased its profitability substantially by hiring Dr. George Dantzig, then of the University of California, as a consultant. He supervised the development and implementation of LP models to optimize the production of different types of crude oils, their refining, and the marketing of some of their principal products. As a result of this effort, an operations research (OR) department was started in the company with the responsibility of continuing to review the firm's operations to find other areas where costs might be decreased or profits increased by applications of OR.

Now attention is being focused on another aspect of one of the company's small California refinery operations: the production of three types of aviation gasoline from the Saudi Arabian crude oil available. Recently, the marketing of petroleum products to the airline industry has become a rather substantial portion of AMARCO's business. As shown in Figure 4.45, the three aviation gasolines, A, B, and C, are made by blending four feedstocks: Alkylate, Catalytic Cracked Gasoline, Straight Run Gasoline, and Isopentane.

In Table 4.14, TEL stands for tetraethyl lead, which is measured in units of milliliters per gallon (ml/gal). Thus, a TEL of 0.5 means there is 0.5 milliliter of tetraethyl lead per gallon of feedstock. Table 4.14 shows that TEL does influence the octane number but does not influence the Reid Vapor Pressure.

Each type of aviation gasoline has a maximum permissible Reid Vapor Pressure of 7. Aviation gasoline A has a TEL level of 0.5 ml/gal and has a minimum octane number of 80. The TEL level of aviation gasolines B and C is 4 ml/gal, but the former has a minimum octane number of 91, whereas the latter has a minimum of 100.

[10] This case was written by William D. Whisler, California State University, Hayward.

Assume that all feedstocks going into aviation gasoline A are leaded at a TEL level of 0.5 ml/gal and that those going into aviation gasolines B and C are leaded at a TEL level of 4 ml/gal. Table 4.15 gives the aviation gasoline data. A final condition is that marketing requires that the amount of aviation gas A produced be at least as great as the amount of aviation gas B.

**Figure 4.45**

The Production of Aviation Gasoline

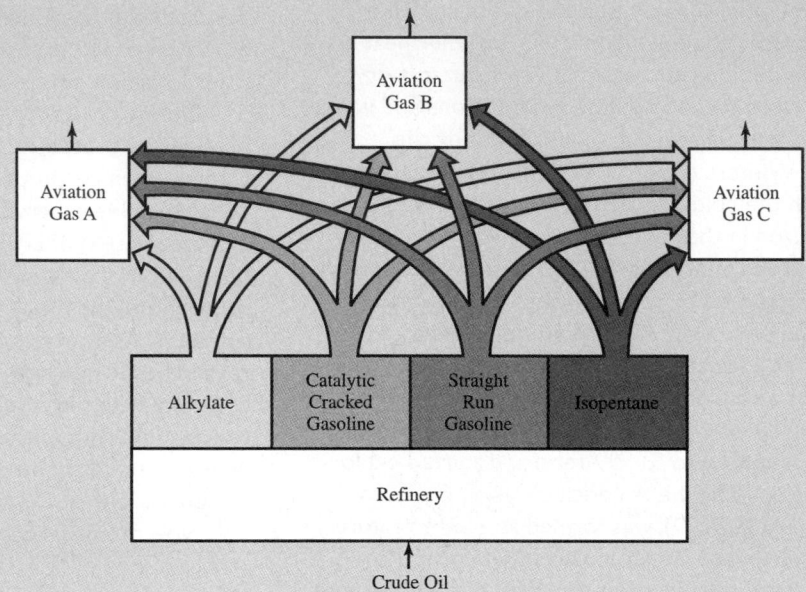

## Table 4.14 Stock Availabilities[a]

| Characteristic | | Feedstock | | |
| --- | --- | --- | --- | --- |
| | Alkylate | Catalytic Cracked Gasoline | Straight Run Gasoline | Isopentane |
| Reid Vapor Pressure | 5 | 8 | 4 | 20 |
| Octane Number | | | | |
|   If TEL is 0.5 | 94 | 83 | 74 | 95 |
|   If TEL is 4.0 | 107.5 | 93 | 87 | 108 |
| Available (Bbl/day) | 14,000 | 13,000 | 14,000 | 11,000 |
| Value ($/Bbl) | 17.00 | 14.50 | 13.50 | 14.00 |

[a]Some of the data in this case have been adapted from Walter W. Garvin, *Introduction to Linear Programming* (New York: McGraw-Hill, 1960), Chapter 5.

## Table 4.15 Aviation Gasoline Data

| Characteristic | Aviation Gasoline | | |
| --- | --- | --- | --- |
| | A | B | C |
| Minimum requirements (Bbl/day) | 12,000 | 13,000 | 12,000 |
| Price ($/Bbl) | 15.00 | 16.00 | 16.50 |

## Questions

1. AMARCO's planners want to determine how the three grades of aviation gasoline should be blended from the available input streams so that the specifications are met and the income is maximized. Develop an LP spreadsheet model of the company's problem.

2. Solve the linear programming model formulated in Question 1.

*The following questions should be attempted only after Questions 1 and 2 have been answered correctly.*

3. Suppose that a potential supply shortage of Saudi Arabian petroleum products exists in the near future due to possible damage to AMARCO's oil production facilities from Iraqi attacks. This could cause the prices of the three types of aviation gasolines to double (while the values of the stocks remain the same, because they are currently on hand). How would this affect the refinery's operations? If, after current stocks are exhausted, additional quantities must be obtained at values double those given in Table 4.14, how might AMARCO's plans be affected?

4. Suppose that because of the new Iraqi crisis, the supply of alkylate is decreased by 1,800 bbl/day, catalytic cracked gas is decreased by 2,000 bbl/day, and straight run gasoline is decreased by 5,000 bbl/day. How does this affect AMARCO's operations?

5. AMARCO is considering trying to fill the aviation gasoline shortage created by the new Iraqi crisis by increasing its own production. If additional quantities of alkylate, catalytic cracked gasoline, straight run gasoline, and isopentane are available, should they be processed? If so, how much of them should be processed, and how do their values affect the situation?

6. Due to the uncertainty about both the U.S. economy and the world economy resulting from the Iraqi crisis, AMARCO's economists are considering doing a new market research study to reestimate the minimum requirement forecasts. With the economy continually weakening, it is felt that demand will decrease, possibly drastically, in the future. However, because such marketing research is expensive, management is wondering whether it would be worthwhile. That is, do changes in the minimum requirements have a significant effect on AMARCO's operations? What is the change in profit from an increase or a decrease in the minimum requirements? Over what ranges of demand do these profit changes apply?

7. Suppose that the Middle East crisis ends and a flood of oil fills the marketplace, causing the prices of aviation gasoline to drop to $10.00, $11.00, and $11.50, respectively, for A, B, and C. How would this affect the company's plans?

8. Suppose that the U.S. government is considering mandating the elimination of lead from aviation gasoline to decrease air pollution. This law would be based on new technology that allows jet engines to burn unleaded gasoline efficiently at any octane level. Thus, there would no longer be any need for constraints on octane level. How would such a new law affect AMARCO?

9. The Environmental Protection Agency is proposing regulations to decrease air pollution. It plans to improve the quality of aviation gasolines by decreasing the requirement on Reid Vapor Pressure from 7 to 6. Management is concerned about this regulation and wonders how it might affect AMARCO's profitability. Analyze and make a recommendation.

10. The Marketing Department indicates that AMARCO will be able to increase its share of the market substantially with a new contract being negotiated with a new customer. The difficulty is that this contract will require that the amount of aviation gas A plus the amount of B must be at least as great as the amount of C produced. Because aviation gasolines A and B are least profitable of the three, this could cause a big decrease in profit for the company. However, marketing indicates that this is a short-run view, because the "large" increase in market share with the concomitant long-run profit increases will more than offset the "temporary small decrease" in profits because of the additional restriction. What do you recommend? Why? ∎

American Office Systems, Inc., was established by the late R. J. Miller, Sr., in 1939. It started as an office supply story in Mountain View, California, and expanded slowly over the years into the manufacture of small office equipment, overhead projectors, and bookkeeping machines. In the 1950s, computers started eroding its market for bookkeeping machines, so the company diversified into the copy machine market. However, it never captured a large market share because bigger firms such as Xerox, Canon, Sharp, and A. B. Dick were so firmly entrenched.

A few years ago, American Office Systems' engineering staff developed an adapter that links a standard copy machine to personal computers, allowing a copy machine to be used as a laser printer, scanner, and fax. The adapters show great promise for both home and office use. However, the company is not well known by either the financial community or the copy machine market, principally due to its small size and rather lackluster record, so it could secure only $15 million in initial financial backing for the adapters. The $15 million was used to finance the construction of a small production facility and of administrative offices in 1994, and in 1995 production and sales began. Two versions of the adapter exist, one for IBM-compatible computers and one for Macintosh computers. The former sells for $175 and the latter for $200.

At the beginning of December 1995, Dr. R. J. Miller, II, President, convened a meeting about the coming year's plans for the adapters. Rob Olsen, Vice President of Production, argued that production facilities should be expanded: "Until we have sufficient capacity to produce the adapters," he said, "there is no use advertising." Sue Williams, Director of Marketing, replied, "On the contrary, without any demand for the adapters, there is no reason to produce them. We need to focus on advertising first." J.T. Howell, the Comptroller, pointed out that Olsen and Williams were talking about the situation as if it only involved a decision between production and marketing: "Yes, funds need to be allocated between production and advertising. However, more important than both is the cash flow difficulty that the company has been

experiencing. As you know, it was only yesterday that, finally, I was able to secure a $750,000 line of credit for the coming year from Citibank. I might add that it is at a very favorable interest rate of 16%. This will partially solve our cash flow problems and it will have a big effect on both production and advertising decisions. In addition, there are financial and accounting factors that must be allowed for in any decision about the adapters." Olsen interjected, "Wow, this is more complicated than I anticipated originally. Before we make a decision, I think we ought to use some modern management science techniques to be sure that all the relevant factors are considered. Last week I hired Carlos Garcia from Stanford. He has a Master's Degree in Operations Research. I think this would be a good project for him." However, Williams said that she thinks that an executive, judgmental decision would be much better. "Let's not get carried away with any of the quantitative mumbo-jumbo that Rob is always suggesting. Besides, his studies always take too much time and are so technical that no one can understand them. We need a decision by the end of next week." After listening to the discussion, Miller decided to appoint an executive action team to study the problem and make a recommendation at next week's meeting. "Rob and Sue, I want both of you to document your arguments in more detail. J.T., be more precise with your comments about the cash flow, accounting, and financial problems. And, by the way Rob, have Carlos look into a model to see if it might produce some insights."

Most of the $15 million initial financing was used to build a five-story building in Mountain View, south of San Francisco. Although currently only about 90% complete, it is being used. The first floor contains the production and shipping facilities plus a small storage area. A larger warehouse, already owned by the company, is located across the street. The other four floors of the building are for the engineering department (second floor), a research lab (third floor), and administration (top two floors). The production facility operates two shifts per day and has a production capacity of 30 IBM adapters and 10 Macintosh adapters per hour. Olsen uses 20 production days per month in his planning. Usually there are a few more, but these are reserved for maintenance and repairs. The last stage of the initial construction will

[11] This case was written by William D. Whisler, California State University, Hayward.

be finished by the beginning of the fourth quarter, making the building 100% finished. This will increase the production capacity rates by 10%.

Howell normally does the company's financial planning monthly, and he assumes that cash flows associated with all current operating expenses, sales revenues (taking collections into account), advertising costs, loans from the line of credit, investments of excess cash in short-term government securities, and so forth, occur at the end of the corresponding month. Because he needs information for the meeting next week, however, he decides to do a rough plan on a quarterly basis. This means that all the just mentioned cash flows, and so on, will be assumed to occur at the end of the quarter. After the meeting, when more time is available, the plan will be expanded to a monthly basis. To get started, one of his senior financial analysts prepares the list of quarterly fixed operating expenses shown in Table 4.16. In addition, the accounting department calculates that the variable costs of the adapters are $100 each for the IBM version and $110 each for the Macintosh version.

**Table 4.16  Quarterly Fixed Operating Expenses**

| Expense | Cost |
| --- | --- |
| Administrative expense | $1,500,000 |
| Fixed manufacturing costs | 750,000 |
| Sales agents' salaries | 750,000 |
| Depreciation | 100,000 |

At present, American Office Systems is experiencing a cash flow squeeze due to the large cash requirements of the startup of the adapter production, advertising, and sales costs. If excess cash is available in any quarter, however, Howell says that the company policy is to invest it in short-term government securities, such as treasury bills. He estimates that during the coming year these investments will yield a return of 6%.

Olsen asks Garcia to look into the production and inventory aspects of the situation first, because this area was his specialty at Stanford. Then he says that he wants him to think about a programming model that might integrate all components of the problem—production, sales, advertising, inventory, accounting, and finance. A mixed-integer programming model appears to be the most appropriate; however, he asks Garcia to use linear programming as an approximation due to the time limitations and Williams's concern about his ideas always being too technical. "There will be more time after next week's meeting to refine the model," he says.

After discussions with Olsen and Williams, Garcia feels that something needs to be done to help the company handle the uncertainty surrounding future sales of the adapters. He points out that it is impossible to guarantee that the company will never be out of stock. However, it is possible to decrease shortages so that any difficulties associated with them would be small and they would not cause major disruptions or additional management problems, such as excess time and cost spent expediting orders, and so forth. Thus, Garcia formulates an inventory model. To be able to solve the model, he has to check the inventory levels of the adapters currently on hand in the warehouse. From these quantities, he calculates that there will be 10,000 IBM and 5,000 Macintosh adapters on hand at the beginning of 1996. Based on the results of the model, he recommends that a simple rule of thumb be used: production plus the end-of-period inventory for the adapters should be at least 10% larger than the estimated sales for the next period. This would be a safety cushion to help prevent shortages of the adapters. In addition, to provide a smooth transition to 1997, the inventory level plus production at the end of the fourth quarter of 1996 should be at least twice the maximum expected sales for that quarter. Garcia says that using these rules of thumb will minimize annual inventory costs. When explaining the inventory model to Olsen, Garcia emphasizes the importance of including inventory carrying costs as part of any analysis, even though such costs frequently are not out-of-pocket. He says that his analysis of data provided by the accounting department yielded a 1% per month inventory carry cost, and this is what he used in his model.

Sales during the first year (1995) for the adapters are shown in Table 4.17. Next year's sales are uncertain. One reason for the uncertainty is that they depend on the advertising. To begin the analysis, Williams asks her marketing research analyst, Debra Lu, to estimate the maximum sales levels for the coming four quarters if no advertising is done. Since last year's sales of both models showed a steady increase throughout the year, Lu projects a continuation of the trend. She forecasts that the company will be able to sell any number of adapters up to the maximum expected sales amounts shown in Table 4.17.

**Table 4.17** 1995 Adapter Sales and Maximum Expected 1996 Sales

| | 1995 Sales | | 1996 Maximum Expected Sales | |
| Quarter | IBM Adapters | Macintosh Adapters | IBM Adapters | Macintosh Adapters |
| --- | --- | --- | --- | --- |
| 1 | 5,000 | 1,000 | 9,000 | 1,800 |
| 2 | 6,000 | 1,200 | 10,000 | 2,000 |
| 3 | 7,000 | 1,400 | 11,000 | 2,200 |
| 4 | 8,000 | 1,600 | 12,000 | 2,400 |

Miller suggests that advertising in magazines such as *PC World* and *Home Office* will increase consumer awareness of both the company and adapters. The next day, Williams has a meeting with several staff members of a San Francisco advertising agency. They show her recommendations for two types of ads (one for the IBM adapters and one for the Macintosh adapters), give her cost information, and the estimated effectiveness of an advertising campaign. Armed with this information and some data from Lu, Williams prepares a brief report for Miller setting out her reasons for thinking that each $10 spent on advertising will sell an additional IBM adapter; the same relationship holds true for the Macintosh adapter.

Based on an analysis of 1995 sales and accounts receivable, the accounting department determines that collection experience is as shown in Table 4.18. For example, 75% of the IBM adapters sold in a quarter are paid for during the quarter, 20% are paid for during the following quarter, and 3% are paid for during

the third quarter. The remaining 2% are written off and sold to a collection agency for $0.50 on the dollar.

**Table 4.18** Collections

| Quarter | IBM Adapters | Macintosh Adapters |
| --- | --- | --- |
| 1 | 0.75 | 0.80 |
| 2 | 0.20 | 0.11 |
| 3 | 0.03 | 0.05 |

## Questions

1. Suppose that you are Garcia. Develop an LP spreadsheet model of the situation to help the executive action team make a decision about how to allocate funds between production and advertising so that all the cash flow, financial, accounting, marketing, inventory, and production considerations are taken into account and American Office Systems' profits are maximized. Use the data collected and the estimates made by the members of the executive action team.

2. Solve the LP model formulated in Question 1.

*The executive action team has assembled to reconsider the plans for the adapters for the coming year. Garcia, who developed the LP model, concludes his presentation by saying, "As everyone can see, the model gives the optimal solution that maximizes profits. Since I have incorporated the estimates and assumptions that all of you made, clearly it is the best solution. No other alternative can give a higher profit." Even Williams, who initially was skeptical of using quantitative models for making executive-level decisions, is impressed and indicates that she will go along with the results.*

*Miller says, "Good work, Carlos! This is a complex problem but your presentation made it all seem so simple. However, remember that those figures you used were based on estimates made by all of us. Some were little better than guesses. What happens if they are wrong? In other words, your presentation has helped me get a handle on the problem we are facing, and I know that models are useful where hard, accurate, data exist. However, with all the uncertainty in our situation and the many rough estimates made, it seems to me that I will still have to make a* *judgment call when it comes down to making a final decision. Also, there has been a new development. J.T. tells me that we might be able to get another $1 million line of credit from a Bahamian bank. It will take a while to work out the details and maybe it will cost us a little. I am wondering if it is worth it. What would we do with the $1 million if we got it?" T. J. responds, "We really need the $1 million. But it is a drop in the bucket. My analysis shows that we really need another $8 million line of credit."*

*Analyze, as Garcia is going to do, the effect of uncertainty and errors on the results of Questions 1 and 2 by answering the following questions. They should be attempted only after Questions 1 and 2 have been answered correctly.*

3. One area where assumptions were made is adapter price.
   a. What happens if the prices for the adapters are a little weak and they decrease to $173 for the IBM version and $198 for the Macintosh version? Does this make any difference?
   b. What about decreases to $172 and $197, respectively, for the IBM and Macintosh versions? Explain the answers in terms that Miller will understand.
   c. Suppose that American Office Systems can increase the price of the adapters to $180 and $205. How would this affect the original solution?

4. Another potential variable is adapter production cost.
   a. Suppose that an error was made in determining the costs of the adapters and that they really should have been $102 for the IBM version and $112 for the Macintosh version. What is the effect of this error?
   b. What about costs of $105 and $115? Explain the answers in terms that Miller will understand.

5. Howell notes that one of the contributing factors to American Office Systems' cash squeeze is the slow collection of accounts receivable. He is considering adopting a new collection procedure recommended by a consulting company. It will

cost $100,000 and will change the collection rates to those given in Table 4.19.
   a. Analyze the effect of this new collection policy and make a recommendation to Howell about whether to implement the new procedure. As before, any accounts receivable not collected by the end of the third quarter will be sold to a collection agency for $0.50 on the dollar.
   b. Howell wonders whether switching to selling adapters for all cash is worth the effort. This would ameliorate the cash squeeze because it would eliminate not only the slow collections but also the use of the collection agency for accounts that remain unpaid after 9 months. It would cost about $90,000 more than at present to implement the all-cash policy because the accounting system would need to be modified and personnel would have to be retrained. Analyze this possibility and make a recommendation to Howell.

| Table 4.19 | New Collections | |
|---|---|---|
| Quarter | IBM Adapters | Macintosh Adapters |
| 1 | 0.90 | 0.92 |
| 2 | 0.07 | 0.03 |
| 3 | 0.01 | 0.01 |

6. Yet another variable is advertising effectiveness.
   a. Suppose that Williams overestimated the effectiveness of advertising. It now appears that $100 is needed to increase sales by one adapter. How will this affect the original solution? Explain the answer in terms that Miller will understand.
   b. What happens if the required advertising outlay is $12.50 per additional adapter sold?

7. Suppose that the line of credit from Citibank that Howell thought he had arranged did not work out because of the poor financial situation of the company. The company can obtain one for the same amount from a small local bank; however, the interest rate is much higher, 24%. Analyze how this change affects American Office Systems.

8. The safety cushion for inventory is subject to revision.

   **a.** Suppose that Garcia finds a bug in his original inventory model. Correcting it results in a safety cushion of 15% instead of the 10% he suggested previously. Determine whether this is important.

   **b.** What if the error is 20%? Explain the answers in terms that Miller will understand.

9. Production capacity is scheduled to increase by 10% in the fourth quarter.

   **a.** Suppose that Miller is advised by the construction company that the work will not be finished until the following year. How will this delay affect the company's plans?

   **b.** In addition to the delay in part **a**, suppose that an accident in the production facility damages some of the equipment so that the capacity is decreased by 10% in the fourth quarter. Analyze how this will affect the original solution.

10. Williams is worried about the accuracy of Lu's 1996 maximum expected sales forecasts. If errors in these forecasts have a big effect on the company profits, she is thinking about hiring a San Francisco marketing research firm to do a more detailed analysis. They would charge $50,000 for a study. Help Williams by analyzing what would happen if Lu's forecasts are in error by 1,000 for IBM adapters and 200 for Macintosh adapters each quarter. Should she hire the marketing research firm?

11. **a.** To determine whether the extra $1 million line of credit is needed, analyze its effect on the original solution given in Question 2.

    **b.** To fully understand the ramifications of the extra $1,000,000 line of credit, redo (1) Question 3b, (2) Question 4b, (3) Question 6a, and (4) Question 8b. Summarize your results.

    **c.** What about Howell's claim that an extra $8,000,000 line of credit is necessary? Use that adjustment and redo Question 6a. ∎

Lakefield Corporation's oil trading desk buys and sells oil products (crude oil and refined fuels), options, and futures in international markets. The trading desk is responsible for buying raw material for Lakefield's refining and blending operations and for selling final products. In addition to trading for the company's operations, the desk also takes speculative positions. In speculative trades, the desk attempts to profit from its knowledge and information about conditions in the global oil markets.

One of the traders, Lisa Davies, is responsible for transactions in the cash market (as opposed to the futures or options markets). Lisa has been trading for several years and has seen the prices of oil-related products fluctuate tremendously. Figure 4.46 shows the prices of heating oil #2 and unleaded gasoline from January 1986 through July 1992. Although excessive volatility of oil prices is undesirable for most businesses, Lakefield's oil trading desk often makes substantial profits in periods of high volatility.

The prices of various oil products tend to move together over long periods of time. Because finished oil products are refined from crude oil, the prices of all finished products tend to rise if the price of crude increases. Because finished oil products are not perfect substitutes, the prices of individual products do not move in lockstep. In fact, over short time periods, the price movements of two products can have a low correlation. For example, in late 1989 and early 1990, there was a severe cold wave in the northeastern United States. The price of heating oil rose from $0.60 per gallon to over $1 per gallon. In the same time period, the price of gasoline rose just over $0.10 per gallon.

Lisa Davies believes that some mathematical analysis might be helpful to spot trading opportunities in the cash markets. The next section provides background about a few important characteristics of fuel oils, along with a discussion of the properties of blended fuels and some implications for pricing.

## Characteristics of Hydrocarbon Fuels

The many varieties of hydrocarbon fuels include heating oil, kerosene, gasoline, and diesel oil. Each type of fuel has many characteristics, for example, heat content, viscosity, freeze point, luminosity,

**Figure 4.46**

Price of Heating Oil #2 and Unleaded Gasoline

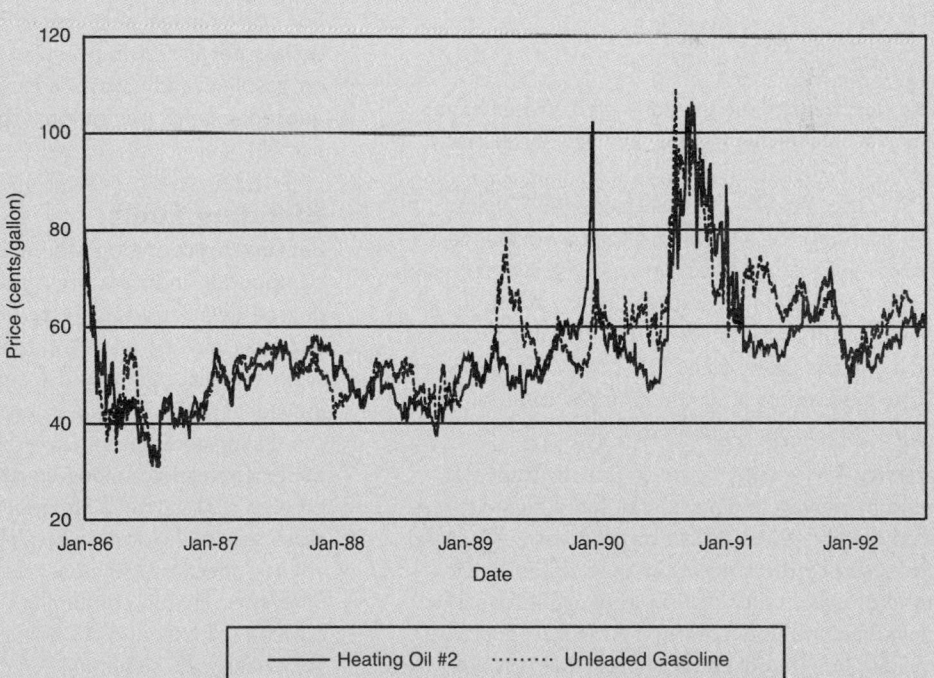

volatility (speed of vaporization), and so on. The relative importance of each characteristic depends on the intended use of the fuel. For example, octane rating is one of the most important characteristics of gasoline. Octane is a measure of resistance to ignition under pressure. An engine burning low-octane fuel is susceptible to "engine knock," which reduces its power output. Surprisingly, octane rating is more important than heat content for gasoline. In contrast, the most important characteristic of kerosene jet fuel is its heat content, but viscosity is also important. High viscosity fuels do not flow as smoothly through fuel lines.

For the types of fuels Lisa Davies usually trades, the most important characteristics are density, viscosity, sulfur content, and flash point, which are described next. When trading and blending other fuels, characteristics besides these four are important to consider.

**Density**   The density of a substance is its mass per unit volume (e.g., grams per cubic centimeter). The density of water is 1 g/cc. A related measure is American Petroleum Institute gravity (API), which is measured in degrees. API is related to density by

$$API = \frac{141.5}{D} - 131.5$$

where $D$ is density measured in g/cc. Water has an API of 10°. Note that density and API are *inversely* related.

The specifications for kerosene jet fuel are nearly identical for all civilian airlines worldwide. Kerosene jet fuel should have an API gravity between 37° and 51. Diesel fuel and heating oil are required to have an API not less than 30. API is important for controlling the flow of fuel in a combustion engine. It can also be used to limit the concentration of heavy hydrocarbon compounds in the fuel.

**Viscosity**   Viscosity refers to the resistance of a liquid to flow. A highly viscous liquid, such as ketchup or molasses, does not pour easily. Viscosity is measured by the amount of time a specified volume of liquid takes to flow through a tube of a certain diameter. It is commonly measured in units of centistokes (hundredths of stokes). Most fuel

specifications place upper limits on viscosity. Less viscous fuel flows easily through lines and atomizes easily for efficient combustion. More viscous fuels must be heated initially to reduce viscosity.

**Sulfur Content**   The content of sulfur is measured in percentage of total sulfur by weight. For example, a fuel with 2% sulfur content has 2 grams of sulfur for every 100 grams of fuel. Sulfur causes corrosion and abrasion of metal surfaces. Low sulfur content is important for maintaining the proper operation of equipment.

**Flash Point**   The flash point of a substance is the lowest temperature at which the substance ignites when exposed to a flame. The product description of kerosene jet fuel from the American Society for Testing and Materials specifies a flash point of at least 100°F. The New York Mercantile Exchange futures contract for heating oil #2 specifies a flash point of at least 130°F. Flash-point restrictions are often prescribed for safety reasons.

Table 4.20 gives a description of some fuels and their prices on a given day. In Table 4.20, the units of viscosity are centistokes, sulfur is given in percentage by weight, and flash point is in degrees Fahrenheit. For convenience, all prices in Table 4.20 are given in dollars per barrel. In practice, the prices of heating oil, gasoline, and kerosene jet fuel are typically quoted in cents per gallon. (There are 42 gallons in a barrel.)

## Blending Fuels

Because hydrocarbon fuels are made of similar compounds and have similar characteristics, a certain degree of substitutability exists among fuels. Different fuels can also be blended to form a new fuel. Next we describe how the characteristics of the individual fuels combine in the blended fuel.

Sulfur combines linearly by weight. This means, for example, that mixing equal weights of a 1% sulfur oil with a 3% sulfur oil produces a 2% sulfur oil. To a close approximation, sulfur combines linearly by volume (because the densities of oils are not very different). That is, combining 0.5 barrel of 1% sulfur oil with 0.5 barrel of 3% sulfur oil gives 1 barrel of very nearly 2% sulfur oil.

## Table 4.20 Description of Available Fuels

| | Fuel 1 1% Sulfur Fuel Oil | Fuel 2 3% Sulfur Fuel Oil | Fuel 3 0.7% Sulfur Fuel Oil | Fuel 4 Heating Oil | Fuel 5 1% Vacuum Gas Oil | Fuel 6 2% Vacuum Gas Oil |
|---|---|---|---|---|---|---|
| API | 10.50 | 10.50 | 10.50 | 34.00 | 25.00 | 25.00 |
| Viscosity | 477.00 | 477.00 | 477.00 | 3.50 | 25.00 | 25.00 |
| Sulfur | 1.00 | 3.00 | 0.70 | 0.20 | 1.00 | 2.00 |
| Flash point | 140.00 | 140.00 | 140.00 | 130.00 | 200.00 | 200.00 |
| Price | 16.08 | 13.25 | 17.33 | 24.10 | 20.83 | 20.10 |

| | Fuel 7 0.5% Vacuum Gas Oil | Fuel 8 Straight Run (Low Sulfur) | Fuel 9 Straight Run (High Sulfur) | Fuel 10 Kerosene Jet Fuel | Fuel 11 Diesel Fuel | Fuel 12 Slurry |
|---|---|---|---|---|---|---|
| API | 25.00 | 21.00 | 17.00 | 46.000 | 35.00 | −4.50 |
| Viscosity | 25.00 | 212.00 | 212.00 | 1.500 | 2.50 | 261.00 |
| Sulfur | 0.50 | 0.30 | 2.75 | 0.125 | 0.20 | 2.37 |
| Flash point | 200.00 | 250.00 | 250.00 | 123.000 | 150.00 | 109.00 |
| Price | 21.46 | 21.00 | 20.00 | 25.520 | 24.30 | 11.50 |

In general, to say that a certain property of oil combines linearly (by volume) means the following: Suppose $x_j$ barrels of oil $j$ (for $j = 1, 2, \ldots, n$) are blended together to form one barrel of oil; that is, $\sum_{j=1}^{n} x_j = 1$. Also suppose that $c_j$ is the measure of the property of oil $j$. Then if the property combines linearly, the measure of the property for the blended oil is a linear combination of the $c_j$'s; that is, $\sum_{j=1}^{n} c_j x_j$.

API gravity does not combine linearly, but density does combine linearly. For example, consider blending 0.5 barrel of oil that has a density of 0.8 g/cc with 0.5 barrel of oil with a density of 1.2 g/cc. The resulting barrel of oil has a density of 1.0 (= 0.8[0.5] + 1.2[0.5]). The 0.8 g/cc density oil has an API of 45.38 , and the 1.2 g/cc density oil has an API of −13.58°. If API combined linearly, the blended barrel of oil would have an API of 15.90°(= 45.38 [0.5] −13.58 [0.5]). However, an API of 15.90 corresponds to a density of 0.96 g/cc, not 1.0 g/cc.[12]

Viscosity, measured in centistokes, does not combine linearly. However, chemical engineers have determined that viscosity can be transformed to another measure, called linear viscosity, which (nearly) combines linearly.[13] Similarly, flash points measured in degrees Fahrenheit do not combine linearly. But chemical engineers defined a new measure, termed linear flash point, which does combine linearly.[14] Table 4.21 summarizes the properties of the 12 fuels measured in units that combine linearly.

## Implications for Pricing

Sulfur in oil is a contaminant. Therefore, oil with a low sulfur content is more valuable than oil with a higher sulfur content, all other characteristics being equal. This relationship can be seen in Table 4.20 by comparing the prices of fuels 1, 2, and 3 and fuels 5,

---

[12] To convert API to density, use $D = 141.5/(API + 131.5)$.

[13] Let $vs$ represent viscosity measured in centistokes. Then linear viscosity, denoted $v$, is defined $v = \ln(\ln[vs + 0.08])$.

[14] Let $fp$ denote flash point measured in degrees Fahrenheit. Then linear flash point is defined $f = 10^{42}(fp + 460)^{-14.286}$. Empirical analysis of oil blending data confirms that the measure $f$ combines nearly linearly.

## Table 4.21    Properties of Available Fuels Measured in Units That Combine Linearly

| | Fuel 1<br>1% Sulfur<br>Fuel Oil | Fuel 2<br>3% Sulfur<br>Fuel Oil | Fuel 3<br>0.7% Sulfur<br>Fuel Oil | Fuel 4<br>Heating<br>Oil | Fuel 5<br>1% Vacuum<br>Gas Oil | Fuel 6<br>2% Vacuum<br>Gas Oil |
|---|---|---|---|---|---|---|
| Density | 0.996 | 0.996 | 0.996 | 0.855 | 0.904 | 0.904 |
| Linear visc. | 1.819 | 1.819 | 1.819 | 0.243 | 1.170 | 1.170 |
| Sulfur | 1.000 | 3.000 | 0.700 | 0.200 | 1.000 | 2.000 |
| Linear flash | 204.800 | 204.800 | 204.800 | 260.400 | 52.500 | 52.500 |
| Price | 16.080 | 13.250 | 17.330 | 24.100 | 20.830 | 20.100 |

| | Fuel 7<br>0.5% Vacuum<br>Gas Oil | Fuel 8<br>Straight Run<br>(Low Sulfur) | Fuel 9<br>Straight Run<br>(High Sulfur) | Fuel 10<br>Kerosene<br>Jet Fuel | Fuel 11<br>Diesel<br>Fuel | Fuel 12<br><br>Slurry |
|---|---|---|---|---|---|---|
| Density | 0.904 | 0.928 | 0.953 | 0.797 | 0.850 | 1.114 |
| Linear visc. | 1.170 | 1.678 | 1.678 | −.782 | −.054 | 1.716 |
| Sulfur | 0.500 | 0.300 | 2.750 | 0.125 | 0.200 | 2.370 |
| Linear flash | 52.500 | 18.500 | 18.500 | 308.800 | 161.700 | 437.000 |
| Price | 21.460 | 21.000 | 20.000 | 25.520 | 24.300 | 11.500 |

6, and 7. Lower-density oils are generally preferred to higher-density oils, because energy per unit mass is higher for low-density fuels, which reduces the weight of the fuel. Lower-viscosity oils are preferred because they flow more easily through fuel lines than oils with higher viscosities. High flash points are preferred for safety reasons. However, because flash point and linear flash point are inversely related, this means that oils with lower linear flash point are preferred to oils with higher linear flash point.

That fuels can be blended cheaply to form new fuels affects price as well. For example, fuel 2 and fuel 3 from Table 4.20 can be blended to form a fuel with the same API, viscosity, sulfur, and flash point as fuel 1. In particular, 0.1304 barrel of fuel 2 and 0.8696 barrel of fuel 3 can be blended to form 1 barrel of a new fuel, which, in terms of the four main characteristics, is identical to fuel 1. Because the cost of blending is small, prices combine nearly linearly. The cost to create the blended fuel is $16.80 per barrel ($16.80 = 0.1304[13.25] + 0.8696[17.33]). If the price of fuel 1 were greater than $16.80, say $17.10, Lisa Davies could create an arbitrage. She could buy fuels 2 and 3 in the appropriate proportions,

Lakefield Corporation could blend them together, and Lisa could sell the blend at the price of fuel 1. The profit would be $0.30 per barrel minus any blending and transaction costs. However, the actual price of fuel 1 is $16.08, so this plan does not represent an arbitrage opportunity.

The *no-arbitrage pricing principle* is simply a generalization of the previous example. No arbitrage means that the price of any fuel must be less than or equal to the cost of any blend of fuels of equal or better quality. As mentioned earlier, better means larger API, lower viscosity, lower sulfur content, and higher flash point. In terms of linear properties, better means lower density, lower linear viscosity, lower sulfur content, and lower linear flash point. Any number of fuels (not just two) can be blended together.

Lisa Davies would like to develop a system that automatically checks the no-arbitrage pricing condition for all of the fuels. If the condition is violated, she would like to know the appropriate amounts of the fuels to buy to create the arbitrage, the profit per barrel of the blended fuel, and the characteristics of the blended fuel.

## Questions

1. Suppose that 0.3 barrel of fuel 2, 0.3 barrel of fuel 3, and 0.4 barrel of fuel 4 are blended together. What is the cost of the blended fuel? What are the (linear) properties of the blended fuel (i.e., density, linear viscosity, sulfur content, and linear flash point)?

2. Using the data from Table 4.21, check whether any of the fuels violate the no-arbitrage pricing condition. If no fuel violates the condition, which fuel's price comes the closest to the no-arbitrage upper bound? If there is a violation, give the explicit recipe.

3. What modifications would you make to the analysis to account for blending costs?

4. What would be the important issues or steps involved in creating a real system for this problem? ∎

Daily trading volume in the foreign exchange markets often exceeds $1 trillion. Participants trade in the spot currency markets, forward markets, and futures markets. In addition, currency options, currency swaps, and other derivative contracts are traded. For simplicity, this case focuses on the spot currency market only. A spot currency transaction is simply an agreement to buy some amount of one currency using another currency.[15] For example, a British company might need to pay a Japanese supplier 150 million yen. Suppose that the spot yen/pound rate is 195.07. Then the British company could use the spot currency market to buy 150 million yen at a cost of 768,954.7 (=150,000,000/ 195.07) British pounds. A sample of today's cross-currency spot rates is given in Table 4.22. (See also the file **Currency Rates.xlsx**.)

To continue the example, suppose the company canceled the order from the supplier and wanted to convert the 150 million yen back into British pounds. From Table 4.22, the pound/yen spot rate is 0.005126. So the company could use the 150 million yen to buy 768,900 (=150,000,000 × 0.005126) pounds. Note that the 768,900 pounds is less than the original 768,954.7 pounds. The difference is the result of the bid-offer spread: The price to buy yen (the bid price) is greater than the price to sell yen (the offer price). The bid-offer spread represents a transaction cost to the company.

Occasionally, market prices may become "out of line" in the sense that there are arbitrage opportunities. In this context, arbitrage means that there is a set of spot currency transactions that creates positive wealth but does not require any funds to initiate—that is, it is a "money pump." When such pure arbitrage opportunities exist, supply and demand forces will generally move prices to eliminate the opportunities. Hence, it is desirable to quickly identify arbitrage opportunities when they do exist and to take advantage of them to the greatest extent possible.

## Questions

1. Formulate a decision model to determine whether there are any arbitrage opportunities with the spot currency rates given in Table 4.22. Note that an arbitrage opportunity could involve several currencies. If there is an arbitrage opportunity, your model should specify the exact set of transactions to achieve it.

2. Find the cross-currency rates in a recent paper— for example, in the *Wall Street Journal*—or on the Web at http://www.oanda.com/convert/classic. Check the numbers for an arbitrage opportunity. If you find one, do you think it represents a real arbitrage opportunity? Why or why not? ∎

**Table 4.22  Cross-Currency Spot Rates**

|  |  | To US Dollar | British Pound | Euro | Japanese Yen | Brazilian Real |
|---|---|---|---|---|---|---|
| From | US Dollar | 1 | 0.60639 | 0.88363 | 118.27 | 2.9092 |
|  | British Pound | 1.6491 | 1 | 1.45751 | 195.07 | 4.79931 |
|  | Euro | 1.1317 | 0.6861 | 1 | 133.77 | 3.29496 |
|  | Japanese Yen | 0.008455 | 0.005126 | 0.007476 | 1 | 0.02462 |
|  | Brazilian Real | 0.34374 | 0.20836 | 0.30349 | 40.62285 | 1 |

[15] A spot transaction agreed to today is *settled* (i.e., the money changes hands) two business days from today. By contrast, a three-month forward transaction agreed to today is settled (approximately) three months from today.

# Network Models

© FRANK RUMPENHORST/DPA/Landov

## RESTRUCTURING BASF NORTH AMERICA'S DISTRIBUTION SYSTEM

A quick look through *Interfaces,* the journal that chronicles management science success stories from real applications, indicates that many of these success stories involve network optimization, the subject of this chapter. A typical example appears in Sery et al. (2001). The authors describe their efforts to restructure BASF North America's distribution system. The BASF Group, with headquarters in Germany, is one of the world's leading chemical companies, with annual sales over $30 billion and more than 100,000 employees worldwide. BASF offers a variety of chemical and chemical-based products to customers in Europe, the NAFTA region, South America, and Asia. You probably know the company from its catchy slogan, "We don't make a lot of the products you buy. We make a lot of the products you buy better." Its diverse product mix includes chemicals, polymers, automotive coatings, colors, dyes, pharmaceuticals, nylon fibers, and agricultural products.

In the mid-1990s, BASF examined its distribution of packaged goods in the North America region and discovered that it shipped 1.6 billion pounds of finished goods annually to customers from a network of 135 locations at an annual cost, including transportation and warehousing, of nearly $100 million. The majority (86) of the 135 locations were distribution centers (DCs), although almost a billion pounds were shipped directly from plants to customers. Unfortunately, there had never been any systematic attempt to optimize this network configuration; it had just evolved over the years. The authors of the study were asked to make recommendations that would (1) decrease logistics costs and (2) increase customer service, defined as the percentage of shipments that reach the customer on the same day or the next day. (This percentage was about 77% before the study.) The authors developed a linear programming model that, when implemented, was able to (1) reduce the number of DCs from 86 to 12; (2) reduce the annual transport, facility, and inventory carrying costs by 6%; (3) achieve a one-time 9% improvement in cash flows from a reduction in the working capital tied up in inventory; and (4) increase the customer service measure to 90%. The redesign worked so well that BASF later developed similar models for its European, Scandinavian, and Far East distribution systems.

The article's description of the study is a virtual textbook example of the modeling process described in Chapter 1 of this book. The problem was first identified as follows: "Define the optimal number and location of warehouses and the corresponding material flows needed to meet anticipated customer demand and required delivery service times at the lowest overall cost." The project team next performed the arduous task of collecting the various demands and costs required for the optimization model. Although we try to indicate "Where Do the Numbers Come From?" in the examples in this book, the authors of the study describe just how difficult data collection can be, particularly when the data is stored in a variety of legacy systems that use a wide range of data definitions. Next, the authors developed a verbal statement of the model, including all assumptions they made, which was then translated in a straightforward manner into the network optimization model itself. The next step was to build a decision support system to implement the model. This user-friendly system allowed BASF management to become comfortable with the model (and learn to trust it) by running it repeatedly under different scenarios to answer all sorts of what-if questions. Finally, the model's recommendations were used to redesign the distribution system in North America, and an honest evaluation of its effects—reduced costs and increased customer service—was made. ■

## 5.1 INTRODUCTION

Many important optimization models have a natural graphical network representation. In this chapter, we discuss some specific examples of network models. There are several reasons for distinguishing network models from other LP models:

- The network structure of these models allows us to represent them graphically in a way that is intuitive to users. We can then use this graphical representation as an aid in the spreadsheet model development. In fact, for a book at this level, the best argument for singling out network problems for special consideration is the fact that they can be represented graphically.

- Many companies have real problems, often extremely large, that can be represented as network models. In fact, many of the best management science success stories have involved large network models. For example, Delta Airlines developed a network model to schedule its entire fleet of passenger airplanes. A few other real applications of network-based models are listed throughout the chapter, but the list is by no means exhaustive. A quick scan of the articles in the *Interfaces* journal indicates that there are probably more network-based applications reported than any other type.

■ Specialized solution techniques have been developed specifically for network models. Although we do not discuss the details of these solution techniques—and they are *not* implemented in Excel's Solver—they are important in real-world applications because they allow companies to solve huge problems that could not be solved by the usual LP algorithms.

# 5.2 TRANSPORTATION MODELS

In many situations, a company produces products at locations called **origins** and ships these products to customer locations called **destinations.** Typically, each origin has a limited amount that it can ship, and each customer destination must receive a required quantity of the product. Spreadsheet optimization models can be used to determine the minimum-cost shipping plan for satisfying customer demands.

For now, we assume that the only possible shipments are those directly from an origin to a destination. That is, no shipments between origins or between destinations are possible. This problem—generally called the **transportation problem**—has been studied extensively in management science. In fact, it was one of the first management science models developed, more than a half century ago. The following is a typical example of a small transportation problem.

| EXAMPLE | **5.1 SHIPPING CARS FROM PLANTS TO REGIONS OF THE COUNTRY** |

The Grand Prix Automobile Company manufactures automobiles in three plants and then ships them to four regions of the country. The plants can supply the amounts listed in the right column of Table 5.1. The customer demands by region are listed in the bottom row of this table, and the unit costs of shipping an automobile from each plant to each region are listed in the middle of the table. Grand Prix wants to find the lowest-cost shipping plan for meeting the demands of the four regions without exceeding the capacities of the plants.

**Table 5.1   Input Data for Grand Prix Example**

|  | Region 1 | Region 2 | Region 3 | Region 4 | Capacity |
|---|---|---|---|---|---|
| **Plant 1** | 131 | 218 | 266 | 120 | 450 |
| **Plant 2** | 250 | 116 | 263 | 278 | 600 |
| **Plant 3** | 178 | 132 | 122 | 180 | 500 |
| **Demand** | 450 | 200 | 300 | 300 | |

**Objective**   To develop a spreadsheet optimization model that finds the least-cost way of shipping the automobiles from plants to regions that stays within plant capacities and meets regional demands.

A typical transportation problem requires three sets of numbers: capacities (or supplies), demands (or requirements), and unit shipping (and possibly production) costs:

- The *capacities* indicate the most each plant can supply in a given amount of time—a month, say—under current operating conditions. In some cases, it might be possible to increase the "base" capacities by using overtime, for example. In such cases, we could modify the model to determine the amounts of additional capacity to use (and pay for).

- The customer demands are typically estimated from some type of forecasting model (as discussed in Chapter 16). The forecasts are often based on historical customer demand data.

- The unit shipping costs come from a transportation cost analysis—how much does it really cost to send a single automobile from any plant to any region? This is not an easy question to answer, and it requires an analysis of the best *mode* of transportation (railroad, plane, ship, or truck). However, companies typically have the required data. Actually, the unit "shipping" cost can also include the unit production cost at each plant. However, if this cost is the same across all plants, as we are tacitly assuming here, it can be omitted from the model.

## Solution

The variables and constraints required for this model are listed in Table 5.2. We must know the amounts sent out of the plants and the amounts sent to the regions. However, these aggregate quantities are not directly the decision variables. The company must decide exactly the number of autos to send from each plant to each region—a shipping plan.

---

**Table 5.2  Variables and Constraints for the Transportation Model**

| | |
|---|---|
| **Input variables** | Plant capacities, regional demands, unit shipping costs |
| **Decision variables** (changing cells) | Number of autos sent from each plant to each region |
| **Objective (target cell)** | Total shipping cost |
| **Other calculated variables** | Number sent out of each plant, number sent to each region |
| **Constraints** | Number sent out of each plant must be less than or equal to Plant capacity |
| | Number sent to each region must be greater than or equal to Region demand |

---

*In a transportation problem, all flows go from left to right—from origins to destinations. More complex network structures are discussed in Section 5.4.*

*The common feature of models in this chapter is that they can be represented graphically, as in Figure 5.1.*

### Representing as a Network Model

A network diagram of this model appears in Figure 5.1. This diagram is typical of network models. It consists of nodes and arcs. A **node,** indicated by a circle, generally represents a geographical location. In this case, the nodes on the left correspond to plants, and the nodes on the right correspond to regions. An **arc,** indicated by an arrow, generally represents a route for getting a product from one node to another. Here, the arcs all go from a plant node to a region node—from left to right.

The problem data fit nicely on such a diagram. The capacities are placed next to the plant nodes, the demands are placed next to the region nodes, and the unit shipping costs are placed on the arcs. The decision variables are usually called **flows.** They represent the amounts shipped on the various arcs. Sometimes (although not in this problem), there are upper limits on the flows on some or all of the arcs. These upper limits are called **arc capacities,** and they can also be shown on the diagram.[1]

**Figure 5.1**

Network Representation of Grand Prix Problem

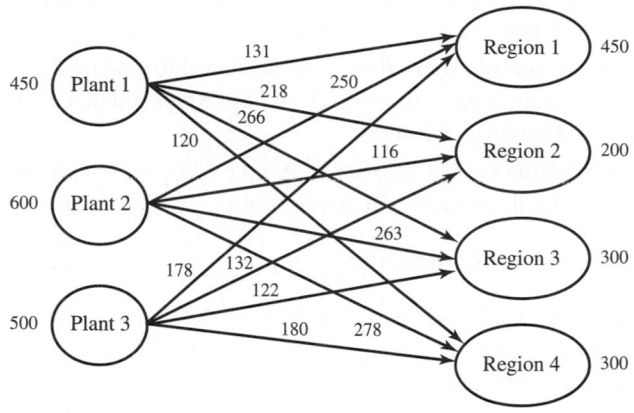

## DEVELOPING THE SPREADSHEET MODEL

The spreadsheet model appears in Figure 5.2. (See the file **Transportation 1.xlsx.**) To develop this model, perform the following steps.

**Figure 5.2**  Grand Prix Transportation Model

| | A | B | C | D | E | F | G | H | I | J | K |
|---|---|---|---|---|---|---|---|---|---|---|---|
| 1 | Grand Prix transportation model | | | | | | | | Range names used: | | |
| 2 | | | | | | | | | Capacity | =Model!$I$13:$I$15 | |
| 3 | Unit shipping costs | | | | | | | | Demand | =Model!$C$18:$F$18 | |
| 4 | | | To | | | | | | Shipping_Plan | =Model!$C$13:$F$15 | |
| 5 | | | Region 1 | Region 2 | Region 3 | Region 4 | | | Total_cost | =Model!$B$21 | |
| 6 | From | Plant 1 | $131 | $218 | $266 | $120 | | | Total_received | =Model!$C$16:$F$16 | |
| 7 | | Plant 2 | $250 | $116 | $263 | $278 | | | Total_shipped | =Model!$G$13:$G$15 | |
| 8 | | Plant 3 | $178 | $132 | $122 | $180 | | | | | |
| 9 | | | | | | | | | | | |
| 10 | Shipping plan, and constraints on supply and demand | | | | | | | | | | |
| 11 | | | To | | | | | | | | |
| 12 | | | Region 1 | Region 2 | Region 3 | Region 4 | Total shipped | | Capacity | | |
| 13 | From | Plant 1 | 150 | 0 | 0 | 300 | 450 | <= | 450 | | |
| 14 | | Plant 2 | 100 | 200 | 0 | 0 | 300 | <= | 600 | | |
| 15 | | Plant 3 | 200 | 0 | 300 | 0 | 500 | <= | 500 | | |
| 16 | | Total received | 450 | 200 | 300 | 300 | | | | | |
| 17 | | | >= | >= | >= | >= | | | | | |
| 18 | | Demand | 450 | 200 | 300 | 300 | | | | | |
| 19 | | | | | | | | | | | |
| 20 | Objective to minimize | | | | | | | | | | |
| 21 | Total cost | $176,050 | | | | | | | | | |

**❶ Inputs.**[2] Enter the unit shipping costs, plant capacities, and region demands in the shaded ranges.

**❷ Shipping plan.** Enter *any* trial values for the shipments from plants to regions in the Shipping_plan range. These are the changing cells. Note that this is modeled as a

---

[1] There can even be *lower* limits, other than 0, on certain flows, but we do not consider any such models here.
[2] From here on, we won't remind you about creating range names, but we continue to list our suggested range names on the spreadsheet.

rectangular range with exactly the same shape (3 rows, 4 columns) as the range where the unit shipping costs are entered. This is natural, and it simplifies the formulas in the following steps.

**3** **Numbers shipped from plants.** We need to calculate the amount shipped out of each plant with row sums in the range G13:G15. To do this most easily, highlight this range and click on the summation ($\Sigma$) toolbar button.

**4** **Amounts received by regions.** We also need to calculate the amount shipped to each region with column sums in the range C16:F16. Again, do this by highlighting the range and clicking on the summation button.

**5** **Total shipping cost.** Calculate the total cost of shipping power from the plants to the regions in the Total_cost cell with the formula

**=SUMPRODUCT(C6:F8,Shipping_plan)**

This formula sums all products of unit shipping costs and amounts shipped. The benefit of placing unit shipping costs and amounts shipped in similar-size rectangular ranges is that it allows us to use the SUMPRODUCT function.

## USING SOLVER

Invoke Solver with the settings shown in Figure 5.3. As usual, check the Assume Linear Model and Assume Non-Negative options before optimizing.

**Figure 5.3**

Solver Dialog Box for the Transportation Model

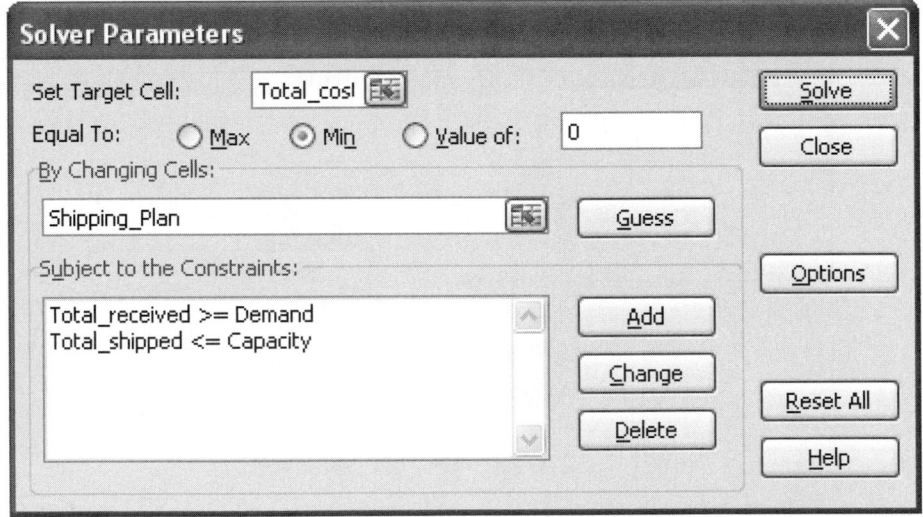

### Discussion of the Solution

*Typically in transportation models, especially large models, only a relatively few of the possible routes are used.*

The Solver solution appears in Figure 5.2 and is illustrated graphically in Figure 5.4. The company incurs a total shipping cost of $176,050 by using the shipments listed in Figure 5.4. Except for the six routes shown, no other routes are used. Most of the shipments occur on the low-cost routes, but this is not always the case. For example, the route from plant 2 to region 1 is relatively expensive, but it *is* used. On the other hand, the route from plant 3 to region 2 is relatively cheap, but it is *not* used. A good shipping plan tries to use cheap routes, but it is constrained by capacities and demands.

**Figure 5.4**

Graphical Representation of Optimal Solution

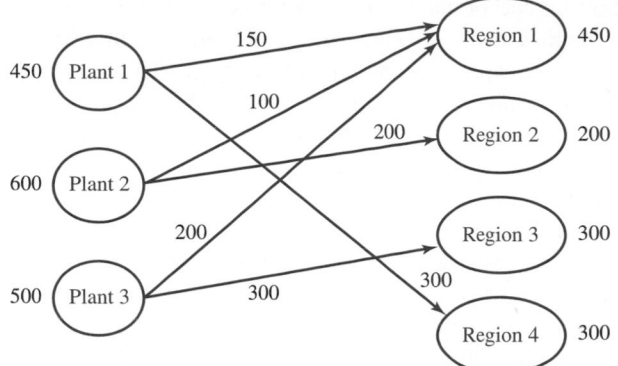

Note that the available capacity is not all used. The reason is that total capacity is 1550, whereas total demand is only 1250. Even though we constrained the demand constraints to be of the "≥" type, there is clearly no reason to send the regions *more* than the regions request because it only increases shipping costs. Therefore, we send them the minimal amounts they request and no more. In fact, we could have expressed the demand constraints as "=" constraints, and we would have obtained exactly the same solution.

### Sensitivity Analysis

We could perform many sensitivity analyses on the basic transportation model. For example, we could vary any one of the unit shipping costs, capacities, or demands. The effect of any such change in a single input is captured nicely in Solver's sensitivity report, shown in Figure 5.5. The top part indicates the effects of changes in the unit shipping costs. The results here are typical. For all routes with positive flows, the corresponding reduced cost is 0, whereas for all routes not currently being used, the reduced cost indicates how much less the unit shipping cost would have to be before the company would start shipping along it. For example, if the unit shipping cost from plant 2 to region 3 decreased by more than $69, then this route would become attractive.

**Figure 5.5**

Solver's Sensitivity Report for the Transportation Model

| | A | B | C | D | E | F | G | H |
|---|---|---|---|---|---|---|---|---|
| 6 | | Adjustable Cells | | | | | | |
| 7 | | | | Final | Reduced | Objective | Allowable | Allowable |
| 8 | | Cell | Name | Value | Cost | Coefficient | Increase | Decrease |
| 9 | | $C$13 | Plant 1 Region 1 | 150 | 0 | 131 | 119 | 13 |
| 10 | | $D$13 | Plant 1 Region 2 | 0 | 221 | 218 | 1E+30 | 221 |
| 11 | | $E$13 | Plant 1 Region 3 | 0 | 191 | 266 | 1E+30 | 191 |
| 12 | | $F$13 | Plant 1 Region 4 | 300 | 0 | 120 | 13 | 239 |
| 13 | | $C$14 | Plant 2 Region 1 | 100 | 0 | 250 | 39 | 72 |
| 14 | | $D$14 | Plant 2 Region 2 | 200 | 0 | 116 | 88 | 116 |
| 15 | | $E$14 | Plant 2 Region 3 | 0 | 69 | 263 | 1E+30 | 69 |
| 16 | | $F$14 | Plant 2 Region 4 | 0 | 39 | 278 | 1E+30 | 39 |
| 17 | | $C$15 | Plant 3 Region 1 | 200 | 0 | 178 | 13 | 69 |
| 18 | | $D$15 | Plant 3 Region 2 | 0 | 88 | 132 | 1E+30 | 88 |
| 19 | | $E$15 | Plant 3 Region 3 | 300 | 0 | 122 | 69 | 194 |
| 20 | | $F$15 | Plant 3 Region 4 | 0 | 13 | 180 | 1E+30 | 13 |
| 21 | | | | | | | | |
| 22 | | Constraints | | | | | | |
| 23 | | | | Final | Shadow | Constraint | Allowable | Allowable |
| 24 | | Cell | Name | Value | Price | R.H. Side | Increase | Decrease |
| 25 | | $C$16 | Total received Region 1 | 450 | 250 | 450 | 300 | 100 |
| 26 | | $D$16 | Total received Region 2 | 200 | 116 | 200 | 300 | 200 |
| 27 | | $E$16 | Total received Region 3 | 300 | 194 | 300 | 200 | 100 |
| 28 | | $F$16 | Total received Region 4 | 300 | 239 | 300 | 150 | 100 |
| 29 | | $G$13 | Plant 1 Total shipped | 450 | -119 | 450 | 100 | 150 |
| 30 | | $G$14 | Plant 2 Total shipped | 300 | 0 | 600 | 1E+30 | 300 |
| 31 | | $G$15 | Plant 3 Total shipped | 500 | -72 | 500 | 100 | 200 |

The bottom part of this report is useful because of its shadow prices. For example, we know that plants 1 and 3 are shipping all of their capacity, so the company would benefit from having more capacity at these plants. In particular, the report indicates that each extra unit of capacity at plant 1 is worth $119, and each extra unit of capacity at plant 3 is worth $72. However, because the allowable increase for each of these is 100, we know that after an increase in capacity of 100 at either plant, further increases will probably be worth *less* than the stated shadow prices.

*The key to this sensitivity analysis is to modify the model slightly before running SolverTable.*

One interesting analysis that cannot be performed with Solver's sensitivity report is to keep shipping costs and capacities constant and allow *all* the demands to change by a certain percentage (positive or negative). To perform this analysis, we use SolverTable, with the varying percentage as the single input. Then we can keep track of the total cost and any particular amounts shipped of interest. The key to doing this correctly is to modify the model slightly before running SolverTable. The appropriate modifications appear in Figure 5.6. Now we store the original demands in row 10, we enter a percent increase in cell I10, and we enter *formulas* in the Demand range in row 20. For example, the formula in cell C20 is =C10*(1+$I$10). Then we run SolverTable with cell I10 as the single input cell, allowing it to vary from –20% to 40% in increments of 5%, and keep track of total cost. As the table shows, the total shipping cost increases at an increasing rate as the demands increase. However, at some point, the problem becomes infeasible. As soon as the total demand is greater than the total capacity, it is impossible to meet all demand.

**Figure 5.6**

Sensitivity Analysis to Percentage Changes in All Demands

| | A | B | C | D | E | F | G | H | I |
|---|---|---|---|---|---|---|---|---|---|
| 1 | Grand Prix transportation model | | | | | | | | |
| 2 | | | | | | | | | |
| 3 | Unit shipping costs | | | | | | | | |
| 4 | | | To | | | | | | |
| 5 | | | Region 1 | Region 2 | Region 3 | Region 4 | | | |
| 6 | From | Plant 1 | $131 | $218 | $266 | $120 | | | |
| 7 | | Plant 2 | $250 | $116 | $263 | $278 | | | |
| 8 | | Plant 3 | $178 | $132 | $122 | $180 | | | |
| 9 | | | | | | | | Input for SolverTable | |
| 10 | Original demands | | 450 | 200 | 300 | 300 | | % change | 0% |
| 11 | | | | | | | | | |
| 12 | Shipping plan, and constraints on supply and demand | | | | | | | | |
| 13 | | | To | | | | | | |
| 14 | | | Region 1 | Region 2 | Region 3 | Region 4 | Total shipped | | Capacity |
| 15 | From | Plant 1 | 150 | 0 | 0 | 300 | 450 | <= | 450 |
| 16 | | Plant 2 | 100 | 200 | 0 | 0 | 300 | <= | 600 |
| 17 | | Plant 3 | 200 | 0 | 300 | 0 | 500 | <= | 500 |
| 18 | | Total received | 450 | 200 | 300 | 300 | | | |
| 19 | | | >= | >= | >= | >= | | | |
| 20 | | Demand | 450 | 200 | 300 | 300 | | | |
| 21 | | | | | | | | | |
| 22 | Objective to minimize | | | | | | | | |
| 23 | Total cost | $176,050 | | | | | | | |
| 24 | | | | | | | | | |
| 25 | Sensitivity of total cost to percentage change in each of the demands | | | | | | | | |
| 26 | | $B$23 | | | | | | | |
| 27 | -20% | $130,850 | | | | | | | |
| 28 | -15% | $140,350 | | | | | | | |
| 29 | -10% | $149,850 | | | | | | | |
| 30 | -5% | $162,770 | | | | | | | |
| 31 | 0% | $176,050 | | | | | | | |
| 32 | 5% | $189,330 | | | | | | | |
| 33 | 10% | $202,610 | | | | | | | |
| 34 | 15% | $215,890 | | | | | | | |
| 35 | 20% | $229,170 | | | | | | | |
| 36 | 25% | Not feasible | | | | | | | |
| 37 | 30% | Not feasible | | | | | | | |

## An Alternative Model

The transportation model in Figure 5.2 is very natural. From the graphical representation in Figure 5.1, we can see that all arcs go from left to right, that is, from plants to regions. Therefore, the rectangular range of shipments allows us to calculate shipments out of plants as row sums and shipments into regions as column sums. In anticipation of later models in this chapter, however, where the graphical network can be more complex, we present an alternative model of the transportation problem. (See the file **Transportation 2.xlsx.**)

First, it is useful to introduce some additional network terminology. We already defined flows as the amounts shipped on the various arcs. The direction of the arcs indicates which way the flows are allowed to travel. An arc pointed into a node is called an **inflow,** whereas an arrow pointed out of a node is called an **outflow.** In the basic transportation model, all outflows originate from suppliers, and all inflows go toward demanders. However, general networks can have both inflows and outflows for *any* given node.

*Although this model is possibly less natural than the original model, it generalizes much better to other network models.*

With this general structure in mind, the typical network model has one changing cell per arc. It indicates how much (if any) to send along that arc in the direction of the arrow. Therefore, it is often useful to model network problems by listing all of the arcs and their corresponding flows in one long list. Then we can deal with constraints in a separate section of the spreadsheet. Specifically, for each node in the network, there is a **flow balance constraint.** These flow balance constraints for the basic transportation model are simply the supply and demand constraints we have already discussed, but they can be more general for other network models, as we will discuss in later sections.

The alternative model of the Grand Prix problem appears in Figure 5.7. In the range A5:C16, we manually enter the plant and region indexes and the associated unit shipping costs. Each row in this range corresponds to an arc in the network. For example, row 12 corresponds to the arc from plant 2 to region 4, with unit shipping cost $278. Then we create a column of changing cells for the flows in column D. (If there were arc capacities, we would place them to the right of the flows, as illustrated in later examples.)

**Figure 5.7** Alternative Model of the Transportation Problem

| | A | B | C | D | E | F | G | H | I | J | K | L | M |
|---|---|---|---|---|---|---|---|---|---|---|---|---|---|
| 1 | Grand Prix transportation model: a more general network formulation | | | | | | | | | | Range names used: | | |
| 2 | | | | | | | | | | | Capacity | =Model!$I$6:$I$8 | |
| 3 | Network structure and flows | | | | | Flow balance constraints | | | | | Demand | =Model!$I$12:$I$15 | |
| 4 | Origin | Destination | Unit cost | Flow | | Capacity constraints | | | | | Destination | =Model!$B$5:$B$16 | |
| 5 | 1 | 1 | 131 | 150 | | Plant | Outflow | | Capacity | | Flow | =Model!$D$5:$D$16 | |
| 6 | 1 | 2 | 218 | 0 | | 1 | 450 | <= | 450 | | Inflow | =Model!$G$12:$G$15 | |
| 7 | 1 | 3 | 266 | 0 | | 2 | 300 | <= | 600 | | Origin | =Model!$A$5:$A$16 | |
| 8 | 1 | 4 | 120 | 300 | | 3 | 500 | <= | 500 | | Outflow | =Model!$G$6:$G$8 | |
| 9 | 2 | 1 | 250 | 100 | | | | | | | Total_Cost | =Model!$B$19 | |
| 10 | 2 | 2 | 116 | 200 | | Demand constraints | | | | | | | |
| 11 | 2 | 3 | 263 | 0 | | Region | Inflow | | Demand | | | | |
| 12 | 2 | 4 | 278 | 0 | | 1 | 450 | >= | 450 | | | | |
| 13 | 3 | 1 | 178 | 200 | | 2 | 200 | >= | 200 | | | | |
| 14 | 3 | 2 | 132 | 0 | | 3 | 300 | >= | 300 | | | | |
| 15 | 3 | 3 | 122 | 300 | | 4 | 300 | >= | 300 | | | | |
| 16 | 3 | 4 | 180 | 0 | | | | | | | | | |
| 17 | | | | | | | | | | | | | |
| 18 | Objective to minimize | | | | | | | | | | | | |
| 19 | Total Cost | $176,050 | | | | | | | | | | | |

The flow balance constraints are conceptually straightforward. Each cell in the Outflow and Inflow ranges in column G contains the appropriate sum of flows. For example, cell G6, the outflow from plant 1, represents the sum of cells D5 through D8, whereas cell G12, the inflow to plant 1, represents the sum of cells D5, D9, and D13. Fortunately, we can *easily* enter these summation formulas by using Excel's built-in SUMIF function in the form =SUMIF(*CompareRange,Criteria,SumRange*).[3] For example, the formula in cell G6 is

**=SUMIF(Origin,F6,Flow)**

This formula compares the plant number in cell F6 to the Origin range in column A and sums all flows where they are equal—that is, it sums all flows out of plant 1. By copying this formula down to cell G8, we obtain the flows out of the other plants. For flows into regions, we enter the similar formula

**=SUMIF(Destination,F12,Flow)**

in cell G12 to sum all flows into region 1, and we copy it down to cell G15 for flows into the other regions. In general, the SUMIF function finds all cells in the first argument that satisfy the criterion in the second argument and then sums the corresponding cells in the third argument. It is a *very* handy function, especially for network modeling.

### Excel Function: *SUMIF*
*The SUMIF function is useful for summing values in a certain range if cells in a related range satisfy given conditions. It has the syntax* =SUMIF(compareRange,criterion, sumRange), *where* compareRange *and* sumRange *are similar-size ranges. This formula checks each cell in* compareRange *to see whether it satisfies the criterion. If it does, it adds the corresponding value in* sumRange *to the overall sum. For example,* =SUMIF(A12:A23,1,D12:D23) *sums all values in the range D12:D23 where the corresponding cell in the range A12:A23 has the value 1.*

This use of the SUMIF function, along with the list of origins, destinations, unit costs, and flows in columns A through D, is the key to the network formulation. From there on, the model is straightforward. We calculate the total cost as the SUMPRODUCT of unit costs and flows, and we set up the Solver dialog box as in Figure 5.8.

**Figure 5.8**
Solver Dialog Box for the Alternative Transportation Model

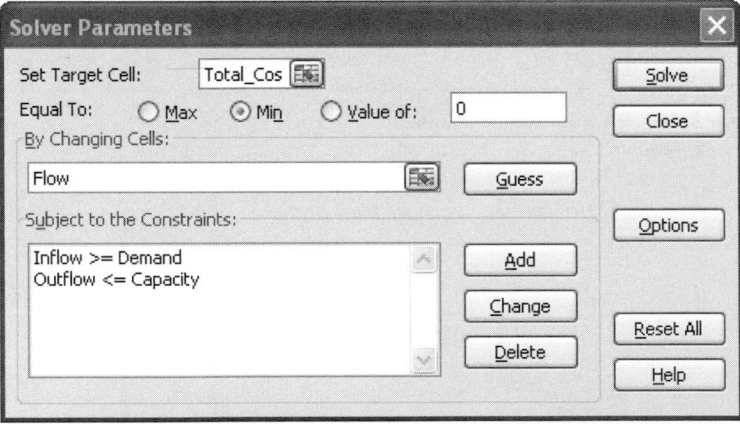

*The alternative network model not only accommodates more general networks, but it also has the fewest number of changing cells.*

Several similar formulations appear throughout this chapter. To a certain extent, this makes all network models look alike. There is an additional benefit from this model formulation. Suppose that, for whatever reason, flows from certain plants to certain regions are not allowed. (Maybe no roads exist.) Disallowing such routes in the original model

---

[3] Try entering these formulas manually, even for a 3 × 4 transportation model, and you'll see why we use the SUMIF function!

isn't easy. The usual trick is to allow the "disallowed" routes but to impose extremely large unit shipping costs on them. This works, but it is wasteful because it adds changing cells that do not really belong in the model. In contrast, the alternative network model omits arcs that are not allowed. For example, if the route from plant 2 to city 4 is not allowed, we simply omit the data in the range A12:D12. This creates a model with exactly as many changing cells as allowable arcs. This additional benefit can be very valuable when the number of potential arcs in the network is huge—even though the vast majority of them are disallowed—and this is exactly the situation in most large network models.

We do not necessarily recommend this more general network model for simple transportation problems. In fact, it is less natural than the original model in Figure 5.2. However, it paves the way for the more complex network problems discussed later in the chapter. ∎

## MODELING ISSUES

*Depending on how you treat the demand constraints, you can get several varieties of the basic transportation model.*

1. The customer demands in typical transportation problems can be handled in one of two ways. First, we can think of these forecasted demands as *minimal* requirements that must be sent to the customers. This is how we treated regional demands here. For example, the amount shipped to region 1 was constrained to be *at least* 450. Alternatively, we could consider the demands as *maximal* sales quantities, the most each region can sell. Then we would constrain the amounts sent to the regions to be less than or equal to the forecasted demands. Whether we express the demand constraints as "≥" or "≤" (or even "=") constraints depends on the context of the problem—do the dealers need at least this many, do they need exactly this many, or can they sell only this many?

2. If all the supplies and demands for a transportation problem are integers, then the optimal Solver solution automatically has integer-valued shipments. We do *not* have to add explicit integer constraints. This is a very important benefit because it allows us to use the "fast" simplex method rather than the much slower branch and bound algorithms used for integer programming.

3. Shipping costs are often nonlinear (and nonsmooth) due to quantity discounts. For example, if it costs $3 per item to ship up to 100 items between locations and $2 per item for each additional item, the proportionality assumption of LP is violated, and the transportation models we have developed are nonlinear. Shipping problems that involve quantity discounts are generally difficult to solve.

4. Excel's Solver uses the simplex method to solve transportation problems. The streamlined version of the simplex method, called the **transportation simplex method,** is much more efficient than the ordinary simplex method for transportation problems. Large transportation problems are usually solved with the transportation simplex method. See Winston (2003) for a discussion of the transportation simplex method.

5. LeBlanc and Galbreth (2007a, 2007b) discuss a large network model they developed for a client. They indicate that our SUMIF method can be inefficient for really large models. They recommend writing a macro in VBA to sum the appropriate flows in and out of nodes. ∎

Extending the basic Grand Prix transportation model is fairly easy, even when the cost structure is considerably more complex. We illustrate one such extension in the following example.

## 5.2 Production and Shipment of Automobiles with Varying Tax Rates

Consider again Grand Prix's problem of shipping automobiles from three plants to four regions. However, the problem is now extended in two directions. First, we assume that Grand Prix not only ships the autos, but it manufactures them at the plants and sells them in the various regions. Second, we assume that this problem takes place in a global context. The effect is that the unit production costs vary by plant, the unit selling prices vary by region, and the tax rates on profits vary according to the plant at which the autos are produced (regardless of where they are sold). The capacities of the plants, the demands of the regions, and the unit shipping costs are the same as before, as shown earlier in Table 5.1. In addition, the unit production costs and tax rates are given in Table 5.3, and the unit selling prices in Table 5.4. For example, if plant 1 produces an auto and ships it to region 2, where it is sold, the profit before taxes is \$20,520 − \$14,350 − \$218 = \$5,952. This is taxed at plant 1's rate of 30%, so the after-tax profit is \$5,952(1 − 0.3) = \$4,166.40. The company now needs to find a production and shipping plan that maximizes its after-tax profit.

**Table 5.3** Plant Production Costs and Tax Rates for the Grand Prix Problem

| Plant | Unit Production Cost | Tax Rate |
|---|---|---|
| 1 | \$14,350 | 30% |
| 2 | \$16,270 | 35% |
| 3 | \$16,940 | 22% |

**Table 5.4** Selling Prices in Regions

| Region | Unit Selling Price |
|---|---|
| 1 | \$19,290 |
| 2 | \$20,520 |
| 3 | \$17,570 |
| 4 | \$18,320 |

**Objective** To extend the previous Grand Prix transportation model to take into account varying production costs, selling prices, and tax rates.

### Where do the numbers come from?

We leave it to the cost accountants to derive the numbers in Table 5.3 and Table 5.4. This is no easy task, particularly in a global setting, but the numbers should be available.

## Solution

In addition to the variables required for the original transportation model in Example 5.1, we require one extra set of calculations. In particular, we need the after-tax profit per automobile produced in a given plant and sold in a given region. After we find these unit after-tax profits, it is straightforward to calculate the total after-tax profit from any production/shipping plan, and this becomes the objective we maximize. The details are next.

## DEVELOPING THE SPREADSHEET MODEL

The completed spreadsheet model appears in Figure 5.9. (See the file **Transportation 3.xlsx**.) Because the only differences from the previous example are in the monetary section, from row 25 down, we need only the following two steps to extend the model in Figure 5.2.

**Figure 5.9**    Spreadsheet Model for the Extended Grand Prix Problem

| | A | B | C | D | E | F | G | H | I | J | K | L | M |
|---|---|---|---|---|---|---|---|---|---|---|---|---|---|
| 1 | Grand Prix transportation model with taxes | | | | | | | | | | | | |
| 2 | | | | | | | | | | | | | |
| 3 | Input data | | | | | | | | | | Range names used: | | |
| 4 | Unit shipping costs (shipping only) | | | | | | | | | | After_tax_profit | =Model!$B$31 | |
| 5 | | | To | | | | | Plant data | | | Capacity | =Model!$I$16:$I$18 | |
| 6 | | | Region 1 | Region 2 | Region 3 | Region 4 | | Unit cost | Tax rate | | Demand | =Model!$C$21:$F$21 | |
| 7 | From | Plant 1 | $131 | $218 | $266 | $120 | | $14,350 | 30% | | Shipping_plan | =Model!$C$16:$F$18 | |
| 8 | | Plant 2 | $250 | $116 | $263 | $278 | | $16,270 | 35% | | Total_received | =Model!$C$19:$F$19 | |
| 9 | | Plant 3 | $178 | $132 | $122 | $180 | | $16,940 | 22% | | Total_shipped | =Model!$G$16:$G$18 | |
| 10 | | | | | | | | | | | | | |
| 11 | Unit selling prices at regions | | $19,290 | $20,520 | $17,570 | $18,320 | | | | | | | |
| 12 | | | | | | | | | | | | | |
| 13 | Shipping plan, and constraints on supply and demand | | | | | | | | | | | | |
| 14 | | | To | | | | | | | | | | |
| 15 | | | Region 1 | Region 2 | Region 3 | Region 4 | Total shipped | | Capacity | | | | |
| 16 | From | Plant 1 | 450 | 0 | 0 | 0 | 450 | <= | 450 | | | | |
| 17 | | Plant 2 | 0 | 0 | 300 | 300 | 600 | <= | 600 | | | | |
| 18 | | Plant 3 | 0 | 500 | 0 | 0 | 500 | <= | 500 | | | | |
| 19 | | Total received | 450 | 500 | 300 | 300 | | | | | | | |
| 20 | | | >= | >= | >= | >= | | | | | | | |
| 21 | | Demand | 450 | 200 | 300 | 300 | | | | | | | |
| 22 | | | | | | | | | | | | | |
| 23 | Monetary outputs | | | | | | | | | | | | |
| 24 | After-tax profit per unit produced in given plant and sold in given region | | | | | | | | | | | | |
| 25 | | | Region 1 | Region 2 | Region 3 | Region 4 | | | | | | | |
| 26 | | Plant 1 | $3,366.30 | $4,166.40 | $2,067.80 | $2,695.00 | | | | | | | |
| 27 | | Plant 2 | $1,800.50 | $2,687.10 | $674.05 | $1,151.80 | | | | | | | |
| 28 | | Plant 3 | $1,694.16 | $2,689.44 | $396.24 | $936.00 | | | | | | | |
| 29 | | | | | | | | | | | | | |
| 30 | Objective to maximize | | | | | | | | | | | | |
| 31 | After-tax profit | $3,407,310 | | | | | | | | | | | |

*This is another example of how the careful planning of spreadsheet layout simplifies the development of the model.*

**1**   **Unit after-tax profits.** The after-tax profit is the unit selling price minus the production cost minus the shipping cost, all multiplied by 1 minus the tax rate. Calculate this for the plant 1, region 1 combination in cell C26 with the formula

**=(C$11-$H7-C7)*(1-$I7)**

and copy it to the range C26:F28 for the other combinations. Note how we can use a single formula to fill this entire range. This takes careful modeling (entering the plant production cost and tax rate data in columns, and the region selling price data in a row) and appropriate use of absolute and relative addresses, but it is more efficient and certainly less likely to cause errors.

**2**   **Total after-tax profit.** Calculate the total after-tax profit in cell B31 with the formula

**=SUMPRODUCT(C26:F28,Shipping_plan)**

## USING SOLVER

The Solver setup is practically the same as before, as shown in Figure 5.10. However, don't forget to check the Maximize option—you do not want to *minimize* after-tax profit!

**Figure 5.10**

Solver Dialog Box
for the Extended
Grand Prix Model

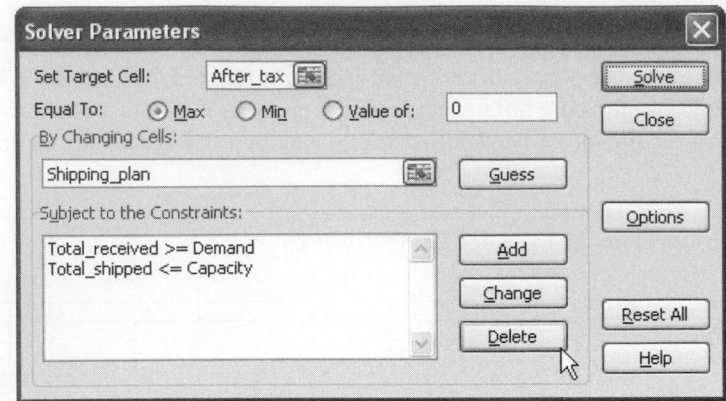

## Discussion of the Solution

The optimal solution shown in Figure 5.9 uses only 4 of the possible 12 routes, and, surprisingly, these are not the 4 routes with the largest unit after-tax profits. In fact, the route with the largest after-tax profit, from plant 1 to region 2, is not used at all. The reason for this is that if we used this route to its fullest extent, we would have to satisfy region 1's demand from plant 2 or 3, and both of these routes have very low unit after-tax profits. Of course, Solver figures this out for us.

Note also that the demand constraints cannot now be changed to "=" constraints. In the previous example, there was no incentive to use all plant capacity, but now there is. The selling prices are large enough that every automobile sale adds to after-tax profit, so the company sells as many as it can. Of course, this raises the question of how many automobiles each region can *really* sell. It might be more realistic to keep the lower bounds on sales (the current demand constraints) but to impose upper limits on sales as well. We ask you to explore this in one of the problems. ∎

---

# PROBLEMS

*Solutions for problems whose numbers appear within a color box can be found in the Student Solutions Files. Order your copy today at the Winston/Albright product Web site, academic.cengage.com/decisionsciences/winston.*

## Skill-Building Problems

**1.** In the original Grand Prix example, the total capacity of the three plants is 1550, well above the total customer demand. Would it help to have 100 more units of capacity at plant 1? What is the most Grand Prix would be willing to pay for this extra capacity? Answer the same questions for plant 2 and for plant 3. Explain why extra capacity can be valuable even though the company already has more total capacity than it requires.

**2.** The optimal solution to the original Grand Prix problem indicates that with a unit shipping cost of $132, the route from plant 3 to region 2 is evidently too expensive—no autos are shipped along this route. Use SolverTable to see how much this unit shipping

cost would have to be reduced before some autos would be shipped along this route.

**3.** Suppose in the original Grand Prix example that the routes from plant 2 to region 1 and from plant 3 to region 3 are not allowed. (Perhaps there are no railroad lines for these routes.) How would you modify the original model (Figure 5.2) to rule out these routes? How would you modify the alternative model (Figure 5.7) to do so? Discuss the pros and cons of these two approaches.

**4.** In the Grand Prix example with varying tax rates, the optimal solution more than satisfies customer demands. Modify the model so that regions have not only lower limits on the amounts they require, but upper limits on the amounts they can sell. Assume these upper limits are 50 autos above the required lower limits. For example, the lower and upper limits for region 1 are 450 and 500. Modify the model and find the optimal solution. How does it differ from the solution without upper limits?

**5.** In the Grand Prix example with varying tax rates, the optimal solution uses all available plant capacity and more than satisfies customer demands. Will this always be the case? Experiment with the unit selling prices and/or tax rates to see whether the company ever uses less than its total capacity.

## Skill-Extending Problems

**6.** Here is a problem to challenge your intuition. In the original Grand Prix example, reduce the capacity of plant 2 to 300. Then the total capacity is equal to the total demand. Reoptimize the model. You should find that the optimal solution uses all capacity and exactly meets all demands with a total cost of $176,050. Now increase the capacity of plant 1 and the demand at region 2 by 1 automobile each, and optimize again. What happens to the optimal total cost? How can you explain this "more for less" paradox?

**7.** Continuing the previous problem (with capacity 300 at plant 2), suppose we want to see how much extra capacity and extra demand we can add to plant 1 and region 2 (the same amount to each) before the total shipping cost stops decreasing and starts *increasing*. Use SolverTable appropriately to find out. (You will probably need to use some trial and error on the range of input values.) Can you explain intuitively what causes the total cost to stop decreasing and start increasing?

**8.** Modify the original Grand Prix example as follows. Increase the demands at the regions by 200 each, so that total demand is well above total plant capacity. However, now interpret these "demands" as "maximum sales," the most each region can accommodate, and change the "demand" constraints to become "≤" constraints, not "≥" constraints. How does the optimal solution change? Does it make realistic sense? If not, how might you change the model to obtain a realistic solution?

**9.** Modify the original Grand Prix example as follows. Increase the demands at the regions by 200 each, so that total demand is well above total plant capacity. This means that some demands cannot be supplied. Suppose there is a unit "penalty" cost at each region for not supplying an automobile. Let these unit penalty costs be $600, $750, $625, and $550 for the four regions. Develop a model to minimize the sum of shipping costs and penalty costs for unsatisfied demands. (*Hint:* This requires a trick. Introduce a fourth plant with plenty of capacity, and set its "unit shipping costs" to the regions equal to the unit penalty costs. Then interpret an auto shipped from this fictitious plant to a region as a unit of demand not satisfied.)

## 5.3 ASSIGNMENT MODELS

In this section, we examine a class of network models called **assignment models.** Assignment models are used to assign, on a one-to-one basis, members of one set to members of another set in a least-cost (or least-time) manner. The prototype assignment model is the assignment of machines to jobs. For example, suppose there are four jobs and five machines. Every pairing of a machine and a job has a given job completion time. The problem is to assign the machines to the jobs so that the total time to complete all jobs is minimized.

*Assignment models are special cases of transportation models where all flows are 0 or 1.*

To see how this is a network problem, recall the transportation problem of sending goods from suppliers to customers. Now think of the machines as the suppliers, the jobs as the customers, and the job completion times as the unit shipping costs. The capacity of any machine represents the most jobs it can handle. The "demand" of any job is the number of times it must be done, usually 1. Finally, there is an arc from every machine to every job it can handle, and the allowable flows on these arcs are all 0 or 1—a particular machine is either paired with a particular job (a flow of 1) or it isn't (a flow of 0). Therefore, we can model this assignment problem *exactly* like we modeled the Grand Prix transportation problem in Example 5.1 by using the appropriate input values.

An example of this model appears in Figures 5.11 and 5.12. (See the file **Assignment.xlsx**.) Here, we see that four jobs must be completed by five machines. Machines 1, 3, and 5 can handle at most one job apiece, whereas machines 2 and 4 can handle two jobs apiece. The spreadsheet model in Figure 5.12 is identical to the transportation model discussed previously, except with different inputs. The only minor difference, as indicated in the Solver dialog box in Figure 5.13, is that we make the demand constraints "=" constraints, because we want each job to be completed exactly once.

## Figure 5.11

Network
Representation of
Assignment of
Machines to Jobs

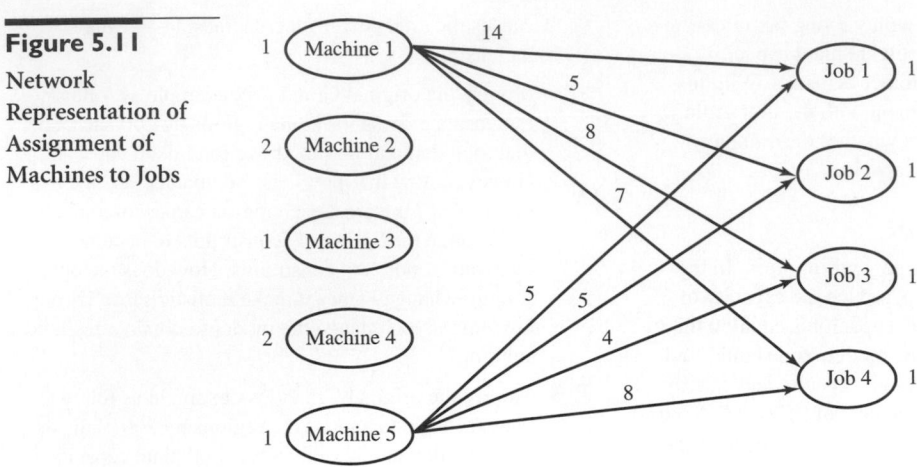

*Note*: Similar arcs exist out of machines 2, 3, and 4.

## Figure 5.12  Spreadsheet Model of the Assignment Problem

| | A | B | C | D | E | F | G | H | I | J | K |
|---|---|---|---|---|---|---|---|---|---|---|---|
| 1 | Assignment of jobs to machines | | | | | | | | | | |
| 2 | | | | | | | | | | | |
| 3 | Times to perform jobs on various machines | | | | | | | | Range names used: | | |
| 4 | | | Job | | | | | | Assignments | =Model!$C$15:$F$19 | |
| 5 | | | 1 | 2 | 3 | 4 | | | Jobs_on_machine | =Model!$G$15:$G$19 | |
| 6 | Machine | 1 | 14 | 5 | 8 | 7 | | | Machine_capacity | =Model!$I$15:$I$19 | |
| 7 | | 2 | 2 | 12 | 6 | 5 | | | Machines_on_job | =Model!$C$20:$F$20 | |
| 8 | | 3 | 7 | 8 | 3 | 9 | | | Total_time | =Model!$B$25 | |
| 9 | | 4 | 2 | 4 | 6 | 10 | | | | | |
| 10 | | 5 | 5 | 5 | 4 | 8 | | | | | |
| 11 | | | | | | | | | | | |
| 12 | Assignments, and constraints on machine capacities and job completion requirements | | | | | | | | | | |
| 13 | | | Job | | | | | | | | |
| 14 | | | 1 | 2 | 3 | 4 | Jobs on machine | | Machine capacity | | |
| 15 | Machine | 1 | 0 | 0 | 0 | 0 | 0 | <= | 1 | | |
| 16 | | 2 | 0 | 0 | 0 | 1 | 1 | <= | 2 | | |
| 17 | | 3 | 0 | 0 | 1 | 0 | 1 | <= | 1 | | |
| 18 | | 4 | 1 | 1 | 0 | 0 | 2 | <= | 2 | | |
| 19 | | 5 | 0 | 0 | 0 | 0 | 0 | <= | 1 | | |
| 20 | | Machines on job | 1 | 1 | 1 | 1 | | | | | |
| 21 | | | = | = | = | = | | | | | |
| 22 | | Required | 1 | 1 | 1 | 1 | | | | | |
| 23 | | | | | | | | | | | |
| 24 | Objective to minimize | | | | | | | | | | |
| 25 | Total time | 14 | | | | | | | | | |

## Figure 5.13

Solver Dialog Box
for the Assignment
Model

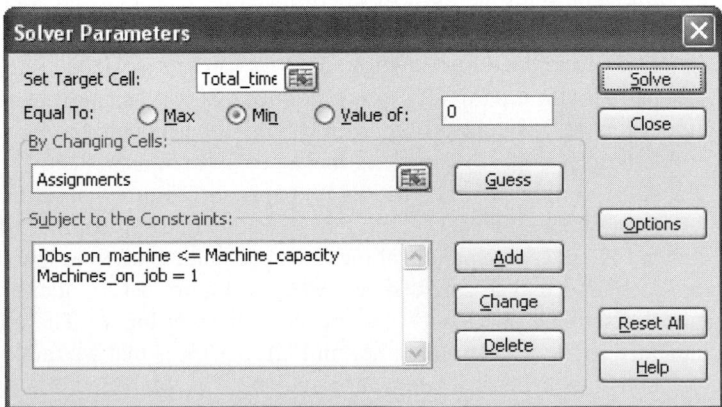

The optimal solution in Figure 5.12 indicates, by the 1's and 0's in the changing cells, which machines are assigned to which jobs. Specifically, machine 2 is assigned to job 4, machine 3 is assigned to job 3, machine 4 is assigned to jobs 1 and 2, and machines 1 and 5 are not assigned to any jobs. With this optimal assignment, it takes 14 time units to complete all jobs.

The following example is a somewhat different and less obvious type of assignment problem.

---

## EXAMPLE 5.3 ASSIGNING SCHOOL BUSES TO ROUTES AT SPRING VIEW

The city of Spring View is taking bids from six bus companies on the eight routes that must be driven in the surrounding school district. Each company enters a bid of how much it will charge to drive selected routes, although not all companies bid on all routes. The data are listed in Table 5.5. (If a company does not bid on a route, the corresponding entry is blank.) The city must decide which companies to assign to which routes with the specifications that (1) if a company does not bid on a route, it cannot be assigned to that route; (2) exactly one company must be assigned to each route; and (3) a company can be assigned to at most two routes. The objective is to minimize the total cost of covering all routes.

**Table 5.5** Bids on Bus Routes

| Company | Route 1 | Route 2 | Route 3 | Route 4 | Route 5 | Route 6 | Route 7 | Route 8 |
|---------|---------|---------|---------|---------|---------|---------|---------|---------|
| 1 |      | 8200 | 7800 | 5400 |      | 3900 |      |      |
| 2 | 7800 | 8200 |      | 6300 |      | 3300 | 4900 |      |
| 3 |      | 4800 |      |      |      | 4400 | 5600 | 3600 |
| 4 |      |      | 8000 | 5000 | 6800 |      | 6700 | 4200 |
| 5 | 7200 | 6400 |      | 3900 | 6400 | 2800 |      | 3000 |
| 6 | 7000 | 5800 | 7500 | 4500 | 5600 |      | 6000 | 4200 |

**Objective** To use a network model to assign companies to bus routes so that each route is covered at minimum cost to the city and no company is assigned to more than two routes.

### WHERE DO THE NUMBERS COME FROM?

This is straightforward. The companies involved make the bids, and the city probably decides that it isn't physically possible (or safe) for any company to handle more than two routes.

## Solution

The variables and constraints for this model are given in Table 5.6. As in the machine-to-job assignment model in Figure 5.12, the changing cells will all contain 0's or 1's. The 1's will indicate which assignments are made.

*All arcs go from company nodes to bus route nodes, and the allowable flows are all 0 or 1.*

We model this problem in the "network" way. Although we do not show the rather large network, you can imagine nodes for the bus companies on the left, nodes for the bus routes on the right, and all arrows going from left to right. All flows are 0 or 1—a company is either assigned to a bus route or it isn't. The constraint that a company can be assigned to at most two bus routes is handled by constraining the outflow from any company node to be at most 2. To ensure that each bus route is covered by exactly one company, we constrain the inflow to each bus route node to be 1.

### Table 5.6 Variables and Constraints for the Assignment Model

| | |
|---|---|
| **Input variables** | Bids for routes, maximum number of bus routes per company |
| **Decision variables (changing cells)** | Assignments of companies to bus routes |
| **Objective (target cell)** | Total cost |
| **Other calculated variables** | Number of bus routes assigned to each company, number of companies assigned to each bus route |
| **Constraints** | Number of bus routes assigned to each company is less than or equal to Maximum number of routes per company<br>Number of companies assigned to each bus route equals 1 |

## DEVELOPING THE SPREADSHEET MODEL

Because this is essentially a transportation model (with some disallowed arcs, the ones where a company doesn't bid on a route), we could mimic the transportation models in Figure 5.2 and Figure 5.12, or we could mimic the more general formulation in Figure 5.7. For efficiency, we do the latter. This actually has two advantages. It doesn't force us to include changing cells for disallowed assignments, and it gets us ready for the more general network model in the next section.

The model appears in Figure 5.14. (See the file **Bus Routes.xlsx**.) Because this model is so similar to the Grand Prix transportation model in Figure 5.7, we do not repeat all the details here. The key steps are as follows. (For help on the SUMIF function, revisit the discussion of the alternative model in Example 5.1.)

### Figure 5.14 Bus Route Assignment Model

| | A | B | C | D | E | F | G | H | I | J | K | L | M |
|---|---|---|---|---|---|---|---|---|---|---|---|---|---|
| 1 | Assignment of bus companies to routes | | | | | | | | | | | | |
| 2 | | | | | | | | | | | | | |
| 3 | Input data | | | | | | | | | | Range names used: | | |
| 4 | Maximum routes per company | 2 | | | | | | | | | Companies_assigned | =Model!$I$25:$I$32 | |
| 5 | | | | | | | | | | | Cost | =Model!$C$17:$C$47 | |
| 6 | Network setup, flows, and arc capacity constraints | | | | | Flow balance constraints | | | | | Destination | =Model!$B$17:$B$47 | |
| 7 | | Origin | Destination | Cost | Flow | | Company | Routes assigned | | Maximum allowed | Flow | =Model!$D$17:$D$47 | |
| 8 | | 1 | 2 | 8200 | 0 | | 1 | 1 | <= | 2 | Maximum_allowed | =Model!$K$17:$K$22 | |
| 9 | | 1 | 3 | 7800 | 1 | | 2 | 2 | <= | 2 | Origin | =Model!$A$17:$A$47 | |
| 10 | | 1 | 4 | 5400 | 0 | | 3 | 1 | <= | 2 | Routes_assigned | =Model!$I$17:$I$22 | |
| 11 | | 1 | 6 | 3900 | 0 | | 4 | 0 | <= | 2 | Total_cost | =Model!$B$50 | |
| 12 | | 2 | 1 | 7800 | 0 | | 5 | 2 | <= | 2 | | | |
| 13 | | 2 | 2 | 8200 | 0 | | 6 | 2 | <= | 2 | | | |
| 14 | | 2 | 4 | 6300 | 0 | | | | | | | | |
| 15 | | 2 | 6 | 3300 | 1 | | Route | Companies assigned | | Required | | | |
| 16 | | 2 | 7 | 4900 | 1 | | 1 | 1 | = | 1 | | | |
| 17 | | 3 | 2 | 4800 | 1 | | 2 | 1 | = | 1 | | | |
| 18 | | 3 | 6 | 4400 | 0 | | 3 | 1 | = | 1 | | | |
| 19 | | 3 | 7 | 5600 | 0 | | 4 | 1 | = | 1 | | | |
| 20 | | 3 | 8 | 3600 | 0 | | 5 | 1 | = | 1 | | | |
| 21 | | 4 | 3 | 8000 | 0 | | 6 | 1 | = | 1 | | | |
| 22 | | 4 | 4 | 5000 | 0 | | 7 | 1 | = | 1 | | | |
| 23 | | 4 | 5 | 6800 | 0 | | 8 | 1 | = | 1 | | | |
| 24 | | 4 | 7 | 6700 | 0 | | | | | | | | |
| 25 | | 4 | 8 | 4200 | 0 | | | | | | | | |
| 26 | | 5 | 1 | 7200 | 0 | | | | | | | | |
| 27 | | 5 | 2 | 6400 | 0 | | | | | | | | |
| 28 | | 5 | 4 | 3900 | 1 | | | | | | | | |
| 29 | | 5 | 5 | 6400 | 0 | | | | | | | | |
| 30 | | 5 | 6 | 2800 | 0 | | | | | | | | |
| 31 | | 5 | 8 | 3000 | 1 | | | | | | | | |
| 32 | | 6 | 1 | 7000 | 1 | | | | | | | | |
| 33 | | 6 | 2 | 5800 | 0 | | | | | | | | |
| 34 | | 6 | 3 | 7500 | 0 | | | | | | | | |
| 35 | | 6 | 4 | 4500 | 0 | | | | | | | | |
| 36 | | 6 | 5 | 5600 | 1 | | | | | | | | |
| 37 | | 6 | 7 | 6000 | 0 | | | | | | | | |
| 38 | | 6 | 8 | 4200 | 0 | | | | | | | | |
| 39 | | | | | | | | | | | | | |
| 40 | Objective to minimize | | | | | | | | | | | | |
| 41 | Total cost | | 40300 | | | | | | | | | | |

**1** **Arc lists.** The list of arcs (company–bus route pairs) in rows 8 to 38 corresponds to the nonblank cells in Table 5.5. There is no point in including arcs that correspond to disallowed assignments. Enter the data in columns A and B manually, referring to Table 5.5.

**2** **Inputs.** Enter the costs from the (nonblank) cells in Table 5.5 in the range C8:C38. Also, enter the maximum number of routes per company in cell B4.

**3** **Assignments.** Enter *any* values in the Flow range. Although these will eventually be 0's and 1's to indicate which assignments are made, any values can be used initially. Solver will eventually find the optimal values.

**4** **Inflows and outflows.** In column G, we need *outflows* (numbers of routes assigned) for company nodes and *inflows* (numbers of companies assigned) for bus route nodes. To calculate these, enter the formulas

=SUMIF(Origin,F8,Flow)

and

=SUMIF(Destination,F16,Flow)

in cells G8 and G16, respectively, and copy them down their respective ranges.

**5** **Requirements on flows.** Enter a link to cell B4 in each cell of the range I8:I13. This is used to prevent any company from being assigned to more than two routes. Also, enter 1 in each cell of the range I16:I23 to reflect that each route must be assigned to exactly one company.

**6** **Total cost.** Calculate the total cost to the city in cell B41 with the formula

=SUMPRODUCT(Cost,Flow)

## USING SOLVER

The Solver setup should appear as in Figure 5.15. As usual, check the Assume Linear Model and Assume Non-Negative options before optimizing.

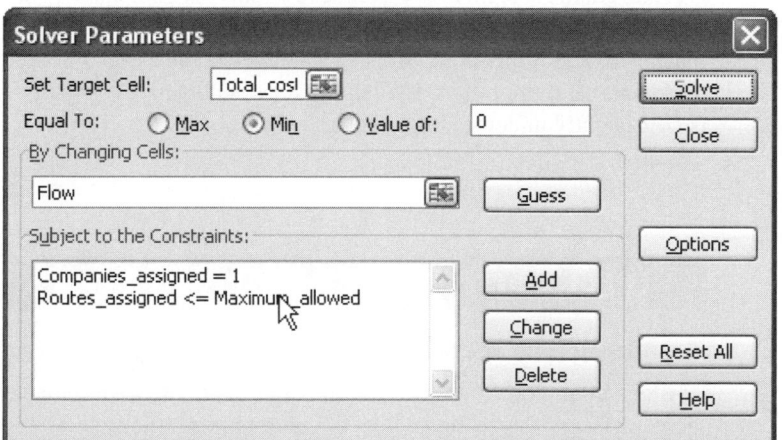

### Discussion of the Solution

The optimal solution in Figure 5.14 indicates that the city should make the following assignments: company 1 covers bus route 3, company 2 covers bus routes 6 and 7, company 3 covers bus route 2, company 5 covers bus routes 4 and 8, and company 6 covers bus routes

1 and 5. The total cost to the city of this assignment is $40,300. Note that company 4 is not assigned to any bus routes. There is no constraint that every company must be assigned to at least one bus route, and company 4 is evidently underbid by at least one company for all bus routes. If the city wanted to require that *all* companies be assigned to at least one bus route, we would simply add a *lower* bound of 1 on all of the outflows from the company nodes (in rows 8 to 13). Of course, this would probably increase the total cost to the city.

### Sensitivity Analysis

One interesting sensitivity analysis is to see what effect the upper bound constraint on the maximum routes has on the total cost. Presumably, if we allow more bus routes per company (assuming this is physically possible for the companies), the companies who tend to bid lowest will be assigned to the bulk of the bus routes, and the total cost will probably decrease. Using SolverTable, the analysis itself is straightforward with no modifications to the model necessary. We specify cell B4 as the single input cell, allow it to vary, say, from 1 to 7 in increments of 1, and keep track of total cost. The resulting output appears in Figure 5.16.

**Figure 5.16**

Sensitivity to the Maximum Number of Routes

| | A | B | C | D | E | F | G |
|---|---|---|---|---|---|---|---|
| 43 | Sensitivity of total cost to maximum routes per company | | | | | | |
| 44 | | $B$41 | | | | | |
| 45 | 1 | Not feasible | | The first problem is clearly infeasible because | | | |
| 46 | 2 | 40300 | | there are only 6 companies and there are 8 | | | |
| 47 | 3 | 39500 | | routes. There is a cost savings from being allowed | | | |
| 48 | 4 | 39500 | | to assign 3 (rather than 2) routes to a | | | |
| 49 | 5 | 39500 | | company, but there is no incentive to assign more | | | |
| 50 | 6 | 39500 | | than 3 routes to any company. | | | |
| 51 | 7 | 39500 | | | | | |

If each company can be assigned to only one route, there is no feasible solution. But this is clear: There are eight routes to cover and only six companies! For larger values of the maximum routes allowed, the total cost begins to decrease, but only until this input value reaches 3. From this point, the city achieves no additional flexibility by allowing companies to travel more routes. Evidently, there is no single company or pair of companies that is consistently underbidding all others. ■

## ADDITIONAL APPLICATIONS

### Assigning Managers at Heery International

LeBlanc et al. (2000) used an optimization model to assign managers to construction projects for Heery International. Heery contracts with the state of Tennessee for projects such as hospitals, office buildings, state park facilities (hotels and cabins), higher-education facilities (libraries, classrooms, and dormitories), armories, and prisons. The assignment model is used for problems with up to 114 projects and 7 managers. As a result of the model, Heery has managed its projects without replacing a manager who resigned and has reduced travel costs. ■

## Skill-Building Problems

**10.** Modify the machine-to-job assignment model under the assumption that only three of the four jobs must be completed. In other words, one of the four jobs does not have to be assigned to any machine. What is the new optimal solution?

**11.** One possible solution method for the machine-to-job assignment problem is the following heuristic procedure. Assign the machine to job 1 that completes job 1 quickest. Then assign the machine to job 2 that, among all machines that still have some capacity, completes job 2 quickest. Keep going until a machine has been assigned to all jobs. Does this heuristic procedure yield the optimal solution for this problem? If it does, see whether you can change the job times so that the heuristic does *not* yield the optimal solution.

**12.** In the machine-to-job assignment problem, the current capacities of the machines are 1, 2, 1, 2, and 1. If you could increase one of these capacities by 1, which would you increase? Why?

**13.** Modify the bus route assignment model, assuming that company 1 decides to place bids on routes 7 and 8 (in addition to its current bids on other routes). The bids on these two routes are $5200 and $3300. Does the optimal solution change?

**14.** We modeled the bus route assignment problem with the alternative form of the transportation model (as in Figure 5.7). Model it instead with the "standard" form (as in Figure 5.2). Discuss the pros and cons of these two approaches for this particular example.

## Skill-Extending Problems

**15.** In the optimal solution to the machine-to-job assignment problem, jobs 1 and 2 are both assigned to machine 4. Suppose we impose the restriction that jobs 1 and 2 must be assigned to *different* machines. Change the model to accommodate this restriction and find the new optimal solution.

**16.** In the optimal solution to the machine-to-job assignment problem, jobs 3 and 4 are assigned to different machines. Suppose we impose the restriction that these jobs must be assigned to the *same* machine. Change the model to accommodate this restriction and find the new optimal solution.

**17.** In the optimal solution to the bus route assignment problem, company 2 is assigned to bus routes 6 and 7. Suppose these two routes are far enough apart that it is infeasible for one company to service both of them. Change the model to accommodate this restriction and find the new optimal solution.

**18.** When we (the authors) originally developed the bus route assignment model, we included an arc capacity constraint: Flow $\leq 1$. After giving this further thought, we deleted this constraint as being redundant. Why could we do this? Specifically, why can't one or more of the flows found by Solver be greater than 1? (*Hint:* Think in terms of flows out of and into the nodes in the network diagram.)

# 5.4 MINIMUM COST NETWORK FLOW MODELS

The objective of many real-world network models is to ship goods from one set of locations to another set of locations at minimum cost, subject to various constraints. There are many variations of these models. The simplest models include a single product that must be shipped via one mode of transportation (truck, for example) in a particular period of time. More complex models—and much larger ones—can include multiple products, multiple modes of transportation, and/or multiple time periods. This general class of problems is referred to as a **minimum cost network flow** problem. We discuss several examples of such problems in this section.

The general minimum cost network flow problem is similar to the transportation problem except for two possible differences. First, arc capacities are often imposed on some or all of the arcs. These become simple upper bound constraints in the model. Second and more significant, inflows *and* outflows can be associated with any node. Nodes are generally categorized as **suppliers, demanders,** and **transshipment points.** A supplier is a location that starts with a certain supply (or possibly a capacity for supplying). A demander is the opposite; it requires a certain amount to end up there. A transshipment point is a location where goods simply pass through.

The best way to think of these categories is in terms of **net inflow** and **net outflow.** The net inflow for any node is defined as total inflow minus total outflow for that node. The net outflow is the negative of this, total outflow minus total inflow. Then a supplier is a node with positive net outflow, a demander is a node with positive net inflow, and a transshipment point is a node with net outflow (and net inflow) equal to 0. It is important to realize that inflows are sometimes allowed to suppliers, but their *net* outflows must be positive. Similarly, outflows from demanders are sometimes allowed, but their *net* inflows must be positive. For example, if Cincinnati and Memphis are manufacturers (suppliers) and Dallas and Phoenix are retail locations (demanders), then flow could go from Cincinnati to Memphis to Dallas to Phoenix.

There are typically two types of constraints in minimum cost network flow models (other than nonnegativity of flows). The first type represents the arc capacity constraints, which are simple upper bounds on the arc flows. The second type represents the flow balance constraints, one for each node. For a supplier, this constraint is typically of the form Net Outflow = Original Supply or possibly Net Outflow $<=$ Capacity. For a demander, it is typically of the form Net Inflow $>=$ Demand or possibly Net Inflow = Demand. For a transshipment point, it is of the form Net Inflow = 0 (which is equivalent to Net Outflow = 0).

If the network is represented graphically, then it is easy to "see" these constraints. We simply examine the flows on the arrows leading into and out of the various nodes. The typical situation is illustrated in the following example.

---

### FUNDAMENTAL INSIGHT

**Flow Balance Constraints**

All network optimization models have some form of flow balance constraints at the various nodes of the network. This flow balance relates the amount that enters the node to the amount that leaves the node. In many network models, the simple structure of these flow balance constraints guarantees that the optimal solutions have integer values. It also enables specialized network versions of the simplex method to solve the huge network models typically encountered in real logistics applications.

---

### EXAMPLE | 5.4 PRODUCING AND SHIPPING TOMATO PRODUCTS AT REDBRAND

The RedBrand Company produces a tomato product at three plants. This product can be shipped directly to the company's two customers, or it can first be shipped to the company's two warehouses and then to the customers. Figure 5.17 is a network representation of RedBrand's problem. Nodes 1, 2, and 3 represent the plants (these are the suppliers, denoted by S), nodes 4 and 5 represent the warehouses (these are the transshipment points, denoted by T), and nodes 6 and 7 represent the customers (these are the demanders, denoted by D). Note that we allow the possibility of some shipments among plants, among warehouses, and among customers. Also, some arcs have arrows on both ends, which means that flow is allowed in either direction.

**Figure 5.17**

Graphical
Representation
of the RedBrand
Logistics Model

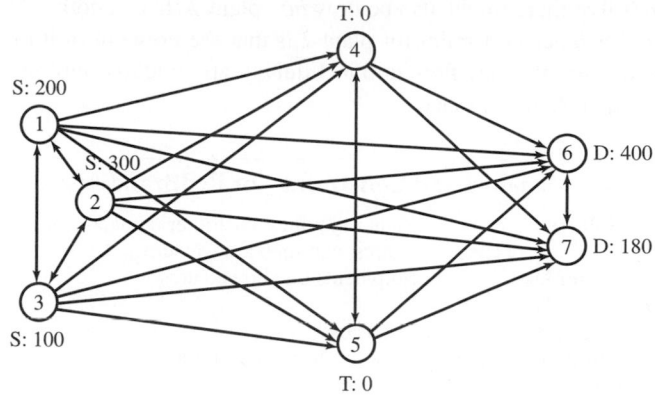

The cost of producing the product is the same at each plant, so RedBrand is concerned with minimizing the total shipping cost incurred in meeting customer demands. The production capacity of each plant (in tons per year) and the demand of each customer are shown in Figure 5.17. For example, plant 1 (node 1) has a capacity of 200, and customer 1 (node 6) has a demand of 400. In addition, the cost (in thousands of dollars) of shipping a ton of the product between each pair of locations is listed in Table 5.7, where a blank indicates that RedBrand cannot ship along that arc. We also assume that at most 200 tons of the product can be shipped between any two nodes. This is the common arc capacity. RedBrand wants to determine a minimum-cost shipping schedule.

**Table 5.7** **Shipping Costs for the RedBrand Example**

| | | *To node* | | | | | |
|---|---|---|---|---|---|---|---|
| | 1 | 2 | 3 | 4 | 5 | 6 | 7 |
| **From node 1** | | 5.0 | 3.0 | 5.0 | 5.0 | 20.0 | 20.0 |
| 2 | 9.0 | | 9.0 | 1.0 | 1.0 | 8.0 | 15.0 |
| 3 | 0.4 | 8.0 | | 1.0 | 0.5 | 10.0 | 12.0 |
| 4 | | | | | 1.2 | 2.0 | 12.0 |
| 5 | | | | 0.8 | | 2.0 | 12.0 |
| 6 | | | | | | | 1.0 |
| 7 | | | | | | 7.0 | |

**Objective** To find the minimum-cost way to ship the tomato product from suppliers to customers, possibly through warehouses, so that customer demands are met and supplier capacities are not exceeded.

## WHERE DO THE NUMBERS COME FROM?

The network configuration itself would come from geographical considerations—which routes are physically possible (or sensible) and which are not. The numbers would be derived as in the Grand Prix automobile example. (See Example 5.1 for further discussion.)

### Solution

*Other than arc capacity constraints, the only constraints are flow balance constraints.*

The variables and constraints for RedBrand's model are listed in Table 5.8. The key to the model is handling the flow balance constraints. We explain how to implement these in the step-by-step instructions for developing the spreadsheet model. However, it isn't enough, say, to specify that the flow out of plant 2 is less than or equal to the capacity of plant 2. The reason is that there might also be flow *into* plant 2 (from another plant). Therefore, the correct flow balance constraint for plant 2 is that the flow out of it must be less than or equal to its capacity plus any flow into it. Equivalently, the *net* outflow for plant 2 must be less than or equal to its capacity.

**Table 5.8** Variables and Constraints for RedBrand Logistics Model

| | |
|---|---|
| **Input variables** | Plant capacities, customer demands, unit shipping costs on allowable arcs, common arc capacity |
| **Decision variables (changing cells)** | Shipments on allowed arcs |
| **Objective (target cell)** | Total cost |
| **Other calculated variables** | Flows into and out of nodes |
| **Constraints** | Flow on each arc must be less than or equal to Common arc capacity |
| | Flow balance at each node |

## DEVELOPING THE SPREADSHEET MODEL

To set up the spreadsheet model, proceed as follows. (See Figure 5.18 and the file **RedBrand Logistics 1.xlsx**. Also, refer to the network in Figure 5.17.)

**Figure 5.18** Spreadsheet Model for the RedBrand Problem

| | A | B | C | D | E | F | G | H | I | J | K |
|---|---|---|---|---|---|---|---|---|---|---|---|
| 1 | RedBrand shipping model | | | | | | | | | | |
| 2 | | | | | | | | | | | |
| 3 | Inputs | | | | | | | | | | |
| 4 | Common arc capacity | 200 | | | | | | | | | |
| 5 | | | | | | | | | | | |
| 6 | Network structure, flows, and arc capacity constraints | | | | | | | Node balance constraints | | | |
| 7 | Origin | Destination | Unit Cost | Flow | | Arc Capacity | | Plant constraints | | | |
| 8 | 1 | 2 | 5 | 0 | <= | 200 | | Node | Plant net outflow | | Plant capacity |
| 9 | 1 | 3 | 3 | 180 | <= | 200 | | 1 | 180 | <= | 200 |
| 10 | 1 | 4 | 5 | 0 | <= | 200 | | 2 | 300 | <= | 300 |
| 11 | 1 | 5 | 5 | 0 | <= | 200 | | 3 | 99.99999997 | <= | 100 |
| 12 | 1 | 6 | 20 | 0 | <= | 200 | | | | | |
| 13 | 1 | 7 | 20 | 0 | <= | 200 | | Warehouse constraints | | | |
| 14 | 2 | 1 | 9 | 0 | <= | 200 | | Node | Warehouse net outflow | | Required |
| 15 | 2 | 3 | 9 | 0 | <= | 200 | | 4 | 2.54659E-08 | = | 0 |
| 16 | 2 | 4 | 1 | 120 | <= | 200 | | 5 | 1.89488E-10 | = | 0 |
| 17 | 2 | 5 | 1 | 0 | <= | 200 | | | | | |
| 18 | 2 | 6 | 8 | 180 | <= | 200 | | Customer constraints | | | |
| 19 | 2 | 7 | 15 | 0 | <= | 200 | | Node | Customer net inflow | | Customer demand |
| 20 | 3 | 1 | 0.4 | 0 | <= | 200 | | 6 | 400 | >= | 400 |
| 21 | 3 | 2 | 8 | 0 | <= | 200 | | 7 | 180 | >= | 180 |
| 22 | 3 | 4 | 1 | 80 | <= | 200 | | | | | |
| 23 | 3 | 5 | 0.5 | 200 | <= | 200 | | Range names used | | | |
| 24 | 3 | 6 | 10 | 0 | <= | 200 | | Arc_Capacity | =Model!$F$8:$F$33 | | |
| 25 | 3 | 7 | 12 | 0 | <= | 200 | | Customer_demand | =Model!$K$20:$K$21 | | |
| 26 | 4 | 5 | 1.2 | 0 | <= | 200 | | Customer_net_inflow | =Model!$I$20:$I$21 | | |
| 27 | 4 | 6 | 2 | 200 | <= | 200 | | Destination | =Model!$B$8:$B$33 | | |
| 28 | 4 | 7 | 12 | 0 | <= | 200 | | Flow | =Model!$D$8:$D$33 | | |
| 29 | 5 | 4 | 0.8 | 0 | <= | 200 | | Origin | =Model!$A$8:$A$33 | | |
| 30 | 5 | 6 | 2 | 200 | <= | 200 | | Plant_capacity | =Model!$K$9:$K$11 | | |
| 31 | 5 | 7 | 12 | 0 | <= | 200 | | Plant_net_outflow | =Model!$I$9:$I$11 | | |
| 32 | 6 | 7 | 1 | 180 | <= | 200 | | Total_cost | =Model!$B$36 | | |
| 33 | 7 | 6 | 7 | 0 | <= | 200 | | Unit_Cost | =Model!$C$8:$C$33 | | |
| 34 | | | | | | | | Warehouse_net_outflow | =Model!$I$15:$I$16 | | |
| 35 | Objective to minimize | | | | | | | | | | |
| 36 | Total cost | $3,260 | | | | | | | | | |

❶ **Origins and destinations.** Enter the node numbers (1 to 7) for the origins and destinations of the various arcs in the range A8:B33. Note that the disallowed arcs are not entered in this list.

❷ **Input data.** Enter the unit shipping costs (in thousands of dollars), the common arc capacity, the plant capacities, and the customer demands in the shaded ranges. Again, only the nonblank entries in Table 5.7 are used to fill up the column of unit shipping costs.

❸ **Flows on arcs.** Enter *any* initial values for the flows in the range D8:D33. These are the changing cells.

**4** **Arc capacities.** To indicate a common arc capacity for all arcs, enter the formula

=$B$4

in cell F8 and copy it down column F.

**5** **Flow balance constraints.** Nodes 1, 2, and 3 are supply nodes; nodes 4 and 5 are transshipment points; and nodes 6 and 7 are demand nodes. Therefore, set up the left sides of the flow balance constraints appropriately for these three cases. Specifically, enter the net *outflow* for node 1 in cell I9 with the formula

=SUMIF(Origin,H9,Flow)-SUMIF(Destination,H9,Flow)

and copy it down to cell I11. This formula subtracts flows into node 1 from flows out of node 1 to obtain net outflow for node 1. Next, copy this *same* formula to cells I15 and I16 for the warehouses. (Remember that for transshipment nodes, the left side of the constraint can be net outflow *or* net inflow, whichever you prefer. The reason is that if net outflow is 0, then net inflow must also be 0.) Finally, enter the net *inflow* for node 6 in cell I20 with the formula

=SUMIF(Destination,H20,Flow)-SUMIF(Origin,H20,Flow)

and copy it to cell I21. This formula subtracts flows out of node 6 from flows into node 6 to obtain the net inflow for node 6.

**6** **Total shipping cost.** Calculate the total shipping cost (in thousands of dollars) in cell B36 with the formula

=SUMPRODUCT(Unit_cost,Flow)

## USING SOLVER

The Solver dialog box should be set up as in Figure 5.19. We want to minimize total shipping costs, subject to the three types of flow balance constraints and the arc capacity constraints.

**Figure 5.19**

Solver Dialog Box for the RedBrand Model

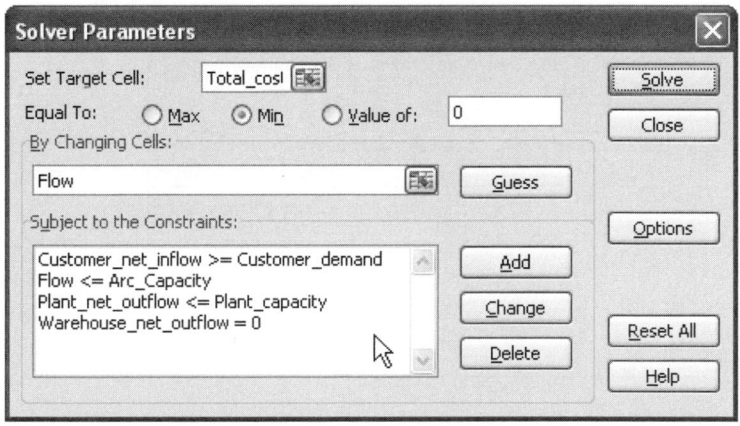

### Discussion of the Solution

The optimal solution in Figure 5.18 indicates that RedBrand's customer demand can be satisfied with a shipping cost of $3,260,000. This solution appears graphically in Figure 5.20. Note in particular that plant 1 produces 180 tons (under capacity) and ships it all to plant 3, not directly to warehouses or customers. Also, note that all shipments from the warehouses go directly to customer 1. Then customer 1 ships 180 tons to customer 2. We purposely chose unit shipping costs (probably unrealistic ones) to produce this type of behavior, just to show that it *can* occur. The costs of shipping from plant 1 directly to warehouses or customers are relatively large compared to the cost of shipping directly to plant 3. Similarly, the costs of shipping from plants or warehouses directly to customer 2 are prohibitive. Therefore, RedBrand should ship to customer 1 and let customer 1 forward some of its shipment to customer 2.

**Figure 5.20**

Optimal Flows for the RedBrand Example

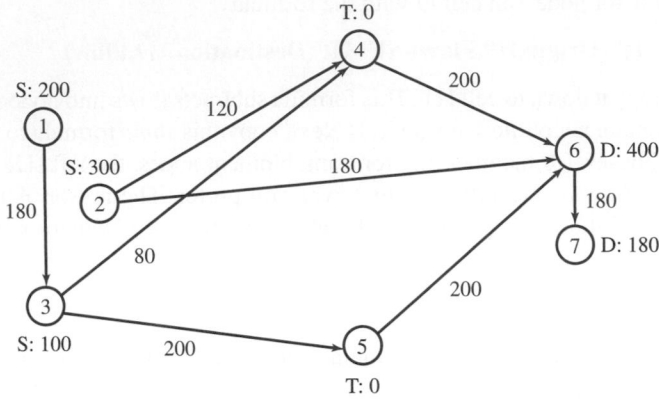

## Sensitivity Analysis

*There are endless variations of this basic minimum cost network flow model, corresponding to the many types of real-world shipping problems.*

How much effect does the arc capacity have on the optimal solution? Currently, three of the arcs with positive flow are at the arc capacity of 200. We can use SolverTable to see how sensitive this number and the total cost are to the arc capacity.[4] In this case, the single input cell for SolverTable is cell B4, which is varied from 150 to 300 in increments of 25. We keep track of two outputs: total cost and the number of arcs at arc capacity. As before, if we want to keep track of an output that does not already exist, we create it with an appropriate formula in a new cell before running SolverTable. This is shown in Figure 5.21. The formula in cell B39 is =COUNTIF(Flow,B4). This formula counts the arcs with flow equal to arc capacity. (See the finished version of the file for a note about this formula.)

**Figure 5.21**

Sensitivity to Arc Capacity

| | A | B | C |
|---|---|---|---|
| 38 | Additional output variable (for sensitivity analysis) | | |
| 39 | Arcs at capacity | 2 | |
| 40 | | | |
| 41 | Sensitivity of total cost and arcs at capacity to arc capacity | | |
| 42 | | $B$36 | $B$39 |
| 43 | 150 | $4,120 | 6 |
| 44 | 175 | $3,643 | 6 |
| 45 | 200 | $3,260 | 3 |
| 46 | 225 | $2,998 | 3 |
| 47 | 250 | $2,735 | 3 |
| 48 | 275 | $2,473 | 3 |
| 49 | 300 | $2,320 | 2 |

## Excel Function: *COUNTIF*

*The COUNTIF function counts the number of values in a given range that satisfy some criterion. The syntax is =COUNTIF(range,criterion). For example, the formula =COUNTIF(D8:D33,150) counts the number of cells in the range D8:D33 that contain the*

---

[4] Note that Solver's sensitivity report would not answer our question. This report is useful only for one-at-a-time changes in inputs, and here we are simultaneously changing the upper limit for *each* flow. However, this report (its bottom section) could be used to assess the effects of changes in plant capacities or customer demands.

*value 150. This formula can also be entered as =COUNTIF(D8:D33,"=150"). Similarly, the formula =COUNTIF(D8:D33,">=100") counts the number of cells in this range with values greater than or equal to 100.*

The SolverTable output is what we would expect. As the arc capacity decreases, more flows bump up against it, and the total cost increases. But even when the arc capacity is increased to 300, two flows are constrained by it. In this sense, even this large an arc capacity costs RedBrand money.

### Variations of the Model

There are many variations of the RedBrand shipping problem that can be handled by a network model. We briefly consider two possible variations. First, suppose that RedBrand ships two products along the given network. Assume that the unit shipping costs are the same for both products (although this assumption could easily be relaxed), but the arc capacity, which is now changed to 300, represents the maximum flow of *both* products that can flow on any arc. In this sense, the two products are competing for arc capacity. Each plant has a separate production capacity for each product, and each customer has a separate demand for each product.

The spreadsheet model for this variation appears in Figure 5.22. (See the file **RedBrand Logistics 2.xlsx**.) Very little in the original model needs to be changed. We need to (1) have two columns of changing cells (columns D and E), (2) apply the previous logic to both products separately in the flow balance constraints, and (3) apply the arc capacities to the *total* flows in column F (which are the sums of flows in columns D and E). The modified Solver dialog box is shown in Figure 5.23. Note that we have range-named blocks of cells for the flow balance constraints. For example, the ranges K9:L11 and N9:O11 are named Plant_net_outflow and Plant_capacity. Then we can use these entire blocks to specify the capacity constraints for both products with the single entry **Plant_net_outflow <= Plant_capacity** in the Solver dialog box. This is another example of planning the spreadsheet layout so that the resulting model is both efficient and readable.

**Figure 5.22** RedBrand Model with Two Products

*A RedBrand shipping model with two products competing for arc capacity*

Network structure, flows, and arc capacity constraints:

| Origin | Destination | Unit Cost | Flow product 1 | Flow product 2 | Total flow | | Arc Capacity |
|---|---|---|---|---|---|---|---|
| 1 | 2 | 5 | 0 | 0 | 0 | <= | 300 |
| 1 | 3 | 3 | 160 | 140 | 300 | <= | 300 |
| 1 | 4 | 5 | 20 | 0 | 20 | <= | 300 |
| 1 | 5 | 5 | 0 | 0 | 0 | <= | 300 |
| 1 | 6 | 20 | 0 | 0 | 0 | <= | 300 |
| 1 | 7 | 20 | 0 | 0 | 0 | <= | 300 |
| 2 | 1 | 9 | 0 | 0 | 0 | <= | 300 |
| 2 | 3 | 9 | 0 | 0 | 0 | <= | 300 |
| 2 | 4 | 1 | 100 | 0 | 100 | <= | 300 |
| 2 | 5 | 1 | 0 | 0 | 0 | <= | 300 |
| 2 | 6 | 8 | 200 | 100 | 300 | <= | 300 |
| 2 | 7 | 15 | 0 | 0 | 0 | <= | 300 |
| 3 | 1 | 0.4 | 0 | 0 | 0 | <= | 300 |
| 3 | 2 | 8 | 0 | 0 | 0 | <= | 300 |
| 3 | 4 | 1 | 0 | 180 | 180 | <= | 300 |
| 3 | 5 | 0.5 | 240 | 60 | 300 | <= | 300 |
| 3 | 6 | 10 | 0 | 0 | 0 | <= | 300 |
| 3 | 7 | 12 | 20 | 0 | 20 | <= | 300 |
| 4 | 5 | 1.2 | 0 | 0 | 0 | <= | 300 |
| 4 | 6 | 2 | 120 | 180 | 300 | <= | 300 |
| 4 | 7 | 12 | 0 | 0 | 0 | <= | 300 |
| 5 | 4 | 0.8 | 0 | 0 | 0 | <= | 300 |
| 5 | 6 | 2 | 240 | 60 | 300 | <= | 300 |
| 5 | 7 | 12 | 0 | 0 | 0 | <= | 300 |
| 6 | 7 | 1 | 160 | 140 | 300 | <= | 300 |
| 7 | 6 | 7 | 0 | 0 | 0 | <= | 300 |

Inputs: Common arc capacity = 300

Node balance constraints:

Plant constraints

| Node | Net outflow product 1 | Net outflow product 2 | | Capacity product 1 | Capacity product 2 |
|---|---|---|---|---|---|
| 1 | 180 | 140 | <= | 200 | 200 |
| 2 | 300 | 100 | <= | 300 | 100 |
| 3 | 100 | 100 | <= | 100 | 100 |

Warehouse constraints

| Node | Net outflow product 1 | Net outflow product 2 | | Required product 1 | Required product 2 |
|---|---|---|---|---|---|
| 4 | 0 | 0 | = | 0 | 0 |
| 5 | 0 | 0 | = | 0 | 0 |

Customer constraints

| Node | Net inflow product 1 | Net inflow product 2 | | Demand product 1 | Demand product 2 |
|---|---|---|---|---|---|
| 6 | 400 | 200 | >= | 400 | 200 |
| 7 | 180 | 140 | >= | 180 | 140 |

Objective to minimize: Total cost = $5,570

**Figure 5.23**
Solver Dialog Box for the Two-Product Model

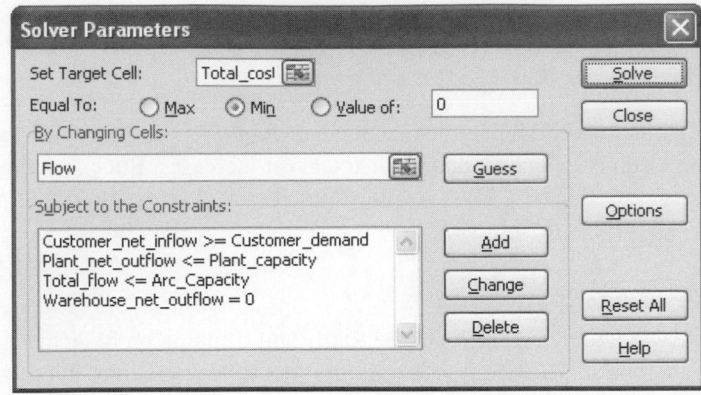

A second variation of the model is appropriate for perishable goods, such as fruit. (See the file **RedBrand Logistics 3.xlsx**.) We again assume that there is a single product, but some percentage of the product that is shipped to warehouses perishes and cannot be sent to customers. This means that the total inflow to a warehouse is *greater than* the total outflow from the warehouse. This behavior is modeled as shown in Figure 5.24. (The corresponding Solver dialog box, not shown here, is the same as in the original RedBrand model.) The "shrinkage factor" in cell B5, the percentage that does *not* spoil in the warehouses, becomes a new input. It is then incorporated into the warehouse flow balance constraints by entering the formula

=SUMIF(Origin,H16,Flow)-$B$5*SUMIF(Destination,H16,Flow)

---

**Figure 5.24**  RedBrand Model with Shrinkage

| | A | B | C | D | E | F | G | H | I | J | K |
|---|---|---|---|---|---|---|---|---|---|---|---|
| 1 | RedBrand shipping model with shrinkage at warehouses | | | | | | | | | | |
| 2 | | | | | | | | | | | |
| 3 | Inputs | | | | | | | | | | |
| 4 | Common arc capacity | 200 | | | | | | | | | |
| 5 | Shrinkage factor | 90% | | | | | | | | | |
| 6 | | | | | | | | | | | |
| 7 | Network formulation | | | | | | | Node balance constraints | | | |
| 8 | | Origin | Destination | Unit Cost | Flow | | Arc Capacity | Plant constraints | | | |
| 9 | | 1 | 2 | 5 | 0 | <= | 200 | Node | Plant net outflow | | Plant capacity |
| 10 | | 1 | 3 | 3 | 200 | <= | 200 | 1 | 200 | <= | 200 |
| 11 | | 1 | 4 | 5 | 0 | <= | 200 | 2 | 300 | <= | 300 |
| 12 | | 1 | 5 | 5 | 0 | <= | 200 | 3 | 100 | <= | 100 |
| 13 | | 1 | 6 | 20 | 0 | <= | 200 | | | | |
| 14 | | 1 | 7 | 20 | 0 | <= | 200 | Warehouse constraints | | | |
| 15 | | 2 | 1 | 9 | 0 | <= | 200 | Node | Warehouse net outflow | | Required |
| 16 | | 2 | 3 | 9 | 0 | <= | 200 | 4 | 0 | = | 0 |
| 17 | | 2 | 4 | 1 | 0 | <= | 200 | 5 | 0 | = | 0 |
| 18 | | 2 | 5 | 1 | 100 | <= | 200 | | | | |
| 19 | | 2 | 6 | 8 | 200 | <= | 200 | Customer constraints | | | |
| 20 | | 2 | 7 | 15 | 0 | <= | 200 | Node | Customer net inflow | | Customer demand |
| 21 | | 3 | 1 | 0.4 | 0 | <= | 200 | 6 | 400 | >= | 400 |
| 22 | | 3 | 2 | 8 | 0 | <= | 200 | 7 | 180 | >= | 180 |
| 23 | | 3 | 4 | 1 | 0 | <= | 200 | | | | |
| 24 | | 3 | 5 | 0.5 | 100 | <= | 200 | | | | |
| 25 | | 3 | 6 | 10 | 200 | <= | 200 | | | | |
| 26 | | 3 | 7 | 12 | 0 | <= | 200 | | | | |
| 27 | | 4 | 5 | 1.2 | 0 | <= | 200 | | | | |
| 28 | | 4 | 6 | 2 | 0 | <= | 200 | | | | |
| 29 | | 4 | 7 | 12 | 0 | <= | 200 | | | | |
| 30 | | 5 | 4 | 0.8 | 0 | <= | 200 | | | | |
| 31 | | 5 | 6 | 2 | 180 | <= | 200 | | | | |
| 32 | | 5 | 7 | 12 | 0 | <= | 200 | | | | |
| 33 | | 6 | 7 | 1 | 180 | <= | 200 | | | | |
| 34 | | 7 | 6 | 7 | 0 | <= | 200 | | | | |
| 35 | | | | | | | | | | | |
| 36 | Objective to minimize | | | | | | | | | | |
| 37 | Total cost | $4,890 | | | | | | | | | |

in cell I16 and copying to cell I17. This formula says that what goes out (the first term) is 90% of what goes in. The other 10% perishes. Of course, shrinkage results in a larger total cost—50% larger—than in the original RedBrand model.

Interestingly, however, some units are still sent to both warehouses, and the entire capacity of all plants is now used. Finally, you can check that a feasible solution exists even for a shrinkage factor of 0% (where everything sent to the warehouses disappears). As you might guess, the solution then is to send everything directly from plants to customers—at a steep cost. ■

## MODELING ISSUES

1. Excel's Solver uses the simplex method to solve network flow models. However, the simplex method can be simplified dramatically for these types of models. The simplified version of the simplex method, called the **network simplex method,** is much more efficient than the ordinary simplex method. Specialized computer codes have been written to implement the network simplex method, and all large network flow problems are solved by using the network simplex method. This is fortunate because real network models can be extremely large. See Winston (2003) for a discussion of this method.

2. If the given supplies and demands for the nodes are integers and all arc capacities are integers, the network flow model always has an optimal solution with all integer flows. Again, this is very fortunate for large problems—we get integer solutions "for free" without having to use an integer programming algorithm. Note, however, that this "integers for free" benefit is guaranteed only for the "basic" network flow model, as in the original RedBrand model. When we modify the model, by adding a shrinkage factor, say, the optimal solution is no longer guaranteed to be integer-valued. ■

## ADDITIONAL APPLICATIONS

### Distribution in Nu-kote International's Network

Nu-kote International, a manufacturer of imaging supplies, used linear programming like the model in this section to reduce costs in its global supply chain. Nu-kote's successful modeling projects, involving as many as 68,000 variables, were completed entirely within Excel and met aggressive timelines—a tribute to the efficiency and user-friendliness of Excel. Details of Nu-kote's Excel modeling projects, which have resulted in over $1 million in annual savings, can be found in LeBlanc et al. (2004), LeBlanc and Galbreth (2007a), and LeBlanc and Galbreth (2007b). ■

## PROBLEMS

### Skill-Building Problems

19. In the original RedBrand problem, suppose the plants cannot ship to each other and the customers cannot ship to each other. Modify the model appropriately and reoptimize. How much does the total cost increase because of these disallowed routes?

20. Modify the original RedBrand problem so that all flows must be from plants to warehouses and from warehouses to customers. Disallow all other arcs. How much does this restriction cost RedBrand, relative to the original optimal shipping cost?

21. In the original RedBrand problem, the costs for shipping from plants or warehouses to customer 2 were purposely made high so that it would be optimal to ship to customer 1 and then let customer 1 ship to

customer 2. Use SolverTable appropriately to do the following. Decrease the unit shipping costs from plants and warehouses to customer 1, all by the same amount, until it is no longer optimal for customer 1 to ship to customer 2. Describe what happens to the optimal shipping plan at this point.

22. In the original RedBrand problem, we assume a constant arc capacity, the same for all allowable arcs. Modify the model so that each arc has its own arc capacity. You can make up the required arc capacities.

23. Continuing the previous problem, make the problem even more general by allowing upper bounds (arc capacities) *and* lower bounds for the flows on the allowable arcs. Some of the upper bounds can be very large numbers, effectively indicating that there is no arc capacity for these arcs, and the lower bounds can be 0 or positive. If they are positive, then they indicate that some positive flow must occur on these arcs. Modify the model appropriately to handle these upper and lower bounds. You can make up the required bounds.

24. Expand the RedBrand two-product spreadsheet model so that there are now three products competing for the arc capacity. You can make up the required input data.

25. In the RedBrand two-product problem, we assumed that the unit shipping costs are the same for both products. Modify the spreadsheet model so that each product has its own unit shipping costs. You can assume that the original unit shipping costs apply to product 1, and you can make up new unit shipping costs for product 2.

## Skill-Extending Problems

26. How difficult is it to expand the original RedBrand model? Answer this by adding a new plant, two new warehouses, and three new customers, and modify the spreadsheet model appropriately. You can make up the required input data.

27. In the RedBrand problem with shrinkage, change the assumptions. Now instead of assuming that there is some shrinkage at the warehouses, assume that there is shrinkage in delivery along each route. Specifically, assume that a certain percentage of the units sent along each arc perish in transit—from faulty refrigeration, say—and this percentage can differ from one arc to another. Modify the model appropriately to take this type of behavior into account. You can make up the shrinkage factors, and you can assume that arc capacities apply to the amounts *originally* shipped, not to the amounts after shrinkage. (Make sure your input data permit a *feasible* solution. After all, if there is too much shrinkage, it will be impossible to meet demands with available plant capacity. Increase the plant capacities if necessary.)

28. Consider a modification of the original RedBrand problem where there are $N$ plants, $M$ warehouses, and $L$ customers. Assume that the only allowable arcs are from plants to warehouses and from warehouses to customers. If *all* such arcs are allowable—all plants can ship to all warehouses and all warehouses can ship to all customers—how many changing cells are in the spreadsheet model? Keeping in mind that Excel's Solver can handle at most 200 changing cells, give some combinations of $N$, $M$, and $L$ that will just barely stay within Solver's limit.

29. Continuing the previous problem, develop a sample model with your own choices of $N$, $M$, and $L$ that barely stay within Solver's limit. You can make up any input data. The important point here is the layout and formulas of the spreadsheet model.

# 5.5 SHORTEST PATH MODELS

In many applications, we need to find the shortest path between two points in a network. Sometimes this problem occurs in a geographical context where, for example, we want to find the shortest path on interstate freeways from Seattle to Miami. There are also problems that do not look like shortest path problems but can be modeled in the same way. We look at one possibility where we find an optimal schedule for replacing equipment.

The typical shortest path problem is a special case of the minimum cost network flow problem from the previous section. To see why this is the case, suppose that we want to find the shortest path between node 1 and node $N$ in a network. To find this shortest path, we create a network flow model where the supply for node 1 is 1, and the demand for node $N$ is 1. All other nodes are transshipment nodes. If an arc joins two nodes in the network, the "shipping cost" is equal to the length of the arc. The "flow" through each arc in the network (in the optimal solution) is either 1 or 0, depending on whether the shortest path includes the arc. No arc capacities are required in the model. The value of the objective is then equal to the sum of the distances of the arcs involved in the path.

### Shortest Path Problems as Network Flow Models

Shortest route problems can be modeled as a special case of more general minimum cost network flow models, using a "supply" of 1 at the origin node and a "demand" of 1 at the destination node. Because specialized algorithms can solve these more general models very quickly, shortest route problems inherit this attractive feature. This is a favorite trick of management scientists. They always try to model a specific problem as a special case of a more general problem that has been well studied and can be solved relatively easily.

## Geographical Shortest Path Models

The following example illustrates the shortest path model in the context of a geographic network.

**EXAMPLE** | **5.5 SHORTEST WALK ACROSS THE STATE**

Maude Jenkins, a 90-year-old woman, is planning to walk across the state, west to east, to gain support for a political cause she favors.[5] She wants to travel the shortest distance to get from city 1 to city 10, using the arcs (roads) shown in Figure 5.25. The numbers on the arcs are miles. Arcs with double-headed arrows indicate that travel is possible in both directions (with the same distance in both directions). What route should Maude take?

**Figure 5.25**

Network for the Shortest Path Problem

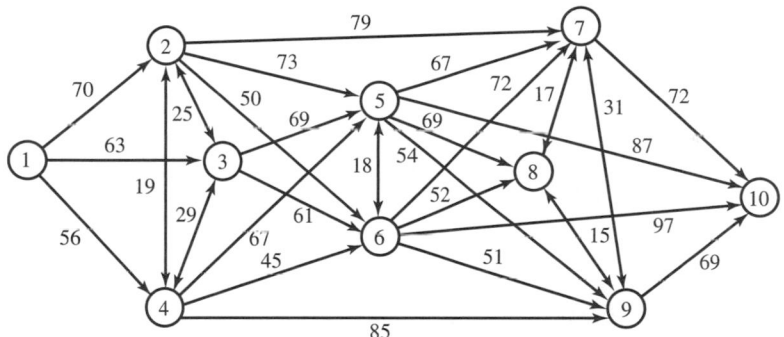

**Objective** To specialize the general network flow model so that we can find a shortest path from node 1 to node 10 for Maude's trip across the state.

### WHERE DO THE NUMBERS COME FROM?

*The "distances" in shortest path models are sometimes costs.*

The distances on the arcs are presumably listed on state maps for the roads Maude is considering. Note, however, that in shortest path problems such as this, the objective is sometimes total *cost*, not distance. Although the cost of an arc might be proportional to its distance, it might not be. For example, a steep uphill route might be more "costly" than a flat stretch of similar length. In such cases, the arc costs would be a bit more difficult to obtain.

[5] Far-fetched? This is based on a real 90-year-old woman who reportedly decided to walk across the *country*. We assume she finished!

# Solution

The variables and constraints for this model are listed in Table 5.9. This network model is exactly like the general minimum cost network flow model in the previous section. All we need to specify is that node 1 has a supply of 1 (you can think of it as Maude herself), node 10 has a demand of 1, and all other nodes are transshipment nodes.

### Table 5.9   Variables and Constraints for Maude's Shortest Path Model

| | |
|---|---|
| Input variables | Network structure and arc distances |
| Decision variables (changing cells) | Flows on arcs (1 if arc is used, 0 otherwise) |
| Objective (target cell) | Total distance |
| Other calculated variables | Flows into and out of arcs |
| Constraints | Flow balance at each node |

## DEVELOPING THE SPREADSHEET MODEL

The completed model and associated Solver dialog box appear in Figures 5.26 and 5.27. (See the file **Shortest Path.xlsx**.) Because this is so similar to the general minimum cost network flow model, we omit most of the details. However, the following points are important.

**Figure 5.26**   Shortest Path Model

| | A | B | C | D | E | F | G | H | I | J | K | L | M |
|---|---|---|---|---|---|---|---|---|---|---|---|---|---|
| 1 | Shortest path model | | | | | | | | | | | | |
| 2 | | | | | | | | | | | | | |
| 3 | Network structure and flows | | | | | Flow balance constraints | | | | | Range names used: | | |
| 4 | Origin | Destination | Distance | Flow | | Node | Net outflow | | Required net outflow | | Destination | =Model!$B$5:$B$39 | |
| 5 | 1 | 2 | 70 | 0 | | 1 | 1 | = | 1 | | Distance | =Model!$C$5:$C$39 | |
| 6 | 1 | 3 | 63 | 0 | | 2 | 0 | = | 0 | | Flow | =Model!$D$5:$D$39 | |
| 7 | 1 | 4 | 56 | 1 | | 3 | 0 | = | 0 | | Net_outflow | =Model!$G$5:$G$14 | |
| 8 | 2 | 3 | 25 | 0 | | 4 | 0 | = | 0 | | Origin | =Model!$A$5:$A$39 | |
| 9 | 2 | 4 | 19 | 0 | | 5 | 0 | = | 0 | | Required_net_outflow | =Model!$I$5:$I$14 | |
| 10 | 2 | 5 | 73 | 0 | | 6 | 0 | = | 0 | | Total_distance | =Model!$B$42 | |
| 11 | 2 | 6 | 50 | 0 | | 7 | 0 | = | 0 | | | | |
| 12 | 2 | 7 | 79 | 0 | | 8 | 0 | = | 0 | | | | |
| 13 | 3 | 2 | 25 | 0 | | 9 | 0 | = | 0 | | | | |
| 14 | 3 | 4 | 29 | 0 | | 10 | -1 | = | -1 | | | | |
| 15 | 3 | 5 | 69 | 0 | | | | | | | | | |
| 16 | 3 | 6 | 61 | 0 | | | | | | | | | |
| 17 | 4 | 2 | 19 | 0 | | | | | | | | | |
| 18 | 4 | 3 | 29 | 0 | | | | | | | | | |
| 19 | 4 | 5 | 67 | 0 | | | | | | | | | |
| 20 | 4 | 6 | 45 | 1 | | | | | | | | | |
| 21 | 4 | 9 | 85 | 0 | | | | | | | | | |
| 22 | 5 | 6 | 18 | 0 | | | | | | | | | |
| 23 | 5 | 7 | 67 | 0 | | | | | | | | | |
| 24 | 5 | 8 | 69 | 0 | | | | | | | | | |
| 25 | 5 | 9 | 54 | 0 | | | | | | | | | |
| 26 | 5 | 10 | 87 | 0 | | | | | | | | | |
| 27 | 6 | 5 | 18 | 0 | | | | | | | | | |
| 28 | 6 | 7 | 72 | 0 | | | | | | | | | |
| 29 | 6 | 8 | 52 | 0 | | | | | | | | | |
| 30 | 6 | 9 | 51 | 0 | | | | | | | | | |
| 31 | 6 | 10 | 97 | 1 | | | | | | | | | |
| 32 | 7 | 8 | 17 | 0 | | | | | | | | | |
| 33 | 7 | 9 | 31 | 0 | | | | | | | | | |
| 34 | 7 | 10 | 72 | 0 | | | | | | | | | |
| 35 | 8 | 7 | 17 | 0 | | | | | | | | | |
| 36 | 8 | 9 | 15 | 0 | | | | | | | | | |
| 37 | 9 | 7 | 31 | 0 | | | | | | | | | |
| 38 | 9 | 8 | 15 | 0 | | | | | | | | | |
| 39 | 9 | 10 | 69 | 0 | | | | | | | | | |
| 40 | | | | | | | | | | | | | |
| 41 | Objective to minimize | | | | | | | | | | | | |
| 42 | Total distance | 198 | | | | | | | | | | | |

**Figure 5.27**

Solver Dialog Box
for the Shortest
Path Model

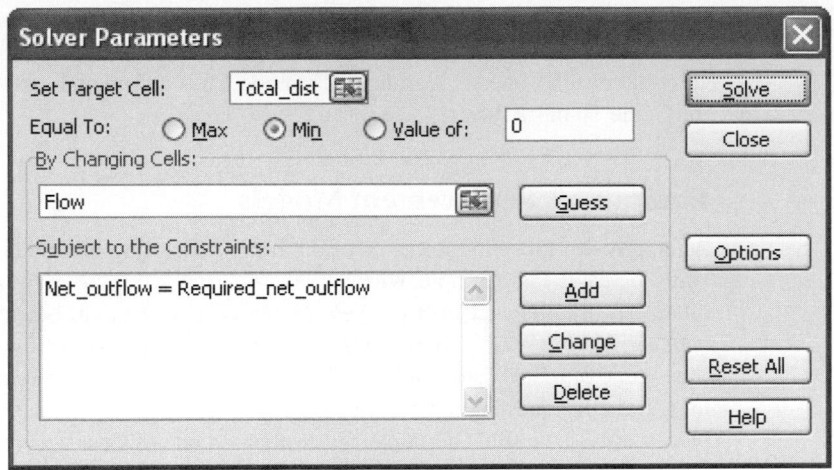

**1** **Arc list.** There is an arc listed in columns A and B for each arc in the graphical network. If the arc goes in both directions, it is listed twice (2 to 4 and 4 to 2, for example) with the same distance in both directions.

**2** **Net outflows.** We list all types of nodes in a single block in the flow balance constraint section. Node 1 is a supplier with a supply of 1, and it has only outflows. Similarly, node 10 is a demander with demand 1, and it has only inflows. The intermediate nodes are all transshipment nodes. We can treat all of the nodes similarly by calculating the net *outflow* from each. To do so, enter the formula

**=SUMIF(Origin,F5,Flow)-SUMIF(Destination,F5,Flow)**

in cell G5 and copy it down for the other nodes. For node 1, this net outflow is really just the outflow, so it should be 1. For node 10, this net outflow is really just the *negative* of the inflow, so it should be –1. For all intermediate nodes, the net outflow should be 0. This explains the values in column I.

**3** **Total distance.** The objective to minimize is total distance, calculated in cell B42 with the formula

**=SUMPRODUCT(Distance,Flow)**

### Discussion of the Solution

After Solver finds the optimal flows, which are 0's and 1's, it is easy to identify the shortest path—just follow the 1's. According to Figure 5.26, Maude first goes from node 1 to node 4 (see row 7), then she goes from node 4 to node 6 (see row 20), and finally she goes from node 6 to node 10 (see row 31). Using this route from 1 to 10, Maude must walk 198 miles, the sum of the distances on the three arcs she traverses.

   Make sure you understand exactly how this model works. There are really two parts: the total distance and the balance of inflows and outflows. For any solution of 0's and 1's in the Flow column, the SUMPRODUCT for total distance simply "picks up" the distances in column C corresponding to the arcs traversed. This accurately reflects the total distance Maude walks.

   For flow balance, consider any intermediate node. If Maude's route goes through it, such as with node 6, then the two SUMIF functions in column G for this node both evaluate to 1—that is, one of the arcs leading into node 6 has a flow of 1, and one of the arcs leading out of node 6 has a flow of 1. On the other hand, if Maude's route doesn't go through

*All flows in a shortest path model are either 0 or 1; a route is either used or it isn't.*

the node, such as with node 3, then the two SUMIF functions for this node both evaluate to 0—no flow in and no flow out. Finally, the flow balance constraints for nodes 1 and 10 ensure that exactly one arc leading out of node 1 has a flow of 1, and exactly one arc leading into node 10 has a flow of 1. ∎

## Equipment Replacement Models

Although shortest path problems often involve traveling through a network, this is not always the case. For example, when should you trade your car in for a new car? As a car gets older, the maintenance cost per year increases, and it might become worthwhile to buy a new car. If your goal is to minimize the average annual cost of owning a car (ignoring the time value of money), then it is possible to set up a shortest path representation of this problem. Actually, the method we discuss can be used in any situation where equipment replacement is an issue. Of course, many people trade in a car because they like the "feel" of a new car. This aspect is not modeled in the problem; we consider only the financial aspects. The following is an example of how equipment replacement can be modeled as a shortest path problem.

---

**EXAMPLE** | **5.6 EQUIPMENT REPLACEMENT AT VANBUREN METALS**

VanBuren Metals is a manufacturing company that uses many large machines to work on metals. These machines require frequent maintenance because of wear and tear, and VanBuren finds that it is sometimes advantageous, from a cost standpoint, to replace machines rather than continue to maintain them. For one particular class of machines, the company has estimated the quarterly costs of maintenance, the salvage value from reselling an old machine, and the cost to purchase a new machine.[6] We assume that the maintenance cost and the salvage value depend on the *age* of the current machine (at the beginning of the quarter). However, we assume that the maintenance costs, the salvage values, and the purchase cost do *not* depend on time. In other words, we assume no inflation. Specifically, we assume the following:

- The purchase cost of a new machine is always $3530.

- The maintenance cost of a machine in its first quarter of use is $100. For each succeeding quarter, the maintenance cost increases by $65. This reflects the fact that machines require more maintenance as they age.

- The salvage value of a machine after one quarter of use is $1530. After each succeeding quarter of use, the salvage value decreases by $110.

VanBuren wants to devise a strategy for purchasing machines over the next five years. As a matter of policy, the company never sells a machine that is less than one year old, and it never keeps a machine that is more than three years old. Also, the machine in use at the beginning of the current quarter is brand new.

**Objective** To find the optimal replacement strategy by modeling the problem as an equivalent shortest path problem.

---

[6] One issue in these types of models is the time period to use. We assume that VanBuren uses quarters. Therefore, the only times it considers purchasing new machines are beginnings of quarters.

In general, a company would gather historical data on maintenance costs and salvage values for similar machines and fit appropriate curves to the data (probably using regression, as discussed in Chapter 16).

## Solution

The variables and constraints required for this machine replacement model appear in Table 5.10. We claimed that this problem can be modeled as a shortest path model, which is probably far from obvious. There are two keys to understanding why this is possible: (1) the meaning of nodes and arcs, and (2) the calculation of costs on arcs. After you understand this, the modeling details are *exactly* as in the previous example.

---

**Table 5.10    Variables and Constraints for the Equipment Replacement Model**

| | |
|---|---|
| **Input variables** | Purchase cost, maintenance costs as a function of age, salvage values as a function of age |
| **Decision variables (changing cells)** | Flows on arcs (1 if arc is used, 0 otherwise), which determine the replacement schedule |
| **Objective (target cell)** | Total (net) cost |
| **Other output cells** | Flows into and out of arcs |
| **Constraints** | Flow balance at each node |

---

The network is constructed as follows. There is a node for each quarter, including the current quarter and the quarter exactly 5 years (20 quarters) from now. (Remember that VanBuren uses a 5-year planning horizon.) These nodes are labeled 1 through 21, where node 1 is the current quarter, node 2 is the next quarter, and so on. There is an arc from each node to each *later* node that is at least 4 quarters ahead but no more than 12 quarters ahead. (This is because VanBuren never sells a machine less than 1 year old, and never keeps a machine more than 3 years.) Several of these arcs are shown in Figure 5.28. (Many nodes and arcs do *not* appear in this figure.)

**Figure 5.28**

Selected Nodes and Arcs for the Machine Replacement Network

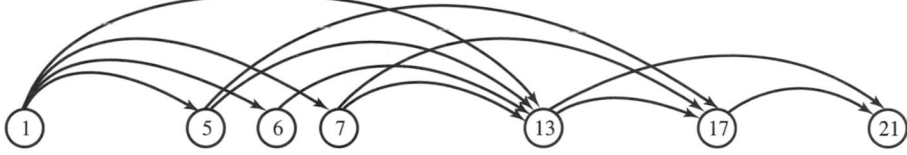

*An arc from any node to a later node corresponds to keeping a machine for a certain period of time and then trading it in for a new machine.*

Consider the arc from node 9 to node 17, for example. "Using" this arc on the shortest path—that is, putting a flow of 1 on it—corresponds to starting with a new machine in quarter 9, keeping it for 8 quarters, selling it, and purchasing another new machine at the beginning of quarter 17. An entire strategy for the 5-year period is a string of such arcs. For example, with the path 1–9–17–21, VanBuren keeps the first machine for 8 quarters, trades it in for a second machine at the beginning of quarter 9, keeps the second machine for 8 quarters, trades it in for a third machine at the beginning of quarter 17, keeps the third machine for 4 quarters, and finally trades it in for a fourth machine at the beginning of quarter 21.

*An arc cost is a sum of maintenance costs minus a salvage value plus the cost of a new machine.*

Given the meaning of the arcs, the calculation of arc costs is a matter of careful bookkeeping. Again, consider the arc from node 9 to node 17. The cost on this arc is the total maintenance cost for this machine during the 8 quarters it is kept, minus the salvage value of an 8-quarter-old machine sold in quarter 17, plus the cost of the replacement machine purchased at the beginning of quarter 17. The total maintenance cost for this machine is the maintenance cost of a machine in its first quarter of use, plus the maintenance cost of a machine in its second quarter of use, plus the maintenance cost of a machine in its third quarter of use, and so on. The first of these is $100, the second is $165, the third is $230, and so on, for the 8 quarters it is kept. You can check that the sum of these 8 costs is $2620. The salvage value at the end of quarter 17 is $1530 − 7($110) = $760, and the cost of the replacement machine is $3530. Therefore, the (net) cost on this arc is $2620 − $760 + $3530 = $5390.

## DEVELOPING THE SPREADSHEET MODEL

The information about arcs in the spreadsheet model is given in Figure 5.29, where rows 27 through 124 have been hidden. (See the file **Machine Replacement.xlsx**.) This part of the model can be completed with the following steps:

**Figure 5.29** Arc Information in the Machine Replacement Model

| | A | B | C | D | E | F | G | H | I | J | K | L | M | N | O | P | Q | R | S |
|---|---|---|---|---|---|---|---|---|---|---|---|---|---|---|---|---|---|---|---|
| 1 | Machine replacement model - shortest path formulation | | | | | | | | | | | | | | | | | | |
| 2 | | | | | | | | | | | | | | | | | | | |
| 3 | Inputs | | | Range names used: | | | | | | | | | | | | | | | |
| 4 | Purchase cost | 3530 | | Destination | =Model!$B$14:$B$130 | | | | | | | | | | | | | | |
| 5 | Maintenance cost | | | Flow | =Model!$S$14:$S$130 | | | | | | | | | | | | | | |
| 6 | In first quarter | 100 | | Net_outflow | =Model!$V$14:$V$34 | | | | | | | | | | | | | | |
| 7 | Increase per quarter | 65 | | Origin | =Model!$A$14:$A$130 | | | | | | | | | | | | | | |
| 8 | Salvage value | | | Required | =Model!$X$14:$X$34 | | | | | | | | | | | | | | |
| 9 | After one quarter | 1530 | | Total_cost | =Model!$V$36 | | | | | | | | | | | | | | |
| 10 | Decrease per quarter | 110 | | | | | | | | | | | | | | | | | |
| 11 | | | | | | | | | | | | | | | | | | | |
| 12 | Network arcs | | | | Maintenance costs in quarter of use: | | | | | | | | | | | | | | |
| 13 | | Origin | Destination | Quarters to keep | 1 | 2 | 3 | 4 | 5 | 6 | 7 | 8 | 9 | 10 | 11 | 12 | Salvage value | Purchase cost | Total cost | Flow |
| 14 | 1 | 5 | 4 | 100 | 165 | 230 | 295 | 0 | 0 | 0 | 0 | 0 | 0 | 0 | 0 | 1200 | 3530 | 3120 | 0 |
| 15 | 1 | 6 | 5 | 100 | 165 | 230 | 295 | 360 | 0 | 0 | 0 | 0 | 0 | 0 | 0 | 1090 | 3530 | 3590 | 0 |
| 16 | 1 | 7 | 6 | 100 | 165 | 230 | 295 | 360 | 425 | 0 | 0 | 0 | 0 | 0 | 0 | 980 | 3530 | 4125 | 1 |
| 17 | 1 | 8 | 7 | 100 | 165 | 230 | 295 | 360 | 425 | 490 | 0 | 0 | 0 | 0 | 0 | 870 | 3530 | 4725 | 0 |
| 18 | 1 | 9 | 8 | 100 | 165 | 230 | 295 | 360 | 425 | 490 | 555 | 0 | 0 | 0 | 0 | 760 | 3530 | 5390 | 0 |
| 19 | 1 | 10 | 9 | 100 | 165 | 230 | 295 | 360 | 425 | 490 | 555 | 620 | 0 | 0 | 0 | 650 | 3530 | 6120 | 0 |
| 20 | 1 | 11 | 10 | 100 | 165 | 230 | 295 | 360 | 425 | 490 | 555 | 620 | 685 | 0 | 0 | 540 | 3530 | 6915 | 0 |
| 21 | 1 | 12 | 11 | 100 | 165 | 230 | 295 | 360 | 425 | 490 | 555 | 620 | 685 | 750 | 0 | 430 | 3530 | 7775 | 0 |
| 22 | 1 | 13 | 12 | 100 | 165 | 230 | 295 | 360 | 425 | 490 | 555 | 620 | 685 | 750 | 815 | 320 | 3530 | 8700 | 0 |
| 23 | 2 | 6 | 4 | 100 | 165 | 230 | 295 | 0 | 0 | 0 | 0 | 0 | 0 | 0 | 0 | 1200 | 3530 | 3120 | 0 |
| 24 | 2 | 7 | 5 | 100 | 165 | 230 | 295 | 360 | 0 | 0 | 0 | 0 | 0 | 0 | 0 | 1090 | 3530 | 3590 | 0 |
| 25 | 2 | 8 | 6 | 100 | 165 | 230 | 295 | 360 | 425 | 0 | 0 | 0 | 0 | 0 | 0 | 980 | 3530 | 4125 | 0 |
| 125 | 15 | 19 | 4 | 100 | 165 | 230 | 295 | 0 | 0 | 0 | 0 | 0 | 0 | 0 | 0 | 1200 | 3530 | 3120 | 0 |
| 126 | 15 | 20 | 5 | 100 | 165 | 230 | 295 | 360 | 0 | 0 | 0 | 0 | 0 | 0 | 0 | 1090 | 3530 | 3590 | 0 |
| 127 | 15 | 21 | 6 | 100 | 165 | 230 | 295 | 360 | 425 | 0 | 0 | 0 | 0 | 0 | 0 | 980 | 3530 | 4125 | 0 |
| 128 | 16 | 20 | 4 | 100 | 165 | 230 | 295 | 0 | 0 | 0 | 0 | 0 | 0 | 0 | 0 | 1200 | 3530 | 3120 | 0 |
| 129 | 16 | 21 | 5 | 100 | 165 | 230 | 295 | 360 | 0 | 0 | 0 | 0 | 0 | 0 | 0 | 1090 | 3530 | 3590 | 0 |
| 130 | 17 | 21 | 4 | 100 | 165 | 230 | 295 | 0 | 0 | 0 | 0 | 0 | 0 | 0 | 0 | 1200 | 3530 | 3120 | 0 |

**1 Inputs.** Enter the inputs for the purchase cost, maintenance costs, and salvage values in the blue ranges.

*The allowable arcs are determined by the company's trade-in policy.*

**2 Arcs.** In the bottom section, columns A and B indicate the arcs in the network. Enter these "origins" and "destinations" manually. Just make sure that the difference between them is at least 4 and no greater than 12 (because of the company's trade-in policy). Also, make sure that the origin is at least 1 and the destination is no more than 21.

**3 Quarters to keep.** Calculate the differences between the values in columns B and A in column C. These differences indicate how many quarters the machine is kept for each arc.

**4 Maintenance costs.** Calculate the quarterly maintenance costs in columns D through O. First, you need to realize why there are so many columns. The maintenance cost for any arc is the *total* maintenance cost for a machine until it's traded in. Because the company can keep a machine for up to 12 quarters, we need 12 columns. For example, for the arc from 1 to 5 in row 14, cell D14 contains the maintenance cost in the first quarter of this period, cell E14 contains the maintenance cost in the second quarter of this period, and so on. Fortunately, we can calculate all of these maintenance costs at once by entering the formula

**=IF(D$13>$C14,0,$B$6+$B$7*(D$13-1))**

in cell D14 and copying it to the range D14:O130. The IF function ensures that no maintenance costs for this machine are incurred unless the machine is still in use. Pay particular attention to the way age is incorporated in this formula. The reference numbers in the range D13:O13 indicate the quarter of use, 1 through 12. For example, consider the situation in cell F24. A new machine was purchased in quarter 2 and is now in its third quarter of use. Therefore, its maintenance cost is $100 + 2($65) = $230.

**5 Salvage values.** In a similar way, calculate the salvage values in column P by entering the formula

**=$B$9-$B$10*(C14-1)**

in cell P14 and copying down column P. For example, the salvage value in row 24 is for a machine that is sold after its fifth year of use. This is $1530 − 4($110) = $1090.

**6 Purchase cost.** The purchase cost of a new machine never changes, so put an absolute link to cell B4 in cell Q14, and copy it down column Q.

**7 Total arc costs.** Calculate the total costs on the arcs as total maintenance cost minus salvage value plus purchase cost. To do this, enter the formula

**=SUM(D14:O14)-P14+Q14**

in cell R14, and copy it down column R.

**8 Flows.** Enter *any* flows on the arcs in column S. As usual, Solver will eventually find flows that are equal to 0 or 1.

## USING SOLVER

From this point, the model is developed *exactly* as in the shortest path model in Example 5.5, with node 1 as the "origin" node and node 21 as the "destination" node. Because we create the flow balance constraints, calculate the total network cost, and use Solver exactly as before, the details are not repeated here (see Figure 5.30).

Figure 5.30

Constraints and
Objective for the
Machine Replace-
ment Model

| | U | V | W | X |
|---|---|---|---|---|
| 12 | Flow balance constraints | | | |
| 13 | Node | Net outflow | | Required |
| 14 | 1 | 1 | = | 1 |
| 15 | 2 | 0 | = | 0 |
| 16 | 3 | 0 | = | 0 |
| 17 | 4 | 0 | = | 0 |
| 18 | 5 | 0 | = | 0 |
| 19 | 6 | 0 | = | 0 |
| 20 | 7 | 0 | = | 0 |
| 21 | 8 | 0 | = | 0 |
| 22 | 9 | 0 | = | 0 |
| 23 | 10 | 0 | = | 0 |
| 24 | 11 | 0 | = | 0 |
| 25 | 12 | 0 | = | 0 |
| 26 | 13 | 0 | = | 0 |
| 27 | 14 | 0 | = | 0 |
| 28 | 15 | 0 | = | 0 |
| 29 | 16 | 0 | = | 0 |
| 30 | 17 | 0 | = | 0 |
| 31 | 18 | 0 | = | 0 |
| 32 | 19 | 0 | = | 0 |
| 33 | 20 | 0 | = | 0 |
| 34 | 21 | -1 | = | -1 |
| 35 | | | | |
| 36 | Total cost | $13,575 | | |

## Discussion of the Solution

After we use Solver to find the shortest path, we can follow the 1's in the Flow range to identify the optimal equipment replacement policy. Although not all of the rows appear in Figure 5.29 (shown earlier), you can check in the finished version of the file that only three arcs have a flow of 1: arcs 1–7, 7–14, and 14–21. This solution indicates that VanBuren should keep the current machine for 6 quarters, trade it in for a new machine at the beginning of quarter 7, keep the second machine for 7 quarters, trade it in for a new machine at the beginning of quarter 14, keep the third machine for 7 quarters, and finally trade it in for a new machine at the beginning of quarter 21. The total (net) cost of this strategy is $13,575.

Although Solver finds the minimum-cost replacement strategy, this might be a good time for you to try your own strategy, just to make sure you understand how the network works. For example, see if you can enter the appropriate flows for the strategy that replaces the machine in quarters 6, 11, 17, and 21. Your flows should automatically satisfy the flow balance constraints, and your total cost should be $14,425. Of course, this is a suboptimal solution; its cost is larger than the minimum cost we found with Solver. ■

## MODELING ISSUES

1.  There is no inflation in this model, which means that monetary values do not increase through time. Inflation could certainly be built in, but we would need to estimate exactly how inflation affects the costs and salvage values, and we would have to build this behavior into the spreadsheet formulas in the model.

2.  As the model now stands, VanBuren is *forced* to resell the current machine and purchase a new one at the end of the 5-year period. This is because the cost of every arc leading into the last node, node 21, includes a salvage value *and* a purchase cost. This feature of the model is not as bad as it might seem. *Every* path from node 1 to node

21 includes the purchase cost in quarter 21, so this cost has no effect on which path is best. The effect of including the salvage value in arcs into node 21 is to penalize strategies that end with old machines after 5 years. Regardless of how we model the problem, we probably *ought* to penalize such strategies in some way. In addition, VanBuren will probably use a rolling planning horizon—that is, it will implement only short-term decisions from the model. The way we model the end of the 5-year horizon should have little effect on these early decisions. ∎

## ADDITIONAL APPLICATIONS

### Periodic Maintenance at Schindler Elevator

Schindler, the world's largest escalator company and second-largest elevator company, maintains tens of thousands of elevators and escalators throughout North America. Thousands of technicians work each day to maintain, repair, and help in emergencies. Blakeley et al. (2003) describe how they developed an automated route-scheduling and planning system to optimize Schindler's preventive maintenance operations. The system uses a series of algorithms to assign maintenance work to technicians and route them to where they are needed. The estimated savings from the optimization system is over $1 million annually. ∎

## PROBLEMS

### Skill-Building Problems

**30.** In Maude's shortest path problem, suppose all arcs in the current network from higher-numbered nodes to lower-numbered nodes, such as from node 6 to node 5, are disallowed. Modify the spreadsheet model and find the shortest path from node 1 to node 10. Is it the same as before? Should you have known the answer to this question before making any changes to the original model? Explain.

**31.** In Maude's shortest path problem, suppose all arcs in the network are "double-arrowed," that is, Maude can travel along each arc (with the same distance) in either direction. Modify the spreadsheet model appropriately. Is her optimal solution still the same?

**32.** Continuing the previous problem, suppose again that all arcs go in both directions, but suppose Maude's objective is to find the shortest path from node 1 to node 7 (not node 10). Modify the spreadsheet model appropriately and solve.

**33.** How difficult is it to add nodes and arcs to an existing shortest path model? Answer by adding a new node, node 11, to Maude's network. Assume that node 11 is at the top of the network, geographically, with double-arrowed arcs joining it to nodes 2, 5, and 7 with distances 45, 22, and 10. Assume that Maude's

objective is still to get from node 1 to node 10. Does the new optimal solution go through node 11?

**34.** In the VanBuren machine replacement problem, we assumed that the maintenance cost and salvage values are *linear* functions of age. Suppose instead that the maintenance cost increases by 50% each quarter and that the salvage value decreases by 10% each quarter. Rework the model with these assumptions. What is the optimal replacement schedule?

**35.** In the VanBuren machine replacement problem, the company's current policy is to keep a machine at least 4 quarters but no more than 12 quarters. Suppose this policy is instead to keep a machine at least 5 quarters but no more than 10 quarters. Modify the spreadsheet model appropriately. Is the new optimal solution the same as before?

**36.** In the VanBuren machine replacement problem, the company's current policy is to keep a machine at least 4 quarters but no more than 12 quarters. Suppose instead that the company imposes no upper limit on how long it will keep a machine; its only policy requirement is that a machine must be kept at least 4 quarters. Modify the spreadsheet model appropriately. Is the new optimal solution the same as before?

## Skill-Extending Problems

**37.** In the VanBuren machine replacement problem, suppose the company starts with a machine that is eight quarters old at the beginning of the first quarter. Modify the model appropriately, keeping in mind that this initial machine must be sold no more than four quarters from now.

**38.** We illustrated how a machine replacement problem can be modeled as a shortest path problem. This is probably not the approach most people would think of when they first see a machine replacement problem. In fact, most people would probably never think in terms of a network. How would *you* model the problem? Does your approach result in an LP model?

## 5.6 OTHER NETWORK MODELS

We conclude this chapter with two network models that apply to the airline industry. (The airline industry is famous for using management science in a variety of ways to help manage operations and save on costs.) Neither of these problems looks like a network at first glance, but some creative thinking reveals underlying network structures. The first problem turns out to be an assignment model; the second is similar to the RedBrand minimum-cost network flow model. Note that these two examples are considerably more difficult than any covered so far in this chapter. They indicate that it is not always straightforward to translate a real-world problem into a spreadsheet model!

EXAMPLE | **5.7 CREW SCHEDULING AT BRANEAST AIRLINES**

Braneast Airlines must staff the daily flights between New York and Chicago shown in Table 5.11.[7] Braneast's crews live in either New York or Chicago. Each day, a crew must fly one New York–Chicago flight and one Chicago–New York flight with at least one hour of downtime between flights. For example, a Chicago-based crew can fly the 9–13 Chicago–New York flight and return on the 14–16 New York–Chicago flight. This incurs a downtime of one hour. Braneast wants to schedule crews to cover all flights and minimize the total downtime.

**Table 5.11    Flight Data for Braneast Problem**

| Flight | Leave Chicago | Arrive N.Y. | Flight | Leave N.Y. | Arrive Chicago |
|--------|---------------|-------------|--------|------------|----------------|
| 1 | 6 A.M. | 10 A.M. | 1 | 7 A.M. | 9 A.M. |
| 2 | 9 A.M. | 1 P.M. | 2 | 8 A.M. | 10 A.M. |
| 3 | Noon | 4 P.M. | 3 | 10 A.M. | Noon |
| 4 | 3 P.M. | 7 P.M. | 4 | Noon | 2 P.M. |
| 5 | 5 P.M. | 9 P.M. | 5 | 2 P.M. | 4 P.M. |
| 6 | 7 P.M. | 11 P.M. | 6 | 4 P.M. | 6 P.M. |
| 7 | 8 P.M. | Midnight | 7 | 7 P.M. | 8 P.M. |

**Objective**    To schedule crews without violating the one-hour downtime restriction so that total downtime is minimized.

### WHERE DO THE NUMBERS COME FROM?

The flight data are part of the airline's overall flight schedule. The one-hour downtime restriction is for safety reasons and is probably built into a union contract.

[7] All times in the spreadsheet model are represented as military time. For example, time 13 corresponds to 1 P.M. Also, all times listed are Eastern Standard Time.

## Solution

The trick is to set this up as an assignment model. The variables and constraints required are listed in Table 5.12. The discussion following this table describes how the assignment model works.

**Table 5.12  Variables and Constraints for the Crew Scheduling Model**

| Input Variables | Flight Schedule Data |
| --- | --- |
| Decision variables (changing cells) | Flows on arcs (0–1 variables indicating assignments of crews to pairs of flights) |
| Objective (target cell) | Total downtime |
| Other output cells | Downtimes for crews assigned to flights flows in and out of nodes |
| Constraints | Flow balance |

The network is constructed as follows. There are two sets of nodes, one for flights departing from Chicago and one for flights departing from New York. There is an arc from a Chicago-based node to a New York-based node if the Chicago flight leaves early, the New York flight leaves later, and there is at least one hour of downtime if a crew is assigned to this pair of flights. For example, flight 1 from Chicago leaves at 6 A.M. and arrives at 10 A.M. in New York. Therefore, there is an arc from this flight's node to the node of each New York-based flight that leaves 11 A.M. or after. This includes the last four flights leaving from New York (see Figure 5.31). All such arcs—those that pair an early flight out of Chicago with a later flight out of New York (that then flies back to Chicago)—must be staffed by a Chicago-based crew. A similar set of arcs go in the opposite direction, from New York to Chicago and then back to New York, which must be staffed by a New York-based crew.

**Figure 5.31**

Network for Airline Crew Scheduling Model

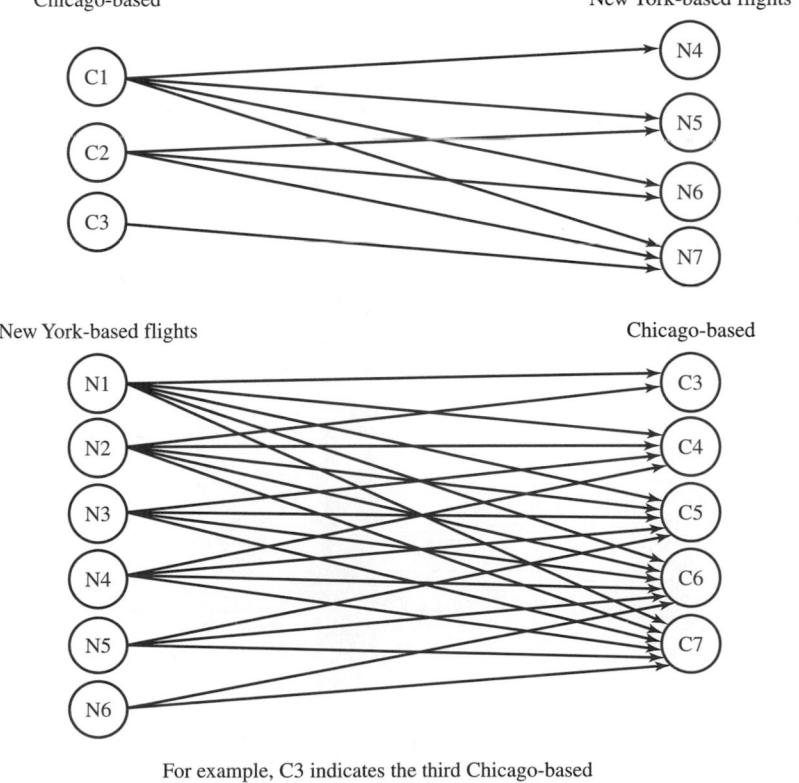

For example, C3 indicates the third Chicago-based flight, N2 indicates the second New York-based flight.

Given this network structure, we can now specify the model. First, the flow on any arc is 0 or 1. It is a 1 only if a crew is assigned to that pair of flights. Second, the "cost" on any arc is the downtime for that pair of flights if a crew is assigned to it. For example, the cost on the top arc in Figure 5.31 (flight 1 out of Chicago paired with flight 4 out of New York) is two hours because the Chicago flight gets in at 10 A.M. and the New York flight leaves at noon. Third, each flight leaving from one city must be paired with exactly one flight leaving the other city. This implies that the total flow out of any node must be 1, and the total flow into any node must be 1. This fact implies that we have an *assignment* model. Finally, it takes exactly seven crews, some based in Chicago and some based in New York, to cover the flights. The solution to the model indicates how many Chicago-based crews and New York-based crews are required.

### DEVELOPING THE SPREADSHEET MODEL

After you understand the conceptual idea, the implementation in Excel is fairly straightforward. The completed spreadsheet model appears in Figure 5.32. (See the file **Crew Scheduling.xlsx**.) The model is formed with the following steps:

**Figure 5.32**

The Airline Crew Scheduling Model

| | A | B | C | D | E | F | G | H | I | J | K |
|---|---|---|---|---|---|---|---|---|---|---|---|
| 1 | Crew scheduling model | | | | | | | | | | |
| 2 | | | | | | | | | | | |
| 3 | **Flight information** | | | | | | | | | | |
| 4 | Chicago-NY flights | | | | NY-Chicago flights | | | | | | |
| 5 | Flight | Departs | Arrives | | Flight | Departs | Arrives | | | | |
| 6 | C1 | 6 | 10 | | N1 | 7 | 9 | | | | |
| 7 | C2 | 9 | 13 | | N2 | 8 | 10 | | | | |
| 8 | C3 | 12 | 16 | | N3 | 10 | 12 | | | | |
| 9 | C4 | 15 | 19 | | N4 | 12 | 14 | | | | |
| 10 | C5 | 17 | 21 | | N5 | 14 | 16 | | | | |
| 11 | C6 | 19 | 23 | | N6 | 16 | 18 | | | | |
| 12 | C7 | 20 | 24 | | N7 | 19 | 20 | | | | |
| 13 | | | | | | | | | | | |
| 14 | **Network formulation** | | | | | **Flow balance constraints** | | | | | |
| 15 | Chicago-based crews | | | | | | | | | | |
| 16 | C Origin | N Destination | C Downtime | C Flow | | Node | Flow Out | Flow In | Total flow | | Required |
| 17 | C1 | N4 | 2 | 1 | | C1 | 1 | 0 | 1 | = | 1 |
| 18 | C1 | N5 | 4 | 0 | | C2 | 1 | 0 | 1 | = | 1 |
| 19 | C1 | N6 | 6 | 0 | | C3 | 0 | 1 | 1 | = | 1 |
| 20 | C1 | N7 | 9 | 0 | | C4 | 0 | 1 | 1 | = | 1 |
| 21 | C2 | N5 | 1 | 0 | | C5 | 0 | 1 | 1 | = | 1 |
| 22 | C2 | N6 | 3 | 0 | | C6 | 0 | 1 | 1 | = | 1 |
| 23 | C2 | N7 | 6 | 1 | | C7 | 0 | 1 | 1 | = | 1 |
| 24 | C3 | N7 | 3 | 0 | | N1 | 1 | 0 | 1 | = | 1 |
| 25 | | | | | | N2 | 1 | 0 | 1 | = | 1 |
| 26 | NY-based crews | | | | | N3 | 1 | 0 | 1 | = | 1 |
| 27 | N Origin | C Destination | N Downtime | N Flow | | N4 | 0 | 1 | 1 | = | 1 |
| 28 | N1 | C3 | 3 | 0 | | N5 | 1 | 0 | 1 | = | 1 |
| 29 | N1 | C4 | 6 | 1 | | N6 | 1 | 0 | 1 | = | 1 |
| 30 | N1 | C5 | 8 | 0 | | N7 | 0 | 1 | 1 | = | 1 |
| 31 | N1 | C6 | 10 | 0 | | | | | | | |
| 32 | N1 | C7 | 11 | 0 | | **Range names used** | | | | | |
| 33 | N2 | C3 | 2 | 1 | | C_Destination | =Model!$B$28:$B$50 | | | | |
| 34 | N2 | C4 | 5 | 0 | | C_Downtime | =Model!$C$17:$C$24 | | | | |
| 35 | N2 | C5 | 7 | 0 | | C_Flow | =Model!$D$17:$D$24 | | | | |
| 36 | N2 | C6 | 9 | 0 | | C_Origin | =Model!$A$17:$A$24 | | | | |
| 37 | N2 | C7 | 10 | 0 | | C_Table | =Model!$A$6:$C$12 | | | | |
| 38 | N3 | C4 | 3 | 0 | | N_Destination | =Model!$B$17:$B$24 | | | | |
| 39 | N3 | C5 | 5 | 0 | | N_Downtime | =Model!$C$28:$C$50 | | | | |
| 40 | N3 | C6 | 7 | 1 | | N_Flow | =Model!$D$28:$D$50 | | | | |
| 41 | N3 | C7 | 8 | 0 | | N_Origin | =Model!$A$28:$A$50 | | | | |
| 42 | N4 | C4 | 1 | 0 | | N_Table | =Model!$E$6:$G$12 | | | | |
| 43 | N4 | C5 | 3 | 0 | | Total_downtime | =Model!$B$52 | | | | |
| 44 | N4 | C6 | 5 | 0 | | Total_flow | =Model!$I$17:$I$30 | | | | |
| 45 | N4 | C7 | 6 | 0 | | | | | | | |
| 46 | N5 | C5 | 1 | 1 | | | | | | | |
| 47 | N5 | C6 | 3 | 0 | | | | | | | |
| 48 | N5 | C7 | 4 | 0 | | | | | | | |
| 49 | N6 | C6 | 1 | 0 | | | | | | | |
| 50 | N6 | C7 | 2 | 1 | | | | | | | |
| 51 | | | | | | | | | | | |
| 52 | **Total downtime** | 26 | | | | | | | | | |

**1** **Enter inputs.** Enter the given flight information in the ranges B6:C12 and F6:G12. Because we plan to use this information with lookup functions later on, we have named the ranges A6:C12 and E6:G12 as C_Table and N_Table, respectively. The labels in columns A and E serve only to identify the various flights.

**2** **Find feasible assignments.** To fill in the Chicago-based crews section, find each early flight leaving from Chicago that can be paired with a later flight leaving from New York so that at least one hour of downtime occurs in between. (These correspond to the arcs in the top section of Figure 5.31.) Then enter the flight codes of all such pairs of flights in columns A and B. Do the same for the pairs that could be handled by New York-based crews. (These correspond to the arcs in the bottom section of Figure 5.31.) Note that all this information is entered *manually*—no formulas are involved.

**3** **Downtimes for feasible assignments.** Calculate the downtime for each feasible pair of flights by using lookup functions to extract the information from the flight schedules. Specifically, enter the formula

**=VLOOKUP(B17,N_Table,2)-VLOOKUP(A17,C_Table,3)**

in cell C17 and copy it down for other flight pairs starting in Chicago. This subtracts the beginning time of the second flight in the pair from the ending time of the first flight in the pair. (Do you see why we use military time?) Similarly, enter the formula

**=VLOOKUP(B28,C_Table,2)-VLOOKUP(A28,N_Table,3)**

in cell C28 and copy it down for other flight pairs starting in New York.

**4** **Flows.** Enter *any* flows in the C_Flow and N_Flow ranges in column D. Remember that these will eventually be 0's and 1's, indicating that a crew is either assigned to a pair of flights or it isn't.

**5** **Flow balance constraints.** There is a node in the network for each flight and a flow balance constraint for each node—hence 14 flow balance constraints. However, things get a bit tricky because each flight could be either the first or second flight in a given flight pair. For example, consider flight C3. From Figure 5.31 (or Figure 5.32), we see that flight C3 is the later flight for two flight pairs (corresponding to rows 28 and 33 of the model), and it is the earlier flight for another flight pair (corresponding to row 24 of the model). Now comes the key observation for this particular model. Flight C3 must be flown exactly once, so exactly one of these arrows must have flow 1, and the others must have flow 0. Therefore, we *add* this node's total inflow to its total outflow and constrain this sum to be 1.[8] To implement this, enter the formulas

**=SUMIF(C_Origin,F17,C_Flow)**

and

**=SUMIF(C_Destination,F17,N_Flow)**

in cells G17 and H17, and copy them to the range G18:H23 to take care of the flights leaving from Chicago. Then enter the formulas

**=SUMIF(N_Origin,F24,N_Flow)**

and

**=SUMIF(N_Destination,F24,C_Flow)**

---

[8] Admittedly, this is not the usual flow balance constraint, but it works here. You might want to search for an alternative way of constructing the network.

in cells G24 and H24, and copy them to the range G25:H30 to take care of the flights leaving from New York. Finally, add these inflows and outflows in column I (in the Total_flow range). As the spreadsheet model indicates (with equal signs and 1's in columns J and K), we eventually constrain these sums to be 1.

**6** **Total downtime.** Calculate the total downtime in the Total_downtime cell with the formula

=SUMPRODUCT(C_Downtime,C_Flow)

+SUMPRODUCT(N_Downtime,N_Flow)

## USING SOLVER

The Solver dialog box should appear as in Figure 5.33. Note that the *only* constraints (other than nonnegativity of the changing cells) are that the total flow into and out of each node must be 1. This, plus the fact that network models with integer inputs automatically have integer solutions, implies that the flows on all arcs will be 0 or 1.

**Figure 5.33**

Solver Dialog Box for Crew Scheduling Model

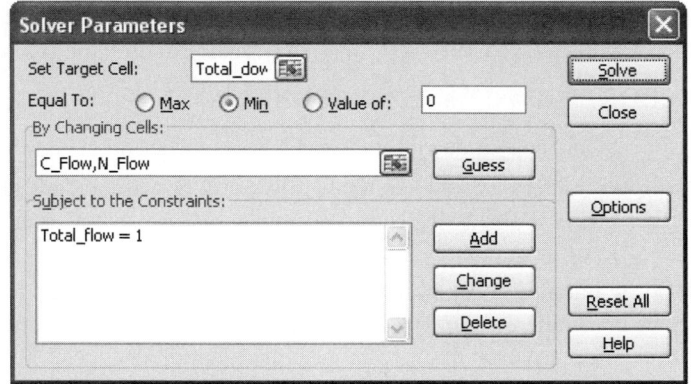

**Figure 5.34**

Modified Input Section to Allow for a Delay

| | A | B | C | D | E | F | G | H | I | J | K |
|---|---|---|---|---|---|---|---|---|---|---|---|
| 3 | **Flight information** | | | | | | | | | | |
| 4 | Chicago-NY flights | | | | NY-Chicago flights | | | | Original C1 flight times | | |
| 5 | Flight | Departs | Arrives | | Flight | Departs | Arrives | | Departs | Arrives | |
| 6 | C1 | 9 | 13 | | N1 | 7 | 9 | | 6 | 10 | |
| 7 | C2 | 9 | 13 | | N2 | 8 | 10 | | | | |
| 8 | C3 | 12 | 16 | | N3 | 10 | 12 | | Delay (hours) for flight C1 | | |
| 9 | C4 | 15 | 19 | | N4 | 12 | 14 | | 3 | | |
| 10 | C5 | 17 | 21 | | N5 | 14 | 16 | | | | |
| 11 | C6 | 19 | 23 | | N6 | 16 | 18 | | | | |
| 12 | C7 | 20 | 24 | | N7 | 19 | 20 | | | | |

### Discussion of the Solution

The optimal solution shown earlier in Figure 5.32 indicates that there should be two Chicago-based crews and five New York-based crews. This is because there are two 1's in the C_Flow range and five 1's in the N_Flow range. These 1's indicate the crew assignments. For example, one Chicago-based crew flies the C1 and N4 flights, and the other flies the C2 and N7 flights. The total downtime for all seven crews is 26 hours.

### Sensitivity Analysis

The only inputs to Braneast's model are the flight times, so we consider one possible sensitivity analysis involving these flight times. Suppose the C1 flight from Chicago is delayed by one or more hours. How will this affect the optimal solution? We need to vary the input section, as shown in Figure 5.34. The original flight times are entered in cells I6 and J6, a flight delay is entered in cell I9, and formulas are entered in cells B6 and C6. (The formula in B6 is =I6+$I$9, which is copied to C6.) After running SolverTable, allowing the delay to vary from 0 to 3 in increments of 1 and keeping track of the total downtime and the numbers of crews based in each city, we obtain the results in Figure 5.35. Unfortunately, there is a subtle problem we forgot to take care of. (Before reading on, see if you can spot it.)

**Figure 5.35**
SolverTable Output for Sensitivity to Flight Delay

| | A | B | C | D | E | F | G | H | I | J | K |
|---|---|---|---|---|---|---|---|---|---|---|---|
| 52 | Total downtime | 23 | | | | | | | | | |
| 53 | | | | | | | | | | | |
| 54 | Number of crews | | | | | | | | | | |
| 55 | Chicago-based | 2 | | | | | | | | | |
| 56 | New York-based | 5 | | | | | | | | | |
| 57 | | | | | | | | | | | |
| 58 | Sensitivity of total downtime and number of crews to delay in flight C1 | | | | | | | | | | |
| 59 | | $B$52 | $B$55 | $B$56 | | | | | | | |
| 60 | 0 | 26 | 2 | 5 | | | | | | | |
| 61 | 1 | 25 | 2 | 5 | | | | | | | |
| 62 | 2 | 24 | 2 | 5 | | | | | | | |
| 63 | 3 | 23 | 2 | 5 | | | | | | | |

However, as explained in the text, we've "cheated" in this table. When the delay becomes 2 or 3 hours, flight pairs that were previously feasible are no longer feasible (because of the 1-hour downtime restriction), but the optimal solutions might be using them!

The problem is that when we delay flight C1, one or more flight pairings that had at least one hour of downtime originally might no longer have this minimal required downtime. In fact, the Solver solution when the delay is 3 hours schedules a crew to the pairing C1–N4. But this is infeasible—the C1 flight gets into New York at time 13, and the N4 flight leaves New York at time 12. So the SolverTable solution reported for delays of 3 (and 2) corresponds to infeasible schedules. Unfortunately, there is no easy fix for running this sensitivity analysis. Recall that we *manually* entered the pairings (in columns A and B, rows 17 to 50 of Figure 5.32) that have downtime of at least 1. To run this sensitivity analysis with SolverTable correctly, we need to modify the original model so that Solver gets to choose from all *possible* pairings, with the constraint that a pairing can be chosen only if its downtime is at least 1. The model grows larger and somewhat more complex, but it can be done. ∎

We finish this section with a model that is realistic, complex, and not at all an obvious network model. However, after we see the network structure lurking in the background, the model simplifies tremendously. If you don't believe us, just try modeling the problem in any way *other* than as a network model.

---

**EXAMPLE** | **5.8 Scheduling Flights at TriCities Airlines**

TriCities Airlines flies several daily commuter flights to and from New York City, Washington, D.C., and Boston. The company has been flying a fixed daily schedule of flights, but it is now deciding whether to change this schedule. Each potential flight has an estimated net revenue based on the typical number of passengers for the flight. (See Figure 5.37 for a listing of all potential flights and their net revenues.) The company owns 4 airplanes, and it does not anticipate buying any more. There is a fixed cost of $1500 per plane per day that flies any flights. However, a plane that is not used does not incur this fixed cost. We assume (although this could be relaxed) that there is no required delay time on the ground; therefore, if a flight arrives in Boston at time 10, it can leave on a new flight at time 10. (We measure time in military time.) Also, any plane that arrives in a city after its last flight of the day has two options. It can sit overnight in that city, or, at a cost of $500, it can be flown empty to another city overnight. The company's objective is to maximize its net profit per day, which equals net revenues from flights flown, minus fixed costs of flying planes, minus overnight costs of flying empty.

**Objective**    To develop a network model for scheduling the airline's flights, given its available aircraft, to maximize net profit from the flights.

**WHERE DO THE NUMBERS COME FROM?**

In a real setting, the airline would first have to decide which flights, including flight times, to include in the potential list of flights. This is presumably based on customer demands. The financial inputs are obtained from accounting records. For example, the net revenue for a flight is based on the number of passengers who typically take the flight, ticket prices, personnel costs, and fuel costs. The fixed cost of operating a plane includes any costs that do not depend directly on the amount of time the plane spends in the air.

## Solution

We first discuss how this problem can be modeled as a minimum cost network flow model (MCNFM)—which is certainly not obvious. The trick is to have a node for each city/time combination. Because we allow flights on the half-hour, this means having nodes of the form Boston8, Boston8.5, and so on, up toWashDC20 (assuming that the earliest flight leaves at time 8 and the latest flight arrives at time 20). There are three types of arcs. The most obvious type is a "flight" arc. For example, if there is a flight from Boston at time 12.5 that arrives at Washington, D.C., at time 14, then there is a flight arc from node Boston12.5 to node WashDC14. The flow on such an arc represents the number of planes that fly this flight. Because each flight can be flown at most once, we impose a capacity of 1 on all such flight arcs. The "cost" on a flight arc is the net revenue for flying the flight. (In this model, it is more natural to use net revenues as the arc "costs," so that we will actually be finding the *maximum* "net profit" network flow.)

The other arcs are less obvious. If a flight arrives in New York, say, at time 13, it might sit on the ground until time 14.5, at which time it leaves for another city. We model this with the "ground" arcs NY13–NY13.5, NY13.5–NY14, and NY14–NY14.5. In general, the flow on any ground arc represents the number of planes sitting on the ground in that city for that half-hour period. These ground arcs have no capacities and no costs.

Finally, the real trick involves relating one day to the next. Suppose one or more planes end up in New York at the end of the day, at time 20. They can either sit overnight in New York, or they can be flown to another city, where they will be available at time 8 the next morning. To model this, we use "overnight" arcs. The flow on an overnight arc such as NY20–NY8 represents the number of planes that sit overnight in New York. It has no capacity and a cost equal to the fixed cost of operating a plane. (By attaching the fixed costs of operating planes to the overnight arcs, rather than to the flight or ground arcs, we avoid double-counting fixed costs.) In contrast, the flow on an overnight arc such as NY20–Boston8 represents the number of planes flown overnight from New York to Boston. It has no capacity and a cost equal to the fixed cost of operating a plane plus the cost of flying a plane empty overnight. Note that the total flow on all overnight arcs equals the total number of planes being used—all planes being used must be *somewhere* overnight. In fact, we constrain this total—it must be less than or equal to the number of planes owned, 4.

A few of the nodes and arcs for this network are shown in Figure 5.36. The flight arcs are the diagonal arcs, the ground arcs all point one step to the right, and the overnight arcs go backward from right to left.

With this network, flow balance (inflow equals outflow) exists at *every* node. This indicates *conservation of planes*. The same planes continue to circulate through the network day after day. Of course, if we want *different* schedules on different days of the week, we have to change the model, and it becomes considerably more complex.

**Figure 5.36**

Selected Nodes and Arcs for Flights Model

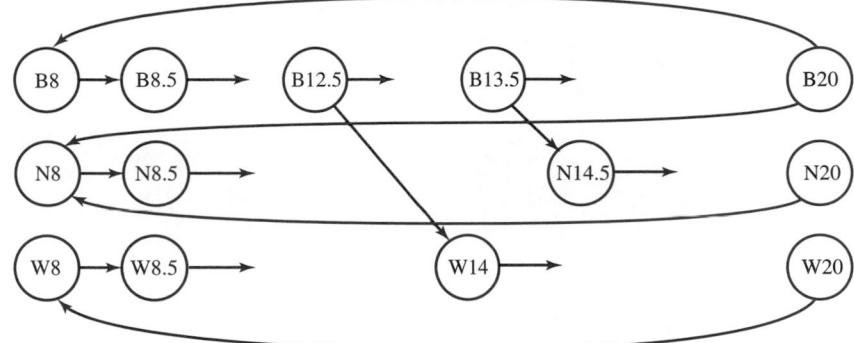

With the preceding discussion in mind, the variables and constraints for the model are listed in Table 5.13.

**Table 5.13    Variables and Constraints for Flight Scheduling Model**

| | |
|---|---|
| **Input variables** | Planes owned, fixed cost per plane used, overnight cost for flying a plane empty, flight information about potential flights (including net revenues for flights) |
| **Decision variables (changing cells)** | Flows (0-1 variables to indicate which flights are selected, when planes are on the ground, when planes are flying overnight empty) |
| **Objective (target cell)** | Net profit |
| **Other output cells** | Net outflows on arcs, number of planes used |
| **Constraints** | Planes used are less than or equal to Planes owned |
| | Flows (for flight arcs) are less than or equal to 1 |
| | Net outflows (for all arcs) equal 0 |

### DEVELOPING THE SPREADSHEET MODEL

The finished model is large, so we show it in pieces. (See the file **Flight Scheduling.xlsx.**) Figure 5.37 shows the *potential* flight schedule, plus the other inputs. Recall that TriCities wants to select the appropriate *subset* of these flights to fly, which could be all of them. (All monetary values are expressed in hundreds of dollars.) Note that the cost of flying a plane empty overnight is a constant. We could easily allow this cost to depend on the origin and destination of the flight.

The information on the three types of arcs appears in Figures 5.38, 5.39, and 5.40. The flight arcs correspond exactly to the available flights in Figure 5.37. Note that each flight arc has a capacity of 1. There are many ground arcs (note the hidden rows in Figure 5.39), each extending one half-hour into the day, and their costs are all 0. Finally, there are only nine ground arcs. Each has a fixed cost, and those that represent empty overnight flights also have an overnight cost.

**Figure 5.37**   Inputs for Flights Problem

| | A | B | C | D | E | F | G | H | I | J |
|---|---|---|---|---|---|---|---|---|---|---|
| 1 | Flight scheduling model | | | | | | | | | |
| 2 | | | | | | | | | | |
| 3 | Input data | | | | | | | Range names used: | | |
| 4 | Planes owned | 4 | | | | | | Flight_destination | =Model!$B$37:$B$59 | |
| 5 | Fixed cost per plane | 15 | | | | | | Flight_flow | =Model!$D$37:$D$59 | |
| 6 | Overnight cost | 5 | | | | | | Flight_net_revenue | =Model!$C$37:$C$59 | |
| 7 | | | | | | | | Flight_origin | =Model!$A$37:$A$59 | |
| 8 | Flight information | | | | | | | Ground_destination | =Model!$B$63:$B$134 | |
| 9 | Flight Number | Origin | Destination | Departs | Arrives | Net Revenue | | Ground_flow | =Model!$D$63:$D$134 | |
| 10 | 1357 | Boston | NY | 8 | 9 | 25 | | Ground_origin | =Model!$A$63:$A$134 | |
| 11 | 8322 | Boston | NY | 9.5 | 10.5 | 30 | | Net_outflow | =Model!$I$37:$I$111 | |
| 12 | 5903 | Boston | WashDC | 12.5 | 14 | 39 | | Net_profit | =Model!$B$156 | |
| 13 | 1207 | Boston | WashDC | 13.5 | 15 | 24 | | Number_owned | =Model!$D$150 | |
| 14 | 1671 | Boston | NY | 13.5 | 14.5 | 24 | | Number_used | =Model!$B$150 | |
| 15 | 5671 | Boston | WashDC | 16 | 17.5 | 35 | | Overnight_destination | =Model!$B$138:$B$146 | |
| 16 | 7133 | Boston | NY | 16.5 | 17.5 | 29 | | Overnight_flow | =Model!$E$138:$E$146 | |
| 17 | 4166 | NY | Boston | 9.5 | 11 | 28 | | Overnight_origin | =Model!$A$138:$A$146 | |
| 18 | 3842 | NY | Boston | 12 | 13.5 | 13 | | | | |
| 19 | 1537 | NY | WashDC | 13 | 14.5 | 18 | | | | |
| 20 | 9320 | NY | Boston | 14 | 16 | 22 | | | | |
| 21 | 3042 | NY | Boston | 16.5 | 18 | 28 | | | | |
| 22 | 3752 | NY | Boston | 18 | 19.5 | 34 | | | | |
| 23 | 9677 | NY | WashDC | 18 | 20 | 39 | | | | |
| 24 | 6212 | NY | Boston | 18.5 | 20 | 15 | | | | |
| 25 | 6811 | WashDC | NY | 9 | 11 | 12 | | | | |
| 26 | 9195 | WashDC | NY | 12.5 | 14 | 28 | | | | |
| 27 | 8350 | WashDC | NY | 13 | 15 | 13 | | | | |
| 28 | 9480 | WashDC | Boston | 13.5 | 15.5 | 18 | | | | |
| 29 | 7555 | WashDC | NY | 14 | 15.5 | 33 | | | | |
| 30 | 9041 | WashDC | Boston | 14 | 15.5 | 28 | | | | |
| 31 | 7539 | WashDC | Boston | 14.5 | 16.5 | 19 | | | | |
| 32 | 2710 | WashDC | Boston | 16 | 17.5 | 15 | | | | |

**Figure 5.38**

Flight Arcs

| | A | B | C | D | E | F |
|---|---|---|---|---|---|---|
| 35 | Flight arcs | | | | | |
| 36 | Flight origin | Flight destination | Flight net revenue | Flight flow | | Flight capacity |
| 37 | Boston8 | NY9 | 25 | 1 | <= | 1 |
| 38 | Boston9.5 | NY10.5 | 30 | 1 | <= | 1 |
| 39 | Boston12.5 | WashDC14 | 39 | 1 | <= | 1 |
| 40 | Boston13.5 | WashDC15 | 24 | 0 | <= | 1 |
| 41 | Boston13.5 | NY14.5 | 24 | 1 | <= | 1 |
| 42 | Boston16 | WashDC17.5 | 35 | 1 | <= | 1 |
| 43 | Boston16.5 | NY17.5 | 29 | 1 | <= | 1 |
| 44 | NY9.5 | Boston11 | 28 | 1 | <= | 1 |
| 45 | NY12 | Boston13.5 | 13 | 1 | <= | 1 |
| 46 | NY13 | WashDC14.5 | 18 | 1 | <= | 1 |
| 47 | NY14 | Boston16 | 22 | 1 | <= | 1 |
| 48 | NY16.5 | Boston18 | 28 | 1 | <= | 1 |
| 49 | NY18 | Boston19.5 | 34 | 1 | <= | 1 |
| 50 | NY18 | WashDC20 | 39 | 1 | <= | 1 |
| 51 | NY18.5 | Boston20 | 15 | 0 | <= | 1 |
| 52 | WashDC9 | NY11 | 12 | 1 | <= | 1 |
| 53 | WashDC12.5 | NY14 | 28 | 1 | <= | 1 |
| 54 | WashDC13 | NY15 | 13 | 0 | <= | 1 |
| 55 | WashDC13.5 | Boston15.5 | 18 | 0 | <= | 1 |
| 56 | WashDC14 | NY15.5 | 33 | 1 | <= | 1 |
| 57 | WashDC14 | Boston15.5 | 28 | 0 | <= | 1 |
| 58 | WashDC14.5 | Boston16.5 | 19 | 1 | <= | 1 |
| 59 | WashDC16 | Boston17.5 | 15 | 0 | <= | 1 |

The rest is straightforward. As usual, we fill out a table of flow balance constraints, as shown in Figure 5.41. (Note that many rows have been hidden.) There is a constraint for each node—that is, each city/time combination. The typical formula for net outflow in cell I37, which can be copied down column I, is

=SUMIF(Flight_origin,H37,Flight_flow)+SUMIF(Ground_origin,H37,Ground_flow)

+SUMIF(Overnight_origin,H37,Overnight_flow)
-(SUMIF(Flight_destination,H37,Flight_flow)

+SUMIF(Ground_destination,H37,Ground_flow)
+SUMIF(Overnight_destination,H37,Overnight_flow))

**Figure 5.39**

Ground Arcs

| | A | B | C | D |
|---|---|---|---|---|
| 61 | Ground arcs | | | |
| 62 | Ground origin | Ground destination | Ground cost | Ground flow |
| 63 | Boston8 | Boston8.5 | 0 | 1 |
| 64 | Boston8.5 | Boston9 | 0 | 1 |
| 65 | Boston9 | Boston9.5 | 0 | 1 |
| 66 | Boston9.5 | Boston10 | 0 | 0 |
| 67 | Boston10 | Boston10.5 | 0 | 0 |
| 68 | Boston10.5 | Boston11 | 0 | 0 |
| 69 | Boston11 | Boston11.5 | 0 | 1 |
| 70 | Boston11.5 | Boston12 | 0 | 1 |
| 71 | Boston12 | Boston12.5 | 0 | 1 |
| 72 | Boston12.5 | Boston13 | 0 | 0 |
| 73 | Boston13 | Boston13.5 | 0 | 0 |
| 74 | Boston13.5 | Boston14 | 0 | 0 |
| 75 | Boston14 | Boston14.5 | 0 | 0 |
| 125 | WashDC15 | WashDC15.5 | 0 | 0 |
| 126 | WashDC15.5 | WashDC16 | 0 | 0 |
| 127 | WashDC16 | WashDC16.5 | 0 | 0 |
| 128 | WashDC16.5 | WashDC17 | 0 | 0 |
| 129 | WashDC17 | WashDC17.5 | 0 | 0 |
| 130 | WashDC17.5 | WashDC18 | 0 | 1 |
| 131 | WashDC18 | WashDC18.5 | 0 | 1 |
| 132 | WashDC18.5 | WashDC19 | 0 | 1 |
| 133 | WashDC19 | WashDC19.5 | 0 | 1 |
| 134 | WashDC19.5 | WashDC20 | 0 | 1 |

**Figure 5.40**

Overnight Arcs

| | A | B | C | D | E |
|---|---|---|---|---|---|
| 136 | Overnight arcs | | | | |
| 137 | Overnight origin | Overnight destination | Fixed cost | Overnight cost | Overnight flow |
| 138 | Boston20 | Boston8 | 15 | 0 | 2 |
| 139 | Boston20 | NY8 | 15 | 5 | 0 |
| 140 | Boston20 | WashDC8 | 15 | 5 | 0 |
| 141 | NY20 | Boston8 | 15 | 5 | 0 |
| 142 | NY20 | NY8 | 15 | 0 | 0 |
| 143 | NY20 | WashDC8 | 15 | 5 | 0 |
| 144 | WashDC20 | Boston8 | 15 | 5 | 0 |
| 145 | WashDC20 | NY8 | 15 | 5 | 0 |
| 146 | WashDC20 | WashDC8 | 15 | 0 | 2 |

**Figure 5.41**

Flow Balance Constraints for Flights Model

| | H | I | J | K |
|---|---|---|---|---|
| 34 | **Flow balance constraints** | | | |
| 35 | | | | |
| 36 | Node | Net outflow | | Required |
| 37 | Boston8 | 0 | = | 0 |
| 38 | Boston8.5 | 0 | = | 0 |
| 39 | Boston9 | 0 | = | 0 |
| 40 | Boston9.5 | 0 | = | 0 |
| 41 | Boston10 | 0 | = | 0 |
| 42 | Boston10.5 | 0 | = | 0 |
| 43 | Boston11 | 0 | = | 0 |
| 44 | Boston11.5 | 0 | = | 0 |
| 45 | Boston12 | 0 | = | 0 |
| 46 | Boston12.5 | 0 | = | 0 |
| 47 | Boston13 | 0 | = | 0 |
| 48 | Boston13.5 | 0 | = | 0 |
| 102 | WashDC15.5 | 0 | = | 0 |
| 103 | WashDC16 | 0 | = | 0 |
| 104 | WashDC16.5 | 0 | = | 0 |
| 105 | WashDC17 | 0 | = | 0 |
| 106 | WashDC17.5 | 0 | = | 0 |
| 107 | WashDC18 | 0 | = | 0 |
| 108 | WashDC18.5 | 0 | = | 0 |
| 109 | WashDC19 | 0 | = | 0 |
| 110 | WashDC19.5 | 0 | = | 0 |
| 111 | WashDC20 | 0 | = | 0 |

This looks complex, but it's simply the sum of outflows from the three types of arcs minus the sum of inflows from the three types of arcs. Because there must be flow balance at each node, we constrain each net outflow to be 0. (Also, keep in mind that all of the range names in this model can be created quickly with the Create from Selection shortcut, provided that you supply "nice" labels for headings.)

Figures 5.42 and 5.43 show the rest of the model and the Solver dialog box. To find the number of planes used, we sum the flows on all overnight arcs in cell B150 with the formula

=SUM(Overnight_flow)

Then we calculate the various monetary values with the usual SUMPRODUCT functions. For example, the formula for total net revenue from flights is

=SUMPRODUCT(Flight_net_revenue,Flight_flow)

Finally, we combine these into a profit objective in cell B156 with the formula

**B153-B154-B155**

The Solver dialog box follows easily—and is remarkably compact for such a large and complex model.

**Figure 5.42**

Rest of Flights Model

| | A | B | C | D |
|---|---|---|---|---|
| 148 | **Constraint on planes** | | | |
| 149 | | Number used | | Number owned |
| 150 | | 4 | <= | 4 |
| 151 | | | | |
| 152 | **Monetary values** | | | |
| 153 | Net revenues | 456 | | |
| 154 | Fixed costs | 60 | | |
| 155 | Overnight costs | 0 | | |
| 156 | Net profit | 396 | | |

**Figure 5.43**

Solver Dialog Box for Flights Model

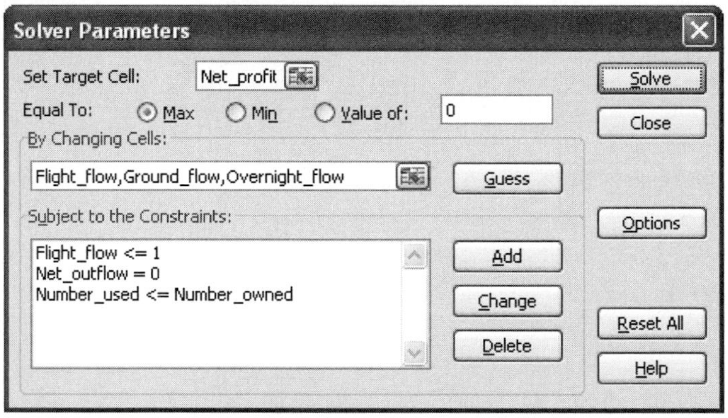

Solver Parameters

Set Target Cell: Net_profit

Equal To: ⦿ Max ◯ Min ◯ Value of: 0

By Changing Cells:
Flight_flow,Ground_flow,Overnight_flow

Subject to the Constraints:
Flight_flow <= 1
Net_outflow = 0
Number_used <= Number_owned

Solve | Close | Guess | Options | Add | Change | Delete | Reset All | Help

## Discussion of the Solution

The optimal solution can be seen primarily from Figures 5.38 and 5.40. The former indicates that TriCities should fly only 17 of the potential 23 flights. The latter shows that no overnight flights should be flown. It also shows that all 4 planes are used. Two of these sit overnight in Boston, and the other two sit overnight in Washington, D.C. No overnight flights are flown, evidently because the cost of doing so is too large. The daily profit from this solution is $39,600.

## Sensitivity Analysis

We could run many interesting sensitivity analyses. For example, what if TriCities had more planes? To answer this, we run SolverTable with cell B4 as the single input cell, allowing it to vary from 4 to 8 in increments of 1, and we keep track of the monetary values, as well as the number of flights flown. (This latter output is calculated in cell B158 with the formula **=SUM(Flight_flow)**.) The results appear in Figure 5.44. As expected, profit and the number of flights flown both increase when the company owns more planes, but this analysis does not take the cost of *purchasing* more planes into account. TriCities would need to trade off the cost of new planes with this increased profit.

**Figure 5.44**

Sensitivity to
Planes Owned

| | A | B | C | D | E | F | G |
|---|---|---|---|---|---|---|---|
| 158 | Flights flown | 17 | | | | | |
| 159 | | | | | | | |
| 160 | **Sensitivity of monetary values and flights flown to planes owned** | | | | | | |
| 161 | | | $B$153 | $B$154 | $B$155 | $B$156 | $B$158 |
| 162 | | 4 | 456 | 60 | 0 | 396 | 17 |
| 163 | | 5 | 495 | 75 | 0 | 420 | 19 |
| 164 | | 6 | 523 | 90 | 5 | 428 | 21 |
| 165 | | 7 | 551 | 105 | 10 | 436 | 22 |
| 166 | | 8 | 551 | 105 | 10 | 436 | 22 |

From Figure 5.44, we see that TriCities still does not fly all 23 potential flights, even with 8 planes. Could it? We can answer this question easily by changing the objective from maximizing profit to maximizing the number of flights flown (in cell B158) and rerunning Solver. If you do so, you will find that the maximum is 23. Therefore, TriCities *could* fly all 23 flights with 8 planes, but the cost structure makes it more profitable to fly only 22. The driving factor here is evidently the fixed cost per plane. When TriCities owns 8 planes, the optimal profit solution *uses* only 7 of these planes.

A final sensitivity analysis involves empty overnight flights. When TriCities owns 7 planes, Figure 5.44 indicates (see cell E165) that it flies 2 empty overnight flights. (These are both from Boston to Washington, D.C.) What happens to this solution if, as a matter of company policy, empty overnight flights are not allowed? We can modify the model in three ways to answer this question. First, we can impose a huge cost on overnight flights, effectively ruling them out. Second, we can impose capacities of 0 on the overnight flight arcs (in Figure 5.40). Third, we can simply eliminate these arcs. We used the first method, with the results shown in Figure 5.45. The solution changes fairly dramatically. Now TriCities uses only 5 of its 7 planes, it flies only 19 (instead of 22) flights, and its profit decreases from $43,600 to $42,000. ∎

**Figure 5.45**

Model with
Overnight Flights
Disallowed

| | A | B | C | D |
|---|---|---|---|---|
| 148 | **Constraint on planes** | | | |
| 149 | | Number used | | Number owned |
| 150 | | 5 | <= | 7 |
| 151 | | | | |
| 152 | **Monetary values** | | | |
| 153 | Net revenues | 495 | | |
| 154 | Fixed costs | 75 | | |
| 155 | Overnight costs | 0 | | |
| 156 | Net profit | 420 | | |
| 157 | | | | |
| 158 | Flights flown | 19 | | |

# ADDITIONAL APPLICATIONS

As stated previously, airlines are heavy users of management science. A quick look through recent issues of the *Interfaces* journal confirms this. Here are some examples. Virtually all of these examples describe optimization models that employ network and integer programming algorithms.

### Improving Fractional Aircraft Ownership Operations at Flexjet

Fractional aircraft ownership programs allow individuals to buy shares in a business jet at a fraction of the cost of full ownership. The fractional aircraft market is the fastest growing segment of the business aircraft market. Hicks et al. (2005) describe how they used large-scale, mixed-integer, nonlinear optimization models to maximize the use of aircraft, crew, and facilities for Flexjet's fractional aircraft ownership operations. Since inception, the system has generated savings in excess of $54 million with projected additional savings of $27 million annually.

### Optimizing Pilot Staffing and Training at Continental Airlines

Yu et al. (2004) describe how they developed the Crew ResourceSolver decision-support system for Continental Airlines. This system employs advanced optimization modeling and solution techniques to solve large, complex pilot staffing and training problems. The authors estimate that the system has saved Continental over $10 million annually.

### UPS Optimizes Its Air Network

Armacost et al. (2004) describe how a team of operations research analysts at UPS and Massachusetts Institute of Technology (MIT) created a system to optimize the design of service networks for delivering express packages. The system determines aircraft routes, fleet assignments, and package routings to ensure overnight delivery at minimum cost. UPS credits the system with savings in excess of $87 million between 2000 and 2002, and it anticipates future savings to be in the hundreds of millions of dollars.

### Optimizing On-Demand Aircraft Schedules for Fractional Aircraft Operators

Martin et al. (2003) describe how Bitwise Solutions developed a flexible, integrated decision-support system to help fractional management companies (companies that manage fractional aircraft ownership programs) optimize their fleet schedules. The system handles all aspects of fractional fleet management: reservations, scheduling, dispatch, aircraft maintenance, and crew requirements. In November 2000, Raytheon Travel Air began using the system and reported a $4.4 million savings in the first year of use.

### Delta Optimizes Continuing-Qualification-Training Schedules for Pilots

The downturn in airline business after the terrorist bombings on 9/11 forced airlines to modify their operations. Sohoni et al. (2003) describe modifications at Delta Airlines, which had to reduce its workforce and modify its requirements for scheduling pilot training. To minimize Delta's costs and automate the scheduling process under a rigid planning time line, the authors developed an optimization system that builds and assigns training schedules based on individual pilot's requirements. Delta expects to save $7.5 million in annual operating costs by using the system to schedule continuing qualification training for its pilots.

### Crew Recovery at Continental Airlines

Due to unexpected events such as inclement weather, airline crews may not be in position to service their remaining scheduled flights. Airlines must reassign crews quickly to cover open flights and return them to their original schedules in a cost-effective manner that honors various regulations. Yu et al. (2003) describe how they developed a decision-support system for Continental Airlines to generate optimal or nearly optimal crew-recovery solutions. Since its implementation, the system has dealt successfully with several disruptive events, including snowstorms, a flood, and the 9/11 terrorist attacks. Continental estimates that the system was responsible for savings of approximately $40 million for major disruptions only. ■

## PROBLEMS

### Skill-Building Problems

**39.** In the crew-scheduling problem, suppose (as in the sensitivity analysis we discussed) that the first Chicago flight, C1, is delayed by 2 hours—that is, its departure and arrival times move up to 8 A.M. and 12 P.M., respectively. How does the model need to be modified? What is the new optimal solution? Is it the same as the solution indicated by SolverTable in Figure 5.35? If not, why not?

**40.** The required downtime in the crew-scheduling problem is currently assumed to be 1 hour. Suppose we instead require it to be 2 hours. How does the model need to be modified? What is the new optimal solution?

**41.** In the crew-scheduling problem, suppose that two extra flights are added to the current list. The first leaves Chicago at 11 A.M. and arrives in New York at 2 P.M. The second leaves New York at 6 P.M. and arrives in Chicago at 8 P.M. (Remember that all quoted times are EST.) Modify the model to incorporate these two new flights. What is the new optimal solution?

**42.** In the flight-scheduling model, use SolverTable to examine the effect of decreasing all net revenues by the *same* percentage, assuming that the company owns 6 planes. Let this percentage vary from 0% to 50% in increments of 10%. Discuss the changes that occur in the optimal solution.

**43.** In the flight-scheduling model, use SolverTable to examine the effect of increasing both the fixed cost per plane and the overnight cost by the *same* percentage, assuming that the company owns 8 planes. Let this percentage vary from 0% to 50% in increments of 10%. Discuss the changes that occur in the optimal solution.

### Skill-Extending Problems

**44.** One rather unrealistic assumption in the flight-scheduling model is that a given plane can fly two consecutive flights with no downtime. For example, it could fly flight 5903 that gets into Washington, D.C. at time 14 and then fly flight 7555 that leaves Washington, D.C. at time 14. Modify the model so that there must be at least 1 hour of downtime between consecutive flights.

**45.** In the crew-scheduling model, there are exactly as many flights departing from Chicago as departing from New York. Suppose more flights are departing from one city than from the other. How would you model this? Illustrate by assuming that there is an extra flight from Chicago that leaves at 11 A.M. and arrives at New York at 2 P.M. (Remember that all quoted times are EST.)

## 5.7 CONCLUSION

In this chapter, we have discussed a number of management science problems that can be formulated as network models. Often these problems are of a logistics nature—shipping goods from one set of locations to another. However, we have also seen that problems that do not involve shipping or traveling along a physical network can sometimes be formulated as network models. Examples include the bus route assignment and machine replacement problems.

Formulating a problem as a network model has at least two advantages. First, although Excel's Solver doesn't employ them, fast special-purpose algorithms exist for various forms of network models. These enable companies to solve extremely large problems that might not be solvable with ordinary LP algorithms. Second, the graphical representation of network models often makes them easier to visualize. When a problem can be visualized graphically, it is often simpler to model (in a spreadsheet or otherwise) and ultimately to optimize.

## Summary of Key Management Science Terms

| Term | Explanation | Page |
|---|---|---|
| Network models | Class of optimization models that can be represented graphically as a network; typically (but not always) involves shipping goods from one set of locations to another at minimum cost | 222 |
| Nodes | Points in a network representation; often correspond to locations | 224 |
| Arcs | Arrows in a network representation; often correspond to routes connecting locations | 224 |
| Flows | Decision variables that represent the amounts sent along arcs | 224 |
| Arc capacities | Upper bounds on flows on some or all arcs | 225 |
| Flow balance constraints | Constraints that force the amount sent into a node to equal the amount sent out, except possibly for amounts that start out or end up at the node | 229 |
| Transshipment node | A node where nothing starts out or ends up; flow into node equals flow out of node | 242 |
| Shortest path models | Network models where the goal is to get from an "origin" node to a "destination" node at minimal distance (or cost) | 250 |

## Summary of Key Excel Terms

| Term | Explanation | Excel | Page |
|---|---|---|---|
| SUMIF function | Sums values in one range corresponding to cells in a related range that satisfy a criterion | =SUMIF(*compareRange, criterion, sumRange*) | 230 |
| COUNTIF function | Counts values in one range that satisfy a criterion | =COUNTIF(*range,criterion*) | 246 |

# PROBLEMS

## Skill-Building Problems

**46.** The 7th National Bank has two check-processing sites. Site 1 can process 10,000 checks per day, and site 2 can process 6000 checks per day. The bank processes three types of checks: vendor, salary, and personal. The processing cost per check depends on the site, as listed in the file **P05_46.xlsx**. Each day, 5000 checks of each type must be processed. Determine how to minimize the daily cost of processing checks.

**47.** The government is auctioning off oil leases at two sites: 1 and 2. At each site, 100,000 acres of land are to be auctioned. Cliff Ewing, Blake Barnes, and Alexis Pickens are bidding for the oil. Government rules state that no bidder can receive more than 40% of the land being auctioned. Cliff has bid $1000 per acre for site 1 land and $2000 per acre for site 2 land. Blake has bid $900 per acre for site 1 land and $2200 per acre for site 2 land. Alexis has bid $1100 per acre for site 1 land and $1900 per acre for site 2 land.

**a.** Determine how to maximize the government's revenue with a transportation model.

**b.** Use SolverTable to see how changes in the government's rule on 40% of all land being auctioned affect the optimal revenue. Why can the optimal revenue not decrease if this percentage required increases? Why can the optimal revenue not increase if this percentage required decreases?

48. The Amorco Oil Company controls two oil fields. Field 1 can produce up to 40 million barrels of oil per day, and field 2 can produce up to 50 million barrels of oil per day. At field 1, it costs $37.50 to extract and refine a barrel of oil; at field 2 the cost is $41.20. Amorco sells oil to two countries: United Kingdom and Japan. The shipping costs per barrel are shown in the file **P05_48.xlsx**. Each day, the United Kingdom is willing to buy up to 40 million barrels at $65.80 per barrel, and Japan is willing to buy up to 30 million barrels at $68.40 per barrel. Determine how to maximize Amorco's profit.

**49.** Touche Young has three auditors. Each can work up to 160 hours during the next month, during which time three projects must be completed. Project 1 takes 130 hours, project 2 takes 140 hours, and project 3 takes 160 hours. The amount per hour that can be billed for assigning each auditor to each project is given in the file **P05_49.xlsx**. Determine how to maximize total billings during the next month.

50. Five employees are available to perform four jobs. The time it takes each person to perform each job is given in the file **P05_50.xlsx**. Determine the assignment of employees to jobs that minimizes the total time required to perform the four jobs. (A dash indicates that a person cannot do that particular job.)

51. Based on Machol (1970). Doc Councilman is putting together a relay team for the 400-meter relay. Each swimmer must swim 100 meters of breaststroke, backstroke, butterfly, or freestyle, and each swimmer can swim only one race. Doc believes that each swimmer will attain the times given in the file **P05_51.xlsx**. To minimize the team's time for the race, which swimmers should swim which strokes?

52. A company is taking bids on four construction jobs. Three contractors have placed bids on the jobs. Their bids (in thousands of dollars) are given in the file **P05_52.xlsx**. (A dash indicates that the contractor did not bid on the given job.) Contractor 1 can do only one job, but contractors 2 and 3 can each do up to two jobs. Determine the minimum cost assignment of contractors to jobs.

**53.** Widgetco manufactures widgets at two factories, one in Memphis and one in Denver. The Memphis factory can produce up to 150 widgets per day, and the Denver factory can produce up to 200 widgets per day. Widgets are shipped by air to customers in Los Angeles and Boston. The customers in each city require 130 widgets per day. Because of the deregulation of airfares, Widgetco believes that it might be cheaper to first fly some widgets to New York or Chicago and then fly them to their final destinations.

The costs of flying a widget are shown in the file **P05_53.xlsx**.
a. Determine how to minimize the total cost of shipping the required widgets to the customers.
b. Suppose the capacities of both factories are reduced in increments of 10 widgets per day. Use SolverTable to see how much the common reduction can be before the total cost increases; before there is no feasible solution.

54. General Ford produces cars in Los Angeles and Detroit and has a warehouse in Atlanta. The company supplies cars to customers in Houston and Tampa. The costs of shipping a car between various points are listed in the file **P05_54.xlsx**, where a dash means that a shipment is not allowed. Los Angeles can produce up to 1100 cars, and Detroit can produce up to 2900 cars. Houston must receive 2400 cars, and Tampa must receive 1500 cars.
a. Determine how to minimize the cost of meeting demands in Houston and Tampa.
b. Modify the answer to part **a** if shipments between Los Angeles and Detroit are not allowed.
c. Modify the answer to part **a** if shipments between Houston and Tampa are allowed at a cost of $5 per car.

55. Sunco Oil produces oil at two wells. Well 1 can produce up to 150,000 barrels per day, and well 2 can produce up to 200,000 barrels per day. It is possible to ship oil directly from the wells to Sunco's customers in Los Angeles and New York. Alternatively, Sunco could transport oil to the ports of Mobile and Galveston and then ship it by tanker to New York or Los Angeles. Los Angeles requires 160,000 barrels per day, and New York requires 140,000 barrels per day. The costs of shipping 1000 barrels between various locations are shown in the file **P05_55.xlsx**, where a dash indicates shipments that are not allowed. Determine how to minimize the transport costs in meeting the oil demands of Los Angeles and New York.

56. Nash Auto has two plants, two warehouses, and three customers. The plants are in Detroit and Atlanta, the warehouses are in Denver and New York, and the customers are in Los Angeles, Chicago, and Philadelphia. Cars are produced at plants, then shipped to warehouses, and finally shipped to customers. Detroit can produce 150 cars per week, and Atlanta can produce 100 cars per week. Los Angeles requires 80 cars per week, Chicago requires 70, and Philadelphia requires 60. It costs $10,000 to produce a car at each plant. The costs of shipping a car between various cities are listed in the file **P05_56.xlsx**. Assume that during a week, at most 50 cars can be shipped from a warehouse to any particular city. Determine how to meet Nash's weekly demands at minimum cost.

**57.** Fordco produces cars in Detroit and Dallas. The Detroit plant can produce up to 6500 cars, and the Dallas plant can produce up to 6000 cars. Producing a car costs $2000 in Detroit and $1800 in Dallas. Cars must be shipped to three cities. City 1 must receive 5000 cars, city 2 must receive 4000 cars, and city 3 must receive 3000 cars. The costs of shipping a car from each plant to each city are given in the file **P05_57.xlsx**. At most 2700 cars can be sent from a given plant to a given city. Determine how to minimize the cost of meeting all demands.

**58.** Each year, Data Corporal produces up to 400 computers in Boston and up to 300 computers in Raleigh. Los Angeles customers must receive 400 computers, and 300 computers must be supplied to Austin customers. Producing a computer costs $350 in Boston and $400 in Raleigh. Computers are transported by plane and can be sent through Chicago. The costs of sending a computer between pairs of cities are shown in the file **P05_58.xlsx**.
  **a.** Determine how to minimize the total (production plus distribution) cost of meeting Data Corporal's annual demand.
  **b.** How would you modify the model in part **a** if at most 200 units could be shipped through Chicago?

**59.** Suppose it costs $10,000 to purchase a new car. The annual operating cost and resale value of a used car are shown in the file **P05_59.xlsx**. Assume that you presently have a new car. Determine a replacement policy that minimizes your net costs of owning and operating a car for the next six years.

**60.** It costs $200 to buy a lawn mower from a lawn supply store. Assume that I can keep a lawn mower for at most 5 years and that the estimated maintenance cost each year of operation is as follows: year 1, $50; year 2, $80; year 3, $140; year 4, $160; year 5, $180. I have just purchased a new lawn mower. Assuming that a lawn mower has no salvage value, determine the strategy that minimizes the total cost of purchasing and operating a lawn mower for the next 10 years.

**61.** At the beginning of year 1, a new machine must be purchased. The cost of maintaining a machine, depending on its age, is given in the file **P05_61.xlsx**. The cost of purchasing a machine at the beginning of each year is given in this same file. There is no trade-in value when a machine is replaced. The goal is to minimize the total (purchase plus maintenance) cost of having a machine for 5 years. Determine the years in which a new machine should be purchased.

**62.** The town of Busville has three school districts. The numbers of black students and white students in each district are shown in the file **P05_62.xlsx**. The Supreme Court requires the schools in Busville to be racially balanced. Thus, each school must have exactly 300 students, and each school must have the same number of black students. The distances between districts are also shown in the file **P05_62.xlsx**. Determine how to minimize the total distance that students must be bussed while still satisfying the Supreme Court's requirements. Assume that a student who remains in his or her own district does not need to be bussed.

**63.** Delko is considering hiring people for four types of jobs. The company would like to hire the number of people listed in the file **P05_63.xlsx** for each type of job. Delko can hire four types of people. Each type is qualified to perform two types of jobs, as shown in this same file. A total of 20 type 1, 30 type 2, 40 type 3, and 20 type 4 people have applied for jobs. Determine how Delko can maximize the number of employees assigned to suitable jobs, assuming that each person can be assigned to at most one job. (*Hint:* Set this up as a transportation model where the "supplies" are the applicants.)

**64.** A truck must travel from New York to Los Angeles. As shown in Figure 5.46, several routes are available. The number associated with each arc is the number of gallons of fuel required by the truck to traverse the arc. Determine the route from New York to Los Angeles that uses the minimum amount of gas.

**Figure 5.46**

Network for Truck Problem

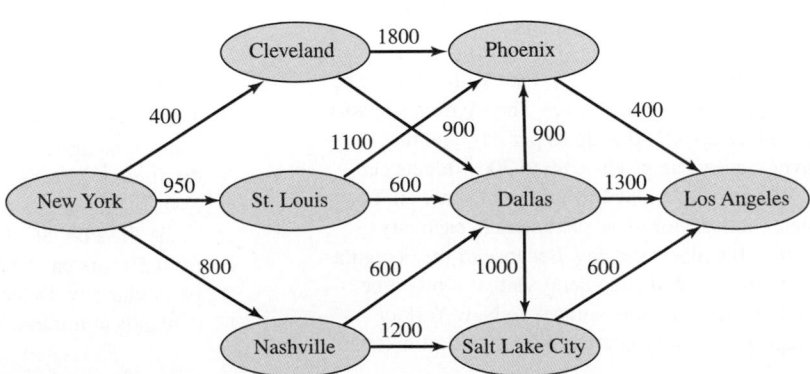

**65.** We are trying to help the MCSCC (Monroe County School Corporation) determine the appropriate high school district for each housing development in Bloomington. For each development, we are given the number of students, the mean family income, the percentage of minorities, and the distance to each high school (South and North). These data are listed in the file **P05_65.xlsx**. In assigning the students, MCSCC wants to minimize total distance traveled subject to the following constraints:

- Each school must have at least 1500 students.
- The mean family income must be at least $85,000 for students of each school.
- Each school must have at least 10% minorities.

Determine an optimal assignment of students to schools. Then provide a one-paragraph summary of how the optimal solution changes as the required minority percentage varies from 5% to 11%.

**66.** A school system has 16 bus drivers that must cover 12 bus routes. Each driver can cover at most one route. The driver's bids for the various routes are listed in the file **P05_66.xlsx**. Each bid indicates the amount the driver will charge the school system to drive that route. How should the drivers be assigned to the routes to minimize the school system's cost? After you find the optimal assignments, use conditional formatting so that the cost the school system pays for each route is highlighted in red and whenever the cheapest bid is not used for a route, that bid is highlighted in green.

## Skill-Extending Problems

**67.** Allied Freight supplies goods to three customers, who each require 30 units. The company has two warehouses. In warehouse 1, 40 units are available, and in warehouse 2, 30 units are available. The costs of shipping one unit from each warehouse to each customer are shown in the file **P05_67.xlsx**. There is a penalty for each unsatisfied customer unit of demand—with customer 1, a penalty cost of $90 is incurred; with customer 2, $80; and with customer 3, $110.

  **a.** Determine how to minimize the sum of penalty and shipping costs.

  **b.** Use SolverTable to see how a change in the unit penalty cost of customer 3 affects the optimal cost.

  **c.** Use SolverTable to see how a change in the capacity of warehouse 2 affects the optimal cost.

**68.** Referring to the previous problem, suppose that Allied Freight can purchase and ship extra units to either warehouse for a total cost of $100 per unit and that all customer demand must be met. Determine how to minimize the sum of purchasing and shipping costs.

**69.** Based on Glover and Klingman (1977). The government has many computer files that must be merged frequently. For example, consider the Survey of Current Income (SCI) and the Consumer Price Service (CPS) files, which keep track of family income and family size. The breakdown of records in each file is given in the file **P05_69.xlsx**. SCI and CPS files contain other pieces of data, but the only variables common to the two files are income and family size. Suppose that the SCI and CPS files must be merged to create a file that will be used for an important analysis of government policy. How should the files be merged? We would like to lose as little information as possible in merging the records. For example, merging an SCI record for a family with income $25,000 and family size 2 with a CPS record for a family with income $26,000 and family size 2 results in a smaller loss of information than if an SCI record for a family with income $25,000 and family size 2 is merged with a CPS record for a family with income $29,000 and family size 3. Let the "cost" of merging an SCI record with a CPS record be $|I_{SCI} - I_{CPS}| + |FS_{SCI} - FS_{CPS}|$ where $I_{SCI}$ and $I_{CPS}$ are the incomes from the SCI and CPS records, and $FS_{SCI}$ and $FS_{CPS}$ are the family sizes. Determine the least expensive way to merge the SCI and CPS records.

**70.** Based on Evans (1984). Currently, State University can store 200 files on hard disk, 100 files in computer memory, and 300 files on tape. Users want to store 300 word-processing files, 100 packaged-program files, and 100 data files. Each month a typical word processing file is accessed eight times; a typical packaged-program file, four times; and a typical data file, two times. When a file is accessed, the time it takes for the file to be retrieved depends on the type of file and on the storage medium. The times are listed in the file **P05_70.xlsx**. The goal is to minimize the total time per month that users spend accessing their files. Determine where files should be stored.

**71.** Bloomington has two hospitals. Hospital 1 has four ambulances, and hospital 2 has two ambulances. Ambulance service is deemed adequate if there is only a 10% chance that no ambulance will be available when an ambulance call is received by a hospital. The average length of an ambulance service call is 20 minutes. Given this information, queueing theory tells us that hospital 1 can be assigned up to 4.9 calls per hour and that hospital 2 can be assigned up to 1.5 calls per hour. Bloomington has been divided into 12 districts. The average number of calls per hour emanating from each district is given in the file **P05_71.xlsx**. This file also shows the travel time (in minutes) needed to get from each district to each hospital. The objective is to minimize the average travel time needed to respond to a call. Determine the proper assignment of districts to hospitals. (*Hint:* Be careful about defining the supply points!)

**72.** In Problem 55, assume that before being shipped to Los Angeles or New York, all oil produced at the wells must be refined at either Galveston or Mobile. To refine 1000 barrels of oil costs $5780 at Mobile and $6250 at Galveston. Assuming that both Mobile and Galveston have infinite refinery capacity, determine how to minimize the daily cost of transporting and refining the oil requirements of Los Angeles and New York.

**73.** Rework the previous problem under the assumption that Galveston has a refinery capacity of 150,000 barrels per day and Mobile has a refinery capacity of 180,000 barrels per day.

**74.** Oilco has oil fields in San Diego and Los Angeles. The San Diego field can produce up to 500,000 barrels per day, and the Los Angeles field can produce up to 400,000 barrels per day. Oil is sent from the fields to a refinery, either in Dallas or in Houston. (Assume that each refinery has unlimited capacity.) To refine 1000 barrels costs $5700 at Dallas and $6000 at Houston. Refined oil is shipped to customers in Chicago and New York. Chicago customers require 400,000 barrels per day, and New York customers require 300,000 barrels per day. The costs of shipping 100,000 barrels of oil (refined or unrefined) between cities are shown in the file **P05_74.xlsx**.
   **a.** Determine how to minimize the total cost of meeting all demands.
   **b.** If each refinery had a capacity of 380,000 barrels per day, how would you modify the model in part **a**?

**75.** At present, 500 long-distance calls must be routed from New York to Los Angeles (L.A.), and 400 calls must be routed from Philadelphia to L.A. On route to L.A. from Philadelphia or New York, calls are sent through Indianapolis or Cleveland, then through Dallas or Denver, and finally to L.A. The number of calls that can be routed between any pair of cities is shown in the file **P05_75.xlsx**. The phone company wants to know how many of the $500 + 400 = 900$ calls originating in New York and Philadelphia can be routed to L.A. Set this up as a minimum cost network flow model—that is, specify the nodes, arcs, shipping costs, and arc capacities. Then solve it.

**76.** Eight students need to be assigned to four dorm rooms at Faber College. Based on "incompatibility measurements," the cost incurred for any pair of students rooming together is shown in the file **P05_76.xlsx**. How should the students be assigned to the four rooms to minimize the total incompatibility cost?

**77.** Based on Ravindran (1971). A library must build shelving to shelve 200 4-inch-high books, 100 8-inch-high books, and 80 12-inch-high books. Each book is 0.5 inch thick. The library has several ways to store the books. For example, an 8-inch-high shelf can be built to store all books of height less than or equal to 8 inches, and a 12-inch-high shelf can be built for the 12-inch books. Alternatively, a 12-inch-high shelf can be built to store all books. The library believes it costs $2300 to build a shelf and that a cost of $5 per square inch is incurred for book storage. (Assume that the area required to store a book is given by the height of the storage area multiplied by the book's thickness.) Determine how to shelve the books at minimum cost. (*Hint:* Create nodes 0, 4, 8, and 12, and make the cost associated with the arc joining nodes $i$ and $j$ equal to the total cost of shelving all books of height greater than $i$ and less than or equal to $j$ on a single shelf.)

**78.** In the original RedBrand problem (Example 5.4), suppose that the company could add up to 100 tons of capacity, in increments of 10 tons, to any *single* plant. Use SolverTable to determine the yearly savings in cost from having extra capacity at the various plants. Assume that the capacity will cost $28,000 per ton right now. Also, assume that the annual cost savings from having the extra capacity will extend over 10 years, and that the total 10-year savings will be discounted at an annual 10% interest rate. How much extra capacity should the company purchase, and which plant should be expanded? (*Hint:* Use the PV function to find the present value of the total cost saving over the 10-year period. You can assume that the costs occur at the *ends* of the respective years.)

**79.** Based on Jacobs (1954). The Carter Caterer Company must have the following number of clean napkins available at the beginning of each of the next 4 days: day 1, 1500; day 2, 1200; day 3, 1800; day 4, 600. After being used, a napkin can be cleaned by one of two methods: fast service or slow service. Fast service costs 10 cents per napkin, and a napkin cleaned via fast service is available for use the day after it is last used. Slow service costs 6 cents per napkin, and these napkins can be reused 2 days after they are last used. New napkins can be purchased for a cost of 20 cents per napkin. Determine how to minimize the cost of meeting the demand for napkins during the next 4 days. (*Note:* There are at least two possible modeling approaches, one network and one nonnetwork. See if you can model it each way.)

**80.** Kellwood, a company that produces a single product, has three plants and four customers. The three plants will produce 3000, 5000, and 5000 units, respectively, during the next time period. Kellwood has made a commitment to sell 4000 units to customer 1, 3000 units to customer 2, and at least 3000 units to customer 3. Both customers 3 and 4 also want to buy as many of the remaining units as possible. The profit associated with shipping a unit from each plant to each customer is given in the file **P05_80.xlsx**. Determine how to maximize Kellwood's profit.

81. I have put four valuable paintings up for sale. Four customers are bidding for the paintings. Customer 1 is willing to buy two paintings, but each other customer is willing to purchase at most one painting. The prices that each customer is willing to pay are given in the file **P05_81.xlsx**. Determine how to maximize the total revenue received from the sale of the paintings.

82. Powerhouse produces capacitors at three locations: Los Angeles, Chicago, and New York. Capacitors are shipped from these locations to public utilities in five regions of the country: northeast (NE), northwest (NW), midwest (MW), southeast (SE), and southwest (SW). The cost of producing and shipping a capacitor from each plant to each region of the country is given in the file **P05_82.xlsx**. Each plant has an annual production capacity of 100,000 capacitors. Each year, each region of the country must receive the following number of capacitors: NE, 55,000; NW, 50,000; MW, 60,000; SE, 60,000; SW, 45,000. Powerhouse believes that shipping costs are too high, and it is therefore considering building one or two more production plants. Possible sites are Atlanta and Houston. The costs of producing a capacitor and shipping it to each region of the country are also given in the file **P05_82.xlsx**. It costs $3 million (in current dollars) to build a new plant, and operating each plant incurs a fixed cost (in addition to variable shipping and production costs) of $50,000 per year. A plant at Atlanta or Houston will have the capacity to produce 100,000 capacitors per year. Assume that future demand patterns and production costs will remain unchanged. If costs are discounted at a rate of 12% per year, how can Powerhouse minimize the net present value (NPV) of all costs associated with meeting current and future demands?

83. Based on Hansen and Wendell (1982). During the month of July, Pittsburgh resident Bill Fly must make four round-trip flights between Pittsburgh and Chicago. The dates of the trips are shown in the file **P05_83.xlsx**. Bill must purchase four round-trip tickets. Without a discounted fare, a round-trip ticket between Pittsburgh and Chicago costs $500. If Bill's stay in a city includes a weekend, he gets a 20% discount on the round-trip fare. If his stay is more than 10 days, he receives a 30% discount, and if his stay in a city is at least 21 days, he receives a 35% discount. However, at most one discount can be applied toward the purchase of any ticket. Determine how to minimize the total cost of purchasing the four round-trip tickets. (*Hint:* It might be beneficial to pair one half of one round-trip ticket number with half of another round-trip ticket.)

84. Three professors must be assigned to teach six sections of finance. Each professor must teach two sections of finance, and each has ranked the six time periods during which finance is taught, as shown in the file **P05_84.xlsx**. A ranking of 10 means that the professor wants to teach at that time, and a ranking of 1 means that he or she does not want to teach at that time. Determine an assignment of professors to sections that maximizes the total satisfaction of the professors.

85. Based on Denardo et al. (1988). Three fires have just broken out in New York. Fires 1 and 2 each require two fire engines, and fire 3 requires three fire engines. The "cost" of responding to each fire depends on the time at which the fire engines arrive. Let $t_{ij}$ be the time in minutes when the engine $j$ arrives at fire $i$ (if it is dispatched to that location). Then the cost of responding to each fire is as follows: fire 1, $6t_{11} + 4t_{12}$; fire 2, $7t_{21} + 3t_{22}$; fire 3, $9t_{31} + 8t_{32} + 5t_{33}$. There are three fire companies that can respond to the three fires. Company 1 has three engines available, and companies 2 and 3 each have two engines available. The time (in minutes) it takes an engine to travel from each company to each fire is shown in the file **P05_85.xlsx**.
   a. Determine how to minimize the cost associated with assigning the fire engines. (*Hint:* A network with seven destination nodes is necessary.)
   b. Would the formulation in part **a** still be valid if the cost of fire 1 were $4t_{11} + 6t_{12}$?

## Modeling Problems

86. A company produces several products at several different plants. The products are then shipped to two warehouses for storage and are finally shipped to one of many customers. How would you use a network flow model to help the company reduce its production and distribution costs? Pay particular attention to discussing the data you would need to implement a network flow model.

87. You want to start a campus business to match compatible male and female students for dating. How would you use the models in this chapter to help you run your business?

88. You have been assigned to ensure that each high school in the Indianapolis area is racially balanced. Explain how you would use a network model to help attain this goal.

89. In the crew-scheduling model in Example 5.7, there are only two cities. Suppose there are more than two cities. Is it possible to modify the network approach appropriately? Discuss how you would do it.

International Textile Company, Ltd., is a Hong
Kong–based firm that distributes textiles world-
wide. The company is owned by the Lao family.
Present plans are to remain in Hong Kong through
the transition in governments. Should the People's
Republic of China continue its economic renaissance,
the company hopes to use its current base to
expand operations to the mainland. International
Textile has mills in the Bahamas, Hong Kong, Korea,
Nigeria, and Venezuela, each weaving fabrics out of
two or more raw fibers: cotton, polyester, and/or silk.
The mills service eight company distribution centers
located near the customers' geographical centers of
activity.

Because transportation costs historically have
been less than 10% of total expenses, management
has paid little attention to extracting savings through
judicious routing of shipments. Ching Lao is returning
from the United States, where he has just completed
his bachelor's degree in marketing. He believes that

each year he can save International Textile hundreds
of thousands of dollars—perhaps millions—just by
better routing of fabrics from mills to distribution
centers. One glaring example of poor routing is the
current assignment of fabric output to the Mexico
City distribution center from Nigeria instead of from
Venezuela, less than a third the distance. Similarly, the
Manila center now gets most of its textiles from
Nigeria and Venezuela, although the mills in Hong
Kong itself are much closer.

Of course, the cost of shipping a bolt of cloth
does not depend on distance alone. Table 5.14
provides the actual costs supplied to Lao from company headquarters. Distribution center demands are
seasonal, so a new shipment plan must be made each
month. Table 5.15 provides the fabric requirements
for the month of March. International Textile's mills
have varying capacities for producing the various
types of cloth. Table 5.16 provides the quantities that
apply during March.

**Table 5.14 Shipping Cost Data (Dollars Per Bolt)**

| Mill | Distribution Center | | | | | | | |
|------|------------|---------|--------|------------|--------|------|-------|----------|
| | Los Angeles | Chicago | London | Mexico City | Manila | Rome | Tokyo | New York |
| Bahamas | 2 | 2 | 3 | 3 | 7 | 4 | 7 | 1 |
| Hong Kong | 6 | 7 | 8 | 10 | 2 | 9 | 4 | 8 |
| Korea | 5 | 6 | 8 | 11 | 4 | 9 | 1 | 7 |
| Nigeria | 14 | 12 | 6 | 9 | 11 | 7 | 5 | 10 |
| Venezuela | 4 | 3 | 5 | 1 | 9 | 6 | 11 | 4 |

**Table 5.15 Fabric Demands for March (Bolts)**

| Fabric | Distribution Center | | | | | | | |
|--------|------------|---------|--------|------------|--------|------|-------|----------|
| | Los Angeles | Chicago | London | Mexico City | Manila | Rome | Tokyo | New York |
| Cotton | 500 | 800 | 900 | 900 | 800 | 100 | 200 | 700 |
| Polyester | 1,000 | 2,000 | 3,000 | 1,500 | 400 | 700 | 900 | 2,500 |
| Silk | 100 | 100 | 200 | 50 | 400 | 200 | 700 | 200 |

[9] This case was written by Lawrence L. Lapin, San Jose State
University.

## Table 5.16  March Production Capacities (Bolts)

| Mill | Production Capacity | | |
| | Cotton | Polyester | Silk |
|---|---|---|---|
| Bahamas | 1,000 | 3,000 | 0 |
| Hong Kong | 2,000 | 2,500 | 1,000 |
| Korea | 1,000 | 3,500 | 500 |
| Nigeria | 2,000 | 0 | 0 |
| Venezuela | 1,000 | 2,000 | 0 |

Lao wants to schedule production and shipments in such a way that the most costly customers are shorted when there is insufficient capacity, and the least-efficient plants operate at less than full capacity when demand falls below maximum production capacity.

You have been retained by International to assist Lao.

## Questions

1. Find the optimal March shipment schedule and its total transportation cost for each of the following:
   a. cotton
   b. polyester cloth
   c. silk

2. The company will be opening a silk-making department in the Nigeria mill. Although it will not be completed for several months, a current capacity of 1,000 bolts for that fabric might be used during March for an added one-time cost of $2,000. Find the new optimal shipment schedule and the total cost for that fabric. Should the Nigeria mill process silk in March?

3. Lao learns that changes might have to be made to the March plans. If a new customer is obtained, the cotton demand in Manila and in Mexico City will increase by 10% at each location. Meanwhile, a big New York customer might cut back, which would reduce polyester demand by 10% in both New York and Chicago. Find the contingent optimal schedules and total costs (a) for cotton and (b) for polyester.

4. International Textile loses a profit of $10 for each bolt of cotton it falls short of meeting the distribution center's demand. For polyester, the loss is $20 per bolt; for silk, it is a whopping $50 per bolt. By running the mills on overtime, the company can produce additional bolts at the additional costs shown in Table 5.17. Using only the original data from Tables 5.14 through 5.16 and the information in Table 5.17, determine new production schedules to maximize overall profit for successively (a) cotton, (b) polyester, and (c) silk. Which fabrics and locations involve overtime production, and what are the overtime quantities?

5. Without making any calculations, offer Lao other suggestions for reducing costs of transportation.

## Table 5.17  Overtime Production Costs

| Mill | Cost per Bolt | | |
| | Cotton | Polyester | Silk |
|---|---|---|---|
| Bahamas | $10 | $10 | N.A. |
| Hong Kong | 15 | 12 | $25 |
| Korea | 5 | 8 | 22 |
| Nigeria | 6 | N.A. | N.A. |
| Venezuela | 7 | 6 | N.A. |

■

A typical paper mill might produce 1200 tons of paper per day to fill orders from 250 customers. Sending 100 truckload shipments per day would not be unusual for a mill served by 20 motor carriers. The carriers will generally accept shipments to any destination that they serve, subject to daily volume commitments and equipment availability. Each carrier has a different and somewhat complex rate structure. Given a pool of orders that must be shipped on a given day, the mill's problem is to assign truckloads to carriers to minimize its total shipping cost.

## Westvaco Company Overview

Each year, Westvaco sells more than $2 billion worth of manufactured paper, paperboard, and specialty chemicals. Production occurs at five domestic paper mills and four chemical plants. In addition, Westvaco has many converting locations, which manufacture liquid packaging, envelopes, folding cartons, and corrugated boxes. Some of Westvaco's products include the following:

- Fine papers, often used in printing applications (magazines and annual reports)
- Bleached paperboard, used in packaging (milk and juice cartons, freezer to oven entrees, and so forth)
- Kraft paper, used for corrugated boxes and decorative laminates (such as Formica)
- Chemicals, including activated carbon printing ink resins

## Transportation Function

The corporate transportation function has a dual role at Westvaco. It supports the operating locations by negotiating freight rates and service commitments with rail, truck, and ocean carriers. In addition, it serves as an internal consulting group for reviewing operations in the field and making recommendations on streamlining tasks, making organizational changes to support changing customer requirements, and supporting the implementation of new technology.

Local traffic departments are responsible for day-to-day operations of mills and plants, including carrier assignments, dispatching, and switching lists for the railroads.

## Production Overview

The production cycle is summarized in Figure 5.47.

---

**Figure 5.47**   Production Cycle Overview

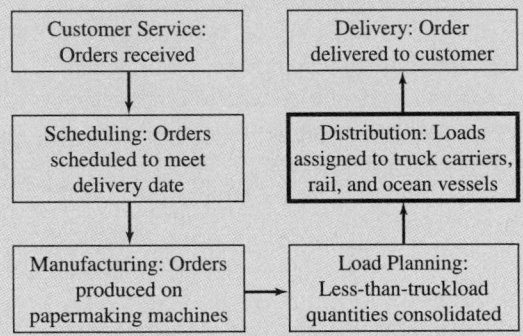

**Orders**   The majority of paper orders are for rolls, where customers request a specific grade and size of paper (diameter and width), amount (pounds, or linear or square feet), and delivery date. The orders typically range in width from 8 to 70 inches. With greater emphasis on just-in-time production by Westvaco's customers, delivery dates are sometimes specified in half-hour time windows. Orders that arrive before or after the time window are not accepted.

**Scheduling**   After orders are received, they are scheduled on paper machines up to 200 inches wide. The paper business is heavily capital intensive: new machines can cost more than $400 million each. Machines usually run 24 hours a day and scheduling is done to minimize waste while meeting shipping date requirements. After production of a "parent" roll, the orders are cut on a rewinder into the exact order size.

**Load Planning** Each morning, a load planner must review the previous day's production to divide large orders and consolidate less-than-truckload (LTL) orders into truckload quantities. Special attention is necessary to ensure that delivery requirements are met for orders that are consolidated. Orders typically weigh between 1000 and 150,000 pounds. A truck can generally pull a trailer with 46,000 to 48,000 pounds of paper. Depending on the construction of the trailer, this is the maximum weight limit that can be loaded while remaining under federal weight limits. Some care must also be taken to remain within axle weight limits. The goal of the load planner is to maximize the weight on a trailer while determining a route that minimizes the total number of miles traveled per day, with no truck making more than four stops (three stops plus the final destination).

**Distribution** This case focuses on the distribution problem shown in the bold box in Figure 5.47. After loads are planned, they are turned over to a transportation planner to assign carriers to loads. The planner has a contract for each carrier that gives the rates to each destination served (state or zip code range). The rates include a mileage charge, a stop-off charge, and a minimum charge per truckload. The transportation planner also has a list of the trailers available for each carrier. The planner will select a carrier for a given shipment based on the knowledge of the best carriers for a given traffic lane, subject to availability. Some carriers have minimum daily volume commitments that must be met.

After the carrier is selected for a given load, the planner updates the information in the mill's mainframe computer and displays this information in the shipping area. The selected carrier's trailer is spotted and brought to the loading dock and loading commences. The shipment information is then phoned or faxed to the carrier.

**A Sample Distribution Problem** Table 5.18 contains a scaled-down version of a typical distribution problem faced by a transportation planner at Westvaco's paper mill in Wickliffe, Kentucky. The load planner has determined that 32 truckloads are needed to distribute last night's production. In the shipping area, 33 drivers from 6 carriers are waiting for their trucks to be loaded. One truck will not be needed today. The carrier PSST has 4 trucks in the shipping area, and Westvaco has a contractual obligation to use all 4 of these trucks today. (In practice, it would not be unusual for a transportation planner to assign 25 truckloads to 20 carriers in a single day.)

The mileage numbers in Table 5.18 represent the total number of miles for the trip from Wickliffe to the final destination, including any intermediate stops. The total charge is calculated as follows. Suppose that the Roseville, Minnesota, trip is assigned to carrier IRST. The cost to Westvaco would be $600(1.13) + 3(75) = \$903$. (If the cost calculated this way were less than IRST's minimum truckload charge of \$400, the cost to Westvaco would be \$400.) Stop-off charges apply only to intermediate stops and not the final destination. Four truckloads are needed to go to Atlanta, Georgia. These truckloads can be assigned to a single carrier, or they can be split among several carriers. If carrier MRST is assigned one of these truckloads, the cost is $612(0.87) = \$532$.

## Question

For the distribution data shown in Table 5.18, what is the least-cost assignment of truckloads to carriers that meets the necessary requirements? What is the cost of this distribution plan?

**Epilogue** Carrier selection at Westvaco was done manually (with pencil and paper!) by transportation planners in the past. A side-by-side test of a spreadsheet LP solution versus manual selection indicated daily savings in the range of 3% to 6%, and so the project was approved. With annual trucking costs of about \$15 million, the total savings with the new approach have been significant. In addition to this benefit, there have been a number of serendipitous side effects. The optimization technique removes the guesswork from carrier selection, especially on weekends, where revolving coverage added

**Table 5.18** Current Distribution Data for Westvaco Case Study

| | | | | | Carrier | | | | | |
|---|---|---|---|---|---|---|---|---|---|---|
| Destination | State | Trips | Stops | Miles | ABCT | IRST | LAST | MRST | NEST | PSST |
| Atlanta | GA | 4 | 0 | 612 | * | 0.88 | 1.15 | 0.87 | 0.95 | 1.05 |
| Everett | MA | 1 | 3 | 612 | * | 1.18 | 1.27 | 1.39 | 1.35 | 1.28 |
| Ephrata | PA | 3 | 0 | 190 | * | 3.42 | 1.73 | 1.71 | 1.82 | 2.00 |
| Riverview | MI | 5 | 0 | 383 | 0.79 | 1.01 | 1.25 | 0.96 | 0.95 | 1.11 |
| Carson | CA | 1 | 2 | 3063 | * | 0.80 | 0.87 | * | 1.00 | * |
| Chamblee | GA | 1 | 0 | 429 | * | 1.23 | 1.61 | 1.22 | 1.33 | 1.47 |
| Roseville | MN | 1 | 3 | 600 | 1.24 | 1.13 | 1.89 | 1.32 | 1.41 | 1.41 |
| Hanover | PA | 1 | 0 | 136 | * | 4.78 | 2.23 | 2.39 | 2.26 | 2.57 |
| Sparks | NV | 2 | 0 | 2439 | * | 1.45 | * | 1.20 | * | * |
| Parsippany | NJ | 1 | 1 | 355 | * | 1.62 | 1.36 | 1.39 | 1.03 | 1.76 |
| Effingham | IL | 5 | 0 | 570 | 0.87 | 0.87 | 1.25 | 0.87 | 0.90 | 1.31 |
| Kearny | NJ | 7 | 0 | 324 | * | 2.01 | 1.54 | 1.53 | 1.28 | 1.95 |
| | | | | | | | | | | |
| | | Minimum charge per truckload | | | 350 | 400 | 350 | 300 | 350 | 300 |
| | | Stop-off charge | | | 50 | 75 | 50 | 35 | 50 | 50 |
| | | Available pulls | | | 4 | 8 | 7 | 7 | 3 | 4 |
| | | Commitment | | | 1 | 7 | 6 | 0 | 0 | 4 |

*Note:* Asterisks (*) indicate carrier does not travel to the destination; rates in dollars/mile.

significant variability to the carrier selection process. The technique adds accountability to the transportation planner's position and, tied to a reason code for changing the carrier, offers a clear answer to management questions regarding carrier selection. Finally, the time savings have also been significant. The carrier assignment portion of the transportation planner's job can be done much faster than before.[10]

∎

[10] This case was co-authored with Dave Rimple, who identified and implemented this project at Westvaco.

# Optimization Models with Integer Variables

© JOSHUA GATES WEISBERG/EPA/Landov

## U.S. AIR FORCE SPACE COMMAND'S LONG-TERM INVESTMENT IN SPACE SYSTEMS

The U.S. Air Force created Space Command in 1982 to enhance defense in the United States through space superiority and to protect the country from weapons of mass destruction. Space Command spends billions of dollars each year procuring and deploying launch vehicles and space systems required for mission area tasks. Space Command includes a space and missile optimization analysis (SAMOA) group to determine the best use of funds to satisfy requirements over a 24-year time horizon. Brown et al. (2003) describe their role within SAMOA to develop a strategic plan that was presented to Congress in 1999 as part of the military's overall strategic plan. The authors of the plan developed an integer programming model, similar to the capital budgeting model in this chapter but *much* larger in scale, to determine the best set of space projects to undertake over the planning horizon. This plan tries to achieve the various missions of Space Command as fully as possible while staying within budget. Like everything in the military, the model has an acronym, SCOUT (space command optimizer of utility toolkit).

The overall planning process within SAMOA is extremely complex. The process consists of five steps: (1) mission area assessment, (2) mission needs analysis, (3) mission solution analysis, (4) portfolio selection, and (5) refined-portfolio selection. The first three steps are essentially steps 1 and 2 of the seven-step modeling process described in Chapter 1. They define the tasks that Space Command needs to accomplish to achieve its missions, the current and future needs—over and above what already exists—to accomplish these tasks, and the required data on candidate systems being considered. This data includes (1) scores for how each system, or combination of systems, accomplishes various tasks; (2) possible starting and ending times for the system (where the possible starting times can be several years in the future, due to the time required for R&D); (3) expected system costs, including development and operating costs over a multiyear period; (4) various precedence relations and side constraints (for example, system B can't be selected unless project A is selected); (5) launch requirements and per-launch costs; and (6) budgetary restrictions.

The last two steps build the integer programming model and then refine it, based on nonquantitative considerations such as political pressures. The model itself has a large number of integer decision variables. There is a binary variable for each combination of system and starting and ending years. For example, if a given system can be started any year from 2005 until 2010 and then end 12 years later, there will be 6 binary variables, one for each potential starting year. There are also integer variables for the number of launches by each selected system each year. The constraints are mostly of the "logical" type. For example, they enforce all precedence relations and side constraints, and they allow a given system to be selected for only one start-end time combination. The authors use a "penalty" type of objective. That is, the objective is total discounted penalty dollars, with penalties for not completely achieving task performance and for violating budget constraints. This allows solutions to violate constraints slightly (they can be slightly over budget, say), which provides more flexibility. The discounting is done in the usual financial sense, to make violations in the distant future less important.

The strategic master plan, the result of the SCOUT model and its refinements, was submitted to Congress in 1999. The plan included planned investments totaling about $310 billion. As the authors state, "This planning effort is the best-staffed and most scrupulously managed example of optimization-based capital planning that we have ever seen." Since 1999, Space Command and several other military units have used SAMOA to help create their strategic master plans. We recommend both this article and a somewhat more general article about military capital planning by Brown et al. (2004). They are both excellent examples of how integer programming can be used to make important and costly capital budgeting decisions. They also indicate the differences between capital budgeting in the military versus capital budgeting in civilian organizations. ∎

# 6.1 INTRODUCTION

In this chapter, we see how many complex problems can be modeled using 0–1 variables and other variables that are constrained to have integer values. A **0–1 variable** is a decision variable that must equal 0 or 1. Usually a 0–1 variable corresponds to an activity that either is or is not undertaken. If the 0–1 variable corresponding to the activity equals 1, then the activity is undertaken; if it equals 0, the activity is not undertaken. A 0–1 variable is also called a **binary variable.**

Optimization models in which some or all of the variables must be integers are known as **integer programming** (IP) models.[1] In this chapter, we illustrate many of the modeling techniques that are needed to formulate IP models of complex situations. You should be aware that a spreadsheet Solver typically has a much harder time solving an IP problem than an LP problem. In fact, a spreadsheet Solver is sometimes unable to solve an IP problem, even if the IP problem has an optimal solution. The reason is that these problems are inherently difficult to solve, no matter what software package is used. However, as we see in this chapter, our ability to *model* complex problems increases tremendously when we use binary variables.

IP models come in many forms. We saw examples in Chapter 4 where the decision variables are naturally integer-valued. For example, when scheduling postal workers (Example 4.2), it's natural to require the numbers of workers to be integers. In examples like this, where we do not want certain decision variables to have fractional values, the problems are basically LP models with integer constraints added at the last minute. In many such examples, if we ignore the integer constraints, optimize with Solver, and then round to the nearest integers, chances are the resulting integer solution will be close to optimal—although admittedly at times the rounded solution is not optimal.

The "integer" models in Chapter 4 are not the types of IP models we discuss in this chapter. If it were simply a matter of adding integer constraints to decision variables, such as the numbers of workers, we would not have included this chapter at all. However, many inherently *nonlinear* problems can be transformed into linear models with the use of binary variables. These are the types of models we discuss here. The clever use of binary variables allows us to solve many interesting and difficult problems that LP algorithms are incapable of solving.

*Except for binary or integer constraints on some changing cells, all models in this chapter are linear.*

All the models we develop in this chapter are, aside from binary or integer changing cells, *linear* models. As in previous chapters, this means that if we look at the target cell, it is ultimately a sum of products of constants and changing cells. The same goes for both sides of all constraints. In other words, the models in this chapter *look* much like the models in the previous three chapters. The only difference is that some of the changing cells are now constrained to be binary or integer. Although the basic algorithm that Solver uses for such models is fundamentally different—because of the binary or integer variables—it still helps that the models are linear. They would present even more of a challenge to Solver if they were nonlinear.

## 6.2 OVERVIEW OF OPTIMIZATION WITH INTEGER VARIABLES

When Excel's Solver solves a linear model without integer constraints, it uses a very efficient algorithm, the simplex method, to perform the optimization. As discussed in Chapter 3, this method examines the "corner" points of the feasible region and returns the best corner point as the optimal solution. The simplex method is efficient because it typically examines only a very small fraction of the hundreds, thousands, or even millions of possible corner points before determining the best corner point.

The main difference between LP and IP models is that LP models allow fractional values, such as 0.137 and 5.3246, in the changing cells, whereas IP models allow only integer values in integer-constrained changing cells. In fact, if changing cells are constrained to be binary, then the only allowable values are 0 and 1. This suggests that IP models should be

---

[1] Many problems in the literature are described as mixed integer linear programming (MILP) models, which indicates that some of the changing cells are constrained to be integers and others are not. Although we do use this acronym, some of our models are of this type.

easier to solve. After all, there are many fewer integer values in a given region than there are continuous values, so searching through the integers should be quicker—especially if their only possible values are 0 and 1. However, IP models are actually *much* more difficult to solve than LP models, primarily because we cannot rely on the simplex method. Although several solution methods have been suggested by researchers—and new methods for specialized problems are still being developed—the solution procedure used by Solver is called **branch and bound.** Although we do not go into the details of the algorithms, we discuss briefly what Solver is doing. This way you can appreciate some of the difficulties with IP models, and you might also understand some of the messages you see in the status bar as Solver performs its optimization.

---

### FUNDAMENTAL INSIGHT

#### Difficulty of Integer Programming Models

You might suspect that IP models are *easier* to solve than LP models. After all, there are only a finite number of feasible integer solutions in an IP model, whereas there are infinitely many feasible (integer and noninteger) solutions in an LP model. However, exactly the opposite is true. As stated previously, IP models are *much* more difficult to solve than LP models. All IP algorithms try to perform an efficient search through the typically huge number of feasible integer solutions. General-purpose algorithms such as branch and bound can be very effective for modest-size problems, but they can fail (or take days of computing time) on the large problems often faced in real applications. In such cases, analysts must develop special-purpose optimization algorithms, or perhaps even heuristics, to find "good" but not necessarily optimal solutions.

---

## Branch and Bound Algorithm

Consider a model with 100 changing cells, all constrained to be binary. Because there are only two values for each binary variable—0 and 1—there are potentially $2^{100}$ feasible solutions, although many of these might not satisfy all the constraints. Unfortunately, $2^{100}$ is an *extremely* large number, so it would take even a very fast computer a long time to check each one of them. Therefore, the naive method of **complete enumeration** of all possible solutions—look at each solution and select the best—is usually impractical. However, **implicit enumeration** is often very practical. This approach examines only a fraction of all $2^{100}$ potential solutions, hopefully a very small fraction, and in doing so, it guarantees that solutions not examined have no chance of being optimal. To see how this works, suppose we find a feasible solution with a profit of $500. If we can somehow guarantee that each solution in a particular subset of solutions has profit *less* than $500, we can ignore this entire subset because it cannot possibly contain the profit-maximizing solution.

This general idea is the essence of the branch and bound method used by the Solver in IP models. The *branching* part means that the algorithm systematically searches through the set of all feasible integer solutions, creating branches, or subsets, of solutions as it goes. For example, if $x_1$ is a binary variable, one branch might have $x_1 = 0$ and another branch might have $x_1 = 1$. Then if $x_2$ is another binary variable, two branches might be created off the $x_1 = 0$ branch—one with $x_2 = 0$ and one with $x_2 = 1$. By forming enough branches, we eventually sweep out all possible integer solutions.

The key, however, is the *bounding* part of the algorithm. Suppose, for the sake of argument, that the objective is to maximize profit. Also, suppose that partway through the solution procedure, the *best* feasible integer solution so far has a profit of $500. This is called the **incumbent** solution—the best so far. Its profit represents a *lower bound* on the optimal profit. That is, we know the optimal solution has profit of at least $500 because we *have* a feasible solution with a profit of $500. This is the easy part of the bounding procedure. We use the best profit found so far as a lower bound on the optimal profit.

The hard part is finding suitable *upper* bounds. Suppose we are considering the branch where $x_1 = 0$ and $x_2 = 1$. If we can somehow show that *any* solution that has $x_1 = 0$ and $x_2 = 1$ can have profit at most $490 (or any number less than our incumbent, $500), then we can ignore this entire branch. Therefore, we want to find an upper bound for each branch that (1) is easy to find in terms of computing time and (2) is as low as possible. Why do we want as low an upper bound as possible? Suppose the upper bound we find for the $x_1 = 0$ and $x_2 = 1$ branch is $515. Then because the incumbent's profit is only $500, this branch might have some potential. That is, it might contain a solution with profit greater than the incumbent. Therefore, we have to pursue it, which costs computer time. The lower the upper bounds we can produce, the quicker we can "prune" branches and the faster the algorithm will be.

The procedures used to find "good" upper bounds for branches are beyond the level of this book. Fortunately, Solver takes care of the details. However, you should now understand some of the messages you'll see in the status bar when you run Solver on IP models. For example, try running Solver on the cutting stock model in Example 6.7 with a tolerance of 0%. You will see plenty of these messages, where the incumbent objective value and the current subproblem (or branch) quickly flash by. For this particular cutting stock model, Solver quickly finds an incumbent solution that is optimal, but it must examine literally thousands of branches before it can *guarantee* that the incumbent is optimal. After a minute or two of computing, we had seen results for 10,000 branches, and there was no end in sight!

## The Solver Tolerance Setting

The Solver Options dialog box contains a **Tolerance** setting, which is relevant for integer-constrained models. Excel's default tolerance is 5%. To explain the Tolerance option, we must first define the **LP relaxation** of an IP model. This is the same model as the IP model, except that all integer constraints are omitted. In particular, cells that are originally constrained to be binary are allowed under the LP relaxation to have *any* fractional values between 0 and 1 (including 0 and 1). The LP relaxation is easy to solve (using the simplex method), and it provides a bound for the IP model. For example, consider a maximization problem where the optimal solution to the LP relaxation has an optimal objective value of $48,214. Then we know that the optimal objective for the original integer-constrained problem can be no larger than $48,214, so that this value represents an upper bound for the original problem.

A tolerance setting of 5% means that Solver stops as soon as it finds a feasible (integer) solution to the IP model that is within 5% of the current upper bound. Initially, the optimal objective value of the LP relaxation serves as the upper bound. As Solver proceeds to find solutions that satisfy the integer constraints, it keeps updating the upper bound. The exact details need not concern us. The important point is that when Solver stops, it guarantees an integer solution that is within at least 5% of the "true" optimal integer solution.

*To guarantee an optimal integer solution, change the Solver tolerance setting to 0%. The disadvantage of this approach is that Solver can run considerably longer on large models.*

The implication is that if we set the tolerance to 0%, Solver will (in theory) run until it finds the *optimal* integer solution. So why don't we always use a tolerance setting of 0%? The reason is that for many IP models, especially large models, it can take Solver a long time to find the optimal solution (or guarantee that the best solution found so far *is* optimal). On the other hand, a solution that is *close* to optimal—within 5%, say—can often be found quickly. This explains why Frontline Systems, the developer of Solver, chose the default tolerance setting of 5%.

We use a tolerance of 0% for all the models in this chapter, simply to guarantee an optimal solution. Therefore, if you use the default tolerance of 5%, you *might* get a solution that is slightly worse than ours.

### Recognizing the Optimal Integer Solution

IP algorithms such as brand and bound often find a very good integer solution very quickly. So why do they sometimes run so long? This is due to the *implicit enumeration* aspect of the algorithms. They have difficulty ruling out large numbers of potential solutions until they have searched all regions of the solution space. In other words, they have difficulty recognizing that they might have found the optimal solution because there are many potential solutions they haven't yet explored. When you run Solver on a reasonably large IP model, watch the status bar. Often a very good incumbent solution, the best solution found so far, is found within seconds, but then Solver spins its wheels for minutes or even hours trying to verify that this solution is optimal.

## 6.3 CAPITAL BUDGETING MODELS

Perhaps the simplest binary IP model is the following capital budgeting example, which illustrates the "go–no go" nature of many IP models.

## EXAMPLE 6.1 SELECTING INVESTMENTS AT TATHAM

The Tatham Company is considering seven investments. The cash required for each investment and the net present value (NPV) each investment adds to the firm are listed in Table 6.1. The cash available for investment is $15,000. Tatham wants to find the investment policy that maximizes its NPV. The crucial assumption here is that if Tatham wants to take part in any of these investments, it must go "all the way." It cannot, for example, go halfway in investment 1 by investing $2500 and realizing an NPV of $8000. In fact, if partial investments were allowed, we wouldn't need IP; we could use LP.

**Table 6.1  Data for the Capital Budgeting Example**

| Investment | Cash Required | NPV |
|---|---|---|
| 1 | $5,000 | $16,000 |
| 2 | $2,500 | $8,000 |
| 3 | $3,500 | $10,000 |
| 4 | $6,000 | $19,500 |
| 5 | $7,000 | $22,000 |
| 6 | $4,500 | $12,000 |
| 7 | $3,000 | $7,500 |

**Objective**   To use binary IP to find the set of investments that stays within budget and maximizes total NPV.

### WHERE DO THE NUMBERS COME FROM?

The initial required cash and the available budget are easy to obtain. Obtaining the NPV for each investment is undoubtedly harder. Here we require a time sequence of anticipated cash inflows from the investments, and we need a discount factor. We might even use simulation to estimate these NPVs. In any case, financial analysts must provide the estimations of the required NPVs.

## Solution

The variables and constraints required for this model are listed in Table 6.2. The most important part is that the decision variables must be binary, where a 1 means an investment is chosen and a 0 means it isn't. These variables cannot have fractional values such as 0.5, because we do not allow partial investments—the company has to go all the way or not at all. Note that we specify the binary restriction in the second row, not the last row. We do this throughout the chapter. However, when we set up the Solver dialog box, we must add explicit binary constraints in the Constraints section.

**Table 6.2**  Variables and Constraints for the Capital Budgeting Model

| | |
|---|---|
| Input variables | Initial cash required for investments, NPVs from investments, budget |
| Decision variables (changing cells) | Whether to invest (binary variables) |
| Objective (target cell) | Total NPV |
| Other calculated variables | Total initial cash required |
| Constraints | Total initial cash required must be less than or equal to Budget |

### DEVELOPING THE SPREADSHEET MODEL

To form the spreadsheet model, which is shown in Figure 6.1, proceed as follows. (See the file **Capital Budgeting 1.xlsx**.)

**Figure 6.1**  Capital Budgeting Model

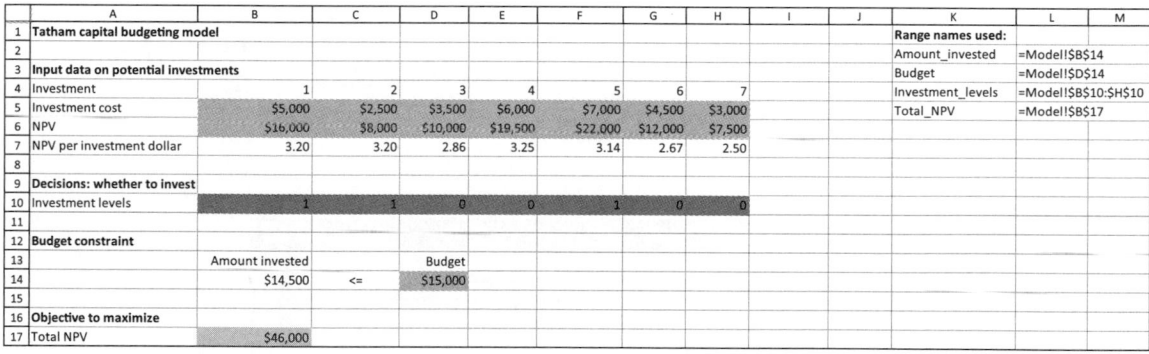

| | A | B | C | D | E | F | G | H | I | J | K | L | M |
|---|---|---|---|---|---|---|---|---|---|---|---|---|---|
| 1 | Tatham capital budgeting model | | | | | | | | | | Range names used: | | |
| 2 | | | | | | | | | | | Amount_invested | =Model!$B$14 | |
| 3 | Input data on potential investments | | | | | | | | | | Budget | =Model!$D$14 | |
| 4 | Investment | 1 | 2 | 3 | 4 | 5 | 6 | 7 | | | Investment_levels | =Model!$B$10:$H$10 | |
| 5 | Investment cost | $5,000 | $2,500 | $3,500 | $6,000 | $7,000 | $4,500 | $3,000 | | | Total_NPV | =Model!$B$17 | |
| 6 | NPV | $16,000 | $8,000 | $10,000 | $19,500 | $22,000 | $12,000 | $7,500 | | | | | |
| 7 | NPV per investment dollar | 3.20 | 3.20 | 2.86 | 3.25 | 3.14 | 2.67 | 2.50 | | | | | |
| 8 | | | | | | | | | | | | | |
| 9 | Decisions: whether to invest | | | | | | | | | | | | |
| 10 | Investment levels | 1 | 1 | 0 | 0 | 1 | 0 | 0 | | | | | |
| 11 | | | | | | | | | | | | | |
| 12 | Budget constraint | | | | | | | | | | | | |
| 13 | | Amount invested | | Budget | | | | | | | | | |
| 14 | | $14,500 | <= | $15,000 | | | | | | | | | |
| 15 | | | | | | | | | | | | | |
| 16 | Objective to maximize | | | | | | | | | | | | |
| 17 | Total NPV | $46,000 | | | | | | | | | | | |

**①** **Inputs.** Enter the initial cash requirements, the NPVs, and the budget in the shaded ranges.

**②** **0–1 values for investments.** Enter *any* trial 0–1 values for the investments in the Investment_levels range. Actually, we can even enter fractional values such as 0.5 in these cells. The Solver binary constraints will eventually force them to be 0 or 1.

*A SUMPRODUCT formula, where one of the ranges includes 0's and 1's, just sums the values in the other range that match up with the 1's.*

**③** **Cash invested.** Calculate the total cash invested in cell B14 with the formula

**=SUMPRODUCT(B5:H5,Investment_levels)**

Note that this formula "picks up" the costs *only* for those investments with 0–1 variables equal to 1. To see this, think how the SUMPRODUCT function works when one of its ranges is a range of 0's and 1's. It effectively sums the cells in the other range corresponding to the 1's.

**④ NPV contribution.** Calculate the NPV contributed by the investments in cell B17 with the formula

**=SUMPRODUCT(B6:H6,Investment_levels)**

Again, this picks up only the NPVs of the investments with 0–1 variables equal to 1.

*Solver makes it easy to specify binary constraints, by clicking on the bin option.*

## USING SOLVER

The Solver dialog box appears in Figure 6.2. We want to maximize the total NPV, subject to staying within the budget. However, we also need to *constrain* the changing cells to be 0–1. Fortunately, Solver makes this simple, as shown in Figure 6.3. We add a constraint with Investments_levels in the left box and choose the bin option in the middle box. The binary in the right box is then added automatically. Note that if *all* changing cells are binary, we do not need to check Solver's Assume Non-Negative option (because 0 and 1 are certainly nonnegative), but we should still check the Assume Linear Model option if the model is linear, as it is here.[2]

**Figure 6.2**

Solver Dialog Box for the Capital Budgeting Model

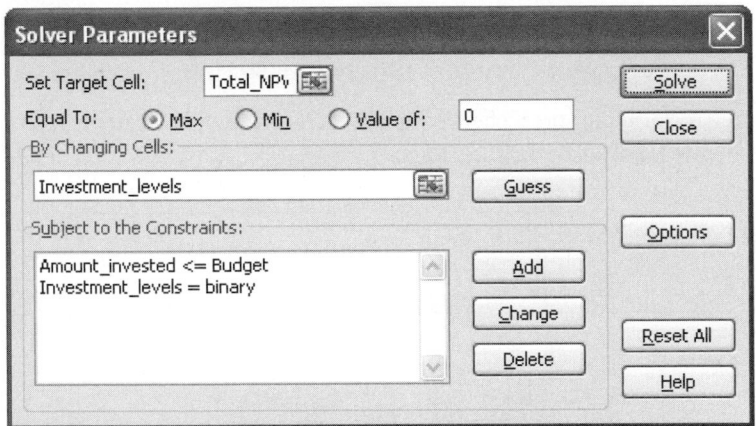

**Figure 6.3**

Specifying a Binary Constraint

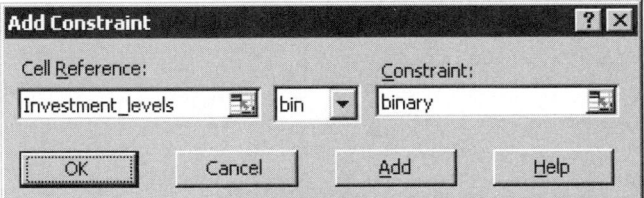

### Discussion of the Solution

The optimal solution in Figure 6.1 indicates that Tatham can obtain a maximum NPV of $46,000 by selecting investments 1, 2, and 5. These three investments consume only $14,500 of the available budget, with $500 left over. However, this $500 is not enough—because of the "investing all the way" requirement—to invest in any of the remaining investments.

---

[2] All the models in this chapter satisfy two of the three linearity assumptions in Chapter 3: proportionality and additivity. Even though they clearly violate the third assumption, divisibility, which precludes integer constraints, they are still considered linear by Solver. Therefore, we gain efficiency by checking the Assume Linear Model option.

If we rank Tatham's investments on the basis of NPV per dollar invested (see row 7 of Figure 6.1), the ranking from best to worst is 4, 1, 2, 5, 3, 6, 7. Using your economic intuition, you might expect the investments to be chosen in this order—until the budget runs out. However, the optimal solution does not do this. It selects the second-, third-, and fourth-best investments, but it ignores the best. To understand why it does this, imagine investing in the order from best to worst, according to row 7, until the budget allows no more. By the time you have invested in investments 4, 1, and 2, you will have consumed $13,500 of the budget, and the remainder, $1500, is not sufficient to invest in any of the rest. This strategy provides an NPV of only $43,500. A smarter strategy, the optimal solution from Solver, gains you an extra $2500 in NPV.

## Sensitivity Analysis

SolverTable can be used on models with binary variables exactly as we have used it in previous models.[3] Here we see how the total NPV varies as the budget increases. We select the Budget cell as the single input cell, allow it to vary from $15,000 to $25,000 in increments of $1000, and keep track of the total NPV, the amount of the budget used, and the binary variables. The results are given in Figure 6.4. Clearly, Tatham can achieve a larger NPV with a larger budget, but as the numbers and the chart show, each extra $1000 of budget

---

**Figure 6.4** Sensitivity to Budget

| | A | B | C | D | E | F | G | H | I | J |
|---|---|---|---|---|---|---|---|---|---|---|
| 19 | Sensitivity of total NPV, amount invested, and investments to budget | | | | | | | | | |
| 20 | Budget | Total NPV | Amt invested | Invest1 | Invest2 | Invest3 | Invest4 | Invest5 | Invest6 | Invest7 |
| 21 | | $B$17 | $B$14 | $B$10 | $C$10 | $D$10 | $E$10 | $F$10 | $G$10 | $H$10 |
| 22 | 15000 | $46,000 | $14,500 | 1 | 1 | 0 | 0 | 1 | 0 | 0 |
| 23 | 16000 | $49,500 | $15,500 | 0 | 1 | 0 | 1 | 1 | 0 | 0 |
| 24 | 17000 | $53,500 | $17,000 | 1 | 1 | 1 | 1 | 0 | 0 | 0 |
| 25 | 18000 | $57,500 | $18,000 | 1 | 0 | 0 | 1 | 1 | 0 | 0 |
| 26 | 19000 | $59,500 | $19,000 | 0 | 1 | 1 | 1 | 1 | 0 | 0 |
| 27 | 20000 | $61,500 | $20,000 | 0 | 1 | 0 | 1 | 1 | 1 | 0 |
| 28 | 21000 | $65,500 | $20,500 | 1 | 1 | 0 | 1 | 1 | 0 | 0 |
| 29 | 22000 | $67,500 | $21,500 | 1 | 0 | 1 | 1 | 1 | 0 | 0 |
| 30 | 23000 | $69,500 | $22,500 | 1 | 0 | 0 | 1 | 1 | 1 | 0 |
| 31 | 24000 | $75,500 | $24,000 | 1 | 1 | 1 | 1 | 1 | 0 | 0 |
| 32 | 25000 | $77,500 | $25,000 | 1 | 1 | 0 | 1 | 1 | 1 | 0 |
| 33 | | | | | | | | | | |
| 34 | | | | | | | | | | |
| 35 | | | | | | | | | | |

Total NPV versus Budget

---

[3] As mentioned in Chapter 4, Solver's sensitivity report is not even available for models with integer constraints because the mathematical theory behind the report changes significantly when variables are constrained to be integers.

does *not* have the same effect on total NPV. The first $1000 increase to the budget adds $3500 to total NPV, the next two $1000 increases add $4000 each, the next two $1000 increases add $2000 each, and so on. Note also how the selected investments vary a lot as the budget increases. This somewhat strange behavior is due to the "lumpiness" of the inputs and the all-or-nothing nature of the problem.

### Effect of Solver Tolerance Setting

*When the Tolerance setting is 5% instead of 0%, Solver's solution might not be optimal, but it will be close.*

To illustrate the effect of the Solver Tolerance setting, compare the SolverTable results in Figure 6.5 with those in Figure 6.4. Each is for the Tatham capital budgeting model, but Figure 6.5 uses Solver's default tolerance of 5%, whereas Figure 6.4 uses a tolerance of 0%. The four shaded cells in Figure 6.5 indicate *lower* total NPVs than the corresponding cells in Figure 6.4. In these four cases, Solver stopped short of finding the true optimal solutions because it found solutions within the 5% tolerance and then quit. (You might get slightly different results. It all depends on the starting solution in your model.)

**Figure 6.5**  Results with Tolerance at 5%

| | A | B | C | D | E | F | G | H | I | J |
|---|---|---|---|---|---|---|---|---|---|---|
| 19 | Sensitivity of total NPV, amount invested, and investments to budget | | | | | | | | | |
| 20 | | Budget | Total NPV | Amt invested | Invest1 | Invest2 | Invest3 | Invest4 | Invest5 | Invest6 | Invest7 |
| 21 | | | $B$17 | $B$14 | $B$10 | $C$10 | $D$10 | $E$10 | $F$10 | $G$10 | $H$10 |
| 22 | | 15000 | $45,500 | $15,000 | 1 | 0 | 0 | 0 | 1 | 0 | 1 |
| 23 | | 16000 | $49,500 | $15,500 | 0 | 1 | 0 | 1 | 1 | 0 | 0 |
| 24 | | 17000 | $53,500 | $17,000 | 1 | 1 | 1 | 1 | 0 | 0 | 0 |
| 25 | | 18000 | $57,500 | $18,000 | 1 | 0 | 0 | 1 | 1 | 0 | 0 |
| 26 | | 19000 | $59,500 | $19,000 | 0 | 1 | 1 | 1 | 1 | 0 | 0 |
| 27 | | 20000 | $60,000 | $20,000 | 1 | 0 | 1 | 0 | 1 | 1 | 0 |
| 28 | | 21000 | $65,500 | $20,500 | 1 | 1 | 0 | 1 | 1 | 0 | 0 |
| 29 | | 22000 | $65,500 | $20,500 | 1 | 1 | 0 | 1 | 1 | 0 | 0 |
| 30 | | 23000 | $68,000 | $22,500 | 1 | 1 | 1 | 0 | 1 | 1 | 0 |
| 31 | | 24000 | $75,500 | $24,000 | 1 | 1 | 1 | 1 | 1 | 0 | 0 |
| 32 | | 25000 | $77,500 | $25,000 | 1 | 1 | 0 | 1 | 1 | 1 | 0 |

■

## MODELING ISSUES

1. The following modifications of the capital budgeting example can be handled easily. You are asked to explore similar modifications in the problems.

   ■ Suppose that at most 2 projects can be selected. In this case, we add a constraint that the sum of the 0–1 variables for the investments is less than or equal to 2. This constraint is satisfied if 0, 1, or 2 investments are chosen, but it is violated if 3 or more investments are chosen.

   ■ Suppose that if investment 2 is selected, then investment 1 must also be selected. In this case, we add a constraint saying that the 0–1 variable for investment 1 is greater than or equal to the 0–1 variable for investment 2. This constraint rules out the one possibility that is not allowed—where investment 2 is selected but investment 1 is not.

   ■ Suppose that either investment 1 or investment 3 (or both) *must* be selected. In this case, we add a constraint that the *sum* of the 0–1 variables for investments 1 and 3 must be greater than or equal to 1. This rules out the one possibility that is not allowed—where both of these 0–1 variables are 0, so that neither investment is selected.

2. Capital budgeting models with multiple periods can also be handled. Figure 6.6 shows one possibility. (See the **Capital Budgeting 2.xlsx** file.) The costs in rows 5 and 6 are *both* incurred if any given investment is selected. Now there are two budget constraints, one in each year, but otherwise the model is exactly as before. Note that some investments can have a cost of 0 in year 1 and a positive cost in year 2. This effectively means that these investments are undertaken in year 2 rather than year 1. Also, it is easy to modify the model to incorporate costs in years 3, 4, and so on.

---

**Figure 6.6** A Two-Period Capital Budgeting Model

| | A | B | C | D | E | F | G | H | I | J | K | L |
|---|---|---|---|---|---|---|---|---|---|---|---|---|
| 1 | Tatham two-period capital budgeting model | | | | | | | | | Range names used: | | |
| 2 | | | | | | | | | | Amount_invested | =Model!$B$14:$B$15 | |
| 3 | Input data on potential investments | | | | | | | | | Budget | =Model!$D$14:$D$15 | |
| 4 | Investment | 1 | 2 | 3 | 4 | 5 | 6 | 7 | | Investment_levels | =Model!$B$10:$H$10 | |
| 5 | Year 1 cost | $5,000 | $2,500 | $3,500 | $6,500 | $7,000 | $4,500 | $3,000 | | Total_NPV | =Model!$B$18 | |
| 6 | Year 2 cost | $2,000 | $1,500 | $2,000 | $0 | $500 | $1,500 | $0 | | | | |
| 7 | NPV | $16,000 | $8,000 | $10,000 | $20,000 | $22,000 | $12,000 | $8,000 | | | | |
| 8 | | | | | | | | | | | | |
| 9 | Decisions: whether to invest | | | | | | | | | | | |
| 10 | Investment levels | 1 | 1 | 0 | 1 | 0 | 0 | 0 | | | | |
| 11 | | | | | | | | | | | | |
| 12 | Budget constraints | | | | | | | | | | | |
| 13 | | Amount invested | | Budget | | | | | | | | |
| 14 | | $14,000 | <= | $14,000 | | | | | | | | |
| 15 | | $3,500 | <= | $4,500 | | | | | | | | |
| 16 | | | | | | | | | | | | |
| 17 | Objective to maximize | | | | | | | | | | | |
| 18 | Total NPV | $44,000 | | | | | | | | | | |

3. If Tatham could choose a *fractional* amount of an investment, then we could maximize its NPV by deleting the binary constraint. The optimal solution to the resulting LP model has a total NPV of $48,714. All of investments 1, 2, and 4, and 0.214 of investment 5 are chosen.[4] Note that there is no way to round the changing cell values from this LP solution to obtain the optimal IP solution. Sometimes the solution to an IP model *without* the integer constraints bears little resemblance to the optimal IP solution.

4. Any IP involving 0–1 variables with only one constraint is called a **knapsack problem.** Think of the problem faced by a hiker going on an overnight hike. For example, imagine that the hiker's knapsack can hold only 14 pounds, and she must choose which of several available items to take on the hike. The benefit derived from each item is analogous to the NPV of each project, and the weight of each item is analogous to the cash required by each investment. The single constraint is analogous to the budget constraint—that is, only 14 pounds can fit in the knapsack. In a knapsack problem, the goal is to get the most value in the knapsack without overloading it. ■

---

## ADDITIONAL APPLICATIONS

### Impact of Check Sequencing on NSF (Not Sufficient Funds) Fees

Apte et al. (2004) report an interesting application in the banking industry that can be modeled very much like the classical knapsack problem. When a bank receives checks on a customer's account, it can process these in any order. If the total of these checks is greater than the customer's checking balance, the order in which the checks are processed can affect the *number* of checks that cannot be honored. For each such check that bounces, the bank

---

[4] If you try this with the **Capital Budgeting 1.xlsx** file, delete the binary constraint, but don't forget to constrain the Investment_levels range to be nonnegative and less than or equal to 1.

charges the customer an NSF fee of about $20 on average. For example, suppose the customer's balance is $200, and checks in the amounts $150, $100, $75, and $25 are presented. If the bank processes them in low-to-high order, then there is only one NSF fee, for the $150 check. However, if it processes them in high-to-low order, there is an NSF fee for each of the three smallest checks. This is *not* a small problem. There is some evidence that by using high-to-low order rather than the opposite, the banking industry stands to gain as much as $1.5 *billion* annually in extra NSF fees. At the time of the article, banks were involved in several lawsuits brought by customers who claimed that the deliberate use of high-to-low order is an unfair practice. ■

# PROBLEMS

*Solutions for problems whose numbers appear within a color box can be found in the Student Solutions Files. Order your copy today at the Winston/Albright product Web site, academic.cengage.com/decisionsciences/winston.*

## Skill-Building Problems

1. Solve the following modifications of the capital budgeting model in Figure 6.1. (Solve each part independently of the others.)
   a. Suppose that at most two of projects 1 through 5 can be selected.
   b. Suppose that if investment 1 is selected, then investment 3 must also be selected.
   c. Suppose that at least one of investments 6 and 7 *must* be selected.
   d. Suppose that investment 2 can be selected only if *both* investments 1 and 3 are selected.

2. In the capital budgeting model in Figure 6.1, we supplied the NPV for each investment. Suppose instead that you are given only the streams of cash inflows from each investment shown in the file **P06_02.xlsx**. This file also shows the cash requirements and the budget. You can assume that (1) all cash outflows occur at the beginning of year 1, (2) all cash inflows occur at the ends of their respective years, and (3) the company uses a 10% discount rate for calculating its NPVs. Which investments should the company make?

3. Solve the previous problem using the input data in the file **P06_03.xlsx**.

4. Solve Problem 2 with the extra assumption that the investments can be grouped naturally as follows: 1–4, 5–8, 9–12, 13–16, and 17–20.
   a. Find the optimal investments when at most one investment from each group can be selected.
   b. Find the optimal investments when at least one investment from each group must be selected. (If the budget isn't large enough to permit this, increase the budget to a larger value.)

5. In the capital budgeting model in Figure 6.1, investment 4 has the largest ratio of NPV to cash require-

ment, but it is not selected in the optimal solution. How much NPV will be lost if Tatham is *forced* to select investment 4? Answer by solving a suitably modified model.

6. As it currently stands, investment 7 in the capital budgeting model in Figure 6.1 has the lowest ratio of NPV to cash requirement, 2.5. Keeping this same ratio, can you change the cash requirement and NPV for investment 7 so that it *is* selected in the optimal solution? Does this lead to any general insights? Explain.

7. Expand and then solve the capital budgeting model in Figure 6.1 so that 20 investments are now possible. You can make up the data on cash requirements, NPVs, and the budget, but use the following guidelines:
   ■ The cash requirements and NPVs for the various investments can vary widely, but the ratio of NPV to cash requirement should be between 2.5 and 3.5 for each investment.
   ■ The budget should allow somewhere between 5 and 10 of the investments to be selected.

8. Suppose in the capital budgeting model in Figure 6.1 that each investment requires $2000 during year 2, and only $5000 is available for investment during year 2.
   a. Assuming that available money uninvested at the end of year 1 cannot be used during year 2, what combination of investments maximizes NPV?
   b. Suppose that any uninvested money at the end of year 1 is available for investment in year 2. Does your answer to part **a** change?

## Skill-Extending Problems

9. The models in this chapter are often called *combinatorial* models because each solution is a combination of the various 0's and 1's, and only a finite number of such combinations exist. For the capital budgeting model in Figure 6.1, there are 7 investments, so there are $2^7 = 128$ possible solutions (some of which are infeasible). This is a fairly large number, but not *too* large. Solve the model *without* Solver by listing all 128 solutions. For each, calculate the total cash

requirement and total NPV for the model. Then manually choose the one that stays within the budget and has the largest NPV.

10. Make up an example, as described in Problem 7, with 20 possible investments. However, do it so the ratios of NPV to cash requirement are in a very tight range, from 3 to 3.2. Then use Solver to find the optimal solution when the Solver tolerance is set to its default value of 5%, and record the solution. Next, solve again with the tolerance set to 0%. Do you get the same solution? Try this on a few more instances of the model, where you keep tinkering with the inputs. The question is whether the tolerance matters in these types of "close call" problems.

## 6.4 FIXED-COST MODELS

In many situations, a fixed cost is incurred if an activity is undertaken at any *positive* level. This cost is independent of the level of the activity and is known as a **fixed cost** (or **fixed charge**). Here are three examples of fixed costs:

- The construction of a warehouse incurs a fixed cost that is the same whether the warehouse is built with a low- or a high-capacity level.

- A cash withdrawal from a bank incurs a fixed cost, independent of the size of the withdrawal.

- A machine that is used to produce several products must be set up for the production of each product. Regardless of the batch size produced, the same fixed cost (lost production due to the setup time) is incurred.

In these examples, a fixed cost is incurred if an activity is undertaken at any positive level, whereas no fixed cost is incurred if the activity is not undertaken at all. Although it might not be obvious, this feature makes the problem inherently *nonlinear,* which means that a straightforward application of LP is not possible. However, a clever use of 0–1 variables can result in a model with linear constraints and a linear objective.

*Unless we use binary variables to handle the logic, fixed-cost models are nonlinear and difficult to solve.*

It is important to realize that compared to the previous capital budgeting model and the integer-constrained models in Chapter 4, the type of model we discuss here and throughout the rest of the chapter (except for Example 6.7) is fundamentally different. We do not simply create an LP model and then add integer constraints. Instead, we use 0–1 variables to *model the logic.* The logic in this section is that if a certain activity is done at any *positive* level, a fixed cost is incurred. However, no fixed cost is incurred if the activity is not done at all. Your first instinct might be to handle such logic with IF functions. However, Solver cannot handle IF functions predictably. This is not really a weakness of Solver. These types of problems are inherently difficult. Fortunately, Solver *is* able to handle linear models with binary variables, so this is the approach we take whenever possible. By using 0–1 variables appropriately, we are able to solve a whole new class of difficult problems. The following example is typical.

---

### FUNDAMENTAL INSIGHT

#### Binary Variables for Modeling

Binary variables are often used to transform a nonlinear model into a linear (integer) model. For example, a fixed cost is not a linear function of the level of some activity; it is either incurred or it isn't incurred. This type of on-off behavior is difficult for nonlinear solvers to handle. However, this behavior can often be handled easily when binary variables are used to make the model linear. Still, large models with many binary variables can be difficult to solve. One approach is to solve the model without integer constraints and then round fractional values to the nearest integer (0 or 1). Unfortunately, this approach is typically not very good because the rounded solution is often infeasible. Even if it is feasible, its objective value can be considerably worse than the optimal objective value.

EXAMPLE | **6.2 TEXTILE MANUFACTURING AT GREAT THREADS**

The Great Threads Company is capable of manufacturing shirts, shorts, pants, skirts, and jackets. Each type of clothing requires that Great Threads have the appropriate type of machinery available. The machinery needed to manufacture each type of clothing must be rented at the weekly rates shown in Table 6.3. This table also lists the amounts of cloth and labor required per unit of clothing, as well as the sales price and the unit variable cost for each type of clothing. In a given week, 4000 labor hours and 4500 square yards (sq yd) of cloth are available. The company wants to find a solution that maximizes its weekly profit.

**Table 6.3   Data for the Great Threads Example**

|  | Rental Cost | Labor Hours | Cloth (sq yd) | Sales Price | Unit Variable Cost |
|---|---|---|---|---|---|
| **Shirts** | $1500 | 2.0 | 3.0 | $35 | $20 |
| **Shorts** | $1200 | 1.0 | 2.5 | $40 | $10 |
| **Pants** | $1600 | 6.0 | 4.0 | $65 | $25 |
| **Skirts** | $1500 | 4.0 | 4.5 | $70 | $30 |
| **Jackets** | $1600 | 8.0 | 5.5 | $110 | $35 |

**Objective**   To develop a linear model with binary variables that can be used to maximize the company's profit, correctly accounting for fixed costs and staying within resource availabilities.

### WHERE DO THE NUMBERS COME FROM?

Except for the fixed costs, this is the same basic problem as the product mix problem (Example 3.2) in Chapter 3. Therefore, the same discussion there about input variables applies here. The fixed costs are the given rental rates for the machinery.

## Solution

*Fixed costs imply that the proportionality assumption of linear models no longer holds.*

The variables and constraints required for this model are listed in Table 6.4. We first note that the cost of producing $x$ shirts during a week is 0 if $x = 0$, but it is $1500 + 20x$ if $x > 0$. This cost structure violates the proportionality assumption (discussed in Chapter 3) that is needed for a linear model. If proportionality were satisfied, then the cost of making, say, 10 shirts would be double the cost of making 5 shirts. However, because of the fixed cost, the total cost of making 5 shirts is $1600, and the cost of making 10 shirts is only $1700. This violation of proportionality requires us to resort to 0–1 variables to obtain a *linear* model. These 0–1 variables allow us to model the fixed costs correctly.

**Table 6.4   Variables and Constraints for the Fixed-Cost Model**

| | |
|---|---|
| **Input variables** | Fixed rental costs, resource usages (labor hours, cloth) per unit of clothing, sales prices, unit variable costs, resource availabilities |
| **Decision variables (changing cells)** | Whether to produce any of each clothing (binary), how much of each clothing to produce |
| **Objective (target cell)** | Profit |
| **Other calculated variables** | Resources used, upper limits on amounts to produce, total revenue, total variable cost, total fixed cost |
| **Constraints** | Amount produced must be less than or equal to Logical upper limit (capacity) |
| | Resources used must be less than or equal to Resources available |

## DEVELOPING THE SPREADSHEET MODEL

The spreadsheet model, shown in Figure 6.7, can now be formulated as follows. (See the file **Fixed Cost Manufacturing.xlsx**.)

**Figure 6.7** Fixed-Cost Clothing Model

| | A | B | C | D | E | F | G | H | I | J | K |
|---|---|---|---|---|---|---|---|---|---|---|---|
| 1 | Great Threads fixed cost clothing model | | | | | | | | Range names used: | | |
| 2 | | | | | | | | | Logical_upper_limit | =Model!$B$18:$F$18 | |
| 3 | Input data on products | | | | | | | | Produce_any? | =Model!$B$14:$F$14 | |
| 4 | | Shirts | Shorts | Pants | Skirts | Jackets | | | Profit | =Model!$B$29 | |
| 5 | Labor hours/unit | 2 | 1 | 6 | 4 | 8 | | | Resource_available | =Model!$D$22:$D$23 | |
| 6 | Cloth (sq. yd.)/unit | 3 | 2.5 | 4 | 4.5 | 5.5 | | | Resource_used | =Model!$B$22:$B$23 | |
| 7 | | | | | | | | | Units_produced | =Model!$B$16:$F$16 | |
| 8 | Selling price/unit | $35 | $40 | $65 | $70 | $110 | | | | | |
| 9 | Variable cost/unit | $20 | $10 | $25 | $30 | $35 | | | | | |
| 10 | Fixed cost for equipment | $1,500 | $1,200 | $1,600 | $1,500 | $1,600 | | | | | |
| 11 | | | | | | | | | | | |
| 12 | Production plan, constraints on capacity | | | | | | | | | | |
| 13 | | Shirts | Shorts | Pants | Skirts | Jackets | | | | | |
| 14 | Produce any? | 0 | 1 | 0 | 0 | 1 | | | | | |
| 15 | | | | | | | | | | | |
| 16 | Units produced | 0 | 965.52 | 0 | 0 | 379.31 | | | | | |
| 17 | | <= | <= | <= | <= | <= | | | | | |
| 18 | Logical upper limit | 0.00 | 1800.00 | 0.00 | 0.00 | 500.00 | | | | | |
| 19 | | | | | | | | | | | |
| 20 | Constraints on resources | | | | | | | | | | |
| 21 | | Resource used | | | Available | | | | | | |
| 22 | Labor hours | 4000.00 | <= | | 4000 | | | | | | |
| 23 | Cloth | 4500.00 | <= | | 4500 | | | | | | |
| 24 | | | | | | | | | | | |
| 25 | Monetary outputs | | | | | | | | | | |
| 26 | Revenue | $80,345 | | | | | | | | | |
| 27 | Variable cost | $22,931 | | | | | | | | | |
| 28 | Fixed cost for equipment | $2,800 | | | | | | | | | |
| 29 | Profit | $54,614 | ← | Objective to maximize | | | | | | | |

**①** **Inputs.** Enter the given inputs in the blue ranges.

**②** **Binary values for clothing types.** Enter *any* trial values for the 0–1 variables for the various clothing types in the Produce_any? range. For example, if we enter a 1 in cell C14, we are implying that the machinery for making shorts is rented and its fixed cost is incurred.

**③** **Production quantities.** Enter *any* trial values for the numbers of the various clothing types produced in the Units_produced range. At this point, we could enter "illegal" values, such as 0 in cell B14 and a positive value in cell B16. We say this is illegal because it implies that the company produces some shirts but avoids the fixed cost of the machinery for shirts. However, Solver will eventually disallow such illegal combinations.

**④** **Labor and cloth used.** In cell B22 enter the formula

**=SUMPRODUCT(B5:F5,Units_produced)**

to calculate total labor hours, and copy this to cell B23 for cloth.

**⑤** **Effective capacities.** Now we come to the tricky part of the model. We need to ensure that if any of a given type of clothing is produced, its 0–1 variable equals 1. This ensures that the model incurs the fixed cost of renting the machine for this type of clothing. We could easily implement these constraints with IF statements. For example, to implement the constraint for shirts, we could enter the following formula in cell B14:

**=IF(B16>0,1,0)**

However, Excel's Solver is unable to deal with IF functions predictably. Therefore, we instead model the fixed-cost constraints as shown in inequality (6.1).

$$\text{Shirts produced} \leq \text{Maximum capacity} \times (0\text{–}1 \text{ variable for shirts})\qquad\textbf{(6.1)}$$

Similar inequalities exist for the other types of clothing.

The effect of binary variables is to force the model to incur the fixed costs if positive production levels are used.

Here is the logic behind inequality (6.1). If the 0–1 variable for shirts is 0, then the right-hand side of the inequality is 0, which means that the left-hand side must be 0—no shirts can be produced. That is, if the 0–1 variable for shirts is 0 so that no fixed cost for shirts is incurred, inequality (6.1) does not allow Great Threads to "cheat" and produce a positive number of shirts. On the other hand, if the 0–1 variable for shirts is 1, the inequality is certainly true and is essentially redundant. It simply states that the number of shirts produced must be no greater than the *maximum* number that could be produced. Inequality (6.1) rules out the one case we want it to rule out—namely, that Great Threads produces shirts but avoids the fixed cost.

To implement inequality (6.1), we need a maximum capacity—an upper limit on the number of shirts that *could* be produced. To obtain this, suppose the company puts all of its resources into producing shirts. Then the number of shirts that can be produced is limited by the smaller of

The point of these ratios is to provide an upper limit on production of any product when no "natural" upper limit is available.

$$\frac{\text{Available labor hours}}{\text{Labor hours per shirt}}$$

and

$$\frac{\text{Available square yards of cloth}}{\text{Square yards of cloth per shirt}}$$

Therefore, the smaller of these—the most limiting—can be used as the maximum needed in inequality (6.1).

To implement this logic, calculate the "effective capacity" for shirts in cell B18 with the formula

**=B14*MIN($D$22/B5,$D$23/B6)**

Then copy this formula to the range C18:F18 for the other types of clothing.[5] By the way, this MIN formula causes no problems for Solver because it involves only input cells, not *changing* cells.

**6** **Monetary values.** Calculate the total sales revenue and the total variable cost by entering the formula

**=SUMPRODUCT(B8:F8,Units_produced)**

in cell B26 and copying it to cell B27. Then calculate the total fixed cost in cell B28 with the formula

**=SUMPRODUCT(B10:F10,Produce_any?)**

Note that this formula picks up the fixed costs only for those products with 0–1 variables equal to 1. Finally, calculate the total profit in cell B29 with the formula

**=B26-B27-B28**

## USING SOLVER

The Solver dialog box is shown in Figure 6.8. We maximize profit, subject to using no more labor hours or cloth than are available, and we ensure that production is less than or equal to "effective" capacity. The key is that this effective capacity is 0 if we decide not to rent the machinery for a given type of clothing. As usual, check the Assume Linear Model and Assume Non-Negative boxes under Solver options, and set the tolerance to 0.

---

[5] Why not set the upper limit on shirts equal to a huge number like 1,000,000? The reason is that Solver works most efficiently when the upper limit is as "tight"—that is, as low—as possible. A tighter upper limit means fewer potential feasible solutions for Solver to search through. Here's an analogy. If you were trying to locate a criminal, which would be easier: (1) if you were told that he was somewhere in Texas, or (2) if you were told he was somewhere in Dallas?

**Figure 6.8**

Solver Dialog Box for the Fixed-Cost Model

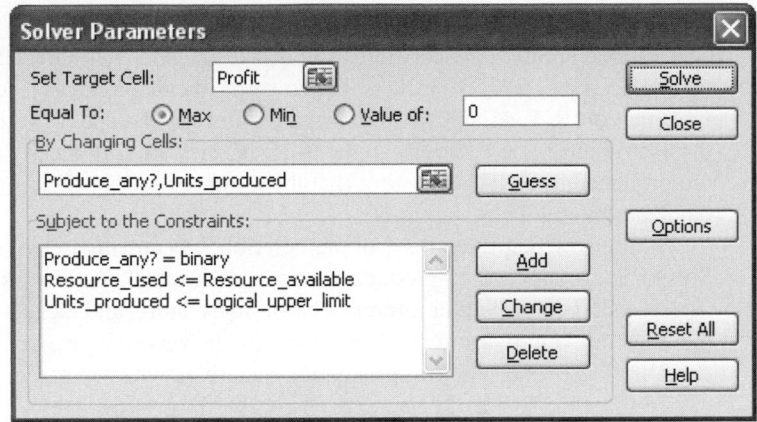

Although Solver finds the optimal solution automatically, you should understand the effect of the logical upper bound constraint on production. It rules out a solution such as the one shown in Figure 6.9. This solution calls for a positive production level of pants but does not incur the fixed cost of the pants equipment. The logical upper bound constraint rules this out because it prevents a positive value in row 16 if the corresponding binary value in row 14 is 0. In other words, if the company wants to produce some pants, then the constraint in inequality (6.1) forces the associated binary variable to be 1, thus incurring the fixed cost for pants.

**Figure 6.9** An Illegal (and Nonoptimal) Solution

| | A | B | C | D | E | F | G | H | I | J | K |
|---|---|---|---|---|---|---|---|---|---|---|---|
| 1 | Great Threads fixed cost clothing model | | | | | | | | Range names used: | | |
| 2 | | | | | | | | | Logical_upper_limit | =Model!$B$18:$F$18 | |
| 3 | Input data on products | | | | | | | | Produce_any? | =Model!$B$14:$F$14 | |
| 4 | | Shirts | Shorts | Pants | Skirts | Jackets | | | Profit | =Model!$B$29 | |
| 5 | Labor hours/unit | 2 | 1 | 6 | 4 | 8 | | | Resource_available | =Model!$D$22:$D$23 | |
| 6 | Cloth (sq. yd.)/unit | 3 | 2.5 | 4 | 4.5 | 5.5 | | | Resource_used | =Model!$B$22:$B$23 | |
| 7 | | | | | | | | | Units_produced | =Model!$B$16:$F$16 | |
| 8 | Selling price/unit | $35 | $40 | $65 | $70 | $110 | | | | | |
| 9 | Variable cost/unit | $20 | $10 | $25 | $30 | $35 | | | | | |
| 10 | Fixed cost for equipment | $1,500 | $1,200 | $1,600 | $1,500 | $1,600 | | | | | |
| 11 | | | | | | | | | | | |
| 12 | Production plan, constraints on capacity | | | | | | | | | | |
| 13 | | Shirts | Shorts | Pants | Skirts | Jackets | | | | | |
| 14 | Produce any? | 0 | 1 | 0 | 1 | 1 | | | | | |
| 15 | | | | | | | | | | | |
| 16 | Units produced | 0 | 965.52 | 450 | 0 | 379.31 | | | | | |
| 17 | | <= | <= | <= | <= | <= | | | | | |
| 18 | Logical upper limit | 0.00 | 1800.00 | 0.00 | 1000.00 | 500.00 | | | | | |
| 19 | | | | | | | | | | | |
| 20 | Constraints on resources | | | | | | | | | | |
| 21 | | Resource used | | Available | | | | | | | |
| 22 | Labor hours | 6700.00 | <= | 4000 | | | | | | | |
| 23 | Cloth | 6300.00 | <= | 4500 | | | | | | | |
| 24 | | | | | | | | | | | |
| 25 | Monetary outputs | | | | | | | | | | |
| 26 | Revenue | $109,595 | | | | | | | | | |
| 27 | Variable cost | $34,181 | | | | | | | | | |
| 28 | Fixed cost for equipment | $4,300 | | | | | | | | | |
| 29 | Profit | $71,114 | ← | Objective to maximize | | | | | | | |

*There is no point to setting a binary variable equal to 1—and Solver will never do it—unless there is positive production of that product.*

Note that inequality (6.1) does *not* rule out the situation we see for skirts in Figure 6.9, where the binary value is 1 and the production level is 0. However, Solver will never choose this type of solution as optimal. Solver recognizes that the binary value in this case can be changed to 0, so that no skirt equipment is rented and its fixed cost is not incurred.

## Discussion of the Solution

The optimal solution appears in Figure 6.7. It indicates that Great Threads should produce about 966 shorts and 379 jackets, but no shirts, pants, or skirts. The total profit is $54,614. Note that the 0–1 variables for shirts, pants, and skirts are all 0, which forces production of these products to be 0. However, the 0–1 variables for shorts and jackets, the products that are produced, are 1. This ensures that the fixed cost of producing shorts and jackets is included in the total cost.

It might be helpful to think of this solution as occurring in two stages. In the first stage, Solver determines which products to produce—in this case, shorts and jackets only. Then in the second stage, Solver figures out how *many* shorts and jackets to produce. If we know that the company plans to produce shorts and jackets only, we could then ignore the fixed costs and determine the best production quantities with the same product mix model discussed in Example 3.2 of Chapter 3. Of course, these two stages—deciding which products to produce and how many of each to produce—are interrelated, and Solver considers both of them in its solution process.

*Because of fixed costs, the optimal solution might call for only a small subset of products to be produced. Only extra side constraints can force more products to be produced.*

The Great Threads management might not be too excited about producing shorts and jackets only. Suppose the company wants to ensure that at least three types of clothing are produced at positive levels. One approach is to add another constraint—namely, that the sum of the 0–1 values in row 14 is greater than or equal to 3. You can check, however, that when this constraint is added and Solver is rerun, the 0–1 variable for skirts becomes 1, but no skirts are produced! Shorts and jackets are more profitable than skirts, so only shorts and jackets are produced (see Figure 6.10). The new constraint forces Great Threads to rent an extra piece of machinery (for skirts), but it doesn't force the company to use it. To force the company to produce some skirts, we also need to add a constraint on the value in E16, such as E16>=100. Any of these additional constraints will cost Great Threads money, but if, as a matter of policy, the company wants to produce more than two types of clothing, this is its only option.

---

**Figure 6.10** The Great Threads Model with Extra Constraint

| | A | B | C | D | E | F | G | H | I |
|---|---|---|---|---|---|---|---|---|---|
| 1 | Great Threads fixed cost clothing model | | | | | | | | |
| 2 | | | | | | | | | |
| 3 | Input data on products | | | | | | | | |
| 4 | | Shirts | Shorts | Pants | Skirts | Jackets | | | |
| 5 | Labor hours/unit | 2 | 1 | 6 | 4 | 8 | | | |
| 6 | Cloth (sq. yd.)/unit | 3 | 2.5 | 4 | 4.5 | 5.5 | | | |
| 7 | | | | | | | | | |
| 8 | Selling price/unit | $35 | $40 | $65 | $70 | $110 | | | |
| 9 | Variable cost/unit | $20 | $10 | $25 | $30 | $35 | | | |
| 10 | Fixed cost for equipment | $1,500 | $1,200 | $1,600 | $1,500 | $1,600 | | | |
| 11 | | | | | | | | | |
| 12 | Production plan, constraints on capacity | | | | | | | | |
| 13 | | Shirts | Shorts | Pants | Skirts | Jackets | Sum | | Required |
| 14 | Produce any? | 0 | 1 | 0 | 1 | 1 | 3 | >= | 3 |
| 15 | | | | | | | | | |
| 16 | Units produced | 0 | 965.52 | 0 | 0 | 379.31 | | | |
| 17 | | <= | <= | <= | <= | <= | | | |
| 18 | Logical upper limit | 0.00 | 1800.00 | 0.00 | 1000.00 | 500.00 | | | |
| 19 | | | | | | | | | |
| 20 | Constraints on resources | | | | | | | | |
| 21 | | Resource used | | | Available | | | | |
| 22 | Labor hours | 4000.00 | <= | | 4000 | | | | |
| 23 | Cloth | 4500.00 | <= | | 4500 | | | | |
| 24 | | | | | | | | | |
| 25 | Monetary outputs | | | | | | | | |
| 26 | Revenue | $80,345 | | | | | | | |
| 27 | Variable cost | $22,931 | | | | | | | |
| 28 | Fixed cost for equipment | $4,300 | | | | | | | |
| 29 | Profit | $53,114 | ← | Objective to maximize | | | | | |

## Sensitivity Analysis

Because the optimal solution currently calls for only shorts and jackets to be produced, an interesting sensitivity analysis is to see how much incentive is required for other products to be produced. One way to check this is to increase the sales price for a nonproduced product such as skirts in a one-way SolverTable. We did this, keeping track of all binary variables and profit, with the results shown in Figure 6.11. When the sales price for skirts is $85 or less, the company continues to produce only shorts and jackets. However, when the sales price is $90 or greater, the company stops producing shorts and jackets and produces *only* skirts. You can check that the optimal production quantity of skirts is 1000 when the sales price of skirts is any value $90 or above. The only reason that the profits in Figure 6.11 increase from row 37 down is that the revenues from these 1000 skirts keep increasing.

**Figure 6.11**

Sensitivity of Binary Variables to Unit Revenue of Skirts

|    | A | B | C | D | E | F | G |
|----|---|---|---|---|---|---|---|
| 31 | Sensitivity of binary variables and profit to unit revenue from skirts | | | | | | |
| 32 |   | $B$14 | $C$14 | $D$14 | $E$14 | $F$14 | $B$29 |
| 33 | 70 | 0 | 1 | 0 | 0 | 1 | $54,614 |
| 34 | 75 | 0 | 1 | 0 | 0 | 1 | $54,614 |
| 35 | 80 | 0 | 1 | 0 | 0 | 1 | $54,614 |
| 36 | 85 | 0 | 1 | 0 | 0 | 1 | $54,614 |
| 37 | 90 | 0 | 0 | 0 | 1 | 0 | $58,500 |
| 38 | 95 | 0 | 0 | 0 | 1 | 0 | $63,500 |
| 39 | 100 | 0 | 0 | 0 | 1 | 0 | $68,500 |

## A Model with IF Functions

In case you are still not convinced that the binary variable approach is required, and you think IF functions could be used instead, take a look at the finished version of the file. The resulting model *looks* the same as in Figure 6.8, but it incorporates the following changes:

- We no longer use the binary range as part of the changing cells range. Instead, we enter the formula **=IF(B16>0,1,0)** in cell B14 and copy it across to cell F14. Logically, this probably appears more natural. If a production quantity is positive, a 1 is entered in row 14, which means that the fixed cost is incurred.

- We model the effective capacities in row 18 with IF functions. Specifically, we enter the formula **=IF(B16>0,MIN($D$22/B5,$D$23/B6),0)** in cell B18 and copy it across to cell F18. (Actually, this constraint isn't even necessary now. Why?)

- We change the Solver dialog box so that it appears as shown in Figure 6.12. The Produce_any? range is not part of the changing cells range, and there is no binary constraint. We also uncheck the Assume Linear Model box in Solver's options because the IF functions make the model nonlinear.

**Figure 6.12**

Solver Dialog Box When IF Functions Are Used

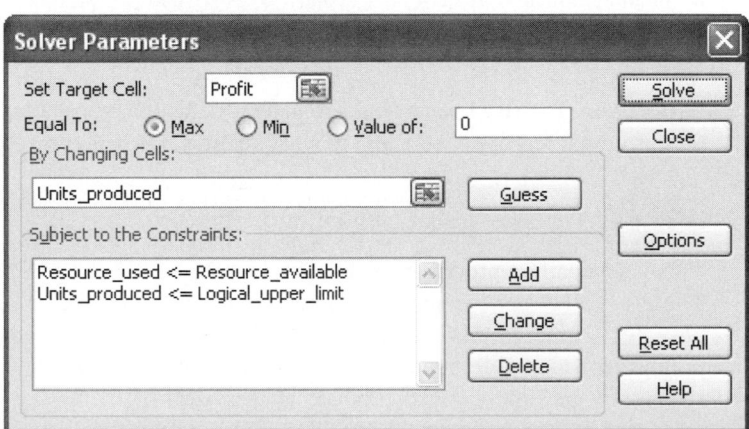

When we ran Solver on this modified model, we found inconsistent results, depending on the initial production quantities entered in row 16. For example, when we entered initial values all equal to 0, the Solver solution was exactly that—all 0's. Of course, this solution is *terrible* because it leads to a profit of $0. However, when we entered initial production quantities all equal to 100, Solver found the correct optimal solution, the same as in Figure 6.7. Was this just lucky? To check, we tried another initial solution, where the production quantities for shorts and jackets were 0, and the production quantities for shirts, pants, and skirts were all 500. In this case, Solver found a solution where only skirts are produced. Of course, we know this is not optimal.

The moral is that the IF-function approach is not the way to go. Its success depends strongly on the initial values we enter in the changing cells, and this requires us to make very good guesses. The binary approach ensures that we get the correct solution. ∎

The following example is similar to the Great Threads example in that there is a fixed cost for any positive level of production of a given product. However, an additional requirement states that if the company produces *any* of a given product, then (possibly for economies of scale) it must produce at least some minimal level such as 1000. This is a typical example of a problem with **either–or constraints:** The company's level of production must either be 0 or at least 1000. In the next example, we show how the use of binary variables allows us to model the either–or constraints in a linear manner.

## EXAMPLE | 6.3 MANUFACTURING AT DORIAN AUTO

Dorian Auto is considering manufacturing three types of cars (compact, midsize, and large) and two types of minivans (midsize and large). The resources required and the profit contributions yielded by each type of vehicle are shown in Table 6.5. At present, 6500 tons of steel and 65,000 hours of labor are available. If any vehicles of a given type are produced, production of that type of vehicle is economically feasible only if at least a minimal number of that type are produced. These minimal numbers are also listed in Table 6.5. Dorian wants to find a production schedule that maximizes its profit.

**Table 6.5** Data for the Dorian Car Example

| Vehicle Type | Compact Car | Midsize Car | Large Car | Midsize Minivan | Large Minivan |
|---|---|---|---|---|---|
| Steel (tons)/unit | 1.5 | 3 | 5 | 6 | 8 |
| Labor hours/unit | 30 | 25 | 40 | 45 | 55 |
| Minimum production (if any) | 1000 | 1000 | 1000 | 200 | 200 |
| Profit contribution/unit | $2,000 | $2,500 | $3,000 | $5,500 | $7,000 |

**Objective**  To use a binary model to determine which types of vehicles to produce (above their minimal requirements), and in what quantities, to maximize profit.

### WHERE DO THE NUMBERS COME FROM?

This is basically a product mix problem, similar to the one in Example 3.2 of Chapter 3. Therefore, the same comments about inputs discussed there apply here as well. The only new inputs in this problem are the minimal production quantities. These might be policy decisions determined by Dorian—management sees no reason to produce midsize minivans unless it can produce at least 200 of them, say—but these policy decisions are undoubtedly based on costs. Presumably, the fixed costs of product design, manufacturing, and marketing are prohibitive unless a minimal number of any vehicle type is produced.

## Solution

The variables and constraints for the Dorian model are listed in Table 6.6. Dorian must decide not only how many of each type of vehicle to produce, but also which types to produce. Of course, after it decides to produce small minivans, say, then it must produce at least 200 of them. The constraints include the usual resource availability constraints. In addition, there are lower and upper limits on the production quantities of any vehicle type. The lower limit is 0 or the minimal production quantity, depending on whether that vehicle type is produced. The upper limit is similar to the upper limit in the Great Thread's fixed-cost model in Example 6.2. That is, it is either 0, if the vehicle type is not produced at all, or it is some suitable large number. As in Example 6.2, we let this large number be the number of that type of vehicle that could be produced if *all* of the steel and labor hours were devoted to it alone.

**Table 6.6** Variables and Constraints for the Dorian Manufacturing Model

| | |
|---|---|
| Input variables | Resources (steel and labor hours) consumed by each vehicle type, profit contribution for each vehicle type, minimal production quantity for each vehicle type, resource availabilities |
| Decision variables (changing cells) | Whether to produce any of each vehicle type (binary), units produced of each vehicle type |
| Objective (target cell) | Profit |
| Other calculated variables | Logical lower and upper bounds on production quantities, resources used |
| Constraints | Production quantities must be greater than or equal to Logical lower bounds |
| | Production quantities must be less than or equal to Logical upper bounds |
| | Resources used must be less than or equal to Resources available |

### DEVELOPING THE SPREADSHEET MODEL

The example can be modeled with the following steps. (See Figure 6.13 and the file **Either Or Manufacturing.xlsx**.)

**Figure 6.13** The Dorian Auto Production Model

| | A | B | C | D | E | F | G | H | I | J |
|---|---|---|---|---|---|---|---|---|---|---|
| 1 | Dorian Auto production model with either-or constraints | | | | | | | | | |
| 2 | | | | | | | | | | |
| 3 | Inputs | | | | | | | Range names used: | | |
| 4 | Vehicle type | Compact car | Midsize car | Large car | Midsize minivan | Large minivan | | Logical_capacity | =Model!$B$19:$F$19 | |
| 5 | Steel (tons)/unit | 1.5 | 3 | 5 | 6 | 8 | | Minimum_production | =Model!$B$15:$F$15 | |
| 6 | Labor hours/unit | 30 | 25 | 40 | 45 | 55 | | Produce_at_least_minimum? | =Model!$B$13:$F$13 | |
| 7 | Minimum production (if any) | 1000 | 1000 | 1000 | 200 | 200 | | Profit | =Model!$B$27 | |
| 8 | | | | | | | | Resource_available | =Model!$D$23:$D$24 | |
| 9 | Profit contribution/unit | $2,000 | $2,500 | $3,000 | $5,500 | $7,000 | | Resource_used | =Model!$B$23:$B$24 | |
| 10 | | | | | | | | Units_produced | =Model!$B$17:$F$17 | |
| 11 | Production plan and bounds on production quantities | | | | | | | | | |
| 12 | Type of car | Compact car | Midsize car | Large car | Midsize minivan | Large minivan | | | | |
| 13 | Produce at least minimum? | 1 | 0 | 0 | 1 | 1 | | | | |
| 14 | | | | | | | | | | |
| 15 | Minimum production | 1000 | 0 | 0 | 200 | 200 | | | | |
| 16 | | <= | <= | <= | <= | <= | | | | |
| 17 | Units produced | 1000 | 0 | 0 | 200 | 473 | | | | |
| 18 | | <= | <= | <= | <= | <= | | | | |
| 19 | Logical capacity | 2167 | 0 | 0 | 1083 | 813 | | | | |
| 20 | | | | | | | | | | |
| 21 | Constraints on resources | | | | | | | | | |
| 22 | | Resource used | | Resource available | | | | | | |
| 23 | Steel | 6482 | <= | 6500 | | | | | | |
| 24 | Labor hours | 65000 | <= | 65000 | | | | | | |
| 25 | | | | | | | | | | |
| 26 | Objective to maximize | | | | | | | | | |
| 27 | Profit | $6,409,091 | | | | | | | | |

**1 Inputs.** Enter the input data in the blue ranges.

**2 Number of vehicles produced.** Enter *any* trial values for the number of vehicles of each type produced in the Units_produced range.

**3 Binary variables for minimum production.** Enter *any* trial 0–1 values in the Produce_at_least_minimum? range. If a value in this range is 1, this means that Dorian must produce at least the minimum number of the corresponding vehicle type. A value of 0 in this range means that Dorian does not produce any of the corresponding vehicle type.

**4 Lower limits on production.** The either–or constraints are implemented with the binary variables in row 13 and the inequalities indicated in rows 15 through 19. To obtain the lower limits on production, enter the formula

**=B7*B13**

in cell B15 and copy it across row 15. This lower limit implies that if the binary variable in row 13 is 1, then Dorian must produce at least the minimum number of that vehicle type. However, if the binary variable is 0, then the lower bound in row 15 is 0 and is essentially redundant—it just says that production must be nonnegative.

**5 Upper limits on production.** To obtain upper limits on production, enter the formula

**B13*MIN($D$23/B5,$D$24/B6)**

in cell B19 and copy it across row 19. Note that the MIN term in this formula is the maximum number of compact cars Dorian could make if it devoted *all* of its resources to compact cars. (A similar upper limit was used in the Great Threads model in Example 6.2.) If the binary variable in row 13 is 1, this upper limit is essentially redundant—production can never be greater than this in any case. But if the binary variable is 0, this upper limit is 0, which prevents Dorian from making any vehicles of this type.

To summarize the lower and upper limits, if the binary variable is 1, the production limits become

Minimum production required ≤ Production ≤ Maximum production possible

On the other hand, if the binary variable is 0, the limits become

0 ≤ Production ≤ 0

*The trick is in getting the constraints to allow what we want to allow, but to disallow "illegal " solutions.*

Of course, these latter inequalities imply that production is 0. Exactly one of these cases must hold for each car type, so they successfully implement the either–or constraints. These lower and upper limits are the keys to the model.

**6 Steel and labor used.** Calculate the tons of steel and number of labor hours used in the Resources_used range by entering the formula

**=SUMPRODUCT(B5:F5,Units_produced)**

in cell B23 and copying it to cell B24.

**7 Profit.** Calculate the profit in cell B27 with the formula

**=SUMPRODUCT(B9:F9,Units_produced)**

## USING SOLVER

The completed Solver dialog box is shown in Figure 6.14. The objective is to maximize profit, the changing cells are the production quantities and the binary variables, and the constraints specify the production limits and resource availabilities. Note that we do not constrain the production quantities to be integers, although we could do so. Extra integer constraints only make the model more difficult to optimize, and if the optimal number of some vehicle type turns out to be 472.7, say, it is probably acceptable to round this up to 473 or down to 472.

**Figure 6.14**
Solver Dialog Box for the Dorian Production Model

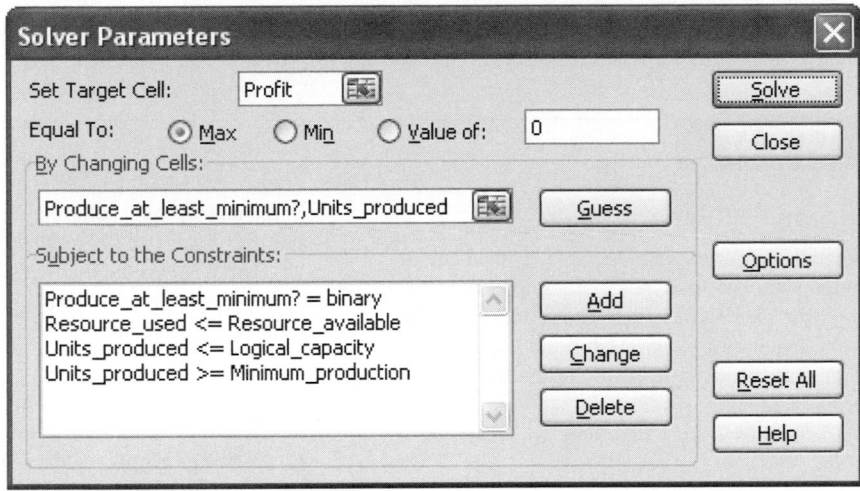

## Discussion of the Solution

The optimal solution in Figure 6.13 indicates, by the 0 values in row 13, that Dorian should not produce any midsize or large cars. The number of 1's in this row, however, indicates that Dorian *must* produce at least the minimum number (1000) of compact cars and the minimum number (200) of each type of minivan. More specifically, the company should produce just enough compact cars and midsize minivans to meet the minimal production quantities. These vehicle types are relatively profitable, given the resources they use. However, they are evidently not as profitable as large minivans. The company should make as many of these as it can, after producing the compact cars and midsize minivans, until it runs out of labor hours.

This solution is certainly not intuitive. (For example, if large minivans are so profitable, why doesn't the company produce all large minivans and nothing else? Do you see why?) Also, this solution appears to be very sensitive to the inputs. Although we do not present any formal sensitivity analysis with SolverTable, we urge you to try different values for the minimal production quantities, the unit profit contributions, and/or the resource availabilities. We found that even small changes in these can yield a very different optimal production policy. For example, you can check that if the availability of steel decreases to 6000 tons, only compact cars and midsize minivans are produced, both above their minimal levels, and *no* large minivans are produced! ∎

# ADDITIONAL APPLICATIONS

## Locating Distribution Centers

When Dow Consumer Products (a manufacturer of food-care products) acquired the Texize home-care product lines of Morton Thiokol in 1985 to form DowBrands, Inc., the distribution channels of the two organizations remained, for the most part, separate. Each had its own district and regional distribution centers for storing and then shipping products to the customer regions. This led to possible inefficiencies in a business where keeping logistics costs low is the key to survival. Robinson et al. (1993), acting as consultants for

DowBrands, modeled the problem as a fixed-cost network problem—which distribution centers to keep open and which routes to use to satisfy which customers with which products. The study was highly successful and convinced DowBrands to close a significant number of distribution centers to reduce costs. ∎

## PROBLEMS

### Skill-Building Problems

**11.** How difficult is it to expand the Great Threads model to accommodate another type of clothing? Answer by assuming that the company can also produce sweatshirts. The rental cost for sweatshirt equipment is $1100; the variable cost per unit and the selling price are $15 and $45, respectively; and each sweatshirt requires 1 labor hour and 3.5 square yards of cloth.

**12.** Referring to the previous problem, if it is optimal for the company to produce sweatshirts, use SolverTable to see how much larger the fixed cost of sweatshirt machinery would have to be before the company would *not* produce any sweatshirts. However, if the solution to the previous problem calls for no sweatshirts to be produced, use SolverTable to see how much lower the fixed cost of sweatshirt machinery would have to be before the company would start producing sweatshirts.

**13.** In the Great Threads model, we didn't constrain the production quantities in row 16 to be integers, arguing that any fractional values could be safely rounded to integers. See whether this is true. Constrain these quantities to be integers and then run Solver. Are the optimal integer values the same as the rounded fractional values in Figure 6.7?

**14.** In the optimal solution to the Great Threads model, the labor hour and cloth constraints are both binding—the company is using all it has.
  **a.** Use SolverTable to see what happens to the optimal solution when the amount of available cloth increases from its current value. (You can choose the range of input values to use.) Capture all of the changing cells, the labor hours and cloth used, and the profit as outputs in the table. The real issue here is whether the company can profitably use more cloth when it is already constrained by labor hours.
  **b.** Repeat part **a**, but reverse the roles of labor hours and cloth. That is, use the available labor hours as the input for SolverTable.

**15.** In the optimal solution to the Great Threads model, no pants are produced. Suppose Great Threads has an order for 300 pairs of pants that *must* be produced. Modify the model appropriately and use Solver to find the new optimal solution. (Is it enough to put a lower bound of 300 on the production quantity in cell D16? Will this automatically force the binary value in cell D14 to be 1? Explain.) How much profit does the company lose because of having to produce pants?

**16.** In the Dorian production model, the optimal solution calls for the minimum number of compact cars and midsize minivans to be produced, but for *more* than the minimum number of large minivans to be produced. If the large minivans are evidently that profitable, why doesn't Dorian discontinue making compact cars and midsize minivans and instead produce even more large minivans?

**17.** The optimal solution to the Dorian production model appears to be sensitive to the model inputs. For each of the following inputs, create a one-way SolverTable that captures all changing cells and the target cell as outputs. You can choose the ranges of these inputs to make the results "interesting." Comment on your results.
  **a.** The steel available
  **b.** The labor hours available
  **c.** The unit profit contribution of large minivans
  **d.** The minimum production level (currently 200) of large minivans
  **e.** The minimum production level (currently 1000) of compact cars

**18.** As the Dorian production model is currently stated, each vehicle type has a minimum production level; if this type is produced at all, its production quantity must be at least this minimum. Suppose that for large minivans, there is also a *maximum* production level of 400. If large minivans are produced, the production level must be from 200 to 400. Modify the model as necessary and use Solver to find the new optimal solution. How do you know that the current optimal solution is not optimal for the modified model?

**19.** If Solver could handle IF functions correctly, how would you use them in the Dorian production example to create an arguably more natural model—without binary variables? Run Solver on your modified model. Do you get the correct solution? (*Note:* You will have to uncheck the Assume Linear Model box.)

## Skill-Extending Problems

**20.** In the Great Threads model, we found an upper bound on production of any clothing type by calculating the amount that could be produced if *all* of the resources were devoted to this clothing type.

    **a.** What if we instead used a very large value such as 1,000,000 for this upper bound? Try it and see whether you get the same optimal solution.

    **b.** Explain why *any* such upper bound is required. Exactly what role does it play in the model as we have formulated it?

**21.** In the last sheet of the file **Fixed Cost Manufacturing.xlsx**, we illustrated one way to model the Great Threads problem with IF functions that didn't work. Try a slightly different approach here. Eliminate the binary variables in row 14 altogether, and eliminate the upper bounds in row 18 and the corresponding upper bound constraints in the Solver dialog box. (The only constraints will now be the resource availability constraints.) However, use IF functions to calculate the total fixed cost of renting equipment, so that if the amount of any clothing type is positive, then its fixed

cost is added to the total fixed cost. Is Solver able to handle this model? Does it depend on the initial values in the changing cells? (Don't forget to uncheck the Assume Linear Model box.)

**22.** In the Dorian production model, suppose that the production quantity of compact cars must either be less than or equal to 100 (a small batch) or greater than or equal to 1000 (a large batch). The same statements hold for the other vehicle types as well, except that the small and large batch limits for both sizes of minivans are 50 and 200. Modify the model appropriately and use Solver to find the optimal solution.

**23.** Suppose in the Dorian production model that no minimum production limits are placed on the individual vehicle types. However, minimum production limits are placed on *all* cars and on *all* minivans. Specifically, if Dorian produces *any* cars, regardless of size, it must produce at least 1500 cars total. Similarly, if the company produces *any* minivans, it must produce at least 1000 minivans total. Modify the model appropriately and use Solver to find the optimal solution.

# 6.5 SET-COVERING AND LOCATION-ASSIGNMENT MODELS

Many companies have geographically dispersed customers that they must service in some way. To do this, they create service center facilities at selected locations and then assign each customer to one of the service centers. Various costs are incurred, including (1) fixed costs of locating service centers in particular locations; (2) operating costs, depending on the service centers' locations; and (3) transportation costs, depending on the distances between customers and their assigned service centers. In this section, we illustrate several examples of this basic problem.

We first examine a particular type of location model called a **set-covering** model. In a set-covering model, each member of a given set (set 1) must be "covered" by an acceptable member of another set (set 2). The objective in a set-covering problem is to minimize the number of members in set 2 that are needed to cover all the members in set 1. For example, set 1 might consist of all cities in a county, and set 2 might consist of the cities where a fire station is located. A fire station "covers" a city if the fire station is located, say, within 10 minutes of the city. The goal is to minimize the number of fire stations needed to cover all cities. Set-covering models have been applied to areas as diverse as airline crew scheduling, truck dispatching, political redistricting, and capital investment. The following example presents a typical set-covering model.

---

EXAMPLE | **6.4 HUB LOCATION AT WESTERN AIRLINES**

Western Airlines wants to design a hub system in the United States. Each hub is used for connecting flights to and from cities within 1000 miles of the hub. Western runs flights among the following cities: Atlanta, Boston, Chicago, Denver, Houston, Los Angeles, New Orleans, New York, Pittsburgh, Salt Lake City, San Francisco, and Seattle. The company wants to determine the smallest number of hubs it needs to cover all these cities, where a city is covered if it is within 1000 miles of at least one hub. Table 6.7 lists which cities are within 1000 miles of other cities.

**Table 6.7    Data for the Western Set-Covering Example**

| | Cities Within 1000 Miles |
|---|---|
| **Atlanta (AT)** | AT, CH, HO, NO, NY, PI |
| **Boston (BO)** | BO, NY, PI |
| **Chicago (CH)** | AT, CH, NY, NO, PI |
| **Denver (DE)** | DE, SL |
| **Houston (HO)** | AT, HO, NO |
| **Los Angeles (LA)** | LA, SL, SF |
| **New Orleans (NO)** | AT, CH, HO, NO |
| **New York (NY)** | AT, BO, CH, NY, PI |
| **Pittsburgh (PI)** | AT, BO, CH, NY, PI |
| **Salt Lake City (SL)** | DE, LA, SL, SF, SE |
| **San Francisco (SF)** | LA, SL, SF, SE |
| **Seattle (SE)** | SL, SF, SE |

**Objective**   To develop a binary model to find the minimum number of hub locations that can cover all cities.

## WHERE DO THE NUMBERS COME FROM?

Western has evidently made a policy decision that its hubs will cover only cities within a 1000-mile radius. Then the cities covered by any hub location can be found from a map. (In a later sensitivity analysis, we explore how the solution changes when we allow the coverage distance to vary.)

## Solution

The variables and constraints for this set-covering model are listed in Table 6.8. The model is straightforward. We use a binary variable for each city to indicate whether a hub is located there. Then we calculate the number of hubs that cover each city and require it to be at least 1. There are no monetary costs in this version of the problem. We simply minimize the number of hubs.

**Table 6.8    Variables and Constraints for the Set-Covering Model**

| | |
|---|---|
| **Input variables** | Cities within 1000 miles of one another |
| **Decision variables (changing cells)** | Locations of hubs (binary) |
| **Objective (target cell)** | Number of hubs |
| **Other calculated variables** | Number of hubs covering each city |
| **Constraints** | Number of hubs covering a city must be greater than or equal to 1 |

## DEVELOPING THE SPREADSHEET MODEL

The spreadsheet model for Western is shown in Figure 6.15. (See the file **Locating Hubs 1.xlsx**.) The model can be developed as follows:

**Figure 6.15** The Airline Hub Set-Covering Model

| | A | B | C | D | E | F | G | H | I | J | K | L | M | N | O | P | Q |
|---|---|---|---|---|---|---|---|---|---|---|---|---|---|---|---|---|---|
| 1 | Western Airlines hub location model | | | | | | | | | | | | | | | | |
| 2 | | | | | | | | | | | | | | | | | |
| 3 | Input data: which cities are covered by which potential hubs | | | | | | | | | | | | | | Range names used: | | |
| 4 | | Potential hub | | | | | | | | | | | | | Hubs_covered_by | =Model!$B$25:$B$36 | |
| 5 | City | AT | BO | CH | DE | HO | LA | NO | NY | PI | SL | SF | SE | | Total_hubs | =Model!$B$39 | |
| 6 | AT | 1 | 0 | 1 | 0 | 1 | 0 | 1 | 1 | 1 | 0 | 0 | 0 | | Used_as_hub? | =Model!$B$21:$M$21 | |
| 7 | BO | 0 | 1 | 0 | 0 | 0 | 0 | 0 | 1 | 1 | 0 | 0 | 0 | | | | |
| 8 | CH | 1 | 0 | 1 | 0 | 0 | 0 | 1 | 1 | 1 | 0 | 0 | 0 | | | | |
| 9 | DE | 0 | 0 | 0 | 1 | 0 | 0 | 0 | 0 | 0 | 1 | 0 | 0 | | | | |
| 10 | HO | 1 | 0 | 0 | 0 | 1 | 0 | 1 | 0 | 0 | 0 | 0 | 0 | | | | |
| 11 | LA | 0 | 0 | 0 | 0 | 0 | 1 | 0 | 0 | 0 | 1 | 1 | 0 | | | | |
| 12 | NO | 1 | 0 | 1 | 0 | 1 | 0 | 1 | 0 | 0 | 0 | 0 | 0 | | | | |
| 13 | NY | 1 | 1 | 0 | 0 | 0 | 0 | 0 | 1 | 1 | 0 | 0 | 0 | | | | |
| 14 | PI | 1 | 1 | 1 | 0 | 0 | 0 | 0 | 1 | 1 | 0 | 0 | 0 | | | | |
| 15 | SL | 0 | 0 | 0 | 1 | 0 | 1 | 0 | 0 | 0 | 1 | 1 | 1 | | | | |
| 16 | SF | 0 | 0 | 0 | 0 | 0 | 1 | 0 | 0 | 0 | 1 | 1 | 1 | | | | |
| 17 | SE | 0 | 0 | 0 | 0 | 0 | 0 | 0 | 0 | 0 | 1 | 1 | 1 | | | | |
| 18 | | | | | | | | | | | | | | | | | |
| 19 | Decisions: which cities to use as hubs | | | | | | | | | | | | | | | | |
| 20 | | AT | BO | CH | DE | HO | LA | NO | NY | PI | SL | SF | SE | | | | |
| 21 | Used as hub? | 0 | 0 | 0 | 0 | 1 | 0 | 0 | 1 | 0 | 1 | 0 | 0 | | | | |
| 22 | | | | | | | | | | | | | | | | | |
| 23 | Constraints that each city must be covered by at least one hub | | | | | | | | | | | | | | | | |
| 24 | City | Hubs covered by | | Required | | | | | | | | | | | | | |
| 25 | AT | 2 | >= | 1 | | | | | | | | | | | | | |
| 26 | BO | 1 | >= | 1 | | | | | | | | | | | | | |
| 27 | CH | 1 | >= | 1 | | | | | | | | | | | | | |
| 28 | DE | 1 | >= | 1 | | | | | | | | | | | | | |
| 29 | HO | 1 | >= | 1 | | | | | | | | | | | | | |
| 30 | LA | 1 | >= | 1 | | | | | | | | | | | | | |
| 31 | NO | 1 | >= | 1 | | | | | | | | | | | | | |
| 32 | NY | 1 | >= | 1 | | | | | | | | | | | | | |
| 33 | PI | 1 | >= | 1 | | | | | | | | | | | | | |
| 34 | SL | 1 | >= | 1 | | | | | | | | | | | | | |
| 35 | SF | 1 | >= | 1 | | | | | | | | | | | | | |
| 36 | SE | 1 | >= | 1 | | | | | | | | | | | | | |
| 37 | | | | | | | | | | | | | | | | | |
| 38 | Objective to minimize | | | | | | | | | | | | | | | | |
| 39 | Total hubs | 3 | | | | | | | | | | | | | | | |

Note that there are multiple optimal solutions to this model, all of which require a total of 3 hubs. You might get a different solution from the one shown here.

**1** **Inputs.** Enter the information from Table 6.7 in the blue range. A 1 in a cell indicates that the column city covers the row city, whereas a 0 indicates that the column city does not cover the row city. For example, the three 1's in row 7 indicate that Boston, New York, and Pittsburgh are the only cities within 1000 miles of Boston.

**2** **0–1 values for hub locations.** Enter *any* trial values of 0's or 1's in the Used_as_hub? range to indicate which cities are used as hubs. These are the changing cells.

*A SUMPRODUCT of two 0–1 ranges just finds the number of matches of 1's in the two ranges. Here it calculates the number of hubs that cover a given city.*

**3** **Cities covered by hubs.** We now determine the number of hubs that cover each city. Specifically, calculate the total number of hubs within 1000 miles of Atlanta in cell B25 with the formula

**=SUMPRODUCT(B6:M6,Used_as_hub?)**

For any 0–1 values in the changing-cells range, this formula "picks up" the number of hubs that cover Atlanta. Then copy this to the rest of the Hubs_covered_by range. Note that a value in the Hubs_covered_by range can be 2 or greater. This indicates that a city is within 1000 miles of multiple hubs.

**4** **Number of hubs.** Calculate the total number of hubs used in cell B39 with the formula

**=SUM(Used_as_hub?)**

## USING SOLVER

The Solver dialog box is shown in Figure 6.16. We minimize the total number of hubs, subject to covering each city by at least one hub and ensuring that the changing cells are binary. As usual, the Assume Linear Model option should be checked.

**Figure 6.16**

Solver Dialog Box for the Set-Covering Model

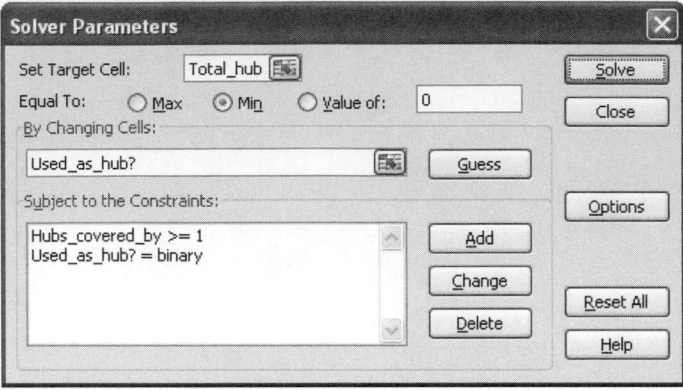

### Discussion of the Solution

Figure 6.17 is a graphical representation of the optimal solution, where the double ovals indicate hub locations and the large circles indicate ranges covered by the hubs. (These large circles are not drawn to scale. In reality, they should be circles of radius 1000 miles centered at the hubs.) Three hubs—in Houston, New York, and Salt Lake City—are needed.[6] Would you have guessed this? The Houston hub covers Houston, Atlanta, and New Orleans. The New York hub covers Atlanta, Pittsburgh, Boston, New York, and Chicago. The Salt Lake City hub covers Denver, Los Angeles, Salt Lake City, San Francisco, and Seattle. Note that Atlanta is the only city covered by two hubs; it can be serviced by New York or Houston.

**Figure 6.17**

Graphical Solution to the Set-Covering Model

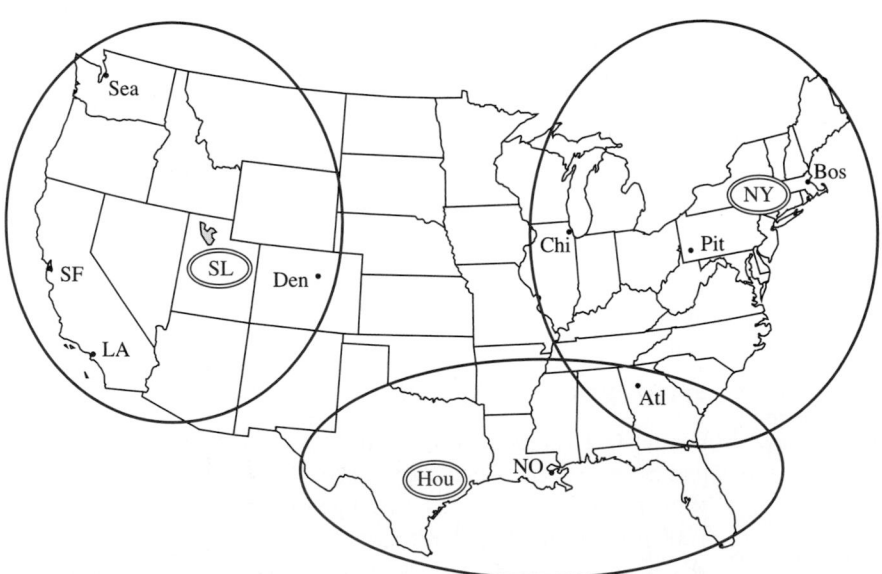

---

[6] Multiple optimal solutions exist for this model, all requiring three hubs, so you might obtain a different solution from ours.

## Sensitivity Analysis

An interesting sensitivity analysis for Western's problem is to see how the solution is affected by the mile limit. Currently, a hub can service all cities within 1000 miles. What if the limit were 800 or 1200 miles, say? To answer this question, we must first collect data on actual distances among all the cities. After we have a matrix of these distances, we can build the 0–1 matrix, corresponding to the range B6:M17 in Figure 6.15, with IF functions. The modified model appears in Figure 6.18. (See the file **Locating Hubs 2.xlsx**.) The typical formula in B24 is **=IF(B8<=$B$4,1,0)**, which is then copied to the rest of the B24:M35

**Figure 6.18**   Sensitivity to Mile Limit

| | A | B | C | D | E | F | G | H | I | J | K | L | M | N | O | P | Q |
|---|---|---|---|---|---|---|---|---|---|---|---|---|---|---|---|---|---|
| 1 | Western Airlines hub location model with distances | | | | | | | | | | | | | | Range names used: | | |
| 2 | | | | | | | | | | | | | | | Hubs_covered_by | =Model!$B$43:$B$54 | |
| 3 | Input data | | | | | | | | | | | | | | Total_hubs | =Model!$B$57 | |
| 4 | Mile limit | 1000 | | | | | | | | | | | | | Used_as_hub? | =Model!$B$39:$M$39 | |
| 5 | | | | | | | | | | | | | | | | | |
| 6 | Distance from each city to each other city | | | | | | | | | | | | | | | | |
| 7 | | AT | BO | CH | DE | HO | LA | NO | NY | PI | SL | SF | SE | | | | |
| 8 | AT | 0 | 1037 | 674 | 1398 | 789 | 2182 | 479 | 841 | 687 | 1878 | 2496 | 2618 | | | | |
| 9 | BO | 1037 | 0 | 1005 | 1949 | 1804 | 2979 | 1507 | 222 | 574 | 2343 | 3095 | 2976 | | | | |
| 10 | CH | 674 | 1005 | 0 | 1008 | 1067 | 2054 | 912 | 802 | 452 | 1390 | 2142 | 2013 | | | | |
| 11 | DE | 1398 | 1949 | 1008 | 0 | 1019 | 1059 | 1273 | 1771 | 1411 | 504 | 1235 | 1307 | | | | |
| 12 | HO | 789 | 1804 | 1067 | 1019 | 0 | 1538 | 356 | 1608 | 1313 | 1438 | 1912 | 2274 | | | | |
| 13 | LA | 2182 | 2979 | 2054 | 1059 | 1538 | 0 | 1883 | 2786 | 2426 | 715 | 379 | 1131 | | | | |
| 14 | NO | 479 | 1507 | 912 | 1273 | 356 | 1883 | 0 | 1311 | 1070 | 1738 | 2249 | 2574 | | | | |
| 15 | NY | 841 | 222 | 802 | 1771 | 1608 | 2786 | 1311 | 0 | 368 | 2182 | 2934 | 2815 | | | | |
| 16 | PI | 687 | 574 | 452 | 1411 | 1313 | 2426 | 1070 | 368 | 0 | 1826 | 2578 | 2465 | | | | |
| 17 | SL | 1878 | 2343 | 1390 | 504 | 1438 | 715 | 1738 | 2182 | 1826 | 0 | 752 | 836 | | | | |
| 18 | SF | 2496 | 3095 | 2142 | 1235 | 1912 | 379 | 2249 | 2934 | 2578 | 752 | 0 | 808 | | | | |
| 19 | SE | 2618 | 2976 | 2013 | 1307 | 2274 | 1131 | 2574 | 2815 | 2465 | 836 | 808 | 0 | | | | |
| 20 | | | | | | | | | | | | | | | | | |
| 21 | Which cities are covered by which potential hubs with this mile limit | | | | | | | | | | | | | | | | |
| 22 | | Potential hub | | | | | | | | | | | | | | | |
| 23 | City | AT | BO | CH | DE | HO | LA | NO | NY | PI | SL | SF | SE | | | | |
| 24 | AT | 1 | 0 | 1 | 0 | 1 | 0 | 1 | 1 | 1 | 0 | 0 | 0 | | | | |
| 25 | BO | 0 | 1 | 0 | 0 | 0 | 0 | 0 | 1 | 1 | 0 | 0 | 0 | | | | |
| 26 | CH | 1 | 0 | 1 | 0 | 0 | 0 | 1 | 1 | 1 | 0 | 0 | 0 | | | | |
| 27 | DE | 0 | 0 | 0 | 1 | 0 | 0 | 0 | 0 | 0 | 1 | 0 | 0 | | | | |
| 28 | HO | 1 | 0 | 0 | 0 | 1 | 0 | 1 | 0 | 0 | 0 | 0 | 0 | | | | |
| 29 | LA | 0 | 0 | 0 | 0 | 0 | 1 | 0 | 0 | 0 | 1 | 1 | 0 | | | | |
| 30 | NO | 1 | 0 | 1 | 0 | 1 | 0 | 1 | 0 | 0 | 0 | 0 | 0 | | | | |
| 31 | NY | 1 | 1 | 1 | 0 | 0 | 0 | 0 | 1 | 1 | 0 | 0 | 0 | | | | |
| 32 | PI | 1 | 1 | 1 | 0 | 0 | 0 | 0 | 1 | 1 | 0 | 0 | 0 | | | | |
| 33 | SL | 0 | 0 | 0 | 1 | 0 | 1 | 0 | 0 | 0 | 1 | 1 | 1 | | | | |
| 34 | SF | 0 | 0 | 0 | 0 | 0 | 1 | 0 | 0 | 0 | 1 | 1 | 1 | | | | |
| 35 | SE | 0 | 0 | 0 | 0 | 0 | 0 | 0 | 0 | 0 | 1 | 1 | 1 | | | | |
| 36 | | | | | | | | | | | | | | | | | |
| 37 | Decisions: which cities to use as hubs | | | | | | | | | | | | | | | | |
| 38 | | AT | BO | CH | DE | HO | LA | NO | NY | PI | SL | SF | SE | | | | |
| 39 | Used as hub? | 0 | 0 | 0 | 0 | 1 | 0 | 0 | 1 | 0 | 1 | 0 | 0 | | | | |
| 40 | | | | | | | | | | | | | | | | | |
| 41 | Constraints that each city must be covered by at least one hub | | | | | | | | | | | | | | | | |
| 42 | City | Hubs covered by | | Required | | | | | | | | | | | | | |
| 43 | AT | 2 | >= | 1 | | | | | | | | | | | | | |
| 44 | BO | 1 | >= | 1 | | | | | | | | | | | | | |
| 45 | CH | 1 | >= | 1 | | | | | | | | | | | | | |
| 46 | DE | 1 | >= | 1 | | | | | | | | | | | | | |
| 47 | HO | 1 | >= | 1 | | | | | | | | | | | | | |
| 48 | LA | 1 | >= | 1 | | | | | | | | | | | | | |
| 49 | NO | 1 | >= | 1 | | | | | | | | | | | | | |
| 50 | NY | 1 | >= | 1 | | | | | | | | | | | | | |
| 51 | PI | 1 | >= | 1 | | | | | | | | | | | | | |
| 52 | SL | 1 | >= | 1 | | | | | | | | | | | | | |
| 53 | SF | 1 | >= | 1 | | | | | | Note: There are multiple optimal solutions to these | | | | | | |
| 54 | SE | 1 | >= | 1 | | | | | | problems, so don't be surprised if you don't get exactly | | | | | | |
| 55 | | | | | | | | | | the same hub locations as shown here. | | | | | | | |
| 56 | Objective to minimize | | | | | | | | | | | | | | | | |
| 57 | Total hubs | 3 | | | | | | | | | | | | | | | |
| 58 | | | | | | | | | | | | | | | | | |
| 59 | Sensitivity of total hubs and their locations to the mile limit | | | | | | | | | | | | | | | | |
| 60 | Mile limit | AT | BO | CH | DE | HO | LA | NO | NY | PI | SL | SF | SE | Total | | | |
| 61 | | $B$39 | $C$39 | $D$39 | $E$39 | $F$39 | $G$39 | $H$39 | $I$39 | $J$39 | $K$39 | $L$39 | $M$39 | $B$57 | | | |
| 62 | 800 | 1 | 1 | 0 | 0 | 0 | 0 | 0 | 0 | 0 | 1 | 0 | 1 | 4 | | | |
| 63 | 900 | 0 | 0 | 0 | 0 | 1 | 0 | 0 | 1 | 0 | 1 | 0 | 0 | 3 | | | |
| 64 | 1000 | 0 | 0 | 1 | 0 | 0 | 0 | 1 | 0 | 0 | 1 | 0 | 0 | 3 | | | |
| 65 | 1100 | 0 | 0 | 1 | 0 | 0 | 0 | 0 | 0 | 0 | 0 | 1 | 0 | 2 | | | |
| 66 | 1200 | 0 | 0 | 1 | 0 | 0 | 0 | 0 | 0 | 0 | 0 | 0 | 1 | 2 | | | |

range.[7] We then run SolverTable, selecting cell B4 as the single input cell, letting it vary from 800 to 1200 in increments of 100, and keeping track of where the hubs are located and the number of hubs. The SolverTable results at the bottom show the effect of the mile limit. When this limit is lowered to 800 miles, 4 hubs are required, but when it's increased to 1100 or 1200, only 2 hubs are required. By the way, the solution shown for the 1000-mile limit is different from the previous solution in Figure 6.15 (because of multiple optimal solutions), but it still requires 3 hubs. ■

## ADDITIONAL APPLICATIONS

### Station Staffing at Pan Am

Like many other airlines, Pan Am has used management science to determine optimal staffing levels for its support staff (for ticket counters, baggage loading and unloading, mechanical maintenance, and so on). Schindler and Semmel (1993) describe how Pan Am used a set-covering model to determine flexible shifts of full-time and part-time personnel in the United States, Central and South America, and Europe. The model allowed the company to reduce its deployment of staff by up to 11% in work-hour requirements and suggested how existing staff could be used more efficiently.

### Locating Florida Disaster Recovery Centers

In 2001, the Federal Emergency Management Agency (FEMA) required every Florida county to identify potential locations for disaster recovery centers (DRCs). Dekle et al. (2005) describe a study sponsored by Alachua County in north-central Florida to identify potential DRC sites. The authors developed a version of the set-covering model with a two-stage approach. The first stage required each resident to be within 20 miles of the closest DRC. It identified a solution with three DRC locations. The second stage then refined this solution to relax the 20-mile requirement and include evaluation criteria not included in stage 1. The final results provided significant improvements over the original FEMA location criteria, and it maintained acceptable travel distances to the nearest DRC.

### Selecting Receiver Locations for Automated Meter Reading

Gavirneni et al. (2004) developed and solved a set-covering model for Schlumberger, a utility company. The company needed to deploy its receivers on utility poles so that all wireless meters in the region can transmit their readings to at least one receiver. Gavirneni et al. solved a large-scale model with 116,600 meters and 20,636 utility poles. ■

The following example is similar to a set-covering model, but it also has an assignment component.

### EXAMPLE | 6.5 LOCATING AND ASSIGNING SERVICE CENTERS AT UNITED COPIERS

United Copiers sells and services copy machines to customers in 11 cities throughout the country. The company wants to set up service centers in three of these cities. After United Copiers chooses the location of the service centers, it must assign customers in each city to one of the service centers. For example, if it decides to locate a service center in

---

[7] We have warned you about using IF functions in Solver models. However, the current use affects only the *inputs* to the problem, not quantities that depend on the changing cells. Therefore, it causes no problems.

New York and then assigns its Boston customers to the New York service center, a service representative from New York will travel from Boston when services are required there. The distances (in miles) between the cities are listed in Table 6.9. The estimated annual numbers of trips to the various customers are listed in Table 6.10. What should United Copiers do to minimize the total annual distance traveled by its service representatives?

**Table 6.9**   Distances for the Service Center Example

|  | Boston | Chicago | Dallas | Denver | Los Angeles | Miami | New York | Phoenix | Pittsburgh | San Francisco | Seattle |
|---|---|---|---|---|---|---|---|---|---|---|---|
| Boston | 0 | 983 | 1815 | 1991 | 3036 | 1539 | 213 | 2664 | 792 | 2385 | 2612 |
| Chicago | 983 | 0 | 1205 | 1050 | 2112 | 1390 | 840 | 1729 | 457 | 2212 | 2052 |
| Dallas | 1815 | 1205 | 0 | 801 | 1425 | 1332 | 1604 | 1027 | 1237 | 1765 | 2404 |
| Denver | 1991 | 1050 | 801 | 0 | 1174 | 2041 | 1780 | 836 | 1411 | 1765 | 1373 |
| Los Angeles | 3036 | 2112 | 1425 | 1174 | 0 | 2757 | 2825 | 398 | 2456 | 403 | 1909 |
| Miami | 1539 | 1390 | 1332 | 2041 | 2757 | 0 | 1258 | 2359 | 1250 | 3097 | 3389 |
| New York | 213 | 840 | 1604 | 1780 | 2825 | 1258 | 0 | 2442 | 386 | 3036 | 2900 |
| Phoenix | 2664 | 1729 | 1027 | 836 | 398 | 2359 | 2442 | 0 | 2073 | 800 | 1482 |
| Pittsburgh | 792 | 457 | 1237 | 1411 | 2456 | 1250 | 386 | 2073 | 0 | 2653 | 2517 |
| San Francisco | 2385 | 2212 | 1765 | 1765 | 403 | 3097 | 3036 | 800 | 2653 | 0 | 817 |
| Seattle | 2612 | 2052 | 2404 | 1373 | 1909 | 3389 | 2900 | 1482 | 2517 | 817 | 0 |

**Table 6.10**   Estimated Numbers of Annual Trips to Customers

| Boston | Chicago | Dallas | Denver | Los Angeles | Miami | New York | Phoenix | Pittsburgh | San Francisco | Seattle |
|---|---|---|---|---|---|---|---|---|---|---|
| 885 | 760 | 1124 | 708 | 1224 | 1152 | 1560 | 1222 | 856 | 1443 | 612 |

**Objective**   To develop a linear model, using binary variables, that determines the locations of service centers and then assigns customers to these service centers to minimize the total annual distance traveled.

## WHERE DO THE NUMBERS COME FROM?

The distances come directly from a map. The numbers of annual trips could be estimated in several ways. For example, the company could multiply the number of customers in each city by the estimated number of trips required per year per customer. However, this might overestimate the total number of trips because a single trip can service multiple customers. More likely, the company would estimate the numbers of trips in Table 6.10 directly from historical records. Finally, the number of service centers to use, in this case three, is probably a policy decision based on cost. However, this number is an obvious candidate for sensitivity analysis.

## Solution

*If we already knew where the service centers were located, this would just be an assignment problem of the type discussed in the previous chapter.*

The variables and constraints for this location-assignment model are listed in Table 6.11. The keys to this model are the binary decision variables and the logical constraints. For each city, we use a binary variable to indicate whether a service center is located there. Also, for each pair of cities, we use a binary variable to indicate whether a service center in the first city is assigned to the customer in the second city. Using these binary variables, the first two constraints in the table are straightforward: Three cities should include service centers, and each city should be assigned to exactly one service center. The last constraint in the table is less obvious. It states that a customer can be assigned to a service center location only if this location has a service center. For example, if no service center is located in Pittsburgh (its binary variable is 0), then no customers can be assigned to a service center in Pittsburgh.

**Table 6.11  Variables and Constraints for the Service Center Model**

| | |
|---|---|
| Input variables | Distances between cities, annual number of trips to each city, number of service centers to locate |
| Decision variables (changing cells) | Whether each city includes a service center (binary), whether a city is assigned to a particular service center (binary) |
| Objective (target cell) | Total distance traveled annually |
| Other calculated variables | Number of service center locations chosen, number of service centers assigned to each customer, total distance traveled to each customer |
| Constraints | Number of service center locations chosen must equal 3 |
| | Number of service centers assigned to each customer must equal 1 |
| | Binary variable for assignment must be less than or equal to Binary variable for service center |

## DEVELOPING THE SPREADSHEET MODEL

The spreadsheet can be developed with the following steps. (See Figure 6.19 and the file **Locating Service Centers 1.xlsx**.)

**Figure 6.19**  Spreadsheet Model for the Service Center Problem

**Distances between cities**

| | Boston | Chicago | Dallas | Denver | Los Angeles | Miami | New York | Phoenix | Pittsburgh | San Francisco | Seattle |
|---|---|---|---|---|---|---|---|---|---|---|---|
| Boston | 0 | 983 | 1815 | 1991 | 3036 | 1539 | 213 | 2664 | 792 | 2385 | 2612 |
| Chicago | 983 | 0 | 1205 | 1050 | 2112 | 1390 | 840 | 1729 | 457 | 2212 | 2052 |
| Dallas | 1815 | 1205 | 0 | 801 | 1425 | 1332 | 1604 | 1027 | 1237 | 1765 | 2404 |
| Denver | 1991 | 1050 | 801 | 0 | 1174 | 2041 | 1780 | 836 | 1411 | 1765 | 1373 |
| Los Angeles | 3036 | 2112 | 1425 | 1174 | 0 | 2757 | 2825 | 398 | 2456 | 403 | 1909 |
| Miami | 1539 | 1390 | 1332 | 2041 | 2757 | 0 | 1258 | 2359 | 1250 | 3097 | 3389 |
| New York | 213 | 840 | 1604 | 1780 | 2825 | 1258 | 0 | 2442 | 386 | 3036 | 2900 |
| Phoenix | 2664 | 1729 | 1027 | 836 | 398 | 2359 | 2442 | 0 | 2073 | 800 | 1482 |
| Pittsburgh | 792 | 457 | 1237 | 1411 | 2456 | 1250 | 386 | 2073 | 0 | 2653 | 2517 |
| San Francisco | 2385 | 2212 | 1765 | 1765 | 403 | 3097 | 3036 | 800 | 2653 | 0 | 817 |
| Seattle | 2612 | 2052 | 2404 | 1373 | 1909 | 3389 | 2900 | 1482 | 2517 | 817 | 0 |

**Range names used:**

| | |
|---|---|
| Allowed | =Model!$O$19 |
| Assignments | =Model!$B$23:$L$33 |
| Included? | =Model!$B$19:$L$19 |
| Included?_copies | =Model!$B$35:$L$45 |
| Locations_assigned_to | =Model!$M$23:$M$33 |
| Total_distance | =Model!$B$62 |
| Total_service_centers | =Model!$M$19 |

**Locations of service centers**

| | Boston | Chicago | Dallas | Denver | Los Angeles | Miami | New York | Phoenix | Pittsburgh | San Francisco | Seattle | Total service centers | | Allowed |
|---|---|---|---|---|---|---|---|---|---|---|---|---|---|---|
| Included? | 0 | 0 | 1 | 0 | 0 | 0 | 1 | 0 | 0 | 1 | 0 | 3 | <= | 3 |

**Assignments (1 if customers along side are serviced by service center along top, 0 otherwise)**

| | Boston | Chicago | Dallas | Denver | Los Angeles | Miami | New York | Phoenix | Pittsburgh | San Francisco | Seattle | Locations assigned to | | Required |
|---|---|---|---|---|---|---|---|---|---|---|---|---|---|---|
| Boston | 0 | 0 | 0 | 0 | 0 | 0 | 1 | 0 | 0 | 0 | 0 | 1 | = | 1 |
| Chicago | 0 | 0 | 0 | 0 | 0 | 0 | 1 | 0 | 0 | 0 | 0 | 1 | = | 1 |
| Dallas | 0 | 0 | 1 | 0 | 0 | 0 | 0 | 0 | 0 | 0 | 0 | 1 | = | 1 |
| Denver | 0 | 0 | 1 | 0 | 0 | 0 | 0 | 0 | 0 | 0 | 0 | 1 | = | 1 |
| Los Angeles | 0 | 0 | 0 | 0 | 0 | 0 | 0 | 0 | 0 | 1 | 0 | 1 | = | 1 |
| Miami | 0 | 0 | 0 | 0 | 0 | 0 | 1 | 0 | 0 | 0 | 0 | 1 | = | 1 |
| New York | 0 | 0 | 0 | 0 | 0 | 0 | 1 | 0 | 0 | 0 | 0 | 1 | = | 1 |
| Phoenix | 0 | 0 | 0 | 0 | 0 | 0 | 0 | 0 | 0 | 1 | 0 | 1 | = | 1 |
| Pittsburgh | 0 | 0 | 0 | 0 | 0 | 0 | 1 | 0 | 0 | 0 | 0 | 1 | = | 1 |
| San Francisco | 0 | 0 | 0 | 0 | 0 | 0 | 0 | 0 | 0 | 1 | 0 | 1 | = | 1 |
| Seattle | 0 | 0 | 0 | 0 | 0 | 0 | 0 | 0 | 0 | 1 | 0 | 1 | = | 1 |
| | <= | <= | <= | <= | <= | <= | <= | <= | <= | <= | <= | | | |

**Copies of "Included?" row**

| Boston | Chicago | Dallas | Denver | Los Angeles | Miami | New York | Phoenix | Pittsburgh | San Francisco | Seattle |
|---|---|---|---|---|---|---|---|---|---|---|
| 0 | 0 | 1 | 0 | 0 | 0 | 1 | 0 | 0 | 1 | 0 |
| 0 | 0 | 1 | 0 | 0 | 0 | 1 | 0 | 0 | 1 | 0 |
| 0 | 0 | 1 | 0 | 0 | 0 | 1 | 0 | 0 | 1 | 0 |
| 0 | 0 | 1 | 0 | 0 | 0 | 1 | 0 | 0 | 1 | 0 |
| 0 | 0 | 1 | 0 | 0 | 0 | 1 | 0 | 0 | 1 | 0 |
| 0 | 0 | 1 | 0 | 0 | 0 | 1 | 0 | 0 | 1 | 0 |
| 0 | 0 | 1 | 0 | 0 | 0 | 1 | 0 | 0 | 1 | 0 |
| 0 | 0 | 1 | 0 | 0 | 0 | 1 | 0 | 0 | 1 | 0 |
| 0 | 0 | 1 | 0 | 0 | 0 | 1 | 0 | 0 | 1 | 0 |
| 0 | 0 | 1 | 0 | 0 | 0 | 1 | 0 | 0 | 1 | 0 |
| 0 | 0 | 1 | 0 | 0 | 0 | 1 | 0 | 0 | 1 | 0 |

*The logical constraint is that a customer cannot be assigned to a service center unless that service center exists.*

**Numbers of annual trips to customers, and total distances (1000s of miles) traveled annually to customers**

| | Annual trips | Total distance |
|---|---|---|
| Boston | 885 | 189 |
| Chicago | 760 | 638 |
| Dallas | 1124 | 0 |
| Denver | 706 | 567 |
| Los Angeles | 1224 | 493 |
| Miami | 1152 | 1449 |
| New York | 1560 | 0 |
| Phoenix | 1222 | 978 |
| Pittsburgh | 856 | 330 |
| San Francisco | 1443 | 0 |
| Seattle | 612 | 500 |

*These distances are 0 because the optimal solution locates service centers in these cities.*

**Objective to minimize (1000s of miles)**

| | |
|---|---|
| Total distance | 5,145 |

**1  Inputs.** Enter the given data in the blue ranges.

**2  Service center location decisions.** Enter *any* trial 0–1 values in the Included? range. For example, a 1 in cell D19 means a service center is located in Dallas, whereas a 0 in cell E19 means no service center is located in Denver.

**3  Assignment decisions.** Enter *any* 0–1 trial values in the Assignments range. For example, a 1 in cell D26 means that Denver is serviced by the center in Dallas, whereas a 0 in cell D27 means that Los Angeles is not serviced by the center in Dallas. At this point, you might ask what these mean if there *is* no service center in Dallas. This is where the logical constraints are necessary, as explained shortly. For now, we simply state that if there is a 1 in some column of the Assignments range, then the corresponding city *will* eventually include a service center.

**4  Number of service centers.** Calculate the number of service centers with the formula

=SUM(Included?)

in cell M19. This just sums 0's and 1's, so it equals the number of 1's.

**5  Number of service centers assigned to each city.** Calculate the number of service centers assigned to each city with row sums in the Number_assigned_to range in column M. That is, enter the formula

=SUM(B23:L23)

in cell M23 and copy it down to cell M33. We eventually constrain these row sums to 1 to ensure that exactly one service center is assigned to each city.

*Always be careful to convert to appropriate units of measurement, if necessary. A factor such as 100 or 1000 in a formula is often evidence of a measurement conversion.*

**6  Total annual distances.** Calculate the total annual distance traveled (in 1000s of miles) to each city by entering the formula

=B49*SUMPRODUCT(B5:L5,B23:L23)/1000

in cell C49 for Boston and copying it down to cell C59 for the other cities. Note that this SUMPRODUCT includes a row of distances from Boston and a row of assignments to customers in Boston. We know, however, that this row of assignments will eventually include only a *single* 1—only a single service center will be assigned to customers in Boston. Therefore, this SUMPRODUCT will be the distance between Boston and the service center assigned to Boston. Then we multiply it by the annual trips to Boston (cell B49) to obtain the total annual distance traveled to Boston, and we divide by 1000 to convert to thousands of miles.

**7  Copies of 0–1 variables.** We need to ensure that only existing service locations can be assigned to customers. Essentially, *each* row of the Assignments range must be less than or equal to the Included? range. For example, if there is a 0 for Denver in the Included? range, there cannot be a 1 in any cell of the Denver column of the Assignments range. The easiest way to implement this constraint is to make 11 copies of the Included? range right below the Assignments range. To do this, enter the formula

=B$19

in cell B35 and copy it to the range B35:L45. We eventually constrain the Assignment range to be less than or equal to this "copy" range.

**8  Total annual distance traveled.** Calculate the total distance traveled annually (in 1000s of miles) in cell B62 with the formula

=SUM(C49:C59)

**USING SOLVER**

The completed Solver dialog box is shown in Figure 6.20. We also check the Assume Linear Model option and set the Solver tolerance to 0%. (There is no need to check the Assume Non-Negative option because all changing cells are binary and hence non-negative.) It is important to understand the first constraint in the list: Assignments <= Included?_copies. Because all cells in these ranges are binary, the constraint effectively says that if an Assignment cell is 1, then the corresponding Included?_copies cell must also be 1. For example, if an assignment is made of the Denver customer to the Dallas service center, so that cell D26 contains 1, then the copy of the Dallas service center binary in cell D38 must be 1. This means that the original Dallas service center binary in cell D19 must be 1, which means a service center must be located in Dallas. This is exactly the behavior we want the model to enforce.

**Figure 6.20**

Solver Dialog Box for the Service Center Model

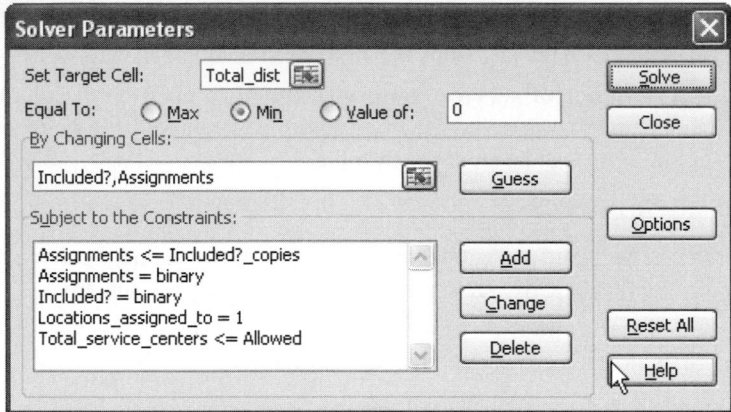

### Discussion of the Solution

The optimal solution in Figure 6.19 indicates that United Copiers should locate service centers in Dallas, New York, and San Francisco. Of course, each of these centers services the customers in its own city. In addition, the Dallas center services customers in Denver, the New York center services customers in Boston, Chicago, Miami, and Pittsburgh, and the San Francisco center services customers in Los Angeles, Phoenix, and Seattle. The total distance traveled annually is slightly over 5.1 million miles.

### Solver Message

When we solved this model, we obtained the Solver message in Figure 6.21. This message can easily occur with reasonably large IP models. It means that the Solver algorithm has already done a lot of calculations but is still not finished. Our recommendation is to click on the Continue button. Alternatively, you can change Solver's default maximum number of iterations in the Options dialog box from 100 to a larger number such as 500 before you run Solver.

**Figure 6.21**

Maximum Iteration Limit Message from Solver

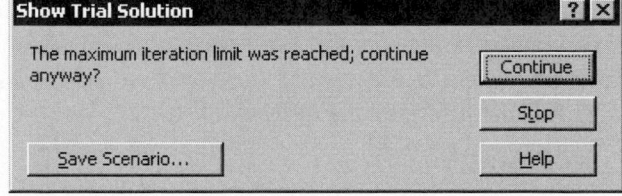

## Sensitivity Analysis

A natural sensitivity analysis is to see how the service center locations and the total annual distance change as we vary the number of required service centers. This is straightforward with SolverTable. We use cell O19 as the single input cell, vary it from 1 to 11 in increments of 1, and keep track of the binary values in row 19 and the target cell. The results are shown in Figure 6.22. As we see, service centers are typically located in Dallas, New York, and San Francisco, but not always. In particular, if only one service center is allowed, it should be located in Dallas, but if two service centers are allowed, they should be located in New York and Phoenix. Of course, as we create more service centers, less traveling is required. At the extreme, if a service center is located in every city, the required traveling distance is 0!

**Figure 6.22** Sensitivity to Number of Service Centers Allowed

| | A | B | C | D | E | F | G | H | I | J | K | L | M |
|---|---|---|---|---|---|---|---|---|---|---|---|---|---|
| 64 | Sensitivity of location binaries and total distance to number of service center locations | | | | | | | | | | | | |
| 65 | | $B$19 | $C$19 | $D$19 | $E$19 | $F$19 | $G$19 | $H$19 | $I$19 | $J$19 | $K$19 | $L$19 | $B$62 |
| 66 | 1 | 0 | 0 | 1 | 0 | 0 | 0 | 0 | 0 | 0 | 0 | 0 | 15,202 |
| 67 | 2 | 0 | 0 | 0 | 0 | 0 | 0 | 1 | 1 | 0 | 0 | 0 | 6,901 |
| 68 | 3 | 0 | 0 | 1 | 0 | 0 | 0 | 1 | 0 | 0 | 1 | 0 | 5,145 |
| 69 | 4 | 0 | 0 | 1 | 0 | 0 | 1 | 1 | 0 | 0 | 1 | 0 | 3,695 |
| 70 | 5 | 0 | 0 | 1 | 0 | 1 | 1 | 1 | 0 | 0 | 1 | 0 | 2,711 |
| 71 | 6 | 0 | 1 | 1 | 0 | 1 | 1 | 1 | 0 | 0 | 1 | 0 | 2,072 |
| 72 | 7 | 0 | 1 | 1 | 1 | 1 | 1 | 1 | 0 | 0 | 1 | 0 | 1,505 |
| 73 | 8 | 0 | 1 | 1 | 1 | 1 | 1 | 1 | 0 | 0 | 1 | 1 | 1,005 |
| 74 | 9 | 0 | 1 | 1 | 1 | 1 | 1 | 1 | 1 | 0 | 1 | 1 | 519 |
| 75 | 10 | 0 | 1 | 1 | 1 | 1 | 1 | 1 | 1 | 1 | 1 | 1 | 189 |
| 76 | 11 | 1 | 1 | 1 | 1 | 1 | 1 | 1 | 1 | 1 | 1 | 1 | 0 |

## MODELING ISSUES

To ensure that no city is serviced by a center that does not exist, we created several copies of the Included? row and then constrained the Assignments range to be less than or equal to the copy block. There is at least one other way to model this logical constraint. If we calculate the column sums of the Assignments range, each such sum represents the number of cities assigned to a certain service center. This number is certainly no greater than 11, the number of cities total, and it must logically be 0 if the service center doesn't exist. Therefore, an upper limit on each column sum is 11 multiplied by the corresponding service center binary value.

The resulting model is shown in Figure 6.23. (See the file **Locating Service Centers 2.xlsx**.) Each value in row 34 is a column sum of the binary values above it, and each value in row 36 is 11 multiplied by the corresponding binary value in row 19. This is a perfectly valid way of modeling this constraint. If a service center is not opened, then the corresponding column sum is forced to 0. If a service center is opened, then the corresponding column must not exceed 11—no real constraint because there are only 11 cities. However, if you run Solver on this version of the model—or worse yet, if you run SolverTable on it—you'll notice that it takes considerably more time to solve. There is a technical reason for this that is beyond the level of the book. However, it points out that not all IP models are equal. Some models *look* just as good as others, but they can take Solver considerably more time to solve. Unfortunately, it is difficult to know which models are more efficient than others. ■

*In binary IP models, the way a constraint is modeled can have a large effect on solution times. Even if two constraints are equivalent in a logical sense, one can lead to a much quicker solution than the other.*

**Figure 6.23** An Alternative Way to Model the Logical Constraint

| | A | B | C | D | E | F | G | H | I | J | K | L | M | N | O |
|---|---|---|---|---|---|---|---|---|---|---|---|---|---|---|---|
| 1 | Locating service centers and assigning service centers to customers - an alternative way of modeling the logical constraint | | | | | | | | | | | | | | |
| 2 | | | | | | | | | | | | | | | |
| 3 | Distances between cities | | | | | | | | | | | | Range names used: | | |
| 4 | | Boston | Chicago | Dallas | Denver | Los Angeles | Miami | New York | Phoenix | Pittsburgh | San Francisco | Seattle | Assignments | =Model!$B$23:$L$33 | |
| 5 | Boston | 0 | 983 | 1815 | 1991 | 3036 | 1539 | 213 | 2664 | 792 | 2385 | 2612 | Centers_allowed | =Model!$O$19 | |
| 6 | Chicago | 983 | 0 | 1205 | 1050 | 2112 | 1390 | 840 | 1729 | 457 | 2212 | 2052 | Included? | =Model!$B$19:$L$19 | |
| 7 | Dallas | 1815 | 1205 | 0 | 801 | 1425 | 1332 | 1604 | 1027 | 1237 | 1765 | 2404 | Locations_assigned_to | =Model!$M$23:$M$33 | |
| 8 | Denver | 1991 | 1050 | 801 | 0 | 1174 | 2041 | 1780 | 836 | 1411 | 1765 | 1373 | Logical_capacity | =Model!$B$36:$L$36 | |
| 9 | Los Angeles | 3036 | 2112 | 1425 | 1174 | 0 | 2757 | 2825 | 398 | 2456 | 403 | 1909 | Number_serviced_by | =Model!$B$34:$L$34 | |
| 10 | Miami | 1539 | 1390 | 1332 | 2041 | 2757 | 0 | 1258 | 2359 | 1250 | 3097 | 3389 | Service_centers | =Model!$M$19 | |
| 11 | New York | 213 | 840 | 1604 | 1780 | 2825 | 1258 | 0 | 2442 | 386 | 3036 | 2900 | Total_distance | =Model!$B$53 | |
| 12 | Phoenix | 2664 | 1729 | 1027 | 836 | 398 | 2359 | 2442 | 0 | 2073 | 800 | 1482 | | | |
| 13 | Pittsburgh | 792 | 457 | 1237 | 1411 | 2456 | 1250 | 386 | 2073 | 0 | 2653 | 2517 | | | |
| 14 | San Francisco | 2385 | 2212 | 1765 | 1765 | 403 | 3097 | 3036 | 800 | 2653 | 0 | 817 | | | |
| 15 | Seattle | 2612 | 2052 | 2404 | 1373 | 1909 | 3389 | 2900 | 1482 | 2517 | 817 | 0 | | | |
| 16 | | | | | | | | | | | | | | | |
| 17 | Locations of service centers | | | | | | | | | | | | | | |
| 18 | | Boston | Chicago | Dallas | Denver | Los Angeles | Miami | New York | Phoenix | Pittsburgh | San Francisco | Seattle | Service centers | | Centers allowed |
| 19 | Included? | 0 | 0 | 1 | 0 | 0 | 0 | 1 | 0 | 0 | 1 | 0 | 3 | <= | 3 |
| 20 | | | | | | | | | | | | | | | |
| 21 | Assignments (1 if customers along side are serviced by service center along top, 0 otherwise | | | | | | | | | | | | | | |
| 22 | | Boston | Chicago | Dallas | Denver | Los Angeles | Miami | New York | Phoenix | Pittsburgh | San Francisco | Seattle | Locations assigned to | | Required |
| 23 | Boston | 0 | 0 | 0 | 0 | 0 | 0 | 1 | 0 | 0 | 0 | 0 | 1 | = | 1 |
| 24 | Chicago | 0 | 0 | 0 | 0 | 0 | 0 | 1 | 0 | 0 | 0 | 0 | 1 | = | 1 |
| 25 | Dallas | 0 | 0 | 1 | 0 | 0 | 0 | 0 | 0 | 0 | 0 | 0 | 1 | = | 1 |
| 26 | Denver | 0 | 0 | 1 | 0 | 0 | 0 | 0 | 0 | 0 | 0 | 0 | 1 | = | 1 |
| 27 | Los Angeles | 0 | 0 | 0 | 0 | 0 | 0 | 0 | 0 | 0 | 1 | 0 | 1 | = | 1 |
| 28 | Miami | 0 | 0 | 0 | 0 | 0 | 0 | 1 | 0 | 0 | 0 | 0 | 1 | = | 1 |
| 29 | New York | 0 | 0 | 0 | 0 | 0 | 0 | 1 | 0 | 0 | 0 | 0 | 1 | = | 1 |
| 30 | Phoenix | 0 | 0 | 0 | 0 | 0 | 0 | 0 | 0 | 0 | 1 | 0 | 1 | = | 1 |
| 31 | Pittsburgh | 0 | 0 | 0 | 0 | 0 | 0 | 1 | 0 | 0 | 0 | 0 | 1 | = | 1 |
| 32 | San Francisco | 0 | 0 | 0 | 0 | 0 | 0 | 0 | 0 | 0 | 1 | 0 | 1 | = | 1 |
| 33 | Seattle | 0 | 0 | 0 | 0 | 0 | 0 | 0 | 0 | 0 | 1 | 0 | 1 | = | 1 |
| 34 | Number serviced by | 0 | 0 | 2 | 0 | 0 | 0 | 5 | 0 | 0 | 4 | 0 | | | |
| 35 | | <= | <= | <= | <= | <= | <= | <= | <= | <= | <= | <= | | | |
| 36 | Logical capacity | 0 | 0 | 11 | 0 | 0 | 0 | 11 | 0 | 0 | 11 | 0 | | | |
| 37 | | | | | | | | | | | | | | | |
| 38 | Numbers of annual trips to customers, and total distances (1000s of miles) traveled annually to customer | | | | | | | | | | | | | | |
| 39 | | Annual trips | Total distance | | | | | | | | | | | | |
| 40 | Boston | 865 | 189 | | | | | | | | | | | | |
| 41 | Chicago | 760 | 638 | | | | | | | | | | | | |
| 42 | Dallas | 1124 | 0 | | | | | | | | | | | | |
| 43 | Denver | 708 | 567 | | | | | | | | | | | | |
| 44 | Los Angeles | 1224 | 493 | | | | | | | | | | | | |
| 45 | Miami | 1152 | 1449 | | | | | | | | | | | | |
| 46 | New York | 1560 | 0 | | | | | | | | | | | | |
| 47 | Phoenix | 1222 | 978 | | | | | | | | | | | | |
| 48 | Pittsburgh | 856 | 330 | | | | | | | | | | | | |
| 49 | San Francisco | 1443 | 0 | | | | | | | | | | | | |
| 50 | Seattle | 612 | 500 | | | | | | | | | | | | |
| 51 | | | | | | | | | | | | | | | |
| 52 | Objective to minimize (1000s of miles) | | | | | | | | | | | | | | |
| 53 | Total distance | 5145 | | | | | | | | | | | | | |

(Annotation box pointing to Dallas, New York, and San Francisco total distances: "These distances are 0 because the optimal solution locates service centers in these cities.")

The final example in this section is structurally similar to the service center location model, but it arises in a slightly different business context.[8]

---

EXAMPLE

## 6.6 MANUFACTURING AND DISTRIBUTING FERTILIZER AT GREEN GRASS

*Like the previous example, this example is basically a fixed-cost location–assignment model. However, one difference here is that not all customers need to be assigned.*

The Green Grass Company manufactures and distributes a fertilizer product. The company sells its product to high-volume customers in various U.S. cities where it has manufacturing plants, but it can decide to operate only some of these plants in any given month. The fixed monthly cost for operating any plant is $60,000, the plant capacity for any operating plant is 2500 pounds per month, and the production cost at any operating plant is $10.25 per pound. After the product is manufactured, it is shipped to customers at a rate of $0.02 per pound per mile. The cities and the distances between them are listed in Table 6.12. The customers submit order sizes and price bids to Green Grass, as listed in Table 6.13. For example, the customer in Boston requires an order of 1430 pounds this month and is willing to pay $75,740 for it. Green Grass can decide to fill this order or not. If not, we assume that the customer takes its business to another company. For the current month, Green Grass must decide which plants to operate and which customers to service from which operating plants to maximize its monthly profit.

---

[8] This example is based on a real problem one of the authors was asked to solve during a consulting experience with a major U.S. manufacturing company.

**Table 6.12**  Distances Between Cities for the Green Grass Example

|  | Boston | Chicago | Dallas | Denver | Los Angeles | Miami | New York | Phoenix |
|---|---|---|---|---|---|---|---|---|
| Boston | 0 | 983 | 1815 | 1991 | 3036 | 1539 | 213 | 2664 |
| Chicago | 983 | 0 | 1205 | 1050 | 2112 | 1390 | 840 | 1729 |
| Dallas | 1815 | 1205 | 0 | 801 | 1425 | 1332 | 1604 | 1027 |
| Denver | 1991 | 1050 | 801 | 0 | 1174 | 2065 | 1780 | 836 |
| Los Angeles | 3036 | 2112 | 1425 | 1174 | 0 | 2757 | 2825 | 398 |
| Miami | 1539 | 1390 | 1332 | 2065 | 2757 | 0 | 1258 | 2359 |
| New York | 213 | 840 | 1604 | 1780 | 2825 | 1258 | 0 | 2442 |
| Phoenix | 2664 | 1729 | 1027 | 836 | 398 | 2359 | 2442 | 0 |

**Table 6.13**  Orders and Price Bids for the Green Grass Example

|  | Quantity | Price |
|---|---|---|
| Boston | 1430 | $75,740 |
| Chicago | 870 | $44,370 |
| Dallas | 770 | $46,320 |
| Denver | 1140 | $87,780 |
| Los Angeles | 700 | $43,850 |
| Miami | 830 | $21,000 |
| New York | 1230 | $74,850 |
| Phoenix | 1070 | $83,980 |

**Objective**   To develop a binary model to help Green Grass decide which manufacturing plants to operate and which customer orders to fill from which operating plants.

## WHERE DO THE NUMBERS COME FROM?

The distances in Table 6.12 are well known, and the customers can supply the data in Table 6.13. Cost accountants can supply the fixed cost of operating a plant, the variable production cost per pound, and the unit shipping cost per mile.

## Solution

The variables and constraints for the Green Grass model are listed in Table 6.14. As in the previous example, there are two sets of binary variables. The first set indicates which plants are open for operation. The second set indicates which customers are supplied by which plants. The first constraint in the table ensures that no customer is supplied by more than one plant. However, it allows the possibility that the customer is not supplied by *any* Green Grass plant. The second constraint ensures that no plant produces and ships more than its "logical capacity." This logical capacity is 0 if the plant is not opened at all, and it is the 2500-pound limit if the plant is opened. With these changing cells and constraints, we see which plants to open and which customers to supply from which open plants to maximize profit.

**Table 6.14**    Variables and Constraints for the Green Grass Model

| | |
|---|---|
| **Input variables** | Fixed cost of operating a plant, production cost per pound, shipping cost per pound per mile, plant capacities, distance matrix, customer order sizes, and price bids |
| **Decision variables (changing cells)** | Which plants to open (binary), which customers to supply from which open plants (binary) |
| **Objective (target cell)** | Monthly profit |
| **Other calculated variables** | Pounds shipped out of each plant, logical capacity of each plant, number of plants shipping to each customer, revenue minus production and shipping cost for each plant/customer pair, total fixed plant cost |
| **Constraints** | Plants supplying each customer msut be less than or equal to 1 <br> Pounds shipped out of each plant must be less than or equal to Logical plant capacity |

## DEVELOPING THE SPREADSHEET MODEL

The completed spreadsheet model appears in Figure 6.24. (See the file **Fixed Cost Transportation.xlsx**.) It can be developed with the following steps:

**Figure 6.24**    Green Grass Production/Shipping Model

| | A | B | C | D | E | F | G | H | I | J | K | L | M |
|---|---|---|---|---|---|---|---|---|---|---|---|---|---|
| 1 | Fixed cost logistics model with customer bids for orders | | | | | | | | | | Range names used: | | |
| 2 | | | | | | | | | | | Assignments | =Model!$B$26:$I$33 | |
| 3 | Inputs | | | | | | | | | | Logical_capacity | =Model!$B$36:$I$36 | |
| 4 | Production cost per pound | $10.25 | | | | | | | | | Number_serviced_by | =Model!$J$26:$J$33 | |
| 5 | Shipping cost per pound per mile | $0.02 | | | | | | | | | Open? | =Model!$B$22:$I$22 | |
| 6 | Monthly plant fixed cost | $60,000 | | | | | | | | | Pounds_shipped_out_of | =Model!$B$34:$I$34 | |
| 7 | Plant capacity (pounds) | 2500 | | | | | | | | | Total_monthly_profit | =Model!$B$51 | |
| 8 | | | | | | | | | | | | | |
| 9 | Distance matrix | | | | | | | | | | Quantities required and prices bid by customers | | |
| 10 | | Boston | Chicago | Dallas | Denver | LA | Miami | NY | Phoenix | | | Quantity | Price |
| 11 | Boston | 0 | 983 | 1815 | 1991 | 3036 | 1539 | 213 | 2664 | | Boston | 1430 | $75,740 |
| 12 | Chicago | 983 | 0 | 1205 | 1050 | 2112 | 1390 | 840 | 1729 | | Chicago | 870 | $44,370 |
| 13 | Dallas | 1815 | 1205 | 0 | 801 | 1425 | 1332 | 1604 | 1027 | | Dallas | 770 | $46,320 |
| 14 | Denver | 1991 | 1050 | 801 | 0 | 1174 | 2065 | 1780 | 836 | | Denver | 1140 | $87,780 |
| 15 | LA | 3036 | 2112 | 1425 | 1174 | 0 | 2757 | 2825 | 398 | | LA | 700 | $43,850 |
| 16 | Miami | 1539 | 1390 | 1332 | 2065 | 2757 | 0 | 1258 | 2359 | | Miami | 830 | $21,000 |
| 17 | NY | 213 | 840 | 1604 | 1780 | 2825 | 1258 | 0 | 2442 | | NY | 1230 | $74,850 |
| 18 | Phoenix | 2664 | 1729 | 1027 | 836 | 398 | 2359 | 2442 | 0 | | Phoenix | 1070 | $83,980 |
| 19 | | | | | | | | | | | | | |
| 20 | Which plants to open | | | | | | | | | | | | |
| 21 | | Boston | Chicago | Dallas | Denver | LA | Miami | NY | Phoenix | | | | |
| 22 | Open? | 1 | 0 | 0 | 1 | 0 | 0 | 1 | 1 | | | | |
| 23 | | | | | | | | | | | | | |
| 24 | Which customers (along side) to ship to from which plants (along top) | | | | | | | | | | | | |
| 25 | | Boston | Chicago | Dallas | Denver | LA | Miami | NY | Phoenix | Number supplied by | | Allowed | |
| 26 | Boston | 1 | 0 | 0 | 0 | 0 | 0 | 0 | 0 | 1 | <= | 1 | |
| 27 | Chicago | 0 | 0 | 0 | 0 | 0 | 0 | 1 | 0 | 1 | <= | 1 | |
| 28 | Dallas | 0 | 0 | 0 | 1 | 0 | 0 | 0 | 0 | 1 | <= | 1 | |
| 29 | Denver | 0 | 0 | 0 | 1 | 0 | 0 | 0 | 0 | 1 | <= | 1 | |
| 30 | LA | 0 | 0 | 0 | 0 | 0 | 0 | 0 | 1 | 1 | <= | 1 | |
| 31 | Miami | 0 | 0 | 0 | 0 | 0 | 0 | 0 | 0 | 0 | <= | 1 | |
| 32 | NY | 0 | 0 | 0 | 0 | 0 | 0 | 1 | 0 | 1 | <= | 1 | |
| 33 | Phoenix | 0 | 0 | 0 | 0 | 0 | 0 | 0 | 1 | 1 | <= | 1 | |
| 34 | Pounds shipped out of | 1430 | 0 | 0 | 1910 | 0 | 0 | 2100 | 1770 | | | | |
| 35 | | <= | <= | <= | <= | <= | <= | <= | <= | | | | |
| 36 | Logical capacity | 2500 | 0 | 0 | 2500 | 0 | 0 | 2500 | 2500 | | | | |
| 37 | | | | | | | | | | | | | |
| 38 | Monetary outputs | | | | | | | | | | | | |
| 39 | Matrix of revenue minus sum of production and shipping cost for each customer (along side) and plant (along top) pair | | | | | | | | | | | | |
| 40 | | Boston | Chicago | Dallas | Denver | LA | Miami | NY | Phoenix | | | | |
| 41 | Boston | $61,083 | $0 | $0 | $0 | $0 | $0 | $0 | $0 | | | | |
| 42 | Chicago | $0 | $0 | $0 | $0 | $0 | $0 | $20,837 | $0 | | | | |
| 43 | Dallas | $0 | $0 | $0 | $26,092 | $0 | $0 | $0 | $0 | | | | |
| 44 | Denver | $0 | $0 | $0 | $76,095 | $0 | $0 | $0 | $0 | | | | |
| 45 | LA | $0 | $0 | $0 | $0 | $0 | $0 | $0 | $31,103 | | | | |
| 46 | Miami | $0 | $0 | $0 | $0 | $0 | $0 | $0 | $0 | | | | |
| 47 | NY | $0 | $0 | $0 | $0 | $0 | $0 | $62,243 | $0 | | | | |
| 48 | Phoenix | $0 | $0 | $0 | $0 | $0 | $0 | $0 | $73,013 | | | | |
| 49 | | | | | | | | | | | | | |
| 50 | Monthly fixed cost | $240,000 | | | | | | | | | | | |
| 51 | Total monthly profit | $110,464 | | | | | | | | | | | |

**1** **Inputs.** Enter the inputs in the blue ranges.

**2** **Plant opening decisions.** Enter *any* set of 0's and 1's in the Open? range. These changing cells indicate which plants to open.

**3** **Assignment decisions.** Enter *any* set of 0's and 1's in the Assignments range. Each changing cell in this range indicates whether a particular plant supplies a particular customer.

**4** **Plants supplying customers.** Each customer can be supplied by at most one plant. To see how many plants are supplying each customer, create row sums of the Assignments range. That is, enter the formula

**=SUM(B26:I26)**

in cell J26 and copy it down to cell J33. Each such sum is just the number of 1's in that row of the Assignments range.

**5** **Amounts produced at plants.** We assume that if a plant is assigned to supply any customer, its production for that customer equals the customer's order requirement. This allows us to calculate the total produced (and shipped out) for each plant, given the 0–1 assignments. To implement this idea, enter the formula

**=SUMPRODUCT(B26:B33,$L$11:$L$18)**

in cell B34 for the first plant and copy it across row 34 for the other plants.

**6** **Logical plant capacities.** If a plant is not open, its capacity is 0. If it is open, its capacity is 2500. To calculate these effective plant capacities, enter the formula

**=$B$7*B22**

in cell B36 for the first plant, and copy it across row 36 for the other plants. The binary value in this formula reduces effective capacity to 0 or keeps it at 2500. (Note that the logic used here is very similar to the logic in the Great Threads fixed-cost model in Example 6.2. The only difference is that we now have a natural capacity, 2500, in case the plant is opened. In the Great Threads example, we had to calculate a suitable upper limit on production.)

**7** **Revenues and variable costs.** If any particular plant–customer assignment is made, we can calculate the revenue minus production and shipping costs for satisfying that customer's order from that plant. To calculate these, enter the formula

**=B26*($M11-$L11*($B$4+$B$5*B11))**

in cell B41 and copy it to the range B41:I48. The first term in this formula is the binary assignment variable. If it is 0, no revenues or costs are incurred on this route because the route isn't used. However, if this binary value is 1, the formula subtracts costs from revenue. (Be careful to check the measurement units in these types of calculations. The production cost is pounds multiplied by cost per pound. The shipping cost is pounds multiplied by miles multiplied by cost per pound per mile.)

**8** **Fixed costs.** Each 1 in the Open? range adds a fixed cost. To calculate the total fixed cost, enter the formula

**=B6*SUM(Open?)**

in cell B50. This is the number of open plants multiplied by the fixed cost per plant.

**9** **Monthly profit.** Calculate the monthly profit in cell B51 with the formula

**=SUM(B41:I48)-B50**

## USING SOLVER

The Solver dialog box is shown in Figure 6.25. As usual, you should check the Assume Linear Model option, but you do not need to check the Assume Non-Negative option because all changing cells are constrained to be binary, hence nonnegative. In words, we want to choose the binary values for plant openings and customer assignments to maximize profit. We must ensure that each plant produces 0 if it isn't open, or no more than its capacity if it is open. Also, we ensure that each customer's demand is satisfied by at most one plant. Of course, this allows the possibility that a customer's demand is not satisfied by Green Grass at all.

**Figure 6.25**

Solver Dialog Box for the Green Grass Model

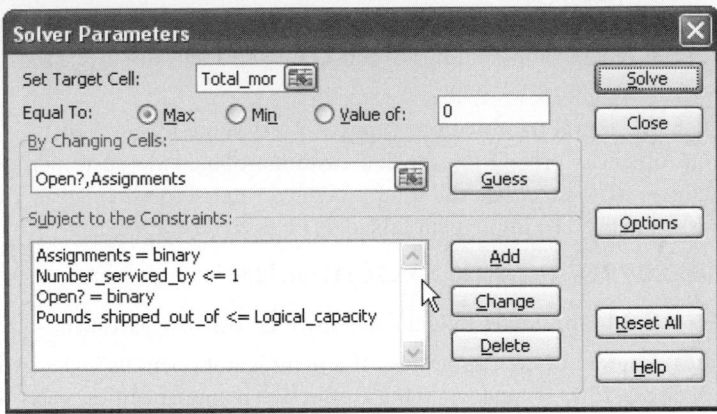

### Discussion of the Solution

The optimal solution in Figure 6.24 indicates that the company should open four plants: Boston (to supply the Boston customer), Denver (to supply the Denver and Dallas customers), New York (to supply the New York and Chicago customers), and Phoenix (to supply the Phoenix and Los Angeles customers). In addition, the model indicates that Green Grass should not supply the Miami customer at all. You can see the main reason for this if you calculate the ratio of order size to price bid for each customer. Miami's ratio is well below the others. Therefore, it is evidently not profitable to supply the Miami customer.

### Sensitivity Analysis

One possible sensitivity analysis is to see how much larger Miami's price bid needs to be before Green Grass supplies it. We tried this, varying Miami's price bid and keeping track of the row sum in cell J31 that indicates whether Miami is supplied. The results (after some trial and error to find the "interesting" price bid range) appear in Figure 6.26. When the Miami price bid increases to some value between $31,000 and $32,000, it becomes profitable to supply Miami. (You can check, by rerunning Solver, that Miami is then supplied by New York.)

**Figure 6.26**

Sensitivity to Miami's Price Bid

|  | A | B | C | D |
|---|---|---|---|---|
| 53 | Sensitivity of whether Miami is supplied to Miami's bid price | | | |
| 54 | | $J$31 | | |
| 55 | 28000 | 0 | | |
| 56 | 29000 | 0 | | |
| 57 | 30000 | 0 | | |
| 58 | 31000 | 0 | | |
| 59 | 32000 | 1 | | |
| 60 | 33000 | 1 | | |
| 61 | 34000 | 1 | | |
| 62 | 35000 | 1 | | |

Another possible sensitivity analysis is on the common plant capacity, currently 2500 pounds. The optimal solution in Figure 6.24 indicates that capacity is not currently a constraining factor. Four of the plants are open, and all are operating well under capacity. Therefore, an *increase* in the common capacity has absolutely no effect, and a slight *decrease* (down to 2100, the highest plant production) also has no effect. However, any decrease below 2100 should have an effect. We explore this in Figure 6.27, where we vary the common plant capacity and keep track of the optimal total fixed cost and profit. As you can see, if the capacity is below 2100, the total profit decreases. However, the total fixed cost remains constant, at least for this range of capacities. This implies that all of these solutions keep four plants open. How does the optimal solution change? Although the results in Figure 6.27 do not provide the answer, you can rerun Solver with any of these capacities to find out. It turns out that the *same* four plants stay open but supply fewer customers. For example, when the common capacity is 1500 or 1750, the four plants supply *only* the customers in their respective cities.

**Figure 6.27**
Sensitivity to Common Plant Capacity

| | A | B | C | D |
|---|---|---|---|---|
| 64 | Sensitivity of total fixed cost and profit to common plant capacity | | | |
| 65 | | $B$50 | $B$51 | |
| 66 | 1500 | $240,000 | $32,433 | |
| 67 | 1750 | $240,000 | $32,433 | |
| 68 | 2000 | $240,000 | $89,628 | |
| 69 | 2250 | $240,000 | $110,464 | |
| 70 | 2500 | $240,000 | $110,464 | |

If you run these sensitivity analyses with SolverTable, you will immediately notice the longer computing times. These are *difficult* problems, even for Solver, and you won't get the immediate solutions you've become accustomed to. Each problem has $2^{72}$ possible binary solutions (because there are 72 binary changing cells), which is an enormous number of potential solutions for Solver to sort through with its branch and bound algorithm. Although a binary model of this type and size are still well within Solver's capabilities, this example should convince you that not all management science optimization models are easy to solve! ∎

# MODELING ISSUES

1.  We have assumed that all possible plant locations are in the same cities as the customers. This is not necessary. We could have any number of customers at one set of locations and any other number of plant locations at another set of locations. As long as we know the distance from each plant to each customer, the model changes hardly at all.

2.  We have assumed that the inputs in the range B4:B7 (see Figure 6.24) are constant, the same for each plant or plant–customer pair. This is also not necessary. If these inputs differ across plants or plant–customer pairs, more input values must be estimated by the cost accountants, but modifications to the model itself are minimal.

3.  We currently assume that the plants in the various locations are already built, and it is just a matter of which to open each month. Suppose instead that the company is expanding and must decide where (or whether) to build *new* plants. Then there is a one-time fixed cost of building each new plant, in addition to the fixed cost of opening an existing plant that we saw in the example. Unfortunately, combining these costs is not a trivial matter. The fixed cost of building must be amortized over some period of time so that it can be combined correctly with the *monthly* revenues and costs in the current model. ∎

## PROBLEMS

### Skill-Building Problems

**24.** In the original Western set-covering model in Figure 6.15, we assumed that each city must be covered by at least one hub. Suppose that for added flexibility in flight routing, Western requires that each city must be covered by at least two hubs. How do the model and optimal solution change?

**25.** In the original Western set-covering model in Figure 6.15, we used the number of hubs as the objective to minimize. Suppose instead that there is a fixed cost of locating a hub in any city, where these fixed costs can possibly vary across cities. Make up some reasonable fixed costs, modify the model appropriately, and use Solver to find the solution that minimizes the sum of fixed costs.

**26.** Set-covering models such as the original Western model in Figure 6.15 often have multiple optimal solutions. See how many alternative optimal solutions you can find. Of course, each must use three hubs because we know this is optimal. (*Hint:* Use various initial values in the changing cells and then run Solver repeatedly.)[9]

**27.** How hard is it to expand a set-covering model to accommodate new cities? Answer this by modifying the model in Figure 6.18. (See the file **LocatingHubs2.xlsx**.) Add several cities that must be served: Memphis, Dallas, Tucson, Philadelphia, Cleveland, and Buffalo. You can look up the distances from these cities to each other and to the other cities in a reference book (or on the Web), or you can make up approximate distances.
   **a.** Modify the model appropriately, assuming that these new cities must be covered *and* are candidates for hub locations.
   **b.** Modify the model appropriately, assuming that these new cities must be covered but are *not* candidates for hub locations.

**28.** In the United Copiers service center model, we assumed that the potential locations of service centers are the same as existing customer locations. Change the model so that the customer locations are the ones given, but the only potential service center locations are in Memphis, Houston, Cleveland, Buffalo, Minneapolis, St. Louis, and Kansas City. You can look up the distances from these cities to the customer cities in a reference book (or on the Web), or you can make up

---

[9] One of our colleagues at Indiana University, Vic Cabot, now deceased, worked for years trying to develop a general algorithm (other than trial and error) for finding *all* alternative optimal solutions to optimization models. It turns out that this is a very difficult problem—and one that Vic never totally solved.

approximate distances. Use Solver to find the optimal solution.

**29.** In the United Copiers service center model, we used total distance traveled as the objective to minimize. Suppose in addition that there is an annual fixed cost of locating a service center in any city, where this fixed cost can vary across cities. There is also a cost per mile of traveling. Modify the current model to make total annual cost the objective to minimize. You can make up reasonable fixed costs and unit traveling costs.

**30.** In the Green Grass shipping model, we assumed that certain inputs (see the range B4:B7 in Figure 6.24) are the same for all plants or plant–customer combinations. Change this so that the unit production cost, the monthly fixed cost, and the monthly capacity can vary by plant, and the unit shipping cost can vary by plant–customer combination. (You can make up data that vary around the values in the B4:B7 range.) Use Solver to find the new optimal solution.

**31.** In the optimal solution to the Green Grass shipping model, the Miami customer's order is not satisfied. Suppose that Green Grass decides, as a matter of policy, to satisfy *each* customer's order (at the customer's bid price). How much profit will the company lose from this policy decision?

**32.** In the Green Grass shipping model, use SolverTable to perform a sensitivity analysis on the fixed cost of opening a plant, letting it vary over some reasonable range that extends below and above the current value of $60,000. Keep track of enough outputs so that you can see the effect on the plants that are opened and the customers whose orders are satisfied, as well as on the total profit. Summarize your findings in words.

### Skill-Extending Problems

**33.** In the United Copiers service center model, we assumed that a customer is serviced totally by a single service center. Suppose a customer can be serviced partly by multiple service centers. For example, the customer in Denver could get half of its service from Dallas and the other half from San Francisco. In this case, we assume that half of Denver's annual trips would be made from Dallas reps and half by San Francisco reps. Modify the model appropriately and then solve it with Solver. How do you interpret the optimal solution? (*Hint:* Allow the changing cells in the Assignments range to be fractional values between 0 and 1.)

**34.** In the Green Grass shipping model, we currently assume that if a customer's order is satisfied, it must be satisfied from a *single* plant. Suppose instead that it can be satisfied from more than one plant. For example, if the company decides to satisfy Dallas's order, it could ship part of this order from Denver and part from Phoenix (or some other combination of open plants). Continue to assume, however, that the company must satisfy either *all* or *none* of each customer's order. Modify the model appropriately and use Solver to solve it. Does the solution change?

35. In the Green Grass shipping model, we assumed that the plants are already built, so that in each month, the only decision is whether to open particular plants (at a monthly fixed cost). Consider instead a general location–shipping model of this type where the plants are not yet built. The company must first decide where to build plants, then how much to produce at the plants, and finally which customers to service from them. The problem is that the building costs are one-time costs, whereas other costs are monthly. How can you reconcile these two types of costs? What should you use as an objective to minimize? Illustrate your procedure on the Green Grass example, where the plant opening fixed costs are ignored—we assume that all plants that are built will remain open—but building costs (which you can make up) are given.

# 6.6 CUTTING STOCK MODELS

The final model we discuss in this chapter has found many real-world applications, especially in manufacturing. The model is relevant in situations where a product is produced in a standard size, which must then be cut into one of several patterns to satisfy customer orders. In contrast to the other models in this chapter, this cutting stock model does not have *binary* variables, but it does have *integer* variables. The problem is relatively easy to model, but it can be very time-consuming for Solver to solve. We warned you earlier that IP models are inherently more difficult to solve than general LP problems. The model in the following example illustrates that this is definitely the case.

EXAMPLE | **6.7 CUTTING PAPER ROLLS AT RHEEM PAPER**

The Rheem Paper Company produces rolls of paper of various types for its customers. One type is produced in standard rolls that are 60 inches wide and (when unwound) 200 yards long. Customers for this type of paper order rolls that are all 200 yards long, but can have any of the widths 12, 15, 20, 24, 30, or 40 inches. In a given week, Rheem waits for all orders and then decides how to cut its 60-inch rolls to satisfy the orders. For example, if there are 5 orders for 15-inch widths and 2 orders for 40-inch widths, Rheem could satisfy the order by producing 3 rolls, cutting each of the first two into a 40-inch and a 15-inch cut (with 5 inches left over) and cutting the third into 4 15-inch cuts (with one of these left over). Each week, Rheem must decide how to cut its rolls in the most economical way to meet its orders. Specifically, it wants to produce as few rolls as possible.

**Objective**  To find a way of cutting paper rolls in various widths so as to satisfy all customer orders and minimize the total number of rolls cut.

### WHERE DO THE NUMBERS COME FROM?

The company knows the various widths its customers need, and it knows the orders for the various widths in the current week.

## Solution

Given the width of the rolls (60 inches) and the available widths (12, 15, 20, 24, 30, and 40), the first thing we must do in this model is "preprocess" the patterns that might be used. For example, one reasonable pattern is to cut a roll into 4 15-inch cuts. In fact, this is perfect—there is no waste. Another pattern is to cut a roll into a 12-inch, a 15-inch, and a 24-inch cut, with 9 inches left over and unusable. The only patterns we consider (the feasible patterns) are the ones with no leftover paper that could be used for customer orders. For example, the pattern of a 12-inch cut and a 30-inch cut is not worth considering because we could still get another 12-inch (or 15-inch) cut from the remainder. We do not present a model for determining all feasible patterns. We simply go through all the possibilities in a systematic way. After we have listed all possible patterns, the problem is then to decide how many rolls to cut into each pattern.

With this in mind, Table 6.15 lists the variables and constraints required for this model.

**Table 6.15   Table of Variables and Constraints for the Cutting Stock Model**

| | |
|---|---|
| **Input variables** | Width of roll, number of rolls of possible widths required by customers, list of patterns roll can be cut into (must be obtained manually) |
| **Decision variables (changing cells)** | Number of rolls cut for each pattern (integer) |
| **Objective (target cell)** | Number of rolls cut total |
| **Other output cells** | Number of each width obtained |
| **Constraints** | Number of each width obtained must be greater than or equal to Number of each width required |

### DEVELOPING THE SPREADSHEET MODEL

The spreadsheet model appears in Figure 6.28. (See the file **Cutting Stock.xlsx**.) To develop it, follow these steps:

**1  Inputs.** Enter the roll width, the available widths, and the number of orders for each width in the blue ranges. The orders we entered in the Required range (row 42) will change from week to week, but the same model can handle any values in this range.

**2  Patterns.** Enter the feasible patterns in columns B through G, starting in row 10. The numbers in each row indicate how many of each width is in the pattern. For example, the first pattern has 5 12-inch cuts with no waste. We calculate the waste in column H by entering the formula

**=$B$3-SUMPRODUCT(B$9:G$9,B10:G10)**

and copying down. This waste column is useful as we try to list all feasible patterns. Specifically, the waste must be nonnegative, and it must be no greater than 12, the smallest available width. (If the waste were 12 or greater, we could get another usable cut from the pattern.) For this particular roll width and this particular set of available widths, there are 26 feasible patterns. (You have to be careful when listing them. It's easy to miss some.)

**3  Decision variables.** Enter *any* values into the Rolls_cut range. These are the decision variables in this model. They indicate how many rolls we should cut into the various patterns.

**4  Widths obtained.** Calculate the number of each width obtained by entering the formula

**=SUMPRODUCT(Rolls_cut,B10:B35)**

**Figure 6.28** The Cutting Stock Model

| | A | B | C | D | E | F | G | H | I | J | K |
|---|---|---|---|---|---|---|---|---|---|---|---|
| 1 | Cutting stock model | | | | | | | | Range names used: | | |
| 2 | | | | | | | | | Obtained | =Model!$B$40:$G$40 | |
| 3 | Width of roll | 60 | inches | | | | | | Required | =Model!$B$42:$G$42 | |
| 4 | | | | | | | | | Rolls_cut | =Model!$K$10:$K$35 | |
| 5 | Widths available | 12 | 15 | 20 | 24 | 30 | 40 | | Total_rolls_cut | =Model!$B$45 | |
| 6 | | | | | | | | | | | |
| 7 | Feasible ways of cutting up a roll | | | | | | | | | | |
| 8 | | | | Width | | | | | | Decisions | |
| 9 | Pattern | 12 | 15 | 20 | 24 | 30 | 40 | Waste | | Pattern | Rolls cut |
| 10 | 1 | 5 | 0 | 0 | 0 | 0 | 0 | 0 | | 1 | 0 |
| 11 | 2 | 3 | 1 | 0 | 0 | 0 | 0 | 9 | | 2 | 0 |
| 12 | 3 | 3 | 0 | 1 | 0 | 0 | 0 | 4 | | 3 | 0 |
| 13 | 4 | 3 | 0 | 0 | 1 | 0 | 0 | 0 | | 4 | 11 |
| 14 | 5 | 2 | 2 | 0 | 0 | 0 | 0 | 6 | | 5 | 0 |
| 15 | 6 | 2 | 1 | 1 | 0 | 0 | 0 | 1 | | 6 | 2 |
| 16 | 7 | 2 | 0 | 0 | 0 | 1 | 0 | 6 | | 7 | 0 |
| 17 | 8 | 1 | 3 | 0 | 0 | 0 | 0 | 3 | | 8 | 0 |
| 18 | 9 | 1 | 1 | 0 | 1 | 0 | 0 | 9 | | 9 | 0 |
| 19 | 10 | 1 | 1 | 0 | 0 | 1 | 0 | 3 | | 10 | 2 |
| 20 | 11 | 1 | 0 | 2 | 0 | 0 | 0 | 8 | | 11 | 0 |
| 21 | 12 | 1 | 0 | 1 | 1 | 0 | 0 | 4 | | 12 | 0 |
| 22 | 13 | 1 | 0 | 0 | 2 | 0 | 0 | 0 | | 13 | 10 |
| 23 | 14 | 1 | 0 | 0 | 0 | 0 | 1 | 8 | | 14 | 0 |
| 24 | 15 | 0 | 4 | 0 | 0 | 0 | 0 | 0 | | 15 | 0 |
| 25 | 16 | 0 | 2 | 1 | 0 | 0 | 0 | 10 | | 16 | 0 |
| 26 | 17 | 0 | 2 | 0 | 1 | 0 | 0 | 6 | | 17 | 0 |
| 27 | 18 | 0 | 2 | 0 | 0 | 1 | 0 | 0 | | 18 | 7 |
| 28 | 19 | 0 | 1 | 2 | 0 | 0 | 0 | 5 | | 19 | 0 |
| 29 | 20 | 0 | 1 | 1 | 1 | 0 | 0 | 1 | | 20 | 1 |
| 30 | 21 | 0 | 1 | 0 | 0 | 0 | 1 | 5 | | 21 | 0 |
| 31 | 22 | 0 | 0 | 3 | 0 | 0 | 0 | 0 | | 22 | 4 |
| 32 | 23 | 0 | 0 | 1 | 0 | 1 | 0 | 10 | | 23 | 0 |
| 33 | 24 | 0 | 0 | 1 | 0 | 0 | 1 | 0 | | 24 | 7 |
| 34 | 25 | 0 | 0 | 0 | 1 | 1 | 0 | 6 | | 25 | 0 |
| 35 | 26 | 0 | 0 | 0 | 0 | 2 | 0 | 0 | | 26 | 3 |
| 36 | | | | | | | | | | | |
| 37 | Constraint on satisfying orders | | | | | | | | | | |
| 38 | | | | Width | | | | | | | |
| 39 | | 12 | 15 | 20 | 24 | 30 | 40 | | | | |
| 40 | Obtained | 49 | 19 | 22 | 32 | 15 | 7 | | | | |
| 41 | | >= | >= | >= | >= | >= | >= | | | | |
| 42 | Required | 48 | 19 | 22 | 32 | 14 | 7 | | | | |
| 43 | | | | | | | | | | | |
| 44 | Objective to minimize | | | | | | | | | | |
| 45 | Total rolls cut | 47 | | | | | | | | | |

in cell B40 and copying it to the rest of the Obtained range. For example, the value in cell B40 is the number of rolls of width 12 inches obtained from *all* possible patterns.

**5** **Rolls cut.** Calculate the number of rolls cut in cell B45 with the formula

=SUM(Rolls_cut)

## USING THE SOLVER

Fill out the Solver dialog box as indicated in Figure 6.29. We want to minimize the number of rolls produced, subject to meeting customer orders. Also, the number cut according to each pattern must be an integer (but not binary), and the Assume Linear Model and Assume Non-Negative options should be checked.

Figure 6.29

Solver Dialog Box
for the Cutting Stock
Model

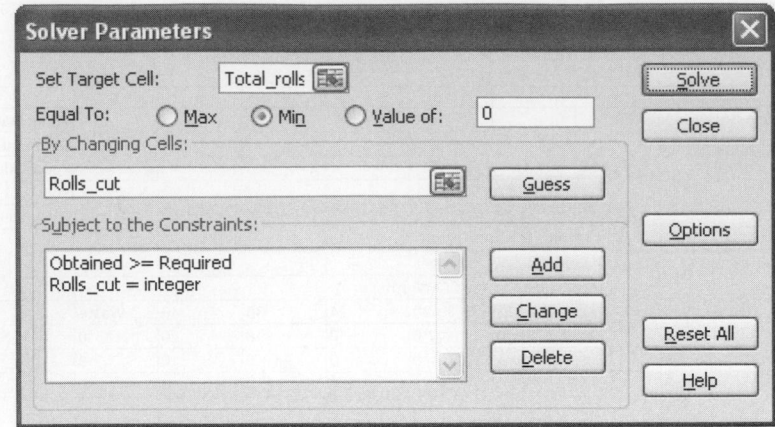

### Discussion of the Solution

The solution indicates that Rheem can meet its customer orders this week with 47 rolls, cut as specified in rows 10 through 35. For example, 11 of the 47 rolls should be cut according to pattern 4, each with three 12-inch rolls and one 24-inch roll. Note that there are two sources of "waste" in this solution. First, there is the unusable waste from all leftover rolls with width less than 12 inches. For example, there is a 1-inch roll left over from the one roll cut into pattern 20. Second, there is some waste from the usable rolls that are not needed in this week's orders. Fortunately, it is minimal—only one 12-inch roll and one 30-inch roll are left over. Actually, if Rheem solves this model on a weekly basis, the model could easily incorporate the inventory of usable leftover rolls from *previous* weeks.

### Solver Tolerance Setting

Until now, we have suggested setting the Solver tolerance to 0%. This guarantees *the* optimal solution. However, this example illustrates why the default tolerance setting is 5% (or at least not 0%). When we set the tolerance to 0% and click on Solve, Solver quickly gets to a solution that requires 47 rolls, but then it runs and runs and runs. (We got tired of waiting, so we pressed the Ctrl+Break key combination to stop it prematurely.) After some experimenting, we found that with the tolerance set at 2% or above, the solution is obtained almost instantaneously, but with the tolerance set at 1% or 0%, it runs seemingly forever. This behavior is not at all uncommon in IP models. Solver often finds a very good or even optimal solution very quickly, but then it takes a long time to verify that it is optimal (or to find something slightly better). The moral is clear. If you set the tolerance to a low value and find that the Solver is taking forever without getting anywhere, press Ctrl+Break to get out. By that time, you probably already have a very good or even optimal solution. ∎

## MODELING ISSUES

We did not perform any sensitivity analysis on this model because there is no obvious sensitivity analysis to perform. The only inputs are the roll width, the set of available widths, and the order amounts. Although it would make sense to perform sensitivity analysis on the order amounts, it would make more sense (in a realistic setting) to wait for next week's orders and simply solve the problem again. Note that the model is *not* set up to perform sensitivity analysis (with SolverTable) on the roll width or the set of available widths. If these change, the entire table of patterns must be recreated by hand. For example, if the roll width changes to 64 inches, patterns 2, 9, 11, 14, 16, and 23 are no longer in the list (why not?), and several new patterns enter the list (what are they?). ∎

## PROBLEMS

### Skill-Building Problems

**36.** In the cutting stock example, we minimized the total number of rolls cut. Do you get the same solution if you minimize the total inches of waste? For example, given the solution in Figure 6.28, this waste includes 2 inches from pattern 6, 12 inches from the extra 12-inch roll produced (in cell B40), and a couple others. Solve the problem with this objective.

**37.** Woodco sells 3-foot, 5-foot, and 9-foot pieces of lumber. Woodco's customers demand 25 3-foot boards, 20 5-foot boards, and 15 9-foot boards. Woodco meets its demands by cutting up 17-foot boards. How can it satisfy its customers' demands with the least amount of waste? Assume that all boards are the same width and thickness.

### Skill-Extending Problem

**38.** The Mayfree Appliance Company requires sheet metal for its appliances. The company can purchase long coils of sheet metal in two different widths: 65 inches and 40 inches. The company must purchase the coils by linear foot of length: $1.20 per foot for a 64-inch coil and $1.00 per foot for a 40-inch coil. (This implies that a square foot, say, of the wider coil is less expensive.) Up to 4000 feet of the 65-inch coil is available, and up to 6000 feet of the 40-inch coil is available. There are manufacturing requirements for six different widths: 50, 45, 40, 35, 20, and 10 inches. Mayfree's requirements are expressed as lengths of the various widths. The company requires 1000 feet of 50-inch width, 2500 feet of 45-inch width, 3000 feet of 40-inch width, 2300 feet of 35-inch width, 1300 feet of 20-inch width, and 2000 feet of 10-inch width. Determine how much of each width coil Mayfree should purchase and how it should cut the coils into various widths to meet its requirements at minimal cost. (*Hint:* First, list all patterns that can be cut from a 65-inch coil, and do the same for a 40-inch coil. Then have a changing cell for each pattern that designates the number of linear feet to be cut in this pattern.)

## 6.7 CONCLUSION

Three important points emerge from this chapter.

- A wide variety of important problems can be modeled as IP problems with binary variables. These can generally be identified as problems where at least some of the activities (such as making a particular investment, opening a particular plant, or supplying a customer from a particular plant) must be done or not done; there is no in-between. Regular LP models cannot handle these problems; IP models with binary variables can.

- Some IP models are simply LP models with integer constraints on the variables. For example, we might constrain the number of refrigerators produced to be an integer. These problems can often be solved by solving the associated LP model and then rounding the solution to integer values. Although there is no guarantee that the rounded solution is optimal, it is often close enough. In contrast, most of the problems discussed in this chapter introduce binary decision variables that specify whether an activity is done or not. If we ignore the binary constraints and only constrain these variables to be *between* 0 and 1, it is generally impossible to find the optimal solution by rounding.

- The solution approach required for IP problems, especially those with 0–1 variables, is inherently more difficult than the simplex method for LP problems. The relatively small examples in this chapter might give the impression that a spreadsheet Solver can handle IP models just as easily as it handles LP models, but this is definitely not the case. In fact, even with the most sophisticated IP computer codes on the most powerful computers, there are IP problems—from real applications—that defy solution. Analysts typically employ heuristic methods on these really difficult problems.

## Summary of Key Management Science Terms

| Term | Explanation | Page |
|---|---|---|
| Binary variables | Variables constrained to have values 1 or 0; usually used to indicate whether an activity is undertaken or not | 286 |
| IP models | Optimization models where some or all of the decision variables are constrained to have integer values | 287 |
| Branch and bound algorithm | A general algorithm for searching through all integer solutions in an IP model | 288 |
| Fixed-cost models | Difficult-to-solve models where certain costs are fixed at some positive level if an activity is undertaken at any level, and are 0 otherwise | 297 |
| Either–or constraints | Constraints where one of mutually exclusive conditions must be satisfied | 304 |
| Set-covering models | Models where members of one set (such as ambulances) must be located so that they "cover" members of another set (such as city districts) | 309 |
| Location models | Models where items (such as branch offices) must be located to provide required services at minimal cost | 309 |

## Summary of Key Excel Terms

| Term | Explanation | Excel | Page |
|---|---|---|---|
| Solver tolerance setting | Setting that specifies whether Solver will stop at a near-optimal integer solution or will continue to optimality | Specify under Solver Options (default 5% doesn't guarantee optimality; 0% does) | 289 |

## PROBLEMS

### Skill-Building Problems

39. Four projects are available for investment. The projects require the cash flows and yield the net present values (in millions) shown in the file **P06_39.xlsx**. If $6 million is available now for investment, find the investment plan that maximizes NPV.

40. You are given a group of possible investment projects for your company's capital. For each project, you are given the NPV the project would add to the firm, as well as the cash outflow required by each project during each year. Given the information in the file **P06_40.xlsx**, determine the investments that maximize the firm's NPV. The firm has $30 million available during each of the next 5 years. All numbers are in millions of dollars.

41. I am moving from New Jersey to Indiana and have rented a truck that can haul up to 1100 cubic feet of furniture. The volume and value of each item I am considering moving on the truck are given in the file **P06_41.xlsx**. Which items should I bring to Indiana?

42. NASA must determine how many of three types of objects to bring on board the space shuttle. The weight and benefit of each of the items are given in the file **P06_42.xlsx**. If the space shuttle can carry up to 2600 pounds of items 1 through 3, which items should be taken on the space shuttle?

43. Coach Night is trying to choose the starting lineup for the basketball team. The team consists of seven players who have been rated on a scale of 1 (poor) to 3 (excellent) according to their ball handling, shooting, rebounding, and defensive abilities. The positions that each player is allowed to play and the players' abilities are listed in the file **P06_43.xlsx**. The five-player starting lineup must satisfy the following restrictions:

- At least four members must be able to play guard (G), at least two members must be able to play forward (F), and at least one member must be able to play center (C).
- The average ballhandling, shooting, and rebounding level of the starting lineup must each be at least 1.8.
- Either player 2 or player 3 (or both) must start. Given these constraints, Coach Night wants to maximize the total defensive ability of the starting team. Use Solver to determine his starting team.

**44.** To graduate from Southeastern University with a major in operations research (OR), a student must complete at least two math courses, at least two OR courses, and at least two computer courses. Some courses can be used to fulfill more than one requirement: Calculus can fulfill the math requirement; Operations Research can fulfill the math and OR requirements; Data Structures can fulfill the computer and math requirements; Business Statistics can fulfill the math and OR requirements; Computer Simulation can fulfill the OR and computer requirements; Introduction to Computer Programming can fulfill the computer requirement; and Forecasting can fulfill the OR and math requirements. Some courses are prerequisites for others: Calculus is a prerequisite for Business Statistics; Introduction to Computer Programming is a prerequisite for Computer Simulation and for Data Structures; and Business Statistics is a prerequisite for Forecasting. Determine how to minimize the number of courses needed to satisfy the major requirements. (*Hint:* Because Calculus is a prerequisite for Business Statistics, for example, you will need a constraint that ensures that the changing cell for Calculus is greater than or equal to the changing cell for Business Statistics.)

**45.** Based on Bean et al. (1987). Boris Milkem's firm owns six assets. The expected selling price (in millions of dollars) for each asset is given in the file **P06_45.xlsx**. For example, if asset 1 is sold in year 2, the firm receives $20 million. To maintain a regular cash flow, Milkem must sell at least $20 million of assets during year 1, at least $30 million worth during year 2, and at least $35 million worth during year 3. Determine how Milkem can maximize his total revenue from assets sold during the next 3 years. In implementing this model, how might the idea of a rolling planning horizon be used?

**46.** The Cubs are trying to determine which of the following free-agent pitchers should be signed: Rick Sutcliffe (RS), Bruce Sutter (BS), Dennis Eckersley (DE), Steve Trout (ST), or Tim Stoddard (TS). (Feel free to substitute your own set of players for these "old" guys!) The cost of signing each pitcher and the predicted number of victories each pitcher will add to the Cubs are listed in the file **P06_46.xlsx**. The Cubs want to sign the pitchers who will add the most victories to the team. Determine who the Cubs should sign based on the following restrictions:
- At most, $12 million can be spent.
- At most, two right-handed pitchers can be signed.
- The Cubs cannot sign both BS and RS.

**47.** Based on Sonderman and Abrahamson (1985). In treating a brain tumor with radiation, physicians want the maximum amount of radiation possible to bombard the tissue containing the tumors. The constraint is, however, that there is a maximum amount of radiation that normal tissue can handle without suffering tissue damage. Physicians must therefore decide how to aim the radiation to maximize the radiation that hits the tumor tissue subject to the constraint of not damaging the normal tissue. As a simple example of this situation, suppose six types of radiation beams (beams differ in where they are aimed and their intensity) can be aimed at a tumor. The region containing the tumor has been divided into six regions: three regions contain tumors and three contain normal tissue. The amount of radiation delivered to each region by each type of beam is shown in the file **P06_47.xlsx**. If each region of normal tissue can handle at most 60 units of radiation, which beams should be used to maximize the total amount of radiation received by the tumors?

**48.** Because of excessive pollution on the Momiss River, the state of Momiss is going to build some pollution control stations. Three sites (1, 2, and 3) are under consideration. Momiss is interested in controlling the pollution levels of two pollutants (1 and 2). The state legislature requires that at least 80,000 tons of pollutant 1 and at least 50,000 tons of pollutant 2 be removed from the river. The relevant data for this problem are shown in the file **P06_48.xlsx**. (The last two rows indicate the number of tons of pollutants removed per ton treated.)
a. Determine how to minimize the cost of meeting the state legislature's goals.
b. Use SolverTable to analyze how a change in the requirement for pollutant 1 changes the optimal solution. Do the same for pollutant 2.

**49.** A manufacturer can sell product 1 at a profit of $2 per unit and product 2 at a profit of $5 per unit. Three units of raw material are needed to manufacture 1 unit of product 1, and 6 units of raw material are needed to manufacture 1 unit of product 2. A total of 120 units of raw material are available. If any product 1 is produced, a setup cost of $10 is incurred; if any product 2 is produced, a setup cost of $20 is incurred.
a. Determine how to maximize the manufacturer's profit.
b. Use SolverTable to analyze how a change in the setup cost for product 1 affects the optimal solution. Do the same for the setup cost for product 2.

**50.** A company is considering opening warehouses in four cities: New York, Los Angeles, Chicago, and Atlanta. Each warehouse can ship 100 units per week. The weekly fixed cost of keeping each warehouse open is $400 for New York, $500 for Los Angeles, $300 for Chicago, and $150 for Atlanta. Region 1 of the country requires 80 units per week, region 2 requires 70 units per week, and region 3 requires 40 units per week. The costs (including production and shipping costs) of sending 1 unit from a warehouse to a region are shown in the file **P06_50.xlsx**. The company wants to meet weekly demands at minimum cost, subject to the preceding information and the following restrictions:

- If the New York warehouse is opened, then the Los Angeles warehouse must be opened.
- At most two warehouses can be opened.
- Either the Atlanta or the Los Angeles warehouse must be opened.

**51.** Glueco produces three types of glue on two different production lines. Each line can be used by up to seven workers at a time. Workers are paid $500 per week on production line 1 and $900 per week on production line 2. For a week of production, it costs $1000 to set up production line 1 and $2000 to set up production line 2. During a week on a production line, each worker produces the number of units of glue shown in the file **P06_51.xlsx**. Each week, at least 120 units of glue 1, at least 150 units of glue 2, and at least 200 units of glue 3 must be produced. Determine how to minimize the total cost of meeting weekly demands.

**52.** Fruit Computer produces two types of computers: Pear computers and Apricot computers. The relevant data are given in the file **P06_52.xlsx**. The equipment cost is a fixed cost that is incurred if any of this type of computer is produced. A total of 3000 chips and 1200 hours of labor are available.
   **a.** Determine how Fruit can maximize its profit.
   **b.** Use SolverTable to analyze the effect on the optimal solution of a change in the selling price of Pear computers. Do the same for the selling price of Apricot computers.

**53.** Consider the Pigskin example (Example 3.3) from Chapter 3. Find Pigskin's optimal production policy if, in addition to the given production and holding costs, there is a fixed cost of $5000 during any month in which there is positive production. Assume now that storage capacity is 200 (hundreds of) footballs.

**54.** A product can be produced on four different machines. Each machine has a fixed setup cost, variable production cost per unit processed, and a production capacity, given in the file **P06_54.xlsx**. A total of 2000 units of the product must be produced. Determine how to minimize the total cost.

**55.** Bookco Publishers is considering publishing five textbooks. The maximum number of copies of each textbook that can be sold, the variable cost of producing each textbook, the selling price of each textbook, and the fixed cost of a production run for each book are given in the file **P06_55.xlsx**. For example, producing 2000 copies of book 1 brings in a revenue of $(2000)(50) = \$100,000$ but costs $80,000 + 25(2000) = \$130,000$.
   **a.** Determine how Bookco can maximize its profit if it can produce at most 10,000 books.
   **b.** Use SolverTable to analyze the effect on the optimal solution of a change in the demand for book 1. Repeat for the demands for the other books.

**56.** Comquat owns four production plants at which computer workstations are produced. Comquat can sell up to 20,000 computers per year at a price of $3500 per computer. For each plant, the production capacity, the production cost per computer, and the fixed cost of operating a plant for a year are given in the file **P06_56.xlsx**. Determine how Comquat can maximize its yearly profit from computer production.

**57.** Eastinghouse sells air conditioners. The annual demand for air conditioners in each region of the country is as follows: East, 100,000; South, 150,000; Midwest, 110,000; and West, 90,000. Eastinghouse is considering building its air conditioners in four different cities: New York, Atlanta, Chicago, and Los Angeles. The cost of producing an air conditioner in a city and shipping it to a region of the country is given in the file **P06_57.xlsx**. Any factory can produce up to 150,000 air conditioners per year. The annual fixed cost of operating a factory in each city is also given in the file **P06_57.xlsx**. At least 50,000 units of the Midwest demand for air conditioners must come from New York, and at least 50,000 units of the Midwest demand must come from Atlanta. Determine how Eastinghouse can minimize the annual cost of meeting demand for air conditioners.

**58.** During the next five periods, the demands listed in the file **P06_58.xlsx** must be met on time. At the beginning of period 1, the inventory level is 0. During each period when production occurs, a setup cost of $250 and a per-unit production cost of $2 are incurred. At the end of each period, a per-unit holding cost of $1 is incurred. Determine the cost-minimizing production schedule.

**59.** Ford has four automobile plants. Each is capable of producing the Focus, Mustang, or Crown Victoria, but it can produce only one of these cars. The fixed cost of operating each plant for a year and the variable cost of producing a car of each type at each plant are given in the file **P06_59.xlsx**. Ford faces the following restrictions:

- Each plant can produce only one type of car.
- The total production of each type of car must be at a single plant. For example, if any Mustangs are

made at plant 1, then all Mustangs must be made there.

- Each year, Ford must produce 5 million of each type of car.
    a. Determine how to minimize the annual cost of producing these cars.
    b. Use SolverTable to see how a change in the demand for a type of car changes the optimal solution. Do this separately for each type of car.
    c. Use SolverTable to see how the optimal solution is affected by a change in the variable cost of producing a Focus at plant 4.

**60.** At a machine tool plant, five jobs must be completed each day. The time it takes to do each job depends on the machine used to do the job. If a machine is used at all, a setup time is required. The relevant times (in minutes) are given in the file **P06_60.xlsx**.
a. Determine how to minimize the sum of the setup and machine operation times needed to complete all jobs.
b. Use SolverTable to see how a change in the setup time for machine 4 changes the optimal solution.
c. Use SolverTable to see how a change in the required time for machine 1 to complete job 3 changes the optimal solution.

**61.** Heinsco produces tomato sauce at five different plants. The tomato sauce is then shipped to one of three warehouses, where it is stored until it is shipped to one of the company's four customers. The following inputs for the problem are given in the file **P06_61.xlsx**:
- The plant capacities (in tons)
- The cost per ton of producing tomato sauce at each plant and shipping it to each warehouse
- The cost of shipping a ton of sauce from each warehouse to each customer
- The customer requirements (in tons) of sauce
- The fixed annual cost of operating each plant and warehouse

Heinsco must decide which plants and warehouses to open, and which routes from plants to warehouses and from warehouses to customers to use. All customer demand must be met. A given customer's demand can be met from more than one warehouse, and a given plant can ship to more than one warehouse.
a. Determine the minimum-cost method for meeting customer demands.
b. Use SolverTable to see how a change in the capacity of plant 1 affects the total cost.
c. Use SolverTable to see how a change in the customer 2 demand affects the total cost.

**62.** Suppose in the previous problem that each customer's demand must be met from a *single* warehouse. Solve the problem with this restriction.

**63.** Based on Walker (1974). The Smalltown Fire Department currently has seven conventional ladder companies and seven alarm boxes. The two closest ladder companies to each alarm box are listed in the file **P06_63.xlsx**. The town council wants to maximize the number of conventional ladder companies that can be replaced with "tower" ladder companies. Unfortunately, political considerations dictate that a conventional company can be replaced only if, after replacement, at least one of the two closest companies to each alarm box is still a conventional company. Determine how to maximize the number of conventional companies that can be replaced by tower companies.

**64.** At Blair General Hospital, six types of surgical operations are performed. The types of operations each surgeon is qualified to perform (indicated by an X) are listed in the file **P06_64.xlsx**. Suppose that surgeons 1 and 2 dislike each other and cannot be on duty at the same time. Determine the minimum number of surgeons required so that the hospital can perform all types of surgery.

**65.** State University must purchase 1100 computers from three vendors. Vendor 1 charges $500 per computer plus a total delivery charge of $5000. Vendor 2 charges $350 per computer plus a total delivery charge of $4000. Vendor 3 charges $250 per computer plus a total delivery charge of $6000. Vendor 1 will sell the university at most 500 computers, vendor 2, at most 900, and vendor 3, at most 400. The minimum order from a vendor is 200 computers. Determine how to minimize the cost of purchasing the needed computers.

**66.** Eastinghouse ships 12,000 capacitors per month to its customers. The capacitors can be produced at three different plants. The production capacity, fixed monthly cost of operation, and variable cost of producing a capacitor at each plant are given in the file **P06_66.xlsx**. The fixed cost for a plant is incurred only if the plant is used to make any capacitors. If a plant is used at all, at least 3000 capacitors per month must be produced at the plant. Determine how to minimize the company's monthly costs of meeting its customers' demands.

**67.** Based on Liggett (1973). A court decision has stated that the enrollment of each high school in Metropolis must be at least 20% black. The numbers of black students and white students in each of the city's five school districts are listed in the file **P06_67.xlsx**. The distance (in miles) that a student in each district must travel to each high school is also shown in the file **P06_67.xlsx**. School board policy requires that all students in a given district must attend the same school. Assuming that each school must have an enrollment of at least 150 students, determine how to minimize the total distance that Metropolis students must travel to high school.

**68.** Based on Westerberg, Bjorklund, and Hultman (1977). Newcor's steel mill has received an order for 25 tons of steel. The steel must be 5% carbon and 5% molybdenum by weight. The steel is manufactured by combining three types of metal: steel ingots, scrap steel, and alloys. Four individual steel ingots are available. At most, one of each can be purchased. The weight (in tons), cost per ton, and the carbon and molybdenum content of each ingot are given in the file **P06_68.xlsx**. Three types of alloys can be purchased. The cost per ton and chemical makeup of each alloy are also given in the file **P06_68.xlsx**. Steel scrap can be purchased at a cost of $100 per ton. Steel scrap contains 3% carbon and 9% molybdenum. Determine how Newcor can minimize the cost of filling its order.

69. Based on Boykin (1985). Chemco annually produces 359 million pounds of the chemical maleic anhydride. A total of four reactors are available to produce maleic anhydride. Each reactor can be run on one of three settings. The cost (in thousands of dollars) and pounds produced (in millions) annually for each reactor and each setting are given in the file **P06_69.xlsx**. A reactor can be run on only one setting for the entire year. Determine how Chemco can minimize the cost of meeting its annual demand for maleic anhydride.

70. Based on Zangwill (1992). Hallco runs a day shift and a night shift. Regardless of the number of units produced, the only production cost during a shift is a setup cost. It costs $8000 to run the day shift and $4500 to run the night shift. Demand for the next two days is as follows: day 1, 2000; night 1, 3000; day 2, 2000; night 2, 3000. It costs $1 per unit to hold a unit in inventory for a shift.
   a. Determine a production schedule that minimizes the sum of setup and inventory costs. All demand must be met on time. (*Note:* Not all shifts have to be run.)
   b. After listening to a seminar on the virtues of the Japanese theory of production, Hallco has cut the setup cost of its day shift to $1000 per shift and the setup cost of its night shift to $3500 per shift. Now determine a production schedule that minimizes the sum of setup and inventory costs. All demand must be met on time. Show that the decrease in setup costs has actually raised the average inventory level. Is this reasonable?

71. Based on Fitzsimmons and Allen (1983). The State of Texas frequently audits companies doing business in Texas. Because these companies often have headquarters located outside the state, auditors must be sent to out-of-state locations. Each year, auditors must make 500 trips to cities in the Northeast, 400 trips to cities in the Midwest, 300 trips to cities in the West, and 400 trips to cities in the South. Texas is considering basing auditors in Chicago, New York, Atlanta, and Los Angeles. The annual cost of basing auditors in any city is $100,000. The cost of sending an auditor from any

of these cities to a given region of the country is given in the file **P06_71.xlsx**. Determine how to minimize the annual cost of conducting out-of-state audits.

## Skill-Extending Problems

72. You have been assigned to arrange the songs on the cassette version of Madonna's latest album. (Feel free to substitute your own favorite rock star for Madonna!) A cassette tape has two sides (1 and 2). The songs on each side of the cassette must total between 14 and 16 minutes in length. The length and type of each song are given in the file **P06_72.xlsx**. The assignment of songs to the tape must satisfy the following conditions:
   - Each side must have exactly two ballads.
   - Side 1 must have at least three hit songs.
   - Either song 5 or song 6 must be on side 1. Determine whether there is an arrangement of songs satisfying these restrictions. (*Hint:* You do not need a target cell when using Solver. In the Solver dialog box, just leave the Target Cell box empty.)

73. Cousin Bruzie of radio station WABC schedules radio commercials in 60-second blocks. This hour, the station has sold time for commercials of 15, 16, 20, 25, 30, 35, 40, and 50 seconds. Determine the minimum number of 60-second blocks of commercials that must be scheduled to fit in all the current hour's commercials. (*Hint:* Certainly no more than eight blocks of time are needed.)

74. Based on Bean et al. (1988). Simon's Mall has 10,000 square feet of space to rent and wants to determine the types of stores that should occupy the mall. The minimum number and maximum number of each type of store (along with the square footage of each type) are given in the file **P06_74.xlsx**. The annual profit made by each type of store depends on how many stores of that type are in the mall. This dependence is also given in the file **P06_74.xlsx** (where all profits are in units of $10,000). For example, if two department stores are in the mall, each department store will earn $210,000 profit per year. Each store pays 5% of its annual profit as rent to Simon's. Determine how Simon can maximize its rental income from the mall.

75. Indiana University's Business School has two rooms that seat 50 students, one room that seats 100 students, and one room that seats 150 students. Classes are held 5 hours a day. At present, the four types of requests for rooms are listed in the file **P06_75.xlsx**. The business school must decide how many requests of each type to assign to each type of room. Suppose that classes that cannot be assigned to a business school room are assigned to another campus building. Determine how to assign classes to minimize the number of hours students spend each week outside the business building.

**76.** Based on Efroymson and Ray (1966). Breadco Bakeries is a new bakery chain that sells bread to customers throughout the state of Indiana. Breadco is considering building bakeries in three locations: Evansville, Indianapolis, and South Bend. Each bakery can bake up to 900,000 loaves of bread each year. The cost of building a bakery at each site is $5 million in Evansville, $4 million in Indianapolis, and $4.5 million in South Bend. To simplify the problem, we assume that Breadco has only three customers. Their demands each year are 700,000 loaves (customer 1); 400,000 loaves (customer 2); and 300,000 loaves (customer 3). The total cost of baking and shipping a loaf of bread to a customer is given in the file **P06_76.xlsx**. Assume that future shipping and production costs are discounted at a rate of 12% per year. Assume that once built, a bakery lasts forever. How would you minimize Breadco's total cost of meeting demand, present and future? (*Note:* Although your model is actually linear, Solver might report that "the conditions for Assume Linear Model are not satisfied" if you do not scale your changing cells and costs in "natural" units, as discussed in Chapter 3. For example, costs can be expressed in units of $1 million or $100,000, and annual shipments can be expressed in units of 100,000 loaves.)

**77.** On Monday morning, you have $3000 in cash on hand. For the next seven days, the following cash requirements must be met: Monday, $5000; Tuesday, $6000; Wednesday, $9000; Thursday, $2000; Friday, $7000; Saturday, $2000; Sunday, $3000. At the beginning of each day, you must decide how much money (if any) to withdraw from the bank. It costs $10 to make a withdrawal of any size. You believe that the opportunity cost of having $1 of cash on hand for a year is $0.20. Assume that opportunity costs are incurred on each day's ending balance. Determine how much money you should withdraw from the bank during each of the next seven days.

**78.** Based on Eaton et al. (1985). Gotham City has been divided into eight districts. The time (in minutes) it takes an ambulance to travel from one district to another is shown in the file **P06_78.xlsx**. The population of each district (in thousands) is as follows: district 1, 40; district 2, 30; district 3, 35; district 4, 20; district 5, 15; district 6, 50; district 7, 45; district 8, 60. Suppose Gotham City has $n$ ambulance locations. Determine the locations of ambulances that maximize the number of people who live within two minutes of an ambulance. Do this separately for $n = 1$; $n = 2$; $n = 3$; $n = 4$. (*Hint:* Set it up so that SolverTable can solve all four problems simultaneously.)

**79.** Arthur Ross, Inc., must complete many corporate tax returns during the period February 15 to April 15. This year, the company must begin and complete the five jobs shown in the file **P06_79.xlsx** during this 8-week period. Arthur Ross employs 4 full-time accountants who normally work 40 hours per week. If necessary, however, they can work up to 20 hours of overtime per week for which they are paid $100 per hour. Determine how Arthur Ross can minimize the overtime cost incurred in completing all jobs by April 15.

**80.** Based on Muckstadt and Wilson (1968). PSI believes it will need the amounts of generating capacity (in millions of kwh) shown in the file **P06_80.xlsx** during the next five years. The company has a choice of building (and then operating) power plants with the capacities (in millions of kwh) and costs (in millions of dollars) also shown in the file **P06_80.xlsx**. Determine how to minimize the total cost of meeting PSI's generating capacity requirements for the next five years.

**81.** Houseco Developers is considering erecting three office buildings. The time (in years) required to complete each of them and the number of workers required to be on the job at all times are shown in the file **P06_81.xlsx**. After a building is completed, it brings in the following amount of rent per year: building 1, $50,000; building 2, $30,000; building 3, $40,000. Houseco faces the following constraints:

- During each year, 60 workers are available.
- At most, one building can be started during any year.
- Building 2 must be completed by the end of year 4.

Determine the maximum total rent that can be earned by Houseco by the end of year 4.

**82.** Four trucks are available to deliver milk to five grocery stores. The capacity and daily operating cost of each truck are shown in the file **P06_82xlsx**. The demand of each grocery store can be supplied by only one truck, but a truck can deliver to more than one grocery. The daily demands of each grocery are as follows: grocery 1, 100 gallons; grocery 2, 200 gallons; grocery 3, 300 gallons; grocery 4, 500 gallons; grocery 5, 800 gallons. Determine how to minimize the daily cost of meeting the demands of the five groceries.

**83.** A county is going to build two hospitals. There are nine cities in which the hospitals can be built. The number of hospital visits per year made by people in each city and the $x$-$y$ coordinates of each city are listed in the file **P06_83.xlsx**. The county's goal is to minimize the total distance that patients must travel to hospitals. Where should it locate the hospitals? (*Hint:* You will need to determine the distance between each pair of cities. An easy way to do this is with lookup tables.)

**84.** It is currently the beginning of 2006. Gotham City is trying to sell municipal bonds to support improvements in recreational facilities and highways. The face values (in thousands of dollars) of the bonds and the due dates at which principal comes due are listed in the file **P06_84.xlsx**. (The due dates are the *beginnings* of the years listed.) The Gold and Silver Company (GS) wants to underwrite Gotham City's bonds. A proposal to Gotham for underwriting this issue consists of the following: (1) an interest rate, 3%, 4%, 5%, 6%, or 7%, for each bond, where coupons are paid annually; and (2) an upfront premium paid by GS to Gotham City. GS has determined the set of fair prices (in thousands of dollars) for the bonds listed in the file **P06_84.xlsx**. For example, if GS underwrites bond 2 maturing in 2009 at 5%, it would charge Gotham City $444,000 for that bond. GS is constrained to use at most three different interest rates. GS wants to make a profit of at least $46,000, where its profit is equal to the sale price of the bonds minus the face value of the bonds minus the premium GS pays to Gotham City. To maximize the chance that GS will get Gotham City's business, GS wants to minimize the total cost of the bond issue to Gotham City, which is equal to the total interest on the bonds minus the premium paid by GS. For example, if the year 2008 bond (bond 1) is issued at a 4% rate, then Gotham City must pay 2 years of coupon interest: 2(0.04)($700,000) = $56,000. What assignment of interest rates to each bond and upfront premiums ensure that GS will make the desired profit (assuming it gets the contract) and maximize the chance of GS getting Gotham City's business?

85. Based on Spencer et al. (1990). When you lease 800 phone numbers from AT&T for telemarketing, AT&T uses an optimization model to tell you where you should locate calling centers to minimize your operating costs over a 10-year horizon. To illustrate the model, suppose you are considering seven calling center locations: Boston, New York, Charlotte, Dallas, Chicago, Los Angeles, and Omaha. You know the average cost (in dollars) incurred if a telemarketing call is made from any of these cities to any region of the country. You also know the hourly wage that you must pay workers in each city. This information is listed in the file **P06_85.xlsx**. Assume that an average call requires 4 minutes of labor. You make calls 250 days per year, and the average number of calls made per day to each region of the country is also listed in the file **P06_85.xlsx**. The cost (in millions of dollars) of building a calling center in each possible location is also listed in this file. Each calling center can make up to 5000 calls per day. Given this information, how can you minimize the discounted cost (at 10% per year) of running the telemarketing operation for 10 years? Assume all wage and calling costs are paid at the *ends* of the respective years.

86. Consider the following puzzle. You are to select four three-letter "words" from the following list: DBA DEG ADI FFD GHI BCD FDF BAI. For each word, you earn a score equal to the position of the word's third letter in the alphabet. For example, DBA earns a score of 1, DEG earns a score of 7, and so on. Your goal is to choose the four words that maximize your total score, subject to the following constraint: The sum of the positions in the alphabet for the first letters of the four words chosen must be at least as large as the sum of the positions in the alphabet for the second letters of the words chosen. Use Solver to solve this problem.

87. Powerco needs to determine a capacity expansion plan to meet Bloomington's power needs for the next 20 years. The current capacity is 5000 kwh. The demand for the current year is 4000 kwh, and demand is expected to increase by 1000 kwh in each succeeding year. At the beginning of each year, Powerco must determine the amount of capacity to add, given the following inputs:

- Any year in which capacity is added, a fixed cost of $120,000 is incurred plus a cost of $120 per kwh of capacity.
- At most 10,000 kwh of capacity can be added in a single year.
- It costs $25 per year to maintain a unit of capacity.
- It costs $12 per year to produce a kwh.
- If production does not meet demand, a shortage cost of $80 per kwh short is incurred.

Develop a linear integer model to help Powerco minimize its costs for the next 20 years.

88. Based on Angel et al. (2003). A fertilizer company is trying to determine the cheapest fertilizer mix that provides desired amounts of nutrients. The mix is made by combining the following fertilizers: SSA, SPO, GUR, TSP, KCI, FERT, and SPF. The mix cannot contain both GUR and TSP. The percentage of potassium (K), sulfur (S), calcium (Ca), sodium (Na) and phosphorus (P) in each fertilizer is listed in the file **P06_88.xlsx**. For example, a pound of SSA is 16% K and 26% Na. The mix must contain at least 200 pounds of K, 220 pounds of S, 240 pounds of Ca, 260 pounds of Na, and 280 pounds of P. The mix cannot contain both GUR and TSP, because if both are present in the mix, the affect of other fertilizers is nullified. The cost per pound (in cents) of each fertilizer is also listed in the file **P06_88.xlsx**. Develop a linear integer model to find the minimum cost fertilizer mixture that meets the stated chemical requirements.

89. Based on Kalvaitishi and Posgay (1974). A direct mail company must determine which of 10 mailing lists to use this month to generate a catalog mailing. The number of names in each list, the mainframe computer time (in hours) needed to process the list, the labor time per letter mailed for each list (in minutes), the number of names (in hundreds of thousands) on each list, the response rate from each list, and the average

profit per order from each list are given in the file **P06_89.xlsx**. It costs $100,000 per month to rent a mainframe computer. A rented computer can be used for up to 100 hours in any given month. The company has 400 employees who each work 160 hours per month. Develop a linear integer model to help the company maximize its monthly profit.

90. A single-shelf bookcase can hold books that are a total of 24 feet wide. We need to store 19 books of the widths (in feet) listed in the file **P06_90.xlsx**. Develop a linear integer model to determine the minimum number of bookcases that are needed to store all 19 books.

91. We are scheduling company interviews at the annual university career fair. Five interview rooms are available. Interviews are conducted from 9 AM to 5 PM. Each company wants all its interviews conducted in a single room. The time preferences for the companies are listed in the file **P06_91.xlsx**. Develop a linear integer model to determine whether five rooms are sufficient to complete the interviews.

92. The file **P06_92.xlsx** lists the distances between 21 U.S. cities. We want to locate liver transplant centers in a subset of these 21 cities.
    a. Suppose we plan to build four liver transplant centers and our goal is to minimize the maximum distance a person in any of these cities has to travel to a center. In which cities should the centers be located?
    b. How many centers are needed, and in which cities should they be located, so that residents of all cities are within 800 miles of a transplant center? (The model must be linear.)
    c. We know that a transplant center is sometimes filled to capacity. With this in mind, we would like everyone to be relatively close to two transplant centers. How many centers are needed, and in which cities should the centers be located, to ensure that residents of all cities are within 800 miles of *two* transplant centers? (Again, the model must be linear.)
    d. The file **P06_92.xlsx** also lists the number of people (in millions) living in each city's metropolitan area. Where should we locate three transplant centers to maximize the number of people within 800 miles of a transplant center?

93. This problem is based on Motorola's online method for choosing suppliers. Suppose Motorola solicits bids from five suppliers for eight products. The list price for each product and the quantity of each product that Motorola needs to purchase during the next year are listed in the file **P06_93.xlsx**. Each supplier has submitted the percentage discount it will offer on each product. These percentages are also listed in the file. For example, supplier 1 offers a 7% discount on product 1

and a 30% discount on product 2. The following considerations also apply:
- There is an administrative cost of $5000 associated with setting up a supplier's account. For example, if Motorola uses three suppliers, it incurs an administrative cost of $15,000.
- To ensure reliability, no supplier can supply more than 80% of Motorola's demand for any product.
- A supplier must supply an integer amount of each product it supplies.

Develop a linear integer model to help Motorola minimize the sum of its purchase and administrative costs.

94. An aged merchant of Baghdad was much respected by all who knew him. He had three sons, and it was a rule of his life to treat them equally. Whenever one son received a present, the other two each received a present of equal value. One day this worthy man fell sick and died, bequeathing all of his possessions to his three sons in equal shares. The only difficulty that arose was over the stock of honey. There were exactly 21 barrels. The old man left instructions that each son should not only receive an equal quantity of honey, but each son should receive exactly the same number of barrels, and no honey should be transferred from barrel to barrel on account of the waste involved. Now, as 7 of these barrels were full of honey, 7 were half full, and 7 were empty, this was quite a puzzle, especially because each brother objected to taking more than 4 barrels of the same description (full, half full, or empty). Develop a linear integer model to solve this puzzle.

95. In the equation SEND + MORE = MONEY, each letter represents a different digit (0–9). The addition is done in the usual way from right to left, first adding D and E to obtain Y (possibly with a carry-over), then adding N and R, and so on. Develop a linear integer model to determine the digit represented by each letter.

96. You are moving away from Bloomington and need to load a truck. The items that will go on the truck must all be packed in boxes. The size (in cubic feet) of each item and each available box are listed in the file **P06_96.xlsx**. For example, the first item requires 87 cubic feet, and the first box can hold 126 cubic feet of stuff. Develop a linear integer model to find the minimum amount of cubic feet needed to pack all items in boxes.

97. Suppose you own 11 bronze coins worth a total of $150, 11 silver coins worth a total of $160, and 11 gold coins worth a total of $170. Develop a linear integer model to find a combination of coins worth exactly $110.

98. Based on McBride and Zufryden (1988). A company is trying to determine which of five possible products to include in its product line. The fixed cost of

producing each product and the unit profit for each product are listed in the file **P06_98.xlsx**. There are five customer segments. The number of customers in each segment and the utility each customer segment associates with each product are also listed in this file. If a consumer believes that all available products have a negative utility, this customer will buy nothing. Otherwise, each customer will buy the available product that has the largest utility. For example, if products 1, 2, and 3 are available, customer segment 4 will purchase product 3. Determine which products the company should produce to maximize its profit. (*Hint:* Use a binary changing cell for each product and a binary changing cell for each customer segment/product combination. To ensure that a customer buys only the product with the largest utility, include the following constraint for each combination of product and customer segment:

$$U_{cj}x_j \geq U_{ci}x_i - M(1 - y_{cj}) \text{ for each } i, j, c$$

Here, $U_{cj}$ is the utility for customer segment $c$ buying product $j$, $x_j$ is a binary for product $j$ being offered, $y_{cj}$ is a binary for customer segment $c$ buying product $j$, and $M$ is a large number ($M$ equal to the largest product utility will work). This constraint ensures that the $y_{cj}$ binary can equal 1 only if the binary $x_j$ equals 1, that is, customer segment $c$ can buy product $j$ only if it is included in the product line. Note that if $y_{cj}$ is 0, then this inequality is automatically satisfied.)

## Modeling Problems

99. Suppose that you want to divide a state containing 12 cities into 5 congressional districts. How might you use IP to assign cities to districts?

100. The Wanderers Insurance Company has hired you to determine the number of sales divisions into which the country should be divided. Each division will need a president, a vice president, and a divisional staff. The time needed to call on a client will depend on the distance of the salesperson from the client. Discuss how you would determine the optimal number of sales divisions and the allocation of the company's salesforce to the various divisions.

101. Ten different types of brownies are sold. You are thinking of developing a new brownie for sale. Brownies are rated on the basis of 5 qualities: price, chocolate flavor, chewiness, sweetness, and ease of preparation. You want to group the 10 brownies on the market into 3 clusters. Each cluster should contain brownies that are relatively similar.
    a. Why would this be useful to you?
    b. How would you do it?

102. Telco, a national telemarketing firm, usually picks a number of sites around the country from which it makes its calls. As a service, AD&D's telecommunication marketing department wants to help Telco choose the number and location of its sites. How can IP be used to approach this problem?

This case deals with strategic planning issues for a large company. The main issue is planning the company's production capacity for the coming year. At issue is the overall level of capacity and the type of capacity—for example, the degree of *flexibility* in the manufacturing system. The main tool used to aid the company's planning process is a mixed integer linear programming (MILP) model. A *mixed* integer program has both integer and continuous variables.

## Problem Statement

The Giant Motor Company (GMC) produces three lines of cars for the domestic (U.S.) market: Lyras, Libras, and Hydras. The Lyra is a relatively inexpensive subcompact car that appeals mainly to first-time car owners and to households using it as a second car for commuting. The Libra is a sporty compact car that is sleeker, faster, and roomier than the Lyra. Without any options, the Libra costs slightly more than the Lyra; additional options increase the price. The Hydra is the luxury car of the GMC line. It is significantly more expensive than the Lyra and Libra, and it has the highest profit margin of the three cars.

## Retooling Options for Capacity Expansion

Currently GMC has three manufacturing plants in the United States. Each plant is dedicated to producing a single line of cars. In its planning for the coming year, GMC is considering the retooling of its Lyra and/or Libra plants. Retooling either plant would

represent a major expense for the company. The retooled plants would have significantly increased production capacities. Although having greater *fixed* costs, the retooled plants would be more efficient and have lower *marginal* production costs—that is, higher *marginal* profit contributions. In addition, the retooled plants would be *flexible*—they would have the capability of producing more than one line of cars.

The characteristics of the current plants and the retooled plants are given in Table 6.16. The retooled Lyra and Libra plants are prefaced by the word *new*. The fixed costs and capacities in Table 6.16 are given on an annual basis. A dash in the profit margin section indicates that the plant cannot manufacture that line of car. For example, the new Lyra plant would be capable of producing both Lyras and Libras but not Hydras. The new Libra plant would be capable of producing any of the three lines of cars. Note, however, that the new Libra plant has a slightly lower profit margin for producing Hydras than the Hydra plant. The flexible new Libra plant is capable of producing the luxury Hydra model but is not as efficient as the current Hydra plant that is dedicated to Hydra production.

The fixed costs are annual costs incurred by GMC, independent of the number of cars produced by the plant. For the current plant configurations, the fixed costs include property taxes, insurance, payments on the loan that was taken out to construct the plant, and so on. If a plant is retooled, the fixed costs will include the previous fixed costs plus the additional cost of the renovation. The additional

**Table 6.16** Plant Characteristics

|  | Lyra | Libra | Hydra | New Lyra | New Libra |
|---|---|---|---|---|---|
| Capacity (in 1000s) | 1000 | 800 | 900 | 1600 | 1800 |
| Fixed cost (in $millions) | 2000 | 2000 | 2600 | 3400 | 3700 |
| Profit Margin by Car Line (in $1000s) | | | | | |
| Lyra | 2 | — | — | 2.5 | 2.3 |
| Libra | — | 3 | — | 3.0 | 3.5 |
| Hydra | — | — | 5 | — | 4.8 |

renovation cost will be an annual cost representing the cost of the renovation amortized over a long period.

## Demand for GMC Cars

Short-term demand forecasts have been very reliable in the past and are expected to be reliable in the future. The demand for GMC cars for the coming year is given in Table 6.17.

**Table 6.17** Demand for GMC Cars

|       | Demand (in 1000s) |
|-------|-------------------|
| Lyra  | 1400              |
| Libra | 1100              |
| Hydra | 800               |

A quick comparison of plant capacities and demands in Table 6.16 and Table 6.17 indicates that GMC is faced with insufficient capacity. Partially offsetting the lack of capacity is the phenomenon of **demand diversion.** If a potential car buyer walks into a GMC dealer showroom wanting to buy a Lyra but the dealer is out of stock, frequently the salesperson can convince the customer to purchase the better Libra car, which is in stock. Unsatisfied demand for the Lyra is said to be *diverted* to the Libra. Only rarely in this situation can the salesperson convince the customer to switch to the luxury Hydra model.

From past experience, GMC estimates that 30% of unsatisfied demand for Lyras is diverted to demand for Libras and 5% to demand for Hydras. Similarly, 10% of unsatisfied demand for Libras is diverted to demand for Hydras. For example, if the demand for Lyras is 1,400,000 cars, then the unsatisfied demand will be 400,000 if no capacity is added. Out of this unsatisfied demand, 120,000 ($= 400,000 \times 0.3$) will materialize as demand for Libras, and 20,000 ($= 400,000 \times 0.05$) will materialize as demand for Hydras. Similarly, if the demand for Libras is 1,220,000 cars (1,100,000 original demand plus 120,000 demand diverted from Lyras), then the unsatisfied demand for Lyras would be 420,000 if no capacity is added. Out of this unsatisfied demand, 42,000 ($= 420,000 \times 0.1$) will materialize as demand for Hydras. All other unsatisfied demand is lost to competitors. The pattern of demand diversion is summarized in Table 6.18.

**Table 6.18** Demand Diversion Matrix

|       | Lyra | Libra | Hydra |
|-------|------|-------|-------|
| Lyra  | NA   | 0.3   | 0.05  |
| Libra | 0    | NA    | 0.10  |
| Hydra | 0    | 0.0   | NA    |

## Question

GMC wants to decide whether to retool the Lyra and Libra plants. In addition, GMC wants to determine its production plan at each plant in the coming year. Based on the previous data, formulate a MILP model for solving GMC's production planning–capacity expansion problem for the coming year. ∎

# 6.2 SELECTING TELECOMMUNICATION CARRIERS TO OBTAIN VOLUME DISCOUNTS[10]

During 2001, many European markets for mobile phones reached saturation. Because of this, mobile phone operators started to shift their focus from growth and market share to cutting costs. One way to do this is to reduce spending on international calls. These calls are routed through network operating companies called carriers. The carriers charge per call-minute for each destination, and they often use a discount on total business volume to price their services. A mobile phone operator must decide how to allocate destinations to carriers.

V-Mobile, a mobile phone operator in Denmark, must make such a decision for a $T$-month planning horizon when it has $C$ carriers to choose from, $D$ destinations for its customers' calls, and there are $I$ price intervals for a typical carrier. (These intervals define a carrier's discount structure.) The inputs include the following:

- The price per call-minute for destination $d$ from carrier $c$ in price interval $i$ in month $t$
- The (forecasted) number of call-minutes for destination $d$ in month $t$
- The lower and upper limits for carrier $c$ in price interval $i$

- The lower and upper limits on capacity (number of call-minutes) for carrier $c$ in month $t$
- The penalty per call-minute (to discourage poor-quality options) for carrier $c$ to destination $d$ in month $t$

V-Mobile wants to find a least-cost way of routing its call-minutes through the various carriers. Of course, it hopes to take advantage of price discounts offered by the carriers.

The file **Carrier Selection.xlsx** provides inputs for one version of V-Mobile's problem. This version has $T = 2, C = 3, D = 5,$ and $I = 3$. The decision variables (changing cells) should include the following:

- The number of call-minutes routed through carrier $c$ to destination $d$ in price interval $i$ in month $t$
- A binary variable for each carrier $c$ and price interval $i$ combination that equals 1 if the total call-minutes for this carrier (over all destinations and months) falls in price interval $i$, and equals 0 otherwise.

Develop an optimization model that helps V-Mobile allocate its international calls in a cost-efficient manner. Then write a brief memo stating (1) how V-Mobile should implement your results for this particular version of the problem, and (2) how the model would need to be modified for other potential problem parameters. ∎

---

[10] This case is based on van de Klundert et al. (2005).

# Nonlinear Optimization Models

## PORTFOLIO OPTIMIZATION AT GE

Portfolio optimization, one of the models discussed in this chapter, is big business. This is illustrated in the article by Chalermkraivuth et al. (2005). They describe how GE Asset Management Incorporated (GEAM), a wholly owned subsidiary of General Electric Company (GE), manages investment portfolios on behalf of various GE units and more than 200 unaffiliated clients worldwide worth billions of dollars. GEAM manages portfolios of assets produced by various insurance businesses, and its investments are primarily in corporate and government bonds. The authors developed a special-purpose algorithm for finding optimal portfolios. Since 2003, their algorithm has been used to optimize more than 30 portfolios valued at over $30 billion. They estimate that, based on $100 billion of assets, the present value of potential benefits from their approach is approximately $75 million over a five-year period.

As in most portfolio optimization problems, GEAM wants to find portfolios that provide appropriate risk/return trade-offs (preferably higher expected returns and lower risk). However, the insurance industry is more complex than this, where portfolio managers must choose the assets within a portfolio so that their characteristics match those of the firms' liabilities. They try to do this in such a way that the bonds and other financial instruments in the portfolio are "immunized" against changes in the interest rates—one main source of risk in bond portfolios. This can be done through a well-developed financial theory of matching the "duration" and "convexity" of the assets and liabilities within an acceptable tolerance. [See Luenberger

345

(1998), for example, for a discussion of the financial theory.] Using this theory, the authors formulated a portfolio optimization model using the variance of economic surplus as a measure of risk, where economic surplus is the difference between the market value of assets and liabilities.

Unfortunately, most GEAM portfolios consist of a large number of securities, and the risk measure is inherently nonlinear. This combination—a large model with inherent nonlinearity—is extremely difficult for even the best commercial solvers. Therefore, the authors developed their own algorithm to locate the efficient frontier, that is, the set of portfolios that provide the maximum expected return for a given level of risk. This approach is typical in the management science field. If analysts encounter a problem that is either too large or too difficult to solve with existing algorithms, they try to develop a new algorithm, usually specific to the problem, which can do the job. In the authors' algorithm, they first find the point on the efficient frontier that maximizes the expected return, without any regard for risk. The result is typically a very risky portfolio. Then, in general, given a set of portfolios on the efficient frontier, they find a nearby portfolio with slightly less risk and slightly less expected return than the previous one. To do this, they approximate the nonlinear portfolio variance by a *linear* function. This approximation has two properties that recommend it: (1) it is a very good approximation in the area of the previous optimal portfolio, and (2) it yields a *linear* programming model that can be solved fairly quickly.

In the modern spirit of management science, the authors went one step further. They not only developed an algorithm that could be used to solve GEAM's large problems, but they also developed a Web-based implementation that is easy for their clients to use. With this system, which has been in place for several years, users do not need to install software on their desktops. They can instead interact via the Web, which provides the user interface. The Web application processes user inputs and requests and displays results. An optimization engine called MATLAB handles all of the heavy number crunching on a centralized application server, and the required data is stored and accessed from an Oracle database. Obviously, this is a complex setup, and months went into its development. But this is a small price to pay for the benefits the portfolio optimization model provides to GE and its customers. ■

## 7.1 INTRODUCTION

In many complex optimization problems, the objective and/or the constraints are nonlinear functions of the decision variables. Such optimization problems are called **nonlinear programming** (NLP) problems. In this chapter, we discuss a variety of interesting problems with inherent nonlinearities, from product pricing to portfolio optimization to rating sports teams.

A model can become nonlinear for several reasons, including the following:

■ There are nonconstant returns to scale, which means that the effect of some input on some output is nonlinear. For example, consider the effect of advertising on sales. Advertising typically creates a saturation effect, so that beyond some level, extra advertising dollars have very little effect on sales—much less than the effect of initial advertising dollars. This violates the proportionality assumption of linear models discussed in Chapter 3.

- In pricing models, where we try to maximize revenue (or profit), revenue is price multiplied by quantity sold, and price is typically the decision variable. Because quantity sold is related to price through a demand function, revenue is really price multiplied by a function of price, and this product is a nonlinear function of price. For example, even if the demand function is linear in price, the product of price and demand is quadratic in price because it includes a squared price term.

- We often try to find the model that best fits observed data. To measure the goodness of the fit, we typically sum the squared differences between the observed values and the model's predicted values. Then we attempt to minimize this sum of squared differences. The squaring introduces nonlinearity.

- In one of the most used financial models, the portfolio optimization model, we try to invest in various securities to achieve high return and low risk. The risk is typically measured as the variance (or standard deviation) of the portfolio, and it is inherently a nonlinear function of the decision variables (the investment amounts).

*Nonlinear models are often more realistic than linear models, but they are also more difficult to solve.*

As these examples illustrate, nonlinear models are common in the real world. In fact, it is probably more accurate to state that truly *linear* models are hard to find. The real world often behaves in a nonlinear manner, so when we model a problem with LP, we are typically *approximating* reality. By allowing nonlinearities in our models, we can often create more realistic models. Unfortunately, this comes at a price—nonlinear optimization models are more difficult to solve.

## 7.2 BASIC IDEAS OF NONLINEAR OPTIMIZATION

When we solve an LP problem with Solver, we can guarantee that the Solver solution is optimal. When we solve an NLP problem, however, Solver sometimes obtains a *suboptimal* solution. For example, if we use Solver to maximize the function in Figure 7.1, it might have difficulty. For the function graphed in this figure, points A and C are called **local maxima** because the function is larger at A and C than at nearby points. However, only point A actually maximizes the function; it is called the **global maximum.** The problem is that Solver can get stuck near point C, concluding that C maximizes the function, and not find point A. Similarly, points B and D are **local minima** because the function has a lower value at B and D than at nearby points. However, only point D is a **global minimum.** If we ask Solver to *minimize* this function, it might conclude—incorrectly—that point B is optimal.

A **local** optimum is better than all nearby points. A **global** optimum is the best point in the entire feasible region. For some NLP problems, Solver can get stuck at a local optimum and never find the global optimum.

**Figure 7.1**

Function with Local Maxima and Minima

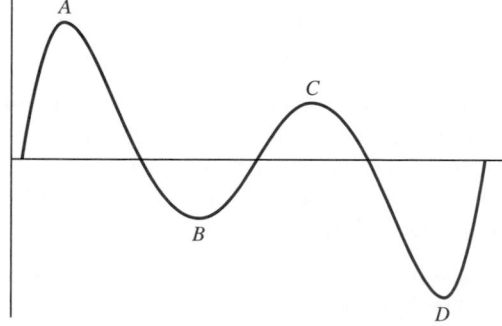

## Convex and Concave Functions

Fortunately, Solver is guaranteed to solve certain types of NLPs correctly. To describe these NLPs, we need to define *convex* and *concave* functions. A function of one variable is **convex** in a region if its slope (rate of change) in that region is always nondecreasing. Equivalently, a function of one variable is **convex** if a line drawn connecting two points on the curve never lies below the curve.[1] Figures 7.2 and 7.3 illustrate two examples of convex functions. In Figure 7.2, the function first decreases and then increases, but the slope is always increasing, first becoming less and less negative and then becoming more and more positive. In contrast, the function in Figure 7.3 is always decreasing, but again the slope is constantly increasing: It is becoming less and less negative.

> A function is **convex** if its slope is always nondecreasing.
> A function is **concave** if its slope is always nonincreasing.

**Figure 7.2**

A Convex Function with a Global Minimum

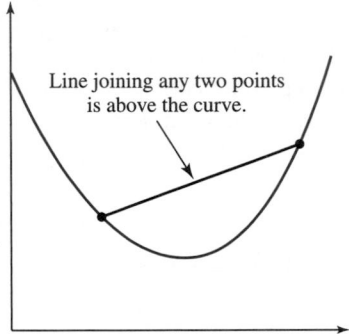

Line joining any two points is above the curve.

**Figure 7.3**

A Decreasing Convex Function

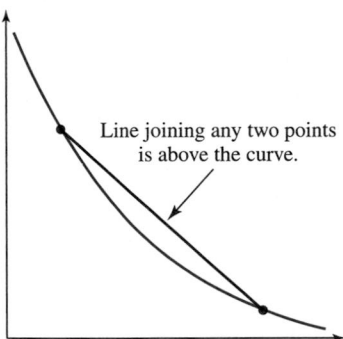

Line joining any two points is above the curve.

The following are common examples of convex functions, although they are by no means the *only* functions that are convex:

$$y = cx^a, \text{ where } a \geq 1,\, c \geq 0 \text{ and } x \geq 0$$
$$y = ce^x, \text{ where } c \geq 0$$

Similarly, a function of one variable is *concave* in a region if its slope is always nonincreasing. Equivalently, a function of one variable is concave if a line drawn connecting two points on the curve never lies above the curve. Figures 7.4 and 7.5 illustrate typical concave functions. The first has a global maximum and the second is increasing, but the slopes of both are constantly decreasing.

[1] For functions of several variables, the precise definition of convexity is more difficult to state. However, the geometric idea of convexity given here suffices for this book.

**Figure 7.4**

A Concave Function
with a Global
Maximum

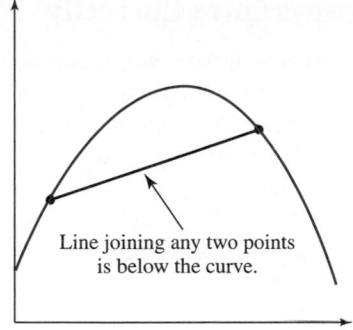

**Figure 7.5**

An Increasing
Concave Function

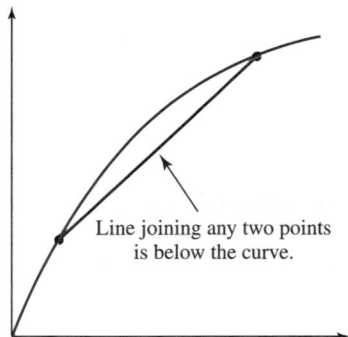

The following are common examples of concave functions, where $\ln(x)$ denotes the natural logarithm of $x$:

$$y = c \ln(x), \text{ where } c \geq 0 \text{ and } x > 0$$
$$y = cx^a, \text{ where } 0 < a \leq 1, c \geq 0 \text{ and } x \geq 0$$

Note that a linear function ($y = ax + b$) is both convex and concave because the slope of a linear function is constant.

For a more intuitive way to think about convex and concave functions, imagine you are walking up a hill. If you are on a stretch where the hill keeps getting steeper every step you take, you are on the *convex* part of the hill. If it keeps getting less steep, then you are on the *concave* part of the hill. Alternatively, if you are walking down a hill and it is getting less steep with every step you take, you are on the *convex* part of the hill; if it is getting steeper, you are on the *concave* part. In either case (walking uphill or downhill), if the steepness is not changing, you are on the linear part of the hill, which means it is both convex and concave.[2]

It can be shown that the sum of convex functions is convex and the sum of concave functions is concave. Also, if you multiply any convex function by a positive constant, the result is still convex, and if you multiply any concave function by a positive constant, the result is still concave. However, if you multiply a convex function by a *negative* constant, the result is concave, and if you multiply a concave function by a negative constant, the result is convex.

---

[2] As still one more way of distinguishing convex and concave functions, convex functions "hold water" (see Figure 7.2), and concave functions don't hold water (see Figure 7.4).

## Problems That Solvers Always Solve Correctly

*Unfortunately, the conditions listed here are often difficult to check without a solid background in calculus.*

As Figure 7.2 suggests, Solver performs well for a *minimization* problem if the objective function is convex. This is because convex functions cannot have a local minimum that is not the global minimum. Similarly, Figure 7.4 suggests that Solver performs well for a *maximization* problem if the objective function is concave. These statements can be generalized to the situation where there are many decision variables and constraints. In fact, if the following conditions hold, Solver is guaranteed to find the global minimum or global maximum if it exists.[3] (There are actually more general conditions than these, but they are beyond the level of this book.)

### Conditions for Maximization Problems

Solver is guaranteed to find the global maximum (if it exists) if the following are both true:

1. The objective function is concave or the logarithm of the objective function is concave.
2. The constraints are linear.

### Conditions for Minimization Problems

Solver is guaranteed to find the global minimum (if it exists) if the following are both true:

1. The objective function is convex.
2. The constraints are linear.

Therefore, if the constraints are linear, we need only check for the appropriate concavity or convexity of the objective to assure that Solver will find the optimal solution (instead of a local, nonglobal optimum).

### When the Assumptions Do Not Hold

There are many problems for which the conditions outlined previously do not hold or cannot be verified. Because we are then not sure whether Solver's solution is the optimal solution, the best strategy is to (1) try several possible starting values for the changing cells, (2) run Solver from each of these, and (3) take the best solution Solver finds.

For example, consider the following NLP:

$$\text{Maximize } (x - 1)(x - 2)(x - 3)(x - 4)(x - 5) \tag{7.1}$$

$$\text{Subject to:}$$

$$x \geq 1 \text{ and } x \leq 5$$

*When an objective function has multiple local optima, the solution Solver finds can depend on the starting solution in the changing cells.*

This is the function shown in Figure 7.1, where the graph extends from $x = 1$ to $x = 5$. Obviously, this function equals 0 when $x$ equals 1, 2, 3, 4, or 5. (Just substitute any of these values for $x$ into the function.) From the graph, we see that the global maximum is between $x = 1$ and $x = 2$, but that there is a local maximum between $x = 3$ and $x = 4$. The spreadsheet in Figure 7.6 shows the results of using Solver to solve this problem. (See the file **Local Maxima Finished.xlsx**.) In columns A and B, we show what happens when the starting value in the changing cell is $x = 1.5$. Solver eventually finds $x = 1.355567$ with a corresponding objective value of 3.631432. (The objective in cell B11 is the product of the

---

[3] The following discussion assumes that your spreadsheet contains no IF, MAX, MIN, or ABS statements that depend on changing cells. Current-generation spreadsheet Solvers are not equipped to deal with these functions, and errors often occur if they are present.

five numbers above it, and the constraints are B5 ≤ 5 and B5 ≥ 1.) However, given the identical setup in columns D and E, but with a starting value of $x = 3.5$, Solver finds the local maximum $x = 3.543912$ and its corresponding objective value of $1.418697$. This second solution is not the correct solution to the problem in equation (7.1), but Solver finds it because of an "unlucky" starting value of $x$.

**Figure 7.6**

Function with Local and Global Maxima

| | A | B | C | D | E |
|---|---|---|---|---|---|
| 1 | Function with local and global maxima | | | | |
| 2 | | | | | |
| 3 | The function is: y=(x-1)(x-2)(x-3)(x-4)(x-5) | | | | |
| 4 | | | | | |
| 5 | x | 1.355567 | | x | 3.543912 |
| 6 | x-1 | 0.355567 | | x-1 | 2.543912 |
| 7 | x-2 | -0.64443 | | x-2 | 1.543912 |
| 8 | x-3 | -1.64443 | | x-3 | 0.543912 |
| 9 | x-4 | -2.64443 | | x-4 | -0.45609 |
| 10 | x-5 | -3.64443 | | x-5 | -1.45609 |
| 11 | Product | 3.631432 | | Product | 1.418697 |

In general, if you try several starting combinations for the changing cells and Solver obtains the same optimal solution in all cases, you can be fairly confident—but still not absolutely sure—that you have found the optimal solution to the NLP. On the other hand, if you try different starting values for the changing cells and obtain several different solutions, then the best you can do is keep the "best" solution you have found and hope that it is indeed optimal.

**FUNDAMENTAL INSIGHT**

**Local Optima versus Global Optima**

Nonlinear objective functions can behave in many ways that make them difficult to optimize. In particular, they can have local optima that are not the global optimum we are searching for, and nonlinear optimization algorithms can get stuck at such local optima. The important property of linear objectives that makes the simplex method so successful—namely, that the optimal solution is a corner point—no longer holds for nonlinear objectives. Now any point in the feasible region can conceivably be optimal. This not only makes the search for the optimal solution more difficult, but it also makes it much more difficult to recognize whether a promising solution (a local optimum) is indeed the global optimum. This is why researchers have spent so much effort trying to obtain conditions that, when true, guarantee that a local optimum must be a global optimum. Unfortunately, these conditions are often difficult to check.

# 7.3 PRICING MODELS

Setting prices on products and services is becoming a critical decision for many companies. A good example is pricing hotel rooms and airline tickets. To many airline customers, ticket pricing appears to be madness on the part of the airlines (how can it cost less to fly thousands of miles to London than to fly a couple of hundred miles within the United States?), but there is some method to the madness. In this section, we examine several pricing problems that can be modeled as NLPs.

EXAMPLE | **7.1 PRICING DECISIONS AT MADISON**

The Madison Company manufactures and retails a certain product. The company wants to determine the price that maximizes its profit from this product. The unit cost of producing and marketing the product is $50. Madison will certainly charge at least $50 for the product to ensure that it makes *some* profit. However, there is a very competitive market for this product, so that Madison's demand falls sharply when it increases its price. How should the company proceed?[4]

**Objective** To use a demand function in a nonlinear model to find the price that maximizes the company's profit.

### WHERE DO THE NUMBERS COME FROM?

Cost accountants should be able to supply the unit cost. Historical data on demands and prices of the product are needed to estimate the demand function, as discussed next.

## Solution

The variables and constraints for this model are listed in Table 7.1. The unit price drives everything. Through a demand function, price determines demand, and these combine to determine the revenue, cost, and profit. (We assume the company produces only what it can sell—that is, it observes its demand and then produces exactly this much.) The only constraint is that the company doesn't want to charge a price less than its unit cost.

**Table 7.1** Variables and Constraints for Madison's Pricing Model

| | |
|---|---|
| **Input variables** | Unit cost, demand function (or points on demand function) |
| **Decision variables (changing cells)** | Unit price to charge |
| **Objective (target cell)** | Profit |
| **Other output variables** | Revenue, cost |
| **Constraints** | Unit price is greater than or equal to Unit cost |

More specifically, if Madison charges $P$ dollars per unit, then its profit is $(P - 50)D$, where $D$ is the number of units demanded. The problem, however, is that $D$ depends on $P$. As the price $P$ increases, the demand $D$ decreases. Therefore, the first step is to estimate how $D$ varies with $P$—that is, we have to estimate the demand function. In fact, this is the first step in almost all pricing problems. We illustrate two possibilities: a *linear* demand function of the form $D = a - bP$, and a *constant elasticity* demand function of the form $D = aP^b$.

### Estimating the Demand Function

*The elasticity of demand measures the sensitivity of demand to changes in price.*

You might recall from microeconomics that the *elasticity* of demand is the percentage change in demand caused by a 1% increase in price. The larger the (magnitude of) elasticity, the more demand reacts to price changes. The advantage of the constant elasticity demand function is that the elasticity remains constant over all points on the demand curve. For example, the elasticity of demand is the same when the price is $60 as when the price is $70. Actually, the exponent $b$ is approximately equal to this constant elasticity. For

---

[4] This example and the next two are based on Dolan and Simon (1996).

example, if $b = -2.5$, then demand decreases by about 2.5% when price increases by 1%. In contrast, the elasticity *changes* for different price levels if the demand function is linear. Nevertheless, both forms of demand functions are commonly used in economic models, and we could use either in our pricing model.

Regardless of the *form* of the demand function, the parameters of the function ($a$ and $b$) must be estimated before any price optimization can be performed. This can be done with Excel trendlines. (Trendlines were introduced in Chapter 2 and are discussed in more detail in Chapter 16.) Suppose that Madison can estimate two points on the demand curve. (At least two are required. More than two can be used in the same way.) Specifically, suppose the company estimates demand to be 400 units when price equals $70 and 300 units when price equals $80. Then we create a scatter chart of demand versus price from these two points, select either chart, and use Excel's Trendline tool with the option to list the equation of the trendline on the chart. For a linear demand curve, we select the Linear trendline option, and for the constant elasticity demand curve, we select the Power trendline option. (The relevant dialog box appears in Figure 7.7. To get to it, select the chart and then select More Trendline Options from the Trendline dropdown on the Chart Tools Layout ribbon.

**Figure 7.7**

Excel's Add Trendline Dialog Box

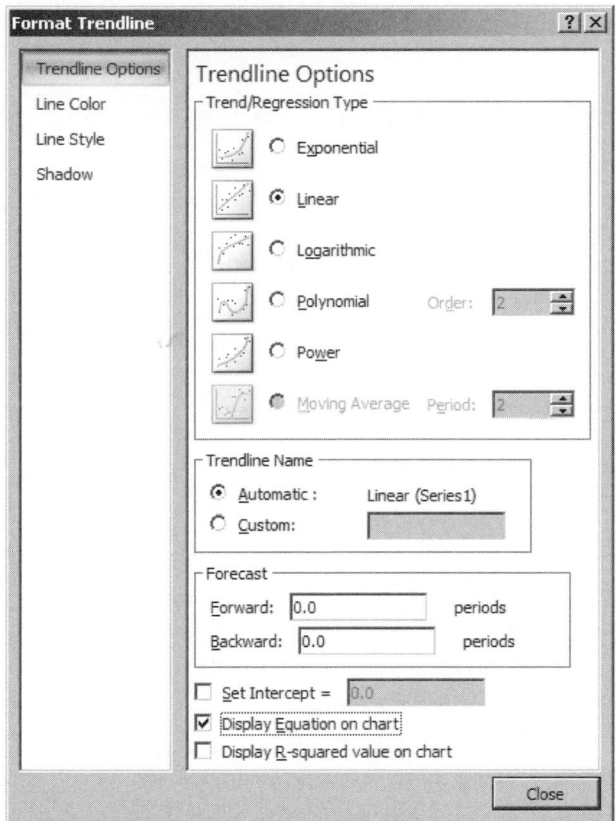

The results are presented in Figure 7.8, where we show both the linear estimate and the constant elasticity estimate. (When you do this, the constant for the constant elasticity curve might appear as 4E+06. To get more significant digits, just click on the equation and then use the Format menu and the Number tab to format the number appropriately.) We can use either of these trendline equations as an estimate of the demand function for the pricing model.

**Figure 7.8** Determining Parameters of Demand Functions

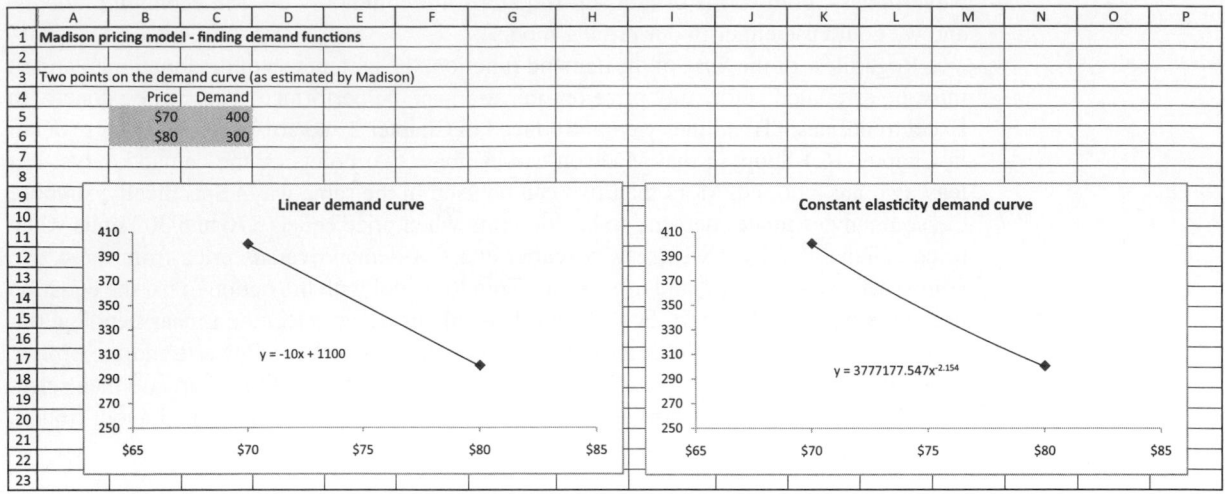

## DEVELOPING THE SPREADSHEET MODEL

Given a demand function, the pricing decision is straightforward, as shown in Figure 7.9. (See the file **Basic Pricing.xlsx**.) Here we have used the constant elasticity demand curve. (The model for linear demand is similar. The finished version of the file illustrates both cases.) The model requires the following steps:

**Figure 7.9**

Pricing Model with Constant Elasticity Demand

| | A | B | C | D | E | F | G | H | I | J | K |
|---|---|---|---|---|---|---|---|---|---|---|---|
| 1 | Madison pricing model with constant elasticity demand function | | | | | | | Range names used: | | | |
| 2 | | | | | | | | Price2 | ='Constant Elasticity'!$B$10 | | |
| 3 | Unit cost | $50 | | | | | | Profit2 | ='Constant Elasticity'!$B$12 | | |
| 4 | | | | | | | | Unit_cost2 | ='Constant Elasticity'!$B$3 | | |
| 5 | Parameters of constant elasticity demand function (from first sheet) | | | | | | | | | | |
| 6 | | Constant | Elasticity | | | | | | | | |
| 7 | | 3777178 | -2.154 | | | | | | | | |
| 8 | | | | | | | | | | | |
| 9 | Pricing model | | | | | | | | | | |
| 10 | Price | $93.31 | | | | | | | | | |
| 11 | Demand | $215.33 | | | | | | | | | |
| 12 | Profit | $9,326 | | | | | | | | | |
| 13 | | | | | | | | | | | |
| 14 | Verification with a data table and corresponding chart | | | | | | | | | | |
| 15 | | Price | Profit | | | | | | | | |
| 16 | | | $9,326 | | | | | | | | |
| 17 | | $55 | $3,363 | | | | | | | | |
| 18 | | $60 | $5,576 | | | | | | | | |
| 19 | | $65 | $7,039 | | | | | | | | |
| 20 | | $70 | $8,000 | | | | | | | | |
| 21 | | $75 | $8,619 | | | | | | | | |
| 22 | | $80 | $9,000 | | | | | | | | |
| 23 | | $85 | $9,214 | | | | | | | | |
| 24 | | $90 | $9,311 | | | | | | | | |
| 25 | | $95 | $9,323 | | | | | | | | |
| 26 | | $100 | $9,275 | | | | | | | | |
| 27 | | $105 | $9,184 | | | | | | | | |
| 28 | | $110 | $9,064 | | | | | | | | |

**1 Inputs.** The inputs for this model are the unit cost and the parameters of the demand function found previously. Enter them as shown.

**2 Price.** Enter any trial value for price. It is the single changing cell.

**3 Demand.** Calculate the corresponding demand from the demand function by entering the formula

**=B7\*Price2^C7**

in cell B11. (To minimize range name conflicts, we used the names Price1, Unit_cost1, and Profit1 for the linear demand model, and we used Price2, Unit_cost2, and Profit2 for the constant elasticity model.)

**4 Profit.** Calculate the profit as unit contribution (price minus unit cost) multiplied by demand with the formula

**=(Price2-Unit_cost2)\*B11**

in cell B12.

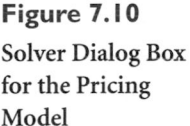

## USING SOLVER

*If you check the Assume Linear Model box for any model in this chapter, you will get an error message. This is because Solver automatically recognizes that these models are nonlinear.*

The relevant Solver dialog box is shown in Figure 7.10. We maximize profit subject to the constraint that price must be at least as large as unit cost, with price as the only decision variable. However, we do *not* check the Assume Linear Model box under Solver options. This model is nonlinear for two reasons. First, the demand function is nonlinear in price because price is raised to a power. But even if the demand function were linear, profit would still be nonlinear because it involves the *product* of price and demand, and demand is a function of price. This nonlinearity can be seen easily with the data table and corresponding chart in Figure 7.9. These show how profit varies with price—the relationship is clearly nonlinear. Profit increases to a maximum, and then declines slowly. (This type of data table and chart are useful in nonlinear models with a *single* changing cell. They show exactly how the objective changes as the changing cell changes. We employ these data tables in other nonlinear examples whenever possible.)

**Figure 7.10**

Solver Dialog Box for the Pricing Model

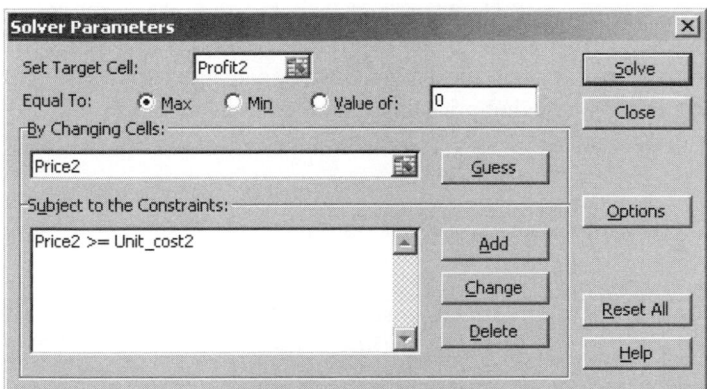

### Solver Technical Note: Nonlinear Solver Settings

When you use Solver on a nonlinear model and do *not* check the Assume Linear Model option, Solver uses a totally different algorithm called GRG (generalized reduced gradient). If you click on Options in the Solver dialog box, you will see several options at

*Solver's nonlinear algorithm can be sensitive to the settings you choose, but these suggestions should help.*

the bottom that are relevant for Solver's GRG algorithm. We always left these at their default settings: Tangent, Forward, and Newton. However, one of our colleagues, Harvey Wagner, a pioneer in the management science field, suggests that he has more luck with the settings Quadratic, Central, and Newton. He also suggests, and we agree based on our own experience, that when Solver terminates, you can sometimes get a better solution by starting Solver again, maybe even several times. Solver quits when it thinks it can't improve on the current solution, but surprisingly, if you then start it again from this solution, Solver sometimes moves to a better solution.

### Discussion of the Solution

*Pricing problems are inherently nonlinear, and the trade-off between selling a lot of units at a low price and selling fewer units at a higher price is difficult to make.*

Guessing the optimal price in this type of model is usually not easy. As the company increases its price, it makes more money on each unit sold, but it sells fewer units. Therefore, the trade-off is always between selling a few relatively high-priced units and selling a lot of relatively low-priced units. Complicating the matter is the fact that as price increases, total cost decreases (because fewer units are demanded). In the present case, we see from the graph in Figure 7.9 that profit increases fairly quickly as price goes from \$55 to about \$85. After this point, profit is almost unaffected by price (at least for the range of prices shown), and any price from \$85 to about \$110 results in a profit within \$200 of the optimal profit. Of course, Solver does better than this; it finds the *optimal* price, \$93.31.

### Is the Solver Solution Optimal?

In general, there is no guarantee that profit is a concave function for all possible inputs to this model. However, the graph in Figure 7.9 indicates that it is concave for the particular inputs we have used and that the Solver solution is indeed optimal (because there is no local maximum that isn't a global maximum).

### Sensitivity Analysis

From an economic point of view, it should be interesting to see how the profit-maximizing price varies with the elasticity of the demand function. To do this, we use SolverTable with the elasticity in cell C7 as the single input cell, allowing it to vary from $-2.4$ to $-1.8$ in increments of 0.1.[5] (Note that when the range of input values is negative, the one with the largest magnitude must be entered first in the SolverTable dialog box.) The results are shown in Figure 7.11. When the demand is most elastic (at the top of the table), increases in price have a greater effect on demand. Therefore, the company should not set the price as high in this case. Interestingly, when demand is least elastic, the company should not only charge a higher price, but this price results in a much higher profit. Would you have guessed this?

**Figure 7.11**
**Sensitivity to Elasticity of Demand**

| | A | B | C | D |
|---|---|---|---|---|
| 31 | Sensitivity of optimal solution to elasticity | | | |
| 32 | | Price | Demand | Profit |
| 33 | | \$B\$10 | \$B\$11 | \$B\$12 |
| 34 | -2.4 | \$85.71 | 86.66 | \$3,095 |
| 35 | -2.3 | \$88.46 | 125.79 | \$4,838 |
| 36 | -2.2 | \$91.67 | 182.10 | \$7,587 |
| 37 | -2.1 | \$95.45 | 262.78 | \$11,945 |
| 38 | -2.0 | \$100.00 | 377.72 | \$18,886 |
| 39 | -1.9 | \$105.56 | 540.20 | \$30,011 |
| 40 | -1.8 | \$112.50 | 767.53 | \$47,970 |

■

[5] Solver *does* provide a sensitivity report for nonlinear models. However, the mathematical theory behind this report is significantly more complex than for linear models, so we present only SolverTable outputs in this chapter.

## 7.2 Pricing with Exchange Rate Considerations at Madison

We continue Example 7.1, but we now assume that Madison manufactures its product in the United States and sells it in the United Kingdom (UK). Given the prevailing exchange rate in dollars per pound, Madison wants to determine the price in pounds it should charge in the UK so that its profit in dollars is maximized. The company also wants to see how the optimal price and the optimal profit depend on exchange rate fluctuations.

**Objective**   To use a nonlinear model to find the price in pounds that maximizes the profit in dollars.

### Where do the numbers come from?

The only new input in this model is the exchange rate, which is readily available. For example, you can find exchange rates at http://www.oanda.com/convert/classic.

## Solution

The model is shown in Figure 7.12. (See the file **Pricing Globally.xlsx**.) It is very similar to the previous model, so we highlight only the new features. The exchange rate in cell B4 indicates the number of dollars required to purchase one pound. For example, with an exchange rate of 2.04, it takes \$2.04 to purchase one pound. Alternatively, $1/2.04 = 0.490$ £ is required to purchase one dollar. As this exchange rate decreases, we say that the dollar gets stronger; as it increases, the dollar gets weaker. Note that we *divide* by the exchange rate to convert dollars to pounds, and we *multiply* by the exchange rate to convert pounds to dollars. With this in mind, the model development is straightforward.

**Figure 7.12**

The Pricing Model in a Foreign Market

| | A | B | C | D | E | F | G | H | I |
|---|---|---|---|---|---|---|---|---|---|
| 1 | Madison pricing problem in a UK market | | | | | | | | |
| 2 | | | | | | | | | |
| 3 | Unit cost ($) | 50 | | | | Range names used: | | | |
| 4 | Exchange rate ($/£) | 2.04 | | | | Price_Pounds | =Model!$B$13 | | |
| 5 | | | | | | Profit_Dollars | =Model!$B$15 | | |
| 6 | Equivalent unit cost in pounds | 24.510 | | | | UnitCost_Pounds | =Model!$B$6 | | |
| 7 | | | | | | | | | |
| 8 | Parameters of demand function in UK market | | | | | | | | |
| 9 | | Constant | Elasticity | | | | | | |
| 10 | | 27556760 | -2.4 | | | | | | |
| 11 | | | | | | | | | |
| 12 | Pricing model (finding the right price in £ to maximize profit in $) | | | | | | | | |
| 13 | Price (£) | 42.02 | | | | | | | |
| 14 | Demand (in UK) | 3499.56 | | | | | | | |
| 15 | Profit ($) | 124984.11 | | | | | | | |
| 16 | | | | | | | | | |
| 17 | Verification with a data table and corresponding chart | | | | | | | | |
| 18 | Price (£) | $B$13 | | | | | | | |
| 19 | | 124984.11 | | | | | | | |
| 20 | 25 | 12166.67 | | | | | | | |
| 21 | 30 | 87974.16 | | | | | | | |
| 22 | 35 | 116112.40 | | | | | | | |
| 23 | 40 | 124443.22 | | | | | | | |
| 24 | 45 | 124077.88 | | | | | | | |
| 25 | 50 | 119868.06 | | | | | | | |
| 26 | 55 | 114063.86 | | | | | | | |
| 27 | 60 | 107746.63 | | | | | | | |
| 28 | 65 | 101441.61 | | | | | | | |
| 29 | 70 | 95398.34 | | | | | | | |
| 30 | 75 | 89726.00 | | | | | | | |
| 31 | 80 | 84461.46 | | | | | | | |

Profit versus Price chart (Profit ($) versus Price (£))

### DEVELOPING THE SPREADSHEET MODEL

The following steps are required:

**1 Inputs.** The inputs are the unit cost (in dollars), the exchange rate, and the parameters of the company's demand function for the UK market. These latter values would need to be estimated exactly as we discussed in the previous example. We chose "reasonable" values for this example, as shown in row 10.

**2 Unit cost in pounds.** Although Madison's unit cost occurs in the United States and is expressed in dollars, it is convenient to express it in pounds. Do this in cell B6 with the formula

**=B3/B4**

(The only reason we calculate this is to form a constraint on the price: the unit price in pounds must be no less than the unit cost, measured in the same currency.)

**3 Price, demand.** As in the previous example, enter any price in cell B13 (which is now in pounds), and calculate the demand in cell B14 from the demand function with the formula

**=B10*Price_Pounds^C10**

**4 Profit.** The profit should be in dollars, so enter the formula

**=(Price_Pounds*B4-B3)*B14**

in cell B15. Note that the unit cost is already in dollars, but the UK price must be converted to dollars.

### USING SOLVER

The Solver dialog box (not shown here) is set up exactly as in Figure 7.10, except that the constraint on price is now Price_Pounds ≥ UnitCost_Pounds, so that pounds are compared to pounds. In fact, the specification of this constraint is the only place where the value in cell B6 enters the model.

### Discussion of the Solution

The optimal solution, with an exchange rate of 2.04, says that Madison should charge 42.02 £ per unit in the UK. This creates demand for about 3500 units. Each of these costs $50 to produce, and the dollar revenue from each of them is 42.02(2.04), or $85.71. The resulting profit in dollars is approximately $124,984. The graph in Figure 7.12, created from a data table of profit versus price, shows how profit declines on either side of the optimal price.

### Is the Solver Solution Optimal?

As in the previous example, the objective is not necessarily a concave function of price for all possible values of the input parameters. However, the graph in Figure 7.12 indicates that it is concave for our particular input parameters and that the Solver solution is indeed optimal.

### Sensitivity Analysis

What happens when the dollar gets stronger or weaker? We use SolverTable with exchange rate as the single input, allowing it to vary from 1.75 to 2.25 in increments of 0.05, and we keep track of price, demand, and profit. The results in Figure 7.13 indicate that as the dollar strengthens (the exchange rate decreases), Madison charges more in pounds for the product but obtains a lower profit. The opposite is true when the dollar weakens. Are these results in line with your economic intuition? Note that when the dollar strengthens, pounds are not worth as much to a U.S. company. Therefore, when we convert the pound revenue to dollars in the profit cell, the profit tends to decrease. But in this case, why does the optimal price in pounds *increase?* We'll say no more here—except that this should be a good question for class discussion.

**Figure 7.13**

Sensitivity of the
Optimal Solution to
the Exchange Rate

| | A | B | C | D |
|---|---|---|---|---|
| 33 | Sensitivity of price, demand, and profit to exchange rate | | | |
| 34 | | $B$13 | $B$14 | $B$15 |
| 35 | 1.75 | 48.98 | 2422.10 | 86503.51 |
| 36 | 1.80 | 47.62 | 2591.52 | 92554.26 |
| 37 | 1.85 | 46.33 | 2767.66 | 98844.97 |
| 38 | 1.90 | 45.11 | 2950.59 | 105378.26 |
| 39 | 1.95 | 43.96 | 3140.39 | 112156.77 |
| 40 | 2.00 | 42.86 | 3337.12 | 119183.02 |
| 41 | 2.05 | 41.81 | 3540.87 | 126459.56 |
| 42 | 2.10 | 40.82 | 3751.69 | 133988.85 |
| 43 | 2.15 | 39.87 | 3969.66 | 141773.40 |
| 44 | 2.20 | 38.96 | 4194.84 | 149815.54 |
| 45 | 2.25 | 38.10 | 4427.30 | 158117.69 |

Many products create add-ons to other products. For example, if you own a men's clothing store, you should recognize that when a person buys a suit, he often buys a shirt or a tie. Failure to take this into account causes you to price your suits too high—and lose potential sales of shirts and ties. The following example illustrates the idea.

## EXAMPLE 7.3 PRICING SUITS AT SULLIVAN'S

Sullivan's is a retailer of upscale men's clothing. Suits cost Sullivan's $320. The current price of suits to customers is $350, which leads to annual sales of 300 suits. The elasticity of the demand for men's suits is estimated to be $-2.5$ and assumed to be constant over the relevant price range. Each purchase of a suit leads to an average of 2 shirts and 1.5 ties being sold. Each shirt contributes $25 to profit, and each tie contributes $15 to profit. Determine a profit-maximizing price for suits.

**Objective**  To use a nonlinear model to price men's suits optimally, taking into account the purchases of shirts and ties that typically accompany purchases of suits.

### WHERE DO THE NUMBERS COME FROM?

The dollar figures are likely supplied by a cost accountant. The elasticity of demand can be estimated from historical data on demands and prices, as discussed in Example 7.1. Finally, the average numbers of shirts and ties sold with suit purchases are available from historical data, assuming the company keeps track of such complementary purchases. (If the company doesn't keep track of such data, it should!)

## Solution

The variables and constraints for this pricing model are listed in Table 7.2. As in the previous two examples, we must first determine the demand function for suits. Although this could be a linear function or some other form, we again assume a constant elasticity function of the form $D = aP^b$, where the exponent $b$ is the elasticity. The solution from this point is practically the same as the solution to Example 7.1 except for the profit function. Each suit sold also generates demand for 2 shirts and 1.5 ties (on average), which contributes $2(25) + 1.5(15)$ extra dollars in profit. Therefore, it makes sense that the profit-maximizing price for suits is *lower* than in the absence of shirts and ties. The company wants to generate more demand for suits so that it can reap the benefits from shirts and ties. The only constraint is that the price of suits should be at least as large as the unit cost of suits. (Is this constraint really necessary? We discuss this question shortly.)

---

**Table 7.2    Variables and Constraints for the Suit Pricing Model**

| | |
|---|---|
| **Input variables** | Unit cost of suit, current price of suit, current demand for suits, elasticity of demand, ties and shirts purchased per suit, unit profits from a tie and a shirt |
| **Decision variables (changing cells)** | Price to charge for a suit |
| **Objective (target cell)** | Total profit |
| **Other output variables** | Constant in demand function, demand for suits, profit from suits alone, profit from ties and shirts |
| **Constraints** | Price of suit must be greater than or equal to Unit cost of suit (necessary?) |

---

## DEVELOPING THE SPREADSHEET MODEL

The spreadsheet solution appears in Figure 7.14. (See the file **Pricing with Add-Ons.xlsx**.) Instead of solving a single model, we actually solve two: the one stated previously and one where we ignore shirts and ties. This way we can gauge the effect that shirts and ties have on the optimal price of suits. We could set this up as two distinct models, but a clever use of SolverTable allows us to treat both cases in a single model. The following steps are required:

**Figure 7.14**

The Pricing Model with Complementary Products

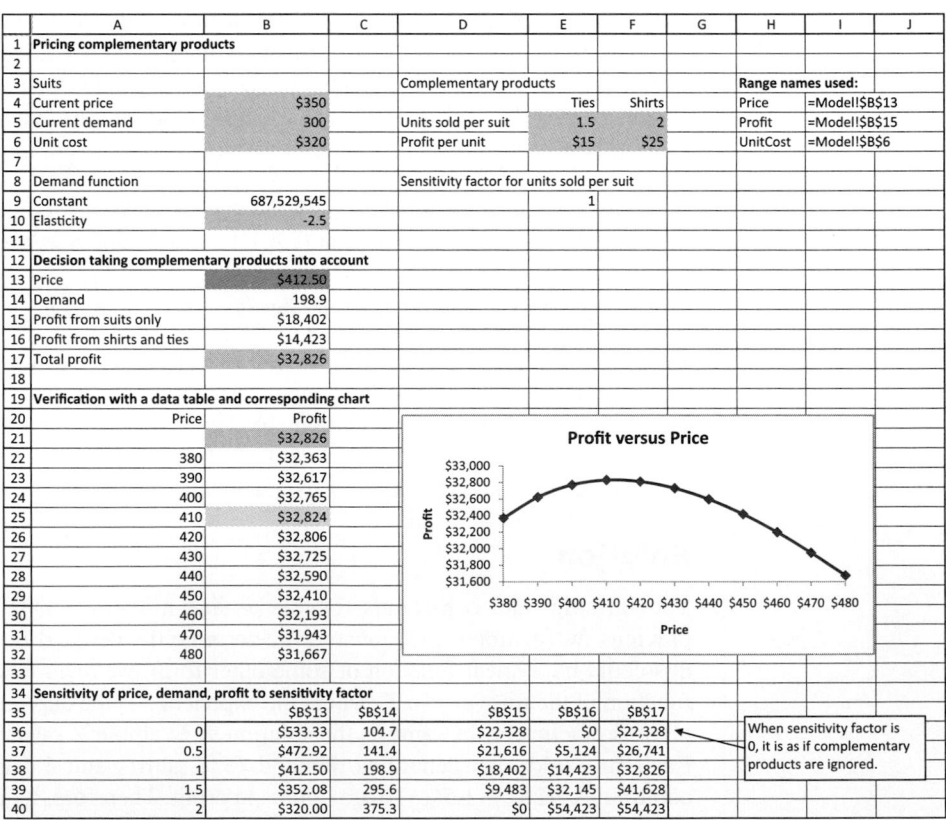

**1** **Inputs.** Enter all inputs in the blue regions.

**2** **Constant for demand function.** The demand function is of the form $D = aP^b$. We can find the constant $a$ from the current demand and price for suits: $300 = a(350^{-2.5})$, so that $a = 300/350^{-2.5}$. Therefore, calculate this constant $a$ in cell B9 with the formula

**=B5/B4^B10**

**3** **Sensitivity factor.** We treat both cases, when shirts and ties are ignored and when they are not, by using SolverTable with a "sensitivity factor" as the input cell. When this factor is 0, the complementary products are ignored; when it is positive, they are taken into consideration. Enter **1** in the sensitivity factor cell E9 for now. In general, this factor determines the average number of shirts and ties purchased with the purchase of a suit—we multiply this factor by the values in the E5:F5 range. When this factor is 1, we get the values in the statement of the problem. When it is 0, no shirts and ties are purchased with a suit.

**4** **Price, demand.** Enter *any* price in cell B13, and calculate the corresponding demand for suits in cell B14 with the formula

**=B9*B13^B10**

**5** **Profits.** The total profit is the profit from suits alone, plus the extra profit from shirts and ties that are purchased along with suits. Calculate the first of these in cell B15 with the formula

**=(Price-Unit cost)*B14**

and calculate the second in cell B16 with the formula

**=E9*SUMPRODUCT(E5:F5,E6:F6)*B14**

Then sum them to get the total profit in cell B17. Note that the sensitivity factor in cell E9 scales the extra profit, depending on how many ties and shirts per suit are sold. If the value in cell E9 is 0, then no shirts and ties are sold; if this value is 1, then the numbers of shirts and ties stated in the problem are sold.

*As this example illustrates, a clever use of SolverTable sometimes enables us to solve multiple problems at once.*

## USING SOLVER

The Solver setup, not shown here, is the same as in Example 7.1. We maximize profit, with the price of suits as the only changing cell, and we constrain this price to be at least as large as the unit cost of suits.

### Discussion of the Solution

The solution in Figure 7.14 uses a sensitivity factor of 1 in cell E9, which means that every suit sale is accompanied (on average) by the sale of 2 shirts and 1.5 ties. This induces the company to keep the suit price relatively low, at $412.50, so that it can sell a lot of suits and therefore a lot of shirts and ties. In fact, we see that the total profit is nearly evenly divided between the profit from suits and the profit from shirts and ties.

To see the effect of complementary products, we then run SolverTable with cell E9 as the single input cell, varied, say, from 0 to 2 (or any other upper limit you like) in increments of 0.5, and keep track of price, demand, and profit (see Figure 7.14). The SolverTable results show that when the company ignores shirts and ties (or, equivalently, suits do not generate any demand for shirts and ties), the optimal price is set high, at $533.33. However, as more ties and shirts are purchased by purchasers of suits, the optimal price of suits decreases fairly dramatically. As we would expect, as more shirts and ties are purchased with suits, the company makes more profit—if it takes shirts and ties into account and prices suits properly. Interestingly, if the sensitivity factor increases to 2,

*The potential sales of complementary products induces a company to price its main product lower than if there were no complementary products.*

so that customers on average buy 3 ties and 4 shirts with every suit, then the company sets its price so that it just breaks even on suits and makes all of its profit on ties and shirts. (If you are skeptical of this result, read the "Is the Constraint Needed?" section that follows.)

For the situation in the problem statement, how much profit does the company lose if it ignores shirts and ties? You can answer this by entering $533.33 in the Price cell, keeping the sensitivity factor equal to 1. You will find that profit decreases from $32,826 to $29,916, which is a drop of about 9%. This is the penalty of pricing in a way that ignores shirts and ties.

### Is the Solver Solution Optimal?

As in the preceding two examples, the graph in Figure 7.14, formed from a data table of profit versus price, indicates that the Solver solution is optimal—there are no local maxima.

### Is the Constraint Needed?

In pricing models, we hardly think twice before constraining the price to be at least as large as the unit cost. However, it might make sense to price a product *below* cost if sales of this product lead to sales—and profits—from other products. Therefore, we deleted the constraint on price in the example and reran SolverTable. The results appear in Figure 7.15. The only change is in row 25, where the sensitivity factor is 2. We now price the suits below cost, just to sell more shirts and ties. In fact, the only reason we priced to break even in this row before was the constraint—we didn't allow a price below the unit cost. When we allow this behavior, the profit increases from its earlier value of $54,423 to $55,210.

**Figure 7.15**  Solution with Pricing Below Cost Allowed

| | A | B | C | D | E | F | G | H | I | J |
|---|---|---|---|---|---|---|---|---|---|---|
| 34 | Sensitivity of price, demand, profit to sensitivity factor | | | | | | | | | |
| 35 | | $B$13 | $B$14 | $B$15 | $B$16 | $B$17 | | | | |
| 36 | 0 | $533.33 | 104.7 | $22,328 | $0 | $22,328 | | | | |
| 37 | 0.5 | $472.92 | 141.4 | $21,616 | $5,124 | $26,741 | | | | |
| 38 | 1 | $412.50 | 198.9 | $18,402 | $14,423 | $32,826 | | Pricing below cost is indeed | | |
| 39 | 1.5 | $352.08 | 295.6 | $9,483 | $32,145 | $41,628 | | optimal in this last row. | | |
| 40 | 2 | $291.67 | 473.2 | -$13,408 | $68,619 | $55,210 | | | | |

Automobile and appliance dealers who profit from maintenance contracts could probably increase their profits significantly if they factored the profits from the maintenance agreements into the determination of prices of their major products. That is, we suspect that the prices of their major products are set too high—not from the customers' standpoint but from the dealers'. Probably the ultimate tie-in reduction in price is the fact that many companies now provide free software. They are hoping, of course, that the receiver of free software will later buy the tie-in product, which is the upgrade. ∎

In many situations, there are peak-load and off-peak demands for a product. In such a situation, it might be optimal for a producer to charge a larger price for peak-load service than for off-peak service. The following example illustrates this situation.

# 7.4 PEAK-LOAD PRICING AT FLORIDA POWER AND LIGHT

Florida Power and Light (FPL) faces demands during both peak-load and off-peak times. FPL must determine the price per kilowatt hour (kwh) to charge during both peak-load and off-peak periods. The daily demand for power during each period (in kwh) is related to price as follows:

$$D_p = 60 - 0.5P_p + 0.1P_o \tag{7.2}$$

$$D_o = 40 - P_o + 0.1P_p \tag{7.3}$$

Here, $D_p$ and $P_p$ are demand and price during peak-load times, whereas $D_o$ and $P_o$ are demand and price during off-peak times. Note that we are now using *linear* demand functions, not the constant elasticity demand functions from the previous examples. (We do this for the sake of variety. The model would not differ substantially if we used constant elasticity demand functions.) Also, note from the signs of the coefficients that an increase in the peak-load price decreases the demand for power during the peak-load period but *increases* the demand for power during the off-peak period. Similarly, an increase in the price for the off-peak period decreases the demand for the off-peak period but *increases* the demand for the peak-load period. In economic terms, this implies that peak-load power and off-peak power are *substitutes* for one another. In addition, it costs FPL $10 per day to maintain 1 kwh of capacity. The company wants to determine a pricing strategy and a capacity level that maximize its daily profit.

**Objective** To use a nonlinear model to determine prices and capacity when there are two different daily usage patterns: peak-load and off-peak.

## WHERE DO THE NUMBERS COME FROM?

As usual, a cost accountant should be able to estimate the unit cost of capacity. The real difficulty here is estimating the demand functions in equations (7.2) and (7.3). This requires either sufficient historical data on prices and demands (for both peak-load and off-peak periods) or educated guesses from management.

## Solution

The variables and constraints for this model are listed in Table 7.3. The company must decide on two prices and must determine the amount of capacity to maintain. Because this capacity level, once determined, is relevant for peak-load and off-peak periods, it must be large enough to meet demands for both periods. This is the reasoning behind the constraint.

**Table 7.3 Variables and Constraints for the Peak-Load Pricing Model**

| | |
|---|---|
| **Input variables** | Parameters of demand functions, unit cost of capacity |
| **Decision variables (changing cells)** | Peak-load and off-peak prices, capacity |
| **Objective (target cell)** | Profit |
| **Other output variables** | Peak-load and off-peak demands, revenue, cost of capacity |
| **Constraints** | Demands must be less than or equal to Capacity |

Due to the relationships between the demand and price variables, it is not obvious what FPL should do. The pricing decisions determine demand, and larger demand requires larger capacity, which costs money. In addition, revenue is price multiplied by demand, so it is not clear whether price should be low or high to increase revenue.

## DEVELOPING THE SPREADSHEET MODEL

The spreadsheet model appears in Figure 7.16. (See the file **Peak-Load Pricing.xlsx**.) It can be developed as follows:

---

**Figure 7.16**   The Peak-Load Pricing Model

| | A | B | C | D | E | F | G | H | I |
|---|---|---|---|---|---|---|---|---|---|
| 1 | Florida Power & Light peak-load pricing model | | | | | | | | |
| 2 | | | | | | | | | |
| 3 | Input data | | | | | Range names used: | | | |
| 4 | Coefficients of demand functions | | | | | Capacity | =PeakLoad!$B$15 | | |
| 5 | | Constant | Peak price | Off-peak price | | Common_Capacity | =PeakLoad!$B$21:$C$21 | | |
| 6 | Peak-load demand | 60 | -0.5 | 0.1 | | Demands | =PeakLoad!$B$19:$C$19 | | |
| 7 | Off-peak demand | 40 | 0.1 | -1 | | Prices | =PeakLoad!$B$13:$C$13 | | |
| 8 | | | | | | Profit | =PeakLoad!$B$26 | | |
| 9 | Cost of capacity/kwh | $10 | | | | | | | |
| 10 | | | | | | | | | |
| 11 | Decisions | | | | | | | | |
| 12 | | Peak-load | Off-peak | | | | | | |
| 13 | Prices | $70.31 | $26.53 | | | | | | |
| 14 | | | | | | | | | |
| 15 | Capacity | 27.50 | | | | | | | |
| 16 | | | | | | | | | |
| 17 | Constraints on demand | | | | | | | | |
| 18 | | Peak-load | Off-peak | | | | | | |
| 19 | Demand | 27.50 | 20.50 | | | | | | |
| 20 | | <= | <= | | | | | | |
| 21 | Capacity | 27.50 | 27.50 | | | | | | |
| 22 | | | | | | | | | |
| 23 | Monetary summary | | | | | | | | |
| 24 | Revenue | $2,477.30 | | | | | | | |
| 25 | Cost of capacity | $275.00 | | | | | | | |
| 26 | Profit | $2,202.30 | | | | | | | |

---

**❶ Inputs.** Enter the parameters of the demand functions and the cost of capacity in the blue ranges.

**❷ Prices and capacity level.** Enter *any* trial prices (per kwh) for peak-load and offpeak power in the Prices range, and enter *any* trial value for the capacity level in the Capacity cell. These are the three values FPL has control over, so they become the changing cells.

**❸ Demands.** Calculate the demand for the peak-load period by substituting into equation (7.2). That is, enter the formula

=B6+SUMPRODUCT(Prices,C6:D6)

in cell B19. Similarly, enter the formula

=B7+SUMPRODUCT(Prices,C7:D7)

in cell C19 for the off-peak demand.

**❹ Copy capacity.** To indicate the capacity constraints, enter the formula

=Capacity

in cells B21 and C21. The reason for creating these links is that we want the two demand cells in row 19 to be paired with two capacity cells in row 21, so that we can specify the Solver constraints appropriately. (Solver doesn't allow a "two versus one" constraint such as B19:C19 <= B15.)

**⑤ Monetary values.** Calculate the daily revenue, cost of capacity, and profit in the corresponding cells with the formulas

**=SUMPRODUCT(Demands,Prices)**

**=Capacity*B9**

and

**=B24-B25**

## USING SOLVER

The Solver dialog box should be filled in as shown in Figure 7.17. We maximize profit by setting appropriate prices and capacity, and we ensure that demand never exceeds the capacity. We should also check Solver's Assume Non-Negative box (prices and capacity cannot be negative), but we should *not* check the Assume Linear Model box. Again, this is because we are multiplying prices by demands, which are functions of prices, so that profit is a nonlinear function of the prices.

**Figure 7.17**

Solver Dialog Box for the Peak-Load Pricing Model

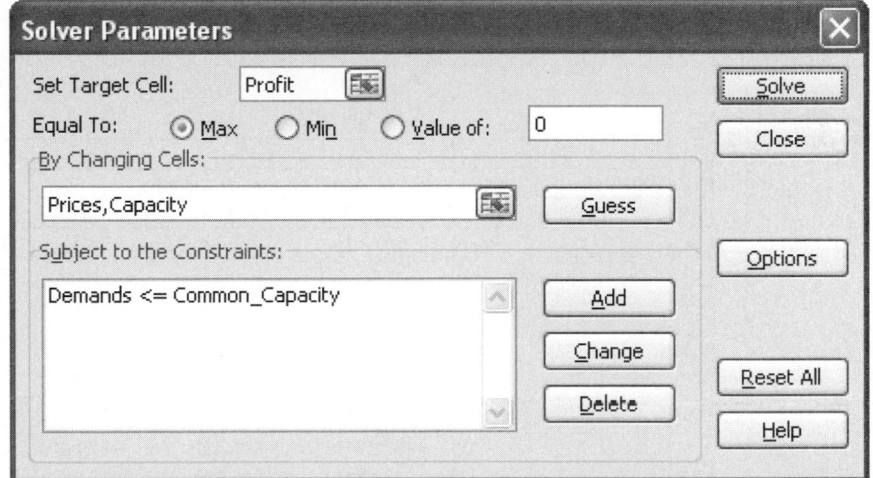

### Discussion of the Solution

The Solver solution in Figure 7.16 indicates that FPL should charge $70.31 per kwh during the peak-load period and $26.53 during the off-peak-load period. These prices generate demands of 27.5 (peak-load) and 20.5 (off-peak), so that a capacity of 27.5 kwh is required. The cost of this capacity is $275. When this is subtracted from the revenue of $2477.30, the daily profit becomes $2202.30.

*Varying the changing cells slightly from their optimal values sometimes provides insight into the optimal solution.*

To gain some insight into this solution, consider what happens if FPL changes the peak-load price slightly from its optimal value of $70.31. If FPL decreases the price to $70, say, you can check that the peak-load demand increases to 27.65 and the off-peak demand decreases to 20.47. The net effect is that revenue increases slightly, to $2478.78. However, the peak-load demand is now greater than capacity, so FPL must increase its capacity from 27.50 to 27.65. This costs an extra $1.50, which more than offsets the increase in revenue. A similar chain of effects occurs if FPL increases the peak price to $71. In this case, peak-load demand decreases, off-peak demand increases, and total revenue decreases. Although FPL can get by with lower capacity, the net effect is slightly less profit. Fortunately, Solver evaluates all of these trade-offs for us when it finds the optimal solution.

## Is the Solver Solution Optimal?

All of the constraints in this example are linear, so they certainly meet the assumptions for a maximization problem. Also, it can be shown that the objective (daily profit) is a concave function of peak-load price, off-peak price, and capacity level—although this is far from obvious. (It requires calculus to verify.) Algebraically, this objective function is called **quadratic,** meaning that it is a sum of linear terms (such as $P_p$), squared terms (such as $P_p^2$), and cross-product terms (such as $P_p P_o$). Not all quadratic functions are concave, but there is a test to check whether a given quadratic function is concave. (Although the details of this test are not presented here, we assure you that the quadratic function for this example passes the test.) Therefore, the assumptions for a maximization problem are satisfied, and the Solver solution is guaranteed to be optimal.

## Sensitivity Analysis

To gain even more insight, we use SolverTable to see the effects of changing the unit cost of capacity, which we allow to vary from $5 to $15 in increments of $1. The results appear in Figure 7.18. They indicate that as the cost of capacity increases, the peak-load price increases, the off-peak price stays constant, the amount of capacity decreases, and profit decreases. The latter two effects are probably intuitive, but we challenge you to explain the effects on price. In particular, why does the peak-load price *increase,* and why doesn't the off-peak price increase as well?

**Figure 7.18**

Sensitivity to Cost of Capacity

| | A | B | C | D | E |
|---|---|---|---|---|---|
| 28 | Sensitivity of changing cells and profit to cost of capacity | | | | |
| 29 | | $B$13 | $C$13 | $B$15 | $B$26 |
| 30 | 5 | $67.81 | $26.53 | 28.75 | $2,342.92 |
| 31 | 6 | $68.31 | $26.53 | 28.50 | $2,314.30 |
| 32 | 7 | $68.81 | $26.53 | 28.25 | $2,285.92 |
| 33 | 8 | $69.31 | $26.53 | 28.00 | $2,257.80 |
| 34 | 9 | $69.81 | $26.53 | 27.75 | $2,229.92 |
| 35 | 10 | $70.31 | $26.53 | 27.50 | $2,202.30 |
| 36 | 11 | $70.81 | $26.53 | 27.25 | $2,174.92 |
| 37 | 12 | $71.31 | $26.53 | 27.00 | $2,147.80 |
| 38 | 13 | $71.81 | $26.53 | 26.75 | $2,120.92 |
| 39 | 14 | $72.31 | $26.53 | 26.50 | $2,094.30 |
| 40 | 15 | $72.81 | $26.53 | 26.25 | $2,067.92 |

# ADDITIONAL APPLICATIONS

## Pricing Analysis at Merrill Lynch

In the late 1990s, Merrill Lynch and other full-service financial service firms were losing business due to electronic trading and the commoditization of trading. Management decided to offer investors more choices for doing business with Merrill Lynch. A cross-functional team evaluated various alternatives, including pricing strategies, and constructed models to assess individual client's choice behavior. The results enabled Merrill Lynch to change the financial services landscape and mitigate its revenue risk. As of year-end 2000, net new assets to the firm totaled $22 billion, and incremental revenue grew to $80 million. ∎

## Skill-Building Problems

**1.** In Example 7.1, we assumed that two points on the demand curve were given (see Figure 7.8). Suppose three additional points are estimated by Madison: (1) demand of 460 when price is $65, (2) demand of 355 when price is $75, and (3) demand of 275 when price is $85. With these new points and the original two points, estimate and interpret the best-fitting linear demand curve; do the same for the best-fitting constant elasticity demand curve.

**2.** Continuing the previous problem, calculate the mean absolute percentage error (MAPE) for each of the two fits, linear and constant elasticity, where each MAPE is the average of the absolute percentage errors for the five points. On the basis of MAPE, which curve provides the better fit?

**3.** In the pricing model in Example 7.1 with the constant elasticity demand function, the assumption is that all units demanded are sold. Suppose the company has the capacity to produce only 200 units. If demand is less than capacity, all of demand is sold. If demand is greater than or equal to capacity, only 200 units are sold. Use Solver to find the optimal price and the corresponding profit. Then use SolverTable to see how sensitive these answers are to the production capacity, letting it vary from 170 to 230 in increments of 10. Discuss your findings relative to the original solution in Example 7.1. In other words, what is the effect of capacity on the optimal price and profit?

**4.** Continuing the previous problem, create a two-way data table similar to the one-way data table in Figure 7.9. This time, however, allow price to vary down a column and allow the capacity to vary across a row. Each cell of the data table should capture the corresponding profit. Explain how the values in the data table confirm the findings from SolverTable in the previous problem.

**5.** Continuing Problem 3 in a slightly different direction, create a two-way SolverTable where the inputs are the elasticity and the production capacity, and the outputs are the optimal price and the optimal profit. (This actually creates two tables, one for each output.) Discuss your findings.

**6.** Change the exchange rate model in Example 7.2 slightly so that the company is now a UK manufacturing company producing for a U.S. market. Assume that the unit cost is now 75 £, the demand function has the same parameters as before (although the price for this demand function is now in dollars), and the exchange rate is the same as before. Your Solver solution should now specify the optimal price to charge in dollars and the optimal profit in £.

**7.** In the exchange rate model in Example 7.2, suppose the company continues to manufacture its product in the United States, but now it sells its product in the United States, the United Kingdom, and possibly other countries. The company can independently set its price in each country where it sells. For example, the price could be $150 in the United States and 110 £ in the United Kingdom. You can assume that the demand function in each country is of the constant elasticity form, each with its own parameters. The question is whether the company can use Solver *independently* in each country to find the optimal price in this country. (You should be able to answer this question without actually running any Solver model(s), but you might want to experiment, just to verify your reasoning.)

**8.** In the exchange rate model in Example 7.2, we found that the optimal unit revenue, when converted to dollars, is $85.71. Now change the problem so that the company is selling in Japan, not the United Kingdom. Assume that the exchange rate is 0.00821 ($/¥) and that the constant in the demand function is 161,423,232,300, but everything else, including the elasticity of the demand function, remains the same. What is the optimal price in yen? What is the optimal unit revenue when converted to dollars? Is it still $85.71? Do you have an intuitive explanation for this?

**9.** In the complementary-product pricing model in Example 7.3, the elasticity of demand for suits is currently $-2.5$. Use SolverTable to see how the optimal price of suits and the optimal profit vary as the elasticity varies from $-2.7$ to $-1.8$ in increments of 0.1. Are the results intuitive? Explain.

**10.** In the complementary-product pricing model in Example 7.3, the SolverTable results in Figure 7.15 indicate that the company can sometimes increase overall profit by selling suits below cost. How far might this behavior continue? Answer by extending the SolverTable to larger values of the sensitivity factor, so that more and more shirts and ties are being purchased per suit. Does there appear to be a lower limit on the price that should be charged for suits? Might it reach a point where the company *gives* them away? (Of course, this would require an unrealistically large purchase of shirts and ties, but is it mathematically possible?)

**11.** In the peak-load pricing model in Example 7.4, the demand functions have positive and negative coefficients of prices. The negative coefficients indicate that as the price of a product increases, demand for *that* product decreases. The positive coefficients indicate that as the price of a product increases, demand for the *other* product increases.

a. Increase the magnitudes of the negative coefficients from $-0.5$ and $-1$ to $-0.7$ and $-1.2$, and then rerun Solver. Do the changes in the optimal solution go in the direction you would expect? Explain.

b. Increase the magnitudes of the positive coefficients from 0.1 and 0.1 to 0.3 and 0.3, and then rerun Solver. Do the changes in the optimal solution go in the direction you would expect? Explain.

c. Make the changes in parts **a** and **b** simultaneously, and then rerun Solver. What happens now?

**12.** In the peak-load pricing model in Example 7.4, we assumed that the capacity level is a decision variable. Assume now that capacity has already been set at 30 kwh. (Note that the cost of capacity is now a sunk cost, so it is irrelevant to the decision problem.) Change the model appropriately and run Solver. Then use SolverTable to see how sensitive the optimal solution is to the capacity level, letting it vary over some relevant range. Does it appear that the optimal prices are set so that demand always equals capacity for at least one of the two periods of the day?

## Skill-Extending Problems

**13.** Continuing Problem 7, suppose the company is selling in the United States, the United Kingdom, and Japan. Assume the unit production cost is $50, and the exchange rates are 1.56 ($/£) and 0.00821 ($/¥). Each country has its own constant elasticity demand function. The parameters for the United States are 19,200,000 and $-2$; the parameters for the United Kingdom are 10,933,620 and $-2.2$; and the parameters for Japan are 15,003,380,400 and $-1.9$. The company has a production capacity of 3000. Therefore, the company can sell only as many units, in total, to all three countries as it can produce.

a. Develop a spreadsheet model that determines the prices the company should charge and the numbers of units it should sell in each of the three countries to maximize its total profit in dollars. (Note that if total demand is greater than capacity, the company

has to decide how much to sell in each country. Therefore, the amounts to sell become changing cells.)

b. When the capacity is 3000, is all of this capacity used? Answer the same question if the capacity is increased to 4000.

c. Discuss the customer behavior that might result from the solution to the model in part **a**. If the company sets its price in one country relatively low compared to its price in another country, what might customers do?

**14.** In the complementary-product pricing model in Example 7.3, we have assumed that the profit per unit from shirts and ties is given. Presumably this is because the prices of these products have already been set. Change the model so that the company must determine the prices of shirts and ties, as well the price of suits. Assume that the unit costs of shirts and ties are, respectively, $20 and $15. Continue to assume that, on average, 2 shirts and 1.5 ties are sold along with every suit (regardless of the prices of shirts and ties), but that shirts and ties have their own separate demand functions. These demands are for shirts and ties purchased separately from suit purchases. Assume constant elasticity demand functions for shirts and ties with parameters 288,500 and $-1.7$ (shirts), and 75,460 and $-1.6$ (ties). Assume the same unit cost and demand function for suits as in Example 7.3.

a. How much should the company charge for suits, shirts, and ties to maximize the profit from all three products?

b. The assumption that customers will always buy, on average, the *same* number of shirts and ties per suit purchase, regardless of the prices of shirts and ties, is not very realistic. How might you change this assumption, and change your model from part **a** accordingly, to make it more realistic?

**15.** Continuing the previous problem (the model in part **a**) one step further, assume that shirts and ties are also complementary. Specifically, assume that each time a shirt is purchased (and is *not* accompanied by a suit purchase), 1.3 ties, on average and regardless of the price of ties, are also purchased. Modify the model from part **a** of the previous problem to find the prices of suits, shirts, and ties to maximize overall profit.

## 7.4 ADVERTISING RESPONSE AND SELECTION MODELS

In Chapter 4, we discussed an advertising allocation model (Example 4.1), where the problem was basically to decide how many ads to place on various television shows to reach the required number of viewers. One assumption of that model was that the "advertising response"—that is, the number of exposures—is *linear* in the number of ads. This means that if one ad gains, say, 1 million exposures, then 10 ads will gain 10 million exposures. This is a questionable assumption at best. More likely, there is a decreasing marginal effect at work, where each extra ad gains *fewer* exposures than the previous ad. In fact, there might even be a saturation effect, where there is an upper limit on the number of exposures possible and, after sufficiently many ads, this saturation level is reached.

In this section, we look at two related examples. In the first example, a company uses historical data to estimate its advertising response function—the number of exposures it gains from a given number of ads. This is a nonlinear optimization model. This type of advertising response function is used in the second example to solve a nonlinear version of the advertising selection problem from Chapter 4. Because the advertising response functions are nonlinear, the advertising selection problem is also nonlinear.

---

## EXAMPLE | 7.5 ESTIMATING AN ADVERTISING RESPONSE FUNCTION

Recall that the General Flakes Company from Example 4.1 of Chapter 4 sells a brand of low-fat breakfast cereal that appeals to people of all age groups and both genders. The company has advertised this product in various media for a number of years and has accumulated data on its advertising effectiveness. For example, the company has tracked the number of exposures to young men from ads placed on a particular television show for five different time periods. In each of these time periods, a different number of ads was used. Specifically, the numbers of ads were 1, 8, 20, 50, and 100. The corresponding numbers of exposures (in millions) were 4.7, 22.1, 48.7, 90.3, and 130.5. What type of nonlinear response function might fit these data well?

**Objective**  To use nonlinear optimization to find the response function (from a given class of functions) that best fits the historical data.

### WHERE DO THE NUMBERS COME FROM?

The question here is how the company measures the number of exposures a given number of ads has achieved. In particular, what does the company mean by "exposures?" If one person sees the same ad 10 times, does this mean 10 exposures? Is it the same thing as 10 people seeing the same ad once each? Although we defer to the marketing experts here, we suggest that one person seeing the same ad 10 times results in fewer "exposures" than 10 people seeing the same ad once each. However the marketing experts decide to count "exposures," it should then lead to the decreasing marginal effects we have built into this example.

## Solution

The chart in Figure 7.19 is a scatter chart of the historical data (with the dots connected). The chart clearly indicates a nonlinear pattern, where extra ads have less effect than the first few ads. Many mathematical functions have this basic shape, and we could use any of them. However, we settle here for one of the simplest, a function of the form

*The function in equation (7.4) is only one of several nonlinear functions that exhibits the type of behavior (increasing at a decreasing rate) we want.*

$$f(n) = a(1 - e^{-bn}) \qquad (7.4)$$

Here, $n$ is the number of ads placed, $f(n)$ is the resulting number of exposures, $a$ and $b$ are constants to estimate, and $e$ is the special number approximately equal to 2.718. This function has some nice properties: (1) it is 0 when $n = 0$; (2) it increases at a decreasing rate when $b > 0$; and (3) it increases to $a$ as $n$ gets large. This latter property is the saturation effect we mentioned previously. The only question, then, is which values of $a$ and $b$ to use to match the historical data in Figure 7.19 as well as possible.

**Figure 7.19** Graph of Historical Data

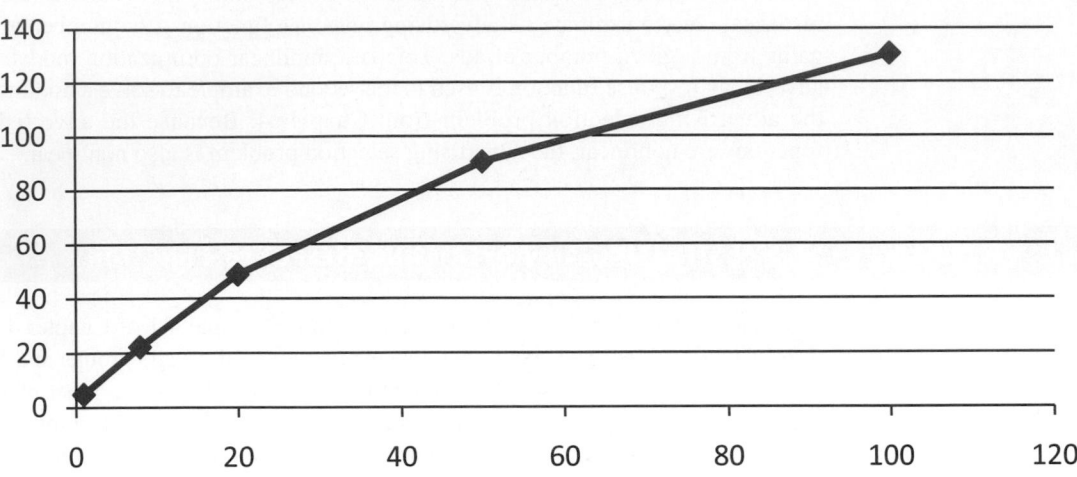

**Historical data**

*The squared differences in the goodness-of-fit measure make this a nonlinear model.*

To do this, we use a standard estimation procedure. Although the spreadsheet details are given shortly, it is worth discussing the idea behind this procedure first. Using the model in equation (7.4) with *any* values of *a* and *b*, we predict the number of exposures we would obtain for 1, 8, 20, 50, or 100 ads. Then we compare these to the actual exposures observed, using a *goodness-of-fit* measure. The specific goodness-of-fit measure used here is the sum of squared differences between actual and predicted exposures. This measure has been used most frequently in estimation problems, so we continue to use it here. Specifically, we use Solver to find the constants *a* and *b* that minimize the sum of squared prediction errors. Of course, the *squares* make this a nonlinear optimization model.

**FUNDAMENTAL INSIGHT**

**Least Squares Estimation**

In many situations, we try to fit a curve of a certain functional form to a set of observed data. Although goodness of fit can be measured in several alternative ways, the most popular method is to use the sum of squared prediction errors as the criterion to minimize. The resulting optimization problem is often unconstrained; we simply want the parameters of the curve that provides the best fit. Because of the *squared* prediction errors, this problem is inherently nonlinear, but it is usually very amenable to analysis. Least squares estimation appears in many areas. For example, we use it later in this chapter to estimate football ratings and to estimate the beta of a stock, and it is the basis for the regression analysis we discuss in Chapter 16.

## DEVELOPING THE SPREADSHEET MODEL

The completed spreadsheet model is shown in Figure 7.20. (See the file **Advertising Response.xlsx**.) The model can be created with the following steps:

**Figure 7.20**  Estimation of Response Function

| | A | B | C | D | E | F | G | H | I | J |
|---|---|---|---|---|---|---|---|---|---|---|
| 1 | Fitting an advertising response curve | | | | | | | | | |
| 2 | | | | | | | | | | |
| 3 | Parameters of response curve | | | | | Range names used: | | | | |
| 4 | Constant | 155.03 | | | | Parameters | =Model!$B$4:$B$5 | | | |
| 5 | Coefficient in exponent | 0.0181 | | | | RMSE | =Model!$D$14 | | | |
| 6 | | | | | | | | | | |
| 7 | Historical data | | | | | | | | | |
| 8 | | Ads | Exposures | Predicted | Squared error | | | | | |
| 9 | | 1 | 4.7 | 2.787 | 3.660 | | | | | |
| 10 | | 8 | 22.1 | 20.942 | 1.341 | | | | | |
| 11 | | 20 | 48.7 | 47.172 | 2.334 | | | | | |
| 12 | | 50 | 90.3 | 92.440 | 4.580 | | | | | |
| 13 | | 100 | 130.5 | 129.761 | 0.547 | | | | | |
| 14 | | | | | 1.579 | ← | Root mean squared error, objective to minimize | | | |

**1  Inputs.** Enter the historical data in the blue region. There are no other inputs.

**2  Parameters of response function.** Enter *any* values for the constants *a* and *b* of the advertising response function in cells B4 and B5. These become the changing cells.

**3  Predicted exposures.** Use equation (7.4), with the values of *a* and *b* in cells B4 and B5, to calculate the predicted number of exposures for each number of ads. To do this, enter the formula

**=$B$4*(1-EXP(-$B$5*A9))**

in cell C9, and copy it down to cell C13.

**4  Squared errors.** Calculate the squared difference between actual and predicted exposures by entering the formula

**=(B9-C9)^2**

in cell D9 and copying it down to cell D13.

*RMSE is the square root of the average of the squared errors.*

**5  Objective to minimize.** We said previously that we want to minimize the sum of squared errors. Actually, this is equivalent to minimizing the root mean squared error (RMSE), which is the *square root* of the average of the squared errors. We use RMSE as the objective to minimize, so enter the formula

**=SQRT(AVERAGE(D9:D13))**

in cell D14. (One reason to use RMSE as the objective, rather than the sum of squared errors, is that RMSE is a smaller number and is less likely to give Solver numerical problems. In any case, we should get the same solution either way. Besides, RMSE has historically been a popular measure to minimize.)

## USING SOLVER

This is a particularly simple Solver setup. As Figure 7.21 indicates, we minimize RMSE using cells B4 and B5 (jointly range-named Parameters) as the changing cells. There are no constraints, not even nonnegativity constraints.[6] An optimization model with no constraints is called an **unconstrained model.**

*In an unconstrained optimization model, there are no infeasible points—all points qualify.*

[6] Actually, by the increasing nature of the historical data and the form of the response function in equation (7.4), we expect *a* and *b* to be nonnegative, but it is not necessary to *constrain* them to be nonnegative.

**Figure 7.21**

Solver Dialog Box
for the Estimation
Problem

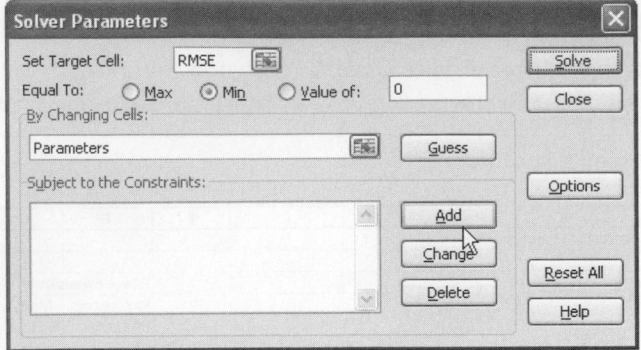

## Discussion of the Solution

The Solver solution in Figure 7.20 indicates that when we use $a = 155.03$ and $b = 0.0181$ in equation (7.4), we get the best possible fit to the historical data. A glance at the Actual and Predicted columns in rows 9 to 13 indicates that this fit is quite good. We can then see what this version of equation (7.4) looks like, as well as the number of exposures it would predict for other numbers of ads. We do this numerically and graphically in Figure 7.22. For example, the formula in cell B18 is **=$B$4\*(1-EXP(-$B$5\*A18))**, which is copied down. We then plot the values in columns A and B to obtain the curve in the figure. The response function increases at a decreasing rate and approaches $a = 155.03$ as the number of ads gets large.

**Figure 7.22**    Estimated Response Function

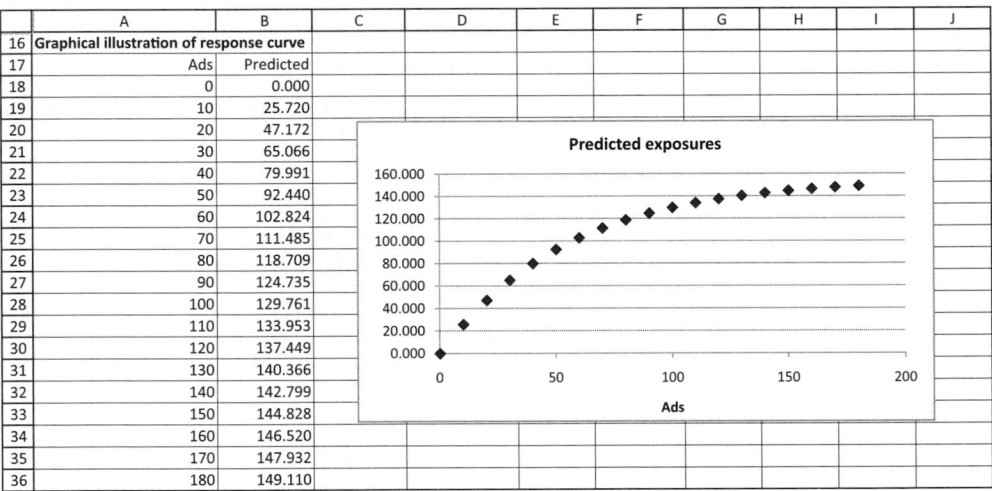

| | A | B | C | D | E | F | G | H | I | J |
|---|---|---|---|---|---|---|---|---|---|---|
| 16 | Graphical illustration of response curve | | | | | | | | | |
| 17 | Ads | Predicted | | | | | | | | |
| 18 | 0 | 0.000 | | | | | | | | |
| 19 | 10 | 25.720 | | | | | | | | |
| 20 | 20 | 47.172 | | | | | | | | |
| 21 | 30 | 65.066 | | | | | | | | |
| 22 | 40 | 79.991 | | | | | | | | |
| 23 | 50 | 92.440 | | | | | | | | |
| 24 | 60 | 102.824 | | | | | | | | |
| 25 | 70 | 111.485 | | | | | | | | |
| 26 | 80 | 118.709 | | | | | | | | |
| 27 | 90 | 124.735 | | | | | | | | |
| 28 | 100 | 129.761 | | | | | | | | |
| 29 | 110 | 133.953 | | | | | | | | |
| 30 | 120 | 137.449 | | | | | | | | |
| 31 | 130 | 140.366 | | | | | | | | |
| 32 | 140 | 142.799 | | | | | | | | |
| 33 | 150 | 144.828 | | | | | | | | |
| 34 | 160 | 146.520 | | | | | | | | |
| 35 | 170 | 147.932 | | | | | | | | |
| 36 | 180 | 149.110 | | | | | | | | |

## Is the Solver Solution Optimal?

*In some nonlinear models, such as this one, Solver finds the optimal solution only if the starting solution is reasonably close to the optimal solution.*

Verifying whether RMSE is a concave function of the two parameters $a$ and $b$ is difficult—even for mathematicians! Therefore, the best approach is to try several starting solutions in cells B4 and B5 and see whether Solver converges to the *same* solution in each case. We tried this, and it works—unless the starting solution is way off. For example, if the starting solution has 200 and 0.1 in cells B4 and B5, respectively, Solver finds the solution in Figure 7.20. However, if the starting solution has 0 and 0 in these cells, Solver stops at a very different solution. In fact, it *stays* at this 0–0 solution. This is typical of many nonlinear optimization models. Unless the starting solution is "reasonably close" to the optimal solution, Solver can go to a completely wrong solution. ∎

## MODELING ISSUES

We used the popular sum-of-squared-errors measure (or its RMSE equivalent) to find the best-fitting response function. Another possibility is to use the sum (or average) of the *absolute* errors. Still another possibility is to use the *maximum* of the absolute errors. All of these have been used in estimation problems, and all lead to nonlinear optimization models. They typically lead to similar, but not necessarily identical, solutions. We used the sum-of-squared-errors measure because it has historically been the most frequently used measure and leads to a smooth nonlinear model—the kind that Solver handles best. ∎

Now that we know how a company can estimate the advertising response function for any type of ad to any group of customers, we use this type of response function in an advertising selection model.

EXAMPLE | **7.6 ADVERTISING SELECTION WITH NONLINEAR RESPONSE FUNCTIONS**

*In this model, each customer group has its own nonlinear advertising response function to each television show.*

In this example, we revisit the problem faced by the General Flakes Company in Example 4.1 of Chapter 4. The company must decide how many ads to place on each of several television shows to meet exposure constraints for each of six groups of customers. (Refer to Figure 7.23 and the file **Advertising Selection.xlsx** for the specific inputs.) The difference now is that each combination of television show and customer group has its own advertising response function of the form in equation (7.4). That is, there are constants $a$ and $b$ of the response function for *each* such combination. (These constants appear in rows 5 to 10 and 14 to 19 of the file.) The company wants to find the selection of ads that minimizes its total cost of meeting all exposure requirements.

**Objective** To use a nonlinear model to find a minimum-cost way of meeting all exposure requirements.

### WHERE DO THE NUMBERS COME FROM?

We already discussed where many of the inputs come from in Example 4.1 of Chapter 4. The new inputs, the parameters of the various response functions, come from fitting response functions, exactly as we illustrated in the previous example, for each combination of television show and customer group. Of course, this assumes the company has enough historical data to carry out this procedure. The numbers we have used are for illustration only, although they are reasonable.

## Solution

The variables and constraints for this model are listed in Table 7.4. Except for the new inputs from the advertising response functions, this table is exactly like the table for Example 4.1 of Chapter 4.

## Table 7.4  Variables and Constraints for the Advertising Model

| | |
|---|---|
| Input variables | Cost per ad, minimal required exposures, parameters of advertising response functions |
| Decision variables (changing cells) | Numbers of ads to place on various types of shows |
| Objective (target cell) | Total advertising cost |
| Other output variables | Total exposures to each viewer group |
| Constraints | Actual exposures must be greater than or equal to Required exposures |

### DEVELOPING THE SPREADSHEET MODEL

The spreadsheet model is shown in Figure 7.23 and in the file **Advertising Selection.xlsx**. The model can be developed with the following steps:

**Figure 7.23**  Spreadsheet Model for Advertising Selection

| | A | B | C | D | E | F | G | H | I |
|---|---|---|---|---|---|---|---|---|---|
| 1 | Advertising model with nonlinear response functions | | | | | | | | |
| 2 | | | | | | Note: All monetary values are in $1000s, and all exposures to ads are in millions of exposures | | | |
| 3 | Constant in advertising response function for various groups for different shows | | | | | | | | |
| 4 | | Desperate Housewives | MNF | Malcolm in Middle | Sports Center | The Real World | Lifetime movie | CNN | Law & Order |
| 5 | Men 18-35 | 93.061 | 116.808 | 84.772 | 43.647 | 26.711 | 11.99 | 11.793 | 79.534 |
| 6 | Men 36-55 | 61.129 | 76.527 | 61.528 | 47.749 | 19.655 | 10.281 | 9.982 | 89.217 |
| 7 | Men >55 | 33.376 | 57.84 | 9.913 | 30.075 | 10.751 | 11.51 | 22.218 | 65.543 |
| 8 | Women 18-35 | 105.803 | 40.113 | 66.998 | 22.101 | 42.451 | 29.403 | 8.236 | 72.145 |
| 9 | Women 36-55 | 71.784 | 26.534 | 46.146 | 16.151 | 34.609 | 24.276 | 10.426 | 92.831 |
| 10 | Women >55 | 56.828 | 17.209 | 8.887 | 9.101 | 8.46 | 31.149 | 23.105 | 71.321 |
| 11 | | | | | | | | | |
| 12 | Coefficient of exponent in advertising response function for various groups for different shows | | | | | | | | |
| 13 | | Desperate Housewives | MNF | Malcolm in Middle | Sports Center | The Real World | Lifetime movie | CNN | Law & Order |
| 14 | Men 18-35 | 0.029 | 0.055 | 0.093 | 0.071 | 0.087 | 0.038 | 0.029 | 0.045 |
| 15 | Men 36-55 | 0.084 | 0.050 | 0.085 | 0.094 | 0.018 | 0.090 | 0.054 | 0.051 |
| 16 | Men >55 | 0.071 | 0.068 | 0.077 | 0.027 | 0.039 | 0.051 | 0.013 | 0.036 |
| 17 | Women 18-35 | 0.035 | 0.063 | 0.069 | 0.074 | 0.060 | 0.012 | 0.039 | 0.035 |
| 18 | Women 36-55 | 0.089 | 0.057 | 0.061 | 0.055 | 0.014 | 0.022 | 0.046 | 0.040 |
| 19 | Women >55 | 0.010 | 0.033 | 0.078 | 0.078 | 0.035 | 0.050 | 0.072 | 0.030 |
| 20 | | | | | | | | | |
| 21 | Cost per ad | 140 | 100 | 80 | 9 | 13 | 15 | 8 | 140 |
| 22 | | | | | | | | | |
| 23 | Advertising plan | | | | | | | | |
| 24 | | Desperate Housewives | MNF | Malcolm in Middle | Sports Center | The Real World | Lifetime movie | CNN | Law & Order |
| 25 | Number ads purchased | 4.836 | 0.000 | 2.794 | 21.852 | 16.284 | 8.285 | 15.289 | 0.000 |
| 26 | | | | | | | | | |
| 27 | Exposures to each group from each show | | | | | | | | |
| 28 | | Desperate Housewives | MNF | Malcolm in Middle | Sports Center | The Real World | Lifetime movie | CNN | Law & Order |
| 29 | Men 18-35 | 12.178 | 0.000 | 19.398 | 34.397 | 20.233 | 3.238 | 4.223 | 0.000 |
| 30 | Men 36-55 | 20.408 | 0.000 | 13.006 | 41.627 | 4.994 | 5.403 | 5.610 | 0.000 |
| 31 | Men >55 | 9.700 | 0.000 | 1.919 | 13.403 | 5.054 | 3.966 | 4.005 | 0.000 |
| 32 | Women 18-35 | 16.476 | 0.000 | 11.747 | 17.714 | 26.472 | 2.783 | 3.699 | 0.000 |
| 33 | Women 36-55 | 25.108 | 0.000 | 7.231 | 11.295 | 7.055 | 4.045 | 5.266 | 0.000 |
| 34 | Women >55 | 2.683 | 0.000 | 1.740 | 7.446 | 3.675 | 10.564 | 15.420 | 0.000 |
| 35 | | | | | | | | | |
| 36 | Constraints on numbers of exposures | | | | | | Range names used: | | |
| 37 | | Actual exposures | | Required exposures | | | Actual_exposures | =Sheet1!$B$38:$B$43 | |
| 38 | Men 18-35 | 93.667 | >= | 60 | | | Number_ads_purchased | =Sheet1!$B$25:$I$25 | |
| 39 | Men 36-55 | 91.049 | >= | 60 | | | Required_exposures | =Sheet1!$D$38:$D$43 | |
| 40 | Men >55 | 38.048 | >= | 28 | | | Total_cost | =Sheet1!$B$46 | |
| 41 | Women 18-35 | 78.890 | >= | 60 | | | | | |
| 42 | Women 36-55 | 60.000 | >= | 60 | | | | | |
| 43 | Women >55 | 41.529 | >= | 28 | | | | | |
| 44 | | | | | | | | | |
| 45 | Objective to minimize | | | | | | | | |
| 46 | Total cost | $1,555.535 | | | | | | | |

**1 Inputs.** Enter the inputs in the blue cells. These include the parameters of the advertising response functions in rows 5 to 10 and 14 to 19. Again, we made up these inputs, but they would typically be estimated from historical data.

**2 Ads purchased.** Enter *any* trial values of the numbers of ads purchased for the various shows in row 25. These cells become the changing cells.

**3** **Exposures from each show to each group.** Use the advertising response functions to calculate the numbers of exposures to each customer group from each show. To do this, enter the formula

**=B5*(1-EXP(-B14*B$25))**

in cell B29 and copy it to the range B29:I34. Note that row 25 must be kept absolute for copying to work correctly because the numbers of ads are always in row 25.

**4** **Total exposures to each group.** Calculate the numbers of exposures to each group by entering the formula

**=SUM(B29:I29)**

in cell B38 and copying it down to cell B43. This formula sums overexposures from the various television shows.

**5** **Total cost.** Calculate the total cost of advertising in cell B46 with the formula

**=SUMPRODUCT(B21:I21,Number_ads_purchased)**

## USING SOLVER

*Integer constraints can be added, but they do not affect the optimal solution to a great extent.*

The Solver dialog box is straightforward to complete, as illustrated in Figure 7.24. Just remember to check the Assume Non-Negative box under Solver options, but do *not* check the Assume Linear Model box. The nonlinear advertising response functions make the model nonlinear. Note that we could also constrain the changing cells to be integers. This would make the model more difficult for Solver to solve, but it would also make the solution more realistic. (However, you can check that it doesn't change the optimal solution by much.)

**Figure 7.24**

Solver Dialog Box for the Advertising Selection Model

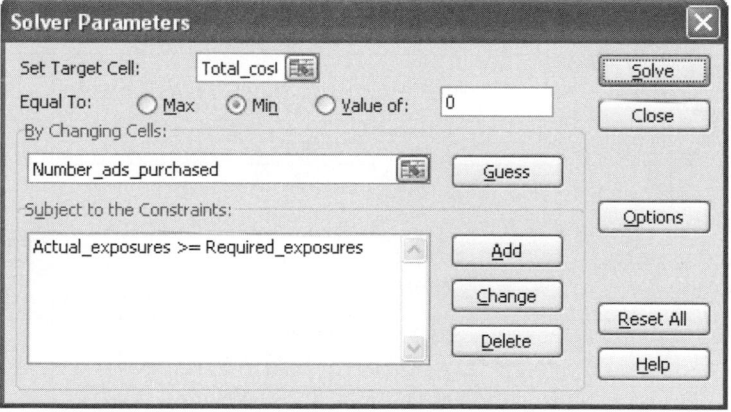

### Discussion of the Solution

First, note that the constants in rows 5 to 10 of the advertising response functions indicate the maximum numbers of exposures possible to each group from each show. The coefficients in rows 14 to 19 indicate how fast the response functions approach these maximum limits: When one of these coefficients increases, fewer ads are needed to approach the saturation level. Together, these two sets of constants indicate which types of ads are most effective to the various customer groups. Solver uses this information in its intricate algorithm to decide how many ads to place on each show. Perhaps surprisingly, no ads are placed on "Monday Night Football," although many exposures to men under 55 would be achieved from these ads. Evidently these ads are too expensive, and exposures to men in these groups can be achieved with cheaper ads on other shows. Note also that the women in the 36 to 55 group are evidently the "bottleneck" group. (Check the differences between the two sides of the exposure constraints.) To achieve the required exposures for this group, many more ads are required than are needed to achieve the required exposures to the other groups.

### Is the Solver Solution Optimal?

It can be shown (with calculus) that this model satisfies the conditions necessary to ensure a single local minimum. Therefore, we know that the Solver solution is optimal. If you didn't know this, however, you could try running Solver several times, each from a different starting solution in row 25. You should find that they all converge to the solution in Figure 7.23.

### Sensitivity Analysis

An interesting sensitivity analysis for this nonlinear model is to see how the optimal cost varies if we change all of the required exposures by the *same* percentage. If we did this in a linear model (and there were no other constraints to worry about), the optimal cost would change by the same percentage due to the proportionality property of linear models. For example, if we increased the right-hand sides of all constraints by 10%, we would expect the optimal cost to increase by 10% in a linear model. However, this is not true in a nonlinear model, as Figure 7.25 indicates. Here we changed the model slightly so that we can vary the single percentage in cell F44. The original required exposures are now in column F, and the formula in cell D38 is **=F38\*(1+$F$44)**, which is copied down.

**Figure 7.25** Sensitivity of Total Cost to Percentage Change in Exposures Required

| | A | B | C | D | E | F |
|---|---|---|---|---|---|---|
| 36 | **Constraints on numbers of exposures** | | | | | |
| 37 | | Actual exposures | | Required exposures | | Originally required |
| 38 | Men 18-35 | 93.667 | >= | 60 | | 60 |
| 39 | Men 36-55 | 91.049 | >= | 60 | | 60 |
| 40 | Men >55 | 38.048 | >= | 28 | | 28 |
| 41 | Women 18-35 | 78.890 | >= | 60 | | 60 |
| 42 | Women 36-55 | 60.000 | >= | 60 | | 60 |
| 43 | Women >55 | 41.529 | >= | 28 | | 28 |
| 44 | | | | | Percentage change | 0% |
| 45 | **Objective to minimize** | | | | | |
| 46 | Total cost | $1,555.535 | | | | |
| 47 | | | | | | |
| 48 | **Sensitivity of total cost to percentage change in all required exposures** | | | | | |
| 49 | | $B$46 | Percentage increase | | | |
| 50 | 0% | $1,555.540 | | | | |
| 51 | 10% | $1,762.090 | 13.3% | | | |
| 52 | 20% | $1,977.880 | 27.2% | | | |
| 53 | 30% | $2,203.260 | 41.6% | | | |
| 54 | 40% | $2,435.570 | 56.6% | | | |
| 55 | 50% | $2,674.540 | 71.9% | | | |

We then used SolverTable to see how sensitive the total cost is to the percentage increase in the required exposures to each group. The percentage increases in total cost, relative to the original cost, are calculated manually (not with SolverTable) in column C. Because of the decreasing marginal effect of extra ads, it takes larger percentage increases in cost to achieve a given percentage increase in exposures. For example, if we need 40% more exposures to each group, we require a 56.6% increase in total cost. This illustrates in a very real way a consequence of nonlinearity. ∎

## PROBLEMS

### Skill-Building Problems

**16.** In estimating the advertising response function in Example 7.5, we indicated that the sum of squared prediction errors *or* RMSE could be used as the objective, and we used RMSE. Try using the sum of squared prediction errors instead. Does Solver find the same solution as in the example? Try running Solver several times, each time from a diffcrent starting solution in the changing cells, and report what happens.

**17.** The best-fitting advertising response function in Example 7.5 fits the observed data. This is because we rigged the observed data to fall close to a curve of the form in equation (7.4). See what happens when one of the observed points is an outlier—that is, it doesn't fit the pattern of the others.
    **a.** Specifically, change the number of exposures corresponding to 50 ads from 90.3 to 125, and then rerun Solver. Do you get essentially the same response function as before, or does this one outlier exert a large influence on the estimated response function?
    **b.** Repeat part **a**, but now change the number of exposures corresponding to 50 ads from 90.3 to 55.

**18.** In judging the fit of the estimated response function in Example 7.5, we could use MAD (mean absolute deviation) instead of RMSE. MAD is the average of the *absolute* prediction errors.
    **a.** When you run Solver with MAD as your objective, do you get approximately the same estimated response function as with RMSE?
    **b.** Repeat part **a**, but do it with the outliers in parts **a** and **b** of the previous problem. Report your results in a brief memo.

**19.** As we mentioned, the advertising response function in equation (7.4) is only one of several nonlinear functions we could have used to get the same "increasing at a decreasing rate" behavior we want in Example 7.5. Another possibility is the function $f(n) = an^b$, where $a$ and $b$ are again constants to be determined. Using the same data as in Example 7.5 and RMSE as the fitting criterion, find the best fit to this type of function. In terms of RMSE, which function appears to fit the data better, the one here or the one in the example? Can you spot any qualitative difference between the two types of functions?

**20.** Starting with the solution to the advertising selection problem in Example 7.6, suppose the company, for whatever reason, cannot place ads on "Sports Center." Make the appropriate changes in the model and rerun Solver. Comment on the changes to the changing cells.

Then comment on the change to the total cost. In particular, explain how the total cost can change so much in the direction it changes.

**21.** The preceding problem indicates how fewer alternatives can cause total cost to increase. This problem indicates the opposite. Starting with the solution to the advertising selection problem in Example 7.6, add a new show, "The View," that appeals primarily to women. Use the following constants and coefficients of exponents for the response functions to the various customer groups for this show: 5, 7, 10, 15, 35, 35 (constants); and 0.03, 0.03, 0.03, 0.08, 0.08, 0.08 (coefficients of exponents). Assume that each ad on "The View" costs $10,000. Make the appropriate changes in the model and rerun Solver. Comment on the changes to the changing cells. Then comment on the change to the total cost. In particular, explain how the total cost can change so much in the direction it changes.

**22.** In the solution to the advertising selection model in Example 7.6, we indicated that the women 36 to 55 group is a "bottleneck" in the sense that the company needs to spend a lot more than it would otherwise have spent to meet the constraint for this group. Form a SolverTable to see how much this group's exposure constraint is costing the company. Vary the required exposures to this group from 30 to 60 in increments of 5, and keep track of the total advertising cost. Comment on your results.

### Skill-Extending Problem

**23.** In Example 7.5, we implied that each of the five observations was from one period of time, such as a particular week. Suppose instead that each is an *average* over several weeks. For example, the 4.7 million exposures corresponding to 1 ad might really be an average over 15 different weeks where 1 ad was shown in each of these weeks. Similarly, the 90.3 million exposures corresponding to 50 ads might really be an average over only 3 different weeks where 50 ads were shown in each of these weeks. If the observations are really averages over *different* numbers of weeks, then simply summing the squared prediction errors doesn't seem appropriate. For example, it seems more appropriate that an average over 15 weeks should get 5 times as much weight as an average over only 3 weeks. Assume the five observations in the example are really averages over 15, 10, 4, 3, and 1 weeks, respectively. Devise an appropriate fitting function, to replace sum of squared errors or RMSE, and use it to find the best fit.

# 7.5 FACILITY LOCATION MODELS

Suppose you need to find a location for a facility such as a warehouse, a tool crib in a factory, or a fire station. Your goal is to locate the facility to minimize the total distance that must be traveled to provide required services. Facility location problems such as these can usually be set up as NLP models. The following example is typical.

---

EXAMPLE | **7.7 WAREHOUSE LOCATION AT LAFFERTY**

The Lafferty Company wants to locate a warehouse from which it will ship products to four customers. The location (in the $x$-$y$ plane) of the four customers and the number of shipments per year needed by each customer are given in Table 7.5. (All coordinates are in miles, relative to the point $x = 0$ and $y = 0$.) A single warehouse must be used to service all of the customers. Lafferty wants to determine the location of the warehouse that minimizes the total distance traveled from the warehouse to the customers.

**Table 7.5** Data for the Lafferty Example

| Customer | x-coordinate | y-coordinate | Shipments per Year |
|----------|--------------|--------------|--------------------|
| 1 | 5 | 10 | 200 |
| 2 | 10 | 5 | 150 |
| 3 | 0 | 12 | 200 |
| 4 | 12 | 0 | 300 |

**Objective** To find the warehouse location, using NLP, that minimizes the total annual distance traveled from the warehouse to the customers.

## WHERE DO THE NUMBERS COME FROM?

The data for this problem are self-explanatory. Of course, at the time the model is solved, the annual shipments for the various customers are probably forecasts.

## Solution

The variables and constraints for this model are listed in Table 7.6. There are no constraints in this model, not even nonnegativity. We can locate the warehouse at *any x-y* coordinate.

**Table 7.6** Variables and Constraints for the Warehouse Location Problem

| | |
|---|---|
| **Input variables** | Customer coordinates, annual customer shipments |
| **Decision variables (changing cells)** | Coordinates of warehouse location |
| **Objective (target cell)** | Total annual distance traveled to the customers from the warehouse |
| **Other output variables** | Distances from customers to warehouse |
| **Constraints** | None |

## DEVELOPING THE SPREADSHEET MODEL

To develop the spreadsheet model, use the following steps (see Figure 7.26 and the file **Warehouse Location.xlsm**)[7]:

**Figure 7.26**

The Facility Location Model

| | A | B | C | D | E | F | G |
|---|---|---|---|---|---|---|---|
| 1 | Lafferty facility location model | | | | | | |
| 2 | | | | | | | |
| 3 | Customer data | | | | | | |
| 4 | | X-coordinate | Y-coordinate | | Annual shipments | | |
| 5 | Customer 1 | 5 | 10 | | 200 | | |
| 6 | Customer 2 | 10 | 5 | | 150 | | |
| 7 | Customer 3 | 0 | 12 | | 200 | | |
| 8 | Customer 4 | 12 | 0 | | 300 | | |
| 9 | | | | | | | |
| 10 | Warehouse location | X-coordinate | Y-coordinate | | Range names used: | | |
| 11 | | 9.314 | 5.029 | | Location | =Model!$B$11:$C$11 | |
| 12 | | | | | Total_annual_distance | =Model!$B$19 | |
| 13 | Customer distances from warehouse | | | | | | |
| 14 | Customer 1 | 6.582 | | | | | |
| 15 | Customer 2 | 0.686 | | | | | |
| 16 | Customer 3 | 11.634 | | | | | |
| 17 | Customer 4 | 5.701 | | | | | |
| 18 | | | | | | | |
| 19 | Total annual distance | 5456.540 | | | | | |
| 20 | | | | | | | |
| 21 | Testing optimality | | | | | | |
| 22 | Is this solution optimal?  Test it yourself.  Click on the left button to generate a "random" set of starting values for | | | | | | |
| 23 | the changing cells.  Then click on the right button to run Solver.  Does it always take you to the same solution? | | | | | | |
| 24 | | | | | | | |
| 25 | | | Generate random values | | | Run Solver | |
| 26 | | | | | | | |
| 27 | | | | | | | |

**❶ Inputs.** Enter the given customer data in the shaded ranges.

**❷ Coordinates of warehouse.** Enter *any* trial values in the Location range for the *x-y* coordinates of the warehouse.

**❸ Distances from warehouse to customers.** Calculate the distances from the warehouse to the customers in the range B14:B17. To do so, recall from the Pythagorean theorem that the (straight-line) distance between the two points $(a, b)$ and $(c, d)$ is $\sqrt{(c-a)^2 + (d-b)^2}$. Therefore, enter the formula

**=SQRT(SUMXMY2(B5:C5,Location))**

in cell B14 and copy it down to cell B17.

### Excel Function: *SUMXMY2*
*Microsoft realized that we often want to sum squared differences between two ranges, so it provided the Excel function SUMXMY2 (read "sum of x minus y squared"). This function has the syntax =SUMXMY2(xRange,yRange). For our example, it is equivalent to the longer form (B5-$B$11)^2+(C5-$C$11)^2. We can then take the square root to get distance.*

**❹ Total annual distance.** The total annual distance traveled from the warehouse to meet the demands of all customers is the sum over all customers of the distance from the warehouse to the customer multiplied by the annual shipments for the customer. Therefore, calculate the total annual distance traveled in cell B19 with the formula

**=SUMPRODUCT(E5:E8,B14:B17)**

---

[7] This file contains a macro, hence the **.xlsm** extension ("m" for macro). When you open the file, a message bar should appear allowing you to enable the macro. The macro won't function unless you enable it.

## USING SOLVER

The Solver setup for this model is shown in Figure 7.27. All we need to specify is that total annual distance should be minimized and the Location range contains the changing cells. There are no constraints, not even nonnegativity constraints. Also, because of the squares in the straight-line distance formula, this model is nonlinear, so the Assume Linear Model option should *not* be checked.

**Figure 7.27**

Solver Dialog Box for the Warehouse Location Model

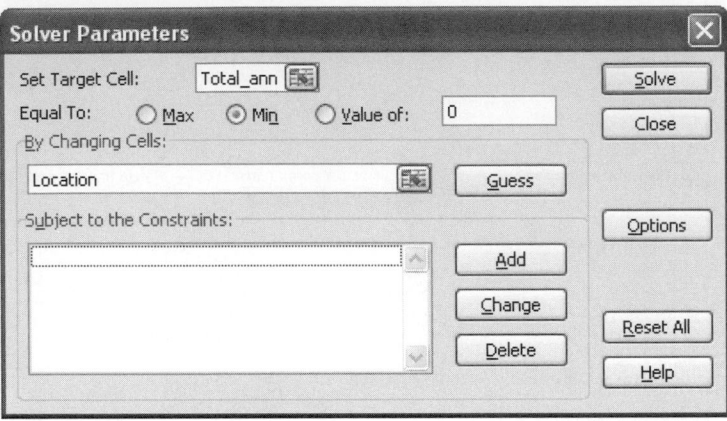

### Discussion of the Solution

The Solver solution in Figure 7.26 is represented graphically in Figure 7.28. The warehouse should be located at $x = 9.32$ and $y = 5.03$. Each year, a total of 5456.54 miles will be traveled from the warehouse to the customers. This solution represents a compromise. On the one hand, Lafferty would like to position the facility near customer 4 because the most trips are made to customer 4. However, because customer 4 is fairly far from the other customers, the warehouse is located in a more central position.

**Figure 7.28**

Graph of Solution to the Warehouse Location Example

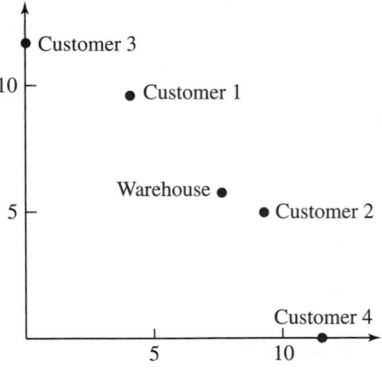

### Sensitivity Analysis

*As the number of shipments to any customer increases, the optimal warehouse location gets closer to that customer.*

One possible sensitivity analysis is to see how the optimal location of the warehouse changes as the annual number of shipments to any particular customer increases. We did this for customer 4 in Figure 7.29. We ran SolverTable with the number of shipments to customer 4 (cell E8) as the single input cell, allowing it to vary from 300 to 700 in increments of 50, and we kept track of the total annual distance and the warehouse location coordinates. As expected, the total annual distance increases as the annual shipments to customer 4 increase. Also, the warehouse gradually gets closer to customer 4. In fact, when the number of annual shipments to customer 4 is 600 or above, the optimal location for the warehouse is *at* customer 4.

**Figure 7.29**

Sensitivity Analysis for Warehouse Location

| | A | B | C | D | E |
|---|---|---|---|---|---|
| 28 | Sensitivity of total distance and warehouse coordinates to shipments to customer 4 | | | | |
| 29 | | $B$19 | $B$11 | $C$11 | |
| 30 | 300 | 5456.540 | 9.314 | 5.029 | |
| 31 | 350 | 5732.969 | 9.634 | 4.877 | |
| 32 | 400 | 6000.839 | 9.690 | 4.762 | |
| 33 | 450 | 6260.753 | 9.680 | 4.510 | |
| 34 | 500 | 6501.694 | 9.788 | 3.846 | |
| 35 | 550 | 6643.198 | 12.000 | 0.000 | |
| 36 | 600 | 6643.199 | 12.000 | 0.000 | |
| 37 | 650 | 6643.199 | 12.000 | 0.000 | |
| 38 | 700 | 6643.200 | 12.000 | 0.000 | |

### Is the Solver Solution Optimal?

The Lafferty model has no constraints. Therefore, we know that the Solver will find an optimal solution if the objective is a convex function of the coordinates of the warehouse. It can be shown (with some difficulty) that the annual distance traveled is a convex function of the coordinates of the warehouse. Therefore, we know that the Solver solution is optimal.

*The buttons in this file let you experiment with randomly generated starting values in the changing cells.*

However, what if you do not know whether the objective is a convex function of the coordinates? Then the best strategy is to try different starting solutions in the Location range, run Solver on each of them, and see whether they all take you to the same solution. In fact, we have made this easy for you in the **Warehouse Location.xlsm** file (see Figure 7.26). We have written two short macros that are automated by clicking buttons. You can click on the left button to randomly generate a new starting location in the changing cells. Then you can click on the right button to run Solver. They should always take you to the same solution.[8] ■

## MODELING ISSUES

1. The straight-line distance function we used in the Lafferty example is relevant if the company is shipping by air. However, if the company is shipping by road, we must take into account that most roads are built in a north–south or east–west direction. Then the relevant distance between points $(a, b)$ and $(c, d)$ is $|a - c| + |b - d|$ (the sum of the absolute differences), and this objective should be used in place of the square root objective. Because of absolute values, it is *still* nonlinear.

2. Besides assuming straight-line distance, we made two other assumptions in the Lafferty example: (1) exactly one warehouse will be built, and (2) this warehouse can be built *anywhere*. In real-world facility location problems, it is often necessary to modify these assumptions. First, it might be possible to build several warehouses. Second, the *possible* locations might be restricted to a certain subset of geographical locations. And third, the distances from all potential warehouse locations to customers might be given by a distance matrix, rather than calculated from some formula. In this situation, an IP model with binary variables is more suitable. There is a 0–1 variable for each potential warehouse location (either build there or don't) and a 0–1 variable for each warehouse–customer pair (either supply that customer from that warehouse or don't). We ask you to model such a version of the warehouse location problem in one of the problems.

[8] If you would like to have similar macros for other NLP models, it is fairly easy. With the **Warehouse Location.xlsm** file open, press the Alt+F11 key combination to see the Visual Basic screen. The code for the macros is in the Module sheet for this file. Except for the line indicated in the code and the range name of the changing cells, these macros can be used for other problems with no changes.

## PROBLEMS

### Skill-Building Problems

24. Modify the warehouse location model so that there is an extra customer. This customer has 250 shipments per year. Try placing this new customer at various locations (see Figure 7.28 for guidance). For example, try placing the customer way up to the right, or way down to the left, or near a current customer, and so on. For each such location, find the optimal warehouse location. Discuss the effect of this new customer and its location on the optimal warehouse location.

**25.** Modify the warehouse location model so that customers always travel in horizontal or vertical directions. For example, this means that if a customer's coordinates are (5, 10) and a warehouse is located at (7, 7), then the traveling distance is $|5 - 7| + |10 - 7| = 5$.

26. Use SolverTable in the warehouse location model to see the effect on the optimal solution of moving one customer farther and farther away from the others. Specifically, let customer 1's coordinates be of the form (5c, 10c), where the factor $c$ is allowed to vary from 1 to 10 in increments of 1. Keep track of the changing cells and the target cell.

### Skill-Extending Problem

27. Modify the warehouse location model as suggested in Modeling Issue 2. Specifically, assume that the same four customers have the same annual shipments, but now, there are only two possible warehouse locations, each with distances to the various customers. (These distances, along with other inputs, are in the file **P07_27.xlsx**.) The company can build either or both of these warehouses. The cost to build a warehouse is $50,000. (You can assume that this cost has been annualized. That is, the company incurs a building cost that is equivalent to $50,000 per year.) If only one warehouse is built, it will ship to all customers. However, if both warehouses are built, then the company must decide which warehouse will ship to each customer. There is a traveling cost of $1 per mile.
   a. Develop an appropriate model to minimize total annual cost, and then use Solver to optimize it. Is this model an NLP or an IP model (or both)?
   b. Use SolverTable with a single input, the traveling cost per mile, to see how large this cost must be before the company builds both warehouses rather than just one.

## 7.6 MODELS FOR RATING SPORTS TEAMS

Sports fans always wonder which team is best in a given sport. Was USC, LSU, or Oklahoma number one during the 2003 NCAA football season? You might be surprised to learn that Solver can be used to rate sports teams. We examine one method for doing this in the following example.

EXAMPLE | **7.8 RATING NFL TEAMS[9]**

We obtained the results of the 256 regular-season NFL games from the 2006 season and entered the data into a spreadsheet, shown at the bottom of Figure 7.30 (see the file **NFL Ratings 2006.xlsx**). (Some of these results are hidden in Figure 7.30 to conserve space.) The teams are indexed 1 to 32, as shown at the top of the sheet. For example, team 1 is Arizona, team 2 is Atlanta, and so on. The first game entered (row 6) is team 25 Pittsburgh versus team 17 Miami, played at Pittsburgh. Pittsburgh won the game by a score of 28 to 17, and the point spread (home team score minus visitor team score) is calculated in column J. A positive point spread in column J means that the home team won; a negative point spread indicates that the visiting team won. Our goal is to determine a set of ratings for the 32 NFL teams that most accurately predicts the actual outcomes of the games played.

[9] The procedure used in this example is practically identical to the procedure used by the nationally syndicated Jeff Sagarin to rate various sports teams. You can see his ratings at http://www.usatoday.com/sports/sagarin.htm.

# Figure 7.30 The NFL Ratings Model

| # | A | B | C | E | F | G | H | I | J | K | L |
|---|---|---|---|---|---|---|---|---|---|---|---|
| 1 | Rating NFL teams in 2006 | | | Objective to minimize | | | | | | | |
| 2 | | | | Sum squared errors | 37405.71 | | | | | | |
| 3 | Ratings of teams | | | | | | | | | | |
| 4 | Index | Team name | Rating | Results of games | | | | | | Model predictions and errors | |
| 5 | 1 | Arizona Cardinals | 78.07 | Week | Home team index | Visiting team index | Home team score | Visiting team score | Point spread | Predicted spread | Squared error |
| 6 | 2 | Atlanta Falcons | 81.98 | 1 | 25 | 17 | 28 | 17 | 11 | 3.5812 | 55.0383 |
| 7 | 3 | Baltimore Ravens | 94.35 | 1 | 19 | 4 | 19 | 17 | 2 | 8.8952 | 47.5441 |
| 8 | 4 | Buffalo Bills | 87.19 | 1 | 21 | 14 | 21 | 26 | -5 | -4.9456 | 0.0030 |
| 9 | 5 | Carolina Panthers | 82.33 | 1 | 5 | 2 | 6 | 20 | -14 | 1.1942 | 230.8625 |
| 10 | 6 | Chicago Bears | 92.90 | 1 | 15 | 9 | 24 | 17 | 7 | 4.6752 | 5.4045 |
| 11 | 7 | Cincinnati Bengals | 89.08 | 1 | 8 | 20 | 14 | 19 | -5 | -9.0381 | 16.3062 |
| 12 | 8 | Cleveland Browns | 79.16 | 1 | 30 | 3 | 0 | 27 | -27 | -16.4287 | 111.7517 |
| 13 | 9 | Dallas Cowboys | 88.66 | 1 | 11 | 29 | 6 | 9 | -3 | -1.9339 | 1.1365 |
| 14 | 10 | Denver Broncos | 86.32 | 1 | 31 | 22 | 16 | 23 | -7 | -2.4589 | 20.6214 |
| 15 | 11 | Detroit Lions | 78.65 | 1 | 12 | 6 | 0 | 26 | -26 | -11.4700 | 211.1195 |
| 16 | 12 | Green Bay Packers | 80.58 | 1 | 26 | 10 | 18 | 10 | 8 | -4.4234 | 154.3399 |
| 17 | 13 | Houston Texans | 80.50 | 1 | 16 | 7 | 10 | 23 | -13 | -2.2433 | 115.7060 |
| 18 | 14 | Indianapolis Colts | 90.88 | 1 | 13 | 24 | 10 | 24 | -14 | -7.0466 | 48.3496 |
| 19 | 15 | Jacksonville Jaguars | 92.49 | 1 | 1 | 28 | 34 | 27 | 7 | 2.6369 | 19.0367 |
| 20 | 16 | Kansas City Chiefs | 85.99 | 1 | 32 | 18 | 16 | 19 | -3 | 0.8930 | 15.1554 |
| 21 | 17 | Miami Dolphins | 85.68 | 1 | 23 | 27 | 0 | 27 | -27 | -18.9516 | 64.7761 |
| 22 | 18 | Minnesota Vikings | 80.91 | 2 | 22 | 19 | 17 | 24 | -7 | -7.3659 | 0.1339 |
| 23 | 19 | New England Patriots | 95.24 | 2 | 24 | 21 | 24 | 30 | -6 | 4.1549 | 103.1230 |
| 24 | 20 | New Orleans Saints | 89.04 | 2 | 3 | 23 | 28 | 6 | 22 | 19.7966 | 4.8549 |
| 25 | 21 | New York Giants | 85.08 | 2 | 17 | 4 | 6 | 16 | -10 | -0.6600 | 87.2360 |
| 26 | 22 | New York Jets | 87.02 | 2 | 2 | 30 | 14 | 3 | 11 | 5.7581 | 27.4776 |
| 27 | 23 | Oakland Raiders | 75.40 | 2 | 7 | 8 | 34 | 17 | 17 | 10.7695 | 38.8188 |
| 28 | 24 | Philadelphia Eagles | 88.39 | 2 | 14 | 13 | 43 | 24 | 19 | 11.2279 | 60.4062 |
| 29 | 25 | Pittsburgh Steelers | 88.42 | 2 | 6 | 11 | 34 | 7 | 27 | 15.0983 | 141.6501 |
| 30 | 26 | St. Louis Rams | 81.05 | 2 | 12 | 20 | 27 | 34 | -7 | -7.6147 | 0.3779 |
| 31 | 27 | San Diego Chargers | 95.20 | 2 | 18 | 5 | 16 | 13 | 3 | -0.5731 | 12.7668 |
| 32 | 28 | San Francisco 49ers | 76.28 | 2 | 9 | 32 | 27 | 10 | 17 | 8.5567 | 71.2893 |
| 33 | 29 | Seattle Seahawks | 81.43 | 2 | 10 | 16 | 9 | 6 | 3 | 1.1779 | 3.3202 |
| 34 | 30 | Tampa Bay Buccaneers | 77.07 | 2 | 27 | 31 | 40 | 7 | 33 | 12.3263 | 427.4010 |
| 35 | 31 | Tennessee Titans | 83.72 | 2 | 29 | 1 | 21 | 10 | 11 | 4.2095 | 46.1114 |
| 36 | 32 | Washington Redskins | 80.95 | 2 | 28 | 26 | 20 | 13 | 7 | -3.9214 | 119.2778 |
| 37 | | | | 2 | 15 | 25 | 9 | 0 | 9 | 4.9193 | 16.6520 |
| 38 | Home team advantage | 0.85 | | 3 | 19 | 10 | 7 | 17 | -10 | 9.7665 | 390.7158 |
| 39 | | | | 3 | 4 | 22 | 20 | 28 | -8 | 1.0136 | 81.2455 |
| 40 | Constraint on average rating (any nominal value could be used) | | | 3 | 25 | 7 | 20 | 28 | -8 | 0.1841 | 66.9797 |
| 41 | Actual average | 85.0 | | 3 | 17 | 31 | 13 | 10 | 3 | 2.8126 | 0.0351 |
| 42 | | = | | 3 | 8 | 3 | 14 | 15 | -1 | -14.3405 | 177.9698 |
| 43 | Nominal average | 85 | | 3 | 30 | 5 | 24 | 26 | -2 | -4.4093 | 5.8047 |
| 44 | | | | 3 | 11 | 12 | 24 | 31 | -7 | -1.0853 | 34.9837 |
| 45 | Range names used: | | | 3 | 14 | 15 | 21 | 14 | 7 | -0.7638 | 60.2766 |
| 46 | Actual_average | =Model!$B$41 | | 3 | 18 | 6 | 16 | 19 | -3 | -11.1454 | 66.3474 |
| 47 | Home_team_advantage | =Model!$B$38 | | 3 | 13 | 32 | 15 | 31 | -16 | 0.3926 | 268.7180 |
| 48 | Nominal_average | =Model!$B$43 | | 3 | 1 | 26 | 14 | 16 | -2 | -2.1322 | 0.0175 |
| 49 | Rating | =Model!$C$5:$C$36 | | 3 | 29 | 21 | 42 | 30 | 12 | -2.8056 | 219.2067 |
| 50 | RatingTable | =Model!$A$5:$C$36 | | 3 | 28 | 24 | 24 | 38 | -14 | -11.2640 | 7.4859 |
| 51 | Sum_squared_errors | =Model!$F$2 | | 3 | 20 | 2 | 23 | 3 | 20 | 7.9112 | 146.1397 |

**Objective**   To use NLP to find the ratings that best predict the actual point spreads observed.

## WHERE DO THE NUMBERS COME FROM?

Sports fans thank heaven for the Web. The results of NFL games, as well as NBA, MLB, and other sporting games, can be found on a number of Web sites. Check out http://www.sportingnews.com, for example. To see much more about sports ratings, go to Jeff Sagarin's page at http://www.usatoday.com/sports/sagarin.htm. Of course, if you are an avid sports fan, you probably already know the good Web sites!

## Solution

We first need to explain the methodology used to rate teams. Suppose that a team plays at home against another team. Then our prediction for the point spread of the game (home team score minus visitor team score) is

Predicted point spread

= Home team rating − Visitor team rating + Home team advantage

The home team advantage is the number of points extra for the home team because of the psychological (or physical) advantage of playing on its home field. Football experts claim that this home team advantage in the NFL is about 3 points. However, we will estimate it, as well as the ratings.

We define the prediction error to be

$$\text{Prediction error} = \text{Actual point spread} - \text{Predicted point spread}$$

*The ratings are chosen so that the predicted point spreads match the actual point spreads as closely as possible.*

We determine ratings that minimize the sum of squared prediction errors.[10] To get a unique answer to the problem, we need to "normalize" the ratings—that is, fix the average rating at some nominal value. Because the well-known Sagarin ratings use a nominal value in the mid-80s, we use a nominal value of 85. (Any nominal value could be used to produce exactly the same *relative* ratings.) Then what do ratings of, say, 82 and 91 really mean? They mean that if two teams with these ratings played each other on a neutral field, the higher rated team would be predicted to win by 9 points.

## DEVELOPING THE SPREADSHEET MODEL

To produce the model in Figure 7.30, proceed as follows:

**1** **Input game data.** If you want to determine the ratings for another NFL (or NBA or MLB) season, you have to get the data from the Web. (We are fortunate to have an inside contact—Winston's best friend is Jeff Sagarin!)

**2** **Changing cells.** Enter *any* value for the home field advantage and the 32 team ratings in the Home_team_advantage and Rating ranges. These comprise the changing cells. Note that it would be possible to use a "given" value for the home team advantage, such as 3, but we let Solver choose the home team advantage that best fits the data.

**3** **Average rating.** Enter the nominal average rating in cell B43, and average the ratings in cell B41 with the formula

**=AVERAGE(Rating)**

**4** **Actual point spreads.** Enter the actual point spreads in column J as differences between columns H and I.

*The VLOOKUP functions let us find the ratings to use for the predicted point spread.*

**5** **Predictions.** We have entered the data on games played by referring to the team index numbers. This allows us to use lookup functions to predict the point spreads. To do this, enter the formula

**=Home_team_advantage+VLOOKUP(F6,RatingTable,3)-VLOOKUP(G6,RatingTable,3)**

in cell K6 for the first game, and copy it down column K for the rest of the games. The VLOOKUP functions simply look up the ratings of the home and visiting teams. (We used the range name RatingTable for the range A5:C36.)

**6** **Prediction errors.** We want to minimize the sum of squared prediction errors. Therefore, enter the formula

**=(J6-K6)^2**

in cell L6, and copy it down. Then sum the squared errors in cell F2.

## USING SOLVER

The completed Solver dialog box is shown in Figure 7.31. We find the ratings and home field advantage that minimize the sum of squared prediction errors. The only constraint is to make the ratings average to the nominal rating. Because of the *squared* errors, this is a nonlinear model, so the Assume Linear Model option should not be checked. Also, there is no need to check the Assume Non-Negative option.

[10] Why *squared* errors? Admittedly, we could minimize the sum of the *absolute* prediction errors, but minimizing the sum of squared errors has a long tradition in statistics.

**Figure 7.31**

Solver Dialog Box
for the NFL Ratings
Model

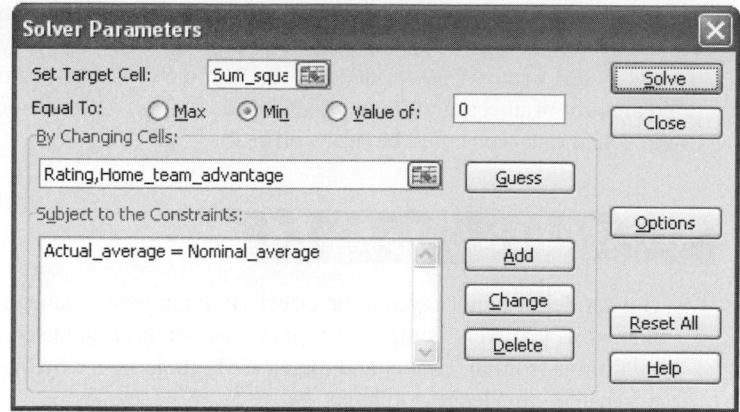

## Discussion of the Solution

The solution in Figure 7.30 shows that a home team advantage of 2.30 provides the best fit, at least for the 2006 season. To provide a better picture of the ratings, we have sorted them from best to worst in Figure 7.32. You might recall that Indianapolis won the Super Bowl, beating Chicago. The ratings ranked Indianapolis number 6 and Chicago about 2 point favorites (based on regular-season games only). The ratings support the playoff picture fairly well. We indicate the 12 playoff teams with color shading. Most of the highly rated teams made the playoffs. However, there are some clear anomalies. Why, for example, did the Seahawks make it in, whereas the Jaguars and Bengals didn't? Of course, the answer is that the NFL has its own way of deciding which teams make the playoffs. It doesn't just go according to the Sagarin ratings!

**Figure 7.32**

Sorted NFL Ratings

| | A | B | C | D | E | F |
|---|---|---|---|---|---|---|
| 1 | Sorted from best to worst | | | | | |
| 2 | | | | | | |
| 3 | Index | Team name | Rating | | | |
| 4 | 19 | New England Patriots | 95.24 | | | |
| 5 | 27 | San Diego Chargers | 95.20 | | | |
| 6 | 3 | Baltimore Ravens | 94.35 | | | |
| 7 | 6 | Chicago Bears | 92.90 | ← | Loser in Super Bowl | |
| 8 | 15 | Jacksonville Jaguars | 92.49 | | | |
| 9 | 14 | Indianapolis Colts | 90.88 | ← | Super Bowl Champion | |
| 10 | 7 | Cincinnatti Bengals | 89.08 | | | |
| 11 | 20 | New Orleans Saints | 89.04 | | | |
| 12 | 9 | Dallas Cowboys | 88.66 | | | |
| 13 | 25 | Pittsburgh Steelers | 88.42 | | All playoff teams | |
| 14 | 24 | Philadelphia Eagles | 88.39 | | shown in green. | |
| 15 | 4 | Buffalo Bills | 87.19 | | | |
| 16 | 22 | New York Jets | 87.02 | | | |
| 17 | 10 | Denver Broncos | 86.32 | | | |
| 18 | 16 | Kansas City Chiefs | 85.99 | | | |
| 19 | 17 | Miami Dolphins | 85.68 | | | |
| 20 | 21 | New York Giants | 85.08 | | | |
| 21 | 31 | Tennessee Titans | 83.72 | | | |
| 22 | 5 | Carolina Panthers | 82.33 | | | |
| 23 | 2 | Atlanta Falcons | 81.98 | | | |
| 24 | 29 | Seattle Seahawks | 81.43 | | | |
| 25 | 26 | St. Louis Rams | 81.05 | | | |
| 26 | 32 | Washington Redskins | 80.95 | | | |
| 27 | 18 | Minnesota Vikings | 80.91 | | | |
| 28 | 12 | Green Bay Packers | 80.58 | | | |
| 29 | 13 | Houston Texans | 80.50 | | | |
| 30 | 8 | Cleveland Browns | 79.16 | | | |
| 31 | 11 | Detroit Lions | 78.65 | | | |
| 32 | 1 | Arizona Cardinals | 78.07 | | | |
| 33 | 30 | Tampa Bay Buccaneers | 77.07 | | | |
| 34 | 28 | San Francisco 49ers | 76.28 | | | |
| 35 | 23 | Oakland Raiders | 75.40 | | | |

Remember that the actual values of the ratings are not as important as the *differences* between teams' ratings. For example, we predict that if Dallas played Arizona at Arizona, Arizona would win by $2.30 + (80.03 - 76.71) \approx 5.6$ points. Of course, there is a considerable amount of uncertainty in any game. We might *predict* Arizona to win by 5.6 points, but the actual outcome could be much different.[11] ∎

## MODELING ISSUES

1.  This model does not capture the effect of "intangibles," such as injuries to key players. If you were going to bet real money on NFL games, you might start with the ratings from the model and then modify them in a subjective fashion to capture any inside knowledge you have.

2.  We can improve the future predictive accuracy by giving more weight to more recent games. To do this, we could multiply the squared error for a game $k$ weeks ago by a factor such as $(0.95)^k$. As an indication of how this "discounts" the importance of past games, this weighting gives a game from 5 weeks ago about 77% of the weight given to this week's game.

3.  We can also use Solver to find the set of ratings that minimizes the sum of *absolute* prediction errors. This shouldn't have much effect on the relative rankings.

4.  Why did Indianapolis have such a low rating? The reason is that it lost one game to Jacksonville by a large margin, 44 to 17. Remember that we *square* the differences between actual and predicted point spreads, thus magnifying unexpected ones. The effect is that this one outlier really lowered Indy's rating. Try running the model without this game to see how the ratings change.

## PROBLEMS

### Skill-Building Problems

28. The file **P07_28.xlsx** lists the scores of all NFL games played during the 1996 season. Use this data set to rank the NFL teams from best to worst.

29. The file **P07_29.xlsx** lists the scores of all NFL games played during the 1997 season. Using all data except for the last game (the Super Bowl), rank the NFL teams from best to worst. Then make a forecast for this Super Bowl. (Note that the bookmakers favored Green Bay by 11 in this game, which Denver won, but you should find that our model is right on the money!)

30. Carry out the suggestion in Modeling Issue 3. That is, find the ratings of the 2004 NFL teams using the sum of absolute prediction errors as the criterion to minimize. Discuss any differences in ratings from this method and the method used in Example 7.8.

31. Carry out the suggestion in Modeling Issue 2. That is, use a weighted sum of squared prediction errors, where the weight on any game played $k$ weeks ago

is $0.95^k$. You can assume that the ratings are being made right after the final regular games of the season (in week 17), so for these final games, $k = 0$. Discuss how the ratings change when early-season games are discounted heavily.

32. The file **P07_32.xlsx** contains scores on all of the regular-season games in the NBA for the 2001–2002 basketball season. Use the same procedure as in Example 7.8 to rate the teams. Then sort the teams based on the ratings. Do these ratings appear to be approximately correct? (You might recall that the Lakers beat the Nets in the finals.) What does the model estimate the home court advantage to be?

33. The file **P07_33.xlsx** contains the scores of the 1994 Big Ten basketball season. Develop ratings for the 11 teams. Which was the best team? Which was the worst team? What is the estimated home court advantage? If you are an Indiana fan, try it again after deleting Indiana's huge loss to Minnesota. See how much this outlier affects the results.

[11] If we were going to *simulate* NFL games based on these ratings, we would simulate a normally distributed point spread with the mean equal to the predicted point spread and standard deviation equal to about 14 points. Yes, there is this much variability in NFL games!

## Skill-Extending Problem

**34.** The method for rating teams in Example 7.8 is based on actual and predicted *point spreads*. This method can be biased if some teams "run up the score" in a few games. An alternative possibility is to base the ratings only on wins and losses. For each game, we observe whether the home team wins. Then from the proposed ratings, we predict whether the home team will win. (We predict the home team will win if the home team advantage plus the home team's rating is greater than the visitor team's rating.) We want the ratings such that the number of predictions that match the actual outcomes is maximized. Try modeling this. Do you run into difficulties? (Remember that Solver doesn't like IF functions.)

## 7.7 PORTFOLIO OPTIMIZATION MODELS

Given a set of investments, how do financial analysts determine the portfolio that has the lowest risk and yields a high expected return? This question was answered by Harry Markowitz in the 1950s. For his work on this and other investment topics, he received the Nobel Prize in economics in 1990. The ideas discussed in this section are the basis for most methods of *asset allocation* used by Wall Street firms. Asset allocation models are used, for example, to determine the percentage of assets to invest in stocks, gold, and Treasury bills. Before proceeding, however, we need to discuss some important formulas involving the expected value and variance of sums of random variables; these formulas are the basis for most asset allocation models.

### Weighted Sums of Random Variables

Let $R_i$ be the (random) return earned during a year on a dollar invested in investment $i$. For example, if $R_i = 0.10$, a dollar invested at the beginning of the year grows to \$1.10 at the end of the year, whereas if $R_i = -0.20$, a dollar invested at the beginning of the year decreases in value to \$0.80. We assume that $n$ investments are available. Let $x_i$ be the fraction of our money invested in investment $i$. We assume that $x_1 + x_2 + \cdots + x_n = 1$, so that all of our money is invested. (To prevent shorting a stock—that is, selling shares we don't own—we assume that $x_i \geq 0$.) Then the annual return on our investments is given by the random variable $R_p$, where

$$R_p = R_1 x_1 + R_2 x_2 + \cdots + R_n x_n$$

(The subscript $p$ stands for "portfolio.")

Let $\mu_i$ be the expected value (also called the mean) of $R_i$, let $\sigma_i^2$ be the variance of $R_i$ (so that $\sigma_i$ is the standard deviation of $R_i$), and let $\rho_{ij}$ be the correlation between $R_i$ and $R_j$. To do any work with investments, you must understand how to use the following formulas, which relate the data for the individual investments to the expected return and the variance of return for a *portfolio* of investments.

$$\text{Expected value of } R_p = \mu_1 x_1 + \mu_2 x_2 + \cdots + \mu_n x_n \tag{7.5}$$

$$\text{Variance of } R_p = \sigma_1^2 x_1^2 + \sigma_2^2 x_2^2 + \cdots + \sigma_n^2 x_n^2 + \sum_{i \neq j} \rho_{ij} \sigma_i \sigma_j x_i x_j \tag{7.6}$$

The latter summation in the variance formula is over all pairs of investments. The quantities in equations (7.5) and (7.6) are extremely important in portfolio selection because of the risk–return trade-off investors need to make. All investors want to choose portfolios with high return, measured by the expected value in equation (7.5), but they also want portfolios with low risk, usually measured by the variance in equation (7.6).

Because we never actually know the true expected values ($\mu_i$'s), variances ($\sigma_i^2$'s), and correlations ($\rho_{ij}$'s), we must estimate them. If historical data is available, we can proceed as follows:

1. Estimate $\mu_i$ by $\overline{X}_i$, the sample average of returns on investment $i$ over several previous years. You can use Excel's AVERAGE function to calculate $\overline{X}_i$.

2. Estimate $\sigma_i^2$ by $s_i^2$, the sample variance of returns on investment $i$ over several previous years. You can use Excel's VAR function to calculate $s_i^2$.

3. Estimate $\sigma_i$ by $s_i$, the sample standard deviation of returns on investment $i$. You can calculate $s_i$ with Excel's STDEV function. (Alternatively, you can calculate $s_i$ as the square root of $s_i^2$.)

4. Estimate $\rho_{ij}$ by $r_{ij}$, the sample correlation between past returns on investments $i$ and $j$. You can calculate the $r_{ij}$'s by using Excel's CORREL function.

We now estimate the mean and variance of the return on a portfolio by replacing each parameter in equations (7.5) and (7.6) with its sample estimate. This yields

$$\text{Estimated expected value of } R_p = \overline{X}_1 x_1 + \overline{X}_2 x_2 + \cdots + \overline{X}_n x_n \qquad \textbf{(7.7)}$$

$$\text{Estimated variance of } R_p = s_1^2 x_1^2 + s_2^2 x_2^2 + \cdots + s_n^2 x_n^2 + \sum_{i \neq j} r_{ij} s_i s_j x_i x_j \qquad \textbf{(7.8)}$$

In keeping with common practice, the annual return on investments is expressed in decimal form. Thus, a return of 0.10 on a stock means that the stock has increased in value by 10%.

*Covariances indicate relationships between variables, but unlike correlations, covariances are affected by the units in which the variables are measured.*

We can rewrite equation (7.8) slightly by using *covariances* instead of correlations. The covariance between two stock returns is another measure of the relationship between the two returns, but unlike a correlation, it is *not* scaled to be between $-1$ and $+1$.

Although a covariance is a somewhat less intuitive measure than a correlation, financial analysts use it so frequently that we use it here as well. If $c_{ij}$ is the estimated covariance between stocks $i$ and $j$, then $c_{ij} = r_{ij} s_i s_j$. Using this equation and the fact that the correlation between any stock and itself is 1, we can also write $c_{ii} = s_i^2$ for each stock $i$. Therefore, an equivalent form of equation (7.8) is the following:

$$\text{Estimated variance of } R_p = \sum_{i,j} c_{ij} x_i x_j \qquad \textbf{(7.9)}$$

As shown in the portfolio optimization example, this allows us to calculate the estimated portfolio variance very easily with Excel's matrix functions.

## Matrix Functions in Excel

Equation (7.8) or (7.9) for the variance of portfolio return looks intimidating, particularly if there are many potential investments. Fortunately, we can take advantage of two built-in Excel matrix functions to simplify our work. In this section, we illustrate how to use Excel's MMULT (matrix multiplication) and TRANSPOSE functions. Then in the next section, we put these to use in the portfolio selection model.

A **matrix** is a rectangular array of numbers. A matrix is an $i \times j$ matrix if it has $i$ rows and $j$ columns. For example,

$$A = \begin{pmatrix} 1 & 2 & 3 \\ 4 & 5 & 6 \end{pmatrix}$$

is a $2 \times 3$ matrix, and

$$B = \begin{pmatrix} 1 & 2 \\ 3 & 4 \\ 5 & 6 \end{pmatrix}$$

is a $3 \times 2$ matrix. If the matrix has only a single row, it is a **row vector.** Similarly, if it has only a single column, it is a **column vector.**

If matrix $A$ has the same number of columns as matrix $B$ has rows, then we can construct the **matrix product** of $A$ and $B$, denoted $AB$. The entry in row $i$, column $j$ of the product $AB$ is obtained by summing the products of the elements in row $i$ of $A$ with the corresponding elements in column $j$ of $B$. If $A$ is an $i \times k$ matrix and $B$ is a $k \times j$ matrix, then $AB$ is an $i \times j$ matrix.

For example, if

$$A = \begin{pmatrix} 1 & 2 & 3 \\ 2 & 4 & 5 \end{pmatrix}$$

and

$$B = \begin{pmatrix} 1 & 2 \\ 3 & 4 \\ 5 & 6 \end{pmatrix}$$

then $AB$ is the following $2 \times 2$ matrix:

$$AB = \begin{pmatrix} 1(1) + 2(3) + 3(5) & 1(2) + 2(4) + 3(6) \\ 2(1) + 4(3) + 5(5) & 2(2) + 4(4) + 5(6) \end{pmatrix} = \begin{pmatrix} 22 & 28 \\ 39 & 50 \end{pmatrix}$$

The Excel MMULT function performs matrix multiplication in a single step. The spreadsheet in Figure 7.33 indicates how to multiply matrices of different sizes. (See the file **Matrix Multiplication.xlsx**.) For example, to multiply matrix 1 by matrix 2 (which is possible because matrix 1 has 3 columns, and matrix 2 has 3 rows), we select the range B13:C14, type the formula

**=MMULT(B4:D5,B7:C9)**

and press Ctrl+Shift+Enter (all three keys at once). Note that we select a range with 2 rows because matrix 1 has 2 rows, and we select a range with 2 columns because matrix 2 has 2 columns.

**Figure 7.33** Examples of Matrix Multiplication in Excel

| | A | B | C | D | E | F | G | H | I | J | K | L | M | N |
|---|---|---|---|---|---|---|---|---|---|---|---|---|---|---|
| 1 | Matrix multiplication in Excel | | | | | | | | | | | | | |
| 2 | | | | | | | | | | | | | | |
| 3 | Typical multiplication of two matrices | | | | | | | Multiplication of a matrix and a column | | | | | | |
| 4 | Matrix 1 | 1 | 2 | 3 | | | | Column 1 | 2 | | | | | |
| 5 | | 2 | 4 | 5 | | | | | 3 | | | | | |
| 6 | | | | | | | | | 4 | | | | | |
| 7 | Matrix 2 | 1 | 2 | | | | | | | | | | | |
| 8 | | 3 | 4 | | | | | Matrix 1 times Column 1, with formula =MMULT(B4:D5,I4:I6) | | | | | | |
| 9 | | 5 | 6 | | | | | Select range with 2 rows, 1 column, enter formula, press Ctrl-Shift-Enter | | | | | | |
| 10 | | | | | | | | | 20 | | | | | |
| 11 | Matrix 1 times Matrix 2, with formula =MMULT(B4:D5,B7:C9) | | | | | | | | 36 | | | | | |
| 12 | Select range with 2 rows, 2 columns, enter formula, press Ctrl-Shift-Enter. | | | | | | | | | | | | | |
| 13 | | 22 | 28 | | | | | Multiplication of a row and a matrix | | | | | | |
| 14 | | 39 | 50 | | | | | Row 1 | | 4 | 5 | | | |
| 15 | | | | | | | | | | | | | | |
| 16 | Multiplication of a quadratic form (row times matrix times column) | | | | | | | Row 1 times Matrix 1, with formula =MMULT(I14:J14,B4:D5) | | | | | | |
| 17 | Matrix 3 | 2 | 1 | 3 | | | | Select range with 1 row, 3 columns, enter formula, press Ctrl-Shift-Enter | | | | | | |
| 18 | | 1 | -1 | 0 | | | | | 14 | 28 | 37 | | | |
| 19 | | 3 | 0 | 4 | | | | | | | | | | |
| 20 | | | | | | | | Multiplication of a row and a column | | | | | | |
| 21 | Transpose of Column 1 times Matrix 3 times Column 1 | | | | | | | Row 2 | 1 | 6 | 3 | | | |
| 22 | Formula is =MMULT(TRANSPOSE(I4:I6),MMULT(B17:D19,I4:I6)) | | | | | | | | | | | | | |
| 23 | Select range with 1 row, 1 column, enter formula, press Ctrl-Shift-Enter | | | | | | | Row 2 times Column 1, with formula =MMULT(I22:K22,I4:I6) | | | | | | |
| 24 | | 123 | | | | | | Select range with 1 row, 1 column, enter formula, press Ctrl-Shift-Enter | | | | | | |
| 25 | | | | | | | | | 32 | | | | | |
| 26 | Notes on quadratic form example: | | | | | | | | | | | | | |
| 27 | Two MMULT's are required because MMULT works on only two ranges at a time. | | | | | | | | | | | | | |
| 28 | TRANSPOSE is needed to change a column into a row. | | | | | | | | | | | | | |

The matrix multiplication in cell B24 indicates that (1) we can multiply three matrices together by using MMULT twice, and (2) we can use the TRANSPOSE function to convert a column vector to a row vector (or vice versa), if necessary. Here, we want to multiply Column 1 by the product of Matrix 3 and Column 1. However, Column 1 is $3 \times 1$, and Matrix 3 is $3 \times 3$, so Column 1 times Matrix 3 doesn't work. Instead, we must transpose Column 1 to make it $1 \times 3$. Then the result of multiplying all three together is a $1 \times 1$ matrix (a number). We calculate it by selecting cell B24, typing the formula

**=MMULT(TRANSPOSE(I4:I6),MMULT(B17:D19,I4:I6))**

and pressing Ctrl+Shift+Enter. MMULT is used twice in this formula because this function can multiply only *two* matrices at a time.

## Excel Function: *MMULT*

*The MMULT and TRANSPOSE functions are useful for matrix operations. They are called array functions because they return results to an entire range, not just a single cell. The MMULT function multiplies two matrices and has the syntax =MMULT(range1,range2), where range1 must have as many columns as range2 has rows. To use this function, highlight a range that has as many rows as range1 and as many columns as range2, type the formula, and press Ctrl+Shift+Enter. The resulting formula will have curly brackets around it in the Excel Formula Bar. You should not type these curly brackets. Excel enters them automatically to remind you that this is an array formula.*

## The Portfolio Selection Model

Most investors have two objectives in forming portfolios: to obtain a large expected return and to obtain a small variance (to minimize risk). The problem is inherently nonlinear because variance is a nonlinear function of the investment amounts. The most common way of handling this two-objective problem is to require a minimal expected return and then minimize the variance subject to the constraint on the expected return. The following example illustrates how we can accomplish this in Excel.

### EXAMPLE | 7.9 PORTFOLIO SELECTION AT PERLMAN & BROTHERS

Perlman & Brothers, an investment company, intends to invest a given amount of money in three stocks. From past data, the means and standard deviations of annual returns have been estimated as shown in Table 7.7. The correlations among the annual returns on the stocks are listed in Table 7.8. The company wants to find a minimum-variance portfolio that yields an expected annual return of at least 0.12.

**Table 7.7** Estimated Means and Standard Deviations of Stock Returns

| Stock | Mean | Standard Deviation |
|-------|------|--------------------|
| 1 | 0.14 | 0.20 |
| 2 | 0.11 | 0.15 |
| 3 | 0.10 | 0.08 |

**Table 7.8** Estimated Correlations Among Stock Returns

| Combination | Correlation |
|-------------|-------------|
| Stocks 1 and 2 | 0.6 |
| Stocks 1 and 3 | 0.4 |
| Stocks 2 and 3 | 0.7 |

**Objective**   To use NLP to find the portfolio of the three stocks that minimizes the risk, measured by portfolio variance, subject to achieving an expected return of at least 0.12.

### WHERE DO THE NUMBERS COME FROM?

Financial analysts typically estimate the required means, standard deviations, and correlations for stock returns from historical data, as discussed at the beginning of this section. However, you should be aware that there is no guarantee that these estimates, based on *historical* return data, are relevant for *future* returns. If the analysts have new information about the stocks, they should incorporate this new information into their estimates.

## Solution

The variables and constraints for this model are listed in Table 7.9. One interesting aspect of this model is that we do *not* have to specify the amount of money invested—it could be $100, $1000, $1,000,000, or any other amount. The model determines the *fractions* of this amount to invest in the various stocks, and these fractions are then relevant for any investment amount. All we require is that the fractions sum to 1, so that all of the money is invested. Besides this, we require *nonnegative* fractions to prevent shorting stocks.[12] We also require that the expected return from the portfolio be at least as large as the specified minimal required expected return.

**Table 7.9** Variables and Constraints for the Portfolio Selection Model

| | |
|---|---|
| **Input variables** | Estimates of means, standard deviations, and correlations for stock returns, minimum required expected portfolio return |
| **Decision variables (changing cells)** | Fractions invested in the various stocks |
| **Objective (target cell)** | Portfolio variance (minimize) |
| **Other output variables** | Covariances between stock returns, total fraction of money invested, expected portfolio return |
| **Constraints** | Total fraction invested must equal 1 |
| | Expected portfolio return must be greater than or equal to Minimum required expected portfolio return |

### DEVELOPING THE SPREADSHEET MODEL

The following are the individual steps required (see Figure 7.34 and the file **Portfolio Selection.xlsx**):

**Figure 7.34** The Portfolio Selection Model

| | A | B | C | D | E | F | G | H | I |
|---|---|---|---|---|---|---|---|---|---|
| 1 | **Portfolio selection model** | | | | | Range names used: | | | |
| 2 | | | | | | Actual_return | =Model!$B$23 | | |
| 3 | **Stock input data** | | | | | Fractions_to_invest | =Model!$B$15:$D$15 | | |
| 4 | | Stock 1 | Stock 2 | Stock 3 | | Portfolio_variance | =Model!$B$25 | | |
| 5 | Mean return | 0.14 | 0.11 | 0.1 | | Required_return | =Model!$D$23 | | |
| 6 | StDev of return | 0.2 | 0.15 | 0.08 | | Total_invested | =Model!$B$19 | | |
| 7 | | | | | | | | | |
| 8 | Correlations | Stock 1 | Stock 2 | Stock 3 | | Covariances | Stock 1 | Stock 2 | Stock 3 |
| 9 | Stock 1 | 1 | 0.6 | 0.4 | | Stock 1 | 0.04 | 0.018 | 0.0064 |
| 10 | Stock 2 | 0.6 | 1 | 0.7 | | Stock 2 | 0.018 | 0.0225 | 0.0084 |
| 11 | Stock 3 | 0.4 | 0.7 | 1 | | Stock 3 | 0.0064 | 0.0084 | 0.0064 |
| 12 | | | | | | | | | |
| 13 | **Investment decisions** | | | | | | | | |
| 14 | | Stock 1 | Stock 2 | Stock 3 | | | | | |
| 15 | Fractions to invest | 0.500 | 0.000 | 0.500 | | | | | |
| 16 | | | | | | | | | |
| 17 | **Constraint on investing everything** | | | | | | | | |
| 18 | | Total invested | | Required value | | | | | |
| 19 | | 1.00 | = | 1 | | | | | |
| 20 | | | | | | | | | |
| 21 | **Constraint on expected portfolio return** | | | | | | | | |
| 22 | | Actual return | | Required return | | | | | |
| 23 | | 0.12 | >= | 0.12 | | | | | |
| 24 | | | | | | | | | |
| 25 | **Portfolio variance** | 0.0148 | | | | | | | |
| 26 | Portfolio stdev | 0.1217 | | | | | | | |

[12] If you want to allow shorting, do not check the Assume Non-Negative box in Solver options.

**①  Inputs.** Enter the inputs in the blue ranges. These include the estimates of means, standard deviations, and correlations, as well as the minimal required expected return.

**②  Fractions invested.** Enter *any* trial values in the Fractions_to_invest range for the fractions of Perlman's money placed in the three investments. Then sum these with the SUM function in cell B19.

**③  Expected annual return.** Use equation (7.7) to compute the expected annual return in cell B23 with the formula

**=SUMPRODUCT(B5:D5,Fractions_to_invest)**

**④  Covariance matrix.** We want to use equation (7.9) to calculate the portfolio variance. To do this, we must first calculate a matrix of covariances. Using the general formula for covariance, $c_{ij} = r_{ij} s_i s_j$ (which holds even when $i = j$ because $r_{ii} = 1$), we can calculate these from the inputs using lookups. Specifically, enter the formula

**=HLOOKUP($F9,$B$4:$D$6,3)\*B9\*HLOOKUP(G$8,$B$4:$D$6,3)**

in cell G9, and copy it to the range G9:I11. (This formula is a bit tricky, so take a close look at it. The term B9 captures the relevant correlation. The two HLOOKUP terms capture the appropriate standard deviations.)

**⑤  Portfolio variance.** Although we don't go into the mathematical details, it can be shown that the summation in equation (7.9) is really the product of three matrices: a row of fractions invested, the covariance matrix, and a column of fractions invested. To calculate it, enter the formula

**=MMULT(Fractions_to_invest,MMULT(G9:I11,TRANSPOSE(Fractions_to_ invest)))**

*The MMULT function can multiply only two matrices at a time.*

in cell B25 and press Ctrl+Shift+Enter. (Remember that Excel puts curly brackets around this formula when you press Ctrl+Shift+Enter. You should *not* type these curly brackets.) Note that this formula uses two MMULT functions. Again, this is because MMULT can multiply only two matrices at a time. Therefore, we first multiply the last two matrices and then multiply this product by the first matrix.

**⑥  Portfolio standard deviation.** Most financial analysts talk in terms of portfolio *variance*. However, it is probably more intuitive to talk about portfolio *standard deviation* because it is in the same units as the returns. We calculate the standard deviation in cell B26 with the formula

**=SQRT(Portfolio_variance)**

Actually, we could use either cell B25 or B26 as the target cell to minimize. Minimizing the square root of a function is equivalent to minimizing the function itself.

## USING SOLVER

The completed Solver dialog box is shown in Figure 7.35. The constraints specify that the expected return must be at least as large as the minimum required expected return, and all of the company's money must be invested. We constrain the changing cells to be nonnegative (to avoid short selling), but because of the squared terms in the variance formula, we do *not* check the Assume Linear Model option.

**Figure 7.35**

Solver Dialog Box
for the Basic
Portfolio Model

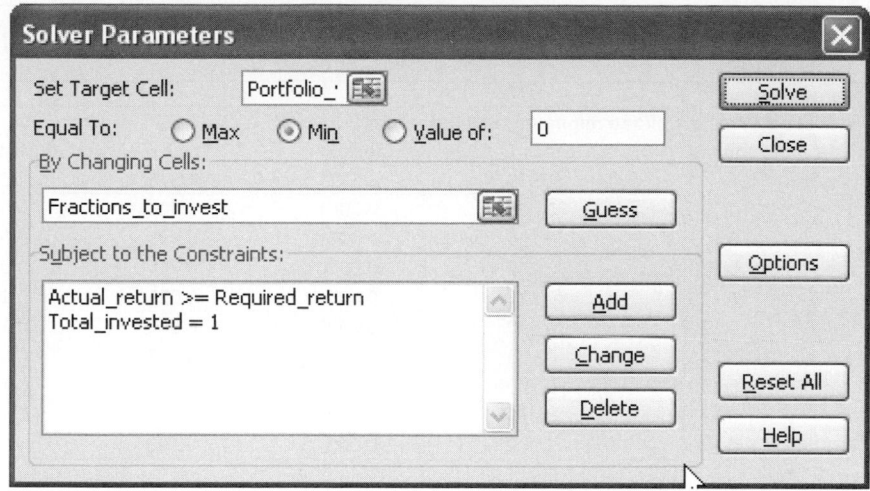

*Guessing the best
allocation in portfolio
optimization models is
difficult because it
depends not only on
expected returns and
standard deviations
of returns, but also
on correlations
between returns.*

### Discussion of the Solution

The solution in Figure 7.34 indicates that the company should put half of its money in each of stocks 1 and 3, and it should not invest in stock 2 at all. This might be somewhat surprising, given that the ranking of riskiness of the stocks is 1, 2, 3, with stock 1 being the most risky but also having the highest expected return. However, the correlations play an important role in portfolio selection, so we can usually not guess the optimal portfolio on the basis of the means and standard deviations of stock returns alone.

We can interpret the portfolio standard deviation of 0.1217 in a probabilistic sense. Specifically, if stock returns are approximately *normally* distributed, then the probability is about 0.68 that the actual portfolio return will be within 1 standard deviation of the expected return, and the probability is about 0.95 that the actual portfolio return will be within 2 standard deviations of the expected return. Given that the expected return is 0.12, this implies a lot of risk—2 standard deviations below this mean is a *negative* return (or loss) of slightly more than 12%!

### Is the Solver Solution Optimal?

The constraints for this model are linear, and it can be shown that the portfolio variance is a convex function of the investment fractions. Therefore, we are guaranteed that the Solver solution is optimal.

### Sensitivity Analysis

This model begs for a sensitivity analysis on the minimum required expected return. When the company requires a larger expected return, it must incur a larger risk, as shown in Figure 7.36. We use SolverTable with cell D23 as the single input cell, allowing it to vary from 0.10 to 0.14 in increments of 0.005. Note that values outside this range are of no interest. Stock 3 has the lowest expected return, 0.10, and stock 1 has the highest expected return, 0.14, so no portfolio can have an expected return outside of this range.

**Figure 7.36** The Efficient Frontier

| | A | B | C | D | E | F |
|---|---|---|---|---|---|---|
| 28 | Sensitivity of optimal portfolio to minimum required return | | | | | |
| 29 | Required | Stock 1 | Stock 2 | Stock 3 | Port stdev | Exp return |
| 30 | | $B$15 | $C$15 | $D$15 | $B$26 | $B$23 |
| 31 | 0.100 | 0.000 | 0.000 | 1.000 | 0.0800 | 0.10 |
| 32 | 0.105 | 0.125 | 0.000 | 0.875 | 0.0832 | 0.11 |
| 33 | 0.110 | 0.250 | 0.000 | 0.750 | 0.0922 | 0.11 |
| 34 | 0.115 | 0.375 | 0.000 | 0.625 | 0.1055 | 0.12 |
| 35 | 0.120 | 0.500 | 0.000 | 0.500 | 0.1217 | 0.12 |
| 36 | 0.125 | 0.625 | 0.000 | 0.375 | 0.1397 | 0.13 |
| 37 | 0.130 | 0.750 | 0.000 | 0.250 | 0.1591 | 0.13 |
| 38 | 0.135 | 0.875 | 0.000 | 0.125 | 0.1792 | 0.14 |
| 39 | 0.140 | 1.000 | 0.000 | 0.000 | 0.2000 | 0.14 |
| 40 | | | | | | |
| 41 | | | | | | |
| 42 | | | | | | |
| 43 | | | | | | |
| 44 | | | | | | |
| 45 | | | | | | |
| 46 | | | | | | |
| 47 | | | | | | |
| 48 | | | | | | |
| 49 | | | | | | |
| 50 | | | | | | |
| 51 | | | | | | |

The results indicate that the company should put more and more into risky stock 1 as the required expected return increases—and stock 2 continues to be unused. The accompanying scatter chart (with the option to "connect the dots") shows the risk–return trade-off. As the company assumes more risk, as measured by portfolio standard deviation, the expected return increases, but at a decreasing rate.

*Financial analysts typically put risk on the horizontal axis and expected return on the vertical axis in this type of risk–return chart.*

The curve in this chart is called the **efficient frontier.** Points on the efficient frontier can be achieved by appropriate portfolios. Points below the efficient frontier can be achieved, but they are not as good as points on the efficient frontier because they have a lower expected return for a given level of risk. In contrast, points above the efficient frontier are unachievable—the company cannot achieve an expected return this high for a given level of risk. An investor typically chooses a point on the efficient frontier that is most appropriate for his or her attitude toward risk. ■

## MODELING ISSUES

1. Typical real-world portfolio selection problems involve a large number of potential investments, certainly many more than three. This admittedly requires more input data, particularly for the correlation matrix, but the basic model does not change at all. In particular, the matrix formula for portfolio variance shows the power of using Excel's matrix functions. Without them, the formula for portfolio variance would be a long involved sum.

2. If Perlman is allowed to short a stock, we allow the fraction invested in that stock to be negative. To implement this, we eliminate the nonnegativity constraints on the changing cells.

3. An alternative objective is to minimize the probability that the portfolio loses money. You are asked to explore this possibility in one of the problems.

4. Sometimes analysts use a "scenario approach" to portfolio analysis as an alternative to the approach used here. See the file **Portfolio Scenario Finished.xlsx** for an example of how this works.

5. There are no transactions costs in Perlman's model. Suppose that for every $1 traded in stock 1 or 2, Perlman must pay $0.01, and for every dollar traded in stock 3, it must pay $0.005. Also, suppose the company begins with 10% of its money invested in stock 1, 40% in stock 2, and 50% in stock 3. The file **Portfolio Transactions Finished.xlsx** illustrates how the transactions costs (from buying and selling) can be accounted for in the model.

## ADDITIONAL APPLICATIONS

### Investment Decision Support for Bank Hapoalim Customers

Avriel et al. (2004) describe the Opti-Money decision support system for allocating assets they developed for Bank Hapoalim, Israel's largest bank. They solved a Markowitz-type NLP model to produce optimal tailor-made investment portfolios in terms of asset classes. In 2002, the bank held 133,000 consultation sessions with 63,000 customers in which Opti-Money was used. The system obtained net income that was 88% higher in customer accounts that used Opti-Money than in accounts where it was not used. In that same year, the annual income for the bank directly attributed to Opti-Money exceeded $31 million. ∎

## PROBLEMS

### Skill-Building Problems

35. For each of the following, answer whether it makes sense to multiply the matrices of the given sizes. In each case where it makes sense, demonstrate an example in Excel, where you can make up the numbers.
    a. $AB$, where $A$ is $3 \times 4$ and $B$ is $4 \times 1$
    b. $AB$, where $A$ is $1 \times 4$ and $B$ is $4 \times 1$
    c. $AB$, where $A$ is $4 \times 1$ and $B$ is $1 \times 4$
    d. $AB$, where $A$ is $1 \times 4$ and $B$ is $1 \times 4$
    e. $ABC$, where $A$ is $1 \times 4$, $B$ is $4 \times 4$, and $C$ is $4 \times 1$
    f. $ABC$, where $A$ is $3 \times 3$, $B$ is $3 \times 3$, and $C$ is $3 \times 1$
    g. $A^TB$, where $A$ is $4 \times 3$ and $B$ is $4 \times 3$, and $A^T$ denotes the transpose of $A$

36. Add a new stock, stock 4, to the model in Example 7.9. Assume that the estimated mean and standard deviation of return for stock 4 are 0.125 and 0.175, respectively. Also, assume the correlations between stock 4 and the original three stocks are 0.3, 0.5, and 0.8. Run Solver on the modified model, where the required expected portfolio return is again 0.12. Is stock in the optimal portfolio? Then run SolverTable as in the example. Is stock 4 in any of the optimal portfolios on the efficient frontier?

37. In the model in Example 7.9, stock 2 is not in the optimal portfolio. Use SolverTable to see whether it ever enters the optimal portfolio as its correlations with stocks 1 and 3 vary. Specifically, use a two-way SolverTable with two inputs, the correlations between stock 2 and stocks 1 and 3, each allowed to vary from 0.1 to 0.9 in increments of 0.1. Capture as outputs the three changing cells. Discuss the results. (*Note:* You'll have to change the model slightly. For example, if you use cells B10 and C11 as the two SolverTable input cells, you'll have to ensure that cells C9 and D10 change accordingly. This is easy. Just put formulas in these latter two cells.)

38. The stocks in Example 7.9 are all *positively* correlated. What happens when they are *negatively* correlated? Answer for each of the following scenarios. In each case, two of the three correlations are the negatives of their original values. Discuss the differences between the optimal portfolios in these three scenarios.
    a. Change the signs of the correlations between stocks 1 and 2 and between stocks 1 and 3. (Here, stock 1 tends to go in a different direction from stocks 2 and 3.)
    b. Change the signs of the correlations between stocks 1 and 2 and between stocks 2 and 3. (Here,

stock 2 tends to go in a different direction from stocks 1 and 3.)

   **c.** Change the signs of the correlations between stocks 1 and 3 and between stocks 2 and 3. (Here, stock 3 tends to go in a different direction from stocks 1 and 2.)

**39.** The file **P07_39.xlsx** contains historical monthly returns for 28 companies. For each company, calculate the estimated mean return and the estimated variance of return. Then calculate the estimated correlations between the companies' returns. Note that "return" here means *monthly* return. (*Hint:* Make life easy for yourself by using StatTools' Summary Statistics capabilities.)

**40.** This problem continues using the data from the previous problem. The file **P07_40.xlsx** includes all of the previous data and contains fractions in row 3 for creating a portfolio. These fractions are currently all equal to 1/28, but they can be changed to any values you like, as long as they continue to sum to 1. For any such fractions, find the estimated mean, variance, and standard deviation of the resulting portfolio return.

## Skill-Extending Problems

**41.** Continuing the previous problem, find the portfolio that achieves an expected monthly return of at least 0.01% and minimizes portfolio variance. Then use SolverTable to sweep out the efficient frontier, as in Example 7.9. Create a chart of this efficient frontier from your SolverTable results. What are the relevant lower and upper limits on the required expected monthly return?

**42.** In many cases, we can assume that the portfolio return is at least approximately *normally* distributed. Then we can use Excel's NORMDIST function to calculate the probability that the portfolio return is negative. The relevant formula is =**NORMDIST(0,*mean,stdev*,1)**, where *mean* and *stdev* are the expected portfolio return and standard deviation of portfolio return, respectively.

   **a.** Modify the model in Example 7.9 slightly, and then run Solver to find the portfolio that achieves at least a 0.12 expected return and minimizes the probability of a negative return. Do you get the same optimal portfolio as before? What is the probability that the return from this portfolio will be negative?

   **b.** Using the model in part **a**, proceed as in Example 7.9 to use SolverTable and create a chart of the efficient frontier. However, this time, put the probability of a negative return on the horizontal axis.

# 7.8 ESTIMATING THE BETA OF A STOCK

For financial analysts, it is important to be able to predict the return on a stock from the return on the market, that is, on a market index such as the S&P 500 index. Here, the **return** on an investment over a time period is the percentage change in its value over the time period. It is often hypothesized that

$$r_s = \alpha + \beta r_m + \varepsilon \qquad (7.10)$$

where $r_s$ is the return on a stock during a time period, $r_m$ is the return on the market during the same time period, $\varepsilon$ is a random error term, and $\alpha$ and $\beta$ are constants that must be estimated. The true value of $\beta$ in equation (7.10), which we will never know but can only estimate, is called the **beta** of the stock. From equation (7.10), we see that an increase in the market return of 1% increases the return on the stock by $\beta$% (on average). Therefore, $\beta$ is a measure of the responsiveness of a stock's return to changes in the market return. The returns on stocks with large positive or negative $\beta$'s are highly sensitive to the business cycle.

Sharpe's **capital asset pricing model** (CAPM) implies that stocks with large beta values are riskier and therefore must yield higher returns than those with small beta values. This implies that if you can estimate beta values more accurately than people on Wall Street, you can better identify overvalued and undervalued stocks and make a lot of money!

How do people usually estimate the beta of a stock? Most often, they run a regression analysis with the monthly return on the stock as the dependent variable and the monthly return on the market as the explanatory (or independent) variable. Because we have not yet covered regression analysis (see Chapter 16), we explore other methods for estimating betas in this section. Specifically, we discuss four methods that (in conjunction with Solver) can be used to estimate $\alpha$ and $\beta$ in equation (7.10). This requires a set of observations, where an observation lists both the market return and the return on the stock during a particular time period. (We use monthly data.)

Let $a$ and $b$ denote potential estimates of the unknown parameters $\alpha$ and $\beta$. Then for month $i$, we generate a prediction of the return on the stock with the equation

$$\hat{r}_{si} = a + br_{mi} \tag{7.11}$$

Here, $\hat{r}_{si}$ is the predicted stock return for period $i$, and $r_{mi}$ is the actual market return for period $i$. The *error* for period $i$, labeled $e_i$, is defined as

$$e_i = r_{si} - \hat{r}_{si} \tag{7.12}$$

That is, the error is the actual return of the stock minus the predicted return. If our predictions were perfect, then all of the errors in equation (7.12) would equal 0. However, this is generally impossible, so we instead try to choose the estimates $a$ and $b$ to make the errors close to 0. The following sections discuss four possible criteria for choosing these estimates.

## Criterion 1: Sum of Squared Errors (Least Squares)

Here we try to minimize the sum of the squared errors over all observations, the same criterion we have used elsewhere in this chapter. The sum of the squared errors is a convex function of the estimates $a$ and $b$, so Solver is guaranteed to find the (unique) estimates of $\alpha$ and $\beta$ that minimize the sum of squared errors. The main problem with the least squares criterion is that outliers, points for which the error in equation (7.12) is especially large, exert a disproportionate influence on the estimates of $\alpha$ and $\beta$.[13]

## Criterion 2: Weighted Sum of Squared Errors

Criterion 1 gives equal weights to older and more recent observations. It seems reasonable that more recent observations have more to say about the beta of a stock, at least for future predictions, than older observations. To incorporate this idea, we can give a smaller weight to the squared errors for older observations. Although this method usually leads to more accurate predictions of the future than least squares, the least squares method has many desirable statistical properties that weighted least squares estimates do not possess.

## Criterion 3: Sum of Absolute Errors (SAE)

Instead of minimizing the sum of the squared errors, we can minimize the sum of the absolute errors for all observations. This is often called the **sum of absolute errors** (SAE) approach. This method has the advantage of not being greatly affected by outliers. Unfortunately, less is known about the statistical properties of SAE estimates. Another drawback to SAE is that there can be more than one combination of $a$ and $b$ that minimizes SAE. However, SAE estimates have the advantage that they can be obtained with *linear* programming.

## Criterion 4: Minimax

Here we try to minimize the maximum absolute error over all observations. This method might be appropriate for a highly risk-averse decision maker. (See Chapter 10 for a discussion of risk aversion.) This **minimax** criterion can also be implemented using LP.

The following example illustrates how the Solver can be used to obtain estimates of $\alpha$ and $\beta$ for these four criteria.

---

[13] This is the criterion most financial analysts use, and they implement it through regression, not optimization per se. The regression approach enables them to see the important effects of stock volatility and correlation with the market.

EXAMPLE | **7.10 ESTIMATING BETAS OF PROMINENT COMPANIES**

We obtained close to nine years of monthly closing price data for 30 company stocks, along with data for the S&P 500 market index over the same months. (We got these data from Yahoo!'s finance Web page. Fortunately, the downloaded data are automatically adjusted for stock splits and dividends.) The data extend from January 1999 to September 2007. Do the betas for these stocks depend on the criterion used to estimate them? Are the estimates the same if we base them on only the most recent *three* years of data, rather than on all of the data?

## Solution

The data are in the file **Stock Beta.xlsx**. There is one worksheet named Data that contains the monthly closing prices and corresponding returns for all stocks and the S&P 500 market index. (See Figure 7.37, where a number of rows have been hidden.) We perform our calculations in a sheet named Model, as shown in Figure 7.38. For any selected company, we set up the sheet so that we can use any of the four criteria and either the most recent three years of data or all of the data simply by changing the target cell in the Solver dialog box. The following steps are required:

**1** **Calculate returns.** The downloaded data from the Web are closing *prices,* not returns. To calculate the returns (in Figure 7.37), enter the formula

**=(B4-B5)/B5**

in cell B113 and copy down and across through cell AF216. (Note that there are no returns for January 1999 because we do not have the closing prices from December 1998.)

**Figure 7.37**

Stock Prices and Returns

| | A | B | C | D | E |
|---|---|---|---|---|---|
| 1 | Monthly closing prices from Jan-1999 to Sep-2007 | | | | |
| 2 | | | | | |
| 3 | Month | S&P 500 | MMM | AA | MO |
| 4 | Sep-07 | 1526.75 | 93.58 | 39.12 | 69.5300 |
| 5 | Aug-07 | 1473.99 | 90.99 | 36.53 | 68.6400 |
| 6 | Jul-07 | 1455.27 | 88.44 | 38.03 | 65.7300 |
| 7 | Jun-07 | 1503.35 | 86.32 | 40.35 | 69.3600 |
| 8 | May-07 | 1530.62 | 87.48 | 41.10 | 69.6200 |
| 9 | Apr-07 | 1482.37 | 81.86 | 35.16 | 67.4900 |
| 10 | Mar-07 | 1420.86 | 75.59 | 33.58 | 64.5300 |
| 104 | May-99 | 1301.84 | 35.90 | 23.42 | 18.7600 |
| 105 | Apr-99 | 1335.18 | 37.03 | 26.42 | 17.0500 |
| 106 | Mar-99 | 1286.37 | 29.43 | 17.48 | 17.1200 |
| 107 | Feb-99 | 1238.33 | 30.81 | 17.19 | 18.8300 |
| 108 | Jan-99 | 1279.64 | 32.05 | 17.65 | 22.5500 |
| 109 | | | | | |
| 110 | Monthly returns from Feb-1999 to Sep-2007 | | | | |
| 111 | | | | | |
| 112 | Month | S&P 500 | MMM | AA | MO |
| 113 | Sep-07 | 0.0358 | 0.0285 | 0.0709 | 0.0130 |
| 114 | Aug-07 | 0.0129 | 0.0288 | -0.0394 | 0.0443 |
| 115 | Jul-07 | -0.0320 | 0.0246 | -0.0575 | -0.0523 |
| 116 | Jun-07 | -0.0178 | -0.0133 | -0.0182 | -0.0037 |
| 117 | May-07 | 0.0325 | 0.0687 | 0.1689 | 0.0316 |
| 118 | Apr-07 | 0.0433 | 0.0829 | 0.0471 | 0.0459 |
| 119 | Mar-07 | 0.0100 | 0.0317 | 0.0145 | 0.0523 |
| 213 | May-99 | -0.0250 | -0.0305 | -0.1136 | 0.1003 |
| 214 | Apr-99 | 0.0379 | 0.2582 | 0.5114 | -0.0041 |
| 215 | Mar-99 | 0.0388 | -0.0448 | 0.0169 | -0.0908 |
| 216 | Feb-99 | -0.0323 | -0.0387 | -0.0261 | -0.1650 |

**Figure 7.38** The Beta Estimation Model

| | A | B | C | D | E | F | G | H | I | J | K | L |
|---|---|---|---|---|---|---|---|---|---|---|---|---|
| 1 | Estimation model for McDonalds: 3-year period, sum of squared errors estimation method | | | | | | | | | | | |
| 2 | | | | Possible objectives | | | | | | | | |
| 3 | Parameters | | | | 3-year | All data | | | | | | |
| 4 | Alpha | 0.0052 | | SSE | 0.0360 | 0.5758 | | | | | | |
| 5 | Beta | 1.8242 | | WSSE | 0.0323 | 0.4008 | | | | | | |
| 6 | | | | SAE | 0.8700 | 5.6560 | | | | | | |
| 7 | Weighting constant | 0.995 | | MaxAE | 0.1083 | 0.2296 | | | | | | |
| 8 | | | | | | | | | | | | |
| 9 | Date | Mkt return | Stock return | Predicted | Error | SqError | AbsError | Weight | | Range names used: | | |
| 10 | Sep-07 | 0.0358 | 0.1060 | 0.0705 | 0.0355 | 0.00126 | 0.0355 | 1 | | Alpha | =Model!$B$4 | |
| 11 | Aug-07 | 0.0129 | 0.0288 | 0.0287 | 0.0001 | 0.00000 | 0.0001 | 0.9950 | | Beta | =Model!$B$5 | |
| 12 | Jul-07 | -0.0320 | -0.0569 | -0.0531 | -0.0038 | 0.00001 | 0.0038 | 0.9900 | | MaxAE_3 | =Model!$E$7 | |
| 13 | Jun-07 | -0.0178 | 0.0042 | -0.0273 | 0.0314 | 0.00099 | 0.0314 | 0.9851 | | MaxAE_All | =Model!$F$7 | |
| 14 | May-07 | 0.0325 | 0.0470 | 0.0646 | -0.0176 | 0.00031 | 0.0176 | 0.9801 | | SAE_3 | =Model!$E$6 | |
| 15 | Apr-07 | 0.0433 | 0.0717 | 0.0842 | -0.0125 | 0.00016 | 0.0125 | 0.9752 | | SAE_All | =Model!$F$6 | |
| 16 | Mar-07 | 0.0100 | 0.0311 | 0.0234 | 0.0077 | 0.00006 | 0.0077 | 0.9704 | | SSE_3 | =Model!$E$4 | |
| 17 | Feb-07 | -0.0218 | -0.0149 | -0.0346 | 0.0197 | 0.00039 | 0.0197 | 0.9655 | | SSE_All | =Model!$F$4 | |
| 18 | Jan-07 | 0.0141 | 0.0005 | 0.0309 | -0.0304 | 0.00093 | 0.0304 | 0.9607 | | WSSE_3 | =Model!$E$5 | |
| 19 | Dec-06 | 0.0126 | 0.0562 | 0.0282 | 0.0280 | 0.00078 | 0.0280 | 0.9559 | | | | |
| 20 | Nov-06 | 0.0165 | 0.0257 | 0.0353 | -0.0096 | 0.00009 | 0.0096 | 0.9511 | | | | |
| 21 | Oct-06 | 0.0315 | 0.0715 | 0.0627 | 0.0088 | 0.00008 | 0.0088 | 0.9464 | | | | |
| 22 | Sep-06 | 0.0246 | 0.0899 | 0.0500 | 0.0399 | 0.00159 | 0.0399 | 0.9416 | | | | |
| 23 | Aug-06 | 0.0213 | 0.0142 | 0.0440 | -0.0299 | 0.00089 | 0.0299 | 0.9369 | | | | |

**2** **Alpha, beta.** (From here on, all instructions relate to the Model sheet, shown in Figure 7.38.) Enter any values of alpha and beta in cells B4 and B5. These can be negative or positive.

**3** **Copy returns.** Copy the S&P 500 returns to column B of the Model sheet, and copy the returns from *any* selected stock to column C of the Model sheet. We suggest that you paste them as values. (Use the Paste Values option under the Paste dropdown.)

**4** **Predictions.** Predict the stock returns from equation (7.11) by entering the formula

=Alpha+Beta*B10

in cell D10 and copying down.

**5** **Errors, squared errors, and absolute errors.** The error in any row is the actual stock return minus the predicted stock return. Therefore, enter the formulas

=C10-D10

=E10^2

=ABS(E10)

in cells E10, F10, and G10, respectively, and copy these down.

**6** **Weights.** (This is for the weighted sum of squares criterion only.) Enter a desired weighting constant in cell B7. Then enter **1** in cell H10, enter the formula

=$B$7*H10

in cell H11, and copy this formula down column H. This makes each weight a constant fraction of the previous weight, so that more recent data are weighted more heavily.

**7** **Objectives.** We set up eight possible objectives in the range B117:C120. Enter the formulas

=SUM(F10:F45)

=SUMPRODUCT(F10:F45,H10:H45)

=SUM(G10:G45)

=MAX(G10:G45)

in cells B117 through B120, and enter similar formulas using *all* of the data in columns F to H in cells C117 through C120.

## USING SOLVER

The completed Solver dialog box should look similar to Figure 7.39, except that *any* of the eight possible objective cells can be used as the target cell. There are no constraints, not even nonnegativity constraints, and the Assume Linear Model box should *not* be checked.

### Discussion of the Solution

The solution in Figure 7.38 indicates that McDonald's is fairly sensitive to the market, having a beta greater than 1 for the sum of squared errors criterion when the most recent 3 years of data are used. If you change the objective, the beta for McDonald's ranges from about 1.58 to 1.82 across the four criteria (using the weight 0.995 for weighted sum of squares) when the most recent 3 years of data are used, and it ranges from about 0.82 to 1.04 when all of the data are used. These results are shown in Figure 7.40, where each is the optimal beta for a different Solver run, each using a different objective. Clearly, a stock's beta can depend not only on which optimality criterion we use but also on the time period we select.

To run this analysis for any other stock, copy its returns to column C of the Model sheet and rerun Solver with one of the possible objectives. You will find that the betas for different companies can vary widely.

**Figure 7.39**

Solver Dialog Box for the Beta Estimation Model

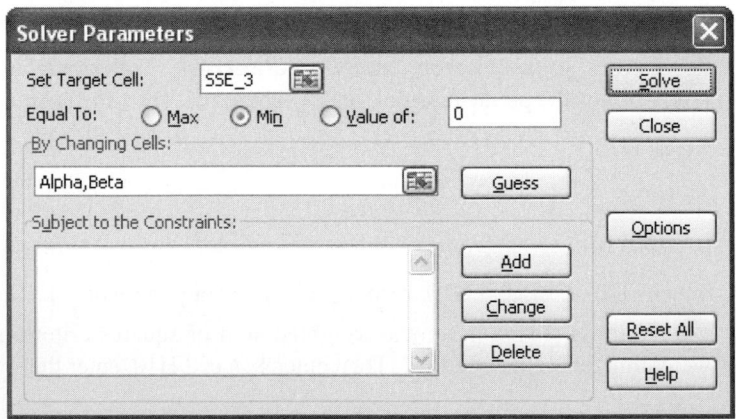

**Figure 7.40**

Optimal Betas for McDonald's Using Various Objective

|   | H | I | J | K |
|---|---|---|---|---|
| 2 | Betas for various objectives for McDonald's | | | |
| 3 |  | 3-year | All data |  |
| 4 | SSE | 1.8242 | 0.8743 |  |
| 5 | WSSE | 1.8203 | 0.9331 |  |
| 6 | SAE | 1.5830 | 1.0419 |  |
| 7 | MaxAE | 1.7519 | 0.8204 |  |

### Alternative Modeling Approaches

You might have noticed that we ignored one of our own warnings in this example. Specifically, the SAE and minimax objectives we used depend on the ABS and MAX functions. Does Solver provide the correct solution for these two criteria? We cannot answer with a definitive "yes," but it appears that the solutions are correct for the problems we solved. Basically, Solver has difficulty with ABS and MAX functions when the objective or constraints are not sufficiently smooth, and it appears that the objectives used here pass the smoothness test. However, it is possible to develop alternative models for these two objectives that are *linear*. The advantage, of course, is that we can then check Solver's Assume Linear Model option, which means that it uses the simplex method and guarantees that an optimal solution is found. In the interest of space, we do not include a full discussion of these alternative models, but you can see them in the files **Stock Beta 3 Alternative Finished.xlsx** and **Stock Beta 4 Alternative Finished.xlsx**. The only drawback to these models is that they are somewhat more difficult to understand, relying as they do on modeling tricks. ∎

## PROBLEMS

### Skill-Building Problems

**43.** Given the data in the file **Stock Beta.xlsx**, estimate the beta (and alpha) for GM. Do this for each criterion and each period of time to obtain a table analogous to that in Figure 7.40. What do you conclude about GM?

**44.** Repeat the previous problem, but analyze IBM instead of GM.

## 7.9 CONCLUSION

A large number of real-world problems can be approximated well by linear models. However, many problems are also inherently nonlinear. We have analyzed several such problems in this chapter, including the important class of portfolio selection problems where the risk, usually measured by portfolio variance, is a nonlinear function of the decision variables. We have purposely neglected much of the mathematics behind nonlinear optimization because of its technical difficulty. However, it is important to realize that nonlinear models present many more hazards for spreadsheet Solvers (or any other software) than linear models. Unless we can verify that the assumptions for a minimization or maximization problem are satisfied—and this can be very difficult to do—there is no guarantee that Solver will converge to the optimal solution (or even converge at all). The examples in this chapter were purposely kept small and "nice" so that Solver could handle them and produce optimal solutions. Larger and more complex nonlinear models are not always so accommodating and frequently require solution methods well beyond the level of this book.

## Summary of Key Management Science Terms

| Term | Explanation | Page |
|------|-------------|------|
| Nonlinear programming (NLP) models | Models with nonlinearities in the objective and/or the constraints | 346 |
| Global optimum | Solution that is guaranteed to be *the* optimal solution | 347 |
| Local optimum | Solution that is better than all nearby solutions, but might not be the best overall | 347 |

| Term | Explanation | Page |
|------|-------------|------|
| Convex function | Function with a nondecreasing slope | 348 |
| Concave function | Function with a nonincreasing slope | 348 |
| Optimality guarantee for NLP models | No package, including Solver, can guarantee that the solution it stops at will be the global optimum unless certain convexity/concavity conditions are satisfied | 350 |
| Demand function | A function that relates demand for a product to its price | 352 |
| Constant elasticity demand function | A demand function where elasticity (% change in demand for a 1% change in price) is constant for any price | 352 |
| Minimizing sum of squared errors | A popular method of fitting a curve of some form to a set of points; the errors are the differences between observed and predicted values | 370 |
| Unconstrained models | An optimization model with no constraints | 371 |
| Weighted sum of random variables | An important quantity in financial portfolio analysis; random variables are returns from investments, weights are fractions put in investments | 387 |
| Return, risk measures of portfolio models | Portfolio models try to maximize expected return and minimize variance of return (risk); formulas for these involve correlations or covariances among investment returns | 387 |
| Matrix | A rectangular array of numbers; often useful for simplifying complex summation formulas | 388 |
| Efficient frontier | Curve that shows the largest expected portfolio return possible for a given level of risk | 394 |
| Beta of a stock | A value that indicates the responsiveness of a stock's return to changes in the return of the market | 396 |

## Summary of Key Excel Terms

| Term | Explanation | Excel | Page |
|------|-------------|-------|------|
| SUMXMY2 function | Useful for calculating distance between two points | =SUMXMY2(*xRange,yRange*) | 379 |
| MMULT function | An array function that multiplies two matrices stored in Excel ranges | Highlight result range, type =MMULT(*range1,range2*), press Ctrl-Shift-Enter | 390 |

# PROBLEMS

## Skill-Building Problems

**45.** Suppose Ford currently sells 250,000 Ford Mustangs annually. The unit cost of a Taurus, including the delivery cost to a dealer, is $16,000. The current Mustang price is $20,000, and the current elasticity of demand for the Mustang is $-1.5$.

    **a.** Determine a profit-maximizing price for a Mustang. Do this when the demand function is of the constant elasticity type. Do it when the demand function is linear.

    **b.** Suppose Ford makes an average profit of $800 from servicing a Mustang purchased from a Ford dealer. (This is an average over the lifetime of the car.) How do your answers to part **a** change?

**46.** Suppose the current exchange rate is 100 yen per dollar. We currently sell 100 units of a product for 700 yen. The cost of producing and shipping the product to Japan is $5, and the current elasticity of demand is $-3$. Find the optimal price to charge for the product (in yen) for each of the following exchange rates: 60 yen/$, 80 yen/$, 100 yen/$, 120 yen/$, 140 yen/$, and 160 yen/$. Assume the demand function is linear.

**47.** Another way to derive a demand function is to break the market into segments and identify a low price, a medium price, and a high price. For each of these prices and market segments, we ask company experts to estimate product demand. Then we use Excel's trend curve fitting capabilities to fit a *quadratic* function that represents that segment's demand function. Finally, we add the segment demand curves to derive an aggregate demand curve. Try this procedure for pricing a candy bar. Assume the candy bar costs $0.55 to produce. The company plans to charge between $1.10 and $1.50 for this candy bar. Its marketing department estimates the demands shown in the file **P07_47.xlsx** (in thousands) in the three regions of the country where the candy bar will be sold. What is the profit-maximizing price, assuming that the *same* price will be charged in all three regions?

**48.** Widgetco produces widgets at plants 1 and 2. It costs $20x^{1/2}$ dollars to produce $x$ units at plant 1 and $40x^{1/3}$ dollars to produce $x$ units at plant 2. Each plant can produce up to 70 units. Each unit produced can be sold for $10. At most 120 widgets can be sold. Determine how Widgetco can maximize its profit.

**49.** If a monopolist produces $q$ units, she can charge $100 - 4q$ dollars per unit. The fixed cost of production is $50 and the variable cost is $2 per unit.
   **a.** How can the monopolist maximize her profit?
   **b.** If the monopolist must pay a sales tax of $2 per unit, will she increase or decrease production (relative to the situation with no sales tax)?
   **c.** Continuing part **b**, use SolverTable to see how a change in the sales tax affects the optimal solution.
   **d.** Again continuing part **b**, use SolverTable to see how simultaneous changes in the fixed and variable costs of production affect the optimal output level. (Use a two-way table.)

**50.** It costs a company $12 to purchase an hour of labor and $15 to purchase an hour of capital. If $L$ hours of labor and $K$ units of capital are available, then $L^{2/3}K^{1/3}$ machines can be produced. Suppose the company has $10,000 to purchase labor and capital.
   **a.** What is the maximum number of machines it can produce?
   **b.** Use SolverTable to see how a change in the price of labor changes the optimal solution.
   **c.** Use SolverTable to see how a change in the price of capital changes the optimal solution.
   **d.** Use SolverTable to see how a change in the amount of money available changes the optimal solution.

**51.** In the previous problem, what is the minimum-cost method of producing 100 machines? (Ignore the $10,000 budget constraint.)

**52.** The cost per day of running a hospital is $200,000 + 0.002x^2$ dollars, where $x$ is the number of patients served per day. What number of patients served per day minimizes the cost per patient of running the hospital?

**53.** Two firms are producing widgets. It costs the first firm $q_1^2$ dollars to produce $q_1$ widgets and the second firm $0.5q_2^2$ dollars to produce $q_2$ widgets. If a total of $q$ widgets are produced, consumers will pay $200 - q$ dollars for each widget. If the two manufacturers want to collude in an attempt to maximize the sum of their profits, how many widgets should each company produce? (The model for this type of problem is called a **collusive duopoly model**.)

**54.** A company manufactures two products. If it charges price $p_i$ for product $i$, it can sell $q_i$ units of product $i$, where $q_1 = 60 - 3p_1 + p_2$ and $q_2 = 80 - 2p_2 + p_1$. It costs $25 to produce a unit of product 1 and $72 to produce a unit of product 2. How many units of each product should the company produce, and what prices should it charge, to maximize its profit?

**55.** Q&H Company advertises during soap operas and football games. Each soap opera ad costs $50,000, and each football game ad costs $100,000. If $S$ soap opera ads are purchased, they will be seen by $5S^{1/2}$ million men and $20S^{1/2}$ million women. If $F$ football ads are purchased, they will be seen by $17F^{1/2}$ million men and $7F^{1/2}$ million women. The company wants at least 40 million men and at least 60 million women to see its ads.
   **a.** Determine how to minimize Q&H's cost of reaching the required number of viewers.
   **b.** How does this model violate the proportionality and additivity assumptions of LP?
   **c.** Suppose that the number of women (in millions) reached by $F$ football ads and $S$ soap opera ads is $7F^{1/2} + 20S^{1/2} - 0.2(FS)^{1/2}$. Why might this be a more realistic representation of the number of women viewers seeing Q&H's ads?

**56.** Beerco has $100,000 to spend on advertising in four markets. The sales revenue (in thousands of dollars) that can be created in each market by spending $x_i$ thousand dollars in market $i$ is given in the file **P07_56.xlsx**.
   **a.** To maximize its sales revenue, how much money should Beerco spend in each market?
   **b.** Use SolverTable to see how a change in the advertising budget affects the optimal sales revenue.

**57.** A beer company has divided Bloomington into two territories. If the company spends $x_1$ dollars on promotion in territory 1, it can sell $60x_1^{1/2}$ cases of beer there; and if it spends $x_2$ dollars on promotion in territory 2, it can sell $40x_2^{1/2}$ cases of beer there. Each case of beer sold in territory 1 sells for $10 and incurs $5 in shipping and production costs. Each case of beer sold in territory 2 sells for $9 and incurs $4 in shipping and production costs. A total of $5000 is available for promotion.

a. How can the beer company maximize its profit?
b. If an extra dollar could be spent on promotion, by approximately how much would the company's profit increase? By how much would its revenue increase?
c. Use SolverTable to see how a change in the price of beer 1 affects the optimal solution. Do the same for a change in the price of beer 2.

**58.** A firm is planning to spend $10,000 on advertising. It costs $3000 per minute to advertise on television and $1000 per minute to advertise on radio. If the firm buys $x$ minutes of television advertising and $y$ minutes of radio advertising, its revenue in thousands of dollars is given by $-2x^2 - y^2 + xy + 8x + 3y$. How can the firm maximize its revenue?

**59.** Proctor and Ramble has given you $12 million to spend on advertising Huggys diapers during the next 12 months. At the beginning of January, Huggys has a 30% market share. During any month, 10% of the people who purchase Huggys defect to brand X, and a fraction $0.2a^{1/2}$ of customers who usually buy brand X switch to Huggys, where $a$ is the amount spent on advertising in millions of dollars. For example, if you spend $4 million during a month, 40% of brand X's customers switch to Huggys. Your goal is to maximize Proctor and Ramble's average market share during the next 12 months, where the average is computed from each month's ending share. Determine an appropriate advertising policy. (*Hint:* Make sure you enter a nonzero trial value for each month's advertising expense or Solver might give you an error message.)

**60.** Based on Kolesar and Blum (1973). Suppose that a company must service customers lying in an area of $A$ square miles with $n$ warehouses. Kolesar and Blum showed that when the warehouse(s) are located properly, the average distance between a warehouse and a customer is $(A/n)^{1/2}$. Assume that it costs the company $60,000 per year to maintain a warehouse and $400,000 to build a warehouse. Also, assume that a $400,000 building cost is equivalent to incurring a cost of $40,000 per year indefinitely. The company fills 160,000 orders per year, and the shipping cost per order is $1 per mile. If the company serves an area of 100 square miles, how many warehouses should it have?

**61.** A company has five factories. The $x$- and $y$-coordinates of the location of each factory are given in the file **P07_61.xlsx**. The company wants to locate a warehouse at a point that minimizes the sum of the squared distances of the plants from the warehouse. Where should the warehouse be located?

**62.** Monroe County is trying to determine where to place the county fire station. The locations of the county's

four major towns are as follows: (10, 20), (60, 20), (40, 30), and (80, 60) (see Figure 7.41). Town 1 averages 20 fires per year; town 2, 30 fires; town 3, 40 fires; and town 4, 25 fires. The county wants to build the fire station in a location that minimizes the average distance that a fire engine must travel to respond to a fire. Because most roads run in either an east–west or a north–south direction, we assume that the fire engine must do the same. For example, if the fire station is located at (30, 40) and a fire occurs at town 4, the fire engine has to travel $|80 - 30| + |60 - 40| = 70$ miles to the fire.

**Figure 7.41** Existing Locations for the Fire Station Problem

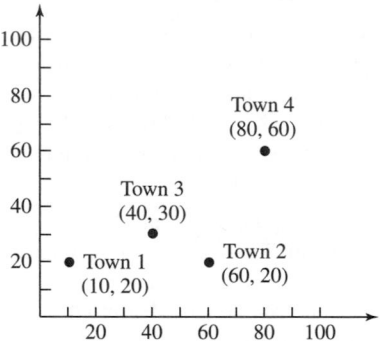

a. Determine where the fire station should be located.
b. Use SolverTable to see how the optimal location of the fire station changes as the number of fires at town 3 changes.

**63.** Consider three investments. You are given the following means, standard deviations, and correlations for the annual return on these three investments. The means are 0.12, 0.15, and 0.20. The standard deviations are 0.20, 0.30, and 0.40. The correlation between stocks 1 and 2 is 0.65, between stocks 1 and 3 is 0.75, and between stocks 2 and 3 is 0.41. You have $10,000 to invest and can invest no more than half of your money in any single stock. Determine the minimum-variance portfolio that yields an expected annual return of at least 0.14.

**64.** I have $1000 to invest in three stocks. Let $R_1$ be the random variable representing the annual return on $1 invested in stock $i$. For example, if $R_i = 0.12$, then $1 invested in stock $i$ at the beginning of a year is worth $1.12 at the end of the year. The means are $E(R_1) = 0.14$, $E(R_2) = 0.11$, and $E(R_3) = 0.10$. The variances are $Var\ R_1 = 0.20$, $Var\ R_2 = 0.08$, and $Var\ R_3 = 0.18$. The correlations are $r_{12} = 0.8$, $r_{13} = 0.7$, and $r_{23} = 0.9$. Determine the minimum-variance portfolio that attains an expected annual return of at least 0.12.

**65.** Oilco must determine how many barrels of oil to extract during each of the next 2 years. If Oilco extracts $x_1$ million barrels during year 1, each barrel can be sold for $80 - x_1$ dollars. If Oilco extracts $x_2$ million barrels during year 2, each barrel can be sold for $85 - x_2$ dollars. The cost of extracting $x_1$ million barrels during year 1 is $2x_1^2$ million dollars, and the cost of extracting $x_2$ million barrels during year 2 is $3x_2^2$ million dollars. A total of 20 million barrels of oil are available, and at most \$250 million can be spent on extraction. Determine how Oilco can maximize its profit (revenues less costs) for the next 2 years.

**66.** Suppose that we are hiring a weather forecaster to predict the probability that next summer will be rainy or sunny. The following suggests a method that can be used to ensure that the forecaster is accurate. Suppose that the actual probability of next summer being rainy is 0.6. (For simplicity, we assume that the summer can only be rainy or sunny.) If the forecaster announces a probability $p$ that the summer will be rainy, he receives a payment of $1 - (1 - p)^2$ if the summer is rainy and a payment of $1 - p^2$ if the summer is sunny. Show that the forecaster will maximize his expected profit by announcing that the probability of a rainy summer is 0.6.

**67.** The cost of producing $x$ units of a product during a month is $x^{1/2}$ dollars. Show that the minimum-cost method of producing 40 units during the next 2 months is to produce all 40 units during a single month.

**68.** A company uses raw material to produce two products. For \$15, a unit of raw material can be purchased and processed into four units of product 1 and two units of product 2. If $x_1$ units of product 1 are produced, they can be sold at $25 - x_1$ dollars per unit. If $x_2$ units of product 2 are produced, they can be sold at $14 - x_2$ dollars per unit. (Negative prices are not permitted.) The company can choose the number of units of raw material that are purchased and processed. How can the company maximize its profit?

## Skill-Extending Problems

**69.** Most economies have a goal of maximizing the average consumption per period. Assume that during each year, an economy saves the same (to be determined) percentage $S$ of its production. During a year in which the beginning capital level is $K$, a quantity $K^{1/2}$ of capital is produced. If the economy saves a percentage $S$ of its capital, then during the current year it consumes $(1 - S)K$ units of capital and, through savings, adds $(SK)^{1/2}$ units of capital. Also, during any year, 10% of all capital present at the beginning of the year depreciates or wears out.

**a.** What annual savings percentage $S$ maximizes the long-run average consumption level? Assume that year 50 represents the long run, so that the objective is the consumption level in year 50. You can assume the initial capital is 1 (for some appropriate measurement unit).

**b.** Use SolverTable to see how the optimal value of $S$ depends on the annual depreciation rate.

**70.** Each morning during rush hour, 10,000 people want to travel from New Jersey to New York City. If a person takes the commuter train, the trip lasts 40 minutes. If $x$ thousand people per morning drive to New York, it takes $20 + 5x$ minutes to make the trip. This problem illustrates a basic fact of life: If people make their decisions individually, they will cause more congestion than is actually necessary!

**a.** Show that if people make their decisions individually, an average of 4000 people will travel by road from New Jersey to New York. Here you should assume that people will divide up between the trains and roads in a way that makes the average travel time by road equal to the travel time by train. When this "equilibrium" occurs, nobody has an incentive to switch from the road to the train or vice versa.

**b.** Show that the average travel time per person is minimized if 2000 people travel by road.

**71.** Based on Grossman and Hart (1983). A salesperson for Fuller Brush has three options: (1) quit, (2) put forth a low effort level, or (3) put forth a high effort level. Suppose for simplicity that each salesperson will sell \$0, \$5000, or \$50,000 worth of brushes. The probability of each sales amount depends on the effort level as described in the file **P07_71.xlsx**. If a salesperson is paid $w$ dollars, he or she earns a "benefit" of $w^{1/2}$ units. In addition, low effort costs the salesperson 0 benefit units, whereas high effort costs 50 benefit units. If a salesperson were to quit Fuller and work elsewhere, he or she could earn a benefit of 20 units. Fuller wants all salespeople to put forth a high effort level. The question is how to minimize the cost of encouraging them to do so. The company cannot observe the level of effort put forth by a salesperson, but it can observe the size of his or her sales. Thus, the wage paid to the salesperson is completely determined by the size of the sale. This means that Fuller must determine $w_0$, the wage paid for sales of \$0; $w_{5000}$, the wage paid for sales of \$5000; and $w_{50,000}$, the wage paid for sales of \$50,000. These wages must be set so that the salespeople value the expected benefit from high effort more than quitting and more than low effort. Determine how to minimize the expected cost of ensuring that all salespeople put forth high effort. (This problem is an example of **agency theory**.)

**72.** Kellpost Cereal Company sells four products: (1) Special L (a low-calorie, high-nutrition cereal); (2) Corn Bran (another low-calorie, high-nutrition cereal);

(3) Admiral Smacks (a sugary cereal pitched at the children's market); and (4) Honey Pops (another sweet cereal pitched at the children's market). Kellpost has sufficient production capacity to produce a total of 10,000 boxes of cereal per month. For each of the past 16 months, Kellpost has kept track of the price and sales of each product. (These data are listed in the file **P07_72.xlsx**.) Market executives believe that Special L and Corn Bran might be substitutes for each other, as might be Admiral Smacks and Honey Pops. For example, this means that an increase in the price of Special L might raise the sales of Corn Bran. The variable cost of bringing a box of each cereal to market is as follows: Special L, $2.00; Corn Bran, $2.20; Admiral Smacks, $2.30; Honey Pops, $2.40.

  a. Use the given information to determine the price for each cereal that will enable Kellpost to maximize profits.

  b. Now suppose that Kellpost can increase its monthly production capacity. The cost (per year) of doing this is $20,000 per thousand boxes of added monthly capacity. Can you determine an optimal capacity level?

73. Find the minimum perimeter rectangle having area 64 square feet. Can you generalize this result?

74. You are given that the two nonhypotenuse sides of a right triangle add up to 10 inches. What is the maximum area of the triangle? Can you generalize this result?

75. A cylindrical soda can has a volume of 20 cubic inches. What height and diameter minimize the surface area of the can? Can you generalize this result?

76. City B is 10 miles downstream from city A. City A is 5 miles south of the river, and city B is 20 miles north of the river. The river is 2 miles wide. Where should we build a bridge across the river to make the travel distance between cities A and B as small as possible? Can you generalize this result?

77. I can swim 2 miles per hour and run 6 miles per hour. I am walking north along South Beach and see someone drowning 0.5 mile out in the ocean and 1 mile north of me. What combination of running and swimming is the quickest way to reach the swimmer?

78. A triangle has a 5-inch side and a 12-inch side. To maximize the area of the triangle what should the third side be? Can you generalize this result?

79. Four items are for sale in the Dollar Value store. The product and sum of their prices is $7.11. What is the price of each item?

## Modeling Problems

80. For the product mix example (Example 3.2 in Chapter 3), discuss where you think the assumptions of a linear model are most likely to break down. How might an NLP model look in this situation?

81. For the Chandler Oil blending example (Example 4.4 in Chapter 4), discuss where you think the assumptions of a linear model are most likely to break down. How might an NLP model look in this situation?

82. For the SureStep aggregate planning example (Example 4.3 in Chapter 4), is it likely that the cost per worker of changing the size of the workforce during a month would be constant (as we assumed)? How could an NLP model account for a situation in which the cost per worker of changing the size of the workforce is not constant?

83. Consider the sports ratings model in Section 7.6. If you were going to give more recent games more weight, how might you determine whether the weight given to a game from $k$ weeks ago should be, say, $(0.95)^k$ or $(0.9)^k$?

84. Consider the sports ratings model in Section 7.6. If you were going to use the approach used there to forecast future sports contests, what problems might you encounter early in the season? How might you resolve these problems?

85. UE is going to invest $400 million to acquire companies in the auto and/or electronics industry. How would you apply portfolio optimization to determine which companies should be purchased?

86. Your family owns a large farm that can grow wheat, corn, cotton, alfalfa, barley, pears, and apples. Each product requires a certain amount of labor each month and a certain number of hours of machine time. You have just studied portfolio optimization and want to help your family run its farm. What would you do?

87. Your company is about to market a new golf club. You have convened a focus group of 100 golfers and asked them to compare your club to the clubs produced by your competitors. You have found, for example, that 30 customers in the focus group would purchase your club if you charged $120, 28 customers would purchase your club if you charged $130, and so on. How could you use this information to determine the price at which your club should be sold?

Kate Torelli, a security analyst for Lion-Fund, has identified a gold mining stock (ticker symbol GMS) as a particularly attractive investment. Torelli believes that the company has invested wisely in new mining equipment. Furthermore, the company has recently purchased mining rights on land that has high potential for successful gold extraction. Torelli notes that gold has underperformed the stock market in the last decade and believes that the time is ripe for a large increase in gold prices. In addition, she reasons that conditions in the global monetary system make it likely that investors may once again turn to gold as a safe haven in which to park assets. Finally, supply and demand conditions have improved to the point where there could be significant upward pressure on gold prices.

GMS is a highly leveraged company, so it is a risky investment by itself. Torelli is mindful of a passage from the annual report of a competitor, Baupost, which has an extraordinarily successful investment record: "Baupost has managed a decade of consistently profitable results despite, and perhaps in some respect due to, consistent emphasis on the avoidance of downside risk. We have frequently carried both high cash balances and costly market hedges. Our results are particularly satisfying when considered in the light of this sustained risk aversion." She would therefore like to *hedge* the stock purchase—that is, reduce the risk of an investment in GMS stock.

Currently GMS is trading at $100 per share. Torelli has constructed seven scenarios for the price of GMS stock one month from now. These scenarios and corresponding probabilities are shown in Table 7.10.

To hedge an investment in GMS stock, Torelli can invest in other securities whose prices tend to move in the direction opposite to that of GMS stock. In particular, she is considering over-the-counter put options on GMS stock as potential hedging instruments. The value of a put option increases as the price of the underlying stock decreases. For example, consider a put option with a strike price of $100 and a time to expiration of one month. This means that the owner of the put has the right to sell GMS stock at $100 per share one month in the future. Suppose that the price of GMS falls to $80 at that time. Then the holder of the put option can exercise the option and receive $20 (=100 − 80). If the price of GMS falls to $70, the option would be worth $30 (=100 − 70). However, if the price of GMS rises to $100 or more, the option expires worthless.

Torelli called an options trader at a large investment bank for quotes. The prices for three (European-style) put options are shown in Table 7.11. Torelli wants to invest $10 million in GMS stock and put options.

### Table 7.11 Put Option Prices (Today) for the GMS Case Study

| | Put Option A | Put Option B | Put Option C |
|---|---|---|---|
| Strike price | 90 | 100 | 110 |
| Option price | $2.20 | $6.40 | $12.50 |

### Questions

1. Based on Torelli's scenarios, what is the expected return of GMS stock? What is the standard deviation of the return of GMS stock?

2. After a cursory examination of the put option prices, Torelli suspects that a good strategy is to buy one put option A for each share of GMS stock purchased. What are the mean and standard deviation of return for this strategy?

### Table 7.10 Scenarios and Probabilities for GMS Stock in One Month

| | Scenario 1 | Scenario 2 | Scenario 3 | Scenario 4 | Scenario 5 | Scenario 6 | Scenario 7 |
|---|---|---|---|---|---|---|---|
| Probability | 0.05 | 0.10 | 0.20 | 0.30 | 0.20 | 0.10 | 0.05 |
| GMS stock price | 150 | 130 | 110 | 100 | 90 | 80 | 70 |

3. Assuming that Torelli's goal is to minimize the standard deviation of the portfolio return, what is the optimal portfolio that invests all $10 million? (For simplicity, assume that fractional numbers of stock shares and put options can be purchased. Assume that the amounts invested in each security must be nonnegative. However, the number of options purchased need *not* equal the number of shares of stock purchased.) What are the expected return and standard deviation of return of this portfolio? How many shares of GMS stock and how many of each put option does this portfolio correspond to?

4. Suppose that short selling is permitted—that is, the nonnegativity restrictions on the portfolio weights are removed. Now what portfolio minimizes the standard deviation of return? (*Hint:* A good way to attack this problem is to create a table of security returns, as indicated in Table 7.12. Only a few of the table entries are shown. To correctly compute the standard deviation of portfolio return, you will need to incorporate the scenario probabilities. If $r_i$ is the portfolio return in scenario $i$, and $p_i$ is the probability of scenario $i$, then the standard deviation of portfolio return is

$$\sqrt{\sum_{i=1}^{7} p_i(r_i - \mu)^2}$$

where $\mu = \sum_{i=1}^{7} p_i r_i$ is the expected portfolio return.)

**Table 7.12** Table of Security Returns

|  | GMS Stock | Put Option A | Put Option B | Put Option C |
|---|---|---|---|---|
| **Scenario 1** |  |  | −100% |  |
| 2 | 30% |  |  |  |
| ⋮ |  |  |  |  |
| 7 |  |  |  | 220% |

∎

Durham Asset Management (DAM) is a small firm with 50 employees that manages the pension funds of small- to medium-sized companies. Durham was founded in 1975 and has grown considerably throughout the years. Initially, DAM managed the pension funds of three small companies whose asset values totaled $30 million. By 1991, DAM's funds under management were valued at $2 billion.

James Franklin is a senior vice president at DAM, in charge of managing the equity portion of one of its largest pension funds. Franklin meets on a quarterly basis with company officials who supervise his decisions and oversee his performance. His work is measured on several levels, including both subjective and objective criteria. The subjective criteria include estimates of the quality of research reports. The objective criteria include the actual performance of Franklin's portfolio relative to a customized index of companies in DAM's investment universe. Franklin attempts to beat the index not by trying to time market moves, but by investing more heavily in those companies he expects to outperform the customized index and less heavily in those companies he expects to underperform the index.

Franklin has several research analysts who are charged with following the performance of several companies within specific industries. The research analysts prepare reports that analyze the past performance of the companies and prepare projections of future performance. The projections include assessments of the most likely or average performance anticipated over the next month.

Franklin analyzes their findings and often asks for additional information or suggests modifications to the analyses. After a period of careful review, the final forecasts for the next month are assembled and summarized. Each month, the analysts' forecasts are compared to the actual results. Annual bonuses for the analysts are based in part on the comparison of these numbers.

It is now late December 1991, and the projections for January 1992 are indicated in Table 7.13.

**Table 7.13** Projections for January 1992 for the DAM Case Study

| Company | Forecasted Mean Return |
|---|---|
| Aluminum Co. of America (ALCOA) | 0.6% |
| Reynolds Metals | 0.9% |
| Alcan Aluminum, Ltd. | 0.8% |
| Wal-Mart Store, Inc. | 1.5% |
| Sears, Roebuck & Co. | 0.8% |
| Kmart Corporation | 1.3% |
| International Business Machines (IBM) | 0.4% |
| Digital Equipment Corporation (DEC) | 1.1% |
| Hewlett Packard Co. (HP) | 0.7% |
| General Motors Corp. (GM) | 1.2% |
| Ford Motor Co. (FORD) | 0.9% |
| Chrysler Corp. | 1.3% |
| Boeing Co. | 0.3% |
| McDonnell Douglas Corp. | 0.2% |
| United Technologies Corp. | 0.7% |

The projections have been made for 15 U.S. companies divided into five industry groups. The five industry groups are metals, retail, computer, automotive, and aviation.

Franklin wants to use the portfolio optimization approach to see what portfolios it would recommend. He has data containing end-of-month prices for the past two years for each of the companies. The data are contained in the spreadsheet **Durham Asset Management.xlsx**. Also included in the spreadsheet is information about dividends and stock splits. Using these data, James constructs a history of 24 monthly returns for each of the 15 companies.

The past data provide useful information about the volatility (standard deviation) of stock returns. They also give useful information about the degree of association (correlation) of returns between pairs of stocks. However, average returns from the past do not tend to be good predictors of future average returns. Rather than using the raw historical data directly, Franklin creates 24 future return scenarios by adjusting the 24 historical returns. The adjustments are made so that the means of the future scenario returns are consistent with the forecasts from Table 7.13. The adjustments are also made so that the volatilities and correlations of the future scenario returns are the same as in the historical data.

The exact procedure that Franklin uses for developing future scenario returns is described next. Let $r_{ij}^0$ denote the historical return of security $j$ in month $i$ (for $j = 1, \ldots, 15$ and $i = 1, \ldots, 24$). Suppose that the average historical return of security $j$ is $\mu_j^0$. For security $j$, denote the forecasted mean return in Table 7.13 by $\mu_j$. (For example, $\mu_1 = 0.6\%$ and $\mu_2 = 0.9\%$, where the index 1 refers to ALCOA, and 2 refers to Reynolds Metals.) Franklin creates the future scenario return $r_{ij}$ for security $j$ in scenario $i$ using the following equation:

$$r_{ij} = r_{ij}^0 + \mu_j - \mu_j^0 \qquad (7.13)$$

Franklin assumes that any of the scenarios defined by equation (7.13) can occur with equal probability. DAM's policy is never to invest more than 30% of the funds in any one industry group. Franklin measures the risk of a portfolio by its standard deviation of return. He then solves a portfolio optimization model for various minimum levels of mean return to see which portfolios are recommended. After analyzing the trade-off between risk and return, Franklin makes a judgment as to which portfolio to hold for the coming month.

## Questions

1. Use the information in the file **Durham Asset Management.xlsx** to create a history of 24 monthly returns for the 15 companies. Compute the historical average return of each stock. In particular, what was the historical return of ALCOA from 12/29/89 to 1/31/90? What was the historical return of Boeing from 5/31/90 to 6/29/90? Explain how you account for dividends and stock splits in computing monthly returns.

2. Develop 24 future scenario returns using equation (7.13). What is the explanation underlying it? In particular, what is the return of ALCOA if scenario 1 occurs? What is the return of Reynolds Metals if scenario 3 occurs?

3. Compute and graph the mean–standard deviation efficient frontier. Compute at least six points on the efficient frontier (including the minimum standard deviation and maximum expected return points). Create a table of results showing the following for each of your points on the efficient frontier: (1) the optimal portfolio weights, (2) mean portfolio return, and (3) standard deviation. (Briefly explain the equations and optimization model used in the spreadsheet.)[14] ∎

[14] Acknowledgment: Thanks to Ziv Katalan and Aliza Schachter for assistance in developing this case.

# Evolutionary Solver: An Alternative Optimization Procedure

© Getty Images/PhotoDisc

## DEVELOPING AN OPERATING-PLAN MODEL AT SANTA FE RAILWAY

Like many other companies, Santa Fe Railway faces increasing demands for customer service, cost pressures, and changing market conditions. This Is particularly true in its intermodal business area, in which traffic moves on some combination of ship or truck and train. The company averaged almost 8% growth per year in intermodal traffic handled during the period from 1989 to 1996. This increased growth and changing patterns of customer traffic has created difficult problems for Santa Fe, as described in Gorman (1998). The company needs to use its trains and rail lines efficiently from a cost standpoint, but it must also provide customers with high-quality service. In addition, the company must be flexible to change its operating plan quickly in response to changing customer traffic patterns.

Historically, Santa Fe's service design was rather myopic. The service designers tried their best to make incremental refinements to current operations, but their thinking was based too much on historical procedures and could not adapt sufficiently to changing customer needs. They eventually decided to create an operating-plan model capable of building an operating plan for the intermodal business unit from scratch, one that could best adapt to the current and expected traffic patterns and would not be constrained by traditional patterns or historical schedules. As inputs, this model requires customer service requirements, engineering capabilities, and physical plant constraints. As outputs, it provides a weekly train timetable, traffic-to-train assignments, yard and railway line schedules, and equipment and locomotive flows. It simultaneously allocates physical rail network resources to trains and allocates scarce train space to traffic flows in a way that minimizes operating costs while meeting customer requirements.

The operating-plan problem can be decomposed into two problems: the train timetable problem and the traffic assignment problem. The former prescribes which trains will travel on which lines at which times. Given this information, the latter problem prescribes which customer loads are assigned to which trains. Each problem is huge, and much ingenuity was required to model and solve these problems. For the timetable problem, the original model represented each hour of the week for every possible train as a binary decision variable, where 1 indicates a train and 0 indicates no train. This model was impossibly large, so the service design team reduced its size by specifying a menu of allowable train routes (about 200) from which the model could choose. Even this reduced problem was much too large for traditional integer programming algorithms to solve, so the analysts did what is becoming more common in large optimization models: they turned to newer, emerging types of algorithms. In particular, they tried the genetic "survival of the fittest" algorithms we discuss in this chapter, where they mix schedules from a given population of schedules to carry over the best characteristics of these schedules to the next generation of schedules. Unfortunately, genetic algorithms alone were painfully slow at producing useful populations of train schedules for this large problem. Therefore, the authors combined genetic algorithms with another type of algorithm, called *tabu search,* to speed up the process. (Tabu search is also a fairly new idea. It uses information from previous iterations to search in a promising direction. However, a *tabu list* prohibits the algorithm from undoing recent changes to the schedule or revisiting recent solutions.) This method of combining algorithms worked and enabled Santa Fe to solve the timetable problem reasonably quickly. The company was then able to solve the traffic assignment problem by a clever priority-based, shortest-path heuristic.

Santa Fe Intermodal has used its operating-plan model to study many major changes in rail operations: to predict train volumes based on long-term forecasts, to quantify the impact of containerization of intermodal business on train operations, and to develop a cost basis in contract negotiations for large amounts of incremental business. The model has shown the potential to improve global service by 4% while reducing costs by 6% over the previous operating plan. As R. Mark Schmidt, an analyst at Santa Fe, states, "Obviously, as with any major deviation from traditional processes, the acceptance of the operating-plan model has been a gradual one. Recent successes of the model are building confidences and as a result, the model is being interwoven into the intermodal service design process at Santa Fe." ■

## 8.1 INTRODUCTION

In Chapters 3 through 7, we used Excel's Solver to solve many interesting and important problems. Unfortunately, there are many optimization problems for which Solver is ill suited to find optimal solutions. However, genetic algorithms often perform well on optimization problems where Solver performs poorly. The purpose of this chapter is to illustrate some interesting models that cannot be solved by the standard Solver, at least not easily or without tricks, but can be solved with genetic algorithms in a reasonably straight-forward manner. In short, the methods in this chapter enable you to solve a much wider range of optimization models.

Fortunately, the developer of the Excel Solver, Frontline Systems (http://www.frontsys.com), has developed a Premium Solver that uses genetic algorithms to find good solutions to many optimization problems that cannot be solved with the standard Excel Solver. Premium Solver, included in the CD-ROM that accompanies this book (but not included in Microsoft Office), contains three separate "solvers":

- The Standard Simplex LP Solver is used to solve linear models, including models where some or all of the changing cells are restricted to be binary and/or integer.

- The Standard GRG Nonlinear Solver is used to solve nonlinear models when the target cell and constraints are "smooth" functions of the changing cells.

- The Evolutionary Solver uses genetic algorithms to find good (close to optimal) solutions to more difficult problems, including those where the target cell and/or constraints are nonsmooth functions of the changing cells.

The first two implement essentially the same versions of the algorithms we have been using in the previous chapters to solve linear, integer, and nonlinear problems. Therefore, for the problems we have been solving, switching to Premium Solver provides no real advantage; the standard Excel Solver works fine. However, you might recall that the standard Solver cannot always handle models with IF, MAX, MIN, and several other Excel functions. The problem is that such models often contain nonsmooth functions in the target cell and/or the constraint cells. To use the standard Excel Solver on these models (if possible), we have to resort to various tricks to get them in smooth form. Fortunately, this is *not* necessary with Evolutionary Solver, as we illustrate in this chapter. Evolutionary Solver uses a type of algorithm called a genetic algorithm, which is much more flexible.

Before discussing genetic algorithms and Evolutionary Solver, we discuss the strengths and weaknesses of the standard Excel Solver.[1]

Consider an optimization model where the target cell is a linear function of the changing cells, the left and right sides of all constraints are linear functions of the changing cells, and all changing cells are allowed to contain fractional values—that is, there are no integer constraints. For such models, called linear models, Solver is guaranteed to find an optimal solution (if an optimal solution exists). We have discussed many linear models in Chapters 3 through 5. Solver is an excellent tool to use for any optimization problem that can be set up as a linear model, provided that the model does not exceed Solver's size constraints—up to 200 changing cells and 100 constraints. Most larger linear models are difficult to handle in a spreadsheet format. These larger models are often solved using a modeling language such as LINGO, GAMS, or AMPL. With a modeling language, a user can generate, say, 10,000 supply constraints for a transportation model with one line of computer code. This makes it easy to compactly represent and solve large models. (We should also mention that Frontline Systems has developed a commercial large-scale Solver capable of solving very large spreadsheet models.)

In Chapter 6, we considered linear models where some or all of the changing cells are constrained to be integers. In theory, Solver should be able to find optimal solutions to these problems, but in practice it can take hours, days, or even weeks to find optimal solutions to integer-constrained models. This is not necessarily a weakness of Solver—integer-constrained models are inherently difficult for *any* optimization software package—but algorithms other than the algorithm used by Solver work better for some integer models.

---

[1] From here on in this chapter, when we refer to "Solver" or the "standard Solver," we are referring to the Solver that ships with Excel. To refer to Premium or Evolutionary Solver, we include the Premium or Evolutionary names. Note that Premium Solver for Excel 2007 is different from Premium Solver for earlier versions of Excel. So if you have a previous version of Premium Solver installed, make sure you install the version (7.0) that accompanies this book.

In the previous chapter, we discussed nonlinear models and saw that the standard Solver's nonlinear algorithm is capable of solving many of these. However, nonlinear models present two problems. First, as we learned in Section 7.2 of Chapter 7, Solver can get stuck at a local maximum or a local minimum to a problem and never find the global maximum or minimum to the problem. The function shown in Figure 7.6 illustrates this situation. In this example, Solver fails to find the global optimal solution for certain starting solutions.

Second, we have emphasized that if a spreadsheet model uses IF, ABS, MAX, or MIN functions that depend on any of the model's changing cells, then the model is typically nonsmooth, and Solver might have difficulty finding an optimal solution. We illustrate one possibility in Figure 8.1 that could be caused by an IF function. The context here might be ordering a product with a quantity discount, so that the order quantity is on the horizontal axis and the total cost (ordering cost plus inventory holding cost) is on the vertical axis. The IF function specifies that if the order quantity is less than *A*, then one function specifies the total cost. If the order quantity is between *A* and *B*, another function specifies the total cost. Finally, if the order quantity is greater than *B*, a third function specifies the total cost. The resulting graph is not only nonlinear, but it has **discontinuities** at *A* and *B*, where the total cost jumps from one value to another. The overall cost-minimizing order quantity is to the right of *B*, and if you select an initial solution to the right of *B*, the standard nonlinear Solver will locate the correct optimal solution. However, if you start at a point to the left of *B*, the standard Solver will almost certainly not be able to locate the optimal solution.

**Figure 8.1**

A Cost Function with Discontinuities

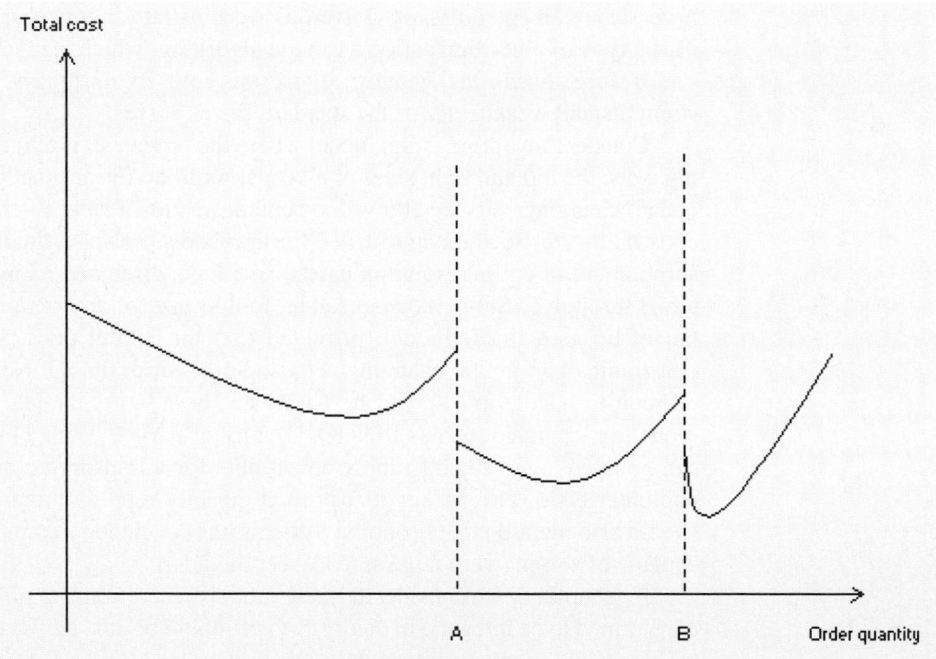

The point of this discussion is that although the standard Solver can handle many models with no difficulty, Solver is not well suited to finding optimal solutions for certain types of models. We now discuss a completely different solution method that is sometimes more successful at solving these difficult problems.

## 8.2 INTRODUCTION TO GENETIC ALGORITHMS

*In GA terms, a chromosome is a binary (0-1) representation of a potential solution.*

In the early 1970s, John Holland of the University of Michigan realized that many features espoused in the theory of natural evolution (such as survival of the fittest and mutation) could be used to help solve difficult optimization problems.[2] Because his methods were based on behavior observed in nature, Holland coined the term *genetic algorithm* to describe his algorithm. Simply stated, a **genetic algorithm** (GA) provides a method of intelligently searching an optimization model's feasible region for an optimal solution. Biological terminology is used to describe the algorithm. The target cell is called a **fitness function,** and a specification of values for all changing cells is called a **chromosome.** For most problems, a GA codes changing cells in binary notation. For example, 1001 represents

$$1(2^3) + 0(2^2) + 0(2^1) + 1(2^0) = 8 + 1 = 9$$

The following is a rough outline of how a GA might work. Suppose a company must decide how many units of each of two products to order. Because of quantity discounts, the function that represents total cost has discontinuities of the type observed in Figure 8.1. Actually, the total cost is even more complex than in Figure 8.1, because there are two products, not just one. However, the only requirement of the algorithm is that total cost $TC(Q_1, Q_2)$ can be calculated for any combination of the order quantities $Q_1$ and $Q_2$. Suppose $Q_1$ and $Q_2$ must each be between 0 and 500. (In this discussion, we assume the model has no constraints other than lower bounds and upper bounds on each changing cell. Later we discuss how a GA can handle other types of constraints.) Then the GA uses the following steps:

1. **Generate a population.** The GA randomly samples values of the changing cells between the lower and upper bounds to generate a set of (usually at least 50) chromosomes. The initial set of chromosomes is called the **population.** For example, two members of the population might be

   - **Chromosome 1:** $Q_1 = 100$ and $Q_2 = 400$ (or in binary, $Q_1 = 001100100$ and $Q_2 = 110010000$)
   - **Chromosome 2:** $Q_1 = 300$ and $Q_2 = 200$ (or in binary, $Q_1 = 100101100$ and $Q_2 = 011001000$)

   The initial population is constructed by randomly choosing points from the problem's feasible region. (Note that 9 binary digits are sufficient to represent any order quantity from 0 to 500.)

2. **Create a new generation.** Create a new generation of chromosomes in the hope of finding improvement. In the new generation, chromosomes with a smaller fitness function (in a minimization problem) have a greater chance of surviving to the next generation. Suppose in our example that chromosome 1 has a fitness value (total cost) of $2560, and chromosome 2 has a fitness value of $3240. Then chromosome 1 should have a larger chance of surviving to the next generation. **Crossover** and **mutation** are also used to generate chromosomes for the next generation.

   a. Crossover (fairly common) splices together two chromosomes at a prespecified point. For example, if chromosomes 1 and 2 are combined by crossover and the crossover point is between the fourth and fifth digits (from the right), the resulting chromosomes (in binary) are

      - **New chromosome 1:** $Q_1 = 100100100$ and $Q_2 = 011000000$ (or $Q_1 = 292$ and $Q_2 = 192$)
      - **New chromosome 2:** $Q_1 = 001101100$ and $Q_2 = 110011000$ (or $Q_1 = 108$ and $Q_2 = 408$)

[2] Goldberg (1989), Davis (1991), and Holland (1975) are good references on genetic algorithms.

Note that the two original $Q_1$'s are used to create the two new $Q_1$'s and similarly for the $Q_2$'s. For example, $Q_1$ for the new chromosome 1 splices together the left digits 10010 from $Q_1$ of the original chromosome 2 and the right digits 0100 from $Q_1$ of the original chromosome 1.

b. Mutation (very rare) randomly selects a digit and changes it from 0 to 1 or vice versa. For example, if we mutate the left digit of $Q_1$ in chromosome 2, the new $Q_1$ in chromosome 2 becomes $Q_1 = 000101100$ (or $Q_1 = 44$). As this example indicates, mutation can provide a dramatic effect, taking us to a completely different location in the feasible region. Therefore, an occasional mutation is useful for getting the algorithm "unstuck."

3. **Stopping condition.** At each generation, the best value of the fitness function in the generation is recorded, and the algorithm repeats step 2. If no improvement in the best fitness value is observed after many consecutive generations, the GA terminates.

To handle a constraint such as $Q_1 + Q_2 \leq 700$, the GA adds (in a minimization problem), $M(Q_1 + Q_2 - 700)$ to the fitness function, where $M$ is a suitably large number such as 1,000,000. Now any chromosome that violates the constraint has a high value of the fitness function because the "penalty" $M(Q_1 + Q_2 - 700)$ greatly increases the value of the new fitness function. This causes the GA to avoid chromosomes that violate the constraint.

## Strengths and Weaknesses of GAs

*GAs have a particular advantage on non-smooth problems—those with discontinuities, for example. However, they are much less efficient than traditional algorithms such as the simplex method on "nice" problems.*

If you let a GA run long enough, it is *guaranteed* to find the solution to any optimization problem. The problem is that the sun could explode before the GA finds the optimal solution! In general, we never know how long to run a GA. For the problems discussed in this chapter, an optimal solution is usually found within 5 minutes or less, although timing depends on the problem, and some experimentation is invariably necessary. Therefore, we usually let Evolutionary Solver run for a few minutes and report the best solution found. Unfortunately, we do not know if the best solution we have found is optimal, but it is usually a "good" solution—that is, very close to being optimal.

As a rule, GAs do very well in problems with few constraints (excluding bounds on changing cells). In addition, the complexity of the target cell does not bother a GA. For example, a GA can easily handle MIN, MAX, IF, and ABS functions in spreadsheet models. This is the key advantage of GAs. On the other hand, GAs do not usually perform as well on problems that have many constraints. For example, the standard Solver has no difficulty with the multiple-constraint linear models in Chapters 3 through 5, but GAs do not perform nearly as well on them.

## 8.3 INTRODUCTION TO EVOLUTIONARY SOLVER

GAs have been available for several years and have been implemented in several software packages. However, they have been available as Excel add-ins only recently. In this chapter, we use the Evolutionary Solver developed by Frontline Systems and available as part of the Premium Solver included on the CD-ROM in this book.[3] To get started with Evolutionary Solver, we examine a simple nonlinear function of a single variable.

---

[3] With two exceptions (in Chapters 13 and 15), this is the only place in this book where Premium Solver is required. For all other optimization models in this book, the standard Solver that ships with Excel is sufficient. However, the standard Solver does *not* include Evolutionary Solver. Therefore, to solve the models in this chapter, you must install Premium Solver.

EXAMPLE | **8.1 MAXIMIZING A NONLINEAR FUNCTION WITH LOCAL MAXIMA**

To see how Evolutionary Solver works, we consider a simple function that is difficult for the standard Solver's nonlinear algorithm. This example, analyzed in Chapter 7, is a function of a single variable $x$: $f(x) = (x - 1)(x - 2)(x - 3)(x - 4)(x - 5)$ for $1 \leq x \leq 5$. We want to maximize $f(x)$ over this range. However, the graph of this function shown in Figure 8.2 indicates that there are two local maxima: one at around $x = 3.5$ and the other at $x = 5$. The global maximum, the one we want, is near $x = 1.5$. How do we find it with Excel?

**Figure 8.2**

Function with Local Maxima

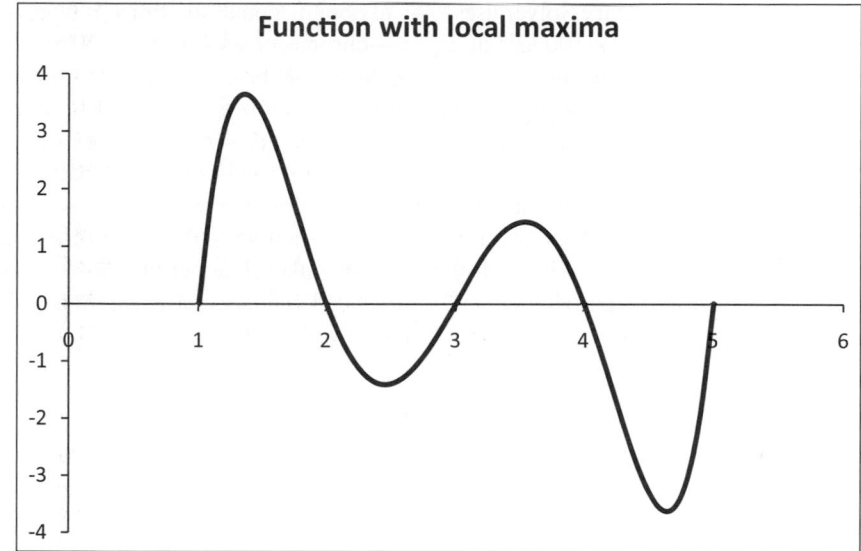

**Objective**   To illustrate how Evolutionary Solver works and to see how it can successfully find a global maximum for a function with several local maxima.

## Solution

The model is particularly simple. (See Figure 8.3 and the file **Local Maxima.xlsx**.) To set it up, enter any value in cell B5 (the only changing cell), enter the formula **=B5-1** in cell B6, copy this down to cell B10, and enter the formula **=PRODUCT(B6:B10)** in cell B11. We want to maximize the value in cell B11 while constraining the value in cell B5 to be between 1 and 5.

**Figure 8.3**

Model for Evaluating the Function

|  | A | B | C | D |
|---|---|---|---|---|
| 1 | Function with local maxima | | | |
| 2 | | | | |
| 3 | The function is: y=(x-1)(x-2)(x-3)(x-4)(x-5) | | | |
| 4 | | | | |
| 5 | x | 1.355567 | | |
| 6 | x-1 | 0.355567 | | |
| 7 | x-2 | -0.64443 | | |
| 8 | x-3 | -1.64443 | | |
| 9 | x-4 | -2.64443 | | |
| 10 | x-5 | -3.64443 | | |
| 11 | Product | 3.631432 | | |

If we use the standard Solver, without checking the Assume Linear Model option, you can check that the solution depends on the starting value in cell B6. If this starting point is near 5, the Solver solution is 5, corresponding to the local maximum at $x = 5$. If the starting point is near 3.5, then the Solver solution is 3.54, corresponding to the local maximum at $x = 3.54$. Only if the starting point is sufficiently small does Solver correctly find the global maximum at $x = 1.356$. This is disturbing because if you didn't have a graph of the function to lead you in the right direction, how would you know where to start? Whatever starting point you use, how would you know whether Solver had found the global maximum? We now see how Evolutionary Solver can help solve this problem.[4]

## USING EVOLUTIONARY SOLVER

Evolutionary Solver uses GAs to obtain "good" solutions. It begins with a population containing, say, 100 sets of values—chromosomes—for the changing cells. For example, one chromosome might be 3.778. (This would be coded in binary form by the algorithm.) This chromosome represents the value of $x$ in this example, but it generally represents a set of values in the changing cells. Chromosomes that yield large objective values have more chance of surviving to the next generation of chromosomes. Chromosomes that yield small objective values have little chance of surviving to the next generation. Occasionally, Evolutionary Solver drastically changes—mutates—the value of a changing cell. Usually we stop Evolutionary Solver after a specified time period (say 1 minute) or when there has been no improvement in the target cell value after a given time. Following is some general information about Evolutionary Solver:

- Evolutionary Solver usually finds a good solution, but there is no guarantee that it will find the *best* solution.

*Evolutionary Solver doesn't handle constraints well. It is usually better to penalize constraint violations and include the penalties in the objective.*

- Evolutionary Solver is not very efficient at handling constraints. The best way to handle constraints is to penalize a violation of a constraint. The penalty is then included in the target cell. We do not use penalties in this example, but we illustrate them in a later example.

- A good starting solution—the values you place in the changing cells—usually helps Evolutionary Solver in its search for an optimal solution. However, the starting solution is not absolutely critical to success.

- Evolutionary Solver places more of a burden on you to specify certain parameters of the algorithm. These parameters are specified in Options dialog boxes, as we illustrate shortly. Unfortunately, these parameters are not very intuitive to most users, and some experimentation is necessary to find the best settings of these parameters for any given model. Nevertheless, if you use the default settings or the settings we suggest, they should work reasonably well.

*Evolutionary Solver uses random numbers in its search; therefore, two different runs can lead to different solutions.*

- Much of the solution process is driven by random numbers that direct the search. Therefore, two people can get different solutions to the same problem. In fact, running Evolutionary Solver a second time can possibly yield a different solution! You can set a random seed parameter to ensure the same solution on two successive runs.

- After Evolutionary Solver has found a good solution, you can use the GRG Nonlinear Solver (the nonlinear algorithm included with the Premium Solver software) to try to find a slightly better solution. If there is no improvement, you can probably infer that the solution found by Evolutionary Solver is optimal or close to optimal.

---

[4] Both Premium Solver and the standard Solver can solve nonlinear models, but Premium Solver's GRG Nonlinear algorithm for Excel 2007 has a new feature: Multistart Search. This feature is *great* for problems with local maxima. In fact, it makes Evolutionary Solver unnecessary for this particular problem. Our claim from the previous edition of the book is still true: GRG Nonlinear is good for "smooth" problems, whereas Evolutionary is required for "nonsmooth" problems. But with Multistart, GRG Nonlinear is even better than before.

In general, use the following steps to implement Evolutionary Solver:

**1 Start Premium Solver.** Assuming you have installed Premium Solver, you find it under the Add-Ins tab. The standard Solver is still under the Data tab, but you don't go there to run Premium Solver; you go to the Add-Ins tab. (This is quite different from Excel 2003 and earlier versions.)

**2 Specify the target cell, changing cells, and constraints.** This is done in the usual way. The only difference is that you should put lower and upper bounds on all changing cells—in addition to any other constraints that might be in the model. At this point, the Solver dialog box should appear as in Figure 8.4.

**Figure 8.4**

Filling Out the Solver Dialog Box

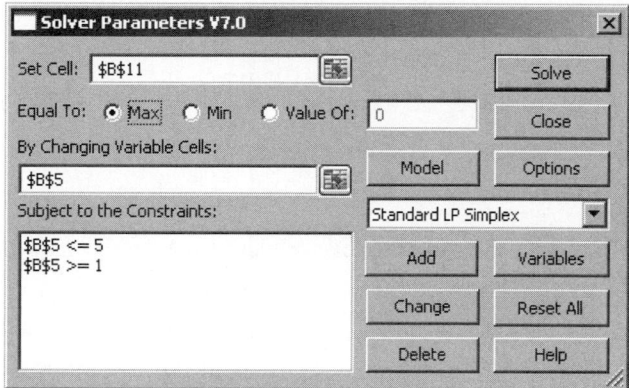

**3 Select Evolutionary Solver.** Click on the drop-down list of available algorithms to select Evolutionary Solver (see Figure 8.5). This is the option we use throughout this chapter, but you can also experiment with the GRG Nonlinear option, especially after Evolutionary Solver finds a good solution.

**Figure 8.5**

Selecting Evolutionary Solver

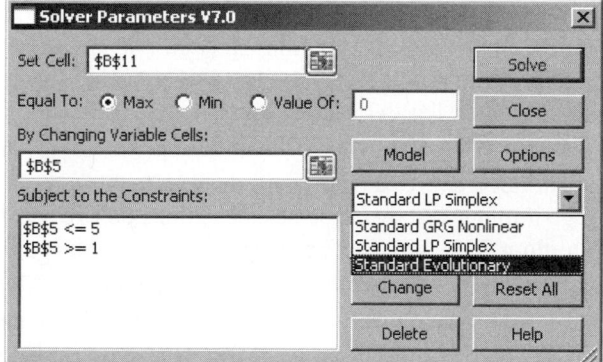

**4 Solver Options.** Click on the Options button to show the Solver Options dialog box in Figure 8.6. This dialog box allows you to fine-tune the way the GA works. Some of the settings are not as crucial as others, and you can leave these at their default values. However, you might want to experiment with some of the others. Unfortunately, the settings that work best for one type of model are not necessarily best for another type of model. Here are some recommendations. (We found this information, plus much more, by clicking on the Help button.)

- **Max Time** is not important. However, if you want Solver to run unattended, set this to a large value such as 10,000 seconds. Otherwise, Solver will beep at you early, and you will have to click a button to make it proceed.

**Figure 8.6**

Evolutionary Solver
Options Dialog Box

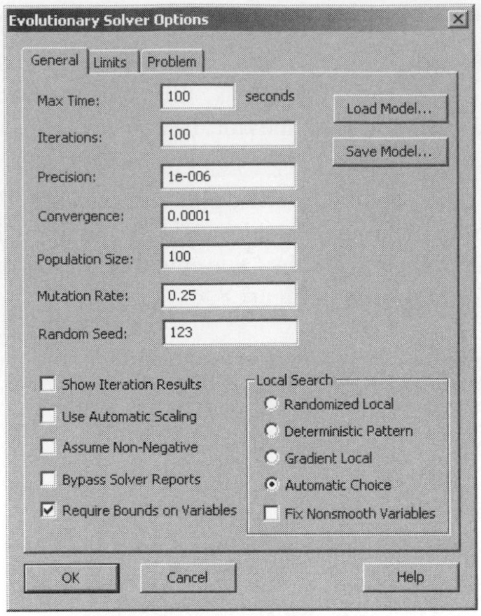

- **Iterations** is not important. You can leave it at its default value.

- **Precision** governs how close the constraint values must be to their bounds, and **Convergence** is concerned with the rate of change of the objective. You can leave these at their default values.

- **Population size** is the number of candidate solutions (chromosomes) at any point in time, and the default value of 100 should work well although we sometimes increase it to 150. Note that the initial population is chosen randomly, but it includes at least one instance of the starting solution you specify in the changing cells.

- **Mutation rate** governs the frequency at which mutations are introduced into the population of solutions. Mutations shouldn't be introduced too often, but by introducing them every now and then, the GA gets a chance to explore a completely different area of the feasible region. You can leave this setting at its default value, but we have had success at increasing it to 0.25.

- Evolutionary Solver uses a random mechanism to perform its search, but you can make it go through exactly the same calculations on two separate runs if you use the same **Random Seed** (any integer) on each run. You can leave this box blank, in which case Evolutionary Solver bases the seed on the system clock.

- The check boxes at the lower left are much like the ones of the same names in the standard Solver. However, you *should* check the **Require Bounds on Variables** option. This forces you to enter explicit upper and lower bounds on all changing cells (as shown in Figure 8.4), which aids Evolutionary Solver in its search process.

*Some experimentation with Evolutionary Solver's settings may be necessary. No single group of settings works best on every problem.*

- The radio buttons under **Local Search** and the **Fix Nonsmooth Variables** option are technical. At each step of the GA, Evolutionary Solver performs a local search in the neighborhood of the best solution found so far (the "incumbent") to find better nearby solutions. The options here govern the way this local search is performed. If you believe the objective behaves linearly in the neighborhood of a solution, **Local Linear Gradient** is a good option. If you believe it behaves smoothly but nonlinearly, **Nonlinear Gradient** is a good option. Otherwise, you can try one of the other two options. The choice is problem dependent, so you need to experiment.

**Figure 8.7**

Evolutionary Solver
Limit Options
Dialog Box

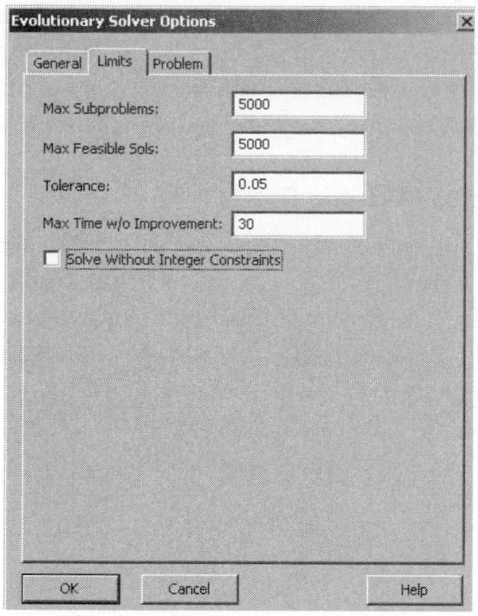

**5** **Limit Options.** Click on the Limits tab to bring up the dialog box in Figure 8.7. This dialog box provides the following additional options.

- **Max Subproblems** and **Max Feasible Sols** both have to do with the length of time Evolutionary Solver runs before asking you whether you want to stop or continue. If you want Solver to continue, unattended, for a long time, set these to large values such as 500,000.

- **Tolerance** and **Max Time w/o Improvement** work in tandem to specify when Evolutionary Solver should stop. Specifically, if the percentage improvement in the best solution's objective value is less than the Tolerance value for the number of seconds in the Max Time without Improvement box, Evolutionary Solver stops and declares the best solution so far as optimal. We recommend leaving Tolerance at its default value but possibly increasing Max Time w/o Improvement to, say, 100 seconds. However, this might just let the algorithm spin its wheels at the same solution for a longer period of time.

- **Solve Without Integer Constraints** allows you to ignore integer constraints, at least temporarily, to get a good noninteger solution. Then you can recheck this box to add back the integer constraints. The search for the best integer solution, starting from the best noninteger solution, should hopefully then go more quickly.

**6** **Problem tab.** The Problem tab can be ignored. It simply shows some information about your problem setup and some limits imposed by Premium Solver.

**7** **Solve.** Back your way out to the beginning Solver dialog box and click on Solve. You can watch the progress of the solution process in the status bar of your screen. In particular, watch the "incumbent," which is the current best value of the target cell. Typically, this value decreases (for a minimization problem) rapidly at first, and then very slowly. If you get the sense that it is going nowhere after a minute or two (and you are tired of waiting), you can press the Esc key a few times to stop the process. (Don't be impatient. Premium Solver tends to keep running for awhile even after you press Esc.) From there, you can either let the process continue or accept the best solution to this point. Don't be surprised if the solution process takes *much* longer than you have experienced for Solver models in previous chapters. GAs are not guaranteed to be fast, but they make up for it by being more flexible.

For this particular model, Evolutionary Solver gets to the solution shown earlier in Figure 8.2 almost instantaneously. Then it runs for 30 seconds (the time we specified in the Limit Options dialog box) without being able to find a better solution, at which time it quits. Note that this solution is indeed the global optimal solution (refer to Figure 8.2), and

*If you get the sense that Evolutionary Solver is getting nowhere, press the Esc key to stop it.*

Evolutionary Solver finds it almost immediately, even when we start at a solution, such as 3.5 or 4.9, that is close to a local maximum. This is because Evolutionary Solver looks all over the feasible region for potentially good solutions. Therefore, Evolutionary Solver is not as likely to get stuck at a local optimum as the standard nonlinear Solver. ∎

### Limits on Changing Cells: Required?

*When using Evolution-ary Solver, it is always a good idea to add explicit upper-bound and lower-bound constraints on the changing cells.*

In the Evolutionary Solver Options dialog box in Figure 8.6, we checked the Required Bounds on Variables box, which forces us to include constraints with lower and upper bounds on the changing cells. Is it possible to leave this box unchecked and ignore bounds on the changing cells? Evidently, the answer is yes, but it is not a good idea—the GA will not work as well. Therefore, always check this box and always include bounds on the changing cells in your list of constraints.

## PROBLEMS

*Solutions for problems whose numbers appear within a color box can be found in the Student Solutions Files. Order your copy today at the Winston/Albright product Web site, academic.cengage.com/decisionsciences/winston.*

### Skill-Building Problems

**1.** Modify the function in Example 8.1 so that it becomes $f(x) = (x-1)(x-2)(x-3)(x-4)(x-5)(x-6)(x-7)$ for $1 \le x \le 7$. Plot a lot of points from 1 to 7 to see what the graph of this function looks like. Then use the standard nonlinear Solver to find its maximum. Try the following starting points: 1, 3, 5, 6, and 6.9.

Report what you find. Then try Evoluationary Solver. Does it get the correct solution?

**2.** Modify the function in Example 8.1 so that it becomes $f(x) = x \sin(x)$ for $0 \le x \le 30$. (Here, $\sin(x)$ is the sine funtion from trigonometry. You can evaluate it with Excel's SIN function.) Plot a lot of points from 0 to 30 to see what the graph of this function looks like. Then use the standard nonlinear Solver to find its maximum. Try the following starting points: 1, 6, 15, 20, and 27. Report what you find. Then try Evoluationary Solver. Does it get the correct solution?

## 8.4 NONLINEAR PRICING MODELS

We examined several pricing models in the previous chapter. We now examine one more such model, where customers of a certain product place less and less value on each succeeding item of the product. We see that if the company selling the product sets a constant price per item, it earns considerably less profit than if it uses a more imaginative pricing scheme, called a **two-part tariff.** In this pricing scheme, each customer pays a fixed amount each time she buys *any* amount of the product. In addition, she pays a variable amount per item purchased.

### EXAMPLE | 8.2 PRICING MENTHOS CANDY

*Piecewise linear objectives, imple-mented with IF logic, are good candidates for Evolutionary Solver.*

Suppose we sell Menthos candy. Most people value the first pack of Menthos they purchase more than the second pack. They also value the second pack more than the third pack, and so on. How can we take advantage of this when pricing Menthos? If we charge a single price for each pack of Menthos, few people are going to buy more than one or two packs. Alternatively, however, we can try the two-part tariff approach, in which we charge an "entry fee" to anyone who buys Menthos, plus a reduced price per pack purchased. For example, if a reasonable *single* price per pack is $1.10, then a reasonable two-part tariff might be an entry fee of $1.50 and a price of $0.50 per pack. This gives some customers an incentive to purchase many packs of Menthos. Because the total cost of purchasing *n* packs of Menthos is no longer a linear function of $n$—it is now "piecewise linear"—we refer to the two-part tariff as a nonlinear pricing strategy.

As usual with pricing models, the key input is customer sensitivity to price. Rather than having a single demand function, however, we now assume that each customer has a unique sensitivity to price. To keep the example fairly small, we assume that four typical customers from the four market segments for the product have been asked what they would pay for each successive pack of Menthos, with the results listed in Figure 8.8. For example, customer 1 is willing to pay $1.24 for the first pack of Menthos, $1.03 for the second pack, and only $0.35 for the tenth pack. These four customers are considered representative of the market. If it costs $0.40 to produce a pack of Menthos, determine a profit-maximizing single price and a profit-maximizing two-part tariff. Assume that the four market segments have 10,000, 5000, 7500, and 15,000 customers, respectively, and that the customers within a market segment all respond identically to price.

**Figure 8.8**

Price Sensitivity of
Four Representative
Customers

| | A | B | C | D | E |
|---|---|---|---|---|---|
| 1 | Pricing Menthos - single price model | | | | |
| 2 | | | | | |
| 3 | Price sensitivity of four types of customers | | | | |
| 4 | | Price willing to pay (or marginal value of packs) | | | |
| 5 | Pack # | Customer 1 | Customer 2 | Customer 3 | Customer 4 |
| 6 | 1 | 1.24 | 0.92 | 1.27 | 1.49 |
| 7 | 2 | 1.03 | 0.85 | 1.11 | 1.24 |
| 8 | 3 | 0.89 | 0.69 | 0.96 | 1.10 |
| 9 | 4 | 0.80 | 0.58 | 0.85 | 0.97 |
| 10 | 5 | 0.77 | 0.50 | 0.73 | 0.81 |
| 11 | 6 | 0.66 | 0.43 | 0.63 | 0.71 |
| 12 | 7 | 0.59 | 0.36 | 0.51 | 0.63 |
| 13 | 8 | 0.51 | 0.32 | 0.45 | 0.53 |
| 14 | 9 | 0.42 | 0.26 | 0.39 | 0.42 |
| 15 | 10 | 0.35 | 0.22 | 0.32 | 0.35 |

**Objective**  To use Evolutionary Solver to find the best pricing strategies for customers who value each succeeding unit of a product less than the previous unit.

## WHERE DO THE NUMBERS COME FROM?

The price sensitivity data listed in Figure 8.8 would be the most difficult to find. However, a well-studied technique in marketing research called *conjoint analysis* can be used to estimate such data. See Green et al. (2001) for a nontechnical discussion of conjoint analysis.

## Solution

We first set up the single-price model. Then, with very little modification, we formulate the two-part tariff model. The approach for each model is as follows.

For any pricing scheme, we calculate the customer's cost if he purchases $n$ packs. Then we compare this cost to the corresponding value in the appropriate column in Figure 8.8. As an example, suppose we charge a single price of $0.80 per pack. If a customer of type 2 purchases 3 packs, the **surplus value** to this customer is the total value to him of the 3 packs, $0.92 + $0.85 + $0.69 = $2.46, minus the cost of the packs, $2.40. Because the value is greater than the cost, a purchase of 3 packs is attractive to this customer. We assume that a customer of a given type will purchase the quantity $n$ that provides the *largest* surplus value. In simple terms, we assume each customer buys the quantity that provides the largest difference between value and cost. However, if the surplus value is always negative for the customer, we assume he doesn't purchase any packs.

By knowing how many packs each customer segment will purchase at each price, we can then maximize the company's profit by setting the price accordingly.

## DEVELOPING THE SINGLE-PRICE MODEL

The single-price model appears in Figure 8.9. (See the **Single Price.xlsx** file.) It can be formed with the following steps:

---

**Figure 8.9** Single-Price Model

| | A | B | C | D | E | F | G | H | I | J | K |
|---|---|---|---|---|---|---|---|---|---|---|---|
| 1 | Pricing Menthos - single price model | | | | | | | | | | |
| 2 | | | | | | | | | | | |
| 3 | Price sensitivity of four types of customers | | | | | | Total value of purchases | | | | |
| 4 | | Price willing to pay (or marginal value of packs) | | | | | | Total value from this many packs | | | |
| 5 | Pack # | Customer 1 | Customer 2 | Customer 3 | Customer 4 | | # of packs | Customer 1 | Customer 2 | Customer 3 | Customer 4 |
| 6 | 1 | 1.24 | 0.92 | 1.27 | 1.49 | | 1 | 1.24 | 0.92 | 1.27 | 1.49 |
| 7 | 2 | 1.03 | 0.85 | 1.11 | 1.24 | | 2 | 2.27 | 1.77 | 2.38 | 2.73 |
| 8 | 3 | 0.89 | 0.69 | 0.96 | 1.10 | | 3 | 3.16 | 2.46 | 3.34 | 3.83 |
| 9 | 4 | 0.80 | 0.58 | 0.85 | 0.97 | | 4 | 3.96 | 3.04 | 4.19 | 4.80 |
| 10 | 5 | 0.77 | 0.50 | 0.73 | 0.81 | | 5 | 4.73 | 3.54 | 4.92 | 5.61 |
| 11 | 6 | 0.66 | 0.43 | 0.63 | 0.71 | | 6 | 5.39 | 3.97 | 5.55 | 6.32 |
| 12 | 7 | 0.59 | 0.36 | 0.51 | 0.63 | | 7 | 5.98 | 4.33 | 6.06 | 6.95 |
| 13 | 8 | 0.51 | 0.32 | 0.45 | 0.53 | | 8 | 6.49 | 4.65 | 6.51 | 7.48 |
| 14 | 9 | 0.42 | 0.26 | 0.39 | 0.42 | | 9 | 6.91 | 4.91 | 6.90 | 7.90 |
| 15 | 10 | 0.35 | 0.22 | 0.32 | 0.35 | | 10 | 7.26 | 5.13 | 7.22 | 8.25 |
| 16 | | | | | | | | | | | |
| 17 | Unit cost | $0.40 | | Total cost of packs | | | Surplus (value minus cost) from purchasing | | | | |
| 18 | | | | # of packs | Cost | | # of packs | Customer 1 | Customer 2 | Customer 3 | Customer 4 |
| 19 | Unit price | $0.80 | | 1 | 0.80 | | 1 | 0.44 | 0.12 | 0.47 | 0.69 |
| 20 | | | | 2 | 1.60 | | 2 | 0.67 | 0.17 | 0.78 | 1.13 |
| 21 | | | | 3 | 2.40 | | 3 | 0.76 | 0.06 | 0.94 | 1.43 |
| 22 | | | | 4 | 3.20 | | 4 | 0.76 | -0.16 | 0.99 | 1.60 |
| 23 | | | | 5 | 4.00 | | 5 | 0.73 | -0.46 | 0.92 | 1.61 |
| 24 | | | | 6 | 4.80 | | 6 | 0.59 | -0.83 | 0.75 | 1.52 |
| 25 | | | | 7 | 5.60 | | 7 | 0.38 | -1.27 | 0.46 | 1.35 |
| 26 | | | | 8 | 6.40 | | 8 | 0.09 | -1.75 | 0.11 | 1.08 |
| 27 | | | | 9 | 7.20 | | 9 | -0.29 | -2.29 | -0.30 | 0.70 |
| 28 | | | | 10 | 8.00 | | 10 | -0.74 | -2.87 | -0.78 | 0.25 |
| 29 | | | | | | | | | | | |
| 30 | Customer behavior | | | | | | Range names used: | | | | |
| 31 | | Customer 1 | Customer 2 | Customer 3 | Customer 4 | | Profit | =Model!$B$37 | | | |
| 32 | Max surplus | 0.76 | 0.17 | 0.99 | 1.61 | | Unit_cost | =Model!$B$17 | | | |
| 33 | # purchased | 4 | 2 | 4 | 5 | | Unit_price | =Model!$B$19 | | | |
| 34 | Market size (1000s) | 10 | 5 | 7.5 | 15 | | | | | | |
| 35 | | | | | | | | | | | |
| 36 | Total purchased (1000s) | 155 | | | | | | | | | |
| 37 | Profit ($1000s) | 62.000 | | | | | | | | | |

**1 Inputs.** Enter the inputs in the blue ranges. Note that the large blue range is the price sensitivity table from Figure 8.8.

**2 Price.** The *only* decision variable in this model is the single price charged for every pack of Menthos sold. Enter any value in this Unit_price cell.

**3 Total value table.** The values in the shaded price sensitivity range are *marginal* values, the most each customer would pay for the next pack of Menthos. In the range H6:K15, calculate the *total* value of *n* packs for each customer (for *n* from 1 to 10). First, enter the formula

**=B6**

in cell H6 and copy it across row 6. Then enter the formula

**=H6+B7**

in cell H7 and copy it to the range H7:K15.

**4** **Total cost column.** Using the single-price scheme, each customer must pay *np* for *n* packs if the price is *p*. Calculate these amounts in the range E19:E28 by entering the formula

=Unit_price*D19

in cell E19 and copying down.

**5** **Surplus table.** This is the key to the model. We calculate the surplus for any customer from buying *n* packs as the total value of *n* packs minus the total cost of *n* packs, and we assume that the customer buys the number of packs with the largest surplus. This makes sense economically. If a customer places more value on *n* packs than it costs to buy *n* packs, then presumably the customer will consider purchasing *n* packs. But a customer will not purchase *n* packs if they cost more than she values them. To calculate these surplus values, enter the formula

=H6-$E19

in cell H19 and copy it to the range H19:K28.

**6** **Maximum surplus.** Calculate the maximum surplus for each customer by entering the formula

=MAX(H19:H28)

in cell B32 and copying it across row 32.

**7** **Packs purchased.** For each customer, we need to find the number of packs that corresponds to the maximum surplus. This can be done best with Excel's MATCH function. Specifically, enter the formula

=IF(B32<0,0,MATCH(B32,H19:H28,0))

in cell B33 and copy it across row 33. This formula says that if the maximum surplus is negative, the customer will not purchase any packs at all. Otherwise, it matches the maximum surplus to the entries in the range H19:H28 and returns the index of the cell where the match occurs. In this example, the match for customer 1 occurs in the fourth cell of the range H19:H28, so the MATCH function returns 4. (Note that the last argument of the MATCH function is 0 if we want an *exact* match, as we do here.) Then calculate the total number of packs purchased by *all* customers with the formula

=SUMPRODUCT(B34:E34,B33:E33)

in cell B36.

**Excel Function:** *MATCH*
*The MATCH function, with the syntax MATCH*(Value,Range,Type), *returns the position (as an integer) of the first match to* Value *in the given* Range. *For example, if* Value *is 6 and the values in the given* Range *are 8, 7, 6, 5, 6, 5, 8, then the MATCH function returns 3. We usually set the* Type *argument to 0, meaning that we want an exact match. Other options for the* Type *parameter can be found in Excel's online help.*

**8** **Profit.** Calculate the profit in cell B37 with the formula

=(Unit_price-Unit_cost)*B36

## USING EVOLUTIONARY SOLVER

First, note that the standard Solver has trouble with this model because of the MAX, IF, and MATCH functions. However, these functions present no difficulties to Evolutionary Solver. We set it up as shown in Figure 8.10, using the same values for the various options as in the previous example. Note that we use an upper limit of $1.50 for the unit price. This suffices because the most any customer will pay for *any* pack of Menthos is $1.49.

**Figure 8.10**

Solver Dialog Box
for the Single-Price
Model

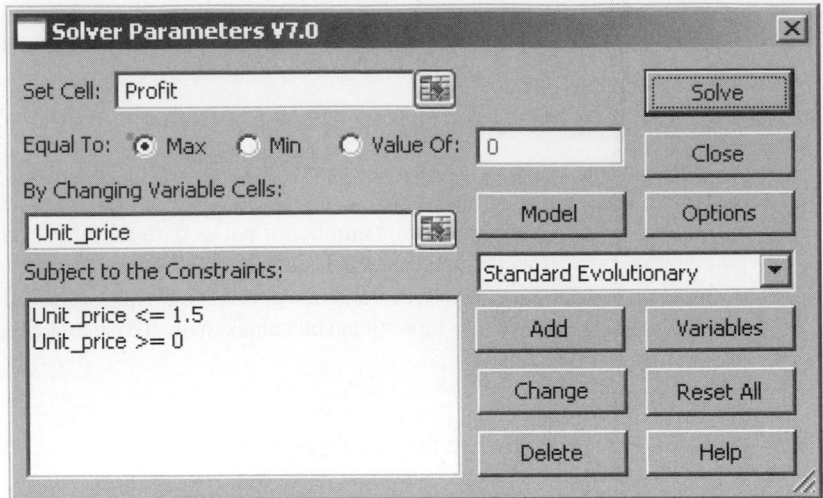

## Discussion of the Solution

Again, Evolutionary Solver converges to the solution in Figure 8.9 quickly and then tries for a long time—unsuccessfully—to find a better solution. We can be fairly certain that this solution is optimal, but this is not guaranteed. The single price of $0.80 produces a profit of $62,000. It strikes the best balance for these four market segments. A lower price would needlessly sacrifice revenue, whereas a higher price would cause at least one market segment to buy fewer packs.

### DEVELOPING THE TWO-PART TARIFF MODEL

The two-part tariff model is so similar that we made a copy of the **Single Price.xlsx** file and then made the following modifications. (See Figure 8.11 and the **Two-Part Tariff.xlsx** file.) The steps that are the same as before are omitted.

**1** **Decision variables.** Now there are two decision variables—the fixed entry fee and the variable cost per pack. Enter any values for these in cells B20 and B21.

**2** **Total cost column.** The total cost of purchasing *n* packs is now the fixed entry fee plus the variable cost times *n*. Calculate this in the range E19:E28 by entering the formula

**=Fixed_price+Variable_price*D19**

in cell E19 and copying it to the rest of the range.

**3** **Revenues.** Calculate the amount paid by the customers in row 34 by entering the formula

**=IF(B33>0,Fixed_price+Variable_price*B33,0)**

in cell B34 and copying it across. Note that the entry fee is evidently too high for customer 2, so she does not purchase any packs, and there is no corresponding revenue.

**4** **Profit.** Calculate the profit in the Profit cell with the formula

**=SUMPRODUCT(B34:E34:B35:E35)-Unit_cost*B37**

The Evolutionary Solver setup is almost the same as before. However, we now select both the Fixed_price and Variable_price cells as changing cells, and we put upper limits on each of them. (We used $10 as an upper limit on Fixed_price and $1.50 for Variable_price, reasoning that these would almost certainly be large enough.)

## Figure 8.11 The Two-Part Tariff Model

| | A | B | C | D | E | F | G | H | I | J | K |
|---|---|---|---|---|---|---|---|---|---|---|---|
| 1 | Pricing Menthos - two-part tariff model | | | | | | | | | | |
| 2 | | | | | | | | | | | |
| 3 | Price sensitivity of four typical customers | | | | | | Total value of purchases | | | | |
| 4 | | Price willing to pay (or marginal value of packs) | | | | | | Total value from this many packs | | | |
| 5 | Pack # | Customer 1 | Customer 2 | Customer 3 | Customer 4 | | # of packs | Customer 1 | Customer 2 | Customer 3 | Customer 4 |
| 6 | 1 | 1.24 | 0.92 | 1.27 | 1.49 | | 1 | 1.24 | 0.92 | 1.27 | 1.49 |
| 7 | 2 | 1.03 | 0.85 | 1.11 | 1.24 | | 2 | 2.27 | 1.77 | 2.38 | 2.73 |
| 8 | 3 | 0.89 | 0.69 | 0.96 | 1.10 | | 3 | 3.16 | 2.46 | 3.34 | 3.83 |
| 9 | 4 | 0.80 | 0.58 | 0.85 | 0.97 | | 4 | 3.96 | 3.04 | 4.19 | 4.80 |
| 10 | 5 | 0.77 | 0.50 | 0.73 | 0.81 | | 5 | 4.73 | 3.54 | 4.92 | 5.61 |
| 11 | 6 | 0.66 | 0.43 | 0.63 | 0.71 | | 6 | 5.39 | 3.97 | 5.55 | 6.32 |
| 12 | 7 | 0.59 | 0.36 | 0.51 | 0.63 | | 7 | 5.98 | 4.33 | 6.06 | 6.95 |
| 13 | 8 | 0.51 | 0.32 | 0.45 | 0.53 | | 8 | 6.49 | 4.65 | 6.51 | 7.48 |
| 14 | 9 | 0.42 | 0.26 | 0.39 | 0.42 | | 9 | 6.91 | 4.91 | 6.90 | 7.90 |
| 15 | 10 | 0.35 | 0.22 | 0.32 | 0.35 | | 10 | 7.26 | 5.13 | 7.22 | 8.25 |
| 16 | | | | | | | | | | | |
| 17 | Unit cost | $0.40 | | Total cost of packs | | | Surplus (value minus cost) from purchasing | | | | |
| 18 | | | | # of packs | Cost | | # of packs | Customer 1 | Customer 2 | Customer 3 | Customer 4 |
| 19 | Price parameters | | | 1 | 3.65 | | 1 | -2.41 | -2.73 | -2.38 | -2.16 |
| 20 | Fixed price | $3.24 | | 2 | 4.06 | | 2 | -1.79 | -2.29 | -1.68 | -1.33 |
| 21 | Variable price | $0.41 | | 3 | 4.46 | | 3 | -1.30 | -2.00 | -1.12 | -0.63 |
| 22 | | | | 4 | 4.87 | | 4 | -0.91 | -1.83 | -0.68 | -0.07 |
| 23 | | | | 5 | 5.28 | | 5 | -0.55 | -1.74 | -0.36 | 0.33 |
| 24 | | | | 6 | 5.69 | | 6 | -0.30 | -1.72 | -0.14 | 0.63 |
| 25 | | | | 7 | 6.09 | | 7 | -0.11 | -1.76 | -0.03 | 0.86 |
| 26 | | | | 8 | 6.50 | | 8 | -0.01 | -1.85 | 0.01 | 0.98 |
| 27 | | | | 9 | 6.91 | | 9 | 0.00 | -2.00 | -0.01 | 0.99 |
| 28 | | | | 10 | 7.32 | | 10 | -0.06 | -2.19 | -0.10 | 0.93 |
| 29 | | | | | | | | | | | |
| 30 | Customer behavior | | | | | | Range names used: | | | | |
| 31 | | Customer 1 | Customer 2 | Customer 3 | Customer 4 | | Fixed_price | =Model!$B$20 | | | |
| 32 | Max surplus | 0.00 | -1.72 | 0.01 | 0.99 | | Profit | =Model!$B$38 | | | |
| 33 | # purchased | 9 | 0 | 8 | 9 | | Unit_cost | =Model!$B$17 | | | |
| 34 | Amount paid | 6.910 | 0.000 | 6.502 | 6.910 | | Variable_price | =Model!$B$21 | | | |
| 35 | Market size (1000s) | 10 | 5 | 7.5 | 15 | | | | | | |
| 36 | | | | | | | | | | | |
| 37 | Total purchased (1000s) | 285 | | | | | | | | | |
| 38 | Profit ($1000s) | 107.517 | | | | | | | | | |

### Discussion of the Solution

The solution in Figure 8.11 was found after about a minute. The solution indicates that the company should charge all customers $3.24 plus $0.41 for each pack purchased. This pricing scheme is too high for the second market segment, which doesn't buy any packs, but it entices segments 1, 3, and 4 to purchase many more packs than they purchased with the single price of $0.80. (Check the price sensitivity columns for these segments. Can you see why they are willing to purchase so many packs with this particular two-part tariff?) More important, it yields a profit of $107,517, about 73% more than the profit from the single-price policy. The moral is clear—clever pricing schemes can make companies significantly larger profits than the simple pricing schemes we are accustomed to. ∎

### Other Forms of Nonlinear Pricing

There are many other forms of nonlinear pricing, such as the following:

- Sell only single-item packs or packs with 6 items.
- Charge one price for the first $n$ packs and another price for the rest.

With Evolutionary Solver, it is easy to experiment with these types of nonlinear pricing schemes and determine the profit earned by each of them. For example, if we allow Menthos to be sold only in a one-pack or a six-pack, it turns out that we can earn a profit of $97,175 by charging $5.39 for a six-pack and virtually any price for a one-pack. Then we will sell three customer segments a six-pack and make $5.39 − $2.40 = $2.99 per customer. Similarly, the best form of the "charge one price for first *n* packs and another price for remaining packs" scheme (where *n* is also a decision variable) is to sell up to four packs at $1.28 and $0.40 for each additional pack. See the book by Dolan and Simon (1996) for further discussion and applications of pricing models.

## PROBLEMS

### Skill-Building Problems

**3.** In Example 8.2, determine the optimal pricing policy if Menthos are sold in only a one-pack or a six-pack.

**4.** In Example 8.2, determine the best pricing policy if quantity discounts with a single-price breakpoint are used.

**5.** Based on Schrage (1997). The file **P08_05.xlsx** lists the size of the four main markets for Excel, Word, and the bundle of Excel and Word. It also shows how much members of each group are willing to pay for each product combination. How can Microsoft maximize the revenue earned from these products? You should consider the following options:

- No bundling, where Word and Excel are sold separately
- Pure bundling, where purchasers can buy only Word and Excel together
- Mixed bundling, where purchasers can buy Word or Excel separately, or they can buy them as a bundle

## 8.5 COMBINATORIAL MODELS

Consider the following situations:

- Xerox must determine where to place maintenance facilities. The more maintenance facilities selected, the more copiers the company will sell due to better availability of maintenance. How can the company locate maintenance facilities to maximize total profit?

- A gasoline company is loading three different products on a tanker truck with five compartments. Each compartment can handle at most one product. How should the company load the truck to come as close as possible to meeting its delivery requirements?

- Fox has 30 different ads of different lengths that must be assigned to 10 different 2-minute commercial breaks. How should the company assign ads to maximize its total ad revenue?

- John Deere must schedule its production of lawn mowers over the next four weeks. The company wants to meet its forecasted demands, keep production hours fairly constant from week to week, and avoid model changeovers as much as possible. How should the company schedule its production?

*Combinatorial problems have only a finite number of feasible solutions. However, they can still be very difficult because this finite number is often enormous.*

Each of these problems is a **combinatorial** optimization problem that requires us to choose the best of many different combinations available. Although combinatorial optimization problems can often be handled as linear Solver models with 0–1 changing cells, the formulation of the constraints needed to keep the model linear is often difficult. (We saw examples of the tricks required in Chapter 6.) With Evolutionary Solver, however, it doesn't matter whether the constraints or the objective are linear. The SUMIF and

COUNTIF functions often prove useful in such problems. The two examples in this section illustrate typical combinatorial optimization problems.

## Loading Products on a Truck

The following example might possibly appear simple when you first read it. It is not! The number of possible solutions is enormous, and it can take a Solver, even Evolutionary Solver, a long time to find an optimal (or nearly optimal) solution.

---

**EXAMPLE**  **8.3 LOADING A GAS STORAGE TRUCK**

A gas truck contains five compartments with the capacities listed in Table 8.1. Three products must be shipped on the truck, and there can be at most one product per compartment. The demand for each product, the shortage cost per gallon, and the maximum allowable shortage for each product are listed in Table 8.2. How can we load the truck to minimize the shortage costs?

**Table 8.1** Truck Capacities

| Compartment | Capacity (Gallons) |
| --- | --- |
| 1 | 2700 |
| 2 | 2800 |
| 3 | 1100 |
| 4 | 1800 |
| 5 | 3400 |

**Table 8.2** Demand and Shortage Data

| Product | Demand | Max Shortage Allowed | Cost per Gallon Short |
| --- | --- | --- | --- |
| 1 | 2900 | 900 | $10 |
| 2 | 4000 | 900 | $8 |
| 3 | 4900 | 900 | $6 |

**Objective**  To use Evolutionary Solver to find the combination of products to compartments that minimizes the total shortage cost.

### WHERE DO THE NUMBERS COME FROM?

The data would be based on the truck dimensions and presumably on contracts the company has with its customers.

## Solution

The objective in this problem is to minimize the total shortage cost. The decision variables indicate the type of product stored in each compartment and the amount of that product to load in the compartment. The constraints must ensure that we do not overfill any compartment and that we do not exceed the maximum allowable shortage.

### DEVELOPING THE SPREADSHEET MODEL

The completed model appears in Figure 8.12. (See the file **Loading Truck.xlsx**.) It can be developed as follows:

**Figure 8.12**   The Truck Loading Model

| | A | B | C | D | E | F | G | H | I |
|---|---|---|---|---|---|---|---|---|---|
| 1 | Storing gas products in compartments | | | | | | | | |
| 2 | | | | | | | | | |
| 3 | Unit shortage costs and penalty cost for violating shortage constraints | | | | | | Range names used | | |
| 4 | Product | Cost/gallon | | | | | Amount | =Model!$C$13:$C$17 | |
| 5 | 1 | $10.00 | | | | | Capacity | =Model!$E$13:$E$17 | |
| 6 | 2 | $8.00 | | | | | Product | =Model!$B$13:$B$17 | |
| 7 | 3 | $6.00 | | | | | Total_cost | =Model!$B$28 | |
| 8 | | | | | | | | | |
| 9 | Shortage penalty | $100 | | | | | | | |
| 10 | | | | | | | | | |
| 11 | Storing decisions | | | | | | | | |
| 12 | Compartment | Product | Amount | | Capacity | | | | |
| 13 | 1 | 2 | 2700.0 | <= | 2700 | | | | |
| 14 | 2 | 1 | 2800.0 | <= | 2800 | | | | |
| 15 | 3 | 2 | 1100.0 | <= | 1100 | | | | |
| 16 | 4 | 3 | 1677.8 | <= | 1800 | | | | |
| 17 | 5 | 3 | 3400.0 | <= | 3400 | | | | |
| 18 | | | | | | | | | |
| 19 | Shortages | | | | | | | | |
| 20 | Product | Amount Stored | Demand | Shortage | Max Shortage | Shortage Violation | | | |
| 21 | 1 | 2800.0 | 2900 | 100.0 | 900 | 0.0 | | | |
| 22 | 2 | 3800.0 | 4000 | 200.0 | 900 | 0.0 | | | |
| 23 | 3 | 5077.8 | 4900 | 0.0 | 900 | 0.0 | | | |
| 24 | | | | | | | | | |
| 25 | Costs and penalties | | | | | | | | |
| 26 | Shortage cost | $2,600.00 | | | | | | | |
| 27 | Penalty cost | $0.00 | | | | | | | |
| 28 | Total cost | $2,600.00 | | | | | | | |

**1** **Inputs.** Enter the inputs from Tables 8.1 and 8.2 into the shaded ranges.

**2** **Decision variables.** Enter any integer values (from 1 to 3) in the Product range and any values (integer or noninteger) in the Amount range. These two ranges represent the changing cells.

**3** **Amounts stored total.** We need to know how many gallons of each product are stored on the truck. To calculate these from the information in the changing cells, we use the SUMIF function. Specifically, enter the formula

**=SUMIF(Product,A21,Amount)**

in cell B21. This formula sums the values in the Amount range for all rows where the product index, 1, in cell A21 matches the index in the Product range. Therefore, it calculates the total amount of product 1 stored on the truck. Copy this formula down for the other two products.

**4** **Shortages.** To calculate the shortages, enter the formula

**=IF(B21<C21,C21-B21,0)**

in cell D21 and copy it down. Note that we have dealt with shortages in previous chapters, but they always required some tricks to keep the models linear. Now we use straightforward IF functions, which present no difficult for Evolutionary Solver.

**5** **Shortage violations.** We could *constrain* the shortages to be less than the maximum allowable shortages, but because the Evolutionary Solver works best with as few constraints as possible, we try another approach. (We use this approach in the following example as well.) We calculate the amount by which each maximum storage constraint is violated (if at all) and then add these violations, multiplied by a suitably large penalty, to the cost objective. Because we eventually minimize total cost, Evolutionary Solver tries to stay away from solutions where this penalty is positive. Therefore, it favors solutions where the maximum storage constraints are satisfied. To implement this strategy, calculate the maximum storage violations in column F by entering the formula

=IF(D21>E21,D21-E21,0)

in cell F21 and copying it down. The solution shown in Figure 8.12 does not have any violations, but the values in column F would be positive if any shortages in column D were greater than 900.

**6**  **Costs.**  Calculate the total shortage cost in cell B26 with the formula

=SUMPRODUCT(B5:B7,D21:D23)

Then calculate the penalty cost from maximum shortage violations in B27 with the formula

=B9*SUM(F21:F23)

Note that we have chosen a penalty of $100 per unit shortage above the maximum allowed. Any large dollar value would suffice here. Finally, calculate the total cost in cell B28 by summing the values in cells B26 and B27.

*This example illustrates how we can incorporate violations of constraints into the objective in the form of penalties.*

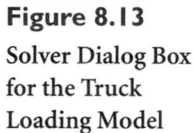

## USING EVOLUTIONARY SOLVER

The Solver setup for this model is straightforward, as shown in Figure 8.13. Unlike some previous models, there are now natural lower limits and upper limits for the changing cells. The Product range must be between 1 and 3 (and they must be integers) because there are only three products. The Amount range must be between 0 and the given capacities of the compartments.

### Discussion of the Solution

The solution in Figure 8.12 shows that product 1 should be stored in compartment 2, product 2 should be stored in compartments 1 and 3, and product 3 should be stored in compartments 4 and 5, the only compartments that end up with excess capacity. The demands for products 1 and 2 are not quite met, and the total shortage cost is $2600, but the shortages are well below the maximum shortages allowed. Therefore, there is no penalty cost for violating the maximum shortage constraints.

**Figure 8.13**

Solver Dialog Box for the Truck Loading Model

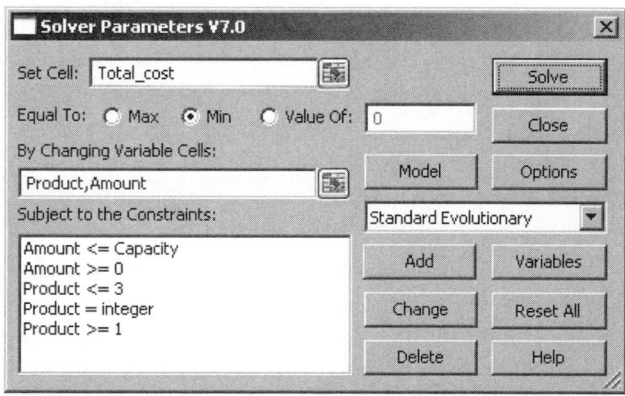

This model is not easy for Evolutionary Solver, in spite of its rather small size, and its success depends a lot on the starting solution. For example, we tried one solution with all 3's in the Product range and all 1000's in the Amount range. It quickly got to a solution with objective value $3200, but then it spun its wheels for a long time before improving. In contrast, when we entered a random combination of 1, 2, and 3 in the Product range and all 0's in the Amount range, the optimal solution was found very quickly.

### Sensitivity Analysis with SolverTable

Nothing prevents us from using SolverTable on an Evolutionary Solver model—except time. We fill in the SolverTable dialog box exactly as before. The only difference is that Evolutionary Solver can take a lot of time to solve *one* problem, let alone a whole series of problems. Also, to provide some assurance that it does not stop prematurely at a suboptimal solution for at least one of the problems, we need to experiment with the Evolutionary Solver settings in the Options dialog boxes, because the appropriate settings are not always obvious.

We tried a sensitivity analysis on the capacity of compartment 3 for this example, allowing it to vary from 300 to 1100 in multiples of 200, and we obtained the results in Figure 8.14. We are not really sure whether these results are optimal. (The equal objective values for capacities of 700 and 900 are somewhat suspicious.) However, we ran this same SolverTable several times, with different Solver option settings and different starting solutions, and we usually obtained *worse* results than in Figure 8.14 on at least one problem. This is not the fault of SolverTable or even the fault of Evolutionary Solver. This storage problem, like many combinatorial problems, is difficult, and unless we allow Evolutionary Solver to run for a very long time, it can easily get stuck at a suboptimal solution fairly far from the optimal solution. For this reason, we do not mention SolverTable again in this chapter, but there is nothing to prevent you from trying it. You just need to be patient!

**Figure 8.14**   SolverTable Results for the Truck Loading Model

| | A | B | C | D | E | F | G | H | I | J | K | L |
|---|---|---|---|---|---|---|---|---|---|---|---|---|
| 30 | Sensitivity of solution to capacity of compartment 3 | | | | | | | | | | | |
| 31 | | | | | | | | | | | | |
| 32 | | $B$13 | $C$13 | $B$14 | $C$14 | $B$15 | $C$15 | $B$16 | $C$16 | $B$17 | $C$17 | $B$28 |
| 33 | 300 | 3 | 2700.0 | 1 | 2800.0 | 2 | 300.0 | 3 | 1800.0 | 2 | 3392.5 | $5,860.33 |
| 34 | 500 | 3 | 2700.0 | 1 | 2800.0 | 2 | 500.0 | 3 | 1800.0 | 2 | 3400.0 | $4,200.00 |
| 35 | 700 | 3 | 2700.0 | 1 | 2800.0 | 2 | 669.5 | 3 | 1800.0 | 2 | 3400.0 | $3,400.00 |
| 36 | 900 | 3 | 2700.0 | 1 | 2800.0 | 2 | 669.5 | 3 | 1800.0 | 2 | 3400.0 | $3,400.00 |
| 37 | 1100 | 2 | 2700.0 | 1 | 2800.0 | 2 | 1100.0 | 3 | 1800.0 | 3 | 3399.1 | $2,600.00 |

## Finding a Good Production Schedule

Determining a monthly production schedule at a manufacturing facility such as a John Deere manufacturing plant is very difficult. Many conflicting objectives must be balanced. The following example illustrates how these competing objectives can be modeled.[5]

---

EXAMPLE | **8.4 Scheduling Production of Lawn Mowers at Easyride**

EasyRide, a lawn mower manufacturer, needs to set its weekly production schedule for the next four weeks. The company produces seven models of lawn mowers. At the beginning of each month, the company has reasonably accurate forecasts for the demand of each model for the month. It also has forecasts for the portion of this demand from customers who will drive to the plant to pick up their lawn mowers. The company has four competing objectives regarding its production schedule.

■ Avoid costly model changeovers during each week as much as possible.

---

[5] This example is based on a model actually developed by John Deere, as described to the authors by John Deere managers.

- Come as close as possible to producing the mowers demanded by customers during week 1 (assuming the "pickup" customers, those who drive to the plant to pick up their mowers, typically arrive during week 1).

- Keep weekly production hours as constant as possible across weeks at each of the three machining centers that the models go through.

- Come as close as possible to producing as many mowers of each model as its monthly forecasts require.

**Objective** To use Evolutionary Solver to find a production schedule that achieves the company's goals as fully as possible.

## WHERE DO THE NUMBERS COME FROM?

As in other production scheduling models we have discussed, the most crucial inputs are the demand forecasts. The company presumably has a method for forecasting demands, probably based on historical data and orders already on the books.

## Solution

It is typically not possible to satisfy all of EasyRide's objectives. Therefore, think of the objectives as targets. If any solution falls short of the target, we penalize it—the farther from the target, the larger the penalty. This is an especially useful technique when using Evolutionary Solver, which thrives on messy objective functions but does less well with a lot of constraints. Therefore, instead of using constraints, we penalize deviations from targets, and we use the total of penalties as the objective to minimize.

The data for the problem appear in Figure 8.15 (see the file **Lawnmower Production.xlsx**). Rows 5 and 6 indicate the forecasts of customer pickups and monthly totals, and rows 10 through 12 indicate the number of hours required at each machine center to produce a mower of each model. The unit penalty costs in rows 15 to 18 are not really "givens." They must be estimated by EasyRide to reflect trade-offs among the competing objectives. They imply the following:

- A changeover penalty of 200 is incurred for each model produced at any *positive* level during a week. For example, if 3 models are produced the first week, 4 the second, 3 the third, and 5 the fourth, the total changeover penalty is $(3 + 4 + 3 + 5)(200) = 3000$.

**Figure 8.15**

Inputs for the Lawn Mower Production Model

| | A | B | C | D | E | F | G | H |
|---|---|---|---|---|---|---|---|---|
| 1 | Lawnmower production model | | | | | | | |
| 2 | | | | | | | | |
| 3 | Forecasts of demand | | | | | | | |
| 4 | | Model 1 | Model 2 | Model 3 | Model 4 | Model 5 | Model 6 | Model 7 |
| 5 | Pickups | 30 | 20 | 15 | 30 | 23 | 12 | 12 |
| 6 | Total | 110 | 90 | 100 | 115 | 80 | 60 | 80 |
| 7 | | | | | | | | |
| 8 | Hours per mower required in the machine centers | | | | | | | |
| 9 | | Model 1 | Model 2 | Model 3 | Model 4 | Model 5 | Model 6 | Model 7 |
| 10 | Center 1 | 3 | 2 | 2 | 2 | 2 | 4 | 2 |
| 11 | Center 2 | 1 | 2 | 1 | 3 | 3 | 3 | 4 |
| 12 | Center 3 | 2 | 3 | 0 | 4 | 3 | 3 | 2 |
| 13 | | | | | | | | |
| 14 | Unit penalty "costs" | | | | Range names used: | | | |
| 15 | Model changeover | 200 | | | Production | =Sheet1!$B$22:$H$25 | | |
| 16 | Satisfy pickups | 50 | | | Total_penalty | =Sheet1!$B$46 | | |
| 17 | Smooth production | 1 | | | | | | |
| 18 | Meet forecasts | 10 | | | | | | |

- A pickup shortage penalty of 50 is incurred for each unit of pickup demand not satisfied during week 1. For example, if 20 units of model 1 are produced during week 1, the pickup penalty for this model is (10)(50) = 500 because 20 is 10 short of the required 30.

- A smoothing production penalty of 1 is incurred during each week at each machine center per hour of deviation from the required weekly average at that center. Here, the required weekly average is based on the production levels needed to meet monthly forecasts. We explain how this is implemented shortly.

- A meeting monthly forecasts penalty of 10 is incurred per unit of each model produced above *or* below the monthly forecast. For example, if the total monthly production of model 1 is 105 or 115 (a deviation of 5 below or 5 above the monthly forecast), the penalty in either case is (5)(10) = 50.

Again, these unit penalties are not givens, and they must be chosen carefully by EasyRide, perhaps on the basis of a sensitivity analysis. Clearly, if one unit penalty is too large, its corresponding objective tends to dominate the solution. In the same way, if a unit penalty is too small, its corresponding objective is practically ignored. We have tried to choose unit penalties that produce a reasonable solution, but you might want to experiment with others.

## DEVELOPING THE SPREADSHEET MODEL

The completed model appears in Figure 8.16. It can be developed with the following steps:

**1 Production schedule.** The decision variables are the weekly production levels of each model. Enter *any* values for these in the Production range. (Refer to Figure 8.15 for range names used.)

---

**Figure 8.16** Model for Lawn Mower Production

| | A | B | C | D | E | F | G | H | I | J | K |
|---|---|---|---|---|---|---|---|---|---|---|---|
| 20 | **Weekly production levels** | | | | | | | | | | |
| 21 | | Model 1 | Model 2 | Model 3 | Model 4 | Model 5 | Model 6 | Model 7 | Models | | |
| 22 | Week 1 | 31 | 21 | 19 | 30 | 29 | 14 | 14 | 7 | | |
| 23 | Week 2 | 0 | 69 | 81 | 42 | 0 | 0 | 0 | 3 | | |
| 24 | Week 3 | 79 | 0 | 0 | 0 | 51 | 0 | 32 | 3 | | |
| 25 | Week 4 | 0 | 0 | 0 | 43 | 0 | 46 | 34 | 3 | | |
| 26 | Mowers produced | 110 | 90 | 100 | 115 | 80 | 60 | 80 | | | |
| 27 | Deviations from forecasts | 0 | 0 | 0 | 0 | 0 | 0 | 0 | | | |
| 28 | Shortages for pickups | 0 | 0 | 0 | 0 | 0 | 0 | 0 | | | |
| 29 | | | | | | | | | | | |
| 30 | **Average hours need per week to meet monthly forecasts** | | | | | | | | | | |
| 31 | Center 1 | 375 | | | | | | | | | |
| 32 | Center 2 | 368.75 | | | | | | | | | |
| 33 | Center 3 | 382.5 | | | | | | | | | |
| 34 | | | | | | | | | | | |
| 35 | **Hours used each week in each center** | | | | | **Deviations from hourly targets** | | | | | |
| 36 | | Week 1 | Week 2 | Week 3 | Week 4 | | | Week 1 | Week 2 | Week 3 | Week 4 |
| 37 | Center 1 | 375 | 384 | 403 | 338 | | Center 1 | 0.00 | 9.00 | 28.00 | 37.00 |
| 38 | Center 2 | 367 | 345 | 360 | 403 | | Center 2 | 1.75 | 23.75 | 8.75 | 34.25 |
| 39 | Center 3 | 402 | 375 | 375 | 378 | | Center 3 | 19.50 | 7.50 | 7.50 | 4.50 |
| 40 | | | | | | | | | | | |
| 41 | **Penalty costs** | | | | | | | | | | |
| 42 | Model changeover | 3200 | | | | | | | | | |
| 43 | Satisfy pickups | 0 | | | | | | | | | |
| 44 | Smooth production | 182 | | | | | | | | | |
| 45 | Meet forecasts | 0 | | | | | | | | | |
| 46 | Total penalty | 3382 | | | | | | | | | |
| 47 | | | | | | | | | | | |
| 48 | | | | | | | | | | | |
| 49 | | | | | | | | | | | |
| 50 | | | | | | | | | | | |

Production Hours across Weeks — Center 1, Center 2, Center 3 (Production Hours vs Week 1, Week 2, Week 3, Week 4)

**2** **Models produced.** For the model changeover objective, we need to know how many different models are produced each week. Therefore, enter the formula

=COUNTIF(B22:H22,">0")

in cell I22 and copy it down.

**3** **Deviations from forecasts.** For the objective of meeting forecasts, we need to calculate the total monthy production levels for each model and see how much they deviate from the monthly forecasts. To do this, enter the formulas

=SUM(B22:B25)

and

=ABS(B6-B26)

in cells B26 and B27 for model 1, and copy these across for the other models. (Recall that ABS is Excel's absolute value function.)

**4** **Pickup shortages.** Here we need to see how much week 1 production of each model is short (if any) of the pickup demand. To do this, enter the formula

=IF(B22<B5,B5-B22,0)

in cell B28 and copy it across.

**5** **Hourly smoothing.** This is the trickiest objective. We want to keep production hours at each machine center as constant as possible across weeks. Although there are undoubtedly other ways to implement this, we suggest the following approach. First, calculate the weekly average hours required at each machine center *if* we produce exactly enough in the month to meet monthly forecasts. To do this, enter the formula

=SUMPRODUCT($B$6:$H$6,B10:H10)/4

in cell B31 for center 1 and copy it down for the other two centers. (Note that we divide by 4 to obtain a weekly average.) These weekly averages become our targets. Next, calculate the *actual* hours used at each center each week in the range B37:E39. Unfortunately, there is no way to enter a *single* formula and then copy it to the rest of the range. However, you can try the following. Enter the formula

=SUMPRODUCT($B$22:$H$22,$B10:$H10)

in cell B37 and copy it down to cell B39. Then copy the range B37:B39 to the range C37:E39. The resulting formulas for weeks 2 to 4 in columns C to E will not be quite correct, but they can be modified easily. Specifically, change the 22's in the column C formulas to 23's, change them to 24's in column D, and change them to 25's in column E. The point is that when copying is not possible, sometimes copying a formula and then modifying it is easier than entering new formulas from scratch. Finally, calculate the deviations from targets in the range H37:K39 by entering the formula

=ABS(B37-$B31)

in cell H37 and copying it to the rest of the range. (Here, copying *is* possible.)

**6** **Penalties.** Calculate the various penalties in the range B42:B45. To do so, enter the formulas

=B15*SUM(I22:I25)

=B16*SUM(B28:H28)

=B17*SUM(H37:K39)

and

=B18*SUM(B27:H27)

in cells B42 through B45. Then calculate the total penalty as their sum in cell B46.

## USING EVOLUTIONARY SOLVER

The Solver setup for this model appears in Figure 8.17. The objective is to minimize the total of penalties, the changing cells are the production levels, and there are no constraints other than lower and upper bounds and integer constraints on the production levels. As for the upper bounds, we chose 150 fairly arbitrarily. The largest monthly forecast for any model is 115, but we might want production to exceed this forecast. Therefore, we build in some "padding" with the upper limit of 150.

**Figure 8.17**

Solver Setup for the Lawn Mower Production Model

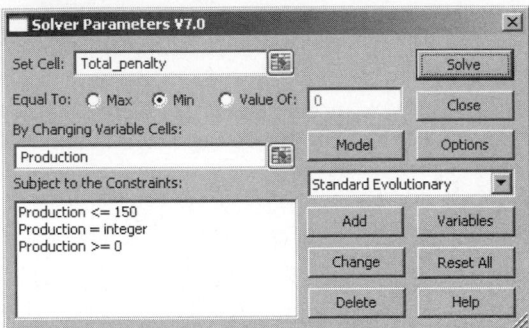

After some experimenting, we find that this is a difficult problem even for Evolutionary Solver. Depending on the starting solution, it can take some time to find as good a solution as the one in Figure 8.16. Therefore, make sure to enter large values in the Solver Options and Limits dialog boxes for Max Time, Max Subproblems, Max Feasible Solns, and Max Time w/o Improvement. Otherwise, Evolutionary Solver might quit prematurely at a solution far from optimal. Another possible strategy is to drop the integer constraint by checking the box in Figure 8.18. This will find a "good" noninteger solution relatively quickly. Then you can run the Solver again, starting from this noninteger solution, with the box unchecked to find a good integer solution.

**Figure 8.18**

Option to Ignore Integer Constraints

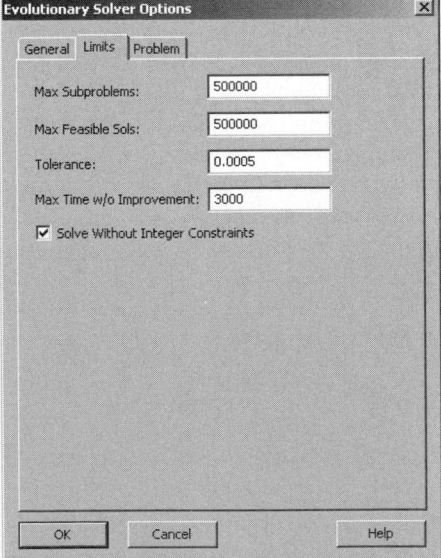

### Discussion of the Solution

The solution in Figure 8.16 represents the best compromise we could find. It produces all seven models during week 1 to keep the pickup shortages low. In fact, it has no pickup shortages. After that, it produces only three separate models each week to keep the changeover penalties low. This solution produces exactly to the monthly forecasts. Finally, all of this is done in a way to keep the production hours as constant as possible across weeks. Even so, the chart in Figure 8.16, based on the data in the range B37:E39, shows that the production hours still vary to some extent across weeks at each machine center. Of course, if you change the unit penalties to reflect different priorities on the objectives and then rerun Evolutionary Solver, you could get a much different solution. For example, if EasyRide decides that pickup shortages are not such an important concern, it could reduce the unit shortage penalty from 50 to, say, 25 or even 5. Then the production schedule might change so that all seven models are *not* produced in week 1. ■

## PROBLEMS

### Skill-Building Problems

6. In the truck-loading problem in Example 8.3, we assumed that any product could be loaded into any compartment. Suppose the following are *not* allowed: product 1 in compartment 2, product 2 in compartment 1, and product 3 in compartment 4. Modify the model appropriately, and then use Evolutionary Solver to find the new optimal solution. (*Hint*: Add a penalty to the objective for violating these new constraints.)

7. In the lawn mower production problem in Example 8.4, the model changeover cost dominates in the optimal objective value. Is this because we assumed such a large unit penalty cost, 200, for each model changeover? Explore this question by changing this unit penalty cost to lower values such as 100 and 50 (or even smaller). What happens to the optimal solution?

8. In the lawn mower production problem in Example 8.4, experiment with the penalty cost for unsatisfied pickups in week 1. If this cost is sufficiently small, does the company ever produce fewer than seven models in week 1 and allow some week 1 pickups to be unsatisfied?

## 8.6 FITTING AN S-SHAPED CURVE

Suppose we want to see how a company's revenue from sales is related to its sales force effort. If $R$ is revenue and $E$ is sales force effort, marketing researchers have found that the relationship between $R$ and $E$ is often well described by a function of the form in equation (8.1)

$$R = a + \frac{(b - a)E^c}{d + E^c} \tag{8.1}$$

for suitable constants $a$, $b$, $c$, and $d$. This function can exhibit diminishing returns, where each extra unit of $E$ contributes less and less to $R$, or it can look like an S-shaped curve, as in Figure 8.19. An S-shaped curve starts out flat, gets steep, and then flattens out. This shape is appropriate if sales effort needs to exceed some critical value to generate significant sales. The following example illustrates how we can use Evolutionary Solver to estimate this type of curve.[6]

---

[6] The model in this section has smooth functions, and it can be solved successfully with the nonlinear algorithm in the standard Solver *if* the initial solution is not too far from the optimal solution. Alternatively, the GRG Nonlinear algorithm in Premium Solver, with the Multistart option, works great. However, we still illustrate Evolutionary Solver as another alternative.

Figure 8.19

An S-Shaped Sales
Response Curve

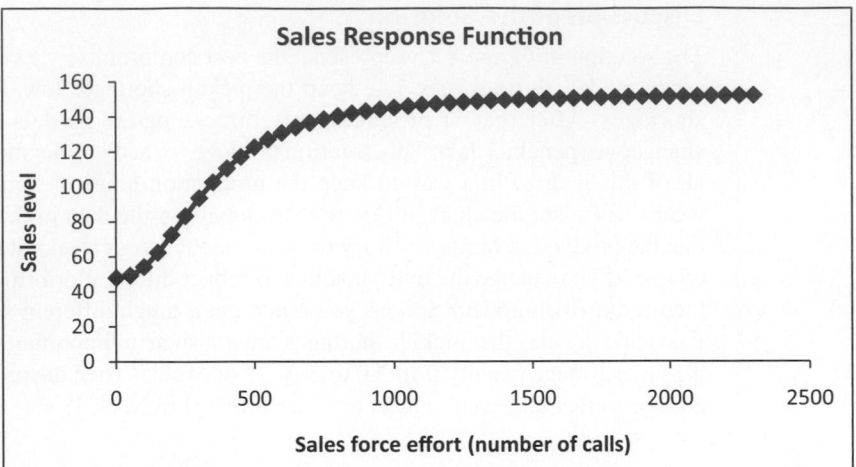

**Sales Response Function**

EXAMPLE

## 8.5 ESTIMATING THE SALES RESPONSE FUNCTION₀ AT LYNTEX LABS

Lyntex Labs wants to estimate its sales response function that relates the revenue from sales of a certain drug to the number of sales calls made. Company experts estimate the revenue that would be obtained in the following five scenarios:

- No sales effort is assigned to the drug.
- Sales effort assigned to the drug is cut in half.
- Sales force effort stays at the current level.
- Sales force effort is increased by 50%.
- Sales force effort saturates the market.

The resulting estimates appear in Table 8.3. Note that the current sales effort is 350,000 sales calls. Also, all sales revenue estimates are expressed relative to an "index" of 100, where 100 represents the current level of sales revenue. For example, the experts estimate that if sales effort is cut in half, sales revenue from the drug will decrease to 68% of the current level. Lyntex assumes that its sales revenue function is of the form in equation (8.1). It wants to find the constants $a$, $b$, $c$, and $d$ that provide the best fit to the estimates in Table 8.3.

**Table 8.3**   Estimated Sales Revenues

| Sales Calls (1000s) | Sales Revenue |
|---|---|
| 0 | 47 |
| 175 | 68 |
| 350 | 100 |
| 525 | 126 |
| 3500 | 152 |

**Objective**   To use Evolutionary Solver to estimate the assumed S-shaped relationship between revenue and sales force effort, as measured by the number of sales calls.

### WHERE DO THE NUMBERS COME FROM?

The required data in Table 8.3 could be historical data, based on various levels of sales force effort the company has used in the past, or, as suggested in the problem statement, they could be educated guesses by people in the marketing department.

## Solution

The model development is basically the same as for Example 7.5 from the previous chapter. (See Figure 8.20 and the file **Sales Response.xlsx**.) We again find the model parameters that minimize the sum of squared errors between the actual revenues and the revenues predicted from the sales response function.

**Figure 8.20** Sales Response Function Estimation

| | A | B | C | D | E | F | G | H |
|---|---|---|---|---|---|---|---|---|
| 1 | Estimating the sales response function at Lyntex Labs | | | | | | | |
| 2 | | | | | | | | |
| 3 | Assumed sales response function: | | | | | | Range names used: | |
| 4 | Estimate sales level when x sales calls (in 1000s) are made is a+(b-a)x$^c$/(d+x$^c$) | | | | | | a | =Estimation!$B$7 |
| 5 | | | | | | | b | =Estimation!$C$7 |
| 6 | Model parameters | | a | b | c | d | c_ | =Estimation!$D$7 |
| 7 | | 47.480 | 152.914 | 2.264 | 534155 | | d | =Estimation!$E$7 |
| 8 | | | | | | | Sum_of_squared_errors | =Estimation!$B$17 |
| 9 | Estimates from management | | | | | | | |
| 10 | | Sales calls (1000s) | Sales level | Sales estimate | Error | | | |
| 11 | | 0 | 47 | 47.480 | -0.480 | | | |
| 12 | | 175 | 68 | 66.747 | 1.253 | | | |
| 13 | | 350 | 100 | 102.070 | -2.070 | | | |
| 14 | | 525 | 126 | 124.327 | 1.673 | | | |
| 15 | | 3500 | 152 | 152.381 | -0.381 | | | |
| 16 | | | | | | | | |
| 17 | Sum of squared errors | 9.028 | | | | | | |

### DEVELOPING THE SPREADSHEET MODEL

To develop the spreadsheet model, use the following steps:

**1** **Inputs.** Enter the data in the blue region from Table 8.3.

**2** **Decision variables.** The only decision variables are the constants *a*, *b*, *c*, and *d* of the sales response function. Enter any values for these. [Note that we tried to give the corresponding cells range names of a, b, c, and d. However, Excel doesn't allow the range name c. (It also doesn't allow the range name r.) Instead, it changes this name to c_].

**3** **Predicted sales revenues.** In column D, calculate the sales revenue levels (remember that these are relative to 100) predicted from equation (8.1). To do so, enter the formula

**=a+((b-a)\*B11^c_)/(d+B11^c_)**

in cell D11 and copy it down to cell D15.

**4** **Prediction errors.** For a good fit, we want the predictions in column D to match the experts' estimates in column C as closely as possible. Therefore, we minimize the sum of squared differences between the two columns. First, calculate the errors in column E by entering the formula

**=C11-D11**

in cell E11 and copying down. Then calculate the sum of squared errors in cell B17 with the formula

**=SUMSQ(E11:E15)**

PREMIUM SOLVER

### USING EVOLUTIONARY SOLVER

No IF, ABS, MAX, or MIN functions are used in this model, so we might try the standard Excel Solver (with the Assume Linear Model box unchecked), just as we did throughout the previous chapter. However, there might be *local* minima in this model that are not *globally* optimal. The standard Solver could easily get stuck at such a local minimum and never find the global minimum. Therefore, we use Evolutionary Solver, which searches the entire feasible region and is less likely to get stuck at such a local minimum. (Again, we could also use Premium Solver's GRG Nonlinear algorithm with the Multistart option.) The only problem is to find a "decent" starting solution and to find reasonable lower and upper limits for the changing cells. It is difficult to tell, just by looking at equation (8.1), what reasonable values for $a$, $b$, $c$, and $d$ might be. Must they be positive? How large can they be? The answers are certainly not obvious.

Therefore, some analysis of equation (8.1) is useful before turning to Solver. First, note that when $E = 0$, estimated sales $R$ equals $a$. Therefore, $a$ should be positive. Second, the fraction in equation (8.1) approaches $b - a$ as $E$ get large, so $b$ is the limiting value of $R$ as $E$ gets large. Third, we want $E^c$ to increase when $E$ increases, so that $R$ will increase with $E$. This occurs only if $c$ is positive. Finally, to keep the denominator positive for all values of $E$, we need $d$ to be positive.

If this analysis is not convincing, another strategy is to graph equation (8.1) and then *watch* how the graph changes as we manually change $a$, $b$, $c$, and $d$ (see Figure 8.21). This chart is an XY chart (where the dots are connected with lines) that plots the actual sales (the experts' estimates) in column C and the predicted values from the sales response function in column D. By changing the constants in row 4 and seeing when the fit between the two curves gets fairly good, we can quickly see that $a$ should be around 47, $b$ should be somewhere between 150 and 160, the exponent $c$ should be somewhere 1.5 and 5, and the constant $d$ should be a large positive number.

**Figure 8.21** Graph of Sales Response Function

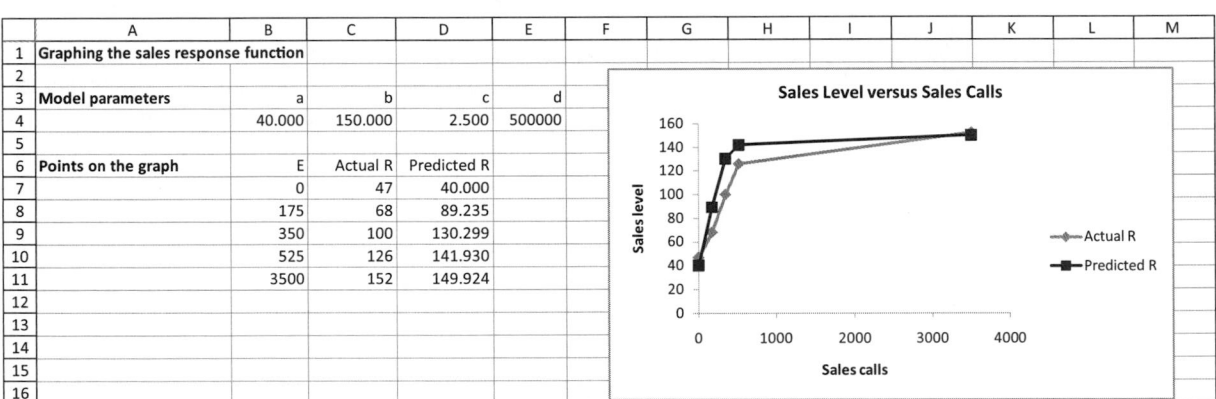

| | A | B | C | D | E | F | G | H | I | J | K | L | M |
|---|---|---|---|---|---|---|---|---|---|---|---|---|---|
| 1 | Graphing the sales response function | | | | | | | | | | | | |
| 2 | | | | | | | | | | | | | |
| 3 | Model parameters | a | b | c | d | | | | | | | | |
| 4 | | 40.000 | 150.000 | 2.500 | 500000 | | | | | | | | |
| 5 | | | | | | | | | | | | | |
| 6 | Points on the graph | E | Actual R | Predicted R | | | | | | | | | |
| 7 | | 0 | 47 | 40.000 | | | | | | | | | |
| 8 | | 175 | 68 | 89.235 | | | | | | | | | |
| 9 | | 350 | 100 | 130.299 | | | | | | | | | |
| 10 | | 525 | 126 | 141.930 | | | | | | | | | |
| 11 | | 3500 | 152 | 149.924 | | | | | | | | | |
| 12 | | | | | | | | | | | | | |
| 13 | | | | | | | | | | | | | |
| 14 | | | | | | | | | | | | | |
| 15 | | | | | | | | | | | | | |
| 16 | | | | | | | | | | | | | |

These are fairly liberal ranges, but all we are trying to obtain at this point are reasonable lower and upper limits for the Solver dialog box.

Using this (somewhat inexact) information, we fill in the Solver dialog box as shown in Figure 8.22. (The bounds on c_ and d that do not appear in this figure are c_>=1.5, d<=1000000, and d>=500.)

### Discussion of the Solution

The best solution found by Evolutionary Solver appears earlier in Figure 8.20. Of course, there is nothing very intuitive about these particular values of $a$, $b$, $c$, and $d$. However, if you substitute them into row 4 of Figure 8.21, you will see that they provide a very good fit. In other words, the sales response function with these parameters should provide very useful predictions of sales levels.

Figure 8.22

Solver Dialog Box
for Sales Response
Estimation

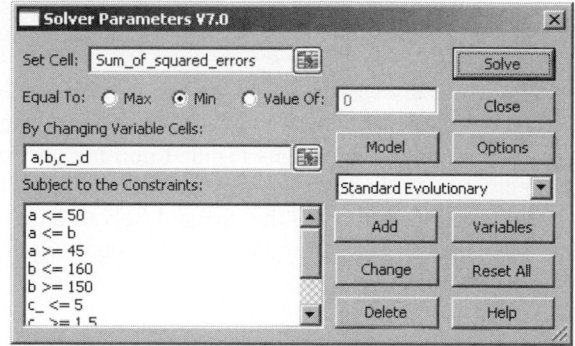

It is interesting to compare Evolutionary Solver with the standard nonlinear Solver for this smooth model. For example, we started each of them at a fairly poor solution: $a=40$, $b=100$, $c=1$, and $d=5000$. (The sum of squared errors for this solution is almost 18,000.) Evolutionary Solver found the solution in Figure 8.20 almost immediately. The standard nonlinear Solver also found a solution almost immediately, but the *wrong* solution. Its objective was about 190, well above the minimum value in Figure 8.20. Again, this is because Evolutionary Solver does a more thorough job of searching the entire feasible region and not getting stuck at a local minimum. (To be fair, Premium Solver's GRG Nonlinear algorithm with the Multistart option also found the solution quickly, even after starting from the poor solution.) ∎

# PROBLEMS

## Skill-Building Problems

9. You are given the following information concerning how a change in sales force effort impacts sales:
   - A 50% cut in sales force effort reduces sales to 48% of its current value.
   - Sales force effort of 0 reduces sales to 15% of its current value.
   - A 50% increase in sales force effort increases sales by 20%.
   - A saturation of sales effort (a 10-fold increase) increases sales by 35%.

   Fit an S-shaped curve as described by equation (8.1) to these data.

10. The file **P08_10.xlsx** contains data on annual advertising (per capita) and annual unit sales (per capita) in different regions of the country. Determine an S-shaped curve as described by equation (8.1) that can be used to determine how advertising influences sales.

11. The adoption level of a new product often can be modeled as an S-shaped curve called the Pearl (or logistic) curve. The equation of this curve is

$$Y = \frac{L}{1 + ae^{-bt}}$$

where $Y$ is the adoption level, $L$ is an (unknown) upper limit on adoptions, and $a$ and $b$ are parameters to be estimated. The file **P08_11.xlsx** lists information on

U.S. cell phones since 1990 (which corresponds to year 1). For this problem, define $Y$ as the number of cell phones per capita. As $t$ increases, $Y$ approaches the limit $L$. Hence we can use this curve to estimate the upper limit on U.S. cell phones per person. Use Evolutionary Solver to estimate the eventual number of cell phones per person in the United States.

## Skill-Extending Problem

12. Sales of a product over time often follow an S-shaped curve. Two functions that yield S-shaped curves are the Pearl (or logistic) curve

$$Y = \frac{L}{1 + ae^{-bt}}$$

and the Gompertz curve

$$Y = Le^{-be^{-kt}}$$

Here, $Y$ is annual sales, $t$ is time (in years), $L$ is the upper limit on sales, and $a$, $b$, and $k$ are parameters to be estimated. (Actually, $L$ must also be estimated.) The file **P08_12.xlsx** contains data for sales of answering machines in the United States. Use the Evolutionary Solver to fit a Pearl and a Gompertz curve to these data. Let $t = 0$ correspond to 1983. Which curve provides the better fit? (*Hint:* You need to use reasonable bounds for the parameters for each curve. For example, $L \geqslant 14.5$ is reasonable.)

## 8.7 PORTFOLIO OPTIMIZATION

In the previous chapter, we discussed one approach to portfolio optimization. The objective in that chapter was to minimize the portfolio variance subject to keeping the mean portfolio return above some required level. This resulted in a nonlinear model (because of the squares and product terms in the portfolio variance formula), but this nonlinear objective was sufficiently smooth to permit using the standard Solver. Now we look at another possible objective. This objective is *not* smooth, so Evolutionary Solver is necessary.

---

EXAMPLE | **8.6 BEATING THE S&P INDEX AT E.T. BARNEY**

E. T. Barney, an investment company, wants to form a portfolio consisting of a number of well-known stocks. The objective is to find the appropriate portfolio that, based on historical data, has the largest probability of beating the S&P 500 market index. How should the company proceed?[7]

**Objective**   To use Evolutionary Solver to find the portfolio that has the highest chance of beating the S&P 500 Index.

### WHERE DO THE NUMBERS COME FROM?

The historical returns from the stocks and the market index are widely available on the Web.

### Solution

The file **Beating S&P 500.xlsx** contains monthly returns for a period of more than 8 years for 29 large companies. See the blue area in Figure 8.23. (Note that there are many hidden

---

**Figure 8.23**   The Portfolio Optimization Model

| | A | B | C | D | E | F | G | H | I | AB | AC | AD | AE | AF | AG |
|---|---|---|---|---|---|---|---|---|---|---|---|---|---|---|---|
| 1 | Maximizing the probability of beating the S&P 500 | | | | | | | | | | | | | | |
| 2 | | | | | | | | | | | | | | | |
| 3 | Weights on stocks for portfolio | | | | | | | | | | | | | | |
| 4 | | MMM | AA | MO | AXP | AIG | BA | CAT | C | VZ | WMT | DIS | | | |
| 5 | | 0.226844 | 0.247194 | 0 | 0.220331 | 0 | 0 | 0 | 0 | 0 | 0 | 0 | | | |
| 6 | | | | | | | | | | | | | | | |
| 7 | Constraint on weights | | | | | Percent of months beating S&P 500 | | | | | | | | | |
| 8 | Sum weights | | | Required | | Old Pct | 70.83% | | | | | | | | |
| 9 | | 1 | = | | 1 | Recent Pct | 48.21% | | | | | | | | |
| 10 | | | | | | | | | | | | | | | |
| 11 | Historical data on returns | | | | | | | | | | | | | | |
| 12 | Month | MMM | AA | MO | AXP | AIG | BA | CAT | C | VZ | WMT | DIS | S&P 500 | Portfolio Return | Beat S&P? |
| 13 | Feb-99 | -0.0387 | -0.0261 | -0.1650 | 0.0548 | 0.1068 | 0.0311 | 0.0520 | 0.0481 | -0.0396 | 0.0015 | 0.0662 | -0.0323 | -0.0100 | Yes |
| 14 | Mar-99 | -0.0448 | 0.0169 | -0.0908 | 0.0870 | 0.0591 | -0.0458 | 0.0081 | 0.0873 | -0.1031 | 0.0715 | -0.1156 | 0.0388 | 0.0384 | No |
| 15 | Apr-99 | 0.2582 | 0.5114 | -0.0041 | 0.1100 | -0.0299 | 0.1952 | 0.4085 | 0.1752 | 0.1233 | -0.0021 | 0.0202 | 0.0379 | 0.2067 | Yes |
| 16 | May-99 | -0.0305 | -0.1136 | 0.1003 | -0.0738 | -0.0230 | 0.0385 | -0.1477 | -0.1149 | -0.0501 | -0.0732 | -0.0828 | -0.0250 | -0.0574 | No |
| 17 | Jun-99 | 0.0139 | 0.1251 | 0.0533 | 0.0769 | 0.0263 | 0.0460 | 0.0933 | 0.0752 | 0.1939 | 0.1332 | 0.0579 | 0.0544 | 0.0406 | No |
| 18 | Jul-99 | 0.0115 | -0.0323 | -0.0734 | 0.0124 | -0.0097 | 0.0313 | -0.0175 | -0.0591 | -0.0148 | -0.1244 | -0.1053 | -0.0320 | 0.0052 | Yes |
| 19 | Aug-99 | 0.0807 | 0.0816 | 0.0049 | 0.0438 | -0.0022 | 0.0015 | -0.0339 | -0.0028 | -0.0422 | 0.0490 | 0.0067 | -0.0063 | 0.0758 | Yes |
| 20 | Sep-99 | 0.0166 | -0.0384 | -0.0750 | -0.0182 | -0.0616 | -0.0591 | -0.0321 | -0.0096 | 0.0979 | 0.0744 | -0.0628 | -0.0286 | -0.0273 | Yes |
| 21 | Oct-99 | -0.0104 | -0.0211 | -0.2286 | 0.1425 | 0.1841 | 0.0804 | 0.0150 | 0.2362 | -0.0294 | 0.1838 | 0.0212 | 0.0625 | 0.0540 | No |
| 112 | May-07 | 0.0687 | 0.1689 | 0.0316 | 0.0711 | 0.0371 | 0.0857 | 0.0820 | 0.0265 | 0.1402 | -0.0021 | 0.0132 | 0.0325 | 0.0735 | Yes |
| 113 | Jun-07 | -0.0133 | -0.0182 | -0.0037 | -0.0585 | -0.0319 | -0.0441 | -0.0036 | -0.0587 | -0.0543 | 0.0108 | -0.0367 | -0.0178 | -0.0285 | No |
| 114 | Jul-07 | 0.0246 | -0.0575 | -0.0523 | -0.0408 | -0.0835 | 0.0757 | 0.0106 | -0.0921 | 0.0454 | -0.0449 | -0.0334 | -0.0320 | -0.0152 | Yes |
| 115 | Aug-07 | 0.0288 | -0.0394 | 0.0443 | 0.0014 | 0.0283 | -0.0619 | -0.0385 | 0.0185 | -0.0174 | -0.0457 | 0.0182 | 0.0129 | 0.0126 | No |
| 116 | Sep-07 | 0.0285 | 0.0709 | 0.0130 | 0.0128 | 0.0281 | 0.0857 | 0.0351 | -0.0045 | 0.0573 | 0.0005 | 0.0235 | 0.0358 | 0.0476 | Yes |

---

[7] We have not seen this particular objective discussed in finance books or articles, but it is clear from discussions with investors that the goal of "beating the market" is important. For an excellent discussion of investment models in general, read the book by Luenberger (1997).

rows and columns in this figure.) We decided to base the optimization on the earliest 3 years of data. Then we can see how the portfolio based on this data performs on the most recent 2 years of data.

## DEVELOPING THE SPREADSHEET MODEL

You can create the model with the following steps:

**1** **Enter weights.** As in the previous chapter, the portfolio is based on the fractions of each dollar invested in the various stocks. We call these the weights. Enter *any* values for the weights in the Weights range. We eventually constrain these weights to be between 0 and 1. Then calculate the sum of the weights in cell B9 with the SUM function.

**2** **Portfolio returns.** For the historical period, the period of the data, calculate the portfolio returns by weighting the actual returns by the weights. To do this, enter the formula

**=SUMPRODUCT(Weights,B13:AD13)**

in cell AF13 and copy it down.

**3** **Beats S&P 500?** The returns from the S&P 500 market index appear in column AE. (These are given. As with the stock returns, they can be found on the Web.) For each month, see whether the portfolio beats the S&P 500 by entering the formula

**=IF(AF13>AE13,"Yes","No")**

in cell AG13 and copying down.

**4** **Objective.** Calculate the fraction of months during the earliest four years where the portfolio beats the S&P 500. Do this in cell G8 with the formula

**=COUNTIF(AG13:AG60,"Yes")/48**

This is the objective we attempt to maximize. Note that it contains the COUNTIF function. This is the feature that necessitates Evolutionary Solver. For comparison, calculate the similar fraction for the most recent four-plus years in cell G9 with the formula

**=COUNTIF(AG61:AG116,"Yes")/56**

## USING EVOLUTIONARY SOLVER

The Solver setup appears in Figure 8.24. We constrain the sum of the weights to be 1 so that all of our money is invested. We constrain the weights to be within 0 and 1 so that the investment in each stock is a positive fraction of the total investment. (We can allow negative weights if short selling is permitted.)

### Discussion of the Solution

There are several things to note about the optimal solution found in Figure 8.23. First, this portfolio puts most of the weight on four companies: 3M (22.7%), Alcoa (24.7%), American Express (22.0%), and Procter & Gamble (21.3%). The rest of the weight is divided among four other companies, and the rest of the companies are not in the portfolio at all. Second, this solution represents the portfolio that beats the S&P 500 most frequently *in the optimization period*—that is, the earliest four years. Whenever we base an optimization on a historical period, there is no guarantee that this solution will work as well in the *future*. We illustrate this by seeing how well the portfolio does in the most recent four-plus years where we have data. Clearly, it does not do as well. The portfolio beats the S&P 500 about 71% of the time during the earliest four years, but only about 48% of the time during the most recent four-plus years. Any time we use historical data to forecast what might happen

**Figure 8.24**

Solver Dialog Box
for the Portfolio
Optimization Model

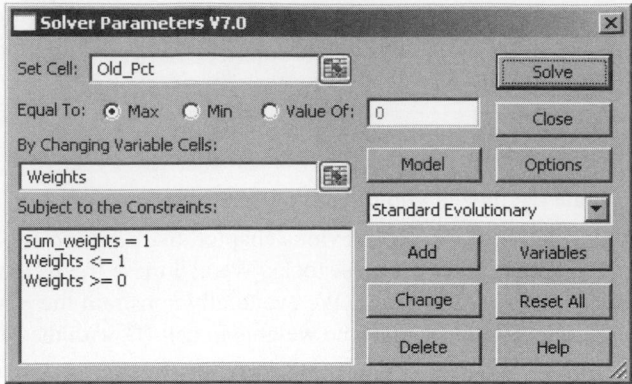

in the future, we are making the implicit assumption that historical patterns will repeat themselves. As many forecasters have discovered to their dismay, this assumption is not always correct.

Finally, this is the best solution we found after experimenting with several random number seeds and several starting solutions for the weights. Some of these converged to a solution with an objective *less than* 75%, which is clearly suboptimal. This is due to the randomness component built into GAs. Different runs can have varying levels of success depending on the "luck of the draw." ■

Is this method of portfolio optimization any better or worse than the variance-minimizing method discussed in the previous chapter? The answer probably depends on the investor's attitude toward risk. There is no guarantee that the probability-maximizing model in this chapter will achieve any particular expected return, although if it beats the market index consistently, it seems that it should provide a decent return. Also, there is no guarantee that this portfolio will provide an acceptable risk—measured by a small variance. Nevertheless, this model might have an intuitive appeal to many investors. If you can beat the S&P 500 consistently, you must be doing a good job!

## PROBLEMS

### Skill-Building Problems

**13.** Visit http://www.yahoo.com. Under Finance, then Stock Research, and finally Historical Quotes, download the monthly returns on any four stocks for years 2000 to 2005 (or as recent a period as you can find) and determine the portfolio that maximizes the chance of beating the S&P 500 for those years. (Note that the ticker symbol for the S&P 500 is ^SPX. Also, this Web site gives closing prices, which you will need to convert to returns.)

**14.** Continuing the previous problem, determine the portfolio that minimizes the chance that you will lose money during any month, subject to the constraint that your expected monthly return is at least 1%.

## 8.8 CLUSTER ANALYSIS

Marketers often want to group objects into clusters of similar objects. For example, identifying similar customers can help a company identify market segments. Identifying a cluster of similar products can help a company identify its main competitors. Here are two actual examples of how the United States is divided into clusters.[8]

---

[8] The book by Johnson and Wichern (2002) has an excellent, although somewhat mathematically advanced, discussion of cluster analysis and the topic of the next section, discriminant analysis.

- Claritas divides each block of the United States into one of 62 clusters. These include Blue Blood Estates, New Homesteaders, Middle America, God's Country, and so on. For example, Blue Blood Estates consists primarily of America's richest suburbs. (Over 1 in 10 residents of Blue Blood Estates is a millionaire.) This is valuable information for marketers. For example, Blue Blood Estates residents consume imported beer at a rate nearly three times the national average.

- SRI clusters families based on their financial status and demographics. For example, the cluster Bank Traditionalists consists of upper-middle-class families of larger than average size with school-age children. This cluster is a natural prospecting ground for life insurance salespeople.

The following example illustrates how we can use Evolutionary Solver to cluster cities. The same method could be use to cluster people, products, or other entities.

---

EXAMPLE | **8.7 CLUSTERING LARGE CITIES IN THE UNITED STATES**

The file **City Clusters.xlsx** contains demographic data on 49 of the largest cities in the United States. Some of the data appear in the shaded region of Figure 8.25. For example, Atlanta is 67% African American, 2% Hispanic, and 1% Asian. It has a median age of 31, a 5% unemployment rate, and a per-capita income of $22,000. We would like to group these 49 cities into 4 clusters of cities that are demographically similar. (We could then experiment with the number of clusters. For this discussion, we fix the number at 4.) The basic idea is to choose a city to anchor, or center, each cluster. We then assign each city to the nearest cluster center, where *nearest* is defined in terms of the six demographic variables. The objective is to minimize the sum of the squared distances from each city to its cluster anchor.

---

**Figure 8.25**  Demographic Data for Selected Cities

| | A | B | C | D | E | F | G | H | I | J | K | L | M | N |
|---|---|---|---|---|---|---|---|---|---|---|---|---|---|---|
| 13 | City data | | | | | | | | Standardized | | | | | |
| 14 | Index | City | PctAfrAmer | PctHispanic | PctAsian | MedianAge | UnempRate | PCIncome | PctAfrAmer | PctHispanic | PctAsian | MedianAge | UnempRate | PCIncome |
| 15 | 1 | Albuquerque | 3 | 35 | 2 | 32 | 5 | 18 | -1.179 | 1.239 | -0.363 | 0.061 | -0.751 | -0.875 |
| 16 | 2 | Atlanta | 67 | 2 | 1 | 31 | 5 | 22 | 2.355 | -0.764 | -0.452 | -0.440 | -0.751 | 0.324 |
| 17 | 3 | Austin | 12 | 23 | 3 | 29 | 3 | 19 | -0.682 | 0.510 | -0.273 | -1.442 | -1.495 | -0.575 |
| 18 | 4 | Baltimore | 59 | 1 | 1 | 33 | 11 | 22 | 1.913 | -0.825 | -0.452 | 0.562 | 1.480 | 0.324 |
| 19 | 5 | Boston | 26 | 11 | 5 | 30 | 5 | 24 | 0.091 | -0.218 | -0.093 | -0.941 | -0.751 | 0.924 |
| 20 | 6 | Charlotte | 32 | 1 | 2 | 32 | 3 | 20 | 0.423 | -0.825 | -0.363 | 0.061 | -1.495 | -0.275 |
| 21 | 7 | Chicago | 39 | 20 | 4 | 31 | 9 | 24 | 0.809 | 0.328 | -0.183 | -0.440 | 0.736 | 0.924 |
| 22 | 8 | Cincinnati | 38 | 1 | 1 | 31 | 8 | 21 | 0.754 | -0.825 | -0.452 | -0.440 | 0.364 | 0.024 |
| 23 | 9 | Cleveland | 47 | 5 | 1 | 32 | 13 | 22 | 1.251 | -0.582 | -0.452 | 0.061 | 2.224 | 0.324 |
| 24 | 10 | Columbus | 23 | 1 | 2 | 29 | 3 | 13 | -0.074 | -0.825 | -0.363 | -1.442 | -1.495 | -2.375 |
| 25 | 11 | Dallas | 30 | 21 | 2 | 30 | 9 | 22 | 0.312 | 0.389 | -0.363 | -0.941 | 0.736 | 0.324 |
| 26 | 12 | Denver | 13 | 23 | 2 | 34 | 7 | 23 | -0.627 | 0.510 | -0.363 | 1.063 | -0.008 | 0.624 |
| 27 | 13 | Detroit | 76 | 3 | 1 | 31 | 9 | 21 | 2.852 | -0.704 | -0.452 | -0.440 | 0.736 | 0.024 |
| 28 | 14 | El Paso | 3 | 69 | 1 | 29 | 11 | 13 | -1.179 | 3.303 | -0.452 | -1.442 | 1.480 | -2.375 |
| 29 | 15 | Fort Worth | 22 | 20 | 2 | 30 | 9 | 20 | -0.130 | 0.328 | -0.363 | -0.941 | 0.736 | -0.275 |
| 30 | 16 | Fresno | 9 | 30 | 13 | 28 | 13 | 16 | -0.847 | 0.935 | 0.624 | -1.942 | 2.224 | -1.475 |

**Objective**  To use Evolutionary Solver to find four cities to be used as cluster centers and to assign all other cities to one of these cluster centers.

**WHERE DO THE NUMBERS COME FROM?**

This basic demographic data on cities is widely available. Note that the data used here is several years old.

## Solution

The first problem is that if we use raw units, percentage African American and Hispanic will drive everything because these values are more spread out than the other demographic attributes. We can see this by calculating means and standard deviations of the characteristics. (See Figure 8.26, which also includes correlations between the attributes.) To remedy this problem, we standardize each demographic attribute by subtracting the attribute's mean and dividing the difference by the attribute's standard deviation. For example, the average city has 24.35% African Americans with a standard deviation of 18.11%. Thus on a standardized basis, Atlanta is larger by $(67 - 24.35)/18.11 = 2.355$ standard deviations on the African-American attribute than a typical city. By working with standardized values for each attribute, we ensure that the analysis is unit-free. To create the standardized values shown in Figure 8.25, enter the formula

$$=(C15-AVERAGE(C\$15:C\$63))/STDEV(C\$15:C\$63)$$

in cell I15 and copy it across to column N and down to row 63.

---

**Figure 8.26** Summary Data for Demographic Attributes

| | A | B | C | D | E | F | G |
|---|---|---|---|---|---|---|---|
| 7 | | PctAfrAmer | PctHispanic | PctAsian | MedianAge | UnempRate | PCIncome |
| 8 | *One Variable Summary* | Data Set #1 | Data Set #1 | Data Set #1 | Data Set #1 | Data Set #1 | Data Set #1 |
| 9 | Mean | 24.35 | 14.59 | 6.04 | 31.878 | 7.020 | 20.918 |
| 10 | Std. Dev. | 18.11 | 16.47 | 11.14 | 1.996 | 2.689 | 3.334 |
| 11 | | | | | | | |
| 12 | | PctAfrAmer | PctHispanic | PctAsian | MedianAge | UnempRate | PCIncome |
| 13 | *Correlation Table* | Data Set #1 | Data Set #1 | Data Set #1 | Data Set #1 | Data Set #1 | Data Set #1 |
| 14 | PctAfrAmer | 1.000 | | | | | |
| 15 | PctHispanic | -0.404 | 1.000 | | | | |
| 16 | PctAsian | -0.317 | 0.000 | 1.000 | | | |
| 17 | MedianAge | 0.010 | -0.221 | 0.373 | 1.000 | | |
| 18 | UnempRate | 0.308 | 0.341 | -0.001 | -0.007 | 1.000 | |
| 19 | PCIncome | 0.126 | -0.298 | 0.374 | 0.480 | 0.014 | 1.000 |

---

## DEVELOPING THE SPREADSHEET MODEL

Now that we have standardized values for all of the attributes, we can develop the spreadsheet model as follows. It is shown in two parts in Figures 8.27 and 8.28.

---

**Figure 8.27** Decision Variables and Target Cell

| | A | B | C | D | E | F | G | H | I | J | K | L |
|---|---|---|---|---|---|---|---|---|---|---|---|---|
| 1 | Clustering cities | | | | | | | | | | | |
| 2 | | | | | | | | | | | | |
| 3 | Cluster centers and standardized values | | | | | | | | | Range names used | | |
| 4 | | Column offset: | 9 | 10 | 11 | 12 | 13 | 14 | | City_index | =Model!$B$6:$B$9 | |
| 5 | Cluster center | City index | PctAfrAmer | PctHispanic | PctAsian | MedianAge | UnempRate | PCIncome | | Cluster_center | =Model!$A$6:$A$9 | |
| 6 | Memphis | 25 | 1.693 | -0.825 | -0.452 | 0.061 | 0.736 | -0.275 | | LookupTable | =Model!$A$15:$N$63 | |
| 7 | Omaha | 34 | -0.627 | -0.704 | -0.452 | 0.061 | -0.751 | -0.275 | | SumSqDists | =Model!$B$11 | |
| 8 | San Francisco | 43 | -0.737 | -0.036 | 2.060 | 2.065 | -0.380 | 3.024 | | | | |
| 9 | Los Angeles | 24 | -0.571 | 1.542 | 0.355 | -0.440 | 1.480 | 0.024 | | | | |
| 10 | | | | | | | | | | | | |
| 11 | Sum Square Distances | 165.348 | | | | | | | | | | |

**Figure 8.28**  Other Calculations for Cluster Analysis

| | I | J | K | L | M | N | O | P | Q | R | S | T | U | V |
|---|---|---|---|---|---|---|---|---|---|---|---|---|---|---|
| 13 | Standardized | | | | | | | Squared distances to centers | | | | | Assigned to | |
| 14 | PctAfrAmer | PctHispanic | PctAsian | MedianAge | UnempRate | PCIncome | | To 1 | To 2 | To 3 | To 4 | Minimum | Index | Center |
| 15 | -1.179 | 1.239 | -0.363 | 0.061 | -0.751 | -0.875 | | 15.086 | 4.447 | 27.044 | 7.017 | 4.447 | 2 | Omaha |
| 16 | 2.355 | -0.764 | -0.452 | -0.440 | -0.751 | 0.324 | | 3.267 | 9.505 | 30.102 | 19.609 | 3.267 | 1 | Memphis |
| 17 | -0.682 | 0.510 | -0.273 | -1.442 | -1.495 | -0.575 | | 14.782 | 4.411 | 32.238 | 11.689 | 4.411 | 2 | Omaha |
| 18 | 1.913 | -0.825 | -0.452 | 0.562 | 1.480 | 0.324 | | 1.213 | 12.057 | 26.962 | 13.526 | 1.213 | 1 | Memphis |
| 19 | 0.091 | -0.218 | -0.093 | -0.941 | -0.751 | 0.924 | | 7.718 | 3.323 | 18.937 | 9.780 | 3.323 | 2 | Omaha |
| 20 | 0.423 | -0.825 | -0.363 | 0.061 | -1.495 | -0.275 | | 6.601 | 1.677 | 23.980 | 16.303 | 1.677 | 2 | Omaha |
| 21 | 0.809 | 0.328 | -0.183 | -0.440 | 0.736 | 0.924 | | 3.874 | 7.102 | 19.481 | 5.032 | 3.874 | 1 | Memphis |
| 22 | 0.754 | -0.825 | -0.452 | -0.440 | 0.364 | 0.024 | | 1.360 | 3.506 | 24.979 | 9.259 | 1.360 | 1 | Memphis |
| 23 | 1.251 | -0.582 | -0.452 | 0.061 | 2.224 | 0.324 | | 2.827 | 12.753 | 28.641 | 9.381 | 2.827 | 1 | Memphis |
| 24 | -0.074 | -0.825 | -0.363 | -1.442 | -1.495 | -2.375 | | 14.776 | 7.547 | 49.615 | 21.982 | 7.547 | 2 | Omaha |
| 25 | 0.312 | 0.389 | -0.363 | -0.941 | 0.736 | 0.324 | | 4.751 | 5.660 | 24.715 | 3.521 | 3.521 | 4 | Los Angeles |
| 26 | -0.627 | 0.510 | -0.363 | 1.063 | -0.008 | 0.624 | | 9.537 | 3.849 | 13.078 | 6.415 | 3.849 | 2 | Omaha |
| 27 | 2.852 | -0.704 | -0.452 | -0.440 | 0.736 | 0.024 | | 1.700 | 14.656 | 36.153 | 17.971 | 1.700 | 1 | Memphis |
| 28 | -1.179 | 3.303 | -0.452 | -1.442 | 1.480 | -2.375 | | 32.506 | 28.005 | 62.553 | 10.881 | 10.881 | 4 | Los Angeles |
| 29 | -0.130 | 0.328 | -0.363 | -0.941 | 0.736 | -0.275 | | 5.663 | 4.537 | 27.534 | 3.079 | 3.079 | 4 | Los Angeles |
| 30 | -0.847 | 0.935 | 0.624 | -1.942 | 2.224 | -1.475 | | 18.378 | 18.203 | 46.094 | 5.578 | 5.578 | 4 | Los Angeles |
| 31 | -1.289 | -0.582 | 5.829 | 2.566 | -0.751 | 0.924 | | 58.327 | 47.617 | 19.602 | 49.812 | 19.602 | 3 | San Francisco |

**①** **Lookup table.** One key to the model is to have an index (1 to 49) for the cities so that we can refer to them by index and then look up their characteristics with a VLOOKUP function. Therefore, name the range A15:N63 as LookupTable.

**②** **Decision variables.** The only changing cells appear in the City_index range of Figure 8.27. They are the indices of the four cities chosen as cluster centers. Enter any four integers from 1 to 49 in these cells.

**③** **Corresponding cities and standardized attributes.** We find the names and standardized attributes of the cluster centers with VLOOKUP functions. First, enter the function

=VLOOKUP(B6,LookupTable,2)

in cell A6 and copy it to the range A6:A9. Then enter the formula

=VLOOKUP($B6,LookupTable,C$4)

in C6 and copy it to the range C6:H9. Note, for example, that the standardized PctAfrAmer is the 9th column of the lookup table. This explains the "column offset" entries in row 4.

**④** **Squared distances to centers.** The next step is to see how far each city is from each of the cluster centers. Let $z_i$ be standardized attribute $i$ for a typical city, and let $c_i$ be standardized attribute $i$ for a typical cluster center. We measure the distance from this city to this cluster center with the usual Euclidean distance formula

$$\text{Distance} = \sqrt{\sum_i (z_i - c_i)^2}$$

where the sum is over all six attributes. We can work just as well with *squared* distances, so we ignore the square root sign in this formula.[9] These squared distances appear in columns P through S of Figure 8.28. For example, the value in cell P15 is the squared distance from Albuquerque to the first cluster center (Memphis), the value in Q15 is the squared distance

---

[9] Minimizing squared distances provides the same solution as minimizing distances.

from Albuquerque to the second cluster center (Omaha), and so on. These calculations can be performed in several equivalent ways. Probably the quickest way is to enter the formula

=SUMXMY2($I15:$N15,$C$6:$H$6)

in cell P15 and copy it to the range P15:S63. (The function SUMXMY2 calculates the differences between the elements of the two range arguments and then sums the squares of these differences—exactly what we want.) The copied versions in columns Q, R, and S then have to be modified slightly. The 6's in the second range argument need to be changed to 7's in column Q, 8's in column R, and 9's in column S.

**5** **Assignments to cluster centers.** Each city is assigned to the cluster center that has the smallest squared distance. Therefore, find the minimum squared distances in column T by entering the formula

=MIN(P15:S15)

in cell T15 and copying it down. Then identify the cluster index (1 through 4) and city name of the cluster center that yields the minimum. We can use the MATCH function to obtain the cluster index. Enter the formula

=MATCH(T15,P15:S15,0)

in cell U15 and copy it down. For example, the 4.447 minimum squared distance for Albuquerque corresponds to the second squared distance, so Albuquerque is assigned to the second cluster center. Finally, to get the *name* of the second cluster center, we can use the INDEX function. Enter the formula

=INDEX(Cluster_center,U15,1)

in cell V15 and copy it down. This formula returns the name in the second row and first (only) column of the Cluster_center range (in Figure 8.27).

### Excel Function: *INDEX*
*The function INDEX, using the syntax INDEX(Range,Row,Column), is usually used to return the value in a given row and column of a specified range. For example, INDEX(A5:C10,3, 2) returns the value in the third row and second column of the range A5:C10, that is, the value in cell B7. If the given range is a single row, the row argument can be omitted. If the given range is a single column, the column argument can be omitted.*

**6** **Sum of squared distances.** The objective is to minimize the sum of squared distances from all cities to the cluster centers to which they are assigned. Calculate this objective in cell B11 (in Figure 8.27) with the formula

=SUM(T15:T63)

## USING EVOLUTIONARY SOLVER

The Solver dialog box should be set up as shown in Figure 8.29. Because the changing cells represent *indices* of cluster centers, they must be integer-constrained, and suitable lower and upper limits are 1 and 49 (the number of cities). Make sure you set the Evolutionary Solver options as we described in Example 8.1. This problem is considerably more difficult to solve, and we want to allow Evolutionary Solver plenty of time to search through a lot of potential solutions.

**Figure 8.29**

Solver Dialog Box
for the Cluster
Model

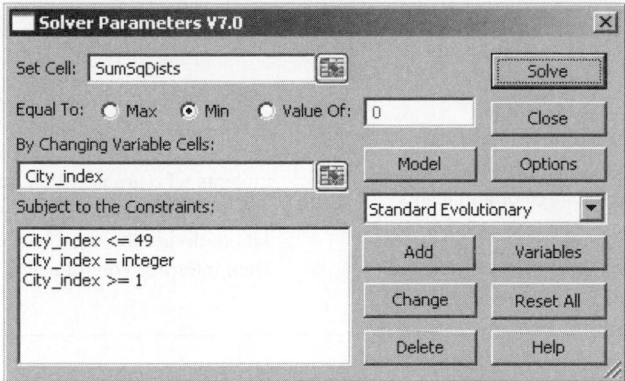

### Discussion of the Solution

*In cluster analysis, we typically do not know the number of clusters ahead of time. Some experimentation with the number of clusters is usually required.*

The solution in Figure 8.27, which uses Memphis, Omaha, San Francisco, and Los Angeles, is the best we found. You might find a slightly different solution, depending on your Solver settings and how long you let Solver run, but you should obtain a similar value in the target cell. If you look closely at the cities assigned to each cluster center, this solution begins to make intuitive sense (see Figure 8.30). The San Francisco cluster consists of rich, older, highly Asian cities. The Memphis cluster consists of highly African-American cities with high unemployment rates. The Omaha cluster consists of average income cities with few minorities. The Los Angeles cluster consists of highly Hispanic cities with high unemployment rates.

Why 4 clusters? We could easily try 3 clusters or 5 clusters. Note that when we *add* a cluster, the sum of squared distances will certainly decrease. In fact, we could obtain an objective value of 0 by using 49 clusters, one for each city, but this would hardly provide much information! Therefore, to choose the "optimal" number of clusters, we stop adding clusters when the sum of squared distances fails to decrease by a substantial amount.

**Figure 8.30**

Clusters in the
Solver Solution

|    | W | X | Y | Z | AA |
|----|---|---|---|---|----|
| 13 | **Clusters** | | | | |
| 14 | Center: | Los Angeles | Memphis | Omaha | San Francisco |
| 15 | | Dallas | Atlanta | Albuquerque | Honolulu |
| 16 | | El Paso | Baltimore | Austin | San Francisco |
| 17 | | Fort Worth | Chicago | Boston | Seattle |
| 18 | | Fresno | Cincinnati | Charlotte | |
| 19 | | Houston | Cleveland | Columbus | |
| 20 | | Long Beach | Detroit | Denver | |
| 21 | | Los Angeles | Memphis | Indianapolis | |
| 22 | | Miami | New Orleans | Jacksonville | |
| 23 | | NY | Oakland | Kansas City | |
| 24 | | San Antonio | Philadelphia | Las Vegas | |
| 25 | | San Diego | St. Louis | Milwaukee | |
| 26 | | San Jose | | Minneapolis | |
| 27 | | | | Nashville | |
| 28 | | | | Oklahoma City | |
| 29 | | | | Omaha | |
| 30 | | | | Phoenix | |
| 31 | | | | Pittsburgh | |
| 32 | | | | Portland | |
| 33 | | | | Sacramento | |
| 34 | | | | Toledo | |
| 35 | | | | Tucson | |
| 36 | | | | Tulsa | |
| 37 | | | | Virginia Beach | |

## Skill-Building Problem

15. The file **P08_15.xlsx** contains the following information about the top 25 MBA programs (according to the 1997 Business Week Guide): percentage of applicants accepted, percentage of accepted applicants who enroll, mean GMAT score of enrollees, mean undergraduate GPA of enrollees, annual cost of school (for state schools, this is the cost for out-of-state students), percentage of students who are minorities, percentage of students who are non-U.S. residents, and mean starting salary of graduates (in thousands of dollars). Use these data to divide the top 25 schools into four clusters. Then interpret your clusters.

# 8.9 DISCRIMINANT ANALYSIS

*In classification examples such as these, we typically create an optimization model on a "training" data set and then apply it to a new data set to predict group membership.*

Discriminant analysis is a statistical tool used by analysts in marketing and other fields of business. Although somewhat similar to cluster analysis, it is also quite different. In cluster analysis, there are no predefined clusters. We look at the information on the different members of the population (cities, products, or whatever) to see which members should be clustered together because of similar characteristics. We do not even know the *number* of clusters to use. In discriminant analysis, however, the clusters (usually called groups) are predefined. For example, there might be two groups: users of a particular product and nonusers. We collect data on a sample (often called a **training sample**) of users and nonusers—their income, their ages, and other possibly relevant data—and we use this data to classify the customers as users or nonusers. The analysis is successful if we can correctly classify a large percentage of the customers in the training sample. Of course, we already know which group each customer in the training sample is in. Therefore, the real purpose is to see whether we can correctly classify a large percentage of customers outside of the training sample on the basis of their income, age, and so on.

Discriminant analysis has been used in several situations, including the following:

- Based on gender, age, income, and residential location, we can classify a consumer as a user or nonuser of a new breakfast cereal.

- Based on income, type of residence, credit card debt, and other information, we can classify a consumer as a good or bad credit risk.

- Based on financial ratios, we can classify a company as a likely or unlikely candidate for bankruptcy.

In general, discriminant analysis can be used to classify members of two or more groups. We focus only on two-group discriminant analysis. In this case, we form a weighted combination of the data for each member, called a **discriminant score,** and classify the member into group 1 or group 2 depending on which side of a cutoff score the member's discriminant score falls. The problem is to find the appropriate weights for the discriminant scores and the appropriate cutoff score that maximize the percentage of correct classifications in the training sample. The following example illustrates the procedure.

EXAMPLE | **8.8 CLASSIFYING SUBSCRIBERS AND NONSUBSCRIBERS TO THE *WALL STREET JOURNAL***

The file **WSJ Subscribers.xlsx** contains the annual income and size of investment portfolio (both in thousands of dollars) for 84 people. It also indicates whether or not each of these people subscribes to the *Wall Street Journal*. Using income and size of investment portfolio, determine a classification rule that maximizes the number of people correctly classified as subscribers or nonsubscribers.

**Objective** To use Evolutionary Solver to find a function of income and investment that does the best job of classifying subscribers and nonsubscribers.

## WHERE DO THE NUMBERS COME FROM?

In a general discriminant analysis, we collect as much useful financial and demographic data as possible about the people (or companies) to be classified.

## Solution

The model is actually simpler than the cluster analysis model. Using appropriate weights, we create a discriminant score for each of the 84 customers. Then based on a cutoff score, we classify each customer as a subscriber or nonsubscriber, and we tally the number of correct classifications.

## DEVELOPING THE SPREADSHEET MODEL

The model appears (with several hidden rows) in Figure 8.31 and can be developed as follows:

**Figure 8.31** The Discriminant Analysis Model

| | A | B | C | D | E | F | G | H | I | J | K | L | M | N |
|---|---|---|---|---|---|---|---|---|---|---|---|---|---|---|
| 1 | Discriminant analysis | | | | | | | | | | | | | |
| 2 | | | | | | | | | | | | | | |
| 3 | Weights for discriminant function | | | | | Range names used: | | | | | | | | |
| 4 | | Income | InvestAmt | | | Cutoff | =Model!$B$8 | | | | | | | |
| 5 | | -0.094 | 0.950 | | | Pct_correct | =Model!$L$16 | | | | | | | |
| 6 | | | | | | Weights | =Model!$B$5:$C$5 | | | | | | | |
| 7 | Cutoff value for classification | | | | | | | | | | | | | |
| 8 | | 33.545 | | | | | | | | | | | | |
| 9 | | | | | | | | | | | Classification matrix | | | |
| 10 | Customer data | | | | | | | | | | (Actual along side, predicted along top) | | | |
| 11 | Person | Income | InvestAmt | WSJSubscriber | Score | Classified as | Correct? | Correct Yes? | Correct No? | | | Yes | No | |
| 12 | 1 | 59.7 | 14.9 | No | 8.6 | No | Yes | | Yes | | Yes | 23 | 4 | |
| 13 | 2 | 60.9 | 25.8 | No | 18.8 | No | Yes | | Yes | | No | 2 | 55 | |
| 14 | 3 | 67.6 | 37.6 | Yes | 29.4 | No | No | No | | | | | | |
| 15 | 4 | 86.6 | 37.0 | No | 27.0 | No | Yes | | Yes | | Percent correct classifications | | | |
| 16 | 5 | 90.4 | 21.4 | No | 11.8 | No | Yes | | Yes | | | 92.86% | | |
| 17 | 6 | 67.2 | 26.4 | No | 18.8 | No | Yes | | Yes | | | | | |
| 18 | 7 | 85.1 | 59.8 | Yes | 48.8 | Yes | Yes | Yes | | | | | | |
| 19 | 8 | 89.9 | 46.2 | No | 35.5 | Yes | No | | No | | | | | |
| 20 | 9 | 100.3 | 55.5 | Yes | 43.3 | Yes | Yes | Yes | | | | | | |
| 21 | 10 | 57.6 | 22.2 | No | 15.7 | No | Yes | | Yes | | | | | |
| 22 | 11 | 88.4 | 34.5 | No | 24.5 | No | Yes | | Yes | | | | | |
| 23 | 12 | 41.9 | 5.0 | No | 0.8 | No | Yes | | Yes | | | | | |

**1** **Customer data.** Enter the customer data in the blue range. This includes the data on the variables used for classification (income and investment amount), as well as an indication of which group each customer is in. These 84 customers represent the training sample, so we know which group (subscriber or nonsubscriber) each of them is in.

**2** **Decision variables.** The decision variables are the weights used to form discriminant scores and the cutoff value for classification. Enter any values for these in the Weights and Cutoff ranges.

**3** **Discriminant scores.** Each discriminant score is a weighted combination of the person's income and investment amount. To calculate these in column E, enter the formula

**=SUMPRODUCT(Weights,B12:C12)**

in cell E12 and copy it down.

**4 Classifications.** We classify a person as a nonsubscriber if the person's discriminant score is *below* the cutoff value; otherwise, the person is classified as a subscriber. Therefore, enter the formula

**=IF(E12<Cutoff,"No","Yes")**

in cell F12 and copy it down. (We could do it the opposite way, where people *above* the cutoff are classified as subscribers, and the results would be equivalent.)

**5 Correct?** Check whether each classification is correct by entering the formula

**=IF(D12=F12,"Yes","No")**

in cell G12 and copying it down.

**6 Tallies.** It is customary to tally the classifications in a classification matrix. This is actually a bit trickier than you might think. We suggest doing it as follows, although there are other ways. First, note that column H indicates which subscribers are classified correctly, and column I does the same for nonsubscribers. To fill these columns, enter the formulas

**=IF(D12="Yes",IF(F12="Yes","Yes","No")," ")**

and

**=IF(D12="No",IF(F12="No","Yes","No")," ")**

in cells H12 and I12, and copy them down. Note that blanks are entered for nonsubscribers in column H and for subscribers in column I. Next, to form the top row of the classification matrix, enter the formulas

**=COUNTIF(H12:H95,"Yes")**

and

**=COUNTIF(D12:D95,"Yes")-L12**

in cells L12 and M12. Similarly, to form the bottom row, enter the formulas

**=COUNTIF(D12:D95,"No")-M13**

and

**=COUNTIF(I12:I95,"Yes")**

in cells L13 and M13. Finally, calculate the percentage of *all* people classified correctly in cell L16 with the formula

**=COUNTIF(G12:G95,"Yes")/COUNTA(G12:G95)**

This is the objective we want to minimize.

## USING EVOLUTIONARY SOLVER

First, note that Evolutionary Solver is required because of the IF (and COUNTIF and COUNTA) functions used to make and tally the classifications. The completed Solver dialog box appears in Figure 8.32 and is straightforward except for the lower and upper limits on the changing cells. There are no natural weights or cutoff values to use. However, we can always constrain the weights to be between −1 and 1. (The reasoning is that if we solve the problem with weights equal to, say, −15 and 15, we can divide them *and* the resulting cutoff score by 15 and obtain exactly the same classifications.) To obtain lower and upper limits on the cutoff value, we first calculated the maximum sum of income and investment

**Figure 8.32**

Solver Dialog Box
for Discriminant
Analysis

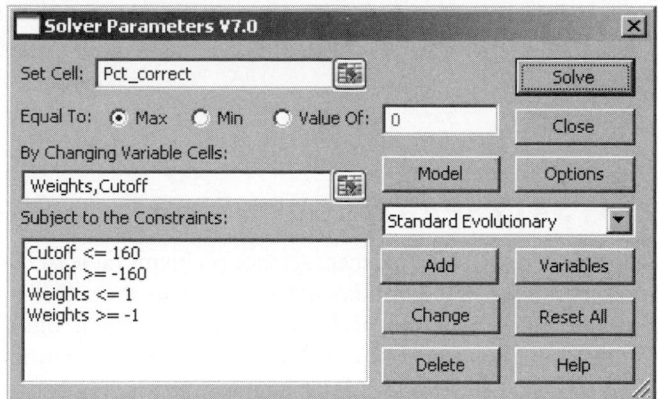

amount for any customer, which is slightly less than 160. This means that the largest discriminant score, using weights of 1, is no larger than 160, and the smallest discriminant score, using weights of –1, is no less than –160. Therefore, there is no need to consider cutoff values below –160 or above 160.

### Discussion of the Solution

*The classification matrix, often called the **confusion matrix**, lets us see how well we classify the members of the training data set. However, there is no guarantee that the model will classify members of a new data set as accurately.*

The solution shown in Figure 8.31 is certainly not unique. Many other sets of weights and cutoff values can obtain a 92.86% correct classification rate, and you will probably obtain a different solution from ours. Note that only 6 of the 84 people are misclassified—4 subscribers are misclassified as nonsubscribers and 2 nonsubscribers are misclassified as subscribers. Also, we see from the weights that the classification is based primarily on the investment amount, with very little weight placed on income. Because of the *positive* weight on the investment amount, people with large investment amounts are classified as subscribers. Therefore, a subscriber such as person 3 is misclassified because his investment amount is abnormally small relative to other subscribers. On the other hand, a nonsubscriber such as person 8 is misclassified because his investment amount is abnormally large relative to other nonsubscribers.

In a real application, we would use this analysis for people other than the 84 in the training sample. That is, we would calculate a discriminant score for each such person and then classify each as a nonsubscriber if her discriminant score is less than the cutoff value. However, the percentage correctly classified would typically be less—maybe considerably less—than the 92.86% rate we obtained in the training sample. The reason is that the optimization procedure takes advantage of all the data for these particular 84 people to derive the weights and the cutoff score. Unfortunately, there is no reason to believe that these will work as well for *another* group of people. ■

## PROBLEMS

### Skill-Building Problems

**16.** For the data in the file **P08_16.xlsx**, develop a classification rule to classify students as likely admits, likely rejects, or borderline.

**17.** For data in the file **P08_17.xlsx**, develop a rule to predict whether a person is likely to purchase our lasagna product. What variables appear to be the most useful?

**18.** The file **P08_18.xlsx** contains information on the following items about 24 companies: EBITASS (earnings before income and taxes, divided by total assets), ROTC (return on total capital), and Group (1 for most admired companies and 2 for least admired companies). Use these data to develop a rule that can be used to classify a company as a most admired or least admired company. Which variable appears to be most important for this classification?

19. The file **P08_19.xlsx** contains the following information for a random sample of 24 U.S. families: income (in thousands of dollars), lawn size (in thousands of square feet), and Group (1 for rider mower owners and 0 for others). Use these data to develop a rule for predicting whether a family is a rider mower owner. Which variable appears to be most important for this classification?

# 8.10 THE TRAVELING SALESPERSON PROBLEM

*Because of its combinatorial nature, traveling salesperson problems with even a moderate number of cities, such as 20 to 30, can be difficult to solve.*

One of the most studied management science problems (at least by academics) is called the traveling salesperson problem. Although easy to state, the problem is very difficult to solve. A salesperson must travel from his home base to a number of other cities, visiting each city exactly once, and finally return to his home base. We want to find the route that has the shortest total distance. Note that a potential solution is simple to describe. If we index the home base as 0 and the cities to be visited as 1 through $n$, then any solution is a permutation of the numbers 1 through $n$. For example, if $n = 8$, then a potential solution is 2, 5, 7, 1, 3, 8, 4, 6. The salesperson goes from 0 to 2, from 2 to 5, and so on, finishing by going from 6 back to 0. Because there are $n!$ permutations of the numbers 1 through $n$, you might think that checking each of them and choosing the best is easy. However, $n!$ grows extremely fast as $n$ increases. For example, 8! is "only" 43,020, but 16! is close to 21 *trillion*. This explosion in the number of permutations is what makes the problem so difficult. Nevertheless, it is easy to model the problem in such a way that Evolutionary Solver can be used to find good, and possibly even optimal, solutions. The following example illustrates the method.

EXAMPLE | **8.9 MINIMIZING A SALESPERSON'S DISTANCE TRAVELED**

Willie Lowman is a salesman who lives in Boston. He needs to visit each of the cities listed in Figure 8.33 (see the file **Traveling Salesperson.xlsx**) and then return to Boston. In what order should Willie visit the cities to minimize the total distance traveled?

**Figure 8.33** Distance Matrix

| | A | B | C | D | E | F | G | H | I | J | K | L |
|---|---|---|---|---|---|---|---|---|---|---|---|---|
| 1 | Traveling salesperson problem | | | | | | | | | | | |
| 2 | | | | | | | | | | | | |
| 3 | Distance matrix | | | | | | | | | | | |
| 4 | | Boston | Chicago | Dallas | Denver | Los Angeles | Miami | New York | Phoenix | Pittsburgh | San Francisco | Seattle |
| 5 | Boston | 0 | 983 | 1815 | 1991 | 3036 | 1539 | 213 | 2664 | 792 | 2385 | 2612 |
| 6 | Chicago | 983 | 0 | 1205 | 1050 | 2112 | 1390 | 840 | 1729 | 457 | 2212 | 2052 |
| 7 | Dallas | 1815 | 1205 | 0 | 801 | 1425 | 1332 | 1604 | 1027 | 1237 | 1034 | 2404 |
| 8 | Denver | 1991 | 1050 | 801 | 0 | 1174 | 2057 | 1780 | 836 | 1411 | 1765 | 1373 |
| 9 | Los Angeles | 3036 | 2112 | 1425 | 1174 | 0 | 2757 | 2825 | 398 | 2456 | 403 | 1919 |
| 10 | Miami | 1539 | 1390 | 1332 | 2057 | 2757 | 0 | 1258 | 2359 | 1250 | 3097 | 3389 |
| 11 | New York | 213 | 840 | 1604 | 1780 | 2825 | 1258 | 0 | 2442 | 386 | 3036 | 2900 |
| 12 | Phoenix | 2664 | 1729 | 1027 | 836 | 398 | 2359 | 2442 | 0 | 2073 | 800 | 1482 |
| 13 | Pittsburgh | 792 | 457 | 1237 | 1411 | 2456 | 1250 | 386 | 2073 | 0 | 2653 | 2517 |
| 14 | San Francisco | 2385 | 2212 | 1765 | 1034 | 403 | 3097 | 3036 | 800 | 2653 | 0 | 817 |
| 15 | Seattle | 2612 | 2052 | 2404 | 1373 | 1919 | 3389 | 2900 | 1482 | 2517 | 817 | 0 |

**Objective** To use Evolutionary Solver, with a special kind of constraint, to find the shortest route that starts and ends in Boston and visits each of the other 10 cities exactly once.

## WHERE DO THE NUMBERS COME FROM?

The numbers in this example could be found from a map. In general, we need the distances from each city to each other city, where distance can be interpreted as a cost. For example, if Willie is flying from city to city, the costs of the various flights is the more relevant "distance" measure, and as we all know, these costs are not necessarily proportional to the actual distances.

## Solution

This problem is surprisingly easy to model in a spreadsheet. We simply need a way to specify that any potential solution is a permutation of the numbers 1 through 10. Fortunately, Evolutionary Solver has a special type of constraint developed specifically for this kind of problem that is called an *alldifferent* constraint. We constrain the indexes of the cities visited to be between 1 and 10, and we also constrain them to be all different. Of course, the only way this can occur is if they are a permutation of the numbers 1 through 10. With this in mind, the model is straightforward.

### DEVELOPING THE SPREADSHEET MODEL

The completed model appears in Figure 8.34 and can be developed with the following steps:

---

**Figure 8.34** The Traveling Salesperson Model

| | A | B | C | D | E | F | G | H | I | J | K | L |
|---|---|---|---|---|---|---|---|---|---|---|---|---|
| 1 | Traveling salesperson problem | | | | | | | | | | | |
| 2 | | | | | | | | | | | | |
| 3 | Distance matrix | | | | | | | | | | | |
| 4 | | Boston | Chicago | Dallas | Denver | Los Angeles | Miami | New York | Phoenix | Pittsburgh | San Francisco | Seattle |
| 5 | Boston | 0 | 983 | 1815 | 1991 | 3036 | 1539 | 213 | 2664 | 792 | 2385 | 2612 |
| 6 | Chicago | 983 | 0 | 1205 | 1050 | 2112 | 1390 | 840 | 1729 | 457 | 2212 | 2052 |
| 7 | Dallas | 1815 | 1205 | 0 | 801 | 1425 | 1332 | 1604 | 1027 | 1237 | 1034 | 2404 |
| 8 | Denver | 1991 | 1050 | 801 | 0 | 1174 | 2057 | 1780 | 836 | 1411 | 1765 | 1373 |
| 9 | Los Angeles | 3036 | 2112 | 1425 | 1174 | 0 | 2757 | 2825 | 398 | 2456 | 403 | 1919 |
| 10 | Miami | 1539 | 1390 | 1332 | 2057 | 2757 | 0 | 1258 | 2359 | 1250 | 3097 | 3389 |
| 11 | New York | 213 | 840 | 1604 | 1780 | 2825 | 1258 | 0 | 2442 | 386 | 3036 | 2900 |
| 12 | Phoenix | 2664 | 1729 | 1027 | 836 | 398 | 2359 | 2442 | 0 | 2073 | 800 | 1482 |
| 13 | Pittsburgh | 792 | 457 | 1237 | 1411 | 2456 | 1250 | 386 | 2073 | 0 | 2653 | 2517 |
| 14 | San Francisco | 2385 | 2212 | 1765 | 1034 | 403 | 3097 | 3036 | 800 | 2653 | 0 | 817 |
| 15 | Seattle | 2612 | 2052 | 2404 | 1373 | 1919 | 3389 | 2900 | 1482 | 2517 | 817 | 0 |
| 16 | | | | | | | | | | | | |
| 17 | Indexes of cities | | | Route to travel | | | Range names used: | | | | | |
| 18 | City | Index | | Index | Distance | | Distance_matrix | =Model!$B$5:$L$15 | | | | |
| 19 | Boston | 0 | | 0 | | | Route | =Model!$D$20:$D$29 | | | | |
| 20 | Chicago | 1 | | 6 | 213 | | Total_distance | =Model!$B$32 | | | | |
| 21 | Dallas | 2 | | 8 | 386 | | | | | | | |
| 22 | Denver | 3 | | 1 | 457 | | | | | | | |
| 23 | Los Angeles | 4 | | 3 | 1050 | | | | | | | |
| 24 | Miami | 5 | | 10 | 1373 | | | | | | | |
| 25 | New York | 6 | | 9 | 817 | | | | | | | |
| 26 | Phoenix | 7 | | 4 | 403 | | | | | | | |
| 27 | Pittsburgh | 8 | | 7 | 398 | | | | | | | |
| 28 | San Francisco | 9 | | 2 | 1027 | | | | | | | |
| 29 | Seattle | 10 | | 5 | 1332 | | | | | | | |
| 30 | | | | 0 | 1539 | | | | | | | |
| 31 | | | | | | | | | | | | |
| 32 | Total distance | 8995 | | | | | | | | | | |

---

**1  Distance matrix.** Enter the distance matrix in the blue range.

**2  Index cities.** We need to refer to the cities by numerical indexes rather than names, so enter appropriate indexes in the range B19:B29. These indexes are based on alphabetical order, but any order could be used. Still, it is convenient to index the home city, Boston, as 0.

**3  Specify route.** Enter any route in the Route range. Note that we enter 0 in cells B19 and B30 because we know the route must start and end in Boston. However, the numbers in between can be any permutation of the numbers 1 through 10. This Route range becomes the changing cell range.

**④ Calculate distances.** To calculate the distances on the various legs of the trip, we can use the INDEX function to perform a lookup in the distance matrix. Specifically, enter the formula

=INDEX(Distance_matrix,D19+1,D20+1)

in cell E20 and copy it down to cell E30. This formula looks up the appropriate distance in the distance matrix. (The +1's are necessary because we have indexed the cities from 0 to 10, not from 1 to 11.) Then calculate the total distance in cell B32 with the SUM function.

*In models such as this, where a solution is a list of indexes, the INDEX and/or VLOOKUP functions are very handy.*

PREMIUM SOLVER

## USING EVOLUTIONARY SOLVER

The Solver dialog box should be set up as shown in Figure 8.35. We want to minimize the total distance traveled, subject to the constraints that all indexes on the route (other than Boston's) are between 1 and 10, and they must be all different. Specifying this alldifferent constraint is similar to specifying an integer or binary constraint. When you choose Evolutionary Solver, a "dif" option is available when you add a constraint. (See Figure 8.36.) It is useful in exactly this type of model, where the numbers in a permutation must all be different.

**Figure 8.35**

Solver Dialog Box with the alldifferent Constraint

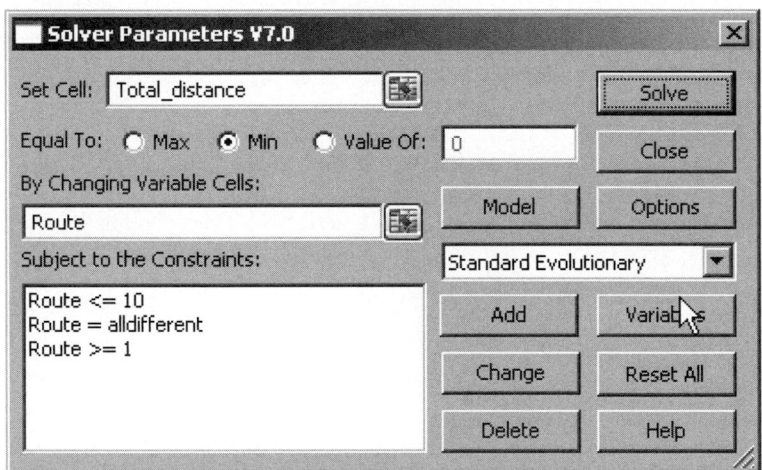

**Figure 8.36**

Specifying an alldifferent Constraint

### Discussion of the Solution

The optimal solution appears in Figure 8.34. Willie should go from Boston to New York to Pittsburgh to Chicago to Denver to Seattle to San Francisco to Los Angeles to Phoenix to Dallas to Miami and finally to Boston. Essentially, Willie should travel around the country in a counter-clockwise manner. The distance of this route is 8995 miles. Is this solution unique? It definitely is not. Willie could travel in a clockwise direction instead: Boston to

Miami to Dallas and so on. Because the distance matrix is symmetric, this clockwise route is bound to have the same total distance as the counter-clockwise route.

### Other Uses for the AllDifferent Constraint

We introduced the alldifferent constraint in the context of the traveling salesperson problem, but it has applications in many other problems. Specifically, it can be used in any model where the solution is defined by a permutation of integers from 1 to $n$. You are asked to explore some possibilities in the problems. ∎

## ADDITIONAL APPLICATIONS

### Sequence-Dependent Scheduling at Baxter International

Two of the problems discussed in this chapter, cluster analysis and the traveling salesperson problem, do not appear to have much in common. However, Moss et al. (2000) describe how they used both of these methodologies to sequence products through production at Baxter International, a large manufacturer of medical supplies. The problem is to reduce setup costs and setup time. Each product in its intravenous (IV) class of products requires a set of components to be present on the production line, and some of these components are common to various products. When production of one product follows the production of another product, components for the previous product not used by the new product have to be repackaged and stored, and components required by the new product but not used by the previous product have to be set up. Therefore, it makes sense to schedule products that use common components next to one another. The authors attacked this problem with cluster analysis (find clusters of products that are similar in terms of the components they require) and the traveling salesperson problem (find a permutation of the products to schedule through production). They estimate that their study saved Baxter about $165,000 annually by reducing setup times. ∎

## PROBLEMS

### Skill-Building Problems

**20.** The traveling salesperson problem is notoriously difficult when the number of cities is even of moderate size. The file **P08_20.xlsx** contains two sheets, one with a distance matrix for a 30-city problem and the other with a distance matrix for a 45-city problem. See whether Evolutionary Solver can successfully solve these problems. How will you know if it is successful?

**21.** An important problem in operations management is the job sequencing problem. Actually, there are many versions of this problem, but they all basically attempt to find the proper sequencing of jobs on a machine. Here is one version of the problem. There are 10 jobs to perform on a single machine. Each job has a given batch size (items to produce), and each item in the batch takes a certain time to perform. Also, each job (the whole batch) has a given due date. These data are listed in the file **P08_21.xlsx**. The "lateness" of any job is 0 if the job is finished on or before its due date, but it is the finish time minus the due date otherwise. The objective is to sequence the jobs to minimize the total lateness. Use Evolutionary Solver to find an optimal sequence of jobs.

### Skill-Extending Problems

**22.** Repeat the previous problem, but now assume there is a setup time for changing from any job to another job, and this setup time can depend on the jobs. For example, the setup time when changing from job 2 to job 4 can be different from the setup time when changing from job 3 to job 4. The data from the previous problem, plus the setup times, are listed in the file **P08_22.xlsx**. Use Evolutionary Solver to find an optimal sequence of jobs.

**23.** You are operating a web site to match up sellers and buyers of a product. 35 sellers and 35 buyers have input their reservation prices, as listed in the file **P08_23.xlsx**. For example, buyer 1 is willing to pay up to $8 for an item, and seller 1 is willing to accept $9 or more for an item. This means that buyer 1 and seller 1 cannot be matched. The goal of http://www.Split-TheDifference.com (there is such a Web site run by Yale professor Barry Nalebuff) is to pair buyers with sellers to maximize the sum of buyers' and sellers' surplus. For example, if buyer 31 and seller 31 are matched, a deal can be made by splitting the difference with a price of $57. Then buyer 31 earns a surplus of $60 − 57 = \$3$, and seller 31 earns a surplus of $57 − 54 = \$3$. What is the maximum sum of buyers' and sellers' surplus that can be obtained?

24. The 30 teams in the NBA are each assigned to one of 6 divisions, where each division has 5 teams. Suppose we want to assign the teams to divisions so that the average distance among teams in the divisions is minimized. In other words, we want to make the assignments so that teams within a division are close to one another. The file **P08_24.xlsx** contains distances between all NBA cities. Use Evolutionary Solver to find an optimal assignment of teams to divisions. Does it turn out that your assignments to divisions are the same as the NBA's? (*Hint:* Arrange the 30 teams into 6 contiguous blocks of 5 teams each. Each block will have 5 team indexes. With an alldifferent constraint, you can ensure that the 30 team indexes are all different. For each block, use lookups to find all distances between pairs of teams in that block and average these. Then average these averages over the 6 divisions to get the objective value.)

## 8.11 CONCLUSION

This chapter contains cutting-edge material. The standard Solver has been available for several years to solve many linear, integer, and nonlinear problems. However, it has not been able to solve the types of problems we have discussed in this chapter, except possibly by employing tricks or by using a lucky initial solution. With Evolutionary Solver now available to a large audience, we are able to solve a much wider variety of problems, and the spreadsheet models are usually straightforward—they do not require tricks. Evolutionary Solver is typically much slower than the standard Solver, especially for linear models with many constraints, because it uses a totally different search procedure. Because of this, we do not recommend that you try Evolutionary Solver unless your model contains functions such as IF, COUNT, COUNTIF, SUMIF, MIN, MAX, and ABS that the standard Solver cannot handle reliably. But if your model is formulated more naturally by using such functions, or if you can think of no other way of formulating it, then Evolutionary Solver can be very useful.

## Summary of Key Management Science Terms

| Term | Explanation | Page |
|---|---|---|
| Genetic algorithm (GA) | Optimization search procedure that mimics the theory of evolution, using crossovers, mutations, and the survival of the fittest | 415 |
| Penalties | Often used in Evolutionary Solver models to handle constraints; penalties are included in objective for violating constraints | 418 |
| Two-part tariff | One of several pricing schemes that can be used to increase revenue; includes a fixed price and a variable price | 422 |
| Surplus value (to customer) | Value to customer of purchasing product minus purchase cost; assumption is that customer purchases the amount that maximizes surplus value | 423 |
| Combinatorial problems | Optimization problems where there are a finite number of feasible solutions (combinations); often difficult because this finite number is huge | 428 |
| Cluster analysis | General method of grouping people, products, cities, and so on, so that members within a cluster are similar and members in different clusters are dissimilar | 444 |

| Term | Explanation | Page |
|------|-------------|------|
| Discriminant analysis | One (of several) methods used to classify people, products, cities, and so on, into well-defined groups based on data about the members | 450 |
| Traveling salesperson problem | Famous difficult management science problem; tries to find optimal route for a salesperson who starts and ends in a given city and visits all other cities exactly once | 454 |

## Summary of Key Excel Terms

| Term | Explanation | Excel | Page |
|------|-------------|-------|------|
| Premium Solver | More powerful version of Solver than Excel's built-in Solver; sold commercially by Frontline Systems | Select Premium Solver from Add-Ins ribbon | 413 |
| Evolutionary Solver | Premium Solver's implementation of GA | Get into Premium Solver, choose Standard Evolutionary item | 416 |
| Evolutionary Solver settings | Various settings that control the way the GA works (see text for details) | Choose Standard Evolutionary, then General Options and Limits Options | 432 |
| alldifferent constraint | Type of constraint available in Evolutionary Solver; useful for models where potential solutions are permutations of integers 1 through $n$ | One of several options for constraint type in Add Constraint dialog box | 455 |

# PROBLEMS

## Skill-Building Problems

25. Fourteen jobs must be assigned to one of three identical machines. The goal is to minimize the total time needed to complete all 14 jobs. The machine capacities and times needed for the jobs are given in file **P08_25.xlsx**. For example, job 8 requires 3 units of capacity on a machine for 2 hours. At any given time, a machine has 5 units of capacity. How should you assign the jobs to machines to ensure the earliest possible completion of all jobs?

26. Nine jobs need to be completed within 8 weeks. The number of weeks required to complete each job is given in the file **P08_26.xlsx**. For example, job 2 requires 3 weeks. Each week, 160 hours of regular time labor are available. Up to 40 hours of overtime labor can be purchased each week at a cost of $10 per hour. Additional overtime hours cost $20 per hour.
    a. Determine how to minimize the overtime cost incurred in completing the jobs within 8 weeks.
    b. The file **P08_26.xlsx** also lists the due date for each job. For example, job 2 should be completed within 6 weeks. A penalty of $500 is incurred for each day a job is late. Determine how to minimize the sum of overtime and due date penalties.

27. The costs of producing product A, product B, or products A and B bundled together are $50, $90, and $140, respectively. The file **P08_27.xlsx** lists the sizes of the three market segments for these products and how much each of the segments is willing to pay for A alone, B alone, or the bundle. Under the assumptions that a market segment will buy the product combination that yields the maximum nonnegative surplus (value minus cost), and a segment will buy no product if no product has a nonnegative surplus, determine an optimal set of product prices. Should the company offer all products for sale?

28. Eight students need to be assigned to four dorm rooms (two students to a room) at Faber College. Based on incompatibility measures, the "cost" incurred if two students room together is shown in the file **P08_28.xlsx**. How would you assign these students to rooms?

29. Cook County needs to build two hospitals. There are nine cities where the hospitals can be built. The number of hospital visits made annually by the inhabitants of each city and the $x$ and $y$ coordinates of each city are listed in the file **P08_29.xlsx**. To minimize the total distance that patients must travel to hospitals, where should the hospitals be located? Solve the problem when people can travel in straight lines ("as the crow flies") between cities. Then solve it when people must travel along a horizontal/vertical grid of roads. (*Hint:* Use lookup functions to generate the distances between each pair of cities.)

30. The file **P08_30.xlsx** contains quarterly revenue for Nike for the years 1991 to 1998. It also contains quarterly "indicator" variables Q1, Q2, and Q3. Here Q1 is 1 for the first quarter of a fiscal year (July–September) and 0 otherwise. Q2 and Q3 are defined similarly for the second and third quarters of the fiscal year (October–December and January–March). The "Quarter #" variable is simply the chronological number of the quarter, 1 to 32. We would like to build a quantitative model to explain the variation in quarterly revenue. A reasonable model is as follows:

$$\text{Predicted Sales} = ab^{Quarter\#}c^{Q_1}d^{Q_2}e^{Q_3}$$

where $a$, $b$, $c$, $d$, and $e$ are parameters to estimate.
   a. Find the values of $a$, $b$, $c$, $d$, and $e$ that best fit this model.
   b. What does your model say about the trend and seasonal aspects of Nike sales? (*Hint:* The trend effect is captured by the term involving Quarter #. Seasonal effects may be interpreted relative to the quarter, Q4, that we have omitted from the analysis.)

31. Music radio WABC has commercials of the following lengths (in seconds): 15, 15, 20, 25, 30, 35, 40, 57. The commercials must be assigned to 60-second breaks. What is the fewest number of breaks that are needed to air all of the commercials?

32. A Wall Street firm is trying to package nine mortgages for sale. The sizes of the mortgages (in thousands of dollars) are listed in the file **P08_32.xlsx**. To be sold, each package must consist of at least $1,000,000 in mortgages. What is the largest number of packages that can be created?

33. During the next 12 months, the amounts of electric power needed (in thousands of kwh) are listed in the file **P08_33.xlsx**. This power can be supplied using four generators. The generating capacity (in thousands of kwh), the operating cost, the startup cost, and the shutdown cost (all costs in thousands of dollars) are also listed in the file **P08_33.xlsx**. At the beginning of month 1, generators 1 and 2 are in operation. At the end of each month, we can either shut down an operating generator or start up a shutdown generator. How can we minimize the cost of meeting demand for power during the next 12 months?

34. Bus 99 serves towns 1 through 10. We assume that town $k$ is $|k - j|$ miles from town $j$. The numbers of people in the towns who want to take the bus each hour are listed in the file **P08_34.xlsx**. Bus 99 will make two stops and anyone who wants to take the bus will walk to the closest bus stop.
   a. If the goal is to minimize the total distance people walk, where should we stop the bus?
   b. If the bus made three stops, how much would the total walking distance be reduced?

35. Ten data sets must be assigned for storage to one of three disk drives. Each disk drive can store 885 MB. The sizes of the data sets (in MB) are listed in the file **P08_35.xlsx**. When many people access a disk drive, there is a significant reduction in the speed at which the data are retrieved. To reduce the number of people accessing a disk drive, we strive to make the data sets on each disk drive as different as possible. To achieve this goal, we have assigned penalties for assigning similar data sets to the same disk drive. These penalties are also listed in the **P08_35.xlsx** file. For example, if data sets 9 and 10 are assigned to the same drive, a penalty of 221 is incurred, whereas if disks 8 and 10 are assigned to the same drive, a penalty of only 35 is incurred. You can think of the penalty as the number of times two data sets are accessed at the same time. Assign the data sets to disk drives to minimize total penalties.

36. Xerox is trying to determine how many maintenance centers are needed in the mid-Atlantic states. Xerox earns $500 profit (excluding the cost of running maintenance centers) on each copier sale. The sales of copiers in each major market (Boston, New York, Philadelphia, Washington, Providence, and Atlantic City) depend on the proximity of the nearest maintenance facility. If a maintenance facility is within 100 miles of a city, sales will be high; if a maintenance facility is within 150 miles of a city, sales will be medium; otherwise, sales will be low. The predicted annual sales (that is, the meaning of low, medium, and high) are listed in the file **P08_36.xlsx**.

   It costs $200,000 per year to place a maintenance representative in a city. It is possible to locate a representative in any city except for Atlantic City and Providence. The distances between the cities are also listed in the file **P08_36.xlsx**. Where should maintenance representatives be located?

## Skill-Extending Problems

37. You are the Democratic campaign manager for the state of Indiana. There are 15 cities in the state of Indiana. The numbers of Democrats and Republican voters in these cities (in thousands) are listed in the file **P08_37.xlsx**. The Democrats control the state legislature, so they can redistrict as they wish. There will be eight congressional districts. Each city must be assigned in its entirety to a single district. Each district must contain between 150,000 and 250,000 voters. Use Evolutionary Solver to assign voters to districts in a way that maximizes the number of districts that will vote Democratic. (*Hint:* You might find it convenient to use the SUMIF function. This function was used frequently in Chapter 5.)

38. Steelco needs to cool 17 pieces of steel. The weight and due date for each piece are listed in the file

**P08_38.xlsx**. Processing and cooling a batch in the furnace takes 5 minutes regardless of the weight in the furnace. The furnace can handle up to 1000 pounds at a time. Jobs 6 and 7 (size 640 and 450, respectively) must be completed on time. How can the company minimize the total time the jobs are late?

39. Suppose you are the ad manager for Fox NFL football. Thirty bids for ads on today's game between the Packers and the Colts have been submitted. Information on these ads is given in the file **P08_39.xlsx**. For example, ad 1 is 23 seconds in length and will bring in $53,000 in revenues. During the game, 14 1-minute slots are available for ads. Determine how Fox can maximize the revenue earned from game ads.

40. Assume that a consumer's purchase decision on an electric razor is based on four attributes, each of which can be set at one of three levels (1, 2, or 3). Using conjoint analysis (a type of analysis used in marketing research), our analysts have divided the market into five segments (labeled as customers 1, 2, 3, 4, and 5) and have determined the "part-worth" that each customer gives to each level of each attribute. These are listed in the file **P08_40.xlsx**. Conjoint analysis usually assumes the customer buys the product yielding the highest total part-worth. Currently there is a single product in the market that sets all four attributes equal to 1. You are going to sell two types of electric razors. Design a product line that maximizes the number of market segments that will buy your product. For example, if you design a product that is level 2 of each attribute, then customer 1 will not buy the product because he values the current product at $1 + 4 + 4 + 4 = 13$ and values your product at $1 + 1 + 1 + 2 = 5$. Assume that in the case of a tie, the consumer does not purchase your product.

41. An important problem in manufacturing is the assembly line balancing problem. When setting up a manufacturing line, activities must be assigned to workstations. The maximum time spent at a workstation is called the cycle time. Minimizing the cycle time translates to maximizing the number of items that can be produced each hour. Here is a typical assembly line balancing problem that can be solved with the Evolutionary Solver. Manufacture of a product consists of 10 activities (A–J) that require the times (in seconds) in the file **P08_41.xlsx** to complete. Certain activities must be completed before others. These precedence relations are also given in the file **P08_41.xlsx**. For example, activity A cannot be performed on a higher numbered workstation than activity B. Use Evolutionary Solver to determine an assignment of activities to workstations that minimizes the total cycle time.

42. A common approach to clustering is called **multidimensional scaling** (MDS). To apply MDS, we rank each pair of objects we want to cluster from least similar (higher number) to most similar (lower number). For example, in the file **P08_42.xlsx**, we compared the similarity of 10 banks and found banks 5 and 10 to be most similar and banks 9 and 10 to be least similar. We now assign a location in the x-y plane to each bank. The goal is to ensure that when we rank the distances between pair of banks, the ordering of these distances matches (as closely as possible) the similarity rankings of the banks.

   a. Constrain each bank to have an x and y coordinate between $-1$ and $+1$ and determine the "location" of each bank. (*Hint:* Use Excel's RANK function to rank the distances from smallest to largest.)
   b. How does this method lead to a natural clustering of banks?
   c. How could you determine whether you need more than two dimensions to adequately locate the banks?

43. Based on Meneses et al. (2004). A string is a list of characters such as "1differ%". The length of the string is the number of characters in the string. The distance between two strings is the number of positions in which the two strings differ. For example, the distance between the strings "1differ%" and "1dizzzr%" is 3. Given a set of strings of the same length, the closest string problem is to find a string of the same length that minimizes the maximum distance between the chosen string and the given list of strings. Consider the following four strings: "median," "differ," "length," and "medium," all with 6 characters. Find a closest string to these strings. (*Hint:* There are many alternative solutions.)

## Modeling Problems

44. The discussion at the beginning of Section 8.8 mentions Claritas. If you were in the direct-mail business, how would you use the information sold by Claritas to improve your profitability?

45. How would you use cluster analysis to help test market a consumer goods product?

46. Your company sells credit card services, and you are concerned with churn. (*Churn* occurs when your customers go to a different company.) Describe how you could use discriminant analysis to learn what distinguishes the customers who switch to another company from those who stay loyal to your company. How might you use such a model?

47. Your company provides credit to customers. Some of these customers default on their loans, with very negative implications for you. Describe how you could use discriminant analysis to learn what distinguishes the customers who default on their loans from those who pay back their loans. How might you use such a model?

The MBA program at State University has approximately 260 incoming students each fall semester. These students are divided into cohorts of approximately 65 students each, and the students in each cohort sit through exactly the same set of fall courses together. Much of the work in these courses is done in teams. To ensure that the teams are comparable, the MBA Office tries to divide the students in each cohort into 14 teams so that each team has the following qualities:

- Four or five members
- At least one member with a CPA
- At least one member with quantitative expertise

- At least one female
- At least one minority student
- At least one international student

The file **MBA Teams.xlsx** indicates the characteristics of the students in a particular cohort of this year's incoming class. Your job is to use the Evolutionary Solver to see if you can create teams that have all of the desired properties. It is not clear whether this will be possible—for example, there might not be enough minority students to go around—so you should create penalties for failing to meet the various goals, where the penalties can be different for different goals. ■

# Multiobjective Decision Making

© EPA/Landov

## EVALUATING AND PRIORITIZING PROJECTS AT NASA

More public pressure than ever before is on NASA to justify its choice of projects to undertake. There is demand for accountability, pressure to cut costs, and an increasing number of potential projects to choose from. In the past, a committee of 15 members from NASA met once a year to review the 30 to 50 proposals submitted by contractors and divisions with the Kennedy Space Center. The five voting members (the decision makers, or DMs) gave each proposal a score from 1 to 10, the scores were averaged over the five DMs, and the top scoring proposals were selected until the budget was exceeded. Because the process was viewed as intuitive, management expressed concern about its subjectivity and consistency. It wanted to replace this process with a more comprehensive and structured process. Tavana (2003) describes the system he developed to meet these needs. He calls it consensus-ranking organizational-support system (CROSS).

The selection of projects at NASA is clearly a multiobjective decision-making problem. As Tavana describes, there are a number of stakeholders for each project. Essentially, they are the different departments within NASA—including Safety, Systems Engineering, Reliability, and others—and each has its own criteria for a successful project. For example, Safety might be concerned about eliminating the possibility of death or serious injury, Systems Engineering might be concerned about eliminating reliance on identified obsolete technology, and Reliability might be concerned about increasing the mean time between failures. CROSS uses AHP (Analytic Hierarchy Process, discussed later in this chapter) to obtain the information each DM needs to obtain a score for each project. It then combines the DMs' scores to get an overall consensus ranking of projects. Finally, it uses this consensus ranking, along with project costs and the overall budget, to select the projects to be funded.

More specifically, the system first asks each DM to use AHP to evaluate the importance of the various stakeholders. For example, one DM might give Safety an importance weight of 0.5, whereas another might give Safety a weight of 0.4. In the next step, each stakeholder is asked to use AHP to evaluate the importance of its various criteria. This leads to a set of weights for each stakeholder–criterion combination. The stakeholders are also asked to estimate the probability that each potential project will be successful in satisfying each criterion. The system uses these probabilities to adjust the previous weights. Next, all of the weights from AHP are used to calculate a project-success factor for each project, as assessed by each DM, and these factors are used to obtain each DM's rankings of the projects. Finally, the system attempts to reach consensus in the rankings using another (non-AHP) methodology.

The system is now being used successfully to select NASA projects. As a measure of its perceived quality, 71 projects were submitted during the first two years of implementation of CROSS. Using this system, the DMs chose 21 projects of the 71, and management subsequently approved all 21 choices. ∎

## 9.1 INTRODUCTION

In many of your classes, you have probably discussed how to make good decisions. Usually, you assume that the correct decision optimizes a *single* objective, such as profit maximization or cost minimization. In most situations you encounter in business and life, however, more than one relevant objective exists. For example, when you graduate, many of you will receive several job offers. Which should you accept? Before deciding which job offer to accept, you might consider how each job "scores" on several objectives, such as salary, interest in work, quality of life in the city you will live in, and nearness to family. In this situation, combining your multiple objectives into a single objective is difficult. Similarly, in determining an optimal investment portfolio, you want to maximize expected return, but you also want to minimize risk. How do you reconcile these conflicting objectives? In this chapter, we discuss three tools, goal programming, trade-off curves, and the Analytic Hierarchy Process (AHP), that decision makers (DMs) can use to solve multiobjective problems. We show how to implement all three of these tools in a spreadsheet.

### FUNDAMENTAL INSIGHT

#### Optimizing with Multiple Objectives

When there are multiple objectives, we can proceed in several fundamental ways. First, we can prioritize the objectives. This is done in goal programming, where we first optimize the highest priority objective, then the second, and so on. Second, we can optimize one objective while constraining the others to be no worse than specified values. This approach is used to find trade-off curves between the objectives. Finally, we can attempt to weight the objectives to measure their importance relative to one another. This is the approach taken by the Analytic Hierarchy Process (AHP). All of these approaches have their critics, but they can all be used to make difficult decision problems manageable.

# 9.2 GOAL PROGRAMMING

In many situations, a company wants to achieve several objectives. Given limited resources, it may prove impossible to meet all objectives simultaneously. If the company can prioritize its objectives, then **goal programming** can be used to make good decisions. The following media selection problem is typical of the situations in which goal programming is useful. This example presents a variation of the advertising model we discussed in Chapters 4 and 7.

---

**EXAMPLE** | **9.1 DETERMINING AN ADVERTISING SCHEDULE AT LEON BURNIT**

The Leon Burnit Ad Agency is trying to determine a TV advertising schedule for a client. The client has three goals (listed here in descending order of importance) concerning whom it wants its ads to be seen by:

- Goal 1: at least 65 million high-income men (HIM)
- Goal 2: at least 72 million high-income women (HIW)
- Goal 3: at least 70 million low-income people (LIP)

Burnit can purchase several types of TV ads: ads shown on live sports shows, on game shows, on news shows, on sitcoms, on dramas, and on soap operas. At most $700,000 total can be spent on ads. The advertising costs and potential audiences (in millions of viewers) of a 1-minute ad of each type are shown in Table 9.1. As a matter of policy, the client requires that at least 2 ads each be placed on sports shows, on news shows, and on dramas. Also, it requires that no more than 10 ads be placed on any single type of show. Burnit wants to find the advertising plan that best meets its client's goals.

---

**Table 9.1    Data for the Advertising Example**

| Ad Type | HIM | HIW | LIP | Cost |
|---|---|---|---|---|
| Sports show | 7 | 4 | 8 | $120,000 |
| Game show | 3 | 5 | 6 | $40,000 |
| News | 6 | 5 | 3 | $50,000 |
| Sitcom | 4 | 5 | 7 | $40,000 |
| Drama | 6 | 8 | 6 | $60,000 |
| Soap opera | 3 | 4 | 5 | $40,000 |

---

**Objective**   To use goal programming to meet the company's goals of reaching various target audiences as much as possible, while staying within an advertising budget.

### WHERE DO THE NUMBERS COME FROM?

As in previous advertising models, the company needs to estimate the number of viewers reached by each type of ad, and it needs to know the cost of each ad. Beyond this, however, management determines the goals. They can set whatever goals they believe are in the company's best interests, and they can prioritize these goals.

## Solution

The variables and constraints for this advertising model are shown in Table 9.2. Most of this is the same as in optimization models in previous chapters. However, the objective is not obvious, and the table includes "deviations from goals" and "balances for goals." We need to see how these fit into the goal programming methodology. We get there one step at a time. We first check whether the company can meet all of its goals simultaneously. To do so, we set up a linear programming (LP) model with *no* objective. We simply want to see whether any solution satisfies all of the constraints, including the goals.

---

**Table 9.2** **Variables and Constraints for the Advertising Model**

| | |
|---|---|
| **Input variables** | Advertising data (potential audiences and cost for each type of ad), advertising budget, goals (lower limits) on various target audiences |
| **Decision variables (changing cells)** | Numbers of ads of various types, deviations from goals |
| **Objective (target cell)** | Multiple (see text) |
| **Other output cells** | Total cost of ads, balances for goals |
| **Constraints** | Ads on sports shows must be greater than or equal to 2 |
| | Ads on news shows must be greater than or equal to 2 |
| | Ads on dramas must be greater than or equal to 2 |
| | Ads on any type of show must be less than or equal to 10 |
| | Total cost of ads must be less than or equal to Advertising budget |
| | Meet goals as well as possible |

---

## DEVELOPING THE LP MODEL

The LP model that checks whether all goals can be met can be developed as follows. (See Figure 9.1 and the LP Model sheet of the file **Advertising Goals.xlsx**.)

---

**Figure 9.1**   Feasibility of Meeting All Goals

| | A | B | C | D | E | F | G | H | I | J |
|---|---|---|---|---|---|---|---|---|---|---|
| 1 | LP model - possible to meet all goals? | | | | | | | | | |
| 2 | | | | Note: All monetary values are in $1000s, and all | | | | | | |
| 3 | | | | exposures to ads are in millions of exposures. | | | | | | |
| 4 | | | | | | | | | | |
| 5 | Exposures to various groups per unit of advertising | | | | | | | | Range names used: | |
| 6 | | Sports ad | Game show ad | News show ad | Sitcom ad | Drama ad | Soap opera ad | | Budget | ='LP Model'!$D$22 |
| 7 | High-income men | 7 | 3 | 6 | 4 | 6 | 3 | | Exposures | ='LP Model'!$B$26:$B$28 |
| 8 | High-income women | 4 | 5 | 5 | 5 | 8 | 4 | | Goal | ='LP Model'!$D$26:$D$28 |
| 9 | Low-income people | 8 | 6 | 3 | 7 | 6 | 5 | | Maximum_ads_allowed | ='LP Model'!$B$19:$G$19 |
| 10 | | | | | | | | | Minimum_ads_required | ='LP Model'!$B$15:$G$15 |
| 11 | Cost/unit | 120 | 40 | 50 | 40 | 60 | 40 | | Number_purchased | ='LP Model'!$B$17:$G$17 |
| 12 | | | | | | | | | Total_cost | ='LP Model'!$B$22 |
| 13 | Advertising plan | | | | | | | | | |
| 14 | | Sports ad | Game show ad | News show ad | Sitcom ad | Drama ad | Soap opera ad | | | |
| 15 | Minimum ads required | 2 | 0 | 2 | 0 | 2 | 0 | | | |
| 16 | | <= | <= | <= | <= | <= | <= | | | |
| 17 | Number purchased | 2.000 | 0.000 | 2.000 | 4.000 | 3.333 | 0.000 | | | |
| 18 | | <= | <= | <= | <= | <= | <= | | | |
| 19 | Maximum ads allowed | 10 | 10 | 10 | 10 | 10 | 10 | | | |
| 20 | | | | | | | | | | |
| 21 | Budget constraint | Total cost | | Budget | | | | | | |
| 22 | | $700 | <= | $700 | | | | | | |
| 23 | | | | | Use Solver, with no objective, to | | | | | |
| 24 | Goals for numbers of exposures | | | | see whether all | | | | | |
| 25 | | Exposures | | Goal | constraints, including goals, can | | | | | |
| 26 | High-income men | 62.000 | >= | 65 | | | | | | |
| 27 | High-income women | 64.667 | >= | 72 | | | | | | |
| 28 | Low-income people | 70.000 | >= | 70 | | | | | | |

---

**①** **Inputs.** Enter all inputs in the blue ranges.

**②** **Numbers of ads.** Enter *any* trial values for the numbers of ads in the Number_purchased range.

**③** **Total cost.** Calculate the total amount spent on ads in cell B22 with the formula

**=SUMPRODUCT(B11:G11,Number_purchased)**

SOLVER

**4** **Exposures obtained.** Calculate the number of people (in millions) in each group that the ads reach in the Exposures range. Specifically, enter the formula

**=SUMPRODUCT(B7:G7,Number_purchased)**

in cell B26 for the HIM group, and copy this to the rest of the Exposures range for the other two groups.

## USING SOLVER

The completed Solver dialog box is shown in Figure 9.2. At this point, there is no objective to maximize or minimize. We are simply looking for *any* solution that meets all of the constraints. When we click on Solve, we get the message that there is no feasible solution because it is impossible to meet all of the client's goals and stay within the budget. To see how large the budget must be to meet all goals, we ran SolverTable with the Budget cell as the single input cell, varied from 700 to 850, and *any* cells as the output cells. (We chose the numbers of exposures cells as output cells.) The results appear in Figure 9.3. They show that unless the budget is greater than $750,000, it is impossible to meet all of the client's goals.

**Figure 9.2**

**Solver Dialog Box for Finding a Feasible Solution**

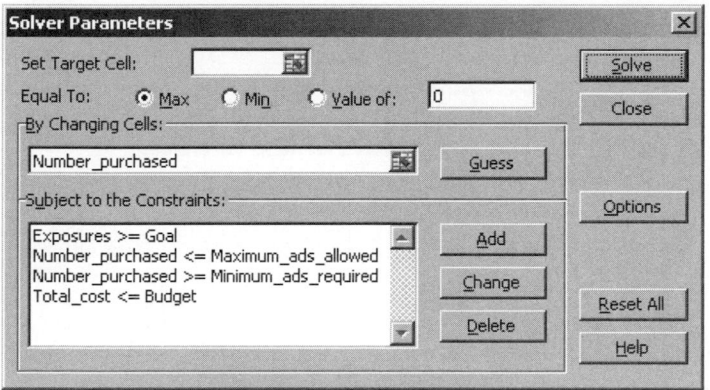

**Figure 9.3**

**Checking How Large the Budget Must Be**

| | A | B | C | D |
|---|---|---|---|---|
| 30 | Sensitivity to budget (to see how large it must be to meet all goals) | | | |
| 31 | | $B$26 | $B$27 | $B$28 |
| 32 | 700 | Not feasible | | |
| 33 | 725 | Not feasible | | |
| 34 | 750 | Not feasible | | |
| 35 | 775 | 65.000 | 72.000 | 70.000 |
| 36 | 800 | 65.000 | 72.000 | 70.000 |
| 37 | 825 | 65.000 | 72.000 | 70.000 |
| 38 | 850 | 65.000 | 72.000 | 70.000 |

*Hard constraints must be satisfied. Soft constraints can be violated to some extent. In goal programming, the soft constraints are prioritized.*

Now that we know that a $700,000 budget is not sufficient to meet all of the client's goals, we use goal programming to see how close Burnit can come to these goals. First, we introduce some terminology. The upper limits and lower limits on the ads of each type and the budget constraints are considered **hard constraints** in this model. This means that they cannot be violated under any circumstances. The goals on exposures, on the other hand, are considered **soft constraints.** The client certainly wants to satisfy these goals but is willing to come up somewhat short—in fact, it must because of the limited budget. In goal programming models, the soft constraints are prioritized. We first try to satisfy the goals with the highest priority (in this case, HIM exposures). If there is still any room to maneuver, we then try to satisfy the goals with the next highest priority (HIW exposures). If there is *still* room to maneuver, we move on to the goals with the third highest priority, and so on.

## DEVELOPING THE GOAL PROGRAMMING MODEL

In general, goal programming requires several consecutive Solver runs, one for each priority level. However, the model can be set up so that we can make these consecutive runs with only minor modifications from one run to the next. We illustrate the procedure in Figure 9.4. (See the GP Model sheet of the file **Advertising Goals.xlsx**.) To develop this model, first make a copy of the original LP Model sheet shown earlier in Figure 9.1. Then modify it using the following steps:

**Figure 9.4** Minimizing Deviation for Highest Priority (HIM) Goal

| | A | B | C | D | E | F | G | H | I | J |
|---|---|---|---|---|---|---|---|---|---|---|
| 1 | Goal programming model | | | | | | | | | |
| 2 | | | | Note: All monetary values are in $1000s, and all | | | | | | |
| 3 | | | | exposures to ads are in millions of exposures. | | | | | | |
| 4 | | | | | | | | | | |
| 5 | Exposures to various groups per unit of advertising | | | | | | | | Range names used: | |
| 6 | | Sports ad | Game show ad | News show ad | Sitcom ad | Drama ad | Soap opera ad | | Already_obtained | ='GP Model'!$D$32:$D$34 |
| 7 | High-income men | 7 | 3 | 6 | 4 | 6 | 3 | | Amt_over_goal | ='GP Model'!$D$26:$D$28 |
| 8 | High-income women | 4 | 5 | 5 | 5 | 8 | 4 | | Amt_under_goal | ='GP Model'!$C$26:$C$28 |
| 9 | Low-income people | 8 | 6 | 3 | 7 | 6 | 5 | | Balance | ='GP Model'!$E$26:$E$28 |
| 10 | | | | | | | | | Budget | ='GP Model'!$D$22 |
| 11 | Cost/unit | 120 | 40 | 50 | 40 | 60 | 40 | | Deviation_under | ='GP Model'!$B$32:$B$34 |
| 12 | | | | | | | | | Exposures | ='GP Model'!$B$26:$B$28 |
| 13 | Advertising plan | | | | | | | | Goal | ='GP Model'!$G$26:$G$28 |
| 14 | | Sports ad | Game show ad | News show ad | Sitcom ad | Drama ad | Soap opera ad | | HIM_deviation | ='GP Model'!$B$32 |
| 15 | Minimum ads required | 2 | 0 | 2 | 0 | 2 | 0 | | HIW_deviation | ='GP Model'!$B$33 |
| 16 | | <= | <= | <= | <= | <= | <= | | LIP_deviation | ='GP Model'!$B$34 |
| 17 | Number purchased | 2.000 | 0.000 | 5.000 | 2.250 | 2.000 | 0.000 | | Maximum_ads_allowed | ='GP Model'!$B$19:$G$19 |
| 18 | | <= | <= | <= | <= | <= | <= | | Minimum_ads_required | ='GP Model'!$B$15:$G$15 |
| 19 | Maximum ads allowed | 10 | 10 | 10 | 10 | 10 | 10 | | Number_purchased | ='GP Model'!$B$17:$G$17 |
| 20 | | | | | | | | | Total_cost | ='GP Model'!$B$22 |
| 21 | Budget constraint | Total cost | | Budget | | | | | | |
| 22 | | $700 | <= | $700 | | | | | | |
| 23 | | | | | | | | | | |
| 24 | Goals for numbers of exposures | | | | | | | | | |
| 25 | | Exposures | Amt under goal | Amt over goal | Balance | | Goal | | | |
| 26 | High-income men | 65.000 | 0 | 0 | 65.000 | = | 65 | | | |
| 27 | High-income women | 60.250 | 11.75 | 0 | 72.000 | = | 72 | | | |
| 28 | Low-income people | 58.750 | 11.25 | 0 | 70.000 | = | 70 | | | |
| 29 | | | | | | | | | | |
| 30 | Deviations from goals (amounts below goals, or 0 if currently meeting goal) | | | | Initially, enter large values in these cells | | | | | |
| 31 | | Deviation under | | Already obtained | (such as the original goals). Then, as high | | | | | |
| 32 | HIM deviation | 0.000 | <= | 65.000 | priority goals are met or partially | | | | | |
| 33 | HIW deviation | 11.750 | <= | 72.000 | met, enter the actual deviations obtained | | | | | |
| 34 | LIP deviation | 11.250 | <= | 70.000 | here (one at a time). | | | | | |

**①** **New changing cells.** The exposure constraints are no longer shown as hard constraints. Instead, we introduce changing cells in the Amt_under_goal and Amt_over_goal ranges to indicate how much under or over each goal we are. These are the "deviations from goals" mentioned in Table 9.2. Enter any values in these ranges. (We entered 0's to get started.) Note that in the Solver solution, at least one of these two types of deviations will always be 0 for each goal—we will either be below the goal or above the goal, but not both.

**②** **Balance equations.** To tie these new changing cells to the rest of the model, we create "balances" in column E that must logically equal the goals in column G. To do this, enter the formula

=B26+C26-D26

in cell E26 and copy it down. The balance equation for each group specifies that the actual number of exposures, plus the number under the goal, minus the number over the goal, *must* equal the goal.

**3 Constraints on deviations under.** The client is concerned only with too *few* exposures, not with too many. Therefore, we set up constraints on the "under" deviations in rows 32 to 34. On the left side, in column B, enter links to the Amt_under_goals range by entering the formula

=C26

in cell B32 and copying down.

**4 Highest priority goal.** The first Solver run tries to achieve the highest priority goal (HIM exposures). To do so, we minimize cell B32, the amount *under* the HIM goal. Do this as shown in Figure 9.4. Then set up the Solver dialog box as shown in Figure 9.5. (Also, check the Assume Linear Model and Assume Non-Negative boxes.) The constraints include the hard constraints, the balance constraint, and the Deviation_under <= Already_obtained constraint. Note that we have entered the goals themselves in the Already_obtained range. Therefore, the Deviation_under <= Already_obtained constraint at this point is essentially redundant—the under deviations cannot possibly be greater than the goals themselves. We include this constraint because it becomes important in later Solver runs, which then require only minimal modifications. The solution from this Solver run is shown in Figure 9.4. It shows that Burnit can satisfy the HIM goal completely. However, the other two goals are not satisfied because their under deviations are positive.

**Figure 9.5**

Solver Dialog Box for the Highest Priority Goal

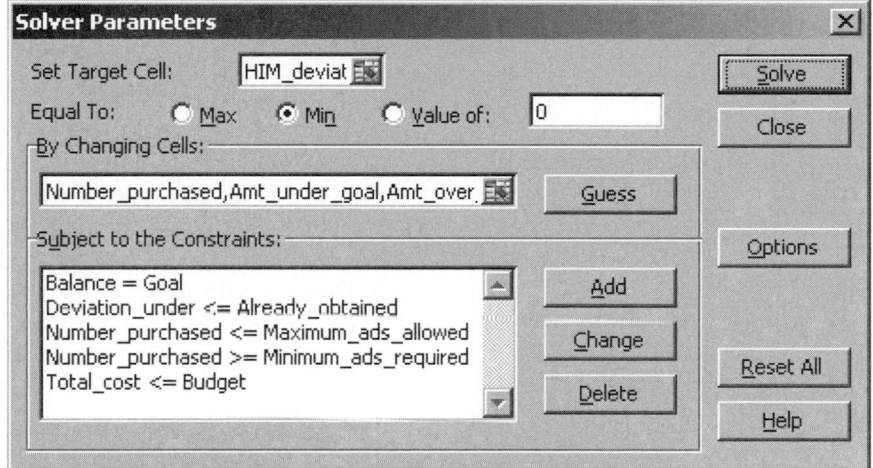

**5 Second highest priority goal.** Now we come to the key aspect of goal programming. After a high priority goal is satisfied as fully as possible, we move on to the next highest priority goal. However, we do not want to lose what we already gained with the high priority goal. Therefore, we constrain its under deviation to be no greater than what we have already achieved. In this case, we achieved a deviation of 0 in step 4, so enter 0 in cell D32 for the upper limit of the HIM under deviation. Then run Solver again, changing only one thing in the Solver dialog box—make cell B33 the target cell. Effectively, we are constraining the under deviation for the HIM group to remain at 0, and we are then minimizing the under deviation for the HIW group. The solution from this second Solver run appears in Figure 9.6. As we promised, the HIM goal has not suffered at all, but we are now a little closer to the HIW goal than before. It was under by 11.75 before, and now it is under by only 11. The lowest priority goal (for the LIP group) essentially comes along for the ride in this step as it could either improve or get worse. It happened to get worse, moving from under by 11.25 to under by 18.

**Figure 9.6** Minimizing Deviation for Second Priority Goal

| | A | B | C | D | E | F | G | H | I | J |
|---|---|---|---|---|---|---|---|---|---|---|
| 1 | Goal programming model | | | | | | | | | |
| 2 | | | | Note: All monetary values are in $1000s, and all | | | | | | |
| 3 | | | | exposures to ads are in millions of exposures. | | | | | | |
| 4 | | | | | | | | | | |
| 5 | Exposures to various groups per unit of advertising | | | | | | | | Range names used: | |
| 6 | | Sports ad | Game show ad | News show ad | Sitcom ad | Drama ad | Soap opera ad | | Already_obtained | ='GP Model'!$D$32:$D$34 |
| 7 | High-income men | 7 | 3 | 6 | 4 | 6 | 3 | | Amt_over_goal | ='GP Model'!$D$26:$D$28 |
| 8 | High-income women | 4 | 5 | 5 | 5 | 8 | 4 | | Amt_under_goal | ='GP Model'!$C$26:$C$28 |
| 9 | Low-income people | 8 | 6 | 3 | 7 | 6 | 5 | | Balance | ='GP Model'!$E$26:$E$28 |
| 10 | | | | | | | | | Budget | ='GP Model'!$D$22 |
| 11 | Cost/unit | 120 | 40 | 50 | 40 | 60 | 40 | | Deviation_under | ='GP Model'!$B$32:$B$34 |
| 12 | | | | | | | | | Exposures | ='GP Model'!$B$26:$B$28 |
| 13 | Advertising plan | | | | | | | | Goal | ='GP Model'!$G$26:$G$28 |
| 14 | | Sports ad | Game show ad | News show ad | Sitcom ad | Drama ad | Soap opera ad | | HIM_deviation | ='GP Model'!$B$32 |
| 15 | Minimum ads required | 2 | 0 | 2 | 0 | 2 | 0 | | HIW_deviation | ='GP Model'!$B$33 |
| 16 | | <= | <= | <= | <= | <= | <= | | LIP_deviation | ='GP Model'!$B$34 |
| 17 | Number purchased | 2.000 | 0.000 | 5.000 | 0.000 | 3.500 | 0.000 | | Maximum_ads_allowed | ='GP Model'!$G$19 |
| 18 | | <= | <= | <= | <= | <= | <= | | Minimum_ads_required | ='GP Model'!$G$15 |
| 19 | Maximum ads allowed | 10 | 10 | 10 | 10 | 10 | 10 | | Number_purchased | ='GP Model'!$G$17 |
| 20 | | | | | | | | | Total_cost | ='GP Model'!$B$22 |
| 21 | Budget constraint | Total cost | | Budget | | | | | | |
| 22 | | $700 | <= | $700 | | | | | | |
| 23 | | | | | | | | | | |
| 24 | Goals for numbers of exposures | | | | | | | | | |
| 25 | | Exposures | Amt under goal | Amt over goal | Balance | | Goal | | | |
| 26 | High-income men | 65.000 | 0 | 0 | 65.000 | = | 65 | | | |
| 27 | High-income women | 61.000 | 11 | 0 | 72.000 | = | 72 | | | |
| 28 | Low-income people | 52.000 | 18 | 0 | 70.000 | = | 70 | | | |
| 29 | | | | | | | | | | |
| 30 | Deviations from goals (amounts below goals, or 0 if currently meeting goal) | | | | | | | | | |
| 31 | | Deviation under | | Already obtained | | | | | | |
| 32 | HIM deviation | 0.000 | <= | 0.000 | | | | | | |
| 33 | HIW deviation | 11.000 | <= | 72.000 | | | | | | |
| 34 | LIP deviation | 18.000 | <= | 70.000 | | | | | | |

Initially, enter large values in these cells (such as the original goals). Then, as high priority goals are met or partially met, enter the actual deviations obtained here (one at a time).

**6 Lowest priority goal.** You can probably guess the last step by now. We minimize cell B34, the deviation for the LIP group, while ensuring that the two higher priority goals are achieved as fully as in steps 4 and 5. As the model is set up, only two changes are necessary—enter 11 in cell D33 and change the Solver target cell to cell B34. When you run Solver this time, however, you will find no room left to maneuver. The solution remains exactly the same as in Figure 9.6. This occurs frequently in goal programming models. After satisfying the first goal or two as fully as possible, there is often no room to improve later goals.

### Discussion of the Solution

To summarize Burnit's situation, the budget of $700,000 allows it to satisfy the client's HIM goal, miss the HIW goal by 11 million, and miss the LIP goal by 18 million. Given the priorities on these three goals, this is the best possible solution. Note that all of the hard constraints are satisfied, as they must be. For example, no more than 10 ads of any type are used, and the budget is not exceeded. Note also that the amounts *over* the goals are all 0. This is not guaranteed to happen, but it did in this example.

### Sensitivity Analysis

Sensitivity analysis should be a part of goal programming just as it is for previous models we have discussed. However, there is no quick way to do it (at least none we know of). SolverTable works on only a *single* objective, whereas goal programming requires a sequence of objectives. Therefore, if we want to see how the solution to Burnit's model changes with different budgets, say, we need to go through the preceding steps several times and keep track of the results manually. This is certainly possible, but it is tedious.

### Effect of Changing Priorities

With three goals, six orderings of the goals are possible. The goal programming solutions corresponding to these orderings are listed in Figure 9.7. Row 4 corresponds to the ordering we used in the example. Clearly, the solution can change if the priorities of the goals change. For example, when we give the HIW goal the highest priority (rows 6, 7), *none* of the goals are achieved completely. (Problem 1 asks you to verify the details.)

**Figure 9.7** Effect of Changing Priorities

| | A | B | C | D | E | F | G | H | I | J | K | L |
|---|---|---|---|---|---|---|---|---|---|---|---|---|
| 1 | Results from changing priorities | | | | | | | | | | | |
| 2 | | | | | | | | | | | | |
| 3 | Priority 1 | Priority 2 | Priority 3 | HIM deviation | HIW deviation | LIP deviation | Sports ad | Game show ad | News show ad | Sitcom ad | Drama ad | Soap opera ad |
| 4 | HIM | HIW | LIP | 0 | 11 | 18 | 2 | 0 | 5 | 0 | 3.5 | 0 |
| 5 | HIM | LIP | HIW | 0 | 11.75 | 11.25 | 2 | 0 | 5 | 2.25 | 2 | 0 |
| 6 | HIW | HIM | LIP | 3 | 6 | 12 | 2 | 0 | 2 | 0 | 6 | 0 |
| 7 | HIW | LIP | HIM | 3 | 6 | 12 | 2 | 0 | 2 | 0 | 6 | 0 |
| 8 | LIP | HIM | HIW | 1.956 | 9.304 | 0 | 2 | 0 | 3.043 | 4.696 | 2 | 0 |
| 9 | LIP | HIW | HIM | 3 | 7.333 | 0 | 2 | 0 | 2 | 4 | 3.333 | 0 |

■

## MODELING ISSUES

1.  The results for the Burnit model are based on allowing the numbers of ads to have noninteger values. They can easily be constrained to integer values, and the solution method remains exactly the same. However, the goals might not be met as fully as before because of the extra integer constraints.

2.  Each priority level in the Burnit model contains exactly one goal. It is easy to generalize to the case where a given priority level can have multiple goals, each modeled with a certain deviation from a target. When we run Solver for this priority level, we use a weighted average of these deviations as the objective to minimize, where the decision maker can choose appropriate weights.

3.  All of the deviations in the objectives of the Burnit model are *under* deviations. However, it is certainly possible to include *over* deviations as objectives. For example, if the budget constraint were treated as a soft constraint, we would try to minimize its over deviation to stay as little over the budget as possible. It is even possible for *both* the under and over deviations of some goal to be included as objectives. This occurs in situations where we want to come as close as possible to some target value—neither under nor over.

4.  The use of changing cells for the under and over deviations might not be intuitive; however, it serves two purposes. First, it provides exactly the information we need for the objectives in goal programming. Second, it keeps the model linear. We tried using an IF function instead (without the under and over cells) to capture the under deviations. It looks great, but even when we uncheck the Assume Linear Model box, the Solver obtains the wrong answer! ■

## Skill-Building Problems

1. For each set of priorities of goals, solve the Burnit problem and verify that the values in Figure 9.7 are correct.

2. Gotham City must determine how to allocate ambulances during the next year. It costs $5000 per year to run an ambulance. Each ambulance must be assigned to one of two districts. Let $x_i$ be the number of ambulances assigned to district $i$, $i = 1$, 2. The average time (in minutes) it takes for an ambulance to respond to a call from district 1 is $40 - 3x_1$; for district 2, the time is $50 - 4x_2$. Gotham City has three goals (listed in order of priority):
   - Goal 1: At most $100,000 per year should be spent on ambulance service.
   - Goal 2: Average response time in district 1 should be at most five minutes.
   - Goal 3: Average response time in district 2 should be at most five minutes.
   a. Use goal programming to determine how many ambulances to assign to each district.
   b. How does your answer change if goal 2 has the highest priority, then goal 3, and then goal 1?

3. Fruit Computer Company is ready to make its annual purchase of computer chips. Fruit can purchase chips (in lots of 100) from three suppliers. Each chip's quality is rated as excellent, good, or mediocre. During the coming year, Fruit needs 5000 excellent chips, 3000 good chips, and 1000 mediocre chips. The characteristics of the chips purchased from each supplier are shown in the file **P09_03.xlsx**. Each year, Fruit has budgeted $28,000 to spend on chips. If Fruit does not obtain enough chips of a given quality, it can special-order additional chips at $10 per excellent chip, $6 per good chip, and $4 per mediocre chip. Fruit assesses a penalty of $1 for each dollar it goes over the annual budget (in payments to suppliers). Determine how Fruit can minimize the penalty associated with meeting the annual chip requirements. Also use goal programming to determine a purchasing strategy. Let the budget constraint have the highest priority, followed in order by the restrictions on excellent, good, and mediocre chips.

4. Hiland Appliance must determine how many TVs and DVD players to stock. It costs Hiland $300 to purchase a TV and $200 to purchase a DVD player. A TV requires 3 square yards of storage space, and a DVD player requires 1 square yard. The sale of a TV earns Hiland a profit of $150, and each DVD player sale earns a profit of $100. Hiland has set the following goals (listed in order of importance):
   - Goal 1: A maximum of $20,000 can be spent on purchasing TVs and DVD players.
   - Goal 2: Highland should earn at least $11,000 profit from the sale of TVs and DVD players.
   - Goal 3: TVs and DVD players should not use up more than 200 square yards of storage space.

   Use a goal programming model to determine how many TVs and DVD players Hiland should order. How can you modify the model if Hiland's second goal is to have a profit of *exactly* $11,000?

5. Each week, Stockco produces two products. Relevant information for each product is shown in the file **P09_05.xlsx**. Stockco has a goal of $48 in weekly profit and incurs a $1 penalty for each dollar it falls short of this goal. A total of 32 hours of labor are available. A $2 penalty is incurred for each hour of overtime (labor over 32 hours) used, and a $1 penalty is incurred for each hour of available labor that is unused. Marketing considerations require that at least 7 units of product 1 be produced and at least 10 units of product 2 be produced. For each unit (of either product) by which production falls short of demand, a penalty of $5 is assessed.
   a. Determine how to minimize the total penalty incurred by Stockco.
   b. Suppose the company sets (in order of importance) the following goals:
      - Goal 1: Avoid underuse of labor.
      - Goal 2: Meet demand for product 1.
      - Goal 3: Meet demand for product 2.
      - Goal 4: Do not use any overtime.

   Use goal programming to determine an optimal production schedule.

6. Based on Steuer (1984). Deancorp produces sausage by blending beef head, pork chuck, mutton, and water. The cost per pound, fat per pound, and protein per pound for these ingredients are listed in the file **P09_06.xlsx**. Deancorp needs to produce 100 pounds of sausage and has set the following goals, listed in order of priority:
   - Goal 1: Sausage should consist of at least 15% protein.
   - Goal 2: Sausage should consist of at most 8% fat.
   - Goal 3: Cost per pound of sausage should not exceed $0.08.

   Use a goal programming model to determine the composition of sausage.

7. Based on Welling (1977). The Touche Young accounting firm must complete three jobs during the next month. Job 1 will require 500 hours of work, job 2 will require 300 hours, and job 3 will require 100 hours. At present, the firm consists of 5 partners, 5 senior employees, and 5 junior employees, each of whom can work up to 40 hours per week. The dollar amount (per hour) that the company can bill depends on the type of accountant assigned to each job, as shown in the file **P09_07.xlsx**. (The "X" indicates that a junior employee does not have enough experience to work on job 1.) All jobs must be completed. Touche Young has also set the following goals, listed in order of priority:
   - Goal 1: Monthly billings should exceed $74,000.
   - Goal 2: At most one partner should be hired.
   - Goal 3: At most three senior employees should be hired.
   - Goal 4: At most one junior employee should be hired.

   Use goal programming to help Touche solve its problem.

8. There are 4 teachers in the Faber College Business School. Each semester, 200 students take each of the following courses: Marketing, Finance, Production, and Statistics. The "effectiveness" of each teacher in teaching each course is given in the file **P09_08.xlsx**. Each teacher can teach a total of 200 students during the semester. The dean has set a goal of obtaining an average teaching effectiveness level of at least 6 in each course. Deviations from this goal in any course are considered equally important. Determine the semester's teaching assignments.

9. The city of Bloomington has 17 neighborhoods. The number of high school students in each neighborhood and the time required to drive from each neighborhood to each of the city's two high schools (North and South) are listed in the file **P09_09.xlsx**. The Bloomington Board of Education needs to determine how to assign students to high schools. All students in a given neighborhood must be assigned to the same high school. The Board has set (in order of priority, from highest to lowest) the following goals:
   - Goal 1: Ensure that the difference in enrollment at the two high schools differs by at most 50.
   - Goal 2: Ensure that average student travel time is at most 13 minutes.
   - Goal 3: Ensure that at most 4% of the students must travel at least 25 minutes to school.
   a. Determine an optimal assignment of students to high schools.
   b. If the enrollment at the two high schools can differ by at most 100 (a change in goal 1), how does your answer change?

## Skill-Extending Problems

10. Based on Lee and Moore (1974). Faber College is admitting students for the class of 2007. Data on its applicants are shown in the file **P09_10.xlsx**. Each row indicates the number of in-state or out-of-state applicants with a given SAT score who plan to be business or nonbusiness majors. For example, 1900 of its in-state applicants have a 700 SAT score, and 1500 of these applicants plan to major in business. Faber has set four goals for this class, listed in order of priority:
    - Goal 1: The entering class should include at least 5000 students.
    - Goal 2: The entering class should have an average SAT score of at least 640.
    - Goal 3: The entering class should consist of at least 25% out-of-state students.
    - Goal 4: At least 2000 members of the entering class should not be business majors.

    Use goal programming to determine how many applicants of each type to admit. Assume that all applicants who are admitted will decide to attend Faber.

11. During the next 4 quarters, Wivco faces the following demands for globots: quarter 1, 13; quarter 2, 14; quarter 3, 12; quarter 4, 15. Globots can be produced by regular-time labor or by overtime labor. Production capacity (number of globots) and production costs during the next 4 quarters are shown in the file **P09_11.xlsx**. Wivco has set the following goals in order of importance:
    - Goal 1: Each quarter's demand should be met on time.
    - Goal 2: Inventory at the end of each quarter should not exceed 3 units.
    - Goal 3: Total production cost should be no greater than $250.

    Use a goal programming model to determine Wivco's production schedule for the next 4 quarters. Assume that at the beginning of the first quarter, 1 globot is in inventory.

12. Lucy's Music Store at present employs 5 full-time employees and 3 part-time employees. The normal workload is 40 hours per week for full-time employees and 20 hours per week for part-time employees. Each full-time employee is paid $6 per hour for work up to 40 hours per week and can sell 5 recordings per hour. A full-time employee who works overtime is paid $10 per hour. Each part-time employee is paid $3 per hour and can sell 3 recordings per hour. It costs Lucy $6 to buy a recording, and each recording sells for $9. Lucy has weekly fixed expenses of $500. She has established the following weekly goals, in order of priority:
    - Goal 1: Sell at least 1600 recordings per week.
    - Goal 2: Earn a profit of at least $2200 per week.

- Goal 3: Full-time employees should work at most 100 hours of overtime.
- Goal 4: To promote a sense of job security, the number of hours by which each full-time employee fails to work 40 hours should be minimized.

Use a goal programming model to determine how many hours per week each employee should work.

13. Based on Taylor and Keown (1984). Gotham City is trying to determine the type and location of recreational facilities to build during the next decade. Four types of facilities are under consideration: golf courses, swimming pools, gymnasiums, and tennis courts. Six sites are under consideration. If a golf course is built, it must be built at either site 1 or site 6. Other facilities can be built at sites 2 through 5. The amounts of available land (in thousands of square feet) at sites 2 through 5 are given in the file **P09_13.xlsx**. The cost of building each facility (in thousands of dollars), the annual maintenance cost (in thousands of dollars) for each facility, and the land (in thousands of square feet) required for each facility are also given in the file **P09_13.xlsx**. The number of user days (in thousands) for each type of facility, also shown in this file, depends on where it is built.

   a. Consider the following set of priorities:
   - Priority 1: The amount of land used at each site should be no greater than the amount of land available.
   - Priority 2: Construction costs should not exceed $1.2 million.
   - Priority 3: User days should exceed 200,000.
   - Priority 4: Annual maintenance costs should not exceed $200,000.

   For this set of priorities, use goal programming to determine the type and location of recreation facilities in Gotham City.

   b. Consider the following set of priorities:
   - Priority 1: The amount of land used at each site should be no greater than the amount of land available.
   - Priority 2: User days should exceed 200,000.
   - Priority 3: Construction costs should not exceed $1.2 million.
   - Priority 4: Annual maintenance costs should not exceed $200,000.

   For this set of priorities, use goal programming to determine the type and location of recreation facilities in Gotham City.

14. A small aerospace company is considering eight projects:
   - Project 1: Develop an automated test facility.
   - Project 2: Bar code all inventory and machinery.
   - Project 3: Introduce a CAD/CAM system.
   - Project 4: Buy a new lathe and deburring system.
   - Project 5: Institute an FMS (Flexible Manufacturing System).
   - Project 6: Install a LAN (Local Area Network).
   - Project 7: Develop an AIS (Artificial Intelligence Simulation).
   - Project 8: Set up a TQM (Total Quality Management) program.

   Each project has been rated on five attributes: return on investment (ROI), cost, productivity improvement, workforce requirements, and degree of technological risk. These ratings are given in the file **P09_14.xlsx**. The company has set the following five goals (listed in order of priority):
   - Goal 1: Achieve an ROI of at least $3250.
   - Goal 2: Limit cost to $1300.
   - Goal 3: Achieve a productivity improvement of at least 6.
   - Goal 4: Limit workforce use to 108.
   - Goal 5: Limit technological risk to a total of 4.

   Use goal programming to determine which projects should be undertaken.

15. A new president has just been elected and has set the following economic goals (listed from highest to lowest priority):
   - Goal 1: Balance the budget (this means revenues are at least as large as costs).
   - Goal 2: Cut spending by at most $150 billion.
   - Goal 3: Raise at most $550 billion in taxes from the upper class.
   - Goal 4: Raise at most $350 billion in taxes from the lower class.

   Currently the government spends $1 trillion per year. Revenue can be raised in two ways: through a gas tax and through an income tax. You must determine $G$, the per-gallon tax rate (in cents); $T_1$, the tax rate charged on the first $30,000 of income; $T_2$, the tax rate charged on any income earned over $30,000; and $C$, the cut in spending (in billions). If the government chooses $G$, $T_1$, and $T_2$, then we assume that the revenue given in the file **P09_15.xlsx** (in billions of dollars) is raised. Of course, the tax rate on income over $30,000 must be at least as large as the tax rate on the first $30,000 of income. Use goal programming to help the president meet his goals.

16. The HAL computer must determine which of eight research and development (R&D) projects to undertake. For each project, four quantities are of interest: (1) the net present value (NPV, in millions of dollars) of the project; (2) the annual growth rate in sales generated by the project; (3) the probability that the project will succeed; and (4) the cost (in millions of dollars) of the project. The relevant information is

given in the file **P09_16.xlsx**. HAL has set the following four goals:

- Goal 1: The total NPV of all chosen projects should be at least $200 million.
- Goal 2: The average probability of success for all projects chosen should be at least 0.75.
- Goal 3: The average growth rate of all projects chosen should be at least 15%.
- Goal 4: The total cost of all chosen projects should be at most $1 billion.

For the following sets of priorities, use (integer) goal programming to determine the projects that should be selected.
  **a.** Goal 2, Goal 4, Goal 1, Goal 3.
  **b.** Goal 1, Goal 3, Goal 4, Goal 2.

17. Based on Klingman and Phillips (1984). The Marines need to fill three types of jobs in two cities (Los Angeles and Chicago). The numbers of jobs of each type that must be filled in each city are shown in the file **P09_17.xlsx**. The Marines available to fill these jobs have been classified into six groups according to the types of jobs each person is capable of doing, the type of job each person prefers, and the city in which each person prefers to live. The data for each of these six groups are also listed in this file. The Marines have the following three goals, listed from highest priority to lowest priority:

- Goal 1: Ensure that all jobs are filled by qualified workers.

- Goal 2: Ensure that at least 8000 employees are assigned to the jobs they prefer.
- Goal 3: Ensure that at least 8000 employees are assigned to their preferred cities.

Determine how the Marines should assign their workers. (*Note:* You may allow fractional assignments of workers.)

18. Based on Vasko et al. (1987). Bethlehem Steel can fill orders using five different types of steel molds. Up to three different molds of each type can be purchased. Each individual mold can be used to fill up to 100 orders per year. Six different types of orders must be filled during the coming year. The waste (in tons) incurred if a type of mold is used to fill an order is shown in the file **P09_18.xlsx** (where an "x" indicates that a type of mold cannot be used to fill an order). The number of each order type that must be filled during the coming year is also shown in this file. Bethlehem Steel has the following two goals, listed in order of priority.

- Goal 1: Because molds are very expensive, Bethlehem wants to use at most five molds.
- Goal 2: Bethlehem wants to have at most 600 tons of total waste.

Use goal programming to determine how Bethlehem should fill the coming year's orders.

## 9.3 PARETO OPTIMALITY AND TRADE-OFF CURVES

In a multiobjective problem with no uncertainty, we often search for Pareto optimal solutions. We assume that the decision maker has exactly two objectives and that the set of feasible points under consideration must satisfy a prescribed set of constraints.

First, we need to define some terms. A solution (call it *A*) to a multiobjective problem is called **Pareto optimal** if no other feasible solution is at least as good as *A* with respect to every objective and strictly better than *A* with respect to at least one objective. A related concept is **domination.** We say a feasible solution *B* **dominates** a feasible solution *A* to a multiobjective problem if *B* is at least as good as *A* on every objective and is strictly better than *A* on at least one objective. From this definition, it follows that Pareto optimal solutions are feasible solutions that are not dominated.

If we graph the "score" of all Pareto optimal solutions in the *x–y* plane with the *x*-axis score being the score on objective 1 and the *y*-axis score being the score on objective 2, the graph is called a **trade-off curve.** It is also called the **efficient frontier.** To illustrate, suppose that the set of feasible solutions for a multiobjective problem is the shaded region bounded by the curve *AB* and the axes in Figure 9.8. If we want to maximize both objectives 1 and 2, then the curve *AB* is the set of Pareto optimal points. All points below the *AB* curve are dominated by points on the curve.

**Figure 9.8**

Trade-off Curve for Maximizing Two Objectives

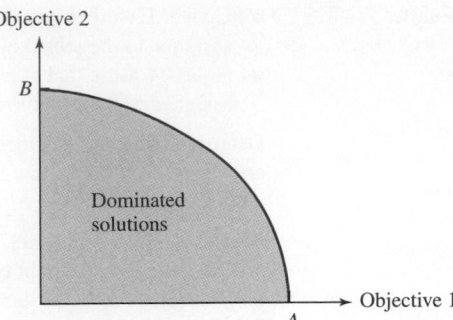

As another illustration, suppose the set of feasible solutions for a multiple-objective problem is all shaded points in the first quadrant bounded from below by the curve *AB* in Figure 9.9. If our goal is to maximize objective 1 and minimize objective 2, then the curve *AB* is the set of Pareto optimal points. In this case, all points to the left of the curve are dominated by points on the curve.

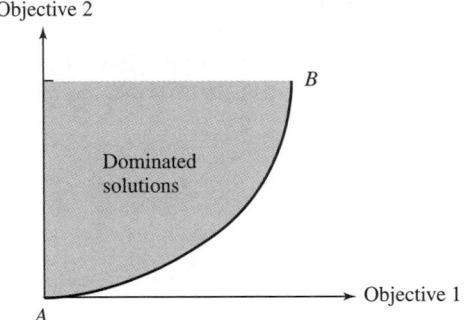

## Finding a Trade-off Curve

To find a trade-off curve, we can proceed according to the following steps.

1.  Choose an objective, say objective 1, and determine its best attainable value $V_1$. For the solution attaining $V_1$, find the value of objective 2 and label it $V_2$. Then $(V_1, V_2)$ is a point on the trade-off curve.

2.  For values $V$ of objective 2 that are better than $V_2$, solve the optimization problem in step 1 with the additional constraint that the value of objective 2 is at least as good as $V$. Varying $V$ (over values of $V$ preferred to $V_2$) yields other points on the trade-off curve.

3.  Step 1 located one endpoint of the trade-off curve. Now determine the best value of objective 2 that can be attained, to obtain the other endpoint of the trade-off curve.

We illustrate the concept of Pareto optimality (and how to determine Pareto optimal solutions) with the following example.

EXAMPLE | **9.2 MAXIMIZING PROFIT AND MINIMIZING POLLUTION AT CHEMCON**

Chemcon plans to produce eight products. The profit per unit, the labor and raw material used per unit produced, and the pollution emitted per unit produced are given in Table 9.3. This table also includes lower and upper limits on production that Chemcon has imposed. Currently 1300 labor hours and 1000 units of raw material are available. Chemcon's two objectives are to maximize profit and minimize pollution produced. Chemcon wants to graph the trade-off curve for this problem.

**Table 9.3** Data for the Chemcon Example

| Product | 1 | 2 | 3 | 4 | 5 | 6 | 7 | 8 |
|---|---|---|---|---|---|---|---|---|
| Labor hrs/unit | 5 | 5 | 1 | 4 | 3.5 | 4 | 2 | 3.5 |
| Raw material/unit | 3 | 4.5 | 5 | 5 | 4.5 | 2 | 3.5 | 3 |
| Pollution/unit | 25 | 29 | 35 | 26 | 17 | 25 | 28 | 6 |
| Profit/unit | 53 | 69 | 73 | 69 | 51 | 49 | 71 | 40 |
| Min production | 0 | 30 | 0 | 10 | 20 | 50 | 30 | 0 |
| Max production | 190 | 110 | 140 | 140 | 190 | 190 | 110 | 150 |

**Objectives**   To find the trade-off curve between pollution and profit by solving a number of LP problems.

## WHERE DO THE NUMBERS COME FROM?

The required data here is basically the same as in the product mix problem from Chapter 3. Of course, the company also needs to find how much pollution each product is responsible for, which requires some scientific investigation.

## Solution

*Get the two extreme points on the trade-off curve by maximizing profit, ignoring pollution, and then minimizing pollution, ignoring profit.*

The model itself is a straightforward version of the product mix model from Chapter 3. We want the product mix that stays within the lower and upper production limits, uses no more labor or raw material than are available, keeps pollution low, and keeps profit high. None of the formulas in the spreadsheet model (see Figure 9.10 and the file **Pollution Tradeoff.xlsx**) presents anything new, so we focus instead on the solution procedure.

Referring to the general three-step procedure for finding the trade-off curve, we let profit be objective 1 and pollution be objective 2. To obtain one endpoint of the curve (step 1), we maximize profit and *ignore* pollution. That is, we maximize the Profit cell and delete the constraint indicated in row 26 from the Solver dialog box. You can check that the solution has profit $20,089 and pollution level 9005.[1] (This is *not* the solution shown in the figure.) At the other end of the spectrum (step 3), we can minimize the pollution in cell B26 and ignore any constraint on profit. You can check that this solution has pollution level 3560 and profit $8360. In other words, profit can get as high as $20,089 by ignoring pollution or as low as $8360, and pollution can get as low as 3560 or as high as 9005. These establish the extremes. Now we search for points in between (step 2).

---

[1] Actually, this is not quite true, as one user pointed out. If we maximize profit and *ignore* pollution, the resulting pollution level is 8980. To find the maximum pollution we could ever get, we need to *maximize* pollution. The resulting pollution level is 9005. Surprisingly, the profit from this solution is *less* than the maximum profit, $20,089.

*Get other points on the trade-off curve by maximizing profit, constraining pollution with varying upper bounds.*

Fortunately, SolverTable is just what we need. According to step 2, we need to constrain pollution to various degrees and see how large profit can be. This is indicated in Figure 9.10, where the objective is to maximize profit with an upper limit on pollution. (We get the same effect by minimizing pollution and putting a *lower* limit on profit.) The only upper limits on pollution we need to consider are those between the extremes, 3560 and 9005. Therefore, we use SolverTable with the setup shown in Figure 9.11. Note that we have used the option to enter nonequally spaced inputs: 3560, 4000, 4500, and so on, ending with 9005. Alternatively, equally spaced inputs could be used. All we require is a representative set of values between the extremes. The results appear in Figure 9.12.

**Figure 9.10**  The Chemcon Model

| | A | B | C | D | E | F | G | H | I | J | K | L |
|---|---|---|---|---|---|---|---|---|---|---|---|---|
| 1 | Chemcon profit versus pollution model | | | | | | | | | | | |
| 2 | | | | | | | | | | | | |
| 3 | Input data | | | | | | | | | | Range names used: | |
| 4 | Product | 1 | 2 | 3 | 4 | 5 | 6 | 7 | 8 | | Actual_pollution | =Model!$B$26 |
| 5 | Labor hours/unit | 5 | 5 | 1 | 4 | 3.5 | 4 | 2 | 3.5 | | Max_production | =Model!$B$17:$I$17 |
| 6 | Raw material/unit | 3 | 4.5 | 5 | 5 | 4.5 | 2 | 3.5 | 3 | | Min_production | =Model!$B$13:$I$13 |
| 7 | | | | | | | | | | | Pollution_upper_bound | =Model!$D$26 |
| 8 | Pollution/unit | 25 | 29 | 35 | 26 | 17 | 25 | 28 | 6 | | Profit | =Model!$B$29 |
| 9 | Profit/unit | $53 | $69 | $73 | $69 | $51 | $49 | $71 | $40 | | Resources_available | =Model!$D$21:$D$22 |
| 10 | | | | | | | | | | | Resources_used | =Model!$B$21:$B$22 |
| 11 | Production plan | | | | | | | | | | Units_produced | =Model!$B$15:$I$15 |
| 12 | Product | 1 | 2 | 3 | 4 | 5 | 6 | 7 | 8 | | | |
| 13 | Min production | 0 | 30 | 0 | 10 | 20 | 50 | 30 | 0 | | | |
| 14 | | <= | <= | <= | <= | <= | <= | <= | <= | | | |
| 15 | Units produced | 0.0 | 30.0 | 0.0 | 10.0 | 21.1 | 50.0 | 48.6 | 150.0 | | | |
| 16 | | <= | <= | <= | <= | <= | <= | <= | <= | | | |
| 17 | Max production | 190 | 110 | 140 | 140 | 190 | 190 | 110 | 150 | | | |
| 18 | | | | | | | | | | | | |
| 19 | Constraints on resources | | | | | | | | | | | |
| 20 | | Resources used | | Resources available | | | | | | | | |
| 21 | Labor hours | 1086.0 | <= | 1300 | | | | | | | | |
| 22 | Raw material | 1000.0 | <= | 1000 | | | | | | | | |
| 23 | | | | | | | | | | | | |
| 24 | Constraint on pollution | | | | | | | | | | | |
| 25 | | Actual pollution | | Pollution upper bound | | | | | | | | |
| 26 | | 5000.0 | <= | 5000 | | | | | | | | |
| 27 | | | | | | | | | | | | |
| 28 | Objective to maximize | | | | | | | | | | | |
| 29 | Profit | $15,738 | | | | | | | | | | |

**Figure 9.11**

SolverTable
Dialog Box

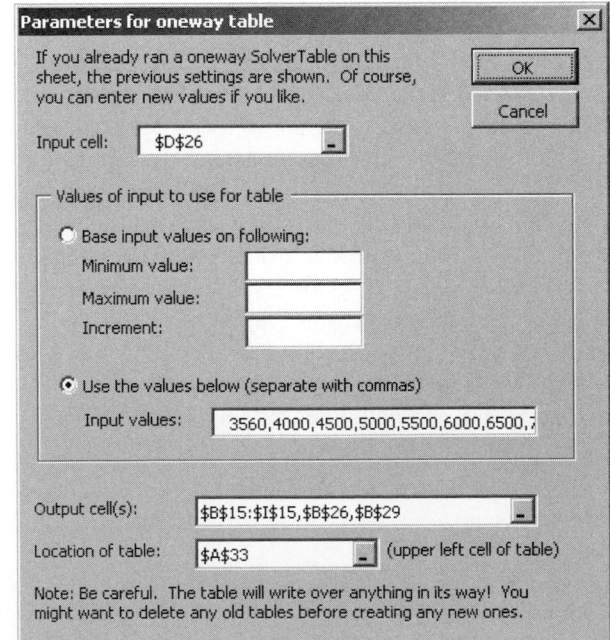

Parameters for oneway table

If you already ran a oneway SolverTable on this sheet, the previous settings are shown. Of course, you can enter new values if you like.

OK

Cancel

Input cell: $D$26

Values of input to use for table

○ Base input values on following:
  Minimum value:
  Maximum value:
  Increment:

● Use the values below (separate with commas)
  Input values: 3560,4000,4500,5000,5500,6000,6500,7

Output cell(s): $B$15:$I$15,$B$26,$B$29

Location of table: $A$33  (upper left cell of table)

Note: Be careful. The table will write over anything in its way! You might want to delete any old tables before creating any new ones.

Figure 9.12    SolverTable Results

| | A | B | C | D | E | F | G | H | I | J | K |
|---|---|---|---|---|---|---|---|---|---|---|---|
| 31 | **Sensitivity of units produced, pollution, and profit to upper bound on pollution** | | | | | | | | | | |
| 32 | Upper bound | Product1 | Product2 | Product3 | Product4 | Product5 | Product6 | Product7 | Product8 | Pollution | Profit |
| 33 | | $B$15 | $C$15 | $D$15 | $E$15 | $F$15 | $G$15 | $H$15 | $I$15 | $B$26 | $B$29 |
| 34 | 3560 | 0.0 | 30.0 | 0.0 | 10.0 | 20.0 | 50.0 | 30.0 | 0.0 | 3560.0 | $8,360 |
| 35 | 4000 | 0.0 | 30.0 | 0.0 | 10.0 | 20.0 | 50.0 | 30.0 | 73.3 | 4000.0 | $11,293 |
| 36 | 4500 | 0.0 | 30.0 | 0.0 | 10.0 | 22.4 | 50.0 | 30.0 | 150.0 | 4500.0 | $14,480 |
| 37 | 5000 | 0.0 | 30.0 | 0.0 | 10.0 | 21.1 | 50.0 | 48.6 | 150.0 | 5000.0 | $15,738 |
| 38 | 5500 | 0.0 | 30.0 | 0.0 | 10.0 | 20.0 | 50.0 | 72.9 | 123.3 | 5500.0 | $16,336 |
| 39 | 6000 | 0.0 | 30.0 | 0.0 | 10.0 | 20.0 | 50.0 | 96.7 | 95.6 | 6000.0 | $16,916 |
| 40 | 6500 | 0.0 | 30.0 | 0.0 | 10.0 | 20.0 | 60.5 | 110.0 | 73.0 | 6500.0 | $17,474 |
| 41 | 7000 | 0.0 | 30.0 | 0.0 | 10.0 | 20.0 | 84.3 | 110.0 | 57.1 | 7000.0 | $18,006 |
| 42 | 7500 | 0.0 | 30.0 | 0.0 | 10.0 | 20.0 | 108.1 | 110.0 | 41.3 | 7500.0 | $18,537 |
| 43 | 8000 | 0.0 | 30.0 | 0.0 | 10.0 | 20.0 | 131.9 | 110.0 | 25.4 | 8000.0 | $19,069 |
| 44 | 8500 | 0.0 | 30.0 | 0.0 | 10.0 | 20.0 | 155.7 | 110.0 | 9.5 | 8500.0 | $19,601 |
| 45 | 9005 | 0.0 | 30.0 | 0.0 | 10.0 | 20.0 | 190.0 | 98.6 | 0.0 | 8980.0 | $20,089 |

## Discussion of the Solution

These results show that as we allow more pollution, profit increases. Also, the product mix shifts considerably. Product 8, a low polluter with a low profit margin, eventually leaves the mix when pollution is allowed to increase, which makes sense. It is less clear why the level of product 6 increases so dramatically. Product 6 is only a moderate polluter and has a moderate profit margin, so the key is evidently that it requires low levels of labor and raw materials. The trade-off curve is created as a scatter chart (with the points connected) directly from columns J and K of the table. This curve appears in Figure 9.13. It indicates that profit indeed increases as Chemcon allows more pollution, but at a decreasing rate. For example, when pollution is allowed to increase from 4000 to 4500, Chemcon can make an extra $3187 in profit. However, when pollution is allowed to increase from 8000 to 8500, the extra profit is only $532. All points below the curve are dominated—for a given level of pollution, the company can achieve a larger profit—and all points above the curve are unattainable.

**Figure 9.13**

Trade-off Curve for Profit versus Pollution

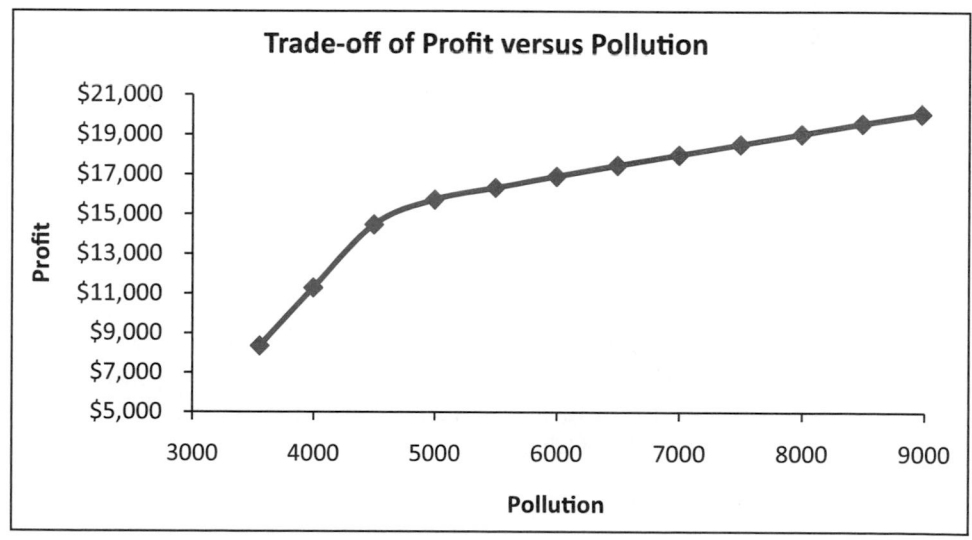

Trade-off curves are not confined to linear models. The following example illustrates a trade-off curve in a situation where the objective is a nonlinear function of the changing cells.

EXAMPLE

## 9.3 TRADE-OFFS BETWEEN EXPOSURES TO MEN AND WOMEN AT LEON BURNIT

This example is a modification of the Burnit advertising example in Example 9.1. Now we assume that Burnit's client is concerned only with *two* groups of people, men and women. Also, the number of exposures to these groups is now a nonlinear square root function of the number of ads placed of any particular type. This implies a marginal decreasing effect of ads—each extra ad of a particular type reaches fewer extra people than the previous ad of this type.[2]

The data for this problem appear in Tables 9.4 and 9.5. The first of these specifies the proportionality constants for the square root exposure functions. For example, if five ads are placed in sports shows, this will achieve $15\sqrt{5} = 33.541$ million exposures to men, but only $5\sqrt{5} = 11.180$ million exposures to women. Evidently, what works well for men does not work so well for women, and vice versa. Given a budget of $1.5 million, find the trade-off curve for exposures to men versus exposures to women.

**Table 9.4** Proportionality Constants for Square Root Exposure Functions

|       | Sports Show | Game Show | News Show | Sitcom | Drama | Soap Opera |
|-------|-------------|-----------|-----------|--------|-------|------------|
| Men   | 15          | 3         | 7         | 7      | 8     | 1          |
| Women | 5           | 5         | 6         | 10     | 9     | 4          |

**Table 9.5** Data on Ads for the Burnit Example

|                 | Sports Show | Game Show | News Show | Sitcom | Drama | Soap Opera |
|-----------------|-------------|-----------|-----------|--------|-------|------------|
| Cost/ad ($1000s) | 120         | 40        | 50        | 40     | 60    | 20         |
| Lower limit     | 2           | 0         | 2         | 0      | 2     | 0          |
| Upper limit     | 10          | 5         | 10        | 5      | 10    | 5          |

**Objective**  To find the trade-off curve for exposures to men versus exposures to women by solving a number of NLP problems.

### WHERE DO THE NUMBERS COME FROM?

We have discussed these same types of numbers in previous examples. Specifically, the parameters in Table 9.4 can be estimated from historical data, exactly as we described in Example 7.5 of Chapter 7.

---

[2] The square root function is an alternative to the exponential advertising response function we used in Example 7.5 of Chapter 7. Each increases at a decreasing rate.

## Solution

Again, the model itself is straightforward, as shown in Figure 9.14. (See the file **Advertising Tradeoff.xlsx**.) We calculate the exposures achieved in rows 22 and 23 by entering the formula

**=B8*SQRT(B$17)**

in cell B22 and copying it to the range B22:G23. We then sum these in cells B30 and B33, and we calculate the total cost in the usual way with the SUMPRODUCT function.

For the three-step trade-off curve procedure, we designate exposures to men as objective 1 and exposures to women as objective 2. For step 1, we maximize exposures to men and ignore women. That is, we do *not* include the constraint in row 30 in the Solver dialog box. You can check that the corresponding solution achieves 89.515 million exposures to men and 79.392 million exposures to women. Reversing the roles of men and women (step 3), you can check that if we maximize exposures to women and ignore men, we achieve 89.220 million exposures to women and only 84.899 million exposures to men.

All other points on the trade-off curve are between these two extremes, and they can again be found easily with SolverTable. We now set up the Solver to maximize exposures to men, and we include the lower limit constraint on exposures to women in the Solver dialog box. (Do you see why it is a *lower* limit constraint in this example, whereas it was an upper limit constraint in the previous example? There we wanted to make pollution low. Here we want to make exposures to women high.) The lower limit cell (D30) becomes the single input cell for SolverTable, and we allow it to vary from (slightly greater than) 79.392 to (slightly less than) 89.220 with suitable values in between. The results appear in table form in Figure 9.15 and in graphical form in Figure 9.16.

**Figure 9.14** The Advertising Trade-off Model

| | A | B | C | D | E | F | G | H | I | J |
|---|---|---|---|---|---|---|---|---|---|---|
| 1 | Burnit nonlinear advertising model | | | | | | | | | |
| 2 | | | | Assumption: The number of exposures (in millions) to each | | | | | | |
| 3 | | | | group is proportional to the square root of the number of ads | | | | | | |
| 4 | | | | of a particular type shown. | | | | | | |
| 5 | | | | | | | | | | |
| 6 | Proportionality constants for exposure functions | | | | | | | | Range names used: | |
| 7 | | Sports ad | Game show ad | News show ad | Sitcom ad | Drama ad | Soap opera ads | | Budget | =Model!$D$26 |
| 8 | Exposures to men | 15 | 3 | 7 | 7 | 8 | 1 | | Exposures_to_men | =Model!$B$33 |
| 9 | Exposures to women | 5 | 5 | 6 | 10 | 9 | 4 | | Exposures_to_women | =Model!$B$30 |
| 10 | | | | | | | | | Maximum_ads_allowed | =Model!$B$19:$G$19 |
| 11 | Cost/ad ($1,000s) | 120 | 40 | 50 | 40 | 60 | 20 | | Minimum_ads_required | =Model!$B$15:$G$15 |
| 12 | | | | | | | | | Number_purchased | =Model!$B$17:$G$17 |
| 13 | Advertising plan | | | | | | | | Total_cost | =Model!$B$26 |
| 14 | | Sports ad | Game show ad | News show ad | Sitcom ad | Drama ad | Soap opera ad | | Women_lower_bound | =Model!$D$30 |
| 15 | Minimum ads required | 2 | 0 | 2 | 0 | 2 | 0 | | | |
| 16 | | <= | <= | <= | <= | <= | <= | | | |
| 17 | Number purchased | 2.000 | 5.000 | 5.387 | 5.000 | 8.177 | 5.000 | | | |
| 18 | | <= | <= | <= | <= | <= | <= | | | |
| 19 | Maximum ads allowed | 10 | 5 | 10 | 5 | 10 | 5 | | | |
| 20 | | | | | | | | | | |
| 21 | Exposures obtained | Sports ad | Game show ad | News show ad | Sitcom ad | Drama ad | Soap opera ad | | | |
| 22 | Men | 21.213 | 6.708 | 16.247 | 15.652 | 22.877 | 2.236 | | | |
| 23 | Women | 7.071 | 11.180 | 13.926 | 22.361 | 25.737 | 8.944 | | | |
| 24 | | | | | | | | | | |
| 25 | Budget constraint | Total cost | | Budget | | | | | | |
| 26 | | 1500.000 | <= | 1500 | | | | | | |
| 27 | | | | | | | | | | |
| 28 | Constraint on minimal exposures to women | | | | | | | | | |
| 29 | | Exposures to women | | Women lower bound | | | | | | |
| 30 | | 89.219 | >= | 89.219 | | | | | | |
| 31 | | | | | | | | | | |
| 32 | Objective to maximize | | | | | | | | | |
| 33 | Exposures to men | 84.934 | | | | | | | | |

**Figure 9.15**   SolverTable Results for the Advertising Trade-off Model

| | A | B | C | D | E | F | G | H | I |
|---|---|---|---|---|---|---|---|---|---|
| 35 | Sensitivity of ads purchased, exposures to women, and exposures to men to lower bound on exposures to women | | | | | | | | |
| 36 | | Sports ad | Game show ad | News show ad | Sitcom ad | Drama ad | Soap opera ad | To women | To men |
| 37 | | $B$17 | $C$17 | $D$17 | $E$17 | $F$17 | $G$17 | $B$30 | $B$33 |
| 38 | 79.393 | 4.839 | 1.744 | 6.072 | 5.000 | 5.508 | 0.776 | 79.393 | 89.515 |
| 39 | 80 | 4.715 | 1.835 | 6.100 | 5.000 | 5.620 | 0.928 | 80.000 | 89.506 |
| 40 | 81 | 4.503 | 1.994 | 6.143 | 5.000 | 5.807 | 1.215 | 81.000 | 89.449 |
| 41 | 82 | 4.280 | 2.163 | 6.178 | 5.000 | 5.997 | 1.555 | 82.000 | 89.336 |
| 42 | 83 | 4.048 | 2.347 | 6.204 | 5.000 | 6.186 | 1.954 | 83.000 | 89.156 |
| 43 | 84 | 3.801 | 2.538 | 6.220 | 5.000 | 6.383 | 2.421 | 84.000 | 88.900 |
| 44 | 85 | 3.540 | 2.745 | 6.228 | 5.000 | 6.578 | 2.969 | 85.000 | 88.554 |
| 45 | 86 | 3.262 | 2.976 | 6.217 | 5.000 | 6.777 | 3.604 | 86.000 | 88.096 |
| 46 | 87 | 2.964 | 3.225 | 6.189 | 5.000 | 6.979 | 4.357 | 87.000 | 87.500 |
| 47 | 88 | 2.600 | 3.580 | 6.173 | 5.000 | 7.269 | 5.000 | 88.000 | 86.713 |
| 48 | 89 | 2.057 | 4.276 | 6.207 | 5.000 | 7.863 | 5.000 | 89.000 | 85.478 |
| 49 | 89.219 | 2.000 | 5.000 | 5.387 | 5.000 | 8.177 | 5.000 | 89.219 | 84.934 |

**Figure 9.16**

Trade-off Curve
for the Advertising
Example

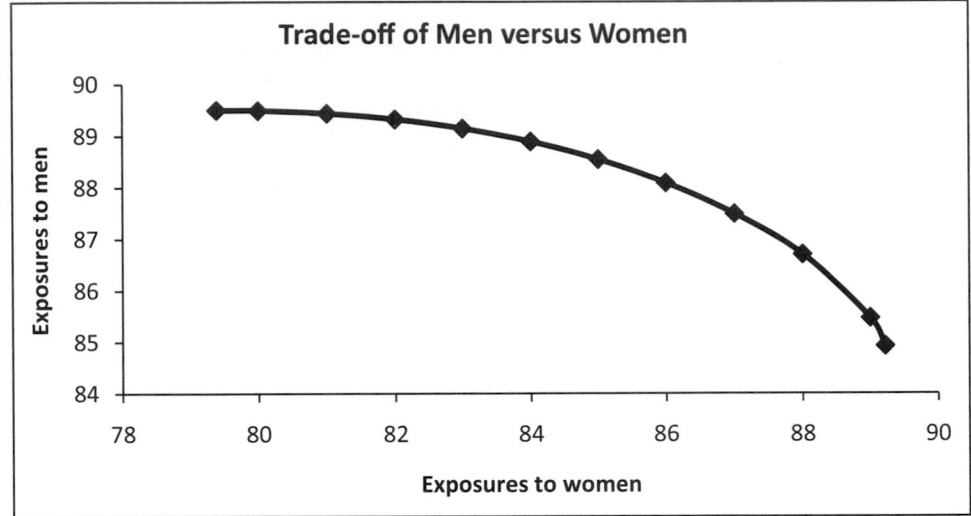

**Discussion of the Solution**

As we go down the table (or to the right in the chart), we require more exposures to women, which has an increasingly negative effect on exposures to men. Not surprisingly, the corresponding solutions place more ads in the shows watched predominantly by women (game shows, dramas, and soaps) and fewer ads in sports and news shows. The upper limit of 5 placed on sitcom ads prevents us from seeing how the number of sitcom ads would change if it were not constrained. It would probably change fairly dramatically, given that these ads are relatively cheap and they tend to reach more women than men.

**Technical Note**

We ran into two problems that you might experience. First, depending on the starting solution, one of the changing cells might become slightly negative (due to numerical roundoff), in which case the SQRT function is undefined, and you get an error message. To remedy this, add a constraint such as Ads>=0.0001. Second, when we ran SolverTable, it indicated "no feasible solution" to the problem in row 49 of Figure 9.15, although we know there is a feasible solution. This can sometimes occur with nonlinear models, depending on the starting solution used. SolverTable uses the solution from the previous problem as the starting solution for the next problem. This seems reasonable, but it *can* produce this error. If it does, try running the Solver on this particular problem again with your own initial solution (such as all 0's). This is what we did to get the values in row 49. ∎

## MODELING ISSUES

1. A trade-off curve is useful because it gives the ultimate decision maker many undominated solutions to choose from. However, it does *not* specify a "best" solution. The decision maker still has to make the difficult decision of which solution from the trade-off curve to implement. This can be done subjectively or with the help of a **multiattribute utility function.** However, estimating these types of functions is difficult, so their use in real-world applications has been limited.

2. We can generalize to a situation where there are more than two objectives by constructing trade-off curves between each *pair* of objectives. ∎

## PROBLEMS

### Skill-Building Problems

**19.** Widgetco produces two types of widgets. Each widget is made of steel and aluminum and is assembled with skilled labor. The resources used and the per-unit profit contribution (ignoring cost of overtime labor purchased) for each type of widget are given in the file **P09_19.xlsx**. At present, 200 pounds of steel, 300 pounds of aluminum, and 300 hours of labor are available. Extra overtime labor can be purchased for $10 per hour. Construct a trade-off curve between the objectives of maximizing profit and minimizing overtime labor.

**20.** Plantco produces three products. Three workers work for Plantco, and the company must determine which product(s) each worker should produce. The number of units each worker would produce if he or she spent the whole day producing each type of product is given in the file **P09_20.xlsx**. The company is also interested in maximizing the happiness of its workers. The amount of happiness "earned" by a worker who spends the entire day producing a given product is also given in this file. Construct a trade-off curve between the objectives of maximizing total units produced daily and total worker happiness.

**21.** If a company spends $a$ on advertising (measured in thousands of dollars) and charges a price of $p$ dollars per unit, then it can sell $1000 - 10p + 20a^{1/2}$ units of the product. The cost per unit of producing the product is $6. Construct a trade-off curve between the objectives of maximizing profit and maximizing the number of units sold.

**22.** GMCO produces three types of cars: compact, medium, and large. The variable cost per car and production capacity (per year) for each type of car are given in the file **P09_22.xlsx**. The annual demand for each type of car depends on the prices of the three types of cars, also given in this file. In this latter table, $P_C$ is the price charged for a compact car (in thousands of dollars). The variables $P_M$ and $P_L$ are defined similarly for medium and large cars. Suppose that each compact car gets 30 mpg, each medium car gets 25 mpg, and each large car gets 18 mpg. GMCO wants to keep the planet pollution free, so in addition to maximizing profit, it wants to maximize the average miles per gallon attained by the cars it sells. Construct a trade-off curve between these two objectives.

**23.** In the capital budgeting example from Chapter 6 (see Example 6.1), we maximized NPV for a given budget. Now find a trade-off curve for NPV versus budget. Specifically, minimize the amount invested, with a lower bound constraint on the NPV obtained. What lower bounds should you use? Do you get the same trade-off curve as in Figure 6.4?

**24.** Referring to the portfolio optimization example from Chapter 7 (see Example 7.9), we constructed the efficient frontier by minimizing portfolio variance, with a lower bound constraint on the expected return. Do it the opposite way. That is, calculate the efficient frontier by maximizing the expected return, with an *upper* bound on the portfolio variance. Do you get the same results as in Example 7.9?

# 9.4 THE ANALYTIC HIERARCHY PROCESS (AHP)

When multiple objectives are important to a decision maker, choosing between alternatives can be difficult. For example, if you are choosing a job, one job might offer the highest starting salary but rate poorly on other objectives such as quality of life in the city where the job is located and the nearness of the job to your family. Another job offer might rate highly on these latter objectives but have a relatively low starting salary. In this case, it can be difficult for you to choose between job offers. The **Analytic Hierarchy Process (AHP),** developed originally by Thomas Saaty, is a powerful tool that can be used to make decisions in situations where multiple objectives are present. We present an example to illustrate such a case.[3] (*Note:* We use matrix notation and matrix multiplication in this section. You may need to review the discussion of matrices in Section 7.7.)

---

EXAMPLE | **9.4 USING AHP TO SELECT A JOB**

Jane is about to graduate from college and is trying to determine which job to accept. She plans to choose among the offers by determining how well each job offer meets the following four objectives:

- Objective 1: High starting salary
- Objective 2: Quality of life in city where job is located
- Objective 3: Interest of work
- Objective 4: Nearness of job to family

**Objective**   To use the AHP method to help Jane select a job that is best in terms of the various job criteria.

### WHERE DO THE NUMBERS COME FROM?

As we discuss, Jane must make a number of trade-offs during the implementation of AHP. In this case, the decision maker supplies the data!

## Solution

To illustrate how AHP works, suppose that Jane is facing three job offers and must determine which offer to accept. In this example, there are four objectives, as listed previously. For each objective, AHP generates a weight (by a method to be described shortly). By convention, the weights are always chosen so that they sum to 1. Suppose that Jane's weights are $w_1 = 0.5115$, $w_2 = 0.0986$, $w_3 = 0.2433$, and $w_4 = 0.1466$. These weights indicate that a high starting salary is the most important objective, followed by interest of work, nearness to family, and quality of life.

Next, suppose that Jane determines (again by a method to be described shortly) how well each job "scores" on each objective. For example, suppose these scores are those listed in Table 9.6. We see from this table that job 1 best meets the objective of a high starting salary, but scores worst on all other objectives. Note that the scores of the jobs on each objective are normalized, which means that for each objective, the sum of the scores of the jobs on that objective is 1.

---

[3] The leading software package for implementing AHP is Expert Choice, developed by Expert Choice Inc.

**Table 9.6** Job Scores on Objectives in the AHP Example

|  | **Salary** | **Quality of Life** | **Interest of Work** | **Nearness to Family** |
|---|---|---|---|---|
| Job 1 | 0.5714 | 0.1593 | 0.0882 | 0.0824 |
| Job 2 | 0.2857 | 0.2519 | 0.6687 | 0.3151 |
| Job 3 | 0.1429 | 0.5889 | 0.2431 | 0.6025 |

*AHP is essentially a process of rating the importance of each objective and then rating how well each possible decision meets each objective. The result is a score for each possible decision, with higher scores preferred.*

Given the weights for the objectives and the scores shown in Table 9.6, Jane can now determine which job offer to accept. Specifically, for each job we calculate an overall score that is a weighted sum of the scores for that job, using the $w$'s as weights. For example, the overall score for job 1 weights the scores in the first row of Table 9.6:

$$\text{Job 1 score} = 0.5115(0.5714) + 0.0986(0.1593) + 0.2433(0.0882) + 0.1466(0.0824)$$
$$= 0.3415$$

Similarly, the overall scores for jobs 2 and 3 are obtained by weighting the scores in the second and third rows of Table 9.6:

$$\text{Job 2 score} = 0.5115(0.2857) + 0.0986(0.2519) + 0.2433(0.6687) + 0.1466(0.3151)$$
$$= 0.3799$$

$$\text{Job 3 score} = 0.5115(0.1429) + 0.0986(0.5889) + 0.2433(0.2431) + 0.1466(0.6025)$$
$$= 0.2786$$

Because the overall score for job 2 is the largest, AHP suggests that Jane should accept this job.

The following discussion on how AHP actually works is technical and is not really necessary for *using* the method. We have included the file **Choosing Jobs with VBA.xlsm** that implements AHP as a decision support system with VBA macros. We urge you to try it out, especially if you are currently making a job decision. You don't need to understand the details behind AHP to run the application. You simply need to make a number of pairwise comparisons, as indicated in a number of dialog boxes. However, if you really *do* want to understand how AHP works, then read on. By the way, the term *criterion* is commonly used instead of objective when discussing AHP. The file **Choosing Jobs with VBA.xlsm** uses this term consistently.

### Pairwise Comparison Matrices

To obtain the weights for the various objectives, we begin by forming a matrix $A$, known as the pairwise comparison matrix. The entry in row $i$ and column $j$ of $A$, labeled $a_{ij}$, indicates how much more (or less) important objective $i$ is than objective $j$ to the decision maker. "Importance" is measured on an integer-valued scale from 1 to 9, with each number having the interpretation shown in Table 9.7. The phrases in this table, such as "strongly more important than," are suggestive only. They simply indicate discrete points on a continuous scale that can be used to compare the relative importance of any two objectives.

**Table 9.7** Interpretation of Values in the Pairwise Comparison Matrix

| Value of $a_{ij}$ | Interpretation |
|---|---|
| 1 | Objectives $i$ and $j$ are equally important. |
| 3 | Objective $i$ is slightly more important than $j$. |
| 5 | Objective $i$ is strongly more important than $j$. |
| 7 | Objective $i$ is very strongly more important than $j$. |
| 9 | Objective $i$ is absolutely more important than $j$. |

For example, if $a_{13} = 3$, then objective 1 is slightly more important to Jane than objective 3. If $a_{ij} = 4$, a value not in the table, then objective $i$ is somewhere between slightly and strongly more important than objective $j$. If objective $i$ is *less* important to Jane than objective $j$, we use the reciprocal of the appropriate index. For example, if objective $i$ is slightly less important than objective $j$, then $a_{ij} = 1/3$. Finally, for all objectives $i$, we use the convention that $a_{ii} = 1$.

For consistency, it is necessary to set $a_{ji} = 1/a_{ij}$. For example, if $a_{13} = 3$, then it is necessary to have $a_{31} = 1/3$. This simply states that if objective 1 is slightly more important than objective 3, then objective 3 is slightly less important than job 1. It is usually easier to determine all $a_{ij}$'s that are greater than 1 and then use the relationship $a_{ji} = 1/a_{ij}$ to determine the remaining entries in the pairwise comparison matrix.

To illustrate, suppose that Jane has identified the following pairwise comparison matrix for her four objectives:

$$A = \begin{bmatrix} 1 & 5 & 2 & 4 \\ 1/5 & 1 & 1/2 & 1/2 \\ 1/2 & 2 & 1 & 2 \\ 1/4 & 2 & 1/2 & 1 \end{bmatrix}$$

The rows and columns of $A$ each correspond to Jane's four objectives: salary, quality of life, interest of work, and nearness to family. Considering the first row, for example, she believes that salary is more important, in various degrees, than quality of life, interest of work, and nearness to family.

The entries in this matrix have built-in pairwise consistency because we require $a_{ij} = 1/a_{ij}$ for each $i$ and $j$. However, they might not be consistent when three (or more) alternatives are considered simultaneously. For example, Jane claims that salary is strongly more important than quality of life ($a_{12} = 5$) and that salary is very slightly more important than interesting work ($a_{13} = 2$). But she also says that interesting work is very slightly more important than quality of life ($a_{32} = 2$). The question is whether these ratings are all consistent with one another. They are not, at least not exactly. It can be shown that some of Jane's pairwise comparisons are slightly inconsistent. When a person is asked to make a number of pairwise comparisons, slight inconsistencies are common and fortunately do not cause serious difficulties. An index that can be used to measure the consistency of Jane's preferences is discussed later in this section.

### Determining the Weights

Although the ideas behind AHP are fairly intuitive, the mathematical reasoning required to derive the weights for the objectives is advanced. Therefore, we simply describe how it is done.

Starting with the pairwise comparison matrix $A$, we find the weights for Jane's four objectives using the following two steps:

1. For each of the columns of $A$, divide each entry in the column by the sum of the entries in the column. This yields a new matrix (call it $A_{\text{norm}}$, for "normalized") in which the sum of the entries in each column is 1. For Jane's pairwise comparison matrix, this step yields

$$A_{\text{norm}} = \begin{bmatrix} 0.5128 & 0.5000 & 0.5000 & 0.5333 \\ 0.1026 & 0.1000 & 0.1250 & 0.0667 \\ 0.2564 & 0.2000 & 0.2500 & 0.2667 \\ 0.1282 & 0.2000 & 0.1250 & 0.1333 \end{bmatrix}$$

**2.** Estimate $w_i$, the weight for objective $i$, as the average of the entries in row $i$ of $A_{norm}$. For Jane's matrix this yields

$$w_1 = \frac{0.5128 + 0.5000 + 0.5000 + 0.5333}{4} = 0.5115$$

$$w_2 = \frac{0.1026 + 0.1000 + 0.1250 + 0.0667}{4} = 0.0986$$

$$w_3 = \frac{0.2564 + 0.2000 + 0.2500 + 0.2667}{4} = 0.2433$$

$$w_4 = \frac{0.1282 + 0.2000 + 0.1250 + 0.1333}{4} = 0.1466$$

Intuitively, why does $w_1$ approximate the weight for objective 1 (salary)? Here is the reasoning. The proportion of weight that salary is given in pairwise comparisons of each objective to salary is 0.5128. Similarly, 0.50 represents the proportion of total weight that salary is given in pairwise comparisons of each objective to quality of life. Therefore, we see that each of the four numbers averaged to obtain $w_1$ represents a measure of the total weight attached to salary. Averaging these numbers should give a good estimate of the proportion of the total weight given to salary.

### Determining the Score of Each Decision Alternative on Each Objective

Now that we have determined the weights for the various objectives, we need to determine how well each job scores on each objective. To determine these scores, we use the same scale described in Table 9.7 to construct a pairwise comparison matrix for each objective. Consider the salary objective, for example. Suppose that Jane assesses the following pairwise comparison matrix. We denote this matrix as $A_1$ because it reflects her comparisons of the three jobs with respect to the first objective, salary.

$$A_1 = \begin{bmatrix} 1 & 2 & 4 \\ 1/2 & 1 & 2 \\ 1/4 & 1/2 & 1 \end{bmatrix}$$

The rows and columns of this matrix correspond to the three jobs. For example, the first row means that Jane believes job 1 is superior to job 2 (and even more superior to job 3) in terms of salary. To find the relative scores of the three jobs on salary, we now apply the *same* two-step procedure as previously discussed to the salary pairwise comparison matrix $A_1$. That is, we first divide each column entry by the column sum to obtain

$$A_{1,norm} = \begin{bmatrix} 0.5714 & 0.5714 & 0.5714 \\ 0.2857 & 0.2857 & 0.2857 \\ 0.1429 & 0.1429 & 0.1429 \end{bmatrix}$$

Then we average the numbers in each row to obtain the vector of scores for the three jobs on salary, denoted by $S_1$:

$$S_1 = \begin{bmatrix} 0.5714 \\ 0.2857 \\ 0.1429 \end{bmatrix}$$

That is, the scores for jobs 1, 2, and 3 on salary are 0.5714, 0.2857, and 0.1429. In terms of salary, job 1 is clearly the favorite.

Next, we repeat these calculations for Jane's other objectives. Each of these objectives requires a pairwise comparison matrix, which we will denote as $A_2$, $A_3$, and $A_4$. Suppose that Jane's pairwise comparison matrix for quality of life is

$$A_2 = \begin{bmatrix} 1 & 1/2 & 1/3 \\ 2 & 1 & 1/3 \\ 3 & 3 & 1 \end{bmatrix}$$

Then the corresponding normalized matrix is

$$A_{2,\text{norm}} = \begin{bmatrix} 0.1667 & 0.1111 & 0.2000 \\ 0.3333 & 0.2222 & 0.2000 \\ 0.5000 & 0.6667 & 0.6000 \end{bmatrix}$$

and by averaging, we obtain

$$S_2 = \begin{bmatrix} 0.1593 \\ 0.2519 \\ 0.5889 \end{bmatrix}$$

Here, job 3 is the clear favorite. However, this does not have much impact because Jane puts relatively little weight on quality of life.

For interest of work, suppose the pairwise comparison matrix is

$$A_3 = \begin{bmatrix} 1 & 1/7 & 1/3 \\ 7 & 1 & 3 \\ 3 & 1/3 & 1 \end{bmatrix}$$

Then the same types of calculations show that the scores for jobs 1, 2, and 3 on interest of work are

$$S_3 = \begin{bmatrix} 0.0882 \\ 0.6687 \\ 0.2431 \end{bmatrix}$$

Finally, suppose the pairwise comparison matrix for nearness to family is

$$A_4 = \begin{bmatrix} 1 & 1/4 & 1/7 \\ 4 & 1 & 1/2 \\ 7 & 2 & 1 \end{bmatrix}$$

In this case, the scores for jobs 1, 2, and 3 on nearness to family are

$$S_4 = \begin{bmatrix} 0.0824 \\ 0.3151 \\ 0.6025 \end{bmatrix}$$

## Determining the Best Alternative

Let's summarize what we have determined so far. Jane first assesses a pairwise comparison matrix $A$ that measures the relative importance of each of her objectives to one another. From this matrix, we obtain a vector of weights that summarizes the relative importance of the objectives. Next, Jane assesses a pairwise comparison matrix $A_i$ for each objective $i$. This matrix measures how well each job compares to other jobs with regard to this objective. For each matrix $A_i$, we obtain a vector of scores $S_i$ that summarizes how the jobs compare in terms of achieving objective $i$.

The final step is to combine the scores in the $S_i$ vectors with the weights in the $w$ vector. Actually, we have already done this. Note that the columns of Table 9.6 are the $S_i$ vectors we just obtained. If we form a matrix $S$ of these score vectors and multiply this matrix by $w$, we obtain a vector of overall scores for each job, as shown here:

$$Sw = \begin{bmatrix} 0.5714 & 0.1593 & 0.0882 & 0.0824 \\ 0.2857 & 0.2519 & 0.6687 & 0.3151 \\ 0.1429 & 0.5889 & 0.2431 & 0.6025 \end{bmatrix} \times \begin{bmatrix} 0.5115 \\ 0.0986 \\ 0.2433 \\ 0.1466 \end{bmatrix} = \begin{bmatrix} 0.3415 \\ 0.3799 \\ 0.2786 \end{bmatrix}$$

These are the same overall scores that we obtained earlier. As before, the largest of these overall scores is for job 2, so AHP suggests that Jane should accept this job. Job 1 follows closely behind, with job 3 somewhat farther behind.

### Checking for Consistency

As mentioned earlier, any pairwise comparison matrix can suffer from inconsistencies. We now describe a procedure to check for inconsistencies. We illustrate this on the $A$ matrix and its associated vector of weights $w$. The same procedure can be used on any of the $A_i$ matrices and their associated weights vector $S_i$:

1. Compute $Aw$. For the example, we obtain

$$Aw = \begin{bmatrix} 1 & 5 & 2 & 4 \\ 1/5 & 1 & 1/2 & 1/2 \\ 1/2 & 2 & 1 & 2 \\ 1/4 & 2 & 1/2 & 1 \end{bmatrix} \times \begin{bmatrix} 0.5115 \\ 0.0986 \\ 0.2433 \\ 0.1466 \end{bmatrix} = \begin{bmatrix} 2.0774 \\ 0.3958 \\ 0.9894 \\ 0.5933 \end{bmatrix}$$

2. Find the ratio of each element of $Aw$ to the corresponding weight in $w$ and average these ratios. For the example, this calculation is

$$\frac{\dfrac{2.0774}{0.5115} + \dfrac{0.3958}{0.0986} + \dfrac{0.9894}{0.2433} + \dfrac{0.5933}{0.1466}}{4} = 4.0477$$

3. Compute the consistency index (labeled $CI$) as

$$CI = \frac{(\text{Step 2 result}) - n}{n - 1}$$

where $n$ is the number of objectives. For the example this is $CI = \dfrac{4.0477 - 4}{4 - 1} = 0.0159$.

4. Compare $CI$ to the random index (labeled $RI$) in Table 9.8 for the appropriate value of $n$.

**Table 9.8**  **Random Indices for Consistency Check for the AHP Example**

| $n$ | 2 | 3 | 4 | 5 | 6 | 7 | 8 | 9 | 10 |
|-----|---|------|------|------|------|------|------|------|------|
| $RI$ | 0 | 0.58 | 0.90 | 1.12 | 1.24 | 1.32 | 1.41 | 1.45 | 1.51 |

To be a perfectly consistent DM, each ratio in step 2 should equal $n$. This implies that a perfectly consistent decision maker has $CI = 0$. The values of $RI$ in Table 9.8 give the average value of $CI$ if the entries in $A$ were chosen at random (subject to the constraints that $a_{ij}$'s must equal 1, and $a_{ij} = 1/a_{ji}$). If the ratio of $CI$ to $RI$ is sufficiently small, then the decision maker's comparisons are probably consistent enough to be useful. Saaty suggests that if $CI/RI < 0.10$, then the degree of consistency is satisfactory, whereas if $CI/RI > 0.10$, serious inconsistencies exist, and AHP may not yield meaningful results. In Jane's example, $CI/RI = 0.0159/0.90 = 0.0177$, which is much less than 0.10. Therefore, Jane's pairwise comparison matrix $A$ does not exhibit any serious inconsistencies. (You can check that the same is true of her other pairwise comparison matrices $A_1$ through $A_4$.)

## DEVELOPING THE SPREADSHEET MODEL

We now show how to implement AHP on a spreadsheet. (See Figure 9.17 and the file **Choosing Jobs.xlsx**.)

**Figure 9.17** The AHP Job Selection Model

| | A | B | C | D | E | F | G | H | I | J | K | L |
|---|---|---|---|---|---|---|---|---|---|---|---|---|
| 1 | Job selection using analytical hierarchy process | | | | | | | | | | | |
| 2 | | | | | | | | | | | | |
| 3 | Pairwise comparisons among objectives | | | | | | Normalized matrix | | | | | Weights |
| 4 | | Salary | Life quality | Work interest | Near family | | | | | | | |
| 5 | Salary | 1 | 5 | 2 | 4 | | 0.5128 | 0.5000 | 0.5000 | 0.5333 | | 0.5115 |
| 6 | Life quality | 1/5 | 1 | 1/2 | 1/2 | | 0.1026 | 0.1000 | 0.1250 | 0.0667 | | 0.0986 |
| 7 | Work interest | 1/2 | 2 | 1 | 2 | | 0.2564 | 0.2000 | 0.2500 | 0.2667 | | 0.2433 |
| 8 | Near family | 1/4 | 2 | 1/2 | 1 | | 0.1282 | 0.2000 | 0.1250 | 0.1333 | | 0.1466 |
| 9 | | | | | | | | | | | | |
| 10 | Pairwise comparisons among jobs on salary | | | | | | Normalized matrix | | | | | Scores |
| 11 | | Job 1 | Job 2 | Job 3 | | | | | | | | |
| 12 | Job 1 | 1 | 2 | 4 | | | 0.5714 | 0.5714 | 0.5714 | | | 0.5714 |
| 13 | Job 2 | 1/2 | 1 | 2 | | | 0.2857 | 0.2857 | 0.2857 | | | 0.2857 |
| 14 | Job 3 | 1/4 | 1/2 | 1 | | | 0.1429 | 0.1429 | 0.1429 | | | 0.1429 |
| 15 | | | | | | | | | | | | |
| 16 | Pairwise comparisons among jobs on quality of life | | | | | | Normalized matrix | | | | | Scores |
| 17 | | Job 1 | Job 2 | Job 3 | | | | | | | | |
| 18 | Job 1 | 1 | 1/2 | 1/3 | | | 0.1667 | 0.1111 | 0.2000 | | | 0.1593 |
| 19 | Job 2 | 2 | 1 | 1/3 | | | 0.3333 | 0.2222 | 0.2000 | | | 0.2519 |
| 20 | Job 3 | 3 | 3 | 1 | | | 0.5000 | 0.6667 | 0.6000 | | | 0.5889 |
| 21 | | | | | | | | | | | | |
| 22 | Pairwise comparisons among jobs on interest of work | | | | | | Normalized matrix | | | | | Scores |
| 23 | | Job 1 | Job 2 | Job 3 | | | | | | | | |
| 24 | Job 1 | 1 | 1/7 | 1/3 | | | 0.0909 | 0.0968 | 0.0769 | | | 0.0882 |
| 25 | Job 2 | 7 | 1 | 3 | | | 0.6364 | 0.6774 | 0.6923 | | | 0.6687 |
| 26 | Job 3 | 3 | 1/3 | 1 | | | 0.2727 | 0.2258 | 0.2308 | | | 0.2431 |
| 27 | | | | | | | | | | | | |
| 28 | Pairwise comparisons among jobs on nearness to family | | | | | | Normalized matrix | | | | | Scores |
| 29 | | Job 1 | Job 2 | Job 3 | | | | | | | | |
| 30 | Job 1 | 1 | 1/4 | 1/7 | | | 0.0833 | 0.0769 | 0.0870 | | | 0.0824 |
| 31 | Job 2 | 4 | 1 | 1/2 | | | 0.3333 | 0.3077 | 0.3043 | | | 0.3151 |
| 32 | Job 3 | 7 | 2 | 1 | | | 0.5833 | 0.6154 | 0.6087 | | | 0.6025 |
| 33 | | | | | | | | | | | | |
| 34 | Determining best job | | | | | | | | | | | |
| 35 | Matrix of scores | | | | | | Weighted scores | | | | | |
| 36 | | Salary | Life quality | Work interest | Near family | | | | | | | |
| 37 | Job 1 | 0.5714 | 0.159 | 0.088 | 0.082 | | 0.3415 | | | | | |
| 38 | Job 2 | 0.2857 | 0.252 | 0.669 | 0.315 | | 0.3799 | ← Job 2 has the highest score | | | | |
| 39 | Job 3 | 0.1429 | 0.589 | 0.243 | 0.602 | | 0.2786 | | | | | |

**1 Inputs.** Enter the pairwise comparison matrices in the shaded ranges. (Note that you can enter fractions such as 1/7 in cell C24, and have them appear as fractions by formatting the cells with the Fraction option.)

**2 Normalized matrix.** Calculate the normalized matrix for the first pairwise comparison matrix in the range G5:J8. This can be done quickly as follows. Starting with the cursor in cell G5, highlight the range G5:J8. Then type the formula

**=B5/SUM(B$5:B$8)**

and press Control+Enter (both keys at once). We introduced this shortcut in an earlier chapter as a quick way to enter the same formula in an entire range. It's really useful!

**3 Weights of objectives.** In the range L5:L8, calculate the weights for each objective. Again, do this the quick way. Starting with the cursor in cell L5, highlight the range L5:L8. Then type the formula

**=AVERAGE(G5:J5)**

and press Control+Enter.

**4 Scores for jobs on objectives.** Repeat the same calculations in steps 2 and 3 for the other pairwise comparison matrices to obtain the normalized matrices in columns G through I and scores vectors in column L.

**5 Overall job scores.** In the range B37:E39, form a matrix of job scores on the various objectives. To get the score vector in the range L12:L14 into the range B37:B39, for example, highlight this latter range, type the formula

**=L12**

and press Control+Enter. Do likewise for the other three scores vectors in column L. Then to obtain the overall job scores (from the matrix product $Sw$), highlight the range G37:G39, type the formula

**=MMULT(B37:E39,L5:L8)**

and press Control+Shift+Enter. (Remember that Control+Shift+Enter is used to enter a matrix function. In contrast, Control+Enter is equivalent to copying a formula to a highlighted range.)

Again we see that job 2 is the most preferred of the three jobs.

### Calculating the Consistency Index

We now show how to compute the consistency index $CI$ for each of the pairwise comparison matrices. (See Figure 9.18, which is also part of the file **AHPJobs.xlsx**. Note that we have hidden columns G through K to save space. These contain the normalized matrices from step 2 in the previous section.) The following steps are relevant for the first pairwise comparison matrix. The others are done in analogous fashion.

**1 Product of comparison matrix and vector of weights (or scores).** Calculate the product of the first pairwise comparison matrix and the weights vector in the range N5:N8 by highlighting this range, typing

**=MMULT(B5:E8,L5:L8)**

and pressing Ctrl+Shift+Enter.

**Figure 9.18** Checking for Consistency

| | A | B | C | D | E | F | L | M | N | O |
|---|---|---|---|---|---|---|---|---|---|---|
| 1 | Job selection using analytical hierarchy process | | | | | | | | | |
| 2 | | | | | | | | | | |
| 3 | Pairwise comparisons among objectives | | | | | | Weights | | Product | Ratios |
| 4 | | Salary | Life quality | Work interest | Near family | | | | | |
| 5 | Salary | 1 | 5 | 2 | 4 | | 0.5115 | | 2.0774 | 4.0611 |
| 6 | Life quality | 1/5 | 1 | 1/2 | 1/2 | | 0.0986 | | 0.3958 | 4.0161 |
| 7 | Work interest | 1/2 | 2 | 1 | 2 | | 0.2433 | | 0.9894 | 4.0672 |
| 8 | Near family | 1/4 | 2 | 1/2 | 1 | | 0.1466 | | 0.5933 | 4.0459 |
| 9 | | | | | | | | | CI | 0.0159 |
| 10 | Pairwise comparisons among jobs on salary | | | | | | Scores | | CI/RI | 0.0176 |
| 11 | | Job 1 | Job 2 | Job 3 | | | | | | |
| 12 | Job 1 | 1 | 2 | 4 | | | 0.5714 | | 1.7143 | 3 |
| 13 | Job 2 | 1/2 | 1 | 2 | | | 0.2857 | | 0.8571 | 3 |
| 14 | Job 3 | 1/4 | 1/2 | 1 | | | 0.1429 | | 0.4286 | 3 |
| 15 | | | | | | | | | CI | 0 |
| 16 | Pairwise comparisons among jobs on quality of life | | | | | | Scores | | CI/RI | 0.0000 |
| 17 | | Job 1 | Job 2 | Job 3 | | | | | | |
| 18 | Job 1 | 1 | 1/2 | 1/3 | | | 0.1593 | | 0.4815 | 3.0233 |
| 19 | Job 2 | 2 | 1 | 1/3 | | | 0.2519 | | 0.7667 | 3.0441 |
| 20 | Job 3 | 3 | 3 | 1 | | | 0.5889 | | 1.8222 | 3.0943 |
| 21 | | | | | | | | | CI | 0.0270 |
| 22 | Pairwise comparisons among jobs on interest of work | | | | | | Scores | | CI/RI | 0.0465 |
| 23 | | Job 1 | Job 2 | Job 3 | | | | | | |
| 24 | Job 1 | 1 | 1/7 | 1/3 | | | 0.0882 | | 0.2648 | 3.0018 |
| 25 | Job 2 | 7 | 1 | 3 | | | 0.6687 | | 2.0154 | 3.0139 |
| 26 | Job 3 | 3 | 1/3 | 1 | | | 0.2431 | | 0.7306 | 3.0054 |
| 27 | | | | | | | | | CI | 0.0035 |
| 28 | Pairwise comparisons among jobs on nearness to family | | | | | | Scores | | CI/RI | 0.0061 |
| 29 | | Job 1 | Job 2 | Job 3 | | | | | | |
| 30 | Job 1 | 1 | 1/4 | 1/7 | | | 0.0824 | | 0.2473 | 3.0005 |
| 31 | Job 2 | 4 | 1 | 1/2 | | | 0.3151 | | 0.9460 | 3.0019 |
| 32 | Job 3 | 7 | 2 | 1 | | | 0.6025 | | 1.8096 | 3.0035 |
| 33 | | | | | | | | | CI | 0.0010 |
| 34 | Determining best job | | | | | | | | CI/RI | 0.0017 |

**②** **Ratios.** In cell O5, calculate the ratio of the two cells to its left with the formula

=N5/L5

and copy this to the range O6:O8.

**③** **Consistency index.** Calculate the consistency index *CI* in cell O9 with the formula

=(AVERAGE(O5:O8)–4)/3

Then in cell O10, calculate the ratio of *CI* to *RI* (for *n* = 4) with the formula

=O9/0.90

(The 0.90 comes from Table 9.8 earlier in the chapter. For the other four pairwise comparison matrices in Figure 9.18, we use *n* = 3 and *RI* = 0.58.)

As Figure 9.18 illustrates, all of the pairwise comparison matrices are sufficiently consistent—the *CI/RI* ratio for each is well less than 0.10. ■

## MODELING ISSUES

1. In Jane's job selection example, suppose that quality of life depends on two subobjectives: recreational facilities and educational facilities. Then we need a pairwise comparison matrix to calculate the proportion of the quality of life score that is determined by recreational facilities and the proportion that is determined by educational

facilities. Next, we need to determine how each job scores (separately) on recreational facilities and educational facilities. Then we can again determine a quality of life score for each job and proceed with AHP as before. Using this idea, AHP can handle a *hierarchy* of objectives and subobjectives—hence the term "hierarchy" in the name of the procedure.

2. Although the finished version of the **Choosing Jobs.xlsx** file can be used as a template for other AHP problems, it is clear by now that typical users would not want to go to all this trouble to create a spreadsheet model, certainly not from scratch. If you intend to make any real decisions with AHP, you will want to acquire special-purpose software such as Expert Choice. Alternatively, you can use the file **Choosing Jobs with VBA.xlsm** mentioned earlier. ∎

## ADDITIONAL APPLICATIONS

### Automated Manufacturing Decisions Using AHP

Weber (1993) reports the successful use of AHP in deciding which of several technologies to purchase for automated manufacturing. As he discusses, these decisions can have several types of impacts: quantitative financial (such as purchase cost), quantitative nonfinancial (such as throughput, cycle time, and scrap, which are difficult to translate directly into dollars), and qualitative (such as product quality and manufacturing flexibility, which are also difficult to translate into dollars). When the decision maker is trying to rate the different technologies along nonmonetary criteria, then he or she should use the method discussed in this section. (For example, how much more do you prefer technology 1 to technology 2 in the area of product quality?) However, he advises that when quantitative financial data are available (for example, technology 1 costs twice as much as technology 2), then this objective information should be used in the AHP preference matrices. Weber developed a software package called AutoMan to implement the AHP method. This software has been purchased by more than 800 customers since its first release in 1989.

### AHP in Saudi Arabia

Bahurmoz (2003) designed and implemented a system based on AHP to select the best candidates to send overseas to do graduate studies and eventually become teachers at the Dar Al-Hekma women's college in Saudi Arabia.

### Other Applications of AHP

AHP has been used by companies in many areas, including accounting, finance, marketing, energy resource planning, microcomputer selection, sociology, architecture, and political science. See Zahedi (1986), Golden et al. (1989), and Saaty (1988) for a discussion of applications of AHP. ∎

## PROBLEMS

### Skill-Building Problems

**25.** Each professor's annual salary increase is determined by his or her performance in three areas: teaching, research, and service to the university. The administration has assessed the pairwise comparison matrix for these objectives as shown in the file **P09_25.xlsx**. The administration has compared two professors with regard to their teaching, research, and service over the past year. The pairwise comparison matrices are also shown in this file.

a. Which professor should receive a bigger raise?

b. Does AHP indicate how large a raise each professor should be given?

c. Check the pairwise comparison matrix for consistency.

26. Your company is about to purchase a new PC. Three objectives are important in determining which computer you should purchase: cost, user friendliness, and software availability. The pairwise comparison matrix for these objectives is shown in the file **P09_26.xlsx**. Three computers are being considered for purchase. The performance of each computer with regard to each objective is indicated by the pairwise comparison matrices also shown in this file.

   a. Which computer should you purchase?

   b. Check the pairwise comparison matrices for consistency.

**27.** You are ready to select your mate for life and have determined that physical attractiveness, intelligence, and personality are key factors in selecting a satisfactory mate. Your pairwise comparison matrix for these objectives is shown in the file **P09_27.xlsx**. Three people (Chris, Jamie, and Pat) are begging to be your mate. (This problem attempts to be gender-neutral!) Your view of these people's attractiveness, intelligence, and personality is given in the pairwise comparison matrices also shown in this file.

   a. Who should you choose as your lifetime mate?

   b. Evaluate all pairwise comparison matrices for consistency.

28. In determining where to invest your money, two objectives, expected rate of return and degree of risk, are considered to be equally important. Two investments (1 and 2) have the pairwise comparison matrices shown in the file **P09_28.xlsx**.

   a. How would you rank these investments?

   b. Now suppose another investment (investment 3) is available. The pairwise comparison matrices for these investments are also shown in this file. (Observe that the entries in the comparison matrices for investments 1 and 2 have not changed.) How would you now rank the investments? Contrast your ranking of investments 1 and 2 with your answer from part **a**.

29. You are trying to determine which MBA program to attend. You have been accepted at two schools: Indiana and Northwestern. You have chosen three attributes to use in helping you make your decision: cost, starting salary for graduates, and ambience of school (can we party there?). Your pairwise comparison matrix for these attributes is shown in the file **P09_29.xlsx**. For each attribute, the pairwise comparison matrix for Indiana and Northwestern is also shown in this file. Which MBA program should you attend?

30. You are trying to determine which of two secretarial candidates (John or Sharon) to hire. The three objectives that are important to your decision are personality, typing ability, and intelligence. You have assessed the pairwise comparison matrix for the three objectives in the file **P09_30.xlsx**. The score of each employee on each objective is also shown in this file. If you follow the AHP method, which employee should you hire?

## Skill-Extending Problems

31. A consumer is trying to determine which type of frozen dinner to eat. She considers three attributes to be important: taste, nutritional value, and price. Nutritional value is considered to be determined by cholesterol and sodium level. Three types of dinners are under consideration. The pairwise comparison matrix for the three attributes is shown in the file **P09_31.xlsx**. Among the three frozen dinners, the pairwise comparison matrix for each attribute is also shown in this file. To determine how each dinner rates on nutrition, you will need the pairwise comparison matrix for cholesterol and sodium also shown in this file. Which frozen dinner would the consumer prefer? (*Hint:* The nutrition score for a dinner equals the score of the dinner on sodium multiplied by the weight for sodium plus the score for the dinner on cholesterol multiplied by the weight for cholesterol.)

32. Based on Lin et al. (1984). You have been hired by Arthur Ross to determine which of the following accounts receivable methods should be used in an audit of the Keating Five and Dime Store: analytic review (method 1), confirmations (method 2), or test of subsequent collections (method 3). The three criteria used to distinguish among the methods are reliability, cost, and validity. The pairwise comparison matrix for the three criteria is shown in the file **P09_32.xlsx**. The pairwise comparison matrices of the three accounting methods for the three criteria are shown in this file. Use AHP to determine which auditing procedure should be used. Also check the first pairwise comparison matrix for consistency.

# 9.5 CONCLUSION

Whenever we face a problem with multiple competing objectives, as is the case in many real-world problems, we are forced to make trade-offs between these objectives. This is usually a very difficult task, and not all management scientists agree on the best way to proceed. When the objectives are very different in nature, no method can disguise the inherent complexity of comparing "apples to oranges." Although one method, finding Pareto optimal solutions and drawing the resulting trade-off curve, locates solutions that are not dominated by any others, we still face the problem of choosing one of the (many) Pareto optimal solutions to implement. The other two methods we discussed in this chapter, goal programming and AHP, make trade-offs and ultimately locate an "optimal" solution. These methods have their critics, but when they are used carefully, they have the potential to help solve some difficult and important real-world problems.

## Summary of Key Management Science Terms

| Term | Explanation | Page |
|------|-------------|------|
| Goal programming | Optimization method that prioritizes multiple objectives (goals); tries to achieve higher priority goals before considering lower priority goals | 465 |
| Pareto optimal solution | Solution that is not dominated, that is, no other solution is at least as good on all objectives and better on at least one objective | 475 |
| Trade-off curve | Curve showing Pareto optimal solutions, used primarily to show the trade-offs between two competing objectives | 475 |
| Analytical Hierarchy Process (AHP) | Method used to find best decision when a decision maker faces multiple criteria; requires a series of pairwise comparisons between criteria and between alternative decisions for each criterion | 484 |

## PROBLEMS

### Skill-Building Problems

**33.** The Pine Valley Board of Education must hire teachers for the coming school year. The types of teachers and the salaries that must be paid are given in the file **P09_33.xlsx**. For example, 20 teachers who are qualified to teach history and science have applied for jobs, and each of these teachers must be paid an annual salary of $21,000. Each teacher who is hired teaches the two subjects he or she is qualified to teach. Pine Valley needs to hire 35 teachers qualified to teach history, 30 teachers qualified to teach science, 40 teachers qualified to teach math, and 32 teachers qualified to teach English. The board has $1.4 million to spend on teachers' salaries. A penalty cost of $1 is incurred for each dollar the board goes over budget. For each teacher by which Pine Valley's goals are unmet, the following costs are incurred (because of the lower quality of education): science, $30,000; math, $28,000; history, $26,000; and English, $24,000. Determine how the board can minimize its total cost due to unmet goals.

**34.** Stockco fills orders for three products for a local warehouse. Stockco must determine how many of each product should be ordered at the beginning of the current month. This month, 400 units of product 1,
500 units of product 2, and 300 units of product 3 will be demanded. The cost and space taken up by 1 unit of each product are shown in the file **P09_34.xlsx**. If Stockco runs out of stock before the end of the month, the stockout costs also shown in this file are incurred. Stockco has $17,000 to spend on ordering products and has 3700 square feet of warehouse space. A $1 penalty is assessed for each dollar spent over the budget limit, and a $10 cost is assessed for every square foot of warehouse space needed.

**a.** Determine Stockco's optimal ordering policy.

**b.** Suppose that Stockco has set the following goals, listed in order of priority:
- Goal 1: Spend at most $17,000.
- Goal 2: Use at most 3700 square feet of warehouse space.
- Goal 3: Meet demand for product 1.
- Goal 4: Meet demand for product 2.
- Goal 5: Meet demand for product 3.

Develop a goal programming model for Stockco.

**35.** BeatTrop Foods is trying to choose one of three companies to merge with. Seven factors are important in this decision:
- Factor 1: Contribution to profitability
- Factor 2: Growth potential

- Factor 3: Labor environment
- Factor 4: R&D ability of company
- Factor 5: Organizational fit
- Factor 6: Relative size
- Factor 7: Industry commonality

The pairwise comparison matrix for these factors is shown in the file **P09_35.xlsx**. The three contenders for merger have the pairwise comparison matrices for each factor also shown in this file.

Use AHP to determine the company that BeatTrop should merge with.

**36.** Productco produces three products. Each product requires labor, lumber, and paint. The resource requirements, unit price, and variable cost (exclusive of raw materials) for each product are given in the file **P09_36.xlsx**. At present, 900 labor hours, 1550 gallons of paint, and 1600 board feet of lumber are available. Additional labor can be purchased at $6 per hour. Additional paint can be purchased at $2 per gallon. Additional lumber can be purchased at $3 per board foot. For the following two sets of priorities, use goal programming to determine an optimal production schedule. For set 1:
- Priority 1: Obtain profit of at least $10,500.
- Priority 2: Purchase no additional labor.
- Priority 3: Purchase no additional paint.
- Priority 4: Purchase no additional lumber.

For set 2:
- Priority 1: Purchase no additional labor.
- Priority 2: Obtain profit of at least $10,500.
- Priority 3: Purchase no additional paint.
- Priority 4: Purchase no additional lumber.

## Skill-Extending Problems

**37.** Jobs at Indiana University are rated on three factors:
- Factor 1: Complexity of duties
- Factor 2: Education required
- Factor 3: Mental and/or visual demands

For each job at IU, the requirement for each factor has been rated on a scale of 1 to 4, with a 4 in factor 1 representing high complexity of duty, a 4 in factor 2 representing high educational requirement, and a 4 in factor 3 representing high mental and/or visual demands. IU wants to determine a formula for grading each job. To do this, it will assign a point value to the score for each factor that a job requires. For example, suppose that level 2 of factor 1 yields a point total of 10, level 3 of factor 2 yields a point total of 20, and level 3 of factor 3 yields a point total of 30. Then a job with these requirements has a point total of 10 + 20 + 30 = 60. A job's hourly salary equals half its point total. IU has two goals (listed in order of priority) in

setting up the points given to each level of each job factor.
- Goal 1: When increasing the level of a factor by 1, the points should increase by at least 10. For example, level 2 of factor 1 should earn at least 10 more points than level 1 of factor 1. Goal 1 is to minimize the sum of deviations from this requirement.
- Goal 2: For the benchmark jobs referred to in the file **P09_37.xlsx**, the actual point total for each job should come as close as possible to the point total listed in the table. Goal 2 is to minimize the sum of the absolute deviations of the point totals from the desired scores.

Use goal programming to find appropriate point totals. What salary should a job with skill levels of 3 for each factor be paid?

**38.** A hospital outpatient clinic performs four types of operations. The profit per operation, as well as the minutes of X-ray time and laboratory time used, are given in the file **P09_38.xlsx**. The clinic has 500 private rooms and 500 intensive care rooms. Type 1 and type 2 operations require a patient to stay in an intensive care room for one day, whereas type 3 and type 4 operations require a patient to stay in a private room for one day. Each day, the hospital is required to perform at least 100 operations of each type. The hospital has set the following goals (listed in order of priority):
- Goal 1: Earn a daily profit of at least $100,000.
- Goal 2: Use at most 50 hours daily of X-ray time.
- Goal 3: Use at most 40 hours daily of laboratory time.

Use goal programming to determine the types of operations that should be performed.

**39.** You are trying to determine which city to live in. New York and Chicago are under consideration. Four objectives will determine your decision: housing cost, cultural opportunities, quality of schools and universities, and crime level. The weight for each objective is in the file **P09_39.xlsx**. For each objective (except for quality of schools and universities), New York and Chicago scores are also given in this file. Suppose that the score for each city on the quality of schools and universities depends on two things: a score on public school quality and a score on university quality. The pairwise comparison matrix for public school and university quality is also shown in this file. To see how each city scores on public school quality and university quality, use the pairwise comparison matrices also shown in this file. You should be able to derive a score for each city on the quality of schools and universities objective. Then use AHP to determine where you should live.

**40.** At Lummins Engine Corporation, production employees work 10 hours per day, 4 days per week. Each day of the week, at least the following number of employees must be working: Monday through Friday, 7 employees; Saturday and Sunday, 3 employees. Lummins has set the following goals, listed in order of priority:

- Goal 1: Meet employee requirements with 11 workers.
- Goal 2: The average number of weekend days off per employee should be at least 1.5 days.
- Goal 3: The average number of consecutive days off an employee gets during the week should not exceed 2.8 days.

Use goal programming to determine how to schedule Lummins employees.

**41.** You are the mayor of Gotham City and you must determine a tax policy for the city. Five types of taxes are used to raise money:

- Property taxes. Let $p$ be the property tax rate.
- A sales tax on all items except food, drugs, and durable goods. Let $s$ be the sales tax rate.
- A sales tax on durable goods. Let $d$ be the durable goods sales tax rate.
- A gasoline sales tax. Let $g$ be the gasoline sales tax rate.
- A sales tax on food and drugs. Let $f$ be the sales tax on food and drugs.

The city consists of three groups of people: low income (LI), middle income (MI), and high income (HI). The amount of revenue (in millions of dollars) raised from each group by setting a particular tax at a 1% level is given in the file **P09_41.xlsx**. For example, a 3% tax on durable good sales will raise 360 million dollars from low-income people. Your tax policy must satisfy the following restrictions:

- Restriction 1: The tax burden on MI people cannot exceed $2.8 billion.
- Restriction 2: The tax burden on HI people cannot exceed $2.4 billion.
- Restriction 3: The total revenue raised must exceed the current level of $6.5 billion.
- Restriction 4: $s$ must be between 1% and 3%.

Given these restrictions, the city council has set the following three goals (listed in order of priority):

- Goal 1: Limit the tax burden on LI people to $2 billion.
- Goal 2: Keep the property tax rate under 3%.
- Goal 3: If their tax burden becomes too high, 20% of the LI people, 20% of the MI people, and 40% of the HI people may consider moving to the suburbs. Suppose that this will happen if their total tax burden exceeds $1.5 billion. To discourage this

exodus, goal 3 is to keep the total tax burden on these people below $1.5 billion.

Use goal programming to determine an optimal tax policy.

**42.** Based on Sartoris and Spruill (1974). Wivco produces two products, which it sells on both a cash and credit basis. Revenues from credit sales will not have been received but are included in determining profit earned during the current 6-month period. Sales during the next 6 months can be made either from units produced during the next 6 months or from beginning inventory. Relevant information about products 1 and 2 is as follows.

- During the next 6 months, at most 150 units of product 1 can be sold on a cash basis, and at most 100 units of product 1 can be sold on a credit basis. It costs $35 to produce each unit of product 1, and each sells for $40. A credit sale of a unit of product 1 yields $0.50 less profit than a cash sale (because of delays in receiving payment). Two hours of production time are needed to produce each unit of product 1. At the beginning of the 6-month period, 60 units of product 1 are in inventory.
- During the next 6 months, at most 175 units of product 2 can be sold on a cash basis, and at most 250 units of product 2 can be sold on a credit basis. It costs $45 to produce each unit of product 2, and each sells for $52.50. A credit sale of a unit of product 2 yields $1.00 less profit than a cash sale. Four hours of production time are needed to produce each unit of product 2. At the beginning of the 6-month period, 30 units of product 2 are in inventory.
- During the next 6 months, Wivco has 1000 hours for production available. At the end of the next 6 months, Wivco incurs a 10% holding cost on the value of ending inventory (measured relative to production cost). An opportunity cost of 5% is also assessed against any cash on hand at the end of the 6-month period.

**a.** Develop and solve an LP model that yields Wivco's maximum profit during the next 6 months. What is Wivco's ending inventory position? Assuming an initial cash balance of $0, what is Wivco's ending cash balance?

**b.** Because an ending inventory and cash position of $0 is undesirable (for ongoing operations), Wivco is considering other options. At the beginning of the 6-month period, Wivco can obtain a loan (secured by ending inventory) that incurs an interest cost equal to 5% of the value of the loan. The maximum value of the loan is 75% of the value of the ending inventory. The loan will be repaid one year from now. Wivco has the following goals (listed in order of priority):

- Goal 1: Make the ending cash balance of Wivco come as close as possible to $75.
- Goal 2: Make profit come as close as possible to the profit level obtained in part **a**.
- Goal 3: At any time, Wivco's current ratio is defined to be

$$\text{Current ratio} = \frac{\text{Wivco's assets}}{\text{Wivco's liabilities}}$$

Assuming initially that current liabilities equal $150, 6 months from now Wivco's current ratio will equal

$$\text{Current ratio} = \frac{CR + AR + EI}{150 + \text{Size of loan}}$$

where CB is the ending cash balance, AR is the value of accounts receivable, and EI is the value of the ending inventory. Six months from now, Wivco wants the current ratio to be as close as possible to 2.

Use goal programming to determine Wivco's production and financial strategy.

## Modeling Problems

**43.** How might you use goal programming to help Congress balance the budget?

**44.** A company is considering buying up to five other businesses. Given knowledge of the company's view of the trade-off between risk and return, how could trade-off curves be used to determine the companies that should be purchased?

**45.** How would you use AHP to determine the greatest sports record of all time? (Many believe it is Joe DiMaggio's 56-game hitting streak.)

**46.** You are planning to renovate a hospital. How would you use AHP to help determine what improvements to include in the renovation?

**47.** You are planning to overhaul a hospital computer system. How would you use AHP to determine the type of computer system to install?

**48.** You have been commissioned to assign 100 remedial education teachers to the 40 schools in the St. Louis School System. What are some objectives you might consider in assigning the teachers to schools?

**49.** You have been hired as a consultant to help design a new airport in northern Indiana that will supplant O'Hare as Chicago's major airport. Discuss the objectives you consider important in designing and locating the airport.

**50.** In the Indiana MBA program we need to divide a class of 60 students into 10 6-person teams. In the interest of diversity, we have the following goals (listed in descending order of importance):

- At least one woman per team
- At least one member of a minority per team
- At least one student with a financial or accounting background per team
- At least one engineer per team

Explain how you could use the material in this chapter to develop a model to assign students to teams.

# CASE | 9.1 PLAY TIME TOY COMPANY

Play Time Toy faces a highly seasonal pattern of sales. In the past, Play Time has used a *seasonal* production schedule, where the amount produced each month matches the sales for that month. Under this production plan, inventory is maintained at a constant level. The production manager, Thomas Lindop, is proposing a switch to a *level*, or constant, production schedule. This schedule would result in significant savings in production costs but would have higher storage and handling costs, fluctuating levels of inventories, and implications for financing. Jonathan King, president of Play Time Toy, has been reviewing pro forma income statements, cash budgets, and balance sheets for the coming year under the two production scenarios. Table 9.9 shows the pro forma analysis under seasonal production, and Table 9.10 shows the pro forma analysis under level production.

---

**Table 9.9**   Seasonal Production

**Annual net profit**   237         **Play Time Toy Company**

|  | Actual Dec 2006 | Projected for 2007 | | | | | | | | | | | | |
|---|---|---|---|---|---|---|---|---|---|---|---|---|---|---|
|  |  | Jan | Feb | Mar | Apr | May | June | July | Aug | Sept | Oct | Nov | Dec | Total |
| Production (sales value) | 850 | 108 | 126 | 145 | 125 | 125 | 125 | 145 | 1,458 | 1,655 | 1,925 | 2,057 | 1,006 | 9000 |
| Inventory (sales value) | 813 | 813 | 813 | 813 | 813 | 813 | 813 | 813 | 813 | 813 | 813 | 813 | 813 | |

| INCOME STATEMENT | | Jan | Feb | Mar | Apr | May | June | July | Aug | Sept | Oct | Nov | Dec | Total |
|---|---|---|---|---|---|---|---|---|---|---|---|---|---|---|
| Net sales | | 108 | 126 | 145 | 125 | 125 | 125 | 145 | 1,458 | 1,655 | 1,925 | 2,057 | 1,006 | 9,000 |
| Cost of goods sold | | | | | | | | | | | | | | |
|   Materials and regular wages | | 70 | 82 | 94 | 81 | 81 | 81 | 94 | 950 | 1,079 | 1,254 | 1,340 | 656 | 5,865 |
|   Overtime wages | | 0 | 0 | 0 | 0 | 0 | 0 | 0 | 61 | 91 | 131 | 151 | 0 | 435 |
| Gross profit | | 38 | 44 | 51 | 44 | 44 | 44 | 51 | 447 | 486 | 539 | 565 | 350 | 2,700 |
| Operating expenses | | 188 | 188 | 188 | 188 | 188 | 188 | 188 | 188 | 188 | 188 | 188 | 188 | 2,256 |
| Inventory cost | | 0 | 0 | 0 | 0 | 0 | 0 | 0 | 0 | 0 | 0 | 0 | 0 | 0 |
| Profit before interest and taxes | | (150) | (144) | (137) | (144) | (144) | (144) | (137) | 259 | 298 | 351 | 377 | 162 | 444 |
| Net interest payments | | 10 | 2 | 1 | 1 | 2 | 2 | 2 | 3 | 7 | 18 | 19 | 19 | 86 |
| Profit before taxes | | (160) | (146) | (138) | (146) | (146) | (147) | (140) | 256 | 290 | 333 | 359 | 144 | 358 |
| Taxes | | (55) | (50) | (47) | (50) | (50) | (50) | (48) | 87 | 99 | 113 | 122 | 49 | 122 |
| Net profit | | (106) | (97) | (91) | (96) | (97) | (97) | (92) | 169 | 192 | 220 | 237 | 95 | 237 |

| BALANCE SHEET | Actual Dec 2006 | Projected for 2007 | | | | | | | | | | | |
|---|---|---|---|---|---|---|---|---|---|---|---|---|---|
|  |  | Jan | Feb | Mar | Apr | May | June | July | Aug | Sept | Oct | Nov | Dec |
| Cash | 175 | 782 | 1,365 | 1,116 | 934 | 808 | 604 | 450 | 175 | 175 | 175 | 175 | 175 |
| Accts receivable | 2,628 | 958 | 234 | 271 | 270 | 250 | 250 | 270 | 1,603 | 3,113 | 3,580 | 3,982 | 3,063 |
| Inventory | 530 | 530 | 530 | 530 | 530 | 530 | 530 | 530 | 530 | 530 | 530 | 530 | 530 |
| Net P/E | 1,070 | 1,070 | 1,070 | 1,070 | 1,070 | 1,070 | 1,070 | 1,070 | 1,070 | 1,070 | 1,070 | 1,070 | 1,070 |
| Total Assets | 4,403 | 3,340 | 3,199 | 2,987 | 2,804 | 2,658 | 2,454 | 2,320 | 3,378 | 4,888 | 5,355 | 5,757 | 4,838 |
| Accts payable | 255 | 32 | 38 | 44 | 38 | 38 | 38 | 44 | 437 | 497 | 578 | 617 | 302 |
| Notes payable | 680 | 0 | 0 | 0 | 0 | 0 | 0 | 0 | 408 | 1,600 | 1,653 | 1,656 | 966 |
| Accrued taxes | 80 | 25 | (24) | (151) | (232) | (282) | (363) | (411) | (324) | (256) | (143) | (21) | (4) |
| Long term debt | 450 | 450 | 450 | 450 | 450 | 450 | 425 | 425 | 425 | 425 | 425 | 425 | 400 |
| Equity | 2,938 | 2,832 | 2,736 | 2,644 | 2,548 | 2,452 | 2,355 | 2,263 | 2,431 | 2,623 | 2,843 | 3,080 | 3,175 |
| Total liability and equity | 4,403 | 3,340 | 3,199 | 2,987 | 2,804 | 2,658 | 2,454 | 2,320 | 3,378 | 4,888 | 5,355 | 5,757 | 4,838 |

## Table 9.10  Level Production

Annual net profit    373          Play Time Toy Company

| | Actual Dec 2006 | Jan | Feb | Mar | Apr | May | June | July | Aug | Sept | Oct | Nov | Dec | Total |
|---|---|---|---|---|---|---|---|---|---|---|---|---|---|---|
| | | **Projected for 2007** | | | | | | | | | | | | |
| Production (sales value) | 850 | 750 | 750 | 750 | 750 | 750 | 750 | 750 | 750 | 750 | 750 | 750 | 750 | 9000 |
| Inventory (sales value) | 813 | 1455 | 2079 | 2684 | 3309 | 3934 | 4559 | 5164 | 4456 | 3551 | 2376 | 1069 | 813 | |

| INCOME STATEMENT | | Jan | Feb | Mar | Apr | May | June | July | Aug | Sept | Oct | Nov | Dec | Total |
|---|---|---|---|---|---|---|---|---|---|---|---|---|---|---|
| Net sales | | 108 | 126 | 145 | 125 | 125 | 125 | 145 | 1,458 | 1,655 | 1,925 | 2,057 | 1,006 | 9,000 |
| Cost of goods sold | | | | | | | | | | | | | | |
|   Materials and regular wages | | 70 | 82 | 94 | 81 | 81 | 81 | 94 | 950 | 1,079 | 1,254 | 1,340 | 656 | 5,865 |
|   Overtime wages | | 0 | 0 | 0 | 0 | 0 | 0 | 0 | 0 | 0 | 0 | 0 | 0 | 0 |
| Gross profit | | 38 | 44 | 51 | 44 | 44 | 44 | 51 | 508 | 576 | 671 | 717 | 350 | 3,135 |
| Operating expenses | | 188 | 188 | 188 | 188 | 188 | 188 | 188 | 188 | 188 | 188 | 188 | 188 | 2,256 |
| Inventory cost | | 0 | 2 | 6 | 10 | 13 | 17 | 20 | 16 | 11 | 4 | 0 | 0 | 100 |
| Profit before interest and taxes | | (150) | (147) | (143) | (154) | (158) | (161) | (158) | 304 | 377 | 478 | 529 | 162 | 779 |
| Net interest payments | | 10 | 3 | 2 | 5 | 10 | 15 | 21 | 26 | 32 | 37 | 31 | 22 | 214 |
| Profit before taxes | | (160) | (149) | (146) | (159) | (168) | (177) | (179) | 277 | 346 | 441 | 498 | 141 | 565 |
| Taxes | | (55) | (51) | (50) | (54) | (57) | (60) | (61) | 94 | 118 | 150 | 169 | 48 | 192 |
| Net profit | | (106) | (99) | (96) | (105) | (111) | (117) | (118) | 183 | 228 | 291 | 329 | 93 | 373 |

| BALANCE SHEET | Actual Dec 2006 | Jan | Feb | Mar | Apr | May | June | July | Aug | Sept | Oct | Nov | Dec |
|---|---|---|---|---|---|---|---|---|---|---|---|---|---|---|
| | | **Projected for 2007** | | | | | | | | | | | | |
| Cash | 175 | 556 | 724 | 175 | 175 | 175 | 175 | 175 | 175 | 175 | 175 | 175 | 175 |
| Accts receivable | 2,628 | 958 | 234 | 271 | 270 | 250 | 250 | 270 | 1,603 | 3,113 | 3,580 | 3,982 | 3,063 |
| Inventory | 530 | 948 | 1,355 | 1,749 | 2,157 | 2,564 | 2,971 | 3,365 | 2,904 | 2,314 | 1,549 | 697 | 530 |
| Net P/E | 1,070 | 1,070 | 1,070 | 1,070 | 1,070 | 1,070 | 1,070 | 1,070 | 1,070 | 1,070 | 1,070 | 1,070 | 1,070 |
| Total Assets | 4,403 | 3,533 | 3,383 | 3,265 | 3,672 | 4,059 | 4,466 | 4,880 | 5,752 | 6,672 | 6,374 | 5,924 | 4,838 |
| Accts payable | 255 | 225 | 225 | 225 | 225 | 225 | 225 | 225 | 225 | 225 | 225 | 225 | 225 |
| Notes payable | 680 | 0 | 0 | 108 | 704 | 1,259 | 1,900 | 2,493 | 3,087 | 3,693 | 2,953 | 2,005 | 836 |
| Accrued taxes | 80 | 25 | (25) | (155) | (240) | (297) | (389) | (450) | (355) | (269) | (119) | 50 | 66 |
| Long term debt | 450 | 450 | 450 | 450 | 450 | 450 | 425 | 425 | 425 | 425 | 425 | 425 | 400 |
| Equity | 2,938 | 2,832 | 2,734 | 2,637 | 2,533 | 2,422 | 2,305 | 2,187 | 2,370 | 2,599 | 2,890 | 3,218 | 3,311 |
| Total liability and equity | 4,403 | 3,533 | 3,383 | 3,265 | 3,672 | 4,059 | 4,466 | 4,880 | 5,752 | 6,672 | 6,374 | 5,924 | 4,838 |

Greg Cole, chief financial officer of Play Time, prepared the two tables. He explained that the pro forma analyses in Tables 9.9 and 9.10 take fully into account the 11% interest payments on the unsecured loan from Bay Trust Company and the 3% interest received from its cash account. An interest charge of 11%/12 on the balance of the loan at the end of a month must be paid the next month.

Similarly, an interest payment of 3%/12 on the cash balance at the end of a month is received in the next month.

The inventory available at the end of December 2006 is $530,000 (measured in terms of cost to produce). Mr. Cole assumed that this inventory represents a sales value of $530,000/0.651667 = $813,300.

## Table 9.11  Play Time Cost Information

- **Gross margin.** The cost of goods sold (excluding overtime costs) is 65.1667% of sales under any production schedule. Materials costs are 30% of sales. All other nonmaterials costs, including regular wages but excluding overtime wages, are 35.1667% of sales.
- **Overtime cost.** Running at capacity but without using any overtime, the plant can produce $1,049,000 of monthly sales. Units produced in excess of this capacity in a month incur an additional overtime cost of 15% of sales. (The monthly production capacity of the plant running on full overtime is $2,400,000 of sales. Since November has the maximum level of projected sales at $2,057,000, the capacity on full overtime should never pose a problem.)
- **Inventory cost.** The plant has a limited capacity to store finished goods. It can store $1,663,000 worth of sales at the plant. Additional units must be moved and stored in rented warehouse space. The cost of storage, handling, and insurance of finished goods over this capacity is 7% of the sales value of the goods per year, or 7%/12 per month.

The inventory and overtime costs in Tables 9.9 and 9.10 are based on the cost information developed by Mr. Lindop. This information is summarized in Table 9.11.

Mr. Cole further explained how the cost information was used in the pro forma analyses. For example, in Table 9.9, the production in August is $1,458,000. The overtime cost in August is therefore calculated to be $61,000 (= 0.15 × (1,458,000 − 1,049,000)). Play Time uses LIFO (last-in, first-out) accounting, so overtime costs are always charged in the month that they occur.[4] The annual overtime cost for the seasonal production plan is $435,000. In Table 9.10, under level production, finished goods worth $5,164,000 are in inventory at the end of July. The inventory cost for the month is $20,000 (= 0.07/12 × (5,164,000 − 1,663,000)). The annual-inventory cost for the level production plan is $100,000.

Mr. Lindop felt that a minimum of $813,300 of inventory (measured in terms of sales value, or $530,000 measured in terms of cost to produce) must be kept on hand at the end of each month. This inventory level represents a reasonable safety stock, which is required because orders do not occur uniformly during a month.

Mr. King was impressed at the possible increase in profit from $237,000 under the seasonal production plan to $373,000 under level production. While studying the pro forma projections, Mr. King realized that some combination of the two production plans might be even better. He asked Mr. Lindop to try to find a production plan with a higher profit than the seasonal and level plans.

Mr. Lindop proceeded to develop a spreadsheet based LP model to maximize annual net profit.

## Question

*Note:* Mr. Lindop's model is contained in the file. **Play Time.xlsx.** The spreadsheet is ready to be optimized, but it has not been optimized yet.

1. Run the optimization model in this file. What is the optimal production plan? What is the optimal annual net profit? How does this optimal production plan compare to the seasonal and level production plans?

2. Suppose that Play Time's bankers will not extend any credit over $1.9 million—in other words, the loan balance in any month cannot exceed $1.9 million. Modify the spreadsheet model to take into account this restriction. What is the optimal production plan in this case? What is the optimal annual net profit?

3. Annual profit is a measure of reward for Play Time Toy. The maximum loan balance is a measure of risk for the bank. Construct a trade-off curve between optimal annual profit and the maximum loan balance. ∎

---

[4] This assumes that overtime production is used only to satisfy current demand and not to build up inventory.

# Decision Making Under Uncertainty

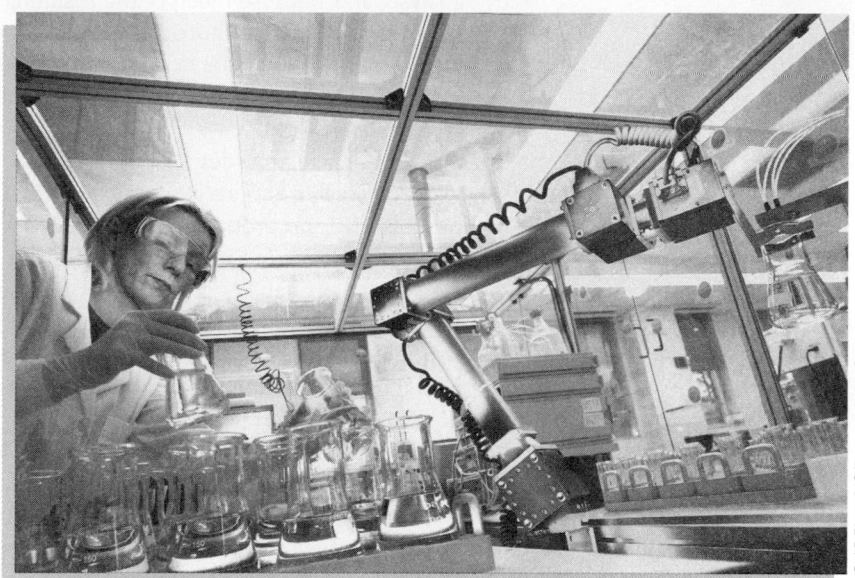

© AP Photo/HO/Photo: Bayer AG

## DECIDING WHETHER TO DEVELOP
## NEW DRUGS AT BAYER

The formal decision-making process discussed in this chapter is often used to make difficult decisions in the face of much uncertainty, large monetary values, and long-term consequences. Stonebraker (2002) chronicles one such decision-making process he performed for Bayer Pharmaceuticals in 1999. The development of a new drug is a time-consuming and expensive process that is filled with risks along the way. A pharmaceutical company must first get the proposed drug through preclinical trials, where the drug is tested on animals. Assuming this stage is successful (and only about half are), the company can then file an application with the Food and Drug Administration (FDA) to conduct clinical trials on humans. These clinical trials have three phases. Phase 1 is designed to test the safety of the drug on a small sample of healthy patients. Phase 2 is designed to identify the optimal dose of the new drug on patients with the disease. Phase 3 is a statistically designed study to prove the efficacy and safety of the new drug on a larger sample of patients with the disease. Failure at any one of these phases means that further testing stops and the drug is never brought to market. Of course, this means that all costs up to the failure point are lost. If the drug makes it through the clinical tests (and only about 25% of all drugs do so), the company can then apply to the FDA for permission to manufacture and market its drug in the United States. After the FDA approves, the company is free to launch the drug in the marketplace.

The study involved the evaluation of a new drug for busting blood clots called BAY 57-9602, and it commenced at a time just prior to the first decision point: whether to conduct preclinical tests. This was the company's first formal use of decision making for evaluating a new drug, so to convince the company of the worth of such a study, Stonebraker did exactly what a successful management science study should do. He formulated the problem and its objectives; he identified risks, costs, and benefits; he involved key people in the organization to help provide the data needed for the decision analysis; and, because much of the resulting data were educated guesses at best, he performed a thorough sensitivity analysis on the inputs. Although we are not told in the article how everything turned out, the analysis did persuade Bayer management to proceed in January 2000 with preclinical testing of the drug.

The article provides a fascinating look at how such a study should proceed. Because there is so much uncertainty, the key is determining probabilities and probability distributions for the various inputs. First, there are uncertainties in the various phases of testing. Each of these can be modeled with a probability of success. For example, the chance of making it through preclinical testing was assessed to be about 65% for BAY 57-9602, although management preferred to use the more conservative benchmark of 50% (based on historical data on other drugs) for the decision analysis. Many of the other uncertain quantities, such as the eventual market share, are continuous random variables. Because the decision tree approach discussed in this chapter requires discrete random variables, usually with only a few possible values, Stonebraker used a popular three-point approximation for all continuous quantities. He asked experts to assess the 10th percentile, the 50th percentile, and the 90th percentile, and he assigned probabilities 0.3, 0.4, and 0.3 to these three values. [The validity of such an approximation is discussed in Keefer and Bodily (1983).]

After getting all such estimates of uncertain quantities from the company experts, the author examined the expected net present value (NPV) of all costs and benefits from developing the new drug. To see which of the various uncertain quantities affected the expected NPV most, he varied each such quantity, one at a time, from its 10th percentile to its 90th percentile, leaving the other inputs at their base 50th percentile values. This identified several quantities that the expected NPV was most sensitive to, including the peak product share and price per treatment in the United States, and the annual growth rate. The expected NPV was not nearly as sensitive to other uncertain inputs, including the product launch date and the production process yield. Therefore, in the final decision analysis, Stonebraker treated the sensitive inputs as uncertain and the less sensitive inputs as certain at their base values. He also calculated the risk profile from developing the drug. This indicates the probability distribution of NPV, taking all sources of uncertainty into account. Although this risk profile was not exactly optimistic (90% chance of losing money using the conservative probabilities of success, 67% chance of losing money with the more optimistic product-specific probabilities of success), this risk profile compared favorably with Bayer's other potential projects. This evaluation, plus the rigor and defensibility of the study, led Bayer management to give the go-ahead on preclinical testing. ■

# 10.1 INTRODUCTION

In this chapter, we provide a formal framework for analyzing decision problems that involve uncertainty. We discuss the following:

- Criteria for choosing among alternative decisions
- How probabilities are used in the decision-making process
- How early decisions affect decisions made at a later stage
- How the value of information can be quantified
- How attitudes toward risk can affect the analysis

Throughout, we employ a powerful graphical tool—a decision tree—to guide the analysis. A decision tree enables the decision maker to view all important aspects of the problem at once: the decision alternatives, the uncertain outcomes and their probabilities, the economic consequences, and the chronological order of events. We show how to implement decision trees in Excel by taking advantage of a very powerful and flexible add-in from Palisade called PrecisionTree.

Many examples of decision making under uncertainty exist in the business world, including the following:

- Whenever a company must decide whether to develop and then market a new product, a number of uncertainties affect the decision, including the customers' reaction to this product and, in situations like the one described in the chapter opener, the technical success of the product. If the product makes it to market and then generates high customer demand, the company will make a large profit. But if the product is technically unsuccessful, or if it makes it to market and demand is low—both very real possibilities for most new products—the company might not even recoup its development costs. Decision analysis helps a company decide whether to continue developing and marketing a new product at the various stages of the product's life cycle.

- Borison (1995) describes an application of formal decision analysis by Oglethorpe Power Corporation (OPC), a Georgia-based electricity supplier. The basic decision OPC faced was whether to build a new transmission line to supply large amounts of electricity to parts of Florida and, if the company decided to build it, how to finance this project. OPC had to deal with several sources of uncertainty: the cost of building new facilities, the demand for power in Florida, and various market conditions, such as the spot price of electricity.

- Utility companies must make many decisions that have significant environmental and economic consequences. [Balson et al. (1992) provide a good discussion of such consequences.] For these companies, it is not necessarily enough to conform to federal or state environmental regulations. Recent court decisions have found companies liable—for huge settlements—when accidents occurred, even though the companies followed all existing regulations. Therefore, when utility companies decide, say, whether to replace equipment or mitigate the effects of environmental pollution, they must take into account the possible environmental consequences (such as injuries to people) as well as economic consequences (such as lawsuits). An aspect of these situations that makes decision analysis particularly difficult is that the potential disasters are often extremely improbable; hence, their likelihoods are difficult to assess accurately.

- Butler et al. (2005) describe how a team of analysts used decision analysis to help U.S. government agencies develop a model to evaluate the alternatives for the disposition of excess plutonium in Russia left after dismantling weapons. Russian scientists modified the model with the aid of the U.S. team to evaluate Russia's disposition alternatives. In another article on a similar topic, Keisler et al. (2004) describe how they used decision analysis to allocate risks between vendors and the Department of Energy in the cleanup of nuclear waste tanks at the Hanford site in Washington state. In still another related article, Dunning et al. (2001) describe how the New York Power Authority used decision analysis to schedule refueling of one of its nuclear power plants.

- Clemen and Kwit (2001) describe the use of decision analysis at Eastman Kodak from 1990 to 1999. They estimate that decision analysis contributed approximately a billion dollars to the company over this time. Besides its contributions to the bottom line, decision analysis also promoted careful thinking about the strategies and alternatives at Kodak and improved the managers' understanding of risk.

## 10.2 ELEMENTS OF A DECISION ANALYSIS

Decision making under uncertainty occurs in a variety of contexts, but all problems have three common elements: (1) the set of decisions (or strategies) available to the decision maker, (2) the set of possible outcomes and the probabilities of these outcomes, and (3) a value model that prescribes monetary values for the various decision–outcome combinations. After these elements are known, the decision maker can find an "optimal" decision, depending on the optimality criterion chosen.

We first discuss the basic elements of any decision analysis for a very simple problem. We assume that a decision maker must choose among three decisions, labeled $D1$, $D2$, and $D3$. Each of these decisions has three possible outcomes, labeled $O1$, $O2$, and $O3$.

### Payoff Tables

At the time the decision must be made, the decision maker does *not* know which outcome will occur. However, after the decision is made, the outcome is eventually revealed, and a corresponding payoff is received. This payoff might actually be a cost, in which case it is indicated as a negative value. The listing of payoffs for all decision–outcome pairs is called a **payoff table**.[1] For this simple decision problem, the payoff table appears in Table 10.1. For example, if the decision maker chooses decision $D2$ and outcome $O3$ then occurs, a payoff of $40 is received.

**Table 10.1   Payoff Table for the Simple Decision Problem**

|  |  | *Outcome* | | |
| --- | --- | --- | --- | --- |
|  |  | *O1* | *O2* | *O3* |
| **Decision** | *D1* | 10 | 10 | 10 |
|  | *D2* | −10 | 20 | 40 |
|  | *D3* | −30 | 30 | 70 |

> A **payoff table** lists the payoff for each decision–outcome pair. Positive values correspond to rewards (or gains), and negative values correspond to costs (or losses).

[1] In situations where all monetary consequences are costs, it is customary to list these costs in a **cost table.** In this case, all monetary values are shown as *positive* costs.

*A decision maker gets to decide which row of the payoff table she wants. However, she does not get to choose the column.*

This table shows that the decision maker can play it safe by choosing decision $D1$. This provides a sure $10 payoff. With decision $D2$, rewards of $20 or $40 are possible, but a loss of $10 is also possible. Decision $D3$ is even riskier; the possible loss is greater, and the maximum gain is also greater. Which decision would you choose? Would your choice change if the values in the payoff table were really measured in *thousands* of dollars? The answers to these questions are what this chapter is all about. We need a criterion for making choices, and we need to evaluate this criterion so that we can identify the "best" decision. As we will see, it is customary to use one particular criterion for decisions involving "moderate" amounts of money.

Before proceeding, we need to emphasize one very important point. In any decision-making problem with uncertainty, the optimal decision can always have less than optimal results—that is, we can be unlucky. Regardless of which decision we choose, we might get an outcome that, in hindsight, makes us wish we had made a different decision. For example, if we make decision $D3$, hoping for a large reward, we might get outcome $O1$, in which case, we will wish we had chosen decision $D1$ or $D2$. Or if we choose decision $D2$, hoping to limit possible losses, we might get outcome $O3$, in which case we will wish we had chosen decision $D3$. The point is that decision makers must make rational decisions, based on the information they have when the decisions must be made, and then live with the consequences. Second guessing these decisions, just because of unlucky outcomes, is not a fair criticism.

## FUNDAMENTAL INSIGHT

### What Is a "Good" Decision?

In the context of decision making under uncertainty, a "good" decision is one that is based on the sound decision-making principles discussed in this chapter. Because the decision must usually be made before uncertainty is resolved, a good decision might have unlucky consequences. However, decision makers should not be criticized for unlucky outcomes. They should be criticized only if their analysis *at the time the decision has to be made* is faulty.

## Possible Decision Criteria

What do we mean by an optimal decision? We will eventually settle on one particular criterion for making decisions, but we first explore some possibilities. With respect to Table 10.1, one possibility is to choose the decision that maximizes the *worst* payoff. This criterion, called the **maximin** criterion, is appropriate for a very conservative (or pessimistic) decision maker. The worst payoffs for the three decisions are the minimums in the three rows: 10, $-10$, and $-30$. The maximin decision maker chooses the decision corresponding to the best of these: decision $D1$ with payoff 10. Clearly, such a criterion tends to avoid large losses, but it fails to even consider large rewards. Hence, this criterion is typically *too* conservative and is not commonly used.

> The **maximin** criterion finds the worst payoff in each row of the payoff table and chooses the decision corresponding to the maximum of these.

*The maximin and maximax criteria make sense in some situations, but they are generally not used in real decision-making problems.*

At the other extreme, the decision maker might choose the decision that maximizes the *best* payoff. This criterion, called the **maximax** criterion, is appropriate for a risk taker (or optimist). The best payoffs for the three decisions are the maximums in the three rows: 10, 40, and 70. The maximax decision maker chooses the decision corresponding to the best of these: decision $D3$ with payoff 70. This criterion looks tempting because it focuses on large gains, but its very serious downside is that it ignores possible losses. Because this type of decision making could eventually bankrupt a company, the maximax criterion is also seldom used.

> The **maximax** criterion finds the best payoff in each row of the payoff table and chooses the decision corresponding to the maximum of these.

## Expected Monetary Value (EMV)

We have introduced the maximin and maximax criteria because (1) they are occasionally used to make decisions, and (2) they illustrate that there are several reasonable criteria for making decisions. In fact, a number of other possible criteria are available that we do not discuss. Instead, we now focus on a criterion that is generally regarded as the preferred criterion in most decision problems: the **expected monetary value** (**EMV**) criterion. To motivate the EMV criterion, we first note that the maximin and maximax criteria make no reference to how *likely* the various outcomes are. However, decision makers typically have at least some idea of these likelihoods, and they ought to use this information in the decision-making process. After all, if outcome $O1$ in our problem is extremely unlikely, then the pessimist who uses maximin is being overly conservative. Similarly, if outcome $O3$ is very unlikely, then the optimist who uses maximax is taking an unnecessary risk.

In the EMV approach, we assess probabilities for each outcome of each decision and then calculate the *expected* payoff from each decision based on these probabilities. This expected payoff, or EMV, is a weighted average of the payoffs in any given row of the payoff table, weighted by the probabilities of the outcomes. We calculate the EMV for each decision, and we choose the decision with the largest EMV.

> The **EMV** for any decision is a weighted average of the possible payoffs for this decision, weighted by the probabilities of the outcomes. Using the EMV criterion, we choose the decision with the largest EMV. This is sometimes called "playing the averages."

## Assessing the Required Probabilities

Where do the probabilities come from? This is a difficult question to answer in general because it depends on each specific problem. In some cases, the current decision problem is similar to those a decision maker has faced many times in the past. Then the probabilities can be estimated from the knowledge of previous outcomes. If a certain type of outcome occurred, say, in about 30% of previous situations, we might estimate its current probability as 0.30.

*A subjective element almost always exists in assessing the probabilities for real decision-making problems. A single "correct" assessment is extremely rare.*

However, many decision problems have no parallels in the past. In such cases, a decision maker must use whatever information is available, plus some intuition, to assess the probabilities. For example, if the problem involves a new product decision, and one possible outcome is that a competitor will introduce a similar product in the coming year, the decision maker must rely on his knowledge of the market and the competitor's situation to assess the probability of this outcome. Note that this assessment can be very subjective. Two decision makers can easily assess the probability of the *same* outcome as 0.30 and 0.45, depending on their information and feelings, and neither is necessarily wrong. This is the nature of assessing probabilities subjectively in real business situations.

In addition to the issue of subjective probabilities, there is also an issue of continuous versus discrete probability distributions. Many uncertain quantities, such as demand for a product or the amount of a patient's prescription drug expenses, are basically continuous random variables. However, the decision tree methodology discussed in this chapter works best with discrete random variables, preferably those with only a few possible values. Researchers have suggested ways of "discretizing" a continuous distribution for use in a decision tree. All of these methods select a few representative values of the uncertain quantity, along with appropriate probabilities, to approximate the continuous distribution. Surprisingly, these discrete approximations often work well. For example, the three-point method from Keefer and Bodily (1983) mentioned in the chapter opener is popular. It requires the decision maker to assess the 10th percentile, the 50th percentile, and the 90th percentile of the continuous distribution. This method uses these three values as its representative values and assigns them probabilities 0.3, 0.4, and 0.3.

For example, suppose that the demand for some product in the coming month is uncertain. The actual probability distribution of this demand is undoubtedly continuous over some range, but a continuous distribution is not easy to implement in a decision tree. Suppose the decision maker assesses the following: (1) demand has a 10% chance of being less than 200, (2) demand has a 50% chance of being less than 280, and (3) demand has a 90% chance of being less than 390. Then the Keefer-Bodily approximation uses a discrete distribution for demand. The possible values are 200, 280, and 390, and their probabilities are 0.3, 0.4, and 0.3. This approximation and similar approximations are not simply wild guesses. Researchers such as Keefer and Bodily have demonstrated that they result in similar decisions to those using the underlying continuous distributions.

## Calculating and Interpreting EMV

With this general framework in mind, let's assume that a decision maker assesses the probabilities of the three outcomes in Table 10.1 as 0.4, 0.4, and 0.2.[2] Then it is simple to calculate the EMV for each decision as the sum of products of payoffs and probabilities:

$$\text{EMV for } D1 : 10(0.4) + 10(0.4) + 10(0.2) = 10$$
$$\text{EMV for } D2 : -10(0.4) + 20(0.4) + 40(0.2) = 12$$
$$\text{EMV for } D3 : -30(0.4) + 30(0.4) + 70(0.2) = 14$$

These calculations lead to the optimal decision: Choose decision $D3$ because it has the largest EMV.

*The EMV is a weighted average of possible monetary values. It is usually not a monetary value that can actually occur.*

It is important to understand what the EMV of a decision represents—and what it doesn't represent. For example, the EMV of 14 for decision $D3$ does *not* mean that we expect to gain $14 from this decision. The payoff table indicates that the result from $D3$ will be a loss of $30, a gain of $30, or a gain of $70; it will *never* be a gain of $14. The EMV is only a weighted average of the possible payoffs. As such, it can be interpreted in one of two ways. First, suppose we can imagine the problem occurring many times, not just once. If we use decision $D3$ each time, then *on average,* we will make a gain of about $14. About 40% of the time, we will lose $30; about 40% of the time, we will gain $30; and about 20% of the time, we will gain $70. These average to $14. This is why the use of the EMV criterion is sometimes referred to as "playing the averages."

But what if the current problem is a "one-shot deal" that will *not* occur many times in the future? Then the second interpretation of EMV is still relevant. It states that the EMV is a "reasonable" criterion for making decisions under uncertainty. This is actually a point that has been debated in intellectual circles for years—what is the best criterion for making decisions? However, researchers have generally concluded that EMV makes sense, even

---

[2] We always express probabilities as numbers between 0 and 1 that sum to 1. However, they are often expressed in more intuitive, but equivalent, ways. For example, we might assess that outcomes $O1$ and $O2$ are equally likely and that each of these is twice as likely as outcome $O3$. This assessment leads to the same probabilities: 0.4, 0.4, and 0.2.

for one-shot deals, as long as the monetary values are not too large. For situations where the monetary values are extremely large, we introduce an alternative criterion in the last section of this chapter. Until then, however, we continue to use EMV.

This is the gist of decision-making uncertainty. We develop a payoff table, assess probabilities of outcomes, calculate EMVs, and choose the decision with the largest EMV. However, before proceeding to examples, we need to introduce a few other concepts: sensitivity analysis, decision trees, and risk profiles.

---

### FUNDAMENTAL INSIGHT

#### What It Means to Be an EMV Maximizer

An EMV maximizer, by definition, is indifferent between entering a gamble that has a certain EMV and receiving a sure dollar amount in the amount of the EMV. For example, consider a gamble where you flip a fair coin and win $0 or $1000 depending on whether you get a head or a tail. If you are an EMV maximizer, you are indifferent between entering this gamble,

which has EMV $500, and receiving $500 for sure. Similarly, if the gamble is between losing $1000 and winning $500, based on the flip of the coin, and you are an EMV maximizer, you are indifferent between entering this gamble, which has EMV −$250, and *paying* a sure $250 to avoid the gamble. (This latter scenario is the basis of insurance.)

---

## Sensitivity Analysis

Some of the quantities in a decision analysis, particularly the probabilities, are often intelligent guesses at best. It is important, especially in real-world business problems, to accompany any decision analysis with a sensitivity analysis. Here we systematically vary inputs to the problem to see how (or if) the outputs—the EMVs and the optimal decision—change. For our simple decision problem, this is easy to do in a spreadsheet. We first develop the spreadsheet model shown in Figure 10.1. (See the file **Simple Decision Problem.xlsx**.)

**Figure 10.1**

Spreadsheet Model of the Simple Decision Problem

|   | A | B | C | D | E | F |
|---|---|---|---|---|---|---|
| 1 | Simple decision problem under uncertainty | | | | | |
| 2 | | | | | | |
| 3 | | | Outcome | | | |
| 4 | | | O1 | O2 | O3 | EMV |
| 5 | Decision | D1 | 10 | 10 | 10 | 10 |
| 6 | | D2 | -10 | 20 | 40 | 12 |
| 7 | | D3 | -30 | 30 | 70 | 14 |
| 8 | Probability | | 0.4 | 0.4 | 0.2 | |

*Usually, the most important information from a sensitivity analysis is whether the optimal decision continues to be optimal as one or more inputs change.*

After entering the payoff table and probabilities, we calculate the EMVs in column F as a sum of products, using the formula

**=SUMPRODUCT(C5:E5,$C$8:$E$8)**

in cell F5 and copying it down. Then it is easy to change any of the inputs and see whether the optimal decision continues to be *D3*. For example, you can check that if the probabilities change only slightly to 0.5, 0.4, and 0.1, the EMVs change to 10, 7, and 4. Now *D3* is the worst decision, and *D1* is the best, so that it appears that the optimal decision is quite sensitive to the assessed probabilities. As another example, if the probabilities remain the same, but the last payoff for *D2* changes from 40 to 55, then its EMV changes to 15, and *D2* becomes the best decision.

Given a simple spreadsheet model, it is easy to make a number of ad hoc changes to inputs, as we have done here, to answer specific sensitivity questions. However, conducting a more systematic sensitivity analysis is often useful, and we explain how to do this later in the chapter. The important thing to realize at this stage is that a sensitivity analysis is not an afterthought to the overall analysis; it is a key component of the analysis.

## Decision Trees

The decision problem we have been analyzing is very basic. We make a decision, observe an outcome, receive a payoff, and that is the end of it. Many decision problems are of this basic form, but many are more complex. In these more complex problems, we make a decision, observe an outcome, make a second decision, observe a second outcome, and so on. A graphical tool called a **decision tree** has been developed to represent decision problems. Decision trees can be used for any decision problems, but they are particularly useful for the more complex types. They clearly show the sequence of events (decisions and outcomes), as well as probabilities and monetary values. The decision tree for our simple problem appears in Figure 10.2. This tree is based on one we drew by hand and calculated with a hand calculator. We urge you to try this on your own, at least once. However, later in the chapter, we introduce an Excel add-in that automates the procedure.

**Figure 10.2**

Decision Tree for the Simple Decision Problem

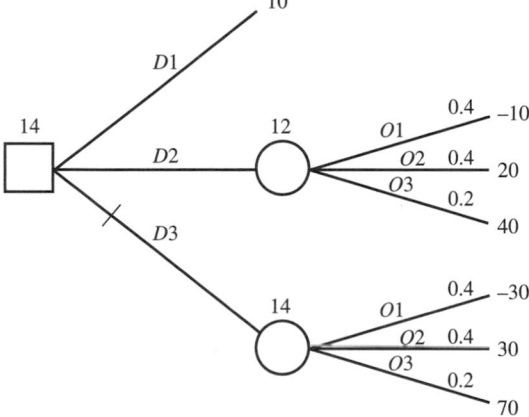

To understand this decision tree, we need to introduce a number of decision tree conventions that have become standard.

### Decision Tree Conventions

- Decision trees are composed of **nodes** (circles, squares, and triangles) and **branches** (lines).

- The nodes represent points in time. A **decision node** (a square) represents a time when the decision maker makes a decision. A **probability node** (a circle) represents a time when the result of an uncertain outcome becomes known. An **end node** (a triangle) indicates that the problem is completed—all decisions have been made, all uncertainty has been resolved, and all payoffs and costs have been incurred. (When people draw decision trees by hand, they often omit the actual triangles, as we have done in Figure 10.2. However, we still refer to the right-hand tips of the branches as the end nodes.)

- Time proceeds *from left to right*. This means that any branches leading into a node (from the left) have already occurred. Any branches leading out of a node (to the right) have not yet occurred.

- Branches leading out of a decision node represent the possible decisions; the decision maker can choose the preferred branch. Branches leading out of probability nodes represent the possible outcomes of uncertain events; the decision maker has no control over which of these will occur.

- Probabilities are listed on probability branches. These probabilities are *conditional* on the events that have already been observed (those to the left). Also, the probabilities on branches leading out of any probability node must sum to 1.

- Monetary values are shown to the right of the end nodes. (As we discuss shortly, some monetary values are also placed next to the branches where they occur in time.)

- EMVs are calculated through a **folding-back** process, discussed next. They are shown above the various nodes. It is then customary to mark the optimal decision branch(es) in some way. We have marked ours with a small notch.

The decision tree in Figure 10.2 follows these conventions. The decision node comes first (to the left) because the decision maker must make a decision *before* observing the uncertain outcome. The probability nodes then follow the decision branches, and the probabilities appear above their branches. (Actually, there is no need for a probability node after the $D1$ branch, because the monetary value is 10 for each outcome.) The ultimate payoffs appear next to the end nodes, to the right of the probability branches. The EMVs above the probability nodes are for the various decisions. For example, if we go along the $D2$ branch, the EMV is 12. The maximum of the EMVs is written above the decision node. Because it corresponds to $D3$, we put a notch on the $D3$ branch to indicate that this decision is optimal.

This decision tree is almost a direct translation of the spreadsheet model in Figure 10.1. In fact, the decision tree is arguably overkill for such a simple problem; the spreadsheet model provides all of the information we need in a more compact form. However, decision trees are very useful in business problems. First, they provide a manager with a graphical view of the whole problem. This can be useful in its own right for the insights it provides, especially in more complex problems. Second, the decision tree provides a framework for doing all of the EMV calculations. Specifically, it allows us to use the following folding-back procedure to find the EMVs and the optimal decision.

### Folding-Back Procedure

Starting from the right of the decision tree and working back to the left:

1. At each probability node, calculate an EMV—a sum of products of monetary values and probabilities.

2. At each decision node, take a maximum of EMVs to identify the optimal decision.

*The folding-back process is a systematic way of calculating EMVs in a decision tree and thereby identifying the optimal decision strategy.*

This is exactly what we did in Figure 10.2. At each probability node, we calculated EMVs in the usual way and wrote them above the nodes. Then at the decision node, we took the maximum of the three EMVs and wrote it above this node. Although this procedure entails more work for more complex decision trees, the same two steps—taking EMVs at probability nodes and taking maximums at decision nodes—are the only ones required. In addition, we introduce an Excel add-in in the next section that does the calculations for us.

### Risk Profiles

In our small example, each decision leads to three possible monetary payoffs with various probabilities. In more complex problems, the number of outcomes can be larger, maybe considerably larger. It is then useful to represent the probability distribution of the monetary values for any decision graphically. Specifically, we show a bar chart, where the bars are located at the possible monetary values, and the heights of the bars correspond to the probabilities. In decision-making contexts, this type of chart is called a **risk profile.** By looking at the risk profile for a particular decision, we see the risks and rewards involved. By comparing risk profiles for different decisions, we gain more insight into their relative strengths and weaknesses.

> The **risk profile** for a decision is a bar chart that represents the probability distribution of monetary outcomes for this decision.

The risk profile for decision $D3$ appears in Figure 10.3. It shows that a loss of $30 and a gain of $30 are equally likely with probability 0.4 each, and that a gain of $70 has probability 0.2. The risk profile for decision $D2$ is similar, except that its bars are over the values −10, 20, and 40, and the risk profile for decision $D1$ is a single bar of height 1 over the value 10. (The file Simple Decision **Problem.xlsx** provides instructions for constructing such a chart with Excel 2007 tools.)

**Figure 10.3**

Risk Profile for Decision $D3$

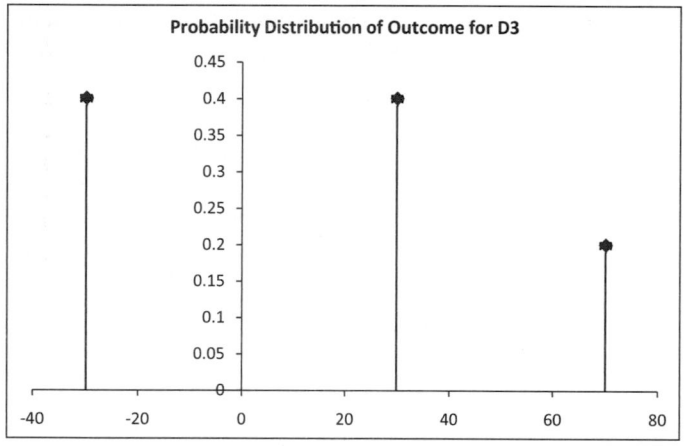

Probability Distribution of Outcome for D3

*A risk profile shows the probability distribution of monetary outcomes, but we typically use only its mean, the EMV, for making decisions.*

Note that the EMV for any decision is a summary measure from the risk profile—it is the *mean* of the corresponding probability distribution. Therefore, when we use the EMV criterion for making decisions, we are not using *all* of the information in the risk profiles; we are comparing only their means. Nevertheless, risk profiles can be useful as extra information for making decisions. For example, a manager who sees too much risk in the risk profile of the EMV-maximizing decision can override this decision and instead choose a somewhat less risky alternative.

We now apply all of these concepts to the following example.

---

## EXAMPLE | 10.1 BIDDING FOR A GOVERNMENT CONTRACT AT SCITOOLS

S ciTools Incorporated, a company that specializes in scientific instruments, has been invited to submit a bid on a government contract. The contract calls for a specific number of these instruments to be delivered during the coming year. The bids must be sealed (so that no company knows what the others are bidding), and the low bid wins the contract. SciTools estimates that it will cost $5000 to prepare a bid and $95,000 to supply the instruments if it wins the contract. On the basis of past contracts of this type, SciTools believes that the possible low bids from the competition, if there is any competition, and the associated probabilities are those shown in Table 10.2. In addition, SciTools believes there is a 30% chance that there will be *no* competing bids. What should SciTools bid to maximize its EMV?

**Table 10.2    Data for the Bidding Example**

| Low Bid | Probability |
| --- | --- |
| Less than $115,000 | 0.2 |
| Between $115,000 and $120,000 | 0.4 |
| Between $120,000 and $125,000 | 0.3 |
| Greater than $125,000 | 0.1 |

**Objective**    To develop a decision model that finds the EMV for various bidding strategies and indicates the best bidding strategy.

### WHERE DO THE NUMBERS COME FROM?

The company has probably done a thorough cost analysis to estimate its cost to prepare a bid and its cost to manufacture the instruments if it wins the contract. Its estimates of whether, or how, the competition will bid are probably based on previous bidding experience and some subjectivity. This is discussed in more detail next.

## Solution

Let's examine the three elements of SciTools' problem. First, SciTools has two basic strategies: submit a bid or do not submit a bid. If SciTools submits a bid, then it must decide how much to bid. Based on SciTools' cost to prepare the bid and its cost to supply the instruments, there is clearly no point in bidding less than $100,000—SciTools wouldn't make a profit even if it won the bid. Although any bid amount over $100,000 might be considered, the data in Table 10.2 suggests that SciTools can limit its choices to $115,000, $120,000, and $125,000.[3]

The next element of the problem involves the uncertain outcomes and their probabilities. We have assumed that SciTools knows exactly how much it will cost to prepare a bid and how much it will cost to supply the instruments if it wins the bid. (In reality, these are probably only estimates of the actual costs, and a follow-up study could treat these costs as additional uncertain quantities.) Therefore, the only source of uncertainty is the behavior of the competitors—will they bid, and if so, how much? From SciTools' standpoint, this is difficult information to obtain. The behavior of the competitors depends on (1) how many competitors are likely to bid and (2) how the competitors assess *their* costs of supplying the instruments. Nevertheless, we assume that SciTools has been involved in similar bidding contests in the past and can predict competitor behavior from past competitor behavior. The result of such prediction is the assessed probability distribution in Table 10.2 and the 30% probability of no competing bids.

The last element of the problem is the *value* model that transforms decisions and outcomes into monetary values for SciTools. The value model is straightforward in this example. If SciTools decides not to bid, then its monetary value is $0—no gain, no loss. If it makes a bid and is underbid by a competitor, then it loses $5000, the cost of preparing the bid. If it bids $B$ dollars and wins the contract, then it makes a profit of $B$ minus $100,000— that is, $B$ dollars for winning the bid, minus $5000 for preparing the bid and $95,000 for supplying the instruments. For example, if it bids $115,000 and the lowest competing bid, if any, is greater than $115,000, then SciTools makes a profit of $15,000.

---

[3] The problem with a bid such as $117,000 is that the data in Table 10.2 make it impossible to calculate the probability of SciTools winning the contract if it bids this amount. Other than this, however, there is nothing that rules out such "in-between" bids.

## Developing the Payoff Table

The corresponding payoff table, along with probabilities of outcomes, appears in Table 10.3. At the bottom of the table, we list the probabilities of the various outcomes. For example, the probability that the competitors' low bid is less than $115,000 is 0.7 (the probability of at least one competing bid) multiplied by 0.2 (the probability that the lowest competing bid is less than $115,000).

**Table 10.3** Payoff Table for the SciTools Bidding Example

| | | *Competitors' Low Bid ($1000s)* | | | | |
|---|---|---|---|---|---|---|
| | | **No bid** | **<115** | **>115, <120** | **>120, <125** | **>125** |
| **SciTools' Bid** | **No** | 0 | 0 | 0 | 0 | 0 |
| **($1000s)** | **bid** | | | | | |
| | **115** | 15 | −5 | 15 | 15 | 15 |
| | **120** | 20 | −5 | −5 | 20 | 20 |
| | **125** | 25 | −5 | −5 | −5 | 25 |
| **Probability** | | 0.3 | 0.7(0.2) = 0.14 | 0.7(0.4) = 0.28 | 0.7(0.3) = 0.21 | 0.7(0.1) = 0.07 |

Sometimes payoff tables can be simplified to better understand the essence of the problem. In the present example, if SciTools bids, the only necessary information about the competitors' bid is whether it is lower or higher than SciTools' bid. That is, SciTools really only cares whether it wins the contract. Therefore, an alternative way of presenting the payoff table is shown in Table 10.4. (See the file **SciTools Bidding Decision 1.xlsx** for these and other calculations. However, we urge you to work this problem on a piece of paper with a hand calculator, just for practice with the concepts.)

**Table 10.4** Alternative Payoff Table for the SciTools Bidding Example

| | | *Monetary Value* | | *Probability That* |
|---|---|---|---|---|
| | | **SciTools Wins** | **SciTools Loses** | *SciTools Wins* |
| **SciTools' Bid ($1000s)** | **No Bid** | NA | 0 | 0.00 |
| | **115** | 15 | −5 | 0.86 |
| | **120** | 20 | −5 | 0.58 |
| | **125** | 25 | −5 | 0.37 |

The third and fourth columns of this table indicate the payoffs to SciTools, depending on whether it wins or loses the bid. The rightmost column shows the probability that SciTools wins the bid for each possible decision. For example, if SciTools bids $120,000, then it wins the bid if there are no competing bids (probability 0.3) *or* if there are competing bids but the lowest of these is greater than $120,000 [probability 0.7(0.3 + 0.1) = 0.28]. In this case, the total probability that SciTools wins the bid is 0.3 + 0.28 = 0.58.

## Developing the Risk Profiles

From Table 10.4, we can obtain risk profiles for each of SciTools' decisions. Again, this risk profile simply indicates all possible monetary values and their corresponding probabilities in a bar chart. For example, if SciTools bids $120,000, two monetary values are possible, a profit of $20,000 and a loss of $5000, and their probabilities are 0.58 and 0.42, respectively. The corresponding risk profile, shown in Figure 10.4, is a bar chart with two bars, one above −$5000 with height 0.42 and one above $20,000 with height 0.58. On the other hand, if SciTools decides not to bid, there is a sure monetary value of $0—no profit, no loss. The risk profile for the "no bid" decision, not shown here, is even simpler. It has a single bar above $0 with height 1.

**Figure 10.4**

Risk Profile for a
Bid of $120,000

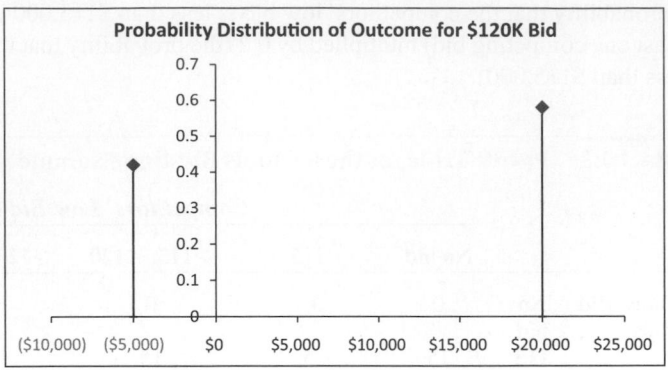

## Calculating EMVs

The EMVs for SciTools' problem are listed in Table 10.5. As always, each EMV (other than the EMV of $0 for not bidding) is a sum of products of monetary outcomes and probabilities. These EMVs indicate that if SciTools uses the EMV criterion for making its decision, it should bid $115,000. The EMV from this bid, $12,200, is the largest of the EMVs.

**Table 10.5** EMVs for the SciTools Bidding Example

| Alternative | EMV Calculation | EMV |
| --- | :---: | --- |
| No bid | 0(1) | $0 |
| Bid $115,000 | $15,000(0.86) + (-5000)(0.14)$ | $12,200 |
| Bid $120,000 | $20,000(0.58) + (-5000)(0.42)$ | $9,500 |
| Bid $125,000 | $25,000(0.37) + (-5000)(0.63)$ | $6,100 |

As discussed previously, it is very important to understand what an EMV implies and what it does not imply. If SciTools bids $115,000, its EMV is $12,200. However, SciTools will definitely *not* earn a profit of $12,200. It will earn $15,000, or it will lose $5000. The EMV of $12,200 represents a weighted average of these two possible values. Nevertheless, we use this value as our decision criterion.

## Developing the Decision Tree

The corresponding decision tree for this problem is shown in Figure 10.5. This is a direct translation of the payoff table and EMV calculations. The company first makes a bidding decision; then observes what the competition bids, if anything; and finally receives a payoff. The folding-back process is equivalent to the calculations shown in Table 10.5.

**Figure 10.5**

Decision Tree for
the SciTools Bidding
Example

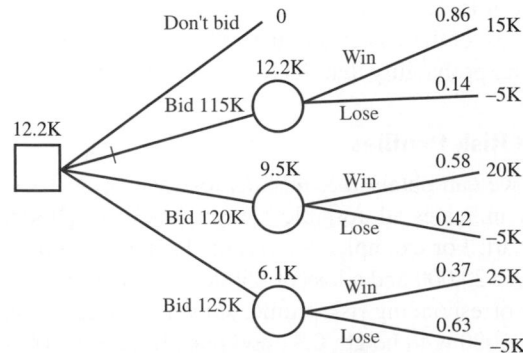

**Figure 10.6**

Equivalent Decision Tree for the SciTools Bidding Example

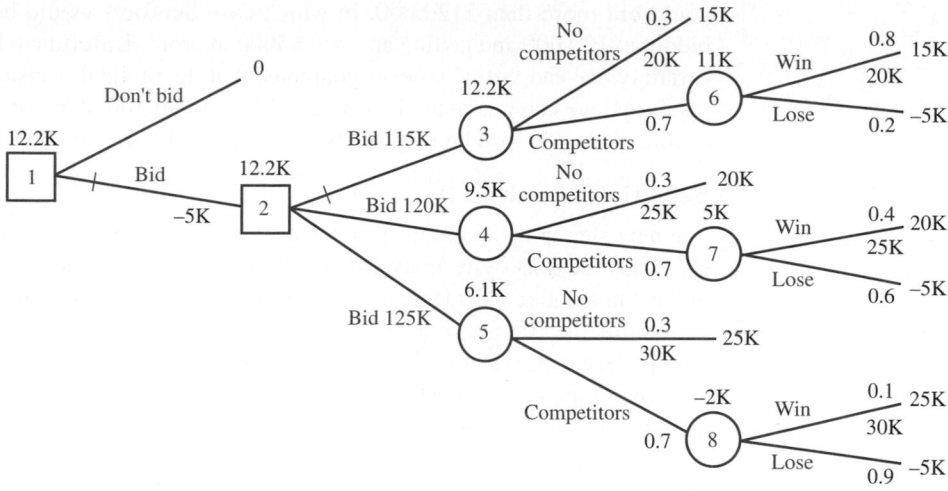

*Placing monetary values below the branches where they occur in time is common.*

As long as we follow the decision tree conventions, there are often equivalent ways to structure a decision tree. One alternative for this example is shown in Figure 10.6. This tree shows exactly how the problem unfolds. The company first decides whether to bid at all. If the company does not make a bid, the profit is a sure $0. Otherwise, the company then decides how much to bid. Note that if the company decides to bid, it incurs a sure cost of $5000, so we place this cost under the Bid branch. This is a common procedure, to place the monetary values on the branches where they occur in time, and it is followed by the PrecisionTree add-in we examine in the next section. After the company decides how much to bid, it then observes whether there is any competition. If there isn't any, the company wins the bid for sure and makes a corresponding profit. Otherwise, if there is competition, the company eventually discovers whether it wins or loses the bid, with the corresponding probabilities and payoffs. Note that we place these payoffs below the branches where they occur in time. Also, we place the *cumulative* payoffs at the ends of the branches. Each cumulative payoff is the sum of all payoffs (or costs) on branches that lead to that end node.

### Folding Back the Decision Tree

The folding-back procedure is a bit more complex than it was for the smaller tree in Figure 10.5. To illustrate, we have numbered the nodes in Figure 10.6 for reference. The EMVs above a selected few of these nodes are calculated as follows:

- Node 7: EMV = 20000(0.40) + (−5000)(0.60) = $5000 (uses monetary values from end nodes)

- Node 4: EMV = 20000(0.30) + (5000)(0.70) = $9500 (uses monetary value from an end node and the EMV from node 7)

- Node 2: EMV = max(12200, 9500, 6100) = $12,200 (uses EMVs from nodes 3, 4, and 5)

- Node 1: EMV = max(0, 12200) = $12,200 (uses monetary value from an end node and EMV from node 2)

The results are the same, regardless of whether we use the table of EMVs in Table 10.5, the decision tree in Figure 10.5, or the decision tree in Figure 10.6 because they all calculate the same EMVs in equivalent ways. In each case, we see that the company should bid $115,000, with a resulting EMV of $12,200. Of course, this decision is not *guaranteed* to produce a good outcome for the company. For example, the competition could bid less than $115,000, in which case SciTools would be out $5000. Alternately, the competition could bid more than $120,000, in which case SciTools would be kicking itself for not bidding $120,000 and getting an extra $5000 in profit. Unfortunately, in problems with uncertainty, we can virtually never guarantee that the optimal decision will produce the best result. All we can guarantee is that the EMV-maximizing decision is the most rational decision, given what we know when we must make the decision.

## Sensitivity Analysis

The next step in the SciTools decision analysis is to perform a sensitivity analysis. We can either use the sensitivity analysis tools of the PrecisionTree add-in, to be discussed shortly, or we can use Excel data tables. One possibility is shown in Figure 10.7. (See the finished version of the file **SciTools Bidding Decision 1.xlsx**.) We first calculate the EMVs in column G, exactly as described previously. Then we find the maximum of these in cell B21, and we use the following nested IF formula in cell B22 to find the decision from column B that achieves this maximum:

**=IF(G16=B21,B16,IF(G17=B21,B17,IF(G18=B21,B18,B19)))**

This long formula simply checks which EMV in column G matches the maximum EMV in cell B21 and returns the corresponding decision from column B.

**Figure 10.7**   Sensitivity Analysis with a Data Table

| | A | B | C | D | E | F | G |
|---|---|---|---|---|---|---|---|
| 1 | SciTools Bidding Example | | | | | | |
| 2 | | | | | | | |
| 3 | Inputs | | | | | | |
| 4 | Cost to prepare a bid | $5,000 | | Range names used: | | | |
| 5 | Cost to supply instruments | $95,000 | | BidCost | =Data!$B$4 | | |
| 6 | | | | PrNoBid | =Data!$B$7 | | |
| 7 | Probability of no competing bid | 0.3 | | ProdCost | =Data!$B$5 | | |
| 8 | Comp bid distribution (if they bid) | | | | | | |
| 9 | <$115K | 0.2 | | | | | |
| 10 | $115K to $120K | 0.4 | | | | | |
| 11 | $120K to $125K | 0.3 | | | | | |
| 12 | >$125K | 0.1 | | | | | |
| 13 | | | | | | | |
| 14 | EMV analysis | | Monetary outcomes | | Probabilities | | |
| 15 | | | SciTools wins | SciTools loses | SciTools wins | SciTools loses | EMV |
| 16 | | No bid | NA | 0 | 0 | 1 | $0 |
| 17 | SciTools' Bid | $115,000 | $15,000 | -$5,000 | 0.86 | 0.14 | $12,200 |
| 18 | | $120,000 | $20,000 | -$5,000 | 0.58 | 0.42 | $9,500 |
| 19 | | $125,000 | $25,000 | -$5,000 | 0.37 | 0.63 | $6,100 |
| 20 | | | | | | | |
| 21 | Maximum EMV | $12,200 | | | | | |
| 22 | Best decision | $115,000 | | | | | |
| 23 | | | | | | | |
| 24 | Data table for sensitivity analysis | | | | | | |
| 25 | Probability of no competing bid | Maximum EMV | Best decision | | | | |
| 26 | | $12,200 | $115,000 | | | | |
| 27 | 0.2 | $11,800 | $115,000 | | | | |
| 28 | 0.3 | $12,200 | $115,000 | | | | |
| 29 | 0.4 | $12,600 | $115,000 | | | | |
| 30 | 0.5 | $13,000 | $115,000 | | | | |
| 31 | 0.6 | $14,200 | $125,000 | | | | |
| 32 | 0.7 | $16,900 | $125,000 | | | | |

After we have the formulas in cells B21 and B22 set up, the data table is easy. In Figure 10.7, we allow the probability of no competing bid to vary from 0.2 to 0.7. The data table shows how the optimal EMV increases over this range. Also, its third column shows that the $115,000 bid is optimal for small values of the input, but that $125,000 becomes optimal for larger values. The main point here is that if we set up a spreadsheet model that links all of the EMV calculations to the inputs, then using data tables to perform sensitivity analyses on selected inputs is easy. ∎

## The Flaw of Averages

Many people make a common mistake when dealing with uncertainty. Sam Savage from Stanford University calls it the "flaw of averages," and we borrow his term. In decision problems, there is frequently an uncertain quantity $X$, and the monetary value we receive by making some decision is a function of $X$, say, $f(X)$. Using the EMV criterion, we are interested in the expected value of $f(X)$, denoted $E[f(X)]$. This is the weighted average of all possible values of $f(X)$, weighted by their probabilities. The flaw is that many people believe this is the same as the function $f$ evaluated at the mean of $X$. That is, they believe that $E[f(X)] = f[E(X)]$. Unfortunately, this equation is true only in a very special case, when the function $f$ is a linear function. Otherwise, this equation is typically false. We illustrate this flaw in the following example.

---

**EXAMPLE** | **10.2 JOINING A MEDICARE DRUG PRESCRIPTION PLAN**

The Medicare Plan D for prescription drugs for the elderly was announced in late 2005 and went into effect in 2006. The "base" plan is the following. Each person pays $384 per year and is then covered as indicated in Table 10.6 (which comes directly from a Medicare informational Web site). In words, you pay the first $250, the plan pays 75% of the next $2000, you pay *all* of the next $2850, the so-called "coverage gap," and the plan pays 95% of everything over $5100. (There are actually many such plans, all offered by private companies. The government stipulates that each such plan must be "at least as good as" the base plan described here.)

**Table 10.6**  Medicare Drug Benefits At-a-Glance (Calendar Year 2006)

| Prescription Drug Spending— (if you have no drug coverage other than Medicare) | Medicare-Approved Plan Pays | You Pay—(if you have no drug coverage other than Medicare) |
|---|---|---|
| $0–$250 | $0 | Up to $250 deductible |
| $250–$2,250 | 75% of drug costs— Up to $1,500 | 25% of drug costs— Up to $500 |
| $2,250–$5,100 Coverage Gap/Donut Hole | 0% of drug costs—$0 | 100% of drug costs— Up to $2,850 |
| **Subtotal:** | **Up to $1,500** | **Up to $3,600 out-of-pocket** |
| Over $5,100 (Catastrophic Benefit) | 95% | 5% or $2 copay/generic $5 copay/brand name |

Note: Your premium (about $32 per month/$384 per year in 2006) is *not* included in what *you pay* as shown in the chart above.

Suppose you believe that your drug expenses next year will be $2000, $3500, $5000, or $6500 with probabilities 0.2, 0.4, 0.3, and 0.1, respectively. If you join the base plan, what are your expected out-of-pocket expenses for the year?

**Objective**  To illustrate the flaw of averages.

**WHERE DO THE NUMBERS COME FROM?**

The provisions of any such plan are published on Medicare's Web site. The distribution of your expenses is based on the prescriptions you are likely to fill next year.

## Solution

In this example, $X$ corresponds to your actual expenses ($2000, $3500, $5000, or $6500), and $f(X)$ corresponds to your out-of-pocket expenses if you join the plan. We want $E[f(X)]$, your *expected* out-of-pocket expenses, and we want to demonstrate that this is *not* equal to $f[E(X)]$. The required calculations are shown in Figure 10.8. (See the file **Medicare.xlsx**.)

**Figure 10.8**

Calculation of Expenses

| | A | B | C | D | E |
|---|---|---|---|---|---|
| 1 | Medicare plan | | | | |
| 2 | | | | | |
| 3 | Premium | $384 | | | |
| 4 | | | | | |
| 5 | Breakpoint | Amount | % you pay | | |
| 6 | 250 | 250 | 100% | | |
| 7 | 2250 | 2000 | 25% | | |
| 8 | 5100 | 2850 | 100% | | |
| 9 | >5100 | | 5% | | |
| 10 | | | | | |
| 11 | Calculations | | | | |
| 12 | Drug expenses, X | $2,000 | $3,500 | $5,000 | $6,500 |
| 13 | Amount you pay, f(X) | $1,072 | $2,384 | $3,884 | $4,054 |
| 14 | Probability | 0.2 | 0.4 | 0.3 | 0.1 |
| 15 | | | | | |
| 16 | E(X) | $3,950 | | | |
| 17 | f[E(X)] | $2,834 | | | |
| 18 | E[f(X)] | $2,739 | | | |

The premium in cell B3 and the schedule in rows 6 to 9 spell out the provisions of the plan. Your possible expenses are in row 12, and their probabilities are listed in row 14. For any possible expense in row 12, your out-of-pocket expense appears below it in row 13. Because of the complex nature of the plan, the formula in cells B13:E13 for calculating the out-of-pocket expense is a complicated IF function not shown here. However, it is straightforward. For example, if your drug expenses are $3500, as in column C, you pay the $384 premium, the $250 deductible, 25% of the next $2000, and all of the remaining $1250. Your total is $2384. The weighted average of the amounts in row 13, weighted by the probabilities in row 14, is your expected out-of-pocket expense. It is calculated in cell B18 with the formula

**=SUMPRODUCT(B13:E13,B14:E14)**

On the other hand, your expected drug expense is calculated in cell B16 with the formula

**=SUMPRODUCT(B12:E12,B14:E14)**

If we apply the same IF function to this mean drug expense, we obtain the value in cell B17. In other words, if you act as if your drug expenses next year are a *sure* $3950, then you will pay $2834 in out-of-pocket expenses under the plan. However, this is *not* equal to your EMV of out-of-pocket expenses, $2739. Only the latter is relevant for decision-making purposes, such as deciding which of several private plans to sign up for.

To put this flaw of averages in a somewhat more general context, assume that there are a number of uncertain inputs. Using appropriate Excel formulas, we calculate an output that is a function of the inputs (just as we did in the Medicare example with the complex IF function). If we substitute the *mean*

### FUNDAMENTAL INSIGHT

#### The Flaw of Averages

When an output is a nonlinear function of one or more uncertain inputs, the expected value of the output—that is, the EMV we use for decision-making purposes—is generally *not* equal to the output we obtain by using the mean values of the inputs. This latter value is what a naïve analyst would obtain by ignoring the uncertainty and using only "best guesses" for the inputs. It typically provides a misleading estimate, possibly too high and possibly too low, of the true EMV we want.

value of each input in its input cell, the output we see is analogous to $f[E(X)]$. However, it is not the same as the expected value of the output that is relevant for decision-making purposes (unless the output is a linear function of the inputs). We pursue this distinction in the next chapter when we discuss simulation. ∎

## PROBLEMS

*Solutions for problems whose numbers appear within a color box can be found in the Student Solutions Files. Order your copy today at the Winston/Albright product Web site, academic.cengage.com/decisionsciences/winston.*

### Skill-Building Problems

1. In the simple three-decision, three-outcome example, we found that decision $D3$ is the EMV-maximizing decision for the probabilities we used. See whether you can find probabilities that make decision $D1$ the best. See if you can find probabilities that make decision $D2$ the best. Qualitatively, how can you explain the results; that is, which types of probabilities tend to favor the various decisions?

2. Using a data table in Excel, perform a sensitivity analysis on the simple three-decision, three-outcome example. Specifically, continue to assume that outcomes $O1$ and $O2$ are equally likely, each with probability $p$. Because the probabilities of all outcomes must sum to 1, the probability of outcome $O3$ must be $1-2p$. Let $p$ vary from 0 to 0.5, in increments of 0.05. How does the optimal EMV vary? How does the optimal decision vary? Why can't $p$ be greater than 0.5?

3. For the simple three-decision, three-outcome example, are there any probabilities that make the EMV criterion equivalent to the maximin criterion? Are there any probabilities that make the EMV criterion equivalent to the maximax criterion? Explain.

4. In the SciTools example, which decision would a maximin decision maker choose? Which decision would a maximax decision maker choose? Would you defend either of these criteria for this particular example? Explain.

5. In the SciTools example, suppose that we make two changes: all references to $115,000 change to $110,000, and all references to $125,000 change to $130,000. Rework the EMV calculations and the decision tree. What is the best decision and its corresponding EMV?

6. In the SciTools example, the probabilities for the low bid of competitors, given that there is at least one competing bid, are currently 0.2, 0.4, 0.3, and 0.1. Let the second of these be $p$, and let the others sum to $1-p$ but keep the same ratios to one another: 2 to 3 to 1.

Use a one-way data table to see how (or whether) the optimal decision changes as $p$ varies from 0.1 to 0.7 in increments of 0.05. Explain your results.

7. In the SciTools example, use a two-way data table to see how (or whether) the optimal decision changes as the bid cost and the company's production cost change simultaneously. Let the bid cost vary from $2000 to $8000 in increments of $1000, and let the production cost vary from $90,000 to $105,000 in increments of $2500. Explain your results.

### Skill-Extending Problems

8. A decision $d$ is **dominated** by another decision $D$ if, for every outcome, the payoff from $D$ is better than (or no worse than) the payoff from $d$.
   a. Explain why you would never choose a dominated decision, using the maximin criterion; using the maximax criterion; using the EMV criterion.
   b. Are any of the decisions in the simple three-decision, three-outcome example dominated by any others? What about in the SciTools example?

9. Besides the maximin, maximax, and EMV criteria, there are other possible criteria for making decisions. One possibility involves **regret.** The idea behind regret is that if we make any decision and then some outcome occurs, we look at that outcome's column in the payoff table to see how much more we could have made if we had chosen the *best* payoff in that column. For example, if the decision we make and the outcome we observe lead to a $50 payoff, and if the highest payoff in this outcome's column is $80, then our regret is $30. We don't want to look back and see how much more we *could* have made, if only we had made a different decision. Therefore, we calculate the regret for each cell in the payoff table (as the maximum payoff in that column minus the payoff in that cell), calculate the maximum regret in each row, and choose the row with the smallest maximum regret. This is called the **minimax regret** criterion.
   a. Apply this criterion to the simple three-decision, three-outcome example. Which decision do you choose?
   b. Repeat part **a** for the SciTools example.
   c. In general, discuss potential strengths and weaknesses of this decision criterion.

**10.** Referring to the previous problem, another possible criterion is called **expected regret.** Here we calculate the regret for each cell, take a weighted average of these regrets in each row, weighted by the probabilities of the outcomes, and choose the decision with the smallest expected regret.

  **a.** Apply this criterion to the simple three-decision, three-outcome example. Which decision do you choose?

  **b.** Repeat part **a** for the SciTools example.

  **c.** The expected regret criterion is actually *equivalent* to the EMV criterion, in that they always lead to the same decisions. Argue why this is true.

**11.** In the SciTools example, you might argue that there is a *continuum* of possible low competitor bids (given that there is at least one competing bid), not just four possibilities. In fact, assume the low competitor bid in this case is normally distributed with mean $118,000 and standard deviation $4,500. Also, assume that Sci-Tools will still either not bid or bid $115,000, $120,000, or $125,000. Use Excel's NORMDIST function to find the EMV for each of SciTools' alternatives. Which is the best decision now? Why can't this be represented in a decision tree?

## 10.3 THE PRECISIONTREE ADD-IN

Decision trees present a challenge for Excel. We must somehow take advantage of Excel's calculating capabilities (to calculate EMVs, for example) and its graphical capabilities (to depict the decision tree). Fortunately, there is a powerful add-in, PrecisionTree, developed by Palisade Corporation, which makes the process relatively straightforward. This add-in not only enables us to draw and label a decision tree, but it also performs the folding-back procedure automatically and then allows us to perform sensitivity analysis on key input parameters.

The first thing you must do to use PrecisionTree is to "add it in." You do this in two steps. First, you must install the Palisade Decision Tools suite (or at least the PrecisionTree program) with the Setup program on the Palisade CD-ROM that accompanies this book. Of course, you need to do this only once. Then to run PrecisionTree, there are two options (we usually use the first):

- If Excel is not currently running, you can launch Excel *and* PrecisionTree by clicking on the Windows Start button and selecting the PrecisionTree item from the Palisade Decision Tools group in the list of Programs.

- If Excel is currently running, the procedure in the previous bullet launches Precision-Tree on top of Excel.

You know that PrecisionTree is ready for use when you see its tab and the associated ribbon (shown in Figure 10.9) If you want to unload PrecisionTree *without* closing Excel, you can do so from its Utilities dropdown.

**Figure 10.9** PrecisionTree Ribbon

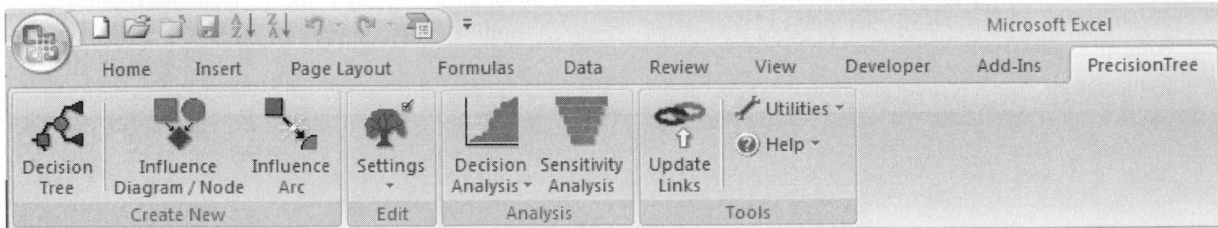

## The Decision Tree Model

PrecisionTree is easy to use—at least its most basic items are. We lead you through the steps for the SciTools example. Figure 10.10 shows the results of this procedure, just so that you can see what you are working toward. (See the file **SciTools Bidding Decision 2.xlsx**.) However, we recommend that you work through the steps on your own, starting with a blank spreadsheet.

---

**Figure 10.10**    Completed Tree from PrecisionTree

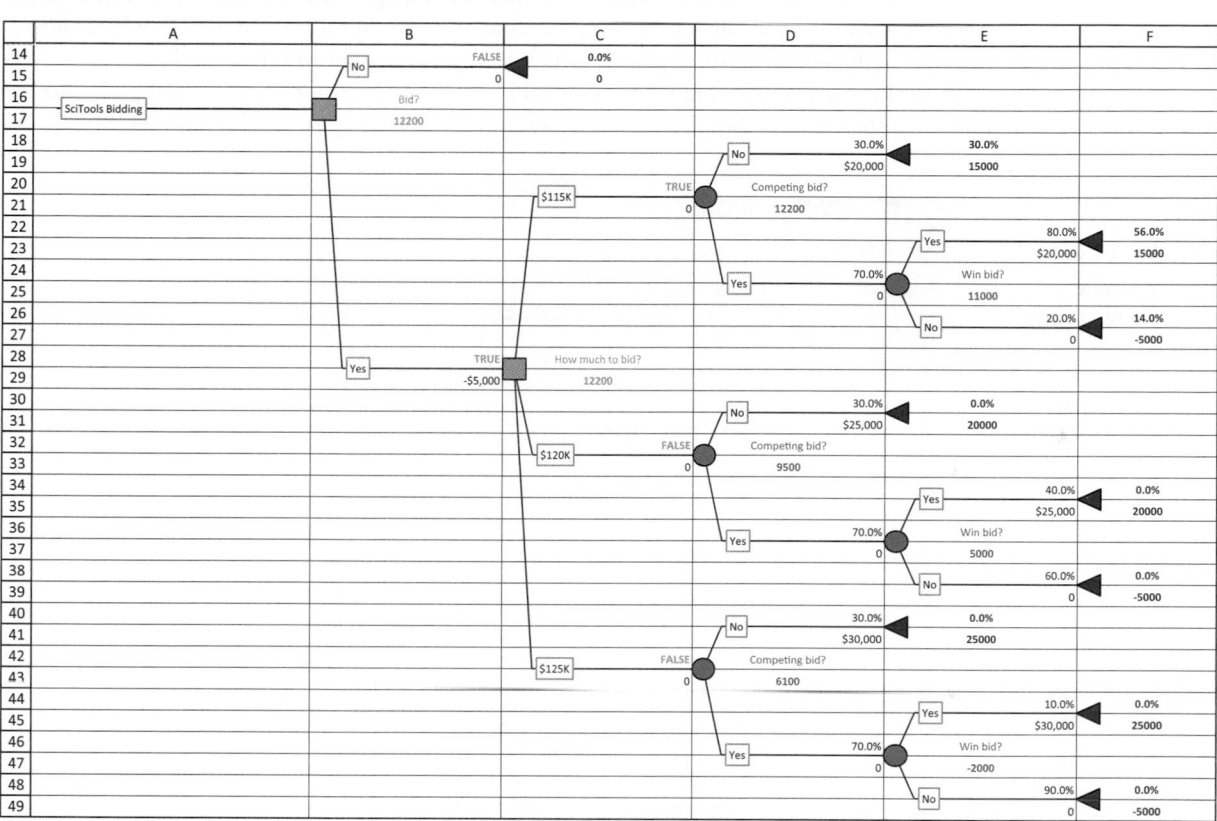

### Building the Decision Tree

**1   Inputs.** Enter the inputs shown in columns A and B of Figure 10.11.

**2   New tree.** Click on the Decision Tree button on the PrecisionTree ribbon, and then click on cell A14 below the input section to start a new tree. You will immediately see a dialog box where, among other things, you can name the tree. Type in a descriptive name

---

**Figure 10.11**

Inputs for the
SciTools Bidding
Example

| | A | B | C | D | E |
|---|---|---|---|---|---|
| 1 | SciTools Bidding Decision | | | | |
| 2 | | | | | |
| 3 | Inputs | | | Range names used: | |
| 4 | Cost to prepare a bid | $5,000 | | BidCost | =Model!$B$4 |
| 5 | Cost to supply instruments | $95,000 | | PrNoBid | =Model!$B$7 |
| 6 | | | | ProductionCost | =Model!$B$5 |
| 7 | Probability of no competing bid | 0.3 | | | |
| 8 | Comp bid distribution (if they bid) | | | | |
| 9 | <$115K | 0.2 | | | |
| 10 | $115K to $120K | 0.4 | | | |
| 11 | $120K to $125K | 0.3 | | | |
| 12 | >$125K | 0.1 | | | |

Figure 10.12

Beginnings of a New
Tree

| | A | B | C |
|---|---|---|---|
| 14 | SciTools Bidding | 100.0% ◀ | |
| 15 | | 0 | |

for the tree, such as SciTools Bidding, and click on OK. You should now see the beginnings of a tree, as in Figure 10.12.

**3** **Decision nodes and branches.** From here on, keep the tree in Figure 10.10 in mind. This is the finished product we eventually want. To obtain decision nodes and branches, click on the (only) triangle end node to open the dialog box in Figure 10.13. Click on the green square to indicate that we want a decision node, and fill in the dialog box as shown. By default, you get two branches, which is what you want in this case. However, if you wanted more than two branches, you would click on the Branches tab and then on Add to get additional branches. The tree expands as shown in Figure 10.14. The boxes that say

Figure 10.13

Dialog Box for
Adding a New
Decision Node and
Branches

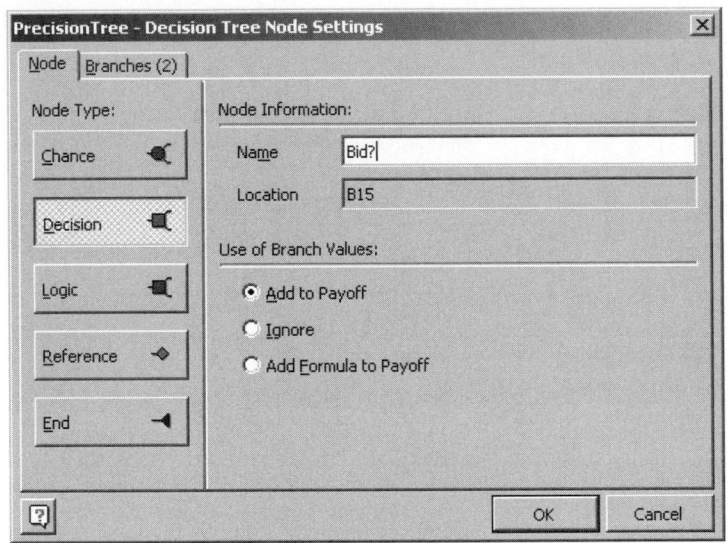

Figure 10.14

Tree with Initial
Decision Node and
Branches

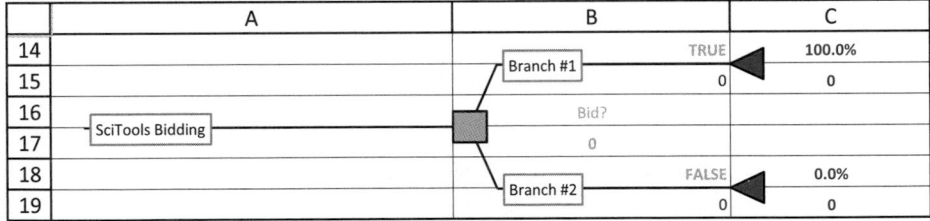

"branch" show the default labels for these branches. Click on either of them to open another dialog box where you can provide a more descriptive name for the branch. Do this to label the two branches "No" and "Yes." Also, you can enter the immediate payoff or cost for either branch right below it. Because there is a $5000 cost of bidding, enter the formula

**=-BidCost**

right below the "Yes" branch in cell B19. (It is negative to reflect a *cost*.) The tree should now appear as in Figure 10.15.

**Figure 10.15**

Decision Tree with
Decision Branches
Labeled

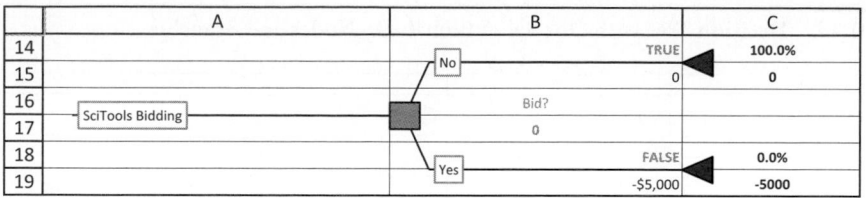

**PRECISIONTREE TIP:** *Allowable Entries*

*On your computer screen, note the color-coding PrecisionTree uses. If you investigate any colored (nonblack) cells, you will see strange formulas that PrecisionTree uses for its own purposes. Do not change these formulas. Enter your own probabilities and monetary values only in the black cells.*

**4 More decision branches.** The top branch is completed; if SciTools does not bid, there is nothing left to do. So click on the bottom end node (the triangle), following Sci-Tools' decision to bid, and proceed as in the previous step to add and label the decision node and three decision branches for the amount to bid (refer to Figure 10.10). The tree to this point should appear as in Figure 10.16. Note that there are no monetary values below these decision branches because no *immediate* payoffs or costs are associated with the bid amount decision.

**Figure 10.16**

Tree with All
Decision Nodes
and Branches

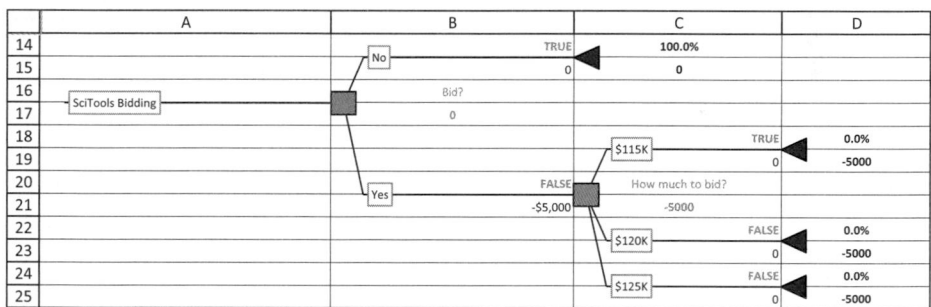

**5 Probability nodes and branches.** We now need a probability node and branches from the rightmost end nodes to capture whether the competition bids. Click on the top one of these end nodes to bring up the same dialog box as shown earlier in Figure 10.13. Now, however, click on the red circle box to indicate that we want a probability node. Label it "Any competing bid?", accept two branches, and click on OK. Then label the two branches "No" and "Yes." Next, repeat this procedure to form another probability node (with two branches) following the "Yes" branch, call it "Win bid?," and label its branches as shown in Figure 10.17.

**6 Copying probability nodes and branches.** You could now repeat the same procedure from the previous step to build probability nodes and branches following the other bid amount decisions, but because they are structurally equivalent, you can save a lot of work by using PrecisionTree's copy and paste feature. Right-click on the leftmost probability node and click on Copy SubTree. Then right-click on either end node below and click on Paste SubTree. Do this again with the other end node. Decision trees can get very "bushy," but this copy and paste feature makes them much less tedious to construct.

**7 Labeling probability branches.** You should now have the decision tree shown in Figure 10.18. It is structurally the same as the completed tree shown earlier in Figure 10.10, but the probabilities and monetary values on the probability branches are incorrect. Note that each probability branch has a value above and below the branch. The value above is the probability (the default values make the branches equally likely), and the value below

**Figure 10.17** Decision Tree with One Set of Probability Nodes and Branches

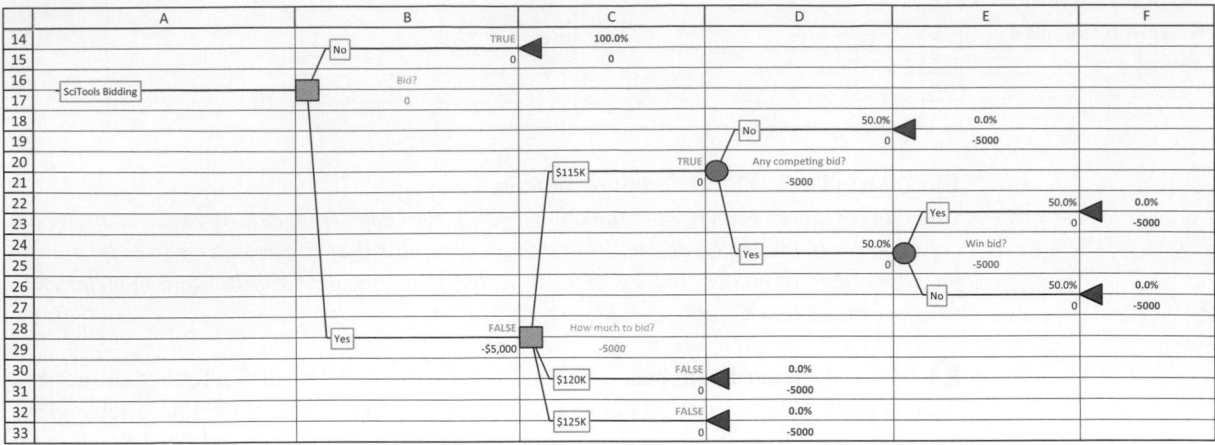

**Figure 10.18** Structure of Completed Tree

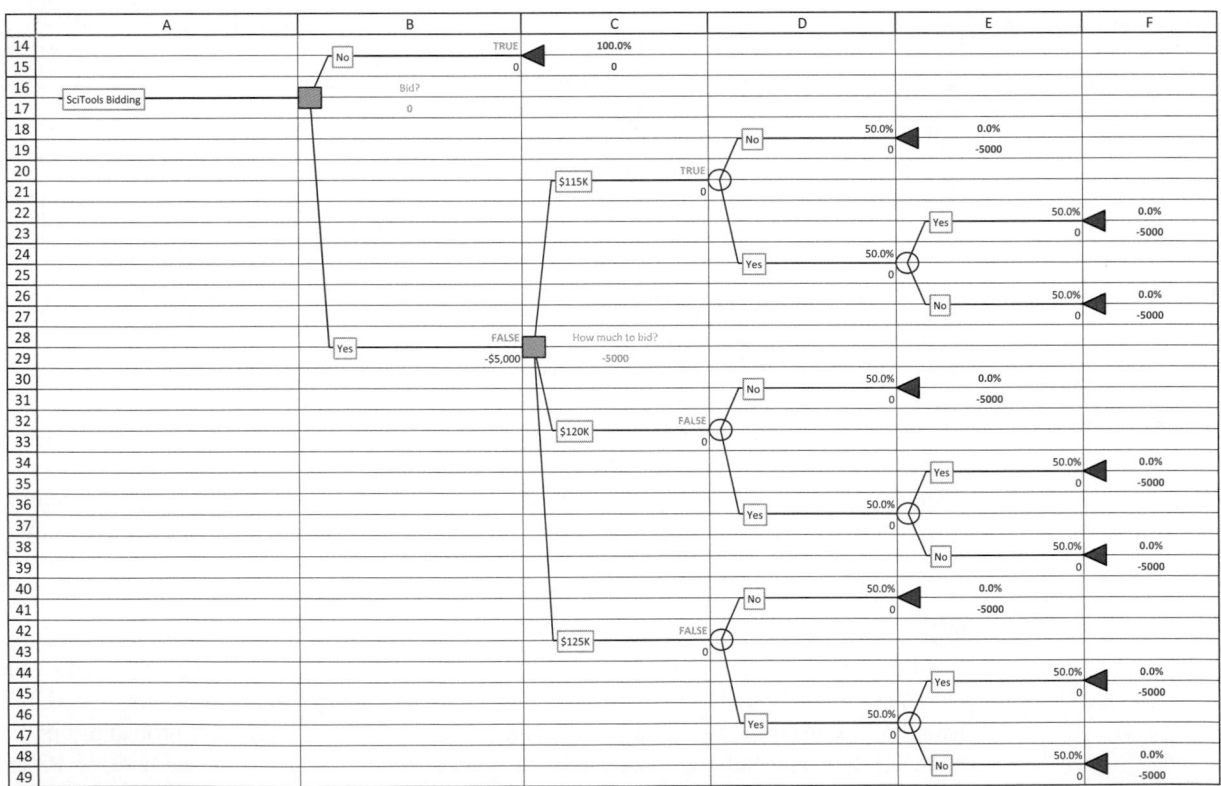

is the monetary value (the default values are 0). You can enter any values or formulas in these cells, exactly as you do in typical Excel worksheets. As usual, it is a good practice to refer to input cells in these formulas whenever possible. In addition, range names can be used instead of cell addresses.

We now get you started with the probability branches following the decision to bid $115,000. First, enter the probability of no competing bid in cell D18 with the formula

=PrNoBid

and enter its complement in cell D24 with the formula

=1-D18

Next, enter the probability that SciTools wins the bid in cell E22 with the formula

=SUM(B10:B12)

and enter its complement in cell E26 with the formula

=1-E22

(Remember that SciTools wins the bid only if the competition bids higher, and in this part of the tree, SciTools is bidding $115,000.) For the monetary values, enter the formula

=115000-ProdCost

in the two cells, D19 and E23, where SciTools wins the contract. Note that we already subtracted the cost of the bid in cell B29, so we should *not* do so again. This would be double-counting, and you should always avoid it in decision trees.

**8** **Enter the other formulas on probability branches.** Using the previous step and Figure 10.10 as a guide, enter formulas for the probabilities and monetary values on the other probability branches, those following the decision to bid $120,000 or $125,000.

## Interpreting the Decision Tree

*To find the optimal decision strategy in any PrecisionTree tree, follow the TRUE labels.*

We are finished! The completed tree shown earlier in Figure 10.10 shows the best strategy and its associated EMV, as we discussed previously. In fact, a comparison of the decision tree in Figure 10.6 that we created manually and the tree from PrecisionTree in Figure 10.10 indicates virtually identical results. The best decision strategy is now indicated by the TRUE and FALSE labels above the decision branches (rather than the notches we entered by hand). Each TRUE corresponds to the optimal decision out of a decision node, whereas each FALSE corresponds to a suboptimal decision. To identify the optimal strategy, we simply follow the TRUE labels. In this case, the company should bid, and its bid amount should be $115,000.

Note that we never have to perform the folding-back procedure manually. Precision-Tree does it for us. Essentially, the tree is completed as soon as we finish entering the relevant inputs. In addition, if we change any of the inputs, the tree reacts automatically. For example, try changing the bid cost in cell B4 from $5000 to some large value such as $20,000. The tree calculations update automatically, and the best decision is then *not* to bid, with an associated EMV of $0.

**PRECISIONTREE TIP:** *Values at End Nodes*
*You will notice that two values follow each triangle end node. The bottom value is the sum of all monetary values on branches leading to this end node. The top value is the probability of getting to this end node when the optimal strategy is used. This explains why many of these probabilities are 0; the optimal strategy never leads to these end nodes.*

## Policy Suggestion and Risk Profile for Optimal Strategy

*The Policy Suggestion shows only the subtree corresponding to the optimal decision strategy.*

After the decision tree is completed, PrecisionTree has several tools we can use to gain more information about the decision analysis. First, we can see a subtree (called a Policy Suggestion) for the *optimal* decision. To do so, click on the Decision Analysis dropdown on the PrecisionTree ribbon and fill in the resulting dialog box as shown in Figure 10.19. (You can experiment with other options.) The Policy Suggestion option shows only that part of the tree that corresponds to the optimal decision, as shown in Figure 10.20.

**Figure 10.19**

Dialog Box for Information About Optimal Decision

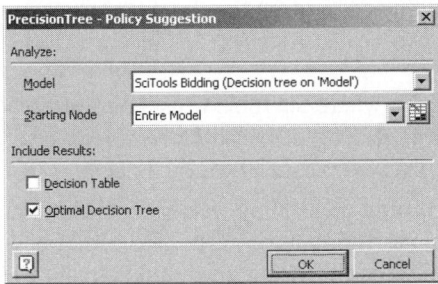

**Figure 10.20**

Subtree for Optimal Decision

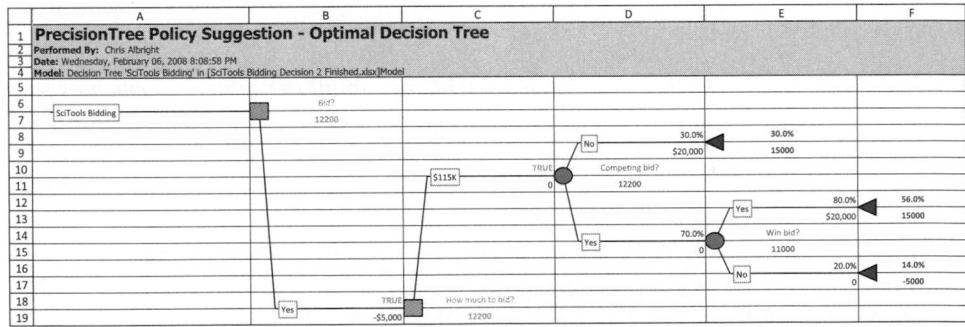

We can also obtain a graphical risk profile of the optimal decision. To get it, select Risk Profile from the Decision Analysis dropdown, and fill in the resulting dialog box as shown in Figure 10.21. (Again, you can experiment with the other options.) As the risk profile in Figure 10.22 indicates, there are only two possible monetary outcomes if SciTools bids $115,000. It either wins $15,000 or loses $5000, and the former is much more likely. (The associated probabilities are 0.86 and 0.14, respectively.) This graphical information is even more useful when there are a larger number of possible monetary outcomes. We can see what they are and how likely they are.

**Figure 10.21**

Risk Profile
Dialog Box

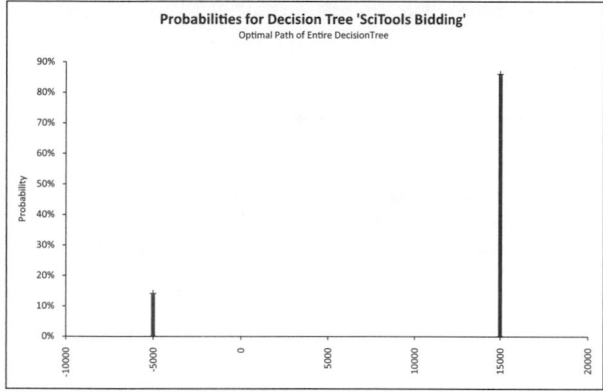

**Figure 10.22**

Risk Profile of
Optimal Decision

## Sensitivity Analysis

*Although it takes some practice and experimenting to get used to PrecisionTree's sensitivity analysis tools, they are powerful and worth learning.*

We have already stressed the importance of sensitivity analysis in any decision problem, and PrecisionTree makes this relatively easy to perform. First, we can enter any values into the input cells and watch how the tree changes. But we can obtain more systematic information by clicking on PrecisionTree's Sensitivity Analysis button. This brings up the dialog box in Figure 10.23. This dialog is fairly "busy," but once you understand the ideas behind it, it is easy to use. Here are the main options and how to use them.

- The Analysis Type dropdown allows you to vary one input (One-Way Sensitivity) or two inputs (Two-Way Sensitivity) simultaneously.

- The Starting Node dropdown lets you choose any node in the tree, and the sensitivity analysis is then performed for the EMV *from that node to the right.* In other words, it assumes you have gotten to that node and are now interested in what will happen from then on. The node selected in the figure, C29, is the leftmost node, so by selecting it, we perform a sensitivity analysis for the EMV of the entire tree. This is the most common setting.

- The Inputs section is where you can add inputs to vary. You can add as many as you like, and whichever inputs are then checked are the ones included in a particular sensitivity analysis. When you add an input to this section, you can specify the range over which you want it to vary. For example, you can vary it by plus or minus 10% in 10 steps from a selected base value, as we did for the production cost in cell B5, or you can vary it from 0 to 0.6 in 12 steps, as we did for the probability of no competing bids in cell B7.

- The Include Results checkboxes provide up to four types of charts you can select, depending on the type of sensitivity analysis. (The bottom two options are disabled for a two-way sensitivity analysis.) You can experiment with these options, but we'll illustrate our favorites shortly.

**Figure 10.23**

Sensitivity Analysis
Dialog Box

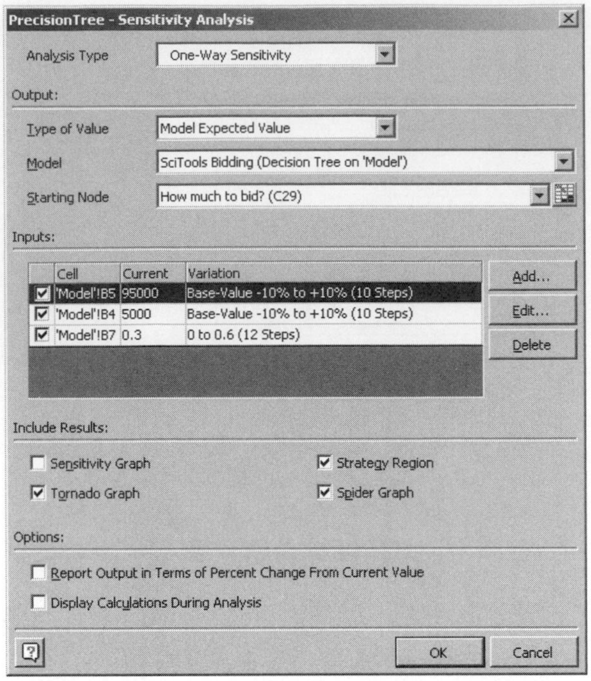

When we click on Run Analysis, PrecisionTree varies each of the checked inputs in the middle section, one at a time if we select the One-Way option, and presents the results in new worksheets. By default, these new worksheets are placed in a new workbook. If you'd rather have them in the same workbook as the model, click on the PrecisionTree Utilities dropdown, select Application Settings, and select Active Workbook from the Replace Reports In option. (This is a global setting. It will take effect for all future PrecisionTree analyses.)

## Strategy Region Charts

*In strategy region charts, we are especially interested in where (or whether) lines cross because this is where decisions change.*

Figure 10.24 illustrates a strategy region chart from a one-way analysis. This chart shows how the EMV varies with the production cost for *both* of the original decisions (bid or don't bid). This type of chart is useful for seeing whether the optimal decision *changes* over the range of the input variable. It does so only if the two lines cross. In this particular graph, the "Bid" decision clearly dominates the "No bid" decision over the production cost range we selected.

## Tornado Chart

A tornado chart shows how sensitive the EMV of the *optimal* decision is to each of the selected inputs over the specified ranges (see Figure 10.25). The length of each bar shows the percentage change in the EMV in either direction, so inputs with longer bars have a greater effect on the selected EMV. (If you checked the next-to-bottom checkbox in Figure 10.23, the lengths of the bars would indicate *percentage* changes from the base value.) The bars are always arranged from longest on top to shortest on the bottom—hence the name *tornado* chart. Here we see that production cost has the largest effect on EMV, and bid cost has the smallest effect.

Figure 10.24

EMV versus Produc-
tion Cost for Each of
Two Decisions

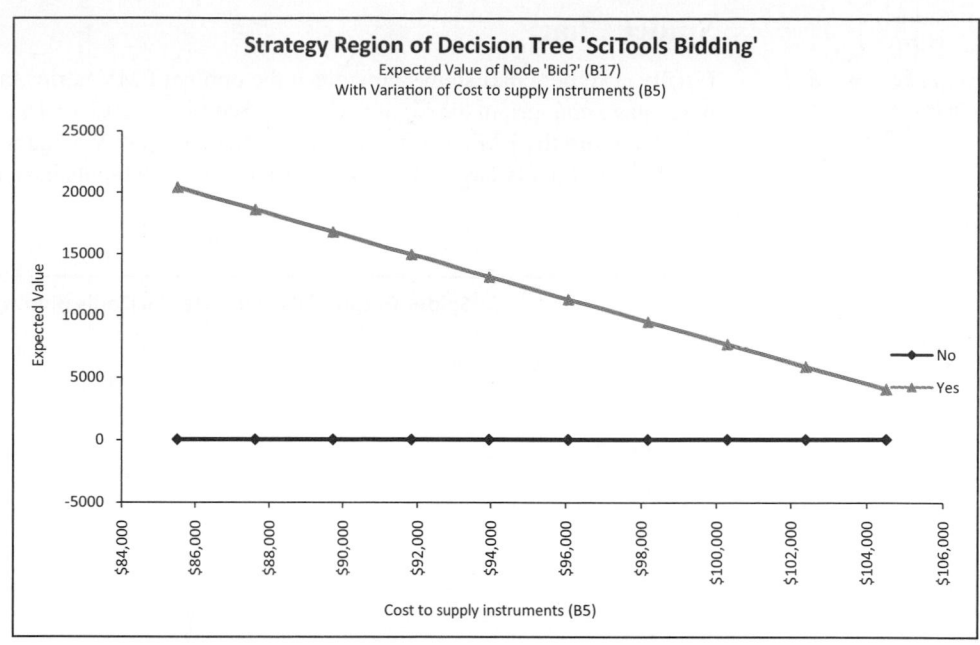

Figure 10.25

Tornado Chart for
SciTools Example

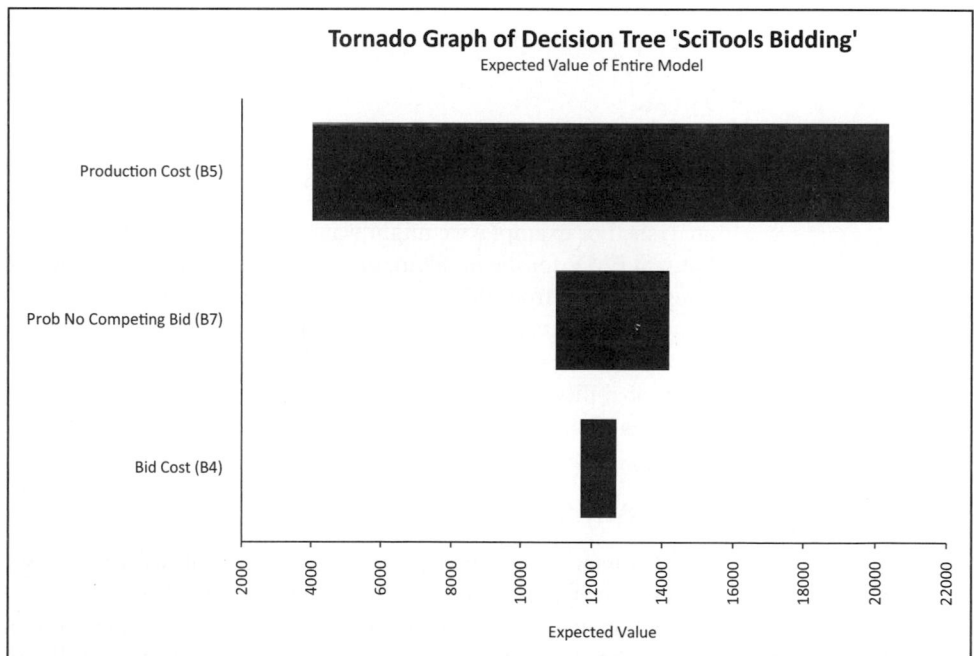

## Spider Chart

*Tornado charts and spider charts indicate which inputs the selected EMV is most sensitive to.*

Finally, a spider chart shows how much the optimal EMV varies in magnitude for various percentage changes in the input variables. (See Figure 10.26.) The steeper the slope of the line, the more the EMV is affected by a particular input. We again see that the production cost has a relatively large effect, whereas the other two inputs have relatively small effects.

**Figure 10.26**

Spider Chart for SciTools Example

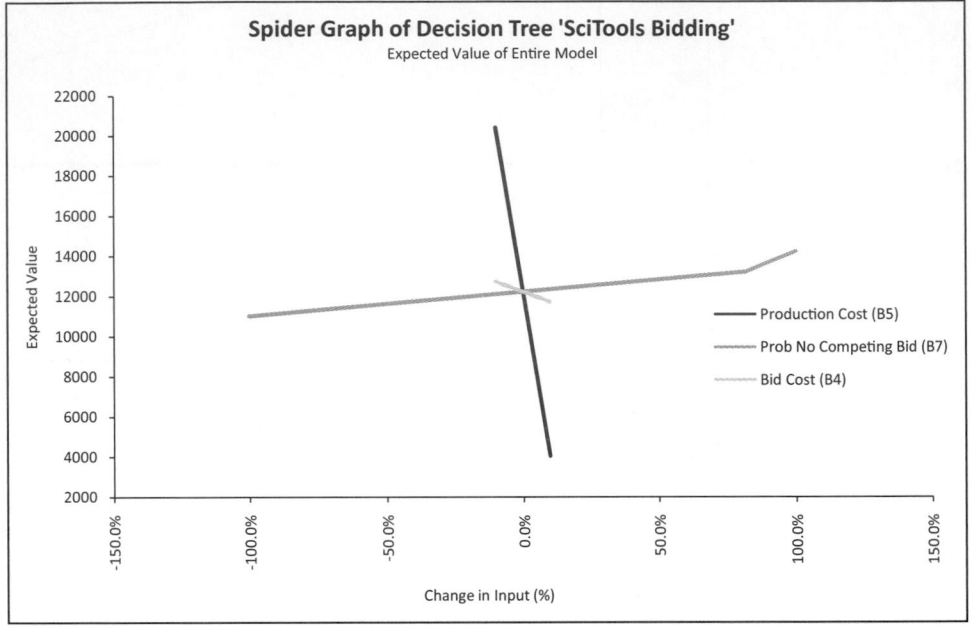

## Another Sensitivity Chart

Each time we click on the Sensitivity Analysis button, we can run a different sensitivity analysis. For example, we might want to choose cell C29 as the cell to analyze. This is the optimal EMV for the problem, given that the company has decided to place a bid. One interesting chart from this analysis is the strategy region chart in Figure 10.27. It indicates how the EMV varies with the probability of no competing bid for *each* of the three bid amount decisions. As we see, the $115,000 bid is best for most of the range, but when the probability of no competing bid is sufficiently large (about 0.55), the $120,000 bid becomes best.

## Two-Way Sensitivity Chart

*A one-way sensitivity analysis varies only one input at a time. A two-way analysis varies two inputs simultaneously.*

Another interesting option is to run a two-way analysis. Then we see how the selected EMV varies as each *pair* of inputs varies simultaneously. We analyzed the EMV in cell C29 with this option, using the same inputs as before. A typical result is shown in Figure 10.28. For each of the possible values of production cost and the probability of no competitor bid, this chart indicates which bid amount is optimal. (By choosing cell C29, we are assuming SciTools will bid; the question is only how much.) As we see, the optimal bid amount remains $115,000 unless the production cost *and* the probability of no competing bid are

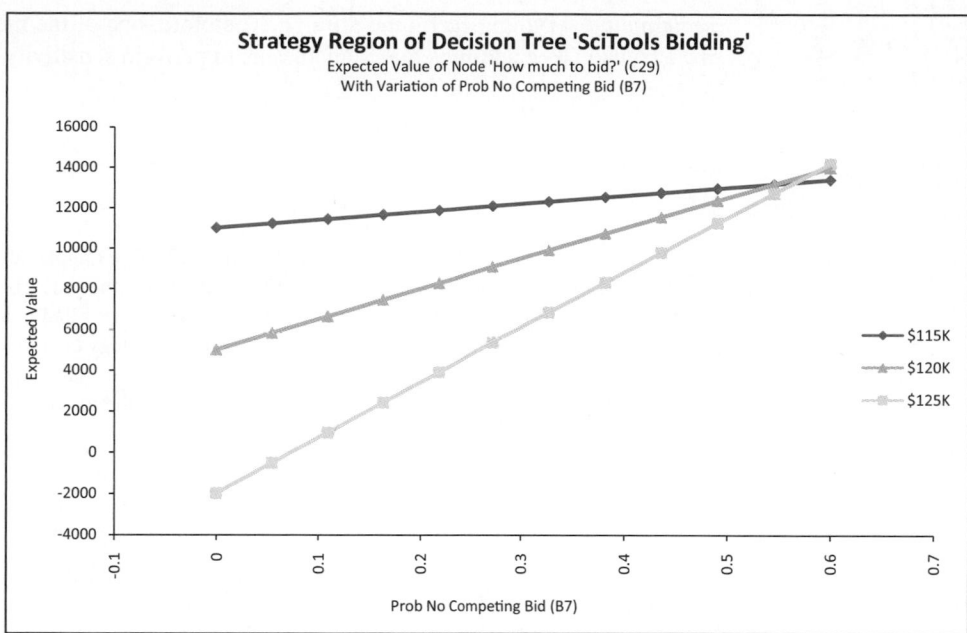

**Figure 10.27**

**Strategy Region Chart for Another EMV Cell**

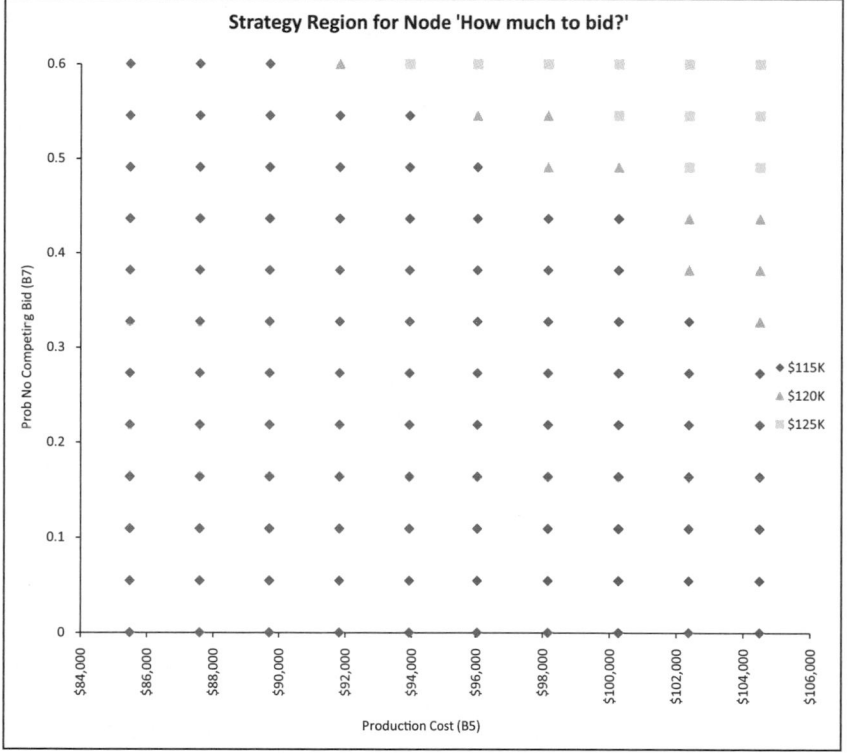

**Figure 10.28**

**Two-Way Sensitivity Analysis**

both large. Then it becomes optimal to bid $120,000 or $125,000. This makes sense intuitively. As the chance of no competing bid increases and a larger production cost must be recovered, it seems reasonable that SciTools should increase its bid.

We reiterate that a sensitivity analysis is always an important component of any real-world decision analysis. If we had to construct decision trees by hand—with paper and pencil—a sensitivity analysis would be virtually out of the question. We would have to recompute everything each time through. Therefore, one of the most valuable features of the PrecisionTree add-in is that it enables us to perform sensitivity analyses in a matter of seconds.

## PROBLEMS

12. In a tree built with PrecisionTree, there are two blue values at each end node, and the top one is a probability. Why are so many of these probabilities 0 in the finished tree in Figure 10.10? What do the remaining (positive) probabilities represent?

**13.** In the SciTools example, we saw that there are two equivalent decision tree structures, shown in Figures 10.5 and 10.6. Use PrecisionTree to create the first of these, and verify that it yields the same EMVs and the same optimal decision as the tree we developed in this section.

14. For the completed decision tree in Figure 10.10, the monetary values in black are those we enter. The monetary values in color are calculated automatically by PrecisionTree. For this particular example, explain exactly how these latter values are calculated (remember the folding-back process) and what they represent. These include the blue values at the end nodes, the red values at the probability nodes, and the green values at the decision nodes.

15. For the SciTools example, after you build the tree as in Figure 10.10 and then run a one-way sensitivity analysis with the dialog box filled in as in Figure 10.23, you obtain three strategy charts. (Try it.) Explain exactly what each of these charts represents. (For this problem, you can ignore the tornado and spider charts.)

16. The tornado chart in Figure 10.25 and the spider chart in Figure 10.26 show basically the same information in slightly different forms. Explain in words exactly what information they provide.

17. Explain in words what information a two-way sensitivity chart, such as the one in Figure 10.28, provides. Demonstrate how you could provide this same information without PrecisionTree's sensitivity tools, using only data tables. (You can still utilize the tree built with PrecisionTree.)

## 10.4 BAYES' RULE

So far, the examples have required a single decision. We now examine multistage problems, where the decision maker must make at least two decisions that are separated in time, such as when a company must first decide whether to buy information that will help it make a second decision. In multistage decision problems, we typically have alternating sets of decision nodes and probability nodes. The decision maker makes a decision, some uncertain outcomes are observed, the decision maker makes another decision, more uncertain outcomes are observed, and so on. Before we can analyze such problems, we must resolve one important probability issue.

*The whole purpose of Bayes' rule is to revise probabilities as new information becomes available.*

In a multistage decision tree, all probability branches at the *right* of the tree are conditional on outcomes that have occurred earlier, to their left. Therefore, the probabilities on these branches are of the form $P(A|B)$, read $A$ given $B$, where $A$ is an event corresponding to a current probability branch, and $B$ is an event that occurs *before* event $A$ in time. However, it is sometimes more natural to *assess* conditional probabilities in the opposite order, that is, $P(B|A)$. Whenever this is the case, we must use **Bayes' rule** to obtain the probabilities needed on the tree. Essentially, Bayes' rule is a mechanism for revising probabilities as new information becomes available.

To develop Bayes' rule, let $A_1$ through $A_n$ be any outcomes. Without any further information, we believe the probabilities of the $A$'s are $P(A_1)$ through $P(A_n)$. These are called **prior probabilities.** We then have the possibility of gaining some information. There are several information outcomes we might observe, a typical one of which is labeled $B$. We assume the probabilities of $B$, given that any of the $A$'s will occur, are known. These probabilities, labeled $P(B|A_1)$ through $P(B|A_n)$, are often called **likelihoods.** Because an information outcome might influence our thinking about the probabilities of the $A$'s, we need to find the conditional probability $P(A_i|B)$ for each outcome $A_i$. This is called the **posterior probability** of $A_i$. This is where Bayes' rule enters the picture. It enables us to calculate posterior probabilities by using the following formula.

---

**Bayes' rule**

$$P(A_i|B) = \frac{P(B|A_i)P(A_i)}{P(B|A_1)P(A_1) + \cdots + P(B|A_n)P(A_n)}$$  **(10.1)**

---

In words, Bayes' rule says that the posterior is the likelihood times the prior, divided by a sum of likelihoods times priors. As a side benefit, the denominator in Bayes' rule is also useful in multistage decision trees. It is the probability $P(B)$ of the information outcome:

---

**Denominator of Bayes' rule**

$$P(B) = P(B|A_1)P(A_1) + \cdots + P(B|A_n)P(A_n)$$  **(10.2)**

---

When there are only two $A$'s, which we relabel as $A$ and Not $A$, Bayes' rules takes the following form:

---

**Bayes' rule for two outcomes**

$$P(A|B) = \frac{P(B|A)P(A)}{P(B|A)P(A) + P(B|\text{Not } A)P(\text{Not } A)}$$  **(10.3)**

---

We illustrate the mechanics of Bayes' rule in the following example. [See Feinstein (1990) for a real application of this example.]

---

**EXAMPLE** | **10.3 DRUG TESTING COLLEGE ATHLETES**

If an athlete is tested for a certain type of drug usage (steroids, say), then the test result is either positive or negative. However, these tests are never perfect. Some athletes who are drug-free test positive, and some who are drug users test negative. The former are called **false positives;** the latter are called **false negatives.** We assume that 5% of all athletes use drugs, 3% of all tests on drug-free athletes yield false positives, and 7% of all tests on drug users yield false negatives. Suppose a typical athlete is tested. If this athlete tests positive, are we sure that he is a drug user? If he tests negative, are we sure he does not use drugs?

**Objective** To use Bayes' rule to revise the probability of being a drug user, given the positive or negative results of the test.

### WHERE DO THE NUMBERS COME FROM?

The estimate that 5% of all athletes are drug users is probably based on a well-known national average. The error rates from the tests are undoubtedly known from extensive experience with the tests. (However, we are not claiming that the numbers used here match reality.)

## Solution

Let $D$ and $ND$ denote that a randomly chosen athlete is or is not a drug user, and let $T+$ and $T-$ indicate a positive or negative test result. (The outcomes $D$ and $ND$ correspond to $A$ and Not $A$ in equation (10.3), and either $T+$ or $T-$ corresponds to $B$.) We are given the following probabilities. First, because 5% of all athletes are drug users, we know that $P(D)$ = 0.05 and $P(ND)$ = 0.95. These are the prior probabilities. They represent the chance that an athlete is or is not a drug user *prior* to the results of a drug test.

Second, from the information on the accuracy of the drug test, we know the conditional probabilities $P(T+|ND)$ = 0.03 and $P(T-|D)$ = 0.07. In addition, a drug-free athlete tests either positive or negative, and the same is true for a drug user. Therefore, we also have the probabilities $P(T-|ND)$ = 0.97 and $P(T+|D)$ = 0.93. These four conditional probabilities of test results given drug user status are the likelihoods of the test results.

Given these priors and likelihoods, we want posterior probabilities such as $P(D|T+)$, the probability that an athlete who tests positive is a drug user, and $P(ND|T-)$, the probability that an athlete who tests negative is drug-free. They are called posterior probabilities because they are assessed *after* the drug test results.

Using Bayes' rule for two outcomes, equation (10.3), we find

$$P(D|T+) = \frac{P(T+|D)P(D)}{P(T+|D)P(D)+P(T+|ND)P(ND)} = \frac{(0.93)(0.05)}{(0.93)(0.05)+(0.03)(0.95)} = 0.620$$

and

$$P(ND|T-) = \frac{P(T-|ND)P(ND)}{P(T-|D)P(D)+P(T-|ND)P(ND)} = \frac{(0.97)(0.95)}{(0.07)(0.05)+(0.97)(0.95)} = 0.996$$

In words, if the athlete tests positive, there is still a 38% chance that he is *not* a drug user, but if he tests negative, we are virtually sure he is not a drug user. The denominators of these two formulas are the probabilities of the test results. We find them from equation (10.2):

$$P(T+) = 0.93(0.05) + 0.03(0.95) = 0.075$$

and

$$P(T-) = 0.07(0.05) + 0.97(0.95) = 0.925$$

This means that if we test a randomly selected athlete, the probability is only 0.075 that he will test positive.

The first Bayes' rule result might surprise you. After all, there is only a 3% chance of a false positive, so if you observe a positive test result, you should be pretty sure that the athlete is a drug user, right? The reason the first posterior probability is "only" 0.620 is that very few athletes in the population are drug users—only 5%. Therefore, we need a lot of evidence to convince us that a particular athlete is a drug user, and a positive test result from a somewhat inaccurate test is not enough evidence to be totally convincing. On the other hand, a negative test result simply adds confirmation to what we already suspected— that a typical athlete is *not* a drug user. This is why $P(ND|T-)$ is so close to 1.

### A More Intuitive Calculation

If you have trouble understanding or implementing Bayes' rule, you are not alone. At least one study has shown that even trained medical specialists have trouble with this type of calculation. Most of us do not think intuitively about conditional probabilities. However, there is an equivalent and more intuitive way to obtain the same result.

*This alternative procedure, using counts instead of probabilities, is equivalent to Bayes' rule and is probably more intuitive.*

Imagine that there are 100,000 athletes. Because 5% of all athletes are drug users, we assume 5000 of our athletes use drugs and the other 95,000 do not. Now we administer the test to all of them. We expect 3%, or 2850, of the nonusers to test positive (because the false positive rate is 3%), and we expect 93%, or 4650, of the drug users to test positive (because the false negative rate is 7%). Therefore, we observe a total of 2850 + 4650 = 7500 positives. If we choose one of these athletes at random, what is the probability that we choose a drug user? It is clearly

$$P(D|T+) = 4650/7500 = 0.620$$

This is the same result we got using Bayes' rule! So if you have trouble with Bayes' rule using probabilities, you can use this alternative method of using *counts*. (By the way, the 100,000 value is irrelevant. We could have used 10,000, 50,000, 1,000,000, or any other convenient value.)

### Spreadsheet Implementation of Bayes' Rule

Bayes' rule is fairly easy to implement in a spreadsheet, as illustrated in Figure 10.29 for the drug example. (See the file **Bayes Rule xlsx**.[4])

**Figure 10.29**

Bayes' Rule for the Drug-Testing Example

| | A | B | C | D | E | F |
|---|---|---|---|---|---|---|
| 1 | Illustration of Bayes' rule using drug example | | | | | |
| 2 | | | | | | |
| 3 | Prior probabilities of drug user status | | | | | |
| 4 | | User | Non-user | | | |
| 5 | | 0.05 | 0.95 | 1 | | |
| 6 | | | | | | |
| 7 | Likelihoods of test results, given drug user status | | | | | |
| 8 | | User | Non-user | | | |
| 9 | Test positive | 0.93 | 0.03 | | | |
| 10 | Test negative | 0.07 | 0.97 | | | |
| 11 | | 1 | 1 | | | |
| 12 | | | | | | |
| 13 | Unconditional probabilities of test results (denominators of Bayes' rule) | | | | | |
| 14 | Test positive | 0.075 | | | | |
| 15 | Test negative | 0.925 | | | | |
| 16 | | 1 | | | | |
| 17 | | | | | | |
| 18 | Posterior probabilities of drug user status (Bayes' rule) | | | | | |
| 19 | | User | Non-user | | | |
| 20 | Test positive | 0.620 | 0.380 | 1 | | |
| 21 | Test negative | 0.004 | 0.996 | 1 | | |

The given priors and likelihoods are listed in the ranges B5:C5 and B9:C10. We first use equation (10.2) to calculate the denominators for Bayes' rule, the unconditional probabilities of the two possible test results, in the range B14:B15. Because each of these is a sum of products of priors and likelihoods, the formula in cell B14 is

**=SUMPRODUCT($B$5:$C$5,B9:C9)**

and this is copied to cell B15. Then we use equation (10.1) to calculate the posterior probabilities in the range B20:C21. Because each of these is a product of a prior and a likelihood, divided by a denominator, the formula in cell B20 is

**=B$5*B9/$B14**

and this is copied to the rest of the B20:C21 range. The various 1's in the margins of Figure 10.29 are row sums or column sums that must equal 1. We show them only as checks of our logic.

As we have noted, a positive drug test still leaves a 38% chance that the athlete is *not* a drug user. Is this a valid argument for not requiring drug testing of athletes? We explore this question in a continuation of the drug-testing example in the next section. Another

[4] The second sheet in this file illustrates how Bayes' rule can be used when there are more than two possible test results and/or drug user categories.

possibility is to administer the drug test a *second* time (at some later date) to any athlete who tests positive. If we can assume that the results of the two tests are probabilistically independent, then it is easy to use Bayes' rule to update the probabilities after a second test. We simply use the posterior probabilities in row 20 as priors. That is, we substitute the probabilities in row 20 for the priors in row 5. If you do so, you will find that the posterior probability of being a drug user, given *two* positive drug tests, increases to 0.981. Now we are over 98% sure that the athlete is a drug user. ∎

# PROBLEMS

## Skill-Building Problems

18. For each of the following, use a one-way data table to see how the posterior probability of being a drug user, given a positive test, varies as the indicated input varies. Write a brief explanation of your results.
    a. Let the input be the prior probability of being a drug user, varied from 0.01 to 0.10 in increments of 0.01.
    b. Let the input be the probability of a false positive from the test, varied from 0 to 0.10 in increments of 0.01.
    c. Let the input be the probability of a false negative from the test, varied from 0 to 0.10 in increments of 0.01.

19. In the drug testing, assume there are three possible test results: positive, negative, and inconclusive. For a drug user, the probabilities of these outcomes are 0.65, 0.06, and 0.29. For a nonuser, they are 0.03, 0.72, and 0.25. Use Bayes' rule to find a table of all posterior probabilities. (The prior probability of being a drug user is still 0.05.) Then answer the following.
    a. What is the posterior probability that the athlete is a drug user, given that her test results are positive; given that her test results are negative; given that her drug results are inconclusive?
    b. What is the probability of observing a positive test result; a negative test result; an inconclusive test result?

20. Referring to the previous problem, find the same probabilities through the counting argument explained in this section. Start with 100,000 athletes and divide them into the various categories.

## Skill-Extending Problem

21. The terms *prior* and *posterior* are relative. Assume that the drug test has been performed, and the outcome is positive, which leads to the posterior probabilities in row 20 of Figure 10.29. Now assume there is a *second* test, probabilistically independent of the first, that can be used as a follow-up. We assume that its false positive and false negative rates are 0.02 and 0.06.
    a. Use the posterior probabilities from row 20 as *prior* probabilities in a second Bayes' rule calculation. (Now *prior* means prior to the second test.) If the athlete also tests positive in this second test, what is the posterior probability that he is a drug user?
    b. We assumed that the two tests are probabilistically independent. Why might this not be realistic? If they are not independent, what kind of additional information would we need about the likelihoods of the test results?

# 10.5 MULTISTAGE DECISION PROBLEMS

In this section, we investigate multistage decision problems. In many such problems, the first stage decision is whether to purchase information that will help make a better second stage decision. The information, if obtained, typically changes the probabilities of later outcomes. To revise the probabilities after the information is obtained, we often (but not always) need to apply Bayes' rule, as discussed in the previous section. In addition, we typically want to learn how much the information is worth. After all, information usually comes at a price, so we want to know whether the information is worth its price. This leads to an investigation of the value of information, an important theme of this section.

We begin with a continuation of the drug-testing example from the previous section. If drug tests are not completely reliable, should they be used? As we see, it all depends on the "costs."[5]

| EXAMPLE | 10.4 DRUG TESTING COLLEGE ATHLETES |
| --- | --- |

The administrators at State University are trying to decide whether to institute mandatory drug testing for athletes. They have the same information about priors and likelihoods as in the previous example, but they now want to use a decision tree approach to see whether the benefits outweigh the costs.[6]

**Objective**   To use a multistage decision framework to determine whether mandatory drug testing can be justified, given a somewhat unreliable test and a set of reasonable monetary values.

### WHERE DO THE NUMBERS COME FROM?

We already discussed the source of the probabilities in the previous example. The monetary values we need are discussed in detail next.

## Solution

We have already discussed the uncertain outcomes and their probabilities. Now we need to discuss the decision alternatives and the monetary values—the other two elements of a decision analysis. We assume that there are only two alternatives: perform drug testing on all athletes or don't perform any drug testing. In the former case, we assume that if an athlete tests positive, this athlete is then barred from athletics.

### Assessing the Monetary Values

The "monetary" values are more difficult to assess. They include the following:

- The benefit $B$ from correctly identifying a drug user and barring this person from athletics
- The cost $C_1$ of the test itself for a single athlete (materials and labor)
- The cost $C_2$ of falsely accusing a nonuser (and barring this person from athletics)
- The cost $C_3$ of not identifying a drug user and allowing this person to participate in athletics
- The cost $C_4$ of violating a nonuser's privacy by performing the test

*Real decision problems often involve nonmonetary benefits and costs. These must be assessed, relative to one another, before rational decisions can be made.*

It is clear that only $C_1$ is a direct monetary cost that is easy to measure. However, the other "costs" and the benefit $B$ are real, and they must be compared on some scale to enable administrators to make a rational decision. We do so by comparing everything to the cost $C_1$, to which we assign value 1. (This does not mean that the cost of testing an athlete is necessarily \$1; it just means that we express all other monetary values as multiples of $C_1$.) Clearly, a lot of subjectivity is involved in making these comparisons, so sensitivity analysis on the final decision tree is a must.

---

[5] It might also depend on whether a second type of test could help confirm the findings of the first test. However, we do not consider such a test.
[6] Again, see Feinstein (1990) for an enlightening discussion of this drug-testing problem at a real university.

## Developing a Benefit–Cost Table

Before developing this decision tree, it is useful to form a benefit–cost table for both alternatives and all possible outcomes. Because we eventually maximize expected net *benefit,* all benefits in this table have a positive sign and all costs have a negative sign. These net benefits are listed in Table 10.7. The first two columns are relevant if no tests are performed; the last four are relevant when testing is performed. For example, if a positive test is obtained for a nonuser and this athlete is barred from athletics, there are three costs: the cost of the test $(C_1)$, the cost of falsely accusing the athlete $(C_2)$, and the cost of violating the athlete's privacy $(C_4)$. The other entries are obtained similarly.

**Table 10.7**   Net Benefits for the Drug-Testing Example

| Ultimate | Don't Test | | Perform Test | | | |
|---|---|---|---|---|---|---|
| decision | D | ND | D and T+ | ND and T+ | D and T− | ND and T− |
| Bar from athletics | B | $-C_2$ | $B - C_1$ | $-(C_1 + C_2 + C_4)$ | $B - C_1$ | $-(C_1 + C_2 + C_4)$ |
| Don't bar | $-C_3$ | 0 | $-(C_1 + C_3)$ | $-(C_1 + C_4)$ | $-(C_1 + C_3)$ | $-(C_1 + C_4)$ |

## DEVELOPING THE DECISION TREE MODEL

The decision model, developed with PrecisionTree and shown in Figures 10.30 and 10.31, is now fairly straightforward. (See the file **Drug Testing Decision.xlsx**.) We first enter all of the benefits and costs in an input section. These, together with the Bayes' rule calculations from the previous example, appear at the top of the spreadsheet in Figure 10.30. Then we use PrecisionTree in the usual way to build the tree in Figure 10.31 and enter the links to the values and probabilities.

**Figure 10.30**   Inputs and Bayes' Rule Calculations for the Drug-Testing Example

| | A | B | C | D | E | F |
|---|---|---|---|---|---|---|
| 1 | Drug testing decision | | | | | |
| 2 | | | | | | |
| 3 | Benefits | | | Given probabilities | | |
| 4 | Identifying user | 25 | | Prior probabilities | | |
| 5 | | | | | User | Non-user |
| 6 | Costs | | | | 0.05 | 0.95 |
| 7 | Test cost | 1 | | | | |
| 8 | Barring non-user | 50 | | Conditional probabilities of test results | | |
| 9 | Not identifying user | 20 | | | User | Non-user |
| 10 | Violation of privacy | 2 | | Positive | 0.93 | 0.03 |
| 11 | | | | Negative | 0.07 | 0.97 |
| 12 | Key probabilities | | | | | |
| 13 | PrUser | 0.05 | | Bayesian revision | | |
| 14 | PrFalseNegative | 0.07 | | Unconditional probabilities of test results | | |
| 15 | PrFalsePositive | 0.03 | | Positive | 0.075 | |
| 16 | | | | Negative | 0.925 | |
| 17 | | | | | | |
| 18 | | | | Posterior probabilities | | |
| 19 | | | | | User | Non-user |
| 20 | | | | Positive | 0.620 | 0.380 |
| 21 | | | | Negative | 0.004 | 0.996 |

It is important to understand the timing (from left to right) in this decision tree. If drug testing is performed, the result of the drug test is observed first (a probability node). Each test result leads to an action (bar from sports or don't), and then the eventual benefit or cost depends on whether the athlete uses drugs (again a probability node). You might argue that the university never knows for certain whether the athlete uses drugs, but we must include this information in the tree to get the correct benefits and costs. On the other hand, if no drug testing is performed, then there is no intermediate test result node or branches.

**Figure 10.31**  Decision Tree for the Drug-Testing Example

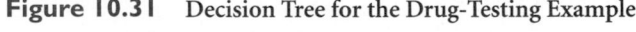

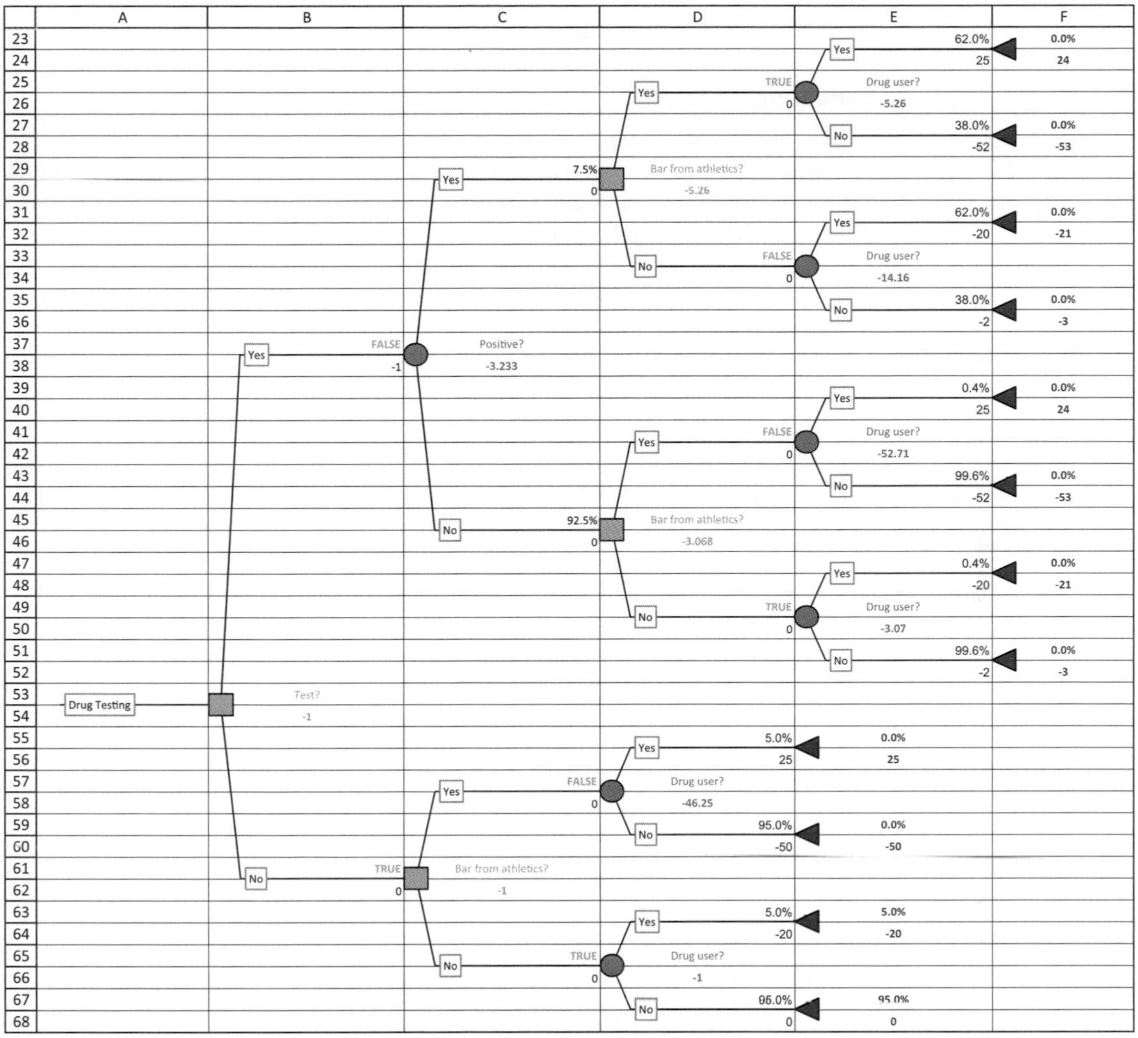

| | A | B | C | D | E | F |
|---|---|---|---|---|---|---|
| | Drug Testing — Test? −1 | | | | | |
| | | | Positive? (FALSE, −1) −3.233 | | | |
| | | Yes | Yes 7.5% / 0 — Bar from athletics? −5.26 | Yes (TRUE, 0) — Drug user? −5.26 | Yes 62.0% / 25 | 0.0% / 24 |
| | | | | | No 38.0% / −52 | 0.0% / −53 |
| | | | | No (FALSE, 0) — Drug user? −14.16 | Yes 62.0% / −20 | 0.0% / −21 |
| | | | | | No 38.0% / −2 | 0.0% / −3 |
| | | | No 92.5% / 0 — Bar from athletics? −3.068 | Yes (FALSE, 0) — Drug user? −52.71 | Yes 0.4% / 25 | 0.0% / 24 |
| | | | | | No 99.6% / −52 | 0.0% / −53 |
| | | | | No (TRUE, 0) — Drug user? −3.07 | Yes 0.4% / −20 | 0.0% / −21 |
| | | | | | No 99.6% / −2 | 0.0% / −3 |
| | | No (TRUE, 0) — Bar from athletics? −1 | Yes (FALSE, 0) — Drug user? −46.25 | Yes 5.0% / 25 | 0.0% / 25 | |
| | | | | No 95.0% / −50 | 0.0% / −50 | |
| | | | No (TRUE, 0) — Drug user? −1 | Yes 5.0% / −20 | 5.0% / −20 | |
| | | | | No 95.0% / 0 | 95.0% / 0 | |

*We require Bayes' rule because it yields exactly those probabilities that are needed in the decision tree.*

Make sure you understand which probabilities are used in the tree. In the lower part, where we don't test, the probabilities are the prior probabilities. We have no test information in this case. In the upper part, where we test, the probabilities for the user and nonuser branches are posterior probabilities, given the results of the test. The reason is that by the time we get to these nodes, the results of the test have already been observed. However, the probabilities for the test results are *unconditional* probabilities, the denominators in Bayes' rule. They are not conditional probabilities such as $P(T+|D)$ because we condition only on information to the *left* of any given branch. In other words, by the time we get to the test result branches, we do not yet know whether the athlete is a drug user.

### Discussion of the Solution

The benefits and costs shown previously in Figure 10.30 were chosen fairly arbitrarily, but with some hope of reflecting reality. The largest cost is falsely accusing (and then barring) a nonuser. This is 50 times as large as the cost of the test. The benefit of identifying a drug user is only half this large, and the cost of not identifying a user is 40% as large as barring a nonuser. The violation of the privacy of a nonuser is twice as large as the cost of the test. Based on these values, the decision tree implies that drug testing should *not* be performed (and no athletes should be barred). The EMVs for testing and for not testing are both negative, indicating that the costs outweigh the benefits for each, but the EMV for not testing is slightly *less* negative.[7]

### Sensitivity Analysis

What would it take to change this decision? We begin with the assumption, probably accepted by most people in our society, that the cost of falsely accusing a nonuser ($C_2$) is the largest of the benefits and costs in the range B4:B10. In fact, because of possible legal costs, we might argue that $C_2$ is *more* than 50 times the cost of the test. But if we increase $C_2$, the scales are tipped even farther in the direction of not testing. On the other hand, if the benefit $B$ from identifying a user and the cost $C_3$ for not identifying a user increase, then testing might be the preferred alternative. We tried this, keeping $C_2$ constant at 50. When $B$ and $C_3$ both had value 45, no testing was still optimal, but when they both increased to 50—the same magnitude as $C_2$—then testing won out by a small margin. However, it would be difficult to argue that $B$ and $C_3$ are of the same magnitude as $C_2$.

*Based on a fairly extensive sensitivity analysis of the relative costs and the error probabilities, it is difficult to make a case for mandatory drug testing.*

Other than the benefits and costs, the only other input we might vary is the accuracy of the test, measured by the error probabilities in cells B14 and B15. Presumably, if the test makes fewer false positives and false negatives, testing might be a more attractive alternative. We tried this, keeping the benefits and costs the same as those in Figure 10.30 but changing the error probabilities. Even when each error probability was decreased to 0.01, however, the no-testing alternative was still optimal—by a fairly wide margin.

In summary, based on a number of reasonable assumptions and parameter settings, this example has shown that it is difficult to make a case for mandatory drug testing. ∎

## The Value of Information

The drug-testing decision problem represents a typical multistage decision problem. We first decide whether to obtain some information that could be useful—the results of a drug test. If we decide not to obtain the information, we make a decision right away (bar the athlete or don't), based on prior probabilities. If we do decide to obtain the information, we first observe the information and *then* make the final decision, based on posterior probabilities.

The questions we ask now are: How much is the information worth, and if it costs a given amount, should we purchase it? Presumably, information that helps us make our ultimate decision should be worth something, but it is not clear how much the information is worth. In addition, even if the information is worth something, it might not be worth as much as its actual price. Fortunately, the answers to our questions are embedded in the decision tree itself.

We actually find the values of two types of information: sample information and perfect information. **Sample information** is the information from the experiment itself. In this example, it is the information from the (less than perfect) drug test. **Perfect information,** on the other hand, is information from a perfect test—that is, a test that tells us with certainty which ultimate outcome will occur. In the drug example, this corresponds to a test that never makes mistakes. Admittedly, perfect information is almost never available at any price, but finding its value is still useful because it provides an upper bound on the value of *any* information. For example, if perfect information is valued at $2000, then *no* information can possibly be worth more than $2000.

---

[7] The university in the Feinstein (1990) study came to the same conclusion.

We will find the **expected value of sample information (EVSI)** and the **expected values of perfect information (EVPI)**. The **EVSI** is the most we would be willing to pay for the sample information.

---

***Formula for EVSI***

$$\text{EVSI} = \text{EMV with (free) sample information} - \text{EMV without information} \quad \textbf{(10.4)}$$

---

The **EVPI** is the most we would be willing to pay for the perfect information.

---

***Formula for EVPI***

$$\text{EVPI} = \text{EMV with (free) perfect information} - \text{EMV without information} \quad \textbf{(10.5)}$$

---

**FUNDAMENTAL INSIGHT**

**The Value of Information**

The amount you should be willing to spend for information is the expected increase in EMV you can obtain from having the information. If the actual price of the information is less than or equal to this amount, you should purchase it; otherwise, the information is not worth its price. In addition, information that never affects your decision is worthless, and it should not be purchased at any price. Finally, the value of *any* information can never be greater than the value of information that would eliminate all uncertainty.

We now see how the value of information can be evaluated in the following typical multistage decision problem.

**EXAMPLE** | **10.5 MARKETING A NEW PRODUCT AT ACME**

The Acme Company is trying to decide whether to market a new product. As in many new-product situations, there is considerable uncertainty about whether the new product will eventually be popular. Acme believes that it might be wise to introduce the product in a regional test market before introducing it nationally. Therefore, the company's first decision is whether to conduct the test market.

Acme estimates that the net cost of the test market is $100,000. We assume this is mostly fixed costs, so that the same cost is incurred regardless of the test market results. If Acme decides to conduct the test market, it must then wait for the results. Based on the results of the test market, it can then decide whether to market the product nationally, in which case it will incur a fixed cost of $7 million. On the other hand, if the original decision is *not* to run a test market, then the final decision—whether to market the product nationally—can be made without further delay. Acme's unit margin, the difference between its selling price and its unit variable cost, is $18. We assume this is relevant only for the national market.

*This is clearly an approximation of the real problem. In the real problem, there would be a continuum of possible outcomes, not just three.*

Acme classifies the results in either the test market or the national market as great, fair, or awful. Each of these results in the national market is accompanied by a forecast of total units sold. These sales volumes (in 1000s of units) are 600 (great), 300 (fair), and 90 (awful). In the absence of any test market information, Acme estimates that probabilities of the three national market outcomes are 0.45, 0.35, and 0.20, respectively.

In addition, Acme has the following historical data from products that were introduced into both test markets and national markets:

- Of the products that eventually did great in the national market, 64% did great in the test market, 26% did fair in the test market, and 10% did awful in the test market.

- Of the products that eventually did fair in the national market, 18% did great in the test market, 57% did fair in the test market, and 25% did awful in the test market.
- Of the products that eventually did awful in the national market, 9% did great in the test market, 48% did fair in the test market, and 43% did awful in the test market.[8]

The company wants to use a decision tree approach to find the best strategy. It also wants to find the expected value of the information provided by the test market.

**Objective**   To develop a decision tree to find the best strategy for Acme, to perform a sensitivity analysis on the results, and to find EVSI and EVPI.

## WHERE DO THE NUMBERS COME FROM?

The fixed costs of the test market and the national market are probably accurate estimates, based on planned advertising and overhead expenses. The unit margin is just the difference between the anticipated selling price and the known unit cost of the product. The sales volume estimates are clearly approximations to reality because the sales from any new product would form a continuum of possible values. Here, the company has "discretized" the problem into three possible outcomes for the national market, and it has estimated the sales for each of these outcomes. As for the probabilities of national market results, given test market results, these are probably based on results from previous products that went through test markets and then national markets.

## Solution

We begin by discussing the three basic elements of this decision problem: the possible strategies, the possible outcomes and their probabilities, and the value model. The possible strategies are clear. Acme must first decide whether to run a test market. Then it must decide whether to introduce the product nationally. However, if Acme decides to run a test market, it can base the national market decision on the results of the test market. In this case, its final strategy is a **contingency plan,** where it conducts the test market, then introduces the product nationally if it receives sufficiently positive test market results and abandons the product if it receives sufficiently negative test market results. The optimal strategies from many multistage decision problems involve similar contingency plans.

Regarding the uncertain outcomes and their probabilities, we note that the given prior probabilities of national market results in the absence of test market results are needed in one part of the tree: where Acme decides not to run a test market. However, the historical percentages we quoted are really likelihoods of test market results, given national market results. For example, one of these is $P$(Great test market | Great national market) = 0.64. Such probabilities are the opposite of what we need in the tree. This is because the event to the right of the given sign, "great national market," occurs in

[8] You can question why the company ever marketed products nationally after awful test market results, but we assume that, for whatever reason, the company made a few such decisions—and that a few turned out to be winners.

time *after* the event to the left of the given sign, "great test market." This is a sure sign that Bayes' rule is required.

The required posterior probabilities of national market results, given test market results, are calculated directly from Bayes' rule, equation (10.1). For example, if *NG*, *NF*, and *NA* represent great, fair, and awful national market results, respectively, and if *TG*, *TF*, and *TA* represent similar events for the test market, than one typical example of a posterior probability calculation is

$$P(NG|TF) = \frac{P(TF|NG)P(NG)}{P(TF|NG)P(NG)+P(TF|NF)P(NF) + P(TF|NA)P(NA)}$$

$$= \frac{0.26(0.45)}{0.26(0.45) + 0.57(0.35) + 0.48(0.20)} = \frac{0.117}{0.4125} = 0.2836$$

This is a reasonable result. In the absence of test market information, we believe the probability of a great national market is 0.45. However, after a test market with only fair results, we revise the probability of a great national market down to 0.2836. The other posterior probabilities are calculated similarly. In addition, the denominator in this calculation, 0.4125, is the unconditional probability of a fair test market. We need such test market probabilities in the tree.

Finally, the monetary values in the tree are straightforward. There are fixed costs of test marketing or marketing nationally, which are incurred as soon as these "go ahead" decisions are made. From that point, if we market nationally, we observe the sales volumes and multiply them by the unit margin to obtain the selling profits.

### Implementing Bayes' Rule

The inputs and Bayes' rule calculations are shown in Figure 10.32. (See the file **Acme Marketing Decisions.xlsx**.) We perform the Bayes' rule calculations exactly as in the drug example. To calculate the unconditional probabilities for test market results, the denominators for Bayes' rule from equation (10.2), enter the formula

**=SUMPRODUCT($B$17:$D$17,B21:D21)**

in cell G16 and copy it down to cell G18. To calculate the posterior probabilities from equation (10.1), enter the formula

**=B$17*B21/$G16**

in cell G22 and copy it to the range G22:I24.

*Bayes' rule is required whenever the probabilities in the statement of the problem are in the "wrong order" relative to what we need in the tree.*

**Figure 10.32** Inputs and Bayes' Rule Calculations for the Acme Marketing Example

| | A | B | C | D | E | F | G | H | I | J | K | L | M | N |
|---|---|---|---|---|---|---|---|---|---|---|---|---|---|---|
| 1 | Acme marketing decisions | | | | | | | | | | | | | |
| 2 | | | | | | | | | | | | | | |
| 3 | Inputs | | | | | | | | | | | | | |
| 4 | Fixed costs ($1000s) | | | | | | | | | | | | | |
| 5 | Test market | 100 | | | | | | | | | | | | |
| 6 | National market | 7000 | | | | | | | | | | | | |
| 7 | | | | | | | | | | | | | | |
| 8 | Unit margin (either market) | $18 | | | | | | | | | | | | |
| 9 | | | | | | | | | | | | | | |
| 10 | Possible quantities sold (1000s of units) in national market | | | | | | | | | | | | | |
| 11 | Great | 600 | | | | | | | | | | | | |
| 12 | Fair | 300 | | | | | | | | | | | | |
| 13 | Awful | 90 | | | | | | | | | | | | |
| 14 | | | | | | | Bayes' rule calculations | | | | | | | |
| 15 | Prior probabilities of national market results | | | | | Unconditional probabilities of test mkt results (denominators of Bayes' rule) | | | | | | | |
| 16 | | Great | Fair | Awful | | Great | 0.3690 | | | | | | | |
| 17 | | 0.45 | 0.35 | 0.20 | | Fair | 0.4125 | | | | | | | |
| 18 | | | | | | Awful | 0.2185 | | | | | | | |
| 19 | Likelihoods of test market results (along side), given national market results (along top) from historical data | | | | | | | | | | | | | |
| 20 | | Great | Fair | Awful | | Posterior probabilities of national mkt results (along top), given test mkt results (along side) | | | | | | | |
| 21 | Great | 0.64 | 0.18 | 0.09 | | | Great | Fair | Awful | | | | | |
| 22 | Fair | 0.26 | 0.57 | 0.48 | | Great | 0.7805 | 0.1707 | 0.0488 | | | | | |
| 23 | Awful | 0.10 | 0.25 | 0.43 | | Fair | 0.2836 | 0.4836 | 0.2327 | | | | | |
| 24 | | | | | | Awful | 0.2059 | 0.4005 | 0.3936 | | | | | |

## DEVELOPING THE DECISION TREE MODEL

The tree is now straightforward to build and label, as shown in Figure 10.33. Note that the fixed costs of test marketing and marketing nationally appear on the decision branches where they occur in time, so that only the selling profits need to be placed on the probability branches. For example, the formula for the selling profit in cell D33 is **=B8*B11**.

Pay particular attention to the probabilities on the branches. The top group are the prior probabilities from the range B17:D17. In the bottom group, the probabilities on the left are unconditional probabilities of test market results from the range G16:G18, and those on the right are posterior probabilities of national market results from the range G22:I24. Again,

**Figure 10.33** Decision Tree for the Acme Marketing Example

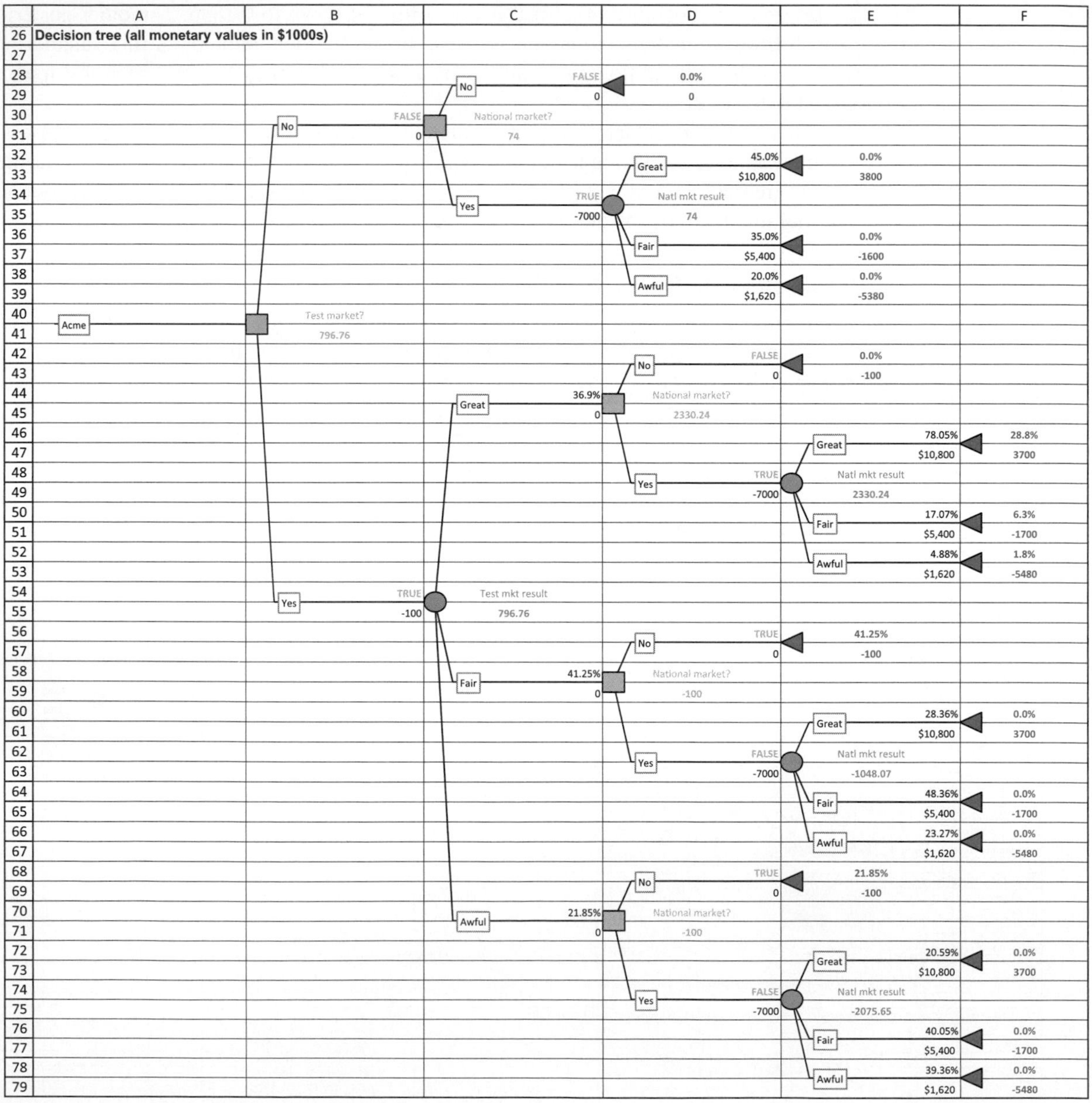

|   | A | B | C | D | E | F |
|---|---|---|---|---|---|---|
| 26 | Decision tree (all monetary values in $1000s) | | | | | |
| 27 | | | | | | |
| 28 | | | No | FALSE 0.0% | | |
| 29 | | | | 0      0 | | |
| 30 | | No | FALSE National market? | | | |
| 31 | | | 0      74 | | | |
| 32 | | | | Great 45.0%  0.0% | | |
| 33 | | | | $10,800  3800 | | |
| 34 | | | Yes TRUE Natl mkt result | | | |
| 35 | | | -7000      74 | | | |
| 36 | | | | Fair 35.0%  0.0% | | |
| 37 | | | | $5,400  -1600 | | |
| 38 | | | | Awful 20.0%  0.0% | | |
| 39 | | | | $1,620  -5380 | | |
| 40 | Acme | Test market? | | | | |
| 41 | | 796.76 | | | | |
| 42 | | | | No FALSE 0.0% | | |
| 43 | | | | 0      -100 | | |
| 44 | | | Great 36.9% National market? | | | |
| 45 | | | 0      2330.24 | | | |
| 46 | | | | | Great 78.05%  28.8% | |
| 47 | | | | | $10,800  3700 | |
| 48 | | | | Yes TRUE Natl mkt result | | |
| 49 | | | | -7000      2330.24 | | |
| 50 | | | | | Fair 17.07%  6.3% | |
| 51 | | | | | $5,400  -1700 | |
| 52 | | | | | Awful 4.88%  1.8% | |
| 53 | | | | | $1,620  -5480 | |
| 54 | | Yes TRUE Test mkt result | | | | |
| 55 | | -100      796.76 | | | | |
| 56 | | | | No TRUE 41.25% | | |
| 57 | | | | 0      -100 | | |
| 58 | | | Fair 41.25% National market? | | | |
| 59 | | | 0      -100 | | | |
| 60 | | | | | Great 28.36%  0.0% | |
| 61 | | | | | $10,800  3700 | |
| 62 | | | | Yes FALSE Natl mkt result | | |
| 63 | | | | -7000      -1048.07 | | |
| 64 | | | | | Fair 48.36%  0.0% | |
| 65 | | | | | $5,400  -1700 | |
| 66 | | | | | Awful 23.27%  0.0% | |
| 67 | | | | | $1,620  -5480 | |
| 68 | | | | No TRUE 21.85% | | |
| 69 | | | | 0      -100 | | |
| 70 | | | Awful 21.85% National market? | | | |
| 71 | | | 0      -100 | | | |
| 72 | | | | | Great 20.59%  0.0% | |
| 73 | | | | | $10,800  3700 | |
| 74 | | | | Yes FALSE Natl mkt result | | |
| 75 | | | | -7000      -2075.65 | | |
| 76 | | | | | Fair 40.05%  0.0% | |
| 77 | | | | | $5,400  -1700 | |
| 78 | | | | | Awful 39.36%  0.0% | |
| 79 | | | | | $1,620  -5480 | |

this corresponds to the standard decision tree convention, where all probabilities on the tree are conditioned on any events that have occurred to the left of them.

### Discussion of the Solution

To interpret this tree, note that each value just below each node name is an EMV. (These are colored red or green by PrecisionTree.) For example, the 796.76 in cell B41 is the EMV for the entire decision problem. It means that Acme's best EMV from acting optimally is $796,760. As another example, the 74 in cell D35 means that if Acme ever gets to that point—there is no test market and the product is marketed nationally—then the EMV is $74,000. Actually, this is the expected selling profit minus the $7 million fixed cost, so the expected selling profit, given that no information from a test market has been obtained, is $7,074,000.

We can also see Acme's optimal strategy by following the TRUE branches from left to right. Acme should first run a test market. If the test market result is great, then the product should be marketed nationally. However, if the test market result is fair or awful, the product should be abandoned. In these cases, the prospects from a national market look bleak, so Acme should cut its losses. (And there *are* losses. In these latter two cases, Acme has already spent $100,000 on the test market and has nothing to show for it.)

After we have done the work to build the tree, we can reap the benefits of PrecisionTree's tools. For example, its policy suggestion and risk profile outputs are shown in Figures 10.34 and 10.35. The policy suggestion shows only the part of the tree corresponding to the optimal strategy. Note that there are two values at each end node. The bottom number is the combined monetary value if we proceed along this sequence of branches, and the top number is the probability of this sequence of branches. This information leads directly to probability distribution in the risk profile. For this optimal strategy, the only possible monetary outcomes are a gain of $3,700,000 and losses of $100,000, $1,700,000, and $5,480,000. Their respective probabilities are 0.288, 0.631, 0.063, and 0.018. Fortunately, the large possible losses are unlikely enough that the EMV is still positive, $796,760.

**Figure 10.34**   Policy Suggestion (Optimal Strategy Branches)

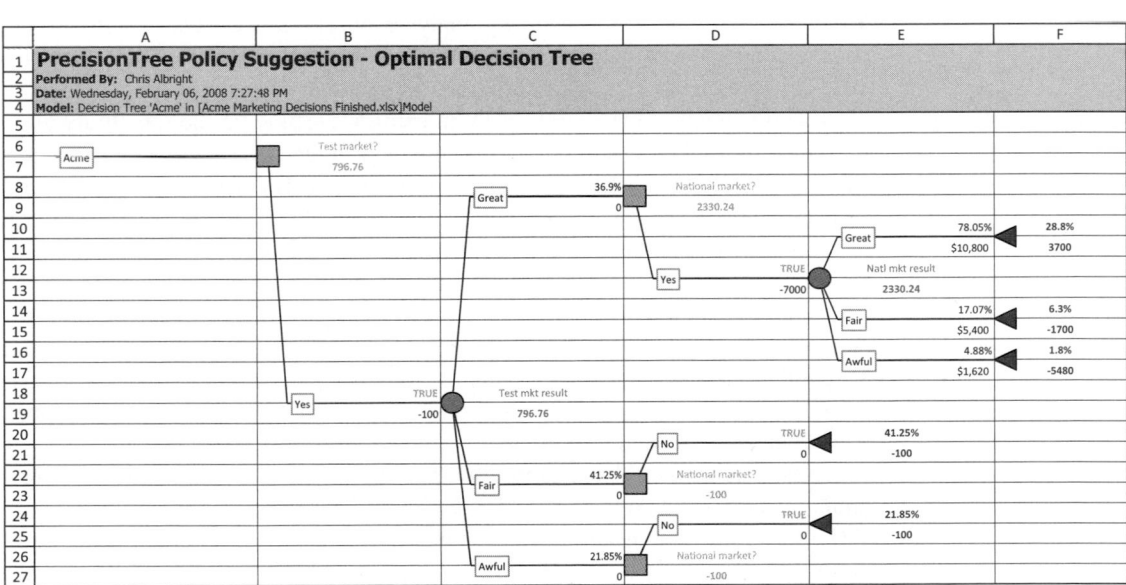

You might argue that the large potential losses and the slightly higher than 70% chance of *some* loss should persuade Acme to abandon the product right away—without a test market. However, this is what "playing the averages" with EMV is all about. Because the EMV of this optimal strategy is greater than 0, the EMV from abandoning the product right away, Acme should go ahead with this optimal strategy if the company is indeed an EMV maximizer. In Section 10.6, we see how this reasoning could change if Acme is a risk-averse decision maker—as it might be with multimillion dollar losses looming in the future!

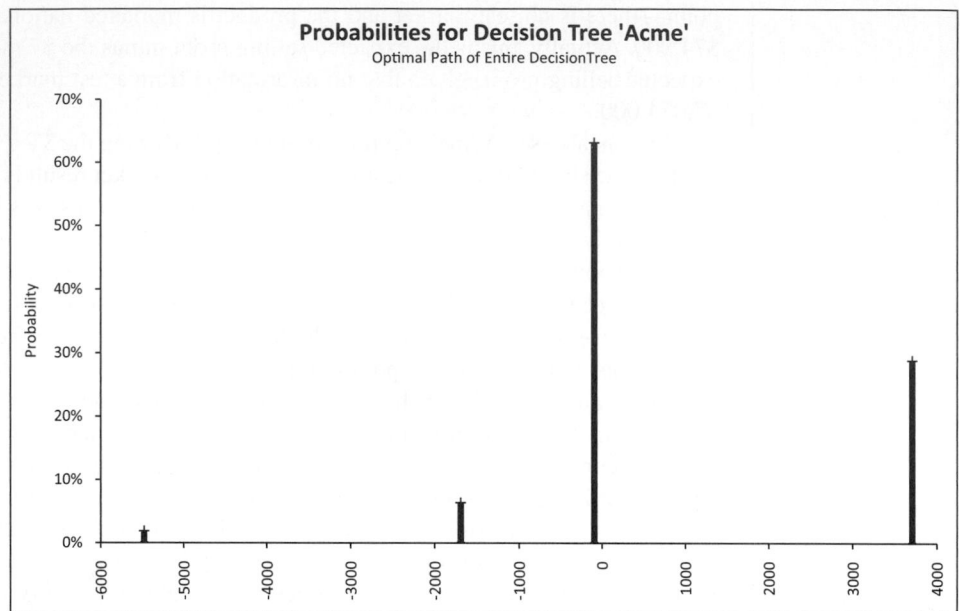

## Sensitivity Analysis

We can perform several sensitivity analyses on this model. We investigate how things change when the unit margin, currently $18, varies from $8 to $28. This can change our decision about whether to run a test market or to market nationally.

We first analyze the overall EMV in cell B41, setting up the sensitivity dialog box as in Figure 10.36. The resulting chart is shown in Figure 10.37. The chart indicates that for small unit margins, it is better *not* to run a test market. The top line, at value 0, corresponds to abandoning the product altogether, whereas the bottom line, at value −100, corresponds to running a test market and then abandoning the product regardless of the results. Similarly, for large unit margins, it is also best not to run a test market. Again, the top line is 100 above the bottom line. However, the reasoning now is different. For large unit margins, the company should market nationally *regardless* of test market results, so there is no reason to spend money on a test market. Finally, for intermediate unit margins, as in our original model, the chart shows that it is best to test market. Clearly, this one single chart provides a lot of information and insight!

By changing the cell to analyze in Figure 10.36, we can gain additional insight. For example, if no test market is available, the EMV for deciding nationally right away, in cell C31, is relevant. The resulting chart is in Figure 10.38. As we see, it is a contest between getting zero profit from abandoning the product, and getting a linearly increasing profit from marketing nationally. The breakpoint appears to be slightly below $18. If the unit margin is above this value, Acme should market nationally; otherwise, it should abandon the product.

**Figure 10.36**

Dialog Box for
Sensitivity Analysis

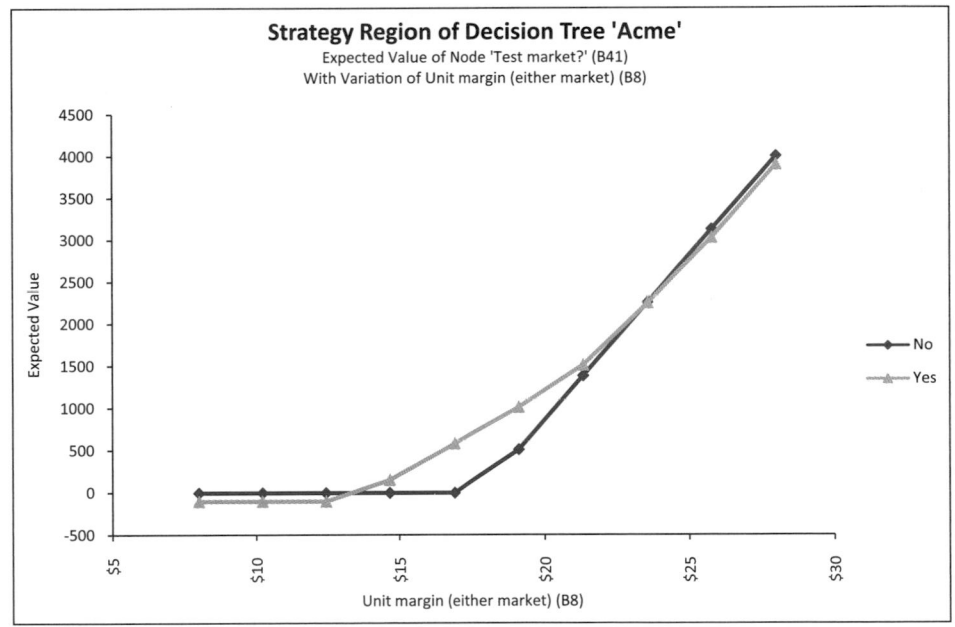

**Figure 10.37**

Sensitivity Analysis
on Overall Profit

We can also choose to analyze any of the EMVs in cells D45, D59, or D71. Each of these is relevant in the case where we have run the test market, we have observed the test market results, and we are about to decide whether to market nationally. For example, if we choose D71 as the cell to analyze, we obtain the chart in Figure 10.39. It indicates that there are indeed situations—where the unit margin is about $26 or more—when the company should market nationally, even though the test market is awful. In contrast, the chart in Figure 10.40, where we analyze cell D45, indicates the opposite behavior. It shows that if the unit margin is low enough—about $13.50 or less—the company should abandon the product nationally, even though the test market results are great. These are very useful insights.

**Figure 10.38**

Sensitivity Analysis
for Deciding
Nationally Right
Away

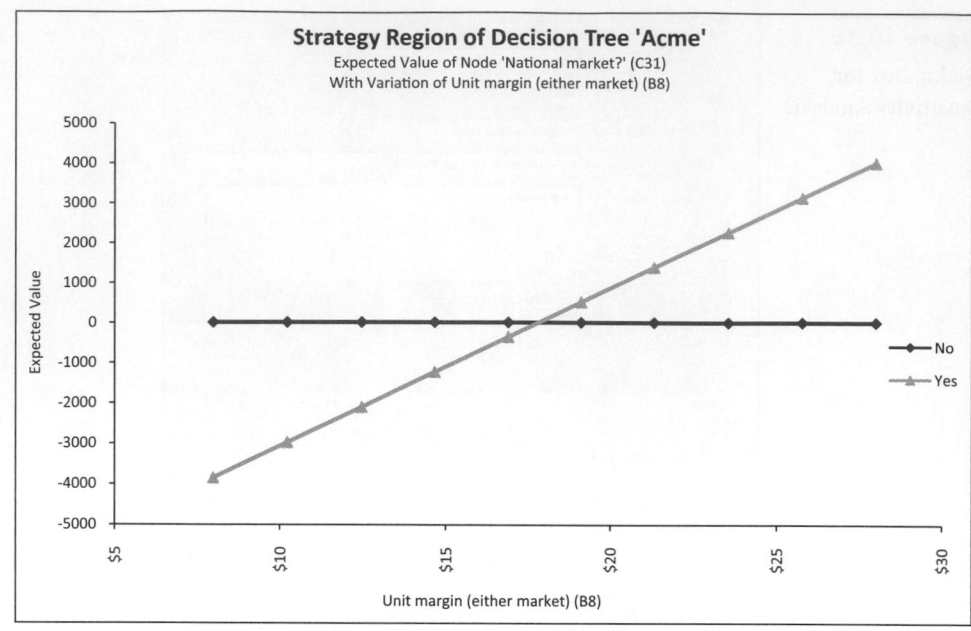

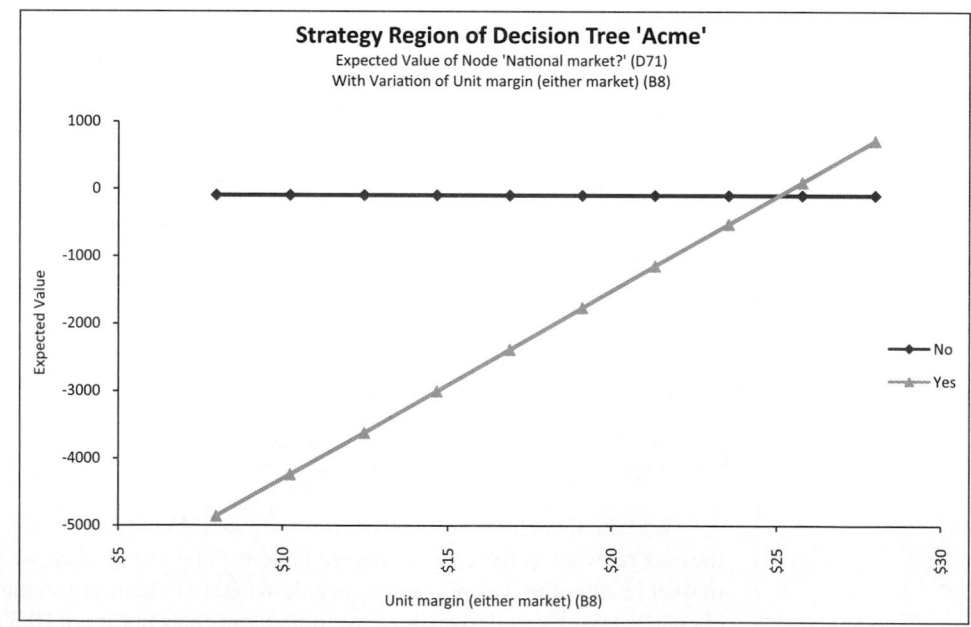

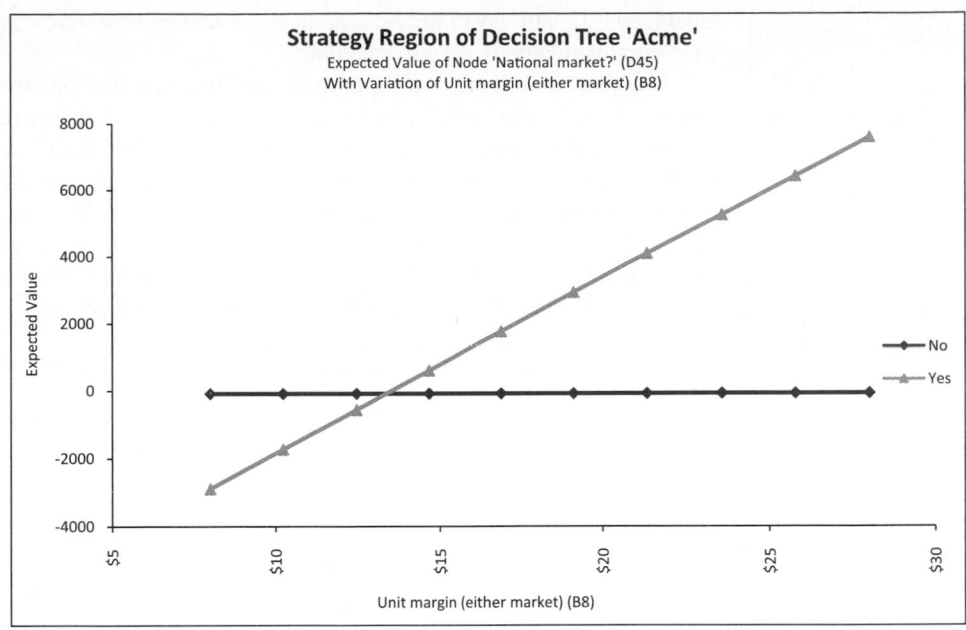

**Strategy Region of Decision Tree 'Acme'**
Expected Value of Node 'National market?' (D45)
With Variation of Unit margin (either market) (B8)

## Expected Value of Sample Information (EVSI)

The role of the test market in this example is to provide information in the form of more accurate probabilities of national market results. Information usually costs something, as it does in Acme's problem. Currently, the fixed cost of the test market is $100,000, which is evidently not too much to pay because Acme's best strategy is to run the test market.

However, we might ask how much this test market is really worth. This is the EVSI, which is simple to obtain from the tree. From Figure 10.33, we see that the EMV from test marketing is $796,760, $100,000 of which is the cost of the test market. Therefore, if we could run this test market for free, the expected profit would be $896,760. On the other hand, the EMV from not running a test market is $74,000 (see cell C31 in the tree). From equation (10.4), the difference is EVSI:

$$\text{EVSI} = \$896{,}760 - \$74{,}000 = \$822{,}760$$

You can check that when you put any value less than 822.76 in cell B5, the test market fixed cost cell, the decision to test market continues to be best.

Intuitively, this test market is worth something because it changes the optimal decision. With no test market information, the optimal decision is to market nationally. (See the top part of the tree in Figure 10.33.) However, with the test market information, the ultimate decision depends on the test market results. Specifically, Acme should market nationally only if the test market result is great. This is what makes information worth something—its outcome affects the optimal decision.

## Expected Value of Perfect Information (EVPI)

We did a lot of work to find EVSI. We had to assess various conditional probabilities, use Bayes' rule, and then build a fairly complex decision tree. In general, Acme has many sources of information to help it make the national decision; the test market we analyzed is just one of them. The question, then, is how much such information *could* be worth. This is answered by EVPI. EVPI provides an upper bound on how much *any* information could be worth and is relatively easy to calculate.

*This perfect information envelope is obviously a fiction, but it helps to explain how perfect information works.*

Imagine that Acme could purchase an envelope that has the true national market result—great, fair, or awful—written inside. Once opened, this envelope would remove all uncertainty, and Acme could make the correct decision. EVPI is what this envelope is worth. To calculate it, we build the tree in Figure 10.41. The key here is that the nodes are reversed in time. We first open the envelope to discover what is inside. This corresponds to the probability node. Then we make the "easy" decision. Given the cost parameters, it is easy to see that Acme should market nationally only if the contents of the envelope reveal that the national market is great. Otherwise, Acme should abandon the product right away.

**Figure 10.41**

**Decision Tree for Evaluating EVPI**

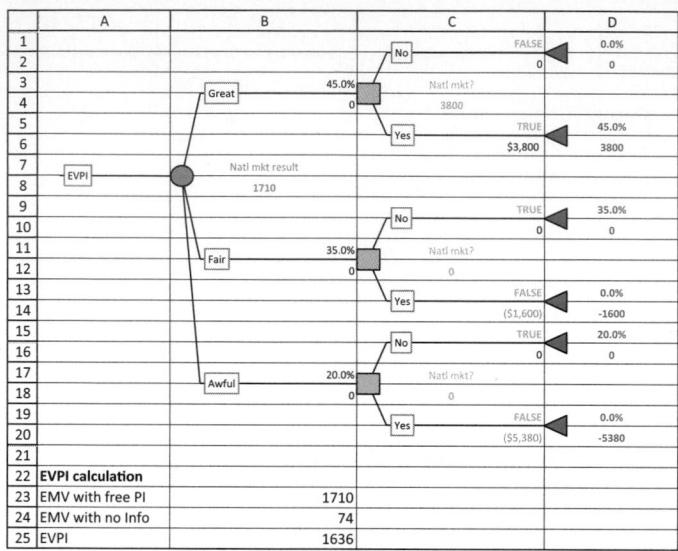

The EVPI calculation is now straightforward. If we get the envelope (perfect information) for free, the tree in Figure 10.41 indicates that the corresponding EMV is $1,710,000. If we have no information, the EMV is, as before, $74,000. Therefore, from equation (10.5):

$$\text{EVPI} = \$1,710,000 - \$74,000 = \$1,636,000$$

No sample information, test market or otherwise, could possibly be worth more than this. So if some hotshot market analyst offers to provide "extremely reliable" market information to Acme for, say, $1.8 million, Acme knows that this information cannot be worth its price. ∎

# PROBLEMS

## Skill-Building Problems

**22.** In deciding whether to perform mandatory drug testing, we claimed that it is difficult to justify such testing under reasonable conditions. Check this yourself in the following questions.

　**a.** Drug testing ought to be more attractive if the test is more reliable. Keeping the costs the same as in the example, use PrecisionTree's two-way sensitivity tool to see whether the optimal decision (test or not test) changes as the probability of a false positive and the probability of a false negative both change. You can let them vary through some reasonable ranges. How do you explain the results?

　**b.** Repeat part **a**, but first double the two monetary values that make the test more attractive: the benefit of identifying a user and the cost of not identifying a user. How do your results differ from those in part **a**?

c. In this part, keep the probabilities of false positives and false negatives the same, but let the benefits and costs vary. Specifically, let the benefit of identifying a user and the cost of not identifying a user be of the form 25a and 20a, where a is some factor that you can vary. Similarly, let the cost of barring a nonuser and the cost of violating privacy be of the form 50b and 2b. The cost of the test is still 1. (The idea is that large values of a and/or small values of b make the testing more attractive.) Use PrecisionTree's two-way sensitivity tool to see whether the optimal decision (test or not test) changes for a reasonable range of values of a and b. Discuss your results.

**23.** In the drug-testing decision, find and interpret EVSI and EVPI. Here, "sample" information refers to the information from the imperfect drug test, whereas "perfect" information refers to completely reliable information on whether the athlete uses drugs.

**24.** Explain in general why EVSI is independent of the actual cost of the information. For example, in the Acme problem, EVSI is the same regardless of whether the actual cost of the test market is $100,000, $200,000, or any other value. Then explain how EVSI, together with the actual cost of the information, leads to the decision about whether to purchase the information.

**25.** Following up on the previous problem, the **expected net gain from information** is defined as the expected amount we gain by having access to the information, at its given cost, as opposed to not having access to the information. Explain how you would calculate this in general. What is its value for the Acme problem?

**26.** Prior probabilities are often educated guesses at best, so it is worth performing a sensitivity analysis on their values. However, we must make sure that we vary them so that all probabilities are nonnegative and sum to 1. For the Acme problem, perform the following sensitivity analyses on the three prior probabilities and comment on the results.
   a. Vary the probability of great in a one-way sensitivity analysis from 0 to 0.6 in increments of 0.1. Do this in such a way that the probabilities of the two other outcomes, fair and awful, stay in the same ratio as they are currently, 7 to 4.
   b. Vary the probabilities of great and fair independently in a two-way sensitivity analysis. You can choose the ranges over which these vary, but you must ensure that the three prior probabilities continue to be nonnegative and sum to 1. (For

example, you couldn't choose ranges where the probabilities of great and fair are 0.6 and 0.5.)

**27.** In the Acme problem, perform a sensitivity analysis on the quantity sold from a great national market (the value in cell B11). Let this value vary over a range of values *greater than* the current value of 600, so that a great national market is even more attractive than before. Does this ever change the optimal strategy? In what way?

**28.** Using trial and error on the prior probabilities in the Acme problem, find values of them that make EVSI equal to 0. These are values where Acme will make the same decision, regardless of the test market results it observes.

## Skill-Extending Problems

**29.** We related EVPI to the value of an envelope that contains the true ultimate outcome. We can extend this concept to "less than perfect" information. For example, in the Acme problem suppose that we could purchase information that would tell us, with certainty, that one of the following two outcomes will occur: (1) the national market will be great, or (2) the national market will not be great. Notice that outcome (2) doesn't tell us whether the national market will be fair or awful; it just tells us that it won't be great. How much should Acme be willing to pay for such information?

**30.** The concept behind EVPI is that we purchase perfect information (the envelope), we then open the envelope to see which outcome occurs, and then we make an easy decision. However, we do *not* get to choose what information the envelope contains. Sometimes a company can pay, not to obtain information, but to influence the outcome. Consider the following version of the Acme problem. There is no possibility of a test market, so Acme must decide right away whether to market nationally. However, suppose Acme can pay to change the probabilities of the national market outcomes from their current values, 0.45, 0.35, and 0.20, to the new values $p$, $(7/11)(1-p)$, and $(4/11)(1-p)$, for some $p$. (In this way, the probabilities of fair and awful stay in the same ratio as before, 7 to 4, but by making $p$ large, the probability of great increases.)
   a. How much should Acme be willing to pay for the change if $p = 0.6$? If $p = 0.8$? If $p = 0.95$?
   b. Are these types of changes realistic? Answer by speculating on the types of actions Acme might be able to take to make the probability of a great national market higher. Do you think such actions would cost more or less than what Acme should be willing to pay for them (from part **a**)?

# 10.6 INCORPORATING ATTITUDES TOWARD RISK

Rational decision makers are sometimes willing to violate the EMV maximization criterion when large amounts of money are at stake. These decision makers are willing to sacrifice some EMV to reduce risk. Are you ever willing to do so personally? Consider the following scenarios.

- You have a chance to enter a lottery where you will win $100,000 with probability 0.1 or win nothing with probability 0.9. Alternatively, you can receive $5000 for certain. How many of you—truthfully—would take the certain $5000, even though the EMV of the lottery is $10,000? Or change the $100,000 to $1,000,000 and the $5000 to $50,000 and ask yourself whether you would prefer the sure $50,000!

- You can either buy collision insurance on your expensive new car or not buy it, where the insurance costs a certain premium and carries some deductible provision. If you decide to pay the premium, you are essentially paying a certain amount to avoid a gamble: the possibility of wrecking your car and not having it insured. You can be sure that the premium is greater than the expected cost of damage; otherwise, the insurance company would not stay in business. Therefore, from an EMV standpoint, you should not purchase the insurance. But how many of you drive without this type of insurance?

These examples, the second of which is certainly realistic, illustrate situations where rational people do not behave as EMV maximizers. Then how do they behave? This question has been studied extensively by many researchers, both mathematically and behaviorally. Although the answer is still not agreed upon universally, most researchers agree that if certain basic behavioral assumptions hold, people are **expected utility** maximizers—they choose the alternative with the largest expected utility. Although we do not go deeply into the subject of expected utility maximization, the discussion in this section acquaints you with the main ideas.

---

### FUNDAMENTAL INSIGHT

#### Risk Averseness

When large amounts of money are at stake, most of us are risk averse. We are willing to sacrifice some EMV to avoid risk. The exact way this is done, using utility functions and expected utility, can be difficult to implement in real situations, but the idea is simple. If you are an EMV maximizer, you are indifferent between a gamble with a given EMV and a sure dollar amount equal to the EMV of the gamble. However, if you are risk averse, you prefer the sure dollar amount to the gamble. In fact, you are willing to accept a sure dollar amount that is somewhat *less than* the EMV of the gamble, just to avoid risk. The more EMV you are willing to give up, the more risk averse you are.

---

## Utility Functions

We begin by discussing an individual's **utility function.** This is a mathematical function that transforms monetary values—payoffs and costs—into **utility values.** Essentially, an individual's utility function specifies the individual's preferences for various monetary payoffs and costs and, in doing so, it automatically encodes the individual's attitudes toward risk. Most individuals are **risk averse,** which means intuitively that they are willing to sacrifice some EMV to avoid risky gambles. In terms of the utility function, this means that every extra dollar of payoff is worth slightly less to the individual than the previous dollar, and every extra dollar of cost is considered slightly more costly (in terms of utility) than the previous dollar. The resulting utility functions are shaped as shown in Figure 10.42. Mathematically, these functions are **increasing** and **concave.** The increasing part means that they go uphill—everyone prefers more money to less money. The concave part means that they increase at a decreasing rate. This is the risk-averse behavior.

**Figure 10.42**
Risk-Averse Utility
Function

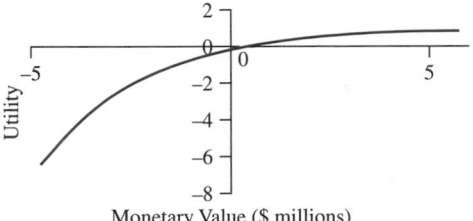

Besides the increasing and concave features of this curve, we mention two of its other aspects. First, we have drawn the curve so that it goes through the origin. This implies that the utilities of negative values (costs) are negative, the utilities of positive values (gains) are positive, and the utility of no gain or loss is 0. Actually, the utility curve does *not* need to go through the origin. It turns out that only *relative* utility values matter. So we could shift the curve upward or downward without changing it for decision-making purposes.

Second, the curve is nearly a straight line in the middle, that is, for "moderate" losses or gains. This is typical. Whenever the possible losses and gains for a problem are within the linear section of the utility curve, the expected utility criterion is equivalent to the EMV criterion. This explains why we have used EMV up to now. Of course, monetary values that are "moderate" for one person are "large" for another. You can bet that Bill Gates' utility curve has a much longer linear section than yours!

There are two aspects of implementing utility maximization in a real decision analysis. First, we must obtain an individual's (or company's) utility function. This time-consuming task, usually carried out by experts in the field, typically involves many trade-offs. (We do not discuss the details of the process here.) Second, we must use the resulting utility function to find the best decision. This second step is relatively straightforward. We simply substitute utility values for monetary values in the decision tree and then fold back as usual. That is, we calculate expected *utilities* at probability branches and take maximums (of expected utilities) at decision branches. We look at a numerical example later in this section.

## Exponential Utility

As we have indicated, utility assessment is tedious. Even in the best of circumstances, when a trained consultant attempts to assess the utility function of a single person, the process requires the person to make a series of choices between hypothetical alternatives involving uncertain outcomes. Unless the person has some training in probability, these choices are probably difficult to understand, let alone make, and the person is unlikely to answer *consistently* as the questioning proceeds. The process is even more difficult when a company's utility function is being assessed. Because company executives typically have different attitudes toward risk, it can be difficult for them to reach a consensus on a common utility function.

For these reasons, classes of ready-made utility functions have been developed. One important class is called **exponential utility** and has been used in many financial investment analyses. An exponential utility function has only one adjustable numerical parameter, called the **risk tolerance,** and there are straightforward ways to discover the most appropriate value of this parameter for a particular individual or company. The advantage of using an exponential utility function is that it is relatively easy to assess. The drawback is that exponential utility functions do not capture all types of attitudes toward risk. Nevertheless, their ease of use has made them popular.

An exponential utility function has the following form:

---

**Exponential utility**

$$U(x) = 1 - e^{-x/R} \tag{10.6}$$

---

Here $x$ is a monetary value (a payoff if positive, a cost if negative), $U(x)$ is the utility of this value, and $R > 0$ is the risk tolerance. As the name suggests, the risk tolerance measures the amount of risk the decision maker is willing to accept. The larger the value of $R$, the less risk averse the decision maker is. That is, a person with a large value of $R$ is more willing to take risks than a person with a small value of $R$.

---

In terms of exponential utility, the **risk tolerance** is a single number that specifies an individual's aversion to risk. The higher the risk tolerance, the less risk averse the individual is.

---

To assess a person's (or company's) exponential utility function, we need to assess the value of $R$. There are a couple of tips for doing this. First, it has been shown that the risk tolerance is approximately equal to the dollar amount $R$ such that the decision maker is indifferent between the following two options:

- Option 1: Obtain no payoff at all.
- Option 2: Obtain a payoff of $R$ dollars or a loss of $R/2$ dollars, depending on the flip of a fair coin.

For example, if you are indifferent between a bet where you win $1000 or lose $500, with probability 0.5 each, and not betting at all, then your $R$ is approximately $1000. From this criterion, it certainly makes intuitive sense that a wealthier person (or company) ought to have a larger value of $R$. This has been found in practice.

*Finding the appropriate risk tolerance value for any company or individual is not necessarily easy, but it is easier than assessing an entire utility function from scratch.*

A second tip for finding $R$ is based on empirical evidence found by Ronald Howard, a prominent decision analyst. Through his consulting experience with large companies, he discovered tentative relationships between risk tolerance and several financial variables: net sales, net income, and equity (Howard, 1988). Specifically, he found that $R$ was approximately 6.4% of net sales, 124% of net income, and 15.7% of equity for the companies he studied. For example, according to this prescription, a company with net sales of $30 million should have a risk tolerance of approximately $1.92 million. Howard admits that these percentages are only guidelines. However, they do indicate that larger and more profitable companies tend to have larger values of $R$, which means that they are more willing to take risks involving large dollar amounts.

We illustrate the use of the expected utility criterion, and exponential utility in particular, with the following example.

EXAMPLE | **10.6 DECIDING WHETHER TO ENTER RISKY VENTURES AT VENTURE LIMITED**

Venture Limited is a company with net sales of $30 million. The company currently must decide whether to enter one of two risky ventures or invest in a sure thing. The gain from the latter is a sure $125,000. The possible outcomes for the less risky venture are a $0.5 million loss, a $0.1 million gain, and a $1 million gain. The probabilities of these outcomes are 0.25, 0.50, and 0.25. The possible outcomes of the more risky venture are a $1 million loss, a $1 million gain, and a $3 million gain. The probabilities of these outcomes are 0.35, 0.60, and 0.05. If Venture Limited must choose exactly one of these alternatives, what should it do?

**Objective**   To see how the company's risk averseness, determined by its risk tolerance in an exponential utility function, affects its decision.

### WHERE DO THE NUMBERS COME FROM?

The outcomes for each of the risky alternatives probably form a continuum of possible values. However, as in Example 10.5, the company has discretized these into a few possibilities and made intelligent estimates of the monetary consequences and probabilities of these discrete possibilities.

## Solution

*Don't worry about the actual utility values (for example, whether they are positive or negative). Only the relative magnitudes matter in terms of decision making.*

We assume that Venture Limited has an exponential utility function. Also, based on Howard's guidelines, we assume that the company's risk tolerance is 6.4% of its net sales, or $1.92 million. (We perform a sensitivity analysis on this parameter later on.) We can substitute into equation (10.6) to find the utility of any monetary outcome. For example, the gain from the riskless alternative (in $1000s) is 125, and its utility is

$$U(125) = 1 - e^{-125/1920} = 1 - 0.9370 = 0.0630$$

(Remember that you can calculate the exponential term in Excel with the EXP function.) As another example, the utility of a $1 million loss is

$$U(-1000) = 1 - e^{-(-1000)/1920} = 1 - 1.6834 = -0.6834$$

These are the values we use (instead of monetary values) in the decision tree.

PRECISION TREE

### DEVELOPING THE DECISION TREE MODEL

Fortunately, PrecisionTree takes care of the details. After we build a decision tree and label it (with monetary values) in the usual way, we click on the name of the tree (the box at the far left of the tree) to open the dialog box in Figure 10.43. We then fill in the information under the Utility Function tab as shown in the figure. This says to use an exponential utility function with risk tolerance 1920, the value in cell B5.[9] (As indicated in the spreadsheet, we are measuring all monetary values in $1000s.) It also indicates that we want expected utilities (as opposed to EMVs) to appear in the decision tree.

*The tree is built and labeled (with monetary values) exactly as before. PrecisionTree then takes care of calculating the expected utilities.*

The completed tree for this example is shown in Figure 10.44. (See the file **Using Exponential Utility.xlsx.**) We build it in exactly the same way as usual and link probabilities and monetary values to its branches in the usual way. For example, there is a link in cell C22 to the monetary value in cell B12. However, the expected values shown in the tree (those shown in color on a computer screen) are expected *utilities,* and the optimal decision is the one with the largest expected utility. In this case, the expected utilities for the riskless

[9] This is a definite improvement over the previous version of PrecisionTree. The "R" value is now linked to a cell, so that it is easy to perform sensitivity analysis on R.

Figure 10.43

Dialog Box for Specifying the Exponential Utility Criterion

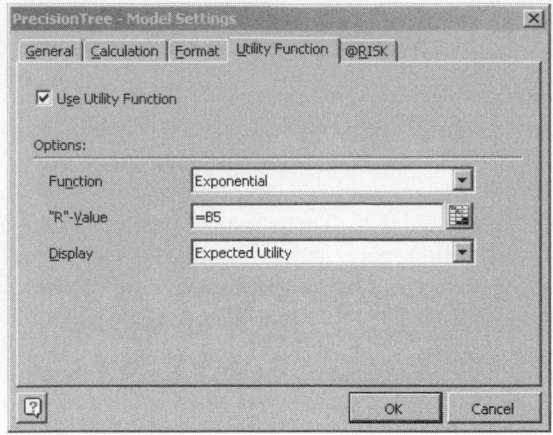

Figure 10.44

Decision Tree for the Risky Venture Example

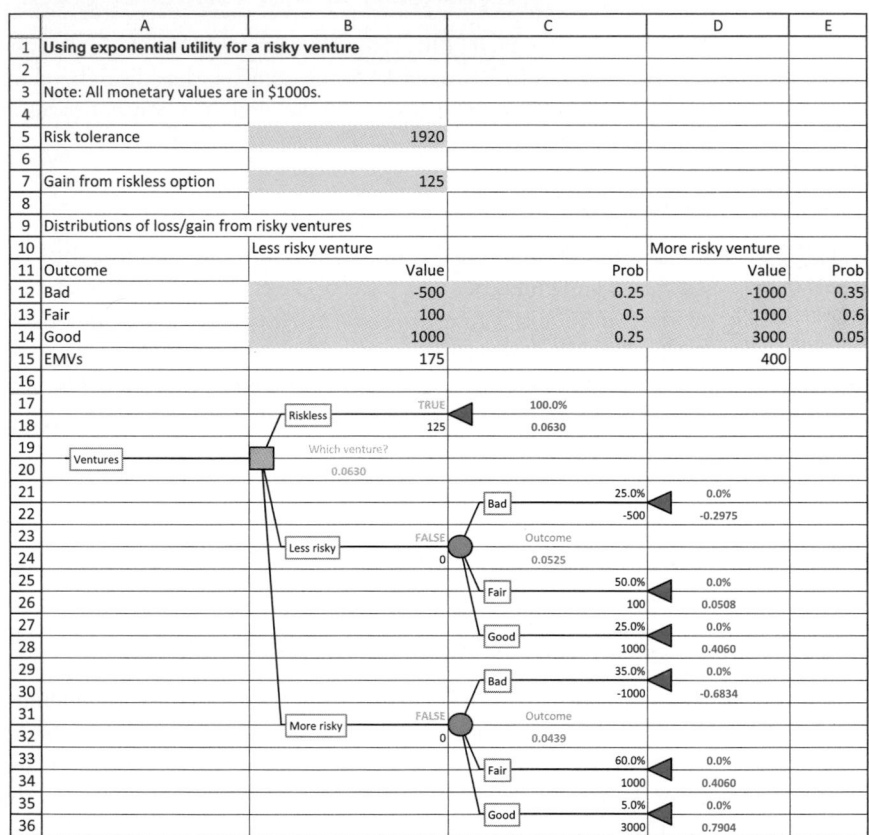

option, investing in the less risky venture, and investing in the more risky venture are 0.0630, 0.0525, and 0.0439, respectively. Therefore, the optimal decision is to take the riskless option.

## Discussion of the Solution

As we see from the tree, the riskless option is best in terms of the expected utility criterion; it has the largest expected utility. However, note that the EMVs of the three decisions are

*A risk-averse decision maker typically gives up EMV to avoid risk—when the stakes are large enough.*

$125,000, $175,000, and $400,000. (The latter two of these are calculated in row 15 as the usual "sumproduct" of monetary values and probabilities.) So from an EMV point of view, the more risky venture is definitely best. In fact, the ordering of the three alternatives using the EMV criterion is exactly the *opposite* of the ordering using expected utility. But Venture Limited is sufficiently risk averse, and the monetary values are sufficiently large, that the company is willing to sacrifice $275,000 of EMV to avoid risk.

### Sensitivity Analysis

How sensitive is the optimal decision to the key parameter, the risk tolerance? We can answer this by changing the risk tolerance and watching how the decision tree changes. You can check that when the company becomes *more* risk tolerant, the more risky venture eventually becomes optimal. In fact, this occurs when the risk tolerance increases to approximately $2.210 million. In the other direction, of course, when the company becomes *less* risk tolerant, the riskless decision continues to be optimal. (The "middle" decision, the less risky alternative, is evidently not optimal for *any* value of the risk tolerance.) The bottom line is that the "optimal" decision depends entirely on the attitude toward risk of Venture Limited's top management.

### Certainty Equivalents

Now suppose that Venture Limited has only two options. It can either enter the less risky venture or receive a *certain* dollar amount $x$ and avoid the gamble altogether. We want to find the dollar amount $x$ so that the company is indifferent between these two options. If it enters the risky venture, its expected utility is 0.0525, calculated earlier. If it receives $x$ dollars for certain, its (expected) utility is

$$U(x) = 1 - e^{-x/1.92}$$

To find the value $x$ where the company is indifferent between the two options, we set $1 - e^{-x/1.92}$ equal to 0.0525, or $e^{-x/1.92} = 0.9475$, and solve for $x$. Taking natural logarithms of both sides and multiplying by 1.92, we get

$$x = -1.92 \ln(0.9475) = \$0.104 \text{ million}$$

This value is called the **certainty equivalent** of the risky venture. The company is indifferent between entering the less risky venture and receiving $104,000 to avoid it. Although the EMV of the less risky venture is $175,000, the company acts as if it is equivalent to a sure $104,000. In this sense, the company is willing to give up the difference in EMV—$71,000—to avoid a gamble.

By a similar calculation, the certainty equivalent of the more risky venture is approximately $86,000. That is, the company acts as if this more risky venture is equivalent to a sure $86,000, when in fact its EMV is a hefty $400,000! In this case, the company is willing to give up the difference in EMV—$314,000—to avoid this particular gamble. Again, the reason is that the company dislikes risk. We can see these certainty equivalents in PrecisionTree by changing the Display box in Figure 10.43 to show Certainty Equivalent. The resulting tree is shown in Figure 10.45. The certainty equivalents we just discussed appear in cells C24 and C32. (Note that we rounded the values in the text to the nearest $1000. The values in the figure are more exact.)

**Figure 10.45**

Decision Tree with
Certainty
Equivalents

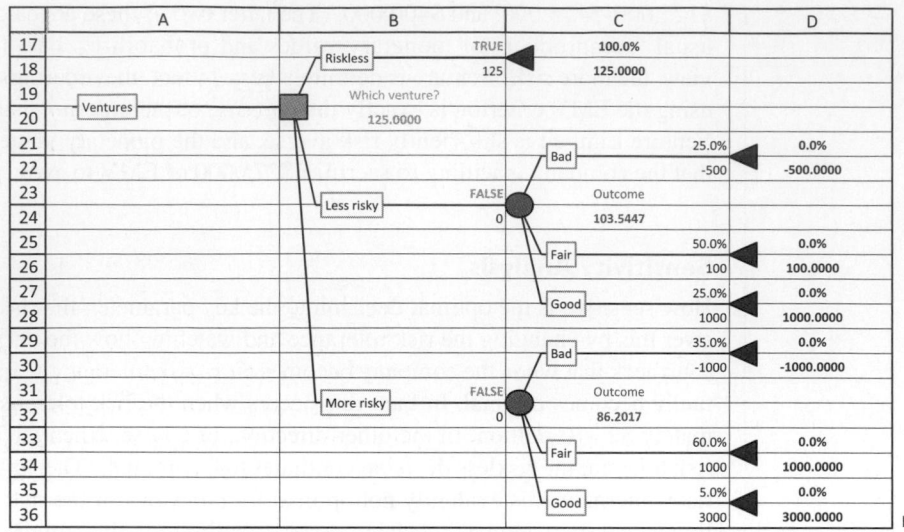

## Is Expected Utility Maximization Used?

The previous discussion indicates that utility maximization is a fairly involved task. The question, then, is whether the effort is justified. Theoretically, expected utility maximization might be interesting to researchers, but is it really used in the business world? The answer appears to be *not very often*. For example, one article on the practice of decision making (Kirkwood, 1992) quotes Ronald Howard—the same person we quoted previously—as having found risk aversion to be of practical concern in only 5% to 10% of business decision analyses. This same article quotes the president of a Fortune 500 company as saying, "Most of the decisions we analyze are for a few million dollars. It is adequate to use expected value (EMV) for these."

## PROBLEMS

### Skill-Building Problems

**31.** For the risky venture example, create a line chart that includes three series, that is, three lines (or curves). Each line should show the expected utility of a particular decision for a sequence of possible risk-tolerance values. (You will have to create the data for the chart manually, by changing the risk tolerance, recording the three expected utilities somewhere on the spreadsheet, changing the risk tolerance again, and so on.) This chart should make it clear when the more risky option becomes optimal and whether the less risky option is ever optimal.

**32.** In the risky venture example, a decision maker with risk tolerance of $1.92 million does not prefer the more risky alternative, in spite of its dominating EMV. Now suppose everything stays the same except for the best monetary outcome of the more risky alternative (the value in cell D14). How much larger must this value be for the decision maker to prefer the more

risky alternative? What is the corresponding EMV at that point?

**33.** In the risky venture example, suppose there is no riskless alternative; the only two possible decisions are the less risky venture and the more risky venture. Explore which of these is the preferred alternative for a range of risk tolerances. Can you find a "cutoff point" for the risk tolerance so that the less risky venture is preferred for risk tolerances below the cutoff and the more risky venture is preferred otherwise?

### Skill-Extending Problem

**34.** Do the absolute magnitudes of the monetary outcomes matter in the risky venture example? Consider the following two possibilities. In each case, multiply all monetary values in the example by a factor of $A$. (For example, double them if $A = 2$.) For each part, briefly explain your findings.

**a.** Currently, an EMV-maximizer would choose the most risky venture. Would this continue to be the case for any factor $A$?

**b.** Currently, an expected utility maximizer with risk tolerance $1.92 million prefers the riskless alternative. Would this continue to be the case for any factor $A$ greater than 1? What about when $A$ is less than 1? You can answer by using trial and error on $A$.

**c.** Referring to the dialog box in Figure 10.43, there is a display dropdown with three options: expected value (EMV), expected utility, and certainty equivalent. The latter is defined for any gamble as the sure monetary amount a risk averse person would take as a trade for the risky gamble. For example, you can check that the certainty equivalent for the more risky alternative is 86.2017 (in thousands of dollars). Explain what this really means by calculating the utility of 86.2017 manually and comparing it to the *expected* utility from the more risky venture (as shown on the tree). How does this explain why the decision maker prefers the riskless alternative to the more risky venture? How does this certainty equivalent change when $A=2$? Discuss whether this change goes in the direction you would expect.

# 10.7 CONCLUSION

In this chapter, we have discussed methods that can be used in decision-making problems where uncertainty is a key element. Perhaps the most important skill you can gain from this chapter is the ability to approach decision problems with uncertainty in a systematic manner. This systematic approach requires you to list all possible decisions or strategies, list all possible uncertain outcomes, assess the probabilities of these outcomes (possibly with the aid of Bayes' rule), calculate all necessary monetary values, and finally do the necessary calculations to obtain the best decision. If large dollar amounts are at stake, you might also need to perform a utility analysis where the decision maker's attitude toward risk is taken into account. After the basic analysis has been completed using best guesses for the various parameters of the problem, you should perform a sensitivity analysis to see whether the best decision continues to be best within a range of problem parameters.

## Summary of Key Management Science Terms

| Term | Explanation | Page |
|---|---|---|
| Payoff (or cost) table | A table that lists the payoffs (or costs) for all combinations of decisions and uncertain outcomes | 506 |
| Maximin criterion | The pessimist's criterion; find the worst possible payoff for each decision, and choose the decision with the best of these | 507 |
| Maximax criterion | The optimist's criterion; find the best possible payoff for each decision, and choose the decision with the best of these | 507 |
| Expected monetary value (EMV) | The weighted average of the possible payoffs from a decision, weighted by their probabilities | 508 |
| EMV criterion | Choose the decision with the maximum EMV | 508 |
| Decision tree | A graphical device for illustrating all the aspects of the decision problem and finding the optimal decision (or decision strategy) | 511 |
| Folding-back procedure | Calculation method for a decision tree; starting at the right, take EMVs at probability nodes, maximums of EMVs at decision nodes | 512 |

*(continued)*

| Term | Explanation | Page |
|------|-------------|------|
| Risk profile | Chart that represents the probability distribution of monetary outcomes for any decision | 512 |
| Bayes' rule | Formula for updating probabilities as new information becomes available; prior probabilities are transformed into posterior probabilities | 534 |
| Expected value of sample information (EVSI) | The most the (imperfect) sample information (such as the results of a test market) is worth | 543 |
| Expected value of perfect information (EVPI) | The most perfect information on some uncertain outcome would be worth; represents an upper bound on *any* EVSI | 543 |
| Contingency plan | A decision strategy where later decisions depend on earlier decisions and outcomes observed in the meantime | 544 |
| Utility function | A mathematical function that encodes an individual's (or company's) attitudes toward risk | 554 |
| Expected utility criterion | Choose the decision that maximizes the expected utility; typically sacrifices EMV to avoid risk when large monetary amounts are at stake | 555 |
| Exponential utility function, risk tolerance | A popular class of utility functions, where only a single parameter, the risk tolerance, has to be specified | 555 |
| Certainty equivalent | The dollar equivalent, in utility terms, of a risky gamble; can be used to see how much EMV a risk averse person is willing to give up to avoid a gamble | 559 |

## Summary of Key Excel Terms

| Term | Explanation | Excel | Page |
|------|-------------|-------|------|
| PrecisionTree add-in | Useful Excel add-in developed by Palisade for building and analyzing decision trees in Excel | Has its own ribbon | 522 |
| PrecisionTree strategy region chart | Useful for seeing how the optimal decision changes as selected inputs vary | Use PrecisionTree Sensitivity Analysis button | 530 |
| PrecisionTree tornado and spider charts | Useful for seeing which inputs affect a selected EMV the most | Use PrecisionTree Sensitivity Analysis button | 530 |

# PROBLEMS

## Skill-Building Problems

**35.** The SweetTooth Candy Company knows it will need 10 tons of sugar 6 months from now to implement its production plans. Jean Dobson, SweetTooth's purchasing manager, has essentially two options for acquiring the needed sugar. She can either buy the sugar at the going market price when she needs it, 6 months from now, or she can buy a futures contract now. The contract guarantees delivery of the sugar in 6 months, but the cost of purchasing it will be based on today's market price. Assume that possible sugar futures contracts available for purchase are for 5 tons or 10 tons only. No futures contracts can be purchased or sold in the intervening months. Thus, SweetTooth's possible decisions are (1) purchase a futures contract for 10 tons of sugar now, (2) purchase a futures contract for 5 tons of sugar now and purchase 5 tons of sugar in 6 months, or (3) purchase all 10 tons of needed sugar in 6 months. The price of sugar bought now for delivery in

6 months is $0.0851 per pound. The transaction costs for 5-ton and 10-ton futures contracts are $65 and $110, respectively. Finally, Ms. Dobson has assessed the probability distribution for the possible prices of sugar 6 months from now (in dollars per pound). The file **P10_35.xlsx** contains these possible prices and their corresponding probabilities.

    **a.** Given that SweetTooth wants to acquire the needed sugar in the least costly way, create a cost table that specifies the cost (in dollars) associated with each possible decision and possible sugar price in the future.

    **b.** Use PrecisionTree to identify the decision that minimizes SweetTooth's expected cost of meeting its sugar demand.

    **c.** Perform a sensitivity analysis on the optimal decision and summarize your findings. In response to which model inputs is the expected cost value most sensitive?

**36.** Carlisle Tire and Rubber, Inc., is considering expanding production to meet potential increases in the demand for one of its tire products. Carlisle's alternatives are to construct a new plant, expand the existing plant, or do nothing in the short run. The market for this particular tire product may expand, remain stable, or contract. Carlisle's marketing department estimates the probabilities of these market outcomes as 0.25, 0.35, and 0.40, respectively. The file **P10_36.xlsx** contains Carlisle's estimated payoff (in dollars) table.

    **a.** Use PrecisionTree to identify the strategy that maximizes this tire manufacturer's expected profit.

    **b.** Perform a sensitivity analysis on the optimal decision and summarize your findings. In response to which model inputs is the expected profit value most sensitive?

**37.** A local energy provider offers a landowner $180,000 for the exploration rights to natural gas on a certain site and the option for future development. This option, if exercised, is worth an additional $1,800,000 to the landowner, but this will occur only if natural gas is discovered during the exploration phase. The landowner, believing that the energy company's interest in the site is a good indication that gas is present, is tempted to develop the field herself. To do so, she must contract with local experts in natural gas exploration and development. The initial cost for such a contract is $300,000, which is lost forever if no gas is found on the site. If gas is discovered, however, the landowner expects to earn a net profit of $6,000,000. Finally, the landowner estimates the probability of finding gas on this site to be 60%.

    **a.** Create a payoff table that specifies the landowner's payoff (in dollars) associated with each possible decision and each outcome with respect to finding natural gas on the site.

    **b.** Use PrecisionTree to identify the strategy that maximizes the landowner's expected net earnings from this opportunity.

    **c.** Perform a sensitivity analysis on the optimal decision and summarize your findings. In response to which model inputs is the expected profit value most sensitive?

**38.** Techware Incorporated is considering the introduction of two new software products to the market. In particular, the company has four options regarding these two proposed products: introduce neither product, introduce product 1 only, introduce product 2 only, or introduce both products. Research and development costs for products 1 and 2 are $180,000 and $150,000, respectively. Note that the first option entails no costs because research and development efforts have not yet begun. The success of these software products depends on the trend of the national economy in the coming year and on the consumers' reaction to these products. The company's revenues earned by introducing product 1 only, product 2 only, or both products in various states of the national economy are given in the file **P10_38.xlsx**. The probabilities of observing a strong, fair, or weak trend in the national economy in the coming year are 0.30, 0.50, and 0.20, respectively.

    **a.** Create a payoff table that specifies Techware's net revenue (in dollars) for each possible decision and each outcome with respect to the trend in the national economy.

    **b.** Use PrecisionTree to identify the strategy that maximizes Techware's expected net revenue from the given marketing opportunities.

    **c.** Perform a sensitivity analysis on the optimal decision and summarize your findings. In response to which model inputs is the expected net revenue value most sensitive?

**39.** Consider an investor with $10,000 available to invest. He has the following options regarding the allocation of his available funds: (1) he can invest in a risk-free savings account with a guaranteed 3% annual rate of return; (2) he can invest in a fairly safe stock, where the possible annual rates of return are 6%, 8%, or 10%; or (3) he can invest in a more risky stock where the possible annual rates of return are 1%, 9%, or 17%. Note that the investor can place all of his available funds in any one of these options, or he can split his $10,000 into two $5000 investments in any two of these options. The joint probability distribution of the possible return rates for the two stocks is given in the file **P10_39.xlsx**.

    **a.** Create a payoff table that specifies this investor's return (in dollars) in one year for each possible decision and each outcome with respect to the two stock returns.

**b.** Use PrecisionTree to identify the strategy that maximizes the investor's expected earnings in one year from the given investment opportunities.

**c.** Perform a sensitivity analysis on the optimal decision and summarize your findings. In response to which model inputs is the expected earnings value most sensitive?

**40.** A buyer for a large department store chain must place orders with an athletic shoe manufacturer 6 months prior to the time the shoes will be sold in the department stores. In particular, the buyer must decide on November 1 how many pairs of the manufacturer's newest model of tennis shoes to order for sale during the upcoming summer season. Assume that each pair of this new brand of tennis shoes costs the department store chain $45. Furthermore, assume that each pair of these shoes can then be sold to the chain's customers for $70. Any shoes remaining unsold at the end of the summer season will be sold in a closeout sale next fall for $35 per pair. The probability distribution of consumer demand for these tennis shoes (in hundreds of pairs) during the upcoming summer season has been assessed by market research specialists and is provided in the file **P10_40.xlsx**. Finally, assume that the department store chain must purchase these tennis shoes from the manufacturer in lots of 100 pairs.

**a.** Create a payoff table that specifies the contribution to profit (in dollars) from the sale of the tennis shoes by this department store chain for each possible purchase decision (in hundreds of pairs) and each outcome with respect to consumer demand.

**b.** Use PrecisionTree to identify the strategy that maximizes the department store chain's expected profit earned by purchasing and subsequently selling pairs of the new tennis shoes.

**c.** Perform a sensitivity analysis on the optimal decision and summarize your findings. In response to which model inputs is the expected earnings value most sensitive?

**41.** Each day, the manager of a local bookstore must decide how many copies of the community newspaper to order for sale in her shop. She must pay the newspaper's publisher $0.40 for each copy, and she sells the newspapers to local residents for $0.50 each. Newspapers that are unsold at the end of day are considered worthless. The probability distribution of the number of copies of the newspaper purchased daily at her shop is provided in the file **P10_41.xlsx**. Employ a decision tree to find the bookstore manager's profit-maximizing daily order quantity.

**42.** Two construction companies are bidding against one another for the right to construct a new community center building in Lewisburg, Pennsylvania. The first construction company, Fine Line Homes, believes that its competitor, Buffalo Valley Construction, will place a

bid for this project according to the distribution shown in the file **P10_42.xlsx**. Furthermore, Fine Line Homes estimates that it will cost $160,000 for its own company to construct this building. Given its fine reputation and long-standing service within the local community, Fine Line Homes believes that it will likely be awarded the project in the event that it and Buffalo Valley Construction submit exactly the same bids. Employ a decision tree to identify Fine Line Homes' profit-maximizing bid for the new community center building.

**43.** Suppose that you have sued your employer for damages suffered when you recently slipped and fell on an icy surface that should have been treated by your company's physical plant department. Specifically, your injury resulting from this accident was sufficiently serious that you, in consultation with your attorney, decided to sue your company for $500,000. Your company's insurance provider has offered to settle this suit with you out of court. If you decide to reject the settlement and go to court, your attorney is confident that you will win the case but is uncertain about the amount the court will award you in damages. He has provided his assessment of the probability distribution of the court's award to you in the file **P10_43.xlsx**. Let $S$ be the insurance provider's proposed out-of-court settlement (in dollars). For which values of $S$ will you decide to accept the settlement? For which values of $S$ will you choose to take your chances in court? Of course, you are seeking to maximize the expected payoff from this litigation.

**44.** Suppose that one of your colleagues has $2000 available to invest. Assume that all of this money must be placed in one of three investments: a particular money market fund, a stock, or gold. Each dollar your colleague invests in the money market fund earns a virtually guaranteed 6% annual return. Each dollar he invests in the stock earns an annual return characterized by the probability distribution provided in the file **P10_44.xlsx**. Finally, each dollar he invests in gold earns an annual return characterized by the probability distribution given in the file.

**a.** If your colleague must place all of his available funds in a single investment, which investment should he choose to maximize his expected earnings over the next year?

**b.** Suppose now that your colleague can place all of his available funds in one of these three investments as before, or he can invest $1000 in one alternative and $1000 in another. Assuming that he seeks to maximize his expected total earnings in one year, how should he allocate his $2000?

**45.** Consider a population of 2000 individuals, 800 of whom are women. Assume that 300 of the women in this population earn at least $60,000 per year, and 200 of the men earn at least $60,000 per year.

**a.** What is the probability that a randomly selected individual from this population earns less than $60,000 per year?

**b.** If a randomly selected individual is observed to earn less than $60,000 per year, what is the probability that this person is a man?

**c.** If a randomly selected individual is observed to earn at least $60,000 per year, what is the probability that this person is a woman?

**46.** Yearly automobile inspections are required for residents of the state of Pennsylvania. Suppose that 18% of all inspected cars in Pennsylvania have problems that need to be corrected. Unfortunately, Pennsylvania state inspections fail to detect these problems 12% of the time. Consider a car that is inspected and is found to be free of problems. What is the probability that there is indeed something wrong that the inspection has failed to uncover?

**47.** Consider again the landowner's decision problem described in Problem 37. Suppose now that, at a cost of $90,000, the landowner can request that a soundings test be performed on the site where natural gas is believed to be present. The company that conducts the soundings concedes that 30% of the time the test will indicate that no gas is present when it actually is. When natural gas is not present in a particular site, the soundings test is accurate 90% of the time.

**a.** Given that the landowner pays for the soundings test and the test indicates that gas is present, what is the landowner's revised estimate of the probability of finding gas on this site?

**b.** Given that the landowner pays for the soundings test and the test indicates that gas is not present, what is the landowner's revised estimate of the probability of not finding gas on this site?

**c.** Should the landowner request the given soundings test at a cost of $90,000? Explain why or why not. If not, when (if ever) would the landowner choose to obtain the soundings test?

**48.** The chief executive officer of a firm in a highly competitive industry believes that one of her key employees is providing confidential information to the competition. She is 90% certain that this informer is the vice president of finance, whose contacts have been extremely valuable in obtaining financing for the company. If she decides to fire this vice president and he is the informer, she estimates that the company will gain $500,000. If she decides to fire this vice president but he is not the informer, the company will lose his expertise and still have an informer within the staff; the CEO estimates that this outcome would cost her company about $2.5 million. If she decides not to fire this vice president, she estimates that the firm will lose $1.5 million regardless of whether he actually is the informer (because in either case the informer is still with the company). Before deciding whether to fire the vice president of finance, the CEO could order lie detector tests. To avoid possible lawsuits, the lie detector tests would have to be administered to all company employees, at a total cost of $150,000. Another problem she must consider is that the available lie detector tests are not perfectly reliable. In particular, if a person is lying, the test will reveal that the person is lying 95% of the time. Moreover, if a person is not lying, the test will indicate that the person is not lying 85% of the time.

**a.** To minimize the expected total cost of managing this difficult situation, what strategy should the CEO adopt?

**b.** Should the CEO order the lie detector tests for all of her employees? Explain why or why not.

**c.** Determine the maximum amount of money the CEO should be willing to pay to administer lie detector tests.

**49.** A customer has approached a bank for a $100,000 1-year loan at a 12% interest rate. If the bank does not approve this loan application, the $100,000 will be invested in bonds that earn a 6% annual return. Without additional information, the bank believes that there is a 4% chance that this customer will default on the loan, assuming that the loan is approved. If the customer defaults on the loan, the bank will lose $100,000. At a cost of $1000, the bank can thoroughly investigate the customer's credit record and supply a favorable or unfavorable recommendation. Past experience indicates that in cases where the customer did not default on the approved loan, 80% received a favorable recommendation on the basis of the credit investigation. Furthermore, in cases where the customer defaulted on the approved loan, 25% received a favorable recommendation on the basis of the credit investigation.

**a.** What course of action should the bank take to maximize its expected profit?

**b.** Compute and interpret the expected value of sample information (EVSI) in this decision problem.

**c.** Compute and interpret the expected value of perfect information (EVPI) in this decision problem.

**50.** A company is deciding whether to market a new product. Assume, for simplicity, that if this product is marketed, there are only two possible outcomes: success or failure. The company assesses that the probabilities of these two outcomes are $p$ and $1 - p$, respectively. If the product is marketed, and it proves to be a failure, the company will lose $450,000. If the product is marketed, and it proves to be a success, the company will gain $750,000. Choosing not to market the product results in no gain or loss for the company. The company is also considering whether to survey prospective buyers of this new product. The results of the consumer survey can be classified as favorable, neutral, or unfavorable. In similar cases where proposed products proved to be market successes, the likelihoods that the survey results were favorable, neutral, or unfavorable were 0.6, 0.3, and 0.1, respectively. In similar cases where proposed products proved to be market failures, the likelihoods that the survey results were favorable, neutral, or unfavorable were 0.1, 0.2, and 0.7, respectively. The total cost of administering this survey is $C$ dollars.

**a.** Let $p = 0.4$. For which values of $C$, if any, would this company choose to conduct the consumer survey?

**b.** Let $p = 0.4$. What is the largest amount that this company would be willing to pay for perfect information about the potential success or failure of the new product?

**c.** Let $p = 0.5$ and $C = \$15,000$. Find the strategy that maximizes the company's expected earnings in this situation. Does the optimal strategy involve conducting the consumer survey? Explain why or why not.

**51.** The U.S. government is attempting to determine whether immigrants should be tested for a contagious disease. Let's assume that the decision will be made on a financial basis. Furthermore, assume that each immigrant who is allowed to enter the United States and has the disease costs the country $100,000. Also, each immigrant who is allowed to enter the United States and does not have the disease will contribute $10,000 to the national economy. Finally, assume that $x$ percent of all potential immigrants have the disease. The U.S. government can choose to admit all immigrants, admit no immigrants, or test immigrants for the disease before determining whether they should be admitted. It costs $T$ dollars to test a person for the disease; the test result is either positive or negative. A person who does not have the disease *always* tests negative. However, 20% of all people who *do* have the disease test negative. The government's goal is to maximize the expected net financial benefits per potential immigrant.

**a.** Let $x = 10$ (i.e., 10%). What is the largest value of $T$ at which the U.S. government will choose to test potential immigrants for the disease?

**b.** How does your answer to the question in part **a** change when $x$ increases to 15?

**c.** Let $x = 10$ and $T = \$100$. Find the government's optimal strategy.

**d.** Let $x = 10$ and $T = \$100$. Compute and interpret the EVPI in this decision problem.

**52.** The senior executives of an oil company are trying to decide whether to drill for oil in a particular field in the Gulf of Mexico. It costs the company $300,000 to

drill in the selected field. Company executives believe that if oil is found in this field, its estimated value will be $1,800,000. At present, this oil company believes there is a 48% chance that the selected field actually contains oil. Before drilling, the company can hire a geologist at a cost of $30,000 to prepare a report that contains a recommendation regarding drilling in the selected field. There is a 55% chance that the geologist will issue a favorable recommendation and a 45% chance that the geologist will issue an unfavorable recommendation. Given a favorable recommendation from the geologist, there is a 75% chance that the field actually contains oil. Given an unfavorable recommendation from the geologist, there is a 15% chance that the field actually contains oil.

**a.** Assuming that this oil company wants to maximize its expected net earnings, determine its optimal strategy through the use of a decision tree.

**b.** Compute and interpret EVSI for this decision problem.

**c.** Compute and interpret EVPI for this decision problem.

**53.** A local certified public accountant must decide which of two copying machines to purchase for her expanding business. The cost of purchasing the first machine is $3100, and the cost of maintaining the first machine each year is uncertain. The CPA's office manager believes that the annual maintenance cost for the first machine will be $0, $150, or $300 with probabilities 0.325, 0.475, and 0.20, respectively. The cost of purchasing the second machine is $3000, and the cost of maintaining the second machine through a guaranteed maintenance agreement is $225 per year. Before the purchase decision is made, the CPA can hire an experienced copying machine repairperson to evaluate the quality of the first machine. Such an evaluation would cost the CPA $100. If the repairperson believes that the first machine is satisfactory, there is a 65% chance that its annual maintenance cost will be $0 and a 35% chance that its annual maintenance cost will be $150. If, however, the repairperson believes that the first machine is unsatisfactory, there is a 60% chance that its annual maintenance cost will be $150 and a 40% chance that its annual maintenance cost will be $300. The CPA's office manager believes that the repairperson will issue a satisfactory report on the first machine with probability 0.50.

**a.** Provided that the CPA wants to minimize the expected total cost of purchasing and maintaining one of these two machines for a one-year period, which machine should she purchase? When, if ever, would it be worthwhile for the CPA to obtain the repairperson's review of the first machine?

**b.** Compute and interpret EVSI for this decision problem.

c. Compute and interpret EVPI for this decision problem.

54. FineHair is developing a new product to promote hair growth in cases of male pattern baldness. If FineHair markets the new product and it is successful, the company will earn $500,000 in additional profit. If the marketing of this new product proves to be unsuccessful, the company will lose $350,000 in development and marketing costs. In the past, similar products have been successful 60% of the time. At a cost of $50,000, the effectiveness of the new restoration product can be thoroughly tested. If the results of such testing are favorable, there is an 80% chance that the marketing efforts of this new product will be successful. If the results of such testing are not favorable, there is a mere 30% chance that the marketing efforts of this new product will be successful. FineHair currently believes that the probability of receiving favorable test results is 0.60.
   a. Identify the strategy that maximizes FineHair's expected net earnings in this situation.
   b. Compute and interpret EVSI for this decision problem.
   c. Compute and interpret EVPI for this decision problem.

55. Hank is considering placing a bet on the upcoming showdown between the Penn State and Michigan football teams in State College. The winner of this contest will represent the Big Ten Conference in the Rose Bowl on New Year's Day. Without any additional information, Hank believes that Penn State has a 0.475 chance of winning this big game. If he wins the bet, he will win $500; if he loses the bet, he will lose $550. Before placing his bet, he may decide to pay his friend Al, who happens to be a football sportswriter for the *Philadelphia Enquirer,* $50 for Al's expert prediction on the game. Assume that Al predicts that Penn State will win similar games 55% of the time and that Michigan will win similar games 45% of the time. Furthermore, Hank believes that when Al predicts that Penn State will win, there is a 70% chance that Penn State will indeed win the football game. Finally, when Al predicts that Michigan will win, Hank believes there is a 20% chance that Penn State will proceed to win the upcoming game.
   a. To maximize his expected profit from this betting opportunity, how should Hank proceed? (You can assume that Hank has three options: to bet on Penn State, to bet on Michigan, or not to bet at all.)
   b. Compute and interpret EVSI for this decision problem.
   c. Compute and interpret EVPI for this decision problem.

56. A product manager at Clean & Brite (C&B) seeks to determine whether her company should market a new brand of toothpaste. If this new product succeeds in the marketplace, C&B estimates that it could earn $1,800,000 in future profits from the sale of the new toothpaste. If this new product fails, however, the company expects that it could lose approximately $750,000. If C&B chooses not to market this new brand, the product manager believes that there would be little, if any, impact on the profits earned through sales of C&B's other products. The manager has estimated that the new toothpaste brand will succeed with probability 0.50. Before making her decision regarding this toothpaste product, the manager can spend $75,000 on a market research study. Such a study of consumer preferences will yield either a positive recommendation with probability 0.50 or a negative recommendation with probability 0.50. Given a positive recommendation to market the new product, the new brand will eventually succeed in the marketplace with probability 0.75. Given a negative recommendation regarding the marketing of the new product, the new brand will eventually succeed in the marketplace with probability 0.25.
   a. To maximize expected profit, what course of action should the C&B product manager take?
   b. Compute and interpret EVSI for this decision problem.
   c. Compute and interpret EVPI for this decision problem.

57. Ford is going to produce a new vehicle, the Pioneer, and wants to determine the amount of annual capacity it should build. Ford's goal is to maximize the profit from this vehicle over the next 10 years. Each vehicle will sell for $13,000 and incur a variable production cost of $10,000. Building 1 unit of annual capacity will cost $3000. Each unit of capacity will also cost $1000 per year to maintain, even if the capacity is unused. Demand for the Pioneer is unknown but marketing estimates the distribution of annual demand to be as shown in the file **P10_57.xlsx**. Assume that the number of units sold during a year is the minimum of capacity and annual demand.
   a. Explain why a capacity of 1,300,000 is not a good choice.
   b. Which capacity level should Ford choose?

58. Pizza King (PK) and Noble Greek (NG) are competitive pizza chains. Pizza King believes there is a 25% chance that NG will charge $6 per pizza, a 50% chance NG will charge $8 per pizza, and a 25% chance that NG will charge $10 per pizza. If PK charges price $p_1$ and NG charges price $p_2$, PK will sell $100 + 25(p_2 - p_1)$ pizzas. It costs PK $4 to make a pizza. PK is considering charging $5, $6, $7, $8, or $9 per pizza. To maximize its expected profit, what price should PK charge for a pizza?

**59.** Many decision problems have the following simple structure. A decision maker has two possible decisions, 1 and 2. If decision 1 is made, a *sure* cost of $c$ is incurred. If decision 2 is made, there are two possible outcomes, with costs $c_1$ and $c_2$ and probabilities $p$ and $1 - p$. We assume that $c_1 < c < c_2$. The idea is that decision 1, the riskless decision, has a "moderate" cost, whereas decision 2, the risky decision, has a "low" cost $c_1$ or a "high" cost $c_2$.

   **a.** Find the decision maker's cost table, that is, the cost for each possible decision and each possible outcome.

   **b.** Calculate the expected cost from the risky decision.

   **c.** List as many scenarios as you can think of that have this structure. (Here's an example to get you started. Think of insurance, where you pay a sure premium to avoid a large possible loss.)

**60.** A nuclear power company is deciding whether to build a nuclear power plant at Diablo Canyon or at Roy Rogers City. The cost of building the power plant is $10 million at Diablo and $20 million at Roy Rogers City. If the company builds at Diablo, however, and an earthquake occurs at Diablo during the next 5 years, construction will be terminated, and the company will lose $10 million (and will still have to build a power plant at Roy Rogers City). Without further expert information, the company believes there is a 20% chance that an earthquake will occur at Diablo during the next 5 years. For $1 million, a geologist can be hired to analyze the fault structure at Diablo Canyon. She will predict either that an earthquake will occur or that an earthquake will not occur. The geologist's past record indicates that she will predict an earthquake on 95% of the occasions for which an earthquake will occur and no earthquake on 90% of the occasions for which an earthquake will not occur. Should the power company hire the geologist? Also, calculate and interpret EVSI and EVPI.

**61.** Consider again Techware's decision problem described in Problem 38. Suppose now that Techware's utility function of net revenue $x$ (measured in dollars), earned from the given marketing opportunities, is $U(x) = 1 - e^{-x/350000}$.

   **a.** Find the course of action that maximizes Techware's expected utility. How does this optimal decision compare to the optimal decision with an EMV criterion? Explain any difference in the two optimal decisions.

   **b.** Repeat part **a** when Techware's utility function is $U(x) = 1 - e^{-x/50000}$.

**62.** Consider again the bank's customer loan decision problem in Problem 49. Suppose now that the bank's utility function of profit $x$ (in dollars) is $U(x) = 1 - e^{-x/150000}$. Find the strategy that maximizes the bank's expected utility in this case. How does this optimal strategy compare to the optimal decision with

an EMV criterion? Explain any difference in the two optimal strategies.

**63.** The Indiana University basketball team trails by 2 points with 8 seconds to go and has the ball. Should it attempt a 2-point shot or a 3-point shot? Assume that the Indiana shot will end the game and that no foul will occur on the shot. Assume that a 3-point shot has a 30% chance of succeeding, and a 2-point shot has a 45% chance of success. Finally, assume that Indiana has a 50% chance of winning in overtime.

## Skill-Extending Problems

**64.** George Lindsey (1959) looked at box scores of more than 1000 baseball games and found the expected number of runs scored in an inning for each on-base and out situation to be as listed in the file **P10_64.xlsx**. For example, if a team has a man on first base with one out, it scores 0.5 run on average until the end of the inning.

   **a.** Use this data to explain why, in most cases, bunting with a man on first base and none out is a bad decision. In what situation might bunting with a man on first base and none out be a good decision?

   **b.** You have a man on first base with one out. What probability of stealing second makes an attempted steal a good idea?

**65.** Mr. Maloy has just bought a new $30,000 sport utility vehicle. As a reasonably safe driver, he believes that there is only about a 5% chance of being in an accident in the coming year. If he is involved in an accident, the damage to his new vehicle depends on the severity of the accident. The probability distribution for the range of possible accidents and the corresponding damage amounts (in dollars) are given in the file **P10_65.xlsx**. Mr. Maloy is trying to decide whether he is willing to pay $170 each year for collision insurance with a $300 deductible. Note that with this type of insurance, he pays the *first* $300 in damages if he causes an accident and the insurance company pays the remainder.

   **a.** Create a payoff table that specifies the cost (in dollars) associated with each possible decision and type of accident.

   **b.** Use PrecisionTree to identify the strategy that minimizes Mr. Maloy's annual expected cost.

   **c.** Perform a sensitivity analysis on the optimal decision and summarize your findings. In response to which model inputs is the expected earnings value most sensitive?

**66.** The purchasing agent for a microcomputer manufacturer is currently negotiating a purchase agreement for a particular electronic component with a given supplier. This component is produced in lots of 1000, and the cost of purchasing a lot is $30,000. Unfortunately, past experience indicates that this supplier has occasionally shipped defective components to its customers. Specifically, the proportion of defective components supplied by this supplier is described by the probability distribution given in the file **P10_66.xlsx**. Although the microcomputer manufacturer can repair a defective component at a cost of $20 each, the purchasing agent is intrigued to learn that this supplier will now assume the cost of replacing defective components in excess of the first 100 faulty items found in a given lot. This guarantee may be purchased by the microcomputer manufacturer prior to the receipt of a given lot at a cost of $1000 per lot. The purchasing agent is interested in determining whether it is worthwhile for her company to purchase the supplier's guarantee policy.

**a.** Create a payoff table that specifies the microcomputer manufacturer's total cost (in dollars) of purchasing and repairing (if necessary) a complete lot of components for each possible decision and each outcome with respect to the proportion of defective items.

**b.** Use PrecisionTree to identify the strategy that minimizes the expected total cost of achieving a complete lot of satisfactory microcomputer components.

**c.** Perform a sensitivity analysis on the optimal decision and summarize your findings. In response to which model inputs is the expected earnings value most sensitive?

**67.** A home appliance company is interested in marketing an innovative new product. The company must decide whether to manufacture this product essentially on its own or employ a subcontractor to manufacture it. The file **P10_67.xlsx** contains the estimated probability distribution of the cost of manufacturing one unit of this new product (in dollars) under the alternative that the home appliance company produces the item on its own. This file also contains the estimated probability distribution of the cost of purchasing one unit of this new product (in dollars) under the alternative that the home appliance company commissions a subcontractor to produce the item.

**a.** Assuming that the home appliance company seeks to minimize the expected unit cost of manufacturing or buying the new product, use PrecisionTree to see whether the company should make the new product or buy it from a subcontractor.

**b.** Perform a sensitivity analysis on the optimal expected cost. Under what conditions, if any, would the home appliance company select an alternative different from the one you identified in part **a**?

**68.** A grapefruit farmer in central Florida is trying to decide whether to take protective action to limit damage to his crop in the event that the overnight temperature falls to a level well below freezing. He is concerned

that if the temperature falls sufficiently low and he fails to make an effort to protect his grapefruit trees, he runs the risk of losing his entire crop, which is worth approximately $75,000. Based on the latest forecast issued by the National Weather Service, the farmer estimates that there is a 60% chance that he will lose his entire crop if it is left unprotected. Alternatively, the farmer can insulate his fruit by spraying water on all of the trees in his orchards. This action, which would likely cost the farmer $C$ dollars, would prevent total devastation but might not completely protect the grapefruit trees from incurring some damage as a result of the unusually cold overnight temperatures. The file **P10_68.xlsx** contains the assessed distribution of possible damages (in dollars) to the insulated fruit in light of the cold weather forecast. Of course, this farmer seeks to minimize the expected total cost of coping with the threatening weather.

**a.** Find the maximum value of $C$ below which the farmer will choose to insulate his crop in hopes of limiting damage as result of the unusually cold weather.

**b.** Set $C$ equal to the value identified in part **a**. Perform sensitivity analysis to determine under what conditions, if any, the farmer would be better off not spraying his grapefruit trees and taking his chances in spite of the threat to his crop.

**69.** A retired partner from Goldman Sachs has 1 million dollars available to invest in particular stocks or bonds. Each investment's annual rate of return depends on the state of the economy in the coming year. The file **P10_69.xlsx** contains the distribution of returns for these stocks and bonds as a function of the economy's state in the coming year. This investor wants to allocate her $1 million to maximize her expected total return 1 year from now.

**a.** If $X = Y = 15\%$ (see the file), find the optimal investment strategy for this investor.

**b.** For which values of $X$ (where $10\% < X < 20\%$) and $Y$ (where $12.5\% < Y < 17.5\%$), if any, will this investor prefer to place all of her available funds in the given stocks to maximize her expected total return one year from now?

**c.** For which values of $X$ (where $10\% < X < 20\%$) and $Y$ (where $12.5\% < Y < 17.5\%$), if any, will this investor prefer to place all of her available funds in the given bonds to maximize her expected total return one year from now?

**70.** A city in Ohio is considering replacing its fleet of gasoline-powered automobiles with electric cars. The manufacturer of the electric cars claims that this municipality will experience significant cost savings over the life of the fleet if it chooses to pursue the conversion. If the manufacturer is correct, the city will save about $1.5 million dollars. If the new technology employed within the electric cars is faulty, as some critics suggest, the conversion to electric cars will cost the city $675,000. A third possibility is that less serious problems will arise and the city will break even with the conversion. A consultant hired by the city estimates that the probabilities of these three outcomes are 0.30, 0.30, and 0.40, respectively. The city has an opportunity to implement a pilot program that would indicate the potential cost or savings resulting from a switch to electric cars. The pilot program involves renting a small number of electric cars for 3 months and running them under typical conditions. This program would cost the city $75,000. The city's consultant believes that the results of the pilot program would be significant but not conclusive; she submits the values in the file **P10_70.xlsx**, a compilation of probabilities based on the experience of other cities, to support her contention. For example, the first row of her table indicates that given that a conversion to electric cars actually results in a savings of $1.5 million, the conditional probabilities that the pilot program will indicate that the city saves money, loses money, and breaks even are 0.6, 0.1, and 0.3, respectively.

   a. What actions should this city take to maximize the expected savings?
   b. Should the city implement the pilot program at a cost of $75,000?
   c. Compute and interpret EVSI for this decision problem.

71. A manufacturer must decide whether to extend credit to a retailer who would like to open an account with the firm. Past experience with new accounts indicates that 45% are high-risk customers, 35% are moderate-risk customers, and 20% are low-risk customers. If credit is extended, the manufacturer can expect to lose $60,000 with a high-risk customer, make $50,000 with a moderate-risk customer, and make $100,000 with a low-risk customer. If the manufacturer decides not to extend credit to a customer, the manufacturer neither makes nor loses any money. Prior to making a credit extension decision, the manufacturer can obtain a credit rating report on the retailer at a cost of $2000. The credit agency concedes that its rating procedure is not completely reliable. In particular, the credit rating procedure will rate a low-risk customer as a moderate-risk customer with probability 0.10 and as a high-risk customer with probability 0.05. Furthermore, the given rating procedure will rate a moderate-risk customer as a low-risk customer with probability 0.06 and as a high-risk customer with probability 0.07. Finally, the rating procedure will rate a high-risk customer as a low-risk customer with probability 0.01 and as a moderate-risk customer with probability 0.05.

   a. Find the strategy that maximizes the manufacturer's expected net earnings.

   b. Should the manufacturer routinely obtain credit rating reports on those retailers who seek credit approval? Why or why not?
   c. Compute and interpret EVSI for this decision problem.

72. A television network earns an average of $1.6 million each season from a hit program and loses an average of $400,000 each season on a program that turns out to be a flop. Of all programs picked up by this network in recent years, 25% turn out to be hits, and 75% turn out to be flops. At a cost of $C$ dollars, a market research firm will analyze a pilot episode of a prospective program and issue a report predicting whether the given program will end up being a hit. If the program is actually going to be a hit, there is a 90% chance that the market researchers will predict the program to be a hit. If the program is actually going to be a flop, there is a 20% chance that the market researchers will predict the program to be a hit.

   a. Assuming that $C = \$160,000$, identify the strategy that maximizes this television network's expected profit in responding to a newly proposed television program.
   b. What is the maximum value of $C$ that this television network should be willing to incur in choosing to hire the market research firm?
   c. Compute and interpret EVPI for this decision problem.

73. A publishing company is trying to decide whether to publish a new business law textbook. Based on a careful reading of the latest draft of the manuscript, the publisher's senior editor in the business textbook division assesses the distribution of possible payoffs earned by publishing this new book. The file **P10_73.xlsx** contains this probability distribution. Before making a final decision regarding the publication of the book, the editor can learn more about the text's potential for success by thoroughly surveying business law instructors teaching at universities across the country. Historical frequencies based on similar surveys administered in the past are also provided in this file.

   a. Find the strategy that maximizes the publisher's expected payoff (in dollars).
   b. What is the most (in dollars) that the publisher should be willing to pay to conduct a new survey of business law instructors?
   c. If the actual cost of conducting the given survey is less than the amount identified in part **a**, what should the publisher do?
   d. Assuming that a survey could be constructed that provides "perfect information" to the publisher, how much should the company be willing to pay to acquire and implement such a survey?

74. Sharp Outfits is trying to decide whether to ship some customer orders now via UPS or wait until after the

threat of another UPS strike is over. If Sharp Outfits decides to ship the requested merchandise now and the UPS strike takes place, the company will incur $60,000 in delay and shipping costs. If Sharp Outfits decides to ship the customer orders via UPS and no strike occurs, the company will incur $4000 in shipping costs. If Sharp Outfits decides to postpone shipping its customer orders via UPS, the company will incur $10,000 in delay costs regardless of whether UPS goes on strike. Let $p$ represent the probability that UPS will go on strike and impact Sharp Outfits' shipments.

    **a.** For which values of $p$, if any, does Sharp Outfits minimize its expected total cost by choosing to postpone shipping its customer orders via UPS?

    **b.** Suppose now that, at a cost of $1000, Sharp Outfits can purchase information regarding the likelihood of a UPS strike in the near future. Based on similar strike threats in the past, the probability that this information indicates the occurrence of a UPS strike is 27.5%. If the purchased information indicates the occurrence of a UPS strike, the chance of a strike actually occurring is 0.105/0.275. If the purchased information does not indicate the occurrence of a UPS strike, the chance of a strike actually occurring is 0.680/0.725. Provided that $p = 0.15$, what strategy should Sharp Outfits pursue to minimize its expected total cost?

    **c.** Continuing part **b**, compute and interpret EVSI when $p = 0.15$.

    **d.** Continuing part **b**, compute and interpret the EVPI when $p = 0.15$.

**75.** An investor has $10,000 in assets and can choose between two different investments. If she invests in the first investment opportunity, there is an 80% chance that she will increase her assets by $590,000 and a 20% chance that she will increase her assets by $190,000. If she invests in the second investment opportunity, there is a 50% chance that she will increase her assets by $1.19 million and a 50% chance that she will increase her assets by $1000. This investor has an exponential utility function for final assets with a risk tolerance parameter equal to $600,000. Which investment opportunity will she prefer?

**76.** City officials in Fort Lauderdale, Florida, are trying to decide whether to evacuate coastal residents in anticipation of a major hurricane that may make landfall near their city within the next 48 hours. Based on previous studies, it is estimated that it will cost approximately $1 million to evacuate the residents living along the coast of this major metropolitan area. However, if city officials choose not to evacuate their residents and the storm strikes Fort Lauderdale, there would likely be some deaths as a result of the hurricane's storm surge along the coast. Although city officials are reluctant to place an economic value on the loss of human life resulting from such a storm, they

realize that it may ultimately be necessary to do so to make a sound judgment in this situation. Prior to making the evacuation decision, city officials consult hurricane experts at the National Hurricane Center in Coral Gables regarding the accuracy of past predictions. They learn that in similar past cases, hurricanes that were *predicted* to make landfall near a particular coastal location actually did so 60% of the time. Moreover, they learn that in past similar cases, hurricanes that were predicted *not* to make landfall near a particular coastal location actually did so 20% of the time. Finally, in response to similar threats in the past, weather forecasters have issued predictions of a major hurricane making landfall near a particular coastal location 40% of the time.

    **a.** Let $L$ be the economic valuation of the loss of human life resulting from a coastal strike by the hurricane. Employ a decision tree to help these city officials make a decision that minimizes the expected cost of responding to the threat of the impending storm as a function of $L$. To proceed, you might begin by choosing an initial value of $L$ and then perform sensitivity analysis on the optimal decision by varying this model parameter. Summarize your findings.

    **b.** For which values of $L$ will these city officials *always* choose to evacuate the coastal residents, regardless of the Hurricane Center's prediction?

**77.** A homeowner wants to decide whether he should install an electronic heat pump in his home. Given that the cost of installing a new heat pump is fairly large, the homeowner would like to do so only if he can count on being able to recover the initial expense over *five* consecutive years of cold winter weather. After reviewing historical data on the operation of heat pumps in various kinds of winter weather, he computes the expected annual costs of heating his home during the winter months with and without a heat pump in operation. These cost figures are shown in the file **P10_77.xlsx**. The probabilities of experiencing a mild, normal, colder than normal, and severe winter are $0.2(1 − x)$, $0.5(1 − x)$, $0.3(1 − x)$, and $x$, respectively.

    **a.** Given that $x = 0.1$, what is the most that the homeowner is willing to pay for the heat pump?

    **b.** If the heat pump costs $500, how large must $x$ be before the homeowner decides it is economically worthwhile to install the heat pump?

    **c.** Given that $x = 0.1$, compute and interpret EVPI when the heat pump costs $500.

    **d.** Repeat part **c** when $x = 0.15$.

**78.** Many men over 50 take the PSA blood test. The purpose of the PSA test is to detect prostate cancer early. Dr. Rene Labrie of Quebec conducted a study to determine whether the PSA test can actually prevent cancer deaths. In 1989, Dr. Labrie randomly divided all male registered voters between 45 and 80 in Quebec City into two groups. Two-thirds of the men were asked to be tested for prostate cancer, and one-third were not asked. Eventually, 8137 men were screened for prostate cancer (PSA plus digital rectal exam) in 1989; 38,056 men were not screened. By 1997, only 5 of the screened men had died of prostate cancer whereas 137 of the men who were not screened had died of prostate cancer (Source: *New York Times,* May 19, 1998).

**a.** Discuss why this study seems to indicate that screening for prostate cancer saves lives.

**b.** Despite the results of this study, many doctors are not convinced that early screening for prostate cancer saves lives. Can you see why they doubt the conclusions of the study?

79. Sarah Chang is the owner of a small electronics company. In 6 months, a proposal is due for an electronic timing system for the next Olympic Games. For several years, Chang's company has been developing a new microprocessor, a critical component in a timing system that would be superior to any product currently on the market. However, progress in research and development has been slow, and Chang is unsure about whether her staff can produce the microprocessor in time. If they succeed in developing the microprocessor (probability $p_1$), there is an excellent chance (probability $p_2$) that Chang's company will win the $1 million Olympic contract. If they do not, there is a small chance (probability $p_3$) that she will still be able to win the same contract with an alternative, inferior timing system that has already been developed. If she continues the project, Chang must invest $200,000 in research and development. In addition, making a proposal (which she will decide whether to do after seeing whether the R&D is successful or not) requires developing a prototype timing system at an additional cost. This additional cost is $50,000 if R&D is successful (so that she can develop the new timing system), and it is $40,000 if R&D is unsuccessful (so that she needs to go with the older timing system). Finally, if Chang wins the contract, the finished product will cost an additional $150,000 to produce.

**a.** Develop a decision tree that can be used to solve Chang's problem. You can assume in this part of the problem that she is using EMV (of her net profit) as a decision criterion. Build the tree so that she can enter any values for $p_1$, $p_2$, and $p_3$ (in input cells) and automatically see her optimal EMV and optimal strategy from the tree.

**b.** If $p_2 = 0.8$ and $p_3 = 0.1$, what value of $p_1$ makes Chang indifferent between abandoning the project and going ahead with it?

**c.** How much would Chang be willing to pay the Olympic organization (now) to guarantee her the contract in the case where her company is successful in developing the contract? (This guarantee is in

force only if she is successful in developing the product.) Assume $p_1 = 0.4$, $p_2 = 0.8$, and $p_3 = 0.1$.

**d.** Suppose now that this a "big" project for Chang. Therefore, she decides to use expected utility as her criterion, with an exponential utility function. Using some trial and error, see which risk tolerance changes her initial decision from "go ahead" to "abandon" when $p_1 = 0.4$, $p_2 = 0.8$, and $p_3 = 0.1$.

80. Suppose an investor has the opportunity to buy the following contract, a stock call option, on March 1. The contract allows him to buy 100 shares of ABC stock at the end of March, April, or May at a guaranteed price of $50 per share. He can exercise this option at most once. For example, if he purchases the stock at the end of March, he can't purchase more in April or May at the guaranteed price. The current price of the stock is $50. Each month, we assume the stock price either goes up by a dollar (with probability 0.6) or goes down by a dollar (with probability 0.4). If the investor buys the contract, he is hoping that the stock price will go up. The reasoning is that if he buys the contract, the price goes up to $51, and he buys the stock (that is, he exercises his option) for $50, then he can turn around and sell the stock for $51 and make a profit of $1 per share. On the other hand, if the stock price goes down, he doesn't have to exercise his option; he can just throw the contract away.

**a.** Use a decision tree to find the investor's optimal strategy (that is, when he should exercise the option), *assuming* he purchases the contract.

**b.** How much should he be willing to pay for such a contract?

81. The Ventron Engineering Company has just been awarded a $2 million development contract by the U.S. Army Aviation Systems Command to develop a blade spar for its Heavy Lift Helicopter program. The blade spar is a metal tube that runs the length of and provides strength to the helicopter blade. Due to the unusual length and size of the Heavy Lift Helicopter blade, Ventron is unable to produce a single-piece blade spar of the required dimensions using existing extrusion equipment and material. The engineering department has prepared two alternatives for developing the blade spar: (1) sectioning or (2) an improved extrusion process. Ventron must decide which process to use. (Backing out of the contract at any point is not an option.) The risk report has been prepared by the engineering department. The information from the report is explained next.

The sectioning option involves joining several shorter lengths of extruded metal into a blade spar of sufficient length. This work will require extensive testing and rework over a 12-month period at a total cost of $1.8 million. Although this process will definitely produce an adequate blade spar, it merely represents an extension of existing technology.

To improve the extrusion process, on the other hand, it will be necessary to perform two steps: (1) improve the material used, at a cost of $300,000, and (2) modify the extrusion press, at a cost of $960,000. The first step will require 6 months of work, and if this first step is successful, the second step will require another 6 months of work. If both steps are successful, the blade spar will be available at that time, that is, a year from now. The engineers estimate that the probabilities of succeeding in steps 1 and 2 are 0.9 and 0.75, respectively. However, if either step is unsuccessful (which will be known only in 6 months for step 1 and in a year for step 2), Ventron will have no alternative but to switch to the sectioning process—and incur the sectioning cost on top of any costs already incurred.

Development of the blade spar must be completed within 18 months to avoid holding up the rest of the contract. If necessary, the sectioning work can be done on an accelerated basis in a 6-month period, but the cost of sectioning will then increase from $1.8 million to $2.4 million. The director of engineering, Dr. Smith, wants to try developing the improved extrusion process. This is not only cheaper (if successful) for the current project, but its expected side benefits for future projects could be sizable. Although these side benefits are difficult to gauge, Dr. Smith's best guess is an additional $2 million. (Of course, these side benefits are obtained only if both steps of the modified extrusion process are completed successfully.)

a. Develop a decision tree to maximize Ventron's EMV. This includes the revenue from this project, the side benefits (if applicable) from an improved extrusion process, and relevant costs. You don't need to worry about the time value of money; that is, no discounting or NPVs are required. Summarize your findings in words in the spreadsheet.

b. What value of side benefits would make Ventron indifferent between the two alternatives?

c. How much would Ventron be willing to pay, right now, for perfect information about both steps of the improved extrusion process? (This information would tell Ventron, right now, the ultimate success and failure outcomes of both steps.)

82. Based on Balson et al. (1992). An electric utility company is trying to decide whether to replace its PCB transformer in a generating station with a new and safer transformer. To evaluate this decision, the utility needs information about the likelihood of an incident, such as a fire; the cost of such an incident; and the cost of replacing the unit. Suppose that the total cost of replacement as a present value is $75,000. If the transformer is replaced, there is virtually no chance of a fire. However, if the current transformer is retained, the probability of a fire is assessed to be 0.0025. If a fire occurs, then the cleanup cost could be high ($80 million) or low ($20 million). The probability of a high cleanup cost, given that a fire occurs, is assessed at 0.2.

a. If the company uses EMV as its decision criterion, should it replace the transformer?

b. Perform a sensitivity analysis on the key parameters of the problem that are difficult to assess, namely, the probability of a fire, the probability of a high cleanup cost, and the high and low cleanup costs. Does the optimal decision from part **a** remain optimal for a "wide" range of these parameters?

c. Do you believe EMV is the correct criterion to use in this type of problem involving environmental accidents?

The Jogger Shoe Company is trying to decide whether to make a change in its most popular brand of running shoes. The new style would cost the same to produce and be priced the same, but it would incorporate a new kind of lacing system that (according to its marketing research people) would make it more popular.

There is a fixed cost of $300,000 for changing over to the new style. The unit contribution to before-tax profit for either style is $8. The tax rate is 35%. Also, because the fixed cost can be depreciated and will therefore affect the after-tax cash flow, we need a depreciation method. We assume it is straight-line depreciation.

The current demand for these shoes is 190,000 pairs annually. The company assumes this demand will continue for the next 3 years if the current style is retained. However, there is uncertainty about demand for the new style, if it is introduced. The company models this uncertainty by assuming a normal distribution in year 1, with mean 220,000 and standard deviation 20,000. The company also assumes that this demand, whatever it is, will remain constant for the next 3 years. However, if demand in year 1 for the new style is sufficiently low, the company can always switch back to the current style and realize an annual demand of 190,000. The company wants a strategy that will maximize the expected NPV of total cash flow for the next 3 years, where a 15% interest rate is used for the purpose of calculating NPV. ■

The Westhouser Paper Company in the state of Washington currently has an option to purchase a piece of good timber forest land. It is now May 1, and the current price of the land is $2.2 million. Westhouser does not actually need the timber from this land until the beginning of July, but its top executives fear that another company might buy the land between now and the beginning of July. They assess that there is 1 chance out of 20 that a competitor will buy the land during May. If this does not occur, they assess that there is 1 chance out of 10 that the competitor will buy the land during June. If Westhouser does not take advantage of its current option, it can attempt to buy the land at the beginning of June or the beginning of July, provided that it is still available.

Westhouser's incentive for delaying the purchase is that its financial experts believe there is a good chance that the price of the land will fall significantly in one or both of the next 2 months. They assess the possible price decreases and their probabilities in Tables 10.8 and 10.9. Table 10.8 shows the probabili-

ties of the possible price decreases during May. Table 10.9 lists the *conditional* probabilities of the possible price decreases in June, *given* the price decrease in May. For example, it indicates that if the price decrease in May is $60,000, then the possible price decreases in June are $0, $30,000, and $60,000 with respective probabilities 0.6, 0.2, and 0.2.

If Westhouser purchases the land, it believes that it can gross $3 million. (This does not count the cost of purchasing the land.) But if it does not purchase the land, Westhouser believes that it can make $650,000 from alternative investments. What should the company do?

**Table 10.8**   Distribution of Price Decrease in May

| Price Decrease | Probability |
|---|---|
| $0 | 0.5 |
| $60,000 | 0.3 |
| $120,000 | 0.2 |

**Table 10.9**   Distribution of Price Decrease in June

| | | | *Price Decrease in May* | | | |
|---|---|---|---|---|---|
| **$0** | | **$60,000** | | **$120,000** | |
| **June Decrease** | **Probability** | **June Decrease** | **Probability** | **June Decrease** | **Probability** |
| $0 | 0.3 | $0 | 0.6 | $0 | 0.7 |
| $60,000 | 0.6 | $30,000 | 0.2 | $20,000 | 0.2 |
| $120,000 | 0.1 | $60,000 | 0.2 | $40,000 | 0.1 |

**B**iotechnical Engineering specializes in developing new chemicals for agricultural applications. The company is a pioneer in using the sterile-male procedure to control insect infestations. It operates several laboratories around the world where insects are raised and then exposed to extra-large doses of radiation, making them sterile. As an alternative to chlorinated hydrocarbon pesticides, such as DDT, the sterile-male procedure has been used more frequently with a good track record of success, most notably with the Mediterranean Fruitfly (or Medfly).

That pest was controlled in California through the release of treated flies on the premise that the sterile male flies would compete with fertile wild males for mating opportunities. Any female that has mated with a sterile fly will lay eggs that do not hatch. The California Medfly campaigns required about five successive releases of sterile males—at intervals timed to coincide with the time for newly hatched flies to reach adulthood—before the Medfly was virtually eliminated. (Only sterile flies were subsequently caught in survey traps.) The effectiveness of the sterile-male procedure was enhanced by the release of malathion poisonous bait just a few days before each release, cutting down on the number of viable wild adults.

More recently, Biotechnical Engineering has had particular success in using genetic engineering to duplicate various insect hormones and pheromones (scent attractants). Of particular interest is the application of such methods against the Gypsy Moth, a notorious pest that attacks trees. The company has developed synthetic versions of both hormones and pheromones for that moth. It has a synthetic sexual attractant that male moths can detect at great distances. Most promising is the synthetic juvenile hormone.

The juvenile hormone controls moth metamorphosis, determining the timing for the transformation of a caterpillar into a chrysalis and then into an adult. Too much juvenile hormone wreaks havoc with this process, causing caterpillars to turn into freak adults that cannot reproduce.

[10] This case was written by Lawrence L. Lapin, San Jose State University.

Biotechnical Engineering has received a government contract to test its new technology in an actual eradication campaign. The company will participate in a small-scale campaign against the Gypsy Moth in the state of Oregon. Because the pest is so damaging, Dr. June Scribner, the administrator in charge, is considering using DDT as an alternative procedure. Of course, that banned substance is only available for government emergency use because of the environmental damage it may cause. In addition to spraying with DDT, two other procedures can be employed: (1) using Biotechnical's scent lure, followed by release of sterile males, and (2) spraying with the company's juvenile hormone to prevent larvae from developing into adults. Dr. Scribner wants to select the method that yields the best expected payoff, as described next.

Although both of the newer procedures are known to work under laboratory conditions, there is some uncertainty about successful propagation of the chemicals in the wild and about the efficacy of the sterile-male procedure with moths.

If the scent-lure program is launched at a cost of $5 million, Biotechnical claims that it will have a 50–50 chance of leaving a low number of native males versus a high number. After the results of that phase are known, a later choice must be made to spray with DDT or to release sterile males; the cost of the sterilization and delivery of the insects to the countryside is an additional $5 million. But if this two-phase program is successful, the NPV of the worth of trees saved is $30 million, including the benefit of avoiding all other forms of environmental damage. The indigenous moth population would be destroyed, and a new infestation could occur only from migrants. Biotechnical's experience with other eradication programs indicates that if the scent lure leaves a small native male population, there is a 90% chance for a successful eradication by using sterile males; otherwise, there is only a 10% chance for success by using sterile males. A failure results in no savings.

The cost of synthesizing enough juvenile hormone is $3 million. Biotechnical maintains that the probability that the hormone can be effectively disseminated is only 0.20. If it works, the worth of the trees saved and environmental damage avoided will be $50 million. This greater level of savings is possible because of the permanent nature of the solution because a successful juvenile hormone can then be applied wherever the moths are known to exist, virtually eliminating the pest from the environment. But if the hormone does not work, the DDT must still be used to save the trees.

DDT constitutes only a temporary solution, and the worth of its savings in trees is far less than the worth of either of the esoteric eradication procedures—if they prove successful. To compare alternatives, Dr. Scribner proposes using the net advantage (crop and environmental savings, minus cost) relative to where she would be were she to decide to use DDT at the outset or were she to be forced to spray with it later. (Regardless of the outcome, Biotechnical will be reimbursed for all expenditures. The decision is hers, not the company's.)

## Questions

1. Under Biotechnical's proposal, the selection of DDT without even trying the other procedures would lead to a neutral outcome for the government, having zero payoff. Discuss the benefits of Dr. Scribner's proposed payoff measure.

2. Construct Dr. Scribner's decision tree diagram, using the proposed payoff measure.

3. What action will maximize Dr. Scribner's expected payoff?

4. Dr. Scribner is concerned about the assumed 50–50 probability for the two levels of surviving native males following the scent-lure program.
   a. Redo the decision tree analysis to find what action will maximize Dr. Scribner's expected payoff when the probability of low native males is, successively, (1) 0.40 or (2) 0.60 instead.
   b. How is the optimal action affected by the probability level assumed for the low native male outcome?

5. Dr. Scribner is concerned about the assumed 0.20 probability for the dissemination success of the juvenile hormone.
   a. Keeping all other probabilities and cash flows at their original levels, redo the decision tree analysis to find what action will maximize Dr. Scribner's expected payoff when the probability of juvenile hormone success is, successively, (1) 0.15 or (2) 0.25 instead.
   b. How is the optimal action affected by the probability level assumed for the juvenile hormone's success?

6. Dr. Scribner is concerned about the assumed probability levels for the success of the sterile-male procedure.
   a. Keeping all other probabilities and cash flows at their original levels, redo the decision tree analysis to find what action will maximize Dr. Scribner's expected payoff when the sterile-male success probabilities are instead as follows:
      (1) 80% for low native males and 5% for high native males
      (2) 70% for low native males and 15% for high native males
   b. How is the optimal action affected by the probability level assumed for the success of the sterile-male procedure?

7. Dr. Scribner is concerned about the assumed levels for the NPV of the worth of trees saved and damage avoided. She believes these amounts are accurate only within a range of ±10%.
   a. Keeping all other probabilities and cash flows at their original levels, redo the decision tree analysis to find what action will maximize Dr. Scribner's expected payoff when the two NPVs are instead, successively, (1) 10% lower or (2) 10% higher than originally assumed.
   b. How is the optimal action affected by the level assumed for the NPVs of the savings from using one of the two esoteric Gypsy Moth eradication procedures? ■

# Introduction to Simulation Modeling

© Getty Images/PhotoDisc

## DEVELOPING BOARDING STRATEGIES AT AMERICA WEST

**M**anagement science often attempts to solve problems that we all experience. One such problem is the boarding process for airline flights. As customers, we all hate to wait while boarders ahead of us store their luggage and block the aisles. But this is also a big problem for the airlines. Airlines lose money when their airplanes are on the ground, so they have a real incentive to reduce the turnaround time from when a plane lands until it departs on its next flight. Of course, the turnaround time is influenced by several factors, including passenger deplaning, baggage unloading, fueling, cargo unloading, airplane maintenance, cargo loading, baggage loading, and passenger boarding. Airlines try to perform all of these tasks as efficiently as possible, but passenger boarding is particularly difficult to shorten. Although the airlines want passengers to board as quickly as possible, they don't want to use measures that might antagonize their passengers.

One study by van den Briel et al. (2005) indicates how a combination of management science methods, including simulation, was used to make passenger boarding more efficient at America West Airlines. America West (to become US Airways in 2006) is a major U.S. carrier based in Phoenix, Arizona. It serves more destinations nonstop than any other airline. The airline's fleet consists of Airbus A320s, Airbus A319s, Boeing 757s, Boeing 737s, and (by the end of 2006) Airbus A318s. The company is a low-fare, full-service airline. It is the only major airline that not only survived but also managed to thrive in the era of air travel deregulation.

At the time of the study, airlines used a variety of boarding strategies, but the predominant strategy was the back-to-front (BF) strategy where, after boarding first-class passengers and passengers with special needs, the rest of the passengers are boarded in groups, starting with rows in the back of the plane. As the authors suspected (and most of us have experienced), this strategy still results in significant congestion. Within a given section of the plane (the back, say), passengers storing luggage in overhead compartments can block an aisle. Also, people in the aisle or middle seat often need to get back into the aisle to let window-seat passengers be seated. The authors developed an integer programming (IP) model to minimize the number of such aisle blockages. The decision variables determined which groups of seats should be boarded in which order. Of course, the BF strategy was one possible feasible solution, but it turned out to be a suboptimal solution. The IP model suggested that the best solution was an outside-in (OI) strategy, where groups of passengers in window seats board first, then groups in the middle seats, and finally groups in aisle seats, with all of these groups going essentially in a back-to-front order.

The authors recognized that their IP model was at best an idealized model of how passengers actually behave. Its biggest drawback is that it ignores the inherent randomness in passenger behavior. Therefore, they followed up their optimization model with a simulation model. As they state, "We used simulation to validate the analytical model and to obtain a finer level of detail." This validation of an approximate or idealized analytical model is a common use for simulation. To make the simulation as realistic as possible, they used two cameras, one inside the plane and one inside the bridge leading to the plane, to tape customer behavior. By analyzing the tapes, they were able to estimate the required inputs to their simulation model, such as the time between passengers, walking speed, blocking time, and time to store luggage in overhead compartments. After the basic simulation model was developed, it was used as a tool to evaluate various boarding strategies suggested by the IP model. It also allowed the authors to experiment with changes to the overall boarding process that might be beneficial. For example, reducing congestion *inside* the airplane is not very helpful if the gate agent at the entrance to the bridge processes passengers too slowly. Their final recommendation, based on a series of simulation experiments, was to add a second gate agent (there had been only one before) and to board passengers in six groups using an OI strategy. The simulation model suggested that this could reduce the boarding time by about 37%.

The authors' recommendations were implemented first in a pilot and then systemwide. The pilot results were impressive, with a 39% reduction in boarding times. By September 2003, the new boarding strategies had been implemented in 80% of Air West's airports, with a decrease in departure delays as much as 60.1%. Besides this obvious benefit to the airline, customers also appear to be happier. Now they can easily understand when to queue up for boarding and they experience less blocking after they get inside the plane. ∎

# 11.1 INTRODUCTION

A simulation model is a computer model that imitates a real-life situation. This model is like other mathematical models, but it explicitly incorporates uncertainty in one or more input variables. When we run a simulation, we allow these random input variables to take on various values, and we keep track of any resulting output variables of interest. In this way, we are able to see how the outputs vary as a function of the varying inputs.

The fundamental advantage of a simulation model is that it shows an entire distribution of results, not simply a single bottom-line result. As an example, suppose an automobile manufacturer is planning to develop and market a new model car. The company is ultimately interested in the net present value (NPV) of the profits from this car over the next 10 years. However, many uncertainties surround this car, including the yearly customer demands, the cost of development, and others. We could develop a spreadsheet model for the 10-year NPV using our *best guesses* for these uncertain quantities. We could then report the NPV based on these best guesses, with the implicit understanding that this best-guess NPV is going to occur. However, this analysis would be incomplete and probably misleading—after all, how can we be certain that any *specific* value of NPV will occur? It is much better to treat the uncertainty explicitly with a simulation model. This involves entering probability distributions for the uncertain quantities and seeing how the NPV varies as the uncertain quantities vary.

Each different set of values for the uncertain quantities can be considered a scenario. Simulation allows us to generate many scenarios, each leading to a particular NPV. In the end, we see a whole distribution of NPVs, not just a single best guess. We can see what the NPV will be on average, and we can also see worst-case and best-case results.

Simulation models are also useful for determining how sensitive a system is to changes in operating conditions. For example, we might simulate the operations of a supermarket. After the simulation model has been developed, we can then run it (with suitable modifications) to ask a number of what-if questions. For example, if the supermarket experiences a 20% increase in business, what will happen to the average time customers must wait for service?

A great benefit of computer simulation is that it enables us to answer these types of what-if questions without actually changing (or building) a physical system. For example, the supermarket might want to experiment with the number of open registers to see the effect on customer waiting times. The only way the supermarket can *physically* experiment with more registers than it currently owns is to purchase more equipment. Then if it determines that this equipment is not a good investment—customer waiting times do not decrease appreciably—the company is stuck with expensive equipment it doesn't need. Computer simulation is a much less expensive alternative because it provides the company with an electronic replica of what would happen *if* the new equipment were purchased. Then, if the simulation indicates that the new equipment is worth the cost, the company can be confident that purchasing it is the right decision. Otherwise, the company can abandon the idea of the new equipment *before* the equipment has been purchased.

Spreadsheet simulation modeling is similar to the other modeling applications in this book. We begin with input variables and then relate these with appropriate Excel formulas to produce output variables of interest. The main difference is that simulation uses *random* numbers to drive the whole process. These random numbers are generated with special functions that we discuss in detail. Each time the spreadsheet recalculates, all of the random numbers change, which enables us to model the logical process once and then use Excel's recalculation ability to generate many different scenarios. By collecting the data from these scenarios, we see which values of the outputs are most likely, and we see the best-case and worst-case scenarios.

In this chapter, we illustrate spreadsheet models that can be developed with the basic Excel package. However, because simulation is becoming such an important tool for analyzing real problems, add-ins to Excel have been developed to streamline the process of developing and analyzing simulation models. Therefore, we also introduce @RISK, one of the most popular simulation add-ins. This add-in not only augments the simulation capabilities of Excel, but it also enables users to analyze models much more quickly and easily.

The purpose of this chapter is to introduce basic simulation concepts, show how simulation models can be developed in Excel, and demonstrate the capabilities of the @RISK add-in. Then in the next chapter, armed with the necessary simulation tools, we explore a number of interesting and useful simulation models.

## 11.2 REAL APPLICATIONS OF SIMULATION

Many simulation applications have been published that cover a wide variety of topics, as we discuss briefly in this section.

Many companies (Cummins Engine, Merck, Procter & Gamble, Kodak, and United Airlines, to name a few) have used simulation to determine which of several possible investment projects they should choose. This is often referred to as **risk analysis.** As an example, consider a situation where a company must choose a single investment. If the future cash flows for each investment project are known with certainty, then most companies advocate choosing the investment with the largest NPV. However, if future cash flows are not known with certainty, then it is not clear how to choose between competing projects. Using simulation, we can obtain a distribution of the NPV for a project. Then we can answer such questions as

- Which project is the riskiest?
- What is the probability that an investment will yield at least a 20% return?
- What is the probability that the NPV of an investment will be less than −$1 billion— that is, a loss of more than $1 billion?

To illustrate the use of simulation in corporate finance, we refer to Norton (1994). This article describes a simulation model that was used by Merck, the world's largest drug company, to determine whether Merck should pay $6.6 billion to acquire Medco, a mail-order drug company. The model's inputs included the following:

- Possible scenarios for the future of the U.S. health-care system, such as a single-payer system, universal coverage, and so on
- Possible future changes in the mix of generic and brand-name drugs
- Probability distributions of profit margins for each product
- Assumptions about competitors' reactions to a merger with Medco

A simulation of the Merck model was performed to see how the merger would perform under various possible scenarios. As Merck's CFO says, "Monte Carlo techniques are a very, very powerful tool to get a more intelligent look at a range of outcomes. It's almost never useful in this kind of environment to build a single bullet forecast." The simulation results indicated that the merger with Medco would benefit Merck regardless of the type of health insurance plan (if any) the federal government enacted.

Other applications of simulation include the following:

- Merrick et al. (2002) developed a simulation model to estimate the risk of accidents involving oil tankers in the Prince William Sound area of Alaska, the region where the *Exxon Valdez* ran aground in 1989. They modeled the behavior of oil tankers, fishing boats, and escort tugs, along with weather conditions, to discover conditions where collisions are more likely to occur. They then used the simulation to introduce measures that might reduce the risk of further oil spills. By the time of their study, measures introduced since the *Exxon Valdez* accident had already reduced the risk of collisions by 75%. The authors estimate, based on their simulation, that the extra measures they proposed would reduce the risk of collisions by an additional 68%.

- So et al. (2003) describe how the Federal Reserve Bank (FRB) needed new mechanisms for providing low-cost, high-quality customer service to remain competitive with other check-processing organizations. To do so, the FRB had to have the right supply of workers at the right time to handle uncertain check arrivals and complete the processing on time. The authors developed two models to help the FRB. The first model, a deterministic optimization model, suggested that the FRB should move from a serial-line configuration to a team structure. The second model, a simulation model, helped show managers how to configure different teams and their work schedules effectively. The implementation of these models, begun in 2000, has enabled the Los Angeles branch of the FRB to save $1 million annually and increase productivity by 24.3%.

- Gavirneni et al. (2004) describe a novel use of simulation. The authors developed the Maxager system, a manufacturing decision-support system consisting of both hardware and software. To sell this system, they had to perform costly and time-intensive pilot studies to demonstrate the benefits of the system to prospective customers. These pilot studies lasted from three to six months and cost hundreds of thousands of dollars. To save time and money, the authors developed a simulation to help them sell Maxager to customers. The simulation essentially let a customer see how Maxager would work on simulated data from the customer's own systems in much less time and expense than a pilot study. In addition, the simulation worked just as effectively in terms of achieving sales as the pilot studies.

- Supply chain management is currently one of the hottest management science topics, both in academic research and in real organizations. The journal *Interfaces* that chronicles real applications of management science ran a special issue in November-December 2003 devoted to closed-loop supply chains, where parts or entire products are cycled back through the organization for refurbishment and possible resales. Of the six applications articles in the issue, four of them, Spengler and Schroter (2003), Kekre et al. (2003), Fleishmann et al. (2003), and Schultmann et al. (2003), describe how they developed simulation models to investigate system behavior of various types. This is not surprising. Supply chain models tend to be very complex, and simulation models stand the best chance of being able to cope with this complexity.

- To avoid road congestion at the Schiphol Airport near Amsterdam, van der Heijden et al. (2002) used simulation to help guide the development of a highly automated underground transport system using automatic guided vehicles (AGVs). They used the simulation to test a number of logistics optimization algorithms and heuristics, including allocating AGVs between terminals, scheduling terminals, and controlling traffic. By using simulation in the planning stages of the project, they were able to reduce the risks of the new technology.

## 11.3 PROBABILITY DISTRIBUTIONS FOR INPUT VARIABLES

In this section, we discuss the "building blocks" of spreadsheet simulation models. All spreadsheet simulation models are similar to the spreadsheet models we have developed in previous chapters. They have a number of cells that contain values of input variables. The other cells contain formulas that embed the logic of the model and eventually lead to the output variable(s) of interest. The primary difference between the spreadsheet models we have developed so far and simulation models is that at least one of the input variable cells in a simulation model contains *random numbers*. We can make these random numbers change by recalculating the spreadsheet. Each time the spreadsheet recalculates, the new random values of the inputs produce new values of the outputs. This is the essence of simulation—seeing how outputs vary as random inputs change.

### Excel Tip: *Recalculation Key*

*The easiest way to make a spreadsheet recalculate is to press the F9 key, which is often called the recalc key.*

Technically speaking, we do not actually enter random numbers in input cells; we enter *probability distributions*. In general, a probability distribution indicates the possible values of a variable and the probabilities of these values. As a very simple example, we might indicate by an appropriate formula (to be described later) that we want a probability distribution with possible values 50 and 100, and corresponding probabilities 0.7 and 0.3. The effect of this is that if we then press the F9 key repeatedly and watch this input cell, we will see the value 50 about 70% of the time and the value 100 about 30% of the time. No other values besides 50 and 100 will appear.

When we enter a given probability distribution in a random input cell, we are describing the possible values and the probabilities of these values that we believe mirror reality. There are many probability distributions to choose from, and we should always attempt to choose an appropriate distribution for each specific problem. This is not necessarily an easy task. Therefore, we address it in this section by answering several key questions:

- What types of probability distributions are available, and why do we choose one probability distribution rather than another in an actual simulation model?
- Which probability distributions can we use in simulation models, and how do we invoke them with Excel formulas?

We also address one additional question: Does the choice of input probability distribution really matter—that is, does it have a large effect on the *outputs* from the simulation?

### FUNDAMENTAL INSIGHT

#### Basic Elements of Spreadsheet Simulation

A spreadsheet simulation model requires three elements: (1) a method for entering random quantities from specified probability distributions in input cells, (2) the usual types of Excel formulas for relating outputs to inputs, and (3) the ability to make the spreadsheet recalculate many times and capture the resulting outputs for statistical analysis. Excel has some capabilities for performing steps (1) and (3), but Excel add-ins such as @RISK provide much better tools for performing these steps.

## Types of Probability Distributions

Think of a toolbox that contains the probability distributions you know and understand. As you gain more experience in simulation modeling, you will naturally add probability distributions to this toolbox that you can then use in *future* simulation models. We begin by adding a few useful probability distributions to this toolbox. However, before adding any specific distributions, we look at some important general characteristics of probability distributions. These include the following categorizations:

- Discrete versus continuous
- Symmetric versus skewed
- Bounded versus unbounded
- Positive versus not necessarily positive

## Discrete versus Continuous

A probability distribution is **discrete** if it has a finite number of possible values.[1] For example, if you throw two dice and look at the sum of the faces showing, there are only 11 discrete possibilities: the integers 2 through 12. In contrast, a probability distribution is **continuous** if its possible values are essentially some continuum. An example is the amount of rain that falls during a month in Indiana. It could be any nonnegative decimal value.

The graph of a discrete distribution is a series of spikes, as shown in Figure 11.1.[2] The height of each spike is the probability of the corresponding value. That's all there is to it. You can have as many possible values as you like, and their probabilities can be any positive numbers that sum to 1.

**Figure 11.1**

A Typical Discrete Probability Distribution

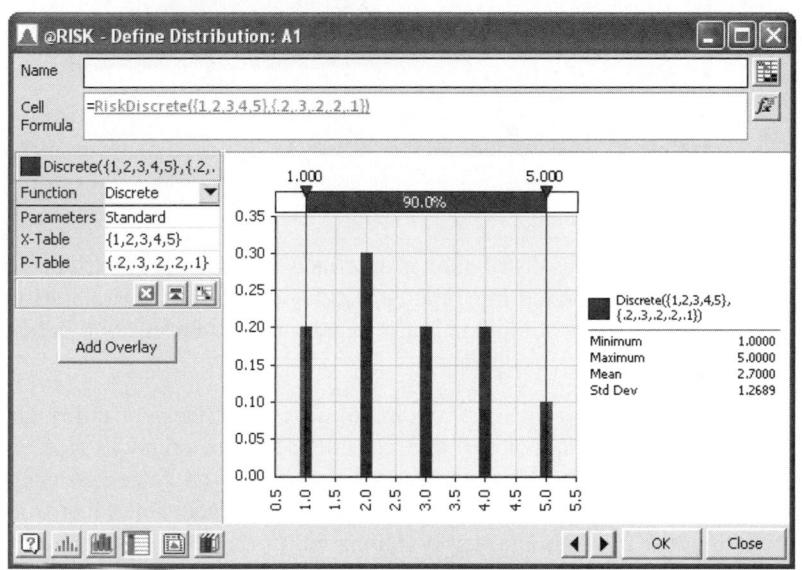

*The heights above a density function are not probabilities, but they still indicate the relative likelihoods of the possible values.*

In contrast, a continuous distribution is characterized by a **density function,** a smooth curve as shown in Figure 11.2. There are two important properties of density functions. First, the height of the density curve above any point is not actually a probability; that is, it is not necessarily between 0 and 1. However, the heights still indicate relative likelihoods. For example, the height of the density above 12 is about 5 times as large as the height above 6 in the figure. Therefore, a random number from this distribution is about 5 times as likely to be near 12 as to be near 6.

Second, probabilities for continuous distributions are found as areas under the density curve. Specifically, the probability of being between 6 and 12 in Figure 11.2 is the shaded area between the vertical lines at 6 and 12. Density functions are always scaled so that the *entire* area under the density is 1. This means that any particular area, such as the area between 6 and 12, is always a value between 0 and 1, that is, a probability. We will not actually calculate areas under particular density functions because this typically requires integral calculus. However, it is important that you understand conceptually that probabilities are areas under the density.

---

[1] Actually, a discrete variable can have a "countably infinite" number of possible values, such as all the nonnegative integers 0, 1, 2, and so on. However, this is not an important distinction for practical applications.
[2] This figure and several later figures are screenshots from Palisade's @RISK program. This program, which is included on the Palisade CD-ROM that accompanies this book, is discussed later in the chapter.

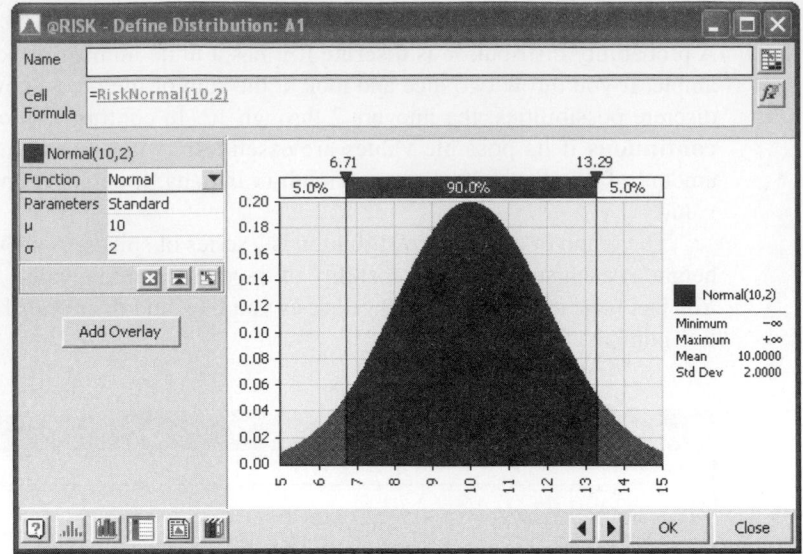

**Figure 11.2**

A Typical Continuous Probability Distribution

---

A continuous distribution is described by a **density function.** Heights above the density function indicate relative likelihoods but are not necessarily values between 0 and 1. Probabilities are found as areas under the density function.

---

Sometimes it is convenient to treat a discrete probability distribution as continuous, and vice versa. For example, consider a student's random score on an exam that has 1000 possible points. If the grader scores each exam to the nearest integer, then even though the score is really discrete with many possible integer values, it is probably more convenient to model its distribution as a continuum. Continuous probability distributions are typically more intuitive and easier to work with than discrete distributions in cases such as this, where there are many possible values. In contrast, we sometimes discretize continuous distributions for simplicity. As an example, consider a random interest rate with possible values in the continuum from 5% to 15%. We might model this with a discrete probability distribution with a few possible values such as 5%, 7.5%, 10%, 12.5%, and 15%. Although this is not as common as going the other way—from discrete to continuous—simulation modelers often do this. (As discussed in the previous chapter, discretizing continuous distributions is more common when building decision trees.)

*A discretized approximation to a continuous distribution uses a few representative values with appropriate probabilities.*

### Symmetric versus Skewed

A probability distribution is **symmetric** around some point if the distribution to the left of the point is a mirror image of the distribution to the right of the point. Otherwise, the distribution is **skewed.** If a distribution is skewed, then we say it is **skewed to the right** (or **positively skewed**) if the longer tail is the right tail. Otherwise, we say the distribution is **skewed to the left** (or **negatively skewed**). The distribution in Figure 11.2 is symmetric, the distribution in Figure 11.3 is skewed to the right, and the distribution in Figure 11.4 is skewed to the left.

We typically choose between a symmetric and skewed distribution on the basis of realism. For example, if we want to model a student's score on a 100-point exam, we should probably choose a left-skewed distribution. This is because a few poorly prepared students typically pull down the curve. On the other hand, if we want to model the time it takes to serve a customer at a bank, we should probably choose a right-skewed distribution. This is

**Figure 11.3**

A Positively Skewed Probability Distribution

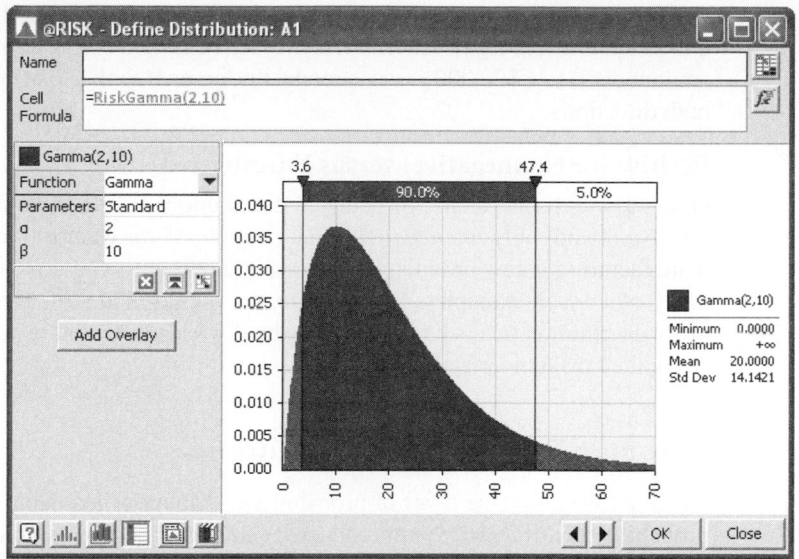

**Figure 11.4**

A Negatively Skewed Probability Distribution

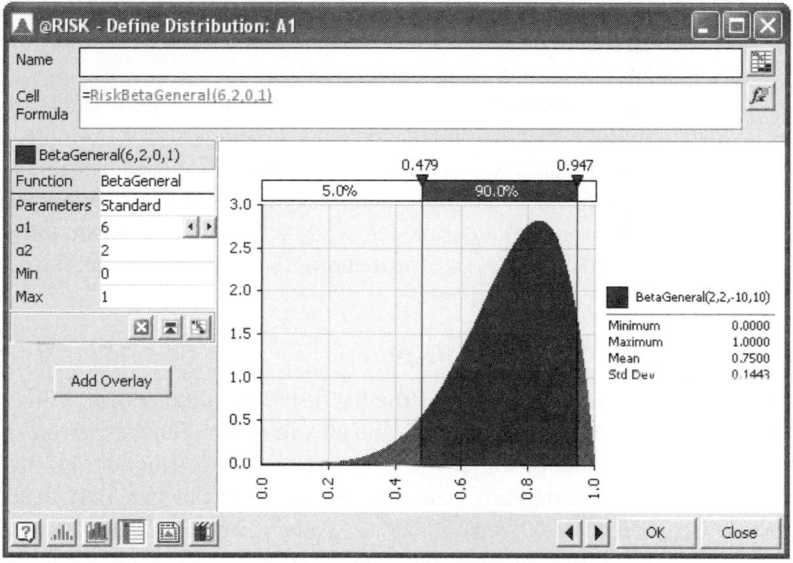

because most customers take only a minute or two, but a few customers take a long time. Finally, if we want to model the monthly return on a stock, we can probably choose a distribution symmetric around 0, reasoning that the stock return is just as likely to be positive as negative, and there is no obvious reason for skewness one way or the other.

### Bounded versus Unbounded

A probability distribution is **bounded** if there are values $A$ and $B$ so that no possible value can be less than $A$ or greater than $B$. The value $A$ is then the *minimum* possible value, and the value $B$ is the *maximum* possible value. The distribution is **unbounded** if there are no such bounds. Actually, a distribution can be bounded in one direction but not the other. As an example, the distribution of scores on a 100-point exam is bounded between 0 and 100. In contrast, the distribution of the amount of damages Mr. Jones submits to his insurance company in a year is bounded on the left by 0, but there is no natural upper bound. Therefore, we might model this amount with a distribution that is bounded on the left by 0 but is unbounded on the right. Alternatively, if we believe there is no possibility of a damage amount over, say, $20,000, we can model this amount with a distribution that is bounded in both directions.

### Positive (or Nonnegative) versus Unrestricted

One important special case of bounded distributions involves variables that are inherently *positive* (or possibly *nonnegative*). For example, if we want to model the random cost of manufacturing a new product, we know for sure that this cost must be positive. There are many other such examples. In each case, we should model the randomness with a probability distribution that is bounded below by 0. We do not want to allow negative values because they make no practical sense.

## Common Probability Distributions

Think of the **Probability Distributions. xlsx** file as a "dictionary" of the most commonly used distributions. Keep it handy for reference.

Now that we know the *types* of probability distributions available, we add some common probability distributions to our toolbox. To help you learn and explore these, we developed the file **Probability Distributions.xlsx**. Each sheet in this file illustrates a particular probability distribution by describing the general characteristics of the distribution; indicating how you can generate random numbers from the distribution, either with Excel's built-in functions or with @RISK functions; and including histograms of these distributions from simulated data to illustrate their shapes.[3]

Each of the following distributions is really a *family* of distributions. Each member of the family is specified by one or more parameters. For example, there is not a *single* normal distribution; there is a normal distribution for each possible mean and standard deviation we specify. Therefore, when we try to find the most appropriate input probability distribution in a simulation model, we first have to choose the most appropriate family, and then we have to select the most appropriate member of that family.

## Uniform Distribution

The uniform distribution is the flat "equally likely" distribution.

The uniform distribution is the flat distribution illustrated in Figure 11.5. It is bounded by a minimum and a maximum, and all values between these two extremes are equally likely. You can think of this as the "I have no idea" distribution. For example, a manager might realize that a building cost is uncertain. If she can state only that, "I know the cost will be between $20,000 and $30,000, but other than this, I have no idea what the cost will be," then a uniform distribution from $20,000 to $30,000 is a natural choice. However, even though some people do use the uniform distribution in such cases, these situations are not very common or realistic. If the manager really thinks about it, she can probably provide more information about the uncertain cost, such as, "The cost is more likely to be close to $25,000 than to either of the extremes." Then some distribution other than the uniform is more appropriate.

The RAND function is Excel's "building block" function for generating random numbers.

Regardless of whether the uniform distribution is an appropriate candidate as an input distribution, it is important for another reason. All spreadsheet packages are capable of generating random numbers uniformly distributed between 0 and 1. These are the "building blocks" of all simulated random numbers, in that random numbers from all other probability distributions are generated from these building blocks.

---

[3] In later sections of this chapter, and all through the next chapter, we discuss much of @RISK's functionality. For this section, the only functionality we use is @RISK's collection of functions, such as RISKNORMAL and RISK-TRIANG, for generating random numbers from various probability distributions. You can skim the details of these functions for now and refer back to them as necessary in later sections.

**Figure 11.5**

The Uniform
Distribution

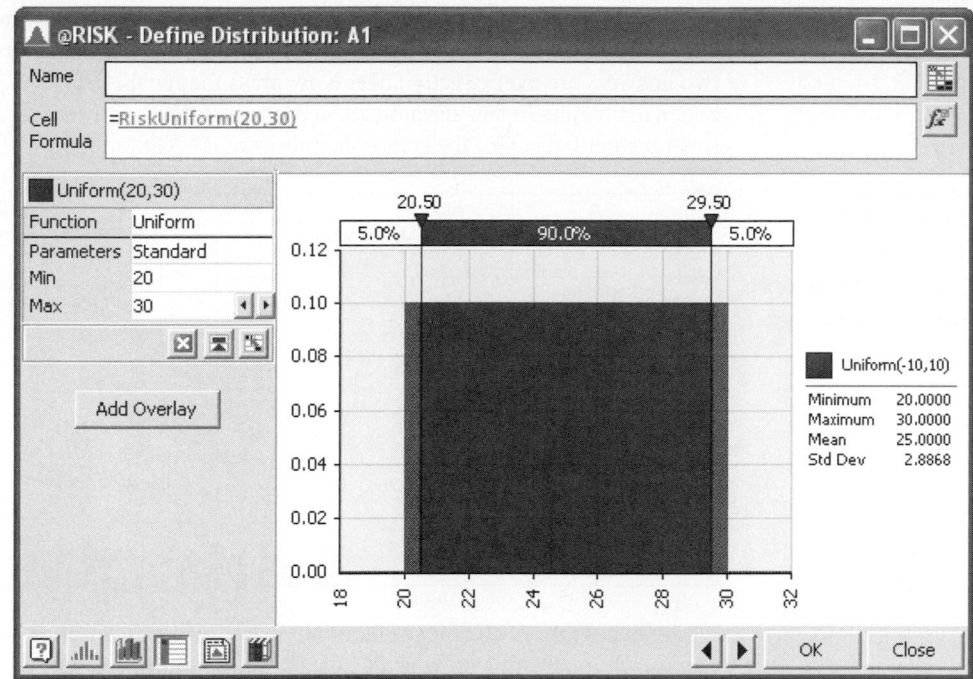

In Excel, we can generate a random number between 0 and 1 by entering the formula

**=RAND()**

in any cell. (The parentheses to the right of RAND indicate that this is an Excel function with no arguments. These parentheses *must* be included.)

**Excel Function:** *RAND*
*To generate a random number equally likely to be anywhere between 0 and 1, enter the formula =RAND() into any cell. Press the F9 key to make it change randomly.*

In addition to being between 0 and 1, the numbers created by this function have two properties that we would expect "random" numbers to have:

- **Uniform property.** Each time we enter the RAND function in a cell, all numbers between 0 and 1 have the same chance of occurring. This means that approximately 10% of the numbers generated by the RAND function are between 0.0 and 0.1; 10% of the numbers are between 0.65 and 0.75; 60% of the numbers are between 0.20 and 0.80; and so on. This property explains why we say the random numbers are *uniformly* distributed between 0 and 1.

- **Independence property.** Different random numbers generated by the computer are *probabilistically independent*. This implies that when we generate a random number in cell A5, say, it has no effect on the values of any other random numbers generated in the spreadsheet. For example, if one call to the RAND function yields a large random number such as 0.98, there is no reason to suspect that the *next* call to RAND will yield an abnormally small (or large) random number; the second random number is unaffected by the value of the first random number.

To illustrate the RAND function, open a new workbook, enter the formula =RAND() in cell A4, and copy it to the range A4:A503. This generates 500 random numbers. Figure 11.6

displays the values we obtained. However, when you try this on your PC, you will undoubtedly obtain *different* random numbers. This is an inherent characteristic of simulation—no two answers are ever exactly alike. Now press the recalc (F9) key. All of the random numbers will change. In fact, each time you press the F9 key or do anything to make your spreadsheet recalculate, all of the cells containing the RAND function will change.

**Figure 11.6**

Uniformly Distributed Random Numbers Generated by the RAND Function

|     | A | B | C | D |
|-----|---|---|---|---|
| 1 | 500 random numbers from RAND function | | | |
| 2 | | | | |
| 3 | Random # | | | |
| 4 | 0.639741246 | | | |
| 5 | 0.977449085 | | | |
| 6 | 0.826336662 | | | |
| 7 | 0.794236038 | | | |
| 8 | 0.326052217 | | | |
| 9 | 0.540446013 | | | |
| 10 | 0.012582316 | | | |
| 501 | 0.868540879 | | | |
| 502 | 0.297930515 | | | |
| 503 | 0.960969187 | | | |

A histogram of the 500 random numbers for our illustration is shown in Figure 11.7. (Again, If you try this on your PC, the shape of your histogram will not be identical to the one shown in Figure 11.7 because it will be based on *different* random numbers.) From property 1, we expect *equal* numbers of observations in the 10 categories. Although the heights of the bars are not exactly equal, the differences are due to chance—not to a faulty random number generator.

**Excel Tool:** *Creating a Histogram*

*A histogram, also called a frequency chart, indicates the number of observations in each of several user-defined categories. We can create a histogram similar to the one in Figure 11.7 with Excel's FREQUENCY function and its chart tools. We explain the somewhat involved procedure in the appendix to this chapter. However, creating histograms with an Excel add-in such as @RISK (or the StatTools add-in that accompanies the book) is considerably easier. We explain how to create histograms in @RISK in Section 11.5.*

**Figure 11.7**

Histogram of the 500 Random Numbers Generated by the RAND Function

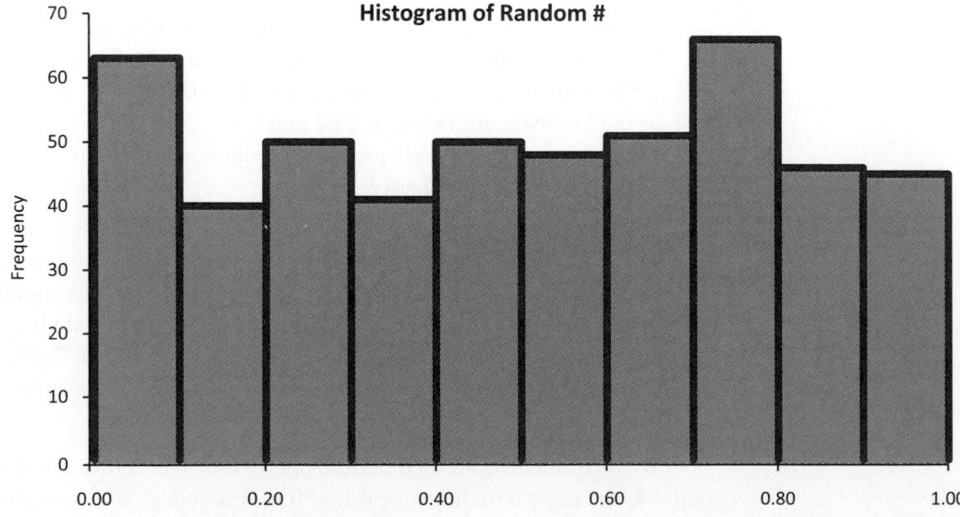

### Technical Excel Note: *Pseudo-random Numbers*

*The "random" numbers generated by the RAND function (or by any other package's random number generator) are not really random. They are sometimes called **pseudo-random numbers.** Each successive random number follows the previous random number by a complex arithmetic operation. If you happen to know the details of this arithmetic operation, you can predict ahead of time exactly which random numbers will be generated by the RAND function. This is very different from using a "true" random mechanism, such as spinning a wheel, to get the next random number—a mechanism that would be impractical to implement on a computer. Mathematicians and computer scientists have studied many ways to produce random numbers that have the two properties we just discussed, and they have developed many competing random number generators such as the RAND function in Excel. The technical details need not concern us. The important point is that these random number generators produce numbers that are useful for simulation modeling.*

Generating a uniformly distributed random number with a minimum and maximum other than 0 and 1 is easy. For example, the formula

**=200+100*RAND()**

generates a number uniformly distributed between 200 and 300. (Make sure you see why.) Alternatively, we could use the @RISK formula[4]

**=RISKUNIFORM(200,300)**

You can take a look at this and other properties of the uniform distribution on the Uniform sheet in the **Probability Distributions.xlsx** file (see Figure 11.8).

**Figure 11.8**
Properties of Uniform Distribution

| | A | B | C | D | E | F | G | H |
|---|---|---|---|---|---|---|---|---|
| 1 | **Uniform distribution** | | | | | | | |
| 2 | | | | | | | | |
| 3 | **Characteristics** | | | This is a flat distribution between two | | | | |
| 4 | Continuous | | | values, labeled here MinVal and MaxVal. Note that | | | | |
| 5 | Symmetric | | | if MinVal=0 and MaxVal=1, then we can just use | | | | |
| 6 | Bounded in both directions | | | Excel's RAND function. | | | | |
| 7 | Not necessarily positive (depends on bounds) | | | | | | | |
| 8 | | | | | | | | |
| 9 | **Parameters** | | | | | | | |
| 10 | MinVal | 50 | | | | | | |
| 11 | MaxVal | 100 | | | | | | |
| 12 | | | | | | | | |
| 13 | **Excel** | | **Example** | | | | | |
| 14 | =MinVal + (MaxVal-MinVal)*RAND() | | 59.903648 | | | | | |
| 15 | | | | | | | | |
| 16 | **@RISK** | | | | | | | |
| 17 | =RISKUNIFORM(MinVal,MaxVal) | | 80.584134 | | | | | |

### @RISK Function: *RISKUNIFORM*

*To generate a random number from any uniform distribution, enter the formula = RISKUNIFORM(MinVal,MaxVal) in any cell. Here, MinVal and MaxVal are the minimum and maximum possible values. Note that if MinVal is 0 and MaxVal is 1, this function is equivalent to Excel's RAND function.*

---

[4] As we have done with other Excel functions, we capitalize the @RISK functions, such as RISKUNIFORM, in the text. However, this is not necessary when you enter the formulas in Excel.

## Freezing Random Numbers

The automatic recalculation of random numbers can be useful sometimes and annoying other times. In some situations, we want the random numbers to stay fixed; that is, we want to "freeze" them at their current values. The following three-step method accomplishes this:

1. Select the range that you want to freeze, such as A4:A503 in Figure 11.6.
2. Press Ctrl+C to copy this range.

*Random numbers that have been frozen do not change when you press the F9 key.*

3. With the same range still selected, select the Paste Values option from the Paste dropdown on the Home ribbon. This procedure pastes a copy of the range onto itself, except that the entries are now *numbers*, not formulas. Therefore, whenever the spreadsheet recalculates, these numbers do not change.

Each sheet in the **Probability Distributions.xlsx** file has a list of 500 random numbers that have been frozen. We created the histograms in the sheets based on the frozen random numbers. However, we encourage you to enter "live" random numbers in column B over our frozen ones and see how the histogram changes when you press F9. (Again, see the appendix to this chapter for instructions on how to create histograms.)

## USING @RISK TO EXPLORE PROBABILITY DISTRIBUTIONS[5]

The **Probability Distributions.xlsx** file illustrates a few frequently used probability distributions, and it shows the formulas required to generate random numbers from these distributions. Another option is to use Palisade's @RISK add-in, which allows you to experiment with probability distributions. Essentially, it allows you to see the shapes of various distributions and calculate probabilities for them, all in a graphical and very user-friendly interface.

To run @RISK, click on the Windows Start button, go to the Programs tab, locate the Palisades DecisionTools suite, and select @RISK. Select a blank cell in your worksheet, and then click on Define Distributions on the @RISK ribbon. Double-click on one of the distributions (we chose uniform, as shown in Figure 11.9) and change the parameters to the ones you want (we chose a minimum of 75 and a maximum of 150). Now you see the shape of the distribution and a few summary measures to the right. For example, you see that the mean and standard deviation of this uniform distribution are 112.5 and 21.651.

From here, everything is interactive. Suppose you want to find the probability that a value from this distribution is less than 95. You can drag the left-hand "slider" in the diagram (the vertical line with the triangle at the top) to the position 95, as shown in Figure 11.9. You see immediately that the left-hand probability is 0.267. Similarly, if you want the probability that a value from this distribution is greater than 125, you can drag the right-hand slider to the position 125 to see that the required probability is 0.3333.

---

[5] Palisade previously offered a stand-alone program called RISKview for exploring probability distributions, and we discussed it in the previous edition. However, Palisade has discontinued RISKview and instead incorporated its functionality into @RISK.

**Figure 11.9**

@RISK Illustration
of Uniform
Distribution

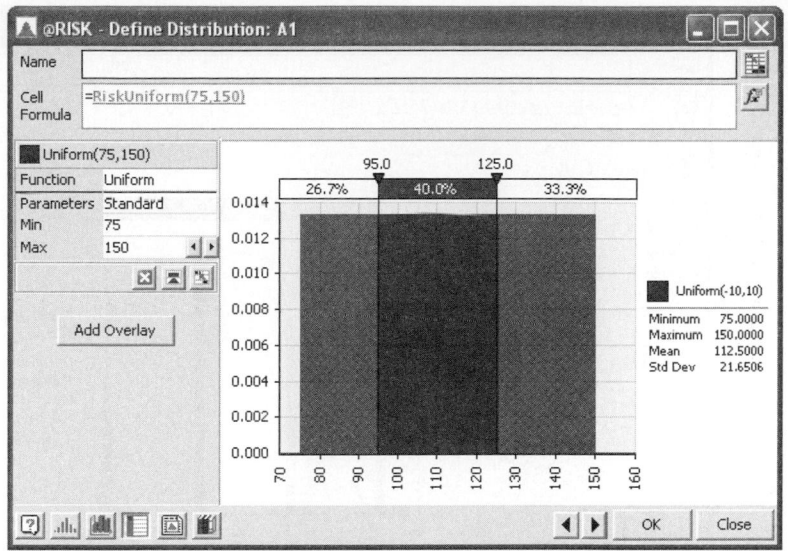

*The interactive capabilities of @RISK's Define Distributions window, with its sliders, make it perfect for finding probabilities or percentiles for any given distribution.*

You can also enter probabilities instead of values. For example, if you want the value so that there is probability 0.10 to the left of it—the 10th percentile—enter 10% in the left space above the chart. You will see that the corresponding value is 82.5. Similarly, if you want the value so that there is probability 0.10 to the right of it, enter 10% in the right space above the chart, and you will see that the corresponding value is 142.5.

We like @RISK's Define Distributions window because it is quick and easy. We urge you to use it and experiment with some of its options. By the way, you can click on the fifth button from the left at the bottom of this window to copy the chart into an Excel worksheet. However, you then lose the interactive capabilities, such as moving the sliders.

## Discrete Distribution

A discrete distribution is useful for many situations, either when the uncertain quantity is not really continuous (the number of televisions demanded, for example) or when you want a discrete approximation to a continuous variable. All you need to do is specify the possible values and their probabilities, making sure that the probabilities sum to 1. Because of this flexibility in specifying values and probabilities, discrete distributions can have practically any shape.

*@RISK's way of generating a discrete random number is much simpler and more intuitive than Excel's "native" method that requires cumulative probabilities and a lookup function.*

As an example, suppose a manager estimates that the demand for a particular brand of television during the coming month will be 10, 15, 20, or 25 with respective probabilities 0.1, 0.3, 0.4, and 0.2. This is a typical discrete distribution, and it is illustrated in Figure 11.10.

The Discrete sheet of the **Probability Distributions.xlsx** file indicates how to work with a discrete distribution (see Figure 11.11). As you see, there are two different ways to generate a random number from this distribution in Excel. We discuss the "Excel" way in detail in Section 11.4. For now, we simply mention that this is one case (of many) where it is much easier to generate random numbers with @RISK functions than with built-in Excel functions. Assuming that @RISK is loaded, all you need to do is enter the function RISKDIS-CRETE with two arguments: a list of possible values, and a list of their probabilities, as in

**=RISKDISCRETE(B11:B14,C11:C14)**

The Excel way, which requires cumulative probabilities and a lookup table, requires more work, is harder to remember, and is certainly less intuitive.

**Figure 11.10**

Discrete Distribution
(from @RISK)

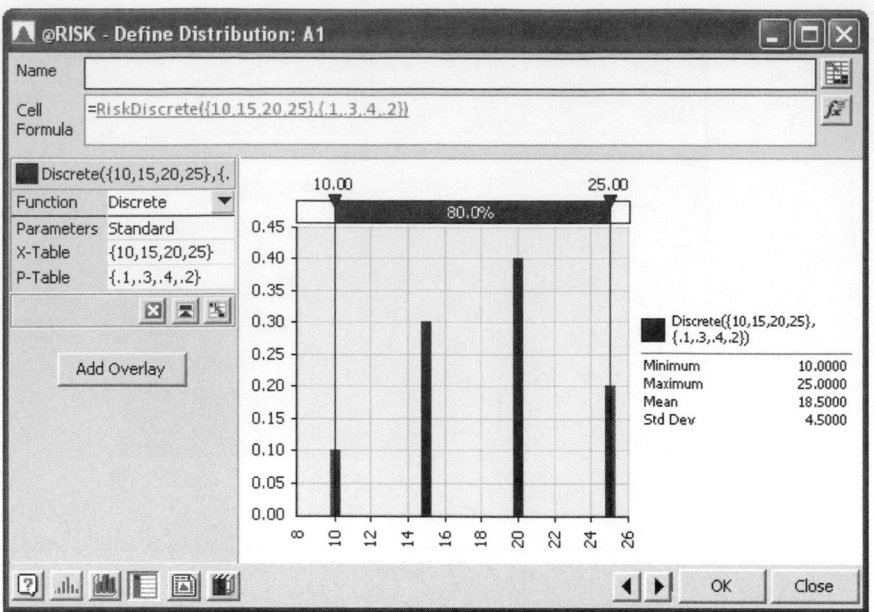

**Figure 11.11**

Properties of
a Discrete
Distribution

|    | A | B | C | D | E | F | G | H | I |
|----|---|---|---|---|---|---|---|---|---|
| 1  | **General discrete distribution** | | | | | | | | |
| 2  | | | | | | | | | |
| 3  | **Characteristics** | | | | | | | | |
| 4  | Discrete | | | | This can have any shape, depending | | | | |
| 5  | Can be symmetric or skewed (or bumpy, i.e., basically any shape) | | | | on the list of possible values and their | | | | |
| 6  | Bounded in both directions | | | | probabilities. | | | | |
| 7  | Not necessarily positive (depends on possible values) | | | | | | | | |
| 8  | | | | | | | | | |
| 9  | **Parameters** | | | | Lookup table required for Excel method | | | | |
| 10 | | Values | Probabilities | | CumProb | Value | | | |
| 11 | | 10 | 0.1 | | 0 | 10 | | | |
| 12 | | 15 | 0.3 | | 0.1 | 15 | | | |
| 13 | | 20 | 0.4 | | 0.4 | 20 | | | |
| 14 | | 25 | 0.2 | | 0.8 | 25 | | | |
| 15 | | | | | | | | | |
| 16 | **Excel** | | **Example** | | | | | | |
| 17 | =VLOOKUP(RAND(),LookupTable,2) | | 10 | | | | | | |
| 18 | | | | | | | | | |
| 19 | **@RISK** | | | | | | | | |
| 20 | =RISKDISCRETE(Values,Probs) | | 20 | | | | | | |

### @RISK Function: *RISKDISCRETE*

*To generate a random number from any discrete probability distribution, enter the formula =RISKDISCRETE(*valRange,probRange*) into any cell. Here* valRange *is the range where the possible values are stored, and* probRange *is the range where their probabilities are stored.*

*The selected input distributions for any simulation model reflect historical data and an analyst's best judgment as to what will happen in the future.*

At this point, a relevant question is, Why would a manager choose this particular discrete distribution? First, it is clearly an approximation. After all, if demands of 20 and 25 are possible, then demands such as 22 or 24 are probably also possible. Here, the manager approximates a discrete distribution with *many* possible values—all integers from 0 to 50, say—with a discrete distribution with a few representative values. This is common in simulation modeling. Second, where do the probabilities come from? They are probably a blend of historical data (perhaps demand was near 15 in 30% of previous months) and the manager's subjective feelings about demand *next* month.

## Normal Distribution

*Normally distributed random numbers are almost always within three standard deviations of the mean.*

The normal distribution is the familiar bell-shaped curve that is the hallmark of statistics (see Figure 11.12). The normal distribution is also useful in simulation modeling as a continuous input distribution, although it is not always the *most* appropriate. The normal distribution is symmetric, which can be a drawback when a skewed distribution is more realistic. Also, it allows negative values, which are not appropriate in many situations. For example, the demand for televisions cannot be negative. Fortunately, this possibility of negative values is often not a problem. The two parameters of a normal distribution are its mean and standard deviation. Suppose you generate a normally distributed random number with mean 100 and standard deviation 20. Then as you might recall from statistics, there is almost no chance of having values more than 3 standard deviations to the left of the mean. Therefore, negative values will virtually never occur in this situation.

**Figure 11.12**

Normal Distribution
(from @RISK)

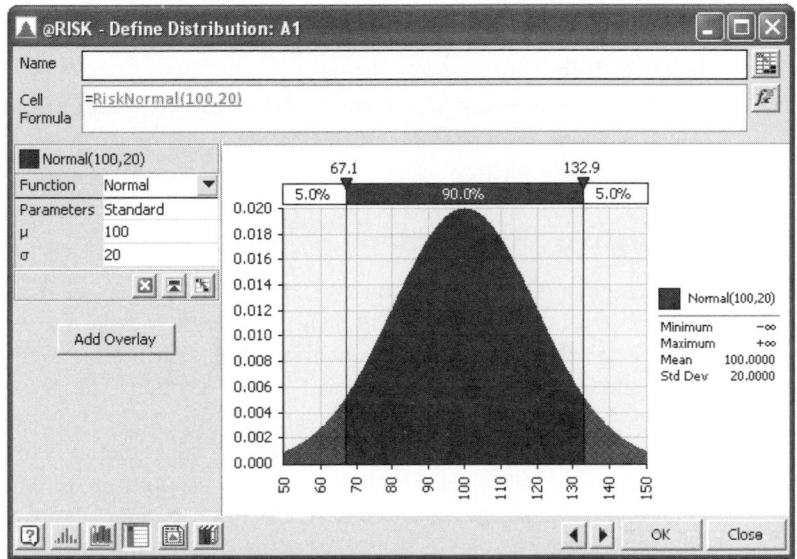

A tip-off that a normal distribution might be an appropriate candidate for an input variable is a statement such as, "We believe the most likely value of demand is 100, the chances are about 95% that demand will be no more than 40 units on either of side of the most likely value, and the shape of the distribution is symmetric around the most likely value." Because a normally distributed value is within 2 standard deviations of its mean with probability 0.95, this statement translates easily to a mean of 100 and a standard deviation of 20. We do not imply that a normal distribution is the *only* candidate for the distribution of demand, but the statement naturally leads us to this distribution.

The Normal sheet in the **Probability Distributions.xlsx** file indicates how we can generate normally distributed random numbers in Excel, either with or without @RISK (see Figure 11.13). This is one case where an add-in is not really necessary—the formula

**=NORMINV(RAND(),*Mean,Stdev*)**

always works. Still, it is not as easy to remember as @RISK's

**=RISKNORMAL(*Mean,Stdev*)**

formula.

Figure 11.13

Properties of the
Normal Distribution

|   | A | B | C | D | E | F | G | H |
|---|---|---|---|---|---|---|---|---|
| 1 | **Normal distribution** | | | | | | | |
| 2 | | | | | | | | |
| 3 | **Characteristics** | | | | | | | |
| 4 | Continuous | | | This is the familiar bell-shaped curve, defined by | | | | |
| 5 | Symmetric (bell-shaped) | | | two parameters: the mean and the standard | | | | |
| 6 | Unbounded in both directions | | | deviation. | | | | |
| 7 | Is both positive and negative | | | | | | | |
| 8 | | | | | | | | |
| 9 | **Parameters** | | | | | | | |
| 10 | Mean | 100 | | | | | | |
| 11 | Stdev | 10 | | | | | | |
| 12 | | | | | | | | |
| 13 | **Excel** | | **Example** | | | | | |
| 14 | =NORMINV(RAND(),Mean,Stdev) | | 90.18632693 | | | | | |
| 15 | | | | | | | | |
| 16 | **@RISK** | | | | | | | |
| 17 | =RISKNORMAL(Mean,Stdev) | | 89.35430818 | | | | | |

### @RISK Function: *RISKNORMAL*

*To generate a normally distributed random number, enter the formula =RISKNORMAL (Mean,Stdev) in any cell. Here, Mean and Stdev are the mean and standard deviation of the normal distribution.*

## Triangular Distribution

*A triangular distribution is a good choice in many simulation models because it is flexible and its parameters are easy to understand.*

The triangular distribution is somewhat similar to the normal distribution in that its density function rises to some point and then falls, but it is more flexible and intuitive than the normal distribution. Therefore, the triangular distribution is an excellent candidate for many continuous input variables, and we use it often. The shape of a triangular density function is literally a triangle, as shown in Figure 11.14. It is specified by three easy-to-understand parameters: the minimum possible value, the most likely value, and the maximum possible value. The high point of the triangle is above the most likely value. Therefore, if a manager states that, "We believe the most likely development cost is $1.5 million, and we don't believe the development cost could possibly be less than $1.2 million or greater than $2.1 million," the triangular distribution with these three parameters is a

Figure 11.14

Triangular Distribution (from @RISK)

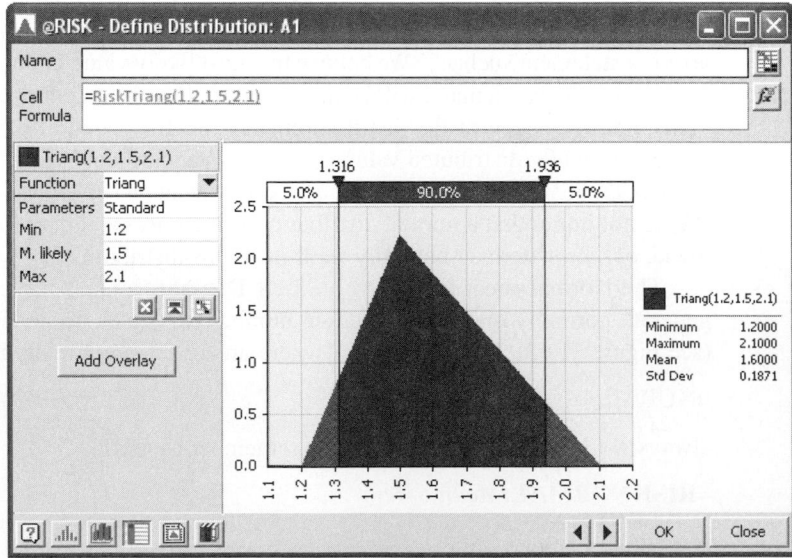

natural choice. Note that, as in this numerical example, the triangular distribution can be skewed if the mostly likely value is closer to one extreme than the other. Of course, it can also be symmetric if the most likely value is right in the middle.

The Triangular sheet of the **Probability Distributions.xlsx** file indicates how to generate random values from this distribution (see Figure 11.15). As we see, there is no way to do it with native Excel (at least not without a lot of trickery). However, it is easy with @RISK, using the RISKTRIANG function, as in

**=RISKTRIANG(B10,B11,B12)**

All you need to feed this function are the minimum value, the most likely value, and the maximum value—in this order and separated by commas. We use this function in many of our examples. Just remember that it has an abbreviated spelling: **RISKTRIANG**, not RISKTRIANGULAR.

**Figure 11.15**
Properties of the Triangular Distribution

| | A | B | C | D | E | F | G | H | I |
|---|---|---|---|---|---|---|---|---|---|
| 1 | Triangular distribution | | | | | | | | |
| 2 | | | | | | | | | |
| 3 | Characteristics | | | The density of this distribution is literally a triangle. The "top" of the | | | | | |
| 4 | Continuous | | | triangle is above the most likely value, and the base of the triangle | | | | | |
| 5 | Can be symmetric or skewed in either direction | | | extends from the minimum value to the maximum value. It is | | | | | |
| 6 | Bounded in both directions | | | intuitive for nontechnical people because the three parameters are | | | | | |
| 7 | Not necessarily positive (depends on bounds) | | | meaningful. | | | | | |
| 8 | | | | | | | | | |
| 9 | Parameters | | | | | | | | |
| 10 | Min | 50 | | | | | | | |
| 11 | MostLikely | 85 | | | | | | | |
| 12 | Max | 100 | | | | | | | |
| 13 | | | | | | | | | |
| 14 | Excel | | | | | | | | |
| 15 | There is no easy way to do it. This is a case where we need an add-in. | | | | | | | | |
| 16 | | | | | | | | | |
| 17 | @RISK | | Example | | | | | | |
| 18 | =RISKTRIANG(Min,MostLikely,Max) | | 75.77332227 | | | | | | |

**@RISK Function: *RISKTRIANG***
*To generate a random number from a triangular distribution, enter the formula = RISKTRIANG(MinVal,MLVal,MaxVal) in any cell. Here, MinVal is the minimum possible value, MLVal is the most likely value, and MaxVal is the maximum value.*

## Binomial Distribution

*A random number from a binomial distribution indicates the number of "successes" in a certain number of identical "trials."*

The binomial distribution is a discrete distribution, but unlike the general discrete distribution we discussed previously, the binomial distribution applies to a very specific situation. This is when a number of independent and identical "trials" occur, where each trial results in a "success" or "failure," and we want to generate the random number of successes in these trials. There are two parameters of this distribution, usually labeled $n$ and $p$. Here, $n$ is the number of trials, and $p$ is the probability of success on each trial.

As an example, suppose an airline company sells 170 tickets for a flight and estimates that 80% of the people with tickets will show up for the flight. How many people will actually show up? You might answer that *exactly* 80% of 170, or 136 people, will show up, but this neglects the inherent randomness. A more realistic way to model this situation is to say that each of the 170 people, independently of one another, will show up with probability 0.8. Then the number of people who actually show up is binomially distributed with $n = 170$ and

$p = 0.8$. (This assumes independent behavior across passengers, which might not be the case, for example, if whole families either show up or don't.) This distribution is illustrated in Figure 11.16.

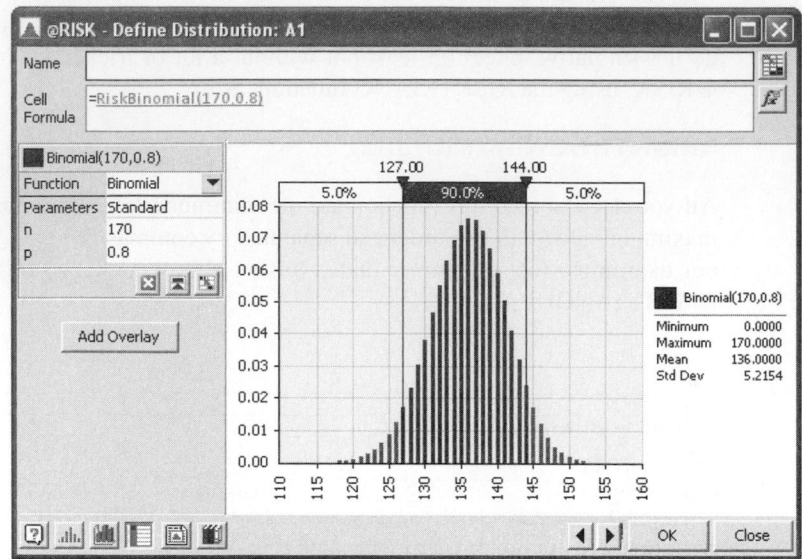

The Binomial sheet of the **Probability Distributions.xlsx** file indicates how to generate random numbers from this distribution (see Figure 11.17). Although we can do this with native Excel by using the built-in CRITBINOM function and the RAND function, it is not very intuitive or easy to remember. Clearly, the @RISK way is preferable. In the airline example, we can generate the number of people who show up with the formula

**=RISKBINOMIAL(170,0.8)**

Note that the histogram in this figure is approximately bell-shaped. This is no accident. When the number of trials $n$ is reasonably large and $p$ is not too close to 0 or 1, the binomial distribution can be well approximated by the normal distribution.

### @RISK Function: *RISKBINOMIAL*

*To generate a random number from a binomial distribution, enter the formula = RISKBINOMIAL(NTrials,PSuccess) in any cell. Here,* NTrials *is the number of trials, and* PSuccess *is the probability of a success on each trial.*

**Figure 11.17**

Properties of the Binomial Distribution

| | A | B | C | D | E | F | G | H |
|---|---|---|---|---|---|---|---|---|
| 1 | **Binomial distribution** | | | | | | | |
| 2 | | | | | | | | |
| 3 | **Characteristics** | | This distribution is of the number of "successes" in a | | | | | |
| 4 | Discrete | | given number of identical, independent trials, when the | | | | | |
| 5 | Can be symmetric or skewed | | probability of success is constant on each trial. | | | | | |
| 6 | Bounded below by 0, bounded above by Ntrials | | | | | | | |
| 7 | Nonnegative | | | | | | | |
| 8 | | | | | | | | |
| 9 | **Parameters** | | | | | | | |
| 10 | NTrials | 170 | | | | | | |
| 11 | PSuccess | 0.8 | | | | | | |
| 12 | | | | | | | | |
| 13 | **Excel** | | **Example** | | | | | |
| 14 | =CRITBINOM(NTrials,PSuccess,RAND()) | | 142 | | | | | |
| 15 | This will generate the number of successes in NTrials, with PSuccess as the probability of success on each trial | | | | | | | |
| 16 | | | | | | | | |
| 17 | **@RISK** | | | | | | | |
| 18 | =RISKBINOMIAL(NTrials,PSuccess) | | 134 | | | | | |

An important special case of the binomial distribution occurs when $n = 1$. In other words, there is only one trial and a certain event either occurs, with probability $p$, or it doesn't occur, with probability $1 - p$. We could use the RISKBINOMIAL function in this case, but there is an easier way. For example, suppose we want to simulate the flip of a fair coin, so that $p = 0.5$. Then we can use the formula **=IF(RAND()<0.5,1,0)**, where 1 corresponds to heads and 0 corresponds to tails (or vice versa). This works because there is a 50-50 chance that the value from RAND will be less than 0.5. Of course, this same type of formula can be used for any probability $p$, not just 0.5.

## Cumul and General Distributions

Two other less well-known, but very useful, distributions are known as the Cumul (short for cumulative) and General distributions. They are useful because the parameters they require are typically the values business people are most likely to understand and feel comfortable with. For this reason, we include a discussion of them in this section.

The Cumul distribution requires minimum and maximum possible values, as well as any number of percentiles. For example, suppose a manager states, in his assessment of the time to complete a project, that "I am sure it will take at least 10 weeks, I am sure that it will take no more than 25 weeks, I am 25% sure that it will take no more than 12 weeks, I am 50% sure that it will take no more than 15 weeks, and I am 75% sure that it will take no more than 19 weeks." Then he has expressed minimum and maximum values as 10 and 25, and he has expressed 25th, 50th, and 75th percentiles as 12, 15, and 19. Given this information, the Cumul distribution is a natural, and it can be implemented by @RISK in the form

**=RISKCUMUL(10,25,{12,15,19},{0.25,0.5,0.75})**

The first two arguments are the minimum and maximum, the next argument is a list of the percentiles in increasing order, and the last argument is a list of the corresponding cumulative probabilities. (If these values and lists are referenced in Excel ranges, the curly brackets should be omitted.) The corresponding distribution in @RISK appears in Figure 11.18. As we see, this density function is flat between the specified percentiles, but all possible values between the minimum and maximum are possible. More information about this distribution appears in the Cumul sheet of the **Probability Distributions.xlsx** file (see Figure 11.19).

**Figure 11.18**
Cumul Distribution

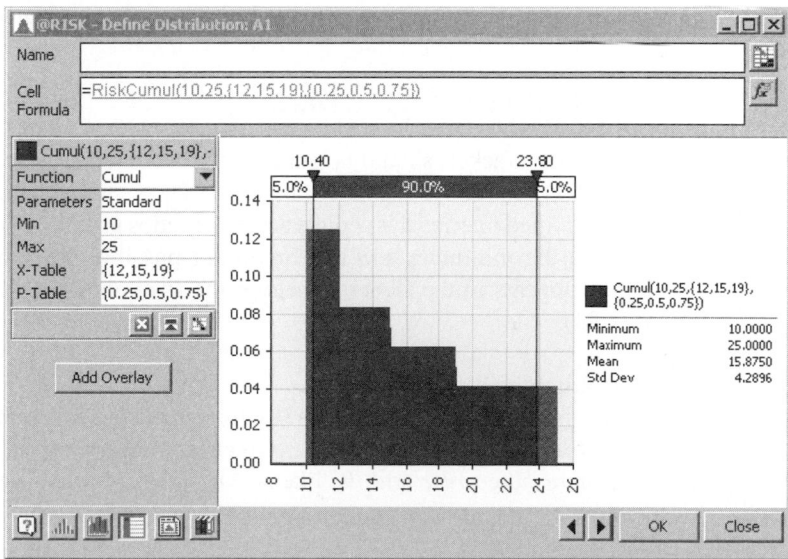

Figure 11.19

Properties of the
Cumul Distribution

| | A | B | C | D | E | F | G | H |
|---|---|---|---|---|---|---|---|---|
| 1 | "CUMUL" distribution | | | | | | | |
| 2 | | | | | | | | |
| 3 | Characteristics | | | This is a general, and natural, distribution when an | | | | |
| 4 | Continuous | | | assessment of an uncertain quantity is expressed as | | | | |
| 5 | Can have any shape | | | a minimum value, a maximum value, and selected | | | | |
| 6 | Bounded in both directions | | | percentiles (values and cumulative probabilities). | | | | |
| 7 | Not necessarily positive (depends on bounds) | | | | | | | |
| 8 | | | | | | | | |
| 9 | Parameters | | | | | | | |
| 10 | Percentiles | Value | Cum prob | | | | | |
| 11 | Min | 10 | 0 | | | | | |
| 12 | | 12 | 0.25 | | | | | |
| 13 | | 15 | 0.5 | | | | | |
| 14 | | 19 | 0.75 | | | | | |
| 15 | Max | 25 | 1 | | | | | |
| 16 | | | | | | | | |
| 17 | Excel | | | | | | | |
| 18 | There is no easy way to do it. This is a case where an add-in is required. | | | | | | | |
| 19 | | | | | | | | |
| 20 | @RISK | | Example | | | | | |
| 21 | =RISKCUMUL(Min,Max,intermediate values in increasing order,cumulative probabilities of intermediate values) | | | | | | | |
| 22 | | | 11.728 | | | | | |

### @RISK Function: *RISKCUMUL*

*To generate a random number with @RISK from the CUMUL distribution, use the syntax =RISKCUMUL(min,max,{valuelist},{problist}), where the* valuelist *are intermediate values in increasing order and the* problist *refers to the corresponding cumulative probabilities. If range references are used for these lists, omit the curly brackets.*

The General distribution also requires a minimum, a maximum, and a set of intermediate values. However, all the user needs to specify are the relative likelihoods of these intermediate values. Now, the manager might state that "I am sure it will take at least 10 weeks, I am sure that it will take no more than 25 weeks, I believe 12 weeks is half as likely as 15 weeks, and I believe 19 weeks is one-fourth as likely as 15 weeks." Then the relative likelihoods of the values of the intermediate values 12, 15, and 19 are in the ratios 2 to 4 to 1. (In our consulting experience with business managers, the General distribution really *is* a natural. Businesspeople tend to think in terms of relative likelihoods.) Given this information, the General distribution is a natural, and it can be implemented with @RISK in the form

### =RISKGENERAL(10,25,{12,15,19},{2,4,1})

Again, the curly brackets should be omitted if range references are used. The corresponding distribution in @RISK appears in Figure 11.20. As we see, the heights of this density above the specified intermediate points are in the ratios given: 2 to 4 to 1. However, *all* values between the minimum and maximum are possible. More information about this distribution appears in the General sheet of the **Probability Distributions.xlsx** file (see Figure 11.21).

### @RISK Function: *RISKGENERAL*

*To generate a random number with @RISK from the GENERAL distribution, use the syntax =RISKGENERAL(min,max,{valuelist},{likelist}), where the* valuelist *are intermediate values in increasing order and the* likelist *are the corresponding relative likelihoods. If range references are used for these lists, omit the curly brackets.*

**Figure 11.20**

General
Distribution

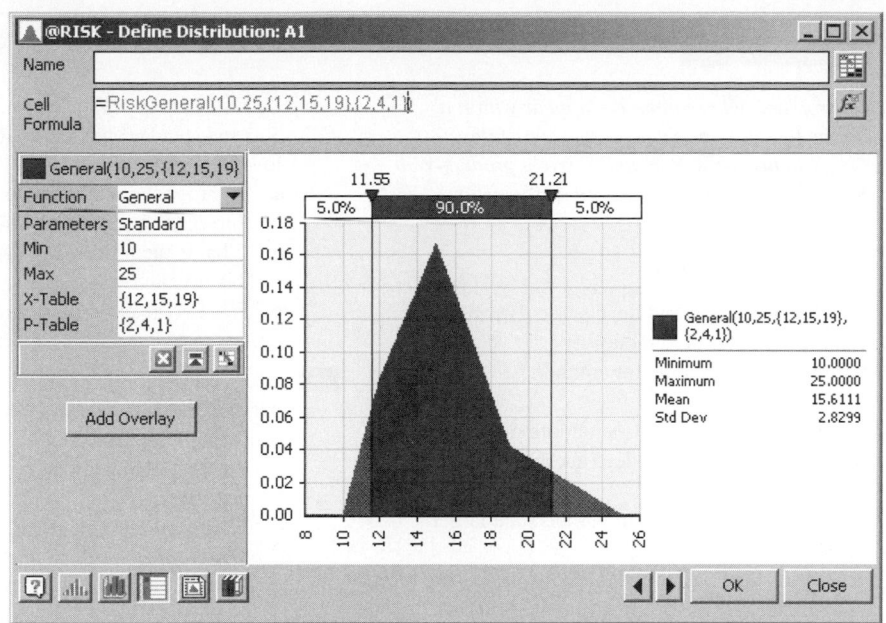

**Figure 11.21**  Properties of the General Distribution

|   | A | B | C | D | E | F | G | H |
|---|---|---|---|---|---|---|---|---|
| 1 | "GENERAL" distribution | | | | | | | |
| 2 | | | | | | | | |
| 3 | **Characteristics** | | | This is a general, and natural distribution, when an | | | | |
| 4 | Continuous | | | assessment of an uncertain quantity is expressed as a | | | | |
| 5 | Can have any shape | | | minimum value, a maximum value, and selected | | | | |
| 6 | Bounded in both directions | | | intermediate values and their relative likelihoods | | | | |
| 7 | Not necessarily positive (depends on bounds) | | | (which do not need to be between 0 and 1). | | | | |
| 8 | | | | | | | | |
| 9 | **Parameters** | | | | | | | |
| 10 | | Value | Relative likelihood | | | | | |
| 11 | Min | 10 | | | | | | |
| 12 | | 12 | 2 | | | | | |
| 13 | | 15 | 4 | | | | | |
| 14 | | 19 | 1 | | | | | |
| 15 | Max | 25 | | | | | | |
| 16 | | | | | | | | |
| 17 | **Excel method** | | | | | | | |
| 18 | There is no easy way to do it. | | | | | | | |
| 19 | | | | | | | | |
| 20 | **@RISK** | | **Example** | | | | | |
| 21 | =RISKGENERAL(Min,Max,intermediate values in increasing order,Relative likelihoods of intermediate values) | | | | | | | |
| 22 | | | 13.774 | | | | | |

Now you have a few commonly used distributions in your toolbox: uniform, discrete, normal, triangular, binomial, cumul, and general. This is plenty for now, but we will introduce a few others in future examples. The more distributions in your toolbox, the more flexible you can be in your simulation models.

# PROBLEMS

## Skill-Building Problems

1. Use the RAND function and the Copy command to generate a set of 100 random numbers.
   a. What fraction of the random numbers are smaller than 0.5?
   b. What fraction of the time is a random number less than 0.5 followed by a random number greater than 0.5?
   c. What fraction of the random numbers are larger than 0.8?
   d. Freeze these random numbers. However, instead of pasting them over the original random numbers, paste them onto a new range. Then press the F9 recalculate key. The original random numbers should change, but the pasted copy should remain the same.

2. Use Excel's functions (not @RISK) to generate 1000 random numbers from a normal distribution with mean 100 and standard deviation 10. Then freeze these random numbers.
   a. Calculate the mean and standard deviation of these random numbers. Are they approximately what you would expect?
   b. Of these random numbers, what fraction is with $k$ standard deviations of the mean? Answer for $k = 1$; for $k = 2$; for $k = 3$. Are the answers close to what they should be (as you learned in your statistics course)?
   c. Create a histogram of the random numbers using 10 to 15 categories of your choice. Does this histogram have approximately the shape you would expect? (See the Appendix to this chapter for instructions on creating a histogram.)

3. Use @RISK to draw a uniform distribution from 400 to 750. Then answer the following questions.
   a. What are the mean and standard deviation of this distribution?
   b. What are the 5th and 95th percentiles of this distribution?
   c. What is the probability that a random number from this distribution is less than 450?
   d. What is the probability that a random number from this distribution is greater than 650?
   e. What is the probability that a random number from this distribution is between 500 and 700?

4. Use @RISK to draw a normal distribution with mean 500 and standard deviation 100. Then answer the following questions.
   a. What is the probability that a random number from this distribution is less than 450?
   b. What is the probability that a random number from this distribution is greater than 650?
   c. What is the probability that a random number from this distribution is between 500 and 700?

5. Use @RISK to draw a triangular distribution with parameters 300, 500, and 900. Then answer the following questions.
   a. What are the mean and standard deviation of this distribution?
   b. What are the 5th and 95th percentiles of this distribution?
   c. What is the probability that a random number from this distribution is less than 450?
   d. What is the probability that a random number from this distribution is greater than 650?
   e. What is the probability that a random number from this distribution is between 500 and 700?

6. Use @RISK to draw a binomial distribution that results from 50 trials with probability of success 0.3 on each trial, and use it to answer the following questions.
   a. What are the mean and standard deviation of this distribution?
   b. You have to be more careful in interpreting @RISK probabilities with a discrete distribution such as this binomial. For example, if you move the left slider to 11, you should find a probability of 0.139 to the left of it. But is this the probability of "less than 11" or "less than or equal to 11"? One way to check is to use Excel's BINOMDIST function. The formula =BINOMDIST($k,n,p,1$) calculates the probability that a binomial random number with parameters $n$ and $p$ is less than or equal to $k$. (The last argument, 1, ensures that you get a *cumulative* probability.) Use this function to interpret the 0.139 value from @RISK.
   c. Using part **b** to guide you, use @RISK to find the probability that a random number from this distribution is greater than 17. Check your answer by using the BINOMDIST function appropriately in Excel.

7. Use @RISK to draw a triangular distribution with parameters 200, 300, and 600. Then superimpose a normal distribution on this drawing, choosing the mean and standard deviation to match those from the

triangular distribution. (Click on the Add Overlay button to get a choice of distributions to superimpose.)

a. What are the 5th and 95th percentiles for these two distributions?

b. What is the probability that a random number from the triangular distribution is less than 400? What is this probability for the normal distribution?

c. Experiment with the sliders to answer other questions like those in part **b**. Would you conclude that these two distributions differ most in the extremes (right or left) or in the middle? Explain.

8. We all hate to bring change to a store. By using random numbers, we could eliminate the need for change and give the store and the customer a fair deal. This problem indicates how it could be done.

a. Suppose that you buy something for $0.20. How could you use random numbers (built into the cash register system) to decide whether you should pay $1.00 or nothing? This would eliminate the need for change!

b. If you bought something for $9.60, how would you use random numbers to eliminate the need for change?

c. In the long run, why is this method fair to both the store and the customers? Would you personally (as a customer) be willing to abide by such a system?

## Skill-Extending Problems

9. A company is about to develop and then market a new product. It wants to build a simulation model for the entire process, and one key uncertain input is the development cost. For each of the following scenarios, choose an appropriate distribution, together with its parameters; justify your choice in words; and use @RISK to draw your chosen distribution.

a. Company experts have no idea what the distribution of the development cost is. All they can state is that "we are 95% sure it will be at least $450,000, and we are 95% sure it will be no more than $650,000."

b. Company experts can still make the same two statements as in part **a**, but now they can also state that "we believe the distribution is symmetric, reasonably bell-shaped, and its most likely value is about $550,000."

c. Company experts can still make the same two statements as in part **a**, but now they can also state that "we believe the distribution is skewed to the right, and its most likely value is about $500,000."

10. Continuing the preceding problem, suppose that another key uncertain input is the development time, which is measured in an *integer* number of months. For each of the following scenarios, choose an appropriate distribution, together with its parameters; justify your choice in words; and use @RISK to draw your chosen distribution.

a. Company experts believe the development time will be from 6 to 10 months, but they have absolutely no idea which of these will result.

b. Company experts believe the development time will be from 6 to 10 months. They believe the probabilities of these five possible values will increase linearly to a most likely value at 8 months and will then decrease linearly.

c. Company experts believe the development time will be from 6 to 10 months. They believe that 8 months is twice as likely as either 7 months or 9 months and that either of these latter possibilities is three times as likely as either 6 months or 10 months.

## 11.4 SIMULATION WITH BUILT-IN EXCEL TOOLS

In this section, we show how spreadsheet simulation models can be developed and analyzed with Excel's built-in tools and without using an add-in. This is certainly possible, but it presents two problems. First, the @RISK functions illustrated in the **Probability Distributions.xlsx** file are not available. We are able to use only Excel's RAND function and transformations of it to generate random numbers from various probability distributions. Second, there is a bookkeeping problem. After we build an Excel model with output cells linked to appropriate random input cells, we can press the F9 key repeatedly to see how the outputs vary. However, how do we keep track of these output values and summarize them? This bookkeeping feature is the real strength of a simulation add-in such as @RISK. It can be done with Excel, usually with data tables, but the summarization of the resulting data is completely up to the user—you!

To illustrate the procedure, we analyze a simple "news vendor" problem. This problem occurs when a company (such as a news vendor) must make a one-time purchase of a product (such as a newspaper) to meet customer demands for a certain period of time. If the company orders too few newspapers, it will lose potential profit by not having enough on hand to satisfy its customers. If it orders too many, it will have newspapers left over at the end of the day that, at best, can be sold at a loss. The following example illustrates this problem in a slightly different context.

---

EXAMPLE | **11.1 ORDERING CALENDARS AT WALTON BOOKSTORE**

In August, Walton Bookstore must decide how many of next year's nature calendars to order. Each calendar costs the bookstore $7.50 and sells for $10. After February 1, all unsold calendars will be returned to the publisher for a refund of $2.50 per calendar. Walton believes that the number of calendars it can sell by February 1 follows the probability distribution shown in Table 11.1. Walton wants to develop a simulation model to help it decide how many calendars to order.

**Table 11.1   Probability Distribution of Demand for Walton Example**

| Demand | Probability |
|--------|-------------|
| 100    | 0.30        |
| 150    | 0.20        |
| 200    | 0.30        |
| 250    | 0.15        |
| 300    | 0.05        |

**Objective**   To use built-in Excel tools—including the RAND function and data tables, but no add-ins—to simulate profit for several order quantities and ultimately choose the "best" order quantity.

---

**WHERE DO THE NUMBERS COME FROM?**

The monetary values are straightforward. The numbers in Table 11.1 are the key to the simulation model. They are discussed in more detail next.

## Solution

We first discuss the probability distribution in Table 11.1. This discrete distribution has only five possible values: 100, 150, 200, 250, and 300. In reality, it is clear that other values of demand are possible. For example, there could be demand for exactly 187 calendars. In spite of its apparent lack of realism, we use this discrete distribution for two reasons. First, its simplicity is a nice feature to get us started with simulation modeling. Second, discrete distributions are often used in real business simulation models. Even though the discrete distribution is only an *approximation* to reality, it can still provide important insights into the actual problem.

As for the probabilities listed in Table 11.1, they are typically drawn from historical data or (if historical data are lacking) educated guesses. In this case, the manager of Walton Bookstore has presumably looked at demands for calendars in previous years, and he has used any information he has about the market for next year's calendars to estimate, for example, that the probability of a demand for 200 calendars is 0.30. The five probabilities in this table must sum to 1. Beyond this requirement, they should be as reasonable and consistent with reality as possible.

Note that this is really a decision problem under uncertainty. Walton must choose an order quantity *before* knowing the demand for calendars. Unfortunately, we cannot use Solver because of the uncertainty.[6] We could use a decision tree, as discussed in the previous chapter, but it would get very "bushy." Therefore, we develop a simulation model for any *fixed* order quantity. Then we run this simulation model with various order quantities to see which one appears to be best.[7]

## DEVELOPING THE SIMULATION MODEL

Now we discuss the ordering model. For any fixed order quantity, we show how Excel can be used to simulate 1000 replications (or any other number of replications). Each replication is an independent replay of the events that occur. To illustrate, suppose we want to simulate profit if Walton orders 200 calendars. Figure 11.22 illustrates the results obtained by simulating 1000 independent replications for this order quantity. (See the file **Walton Bookstore 1.xlsx**.) Note that there are a number of hidden rows in Figure 11.22. (This is the case for several of the spreadsheet figures in this chapter.) To develop this model, use the following steps:

**Figure 11.22**   Walton Bookstore Simulation Model

| | A | B | C | D | E | F | G | H | I | J | K |
|---|---|---|---|---|---|---|---|---|---|---|---|
| 1 | Simulation of Walton's bookstore | | | | | | | | Range names used: | | |
| 2 | | | | | | | | | LookupTable | =Model!$D$5:$F$9 | |
| 3 | Cost data | | | Demand distribution | | | | | Order_quantity | =Model!$B$9 | |
| 4 | Unit cost | $7.50 | | Cum Prob | Demand | Probability | | | Profit | =Model!$G$19:$G$1018 | |
| 5 | Unit price | $10.00 | | 0.00 | 100 | 0.30 | | | Unit_cost | =Model!$B$4 | |
| 6 | Unit refund | $2.50 | | 0.30 | 150 | 0.20 | | | Unit_price | =Model!$B$5 | |
| 7 | | | | 0.50 | 200 | 0.30 | | | Unit_refund | =Model!$B$6 | |
| 8 | Decision variable | | | 0.80 | 250 | 0.15 | | | | | |
| 9 | Order quantity | 200 | | 0.95 | 300 | 0.05 | | | | | |
| 10 | | | | | | | | | | | |
| 11 | Summary measures for simulation below | | | | | | | | | | |
| 12 | Average profit | $204.13 | | 95% confidence interval for expected profit | | | | | | | |
| 13 | Stdev of profit | $328.04 | | Lower limit | $183.79 | | | | | | |
| 14 | Minimum profit | -$250.00 | | Upper limit | $224.46 | | | | | | |
| 15 | Maximum profit | $500.00 | | | | | | | | | |
| 16 | | | | | | | | | | | |
| 17 | Simulation | | | | | | | | Distribution of profit | | |
| 18 | Replication | Random # | Demand | Revenue | Cost | Refund | Profit | | Value | Frequency | |
| 19 | 1 | 0.2249 | 100 | $1,000 | $1,500 | $250 | -$250 | | -250 | 299 | |
| 20 | 2 | 0.6693 | 200 | $2,000 | $1,500 | $0 | $500 | | 125 | 191 | |
| 21 | 3 | 0.4164 | 150 | $1,500 | $1,500 | $125 | $125 | | 500 | 510 | |
| 22 | 4 | 0.7562 | 200 | $2,000 | $1,500 | $0 | $500 | | | | |
| 23 | 5 | 0.1581 | 100 | $1,000 | $1,500 | $250 | -$250 | | | | |
| 24 | 6 | 0.0579 | 100 | $1,000 | $1,500 | $250 | -$250 | | | | |
| 25 | 7 | 0.7452 | 200 | $2,000 | $1,500 | $0 | $500 | | | | |
| 26 | 8 | 0.3717 | 150 | $1,500 | $1,500 | $125 | $125 | | | | |
| 27 | 9 | 0.5077 | 200 | $2,000 | $1,500 | $0 | $500 | | | | |
| 28 | 10 | 0.6669 | 200 | $2,000 | $1,500 | $0 | $500 | | | | |
| 1012 | 994 | 0.7689 | 200 | $2,000 | $1,500 | $0 | $500 | | | | |
| 1013 | 995 | 0.8861 | 250 | $2,000 | $1,500 | $0 | $500 | | | | |
| 1014 | 996 | 0.4036 | 150 | $1,500 | $1,500 | $125 | $125 | | | | |
| 1015 | 997 | 0.4092 | 150 | $1,500 | $1,500 | $125 | $125 | | | | |
| 1016 | 998 | 0.5055 | 200 | $2,000 | $1,500 | $0 | $500 | | | | |
| 1017 | 999 | 0.2457 | 100 | $1,000 | $1,500 | $250 | -$250 | | | | |
| 1018 | 1000 | 0.3484 | 150 | $1,500 | $1,500 | $125 | $125 | | | | |

[6] Palisade Corporation has another Excel add-in called RISKOptimizer that can be used for optimization in a simulation model. We do not discuss this add-in here, but it is included on the Palisade CD-ROM that accompanies the book.

[7] Pfeiffer et al. (2001) discuss the pros and cons of the various approaches to analyzing the news vendor problem. With some reservations, they advocate the simulation approach used here. We discuss another approach in Chapter 13.

**1** **Inputs.** Enter the cost data in the range B4:B6, the probability distribution of demand in the range E5:F9, and the proposed order quantity, 200, in cell B9. Pay particular attention to the way the probability distribution is entered (and compare to the Discrete sheet in the **Probability Distributions.xlsx** file). Columns E and F contain the possible demand values and the probabilities from Table 11.1. It is also necessary (see step 3 for the reasoning) to have the cumulative probabilities in column D. To obtain these, first enter the value 0 in cell D5. Then enter the formula

**=F5+D5**

in cell D6 and copy it to the range D7:D9.

**2** **Generate random numbers.** Enter a random number in cell B19 with the formula

**=RAND()**

and copy this to the range B20:B1018.

**3** **Generate demands.** The key to the simulation is the generation of the customer demands in the range C19:C1018 from the random numbers in column B and the probability distribution of demand. Here is how it works. We divide the interval from 0 to 1 into five segments: 0.0 to 0.3 (length 0.3), 0.3 to 0.5 (length 0.2), 0.5 to 0.8 (length 0.3), 0.8 to 0.95 (length 0.15), and 0.95 to 1.0 (length 0.05). Note that these lengths are the probabilities of the various demands. Then we associate a demand with each random number, depending on which interval the random number falls in. For example, if a random number is 0.5279, this falls in the third interval, so we associate the third possible demand value, 200, with this random number.

The best way to implement this procedure is with a VLOOKUP function. To do this, we create a lookup table in the range D5:E9 (range named LookupTable). This table has the cumulative probabilities in column D and the possible demand values in column E. In fact, the whole purpose of the cumulative probabilities in column D is to allow us to use the VLOOKUP function. To generate the simulated demands, enter the formula

**=VLOOKUP(B19,LookupTable,2)**

in cell C19 and copy it to the range C20:C1018. For each random number in column B, this function compares the random number to the values in D5:D9 and returns the appropriate demand from E5:E9.

This step is the key to the simulation, so make sure you understand exactly what it entails. The rest is bookkeeping, as we illustrate in the following steps. First, however, we note that a separate column for the random numbers in column B is not really necessary. They could be included in the VLOOKUP function directly, as in

**=VLOOKUP(RAND(),LookupTable,2)**

**4** **Revenue.** After the demand is known, the number of calendars sold is the smaller of the demand and the order quantity. For example, if 150 calendars are demanded, 150 will be sold. But if 250 are demanded, only 200 can be sold (because Walton orders only 200). Therefore, to calculate the revenue in cell D19, enter the formula

**=Unit_price*MIN(C19,Order_quantity)**

**5** **Ordering cost.** The cost of ordering the calendars does not depend on the demand; it is the unit cost multiplied by the number ordered. Calculate this cost in cell E19 with the formula

**=Unit_cost*Order_quantity**

*This rather cumbersome procedure for generating a discrete random number is greatly simplified when we use @RISK.*

**6** **Refund.** If the order quantity is greater than the demand, there is a refund of $2.50 for each calendar left over; otherwise, there is no refund. Therefore, enter the refund in cell F19 with the formula

=Unit_refund*MAX(Order_quantity-C19,0)

For example, if demand is 150, then 50 calendars are left over, and this MAX is 50, the larger of 50 and 0. However, if demand is 250, then no calendars are left over, and this MAX is 0, the larger of –50 and 0. (This calculation could also be accomplished with an IF function instead of a MAX function.)

**7** **Profit.** Calculate the profit in cell G19 with the formula

=D19-E19+F19

**8** **Copy to other rows.** Do the same bookkeeping for the other 999 replications by copying the range D19:G19 to the range D20:G1018.

**9** **Summary measures.** Each profit value in column G corresponds to one randomly generated demand. We usually want to see how these vary from one replication to another. First, calculate the average and standard deviation of the 1000 profits in cells B12 and B13 with the formulas

=AVERAGE(Profit)

and

=STDEV(Profit)

Similarly, calculate the smallest and largest of the 1000 profits in cells B14 and B15 with the MIN and MAX functions.

**10** **Confidence interval for expected profit.** Calculate a 95% confidence interval for the expected profit in cells E13 and E14 with the formulas

=B12-1.96*B13/SQRT(1000)

and

=B12+1.96*B13/SQRT(1000)

(See the "Notes About Confidence Intervals" section later in this chapter for details.)

**11** **Distribution of simulated profits.** There are only three possible profits: –$250, $125, or $500 (depending on whether demand is 100, 150, or at least 200—see the following discussion). We can use the COUNTIF function to count the number of times each of these possible profits is obtained. To do so, enter the formula

=COUNTIF(Profit,I19)

in cell J19 and copy it down to cell J21.

## Discussion of the Simulation Results

*For this particular model, the output distribution is also discrete: There are only three possible profits for an order quantity of 200.*

At this point, it is a good idea to stand back and see what we have accomplished. First, in the body of the simulation, rows 19 to 1018, we randomly generated 1000 possible demands and the corresponding profits. Because there are only five possible demand values (100, 150, 200, 250, and 300), there are only five corresponding profit values: –$250, $125, $500, $500, and $500. Also, note that for the order quantity 200, the profit is $500 regardless of whether demand is 200, 250, or 300. (Make sure you understand why.) A tally of the profit values in these rows, including the hidden rows, indicates that 299 rows have profit equal to –$250 (demand 100), 191 rows have profit equal to $125 (demand 150), and 510 rows have profit equal to $500 (demand 200, 250, or 300). The average of these 1000 profits is $204.13, and their standard deviation is $328.04. (Again, remember that your answers will differ from these because your random numbers will almost surely differ from those shown in Figure 11.22.)

Typically, we want a simulation model to capture one or more output variables, such as profit. These output variables depend on random inputs, such as demand. Our goal is to estimate the probability distributions of the outputs. In the Walton simulation, we estimate the probability distribution of profit to be

$$P(\text{Profit} = -\$250) = 299/1000 = 0.299$$
$$P(\text{Profit} = \$125) = 191/1000 = 0.191$$
$$P(\text{Profit} = \$500) = 510/1000 = 0.510$$

The confidence interval provides a measure of accuracy of the mean profit, as estimated from the simulation.

We also estimate the mean of this distribution to be $204.13 and its standard deviation to be $328.04. Note that if the entire simulation were run again with *different* random numbers (such as the ones you might have generated on your PC), the answers would be slightly different. This is the primary reason for the confidence interval in cells E13 and E14. This interval expresses our uncertainty about the *mean* of the profit distribution. Our best guess for this mean is the average of the 1000 profits we happened to observe. However, because the corresponding confidence interval is somewhat wide, from $183.79 to $224.46, we are not at all sure of the *true* mean of the profit distribution. We are only 95% confident that the true mean is within this interval. If we run this simulation again with different random numbers, the average profit will probably be different from the average profit we observed, $204.13, and the other summary statistics will probably also be different.

### Notes about Confidence Intervals

It is common in computer simulations to estimate the mean of some distribution by the average of the simulated observations, just as we estimated the mean of the profit distribution by the average of 1000 profits. The usual practice is then to accompany this estimate with a **confidence interval,** which indicates the accuracy of the estimate. You might recall from statistics that to obtain a confidence interval for the mean, you start with the estimated mean and then add and subtract a multiple of the **standard error** of the estimated mean. If we denote the estimated mean (that is, the average) by $\overline{X}$, we have the following formula.

---

*Confidence interval for the mean*

$$\overline{X} \pm (\text{Multiple} \times \text{Standard Error of } \overline{X})$$

---

The standard error of $\overline{X}$ is the standard deviation of the observations divided by the square root of $n$, the number of observations:

---

*Standard error of $\overline{X}$*

$$s/\sqrt{n}$$

---

Here, $s$ is the standard deviation of the observations. We obtain it with the STDEV function in Excel.

The "multiple" in the confidence interval formula depends on the confidence level and the number of observations. If the confidence level is 95%, the level used most frequently, then the multiple is usually very close to 2, so a good guideline is to go out 2 standard errors on either side of the average to obtain an approximate 95% confidence interval for the mean.

---

*Approximate 95% confidence interval for the mean*

$$\overline{X} \pm 2s/\sqrt{n}$$

---

To be more precise, if $n$ is reasonably large, which is almost always the case in simulations, the central limit theorem from statistics implies that the correct multiple is the number from the standard normal distribution that cuts off probability 0.025 in each tail. This is a famous number in statistics: 1.96. Because 1.96 is very close to 2, for all practical purposes we can use 2 instead of 1.96 when forming the confidence interval. (Note that this would be a different multiple if, say, we were using a 90% or a 99% confidence level rather than a 95% level.)

*The idea is to choose the number of iterations large enough so that the resulting confidence interval is sufficiently narrow.*

Analysts often plan a simulation so that the confidence interval for the mean of some important output is sufficiently narrow. The reasoning is that narrow confidence intervals imply more precision about the estimated mean of the output variable. If the confidence level is fixed at some value such as 95%, the only way to narrow the confidence interval is to simulate more replications. Assuming that the confidence level is 95%, the following value of $n$ is required to ensure that the resulting confidence interval has length approximately equal to some specified value $L$:

---

***Sample size determination***

$$ n = \frac{16 \times (\text{Estimated standard deviation})^2}{L^2} $$

---

To use this formula, we must estimate the standard deviation of the output variable. For example, in the Walton simulation, we saw that with $n = 1000$, the resulting 95% confidence interval for the mean profit has length $224.46 - $183.79 = $40.66. Suppose that we want to reduce this length to $25; that is, we want $L = $25. We do not know the exact standard deviation of the profit distribution, but we can estimate it from the simulation as $328.04. Therefore, to obtain the required confidence interval length $L$, we need to simulate $n$ replications, where

$$ n = \frac{16(328.04)^2}{25^2} \approx 2755 $$

(When this formula produces a noninteger, it is common to round upward.) The claim, then, is that if we rerun the simulation with 2755 replications rather than 1000 replications, the length of the 95% confidence interval for the mean profit will be close to $25.

## Finding the Best Order Quantity

We are not yet finished with the Walton example. So far, we have run the simulation for only a single order quantity, 200. Walton's ultimate goal is to find the *best* order quantity. Even this statement must be clarified. What do we mean by "best?" As in Chapter 10, we use the *expected* profit as our optimality criterion—that is, EMV—but we indicate how other characteristics of the profit distribution could influence our decision. We can obtain the required outputs with a data table. Specifically, we use a data table to rerun the simulation for other order quantities as shown in Figure 11.23. (This is still part of the **Walton Bookstore 1.xlsx** file.)

**Figure 11.23**

Data Table for Walton Bookstore Simulation

| | L | M | N | O |
|---|---|---|---|---|
| 17 | Data table for average profit versus order quantity | | | |
| 18 | Order quantity | AvgProfit | | |
| 19 | | $204.13 | | |
| 20 | 100 | $250.00 | | |
| 21 | 125 | $256.44 | | |
| 22 | 150 | $262.88 | | |
| 23 | 175 | $233.50 | | |
| 24 | 200 | $204.13 | | |
| 25 | 225 | $120.19 | | |
| 26 | 250 | $36.25 | | |
| 27 | 275 | ($76.00) | | |
| 28 | 300 | ($188.25) | | |

To optimize in simulation models, try various values of the decision variable(s) and run the simulation for each of them.

To create this table, enter the trial order quantities shown in the range A1023:A1031, enter the link =B12 to the average profit in cell B19, and select the data table range, L19:M28. Then select Data Table from the What-If Analysis dropdown, specifying that the column input cell is B9 (refer to Figure 11.22). Finally, construct a column chart of the average profits in the data table, as in Figure 11.24. Note that an order quantity of 150 appears to maximize the average profit. Its average profit of $262.88 is slightly higher than the average profits from nearby order quantities and much higher than the profit gained from an order of 200 or more calendars. However, again keep in mind that this is a simulation, so that all of these average profits depend on the particular random numbers we generated. If we rerun the simulation with different random numbers, some other order quantity could be best.

**Figure 11.24**

Average Profit versus Order Quantity

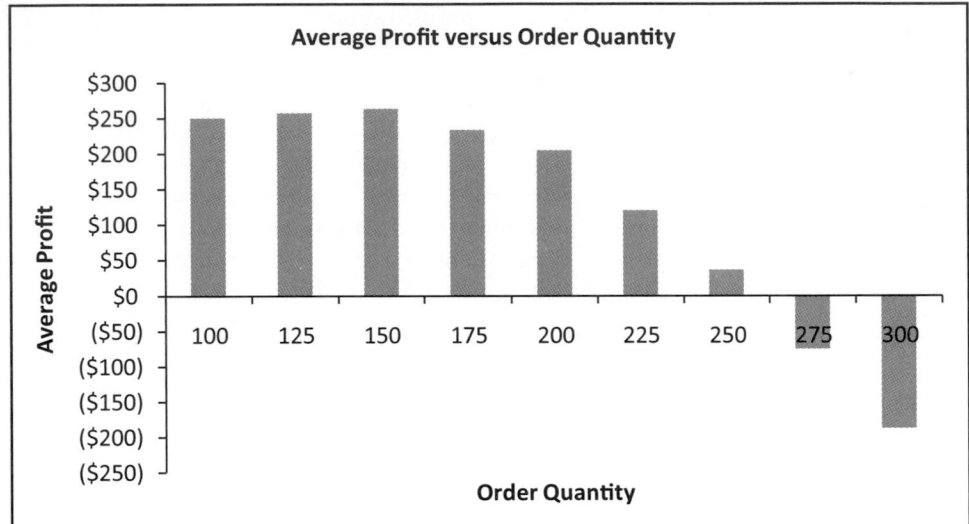

## To Freeze or Not to Freeze

In developing this simulation model, we didn't instruct you to freeze the random numbers in column B. The effect is that every time you press the F9 key or make any change to your spreadsheet model, a new set of simulated answers (including those in the data table) will appear. Depending on the speed of your computer, this recalculation can take a few seconds, even for a relatively small simulation. For larger simulations, the recalculation time can be lengthy, which is one of the primary reasons you might want to freeze your random numbers.

However, the drawback is that after the random numbers are frozen, you are stuck with that particular set of random numbers. We typically do *not* freeze the random numbers. Then we can generate many different scenarios simply by pressing the F9 key.

## Using a Data Table to Repeat Simulations

The Walton simulation is a particularly simple one-line simulation model. We are able to capture all of the logic—generating a demand and calculating the corresponding profit—in a single row. Then to replicate the simulation, we simply copy this row down as far as we like. Many simulation models are significantly more complex and require more than one row to capture the logic. Nevertheless, they still result in one or more output quantities (such as profit) that we want to replicate. We now illustrate another method that is more general (still using the Walton example), which uses a *data table* to generate the replications. Refer to Figure 11.25 and the file **Walton Bookstore 2.xlsx**.

**Figure 11.25**   Using a Data Table to Simulate Replications

| | A | B | C | D | E | F | G | H | I | J | K |
|---|---|---|---|---|---|---|---|---|---|---|---|
| 1 | Simulation of Walton's bookstore | | | | | | | | | | |
| 2 | | | | | | | | | | | |
| 3 | Cost data | | | Demand distribution | | | | Range names used: | | | |
| 4 | Unit cost | $7.50 | | CumProb | Demand | Probability | | LookupTable | =Model!$D$5:$F$9 | | |
| 5 | Unit price | $10.00 | | 0.00 | 100 | 0.30 | | Order_quantity | =Model!$B$9 | | |
| 6 | Unit refund | $2.50 | | 0.30 | 150 | 0.20 | | Profit | =Model!$B$24:$B$1023 | | |
| 7 | | | | 0.50 | 200 | 0.30 | | Unit_cost | =Model!$B$4 | | |
| 8 | Decision variable | | | 0.80 | 250 | 0.15 | | Unit_price | =Model!$B$5 | | |
| 9 | Order quantity | 200 | | 0.95 | 300 | 0.05 | | Unit_refund | =Model!$B$6 | | |
| 10 | | | | | | | | | | | |
| 11 | Summary measures from simulation below | | | | | | | | | | |
| 12 | Average | $203.75 | | 95% confidence interval for expected profit | | | | | | | |
| 13 | StDev | $324.03 | | Lower limit | $183.67 | | | | | | |
| 14 | Minimum | -$250.00 | | Upper limit | $223.83 | | | | | | |
| 15 | Maximum | $500.00 | | | | | | | | | |
| 16 | | | | | | | | | | | |
| 17 | Simulation | | | | | | | | | | |
| 18 | | Demand | Revenue | Cost | Refund | Profit | | | | | |
| 19 | | 100 | $1,000 | $1,500 | $250 | -$250 | | | | | |
| 20 | | | | | | | | | | | |
| 21 | Data table for replications, each shows profit from that replication | | | | | | | | | | |
| 22 | Replication | Profit | | | | | | | | | |
| 23 | | -$250 | | | | | | | | | |
| 24 | 1 | $500 | | | | | | | | | |
| 25 | 2 | -$250 | | | | | | | | | |
| 26 | 3 | $500 | | | | | | | | | |
| 27 | 4 | $500 | | | | | | | | | |
| 28 | 5 | $500 | | | | | | | | | |
| 29 | 6 | -$250 | | | | | | | | | |
| 30 | 7 | -$250 | | | | | | | | | |
| 31 | 8 | -$250 | | | | | | | | | |
| 32 | 9 | -$250 | | | | | | | | | |
| 33 | 10 | $500 | | | | | | | | | |
| 1017 | 994 | -$250 | | | | | | | | | |
| 1018 | 995 | -$250 | | | | | | | | | |
| 1019 | 996 | $500 | | | | | | | | | |
| 1020 | 997 | $500 | | | | | | | | | |
| 1021 | 998 | -$250 | | | | | | | | | |
| 1022 | 999 | -$250 | | | | | | | | | |
| 1023 | 1000 | $500 | | | | | | | | | |

Through row 19, this model is exactly like the previous model. That is, we use the given data at the top of the spreadsheet to construct a typical "prototype" of the simulation in row 19. Actually, we use our earlier suggestion. We eliminate an explicit random number cell and enter the formula

**=VLOOKUP(RAND(),LookupTable,2)**

for demand in cell B19. Also, we use a convention introduced in Chapter 2, in which we color any random quantity, in this case, demand, green. This is optional, but we do it to remind ourselves that this cell contains a random number. (Unfortunately, the green doesn't show correctly in the book. It shows as a light shade of blue.)

The key to simulating many replications in Excel (without an add-in) is to use a data table with any blank cell as the column input cell.

Note that we no longer copy this row 19 down—and we definitely do *not* freeze the cell with the random number, cell B19. Instead, we form a data table in the range A23:B1023 to replicate the basic simulation 1000 times. In column A, we list the replication numbers, 1 to 1000. The formula for the data table in cell B23 is **=F19**. This creates a link to the profit from the prototype row for use in the data table. Then we create a data table and enter *any blank cell* (such as C23) as the column input cell. (No row input cell is necessary, so its box should be left empty.) This tricks Excel into repeating the row 19 calculations 1000 times, each time with a new random number, and reporting the profits in column B of the data table. (If we want to see other simulated quantities, such as revenue, for each replication, we can add extra output columns to the data table.)

### Excel Tip: *How Data Tables Work*
*To understand this procedure, you must understand exactly how data tables work. When we create a data table, Excel takes each value in the left column of the data table (here column A), substitutes it into the cell we designate as the column input cell, recalculates the spreadsheet, and returns the output value (or values) we have requested in the top row of the data table (such as profit). It might seem silly to substitute each replication number from column A into a blank cell such as cell C23, but this part is really irrelevant. The important part is the recalculation. Each recalculation leads to a new random demand and the corresponding profit, and these profits are the quantities we want. Of course, this means that we should not freeze the quantity in cell B19 before forming the data table. The whole point of the data table is to use a different random number for each replication, and this occurs only if the random demand in row 19 is left unfrozen.*

If you create a data table and the output is constant the whole way down its column, press the F9 key to force a recalculation.

### Excel Tip: *Recalculation Mode*
*To speed up recalculation, select the Office button, then Excel Options, and then the Formulas group. Under the Calculation options, click on the Automatic except for data tables option, and click on OK. Now when you change anything in your spreadsheet, everything will recalculate in the usual way except data tables. Data tables will not recalculate until you intentionally press the F9 key. Data tables can require a lot of computing time, so this option can be very useful. However, be aware that if you set this option and then form a data table, you have to press F9 to make the data table recalculate the first time. Otherwise, you see the same output value the whole way down the data table.*

### Using a Two-Way Data Table

We can carry this method one step further to see how the profit depends on the order quantity. Here we use a two-way data table with the replication number along the side and possible order quantities along the top. See Figure 11.26 and the file **Walton Bookstore 3.xlsx**. Now the data table range is A23:J1023, and the driving formula, entered in cell A23, is again the link **=F19**. The column input cell should again be *any blank cell*, but the row input cell should be B9 (the order quantity). Each cell in the body of the data table shows a simulated profit for a particular replication and a particular order quantity, and each is based on a *different* random demand.

By averaging the numbers in each column of the data table (see row 14), we again see that 150 appears to be the best order quantity. It is also helpful to construct a bar chart of these averages, as in Figure 11.27. Now, however, assuming you have not frozen anything, the data table and the corresponding chart will change each time you press the F9 key. To see whether 150 is always the best order quantity, you can press the F9 key and see whether the bar above 150 continues to be the highest. ■

By now you should appreciate the usefulness of data tables in spreadsheet simulations. They allow you to take a "prototype" simulation and replicate its key results as often as you

**Figure 11.26**

Using a Two-Way Data Table for the Simulation Model

| | A | B | C | D | E | F | G | H | I | J |
|---|---|---|---|---|---|---|---|---|---|---|
| 1 | Simulation of Walton's bookstore | | | | | | | | | |
| 2 | | | | | | | | | | |
| 3 | Cost data | | | Demand distribution | | | | Range names used: | | |
| 4 | Unit cost | $7.50 | | CumProb | Demand | Probability | | LookupTable | =Model!$D$5:$F$9 | |
| 5 | Unit price | $10.00 | | 0.00 | 100 | 0.30 | | Order_quantit | =Model!$B$9 | |
| 6 | Unit refund | $2.50 | | 0.30 | 150 | 0.20 | | Unit_cost | =Model!$B$4 | |
| 7 | | | | 0.50 | 200 | 0.30 | | Unit_price | =Model!$B$5 | |
| 8 | Decision variable | | | 0.80 | 250 | 0.15 | | Unit_refund | =Model!$B$6 | |
| 9 | Order quantity | 200 | | 0.95 | 300 | 0.05 | | | | |
| 10 | | | | | | | | | | |
| 11 | Summary measures of simulated profits for each order quantity | | | | | | | | | |
| 12 | | | | | Order quantity | | | | | |
| 13 | | 100 | 125 | 150 | 175 | 200 | 225 | 250 | 275 | 300 |
| 14 | Average profit | $250.00 | $237.50 | $255.00 | $223.75 | $140.00 | $67.50 | $55.00 | -$70.00 | -$300.00 |
| 15 | Stdev profit | $0.00 | $92.79 | $176.70 | $233.54 | $346.85 | $346.69 | $449.74 | $441.70 | $460.84 |
| 16 | | | | | | | | | | |
| 17 | Simulation | | | | | | | | | |
| 18 | | Demand | Revenue | Cost | Refund | Profit | | | | |
| 19 | | 100 | $1,000 | $1,500 | $250 | -$250 | | | | |
| 20 | | | | | | | | | | |
| 21 | Data table showing profit for replications with various order quantities | | | | | | | | | |
| 22 | Replication | | | Order quantity | | | | | | |
| 23 | ($250.00) | 100 | 125 | 150 | 175 | 200 | 225 | 250 | 275 | 300 |
| 24 | 1 | $250 | $313 | $438 | | -$250 | 375 | -500 | 500 | -750 |
| 25 | 2 | $250 | $125 | $0 | -$125 | $500 | -375 | -500 | 500 | -750 |
| 26 | 3 | $250 | $313 | $375 | $438 | -$250 | -375 | 625 | -625 | -750 |
| 27 | 4 | $250 | $125 | $375 | -$125 | -$250 | 0 | -125 | 125 | -750 |
| 28 | 5 | $250 | $313 | $375 | -$125 | $500 | -375 | -500 | -250 | -375 |
| 29 | 6 | $250 | $313 | $375 | $250 | -$250 | 0 | -500 | -625 | 0 |
| 30 | 7 | $250 | $125 | $375 | -$125 | $125 | 562.5 | 250 | 687.5 | 0 |
| 31 | 8 | $250 | $313 | $375 | -$125 | -$250 | 0 | 250 | -625 | -375 |
| 32 | 9 | $250 | $313 | $0 | $250 | $125 | 0 | -500 | 500 | -750 |
| 1019 | 996 | $250 | $125 | $0 | $438 | $500 | 562.5 | -500 | -250 | 0 |
| 1020 | 997 | $250 | $313 | $375 | $438 | $500 | 375 | -125 | 125 | -750 |
| 1021 | 998 | $250 | $313 | $375 | $438 | $500 | -375 | 250 | 125 | 0 |
| 1022 | 999 | $250 | $313 | $375 | $438 | $125 | -375 | -500 | -250 | -750 |
| 1023 | 1000 | $250 | $313 | $375 | $438 | $500 | 375 | -125 | -625 | 0 |

like. This method makes summary statistics (over the entire group of replications) and corresponding charts fairly easy to obtain. Nevertheless, it takes some work to create the data tables, summary statistics, and charts. In the next section, we show how the @RISK add-in does most of this work for us.

# PROBLEMS

## Skill-Building Problems

**11.** Suppose you own an expensive car and purchase auto insurance. This insurance has a $1000 deductible, so that if you have an accident and the damage is less than $1000, you pay for it out of your pocket. However, if the damage is greater than $1000, you pay the first $1000 and the insurance pays the rest. In the current year, there is probability 0.025 of your having an accident. If you have an accident, the damage amount is normally distributed with mean $3000 and standard deviation $750.

a. Use Excel and a one-way data table to simulate the amount you have to pay for damages to your car. Run 5000 iterations. Then find the average amount you pay, the standard deviation of the amounts you

pay, and a 95% confidence interval for the average amount you pay. (Note that many of the amounts you pay will be 0 because you have no accident.)

b. Continue the simulation in part **a** by creating a two-way data table, where the row input is the deductible amount, varied from $500 to $2000 in multiples of $500. Now find the average amount you pay, the standard deviation of the amounts you pay, and a 95% confidence interval for the average amount you pay for *each* deductible amount.

c. Do you think it is reasonable to assume that damage amounts are *normally* distributed? What would you criticize about this assumption? What might you suggest instead?

**Figure 11.27** Chart of Average Profits for Different Order Quantities

12. In August 2007, a car dealer is trying to determine how many 2008 cars to order. Each car ordered in August 2007 costs $10,000. The demand for the dealer's 2008 models has the probability distribution shown in the file **P11_12.xlsx**. Each car sells for $15,000. If demand for 2008 cars exceeds the number of cars ordered in August, the dealer must reorder at a cost of $12,000 per car. Excess cars can be sold at $9000 per car. Use simulation to determine how many cars to order in August. For your optimal order quantity, find a 95% confidence interval for the expected profit.

13. In the Walton Bookstore example, suppose that Walton receives no money for the first 50 excess calendars returned but receives $2.50 for every calendar after the first 50 returned. Does this change the optimal order quantity?

14. A sweatshirt supplier is trying to decide how many sweatshirts to print for the upcoming NCAA basketball championships. The final four teams have emerged from the quarterfinal round, and there is now a week left until the semifinals, which are then followed in a couple of days by the finals. Each sweatshirt costs $10 to produce and sells for $25. However,

in 3 weeks, any leftover sweatshirts will be put on sale for half price, $12.50. The supplier assumes that the demand for his sweatshirts during the next 3 weeks (when interest is at its highest) has the distribution shown in the file **P11_14.xlsx**. The residual demand, after the sweatshirts have been put on sale, has the distribution also shown in this file. The supplier, being a profit maximizer, realizes that every sweatshirt sold, even at the sale price, yields a profit. However, he also realizes that any sweatshirts produced but not sold (even at the sale price) must be thrown away, resulting in a $10 loss per sweatshirt. Analyze the supplier's problem with a simulation model.

## Skill-Extending Problem

15. In the Walton Bookstore example with a discrete demand distribution, explain why an order quantity other than one of the possible demands cannot maximize the expected profit. (*Hint:* Consider an order of 190 calendars. If this maximizes expected profit, then it must yield a higher expected profit than an order of 150 or 100. But then an order of 200 calendars must also yield a larger expected profit than an order of 190 calendars. Why?)

# 11.5 INTRODUCTION TO @RISK

*@RISK provides a number of functions for simulating from various distributions, and it takes care of all the bookkeeping in spreadsheet simulations. Simulating without @RISK in Excel requires much more work for you.*

Spreadsheet simulation modeling has become extremely popular in recent years, both in the academic and corporate communities. Much of the reason for this popularity is due to simulation add-ins such as @RISK. There are two primary advantages to using such an add-in. First, an add-in gives us easy access to many probability distributions we might want to use in simulation models. We already saw in Section 11.3 how the RISKDISCRETE, RISKNORMAL, and RISKTRIANG functions, among others, are easy to use and remember. Second, an add-in allows us to perform simulations much more easily than is possible with Excel alone. To replicate a simulation in Excel, we typically need to build a data table. Then we have to calculate summary statistics, such as averages, standard deviations, and percentiles, with built-in Excel functions. If we want graphs to enhance the analysis, we have to create them. In short, we have to perform a number of time-consuming steps for each simulation. Simulation add-ins such as @RISK perform much of this work for us automatically.

Although we focus on @RISK in this book, other simulation add-ins are available for Excel. A worthy competitor is Crystal Ball, developed by Decisioneering (http://www.decisioneering.com). Crystal Ball has much of the same functionality as @RISK. In addition, because of the relative ease of developing "home-grown" applications in Excel with Excel's built-in macro language Visual Basic for Applications (VBA), some individuals have developed their own simulation add-ins for Excel. However, we have a natural bias for @RISK—we have been permitted by its developer, Palisade Corporation (http://www.palisade.com), to include it in the Palisade CD-ROM that accompanies this book. If it were not included, you would have to purchase it from Palisade at a fairly steep price (hundreds of dollars). Microsoft Office does not include @RISK, Crystal Ball, or any other simulation add-in—you must purchase them separately.

## @RISK Features

The following is an overview of some of @RISK's features. We discuss all of these in more detail later in this section.

- @RISK contains a number of functions, such as RISKNORMAL and RISKDISCRETE, that make it easy to generate observations from the most important probability distributions we discussed in Section 11.3.

- You can specify any cell or range of cells in the simulation model as **output cells.** When you run the simulation, @RISK automatically keeps summary measures (averages, standard deviations, percentiles, and others) from the values generated in these output cells across the replications. It also creates graphs such as histograms based on these values. In other words, @RISK takes care of tedious bookkeeping operations for you.

- @RISK has a special function, RISKSIMTABLE, which allows you to run the same simulation several times using a different value of some key input variable each time. This input variable is typically a decision variable. For example, suppose that you would like to simulate an inventory-ordering policy (as in the Walton Bookstore example). Your ultimate goal is to compare simulation outputs across a number of possible order quantities such as 100, 150, 200, 250, and 300. If you use an appropriate formula involving the RISKSIMTABLE function, the entire simulation is performed for each of these order quantities separately—with one click of a button. You can then compare the outputs to choose the "best" order quantity.

## Loading @RISK

To build simulation models with @RISK, you need to have Excel open with @RISK added in. The first step, if you have not already done so, is to install the Palisade DecisionTools suite with the Setup program on the CD-ROM that is bundled with this book. Then you can load @RISK by clicking on the Windows Start button, selecting the Programs group, selecting the Palisade DecisionTools group, and finally selecting the @RISK item. If Excel is already open, this loads @RISK inside Excel. If Excel is not yet open, this launches Excel and @RISK simultaneously. After @RISK is loaded, you see an @RISK tab and the corresponding @RISK ribbon in Figure 11.28.

**Figure 11.28** @RISK Ribbon

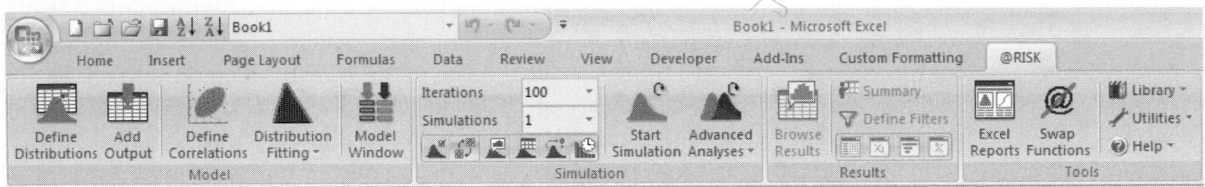

## @RISK Models with a Single Random Input Variable

*The majority of the work (and thinking) goes into developing the model. Setting up @RISK and then running it are easy.*

In the remainder of this section, we illustrate some of @RISK's functionality by revisiting the Walton Bookstore example. Then in the next chapter, we use @RISK to help develop a number of interesting simulation models. Throughout our discussion, you should keep one very important idea in mind. The development of a simulation model is basically a two-step procedure. The first step is to build the model itself. This step requires you to build in all of the logic that transforms inputs (including @RISK functions such as RISKDISCRETE) into outputs (such as profit). This is where most of the work and thinking go, exactly as in models from previous chapters, and @RISK cannot do this for you. It is *your* job to enter the formulas that link inputs to outputs appropriately. However, after this logic has been incorporated, @RISK takes over in the second step. It automatically replicates your model, with different random numbers on each replication, and it reports any requested summary measures in tabular and graphical form. Therefore, @RISK can greatly decrease the amount of "busy work" required, but it is not a magic bullet![8]

We begin by analyzing an example with a single random input variable.

---

[8] If you are used to the previous version (4.5) of @RISK, you are in for some surprises with the new version (5.0) packaged with this book. The main differences are in where you find your results, as we explain shortly. However, the model building step—usually the most time-consuming and difficult step—is no different from before.

**11.2 USING @RISK AT WALTON BOOKSTORE**

*This is the same Walton bookstore model as before, except that we now use a triangular distribution for demand.*

Recall that Walton Bookstore buys calendars for $7.50, sells them at the regular price of $10, and gets a refund of $2.50 for all calendars that cannot be sold. In contrast to Example 11.1, we now assume that Walton estimates a triangular probability distribution for demand, where the minimum, most likely, and maximum values of demand are 100, 175, and 300, respectively. The company wants to use this probability distribution, together with @RISK, to simulate the profit for any particular order quantity. It eventually wants to find the best order quantity.

**Objective** To learn about @RISK's basic functionality by revisiting the Walton bookstore problem.

### WHERE DO THE NUMBERS COME FROM?

The monetary values are the same as before. The parameters of the triangular distribution of demand are probably Walton's best subjective estimates, possibly guided by its experience with previous calendars.

## Solution

We use this example to illustrate the most important features of @RISK. We first see how it helps us to choose an appropriate input probability distribution for demand. Then we use it to build a simulation model for a specific order quantity and generate outputs from this model. Finally, we show how the RISKSIMTABLE function enables us to simultaneously generate outputs from several order quantities so that we can choose a best order quantity.

### DEVELOPING THE SIMULATION MODEL

The spreadsheet model for profit is essentially the same as we developed previously *without* @RISK, as shown in Figure 11.29. (See the file **Walton Bookstore 4.xlsx**.) The only new things to be aware of are the following:

**Figure 11.29**

Simulation Model with a Fixed Order Quantity

| | A | B | C | D | E | F | G | H | I | J |
|---|---|---|---|---|---|---|---|---|---|---|
| 1 | Simulation of Walton's Bookstore using @RISK | | | | | | | Range names used: | | |
| 2 | | | | | | | | Order_quantity | =Model!$B$9 | |
| 3 | Cost data | | | Demand distribution - triangular | | | | Profit | =Model!$F$13 | |
| 4 | Unit cost | $7.50 | | Minimum | 100 | | | Unit_cost | =Model!$B$4 | |
| 5 | Unit price | $10.00 | | Most likely | 175 | | | Unit_price | =Model!$B$5 | |
| 6 | Unit refund | $2.50 | | Maximum | 300 | | | Unit_refund | =Model!$B$6 | |
| 7 | | | | | | | | | | |
| 8 | Decision variable | | | | | | | | | |
| 9 | Order quantity | 200 | | | | | | | | |
| 10 | | | | | | | | | | |
| 11 | Simulation | | | | | | | | | |
| 12 | | Demand | Revenue | Cost | Refund | Profit | | | | |
| 13 | | 189 | $1,890 | $1,500 | $28 | $418 | | | | |
| 14 | | | | | | | | | | |
| 15 | Summary measures of profit from @RISK - based on 1000 iterations | | | | | | | | | |
| 16 | Minimum | -$235.00 | | | | | | | | |
| 17 | Maximum | $500.00 | | | | | | | | |
| 18 | Average | $337.51 | | | | | | | | |
| 19 | Standard deviation | $189.06 | | | | | | | | |
| 20 | 5th percentile | -$47.50 | | | | | | | | |
| 21 | 95th percentile | $500.00 | | | | | | | | |
| 22 | P(profit <= 300) | 0.360 | | | | | | | | |
| 23 | P(profit > 400) | 0.516 | | | | | | | | |

**1 Input distribution.** To generate a random demand, enter the formula

**=ROUND(RISKTRIANG(E4,E5,E6),0)**

in cell B13 for the random demand. This uses the RISKTRIANG function to generate a demand from the given input distribution. (As before, we continue to color random input cells green.) We also use Excel's ROUND function to round demand to the nearest integer. Recall from our discussion in Section 11.3 that Excel has no built-in functions to generate random numbers from a triangular distribution, but it is easy with @RISK.

**2 Output cell.** When we run the simulation, we want @RISK to keep track of profit. In @RISK's terminology, we need to designate the Profit cell, F13, as an **output cell.** To do this, select cell F13 and then click on the Add Output button on the @RISK ribbon (see Figure 11.28). This adds **RISKOUTPUT("label")** + to the cell's formula. (Here, "label" is a name that @RISK uses for its reports. In this case, it makes sense to use "Profit" as the label.) The formula in cell F13 changes from

**=C13+E13-D13**

to

**=RISKOUTPUT("Profit")+C13+E13-D13**

*The RISKOUTPUT function indicates that a cell is an output cell, so that @RISK keeps track of its values throughout the simulation.*

The plus sign following RISKOUTPUT does *not* indicate addition. It is simply @RISK's way of indicating that we want to keep track of the value in this cell (for reporting reasons) as the simulation progresses. Any number of cells can be designated in this way as output cells. They are typically the "bottom line" values of primary interest. We color such cells gray for emphasis.

**3 Summary functions.** There are several places where you can store @RISK results. One possibility is to use @RISK statistical functions to place results right in your model worksheet. @RISK provides several functions for summarizing output values. We illustrate some of these in the range B16:B23 of Figure 11.29. They contain the formulas

**=RISKMIN(Profit)**

**=RISKMAX(Profit)**

**=RISKMEAN(Profit)**

**=RISKSTDDEV(Profit)**

**=RISKPERCENTILE(Profit,0.05)**

*These @RISK summary functions allow you to show simulation results on the same sheet as the model. However, they are totally optional.*

**=RISKPERCENTILE(Profit,0.95)**

**=RISKTARGET(Profit,300)**

and

**=1-RISKTARGET(Profit,400)**

The values in these cells are not meaningful until you run the simulation. However, once the simulation runs, these formulas capture summary statistics of profit. For example, RISKMEAN calculates the average of the 1000 simulated profits, RISKPERCENTILE finds the value such that the specified percentage of simulated profits are less than or equal to this value, and RISKTARGET finds the percentage of simulated profits that are less than or equal to the specified value. Although these same summary statistics also appear in other @RISK reports, it is sometimes handy to have them in the same worksheet as the model.

## Running the Simulation

Now that we have developed the model for Walton, the rest is straightforward. The procedure is always the same: (1) specify simulation settings, (2) run the simulation, and (3) examine the results.

**①** **Simulation settings.** We must first choose some simulation settings. To do so, the buttons on the left of the Simulation group (see Figure 11.30) are useful. We typically do the following:

- Set Iterations to a number such as 1000. (@RISK calls "replications" iterations.) Any number could be used, but because the educational version of @RISK allows only 1000 uninterrupted iterations, we typically choose 1000.

- Set Simulations to 1. In a later section, you'll see why you might want to request multiple simulations.

- Click on the "dice" button so that it becomes orange. This button is actually a toggle for what appears on your worksheet. If it is orange, the setting is called "Monte Carlo" and all random cells appear random (they change when you press the F9 key). If it is blue, only the *means* appear in random input cells and the F9 key has no effect. We prefer the Monte Carlo setting, although it has no effect on how the simulation is actually run.

- Many more settings are available by clicking on the button to the left of the "dice" button, but the ones we mentioned should suffice. In addition, more permanent settings can be chosen from Application Settings under Utilities on the @RISK ribbon. Figure 11.31 shows three particular settings we suggest: (1) Place Reports In: Active Workbook (rather than a new workbook), (2) Iterations: 1000, and (3) Standard Recalc: Random Values (which saves you from having to click on the "dice" button each time).

**Figure 11.30**

Simulation Group on @RISK Ribbon

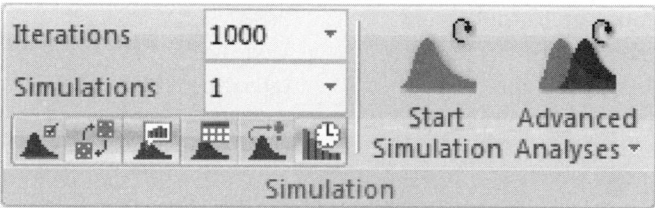

### @RISK TECHNICAL ISSUE: *Latin Hypercube Sampling*

*Leave Latin Hypercube sampling on. It produces more accurate results.*

*One setting you shouldn't change is the Sampling Type (available from the button to the left of the "dice" button). It should remain at the default Latin Hypercube setting. This is a more efficient option than the other (Monte Carlo) option because it produces a more accurate estimate of the profit distribution. In fact, we were surprised how accurate it is. In repeated runs of this model, always using different random numbers, we virtually always got a mean profit within a few pennies of $337.50. It turns out that this is the true mean profit for this input distribution of demand. Amazingly, simulation estimates it correctly—almost exactly—on virtually every run! Unfortunately, this means that a confidence interval for the mean, based on @RISK's outputs and the usual confidence interval formula (which assumes Monte Carlo sampling), is much wider (more pessimistic) than it should be. Therefore, we do not even calculate such confidence intervals from here on.*

**②** **Run the simulation.** To run the simulation, simply click on the Start Simulation on the @RISK ribbon. When you do so, @RISK repeatedly generates a random number for each random input cell, recalculates the worksheet, and keeps track of all output cell

Figure 11.31

Application Settings
Under @RISK
Utilities

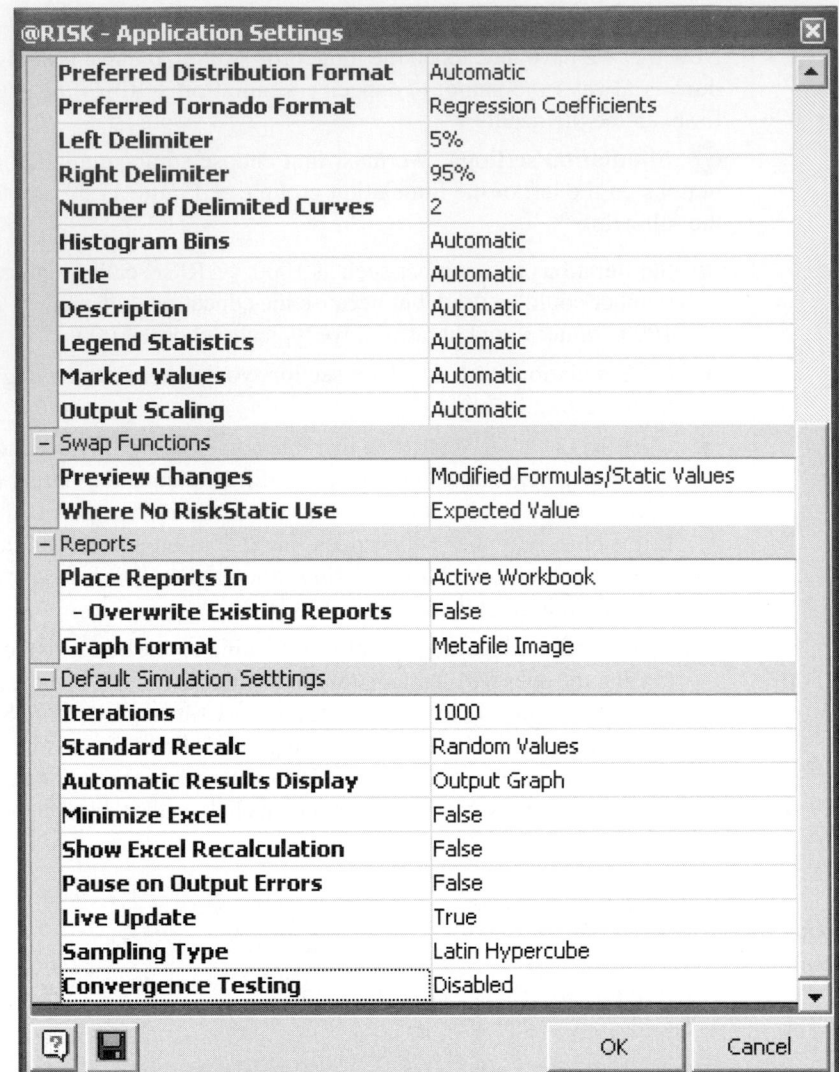

@RISK – Application Settings

| Preferred Distribution Format | Automatic |
| Preferred Tornado Format | Regression Coefficients |
| Left Delimiter | 5% |
| Right Delimiter | 95% |
| Number of Delimited Curves | 2 |
| Histogram Bins | Automatic |
| Title | Automatic |
| Description | Automatic |
| Legend Statistics | Automatic |
| Marked Values | Automatic |
| Output Scaling | Automatic |
| – Swap Functions | |
| Preview Changes | Modified Formulas/Static Values |
| Where No RiskStatic Use | Expected Value |
| – Reports | |
| Place Reports In | Active Workbook |
| – Overwrite Existing Reports | False |
| Graph Format | Metafile Image |
| – Default Simulation Setttings | |
| Iterations | 1000 |
| Standard Recalc | Random Values |
| Automatic Results Display | Output Graph |
| Minimize Excel | False |
| Show Excel Recalculation | False |
| Pause on Output Errors | False |
| Live Update | True |
| Sampling Type | Latin Hypercube |
| Convergence Testing | Disabled |

OK          Cancel

values. You can watch the progress at the bottom left of the screen. (Note: Palisade has informed us that Excel 2007 does repetitive calculations much more slowly than in Excel 2003, so if you're used to @RISK simulations running very quickly, be patient. By the time you read this, the "problem" will hopefully have been fixed in a Microsoft Office service pack.)

**3** **Examine the Results.** The big questions are (1) which results you want and (2) where you want them. @RISK gives you a lot of possibilities, and we mention only our favorites.

- You can ask for summary measures right in your model worksheet by using the @RISK statistical functions, such as RISKMEAN, that we discussed earlier.

*For a quick histogram of an output or input, select the output or input cell and click on @RISK's Browse Results button.*

- The quickest way to get results is to select an input or output cell (we chose the profit cell, F13) and then click on the Browse Results button on the @RISK ribbon. (See Figure 11.32.) This shows an interactive histogram of the selected value, as shown in Figure 11.33. You can move the sliders on this histogram to see probabilities of various outcomes. Note that the window you see from Browse Results is temporary—it goes away when you click on Close. You can make a permanent copy of the chart by clicking on the third button from the left (see the bottom of Figure 11.33) and choosing one of the copy options.

**Figure 11.32**

Results and Tools
Groups on @RISK
Ribbon

### @RISK Tip: *Saving Graphs and Tables*

*When you run a simulation with @RISK and then save your file, it asks whether you want to save your graphs and tables. We suggest that you save them. This makes your file slightly larger, but when you reopen it, the temporary graphs and tables, such as the histogram in Figure 11.32, will still be available. Otherwise, you will have to rerun the simulation.*

**Figure 11.33**

Interactive
Histogram of
Profit Output

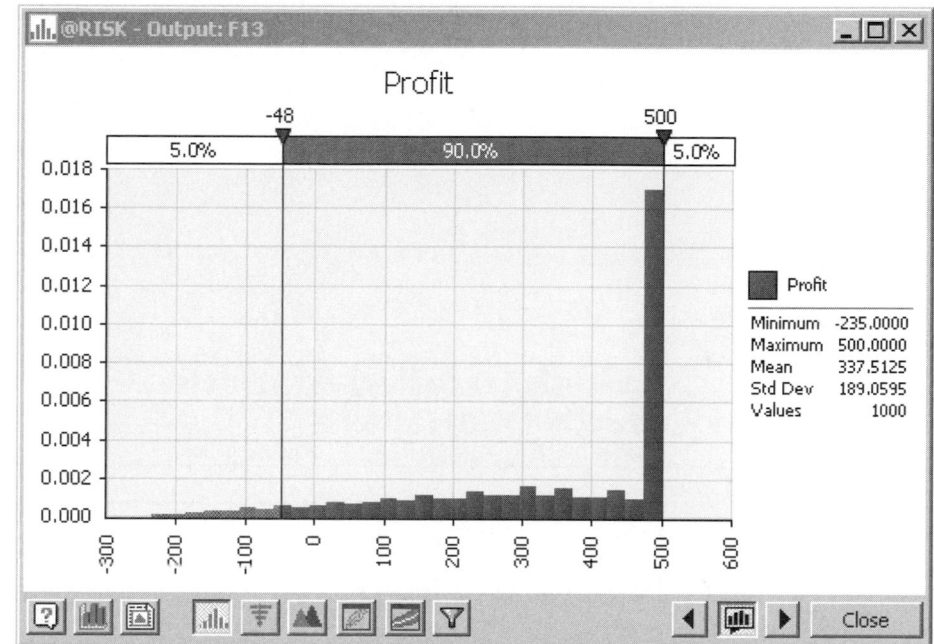

*For a quick (and customizable) report of the results, click on @RISK's Summary button.*

- You can click on the Summary button (again, see Figure 11.32) to see the temporary window in Figure 11.34 with the summary measures for Profit. In general, this report shows the summary for *all* designated inputs and outputs. By default, this Results Summary window shows a mini histogram for each output and a number of numerical summary measures. However, it is easy to customize. If you right-click on this table and choose Columns for Table, you can check or uncheck any of the options. For future screenshots in this book, we elected *not* to show the Graph and Errors columns, but instead to show median and standard deviation columns.

*If you want permanent copies of the simulation results, click on @RISK's Excel Reports buttons and check the reports you want. They will be placed in new worksheets.*

- You can click on the Excel Reports button (again, see Figure 11.32) to choose from a number of reports that are placed on new worksheets. This is a good option if you want permanent (but noninteractive) copies of reports in your workbook. As an example, Figure 11.35 shows (part of) the Detailed Statistics report you can request. It has the same information as the summary report in Figure 11.34, plus a lot more.

### Discussion of the Simulation Results

The strength of @RISK is that it keeps track of any outputs you specify and then allows you to show the corresponding results as graphs or tables, in temporary windows or in

**Figure 11.34** Summary Table of Profit Output

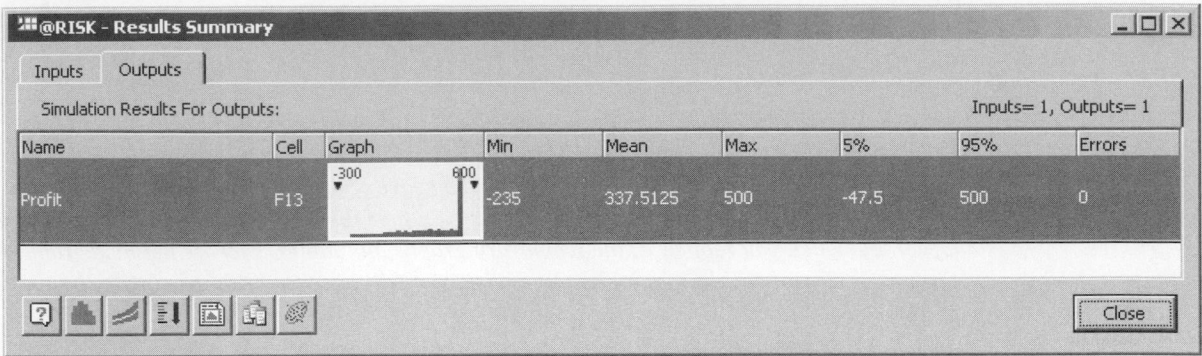

| Name | Cell | Graph | Min | Mean | Max | 5% | 95% | Errors |
|---|---|---|---|---|---|---|---|---|
| Profit | F13 | -300 to 600 | -235 | 337.5125 | 500 | -47.5 | 500 | 0 |

**Figure 11.35**

@RISK Detailed Statistics Report

# @Risk Detailed Statistics

**Performed By:** Chris Albright
**Date:** Monday, October 08, 2007 2:33:55 PM

| | B | C | D |
|---|---|---|---|
| 6 | Name | Profit | Demand |
| 7 | Description | Output | RiskTriang(E4,E5,E6) |
| 8 | Cell | Model!F13 | Model!B13 |
| 9 | Minimum | -235 | 101.946 |
| 10 | Maximum | 500 | 296.6687 |
| 11 | Mean | 337.5125 | 191.6672 |
| 12 | Std Deviation | 189.0595 | 41.2748 |
| 13 | Variance | 35743.51 | 1703.609 |
| 14 | Skewness | -0.9482242 | 0.2363251 |
| 15 | Kurtosis | 2.792944 | 2.404146 |
| 16 | Errors | 0 | 0 |
| 17 | Mode | 290 | 173.9869 |
| 18 | 5% Perc | -47.5 | 127.369 |
| 19 | 10% Perc | 42.5 | 138.6223 |
| 20 | 15% Perc | 102.5 | 147.3225 |
| 21 | 20% Perc | 162.5 | 154.7333 |
| 22 | 25% Perc | 207.5 | 161.1572 |
| 23 | 30% Perc | 252.5 | 166.99 |
| 24 | 35% Perc | 290 | 172.4364 |

permanent worksheets. As we have seen, @RISK provides several options for displaying results, and we encourage you to explore the possibilities. However, don't lose sight of the overall goal: You want to see how outputs vary as the random inputs vary, and you want reports that "tell the story" most effectively. For this particular example, the results in Figures 11.29, 11.33, 11.34, and 11.35 allow us to conclude the following:

- The smallest simulated profit (out of 1000) was −$235, the largest was $500, the average was $337.51, and the standard deviation of the 1000 profits was $189.06. Five percent of the simulated profits were −$47.50 or below, and 95 percent were $500 or above. Also, 36% of the profits were less than or equal to $300, and 51.6% were larger than $400. (See Figure 11.29. These results are also available from the summary table in Figure 11.34 or the detailed statistics report in Figure 11.35. In particular, the bottom of the detailed statistics report, not shown in the figure, allows you to ask for any percentiles or "target" values.)

- The profit distribution, for this particular order quantity, is extremely skewed to the left, with a large bar at $500. (See Figure 11.33.) Do you see why? It's because profit is exactly $500 if demand is greater than or equal to the order quantity, 200. In other words, the probability that profit is $500 equals the probability that demand is at least 200. (This probability is 0.4.) Lower demands result in decreasing profits, which explains the gradual decline in the histogram from right to left.

### Revisiting the Flaw of Averages

In the previous chapter, we discussed the "flaw of averages," a misconception many people have about problems involving uncertainty. In the context of simulation, the flaw is essentially the following: If we substitute *mean* values for the inputs and observe a resulting output, this output value is generally *not* equal to the mean output value we get from running the simulation. This has tremendous importance in real applications. It means that if we ignore uncertainty in the inputs and simply use their means for the spreadsheet model, we can get a very misleading value of the mean output value. To make things worse, we generally can't tell, at least not without performing more analysis, whether the error is on the low side or the high side.

This flaw of averages is very easy to demonstrate in @RISK. We suggested using the Monte Carlo (Random) option (by clicking on the "dice" button to make it orange) instead of Static option (by clicking on the "dice" button again to make it blue). The Monte Carlo option makes the simulation appear random. When you select it and then press the F9 recalc key, all of the random numbers change. However, this setting is completely cosmetic and has no effect on the way @RISK works when you run the simulation. So for now, we use the Static option instead. The effect is that we see the *mean* input value in each input cell. In the Walton model, there is only one input cell, the demand cell, and its mean is 191.67 (see Figure 11.36). [The mean of a triangular distribution is the

**Figure 11.36**

The Walton Model Using the Mean Demand

| | A | B | C | D | E | F |
|---|---|---|---|---|---|---|
| 1 | Simulation of Walton's Bookstore using @RISK | | | | | |
| 2 | | | | | | |
| 3 | Cost data | | | Demand distribution - triangular | | |
| 4 | Unit cost | $7.50 | | Minimum | 100 | |
| 5 | Unit price | $10.00 | | Most likely | 175 | |
| 6 | Unit refund | $2.50 | | Maximum | 300 | |
| 7 | | | | | | |
| 8 | Decision variable | | | | | |
| 9 | Order quantity | 200 | | | | |
| 10 | | | | | | |
| 11 | Simulation | | | | | |
| 12 | | Demand | Revenue | Cost | Refund | Profit |
| 13 | | 192 | $1,920 | $1,500 | $20 | $440 |

average of its three parameters: $(100 + 175 + 300)/3 = 191.67$. The model rounds it to 192.] Using this mean value for the input, we see that the resulting profit is $440. However, we know from running the simulation that the expected profit is about $337. This is the flaw of averages. The mean profit we want, $337, isn't even close to the profit we obtain by using the mean demand in the model. In other words, a deterministic version of this model, one that ignores uncertainty and uses the mean value of demand, gives a very misleading estimate of profit.

Why should the profit from using the mean demand be so different from the mean of the simulated profits? The reason is enlightening. We are using an order quantity of 200 and the (rounded) mean demand, 192, is pretty close to this order quantity. If demand were exactly 192, Walton would sell 192 calendars and have only 8 left over. This is just about as good a scenario as Walton can hope for, given an order quantity of 200. The demand nearly matches the supply. However, when we run the simulation, the demand can vary widely, and many of the simulated scenarios are considerably less attractive than the one where demand is 192. This explains why the mean of the simulated profits is considerably *less* than the profit using the mean demand.

> ### FUNDAMENTAL INSIGHT
>
> **The Flaw of Averages**
>
> If a model contains uncertain inputs, it can be very misleading to build a deterministic model by using the *means* of the inputs to predict an output value. The resulting output can be considerably different—lower *or* higher—than the mean of the outputs obtained from running a simulation with the uncertainty incorporated explicitly.

## Using RISKSIMTABLE

Walton's ultimate goal is to choose an order quantity that provides a large mean profit. We could rerun the simulation model several times, each time with a different order quantity in the order quantity cell, and compare the results. However, this has two drawbacks. First, it takes a lot of time and work. The second drawback is more subtle. Each time we run the simulation, we get a *different* set of random demands. Therefore, one of the order quantities could win the contest just by luck. For a fairer comparison, we should test each order quantity on the *same* set of random demands.

*The RISKSIMTABLE function allows you to run several simulations at once—one for each value of some variable (usually a decision variable).*

The RISKSIMTABLE function in @RISK enables us to obtain a fair comparison quickly and easily. We illustrate this function in Figure 11.37. (See the file **Walton Bookstore 5.xlsx.**) There are two modifications to the previous model. The first is that we have listed order quantities we want to test in row 9. (We chose these as representative order quantities. You could change, or add to, this list.) Second, instead of entering a *number* in cell B9, we enter the *formula*

**=RISKSIMTABLE(D9:H9)**

**Figure 11.37**

Model with a RISKSIMTABLE Function

| | A | B | C | D | E | F | G | H | I | J | K |
|---|---|---|---|---|---|---|---|---|---|---|---|
| 1 | Simulation of Walton's Bookstore using @RISK | | | | | | | | Range names used: | | |
| 2 | | | | | | | | | Order_quantity | =Model!$B$9 | |
| 3 | Cost data | | | Demand distribution - triangular | | | | | Profit | =Model!$F$13 | |
| 4 | Unit cost | $7.50 | | Minimum | 100 | | | | Unit_cost | =Model!$B$4 | |
| 5 | Unit price | $10.00 | | Most likely | 175 | | | | Unit_price | =Model!$B$5 | |
| 6 | Unit refund | $2.50 | | Maximum | 300 | | | | Unit_refund | =Model!$B$6 | |
| 7 | | | | | | | | | | | |
| 8 | Decision variable | | | Order quantities to try | | | | | | | |
| 9 | Order quantity | 150 | | 150 | 175 | 200 | 225 | 250 | | | |
| 10 | | | | | | | | | | | |
| 11 | Simulated quantities | | | | | | | | | | |
| 12 | | Demand | Revenue | Cost | Refund | Profit | | | | | |
| 13 | | 180 | $1,500 | $1,125 | $0 | $375 | | | | | |
| 14 | | | | | | | | | | | |
| 15 | Summary measures of profit from @RISK - based on 1000 iterations for each simulation | | | | | | | | | | |
| 16 | Simulation | 1 | 2 | 3 | 4 | 5 | | | | | |
| 17 | Order quantity | 150 | 175 | 200 | 225 | 250 | | | | | |
| 18 | Minimum | $15.00 | -$110.00 | -$235.00 | -$360.00 | -$485.00 | | | | | |
| 19 | Maximum | $375.00 | $437.50 | $500.00 | $562.50 | $625.00 | | | | | |
| 20 | Average | $354.16 | $367.19 | $337.48 | $270.32 | $175.02 | | | | | |
| 21 | Standard deviation | $58.98 | $121.88 | $189.07 | $247.08 | $287.01 | | | | | |
| 22 | 5th percentile | $202.50 | $77.50 | -$47.50 | -$172.50 | -$297.50 | | | | | |
| 23 | 95th percentile | $375.00 | $437.50 | $500.00 | $562.50 | $625.00 | | | | | |

Note that the list does not need to be entered in the spreadsheet (although this is a good idea). We could instead enter the formula

**=RISKSIMTABLE({150,175,200,225,250})**

where the list of numbers must be enclosed in curly brackets. In either case, the worksheet displays the first member of the list, 150, and the corresponding calculations for this first order quantity. However, the model is now set up to run the simulation for *all* order quantities in the list.

To implement this, only one setting needs to be changed. As before, we enter 1000 for the number of iterations, but this time we enter 5 for the number of simulations. @RISK then runs 5 simulations of 1000 iterations each, one simulation for each order quantity in the list, and it uses the *same* 1000 random demands for each simulation.

### @RISK Function: *RISKSIMTABLE*

*To run several simulations simultaneously, enter the formula =RISKSIMTABLE (InputRange) in any cell. Here, InputRange refers to a list of the values to be simulated, such as various order quantities. Before running the simulation, make sure the number of simulations is set to the number of values in the InputRange list.*

You can again get results from the simulation in various ways. Here are some possibilities.

- You can enter the same @RISK statistical functions in cells in the model worksheet, as shown in rows 18–23 of Figure 11.37. The trick is to realize that each such function can have a last argument that specifies the simulation number. For example, the formulas in cells C20 and C22 are

**=RISKMEAN(Profit,C16)**

and

**=RISKPERCENTILE(Profit,0.05,C16)**

Remember that the results in these cells are meaningless until you run the simulation.

- You can select the Profit cell and click on Browse Results to see a histogram of profits, as shown in Figure 11.38. By default, the histogram shown is for the *first* simulation, where the order quantity is 150. However, if you click on the red button with the pound sign, you can select any of the simulations. As an example, Figure 11.39 shows the histogram of profits for the fifth simulation, where the order quantity is 250. (Do you see why these two histograms are so different? When the order quantity is 150, there is a high probability of selling out; hence the spike on the right is large. But the probability of selling out with an order quantity of 250 is much lower; hence its spike on the right is much less dominant.)

- You can click on the Summary button to get the results from all simulations shown in Figure 11.40. (These results match those in Figure 11.37.)

- You can click on Excel Reports to get any of a number of reports on permanent worksheets. Specifically, we suggest you try Quick Reports. This produces several graphs and summary measures for each simulation, each on a different worksheet. This provides a lot of information for almost no work!

For this particular example, the results in Figures 11.37–11.40 are illuminating. We see that an order quantity of 200 provides the largest *mean* profit. However, is this necessarily the "best" order quantity? This depends on our attitude toward risk. Certainly, larger order quantities incur more risk (their histograms are more spread out, their 5th and 95th percentiles are

**Figure 11.38** Histogram of Profit with Order Quantity 150

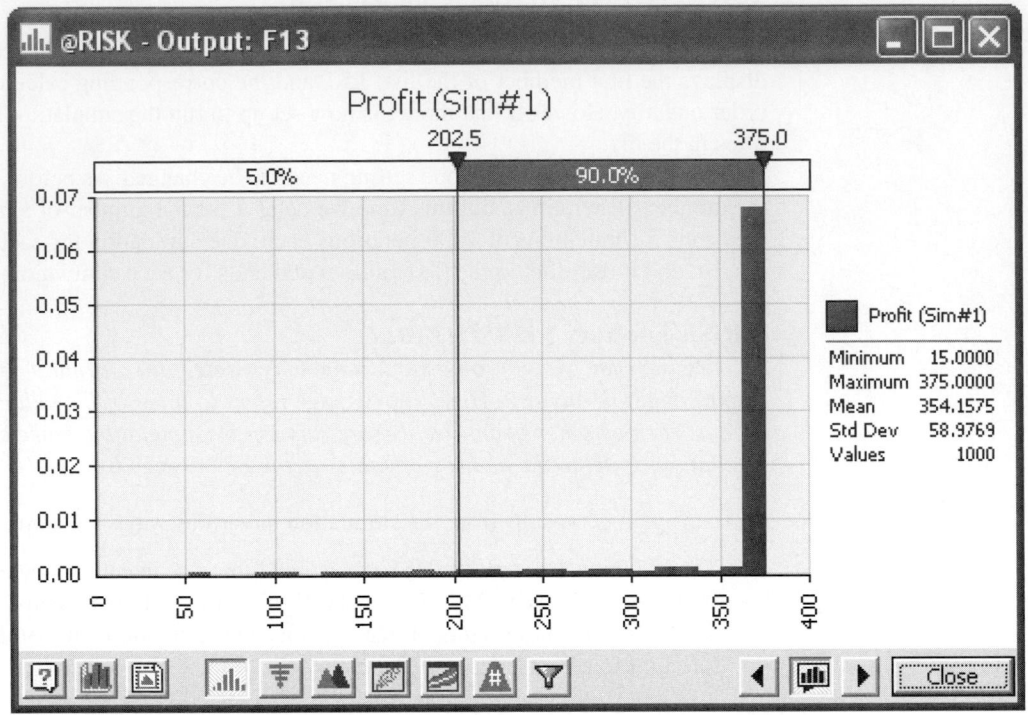

**Figure 11.39** Histogram of Profit with Order Quantity 250

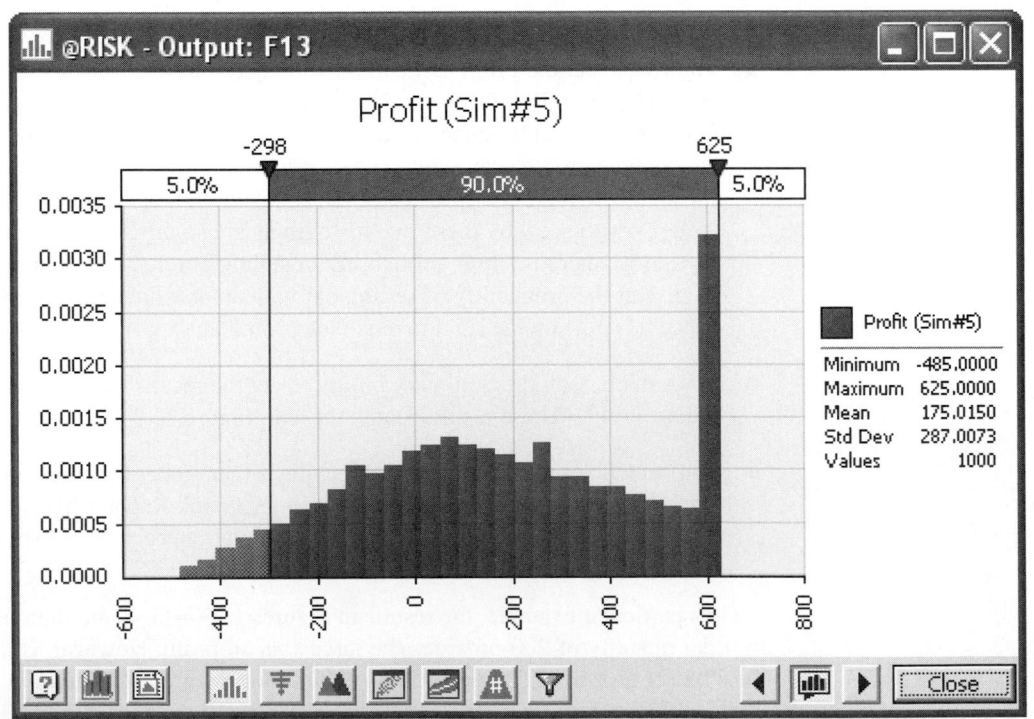

**Figure 11.40** Summary Report for All Five Simulations

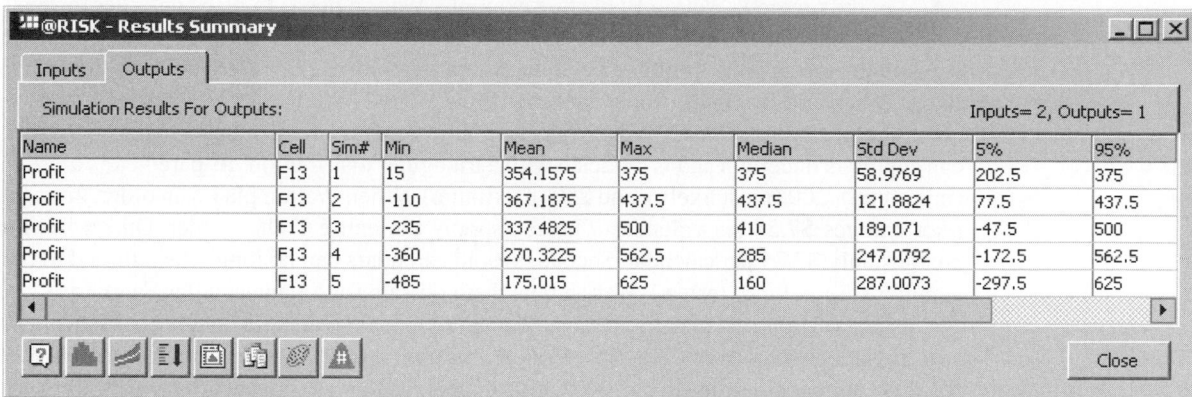

| Name | Cell | Sim# | Min | Mean | Max | Median | Std Dev | 5% | 95% |
|------|------|------|------|---------|-------|--------|---------|--------|-------|
| Profit | F13 | 1 | 15 | 354.1575 | 375 | 375 | 58.9769 | 202.5 | 375 |
| Profit | F13 | 2 | -110 | 367.1875 | 437.5 | 437.5 | 121.8824 | 77.5 | 437.5 |
| Profit | F13 | 3 | -235 | 337.4825 | 500 | 410 | 189.071 | -47.5 | 500 |
| Profit | F13 | 4 | -360 | 270.3225 | 562.5 | 285 | 247.0792 | -172.5 | 562.5 |
| Profit | F13 | 5 | -485 | 175.015 | 625 | 160 | 287.0073 | -297.5 | 625 |

more extreme), but they also have more upside potential. On the other hand, a smaller order quantity, while having a somewhat smaller mean, might be preferable because of less variability. It is *not* an easy choice, but at least the simulation results gives us plenty of information on which base our decision. ■

## Some Limitations of @RISK

The educational version of @RISK included with the book has some limitations you should be aware of. (If you want to spend several hundred dollars, you can purchase the commercial version of @RISK without these limitations.)

■ The simulation model must be contained in a single workbook with at most four worksheets, and each worksheet is limited to 300 rows and 100 columns.

■ The number of @RISK input probability distribution functions, such as RISKNORMAL, is limited to 100.

■ The number of unattended iterations is limited to 1000. You can request more than 1000, but you have to click a button after each 1000 iterations.

*To avoid potential problems, close all other workbooks when running an @RISK model.*

The first limitation shouldn't cause problems, at least not for the model sizes discussed in this book. However, we strongly urge you to close all other workbooks when you are running an @RISK simulation model, *especially* if they also contain @RISK functions. The second limitation can be a problem, especially in multiperiod problems. For example, if you are simulating 52 weeks of a year, and each week requires two random inputs, you are already over the 100-function limit. One way to get around this is to use built-in Excel functions for random inputs rather than @RISK functions whenever possible. For example, if you want to simulate the flip of a fair coin, the formula **=IF(RAND()<0.5,"Heads","Tails")** works just as well as the formula **=IF(RISKUNIFORM(0,1)<0.5,"Heads","Tails")**, but the former doesn't count against the 100-function limit.

## @RISK Models with Several Random Input Variables

We conclude this section with another modification of the Walton Bookstore example. To this point, there has been a single random variable, demand. Often, there are several random variables, each reflecting some uncertainty, and we want to include each of them in the simulation model. The following example illustrates how this can be done, and it also illustrates a very useful feature of @RISK, its sensitivity analysis.

EXAMPLE    11.3 ADDITIONAL UNCERTAINTY AT WALTON BOOKSTORE

As in the previous Walton Bookstore example, Walton needs to place an order for next year's calendar. We continue to assume that the calendars sell for $10, and customer demand for the calendars at this price is triangularly distributed with minimum value, most likely value, and maximum value equal to 100, 175, and 300. However, there are now two other sources of uncertainty. First, the maximum number of calendars Walton's supplier can supply is uncertain and is modeled with a triangular distribution. Its parameters are 125 (minimum), 200 (most likely), and 250 (maximum). When Walton places an order, the supplier charges $7.50 per calendar *if* he can supply the entire Walton order. Otherwise, he charges only $7.25 per calendar. Second, unsold calendars can no longer be returned to the supplier for a refund. Instead, Walton puts them on sale for $5 apiece after February 1. At this price, Walton believes the demand for leftover calendars is triangularly distributed with parameters 0, 50, and 75. Any calendars *still* left over, say, after March 1, are thrown away. Walton again wants to use simulation to analyze the resulting profit for various order quantities.

**Objective**    To develop and analyze a simulation model with multiple sources of uncertainty using @RISK, and to introduce @RISK's sensitivity analysis features.

## WHERE DO THE NUMBERS COME FROM?

As in Example 11.2, the monetary values are straightforward, and the parameters of the triangular distributions would probably be educated guesses, possibly based on experience with previous calendars.

## Solution

As always, we first need to develop the model. Then we can run the simulation with @RISK and examine the results.

## DEVELOPING THE SIMULATION MODEL

The completed model is shown in Figure 11.41. (See the file **Walton Bookstore 6.xlsx**.) The model requires a bit more logic than the previous Walton model. It can be developed with the following steps:

**Figure 11.41**

@RISK Simulation Model with Three Random Inputs

| | A | B | C | D | E | F | G | H | I | J | K | L | M |
|---|---|---|---|---|---|---|---|---|---|---|---|---|---|
| 1 | Simulation of Walton's Bookstore using @RISK | | | | | | | | | | Range names used: | | |
| 2 | | | | | | | | | | | Order_quantity | =Model!$B$10 | |
| 3 | Cost data | | | Demand distribution: triangular | | | | | | | Profit | =Model!$J$14 | |
| 4 | Unit cost 1 | $7.50 | | | Regular price | Sale price | | Supply distribution: triangular | | | Regular_price | =Model!$B$6 | |
| 5 | Unit cost 2 | $7.25 | | Minimum | 100 | 0 | | Minimum | 125 | | Sale_price | =Model!$B$7 | |
| 6 | Regular price | $10.00 | | Most likely | 175 | 50 | | Most likely | 200 | | Unit_cost_1 | =Model!$B$4 | |
| 7 | Sale price | $5.00 | | Maximum | 300 | 75 | | Maximum | 250 | | Unit_cost_2 | =Model!$B$5 | |
| 8 | | | | | | | | | | | | | |
| 9 | Decision variable | | | Order quantities to try | | | | | | | | | |
| 10 | Order quantity | 150 | | | 150 | 175 | 200 | 225 | 250 | | | | |
| 11 | | | | | | | | | | | | | |
| 12 | Simulated quantities | | | | | At regular price | | At sale price | | | | | |
| 13 | | Maximum supply | Actual supply | Cost | Demand | Revenue | Left over | Demand | Revenue | Profit | | | |
| 14 | | 172 | 150 | $1,125 | 192 | $1,500 | 0 | 59 | $0 | $375 | | | |
| 15 | | | | | | | | | | | | | |
| 16 | Summary measures of profit from @RISK - based on 1000 iterations for each simulation | | | | | | | | | | | | |
| 17 | Simulation | 1 | 2 | 3 | 4 | 5 | | | | | | | |
| 18 | Order quantity | 150 | 175 | 200 | 225 | 250 | | | | | | | |
| 19 | Minimum | $15.00 | -$172.50 | -$360.00 | -$394.00 | -$394.00 | | | | | | | |
| 20 | Maximum | $409.75 | $478.50 | $547.25 | $616.00 | $671.00 | | | | | | | |
| 21 | Average | $361.57 | $389.55 | $394.50 | $395.03 | $397.62 | | | | | | | |
| 22 | Standard deviation | $43.51 | $94.74 | $148.51 | $176.27 | $178.58 | | | | | | | |
| 23 | 5th percentile | $265.00 | $182.50 | $55.00 | $11.50 | $14.25 | | | | | | | |
| 24 | 95th percentile | $375.00 | $456.50 | $528.00 | $577.50 | $588.50 | | | | | | | |

**1 Random inputs.** There are three random inputs in this model: the most the supplier can supply Walton, the customer demand when the selling price is $10, and the customer demand for sale-price calendars. Generate these in cells B14, E14, and H14 (using the ROUND function to obtain integers) with the RISKTRIANG function. Specifically, the formulas in cells B14, E14, and H14 are

**=ROUND(RISKTRIANG(I5,I6,I7),0)**

**=ROUND(RISKTRIANG (E5,E6,E7),0)**

and

**=ROUND(RISKTRIANG (F5,F6,F7),0)**

Note that in cell H14, we generate the random *potential* demand for calendars at the sale price even though there might not be any calendars left to put on sale.

**2 Actual supply.** The number of calendars supplied to Walton is the smaller of the number ordered and the maximum the supplier is able to supply. Calculate this value in cell C14 with the formula

**=MIN(B14,Order_quantity)**

**3 Order cost.** Walton gets the reduced price, $7.25, if the supplier cannot supply the entire order. Otherwise, Walton must pay $7.50 per calendar. Therefore, calculate the total order cost in cell D14 with the formula (using the obvious range names)

**=IF(B14>=Order_quantity,Unit_cost_1,Unit_cost_2)*C14**

**4 Other quantities.** The rest of the model is straightforward. Calculate the revenue from regular-price sales in cell F14 with the formula

**=Regular_price*MIN(C14,E14)**

Calculate the number left over after regular-price sales in cell G14 with the formula

**=MAX(C14-E14,0)**

Calculate the revenue from sale-price sales in cell I14 with the formula

**=Sale_price*MIN(G14,H14)**

Finally, calculate profit and designate it as an output cell for @RISK in cell J14 with the formula

**=RISKOUTPUT("Profit")+F14+I14-D14**

We could also designate other cells (the revenue cells, for example) as output cells, but we have chosen to have a single output cell, Profit.

**5 Order quantities.** As before, enter a RISKSIMTABLE function in cell B10 so that Walton can try different order quantities. Specifically, enter the formula

**=RISKSIMTABLE(D10:H10)**

in cell B10.

### Running the Simulation

*On each iteration, @RISK generates a new set of random inputs and calculates the corresponding output(s).*

As always, the next steps are to specify the simulation settings (we chose 1000 iterations and 5 simulations) and run the simulation. It is important to realize what @RISK does when it runs a simulation with several random input cells. For each iteration, @RISK generates a random value for each input variable *independently* of the others. In this example, it generates a maximum supply in cell B14 from one triangular distribution, generates a regular-price demand in cell E14 from another triangular distribution, and generates a sale-price demand in cell H14 from a third triangular distribution. With these input values, @RISK then calculates the profit. Finally, for each order quantity, it iterates this procedure 1000 times, keeping track of the corresponding profits.[9]

## Discussion of the Simulation Results

Selected results are given in Figures 11.41 (at the bottom) and 11.42, the profit histogram for an order quantity of 200. (The histograms for the other order quantities are similar to what we've seen before, with more skewness to the left and a larger spike to the right as the order quantity decreases). For this particular order quantity, they indicate an average profit of about $395, a 5th percentile of $55, a 95th percentile of $528, and a distribution of profits that is again skewed to the left.

**Figure 11.42**

Histogram of
Simulated Profits
for Order
Quantity 200

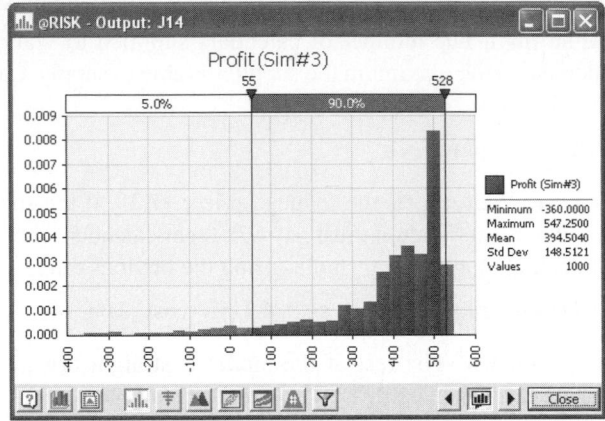

## Sensitivity Analysis

We now demonstrate a feature of @RISK that is particularly useful when there are several random input cells. This feature enables us to see which of these inputs is most related to, or *correlated* with, an output cell. To perform this analysis, select the profit cell, J14, and click on the Browse Results button. You see a histogram of profit in a temporary window, as we've already discussed, with a number of buttons at the bottom of the window. Click on the red button with the pound sign to select a simulation. We chose #3, where the order quantity is 200. Then click on the "tornado" button (the fifth button from the left) and choose Correlation Coefficients. This produces the chart in Figure 11.43.

**Figure 11.43**

Tornado Chart for
Sensitivity Analysis

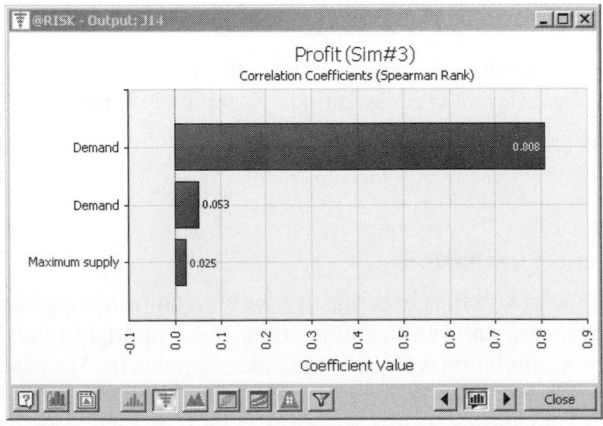

---

[9] It is also possible to *correlate* the inputs, as we demonstrate in the next section.

(The Regression option produces similar results, but the Correlation option is probably easier to understand.)

This figure shows graphically and numerically how each of the random inputs correlates with profit: the higher the (magnitude of the) correlation, the stronger the relationship between that input and profit. In this sense, we see that the regular-price demand has by far the largest effect on profit. The other two inputs, maximum supply and sale-price demand, are nearly uncorrelated with profit, so they are much less important. Identifying important input variables is important for real applications. If a random input is highly correlated with an important output, then it might be worth the time and money to learn more about this input and possibly reduce the amount of uncertainty involving it. ∎

*A tornado chart allows you to see which of the random inputs have the most effect on an output.*

# PROBLEMS

## Skill-Building Problems

**16.** If you add several normally distributed random numbers, the result is normally distributed, where the mean of the sum is the sum of the individual means, and the variance of the sum is the sum of the individual variances. (Remember that variance is the square of standard deviation.) This is a difficult result to prove mathematically, but it is easy to demonstrate with simulation. To do so, run a simulation where you add three normally distributed random numbers, each with mean 100 and standard deviation 10. Your single output variable should be the sum of these three numbers. Verify with @RISK that the distribution of this output is approximately normal with mean 300 and variance 300 (hence, standard deviation $\sqrt{300} = 17.32$).

**17.** In Problem 11, suppose that the damage amount is triangularly distributed with parameters 500, 1500, and 7000. That is, the damage in an accident can be as low as $500 or as high as $7000, the most likely value is $1500, and there is definite skewness to the right. (It turns out, as you can verify in RISKview, that the mean of this distribution is $3000, the same as in Problem 11.) Use @RISK to simulate the amount you pay for damage. Run 5000 iterations. Then answer the following questions. In each case, explain how the indicated event would occur.
   **a.** What is the probability that you pay a positive amount but less than $250?
   **b.** What is the probability that you pay more than $500?
   **c.** What is the probability that you pay exactly $1000 (the deductible)?

**18.** Continuing the previous problem, assume as in Problem 11 that the damage amount is *normally* distributed with mean $3000 and standard deviation $750. Run @RISK with 5000 iterations to simulate the amount you pay for damage. Compare your results with those in the previous problem. Does it appear to matter whether you assume a triangular distribution or a normal distribution

for damage amounts? Why isn't this a totally fair comparison? (*Hint:* Use @RISK to find the standard deviation for the triangular distribution.)

**19.** In Problem 12, suppose that the demand for cars is normally distributed with mean 100 and standard deviation 15. Use @RISK to determine the best order quantity, that is, the one with the largest mean profit. Using the statistics and/or graphs from @RISK, discuss whether this order quantity would be considered best by the car dealer. (The point is that a decision maker can use more than just *mean* profit in making a decision.)

**20.** Use @RISK to analyze the sweatshirt situation in Problem 14. Do this for the discrete distributions given in the problem and then do it for normal distributions. For the normal case, assume that the regular demand is normally distributed with mean 9800 and standard deviation 1300 and that the demand at the reduced price is normally distributed with mean 3800 and standard deviation 1400.

## Skill-Extending Problem

**21.** Although the normal distribution is a reasonable input distribution in many situations, it does have two potential drawbacks: (1) it allows negative values, even though they may be extremely improbable, and (2) it is a symmetric distribution. Many situations are modeled better with a distribution that allows only positive values and is skewed to the right. Two of these are the gamma and lognormal distributions, and @RISK enables you to generate observations from each of these distributions. The @RISK function for the gamma distribution is RISKGAMMA, and it takes two arguments, as in **=RISKGAMMA(3,10)**. The first argument, which must be positive, determines the shape. The smaller the argument, the more skewed the distribution is to the right; the larger the argument, the more symmetric the distribution is. The second argument determines the scale, in the sense that the product of the second argument and the first argument equals the mean of the distribution. (The mean above, when the arguments are 3 and 10, is 30.) Also, the product of the second argument and the square root of the first argument is the standard deviation of the distribution. (When the arguments are 3 and 10, it is $\sqrt{3}(10) = 17.32$.) The @RISK function for the lognormal distribution is RISKLOGNORM. It has two arguments, as in **=RISKLOGNORM(40, 10)**. These arguments are the mean and standard deviation of the distribution. Rework Example 11.2 for the following demand distributions. Do the simulated outputs have any different qualitative properties with these distributions than with the triangular distribution used in the example?

**a.** Gamma distribution with parameters 2 and 85
**b.** Gamma distribution with parameters 5 and 35
**c.** Lognormal distribution with mean 170 and standard deviation 60

## 11.6 THE EFFECTS OF INPUT DISTRIBUTIONS ON RESULTS

In Section 11.3, we discussed input distributions. The randomness in input variables causes the variability in the output variables. We now briefly explore whether the choice of input distribution(s) makes much difference in the distribution of an output variable such as profit. This is an important question. If the choice of input distribution doesn't matter much, then we do not need to agonize over this choice. However, if it *does* make a difference, then we have to be more careful about choosing the most appropriate input distribution for any particular problem. Unfortunately, it is impossible to answer the question definitively. The best we can say in general is that it depends. Some models are more sensitive to changes in the shape or parameters of input distributions than others. Still, the issue is worth exploring.

We discuss two types of sensitivity analysis in this section. First, we see whether the shape of the input distribution matters. In the Walton bookstore example, we have been assuming a triangularly distributed demand with some skewness. Do we get basically the same results if we try another input distribution such as the normal distribution? Second, we see whether the *independence* of input variables is crucial to the output results. Many random quantities in real situations are not independent; they are positively or negatively correlated. Fortunately, @RISK enables us to build correlation into a model. We analyze the effect of this correlation.

### Effect of the Shape of the Input Distribution(s)

We first explore the effect of the shape of the input distribution(s). As the following example indicates, if we make a "fair" comparison, the shape can have a relatively minor effect.

| EXAMPLE | **11.4 EFFECT OF DEMAND DISTRIBUTION AT WALTON'S** |

We continue to explore the demand for calendars at Walton Bookstore. We keep the same unit cost, unit price, and unit refund for leftovers as in Example 11.2. However, in that example, we used a triangular distribution for demand with parameters 100, 175, and 300. Assuming that Walton orders 200 calendars, is the distribution of profit affected if we instead use a *normal* distribution of demand?

**Objective**   To see whether a triangular distribution with some skewness gives the same profit distribution as a normal distribution for demand.

The numbers here are the same as in Example 11.2. However, as discussed next, we will choose the parameters of the normal distribution to provide a fair comparison with the triangular distribution we used earlier.

## Solution

*For a fair comparison of alternative input distributions, the distributions should have (at least approximately) equal means and standard deviations.*

In this type of analysis, it is important to make a fair comparison. When we select a normal distribution for demand, we must choose a mean and standard deviation. Which values should we choose? It seems only fair to choose the *same* mean and standard deviation that the triangular distribution has. To find the mean and standard deviation for a triangular distribution with given minimum, most likely, and maximum values, we can take advantage of @RISK's Define Distributions window. Select any blank cell, click on the Define Distribution button, select the triangular distribution, and enter the parameters 100, 175, and 300. The pane on the right indicates that the mean and standard deviation are 191.67 and 41.248, respectively. Therefore, for a fair comparison, we use the normal distribution with mean 191.67 and standard deviation 41.248. In fact, @RISK allows us to see a comparison of these two distributions, as in Figure 11.44. To get this chart, click on the Add Overlay button, select the normal distribution from the gallery, and enter 191.67 and 41.248 as its mean and standard deviation.

**Figure 11.44**

Triangular and Normal Distributions for Demand

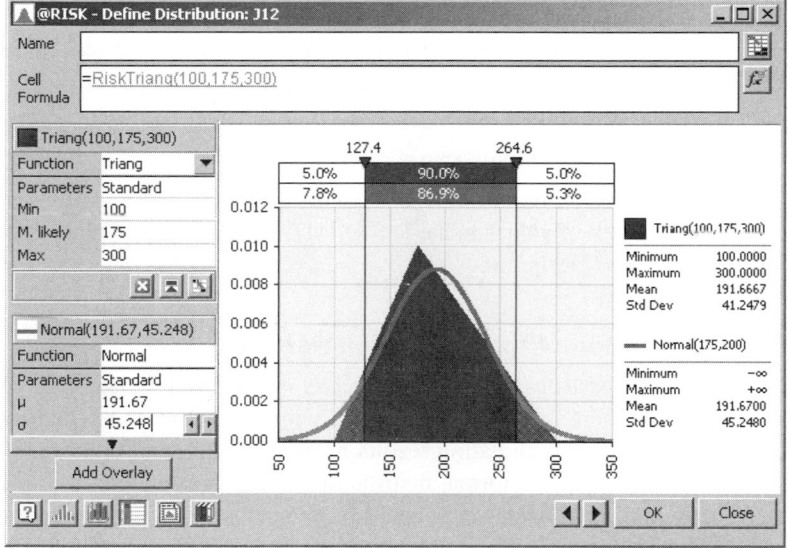

The logic in this model is almost exactly the same as before. (See Figure 11.45 and the file **Walton Bookstore 7.xlsx**.) However, a clever use of the RISKSIMTABLE function allows us to run two simulations at once, one for the triangular distribution and one for the corresponding normal distribution. The two steps required are as follows:

Figure 11.45

@RISK Model for Comparing Two Input Distributions

| | A | B | C | D | E | F | G | H | I | J | K | L | M |
|---|---|---|---|---|---|---|---|---|---|---|---|---|---|
| 1 | Simulation of Walton's Bookstore using @RISK - two possible demand distributions | | | | | | | | | | Range names used: | | |
| 2 | | | | | | | | | | | Order_quantity | =Model!$B$9 | |
| 3 | Cost data | | | Demand distribution 1 - triangular | | | Demand distribution 2 - normal | | | | Profit | =Model!$F$15 | |
| 4 | Unit cost | $7.50 | | Minimum | 100 | | Mean | 191.67 | | | Unit_cost | =Model!$B$4 | |
| 5 | Unit price | $10.00 | | Most likely | 175 | | Stdev | 41.248 | | | Unit_price | =Model!$B$5 | |
| 6 | Unit refund | $2.50 | | Maximum | 300 | | | | | | Unit_refund | =Model!$B$6 | |
| 7 | | | | | | | | | | | | | |
| 8 | Decision variable | | | | | | | | | | | | |
| 9 | Order quantity | 200 | | | | | | | | | | | |
| 10 | | | | | | | | | | | | | |
| 11 | Demand distribution to use | 1 | ← | | Formula is =RiskSimtable({1,2}) | | | | | | | | |
| 12 | | | | | | | | | | | | | |
| 13 | Simulated quantities | | | | | | | | | | | | |
| 14 | | Demand | Revenue | Cost | Refund | Profit | | | | | | | |
| 15 | | 132 | $1,320 | $1,500 | $170 | -$10 | | | | | | | |
| 16 | | | | | | | | | | | | | |
| 17 | Summary measures of profit from @RISK - based on 1000 iterations for each simulation | | | | | | | | | | | | |
| 18 | Simulation | 1 | 2 | | | | | | | | | | |
| 19 | Distribution | Triangular | Normal | | | | | | | | | | |
| 20 | Minimum | -$242.50 | -$640.00 | | | | | | | | | | |
| 21 | Maximum | $500.00 | $500.00 | | | | | | | | | | |
| 22 | Average | $337.52 | $342.79 | | | | | | | | | | |
| 23 | Standard deviation | $189.07 | $201.85 | | | | | | | | | | |
| 24 | 5th percentile | -$47.50 | -$70.00 | | | | | | | | | | |
| 25 | 95th percentile | $500.00 | $500.00 | | | | | | | | | | |

*As you continue to use @RISK, look for ways to use the RISKSIMTABLE function. It can really improve your efficiency because it allows you to run several simulations at once.*

**1** **RISKSIMTABLE function.** We index the two distributions as 1 and 2. To indicate that we want to run the simulation with both of them, enter the formula

**=RISKSIMTABLE({1,2})**

in cell B11. Note that when we enter actual numbers in this function, rather than cell references, @RISK requires us to put curly brackets around the list of numbers.

**2** **Demand.** When the value in cell B11 is 1, we want the demand distribution to be triangular. When it is 2, we want the distribution to be normal. Therefore, enter the formula

**=ROUND(IF(B11=1,RISKTRIANG(E4,E5,E6),RISKNORMAL(H4,H5)),0)**

in cell B15. Again, the effect is that the first simulation uses the triangular distribution; the second uses the normal distribution.

### Running the Simulation

The only @RISK setting to change is the number of simulations. It should now be set to 2, the number of values in the RISKSIMTABLE formula. Other than this, we run the simulation exactly as before.

### Discussion of the Simulation Results

The comparison is shown numerically in Figure 11.46 and graphically in Figure 11.47. As we see, there is more chance of really low profits when the demand distribution is normal, whereas each simulation results in the same maximum profit. Both of these statements make sense. The normal distribution, being unbounded on the left, allows for very low demands, and these occasional low demands result in very low profits. On the other side, Walton's maximum profit is $500 regardless of the input distribution (provided it allows

Figure 11.46

Summary Results for Comparison Model

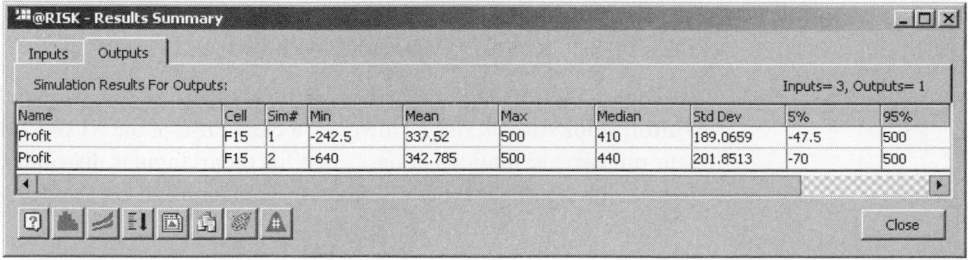

**Figure 11.47** Graphical Results for Comparison Model

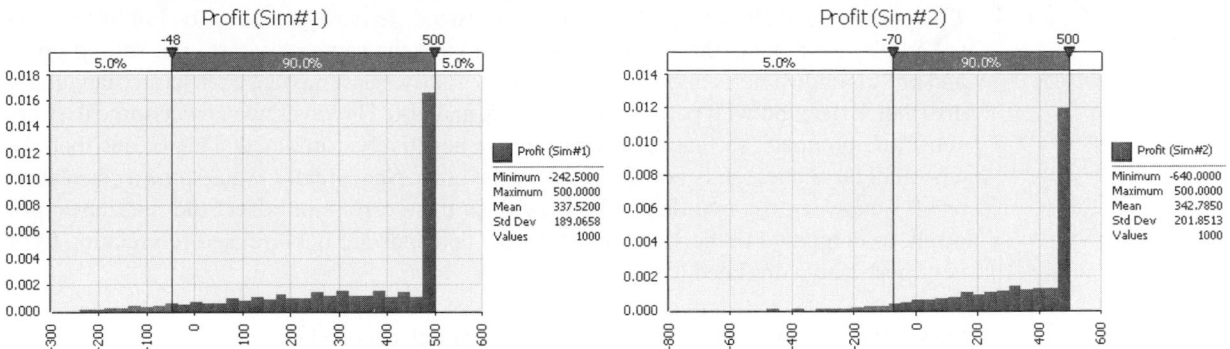

demands greater than the order quantity). This occurs when Walton's sells all it orders, in which case excess demand has no affect on profit.

Nevertheless, the profit distribution in this model is not greatly affected by the choice of demand distribution, at least not when (1) the candidate input distributions have the same mean and standard deviation, and (2) their shapes are not *too* dissimilar. This general conclusion about insensitivity of output distributions to shapes of input distributions can probably be made in many simulation models. However, it is always worth checking, as we have done here, especially if a lot of money is at stake! ■

---

**FUNDAMENTAL INSIGHT**

### Shape of the Output Distribution

Predicting the shape of the output distribution from the shape(s) of the input distribution(s) is difficult. For example, normally distributed inputs don't necessarily produce normally distributed outputs. It is also difficult to predict how sensitive the shape of the output distribution is to the shape(s) of the input distribution(s).

For example, normally and triangularly distributed inputs (with the same means and standard deviations) are likely to lead to similar output distributions, but there could be differences, say, in the tails of the output distributions. In any case, you should examine the *entire* output distribution carefully, not just a few of its summary measures.

---

## Effect of Correlated Input Variables

*Input variables in real-world problems are often correlated, which makes the material in this section particularly important.*

Until now, all of the random numbers we have generated with @RISK functions have been probabilistically independent. This means, for example, that if a random value in one cell is much larger than its mean, the random values in other cells are completely unaffected. They are no more likely to be abnormally large or small than if the first value had been average or less than average. Sometimes, however, independence is unrealistic. Instead, the random numbers should be correlated in some way. If they are positively correlated, then large numbers tend to go with large numbers, and small numbers go with small. If they are negatively correlated, then large numbers tend to go with small, and small numbers go with large. As an example, we might expect daily stock price changes for two companies in the same industry to be positively correlated. If the price of one oil company increases, the price of another oil company probably tends to increase as well. @RISK allows us to build in this correlated behavior with the RISKCORRMAT function, as we illustrate in the following variation of the Walton example.

EXAMPLE | **11.5 CORRELATED DEMANDS FOR TWO CALENDARS AT WALTON'S**

S uppose that Walton Bookstore must order two different calendars. To simplify the example, we assume that the calendars each have the same unit cost, unit selling price, and unit refund value as in previous examples. Also, we assume that each has a triangularly distributed demand with parameters 100, 175, and 300. However, we now assume they are substitute products, so that their demands are negatively correlated. This means that if a customer buys one, she is not likely to buy the other. Specifically, we assume a correlation of –0.9 between the two demands. How does this correlation affect the distribution of profit, as compared to the situation where the demands are uncorrelated (correlation 0) or very positively correlated (correlation 0.9)?

**Objective**   To see how @RISK enables us to simulate correlated demands, and to see the effect of correlated demands on profit.

### WHERE DO THE NUMBERS COME FROM?

The only new input here is the correlation, which is probably negative, assuming that the calendars are substitute products, but it is a difficult number to estimate accurately. This is a good candidate for a sensitivity analysis.

## Solution

The key to building in correlation is @RISK's RISKCORRMAT (correlation matrix) function. To use this function, we must include a correlation matrix in the model, as shown in the range J5:K6 of Figure 11.48. (See the file **Walton Bookstore 8.xlsx**.) A correlation matrix always has 1's along its diagonal (because a variable is always perfectly correlated with itself) and the correlations between variables elsewhere. Also, the matrix is always symmetric, so that the correlations above the diagonal are a mirror image of those below it. (We enforce this by entering the *formula* =**J6** in cell K5.)

**Figure 11.48**
**Simulation Model with Correlations**

| | A | B | C | D | E | F | G | H | I | J | K |
|---|---|---|---|---|---|---|---|---|---|---|---|
| 1 | Simulation of Walton's Bookstore using @RISK - correlated demands | | | | | | | | | | |
| 2 | | | | | | | | | | | |
| 3 | Cost data - same for each product | | | Demand distribution for each product- triangular | | | | | Correlation matrix between demands | | |
| 4 | Unit cost | $7.50 | | Minimum | 100 | | | | | Product 1 | Product 2 |
| 5 | Unit price | $10.00 | | Most likely | 175 | | | | Product 1 | 1 | -0.9 |
| 6 | Unit refund | $2.50 | | Maximum | 300 | | | | Product 2 | -0.9 | 1 |
| 7 | | | | | | | | | | | |
| 8 | Decision variables | | | | | Note RISKSIMTABLE function in cell J6. | | | Possible correlations to try | | |
| 9 | Order quantity 1 | 200 | | | | | | | | -0.9 | 0 | 0.9 |
| 10 | Order quantity 2 | 200 | | | | | | | | | |
| 11 | | | | | | | | | Range names used: | | |
| 12 | Simulated quantities | | | | | | | | Order_quantity_1 | =Model!$B$9 | |
| 13 | | Demand | Revenue | Cost | Refund | Profit | | | Order_quantity_2 | =Model!$B$10 | |
| 14 | Product 1 | 222 | $2,000 | $1,500 | $0 | $500 | | | Profit | =Model!$F$16 | |
| 15 | Product 2 | 216 | $2,000 | $1,500 | $0 | $500 | | | Unit_cost | =Model!$B$4 | |
| 16 | Totals | 438 | $4,000 | $3,000 | $0 | $1,000 | | | Unit_price | =Model!$B$5 | |
| 17 | | | | | | | | | Unit_refund | =Model!$B$6 | |
| 18 | Summary measures of profit from @RISK - based on 1000 iterations | | | | | | | | | | |
| 19 | Simulation | 1 | 2 | 3 | | | | | | | |
| 20 | Correlation | -0.9 | 0 | 0.9 | | | | | | | |
| 21 | Minimum | $272.50 | -$275.00 | -$432.50 | | | | | | | |
| 22 | Maximum | $1,000.00 | $1,000.00 | $1,000.00 | | | | | | | |
| 23 | Average | $675.00 | $675.00 | $675.00 | | | | | | | |
| 24 | Standard deviation | $157.76 | $262.88 | $365.51 | | | | | | | |
| 25 | 5th percentile | $392.50 | $197.50 | -$72.50 | | | | | | | |
| 26 | 95th percentile | $925.00 | $1,000.00 | $1,000.00 | | | | | | | |

To enter random values in any cells that are correlated, we start with a typical @RISK formula, such as

**=RISKTRIANG(E4,E5,E6)**

Then we add an extra argument, the RISKCORRMAT function, as follows:

**=RISKTRIANG(E4,E5,E6,RISKCORRMAT(J5:K6,1))**

*The RISKCORRMAT function is "tacked on" as an extra argument to a typical random @RISK function.*

The first argument of the RISKCORRMAT function is the correlation matrix range. The second is an index of the variable. In this case, the first calendar demand has index 1, and the second has index 2.

### @RISK Function: *RISKCORRMAT*

*This function enables us to correlate two or more input variables in an @RISK model. The function has the form RISKCORRMAT(CorrMat,Index), where* CorrMat *is a matrix of correlations and* Index *is an index of the variable being correlated to others. For example, if there are three correlated variables, Index is 1 for the first variable, 2 for the second, and 3 for the third. The RISKCORRMAT function is not entered by itself. Rather, it is entered as the last argument of a random @RISK function, such as* **=RISKTRIANG(10,15,30, RISKCORRMAT(CorrMat,2)).**

## DEVELOPING THE SIMULATION MODEL

Armed with this knowledge, the simulation model in Figure 11.48 is straightforward. It can be developed as follows:

**1 Inputs.** Enter the inputs in the blue ranges in columns B and D.

**2 Correlation matrix.** For the correlation matrix in the range J5:H6, enter 1's on the diagonal, and enter the formula

**=J6**

in cell K5. Then, because we want to compare the results for several correlations (those in the range I9:K9), enter the formula

**=RISKSIMTABLE(I9:K9)**

in cell J6. This allows us to simultaneously simulate negatively correlated demands, uncorrelated demands, and positively correlated demands.

**3 Order quantities.** We assume the company orders the *same* number of each calendar, 200, so enter this value in cells B9 and B10. However, the simulation is set up so that you can experiment with any order quantities in these cells, including unequal values.

**4 Correlated demands.** Generate correlated demands by entering the formula

**=ROUND(RISKTRIANG(E4,E5,E6,RISKCORRMAT(J5:K6,1)),0)**

in cell B14 for demand 1 and the formula

**=ROUND(RISKTRIANG(E4,E5,E6,RISKCORRMAT(J5:K6,2)),0)**

in cell B15 for demand 2. The only difference between these is the index of the variable being generated. The first has index 1; the second has index 2.

**5 Other formulas.** The other formulas in rows 14 and 15 are identical to ones we developed in previous examples, so we won't discuss them again here. The quantities in row 16 are simply sums of rows 14 and 15. Also, the only @RISK output we specified is the total profit in cell F16.

## Running the Simulation

We set up and run @RISK exactly as before. For this example, we set the number of iterations to 1000 and the number of simulations to 3 (because we are trying three different correlations).

## Discussion of the Simulation Results

Selected numerical and graphical results are shown in Figures 11.49 and 11.50. You will probably be surprised to see that the *mean* total profit is the same, regardless of the correlation. This is no coincidence. In each of the three simulations, @RISK uses the *same* random numbers, but it "shuffles" them in different orders to get the correct correlations. This means that averages are unaffected. (The idea is that the average of the numbers 30, 26, and 48 is the same as the average of the numbers 48, 30, and 26.)

**Figure 11.49**

Summary Results for Correlated Model

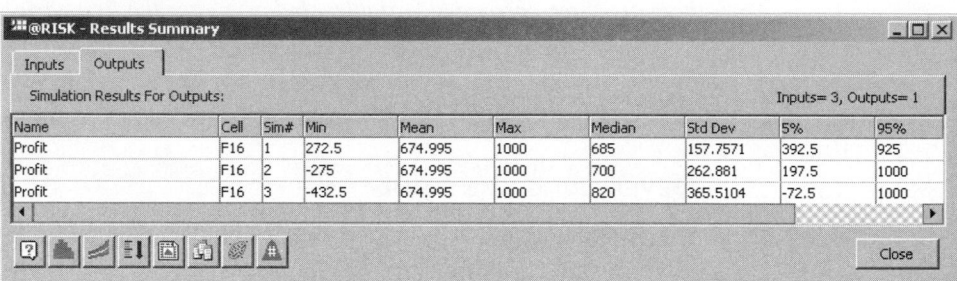

**Figure 11.50**    Graphical Results for Correlated Model

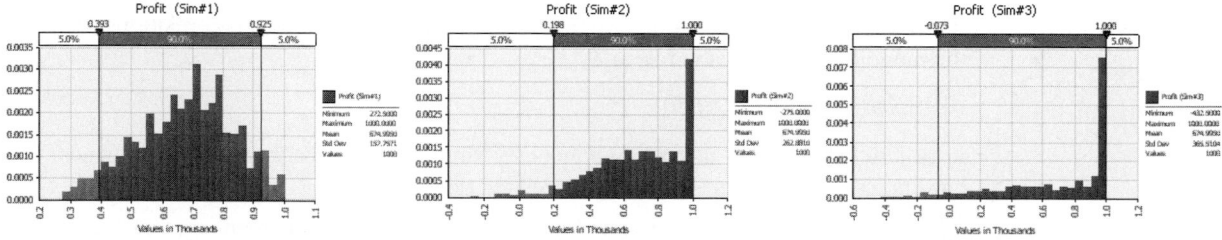

However, the correlation has a definite effect on the *distribution* of total profit. We can see this in Figure 11.49, for example, where the standard deviation of total profit increases as the correlation goes from negative to zero to positive. This same increase in variability is apparent in the histograms in Figure 11.50. Do you see intuitively why this increase in variability occurs? Basically, it is the "Don't put all your eggs in one basket" effect. When the correlation is negative, high demands for one product tend to cancel low demands for the other product, so extremes in profit are rare. However, when the correlation is positive, high demands for the two products tend to go together, as do low demands. These make extreme profits on either end much more likely.

This same phenomenon occurs if we simulate an investment portfolio containing two stocks. When the stocks are positively correlated, the portfolio is much riskier (more variability) than when they are negatively correlated. Of course, this is why investors are advised to diversify their portfolios. ∎

# MODELING ISSUES

We illustrated the RISKCORRMAT function for *triangularly* distributed values. However, it can be used with any of @RISK's distributions by tacking on RISKCORRMAT as a last argument. We can even mix them. For example, assuming that CMat is the range name for a 2×2 correlation matrix, we can enter the formulas

**=RISKNORMAL(10,2,RISKCORRMAT(CMat,1))**

and

**=RISKUNIFORM(100,200,RISKCORRMAT(CMat,2))**

*With the RISKCORRMAT function, we can correlate random numbers from any distributions.*

into cells A4 and B4, say, and then copy them down. In this case @RISK generates a sequence of normally distributed random numbers in column A and another sequence of uniformly distributed random numbers in column B. Then it shuffles them in some complex way until their correlation is approximately equal to the specified correlation in the correlation matrix. ■

# PROBLEMS

## Skill-Building Problems

**22.** Bottleco produces six-packs of soda cans. Each can is supposed to contain at least 12 ounces of soda. If the total weight in a six-pack is under 72 ounces, Bottleco is fined $100 and receives no sales revenue for the six-pack. Each six-pack sells for $3.00. It costs Bottleco $0.02 per ounce of soda put in the cans. Bottleco can control the mean fill rate of its soda-filling machines. The amount put in each can by a machine is normally distributed with standard deviation 0.10 ounce.

   **a.** Assume that the weight of each can in a six-pack has a 0.8 correlation with the weight of the other cans in the six-pack. What mean fill quantity (within 0.05 ounce) maximizes expected profit per six-pack?

   **b.** If the weights of the cans in the six-pack are probabilistically independent, what mean fill quantity (within 0.05 ounce) maximizes expected profit per six-pack?

   **c.** How can you explain the difference in the answers to parts **a** and **b**?

**23.** When you use @RISK's correlation feature to generate correlated random numbers, how can you verify that they are correlated? Try the following. Use the RISKCORRMAT function to generate two normally distributed random numbers, each with mean 100 and standard deviation 10, and with correlation 0.7. To run a simulation, you need an output variable, so sum these two numbers and designate the sum as an output variable. Now run @RISK with 500 iterations. Click on @RISK's Excel Reports button and check the Simulation Data option to see the simulated data.

   **a.** Use Excel's CORREL function to calculate the correlation between the two input variables. It should be close to 0.7. Then draw a scatterplot (XY chart) of these two input variables. The plot should indicate a definite positive relationship.

**b.** Are the two input variables correlated with the output? Use Excel's CORREL function to find out. Interpret your results intuitively.

**24.** Repeat the previous problem, but make the correlation between the two inputs equal to −0.7. Explain how the results change.

**25.** Repeat Problem 23, but now make the second input variable triangularly distributed with parameters 50, 100, and 500. This time, verify not only that the correlation between the two inputs is approximately 0.7, but also that the shapes of the two input distributions are approximately what they should be: normal for the first and triangular for the second. Do this by creating histograms in Excel. The point is that you can use @RISK's RISKCORRMAT function to correlate random numbers from *different* distributions.

**26.** Suppose you are going to invest equal amounts in three stocks. The annual return from each stock is normally distributed with mean 0.01 (1%) and standard deviation 0.06. The annual return on your portfolio, the output variable of interest, is the average of the three stock returns. Run @RISK, using 1000 iterations, on each of the following scenarios.
**a.** The three stock returns are highly correlated. The correlation between each pair is 0.9.
**b.** The three stock returns are practically independent. The correlation between each pair is 0.1.
**c.** The first two stocks are moderately correlated. The correlation between their returns is 0.4. The third stock's return is negatively correlated with the other two. The correlation between its return and each of the first two is −0.8.
**d.** Compare the portfolio distributions from @RISK for these three scenarios. What do you conclude?
**e.** You might think of a fourth scenario, where the correlation between *each* pair of returns is a large negative number such as –0.8. But explain intuitively why this makes no sense. Try running the simulation with these negative correlations to see what happens.

**27.** The effect of the shapes of input distributions on the distribution of an output can depend on the output function. For this problem, assume there are 10 input variables. We want to compare the case where these 10 inputs each has a normal distribution with mean 1000 and standard deviation 250 to the case where each has a triangular distribution with parameters 600, 700, and 1700. (You can check with @RISK's Define Distributions window that even though this triangular distribution is very skewed, it has the same mean and approximately the same standard deviation as the normal distribution.) For each of the following outputs, run @RISK twice, once with the normally distributed inputs and once with the triangularly distributed inputs, and comment on the differences between the resulting output distributions. For each simulation, run 10,000 iterations.
**a.** Let the output be the *average* of the inputs.
**b.** Let the output be the *maximum* of the inputs.
**c.** Calculate the average of the inputs. Let the output be the minimum of the inputs if this average is less than 1000; otherwise, let the output be the maximum of the inputs.

## Skill-Extending Problem

**28.** The Business School at State University currently has three parking lots, each containing 155 spaces. Two hundred faculty members have been assigned to each lot. On a peak day, an average of 70% of all lot 1 parking sticker holders show up, an average of 72% of all lot 2 parking sticker holders show up, and an average of 74% of all lot 3 parking sticker holders show up.
**a.** Given the current situation, estimate the probability that on a peak day, at least one faculty member with a sticker will be unable to find a spot. Assume that the number of people who show up at each lot is independent of the number of people who show up at the other two lots. (*Hint:* Use the RISKBINOMIAL function.)
**b.** Now suppose the numbers of people who show up at the three lots are correlated (correlation 0.9). Does your solution work as well? Why or why not?

# 11.7 CONCLUSION

Simulation has traditionally not received the attention it deserves in management science courses. The primary reason for this has been the lack of easy-to-use simulation software. Now with Excel's built-in simulation capabilities, plus powerful and affordable add-ins such as @RISK, simulation is receiving its rightful emphasis. The world is full of uncertainty, which is what makes simulation so valuable. Simulation models provide important insights that are missing in models that do not incorporate uncertainty explicitly. In addition, simulation models are relatively easy to understand and develop. Therefore, we suspect that simulation models (together with optimization models) will soon be the primary emphasis of many management science courses—if they are not already. In this chapter, we have illustrated the basic ideas of simulation, how to perform simulation with Excel built-in tools, and how @RISK enhances Excel's basic capabilities. In the next chapter, we build on this knowledge to develop and analyze simulation models in a variety of business areas.

## Summary of Key Management Science Terms

| Term | Explanation | Page |
|---|---|---|
| Simulation models | Models with random inputs that affect one or more outputs where the randomness is modeled explicitly | 581 |
| Probability distributions for input variables | Specification of the possible values and their likelihoods for random input variables; these must be specified in any simulation model | 583 |
| Density function | Function that indicates the probability distribution of a continuous random variable; probabilities are areas under the density | 585 |
| Uniform distribution | The flat distribution, where all values in a bounded continuum are equally likely | 588 |
| Histogram | A column chart that shows the numbers of observations in specified categories | 590 |
| Discrete distribution | A general distribution where a discrete number of possible values and their probabilities are specified | 593 |
| Normal distribution | The familiar bell-shaped distribution, specified by a mean and a standard deviation | 595 |
| Triangular distribution | Literally a triangular-shaped distribution, specified by a minimum value, a most likely value, and a maximum value | 596 |
| Binomial distribution | The random number of successes in a given number of independent trials, where each trial has the same probability of success | 597 |
| Confidence interval | An interval around an estimate of some parameter, so that we are very confident that the true value of the parameter is within the interval | 608 |
| Latin Hypercube sampling | An efficient way of simulating random numbers for a simulation model, where the results are more accurate than with other sampling methods | 619 |
| Correlated input variables | Random quantities, such as returns from stocks in the same industry, that tend to go together (or possibly go in opposite directions from one another) | 635 |

## Summary of Key Excel Terms

| Term | Explanation | Excel | Page |
|---|---|---|---|
| F9 key | The recalc key, used to make the spreadsheet recalculate | Press the F9 key | 584 |
| RAND function | Excel's built-in random number generator; generates uniform random numbers between 0 and 1 | =RAND() | 589 |
| Freezing random numbers | Changing "volatile" random numbers into "fixed" numbers | Copy range, paste it onto itself with the Paste Values option | 592 |
| @RISK random functions | A set of functions, including RISKNORMAL and RISKTRIANG, for generating random numbers from various distributions | =RISKNORMAL (*mean,stdev*) or =RISKTRIANG (*min,mostlikely,max*), for example | 596 |
| Replicating with Excel only | Useful when an add-in such as @RISK is not available | Develop simulation model, use a data table with any blank Column Input cell to replicate one or more outputs | 603 |
| @RISK | A useful simulation add-in developed by Palisade | Has its own toolbar in Excel | 615 |
| RISKOUTPUT function | Used to indicate that a cell contains an output that will be tracked by @RISK | =RISKOUTPUT ("Profit")+Revenue-Cost, for example | 618 |
| RISKSIMTABLE function | Used to run an @RISK simulation model for several values of some variable, often a decision variable | =RISKSIMTABLE(*list*) | 625 |
| RISKCORRMAT function | Used to correlate two or more random input variables | =RISKNORMAL(100,10, RISKCORRMAT (*CorrMat*,2)), for example | 636 |
| Creating histograms in Excel | Method for specifying categories (bins) and using Excel's FREQUENCY function as basis for a bar chart | See appendix for details | 646 |

## PROBLEMS

### Skill-Building Problems

**29.** Six months before its annual convention, the American Medical Association (AMA) must determine how many rooms to reserve. At this time, the AMA can reserve rooms at a cost of $100 per room. The AMA believes the number of doctors attending the convention will be normally distributed with a mean of 5000 and a standard deviation of 1000. If the number of people attending the convention exceeds the number of rooms reserved, extra rooms must be reserved at a cost of $160 per room.

**a.** Use simulation with @RISK to determine the number of rooms that should be reserved to minimize the expected cost to the AMA.

**b.** Rework part **a** for the case where the number attending has a triangular distribution with minimum value 2000, maximum value 7000, and most likely value 5000. Does this change the substantive results from part **a**?

**30.** You have made it to the final round of "Let's Make a Deal." You know that there is $1 million prize behind one of the three doors: door 1, door 2, or door 3. It is equally likely that the prize is behind any of the three doors. The two doors without a prize have nothing behind them. You randomly choose door 2. Before you see whether the prize is behind door 2, host Monty Hall opens a door that has no prize behind it. To be specific, suppose that before door 2 is opened, Monty reveals that there is no prize behind door 3. You now have the opportunity to switch and choose door 1. Should you switch? Use a spreadsheet to simulate this situation 1000 times. For each replication, use an @RISK function to generate the door behind which the prize sits. Then use another @RISK function to generate the door that Monty will open. Assume that Monty plays as follows: Monty knows where the prize is and will open an empty door, but he cannot open door 2. If the prize is really behind door 2, Monty is equally likely to open door 1 or door 3. If the prize is really behind door 1, Monty must open door 3. If the prize is really behind door 3, Monty must open door 1.

**31.** A new edition of our management science textbook will be published a year from now. Our publisher currently has 2000 copies on hand and is deciding whether to do another printing before the new edition comes out. The publisher estimates that demand for the book during the next year is governed by the probability distribution in the file **P11_31.xlsx.** A production run incurs a fixed cost of $50,000 plus a variable cost of $50 per book printed. Books are sold for $80 per book. Any demand that cannot be met incurs a penalty cost of $10 per book, due to loss of goodwill.

Half of any leftover books can be sold to Barnes and Noble for $35 per book. Our publisher is interested in maximizing expected profit. The following print-run sizes are under consideration: 0 (no production run), 1000, 2000, 4000, 6000, and 8000. What decision would you recommend? Use simulation with at least 100 replications. For your optimal decision, our publisher can be 90% certain that the actual profit associated with remaining sales of the current edition will be between what two values?

**32.** It is equally likely that annual unit sales for Widgetco's widgets will be low or high. If sales are low (60,000), the company can sell the product for $10 per unit. If sales are high (100,000), a competitor will enter, and Widgetco can sell the product for only $8 per unit. The variable cost per unit has a 25% chance of being $6, a 50% chance of being $7.50, and a 25% chance of being $9. Annual fixed costs are $30,000.
   **a.** Use simulation to estimate Widgetco's expected annual profit.
   **b.** Find an interval that has a 90% chance of containing Widgetco's annual profit.
   **c.** Now suppose that annual unit sales, variable cost, and unit price are equal to their respective expected values; that is, there is no uncertainty. Determine Widgetco's annual profit for this scenario.

   **d.** Can you conclude from the results in parts **a** and **c** that the expected profit from the simulation is equal to the profit from the scenario where each input assumes its expected value? Explain.

**33.** W. L. Brown, a direct marketer of women's clothing, must determine how many telephone operators to schedule during each part of the day. W. L. Brown estimates that the number of phone calls received each hour of a typical 8-hour shift can be described by the probability distribution in the file **P11_33.xlsx.** Each operator can handle 15 calls per hour and costs the company $20 per hour. Each phone call that is not handled is assumed to cost the company $6 in lost profit. Considering the options of employing 6, 8, 10, 12, 14, or 16 operators, use simulation to determine the number of operators that minimizes the expected hourly cost (labor costs plus lost profits).

**34.** Assume that all of your job applicants must take a test, and that the scores on this test are normally distributed. The "selection ratio" is the cutoff point you use in your hiring process. For example, a selection ratio of 20% means that you will accept applicants for jobs who rank in the top 20% of all applicants. If you choose a selection ratio of 20%, the average test score of those selected will be 1.40 standard deviations above average of all applicants. Use simulation to verify this fact, proceeding as follows.
   **a.** Show that if you want to accept only the top 20% of all applicants, you should accept applicants whose test scores are at least 0.842 standard deviation above average. (No simulation is required here. Just use the appropriate Excel normal function.)
   **b.** Now generate 1000 test scores from a normal distribution with mean 0 and standard deviation 1. The average test score of those selected is the average of the scores that are at least 0.842. To determine this, use Excel's DAVERAGE function. To do so, put the heading Score in cell A3, generate the 1000 test scores in the range A4:A1003, and name the range A3:A1003 Data. In cells C3 and C4, enter the *labels* Score and >0.842. (The range C3:C4 is called the *criterion* range.) Then calculate the average of all applicants who will be hired by entering the formula =DAVERAGE(Data, "Score", C3:C4) in any cell. This average should be close to the theoretical average, 1.40. This formula works as follows. Excel finds all observations in the Data range that satisfy the criterion described in the range C3:C4 (Score>0.842). Then it averages the values in the Score column (the second argument of DAVERAGE) corresponding to these entries. Look in online help for more about Excel's database functions.
   **c.** What information would you need to determine an "optimal" selection ratio? How could you determine an optimal selection ratio?

**35.** Lemington's is trying to determine how many Jean Hudson dresses to order for the spring season. Demand for the dresses is assumed to follow a normal distribution with mean 400 and standard deviation 100. The contract between Jean Hudson and Lemington's works as follows. At the beginning of the season, Lemington's reserves $x$ units of capacity. Lemington's must take delivery for at least $0.8x$ dresses and can, if desired, take delivery on up to $x$ dresses. Each dress sells for \$160, and Jean charges \$50 per dress. If Lemington's does not take delivery on all $x$ dresses, it owes Jean a \$5 penalty for each unit of reserved capacity that was unused. For example, if Lemington's orders 450 dresses, and demand is for 400 dresses, then Lemington's will receive 400 dresses and owe Jean 400(\$50) + 50(\$5). How many units of capacity should Lemington's reserve to maximize its expected profit?

**36.** Dilbert's Department Store is trying to determine how many Hanson T-shirts to order. Currently the shirts are sold for \$21.00, but at later dates the shirts will be offered at a 10% discount, then a 20% discount, then a 40% discount, then a 50% discount, and finally a 60% discount. Demand at the full price of \$21.00 is believed to be normally distributed with mean 1800 and standard deviation 360. Demand at various discounts is assumed to be a multiple of full price demand. These multiples, for discounts of 10%, 20%, 40%, 50%, and 60% are, respectively, 0.4, 0.7, 1.1, 2, and 50. For example, if full-price demand is 2500, then at a 10% discount, customers would be willing to buy 1000 T-shirts. The unit cost of purchasing T-shirts depends on the number of T-shirts ordered, as shown in the file **P11_36.xlsx**. Use simulation to see how many T-shirts Dilbert's should order. Model the problem so that Dilbert's first orders some quantity of T-shirts, and then discounts deeper and deeper, as necessary, to sell all of the shirts.

**37.** Target is trying to decide how many Peyton Manning jerseys to order for the upcoming football season. The jerseys sell for \$50, and Target believes that the demand at this price is normally distributed with a most likely value of 200 and a 95% chance of being between 120 and 280. If Target orders 200 jerseys, its cost is \$27.00 per jersey. Every increment of 50 jerseys reduces the unit cost of a jersey by \$1.35. For example, if the order quantity is from 250 jerseys to 299 jerseys, the unit cost for each is \$25.65. After the Super Bowl, the jerseys will be marked down to a sale price of \$20. Historically, demand for sale-price items has followed a normal distribution with mean equal to half the *actual* full price demand and standard deviation equal to 20% of the mean demand at the sale price. How many jerseys (within 10) should Target order to maximize its expected profit? You can assume that any jerseys not sold at the marked-down price have no value.

## Skill-Extending Problems

**38.** The annual return on each of four stocks for each of the next five years is assumed to follow a normal distribution, with the mean and standard deviation for each stock, as well as the correlations between stocks, listed in the file **P11_38.xlsx**. We believe that the stock returns for these stocks in a given year are correlated, according to the correlation matrix given, but we believe the returns in different years are uncorrelated. For example, the returns for stocks 1 and 2 in year 1 have correlation 0.55, but the correlation between the return of stock 1 in year 1 and the return of stock 1 in year 2 is 0, and the correlation between the return of stock 1 in year 1 and the return of stock 2 in year 2 is also 0. The file has the formulas you might expect for this situation entered in the range C20:G23. You can check how the RISKCORRMAT function has been used in these formulas. Just so that we have an @RISK output cell, we calculate the average of all returns in cell B25 and designate it as an @RISK output. (This cell is not really important for the problem, but we include it because @RISK requires at least one output cell.)

  **a.** Using the model exactly as it stands, run @RISK with 1000 iterations. The question is whether the correlations in the simulated data are close to what we expect. To find out, go to @RISK's Report Settings and check the Input Data option before you run the simulation. This will show you all of the simulated returns on a new sheet. Then use Excel's CORREL function to calculate correlations for all pairs of columns in the resulting Inputs Data Report sheet. (This is tedious. We recommend instead that you use the StatTools add-in included with this book or the Analysis ToolPak that ships with Excel to create a matrix of all correlations.) Comment on whether the correlations are different from what you expect.

  **b.** Recognizing that this is a common situation (correlation within years, no correlation across years), @RISK allows you to model it by adding a *third* argument to the RISKCORRMAT function: the year index in row 19 of the **P11_38.xlsx** file. For example, the RISKCORRMAT part of the formula in cell C20 becomes **=RISKNORMAL(\$B5,\$C5, RISKCORRMAT(\$B\$12:\$E\$15,\$B20,C\$19))**. Make this change to the formulas in the range C20:G23, rerun the simulation, and redo the correlation analysis in part **a**. Verify that the correlations between inputs are now more in line with what you expect.

**39.** It is surprising (but true) that if 23 people are in the same room, there is about a 50% chance that at least two people will have the same birthday. Suppose you want to estimate the probability that if 30 people are in the same room, at least two of them will have the same birthday. You can proceed as follows.

a. Generate the birthdays of 30 different people. Ignoring the possibility of a leap year, each person has a 1/365 chance of having a given birthday (call the days of the year 1, 2, . . . , 365). You can use a formula involving the RANDBETWEEN function to generate birthdays.

b. After you have generated 30 people's birthdays, how can you tell whether at least two people have the same birthday? The key here is to use Excel's RANK function. (You can learn how to use this function with Excel's online help.) This function returns the rank of a number relative to a given group of numbers. In the case of a tie, two numbers are given the same rank. For example, if the set of numbers is 4, 3, 2, 5, the RANK function will return 2, 3, 4, 1. If the set of numbers is 4, 3, 2, 4, the RANK function will return 1, 3, 4, 1.

c. After using the RANK function, you should be able to determine whether at least two of the 30 people have the same birthday How?

40. United Electric (UE) sells refrigerators for $400 with a 1-year warranty. The warranty works as follows. If any part of the refrigerator fails during the first year after purchase, UE replaces the refrigerator for an average cost of $100. As soon as a replacement is made, another 1-year warranty period begins for the customer. If a refrigerator fails outside the warranty period, we assume that the customer immediately purchases another UE refrigerator. Suppose that the amount of time a refrigerator lasts follows a normal distribution with a mean of 1.8 years and a standard deviation of 0.3 year.

a. Estimate the average profit per year UE earns from a customer.

b. How could the approach of this problem be used to determine the *optimal* warranty period?

41. A Tax Saver Benefit (TSB) plan allows you to put money into an account at the beginning of the calendar year that can be used for medical expenses. This amount is not subject to federal tax—hence the "Tax Saver." As you pay medical expenses during the year, the administrator of the TSB reimburses you until the TSB account is exhausted. From that point on, you must pay your medical expenses out of your own pocket. On the other hand, if you put more money into your TSB than the medical expenses you incur, this extra money is lost to you. Your annual salary is $80,000 and your federal income tax rate is 30%.

a. Assume that your medical expenses in a year are normally distributed with mean $2000 and standard deviation $500. Build an @RISK model in which the output is the amount of money left to you after paying taxes, putting money in a TSB, and paying any extra medical expenses. Experiment with the amount of money put in the TSB by using a RISKSIMTABLE function.

b. Rework part a, but this time assume a gamma distribution for your annual medical expenses. Use $\alpha = 16$ and $\beta = 125$ as the two parameters of this distribution. These imply the same mean and standard deviation as in part a, but the distribution of medical expenses is now skewed to the right, which is probably more realistic. Using simulation, see whether you should now put more or less money in a TSB than in part a.

42. At the beginning of each week, a machine is in one of four conditions: 1 = excellent; 2 = good; 3 = average; 4 = bad. The weekly revenue earned by a machine in state 1, 2, 3, or 4 is $100, $90, $50, or $10, respectively. After observing the condition of the machine at the beginning of the week, the company has the option, for a cost of $200, of instantaneously replacing the machine with an excellent machine. The quality of the machine deteriorates over time, as shown in the file **P11_42.xlsx**. Four maintenance policies are under consideration:

- Policy 1: Never replace a machine.
- Policy 2: Immediately replace a bad machine.
- Policy 3: Immediately replace a bad or average machine.
- Policy 4: Immediately replace a bad, average, or good machine.

Simulate each of these policies for 50 weeks (using 250 iterations each) to determine the policy that maximizes expected weekly profit. Assume that the machine at the beginning of week 1 is excellent.

43. Simulation can be used to illustrate a number of results from statistics that are difficult to understand with nonsimulation arguments. One is the famous central limit theorem, which says that if you sample enough values from *any* population distribution and then average these values, the resulting average will be approximately normally distributed. Confirm this by using @RISK with the following population distributions (run a separate simulation for each): (a) discrete with possible values 1 and 2 and probabilities 0.2 and 0.8; (b) exponential with mean 1 (use the RISKEXPON function with the single argument 1); (c) triangular with minimum, most likely, and maximum values equal to 1, 9, and 10. Note that each of these distributions is very nonnormal. Run each simulation with 10 values in each average, and run 1000 iterations to simulate 1000 averages. Create a histogram of the averages to see that it is indeed bell-shaped. Then repeat, using 30 values in each average. Are the histograms based on 10 values qualitatively different from those based on 30?

**44.** In statistics, we often use observed data to test a hypothesis about a population or populations. The basic method uses the observed data to calculate a test statistic (a single number). If the magnitude of this test statistic is sufficiently large, we reject the null hypothesis in favor of the research hypothesis. As an example, consider a researcher who believes teenage girls sleep longer than teenage boys on average. She collects observations on $n = 40$ randomly selected girls and $n = 40$ randomly selected boys. (We assume that each observation is the average sleep time over several nights for a given person.) The averages are $\bar{X}_1 = 7.9$ hours for the girls and $\bar{X}_2 = 7.6$ hours for the boys. The standard deviation of the 40 observations for girls is $s_1 = 0.5$ hour; for the boys, it is $s_2 = 0.7$ hour. The researcher, consulting her statistics textbook, then calculates the test statistic

$$\frac{\bar{X}_1 - \bar{X}_2}{\sqrt{s_1^2/40 + s_2^2/40}} = \frac{7.9 - 7.6}{\sqrt{0.25/40 + 0.49/40}} = 2.206$$

Based on the fact that 2.206 is "large," she claims that her research hypothesis is confirmed—girls *do* sleep longer than boys.

You are skeptical of this claim, so you check it out by running a simulation. In your simulation, you assume that girls and boys have the *same* mean and standard deviation of sleep times in the entire population, say, 7.7 and 0.6. You also assume that the distribution of sleep times is normal. Then you repeatedly simulate observations of 40 girls and 40 boys from this distribution and calculate the test statistic. The question is whether the observed test statistic, 2.206, is "extreme." If it is larger than most or all of the test statistics you simulate, then the researcher is justified in her claim; otherwise, this large a statistic could have happened just by chance, even if the girls and boys have *identical* population means. Use @RISK to see which is the case.

## Modeling Problems

**45.** Big Hit Video must determine how many copies of a new video to purchase. Assume that the company's goal is to purchase a number of copies that will maximize its expected profit from the video during the next year. Describe how you would use simulation to solve this problem. To simplify matters, assume that each time a video is rented, it is rented for one day.

**46.** Many people who are involved in a small auto accident do not file a claim because they are afraid their insurance premiums will be raised. Suppose that City Farm Insurance has three rates. If you file a claim, you are moved to the next higher rate. How might you use simulation to determine whether a particular claim should be filed?

**47.** A building contains 1000 light bulbs. Each bulb lasts at most 5 months. The company maintaining the building is trying to decide whether it is worthwhile to practice a "group replacement" policy. Under a group replacement policy, all bulbs are replaced every $T$ months (where $T$ is to be determined). Also, bulbs are replaced when they burn out. Assume that it costs $0.05 to replace each bulb during a group replacement and $0.20 to replace each burned-out bulb if replaced individually. How could you use simulation to determine whether a group replacement policy is worthwhile?

**48.** We are constantly hearing reports on the nightly news about natural disasters—droughts in Texas, hurricanes in Florida, floods in California, and so on. We often hear that one of these was the "worst in over 30 years," or some such statement. This was especially the case in the last half of 2005, with the terrible hurricanes in the southern United States and the deadly earthquake in Pakistan. Are natural disasters getting worse these days, or does it just appear so? How might you use simulation to answer this question? Here is one possible approach. Imagine that there are $N$ areas of the country (or the world) that tend to have, to some extent, various types of weather phenomena each year. For example, hurricanes are always a potential problem for Florida. You might model the severity of the problem for any area in any year by a normally distributed random number with mean 0 and standard deviation 1, where negative values are interpreted as mild years and positive values are interpreted as severe years. (We suggest the normal distribution, but other distributions can be used as well.) Then you could simulate such values for all areas over a period of many years and keep track, say, of whether any of the areas have worse conditions in the current year than they have had in the past 30 years. What might you keep track of? How might you interpret your results?

---

## APPENDIX **CREATING HISTOGRAMS WITH EXCEL TOOLS**

When we generate data for input or output variables, it is useful to create histograms. A histogram, really just a bar chart, lets us see how the data is distributed. We divide the data range into a number of categories, usually called **bins;** count the number of observations in each bin; and then use these counts as the basis for the histogram.

Simulation and statistical software packages, including @RISK, typically have the capability to create a histogram (with automatically chosen bins) with the click of a button. You can also create a histogram with native Excel tools, but you have to do most of the work manually. We lead you through the steps of this process here.

The ingredients for a histogram and the finished product are shown in Figure 11.51. (See the file **Histogram.xlsx**.) The histogram is based on the given data in column A (which really extends down to row 203—that is, 200 observations). We then build the histogram with the following steps:

**Figure 11.51** Creation of Histogram

| | A | B | C | D | E | F | G | H | I | J | K | L | M | N |
|---|---|---|---|---|---|---|---|---|---|---|---|---|---|---|
| 1 | Creating a histogram | | | | | | | | | | | | | |
| 2 | | | | | | | | | | | | | | |
| 3 | Data | | Bins | Labels | Counts | | | | | | | | | |
| 4 | 84.2 | | 10 | 0-10 | 6 | | | | | | | | | |
| 5 | 84.8 | | 20 | 10-20 | 8 | | | | | | | | | |
| 6 | 42.2 | | 30 | 20-30 | 16 | | | | | | | | | |
| 7 | 19.7 | | 40 | 30-40 | 25 | | | | | | | | | |
| 8 | 74.8 | | 50 | 40-50 | 27 | | | | | | | | | |
| 9 | 89.9 | | 60 | 50-60 | 16 | | | | | | | | | |
| 10 | 32.6 | | 70 | 60-70 | 33 | | | | | | | | | |
| 11 | 73.0 | | 80 | 70-80 | 38 | | | | | | | | | |
| 12 | 91.7 | | 90 | 80-90 | 25 | | | | | | | | | |
| 13 | 47.7 | | | >90 | 6 | | | | | | | | | |
| 14 | 50.6 | | | | | | | | | | | | | |
| 15 | 74.0 | | | | | | | | | | | | | |
| 16 | 38.9 | | | | | | | | | | | | | |
| 17 | 71.8 | | | | | | | | | | | | | |
| 18 | 82.3 | | | | | | | | | | | | | |

**1** **Bins.** The choice of bins typically depends on the range of the data and the number of observations. A scan of these data indicates that all observations are in the range 0 to 100. Therefore, we conveniently choose 10 equal-length bins: 0–10, 10–20, and so on, up to 90–100. We designate the first 9 of these by their right-hand endpoints, as shown in column C. The first bin is really "<=10", the second is ">10 and <=20" and so on. We only need to specify the first 9 bins in column C. The 10th is then automatically ">90".

**2** **Bin Labels.** Although this step is not entirely necessary, it is nice to have meaningful labels for the bins on the horizontal axis of the histogram. We enter these labels manually in column D. (We prefix each label with an apostrophe, as in '10–20, to make sure it is interpreted as a label and not as subtraction.)

**3** **Counts.** To get the counts of observations in the various bins in column E, we use Excel's FREQUENCY function. This is an "array" function that fills up an entire range at once. It takes two arguments, the data range and the bins range. To use it, highlight the range E4:E13, type the formula

=**FREQUENCY(A4:A203,C4:C12)**

and press Ctrl+Shift+Enter (all three keys at once). As with all array functions in Excel, you will see curly brackets around the formula in the Formula Bar. However, you should *not* type these curly brackets.

**④ Chart.** To create the histogram, highlight the range of labels and counts, D4:E13, and select the first Column type chart from the Insert ribbon.

**⑤ Gaps and Borders.** The default column chart has gaps between the columns. It is customary to have no gaps in a histogram. To get rid of the gaps, right-click on any bar in the histogram, select the Format Data Series menu item, and set the Gap Width to No Gap. The resulting chart will need some borders around the bars, so with the Format Data Series dialog box still open, change the Border Color to black.

Egress, Inc., is a small company that designs, produces, and sells ski jackets and other coats. The creative design team has labored for weeks over its new design for the coming winter season. It is now time to decide how many ski jackets to produce in this production run. Because of the lead times involved, no other production runs will be possible during the season. Predicting ski jacket sales months in advance of the selling season can be tricky. Egress has been in operation for only 3 years, and its ski jacket designs were quite successful in 2 of those years. Based on realized sales from the last 3 years, current economic conditions, and professional judgment, 12 Egress employees have independently estimated demand for their new design for the upcoming season. Their estimates are listed in Table 11.2.

**Table 11.2   Estimated Demands**

| | |
|--------|--------|
| 14,000 | 16,000 |
| 13,000 | 8,000 |
| 14,000 | 5,000 |
| 14,000 | 11,000 |
| 15,500 | 8,000 |
| 10,500 | 15,000 |

To assist in the decision on the number of units for the production run, management has gathered the data in Table 11.3. Note that $S$ is the price Egress charges retailers. Any ski jackets that do not sell during the season can be sold by Egress to discounters for $V$ per jacket. The fixed cost of plant and equipment is $F$. This cost is incurred irrespective of the size of the production run.

**Table 11.3   Monetary Values**

| | |
|---|---|
| Variable production cost per unit (C): | $80 |
| Selling price per unit (S): | $100 |
| Salvage value per unit (V): | $30 |
| Fixed production cost (F): | $100,000 |

## Questions

1. Egress management believes that a normal distribution is a reasonable model for the unknown demand in the coming year. What mean and standard deviation should Egress use for the demand distribution?

2. Use a spreadsheet model to simulate 1000 possible outcomes for demand in the coming year. Based on these scenarios, what is the expected profit if Egress produces $Q = 7800$ ski jackets? What is the expected profit if Egress produces $Q = 12,000$ ski jackets? What is the standard deviation of profit in these two cases?

3. Based on the same 1000 scenarios, how many ski jackets should Egress produce to maximize expected profit? Call this quantity $Q$.

4. Should $Q$ equal mean demand or not? Explain.

5. Create a histogram of profit at the production level $Q$. Create a histogram of profit when the production level $Q$ equals mean demand. What is the probability of a loss greater than $100,000 in each case? ∎

Management of Ebony, a leading manufacturer of bath soap, is trying to control its inventory costs. The weekly cost of holding one unit of soap in inventory is $30 (one unit is 1000 cases of soap). The marketing department estimates that weekly demand averages 120 units, with a standard deviation of 15 units, and is reasonably well modeled by a normal distribution. If demand exceeds the amount of soap on hand, those sales are lost; that is, there is no backlogging of demand. The production department can produce at one of three levels: 110, 120, or 130 units per week. The cost of changing production from one week to the next is $3000.

Management would like to evaluate the following production policy. If the current inventory is less than $L = 30$ units, then produce 130 units in the next week. If the current inventory is greater than $U = 80$ units, then produce 110 units in the next week. Otherwise, continue at the previous week's production level.

Ebony currently has 60 units of inventory on hand. Last week's production level was 120.

## Questions

1. Create a spreadsheet to simulate 52 weeks of operation at Ebony. Graph the inventory of soap over time. What is the total cost (inventory cost plus production change cost) for the 52 weeks?

2. Use a simulation of 500 iterations to estimate the average 52-week cost with values of $U$ ranging from 30 to 80 in increments of 10. Keep $L = 30$ for every trial.

3. Calculate the sample mean and standard deviation of the 52-week cost under each policy. Graph the average 52-week cost versus $U$. What is the best value of $U$ for $L = 30$?

4. What other production policies might be useful to investigate?

5. There is a lost sales aspect to this case that hasn't been included, at least not explicitly, in the questions. How could you include it explicitly in the analysis? ∎

# Simulation Models

© AP Photo/Mary Altaffer

## MERRILL LYNCH IMPROVES LIQUIDITY RISK MANAGEMENT FOR REVOLVING CREDIT LINES

The Merrill Lynch banking group comprises several Merrill Lynch affiliates, including Merrill Lynch Bank USA (ML Bank USA). ML Bank USA has assets of more than $60 billion (as of June 30, 2005). The bank acts as an intermediary, accepting deposits from Merrill Lynch retail customers and using the deposits to fund loans and make investments. One way ML Bank USA uses these assets is to provide revolving credit lines to institutional and large corporate borrowers. Currently, it has a portfolio of about $13 billion in credit-line commitments with more than 100 companies. When it makes these commitments, it must be aware of the liquidity risk, defined as the ability to meet all cash obligations when due. In other words, if a borrower asks for funds as part of its revolving credit-line agreement, the bank must have the funds available to honor the request, typically on the same day the request is made. This liquidity requirement poses a huge risk to the bank. The bank must keep enough cash or liquid investments (i.e., investments that can be converted to cash quickly) in reserve to honor its customers' requests whenever they occur. If the bank knew when, and in what quantities, these requests would occur, it could manage its cash reserves more prudently, essentially holding a smaller amount in liquid investments for credit requests and investing the rest in other more illiquid and profitable investments.

Duffy et al. (2005) discuss their role as members of Merrill Lynch's Banking Group and Management Science Group in developing a model to manage the liquidity risk for ML Bank USA's revolving credit lines. The revolving credit lines give borrowers access to a specified amount of cash on demand for short-term funding needs in return for a fee paid to the bank. The bank also earns an interest rate on advances that compensates it for the liquidity and other risks it takes. These credit lines are therefore profitable for the bank, but they are not the borrowers' primary sources of funding. Customers typically use these credit lines to retire maturing commercial paper (available at cheaper interest rates) during the process of rolling it over (i.e., attempting to reissue new commercial paper notes), and/or when their credit rating falls. The essence of the problem is that when a customer's credit ratings (measured by the Moody rating scale, for example) fall, the customers are less likely to obtain funds from cheaper sources such as commercial paper, so they then tend to rely on their credit lines from ML Bank USA and other banks. This poses problems for ML Bank USA. It must honor its commitments to the borrowers, as spelled out in the credit-line agreements, but customers with low credit ratings are the ones most likely to default on their loans.

Two other aspects of the problem are important. First, the credit-line agreements often have a "term-out" option, which allows the borrower to use funds for an additional period after expiration, typically for one year. A customer that is experiencing financial difficulties and has seen its credit rating fall is the type most likely to use its term-out option. Second, movements in credit ratings for customers in the same industry or even in different industries tend to be positively correlated because they can all be affected by movements in their industry or the overall economy. This increases the liquidity risk for ML Bank USA because it increases the chance that poor economic conditions will lead many customers to request additional credit.

The authors built a rather complex simulation model to track the demand for usage of these credit facilities. The model simulates monthly credit-line usage for each customer over a five-year period. During this period, some credit lines are renewed, some expire and are not renewed, and some customers exercise their term-out options. The model has several significant features: (1) It models the probabilistic changes in credit ratings for its customers, where a customer's credit rating can move from one level to another level in a given month with specified probabilities; (2) these probabilities are chosen in such a way that movements in credit ratings are positively correlated across customers; and (3) expert-system business rules are used to determine whether the company will renew or terminate expiring lines of credit and whether customers will exercise their term-out options. For example, a typical rule is that the bank does not renew a credit line if the borrower's credit rating is sufficiently low.

The authors developed a user-friendly Excel-based system to run their model. It actually invokes and executes the simulation behind the scenes in a simulation package called Arena. Users of the system can change many of the parameters of the model, such as the business-rule cutoffs, to customize the simulation.

The model has helped ML Bank USA manage its revolving credit lines. The output of the model provides a scientific and robust measure of liquidity risk that the bank has confidence in—and therefore uses. The model has led to two tangible financial benefits. First, the model reduced the bank's liquidity requirement from 50% to 20% of outstanding commitments, thus freeing up about \$4 billion of liquidity for other profitable illiquid investments. Second, during the first 21 months after the system was implemented, the bank's portfolio expanded from \$8 billion in commitments and 80 customers to \$13 billion and more than 100 customers. The bank continues to use the model for its long-range planning. ■

# 12.1 INTRODUCTION

In the previous chapter, we introduced most of the important concepts for developing and analyzing spreadsheet simulation models. We also discussed many of the available features in the powerful simulation add-in, @RISK, which accompanies this book. Now we apply the tools to a wide variety of problems that can be analyzed by simulation. For convenience, we group the applications into four general areas: (1) operations models, (2) financial models, (3) marketing models, and (4) games of chance. The only overriding theme in this chapter is that simulation models can yield important insights in all of these areas. This chapter is admittedly rather long, with many examples. However, you can cover just the ones of most interest to you, and you can cover them in practically any order.

# 12.2 OPERATIONS MODELS

Whether we are discussing the operations of a manufacturing or a service company, there is likely to be uncertainty that can be modeled with simulation. In this section, we look at examples of bidding for a government contract (uncertainty in the bids by competitors), warranty costs (uncertainty in the time until failure of an appliance), drug production (uncertainty in the yield), and quality control (uncertainty in the quality of manufactured parts).[1]

## Bidding for Contracts

In situations where a company must bid against competitors, simulation can often be used to determine the company's optimal bid. Usually the company does not know what its competitors will bid, but it might have an idea about the *range* of the bids its competitors will choose. In this section, we show how to use simulation to determine a bid that maximizes the company's expected profit.[2]

| EXAMPLE | 12.1 BIDDING FOR A GOVERNMENT CONTRACT |

The Miller Construction Company is trying to decide whether to make a bid on a construction project. Miller believes it will cost the company \$10,000 to complete the project (if it wins the contract), and it will cost \$350 to prepare a bid. However, there is uncertainty about each of these. Upon further reflection, Miller assesses that the cost to complete the project has a triangular distribution with minimum, most likely, and maximum values \$9000, \$10,000, and \$15,000. Similarly, Miller assesses that the cost to prepare a bid has a triangular distribution with parameters \$300, \$350, and \$500. (Note the skewness in these distributions. Miller recognizes that cost overruns are much more likely than cost underruns.) Four potential competitors are going to bid against Miller. The lowest

---
[1] Additional simulation models in the operations area are examined in the next three chapters, where we develop simulations for inventory, queueing, and project scheduling problems.
[2] You can compare this to the bidding example, Example 10.1, in Chapter 10.

bid wins the contract, and the winner is then given the winning bid amount to complete the project. Based on past history, Miller believes that each potential competitor will bid, independently of the others, with probability 0.5. Miller also believes that each competitor's bid will be a multiple of its (Miller's) most likely cost to complete the project, where this multiple has a triangular distribution with minimum, most likely, and maximum values 0.9, 1.3, and 1.8, respectively. If Miller decides to prepare a bid, its bid amount will be a multiple of $500 in the range $10,500 to $15,000. The company wants to use simulation to determine which strategy to use to maximize its expected profit.

**Objective**    To simulate the profit to Miller from any particular bid and to see which bid amount is best.

## WHERE DO THE NUMBERS COME FROM?

We already discussed this type of bidding problem in Chapter 10. The new data required here are the parameters of the distributions of Miller's costs, those of the competitors' bids, and the probability that a given competitor will place a bid. Triangular distributions are chosen for simplicity, although Miller could try other types of distributions. The parameters of these distributions are probably educated guesses, possibly based on previous contracts and bidding experience against these same competitors. The probability that a given competitor will place a bid can be estimated from these same competitors' bidding history.

## Solution

The logic is straightforward. We first simulate the number of competitors who will bid and then simulate their bids. Next, for any bid Miller makes, we see whether Miller wins the contract, and if so, what its profit is.

## DEVELOPING THE SIMULATION MODEL

The simulation model appears in Figure 12.1. (See the file **Contract Bidding.xlsx**.) The model can be developed with the following steps. (Note that this model does not check the

**Figure 12.1**   Bidding Simulation Model

| | A | B | C | D | E | F | G | H | I | J | K | L | M |
|---|---|---|---|---|---|---|---|---|---|---|---|---|---|
| 1 | Bidding for a contract | | | | | | | | | | | | |
| 2 | | | | | | | | | | | | | |
| 3 | Inputs | | | | | | | | | | | | |
| 4 | Miller's costs, triangular distributed | Min | Most likely | Max | | | | | | | | | |
| 5 | Cost to prepare a bid | $300 | $350 | $500 | | | | | | | | | |
| 6 | Cost to complete project | $9,000 | $10,000 | $15,000 | | | | | | | | | |
| 7 | | | | | | | | | | | | | |
| 8 | Number of potential competitors | 4 | | | | | | | | | | | |
| 9 | Probability a given competitor bids | 0.5 | | | | | | | | | | | |
| 10 | | | | | | | | | | | | | |
| 11 | Parameters of triangular distributions for each competitor's bid (expressed as multiple of Miller's most likely cost to complete project) | | | | | | | | | | | | |
| 12 | Min | 0.9 | | | | | | | | | | | |
| 13 | Most likely | 1.3 | | | | | | | | | | | |
| 14 | Max | 1.8 | | | | | | | | | | | |
| 15 | | | | Possible bids for Miller | | | | | | | | | |
| 16 | Miller's bid | $10,500 | | $10,500 | $11,000 | $11,500 | $12,000 | $12,500 | $13,000 | $13,500 | $14,000 | $14,500 | $15,000 |
| 17 | | | | | | | | | | | | | |
| 18 | Simulation | | | | | | | | | | | | |
| 19 | Miller's cost to prepare a bid | $359 | | | | | | | | | | | |
| 20 | Miller's cost to complete project | $11,279 | | | | | | | | | | | |
| 21 | Number of competing bids | 1 | | | | | | | | | | | |
| 22 | Competitor index | 1 | 2 | 3 | 4 | | | | | | | | |
| 23 | Competitors' bids | $15,697 | | | | | | | | | | | |
| 24 | Minimum competitor bid | $15,697 | | | | | | | | | | | |
| 25 | | | | | | | | | | | | | |
| 26 | Miller wins bid? (1 if yes, 0 if no) | 1 | | | | | | | | | | | |
| 27 | Miller's profit | -$1,138 | | | | | | | | | | | |

possibility of Miller not bidding at all. But this case is easy. If Miller chooses not to bid, its profit is a certain $0.)

**1** **Inputs.** Enter the inputs in the blue cells.

**2** **Miller's bid.** We can test all of Miller's possible bids simultaneously with the RISKSIMTABLE function. To set up for this, enter the formula

**=RISKSIMTABLE(D15:M15)**

in cell B15. As with all uses of this function, the spreadsheet shows the simulated values for the *first* bid, $10,500. However, when we run the simulation, we see outputs for all of the bids.

**3** **Miller's costs.** Generate Miller's cost to prepare a bid in cell B19 with the formula

**=RISKTRIANG(B5,C5,D5)**

Then copy this to cell B20 to generate Miller's cost to complete the project.

**4** **Competitors and their bids.** First, generate the random number of competitors who bid. This has a binomial distribution with 4 trials and probability of "success" equal to 0.5 for each trial, so enter the formula

**=RISKBINOMIAL(B8,B9)**

in cell B21. Then generate random bids for the competitors who bid in row 23 by entering the formula

**=IF(B22<=$B$21,RISKTRIANG($B$12,$B$13,$B$14)*$C$6,"")**

in cell B23 and copying across. This generates a random bid for all competitors who bid, and it enters a blank for those who don't. (Remember that the random value is the *multiple* of Miller's most likely cost to complete the project.) Calculate the smallest of these (if there are any) in cell B24 with the formula

**=IF(B21>=1,MIN(B23:E23),"")**

Of course, Miller will not see these other bids until it has submitted its own bid.

**5** **Win contract?** See whether Miller wins the bid by entering the formula

**=IF(OR(B16<B24,B21=0),1,0)**

in cell B26. Here, 1 means that Miller wins the bid, and 0 means a competitor wins the bid. Of course, if there are no competing bids, Miller wins for sure. Then designate this cell as an @RISK output cell. Recall that to designate a cell as an @RISK output cell, you select the cell and then click on the Add Output button on @RISK's ribbon. You can then name this output appropriately. We used the name "Win bid."

**6** **Miller's profit.** If Miller submits a bid, the bid cost is lost for sure. Beyond that, the profit to Miller is the bid amount minus the cost of completing the project if the bid is won. Otherwise, Miller makes nothing. So enter the formula

**=IF(B26=1,B16-B20,0)-B19**

in cell B27. Then designate this cell as an additional @RISK output cell. (We named it Profit.)

**Running the Simulation**

We set the number of iterations to 1000, and we set the number of simulations to 10 because Miller wants to test 10 bid amounts.

*Recall that the RISKSIMTABLE function allows you to run a separate simulation for each value in its list.*

## Discussion of the Simulation Results

The summary results appear in Figure 12.2. For each simulation—that is, each bid amount—there are two outputs: 1 or 0 to indicate whether Miller wins the contract, and Miller's profit. The only interesting results for the 0/1 output are in the mean column, which shows the fraction of iterations that resulted in 1's. So we see, for example, that if Miller bids $12,000 (simulation #4), the probability of winning the bid is estimated to be 0.587. This probability clearly decreases as Miller's bid increases.

**Figure 12.2**

Summary Results from @RISK

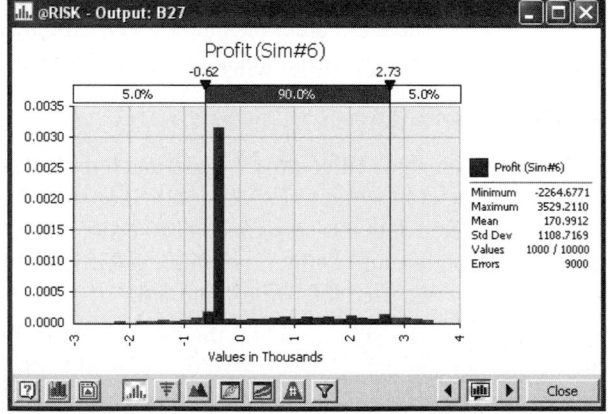

| Name | Cell | Sim# | Min | Mean | Max | Median | Std Dev | 5% | 95% |
|---|---|---|---|---|---|---|---|---|---|
| Wins Bid | B26 | 1 | 0 | 0.881 | 1 | 1 | 0.3239505 | 0 | 1 |
| Wins Bid | B26 | 2 | 0 | 0.787 | 1 | 1 | 0.4096325 | 0 | 1 |
| Wins Bid | B26 | 3 | 0 | 0.689 | 1 | 1 | 0.4631344 | 0 | 1 |
| Wins Bid | B26 | 4 | 0 | 0.581 | 1 | 1 | 0.4936423 | 0 | 1 |
| Wins Bid | B26 | 5 | 0 | 0.475 | 1 | 0 | 0.4996245 | 0 | 1 |
| Wins Bid | B26 | 6 | 0 | 0.359 | 1 | 0 | 0.4799472 | 0 | 1 |
| Wins Bid | B26 | 7 | 0 | 0.272 | 1 | 0 | 0.4452125 | 0 | 1 |
| Wins Bid | B26 | 8 | 0 | 0.213 | 1 | 0 | 0.4096325 | 0 | 1 |
| Wins Bid | B26 | 9 | 0 | 0.168 | 1 | 0 | 0.3740534 | 0 | 1 |
| Wins Bid | B26 | 10 | 0 | 0.134 | 1 | 0 | 0.3408228 | 0 | 1 |
| Profit | B27 | 1 | -4764.677 | -1109.27 | 1029.211 | -747.65 | 1264.907 | -3595.264 | 534.2583 |
| Profit | B27 | 2 | -4264.677 | -640.0039 | 1529.211 | -395.128 | 1178.434 | -2933.573 | 1006.308 |
| Profit | B27 | 3 | -3764.677 | -272.5675 | 2029.211 | -353.8484 | 1100.608 | -2392.814 | 1463.146 |
| Profit | B27 | 4 | -3264.677 | -3.810187 | 2529.211 | -346.4289 | 1058.958 | -1805.828 | 1929.528 |
| Profit | B27 | 5 | -2764.677 | 149.7272 | 3029.211 | -352.5558 | 1075.519 | -1187.955 | 2332.889 |
| Profit | B27 | 6 | -2264.677 | 170.9912 | 3529.211 | -359.0678 | 1108.717 | -616.3383 | 2726.53 |
| Profit | B27 | 7 | -1764.677 | 166.7163 | 4029.211 | -361.9686 | 1153.412 | -464.5716 | 3058.364 |
| Profit | B27 | 8 | -1264.677 | 157.6586 | 4529.211 | -364.9714 | 1225.319 | -460.6413 | 3463.762 |
| Profit | B27 | 9 | -764.6771 | 119.4651 | 5029.211 | -367.4769 | 1261.712 | -459.4841 | 3558.395 |
| Profit | B27 | 10 | -496.554 | 84.26152 | 5529.211 | -369.4244 | 1298.07 | -458.998 | 3723.797 |

**Figure 12.3**

Histogram of Profit for a $13,000 Bid

In terms of net profit, if we concentrate only on the mean column, then a bid amount of $13,000 (simulation #6) is clearly the best. But as the other numbers in this figure indicate, the mean doesn't tell the whole story. For example, if Miller bids $13,000, it could win the bid but still lose a considerable amount of money because of cost overruns. The histogram of profit in Figure 12.3 indicates this more clearly. It shows that in spite of the positive mean, most outcomes are negative!

So what should Miller do? If it doesn't bid at all, its profit is $0 for sure. If Miller is an *expected* profit maximizer, then the fact that several of the means in Figure 12.2 are positive indicates that bidding is better than not bidding, with a bid of \$13,000 being the best bid. However, potential cost overruns and the corresponding losses are certainly a concern. Depending on Miller's degree of risk aversion, the company might decide to (1) not bid at all, or (2) bid higher than \$13,000 to minimize its worse loss. Still, we would caution Miller not to be too conservative. Rather than focusing on the Min (worst case) column in Figure 12.2, we would suggest focusing on the 5% column. This shows nearly how bad things could get (5% of the time it would be worse than this), and this fifth percentile remains nearly constant for higher bids. ∎

## Warranty Costs

When you buy a new product, it usually carries a warranty. A typical warranty might state that if the product fails within a certain period such as 1 year, you will receive a new product at no cost, and it will carry the *same* warranty. However, if the product fails after the warranty period, you have to bear the cost of replacing the product. Due to random lifetimes of products, we need a way to estimate the warranty costs (to the company) of a product. We see how simulation can accomplish this in the next example.

---

**EXAMPLE** | **12.2 Warranty Costs for a Camera**

The Yakkon Company sells a popular camera for \$250. This camera carries a warranty such that if the camera fails within 1.5 years, the company gives the customer a new camera for free. If the camera fails after 1.5 years, the warranty is no longer in effect. Every replacement camera carries exactly the same warranty as the original camera, and the cost to the company of supplying a new camera is always \$185. Use simulation to estimate, for a given sale, the number of replacements under warranty and the NPV of profit from the sale, using a discount rate of 12%.

**Objective**   To use simulation to estimate the number of replacements under warranty and the total NPV of profit from a given sale.

### Where do the numbers come from?

The warranty information is a policy decision made by the company. The hardest input to estimate is the probability distribution of the lifetime of the product. We discuss this next.

## Solution

The only randomness in this problem concerns the time until failure of a new camera. Yakkon could estimate the distribution of time until failure from historical data. This would probably indicate a right-skewed distribution, as shown in Figure 12.4. If you look through the list of distributions available in @RISK under Define Distributions, you will see several with this same basic shape. The one shown in Figure 12.4 is a commonly used distribution called the **gamma** distribution. For variety (and realism), we use this distribution in the example, although other choices such as the triangular are certainly possible.

### Selecting a Gamma Distribution

The gamma distribution is characterized by two parameters, usually denoted by $\alpha$ and $\beta$. These determine its exact shape and location. It can be shown that the mean and standard deviation are $\mu = \alpha\beta$ and $\sigma = \sqrt{\alpha}\beta$. Alternatively, if we estimate the mean and standard deviation, we can solve these equations for $\alpha$ and $\beta$. This leads to $\alpha = \mu^2/\sigma^2$ and $\beta = \sigma^2/\mu$. So, for example, if we want a gamma distribution with mean 2.5 and standard deviation 1 (which in this example would be based on camera lifetime data from the past), we use $\alpha = 2.5^2/1^2 = 6.25$ and $\beta = 1^2/2.5 = 0.4$. These are the values shown in Figure 12.4 and the ones we use for this example. The values in the figure (from @RISK) imply that the probability of failure before 1.5 years is about 0.15, so that the probability of failure out of warranty is about 0.85.

**Figure 12.4**

Right-Skewed
Gamma
Distribution

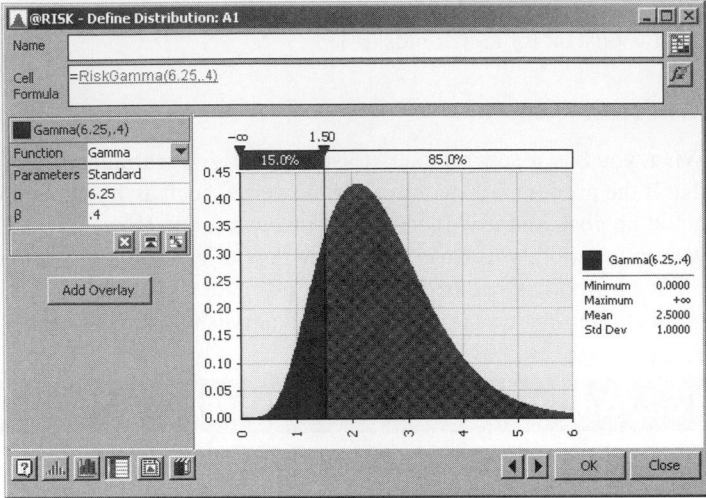

## DEVELOPING THE SIMULATION MODEL

The simulation model appears in Figure 12.5. (See the file **Warranty Costs.xlsx**.) The particular random numbers in this figure indicate an example (a rather unusual one) where there are two failures within warranty. However, because the lifetime of the second replacement (cell D17) is greater than 1.5, the company incurs only two replacement costs, as shown in cells B19 and C19. The model can be developed with the following steps.

**Figure 12.5**

Warranty Simula-
tion Model

| | A | B | C | D | E | F |
|---|---|---|---|---|---|---|
| 1 | **Warranty costs for camera** | | | | | |
| 2 | | | | | | |
| 3 | **Inputs** | | | | | |
| 4 | Parameters of time to failure distribution of any new camera (Gamma) | | | | | |
| 5 | Desired mean | 2.5 | | | | |
| 6 | Desired stdev | 1 | | | | |
| 7 | Implied alpha | 6.250 | | | | |
| 8 | Implied beta | 0.400 | | | | |
| 9 | | | | | | |
| 10 | Warranty period | 1.5 | | | | |
| 11 | Cost of new camera (to customer) | $250 | | | | |
| 12 | Replacement cost (to company) | $185 | | | | |
| 13 | Discount rate | 12% | | | | |
| 14 | | | | | | |
| 15 | **Simulation of new camera and its replacements (if any)** | | | | | |
| 16 | Camera | 1 | 2 | 3 | 4 | 5 |
| 17 | Lifetime | 0.925 | 1.351 | 1.698 | NA | NA |
| 18 | Time of failure | 0.925 | 2.276 | 3.974 | NA | NA |
| 19 | Cost to company | 185 | 185 | 0 | 0 | 0 |
| 20 | Discounted cost | 166.59 | 142.94 | 0.00 | 0.00 | 0.00 |
| 21 | | | | | | |
| 22 | Failures within warranty | 2 | | | | |
| 23 | NPV of profit from customer | ($244.53) | | | | |

**1 Inputs.** Enter the inputs in the blue cells.

**2 Parameters of gamma distribution.** As we discussed previously, if we enter a desired mean and standard deviation (in cells B5 and B6), we have to calculate the parameters of the gamma distribution. Do this by entering the formulas

**=B5^2/B6^2**

and

**=B6^2/B5**

in cells B7 and B8.

**3 Lifetimes and times of failures.** We generate at most 5 lifetimes and corresponding times of failures. Why only 5? We could generate more, but it is extremely unlikely that this same customer will experience more than 5 failures within warranty, so 5 suffices. As soon as a lifetime is greater than 1.5, the warranty period, we do not generate any further lifetimes, since "the game is over"; instead, we record "NA" in row 17. With this in mind, enter the formulas

**=RISKGAMMA(B7,B8)**

**=IF(B17<B10,RISKGAMMA(B7,B8),"NA")**

and

**=IF(C17="NA","NA",IF(C17<$B$10,RISKGAMMA($B$7,$B$8),"NA"))**

in cells B17, C17, and D17, and copy the latter formula to cells E17 and F17. These formulas guarantee that once "NA" is recorded in a cell, all cells to its right also contain "NA." To get the actual times of failures, relative to time 0 when the customer originally purchases the camera, enter the formulas

**=B17**

and

**=IF(C17="NA","NA",B18+C17)**

in cells B18 and C18, and copy the latter across row 18. These values are used for the NPV calculation because we need to know exactly when cash flows occur.

**@RISK Function: *RISKGAMMA***

*To generate a random number from the gamma distribution, use the RISKGAMMA function in the form =RISKGAMMA(Alpha,Beta). The mean and standard deviation of this distribution are $\mu = \alpha\beta$ and $\sigma = \sqrt{\alpha\beta}$. Equivalently, $\alpha = \mu^2/\sigma^2$ and $\beta = \sigma^2/\mu$.*

*Excel's NPV function can be used only for cash flows that occur at the ends of the respective years. Otherwise, you have to discount cash flows "manually."*

**4 Costs and discounted costs.** In row 19, we enter the replacement cost ($185) or 0, depending on whether a failure occurs within warranty, and in row 20, we discount these costs back to time 0, using the failure times in row 18. To do this, enter the formulas

**=IF(B17<B10,B12,0)**

and

**=IF(C17="NA",0,IF(C17<$B$10,$B$12,0))**

in cells B19 and C19, and copy this latter formula across row 19. Then enter the formula

**=IF(B19>0,B19/(1+$B$13)^B18,0)**

in cell B20 and copy it across row 20. This formula uses the well-known fact that the present value of a cash flow at time $t$ is the cash flow multiplied by $1/(1 + r)^t$, where $r$ is the discount rate.

**5** **Outputs.** Calculate two outputs, the number of failures within warranty and the NPV of profit, with the formulas

**=COUNTIF(B19:F19,">0")**

and

**=B11-B12-SUM(B20:F20)**

in cells B22 and B23. Then designate these two cells as @RISK output cells. Note that the NPV is the margin from the sale (undiscounted) minus the sum of the discounted costs from replacements under warranty.

### Running the Simulation

The @RISK setup is typical. We run 1000 iterations of a *single* simulation (because there is no RISKSIMTABLE function).

### Discussion of the Simulation Results

The @RISK summary statistics and histograms for the two outputs appear in Figures 12.6, 12.7, and 12.8. They show a pretty clear picture. About 85% of the time, there are no failures within the warranty period and the company makes a profit of $65, the margin from the camera sale. However, there is about a 12.9% chance of exactly 1 failure under warranty, in which case, the company's NPV of profit is an approximate $100 loss. Additionally, there is about a 2.1% chance that there are even more failures under warranty, in which

**Figure 12.6** @RISK Summary Statistics for Warranty Model

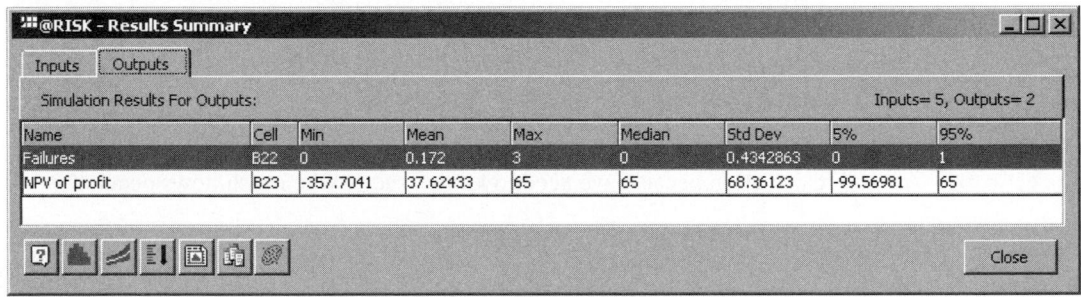

**Figure 12.7**

Histogram of
Number of Failures

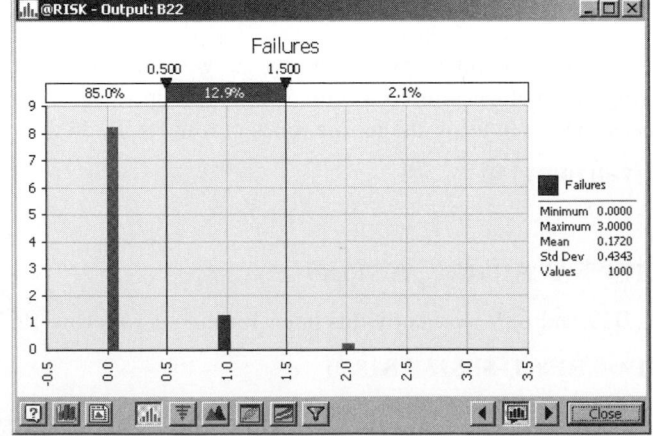

**Figure 12.8**

Histogram of NPV of Profit

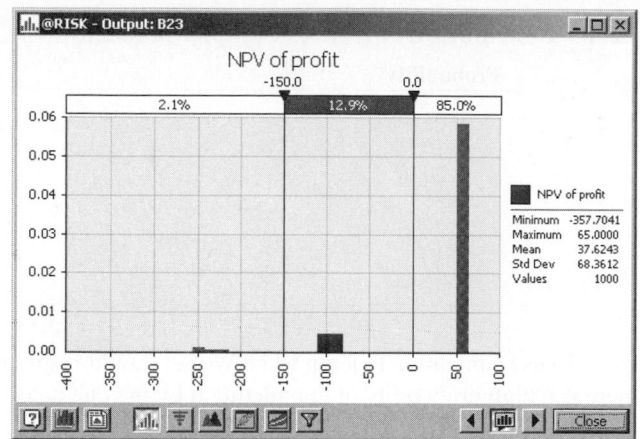

case the loss is even greater. Note that in our 1000 iterations, the maximum number of failures under warranty was 3, and the maximum net loss was $357.70. On average, the NPV of profit was $37.62.

These results indicate that Yakkon is not suffering terribly from warranty costs. However, the company could decrease the effects of warranty costs in several ways. First, it could increase the price of the camera. Second, it could decrease the warranty period, say, from 1.5 years to 1 year. Third, it could change the terms of the warranty. For example, it could stipulate that if the camera fails within a year, the customer gets a new camera for free, whereas if the time to failure is between 1 and 1.5 years, the customer pays some pro rata share of the replacement cost. Finally, it could try to sell the customer an extended warranty—at a hefty price. We ask you to explore these possibilities in the "Problems" section. ■

## Drug Production with Uncertain Yield

In many manufacturing settings, products are produced in batches, and the usable yields from these batches are uncertain. This is particularly true in the drug industry. The following example illustrates how a drug manufacturer can take this uncertainty into account when planning production.

---

**EXAMPLE** | **12.3 MEETING AN ORDER DUE DATE AT WOZAC**

The Wozac Company manufactures drugs. Wozac has recently accepted an order from its best customer for 8000 ounces of a new drug, and Wozac wants to plan its production schedule to meet the customer's promised delivery date of December 1. There are three sources of uncertainty that make planning difficult. First, the drug must be produced in batches, and there is uncertainty in the time required to produce a batch, which could be anywhere from 5 to 11 days. This uncertainty is described by the discrete distribution in Table 12.1. Second, the yield (usable quantity) from any batch is uncertain. Based on historical data, Wozac believes the yield can be modeled by a triangular distribution with minimum, most likely, and maximum values equal to 600, 1000, and 1100 ounces, respectively. Third, all batches must go through a rigorous inspection after they are completed. The probability that a typical batch passes inspection is only 0.8. The probability that the batch fails inspection is 0.2, in which case *none* of it can be used to help fill the order. Wozac wants to use simulation to help decide how many days prior to the due date it should begin production.

**Table 12.1  Distribution of Days to Complete a Batch**

| Days | Probability |
|------|-------------|
| 5  | 0.05 |
| 6  | 0.10 |
| 7  | 0.20 |
| 8  | 0.30 |
| 9  | 0.20 |
| 10 | 0.10 |
| 11 | 0.05 |

**Objective**   To use simulation to learn when Wozac should begin production for this order so that there is a high probability of completing it by the due date.

## WHERE DO THE NUMBERS COME FROM?

The important inputs here are the probability distributions of the time to produce a batch, the yield from a batch, and the inspection result. The probabilities we have assumed would undoubtedly be based on previous production data. For example, the company might have observed that about 80% of all batches in the past passed inspection. Note that a *discrete* distribution is natural for the number of days to produce a batch, and a *continuous* distribution is appropriate for the yield from a batch.

## Solution

The idea is to simulate successive batches—their days to complete, their yields, and whether they pass inspection—and keep a running total of the usable ounces obtained so far. We then use IF functions to check whether the order is complete or another batch is required. We simulate only as many batches as are required to meet the order, and we keep track of the days required to produce all of these batches. In this way, we can "back up" to see when production must begin to meet the due date. For example, if the simulation indicates that the order takes 96 days to complete, then production must begin on August 27, which is 96 days before the due date. (For simplicity, we assume that production occurs 7 days a week.)

## DEVELOPING THE SIMULATION MODEL

The completed model appears in Figure 12.9. (See the file **Drug Production.xlsx**.) The model can be developed as follows:

**1  Inputs.**  Enter all of the inputs in the blue cells.

**2  Batch indexes.**  We do not know ahead of time how many batches will be required to fill the order. We want to have enough rows in the simulation to cover the worst case that is likely to occur. After some experimentation, we found that 25 batches are almost surely enough. Therefore, enter the batch indexes 1 to 25 in column A of the simulation section. (If 25 are not enough, we can always add more rows.) The idea, then, is to fill the *entire* range B25:F49 with formulas. However, we use IF functions in these formulas so that if enough has already been produced to fill the order, blanks are inserted in the remaining cells. For example, the scenario shown in Figure 12.9 requires 12 batches, so blanks appear below row 36.

**3  Days for batches.**  Simulate the days required for batches in column B. To do this, enter the formulas

**=RISKDISCRETE(B9:B15,C9:C15)**

## Figure 12.9  The Drug Production Simulation Model

| | A | B | C | D | E | F | G | H | I | J | K | L |
|---|---|---|---|---|---|---|---|---|---|---|---|---|
| 1 | Planning production of a drug | | | | | | | | | | | |
| 2 | | | | | | | | | | | | |
| 3 | Input section | | | | | | | | | | | |
| 4 | Amount required (ounces) | 8000 | | | | | | | | | | |
| 5 | Promised delivery date | 12/01/08 | | | | | | | | | | |
| 6 | | | | | Assumptions: | | | | | | | |
| 7 | Distribution of days needed to produce a batch (discrete) | | | | The drug is produced in similar-sized batches, although the yield in each | | | | | | | |
| 8 | | Days | Probability | | batch is random.  Also, the number of days to produce a batch is random. | | | | | | | |
| 9 | | 5 | 0.05 | | Each batch is inspected, and if it doesn't pass inspection, none of that batch | | | | | | | |
| 10 | | 6 | 0.10 | | can be used. | | | | | | | |
| 11 | | 7 | 0.20 | | | | | | | | | |
| 12 | | 8 | 0.30 | | | | | | | | | |
| 13 | | 9 | 0.20 | | | | | | | | | |
| 14 | | 10 | 0.10 | | | | | | | | | |
| 15 | | 11 | 0.05 | | | | | | | | | |
| 16 | | | | | | | | | | | | |
| 17 | Distribution of yield (ounces) from each batch (triangular) | | | | | | | | | | | |
| 18 | | Min | Most likely | Max | | | | | | | | |
| 19 | | 600 | 1000 | 1100 | | | | | | | | |
| 20 | | | | | | | | | | | | |
| 21 | Probability of passing inspection | 0.8 | | | | | | | | | | |
| 22 | | | | | | | | | | | | |
| 23 | Simulation model | | | | | | | Summary measures | | | | |
| 24 | Batch | Days | Yield | Pass? | CumYield | Enough? | | Batches required | 12 | | | |
| 25 | 1 | 6 | 982.4 | Yes | 982.4 | Not yet | | Days to complete | 94 | | | |
| 26 | 2 | 8 | 902.4 | Yes | 1884.8 | Not yet | | Day to start | 8/29/08 | | | |
| 27 | 3 | 8 | 887.8 | No | 1884.8 | Not yet | | | | | | |
| 28 | 4 | 5 | 830.6 | Yes | 2715.4 | Not yet | | @Risk summary outputs | | | | |
| 29 | 5 | 10 | 794.2 | Yes | 3509.6 | Not yet | | Max batches reqd | 20 | | | |
| 30 | 6 | 8 | 872.5 | Yes | 4382.1 | Not yet | | | | | | |
| 31 | 7 | 8 | 768.4 | Yes | 5150.5 | Not yet | | Avg days reqd | 94 | 8/29/08 | | |
| 32 | 8 | 8 | 651.0 | Yes | 5801.5 | Not yet | | Min days reqd | 59 | 10/3/08 | | |
| 33 | 9 | 9 | 879.3 | No | 5801.5 | Not yet | | Max days reqd | 160 | 6/24/08 | | |
| 34 | 10 | 7 | 690.6 | Yes | 6492.1 | Not yet | | 5th perc days reqd | 72 | 9/20/08 | | |
| 35 | 11 | 8 | 941.0 | Yes | 7433.0 | Not yet | | 95th perc days reqd | 121 | 8/2/08 | | |
| 36 | 12 | 9 | 897.6 | Yes | 8330.6 | Yes | | | | | | |
| 37 | 13 | | | | | | | Probability of meeting due date for several starting dates | | | | |
| 38 | 14 | | | | | | | | 7/15/08 | 0.991 | | |
| 39 | 15 | | | | | | | | 8/1/08 | 0.954 | | |
| 40 | 16 | | | | | | | | 8/15/08 | 0.845 | | |
| 41 | 17 | | | | | | | | 9/1/08 | 0.469 | | |
| 42 | 18 | | | | | | | | 9/15/08 | 0.120 | | |
| 43 | 19 | | | | | | | | | | | |
| 44 | 20 | | | | | | | | | | | |
| 45 | 21 | | | | | | | | | | | |
| 46 | 22 | | | | | | | | | | | |
| 47 | 23 | | | | | | | | | | | |
| 48 | 24 | | | | | | | | | | | |
| 49 | 25 | | | | | | | | | | | |

and

**=IF(OR(F25="Yes",F25=""),"",RISKDISCRETE($B$9:$B$15,$C$9:$C$15))**

in cell B25 and B26, and copy the latter formula down to cell B49. Note how the IF function enters a blank in this cell if either of two conditions is true: the order was just completed in the previous batch, or it has been completed for some time. Similar logic appears in later formulas.

**4** **Batch yields.** Simulate the batch yields in column C. To do this, enter the formulas

**=RISKTRIANG(B19,C19,D19)**

and

**=IF(OR(F25="Yes",F25= ""), "",RISKTRIANG($B$19,$C$19,$D$19))**

We can use Excel's RAND function inside an IF function to simulate whether some event occurs or does not occur.

in cells C25 and C26, and copy the latter formula down to cell C49.

**5** **Pass inspection?** Check whether each batch passes inspection with the formulas

=IF(RAND()<B21, "Yes","No")

and

=IF(OR(F25="Yes",F25= ""),"",IF(RAND()<$B$21, "Yes","No"))

in cells D25 and D26, and copy the latter formula down to cell D49. Note that we could use @RISK's RISKUNIFORM(0,1) function instead of RAND(), but there is no real advantage to doing so. They are essentially equivalent. (Besides, the educational version of @RISK imposes an upper limit of 100 "RISK" input functions per model, so it is often a good idea to substitute built-in Excel functions when possible.)

**6** **Order filled?** We keep track of the cumulative usable production and whether the order has been filled in columns E and F. First, enter the formulas

=IF(D25="Yes",C25,0)

and

=IF(E25>=B4,"Yes","Not yet")

in cells E25 and F25 for batch 1. Then enter the general formulas

=IF(OR(F25="Yes",F25=""),"",IF(D26="Yes",C26+E25,E25))

and

=IF(OR(F25="Yes",F25=""),"",IF(E26>=$B$4,"Yes","Not yet"))

in cells E26 and F26, and copy them down to row 49. Note that the entry in column F is "Not yet" if the order is not yet complete. In the row that completes the order, it changes to "Yes," and then it is blank in succeeding rows.

**7** **Summary measures.** Calculate the batches and days required in cells I24 and I25 with the formulas

=COUNT(B25:B49)

and

=SUM(B25:B49)

These are the two cells we use as output cells for @RISK, so we designate them as such. Also, calculate the day the order should be started to just meet the due date in cell I26 with the formula

=B5-I25

Date subtraction in Excel allows us to calculate the number of days between two given dates.

This formula uses date subtraction to find an elapsed time. (Again, we assume for simplicity that production occurs every day of the week.)

This completes the simulation model development. The other entries in columns H to J will be explained shortly.

### Dealing with Uncertain Timing

Many simulations that model a process over multiple time periods must deal with uncertain timing of events, such as when the manufacturing of an order will finish, which year sales of a new product will begin, and many others. Essentially, the spreadsheet model must generate random numbers that determine the timing and then "play out" the events. This can require tricky IF functions and possibly other functions. However, the hard work often involves getting the logic correct for the first period or two. Then it is just a matter of copying this logic down for the other periods. In other words, a bit of hard work developing the first row or two can result in a very powerful model.

### Running the Simulation

We set the number of iterations to 1000 and the number of simulations to 1, and then run the simulation as usual.

### Discussion of the Simulation Results

After running the simulation, we obtain the histograms of the number of batches required and the number of days required in Figures 12.10 and 12.11.

**Figure 12.10**

Histogram of Batches Required

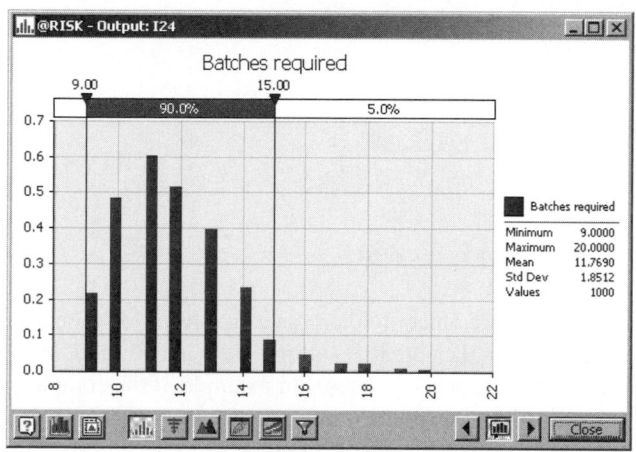

**Figure 12.11**

Histogram of Days Required

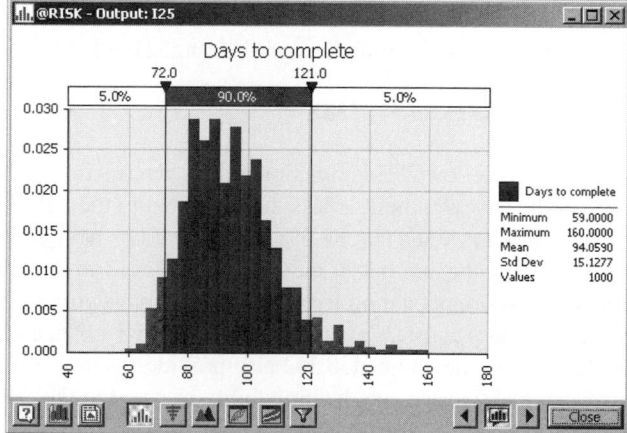

How should Wozac use this information? The key questions are

- How many batches are required?
- When should production start?

To answer these questions, it is helpful to use several of @RISK's statistical functions. Recall that these functions can be entered directly into the Excel model worksheet. (Also, recall that they provide useful information *after* the simulation has been run.) These functions provide no new information we don't already have from other @RISK windows, but they allow us to see (and manipulate) this information directly in the spreadsheet.

For the first question, we enter the formula

**=RISKMAX(I24)**

in cell I29. (Refer to Figure 12.9.) It shows that the worst case from the 1000 iterations, in terms of batches required, is 20 batches. (If this maximum were 25, we would add more rows to the simulation model and run the simulation again!)

We can answer the second question in two ways. First, we can calculate summary measures for days required and then back up from the due date. We do this in the range I31:J35. The formulas in column I are

**=INT(RISKMEAN(I25))**

**=RISKMIN(I25)**

**=RISKMAX(I25)**

**=RISKPERCENTILE(I25,0.05)**

and

**=RISKPERCENTILE(I25,0.95)**

*Using @RISK summary functions, such as RISKMEAN, RISKPERCENTILE, and others, allows us to capture simulation results in the same worksheet as the simulation model. These functions do not provide useful results until after the simulation is run.*

(The first uses the INT function to produce an integer.) We then subtract each of these from the due date to obtain the potential starting dates in column J. Wozac should understand the pros and cons of these starting dates. For example, if the company wants to be 95% sure of meeting the due date, it should start production on August 2. In contrast, if Wozac starts production on September 20, there is only a 5% chance of meeting the due date.

Alternatively, we can get a more direct answer to our question by using @RISK's RISKTARGET function. This allows us to find the probability of meeting the due date for *any* starting date, such as the trial dates in the range H38:H42. We enter the formula

**=RISKTARGET($I$25,$B$4-H38)**

in cell I38 and copy it down. This function returns the fraction of iterations where the (random) value in the first argument is less than or equal to the (fixed) value in the second argument. For example, we see that 84.5% of the iterations have a value of days required less than or equal to 108, the number of days from August 15 to the due date.

What is our recommendation to Wozac? We suggest going with the 95th percentile—begin production on August 2. Then there is only a 5% chance of failing to meet the due date. But the table in the range H38:I42 also provides useful information. For each potential starting date, Wozac can see the probability of meeting the due date if it starts production on that date. ∎

## Deming's Funnel Experiment

Edwards Deming was an American statistician whose views on quality management revolutionized the way companies do business across the world. Deming has been given much of the credit for Japan's spectacular post–World War II economic recovery. He traveled around the United States giving a famous 4-day seminar on quality management. After attending his seminar, many U.S. companies (including Xerox, GM, and Ford) reorganized their businesses to reflect Deming's management philosophy as embraced in his famous 14 points. For example, GM's Saturn plant is run almost completely in accordance with Deming's 14 points. We strongly recommend Deming's book *Out of the Crisis* (1986). It contains some great insights.

An important component of Deming's seminar was his famous funnel experiment. The funnel experiment is designed to show how businesses often greatly overadjust "stable" processes. We illustrate how it works in the following example.

---

**EXAMPLE** | **12.4 TAMPERING WITH A STABLE PROCESS**

---

Suppose that you are in the business of drilling a tiny hole in the exact center of a square piece of wood. In the past, the holes you have drilled were, on average, in the center of the wood, and the $x$- and $y$-coordinates each had a standard deviation of 0.1 inch. Also, the drilling process has been *stable*—that is, the holes average being in the center of the square, and the deviations from the center of the square (measured in both the $x$- and $y$-coordinates) follow a normal distribution with mean 0 and standard deviation 0.1 inch. This means, for example, that the $x$-coordinate is within 0.1 inch of the center for 68% of the holes, the $x$-coordinate is within 0.2 inch of the center for 95% of the holes, and the $x$-coordinate is within 0.3 inch of the center for 99.7% of the holes. This describes the *inherent* variability in the drilling process. Unless you change the hole-drilling process, you must accept this amount of variation.

Now suppose that you drill a hole and its $x$- and $y$-coordinates are $x = 0.1$ and $y = 0$ [where the center of the square has coordinates (0, 0)]. A natural reaction is to reduce the $x$-setting of the drill by 0.1 to correct for the fact that the $x$-coordinate was too high. Then if the next hole has coordinates $x = -0.2$ and $y = 0.1$, you might try to increase the $x$-coordinate by 0.2 and decrease the $y$-coordinate by 0.1. Deming's funnel experiment shows that this method of continually readjusting a stable process—he calls it "tampering"—actually *increases* the variability of the coordinates of the position where the hole is drilled. In other words, tampering generally make a process worse!

To illustrate the effects of tampering, Deming placed a funnel above a target on the floor and dropped small balls through the funnel in an attempt to hit the target. As he demonstrated, many balls did *not* hit the target. His goal, therefore, was to make the balls fall as close to the target as possible. Deming proposed four rules for adjusting the positioning of the funnel.

- **Rule 1.** Never move the funnel. (Don't tamper.)
- **Rule 2.** After each ball is dropped, move the funnel—*relative to its previous position*—to compensate for any error. To illustrate, suppose the target has coordinates (0, 0), and the funnel begins directly over the target. If the ball lands at (0.5, 0.1) on the first drop, we compensate by repositioning the funnel at $(0 - 0.5, 0 - 0.1) = (-0.5, -1)$. If the second drop has coordinates (1, −2), we then reposition the funnel at $(-0.5 - 1, -0.1 - (-2)) = (-1.5, 1.9)$.

- **Rule 3.** Move the funnel—*relative to its original position at* $(0, 0)$—to compensate for any error. For example, if the ball lands at $(0.5, 0.1)$ on the first drop, we compensate by repositioning the funnel at $(0 - 0.5, 0 - 0.1) = (-0.5, -1)$. If the second drop has coordinates $(1, -2)$, we then reposition the funnel at $(0 - 1, 0 - (-2)) = (-1, 2)$.

- **Rule 4.** Always reposition the funnel directly over the last drop. Therefore, if the first ball lands at $(0.5, 1)$, we position the funnel at $(0.5, 1)$. If the second drop has coordinates $(1, 2)$, we position the funnel at $(1, 2)$. (This rule might be followed, for example, by an automobile manufacturer's painting department. With each new batch of paint, they attempt to match the color of the previous batch—regardless of whether the previous color was correct.)

Do you believe any of these latter three rules outperform rule 1, the "leave it alone" rule? Is so, read on—you might be surprised.

**Objective**   To use simulation to see the effect of tampering with a stable process, as opposed to leaving it alone.

## WHERE DO THE NUMBERS COME FROM?

Obviously, we made up the numbers for this experiment (the standard deviations). However, any stable manufacturing process has parameters that can be measured by watching the process over time. In fact, this is exactly what **control charts,** a staple of most manufacturing companies, are designed to do.

## Solution

To see how these rules work, we assume that the *x*-coordinate on each drop is normally distributed with mean equal to the *x*-coordinate of the funnel position and standard deviation of 1. A similar statement holds for the *y*-coordinate. Also, we assume that the *x*- and *y*-coordinates are selected independently of one another. These assumptions describe the inherent variability in the process of dropping the balls.

To see how the rules work, let $F_0$, $X_0$, and $F_1$ be, respectively, the *x*-coordinates of the funnel position on the previous drop, the outcome of the previous drop, and the repositioned funnel position for the next drop. Then rule 1 never repositions, so that $F_1 = F_0$. Rule 2 repositions relative to the previous funnel position, so that $F_1 = F_0 - X_0$. Rule 3 repositions relative to the original position (at 0), so that $F_1 = 0 - X_0 = -X_0$. Finally, rule 4 repositions at the previous drop, so that $F_1 = X_0$. Similar equations hold for the *y*-coordinate.

For the simulation model, we simulate 45 consecutive drops of the ball from each of the four rules. Our single output measure is the (straight-line) distance of the final drop from the target. A rule is presumably a good one if the mean distance is small and the standard deviation of this distance is also small.

## DEVELOPING THE SIMULATION MODEL

Given the repositioning equations for the rules, the simulation model is straightforward. In fact, we can use a RISKSIMTABLE function to test all four rules simultaneously. The completed model appears in Figure 12.12. (See the file **Funnel Experiment.xlsx.**) It can be developed with the following steps:

**1** **Rule.**   Enter the formula

**=RISKSIMTABLE({ 1, 2, 3, 4})**

**Figure 12.12** The Funnel Experiment Simulation Model

| | A | B | C | D | E | F | G | H | I | J | K |
|---|---|---|---|---|---|---|---|---|---|---|---|
| 1 | Deming's funnel experiment | | | | | | | | | | |
| 2 | | | | Range names used: | | | | | | | |
| 3 | Rule | 1 | | Rule | =Model!$B$3 | | | | | | |
| 4 | | | | | | | | | | | |
| 5 | | Funnel positioned at: | | Drop lands at: | | | | | | | |
| 6 | Drop | Xpos | Ypos | Xdrop | Ydrop | | Explanation of rules: | | | | |
| 7 | 1 | 0 | 0 | -0.11 | 0.05 | | Rule 1: Never move the funnel | | | | |
| 8 | 2 | 0.00 | 0.00 | 0.11 | 0.04 | | Rule 2: Move the funnel, relative to its previous | | | | |
| 9 | 3 | 0.00 | 0.00 | 0.00 | -0.03 | | position, to compensate for the previous error. | | | | |
| 10 | 4 | 0.00 | 0.00 | -0.03 | -0.01 | | Rule 3: Move the funnel, relative to its original position, | | | | |
| 11 | 5 | 0.00 | 0.00 | -0.07 | 0.03 | | to compensate for the previous error. | | | | |
| 12 | 6 | 0.00 | 0.00 | 0.10 | -0.09 | | Rule 4: Reposition the funnel over the previous drop. | | | | |
| 13 | 7 | 0.00 | 0.00 | -0.04 | 0.08 | | | | | | |
| 14 | 8 | 0.00 | 0.00 | 0.11 | 0.06 | | Distance of final drop from target | | | | 0.052 |
| 15 | 9 | 0.00 | 0.00 | -0.01 | 0.08 | | | | | | |
| 16 | 10 | 0.00 | 0.00 | -0.11 | 0.03 | | | | | | |
| 47 | 41 | 0.00 | 0.00 | 0.06 | 0.20 | | | | | | |
| 48 | 42 | 0.00 | 0.00 | 0.04 | 0.01 | | | | | | |
| 49 | 43 | 0.00 | 0.00 | -0.10 | -0.09 | | | | | | |
| 50 | 44 | 0.00 | 0.00 | -0.01 | 0.07 | | | | | | |
| 51 | 45 | 0.00 | 0.00 | 0.04 | -0.03 | | | | | | |

in cell B3 to indicate that we want to simulate all four rules. Recall that if individual values are listed in RISKSIMTABLE, they must be enclosed in curly brackets. No curly brackets are used if the list is referenced by a range address.

**2** **Position funnel.** Enter 0 in cells B7 and C7 to indicate that the original funnel position is above the target at (0,0). Then implement the positioning equations by entering the formula

**=IF(Rule=1,0,IF(Rule=2,B7-D7,IF(Rule=3,-D7,D7)))**

in cell B8 and copying it to the range B8:C51. Note how this formula references the location of the previous drop. The IF function captures the logic for all four rules.

**3** **Simulate drops.** Simulate the positions of the drops by entering the formula

**=RISKNORMAL(B7,1)**

in cell D7 and copying it to the range D7:E51. This says that the ball's drop position is normally distributed with mean equal to the funnel's position and standard deviation 1.

**4** **Distance.** Calculate the final distance from the target in cell K14 with the formula

**SQRT(SUMSQ(D51:E51))**

Here we have used the SUMSQ function to get the sum of squares for the distance formula. Then designate this cell as an @RISK output cell.

## Using @Risk

We set the number of iterations to 1000 and the number of simulations to 4 (because of simulating the four rules simultaneously). Selected summary measures for the final distance from the target for all four rules are shown in Figure 12.13. We also show histograms of this distance for rules 1, 2, and 3 in Figures 12.14, 12.15, and 12.16. (The histogram for rule 4 isn't shown because it is practically identical to the one for rule 3.)

**Figure 12.13**

Summary Results for All Rules

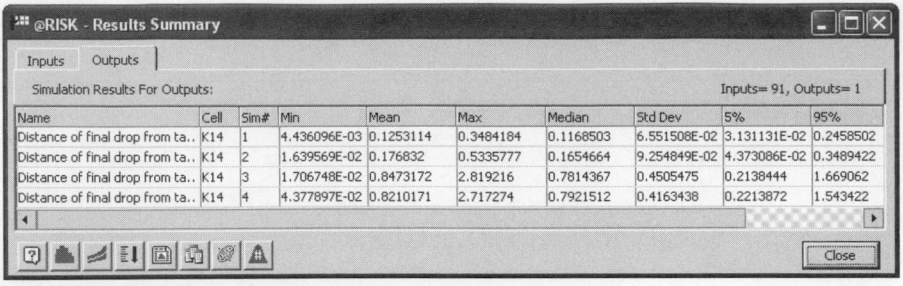

| Name | Cell | Sim# | Min | Mean | Max | Median | Std Dev | 5% | 95% |
|---|---|---|---|---|---|---|---|---|---|
| Distance of final drop from ta.. | K14 | 1 | 4.436096E-03 | 0.1253114 | 0.3484184 | 0.1168503 | 6.551508E-02 | 3.131131E-02 | 0.2458502 |
| Distance of final drop from ta.. | K14 | 2 | 1.639569E-02 | 0.176832 | 0.5335777 | 0.1654664 | 9.254849E-02 | 4.373086E-02 | 0.3489422 |
| Distance of final drop from ta.. | K14 | 3 | 1.706748E-02 | 0.8473172 | 2.819216 | 0.7814367 | 0.4505475 | 0.2138444 | 1.669062 |
| Distance of final drop from ta.. | K14 | 4 | 4.377897E-02 | 0.8210171 | 2.717274 | 0.7921512 | 0.4163438 | 0.2213872 | 1.543422 |

**Figure 12.14**

Histogram of Distance from Target for Rule 1

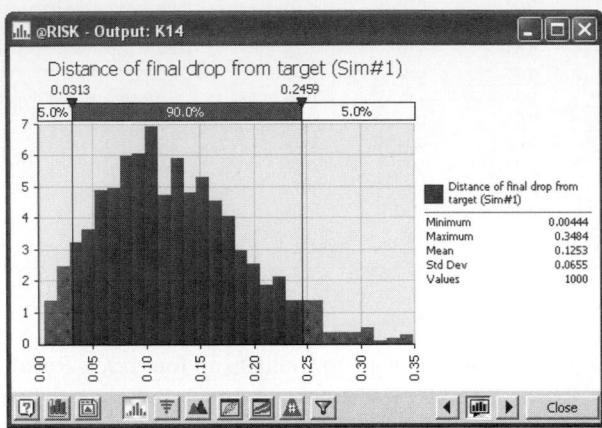

**Figure 12.15**

Histogram of Distance from Target for Rule 2

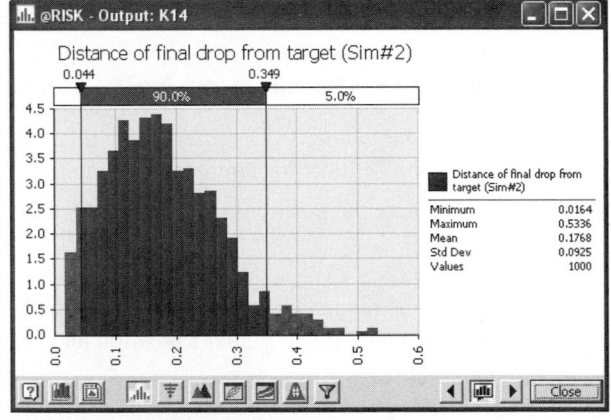

**Figure 12.16**

Histogram of Distance from Target for Rule 3

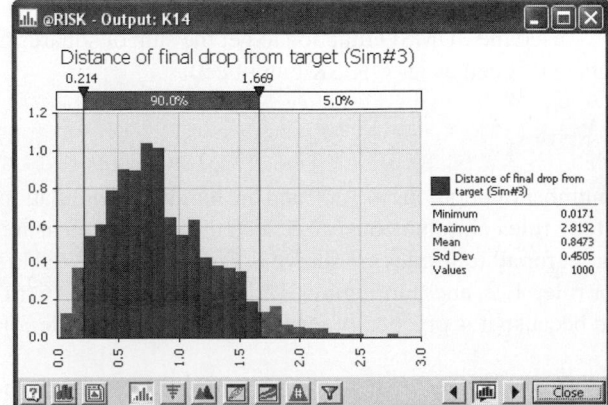

### Discussion of the Simulation Results

These results prove Deming's point about tampering. Rule 2 might not appear to be much worse than rule 1, but its mean distance and standard deviation of distances are both about 45% higher than for rule 1. Rules 3 and 4 are disastrous. Their mean distances are more than six times larger than for rule 1, and their standard deviations are also much larger. (The reason is that the drops for rule 3 tend to swing back and forth—first to the left, then to the right, then to the left, and so on—and the swings tend to increase through time. In contrast, the drops for rule 4 tend to drift away from the target over time.) The moral of the story, as Deming preached, is that you should not tamper with a stable process. If the process is not behaving as desired, then *fundamental* changes to the process are required, not a lot of tinkering. ∎

## PROBLEMS

*Solutions for problems whose numbers appear within a color box can be found in the Student Solutions Files. Order your copy today at the Winston/Albright product Web site, academic.cengage.com/decisionsciences/winston.*

### Skill-Building Problems

1. In Example 12.1, the possible profits vary from negative to positive for each of the 10 possible bids examined.
   a. For each of these, use @RISK's RISKTARGET function to find the probability that Miller's profit is positive. Do you believe these results should have any bearing on Miller's choice of bid?
   b. Use @RISK's RISKPERCENTILE function to find the 10th percentile for each of these bids. Can you explain why the percentiles have the values you obtain?

2. If the number of competitors in Example 12.1 doubles, how does the optimal bid change?

3. Referring to Example 12.1, if the average bid for each competitor who bids stays the same, but their bids exhibit less variability, does Miller's optimal bid increase or decrease? To study this question, assume that each competitor's bid, expressed as a multiple of Miller's cost to complete the project, follows each of the following distributions.
   a. Triangular with parameters 1.0, 1.3, and 2.4.
   b. Triangular with parameters 1.2, 1.3, and 2.2.
   c. Use @RISK's Define Distributions window to see that the distributions in parts **a** and **b** have the same mean as the original triangular distribution in the example, but smaller standard deviations. What is the common mean? Why is it not the same as the most likely value, 1.3?

4. In the warranty example, Example 12.2, we introduced the gamma distribution to model the right skewness of the lifetime distribution. Experiment to see how the results change if you use the triangular distribution instead. Let its minimum value be 0, and choose its most likely and maximum values so that this triangular distribution has approximately the same mean and standard deviation as the gamma distribution in the example. (Use @RISK's Define Distributions window and trial and error to do this.) Then run the simulation and comment on similarities or differences between your outputs and the outputs in the example.

5. See how sensitive the results in the warranty example, Example 12.2, are to the following changes. For each part, make the change indicated, run the simulation, and comment on any differences between your outputs and the outputs in the example.
   a. The cost of a new camera is increased to $300.
   b. The warranty period is decreased to 1 year.
   c. The terms of the warranty are changed. If the camera fails within 1 year, the customer gets a new camera for free. However, if the camera fails between 1 year and 1.5 years, the customer pays a pro rata share of the new camera, going linearly from 0 to full price. For example, if it fails at 1.2 years, which is 40% of the way from 1 to 1.5, the customer pays 40% of the full price.
   d. The customer pays $50 upfront for an extended warranty. This extends the warranty to 3 years. This extended warranty is just like the original, so that if the camera fails within 3 years, the customer gets a new camera for free.

6. In the drug production example, Example 12.3, we commented on the 95th percentile on days required in

cell I35 and the corresponding date in cell J35. If the company begins production on this date, then it is 95% sure to complete the order by the due date. We found this date to be August 2. Do you always get this answer? Find out by (1) running the simulation 10 more times, each with 1000 iterations, and finding the 95th percentile and corresponding date in each, and (2) running the simulation again, but with 10,000 iterations. Comment on the difference between simulations 1 and 2 in terms of accuracy. Given these results, when would you recommend that production should begin?

7. In the drug production example, Example 12.3, suppose we want to run 5 simulations, where we vary the probability of passing inspection from 0.6 to 1.0 in increments of 0.1. Use the RISKSIMTABLE function appropriately to do this. Comment on the effect of this parameter on the key outputs. In particular, does the probability of passing inspection have a big effect on when production should start? (*Note:* When this probability is low, it might be necessary to produce more

than 25 batches, the maximum we built into our model. Check whether this maximum should be increased.)

8. In the simulation of Deming's funnel experiment, the @RISK outputs show how tampering leads to poor results, at least in terms of the mean and standard deviation of the distance of the final drop from the target. However, the results we presented don't show how the tampering rules, particularly rules 3 and 4, go wrong. To get a better idea of this, create two scatterplots (XY charts), one of the *x*-coordinate in column D versus the drop number in column A, and one of the *y*-coordinate in column E versus the *x*-coordinate in column D. (You could also create a third scatterplot, of the *y*-coordinate versus the drop number, but it would be about the same as the first.) Use the chart subtype that "connects the dots" for each scatterplot. To go from one rule to another, enter a number from 1 to 4 in cell B3, not a formula. Then press the F9 key several times to see how the scatterplots change. Describe how the drops seem to evolve over time according to the various rules.

## 12.3 FINANCIAL MODELS

Simulation has been applied to many financial applications. Future cash flows, future stock prices, and future interest rates are some of the many uncertain variables financial analysts must deal with. In every direction they turn, they see uncertainty. In this section, we analyze a few typical financial applications that can benefit from simulation modeling.

### Financial Planning Models

Many companies, such as GM, Eli Lilly, Procter & Gamble, and Pfizer, use simulation in their capital budgeting and financial planning processes. Simulation can be used to model the uncertainty associated with future cash flows. In particular, simulation can be used to answer questions such as the following:

- What are the mean and variance of a project's NPV?
- What is the probability that a project will have a negative NPV?
- What are the mean and variance of a company's profit during the next fiscal year?
- What is the probability that a company will have to borrow more than $2 million during the next year?

The following example illustrates how simulation can be used to evaluate an investment opportunity.

EXAMPLE     12.5 DEVELOPING A NEW CAR AT GF AUTO

General Ford (GF) Auto Corporation is developing a new model of compact car. This car is assumed to generate sales for the next 5 years. GF has gathered information about the following quantities through focus groups with the marketing and engineering departments:

- **Fixed cost of developing car.** This cost is assumed to be $1.4 billion. The fixed cost is incurred at the beginning of year 1, before any sales are recorded.

- **Margin per car.** This is the unit selling price minus the variable cost of producing a car. GF assumes that in year 1, the margin will be $5000. Every other year, GF assumes the margin will decrease by 4%.[3]

- **Sales.** The demand for the car is the uncertain quantity. GF assumes sales—number of cars sold—in the first year are triangularly distributed with parameters 100,000, 150,000, and 170,000. Every year after that, the company assumes that sales will decrease by some percentage, where this percentage is triangularly distributed with parameters 5%, 8%, and 10%. GF also assumes that the percentage decreases in successive years are independent of one another.

- **Depreciation and taxes.** The company depreciates its development cost on a straight-line basis over the lifetime of the car. The corporate tax rate is 40%.

- **Discount rate.** GF figures its cost of capital at 15%.

GF wants to develop a simulation model to evaluate its NPV of after-tax cash flows for this new car over the 5-year time horizon.

**Objective**    To simulate the cash flows from the new car model, from the development time to the end of its life cycle, so that GF can estimate the NPV of after-tax cash flows from this car.

### WHERE DO THE NUMBERS COME FROM?

This problem has many inputs. As we indicated, they are probably obtained from experts within the company and from focus groups of potential customers.

## Solution

This model is like most financial multiyear spreadsheet models. The completed model extends several years to the right, but most of the work is for the first year or two. From that point, we simply copy to the other years to complete the model.

### DEVELOPING THE SIMULATION MODEL

The simulation model for GF appears in Figure 12.17. (See the file **New Car Development. xlsx**.) The model can be formed as follows:

**1** **Inputs.**  Enter the various inputs in the blue cells.

**2** **Unit sales.**  Generate first year sales in cell B12 with the formula

**=RISKTRIANG(E5,F5,G5)**

---

[3] The margin decreases because variable costs tend to increase through time, whereas selling prices tend to remain fairly constant through time.

**Figure 12.17** The GF Auto Simulation Model

| | A | B | C | D | E | F | G |
|---|---|---|---|---|---|---|---|
| 1 | New car simulation | | | | | | |
| 2 | | | | | | | |
| 3 | Inputs | | | Parameters of triangular distributions | | | |
| 4 | Fixed development cost | $1,400,000,000 | | | Min | Most likely | Max |
| 5 | Year 1 contribution | $5,000 | | Year 1 sales | 100000 | 150000 | 170000 |
| 6 | Annual decrease in contribution | 4% | | Annual decay rate | 5% | 8% | 10% |
| 7 | Tax rate | 40% | | | | | |
| 8 | Discount rate | 15% | | | | | |
| 9 | | | | | | | |
| 10 | Simulation | | | | | | |
| 11 | End of year | 1 | 2 | 3 | 4 | 5 | |
| 12 | Unit sales | 129137 | 118721 | 109417 | 102122 | 92835 | |
| 13 | Unit contribution | $5,000 | $4,800 | $4,608 | $4,424 | $4,247 | |
| 14 | Revenue minus variable cost | $645,687,270 | $569,859,933 | $504,193,828 | $451,754,559 | $394,245,786 | |
| 15 | Depreciation | $280,000,000 | $280,000,000 | $280,000,000 | $280,000,000 | $280,000,000 | |
| 16 | Before tax profit | $365,687,270 | $289,859,933 | $224,193,828 | $171,754,559 | $114,245,786 | |
| 17 | After tax profit | $219,412,362 | $173,915,960 | $134,516,297 | $103,052,736 | $68,547,472 | |
| 18 | Cash flow | $499,412,362 | $453,915,960 | $414,516,297 | $383,052,736 | $348,547,472 | |
| 19 | | | | | | | |
| 20 | NPV of cash flows | $42,349,830 | | | | | |

Then generate the reduced sales in later years by entering the formula

**=B12*(1-RISKTRIANG($E$6,$F$6,$G$6))**

in cell C12 and copying it across row 12. Note that each sales figure is a random fraction of the *previous* sales figure.

**3** **Contributions.** Calculate the unit contributions in row 13 by entering the formulas

**=B5**

and

**=B13*(1-$B$6)**

in cells B13 and C13, and copying the latter across. Then calculate the contributions in row 14 as the product of the corresponding values in rows 12 and 13.

*We subtract deprecia-tion to get before-tax profit, but we then add it back after taxes have been deducted.*

**4** **Depreciation.** Calculate the depreciation each year in row 15 as the development cost in cell B4 divided by 5. This is exactly what "straight-line depreciation" means.

**5** **Before-tax and after-tax profits.** To calculate the before-tax profit in any year, we subtract the depreciation from total contribution, so each value in row 16 is the difference be-tween the corresponding values in rows 14 and 15. The reason is that depreciation isn't taxed. To calculate the after-tax profits in row 17, we multiply each before-tax profit by 1 minus the tax rate in cell B7. Finally, each cash flow in row 18 is the sum of the corresponding values in rows 15 and 17. Here we add depreciation back to get the cash flow.

**6** **NPV.** Calculate the NPV of cash flows in cell B20 with the formula

**=-B4+NPV(B8,B18:F18)**

and designate it as an @RISK output cell (the only output cell). Here, we are assuming that the development cost is incurred right now, so that it isn't discounted, and that all other cash flows occur at the ends of the respective years. This allows us to use the NPV function directly.

### Running the Simulation

We set the number of iterations to 1000 and the number of simulations to 1, and then run the simulation as usual.

## Discussion of the Simulation Results

*Financial analysts typically look at VAR to see how bad—or more precisely, almost how bad—things could get.*

After running @RISK, we obtain the summary measures for total NPV in Figure 12.18 and the histogram in Figure 12.19. These results are somewhat comforting but also a cause of concern for GF. On the bright side, the mean NPV is about $135 million, and there is some chance that the NPV could go well above that figure, even up to almost $400 million. However, there is also a dark side as shown by the two sliders in the histogram. We placed one slider over an NPV of 0. As the histogram indicates, there is about an 84% chance of a positive NPV, but there is about a 16% chance of it being negative. The second slider is positioned at its default 5th percentile setting. Financial analysts often call this percentile the **value at risk,** or **VAR,** because it indicates *nearly* the worst possible outcome. From this simulation, we see that GF's VAR is approximately an $87 million loss.

> The **VAR** is the 5th percentile of a distribution, and it is often used in financial models. It indicates nearly the worst possible outcome.

**Figure 12.18**  Summary Measures for Total NPV

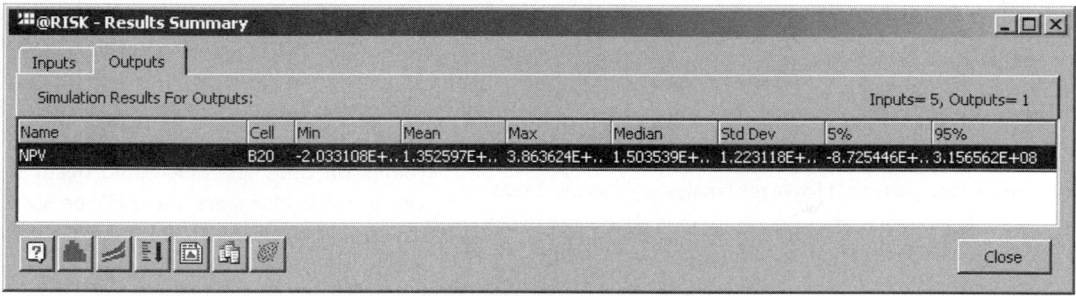

**Figure 12.19**

Histogram of Total NPV

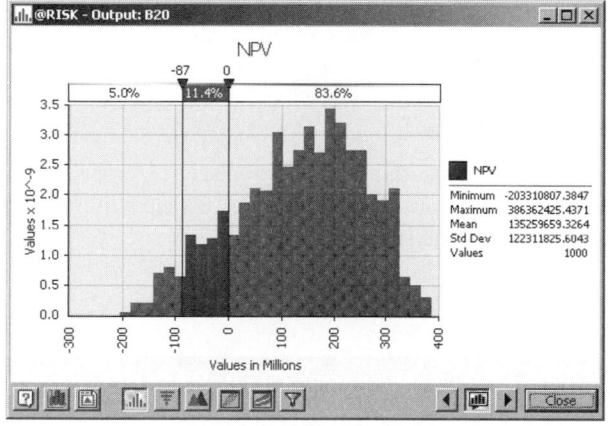

*A tornado chart lets us see which random inputs have the most effect on a specified output.*

What is most responsible for this huge variability in NPV, the variability in first-year sales or the variability in annual sales decreases? We can answer this with @RISK's Tornado Chart (see Figure 12.20). To get this chart, click on the tornado button below the histogram in Figure 12.19 and select the Correlation option. This chart answers our question emphatically. Variability in first-year sales is by far the largest influence on NPV. It correlates almost perfectly with NPV. The annual decreases in sales are not unimportant, but they have much less effect on NPV. If GF wants to get a more favorable NPV distribution, it should do all it can to boost first-year sales—and make the first-year sales distribution less variable.

**Figure 12.20**

Tornado Chart for
NPV

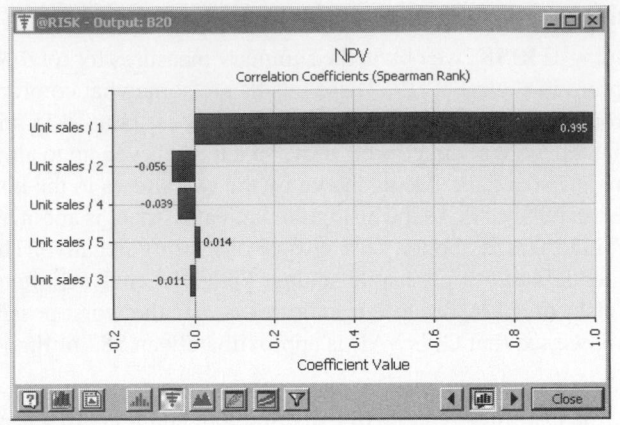

---

### The Mean Isn't Everything

Many discussions of simulation focus on the *mean* of some output variable. This makes sense, given the importance of EMV for decision making as discussed in Chapter 10. After all, EMV is just the mean of a monetary output. However, analysts in many areas, including finance, are often at least as interested in the extreme values of an output distribution. For example, the VAR discussed in this example indicates nearly how bad things could get if unlucky outcomes occur.

If large amounts of money are at stake, particularly potential losses, companies might not be able to "play the averages" by focusing only on the mean. They have to be aware of potential disasters as well. Of course, simulation also shows the bright side, the extremes on the right that could occur if lucky outcomes occur. Managers shouldn't be so conservative that they focus only on the negative outcomes and ignore the upside potential.

## Cash Balance Models

All companies track their cash balance through time. As specific payments come due, companies often need to take out short-term loans to keep a minimal cash balance. The following example illustrates one such application.

---

EXAMPLE | **12.6 MAINTAINING A MINIMAL CASH BALANCE AT ENTSON**

The Entson Company believes that its monthly sales during the period from November of the current year to July of next year are normally distributed with the means and standard deviations given in Table 12.2. Each month Entson incurs fixed costs of $250,000. Taxes of $150,000 must be paid in March, and taxes of $50,000 must be paid in June. Dividends of $50,000 must also be paid in June. Entson estimates that its receipts in a given month are a weighted sum of sales from the current month, the previous month, and two months ago with weights 0.2, 0.6, and 0.2. In symbols, if $R_t$ and $S_t$ represent receipts and sales in month $t$, then

$$R_t = 0.2S_{t-2} + 0.6S_{t-1} + 0.2S_t \qquad (12.1)$$

**Table 12.2  Monthly Sales (in Thousands of Dollars) for Entson**

|  | Nov. | Dec. | Jan. | Feb. | Mar. | Apr. | May | Jun. | Jul. |
|---|---|---|---|---|---|---|---|---|---|
| **Mean** | 1500 | 1600 | 1800 | 1500 | 1900 | 2600 | 2400 | 1900 | 1300 |
| **St Dev** | 70 | 75 | 80 | 80 | 100 | 125 | 120 | 90 | 70 |

The materials and labor needed to produce a month's sales must be purchased one month in advance, and the cost of these averages to 80% of the product's sales. For example, if sales in February are $1,500,000, then the February materials and labor costs are $1,200,000, but these must be paid in January.

At the beginning of January, Entson has $250,000 in cash. The company wants to ensure that each month's ending cash balance never dips below $250,000. This means that Entson might have to take out short-term (one-month) loans. For example, if the ending cash balance at the end of March is $200,000, Entson will take out a loan for $50,000, which it will then pay back (with interest) one month later. The interest rate on a short-term loan is 1% per month. At the beginning of each month, Entson earns interest of 0.5% on its cash balance. The company wants to use simulation to estimate the maximum loan it will need to take out to meet its desired minimum cash balance. Entson also wants to analyze how its loans will vary through time, and it wants to estimate the total interest paid on these loans.

**Objective**  To simulate Entson's cash flows and the loans the company must take out to meet a minimum cash balance.

## WHERE DO THE NUMBERS COME FROM?

Although there are many monetary inputs in the problem statement, they should all be easily accessible. Of course, Entson chooses the minimum cash balance of $250,000 as a matter of company policy.

## Solution

There is a considerable amount of bookkeeping in this simulation, so it is a good idea to list the events in chronological order that occur each month. We assume the following:

- Entson observes its beginning cash balance.
- Entson receives interest on its beginning cash balance.
- Receipts arrive and expenses are paid (including payback of the previous month's loan, if any, with interest).
- If necessary, Entson takes out a short-term loan.
- The final cash balance is observed, which becomes next month's beginning cash balance.

## DEVELOPING THE SIMULATION MODEL

The completed simulation model appears in Figure 12.21. (See the file **Cash Balance. xlsx.**) The model requires the following steps:

**1  Inputs.**  Enter the inputs in the blue cells. Note that we simulate loans (in row 42) only for the period from January to June of next year. However, we need sales figures (in row 28) in November and December from the current year to generate receipts for January and

Figure 12.21
The Cash Balance Simulation Model

| | A | B | C | D | E | F | G | H | I | J |
|---|---|---|---|---|---|---|---|---|---|---|
| 1 | Entson cash balance simulation | | | | | | | | | |
| 2 | | | | | | All monetary values are in $1000s. | | | | |
| 3 | Inputs | | | | | | | | | |
| 4 | Distribution of monthly sales (normal) | | | | | | | | | |
| 5 | | Nov | Dec | Jan | Feb | Mar | Apr | May | Jun | Jul |
| 6 | Mean | 1500 | 1600 | 1800 | 1500 | 1900 | 2600 | 2400 | 1900 | 1300 |
| 7 | St Dev | 70 | 75 | 80 | 80 | 100 | 125 | 120 | 90 | 70 |
| 8 | | | | | | | | | | |
| 9 | Monthly fixed cost | | | 250 | 250 | 250 | 250 | 250 | 250 | |
| 10 | Tax, dividend expenses | | | 0 | 0 | 150 | 0 | 0 | 100 | |
| 11 | | | | | | | | | | |
| 12 | Receipts in any month are of form: A*(sales from 2 months ago)+B*(previous month's sales)+C*(current month's sales), where: | | | | | | | | | |
| 13 | | A | B | C | | | | | | |
| 14 | | 0.2 | 0.6 | 0.2 | | | | | | |
| 15 | | | | | | | | | | |
| 16 | Cost of materials and labor for next month, spent this month, is a percentage of product's sales from next month, where the percentage is: | | | | | | | | | |
| 17 | | 80% | | | | | | | | |
| 18 | | | | | | | | | | |
| 19 | Initial cash in January | 250 | | | | | | | | |
| 20 | Minimum cash balance | 250 | | | | | | | | |
| 21 | | | | | | | | | | |
| 22 | Monthly interest rates | | | | | | | | | |
| 23 | Interest rate on loan | 1.0% | | | | | | | | |
| 24 | Interest rate on cash | 0.5% | | | | | | | | |
| 25 | | | | | | | | | | |
| 26 | Simulation | | | | | | | | | |
| 27 | | Nov | Dec | Jan | Feb | Mar | Apr | May | Jun | Jul |
| 28 | Actual sales | 1488.324 | 1536.407 | 1821.793 | 1454.789 | 2023.135 | 2596.600 | 2449.972 | 2004.528 | 1310.329 |
| 29 | | | | | | | | | | |
| 30 | Cash, receipts | | | | | | | | | |
| 31 | Beginning cash balance | | | 250.000 | 421.286 | 250.000 | 250.000 | 250.000 | 250.000 | |
| 32 | Interest on cash balance | | | 1.250 | 2.106 | 1.250 | 1.250 | 1.250 | 1.250 | |
| 33 | Receipts | | | 1583.867316 | 1691.314966 | 1641.858901 | 2024.158547 | 2452.581126 | 2390.2086 | |
| 34 | Costs | | | | | | | | | |
| 35 | Fixed costs | | | 250 | 250 | 250 | 250 | 250 | 250 | |
| 36 | Tax, dividend expenses | | | 0 | 0 | 150 | 0 | 0 | 100 | |
| 37 | Material, labor expenses | | | 1163.831 | 1618.508 | 2077.280 | 1959.977 | 1603.623 | 1048.263 | |
| 38 | Loan payback (principal) | | | | 0.000 | 3.800 | 838.009 | 1030.958 | 441.059 | 0.000 |
| 39 | Loan payback (interest) | | | | 0.000 | 0.038 | 8.380 | 10.310 | 4.411 | 0.000 |
| 40 | | | | | | | | | | |
| 41 | Cash balance before loan | | | 421.286 | 246.200 | -588.009 | -780.958 | -191.059 | 797.726 | |
| 42 | Loan amount (if any) | | | 0.000 | 3.800 | 838.009 | 1030.958 | 441.059 | 0.000 | |
| 43 | Final cash balance | | | 421.286 | 250.000 | 250.000 | 250.000 | 250.000 | 797.726 | |
| 44 | | | | | | | | | | |
| 45 | Maximum loan | 1030.958 | | | | | | | | |
| 46 | Total intest on loans | 23.138 | | | | | | | | |

February. Also, we need July sales for next year to generate the material and labor costs paid in June.

**2** **Actual sales.** Generate the sales in row 28 by entering the formula

=RISKNORMAL(B6,B7)

in cell B28 and copying across.

**3** **Beginning cash balance.** For January of next year, enter the cash balance with the formula

=B19

in cell D31. Then for the other months enter the formula

=D43

in cell E31 and copy it across row 31. This reflects that the beginning cash balance for one month is the final cash balance from the previous month.

**4** **Incomes.** Entson's incomes (interest on cash balance and receipts) are entered in rows 32 and 33. To calculate these, enter the formulas

=$B$24*D31

and

=SUMPRODUCT($B$14:$D$14,B28:D28)

in cells D32 and D33 and copy them across rows 32 and 33. This latter formula, which is based on equation (12.1), multiplies the fixed weights in row 14 by the relevant sales and adds these products to calculate receipts.

**5** **Expenses.** Entson's expenses (fixed costs, taxes and dividends, material and labor costs, and payback of the previous month's loan) are entered in rows 35 to 39. Calculate these by entering the formulas

=D9

=D10

=$B$17*E28

=D42

and

=D42*$B$23

in cells D35, D36, D37, E38, and E39 and copying these across rows 35 to 39. (For the loan payback, we are assuming that no loan payback is due in January.)

**6** **Cash balance before loan.** Calculate the cash balance before the loan (if any) by entering the formula

=SUM(D31:D33)-SUM(D35:D39)

in cell D41 and copying it across row 41.

*The loan amounts are determined by the random cash inflows and outflows and the fact that Entson's policy is to maintain a minimum cash balance.*

**7** **Amount of loan.** If the value in row 41 is below the minimum cash balance ($250,000), Entson must borrow enough to bring the cash balance up to this minimum. Otherwise, no loan is necessary. Therefore, enter the formula

=MAX($B$20-D41,0)

in cell D42 and copy it across row 42. (We could use an IF function, rather the MAX function, to accomplish the same result.)

**8** **Final cash balance.** Calculate the final cash balance by entering the formula

=D41+D42

in cell D43 and copying it across row 43.

**9** **Maximum loan, total interest.** Calculate the maximum loan from January to June in cell B45 with the formula

=MAX(D42:I42)

Then calculate the total interest paid on all loans in cell B46 with the formula

=SUM(E39:J39)

*An @RISK output range, as opposed to a single output cell, allows us to obtain a summary chart that shows the whole simulated range at once. This range is typically a time series.*

**10** **Output range.** In the usual way, designate cells B45 and B46 as output cells. Also, designate the entire range of loans, D42:I42, as an output range. To do this, highlight this range and click on the @RISK Add Output button. It will ask you for a name of the output. We suggest "Loans." Then a typical formula in this range, such as the formula for cell E42, is

=RISKOUTPUT("Loans",2)+MAX($B$20-E41,0)

This indicates that cell E42 is the second cell in the Loans output range.

## Running the Simulation

We set the number of iterations to 1000 and the number of simulations to 1. We then run the simulation in the usual way.

## Discussion of the Simulation Results

After running the simulation, we obtain the summary results in Figure 12.22. They indicate that the maximum loan varies considerably, from a low of about $461,000 to a high of about $1,534,000. The average is about $952,500. We also see that Entson is spending close to $20,000 on average in interest on the loans, although the actual amounts vary considerably from one iteration to another.

**Figure 12.22**

Summary Measures for Simulation

| | | @RISK - Results Summary | | | | | | |
|---|---|---|---|---|---|---|---|---|

Inputs   Outputs

Simulation Results For Outputs:                  Inputs= 9, Outputs= 8

| Name | Cell | Min | Mean | Max | Median | Std Dev | 5% | 95% |
|---|---|---|---|---|---|---|---|---|
| − Range: Loans | | | | | | | | |
| Loan amount (if any) / Jan | D42 | 0 | 0.3120223 | 64.81628 | 0 | 3.559813 | 0 | 0 |
| Loan amount (if any) / Feb | E42 | 0 | 14.54189 | 351.7782 | 0 | 39.7943 | 0 | 102.3367 |
| Loan amount (if any) / Mar | F42 | 201.7258 | 734.8561 | 1194.72 | 736.7593 | 157.588 | 462.1605 | 992.7601 |
| Loan amount (if any) / Apr | G42 | 461.3435 | 950.9836 | 1534.026 | 955.7982 | 163.0347 | 682.6968 | 1212.633 |
| Loan amount (if any) / May | H42 | 0 | 309.9905 | 826.8547 | 308.2774 | 147.6159 | 60.40136 | 547.5947 |
| Loan amount (if any) / Jun | I42 | 0 | 0 | 0 | 0 | 0 | 0 | 0 |
| − Range: <none> | | | | | | | | |
| Maximum loan | B45 | 461.3435 | 952.5247 | 1534.026 | 955.976 | 161.0774 | 687.219 | 1212.633 |
| Total interest | B46 | 7.421526 | 20.10684 | 33.60012 | 20.13556 | 4.273962 | 13.28679 | 27.12564 |

We can also gain insights from the summary trend chart of the series of loans, shown in Figure 12.23. To get this chart, click on the third button at the bottom of the Results Summary window in Figure 12.22. (This button is also available in any histogram window.) This chart clearly shows how the loans vary through time. The middle line is the mean loan amount. The inner bands extend to 1 standard deviation on each side of the mean, and the outer bands extend to the 5th and 95th percentiles. (@RISK lets you customize these bands in a number of ways by right-clicking on the chart.) We see that the largest loans are required in March and April.

**Figure 12.23**

Summary Chart of Loans Through Time

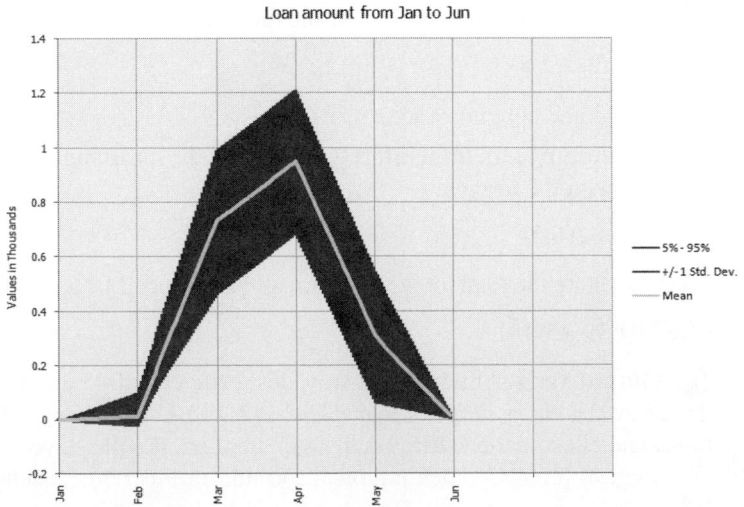

Is it intuitively clear why the required loans peak in March and April? After all, why should Entson need money in months when its sales tend to be relatively high? Two factors are working here. First, Entson has to pay its costs early. For example, it has to pay 80% of its April sales for labor and material expenses in March. Second, most of its receipts arrive late. For example, 80% of its receipts from sales in March are not received until *after* March. Therefore, the answer to our question is that the timing and amounts of loans are fairly complex. Of course, this is why Entson goes to the trouble of building a simulation model! ■

## Investment Models

Individual investors typically want to choose investment strategies that meet some pre-specified goal. The following example is typical. Here, a person wants to meet a retirement goal, starting at an early age.

---

## EXAMPLE | 12.7 INVESTING FOR RETIREMENT

Attorney Sally Evans has just begun her career. At age 25, she has 40 years until retirement, but she realizes that now is the time to start investing. She plans to invest $1000 at the beginning of each of the next 40 years. Each year, she plans to put fixed percentages—the same each year—of this $1000 into stocks, Treasury bonds (T-bonds), and Treasury bills (T-bills). However, she is not sure which percentages to use. (We call these percentages *investment weights*.) She does have historical annual returns from stocks, T-bonds, and T-bills from 1946 to 2001. These are listed in the file **Retirement Planning.xlsx**. This file also includes inflation rates for these years. For example, for 1993 the annual returns for stocks, T-bonds, and T-bills were 9.99%, 18.24%, and 2.90%, respectively, and the inflation rate was 2.75%. Sally would like to use simulation to help decide what investment weights to use, with the objective of achieving a large investment value, in *today's* dollars, at the end of 40 years.

**Objective** To use simulation to estimate the value of Sally's future investments, in today's dollars, from several investment strategies in T-bills, T-bonds, and stocks.

### WHERE DO THE NUMBERS COME FROM?

Historical returns and inflation rates, such as those quoted here, are widely available on the Web. In fact, you might want to get more recent data for use in the model.

## Solution

*We simulate future scenarios by randomly choosing past scenarios, giving higher probabilities to more recent scenarios.*

The most difficult modeling aspect is settling on a way to use historical returns and inflation factors to generate *future* values of these quantities. We use a "scenario" approach. We think of each historical year as a possible scenario, where the scenario specifies the returns and inflation factor for that year. Then for any future year, we randomly choose one of these scenarios. It seems intuitive that more recent scenarios ought to have a greater chance of being chosen. To implement this idea, we give a weight (not to be confused with the investment weights) to each scenario, starting with weight 1 for 2001. Then the weight for any year is a "damping factor" multiplied by the weight from the next year. For example, the weight for 1996 is the damping factor multiplied by the weight for 1997. To change these weights to probabilities, we divide each weight by the sum of all the weights. The damping factor we use is 0.98. Others could be used instead, and we are frankly not sure which produces the most realistic results. (This is an important question for financial research!)

*Without a package like RISKOptimizer, we cannot find the "best" set of investment weights, but the simulation model lets us experiment with various sets of weights.*

The other difficult part of the solution is knowing which investment weights to try. This is really an optimization problem—find three weights that add to one and produce the largest mean final cash. Palisade has another software package, RISKOptimizer, that solves this type of optimization–simulation problem. However, we simply try several sets of weights, where some percentage is put into stocks and the remainder is split evenly between T-bonds and T-bills, and see which does best. You can try other sets if you like.

## DEVELOPING THE SIMULATION MODEL

The historical data and the simulation model (each with some rows hidden) appear in Figures 12.24 and 12.25. (Again, see the **Retirement Planning.xlsx** file.) The model can be developed as follows:

**Figure 12.24**

Historical Data, Inputs, and Probabilities

| | A | B | C | D | E | F | G |
|---|---|---|---|---|---|---|---|
| 18 | **Historical data and probabilities** | | | | | | |
| 19 | Year | T-Bills | T-Bonds | Stocks | Inflation | ProbWts | Probability |
| 20 | 1946 | 0.0035 | -0.0010 | -0.0807 | 0.1817 | 0.3292 | 0.0097 |
| 21 | 1947 | 0.0050 | -0.0263 | 0.0571 | 0.0901 | 0.3359 | 0.0099 |
| 22 | 1948 | 0.0081 | 0.0340 | 0.0550 | 0.0271 | 0.3428 | 0.0101 |
| 23 | 1949 | 0.0110 | 0.0645 | 0.1879 | -0.0180 | 0.3497 | 0.0103 |
| 24 | 1950 | 0.0120 | 0.0006 | 0.3171 | 0.0579 | 0.3569 | 0.0105 |
| 52 | 1978 | 0.0718 | -0.0116 | 0.0656 | 0.0903 | 0.6283 | 0.0186 |
| 53 | 1979 | 0.1038 | -0.0122 | 0.1844 | 0.1331 | 0.6412 | 0.0189 |
| 54 | 1980 | 0.1124 | -0.0395 | 0.3242 | 0.1240 | 0.6543 | 0.0193 |
| 55 | 1981 | 0.1471 | 0.0185 | -0.0491 | 0.0894 | 0.6676 | 0.0197 |
| 56 | 1982 | 0.1054 | 0.4035 | 0.2141 | 0.0387 | 0.6812 | 0.0201 |
| 57 | 1983 | 0.0880 | 0.0068 | 0.2251 | 0.0380 | 0.6951 | 0.0205 |
| 58 | 1984 | 0.0985 | 0.1543 | 0.0627 | 0.0395 | 0.7093 | 0.0209 |
| 59 | 1985 | 0.0772 | 0.3097 | 0.3216 | 0.0377 | 0.7238 | 0.0214 |
| 60 | 1986 | 0.0616 | 0.2444 | 0.1847 | 0.0113 | 0.7386 | 0.0218 |
| 61 | 1987 | 0.0547 | -0.0269 | 0.0523 | 0.0441 | 0.7536 | 0.0223 |
| 62 | 1988 | 0.0635 | 0.0967 | 0.1681 | 0.0442 | 0.7690 | 0.0227 |
| 63 | 1989 | 0.0837 | 0.1811 | 0.3149 | 0.0465 | 0.7847 | 0.0232 |
| 64 | 1990 | 0.0781 | 0.0618 | -0.0317 | 0.0611 | 0.8007 | 0.0236 |
| 65 | 1991 | 0.0560 | 0.1930 | 0.3055 | 0.0306 | 0.8171 | 0.0241 |
| 66 | 1992 | 0.0351 | 0.0805 | 0.0767 | 0.0290 | 0.8337 | 0.0246 |
| 67 | 1993 | 0.0290 | 0.1824 | 0.0999 | 0.0275 | 0.8508 | 0.0251 |
| 68 | 1994 | 0.0390 | -0.0777 | 0.0131 | 0.0267 | 0.8681 | 0.0256 |
| 69 | 1995 | 0.0560 | 0.2348 | 0.3720 | 0.0250 | 0.8858 | 0.0262 |
| 70 | 1996 | 0.0514 | 0.0143 | 0.2382 | 0.0330 | 0.9039 | 0.0267 |
| 71 | 1997 | 0.0491 | 0.0994 | 0.3186 | 0.0170 | 0.9224 | 0.0272 |
| 72 | 1998 | 0.0516 | 0.1492 | 0.2834 | 0.0160 | 0.9412 | 0.0278 |
| 73 | 1999 | 0.0439 | -0.0825 | 0.2089 | 0.0270 | 0.9604 | 0.0284 |
| 74 | 2000 | 0.0537 | 0.1666 | -0.0903 | 0.0340 | 0.9800 | 0.0289 |
| 75 | 2001 | 0.0573 | 0.0557 | -0.1185 | 0.0160 | 1.0000 | 0.0295 |
| 76 | | | | | Sums --> | 33.8702 | 1.0000 |

**Figure 12.25**  The Simulation Model

| | A | B | C | D | E | F | G | H | I | J | K | L | M | N | O | P | Q |
|---|---|---|---|---|---|---|---|---|---|---|---|---|---|---|---|---|---|
| 1 | **Planning for retirement** | | | | | | | | | | | | | | | | |
| 2 | | | | | | | | | | | | | | | | | |
| 3 | **Inputs** | | | | | | | | Range names used: | | | | | | | | |
| 4 | Damping factor | 0.98 | | | | | | | LTable1 | =Model!$A$10:$D$12 | | | | | | | |
| 5 | Yearly investment | $1,000 | | | | | | | LTable2 | =Model!$A$20:$E$75 | | | | | | | |
| 6 | Planning horizon | 40 | years | | | | | | Weights | =Model!$B$16:$D$16 | | | | | | | |
| 7 | | | | | | | | | | | | | | | | | |
| 8 | **Alternative sets of weights to test** | | | | | | | | | | | | | | | | |
| 9 | Index | T-Bills | T-Bonds | Stocks | | | | | | | | | | | | | |
| 10 | 1 | 0.10 | 0.10 | 0.80 | | | | | | | | | | | | | |
| 11 | 2 | 0.20 | 0.20 | 0.60 | | | | | | | | | | | | | |
| 12 | 3 | 0.30 | 0.30 | 0.40 | | | | | | | | | | | | | |
| 13 | | | | | | | | | | | | | | | | | |
| 14 | **Weights used** | | | | | | | | **Output from simulation below** | | | | | | | | |
| 15 | Index | T-Bills | T-Bonds | Stocks | | | | | Final cash (today's dollars) | | $72,757 | | | | | | |
| 16 | 1 | 0.10 | 0.10 | 0.80 | | | | | | | | | | | | | |
| 17 | | | | | | | | | | | | | | Column offset for lookup2 | | | |
| 18 | **Historical data and probabilities** | | | | | | | | **Simulation model** | | | 2 | 3 | 4 | 5 | | |
| 19 | Year | T-Bills | T-Bonds | Stocks | Inflation | ProbWts | Probability | | Future year | Beginning cash | Scenario | T-Bills | T-Bonds | Stocks | Inflation | Ending cash | Deflator |
| 20 | 1946 | 0.0035 | -0.0010 | -0.0807 | 0.1817 | 0.3292 | 0.0097 | | 1 | $1,000 | 1995 | 1.0560 | 1.2348 | 1.3720 | 1.0250 | 1327 | 0.976 |
| 21 | 1947 | 0.0050 | -0.0263 | 0.0571 | 0.0901 | 0.3359 | 0.0099 | | 2 | 2327 | 1988 | 1.0635 | 1.0967 | 1.1681 | 1.0442 | 2677 | 0.934 |
| 22 | 1948 | 0.0081 | 0.0340 | 0.0550 | 0.0271 | 0.3428 | 0.0101 | | 3 | 3677 | 1990 | 1.0781 | 1.0618 | 0.9683 | 1.0611 | 3635 | 0.881 |
| 23 | 1949 | 0.0110 | 0.0645 | 0.1879 | -0.0180 | 0.3497 | 0.0103 | | 4 | 4635 | 1982 | 1.1054 | 1.4035 | 1.2141 | 1.0387 | 5665 | 0.848 |
| 24 | 1950 | 0.0120 | 0.0006 | 0.3171 | 0.0579 | 0.3569 | 0.0105 | | 5 | 6665 | 1968 | 1.0521 | 0.9974 | 1.1106 | 1.0472 | 7287 | 0.809 |
| 52 | 1978 | 0.0718 | -0.0116 | 0.0656 | 0.0903 | 0.6283 | 0.0186 | | 33 | 145741 | 1954 | 1.0086 | 1.0719 | 1.5262 | 0.9950 | 208266 | 0.195 |
| 53 | 1979 | 0.1038 | -0.0122 | 0.1844 | 0.1331 | 0.6412 | 0.0189 | | 34 | 209266 | 1966 | 1.0476 | 1.0365 | 0.8994 | 1.0335 | 194184 | 0.189 |
| 54 | 1980 | 0.1124 | -0.0395 | 0.3242 | 0.1240 | 0.6543 | 0.0193 | | 35 | 195184 | 1983 | 1.0880 | 1.0068 | 1.2251 | 1.0380 | 232183 | 0.182 |
| 55 | 1981 | 0.1471 | 0.0185 | -0.0491 | 0.0894 | 0.6676 | 0.0197 | | 36 | 233183 | 1950 | 1.0120 | 1.0006 | 1.3171 | 1.0579 | 292631 | 0.172 |
| 56 | 1982 | 0.1054 | 0.4035 | 0.2141 | 0.0387 | 0.6812 | 0.0201 | | 37 | 293631 | 1958 | 1.0154 | 0.9390 | 1.4336 | 1.0176 | 394147 | 0.169 |
| 57 | 1983 | 0.0880 | 0.0068 | 0.2251 | 0.0380 | 0.6951 | 0.0205 | | 38 | 395147 | 2000 | 1.0537 | 1.1666 | 0.9097 | 1.0340 | 375307 | 0.163 |
| 58 | 1984 | 0.0985 | 0.1543 | 0.0627 | 0.0395 | 0.7093 | 0.0209 | | 39 | 376307 | 1988 | 1.0635 | 1.0967 | 1.1681 | 1.0442 | 432941 | 0.156 |
| 59 | 1985 | 0.0772 | 0.3097 | 0.3216 | 0.0377 | 0.7238 | 0.0214 | | 40 | 433941 | 1993 | 1.0290 | 1.1824 | 1.0999 | 1.0275 | 477795 | 0.152 |

**1** **Inputs.** Enter the data in the blue regions of Figures 12.24 and 12.25.

**2** **Weights.** The investment weights we will use for the model are in rows 10 to 12. (For example, the first set puts 80% in stocks and 10% in each of T-bonds and T-bills.) We can simulate all three sets of weights simultaneously with a RISKSIMTABLE and VLOOKUP combination as follows. First, enter the formula

**=RISKSIMTABLE({1,2,3})**

in cell A16. Then enter the formula

**=VLOOKUP($A$16,$A$10:$D$12,2)**

in cell B16 and copy it to cells C16 and D16. Then modify the formulas in these latter two cells, changing the last argument of the VLOOKUP to 3 and 4, respectively. For example, the formula in cell D16 should end up as

**=VLOOKUP($A$16,$A$10:$D$12,4)**

The effect is that we run three simulations, one for each set of weights in rows 10 to 12.

**3** **Probabilities.** Enter value 1 in cell F75. Then enter the formula

**=$B$4*F75**

in cell F74 and copy it *up* to cell F20. Sum these values with the SUM function in cell F76. Then to convert them to probabilities (numbers that add to 1), enter the formula

**=F20/$F$76**

in cell G20 and copy it down to cell G75. Note how the probabilities for more recent years are considerably larger. When we randomly select scenarios, the recent years have a greater chance of being chosen. (The SUM formula in cell G76 simply confirms that the probabilities sum to 1.)

**4** **Scenarios.** Moving to the model in Figure 12.25, we want to simulate 40 scenarios in columns K through O, one for each year of Sally's investing. To do this, enter the formulas

**=RISKDISCRETE($A$20:$A$75,$G$20:$G$75)**

and

**=1+VLOOKUP($K20,$A$20:$E$75,L$18)**

in cells K20 and L20, and then copy this latter formula to the range M20:O20. Make sure you understand how the RISKDISCRETE and VLOOKUP functions combine to achieve our goal. The RISKDISCRETE randomly generates a year from column A, using the probabilities in column G. Then the VLOOKUP captures the data from this year. (We add 1 to the VLOOKUP to get a value such as 1.08, rather than 0.08.) This is the key to the simulation. (Do you see why we don't use Excel's RANDBETWEEN function to generate the years in column K? The reason is that this function makes all possible years equally likely, and we want more recent years to be *more* likely.)

**5** **Beginning, ending cash.** The bookkeeping part is straightforward. Begin by entering the formula

**=B5**

in cell J20 for the initial investment. Then enter the formulas

**=J20*SUMPRODUCT($B$16:$D$16,L20:N20)**

and

**=$B$5+P20**

in cells P20 and J21 for ending cash in the first year and beginning cash in the second year. The former shows how the beginning cash grows in a given year. You should think through this formula carefully. The latter formula implies that Sally reinvests her previous money, plus she invests an additional $1000. Copy these formulas down columns J and P.

**6** **Deflators.** We eventually want to deflate future dollars to today's dollars. The proper way to do this is to calculate deflators (also called deflation factors). Do this by entering the formula

=1/O20

in cell Q20. Then enter the formula

=Q20/O21

in cell Q21 and copy it down. The effect is that the deflator for future year 20, say, in cell Q39, is 1 divided by the product of all 20 inflation factors up through that year. (This is similar to discounting for the time value of money, but the relevant discount rate, now the inflation rate, varies from year to year.)

**7** **Final cash.** Calculate the final value *in today's dollars* in cell K15 with the formula

=P59*Q59

Then designate this cell as an @RISK output cell.

### Running the Simulation

Set the number of iterations to 1000 and the number of simulations to 3 (one for each set of investment weights we want to test). Then run the simulation as usual.

### Discussion of the Simulation Results

Summary results appear in Figure 12.26. The first simulation, which invests the most heavily in stocks, is easily the winner. Its mean final cash, close to $181,000 in today's dollars, is much greater than the means for the other two sets of weights. The first simulation also has a *much* larger upside potential (its 95th percentile is well over $400,000). Even its downside is slightly better than the others: its 5th percentile is the best, and its minimum is only slightly worse than the minimum for the third set of weights.

Nevertheless, the histogram for simulation 1 (put 80% in stocks), shown in Figure 12.27, indicates a lot of variability—and skewness—in the distribution of final cash.[4] As in Example 12.5, the concept of VAR is useful. Recall that VAR is defined as the 5th percentile of a distribution and is often the value investors worry about. Perhaps Sally should rerun the simulation with different investment weights, with an eye on the weights that increase her VAR. Right now it is close to $43,000—not too good considering that she invests $40,000 total. She might not like the prospect of a 5% chance of ending up with no more than this! We also encourage you to try running this simulation with other investment weights, both for the 40-year horizon and (after modifying the spreadsheet model slightly) for shorter time horizons such as 10 or 15 years. Even though the stock strategy appears to be best for a long horizon, it is not necessarily guaranteed to dominate for a shorter time horizon.

---

[4] Interestingly, these results are much better than in the same model in the second edition of this book. There we used historical data only through 1994. With the bull market that lasted through most of the late 1990s, and with the most recent years being most likely to be chosen in the simulation, we are now likely to generate better investment outcomes.

**Figure 12.26**

Summary Results
from @RISK

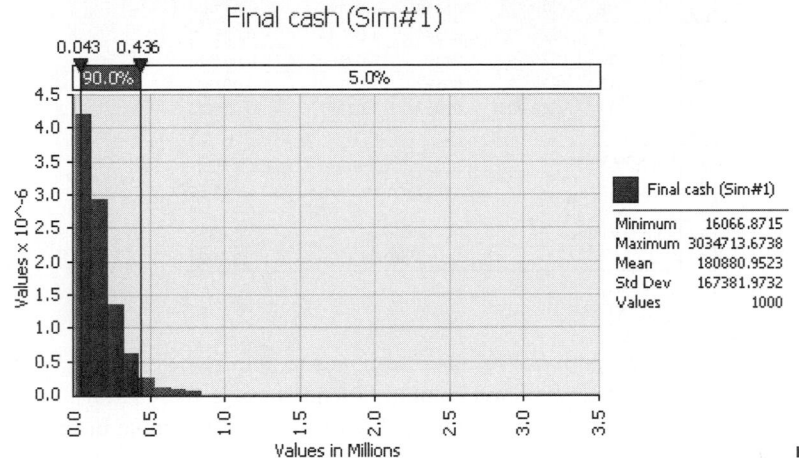

**Figure 12.27**

Histogram of Final
Cash with 80% in
Stocks

## Simulating Stock Prices and Options

In this section, we illustrate how @RISK can be used to simulate stock prices. Then we show how to analyze derivative securities such as call options with simulation.

## Modeling the Price of a Stock

An enormous amount of research has been devoted to discovering the way stock prices change. Although few agree on the best model of stock price changes, one popular model states that price changes follow a lognormal distribution. Essentially, this means that the logarithm of a stock's price at any time is a normally distributed random variable. To be more specific, the stock price $p_t$ at any time $t$ in the future is related to the current price $p_0$ by the formula

$$p_t = p_0 \exp\left[(\mu - 0.5\sigma^2)t + \sigma Z\sqrt{t}\right] \tag{12.2}$$

*The model indicated by equation (12.2) or (12.3) is called the lognormal model of price changes. This model is commonly used by financial analysts.*

Here, $\mu$ is the mean percentage growth rate of the stock; $\sigma$ is the standard deviation of the growth rate, usually called the **volatility;** and $Z$ is a normal random variable with mean 0 and standard deviation 1. Both $\mu$ and $\sigma$ are expressed as decimals, such as $\mu = 0.06$ for a 6% mean growth rate, and all quantities are measured with respect to a common unit of time, such as a year. Another way of stating equation (12.2) is to relate the price at time $t$, $p_t$, to the price $s$ time periods ago, $p_{t-s}$:

$$p_t = p_{t-s} \exp\left[(\mu - 0.5\sigma^2)s + \sigma Z\sqrt{s}\right] \tag{12.3}$$

Essentially, the $t$ inside the brackets in equation (12.2) is replaced by $s$ in equation (12.3). This is because the two prices in the latter equation are separated by a period of length $s$.

The spreadsheet in Figure 12.28 illustrates how to estimate the parameters $\mu$ and $\sigma$ in equation (12.2) from monthly returns. (See the file **Stock Returns.xlsx.**) We first enter the observed closing prices of the stock in column B. The corresponding monthly returns (percentage changes) are calculated in column C. For example, the formula in cell C6 is

Figure 12.28

Calculating Mean
and Standard
Deviation of Stock
Returns

| | A | B | C | D | E |
|---|---|---|---|---|---|
| 1 | Estimating mean and standard deviation of stock returns | | | | |
| 2 | | | | | |
| 3 | Historical data | | | | |
| 4 | Month | Closing | Return | 1+Return | Ln(1+Return) |
| 5 | 0 | $25.00 | | | |
| 6 | 1 | $24.70 | -0.01200 | 0.98800 | -0.01207 |
| 7 | 2 | $23.70 | -0.04049 | 0.95951 | -0.04133 |
| 8 | 3 | $22.90 | -0.03376 | 0.96624 | -0.03434 |
| 9 | 4 | $22.81 | -0.00393 | 0.99607 | -0.00394 |
| 10 | 5 | $22.89 | 0.00351 | 1.00351 | 0.00350 |
| 11 | 6 | $22.56 | -0.01442 | 0.98558 | -0.01452 |
| 12 | 7 | $23.94 | 0.06117 | 1.06117 | 0.05937 |
| 13 | 8 | $24.37 | 0.01796 | 1.01796 | 0.01780 |
| 14 | 9 | $24.99 | 0.02544 | 1.02544 | 0.02512 |
| 15 | 10 | $26.09 | 0.04402 | 1.04402 | 0.04308 |
| 16 | 11 | $26.14 | 0.00192 | 1.00192 | 0.00191 |
| 17 | 12 | $26.90 | 0.02907 | 1.02907 | 0.02866 |
| 18 | | | | | |
| 19 | Monthly values | | | Mean | 0.61% |
| 20 | | | | StDev | 2.88% |
| 21 | | | | | |
| 22 | Annual values | | | Mean | 7.33% |
| 23 | | | | StDev | 9.99% |

=(B6–B5)/B5

The return of –0.012 corresponds to a decrease of 1.2%. We then add 1 to each return in column C to obtain column D, and we take the natural logarithms of the numbers in column D to obtain column E. For example, the formula in cell E6 is

=LN(D6)

The average of the numbers in column E, calculated in cell E19 with the AVERAGE function, represents the mean monthly growth rate. Similarly, the standard deviation calculated in cell E20 represents the standard deviation of the monthly growth rate. (It can be calculated with the STDEV or the STDEVP function with slightly different results; we used the latter.) To obtain the mean yearly growth rate in cell E22, we multiply the mean monthly growth rate by 12. To obtain the standard deviation of the yearly growth rate in cell E23, we multiply the monthly standard deviation by $\sqrt{12}$. Thus, our estimate of the mean yearly growth rate of the stock price is 7.33%. The standard deviation of the growth rate is 9.99%.

Now that we know how analysts find the mean and standard deviation of a stock's growth rate, we use equation (12.2) or (12.3) and simulation to value certain derivative securities.[5]

## Valuing a European Call Option

A **European option** on a stock gives the owner of the option the right to buy (if the option is a **call** option) or sell (if the option is a **put** option) 100 shares of a stock on a particular date for a particular price.[6] The price at which an option holder can buy or sell the stock is called the **exercise price** (or **strike price**) of the option. The date by which the option must be used (or "exercised") is called the **exercise date.**

---

[5] Derivative securities get their name because their value is *derived* from the value of an underlying security such as a stock. A wide variety of derivative securities are available in the market. We discuss some of the simplest ones.

[6] Options are usually for 100 shares of the stock, so we will follow this convention here.

For example, suppose that a stock is currently selling for $50 and you purchase a call option with an exercise price of $56 and a 3-month exercise date. What will you earn from this option? If $T$ represents the exercise date and $p_T$ represents the price of the stock at time $T$, you will earn $0 if $p_T \le 56$, and you will earn $100 (P_T - 56)$ if $p_T > 56$. Here is the reasoning. If $p_T \le 56$, you have the option, if you want to use it, of buying 100 shares of stock for *more* than they are worth. This would be an irrational thing to do, so you will let your option expire—without ever using it. In this case, we say that you are "out of the money." On the other hand, if $p_T > 56$, you could buy 100 shares at the option price of $56, sell them for the current price of $p_T$, and make a profit of $100 (p_T - 56)$ dollars. In this case, you are "in the money."

We have omitted one thing, however. You must pay for the option in the first place. The question is, what is a fair price for such an option? Because option trading is a multi-billion-dollar business, this is an important question! Black and Scholes (1973) were the first to derive a formula for pricing options. Shortly after that, Cox et al. (1979) derived a different but equivalent method for pricing options. We use their method, which is based on the following extremely important result.

### Option Pricing Result

The price of an option on a nondividend-paying stock must be the expected discounted value of the cash flows from an option on a stock having the same standard deviation as the stock on which the option is written and growing at the risk-free rate of interest. Here, discounting is done continuously at the risk-free rate. (If the stock pays dividends, the risk-free rate should be replaced by the difference between the risk-free rate and the dividend rate in what follows.)

One surprising implication of this result is that the price of the option does *not* depend on the mean growth rate of the stock itself, only on the risk-free rate and the standard deviation of the growth rate of the stock.

In the following example, we use @RISK to estimate the price of a European option.

---

EXAMPLE | **12.8 PRICING A EUROPEAN CALL OPTION**

A share of AnTech stock currently sells for $42. A European call option with an expiration date of 6 months and an exercise price of $40 is available. The stock has an annual standard deviation of 20%. The stock price has tended to increase at a rate of 15% per year. The risk-free rate is 10% per year. What is a fair price for this option?

**Objective**    To use simulation to find the price of a European call option.

#### WHERE DO THE NUMBERS COME FROM?

All of this information is publicly available. The mean and standard deviation would probably be found as in Figure 12.28 from historical stock price data. Interestingly, however, financial analysts often infer the standard deviation of the stock's returns from the *known* price of an option on it. They call this standard deviation the *implied volatility*. Essentially, they "back into" the standard deviation that must have caused the option price to be what it is.

## Solution

According to the result of Cox et al., we need to know the mean of the cash flow from this option, discounted to time 0, assuming that the stock price increases at the risk-free rate. Therefore, we simulate many 6-month periods, each time finding the discounted cash flow of the option. The average of these discounted cash flows represents an estimate of the true mean—that is, it estimates the fair price of the option.

## DEVELOPING THE SIMULATION MODEL

The spreadsheet model is fairly simple, as shown in Figure 12.29. (See the file **European Call.xlsx**.) It can be formed as follows:

**Figure 12.29**

Determining the Price of a European Call Option

| | A | B | C | D | E |
|---|---|---|---|---|---|
| 1 | Pricing a European call option with simulation | | | | |
| 2 | | | | | |
| 3 | Input section | | | Range names used: | |
| 4 | Current price | $42 | | Current_price | =Model!$B$4 |
| 5 | Exercise price | $40 | | Duration | =Model!$B$9 |
| 6 | Mean annual return | 15% | | Exercise_price | =Model!$B$5 |
| 7 | Volatility | 20% | | Mean_annual_return | =Model!$B$6 |
| 8 | Risk-free rate | 10% | | Risk_free_rate | =Model!$B$8 |
| 9 | Duration | 0.5 | | Volatility | =Model!$B$7 |
| 10 | | | | | |
| 11 | Simulation section | | | | |
| 12 | Stock price in 6 months (growing at risk-free rate) | $35.15 | | | |
| 13 | Option cash flow at termination | $0.00 | | | |
| 14 | Discounted value of option | $0.00 | | | |
| 15 | | | | | |
| 16 | Value of option (average of discounted value) | $475.94 | | | |

**1** **Inputs.** Enter the inputs in the blue cells. Note that the exercise date is expressed in years. Also, note that we enter the mean growth rate of the stock in cell B6. However, as we noted earlier, this value is not required in the model. (It is common to refer to the standard deviation of stock returns as the **volatility** and the time until the exercise date as the **duration**.)

**2** **Simulated stock price at exercise date.** Using equation (12.2) with $\mu$ replaced by the *risk-free* rate, simulate the stock price in 6 months by entering the formula

**=Current_price*EXP((Risk_free_rate-0.5*Volatility^2)*Duration +Volatility*RiskNormal(0,1)*SQRT(Duration))**

in cell B12.

**3** **Cash flow from option.** Calculate the cash flow from the option by entering the formula

**=100*MAX(B12-Exercise_price,0)**

in cell B13. This says that if the future price in cell B12 is greater than the exercise price in cell B5, we make the difference; otherwise, we never exercise the option and make nothing. Note that we multiply by 100 because the option is for 100 shares of the stock.

**4** **Discount the cash flow.** Discount the cash flow in cell B14 with the formula

**=EXP(-Duration*Risk_free_rate)*B13**

This represents the NPV of the cash flow (if any) realized at the exercise date. Because the price of the option is the average of this discounted value, we designate it as an @RISK output cell.

**5** **Average of output cell.** We can take advantage of @RISK's RISKMEAN function to obtain the eventual price of the option on the spreadsheet itself. To do this, enter the formula

**=RISKMEAN(B14)**

in cell B16.

## USING @RISK

Because this is a small simulation model and we want an accurate average in cell B16, we can afford to run a lot of iterations. Therefore, we set the number of iterations to 10,000 and the number of simulations to 1. After running @RISK, the value $475.94 appears in cell B16. According to the result of Cox et al., this average is an estimate of the fair price for the option. It turns out (from the Black–Scholes formula) that $475.94 is *very* close to the correct price for this option—the simulation got it almost exactly right!

This surprised us initially. After all, from basic statistical inference, we know that it is difficult to estimate a mean exactly. We usually surround the estimated mean by 95% confidence limits to indicate the level of accuracy. However, the effect of using Latin Hypercube sampling is that means can be estimated *much* more accurately. With 10,000 iterations, we evidently get the correct answer to within a few pennies! ■

We now extend the previous example by simulating a portfolio that includes a company's stock and a call option on that stock.

EXAMPLE

## 12.9 RETURN ON A PORTFOLIO WITH A STOCK AND AN OPTION ON THE STOCK

Suppose the investor buys 100 shares of AnTech stock at the current price and one call option on this stock for $475.94, the fair price we calculated in the previous example. Use simulation to find the return on the investor's portfolio as of the exercise date.

**Objective** To use simulation to evaluate a portfolio containing the stock and a call option on the stock.

### WHERE DO THE NUMBERS COME FROM?

Although we used simulation in the previous example to find the price of the option, this price is quoted publicly, as is the price of the stock.

## Solution

The purpose of this simulation is totally different from the previous example. This time, the purpose is to simulate the behavior of a portfolio. Therefore, we now let the stock price grow at *its* mean rate, not the risk-free rate, to generate the stock price in 6 months. The rest is basically bookkeeping.

### DEVELOPING THE SIMULATION MODEL

The spreadsheet model appears in Figure 12.30. (See the file **OptionPortfolio.xlsx**.) The model can be developed as follows:

**1 Inputs.** Enter the values in the shaded range. These are the same as before, but they now include the known price of the call option. We also include the number of shares purchased and the number of options purchased. This adds some flexibility to the model.

**2 Future stock price.** Generate the random stock price in six months in cell B15 with the formula

Figure 12.30
Simulating a
Portfolio Return
Containing a Call
Option

| | A | B | C | D | E |
|---|---|---|---|---|---|
| 1 | Return on a portfolio with stock and a call option on the stock | | | | |
| 2 | | | | | |
| 3 | Input section | | | Range names used: | |
| 4 | Current price | $42 | | Current_price | =Model!$B$4 |
| 5 | Exercise price | $40 | | Duration | =Model!$B$9 |
| 6 | Mean annual return | 15% | | Exercise_price | =Model!$B$5 |
| 7 | Volatility | 20% | | Mean_annual_return | =Model!$B$6 |
| 8 | Risk-free rate | 10% | | Option_price | =Model!$B$12 |
| 9 | Duration | 0.5 | | Options_purchased | =Model!$B$11 |
| 10 | Shares purchased | 100 | | Risk_free_rate | =Model!$B$8 |
| 11 | Options purchased | 1 | | Shares_purchased | =Model!$B$10 |
| 12 | Option price | $475.94 | | Volatility | =Model!$B$7 |
| 13 | | | | | |
| 14 | Simulation section | | | | |
| 15 | Stock price in 6 months (growing at stock's rate) | $41.19 | | | |
| 16 | Cash flow at termination for option | $118.53 | | | |
| 17 | | | | | |
| 18 | Ending portfolio value | $4,237.06 | | | |
| 19 | Investment cost | $4,675.94 | | | |
| 20 | Portfolio return | -9.39% | | | |
| 21 | | | | | |
| 22 | Summary measures from @RISK (based on 10,000 iterations) | | | | |
| 23 | Mean return | 9.4% | | | |
| 24 | Stdev of return | 25.5% | | | |
| 25 | Min return | -49.0% | | | |
| 26 | Max return | 140.0% | | | |
| 27 | 5th percentile of return | -24.0% | | | |
| 28 | 95th percentile of return | 56.4% | | | |
| 29 | Probability of a positive return | 0.591 | | | |

**=Current_price\*EXP((Mean_annual_return-0.5\*Volatility^2)\*Duration +Volatility\*RiskNormal(0,1)\*SQRT(Duration))**

This again uses equation (12.2), but it uses the stock's mean growth rate, not the risk-free rate, for $\mu$.

❸ **Option cash flow.** Calculate the cash flow from the option exactly as before by entering the formula

**=100\*MAX(B15-Exercise_price,0)**

in cell B16.

❹ **Portfolio value.** In 6 months, the portfolio will be worth the value of the stock plus the cash flow from the option. Calculate this in cell B18 with the formula

**=SUMPRODUCT(B10:B11,B15:B16)**

Then in cells B19 and B20, calculate the amount we paid for the portfolio and its return (the percentage change) with the formulas

**=Shares_purchased\*Current_price+Options_purchased\*Option_price**

and

**=(B18-B19)/B19**

Then designate cell B20 as an @RISK output cell.

❺ **@RISK summary statistics.** We again show the basic summary results from @RISK on the spreadsheet by using its RISKMEAN, RISKSTDDEV, RISKMIN, RISKMAX, RISKPERCENTILE, and RISKTARGET functions. For example, the formulas in cells B27 and B29 are

**=RISKPERCENTILE(B20,0.05)**

and

**=1-RISKTARGET(B20,0)**

## USING @RISK

After running @RISK for 10,000 iterations, we obtain the values in the range B23:B29 of Figure 12.30. The mean return from this portfolio is about 9.4%, but there is considerable variability. There is a 5% chance that it will lose at least 24%, and there is a 5% chance that it will gain at least 56.4%. The probability that it will provide a *positive* return is about 0.59.

If you have any intuition for financial portfolios, you have probably noticed that this investor is "putting all her eggs in one basket." If the stock price increases, she gains by owning the shares of stock, and she also gains from holding the options (because she is more likely to be "in the money"). However, if the price of the stock decreases, she loses money on her shares of stock, and her option are worthless. A safer strategy is to **hedge** her bets. She can purchase 100 shares of the stock and purchase one *put* option on the stock. A put option allows her to sell shares of stock for the exercise price at the exercise date. With a put option, the investor hopes the stock price will decrease because she can then sell her shares at the exercise price and immediately buy them back at the decreased stock price, thus earning a profit. Therefore, a portfolio consisting of shares of stock and put options on the stock covers the investor in both directions. It has less upside potential, but it decreases the downside risk. ∎

### Valuing a More Exotic Call Option

The European call option is fairly simple. A variety of other derivative securities are currently available. In fact, their variety and complexity are what make them attractive—and dangerous for the unsuspecting investor. We examine one variation of the basic call option, an **Asian** option. Its payoff depends, not on the price at expiration of the underlying stock, but on the *average* price of the stock over the lifetime of the option. That is, if the exercise price of the option is $p_e$, and the average price of the stock over the lifetime of the option is $p_{avg}$, then the payoff at the expiration date from the option is the larger of $p_{avg} - p_e$ and 0.

To price an Asian option (or any number of other exotic options), we again find the expected discounted value of the cash flow from the option, assuming that the stock grows at the risk-free rate. The following example illustrates how to approximate this expected value with simulation.

---

EXAMPLE | **12.10 PRICING AN ASIAN OPTION**

Consider a stock currently priced at $100 per share. Its mean annual return is 15%, and the standard deviation of its annual return is 30%. What is the value of an Asian option that expires in 52 weeks (1 year) with an exercise price of $110? Assume that the risk-free rate is 9%.

**Objective** To use simulation to estimate the price of a more exotic call option.

## WHERE DO THE NUMBERS COME FROM?

Again, all of the given data is publicly available.

## Solution

To value this option, we base $p_{avg}$ on the average of the weekly (simulated) stock prices, assuming that the stock price grows at the risk-free rate. This requires us to generate weekly stock prices from equation (12.3), using $s = 1/52$. That is, we simulate any week's price from the previous week's price. These two prices are separated by a week, or 1/52 of a year, which means we should use $s = 1/52$ in equation (12.3).

## DEVELOPING THE SIMULATION MODEL

The spreadsheet model appears in Figure 12.31. (See the file **Asian Option.xlsx**.) The model can be developed as follows:

**Figure 12.31**  Determining the Price of an Asian Option

| | A | B | C | D | E | F | G | H | I |
|---|---|---|---|---|---|---|---|---|---|
| 1 | Pricing an Asian call option with simulation | | | | | | | | |
| 2 | | | | | | | | | |
| 3 | Input section | | | Weekly prices (growing at risk-free rate) | | | | Range names used: | |
| 4 | Current price | $100 | | Week | Simulated price | | | Current_price | =Model!$B$4 |
| 5 | Exercise price | $110 | | 0 | $100.00 | | | Duration | =Model!$B$9 |
| 6 | Mean annual return | 15% | | 1 | $111.22 | | | Exercise_price | =Model!$B$5 |
| 7 | Volatility | 30% | | 2 | $114.94 | | | Mean_annual_return | =Model!$B$6 |
| 8 | Risk-free rate | 9.0% | | 3 | $111.21 | | | Risk_free_rate | =Model!$B$8 |
| 9 | Duration | 1.0 | | 4 | $119.71 | | | Volatility | =Model!$B$7 |
| 10 | | | | 5 | $116.78 | | | | |
| 11 | Simulation section | | | 6 | $113.28 | | | | |
| 12 | Average of weekly prices | $115.065 | | 7 | $111.90 | | | | |
| 13 | Option cash flow at termination | $506.468 | | 8 | $114.52 | | | | |
| 14 | Discounted value of option | $462.877 | | 9 | $110.82 | | | | |
| 15 | | | | 10 | $105.90 | | | | |
| 16 | Value of option (average of discounted value) | $458.10 | | 11 | $113.57 | | | | |
| 17 | | | | 12 | $111.50 | | | | |
| 18 | | | | 13 | $114.62 | | | | |
| 55 | | | | 50 | $101.17 | | | | |
| 56 | | | | 51 | $104.43 | | | | |
| 57 | | | | 52 | $103.31 | | | | |

**1** **Inputs.** Enter the inputs in the blue range. As in the valuation of the European call option, we enter the mean growth rate of the stock in cell B6 even though it is not used in the simulation.

**2** **Weekly prices.** Enter the initial price (week 0) in cell E5 with the formula

=Current_price

Then to generate each weekly price from the previous one, enter the formula

=E5*EXP((Risk_free_rate-0.5*Volatility^2)*(1/52)
+Volatility*RiskNormal(0,1)*SQRT(1/52))

in cell E6 and copy it to the range E7:E57. Again, this is based on equation (12.3) with $s = 1/52$.

**3** **Discounted value of option.** Enter the formulas

=AVERAGE(E5:E57)

=100*MAX(B12-Exercise_price,0)

and

=EXP(-Duration*Risk_free_rate)*B13

in cells B12, B13, and B14. These are exactly as in the European call option example, except that the payoff in cell B13 is based on the *average* in cell B12, not on the ending price of the stock. Then designate cell B14 as the @RISK output cell, because the price of the option is estimated by the average value in this cell.

**4** **Average of output cell.** We again show the main @RISK summary measure in the spreadsheet itself. Enter the formula

=RISKMEAN(B14)

in cell B16.

## Using @RISK

After running @RISK for 10,000 iterations, the value in cell B16 is $458.10. This is our estimate for the price of this Asian option. (The actual market price of this particular option is about $468, pretty close to our estimate. We could have gotten a slightly more accurate estimate of the actual price by running more iterations with @RISK.) ∎

# PROBLEMS

## Skill-Building Problems

**9.** Rerun the new car simulation from Example 12.5 but now introduce uncertainty into the fixed development cost. Let it be triangularly distributed with parameters $1.2 billion, $1.3 billion, and $1.7 billion. (You can check that the mean of this distribution is $1.4 billion, the same as the cost given in the example.) Comment on the differences between your outputs and those in the example. Would you say these differences are "important" for the company?

**10.** Rerun the new car simulation from Example 12.5, but now use the RISKSIMTABLE function appropriately to simulate discount rates of 7.5%, 10%, 12.5%, and 15%. Comment on how the outputs change as the discount rate decreases from the value we used, 15%.

**11.** In the cash balance model from Example 12.6, the timing is such that some receipts are delayed by 1 or 2 months, and the payments for materials and labor must be made a month in advance. Change the model so that all receipts are received immediately, and payments made this month for materials and labor are 80% of sales *this* month (not next month). The period of interest is again January to June. Rerun the simulation, and comment on any differences between your outputs and those from the example.

**12.** In the cash balance model from Example 12.6, is the $250,000 minimum cash balance requirement really "costing" the company very much? Find out by rerunning the simulation with minimum required cash balances of $50,000, $100,000, $150,000, and $200,000. Use the RISKSIMTABLE function to run all

simulations at once. Comment on the outputs from these simulations. In particular, comment on whether the company appears to be better off with a lower minimum cash balance.

**13.** Run the retirement model from Example 12.7 with a damping factor of 1.0 (instead of 0.98), again using the same three sets of investment weights. Explain in words what it means, in terms of the simulation, to have a damping factor of 1. Then comment on the differences, if any, between your simulation results and those in the example.

**14.** The simulation output from Example 12.7 indicates that an investment heavy in stocks produces the best results. Would it be better to invest *entirely* in stocks? Find out by rerunning the simulation. Is there any apparent downside to this strategy?

**15.** Modify the model from Example 12.7 so that you use only the years 1970 to 2001 of historical data. Run the simulation for the same three sets of investment weights. Comment on whether your results differ in any important way from those in the example.

**16.** Referring to the retirement example in Example 12.7, rerun the model for a planning horizon of 10 years; 15 years; 25 years. For each, try to find the set of investment weights that maximize the VAR (the 5th percentile) of final cash in today's dollars. Does it appear that a portfolio heavy in stocks is better for long horizons but not for shorter horizons?

**17.** A European put option allows an investor to *sell* a share of stock at the exercise price on the exercise data. For example, if the exercise price is $48, and the stock price is $45 on the exercise date, the investor can sell the stock for $48 and then immediately buy it back (that is, cover his position) for $45, making $3 profit. But if the stock price on the exercise date is greater than the exercise price, the option is worthless at that date. So for a put, the investor is hoping that the price of the stock *decreases*. Using the same parameters as in Example 12.8, find a fair price for a European put option. (*Note:* As discussed in the text, an actual put option is usually for 100 shares.)

18. Modify Example 12.9 so that the portfolio now contains 100 shares of stock and one *put* option on the stock with the same parameters as in the example. You can assume that the price of an option is $81. Discuss in a brief memo how this portfolio differs from the portfolio in the example.

## Skill-Extending Problems

19. Change the new car simulation from Example 12.5 as follows. It is the same as before for years 1 to 5, including depreciation through year 5. However, the car might sell through year 10. Each year *after* year 5, the company examines sales. If fewer than 90,000 cars were sold that year, there is a 50% chance the car won't be sold after that year. Modify the model and run the simulation. Keep track of two outputs: NPV (through year 10) and the number of years of sales.

20. If you own a stock, buying a put option on the stock will greatly reduce your risk. This is the idea behind **portfolio insurance.** To illustrate, consider a stock (Trumpco) that currently sells for $56 and has an annual volatility of 30%. Assume the risk-free rate is 8%, and you estimate that the stock's annual growth rate is 12%.
    a. Suppose you own 100 shares of Trumpco. Use simulation to estimate the probability distribution of the percentage return earned on this stock during a 1-year period.
    b. Now suppose you also buy a put option (for $238) on Trumpco. The option has an exercise price of $50 and an exercise date 1 year from now. Use simulation to estimate the probability distribution of the percentage return on your portfolio over a 1-year period. Can you see why this strategy is called a portfolio insurance strategy?
    c. Use simulation to show that the put option should, indeed, sell for about $238.

21. For the data in the previous problem, the following is an example of a **butterfly spread:** sell two calls with an exercise price of $50, buy one call with an exercise price of $40, and buy one call with an exercise price of $60. Simulate the cash flows from this portfolio.

22. Cryco stock currently sells for $69. The annual growth rate of the stock is 15%, and the stock's annual volatility is 35%. The risk-free rate is currently 5%. You have bought a 6-month European put option on this stock with an exercise price of $70.
    a. Use @RISK to value this option.
    b. Use @RISK to analyze the distribution of percentage returns (for a 6-month horizon) for the following portfolios:
       - **Portfolio 1:** Own 100 shares of Cryco.
       - **Portfolio 2:** Own 100 shares of Cryco and buy the put described in part **a.**

    Which portfolio has the larger expected return? Explain why portfolio 2 is known as portfolio insurance.

23. A **knockout call option** loses all value at the instant the price of the stock drops below a given "knockout level." Determine a fair price for a knockout call option when the current stock price is $20, the exercise price is $21, the knockout price is $19.50, the mean annual growth rate of the stock is 12%, the annual volatility is 40%, the risk-free rate is 10%, and the exercise date is 1 month from now (where we assume there are 21 trading days in the month and 250 in a year).

24. Suppose an investor has the opportunity to buy the following contract (a stock call option) on March 1. The contract allows him to buy 100 shares of ABC stock at the end of March, April, or May at a guaranteed price of $50 per share. He can exercise this option at most once. For example, if he purchases the stock at the end of March, he cannot purchase more in April or May at the guaranteed price. If the investor buys the contract, he is hoping that the stock price will go up. The reasoning is that if he buys the contract, the price goes up to $51, and he buys the stock (that is, he exercises his option) for $50, he can then sell the stock for $51 and make a profit of $1 per share. Of course, if the stock price goes down, he doesn't have to exercise his option; he can just throw the contract away.

    Assume that the stock price change each month is normally distributed with mean 0 and standard deviation 2. The investor uses the following strategy. At the end of March, he exercises the option only if the stock price is above $51.50. At the end of April, he exercises the option (assuming he hasn't exercised it yet) only if the price is above $50.75. At the end of May, he exercises the option (assuming he hasn't exercised it yet) only if the price is above $50.00. (This isn't necessarily his best strategy, but it's a reasonable one.) Simulate 250 replications of this strategy and answer the following:
    a. Estimate the probability that he will exercise his option.
    b. Estimate his net profit with this strategy. (This doesn't include the price of the contract.)
    c. Estimate the probability that he will net over $300.
    d. Estimate the worth of this contract to him.

# 12.4 MARKETING MODELS

Marketing departments have plenty of opportunities to use simulation. They face uncertainty in the brand-switching behavior of customers, the entry of new brands into the market, customer preferences for different attributes of products, the effects of advertising on sales, and so on. We examine some interesting marketing applications of simulation in this section.

## Models of Customer Loyalty

*Churn occurs when customers leave one company and go to another company.*

What is a loyal customer worth to a company? This is an extremely important question for companies and an important part of customer relationship management (CRM), which is currently one of the hottest topics in marketing. Companies know that if customers become dissatisfied with the company's product, they are likely to switch and never return. Marketers refer to this customer loss as **churn.** The loss in profit from churn can be large, particularly because long-standing customers tend to be more profitable in any given year than new customers. The following example uses a reasonable model of customer loyalty and simulation to estimate the worth of a customer to a company. It is based on the excellent discussion of customer loyalty in Reichheld (1996).

---

EXAMPLE | **12.11 THE LONG-TERM VALUE OF A CUSTOMER AT CCAMERICA**

CCAmerica is a credit card company that does its best to gain customers and keep their business in a highly competitive industry. The first year a customer signs up for service typically results in a loss to the company because of various administrative expenses. However, after the first year, the profit from a customer is typically positive, and this profit tends to increase through the years. The company has estimated the mean profit from a typical customer to be as shown in column B of Figure 12.32. For example, the company expects to lose \$40 in the customer's first year but to gain \$87 in the fifth year—provided that the customer stays loyal that long. For modeling purposes, we assume that the *actual* profit from a customer in the customer's $n$th year of service is normally distributed with mean shown in Figure 12.32 and standard deviation equal to 10% of the mean. At the end of each year, the customer leaves the company, never to return, with probability 0.15, the **churn rate.** Alternatively, the customer stays with probability 0.85, the **retention rate.** The company wants to estimate the NPV of the net profit from any such customer who has just signed up for service at the beginning of year 1, at a discount rate of 15%, assuming that the cash flow occurs in the middle of the year.[7] The company also wants to see how sensitive this NPV is to the retention rate.

**Objective**   To use simulation to find the NPV of a customer and to see how this varies with the retention rate.

### WHERE DO THE NUMBERS COME FROM?

The numbers in Figure 12.32 are undoubtedly averages, based on historical records of many customers. To build in randomness for any *particular* customer, we need a probability distribution around the numbers in this figure. We arbitrarily chose a normal distribution

---

[7] This makes the NPV calculation slightly more complex, but it is probably more realistic than our usual assumption that cash flows occur at the *ends* of the years.

**Figure 12.32**

Mean Profit as a
Function of Years as
Customer

| | A | B |
|---|---|---|
| 9 | Estimated means | |
| 10 | Year | Mean Profit(if still here) |
| 11 | 1 | ($40.00) |
| 12 | 2 | $66.00 |
| 13 | 3 | $72.00 |
| 14 | 4 | $79.00 |
| 15 | 5 | $87.00 |
| 16 | 6 | $92.00 |
| 17 | 7 | $96.00 |
| 18 | 8 | $99.00 |
| 19 | 9 | $103.00 |
| 20 | 10 | $106.00 |
| 21 | 11 | $111.00 |
| 22 | 12 | $116.00 |
| 23 | 13 | $120.00 |
| 24 | 14 | $124.00 |
| 25 | 15 | $130.00 |
| 26 | 16 | $137.00 |
| 27 | 17 | $142.00 |
| 28 | 18 | $148.00 |
| 29 | 19 | $155.00 |
| 30 | 20 | $161.00 |
| 31 | 21 | $161.00 |
| 32 | 22 | $161.00 |
| 33 | 23 | $161.00 |
| 34 | 24 | $161.00 |
| 35 | 25 | $161.00 |
| 36 | 26 | $161.00 |
| 37 | 27 | $161.00 |
| 38 | 28 | $161.00 |
| 39 | 29 | $161.00 |
| 40 | 30 | $161.00 |

centered on the historical average and a standard deviation equal to 10% of the average. These are educated guesses. Finally, the churn rate is a number very familiar to marketing people, and it can also be estimated from historical customer data.

## Solution

The idea is to keep simulating profits (or a loss in the first year) for the customer until the customer churns. We simulate 30 years of potential profits.

### DEVELOPING THE SIMULATION MODEL

The simulation model appears in Figure 12.33. (See the file **Customer Loyalty.xlsx**.) The model can be developed with the following steps:

**1** **Inputs.** Enter the inputs in the blue cells.

**2** **Retention rate.** Although an 85% retention rate is given in the statement of the problem, we investigate retention rates from 75% to 95%, as shown in row 4. To run a separate simulation for each of these, enter the formula

=RISKSIMTABLE(D4:H4)

in cell B4.

*As usual, Excel's RAND function can be used inside an IF statement to determine whether a given event occurs.*

**3** **Timing of churn.** In column C, we want to use simulation to discover when the customer churns. This column will contain a sequence of No's, followed by a Yes, and then a sequence of blanks. To generate these, enter the formulas

=IF(RAND()<1-B4, "Yes","No")

and

=IF(OR(C11="",C11="Yes"),"",IF(RAND()<1-$B$4, "Yes","No"))

Figure 12.33   The Customer Loyalty Model

| | A | B | C | D | E | F | G | H | I | J |
|---|---|---|---|---|---|---|---|---|---|---|
| 1 | Customer loyalty model in the credit card industry | | | | | | | | | |
| 2 | | | | | | | | | | |
| 3 | Inputs | | | Retention rates to try | | | | | | |
| 4 | Retention rate | 0.75 | | 0.75 | 0.80 | 0.85 | 0.90 | 0.95 | | |
| 5 | Discount rate | 0.15 | | | | | | | | |
| 6 | Stdev % of mean | 10% | | | | | | | | |
| 7 | | | | | | | | | | |
| 8 | | | | | | | | | | |
| 9 | Estimated means | | Simulation | | | | Outputs | | | |
| 10 | Year | Mean Profit(if still here) | Quits at end of year? | Actual profit | Discounted profit | | NPV | $17.94 | | |
| 11 | 1 | ($40.00) | No | ($43.14) | ($40.23) | | Years loyal | 2 | | |
| 12 | 2 | $66.00 | Yes | $71.74 | $58.17 | | | | | |
| 13 | 3 | $72.00 | | $0.00 | $0.00 | | Means | | | |
| 14 | 4 | $79.00 | | $0.00 | $0.00 | | Simulation | Retention rate | NPV | Years loyal |
| 15 | 5 | $87.00 | | $0.00 | $0.00 | | 1 | 0.75 | $101.74 | 4.10 |
| 16 | 6 | $92.00 | | $0.00 | $0.00 | | 2 | 0.80 | $134.32 | 5.09 |
| 17 | 7 | $96.00 | | $0.00 | $0.00 | | 3 | 0.85 | $182.63 | 6.61 |
| 18 | 8 | $99.00 | | $0.00 | $0.00 | | 4 | 0.90 | $253.87 | 9.68 |
| 19 | 9 | $103.00 | | $0.00 | $0.00 | | 5 | 0.95 | $368.45 | 15.95 |
| 20 | 10 | $106.00 | | $0.00 | $0.00 | | | | | |
| 21 | 11 | $111.00 | | $0.00 | $0.00 | | | | | |
| 22 | 12 | $116.00 | | $0.00 | $0.00 | | | | | |
| 23 | 13 | $120.00 | | $0.00 | $0.00 | | | | | |
| 24 | 14 | $124.00 | | $0.00 | $0.00 | | | | | |
| 25 | 15 | $130.00 | | $0.00 | $0.00 | | | | | |
| 26 | 16 | $137.00 | | $0.00 | $0.00 | | | | | |
| 27 | 17 | $142.00 | | $0.00 | $0.00 | | | | | |
| 28 | 18 | $148.00 | | $0.00 | $0.00 | | | | | |
| 29 | 19 | $155.00 | | $0.00 | $0.00 | | | | | |
| 30 | 20 | $161.00 | | $0.00 | $0.00 | | | | | |
| 31 | 21 | $161.00 | | $0.00 | $0.00 | | | | | |
| 32 | 22 | $161.00 | | $0.00 | $0.00 | | | | | |
| 33 | 23 | $161.00 | | $0.00 | $0.00 | | | | | |
| 34 | 24 | $161.00 | | $0.00 | $0.00 | | | | | |
| 35 | 25 | $161.00 | | $0.00 | $0.00 | | | | | |
| 36 | 26 | $161.00 | | $0.00 | $0.00 | | | | | |
| 37 | 27 | $161.00 | | $0.00 | $0.00 | | | | | |
| 38 | 28 | $161.00 | | $0.00 | $0.00 | | | | | |
| 39 | 29 | $161.00 | | $0.00 | $0.00 | | | | | |
| 40 | 30 | $161.00 | | $0.00 | $0.00 | | | | | |

in cells C11 and C12, and copy the latter formula down column C. Study these formulas carefully to see how the logic works. Note that they do not rely on @RISK functions. Excel's RAND function can be used any time we want to simulate whether an event occurs.

**4 Actual and discounted profits.** Profits (or a loss in the first year) occur as long as there is not a blank in column C. Therefore, simulate the actual profits by entering the formula

**=IF(C11<> "",RISKNORMAL(B11,$B$6*ABS(B11)),0)**

in cell D11 and copying it down. (The absolute value function, ABS, is required in case any of the cash flows are negative. A normal distribution cannot have a *negative* standard deviation.) Then discount these appropriately in column E by entering the formula

**=D11/(1+$B$5)^(A11-0.5)**

*Careful discounting is required if cash flows occur midyear.*

in cell E11 and copying it down. Note how the exponent of the denominator accounts for the cash flow in the *middle* of the year.

**5 Outputs.** We actually keep track of two outputs, the total NPV and the number of years the customer stays with the company. Calculate the NPV in cell H10 by summing the discounted values in column E. (They have already been discounted, so the NPV function is not needed.) To find the number of years the customer is loyal, note that it is always the number of No's in column C, plus 1. Therefore, calculate it in cell H11 with the formula

**=COUNTIF(C11:C40,"No")+1**

Finally, designate both of cells H10 and H11 as @RISK output cells.

### Running the Simulation

Set the number of iterations to 1000 and the number of simulations to 5 (one for each potential retention rate). Then run the simulation as usual.

### Discussion of the Simulation Results

Summary results for all five retention rates and the histogram for an 85% retention rate appear in Figures 12.34 and 12.35. The histogram indicates that there is almost a 14% chance that the NPV will be negative, whereas the chance that it will be above $300 is over 26%. We also see from the summary measures that the mean NPV and the mean number of years loyal are sensitive to the retention rate.

**Figure 12.34**
Summary Results for the Customer Loyalty Model

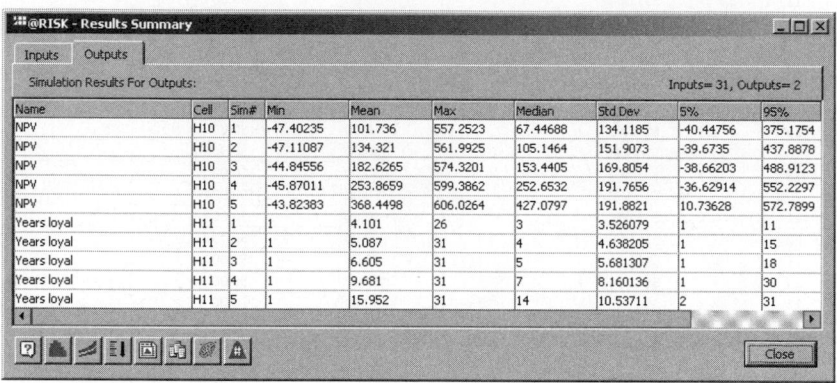

**Figure 12.35**
Histogram of NPV for an 85% Retention Rate

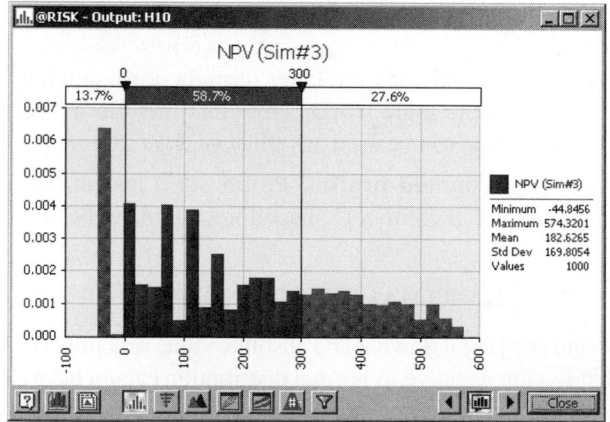

*Varying the retention rate can have a large impact on the value of a customer.*

To follow up on this observation, we used the RISKMEAN function to capture the means in columns I and J of the model sheet and then created a line chart of them as a function of the retention rate (see Figure 12.36). This line chart shows the rather dramatic effect the retention rate can have on the value of a customer. For example, if it increases from the

**Figure 12.36**
Sensitivity of
Outputs to the
Retention Rate

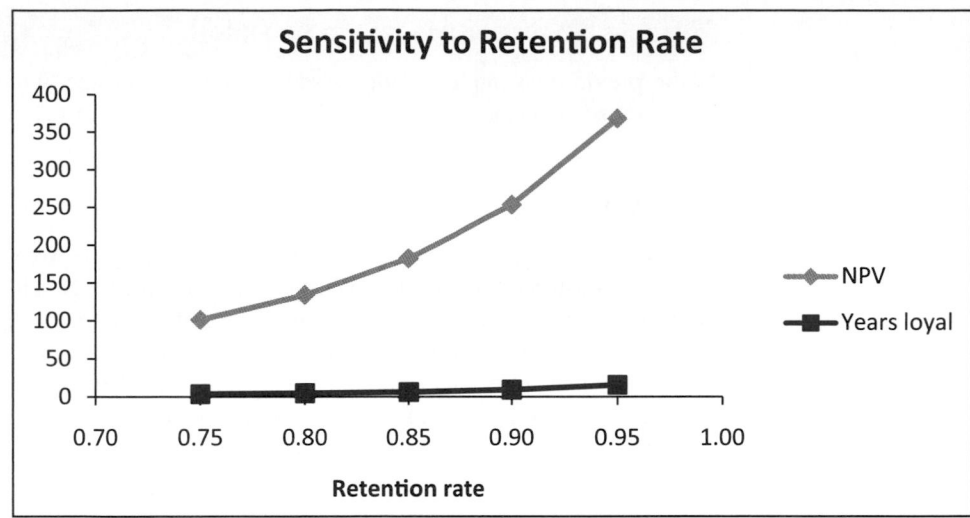

current 85% to 90%, the mean NPV increases by about 39%. If it increases from 85% to 95%, the mean NPV increases by over 100%. In the other direction, if the retention rate decreases from 85% to 80%, the mean NPV decreases by about 27%. This is why credit card companies are so anxious to keep their customers. ∎

The following example is a variation of the previous example. We now investigate the effect of offering a customer an incentive to remain loyal. We also change the model to allow previous customers to rejoin our company.

---

**EXAMPLE** | **12.12 REDUCING CHURN AT AOSN**

We are all aware of the fierce competition by Internet Service Providers (ISPs) to get our business. For example, MSN is always trying to attract AOL's customers, and vice versa. Some are even giving away prizes to entice us to sign up for a guaranteed length of time. This example is based on one such offer. We assume that an ISP named AOSN is willing to give a customer a free PC, at a cost of $700 to AOSN, if the customer signs up for a guaranteed 3 years of service. During that time, the cost of service to the customer is a constant $21.95 per month, or $263.40 annually. After 3 years, we assume the cost of service increases by 3% annually. We assume that in any year after the guaranteed 3 years, the probability is 0.7 that the customer stays with AOSN. As in the previous example, this is the retention rate. We also assume that if a customer has switched to another ISP, there is always a probability of 0.1 that the customer (without any free PC offer) willingly joins AOSN. AOSN wants to see whether, in terms of NPV with a 10% discount rate, this offer makes financial sense. It also wants to see how the NPV varies with the retention rate.

**Objective**   To use simulation to estimate whether it makes sense for an ISP to give away a free PC for a promise of at least 3 years of customer loyalty, and to see how the answer varies with the retention rate.

## WHERE DO THE NUMBERS COME FROM?

In the previous example, we discussed the switching rates, which would be estimated from extensive customer data. The other data in the problem statement are straightforward to obtain.

## Solution

The solution strategy is fairly similar to the previous example. We use IF functions to check whether a customer is currently getting service from AOSN. There are two differences, however. First, we need to modify the logic so that a customer can leave AOSN *or* return. Second, we run two side-by-side simulations: one for a customer who has just accepted a free PC for a guaranteed 3-year subscription and the other for a customer who is not currently an AOSN customer and does *not* accept such an offer. By comparing these, we can see whether the free PC is worth its cost to AOSN.

## DEVELOPING THE SIMULATION MODEL

The completed simulation model appears in Figure 12.37. (See the file **Free PC Value.xlsx**.) The model can be developed with the following steps:

**Figure 12.37**   The Free PC Simulation Model

| | A | B | C | D | E | F | G | H | I | J | K | L | M |
|---|---|---|---|---|---|---|---|---|---|---|---|---|---|
| 1 | Estimating value of giving away free PC to get loyal customer | | | | | | | | | | | | |
| 2 | | | | | | | | | | | | | |
| 3 | Inputs | | | Retention rates to try | | | | | | | | | |
| 4 | Retention rate | 0.5 | | 0.5 | 0.6 | 0.7 | 0.8 | 0.9 | | | | | |
| 5 | Switchback rate | 0.1 | | | | | | | | | | | |
| 6 | Cost of PC | $700 | | | | | | | | | | | |
| 7 | Yearly subscription cost | $263.40 | | | | | | | | | | | |
| 8 | Annual cost increase | 3% | | | | | | | | | | | |
| 9 | Discount rate | 10% | | | | | | | | | | | |
| 10 | | | | | | | | | | | | | |
| 11 | Outputs from simulation below | | | Probability of difference being positive | | | | | | | | | |
| 12 | NPV with PC | $428.79 | | Simulation | 1 | 2 | 3 | 4 | 5 | | | | |
| 13 | NPV without PC | $288.45 | | Retention rate | 0.5 | 0.6 | 0.7 | 0.8 | 0.9 | | | | |
| 14 | Difference | $140.34 | | Pr(positive) | 0.347 | 0.400 | 0.467 | 0.501 | 0.600 | | | | |
| 15 | | | | | | | | | | | | | |
| 16 | Simulation | | | With Free PC | | | | Without free PC | | | | | |
| 17 | | End of year | Subscription cost | With us? | Quit? | Switch to us? | Revenue | With us? | Quit? | Switch to us? | Revenue | | Random numbers for: |
| 18 | 0 | | | | | ($700) | | | | | | | Quitting | Switching |
| 19 | 1 | $263.40 | Yes | No | No | $263.40 | No | No | No | $0.00 | | 0.073137 | 0.819553 |
| 20 | 2 | $263.40 | Yes | No | No | $263.40 | No | No | No | $0.00 | | 0.191073 | 0.788467 |
| 21 | 3 | $263.40 | Yes | No | No | $263.40 | No | No | No | $0.00 | | 0.156098 | 0.539344 |
| 22 | 4 | $271.30 | Yes | Yes | No | $271.30 | No | No | No | $0.00 | | 0.7632 | 0.237589 |
| 23 | 5 | $279.44 | No | No | No | $0.00 | No | No | No | $0.00 | | 0.231037 | 0.970496 |
| 24 | 6 | $287.82 | No | No | No | $0.00 | No | No | No | $0.00 | | 0.035589 | 0.810818 |
| 25 | 7 | $296.46 | No | No | No | $0.00 | No | No | No | $0.00 | | 0.077157 | 0.671465 |
| 26 | 8 | $305.35 | No | No | No | $0.00 | No | No | No | $0.00 | | 0.695741 | 0.670606 |
| 27 | 9 | $314.51 | No | No | No | $0.00 | No | No | No | $0.00 | | 0.393822 | 0.475298 |
| 28 | 10 | $323.95 | No | No | No | $0.00 | No | No | No | $0.00 | | 0.003606 | 0.717069 |
| 29 | 11 | $333.67 | No | No | No | $0.00 | No | No | No | $0.00 | | 0.369943 | 0.284277 |
| 30 | 12 | $343.68 | No | No | Yes | $0.00 | No | No | Yes | $0.00 | | 0.777977 | 0.023854 |
| 31 | 13 | $353.99 | Yes | No | No | $353.99 | Yes | No | No | $353.99 | | 0.053296 | 0.543153 |
| 32 | 14 | $364.61 | Yes | No | No | $364.61 | Yes | No | No | $364.61 | | 0.320396 | 0.77635 |
| 33 | 15 | $375.55 | Yes | Yes | No | $375.55 | Yes | Yes | No | $375.55 | | 0.692112 | 0.38566 |
| 34 | 16 | $386.81 | No | No | No | $0.00 | No | No | No | $0.00 | | 0.322743 | 0.273569 |
| 35 | 17 | $398.42 | No | No | No | $0.00 | No | No | No | $0.00 | | 0.104524 | 0.905263 |
| 36 | 18 | $410.37 | No | No | No | $0.00 | No | No | No | $0.00 | | 0.386579 | 0.454987 |
| 37 | 19 | $422.68 | No | No | No | $0.00 | No | No | No | $0.00 | | 0.878338 | 0.40961 |
| 38 | 20 | $435.36 | No | No | No | $0.00 | No | No | No | $0.00 | | 0.21904 | 0.932583 |
| 39 | 21 | $448.42 | No | No | No | $0.00 | No | No | No | $0.00 | | 0.568445 | 0.115218 |
| 40 | 22 | $461.87 | No | No | No | $0.00 | No | No | No | $0.00 | | 0.310568 | 0.546483 |
| 41 | 23 | $475.73 | No | No | No | $0.00 | No | No | No | $0.00 | | 0.593845 | 0.810983 |
| 42 | 24 | $490.00 | No | No | No | $0.00 | No | No | No | $0.00 | | 0.915499 | 0.378981 |
| 43 | 25 | $504.70 | No | No | No | $0.00 | No | No | No | $0.00 | | 0.371658 | 0.863412 |
| 44 | 26 | $519.84 | No | No | No | $0.00 | No | No | No | $0.00 | | 0.964949 | 0.728986 |
| 45 | 27 | $535.44 | No | No | No | $0.00 | No | No | No | $0.00 | | 0.175341 | 0.88567 |
| 46 | 28 | $551.50 | No | No | No | $0.00 | No | No | No | $0.00 | | 0.596402 | 0.544829 |
| 47 | 29 | $568.05 | No | No | No | $0.00 | No | No | No | $0.00 | | 0.843877 | 0.188536 |
| 48 | 30 | $585.09 | No | No | No | $0.00 | No | No | No | $0.00 | | 0.390914 | 0.963068 |

**1 Inputs.** Enter the given data in the blue cells.

**2 Retention rate.** We will test the retention rates in row 4 with five separate simulations, so enter the formula

**=RISKSIMTABLE(D4:H4)**

in cell B4.

**3 Subscription prices.** Enter a link to the current subscription price from cell B7 in cells B19 to B21. Then calculate the increasing subscription costs with the formula

**=B21*(1+$B$8)**

in cell B22, and copy it down column B. For these latter years, the subscription is increasing by 3% annually.

*Using common random numbers for two side-by-side simulations is a good practice because it results in a fairer comparison.*

**4 Random numbers.** Columns C to F are for a customer who accepts a free PC, whereas columns G to J are for a customer who does not accept such an offer. To compare these fairly, they should use the *same* random numbers for generating switching behavior. Therefore, enter two columns of random numbers with the RAND function in columns L and M. The first set in column L is used to see whether the customer quits AOSN in any year, whereas the second set in column M is used to see whether the customer switches back to AOSN in any given year.

**5 Switching with free PC.** To understand columns C to E, each cell in column C indicates whether the customer is with AOSN during that year. If "Yes," then a "Yes" is possible in column D, meaning that the customer quits AOSN at the end of the year. If "No," then a "Yes" is possible in column E, meaning that the customer switches back to AOSN at the end of the year. (The meaning is the same in columns G to I.) For a customer who accepts a free PC, fill in columns C, D, and E as follows. Enter "Yes" in cells C19 to C21 and "No" in cells D19 to D20 and E19 to E21. (This customer is not *allowed* to switch during the first three years.) Then enter the formulas

**=IF(D21= "Yes","No",IF(E21="Yes","Yes",C21))**

**=IF(L21<B4,"No","Yes")**

and

**=IF(C22="Yes","No",IF(M22<$B$5,"Yes","No"))**

in cells C22, D21, and E22, and copy these down their respective columns. These formulas allow the customer to switch back and forth after 3 years.

**6 Switching with no free PC.** The logic for the customer in columns G to I is almost the same. Now we assume that the customer is not with AOSN in year 0, so enter the formula

**=IF(RAND()<B5,"Yes","No")**

in cell G19 to see whether she might join AOSN of her own accord in year 1. Then enter the same logic for the other cells in columns G to I as in the previous step, referring to the *same* random numbers in columns L and M.

**7 Revenue.** Enter a link to the cost of the PC in cell F18, but make it negative. Then enter the formula

**=IF(C19="Yes",$B19,0)**

in cell F19, and copy it to the ranges F19:F48 and J19:J48—the logic is equivalent for both customers.

**8 NPV.** We assume that all cash flows are at the *ends* of the respective years, so enter the formulas

=F18+NPV(B9,F19:F48)

=NPV(B9,J19:J48)

and

=B12−B13

in cells B12, B13, and B14, and designate each of these as @RISK output cells. Note that the first includes the cost (to AOSN) of the PC, whereas the second does not. We are particularly interested in the difference, in cell B14. If it tends to be positive, then the free PC is worth the cost to AOSN.

### Running the Simulation

Set up @RISK to run 1000 iterations and 5 simulations, one for each retention rate to be tested. Then run the simulation as usual.

### Discussion of the Simulation Results

Selected results appear in Figures 12.38 and 12.39. The summary statistics indicate that the mean difference between the two NPVs is positive except for the lowest retention rate, 0.5. However, in all cases, this difference in NPV varies from more than $1000 negative to more than $1000 positive. This indicates that for some customers, the free PC offer will make money, whereas for others it will lose money. Another way to view the results is by the probabilities of positive differences in NPV, shown in the range E13:I13 of Figure 12.37. (We found these with the RISKTARGET function.) With retention rates of 0.5, 0.6, and 0.7, there is actually less than a 50–50 chance that the difference will be positive. If the actual retention rate is 0.7, perhaps AOSN ought to rethink its free PC strategy. In a purely financial sense, it is not a clear winner.

---

**Figure 12.38**    Summary Statistics from @RISK

**@RISK - Results Summary**

Inputs | Outputs

Simulation Results For Outputs:                                                          Inputs= 1, Outputs= 3

| Name | Cell | Sim# | Min | Mean | Max | Median | Std Dev | 5% | 95% |
|---|---|---|---|---|---|---|---|---|---|
| NPV with PC | B12 | 1 | -44.96318 | 462.9238 | 1588.01 | 425.2642 | 318.2812 | 15.63218 | 1057.47 |
| NPV with PC | B12 | 2 | -44.96318 | 563.7779 | 1786.695 | 519.1096 | 365.9869 | 57.57441 | 1227.422 |
| NPV with PC | B12 | 3 | -44.96318 | 742.6642 | 2242.521 | 702.8228 | 442.1791 | 67.39185 | 1507.819 |
| NPV with PC | B12 | 4 | -44.96318 | 1002.5 | 2373.562 | 953.2783 | 540.6018 | 140.3397 | 1975.322 |
| NPV with PC | B12 | 5 | -44.96318 | 1477.501 | 2373.562 | 1544.087 | 615.0246 | 313.8506 | 2373.562 |
| NPV without PC | B13 | 1 | 0 | 485.2859 | 1988.479 | 421.2366 | 358.1426 | 35.80929 | 1181.173 |
| NPV without PC | B13 | 2 | 0 | 546.7148 | 2187.121 | 479.2117 | 394.0594 | 38.24294 | 1324.52 |
| NPV without PC | B13 | 3 | 0 | 691.3823 | 2645.111 | 607.2047 | 489.261 | 38.24294 | 1583.361 |
| NPV without PC | B13 | 4 | 0 | 879.9634 | 2834.938 | 814.0509 | 591.4378 | 33.53052 | 1987.767 |
| NPV without PC | B13 | 5 | 0 | 1195.121 | 3073.562 | 1139.288 | 752.2802 | 38.24294 | 2512.381 |
| Difference | B14 | 1 | -936.0626 | -22.36205 | 1358.172 | -44.96318 | 292.9265 | -502.1037 | 476.3199 |
| Difference | B14 | 2 | -1175.517 | 17.06311 | 1454.185 | -44.96318 | 347.9307 | -502.1037 | 628.4503 |
| Difference | B14 | 3 | -1345.561 | 51.28196 | 2134.938 | -44.96318 | 417.8629 | -700 | 770.8997 |
| Difference | B14 | 4 | -1544.111 | 122.5365 | 1975.322 | 96.1647 | 542.0587 | -700 | 1146.129 |
| Difference | B14 | 5 | -2175.116 | 282.3794 | 2373.562 | 140.3397 | 677.4404 | -700 | 1544.087 |

Close

**Figure 12.39**

Histogram of the Difference in NPV for a 70% Retention Rate

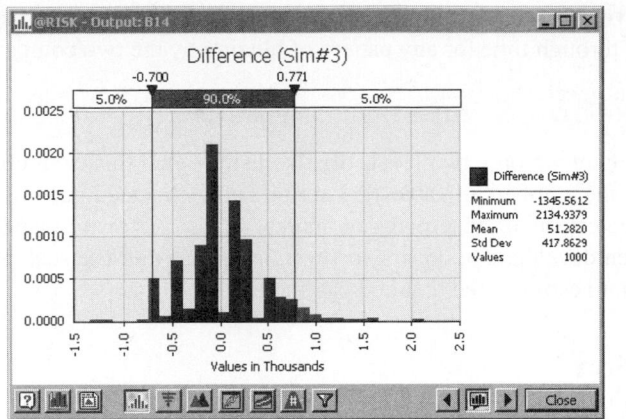

## Market Share Models

We conclude this marketing section with a fairly simple model of market share behavior. This model is based on the type of competition faced by two dominant brands in an industry, such as Coca-Cola and Pepsi. We ignore all other brands. Each quarter, one of the companies wins market share from the other in a random manner, although this behavior depends largely on how much each company promotes its product. The timing of promotions is the key aspect of the model.

---

**EXAMPLE**

## 12.13 ESTIMATING DYNAMIC MARKET SHARE WITH TWO DOMINANT BRANDS

We assume there are two dominant companies in the soft drink industry, "us" and "them." For this example, we view everything from the point of view of us. We start with a 45% market share. During each of the next 20 quarters, each company promotes its product to some extent. To make the model simple, we assume that each company promotes at a "regular" level or at a "blitz" level during each quarter. Depending on each company's promotional behavior in a given quarter, the change in our market share from this quarter to the next is triangularly distributed, with parameters given in Table 12.3. For example, if we blitz and they don't, then we could lose as much as 1% market share, we could gain as much as 6% market share, and our most likely outcome is an increase of 2% market share. We want to develop a simulation model that allows us to gauge the long-term change in our market share for any pattern of blitzing employed by each company.

---

**Table 12.3** Parameters of Market Share Change Distributions

| Blitzer | Minimum | Most Likely | Maximum |
|---------|---------|-------------|---------|
| Neither | −0.03 | 0 | 0.03 |
| Both | −0.05 | 0 | 0.05 |
| Only us | −0.01 | 0.02 | 0.06 |
| Only them | −0.06 | −0.02 | 0.01 |

**Objective** To develop a simulation model that allows us to see how our market share changes through time for any pattern of blitzing by the two companies.

## WHERE DO THE NUMBERS COME FROM?

Even if there are only two levels of advertising—and this is an obvious approximation to reality—the numbers in Table 12.3 are probably educated guesses at best. It is difficult to gauge the effects of advertising on market share, and many management science models have been developed to do so. However, marketers can use such models, along with their intuition, to estimate the required parameters.

## Solution

*The real purpose of the model is to allow us to test various patterns of blitzing by both companies.*

The idea is that we can enter *any* pattern of blitzing, indicated by 0's and 1's, of the two companies, simulate the corresponding changes in market shares, and then track our market share through the 20-quarter period. After the simulation has been developed, we can use it as a tool to analyze various blitzing patterns.

## DEVELOPING THE SIMULATION MODEL

The completed simulation model (with several hidden columns) appears in Figure 12.40. (See the file **Market Share.xlsx**.) The following steps are required to develop the model:

**Figure 12.40** The Market Share Simulation Model

| | A | B | C | D | E | F | G | H | S | T | U |
|---|---|---|---|---|---|---|---|---|---|---|---|
| 1 | Market share model | | | | | | | | | | |
| 2 | | | | | | | | | | | |
| 3 | Inputs | | | | | | | | | | |
| 4 | Our current market share | 45% | | | | | | | | | |
| 5 | | | | | | | | | | | |
| 6 | Parameters of triangular distribution of change in our market share - depends on who has a big promotional campaign | | | | | | | | | | |
| 7 | | Minimum | Most likely | Maximum | | | | | | | |
| 8 | Neither | -0.03 | 0 | 0.03 | | | | | | | |
| 9 | Both | -0.05 | 0 | 0.05 | | | | | | | |
| 10 | Only us | -0.01 | 0.02 | 0.06 | | | | | | | |
| 11 | Only them | -0.06 | -0.02 | 0.01 | | | | | | | |
| 12 | | | | | | | | | | | |
| 13 | Promotional campaigns (1 if promote, 0 if not) - enter any patterns you want to test in the following two rows | | | | | | | | | | |
| 14 | Quarter | 1 | 2 | 3 | 4 | 5 | 6 | 7 | 18 | 19 | 20 |
| 15 | Us | 0 | 1 | 0 | 1 | 0 | 1 | 0 | 1 | 0 | 1 |
| 16 | Them | 1 | 0 | 1 | 0 | 1 | 0 | 1 | 0 | 1 | 0 |
| 17 | | | | | | | | | | | |
| 18 | Simulation | | | | | | | | | | |
| 19 | Possible changes in our market share | | | | | | | | | | |
| 20 | Quarter | 1 | 2 | 3 | 4 | 5 | 6 | 7 | 18 | 19 | 20 |
| 21 | Neither promote | 0.60% | 0.64% | -0.11% | -1.74% | -0.24% | -0.61% | 0.12% | 0.03% | -1.99% | -0.08% |
| 22 | Both promote | 0.96% | -0.20% | -0.53% | 1.91% | 1.95% | -1.15% | 1.62% | -2.04% | -1.24% | -0.43% |
| 23 | Only we promote | 3.65% | 0.70% | 2.84% | 0.19% | 1.27% | 3.07% | 3.44% | 1.23% | 4.79% | -0.73% |
| 24 | Only they promote | -0.10% | -2.03% | -2.18% | -0.91% | -1.07% | -2.58% | 0.05% | -3.85% | -0.13% | -4.06% |
| 25 | | | | | | | | | | | |
| 26 | Tracking our market share | | | | | | | | | | |
| 27 | Beginning market share | 45.00% | 44.90% | 45.61% | 43.43% | 43.62% | 42.55% | 45.62% | 41.79% | 43.02% | 42.89% |
| 28 | Change in our market share | -0.10% | 0.70% | -2.18% | 0.19% | -1.07% | 3.07% | 0.05% | 1.23% | -0.13% | -0.73% |
| 29 | Ending market share | 44.90% | 45.61% | 43.43% | 43.62% | 42.55% | 45.62% | 45.67% | 43.02% | 42.89% | 42.16% |

**❶ Inputs.** Enter the inputs in the blue ranges.

**❷ Blitz pattern.** Enter any sequence of 0's and 1's in rows 15 and 16. The 1's indicate blitz promotions. (In reality, our company has no control over the pattern in row 16, and although we can choose the pattern in row 15, we probably have to choose it *before* observing their pattern in row 16. We arbitrarily entered a pattern where the 1's and 0's alternate for each company, and the two companies are "out of step" with one another. However, this is purely for illustration.)

**3** **Possible market share changes.** It simplifies matters to generate the *possible* market share changes in rows 21 to 24. These are then used as needed in row 28. To generate these random changes, enter the formula

**=RISKTRIANG($B8,$C8,$D8)**

in cell B21, and copy it to the range B21:U24.

**4** **Our market share.** We track our market share in rows 27 to 29. There are really only two ideas here. First, our beginning market share in any quarter is our ending market share from the previous quarter. Second, the change in our market share in any quarter is one of the values in rows 21 to 24, depending on who blitzes that quarter. This requires a nested IF formula. Start by entering a link to our current market share (from cell B4) in cell B27. Then enter the formulas

**=IF(AND(B16=0,B15=0),B21,IF(AND(B16=1,B15=1),B22,IF(AND(B16=0,B15=1),B23,B24)))**

**=B27+B28**

and

**=B29**

in cells B28, B29, and C27, and copy all of these across. Again, the nested IF simply records the appropriate market share change for that quarter from rows 21 to 24.

**5** **Output range.** Designate the entire 20-quarter range in row 29 as an output range. To do so, highlight this range and click on the @RISK Add Output button. We suggest that you name this output range "Market share."

### Running the Simulation

We set @RISK to run 1000 iterations for a single simulation. However, unlike previous examples, the point here is not so much to see results for any particular simulation run, but rather to use the simulation model as a tool for analysis. That is, we can play any "game" we want by seeing how a blitzing strategy for us does against a given blitzing strategy for them. For example, in the file **Market Share Random 10.xlsx**, we entered formulas in their row 16 that guarantee exactly 10 randomly placed 1's.[8] This is relevant if we believe they are going to blitz half of the time, but we have no idea when. Then we can try any strategy we want and run the resulting simulation.

### Discussion of the Simulation Results

*These results represent only one possibility. Other patterns of blitzes will certainly lead to different results.*

Figure 12.41 shows the summary graph of our market share through time when we react to their "random 10" strategy by blitzing in the middle 12 quarters, Q5 to Q16. That is, we blitz 2 more quarters than they do, and we do our blitzing consecutively. The results are not unexpected. Because we blitz 2 more quarters than they do, we tend to gain market share—our average market share after 20 quarters is close to 50%, up from the initial 45%. However, the shape of this summary graph clearly shows what happens to our market share when we do not blitz and there is a chance that they do.

---

[8] These formulas are interesting in their own right. How can we randomly enter 0's and 1's and guarantee that exactly half are 1's? The idea is that if there is a 1 in Q1, then the probability of a 1 in Q2 should be 9/19. However, if there is a 0 in Q1, then the probability of a 1 in Q2 should be 10/19.

**Figure 12.41**

Summary Chart for
Our "Middle 12"
Strategy versus
Their "Random 10"
Strategy

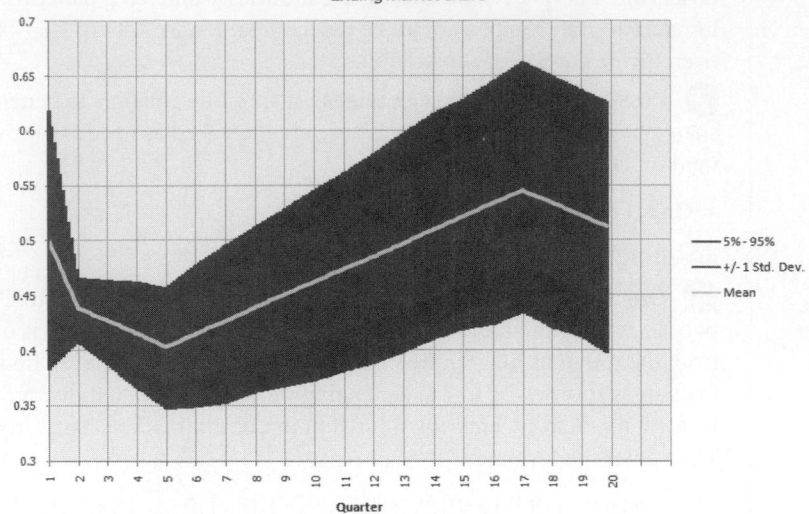

This example clearly indicates how a simulation model can be used as a tool to analyze all sorts of scenarios. In this case, the purpose is not to run a simulation once and then report these specific results. Rather, the purpose is to run the simulation many times, tweaking various parameters on each run, to see what insights we can gain. ■

## FUNDAMENTAL INSIGHT

### Using a Simulation Model as a Tool

The purpose of simulation models in many real applications such as this market share example is to use them as a tool to provide insights. By making the simulation models as general as possible, we can then experiment with various configurations to see their affect on key outputs. For example, we can experiment with advertising strategies to see their affect on market share, with manufacturing strategies to see their effect on throughput and machine utilization, with investment strategies to see their affect on NPVs, with different game strategies to see their affect on the probability of winning football games, and so on. This use of simulation as a tool to gain insights is arguably the most important reason for building simulation models in the first place!

## PROBLEMS

### Skill-Building Problems

25. Suppose that Coke and Pepsi are fighting for the cola market. Each week, each person in the market buys one case of Coke or Pepsi. If the person's last purchase was Coke, there is a 0.90 probability that this person's next purchase will be Coke; otherwise, it will be Pepsi. (We are considering only two brands in the market.) Similarly, if the person's last purchase was Pepsi, there is a 0.80 probability that this person's next purchase will be Pepsi; otherwise, it will be Coke. Currently half of all people purchase Coke, and the other half purchase Pepsi. Simulate 1 year of sales in the cola market and estimate each company's average weekly market share. Do this by assuming that the total market size is fixed at 100 customers. (*Hint:* Use the RISKBINOMIAL function.)

26. Seas Beginning sells clothing by mail order. An important question is when to strike a customer from their mailing list. At present, they strike a customer from their mailing list if a customer fails to order from six consecutive catalogs. They want to know whether striking a customer from their list after a customer fails to order from four consecutive catalogs will result in a higher profit per customer. The following data are available:

■ If a customer placed an order the last time she received a catalog, then there is a 20% chance she will order from the next catalog.

- If a customer last placed an order one catalog ago, there is a 16% chance she will order from the next catalog she receives.
- If a customer last placed an order two catalogs ago, there is a 12% chance she will order from the next catalog she receives.
- If a customer last placed an order three catalogs ago, there is an 8% chance she will order from the next catalog she receives.
- If a customer last placed an order four catalogs ago, there is a 4% chance she will order from the next catalog she receives.
- If a customer last placed an order five catalogs ago, there is a 2% chance she will order from the next catalog she receives.

It costs $1 to send a catalog, and the average profit per order is $15. Assume a customer has just placed an order. To maximize expected profit per customer, would Seas Beginning make more money canceling such a customer after six nonorders or four nonorders?

27. Based on Babich (1992). Suppose that each week, each of 300 families buys a gallon of orange juice from company A, B, or C. Let $p_A$ denote the probability that a gallon produced by company A is of unsatisfactory quality, and define $p_B$ and $p_C$ similarly for companies B and C. If the last gallon of juice purchased by a family is satisfactory, then the next week they will purchase a gallon of juice from the same company. If the last gallon of juice purchased by a family is not satisfactory, then the family will purchase a gallon from a competitor. Consider a week in which A families have purchased juice A, B families have purchased juice B, and C families have purchased juice C. Assume that families that switch brands during a period are allocated to the remaining brands in a manner that is proportional to the current market shares of the other brands. Thus, if a customer switches from brand A, there is probability $B/(B + C)$ that he will switch to brand B and probability $C/(B + C)$ that he will switch to brand C. Suppose that the market is currently divided equally: 100 families for each of the three brands.
    a. After a year, what will the market share for each firm be? Assume $p_A = 0.10$, $p_B = 0.15$, and $p_C = 0.20$. (*Hint:* You will need to use the RISKBINO-MIAL function to see how many people switch from A and then use the RISKBINOMIAL function again to see how many switch from A to B and from A to C.)
    b. Suppose a 1% increase in market share is worth $10,000 per week to company A. Company A believes that for a cost of $1 million per year, it can cut the percentage of unsatisfactory juice cartons in half. Is this worthwhile? (Use the same values of $p_A$, $p_B$, and $p_C$ as in part a.)

## Skill-Extending Problems

28. Suppose that GLC earns a $4000 profit each time a person buys a car. We want to determine how the expected profit earned from a customer depends on the quality of GLC's cars. We assume a typical customer will purchase 10 cars during her lifetime. She will purchase a car now (year 1) and then purchase a car every 5 years—during year 6, year 11, and so on. For simplicity, we assume that Hundo is GLC's only competitor. We also assume that if the consumer is satisfied with the car she purchases, she will buy her next car from the same company, but if she is not satisfied, she will buy her next car from the other company. Hundo produces cars that satisfy 80% of its customers. Currently, GLC produces cars that also satisfy 80% of its customers. Consider a customer whose first car is a GLC car. If profits are discounted at 10% annually, use simulation to estimate the value of this customer to GLC. Also estimate the value of a customer to GLC if it can raise its customer satisfaction rating to 85%; to 90%; to 95%.

29. The Mutron Company is thinking of marketing a new drug used to make pigs healthier. At the beginning of the current year, there are 1,000,000 pigs that might use the product. Each pig will use Mutron's drug or a competitor's drug once a year. The number of pigs is forecasted to grow by an average of 5% per year. However, this growth rate is not a sure thing. Mutron assumes that each year's growth rate is an independent draw from a normal distribution, with probability 0.95 that the growth rate will be between 3% and 7%. Assuming it enters the market, Mutron is not sure what its share of the market will be during year 1, so it models this with a triangular distribution. Its worst-case share is 20%, its most likely share is 40%, and its best-case share is 70%. In the absence of any *new* competitors entering this market (in addition to itself), Mutron believes its market share will remain the same in succeeding years. However, there are three potential entrants (in addition to Mutron). At the beginning of each year, each entrant that has not already entered the market has a 40% chance of entering the market. The year after a competitor enters, Mutron's market share will drop by 20% for each *new* competitor who entered. For example, if two competitors enter the market in year 1, Mutron's market share in year 2 will be reduced by 40% from what it would have been with no entrants. Note that if all three entrants have entered, there will be no more entrants. Each unit of the drug sells for $2.20 and incurs a variable cost of $0.40. Profits are discounted by 10% annually.
    a. Assuming that Mutron enters the market, use simulation to find its NPV for the next 10 years from the drug.
    b. Again assuming that Mutron enters the market, it can be 95% certain that its *actual* NPV from the drug is between what two values?

## 12.5 SIMULATING GAMES OF CHANCE

We realize that this is a book about "business" applications. However, it is instructive (and fun) to see how simulation can be used to analyze games of chance, including sports contests. In fact, many analysts refer to Monte Carlo simulation, and you can guess where that name comes from—the gambling casinos of Monte Carlo. Besides, today's sports and gambling industries are definitely big business!

### Simulating the Game of Craps

Most games of chance are great candidates for simulation because they are, by their very nature, driven by randomness. In this section, we examine one such game that is extremely popular in the gambling casinos: the game of craps. In its most basic form, the game of craps is played as follows. A player rolls two dice and observes the sum of the two sides turned up. If this sum is 7 or 11, the player wins immediately. If the sum is 2, 3, or 12, the player loses immediately. Otherwise, if this sum is any other number (4, 5, 6, 8, 9, or 10), that number becomes the player's "point." Then the dice are thrown repeatedly until the sum is the player's point or 7. In case the player's point occurs before a 7, the player wins. But if a 7 occurs before the point, the player loses. The following example uses simulation to determine the properties of this game.

---

**EXAMPLE** | **12.14 ESTIMATING THE PROBABILITY OF WINNING AT CRAPS**

Joe Gamble loves to play craps at the casinos. He suspects that his chances of winning are less than 50–50, but he wants to find the probability that he wins a single game of craps.

**Objective**   To use simulation to find the probability of winning a single game of craps.

#### WHERE DO THE NUMBERS COME FROM?

There are no input numbers here, only the rules of the game.

### Solution

We simulate a single game. By running this simulation for many iterations, we can estimate the probability that Joe wins a single game of craps. If his intuition is correct (and surely it must be, or the casino could not stay in business), this probability is less than 0.5.

#### DEVELOPING THE SIMULATION MODEL

The simulation model is for a single game. (See Figure 12.42 and the file **Craps.xlsx**.) There is a subtle problem here: We do not know how many tosses of the dice are necessary to determine the outcome of a single game. Theoretically, the game could continue forever, with the player waiting for his point or a 7. However, it is extremely unlikely that more than, say, 40 tosses are necessary in a single game. (This can be shown by a probability argument, but we do not present it here.) Therefore, we simulate 40 tosses and use only those that are necessary to determine the outcome of a single game. The steps required to simulate a single game are as follows:

# Figure 12.42
## Simulation of Craps Game

| | A | B | C | D | E | F | G | H | I | J |
|---|---|---|---|---|---|---|---|---|---|---|
| 1 | Craps Simulation | | | | | | | | | |
| 2 | | | | | | | | | | |
| 3 | Simulated tosses | | | | | | | | | |
| 4 | Toss | Die 1 | Die 2 | Sum | Win on this toss? | Lose on this toss? | Continue? | | Summary results from simulation | |
| 5 | 1 | 4 | 4 | 8 | 0 | 0 | Yes | | Win? (1 if yes, 0 if no) | 0 |
| 6 | 2 | 6 | 6 | 12 | 0 | 0 | Yes | | Number of tosses | 6 |
| 7 | 3 | 4 | 5 | 9 | 0 | 0 | Yes | | | |
| 8 | 4 | 2 | 3 | 5 | 0 | 0 | Yes | | Pr(winning) | 0.491 |
| 9 | 5 | 1 | 2 | 3 | 0 | 0 | Yes | | Expected number of tosses | 3.392 |
| 10 | 6 | 6 | 1 | 7 | 0 | 1 | No | | | |
| 11 | 7 | 1 | 4 | 5 | | | | | | |
| 12 | 8 | 2 | 4 | 6 | | | | | | |
| 13 | 9 | 3 | 4 | 7 | | | | | | |
| 14 | 10 | 3 | 5 | 8 | | | | | | |
| 15 | 11 | 2 | 4 | 6 | | | | | | |
| 16 | 12 | 3 | 5 | 8 | | | | | | |
| 42 | 38 | 6 | 6 | 12 | | | | | | |
| 43 | 39 | 6 | 2 | 8 | | | | | | |
| 44 | 40 | 2 | 2 | 4 | | | | | | |

**1** **Simulate tosses.** Simulate the results of 40 tosses in the range B5:D44 by entering the formula

**=RANDBETWEEN(1,6)**

in cells B5 and C5 and the formula

**=SUM(B5:C5)**

in cell D5. Then copy these to the range B6:D44. (Note: The RANDBETWEEN function is new to Excel 2007. It generates a random integer between the two specified values such that all values are equally likely, so it is perfect for tossing a die. We could also have used @RISK's RISKDUNIFORM function, as we did in the previous edition.)

**Excel Function:** *RANDBETWEEN*
*The function RANDBETWEEN in the form =RANDBETWEEN(N1,N2) generates a random integer from N1 to N2, with each possibility being equally likely.*

**@RISK Function:** *RISKDUNIFORM*
*The @RISK function RISKDUNIFORM in the form =RISKDUNIFORM({List}) generates a random member of a given list, so that each member of the list has the same chance of being chosen. Here* List *is a list of values separated by commas.*

**2** **First toss outcome.** Determine the outcome of the first toss with the formulas

**=IF(OR(D5=7,D5=11),1,0)**

**=IF(OR(D5=2,D5=3,D5=12),1,0)**

and

**=IF(AND(E5=0,F5=0),"Yes","No")**

in cells E5, F5, and G5. Note that we use the OR condition to check whether Joe wins right away (in which case a 1 is recorded in cell E5). Similarly, the OR condition in cell F5 checks whether he loses right away. In cell G5, we use the AND condition to check whether both cells E5 and F5 are 0, in which case the game continues. Otherwise, the game is over.

**3** **Outcomes of other tosses.** Assuming the game continues beyond the first toss, Joe's point is the value in cell D5. Then we are waiting for a toss to have the value in cell D5 or 7, whichever occurs first. To implement this logic, enter the formulas

**=IF(OR(G5="No",G5=""),"",IF(D6=$D$5,1,0))**

**=IF(OR(G5="No",G5=""),"",IF(D6=7,1,0))**

*As in many spreadsheet simulation models, the concepts in this model are simple. The key is careful bookkeeping.*

and

**=IF(OR(G5="No",G5=""),"",IF(AND(E6=0,F6=0),"Yes","No"))**

in cells E6, F6, and G6, and copy these to the range E7:G44. The OR condition in each formula checks whether the game just ended on the previous toss or has been over for some time, in which case blanks are entered. Otherwise, the first two formulas check whether Joe wins or loses on this toss. If both of these return 0, the third formula returns "Yes" (and the game continues). Otherwise, it returns "No" (and the game ends).

**4 Game outcomes.** We keep track of two aspects of the game in @RISK output cells: whether Joe wins or loses and how many tosses are required. To find these, enter the formulas

**=SUM(E5:E44)**

and

**=COUNT(E5:E44)**

in cells J5 and J6, and designate each of these as an @RISK output cell. Note that both functions, SUM and COUNT, ignore blank cells.

*The mean (or average) of a sequence of 0's and 1's is the fraction of 1's in the sequence. This can typically be interpreted as a probability.*

**5 Simulation summary.** Although we get summary measures in the various @RISK results windows when we run the simulation, it is useful to see some key summary measures right on the model sheet. To get these, enter the formula

**=RISKMEAN(J5)**

in cell J8 and copy it to cell J9. As the labels indicate, the RISKMEAN in cell J8, being an average of 0's and 1's, is just the fraction of iterations where Joe wins. The average in cell J9 is the average number of tosses until the game's outcome is determined.

### Running the Simulation

We set the number of iterations to 10,000 (primarily to obtain a very accurate answer) and the number of simulations to 1. Then we run the simulation as usual.

### Discussion of the Simulation Results

*Perhaps surprisingly, the probability of winning in craps is 0.493, only slightly less than 0.5.*

After running @RISK, we obtain the summary results in cells J8 and J9 of Figure 12.42 (among others). Our main interest is in the average in cell J8 because it represents our best estimate of the probability of winning, 0.491. (A probability argument can be used to show that the exact probability of winning in craps is 0.493.) We also see that the average number of tosses needed to determine the outcome of a game was 3.392. (The maximum number of tosses ever needed was 30.) ∎

## Simulating the NCAA Basketball Tournament

Each year the suspense reaches new levels as "March Madness" approaches, the time of the NCAA Basketball Tournament. Which of the 64 teams in the tournament will reach the "Sweet Sixteen," which will go on to the prestigious "Final Four," and which team will be crowned champion? The excitement at Indiana University is particularly high, given its strong basketball tradition, so it has become a yearly tradition at IU (at least for the authors) to simulate the NCAA Tournament right after the 64-team field has been announced. We share that simulation in the following example.

EXAMPLE | 12.15 March Madness

As of press time for this book, the most recent NCAA Basketball Tournament was the 2007 tournament, won by the University of Florida (for the second year in a row). Of course, on the Sunday evening when the 64-team field was announced, we did not know which team would win. All we knew were the pairings (which teams would play which other teams) and the team ratings, based on Jeff Sagarin's nationally syndicated rating system. We show how to simulate the tournament and keep a tally of the winners.

**Objective**  To simulate the 64-team NCAA basketball tournament and keep a tally on how often each team wins the tournament.

## WHERE DO THE NUMBERS COME FROM?

As soon as you learn the pairings for the *next* NCAA tournament, you can visit Sagarin's site at http://www.usatoday.com/sports/sagarin.htm#hoop for the latest ratings.

## Solution

*We model the point spread as normally distributed, with mean equal to the difference between the Sagarin ratings and standard deviation 10.*

We need to make one probabilistic assumption. From that point, it is a matter of "playing out" the games and doing the required bookkeeping. To understand this probabilistic assumption, suppose team A plays team B, and Sagarin's ratings for these teams are, say, 85 and 78. Then Sagarin predicts that the actual point differential in the game (team A's score minus team B's score) will be the difference between the ratings, 7.[9] We take this one step further. We assume the *actual* point differential is normally distributed with mean equal to Sagarin's prediction, 7, and standard deviation 10. (Why 10? This is an estimate based on an extensive analysis of historical data.) Then if the actual point differential is positive, team A wins. If it is negative, team B wins.

## DEVELOPING THE SIMULATION MODEL

We only outline the simulation model. You can see the full details in the file **March Madness.xlsm**. (It includes the data for the 2007 tournament, but you can easily modify it for future tournaments by following the directions on the sheet.) The entire simulation is on a single Model sheet. Columns A to C list team indexes, team names, and Sagarin ratings. If two teams are paired in the first round, they are placed next to one another in the list. Also, all teams in a given region are listed together. (The regions are color-coded.) Columns K to Q contains the simulation. The first round results are at the top, the second round results are below these, and so on. Winners from one round are automatically carried over to the next round with appropriate formulas. Selected portions of the Model sheet appear in Figures 12.43 and 12.44. We now describe the essential features of the model.

❶ **Teams and ratings.** We first enter the teams and their ratings, as shown in Figure 12.43. Most of the teams shown here were in the East regional in the 2007 tournament. North Carolina played Eastern Kentucky in the first round, Marquette played Michigan State, and so on.

❷ **Simulate rounds.** Jumping ahead to the fourth-round simulation in Figure 12.44, we capture the winners from the previous round 3 and then simulate the games in round 4.

[9] In general, there is also a home-court advantage, but we assume all games in the tournament are on neutral courts, so that there is no advantage to either team.

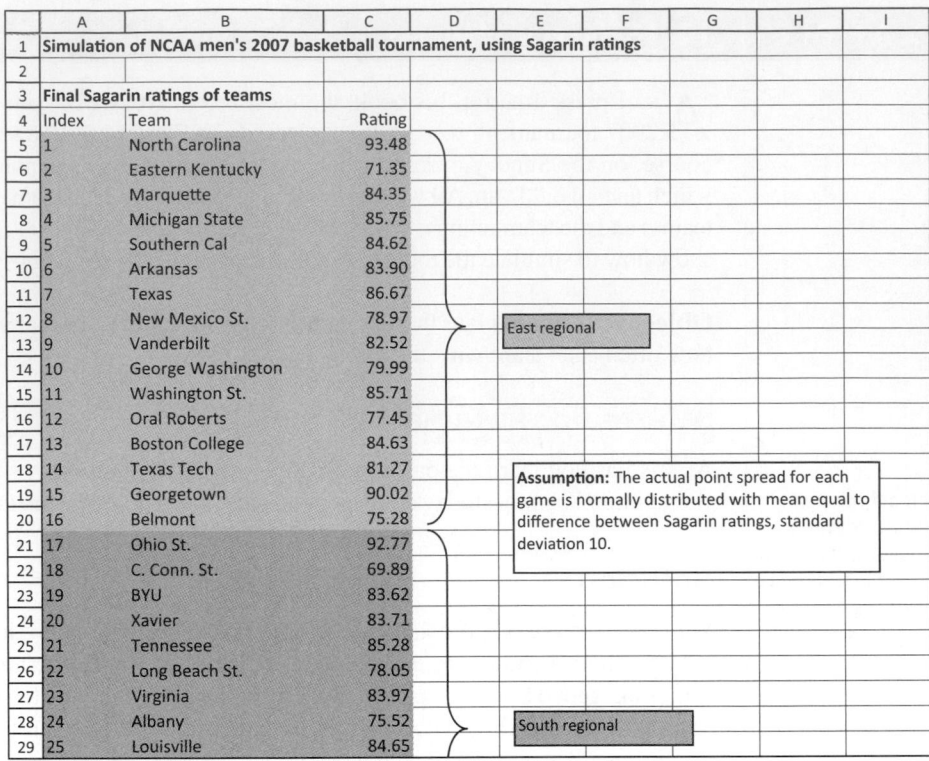

**Figure 12.43**

Teams and Sagarin Ratings

| | A | B | C | D | E | F | G | H | I |
|---|---|---|---|---|---|---|---|---|---|
| 1 | Simulation of NCAA men's 2007 basketball tournament, using Sagarin ratings | | | | | | | | |
| 2 | | | | | | | | | |
| 3 | Final Sagarin ratings of teams | | | | | | | | |
| 4 | Index | Team | Rating | | | | | | |
| 5 | 1 | North Carolina | 93.48 | | | | | | |
| 6 | 2 | Eastern Kentucky | 71.35 | | | | | | |
| 7 | 3 | Marquette | 84.35 | | | | | | |
| 8 | 4 | Michigan State | 85.75 | | | | | | |
| 9 | 5 | Southern Cal | 84.62 | | | | | | |
| 10 | 6 | Arkansas | 83.90 | | | | | | |
| 11 | 7 | Texas | 86.67 | | | | | | |
| 12 | 8 | New Mexico St. | 78.97 | | | East regional | | | |
| 13 | 9 | Vanderbilt | 82.52 | | | | | | |
| 14 | 10 | George Washington | 79.99 | | | | | | |
| 15 | 11 | Washington St. | 85.71 | | | | | | |
| 16 | 12 | Oral Roberts | 77.45 | | | | | | |
| 17 | 13 | Boston College | 84.63 | | | | | | |
| 18 | 14 | Texas Tech | 81.27 | | | | | | |
| 19 | 15 | Georgetown | 90.02 | | | | | | |
| 20 | 16 | Belmont | 75.28 | | | | | | |
| 21 | 17 | Ohio St. | 92.77 | | | | | | |
| 22 | 18 | C. Conn. St. | 69.89 | | | | | | |
| 23 | 19 | BYU | 83.62 | | | | | | |
| 24 | 20 | Xavier | 83.71 | | | | | | |
| 25 | 21 | Tennessee | 85.28 | | | | | | |
| 26 | 22 | Long Beach St. | 78.05 | | | | | | |
| 27 | 23 | Virginia | 83.97 | | | | | | |
| 28 | 24 | Albany | 75.52 | | | South regional | | | |
| 29 | 25 | Louisville | 84.65 | | | | | | |

**Assumption:** The actual point spread for each game is normally distributed with mean equal to difference between Sagarin ratings, standard deviation 10.

**Figure 12.44**

The NCAA Basketball Simulation Model (Last 3 Rounds Only)

| | K | L | M | N | O | P | Q |
|---|---|---|---|---|---|---|---|
| 124 | Results of Round 4 | | | | | | |
| 125 | Game | Indexes | Teams | Predicted | Simulated | Index of winner | Winner |
| 126 | 1 | 5 | Southern Cal | -5.4 | -16.09 | 15 | Georgetown |
| 127 | | 15 | Georgetown | | | | |
| 128 | 1 | 17 | Ohio St. | 7.97 | 10.88 | 17 | Ohio St. |
| 129 | | 30 | Creighton | | | | |
| 130 | 1 | 39 | Maryland | -3.37 | -4.77 | 47 | Wisconsin |
| 131 | | 47 | Wisconsin | | | | |
| 132 | 1 | 51 | Kentucky | -4.76 | 0.67 | 51 | Kentucky |
| 133 | | 63 | UCLA | | | | |
| 134 | | | | | | | |
| 135 | Semifinals | | | | | | |
| 136 | Game | Indexes | Teams | Predicted | Simulated | Index of winner | Winner |
| 137 | 1 | 15 | Georgetown | -2.75 | -5.83 | 17 | Ohio St. |
| 138 | | 17 | Ohio St. | | | | |
| 139 | 2 | 47 | Wisconsin | 4.96 | 11.95 | 47 | Wisconsin |
| 140 | | 51 | Kentucky | | | | |
| 141 | | | | | | | |
| 142 | Finals | | | | | | |
| 143 | Game | Indexes | Teams | Predicted | Simulated | Index of winner | Winner |
| 144 | 1 | 17 | Ohio St. | 1.66 | 4.41 | 17 | Ohio St. |
| 145 | | 47 | Wisconsin | | | | |

The key formulas are in columns N and O. For example, the formulas in cells N126 and O126 are

**=VLOOKUP(L126,LTable,3)-VLOOKUP(L127,LTable,3)**

and

**=RISKNORMAL(N126,10)**

The first of these looks up the ratings of the two teams involved (in this case, Southern Cal and Georgetown) and subtracts them to get the predicted point spread. The second formula simulates a point spread with the predicted point spread as its mean. The rest of the formulas do the appropriate bookkeeping. You can view the details in the file.

**3 Outputs.** As shown by the boxed-in cells in Figure 12.44, we designate seven cells as @RISK output cells: the index of the winner, the indexes of the two finalists, and the indexes of the four semifinalists (the Final Four teams). However, the results we really want are tallies, such as the number of iterations where North Carolina (or any other team) wins the tournament. This takes some planning. In the @RISK Excel Reports dialog box, if we check the Simulation Data option, we get a sheet called Data that lists the values of all @RISK output cells for *each* of the iterations. (We used 1000 iterations.) After we have these, we can use COUNTIF functions to tally the number of wins (or finalist or semifinalist appearances) for each team, right in the original Model sheet.

*The Simulation Data report in @RISK lists the outputs from each iteration of the simulation, which allows us to tally the winners.*

Some of these tallies appear in Figure 12.45. For example, the formula in cell U5 is

**=COUNTIF('Data'!$I$8:$I$1007,S5)**

In this case, the range I8:I1007 of the Data sheet contains the indexes of the 1000 winners, so this formula counts the number of these that are index 1.[10] As you can see, the top-rated team in the East region, North Carolina, won the tournament in 167 of the 1000 iterations and reached the Final Four almost half of the time. In contrast, the lowly rated Eastern Kentucky did not make the Final Four in any of the 1000 iterations.

**Figure 12.45**

Tally of Winners

|  | S | T | U | V | W |
|---|---|---|---|---|---|
| 1 |  | Update formulas for tallies |  |  |  |
| 2 |  |  |  |  |  |
| 3 | Tally of winners, finalists, and semifinalists |  |  |  |  |
| 4 | Index | Team | Winner | Finalist | Semifinalist |
| 5 | 1 | North Carolina | 167 | 275 | 473 |
| 6 | 2 | Eastern Kentucky | 0 | 0 | 0 |
| 7 | 3 | Marquette | 3 | 8 | 33 |
| 8 | 4 | Michigan State | 2 | 7 | 17 |
| 9 | 5 | Southern Cal | 3 | 6 | 26 |
| 10 | 6 | Arkansas | 1 | 4 | 19 |
| 11 | 7 | Texas | 6 | 16 | 62 |
| 12 | 8 | New Mexico St. | 0 | 0 | 0 |
| 13 | 9 | Vanderbilt | 2 | 6 | 18 |
| 14 | 10 | George Washington | 0 | 0 | 8 |
| 15 | 11 | Washington St. | 9 | 21 | 56 |
| 16 | 12 | Oral Roberts | 0 | 0 | 2 |
| 17 | 13 | Boston College | 2 | 10 | 23 |
| 18 | 14 | Texas Tech | 1 | 1 | 4 |
| 19 | 15 | Georgetown | 68 | 137 | 258 |
| 20 | 16 | Belmont | 0 | 0 | 1 |

[10] Unfortunately, each time we rerun the simulation, the Data sheet is deleted and then recreated, which messes up the references in the tally formulas. Therefore, we created a macro to update these formulas. You can run the macro by clicking on the button shown at the top of Figure 12.45.

## Skill-Building Problems

**30.** The game of Chuck-a-Luck is played as follows: You pick a number between 1 and 6 and toss three dice. If your number does not appear, you lose $1. If your number appears $x$ times, you win $x. On the average, how much money will you win or lose on each play of the game? Use simulation to find out.

**31.** A **martingale** betting strategy works as follows. We begin with a certain amount of money and repeatedly play a game in which we have a 40% chance of winning any bet. In the first game, we bet $1. From then on, every time we win a bet, we bet $1 the next time. Each time we lose, we double our previous bet. Currently we have $63. Assume we have unlimited credit, so that we can bet more money than we have. Use simulation to estimate the profit we will have earned after playing the game 50 times.

## Skill-Extending Problems

**32.** Based on Morrison and Wheat (1984). When his team is behind late in the game, a hockey coach usually waits until there is one minute left before pulling the goalie. Actually, coaches should pull their goalies much sooner. Suppose that if both teams are at full strength, each team scores an average of 0.05 goal per minute. Also, suppose that if you pull your goalie, you score an average of 0.08 goal per minute and your opponent scores an average of 0.12 goal per minute.

Suppose you are one goal behind with 5 minutes left in the game. Consider the following two strategies:
- Pull your goalie if you are behind at any point in the last 5 minutes of the game; put him back in if you tie the score.
- Pull your goalie if you are behind at any point in the last minute of the game; put him back in if you tie the score.

Which strategy maximizes your chance of winning or tying the game? Simulate the game using 10-second increments of time. Use the @RISKBINOMIAL function to determine whether a team scores a goal in a given 10-second segment. This is reasonable because the probability of scoring two or more goals in a 10-second period is near 0.

**33.** You are playing Andy Roddick in tennis, and you have a 42% chance of winning each point. (You are *good*!)
  **a.** Use simulation to estimate the probability you will win a particular game. Note that the first player to score at least 4 points and have at least 2 more points than his opponent wins the game.
  **b.** Use simulation to determine your probability of winning a set. Assume that the first player to win 6 games wins the set if he is at least 2 games ahead; otherwise, the first player to win 7 games wins the set.
  **c.** Use simulation to determine your probability of winning a match. Assume that the first player to win 3 sets wins the match.

# 12.6 USING TOPRANK WITH @RISK FOR POWERFUL MODELING

In this section, we illustrate how another Palisade Decision Tools add-in, TopRank, can be used together with @RISK as a very powerful modeling combination. As we have seen, @RISK introduces uncertainty explicitly into a spreadsheet model by allowing several inputs to have probability distributions. Then it simulates random values from these. However, if a model has many inputs, it is often a good idea to determine which inputs have large effects on a key output variable. Those that have a relatively minor effect can be treated as nonrandom, with best guesses used as their values. We can then focus on the more important input variables and model them, with probability distributions, in an appropriate manner.

TopRank is a what-if tool that allows us to see which of many inputs have large effects on an output variable. We first develop a spreadsheet model in the usual way, using best-guess values for all inputs. We then use TopRank to vary each of the inputs through a designated range, while holding the other inputs constant. TopRank reports the corresponding variation of any output we select. We can then see, usually through one of several charts, which inputs are most critical. At this point, we can either conclude the analysis or switch to @RISK and model the key inputs with appropriate probability distributions.

The following example, which illustrates how TopRank and @RISK can work in tandem, is an extremely important one. Simulation in the business world is often used to analyze potential products. The profitability of a new product is highly uncertain because it depends on many uncertain quantities. Many companies we have worked with (including General Motors and Eli Lilly) begin the analysis of every new product by determining the uncertain quantities that can affect the profitability of the product. This analysis is often the deciding factor in whether the product is developed and marketed.

| EXAMPLE | **12.16 NEW PRODUCT DEVELOPMENT AT SIMTEX** |
|---|---|

SimTex, a pharmaceutical company, is in the early stages of developing a new drug called Biathnon. As with most new drugs, the future of Biathnon is highly uncertain. For example, its introduction into the market could be delayed, pending tests by the Food and Drug Administration (FDA). Also, its market could be diminished by a potential rival product from SimTex's competition. SimTex has identified the following key inputs that will affect Biathnon's future profitability:

- Number of years after product is developed until it is produced (due to potential FDA delays)
- Number of years the product sells
- Initial cost incurred in developing the product
- Salvage value obtained from equipment after production of the product has been discontinued
- Fixed production cost incurred during years in which the product is manufactured
- Unit cost of producing the product
- Unit price of the product
- Initial demand for the product during the first year it is sold
- Annual percentage growth in demand for the product
- Percentage of demand for the product that is lost to the competition
- Discount rate used to discount cash flows from the product

These are the inputs to a profitability model for Biathnon. A natural question is how changes in the inputs affect the key output—the NPV of Biathnon over its lifetime. How can SimTex use TopRank and @RISK to analyze this NPV?

**Objective**   To use TopRank to identify the inputs that affect NPV most, and then to use @RISK to model these inputs with probability distributions.

### WHERE DO THE NUMBERS COME FROM?

Most of the inputs in the preceding list are difficult to estimate. However, this is exactly why we are using TopRank: to see how sensitive NPV is to the various input values. Then the company can spend more energy trying to estimate the inputs that really matter.

## Solution

The first step is to develop a profitability model for Biathnon's NPV as a function of the various inputs. For this first step, we use best guess values for the inputs.

## DEVELOPING THE BASIC MODEL

This model appears in Figure 12.46. (See the file **New Product 1.xlsx**.[11]) We spell out the particular assumptions in the text box, list the inputs in rows 13 to 23, and develop the model in rows 27 to 38. Most of the details are as follows:

---

**Figure 12.46** The Basic SimTex Model

| | A | B | C | D | E | F | G | H | AE | AF | AG | AH | AI |
|---|---|---|---|---|---|---|---|---|---|---|---|---|---|
| 1 | Model of new product by SimTex | | | | | | | | | | | | |
| 2 | | | | | | | | | | | | | |
| 3 | Inputs | | | Range names used: | | | | | | | | | |
| 4 | Years delayed | 2 | | Annual_demand_growth | | =Model!$B$21 | | | | | | | |
| 5 | Product lifetime | 12 | | Annual_fixed_cost | | =Model!$B$17 | | | | | | | |
| 6 | Development cost | $120,000 | | Development_cost | | =Model!$B$15 | | | | | | | |
| 7 | Salvage value | $20,000 | | Discount_rate | | =Model!$B$23 | | | | | | | |
| 8 | Annual fixed cost | $6,000 | | Initial_demand | | =Model!$B$20 | | | | | | | |
| 9 | Unit cost | $2 | | Lost_sales | | =Model!$B$22 | | | | | | | |
| 10 | Unit price | $5 | | Product_lifetime | | =Model!$B$14 | | | | | | | |
| 11 | Initial demand | 20000 | | Salvage_value | | =Model!$B$16 | | | | | | | |
| 12 | Annual demand growth | 10% | | Unit_cost | | =Model!$B$18 | | | | | | | |
| 13 | Lost sales | 20% | | Unit_price | | =Model!$B$19 | | | | | | | |
| 14 | Discount rate | 10% | | Years_delayed | | =Model!$B$13 | | | | | | | |
| 15 | | | | | | | | | | | | | |
| 16 | Financial model (shown for any number of years the product *might* live) | | | | | | | | | | | | |
| 17 | | | | | | | | | | | | | |
| 18 | Year | 0 | 1 | 2 | 3 | 4 | 5 | 6 | 29 | 30 | | | |
| 19 | Development cost | $120,000 | | | | | | | | | | | |
| 20 | Producing product? | No | No | No | Yes | Yes | Yes | Yes | No | No | | | |
| 21 | Fixed cost | | $0 | $0 | $6,000 | $6,000 | $6,000 | $6,000 | $0 | $0 | | | |
| 22 | Total demand | | 0 | 0 | 20000 | 22000 | 24200 | 26620 | 0 | 0 | | | |
| 23 | SimTex's demand | | 0 | 0 | 16000 | 17600 | 19360 | 21296 | 0 | 0 | | | |
| 24 | Variable cost | | $0 | $0 | $32,000 | $35,200 | $38,720 | $42,592 | $0 | $0 | | | |
| 25 | Revenue | | $0 | $0 | $80,000 | $88,000 | $96,800 | $106,480 | $0 | $0 | | | |
| 26 | Salvage value | | $0 | $0 | $0 | $0 | $0 | $0 | $0 | $0 | | | |
| 27 | Net profit | -$120,000 | $0 | $0 | $42,000 | $46,800 | $52,080 | $57,888 | $0 | $0 | | | |
| 28 | | | | | | | | | | | | | |
| 29 | NPV of profit | $284,237 | | | | | | | | | | | |

**Assumptions:**
1. Development costs occur at the end of year 0.
2. It takes some years (specified in cell B4) until production begins. Initial demand, fixed costs, variable costs, and revenues begin in this year.
3. The product is produced for the lifetime specified in cell B5. At the end of the product lifetime, the salvage value is obtained.
4. All revenues, costs occur at the ends of the respective years. The NPV is discounted back to the beginning of year 1.

---

**❶ Timing.** The key to this model is the timing in row 20—whether Biathnon is being produced in any year. To allow for general (even noninteger) values in cells B4 and B5, enter the formula

**=IF(AND(B18>Years_delayed,B18<=Years_delayed+Product_lifetime),"Yes","No")**

in cell B20 and copy it across row 20. For example, with the inputs used in this base-case model, Biathnon is produced only in years 3 to 14, so these are the only years (from year 1 on) that contribute to NPV.

---

[11] We split this example into three separate files—one for the base model, one for the TopRank model, and one for the @RISK model.

**2** **Financials and other formulas.** The formulas in the other cells are then straightforward. For year 1 (column C), the formulas in rows 21 to 27 are

**=IF(C20="Yes",Annual_fixed_cost,0)**

**=IF(AND(B20="No",C20="Yes"),Initial_demand,IF(C20="Yes",B22*(1+Annual_ demand_growth),0))**

**=IF(C22=0,0,C22*(1-Lost_sales))**

**=IF(C23=0,0,C23*Unit_cost)**

**=IF(C23=0,0,C23*Unit_Price)**

**=IF(AND(C20="Yes",D20="No"),Salvage_value,0)**

and

**=-C19-C21-C24+C25+C26**

The second of these formulas (in cell C22) might require some explanation. The first IF checks whether production occurs this year but not the previous year. If so, this must be the first year of production, so that the demand is the initial demand. Otherwise, the second IF checks whether production is still occurring. If so, then demand is the previous year's demand plus the growth percentage. Similarly, the formula for salvage value in cell C26 checks whether production occurs this year but not next year. If so, then this must be the year when the salvage value is obtained.

**3** **NPV.** Calculate the NPV (discounted to the beginning of year 0) in cell B29 with the formula

**=NPV(Discount_rate,C27:AF27)+B27**

Note that the fixed cost in cell B27 is *not* discounted.

Now that the model has been developed, we could use trial and error (or data tables) to see how the NPV reacts to changes in the inputs. However, TopRank does this for us. Actually, it can be used in a number of ways. We discuss only one of them, although it appears to us to be the most useful.

## USING TOPRANK

To use TopRank, we leave the model alone but change the input section.[12] Instead of entering *constants* in the input cells, we enter TopRank's RISKVARY function. This function has the syntax

**=RISKVARY(base,minimum,maximum,rangetype,steps,distribution)**

where

- *base* is the base case (best guess) for the input.
- *minimum* is the smallest possible value for the input.
- *maximum* is the largest possible value for the input.
- *rangetype* is 0, 1, or 2 and determines the way *minimum* and *maximum* should be entered (even though 0 is the default value, we use *rangetype* 2—see the TopRank manual for more details).
- *steps* is the number of values from *minimum* to *maximum* to use for this input.
- *distribution* is an optional argument that we omit.

[12] This discussion assumes TopRank is open within Excel. It can be opened exactly like @RISK, from the Start button of Windows.

We set up the input section for TopRank as shown in Figure 12.47. (See the file **New Product 2.xlsx**.) All entries in columns C to E are *constants* (not formulas). For example, for the development cost in row 6, the base case is $120,000, but we want to examine development costs from 90% to 150% of this base case—that is, from $108,000 to $180,000. We then enter the formula

**=RISKVARY(D4,C4\*D4,E4\*D4,2,8)**

in cell B4 and copy it down to cell B14. This formula tells TopRank to vary this input from its minimum to its maximum in 8 steps. (The next-to-last argument, 2, implies that the second and third arguments are the actual minimum and maximum.)

**Figure 12.47**

Inputs for the SimTex Model

| | A | B | C | D | E |
|---|---|---|---|---|---|
| 3 | **Inputs** | Actual | Low | Base | High |
| 4 | Years delayed | 2.12 | 50% | 2 | 300% |
| 5 | Product lifetime | 7.75 | 50% | 12 | 200% |
| 6 | Development cost | $168,539 | 90% | $120,000 | 150% |
| 7 | Salvage value | $23,116 | 0% | $20,000 | 150% |
| 8 | Annual fixed cost | $5,751 | 80% | $6,000 | 125% |
| 9 | Unit cost | $2.04 | 50% | $2 | 150% |
| 10 | Unit price | $3.41 | 60% | $5 | 125% |
| 11 | Initial demand | 18149.54 | 30% | 20000 | 120% |
| 12 | Annual demand growth | 9% | 50% | 10% | 120% |
| 13 | Lost sales | 10% | 0% | 20% | 200% |
| 14 | Discount rate | 16% | 60% | 10% | 200% |

To use TopRank, we proceed in four steps, very much like in @RISK: (1) use the Analysis Settings button (see the TopRank ribbon in Figure 12.48) to make various settings; (2) use the Add Output button to select one or more output cells; (3) use the Report Settings button to indicate the outputs you want and the Utilities dropdown to indicate where you want them to be placed; and (4) use the Run What-if Analysis button to perform the calculations.

**Figure 12.48**

TopRank Ribbon

For step (1), we suggest accepting all of the default settings. For step (2), highlight the NPV cell (B29) and click on the Add Output button. For step (3), click on the Report Settings button. We suggest checking the Tornado Graph, Spider Graph, and Sensitivity Graphs options, although you can experiment with the other options. Then if you want the results to be placed in the same workbook as the model (as we do), click on the Utilities dropdown and then on Application Settings, where you can choose the option to place the reports in the Active Workbook. (These Application Settings will then apply to all future TopRank models unless you change them.) Finally, run the analysis in step (4) by clicking on the Run What-if Analysis button. TopRank varies each input cell from its minimum to its maximum, using the number of steps you specified and keeping the *other* inputs at their base levels, and keeps track of all the NPVs.

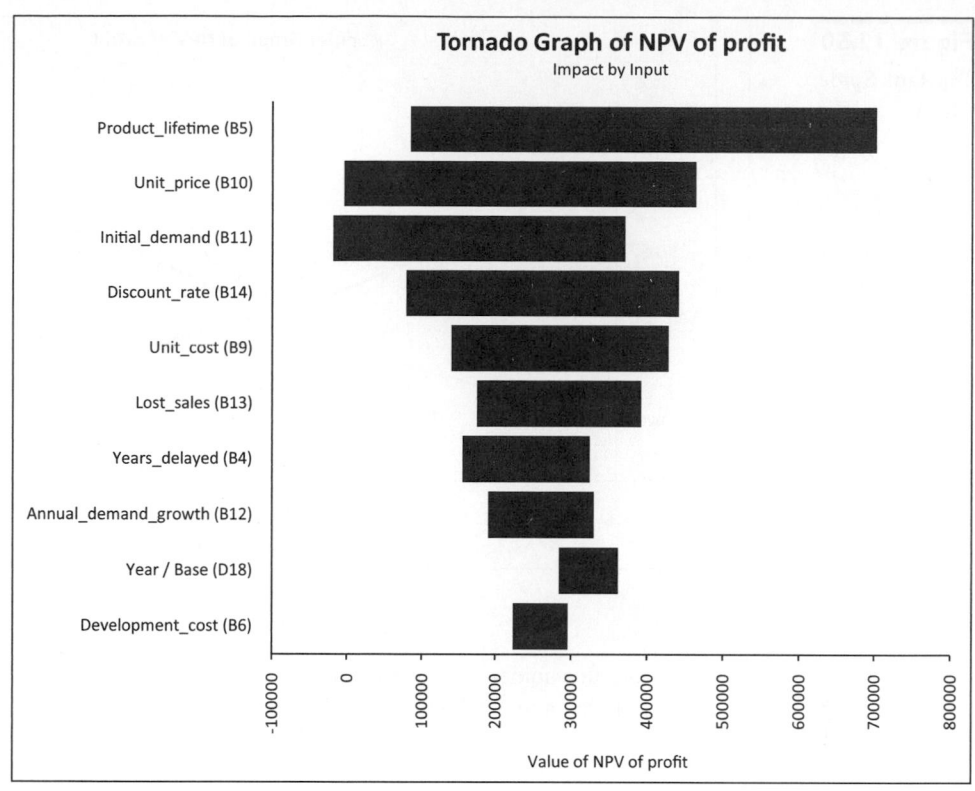

**Figure 12.49**
TopRank Tornado Chart

Perhaps the best way to understand the TopRank results is through the tornado chart in Figure 12.49. Each bar in the chart indicates the variation in NPV as an individual input varies from its minimum to its maximum. For example, NPV decreases by about 70% and increases by about 147% (from its base-case value) when product lifetime varies from its minimum (6 years) to its maximum (24 years). Because the longer bars are always on the top, and the shortest are always on the bottom, the inputs at the top of the chart are always the most important ones. In this case, the five most important inputs are product lifetime, unit price, initial demand, discount rate, and unit production cost.

Clearly, if SimTex is going to simulate the product's NPV, it should spend most of its time accurately assessing the probability distributions of these five key inputs. In contrast, the tornado chart indicates that annual fixed cost and salvage value have very little effect on NPV. Therefore, little effort should be spent trying to estimate their values accurately—the base-case values suffice.

Before proceeding to a simulation, we mention two other chart types available in TopRank: spider charts and sensitivity charts. A spider chart for the SimTex model appears in Figure 12.50. (We altered the original spider chart to make it less cluttered. Specifically, we right-clicked on the chart, then on Select Data, and removed all but the five most important inputs from the tornado chart.) This chart is fairly straightforward. For each of the five inputs shown, a curve shows the percentage change in NPV as a function of the percentage change in the input (over the range we specified for the input).

**Figure 12.50**

TopRank Spider
Chart

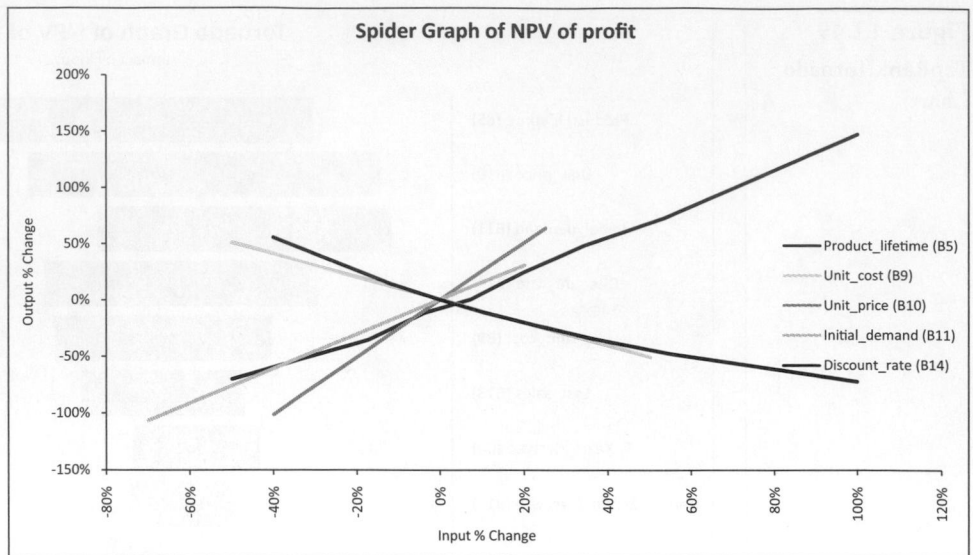

From this spider chart we learn, not surprisingly, that changes in unit price, unit cost, and initial demand result in *linear* changes in NPV. Also, a 1% increase in unit price results in a *larger* percentage increase in NPV than does a 1% percentage increase in initial demand. (Can you see why?) As the discount rate increases, NPV decreases, but the rate of decrease slows; after a while, increases in the discount rate cannot decrease NPV much further. Increases in product lifetime appear to increase product NPV in a slightly nonlinear fashion.

The final TopRank chart type, a sensitivity chart, is similar to a spider chart, except that it shows one input only. Also, it shows *actual* values rather than percentage changes. For example, a graph of NPV versus product lifetime appears in Figure 12.51.

**Figure 12.51**    TopRank Sensitivity Chart

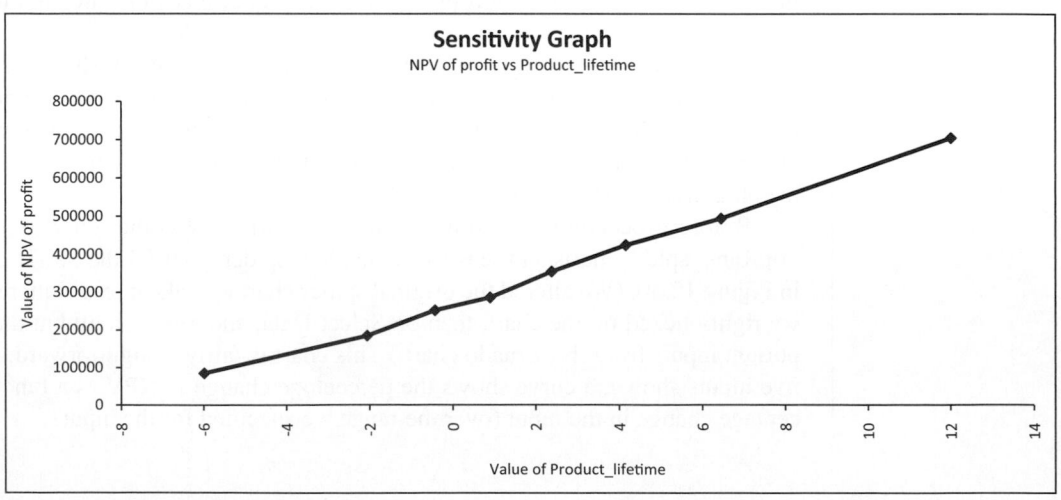

## Running an @RISK Simulation

The sensitivity analysis with TopRank has indicated that the five key drivers of NPV are product lifetime, unit price, unit cost, initial product demand, and discount rate. We now run an @RISK simulation of this model to estimate the distribution of NPV earned from Biathnon. We keep all inputs other than the five key inputs fixed at their base values, and we use @RISK functions for the key inputs. Actually, we use random functions for product lifetime, unit price, unit cost, and initial demand, and we vary discount rate systematically with a RISKSIMTABLE function.[13]

Which probability distributions should we use to model the product lifetime, unit price, unit cost, and initial demand inputs? There are several ways to proceed in general. First, if we have a lot of historical data on any input, we can use the fitting capabilities of @RISK to fit a distribution to the historical data. It is unlikely that SimTex has relevant historical data that pertain to this *new* product, so we will not pursue this approach. Second, we can use @RISK's Model window to examine *shapes* of potential candidate distributions. Finally, we can choose a *simple* distribution that management understands and then assess its parameters.

We use the latter approach, using the triangular distribution for each of the random inputs. The use of a triangular random variable is common at many companies such as General Motors and Eli Lilly. The triangular distribution is often used because, unlike the normal distribution, it makes no assumption that the distribution of the uncertain quantity is symmetric about the mean or most likely value. In fact, the use of the triangular distribution at GM to model uncertain quantities in the analysis of new products grew directly out of deterministic Tornado Chart analysis.

To assess a triangular distribution for any input, all we need are minimum, most likely, and maximum values for the input. We use the same values of these that we used in the TopRank analysis. They are shown in columns E to G of Figure 12.52. (See the file **New Product 3.xlsx**.) Then we enter the usual @RISK formulas in random input cells. For example, the formula in cell B5 is

**=RISKTRIANG(E5,F5,G5)**

Next, we model various discount rates in cell B14 with a RISKSIMTABLE function in the usual way, using the discount rates in the range E14:H14. This allows us to try a discount rate appropriate for a less risky project (6%), a project of average risk (10%), and a project of higher risk (15% or 20%). Finally, we designate the NPV as the single @RISK output cell.

**Figure 12.52**

Parameters for Triangular Distributions and Discount Rates

| | A | B | C | D | E | F | G | H |
|---|---|---|---|---|---|---|---|---|
| 3 | **Inputs** | Actual | | | Parameters for triangular distributions | | | |
| 4 | Years delayed | 2 | nonrandom | | Minimum | Most likely | Maximum | |
| 5 | Product lifetime | 16.39 | triangular | | 6 | 12 | 24 | |
| 6 | Development cost | $120,000 | nonrandom | | | | | |
| 7 | Salvage value | $20,000 | nonrandom | | | | | |
| 8 | Annual fixed cost | $6,000 | nonrandom | | | | | |
| 9 | Unit cost | $2.76 | triangular | | $1.00 | $2.00 | $3.00 | |
| 10 | Unit price | $4.74 | triangular | | $3.00 | $5.00 | $6.25 | |
| 11 | Initial demand | 11095 | triangular | | 6000 | 20000 | 24000 | |
| 12 | Annual demand growth | 10% | nonrandom | | | | | |
| 13 | Lost sales | 20% | nonrandom | | Risksimtable values for discount rate | | | |
| 14 | Discount rate | 6% | use risksimtable | | 6% | 10% | 15% | 20% |

[13] The discount rate used in a typical new product analysis is usually a corporate rate of 10% to 15% and is obtained from the CAPM (Capital Asset Pricing Model). Riskier projects should be discounted at a higher rate than the corporate rate, and less risky projects should be discounted at a lower rate than the corporate rate.

**Figure 12.53**

Selected @RISK
Results

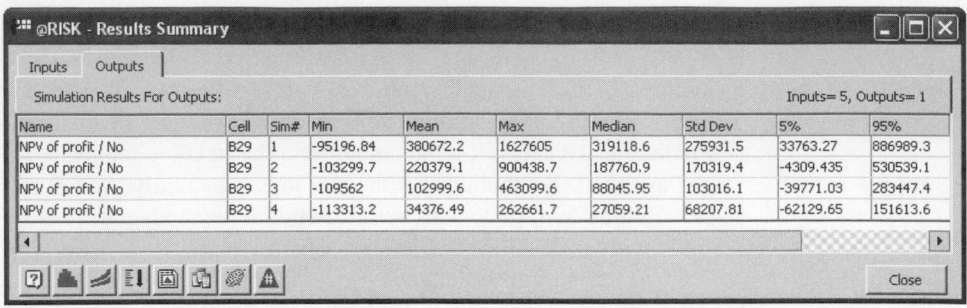

| Name | Cell | Sim# | Min | Mean | Max | Median | Std Dev | 5% | 95% |
|---|---|---|---|---|---|---|---|---|---|
| NPV of profit / No | B29 | 1 | -95196.84 | 380672.2 | 1627605 | 319118.6 | 275931.5 | 33763.27 | 886989.3 |
| NPV of profit / No | B29 | 2 | -103299.7 | 220379.1 | 900438.7 | 187760.9 | 170319.4 | -4309.435 | 530539.1 |
| NPV of profit / No | B29 | 3 | -109562 | 102999.6 | 463099.6 | 88045.95 | 103016.1 | -39771.03 | 283447.4 |
| NPV of profit / No | B29 | 4 | -113313.2 | 34376.49 | 262661.7 | 27059.21 | 68207.81 | -62129.65 | 151613.6 |

We now run @RISK in the usual way, using 1000 iterations and 4 simulations (one for each discount rate). Selected results appear in Figure 12.53. We see that if the project is assessed to be less risky than the company's typical project (justifying a 6% discount rate), the project has a mean NPV (often called the risk-adjusted project NPV) of $380,672, whereas if the project is so risky that it deserves a 20% discount rate, the risk-adjusted NPV is only $34,376. Even if the project is extremely risky, it is still worth doing because it has a positive risk-adjusted NPV.

Note that the standard deviations are fairly large, and there is a possibility that the NPV will be negative. However, given the positive means and high upside potential, most companies would be willing to accept this amount of risk and go ahead with the product. ■

## FUNDAMENTAL INSIGHT

### Identifying Key Inputs

Not all inputs are equally important in terms of their effect on an output. It is essential to identify the key inputs, those that produce the largest changes in the output when they vary over their anticipated ranges. An add-in such as TopRank helps identify the key inputs, although this could also be accomplished with Excel data tables. If an input is identified as being relatively unimportant, it is probably safe to set this equal to a best guess in the model. However, the uncertainty in the key inputs should be modeled explicitly with random functions in a simulation model.

## 12.7 CONCLUSION

We claimed in the previous chapter that spreadsheet simulation, especially together with an add-in such as @RISK, is a very powerful tool. After seeing the examples in this chapter, you should now appreciate how powerful and flexible simulation can be. Unlike Solver optimization models, where we often make simplifying assumptions to achieve linearity, say, we can allow virtually anything in simulation models. All we need to do is relate output cells to input cells with appropriate formulas, where any of the input cells can contain probability distributions to reflect uncertainty. The results of the simulation then show how bad things can get, how good they can get, and what we might expect on average. It is no wonder that companies such as GM, Eli Lilly, and many others are relying more and more on simulation models to analyze their corporate operations.

## Summary of Key Management Science Terms

| Term | Explanation | Page |
|---|---|---|
| Gamma distribution | Right-skewed distribution of nonnegative values useful for many quantities such as the lifetime of an appliance | 657 |
| Value at risk (VAR) | Fifth percentile of distribution of some output, usually a monetary output; indicates nearly how bad the output could be | 675 |
| Stock option | An investment that gives the investor an option to buy or sell stock at a given price at a specified time in the future | 686 |
| Churn | When customers stop buying our product or service and switch to a competitor | 695 |

## Summary of Key Excel Terms

| Term | Explanation | Excel | Page |
|---|---|---|---|
| RISKGAMMA function | Implements the gamma distribution in @RISK | =RISKGAMMA (*alpha, beta*) | 659 |
| RISKDUNIFORM function | Generates a random number from a discrete set of possible values, where each has the same probability | =RISKDUNIFORM ({1,2,3,4}), for example | 709 |
| RANDBETWEEN function | Generates a random integer between two limits, where each is equally likely | =RANDBETWEEN(1,6), for example | 709 |
| TopRank | Used for deterministic what-if analysis, to see which inputs affect an output most | Use TopRank ribbon | 714 |
| RISKVARY function | Used with TopRank to specify that an input should be varied over some range | RISKVARY (*base, minimum, maximum, rangetype, steps, distribution*) | 717 |

## PROBLEMS

### Skill-Building Problems

**34.** Your company assembles two components into a finished product. You get component 1 from one supplier and component 2 from another supplier. You just received an order for the product, so you immediately request a component 1 and a component 2 from the suppliers. The shipping times for the suppliers are independent random variables, each triangularly distributed with minimum 24 hours, most likely value 30 hours, and maximum 60 hours. (Assume for simplicity that your company operates 24 hours a day and can receive a shipment at any time of day.) You can start assembly any time after both components are received. The assembly time takes a triangularly distributed amount of time to complete, with minimum, most likely, and maximum times of 12 hours, 15 hours, and 30 hours, respectively. Finally, you ship the product to the customer, and this shipping time is triangularly distributed with parameters 24, 36, and 60 hours.

**a.** If the random times were not random but were instead replaced by their means, how many hours would it take for the customer to receive the product? (Note: The mean of a triangular distribution is the average of its three parameters.)

**b.** Using simulation, what can you say about the distribution of time (hours) it takes for the customer to receive the product? How does the mean of this distribution compare to your answer from part **a**?

**35.** You now have $3. You will toss a fair coin four times. Before each toss you can bet any amount of your money (including none) on the outcome of the toss. If heads comes up, you win the amount you bet. If tails comes up, you lose the amount you bet. Your goal is to reach $6. It turns out that you can maximize your chance of reaching $6 by betting either the money you have on hand or $6 minus the money you have on hand, whichever is smaller. Use simulation to estimate the probability that you will reach your goal by using this strategy.

**36.** You now have $1000, all of which is invested in a sports team. Each year there is a 60% chance that the value of the team will increase by 60% and a 40% chance that the value of the team will decrease by 60%. Estimate the mean and median value of your investment after 100 years. Explain the large difference between the estimated mean and median.

**37.** Suppose you have invested 25% of your portfolio in four different stocks. The mean and standard deviation of the annual return on each stock are as shown in the file **P12_37.xlsx**. The correlations between the annual returns on the four stocks are also shown in this file.
  **a.** What is the probability that your portfolio's annual return will exceed 20%?
  **b.** What is the probability that your portfolio will lose money during the course of a year?

**38.** A ticket from Indianapolis to Orlando on Deleast Airlines sells for $150. The plane can hold 100 people. It costs Deleast $8000 to fly an empty plane. Each person on the plane incurs variable costs of $30 (for food and fuel). If the flight is overbooked, anyone who cannot get a seat receives $300 in compensation. On average, 95% of all people who have a reservation show up for the flight. To maximize expected profit, how many reservations for the flight should Deleast book? (*Hint:* The function RISKBINOMIAL can be used to simulate the number who show up. It takes two arguments: the number of reservations booked and the probability that any ticketed person shows up.)

**39.** Based on Marcus (1990). The Balboa mutual fund has beaten the Standard and Poor's 500 during 11 of the last 13 years. People use this as an argument that you can beat the market. Here is another way to look at it that shows that Balboa's beating the market 11 out of 13 times is not unusual. Consider 50 mutual funds, each of which has a 50% chance of beating the market during a given year. Use simulation to estimate the probability that over a 13-year period, the best of the 50 mutual funds will beat the market for at least 11 out of 13 years. This probability turns out to exceed 40%, which means that the best mutual fund beating the market 11 out of 13 years is not an unusual occurrence!

**40.** You have been asked to simulate the cash inflows to a toy company for the next year. Monthly sales are independent random variables. Mean sales for the months January to March and October to December are $80,000, and mean sales for the months April to September are $120,000. The standard deviation for each month's sales is 20% of the month's mean sales. We model the method used to collect monthly sales as follows:
  ▪ During each month, a certain fraction of new sales are collected. All new sales not collected become one month overdue.

  ▪ During each month, a certain fraction of one-month overdue sales is collected. The remainder becomes two months overdue.
  ▪ During each month, a certain fraction of two-month overdue sales is collected. The remainder is written off as bad debt.

You are given the information in the file **P12_40.xlsx** from some past months. Using this information, build a simulation model that generates the total cash inflow for each month. Develop a simple forecasting model and build the error of your forecasting model into the simulation. Assuming that there are $120,000 of one-month-old sales outstanding and $140,000 of two-month-old sales outstanding during January, you are 95% sure that total cash inflow for the year will be between what two values?

**41.** Consider a device that requires two batteries to function. If either of these batteries dies, the device will not work. Currently, two brand new batteries are in the device, and we have three extra brand new batteries. Each battery, after it is placed in the device, lasts a random amount of time that is triangularly distributed with parameters 15, 18, and 25 (all expressed in hours). When any of the batteries in the device dies, it is immediately replaced by an extra (if an extra is still available). Use @RISK to simulate the time the device can last with the batteries currently available.

**42.** Consider a drill press containing three drill bits. The current policy (called **individual replacement**) is to replace a drill bit when it fails. The firm is considering changing to a **block replacement** policy in which all three drill bits are replaced whenever a single drill bit fails. Each time the drill press is shut down, the cost is $100. A drill bit costs $50, and the variable cost of replacing a drill bit is $10. Assume that the time to replace a drill bit is negligible. Also, assume that the time until failure for a drill bit follows an exponential distribution with a mean of 100 hours. This can be modeled in @RISK with the formula =RISKEXPON(100). Determine which replacement policy (block or individual replacement) should be implemented.

**43.** Freezco sells refrigerators. Any refrigerator that fails before it is three years old is replaced free. Of all refrigerators, 3% fail during their first year of operation; 5% of all one-year-old refrigerators fail during their second year of operation; and 7% of all two-year-old refrigerators fail during their third year of operation.
  **a.** Estimate the fraction of all refrigerators that will have to be replaced.
  **b.** It costs $500 to replace a refrigerator, and Freezco sells 10,000 refrigerators per year. If the warranty period were reduced to 2 years, how much per year in replacement costs would be saved?

**44.** The annual demand for Prizdol, a prescription drug manufactured and marketed by the NuFeel Company, is normally distributed with mean 50,000 and standard deviation 12,000. We assume that demand during each of the next 10 years is an independent random draw from this distribution. NuFeel needs to determine how large a Prizdol plant to build to maximize its expected profit over the next 10 years. If the company builds a plant that can produce $x$ units of Prizdol per year, it will cost \$16 for each of these $x$ units. NuFeel will produce only the amount demanded each year, and each unit of Prizdol produced will sell for \$3.70. Each unit of Prizdol produced incurs a variable production cost of \$0.20. It costs \$0.40 per year to operate a unit of capacity.

  **a.** Among the capacity levels of 30,000, 35,000, 40,000, 45,000, 50,000, 55,000, and 60,000 units per year, which level maximizes expected profit? Use simulation to answer this question.

  **b.** Using the capacity from your answer to part **a**, NuFeel can be 95% certain that *actual* profit for the 10-year period will be between what two values?

**45.** We are trying to determine the proper capacity level for a new electric car. A unit of capacity gives us the potential to produce one car per year. It costs \$10,000 to build a unit of capacity, and the cost is charged equally over the next 5 years. It also costs \$400 per year to maintain a unit of capacity (whether or not it is used). Each car sells for \$14,000 and incurs a variable production cost of \$10,000. The annual demand for the electric car during each of the next 5 years is believed to be normally distributed with mean 500,000 and standard deviation 100,000. The demands during different years are assumed to be independent. Profits are discounted at a 10% annual interest rate. We are working with a 5-year planning horizon. Capacity levels of 300,000, 400,000, 500,000, 600,000, and 700,000 are under consideration.

  **a.** Assuming we are risk neutral, use simulation to find the optimal capacity level.

  **b.** Using the answer to part **a**, there is a 5% chance that the *actual* discounted profit will exceed what value?

  **c.** Using the answer to part **a**, there is a 5% chance that the *actual* discounted profit will be less than what value?

  **d.** If we are risk averse, how might the optimal capacity level change?

**46.** Based on Kelly (1956). You currently have \$100. Each week, you can invest any amount of money you currently have in a risky investment. With probability 0.4, the amount you invest is tripled (e.g., if you invest \$100, you increase your asset position by \$300), and, with probability 0.6, the amount you invest is lost. Consider the following investment strategies:

- Each week invest 10% of your money.
- Each week invest 30% of your money.
- Each week invest 50% of your money.

Use @RISK to simulate 100 weeks of each strategy 1000 times. Which strategy appears to be best? (In general, if you can multiply your investment by $M$ with probability $p$ and lose your investment with probability $q$, you should invest a fraction $[(p(M-1) - q]/(M-1)$ of your money each week. This strategy maximizes the expected growth rate of your fortune and is known as the **Kelly criterion**.) [*Hint:* If an initial wealth of $I$ dollars grows to $F$ dollars in 100 weeks, then the weekly growth rate, labeled $r$, satisfies $F = (1 + r)^{100} I$, so that $r = (F/I)^{1/100} - 1$.]

**47.** Amanda has 30 years to save for her retirement. At the beginning of each year, she puts \$5000 into her retirement account. At any point in time, all of Amanda's retirement funds are tied up in the stock market. Suppose the annual return on stocks follows a normal distribution with mean 12% and standard deviation 25%. What is the probability that at the end of 30 years, Amanda will have reached her goal of having \$1,000,000 for retirement? Assume that if Amanda reaches her goal *before* 30 years, she will stop investing. (*Hint:* Each year you should keep track of Amanda's beginning cash position—for year 1, this is \$5000—and Amanda's ending cash position. Of course, Amanda's ending cash position for a given year is a function of her beginning cash position and the return on stocks for that year. To estimate the probability that Amanda will meet her goal, use an IF statement that returns 1 if she meets her goal and 0 otherwise.)

## Skill-Extending Problems

**48.** Consider an oil company that bids for the rights to drill in offshore areas. The value of the right to drill in a given offshore area is highly uncertain, as are the bids of the competitors. This problem demonstrates the "winner's curse." The winner's curse states that the optimal bidding strategy entails bidding a substantial amount below your assumed value of the product for which you are bidding. The idea is that if you do not bid under your assumed value, your uncertainty about the actual value of the product will often lead you to win bids for products on which you (after paying your high bid) lose money. Suppose Royal Conch Oil (RCO) is trying to determine a profit-maximizing bid for the right to drill on an offshore oil site. The actual value of the right to drill is unknown, but it is equally likely to be any value between \$10 million and \$110 million. Seven competitors will bid against RCO. Each bidder's (including RCO's) estimate of the value of the drilling rights is equally likely to assume any number between 50% and 150% of the actual value.

Based on past history, RCO believes that each competitor is equally likely to bid between 40% and 60% of its value estimate. Given this information, what fraction (within 0.05) of RCO's estimated value should it bid to maximize its expected profit? (*Note:* Use the RISKUNIFORM function to model the actual value of the field and the competitors' bids.)

49. You begin year 1 with $500. At the beginning of each year, you put half of your money under your mattress and invest the other half in Whitewater stock. During each year, there is a 50% chance that the Whitewater stock will double, and there is a 50% chance that you will lose half of your investment. To illustrate, if the stock doubles during the first year, you will have $375 under the mattress and $375 invested in Whitewater during year 2. You want to estimate your annual return over a 50-year period. If you end with $F$ dollars, then your annual return is $(F/500)^{1/50} - 1$. For example, if you end with $10,000, your annual return is $20^{1/50} - 1 = 0.062$, or 6.2%. Run 1000 replications of an appropriate simulation. Based on the results, you can be 95% certain that your annual return will be between what two values?

50. Mary Higgins is a freelance writer with enough spare time on her hands to play the stock market fairly seriously. Each morning, she observes the change in stock price of a particular stock and decides whether to buy or sell, and if so, how many shares to buy or sell. We assume that on day 1, she has $100,000 cash to invest and that she spends part of this to buy her first 500 shares of the stock at the current price of $50 per share. From that point on, she follows a fairly simple "buy low, sell high" strategy. Specifically, if the price has increased three days in a row, she sells 25% of her shares of the stock. If the price has increased two days in a row (but not three), she sells 10% of her shares. In the other direction, if the price has decreased three days in a row, she buys 25% more shares, whereas if the price has decreased only two days in a row, she buys 10% more shares. We assume a fairly simple model of stock price changes, as described in the file **P12_50.xlsx**. Each day, the price can change by as much as $2 in either direction, and the probabilities depend on the previous price change: decrease, increase, or no change. Build a simulation model of this strategy for a period of 75 trading days. (You can assume that the stock price on each of the previous two days was $49.) Decide on interesting @RISK output cells, and then run @RISK and report your findings.

51. You are considering a 10-year investment project. At present, the expected cash flow each year is $1000. Suppose, however, that each year's cash flow is normally distributed with mean equal to *last* year's actual cash flow and standard deviation $100. For example, suppose that the actual cash flow in year 1 is $1200.

Then year 2 cash flow is normal with mean $1200 and standard deviation $100. Also, at the end of year 1, your best guess is that each later year's expected cash flow will be $1200.

a. Estimate the mean and standard deviation of the NPV of this project. Assume that cash flows are discounted at a rate of 10% per year.

b. Now assume that the project has an abandonment option. At the end of each year, you can abandon the project for the value given in the file **P12_51.xlsx**. For example, suppose that year 1 cash flow is $400. Then at the end of year 1, you expect cash flow for each remaining year to be $400. This has an NPV of less than $6200, so you should abandon the project and collect $6200 at the end of year 1. Estimate the mean and standard deviation of the project with the abandonment option. How much would you pay for the abandonment option? (*Hint:* You can abandon a project at most once. Thus in year 5, for example, you abandon only if the sum of future expected NPVs is less than the year 5 abandonment value, *and* the project has not yet been abandoned. Also, after you abandon the project, the actual cash flows for future years will be 0. So the future cash flows after abandonment should disappear.)

52. Toys For U is developing a new Hannah Montana doll. The company has made the following assumptions:
- It is equally likely that the doll will sell for 2, 4, 6, 8, or 10 years.
- At the beginning of year 1, the potential market for the doll is 1 million. The potential market grows by an average of 5% per year. Toys For U is 95% sure that the growth in the potential market during any year will be between 3% and 7%. It uses a normal distribution to model this.
- The company believes its share of the potential market during year 1 will be at worst 20%, most likely 40%, and at best 50%. It uses a triangular distribution to model this.
- The variable cost of producing a doll during year 1 is equally likely to be $4 or $6.
- Each year the selling price and variable cost of producing the doll will increase by 5%. The current selling price is $10.
- The fixed cost of developing the doll (which is incurred right away, at time 0) is equally likely to be $4, $8, or $12 million.
- Right now, one competitor is in the market. During each year that begins with four or fewer competitors, there is a 20% chance that a new competitor will enter the market.
- We determine year $t$ sales (for $t > 1$) as follows. Suppose that at the end of year $t - 1$, $n$ competitors are present. Then we assume that during year $t$, a fraction $0.9 - 0.1n$ of the company's loyal

customers (last year's purchasers) will buy a doll during the next year, and a fraction $0.2 - 0.04n$ of customers currently in the market who did not purchase a doll last year will purchase a doll from the company this year. We can now generate a prediction for year $t$ sales. Of course, this prediction will not be exactly correct. We assume that it is sure to be accurate within 15%, however. (There are different ways to model this. You can choose any method that is reasonable.)

**a.** Use @RISK to estimate the expected NPV of this project.

**b.** Use the percentiles in @RISK's output to find an interval so that you are 95% certain that the company's *actual* NPV will be within this interval.

**53.** Dord Motors is considering whether to introduce a new model called the Racer. The profitability of the Racer will depend on the following factors:

- The fixed cost of developing the Racer is equally likely to be $3 or $5 billion.
- Year 1 sales are normally distributed with mean 200,000 and standard deviation 50,000. Year 2 sales are normally distributed with mean equal to actual year 1 sales and standard deviation 50,000. Year 3 sales are normally distributed with mean equal to actual year 2 sales and standard deviation 50,000.
- The selling price in year 1 is $13,000. The year 2 selling price will be

$$1.05[\text{year 1 price} + \$30(\% \text{ diff1})]$$

where % *diff*1 is the percentage by which actual year 1 sales differ from expected year 1 sales. The 1.05 factor accounts for inflation. For example, if the year 1 sales figure is 180,000, which is 10% below the expected year 1 sales, then the year 2 price will be

$$1.05[13,000 + 30(-10)] = \$13,335$$

Similarly, the year 3 price will be

$$1.05[\text{year 2 price} + \$30(\% \text{ diff2})]$$

where % diff 2 is the percentage by which actual year 2 sales differ from expected year 2 sales.

- The variable cost is equally likely to be $5000, $6000, $7000, or $8000 during year 1 and is assumed to increase by 5% each year.

**a.** Your goal is to estimate the NPV of the new car during its first 3 years. Assume that cash flows are discounted at 10%. Simulate 1000 trials and estimate the mean and standard deviation of the NPV for the first 3 years of sales. Also, determine an interval so that you are 95% certain that the NPV of the Racer during its first 3 years of operation will be within this interval.

**b.** Rerun the simulation from part **a**, but now assume that the fixed cost of developing the Racer is triangularly distributed with minimum, most likely, and maximum values $3, $4, and $5 billion. Also, assume that the variable cost per car in year 1 is triangularly distributed with minimum, most likely, and maximum values $5000, $7000, and $8000.

**54.** Truckco produces the OffRoad truck. The company wants to gain information about the discounted profits earned during the next three years. During a given year, the total number of trucks sold in the United States is

$$500,000 + 50,000G - 40,000I$$

where $G$ is the percentage increase in gross domestic product during the year and $I$ is the percentage increase in the consumer price index during the year. During the next 3 years, Value Line has made the predictions listed in the file **P12_54.xlsx**. In the past, 95% of Value Line's $G$ predictions have been accurate within 6%, and 95% of Value Line's $I$ predictions have been accurate within 5%. We assume that the actual $G$ and $I$ values are normally distributed each year.

At the beginning of each year, a number of competitors might enter the trucking business. The probability distribution of the number of competitors that will enter the trucking business is also given in the file **P12_54.xlsx**. Before competitors join the industry at the beginning of year 1, there are two competitors. During a year that begins with $n$ competitors (after competitors have entered the business, but before any have left), OffRoad will have a market share given by $0.5(0.9)^n$. At the end of each year, there is a 20% chance that any competitor will leave the industry. The selling price of the truck and the production cost per truck are also given in the file **P12_54.xlsx**. Simulate 1000 replications of Truckco's profit for the next 3 years. Estimate the mean and standard deviation of the discounted 3-year profits, using a discount rate of 10%. You can use Excel's NPV function here. Do the same if there is a 50% chance during each year that any competitor will leave the industry.

**55.** Suppose you buy an electronic device that you operate continuously. The device costs you $100 and carries a 1-year warranty. The warranty states that if the device fails during its first year of use, you get a new device for no cost, and this new device carries exactly the same warranty. However, if it fails after the first year of use, the warranty is of no value. You need this device for the next 6 years. Therefore, any time the device fails outside its warranty period, you must pay $100 for another device of the same kind. (We assume the price does not increase during the 6-year period.) The time until failure for a device is gamma distributed with parameters $\alpha = 2$ and $\beta = 0.5$. (This implies a mean of 1 year.) Use @RISK to simulate the 6-year period. Include as outputs (1) your total cost, (2) the number of failures during the warranty period, and (3) the number of devices owned during the 6-year period.

56. Rework the previous problem for a case in which the 1-year warranty requires you to pay for the new device even if failure occurs during the warranty period. Specifically, if the device fails at time $t$, measured relative to the time it went into use, you must pay $100t$ for a new device. For example, if the device goes into use at the beginning of April and fails 9 months later, at the beginning of January, you must pay $75. The reasoning is that you got 9/12 of the warranty period for use, so you should pay that fraction of the total cost for the next device. As before, however, if the device fails outside the warranty period, you must pay the full $100 cost for a new device.

57. Based on Hoppensteadt and Peskin (1992). The following model (the Reed–Frost model) is often used to model the spread of an infectious disease. Suppose that at the beginning of period 1, the population consists of 5 diseased people (called infectives) and 95 healthy people (called susceptibles). During any period, there is a 0.05 probability that a given infective person will encounter a particular susceptible. If an infective encounters a susceptible, there is a 0.5 probability that the susceptible will contract the disease. An infective survives an average of 10 periods with the disease. To model this, we assume that there is a 0.10 probability that an infective dies during any given period. Use @RISK to model the evolution of the population over 100 periods. Use your results to answer the following questions. [*Hint:* During any period, there is a probability $0.05(0.50) = 0.025$ that an infective will infect a particular susceptible. Thus the probability that a particular susceptible is not infected during a period is $(1 - 0.025)^n$, where $n$ is the number of infectives present at the end of the previous period.]
   a. What is the probability that the population will die out?
   b. What is the probability that the disease will die out?
   c. On the average, what percentage of the population becomes infected by the end of period 100?
   d. Suppose that people use infection protection during encounters. The use of protection reduces the probability that a susceptible will contract the disease during a single encounter with an infective from 0.50 to 0.10. Now answer parts a to c under the assumption that everyone uses protection.

58. Chemcon has taken over the production of Nasacure from a rival drug company. Chemcon must build a plant to produce Nasacure by the beginning of 2007. After the plant is built, the plant's capacity cannot be changed. Each unit sold brings in $10 in revenue. The

fixed cost (in dollars) of producing a plant that can produce $x$ units per year of the drug is $5,000,000 + 10x$. This cost is assumed to be incurred at the end of 2007. In fact, we assume that all cost and sales cash flows are incurred at the ends of the respective years. If a plant of capacity $x$ is built, the variable cost of producing a unit of Nasacure is $6 - 0.1(x - 1,000,000)/100,000$. For example, a plant capacity of 1,100,000 units has a variable cost of $5.90. Each year, a plant operating cost of $1 per unit of capacity is also incurred. Based on a forecasting sales model from the previous 10 years, Chemcon forecasts that demand in year $t$, $D_t$, is related to the demand in the previous year, $D_{t-1}$, by the equation

$$D_t = 67,430 + 0.985D_{t-1} + e_t$$

where $e_t$ is a random term that is normally distributed with mean 0 and standard deviation 29,320. The demand in 2006 was 1,011,000 units. If demand for a year exceeds production capacity, all demand in excess of plant capacity is lost. Chemcon wants to determine a capacity level that will maximize expected discounted profits (using a discount rate of 10%) for the time period 2007 to 2016. Use simulation to help it do so.

59. The Tinkan Company produces 1-pound cans for the Canadian salmon industry. Each year, the salmon spawn during a 24-hour period and must be canned immediately. Tinkan has the following agreement with the salmon industry. The company can deliver as many cans as it chooses. Then the salmon are caught. For each can by which Tinkan falls short of the salmon industry's needs, the company pays the industry a $2 penalty. Cans cost Tinkan $1 to produce and are purchased for $2 per can. If any cans are left over, they are returned to Tinkan and the company reimburses the industry $2 for each extra can. These extra cans are put in storage for next year. Each year a can is held in storage, a carrying cost equal to 20% of the can's production cost is incurred. It is well known that the number of salmon harvested during a year is strongly related to the number of salmon harvested the previous year. In fact, using past data, Tinkan estimates that the harvest size in year $t$, $H_t$ (measured in the number of cans required), is related to the harvest size in the previous year, $H_{t-1}$, by the equation

$$H_t = H_{t-1}e_t$$

where $e_t$ is normally distributed with mean 1.02 and standard deviation 0.10.

Tinkan plans to use the following production strategy. For some value of $x$, it will produce enough cans at the beginning of year $t$ to bring its inventory up to $x + \hat{H}_t$, where $\hat{H}_t$ is the predicted harvest size in year $t$. Then it will deliver these cans to the salmon industry. For example, if it uses $x = 100,000$, the predicted harvest size is 500,000 cans, and 80,000 cans are already in inventory, then Tinkan will produce and deliver 520,000 cans. Given that the harvest size for the previous year was 550,000 cans, use simulation to help Tinkan develop a production strategy that will maximize its expected profit over the next 20 years.

60. You are unemployed, 21 years old, and searching for a job. Until you accept a job offer, the following situation occurs. At the beginning of each year, you receive a job offer. The annual salary associated with the job offer is equally likely to be any number between $20,000 and $100,000. You must immediately choose whether to accept the job offer. If you accept an offer with salary $x$, you receive $x$ per year while you work (we assume you retire at age 70), including the current year. Assume that cash flows are discounted so that a cash flow received 1 year from now has a present value of 0.9. You have adopted the following policy. You will accept the first job offer that exceeds $w$ dollars.
   a. Use simulation to determine the value of $w$ (within $10,000) that maximizes the expected NPV of earnings you will receive the rest of your working life.
   b. Repeat part **a**, assuming now that you get a 3% raise in salary every year after the first year you accept the job.

61. Based on Bukiet et al. (1997). Many Major League teams (including Oakland, Boston, LA Dodgers, and Toronto) use mathematical models to evaluate baseball players. A common measure of a player's offensive effectiveness is the number of runs generated per inning (RPI) if a team were made up of nine identical copies of this player. For example, which team would score more runs: a team with nine copies of Ichiro Suzuki or a team with nine copies of Manny Ramirez? We can use simulation to answer this question. Let's consider a simplified baseball game in which each plate appearance results in one of six outcomes:
   - **Out:** Runners do not advance.
   - **Walk:** Runners advance if forced.
   - **Single:** Runner on first moves to second. All other runners score.
   - **Double:** Runner on first moves to third. All other runners score.
   - **Triple:** All runners on base score.
   - **Home Run:** All runners and batter score.

   A team gets three outs per inning. You are given the data in the file **P12_61.xlsx** on Ichiro Suzuki and Manny Ramirez from the 2004 season. Use simulation to determine which hitter is more valuable according to the RPI criterion.

62. In this version of "dice blackjack," you toss a single die repeatedly and add up the sum of your dice tosses. Your goal is to come as close as possible to a total of 7 without going over. You may stop at any time. If your total is 8 or more, you lose. If your total is 7 or less, the "house" then tosses the die repeatedly. The house stops as soon as its total is 4 or more. If the house totals 8 or more, you win. Otherwise, the higher total wins. If there is a tie, the house wins. Consider the following strategies:
   - Keep tossing until your total is 3 or more.
   - Keep tossing until your total is 4 or more.
   - Keep tossing until your total is 5 or more.
   - Keep tossing until your total is 6 or more.
   - Keep tossing until your total is 7 or more.

   For example, suppose you keep tossing until your total is 4 or more. Here are some examples of how the game might go:
   - You toss a 2 and then a 3 and stop for total of 5. The house tosses a 3 and then a 2. You lose because a tie goes to the house.
   - You toss a 3 and then a 6. You lose.
   - You toss a 6 and stop. The house tosses a 3 and then a 2. You win.
   - You toss a 3 and then a 4 for total of 7. The house tosses a 3 and then a 5. You win.

   Note that only 4 tosses need to be generated for the house, but more tosses might need to be generated for you, depending on your strategy. Develop a simulation and run it for at least 1000 iterations for each of the strategies listed previously. For each strategy, what are the two values so that you are 95% sure that your probability of winning is between these two values? Which of the five strategies appears to be best?

63. It is now May 1, 2006, and GM is deciding whether to produce a new car. The following information is relevant.
   - The fixed cost of developing the car is incurred on January 1, 2007 and is assumed to follow a triangular distribution with smallest possible cost $300 million, most likely cost $400 million, and largest possible cost $700 million. The fixed cost is depreciated on a straight-line base during the years 2008 to 2011. The tax rate is 40%.
   - The car will first come to market during 2008 and is equally likely to sell for 6, 7, or 8 years.
   - The market size during 2008 will be between 20,000 and 90,000 cars. There is a 25% chance that the market size will be less than or equal to 50,000 cars, a 50% chance that it will be less than or equal to 70,000 cars, and a 75% chance that it will be less than or equal to 80,000 cars. After 2008, the market size is assumed to grow by 5% per year.
   - The market share during 2008 is assumed to follow a triangular distribution with most likely value 40%. There is a 5% chance that market share will be 20% or less and a 5% chance that it will be 50% or more. The market share during later years will

remain unchanged unless R&D makes a design improvement.

- There is a 50% chance that R&D will make a design improvement during 2009, a 20% chance that it will make a design improvement during 2010, and a 30% chance that no design improvement will occur. There will be at most one design improvement. During the year (if any) in which a design improvement occurs, GM's market share will increase to 50% above its current value. For example, suppose GM's market share at the beginning of 2009 is 30%. If a design improvement occurs during 2009, its market share during 2009 and all later years will be 45%.
- The car sells for $15,000 each year.
- The cost of producing the first $x$ cars is $10,000x^{0.9}$ dollars. This builds a learning curve into the cost structure.
- During 2008 and later years, cash flows are assumed to occur midyear.
- GM discounts its cash flows at 15% per year.

Use simulation to model GM's situation. Based on the simulation output, GM can be 95% sure that the NPV generated by the car is between what two values? Should GM produce this car? Explain why or why not. What are the two key drivers of the car's NPV? (*Hint*: The way the uncertainty about the market size in 2008 is stated suggests using the Cumul distribution from Section 11.3 in Chapter 11.)

64. It is January 1, 2006, and Lilly is considering developing a new drug called Dialis. We are given the following information
    - On March 15, 2006, Lilly incurs a fixed cost that is assumed to follow a triangular distribution with best case $10 million, most likely case $35 million, and worst case $50 million. This cost will be depreciated on a straight-line basis during the years 2007 to 2012.
    - The product will be sold during the years 2007 to 2012. In years 2007 and 2008, the product will be sold only in the United States, but starting in 2009, Lilly might sell the product overseas. The 2007 market size in the United States is assumed to be between 500,000 and 3,000,000 units. A market size of 1,000,000 units is assumed to be twice as likely as a market size of 700,000, and a market size of 2,000,000 units is assumed to be three times as likely as a market size of 700,000.
    - Lilly's 2007 market share is assumed to follow a triangular distribution with worst case 10%, most likely case 20%, and best case 30%. Lilly assumes that its market share will remain the same unless a competitor enters the market.
    - The growth rate in market size in later years is assumed to be the same each year. In the first year, it is assumed to follow a triangular distribution with worst case 5% annual growth, most likely case 12% annual growth, and best case 14% annual growth.

- A single competitor might enter the market. Each year, the competitor has a 30% chance of entering the market, assuming it has not already entered. The year after entering the market, a competitor causes a permanent loss of 40% of Lilly's market share. For example, suppose the competitor enters in 2008, and Lilly's share was 20%. Then in the years 2009 to 2012, its market share will be 12%.
- At the beginning of 2009, Lilly will decide whether to sell Dialis overseas. If no competitor has entered the market by the end of 2008, there is a 70% chance that Lilly will sell the product overseas. If a competitor has entered the market by the end of 2008, there is only a 30% chance that Lilly will sell the product overseas. Lilly's market share overseas will equal its market share in the United States. It estimates that the overseas market is 25% of world sales for drugs of this type. (The other 75% is U.S. sales.)
- Each year the product sells for $120 and incurs a unit cost of $80.
- Cash flows are discounted at 15% annually, and profits are taxed at 40%.
- Cash flows for years 2007 to 2012 take place midyear.

Use simulation to model Lilly's situation. Based on the simulation output, Lilly can be 95% sure the NPV for this project is between what two numbers? Would you go ahead with this project? Explain why or why not. (*Hint*: The way the uncertainty about the market size in 2007 is stated suggests using the General distribution from Section 11.3 in Chapter 11.)

65. It is January 1, 2006, and Merck is trying to determine whether to continue development of a new drug. The following information is relevant. You can assume that all cash flows occur at the ends of the respective years.
    - Clinical trials (the trials where the drug is tested on humans) are equally likely to be completed in 2007 or 2008.
    - There is an 80% chance that clinical trials will succeed. If these trials fail, the FDA will not allow the drug to be marketed.
    - The cost of clinical trials is assumed to follow a triangular distribution with best case $100 million, most likely case $150 million, and worst case $250 million. Clinical trial costs are incurred at the end of the year clinical trials are completed.
    - If clinical trials succeed, the drug will be sold for five years, earning a profit of $6 per unit sold.
    - If clinical trials succeed, a plant will be built during the same year trials are completed. The cost of the plant is assumed to follow a triangular distribution with best case $1 billion, most likely case

$1.5 billion, and worst case $2.5 billion. The plant cost will be depreciated on a straight-line basis during the five years of sales.

- Sales begin the year after successful clinical trials. Of course, if the clinical trials fail, there are no sales.
- During the first year of sales, Merck believe sales will be between 100 million and 200 million units. Sales of 140 million units are assumed to be three times as likely as sales of 120 million units, and sales of 160 million units are assumed to be twice as likely as sales of 120 million units.
- Merck assumes that for years 2 to 5 that the drug is on the market, the growth rate will be the same each year. The annual growth in sales will be between 5% and 15%. There is a 25% chance that the annual growth will be 7% or less, a 50% chance that it will be 9% or less, and a 75% chance that it will be 12% or less.
- Cash flows are discounted 15% per year, and the tax rate is 40%.

Use simulation to model Merck's situation. Based on the simulation output, would you recommend that Merck continue developing? Explain your reasoning. What are the three key drivers of the project's NPV? (*Hint*: The way the uncertainty about the first year sales is stated suggests using the General distribution from Section 11.3 in Chapter 11. Similarly, the way the uncertainty about the annual growth rate is stated suggests using the Cumul distribution from Section 11.3.)

66. Nucleon is trying to determine whether to produce a new drug that makes pigs healthier. The product will be sold in the years 2007 to 2011. The following information is relevant:
    - A fixed cost is incurred on 1/1/2006 and will be between $1 billion and $5 billion. There is a 20% chance the fixed cost will be less than or equal to $2 billion, a 60% chance that it will be less than or equal to $3 billion, and a 90% chance that it will be less than or equal to $4 billion. The fixed cost is depreciated on a straight-line basis during years 2007 to 2011.
    - The weighted average cost of capital is 15%. This is the rate Nucleon uses for discounting cash flows.
    - The market size in 2007 is 10 million pigs.

- During each of the years 2008 to 2011, the market size will grow at the same rate. This growth rate is assumed to follow a triangular distribution with best case 15%, most likely case 6%, and worst case 1%.
- The selling price is always $100 per unit, and the unit cost of production is always $16 per unit.
- In 2007, the average number of units of the drug sold for each pig will be between 1 and 2, with 1.3 and 1.7 being equally likely, and 1.5 being twice as likely as 1.3.
- There are three potential competitors. During each of the years 2007 to 2011, a competitor who has not entered the market has a 60% chance of entering the market.
- The year after a competitor enters the market, the average units sold per pig of the Nucleon drug drops by 20% for each competitor entering. For example, suppose that sales per pig are 1.5 units in 2007. If two competitors enter the market in 2007, Nucleon sales per pig drop to 0.9 in 2008.
- All cash flows other than the fixed cost on 1/1/2006 are incurred midyear.

Use simulation to model Nucleon's situation. Based on the simulation output, would you go ahead with this project? Explain why or why not? What are the three key drivers of the project's NPV? (*Hint*: The way the uncertainty about the fixed cost is stated suggests using the Cumul distribution from Section 11.3 in Chapter 11. Similarly, the way the uncertainty about the units sold per pig in 2007 is stated suggests using the General distribution from Section 11.3 in Chapter 11.)

67. Suppose you are using an underwater probe to search for a sunken ship. At any time in the search, your probe is located at some point $(x,y)$ in a grid, where the distance between lines in the grid is some convenient unit such as 100 meters. The sunken ship is at some unknown location on the grid, $(X,Y)$. If your probe is at $(x,y)$, you will move it to one of the eight nearby grid points $(x-1,y-1)$, $(x-1,y)$, $(x-1,y+1)$, $(x,y-1)$, $(x,y+1)$, $(x+1,y-1)$, $(x+1,y)$, or $(x+1,y+1)$, with probability 1/8 each, for the next search. If you start at $(0,0)$ and the ship is at $(5,2)$, use simulation to estimate the probability that you will find the ship in 100 moves or fewer.

Your next-door neighbor, Scott Jansen, has a 12-year-old daughter, and he wants to pay the tuition for her first year of college 6 years from now. The tuition for the first year will be $17,500. Scott has gone through his budget and finds that he can invest $200 per month for the next 6 years. Scott has opened accounts at two mutual funds. The first fund follows an investment strategy designed to match the return of the S&P 500. The second fund invests in short-term Treasury bills. Both funds have very low fees.

Scott has decided to follow a strategy in which he contributes a fixed fraction of the $200 to each fund. An adviser from the first fund suggested that each month he invest 80% of the $200 in the S&P 500 fund and the other 20% in the T-bill fund. The adviser explained that the S&P 500 has averaged much larger returns than the T-bill fund. Even though stock returns are risky investments in the short run, the risk would be fairly minimal over the longer 6-year period. An adviser from the second fund recommended just the opposite: invest 20% in the S&P 500 fund and 80% in T-bills, he said. Treasury bills are backed by the U.S. government. If you follow this allocation, he said, your average return will be lower, but at least you will have enough to reach your $17,500 target in 6 years.

Not knowing which adviser to believe, Scott has come to you for help.

## Questions

1. The file **College.xlsx** contains 261 monthly returns of the S&P 500 and Treasury bills from January 1970 through September 1991. (If you can find more recent data on the Web, feel free to use it.) Suppose that in each of the next 72 months (6 years), it is equally likely that any of the historical returns will occur. Develop a spreadsheet model to simulate the two suggested investment strategies over the 6-year period. Plot the value of each strategy over time for a single iteration of the simulation. What is the total value of each strategy after 6 years? Does either of the strategies reach the target?

2. Simulate 1000 iterations of the two strategies over the 6-year period. Create a histogram of the final fund values. Based on your simulation results, which of the two strategies would you recommend? Why?

3. Suppose that Scott needs to have $19,500 to pay for the first year's tuition. Based on the same simulation results, which of the two strategies would you recommend now? Why?

4. What other real-world factors might be important to consider in designing the simulation and making a recommendation? ∎

An investor is considering the purchase of zero-coupon U.S. Treasury bonds. A 30-year zero-coupon bond yielding 8% can be purchased today for $9.94. At the end of 30 years, the owner of the bond will receive $100. The yield of the bond is related to its price by the following equation:

$$P = \frac{100}{(1 + y)^t}$$

Here, $P$ is the price of the bond, $y$ is the yield of the bond, and $t$ is the maturity of the bond measured in years. Evaluating this equation for $t = 30$ and $y = 0.08$ gives $P = 9.94$.

The investor is planning to purchase a bond today and sell it one year from now. The investor is interested in evaluating the *return* on the investment in the bond. Suppose, for example, that the yield of the bond one year from now is 8.5%. Then the price of the bond one year later will be $9.39 [$= 100/(1 + 0.085)^{29}$]. The time remaining to maturity is $t = 29$ because one year has passed. The return for the year is $-5.54\%[=(9.39 - 9.94)/9.94]$.

In addition to the 30-year-maturity zero-coupon bond, the investor is considering the purchase of zero-coupon bonds with maturities of 2, 5, 10, or 20 years. All of the bonds are currently yielding 8.0%. (Bond investors describe this as a *flat yield curve*.) The investor cannot predict the future yields of the bonds with certainty. However, the investor believes that the yield of each bond one year from now can be modeled by a normal distribution with a mean of 8% and a standard deviation of 1%.

## Questions

1. Suppose that the yields of the five zero-coupon bonds are all 8.5% one year from today. What are the returns of each bond over the period?

2. Using a simulation with 1000 iterations, estimate the expected return of each bond over the year. Estimate the standard deviations of the returns.

3. Comment on the following statement: "The expected yield of the 30-year bond one year from today is 8%. At that yield, its price would be $10.73. The return for the year would be 8% [$=(10.73-9.94)/9.94$]. Hence, the average return for the bond should be 8% as well. A simulation isn't really necessary. Any difference between 8% and the answer in Question 2 must be due to simulation error." ∎

You are the CFO for Carco, a small car rental company. You are trying to get some idea of what Carco's financial and income statements will look like during the current year (year 0) and the next five years. The following relationships hold:

- Current assets for each year are a "current assets factor" multiplied by the year's sales, where the current assets factors for different years are independent normal random variables with mean 0.15 and standard deviation 0.02.
- Each year, "fixed assets at cost" equals depreciation plus fixed assets.
- Accumulated depreciation in year 0 equals $330. For year $t$ ($t \geq 1$), the depreciation equals the accumulated depreciation in year $t-1$ plus 10% of the fixed assets at cost for year $t-1$.
- Net fixed assets for year $t$ equals a "net fixed assets factor" multiplied by year $t$ sales, where the net fixed assets factors for different years are independent normal random variables with mean 0.77 and standard deviation 0.04.
- Total assets each year equals net fixed assets plus current assets.
- Current liabilities each year equals a "current liabilities factor" multiplied by the year's sales, where the current liabilities factor for different years are independent normal random variables with mean 0.08 and standard deviation 0.01.
- Long-term debt for year 0 is $280.
- For $t \geq 1$, the long-term debt for year $t$ is the year $t$ debt-equity ratio multiplied by the sum of year $t$ retained earnings and the year $t$ stock. Carco wants to have the following debt-equity ratios in years 1 through 5: 0.48, 0.46, 0.44, 0.42, and 0.40.
- Stock in year 0 is $450. For $t \geq 1$, year $t$ stock equals the sum of year $t-1$ stock and year $t$ new stock.
- Year 0 retained earnings equals $110. For $t \geq 1$, year $t$ retained earnings is the sum of year $t-1$ retained earnings and year $t$ retention.
- Each year, total liabilities is the sum of current liabilities, long-term debt, stock, and retained earnings.

- The amount of new stock issued each year must be enough to make total assets equal to total liabilities.
- The interest rate on current debt is 10.5%, and the interest rate on new debt is 9.5%. During each of the next five years, 20% of the current $280 in long-term debt must be paid off. Then the *total* amount of new debt during year $t$ is the year $t$ long-term debt minus the amount of initial debt still remaining.
- The new debt for year $t$ equals the *total* new debt for year $t$ minus the *total* new debt for year $t-1$.
- Year 0 sales equals $1000, and for $t \geq 1$, year $t$ sales equals a "sales factor" multiplied by year $t-1$ sales, where the sales factors for different years are independent normal random variables with mean 1.1 and standard deviation 0.05. (This does *not* mean that sales during successive years are independent!)
- Year $t$ expense equals an "expense factor" multiplied by year $t$ sales, where the expense factors for different years are independent normal random variables, with mean 0.80 and standard deviation 0.06.
- To calculate yearly interest payments, remember that interest is 10.5% on old debt and 9.5% on new debt.
- Depreciation for year 0 is $0, and for $t \geq 1$, year $t$ depreciation is 10% of the year $t-1$ fixed assets at cost.
- The before-tax profit each year is the sales minus the sum of expenses, interest payments, and depreciation.
- The tax rate is 47%.
- Dividends each year are 70% of after-tax profits.
- Retention each year is 30% of after-tax profits.

Set up a spreadsheet to model the current year (year 0) and next five years of Carco's financial future. Now simulate the firm's future. Use your output to answer the following questions. (*Note:* Your spreadsheet is allowed to contain circular references. There are many of these. For example, stock purchased each year depends on long-term debt, and long-term debt depends on stock. To resolve the circular references, use the Tools/Options menu item, click on the Calculations tab, check the Iterations box, and enter 20 as the Maximum Number of Iterations. This ensures that the spreadsheet will recalculate itself 20 times, which in turn ensures that the values in the spreadsheet will converge to the correct values.)

## Questions

1. There is only a 5% chance that total new debt will exceed what value?

2. On the average, total interest payments for the next five years will equal what value?

3. What is the probability that profit will be negative during year 5? ∎

© AP Photo/Gerry Broome

## INVENTORY DECISIONS IN DELL'S SUPPLY CHAIN

Dell is the largest computer-systems company based on estimates of global market share, and it is also the fastest growing of the major computer-systems companies competing in the business, education, government, and consumer markets. Dell's key to success is its strategy of bypassing retailers and selling its products directly to customers. Inventory management is extremely important to a company such as Dell. It not only incurs the usual costs for holding inventory—loss of interest from capital tied up in inventory and storage costs—but it also incurs huge costs from obsolescence. Because of the rapid changes in technology, many computer components lose from 0.5 to 2.0% of their value per *week*, so that a supply chain filled with yesterday's technology is practically worthless. Although Dell was aware of the costs of holding too much inventory, it didn't employ the types of mathematical models discussed in this chapter for managing its inventory until 1999, when it hired a group from the University of Michigan to study the problem. The results of this study appear in Kapuscinski et al. (2004).

Due to direct sales, Dell actually carries very little inventory. It assembles computer systems at its manufacturing plants in Austin, Texas, and ships them to customers in just a few days. Therefore, the plants carry virtually no inventory of finished goods. The inventory of computer components held at Dell's suppliers is a different story. Many of its suppliers are located in Southeast Asia. Because transportation of components from Asia to Texas can take anywhere from a week to a month, Dell requires its suppliers to keep inventory on hand in *revolvers*, small warehouses located within a few miles of Dell's assembly plants in Austin. Each revolver is shared by several suppliers who pay rents for using them. The key problem is to reduce inventory at the revolvers, while maintaining an adequate service level. (Dell's service level is about 98.8%, meaning that the components it needs are available about 98.8% of the time.) Dell shares its data on demand forecasts and actual demands with its suppliers and provides guidelines on how to manage their inventory levels at the revolvers. The authors recommended using an $(R, Q)$ ordering policy at the revolvers for one particular important component (called XDX in the paper to conceal its identity). This means that when inventory of XDX reaches the reorder point $R$, the supplier orders an amount $Q$.

When we discuss this type of ordering policy later in this chapter, we see that the difficult part is finding the appropriate reorder point $R$. During the time it takes an order to arrive at the revolver, called the *lead time*, Dell experiences demand for the component. To guard against stockouts in case this lead time demand is larger than expected, $R$ contains some safety stock. The amount of safety stock to hold depends on several factors: (1) the variance of demand during lead time, (2) the variance of the length of the lead time, and (3) the desired service levels. The first two of these are caused by uncertainty, whereas the third is based on costs. The authors performed a careful study of the causes of uncertainty. They broke demand into two parts: the aggregate demand for computer systems and the percentage of this aggregate demand for particular components such as XDX. Another source of uncertainty, at least to the suppliers, is the "pull" variance. This occurs when multiple suppliers supply the same component in their revolvers. Dell doesn't "pull" from these suppliers at a uniform rate. It might use supplier A's components for a few days and then use supplier B's for a few days. The authors examined how each of these sources of uncertainty affects the amount of safety stock (and hence excess inventory) prescribed by the model and suggested how better forecasting methods and information sharing can lead to improved results.

In terms of service level, the authors used a critical fractile analysis to determine an optimal service level. This critical fractile, also discussed later in this chapter, is a ratio of the cost of having too little inventory (for example, lost profit from a canceled order and increased shipping cost for not having a component when needed) to the cost of having too much inventory (for example, cost of capital tied up in excess inventory and price erosion from having obsolescent components).

The authors' recommendations went into effect in 1999 and are still being implemented. They estimated that Dell could reduce the current inventory from 10.5 days by about 38%. (Dell thinks of inventory in terms of days of supply rather than units on hand.) By removing approximately 4 days of safety-stock inventory, they estimate that the NPV of savings in XDX passing through the revolvers is about $43 million. Of course, as the authors' system is used for other important components, the savings will only increase. ∎

# 13.1 INTRODUCTION

Inventory management is one of the most important decisions faced by many companies. These companies include not only retailers that stock products for sale to customers like you, but also companies that supply other companies. They all face two competing pressures. The first is the pressure to have enough inventory on hand. The most obvious reason for this is that they do not want to run out of products that customers demand. Another prominent reason, however, is the fixed cost of ordering or producing, as we discuss throughout this chapter. If a fixed cost is incurred each time the company orders from its supplier, or a fixed cost is incurred each time a manufacturer produces a batch, where this cost does not depend on the order or batch size, then the company has an incentive to place large orders or produce large batches to minimize its annual fixed costs.[1]

The second pressure related to inventory management is the pressure to carry as little inventory as possible. The most obvious reasons for this are the cost of storing items and the interest costs involved in tying up money in inventory. If the company has to pay cash for items that end up sitting on the shelf for long periods of time, it loses potential interest on this money that could be invested elsewhere. Storage space is sometimes an issue as well. Some companies simply do not have the space to store as much inventory as they might like. For example, there is fierce competition for shelf space in supermarkets.

These two competing pressures are at the heart of most inventory models. Companies want to order enough, but they do not want to order too much. The balance is typically not easy to find, so we need models to determine the best ordering (or production) policy. An inventory problem can usually be broken up into two parts: (1) *how much* to order on each ordering opportunity and (2) *when* to order. When we assume that customer demand is known, the resulting models are called **deterministic** models. If customer demand is known and the order quantity has been determined, then specifying when the orders should be placed is relatively easy. A more realistic situation occurs when customer demand is uncertain. In this case, the decision on when to place orders becomes more difficult. We want to place them early enough so that the chance of running out before the orders arrive is fairly small. These more difficult problems require **probabilistic** inventory models.

Inventory management as an academic subject falls somewhere between management science and operations management. (We have been told that many instructors who use this book for a management science class do not cover this chapter because it is covered in the operations management course.) However, inventory management has long held an important place in management science, both in theory and in practice. There is plenty of evidence to support this claim. For example, a quick scan of *Interfaces* articles indicates the many real applications of inventory management and supply chain management. To name a few, three articles by Billington et al. (2004), Guide et al. (2005), and Laval et al. (2005) describe supply chain management at Hewlett-Packard; de Kok et al. (2005) describe how Philips Electronics synchronizes its supply chain to minimize the so-called "bullwhip" effect; Troyer et al. (2005) discuss inventory management and order fulfillment at Deere's Commercial and Consumer Equipment Division; and Bangash et al. (2004) discuss inventory requirements planning at Lucent Technologies. (Four of these articles appeared in the prize-winning issues of *Interfaces*.) So regardless of whether inventory management is discussed in a management science course or an operations management course, this topic is extremely important for today's global organizations. Inventory management also uses a variety of management science tools, many of which are described in this chapter.

---

[1] Some companies order products from vendors, whereas other companies produce the products they need. They both face similar inventory decisions. Throughout most of the chapter, we focus on companies that order from vendors, and we talk about order quantities, but similar models apply to companies that produce. They must decide on production quantities, often called batch sizes.

## 13.2 CATEGORIES OF INVENTORY MODELS

Researchers have analyzed many inventory models, both deterministic and probabilistic. We discuss only the most basic of these models, which have been used extensively in real applications. We begin by discussing several important issues and introducing some terminology.[2] Keep in mind, however, that the possible number of real-world situations that require inventory management is virtually unlimited. We list only some of the factors that are common to these situations.

### Deterministic versus Probabilistic Models

We have already mentioned the distinction between deterministic and probabilistic inventory models. In deterministic models, we assume that all inputs to the problem, particularly customer demand, are known when the decisions are made. In reality, a company must always forecast future demands with some type of forecasting model. The outputs of this forecasting model might include a mean demand and a standard deviation of demand. In deterministic models, however, we use only the mean and discard any information about the uncertainty, such as the standard deviation. This makes the resulting models simpler, but usually less realistic. Probabilistic models use this information about uncertainty explicitly. They are typically more difficult to analyze, but they tend to produce better decisions, especially when the level of uncertainty is high.

### External versus Internal Demand

A second factor in inventory modeling is whether demand for the product is generated *externally* or *internally*. **External demand** (or **independent demand**) occurs when the company that sells the product cannot directly control the extent or the timing of customer demand. For example, a retailer who orders products from a supplier and then waits to see how many customers request these products faces external demand. In these situations, we usually assume that ordering decisions are influenced by, but do not affect, customer demand.

In contrast, **internal demand** (or **dependent demand**) occurs in most assembly and manufacturing processes. Consider, for example, a company that manufactures laptop computers. The external demand is for the finished product, but the internal demand is for the components that go into the finished product. After the company forecasts the number of laptops its customers will demand, say, in the next month, it must then determine an appropriate production schedule for producing them. This production schedule will necessitate having inventories of the laptop's component parts and subassemblies on hand at the right time. In short, the production schedule determines, in large part, the inventory required for all of the individual parts and subassemblies. The coordination of all of these—ensuring that everything is on hand when it is needed—is a complex problem that we do not discuss in this book. However, it is a big part of supply chain management, a topic that is receiving more attention than ever from both academics and practitioners. The supply chain needs to ensure that the parts and subassemblies are available at the right time and the right place (and at the cheapest cost) for manufacturers to compete in today's business environment.

---

[2] Entire books, such as Cachon and Terwiesch (2005), discuss the general topic of matching supply with demand in much more depth than we provide here.

## Ordering versus Production

A third factor in inventory modeling is whether the company orders the products from a supplier or produces them internally. If the products are ordered, then there is typically an order **lead time,** the time elapsed from when the order is placed until it arrives. In ordering models, there is also usually a fixed cost (also called a **setup** or **ordering** cost) each time an order is placed, where this cost is independent of the order quantity. In contrast, if products are produced internally, there is also a lead time, the time it takes to produce a batch of items. This time is determined by a production rate, such as 10 units per hour, and possibly by a setup time, the fixed time necessary to set up any machinery to produce a specific type of product. As in ordering models, there can also be a setup cost each time a batch is produced, where this cost is independent of the batch size.

## Continuous versus Periodic Review

A fourth factor in inventory modeling is whether inventory is reviewed continuously or periodically. In **continuous review** models, the inventory is monitored continually and orders can be placed at any time. Typically, there is a **reorder point**—a specific inventory level—so that when the inventory on hand reaches this reorder point, an order is placed immediately. This could happen Wednesday afternoon, Friday morning, or any other time. In contrast, in **periodic review** models, there is some standard time, such as every Monday morning, when the inventory is reviewed and ordering decisions are made. Except possibly for emergency orders, these are the only times when orders are placed. Continuous review models can certainly be implemented, given today's computerized access to inventory levels in real time, and these models can result in lower annual costs than periodic review models. However, when a company stocks many products (hundreds or even thousands), it is often more convenient to order these, say, only on Monday mornings.

## Single-Product versus Multiple-Product Models

A final factor in inventory modeling concerns the number of products involved. Models that consider only a single product are conceptually and mathematically simpler, so we initially analyze single-product models. However, most companies have many different products that must be considered simultaneously. If the company orders these items from a supplier, then it may be wise to synchronize the orders in some way to minimize ordering costs. We look at one such synchronization model in Section 13.4.

# 13.3 TYPES OF COSTS IN INVENTORY MODELS

Companies face a number of costs when they manage inventories. Although the types of costs vary depending on the company and the situation, the following costs are typical.

## Ordering (or Setup) Cost

*The setup cost is independent of the order (or production batch) size.*

We have already mentioned the **ordering** (or **setup**) cost. This is the fixed cost incurred every time an order is placed or a batch is produced. The ordering cost is independent of the amount ordered or produced. This ordering cost includes the cost of paperwork and billing each time an order is placed and could include other costs as well, such as paying a truck driver to deliver the order to the company's warehouse. If the product is produced rather than ordered, this cost can include the cost to set up equipment.

## Unit Purchasing (or Production) Cost

The **unit purchasing** (or **production**) cost is the cost for each additional unit purchased or produced (often referred to as the **variable** cost). For example, to order 100 units, the company might have to pay a setup cost of $500 plus $3 per unit, for a total of $800. Here, $3 is the unit purchasing cost. If the company produces the product, then the unit production cost includes the cost of raw materials and the labor cost for each unit produced. Sometimes the unit purchasing cost is not constant but changes according to a quantity discount schedule. We consider a quantity discount model in Section 13.4.

## Holding (or Carrying) Cost

*A large part of the holding cost is the cost of capital tied up in inventory.*

The **holding** (or **carrying**) cost is the cost that motivates the company to keep less inventory on hand. This cost generally has two components, the **financial holding** cost and the **nonfinancial holding** cost. The nonfinancial holding cost is usually the cost of storing the product. For example, this might be the cost of renting warehouse space. The financial holding cost is the opportunity cost of having money tied up in inventory when that money could instead be earning interest in other investments. There can be other holding costs, such as spoilage, insurance, and overhead, which vary according to the amount and type of inventory on hand.

## Shortage (or Penalty) Cost

We also need to measure the cost of running out of inventory. This **shortage** (or **penalty**) cost is often the most difficult cost to measure. For one thing, it depends on how the company handles shortages. At one extreme, there are **lost sales** models, where any demands that occur when inventory is zero are lost; these customers take their business elsewhere. At the other extreme, there are **complete backlogging** models, where demands that occur when inventory is zero are satisfied as soon as a new order arrives.[3] Both of these models— or any in between, called **partial backlogging** models—have negative effects for the company. There is lost revenue, loss of goodwill, and possibly expedited shipments with higher costs. Unfortunately, it can be difficult to put a dollar value on the "cost" of running out of inventory. An alternative is to specify a **service level,** such as meeting at least 95% of the demand on time.

## Revenue

Finally, there is the **selling price** of the product and the resulting revenue to the company. In many situations, the revenue is a fixed amount that is not affected by any ordering decisions. This occurs when the selling price is constant and the company intends to satisfy all demand eventually. In such cases, we can add the total revenue to the relevant costs, but it does not affect any ordering or production decisions. On the other hand, there are times, such as in lost sales models, when the selling price affects the ordering decision. Here the shortage cost depends on the amount of revenue lost by not having enough inventory on hand, and this clearly depends on the selling price.

---

[3] We also say the excess demand is **backordered.** Both terms, backlog and backorder, mean that these orders are kept on the books and are satisfied when additional shipments arrive.

# 13.4 ECONOMIC ORDER QUANTITY (EOQ) MODELS

We first examine a class of models called **economic order quantity** (EOQ) models. These are the most basic of all the inventory planning models. Developed originally in 1915 by F. W. Harris of Westinghouse Corporation, they are also among the earliest management science models. Despite their simplicity, numerous companies have applied these models, and they continue to play a prominent role in inventory management.

We begin by studying the most basic EOQ model. Then we examine several interesting variations of this basic model. All of these models make the following assumptions:

*A crucial assumption of the basic EOQ model is that demand occurs at a constant known rate through time.*

- A company orders a single product from a supplier and sells this product to its customers.
- Orders can be placed at any time (continuous review).
- There is a constant, known demand rate for the product, usually expressed in units per year (annual demand).
- There is a constant, known lead time for delivery of the product from the supplier.
- There is a fixed ordering cost each time the product is ordered, independent of the size of the order.
- The price the company charges for the product is fixed.
- The annual holding cost is proportional to the average amount of inventory on hand.

The constant demand rate means, for example, that if the yearly demand is 52,000 units, then each week's demand is approximately 1000 units—there are no peaks or valleys during the year. The known lead time means that if the company places an order on Monday and the lead time is 3 days, then the order arrives, with certainty, on Thursday. We discuss the holding cost in more detail shortly.

## The Basic EOQ Model

The most basic EOQ model adds the following two assumptions.

- No stockouts are allowed; that is, the company never allows itself to run out of inventory.
- The unit cost of purchasing the product from the supplier is constant. In particular, no quantity discounts are available.

These assumptions have important implications. Because the demand rate and lead time are assumed known, the company can *ensure* that it always has enough on hand to meet demand on time. The main decision is whether to order small amounts frequently or to order large amounts infrequently. The former results in large fixed costs and small holding costs (less inventory on hand), whereas the latter results in the opposite. The EOQ analysis balances these two competing forces.

We now analyze this basic EOQ model in the following example.

---

**FUNDAMENTAL INSIGHT**

### Importance of EOQ

The basic EOQ model and its variations are among the simplest models discussed in this book, and they have been known for close to a century. However, they capture the essence of many companies' problems, and they are still in wide use today. As with most models for managing inventory, they balance the costs of ordering too frequently and not ordering frequently enough.

---

EXAMPLE | **13.1 ORDERING CAMERAS AT MACHEY'S**

Machey's Department Store sells 1200 cameras per year, and the demand pattern throughout the year is very steady. The store orders its cameras from a regional warehouse, and it usually takes a week for the cameras to arrive after an order has been placed. Each time an order is placed, an ordering cost of $125 is incurred. The store pays $100 for each camera and sells them for $130 apiece. There is no physical storage cost, but the store's annual cost of capital is estimated at 8% per year—that is, it can earn 8% on any excess cash it invests. The store wants to determine how often it should order cameras, when it should place orders, and how many cameras it should order in each order.

**Objective**    To determine when to order and how much to order so that the store never runs out of cameras and profit is maximized.

### WHERE DO THE NUMBERS COME FROM?

Throughout this chapter, we refer you back to Sections 13.2 and 13.3 for a general discussion of the inputs to these inventory problems. For this reason, we do not include this "Where Do the Numbers Come From?" section in later examples.

## Solution

We first discuss some basic quantities and relationships. Let $D = 1200$ be the annual demand. Because demand occurs steadily through the year, Machey's places an order every time its inventory gets sufficiently low. Therefore, there are really two decisions to make: (1) when to order, and (2) how much to order. The first of these is straightforward. Because the lead time is 1 week, and the demand in a week is $D/52$, or about 23, Machey's should place an order when its inventory drops to 23 cameras. This way, the order will arrive just as inventory runs out.

The second decision concerns the amount of each order. We let $Q$ be the quantity ordered each time an order is placed. This is the primary decision variable. After we know $Q$, the number of orders per year is given by

$$\text{Number of orders per year} = D/Q \qquad (13.1)$$

Equivalently, the time between orders (measured as a fraction of a year) is $Q/D$. For example, if $Q = 300$, Machey's places $D/Q = 4$ orders per year, and the time between orders is $Q/D = 0.25$ year (3 months). A graph of the company's inventory through time appears in Figure 13.1. The key aspect in this figure is that the inventory level jumps up to $Q$ whenever an order arrives and decreases linearly (due to demand) until the next order arrives.

**Figure 13.1**

Inventory Level for the Basic EOQ Model

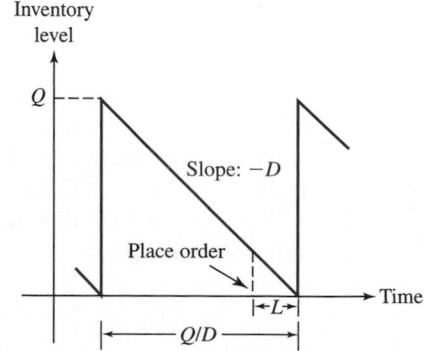

The problem is to find an order quantity $Q$ that maximizes Machey's annual profit. There are several components of the annual profit. First, each time Machey's places an order, it incurs a fixed ordering cost, labeled $K$. For this example, $K = \$125$. Because $D/Q$ orders are placed per year, the annual ordering cost is

$$\text{Annual ordering cost} = KD/Q \qquad (13.2)$$

On top of this, Machey's pays a variable cost, labeled $c$, for each camera it purchases. Here, $c = \$100$. Because the annual demand is $D = 1200$ and all demand must be met, the annual variable cost is $cD = \$120,000$. Note that this cost does *not* depend on $Q$. Similarly, the company's revenue from each camera, labeled $r$, is $r = \$130$, so its annual revenue is $rD$. This is also unaffected by the order quantity $Q$.

Now we consider the annual holding cost. There is no cost for physically storing the cameras, but Machey's loses money from potential investments by having excess cash tied up in inventory. If we let $i$ be Machey's annual cost of capital, where $i = 0.08$ (8%), then it can be shown from a net present value argument that the relevant annual holding cost is $i$ multiplied by the average monetary value of inventory, where this average is over the entire year. Because the inventory decreases linearly from $Q$ to 0 between orders, the average level of inventory at a typical point in time is $(Q + 0)/2 = Q/2$, which implies that the average monetary value of inventory is $cQ/2$. Therefore, the annual holding cost from money tied up in inventory is

$$\text{Annual financial holding cost} = icQ/2 \qquad (13.3)$$

[In general, if there is also a storage cost of $s$ dollars per unit held in storage per year, then the total annual holding cost is $(s + ic)Q/2$. In the inventory literature, the combined unit holding cost, $(s + ic)$, is usually labeled $h$.]

We can now develop a spreadsheet to optimize Machey's annual profit.

## DEVELOPING THE SPREADSHEET MODEL

The spreadsheet model appears in Figure 13.2. (See the file **Basic EOQ.xlsx**.) In the interest of space, we do not list the individual steps for developing this model. All of the formulas are based directly on equations (13.1), (13.2), and (13.3). For example, the annual holding cost, determined by equation (13.3), is calculated in cell B18 with the formula

=Annual_interest_rate*Unit_purchasing_cost*Order_quantity/2

Note that the only changing cell is the Order_quantity cell. It drives all of the quantities below it except for the annual purchase cost and the annual revenue, which do not depend on the order quantity. (They could actually be omitted from the model, although Machey's would then not be able to see its overall profit.) Also, note that we have included the lead time in the spreadsheet model, although it is never used in any formulas. Its only role is to determine *when* to order. We already saw that Machey's should place an order when its inventory drops to 23 cameras.

## USING SOLVER

The Solver setup (not shown) is particularly simple. We maximize annual profit with a single changing cell, the order quantity cell. There are *no* constraints other than nonnegativity of the order quantity. (If you like, you can also constrain the order quantity to be an integer. However, this is not really necessary. For all practical purposes, it suffices to round the Solver solution to the nearest integer.) Also, the Assume Linear Model box should *not* be checked because the decision variable $Q$ appears in the denominator of equation (13.2) for the annual ordering cost. This makes the model nonlinear.

Figure 13.2

The Basic EOQ
Model

| | A | B | C | D | E |
|---|---|---|---|---|---|
| 1 | Machey's EOQ model | | | | |
| 2 | | | | | |
| 3 | Inputs | | | Range names used: | |
| 4 | Fixed ordering cost | $125 | | Annual_demand | =Model!$B$8 |
| 5 | Annual interest rate | 8% | | Annual_interest_rate | =Model!$B$5 |
| 6 | Unit purchasing cost | $100 | | Annual_profit | =Model!$B$21 |
| 7 | Selling price per unit | $130 | | Fixed_ordering_cost | =Model!$B$4 |
| 8 | Annual demand | 1200 | | Order_quantity | =Model!$B$12 |
| 9 | Lead time in years | 1/52 | | Orders_per_year | =Model!$B$13 |
| 10 | | | | Selling_price_per_unit | =Model!$B$7 |
| 11 | Ordering model | | | Unit_purchasing_cost | =Model!$B$6 |
| 12 | Order quantity | 193.65 | | | |
| 13 | Orders per year | 6.20 | | | |
| 14 | Time between orders (days) | 58.90 | | | |
| 15 | | | | | |
| 16 | Monetary values | | | | |
| 17 | Annual fixed ordering cost | $775 | affected by order quantity | | |
| 18 | Annual holding cost | $775 | | | |
| 19 | Annual purchasing cost | $120,000 | unaffected by order quantity | | |
| 20 | Annual revenue | $156,000 | | | |
| 21 | Annual profit | $34,451 | | | |
| 22 | | | | | |
| 23 | Alternative EOQ formula | 193.65 | | | |

## Discussion of the Solution

*Using the optimal order quantity, the annual fixed cost of ordering and the annual holding cost are always equal in the basic EOQ model.*

The Solver solution specifies that Machey's should order about 194 cameras each time it orders. This results in about 6 orders per year or about one order every 59 days. Note that the annual ordering cost and the annual financial holding cost for this optimal solution are equal. This is no coincidence. It always occurs in the basic EOQ model. Because the annual purchasing cost and revenue do not depend on the order quantity, the problem is essentially a trade-off between too many orders (high fixed ordering costs) and too much inventory (high holding costs). Calculus can be used to show that Solver always chooses the order quantity that makes these two costs equal.

## EOQ Formula

A feature of some nonlinear models, including this EOQ model, is that they have no constraints and can be solved with calculus—without the need for a spreadsheet Solver. Although we do not pursue the details, the calculus solution, shown in cell B23 of Figure 13.2, is that the optimal order quantity satisfies

$$Q = \sqrt{2KD/h} \qquad \textbf{(13.4)}$$

*This famous EOQ (or square root) formula is found by using calculus to minimize the total annual cost (or maximize the total annual profit). It indicates exactly how the optimal order quantity is related to the key inputs.*

where in general, $h$ is the combined unit holding cost, in this case $ic$. The advantage of this well-known "square-root formula" is that it gives us immediate insight into the effects of changes in inputs. For example, the effect of quadrupling the annual demand is to double the optimal order quantity. The disadvantage of this formula is that it holds only under the assumptions we have described. If a company wants to modify the EOQ model to meet any special circumstances, it is better to develop a flexible spreadsheet model and then use Solver. ■

## EOQ Models with Quantity Discounts

The next example illustrates one of many possible variations of the basic EOQ model. In this variation, the company placing the order can obtain quantity discounts from its supplier.

EXAMPLE | 13.2 ORDERING THUMB DRIVES WITH QUANTITY DISCOUNTS AT AJ TAYLOR

The accounting firm of AJ Taylor buys USB thumb drives from a distributor of PC supplies. The firm uses approximately 5000 drives per year at a fairly constant rate. The distributor offers the following quantity discount. If fewer than 500 drives are ordered, the cost per drive is $30. If at least 500 but fewer than 800 drives are ordered, the cost per drive is $28. If at least 800 drives are ordered, the cost per drive is $26. The fixed cost of placing an order is $100. The company's cost of capital is 10% per year, and there is no storage cost. The firm wants to find the optimal order quantity and the corresponding total annual cost.

**Objective** To find the order quantity that minimizes the total annual cost of ordering in the face of quantity discounts.

## Solution

A clever use of a lookup table and the SolverTable add-in makes it easy to modify the basic EOQ model to solve this problem. The idea is to solve *three* separate basic EOQ models, one for each region of the purchase cost function. For example, in the second region, the unit purchase cost is specified as $28. We can force the order quantity to be within this region by adding constraints that it must be between 500 and 799. After solving the three models, we take the lowest of the three optimal costs.

### DEVELOPING THE SPREADSHEET MODEL

The completed model appears in Figure 13.3. (See the file **EOQ with Quantity Discounts.xlsx**.) The accompanying Solver dialog box appears in Figure 13.4. Again, we do not spell out all of the details, but only the key points.

**Figure 13.3**

The EOQ Model with Quantity Discounts

| | A | B | C | D | E | F | G |
|---|---|---|---|---|---|---|---|
| 1 | AJ Taylor's EOQ model with quantity discounts | | | | | | |
| 2 | | | | | | | |
| 3 | Inputs | | | | | Range names used: | |
| 4 | Fixed ordering cost | $100 | | | | Annual_demand | =Model!$B$6 |
| 5 | Annual interest rate | 10% | | | | Annual_interest_rate | =Model!$B$5 |
| 6 | Annual demand | 5000 | | | | Fixed_ordering_cost | =Model!$B$4 |
| 7 | | | | | | Max_quantity | =Model!$B$17 |
| 8 | Purchase cost function | | | | | Min_quantity | =Model!$B$16 |
| 9 | Region | 1 | 2 | 3 | | Order_quantity | =Model!$B$20 |
| 10 | Unit purchase cost | $30.00 | $28.00 | $26.00 | | Orders_per_year | =Model!$B$21 |
| 11 | Min quantity | 0 | 500 | 800 | | Total_annual_cost | =Model!$B$28 |
| 12 | Max quantity | 499 | 799 | 2000 | | Unit_purchase_cost | =Model!$B$15 |
| 13 | | | | | | | |
| 14 | Region analyzed | 3 | | | | | |
| 15 | Unit purchase cost | $26.00 | | | | | |
| 16 | Min quantity | 800 | | | | | |
| 17 | Max quantity | 2000 | | | | | |
| 18 | | | | | | | |
| 19 | Ordering model | | | | Using SolverTable to solve in all regions | | |
| 20 | Order quantity | 800.00 | | | Region | Order quantity | Cost |
| 21 | Orders per year | 6.25 | | | | $B$20 | $B$28 |
| 22 | Time between orders (days) | 58.40 | | | 1 | 499.00 | $151,751 |
| 23 | | | | | 2 | 597.61 | $141,673 |
| 24 | Monetary values | | | | 3 | 800.00 | $131,665 |
| 25 | Annual fixed ordering cost | $625 | | | | | |
| 26 | Annual holding cost | $1,040 | | | | | |
| 27 | Annual purchasing cost | $130,000 | | | | | |
| 28 | Total annual cost | $131,665 | | | | | |

**①** **Purchase cost function.** Enter the parameters of the purchase cost function in the range B9:D12. This range is used for a lookup function later on. Note that we have entered a maximum order of 2000 in column D. Any large value can be used here.

**Figure 13.4**

Solver Dialog Box for the Quantity Discount Model

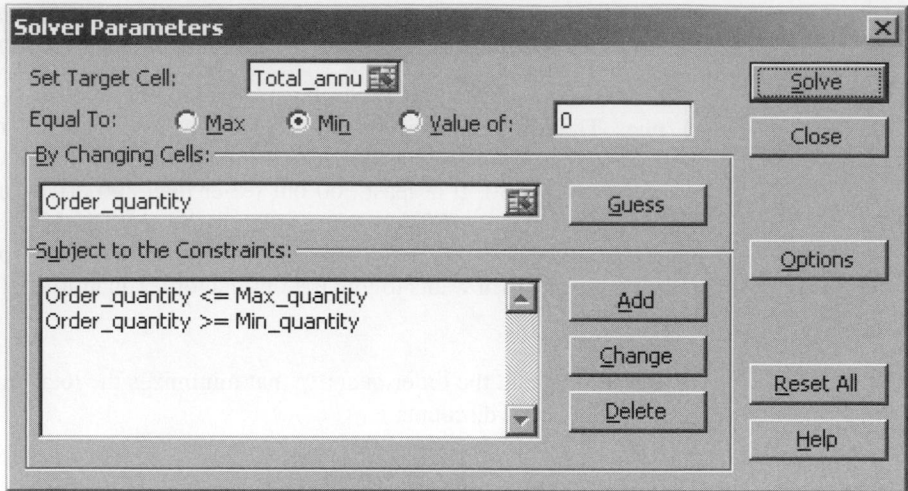

**2 Specify a region.** We set up the model for a particular region of the purchase cost function. In general, enter any value (1, 2, or 3) in cell B14. (We show results for region 3.) Then use the HLOOKUP function to obtain the required information in cells B15 to B17. Specifically, enter the formula

**=HLOOKUP(B14, B9:D12, 2)**

in cell B15, and enter similar formulas in cells B16 and B17, except with third arguments 3 and 4, respectively.

**3 Basic EOQ.** Given the unit purchase cost in cell B15, develop the rest of the EOQ model exactly as in the previous example. (This time, however, note that there is no revenue. Everything is in terms of costs, so that we are minimizing.)

## USING SOLVER

We set up Solver to minimize the total annual cost and specify the order quantity cell as the single changing cell. We also include the constraints Order_quantity>=Min_quantity and Order_quantity<=Max_quantity in the Solver dialog box. This forces the order quantity to be inside the region for which the unit purchase cost is relevant. We then run SolverTable with cell B14 as the single input, varied from 1 to 3 in increments of 1, and keep track of the order quantity and the total annual cost. This is the key. When SolverTable varies the region index in cell B14, it automatically varies the unit purchase cost and the lower and upper limits on the order quantity. So we get three Solver solutions for the price of one!

### Discussion of the Solution

The SolverTable results indicate the minimum annual costs for the three regions. If the company is forced to order in the first region at a unit cost of $30, its minimal cost is $151,751, which is achieved by ordering the maximum order quantity in this region, 499 units. If the company is forced to order in the second region at a unit cost of $28, its minimal cost is $141,673, which is achieved by ordering 598 units. Finally, if the company is forced to order in the third region at a unit cost of $26, its minimal cost is $131,665, which is achieved by ordering the minimum order quantity in this region, 800 units. Therefore, Taylor should use the smallest of these three costs; that is, it should order 800 units for a total annual cost of $131,665. ∎

## EOQ Models with Shortages Allowed

In the basic EOQ model, we assume that the company decides, as a matter of policy, not to allow any shortages. Because the demand rate and the lead time are known, the ordering can be done so that an order arrives just as the inventory level reaches zero. This means that it is possible to *prevent* shortages from occurring. However, it might be in the company's best interests to allow a few shortages if the penalty for a shortage is not too large. As discussed in Section 13.2, this opens up a wide range of possible models.

*There are several reasonable ways to evaluate the cost of not satisfying customer demand on time. Each results in a slightly different model.*

First, are shortages backlogged or are these demands lost? And what about the penalty cost for a shortage? Does the penalty relate only to the number of units short per year or also to the amount of time shortages last? After all, a customer might be twice as unhappy if she has to wait two days instead of one day for her demand to be satisfied. Whatever type of shortage cost we assume, the practical difficulty is then assessing a specific dollar value for this cost. For example, what is the cost of having a customer wait at all? What is the cost of having a customer wait three days?

The following example illustrates a complete backlog model where the penalty cost is charged per unit short per amount of time short. In this case, the annual penalty cost is a constant $p$ multiplied by the product of the average number of units backlogged and the average amount of time a customer has to wait for a backlogged unit. The constant $p$ is the penalty cost charged for each customer who has to wait one unit of time for one backlogged item.

---

EXAMPLE | **13.3 ORDERING AUDIO CDS AT GMB WITH SHORTAGES ALLOWED**

GMB is a mail-order distributor of audio CDs that sells approximately 50,000 CDs per year. Each CD is packaged in a jewel case that GMB buys from a supplier. The fixed cost of placing an order for jewel cases is $200. GMB pays $0.50 for each jewel case, and its cost of capital is 10%. The cost of storing a jewel case for one year is $0.50. GMB believes it can afford to run out of jewel cases from time to time, reasoning that this simply makes the time between customer orders and customer deliveries a bit longer. It knows that there is some cost of doing this—impatient customers can take their business elsewhere—but it is not sure what dollar amount $p$ to attach to this cost. It decides to use a trial value of $p = \$52$, reasoning that this value implies a $1 penalty for each extra week a customer has to wait because of a backlogged jewel case. GMB wants to develop a spreadsheet model to find the optimal order quantity, the optimal amount to backlog, and the optimal annual cost. It also wants to see how sensitive these quantities are to the unit shortage cost $p$.

**Objective** To find the order quantity and the maximum shortage allowed that minimize total annual cost, and to see how sensitive the solution is to the unit shortage cost.

## Solution

*Even though the order quantity is Q, the maximum inventory level is only Q−b because part of the order is used to satisfy backlogged demand.*

As in the basic EOQ model, the first step is to develop the components of the total annual cost. The key is again the saw-toothed graph shown in Figure 13.5. Now there are two decision variables: $Q$, the order quantity, and $b$, the maximum amount backlogged. Each cycle has length $Q/D$, the time to deplete $Q$ units at demand rate $D$. But now a cycle has two parts. During time $(Q - b)/D$ (the time required to deplete the first $Q - b$ units), there is positive inventory and demands are met on time. During the last section of each cycle of length $b/D$ (the time it takes to delete $b$ units), the inventory is negative, which means that shortages exist. The order for $Q$ units is placed so that it arrives precisely when the

**Figure 13.5**

The EOQ Model
with Shortages
Allowed

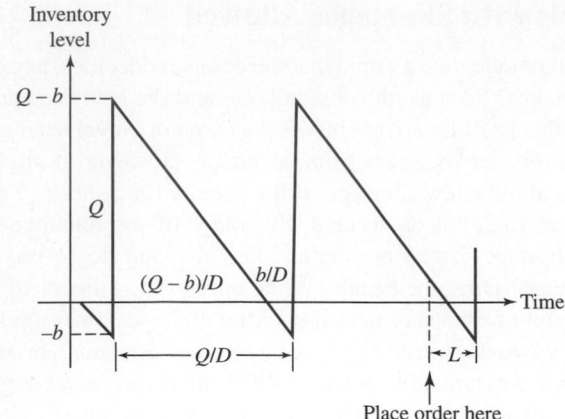

inventory level reaches $-b$. When this order arrives, $b$ units are used immediately to satisfy backlogged demand and the other $Q - b$ units go into on-hand inventory. Therefore, right after any order arrives, there are $Q - b$ units in inventory. Note that if there is an order lead time of $L$, the order should be placed when the inventory level is $DL$ units above its lowest point, $-b$. This is exactly analogous to the basic EOQ model because $DL$ is the amount of demand during the lead time.

The total cost function, a function of both $Q$ and $b$, is now fairly straightforward. The annual setup cost is $KD/Q$, the same as before, because there are $D/Q$ orders per year. The annual purchase cost is $cD$ because all demand is eventually satisfied. (In this section, we assume a constant unit purchasing cost; no quantity discounts are available.) The annual financial holding cost is again the interest rate times half of the purchase cost of an order, $icQ/2$.

To find the annual storage cost, refer to Figure 13.5. The storage cost per order cycle is the unit storage cost $s$ multiplied by the average inventory when inventory is positive, $(Q - b)/2$, multiplied by the amount of time during a cycle when inventory is positive, $(Q - b)/D$. To obtain the annual storage cost, we multiply the cost per cycle by the number of cycles per year, $D/Q$, to obtain

$$\text{Annual storage cost} = s[(Q - b)/2][(Q - b)/D](D/Q) = s(Q - b)^2/(2Q) \quad \textbf{(13.5)}$$

Again referring to Figure 13.5, the average shortage cost per cycle is $p$ multiplied by the average amount short when the inventory level is negative, $b/2$, multiplied by the amount of time during a cycle when inventory is negative, $b/D$. Multiplying the shortage cost per cycle by the number of cycles per year, $D/Q$, gives

$$\text{Annual shortage cost} = p(b/2)(b/D)(D/Q) = pb^2/(2Q) \quad \textbf{(13.6)}$$

## DEVELOPING THE SPREADSHEET MODEL

We can now develop the spreadsheet model for GMB, which appears in Figure 13.6. (See the file **EOQ with Shortages.xlsx**.) We again omit most of the details because all formulas are based directly on the cost equations shown previously. For example, the formula in cell B21 for the annual shortage cost is

    =Shortage_cost_per_unit_per_year*Maximum_backlog^2/(2*Order_quantity)

This follows directly from equation (13.6).

## USING SOLVER

The Solver setup is also straightforward. We minimize the total annual cost, with cells B12 and B13 as the changing cells and the Assume Non-Negative option checked. (We could also constrain the changing cells to be integers, but this is not really necessary—we can always round noninteger solutions to integers with little affect on costs.)

### Discussion of the Solution

The solution indicates that GMB should order 6057 units each time it orders and should plan its ordering so that there is a backlog of about 58 units when an order arrives. For example, if the order lead time is 1 week (1/52 year), then because the demand during lead time is $DL = 50,000/52 \approx 962$, GMB should place an order when the inventory level reaches $962 - 58 = 904$. That way, the backlog will be 58 units by the time the order arrives. The optimal policy indicates that about 8 orders will be placed per year. The total annual cost is \$28,302. However, only \$3302 of this is affected by the ordering policy. The other \$25,000 is the total purchase cost, which is incurred regardless of the timing or quantity of orders.

To see the effect of the unit shortage cost $p$ on the optimal solution, we ran SolverTable with cell B8 as the single input cell, varied from \$10 to \$110 in increments of \$20, and recorded the order quantity, the maximum backlog, and the annual cost as outputs. These results appear in Figure 13.6 from row 26 down. The entries in this table show that $Q$ and the total annual cost are fairly insensitive to $p$. However, the maximum backlog $b$ is quite sensitive to $p$, especially when $p$ is small. This makes sense. Why should GMB worry about making customers wait if it believes the penalty for making them wait is very low? This information should make GMB more comfortable, knowing that its estimate of $p$ is not that crucial, at least not in terms of total annual cost.

**Figure 13.6**

Optimal Solution with Shortages Allowed

| | A | B | C | D | E | F | G |
|---|---|---|---|---|---|---|---|
| 1 | GMB's EOQ model with shortages allowed | | | | | | |
| 2 | | | | | | | |
| 3 | Inputs | | | | Range names used: | | |
| 4 | Fixed ordering cost | $200 | | | Annual_demand | =Model!$B$9 | |
| 5 | Storage cost per unit per year | $0.50 | | | Annual_interest_rate | =Model!$B$6 | |
| 6 | Annual interest rate | 10% | | | Fixed_ordering_cost | =Model!$B$4 | |
| 7 | Unit purchasing cost | $0.50 | | | Maximum_backlog | =Model!$B$13 | |
| 8 | Shortage cost per unit per year | $52 | | | Order_quantity | =Model!$B$12 | |
| 9 | Annual demand | 50000 | | | Orders_per_year | =Model!$B$15 | |
| 10 | | | | | Shortage_cost_per_unit_per_year | =Model!$B$8 | |
| 11 | Ordering model | | | | Storage_cost_per_unit_per_year | =Model!$B$5 | |
| 12 | Order quantity | 6056.5 | | | Time_between_orders | =Model!$B$14 | |
| 13 | Maximum backlog | 57.7 | | | Total_annual_cost | =Model!$B$23 | |
| 14 | Time between orders | 0.121 | | | Unit_purchasing_cost | =Model!$B$7 | |
| 15 | Orders per year | 8.3 | | | | | |
| 16 | | | | | | | |
| 17 | Monetary values | | | | | | |
| 18 | Annual setup cost | $1,651 | | | | | |
| 19 | Annual financial holding cost | $151 | | | | | |
| 20 | Annual storage cost | $1,485 | | | | | |
| 21 | Annual shortage cost | $14 | | | | | |
| 22 | Annual purchasing cost | $25,000 | | | | | |
| 23 | Total annual cost | $28,302 | | | | | |
| 24 | | | | | | | |
| 25 | Sensitivity of order quantity, maximum backlog, and total annual cost to unit shortage cost | | | | | | |
| 26 | | | $B$12 | $B$13 | $B$23 | | |
| 27 | | 10 | 6165 | 294 | $28,244 | | |
| 28 | | 30 | 6076 | 100 | $28,292 | | |
| 29 | | 50 | 6058 | 60 | $28,302 | | |
| 30 | | 70 | 6050 | 43 | $28,306 | | |
| 31 | | 90 | 6045 | 33 | $28,308 | | |
| 32 | | 110 | 6043 | 27 | $28,310 | | |

## Reducing the Setup Cost

There has been a lot of talk in the past few years about striving for zero inventory. The argument is that the less inventory a company carries, the more efficiently it is operating its business.[4] The question is whether this argument can be justified from an economic point of view, at least in the context of the EOQ models we have been discussing. We have seen that the main reason for carrying more inventory is the fixed setup cost $K$. If $K$ is large, it is economical to order in larger quantities, which means that the average inventory level is large. So if this is true, what incentive is there for a company to strive for zero inventory?

One possible answer to this question is to reconsider whether the setup cost is really *fixed*. Is a company automatically stuck with some value of $K$, or is it possible to reduce this value of $K$ and thereby justify smaller order quantities and smaller inventory levels? This is an interesting modeling question. How can we mathematically model the cost of reducing $K$?

One researcher, Evan Porteus, has proposed a model where a company can make a one-time investment to reduce the value of $K$ (Porteus, 1985). Specifically, if the company's current setup cost is $K_0$, he assumes that by investing $f(K)$ dollars, the company can reduce the setup cost from $K_0$ to $K$, where $K < K_0$. Having a smaller value of $K$ implies a lower total annual cost, but this reduction must be weighed against the one-time investment required to reduce the setup cost. Also, the optimal *amount* of setup cost reduction must be determined. Therefore, $K$ becomes a decision variable along with the order quantity $Q$ in the basic EOQ model. (We do not allow quantity discounts or shortages in this section.)

There are two modeling problems here. The first is to choose a reasonable form for the function $f(K)$. The second is to find a way to turn a one-time investment cost, $f(K)$, into an equivalent *annual* cost, so that the cost of reducing the setup cost is comparable to the annual operating costs we have been discussing. For the first problem, Porteus assumes that the investment required to reduce the setup cost from $K_0$ to $K$ is of the form

$$f(K) = a_0 + a_1 \ln(K)$$

for some constants $a_0$ and $a_1$. (Here, ln is the natural logarithm.) This form is not as strange as it might look. It implies that each 10% decrease in $K$ costs a *fixed* dollar amount. (The 10% figure is chosen for convenience; the same argument can be used for any other percentage.) Specifically, it can be shown that the cost of reducing $K$ by 10% is $a_1 \ln(0.9) = -0.1054a_1$ dollars, regardless of whether the reduction is from \$300 to \$270, \$30 to \$27, \$3 to \$2.70, or any other 10% change. This constant cost per 10% decrease is a reasonable property for $f(K)$ to have.

We can fully specify the $f(K)$ function—that is, find $a_0$ and $a_1$—if we are given two inputs: the initial setup cost $K_0$ and the cost of a 10% reduction in $K$. To illustrate, suppose that the initial setup cost is $K_0 = \$500$, and it takes a one-time investment of \$1000 to reduce this by 10%. Then we set $-0.1054a_1 = 1000$ to obtain $a_1 = -9491$. Also, because it costs zero dollars to stay at level $K_0$, we have $f(K_0) = 0$, which implies that

$$0 = a_0 + a_1 \ln(K_0) = a_0 - 9491 \ln(500) = a_0 - 58,984$$

*We need to convert a one-time investment cost into an equivalent annual cost. If the one-time cost is f(K), and i is the annual interest rate, then the equivalent annual cost is the product f(K)i.*

or

$$a_0 = 58,984$$

Now we tackle the second problem. The investment cost $f(K)$ is a one-time investment. However, it is equivalent to an annual investment in perpetuity of $f(K)i$ dollars, where $i$ is the annual interest rate. This follows from an NPV argument that we do not present here. In words, if the company were to pay $f(K)i$ dollars at the beginning of each year

---

[4] See the article by Zangwill (1992) for a discussion of the merits of keeping inventory low.

forever, this would be equivalent in NPV terms to a one-time payment of $f(K)$ dollars. Putting all of this together, the total annual cost to the company is $f(K)i$ plus the annual operating cost from any of our previous models. In addition to any previous decision variables, such as $Q$, we now need to choose $K$, subject to the constraint $K \leq K_0$. We illustrate the procedure in the following example.

---

EXAMPLE | **13.4 REDUCING THE SETUP COST AT COMPSERVE**

The CompServe Company stocks expensive laser printers. The annual demand for this product is 300 units. The cost from CompServe's supplier is $1000 per printer, the cost of capital is 10%, and the storage cost per printer per year is $30. CompServe currently incurs a setup cost of $800 per order, but it believes that by streamlining its ordering and delivery operations, it can reduce this value and thereby achieve smaller inventory levels. Specifically, CompServe estimates that each 10% reduction in setup cost will require a $1500 investment. However, preliminary analysis shows that reducing the setup cost below $50 is physically impossible, regardless of the amount invested. Should the company invest in setup cost reductions, and if so, how does this affect its ordering policy?

**Objective**   To check, in the context of the basic EOQ model, whether it is cost-effective to make a one-time investment in setup cost reduction.

## Solution

We must first find the parameters $a_0$ and $a_1$ of the investment cost function $f(K)$ by using the information on the original setup cost, $800, and the cost per 10% setup cost reduction, $1500. Then we can express all annual costs in terms of the decision variables $K$ and $Q$ and use Solver to optimize. The details are explained next.

**DEVELOPING THE SPREADSHEET MODEL**

The spreadsheet solution shown in Figure 13.7 is very similar to the solution for the basic EOQ model. (See the file **EOQ with Setup Reduction.xlsx**.) We list the key steps here:

**Figure 13.7**

Solution to the Setup Cost Reduction Example

| | A | B | C | D | E |
|---|---|---|---|---|---|
| 1 | CompServe's EOQ model with possible setup cost reduction | | | | |
| 2 | | | | | |
| 3 | Inputs | | | Range names used: | |
| 4 | Initial setup cost | $800 | | Annual_demand | =Model!$B$9 |
| 5 | Minimal setup cost achievable | $50 | | Annual_interest_rate | =Model!$B$7 |
| 6 | Storage cost per unit per year | $30 | | Cost_of_reduction_in_setup_cost | =Model!$B$10 |
| 7 | Annual interest rate | 10% | | Initial_setup_cost | =Model!$B$4 |
| 8 | Unit purchasing cost | $1,000 | | Intercept | =Model!$B$13 |
| 9 | Annual demand | 300 | | Minimal_setup_cost_achievable | =Model!$B$5 |
| 10 | Cost of reduction in setup cost | $1,500 | | Order_quantity | =Model!$B$18 |
| 11 | | | | Orders_per_year | =Model!$B$20 |
| 12 | Parameters of setup cost reduction function | | | Setup_cost_after_reduction | =Model!$B$17 |
| 13 | Intercept | 95168 | | Slope | =Model!$B$14 |
| 14 | Slope | -14237 | | Storage_cost_per_unit_per_year | =Model!$B$6 |
| 15 | | | | Total_annual_cost | =Model!$B$28 |
| 16 | Analysis using the Solver | | | Unit_purchasing_cost | =Model!$B$8 |
| 17 | Setup cost after reduction | $103.94 | | | |
| 18 | Order quantity | 21.9 | | | |
| 19 | Time between orders | 0.346 | | | |
| 20 | Orders per year | 2.89 | | | |
| 21 | | | | | |
| 22 | Monetary values | | | | |
| 23 | One-time investment to reduce setup cost | $29,054 | | | |
| 24 | Equivalent annual cost to reduce setup cost | $2,905 | | | |
| 25 | Annual setup cost | $1,424 | | | |
| 26 | Annual holding cost | $1,424 | | | |
| 27 | Annual purchasing cost | $300,000 | | | |
| 28 | Total annual cost | $305,753 | | | |

**1  Parameters of setup cost reduction function.** Calculate the parameters $a_0$ and $a_1$ of the setup cost reduction function in cells B13 and B14 using the procedure outlined previously. Specifically, calculate the slope $a_1$ with the formula

=Cost_reduction_in_setup_cost/LN(0.9)

Then calculate $a_0$ with the formula

=-Slope*LN(Initial_setup_cost)

This formula ensures that the cost of making *no* setup cost reduction is 0.

**2  Cost of reducing setup cost.** Enter the one-time investment in setup cost reduction in cell B23 with the formula

=Intercept+Slope*LN(Setup_cost_after_reduction)

Then enter the equivalent annual cost in cell B24 with the formula

=B23*Annual_interest_rate

### USING SOLVER

The rest of the model is exactly like the basic EOQ model. To set up Solver, we identify annual cost as the objective to minimize, with cells B17 and B18 as the changing cells. We constrain cell B17 to be less than or equal to cell B4 and greater than or equal to cell B5, and we select the Assume Non-Negative option. (We could also constrain the order quantity to be an integer, but we have not done so.)

### Discussion of the Solution

As Figure 13.7 indicates, CompServe should first invest $29,054 to reduce the setup cost from $800 to $103.94. Then its optimal order quantity is about 22 printers, and the total annual cost, including the investment in setup cost reduction, is $305,753. Of course, only $5753 of this is affected by the decision variables. The other $300,000 is the unavoidable annual purchase cost.

Has setup cost reduction worked? If this example is solved with the basic EOQ model, using the original $800 setup cost, you can check that the optimal order quantity is 61 units, and the annual cost (not counting the $300,000 purchase cost) is approximately $7900. When setup cost reduction is allowed, the company reduces its setup cost from $800 to slightly over $100, and the ordering quantity drops sharply to 22 units. Instead of ordering about 5 times a year (300/61), it now orders almost 14 times a year (300/22). Also, the annual cost decreases by over $2000. Because the company's initial investment of almost $29,000 is equivalent to about $2900 per year, the savings in annual ordering and holding costs is about $4900. In addition, there may be other intangible benefits from holding less inventory, as Zangwill (1992) and many other authors have noted.  ∎

## Synchronizing Orders for Several Products

Until now, we have assumed that a company orders a single product. If the company orders several products, it could calculate the EOQ for each product and order them according to separate schedules. However, there might be economies, particularly reduced setup costs, from synchronizing the orders so that several products are ordered simultaneously. This should be particularly attractive for products that come from the same supplier. Then, for example, the same truck can deliver orders for several products, thereby reducing the setup cost involved with the delivery. We develop a model in this section that takes advantage of synchronization, and we compare it to the "individual EOQs" policy that uses no synchronization. Although this model can be developed for any number of products, we keep things relatively simple by assuming that there are only *two* products. We illustrate the approach in the following example.

---

EXAMPLE | **13.5 SYNCHRONIZED ORDERING AT SLEEPEASE**

Sleepease, a retailer of bedding supplies, orders king-size and queen-size mattresses from a regional supplier. There is a fairly constant demand for each of these products. The annual demand for queens is 2200; the demand for kings is 250. The unit purchasing costs for queen-size and king-size mattresses are $100 and $120, and the company's cost to store either of these for one year is $15. Sleepease's ordering cost is based primarily on the fixed cost of delivering a batch of mattresses. This ordering cost is $500 if either queens or kings are ordered separately, but the ordering cost is only $650 if both are ordered together. Sleepease's cost of capital is 10%. The company wants to know whether synchronizing orders is better than not synchronizing them, and if so, it wants to find the best synchronized ordering policy.

**Objective** To find the optimal synchronized ordering policy, and to compare it to the EOQ policy where orders for the two are not synchronized.

## Solution

The only real cost benefit from synchronization is reduced setup costs. Let $K_1 = \$500$ be the setup cost for ordering queens alone, and define $K_2 = \$500$ similarly for kings. When both products are ordered simultaneously, we denote the setup cost for the order by $K_{12} = \$650$. The important point is that $K_{12}$ is less than $K_1 + K_2$. This reflects the economy of scale achieved when both products are ordered together rather than individually. All other parameters ($s$, $c$, $D$, and $i$) are defined as before, except that each product has its own values of $s$, $c$, and $D$.

To model this problem, consider the graph in Figure 13.8. This depicts a synchronization policy where queens are ordered three times as often as kings. In general, let $t_1$ and $t_2$, respectively, be the time between orders of queens and kings, and let $T$ be the cycle time, defined as the larger of $t_1$ and $t_2$. (In the graph, $t_2 > t_1$, so $T = t_2$.) Also, let $n_1$ and $n_2$, respectively, be the number of times queens and kings are ordered during a cycle. (In the graph, $n_1 = 3$ and $n_2 = 1$.) Then under a synchronization model, $n_1$ and $n_2$ are both positive

**Figure 13.8**

EOQ with Synchronization

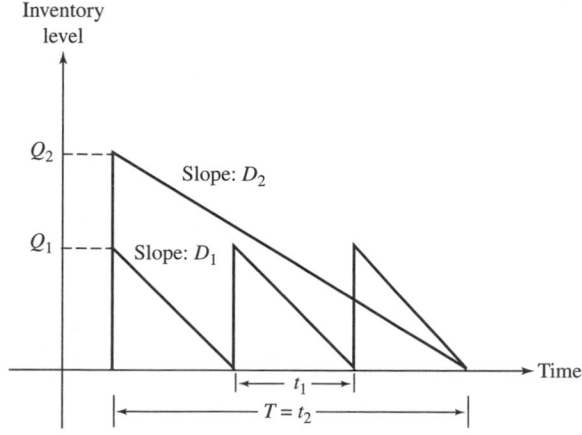

integers, and at least one of them equals 1. (Actually, they could both be 1, in which case queens and kings are always ordered together.)

For the optimization model, it is convenient to let $T$, $n_1$, and $n_2$ be the decision variables—that is, the changing cells in the spreadsheet. We can easily recover the order quantities $Q_1$ and $Q_2$ from these values as follows. First, we know that $t_1$, the time between orders of queens, is $T/n_1$. Similarly, $t_2 = T/n_2$. Then given $t_1$ and $t_2$, the order quantities $Q_1$ and $Q_2$ must be $Q_1 = D_1 t_1$ and $Q_2 = D_2 t_2$ (because we want each $Q$ to decrease to 0 in time $t$ at rate $D$).

To develop the total annual cost, the purchasing and holding costs are exactly as before (for each product). Therefore, we concentrate on the setup cost. During an ordering cycle of length $T$, both products are ordered together exactly once, for a setup cost of $K_{12}$. Then product $j$ (for $j = 1$ or $j = 2$) is ordered $n_j - 1$ times by itself, for a setup cost of $K_j(n_j - 1)$. (For at least one of the two products, this latter term is 0. For example, it is 0 for product 2 in Figure 13.8.) The number of cycles per year is $1/T$, so the total annual setup cost is

$$\text{Annual setup cost} = [K_{12} + (n_1 - 1)K_1 + (n_2 - 1)K_2]/T \qquad \textbf{(13.7)}$$

We are now ready to develop the spreadsheet model.

## DEVELOPING THE SPREADSHEET MODEL

The spreadsheet model appears in Figure 13.9. (See the file **EOQ with Synchronized Ordering.xlsx**.) The top part of the spreadsheet shows the analysis for the synchronized ordering policy. It can be formed as follows:

**Figure 13.9**

Solution to the Synchronized Ordering Example

| | A | B | C | D | E | F | G | H | I |
|---|---|---|---|---|---|---|---|---|---|
| 1 | Synchronized Ordering of Two Products | | | | | | | | |
| 2 | | | | | | | | | |
| 3 | Inputs | | | | | | | Range names used: | |
| 4 | Interest rate | 10% | | | | | | Cycle_time | =Model!$B$17 |
| 5 | Joint setup cost | $650 | | | | | | Interest_rate | =Model!$B$4 |
| 6 | | | | | | | | Joint_setup_cost | =Model!$B$5 |
| 7 | Product | Setup cost (individual) | Storage cost | Purchasing cost | Combined holding cost | Annual demand | | Orders_per_cycle | =Model!$B$14:$B$15 |
| 8 | Queens | $500 | $15 | $100 | $25 | 2200 | | Synchronized_order_quantities | =Model!$E$14:$E$15 |
| 9 | Kings | $500 | $15 | $120 | $27 | 250 | | Total_annual_cost | =Model!$B$23 |
| 10 | | | | | | | | | |
| 11 | Optimal synchronized policy | | | | | | | | |
| 12 | | | | | | | | | |
| 13 | Product | Orders per cycle | Time between orders | Orders per year | Synchronized order quantities | | | | |
| 14 | Queens | 2 | 0.130 | 7.7 | 285 | | | | |
| 15 | Kings | 1 | 0.259 | 3.9 | 65 | | | | |
| 16 | | | | | | | | | |
| 17 | Cycle time | 0.259 | | | | | | | |
| 18 | | | | | | | | | |
| 19 | Costs affected by ordering policy | | | | | | | | |
| 20 | Annual setup cost | $4,438 | | | | | | | |
| 21 | Annual holding cost | $4,438 | | | | | | | |
| 22 | Annual purchasing cost | $250,000 | | | | | | | |
| 23 | Total annual cost | $258,876 | | | | | | | |
| 24 | | | | | | | | | |
| 25 | Optimal policy with no synchronization (using individual EOQs) | | | | | | | | |
| 26 | | | | | | | | | |
| 27 | Product | Separate EOQs | Time between orders | Orders per year | Annual setup costs | Annual holding costs | | | |
| 28 | Queens | 297 | 0.135 | 7.4 | $3,708 | $3,708 | | | |
| 29 | Kings | 96 | 0.385 | 2.6 | $1,299 | $1,299 | | | |
| 30 | Totals | | | | $5,007 | $5,007 | | | |
| 31 | | | | | | | | | |
| 32 | Annual purchasing cost | $250,000 | | | | | | | |
| 33 | Total annual cost | $260,014 | | | | | | | |

**1 Inputs.** Enter the inputs in rows 4, 5, 8, and 9. As usual, note that the combined holding costs in the range E8:E9 are storage costs plus the interest rate multiplied by the purchasing costs.

**2 Orders per cycle and cycle time.** Enter *any* trial values in the cells B14, B15, and B17. The values in cells B14 and B15 correspond to $n_1$ and $n_2$; the value in cell B17 corresponds to $T$.

**3** **Timing of orders.** Calculate the times between orders, $t_1$ and $t_2$, in the range C14:C15 by entering the formula

**=Cycle_time/B14**

in cell C14 and copying it down. Then calculate the orders per year in the range D14:D15 as the reciprocals of the values in C14:C15.

**4** **Order quantities.** Calculate the order quantity for queens in cell E14 with the formula

**=F8*C14**

and copy this to cell E15 for the kings. Again, this expresses the order quantity as the annual demand multiplied by the time between orders.

**5** **Annual setup cost.** Calculate the annual setup cost in cell B20 with the formula

**=(Joint_setup_cost+SUMPRODUCT(Orders_per_cycle-1,B8:B9))/Cycle_time**

This follows directly from equation (13.7). (Note how the term Orders_per_cycle-1 is used inside the SUMPRODUCT function. It takes the values in the Orders_per_cycle range, subtracts 1 from each of them, and multiplies these by the values in the B8:B9 range.)

**6** **Other costs.** Calculate the other costs exactly as in previous EOQ models, except that now the holding and purchasing costs must be summed over the two products, queens and kings.

## USING SOLVER

We can now use Solver to find the optimal synchronized policy. We minimize the annual cost, using cells B14, B15, and B17 as the changing cells. The constraints are that cell B17 should be nonnegative and cells B14 and B15 should be integers and greater than or equal to 1 (to ensure that Sleepease orders each product a positive integer number of times per cycle).

### Discussion of the Solution

We see that there are about four cycles every year (because cycle time is about 1/4 year). Queens are ordered twice every cycle, and kings are ordered only once. The total annual cost (not counting the purchasing cost) from this synchronized ordering policy is $8876. For comparison, the bottom part of the spreadsheet in Figure 13.9 shows the unsynchronized policy from using individual EOQs. Now queens and kings are both ordered slightly less frequently than before, but because the orders are not synchronized, there are more ordering times per year. By comparing setup and holding costs, we see that this unsynchronized policy costs about 12.7% more than the best synchronized policy ($10,014 versus $8876). In addition, there is an important noneconomic advantage of synchronizing orders—the ordering process is easier to manage.

Would you have guessed that queens would be ordered more frequently than kings? The reason is that the number of orders per year for either product is $D/Q$. From the EOQ square-root formula, we know that the optimal number of orders per year is proportional to the square root of $D$. Now, kings and queens have very similar setup costs $K$ (if ordered separately) and holding costs $h$. Therefore, their relative ordering frequencies are determined by their demand rates, and queens have a much larger demand rate. Therefore, it makes sense to order queens more frequently. (The analysis would not be this straightforward if kings and queens had different values for all three parameters $K$, $D$, and $h$). ∎

## More Than Two Products

Virtually the same spreadsheet could be used for more than two products, provided that we make a simplifying assumption. This assumption is that a setup cost reduction is available only when the company places an order for *all* of the products simultaneously. Unfortunately, it is probably more realistic to assume that there is a setup cost reduction when *any* subset of products is ordered simultaneously. To illustrate, suppose that there are four products, product 1 is ordered once per cycle, products 2 and 3 are ordered twice per cycle, and product 4 is ordered four times per cycle (see Figure 13.10). When all four products are ordered together at the beginning of a cycle, there is definitely a setup cost reduction, but there is probably also some setup cost reduction when products 2, 3, and 4 are ordered together in the middle of a cycle. If we allow this possibility, however, and then try to optimize over all possible synchronizations, the problem becomes difficult to model in a spreadsheet. Therefore, we do not pursue this multiple-product model any further here.

**Figure 13.10**

Another Way to Synchronize

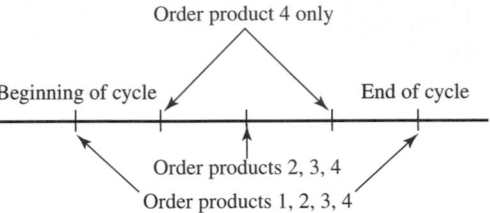

---

# PROBLEMS

*Solutions for problems whose numbers appear within a color box can be found in the Student Solutions Files. Order your copy today at the Winston/Albright product Web site, academic.cengage.com/decisionsciences/winston.*

## Skill-Building Problems

1. In the basic EOQ model in Example 13.1, suppose that the fixed cost of ordering is $500. Use Solver to find the new optimal order quantity. How does it compare to the optimal order quantity in the example? Could you have predicted this from equation (13.4)?

2. If the lead time in Example 13.1 changes from one week to two weeks, how is the optimal policy affected? Does the optimal order quantity change?

3. In the quantity discount model in Example 13.2, suppose we want to see how the optimal order quantity and the total annual cost vary as the fixed cost of ordering varies. Use a *two-way* SolverTable to perform this analysis, allowing the fixed cost of ordering to vary from $50 to $200 in increments of $50. Indicate the optimal ordering policy for each fixed cost of ordering.

**4.** In the quantity discount model in Example 13.2, the minimum total annual cost in region 3 is clearly the best. Evidently, the larger unit purchase costs in the other two regions make these two regions unattractive.

Could region 1 ever be best? What about region 2? To answer these questions, assume that there is no price break at all. Specifically, assume that the unit purchase cost is *always* $26. What is the optimal order quantity with this assumption? How does this help answer the preceding questions?

5. The quantity discount model in Example 13.2 uses one of two possible types of discount structures. It assumes that if the company orders 600 units, say, each unit costs $28. This provides a big incentive to jump up to a higher order quantity. For example, the total purchasing cost of 499 units is 499($30) = $14,970, whereas the total cost of 500 units is only 500($28) = $14,000. Change the discount structure so that the first 499 units cost $30 apiece, the next 300 units cost $28 apiece, and any units from 800 on cost $26 apiece. Now the cost of 500 units is 499($30) + $28 = $14,998. Modify the model to incorporate this structure, and find the optimal order quantity.

6. In Example 13.3, we used SolverTable to show what happens when the unit shortage cost varies. As the table indicates, the company orders more and allows more backlogging as the unit shortage cost decreases. Redo the SolverTable, this time trying even smaller unit shortage costs. Explain what happens when the unit shortage cost is really small. Do you think a company would ever use a really small shortage cost?

Why or why not? Then redo the SolverTable again, this time trying even larger unit shortage costs. How do the results in this case compare to the results from the basic EOQ model with *no* shortages allowed?

7. In Example 13.4, we showed why a company might invest to reduce its setup cost. It all depends on how much this investment costs, as specified (in the model) by the cost of a 10% reduction in the setup cost. Use SolverTable to see how the results change as this cost of a 10% reduction varies. You can choose the range for this cost that makes the results "interesting." Within your range, does the lower limit on setup cost ($50) ever become a binding constraint?

8. Modify the synchronized ordering model in Example 13.5 slightly so that you can use a *two-way* SolverTable on the fixed costs. Specifically, enter a formula in cell B9 so that the fixed cost of ordering kings alone is equal to the fixed cost of ordering queens alone. Then let the two inputs for SolverTable be the fixed cost of ordering queens alone and the joint fixed cost of ordering both kings and queens together. Let these vary over a reasonable range, but make sure that the first input is less than the second, and the second input is less than twice the first. (Otherwise, the model wouldn't be realistic.) Capture the changing cells and the sum of annual setup and holding costs as SolverTable outputs. Describe your findings in a brief report.

## Skill-Extending Problems

**9.** In the basic EOQ model in Example 13.1, suppose that the fixed cost of ordering and the unit purchasing cost are both multiplied by the same factor $f$. Use SolverTable to see what happens to the optimal order quantity and the corresponding annual fixed order cost and annual holding cost as $f$ varies from 0.5 to 5 in increments of 0.25. Could you have discovered the same results algebraically, using equations (13.2) through (13.4)?

10. In the basic EOQ model, revenue is often omitted from the model. The reasoning is that all demand will be sold at the given selling price, so revenue is a fixed quantity that is independent of the order quantity. Change that assumption as follows. Make selling price a decision variable, which must be between $110 and $150. Then assume that annual demand is a nonlinear function of the selling price $p$: Annual Demand = $497000p^{-1.24}$. (This implies a constant elasticity of approximately $-1.24$ for the demand curve.) Modify the model in Example 13.1 as necessary and then use Solver to find the optimal selling price and order quantity. What are the corresponding demand and profit? Which appears to affect profit more in this model, order quantity or selling price?

11. In the quantity discount model in Example 13.2, the minimum total annual cost is region 3 is clearly the best. Evidently, the larger unit purchase costs in the other two regions make these two regions unattractive. When would a switch take place? To answer this question, change the model slightly. First, change the fixed cost of ordering to $40. Second, keep the unit cost in region 3 at $26, but change the unit costs in regions 1 and 2 to $26 + 2k$ and $26 + k$, where you can let $k$ vary. (Currently, $k$ is $2.) Use a *two-way* SolverTable, with $k$ varied over some appropriate range to see how small $k$ must be before it is optimal to order from region 1 or 2. What region is the optimal ordering quantity in if there is no price break at all ($k = 0$)? How do you reconcile this with your SolverTable findings?

# 13.5 PROBABILISTIC INVENTORY MODELS

In most situations, companies that make ordering and production decisions face uncertainty about the future. Probably the most common and important element of uncertainty is customer demand, but there can be others. For example, there can be uncertainty in the amount of lead time between placement and receipt of an order. A company that faces uncertainty has three basic options. First, it can use best guesses for uncertain quantities and proceed according to one of the deterministic models we developed in the previous section (or according to one of the many other deterministic models that exist in the literature). Second, it can develop an analytical (nonsimulation) model to deal with the uncertainty. The advantage to such a model is that we can calculate bottom line results, such as expected cost, and then use Solver to optimize. The disadvantage is that these analytical models tend to be mathematically complex. The third possibility is to develop a simulation model. The advantage of a simulation model is that it is relatively easy to develop, regardless of the complexity of the problem. The disadvantage is that it can be difficult, or at least time-consuming, to find *optimal* ordering policies from a simulation.[5]

We already examined one probabilistic inventory model in Chapter 11, the newsvendor model. The essence of a newsvendor model is that a company must place an order for some product exactly once and then wait to see how large the demand is. If the demand is larger than expected, the company loses sales it could have made. If the demand is smaller than expected, the company must dispose of the excess items or sell them at a marked-down price. This presents a classical trade-off between ordering too few and ordering too many. We used simulation in Chapter 11 to analyze this problem. We now see how it can be solved analytically.

Besides the newsvendor model, we also examine a continuous review model where a company orders a product repeatedly through time. The model we examine is basically the same EOQ model as in the previous section but with one important difference. Now the demand during any period of time is random, and only its probability distribution is known. This is more realistic, but it complicates the analysis. We assume that the company uses an $(R,Q)$ ordering policy, which is used by many companies. This continuous review policy is determined by two numbers, $R$ and $Q$. The value $R$ is the **reorder point.** When the company's inventory level drops to $R$, an order is placed. The order quantity $Q$ specifies the amount to order each time an order is placed.

## Newsvendor Model

The newsvendor model is one of the simplest probabilistic inventory models, but it is also a very important one.[6] It occurs whenever a company must place a one-time order for a product and then wait to see the demand for the product. The assumption is that after this demand occurs, the product is no longer valuable. This could be the case for a daily newspaper (who wants yesterday's newspaper?), a calendar (who wants a 2005 calendar after 2005?), a fashion product that tends to go out of style after the current "season" (what woman wants last year's dress styles?), and so on. Given the single chance to order, the company needs to balance the cost of ordering too much versus the cost of not ordering enough.

To put this problem in a fairly general setting, we let $c_{over}$ and $c_{over}$, respectively, be the cost of having 1 more unit or 1 fewer unit on hand than demand. For example, if demand turns out to be 100 units, $c_{over}$ is the cost if we order 101 units, whereas $c_{under}$ is the cost if we order 99 units. Each of these is a per unit cost, so if we order, say, 110 units, the cost is $10c_{over}$, whereas if we order 90 units, the cost is $10c_{under}$. The example discussed shortly indicates how we find $c_{over}$ and $c_{under}$ from given monetary inputs. For now, we assume they are known.

Now let $D$ be the random demand. We assume that $D$ has a cumulative probability distribution $F(x)$, so that for any potential demand $x$, $F(x)$ is the probability $P(D \leq x)$ that $D$ is less than or equal to $x$. In general, this distribution needs to be estimated, probably from historical data on demands for this product or similar products. Then the best order quantity balances the cost of understocking times the probability of understocking with the cost of overstocking times the probability of overstocking. As an example, suppose the unit cost of understocking, $c_{under}$, is four times as large as the unit cost of overstocking, $c_{over}$. Then it seems reasonable (and it can be proved) that we need the probability of understocking to be

---

[5] Fortunately, this is less true now than it used to be. Palisade, for example, has developed a software package called RISKOptimizer that uses a genetic algorithm to optimize a specified output in a simulation model. This software is included with the Palisade suite that is bundled with the book. We refer to Winston (1999) for a discussion of simulation models that use RISKOptimizer.

[6] The article by Pfeifer et al. (2001) contains an interesting discussion of three alternative methods to analyze the newsvendor problem: decision trees, simulation, and the critical fractile analysis discussed here. Although the authors provide pros and cons of each method, they appear to prefer simulation.

1/4 as large as the probability of overstocking. If $Q$ is the order quantity, the probability of overstocking is $P(D \le Q) = F(Q)$, and the probability of understocking is 1 minus this, $1 - F(Q)$.[7] Because we want the probability of understocking to be 1/4 as large as the probability of overstocking, we set $1 - F(Q) = (1/4)F(Q)$ and solve for $F(Q)$ to obtain $F(Q) = 4/5$.

A similar argument for *any* values of $c_{over}$ and $c_{under}$ leads to the following equation that the optimal order quantity $Q$ must satisfy:

$$F(Q) = \frac{c_{under}}{c_{over} + c_{under}} \qquad (13.8)$$

The fraction on the right side of this equation is called the **critical fractile.** This fraction determines the optimal order quantity through an examination of the demand distribution. For example, if the cost of understocking is four times as large as the cost of overstocking, then the critical fractile is 4/5, so there is an 80% chance that demand is less than or equal to the optimal order quantity value. For any particular demand distribution, we can then appeal to the RISKview program, built-in Excel functions, tables in books, or some other means to find the optimal $Q$. We illustrate the procedure in the following continuation of the Walton Bookstore calendar example from Chapter 11.

---

EXAMPLE | **13.6 ORDERING CALENDARS AT WALTON BOOKSTORE**

Recall that Walton Bookstore buys calendars for $7.50, sells them at the regular price of $10, and gets a refund of $2.50 for all calendars that cannot be sold. As in Example 11.2 of Chapter 11, Walton estimates that demand for the calendar has a triangular distribution with minimum, most likely, and maximum values equal to 100, 175, and 300, respectively. How many calendars should Walton order to maximize expected profit?

**Objective** To use critical fractile analysis to find the optimal order quantity.

## Solution

There are two steps in this analysis. First, we must identify the unit costs of overstocking and understocking, $c_{over}$ and $c_{under}$, so that we can calculate the critical fractile in equation (13.8). Second, we must find the order quantity that achieves this critical fractile.

To find the unit cost of overstocking, assume that demand is 200 (any value would do), and Walton orders 201 calendars. This means one calendar will be left over. Because the calendar costs $7.50 and the eventual refund is only $2.50, the cost of this extra calendar is $c_{over} = \$5$. In other words, Walton loses $5 for each calendar that can't be sold. In the other direction, if 199 calendars are ordered, there is an opportunity cost of not being able to satisfy customer 200. This cost is the profit margin per calendar, $10 − $7.50, so that $c_{under} = \$2.50$. Therefore, the critical fractile is $2.50/(5 + 2.50) = 1/3$.

Now we need to find the value such that the probability of demand being less than or equal to this value is 1/3. This value is easy to find by using @RISK's Define Distribution window (see Figure 13.11). We first choose the appropriate distribution (triangular with parameters 100, 175, and 300) and then enter 33.3% above the chart. The corresponding value is the corresponding order quantity. In this case, it is approximately 171. (See the file **Newsvendor.xlsx**.)

---

[7] Strictly speaking, this requires that $D$ be a continuous random variable, which we assume here. However, a similar argument works when $D$ is discrete.

Figure 13.11

Finding the Optimal
Order Quantity with
@RISK

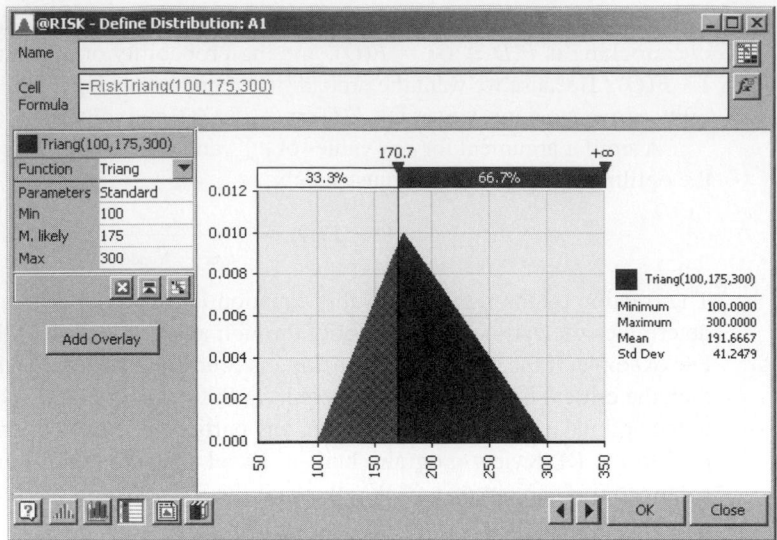

### Discussion of the Solution

Unfortunately, the critical fractile method provides only the optimal order quantity. For this example, it indicates that an order for 171 calendars achieves the best balance between overstocking and understocking. Specifically, the probability of understocking is then 2/3, and the probability of understocking is 1/3. The method does *not* provide a distribution of Walton's net profit, or even its *expected* net profit, from using this order quantity (at least not without a more complex analysis that is beyond the scope of this book). This is exactly the type of information that simulation can provide, as illustrated in Example 11.2 of Chapter 11. In short, simulation enables us to see how net profit is distributed for a given order quantity, but it isn't well suited to finding the *optimal* order quantity. Critical fractile analysis is exactly the opposite in that it enables us to find the optimal order quantity rather easily, but it doesn't provide the distribution of net profit. Further analysis of net profit for this order quantity is best left to simulation.

In spite of its shortcomings, critical fractile analysis does allow us to see how the optimal order quantity depends on (1) the relative values of $c_{over}$ and $c_{under}$, and (2) the shape of the demand distribution. For example, suppose the selling price increases from $10 to $15. This doesn't affect the cost of overstocking, but it increases the cost of understocking to $7.50, the new profit margin. As we would expect, this provides an incentive for Walton to order *more* calendars than before to avoid running out and losing sales. This is exactly what happens. The new critical fractile is $7.50/(5 + 7.50) = 0.6$, which we enter in @RISK's Define Distribution window. You can check that the corresponding order quantity is now 200, the probability of understocking is only 0.4, and the probability of overstocking is 0.6. As another example, suppose the selling price remains at $10, but Walton receives only $1 for leftover calendars. Then the understocking cost is unaffected, but the overstocking cost increases to $6.50, the difference between Walton's unit cost and the salvage value. This provides an incentive to order *fewer* calendars. The critical fractile is now $2.50/(6.50 + 2.50) = 0.278$, the optimal order quantity decreases to about 165, the probability of understocking is 0.722, and the probability of overstocking is 0.278.

We can also easily see how the optimal order quantity depends on the shape of the demand distribution. Suppose, for example, that the demand distribution is normal with the same mean and standard deviation, 191.67 and 41.248, as the triangular distribution we just

**Figure 13.12**

Critical Fractile
Analysis with Nor-
mally Distributed
Demand

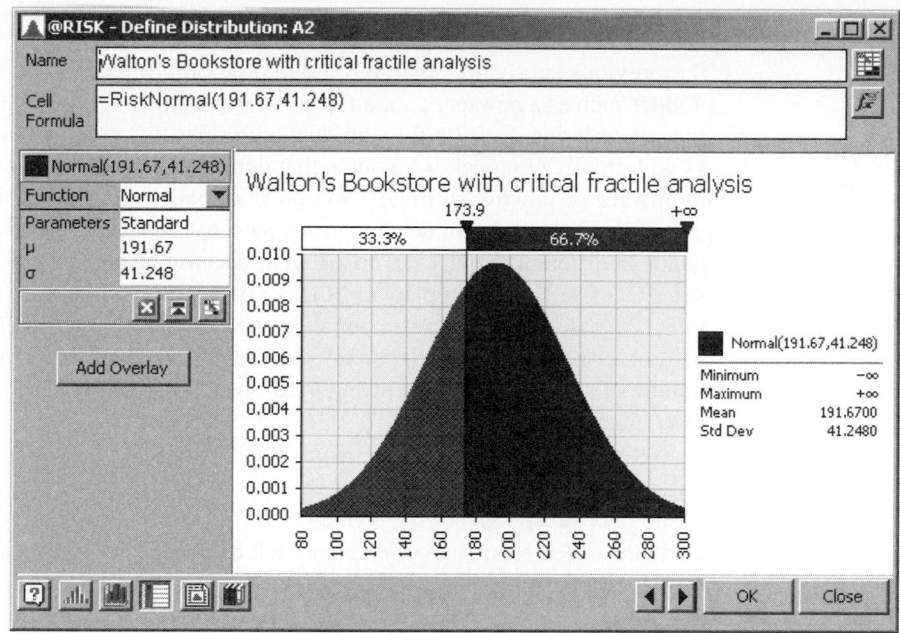

analyzed. Then we can still find the optimal order quantity from @RISK, as shown in Figure 13.12, just by choosing a different distribution. Apparently, this has very little affect on the optimal order quantity, which increases only to about 174. ■

## ADDITIONAL APPLICATIONS

### A Newsvendor Tackles the Newsvendor Model

Koschat et al. (2003) describe a real newsvendor problem experienced by Time Inc. Time is the largest publisher of consumer magazines in the United States, with such titles as *People*, *Sports Illustrated*, *Time*, *Fortune*, and many others. Time Inc. has three problems: (1) how many issues of each magazine to print, (2) how to distribute these to its wholesalers around the country, and (3) how to distribute the magazines from the wholesalers to the many retailers that sell them. Until the time of the study (1998), these decisions were made in an informal manner, using the (sometimes biased and unscientific) judgments of the parties involved. The authors discuss how they analyzed and then implemented the allocation of magazines from publisher to wholesalers to retailers by using the principles we have discussed here for general newsvendor problems. However, they also state that the problems faced by Time Inc. are too complex, due to data requirements and political pressures, to be solved entirely by management science models. Expert judgment and some amount of compromise were required to make the study successful. Still, the authors estimate that their study has generated incremental profits in excess of $3.5 million annually. ■

The critical fractile analysis discussed here is in terms of the newsvendor model, where a company orders exactly once. As discussed in the chapter opener about Dell's supply chain, this same critical fractile analysis can be used to determine an optimal service level for a company. As we see, service levels play an important role in the $(R,Q)$ ordering policies discussed next.

## The $(R,Q)$ Ordering Policy

The previous subsection analyzed a one-time ordering decision, which is relevant for a product such as a newspaper or a fashion item that quickly goes out of style. We now examine an ordering decision for a product with sales that continue into the indefinite future. As with the EOQ model, we assume that demand is more or less constant through time—no upward or downward trends, and no seasonality—but that it is random. That is, the probability distribution of demand in any month, say, is always the same, but the *actual* demands in different months can be different because of randomness. As with the deterministic EOQ model, the company must make two decisions: when to order and how much to order. We assume that it uses a popular type of policy, called an $(R,Q)$ policy, where $R$ is the reorder point and $Q$ is the order quantity. Under this policy, the company continually monitors its inventory. When inventory drops to $R$ or below, the company places an order for $Q$ units.

When a company chooses the reorder point $R$, it must take into account the effects of running out of inventory. If the company believes shortages are very expensive or undesirable, it should choose a relatively large value of $R$. This leads to a relatively large level of **safety stock,** the expected amount of inventory left over—the cushion—by the time the next order arrives. On the other hand, if shortages are not considered too expensive or undesirable, the company can afford to use a lower value of $R$, with a smaller resulting level of safety stock. As in the newsvendor model, we show how to determine an appropriate trade-off between leftovers and shortages.

To specify an $(R,Q)$ policy, we must also determine the appropriate order quantity $Q$. It turns out that the choices of $R$ and $Q$ can be made almost independently. The choice of $R$ depends largely on how we measure shortage costs (or customer service), whereas the choice of $Q$ depends mostly on the same cost factors we considered in the deterministic EOQ models. Specifically, the company wants to order enough to avoid frequent fixed ordering costs but as little as possible to avoid excessive holding costs. We develop a Solver model that can be used to determine $Q$ and $R$ simultaneously, as illustrated in the following example.

---

EXAMPLE | **13.7 ORDERING CAMERAS WITH UNCERTAIN DEMAND AT MACHEY'S**

In Example 13.1, we considered Machey's department store, which sells, on average, 1200 cameras per year. The store pays a setup cost of $125 per order, and the holding cost is $8 per camera per year. It takes 1 week for an order to arrive after it is placed. In that example, the optimal order quantity $Q$ was found to be 194 cameras. Now we assume that the annual demand is normally distributed with mean 1200 and standard deviation 70. Machey's wants to know when to order and how many cameras to order at each ordering opportunity.

**Objective**   To find the $(R,Q)$ policy that minimizes the company's expected annual cost.

## Solution

Suppose the company places an order for $Q$ cameras every time its inventory level drops to $R$. Our goal is to find optimal values of $Q$ and $R$. Two aspects of this model are critical to its solution: demand during lead time and the "cost" of running out of inventory.

### Demand During Lead Time and Safety Stock

*The key to choosing the appropriate reorder point R is the distribution of demand that occurs during an order lead time.*

The most critical probabilistic quantity is the amount of demand during an order lead time. To illustrate, suppose that Machey's uses $R = 30$ as the reorder point. This means that it places an order as soon as the inventory level drops to 30 cameras. This order arrives 1 week later. If the demand during this lead time is 25 cameras, say, then no shortage will occur, and 5 cameras will remain when the order arrives. However, if the demand during this period is 35 cameras, then there will be a shortage of 5 cameras by the time the order arrives. Therefore, the demand during lead time, in conjunction with the choice of $R$, determines the extent of shortages. Before we can continue, we need to analyze this quantity in some detail.

Let $D_{AD}$ be the annual demand, and let $D_{LD}$ be the demand during an order lead time of length $L$. (For clarity, we use subscripts AD for annual demand and LD for lead time demand.) From the statement of the problem, $D_{AD}$ is normally distributed with mean $\mu_{AD} = 1200$ and standard deviation $\mu_{AD} = 70$. By making appropriate probability assumptions, it can be shown that $D_{LD}$ is also normally distributed, and its mean and standard deviation are $\mu_{LD} = L\mu_{AD}$ and $\sigma_{LD} = \sqrt{L}\sigma_{AD}$. Because the lead time is 1 week ($L = 1/52$), Machey's expected demand during lead time is $\mu_{LD} = (1/52)(1200) \approx 23$ cameras, and the standard deviation of demand during lead time is $\sigma_{LD} = \sqrt{1/52}(70) \approx 9.7$ cameras.

Given these values, you might think that Machey's should set its reorder point $R$ equal to 23, the mean demand during lead time. But then there would be a 50–50 chance of stocking out before the order arrives (because the probability that a normal random variable is greater than its mean is 0.5). What if the company instead sets $R$ equal to 1 standard deviation above the mean—that is, $R = 23 + 9.7 \approx 33$? Then the probability of a stockout is $P(D_{LD} > 33)$. This can be found with the NORMDIST function in Excel. (It can also be found with RISKview, but we take advantage of Excel functions here.) The syntax for this function is NORMDIST($x, \mu, \sigma$, 1). It returns the probability that a normal random variable with mean $\mu$ and standard deviation $\sigma$ is less than or equal to a specified value $x$. Therefore, we find $P(D_{LD} > 33)$, the probability of a stockout, with the formula $=1-$NORMDIST (33,23,9.7,1), which is approximately 0.15 (see Figure 13.13).

**Figure 13.13**

Probability Under a Normal Distribution

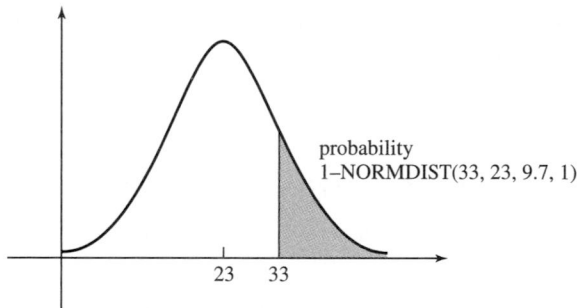

probability
1–NORMDIST(33, 23, 9.7, 1)

23    33

In general, suppose that Machey's decides to set $R$ equal to $k$ standard deviations above the mean, where $k$ is a multiplier that must be determined. That is, it uses the reorder level

$$R = \mu_{LD} + k\sigma_{LD} = \mu_{LD} + \text{safety stock} \tag{13.9}$$

In effect, the multiplier $k$ becomes the decision variable. Usually $k$ is positive (as we require in this section). The term $k\sigma_{LD}$ then becomes the safety stock. To summarize the reasoning, Machey's expects an amount $\mu_{LD}$ to be demanded during the 1-week lead time. However, because shortages are undesirable, it orders when the inventory level is $k\sigma_{LD}$ above $\mu_{LD}$. Therefore, it expects the inventory level to be $k\sigma_{LD}$, a positive value, when the order arrives. This value, the safety stock, is its cushion against larger-than-expected demand. But although the company plans for this safety stock to exist, there is no guarantee that it *will* exist. The previous probability calculation with $k = 1$ shows that there is about a 15% chance that the safety stock of 10 units will be depleted before the order arrives. In this case, a stockout occurs. We want to choose $k$ and the order quantity $Q$ in an optimal manner.

**Finding the Expected Costs** We now develop an expression for Machey's expected total annual cost as a function of the order quantity $Q$ and $k$. In the following discussion, we refer to an **order cycle,** which begins each time an order arrives and ends just before the *next* order arrives (see Figure 13.14).

**Figure 13.14**

Depiction of an
Order Cycle

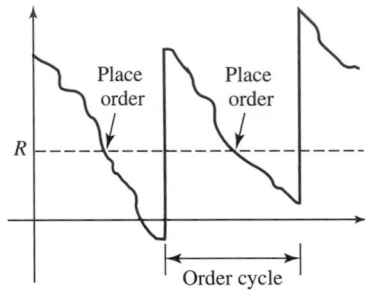

We first consider the annual setup and holding costs. If an order quantity $Q$ is used, it takes an expected amount of time $Q/\mu_{AD}$ to deplete this inventory. (Remember that $\mu_{AD}$ is the expected annual demand. It plays the same role as $D$ in the deterministic EOQ models.) Therefore, there are an expected $\mu_{AD}/Q$ order cycles per year, so the expected annual setup cost is $K\mu_{AD}/Q$. For the holding cost, consider any order cycle. The lowest inventory level during a cycle is expected to be $k\sigma_{LD}$, the safety stock. The highest inventory level occurs when the order arrives and the expected inventory jumps up to $Q + k\sigma_{LD}$. Therefore, the expected average inventory level during a typical cycle is $[k\sigma_{LD} + (Q + k\sigma_{LD})]/2$, and we multiply this by the unit holding cost $h$ to obtain the expected annual holding cost. (Note that we are now using the letter $h$ to refer to the unit holding cost. Comparing to the EOQ section, $h = s + ic$.) Simplifying the algebra slightly leads to the following expressions for expected annual setup and holding costs:

$$\text{Expected annual setup cost} = K\mu_{AD}/Q \qquad \textbf{(13.10)}$$

$$\text{Expected annual holding cost} = h(Q/2 + k\sigma_{LD}) \qquad \textbf{(13.11)}$$

*A company can try to attach a dollar figure to shortages, or it can instead specify a service level such as the fraction of demand satisfied with on-hand inventory. However, the "appropriate" service level is ultimately determined by costs.*

where (for Machey's) $K = \$125$, $h = \$8$, $\mu_{AD} = 1200$, $\sigma_{LD} = 9.7$, and $Q$ and $k$ need to be determined.

**Two Ways to "Cost" Shortages** We now consider two alternative models of "costing" shortages. Neither of these models is clearly superior to the other, so Machey's must decide which model is more in line with the company's goals. Model 1 assumes that there is a shortage cost of $p$ per unit short. In this model, a cycle with a shortage of 5 units is 5 times as costly as a cycle with a shortage of only 1 unit. For example, suppose Machey's uses model 1 with $p = \$10$. If the *average* number of shortages during each of its order cycles is 2, and there are 13 order cycles during the year, then its annual shortage cost is $260.

Model 2 gets around the difficult problem of assessing *dollar* shortage costs by instead specifying a service level. Specifically, it requires that the fraction of demand that can be met from on-hand inventory must be at least $s$, where $s$ is a number between 0 and 1. This fraction is often called the **fill rate.** For example, if Machey's uses model 2 with $s = 0.98$, then it choose its ordering policy so that at least 98% of all customer demand can be met from on-hand inventory. That is, it tries to achieve a fill rate of 98%.

Before we can solve Machey's problem on a spreadsheet, we must develop formulas for the shortage cost (or service level) for these two shortage-costing models.

**Expected Shortage Cost for Model 1**  In model 1, Machey's assesses a shortage cost of $p$ per unit short during any order cycle. Therefore, to evaluate the expected annual shortage cost, we must find the expected number of shortages per order cycle. Let $E(B)$ be the expected number of units short during a typical order cycle. Then the expected shortage cost during this cycle is $pE(B)$, and the expected annual shortage cost is the expected shortage cost per cycle multiplied by the expected number of cycles per year, $\mu_{AD}/Q$. This leads to the following expected total annual shortage cost:

$$\text{Model 1 expected annual shortage cost} = pE(B)\mu_{AD}/Q \qquad (13.12)$$

The problem is to find an expression for $E(B)$. This expected value is related to a well-known quantity called the **normal loss function**. Fortunately, this can be calculated with built-in Excel functions. The formula for $E(B)$ is[8]

$$E(B) = [n(k) - kP(Z > k)]\sigma_{LD} \qquad (13.13)$$

Here, $n(k)$ is the standard normal density function evaluated at $k$, and $Z$ is a standard normal random variable. (Recall that *standard* normal implies mean 0 and standard deviation 1.) We now show how to implement model 1 for the camera example.

### DEVELOPING THE SPREADSHEET FOR MODEL 1

We assume that Machey's decides to use model 1 with $p = \$10$ as the unit shortage cost. The spreadsheet solution appears in Figure 13.15. (See the file **Ordering Cameras 1.xlsx**.) It can be developed as follows:

**1** **Inputs.** Enter the inputs in the blue range.

**2** **Lead time demand.** Calculate the mean and standard deviation of lead time demand in cells B12 and B13 with the formulas

=Lead_time*Expected_annual_demand

 and

=SQRT(Lead_time)*Stdev_of_annual_demand

(Admittedly, we have created a lot of range names to make the formulas more readable, but they can all be created in one step with the Create from Selection shortcut.)

**3** **Decision variables.** Enter any values in cells B16 and B17 for the order quantity $Q$ and the multiplier $k$. These are the changing cells.

**4** **Safety stock and reorder point.** The decision variables determine the safety stock and the reorder point. Calculate them in cells B18 and B19 with the formulas

=Multiple_k*Stdev_lead_time_demand

---

[8] This is one of the few times in this book where you will have to take our word for it. The derivation of this formula is beyond the level of this book. Also, it depends on demand being normally distributed.

Figure 13.15

Optimal Solution
for Model 1

| | A | B | C | D | E |
|---|---|---|---|---|---|
| 1 | Optimal (R,Q) ordering policy for model 1 | | | | |
| 2 | | | | | |
| 3 | Inputs | | | Range names used: | |
| 4 | Setup cost per order | $125 | | Expected_annual_demand | =Model!$B$6 |
| 5 | Holding cost per unit per year | $8 | | Expected_shortage_per_cycle | =Model!$B$20 |
| 6 | Expected annual demand | 1200 | | Holding_cost_per_unit_per_year | =Model!$B$5 |
| 7 | Stdev of annual demand | 70 | | Lead_time | =Model!$B$8 |
| 8 | Lead time | 0.0192 | | Mean_lead_time_demand | =Model!$B$12 |
| 9 | Shortage cost per unit short | $10 | | Multiple_k | =Model!$B$17 |
| 10 | | | | Order_quantity | =Model!$B$16 |
| 11 | Lead time demand | | | Reorder_point | =Model!$B$19 |
| 12 | Mean lead time demand | 23.077 | | Safety_stock | =Model!$B$18 |
| 13 | Stdev lead time demand | 9.707 | | Setup_cost_per_order | =Model!$B$4 |
| 14 | | | | Shortage_cost_per_unit_short | =Model!$B$9 |
| 15 | Ordering policy | | | Stdev_lead_time_demand | =Model!$B$13 |
| 16 | Order quantity | 198.6 | | Stdev_of_annual_demand | =Model!$B$7 |
| 17 | Multiple k | 1.12 | | Total_annual_cost | =Model!$B$25 |
| 18 | Safety stock | 10.8 | | | |
| 19 | Reorder point | 33.9 | | | |
| 20 | Expected shortage per cycle | 0.65 | | | |
| 21 | | | | | |
| 22 | Annual setup cost | $755 | | | |
| 23 | Annual holding cost | $881 | | | |
| 24 | Annual shortage cost | $39 | | | |
| 25 | Total annual cost | $1,675 | | | |

and

**=Mean_lead_time_demand+Safety_stock**

**5** **Expected backorders.** Use equation (13.13) to calculate the expected number of backorders per order cycle, $E(B)$, in cell B20 with the formula

**=Stdev_lead_time_demand*(NORMDIST(Multiple_k,0,1,0)-Multiple_k*(1-NORMSDIST(Multiple_k)))**

Note that this formula uses two related functions, NORMDIST and NORMSDIST. The first of these takes four arguments: a value, the mean, the standard deviation, and 0 or 1. When the fourth argument is 1, the function returns a cumulative (left-hand tail) probability, but when this argument is 0, it returns the value of the density function. Here it is used with a fourth argument equal to 0 to evaluate the standard normal density at value $k$. The second function, the NORMSDIST function, takes only one argument, a value. (The "S" in NORMSDIST stands for *standard* normal.) It returns the probability to the left of this value under the standard normal curve. To obtain the probability to the right of the value $k$, we subtract the NORMSDIST probability from 1 (see Figure 13.16).

**6** **Expected annual costs.** Use equations (13.10) to (13.12) to calculate the expected annual setup, holding, and shortage costs in cells B22 to B24 with the formulas

Figure 13.16

NORMDIST and
NORMSDIST
Functions

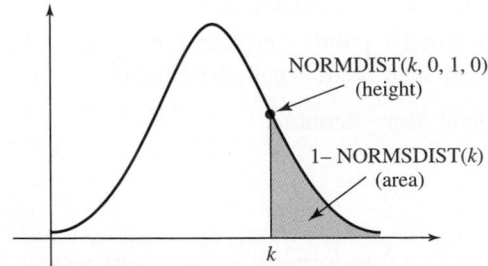

NORMDIST($k$, 0, 1, 0)
(height)

1– NORMSDIST($k$)
(area)

$k$

=Setup_cost_per_order*Expected_annual_demand/Order_quantity

=Holding_cost_per_unit_per_year*(Safety_stock+Order_quantity/2)

and

=Shortage_cost_per_unit_short*Expected_shortage_per_cycle*Expected_annual_
demand/Order_quantity

Then calculate the expected total annual cost in cell B25 by summing the costs in cells B22 to B24.

## USING SOLVER

We set up Solver to minimize the expected total annual cost. The only constraints are non-negativity constraints on the changing cells, B16 and B17. As usual, we do *not* check the Assume Linear Model box. This model is nonlinear in both $Q$ and $k$.

### Discussion of the Solution

The interpretation of the Solver solution in Figure 13.15 is that Machey's should wait until the inventory level drops to approximately 34 cameras and then place an order for 199 cameras. The expected number of backorders is $E(B) = 0.65$, so that the expected shortage cost during any order cycle is $pE(B) = \$6.50$. Multiplying this by the expected number of cycles per year (1200/198.6) gives the expected annual shortage cost of approximately \$39.

Note that the optimal order quantity, 199, is very close to the optimal EOQ, 194, from Example 13.1. This is despite the fact that demand is now random, not assumed known as before. This explains why companies often use the simple EOQ formula to determine the order quantity, even when demand is random.

### Service Level Constraint for Model 2

Model 2 uses a service level constraint instead of a dollar shortage cost. To model this constraint, we need an expression for the fill rate, the fraction of demand met directly from existing inventory. Note that $Q$ items are ordered each cycle, and the expected shortage per cycle is $E(B)$, which we evaluated for model 1. Therefore, the expected fraction of demand met on time is $1 - E(B)/Q$, and the model 2 service level constraint becomes:

$$1 - E(B)/Q \geq s \qquad (13.14)$$

(Note that we are now using the letter $s$ for the service level, not the unit storage cost.)

## DEVELOPING THE SPREADSHEET FOR MODEL 2

The spreadsheet for model 2 appears in Figure 13.17. (See the file **Ordering Cameras 2.xlsx**.) It assumes a service level where at least 99% ($s = 0.99$) of customer demands must be satisfied with existing inventory. This model is very similar to the one shown in Figure 13.15, so we list only the changes.

**1** **Required service level.** There is no unit shortage cost input. Instead, enter the required service level (fill rate) in cell D22.

**2** **Actual service level.** Use the left side of inequality (13.14) to calculate the expected fraction of demand met with existing inventory in cell B22 with the formula

=1-Expected_shortage_per_cycle/Order_quantity

**3** **Expected total annual cost.** The total cost now includes only the setup and holding costs (which are the same as before).

## USING SOLVER

We again minimize the expected total annual cost, but we now add the service level constraint in row 22. There is no longer a shortage *cost* to penalize shortages. Instead, the company requires that 99% of all demand be met from existing inventory.

### Discussion of the Solution

Compared to the solution for model 1, the solution in Figure 13.17 has a slightly larger order quantity $Q$ and a significantly lower multiplier $k$. Therefore, this model specifies that Machey's should order a bit more on each order, and it should hold less safety stock—that is, it should let its inventory drop lower before ordering. Why are the solutions from the two models different? One way to understand the difference is to substitute the optimal values of $Q$ and $k$ from model 1 into the spreadsheet for model 2. If you do this, you will find that $Q$ and $k$ from model 1 lead to a service level (in cell B22) of 0.997 in model 2. This large service level, larger than the 0.99 required, can be attained only with increased safety stock. Evidently, the unit penalty cost of $10 in model 1 is *equivalent* to a required service level of 0.997 in model 2. Alternatively, if we want a service level of 0.99 in model 2, then the equivalent model 1 unit penalty cost must be considerably less than $10.

**Figure 13.17**

Optimal Solution
for Model 2

| | A | B | C | D | E | F | G |
|---|---|---|---|---|---|---|---|
| 1 | Optimal (R,Q) ordering policy for model 2 | | | | | | |
| 2 | | | | | | | |
| 3 | **Inputs** | | | | Range names used: | | |
| 4 | Setup cost per order | $125 | | | Actual_fill_rate | =Model!$B$22 | |
| 5 | Holding cost per unit per year | $8 | | | Expected_annual_demand | =Model!$B$6 | |
| 6 | Expected annual demand | 1200 | | | Expected_shortage_per_cycle | =Model!$B$19 | |
| 7 | Stdev of annual demand | 70 | | | Holding_cost_per_unit_per_year | =Model!$B$5 | |
| 8 | Lead time | 0.0192 | | | Lead_time | =Model!$B$8 | |
| 9 | | | | | Mean_lead_time_demand | =Model!$B$11 | |
| 10 | **Lead time demand** | | | | Multiple_k | =Model!$B$16 | |
| 11 | Mean lead time demand | 23.077 | | | Order_quantity | =Model!$B$15 | |
| 12 | Stdev lead time demand | 9.707 | | | Reorder_point | =Model!$B$18 | |
| 13 | | | | | Required_fill_rate | =Model!$D$22 | |
| 14 | **Ordering policy** | | | | Safety_stock | =Model!$B$17 | |
| 15 | Order quantity | 200.0 | | | Setup_cost_per_order | =Model!$B$4 | |
| 16 | Multiple k | 0.47 | | | Stdev_lead_time_demand | =Model!$B$12 | |
| 17 | Safety stock | 4.6 | | | Stdev_of_annual_demand | =Model!$B$7 | |
| 18 | Reorder point | 27.7 | | | Total_annual_cost | =Model!$B$26 | |
| 19 | Expected shortage per cycle | 2.00 | | | | | |
| 20 | | | | | | | |
| 21 | **Service level constraint** | Actual fill rate | | Required fill rate | | | |
| 22 | | 0.990 | >= | 0.99 | | | |
| 23 | | | | | | | |
| 24 | Annual setup cost | $750 | | | | | |
| 25 | Annual holding cost | $837 | | | | | |
| 26 | Total annual cost | $1,587 | | | | | |

*It is usually easier for a company to specify a service level, but any such service level is really equivalent to some unit shortage cost.*

This is an important concept. Machey's managers probably favor model 2 because a service level constraint is easier to estimate than a unit shortage cost. However, any particular service level in model 2 is really *equivalent* to an appropriate unit shortage cost in model 1. To find the equivalent unit shortage cost $p$ for any required service level $s$, we can use SolverTable on model 1. We first calculate the fill rate as in model 2. We then run SolverTable to see how the fill rate varies with the unit shortage cost (see Figure 13.18). Note that Solver is actually minimizing total expected annual cost, but it is reporting the fill rate. We see, for example, that a fill rate of 99% is equivalent to a unit shortage cost somewhere between $4 and $5. Similarly, a fill rate of 98% is equivalent to a unit shortage cost of approximately $1. The point is that when a company specifies a required fill rate, this is really equivalent to specifying a corresponding unit shortage cost.

| | A | B |
|---|---|---|
| 27 | Fill rate | 99.67% |
| 28 | | |
| 29 | Fill rate as a function of the unit shortage cost | |
| 30 | | $B$27 |
| 31 | 1 | 98.03% |
| 32 | 2 | 98.06% |
| 33 | 3 | 98.38% |
| 34 | 4 | 98.93% |
| 35 | 5 | 99.21% |
| 36 | 6 | 99.38% |
| 37 | 7 | 99.49% |
| 38 | 8 | 99.57% |
| 39 | 9 | 99.63% |
| 40 | 10 | 99.67% |
| 41 | 11 | 99.71% |
| 42 | 12 | 99.74% |
| 43 | 13 | 99.76% |
| 44 | 14 | 99.78% |
| 45 | 15 | 99.80% |

### Random Lead Times

Throughout this section, we have assumed that the lead time for orders is a known quantity. We can easily modify the analysis for the case where the lead time $L$ is random. This is important, because uncertain lead times for ordering in real applications are not uncommon—suppliers might not be able to deliver according to a precise schedule.

When $L$ is random, we need to estimate its mean and standard deviation (from historical lead time data), which we denote by $\mu_L$ and $\sigma_L$. Given these values, the expected demand during lead time becomes

$$\mu_{LD} = \mu_L \, \mu_{AD}$$

and the standard deviation of demand during lead time becomes

$$\sigma_{LD} = \sqrt{\mu_L \sigma_{AD}^2 + \mu_{AD}^2 \sigma_L^2}$$

The first of these is the expected lead time, expressed as a fraction of a year, multiplied by the expected annual demand. The second formula is less intuitive, but as expected, it includes both the uncertainty in annual demand and the uncertainty in lead time.

For example, suppose as before that $\mu_{AD} = 1200$ and $\sigma_{AD} = 70$. However, instead of $L$ being fixed at $1/52$, it is uncertain with mean $\mu_L = 1/52$ and $\sigma_L = 1/104$, so that the standard deviation of the lead time is half a week. Then $\mu_{LD}$ is still 23.077 units $[= (1/52)(1200)]$, but the standard deviation of demand during lead time is

$$\sigma_{LD} = \sqrt{(1/52)70^2 + 1200^2(1/104)^2} = 15.079$$

This is considerably larger than $\sigma_{LD} = 9.7$ when $L$ was known with certainty. Intuitively, we can see that the extra uncertainty about the lead time adds to the uncertainty about the demand during lead time.

After we use these formulas to obtain $\mu_{LD}$ and $\sigma_{LD}$, we can find the optimal $(R,Q)$ exactly as in the nonrandom lead time case. For example, we reran the Solver for model 2 using $\sigma_{LD} = 15.079$ in cell B12. (Nothing else needs to be changed.) The order quantity hardly changed, the safety stock increased from 4.6 to 11.2, the reorder point increased from 27.7 to 34.3, and expected total annual cost increased from \$1587 to \$1640. In short, when the lead time is uncertain, a company needs to order earlier, which means larger safety stock and higher inventory holding costs. ■

# PROBLEMS

## Skill-Building Problems

**12.** Consider each change to the monetary inputs (the purchase cost, the selling price, and the salvage price) one at a time in Example 13.6. For each such change, either up or down, describe how the cost of understocking and the cost of overstocking change, how the critical fractile changes, and how the optimal order quantity changes. Are these changes all intuitive?

**13.** As stated in Example 13.6, the critical fractile analysis is useful for finding the optimal order quantity, but it doesn't (at least by itself) show the probability distribution of net profit. Use @RISK, as in Chapter 11, to explore this distribution. Actually, do it twice, once with the triangular demand distribution and its optimal order quantity and once with the normal demand distribution and its optimal order quantity. What can you say about the resulting distributions of net profit? What can you say about the resulting *expected* net profits? Could you use @RISK to confirm that these order quantities are indeed optimal? Explain how.

**14.** We saw in Example 13.6 that the optimal order quantities with the triangular and normal demand distributions are very similar (171 versus 174). Perhaps this is because these two distributions, with the parameters used in the example, have similar shapes. Explore whether this similarity in optimal order quantities continues as the triangular distribution gets more skewed in one direction or the other. Specifically, keep the same minimum and maximum values (100 and 300), but let the most likely value vary so that the triangular distribution is more or less skewed in one direction or the other. For each most likely value, use RISKview to find the optimal order quantity and compare this to optimal order quantity for a normal demand distribution with the same mean and standard deviation as the triangular distribution with the given most likely value. (In other words, you should pair each triangular distribution with a normal distribution so that they have the same means and standard deviations.) Comment on your results in a brief report.

**15.** In the first $(R,Q)$ model in Example 13.7, the one with a shortage cost, we let both $Q$ and the multiple $k$ be changing cells. However, we stated that the optimal $Q$ depends mainly on the fixed ordering cost, the holding cost, and the expected annual demand. This implies that a good approximation to the optimal $Q$ is the EOQ from equation (13.4), replacing $D$ with the *expected* annual demand and $s + ic$ with the given unit holding cost. Check how good this approximation is by using this EOQ formula to obtain $Q$ and then using Solver with a single changing cell—the multiple $k$—to optimize the expected total annual cost. How close are the results to those in Example 13.7?

**16.** Change the model in the file **Ordering Cameras 2.xlsx** slightly to allow a random lead time with a given mean and standard deviation. If the mean lead time is 2 weeks, and the standard deviation of lead time is half a week, find the optimal solution if the company desires a fill rate of 98.5%. Explain exactly how the company would implement this solution.

**17.** In both $(R,Q)$ models, the one with a shortage cost and the one with a service level constraint, we set up Solver so that the multiple $k$ is constrained to be nonnegative. The effect is that the reorder point $R$ will be no less than the mean demand during lead time, and the expected safety stock will be nonnegative. This seems reasonable, but is it always optimal? Experiment with the service level in the file **Ordering Cameras 2.xlsx**. Change the Solver settings to allow the multiple $k$ to be negative; that is, don't constrain it to be nonnegative. For lower service levels, is it ever optimal to have $k$ negative? Comment briefly why this might or might not be the case and explain the implications for the company.

**18.** In Example 13.7, we discussed the equivalence between the model with shortage costs and the model with a service level constraint. We also showed how to see this equivalence with SolverTable. Extend the SolverTable in the **Ordering Cameras 1.xlsx** file, with the unit shortage cost as the single input varied from $0.50 to $15 in increments of $0.50. As outputs, keep track of the order quantity, the safety stock, the reorder point, the fraction of demand met with existing inventory, and the expected annual setup, holding, and shortage costs. Discuss whether these go in the direction you would expect. Also, discuss how these results relate the two models, one with shortage costs and the other with a service level constraint. (What is equivalent to what?)

## Skill-Extending Problems

**19.** We claimed that the critical fractile formula, equation (13.8), is appropriate because the optimal $Q$ should satisfy $c_{under}(1 - F(Q)) = c_{over} F(Q)$, that is, the cost of understocking times the probability of understocking should equal the cost of overstocking times the probability of overstocking. Assume that $Q$ satisfies this equation [which is equivalent to equation (13.8)]. Use a probability argument to show why $Q - 1$ and $Q + 1$ are both worse than $Q$ in terms of expected cost.

**20.** The first $(R,Q)$ model in this section assumes that the total shortage cost is proportional to the amount of demand that cannot be met from on-hand inventory. Similarly, the second model assumes that the service level constraint is in terms of the fill rate, the fraction of all customer demand that can be met with on-hand inventory. Consider the following variations of these models. The first, labeled model 3, assumes that a shortage cost is incurred on every order cycle that experiences a stockout. This cost is independent of the *size* of the stockout. The second model, labeled model 4, prescribes a service level constraint but now on the fraction of order cycles that experience no stockouts.

**a.** In each of these new models, we need to calculate the probability of a stockout during an order cycle. This is the probability that the demand during lead time is greater than the safety stock. Assuming that demand during lead time is still normally distributed, how can this probability be calculated? (Hint: Use the NORMDIST or NORMSDIST function.)

**b.** Given your method in part **a**, solve the model from Example 13.7 when the cost of having a shortage in any cycle is $100, and all other parameters are as before. What are the optimal reorder point and the safety stock level?

**c.** Continuing part **b**, what model 4 service level constraint is this $100 stockout cost equivalent to?

**21.** Turn the previous problem around. Now assume that the store's service level requirement obligates it to meet customer demand on 99% of all order cycles. In other words, use model 4. What $(R,Q)$ policy should it use? Then find the model 3 cost parameter (the cost per cycle with a shortage) that is equivalent to this service level.

## 13.6 ORDERING SIMULATION MODELS

Analytical models such as those in the previous section are useful and often provide important insights. Unfortunately, they can also often lead to dead ends. As problems become more complex, the required mathematical models become too difficult for most managers to comprehend. In fact, mathematical models do not even exist for many realistic problems. Therefore, it is useful to turn to simulation, where virtually "anything goes." Simulation allows us to combine assumptions about uncertain quantities and ordering policies and then play out the events as they occur through time. We already illustrated a newsvendor simulation model in Chapter 11 when we discussed Walton Bookstore's calendars. The following example illustrates a somewhat more ambitious ordering simulation. It describes a type of ordering policy, an $(s, S)$ policy, that is commonly used in periodic review situations.

**EXAMPLE** | **13.8 SIMULATING ORDERING POLICIES AT HOME REPAIR**

Home Repair is a large hardware retail store that often has to place orders for hammers. The fixed cost for placing an order is $500, independent of the size of the order. The unit cost per hammer is $20. Home Repair estimates that the cost of holding a hammer in inventory for 1 week is $3. The company defines its **inventory position** at the beginning of any week as the number of hammers in inventory, plus any that have already been ordered but have not yet arrived, minus any backorders. The company's ordering policy is an $(s, S)$ policy, a common periodic review policy used by many companies. This policy, defined by two numbers $s$ and $S$, where $s < S$, specifies that if the inventory position at the beginning of the week is at level $x$, and $x$ is less than or equal to $s$, exactly enough hammers are ordered to bring the inventory position up to $S$; that is, Home Repair orders $S - x$ hammers. Otherwise, if the inventory position is greater than $s$, no order is placed that week. If an order is placed, it arrives after a lead time of 1, 2, or 3 weeks with probabilities 0.7, 0.2, and 0.1.

The weekly demand for hammers is uncertain, but it can be described by a normal distribution with mean 300 and standard deviation 75. The company's policy is to satisfy all demand in the week it occurs. If weekly demand cannot be satisfied completely from on-hand inventory, then an emergency order is placed at the end of the week for the shortage. This order arrives virtually instantaneously but at a steep cost of $35 per hammer.

It is currently the beginning of week 1, and the current inventory of hammers, including any that might just have arrived, is 600. No other orders are on the way. Home Repair wants to simulate several (s, S) policies to see which does best in terms of total costs over the next 48 weeks.[9]

**Objective**   To use simulation to analyze costs when the company uses an (s,S) ordering policy.

## Solution

We use @RISK to simulate a 48-week period and keep track of the total costs for this period for each of several (s, S) policies. There is no way to optimize over all possible (s, S) policies (except by using a package such as Palisade's RISKOptimizer), but it is possible to test a number of representative policies and choose the best of these.

### DEVELOPING THE SIMULATION MODEL

The simulation model is shown in Figures 13.19 and 13.20, with a number of hidden rows in the latter figure. (See the file **Order Simulation.xlsx**.) It is mostly a matter of careful bookkeeping, as we describe in the following steps:

**Figure 13.19**   Inputs for the Simulation Model

| | A | B | C | D | E | F | G | H | I |
|---|---|---|---|---|---|---|---|---|---|
| 1 | Evaluating an ordering policy | | | | | | | | |
| 2 | | | | | | | | | |
| 3 | | | | | | | | | |
| 4 | Assumptions: | | | | | | | | |
| 5 | A company uses an ordering policy determined by two integers s (reorder point) and S (order up to quantity). At the beginning of each week, right after any shipments have arrived, its inventory position is examined. This includes on-hand inventory plus any that has been ordered but has not yet arrived. If the inventory position is greater than s, no order is placed. But if it is less than or equal to s, an order is placed to bring the inventory position up to S, and this order arrives after a random lead time of 1 to 3 weeks. All demand is satisfied on time -- one way or the other. Either it is satisfied from onhand inventory, or if demand in any week is greater than on-hand inventory, the demand is met by an emergency shipment (at a high cost). | | | | | | | | |
| 6 | | | | | | | | | |
| 7 | | | | | | | | | |
| 8 | | | | | | | | | |
| 9 | | | | | | | | | |
| 10 | | | | | | | | | |
| 11 | | | | | | | | | |
| 12 | Costs | | | | | Range names used: | | | |
| 13 | Fixed order cost | $500 | | | | Emergency_shi | =Model!$B$16 | | |
| 14 | Variable order cost | $20 | | | | Fixed_order_cc | =Model!$B$13 | | |
| 15 | Inventory holding cost | $3 | | | | Inventory_hold | =Model!$B$15 | | |
| 16 | Emergency shipment cost | $35 | | | | Mean_weekly_ | =Model!$B$25 | | |
| 17 | | | | | | Order_up_to_le | =Model!$B$36 | | |
| 18 | Distribution of order lead time | | | | | Reorder_point_ | =Model!$B$35 | | |
| 19 | | # of weeks | Probability | | | Stdev_weekly_ | =Model!$B$26 | | |
| 20 | | 1 | 0.7 | | | Variable_order | =Model!$B$14 | | |
| 21 | | 2 | 0.2 | | | | | | |
| 22 | | 3 | 0.1 | | | | | | |
| 23 | | | | | | | | | |
| 24 | Distribution of demand in a week - Normal (rounded to nearest integer) | | | | | | | | |
| 25 | Mean weekly demand | 300 | | | | | | | |
| 26 | Stdev weekly demand | 75 | | | | | | | |
| 27 | | | | | Ordering policies to try | | | | |
| 28 | Other inputs | | | | Policy | s | S | | |
| 29 | Initial inventory | 600 | | | 1 | 200 | 500 | | |
| 30 | Due in week 2 | 0 | | | 2 | 350 | 500 | | |
| 31 | Due in week 3 | 0 | | | 3 | 350 | 750 | | |
| 32 | | | | | 4 | 500 | 750 | | |
| 33 | Order parameters | | | | 5 | 400 | 1000 | | |
| 34 | Policy index | 1 | | | 6 | 600 | 1000 | | |
| 35 | Reorder point s | 200 | | | 7 | 500 | 1250 | | |
| 36 | Order up to level S | 500 | | | 8 | 700 | 1250 | | |

[9] Why 48 weeks, not 52? There are 2 random inputs for each week in the model, plus one for the RISKSIMTABLE function, and the maximum number of random inputs allowed by the educational version of @RISK is 100. Therefore, 48 weeks gets us slightly under the limit.

**Figure 13.20**  Simulation of a 48-Week Period

| | A | B | C | D | E | F | G | H | I | J | K | L | M |
|---|---|---|---|---|---|---|---|---|---|---|---|---|---|
| 38 | Summary measures from 48-week simulation below | | | | | | | | | | | | |
| 39 | | Fixed order | Var order | Holding | Emergency | Total | | | | | | | |
| 40 | Cost totals | $11,500 | $186,000 | $22,650 | $164,500 | $384,650 | | | | | | | |
| 41 | | | | | | | | | | | | | |
| 42 | Simulation | | | Inventory and order quantities, and lead time information | | | | | | | Costs | | |
| 43 | Week | Begin on-hand | Due in later | Inv position | Amt ordered | Week order arrives | Demand | End on-hand | Emerg orders | Fixed order | Variable order | Holding | Emergency |
| 44 | 1 | 600 | 0 | 600 | 0 | NA | 300 | 300 | 0 | $0 | $0 | $1,350 | $0 |
| 45 | 2 | 300 | 0 | 300 | 0 | NA | 300 | 0 | 0 | $0 | $0 | $450 | $0 |
| 46 | 3 | 0 | 0 | 0 | 500 | 4 | 300 | 0 | 300 | $500 | $10,000 | $0 | $10,500 |
| 47 | 4 | 500 | 0 | 500 | 0 | NA | 300 | 200 | 0 | $0 | $0 | $1,050 | $0 |
| 48 | 5 | 200 | 0 | 200 | 300 | 6 | 300 | 0 | 100 | $500 | $6,000 | $300 | $3,500 |
| 49 | 6 | 300 | 0 | 300 | 0 | NA | 300 | 0 | 0 | $0 | $0 | $450 | $0 |
| 50 | 7 | 0 | 0 | 0 | 500 | 8 | 300 | 0 | 300 | $500 | $10,000 | $0 | $10,500 |
| 51 | 8 | 500 | 0 | 500 | 0 | NA | 300 | 200 | 0 | $0 | $0 | $1,050 | $0 |
| 52 | 9 | 200 | 0 | 200 | 300 | 10 | 300 | 0 | 100 | $500 | $6,000 | $300 | $3,500 |
| 53 | 10 | 300 | 0 | 300 | 0 | NA | 300 | 0 | 0 | $0 | $0 | $450 | $0 |
| 54 | 11 | 0 | 0 | 0 | 500 | 12 | 300 | 0 | 300 | $500 | $10,000 | $0 | $10,500 |
| 55 | 12 | 500 | 0 | 500 | 0 | NA | 300 | 200 | 0 | $0 | $0 | $1,050 | $0 |
| 87 | 44 | 500 | 0 | 500 | 0 | NA | 300 | 200 | 0 | $0 | $0 | $1,050 | $0 |
| 88 | 45 | 200 | 0 | 200 | 300 | 46 | 300 | 0 | 100 | $500 | $6,000 | $300 | $3,500 |
| 89 | 46 | 300 | 0 | 300 | 0 | NA | 300 | 0 | 0 | $0 | $0 | $450 | $0 |
| 90 | 47 | 0 | 0 | 0 | 500 | 48 | 300 | 0 | 300 | $500 | $10,000 | $0 | $10,500 |
| 91 | 48 | 500 | 0 | 500 | 0 | NA | 300 | 200 | 0 | $0 | $0 | $1,050 | $0 |

**1  Inputs.**  Enter the inputs in the blue ranges in Figure 13.19. These include the various costs, the parameters of the demand distribution, the current inventory situation, and possible combinations of $s$ and $S$ to test. (You can try other, or more, pairs if you like.) Note that the values in cells B30 and B31 are 0 because we have assumed that no orders are currently on the way. However, we develop the model so that it can respond to nonzero values in these cells. These values correspond to orders placed before week 1 but not due in until after week 1.

**2  Ordering policy.**  As usual, we set up the model with a RISKSIMTABLE function so that we can test all of the selected ordering policies simultaneously. To do this, enter the formula

**=RISKSIMTABLE(E29:E36)**

in cell B34. Then enter the formulas

**=VLOOKUP(B34,E29:G36,2)**

and

**=VLOOKUP(B34,E29:G36,3)**

in cells B34 and B35 to capture the values of $s$ and $S$ that are used in the simulation.

**3  Beginning inventory.**  Moving to the simulation model in Figure 13.20, our strategy is the same as in most multiperiod models. We fill in the logic for the first few weeks and then copy down. We begin with column B, which contains the beginning on-hand inventory, right after any order has arrived. For week 1, this is the initial 600 hammers, so enter the formula

**=B29**

in cell B44. For later weeks, we have to sum the final inventory from the previous week and the amount due in, if any, from previous orders. To do this, enter the formulas

**=H44+B30+SUMIF($F$44:F44,A45,$E$44:E44)**

**=H45+B31+SUMIF($F$44:F45,A46,$E$44:E45)**

and

**=H46+SUMIF($F$44:F46,A47,$E$44:E46)**

in cells B45 to B47. This last formula is general, so copy it down to the other weeks. Note how the SUMIF function is used. It sums all previous orders from column E that are due in at the beginning of the current week listed in column A. For example, in week 4, it looks for any due dates in the range F44:F46 that equal 4 and sums the corresponding order quantities.

**4** **Due in later.** In column C, we record the amounts already ordered but not yet in, so that we can calculate the inventory position in column D. Do this by entering the formulas

**=SUM(B30:B31)**
**=B31+SUMIF($F$44:F44, ">"&A45,$E$44:E44)**

and

**=SUMIF($F$44:F45, ">"&A46,$E$44:E45)**

in cells C44 to C46, and copy this latter formula down. The SUMIF function is used essentially as in the previous step, but now we want conditions (the middle argument) such as ">1". To do this in Excel, we must put the greater-than sign in quotes, followed by an ampersand (&), and then a cell reference.

**5** **Inventory position.** The inventory position is the amount on hand plus the amount due in, so enter the formula

**=SUM(B44:C44)**

in cell D44 and copy it down.

**6** **Order.** Following the logic of the $(s, S)$ ordering policy, calculate the order quantity in cell E44 with the formula

**=IF(D44<=Reorder_point_s,Order_up_to_level_S-D44,0)**

and copy it down. Then to see when this order arrives (if there is an order), enter the formula

**=IF(E44>0,A44+RISKDISCRETE($B$20:$B$22,$C$20:$C$22),"NA")**

in cell F44 and copy it down.

**7** **Demand.** Generate random demands in column G (rounded to the nearest integer) by entering the formula

**=ROUND(RISKNORMAL(Mean_weekly_demand,Stdev_weekly_demand),0)**

in cell G44 and copying it down.

**8** **End inventory and emergency orders.** If customer demand is less than on-hand inventory, then ending inventory is the difference; otherwise it is 0. Therefore, enter the formula

**=MAX(B44-G44,0)**

in cell H44 and copy it down. Similarly, there are emergency orders only if customer demand is greater than on-hand inventory, so enter the formula

**=MAX(G44-B44,0)**

in cell I44 and copy it down.

**9** **Weekly costs.** The weekly costs are straightforward. Calculate them for week 1 in cells J44 to M44 with the formulas

**=IF(E44>0,Fixed_order_cost,0)**

**=Variable_order_cost*E44**

=Inventory_holding_cost*(B44+H44)/2

and

=Emergency_shipment_cost*I44

and then copy these down. Note that we are basing the holding cost in any week on the *average* of the beginning and ending inventories for that week. It would be no more difficult to base it on the ending inventory only.

**⑩ Summary measures.** Calculate the total costs of the various types in row 40 and designate them as @RISK output cells. For example, the formula in cell B40 is (remember that the text inside the RISKOUTPUT function is for labeling purposes only)

=RISKOUTPUT("Fixed order")+SUM(J44:J91)

It is important to look carefully at the completed model before running @RISK. Press the F9 key a few times to get new random numbers and check whether all of the logic, particularly in columns B and C, is working the way it should. It is easy to make errors, especially in the timing of order arrivals, in a model as complex as this one, and there is no sense in running @RISK on a model that contains logical errors!

## USING @RISK

We use @RISK exactly as in Chapters 11 and 12. We set the number of iterations to 1000 (each simulates a 48-week period) and the number of simulations to 8 (one for each combination of *s* and *S* we want to test).

### Discussion of the Solution

After running @RISK and copying selected outputs back to Excel, we obtained the results in Figure 13.21. The two shaded cells correspond to the smallest *average* 48-week total costs among all pairs of *s* and *S*. Home Repair might prefer the policy with *s* = 500 and

---

**Figure 13.21** Selected Results from @RISK

| | A | B | C | D | E | F | G | H | I |
|---|---|---|---|---|---|---|---|---|---|
| 93 | Selected @Risk results for total cost (based on 1000 iterations) | | | | | | | | |
| 94 | Simulation | 1 | 2 | 3 | 4 | 5 | 6 | 7 | 8 |
| 95 | Reorder point s | 200 | 350 | 350 | 500 | 400 | 600 | 500 | 700 |
| 96 | Order up to level S | 500 | 500 | 750 | 750 | 1000 | 1000 | 1250 | 1250 |
| 97 | Minimum | $356,541 | $346,636 | $332,586 | $332,629 | $336,452 | $337,006 | $342,045 | $352,927 |
| 98 | Maximum | $461,631 | $461,590 | $449,048 | $434,125 | $440,090 | $428,283 | $442,806 | $433,077 |
| 99 | Mean | $407,807 | $396,686 | $388,237 | $377,528 | $386,467 | $378,010 | $389,556 | $389,416 |
| 100 | Stdev | $17,694 | $17,880 | $17,376 | $16,219 | $16,119 | $14,616 | $14,294 | $12,736 |
| 101 | Percentiles | | | | | | | | |
| 102 | 5% | $379,683 | $367,872 | $360,366 | $351,501 | $361,507 | $355,731 | $366,751 | $369,032 |
| 103 | 10% | $385,767 | $374,292 | $366,243 | $357,424 | $365,954 | $360,370 | $372,600 | $373,472 |
| 104 | 15% | $390,089 | $378,259 | $369,913 | $361,177 | $369,392 | $363,303 | $374,931 | $376,345 |
| 105 | 20% | $392,433 | $381,535 | $373,376 | $364,091 | $372,813 | $365,366 | $377,605 | $378,301 |
| 106 | 25% | $395,282 | $383,945 | $376,643 | $366,386 | $375,644 | $367,662 | $379,454 | $380,381 |
| 107 | 30% | $397,931 | $386,667 | $378,936 | $369,053 | $378,042 | $369,904 | $381,326 | $382,360 |
| 108 | 35% | $400,430 | $389,063 | $381,226 | $370,620 | $380,419 | $371,498 | $383,589 | $384,160 |
| 109 | 40% | $403,193 | $391,708 | $383,837 | $372,539 | $382,118 | $373,231 | $385,236 | $386,014 |
| 110 | 45% | $404,980 | $394,116 | $386,104 | $374,636 | $383,733 | $375,473 | $387,063 | $387,605 |
| 111 | 50% | $407,125 | $396,182 | $388,043 | $376,629 | $385,544 | $377,171 | $388,766 | $389,251 |
| 112 | 55% | $409,715 | $398,894 | $390,382 | $379,321 | $387,704 | $379,055 | $390,895 | $390,870 |
| 113 | 60% | $411,953 | $400,674 | $392,656 | $381,418 | $389,840 | $380,830 | $393,128 | $392,815 |
| 114 | 65% | $414,161 | $403,225 | $395,063 | $383,588 | $391,606 | $382,909 | $395,246 | $394,595 |
| 115 | 70% | $416,864 | $405,801 | $397,014 | $385,753 | $394,092 | $384,988 | $396,851 | $396,166 |
| 116 | 75% | $419,694 | $407,837 | $399,292 | $388,581 | $396,653 | $387,438 | $399,263 | $398,066 |
| 117 | 80% | $422,451 | $411,396 | $402,091 | $391,168 | $399,818 | $390,259 | $401,548 | $400,286 |
| 118 | 85% | $425,846 | $415,285 | $405,793 | $394,226 | $403,551 | $393,795 | $404,327 | $402,137 |
| 119 | 90% | $431,667 | $420,808 | $410,319 | $399,249 | $407,570 | $396,837 | $407,913 | $405,411 |
| 120 | 95% | $438,017 | $427,398 | $417,541 | $404,318 | $414,381 | $404,064 | $414,486 | $410,237 |

$S = 750$ (at least among these particular policies). This policy has the smallest average total cost, it has the smallest 5th percentile, it has the smallest median (50th percentile), and its 95th percentile is close to the smallest. Even with this ordering policy, however, there is still considerable variability—from about $333,000 for the best of the 1000 iterations to about $434,000 for the worst.

We do not claim that this simulation model is particularly easy. The random lead times require some tricky logic. However, an analytical (nonsimulation) model of a situation as complex as Home Repair's would be totally out of the question for all but the most mathematically clever analysts. Simulation brings such complex models within the grasp of non-mathematicians. In addition, the modeling process itself often yields insights, such as why one ordering policy is better than another, that would not be apparent otherwise. ∎

## PROBLEMS

### Skill-Building Problems

**22.** Change the ordering simulation so that the lead time can be 1, 2, 3, or 4 weeks with probabilities 0.5, 0.2, 0.2, and 0.1, respectively. Also, assume that based on previous orders, orders of sizes 350, 0, and 400 are scheduled to arrive at the beginnings of weeks 2, 3, and 4, respectively. Simulate the same $(s, S)$ policies as in the example.

**23.** Change the ordering simulation so that emergency orders are never made. If demand in any week is greater than supply, the excess demand is simply lost. Simulate the same $(s, S)$ policies as in the example.

### Skill-Extending Problem

**24.** Change the ordering simulation so that emergency orders are never made. Instead, assume that all excess demand is backlogged. Now the inventory position is the amount on hand, plus the amount on order, minus the backlog. Simulate the same $(s, S)$ policies as in the example.

## 13.7 SUPPLY CHAIN MODELS

One of today's hottest areas of interest, both for academics and business managers, is supply chain management. This refers to the entire process of getting materials from suppliers, transforming them into finished products, and ultimately getting the finished products to customers. With current computer technology and enterprise resource planning (ERP) software packages available from companies such as SAP, companies are able to interact with their customers and suppliers in a much more integrated manner, thus making their supply chains more efficient than ever before. Efficient supply chains have become a requirement in most industries. Without them, companies cannot compete successfully.

There are numerous interesting and difficult management science problems under the (very wide) supply chain umbrella. (For example, take a look at the July-August 2000 and November-December 2003 issues of *Interfaces*. These are both special issues devoted entirely to supply chain management applications.) We consider one of these in the following example.[10] This is a problem faced by many companies in the fashion industry. When they introduce a new fashion, they are never sure whether it will sell well or not. Therefore, a reasonable strategy is to produce a limited amount early and see how things go. If the product sells well early, they can produce more later on—subject to capacity restrictions. If the product does poorly early, they can cut their losses short.

[10] This is an optimization model that requires the Evolutionary Solver discussed in Chapter 8.

EXAMPLE | 13.9 PLANNING PRODUCTION OF BLOUSES AT SHIRTTAILS

ShirtTails is a clothing manufacturer that operates its own chain of discount retail stores. At the beginning of November 2008, ShirtTails is trying to plan its production of a new blouse that is worn primarily in the warmer months. Based on production constraints from other products, the company knows it has two opportunities to produce this blouse—in November 2008 and later in April 2009. The production capacity (for this blouse) is 1200 in November. In April, the capacity will increase to 2500. By April, demand for the blouses produced in November will be known. Using this information, ShirtTails will then be able to plan its production in April.

The unit cost of producing a blouse is $12, and the selling price will be $14. These remain constant. There is a $1 holding cost per blouse still in inventory after the pre-April demand. By November 2009, any remaining blouses in inventory will be sold at a markdown price of $4. (This is because ShirtTails plans to introduce a new blouse the next year.) Demand for the blouses before April is not known with any certainty, but ShirtTails believes it should be somewhere between 100 and 1000. After April, the demand for blouses is expected to be anywhere from 3 to 7.5 times as large as the demand before April.

What production plan should the company use to maximize the expect profit from these blouses?

**Objective** To develop an optimization model that specifies production quantities of blouses in two time periods, where the second production quantity can be based on demand information from the first period.

## Solution

We first need to recognize that a production plan is really a *contingency plan*. This means that the company will determine a production quantity in November, but it will not commit to a production quantity in April until *after* it observes the pre-April demand. In other words, the contingency plan will specify a single production quantity in November and a production quantity in April for *each* pre-April demand that might be observed.

Before solving anything numerically, we must decide on probability distributions of demand. We will eventually try several, but we initially assume "unimodal" symmetric discrete distributions—essentially the discrete analog of a normal distribution where the probabilities increase and then decrease. We spell out the details shortly.

Finally, we point out explicitly that this is *not* a simulation model, despite the uncertainty. We plan to calculate an expected profit for any given production plan and then use Evolutionary Solver to maximize this expected profit.

### DEVELOPING THE SPREADSHEET MODEL

The completed model appears in Figures 13.22 and 13.23. (See the file **Fashion Production.xlsx**.) It can be developed with the following steps:

**1** **Inputs.** Enter the inputs in the blue ranges in Figure 13.22. These include the given costs, the capacities, and the probability distributions we are initially assuming. Regarding these distributions, rows 13 and 14 indicate the distribution of pre-April demand, which can be any value from 100 to 1000 in increments of 100. Note that the probabilities increase gradually and then decrease—the unimodal property we mentioned. The table in rows 18 to 27 then specifies the distribution of post-April demand, given the pre-April demand. For example, if pre-April demand is 400 (in column E), then post-April demand will be one of the values in the range E18:E27, with the corresponding probabilities in

**Figure 13.22** Inputs for the Fashion Model

| | A | B | C | D | E | F | G | H | I | J | K | L |
|---|---|---|---|---|---|---|---|---|---|---|---|---|
| 1 | Two-stage production for a fashion product | | | | | | | | | | | |
| 2 | | Use the Scenario Manager (under What-If Analysis on the Data ribbon) to view models that incorporate different types of probabilities. When any of these scenarios is "shown," you'll see the optimal production policy for that scenario. | | | | | | | | | | |
| 3 | Inputs | | | | | | | | | | | |
| 4 | Unit production cost | $12 | constant through both periods | | | | | | | | | |
| 5 | Selling price | $14 | constant through both periods | | | | | | | | | |
| 6 | Markdown price | $4 | for any items left over after later period | | | | | | | | | |
| 7 | Holding cost | $1 | charged per unit in inventory after early period | | | | | | | | | |
| 8 | Overcapacity penalty | $500,000 | | | | | | | | | | |
| 9 | Early capacity | 1200 | | | | | | | | | | |
| 10 | Later capacity | 2500 | | | | | | | | | | |
| 11 | | | | | | | | | | | | |
| 12 | Demand during early period | | | | | | | | | | | |
| 13 | Value | 100 | 200 | 300 | 400 | 500 | 600 | 700 | 800 | 900 | 1000 | |
| 14 | Probability | 0.05 | 0.05 | 0.05 | 0.10 | 0.25 | 0.25 | 0.10 | 0.05 | 0.05 | 0.05 | |
| 15 | | | | | | | | | | | | |
| 16 | Distribution of demand during later period (probabilities at right assumed valid for each column separately) | | | | | | | | | | | |
| 17 | Multiple of early demand | Later demand (one column for each possible early demand) | | | | | | | | | | Probability |
| 18 | 3 | 300 | 600 | 900 | 1200 | 1500 | 1800 | 2100 | 2400 | 2700 | 3000 | 0.05 |
| 19 | 3.5 | 350 | 700 | 1050 | 1400 | 1750 | 2100 | 2450 | 2800 | 3150 | 3500 | 0.05 |
| 20 | 4 | 400 | 800 | 1200 | 1600 | 2000 | 2400 | 2800 | 3200 | 3600 | 4000 | 0.05 |
| 21 | 4.5 | 450 | 900 | 1350 | 1800 | 2250 | 2700 | 3150 | 3600 | 4050 | 4500 | 0.10 |
| 22 | 5 | 500 | 1000 | 1500 | 2000 | 2500 | 3000 | 3500 | 4000 | 4500 | 5000 | 0.25 |
| 23 | 5.5 | 550 | 1100 | 1650 | 2200 | 2750 | 3300 | 3850 | 4400 | 4950 | 5500 | 0.25 |
| 24 | 6 | 600 | 1200 | 1800 | 2400 | 3000 | 3600 | 4200 | 4800 | 5400 | 6000 | 0.10 |
| 25 | 6.5 | 650 | 1300 | 1950 | 2600 | 3250 | 3900 | 4550 | 5200 | 5850 | 6500 | 0.05 |
| 26 | 7 | 700 | 1400 | 2100 | 2800 | 3500 | 4200 | 4900 | 5600 | 6300 | 7000 | 0.05 |
| 27 | 7.5 | 750 | 1500 | 2250 | 3000 | 3750 | 4500 | 5250 | 6000 | 6750 | 7500 | 0.05 |

column L (which are also unimodal). Note that the demands in each column of the bottom table range from 3 times to 7.5 times the demand in row 13, as described in the statement of the problem. Of course, this implies that the two periods have highly correlated demands. If pre-April demand is high, post-April demand is also likely to be high. (There is no requirement that the probabilities in row 14 be the same as those in column L. In fact, there is no necessary connection between these two sets of probabilities. We made them equal for illustration only.)

**2** **Production plan.** Moving to the optimization model in Figure 13.23, enter any production quantities in cell B30 and row 32. For example, the particular values in the figure (the optimal values) imply that ShirtTails will produce 600 blouses in November. Then if pre-April demand is 400 (column E), it will produce 1600 more blouses in April. In contrast, if pre-April demand is 600 or more (columns G–K), it will produce at capacity, 2500, in April.

**3** **Production cost.** The total production cost is proportional to the total number of blouses produced. Calculate it in row 35 by entering the formula

=Unit_production_cost*(Early_production+B32)

in cell B35 and copying it across.

**4** **Holding cost.** The holding cost depends only on the November production quantity and pre-April demand. Calculate it in row 37 by entering the formula

=Holding_cost*MAX(Early_production-B13,0)

in cell B37 and copying it across.

**Figure 13.23** The Optimization Model

| | A | B | C | D | E | F | G | H | I | J | K |
|---|---|---|---|---|---|---|---|---|---|---|---|
| 29 | **Production decisions** | | | | | | | | | | |
| 30 | Early production | 600 | | | | | | | | | |
| 31 | | | | | | | | | | | |
| 32 | Later production | 0 | 500 | 1050 | 1600 | 2150 | 2500 | 2500 | 2500 | 2500 | 2500 |
| 33 | | | | | | | | | | | |
| 34 | **Costs, revenues for all scenarios** | | | | | | | | | | |
| 35 | Production cost | $7,200 | $13,200 | $19,800 | $26,400 | $33,000 | $37,200 | $37,200 | $37,200 | $37,200 | $37,200 |
| 36 | | | | | | | | | | | |
| 37 | Holding cost | $500 | $400 | $300 | $200 | $100 | $0 | $0 | $0 | $0 | $0 |
| 38 | | | | | | | | | | | |
| 39 | Sales revenue | $5,600 | $11,200 | $16,800 | $22,400 | $28,000 | $33,600 | $39,200 | $43,400 | $43,400 | $43,400 |
| 40 | | $6,300 | $12,600 | $18,900 | $25,200 | $31,500 | $37,800 | $43,400 | $43,400 | $43,400 | $43,400 |
| 41 | | $7,000 | $14,000 | $21,000 | $28,000 | $35,000 | $42,000 | $43,400 | $43,400 | $43,400 | $43,400 |
| 42 | | $7,700 | $15,400 | $23,100 | $30,800 | $38,500 | $43,400 | $43,400 | $43,400 | $43,400 | $43,400 |
| 43 | | $8,400 | $15,400 | $23,100 | $30,800 | $38,500 | $43,400 | $43,400 | $43,400 | $43,400 | $43,400 |
| 44 | | $8,400 | $15,400 | $23,100 | $30,800 | $38,500 | $43,400 | $43,400 | $43,400 | $43,400 | $43,400 |
| 45 | | $8,400 | $15,400 | $23,100 | $30,800 | $38,500 | $43,400 | $43,400 | $43,400 | $43,400 | $43,400 |
| 46 | | $8,400 | $15,400 | $23,100 | $30,800 | $38,500 | $43,400 | $43,400 | $43,400 | $43,400 | $43,400 |
| 47 | | $8,400 | $15,400 | $23,100 | $30,800 | $38,500 | $43,400 | $43,400 | $43,400 | $43,400 | $43,400 |
| 48 | | $8,400 | $15,400 | $23,100 | $30,800 | $38,500 | $43,400 | $43,400 | $43,400 | $43,400 | $43,400 |
| 49 | Expected sales revenues | $8,015 | $14,980 | $22,470 | $29,960 | $37,450 | $42,560 | $43,190 | $43,400 | $43,400 | $43,400 |
| 50 | | | | | | | | | | | |
| 51 | Markdown revenue | $800 | $1,200 | $1,800 | $2,400 | $3,000 | $2,800 | $1,200 | $0 | $0 | $0 |
| 52 | | $600 | $800 | $1,200 | $1,600 | $2,000 | $1,600 | $0 | $0 | $0 | $0 |
| 53 | | $400 | $400 | $600 | $800 | $1,000 | $400 | $0 | $0 | $0 | $0 |
| 54 | | $200 | $0 | $0 | $0 | $0 | $0 | $0 | $0 | $0 | $0 |
| 55 | | $0 | $0 | $0 | $0 | $0 | $0 | $0 | $0 | $0 | $0 |
| 56 | | $0 | $0 | $0 | $0 | $0 | $0 | $0 | $0 | $0 | $0 |
| 57 | | $0 | $0 | $0 | $0 | $0 | $0 | $0 | $0 | $0 | $0 |
| 58 | | $0 | $0 | $0 | $0 | $0 | $0 | $0 | $0 | $0 | $0 |
| 59 | | $0 | $0 | $0 | $0 | $0 | $0 | $0 | $0 | $0 | $0 |
| 60 | | $0 | $0 | $0 | $0 | $0 | $0 | $0 | $0 | $0 | $0 |
| 61 | Expected markdown revenues | $110 | $120 | $180 | $240 | $300 | $240 | $60 | $0 | $0 | $0 |
| 62 | | | | | | | | | | | |
| 63 | **Expected values** | | | | | | | | | | |
| 64 | Production cost | $31,500 | | | | | | | | | |
| 65 | Holding cost | $105 | | | | | | | | | |
| 66 | Sales revenue | $36,101 | | | | | | | | | |
| 67 | Markdown revenue | $185 | | | | | | | | | |
| 68 | Profit | $4,681 | | | | | | | | | |

**5 Sales revenue.** The total sales revenue (not including markdown sales) depends on both production quantities and both pre-April and post-April demand. Therefore, there is a whole matrix of these quantities, one for each possible combination of demands. Fortunately, these can be calculated with one general formula. To do so, enter the formula

**=Selling_price*MIN(B$13+B18,Early_production+B$32)**

in cell B39 and copy it to the range B39:K48. Note that the first argument of the MIN is the total demand. The second argument is the total production. ShirtTails sells the smaller of these two quantities at the $14 price.

**6 Expected sales revenue.** For each possible pre-April demand—that is, each column from B to K—we need to calculate the expected total sales revenue, where the expected value is over the distribution of post-April demand. To do this, enter the formula

**=SUMPRODUCT(B39:B48,$L$18:$L$27)**

in cell B49 and copy it across row 49. For example, if we are told that pre-April demand is 400 (column E), our best guess for total sales revenue is $29,960.

**7 Markdown revenue.** The calculation of markdown revenue is similar to the previous two steps. First, enter the formula

=Markdown_price*MAX((Early_production+B$32)-(B$13+B18),0)

in cell B51 and copy it to the range B51:K60. These cells show the markdown revenue for each demand combination. Then calculate the expected markdown revenues, given pre-April demand, by entering the formula

=SUMPRODUCT(B51:B60,$L$18:$L$27)

in cell K61 and copying it across row 61.

**8** **Expected revenues, costs, and profits.** At this point, rows 35, 37, 49, and 61 contain revenues and costs for each possible value of pre-April demand. To get overall expected values, we must "SUMPRODUCT" these with the row of pre-April demand probabilities. For example, calculate the overall expected sales revenue in cell B66 with the formula

=SUMPRODUCT(B49:K49,B14:K14)

The others are calculated similarly, and the expected profit is the sum of expected revenues minus the sum of expected costs. These are the values ShirtTails can expect as it looks ahead from November 2000—that is, before any demands have been observed.

## USING EVOLUTIONARY SOLVER

We set up Evolutionary Solver as shown in Figure 13.24. The target cell is the expected profit, the changing cells are the production quantities, and we must constrain them to be within capacity. Of course, the production quantities must also be nonnegative. Note that we use Evolutionary Solver because of the various MAX and MIN functions in the cell formulas. Recall that the standard Solver has problems with such functions, whereas Evolutionary Solver handles them nicely.

**Figure 13.24**

Evolutionary Solver Dialog Box for the Fashion Model

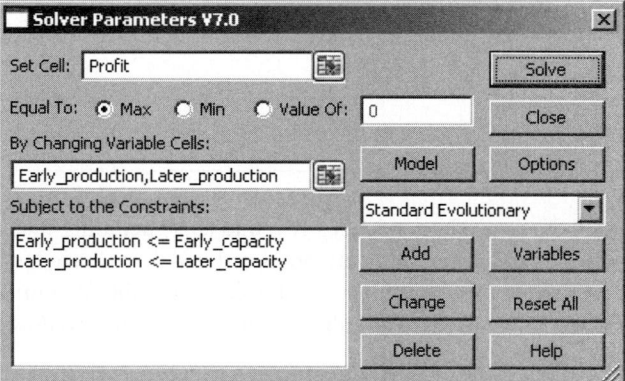

### Discussion of the Solution

The solution in Figure 13.23 is fairly intuitive. ShirtTails could produce up to 1200 units in November, but it holds production to 600 because it is not sure whether these blouses will be popular. After observing the pre-April demand, the company then produces more or less, depending on the success of the blouses to that point. If pre-April demand is its minimum value, 100, then there are already 500 of these "dogs" left in inventory, and the company does not produce any more. But if pre-April demand is sufficiently large, the company recognizes that it has a hot item and produces to capacity in April.

We continue this example by seeing how the shape of the demand distribution affects the optimal production plan. The distribution we have been using assumes a most likely demand in the middle, with less likely demand values on either side—the unimodal property.

We investigate two other possibilities, shown in Figures 13.25 and 13.26. We call the first of these "U-shaped" because the probabilities are large on either end but decrease in the middle. This is reasonable if ShirtTails believes the blouse will be either very popular or very unpopular. The second distribution, in Figure 13.26, has equal probabilities for all

**Figure 13.25** Results for a U-Shaped Probability Distribution

| | A | B | C | D | E | F | G | H | I | J | K | L |
|---|---|---|---|---|---|---|---|---|---|---|---|---|
| 12 | **Demand during early period** | | | | | | | | | | | |
| 13 | Value | 100 | 200 | 300 | 400 | 500 | 600 | 700 | 800 | 900 | 1000 | |
| 14 | Probability | 0.25 | 0.10 | 0.05 | 0.05 | 0.05 | 0.05 | 0.05 | 0.05 | 0.10 | 0.25 | |
| 15 | | | | | | | | | | | | |
| 16 | **Distribution of demand during later period (probabilities at right assumed valid for each column separately)** | | | | | | | | | | | |
| 17 | Multiple of early demand | Later demand (one column for each possible early demand) | | | | | | | | | | Probability |
| 18 | 3 | 300 | 600 | 900 | 1200 | 1500 | 1800 | 2100 | 2400 | 2700 | 3000 | 0.25 |
| 19 | 3.5 | 350 | 700 | 1050 | 1400 | 1750 | 2100 | 2450 | 2800 | 3150 | 3500 | 0.10 |
| 20 | 4 | 400 | 800 | 1200 | 1600 | 2000 | 2400 | 2800 | 3200 | 3600 | 4000 | 0.05 |
| 21 | 4.5 | 450 | 900 | 1350 | 1800 | 2250 | 2700 | 3150 | 3600 | 4050 | 4500 | 0.05 |
| 22 | 5 | 500 | 1000 | 1500 | 2000 | 2500 | 3000 | 3500 | 4000 | 4500 | 5000 | 0.05 |
| 23 | 5.5 | 550 | 1100 | 1650 | 2200 | 2750 | 3300 | 3850 | 4400 | 4950 | 5500 | 0.05 |
| 24 | 6 | 600 | 1200 | 1800 | 2400 | 3000 | 3600 | 4200 | 4800 | 5400 | 6000 | 0.05 |
| 25 | 6.5 | 650 | 1300 | 1950 | 2600 | 3250 | 3900 | 4550 | 5200 | 5850 | 6500 | 0.05 |
| 26 | 7 | 700 | 1400 | 2100 | 2800 | 3500 | 4200 | 4900 | 5600 | 6300 | 7000 | 0.10 |
| 27 | 7.5 | 750 | 1500 | 2250 | 3000 | 3750 | 4500 | 5250 | 6000 | 6750 | 7500 | 0.25 |
| 28 | | | | | | | | | | | | |
| 29 | **Production decisions** | | | | | | | | | | | |
| 30 | Early production | 450 | | | | | | | | | | |
| 31 | | | | | | | | | | | | |
| 32 | Later production | 0 | 352 | 751 | 1154 | 1551 | 1953 | 2352 | 2500 | 2500 | 2500 | |
| 33 | | | | | | | | | | | | |
| 63 | **Expected values** | | | | | | | | | | | |
| 64 | Production cost | $22,478 | | | | | | | | | | |
| 65 | Holding cost | $122 | | | | | | | | | | |
| 66 | Sales revenue | $26,178 | | | | | | | | | | |
| 67 | Markdown revenue | $13 | | | | | | | | | | |
| 68 | Profit | $3,591 | | | | | | | | | | |

**Figure 13.26** Results for Equally Likely Probabilities

| | A | B | C | D | E | F | G | H | I | J | K | L |
|---|---|---|---|---|---|---|---|---|---|---|---|---|
| 12 | **Demand during early period** | | | | | | | | | | | |
| 13 | Value | 100 | 200 | 300 | 400 | 500 | 600 | 700 | 800 | 900 | 1000 | |
| 14 | Probability | 0.10 | 0.10 | 0.10 | 0.10 | 0.10 | 0.10 | 0.10 | 0.10 | 0.10 | 0.10 | |
| 15 | | | | | | | | | | | | |
| 16 | **Distribution of demand during later period (probabilities at right assumed valid for each column separately)** | | | | | | | | | | | |
| 17 | Multiple of early demand | Later demand (one column for each possible early demand) | | | | | | | | | | Probability |
| 18 | 3 | 300 | 600 | 900 | 1200 | 1500 | 1800 | 2100 | 2400 | 2700 | 3000 | 0.10 |
| 19 | 3.5 | 350 | 700 | 1050 | 1400 | 1750 | 2100 | 2450 | 2800 | 3150 | 3500 | 0.10 |
| 20 | 4 | 400 | 800 | 1200 | 1600 | 2000 | 2400 | 2800 | 3200 | 3600 | 4000 | 0.10 |
| 21 | 4.5 | 450 | 900 | 1350 | 1800 | 2250 | 2700 | 3150 | 3600 | 4050 | 4500 | 0.10 |
| 22 | 5 | 500 | 1000 | 1500 | 2000 | 2500 | 3000 | 3500 | 4000 | 4500 | 5000 | 0.10 |
| 23 | 5.5 | 550 | 1100 | 1650 | 2200 | 2750 | 3300 | 3850 | 4400 | 4950 | 5500 | 0.10 |
| 24 | 6 | 600 | 1200 | 1800 | 2400 | 3000 | 3600 | 4200 | 4800 | 5400 | 6000 | 0.10 |
| 25 | 6.5 | 650 | 1300 | 1950 | 2600 | 3250 | 3900 | 4550 | 5200 | 5850 | 6500 | 0.10 |
| 26 | 7 | 700 | 1400 | 2100 | 2800 | 3500 | 4200 | 4900 | 5600 | 6300 | 7000 | 0.10 |
| 27 | 7.5 | 750 | 1500 | 2250 | 3000 | 3750 | 4500 | 5250 | 6000 | 6750 | 7500 | 0.10 |
| 28 | | | | | | | | | | | | |
| 29 | **Production decisions** | | | | | | | | | | | |
| 30 | Early production | 586 | | | | | | | | | | |
| 31 | | | | | | | | | | | | |
| 32 | Later production | 0 | 375 | 784 | 1364 | 1788 | 2232 | 2500 | 2500 | 2500 | 2500 | |
| 33 | | | | | | | | | | | | |
| 63 | **Expected values** | | | | | | | | | | | |
| 64 | Production cost | $26,885 | | | | | | | | | | |
| 65 | Holding cost | $143 | | | | | | | | | | |
| 66 | Sales revenue | $30,991 | | | | | | | | | | |
| 67 | Markdown revenue | $107 | | | | | | | | | | |
| 68 | Profit | $4,070 | | | | | | | | | | |

demand values. This equally likely case is reasonable if ShirtTails has no idea how popular the blouses will be. In comparison with the unimodal scenario, we see some clear differences between the optimal solutions. The equally likely scenario calls for less production in November, generally less production in April, and a somewhat lower expected profit. This pattern is even more evident with the U-shaped scenario, which has the lowest production levels and the lowest expected profit.

These differences make intuitive sense. With a unimodal distribution, the company has the most assurance of what demand is likely to be, and it can plan accordingly. Planning is more difficult with the equally likely "no idea" distribution, and it is even *more* difficult with the U-shaped distribution. With this latter distribution, the company isn't sure whether to produce a lot in case demand is strong or to produce very little in case demand is weak. It stands to lose no matter what it does! Of course, the company cannot simply choose one distribution over another because one produces a larger expected profit. It should choose the distribution most in line with its realistic assessment of future demand. ∎

### Excel Tip: *Scenario Manager*

*As the text box in Figure 13.22 indicates, we used Excel's Scenario feature to save each of the three scenarios under the names Unimodal, U-shaped, and Equally Likely. This feature is useful if you want to store several named scenarios in a single workbook. To do so, enter key inputs values in your spreadsheet that constitute a scenario, including the probabilities and the values in the red cells after running Solver. Then use the Scenario Manager under What-If Analysis on the Data ribbon. This gives you a chance to name a scenario and designate the cells (unfortunately called Changing Cells, but not at all the same concept as Solver's Changing Cells) that include the key inputs. If you ever want to view this scenario later on, just use the Scenario Manager, select the scenario you want from the list of scenarios, and click on View.*

## PROBLEM

### Skill-Building Problem

**25.** The problem in Example 13.9 assumes that the heaviest demand occurs in the second (post-April) phase of selling. It also assumes that capacity is higher in the second production opportunity than in the first. Suppose the situation is reversed, so that the higher capacity and most of the demand occur in the first phase. Make some reasonable assumptions for the resulting input parameters, and then solve for the optimal production plan. Do you get qualitatively different results? Which situation would you rather face if you were ShirtTails?

## 13.8 CONCLUSION

We have examined a variety of inventory/ordering models in this chapter. The general theme is the balance companies try to find between competing costs. If they order frequent, small quantities, they keep inventory low, but they incur large fixed ordering costs. In contrast, if they order infrequent, large quantities, they minimize ordering costs, but they incur large holding costs. The basic EOQ model and its many variations are able to achieve the right balance between these costs. These EOQ models are relatively straightforward and find many uses in today's business world. However, as we introduce complications that real companies face, such as multiple products, uncertain demand, uncertain delivery lead times, and complex supply chain considerations, the models can become extremely difficult. In this case, simulation is often the best alternative; sometimes, it is the *only* alternative.

## Summary of Key Management Science Terms

| Term | Explanation | Page |
|------|-------------|------|
| Lead time | The time between placement of an order and receiving it | 741 |
| Setup cost (or ordering cost) | Fixed cost of placing an order, independent of the size of the order | 741 |
| Continuous review model | Model where order can be placed at any point in time | 741 |
| Reorder point | Inventory level that triggers an order to replenish stock | 741 |
| Periodic review model | Model where order is placed only at discrete points in time, such as the beginning of a week | 741 |
| Holding cost | Cost of holding inventory, could be cost of physical storage or cost of money tied up in inventory | 742 |
| Economic order quantity (EOQ) models | Commonly used models that find the order quantity that trades off setup cost versus holding cost (plus possibly other costs), typified by the famous square root formula | 743 |
| Probabilistic inventory models | Models where demand and possibly other inputs such as lead times are treated as random variables | 759 |
| Safety stock | Extra inventory held in case demand during lead time is larger than expected | 764 |
| $(R,Q)$ ordering policy | Continuous review ordering policy that orders $Q$ when inventory level falls to $R$ | 764 |
| Normal loss function | Function that enables us to calculate the expected shortage during an order cycle, assuming normally distributed demand | 767 |
| Supply chain models | Wide variety of models that model the process of getting goods from suppliers, manufacturing or assembling them, and distributing them to customers | 778 |

# PROBLEMS

## Skill-Building Problems

26. Each month, a gas station sells 4000 gallons of gasoline. Each time the parent company refills the station's tanks, it charges the station $100 plus $2.40 per gallon. The annual cost of holding a gallon of gasoline is $0.30.
    a. How large should the station's orders be?
    b. How many orders per year will the station place?
    c. How long will it be between orders?
    d. Are the EOQ assumptions satisfied in this situation? Why or why not?
    e. If the lead time is 2 weeks, what is the reorder point? If the lead time is 10 weeks, what is the reorder point?

27. A bakery that orders cartons of bread mix has used an EOQ model to determine that an order quantity of 90 cartons per order is economically optimal. The bakery needs 150 cartons per month to meet demand. It takes $L$ days for the bakery's supplier to deliver an order. When should the bakery place its orders when $L = 2$,

when $L = 5$, and when $L = 10$? (Assume that the bakery and its supplier both work 7-day weeks and that there are 30 days per month.)

28. Consider the basic EOQ model. We want to know the sensitivity of (1) the optimal order quantity, (2) the sum of the annual order cost and the annual holding cost (not including the annual purchase cost $cD$), and (3) the time between orders to various parameters of the problem.
    a. How do (1), (2), and (3) change if the setup cost $K$ decreases by 10%?
    b. How do (1), (2), and (3) change if the annual demand doubles?
    c. How do (1), (2), and (3) change if the cost of capital increases by 10%? (For this part, assume that the storage cost $s$ is zero.)
    d. How do (1), (2), and (3) change if the changes in parts **a**, **b**, and **c** all occur simultaneously?

29. Based on Baumol (1952). Money in your savings account earns interest at a 10% annual rate. Each time

you go to the bank, you waste 15 minutes in line, and your time is worth $10 per hour. During each year, you need to withdraw $10,000 to pay your bills.

a. How often should you go to the bank?

b. Each time you go to the bank, how much money should you withdraw?

c. If your need for cash increases, will you go to the bank more often or less often?

d. If the interest rate increases, will you go to the bank more often or less often?

e. If the bank adds more tellers, will you go to the bank more often or less often?

30. The efficiency of an inventory system is often measured by the **turnover ratio.** The turnover ratio ($TR$) is defined by

$$TR = \frac{\text{Cost of goods sold per year}}{\text{Average value of on-hand inventory}}$$

a. Does a high turnover ratio indicate an efficient inventory system?

b. If the EOQ model is being used, determine $TR$ in terms of $K, D, h,$ and $Q$.

c. Suppose that $D$ increases. Show that $TR$ will also increase. Does this make intuitive sense?

31. A consulting firm is trying to determine how to minimize the annual costs associated with purchasing high-quality paper for its printers. Each time an order is placed, an ordering cost of $20 is incurred. The price per ream of printer paper depends on $Q$, the number of reams ordered, as shown in the file **P13_31.xlsx**. The annual holding cost is 20% of the dollar value of inventory. During each month, the consulting firm uses 80 reams of printer paper. Determine the optimal order quantity and the number of orders placed each year.

**32.** Each year, Shopalot Stores sells 10,000 cases of soda. The company is trying to determine how many cases to order each time it orders. It costs $50 to process each order, and the cost of carrying a case of soda in inventory for 1 year is 20% of the purchase price. The soda supplier offers Shopalot the schedule of quantity discounts shown in the file **P13_32.xlsx**, where $Q$ is the number of cases per order. Each time an order is placed, how many cases of soda should the company order?

33. The Gilette Company buys a product using the price schedule given in the file **P13_32.xlsx**. The company estimates the unit holding cost at 10% of the purchase price and the ordering cost at $40 per order. Gilette's annual demand is 460 units.

a. Determine how often the company should order.

b. Determine the optimal order quantity.

c. At what price should the company order?

34. The manager of a hardware store decides to use the EOQ with shortages model to determine the ordering policy for tape measures. Using economic considerations, the manager determines that she should use an order quantity of $Q = 30$ and have a maximum shortage of $b = 3$. The lead time for her supplier to deliver an order is $L$ working days, where there are 6 working days in a week. (Essentially, you can ignore Sundays.) The weekly demand is for 20 tape measures. What reorder point should the manager use if $L = 3$; if $L = 5$; if $L = 10$? (*Hint*: The manager should plan her orders so that the inventory level is $-b$ when an order arrives.)

35. A luxury car dealer must pay $20,000 for each car purchased. The annual holding cost is estimated to be 25% of the dollar value of inventory. The dealer sells an average of 500 cars per year. He is willing to backlog some demand but estimates that if he is short one car for one year, he will lose $20,000 worth of future profits. Each time the dealer places an order for cars, the ordering cost is $10,000. Determine the luxury car dealer's optimal ordering policy. What is the maximum shortage that will occur? Assume it costs $5000 to store a car for a year (this is in addition to the holding cost above).

36. Reconsider Example 13.1. Each time Machey's orders cameras, it incurs a $125 ordering cost. Assume that Machey's could make an investment to decrease this ordering cost. Suppose that any 10% decrease costs a fixed amount, $C$ dollars. Using $i = 0.10$ and Solver, experiment with different values of $C$ to see how Machey's optimal order quantity is affected. Assume the minimum possible ordering cost is $35.

**37.** The particular logarithmic function proposed in Example 13.4 is just one possibility for the cost of a setup cost reduction. In the previous problem, suppose instead that Machey's has only three possibilities. The company can either leave the setup cost as it is, spend $C_1$ dollars to reduce the setup cost to $100, or spend $C_2$ dollars to reduce it to $75. Analyze these possibilities for various values of $C_1$ and $C_2$ to see which is optimal in terms of total annual cost.

38. Chicago Mercy Hospital needs to order drugs that are used to treat heart attack victims. Annually, 500 units of drug 1 and 800 units of drug 2 are used. The unit purchasing cost for drug 1 is $150 per unit, and the unit cost of purchasing drug 2 is $300. It costs $20 to store a unit of each drug for a year. When only drug 1 is ordered, an order for drug 1 costs $400. When only drug 2 is ordered, an order for drug 2 costs $600. If both drugs are ordered at the same time, the cost of placing an order is $800. Chicago Mercy's annual cost of capital is 18%. Determine a cost-minimizing ordering policy.

39. Software EG, a retail company, orders two kinds of software from TeleHard Software. Annually, Software EG sells 800 units of product 1 and 400 units of product 2. The unit purchasing cost is $30 per unit of product 1 and $25 per unit of product 2. It costs $5 to store

a unit of either product for a year. The cost of placing an order for either product separately or both products together is $100. Software EG's annual cost of capital is 14%. Determine a cost-minimizing ordering policy.

40. Customers at Joe's Office Supply Store demand an average of 6000 desks per year. Each time an order is placed, an ordering cost of $300 is incurred. The annual holding cost for a single desk is 25% of the $200 cost of a desk. One week elapses between the placement of an order and the arrival of the order. In parts **a** to **d**, assume that no shortages are allowed.
   a. Each time an order is placed, how many desks should be ordered?
   b. How many orders should be placed each year?
   c. Determine the total annual costs (excluding purchasing costs) of meeting the customers' demands for desks.
   d. If the lead time is 5 weeks, what is the reorder point? (One year equals 52 weeks.)
   e. How do the answers to parts **a** and **b** change if shortages are allowed and a cost of $80 is incurred if Joe's is short one desk for one year?

41. A camera store sells an average of 100 cameras per month. The cost of holding a camera in inventory for a year is 30% of the price the camera shop pays for the camera. It costs $120 each time the camera store places an order with its supplier. The price charged per camera depends on the number of cameras ordered, as specified in the file **P13_41.xlsx**. Each time the camera store places an order, how many cameras should it order?

42. A hospital must order the drug Porapill from Daisy Drug Company. It costs $500 to place an order. Annual demand for the drug is normally distributed with mean 10,000 and standard deviation 3000, and it costs $5 to hold 1 unit in inventory for 1 year. (A unit is a standard container for the drug.) Orders arrive 1 month after being placed. Assume that all shortages are backlogged.
   a. What $(R,Q)$ policy should the company use if it wants to meet 95% of all customer demand from existing inventory?
   b. Suppose the company could pay $C$ dollars per year to decrease its lead time per order from 1 month to half a month. What is the most it would be willing to pay to do this (and still have a 95% service level)?

43. Chicago's Treadway Tires Dealer must order tires from its national warehouse. It costs $10,000 to place an order. Annual tire sales are normally distributed with mean 20,000 and standard deviation 5000. It costs $10 per year to hold a tire in inventory, and the lead time for delivery of an order is normally distributed with mean 3 weeks and standard deviation 1 week. Assume that all shortages are backlogged.

a. Find the $(R,Q)$ policy the company should use to meet a service level where 96% of all demand is met with on-hand inventory.
b. Assume that the company could pay $C$ dollars per year to decrease the variability in lead times to essentially 0. That is, the lead time would then be a certain 3 weeks. What is the most it would be willing to pay (and still meet the service level in part **a**)?

**44.** Suppose the annual demand for Soni DVD players at an appliance store is normally distributed with mean 150 and standard deviation 45. When the store orders these DVD players from its supplier, it takes an amount of time $L$ for the order to arrive, where $L$ is measured as a fraction of a year. In each of the following, find the mean $\mu_{LD}$ and the standard deviation $\sigma_{LD}$ of the demand during lead time.
   a. Assume that $L$ is known to be 3/52, that is, 3 weeks.
   b. Assume that $L$ is uncertain, with mean 3/52 and standard deviation 1/52.

45. In the previous problem, assume that it costs $300 to place an order. The holding cost per DVD player held in inventory per year is $15. The cost each time a customer orders a DVD player that is not in stock is estimated at $40. (All demand is backlogged.)
   a. Find the optimal ordering policy for parts **a** and **b** of the previous problem (when lead time is known for certain and when it is not).
   b. How much more is the expected annual holding cost when $L$ is random than when it is known with certainty? Why is this cost greater in the random case?

46. How do your answers to part **a** of the previous problem change if, instead of incurring a $40 penalty cost for each shortage, the store has a service level requirement of meeting 95% of all customer demands on time? In each case ($L$ known with certainty and $L$ random) what penalty cost $p$ is this service level requirement equivalent to?

47. A hospital orders its blood from a regional blood bank. Each year, the hospital uses an average of 1040 pints of type O blood. Each order placed with the regional blood bank incurs a cost of $250. The lead time for each order is 5 days. It costs the hospital $20 to hold 1 pint of blood in inventory for a year. The stockout cost per pint is estimated to be $50. Annual demand for type O blood is normally distributed with standard deviation 43.26 pints.
   a. Determine the optimal order quantity, reorder point, and safety stock level. Assume that 365 days equal 1 year and that all demand is backlogged.
   b. What service level requirement (from model 2) is equivalent to this $50 stockout cost?

48. A firm experiences demand with a mean of 100 units per day. Lead time demand is normally distributed

with mean 1000 units and standard deviation 200 units. It costs $6 to hold 1 unit for 1 year. If the firm wants to meet 90% of all demand on time, what is the expected annual cost of holding safety stock? Assume that each order costs $50.

**49.** A department store is trying to decide how many JP Desksquirt II printers to order. Because JP is about to come out with a new model in a few months, the store will order only a limited number of model IIs. The cost per printer is $200, and each printer is sold for $230. If any model IIs are still in stock when the next model comes out, they will be sold for $150 apiece. If a customer wants a model II, and there are none left, the store will special order the printer at an extra cost (to the store) of $25. These printers are not in great demand. The store estimates that the number of model IIs that will be demanded during the next few months (before the next model comes out) is equally likely to be any value from 10 to 20, inclusive. Develop a simulation model that can help the store determine the optimal number of printers to order, assuming that only one order will ever be placed.

**50.** Every 4 years, Blockbuster Publishers revises its textbooks. It has been 3 years since the best-selling book *The Joy of Excel* has been revised. At present, 2000 copies of the book are in stock, and Blockbuster must determine how many copies of the book to print for the next year. The sales department believes that sales during the next year are governed by a triangular distribution with parameters 4000, 6000, and 9000. Each copy of *Joy* sold during the next year brings the publisher a revenue of $35. Any copies left at the end of the next year cannot be sold at full price but can be sold for $5 to Bonds Ennoble and Gitano's bookstores. The cost of a printing of the book is $50,000 plus $15 per book printed.

**a.** Use simulation to help the publisher decide how many copies of *Joy* to print.

**b.** How does your answer change if 4000 copies are currently in stock?

**51.** Lowland Appliance replenishes its stock of color TVs three times a year. Each order takes 1/9 of a year to arrive. Annual demand for the color TVs follows a normal distribution with a mean of 990 and a standard deviation of 40. Assume that the cost of holding a TV in inventory for a year is $100. Assume that Lowland begins with 500 TVs in inventory, the cost of a shortage is $150, and the cost of placing an order is $500.

**a.** Suppose that whenever inventory is reviewed, and the inventory level is $I$, an order for $480I$ TVs is placed. Use simulation to estimate the average annual cost of this policy. Such a policy is called an **order-up** policy.

**b.** Use simulation to estimate the average annual cost for order-up policies when Lowland orders up to 200, 400, 600, and 800 TVs.

**52.** Computco sells personal computers. The demand for its computers during a month follows a normal distribution, with a mean of 400 and standard deviation of 100. Each time an order is placed, costs of $600 per order and $1500 per computer are incurred. Computers are sold for $2800, and if Computco does not have a computer in stock, the customer will buy a computer from a competitor. At the end of each month, a holding cost of $10 per computer is incurred. Orders are placed at the end of each month, and they arrive at the beginning of the next month. Four ordering policies are under consideration:

- Policy 1: Place an order for 900 computers whenever the end-of-month inventory is 50 or less.
- Policy 2: Place an order for 600 computers whenever the end-of-month inventory is 200 or less.
- Policy 3: Place an order for 1000 computers whenever end-of-month inventory is 400 or less.
- Policy 4: Place an order for 1200 computers whenever end-of-month inventory is 500 or less.

Using simulation, run 1000 iterations of an appropriate model to determine which ordering policy maximizes expected profit for a 2-year period. To get a more accurate idea of expected profit, you can credit Computco with a salvage value of $1500 for each computer left at the end of the last month. Assume that 400 computers are in inventory at the beginning of the first month.

## Skill-Extending Problems

**53.** Based on Ignall and Kolesar (1972). Father Dominic's Pizza Parlor receives 30 calls per hour for delivery of pizza. It costs Father Dominic's $10 to send out a truck to deliver pizzas. Each minute a customer spends waiting for a pizza costs the pizza parlor an estimated $0.20 in lost future business.

**a.** How often should Father Dominic's send out a truck?

**b.** What would the answer be if a truck could carry only five pizzas?

**54.** Suppose that instead of ordering the amount $Q$ specified by the EOQ formula, we use the order quantity $0.8Q$. Show that the sum of the annual ordering cost and the annual holding cost increases by 2.5%.

**55.** In terms of $K$, $D$, and $h$, what is the average length of time that an item spends in inventory before being used to meet demand? Explain how this result can be used to characterize a fast-moving or slow-moving item.

**56.** A drugstore sells 30 bottles of antibiotics per week. Each time it orders antibiotics, there is a fixed ordering cost of $10 and a cost of $10 per bottle. Assume that the store's cost of capital is 10%, there is no storage cost, and antibiotics spoil and cannot be sold if they spend more than 1 week in inventory. When the drugstore places an order, how many bottles of antibiotics should it order?

**57.** During each year, CSL Computer Company needs to train 27 service representatives. It costs $12,000 to run a training program, regardless of the number of students being trained. Service reps earn a monthly salary of $1500, so CSL does not want to train them before they are needed. Each training session takes 1 month.
  **a.** State the assumptions needed for the EOQ model to be applicable.
  **b.** How many service reps should be in each training group?
  **c.** How many training programs should CSL undertake each year?
  **d.** How many trained service reps will be available when each training program begins?

**58.** A hospital orders its thermometers from a hospital supply firm. The cost per thermometer depends on the order quantity $Q$, as shown in the file **P13_58.xlsx**. The annual holding cost is 25% of the purchasing cost. Let $Q_{80}$ be the optimal EOQ order quantity if the cost per thermometer is $0.80, and let $Q_{79}$ be defined similarly if the cost per thermometer is $0.79.
  **a.** Explain why $Q_{79}$ will be larger than $Q_{80}$.
  **b.** Explain why the optimal order quantity must be $Q_{79}$, $Q_{80}$, or 100.
  **c.** If $Q_{80} > 100$, explain why the optimal order quantity must be $Q_{79}$.
  **d.** If $Q_{80} < 100$ and $Q_{79} < 100$, explain why the optimal order quantity must be $Q_{80}$ or 100.
  **e.** If $Q_{80} < 100$ and $Q_{79} > 100$, explain why the optimal order quantity must be $Q_{79}$.

**59.** In the previous problem, suppose that the cost per order is $1, and the monthly demand is 50 thermometers. What is the optimal order quantity? What is the smallest discount the supplier could offer that would still be accepted by the hospital?

**60.** Suppose that instead of measuring shortage in terms of cost per shortage per year, a cost of $P$ dollars is incurred for each unit the firm is short. This cost does not depend on the length of time before the backlogged demand is satisfied. Determine a new expression for the annual shortage cost as a function of $Q$ and $b$, and solve GMB's problem (Example 13.3) with this way of costing shortages for reasonable values of $P$. (What values of $P$ do you think are reasonable?)

**61.** The penalty cost $p$ used in the shortage model might be very difficult to estimate. Instead, a company might use a service-level constraint, such as, "95% of all demand must be met from on-hand inventory." Solve Problem 35 with this constraint instead of the $20,000 penalty cost. Now the problem is to minimize the total annual ordering and holding costs subject to meeting the service-level constraint.

**62.** A newspaper has 500,000 subscribers who pay $4 per month for the paper. It costs the company $200,000 to bill all its customers. Assume that the company can earn interest at a rate of 20% per year on all revenues. Determine how often the newspaper should bill its customers. (*Hint:* Consider unpaid subscriptions as the inventoried good.)

**63.** A firm knows that the price of the product it is ordering is going to increase permanently by $X$ dollars. It wants to know how much of the product it should order before the price increase goes into effect. Here is one approach to this problem. Suppose the firm places one order for $Q$ units before the price increase goes into effect.
  **a.** What extra holding cost is incurred by ordering $Q$ units now?
  **b.** How much in purchasing costs is saved by ordering $Q$ units now?
  **c.** What value of $Q$ maximizes purchasing cost savings less extra holding costs?
  **d.** Suppose that the annual demand is 1000 units, the holding cost per unit per year is $7.50, and the price of the item is going to increase by $10. How large an order should the firm place before the price increase goes into effect?

**64.** Based on Riccio et al. (1986). The borough of Staten Island has two sanitation districts. In district 1, street litter piles up at an average rate of 2000 tons per week, and in district 2, it piles up at an average rate of 1000 tons per week. Each district has 500 miles of streets. Staten Island has 10 sanitation crews and each crew can clean 50 miles per week of streets. To minimize the average level of the total amount of street litter in the two districts, how often should each district be cleaned? Assume that litter in a district grows at a constant rate until it is picked up, and assume that pickup is instantaneous. (*Hint:* Let $p_i$ equal the average number of times that district $i$ is cleaned per week. Then $p_1 + p_2 = 1$.)

**65.** A company inventories two items. The relevant data are shown in the file **P13_65.xlsx**. Determine the optimal inventory policy if no shortages are allowed and if the average investment in inventory is not allowed to exceed $700. If this constraint could be relaxed by $1, by how much would the company's annual costs decrease? (*Hint:* Use Solver.)

**66.** An **exchange curve** can be used to display the trade-offs between the average investment in inventory and the annual ordering cost. To illustrate the usefulness of a trade-off curve, suppose that a company must order two products with the attributes shown in the file **P13_66.xlsx**.

    a. Draw a curve that displays annual order cost on the horizontal axis and average inventory investment on the vertical axis.

    b. Currently, the firm orders each product 10 times per year. Demonstrate that this is a suboptimal ordering policy.

    c. Suppose management limits the company's average inventory investment to $10,000. Use the exchange curve to determine the best ordering policy.

67. A company currently has two warehouses. Each warehouse services half the company's demand, and the annual demand serviced by each warehouse is normally distributed with mean 10,000 and standard deviation 1000. The lead time for meeting demand is 1/10 year. The company wants to meet 95% of all demand on time. Assume that each warehouse uses the EOQ formula to determine its order quantity and that this leads to $Q = 2000$ for each warehouse.

    a. How much safety stock must be held at each warehouse?

    b. Show that if the company had only one warehouse, it would hold less safety stock than it does when it has two warehouses.

    c. A young MBA argues, "By having one central warehouse, I can reduce the total amount of safety stock needed to meet 95% of all customer demands on time. Therefore, we can save money by having only one central warehouse instead of several branch warehouses." How might this argument be rebutted?

68. In most of the Walton Bookstore examples in Chapter 11, we assumed that there is a single product. Suppose instead that a company sells two competing products. Sales of either product tend to take away sales from the other product. That is, the demands for the two products are negatively correlated. The company first places an order for each product. Then during a period of time, there is demand $D_1$ for product 1 and demand $D_2$ for product 2. These demands are normally distributed with means 1000 and 1200 and standard deviations 250 and 350. The correlation between $D_1$ and $D_2$ is $\rho$, where $\rho$ is a negative number between $-1$ and 0. The unit cost of each product is $7.50, the unit price for each product is $10, and the unit refund for any unit of either product not sold is $2.50. The company must decide how many units of each product to order. Use @RISK to help the company by experimenting with different order quantities. Try this for $\rho = -0.3$, $\rho = -0.5$, and $\rho = -0.7$. What recommendation can you give about the "best" order quantities as the demands become more highly correlated (in a negative direction)?

69. Work the previous problem when the demands are *positively* correlated, as they might be with products such as peanut butter and jelly. Now use $\rho = 0.3$, $\rho = 0.5$, and $\rho = 0.7$ in your simulations.

70. A highly perishable drug spoils after 3 days. A hospital estimates that it is equally likely to need between 1 and 9 units of the drug daily. Each time an order for the drug is placed, a fixed cost of $200 is incurred as well as a purchase cost of $50 per unit. Orders are placed at the end of each day and arrive at the beginning of the following day. It costs no money to hold the drug in inventory, but a cost of $100 is incurred each time the hospital needs a unit of the drug and does not have any available. The following three policies are under consideration:

- If we end the day with fewer than 5 units, order enough to bring the next day's beginning inventory up to 10 units.
- If we end the day with fewer than 3 units, order enough to bring the next day's beginning inventory up to 7 units.
- If we end the day with fewer than 8 units, order enough to bring the next day's beginning inventory up to 15 units.

Use simulation to compare these policies with regard to expected daily costs, expected number of units short per day, and expected number of units spoiling each day. Assume that the hospital begins day 1 with 5 units of the drug on hand. (*Hint:* You will need to keep track of the age distribution of the units on hand at the beginning of each day. Assume that the hospital uses a FIFO [first in, first out] inventory policy. The trick is to get formulas that relate the age of each unit of the drug you have at the beginning of the day to the age of each unit you have at the end of the day.)

## Modeling Problems

71. A trucking firm must decide at the beginning of the year on the size of its trucking fleet. If on a given day the firm does not have enough trucks, the firm will have to rent trucks from Hertz. Discuss how you would determine the optimal size of the trucking fleet?

72. A computer manufacturer produces computers for 40 different stores. To monitor its inventory policies, the manufacturer needs to estimate the mean and standard deviation of its weekly demand. How might it do this?

73. Based on Brout (1981). Planner's Peanuts sells 100 products. The company has been disappointed with the high level of inventory it keeps of each product and its low service level (percentage of demand met on time). Describe how you would help Planner's improve its performance on both these objectives. Pay close attention to the data you would need to collect and how the data would be used.

**74.** Austin (1977) conducted an extensive inventory analysis for the United States Air Force. He found that for over 250,000 items the annual holding cost was assumed to equal 32% of the item's purchase price. He also found that when an order was placed for most items, a fixed cost of over $200 was incurred. The Air Force held 1 month of safety stock for each item. Given this limited information, discuss how you could improve the Air Force's inventory policies.

Riders of the subway system in the city of Metropolis must pay for the ride by purchasing a token. The same token can also be used to ride the buses in Metropolis. A single token is good for a trip to any destination served by the system. (Tokens are also used by millions of commuters for bridge, tunnel, and highway tolls in many areas of the country.)

Late in 1996, Metropolis transit officials announced that they were seeking a fare increase from $1.50 to $2.00. Later negotiations with politicians in the state capital reduced the requested increase to $1.75. It usually takes a few weeks between the announcement of a fare increase and the time that the increase goes into effect. Knowing that an increase will occur gives users of mass transit an opportunity to mitigate the effect of the increase by hoarding tokens—that is, by purchasing a large supply of tokens before the fare increase goes into effect.

There is a clear motivation for hoarding tokens—namely, the purchase of tokens before a fare increase offers a savings over purchasing the same tokens at a higher price after the change in fare. Why wouldn't riders want to purchase a very large supply of tokens? The reason is the inventory cost that arises because of the time value of money.[11] The larger the supply that is hoarded, the longer the time until the tokens are used. Purchasing the supply of tokens represents an immediate cost, but the benefit is only realized over a longer period of time.

Thus, there is a trade-off between the immediate cost and the prolonged benefit. The optimal number of tokens to hoard balances these two effects to maximize the present value of the net benefit of the hoarding strategy.

Suppose that the current price of subway tokens is $p_1 = \$1.50$ and the fare is due to rise to $p_2 = \$1.75$. Suppose that you use the subway to commute 2 times per day, 5 days per week, 50 weeks per year. Also, suppose that you can purchase (or *hoard*) any number of tokens before the price increase takes effect. You will use the hoarded tokens during your normal usage of the mass transit system. After your hoard runs out, you will start purchasing tokens each day at the higher price. Suppose that your cost of capital is 15% per year. This means that you can borrow money to purchase your token supply, but the interest cost on the borrowed money is 15% per year.[12]

## Questions

1. What is the optimal number of tokens to hoard?

2. What is the present value of the savings over not hoarding at all?

3. Suppose that the optimal quantity to hoard is $Q^*$. What is the present value of the savings if you decide to hoard only $0.8Q^*$? ∎

---

[11] We are assuming that the hoarded tokens will be used by the hoarder for rides on the mass transit system, not for the immediate sale to other riders. In fact, such sales are illegal in Metropolis.

[12] Using 250 commuting days per year, you can assume that the daily interest cost is 0.05592% $(=1.15^{(1/250)}-1)$.

# Queueing Models

© CORBIS

## REDUCING WORK-IN-PROGRESS LEVELS AT WOODWARD AIRCRAFT ENGINE SYSTEMS

The previous chapter was all about inventory management, where companies try to achieve the correct balance between holding too much inventory and not holding enough inventory to meet demands. A type of inventory that is particularly important in the manufacturing industry is called work-in-process (WIP) inventory. As its name implies, this is inventory that is partway through the manufacturing process and is not yet a finished good. Manufacturing companies try to keep WIP low, for reasons of space and financial concerns, but they need a certain amount of WIP to keep their processes running smoothly. Srinivasan et al. (2003) discuss a study they performed at Woodward Aircraft Engine Systems to achieve appropriate levels of WIP. Woodward is a leading producer of fuel-control systems and components for aircraft and industrial engines and turbines. With headquarters in Rockford, Illinois, Woodward serves a global market and has about 3600 employees. The Rockford plant manufactures a large variety of products at low volumes, some as low as 100 per year. As these products are manufactured, they flow through *cells,* groups of machines that perform similar operations, and the various products require different routings through these cells depending on their specifications. The company knows (or forecasts) its demands for the various products, so it knows how many of each product it needs to manufacture per time period, the *throughput,* to meet demands. The problem is to determine the amount of WIP required to achieve the desired throughputs.

The authors model the manufacturing system as a closed queueing network (CQN). A *queueing network* is simply a sequence of cells or machines that partially completed products must pass through as they are being manufactured into finished products. Products typically form a queue in front of the machines on their routings, and congestion is very possible, especially when certain machines are bottlenecks. A *closed* queueing network means that there are a *constant* number of partially completed products of a given type in the network at all times. This type of model is often used when a new product of a given type is introduced into the network as soon as a part of that type finishes and leaves the network. Researchers have done much analytical work in the area of queueing networks, and various approximations exist for calculating performance measures of CQNs.

At Woodward, there are essentially two decision variables for any given product type. The first is the batch size, the number of parts on a pallet. A given batch goes through the manufacturing process, that is, through its routing of cells and machines, as a unit. At any machine along the route, there can be a setup time and a processing time per unit. Therefore, larger batch sizes are sometimes beneficial for reducing setups. The second decision variable is the number of batches in the system at any point in time. Because the overall system is modeled as a CQN, this number of batches (for any given product type) is constant. Together, these two decision variables determine the amount of WIP in the system at all times. The problem is to adjust these two decision variables, for all product types, so that the throughputs of all products match the demands for them as closely as possible. The authors developed an approximate algorithm, using results from the vast queueing literature, to do this. Then they implemented this algorithm in Excel with a user-friendly interface so that Woodward employees could use it easily to answer various what-if questions.

Although the details of the algorithm are rather complex, they rely on a very basic formula, called Little's formula, which is discussed in this chapter. Little's formula states that the expected number of parts in a system is equal to the arrival rate of parts to the system multiplied by the average time a part spends in the system. Little's formula can be applied in an amazing variety of situations; the only trick is to see how it applies. In Woodward's situation, the number of parts in the system is fixed because of the CQN assumption; it is the number of pallets of a given product type in the system at all times. The arrival rate of parts to the system is the throughput of a given product type. The reasoning is that the rate at which products leave the system, the throughput rate, must equal the rate at which new products of this type enter the system. Finally, the average time a part spends in the system is known in manufacturing as the *cycle time:* the time it takes to manufacture a typical product. So Little's law relates cycle time to throughput and the number of pallets to use.

The authors' algorithm and spreadsheet implementation have helped Woodward immensely by enabling the company to reduce its WIP inventory from about three weeks of inventory to less than one week of inventory. As Director of Manufacturing, Steven J. Ebbing, states, "The spreadsheet software tool presented in this paper has enabled a smooth flow of products through the various operations in the cells at Woodward, with significant reduction in WIP levels. The what-if analysis is invaluable for setting WIP levels for different products as well as for individual machines." ∎

# 14.1 INTRODUCTION

A basic fact of life is that we all spend a great deal of time waiting in lines (queues). We wait in line at a bank, at a supermarket, at a fast-food restaurant, at a stoplight, and so on. Of course, people are not the only entities that wait in queues. Televisions at a television repair shop, other than the one(s) being repaired, are essentially waiting in line to be repaired. Also, when messages are sent through a computer network, they often must wait in a queue before being processed.

Mathematically, it does not really matter whether the entities waiting are people or televisions or computer messages. The same type of analysis applies to all of these. The purpose of such an analysis is generally twofold. First, we want to examine an *existing* system to quantify its operating characteristics. For example, if a fast-food restaurant currently employs 12 people in various jobs, the manager might be interested in determining the amount of time a typical customer must wait in line or how many customers are typically waiting in line. Second, we want to learn how to make a system better. The manager might find, for example, that the fast-food restaurant would do better, from an economic standpoint, by employing only 10 workers and deploying them in a different manner.

The first objective, analyzing the characteristics of a given system, is difficult from a mathematical point of view. The two basic modeling approaches are **analytical** and **simulation.** With the analytical approach, we search for mathematical *formulas* that describe the operating characteristics of the system, usually in "steady state." The mathematical models are typically too complex to solve unless we make simplifying (and sometimes unrealistic) assumptions. For example, at a supermarket, customers typically join one of several lines (probably the shortest), possibly switch lines if they see that another line is moving faster, and eventually get served by one of the checkout people. Although this behavior is common—and is simple to describe in words—it is *very* difficult to analyze analytically.

The second approach, simulation, allows us to analyze much more complex systems, *without* making many simplifying assumptions. However, the drawback to queueing simulation is that it usually requires specialized software packages or trained computer programmers to implement.

In this chapter, we employ both the analytical approach and simulation. For the former, we discuss several well-known queueing models that describe some—but certainly not all—queueing situations in the real world. These models illustrate how to calculate such operating characteristics as the average waiting time per customer, the average number of customers in line, and the fraction of time servers are busy. These analytical models generally require simplifying assumptions, and even then they can be difficult to understand. Therefore, we also discuss queueing simulations. Unfortunately, queueing simulations are not nearly as straightforward as the simulations we developed in previous chapters. We typically need to generate random times between customer arrivals and random service times and then "play out" the events. This playing out of events is far from easy in a spreadsheet. We provide only a taste of what can be done—and show why commercial software packages are usually used instead of spreadsheets.

The second objective in many queueing studies is optimization, where we attempt to find the "best" system. Of course, to find the best system, we need to be able to analyze each of several competing systems, either analytically or by simulation. But beyond this, we must make difficult choices. For example, if the fast-food restaurant wants to decide how many employees to hire for various times of day, it must analyze the trade-off between more employees (better service, higher wages) and fewer employees (worse service, lower wages). The cost of extra employees is fairly easy to quantify—the marginal cost of one extra employee is the wage rate. However, estimating the "cost" of making a customer wait an extra two minutes in line, for instance, is difficult. In terms of immediate out-of-pocket costs, it costs the restaurant nothing; however, it can have long-range implications: Fewer customers will bring their business to this restaurant. To find the optimal number of employees, the restaurant must estimate the dollar cost of having customers wait in line. Only by estimating this cost can it make an economic choice between the cost of waiting and the cost of more efficient service.

*The formulas that relate queueing inputs to queueing outputs are difficult to derive mathematically. We present a few of these formulas, but we do not derive them.*

The examples in this chapter highlight these two objectives. We show how to find important characteristics, such as expected waiting times, of specific systems, and we also illustrate how to search for economically optimal systems.

This chapter is very different from earlier chapters because of the nature of queueing systems. The models in previous chapters could almost always be developed from "first principles." By using relatively simple formulas involving functions such as SUM, SUMPRODUCT, IF, and so on, we were able to convert inputs into outputs. This is no longer possible with queueing models. The inputs are typically mean customer arrival rates and mean service times. The required outputs are typically mean waiting times in queues, mean queue lengths, the fraction of time servers are busy, and possibly others. Deriving the formulas that relate the inputs to the outputs is mathematically *very difficult,* well beyond the level of this book. Therefore, many times in this chapter you have to take our word for it. Nevertheless, the models we illustrate are very valuable for the important insights they provide.

## 14.2 ELEMENTS OF QUEUEING MODELS

We begin by listing some of the features of queueing systems that distinguish one system from another. Almost all queueing systems are alike in that customers enter a system, possibly wait in one or more queues, get served, and then depart.[1] This general description of a queueing system—customers entering, waiting in line, and being served—hardly suggests the variety of queueing systems that exist. We now discuss some of the key features and their variations.

### Characteristics of Arrivals

*Interarrival times are the times between successive customer arrivals.*

First, we must specify the customer arrival process. This includes the timing of arrivals as well as the types of arrivals. Regarding timing, specifying the probability distribution of **interarrival times,** the times between successive customer arrivals, is most common. These interarrival times might be known—that is, nonrandom. For example, the arrivals at some doctors' offices are scheduled fairly precisely. Much more commonly, however, interarrival times are random with a probability distribution. In real applications, this probability distribution must be estimated from observed customer arrival times. Also, this distribution can vary through time. For example, the rate of arrivals to McDonald's is certainly higher around noon than in the middle of the afternoon.

*We assume customers arrive one at a time and all have the same priority.*

Regarding the types of arrivals, there are at least two issues. First, do customers arrive one at a time or in batches—carloads, for example? The simplest system is when customers arrive one at a time, as we assume in all of the models in this chapter. Second, are all customers essentially alike, or can they be separated into priority classes? At a computer center, for example, certain jobs might receive higher priority and run first, whereas the lower-priority jobs might be sent to the back of the line and run only after midnight. We assume throughout this chapter that all customers have the same priority.

[1] From here on, we refer to the entities requesting service as *customers,* regardless of whether they are actually people. Also, we refer to *servers* performing service on these customers, regardless of the type of work being performed and whether the servers are people, machines, or other types of technology.

Another issue is whether (or how long) customers will wait in line. A customer might arrive to the system, see that too many customers are waiting in line, and decide not to enter the system at all. This is called **balking.** A variation of balking occurs when the choice is made by the system, not the customer. In this case, we assume there is a waiting room size so that if the number of customers in the system equals the waiting room size, newly arriving customers are not allowed to enter the system. We call this a **limited waiting room** system. Another type of behavior, called **reneging,** occurs when a customer already in line becomes impatient and leaves the system before starting service. Systems with balking and reneging are difficult to analyze, so we do not consider any such systems in this chapter. However, we do discuss limited waiting room systems.

## Service Discipline

*We always assume a FCFS discipline.*

When customers enter the system, they might have to wait in line until a server becomes available. In this case, we must specify the **service discipline.** The service discipline is the rule that states which customer, from all who are waiting, goes into service next. The most common service discipline is **first-come-first-served** (FCFS), where customers are served in the order of their arrival. All of the models we discuss use the FCFS discipline. However, other service disciplines are possible, including **service-in-random-order** (SRO), **last-come-first-served** (LCFS), and various priority disciplines (if there are customer classes with different priorities). For example, a type of priority discipline used in some manufacturing plants is called the **shortest-processing-time** (SPT) discipline. In this case, the jobs that are waiting to be processed are ranked according to their eventual processing (service) times, which are assumed to be known. Then the job with the shortest processing time is processed next.

One other aspect of the waiting process is whether there is a *single* line or *multiple* lines. For example, most banks now have a single line. An arriving customer joins the end of the line. When any teller finishes service, the customer at the head of the line goes to that teller. In contrast, most supermarkets have multiple lines. When a customer goes to a checkout counter, she must choose which of several lines to enter. Presumably, she will choose the shortest line, but she might use other criteria in her decision. After she joins a line—inevitably the slowest-moving one, from our experience!—she might decide to move to another line that seems to be moving faster.

## Service Characteristics

In the simplest systems, each customer is served by exactly one server, even when the system contains multiple servers. For example, when you enter a bank, you are eventually served by a single teller, even though several tellers are working. The service times typically vary in some random manner, although constant (nonrandom) service times are sometimes possible. When service times are random, we must specify the probability distribution of a typical service time. This probability distribution can be the same for all customers and servers, or it can depend on the server and/or the customer. As with interarrival times, service time distributions must typically be estimated from service time data in real applications.

In a situation like the typical bank, where customers join a single line and are then served by the first available teller, we say the servers (tellers) are in **parallel** (see Figure 14.1). A different type of service process is found in many manufacturing settings. For example, various types of parts (the "customers") enter a system with several types of machines (the "servers"). Each part type then follows a certain machine routing, such as machine 1, then machine 4, and then machine 2. Each machine has its own service time

**Figure 14.1**

Queueing System
with Servers in
Parallel

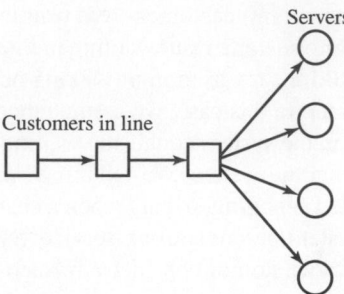

distribution, and a typical part might have to wait in line behind any or all of the machines on its routing. This type of system is called a **queueing network.** The simplest type of queueing network is a **series system**, where all parts go through the machines in numerical order: first machine 1, then machine 2, then machine 3, and so on (see Figure 14.2). We examine mostly parallel systems in this chapter. However, we discuss the simulation of a series system toward the end of the chapter.

**Figure 14.2**

Queueing System
with Servers in
Series

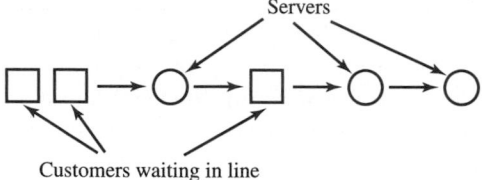

## Short-Run versus Steady-State Behavior

If you run a fast-food restaurant, you are particularly interested in the queueing behavior during your peak lunchtime period. The customer arrival rate during this period increases sharply, and you probably employ more workers to meet the increased customer load. In this case, your primary interest is in the *short-run* behavior of the system—the next hour or two. Unfortunately, short-run behavior is the most difficult to analyze, at least with analytical models. Although we show in Section 14.6 that short-run behavior can be approximated analytically, we usually resort to simulation to understand what happens in the short run.

But how do we draw the line between the *short run* and the *long run*? The answer depends on how long the effects of *initial conditions* persist. In the restaurant example, the initial conditions are determined by the number of customers already in line at the beginning of the lunch period—say, at 11:30. Suppose the restaurant manager is interested in the average number of customers waiting in line over a two-hour peak period. The question then is how much this average is affected by the number of customers in line at 11:30. Specifically, we need to determine whether the effects of the initial conditions get washed out in a period as long as two hours.

Ultimately, the only way to answer this question is with empirical evidence. We might compare a lunch period starting with no people in line at 11:30 to one where 10 people are already in line at 11:30. If the average levels of congestion over the entire 2-hour lunch period are approximately the same in each case, then the initial conditions at 11:30 evidently make little difference, and a *long-run* analysis is permitted. However, if the lunch period that starts with many people in line is never able to overcome this initial load—that is, it tends to stay crowded—then the initial conditions are important, and a *short-run* analysis is required.

Steady-state analysis is relevant for the long run, but the "long run" can sometimes be as short as an hour or two.

Analytical models are best suited for studying long-run behavior. This type of analysis is called **steady-state analysis** and is the focus of much of the chapter. One requirement for steady-state analysis is that the parameters of the system remain constant for the entire time period. In particular, the arrival rate must remain constant. In the restaurant example, if the objective is to study a 2-hour peak lunchtime period where the arrival rate is significantly larger than normal, and if we decide to employ steady-state analysis, then the results of this 2-hour analysis do *not* apply to the rest of the day, when the arrival rate is much lower. If the parameters of the system change from one time period to another, a separate steady-state analysis is required for each time period. Alternatively, we can use simulation, where constant parameters such as the arrival rate are *not* required.

Unless a system is stable, queue lengths will eventually increase without bound.

Another requirement for steady-state analysis is that the system must be **stable.** This means that the servers must serve fast enough to keep up with arrivals—otherwise, the queue can theoretically grow without limit. For example, in a single-server system where all arriving customers join the system, the requirement for system stability is that the arrival rate must be less than the service rate. If the system is not stable, the analytical models discussed in this chapter cannot be used. Again, however, we can use simulation, which does not require system stability.

---

## FUNDAMENTAL INSIGHT

### The Limitations of Steady-State Results

Most queueing results (other than those from simulation) are for steady state. These are based on rather restrictive assumptions, such as a constant arrival rate and a constant service rate. Such results are at best approximate if we need short-run results (how busy will a store be in the next hour) and the parameters are changing through time (the arrival rate is much lower in midmorning than at noon, say). The problem with steady-state results is that they are relevant only when the effects of initial conditions have been washed out by the passage of time, and this can take awhile. Fortunately, short-run results are available, either from an approximation such as the one in Section 14.6 or from simulation.

---

## 14.3 THE EXPONENTIAL DISTRIBUTION

Queueing systems generally contain uncertainty. Specifically, times between customer arrivals (interarrival times) and customer service times are generally modeled as random variables. The most common probability distribution used to model these uncertain quantities is the **exponential** distribution. Many queueing models can be analyzed in a fairly straightforward manner, even on a spreadsheet, if we assume exponentially distributed interarrival times and service times. This exponential assumption buys us a lot in terms of simplified analysis, but it is very strong. Therefore, understanding the exponential distribution and some of its ramifications for queueing applications is important.

A random variable $X$ has an exponential distribution with parameter $\lambda$ (with $\lambda > 0$) if the density function for $X$ has the form

$$f(x) = \lambda e^{-\lambda x} \quad \text{for } x > 0$$

($\lambda$ is the Greek letter *lambda*. Its use is standard in the queueing literature.) The graph of this function appears in Figure 14.3. (We obtained this graph from @RISK, as discussed in Chapter 11.) You might want to compare this density to the more familiar bell-shaped, symmetric normal curve. In contrast to the normal distribution, the exponential distribution is not bell-shaped, and it is heavily skewed to the right. Because this density decreases continually from left to right, its most likely value is at 0. This means that $X$ is more likely to be near 0 than any other value. Equivalently, if we collect many observations from an exponential distribution and draw a histogram of the observed values, we expect it to resemble the smooth curve in Figure 14.3, with the tallest bars to the left.

**Figure 14.3**

Typical Exponential Distribution

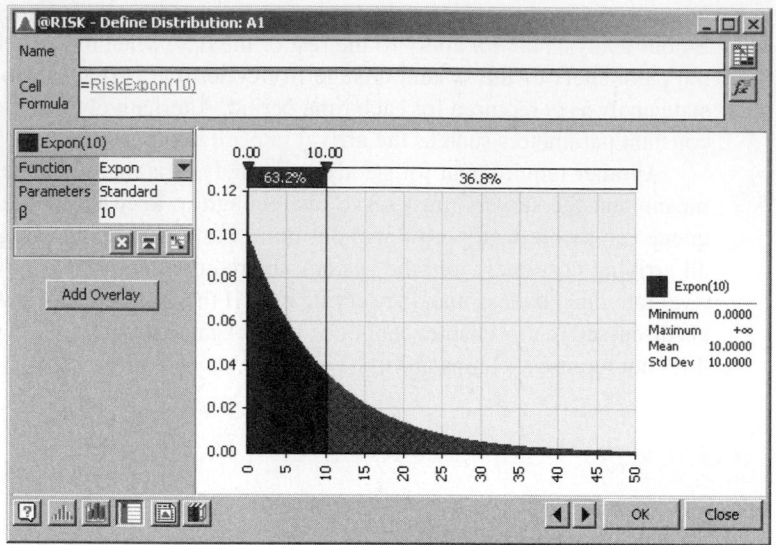

*The mean and standard deviation of an exponential distribution are both equal to the reciprocal of the parameter $\lambda$.*

The mean and standard deviation of this distribution are easy to remember. They are both equal to the *reciprocal* of the parameter $\lambda$. For example, an exponential distribution with parameter $\lambda = 0.1$ has both mean and standard deviation equal to 10.

The random variable $X$ is always expressed in some time unit, such as minutes. For example, $X$ might be the number of minutes it takes to serve a customer. Now, suppose that the mean service time is 3 minutes. Then $1/\lambda = 3$, so that $\lambda = 1/3$. For this reason, $\lambda$ can be interpreted as a *rate*—in this case, 1 customer every 3 minutes (on average). Of course, the value of $\lambda$ depends on the unit of time. If we switch from minutes to hours, say, $\lambda$ changes from $1/3$ (1 every 3 minutes) to $60(1/3) = 20$ (20 every hour). The corresponding mean is then $1/\lambda = 1/20$ hour.

## The Memoryless Property

The property that makes the exponential distribution so useful in queueing models (and in many other management science models) is called the **memoryless property,** which can be stated as follows. Let $x$ and $h$ be any positive numbers that represent amounts of time. Then if $X$ is exponentially distributed, the following equation holds:

$$P(X > x + h \mid X > x) = P(X > h) \tag{14.1}$$

The probability on the left is a conditional probability, the probability that $X$ is greater than $x + h$, given that it is greater than $x$. The memoryless property states that this conditional probability is the same as the unconditional probability that $X$ is greater than $h$. We now interpret this important property in several contexts.

First, suppose that $X$ is the time, measured in hours, until failure of some item such as a light bulb. Now consider two light bulbs with the same exponential distribution of time to failure. The only difference is that the first light bulb has already survived $x = 20$ hours, whereas the second light bulb is brand new. Suppose we want the probabilities that light bulbs 1 and 2 will survive at least $h = 5$ additional hours. The memoryless property says that these probabilities are the *same* for the two light bulbs! In other words, the light bulb that has been in use for 20 hours has the same chance of surviving at least 5 more hours as the brand new light bulb. For this reason, the memoryless property is sometimes called the *no wear-out* property.

As a second example, suppose that $X$ is the time, measured in minutes, until the next customer arrival. Suppose it is currently 3:00 P.M., and the previous arrival occurred at 2:57 P.M. Then we know that $X$ is greater than 3 minutes. Given this information, what is the probability that the *next* arrival will occur after 3:05 P.M.? (Here $x = 3$ and $h = 5$, measured in minutes.) This is the same as the probability that the next arrival would occur after 3:05 P.M. if there were an arrival right now, at 3:00 P.M. That is, as far as the future (after 3:00 P.M.) is concerned, we can forget how long it has been since the last arrival and assume that an arrival just occurred, at 3:00 P.M. This example illustrates why the property is called the *memoryless* property.

These examples indicate why the exponential distribution is attractive from a mathematical point of view. If we observe a process at any time, all exponential times (interarrival times and service times, say) essentially "start over" probabilistically—we do not have to know how long it has been since various events (the last arrival or the beginning of service) occurred. The exponential distribution is the only continuous probability distribution with this property. On the negative side, however, this strong memoryless property makes the exponential distribution inappropriate for many real applications. In the light bulb example, we might dismiss the exponential assumption immediately on the grounds that light bulbs *do* wear out—a light bulb that has been in continuous use for 20 hours is *not* as good as a brand new one. Nevertheless, the ultimate test of appropriateness is whether sample data fit an exponential curve. We illustrate how to check this in the following example.

| EXAMPLE | **14.1 ESTIMATING INTERARRIVAL AND SERVICE TIME DISTRIBUTIONS AT A BANK** |
| --- | --- |

A bank manager would like to use an analytical queueing model to study the congestion at the bank's automatic teller machines (ATMs). A simple model of this system requires that the interarrival times (times between customer arrivals to the machines) and service times (times customers spend with the machines) are exponentially distributed. During a period of time when business is fairly steady, several employees use stopwatches to gather data on interarrival times and service times. The data are listed in Figure 14.4 (with several rows hidden). The bank manager wants to know, based on these data, whether it is reasonable to assume exponentially distributed interarrival times and service times. In each case, the manager also wants to know the appropriate value of $\lambda$.

**Objective** To test the appropriateness of the exponential distribution for interarrival time and service time data at ATMs.

**WHERE DO THE NUMBERS COME FROM?**

We already mentioned employees with stopwatches. Unless the bank has some electronic tracking device, manual recording of the data is the only alternative.

## Solution

To see whether these times are consistent with the exponential distribution, we plot histograms of the interarrival times and the service times. (See the file **Exponential Fit.xlsx**.

Also, see the appendix to Chapter 11 for directions on creating histograms.) The histograms appear in Figures 14.5 and 14.6. The histogram of interarrival times appears to be consistent with the exponential density in Figure 14.3. Its highest bar is at the left, and the remaining bars fall off gradually from left to right. On the other hand, the histogram of

**Figure 14.4**

Interarrival and Service Times for the ATM Example

| | A | B | C | D |
|---|---|---|---|---|
| 1 | **Interarrival times and service times at a bank (in seconds)** | | | |
| 2 | | | | |
| 3 | Averages of data below | | | |
| 4 | | Interarrival Time | Service Time | |
| 5 | | 25.3 | 22.3 | |
| 6 | | | | |
| 7 | Customer | Interarrival Time | Service Time | |
| 8 | 1 | 8 | 11 | |
| 9 | 2 | 33 | 20 | |
| 10 | 3 | 9 | 16 | |
| 11 | 4 | 11 | 8 | |
| 12 | 5 | 5 | 12 | |
| 13 | 6 | 24 | 17 | |
| 14 | 7 | 4 | 41 | |
| 15 | 8 | 46 | 7 | |
| 16 | 9 | 25 | 19 | |
| 17 | 10 | 10 | 43 | |
| 101 | 94 | 3 | 11 | |
| 102 | 95 | 14 | 16 | |
| 103 | 96 | 17 | 30 | |
| 104 | 97 | 17 | 24 | |
| 105 | 98 | 3 | 31 | |
| 106 | 99 | 42 | 59 | |
| 107 | 100 | 112 | 22 | |
| 108 | 101 | 17 | 40 | |
| 109 | 102 | 5 | 11 | |

**Figure 14.5**   Histogram of Interarrival Times for the ATM Example

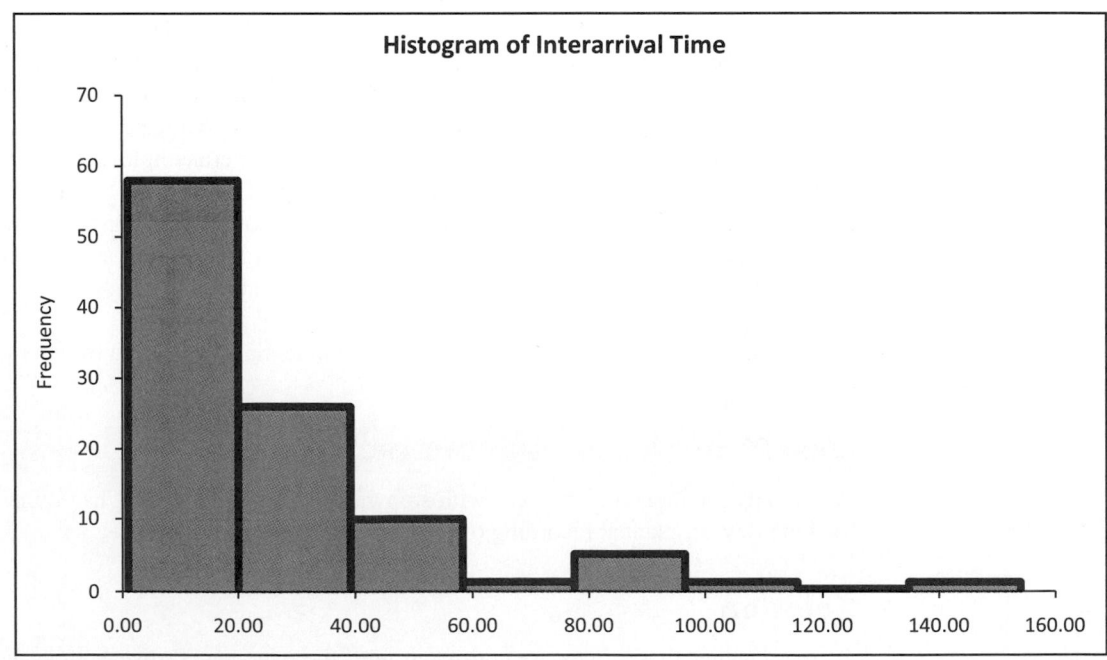

**Figure 14.6**  Histogram of Service Times for the ATM Example

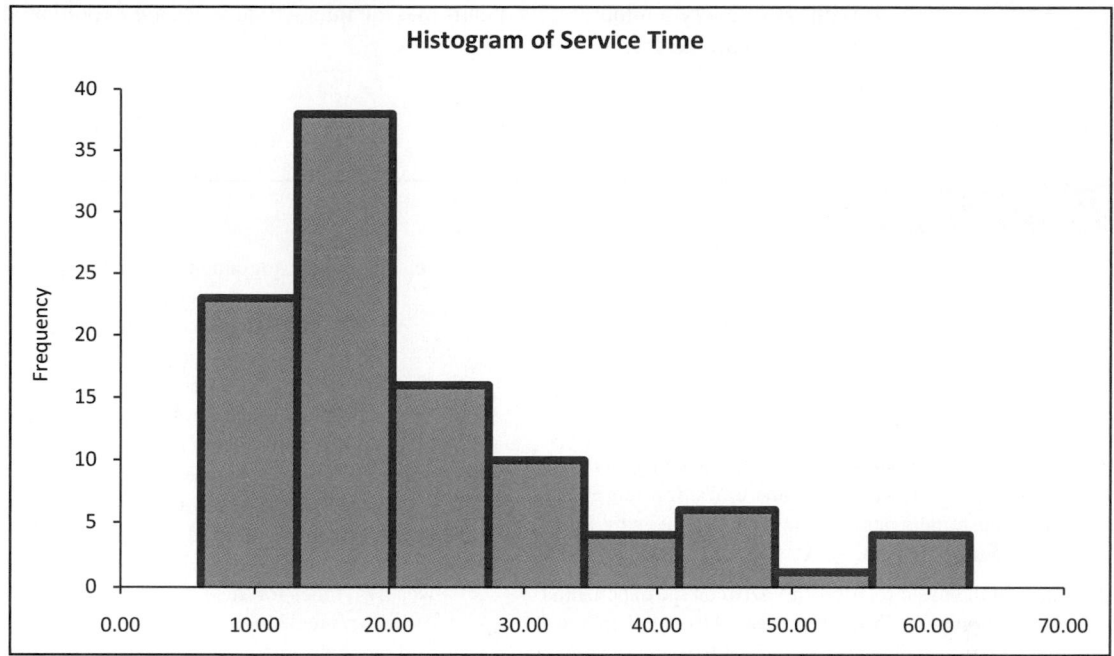

the service times is not shaped like the exponential density. Its highest bar is *not* the one farthest to the left but instead corresponds to the second category. Considering the way automatic teller machines operate, this is not surprising. Some minimum time is required to process any customer, regardless of the task, so that the most likely times are *not* close to 0. Therefore, the exponential assumption for interarrival times is reasonable, but it is questionable for service times.[2]

In either case, if the manager decides to accept the exponential assumption, the parameter $\lambda$ is the rate of arrivals (or services) and is estimated by the reciprocal of the average of the observed times. For interarrival times, this estimate of $\lambda$ is the reciprocal of the average in cell B5 of Figure 14.4: $1/25.3 = 0.0395$—that is, 1 arrival every 25.3 seconds. For service times, the estimated $\lambda$ is the reciprocal of the average in cell C5: $1/22.3 = 0.0448$—that is, 1 service every 22.3 seconds.  ∎

## The Poisson Process Model

*If we say arrivals occur according to a Poisson process, this means the interarrival times are exponentially distributed.*

When the interarrival times are exponentially distributed, we often state that "arrivals occur according to a Poisson process." There is a close relationship between the exponential distribution, which measures *times* between events such as arrivals, and the **Poisson distribution,** which counts the *number* of events in a certain length of time. The details of

---

[2] There are formal statistical procedures for testing whether an exponential fit is reasonable, but this "eye-balling" method often suffices.

this relationship are beyond the level of this book, so we do not explore this topic any further here. However, if we say that customers arrive at a bank according to a Poisson process with rate 1 every 3 minutes, this means that the interarrival times are exponentially distributed with parameter $\lambda = 1/3$.

## PROBLEMS

*Solutions for problems whose numbers appear within a color box can be found in the Student Solutions Files. Order your copy today at the Winston/Albright product Web site, academic.cengage.com/decisionsciences/winston.*

### Skill-Building Problems

1. An extremely important concept in queueing models is the difference between rates and times. If $\lambda$ represents a rate (customers per hour, say), then argue why $1/\lambda$ is a time and vice versa.

2. Explain the basic relationship between the exponential distribution and a Poisson process. Also, explain how the exponential distribution and the Poisson distribution are fundamentally different. (*Hint:* What type of data does each describe?)

**3.** We can easily generate random numbers in a spreadsheet that have an exponential distribution with a given mean. For example, to generate 200 such numbers from an exponential distribution with $\lambda = 1/3$, enter the formula $=-3*LN(RAND())$ in cell A4 and copy it to the range A5:A203. Then select the A4:A203 range, choose the Edit/Copy command, and choose the Edit/Paste Special command with the Values option. (This freezes the random numbers, so that they don't change each time the spreadsheet recalculates.) Explore the properties of these numbers as follows.
   **a.** Find the average of the 200 numbers with the AVERAGE function. What theoretical value should this average be close to?
   **b.** Find the standard deviation of the 200 numbers with the STDEV function. What theoretical value should this standard deviation be close to?

   **c.** Create a histogram of the random numbers, using about 15 categories, each of length 1, where the first category extends from 0 to 1. Does the histogram have the shape you would expect?
   **d.** Suppose you collected the data in column A by timing arrivals at a store. The value in cell A4 is the time (in minutes) until the first arrival, the value in cell A5 is the time between the first and second arrivals, the value in cell A6 is the time between the second and third arrivals, and so on. How might you convince yourself that the interarrival times for this store are indeed exponentially distributed? What is your best guess for the arrival rate (customers per minute)?

### Skill-Extending Problem

4. Do exponentially distributed random numbers have the memoryless property? Here is one way to find out. Generate many exponentially distributed random numbers with mean 3, using the formula in the previous problem. Find the fraction of them that are greater than 1. This estimates the probability $P(X > 1)$. Now find all random numbers that are greater than 4. Among these, find the fraction that are greater than 5. This estimates the probability $P(X > 4 + 1|X > 4)$. According to the memoryless property, these two estimates should be nearly equal. Are they? Try to do this *without* freezing the random numbers, so that you can get repeated estimates of the two probabilities by pressing the F9 key.

## 14.4 IMPORTANT QUEUEING RELATIONSHIPS

As we stated, the calculations required in queueing models are neither simple nor obvious. Fortunately, however, there are several very useful and general relationships that hold for a wide variety of queueing models. We briefly discuss them here so that we can use them in the queueing models in later sections.

We typically calculate two general types of outputs in a queueing model: **time averages** and **customer averages**. Typical time averages are[3]

- $L$, the expected number of customers in the system
- $L_Q$, the expected number of customers in the queue
- $L_S$, the expected number of customers in service
- $P$(all idle), the probability that all servers are idle
- $P$(all busy), the probability that all servers are busy

If you were going to estimate the quantity $L_Q$, for example, you might observe the system at many time points, record the number of customers in the queue at each time point, and then average these numbers. In other words, you would average this measure over *time*. Similarly, to estimate a probability such as $P$(all busy), you would observe the system at many time points, record a 1 each time all servers are busy and a 0 each time at least one server is idle, and then average these 0's and 1's.

In contrast, typical customer averages are

- $W$, the expected time spent in the system (waiting in line or being served)
- $W_Q$, the expected time spent in the queue
- $W_S$, the expected time spent in service

To estimate the quantity $W_Q$, for example, you would observe many customers, record the time in queue for each customer, and then average these times over the number of customers observed. Now you are averaging over *customers*.

## Little's Formula

*Little's formula relates time averages, such as L, to customer averages, such as W. If we can find one of these, then Little's formula gives us the value of the other one.*

**Little's formula** is a famous formula that relates time averages and customer averages in steady state. This formula was first discovered by Little.[4] The formula is easy to state. Consider any queueing system. Let $\lambda$ be the average rate at which customers enter this system, let $L$ be the expected number of customers in the system, and let $W$ be the expected time a typical customer spends in the system. Then Little's formula can be expressed as

$$L = \lambda W \qquad (14.2)$$

It can also be stated in terms of $L_Q$ and $W_Q$ or in terms of $L_S$ and $W_S$. That is, two alternative versions of Little's formula are

$$L_Q = \lambda W_Q \qquad (14.3)$$

and

$$L_S = \lambda W_S \qquad (14.4)$$

The reasoning behind Little's formula is actually very simple. For example, to see why equation (14.3) is true, consider a long time period of length $T$. During this period, we expect about $\lambda T$ customers to enter the system (from the definition of $\lambda$ as a rate), and each of these waits in queue for an expected time $W_Q$. Therefore, the expected total number of customer minutes spent in queue is $\lambda T W_Q$. On the other hand, the expected number of customers in the queue at any time during this period is $L_Q$, so the total number of customer

---

[3] These quantities appear several times throughout this chapter, and we will continue to use this notation.
[4] The original result was published in Little (1961). Numerous extensions of the basic result have been published since, including Brumelle (1971), Stidham (1974), and Heyman and Stidham (1980). It is now known that Little's formula holds in an amazingly wide variety of queueing systems.

minutes spent in the queue can also be calculated as $L_Q T$. Setting $\lambda T W_Q$ equal to $L_Q T$ and canceling $T$, we get equation (14.3). Strictly speaking, this argument is valid only for an extremely large time $T$, which is why Little's formula is a *steady-state* result. When we use simulation for relatively small values of time $T$, Little's formula is only an approximation.

Typically, we use analytical methods to find one of the $L$'s and then appeal to Little's formula to find the corresponding $W$. Alternatively, we can find $L$ from $W$. For example, suppose the arrival rate to a single-server queueing system is 30 customers per hour ($\lambda = 30$). Also, suppose we know (probably from an analytical model) that the expected number of customers in the system is $L = 2.5$. Then equation (14.2) implies that a typical customer spends an expected time $W = L/\lambda = 2.5/30 = 0.0833$ hour = 5 minutes in the system. If we also know that the average number of customers in the queue is $L_Q = 1.8$, then equation (14.3) implies that a typical customer's expected time in the queue is $W_Q = L_Q/\lambda = 1.8/30 = 0.06$ hour = 3.6 minutes.

## Other Relationships

Two other formulas relate these quantities. First, all customers are either in service or in the queue, so we have

$$L = L_Q + L_S \tag{14.5}$$

In the example from the previous paragraph, equation (14.5) implies that $L_S = 2.5 - 1.8 = 0.7$. (For a single-server system this means that exactly one customer is in service 70% of the time and no customers are in service 30% of the time.)

Second, we have

$$W = W_Q + W_S \tag{14.6}$$

Equation (14.6) follows because the time spent in the system is the time spent in the queue plus the time spent in service, and $W_S$ is the expected time in service. In our numerical example, equation (14.6) implies that the expected time a typical customer spends in service is $5.0 - 3.6 = 1.4$ minutes.

One final important queueing measure is called the **server utilization**. The server utilization, denoted by $U$, is defined as the long-run fraction of time a typical server is busy. In a multiple-server system, where there are $s$ identical servers in parallel, server utilization is defined as

$$U = L_S/s$$

*Server utilization is the fraction of time a typical server is busy.*

That is, it is the expected number of busy servers divided by the number of servers. For example, if $s = 3$ and $L_S = 2.55$, then $U = 0.85$. In this case the expected number of busy servers is 2.55, and each of the three servers is busy about 85% of the time.

## Skill-Building Problems

**5.** Assume that parts arrive at a machining center at a rate of 60 parts per hour. The machining center is capable of processing 75 parts per hour—that is, the mean time to machine a part is 0.8 minute. If you are watching these parts *exiting* the machine center, what exit rate do you observe, 60 or 75 per hour? Explain.

**6.** Little's formula applies to an entire queueing system or to a subsystem of a larger system. For example, consider a single-server system composed of two subsystems. The first subsystem is the waiting line, and the second is the service area, where service actually takes place. Let $\lambda$ be the rate that customers enter the system and assume that $\lambda = 60$ per hour.

    **a.** If the expected number of customers waiting in line is 2.5, what does Little's formula applied to the first subsystem tell us?

    **b.** Let $\mu$ be the service rate of the server (in customers per hour). Assuming that $\lambda < \mu$ (so that the server can serve customers faster than they arrive), argue why the rate into the second subsystem must be $\lambda$. Then, letting $\mu = 80$ per hour, what does Little's formula applied to the second subsystem tell us

about the expected number of customers in service?

**7.** Consider a bank where potential customers arrive at rate of 60 customers per hour. However, because of limited space, 1 out of every 4 arriving customers finds the bank full and leaves immediately (without entering the bank). Suppose that the average number of customers waiting in line in the bank is 3.5. How long will a typical *entering* customer have to wait in line? (*Hint:* In Little's formula, $\lambda$ refers only to customers who *enter* the system.)

## Skill-Extending Problem

**8.** Consider a fast-food restaurant where customers enter at a rate of 75 per hour, and 3 servers are working. Customers wait in a single line and go, in FCFS fashion, to the first of the 3 servers who is available. Each server can serve 1 customer every 2 minutes on average. If you are standing at the exit, counting customers as they leave the restaurant, at what rate will you see them leave? On average, how many of the servers are busy?

# 14.5 ANALYTICAL STEADY-STATE QUEUEING MODELS

In this section, we discuss several analytical models for queueing systems. As we stated, these models cannot be developed without a fair amount of mathematical background—more than we assume in this book. Therefore, we must rely on the queueing models that have been developed in the management science literature—and there are literally hundreds or even thousands of these. We will illustrate only the most basic models, and even for these, we provide only the key formulas. In some cases, we even automate these formulas with behind-the-scenes macros. This enable you to focus on the aspects of practical concern: (1) the meaning of the assumptions and whether they are realistic, (2) the relevant input parameters, (3) interpretation of the outputs, and possibly (4) how to use the models for economic optimization.

## The Basic Single-Server Model

*Kendall's notation, such as M/M/1, allows us to describe a variety of queueing systems with a few well-chosen symbols.*

We begin by discussing the most basic single-server model, labeled the $M/M/1$ model. This shorthand notation, developed by Kendall, implies three things. The first $M$ implies that the distribution of interarrival times is exponential.[5] The second $M$ implies that the distribution of service times is also exponential. Finally, the "1" implies that there is a *single* server. Customarily, $\lambda$ denotes the arrival rate, and $\mu$ denotes the service rate. (Here, $\mu$ is the Greek letter *mu*.) This means that $1/\lambda$ is the mean time between arrivals and $1/\mu$ is the

---

[5] The $M$ actually stands for *Markov*, a technical term that is synonymous with the exponential distribution. You can also think of it as an acronym for *memoryless*.

mean service time per customer. The model in this section is sometimes called the *classical M/M/1 queueing model*, which means that *all* customer arrivals join the system and stay until they are eventually served.

The mathematical derivation of the steady-state results for an $M/M/1$ queueing system is rather involved, so we simply list the results, which are surprisingly simple. First, we define $\rho$ (the Greek letter *rho*) by $\rho = \lambda/\mu$. This is called the **traffic intensity,** which is a very useful measure of the congestion of the system. In fact, the system is stable only if $\rho < 1$. If $\rho \geq 1$, so that $\lambda \geq \mu$, then arrivals occur at least as fast as the server can handle them; in the long run, the queue becomes infinitely large—that is, it is unstable. Therefore, we must assume that $\rho < 1$ to obtain steady-state results.

*The formulas presented here are not necessarily intuitive, and it takes a fair amount of mathematics to derive them rigorously. However, you can still use them!*

Assuming that the system is stable, let $p_n$ be the steady-state probability that there are exactly $n$ customer in the system (waiting in line or being served) at any point in time. This probability can be interpreted as the long-run *fraction* of time when there are $n$ customers in the system. For example, $p_0$ is the long-run fraction of time when there are no customers in the system, $p_1$ is the long-run fraction of time when there is exactly one customer in the system, and so on. These steady-state probabilities can be found from the following steady-state equation:

$$p_n = (1 - \rho) \rho^n \quad n \geq 0 \qquad (14.7)$$

From the definition of expected value, the expected number of customers in the system, $L$, is the sum over all $n$ of $n$ multiplied by $p_n$. It can be shown that this sum reduces to

$$L = \frac{\rho}{1 - \rho} = \frac{\lambda}{\mu - \lambda} \qquad (14.8)$$

where the last two expressions are equivalent. Then we can find $W$, $W_Q$, and $L_Q$ from Little's formula and the fact that $1/\mu$ is the expected time in service:

$$W = L/\lambda, \quad W_Q = W - 1/\mu, \quad L_Q = \lambda W_Q \qquad (14.9)$$

Two other results are worth noting. First, the server utilization $U$ is the fraction of time the server is busy. This fraction is $1 - p_0 = \rho$, so that the server utilization is equal to the traffic intensity:

$$U = \rho \qquad (14.10)$$

For example, if $\lambda = 40$ per hour and $\mu = 60$ per hour, then $U = \rho = 2/3$, so that the server is busy 2/3 of the time and is idle 1/3 of the time. Second, it is possible to derive the following explicit expression for the distribution of time spent by a typical customer in the queue:

$$P(\text{Time in queue} > t) = \rho e^{-\mu(1-\rho)t} \quad \text{for any } t > 0 \qquad (14.11)$$

The following example illustrates these results.

EXAMPLE | **14.2 QUEUEING AT A POSTAL BRANCH**

The Smalltown postal branch employs a single clerk. Customers arrive at this postal branch according to a Poisson process at a rate of 30 customers per hour, and the average service time is exponentially distributed with mean 1.5 minutes. All arriving customers enter the branch, regardless of the number already waiting in line. The manager of the postal branch would ultimately like to decide whether to improve the system. To do this, she first needs to develop a queueing model that describes the steady-state characteristics of the current system.

**Objective** To model the postal branch's system as an $M/M/1$ queue and then use the analytical formulas in equations (14.7) to (14.11) to find the system's steady-state characteristics.

The branch manager needs to proceed as in Example 14.1 to estimate the arrival rate and the mean service rate (and verify that the resulting distributions are at least approximately exponential).

## Solution

To begin, we must choose a common unit of time and then express the arrival and service rates ($\lambda$ and $\mu$) in this unit. We could measure time in seconds, minutes, hours, or any other convenient time unit, as long as we are consistent. Here we choose minutes as the unit of time. Then, because 1 customer arrives every 2 minutes, $\lambda = 1/2$. Also, because the mean service *time* is 1.5 minutes, the service *rate* is its reciprocal—that is, $\mu = 1/1.5 = 0.667$. Then the traffic intensity is

$$\rho = \lambda/\mu = (1/2)/(2/3) = 0.75$$

Because this is less than 1, we know that the system is stable and steady state will occur.

### Using the Spreadsheet Model Template

To implement the formulas for the $M/M/1$ model, we developed an $M/M/1$ template file. (See Figure 14.7 and the file **MM1 Template.xlsx**.) We do not provide step-by-step

---

**Figure 14.7** Template for the $M/M/1$ Queue

| | A | B | C | D | E | F | G | H | I |
|---|---|---|---|---|---|---|---|---|---|
| 1 | M/M/1 queue | | | | | | | | |
| 2 | | | | | | | | | |
| 3 | Inputs | | | | | | | | |
| 4 | Unit of time | minute | | | Enter desired inputs in blue cells and | | | | |
| 5 | Arrival rate | 0.500 | customers/minute | | everything recalculates automatically. | | | | |
| 6 | Service rate | 0.667 | customers/minute | | | | | | |
| 7 | | | | | | | | | |
| 8 | Outputs | | | | | | | | |
| 9 | Direct outputs from inputs | | | | Distribution of number in system | | | Distribution of time in queue | |
| 10 | Mean time between arrivals | 2.000 | minutes | | n (customers) | P(n in system) | | t (in minutes) | P(wait > t) |
| 11 | Mean time per service | 1.500 | minutes | | 0 | 0.250 | | 2.000 | 0.537 |
| 12 | Traffic intensity | 0.750 | | | 1 | 0.188 | | | |
| 13 | | | | | 2 | 0.141 | | | |
| 14 | Summary measures | | | | 3 | 0.105 | | | |
| 15 | Expected number in system | 3.000 | customers | | 4 | 0.079 | | | |
| 16 | Expected number in queue | 2.250 | customers | | 5 | 0.059 | | | |
| 17 | Expected time in system | 6.000 | minutes | | 6 | 0.044 | | | |
| 18 | Expected time in queue | 4.500 | minutes | | 7 | 0.033 | | | |
| 19 | Server utilization | 75.0% | | | 8 | 0.025 | | | |
| 20 | | | | | 9 | 0.019 | | | |
| 21 | | | | | 10 | 0.014 | | | |
| 22 | | | | | 11 | 0.011 | | | |
| 23 | | | | | 12 | 0.008 | | | |
| 24 | | | | | 13 | 0.006 | | | |
| 25 | | | | | 14 | 0.004 | | | |
| 26 | | | | | 15 | 0.003 | | | |
| 27 | | | | | 16 | 0.003 | | | |
| 28 | | | | | 17 | 0.002 | | | |
| 29 | | | | | 18 | 0.001 | | | |
| 30 | | | | | 19 | 0.001 | | | |
| 31 | | | | | 20 | 0.001 | | | |
| 32 | | | | | 21 | 0.001 | | | |
| 33 | | | | | 22 | 0.000 | | | |

instructions because we expect that you will use this as a template rather than enter the formulas yourself. However, we make the following points:

**1** All you need to enter are the inputs in cells B4 through B6. Note that the rates in cells B5 and B6 are relative to the time unit you specify in cell B4.

**2** You can enter *numbers* for the rates in cells B5 and B6, or you can base these on observed data. (Example 14.1 illustrated the estimation of arrival and service rates from observed data.)

**3** The value of $L$ in cell B15 is calculated from equation (14.8). Then the values in cells B5, B15, and B17 are related by the equation (14.2) version of Little's formula, $L = \lambda W$; the values in cells B5, B16, and B18 are related by equation (14.3), $L_Q = \lambda W_Q$; and the value in cell B18 is calculated from $W_Q = W - 1/\mu$. From equation (14.10), the server utilization in cell B19 is the same as the traffic intensity in cell B12.

**4** The steady-state probabilities in column F are based on equation (14.7). You can copy these down as far as you like, until the probabilities are negligible.

**5** The waiting time probability in cell I11 is calculated from equation (14.11). You can enter any time $t$ in cell H11 to obtain the probability that a typical customer will wait in the queue at least this amount of time. Alternatively, you can enter other values of $t$ in cells H12, H13, and so on, and then copy the formula in cell I11 down to calculate other waiting time probabilities.

### Discussion of the Results

From Figure 14.7, we see, for example, that when the arrival rate is 0.5 and the service rate is 0.667, the expected number of customers in the queue is 2.25 and the expected time a typical customer spends in the queue is 4.5 minutes. However, cells F11 and I11 indicate that 25% of all customers spend no time in the queue, and 53.7% spend more than 2 minutes in the queue. Also, just for illustration, cell F15 indicates that the steady-state probability of having exactly four customers in the system is 0.079. Equivalently, there are exactly four customers in the system 7.9% of the time.

The branch manager can experiment with other arrival rates or service rates in cells B5 and B6 to see how the various output measures are affected. One particularly important insight can be obtained through a data table, as shown in Figure 14.8. The current server

*The traffic intensity determines the amount of congestion in the system.*

**Figure 14.8**

Effect of Varying Service Rate

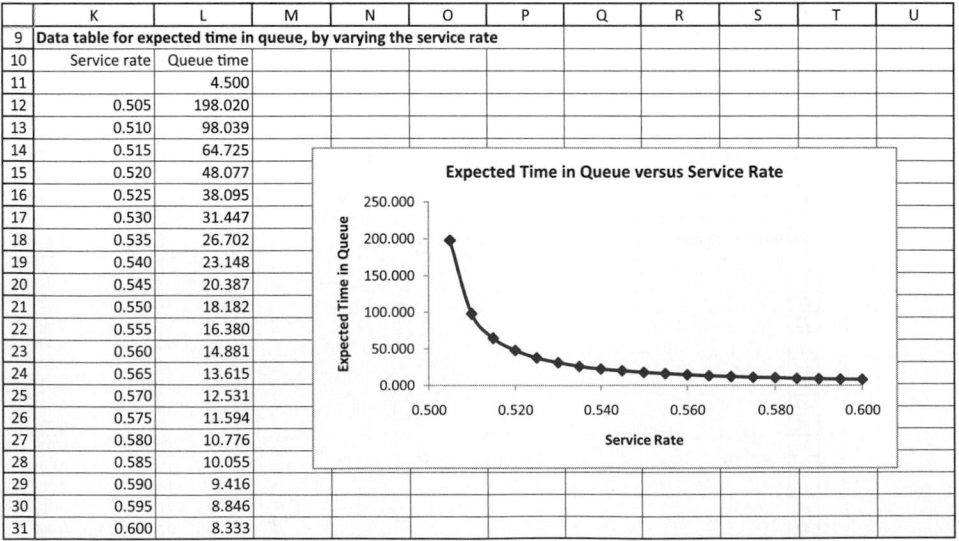

| | K | L | M | N | O | P | Q | R | S | T | U |
|---|---|---|---|---|---|---|---|---|---|---|---|
| 9 | Data table for expected time in queue, by varying the service rate | | | | | | | | | | |
| 10 | Service rate | Queue time | | | | | | | | | |
| 11 | | 4.500 | | | | | | | | | |
| 12 | 0.505 | 198.020 | | | | | | | | | |
| 13 | 0.510 | 98.039 | | | | | | | | | |
| 14 | 0.515 | 64.725 | | | | | | | | | |
| 15 | 0.520 | 48.077 | | | | | | | | | |
| 16 | 0.525 | 38.095 | | | | | | | | | |
| 17 | 0.530 | 31.447 | | | | | | | | | |
| 18 | 0.535 | 26.702 | | | | | | | | | |
| 19 | 0.540 | 23.148 | | | | | | | | | |
| 20 | 0.545 | 20.387 | | | | | | | | | |
| 21 | 0.550 | 18.182 | | | | | | | | | |
| 22 | 0.555 | 16.380 | | | | | | | | | |
| 23 | 0.560 | 14.881 | | | | | | | | | |
| 24 | 0.565 | 13.615 | | | | | | | | | |
| 25 | 0.570 | 12.531 | | | | | | | | | |
| 26 | 0.575 | 11.594 | | | | | | | | | |
| 27 | 0.580 | 10.776 | | | | | | | | | |
| 28 | 0.585 | 10.055 | | | | | | | | | |
| 29 | 0.590 | 9.416 | | | | | | | | | |
| 30 | 0.595 | 8.846 | | | | | | | | | |
| 31 | 0.600 | 8.333 | | | | | | | | | |

The M/M/1 system
gets very congested,
with long waiting
times, when the arrival
rate is just barely less
than the service rate.

utilization is 0.75, and the system is behaving fairly well, with short waits in queue on average. The data table, however, shows how bad things can get when the service rate is just barely above the arrival rate, so that the traffic intensity is just barely below 1. (The single output for this data table is the expected time in queue, from cell B18, and the column input cell is the service rate cell, B6.) The corresponding line chart shows that the expected time in queue increases extremely rapidly as the service rate gets closer to the arrival rate. Whatever else the branch manager learns from this model, she now knows that she does not want a service rate close to the arrival rate, at least not for extended periods of time.

We make one other important comment about this system. Our entire analysis depends on the fact that the arrival rate remains constant at 1 every 2 minutes, on average. Therefore, the results in Figure 14.7 are valid only for the period of time when this arrival rate is in effect. If the arrival rate suddenly changes, as it might during the lunch period or the 5:00 P.M. rush, then a new steady-state analysis must be performed with the new arrival rate. ∎

## The Basic Multiple-Server Model

Many service facilities such as banks and postal branches employ multiple servers. Usually, these servers work in parallel, so that each customer goes to exactly one server for service and then departs. In this section, we analyze the simplest version of this multiple-server parallel system, labeled the $M/M/s$ model. Again, the first $M$ means that interarrival times are exponentially distributed. The second $M$ means that the service times for *each* server are exponentially distributed. (We also assume that each server is identical to the others, in the sense that each has the same mean service time.) Finally, the $s$ in $M/M/s$ denotes the number of servers. (If $s = 1$, the $M/M/s$ and $M/M/1$ models are identical. In other words, the $M/M/1$ system is a special case of the $M/M/s$ system.)

The M/M/s system assumes that all customers wait in a single line and are served in FCFS order.

If you think about the multiple-server facilities you typically enter, such as banks, post offices, and supermarkets, you recognize that there are two types of waiting line configurations. The first, usually seen at supermarkets, is where each server has a separate line. Each customer must decide which line to join (and then either stay in that line or switch later on). The second, seen at most banks and post offices, is where there is a *single* waiting line, from which customers are served in FCFS order. We examine only the second type because it is arguably the more common system in real-world situations and is much easier to analyze mathematically.

There are three inputs to this system: the arrival rate $\lambda$, the service rate (per server) $\mu$, and the number of servers $s$. To ensure that the system is stable, we must also assume that the traffic intensity, now given by $\rho = \lambda/(s\mu)$, is less than 1. In words, we require that the arrival rate $\lambda$ be less than the *maximum* service rate $s\mu$ (which is achieved when all $s$ servers are busy). If the traffic intensity is not less than 1, the length of the queue eventually increases without bound.

Stability in $M/M/s$ model: $\rho = \lambda/(s\mu) < 1$

The steady-state analysis for the $M/M/s$ system is more complex than for the $M/M/1$ system. As before, let $p_n$ be the probability that there are exactly $n$ customers in the system, waiting or in service. Then it turns out that all of the steady-state quantities depend on $p_0$, which can be calculated from the rather complex formula in equation (14.12). Then the other quantities can be calculated from $p_0$, as indicated in equations (14.13) to (14.17).

$$p_0 = \frac{1}{\displaystyle\sum_{n=0}^{s-1} \frac{(s\rho)^n}{n!} + \frac{(s\rho)^s}{s!(1-\rho)}} \tag{14.12}$$

$$p_n = \begin{cases} \dfrac{(s\rho)^n p_0}{n!} & \text{if } 1 \leqslant n \leqslant s \\[3mm] \dfrac{(s\rho)^n p_0}{s! s^{n-s}} & \text{if } n > s \end{cases} \tag{14.13}$$

$$P(\text{All servers busy}) = \frac{(s\rho)^s p_0}{s!(1-\rho)} \tag{14.14}$$

$$L_Q = P(\text{All servers busy})\frac{\rho}{1-\rho} \tag{14.15}$$

$$W_Q = L_Q/\lambda, \quad W = W_Q + 1/\mu, \quad L = \lambda W \tag{14.16}$$

$$P(\text{Wait in queue} > t) = P(\text{All servers busy})e^{-s\mu(1-\rho)t} \quad \text{for any } t > 0 \tag{14.17}$$

These formulas are admittedly complex, so we have implemented them, with the use of a VBA macro, in a template file. The following example illustrates the process.

---

EXAMPLE | **14.3 QUEUEING AT COUNTY BANK**

County Bank has several branch locations. At one of these locations, customers arrive at a Poisson rate of 150 per hour. The branch employs 6 tellers. Each teller takes, on average, 2 minutes to serve a customer, and service times are exponentially distributed. Also, all tellers perform all tasks, so that customers can go to any of the 6 tellers. Customers who arrive and find all 6 tellers busy join a single queue and are then served in FCFS fashion. As a first step, the bank manager wants to develop a queueing model of the current system. Then he wants to find the "best" number of tellers, given that tellers are paid $8 per hour.

**Objective** To develop an $M/M/s$ queueing model for the bank and examine its steady-state properties, and then to find the number of tellers that is best from an economic point of view.

### WHERE DO THE NUMBERS COME FROM?

The same comments as in Example 14.2 apply here. Of course, the $8 figure is just the current hourly wage rate.

## Solution

As with the $M/M/1$ system, we have created a template file that calculates $p_0$ from equation (14.12), using a behind-the-scenes VBA macro, and then implements the formulas in equations (14.13) to (14.17). (See the file **MMs Template.xlsm** and Figure 14.9.)

### Using the Spreadsheet Model Template

*The template file uses a macro to calculate the probability that the system is empty. Built-in formulas then calculate all other steady-state measures. Don't forget to enable the macro when you open the file.*

All you need to do is enter the inputs in cells B4 to B7 and then click on the button. This button runs the macro that calculates $p_0$ in cell B16, and then the formulas in the other cells all recalculate automatically. For this example, the necessary inputs are the unit of time (we have chosen "hour"), the arrival rate (150), the service rate per server (30), and the number of servers (6). We invite you to look at the formulas in the various cells to check that they do indeed implement equations (14.13) to (14.17). As with the $M/M/1$ template, you can copy the probability distribution in columns E and F as far down as you like, until the probabilities are negligible, and you can enter any time $t$ in cell H12 to get the corresponding waiting time probability in cell I12.

## Discussion of the Results

*The server utilization in an M/M/s system—the fraction of time each server is busy—is equal to the traffic intensity.*

From Figure 14.9 we see that when there are 6 tellers, and the traffic intensity is 0.833, the expected number of customers in the system is 7.94, and the expected time a typical customer spends in the system is 0.053 hour (about 3.2 minutes). Also, about 41% of all arriving customers can go immediately into service, whereas about 32% of all customers must wait more than 0.02 hour (about 1.2 minutes) in the queue. Finally, we can find the expected fraction of time each teller is busy as $L_S/s$. We find $L_S$, the expected number of busy tellers, from $L_S = L - L_Q = 7.938 - 2.938 = 5$. Then the expected fraction of time each teller is busy is $L_S/s = 5/6 = 0.833$. If this number doesn't ring a bell, it should—it is the server utilization in cell B13. This is no coincidence. The server utilization in an $M/M/s$ system, calculated as the arrival rate divided by the maximum service rate, is always the expected fraction of time a typical server is busy. That is, the traffic intensity is equal to the server utilization $U$.

**Figure 14.9** Template for the $M/M/s$ Queue

| | A | B | C | D | E | F | G | H | I |
|---|---|---|---|---|---|---|---|---|---|
| 1 | M/M/s Queue | | | | | | | | |
| 2 | | | | | | | | | |
| 3 | Inputs | | | | | | | | |
| 4 | Unit of time | hour | | | | | | | |
| 5 | Arrival rate | 150 | customers/hour | | | | | | |
| 6 | Service rate per server | 30 | customers/hour | | | | | | |
| 7 | Number of servers | 6 | | | | | | | |
| 8 | | | | | | | | | |
| 9 | Outputs | | | | | | | | |
| 10 | Direct outputs from inputs | | | | Distribution of number in system | | | Distribution of time in queue | |
| 11 | Mean time between arrivals | 0.007 | hours | | n (customers) | P(n in system) | | t (in hours) | P(wait > t) |
| 12 | Mean time per service | 0.033 | hours | | 0 | 0.0045 | | 0.020 | 0.322 |
| 13 | Traffic intensity | 0.833 | | | 1 | 0.0226 | | | |
| 14 | | | | | 2 | 0.0564 | | | |
| 15 | Summary measures | | | | 3 | 0.0940 | | | |
| 16 | P(system empty) | 0.005 | | | 4 | 0.1175 | | | |
| 17 | P(all servers busy) | 58.8% | | | 5 | 0.1175 | | | |
| 18 | Expected number in system | 7.938 | customers | | 6 | 0.0979 | | | |
| 19 | Expected number in queue | 2.938 | customers | | 7 | 0.0816 | | | |
| 20 | Expected time in system | 0.053 | hours | | 8 | 0.0680 | | | |
| 21 | Expected time in queue | 0.020 | hours | | 9 | 0.0567 | | | |
| 22 | Percentage who don't wait in queue | 41.2% | | | 10 | 0.0472 | | | |
| 23 | | | | | 11 | 0.0394 | | | |
| 24 | | | | | 12 | 0.0328 | | | |
| 25 | | | | | 13 | 0.0273 | | | |
| 26 | | | | | 14 | 0.0228 | | | |
| 27 | | | | | 15 | 0.0190 | | | |
| 28 | | | | | 16 | 0.0158 | | | |
| 29 | | | | | 17 | 0.0132 | | | |
| 30 | | | | | 18 | 0.0110 | | | |
| 31 | | | | | 19 | 0.0092 | | | |
| 32 | | | | | 20 | 0.0076 | | | |
| 33 | | | | | 21 | 0.0064 | | | |
| 34 | | | | | 22 | 0.0053 | | | |

(Note in spreadsheet, near E2: "After entering inputs in blue cells, click on the button below to run the macro that calculates P(0), the value in cell B16. Everything else recalculates automatically. Do *not* rearrange cells in this template -- this might cause the macro to stop behaving correctly." Button labeled "Do Calculations")

## Economic Analysis

We now turn to the economic analysis. There is a cost and a benefit from adding a teller. The cost is the wage rate paid to the extra teller, $8 per hour. The benefit is that customers wait less time in the bank. Note that adding an extra teller makes both $W$ and $W_Q$ decrease by the *same* amount. This is because $W$ equals $W_Q$ plus the expected service time per customer, and this expected service time does not change with extra tellers. This means that extra tellers decrease only the expected time in line, not the time in service. (The latter would decrease only if we made each teller *faster*, rather than adding tellers.) To see how $W_Q$ changes, try entering 7 and then 8 for the number of tellers in cell B7 of Figure 14.9 and clicking on the button for each change. You should observe that the value of $W_Q$ changes from 0.0196 hour (with 6 tellers) to 0.0054 hour (with 7 tellers) to 0.0019 hour (with 8 tellers). Because the arrival rate is 150 customers per hour, these waiting times translate to 2.94, 0.81, and 0.28 customer-hours spent waiting in line each hour. (Just multiply each expected waiting time in queue by 150.)

The real problem is to evaluate the *cost* of waiting in line. This is not an out-of-pocket cost for the bank, but it does represent an indirect cost: Customers who experience long waits might take their business elsewhere. In any case, the key to the trade-off is assessing a unit cost, $c_Q$, per customer-hour spent waiting in the queue. If the manager can assess this unit cost, then the total expected cost per hour of customer waiting is $c_Q \lambda W_Q$. The reasoning is that $\lambda$ customers arrive per hour, and each waits an expected time $W_Q$ in the queue. Then we can trade off this waiting cost against the cost of hiring extra tellers.

We provide another template in the file **MMs Optimizing Template.xlsm** that helps solve the problem (see Figure 14.10). You now need to provide the arrival rate, the service rate per server, the wage rate per server, and the unit waiting cost per customer per unit time in line. You should *not* enter the number of servers as an input. Instead, the macro—run by clicking on the button—calculates selected summary measures of the system for several choices of the number of servers. Specifically, for each number of servers, the macro does the same calculations we did in the $M/M/s$ template to calculate the value of $W_Q$ in row 17. Then the cost of wages in row 18 is the wage rate multiplied by the number of servers, the queueing cost in row 19 is $c_Q \lambda W_Q$, and the total cost in row 20 is the sum of these two costs.

**Figure 14.10**  A Template for Queueing Optimization

| | A | B | C | D | E | F | G | H | I |
|---|---|---|---|---|---|---|---|---|---|
| 1 | M/M/s Queue - A Template for Optimizing | | | | | | | | |
| 2 | | | | | Directions: | | | | |
| 3 | Inputs | | | | 1. Enter the inputs in cells B4 through B8. | | | | |
| 4 | Unit of time | hour | | | 2. Press the "Do Calculations" button. | | | | |
| 5 | Arrival rate | 150 | custs/hour | | | | | | |
| 6 | Service rate per server | 30 | custs/hour | | | | | | |
| 7 | Wage rate per server | $8.00 | $/hour | | | | | | |
| 8 | Cost per customer for time in queue | $5.50 | $/hour | | | Do Calculations | | | |
| 9 | | | | | | | | | |
| 10 | Minimum number of servers | 6 | | | | | | | |
| 11 | | | | | | | | | |
| 12 | Outputs | | | | | | | | |
| 13 | Number of servers | 6 | 7 | 8 | | | | | |
| 14 | Server utilization | 0.833 | 0.714 | 0.625 | | | | | |
| 15 | P(system empty) | 0.005 | 0.006 | 0.006 | | | | | |
| 16 | Percentage who wait in queue | 0.588 | 0.324 | 0.167 | | | | | |
| 17 | Expected time in queue | 0.0196 | 0.0054 | 0.0019 | | | | | |
| 18 | Wages paid per hour | $48.00 | $56.00 | $64.00 | | | | | |
| 19 | Queueing cost per hour | $16.16 | $4.46 | $1.53 | | | | | |
| 20 | Total cost per hour | $64.16 | $60.46 | $65.53 | | | | | |
| 21 | | | | | | | | | |
| 22 | | Starting with the minimum number of servers in column B, the macro | | | | | | | |
| 23 | | keeps increasing the number of servers until the total cost in row 20 | | | | | | | |
| 24 | | increases. Then the next to last total cost must be the minimum. | | | | | | | |
| 25 | | | | | | | | | |

To optimize, the macro begins by using the smallest number of tellers required to keep the system stable. In this case, 6 tellers are required, as seen in cell B10. Then it keeps adding a teller and calculating the total expected cost for that number of tellers—total wages plus total expected waiting cost—until the total expected cost starts to increase. Given the inputs in Figure 14.10, where the manager assesses customer waiting time at $5.50 per hour, the total expected cost when there are 6 tellers is $64.16. It then decreases to $60.46 with 7 tellers, and then it increases to $65.53 with eight tellers. Because the total expected cost would only continue to increase with more than 8 tellers, the macro quits with 8, implying that 7 tellers is best.

*One of the most difficult aspects of an economic analysis of a queueing system is assessing the cost of making a customer wait in line.*

This procedure requires a value for $c_Q$ in cell B8. Because this value is probably very difficult for a bank manager to assess, we can use an alternative indirect approach. We can find ranges for $c_Q$ where a specific number of servers is economically optimal. To do this, first enter the largest reasonable value of $c_Q$ in cell B8 and run the macro. For example, if the manager knows he would never value customer waiting time at more than $20 per hour, enter $20 in cell B8. Running the macro with this $c_Q$ gives the results in Figure 14.11. They imply that a choice of 8 tellers is optimal when $c_Q = 20$. They also imply that no more than 8 tellers would ever be optimal for any *smaller* value of $c_Q$. (Make sure you understand why this is true.) Given the output in Figure 14.11, we now ask, when is 6 tellers better than seven? The total cost comparison, using the values of $W_Q$ in row 17, shows that 6 tellers is better than 7 when

$$6(\$8) + c_Q(150)(0.0196) < 7(\$8) + c_Q(150)(0.0054)$$

This reduces to $c_Q < \$3.76$. Similarly, 7 tellers is better than eight when

$$7(\$8) + c_Q(150)(0.0054) < 8(\$8) + c_Q(150)(0.0019)$$

This reduces to $c_Q < \$15.24$. These results imply that it is best to use 6 tellers when $c_Q < \$3.76$. Otherwise, if $c_Q < \$15.24$, it is best to use 7 tellers. Finally, for $c_Q$ between $15.24 and $20, it is best to use 8 tellers.

**Figure 14.11**    Output Useful for Sensitivity Analysis on the Unit Waiting Cost

| | A | B | C | D | E | F | G | H | I |
|---|---|---|---|---|---|---|---|---|---|
| 1 | M/M/s Queue - A Template for Optimizing | | | | | | | | |
| 2 | | | | | Directions: | | | | |
| 3 | Inputs | | | | 1. Enter the inputs in cells B4 through B8. | | | | |
| 4 | Unit of time | hour | | | 2. Press the "Do Calculations" button. | | | | |
| 5 | Arrival rate | 150 | custs/hour | | | | | | |
| 6 | Service rate per server | 30 | custs/hour | | | | | | |
| 7 | Wage rate per server | $8.00 | $/hour | | | | | | |
| 8 | Cost per customer for time in queue | $20.00 | $/hour | | | Do Calculations | | | |
| 9 | | | | | | | | | |
| 10 | Minimum number of servers | 6 | | | | | | | |
| 11 | | | | | | | | | |
| 12 | Outputs | | | | | | | | |
| 13 | Number of servers | 6 | 7 | 8 | 9 | | | | |
| 14 | Server utilization | 0.833 | 0.714 | 0.625 | 0.556 | | | | |
| 15 | P(system empty) | 0.005 | 0.006 | 0.006 | 0.007 | | | | |
| 16 | Percentage who wait in queue | 0.588 | 0.324 | 0.167 | 0.081 | | | | |
| 17 | Expected time in queue | 0.0196 | 0.0054 | 0.0019 | 0.0007 | | | | |
| 18 | Wages paid per hour | $48.00 | $56.00 | $64.00 | $72.00 | | | | |
| 19 | Queueing cost per hour | $58.75 | $16.21 | $5.58 | $2.01 | | | | |
| 20 | Total cost per hour | $106.75 | $72.21 | $69.58 | $74.01 | | | | |
| 21 | | | | | | | | | |
| 22 | | Starting with the minimum number of servers in column B, the macro | | | | | | | |
| 23 | | keeps increasing the number of servers until the total cost in row 20 | | | | | | | |
| 24 | | increases. Then the next to last total cost must be the minimum. | | | | | | | |
| 25 | | | | | | | | | |

## A Comparison of Models

Here is a question many of you have probably pondered while waiting in line. Would you rather go to a system with one fast server or a system with several slow servers? In the latter case, we assume that only one waiting line forms, so that you can't get unlucky by joining the "wrong" line. The solution to the question is fairly straightforward, now that we know how to obtain outputs for $M/M/1$ and $M/M/s$ models. In the following example, we make the comparison numerically. For a fair comparison, we assume that (1) the arrival rate is the same for both systems, and (2) the service rate $\mu_{fast}$ for the single fast server is equal to $s\mu_{slow}$, where $\mu_{slow}$ is the service rate for *each* of the $s$ slow servers.

---

EXAMPLE | **14.4 COMPARING ONE FAST SERVER TO SEVERAL SLOW SERVERS**

Which system has the better steady-state characteristics such as $L$, $W$, $L_Q$, and $W_Q$: a single-server system where the single server can serve 30 customers per hour or a five-server system where each of the servers can serve six customers per hour? For each system, we assume that customers arrive according to a Poisson process at rate 25 per hour.

**Objective** To see whether customers should prefer a system with one fast server or a system with several slower servers.

### WHERE DO THE NUMBERS COME FROM?

We can use any representative inputs for the comparison. In fact, it would be useful to try others, just to see whether the qualitative results we discuss next continue to hold.

## Solution

First, note that the two models are comparable in the sense that $\mu_{fast} = s\mu_{slow}$ because $\mu_{fast} = 30$, $s = 5$, and $\mu_{slow} = 6$. Equivalently, the traffic intensity is 5/6 for each. The spreadsheets in Figures 14.12 and 14.13 answer our question. (They were formed from the **MM1 Template.xlsx** and **MMs Template.xlsm** files simply by changing the inputs.) As you can see, the comparison is not entirely clear-cut. The $M/M/1$ system has a smaller $L$ but a

---

**Figure 14.12** $M/M/1$ System with a Single Fast Server

| | A | B | C | D | E | F | G | H | I |
|---|---|---|---|---|---|---|---|---|---|
| 1 | M/M/1 queue | | | | | | | | |
| 2 | | | | | | | | | |
| 3 | Inputs | | | | | | | | |
| 4 | Unit of time | hour | | | Enter desired inputs in blue cells and | | | | |
| 5 | Arrival rate | 25.000 | customers/hour | | everything recalculates automatically. | | | | |
| 6 | Service rate | 30.000 | customers/hour | | | | | | |
| 7 | | | | | | | | | |
| 8 | Outputs | | | | | | | | |
| 9 | Direct outputs from inputs | | | | Distribution of number in system | | | Distribution of time in queue | |
| 10 | Mean time between arrivals | 0.040 | hours | | n (customers) | P(n in system) | | t (in hours) | P(wait > t) |
| 11 | Mean time per service | 0.033 | hours | | 0 | 0.167 | | 0.250 | 0.239 |
| 12 | Traffic intensity | 0.833 | | | 1 | 0.139 | | | |
| 13 | | | | | 2 | 0.116 | | | |
| 14 | Summary measures | | | | 3 | 0.096 | | | |
| 15 | Expected number in system | 5.000 | customers | | 4 | 0.080 | | | |
| 16 | Expected number in queue | 4.167 | customers | | 5 | 0.067 | | | |
| 17 | Expected time in system | 0.200 | hours | | 6 | 0.056 | | | |
| 18 | Expected time in queue | 0.167 | hours | | 7 | 0.047 | | | |
| 19 | Server utilization | 83.3% | | | 8 | 0.039 | | | |

**Figure 14.13** $M/M/s$ System with Several Slow Servers

| | A | B | C | D | E | F | G | H | I |
|---|---|---|---|---|---|---|---|---|---|
| 1 | M/M/s Queue | | | | | | | | |
| 2 | | | | | After entering inputs in blue cells, click on the button below to | | | | |
| 3 | Inputs | | | | run the macro that calculates P(0), the value in cell B16. | | | | |
| 4 | Unit of time | hour | | | Everything else recalculates automatically. Do *not* rearrange | | | | |
| 5 | Arrival rate | 25 | customers/hour | | cells in this template -- this might cause the macro to stop | | | | |
| 6 | Service rate per server | 6 | customers/hour | | behaving correctly. | | | | |
| 7 | Number of servers | 5 | | | | | | | |
| 8 | | | | | | Do Calculations | | | |
| 9 | Outputs | | | | | | | | |
| 10 | Direct outputs from inputs | | | | Distribution of number in system | | | Distribution of time in queue | |
| 11 | Mean time between arrivals | 0.040 | hours | | n (customers) | P(n in system) | | t (in hours) | P(wait > t) |
| 12 | Mean time per service | 0.167 | hours | | 0 | 0.0099 | | 0.020 | 0.561 |
| 13 | Traffic intensity | 0.833 | | | 1 | 0.0411 | | | |
| 14 | | | | | 2 | 0.0857 | | | |
| 15 | Summary measures | | | | 3 | 0.1191 | | | |
| 16 | P(system empty) | 0.010 | | | 4 | 0.1240 | | | |
| 17 | P(all servers busy) | 62.0% | | | 5 | 0.1034 | | | |
| 18 | Expected number in system | 7.267 | customers | | 6 | 0.0861 | | | |
| 19 | Expected number in queue | 3.101 | customers | | 7 | 0.0718 | | | |
| 20 | Expected time in system | 0.291 | hours | | 8 | 0.0598 | | | |
| 21 | Expected time in queue | 0.124 | hours | | 9 | 0.0498 | | | |
| 22 | Percentage who don't wait in queue | 38.0% | | | 10 | 0.0415 | | | |

*Perhaps surprisingly, the choice between these two systems is not entirely clear-cut.*

larger $L_Q$. Similarly, it has a smaller $W$ but a larger $W_Q$. In addition, the $M/M/1$ system is worse in that it has a smaller percentage of customers who experience no waiting in line (16.7% versus 38.0%) and a larger percentage who must wait in line at least 0.25 hour (23.9% versus 17.8%). The basic conclusion is that if you hate to wait in a queue, you should prefer the system with multiple slow servers. However, when it is your turn to be served, you clearly prefer the system with the single fast server. In this latter system, you spend less *total* time in the system, but more of it is spent waiting in line. Take your choice! ∎

## The Effect of the Traffic Intensity

We have mentioned that for an $M/M/1$ or $M/M/s$ system to be stable, the traffic intensity must be less than 1. In words, the system must be able to service the customers faster than they arrive; otherwise, the queue length eventually grows without limit. It is interesting to see what happens to a system when the traffic intensity gets closer and closer to 1 but stays less than 1. As the following continuation of the County Bank example shows, the effects can be disastrous. We already saw this phenomenon for a single-server system in Example 14.2. It is worth seeing again, this time in a multiple-server setting. In fact, this is arguably the most important lesson from this chapter!

**FUNDAMENTAL INSIGHT**

### The Effect of the Traffic Intensity

Queueing models are all about waiting lines and congestion. One of the most fundamental insights about queueing systems is that congestion increases in a very nonlinear manner as the traffic intensity gets closer to 1. More specifically, as the arrival rate gets closer and closer to the maximum rate at which the system can service customers, waiting lines grow extremely rapidly. Therefore, real systems have to have some mechanism, such as turning customers away or adding more servers, to reduce congestion to an acceptable level.

EXAMPLE | **14.5 INCREASINGLY LONG LINES AT COUNTY BANK**

Over a period of time, the County Bank branch office from Example 14.3 has been experiencing a steady increase in the customer arrival rate. This rate has increased from the previous value of 150 customers per hour to 160, then to 170, and it is still increasing. During this time, the number of tellers has remained constant at six, and the mean service time per teller has remained constant at 2 minutes. The bank manager has seen an obvious increase in bank congestion. Is this reinforced by the $M/M/s$ model? What will happen if the arrival rate continues to increase?

**Objective** To see what happens to congestion in a multiple-server system when the traffic intensity gets close to 1.

**WHERE DO THE NUMBERS COME FROM?**

The numbers here are all hypothetical, just to illustrate an effect.

## Solution

*A multiple-server system with a traffic intensity just barely below 1 behaves very badly—customers must wait long times in line.*

Because $s\mu$ has stayed constant at value $6(30) = 180$, the traffic intensity, $\lambda/(s\mu)$, has climbed from $150/180 = 0.833$ to $160/180 = 0.889$ to $170/180 = 0.944$, and it is still climbing. We know that $\lambda$ must stay below 180 or the system will become unstable, but what about values of $\lambda$ slightly below 180? We recalculated the spreadsheet in Figure 14.13 for several values of $\lambda$ and obtained the results in Table 14.1. ($W$ and $W_Q$ are expressed in minutes.) Although each column of this table represents a stable system, the congestion is becoming unbearable. When $\lambda = 178$, the expected line length is over 80 customers, and a typical customer must wait about a half hour in line. Things are twice as bad when $\lambda = 179$.

**Table 14.1    Effects of Increasing Arrival Rate**

| | *Customer Arrival Rate* ($\lambda$) | | | | | |
|---|---|---|---|---|---|---|
| | **150** | **160** | **170** | **175** | **178** | **179** |
| **Traffic intensity** | 0.833 | 0.889 | 0.944 | 0.972 | 0.989 | 0.994 |
| $L$ | 7.94 | 11.04 | 20.14 | 38.18 | 92.21 | 182.22 |
| $L_Q$ | 2.94 | 5.71 | 14.47 | 32.35 | 86.28 | 176.25 |
| $W$ | 3.18 | 4.14 | 7.11 | 13.09 | 31.08 | 61.08 |
| $W_Q$ | 1.18 | 2.14 | 5.11 | 11.09 | 29.08 | 59.08 |

*If you remember nothing else from this chapter, remember that congestion in a system becomes unbearable as the traffic intensity gets close to 1.*

The conclusion should be clear to the bank manager. Something must be done to alleviate the congestion—probably adding extra tellers—and the bank will no doubt take such measures if it wants to stay in business. However, the point of the example is that systems moving toward the borderline of stability become extremely congested. As the results in the table indicate, there is a huge difference between a system with a traffic intensity of 0.9 and a system with a traffic intensity of 0.99! (This phenomenon is exemplified in today's airports in a very real and painful way.) ∎

## Other Exponential Models

The basic $M/M/s$ model and its special case, the $M/M/1$ model, represent only two of the hundreds or even thousands of analytical queueing models that researchers have studied. Some of these are relatively simple extensions of the models we have discussed, and others are much more complex. Two of the relatively simple extensions are the **limited waiting** room and **limited source** models. Both of these continue to assume exponential interarrival times and service times. In the limited waiting room model, we start with the basic $M/M/s$ (or $M/M/1$) model but assume that arrivals are turned away when the number already in the queue is at some maximum level. For example, we might prescribe that at most 10 customers can wait in line. If a customer arrives and 10 customers are already in line, then this new customer must go elsewhere (to another bank branch, say).

In the limited source model, we assume that there are only a finite (fairly small) number of customers in the entire population. The context is usually that the "customers" are machines. Then an "arrival" means that a machine breaks down and arrives to a repair center. A "service" means a machine repair. The unique aspect of this type of system is that the arrival rate to the repair center depends on the number of machines already there. When most of the machines are in repair, the arrival rate to the repair center is necessarily low—there are not very many machines left to break down because most of them are already broken down. Conversely, when the number in the repair shop is low, the arrival rate to the repair shop is higher because most machines are candidates for breakdowns.

*Stability is not an issue when the number of customers allowed in the system is finite.*

One interesting aspect of both systems is that stability is not an issue. That is, there is no need to require that a traffic intensity be less than 1 to ensure steady state. The reason is that only a finite number of customers (or machines) are allowed in the system. Therefore, it is impossible for the congestion in the system to grow without bound. As a result, steady state always occurs, regardless of the relationship between the arrival rate and the service rate. This doesn't mean that these systems necessarily have low degrees of congestion. It just means that their queue length cannot grow without bound.

In the interest of space, we do not discuss examples of these two types of systems. However, we have included templates for them in the files **Limited Queue Template.xlsm** and **Limited Source Template.xlsm**, and several of the problems allow you to explore these templates.

## Erlang Loss Model

All of the results so far are possible because of the exponential distribution and its memoryless property. If we drop the exponential assumption, for either interarrival times or service times, the mathematical derivations become much more difficult, and "nice" results are scarce. In this section, we discuss one of the better-known results for nonexponential systems. Actually, we continue to assume a Poisson arrival process—that is, exponentially distributed interarrival times—but we relax the exponential service time requirement. This is important because many real-world service time distributions are definitely *not* exponential.

The model in this section is called the **Erlang loss model.**[6] The reason for the term *loss* is that there is no waiting room at all, so that customers who arrive when all servers are busy are lost to the system. (They are forced to go elsewhere.) As usual, we let $\lambda$ be the arrival rate, $\mu$ be the service rate per server (so that $1/\mu$ is the mean service time), and $s$ be the number of servers. Then the steady-state distribution is specified by $p_n$, $0 \leq n \leq s$, where $p_n$ is again the probability of exactly $n$ customers in the system, and $n$ cannot be greater than $s$ because no queueing is allowed.

The probability $p_s$ is of particular interest because it is the probability that all $s$ servers are busy, so it represents the fraction of arrivals that are lost to the system. Therefore, the effective arrival rate—the rate at which customers actually *enter* the system—is $\lambda(1 - p_s)$, the usual arrival rate multiplied by the probability that an arrival is able to enter the system.

---

[6] This model is named after Erlang, one of the pioneer researchers in queueing theory. Erlang studied queueing in telephone systems in the early 1900s.

This is the arrival rate we need to use in Little's formula to relate $L$ and $W$. To do this, first note that all time spent in the system is *service* time (no queueing), so $W = 1/\mu$. Then Little's formula reduces to

$$L = \lambda(1-p_s)W = \lambda(1 - p_s)/\mu$$

Of course, $L_Q$ and $W_Q$ are irrelevant for this system because no customers are allowed to wait in a queue.

In the Erlang loss model, the steady-state distribution depends on the service time distribution only through its mean.

A rather remarkable mathematical result states that the steady-state probabilities for this system depend on the service time distribution only through the *mean* service time, $1/\mu$. That is, the *form* of the service time distribution does not matter; it could be exponential or anything else, as long as it has mean $1/\mu$. This allows us to calculate the steady-state distribution as if the service times were exponential. We illustrate the procedure in the following example.

## EXAMPLE | 14.6 REQUESTS FOR FIRE ENGINES

Suppose that a fire department receives an average of 24 requests for fire engines each hour, and that these requests occur according to a Poisson process. Each request causes a fire engine to be unavailable for an average of 20 minutes. To have at least a 99% chance of being able to respond to a request, how many fire engines should the fire department have?

**Objective**   To use the Erlang loss model to find an appropriate number of fire engines so that one is almost always available.

### WHERE DO THE NUMBERS COME FROM?

The arrival rate and the mean service time should be available from historical data. Note that for the service time distribution, we need only the mean, 20 minutes. The Erlang loss model is then relevant, regardless of how the actual service times vary around this mean—they could all be close to 20 minutes or they could vary wildly around 20 minutes.

## Solution

Luckily, we do not need to assume that service times are exponential to get results. This would probably be an unrealistic assumption for this example.

To model this as a queueing problem, we identify the requests for fire engines as customers and the fire engines as servers. Then the key aspect of the problem is that there is no queueing for service. If a request occurs when at least one fire engine is available, an available fire engine services this request. (We assume that each request is serviced by a *single* fire engine.) However, if no fire engine is available, then this request is not serviced at all—it is lost. Therefore, this problem is essentially like the $M/M/s$ model with a waiting room size of 0, where $s$ is the number of fire engines (a value to be determined). The only difference is that we are *not* assuming exponentially distributed service times. All we are told is that the mean service time is 20 minutes. Because there is probably some minimum time that all service times must exceed, the exponential assumption almost certainly does not apply, so it is more realistic to assume nonexponentially distributed service times. However, the mathematical result mentioned previously makes this a moot point; only the *mean* service time matters.

### Using the Spreadsheet Model Template

The main focus here is on $p_s$, the fraction of arriving requests that see no available fire engines. We want this fraction to be no greater than 0.01. We have developed a template to calculate this and other steady-state quantities. (See the file **Erlang Loss Template.xlsm** and Figure 14.14.) As usual, all you need to do is enter the inputs in the shaded range and then click on a macro button to calculate the various quantities. We make the following comments about this template.

**Figure 14.14**   The Erlang Loss Model

| | A | B | C | D | E | F | G | H | I |
|---|---|---|---|---|---|---|---|---|---|
| 1 | Erlang Loss Model | | | | | | | | |
| 2 | | | | | Directions: | | | | |
| 3 | Inputs | | | | 1. Enter the inputs in cells B4 through B7. | | | | |
| 4 | Unit of time | hour | | | 2. Press the "Do Calculations" button. | | | | |
| 5 | Arrival rate | 24 | customers/hour | | | | | | |
| 6 | Service rate | 3 | customers/hour | | | Do Calculations | | | |
| 7 | Number of servers | 15 | | | | | | | |
| 8 | | | | | | | | | |
| 9 | | | | | | | | | |
| 10 | Outputs | | | | | | | | |
| 11 | Summary measures | | | | Steady-state probabilities | | | | |
| 12 | Percentage of requests lost | 0.91% | | | n | P(n) | | | |
| 13 | Entering arrival rate | 23.782 | customers/hour | | 0 | 0.000 | | | |
| 14 | Expected number in system | 7.927 | customers | | 1 | 0.003 | | | |
| 15 | Expected time in system | 0.333 | hours | | 2 | 0.011 | | | |
| 16 | | | | | 3 | 0.029 | | | |
| 17 | | | | | 4 | 0.058 | | | |
| 18 | | | | | 5 | 0.092 | | | |
| 19 | | | | | 6 | 0.123 | | | |
| 20 | | | | | 7 | 0.141 | | | |
| 21 | | | | | 8 | 0.141 | | | |
| 22 | | | | | 9 | 0.125 | | | |
| 23 | | | | | 10 | 0.100 | | | |
| 24 | | | | | 11 | 0.073 | | | |
| 25 | | | | | 12 | 0.049 | | | |
| 26 | | | | | 13 | 0.030 | | | |
| 27 | | | | | 14 | 0.017 | | | |
| 28 | | | | | 15 | 0.009 | | | |

**1** The service rate is entered as an input as usual. For this example, it is three per hour because each service request requires 20 minutes on average. Again, there is no requirement that the service times be *exponential* with this rate; all we need to know is the rate itself.

**2** The macro calculates the steady-state distribution in columns E and F (using rather complex formulas) and reports the last of these in cell B12. This is the fraction of arrivals lost. We can then get the effective arrival rate, $L$, and $W$ with simple formulas in cells B13 to B15, as discussed earlier.

### Discussion of the Results

To ensure that the fire department achieves its goal of meeting at least 99% of all requests, we need to vary the number of fire engines in cell B7 until the percentage of lost requests in cell B12 is no more than 1%. We did this by trial and error; the results appear in Table 14.2. As these results show, the required number of fire engines is 15. Using this value, which appears in Figure 14.14, the arrival rate of requests that can be serviced is 23.782. This is the arrival rate of all requests, 24, multiplied by the probability that at least one fire engine is available, $1 - 0.0091$. Also, we see from cell B14 that the expected number of requests that are being serviced at any time, $L$, is 7.927.

**Table 14.2** Outputs for the Fire Engine Example

| Number of Fire Engines | Percentage of Requests Lost |
|---|---|
| 12 | 5.1% |
| 13 | 3.1 |
| 14 | 1.7 |
| 15 | 0.9 |
| 16 | 0.5 |

■

## ADDITIONAL APPLICATIONS

### Access to Emergency Services on the Phone

The Erlang loss model was originally developed for the telephone industry many years ago, but it is still relevant today. Ramaswami et al (2005) discuss a problem faced by AT&T customers who seek emergency service by dialing 911. The problem is that many of them couldn't get through because of traffic congestion at the carrier's switches (the technology that provides dial tones). Network engineers had analyzed the situation by traditional queueing methods, and they had concluded that there was no reason for congestion because the arrival rates were not very large relative to the service rates. However, the authors of the article probed deeper. It seems that there are two classes of customers, those who talk on the phone and those who use the phone to connect to the Internet. Although this latter group is a small fraction of all callers, their "calls" last a *much* longer time. The authors analyzed a revised version of the Erlang loss model, one that deals with these two classes of customers, and they were able to attribute the failure of emergency calls to get through to the long Internet sessions. By understanding the source of the problem, they were able to recommend solutions. ■

### General Multiple-Server Model[7]

Another interesting variation of the $M/M/s$ model is to allow nonexponential interarrival and/or service times. Then we use the letter $G$ (for general) instead of $M$. Specifically, the $G/G/s$ model allows *any* interarrival time distribution and *any* service time distribution. This more general model is important for two reasons. First, data on interarrival times or service times often indicate that the exponential distribution represents a poor approximation to reality. (This is especially true for service times in real applications.) Second, summary measures such as $W$ or $W_Q$ can be sensitive to the *form* of the interarrival time and service time distributions. Therefore, $M/M/s$ models, even those that use the appropriate *mean* interarrival time and *mean* service time, can give misleading results when the actual distributions are not exponential.

The bad news is that obtaining exact analytical results for the $G/G/s$ model is extremely difficult. The good news is that there is an approximation to this model that gives sufficiently accurate results and can be implemented fairly easily in a spreadsheet. This approximation is attributed to two researchers, Allen and Cunneen, and is referred to as the Allen–Cunneen approximation (Tanner, 1995, p. 218). We illustrate it in the following example.

---

[7] This subsection is somewhat more advanced and can be omitted without any loss in continuity.

## 14.7 REVISITING COUNTY BANK WITH NONEXPONENTIAL TIMES

The bank manager in Example 14.3 doubts that the exponential distribution provides a good approximation to the actual interarrival times and service times. Therefore, he collects data on successive interarrival times and service times on 127 consecutive customers. He then calculates the means and standard deviations of these, with the results shown in rows 5 and 6 of Figure 14.15. (See the Data sheet of the file **GGs Template.xlsx.**) Are these data consistent with exponential interarrival times and service times? If not, how much do summary measures such as $W_Q$ and $L_Q$ change if we use the Allen–Cunneen approximation instead of the $M/M/s$ model? We again assume that there are 6 tellers at the bank.

**Figure 14.15**

Data for Estimating Parameters of Distributions

| Data (in minutes) during peak periods | | |
|---|---|---|
| | | |
| **Summary of data below** | | |
| | Interarrival times | Service times |
| Mean | 0.0064 | 0.0364 |
| Stdev | 0.0069 | 0.0543 |
| Squared CV | 1.1364 | 2.2243 |
| | | |
| **Data** | | |
| Customer | Interarrival times | Service times |
| 1 | 0.0028 | 0.0037 |
| 2 | 0.0043 | 0.0096 |
| 3 | 0.0015 | 0.0330 |
| 4 | 0.0098 | 0.0012 |
| 5 | 0.0235 | 0.0376 |
| 6 | 0.0090 | 0.0127 |
| 7 | 0.0025 | 0.0521 |
| 8 | 0.0021 | 0.0156 |
| 124 | 0.0048 | 0.0267 |
| 125 | 0.0046 | 0.0395 |
| 126 | 0.0051 | 0.0058 |
| 127 | 0.0039 | 0.0181 |

**Objective** To see how an approximation to the general multiple-server model can be implemented, and to see how sensitive steady-state measures are to the forms of the interarrival and service time distributions.

### WHERE DO THE NUMBERS COME FROM?

As in Example 14.1, the manager probably needs to get employees with stopwatches to collect the data.

## Solution

First, note that the estimated arrival rate from the data is the reciprocal of the average interarrival time. Taking the reciprocal of the value in cell B5, we obtain an arrival rate of about 155 customers per hour. Similarly, taking the reciprocal of the average service time in cell C5, we obtain a service rate (per server) of about 27 customers per hour. These are nearly the same rates we used in Example 14.3. But are these times *exponentially* distributed?

One useful measure of a probability distribution of positive quantities is the **squared coefficient of variation,** defined as the squared ratio of the standard deviation to the mean and denoted by *scv.*

*Squared coefficient of variation*

$$scv = (\text{standard deviation}/\text{mean})^2$$

You might recall that the standard deviation of the exponential distribution equals the mean, so that $scv = 1$ for the exponential distribution. Analysts often characterize a distribution as being more or less variable than an exponential distribution by seeing whether its $scv$ is greater than or less than 1. Intuitively, the reason is that if we fix the mean at some value, then $scv$ increases as the standard deviation increases. So if we compare a nonexponential distribution to an exponential distribution, both of which have the same mean, then the nonexponential will exhibit more variability than the exponential if its $scv$ is greater than 1, and it will be less variable if its $scv$ is less than 1. This $scv$ measure is critical because it is not only required by the Allen–Cunneen approximation, but it also has a big impact on the behavior of the queueing system.

### Using the Spreadsheet Model Templates

The $scv$ values for the bank data appear in row 7 of Figure 14.15. For example, the formula in cell B7 is **=(B6/B5)^2**. We see that the interarrival times are slightly more variable and the service times are considerably more variable than they would be for exponentially distributed times. This suggests that the $M/M/s$ model might give misleading results. We check this by comparing the $M/M/s$ results with the $G/G/s$ results. To obtain the $M/M/s$ results, we enter the reciprocals of the averages in row 4 of Figure 14.15 as inputs to the **MMs Template.xlsm** file to obtain Figure 14.16. In particular, we see that $L_Q = 13.793$ and $W_Q = 0.089$ (about 5.3 minutes per customer).

**Figure 14.16**   Results from $M/M/s$ Model

| | A | B | C | D | E | F | G | H | I |
|---|---|---|---|---|---|---|---|---|---|
| 1 | M/M/s Queue | | | | | | | | |
| 2 | | | | | After entering inputs in blue cells, click on the button below to | | | | |
| 3 | **Inputs** | | | | run the macro that calculates P(0), the value in cell B16. | | | | |
| 4 | Unit of time | hour | | | Everything else recalculates automatically. Do *not* rearrange | | | | |
| 5 | Arrival rate | 155.417 | customers/hour | | cells in this template -- this might cause the macro to stop | | | | |
| 6 | Service rate per server | 27.491 | customers/hour | | behaving correctly. | | | | |
| 7 | Number of servers | 6 | | | | | | | |
| 8 | | | | | | | | | |
| 9 | **Outputs** | | | | | Do Calculations | | | |
| 10 | **Direct outputs from inputs** | | | | **Distribution of number in system** | | | **Distribution of time in queue** | |
| 11 | Mean time between arrivals | 0.006 | hours | | n (customers) | P(n in system) | | t (in hours) | P(wait > t) |
| 12 | Mean time per service | 0.036 | hours | | 0 | 0.0011 | | 0.020 | 0.699 |
| 13 | Traffic intensity | 0.942 | | | 1 | 0.0061 | | | |
| 14 | | | | | 2 | 0.0172 | | | |
| 15 | **Summary measures** | | | | 3 | 0.0324 | | | |
| 16 | P(system empty) | 0.001 | | | 4 | 0.0458 | | | |
| 17 | P(all servers busy) | 84.6% | | | 5 | 0.0518 | | | |
| 18 | Expected number in system | 19.446 | customers | | 6 | 0.0488 | | | |
| 19 | Expected number in queue | 13.793 | customers | | 7 | 0.0460 | | | |
| 20 | Expected time in system | 0.125 | hours | | 8 | 0.0434 | | | |
| 21 | Expected time in queue | 0.089 | hours | | 9 | 0.0409 | | | |
| 22 | Percentage who don't wait in queue | 15.4% | | | 10 | 0.0385 | | | |

In contrast, the Allen–Cunneen approximation appears in Figure 14.17. This is from another template file, **GGs Template.xlsx**, that implements this approximation. Its inputs include not only the arrival and service rates (the reciprocals of the mean times) but also the $scv$ values for indicating variability. As we indicate in the figure, these inputs in the shaded cells can be entered as numbers or as links to summary measures from data, as we have done here. (Compare cells B7 and B8 of Figure 14.17 to row 7 of Figure 14.15, for example.) Then the approximation uses rather complex formulas in rows 11 through 20, which we do not list here, to obtain the approximate summary measures in cells B17 through B20. (Note that no macro is required.)

### Discussion of the Results

Comparing the $M/M/s$ results in Figure 14.16 to the $G/G/s$ approximation in Figure 14.17, we note that the values of $L_Q$ and $W_Q$ have changed considerably from the $M/M/s$ model. They are now $L_Q = 23.177$ and $W_Q = 0.149$ (or about 8.9 minutes per customer). The reason is that congestion in a queueing system typically *increases* as the interarrival time and service time distributions exhibit more variability, even if they retain the same means. In particular, the large value of $scv$ for the service time distribution causes considerably longer queue lengths and waiting times in the queue than in a comparable exponential system. In short, if the bank manager uses the $M/M/s$ model in this situation, he will obtain overly optimistic results with respect to congestion.

**Figure 14.17**

The Allen–Cunneen Approximation

**Figure 14.17**

The Allen–Cunneen Approximation

| | A | B | C | D | E | F |
|---|---|---|---|---|---|---|
| 1 | G/G/s template using the Allen-Cunneen approximation | | | | | |
| 2 | | | | | | |
| 3 | **Inputs** | | | | | |
| 4 | Arrival rate | 155.417 | Enter numbers here, or (as in this | | | |
| 5 | Service rate per server | 27.491 | file) enter links to summary data | | | |
| 6 | Number of servers | 6 | from observed interarrival and | | | |
| 7 | scv for interarrival times | 1.136 | service times on another sheet. | | | |
| 8 | scv for service times | 2.224 | | | | |
| 9 | | | | | | |
| 10 | **Calculations of intermediate quantities** | | | | | |
| 11 | Ratio of arrival rate to service rate | 5.653 | The approximation is valid only | | | |
| 12 | Server utilization | 0.942 | when the utilization in cell B12 is | | | |
| 13 | A Poisson quantity | 0.760 | less than 1. Otherwise, it gives | | | |
| 14 | Erlang C-function | 0.846 | meaningless outputs. | | | |
| 15 | | | | | | |
| 16 | **Important outputs** | | | | | |
| 17 | Expected wait in queue | 0.149 | | | | |
| 18 | Expected queue length | 23.177 | | | | |
| 19 | Expected wait in system | 0.186 | | | | |
| 20 | Expected number in system | 28.830 | | | | |

The Allen–Cunneen approximation is evidently not well known, but it is important for the insights it can provide. We saw in the example that, as the variability increases in the interarrival times or the service times, the congestion tends to increase. On the other side, this approximation allows us to see how much better a system might behave if we could *reduce* the variability. For example, suppose the bank has the same means as in the example, but it is somehow able to schedule the arrivals at exactly 1 customer every $1/155.417$ hour—no uncertainty whatsoever in the arrival times. The results appear in Figure 14.18. (The only change we have to make is to enter 0 in cell B7.) The change in the outputs is rather dramatic. The values of $W_Q$ and $L_Q$ were 0.149 and 23.177 in the example. Now they have decreased to 0.099 and 15.340. This is one more example of how variability is the enemy in queueing systems.

## Figure 14.18

Queueing System with No Variability in the Arrival Times

| | A | B | C | D | E | F |
|---|---|---|---|---|---|---|
| 1 | G/G/s template using the Allen-Cunneen approximation | | | | | |
| 2 | | | | | | |
| 3 | **Inputs** | | | | | |
| 4 | Arrival rate | 155.417 | | | | |
| 5 | Service rate per server | 27.491 | | | | |
| 6 | Number of servers | 6 | | | | |
| 7 | scv for interarrival times | 0.000 | | | | |
| 8 | scv for service times | 2.224 | | | | |
| 9 | | | | | | |
| 10 | **Calculations of intermediate quantities** | | | | | |
| 11 | Ratio of arrival rate to service rate | 5.653 | | | | |
| 12 | Server utilization | 0.942 | | | | |
| 13 | A Poisson quantity | 0.760 | | | | |
| 14 | Erlang C-function | 0.846 | | | | |
| 15 | | | | | | |
| 16 | **Important outputs** | | | | | |
| 17 | Expected wait in queue | 0.099 | | | | |
| 18 | Expected queue length | 15.340 | | | | |
| 19 | Expected wait in system | 0.135 | | | | |
| 20 | Expected number in system | 20.993 | | | | |

Enter numbers here, or (as in this file) enter links to summary data from observed interarrival and service times on another sheet.

The approximation is valid only when the utilization in cell B12 is less than 1. Otherwise, it gives meaningless outputs.

## FUNDAMENTAL INSIGHT

### Variation Is the Enemy

Everything else being equal, increased variation in the times between arrivals and/or service times typically means more congestion in the system. If arrivals can be scheduled to occur at regularly spaced intervals, or if service times can be made less variable, there will tend to be fewer periods when long waiting lines develop. For example, imagine a doctor who schedules appointments every 15 minutes and always takes about 12 to 15 minutes per patient. There would be no waiting!

## PROBLEMS

### Skill-Building Problems

**9.** A fast-food restaurant has one drive-through window. On average, 40 customers arrive per hour at the window. It takes an average of 1 minute to serve a customer. Assume that interarrival and service times are exponentially distributed.
   **a.** On average, how many customers are waiting in line?
   **b.** On average, how long does a customer spend at the restaurant (from time of arrival to time service is completed)?
   **c.** What fraction of the time are more than three cars in line? (Here, the line includes the car, if any, being serviced.)

**10.** The Decision Sciences Department is trying to determine whether to rent a slow or a fast copier. The department believes that an employee's time is worth $15 per hour. The slow copier rents for $4 per hour, and it takes an employee an average of 10 minutes to complete copying. The fast copier rents for $15 per

hour, and it takes an employee an average of 6 minutes to complete copying. On average, four employees per hour need to use the copying machine. (Assume the copying times and interarrival times to the copying machine are exponentially distributed.) Which machine should the department rent to minimize expected total cost per hour?

**11.** The **MM1 Template.xlsx** file is now set up so that you can enter any integer in cell E11 and the corresponding probability of that many in the system appears in cell F11. Change this setup so that columns E and F specify the distribution of the number in the *queue* rather than the system. That is, set it up so that if you enter an integer in cell E11, the formula in cell F11 gives the probability of that many customers in the queue. (*Hint:* You don't even need to understand the current formula in cell F11. You only need to understand the relationship between the number in the queue and the number in the system. If *n* are in the system, how many are in the queue?)

12. The **MM1 Template.xlsx** file is now set up so that when you enter any time value in cell H11, the formula in cell I11 gives the probability that the wait in queue will be greater than this amount of time. Suppose that you would like the information to go the other direction. That is, you would like to specify a probability, such as 0.05, in cell I11 and obtain the corresponding time in cell H11. Try doing this as follows with Excel's Goal Seek tool. Use the Tools/Goal Seek menu items to get to a dialog box. Then in this dialog box, enter I11 as the Set cell, enter the desired probability such as 0.05 in the By Value box, and enter H11 as the changing cell. Use this procedure to answer the following. In an $M/M/1$ queue where customers are entering at rate 50 per hour and the mean service time is 1 minute, find the number of minutes $t$ such that there is a 5% chance of having to wait in the queue more than $t$ minutes.

13. Expand the **MM1 Template.xlsx** file so that the steady-state probability distribution of the number in the system is shown in tabular form and graphically. That is, enter values 0, 1, and so on (up to some upper limit you can choose) in the range from cell E11 down and copy the formula in cell F11 down accordingly. Then create a column chart using the data in columns E and F.

14. For an $M/M/1$ queueing system, we know that $L = \lambda/(\mu - \lambda)$. Suppose that $\lambda$ and $\mu$ are both doubled. How does $L$ change? How does $W$ change? How does $W_Q$ change? How does $L_Q$ change? (Remember the basic queueing relationships, including Little's formula.)

15. Suppose that you observe a sequence of interarrival times, such as 1.2, 3.7, 4.2, 0.5, 8.2, 3.1, 1.7, 4.2, 0.7, 0.3, and 2.0. For example, 4.2 is the time between the arrivals of customers 2 and 3. If you average these, what parameter of the $M/M/s$ model are you estimating? Use these numbers to estimate the arrival rate $\lambda$. If instead these numbers were observed service times, what would their average be an estimate of, and what would the corresponding estimate of $\mu$ be?

16. In the $M/M/s$ model, where $\mu$ is the service rate per server, explain why $\lambda < \mu$ is *not* the appropriate condition for steady state, but $\lambda < s\mu$ is.

17. Expand the **MMs Template.xlsm** file so that the steady-state probability distribution of the number in the system is shown in tabular form and graphically. That is, enter values 0, 1, and so on (up to some upper limit you can choose) in the range from cell E12 down and copy the formula in cell F12 down accordingly. Then create a column chart using the data in columns E and F.

18. Each airline passenger and his luggage must be checked to determine whether he is carrying weapons onto the airplane. Suppose that at Gotham City Airport, 10 passengers per minute arrive, on average.

Also, assume that interarrival times are exponentially distributed. To check passengers for weapons, the airport must have a checkpoint consisting of a metal detector and baggage X-ray machine. Whenever a checkpoint is in operation, two employees are required. These two employees work simultaneously to check a *single* passenger. A checkpoint can check an average of 12 passengers per minute, where the time to check a passenger is also exponentially distributed. Under the assumption that the airport has only one checkpoint, answer the following questions.
   a. Why is an $M/M/1$, not an $M/M/2$, model relevant here?
   b. What is the probability that a passenger will have to wait before being checked for weapons?
   c. On average, how many passengers are waiting in line to enter the checkpoint?
   d. On average, how long will a passenger spend at the checkpoint (including waiting time in line)?

19. A supermarket is trying to decide how many cash registers to keep open. Suppose an average of 18 customers arrive each hour, and the average checkout time for a customer is 4 minutes. Interarrival times and service times are exponentially distributed, and the system can be modeled as an $M/M/s$ system. (In contrast to the situation at most supermarkets, we assume that all customers wait in a *single* line.) It costs $20 per hour to operate a cash register, and a cost of $0.25 is assessed for each minute the customer spends in the cash register area (in line or being served). How many registers should the store open to minimize the expected hourly cost?

20. A small bank is trying to determine how many tellers to employ. The total cost of employing a teller is $100 per day, and a teller can serve an average of 60 customers per day. On average, 50 customers arrive per day at the bank, and both service times and interarrival times are exponentially distributed. If the delay cost per customer day is $100, how many tellers should the bank hire?

21. In this problem, all interarrival and service times are exponentially distributed.
   a. At present, the finance department and the marketing department each has its own typists. Each typist can type 25 letters per day. Finance requires that an average of 20 letters per day be typed, and marketing requires that an average of 15 letters per day be typed. For each department, determine the average length of time that elapses between a request for a letter and completion of the letter.
   b. Suppose that the two typists are grouped into a typing pool; that is, each typist is now available to type letters for either department. For this arrangement, calculate the average length of time between a request for a letter and completion of the letter.

**c.** Comment on the results of parts **a** and **b**.

**d.** Under the pooled arrangement, what is the probability that more than 0.2 day will elapse between a request for a letter and start of the letter?

**22.** MacBurger's is attempting to determine how many servers to have available during the breakfast shift. On average, 100 customers arrive per hour at the restaurant. Each server can handle an average of 50 customers per hour. A server costs $5 per hour, and the cost of a customer waiting in line for one hour is $20. Assuming that an $M/M/s$ model is applicable, determine the number of servers that minimizes the expected sum of hourly delay and service costs.

**23.** On average, 100 customers arrive per hour at the Gotham City Bank. The average service time for each customer is 1 minute. Service times and interarrival times are exponentially distributed. The manager wants to ensure that no more than 1% of all customers will have to wait in line for more than 5 minutes. If the bank follows the policy of having all customers join a single line, how many tellers must the bank hire?

**The following four problems are optional. They are based on the limited queue and limited source models in the Limited Queue Template.xlsm and Limited Source Template.xlsm files.**

**24.** A service facility consists of 1 server who can serve an average of 2 customers per hour (service times are exponential). An average of 3 customers per hour arrive at the facility (interarrival times are assumed to be exponential). The system capacity is 3 customers: 2 waiting and 1 being served.

**a.** On average, how many potential customers enter the system each hour?

**b.** What is the probability that the server is busy at a typical point in time?

**25.** On average, 40 cars per hour are tempted to use the drive-through window at the Hot Dog King Restaurant. (We assume that interarrival times are exponentially distributed.) If a total of more than four cars are in line (including the car at the window), a car will not enter the line. It takes an average of 4 minutes (exponentially distributed) to serve a car.

**a.** What is the average number of cars waiting for the drive-through window (not including the car at the window)?

**b.** On average, how many cars will be served per hour?

**c.** I have just joined the line at the drive-through window. On average, how long will it be before I receive my food?

**26.** A laundromat has 5 washing machines. A typical machine breaks down once every five days. A repairman can repair a machine in an average of 2.5 days.

Currently, three repairmen are on duty. The owner of the laundromat has the option of replacing them with a superworker, who can repair a machine in an average of 5/6 of a day. The salary of the superworker equals the pay of the three regular employees. Breakdown and service times are exponential. Should the laundromat replace the three repairers with the superworker?

**27.** The limited source model can often be used to approximate the behavior of a computer's CPU ( central processing unit). Suppose that 20 terminals (assumed to always be busy) feed the CPU. After the CPU responds to a user, the user takes an average of 80 seconds before sending another request to the CPU (this is called the *think time*). The CPU takes an average of 2 seconds to respond to any request. On average, how long will a user have to wait before the CPU acts on the user's request? How will your answer change if there are 30 terminals? What if there are 40 terminals? Of course, you must make appropriate assumptions about the exponential distribution to answer this question.

## Skill-Extending Problems

**28.** Consider an airport where taxis and customers arrive (exponential interarrival times) with respective rates of 1 and 2 per minute. No matter how many other taxis are present, a taxi will wait. If an arriving customer does not find a taxi, the customer immediately leaves.

**a.** Model this system as an $M/M/1$ queue. (*Hint:* Think of the taxis as the "customers.")

**b.** Find the average number of taxis that are waiting for a customer.

**c.** Suppose all customers who use a taxi pay a $2 fare. During a typical hour, how much revenue will the taxis receive?

**29.** A bank is trying to determine which of two machines to rent for check processing. Machine 1 rents for $10,000 per year and processes 1000 checks per hour. Machine 2 rents for $15,000 per year and processes 1600 checks per hour. Assume that machines work 8 hours a day, 5 days a week, 50 weeks a year. The bank must process an average of 800 checks per hour, and the average check processed is for $100. Assume an annual interest rate of 20%. Then determine the cost to the bank (in lost interest) for each hour that a check spends waiting for and undergoing processing. Assuming that interarrival times and service times are exponentially distributed, which machine should the bank rent?

**30.** A worker at the State Unemployment Office is responsible for processing a company's forms when it opens for business. The worker can process an average of four forms per week. In 2006, an average of 1.8 companies per week submitted forms for processing, and the worker had a backlog of 0.45 week. In 2007, an average of 3.9 companies per week submitted forms for processing, and the worker had a 5-week backlog. The poor worker was fired but later sued to get her job back. The court said that because the amount of work submitted to the worker had approximately doubled, the worker's backlog should also have doubled. Because her backlog increased by more than a factor of 10, she must have been slacking off, so the state was justified in firing her. Use queueing theory to defend the worker. (This is based on an actual case!)

31. For the $M/M/1$ queueing model, why do the following results hold? (*Hint:* Remember that $1/\mu$ is the mean service time. Then think how long a typical arrival must wait in the system or in the queue.)
    a. $W = (L + 1)/\mu$
    b. $W_Q = L/\mu$

32. Referring to Problem 18, suppose the airline wants to determine how many checkpoints to operate to minimize operating costs and delay costs over a 10-year period. Assume that the cost of delaying a passenger for one hour is $10 and that the airport is open every day for 16 hours per day. It costs $1 million to purchase, staff, and maintain a metal detector and baggage X-ray machine for a 10-year period. Finally, assume that each passenger is equally likely to enter a given checkpoint, so that the "effective" arrival rate to any checkpoint is the total arrival rate divided by the number of checkpoints. (Assume that each checkpoint has its own waiting line.)

33. The manager of a bank wants to use an $M/M/s$ queueing model to weigh the costs of extra tellers against the cost of having customers wait in line. The arrival rate is 60 customers per hour, and the average service time is 4 minutes. The cost of each teller is easy to gauge at the $8.50 per hour wage rate. However, because estimating the cost per minute of waiting time is difficult, the bank manager decides to hire the minimum number of tellers so that a typical customer has probability 0.05 of waiting more than 5 minutes in line.
    a. How many tellers will the manager use, given this criterion?
    b. By deciding on this many tellers as "optimal," the manager is *implicitly* using some value (or some range of values) for the cost per minute of waiting time. That is, a certain cost (or cost range) would lead to the same number of tellers as suggested in part a. What is this implied cost (or cost range)?

34. On average, 100 customers arrive per hour at Gotham City Bank. It takes a teller an average of 2 minutes to

serve a customer. Interarrival and service times are exponentially distributed. The bank currently has 4 tellers working. The bank manager wants to compare the following two systems with regard to the average number of customers present in the bank and the probability that a customer will spend more than 8 minutes in line.
    ■ **System 1:** Each teller has his or her own line (and no moving between lines is permitted). Arriving customers are equally likely to choose any teller.
    ■ **System 2:** All customers wait in a single line for the first available teller.

If you were the bank manager, which system would you prefer?

35. Consider the following two queueing systems.
    ■ **System 1:** An $M/M/1$ system with arrival rate $\lambda$ and service rate $3\mu$
    ■ **System 2:** An $M/M/3$ system with arrival rate $\lambda$ and each server working at rate $\mu$

    Which system will have the smaller $W$ and $L$?

**The following problems are optional. They are based on the limited queue model in the Limited Queue Template.xlsm file.**

36. Two one-barber shops sit side by side in Dunkirk Square. Each shop can hold a maximum of 4 people, and any potential customer who finds a shop full will not wait for a haircut. Barber 1 charges $11 per haircut and takes an average of 15 minutes to complete a haircut. Barber 2 charges $7 per haircut and takes an average of 10 minutes to complete a haircut. On average, 10 potential customers arrive per hour at each barber shop. Of course, a potential customer becomes an actual customer only if he or she finds that the shop is not full. Assuming that interarrival times and haircut times are exponential, which barber will earn more money?

37. The small mail-order firm Sea's Beginning has one phone line. An average of 60 people per hour call in orders, and it takes an average of 1 minute to handle a call. Time between calls and time to handle calls are exponentially distributed. If the phone line is busy, Sea's Beginning can put up to $c - 1$ people on hold. If $c - 1$ people are on hold, a caller gets a busy signal and calls a competitor (Air's End). Sea's Beginning wants only 1% of all callers to get a busy signal. How many people should it be able to put on hold, that is, what is the required value of $c$?

# 14.6 APPROXIMATING SHORT-RUN BEHAVIOR ANALYTICALLY

Until now, we have concentrated on steady-state results. These are typically long-run results where we assume that the parameters of the system, including the arrival rate, service rate, and number of servers, remain constant. However, in many situations, these parameters vary through time, so that steady-state results do not apply. Here are some examples.

- A fast-food restaurant is likely to experience a much larger arrival rate during the time from noon to 1:30 P.M. than during other hours of the day. Also, the number of servers might also vary during the day, with more servers available during the busier periods.

- Because most heart attacks occur during the morning, a coronary care unit experiences more arrivals during the morning.

- Most voters vote either before or after work, so a polling place tends to be less busy during the middle of the day.

When the parameters defining the queueing system vary over time, we say that the system is **nonstationary.** For example, consider a fast-food restaurant that opens at 6:00 in the morning and closes at midnight. We are interested in the probability distribution of the number of customers present at all times between opening and closing, given that the arrival rate and the number of servers change throughout the day. We call these **transient** probability distributions because they depend on the time of day. For example, the probability of having at least six customers in line is probably greater at noon than in the middle of the afternoon.

Many analysts approximate transient distributions with steady-state distributions. For example, if they are interested in the distribution of line lengths during the peak lunchtime period from, say, 11:30 A.M. until 1:00 P.M., they approximate the arrival rate for this period and use it in the $M/M/s$ steady-state model to see how the lunchtime period behaves. But do steady-state results, which are appropriate for the long run, apply to a period of 1.5 hours? This is a difficult question to answer because it depends on a number of factors. However, many analysts never bother to check; they just apply the steady-state results and hope for the best. In most cases, the only viable alternative has been to create a simulation model of the short run, as discussed in the next section. However, the downside to this is that it requires an analyst to write a fairly complex computer program (or learn a simulation software package).

Fortunately, as pointed out in Winston (2004), there is another alternative for approximating transient behavior of queues. Although the details are a bit messy, this approach can be implemented in a spreadsheet in a very natural way, as we discuss shortly. The only assumptions we require are the following:

1. The arrival rate, the service rate, and the number of servers can depend on time, so we write them as $\lambda(t)$, $\mu(t)$, and $s(t)$, where $t$ stands for time.

2. The probability of an arrival during a short period of time (a second, say) is proportional to the arrival rate, $\lambda(t)$. That is, $\Delta t$ if is a short period of time, the probability of an arrival during the interval from $t$ to $t + \Delta t$ is approximately equal to $\lambda(t)\Delta t$. Also, the probability of *more* than one arrival during this short interval is negligible.

3. Similarly, the probability of a service completion during a short interval from $t$ to $t + \Delta t$ is approximately equal to $b_n(t)\mu(t)\Delta t$, where $b_n(t)$ is the number of busy servers when there are $n$ customers in the system at time $t$. Again, the probability of more than one service completion during this short interval is negligible.

**4.** Arrivals and service completions during different periods of time are probabilistically independent.

Although not obvious, these are equivalent to the exponential assumptions we made in the $M/M/1$ and $M/M/s$ models earlier, except that we then required the arrival rate, the service rate, and the number of servers to remain *constant* through time. Now we are essentially continuing with the memoryless assumption of the exponential distribution, but we are allowing the input parameters to vary through time.

The method works as follows. Let $p_n(t)$ be the probability that $n$ customers are in the system at time $t$. We start with the distribution at time 0, which is presumably known. For example, if there are no customers in the system at time 0, then $p_0(0) = 1$ and $p_n(0) = 0$ for $n > 0$. Alternatively, if five customers are already in the system at time 0, then $p_5(0) = 1$ and $p_n(0) = 0$ for $n \neq 5$. Starting with the known distribution at time 0, we then use a *bootstrap* approach to calculate $p_n(t)$ for times $t$ that are multiples of some short interval $\Delta t$. For example, $\Delta t$ might be 1 second or 5 seconds. We find $p_n(\Delta t)$ from $p_n(0)$, $p_n(2\Delta t)$ from $p_n(\Delta t)$, $p_n(3\Delta t)$, from $p_n(2\Delta t)$, and so on. In other words, we pull ourselves up by our bootstraps.

The logic for calculating these probabilities is fairly straightforward. Suppose, for example, that we want the probability of having $n$ customers in the system at time $t + \Delta t$. Then, ignoring events that have negligible probabilities (two or more events, either arrivals or service completions, in a short time interval), there are only three ways this can happen: (1) there were $n - 1$ customers in the system at time $t$ and an arrival occurred in the interval of length $\Delta t$, (2) there were $n + 1$ customers in the system at time $t$ and a service completion occurred in the interval of length $\Delta t$, or (3) there were $n$ customers in the system at time $t$ and no arrivals or service completions occurred in the interval of length $\Delta t$. Using the preceding assumptions, this allows us to write

$$p_n(t + \Delta t) \simeq \lambda(t)\Delta t p_{n-1}(t) + b_{n+1}(t)\mu(t)\Delta t p_{n+1}(t) + [1 - (\lambda(t) + b_n(t)\mu(t))\Delta t]p_n(t)$$

(A slight variation of this is required for $n = 0$ and for $n = N$, where $N$ represents the maximum number allowed in the system. See Winston [2004] for details.)

Admittedly, this equation is intimidating, but it is perfectly suited for spreadsheet calculations. All we need to specify are (1) the arrival rate function, $\lambda(t)$; (2) the service rate function, $\mu(t)$; (3) the number of servers, $s(t)$, at time $t$; and (4) some small interval of time, $\Delta t$. (Note that the function $b_n(t)$, the number of busy servers, is typically the smaller of $n$ and $s(t)$.) To spare you some of the details, we implemented the procedure in the file **Transient Queue Template.xlsm**, which we discuss in the following example.

---

| EXAMPLE | **14.8 ANALYSIS OF LUNCHTIME RUSH** |
|---|---|

A small fast-food restaurant is trying to model its lunchtime rush period. The restaurant opens at 11 A.M., and all customers wait in one line to have their orders filled by a single server. The arrival rate per hour varies considerably from one half-hour period to the next, as shown in Table 14.3. The restaurant can serve an average of 50 people per hour, and service times are assumed to be exponentially distributed. Management wants to approximate the probability distribution of customers in the store from 11 A.M. through 2 P.M.

**Table 14.3** Arrival Rate

| Time Period | Hourly Arrival Rate |
|---|---|
| 11:00–11:30 | 30 |
| 11:30–Noon | 40 |
| Noon–12:30 | 50 |
| 12:30–1:00 | 60 |
| 1:00–1:30 | 35 |
| 1:30–2:00 | 25 |

**Objective**  To approximate the time-varying distribution of customers during the three-hour lunchtime rush period.

## WHERE DO THE NUMBERS COME FROM?

The data collection process wouldn't be much different in this example from what it was in previous examples. However, each rate in Table 14.3 should be based on observations during that particular half-hour period. For example, if the manager observes 14, 10, 15, 14, 16, 22, 13, 12, 19, and 15 arrivals from 11:00 to 11:30 on 10 consecutive days, he should average these (and then multiply by 2 to convert it to an *hourly* rate) to approximate the first arrival rate in the table.

## Solution

The file **Transient Queue Template.xlsm** has an input section you must fill in, and it has an output section, along with several output charts, that are created by a macro. You run this macro by clicking on a button. The input section is shown in Figure 14.19. As the text boxes indicate, you can enter any arrival rates, service rates, and numbers of servers over any periods of time. You must also enter the number of customers initially present in the system, which we assume to be 0 in this example.

**Figure 14.19**

Inputs for
Lunchtime Rush

| | A | B | C | D | E | F | G | H | I |
|---|---|---|---|---|---|---|---|---|---|
| 1 | Inputs | | | | | | | | |
| 2 | | | | | | | | | |
| 3 | Initial number of customers in system | | | 0 | | | | | |
| 4 | | | | | | | | | |
| 5 | | | | | | | | | |
| 6 | | Enter the initial number of customers in the system above. Then enter the hourly arrival rates below. The times in column B don't have to be equally spaced and can extend down as far as you like. The last time you enter is the "ending" time for the model. Each rate in column C should be the arrival rate for that time until the next time. E.g., the first rate below, 30, indicates that customer arrive at rate 30 per hour during the period from 11:00AM till 11:30AM. | | | | Enter the service rates and numbers of servers below in columns G and H. (Column I, the total rate, is for informational purposes only. It is the product of columns G and H, which you can compare to the arrival rates.) The time intervals don't need to be the same as for the arrival rates to the left, but the starting and ending times should be the same. The rates are interpreted exactly as arrival rates. E.g., the data below indicate that from 11:00AM till 2:00PM, 1 server is serving at rate 50 customers per hour. | | | |
| 7 | | | | | | | | | |
| 8 | | | | | | | | | |
| 9 | | | | | | | | | |
| 10 | | | | | | | | | |
| 11 | | | | | | | | | |
| 12 | | | | | | | | | |
| 13 | | | | | | | | | |
| 14 | | | | | | | | | |
| 15 | | | | | | | | | |
| 16 | | | | | | | | | |
| 17 | | | | | | | | | |
| 18 | | Clock time | Rate | | | Clock time | Rate per server | Number of servers | Total rate |
| 19 | | 11:00 AM | 30 | | | 11:00 AM | 50 | 1 | 50 |
| 20 | | 11:30 AM | 40 | | | 2:00 PM | NA | NA | NA |
| 21 | | 12:00 PM | 50 | | | | | | |
| 22 | | 12:30 PM | 60 | | | | | | |
| 23 | | 1:00 PM | 35 | | | | | | |
| 24 | | 1:30 PM | 25 | | | | | | |
| 25 | | 2:00 PM | NA | | | | | | |

After you enter the inputs and click on the button, the macro uses the bootstrap approach described earlier to calculate the probability distribution for each 5-second interval ($\Delta t = 5$). Some of the results appear in Figure 14.20. (Thousands of rows are not shown in the figure. There are a *lot* of 5-second intervals in a 3-hour period!) Actually, only summary measures of these distributions, not the probabilities themselves, appear in the output. For example, the expected number in the queue and the standard deviation of the number in the queue appear in cells P34 and Q34 for the 5-second interval starting at 11:01:15.

---

**Figure 14.20**   Numerical Outputs for Lunchtime Rush

| | K | L | M | N | O | P | Q | R | S | T | U | V | W | X | Y |
|---|---|---|---|---|---|---|---|---|---|---|---|---|---|---|---|
| 1 | Outputs | | | | | | | | | | | | | | |
| 2 | | | | | | | | | | | | | | | |
| 3 | | | | | | | | | | | | | | | |
| 4 | | | | | | | | | | | | | | | |
| 5 | For each 5-second interval, the program calculates the probability distribution of the | | | | | | | | | | | | | | |
| 6 | line length (number of customers in the system) and uses it to calculate the summary measures below. ExpL and StdevL are the mean and standard deviation of | | | | | | | | | | | | | | |
| 7 | the line length, and LowerL and UpperL are, respectively, 1 standard deviation | | | | | | | | | | | | | | |
| 8 | below the mean and 1 standard deviation above the mean. | | | | | | | | | | | | | | |
| 9 | ExpQ, StdevQ, LowerQ, and UpperQ are similar measures for the number in the | | | | | | | | | | | | | | |
| 10 | queue. (If LowerL or LowerQ would be negative, they are replaced by 0.) PrEmpty is | | | | | | | | | | | | | | |
| 11 | the probability of no one in the system, and PrWait is the probability that all servers | | | | | | | | | | | | | | |
| 12 | are busy, so that an arriving customer must wait. All of these measures are graphed versus time in the charts below. For comparison, the steady-state (SS) measures are | | | | | | | | | | | | | | |
| 13 | also calculated (for each 5-second interval) and are shown in yellow in the charts. If | | | | | | | | | | | | | | |
| 14 | the traffic intensity for any time interval is >= 1, then there is no steady state, and | | | | | | | | | | | | | | |
| 15 | that section of the graphs is missing. | | | | | | | | | | | | | | |
| 16 | | | | | | | | | | | | | | | |
| 17 | | | | | | | | | | | | | | | |
| 18 | Clock time | ExpL | StdevL | LowerL | UpperL | ExpQ | StdevQ | LowerQ | UpperQ | PrEmpty | PrWait | SSExpL | SSExpQ | SSPrEmpty | SSPrWait |
| 19 | 11:00:00 AM | 0.000 | 0.000 | 0.000 | 0.000 | 0.000 | 0.000 | 0.000 | 0.000 | 1.0000 | 0.0000 | 1.5 | 0.9 | 0.39999998 | 0.6 |
| 20 | 11:00:05 AM | 0.042 | 0.200 | 0.000 | 0.241 | 0.000 | 0.000 | 0.000 | 0.000 | 0.9583 | 0.0417 | 1.5 | 0.9 | 0.39999998 | 0.6 |
| 21 | 11:00:10 AM | 0.080 | 0.278 | 0.000 | 0.359 | 0.002 | 0.042 | 0.000 | 0.043 | 0.9213 | 0.0787 | 1.5 | 0.9 | 0.39999998 | 0.6 |
| 22 | 11:00:15 AM | 0.117 | 0.336 | 0.000 | 0.453 | 0.005 | 0.071 | 0.000 | 0.076 | 0.8883 | 0.1117 | 1.5 | 0.9 | 0.39999998 | 0.6 |
| 23 | 11:00:20 AM | 0.151 | 0.383 | 0.000 | 0.534 | 0.009 | 0.098 | 0.000 | 0.108 | 0.8587 | 0.1413 | 1.5 | 0.9 | 0.39999998 | 0.6 |
| 24 | 11:00:25 AM | 0.182 | 0.424 | 0.000 | 0.606 | 0.014 | 0.125 | 0.000 | 0.139 | 0.8321 | 0.1679 | 1.5 | 0.9 | 0.39999998 | 0.6 |
| 25 | 11:00:30 AM | 0.212 | 0.459 | 0.000 | 0.671 | 0.021 | 0.150 | 0.000 | 0.170 | 0.8081 | 0.1919 | 1.5 | 0.9 | 0.39999998 | 0.6 |
| 26 | 11:00:35 AM | 0.241 | 0.491 | 0.000 | 0.732 | 0.027 | 0.174 | 0.000 | 0.201 | 0.7864 | 0.2136 | 1.5 | 0.9 | 0.39999998 | 0.6 |
| 27 | 11:00:40 AM | 0.268 | 0.520 | 0.000 | 0.788 | 0.034 | 0.198 | 0.000 | 0.232 | 0.7667 | 0.2333 | 1.5 | 0.9 | 0.39999998 | 0.6 |
| 28 | 11:00:45 AM | 0.293 | 0.547 | 0.000 | 0.840 | 0.042 | 0.220 | 0.000 | 0.262 | 0.7488 | 0.2512 | 1.5 | 0.9 | 0.39999998 | 0.6 |
| 29 | 11:00:50 AM | 0.317 | 0.572 | 0.000 | 0.889 | 0.050 | 0.242 | 0.000 | 0.292 | 0.7324 | 0.2676 | 1.5 | 0.9 | 0.39999998 | 0.6 |
| 30 | 11:00:55 AM | 0.340 | 0.596 | 0.000 | 0.936 | 0.058 | 0.263 | 0.000 | 0.321 | 0.7174 | 0.2826 | 1.5 | 0.9 | 0.39999998 | 0.6 |
| 31 | 11:01:00 AM | 0.362 | 0.618 | 0.000 | 0.980 | 0.066 | 0.283 | 0.000 | 0.349 | 0.7036 | 0.2964 | 1.5 | 0.9 | 0.39999998 | 0.6 |
| 32 | 11:01:05 AM | 0.383 | 0.639 | 0.000 | 1.022 | 0.074 | 0.303 | 0.000 | 0.377 | 0.6909 | 0.3091 | 1.5 | 0.9 | 0.39999998 | 0.6 |
| 33 | 11:01:10 AM | 0.404 | 0.659 | 0.000 | 1.062 | 0.083 | 0.322 | 0.000 | 0.405 | 0.6791 | 0.3209 | 1.5 | 0.9 | 0.39999998 | 0.6 |
| 34 | 11:01:15 AM | 0.423 | 0.678 | 0.000 | 1.101 | 0.091 | 0.340 | 0.000 | 0.432 | 0.6682 | 0.3318 | 1.5 | 0.9 | 0.39999998 | 0.6 |

For comparison, the macro also calculates similar summary measures based on the steady-state formulas. (These are prefaced by "SS.") Each of these uses the input parameters for its half-hour period. For example, the steady-state results are constant during the first half-hour; they are based on an arrival rate of 30 per hour. As the note in the text box indicates, these steady-state results are reported only for half-hour periods where the system is stable; otherwise they are left blank. (Note that the system is *not* stable from noon until 1:00 because the arrival rate is *not* less than the service rate during this period.)

The numerical output is too "dense" to make much sense to management, so several charts are also provided by the macro. These include charts of (1) the expected number in the system, (2) the expected number in the queue, (3) the probability that all servers are busy, and (4) the probability that all servers are idle. Each is shown as a function of time. For example, Figure 14.21 shows how the expected number in the queue varies through time. It also shows upper and lower limits (plus or minus one standard deviation from the expected value line), so you can see where the *actual* queue length is likely to be at any point in time. (Remember the rule of thumb that says that the actual value has about a 2/3 chance of being within one standard deviation of the mean.) Finally, the chart includes the

**Figure 14.21** Chart of Expected Line Length

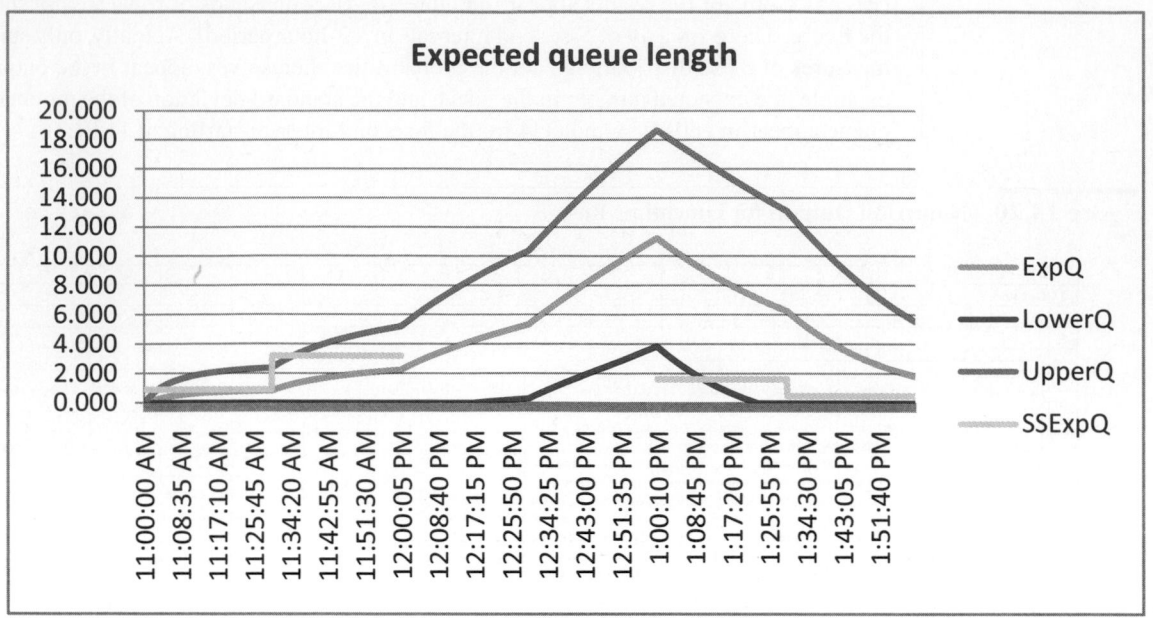

steady-state solutions for comparison. These are the horizontal lines, but they appear only in time periods where the system is stable.

### Discussion of the Results

The outputs from this file can be very useful—and very revealing. First, during periods where the arrival rate is at least as large as the service rate, steady-state results tell us nothing—they don't *exist* for such periods. In contrast, the transient results show how the queue grows during such periods (and then decreases as the arrival rate declines). Second, even when the arrival rate is less than the service rate so that steady-state results exist, the steady-state results can be very different from the transient results. For example, the steady-state results for the period from 1:00 to 2:00 indicate very short queue lengths, whereas the transient results indicate much larger queue lengths. The reason is very simple. The steady-state results fail to account for the customers who are still in line at 1:00. These customers, who are left over from the rush the hour before, are the reason the system doesn't converge to steady-state during the next hour. Therefore, the steady-state results give the manager an overly optimistic picture of the hour from 1:00 to 2:00. In contrast, the transient results take this leftover congestion into account, so they give the manager a much more realistic view of this last hour.

Keep in mind that this approach is *not* simulation. No random numbers are involved, and nothing will change if you press the F9 key. However, because we calculate the probability distributions only on every 5-second interval, the results are only *approximately* correct. We could make them more exact by using a 1-second interval, say, but this would require five times as many calculations (and rows of output). Because not too much can happen in a 5-second interval, this size interval should yield sufficiently accurate results in most situations. ∎

**38.** In the lunchtime rush example, we assumed that the system starts empty and idle at 11 A.M. Assume now that the restaurant opens earlier than 11 A.M., but we are still interested only in the period from 11 A.M. to 2 P.M. How does the initial number of customers present at 11 A.M. affect the results? Run the model six times, varying the initial number of customers from 0 to 10 in increments of 2. Write a short report on your findings.

**39.** In the lunchtime rush example, the arrival rate changed fairly gradually throughout the period of interest. Assume now that the arrival rate first increases and then decreases in a more abrupt manner. Specifically, replace the arrival rates in the example by the following: 15, 20, 70, 85, 30, and 20. Note that the sum of these rates is the same as the sum of the rates in the example, so that we expect the same total number of arrivals, but now they are more concentrated in the noon to 1 P.M. hour. Compare the results with these arrival rates to the results in the example. Write a short report on your findings.

## Skill-Extending Problem

**40.** Using the arrival rates from the lunchtime rush example, it seems sensible to vary the number of servers so that more servers work during the busy hours. In particular, suppose management wants to have an average of three servers working (in parallel) in any half-hour period, but the number working can vary across periods. Also, assume that each server has a service rate of 16 customers per hour. Experiment with ways to deploy the servers, assuming that at least one server must be working each half-hour period. For example, at one extreme, you could have three servers working *each* half-hour period. At the other extreme, you could have a single server working all but one of the half-hour periods, and 13 servers working during the other half-hour period. Defend the deployment you think works best in a brief report.

# 14.7 QUEUEING SIMULATION MODELS

A popular alternative to using the analytical models from the previous two sections is to develop queueing simulations. There are several advantages to using simulation. Probably the most important advantage is that we are not restricted to the assumptions required by the standard analytical queueing models. These models typically require that interarrival times and service times are exponentially distributed, customers wait in a single queue and are served in FCFS fashion, all servers are identical in terms of their service time distributions, there are no customer types with higher priority than others, and so on.[8] When we use simulation, anything goes. If we want nonexponential service times, they are easy to build in. If we want customers to wait in several lines, one behind each server, and we even want to allow them to switch queues (as you might in a supermarket), simulation can handle it. If we want higher-priority customers to be able to "bump" lower-priority customers out of service, this is no problem with simulation. Just about any queueing situation can be simulated.

A second advantage of queueing simulation is that we get to *see* the action through time. Simulation outputs typically include not only summary measures such as the average queue length for some period of time, but they can also include time series graphs of important quantities such as the number of servers busy or the number of customers waiting in line. In this way, we can see how queues build from time to time. In addition, we can run a simulation many times, each time using different random numbers, to see how one day might differ from another.

---

[8] There are analytical models for many "nonstandard" queueing situations, but they are mathematically too complex for most users to understand.

The downside of queueing simulation is that it has traditionally required a clever computer programmer, a specialized software package, or both. Generating all of the random quantities (interarrival times and service times, say) required by a simulation is easy. The difficult part is essentially a bookkeeping problem. Imagine that you are given a list of customer arrival times and their corresponding service times. You must then "play out" the events as they would then occur through time. Say customer 17 arrives at 9:47, sees that four customers are ahead of her in line, and all three of the servers in the system are currently busy with customers. How do you know when customer 17 will enter service and with which server? This is the biggest challenge in a queueing simulation—keeping track of the state of the system as events occur through time. Special queueing software packages are available to do all of the bookkeeping for you, but this software is often expensive and far from trivial to master. Therefore, some people write their own programs, in C, Visual Basic, or some other language to keep track of the events. Unfortunately, even good programmers sometimes struggle when writing queueing simulations. There are numerous details to get straight. One "small" error can make a queueing simulation behave very differently than intended.

We know that most of you are not programmers. You want the insights that a simulation can provide, but you do not want to develop the simulations yourself. Therefore, we have developed two fairly general simulation models that you can run. Each is based on a program, written in Excel's VBA programming language, that runs in the background and does all of the simulation bookkeeping. All you need to do is enter the appropriate input parameters and click a button. The outputs then appear automatically.

The first simulation model we examine is a variation of the $M/M/s$ queueing model we discussed in the Section 14.5. (See the file **Multiserver Simulation.xlsm**.) Customers arrive at a service center according to a Poisson process (exponential interarrival times), they wait (if necessary) in a single queue, and then they are served by the first available server. The simulation model is different in the following respects from the analytical $M/M/s$ model:

- The service times are not necessarily exponentially distributed. The file allows three options: (1) constant (nonrandom) service times, (2) exponentially distributed service times, and (3) gamma distributed service times. This latter option uses the gamma distribution, which is typically shaped as in Figure 14.22. Because its mode is *not* necessarily 0, as with the exponential distribution, it is often more realistic for service times. By allowing three different service time distributions, we can see how different amounts of variability in the service times affect outputs such as waiting times.

- The waiting room is of limited size, where this size is an input parameter. If the queue is already this long and another customer arrives, this new customer is not allowed to enter the system. Of course, you can enter a large value for this input, in which case it is unlikely that any customers will be turned away.

- The simulated runtime is another user input. We might want to run a simulation for 100 hours (of *simulated* time) or only 10 minutes. By varying the runtime, we can

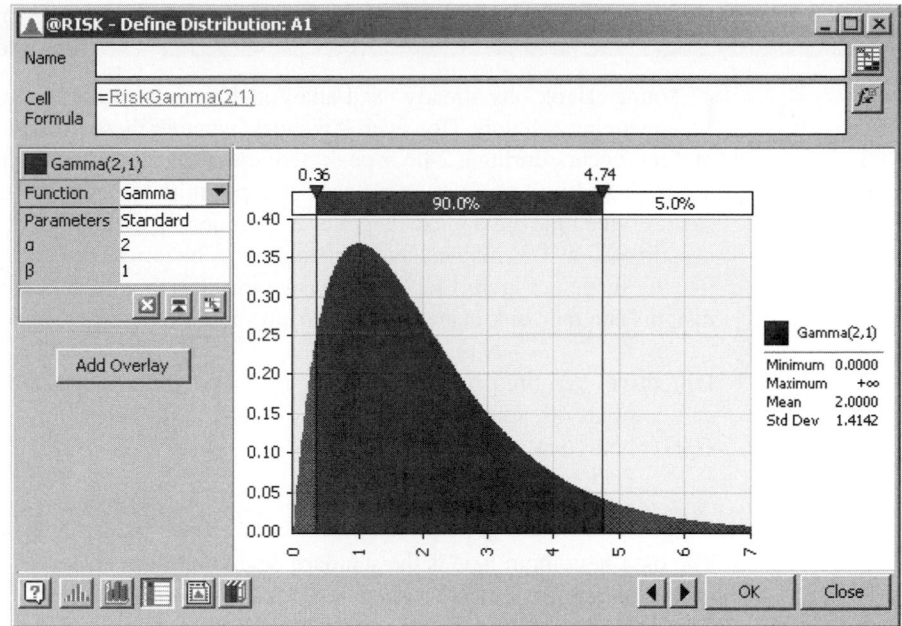

**Figure 14.22**

Typical Gamma Distribution

see how long-run behavior differs from short-run behavior. In addition, there is a *warm-up time* input. The simulation always starts empty and idle—no customers in the system—which might not be very realistic if we want to simulate a peak period, say, that starts with some customers already in the system. Therefore, the purpose of the warm-up period is to allow the system to get to a "typical" busy state. No statistics are collected during the warm-up period. Statistics are collected only during the runtime period. As an example, suppose a bank opens at 9:00 A.M., empty and idle, and we are interested in the period from 11:30 A.M. until 1:30 P.M. Then the warm-up period would be of length 2.5 hours, and the runtime period would be of length 2 hours.

■ Every time you run the simulation, you are asked for a *random number seed*. The actual number you enter is not important. The important part is that if you enter the *same* seed for two different runs, you get the same stream of random numbers. This is often useful for comparing different systems under "like" conditions (the same interarrival times and the same service times, say). Alternatively, if you enter *different* seeds for two different runs, you get a different stream of random numbers on each run. This is useful for seeing how much the system behavior can vary from one run to the next.

These last two points enable some very important insights into queueing systems in general. An analytical model such as the $M/M/s$ model provides summary measures, typically means, in steady state. It might say, for example, that the mean time in queue per customer is 4.85 minutes. But if we simulate such a system for 2 hours, say, and average the times in queue for the simulated customers, will the average be 4.85 minutes? The answer is a very definite "no." First, the average might not be the steady-state value because 2 hours might not be long enough to "get into" steady state. Second, different runs using different random numbers will typically provide different averages. You might be surprised to see how much they can vary.

We now illustrate how the simulation works by revisiting the County Bank queueing situation (see Examples 14.3 and 14.7) with simulation.

EXAMPLE | **14.9 SIMULATING QUEUEING AT COUNTY BANK**

County Bank has already used analytical models to obtain steady-state measures of queueing behavior. However, it wonders whether these provide very realistic estimates of what occurs during a 2-hour peak period at the bank. During this peak period, arrivals occur according to a Poisson process of 2 per minute, there are 6 tellers employed, and each service time has a mean length of 2.7 minutes. The standard deviation of service times is estimated at 1.5 minutes, and a histogram of historical service times has a shape much like the shape in Figure 14.22, so that a gamma distribution appears to be reasonable. What insights can the bank manager obtain from simulation?

**Objective** To simulate the bank's queueing system for a two-hour peak period so that we can compare its actual behavior to the steady-state behavior predicted by $M/M/s$ and $G/G/s$ analytical models.

## WHERE DO THE NUMBERS COME FROM?

The only new input here is the standard deviation of service times. As with the rest of the inputs, it can be estimated from observed data on service times.

## Solution

For comparison, we first show results from the analytical models of Section 14.5. If we use the analytical $M/M/s$ model (ignoring the fact that service times are not really exponentially distributed), we obtain the results in Figure 14.23. (The value in cell B6 is $1/2.7$, the reciprocal of the mean service time.) For example, the mean wait in queue is $W_Q = 3.33$ minutes. If we use the analytical $G/G/s$ model with the Allen–Cunneen approximation, we obtain the results in Figure 14.24. [The values in cells B5 and B8 are $1/2.7$ and $(1.5/2.7)^2$. The value in cell B7 is 1 because the exponential distribution has coefficient of variation 1.] The value of $W_Q$ is now 2.18. Evidently, the gamma distribution, which has a much lower coefficient of variation, results in less time in the queue.

---

**Figure 14.23** Results from the $M/M/s$ Model

| | A | B | C | D | E | F | G | H | I |
|---|---|---|---|---|---|---|---|---|---|
| 1 | M/M/s Queue | | | | | | | | |
| 2 | | | | | After entering inputs in blue cells, click on the button below to | | | | |
| 3 | Inputs | | | | run the macro that calculates P(0), the value in cell B16. | | | | |
| 4 | Unit of time | hour | | | Everything else recalculates automatically. Do *not* rearrange | | | | |
| 5 | Arrival rate | 2 | customers/hour | | cells in this template -- this might cause the macro to stop | | | | |
| 6 | Service rate per server | 0.37037 | customers/hour | | behaving correctly. | | | | |
| 7 | Number of servers | 6 | | | | | | | |
| 8 | | | | | | | | | |
| 9 | Outputs | | | | | Do Calculations | | | |
| 10 | Direct outputs from inputs | | | | Distribution of number in system | | | Distribution of time in queue | |
| 11 | Mean time between arrivals | 0.500 | hours | | n (customers) | P(n in system) | | t (in hours) | P(wait > t) |
| 12 | Mean time per service | 2.700 | hours | | 0 | 0.0021 | | 0.020 | 0.737 |
| 13 | Traffic intensity | 0.900 | | | 1 | 0.0116 | | | |
| 14 | | | | | 2 | 0.0313 | | | |
| 15 | Summary measures | | | | 3 | 0.0564 | | | |
| 16 | P(system empty) | 0.002 | | | 4 | 0.0761 | | | |
| 17 | P(all servers busy) | 74.0% | | | 5 | 0.0822 | | | |
| 18 | Expected number in system | 12.061 | customers | | 6 | 0.0740 | | | |
| 19 | Expected number in queue | 6.661 | customers | | 7 | 0.0666 | | | |
| 20 | Expected time in system | 6.031 | hours | | 8 | 0.0600 | | | |
| 21 | Expected time in queue | 3.331 | hours | | 9 | 0.0540 | | | |
| 22 | Percentage who don't wait in queue | 26.0% | | | 10 | 0.0486 | | | |

Figure 14.24

Results from the

*G/G/s* Model

| | A | B | C | D | E | F |
|---|---|---|---|---|---|---|
| 1 | G/G/s template using the Allen-Cunneen approximation | | | | | |
| 2 | | | | | | |
| 3 | **Inputs** | | | | | |
| 4 | Arrival rate | 2.000 | | | | |
| 5 | Service rate per server | 0.370 | | | | |
| 6 | Number of servers | 6 | | | | |
| 7 | scv for interarrival times | 1.000 | | | | |
| 8 | scv for service times | 0.309 | | | | |
| 9 | | | | | | |
| 10 | **Calculations of intermediate quantities** | | | | | |
| 11 | Ratio of arrival rate to service rate | 5.400 | | | | |
| 12 | Server utilization | 0.900 | | | | |
| 13 | A Poisson quantity | 0.778 | | | | |
| 14 | Erlang C-function | 0.740 | | | | |
| 15 | | | | | | |
| 16 | **Important outputs** | | | | | |
| 17 | Expected wait in queue | 2.179 | | | | |
| 18 | Expected queue length | 4.359 | | | | |
| 19 | Expected wait in system | 4.879 | | | | |
| 20 | Expected number in system | 9.759 | | | | |

Enter numbers here, or (as in this file) enter links to summary data from observed interarrival and service times on another sheet.

The approximation is valid only when the utilization in cell B12 is less than 1. Otherwise, it gives meaningless outputs.

## Using the Spreadsheet Simulation Model

When you open the file **Multiserver Simulation.xlsm**, you see the Explanation sheet in Figure 14.25. By clicking on the button, you see a couple of dialog boxes where you can enter the required inputs. These appear in Figures 14.26 and 14.27. Note that the first of these asks you for a random number seed.

Figure 14.25

Explanation Sheet

### Multiserver Queueing System

This application simulates a multi-server queueing system, such as at a bank, where arriving customers wait in a single line for the first available server. The system starts in the "empty and idle" state and runs for a user-specified amount of time. The user must specify the arrival rate, the service rate per server, the number of (identical) servers, and the maximum number of customers allowed in the system. (If a customer arrives when the system is full, this customer leaves.) The service time distribution can be constant (no randomness), exponential, or gamma (in which case the standard deviation of the service time must also be supplied). The user also needs to specify a warmup time and a run time. The simulation occurs during both of these times, but statistics are collected only during the run time.

You can easily run several simulations with the same or different inputs. Each analysis is shown, along with its inputs, in a separate Report sheet: Report_1, Report_2, and so on. For each run, you are asked for new inputs in a pair of dialog boxes. For convenience, the "default" values shown in these dialog boxes after the first run are those from the *previous* run, which you can then modify as you like.

We suggest that you store this file somewhere safe and then, as you run simulations, save your modified files under different names. That way, you can always start with this original version.

Run the simulation

The simulation results appear in Figure 14.28. Again, we do not discuss all of the details, but when the simulation runs it does the following:

■ Starts with an empty and idle system—no customers are in the bank.

Figure 14.26

First Input Dialog
Box

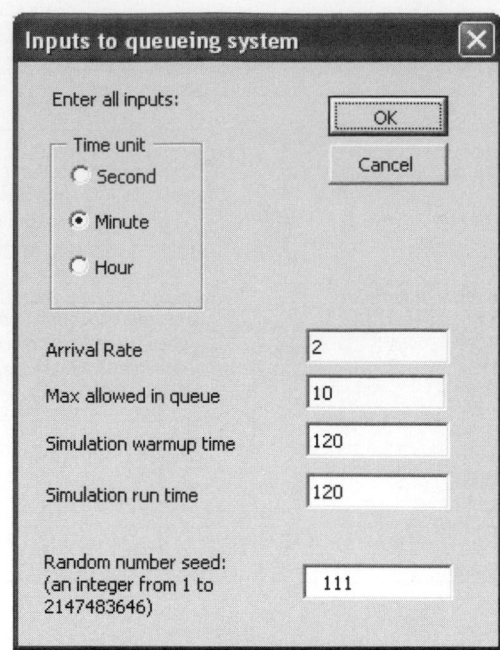

Figure 14.27

Second Input Dialog
Box

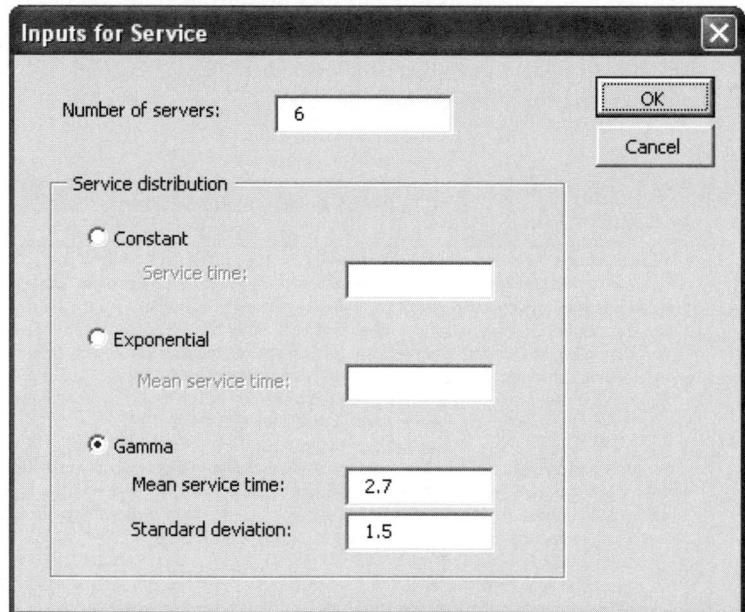

- Keeps simulating customer arrivals and service times, and keeps playing out the events but doesn't keep track of any customer statistics for the first 120 minutes, the warm-up period. It keeps track of statistics only for the next 120 minutes, the runtime period.

- If a customer arrives, and 10 customers are already in line, this customer is turned away (or, if you like, the customer decides not to bother waiting). If we want to ensure that no one is turned away, we can choose a large value for this input.

- Reports the summary measures for this run, as shown in Figure 14.28.

**Figure 14.28**

Simulation Results

| | A | B | C |
|---|---|---|---|
| 1 | **Multiple Server Queueing Simulation** | | |
| 2 | | | |
| 3 | **Inputs** | | |
| 4 | | | |
| 5 | Time unit | minute | |
| 6 | Customer arrival rate | 2.000 | customers/minute |
| 7 | Mean time between arrivals | 0.500 | minute |
| 8 | Number of servers | 6 | |
| 9 | Service time distribution | Gamma | |
| 10 | Mean service time | 2.700 | minutes |
| 11 | Stdev of service times | 1.500 | minutes |
| 12 | Service rate for system | 2.222 | customers/minute |
| 13 | Maximum allowed in queue | 10 | customers |
| 14 | Simulation warmup time | 120 | minutes |
| 15 | Simulation run time | 120 | minutes |
| 16 | Random number seed | 111 | |
| 17 | | | |
| 18 | **Simulation Outputs** | | |
| 19 | | | |
| 20 | Average time in queue per customer | 1.06 | minutes |
| 21 | Maximum time a customer was in queue | 4.23 | minutes |
| 22 | Average number of customers in queue | 1.86 | |
| 23 | Maximum number in queue | 10 | |
| 24 | | | |
| 25 | Average time in system per customer | 3.86 | minutes |
| 26 | Maximum time a customer was in system | 9.45 | minutes |
| 27 | Average number of customers in system | 6.88 | |
| 28 | Maximum number in system | 16 | |
| 29 | | | |
| 30 | Fraction of time each server is busy | 83.4% | |
| 31 | | | |
| 32 | Number of customers processed | 223 | |
| 33 | Number of customers turned away | 2 | |
| 34 | Fraction of customers turned away | 0.9% | |

## Discussion of the Results

The outputs in Figure 14.28 should be self-explanatory. During the 2-hour period, 223 customers entered the bank, and 2 were turned away. Each teller was busy, on average, 83.4% of the time, the average customer waited in the queue for 1.06 minutes, the average length of the queue was 1.86, the maximum queue length was 10, and so on. We also obtain a graph of the queue length distribution, as shown in Figure 14.29. Each bar represents the percentage of simulated time the queue length was equal to any particular value. For example, the bar on the left shows that there was no queue at all about 48% of the time.

Clearly, the average time in queue, 1.06 minutes, is much smaller than $W_Q$ from the $M/M/s$ and $G/G/s$ models. Which is the "correct" value for County Bank's 2-hour peak period? This is not an easy question to answer. The 1.06 value from the simulation depends to a great extent on the random numbers we happened to simulate. To illustrate this, we ran the simulation several more times, each with a different random number seed, and we obtained values ranging from slightly under 0.7 to slightly over 2.1. This shows the bank manager that the average time in queue during any day's 2-hour peak period *depends on the day*. Some days she will get lucky, and other days she won't. This variability from day to day—that is, from run to run—is one of the most important insights we can gain from simulation.

Besides the variability from day to day, the simulation results can depend on the length of the runtime period, and they can be affected by the limited queue size. For example, we ran the simulation for 10,000 minutes. The average time in queue did not change much, but hundreds of customers were turned away. Then we changed the maximum queue size to

**Figure 14.29** Queue Length Distribution

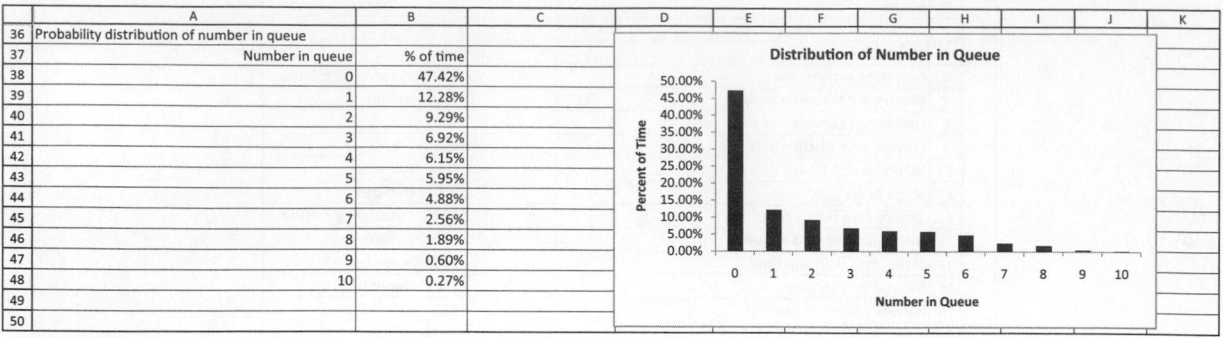

| | A | B | C | D E F G H I J | K |
|---|---|---|---|---|---|
| 36 | Probability distribution of number in queue | | | | |
| 37 | Number in queue | % of time | | | |
| 38 | 0 | 47.42% | | | |
| 39 | 1 | 12.28% | | | |
| 40 | 2 | 9.29% | | | |
| 41 | 3 | 6.92% | | | |
| 42 | 4 | 6.15% | | | |
| 43 | 5 | 5.95% | | | |
| 44 | 6 | 4.88% | | | |
| 45 | 7 | 2.56% | | | |
| 46 | 8 | 1.89% | | | |
| 47 | 9 | 0.60% | | | |
| 48 | 10 | 0.27% | | | |
| 49 | | | | | |
| 50 | | | | | |

*The simulation results can vary widely from one run to the next, due to different random numbers. This often reflects accurately what occurs in the real world.*

100 and ran the simulation again for 10,000 minutes. The average time in queue was now much larger (over 2 minutes), and no customers were turned away. This illustrates that if all customers are allowed to enter the system, the average time in queue increases, whereas if many are turned away, the average time in queue, *for those who enter,* is much smaller. ∎

The next example uses the same simulation model (still the **Multiserver Simulation.xlsm** file) but with different inputs. Specifically, we see the affect on waiting for different service time distributions, all with the same mean. For a given mean, the exponential distribution has the most variability, the constant distribution has the least (none), and the gamma distribution is typically in the middle. We see whether this ordering carries over to average times in the queue.

---

EXAMPLE | **14.10 QUEUEING FOR HELP AT HYTEX**

HyTex is a software company that offers technical support for its customers over the phone. The demand for help is fairly constant throughout the day, with calls arriving at a rate of approximately 10 per minute. HyTex keeps 35 technical support lines open at all times, and it takes 3.5 minutes, on average, to answer a customer's question. Customers who call when all technical support people are busy face two possible situations. If there are fewer than 20 customers already on hold (the phone version of waiting in line), then a new caller is also put on hold. But if 20 customers are already on hold, a new caller gets a busy signal and must hang up. The service times—the times to answer customers' questions—are highly variable. HyTex wants to know how much it is suffering because of this variability.

**Objective** To use simulation to analyze the affect of the shape of the service time distribution on customer waiting times.

### WHERE DO THE NUMBERS COME FROM?

These inputs are estimated from the extensive call data available. However, a subtle issue concerns the arrival rate of 10 per minute. Estimating the arrival rate of *all* calls is not easy because of the difficulty associated with tracking calls that receive a busy signal and are therefore lost.

## Solution

This example is important because it illustrates how we can use a simulation model as a tool to study system behavior with various input parameters.

### Selection of Inputs

If the service times are highly variable, then a histogram of them might resemble an exponential distribution—that is, a lot of short calls but a few really long ones. Therefore, we first simulate the system with exponential service times. The arrival rate is 10, the mean service time is 3.5, the number of servers is 35, and the maximum allowable queue size is 20. With these parameters, we used a warm-up period of 1000 minutes and a runtime period of 2000 minutes for each simulation (you can think of this as several days strung together), and we made five runs with different random number seeds. We then changed the service time distribution to a gamma distribution with mean 3.5 and standard deviation 2.8. (This distribution has a squared coefficient of variation 0.64, so it is not as variable as the exponential distribution, which has squared coefficient of variation 1.) Finally, we changed the service time distribution to be constant with value 3.5. For both the gamma and constant distributions, we made five runs, using the same seeds as in the exponential runs. (If you want to mimic our results, you should use the seeds 111, 222, 333, 444, and 555.)

### Discussion of the Results

Selected results appear in Table 14.4. For each simulation run, we list two quantities: the average time in queue for the customers who did not receive busy signals, and the fraction of callers who received busy signals and were therefore lost. If we look only at the average times in queue, the results sometimes go in the *opposite* direction from what we predicted. The most variable distribution, the exponential, sometimes has the smallest times, whereas the least variable distribution, the constant, always has the largest times. However, there is a reason for this. These averages are only for the customers who were able to enter the system. As the percentages of lost callers show, many more callers were lost with the exponential than with the constant distribution, with the gamma distribution in the middle. (Over a period of 2000 minutes, with an arrival rate of 10 per minute, the system sees about 20,000 callers. An extra 1% lost therefore translates to about 200 callers—not an insignificant number.) With highly variable service times, customers do not wait quite as long in the queue because there are not as many customers to wait—many of them cannot get through at all!

### Table 14.4  Comparison of Models

| Seed | *Average Time in Queue* | | | *Percentage of Callers Lost* | | |
|------|-------------|-------|----------|-------------|-------|----------|
|      | **Exponential** | **Gamma** | **Constant** | **Exponential** | **Gamma** | **Constant** |
| 111 | 0.92 | 0.84 | 0.92 | 4.8 | 3.6 | 3.0 |
| 222 | 0.81 | 0.80 | 0.85 | 4.1 | 3.1 | 2.3 |
| 333 | 0.81 | 0.81 | 0.87 | 4.0 | 3.4 | 2.8 |
| 444 | 0.80 | 0.82 | 0.88 | 4.7 | 3.5 | 2.8 |
| 555 | 0.77 | 0.75 | 0.82 | 3.8 | 2.9 | 2.4 |

So we again see that variability is the enemy. HyTex hates to have unhappy customers, and customers who receive busy signals are probably the unhappiest. The company should try to reduce the variability of service times, even if it cannot reduce the *mean* service time. If this is not possible, there are two other possible remedies: (1) hire more technical support people, and/or (2) rent more trunk lines, so that more customers can be put on hold. ∎

## Simulating a Series System with Blocking

Outputs from one queue are often inputs to another queue. This is particularly true in many manufacturing environments, where a part has to pass through several "stations" in succession. At each station, a machine does a certain operation and then passes the part to the next station. After the part has gone through each station, it goes into finished product inventory. If each part has to pass through station 1, then station 2, and so on, we call the system a **series** system. One possible series system appears in Figure 14.30. This system has three stations. Stations 1 and 3 each have a single machine (labeled M1 and M3), whereas station 2 has two machines (labeled M2,1 and M2,2). Each part has to be processed at M1, then at M2,1 *or* M2,2, and then at M3. There can also be limited **buffers** (spaces for queueing) in front of the stations. In the figure, there is no limit to the queue size in front of station 1 (which we will always assume), but there is room for only three parts in front of station 2 and room for only four parts in front of station 3. These limited buffers can create **blocking.** As an example, suppose the buffers in front of station 2 are all full and a part finishes processing at station 1. Then this part is blocked, which means that it cannot move from machine M1, and this prevents other parts from entering M1 for processing. There can even be a cascading effect, where blocking of a part at M2,1 or M2,2 eventually causes blocking at M1. This blocking can have a serious negative effect on overall operations.

We developed a simulation, again written in VBA, for this type of system. (See the file **Series Simulation.xlsm.**) This simulation allows up to 10 stations in series with any number of machines per station and any numbers of buffers in front of the stations (after station 1, which always has unlimited buffers). Parts arrive to station 1 with a given arrival rate. We allow two possibilities: (1) a constant (nonrandom) arrival process, where parts arrive according to a precise nonrandom schedule; and (2) a Poisson arrival process, where times between arrivals are exponentially distributed. Similarly, the processing (service) times for the different stations can differ, and each can have either a constant (nonrandom) distribution or an exponential distribution. The simulation starts in the empty and idle state, there can be a warm-up period where no statistics are collected, and then the simulation runs for a prescribed number of minutes.

Guessing how this type of system might behave is very difficult. In fact, this is the whole purpose of the simulation. It allows a manufacturer to analyze many what-if scenarios, without actually making changes to the physical system. We illustrate how this might work in the following example.

---

EXAMPLE | 14.11 PROCESSING PARTS AT STREAMLINING

The Streamlining Company manufactures various types of automobile parts. Its factory has several production lines, all versions of the series system in Figure 14.30, with varying numbers of stations and machines. In an effort to improve operations, the company wants to gain some insights into how average throughput times and other output measures are affected by various inputs. (The **throughput** time is the elapsed time from when a part enters the system until it finishes processing at all stations.) Specific questions of interest include the following:

Figure 14.30

A Series System with
Possible Blocking

**3-station system with multiple machines at station 2**

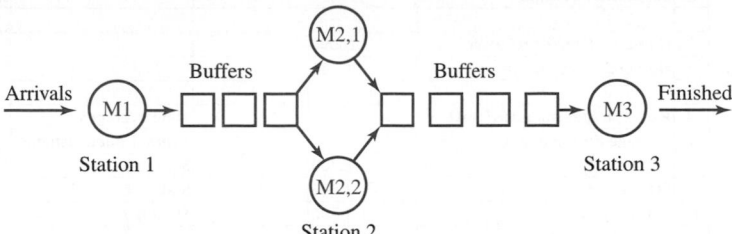

- Is it better to have a single fast machine at each station or multiple slower machines?
- How much does the variability of the arrival process to station 1 affect outputs? What about the variability of processing times at machines?
- The company has experimented with 0 buffers and has found that the resulting blocking can be disastrous. It now wants to create some buffers (which entails a significant cost). Where should it place the buffers?

**Objective**   To use simulation to learn how the inputs to the system, including the configuration of buffers, affect such output measures as throughput times.

## WHERE DO THE NUMBERS COME FROM?

The company should use "reasonable" inputs for the simulation, based on historical observations. However, the whole point of the simulation is to use it as a tool: to learn how outputs are affected by varying inputs.

## Solution

The simulation model in the file **Series Simulation.xlsm** allows us to experiment as much as we like by changing inputs, running the simulation, and examining the outputs. The inputs section appears in Figure 14.31.[9] Note that 1 is the code for constant interarrival or processing times, whereas 2 is the code for exponentially distributed times. Also, cell B14

**Figure 14.31**

**Inputs Section**

|  | A | B | C | D | E | F |
|---|---|---|---|---|---|---|
| 1 | **Inputs for simulation** | | | | | |
| 2 | | | | | | |
| 3 | **Arrival process of parts to station 1:** | | | Enter inputs in all of the blue cells, then click on the button to run the simulation. | | |
| 4 | Distribution (1 for constant, 2 for exponential) | 2 | | | | |
| 5 | Arrival rate to station 1 (parts/minute) | 1.00 | | | | |
| 6 | | | | | | |
| 7 | **Configuration of process (fill in the blue cells):** | | | Run the simulation | | |
| 8 | Number of stations (<= 10) | 3 | | | | |
| 9 | | | | | | |
| 10 | Station | 1 | 2 | 3 | | |
| 11 | Number of parallel machines at stations | 1 | 1 | 1 | | |
| 12 | Distribution of processing time for each machine at station (1 for constant, 2 for exponential) | 2 | 2 | 2 | | |
| 13 | Mean processing time (minutes) per machine | 0.7 | 0.7 | 0.7 | | |
| 14 | Number of buffers in front of stations | | 5 | 5 | | |
| 15 | | | | | | |
| 16 | **Simulation times (minutes)** | | | | | |
| 17 | Warmup time (no statistics collected) | 1000 | | | | |
| 18 | Run time | 10000 | | | | |

[9] The only dialog box in this application is for a random number seed; the other inputs must be entered manually. However, when you change the number of stations in cell B8, the shaded input range in rows 11 to 14 automatically resizes to accommodate the number of stations.

Figure 14.32
Simulation Outputs

|  | A | B | C | D | E |
|---|---|---|---|---|---|
| 1 | Simulation Outputs |  |  |  |  |
| 2 |  |  |  |  |  |
| 3 | Number of items processed | 10090 |  |  |  |
| 4 | Number left at closing | 16 |  |  |  |
| 5 |  |  |  |  |  |
| 6 | Part averages (minutes/part) |  |  | Time averages |  |
| 7 | Average time in queues |  |  | Average queue lengths |  |
| 8 | Station 1 | 2.400 |  | Station 1 | 2.42 |
| 9 | Station 2 | 1.565 |  | Station 2 | 1.58 |
| 10 | Station 3 | 1.302 |  | Station 3 | 1.31 |
| 11 | Total in all stations | 5.267 |  |  |  |
| 12 |  |  |  | Percent time processing |  |
| 13 | Average times being blocked |  |  | Station 1 | 69.70% |
| 14 | Station 1 | 0.056 |  | Station 2 | 71.38% |
| 15 | Station 2 | 0.039 |  | Station 3 | 70.66% |
| 16 | Total in all stations | 0.095 |  |  |  |
| 17 |  |  |  | Percent time blocked |  |
| 18 | Average throughput time | 7.457 |  | Station 1 | 5.65% |
| 19 | Percent time in queue | 70.63% |  | Station 2 | 3.95% |
| 20 | Percent time being blocked | 1.28% |  |  |  |
| 21 | Percent time being processed | 28.09% |  |  |  |

is black to indicate that the number of buffers in front of station 1 is always unlimited. When we run the simulation, we obtain outputs such as those in Figure 14.32. (These are for the inputs in Figure 14.31.) Perhaps the most important part of the outputs is in the range B18:B21. For this particular run, we see that the average part took 7.457 minutes to get through the system. Only 28.09% of this was in processing. The rest was spent in queues or being blocked at station 1 or 2. In addition, we see at the top of the output that 10,090 parts were completed during the runtime period (some of which *entered* the system during the warm-up period), and 16 parts were left uncompleted at the end of the runtime.

Turning to Streamlining's questions, we first examine the trade-off between fast and slow machines. The outputs in Figure 14.33 are typical. (These results were obtained by making multiple runs and copying the outputs from each run to a summary sheet. For each set of inputs, we made three runs with random number seeds 111, 222, and 333.) We keep the arrival rate at 1 part per minute and the mean service rate at 1/0.6 parts per minute at each station. In the first set of runs, there is a single fast machine at each station. Each machine has an exponential processing time with mean 0.6 minute. In the second set of runs, we triple the number of machines at each station and also triple the mean processing time for each machine to achieve equivalent slow machines.

The use of three runs per configuration indicates that different random numbers can produce slightly different results. However, if average throughput time is of primary interest, the fast machines are clearly better. Even so, the results are probably not clear-cut to a manufacturer. For example, manufacturing companies typically like high utilization of their machines. The slow machines have much higher utilization than the fast ones. The fast machines tend to process the parts quickly, but then the parts are often passed to a queue. So it comes down to a trade-off between a lot of time in processing or a lot of time in queues.

This configuration might be described as *low utilization*. Parts arrive at rate 1 per minute, and each mean processing time (for the fast machines) is only 0.6 minute. Figure 14.34 shows the same type of results when the utilization is much higher. Here we increase the mean processing times for the fast machines to 0.9 (and triple them for the slow machines). We also increase the buffer sizes to 10. This system is a disaster—take a look at the average throughput times and the average times spent in queue in front of station 1, for example—but it does indicate a very interesting result. In terms of average throughput

**Figure 14.33** Fast Versus Slow Machines with Low Utilization

| | A | B | C | D | E | F | G | H |
|---|---|---|---|---|---|---|---|---|
| 1 | Inputs (all use arrival rate of 1, exponential interarrival times, 3 stations, warmup time of 1000, run time of 10000) | | | | | | | |
| 2 | | | | | | | | |
| 3 | Station | 1 | 2 | 3 | | 1 | 2 | 3 |
| 4 | Number of parallel machines at stations | 1 | 1 | 1 | | 3 | 3 | 3 |
| 5 | Distribution of processing time for each machine at station (1 for constant, 2 for exponential) | 2 | 2 | 2 | | 2 | 2 | 2 |
| 6 | Mean processing time (minutes) per machine | 0.6 | 0.6 | 0.6 | | 1.8 | 1.8 | 1.8 |
| 7 | Number of buffers in front of stations | | 5 | 5 | | | 5 | 5 |
| 8 | | | | | | | | |
| 9 | **Counts of parts** | Run 1 | Run 2 | Run 3 | | Run 1 | Run 2 | Run 3 |
| 10 | Number of items processed | 10098 | 10045 | 10069 | | 10094 | 10044 | 10067 |
| 11 | Number left at closing | 7 | 2 | 5 | | 14 | 5 | 11 |
| 12 | | | | | | | | |
| 13 | **Part averages (minutes/part)** | | | | | | | |
| 14 | Average time in queues | | | | | | | |
| 15 | Station 1 | 0.978 | 1.057 | 1.138 | | 0.526 | 0.584 | 0.690 |
| 16 | Station 2 | 0.913 | 0.916 | 0.864 | | 0.530 | 0.533 | 0.496 |
| 17 | Station 3 | 0.822 | 0.801 | 0.827 | | 0.500 | 0.486 | 0.497 |
| 18 | Total in all stations | 2.713 | 2.774 | 2.829 | | 1.555 | 1.604 | 1.683 |
| 19 | | | | | | | | |
| 20 | Average times being blocked | | | | | | | |
| 21 | Station 1 | 0.021 | 0.023 | 0.019 | | 0.040 | 0.043 | 0.038 |
| 22 | Station 2 | 0.017 | 0.017 | 0.015 | | 0.032 | 0.031 | 0.029 |
| 23 | Total in all stations | 0.037 | 0.040 | 0.034 | | 0.071 | 0.074 | 0.066 |
| 24 | | | | | | | | |
| 25 | Average throughput time | 4.549 | 4.614 | 4.663 | | 7.022 | 7.075 | 7.151 |
| 26 | Percent time in queue | 59.65% | 60.12% | 60.67% | | 22.15% | 22.66% | 23.54% |
| 27 | Percent time being blocked | 0.82% | 0.87% | 0.72% | | 1.02% | 1.05% | 0.93% |
| 28 | Percent time being processed | 39.53% | 39.01% | 38.61% | | 76.83% | 76.29% | 75.53% |
| 29 | | | | | | | | |
| 30 | **Time averages** | | | | | | | |
| 31 | Average queue lengths | | | | | | | |
| 32 | Station 1 | 0.99 | 1.06 | 1.15 | | 0.53 | 0.59 | 0.70 |
| 33 | Station 2 | 0.92 | 0.92 | 0.87 | | 0.53 | 0.54 | 0.50 |
| 34 | Station 3 | 0.83 | 0.80 | 0.83 | | 0.51 | 0.49 | 0.50 |
| 35 | | | | | | | | |
| 36 | Percent time processing | | | | | | | |
| 37 | Station 1 | 59.79% | 60.24% | 60.04% | | 60.10% | 60.57% | 60.33% |
| 38 | Station 2 | 61.20% | 60.28% | 60.08% | | 61.47% | 60.55% | 60.34% |
| 39 | Station 3 | 60.61% | 60.18% | 61.19% | | 60.58% | 60.16% | 61.19% |
| 40 | | | | | | | | |
| 41 | Percent time blocked | | | | | | | |
| 42 | Station 1 | 2.09% | 2.33% | 1.87% | | 1.03% | 1.10% | 0.98% |
| 43 | Station 2 | 1.69% | 1.72% | 1.52% | | 0.81% | 0.79% | 0.68% |

time, the slow machines are now *better* by quite a margin. Can you see why intuitively? The reason is that when utilization is high, one long processing time on a fast machine—which is always a possibility with an exponential distribution—can back up the whole system for a long time. If there are multiple machines, however, parts can "move around" a machine experiencing a long processing time, and the whole system is not as affected. You might have guessed this before running the simulation, but simulation confirms it.

Streamlining's next question concerns the variability of arrival and processing times. Here we examine a three-station process, with one machine at each station and five buffers in front of stations 2 and 3. Parts arrive at rate 1 per minute, and the average service time is 0.7 minute at each machine. Figure 14.35 lists some results. In columns B and C, interarrival times and processing times are exponential. In columns D and E, interarrival times are constant and processing times are exponential. This might be realistic if the company

**Figure 14.34** Fast versus Slow Machines with High Utilization

| | A | B | C | D | E | F | G | H |
|---|---|---|---|---|---|---|---|---|
| 1 | Inputs (all use arrival rate of 1, exponential interarrival times, 3 stations, warm-up time of 1000, run time of 10000) | | | | | | | |
| 2 | | | | | | | | |
| 3 | Station | 1 | 2 | 3 | | 1 | 2 | 3 |
| 4 | Number of parallel machines at stations | 1 | 1 | 1 | | 3 | 3 | 3 |
| 5 | Distribution of processing time for each machine at station (1 for constant, 2 for exponential) | 2 | 2 | 2 | | 2 | 2 | 2 |
| 6 | Mean processing time (minutes) per machine | 0.9 | 0.9 | 0.9 | | 2.7 | 2.7 | 2.7 |
| 7 | Number of buffers in front of stations | | 10 | 10 | | | 10 | 10 |
| 8 | | | | | | | | |
| 9 | **Counts of parts** | Run 1 | Run 2 | Run 3 | | Run 1 | Run 2 | Run 3 |
| 10 | Number of items processed | 9962 | 9922 | 9965 | | 10076 | 9950 | 10074 |
| 11 | Number left at closing | 163 | 133 | 144 | | 53 | 108 | 23 |
| 12 | | | | | | | | |
| 13 | **Part averages (minutes/part)** | | | | | | | |
| 14 | Average time in queues | | | | | | | |
| 15 | Station 1 | 105.539 | 40.671 | 122.249 | | 41.921 | 29.573 | 46.259 |
| 16 | Station 2 | 6.067 | 5.375 | 5.840 | | 6.219 | 5.104 | 5.708 |
| 17 | Station 3 | 4.347 | 3.996 | 4.372 | | 4.197 | 3.665 | 4.258 |
| 18 | Total in all stations | 115.952 | 50.042 | 132.461 | | 52.337 | 38.343 | 56.225 |
| 19 | | | | | | | | |
| 20 | Average times being blocked | | | | | | | |
| 21 | Station 1 | 0.114 | 0.090 | 0.108 | | 0.306 | 0.223 | 0.265 |
| 22 | Station 2 | 0.055 | 0.047 | 0.054 | | 0.156 | 0.116 | 0.137 |
| 23 | Total in all stations | 0.169 | 0.137 | 0.163 | | 0.462 | 0.340 | 0.402 |
| 24 | | | | | | | | |
| 25 | Average throughput time | 118.644 | 52.780 | 135.160 | | 60.850 | 46.674 | 64.799 |
| 26 | Percent time in queue | 97.73% | 94.81% | 98.00% | | 86.01% | 82.15% | 86.77% |
| 27 | Percent time being blocked | 0.14% | 0.26% | 0.12% | | 0.76% | 0.73% | 0.62% |
| 28 | Percent time being processed | 2.13% | 4.93% | 1.88% | | 13.23% | 17.12% | 12.61% |
| 29 | | | | | | | | |
| 30 | **Time averages** | | | | | | | |
| 31 | Average queue lengths | | | | | | | |
| 32 | Station 1 | 106.39 | 41.07 | 122.72 | | 42.28 | 29.87 | 46.64 |
| 33 | Station 2 | 6.04 | 5.34 | 5.82 | | 6.27 | 5.08 | 5.76 |
| 34 | Station 3 | 4.33 | 3.96 | 4.36 | | 4.23 | 3.65 | 4.29 |
| 35 | | | | | | | | |
| 36 | Percent time processing | | | | | | | |
| 37 | Station 1 | 88.58% | 89.42% | 89.20% | | 93.38% | 92.42% | 93.59% |
| 38 | Station 2 | 90.21% | 89.23% | 89.01% | | 93.32% | 90.97% | 91.87% |
| 39 | Station 3 | 89.61% | 89.04% | 90.66% | | 90.68% | 89.27% | 91.80% |
| 40 | | | | | | | | |
| 41 | Percent time blocked | | | | | | | |
| 42 | Station 1 | 11.39% | 8.96% | 10.78% | | 6.43% | 4.68% | 5.55% |
| 43 | Station 2 | 5.48% | 4.64% | 5.43% | | 3.31% | 2.40% | 2.91% |

releases one part to the line every minute according to a nonrandom schedule. In columns F and G, interarrival times are exponential and processing times are constant. Finally, both are constant in column H. We made two runs for each of the random cases. Of course, only one run is necessary for the nonrandom case. By this time, these results should not come as a surprise. The more the company can do to decrease variability, the better the manufacturing process will operate.

Finally, we analyze the affect of buffers and their placement. We now assume a 10-station process with a single machine at each station. The parts arrive at rate 1 per minute, each machine has a mean processing time of 0.5 minute, and all times are exponentially distributed. You might expect that when parts arrive only half as fast as the machines can process them, there should not be congestion. This is not true, especially if buffers are severely limited. We made several runs, starting with 0 buffers in the system and gradually

Figure 14.35 **Figure 14.35** Constant versus Exponential Times

| | A | B | C | D | E | F | G | H |
|---|---|---|---|---|---|---|---|---|
| 1 | Constant versus exponential interarrival or service times | | | | | | | |
| 2 | | | | | | | | |
| 3 | Each run has arrival rate 1, 3 stations with 1 machine each, mean service time 0.7, 5 buffers at stations 2 and 3, warm-up time 1000, and run time 10000 | | | | | | | |
| 4 | | | | | | | | |
| 5 | | Exp arrivals, Exp services | | Const arrivals, Exp services | | Exp arrivals, Const services | | Both const |
| 6 | Count of parts | Run 1 | Run 2 | Run 1 | Run 2 | Run 1 | Run 2 | Run 1 |
| 7 | Number of items processed | 10090 | 10039 | 10004 | 9999 | 10098 | 10042 | 10000 |
| 8 | Number left at closing | 16 | 8 | 4 | 5 | 3 | 2 | 2 |
| 9 | | | | | | | | |
| 10 | Part averages (minutes/part) | | | | | | | |
| 11 | Average time in queues | | | | | | | |
| 12 | Station 1 | 2.400 | 2.935 | 0.587 | 0.631 | 0.789 | 0.838 | 0.000 |
| 13 | Station 2 | 1.565 | 1.565 | 1.017 | 1.026 | 0.000 | 0.000 | 0.000 |
| 14 | Station 3 | 1.302 | 1.244 | 1.065 | 1.048 | 0.000 | 0.000 | 0.000 |
| 15 | Total in all stations | 5.267 | 5.744 | 2.670 | 2.704 | 0.789 | 0.838 | 0.000 |
| 16 | | | | | | | | |
| 17 | Average times being blocked | | | | | | | |
| 18 | Station 1 | 0.056 | 0.062 | 0.013 | 0.015 | 0.000 | 0.000 | 0.000 |
| 19 | Station 2 | 0.039 | 0.037 | 0.018 | 0.019 | 0.000 | 0.000 | 0.000 |
| 20 | Total in all stations | 0.095 | 0.100 | 0.031 | 0.034 | 0.000 | 0.000 | 0.000 |
| 21 | | | | | | | | |
| 22 | Average throughput time | 7.457 | 7.941 | 4.799 | 4.837 | 2.889 | 2.939 | 2.100 |
| 23 | Percent time in queue | 70.63% | 72.33% | 55.63% | 55.91% | 27.29% | 28.52% | 0.00% |
| 24 | Percent time being blocked | 1.28% | 1.25% | 0.65% | 0.71% | 0.00% | 0.00% | 0.00% |
| 25 | Percent time being processed | 28.09% | 26.42% | 43.72% | 43.39% | 72.71% | 71.48% | 100.00% |
| 26 | | | | | | | | |
| 27 | Time averages | | | | | | | |
| 28 | Average queue lengths | | | | | | | |
| 29 | Station 1 | 2.42 | 2.95 | 0.59 | 0.63 | 0.80 | 0.84 | 0.00 |
| 30 | Station 2 | 1.58 | 1.57 | 1.02 | 1.03 | 0.00 | 0.00 | 0.00 |
| 31 | Station 3 | 1.31 | 1.25 | 1.07 | 1.05 | 0.00 | 0.00 | 0.00 |
| 32 | | | | | | | | |
| 33 | Percent time processing | | | | | | | |
| 34 | Station 1 | 69.70% | 70.27% | 69.16% | 69.94% | 70.69% | 70.30% | 70.01% |
| 35 | Station 2 | 71.38% | 70.27% | 70.58% | 70.03% | 70.69% | 70.30% | 70.01% |
| 36 | Station 3 | 70.66% | 70.16% | 70.01% | 69.90% | 70.69% | 70.30% | 70.01% |
| 37 | | | | | | | | |
| 38 | Percent time blocked | | | | | | | |
| 39 | Station 1 | 5.65% | 6.26% | 1.30% | 1.48% | 0.00% | 0.00% | 0.00% |
| 40 | Station 2 | 3.95% | 3.74% | 1.82% | 1.94% | 0.00% | 0.00% | 0.00% |

adding buffers. Selected results for average throughput times appear in Figure 14.36. When there are no buffers, blocking kills the system. This might not be evident from the percentages listed, because each part spends only a small amount of time being blocked. But there is almost always blocking somewhere in the system, and the effect is that a long queue eventually builds in front of station 1.

Suppose Streamlining has enough funds to build exactly 1 buffer somewhere. Where should the buffer be placed? We made nine runs, placing the single buffer in front of each station, with the results in rows 19 to 22. Clearly, the single buffer should be placed in the *middle* of the line, in front of station 6. Placing it at the front or the back of the line does virtually no good. The reason is probably not intuitive, at least not until we provide the clue. The basic problem with this serial system is the interdependence between stations. A long processing time at one station can have negative effects throughout the entire line. Upstream stations (to the left) become blocked, and downstream stations (to the right) become starved for parts to process. By placing a buffer in the middle of the line, we do the most we can to break the line into two less dependent parts. This effect can be seen by continuing to add buffers one at a time. When there are two buffers, one should be placed about a third of the way down the line, and the other should be placed about two-thirds of the way down, breaking the line into three approximately equal sections. Similarly, when there are three buffers, they should be placed to break the line into four approximately equal sections.

**Figure 14.36**   Buffers and Their Placement

| | A | B | C | D | E | F | G | H | I | J | K |
|---|---|---|---|---|---|---|---|---|---|---|---|
| 1 | Effect on throughput of adding buffers | | | | | | | | | | |
| 2 | | | | | | | | | | | |
| 3 | For each run, arrival process has rate 1, exponential interarrival times, warm-up time 1000, and run time 10000 | | | | | | | | | | |
| 4 | | | | | | | | | | | |
| 5 | Station inputs are as follows, with only the buffers in row 10 changing from one run to the next | | | | | | | | | | |
| 6 | Station | 1 | 2 | 3 | 4 | 5 | 6 | 7 | 8 | 9 | 10 |
| 7 | Number of parallel machines at stations | 1 | 1 | 1 | 1 | 1 | 1 | 1 | 1 | 1 | 1 |
| 8 | Distribution of processing time for each machine at station (1 for constant, 2 for exponential) | 2 | 2 | 2 | 2 | 2 | 2 | 2 | 2 | 2 | 2 |
| 9 | Mean processing time (minutes) per machine | 0.5 | 0.5 | 0.5 | 0.5 | 0.5 | 0.5 | 0.5 | 0.5 | 0.5 | 0.5 |
| 10 | Number of buffers in front of stations | | 0 | 0 | 0 | 0 | 0 | 0 | 0 | 0 | 0 |
| 11 | | | | | | | | | | | |
| 12 | No buffers | | | | | | | | | | |
| 13 | Average throughput time | 837.302 | | | | | | | | | |
| 14 | Percent time in queue | 99.11% | | | | | | | | | |
| 15 | Percent time being blocked | 0.43% | | | | | | | | | |
| 16 | Percent time being processed | 0.47% | | | | | | | | | |
| 17 | | | | | | | | | | | |
| 18 | Exactly 1 buffer in system | At 2 | At 3 | At 4 | At 5 | At 6 | At 7 | At 8 | At 9 | At 10 | |
| 19 | Average throughput time | 774.887 | 717.163 | 668.415 | 645.790 | 637.323 | 646.021 | 689.034 | 736.138 | 781.783 | |
| 20 | Percent time in queue | 99.06% | 98.95% | 98.88% | 98.85% | 98.85% | 98.88% | 98.96% | 99.05% | 99.13% | |
| 21 | Percent time being blocked | 0.48% | 0.52% | 0.54% | 0.54% | 0.52% | 0.49% | 0.45% | 0.42% | 0.41% | |
| 22 | Percent time being processed | 0.46% | 0.53% | 0.58% | 0.61% | 0.63% | 0.63% | 0.59% | 0.53% | 0.46% | |
| 23 | | | | | | | | | | | |
| 24 | Exactly 2 buffers in system | At 2,10 | At 3,9 | At 4,8 | At 5,7 | Both at 6 | | | | | |
| 25 | Average throughput time | 710.386 | 577.575 | 470.710 | 441.238 | 542.693 | | | | | |
| 26 | Percent time in queue | 98.99% | 98.76% | 98.43% | 98.34% | 98.64% | | | | | |
| 27 | Percent time being blocked | 0.47% | 0.55% | 0.66% | 0.70% | 0.59% | | | | | |
| 28 | Percent time being processed | 0.54% | 0.69% | 0.91% | 0.96% | 0.77% | | | | | |
| 29 | | | | | | | | | | | |
| 30 | Exactly 3 buffers in system | At 2,6,10 | At 3,6,9 | At 4,6,8 | At 5,6,7 | | | | | | |
| 31 | Average throughput time | 479.545 | 344.361 | 272.953 | 324.105 | | | | | | |
| 32 | Percent time in queue | 98.46% | 97.86% | 97.29% | 97.74% | | | | | | |
| 33 | Percent time being blocked | 0.64% | 0.86% | 1.06% | 0.92% | | | | | | |
| 34 | Percent time being processed | 0.90% | 1.29% | 1.64% | 1.34% | | | | | | |
| 35 | | | | | | | | | | | |
| 36 | Many buffers in system | 1 at each | 2 at each | 5 at each | 20 at each | | | | | | |
| 37 | Average throughput time | 12.787 | 10.399 | 9.997 | 9.986 | | | | | | |
| 38 | Percent time in queue | 49.68% | 46.89% | 49.58% | 50.02% | | | | | | |
| 39 | Percent time being blocked | 11.32% | 5.13% | 0.49% | 0.00% | | | | | | |
| 40 | Percent time being processed | 39.01% | 47.99% | 49.92% | 49.98% | | | | | | |

The bottom section of Figure 14.36 indicates the *saturation* effect of adding more buffers. The company gets a lot from its money from the first few buffers, but after the first few, blocking becomes a minor problem and more buffers fail to make much of an improvement. If buffers entail significant costs, Streamlining must trade off these costs against lower average throughput times and possibly other considerations. ∎

## ADDITIONAL APPLICATIONS

### Improving Car Body Production at PSA Peugeot Citroen

In 1998, the new CEO of PSA Peugeot Citroen, the French carmaker, decided to set ambitious targets for growth, innovation, and profitability. To meet these targets, PSA decided to focus on the car-body shops, the bottlenecks at its plants. An R&D team conducted a management science study of car-body production, using a number of analytic tools, including a simulation model of series-parallel systems. They used this simulation to analyze a number of different configurations of manufacturing stations and buffers in the manufacturing line, and they were able to persuade PSA to implement the best of these configurations. They estimate that their study contributed $130 million to the bottom line in 2001 alone, with minimal capital investment and no compromise in quality. ∎

# PROBLEMS

## Skill-Building Problems

**41.** The Smalltown Credit Union experiences its greatest congestion on paydays from 11:30 A.M. until 1:00 P.M. During these rush periods, customers arrive according to a Poisson process at rate 2.1 per minute. The credit union employs 10 tellers for these rush periods, and each takes 4.7 minutes to service a customer. Customers who arrive to the credit union wait in a single queue, if necessary, unless 15 customers are already in the queue. In this latter case, arriving customers are too impatient to wait, and they leave the system. Simulate this system to find the average wait in queue for the customers who enter, the average number in queue, the percentage of time a typical teller is busy, and the percentage of arrivals who do not enter the system. Try this simulation under the following conditions and comment on your results. For each condition, make five separate runs, using a different random number seed on each run.

  **a.** Try a warm-up time of 2 hours. Then try no warm-up time. Use exponentially distributed service times for each.

  **b.** Try exponentially distributed service times. Then try gamma-distributed service times, where the standard deviation of a service time is 2.4 minutes. Use a warm-up period of 1 hour for each.

  **c.** Try 10 tellers, as in the statement of the problem. Then try 11, then 12. Use exponentially distributed service times and a warm-up period of 1 hour for each.

  **d.** Why might the use of a long warm-up time bias the results toward *worse* system behavior than would actually be experienced? If you could ask the programmer of the simulation to provide another option concerning the warm-up period, what would it be? (*Hint:* The real rush doesn't begin until 11:30.)

**42.** How long does it take to reach steady state? Use simulation, with the **Multiserver Simulation.xlsm** file, to experiment with the effect of warm-up time and runtime on the key outputs. For each of the following, assume a five-server system with a Poisson arrival rate of 1 per minute and gamma-distributed service times with mean 4.0 minutes and standard deviation 3.1 minutes. For each part, make five separate runs, using a different random number seed on each run.

  **a.** Use a warm-up time of 0 and a runtime of 30 minutes.

  **b.** Use a warm-up time of 0 and a runtime of 180 minutes.

  **c.** Use a warm-up time of 120 minutes and a runtime of 30 minutes.

  **d.** Use a warm-up time of 120 minutes and a runtime of 180 minutes.

  **e.** Repeat parts **a** to **d** when the mean and standard deviation of service times are 4.8 and 4.2 minutes, respectively. (This should produce considerably more congestion.)

**43.** Given the model in the **Multiserver Simulation.xlsm** file, what unit cost parameters should be used if we are interested in "optimizing" the system? Choose representative inputs and unit costs, and then illustrate how to use the simulation outputs to estimate total system costs.

**44.** Simulate the system in Problem 10. Make any assumptions about the warm-up time and runtime you believe are appropriate. Try solving the problem with exponentially distributed copying times. Then try it with gamma-distributed copying times, where the standard deviation is 3.2 minutes. Do you get the same recommendation on which machine to purchase?

**45.** In Example 14.4 of Section 14.5, we examined whether an $M/M/1$ system with a single fast server is better or worse than an $M/M/s$ system with several slow servers. Keeping the same inputs as in the example, use simulation to see whether you obtain the same type of results as with the analytical models. Then repeat, using gamma-distributed service times with standard deviation 6 minutes.

**46.** A telephone-order sales company must determine how many telephone operators are needed to staff the phones during the 9-to-5 shift. It is estimated that an average of 480 calls are received during this time period and that the average call lasts for 6 minutes. There is no "queueing." If a customer calls and all operators are busy, this customer receives a busy signal and must hang up. If the company wants to have at most 1 chance in 100 of a caller receiving a busy signal, how many operators should be hired for the 9-to-5 shift? Base your answer on an appropriate simulation. Does it matter whether the service times are exponentially distributed or gamma distributed? Experiment to find out.

**47.** US Airlines receives an average of 500 calls per hour from customers who want to make reservations, where the times between calls follow an exponential distribution. It takes an average of 3 minutes to handle each call. Each customer who buys a ticket contributes $100 to US Airlines profit. It costs $15 per hour to staff a telephone line. Any customer who receives a busy signal will purchase a ticket from another airline. How many telephone lines should US Airlines have? Base your answer on an appropriate simulation. Does it matter whether the service times are exponentially distributed or gamma distributed? Experiment to find out.

## Skill-Extending Problems

48. Consider a series system of the type in the **Series Simulation.xlsm** file. There are two stations. Each station has three machines, and the mean processing time for each machine is 3.1 minutes. Parts arrive to station 1 at a Poisson rate of 0.8 per minute. The processing times at one station are constant; at the other, they are exponentially distributed. Where would you rather have the constant processing times—at station 1 or station 2? Does the answer depend on the number of buffers in front of station 2? Experiment to find out.

49. A company's warehouse can store up to four units of a good. Each month, an average of 10 orders for the good are received. The times between the receipts of successive orders are exponentially distributed. When an item is used to fill an order, a replacement item is immediately ordered, and it takes an average of one month for a replacement item to arrive. If no items are on hand when an order is received, the order is lost. Use simulation to estimate the fraction of all orders that will be lost due to shortage. (*Hint:* Let the storage space for each item be a "server" and think about what it means for a server to be busy. Then decide on an appropriate definition of "service time".)

## 14.8 CONCLUSION

We have seen that there are two basic approaches for analyzing queueing systems. The first is the analytical approach, where we attempt to find formulas (or possibly algorithms, implemented with macros) to calculate steady-state performance measures of the system. The second is the simulation approach, where we simulate the random elements of the system and then keep track of the events as they occur through time. The advantage of the analytical approach is that, at least for the simplest models, it provides summary measures such as $L_Q$ and $W_Q$ that are relatively simple to interpret. Also, by using template files for these systems, we can easily vary the inputs to see how the outputs change. The main disadvantage of the analytical approach is that the mathematics becomes extremely complex unless we are willing to make simplifying assumptions, some of which can be unrealistic. For example, we must typically assume that service times are exponentially distributed, an unrealistic assumption in many real applications. Also, we must typically assume that the arrival rate remains constant through time and that we are concerned only with steady state (unless we use the approximate approach in Section 14.6).

The simulation approach provides much more flexibility. Also, simulation lets us "see" how the system behaves and how queues can build up through time. The disadvantage of queueing simulation is that it is not well suited to spreadsheets. You have two basic choices: buy (and learn) specialized queueing software packages or write your own queueing simulation in procedural languages such as VBA. Neither possibility is very attractive. However, the two general queueing simulation models we have provided in the **Multiserver Simulation.xlsm** and the **Series Simulation.xlsm** files allow you to experiment with many system configurations to see how inputs and inherent randomness affect system outputs. The insights gained can be extremely valuable.

# Summary of Key Management Science Terms

| Term | Explanation | Page |
|------|-------------|------|
| Analytical queueing models | Models where outputs such as expected waiting time in queue can be calculated directly from inputs such as arrival rate and service rate | 795 |
| Queueing simulation model | Models where the events in a queueing process are "played out" through time, using simulated random numbers and careful bookkeeping | 795 |
| Interarrival times | Times between successive arrivals | 796 |
| Parallel system | Queueing system, such as at a bank, where each customer must be served by exactly one of (usually equivalent) servers | 797 |
| Steady-state analysis | Analysis of the long run, where the effects of initial conditions have been washed out | 799 |
| Stable system | A system where the queue doesn't grow infinitely large in the long run | 799 |
| Exponential distribution, memoryless property | A popular distribution for queueing systems, characterized by the memoryless property where the future, given the current state, is independent of the past | 799 |
| Poisson process model | Series of events, such as customer arrivals, where times between events are exponentially distributed | 803 |
| Time averages | Averages, such as average queue length, taken over time | 805 |
| Customer averages | Averages, such as average waiting time, taken over customers | 805 |
| Little's formula | Important formula that relates time averages to customer averages | 805 |
| Server utilization | Average fraction of time a typical server is busy | 806 |
| $M/M/1$ and $M/M/s$ models | Simplest and most common analytical queueing models, where interarrival times and service times are exponentially distributed, and there is either a single server or multiple servers in parallel | 807 |
| Traffic intensity | A measure of congestion; typically, the arrival rate divided by the maximum service rate | 808 |
| Limited waiting room models | Models where customers are turned away if the number of customers in the system is already at some maximum level | 818 |
| Limited source models | Models where a finite number of customers are in the population, so that the arrival rate depends on how many of them are currently in service | 819 |
| Erlang loss model | Model where no customer arrivals are allowed when all servers are busy | 819 |
| $G/G/s$ model | General multiserver model, where interarrival times and service times are allowed to have *any* probability distributions | 822 |
| Squared coefficient of variation | Measure of variability: squared ratio of standard deviation to mean | 823 |

| Term | Explanation | | Page |
|------|-------------|--|------|
| Transient distribution | Short-run distribution of the state of the system, particularly useful when parameters of the system change through time | | 830 |

## Summary of Key Excel Terms

| Term | Explanation | Excel | Page |
|------|-------------|-------|------|
| Queueing templates | Ready-made spreadsheet files that implement complex queueing models, often with behind-the-scenes macros | See the **MM1 Template.xlsx** file, for example | 809, 812, etc. |

# PROBLEMS

## Skill-Building Problems

50. Referring to the multistation serial system in the **Series Simulation.xlsm** file, let $s_i$ and $1/\mu_i$ be the number of machines and the mean processing time at station $i$. Then the mean processing rate at station $i$ is $s_i\mu_i$. We might expect the system to operate well only if each $s_i\mu_i$ is greater than $\lambda$, the arrival rate to station 1. This problem asks you to experiment with the simulation to gain some insights into congestion. For each of the following parts, assume a Poisson arrival rate of $\lambda = 1$ per minute, and assume that processing times are exponentially distributed. Each part should be answered independently. For each, you should discuss the most important outputs from your simulation.
    a. Each station has $s_i = 1$ and the $\mu_i$'s are constant from station to station. There are 100 (essentially unlimited) buffers in front of all stations after station 1. Each processing time has mean $1/\mu_i = 0.6$ minute and there are three stations.
    b. Same as part **a**, except that there are 10 stations.
    c. Same as part **a**, except that each processing time has mean 0.9 minute.
    d. Same as part **c**, except that there are 10 stations.
    e. Repeat parts **a** to **d** but now assume there are only two buffers in front of each station.

51. Repeat the previous problem, but now assume that $s_i = 3$ at each station. Change the $\mu_i$'s so that the *products* $s_i\mu_i$ are the same as in the previous problem.

52. Continuing Problem 50, we might expect that the system will be only as good as the station with the smallest value of $s_i\mu_i$ (called the **bottleneck** station). This problem asks you to experiment with the simulation to gain some insights into bottlenecks. For each of the following parts, assume a Poisson arrival rate of $\lambda = 1$ per minute, and assume that processing times are exponentially distributed. Each station has $s_i = 1$ and

there are five stations. Each station, except for the bottleneck station, has a processing time mean of $1/\mu_i = 0.6$ minute. The bottleneck station has mean 0.9 minute. Each part should be answered independently. For each, you should discuss the most important outputs from your simulation.
    a. Suppose there are 100 (essentially unlimited) buffers in front of all stations after station 1. Run the simulation when station 1 is the bottleneck. Repeat when it is station 2; station 3; station 4; station 5.
    b. Repeat part **a** when there are only two buffers in front of each station after station 1.
    c. Suppose station 3 is the bottleneck station and you have 4 buffers to allocate to the whole system. Experiment to see where they should be placed.

53. On average, 50 customers arrive per hour at a small post office. Interarrival times are exponentially distributed. Each window can serve an average of 25 customers per hour. Service times are exponentially distributed. It costs $25 per hour to open a window, and the post office values the time a customer spends waiting in line at $15 per customer hour. To minimize expected hourly costs, how many postal windows should be opened?

54. On average, 300 customers arrive per hour at a huge branch of Bank 2. It takes an average of 2 minutes to serve each customer. It costs $10 per hour to keep a teller window open, and the bank estimates that it will lose $50 in future profits for each hour that a customer waits in line. How many teller windows should Bank 2 open?

55. Ships arrive at a port facility at an average rate of two ships every three days. On average, it takes a single crew one day to unload a ship. Assume that interarrival and service times are exponential. The shipping company owns the port facility as well as the ships using that

facility. The company estimates that it costs $1000 per day for each day that a ship spends in port. The crew servicing the ships consists of 100 workers, each of whom is paid an average of $30 per day. A consultant has recommended that the shipping company hire an additional 40 workers and split the employees into two equal-size crews of 70 each. This would give each crew an average unloading or loading time of 1.5 days. Which crew arrangement would you recommend to the company?

**56.** On average, 40 jobs arrive per day at a factory. The time between arrivals of jobs is exponentially distributed. The factory can process an average of 42 jobs per day, and the time to process a job is exponentially distributed.

   **a.** On average, how long does it take before a job is completed (measured from the time the job arrives at the factory)?
   **b.** What fraction of the time is the factory idle?
   **c.** What is the probability that work on a job will begin within two days of its arrival at the factory?

**57.** A printing shop receives an average of one order per day. The average length of time required to complete an order is half a day. At any given time, the print shop can work on at most one job. Interarrival times and service times are exponentially distributed.

   **a.** On average, how many jobs are present in the print shop?
   **b.** On average, how long will a person who places an order have to wait until it is finished?
   **c.** What is the probability that an order will begin work within two days of its arrival?

**58.** At the Franklin Post Office, patrons wait in a single line for the first open window. On average, 100 patrons enter the post office per hour, and each window can serve an average of 45 patrons per hour. The post office estimates a cost of $0.10 for each minute a patron waits in line and believes that it costs $20 per hour to keep a window open. Interarrival times and service times are exponential.

   **a.** To minimize the total expected hourly cost, how many windows should be open?
   **b.** If the post office's goal is to ensure that at most 5% of all patrons will spend more than 5 minutes in line, how many windows should be open?

**59.** The manager of a large group of employees must decide whether she needs another photocopying machine. The cost of a machine is $40 per 8-hour day regardless of whether the machine is in use. On average, four people need to use the copying machine per hour. Each person uses the copier for an average of 10 minutes. Interarrival times and copying times are exponentially distributed. Employees are paid $8 per hour, and we assume that a waiting cost is incurred when a worker is waiting in line or is using the copying machine. How many copying machines should be rented?

**60.** The Newcoat Painting Company has for some time been experiencing high demand for its automobile repainting service. Because it has had to turn away business, management is concerned that the limited space available to store cars awaiting painting has cost them in lost revenue. A small vacant lot next to the painting facility has recently been made available for rental on a long-term basis at a cost of $10 per day. Management believes that each lost customer costs $20 in profit. Current demand is estimated to be 21 cars per day with exponential interarrival times (including those turned away), and the facility can service at an exponential rate of 24 cars per day. Cars are processed on a FCFS basis. Waiting space is now limited to 9 cars but can be increased to 20 cars with the lease of the vacant lot. Newcoat wants to determine whether the vacant lot should be leased. Management also wants to know the expected daily lost profit due to turning away customers if the lot is leased. Only one car can be painted at a time. Try using the **Limited Queue Template.xlsm** file for an analytical solution and the **Multiserver Simulation.xlsm** file for a simulation solution.

**61.** On average, 90 patrons arrive per hour at a hotel lobby (interarrival times are exponential) waiting to check in. At present there are five clerks, and patrons wait in a single line for the first available clerk. The average time for a clerk to service a patron is 3 minutes (exponentially distributed). Clerks earn $10 per hour, and the hotel assesses a waiting time cost of $20 for each hour that a patron waits in line.

   **a.** Compute the expected cost per hour of the current system.
   **b.** The hotel is considering replacing one clerk with an Automatic Clerk Machine (ACM). Management estimates that 20% of all patrons will use an ACM. An ACM takes an average of 1 minute to service a patron. It costs $48 per day (1 day equals 8 hours) to operate an ACM. Should the hotel install the ACM? Assume that all customers who are willing to use the ACM wait in a separate queue.

## Skill-Extending Problem

**62.** The mail order firm of L. L. Pea receives an average of 200 calls per hour, where times between calls are exponentially distributed. It takes an L. L. Pea operator an average of 3 minutes to handle a call. If a caller gets a busy signal, L. L. Pea assumes that he or she will call a competing mail-order company, and L. L. Pea will lose an average of $30 in profit. The cost of keeping a phone line open is $9 per hour. How many operators should L. L. Pea have on duty? Use simulation to answer this question. Does the answer depend on whether the service times are exponentially distributed?

## Modeling Problems

**63.** Bloomington Hospital knows that insurance companies are going to reduce the average length of stay of many types of patients. How can queueing models be used to determine how changes in insurance policies will influence the hospital?

**64.** Excessive delays have recently been noted on New York City's 911 system. Discuss how you would use queueing models to improve the performance of the 911 system.

**65.** Suppose that annually an average of $\lambda$ library patrons want to borrow a book. A patron borrows the book for an average of $1/\mu$ years. Suppose we observe that the book is actually borrowed an average of $R$ times per year. Explain how we can estimate $\lambda$, which is an unobservable quantity. (*Hint:* Let $U$ be the expected number of times per year a patron wants to borrow the book and the book is out. Note that $\lambda = R + U$.)

**66.** Based on Quinn et al. (1991). Winter Riggers handles approximately \$400 million in telephone orders per year. Winter Riggers' system works as follows. Callers are connected to an agent if one is available. Otherwise, they are put on hold (if a "trunk" line is available). A customer can hang up at any time and leave the system. Winter Riggers would like to efficiently manage the telephone system (lines and agents) used to process these orders. Of course, orders are very seasonal and depend on the time of day.
  **a.** What decisions must Winter Riggers make?
  **b.** What would be an appropriate objective for Winter Riggers to minimize (or maximize)? What difficulties do you see in specifying the objective?
  **c.** What data would Winter Riggers need to keep track of to improve its efficiency?

**67.** Zerox has 16 service centers throughout the United States. Zerox is trying to determine how many technicians it should assign to each service center. How would you approach this problem?

**68.** Based on Kolesar et al. (1974). Metropolis PD Precinct 88 must determine the minimum number of police cars required to meet its needs for the next 24 hours. An average call for service requires 30 minutes. The number of calls the police department expects to receive during each hour is shown in the file **P14_68.xlsx**. The Metropolis PD standard of service is that there should be a 90% chance that a car is available to respond to a call. For each of the following, discuss how you might find a solution.
  **a.** Suppose that patrol officer teams assigned to a car work an 8-hour shift beginning at 12 A.M., 8 A.M., or 4 P.M. Officers get an hour off for a meal. This hour can be anytime between the second and fifth hour of their shift. The precinct wants to know how many teams are needed to meet daily demand.
  **b.** Suppose that patrol officer teams assigned to a car begin their 8-hour shifts at 12 A.M., 8 A.M., 12 P.M., 4 P.M., and 8 P.M. An hour off for meals may be taken anytime during a shift. The precinct again wants to know how many teams are needed to meet daily demand.

The Catalog Company is a mail- and phone-order company that sells generic brands of houseware items and clothing. Approximately 95% of customer orders are received by phone; the remaining 5% are received in the mail. Phone orders are accepted at Catalog Company's toll-free 800 number, 800-SAVE-NOW. The number is available 9 hours per day (8 A.M. to 5 P.M.), 5 days a week.

Sarah Walters, a recent graduate of Columbia Business School, has just been hired by Catalog to improve its operations. Sarah would like to impress her boss, Ben Gleason, the president of Catalog Company, with some ideas that would quickly improve the company's bottom line. After spending a week learning about Catalog's operations, Sarah feels that a substantial impact can be made by a closer evaluation of the phone order system.

Currently, Catalog employs a single full-time operator to take orders over the phone. Sarah wonders whether additional operators should be hired to take phone orders. Ben feels that Sarah's time might be better spent studying the catalog mailing lists. Ben reasons that the mailing lists are where customers are generated, and improving the list will bring in more revenue. And besides, Ben says, "Catalog's phone operator, Betty Wrangle, seems to be doing nothing more than half of the time that I walk by. Hiring more operators to do nothing will just waste more money." Although Sarah knows the mailing lists are important, she thinks that a study of the mailing lists will take far more time than a quick evaluation of the phone order system.

Forging ahead, Sarah discovers the following information about the phone order system. The phone operator, Betty Wrangle, is paid $9 per hour in wages and benefits. The average cost to Catalog for a completed 800 number call is $1.50. With only one phone line, any incoming calls that arrive when Betty is on the phone to another customer get a busy signal. The cost of the phone line is $40 per month. The phone company can immediately add up to four additional phone lines using the same 800 number, each at a cost of $40 per month per line. Catalog's phone system is such that it cannot be upgraded in the near future to allow incoming calls to be placed on hold. The average profit on an order (not including the cost of the operator or phone call) is 40% of the amount of the order. For example, an order of $100 brings a profit of $40 to Catalog.

Sarah decided that additional information needed to be collected about the frequency of incoming calls, the length of the calls, and so on. After talking to the phone company, Sarah learned that she could borrow equipment for one day that could detect when a call was coming in, even when Betty was on the phone. The caller would still get a busy signal and be lost, but Sarah would know that a call had been attempted. Sarah collected almost nine hours of data the next day; these data are presented in the file **Catalog Orders.xlsx**. Sarah believes that most of the callers who receive a busy signal take their business elsewhere and are totally lost to Catalog. Sarah does not feel that extending the hours of operation of the 800 number would be beneficial because the hours of operation are printed prominently in all of the catalogs.

The first call arrives 0.036 hour into the day. It takes Betty 0.054 hour to process the call and record the order for $65.21 worth of merchandise. Callers 5 and 6 get busy signals when they call, because Betty was still processing caller 4. Because calls 5 and 6 were lost, no call length information was available and no orders were placed. Data collection was stopped at call number 80.

## Questions
Use the complete information in the file **Catalog Orders.xlsx** to answer the following questions:

1. Approximately what fraction of the time is Betty idle? Is Ben's estimate correct?

2. Approximately how many calls are lost in an average hour due to a busy signal?

3. Use the data to estimate the average arrival rate of all attempted calls to Catalog. Give an approximate 95% confidence interval for the estimate. Plot a frequency histogram of interarrival times. Does the distribution of interarrival times appear to be exponential?

**4.** Use the data to estimate the average service rate of all completed calls. Give an approximate 95% confidence interval for the estimate. Plot a frequency histogram of service times. Does the service time distribution appear to be exponential? Give an approximate 95% confidence interval for the average revenue per call.

**5.** Would you recommend that Catalog acquire additional phone lines and operators? If so, how many? If not, why not? Justify your answer in enough detail so that Ben Gleason would be convinced of your recommendation. ∎

# CASE 14.2 PACIFIC NATIONAL BANK[10]

Pacific National Bank is a medium-size bank with 21 branches in the San Francisco Bay Area. Until very recently, Pacific did not operate its own ATMs; instead, it relied on an outside vendor to operate them. Ninety percent of the ATM customers obtained cash advances with non-Pacific credit cards, so the ATMs did little to directly improve Pacific's own banking business. Operations Vice President Nancy Meisterhaus wants to change that, by having Pacific offer a broader mix of banking services with its own machines tied into its own data-processing network.

The industry consensus is that the ATM appeals to customers in much the same way as the supermarket express line: It minimizes the amount of waiting. But for Pacific, the 24-hour ATM would also have the broader appeal of providing essential banking services at all hours, reaching a segment of the market not currently served. Historically, customers who find standard banking hours inconvenient have been lost to Pacific, so the ATM will increase the bank's market share.

Besides attracting more customers and servicing existing customers better, the ATM operation should offer substantial cost advantages. Fewer human tellers would be required for the same volume of transactions as before. The per transaction cost of the machine, which does need some human attention for restocking and maintenance, should be substantially less. But even if that were not so, its 24-hour readiness would be extremely expensive to duplicate with human tellers, who would have to be given extra protection for dangerous late-night work.

Ms. Meisterhaus selected the Walnut Creek office as the test branch for a captive ATM. Customers from that branch were recruited to sign up for a Pacific ATM card. All residents within the neighboring ZIP codes were offered an incentive to open free checking accounts at Pacific when they also signed up for the card. After a critical mass of ATM card holders was established—but before the banking ATM was installed—statistics were kept. The arrival times in Table 14.5 were determined for various times of the week.

## Table 14.5 Customer Arrivals at the Walnut Creek Office—Before ATM Installation

| Period | Daily Average Number of Arrivals |
|---|---|
| (1) Monday–Friday 10 A.M.–12 P.M. | 155 |
| (2) Monday–Friday 12–1 P.M. | 242 |
| (3) Monday–Friday 1–3 P.M. | 290 |
| (4) Friday 3–6 P.M. | 554 |

The bank opens at 10 A.M. and closes at 3 P.M., except on Friday, when it closes at 6 P.M. Past study shows that, over each period, customers arrive randomly at a stable mean rate, so the assumption of a Poisson process is valid. The mean time required to complete customer transactions is 2 minutes, and the individual service times have a frequency distribution with a pronounced positive skew, so an exponential distribution is a reasonable approximation to reality.

Tellers all work part-time and cost $10 per bank hour. Pacific's experience has established that there will be a significant drop-off in clientele soon after a bout during which customers suffer lengthy delays in getting teller access. The supplier of the ATM equipment claims that other banks of comparable size have experienced a 30% diversion of regular business away from human tellers to the ATM, which produced a further 20% expansion beyond the previous level of overall client transactions—all absorbed by the ATM, half of it outside regular banking hours. The supplier also maintains that ATM traffic is fairly uniform, except between 11 P.M. and 6 A.M., when it is negligible. Ms. Meisterhaus believes that the ATM busy-period arrivals will constitute a single Poisson process.

Industry experience is that the mean service time at an ATM is one-half minute, with an exponential distribution serving as an adequate approximation to the unknown positively skewed unimodal distribution that actually applies. Ms. Meisterhaus believes that, once the ATM is installed, the Walnut Creek human tellers will be left with a greater proportion of the more involved and

---

[10] This case was written by Lawrence L. Lapin, San Jose State University.

lengthy transactions, raising their mean service time to 2.5 minutes.

Ms. Meisterhaus knows that much of the evaluation of the ATM operations will be a queueing exercise. Her knowledge of this subject is a bit rusty, so she has retained you to assist her.

## Questions

1.  Assume that Pacific National Bank remains with human tellers only.
    a. For each time period in Table 14.5, determine the minimum number of tellers needed on station to service the customer stream.
    b. Assume that the number of tellers found in part **a** is used. For each time period, determine the mean customer waiting time.
    c. For each time period, determine the mean customer waiting time when the number of tellers is one more than found in part **a**.

2.  Past experience shows that the drop-off in clientele due to waiting translates into an expected NPV in lost future profits of $0.10 per minute. For each time period in Table 14.5, determine the average hourly queueing system cost (server cost + waiting cost), assuming that the bank uses the following service arrangement:
    a. The minimum number of human tellers necessary to service the arriving customers
    b. One teller more than was found in part **a** of Question 1

3.  Suppose that the ATM is installed and that customers themselves decide whether to use human tellers or to use the ATM, and that two queues form independently for each. Finally, assume that a 10% traffic increase is generated

by the ATM within each open time period and that all of it is for the ATM.
    a. For each period in Table 14.5, determine the mean arrival rate at the human teller windows.
    b. Do the same with regard to the mean arrival rate at the ATM.
    c. Find the minimum number of human tellers required to be on station during each time period.

4.  Assume that the number of human tellers used is one more than that found in part **c** of Question 3. Determine for Ms. Meisterhaus the mean customer waiting time during each open period in Table 14.5 for those customers who seek the following:
    a. Human tellers
    b. Access to the ATM

5.  The hourly cost of maintaining and operating the ATM is $5. Increased customer traffic results in additional bank profit estimated to be $0.20 per transaction. Determine for Ms. Meisterhaus the net hourly queueing system cost, reflecting any profit increase, for operating with the ATM for each of the four periods identified in Table 14.5. Use the mean waiting times from Question 4.

6.  Consider the complete 24-hour, 7-day picture. Incorporate whatever information you need from Questions 1 through 5 and your solutions, plus any additional information in the case and any necessary assumptions, to compare the net cost of operation with and without the ATM. Then give your overall recommendation to Ms. Meisterhaus. ∎

# Project Management

© CORBIS

## SCHEDULING THE NEW-PRODUCT DEVELOPMENT PROCESS AT DOW AGROSCIENCES

Dow AgroSciences, a wholly owned subsidiary of The Dow Chemical Company, is in the business of developing new agricultural products. It subjects product candidates to tests covering safety, efficacy, and environmental impact as well as other tests to validate the biology and confirm that the products will do well in the business market. To beat the competition to market, the company is under pressure to do its testing and use its resources as efficiently as possible. The development schedule is the key. At any time, around 30 products can be going through testing, each of which consists of tens to hundreds of tasks that must be performed. The scheduling of these tasks must take the following data into account: (1) the net present value (NPV) of the cash flows each candidate is expected to generate, depending on its launch date, (2) the costs of tasks in the development process, (3) the technical precedence relationships for tasks, (4) the durations of the tasks, (5) the probability that the candidate will fail a task, resulting in the cancellation of the development process for that candidate, (6) resource requirements and capacities, and others. Many of the required inputs are uncertain, so that probability distributions are needed to model them correctly.

Bassett et al. (2004) describe a simulation-based optimization model they developed to help generate good schedules in this complex environment.

Unlike the rather simple project scheduling examples described in this chapter, the situation at Dow AgroSciences is much larger and considerably more complex. First, there are several projects in process at a given time, not a single project, and they are all competing for scarce resources such as line-item budgets. Second, some tasks can fail for some projects, in which case, these projects do not continue in the development process and therefore free up resources for other projects. Third, precedence relationships are only partly fixed. There are often fixed precedence relationships of the type discussed in this chapter, where, for example, task C cannot start until tasks A and B are finished. However, other precedence relationships can be introduced for strategic reasons. For example, suppose tasks E and F can begin at the same time, but there is a probability that task E will fail. Then it might be better to allow task F to start only when task E is successfully completed. The reason is that if task E fails, the cost of performing task F will be saved. Also, the schedule can impose precedence relationships across projects to reduce the simultaneous use of scarce resources. Finally, due to the seasonal nature of agricultural products, a delay of 1 month that causes a product to miss the growing season might be just as costly as a delay of 10 months.

The authors first tried to formulate their problem as an integer programming (IP) model, as has often been done in the project scheduling literature. However, they found that the size and complexity of the problem made the resulting IP model too difficult to solve in a reasonable amount of time. Therefore, they turned to simulation and heuristic methods for optimizing, using precedence relationships as decision variables. For any proposed solution, that is, any set of precedence relationships within and across projects, they simulate the development of these projects over a multiyear period. The simulation output contains the value of the objective they want to maximize, expected NPV. They then experiment with several heuristic methods, including the genetic algorithms discussed in Chapter 8, to find solutions with larger values of the objective. Of course, each new solution must be simulated to find *its* value of the objective. There is no guarantee that this methodology will find an optimal solution, but it appears to produce very good solutions in an acceptable amount of computing time.

The authors implemented their solution method in a system with an Excel-based user-friendly front end. In the background, the system uses a simulation package, AweSim, plus the authors' own C++ computer code, to implement the simulation and heuristic algorithms. Dow AgroSciences has put this system into practice via their Six Sigma project in Research and Development. From 1998 to 2004, the company has verified savings of several million dollars based on the schedules determined by the system. As Beth Swisher, Manager of R&D Effectiveness at Dow AgroSciences, states, "I feel comfortable stating that more than one million dollars have been saved due to our possession of the technology. In addition to these 'hard' savings, the improved understanding of the overall new-product development process across all the functions in the company has been invaluable." ∎

# 15.1 INTRODUCTION

All organizations have ongoing activities, and they have projects. The distinction is that a *project* has a beginning, an end, and one or more well-defined goals. The project could be the development of a software program, the building of a house or an office building, the development of a new drug, a marketing campaign for a new product, and many others. Typically, a team of employees is assigned to a project, and one member of the team is designated as the project manager. The team is assigned to complete the project within a certain time, within a certain budget, and within certain specifications. At some point in the future, the team will complete the project (or deem it a failure), and the project's life cycle will be finished. The purpose of this chapter is to discuss ways to manage projects successfully. This is an extremely important topic for real organizations. There can be serious consequences when a project is not finished on time, runs over budget, or fails to meet specifications.

As an academic discipline, project management is discussed in management, operations management, and management science. The discussion in management tends to focus on the "soft" skills necessary to manage projects successfully. The project manager must be an effective leader, and team members must communicate successfully, agree on goals, cooperate, report progress clearly, and so on. Although the importance of these people skills is clear, it is not the focus of this chapter.

*CPM usually implies known activity times, and PERT usually implies uncertain activity times.*

Management science (and operations management) tends to focus on the quantitative tools that have been developed to manage projects. These go under the twin acronyms of PERT (Program Evaluation and Review Technique) and CPM (Critical Path Method). These methods were developed independently about a half-century ago. PERT was developed jointly by the U.S. Navy, Lockheed, and the consulting firm of Booz, Allen, and Hamilton in their work on the Polaris nuclear missile. CPM was developed at DuPont and Remington-Rand to improve the construction of new production facilities and the shutdown of existing facilities. The main difference between PERT and CPM is that CPM was developed for projects with a set of commonly performed tasks, where the task times are fairly well known. In contrast, PERT was developed for projects with tasks where scientists had little experience and could not estimate their times with much certainty. In short, the CPM model did not include uncertainty in task times, but the PERT model did.

Over the years, the two methods have tended to merge, so that people now often speak of PERT/CPM models. In either case, the emphasis is on a project that starts at some point and ends some time later. The project consists of a number of tasks that must be completed for the project to be completed. These tasks have durations (the time it takes to complete them, assumed known for CPM, random for PERT), they typically cost money, and they often require nonfinancial resources such as people and facilities. They also have precedence relationships. For example, task G might not be able to start until tasks B, D, and F are finished. These precedence relationships put constraints on what can be done when. In addition, limited resources can place constraints on the tasks that can be done simultaneously. A well-established methodology has been developed to analyze such projects. It involves various charts and some reasonably simple calculations. We explain how it works in this chapter. As we will see, most of it can be accomplished in Excel. However, you might be aware that there is another package in the Microsoft Office family called Microsoft Project.[1] This powerful package is devoted exclusively to managing projects. Of course, power usually implies complexity, and Project is very complex. We include an educational version of Project with the book, and we discuss it briefly at the end of the chapter. However,

---

[1] We tend to think of Microsoft Office as including Excel, Word, Access, PowerPoint, and Outlook, which make up the package you get when you purchase Office. However, Microsoft includes other packages, such as Project, when it discusses its "Office family." Unfortunately, you have to purchase these other packages separately.

a thorough discussion of the Project software is well beyond the scope of this book. We are content to do most of the calculations in Excel.

*The focus of most PERT/CPM discussions is time, but resource usage (money, people, facilities, and so on) is also very important.*

Projects have three dimensions: time, resources, and scope.[2] The usual discussion of PERT/CPM focuses primarily on the *time* dimension. How long will the project take to complete if everything goes according to schedule, which tasks form bottlenecks that prevent the project from being completed earlier, and which tasks have some slack, in the sense that they can be delayed to some extent without delaying the project? These questions are the usual focus of PERT/CPM models, and we too focus primarily on the time dimension. However, we also discuss the *resource* dimension. The tasks in a project almost always compete for resources, whether dollars or nonfinancial resources, and no real project management application can afford to ignore these resources. For example, one version of the problem we analyze is the *crashing* problem. In this problem, we decide how to spend money optimally to speed up (crash) the completion of the project. For example, if we find that the project will not be completed until 16 weeks from now, but we have a deadline of 14 weeks from now, we need to find a way to crash critical tasks to save a couple of weeks.

The third dimension, *scope,* is the most difficult to model quantitatively. Scope involves the deliverable itself—what it is intended to do and what features it should include. For example, if the purpose of the project is to deliver a new version of Excel, the software developers at Microsoft have to control scope. It is all too easy to keep adding features, refining existing features, and generally adding to the scope. (This is undoubtedly why Microsoft's software products often come out later than originally advertised. And Microsoft is certainly not alone!) If the project manager doesn't keep a constant eye on *scope creep,* the project can easily run over budget and/or fail to meet its deadline. Unfortunately, scope is not easy to model, so we do not discuss it any further here.

This chapter provides an introduction to project management. In particular, it discusses the basic deterministic CPM model, where task times are assumed to be known, and it uses simulation to analyze a version of the PERT model, where task times are assumed to be random. However, the opener to this chapter indicates how complex project management can be in the real world. A company such as Dow AgroSciences often needs to juggle *many* projects simultaneously, the timing of eventual revenues needs to be considered, possible failures in testing at some stage along the way can terminate projects and result in lost costs, extra precedence relationships can be introduced to manage costs and other resources, and so on. The problems can quickly become complex, which is all the more reason to employ management science techniques to solve them, as companies such as Dow AgroSciences have learned to their benefit.

Before continuing, we note that many entire books are devoted to project management, and the material we include here is typically found in two or three chapters of such books. This material is certainly an important aspect of project management, but it is not the only aspect. Other aspects include selecting the project in the first place, setting goals and specifications for the project, properly managing people involved in the project (including adequate communication), monitoring the progress of the project (and making changes to the original plan when necessary), knowing when to "pull the plug" on a project that is not making adequate progress, and others. All of these aspects are important for determining whether a real-world project is successful or not, and the failure to manage them properly is the reason why so many projects have been unsuccessful. [One notable failure occurred in the 1990s, when Health Care Financing Administration, the agency that administers Medicare, spent at least $50 million developing a Medicare Transactions system that never became a reality. This failure of this project is described in Friel (2000).] If you are interested in learning more about project management, we recommend the following books: Klastorin (2004), Marchewka (2006), and Gido & Clements (2006).

---

[2] Some people add a fourth dimension, *quality*. However, quality can be encompassed within scope.

## 15.2 THE BASIC CPM MODEL

In this section, we describe the basic CPM procedure for finding the length of time required to complete a project. This approach assumes that we know (1) the activities that comprise the project, (2) the precedence relationships among activities, and (3) the time required to complete each activity.[3] This time, called the activity **duration**, is assumed to be known with certainty. However, even when we relax this assumption in a later section and assume there is a probability distribution for each activity duration, the same basic procedure explained here can still be used as part of a simulation model.

To proceed, we need a list of the activities that comprise the project. The project is complete when all of the activities have been completed. Each activity has a set of activities called its **immediate predecessors** that must be completed before the activity begins. It also has a set of activities called its **immediate successors** that cannot start until it has finished. (The word *immediate* is sometimes omitted.) A project network diagram is usually used to represent the precedence relationships among activities. Two types of diagrams do this, activity-on-node (AON) networks and activity-on-arc (AOA) networks, and proponents of each type have rather strong feelings. We favor AON networks because we believe they are more intuitive, so we do not discuss AOA networks in this book.

In the AON representation of a project, there is a node for each activity. Then there is an arc from node *i* to node *j* if node *i* is an immediate predecessor of node *j*. To illustrate this, consider a project that consists of five activities, labeled A, B, C, D, and E. Activities A and B can start immediately. Activity C cannot start until activity B is finished, activity D cannot start until activity A is finished, and activity E cannot start until activities A and C are both finished. The project is finished when all activities are finished.

*AON networks use nodes for activities and arcs to indicate precedence relationships.*

We indicate the precedence relationships in Table 15.1 and the AON network in Figure 15.1. Table 15.1 also includes the duration for each activity. In an AON network, these durations are placed next to the nodes. In addition, there is typically a Start node and a Finish node in the diagram. These simply indicate the start and the finish of the project.

**Figure 15.1**

AON Network for a Five-Activity Project

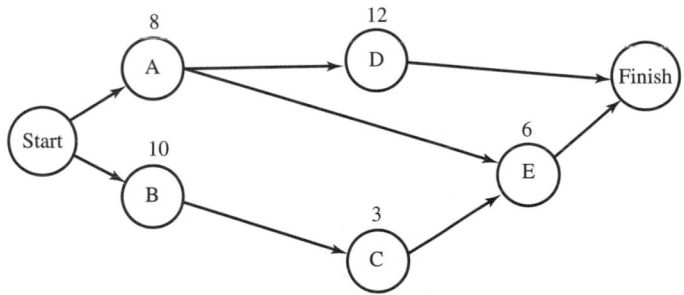

**Table 15.1**  Data for a Five-Activity Project

| Node | Immediate Predecessor(s) | Immediate Successor(s) | Duration |
|------|--------------------------|------------------------|----------|
| A | None | D, E | 8 |
| B | None | C | 10 |
| C | B | E | 3 |
| D | A | None | 12 |
| E | A, C | None | 6 |

[3] Activities are also called *tasks* in the project-management literature. The two terms, activities and tasks, are synonymous.

Note that activity E illustrates what we mean by the term *immediate* predecessor. Clearly, activity B is also a predecessor of activity E—it must be finished before activity E can start—but it is not an immediate predecessor because it will be finished before another predecessor of activity E, activity C, can even begin.

The rules for drawing an AON network are as follows:

- Include a node for each activity and place its duration next to the node.

- Include an arc from node $i$ to node $j$ only if node $i$ is an immediate predecessor of node $j$.

- Include a Start and a Finish node with zero durations. There is an arc from the Start node to each node that has no predecessors. These activities can all start immediately. There is an arc into the Finish node from each node that has no successors. When all of these activities have been finished, the project is finished.

Two problems are typically analyzed in project scheduling. In the first, which we discuss in this subsection, we find the time to complete the project and locate the bottleneck activities. In the second, to be discussed in the next section, we try to find cost-efficient ways to complete the project within a given deadline. In each of these problems, a key concept is a bottleneck activity, called a **critical activity.** This is an activity that prevents the project from being completed any sooner. More precisely, a critical activity is an activity that, if its duration increases, the time to complete the project necessarily increases. The set of critical activities is called the **critical path.** The critical path is important for practical reasons. It identifies the activities that we should attempt to expedite because this will have a beneficial effect on the overall project time. In contrast, if an activity is *not* on the critical path, then speeding it up will not have any beneficial effect on the overall project time.

> An activity is **critical** if, by increasing its duration, the time to complete the project increases. The **critical path** is the set of critical activities.

There are several ways to model project scheduling. The way we describe in this section is called the "traditional" approach because of its widespread use in the project-scheduling field. This approach has the advantages that it is easily implemented in a spreadsheet, and it allows us to simulate projects with *random* durations in a natural way, as we illustrate in Section 15.4. However, another approach is sometimes used that involves a network optimization with Solver, much like the ones we discussed in Chapter 5.

Specifically, you should be able to convince yourself that the critical path through a project network such as the one in Figure 15.1 is the *longest* path from the Start node to the Finish node, using the durations as "distances." If the project network is not too complex, this longest path can be determined easily. For example, there are three paths from Start to Finish in Figure 15.1: Start-->A-->D-->Finish, Start-->A-->E-->Finish, and Start-->B-->C-->E-->Finish. The lengths of these paths are $8 + 12 = 20$, $8 + 6 = 14$, and $10 + 3 + 6 = 19$, respectively. Therefore, the critical path is the longest path, Start-->A-->D-->Finish, the critical activities are A and D, the time to complete the project is 20, and all activities other than A and D have some slack.

Although this "longest path through a network" approach is appealing and can be implemented fairly easily with Solver, it doesn't generalize easily to the case where the activity durations are random. Therefore, we do not pursue this approach here. Instead, we use the traditional approach discussed next.

We first require some basic insights. Let $ES_j$ be the earliest time activity $j$ can start, and let $EF_j$ be the earliest time activity $j$ can finish. Clearly, the earliest an activity can finish is the earliest time it can start plus its duration. For example, if the earliest activity D can start is time 8, and its duration is 12, then the earliest D can finish is time 20. In general, if $d_j$ is the duration of activity $j$, we have

$$EF_j = ES_j + d_j \qquad (15.1)$$

Now, if activity $i$ is an immediate predecessor of activity $j$, then activity $j$ cannot start until activity $i$ finishes. In fact, activity $j$ cannot start until *all* of its immediate predecessors have finished, so the earliest time activity $j$ can start is the *maximum* of the earliest finish times of its immediate predecessors:

$$ES_j = \max(EF_i) \qquad (15.2)$$

Here, the maximum is over all immediate predecessors $i$ of activity $j$.

We use equations (15.1) and (15.2) to find the earliest start times and earliest finish times of all activities, beginning with the fact that the earliest start time for the Start node is 0—it can start right away. A by-product of these calculations is that we automatically obtain the project completion time. It is the earliest start time of the Finish node:

$$\text{Project completion time} = ES_{\text{Finish node}} \qquad (15.3)$$

The reason is that as soon as we reach the Finish node, the entire project is complete.

This calculation of the earliest start and finish times through equations 15.1 to 15.3 is usually called the *forward pass* of the CPM algorithm. The reason for this term is that we do the calculations in "forward" chronological order of the activities.

To find the critical activities and the critical path, we need two other equations. Let $LS_j$ and $LF_j$ be the latest time activity $j$ can start and the latest time it can finish *without increasing the project completion time*. Again, we have, analogous to equation (15.1),

$$LS_j = LF_j - d_j \qquad (15.4)$$

(We write the equation in this form because we find $LF_j$ first and then use it to find $LS_j$.)

Now suppose activity $j$ is an immediate successor of activity $i$. Then activity $i$ must be finished before activity $j$ can start. In fact, a bit of thought should convince you that the latest time activity $i$ can finish is the *minimum* of the latest start times of all its successors:

$$LF_i = \min(LS_j) \qquad (15.5)$$

Here, the minimum is over all immediate successors $j$ of activity $i$.

For example, suppose activity F has two successors, G and H, and we somehow find that the latest start times for G and H are 26 and 30. In this case, the bottleneck, at least for this part of the network, is activity G. The latest it can start without delaying the project is 26; activity H can start later. Therefore, activity G's predecessor, activity F, has to be finished no later than time 26.

We use equations (15.4) and (15.5) to calculate the latest start times and latest finish times for all activities, beginning with the fact that the latest finish time for the Finish node is the project completion time. (Make sure you see why this is true.) This set of calculations is called the *backward pass* of the CPM algorithm because we work through the activities in "backward" chronological order. Then we calculate the **slack** of each activity $j$ as the difference between the latest start time and the earliest start time of activity $j$:

$$\text{Slack of activity } j = LS_j - ES_j \qquad (15.6)$$

The idea behind slack is very simple. If an activity has any positive slack, then this activity has some room to maneuver—it could start a bit later without delaying the project. In fact, its duration could increase by the amount of its slack without delaying the project. However, if an activity has zero slack, then any increase in its duration necessarily delays the project. Therefore, the critical path consists of activities with zero slack.

The following example illustrates how to implement this method.

## EXAMPLE | 15.1 CREATING AN OFFICE LAN

*The lists of activities and their immediate predecessors in such a table are enough to determine the list of immediate successors. Try listing the successors on your own.*

An insurance company has decided to construct a local area network (LAN) in one of its large offices so that its employees can share printers, files, and other conveniences. The project consists of 15 activities, labeled A through O, as listed in Table 15.2. This table indicates the immediate predecessors and immediate successors of each activity, along with each activity's expected duration. (At this point these durations are assumed known.) Note that activity A is the only activity that can start right away, and activity O is the last activity to be completed. This table implies the AON network in Figure 15.2. The company wants to know how long the project will take to complete, and it also wants to know which activities are on the critical path.

**Table 15.2  Data on LAN Activities**

| Description | Activity | Immediate Predecessor(s) | Immediate Successor(s) | Duration (days) |
|---|---|---|---|---|
| Perform needs analysis | A | None | B | 10 |
| Develop specifications | B | A | C, D | 6 |
| Select server | C | B | E, G | 6 |
| Select software | D | B | F, G | 12 |
| Select cables | E | C | F | 4 |
| Purchase equipment | F | D, E | H, I | 3 |
| Develop user manuals | G | C, D | J | 6 |
| Wire offices | H | F | L | 12 |
| Set up server | I | F | K | 3 |
| Develop training program | J | G | M | 14 |
| Install software | K | I | L | 4 |
| Connect network | L | H, K | M, N | 3 |
| Train users | M | J, L | O | 8 |
| Test and debug system | N | L | O | 12 |
| Get management acceptance | O | M, N | None | 4 |

**Objective**  To develop a spreadsheet model of the LAN project so that we can calculate the time required to complete the project and identify the critical activities.

### WHERE DO THE NUMBERS COME FROM?

The computer systems people should be able to obtain the data in the first four columns of Table 15.2. They would know what needs to be done and in which order. However, the data in the last column, the durations, are probably guesses at best. There is usually uncertainty regarding activity times, due to workers not showing up, unavailable components, software

**Figure 15.2** AON Diagram for LAN Project

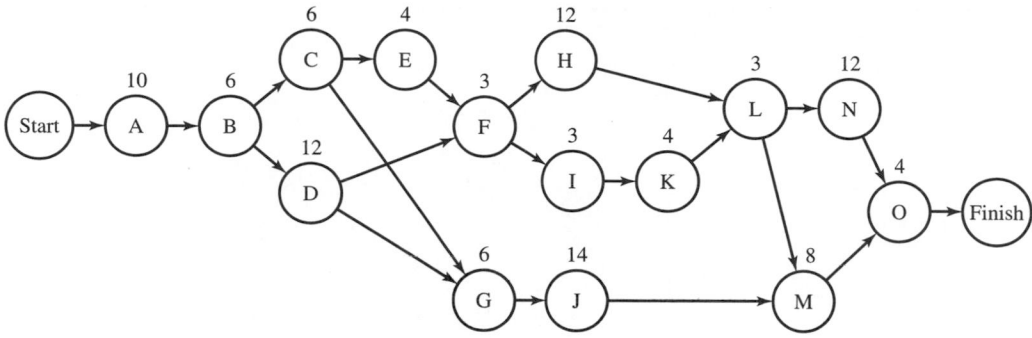

bugs, and so on. We ignore this uncertainty here, but we will deal with it explicitly in Section 15.4, when we discuss simulation of a project.

## Solution

To implement the method, we use equations (15.1) and (15.2) to find the earliest start and finish times of all activities, equation (15.3) to find the project completion time, equations (15.4) and (15.5) to find the latest start and finish times, and finally equation (15.6) to find the slacks and hence the critical activities.

### DEVELOPING THE SPREADSHEET MODEL

The completed spreadsheet model is shown in Figure 15.3 (see the file **Project Scheduling. xlsx**) and can be developed with the following steps:

**1** **Input data.** Enter the predecessors, successors, and durations in the shaded range. Note how we have entered data for the Start and Finish nodes in rows 5 and 21.

**2** **Earliest start and finish times.** Here we implement the forward pass of the algorithm with equations (15.1) and (15.2). To implement equation (15.1), enter the formula

**=B25+E5**

in cell C25 and copy it down to cell C41. To implement equation (15.2), begin by entering 0 in cell B25. This is because the Start node can begin immediately. Then every other earliest start time is the *maximum* of the earliest finish times of its predecessors. Unfortunately, there is no way to enter a single formula and copy it down. We need to specialize each formula to each activity's particular predecessors. For example, the formulas for activities D and G, in cells D29 and D32, are

**=C27**

and

**=MAX(C28:C29)**

*Each earliest start time is the maximum of the earliest finish times of its predecessors.*

This is because activity D has a single predecessor, whereas activity G has two predecessors. The other formulas in column B are similar.

**3** **Project completion time.** The project completion time is given in equation (15.3) as the earliest start time of the Finish node. We record it in cell B43 with the formula

**=B41**

**Figure 15.3** Spreadsheet Model of LAN Project

| | A | B | C | D | E | F | G | H | I | J | K |
|---|---|---|---|---|---|---|---|---|---|---|---|
| 1 | Office LAN project - finding project time and critical path | | | | | | | | | | |
| 2 | | | | | | | | | | | |
| 3 | Data on activity network | | | | | | | | | | |
| 4 | Activity | Label | Predecessors | Successors | Duration | | | | | | |
| 5 | Dummy Start node | Start | None | A | 0 | | | | | | |
| 6 | Perform needs analysis | A | Start | B | 10 | | | | | | |
| 7 | Develop specifications | B | A | C,D | 6 | | | | | | |
| 8 | Select server | C | B | E,G | 6 | | | | | | |
| 9 | Select software | D | B | F,G | 12 | | | | | | |
| 10 | Select cables | E | C | F | 4 | | | | | | |
| 11 | Purchase equipment | F | D,E | H,I | 3 | | | | | | |
| 12 | Develop user manuals | G | C,D | J | 6 | | | | | | |
| 13 | Wire offices | H | F | L | 12 | | | | | | |
| 14 | Set up server | I | F | K | 3 | | | | | | |
| 15 | Develop training program | J | G | M | 14 | | | | | | |
| 16 | Install software | K | I | L | 4 | | | | | | |
| 17 | Connect network | L | H,K | M,N | 3 | | | | | | |
| 18 | Train users | M | J,L | O | 8 | | | | | | |
| 19 | Test & debug system | N | L | O | 12 | | | | | | |
| 20 | Get management acceptance | O | M,N | Finish | 4 | | | | | | |
| 21 | Dummy Finish node | Finish | O | None | 0 | | | | | | |
| 22 | | | | | | | | | | | |
| 23 | Activity start and finish times | | | | | | | | | | |
| 24 | Activity | Earliest start time | Earliest finish time | Latest start time | Latest finish time | Slack | | | | | |
| 25 | Start | 0 | 0 | 0 | 0 | | | | | | |
| 26 | A | 0 | 10 | 0 | 10 | 0 | | | | | |
| 27 | B | 10 | 16 | 10 | 16 | 0 | | | | | |
| 28 | C | 16 | 22 | 18 | 24 | 2 | | | | | |
| 29 | D | 16 | 28 | 16 | 28 | 0 | | | | | |
| 30 | E | 22 | 26 | 24 | 28 | 2 | | | | | |
| 31 | F | 28 | 31 | 28 | 31 | 0 | | | | | |
| 32 | G | 28 | 34 | 30 | 36 | 2 | | | | | |
| 33 | H | 31 | 43 | 31 | 43 | 0 | | | | | |
| 34 | I | 31 | 34 | 36 | 39 | 5 | | | | | |
| 35 | J | 34 | 48 | 36 | 50 | 2 | | | | | |
| 36 | K | 34 | 38 | 39 | 43 | 5 | | | | | |
| 37 | L | 43 | 46 | 43 | 46 | 0 | | | | | |
| 38 | M | 48 | 56 | 50 | 58 | 2 | | | | | |
| 39 | N | 46 | 58 | 46 | 58 | 0 | | | | | |
| 40 | O | 58 | 62 | 58 | 62 | 0 | | | | | |
| 41 | Finish | 62 | 62 | 62 | 62 | | | | | | |
| 42 | | | | | | | | | | | |
| 43 | Project completion time | 62 | | | | | | | | | |

Callout box:
Activities with 0 slack are on critical, i.e., they are on the critical path. Therefore, the critical path is A-B-D-F-H-L-N-O. The durations of the noncritical activities, C, E, G, I, J, K, and M, could be increased slightly without affecting the project completion time.

**4** **Latest start and finish times.** Next, we implement the backward pass of the algorithm with equations (15.4) and (15.5). To implement equation (15.4), enter the formula

**=E25-E5**

in cell D25 and copy it down to cell D41. To implement equation (15.5), begin by entering the formula

**=B43**

in cell E41. By definition, the latest the Finish node can start (or finish because it has 0 duration) is the project completion time. For the other activities, we use equation (15.5) to calculate the latest finish times. Again, there is no way to copy one formula to all cells; it depends on each activity's particular successors. For example, the formulas for activities D and G, in cells E29 and E32, are

**=MIN(D31:D32)**

and

*Each latest finish time is the minimum of the latest start times of its successors.*

**=D35**

This is because activity D has two successors, whereas activity G has only a single successor. The other formulas in column D are similar.

**⑤ Slacks.** Using equation (15.6), enter the formula

**=D26-B26**

in cell F26 and copy it down to cell F40 to calculate the slacks.

### Discussion of the Solution

The solution in Figure 15.3 indicates that the room can be completed in 62 days—but no less—if the various activities are started within their earliest and latest start time ranges. We see, for example, that activity B, which is critical, *must* start at time 10. However, activity C, which is noncritical, can start at any time from 16 to 18. The critical activities are the ones with zero slack: A, B, D, F, H, L, N, and O. (Refer to the AON network in Figure 15.2 to see this path.) If any of the activities on this path is delayed, the project completion time will necessarily increase.

To convince yourself of the difference between critical and noncritical activities, try increasing the duration of any critical activity such as activity D by 1 day. You will see that the project completion time increases by 1 day as well. However, try increasing the duration of any noncritical activity such as activity C by any amount up to its slack. You will see that the project completion time does not increase at all.

*A Gantt chart shows the time line of the project.*

This solution can be depicted best with a **Gantt chart,** as shown in Figure 15.4. This popular type of chart is essentially a time line of when activities start and finish. For example, the horizontal bar for wiring the office indicates that this activity starts 31 days from now and is completed 12 days later. (Keep in mind that the current time is day 0.) From

**Figure 15.4**   Gantt Chart for the LAN Project

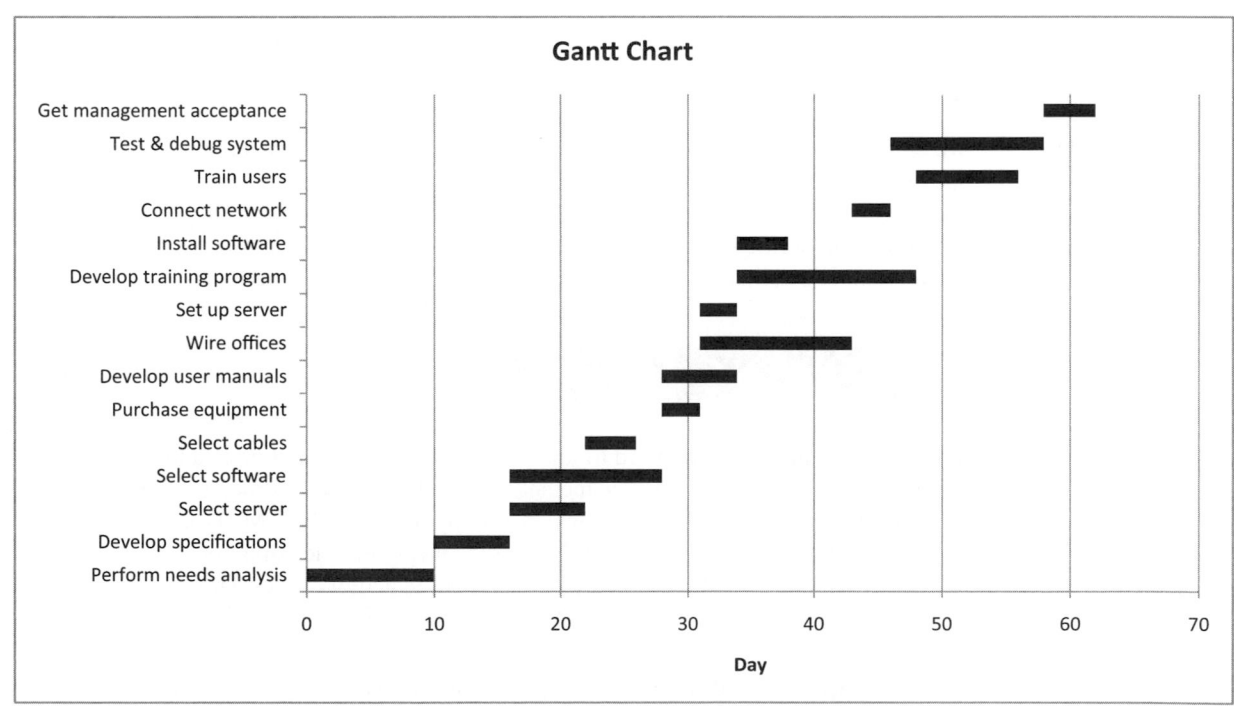

**Figure 15.5** Data for the Gantt Chart

| | A | B | C | D | E | F | G |
|---|---|---|---|---|---|---|---|
| 45 | **Data for Gantt chart** | | | | | | |
| 46 | Activity | Start time | Duration | | | | |
| 47 | Perform needs analysis | 0 | 10 | | | | |
| 48 | Develop specifications | 10 | 6 | | | | |
| 49 | Select server | 16 | 6 | | | | |
| 50 | Select software | 16 | 12 | | | | |
| 51 | Select cables | 22 | 4 | | | | |
| 52 | Purchase equipment | 28 | 3 | | | | |
| 53 | Develop user manuals | 28 | 6 | | | | |
| 54 | Wire offices | 31 | 12 | | | | |
| 55 | Set up server | 31 | 3 | | | | |
| 56 | Develop training program | 34 | 14 | | | | |
| 57 | Install software | 34 | 4 | | | | |
| 58 | Connect network | 43 | 3 | | | | |
| 59 | Train users | 48 | 8 | | | | |
| 60 | Test & debug system | 46 | 12 | | | | |
| 61 | Get management acceptance | 58 | 4 | | | | |

The noncritical activities can have start times anywhere within their earliest to latest start time ranges. There is no such flexibility for the critical activities.

the bars farthest to the right, we see that the project is completed 62 days from now. We created this Gantt chart, using the data shown in Figure 15.5, as explained in the following Excel Tip.

**Excel Tip:** *Creating a Gantt Chart*
*To create a Gantt chart as in Figure 15.4, enter the data in Figure 15.5—the names of the activities, their start times, and their durations—in a three-column range. Highlight this range, click on the Insert tab, and select a stacked horizontal bar chart (the second subtype in the Bar category). You can accept the rest of the default chart settings, except to get rid of the legend. The resulting chart will have two adjacent bars for each activity, one on the left for the start time and one on the right for the duration. Right-click on one of the start time bars and select Format Data Series. Then change the Fill to None. This effectively hides the start time bars and shows only the appropriately placed duration bars.*

*The bars in the Gantt chart for noncritical activities can be adjusted slightly. The bars for critical activities are fixed.*

According to this Excel Tip, we require start times and durations for the Gantt chart. We could use any start times within the earliest and latest start time ranges. The start times shown in Figure 15.5 are the earliest start times, but you can try your own values in column B of Figure 15.3 to see how the Gantt chart changes. Just remember that you have choices only for the noncritical activities: C, E, G, I, J, K, and M. The start times for the critical activities cannot be changed without increasing the overall project time. ∎

## MODELING ISSUES

1. The CPM algorithm we used to find the project completion time and the critical path is only one of several possible methods for finding these. In Problems 6 and 7, we indicate two alternatives, both of which employ Solver. The CPM algorithm is probably the most popular method, and it extends nicely to other situations, particularly when we want to simulate a project with random activity times. However, the Solver models also have their strengths, especially when we want to optimize some sort of cost or reward.

2. The types of precedence relationships we have used are sometimes called **finish-to-start** relationships. For example, task B cannot start until task A finishes. These are the most common types of precedence relationships, but they are not the only types.

Three other possible types are **start-to-start** relationships (task B cannot start until task A has started), **finish-to-finish** relationships (task B cannot finish until task A has finished), and **start-to-finish** relationships (task B cannot finish until task A has started). Problem 8 asks you to explore the first of these. ∎

# PROBLEMS

*Solutions for problems whose numbers appear within a color box can be found in the Student Solutions Files. Order your copy today at the Winston/Albright product Web site, academic.cengage.com/decisionsciences/winston.*

## Skill-Building Problems

**1.** Use a one-way data table to see how sensitive the project completion time in the LAN project is to the duration of activity D (selecting software). Let the duration vary from 10 to 16 days in increments of 1 day.

**2.** Repeat the previous problem, but now keep track of the following outputs in your data table: the project completion time and the slack for each activity. As the duration of activity D changes, do any critical activities become noncritical? Do any noncritical activities become critical?

**3.** Use a two-way data table to see how sensitive the project completion time in the LAN project is to the duration of activities E and H (selecting cables and wiring offices). Let the durations of these activities vary from 3 to 6 days and from 10 to 16 days, respectively, in increments of 1 day each.

**4.** In the LAN project, activities C and D can be done concurrently. Suppose instead that activity C is an immediate predecessor of activity D. (Perhaps they use the same employees, and these employees can perform only one activity at a time.) How does the AON diagram change? How much does the project completion time increase? What is the new critical path? (You can assume that activity E is still an immediate successor of activity C. That is, it doesn't need to wait for activity D to finish.)

**5.** How difficult is it to add new activities to an existing project scheduling model? Answer this question by assuming that there are two other activities, labeled P and Q. Activity P moves selected employees to temporary offices while installation occurs, and activity Q moves them back after installation is finished. Activity P has immediate predecessors D and E, immediate successor H, and duration three days. Activity Q has immediate predecessor L, immediate successor O, and duration three days. Find the new project completion time. Does the critical path change because of the new activity?

**6.** The data in Figure 15.5 for the Gantt chart uses the earliest start times for all activities. These could actually be anywhere between the earliest and latest start times without affecting the project completion time. Enter formulas in the start time cells (column B of Figure 15.5) using Excel's RAND function, which allows these start times to be anywhere between the earliest and latest start times. Then go to the Gantt chart sheet and press the F9 key a few times. The bars for the noncritical activities should slide to the left or right in their allowable ranges, but the project completion time shouldn't change.

## Skill-Extending Problems

**7.** We have illustrated the traditional CPM algorithm for finding the project length and the critical path. An alternative method is sometimes used. It sets up a Solver model for finding a *feasible* solution to a set of constraints, and there is no objective to maximize or minimize. Let $d_j$ be the duration of activity $j$, and let $t_j$ be the start time of activity $j$. Let the $t_j$'s be the changing cells in the Solver model. There is a constraint for each arc in the AON network. Specifically, if there is an arc from activity $i$ to activity $j$, then there is a constraint $t_j \geq t_i + d_i$. This states that activity $j$ cannot start until its predecessor, activity $i$, finishes. Develop this Solver model for the LAN project, making sure that there is no target cell in the Solver dialog box. (Just delete whatever is in the Target Cell box.) Then run Solver to find the project completion time. Can you tell from the solution which activities are critical?

**8.** Expanding on the previous problem, there is a third possible approach for finding the project length and the critical path. We already stated that the critical path is the *longest* path from the Start node to the Finish node. Using the same approach that we used in Chapter 5 to find the *shortest* path through a network, find the project length and the critical path for the LAN project. (*Hint:* The only necessary modification to the shortest path method is to maximize, not minimize.)

**9.** The "Modeling Issues" section described three alternative types of precedence relationships besides the usual finish-to-start relationship. The following questions ask you to explore the first of these alternatives for the LAN project.
  **a.** Start-to-start relationships are sometimes useful for activities that can run parallel to one another. Suppose that there is a start-to-start relationship

between activities J (developing training program) and M (training users). Specifically, activity M cannot start until activity J has started. In general, do the CPM formulas for earliest start times need to be changed when there are start-to-start relationships? What about the formulas for latest finish times? Redo the CPM calculations with this new relationship.

**b.** Repeat part **a**, but now generalize even a bit more. Assume that activity M cannot start until three weeks after activity J starts. This is a *delayed* start-to-start relationship.

**c.** Getting the correct logic for earliest start and latest finish formulas for the relationships in parts **a** and **b** can be a bit tricky. As an alternative, modify the Solver model from Problem 7 for these relationships. This should be more straightforward. Do you get the same results as in parts **a** and **b**? (You should.)

---

# 15.3 MODELING ALLOCATION OF RESOURCES

The basic CPM model presented in the previous section is concerned solely with timing. We assume the activities have known durations, and we then schedule them so that the project is completed as soon as possible. In this section, we discuss another aspect of project scheduling, the allocation of resources. The activities in a project always consume resources, including money, people, and possibly others. When we say that an activity has a duration of 10 days, we are implicitly assuming that certain resources have been allocated to this activity. For example, it might be that five engineers, working at $300 per day per engineer, can complete the activity in 10 days. It is possible, however, that if we used more or fewer than five engineers on the activity (or maybe even paid them more or less than $300 per day), the activity would be finished sooner or later than 10 days. These are trade-offs that must typically be made when scheduling a project.

If you suspect that this is a multiobjective optimization problem, as discussed in Chapter 9, you are absolutely correct. There are typically three primary objectives: (1) to finish the project quickly, (2) to consume as few resources as possible (especially, to minimize costs), and (3) to produce a high-quality project. Because of these three objectives, there are many potential optimization models for project scheduling, and the academic research in this area has explored many of them, including some that are quite complex. We set our sights considerably lower here. We first indicate how a project manager can at least *monitor* resource usage. This is not actually optimization, but optimization models could be built upon it. We then discuss one of the most popular optimization models for project scheduling, called **crashing.** In the crashing model, we are allowed to shorten the activity durations by spending extra money on them—that is, we can *crash* the activities. The problem is to spend as little extra money as possible to complete the project within a given deadline. (We say "extra" because money is presumably already being spent to achieve the given activity durations. We want to spend extra money to speed them up.)

## Monitoring the Use of Resources

Almost all projects require money and people. Therefore, we focus on these two resources here. Of course, other resources such as facilities or equipment could also be monitored. The following extension of the LAN project example from the previous section illustrates how the money and people devoted to the project can be monitored through time in Excel. We mention, however, that this is somewhat tedious. A software package that is devoted to project scheduling, such as Microsoft Project, has much better tools for monitoring resource usage.

EXAMPLE | 15.2 MONITORING RESOURCES FOR THE LAN PROJECT

Recall from Example 15.1 that an insurance company is creating a LAN for one of its large offices. In that example, we provided activity durations for the 15 activities comprising the project, and we showed that with these durations, the project can be completed in 62 days. We now make some assumptions about the money and people resources that are implicit in these activity durations. First, we assume that the various activities require different technical expertise, which comes from five groups of people: engineering, systems, purchasing, installers, and training. To achieve the durations used in Example 15.1, we assume the number of people required per day for the various activities are those shown in Table 15.3. For example, to perform the needs analysis in 10 days, six engineers are required per day. Note that connecting the network is the only activity that requires two different types of people: three systems people and five installers for each of the three days this activity takes to complete. Also, note that the last activity, getting management acceptance, doesn't show any people requirements. In reality, this activity is probably the responsibility of the project manager, who is busy throughout the entire project. (Almost all projects have a project manager.)

**Table 15.3  People Required per Day for Various Activities**

| Activity | Duration | Engineering | Systems | Purchasing | Installers | Training |
|---|---|---|---|---|---|---|
| Perform needs analysis | 10 | 6 | | | | |
| Develop specifications | 6 | 8 | | | | |
| Select server | 6 | | 5 | | | |
| Select software | 12 | | 7 | | | |
| Select cables | 4 | | 3 | | | |
| Purchase equipment | 3 | | | 4 | | |
| Develop user manuals | 6 | | | | | 5 |
| Wire offices | 12 | | | | 8 | |
| Set up server | 3 | | 4 | | | |
| Develop training program | 14 | | | | | 9 |
| Install software | 4 | | 6 | | | |
| Connect network | 3 | | 3 | | 5 | |
| Train users | 8 | | | | | 8 |
| Test and debug system | 12 | | 5 | | | |
| Get management acceptance | 4 | | | | | |

In addition to these people, the various activities require money. It certainly costs money to pay the people, and there are probably other costs as well. We assume the costs per day for the various activities are those shown in Table 15.4. The company wants to see how its people and money are used through time. Also, because some of the activities have some slack, the company wants to see how the resource usages are affected by adjusting the starting times of the noncritical activities.

**Objective**   To create time series charts of the money and people usages, and to see how these are affected by the starting times of the noncritical activities.

### Table 15.4 Costs per Day for the Various Activities

| Activity | Cost per Day |
|---|---|
| Perform needs analysis | $500 |
| Develop specifications | $500 |
| Select server | $400 |
| Select software | $400 |
| Select cables | $400 |
| Purchase equipment | $300 |
| Develop user manuals | $300 |
| Wire offices | $450 |
| Set up server | $400 |
| Develop training program | $300 |
| Install software | $400 |
| Connect network | $450 |
| Train users | $300 |
| Test and debug system | $400 |
| Get management acceptance | $250 |

### WHERE DO THE NUMBERS COME FROM?

The numbers of people required per day, shown in Table 15.3, are probably based on technical considerations of the activities. In fact, these numbers are probably chosen *first,* and activity durations are then based on them. For example, the company might estimate that it takes eight installers to wire the offices properly, and if eight installers are used per day, the wiring can then be completed in 12 days. The costs in Table 15.4 are based on the wage rates of the various types of people, plus any other expenses required to perform the activities.

## Solution

The solution appears in the file **Project Monitoring.xlsx**. To monitor daily costs, we proceed as follows. (See Figures 15.6, 15.7, and 15.8, where Figure 15.7 includes several hidden columns.) We first perform the same CPM calculations as in Example 15.1. These appear in Figure 15.6, along with the given costs per day. We then create a table of daily costs, as shown in Figure 15.7. To do this, we need the starting times for the activities in column B. This figure uses the *earliest* starting times for illustration. The file actually contains a second similar table that uses the *latest* starting times, just for comparison.

Then we fill in the table by entering the formula

=IF(AND($B47<C$46,$B47+$E6>=C$46),$G6,0)

in cell C47 and copying it to the rest of the table. This formula checks whether the day in row 46 is within the duration of the activity. If it is, the formula records the daily cost; otherwise, it records 0. Then we sum the daily costs in row 62.

After we have the total daily costs in row 62, we can create a chart of these costs through time, as shown in Figure 15.8. Here are several notes about this chart:

- We used a scatter chart of cost (row 62) versus day (row 46). You can experiment with other chart types, such as a line chart, but don't go overboard with fancy charts. The point is to indicate the variation in daily cost through time as clearly as possible.

- We actually chart two series in Figure 15.8: one where all activities begin at their earliest start times and one where they all start at their latest start times. There are

**Figure 15.6**  CPM Calculations for the LAN Project

| | A | B | C | D | E | F | G |
|---|---|---|---|---|---|---|---|
| 1 | Office LAN project - monitoring costs | | | | | | |
| 2 | | | | | | | |
| 3 | Data on activity network | | | | | | |
| 4 | Activity | Label | Predecessors | Successors | Duration | | |
| 5 | Dummy Start node | Start | None | A | 0 | | Cost per day |
| 6 | Perform needs analysis | A | Start | B | 10 | | $500 |
| 7 | Develop specifications | B | A | C,D | 6 | | $500 |
| 8 | Select server | C | B | E,G | 6 | | $400 |
| 9 | Select software | D | B | F,G | 12 | | $400 |
| 10 | Select cables | E | C | F | 4 | | $400 |
| 11 | Purchase equipment | F | D,E | H,I | 3 | | $300 |
| 12 | Develop user manuals | G | C,D | J | 6 | | $300 |
| 13 | Wire offices | H | F | L | 12 | | $450 |
| 14 | Set up server | I | F | K | 3 | | $400 |
| 15 | Develop training program | J | G | M | 14 | | $300 |
| 16 | Install software | K | I | L | 4 | | $400 |
| 17 | Connect network | L | H,K | M,N | 3 | | $450 |
| 18 | Train users | M | J,L | O | 8 | | $300 |
| 19 | Test & debug system | N | L | O | 12 | | $400 |
| 20 | Get management acceptance | O | M,N | Finish | 4 | | $250 |
| 21 | Dummy Finish node | Finish | O | None | 0 | | |
| 22 | | | | | | | |
| 23 | Activity start and finish times | | | | | | |
| 24 | Activity | Earliest start time | Earliest finish time | Latest start time | Latest finish time | Slack | |
| 25 | Start | 0 | 0 | 0 | 0 | | |
| 26 | A | 0 | 10 | 0 | 10 | 0 | |
| 27 | B | 10 | 16 | 10 | 16 | 0 | |
| 28 | C | 16 | 22 | 18 | 24 | 2 | |
| 29 | D | 16 | 28 | 16 | 28 | 0 | |
| 30 | E | 22 | 26 | 24 | 28 | 2 | |
| 31 | F | 28 | 31 | 28 | 31 | 0 | |
| 32 | G | 28 | 34 | 30 | 36 | 2 | |
| 33 | H | 31 | 43 | 31 | 43 | 0 | |
| 34 | I | 31 | 34 | 36 | 39 | 5 | |
| 35 | J | 34 | 48 | 36 | 50 | 2 | |
| 36 | K | 34 | 38 | 39 | 43 | 5 | |
| 37 | L | 43 | 46 | 43 | 46 | 0 | |
| 38 | M | 48 | 56 | 50 | 58 | 2 | |
| 39 | N | 46 | 58 | 46 | 58 | 0 | |
| 40 | O | 58 | 62 | 58 | 62 | 0 | |
| 41 | Finish | 62 | 62 | 62 | 62 | | |
| 42 | | | | | | | |
| 43 | Project time | 62 | | | | | |

**Figure 15.7**  Daily Costs for the LAN Project (Using Earliest Start Times)

| | A | B | C | D | E | F | BK | BL |
|---|---|---|---|---|---|---|---|---|
| 45 | Daily costs using earliest starting times | | Day | | | | | |
| 46 | Activity | Starting time | 1 | 2 | 3 | 4 | 61 | 62 |
| 47 | A | 0 | 500 | 500 | 500 | 500 | 0 | 0 |
| 48 | B | 10 | 0 | 0 | 0 | 0 | 0 | 0 |
| 49 | C | 16 | 0 | 0 | 0 | 0 | 0 | 0 |
| 50 | D | 16 | 0 | 0 | 0 | 0 | 0 | 0 |
| 51 | E | 22 | 0 | 0 | 0 | 0 | 0 | 0 |
| 52 | F | 28 | 0 | 0 | 0 | 0 | 0 | 0 |
| 53 | G | 28 | 0 | 0 | 0 | 0 | 0 | 0 |
| 54 | H | 31 | 0 | 0 | 0 | 0 | 0 | 0 |
| 55 | I | 31 | 0 | 0 | 0 | 0 | 0 | 0 |
| 56 | J | 34 | 0 | 0 | 0 | 0 | 0 | 0 |
| 57 | K | 34 | 0 | 0 | 0 | 0 | 0 | 0 |
| 58 | L | 43 | 0 | 0 | 0 | 0 | 0 | 0 |
| 59 | M | 48 | 0 | 0 | 0 | 0 | 0 | 0 |
| 60 | N | 46 | 0 | 0 | 0 | 0 | 0 | 0 |
| 61 | O | 58 | 0 | 0 | 0 | 0 | 250 | 250 |
| 62 | Total cost for each day | | $500 | $500 | $500 | $500 | $250 | $250 |

**Figure 15.8**   Time Series of Daily Costs

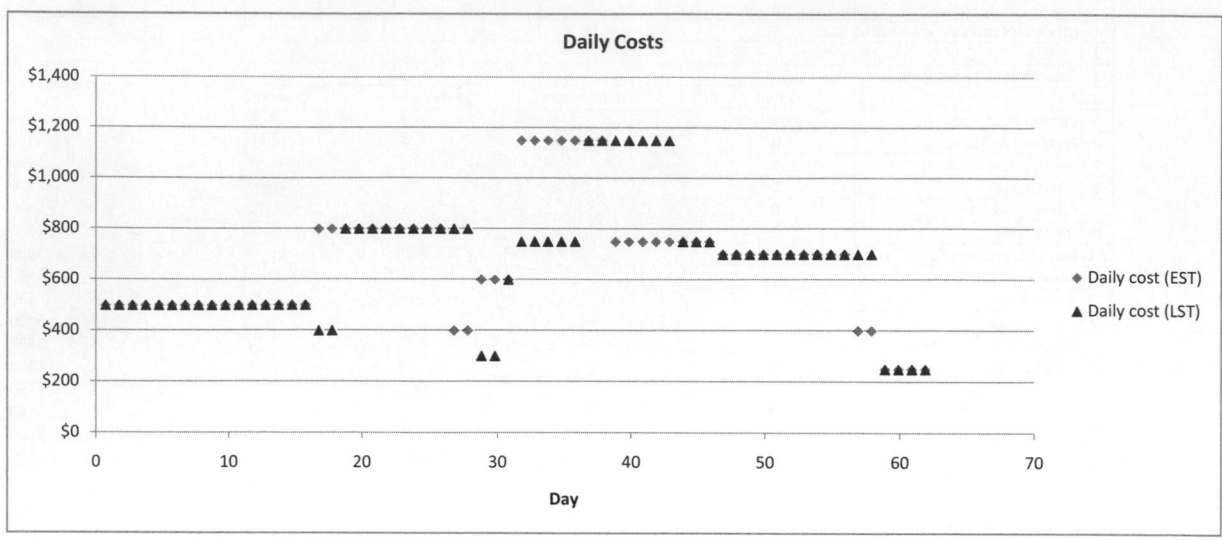

some differences between the two, and the project manager needs to judge how important these differences are. For example, if his goal is to smooth out daily costs as much as possible, each of these series appears to be about equally smooth.

- Regardless of which starting times are used (either the earliest start times, the latest start times, or any times in between), the project manager can see from this chart where the cost requirements peak (somewhere in the middle of the project) and where they are lowest (at the beginning and the end of the project). This is exactly the type of information such a chart is intended to provide.

We can develop a time series chart of people usage in essentially the same way, as indicated in Figures 15.9, 15.10, and 15.11. The first of these again shows the CPM calculations, along with the data on people usage per day. Figure 15.10 (with many hidden columns) shows the daily usage of engineers, assuming that all activities start at their earliest start times. There is a similar table for the other types of people (systems, purchasing, installers, and training), and in each of these, we could replace the earliest start times with the latest start times or any times in between. The typical formula in cell C48 is

**=IF(AND($B48<C$47,$B48+$E6>=C$47),$G6,0)**

which is then copied to the rest of the table. The chart in Figure 15.11 is again a scatter chart of the usage of each type of people versus day. (Remember that this chart is based on the earliest start times. To see how usages vary with start times, we could enter different start times in column B of Figure 15.10.)

We are making an important assumption in these people usage calculations. For example, the chart shows that 12 systems people are required in days 17 through 22. Actually,

Figure 15.9    CPM Calculations for the LAN Project

|  | A | B | C | D | E | F | G | H | I | J | K |
|---|---|---|---|---|---|---|---|---|---|---|---|
| 1 | Office LAN project - monitoring people | | | | | | | | | | |
| 2 | | | | | | | | | | | |
| 3 | Data on activity network | | | | | | | | | | |
| 4 | Activity | Label | Predecessors | Successors | Duration | | Resources (# of people) used per day | | | | |
| 5 | Dummy Start node | Start | None | A | 0 | | Engineering | Systems | Purchasing | Installers | Training |
| 6 | Perform needs analysis | A | Start | B | 10 | | 6 | | | | |
| 7 | Develop specifications | B | A | C,D | 6 | | 8 | | | | |
| 8 | Select server | C | B | E,G | 6 | | | | 5 | | |
| 9 | Select software | D | B | F,G | 12 | | | | 7 | | |
| 10 | Select cables | E | C | F | 4 | | | | 3 | | |
| 11 | Purchase equipment | F | D,E | H,I | 3 | | | | | 4 | |
| 12 | Develop user manuals | G | C,D | J | 6 | | | | | | 5 |
| 13 | Wire offices | H | F | L | 12 | | | | | 8 | |
| 14 | Set up server | I | F | K | 3 | | | 4 | | | |
| 15 | Develop training program | J | G | M | 14 | | | | | | 9 |
| 16 | Install software | K | I | L | 4 | | | 6 | | | |
| 17 | Connect network | L | H,K | M,N | 3 | | | 3 | | 5 | |
| 18 | Train users | M | J,L | O | 8 | | | | | | 8 |
| 19 | Test & debug system | N | L | O | 12 | | | 5 | | | |
| 20 | Get management acceptance | O | M,N | Finish | 4 | | | | | | |
| 21 | Dummy Finish node | Finish | O | None | 0 | | | | | | |
| 22 | | | | | | | | | | | |
| 23 | Activity start and finish times | | | | | | | | | | |
| 24 | Activity | Earliest start time | Earliest finish time | Latest start time | Latest finish time | Slack | | | | | |
| 25 | Start | 0 | 0 | 0 | 0 | | | | | | |
| 26 | A | 0 | 10 | 0 | 10 | 0 | | | | | |
| 27 | B | 10 | 16 | 10 | 16 | 0 | | | | | |
| 28 | C | 16 | 22 | 18 | 24 | 2 | | | | | |
| 29 | D | 16 | 28 | 16 | 28 | 0 | | | | | |
| 30 | E | 22 | 26 | 24 | 28 | 2 | | | | | |
| 31 | F | 28 | 31 | 28 | 31 | 0 | | | | | |
| 32 | G | 28 | 34 | 30 | 36 | 2 | | | | | |
| 33 | H | 31 | 43 | 31 | 43 | 0 | | | | | |
| 34 | I | 31 | 34 | 36 | 39 | 5 | | | | | |
| 35 | J | 34 | 48 | 36 | 50 | 2 | | | | | |
| 36 | K | 34 | 38 | 39 | 43 | 5 | | | | | |
| 37 | L | 43 | 46 | 43 | 46 | 0 | | | | | |
| 38 | M | 48 | 56 | 50 | 58 | 2 | | | | | |
| 39 | N | 46 | 58 | 46 | 58 | 0 | | | | | |
| 40 | O | 58 | 62 | 58 | 62 | 0 | | | | | |
| 41 | Finish | 62 | 62 | 62 | 62 | | | | | | |
| 42 | | | | | | | | | | | |
| 43 | Project time | 62 | | | | | | | | | |

|  | A | B | C | D | E | F | BK | BL |
|---|---|---|---|---|---|---|---|---|
| 45 | Resources consumed using earliest starting times | | | | | | | |
| 46 | Engineering | | Day | | | | | |
| 47 | Activity | Starting time | 1 | 2 | 3 | 4 | 61 | 62 |
| 48 | A | 0 | 6 | 6 | 6 | 6 | 0 | 0 |
| 49 | B | 10 | 0 | 0 | 0 | 0 | 0 | 0 |
| 50 | C | 16 | 0 | 0 | 0 | 0 | 0 | 0 |
| 51 | D | 16 | 0 | 0 | 0 | 0 | 0 | 0 |
| 52 | E | 22 | 0 | 0 | 0 | 0 | 0 | 0 |
| 53 | F | 28 | 0 | 0 | 0 | 0 | 0 | 0 |
| 54 | G | 28 | 0 | 0 | 0 | 0 | 0 | 0 |
| 55 | H | 31 | 0 | 0 | 0 | 0 | 0 | 0 |
| 56 | I | 31 | 0 | 0 | 0 | 0 | 0 | 0 |
| 57 | J | 34 | 0 | 0 | 0 | 0 | 0 | 0 |
| 58 | K | 34 | 0 | 0 | 0 | 0 | 0 | 0 |
| 59 | L | 43 | 0 | 0 | 0 | 0 | 0 | 0 |
| 60 | M | 48 | 0 | 0 | 0 | 0 | 0 | 0 |
| 61 | N | 46 | 0 | 0 | 0 | 0 | 0 | 0 |
| 62 | O | 58 | 0 | 0 | 0 | 0 | 0 | 0 |
| 63 | Total for each day | | 6 | 6 | 6 | 6 | 0 | 0 |

**Figure 15.11**    Time Series of People Usages

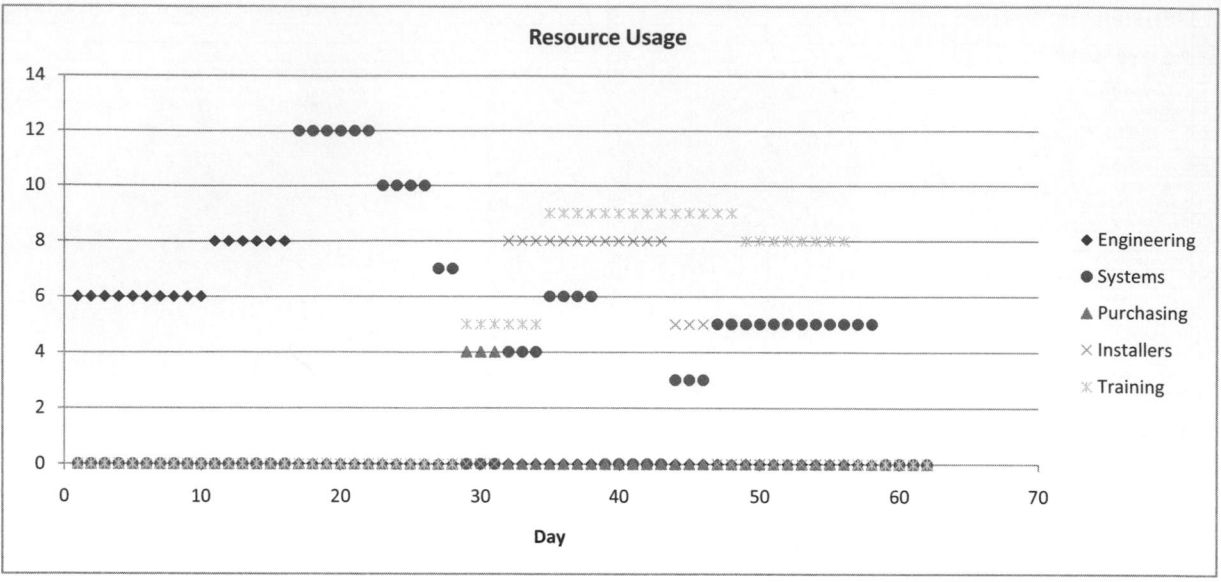

5 of these are required for selecting the server, and 7 are required for selecting the software. But what if fewer than 12 systems people are *available* on days 17 through 22? Then the current schedule is clearly infeasible. There are two options: (1) one of these two activities could be postponed, hence lengthening the time of the project, or (2) some extra systems people could be hired (or borrowed from another project). In any case, the value of such a chart is that it shows potential infeasibilities in the current schedule, so that alternative schedules can be pursued.

In a practical sense, charts such as these are monitored *throughout* the lifetime of the project. As we all know from experience, cost estimates often change (they usually increase) as the project unfolds, and estimates of other resource requirements can change as well. Therefore, the project manager needs to monitor requirements continually to ensure that they stay within allowable limits. ∎

## Crashing the Activities

The objective in many project-scheduling analyses is to find a minimum-cost method of reducing activity times to meet a deadline. The term *crashing the activities* is often used to mean reducing the activity times. Of course, it typically costs money to crash activities—hiring extra workers, using extra equipment, using overtime, and so on—so the problem becomes one of crashing just the right activities in just the right amounts to meet a deadline at minimum cost. We now illustrate how Solver can be used to solve this problem.

EXAMPLE | **15.3 MEETING A DEADLINE FOR THE LAN PROJECT**

From the CPM calculations in Example 15.1, the insurance company knows that if the LAN activities continue to take as long as listed in Table 15.2, the entire project will take 62 working days to complete. Unfortunately, the project manager is under pressure to finish the job in 56 working days. He estimates that each activity could be crashed by a certain amount at a certain cost. Specifically, he estimates the cost per day of activity time reduction and the maximum possible days of reduction for each activity, as shown in Table 15.5. For example, activity A's duration could be reduced from 10 days to 9 days at cost $600, or it could be reduced from 10 days to 8 days at cost $1200. (It is even possible to have a fractional reduction, such as from 10 days to 8.5 days at cost $900.) On the other hand, note that three of the activities cannot be crashed at all, probably due to technical considerations. How can the deadline be met at minimum cost?

**Table 15.5**    Crashing Inputs

| Description | Activity | Cost per Day | Maximum Reduction |
| --- | --- | --- | --- |
| Perform needs analysis | A | $600 | 2 |
| Develop specifications | B | $600 | 1 |
| Select server | C | $480 | 1 |
| Select software | D | $480 | 3 |
| Select cables | E | $480 | 1 |
| Purchase equipment | F | - | 0 |
| Develop user manuals | G | $360 | 1 |
| Wire offices | H | $540 | 4 |
| Set up server | I | - | 0 |
| Develop training program | J | $360 | 4 |
| Install software | K | $480 | 1 |
| Connect network | L | - | 0 |
| Train users | M | $360 | 2 |
| Test and dcbug system | N | $480 | 3 |
| Get management acceptance | O | $300 | 1 |

**Objective**    To use a Solver model to decide how much to crash each activity so that the deadline is met at minimum cost.

### WHERE DO THE NUMBERS COME FROM?

The numbers in Table 15.5 are not necessarily easy to obtain. The project manager probably has some idea of the minimum possible time to perform any activity, regardless of the amount spent. For example, wiring offices takes a minimal amount of time, regardless of how many people are working on it. He probably also has a good idea of what it would take to expedite any activity—extra workers, for example—and the corresponding cost.

## Solution

The required Solver model follows almost immediately from the project scheduling Solver model in Figure 15.3 discussed previously. We need to make only a few changes, as summarized in the following list and in Table 15.6.

## Table 15.6  Variables and Constraints for the Crashing Model

| | |
|---|---|
| **Input variables** | Activity durations (before crashing), precedence relationships, crashing data, deadline |
| **Decision variables (changing cells)** | Crashing amounts of activities |
| **Objective (target cell)** | Total crashing cost |
| **Other calculated variables** | Project length |
| **Constraints** | Precedence constraints |
| | Crashing amount must be less than or equal to Maximum reduction |
| | Project length must be less than or equal to Deadline |

- There are now changing cells to indicate how much crashing to perform.

- There are two constraints: we cannot crash by more than the allowable limits, and we must meet the deadline.

- The objective is to minimize the crashing costs. The project length is not the objective; it is part of the deadline constraint.

## DEVELOPING THE SPREADSHEET MODEL

The spreadsheet model is shown in Figure 15.12. (See the **Project Crashing.xlsx** file.) Because much of this model is identical to the previous project-scheduling model, we discuss only the modifications.

**Figure 15.12**  The Crashing Model (With a Suboptimal Solution)

| | A | B | C | D | E | F | G | H | I | J | K | L | M |
|---|---|---|---|---|---|---|---|---|---|---|---|---|---|
| 1 | Office LAN project - crashing to meet a deadline | | | | | | | | | | | | |
| 2 | | | | | | | | | | | | | |
| 3 | Data on activity network | | | | | | Crashing section | | | | | | |
| 4 | Activity | Label | Predecessors | Successors | Duration | | | | | | | | |
| 5 | Dummy Start node | Start | None | A | 0 | | Original duration | | Crash amount | | Max crash | | Cost per day |
| 6 | Perform needs analysis | A | Start | B | 8.00 | | 10 | | 2.00 | <= | 2 | | $600 |
| 7 | Develop specifications | B | A | C,D | 5.00 | | 6 | | 1.00 | <= | 1 | | $600 |
| 8 | Select server | C | B | E,G | 6.00 | | 6 | | 0.00 | <= | 1 | | $480 |
| 9 | Select software | D | B | F,G | 12.00 | | 12 | | 0.00 | <= | 3 | | $480 |
| 10 | Select cables | E | C | F | 4.00 | | 4 | | 0.00 | <= | 1 | | $480 |
| 11 | Purchase equipment | F | D,E | H,I | 3.00 | | 3 | | 0.00 | <= | 0 | | |
| 12 | Develop user manuals | G | C,D | J | 6.00 | | 6 | | 0.00 | <= | 1 | | $360 |
| 13 | Wire offices | H | F | L | 10.00 | | 12 | | 2.00 | <= | 4 | | $540 |
| 14 | Set up server | I | F | K | 3.00 | | 3 | | 0.00 | <= | 0 | | |
| 15 | Develop training program | J | G | M | 14.00 | | 14 | | 0.00 | <= | 4 | | $360 |
| 16 | Install software | K | I | L | 4.00 | | 4 | | 0.00 | <= | 1 | | $480 |
| 17 | Connect network | L | H,K | M,N | 3.00 | | 3 | | 0.00 | <= | 0 | | |
| 18 | Train users | M | J,L | O | 8.00 | | 8 | | 0.00 | <= | 2 | | $360 |
| 19 | Test & debug system | N | L | O | 12.00 | | 12 | | 0.00 | <= | 3 | | $480 |
| 20 | Get management acceptance | O | M,N | Finish | 3.00 | | 4 | | 1.00 | <= | 1 | | $300 |
| 21 | Dummy Finish node | Finish | O | None | 0 | | | | | | | | |
| 22 | | | | | | | | | | | | | |
| 23 | Activity start and finish times | | | | | | | | | | | | |
| 24 | Activity | Earliest start time | Earliest finish time | Latest start time | Latest finish time | Slack | | | Range names used | | | | |
| 25 | Start | 0 | 0 | 0 | 0 | | | | Cost_per_day | =Model!$M$6:$M$20 | | | |
| 26 | A | 0 | 8 | 0 | 8 | 0 | | | Crash_amount | =Model!$I$6:$I$20 | | | |
| 27 | B | 8 | 13 | 8 | 13 | 0 | | | Crashing_cost | =Model!$B$47 | | | |
| 28 | C | 13 | 19 | 15 | 21 | 2 | | | Deadline | =Model!$D$45 | | | |
| 29 | D | 13 | 25 | 13 | 25 | 0 | | | Max_crash | =Model!$K$6:$K$20 | | | |
| 30 | E | 19 | 23 | 21 | 25 | 2 | | | Project_time | =Model!$B$45 | | | |
| 31 | F | 25 | 28 | 25 | 28 | 0 | | | | | | | |
| 32 | G | 25 | 31 | 25 | 31 | 0 | | | | | | | |
| 33 | H | 28 | 38 | 28 | 38 | 0 | | | | | | | |
| 34 | I | 28 | 31 | 31 | 34 | 3 | | | | | | | |
| 35 | J | 31 | 45 | 31 | 45 | 0 | | | | | | | |
| 36 | K | 31 | 35 | 34 | 38 | 3 | | | | | | | |
| 37 | L | 38 | 41 | 38 | 41 | 0 | | | | | | | |
| 38 | M | 45 | 53 | 45 | 53 | 0 | | | | | | | |
| 39 | N | 41 | 53 | 41 | 53 | 0 | | | | | | | |
| 40 | O | 53 | 56 | 53 | 56 | 0 | | | | | | | |
| 41 | Finish | 56 | 56 | 56 | 56 | | | | | | | | |
| 42 | | | | | | | | | | | | | |
| 43 | Deadline constraint | | | | | | | | | | | | |
| 44 | | Project time | | Deadline | | | | | | | | | |
| 45 | | 56 | <= | 56 | | | | | | | | | |
| 46 | | | | | | | | | | | | | |
| 47 | Crashing cost | $3,180 | | | | | | | | | | | |

**①** **Input data.** In the shaded ranges, enter the three extra inputs: the per-day crashing costs, the upper limits on crashing, and the deadline.

**②** **Reductions.** Enter *any* initial values for the changing cells in column I for the reductions in activity durations.

**③** **Durations.** Calculate the durations *after* crashing in column E by subtracting the reductions in column I from the original durations, which have been moved to column G. Note that these modified durations in column E are then used, via the same CPM calculations as before, to find the project time in cell B45.

**④** **Crashing cost.** To calculate the total cost of crashing, enter the formula

=SUMPRODUCT(Crash_amount,Cost_per_day)

in cell B47.

## USING EVOLUTIONARY SOLVER

The Solver dialog box appears in Figure 15.13. As usual, you should check the Assume Non-Negative option but *not* the Assume Linear Model, before optimizing. We have introduced a subtle nonlinearity into this model that would be easy to miss. For any crashing amounts in the changing cells, the new durations are calculated in column E, and these are used to calculate the project completion time, using the same logic for earliest start and finish times as before. (Actually, we don't really require the latest start and finish times. They are used only to calculate the slacks.)

**Figure 15.13**

Evolutionary Solver Dialog Box for the Crashing Model

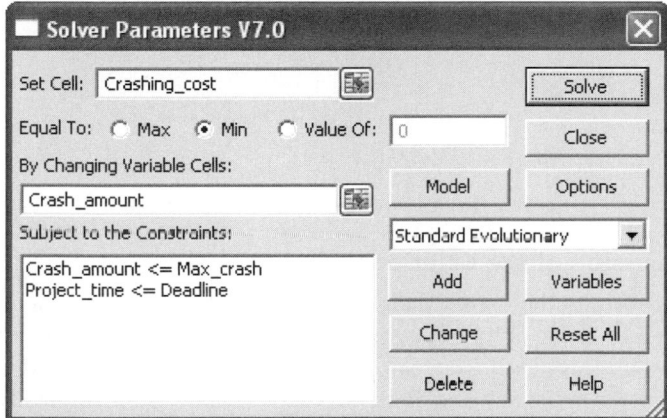

The problem is that some of the formulas in the earliest start time column use the MAX function, which introduces nonlinearity into the model. In fact, it makes the model *nonsmooth*—the same problem we discussed with IF functions in the backlogging aggregate planning model in Chapter 4. So you should be aware that Solver is not totally reliable for this version of the model unless we use Evolutionary Solver, as discussed in Chapter 8. (The **Project Crashing.xlsx** file is set up for Evolutionary Solver.)

### An Alternative Linear Model

A *linear* version of the crashing model is also available, and we have included it for your convenience in the file **Project Crashing Linear.xlsx** (see Figure 15.14). In this model, we handle precedence relationships through constraints. We let the start times of the various activities in row 4 be changing cells. (The reductions in durations in row 7 are also changing cells.) Denote the starting time of activity $i$ by $t_i$ and its duration by $d_i$. Then if activity

$j$ is an immediate successor of activity $i$, we add the constraint $t_j \geq t_i + d_i$ (or alternatively, $t_j - t_i \geq d_i$), which ensures that activity $j$ cannot start until after activity $i$ finishes. There is one such constraint for each arc in the AON network, and they are implemented in rows 15 to 35. The project time is the start time of the Finish node (found in cell T4), and the total cost of crashing is a simple sumproduct of rows 7 and 12. The resulting linear model guarantees a very quick Solver solution because the simplex method can be used. It is also a somewhat more flexible model because it can be generalized for other versions of the basic CPM model.

**Figure 15.14** The Linear Crashing Model

Office LAN project - crashing to meet a deadline: a linear model

| | Start | A | B | C | D | E | F | G | H | I | J | K | L | M | N | O | Finish |
|---|---|---|---|---|---|---|---|---|---|---|---|---|---|---|---|---|---|
| Activity | Start | A | B | C | D | E | F | G | H | I | J | K | L | M | N | O | Finish |
| Start times | 0 | 0 | 9 | 15 | 15 | 21 | 25 | 25 | 28 | 33 | 31 | 36 | 40 | 45 | 43 | 53 | 56 |
| Original duration | | 10 | 6 | 6 | 12 | 4 | 3 | 6 | 12 | 3 | 14 | 4 | 3 | 8 | 12 | 4 | |
| Reduction | | 1 | 0 | 0 | 2 | 0 | 0 | 0 | 0 | 0 | 0 | 0 | 0 | 0 | 2 | 1 | |
| | | <= | <= | <= | <= | <= | <= | <= | <= | <= | <= | <= | <= | <= | <= | <= | |
| Maximum reduction | | 2 | 1 | 1 | 3 | 1 | 0 | 1 | 4 | 0 | 4 | 1 | 0 | 2 | 3 | 1 | |
| Duration after reduction | | 9 | 6 | 6 | 10 | 4 | 3 | 6 | 12 | 3 | 14 | 4 | 3 | 8 | 10 | 3 | |
| Cost per day crashed | | 600 | 600 | 480 | 480 | 480 | | 360 | 540 | | 360 | 480 | | 360 | 480 | 300 | |

| Diff_in_start_times | =Model!$U$15:$U$35 |
|---|---|
| Duration | =Model!$W$15:$W$35 |
| Max_reduction | =Model!$E$9:$S$9 |
| Project_time | =Model!$B$39 |
| Reduction | =Model!$E$7:$S$7 |
| Start_times | =Model!$D$4:$T$4 |

Incident matrix (from AON diagram)

| | | Start | A | B | C | D | E | F | G | H | I | J | K | L | M | N | O | Finish | Diff in start times | | Duration |
|---|---|---|---|---|---|---|---|---|---|---|---|---|---|---|---|---|---|---|---|---|---|
| Start | A | -1 | 1 | | | | | | | | | | | | | | | | 0 | >= | 0 |
| A | B | | -1 | 1 | | | | | | | | | | | | | | | 9 | >= | 9 |
| B | C | | | -1 | 1 | | | | | | | | | | | | | | 6 | >= | 6 |
| B | D | | | -1 | | 1 | | | | | | | | | | | | | 6 | >= | 6 |
| C | E | | | | -1 | | 1 | | | | | | | | | | | | 6 | >= | 6 |
| C | G | | | | -1 | | | | 1 | | | | | | | | | | 10 | >= | 6 |
| D | F | | | | | -1 | | 1 | | | | | | | | | | | 10 | >= | 10 |
| D | G | | | | | -1 | | | 1 | | | | | | | | | | 10 | >= | 10 |
| E | F | | | | | | -1 | 1 | | | | | | | | | | | 4 | >= | 4 |
| F | H | | | | | | | -1 | | 1 | | | | | | | | | 3 | >= | 3 |
| F | I | | | | | | | -1 | | | 1 | | | | | | | | 8 | >= | 3 |
| G | J | | | | | | | | -1 | | | 1 | | | | | | | 6 | >= | 6 |
| H | L | | | | | | | | | -1 | | | | 1 | | | | | 12 | >= | 12 |
| I | K | | | | | | | | | | -1 | | 1 | | | | | | 3 | >= | 3 |
| J | M | | | | | | | | | | | -1 | | | 1 | | | | 14 | >= | 14 |
| K | L | | | | | | | | | | | | -1 | 1 | | | | | 4 | >= | 4 |
| L | M | | | | | | | | | | | | | -1 | 1 | | | | 5 | >= | 3 |
| L | N | | | | | | | | | | | | | -1 | | 1 | | | 3 | >= | 3 |
| M | O | | | | | | | | | | | | | | -1 | | 1 | | 8 | >= | 8 |
| N | O | | | | | | | | | | | | | | | -1 | 1 | | 10 | >= | 10 |
| O | Finish | | | | | | | | | | | | | | | | -1 | 1 | 3 | >= | 3 |

Deadline constraint

| | Project time | | Deadline |
|---|---|---|---|
| | 56 | <= | 56 |

| Total cost of crashing | 2820 |
|---|---|

## Discussion of the Solution

According to the optimal solution in Figure 15.12, the durations for activities D and N should be reduced by 2 days each, and the durations for activities A and O should be reduced by 1 day each. The total cost of this strategy is $2820, and it allows the project to be completed in the required 56 days. Note that none of the originally noncritical activities is crashed. These activities were not bottlenecks in the first place, so it doesn't make much sense to crash these activities. (We do not imply that noncritical activities are *never* crashed. They could eventually become critical as other activities are crashed and then become candidates for crashing. However, this is not the case here.)

## Sensitivity Analysis

Project crashing is ultimately a trade-off between time and cost. We have minimized the crashing cost for a given time deadline. However, this is another perfect opportunity to use SolverTable to see how the crashing cost depends on the deadline. We show this trade-off in Figure 15.15, where the deadline is varied from 45 days to the original 62 days in increments of a day. (Note that we used the *linear* version of the model in the file **Project Crashing Linear.xlsx** to create this table. The Evolutionary Solver model takes too long for use with SolverTable.) Given the limits on the amounts of reduction in the activity durations, we see that a deadline of 47 days or fewer is impossible to meet. For longer deadlines, the table shows the optimal crashing costs. We also calculated the changes in these

**Figure 15.15**  Trade-Off Between Deadline and Crashing Cost

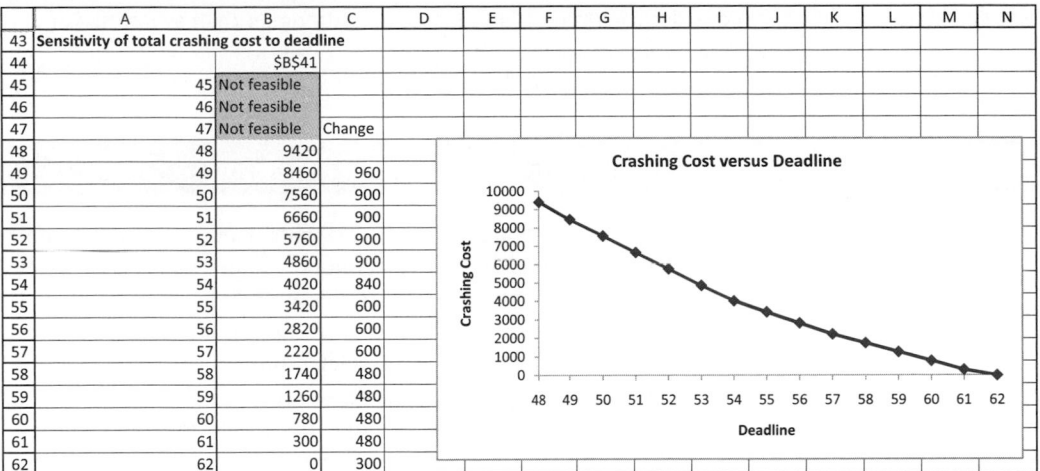

costs in column C. Although a longer deadline always costs less, the changes are clearly not constant. For example, it costs only $300 to reduce the completion time from 62 days to 61 days, but it costs $960 to reduce the completion time from 49 days to 48 days. ∎

## MODELING ISSUES

1.  The crashing cost functions we have used are *linear* in the amount of reduction—each day of reduction (for a given activity) costs the same amount. This is probably unrealistic. Each extra day of reduction typically costs *more* than the previous day. However, if we can specify the nonlinear relationship between amount of reduction and cost (probably by estimating it from historical data), then Evolutionary Solver is able to solve the problem with very little modification to the model. Alternatively, the linear model in **Project Crashing Linear.xlsx** could be modified to have a nonlinear objective. Then the regular (not Evolutionary) Solver could be used with the Assume Linear Model option unchecked.

2.  There might only be discrete crashing opportunities available. For example, there might be two types of equipment we could purchase to reduce some activity's duration, each involving a certain cost and leading to a certain reduction. This kind of discrete choice can be handled with binary (0–1) variables as in Chapter 6. ∎

### Scheduling Multiple Projects

Many organizations have limited labor resources and multiple projects that can (or must) be completed. Selecting the projects to undertake is a very important problem for any company. The company must select a portfolio of projects that is consistent with its overall goals and strategy, provides desired diversification, maintains adequate cash flows, does not exceed resource availabilities, and does not exceed a reasonable level or risk.

In this section, we illustrate one possible model for project portfolio selection. In this model, we assume that each potential project has a worker requirement over some duration and a deadline. If the project is completed by the deadline, the company receives a reward;

otherwise, it receives no reward. We use Evolutionary Solver to determine the projects to undertake and the optimal start time for each project undertaken. To simplify the example, we consider each project as a single activity rather than as a series of activities (as in other sections of this chapter).

| EXAMPLE | 15.4 SCHEDULING PROJECTS AT TIMBURTON |

Timburton Construction has 10 projects that it can (if desired) complete within the next 10 months. Each project earns a certain revenue when it is completed, but only if it is completed within the next 10 months. Otherwise, the project earns no revenue. The number of workers needed each month, the number of months needed to complete each project, and the revenue earned from each completed project are listed in Table 15.7. We assume that after the company begins working on a project, it must work on the project during consecutive months until the project is completed. Timburton has 220 workers available each month. How can it maximize the revenue earned during the next 10 months?

**Table 15.7    Worker Requirements and Revenues**

| Project | Workers per Month | Months | Revenue |
|---------|-------------------|--------|---------|
| 1 | 74 | 5 | 4800 |
| 2 | 98 | 2 | 3330 |
| 3 | 91 | 3 | 4100 |
| 4 | 95 | 4 | 6840 |
| 5 | 59 | 2 | 1650 |
| 6 | 81 | 3 | 3880 |
| 7 | 84 | 4 | 6380 |
| 8 | 78 | 3 | 4200 |
| 9 | 95 | 3 | 4860 |
| 10 | 58 | 5 | 5220 |

**Objective**    To find starting times for the projects so that total revenue is maximized and worker utilization each month is no greater than worker availability.

## WHERE DO THE NUMBERS COME FROM?

The setup here is a simplified version of what might happen in a real company. In reality, each project would probably be composed of well-defined tasks, each of which would require workers (and maybe other resources) over some duration. As for the revenues, the all-or-nothing nature we are assuming here might be built into contracts for the project, where the company gets paid by a client only if it completes the client's project by a certain deadline. Of course, these deadlines could differ across projects. This generalization could easily be incorporated into our model.

## Solution

The completed model is in the file **Scheduling Multiple Projects.xlsx** (see Figure 15.16). We assume that each project can be started at the beginning of any month from 1 to 10. Each changing cell indicates the month a project starts. For example, a changing cell value of 4 for project 5 means that project 5 is started at the beginning of month 4. We also allow each project's changing cell to equal 11. This means that the company does not undertake the project at all. To develop the model, proceed according to the following steps:

# Figure 15.16 Model for Scheduling Multiple Projects

| | A | B | C | D | E | F | G | H | I | J | K |
|---|---|---|---|---|---|---|---|---|---|---|---|
| 1 | Scheduling multiple (overlapping) projects | | | | | | | | | | |
| 2 | | | | | Ranges names used: | | | | | | |
| 3 | Deadline | 10 | | | Start | =Model!$F$7:$F$16 | | | | | |
| 4 | Workers available per month | 220 | | | Target | =Model!$B$35 | | | | | |
| 5 | | | | | | | | | | | |
| 6 | Project | Workers/month | Months | Revenue | | Start | Finish | Earned | | | |
| 7 | 1 | 74 | 5 | 4800 | | 11 | 15 | 0 | | | |
| 8 | 2 | 98 | 2 | 3330 | | 9 | 10 | 3330 | | | |
| 9 | 3 | 91 | 3 | 4100 | | 8 | 10 | 4100 | | | |
| 10 | 4 | 95 | 4 | 6840 | | 4 | 7 | 6840 | | | |
| 11 | 5 | 59 | 2 | 1650 | | 4 | 5 | 1650 | | | |
| 12 | 6 | 81 | 3 | 3880 | | 1 | 3 | 3880 | | | |
| 13 | 7 | 84 | 4 | 6380 | | 11 | 14 | 0 | | | |
| 14 | 8 | 78 | 3 | 4200 | | 1 | 3 | 4200 | | | |
| 15 | 9 | 95 | 3 | 4860 | | 6 | 8 | 4860 | | | |
| 16 | 10 | 58 | 5 | 5220 | | 1 | 5 | 5220 | | | |
| 17 | | | | | | | | | | | |
| 18 | Projects (along side) worked on in various months (along top) | | | | | | | | | | |
| 19 | | 1 | 2 | 3 | 4 | 5 | 6 | 7 | 8 | 9 | 10 |
| 20 | 1 | 0 | 0 | 0 | 0 | 0 | 0 | 0 | 0 | 0 | 0 |
| 21 | 2 | 0 | 0 | 0 | 0 | 0 | 0 | 0 | 0 | 1 | 1 |
| 22 | 3 | 0 | 0 | 0 | 0 | 0 | 0 | 0 | 1 | 1 | 1 |
| 23 | 4 | 0 | 0 | 0 | 1 | 1 | 1 | 1 | 0 | 0 | 0 |
| 24 | 5 | 0 | 0 | 0 | 1 | 1 | 0 | 0 | 0 | 0 | 0 |
| 25 | 6 | 1 | 1 | 1 | 0 | 0 | 0 | 0 | 0 | 0 | 0 |
| 26 | 7 | 0 | 0 | 0 | 0 | 0 | 0 | 0 | 0 | 0 | 0 |
| 27 | 8 | 1 | 1 | 1 | 0 | 0 | 0 | 0 | 0 | 0 | 0 |
| 28 | 9 | 0 | 0 | 0 | 0 | 0 | 1 | 1 | 1 | 0 | 0 |
| 29 | 10 | 1 | 1 | 1 | 1 | 1 | 0 | 0 | 0 | 0 | 0 |
| 30 | Workers used | 217 | 217 | 217 | 212 | 212 | 190 | 190 | 186 | 189 | 189 |
| 31 | Worker capacity exceeded? | 0 | 0 | 0 | 0 | 0 | 0 | 0 | 0 | 0 | 0 |
| 32 | | | | | | | | | | | |
| 33 | Total revenue earned | 34080 | | | | | | | | | |
| 34 | Penalty for exceeding capacity | 0 | | | | | | | | | |
| 35 | Objective to maximize | 34080 | | | | | | | | | |

**1** **Inputs.** Enter the inputs in the blue ranges.

**2** **Project Schedule.** Enter any start times in the range F7:F16. Then calculate the finish times in column G by entering the formula

**=F7+C7-1**

in cell G7 and copying it down. Note the effect of subtracting 1. The projects finish at the *ends* of the months in column G. For example, using the values in Figure 15.16, project 4 starts in month 4 and finishes at the end of month 7, for a duration of 4 months.

**3** **Revenues.** The revenue for a project is obtained only if the project is finished by the deadline, so enter the formula

**=IF(G7<=Deadline,D7,0)**

in cell H7 and copy it down. (This is one of several places where IF functions are required. This explains why we eventually need Evolutionary Solver.)

**4** **Worker utilization.** The table in the middle of the model uses 1's and 0's to indicate which months workers are used or not used by the various projects. To fill it in, enter the formula

**=IF(AND($F7<=B$19,B$19<=$G7),1,0)**

in cell B20 and copy it to the range B20:K29. Then to find the number of workers used each month, enter the formula

**=SUMPRODUCT($B$7:$B$16,B20:B29)**

in cell B30 and copy it across row 30. This formula is based on the assumption that each project uses the *same* number of workers for its entire duration. (It wouldn't be difficult to change this assumption so that worker utilization could change during the project's duration.)

**⑤ Penalties.** Recall from Chapter 8 that Evolutionary Solver does better with penalties for violating constraints than with explicit constraints. Therefore, we check in row 31 whether each month's worker availability is violated with the formula

**=IF(B30>$B$4,1,0)**

in cell B31, copied across row 31. Then we calculate a total penalty for worker constraint violations in cell B34 with the formula

**=100000*SUM(B31:K31)**

(Any suitably large constant could be used here. We just want it to be large relative to the magnitudes of the revenues.)

**⑥ Objective.** Finally, sum the revenues in column H to obtain the total revenue earned in cell B33, and calculate the objective to maximize in cell B35 with the formula

**=B33-B34**

As usual, we subtract the penalty for violating constraints from the "real" objective.

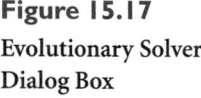

## USING EVOLUTIONARY SOLVER

We now set up the Evolutionary Solver window as shown in Figure 15.17. Note that there are no explicit constraints on worker availabilities because these have been incorporated as penalties in the objective. The only explicit constraints are that the start times must be integers between 1 and the deadline plus 1. (Again, the interpretation of a start time equal to 11 is that this project isn't undertaken at all.)

**Figure 15.17**
Evolutionary Solver
Dialog Box

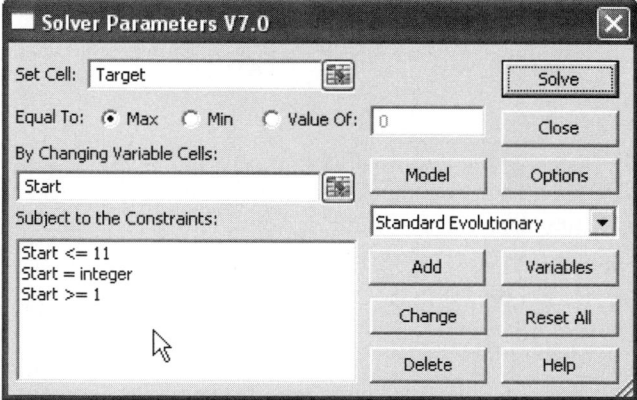

### Discussion of the Solution

It took us a number of tries, using various starting solutions in the changing cells and various Evolutionary Solver settings, to obtain the solution shown in Figure 15.16. This is evidently a difficult combinatorial problem, even though there are only 10 changing cells, each with only 11 possible values. (Keep in mind that this implies $10^{11}$ possible solutions, a *very* large number!) Don't be surprised if you obtain a solution with a slightly smaller objective than we obtained. In fact, there may even be a slightly *better* solution than ours. In any case, our solution indicates that the company can complete all but two of the projects within the deadline without violating worker availability in any month. To achieve this, it has to stagger the starting times of the projects so that they don't overlap too much. You can see that the maximum number of projects ever in process at any time is three. If you compare the worker requirements in the input section to the number of workers available each month, 220, the solution makes sense—four projects never "fit" in a single month, but some combinations of three projects do fit. ∎

# PROBLEMS

## Skill-Building Problems

10. Suppose, after doing the analysis in Example 15.2, the project manager sees a problem with the current setup. Activity C, selecting the server, requires five systems people, and activity D, selecting the software, requires seven systems people. The problem is that these two activities are scheduled concurrently, even though it turns out that four of the five systems people for activity C and four of the seven systems people for activity D are the *same people*. Assuming that a given person can work on only one activity at a time, some changes need to be made.

    **a.** One possible change is to assign two of the four common people to activity C and the other two to activity D. Now three people will be assigned to activity C and five people will be assigned to activity D. Unfortunately, with fewer people assigned, the durations of these activities will increase from 6 days to 9 days for activity C and from 12 days to 14 days for activity D. How much will these changes delay the project?

    **b.** Another possible change is to make activity D a successor to activity C, so that the four common people can continue to be assigned to both activities. How should the AON diagram for the project be redrawn? How much will this change delay the project?

    **c.** What other changes might you suggest?

11. In the Monitoring Costs sheet of the **Project Monitoring.xlsx** file, we created two tables of daily costs, one where all activities start at their earliest start times and one where they start at their latest start times. Then we created a single chart for both of these. As an alternative, do the following. Delete the bottom table (the one that uses latest start times). For the top table, give the user three choices: (1) the start times in column B can be the earliest start times, (2) the start times can be halfway between the earliest and latest start times, and (3) the start times can be the latest start times. Implement this so that the user can input a 1, 2, or 3 in some (currently unused) cell to make the choice. Based on this input, the appropriate start times should appear in the table (from the use of IF formulas), and the chart should show the

associated daily costs graphically. (If you know how, you could also let the user make the choice from one of three radio buttons.)

12. In the LAN crashing model in Example 15.3, suppose that activity D is now an immediate successor to activity C, that is, activity D cannot begin until activity C is finished. Everything else stays the same. (However, note that activity B is no longer an *immediate* predecessor of activity D, and activity G is no longer an *immediate* successor of activity C.) Modify both the **Project Crashing.xlsx** and **Product Crashing Linear.xlsx** files and run the appropriate Solver on each of them to meet a deadline of 58 days. Do you get the same schedule from each of them? (The idea is that the linear model, if set up correctly, should find the optimal solution easily, but the genetic algorithm might have some trouble getting the exact optimal solution.)

13. Modify the multiple project-scheduling model in Example 15.4 so that each project has its own due date. These due dates are listed in the file **P15_13.xlsx** Assume no revenue is earned unless a project is completed by its due date. Assuming that the objective is still to maximize total revenue, when should each project be started?

14. Given the due dates in the previous problem, how would you maximize the number of projects completed on time? (The difference here is that you are ignoring revenues.)

15. Suppose the projects in Example 15.4 are apartment units and the profit is the monthly rent earned from each apartment unit. Assume that rent is paid each month (through month 10) beginning with the month after the project is completed. How can we maximize the profit earned during the next 10 months?

16. In the model in Example 15.4, suppose each project consists of two activities and the second activity for each project cannot begin until the first activity is completed. Assuming the two activities for a given project *could* require different numbers of employees, how would you modify the model developed in Example 15.4? (You can make up any reasonable activity times and employee requirements.)

17. In the crashing model in Example 15.3, we assumed that the cost per day crashed is *constant*. This is often unrealistic. For example, it might cost $300 to decrease the duration of an activity from 10 days to 9 days, but it might cost $450 to reduce it from 9 days to 8 days. One possible way to model this is to assume that the crashing cost, $c(d)$, for reducing the duration by $d$ days is a quadratic: $c(d) = cd^2$ for some constant $c > 0$. This function produces the "increasing cost per day" behavior frequently seen. To try it out in Example 15.3, suppose the crashing cost for activity H, wiring offices, exhibits this quadratic behavior, with $c = 300$. Then, for example, the cost of reducing the duration of activity H from 12 days to 9 days is $c(3) = 300(3)^2 = \$2700$. Modify the **Project Crashing Linear.xlsx** model to accommodate this quadratic function, and then optimize to meet a deadline of 54 days. (You can still assume that activity H can be crashed by a maximum of 4 days.) Make sure you do *not* check the Assume Linear Model box in Solver.

## Skill-Extending Problems

18. In the Monitoring People sheet of the **Project Monitoring.xlsx** file, we created five tables of daily costs, one for each type of people, and we created a chart for all of these. In each table, the start times were the earliest start times. As an alternative, do the following. Delete the bottom four tables. For the top table, give the user three choices for the start times: (1) the start times in column B can be the earliest start times, (2) the start times can be halfway between the earliest and latest start times, and (3) the start times can be the latest start times. Also, let the user choose one type of people to monitor: engineering, systems, purchasing, installers, or training. You can decide on the user interface for making these choices. Based on these choices, the appropriate start times should appear in column B of the table, the body of the table should show daily usages of the type of people selected, and the chart should show these daily usages graphically. (*Hint*: In the formulas in the body of the table, you'll need to refer to one of the columns in the range G6:K20. One useful way to do so is with Excel's OFFSET function. For example, you could offset everything with respect to cell F5 or any other convenient "anchor" cell. Look up the OFFSET function in online help.)

19. Starting with a project schedule where some activities are noncritical, is it ever optimal to crash any of these noncritical activities to meet a given deadline? The idea is that as you keep crashing to meet a tighter and tighter deadline, a noncritical activity could conceivably become critical, and then you might want to crash it. Experiment with the LAN project model to see if you can ever make this occur. Feel free to change the maximum reductions for the activities and/or their crashing costs per day.

## 15.4 MODELS WITH UNCERTAIN ACTIVITY TIMES

*When activity times are random, we typically cannot say for certain whether a given activity will be on the critical path.*

In Section 15.2, we learned how to calculate the required time to complete a project that consists of several activities. We also saw that the critical path consists of the bottleneck activities, those activities that cannot be delayed without delaying the project as a whole. In that section, we assumed that the individual activity times are known with certainty. We now make the more realistic assumption that the activity times are random with given probability distributions, and we find the distribution of the time needed to complete the project. Because of randomness, we can no longer identify *the* critical path. We can only determine the *probability* that any activity is critical.

To illustrate this latter statement, suppose that activities A and B can begin immediately. Activity C can then begin as soon as activities A and B are both completed, and the project is completed as soon as activity C is completed (see Figure 15.18). Activity C is clearly on the critical path, but what about A and B? Let's say that the *expected* activity times of A and B are 10 and 12, respectively. If we use these expected times and ignore any uncertainty about the actual times—that is, if we proceed as in Section 15.2—then activity B is definitely a critical activity because its duration is definitely longer than activity A's duration. However, suppose there is some positive probability that A can have duration 12 and B can have duration 11. Under this scenario, A is a critical activity. Therefore, we cannot say in advance which of the activities, A or B, will be critical. However, we can use simulation to see how *likely* it is that each of these activities is critical. We can also see how long the entire project is likely to take.

**Figure 15.18**

A Simple Project
Network

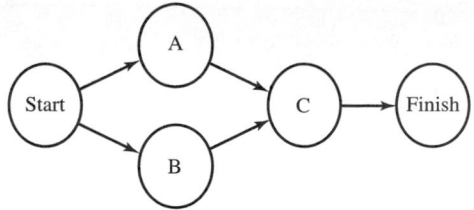

We illustrate the procedure in the following example, which is the same example that we have been discussing (without crashing). We repeat the story here for your convenience.

## EXAMPLE | 15.5 LAN PROJECT WITH UNCERTAIN ACTIVITY TIMES

We again analyze the LAN project from Example 15.1, but we now assume that the activity durations are uncertain, with given probability distributions. The company realizes that the *actual* activity times can vary due to unexpected delays, worker illnesses, and so on. Assuming that the company has a deadline of 60 days, it wants to use simulation to see (1) how long the project is likely to take, (2) how likely it is that the project will be completed by the deadline, and (3) which activities are likely to be critical.

**Objective**   To simulate the time to complete the LAN project, and to estimate the probability that any given activity will be part of the critical path.

### WHERE DO THE NUMBERS COME FROM?

All of the data are the same as in Example 15.1 except for the probability distributions for activity times. We discuss these in some detail here.

## Solution

We first need to choose distributions for the uncertain activity times. Then, given any randomly generated activity times, we illustrate a method for calculating the length of the project and identifying the activities on the critical path.

### The PERT Distribution

As always, we could use several reasonable candidate probability distributions for the random activity times. Here we illustrate a distribution that is popular in project scheduling, called the PERT distribution. As shown in Figure 15.19, it is a curved version of the triangular distribution. Like the triangular distribution, the PERT distribution is specified by three parameters that the company should be able to estimate from past experience: a minimum value, a most likely value, and a maximum value. The distribution in the figure uses the values 4, 5, and 12 for these three values, which implies a mean of 6.[4] We use this distribution for activity B. Its random activity time can be generated with @RISK using the formula

**=RISKPERT(4,5,12)**

---

[4] This distribution is named after the acronym PERT (Program Review and Evaluation Technique), which is synonymous with project scheduling in an uncertain environment. Its mean is always a weighted average of its three parameters, with the most likely value getting four times as much weight as the other two. In this case, the mean is $[1(4) + 4(5) + 1(12)]/(1 + 4 + 1) = 6$.

**Figure 15.19**
PERT Distribution

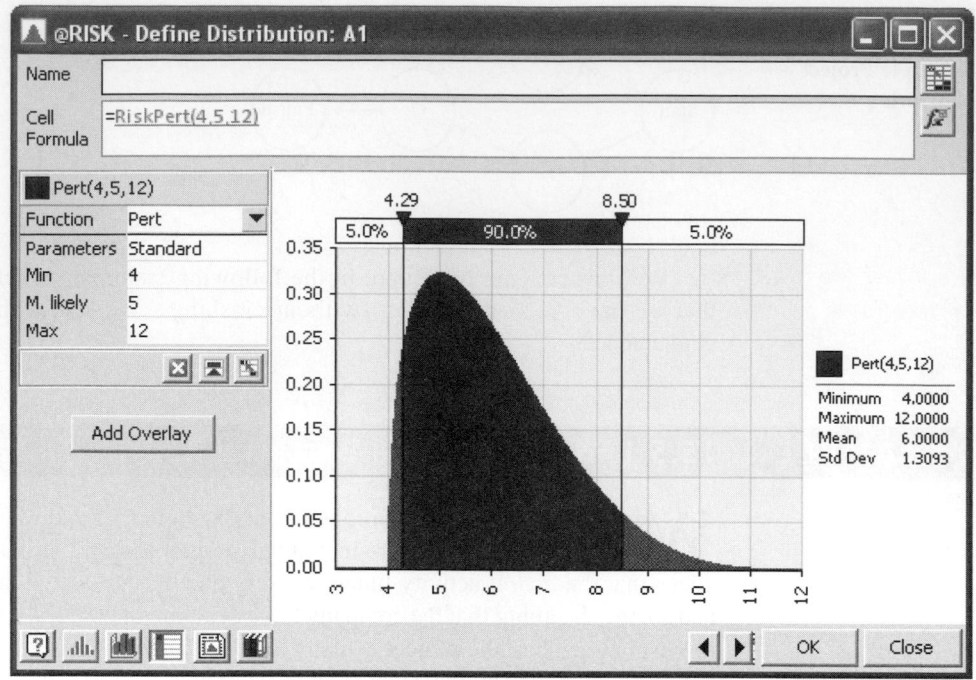

Similarly, for the other activities, we choose parameters for the PERT distribution that lead to the same means as the durations we used in Example 15.1. (In reality, it would be done the other way around. The contractor would estimate the minimum, most likely, and maximum parameters for the various activities, and the means would then follow from these. We want to keep the means the same as the activity times in Example 15.1 for comparison.)

### @RISK Function: *RISKPERT*

*To generate a random number with @RISK from the PERT distribution, a curved version of the triangular distribution, enter the formula =RISKPERT(Min,Most likely,Max).*

### DEVELOPING THE SIMULATION MODEL

We again use the same basic CPM model to calculate the earliest start and finish times, the latest start and finish times, and the slacks for each of the activities, exactly as we did in Section 15.2. This method allow us to calculate the total project time for any *fixed* values of the activity times—that is, for any iteration of the simulation. By looking at the slacks for any iteration, we can see which activities are critical for that iteration (because an activity is critical only if its slack is 0).

The model is a direct extension of the model in Example 15.1, as shown in Figure 15.20 (see the **Project Simulation.xlsx** file), so we describe only the new steps necessary:

**Figure 15.20**  The LAN Project Simulation Model

| | A | B | C | D | E | F | G | H | I |
|---|---|---|---|---|---|---|---|---|---|
| 1 | Office LAN project - simulation with random activity times | | | | | | | | |
| 2 | | | | | | | | | |
| 3 | Data on activity network | | | | | Parameters of PERT distributions | | | |
| 4 | Activity | Label | Predecessors | Successors | Min | Most likely | Max | Implied mean | Duration |
| 5 | Dummy Start node | Start | None | A | | | | | 0 |
| 6 | Perform needs analysis | A | Start | B | 8 | 9 | 16 | 10 | 10.706 |
| 7 | Develop specifications | B | A | C,D | 4 | 5 | 12 | 6 | 8.093 |
| 8 | Select server | C | B | E,G | 5 | 6 | 7 | 6 | 5.417 |
| 9 | Select software | D | B | F,G | 4 | 13 | 16 | 12 | 13.339 |
| 10 | Select cables | E | C | F | 3 | 4 | 5 | 4 | 4.159 |
| 11 | Purchase equipment | F | D,E | H,I | 2 | 3 | 4 | 3 | 3.636 |
| 12 | Develop user manuals | G | C,D | J | 4 | 6 | 8 | 6 | 6.345 |
| 13 | Wire offices | H | F | L | 10 | 11 | 18 | 12 | 11.840 |
| 14 | Set up server | I | F | K | 3 | 3 | 3 | 3 | 3.000 |
| 15 | Develop training program | J | G | M | 12 | 14 | 16 | 14 | 13.221 |
| 16 | Install software | K | I | L | 3 | 4 | 5 | 4 | 3.225 |
| 17 | Connect network | L | H,K | M,N | 2 | 3 | 4 | 3 | 3.363 |
| 18 | Train users | M | J,L | O | 8 | 8 | 8 | 8 | 8.000 |
| 19 | Test & debug system | N | L | O | 6 | 11 | 22 | 12 | 10.088 |
| 20 | Get management acceptance | O | M,N | Finish | 3 | 4 | 5 | 4 | 3.901 |
| 21 | Dummy Finish node | Finish | O | None | | | | | 0 |
| 22 | | | | | | | | | |

> The @RISK statistical measures in columns H and K are meaningless until you run the simulation.

| | A | B | C | D | E | F | G | H | J | K |
|---|---|---|---|---|---|---|---|---|---|---|
| 23 | Activity start and finish times | | | | | | | | | |
| 24 | Activity | Earliest start time | Earliest finish time | Latest start time | Latest finish time | Slack | On critical path? | Pr(critical) | Summary statistics from @RISK for project completion time | |
| 25 | Start | 0.00 | 0.00 | 0.00 | 0.00 | | | | Minimum | 54.45 |
| 26 | A | 0.00 | 10.71 | 0.00 | 10.71 | 0.00 | 1 | 0.972 | Maximum | 75.67 |
| 27 | B | 10.71 | 18.80 | 10.71 | 18.80 | 0.00 | 1 | 0.972 | Mean | 62.83 |
| 28 | C | 18.80 | 24.22 | 22.56 | 27.98 | 3.76 | 0 | 0.158 | Standard deviation | 3.75 |
| 29 | D | 18.80 | 32.14 | 18.80 | 32.14 | 0.00 | 1 | 0.833 | Percentiles | |
| 30 | E | 24.22 | 28.37 | 27.98 | 32.14 | 3.76 | 0 | 0.159 | 5% | 56.96 |
| 31 | F | 32.14 | 35.77 | 32.14 | 35.77 | 0.00 | 1 | 0.725 | 10% | 58.13 |
| 32 | G | 32.14 | 38.48 | 33.50 | 39.84 | 1.36 | 0 | 0.275 | 25% | 60.11 |
| 33 | H | 35.77 | 47.61 | 35.77 | 47.61 | 0.00 | 1 | 0.725 | 50% | 62.64 |
| 34 | I | 35.77 | 38.77 | 41.39 | 44.39 | 5.61 | 0 | 0.000 | 75% | 65.28 |
| 35 | J | 38.48 | 51.70 | 39.84 | 53.06 | 1.36 | 0 | 0.275 | 90% | 67.56 |
| 36 | K | 38.77 | 42.00 | 44.39 | 47.61 | 5.61 | 0 | 0.000 | 95% | 69.27 |
| 37 | L | 47.61 | 50.98 | 47.61 | 50.98 | 0.00 | 1 | 0.725 | Targets (days) | |
| 38 | M | 51.70 | 59.70 | 53.06 | 61.06 | 1.36 | 0 | 0.282 | 60 | 0.237 |
| 39 | N | 50.98 | 61.06 | 50.98 | 61.06 | 0.00 | 1 | 0.718 | 62 | 0.426 |
| 40 | O | 61.06 | 64.97 | 61.06 | 64.97 | 0.00 | 1 | 1.000 | | |
| 41 | Finish | 64.97 | 64.97 | 64.97 | 64.97 | | | | | |
| 42 | | | | | | | | | | |
| 43 | Project completion time | 64.97 | | | | | | | | |

**1** **Inputs.** Enter the information about precedence relationships and the parameters of the PERT activity time distributions in the blue cells. As discussed previously, we actually chose the minimum, most likely, and maximum values to achieve the same *mean* durations as in Example 15.1. Note that some of these distributions are symmetric about the most likely value, whereas others are skewed.

**2** **Activity times.** Generate random activity times in column I by entering the formula

=RISKPERT(E6,F6,G6)

in cell I6 and copying it down. Of course, the durations for the fictitious Start and Finish nodes, in cells I5 and I21, are nonrandom and are equal to 0.

**3** **Critical activities.** To see whether an activity is critical, enter the formula

=IF(F26=0,1,0)

in cell G26 and copy it down. This records a 1 for any activity with 0 slack—that is, for any critical activity. However, if you press the F9 key to generate new random durations, you will see that the critical activities can change from one iteration to another. It is convenient to calculate averages of these 0's and 1's in column H. To do so, enter the formula

=RISKMEAN(G26)

in cell H26 and copy it down. Initially, the values in this column are meaningless. However, after running the simulation, they indicate the fraction of iterations that result in 1. This fraction is an estimate of the probability that the activity is critical.

**④** **Summary measures.** Enter @RISK statistical functions in column K for the project completion time. For example, enter

**=RISKMEAN(B43)**

in cell K27 and

**=RISKPERCENTILE($B$43,J30)**

in cell K30.

### Running the Simulation

We set the number of iterations to 1000 and the number of simulations to 1, and then run the simulation in the usual way.

### Discussion of the Simulation Results

After running the simulation, we request the histogram of project times shown in Figure 15.21. Recall from Example 15.1 that when the activity times are not random, the project time is 62 days. Now it varies from a low of 54.45 days to a high of 75.67 days, with an average of 62.83 days.[5] Because the company is interested in the probability of finishing the project within 60 days, we moved the left slider in the graph to 60. This indicates that there is only about a 23.7% chance of achieving the deadline. In the other direction, we see that there is about a 5% chance that the project will take longer than 69.27 days. This is certainly not good news for the company, and it might have to resort to the crashing we discussed in the previous section.

**Figure 15.21**

Histogram of Project Completion Time

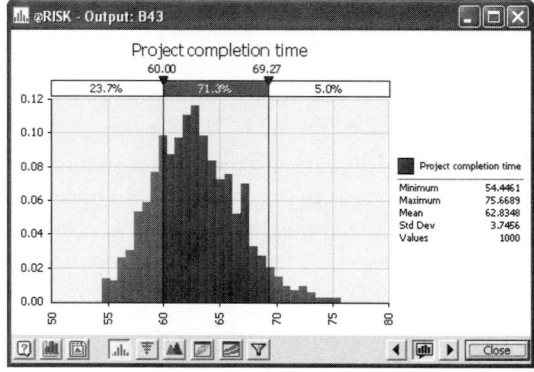

The @RISK averages of 0's and 1's in the range H26:H40 of Figure 15.20 indicate the fraction of iterations where each activity was critical. Several of these fractions, notably for activities A, B, and O, are very close (or equal) to 1. This means that these activities are almost always (or always) critical. Evidently, only very unusual values for the random durations can make these activities noncritical. Similarly, activities I and K are never critical; their fractions are equal to 0. The fractions for the other activities are less extreme. Any one of them could easily be on the critical path. Therefore, we see that there is no *single* critical path. It depends completely on the random durations we happen to observe.

One last observation is that the 0's and 1's in column G are "all or nothing." That is, if the slack changes from 0 to a very small positive number such as 0.00023, then the 0–1 variable in column G changes from 0 to 1 and indicates that the corresponding activity is noncritical. We suspect that this happened in the few iterations where activities A and B were not critical. They were probably still very *close* to being critical. ∎

---

[5] It can be shown mathematically that the expected project time is *always* greater than when the expected activity times are used to calculate the project time (as in Example 15.1). In other words, an assumption of certainty always leads to an underestimation of the true expected project time.

The traditional PERT approach to project scheduling with uncertain activity times does not involve simulation. Instead, it starts with a minimum, most likely, and maximum estimate of each activity's time (just as we did with the PERT distribution). Then it uses formulas to find the mean and standard deviation of each activity time distribution, and finally it uses an *approximate* method to calculate the mean and standard deviation of the time to complete the project. This method has been in use for many years, and it is found in many textbooks on project management. However, we favor the simulation approach used here because it has the following benefits over the traditional approach: (1) it is more straightforward and easier to understand, (2) it permits *any* distributions for the activity times, not just the PERT distributions we used, (3) it provides estimates of the probabilities that the various activities are critical, and (4) it even allows us to build correlation (with the RISKCORRMAT function) into the activity times. In short, the simulation approach is more flexible, and it can be implemented easily with Excel and @RISK. ∎

# PROBLEMS

## Skill-Building Problems

**20.** In the model in Example 15.5, suppose bonuses and penalties are incurred for earliness or lateness. Specifically, suppose a bonus of $2000 is received if the project is completed within 60 days, an *extra* bonus of $1000 is received if the project is completed within 58 days, and a penalty of $1000 is incurred for every full day past a project completion of 64 days. (For example, if the project is completed in 66.7 days, the penalty is $2000— two full days late.) Modify the model appropriately, and then run the simulation to find the distribution of the net monetary outcome (negative if a penalty, positive if a bonus). What is the expected value of this net amount? What is the probability of a $3000 total bonus? What is the probability of a penalty of at least $4000?

**21.** We indicated in Example 15.5 that the mean project length from the simulation is *greater than* the project length of 62 days from substituting the mean activity durations (the ones used in earlier sections). Note that the PERT distributions we used in the example, with the exception of activity D, are either symmetric around the most likely value or skewed to the right. Could this skewness to the right lead to the rather large mean project length from the simulation? Experiment with the parameters of the PERT distributions in the example, always keeping the same *mean* durations. For example, you could change the parameters of activity A from 8, 9, 16 to 7, 10, 13 (to make it symmetric) or to 4, 11, 12 (to make it skewed to the left). Each of these has the same mean, 10, and there are many other combinations that have mean 10 that you could try. Run the simulation with a few such combinations. What effect does it have on the mean project length from the simulation? Does the mean project length continue to be greater

than 62? What effect does it have on the percentiles of the simulation, such as the 5th or 95th percentiles? Do you conclude that the *shapes* of the input distributions, given that they keep the same means, have much effect on the distribution of project length?

## Skill-Extending Problems

**22.** We saw in Chapter 11 how to introduce correlation into an @RISK simulation with RISKCORRMAT functions. We implicitly assumed that the activity durations in Example 15.5 are probabilistically independent. However, it is very possible that some of them would be correlated in a real situation. Specifically, assume activities A and B are positively correlated with correlation 0.7. Also, assume that activities G and J are positively correlated with correlation 0.6. Modify the model appropriately and rerun the simulation. What differences, if any, do you see in the outputs?

**23.** Most of the literature in project scheduling with uncertain activity times advocates the use of the *beta* distribution for activity times. This is a continuous distribution with four parameters: a minimum, a maximum, and two parameters $\alpha_1$ and $\alpha_2$ that control the shape of the distribution. (@RISK calls this the *generalized* beta, or BetaGeneral, distribution because the "standard" beta distribution has minimum 0 and maximum 1.) It turns out that the PERT distribution we have been using is a special case of the generalized beta distribution. However, it has only three parameters: a minimum, a most likely value, and a maximum. To understand this better, try the following. Click on the Windows Start button, Programs, Palisade Decision Tools, Online Manuals, and finally Distribution Function Summary to open a PDF help file. Click on its bookmark tab to see a list of distribution functions and click on the PERT (Beta) bookmark. There you can see how the $\alpha_1$ and $\alpha_2$ parameters are found from the minimum, most likely, and maximum parameters of the PERT distribution. Specifically, they are chosen so that the mean of the PERT distribution is (min + 4 ml + max)/6, where ml is the most likely value. You can also click on the Beta (Generalized) bookmark to see its properties. Now use this information from online help as follows. Suppose the parameters of a PERT distribution are 4, 5, and 12. What is the mean of this distribution? What are the corresponding values of

$\alpha_1$ and $\alpha_2$ for the equivalent beta distribution? According to the online help for the generalized beta distribution, its mean is min + $[\alpha_1/(\alpha_1 + \alpha_2)]$ (max − min). Does this evaluate to the same mean that you got for the PERT distribution? Finally, open RISKview. Select the PERT distribution with parameters 4, 5, and 12, and look at its shape and properties. Then select the equivalent BetaGeneral distribution with the parameters you found earlier. Does it have the same shape and properties as the PERT distribution? It should— they're equivalent.

## 15.5 A BRIEF LOOK AT MICROSOFT PROJECT

The preceding sections have shown how to implement the various features of project scheduling in Excel. Excel is a tremendously flexible tool, so with some creativity, it is possible to implement virtually all of the aspects of project management in a spreadsheet. However, a number of software packages are devoted entirely to project management. These packages are not necessarily as flexible as Excel, but they tend to be very good at their intended purpose: project management. We have included the educational version of Microsoft Project (MS Project) in the software that accompanies this book. MS Project is actually part of the Microsoft Office family of software, but it must be purchased separately from Office. It is arguably one of the most popular project-management software packages and is used by many companies to manage their projects.

The good news is that MS Project is a powerful software package for managing projects. The bad news is that, as with other powerful software packages, it takes some time and practice to learn the many features of the package. There is no way we can provide more than a brief introduction to its capabilities. Nevertheless, it is not too difficult to get started, as we discuss briefly here.

When you open MS Project, you can ask to create a new project. This takes you through a wizard that asks you a few questions, such as when the project can start, and eventually shows you a blank spreadsheet-like window. This is where you can list the project tasks and their durations, as shown in Figure 15.22 for the LAN project we have been discussing. (MS Project allows you to save your work in an mpp file. The file for this project is **LAN Project.mpp**.) Note that the start time for each project is 1/30/2006 (the day this section was written), and the finish times are automatically entered as the start times plus the durations.[6] Note also that MS Project does not require Start and Finish nodes, although you can add these (with 0 durations) if you like.

The next step is to enter the immediate predecessors of the tasks in the Predecessors column. These appear in the next-to-last column of Figure 15.23. For example, the predecessors of activity 6 (purchase equipment) are activities 3 and 4, and we enter them as "3,4" in the Predecessors column. (Note that we have now specified that the project can start on 9/1/2006, and working is permitted on weekends.) As soon as this information on durations and immediate predecessors is entered, MS Project does the required CPM calculations behind the scenes. By right-clicking in the gray row at the top of the window, you can ask for various columns of information to be inserted. As Figure 15.23 indicates, we asked for the early start and finish times, the late start and finish times, the free and total slacks, and the immediate successors. You do not need to do anything to create these columns; all you need

[6] By default, Project skips over the weekends. For example, note that the first activity, with duration 10 days, goes from Monday through Friday and then the next Monday through the next Friday. However, it is possible to change a setting so that work is performed over weekends, as we do in later figures.

## Figure 15.22

Tasks for the LAN Project

| | ⓘ | Task Name | Duration | Start | Finish | Predecessors | Resource Names |
|---|---|---|---|---|---|---|---|
| 1 | ▦ | Perform needs analysis | 10 days | Mon 1/30/06 | Fri 2/10/06 | | |
| 2 | | Develop specifications | 6 days | Mon 1/30/06 | Mon 2/6/06 | | |
| 3 | | Select server | 6 days | Mon 1/30/06 | Mon 2/6/06 | | |
| 4 | | Select software | 12 days | Mon 1/30/06 | Tue 2/14/06 | | |
| 5 | | Select cables | 4 days | Mon 1/30/06 | Thu 2/2/06 | | |
| 6 | | Purchase equipment | 3 days | Mon 1/30/06 | Wed 2/1/06 | | |
| 7 | | Develop user manuals | 6 days | Mon 1/30/06 | Mon 2/6/06 | | |
| 8 | | Wire offices | 12 days | Mon 1/30/06 | Tue 2/14/06 | | |
| 9 | | Set up server | 3 days | Mon 1/30/06 | Wed 2/1/06 | | |
| 10 | | Develop training program | 14 days | Mon 1/30/06 | Thu 2/16/06 | | |
| 11 | | Install software | 4 days | Mon 1/30/06 | Thu 2/2/06 | | |
| 12 | | Connect network | 3 days | Mon 1/30/06 | Wed 2/1/06 | | |
| 13 | | Train users | 8 days | Mon 1/30/06 | Wed 2/8/06 | | |
| 14 | | Test & debug system | 12 days | Mon 1/30/06 | Tue 2/14/06 | | |
| 15 | | Get management acceptar | 4 days | Mon 1/30/06 | Thu 2/2/06 | | |

## Figure 15.23   Tasks and Precedence Relations for LAN Project

| | Task Name | Duration | Start | Finish | Early Start | Early Finish | Late Start | Late Finish | Free Slack | Total Slack | Predecessors | Successors |
|---|---|---|---|---|---|---|---|---|---|---|---|---|
| 1 | Perform needs analysis | 10 days | Fri 9/1/06 | Sun 9/10/06 | Fri 9/1/06 | Sun 9/10/06 | Fri 9/1/06 | Sun 9/10/06 | 0 days | 0 days | | 2 |
| 2 | Develop specifications | 6 days | Mon 9/11/06 | Sat 9/16/06 | Mon 9/11/06 | Sat 9/16/06 | Mon 9/11/06 | Sat 9/16/06 | 0 days | 0 days | 1 | 3,4 |
| 3 | Select server | 6 days | Sun 9/17/06 | Fri 9/22/06 | Sun 9/17/06 | Fri 9/22/06 | Tue 9/19/06 | Sun 9/24/06 | 0 days | 2 days | 2 | 5,7 |
| 4 | Select software | 12 days | Sun 9/17/06 | Thu 9/28/06 | Sun 9/17/06 | Thu 9/28/06 | Sun 9/17/06 | Thu 9/28/06 | 0 days | 0 days | 2 | 6,7 |
| 5 | Select cables | 4 days | Sat 9/23/06 | Tue 9/26/06 | Sat 9/23/06 | Tue 9/26/06 | Mon 9/25/06 | Thu 9/28/06 | 2 days | 2 days | 3 | 6 |
| 6 | Purchase equipment | 3 days | Fri 9/29/06 | Sun 10/1/06 | Fri 9/29/06 | Sun 10/1/06 | Fri 9/29/06 | Sun 10/1/06 | 0 days | 0 days | 4,5 | 8,9 |
| 7 | Develop user manuals | 6 days | Fri 9/29/06 | Wed 10/4/06 | Fri 9/29/06 | Wed 10/4/06 | Sun 10/1/06 | Fri 10/6/06 | 0 days | 2 days | 3,4 | 10 |
| 8 | Wire offices | 12 days | Mon 10/2/06 | Fri 10/13/06 | Mon 10/2/06 | Fri 10/13/06 | Mon 10/2/06 | Fri 10/13/06 | 0 days | 0 days | 6 | 12 |
| 9 | Set up server | 3 days | Mon 10/2/06 | Wed 10/4/06 | Mon 10/2/06 | Wed 10/4/06 | Sat 10/7/06 | Mon 10/9/06 | 0 days | 5 days | 6 | 11 |
| 10 | Develop training program | 14 days | Thu 10/5/06 | Wed 10/18/06 | Thu 10/5/06 | Wed 10/18/06 | Sat 10/7/06 | Fri 10/20/06 | 0 days | 2 days | 7 | 13 |
| 11 | Install software | 4 days | Thu 10/5/06 | Sun 10/8/06 | Thu 10/5/06 | Sun 10/8/06 | Tue 10/10/06 | Fri 10/13/06 | 5 days | 5 days | 9 | 12 |
| 12 | Connect network | 3 days | Sat 10/14/06 | Mon 10/16/06 | Sat 10/14/06 | Mon 10/16/06 | Sat 10/14/06 | Mon 10/16/06 | 0 days | 0 days | 8,11 | 13,14 |
| 13 | Train users | 8 days | Thu 10/19/06 | Thu 10/26/06 | Thu 10/19/06 | Thu 10/26/06 | Sat 10/21/06 | Sat 10/28/06 | 2 days | 2 days | 10,12 | 15 |
| 14 | Test & debug system | 12 days | Tue 10/17/06 | Sat 10/28/06 | Tue 10/17/06 | Sat 10/28/06 | Tue 10/17/06 | Sat 10/28/06 | 0 days | 0 days | 12 | 15 |
| 15 | Get management acceptar | 4 days | Sun 10/29/06 | Wed 11/1/06 | Sun 10/29/06 | Wed 11/1/06 | Sun 10/29/06 | Wed 11/1/06 | 0 days | 0 days | 13,14 | |

to do is ask for them. Note that MS Project shows each Start time (third column) as the Early Start time by default. However, we know that tasks with slack can start anywhere between their early and late start times.

### Technical Note: *Free and Total Slacks*

*The quantity we have called slack is often called total slack. A task's **total slack** is the amount of time the task can be delayed before the project finish date is delayed. For example, task 3, selecting the server, has a total slack of 2 days. It can start as early as Sunday, 9/17/2006, but if it is delayed by 2 days and doesn't start until the following Tuesday, the project as a whole will not be delayed. There is also another slack called the free slack. A task's **free slack** is defined as the amount of time a task can be delayed without delaying its successor tasks. For example, note that task 3's successors, tasks 5 and 7, have early start times Saturday, 9/23/2006 and Friday, 9/29/2006. Task 3's early finish time is Friday, 9/22/2006, so if task 3 is delayed at all, the early start time of one of its successors, task 5, will be delayed. This explains the free slack of 0 for task 3. However, this free slack for task 3 is probably less relevant than its total slack because activity 5 itself has slack and can therefore be delayed without delaying the project.*

MS Project automatically creates a fairly large number of charts that you can view. We show two of them in Figures 15.24 and 15.25. The Gantt chart in Figure 15.24 is essentially the same as the one we constructed in Excel except that the order of tasks from top to

**Figure 15.24** Gantt Chart for the LAN Project

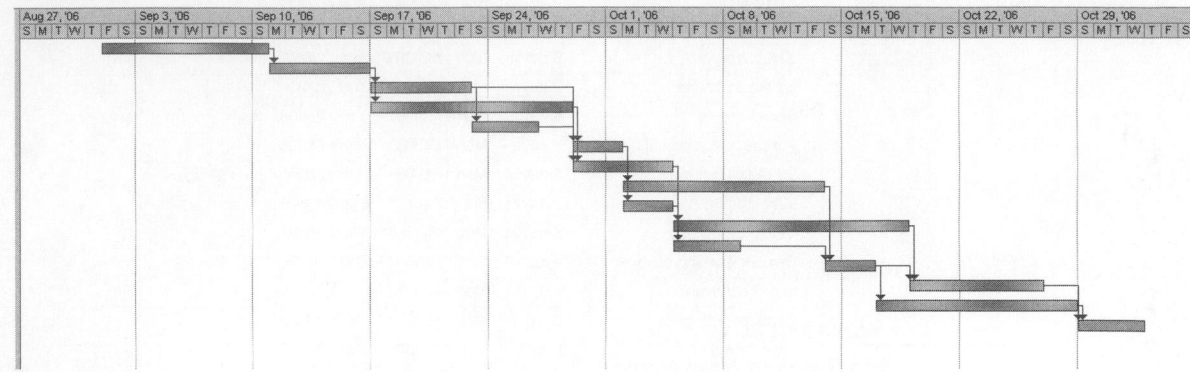

**Figure 15.25** Network Diagram for the LAN Project

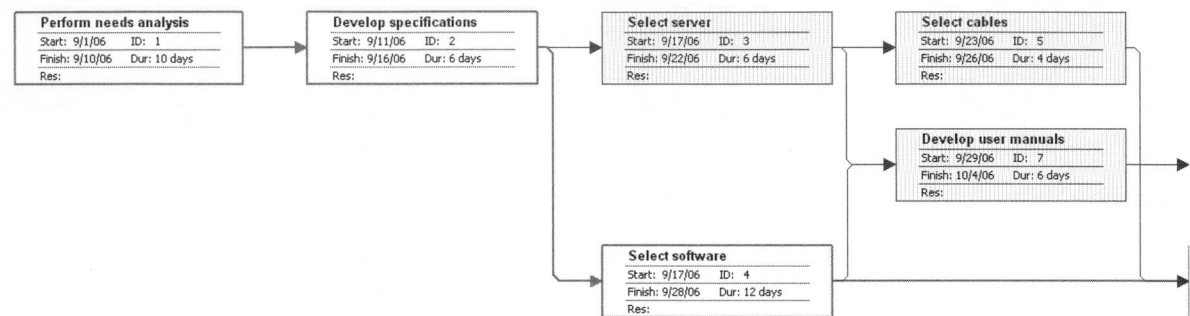

bottom is reversed. (You can hover the cursor over any of these bars to see more information about the associated tasks.) The AON project diagram, part of which appears in Figure 15.25, shows the precedence relationships, as well as the start and finish times, the durations, and information about resources used (which we haven't specified for this project). Although it is not visible in this black and white drawing, the critical activities and noncritical activities appear in different colors on a computer screen.

In addition, you can request many reports. One possibility (not shown here) lists information about the activities on the critical path. Of course, MS Project figures out which activities are on the critical path. All you need to do is ask for the report.

MS Project is a very powerful and feature-rich software package; however, it does have some drawbacks. First, it has no built-in optimizer (such as Solver) to perform any optimization, such as crashing to meet a deadline. Second, it assumes a deterministic world, where the durations of the activities are known with certainty. Of course, you can change any durations manually to see how the project as a whole is affected, but you cannot run a simulation with random durations, as we did with @RISK. In spite of these drawbacks, MS Project and other project management software packages play a prominent role at many organizations, and we wouldn't be surprised if many of you end up using one of these packages in your jobs.

## 15.6 CONCLUSION

As we have indicated in this chapter, project management is an area all in itself. This is due to the importance of managing large and costly projects in most organizations. Many entire books have been written about the various aspects of project management, and the topics we have covered here form only a relatively small percentage of the material in these books. Nevertheless, we have seen that management science offers a number of tools that are useful in scheduling and allocating resources to projects. Among others, these tools include (1) the CPM calculations used to determine the length of a project and its critical path, (2) optimization models for crashing activities to meet a deadline at minimum cost, and (3) simulation models for determining how the length of a project is affected by uncertain task times. Finally, we have seen that a number of software packages, such as MS Project, are devoted entirely to project management. Although these packages lack some of the features available with Excel, notably optimization and simulation, they can be very effective for managing the timing and required resources of real-world projects.

## Summary of Key Management Science Terms

| Term | Explanation | Page |
|---|---|---|
| CPM | Critical Path Method, used to analyze projects with known activity times | 863 |
| PERT | Program and Evaluation Review Technique, used to analyze projects with random activity times | 863 |
| Duration | Time to complete an activity in a project | 865 |
| Immediate predecessor | Activity that must be completed before a given activity can begin | 865 |
| Immediate successor | Activity that can't start until a given activity is completed | 865 |
| Critical activity | Activity whose delay will necessarily delay the completion of the project | 866 |
| Critical path | Set of all critical activities, also called the *bottleneck* path | 866 |
| Slack | Amount a noncritical activity can be delayed without delaying the project | 867 |
| Earliest and latest starting times | Earliest and latest times an activity can start and finish, given the precedence relationships in the project | 868 |
| Earliest and latest finish times | Earliest and latest times an activity can start and finish without delaying the project | 868 |
| Gantt chart | Chart that shows the schedule of activities | 871 |
| Crashing | Reducing activity times (at a cost) to meet a deadline | 880 |

## Summary of Key Excel Terms

| Term | Explanation | Excel | Page |
|---|---|---|---|
| Gantt chart | Way to show activity durations through time in a meaningful way | See Excel Tip | 872 |
| PERT distribution | Useful for simulating activity times | Use RISKPERT function in @RISK | 892 |
| Microsoft Project | Separate from Excel, but a useful package for analyzing multiactivity projects | | 896 |

## PROBLEMS

### Skill-Building Problems

**24.** Before a new product can be introduced at Kehls, the activities shown in the file **P15_24.xlsx** must be completed, where all times are in weeks.
   **a.** Draw the AON project network and determine a critical path and the minimum number of weeks required before the new product can be introduced.
   **b.** The duration of each activity can be reduced by up to 2 weeks at the following cost per week: A, $80; B,

$60; C, $30; D, $60; E, $40; F, $30; G, $20. (Assume that activity H cannot be crashed.) Determine how to minimize the cost of getting the product into the stores for the peak Christmas sales period, assuming that it is now 12 weeks before this period begins.

**25.** A company has a project that consists of 11 activities, described in the file **P15_25.xlsx**. Draw an AON project network and then find the critical path and the minimum number of days required to complete this project. Also, create the associated Gantt chart.

26. The promoters of a rock concert in Indianapolis must perform the tasks shown in the file **P15_26.xlsx** before the concert can be held. (All durations are in days.) Draw the AON project network. Then find the critical path and the minimum number of days needed to prepare for the concert, and create the associated Gantt chart.

27. Consider the (simplified) list of activities and predecessors that are involved in building a house, as shown in the file **P15_27.xlsx**.
   a. Draw an AON project network and find the critical path and the minimum number of days needed to build the house. Also, create the associated Gantt chart.
   b. Suppose that by hiring additional workers, the duration of each activity can be reduced. The costs per day of reducing the duration of the activities are also given in the file **P15_27.xlsx**. Find the strategy that minimizes the cost of completing the project within 20 days.

28. Horizon Cable is about to expand its cable TV offerings in Smalltown by adding MTV and other stations. The activities listed in the file **P15_28.xlsx** must be completed before the service expansion can be completed. Draw the AON project network and find the critical path and the minimum number of weeks needed to complete the project. Also, create the associated Gantt chart.

29. A company is planning to manufacture a product that consists of three parts (A, B, and C). The company anticipates that it will take 5 weeks to design the three parts and determine the way in which these parts must be assembled to make the final product. Then the company estimates that it will take 4 weeks to make part A, 5 weeks to make part B, and 3 weeks to make part C. The company must test part A after it is completed, and the testing takes 2 weeks. The assembly line process will then proceed as follows: assemble parts A and B (2 weeks) and then attach part C (1 week). Then the final product must undergo 1 week of testing. Draw the AON project network. Then find the critical path and the minimum amount of time needed to complete the project, and create the associated Gantt chart.

30. When an accounting firm audits a corporation, the first phase of the audit involves obtaining knowledge of the business. This phase of the audit requires the activities listed in the file **P15_30.xlsx**.
   a. Draw the AON project network and determine the critical path and the minimum number of days needed to complete the first phase of the audit. Also, create the associated Gantt chart.
   b. Assume that the first phase must be completed within 30 days. The duration of each activity can be reduced by incurring the costs listed in the file

**P15_30.xlsx.** Find the strategy that minimizes the cost of meeting this deadline.

31. The city of Bloomington is about to build a new water treatment plant. After the plant is designed (D), we can select the site (S), the building contractor (C), and the operating personnel (P). After the site is selected, we can erect the building (B). We can order the water treatment machine (W) and prepare the operations manual (M) only after the contractor is selected. We can begin training (T) the operators when both the operations manual and operating personnel selection are completed. When the treatment plant and the building are finished, we can install the treatment machine (I). After the treatment machine is installed and operators are trained, we can obtain an operating license (L). Assume that the time (in months) needed to complete each activity is *normally* distributed, with the means and standard deviations given in the file **P15_31.xlsx**. Use simulation to estimate the probability that the project will be completed in (a) under 50 days and (b) more than 55 days. Also estimate the probabilities that B, I, and T are critical activities.

32. To complete an addition to the Business Building, the activities in the file **P15_32.xlsx** must be completed (all times are in months). Assume that all activity times are *normally* distributed with the means and standard deviations given in the file. The project is completed after Room 111 has been destroyed and the main structure has been built.
   a. Estimate the probability that it will take at least three years to complete the addition.
   b. For each activity, estimate the probability that it will be a critical activity.

33. To build Indiana University's new law building, the activities in the file **P15_33.xlsx** must be completed (all times are in months). Assume that all activity times are *normally* distributed with the means and standard deviations given in the file.
   a. Estimate the probability that the project will take less than 30 months to complete.
   b. Estimate the probability that the project will take more than 3 years to complete.
   c. For each of the activities A, B, C, and G, estimate the probability that it is a critical activity.

34. Tom Jacobs, an independent contractor, has agreed to build a new room on an existing house. He plans to begin work on Monday morning, June 1. The main concern is when he will complete the project, given that he works only on weekdays. The work proceeds in stages, labeled A through J, as summarized in the table in the file **P15_34.xlsx**. Three of these activities, wiring, plumbing, and duct work, will be done by separate independent subcontractors.
   a. How long will the project take to complete, given the activity times (durations) in the table? Which are the critical activities.

**b.** Use a one-way data table to see how sensitive the project completion time is to the duration of activity H (hanging dry wall). Let the duration vary from 2 to 8 days in increments of 0.5 day.

**c.** Use a two-way data table to see how sensitive the project completion time is to the duration of activities E and F (electrical wiring and plumbing). Let the durations of each of these activities vary from 2 to 6 days in increments of 0.5 day.

**d.** Tom is currently subcontracting the electrical wiring, plumbing, and duct work. This explains why these three activities can be performed simultaneously. Suppose instead that Tom plans to do the first two of these by himself, and he can work on only one activity at a time—electrical wiring and then plumbing. Modify the critical path model appropriately. How much does the project completion time increase? What is the new critical path?

**e.** Continuing part **d**, where electrical wiring must be done *before* plumbing, suppose Tom must complete the project within a deadline of 17 days. You are given the crashing data in the file **P15_34.xlsx**. What should he do?

**f.** How difficult is it to add new activities to an existing project scheduling model? Answer this question by assuming that Tom must also install bookshelves in the room, and these can be installed only after the drywall has been hung. It typically takes 2.5 days to install the bookshelves. However, he has been instructed to make these bookshelves from a special type of wood, which must be custom ordered. He can place the order right away, and it is likely to take 10 working days to arrive. In addition, he has been instructed to install a wet bar in the room. This cannot be started until the plumbing and electrical wiring are finished, and this wet bar takes an estimated 3.5 days to finish. Find the new project completion time. Does the critical path change because of the new activities?

**35.** In the previous problem, all of Tom's activities have fixed durations. Now assume they have PERT distributions with the parameters listed in the file **P15_35.xlsx**.

**a.** Use @RISK to simulate this project. What is the mean length of time required to complete the project? What is the probability that it will be completed within 20 days? What is the probability that it will require more than 23 days to complete?

**b.** Are there activities that are always (or almost always) critical? Are there activities that are never (or almost never) critical? For each other activity, what is the probability that it is critical?

**c.** For any activities that are never (or almost never) critical, we might expect that the durations of these activities are not highly correlated with the total project time. Use @RISK's sensitivity analysis, with the correlation option, to see whether this is the case. What correlations between the inputs and the output do you find? Can you explain why they turn out as they do?

## Skill-Extending Problems

**36.** Real-world projects often have *milestones* where costs are incurred or payments are received. Usually the costs are incurred relatively early, and the payments are received relatively late. Because of the time value of money, we obviously want to incur the costs as late as possible and receive the payments as early as possible. Consider the AON diagram in Figure 15.26. As before, the circles denote activities, the arrows denote precedence relationships, and the numbers next to the circles are durations (in months). The diamonds denote milestones, and the number next to each milestone denotes the cost incurred (if negative) or the payment received (if positive) when that milestone is reached. The problem is to maximize the NPV of all cash flows (payments minus costs) by choosing the starting times of the activities appropriately. Develop a Solver model

**Figure 15.26**

AON Diagram for a Project with Milestones

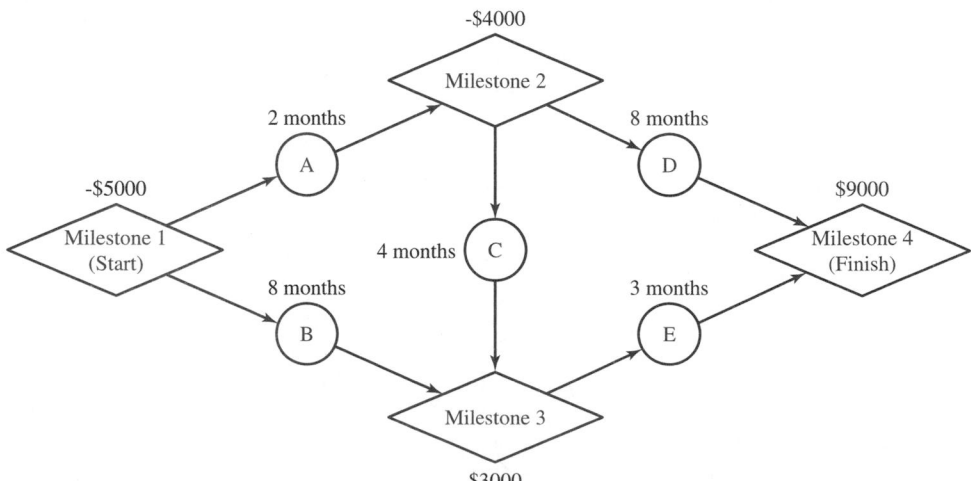

to do so, using an annual discount rate of 10%. (For discounting purposes, you can assume that if a milestone is reached after, say, 10 months of work, then the cost or payment is incurred at the *end* of month 10.)

37. Based on LeBlance et al. (2000). A construction company has eight project managers and has 14 projects scheduled for the next 12 weeks. Each project must be assigned a project manager. The start and finish week for each project as well as the hours per week each project manager would need to spend on a project are given in file **P15_37.xlsx**. For example, project 1 starts at the beginning of week 4 and finishes at the end of week 10, for a duration of 7 weeks. Also note that if manager 2 is assigned to project 1, he will work 50 hours per week on the project. In assigning managers, the company has a policy of not allowing a manager to work more than 70 hours a week. Given this constraint and the fact that all projects must be done, the company wants to minimize the total number of weeks during which managers work more than 50 or less than 30 hours. (Note that, given the data for the problem, working fewer than 30 hours in a week means not working that week at all.) How would you assign managers to projects? (*Hint:* This problem is conceptually fairly simple, but the bookkeeping is difficult. Here is one possibility. Let the changing cells be a column of indexes of the managers assigned to the various projects. For example, the changing cell for project 1 is 4 if we assign manager 4 to project 1. Based on the values in these changing cells, use a lookup function to find the number of hours used by each project. For example, again assuming manager 4 is assigned to project 1, this lookup should return 38 for project 1. Now create a table with weeks along the top and projects along the side. Each entry in the table should indicate how many hours are spent on each project each week. IF functions work here. Finally, create one more table with weeks along the top and managers along the side and use SUMIF functions, based on the data in the previous table, to calculate the number of hours each manager is working each week. As you can probably guess, you'll need to use Evolutionary Solver if you set it up this way. Also, you might have to let Evolutionary Solver run for a *long* time. This is not an easy problem!)

38. Consider a project with six activities. The CPM method has already been implemented, with the results shown in the file **P15_38.xlsx**. (All times are in months.) This file also shows the number of workers of type A, the number of workers of type B, and the material costs per month for each of the activities. Workers of type A receive $1600 per month, and workers of type B receive $2400 per month.

   a. Create a table and then an associated line chart that shows the monthly cash flows through the end of the project when each activity is started at its earliest start time and when it is started at its latest start time. That is, two series should be plotted on the chart.

   b. Suppose the company in charge of this project wants to find the start times for the activities so that the NPV of the cash flows is minimized, using an annual discount rate of 10%. Create a Solver model to do this. The only constraints are that the start times must be within their earliest and latest start time ranges.

39. One problem with our Excel implementation of the CPM method is that the maximum and minimum formulas for the earliest start time and the latest finish times have to be tailored to the specific AON network. That is, we can't enter formulas for a typical activity and then copy them down for the other activities. However, there is a clever way of doing this if you are willing to use some advanced Excel functions.[7] This method is illustrated in the file **Project Scheduling Ragsdale.xlsx** for the LAN project from Example 15.1. The text box in this file explains a few things about the new formulas, including the fact that they deliberately create circular references.

   a. Use online help to learn exactly what the formulas for the earliest start times and latest finish times are doing and why one formula fits all for each. Then explain in words how they work.

   b. Implement this method for the project in Figure 15.27. You can make up any durations for the activities.

---

[7] We thank Cliff Ragsdale, a fellow textbook author, for discovering this method.

**Figure 15.27** The AON Project Network

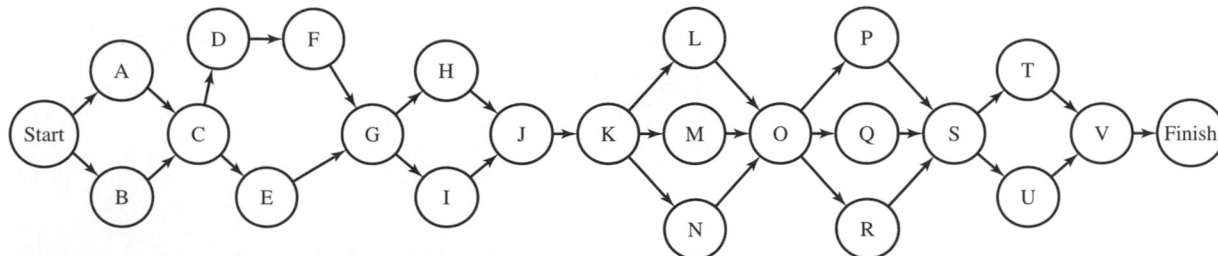

# Regression and Forecasting Models

© Mark Richards/Photo Edit

## FORECASTING AT TACO BELL

How much quantitative analysis occurs at fast-food restaurants? At Taco Bell, a lot! This is described in an article by Huerter and Swart (1998), who explain the approach to labor management that has occurred at Taco Bell restaurants over the past decade. Labor is a large component of costs at Taco Bell. Approximately 30% of every sales dollar goes to labor. However, the unique characteristics of fast-food restaurants make it difficult to plan labor use efficiently. In particular, the Taco Bell product—food—cannot be inventoried; it must be made fresh at the time the customer orders it. Because of shifting demand throughout any given day, where the lunch period accounts for approximately 52% of a day's sales, and as much as 25% of a day's sales can occur during the busiest hour, labor requirements vary greatly throughout the day. If too many workers are on hand during slack times, they are paid for doing practically nothing. Worse than that, however, are the lost sales (and unhappy customers) that occur if too few workers are on hand during peak times. Prior to 1988, Taco Bell made very little effort to manage the labor problem in an efficient, centralized manner. It simply allocated about 30% of each store's sales to the store managers and let them allocate it as best they could—not always with good results.

In 1988, Taco Bell initiated its "value meal" deals, where certain meals were priced as low as 59 cents. This increased demand to the point where management could no longer ignore the labor allocation problem. Therefore, in-store computers were installed, data from all stores were collected, and a team of analysts was assigned the task of developing a cost-efficient labor allocation system. This system, which has been fully integrated into all Taco Bell stores since 1993, is composed of three subsystems: (1) a forecasting subsystem that, for each store, forecasts the arrival rate of customers by 15-minute interval by day of week; (2) a simulation subsystem that, for each store, simulates the congestion and number of lost customers that will occur for any customer arrival rate, given a specific number (and deployment) of workers; and (3) an optimization subsystem that, for each store, indicates the minimum cost allocation of workers, subject to various constraints, such as a minimum service level and a minimum shift length for workers. Although all three of these subsystems are important, the forecasting subsystem is where it all starts. Each store must have a reasonably accurate forecast of future customer arrival rates, broken down by small time intervals (such as 11:15 A.M. to 11:30 A.M. on Friday), before labor requirements can be predicted and labor allocations can be made in an intelligent manner. Like many real-world forecasting systems, Taco Bell's system has two important characteristics: (1) it requires extensive data, which have been made available by the in-store computer systems, and (2) the eventual forecasting method used is mathematically a fairly simple one, namely, 6-week moving averages, which we will study in this chapter.

Simple or not, the forecasts, as well as the other system components, have enabled Taco Bell to cut costs and increase profits considerably. In its first 4 years, 1993 to 1996, the labor management system is estimated to have saved Taco Bell approximately $40.34 million in labor costs. Because the number of Taco Bell stores is constantly increasing, the annual companywide savings from the system will certainly grow in the future. In addition, the focus on quantitative analysis has produced other side benefits for Taco Bell. Its service is now better and more consistent across stores, with many fewer customers leaving because of slow service. Also, the quantitative models developed have enabled Taco Bell to evaluate the effectiveness of various potential productivity enhancements, including self-service drink islands, customer-activated touch screens for ordering, and smaller kitchen areas. So the next time you order food from Taco Bell, you can be assured that there is definitely a method to the madness! ■

## 16.1 INTRODUCTION

Many decision-making applications depend on a forecast of some quantity. Here are several examples:

- When a service organization, such as a fast-food restaurant, plans its staffing over some time period, it must forecast the customer demand as a function of time. This might be done at a very detailed level, such as the demand in successive quarter-hour periods, or at a more aggregate level, such as the demand in successive weeks.

- When a company plans its ordering or production schedule for a product, it must forecast the customer demand for this product so that it can stock appropriate quantities—neither too much nor too little.

- When an organization plans to invest in stocks, bonds, or other financial instruments, it typically attempts to forecast movements in stock prices and interest rates.

- When government representatives plan policy, they attempt to forecast movements in macroeconomic variables such as inflation, interest rates, and unemployment.

Many forecasting methods are available, and all practitioners have their favorites. To say the least, there is little agreement among practitioners or theoreticians as to the *best* forecasting method. The methods can generally be divided into three groups: (1) **judgmental** methods, (2) **regression** methods, and (3) **extrapolation** methods. The first of these is basically nonquantitative and is not discussed here.

**Regression** models, also called **causal** models, forecast a variable by estimating its relationship with other variables. For example, a company might use a regression model to estimate the relationship between its sales and its advertising level, the population income level, the interest rate, and possibly others. The technique of regression is extremely popular, due to its flexibility and power. Regression can estimate relationships between time series variables or cross-sectional variables (those that are observed at a single point in time), and it can estimate linear or nonlinear relationships.

**Extrapolation** methods, also called **time series methods,** use past data of a time series variable—and nothing else—to forecast future values of the variable. Many extrapolation methods are available, including the two we discuss here: moving averages and exponential smoothing. All extrapolation methods search for *patterns* in the historical series and then attempt to extrapolate these patterns into the future. Some try to track long-term upward or downward trends and then project these. Some try to track the seasonal patterns (sales up in November and December, down in other months, for example) and then project these.

Much academic research has been devoted to forecasting methods in the past few decades, and with the advances in computing power, many of the methods described in the academic literature have been developed into complex software packages. Interestingly, however, there is not complete agreement, even among academics, that we can obtain better forecasts today than we could, say, in 1970. An article by Franses (2004) describes a survey of 76 members of the editorial boards of academic journals associated with forecasting. The survey asked several questions about the status of forecasting methods today versus a few decades ago. Most of the respondents believe that the advances in theory and software have resulted in better forecasts, but they are not unanimous in this opinion. They appear to recognize that quantitative forecasting methods can go only so far. Many of the respondents believe that the opinions of experts in the subject area should be used to *complement* the forecasts from software packages. In other words, they don't think human judgment should be omitted from the forecasting process.

Regression analysis and time series analysis are both very broad topics, with many entire books and thousands of research articles devoted to them. We can only scratch the surface of these topics in a single chapter. However, a little can go a long way. By the time you have read this chapter, you will be able to apply some very powerful techniques.

## 16.2 OVERVIEW OF REGRESSION MODELS

Regression analysis is the study of relationships between variables. It is one of the most useful tools for a business analyst because it applies to so many situations. Some potential uses of regression analysis in business address the following questions:

- How do wages of employees depend on years of experience, years of education, and gender?

- How does the current price of a stock depend on its own past values, as well as the current and past values of a market index?

- How does a company's current sales level depend on its current and past advertising levels, the advertising levels of its competitors, the company's own past sales levels, and the general level of the market?

- How does the unit cost of producing an item depend on the total quantity of items that have been produced?

- How does the selling price of a house depend on such factors as the square footage of the house, the number of bedrooms in the house, and perhaps others?

Each of these questions asks how a single variable, such as selling price or employee wages, depends on other relevant variables. If we can estimate this relationship, we can better understand how the world operates and also do a better job of predicting the variable in question. For example, we can understand how a company's sales are affected by its advertising and also use the company's records of current and past advertising levels to predict future sales.

*Regression is capable of dealing with cross-sectional data and time series data.*

We can categorize regression analysis in several ways. One categorization is based on the type of data being analyzed. There are two basic types: cross-sectional data and time series data. Cross-sectional data are usually data gathered from approximately the same period of time from a cross section of a population. The housing and wage examples mentioned previously are typical cross-sectional studies. The first concerns a sample of houses, presumably sold during a short period of time, such as houses sold in Bloomington, Indiana, during the first quarter of 2006. The second concerns a sample of employees observed at a particular point in time, such as a sample of automobile workers observed at the beginning of 2005. In contrast, time series studies involve one or more variables that are observed at several, usually equally spaced, points in time. The stock price example mentioned previously fits this description. We observe the price of a particular stock and possibly the price of a market index at the beginning of every week, say, and then try to explain the movement of the stock's price through time.

*Regression uses one or more explanatory variables to explain a single dependent variable.*

A second categorization of regression analysis involves the number of explanatory variables in the analysis. First, we must introduce some terms. In every regression study, we are trying to explain or predict a particular variable. This is called the **dependent** variable (or the **response** variable) and is often denoted generically as $Y$. To help explain or predict the dependent variable, we use one or more **explanatory** variables. These variables are also called **independent** variables or **predictor** variables, and they are often denoted generically as $X$'s. If there is a single explanatory variable, the analysis is called **simple regression.** If there are several explanatory variables, it is called **multiple regression.**

There are important differences between simple and multiple regression. The primary difference, as the name implies, is that simple regression is simpler. The calculations are simpler, the interpretation of output is somewhat simpler, and fewer complications can occur. We will begin with a simple regression example to introduce the ideas of regression. Then we will move on to the more general topic of multiple regression.

We show how to estimate regression equations that describe relationships between variables. We also discuss the interpretation of these equations, explain numerical measures that indicate the goodness-of-fit of the equations we estimate, and describe how to use the regression equations for prediction.[1]

---

[1] The terms *prediction* and *forecasting* are practically synonyms. Some analysts reserve the term *forecasting* for future values of a time series variable and use the term *prediction* for any type of variable, time series or otherwise. However, we do not make this distinction.

## The Least-Squares Line

The basis for regression is a rather simple idea. If we create a scatterplot of one variable $Y$ versus another variable $X$, we obtain a swarm of points that indicates any possible relationship between these two variables. To quantify this relationship, we try to find the "best-fitting" line (or curve) through the points in the graph. But what do we mean by best-fitting?

Consider the scatterplot in Figure 16.1. The line shown is one possible fit. It appears to be a reasonably good fit, but we need a numerical measure of the goodness-of-fit so that we can compare this fit with the fits of other possible lines.

**Figure 16.1**

Scatterplot with Proposed Regression Line

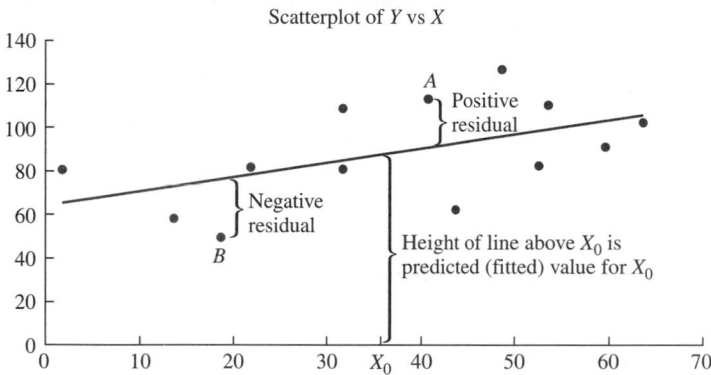

The measure commonly used is the **sum of squared residuals.** Here, a **residual** is defined as the vertical distance from a point to the line, as illustrated for points A and B. If the point is above the line (point A), the residual is positive; if the point is below the line (point B), the residual is negative. To measure the goodness-of-fit, we square all of the residuals and sum them. Intuitively, a good fit should have a small sum of squared residuals. In fact, the line we want is the line with the *minimum* sum of squared residuals, where the minimum is over all possible lines. We call this the **least-squares line.** This is the line that is found by regression. (Why do we *square* the residuals? One reason is to make them all positive. Another is to severely penalize large residuals. The most compelling reason, however, is that this is the way it has been done by statisticians for many years.)

> A **residual** is a prediction error. It is the difference between an observed $Y$ and the predicted $Y$ from the regression line.

> The **least-squares regression line** minimizes the sum of squared residuals.

The details of the procedure used to find the least-squares line are beyond the scope of this book. The procedure is basically a calculus problem. Fortunately, it is done automatically by regression software, including software built into Excel. We rely on this software to find the least-squares line, and we then interpret the results.

## Prediction and Fitted Values

After we find the least-squares line, we can use it for prediction. Geometrically, this is easy. Given any value of $X$, we predict the corresponding value of $Y$ to be the height of the line above this $X$. This is shown in Figure 16.1 for the value $X_0$. The predicted $Y$ value is called the **fitted value.**

> A **fitted value** is a predicted value of $Y$ found by substituting given $X$'s into the regression equation.

In contrast, the height of any point is the **actual value** of $Y$ for this point. Therefore, we have the following important relationship. It states that the residual for any point is the difference between the observed value of $Y$ and the predicted value of $Y$.

> **Relationship between residuals and fitted values**
>
> $$\text{Residual} = \text{Actual value} - \text{Fitted value} \qquad (16.1)$$

In general, we estimate the least-squares line as a regression equation relating $Y$ to one or more $X$'s. For example, this equation might be $Y = 5 + 3X$. To predict $Y$ for any given value of $X$, we simply substitute this value of $X$ into the regression equation. This gives us the fitted value of $Y$. For example, with the proposed equation, if $X = 2$, the fitted (predicted) value of $Y$ is $5 + 3(2) = 11$. If we happen to know that the actual value of $Y$ for this point is 13, say, then the residual is positive: $13 - 11 = 2$. On the other hand, if the actual value is 8, then the residual is negative: $8 - 11 = -3$.

## Measures of Goodness-of-Fit

Besides the sum of squared residuals, other measures of goodness-of-fit typically are quoted in regression analyses. We briefly describe these here and discuss them in more detail in subsequent sections.

### Standard Error of Estimate

The sum of squared residuals is measured in *squared* units of the $Y$ variable. For example, if $Y$ is sales in dollars, then the sum of squared residuals is in squared dollars. It is more meaningful to obtain a related measure in dollars. The resulting measure is called the **standard error of estimate.** This measure is obtained by averaging and then taking the square root, as shown in the following formula. In this formula, $n$ is the number of observations, and $k$ is the number of explanatory variables in the regression equation.

> **Formula for standard error of estimate**
>
> $$\text{Standard error of estimate} = \sqrt{\text{Sum of squared residuals}/(n - k - 1)} \qquad (16.2)$$

*The standard error of estimate is a measure of the magnitude of the prediction errors we are likely to make, based on the regression equation.*

The standard error of estimate is useful because it provides an estimate of the magnitude of the prediction errors we are likely to make. For example, if the standard error of estimate is \$150, then as a ballpark estimate, we expect our predictions to be off by about \$150. More precisely, the standard error of estimate behaves like a standard deviation. Therefore, from the well-known empirical rule of statistics, we expect about 2/3 of our predictions to be no greater than \$150 (one standard error) in magnitude, and we expect about 95% of our predictions to be no greater than \$300 (2 standard errors) in magnitude.

## Multiple $R$ and $R$-Square

Another goodness-of-fit measure is called the **multiple $R$,** which is defined as the correlation between the actual $Y$ values and the fitted $Y$ values. In general, a correlation is a number between $-1$ and $+1$ that measures the goodness-of-fit of the linear relationship between two variables. A correlation close to $-1$ or $+1$ indicates a tight linear fit, whereas a correlation close to 0 tends to indicate no linear fit—usually a shapeless swarm of points. In regression, we want the fitted $Y$ values to be close to the actual $Y$ values, so we want a scatterplot of the actual values versus the fitted values to be close to a 45° line, with the multiple $R$ close to $+1$.

---

**Formula for multiple R**

$$\text{Multiple } R = \text{Correlation between actual } Y\text{'s and fitted } Y\text{'s} \qquad \textbf{(16.3)}$$

---

How large should multiple $R$ be to indicate a "good" fit? This is difficult to answer directly, other than to say "the larger, the better." However, if we square the multiple $R$, we get a measure that has a more direct interpretation. This measure is known simply as **R-square.** It represents the percentage of the variation of the $Y$ values explained by the $X$'s included in the regression equation. For example, if multiple $R$ is 0.8, then $R$-square is 0.64, so we say that 64% of the variation of $Y$ has been explained by the regression. The idea is that the $X$'s included in the regression are presumably related to $Y$, so that they help explain why the $Y$ values vary as they do. Naturally, we want the $X$'s to explain as much of this variation as possible, so we want $R$-square values as close to 1 as possible.

---

**Formula for R-square**

$$\begin{aligned} R\text{-square} &= (\text{multiple } R)^2 \\ &= \text{Percentage of variation of } Y \text{ explained by the regression} \qquad \textbf{(16.4)} \end{aligned}$$

---

*The R-square value can never decrease as more explanatory variables are added to the regression equation.*

Although $R$-square is probably the most frequently quoted measure in regression analyses, some caution is necessary. First, $R$-square values are often disappointingly low. Some variables in business are simply not easy to explain, particularly those in behavioral areas. Regressions in these areas sometimes have $R$-squares in the 10% to 20% range. This does not necessarily mean that these regressions are useless. After all, explaining 20% of the variation in some variable is better than not explaining anything at all. Second, $R$-squares can sometimes be inflated by adding $X$'s to the equation that do not really belong. This is due to the mathematical property that $R$-square can only *increase,* never decrease, when extra $X$'s are added to an equation. In general, we have to avoid the temptation to build large equations with many $X$'s just to pump up $R$-square. It is usually preferable to include only a few "important" $X$'s and omit those that yield only marginal increases in $R$-square. Finding the right set of $X$'s, however, is not easy. In fact, it is probably the biggest challenge to the analyst and takes a good deal of experience.

## 16.3 SIMPLE REGRESSION MODELS

In this section, we discuss how to estimate the regression equation for a dependent variable $Y$ based on a single explanatory variable $X$. (The common terminology is that we "regress $Y$ on $X$.") This is the equation of the least-squares line passing through the scatterplot of $Y$ versus $X$. Because we are estimating a *straight* line, the regression equation is of the form $Y = a + bX$, where, as in basic algebra, $a$ is called the **intercept** and $b$ is called the **slope.**

## Regression-Based Trend Models

A special case of simple regression is when the only explanatory variable is time, usually labeled $t$ (rather than $X$). In this case, the dependent variable $Y$ is some time series variable, such as a company's monthly sales, and the purpose of the regression is to see whether this dependent variable follows a trend through time. If there is a *linear* trend, then the equation for $Y$ has the form $Y = a + bt$. If $b > 0$, then $Y$ tends to increase by $b$ units every time period, whereas if $b < 0$, then $Y$ tends to decrease by $b$ units every time period. Alternatively, if there is an *exponential* trend, the equation for $Y$ has the form $Y = ae^{bt}$. In this case, the variable $Y$ changes by a constant *percentage* each time period, and this percentage is approximately equal to the coefficient in the exponent, $b$. For example, if $b = 0.025$, then $Y$ increases by about 2.5% per period, whereas if $b = -0.025$, then $Y$ decreases by about 2.5% per period.

> With a **linear** trendline, the variable changes by a constant *amount* each period.
>
> With an **exponential** trendline, the variable changes by a constant *percentage* each period.

The following example illustrates how easily trends can be estimated with Excel.

---

## EXAMPLE | 16.1 FORECASTING SALES AT BEST CHIPS

*It is customary to index time from 1 to the number of time periods.*

The Best Chips Company produces and sells potato chips throughout the country. Its sales have been growing steadily over the past 10 years, as shown in Figure 16.2 and the file **Exponential Growth.xlsx**.[2] (Note that we have indexed the years so that year 1 corresponds to 1997.) The company wants to predict its sales for the next couple of years, assuming that the upward trend it has observed in the past 10 years will continue in the future. How should the company proceed?

**Figure 16.2**

Historical Sales at Best Chips

| | A | B |
|---|---|---|
| 1 | **Historical data** | |
| 2 | Year | Sales |
| 3 | 1 | $1,345,000 |
| 4 | 2 | $1,352,000 |
| 5 | 3 | $1,463,000 |
| 6 | 4 | $1,511,000 |
| 7 | 5 | $1,610,000 |
| 8 | 6 | $1,649,000 |
| 9 | 7 | $1,713,000 |
| 10 | 8 | $1,850,000 |
| 11 | 9 | $2,051,000 |
| 12 | 10 | $2,203,000 |

---

[2] We omit the "Where Do the Numbers Come From?" sections in this chapter because the data sources should be obvious.

**Objective** To fit linear and exponential trendlines to the company's historical sales data and to use the better of these trendlines to predict future sales.

## Solution

We begin by using the Chart Wizard to create the scatterplot of Sales versus Year shown in Figure 16.3. (The terms "scatterplot," "scatter chart," and "XY chart" are all used to describe the same thing. We use "scatterplot" in this chapter.) Sales are clearly increasing through time, but it is not absolutely clear whether they are increasing at a constant rate, which would favor a linear trendline, or at an increasing rate, which would favor an exponential trendline. Therefore, we try fitting both of these.

**Figure 16.3**
Time Series Plot
of Sales

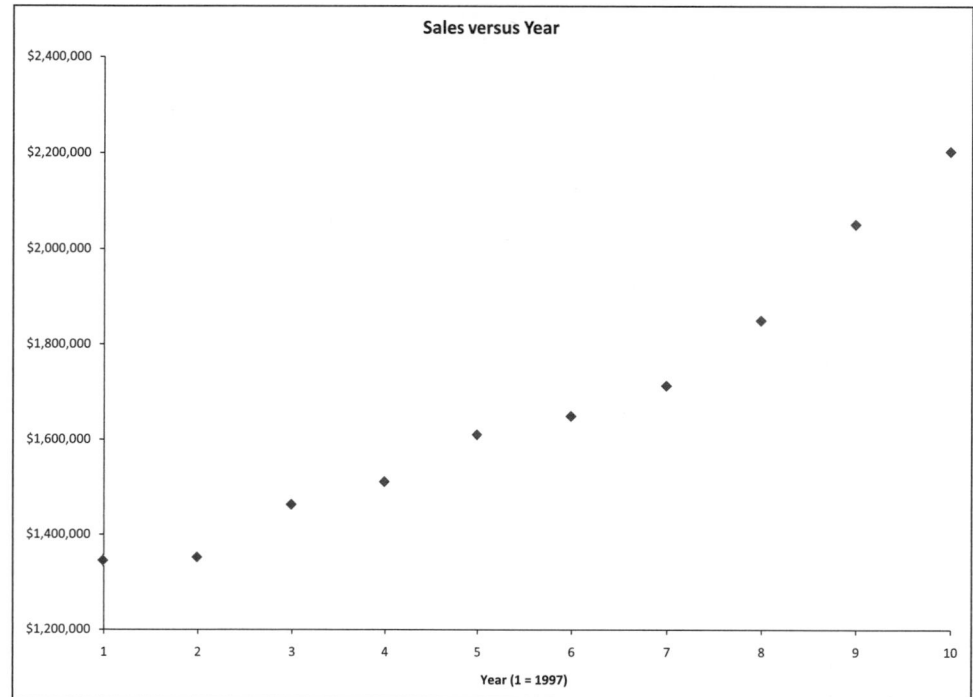

**Excel Tool:** *Creating a Scatterplot with the Chart Wizard*
*To create a scatterplot in Excel, select the two series of data and then select a SCATTER chart of some type from the Insert ribbon. By default, the range on the left will be on the horizontal axis, and the range on the right will be on the vertical axis. If this isn't what you want, select the chart and use the Select Data Source option on the Chart Tools Design ribbon to switch the roles of the two series. This is the key step. You can experiment with other options, but they are mainly for formatting the chart.*

### Fitting a Linear Trendline

To superimpose a linear trendline on any scatterplot, select the chart and then select More Trendline Options from the Trendline dropdown on the Chart Tools Layout ribbon. This brings up the dialog box in Figure 16.4. You can select any of six types of trendlines. For now, select the default Linear option. Also, check the Display Equation on Chart option. (You can also elect to display the $R$-square value if you like.) The result appears in Figure 16.5.

**Figure 16.4**

Dialog Box for
Adding a Trendline

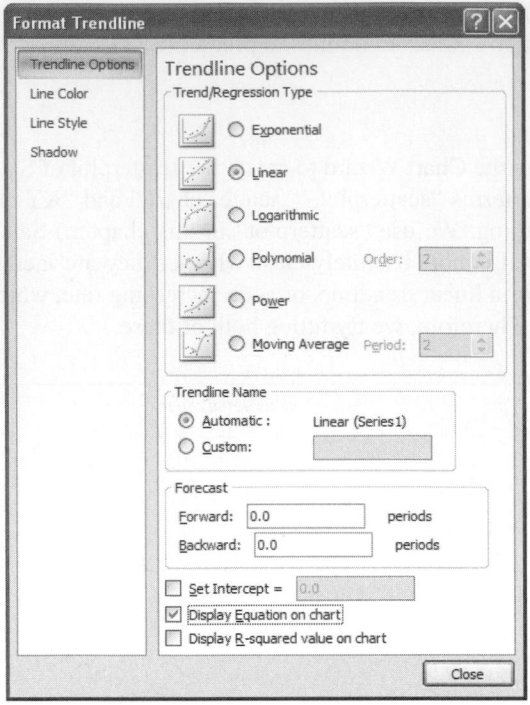

**Excel Tool:** *Inserting Trendlines*

*It is easy to fit any of several types of trendlines to a scatterplot of some variable versus time. To do so, select the chart and then select More Trendline Options from the Trendline dropdown on the Chart Tools Layout ribbon. This brings up a dialog box where you can select one of several types of trendlines. In addition, you can elect to display an equation of the trendline and/or the R-square value on the chart. This equation and/or the R-square value appear in a text box. You can select this text box and move it, change its font size, or change its number format as you like.*

**Figure 16.5**

Plot with Superim-
posed Linear
Trendline

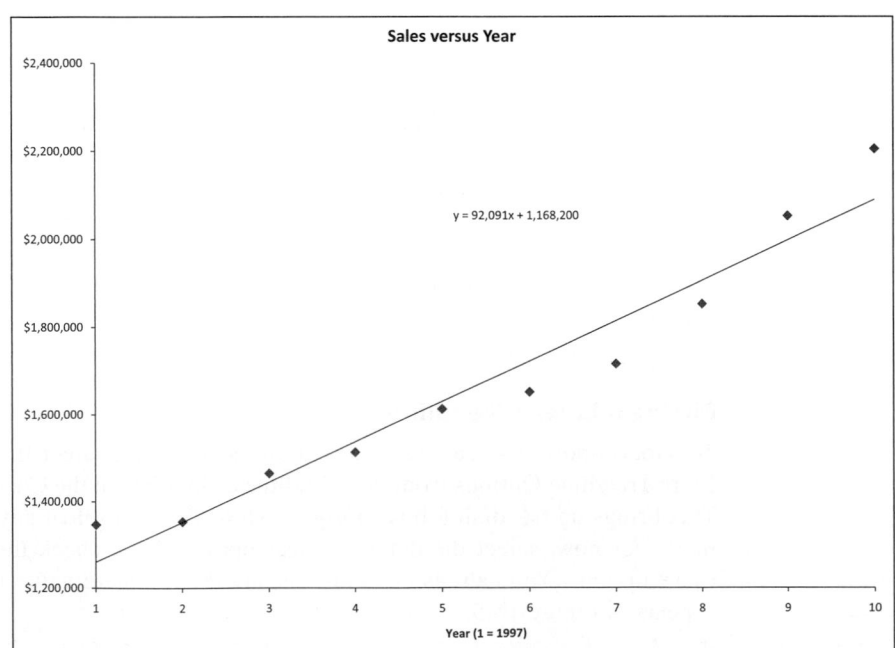

*The coefficient of time in the linear trendline equation represents the change in the variable per time period.*

This figure shows the best-fitting straight line to the points, and it indicates that the equation of this straight line is $y = 92,091x + 1,168,200$. Here, $y$ corresponds to sales and $x$ corresponds to year.[3] The most important part of this equation is the coefficient of $x$, 92,091. It implies that sales are increasing by \$92,091 per year—*if* we believe that the linear trendline provides a good fit.

### Fitting an Exponential Trendline

*The coefficient of time in the exponent of the exponential trendline equation represents the (approximate) percentage change in the variable per time period.*

To obtain an exponential trendline, we go through the same procedure except that we select the Exponential option in Figure 16.4. The resulting *curve* appears in Figure 16.6. The equation for the curve is $y = 1,227,762e^{0.0541x}$. The most important part of this equation is the coefficient in the exponent, 0.0541. It implies that sales are increasing by approximately 5.4% per year. In general, the coefficient in the exponent of an exponential trendline equation, when expressed as a percentage, indicates the approximate percentage by which the series is changing each period. Note that if this coefficient were negative, such as $-0.0325$, then the series would be *decreasing* by approximately 3.25% each period (and the plot would be trending downward). (We say "approximate" because the exact rate is $e^b - 1$ when the coefficient in the exponent is $b$. For example, when $b = 0.0541$, the exact rate is $e^{0.0541} - 1 = 0.0556$, or 5.56%.)

**Figure 16.6**

Plot with Superimposed Exponential Trendline

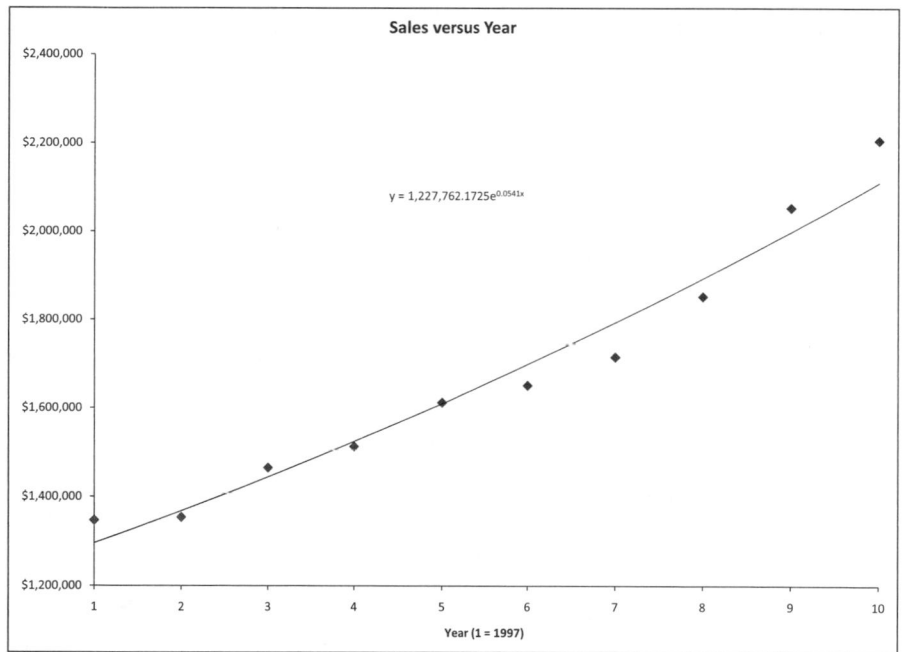

### Measuring the Goodness-of-Fit

Which of these trendlines provides the better fit? We can proceed in two ways. First, we can "eyeball" it. Looking at the superimposed trendlines in Figures 16.5 and 16.6, it appears that the exponential fit is slightly better. However, the typical way to measure fits to a trendline through time is to calculate the historical predictions from each curve and the corresponding absolute percentage errors (APEs). We find the predictions by plugging the year

---

[3] Although we like to use the variable $t$ to denote time, Excel uses the variable $x$ in its trendline equations.

indexes (1 to 10) into the trendline equations. We then calculate the APE for each year from the following equation:

> **Absolute percentage error**
>
> $$\text{APE} = \frac{|\text{Actual sales} - \text{Predicted sales}|}{\text{Actual sales}} \tag{16.6}$$

A measure of goodness-of-fit is then the average of these APE values, denoted by MAPE (mean absolute percentage error).[4] This measure is quite intuitive. For example, if it is 2.1%, then we know that the predicted values for the historical period are off—too low or too high—by 2.1% on average.

> A useful measure of the goodness-of-fit of any trendline through time is **MAPE,** the mean absolute percentage error. It is the average of the APE values calculated from equation (16.6).

All of this is implemented in Figure 16.7. To create the predictions, APEs, and MAPEs, proceed as follows:

**1 Predictions.** Calculate the predictions from the linear trendline by entering the formula

**1168200+92091*A3**

in cell D3 and copying it down to cell D14. (Note that cells D13 and D14 then contain the predictions for 2007 and 2008. There is no way to know how good these future predictions are until we observe actual sales in 2007 and 2008.) Similarly, calculate the predictions from the exponential trendline by entering the formula

**=1227762*EXP(0.0541*A3)**

in cell E3 and copying it down to cell E14. Note that we calculate $e$ to some power in Excel with Excel's EXP function.

**Figure 16.7**

Evaluating the
Goodness-of-Fit of
Each Trendline

|  | A | B | C | D | E | F | G |
|---|---|---|---|---|---|---|---|
| 1 | Historical data | | | **Predictions** | | **Absolute percentage errors** | |
| 2 | Year | Sales | | Linear | Exponential | Linear | Exponential |
| 3 | 1 | $1,345,000 | | $1,260,291 | $1,296,013 | 6.30% | 3.64% |
| 4 | 2 | $1,352,000 | | $1,352,382 | $1,368,059 | 0.03% | 1.19% |
| 5 | 3 | $1,463,000 | | $1,444,473 | $1,444,110 | 1.27% | 1.29% |
| 6 | 4 | $1,511,000 | | $1,536,564 | $1,524,388 | 1.69% | 0.89% |
| 7 | 5 | $1,610,000 | | $1,628,655 | $1,609,129 | 1.16% | 0.05% |
| 8 | 6 | $1,649,000 | | $1,720,746 | $1,698,581 | 4.35% | 3.01% |
| 9 | 7 | $1,713,000 | | $1,812,837 | $1,793,005 | 5.83% | 4.67% |
| 10 | 8 | $1,850,000 | | $1,904,928 | $1,892,678 | 2.97% | 2.31% |
| 11 | 9 | $2,051,000 | | $1,997,019 | $1,997,893 | 2.63% | 2.59% |
| 12 | 10 | $2,203,000 | | $2,089,110 | $2,108,956 | 5.17% | 4.27% |
| 13 | 11 | | | $2,181,201 | $2,226,193 | | |
| 14 | 12 | | | $2,273,292 | $2,349,948 | | |
| 15 | | | | | | | |
| 16 | | | | | **MAPE** | 3.14% | 2.39% |

[4] We will see this measure and two other measures of forecast errors when we study time series forecasting in more detail in Sections 16.5 to 16.7.

**Excel Function:** *EXP*

*The formula* =EXP(value) *is equivalent to the special number* e *raised to the power* value. *(Here,* e *is approximately equal to 2.718.) For example,* $e^{2.5}$ *can be calculated in Excel with the formula* =EXP(2.5), *which evaluates to 12.1825. The EXP function is sometimes called the* antilog *function.*

**2** **APE values.** Calculate all of the APE values at once by entering the formula

**=ABS($B3-D3)/$B3**

in cell F3 and copying it to the range F3:G12. This follows directly from equation (16.6) and Excel's ABS (absolute value) function.

**3** **MAPE values.** Calculate the MAPE for each trendline by entering the formula

**=AVERAGE(F3:F12)**

in cell F16 and copying it to cell G16.

## Discussion of the Results

The MAPE values confirm that the exponential trendline is slightly better than the linear trendline. The exponential trendline is off, on average, by 2.39%, whereas the similar figure for the linear trendline is 3.14%. Using the exponential trendline, we estimate that sales are increasing by slightly more than 5% per year. The predictions in cells E15 and E16 essentially project this 5% increase to the years 2007 and 2008. Again, however, we can't tell how good these future predictions are until we observe *actual* sales in 2007 and 2008.

**Technical Note:** *Estimating an Exponential Trendline with Regression*
*Excel actually uses regression to estimate the exponential trendline. However, regression always estimates* linear *equations of the form Y = a + bX. Therefore, to estimate an equation of the form Y = $ae^{bt}$, a logarithmic transformation is required. By taking logarithms of both sides and using the rules of logarithms, we get ln(Y) = ln(a) + bt, which is linear in time t. [The dependent variable is now ln(Y).] Excel actually makes this transformation behind the scenes when it estimates the exponential trendline, but it hides the details from us.*

## Caution about Exponential Trendlines

Exponential trendlines are often used in predicting sales and other economic quantities. However, we urge caution with such predictions. It is difficult for *any* company to sustain a given percentage increase year after year. For example, we used this same procedure on quarterly sales at the computer chip giant Intel, starting in 1986. Through 1996, Intel sales rose at a staggering rate of approximately 27% per year, and the corresponding exponential fit was quite good. However, since that time, Intel's sales have gone up much more slowly, and in some quarters, they have actually decreased. If we had used the exponential trendline through 1996 to forecast sales after 1996, we would have overpredicted by huge amounts! ∎

## Using an Explanatory Variable Other Than Time

We are not restricted to using time as the explanatory variable in simple regression. Any variable *X* that is related to the dependent variable *Y* is a candidate. The following example illustrates one such possibility. It shows how we can still take advantage of Excel's Add Trendline option, even though the resulting trendline is not what we usually think of with trend—a trend through *time*.

---

**EXAMPLE** | **16.2 ESTIMATING TOTAL COST FOR A SINGLE PRODUCT**

Consider a company that produces a single product. For each of the past 16 months, the company has kept track of the number of units produced as well as the total cost of production. These data appear in Figure 16.8 and in the file **Cost Regression 1.xlsx**. What can simple regression tell us about the relationship between these two variables? How can it be used to predict future production costs?

**Figure 16.8**

Cost and Production Data for a Single Product

|    | A | B | C |
|----|-----|----------------|------------|
| 1 | Month | Units Produced | Total Cost |
| 2 | 1 | 500 | $131,000 |
| 3 | 2 | 600 | $135,000 |
| 4 | 3 | 400 | $104,000 |
| 5 | 4 | 300 | $76,000 |
| 6 | 5 | 800 | $186,000 |
| 7 | 6 | 900 | $190,100 |
| 8 | 7 | 600 | $150,000 |
| 9 | 8 | 400 | $98,000 |
| 10 | 9 | 300 | $78,000 |
| 11 | 10 | 200 | $60,000 |
| 12 | 11 | 400 | $108,000 |
| 13 | 12 | 600 | $152,000 |
| 14 | 13 | 700 | $158,000 |
| 15 | 14 | 500 | $134,380 |
| 16 | 15 | 300 | $86,000 |
| 17 | 16 | 200 | $60,000 |

**Objective** To use simple regression to estimate the relationship between Units Produced and Total Cost, and to use this relationship to predict future total costs.

## Solution

*A scatterplot of Y versus X is always a good place to start in any regression analysis.*

When we try to relate two variables with regression, it is always a good idea to create a scatterplot of the two variables first, just to see whether there is any relationship worth pursuing. This can be done with Excel's chart tools in the usual way, which leads to the

**Figure 16.9** Scatterplot of Total Cost versus Units Produced

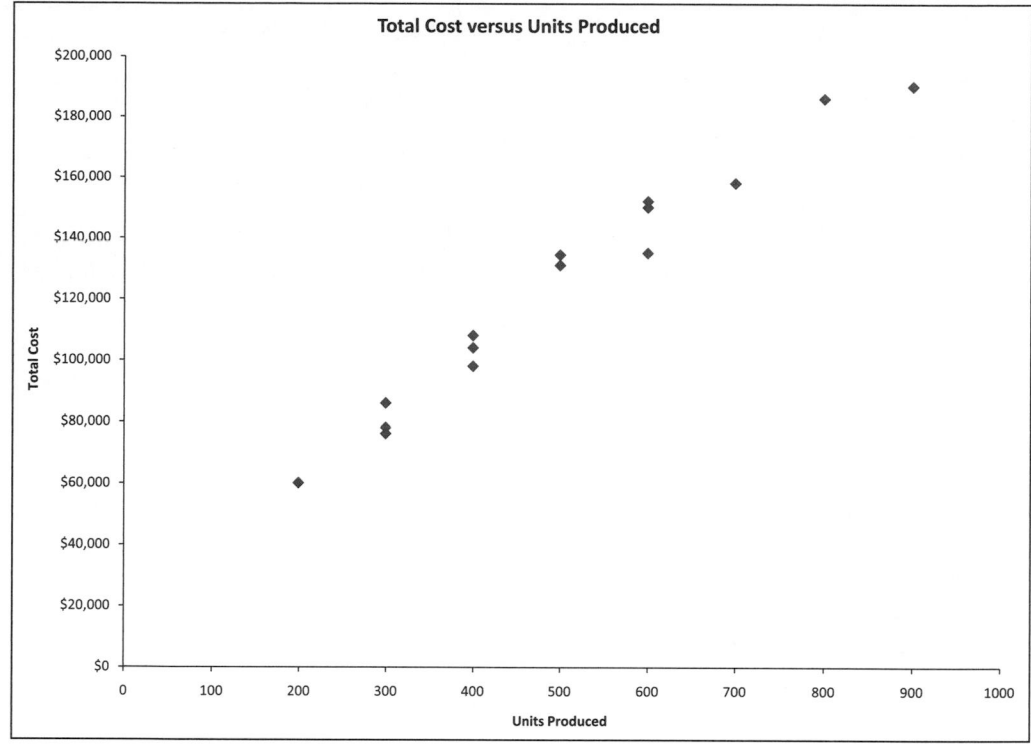

scatterplot in Figure 16.9. This plot indicates a clear linear relationship, where Total Cost increases linearly as Units Produced increases.

### Fitting a Linear Trendline

*Excel's Trendline tool can be used even when the explanatory variable X does not represent time.*

We can now fit a straight line to this plot using Excel's Trendline tool. To do so, select the chart and then select the Chart/Add Trendline menu item. In the resulting dialog box, click on the Type tab and select the Linear option. Then click on the Options tab and check the Display equation and Display *R*-squared boxes. The results appear in Figure 16.10.

### Discussion of the Results

The equation of the straight line has a slope, 198.47, and an intercept, 23,643. For this example, both numbers have a natural interpretation. The slope corresponds to the unit variable cost of production. We estimate that each extra unit produced contributes $198.47 to total cost. The intercept corresponds to the fixed cost of production. We estimate that the fixed cost is $23,643, regardless of the production level.

As discussed previously, the *R*-square value is the percentage of variation of Total Cost explained by Units Produced. In this case, Units Produced explains slightly more than 97% of the variation in Total Cost; only about 3% of this variation is left unexplained. Alternatively, multiple *R*, the square root of *R*-square, is the correlation between the actual Total Cost values and the fitted Total Cost values, as predicted by the regression equation. In this case, multiple *R* is $\sqrt{0.9717} = 0.9858$.

We can now find the fitted values, the residuals, and the standard error of estimate. The results appear in Figure 16.11. (Rows 2 to 17 contain the historical data for the first 16 months. Rows 18 and 19 are used for prediction in the next 2 months.) We first

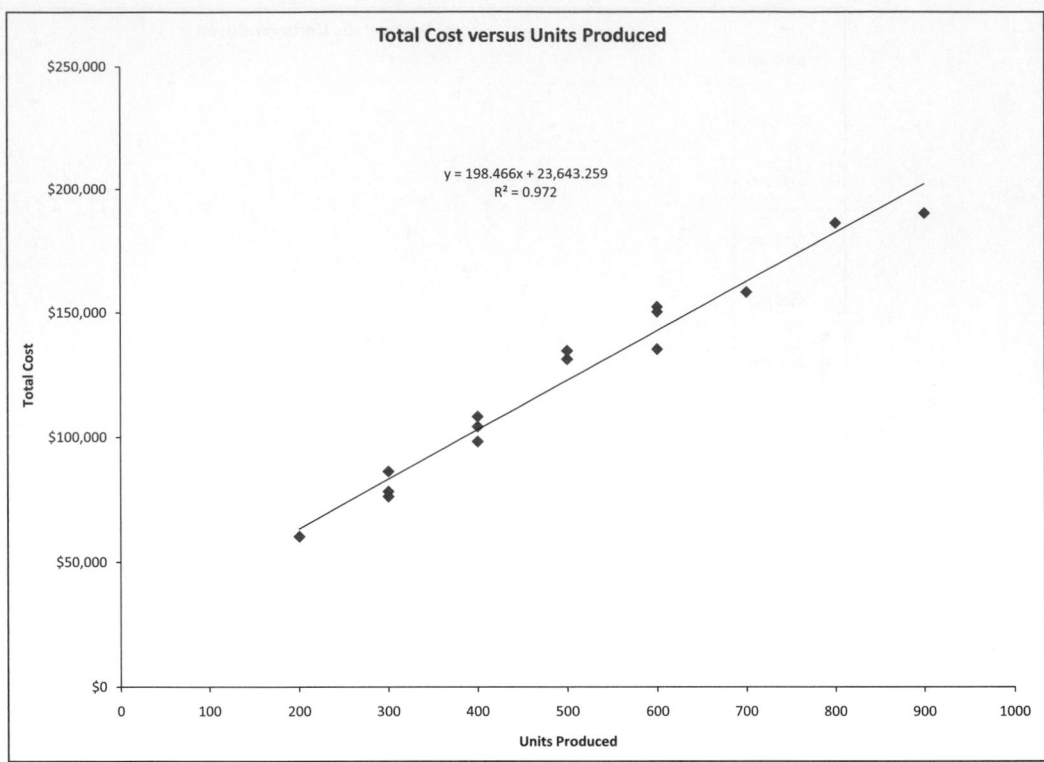

insert the intercept and slope values from the chart in cells F2 and F3. To get the fitted values for any months, we substitute into the regression equation. To do this, enter the formula

**=$F$2+$F$3*B2**

in cell H2 and copy it down to cell H19. Note that the last two of these are actually predictions of future months, given the proposed values of Units Produced in cells B18 and B19.

To calculate the residuals as differences between actual and fitted values, enter the formula

**=C2-H2**

in cell I2 and copy it down to cell H17. (Note that no residuals are available for months 17 and 18 because their *actual* total costs are not yet known.) Then calculate the standard error of estimate in cell F6 with the formula

**=SQRT(SUMSQ(I2:I17)/(16-1-1))**

This formula, based on equation (16.2), uses Excel's SUMSQ function to sum the squares of the residuals, and then it divides by the number of observations minus the number of explanatory variables minus 1.

**Excel Function:** *SUMSQ*
*The SUMSQ function, in the form=SUMSQ(range), returns the sum of the squares of the values in the specified range.*

**Figure 16.11** Simple Regression Output

| | A | B | C | D | E | F | G | H | I |
|---|---|---|---|---|---|---|---|---|---|
| 1 | Month | Units Produced | Total Cost | | Regression parameters from chart | | | Fitted Values | Residuals |
| 2 | 1 | 500 | $131,000 | | Intercept | 23643 | | $122,876 | $8,124 |
| 3 | 2 | 600 | $135,000 | | Slope | 198.466 | | $142,723 | -$7,723 |
| 4 | 3 | 400 | $104,000 | | | | | $103,029 | $971 |
| 5 | 4 | 300 | $76,000 | | Standard error of estimate | $7,262 | | $83,183 | -$7,183 |
| 6 | 5 | 800 | $186,000 | | | | | $182,416 | $3,584 |
| 7 | 6 | 900 | $190,100 | | | | | $202,262 | -$12,162 |
| 8 | 7 | 600 | $150,000 | | | | | $142,723 | $7,277 |
| 9 | 8 | 400 | $98,000 | | | | | $103,029 | -$5,029 |
| 10 | 9 | 300 | $78,000 | | | | | $83,183 | -$5,183 |
| 11 | 10 | 200 | $60,000 | | | | | $63,336 | -$3,336 |
| 12 | 11 | 400 | $108,000 | | | | | $103,029 | $4,971 |
| 13 | 12 | 600 | $152,000 | | | | | $142,723 | $9,277 |
| 14 | 13 | 700 | $158,000 | | | | | $162,569 | -$4,569 |
| 15 | 14 | 500 | $134,380 | | | | | $122,876 | $11,504 |
| 16 | 15 | 300 | $86,000 | | | | | $83,183 | $2,817 |
| 17 | 16 | 200 | $60,000 | | | | | $63,336 | -$3,336 |
| 18 | 17 | 400 | | | | Future predictions | → | $103,029 | |
| 19 | 18 | 800 | | | | | → | $182,416 | |

The most important aspects of the output are the following:

- We estimate that each additional unit produced adds about $198 to total cost.

- The large $R$-square and multiple $R$ values confirm exactly what the scatterplot indicates—that a very strong linear relationship exists between Total Cost and Units Produced.

- The standard error of estimate indicates that the prediction errors based on this regression equation will be in the neighborhood of $7000—many prediction errors will be less than this value and a few will be more. This large an error might sound like a lot, but it is not all that large compared to the magnitudes of total costs, which are often well over $100,000. ∎

# PROBLEMS

*Solutions for problems whose numbers appear within a color box can be found in the Student Solutions Files. Order your copy today at the Winston/Albright product Web site, academic.cengage.com/decisionsciences/winston.*

## Skill-Building Problems

**1.** The file **P16_01.xlsx** contains quarterly sales at Johnson & Johnson from 1991 through the first quarter of 2001. Chart these sales and fit both a linear trendline and an exponential trendline through the points. Then calculate the MAPE for each. Does either provide a

good fit? Which of the two provides the better fit? Interpret the better-fitting trendline.

**2.** The file **P16_02.xlsx** contains quarterly sales at Intel from 1986 through the first quarter of 2001. Chart these sales through the end of 1996 only, and fit an exponential trendline to these points. Interpret the growth rate you find. (Is it annual or quarterly?) Calculate the MAPE for these years. Then use this exponential trendline to predict the quarterly sales from 1997 on, and calculate the MAPE for this period. Describe your results in a concise memo to Intel management.

3. The file **P16_03.xlsx** gives the annual sales for Microsoft (in millions of dollars) for a 10-year period.
   a. Fit an exponential trendline to these data.
   b. By what percentage do you estimate that Microsoft will grow each year?
   c. Why can't a high rate of exponential growth continue for a long time?
   d. Rather than an exponential curve, what type of curve might better represent the growth of a new technology?
   e. If you can find Microsoft sales data since the period shown in the file, check whether its sales continued at the exponential rate from part **b**.

4. The file **P16_04.xlsx** contains monthly data on production levels and production costs during a 4-year period for a company that produces a single product. Use simple regression on all of the data to see how Total Cost is related to Units Produced. Use the resulting equation to predict total cost in month 49, given that the proposed production level for that month is 450 units. Do you see anything "wrong" with the analysis? How should you modify your analysis if your main task is to find an equation useful for predicting *future* costs, and you know that the company installed new machinery at the end of month 18? Write a concise memo to management that describes your findings.

5. Management of a home appliance store in Charlotte wants to understand the growth pattern of the monthly sales of DVD units over the past 2 years. The managers have recorded the relevant data in the file **P16_05.xlsx**. Have the sales of DVD units been growing linearly over the past 24 months? By examining the results of a linear trendline, explain why or why not.

6. Do the sales prices of houses in a given community vary systematically with their sizes (as measured in square feet)? Answer this question by estimating a simple regression model where the sales price of the house is the dependent variable, and the size of the house is the explanatory variable. Use the sample data given in **P16_06.xlsx**. Interpret your estimated model, the associated $R$-square value, and the associated standard error of estimate.

7. The file **P16_07.xlsx** contains observations of the U.S. minimum wage during each of the years from 1950 through 1994. Did the minimum wage grow at roughly a *constant* rate over this period? Use simple linear regression analysis to address this question. Explain your results.

8. Based on the data in the file **P16_08.xlsx** from the U.S. Department of Agriculture, explore the relationship between the number of farms ($X$) and the average size of a farm ($Y$) in the United States between 1950 and 1997. Specifically, generate a simple linear regression model and interpret it.

## Skill-Extending Problems

9. We discussed linear and exponential trendlines. Another popular choice is a *power* trendline, also called a *constant elasticity* trendline. This trendline has the form $y = ax^b$, and it has the property that when $x$ increases by 1%, $y$ changes by a constant *percentage*. In fact, this constant percentage is approximately equal to the exponent $b$ (which could be positive or negative). The power trendline is often cited in the economics literature, where, for example, $x$ might be price and $y$ might be demand. Fortunately, it can be found through Excel's Trendline tool; the power trendline is just another option. Estimate and interpret a power trendline for the data on demand and price of some commodity listed in the file **P16_09.xlsx**. In particular, if price increases by 1%, what do you expect to happen to demand? Calculate the MAPE for this power trendline. Would you say it provides a good fit?

10. Sometimes curvature in a scatterplot can be fit adequately (especially to the naked eye) by several trendlines. We discussed the exponential trendline, and the power trendline is discussed in the previous problem. Still another fairly simple trendline is the *parabola*, a polynomial of order 2 (also called a *quadratic*). For the demand-price data in the file **P16_10.xlsx**, fit all three of these types of trendlines to the data, and calculate the MAPE for each. Which provides the best fit? (*Hint:* Note that a polynomial of order 2 is still another of Excel's Trendline options.)

11. The management of Beta Technologies, Inc., is trying to determine the variable that best explains the variation of employee salaries using a sample of 52 full-time employees; see the file **P16_11.xlsx**. Estimate simple linear regression models to identify which of the following has the *strongest* linear relationship with annual salary: the employee's gender, age, number of years of relevant work experience prior to employment at Beta, number of years of employment at Beta, or number of years of post-secondary education. Provide support for your conclusion.

# 16.4 MULTIPLE REGRESSION MODELS

When we try to explain a dependent variable $Y$ with regression, there are often a multitude of explanatory variables to choose from. In this section, we explore multiple regression, where the regression equation for $Y$ includes a number of explanatory variables, the $X$'s. The general form of this equation is shown in the box. Geometrically, this equation represents a *hyperplane* through a scatter of points in $(k - 1)$-dimensional space ($k$ $X$'s and 1 $Y$). However, unless $k = 1$ or $k = 2$, this hyperplane is impossible to draw. Nevertheless, it is helpful to keep the image of a plane passing through a set of points in mind as you study multiple regression.

> **Multiple regression equation**
>
> $$Y = a + b_1 X_1 + b_2 X_2 + \cdots + b_k X_k \qquad \textbf{(16.7)}$$

In equation (16.7), $a$ is again the $Y$-intercept, and $b_1$ through $b_k$ are the slopes. Collectively, we refer to $a$ and the $b$'s as the **regression coefficients.** Each slope coefficient is the expected change in $Y$ when that particular $X$ increases by 1 unit and the other $X$'s in the equation remain constant. For example, $b_1$ is the expected change in $Y$ when $X_1$ increases by 1 unit and the other $X$'s in the equation, $X_2$ through $X_k$, remain constant. The intercept $a$ is typically less important. Literally, it is the expected value of $Y$ when all of the $X$'s equal 0. However, this makes sense only if it is practical for all of the $X$'s to equal 0, which is rarely the case.

> The **regression coefficients** are the intercept and slopes of the regression equation.

We illustrate these ideas in the following extension of Example 16.2.

## EXAMPLE | 16.3 ESTIMATING TOTAL COST FOR SEVERAL PRODUCTS

Suppose the company in Example 16.2 now produces three different products, A, B, and C. The company has kept track of the number of units produced of each product and the total production cost for the past 15 months. These data appear in Figure 16.12 and in the file **Cost Regression 2.xlsx**. What can multiple regression tell us about the relationship between these variables? How can multiple regression be used to predict future production costs?

**Figure 16.12**

Cost and Production Data for Multiple Products

| | A | B | C | D | E |
|---|---|---|---|---|---|
| 1 | Month | Units A | Units B | Units C | Total Cost |
| 2 | 1 | 696 | 819 | 895 | $58,789 |
| 3 | 2 | 627 | 512 | 925 | $50,276 |
| 4 | 3 | 122 | 323 | 814 | $43,703 |
| 5 | 4 | 313 | 981 | 670 | $50,857 |
| 6 | 5 | 340 | 884 | 356 | $46,397 |
| 7 | 6 | 462 | 599 | 673 | $46,731 |
| 8 | 7 | 269 | 302 | 737 | $40,328 |
| 9 | 8 | 343 | 495 | 878 | $42,368 |
| 10 | 9 | 986 | 191 | 592 | $44,617 |
| 11 | 10 | 555 | 314 | 467 | $40,515 |
| 12 | 11 | 908 | 593 | 749 | $55,546 |
| 13 | 12 | 595 | 115 | 458 | $36,856 |
| 14 | 13 | 557 | 369 | 160 | $35,697 |
| 15 | 14 | 271 | 550 | 457 | $40,130 |
| 16 | 15 | 878 | 750 | 983 | $59,929 |

**Objective**  To use multiple regression to estimate the relationship between units produced of three products and the total production cost, and to use this relationship to predict future total costs.

## Solution

*A useful first step in multiple regression is to create a scatterplot of Y versus each of the X's.*

The dependent variable $Y$ is again Total Cost, but there are now three potential $X$'s, Units A, Units B, and Units C. We are not required to use all three of these, but we do so here. In fact, it is again a good idea to begin with scatterplots of $Y$ versus each $X$ to see which $X$'s are indeed related to $Y$. We did this and obtained three scatterplots; a typical one appears in Figure 16.13. This scatterplot—and the ones for products A and C are similar—indicates a fairly strong linear relationship between Total Cost and Units B.

**Figure 16.13**  Scatterplot of Total Cost versus Units B

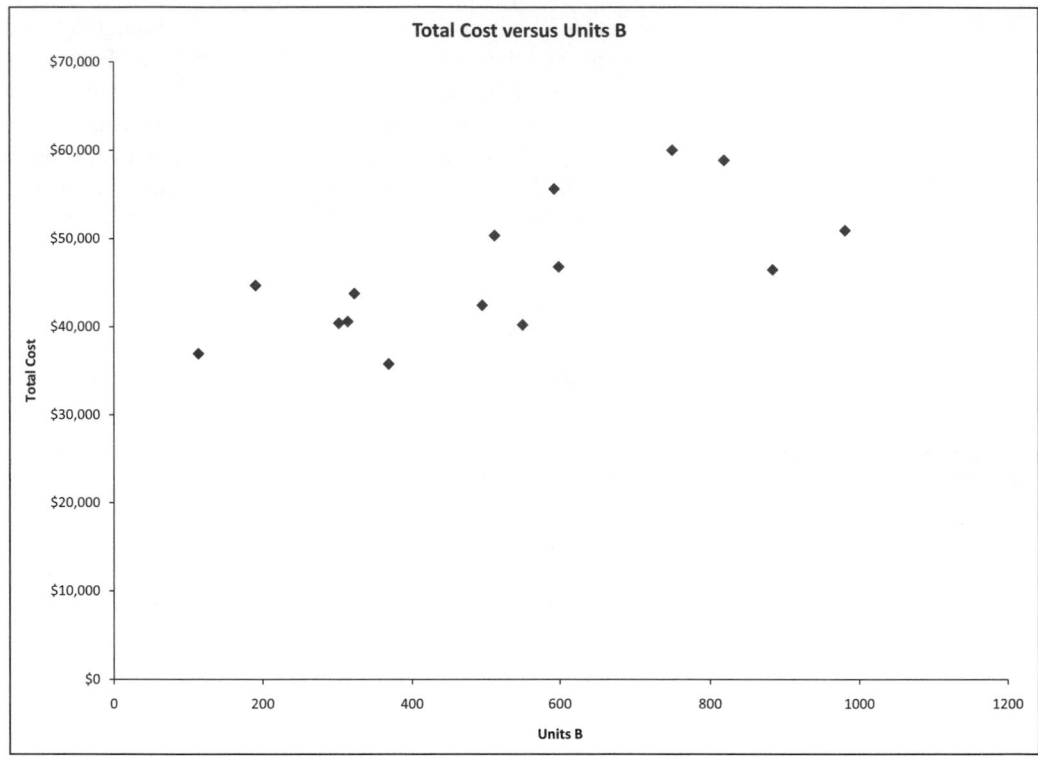

## USING ANALYSIS TOOLPAK

*When there are multiple independent variables, Excel's Trendline option cannot be used to find the regression equation.*

Unfortunately, when there are multiple $X$'s, we cannot estimate the multiple regression equation by using Excel's Trendline option as we did with simple regression. Instead, we must use a statistical software package or an Excel add-in. Fortunately, Excel includes such an add-in, called Analysis ToolPak. (See the following paragraph about loading this add-in.)

**Excel Tool:** *The Analysis ToolPak Add-In*
*The Analysis ToolPak add-in is part of Excel. It performs a number of statistical analyses, including regression. To use it, you must first make sure it is loaded in memory. To do this, select the Office button, then Excel Options, then Add-Ins, then Go, and if necessary, check*

*the Analysis ToolPak item. (You do not need to check the Analysis ToolPak–VBA item. We will not be using it.) You will know the Analysis ToolPak is loaded because a Data Analysis button appears on the Data ribbon.*

To run the regression analysis with Analysis ToolPak, select Data Analysis from the Data ribbon, select Regression from the list of Analysis Tools, and fill out the resulting dialog box as shown in Figure 16.14. The following options are the most important; you can experiment with the other settings.

- The range for the *X*'s must be contiguous. In other words, the data for the explanatory variables must be in adjacent columns. You might have to move the data around to get the *X*'s next to each other, depending on the setup of your data set.

- It is useful for reporting purposes to include the variable names (row 1 in our case) in the *Y* and *X*'s ranges. To do this, you should check the Labels box.

- There are a number of options on where to put the output. We chose cell G1 (of the same worksheet as the data) as the upper-left corner of our output range.

- If you check the Residuals box, you automatically get the fitted (predicted) values of the *Y*'s and the corresponding residuals.

**Figure 16.14**

Regression Dialog Box from Analysis ToolPak

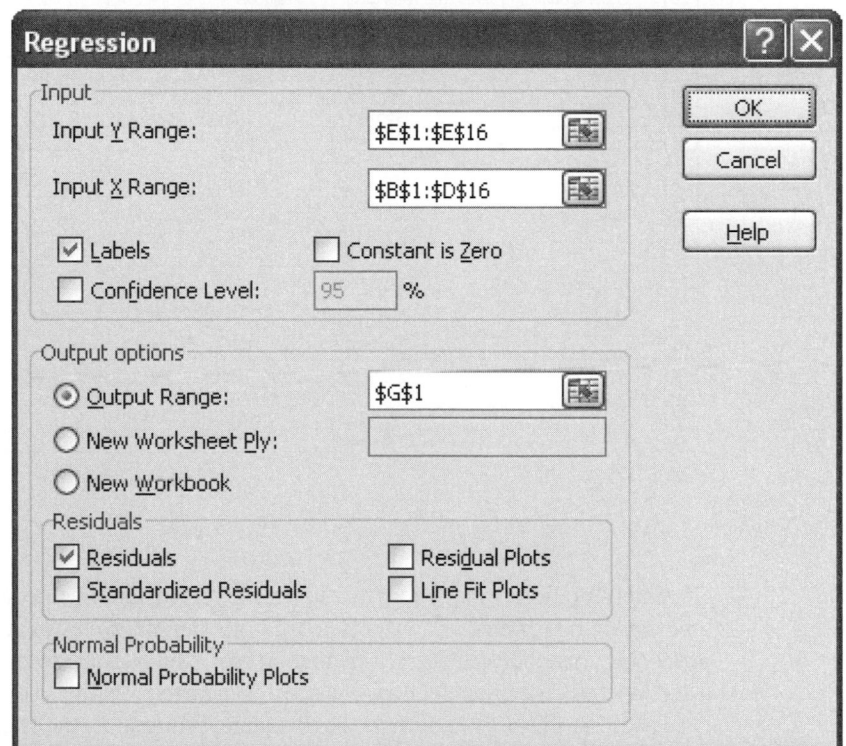

### Discussion of the Results

The resulting output appears in Figure 16.15. We will not explain *all* of this output, but we will focus on the highlights. The most important part is the regression equation itself, which is implied by the values in the H17:H20 range:

Predicted Total Cost = 20,261 + 12.802Units A + 17.691Units B + 15.230Units C

| | G | H | I | J | K | L | M |
|---|---|---|---|---|---|---|---|
| 1 | SUMMARY OUTPUT | | | | | | |
| 2 | | | | | | | |
| 3 | *Regression Statistics* | | | | | | |
| 4 | Multiple R | 0.973 | | | | | |
| 5 | R Square | 0.946 | | | | | |
| 6 | Adjusted R Square | 0.931 | | | | | |
| 7 | Standard Error | 1980.505 | | | | | |
| 8 | Observations | 15 | | | | | |
| 9 | | | | | | | |
| 10 | ANOVA | | | | | | |
| 11 | | *df* | *SS* | *MS* | *F* | *Significance F* | |
| 12 | Regression | 3 | 754480290.6 | 251493430 | 64.11721 | 0.000 | |
| 13 | Residual | 11 | 43146416.96 | 3922401.54 | | | |
| 14 | Total | 14 | 797626707.6 | | | | |
| 15 | | | | | | | |
| 16 | | *Coefficients* | *Standard Error* | *t Stat* | *P-value* | *Lower 95%* | *Upper 95%* |
| 17 | Intercept | 20261.273 | 1968.133 | 10.295 | 0.000 | 15929.442 | 24593.103 |
| 18 | Units A | 12.802 | 2.083 | 6.147 | 0.000 | 8.218 | 17.386 |
| 19 | Units B | 17.691 | 2.137 | 8.278 | 0.000 | 12.988 | 22.395 |
| 20 | Units C | 15.230 | 2.346 | 6.491 | 0.000 | 10.065 | 20.394 |
| 21 | | | | | | | |
| 22 | | | | | | | |
| 23 | | | | | | | |
| 24 | RESIDUAL OUTPUT | | | | | | |
| 25 | | | | | | | |
| 26 | *Observation* | *Predicted Total Cost* | *Residuals* | | | | |
| 27 | 1 | 57291.13 | 1497.87 | | | | |
| 28 | 2 | 51433.51 | -1157.51 | | | | |
| 29 | 3 | 39934.42 | 3768.58 | | | | |
| 30 | 4 | 51827.27 | -970.27 | | | | |
| 31 | 5 | 45674.72 | 722.28 | | | | |
| 32 | 6 | 47022.41 | -291.41 | | | | |
| 33 | 7 | 40272.08 | 55.92 | | | | |
| 34 | 8 | 46781.22 | -4413.22 | | | | |
| 35 | 9 | 45278.99 | -661.99 | | | | |
| 36 | 10 | 40033.67 | 481.33 | | | | |
| 37 | 11 | 53783.37 | 1762.63 | | | | |
| 38 | 12 | 36888.13 | -32.13 | | | | |
| 39 | 13 | 36356.73 | -659.73 | | | | |
| 40 | 14 | 40420.75 | -290.75 | | | | |
| 41 | 15 | 59740.61 | 188.39 | | | | |
| 42 | | | | | | | |
| 43 | Future predictions | | 95% prediction interval | | | | |
| 44 | 16 | 45922.39 | 41961.38 | 49883.40 | | | |
| 45 | 17 | 44906.80 | 40945.79 | 48867.81 | | | |

The interpretation is much like that in simple regression. Each coefficient of a Units variable can be interpreted as a variable cost. For example, we estimate that each extra unit of product B contributes about $17.69 to total cost. The constant term, 20,261, is again the estimated fixed cost of production. This cost is incurred regardless of the level of production.

The other important outputs are $R$-square, multiple $R$, the standard error of estimate, the fitted values, and the residuals:

■ The $R$-square value is the percentage of variation of Total Cost explained by the *combination* of all three explanatory variables. We see that these three Units variables explain about 94.6% of the variation in Total Cost—a fairly high percentage.

■ The multiple $R$, the square root of $R$-square, is the correlation between the actual $Y$'s and fitted values. Because $R$-square is large, the multiple $R$ is also large: 0.973. This high value implies that the points in a scatterplot (not shown) of actual $Y$ values versus fitted values are close to a 45° line.

- The standard error of estimate has exactly the same interpretation as before. It is a ballpark estimate of the magnitude of the prediction errors we are likely to make, based on the regression equation. Here, this value is about $1981—not too bad considering that the total costs vary around $50,000.

- The fitted values are found by substituting each set of $X$'s into the regression equation, and the residuals are the differences between actual total costs and fitted values. Analysis ToolPak calculates these automatically for us in the range H26:I41 (if we check the Residuals box in Figure 16.14). As indicated by the standard error of estimate, most of the residuals are no more than about $2000 in magnitude, and quite a few are considerably less than this.

### A Note about Adjusted R-square

You are probably wondering what the *adjusted* $R$-square value means in the multiple regression output. Although it has no simple interpretation like $R$-square (percentage of variation explained), it is useful for comparing regression equations. The problem with $R$-square is that it can *never* decrease when we add extra explanatory variables to a regression equation. However, there ought to be some penalty for adding variables that don't really belong. This is the purpose of adjusted $R$-square, which acts as a monitor. If we add one or more extra explanatory variables to an already existing equation, adjusted $R$-square *can* decrease. If this occurs, then we have evidence that the extra variables don't really belong in the equation and should probably be deleted.

### Prediction of Future Costs

If we conclude that the fit is good enough to provide useful *future* predictions, we can then substitute future estimates of production levels into the regression equation. We did this for the proposed values of the $X$'s for months 16 and 17 in rows 19 and 20. (These do not appear in Figure 16.12 or Figure 16.15.) Specifically, we enter the formula

**=$H$17+$H$18*B17+$H$19*C17+$H$20*D17**

in cell H44 and copy it to cell H45. Of course, this could be done for *any* assumed production levels in these two months, not just the ones we chose. In each case, the predicted total cost is approximately in the $45,000 to $46,000 range, and the standard error of estimate implies that these predictions are probably not off by more than about $2000.

More specifically, it is common to quote a **95% prediction interval** for each future prediction. We are 95% sure that the actual future value will be inside this interval. Although the exact calculation of a 95% prediction interval is somewhat complex, a good and easy approximation is to go out two standard errors of estimate on either side of the predicted value. For example, an approximate 95% prediction interval for the total cost in month 16 extends (aside from rounding) from $45,922 - 2(1981) = 41,961$ to $45,922 + 2(1981) = 49,883$. We show these prediction intervals in the range I44:J45. Their relatively large widths indicate that even with an excellent fit—an $R$-square of 94.6% is quite good—we cannot ensure completely accurate future predictions. ∎

## Incorporating Categorical Variables

In regression analysis, we are always searching for good explanatory variables to explain some dependent variable $Y$. Often these explanatory variables are quantitative, such as the Units Produced variables in the two previous examples. However, there are often useful, qualitative categorical variables that help explain $Y$, such as gender (male or female), region of country (east, south, west, or north), quarter of year (Q1, Q2, Q3, or Q4), and so on.

Because regression works entirely with numbers, we need a way to transform these categorical variables into numeric variables that can be used in a regression equation. The solution is to use **dummy** variables, also called **0–1** variables or **indicator** variables. For any categorical variable, we create a dummy variable for each possible category. Its value is 1 for each observation in that category, and it is 0 otherwise.

> A **dummy** variable for any category equals 1 for all observations in that category and 0 for all observations not in that category.

For example, the variable Gender has two possible values, Male and Female, so we can create two dummy variables, Male and Female. Male equals 1 for all males and 0 for all females, whereas Female equals 1 for all females and 0 for all males. As another example, if the variable Quarter has possible values Q1, Q2, Q3, and Q4, we can create four dummy variables, one for each quarter. For example, the dummy variable Quarter1 equals 1 for all quarter 1 observations and 0 for all other observations.

*For a categorical variable with m categories, include only m − 1 of the corresponding dummy variables in the regression equation. Any one of them can be omitted.*

There is one technical rule we must follow when using dummy variables in regression. If a categorical variable has $m$ categories, we should use only $m - 1$ of the $m$ possible dummy variables in the regression equation. We can omit *any* one of the dummies, which becomes the **reference** (or **base**) category. We then interpret the regression coefficients of the included dummies with respect to the reference category. For example, if $Y$ is salary, and if we include the dummy variable Male in the equation, then the reference category is female. If the coefficient of Male turns out to be, say, $2000, then the interpretation is that, all else being equal, males average $2000 more in salary than females. If we had included Female instead of Male in the equation, then the coefficient of Female would be –$2000, meaning again that females average $2000 less than males. The point is that one dummy must be omitted, and it doesn't matter which one we omit.

The following example, another extension of Example 16.2, illustrates the use of dummy variables.

---

**FUNDAMENTAL INSIGHT**

### Which Explanatory Variables to Use

Regression outputs contain a lot of numbers and graphs, and it can be difficult to learn what they all mean. However, the biggest challenge in using regression, especially with the abundance of data in today's world, is discovering the best set of explanatory variables to include in a regression equation. Besides the variables in the "raw" data set, you can create dummy variables, nonlinear functions of the original variables (such as logarithms), lagged versions of the original variables, and others. It takes some experience with regression, and with the problem at hand, to find a good set of explanatory variables. It also takes a willingness to experiment. There is almost never one *best* regression equation; there are usually several that are *useful*.

---

**EXAMPLE** | **16.4 ESTIMATING PRODUCTION COSTS AT THREE COMPANY PLANTS**

Suppose the company in Example 16.2 produces a single product at three different manufacturing plants. As in that example, the company wants to regress total cost on units produced, but it suspects that the relationship between these variables might differ across plants. It has monthly data from the past 16 months for each of the plants, some of which appear in Figure 16.16. (See the file **Cost Regression 3.xlsx**.) How can the company use dummy variables to estimate the relationship between Total Cost and Units Produced for all three plants simultaneously?

**Figure 16.16**

Cost Data for Three Plants

| | A | B | C | D |
|---|---|---|---|---|
| 1 | Month | Plant | Units Produced | Total Cost |
| 2 | 1 | 1 | 800 | $190,600 |
| 3 | 1 | 2 | 500 | $142,200 |
| 4 | 1 | 3 | 200 | $46,400 |
| 5 | 2 | 1 | 400 | $99,700 |
| 6 | 2 | 2 | 800 | $194,300 |
| 7 | 2 | 3 | 300 | $74,400 |
| 8 | 3 | 1 | 300 | $82,800 |
| 9 | 3 | 2 | 700 | $171,100 |
| 10 | 3 | 3 | 200 | $50,100 |
| 11 | 4 | 1 | 400 | $104,300 |
| 12 | 4 | 2 | 600 | $158,600 |
| 13 | 4 | 3 | 200 | $52,100 |
| 14 | 5 | 1 | 600 | $148,800 |
| 15 | 5 | 2 | 800 | $201,500 |
| 16 | 5 | 3 | 600 | $132,000 |
| 17 | 6 | 1 | 300 | $81,500 |
| 18 | 6 | 2 | 600 | $155,900 |
| 19 | 6 | 3 | 200 | $45,300 |
| 20 | 7 | 1 | 500 | $129,100 |
| 21 | 7 | 2 | 700 | $179,000 |
| 22 | 7 | 3 | 400 | $86,600 |
| 23 | 8 | 1 | 400 | $105,500 |

**Objective**  To use dummy variables for plants to estimate a single regression equation relating total cost to units produced for all three plants.

## Solution

After we get the data set up properly, we can use Analysis ToolPak to run the regression in the usual way. However, we must first create the dummy variables.

### Creating the Dummy Variables

The simplest way to create dummy variables for the plants is with IF formulas. The results are shown in Figure 16.17. The formulas for the dummies in cells C2, D2, and E2 are

=IF(B2=1,1,0)

=IF(B2=2,1,0)

and

=IF(B2=3,1,0)

**Figure 16.17**

Original Data with Dummy Variables Added

| | A | B | C | D | E | F | G |
|---|---|---|---|---|---|---|---|
| 1 | Month | Plant | Plant1 | Plant2 | Plant3 | Units Produced | Total Cost |
| 2 | 1 | 1 | 1 | 0 | 0 | 800 | $190,600 |
| 3 | 1 | 2 | 0 | 1 | 0 | 500 | $142,200 |
| 4 | 1 | 3 | 0 | 0 | 1 | 200 | $46,400 |
| 5 | 2 | 1 | 1 | 0 | 0 | 400 | $99,700 |
| 6 | 2 | 2 | 0 | 1 | 0 | 800 | $194,300 |
| 7 | 2 | 3 | 0 | 0 | 1 | 300 | $74,400 |
| 8 | 3 | 1 | 1 | 0 | 0 | 300 | $82,800 |
| 9 | 3 | 2 | 0 | 1 | 0 | 700 | $171,100 |
| 10 | 3 | 3 | 0 | 0 | 1 | 200 | $50,100 |
| 11 | 4 | 1 | 1 | 0 | 0 | 400 | $104,300 |
| 12 | 4 | 2 | 0 | 1 | 0 | 600 | $158,600 |
| 13 | 4 | 3 | 0 | 0 | 1 | 200 | $52,100 |
| 14 | 5 | 1 | 1 | 0 | 0 | 600 | $148,800 |
| 15 | 5 | 2 | 0 | 1 | 0 | 800 | $201,500 |
| 16 | 5 | 3 | 0 | 0 | 1 | 600 | $132,000 |
| 17 | 6 | 1 | 1 | 0 | 0 | 300 | $81,500 |
| 18 | 6 | 2 | 0 | 1 | 0 | 600 | $155,900 |
| 19 | 6 | 3 | 0 | 0 | 1 | 200 | $45,300 |
| 20 | 7 | 1 | 1 | 0 | 0 | 500 | $129,100 |
| 21 | 7 | 2 | 0 | 1 | 0 | 700 | $179,000 |
| 22 | 7 | 3 | 0 | 0 | 1 | 400 | $86,600 |
| 23 | 8 | 1 | 1 | 0 | 0 | 400 | $105,500 |

which are then copied down their respective columns. Actually, we need only two of these dummies in the regression equation. Because Analysis ToolPak requires the independent variables to be in adjacent columns, we include the Plant2 and Plant3 dummies, along with the quantitative variable Units Produced, as the explanatory variables. This means that plant 1 is the reference category.

## Discussion of the Results

The regression output from the Analysis ToolPak appears in Figure 16.18. It literally implies the following regression equation for predicting total cost:

$$\text{Predicted Total Cost} = 22,852 + 12,972\text{Plant2} - 15,045\text{Plant3} + 204.15\text{Units Produced}$$

**Figure 16.18**

Regression Output from Analysis Tool-Pak with Dummy Variables Included

| | I | J | K | L | M | N | O |
|---|---|---|---|---|---|---|---|
| 1 | SUMMARY OUTPUT | | | | | | |
| 2 | | | | | | | |
| 3 | | *Regression Statistics* | | | | | |
| 4 | Multiple R | 0.997 | | | | | |
| 5 | R Square | 0.995 | | | | | |
| 6 | Adjusted R Square | 0.994 | | | | | |
| 7 | Standard Error | 3525.057 | | | | | |
| 8 | Observations | 48 | | | | | |
| 9 | | | | | | | |
| 10 | ANOVA | | | | | | |
| 11 | | *df* | *SS* | *MS* | *F* | *Significance F* | |
| 12 | Regression | 3 | 1.05525E+11 | 35175003210 | 2830.75234 | 2.50011E-50 | |
| 13 | Residual | 44 | 546745160.2 | 12426026.37 | | | |
| 14 | Total | 47 | 1.06072E+11 | | | | |
| 15 | | | | | | | |
| 16 | | *Coefficients* | *Standard Error* | *t Stat* | *P-value* | *Lower 95%* | *Upper 95%* |
| 17 | Intercept | 22851.936 | 1607.293 | 14.218 | 4.65979E-18 | 19612.649 | 26091.222 |
| 18 | Plant2 | 12971.974 | 1278.609 | 10.145 | 4.27256E-13 | 10395.107 | 15548.840 |
| 19 | Plant3 | -15045.290 | 1262.500 | -11.917 | 2.2872E-15 | -17589.691 | -12500.889 |
| 20 | Units Produced | 204.146 | 2.688 | 75.938 | 2.64487E-48 | 198.728 | 209.564 |

However, it is more intuitive to think of this as three separate equations, one for each plant. For plant 1, the reference category, the dummies Plant2 and Plant3 are 0, so the equation reduces to

$$\text{Predicted Total Cost (plant 1)} = 22,852 + 204.15\text{Units Produced}$$

For plant 2, the dummy Plant2 is 1 and the dummy Plant3 is 0, so the equation reduces to

$$\text{Predicted Total Cost (plant 2)} = (22,852 + 12,972) + 204.15\text{Units Produced}$$

Finally, for plant 3, the dummy Plant2 is 0 and the dummy Plant3 is 1, so the equation reduces to

$$\text{Predicted Total Cost (plant 3)} = (22,852 - 15,045) + 204.15\text{Units Produced}$$

We see from these equations that the coefficient of Units Produced is 204.15 for each plant. Therefore, if any of the plants produces an extra unit, we expect its total cost to increase by about $204. The only difference between the equations is in their intercepts. Specifically, if plants 1 and 2 produce the same numbers of units, we expect plant 2's total cost to be $12,972 *higher* than plant 1's. Similarly, if plants 1 and 3 produce the same numbers of units, we expect plant 3's total cost to be $15,045 *lower* than plant 1's. In this sense, the coefficients of the dummy variables allow us to compare each plant to the reference plant. Of course, we can also compare *nonreference* plants to one another. If plants 2 and 3 produce the same numbers of units, we expect plant 2's total cost to be ($12,972 + $15,045) higher than plant 3's.

Geometrically, the regression analysis produces three parallel lines for the three plants, as shown in Figure 16.19. Each of the lines has the same slope, 204.15, but they have different intercepts. By including the dummy variables as we have done, we are forcing the regression to estimate parallel lines, so that the effect of Units Produced on Total Cost is the *same* for each plant. If we believe this effect *differs* across plants—that is, we believe the variable costs for the three plants might not be the same—we must include extra explanatory variables, called *interaction* variables, to the regression equation. However, we do not pursue this topic here.

**Figure 16.19**
Estimation of Three Parallel Regression Lines

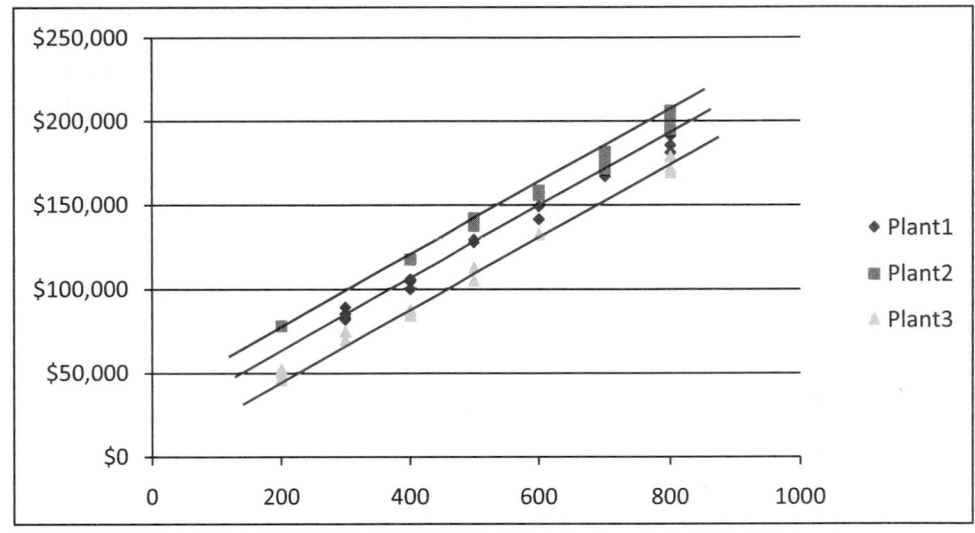

## A Caution about Regression Assumptions

In this brief introduction to regression, we have discussed only the basic elements of regression analysis, and we have omitted many of the technical details that can be found in more complete statistics books. In particular, we have not discussed what can go wrong if various statistical assumptions behind regression analysis are violated. Although there is not room here for a complete discussion of these assumptions and their ramifications, we briefly state a few cautions you should be aware of.

## Multicollinearity

In the best of worlds, we would like the explanatory variables, the $X$'s, to provide nonoverlapping information about the dependent variable $Y$. We do not want them to provide redundant information. However, sometimes redundancy is difficult to avoid. For example, in trying to explain employee salaries, three potential explanatory variables are age, years of seniority with this company, and years of experience with this type of job. These three variables are likely to be highly correlated with one another (as well as with salary), and it is not clear whether we should include all three in a regression equation for salary.

*Multicollinearity makes it difficult to interpret individual regression coefficients, but it does not have a negative effect on predictions.*

When we do include $X$'s that are highly correlated with one another, we introduce a problem called **multicollinearity.** The problem is that when $X$'s are highly correlated, it is virtually impossible to sort out their separate influences on $Y$. This inability to sort out separate effects can even lead to "wrong" signs on the regression coefficients. For example, if age, years of seniority, and years of experience are all entered in an equation for salary, it is possible that one of the three regression coefficients will be *negative,* even though all three variables are positively correlated to salary. Therefore, the presence of multicollinearity makes regression equations difficult to interpret. Fortunately, however, multicollinearity is not a problem if we are concerned only with *prediction* of new $Y$'s.

## Nonlinear Relationships

If scatterplots of $Y$ versus the various $X$'s indicate any nonlinear relationships, then the linear relationship we have been estimating will almost certainly lead to a poor fit and poor predictions. Fortunately, as with the exponential trendline, there are often nonlinear transformations of $Y$ and/or the $X$'s that "straighten out" the scatterplots and allow us to use *linear* regression. We do not discuss such transformations here. We simply warn you that if the scatterplots of the original variables do not appear to be linear, you should not blindly proceed to estimate linear relationships.

## Nonconstant Error Variance

One assumption of regression is that the variation of the $Y$'s above any values of the $X$'s is the same, regardless of the particular values of the $X$'s chosen. Sometimes this assumption is clearly violated. For example, if $Y$ is a household's annual amount spent on vacations and $X$ is the household's annual income, it is very possible that the variation of the $Y$'s for low-income households is considerably less than that for high-income households. The low-income households don't have much to spend on vacations, so their vacation spending is likely to be tightly bunched at low values. In contrast, the high-income households have a lot to spend, but they might or might not elect to spend it on vacations. Typically, nonconstant error variance appears in a scatterplot as a "fan-shape" swarm of points. We simply alert you to this possibility and suggest that you obtain expert help if you spot an obvious fan shape.

## Autocorrelation of Residuals

Autocorrelation means that a variable's values are correlated to its own previous values. This typically occurs in time series variables. For example, we might be using regression to forecast monthly sales. If the residuals are autocorrelated, then an overprediction in January is likely to be followed by an overprediction in February, and an underprediction in June is likely to be followed by an underprediction in July. It is not difficult to detect autocorrelation of residuals (although we do not discuss the measures for doing so), but it is much more difficult to deal with autocorrelation appropriately. Again, you should consult an expert if you believe your time series analysis is subject to autocorrelation.

---

**FUNDAMENTAL INSIGHT**

### Cautions about Regression

Regression is a very powerful method for discovering relationships between variables, and with the software available in today's world, it is very easy to use. Unfortunately, it is also very easy to use incorrectly. Many people are not aware of the assumptions behind the regression model, how to check whether these assumptions hold, or how to modify the analysis if the

assumptions do not hold. This has led to many incorrect interpretations of regression output. Like most powerful tools, regression is easy to misuse if you don't understand some of the theory behind it. Because this theory is fairly complex, don't be afraid to ask a statistical expert for help if you are conducting an important regression analysis.

# PROBLEMS

## Skill-Building Problems

**12.** Suppose you are an analyst for a company that produces four products, and you are trying to decide how much of each product to produce next month. To model this decision problem, you need the unit variable production cost for each product. After some digging, you find the historical data on production levels and costs in the file **P16_12.xlsx**. Use these data to find estimates of the unit costs you need. You should also find an estimate of the fixed cost of production. Will this be of any use to you in deciding how much of each product to produce? Why or why not?

**13.** A trucking company wants to predict the yearly maintenance expense ($Y$) for a truck using the number of miles driven during the year ($X_1$) and the age of the truck ($X_2$, in years) at the beginning of the year. The company has gathered the data given in the file **P16_13.xlsx**. Note that each observation corresponds to a particular truck. Estimate a multiple regression model using the given data. Interpret each of the estimated regression coefficients. Also, interpret the standard error of estimate and the $R$-square value for these data.

**14.** An antique collector believes that the price received for a particular item increases with its age and with the number of bidders. The file **P16_14.xlsx** contains data on these three variables for 32 recently auctioned comparable items. Estimate a multiple regression model using the given data. Interpret each of the estimated regression coefficients. Is the antique collector correct in believing that the price received for the item increases with its age and with the number of bidders? Interpret the standard error of estimate and the $R$-square value for these data.

**15.** Stock market analysts are continually looking for reliable predictors of stock prices. Consider the problem of modeling the price per share of electric utility stocks ($Y$). Two variables thought to influence this stock price are return on average equity ($X_1$) and annual dividend rate ($X_2$). The stock price, returns on equity, and dividend rates on a randomly selected day for 16 electric utility stocks are provided in the file **P16_15.xlsx**. Estimate a multiple regression model using the given data. Interpret each of the estimated regression coefficients. Also, interpret the standard error of estimate and the $R$-square value for these data.

**16.** Consider the enrollment data for *Business Week*'s top 50 U.S. graduate business programs in the file **P16_16.xlsx**. Use these data to estimate a multiple regression model to assess whether a systematic relationship exists between the total number of full-time students and the following explanatory variables: the proportion of female students, the proportion of minority students, and the proportion of international students enrolled at these distinguished business schools.

   **a.** Interpret the coefficients of your estimated regression model. Do any of these results surprise you? Explain.

   **b.** How well does your estimated regression model fit the given data?

**17.** David Savageau and Geoffrey Loftus, the authors of *Places Rated Almanac* (published in 2000 by Macmillan), have ranked 325 metropolitan areas in the United States with consideration of the following aspects of life in each area: cost of living, transportation, jobs, education, climate, crime, arts, health, and recreation. The data are in the file **P16_17.xlsx**. The last column lists the city's overall score, which is the average of the other scores. (You can check this with Excel's AVERAGE function.)

   **a.** Use multiple regression analysis to explore the relationship between the metropolitan area's overall score and the set of potential explanatory variables.

   **b.** Does the given set of explanatory variables do a good job of explaining variation in the overall score? Explain why or why not.

**18.** Suppose that a regional express delivery service company wants to estimate the cost of shipping a package ($Y$) as a function of cargo type, where cargo type includes the following possibilities: fragile, semifragile, and durable. Costs for 15 randomly chosen packages of approximately the same weight and same distance shipped, but of different cargo types, are provided in the file **P16_18.xlsx**.

   **a.** Formulate an appropriate multiple regression model to predict the cost of shipping a given package.

   **b.** Estimate the formulated model using the given sample data, and interpret the estimated regression coefficients.

   **c.** According to the estimated regression model, which cargo type is the *most* costly to ship? Which cargo type is the *least* costly to ship?

   **d.** How well does the estimated model fit the given sample data? How might the model be improved?

   **e.** Given the estimated regression model, predict the cost of shipping a package with semifragile cargo.

## Skill-Extending Problems

**19.** The owner of a restaurant in Bloomington, Indiana, has recorded sales data for the past 19 years. He has also recorded data on potentially relevant variables. The data are listed in the file **P16_19.xlsx**.

a. Estimate a simple regression model involving annual sales (the dependent variable) and the size of the population residing within 10 miles of the restaurant (the explanatory variable). Interpret $R$-square for this regression.

b. Add another explanatory variable—annual advertising expenditures—to the regression model in part **a**. Estimate and interpret this expanded model. How does the $R$-square value for this multiple regression model compare to that of the simple regression model estimated in part **a**? Explain any difference between the two $R$-square values. How can you use the adjusted $R$-squares for a comparison of the two models?

c. Add one more explanatory variable to the multiple regression model estimated in part **b**. In particular, estimate and interpret the coefficients of a multiple regression model that includes the *previous* year's advertising expenditure. How does the inclusion of this third explanatory variable affect the $R$-square, compared to the corresponding values for the model of part **b**? Explain any changes in this value. What does the adjusted $R$-square for the new model tell you?

20. A regional express delivery service company recently conducted a study to investigate the relationship between the cost of shipping a package ($Y$), the package weight ($X_1$), and the distance shipped ($X_2$). Twenty packages were randomly selected from among the large number received for shipment, and a detailed analysis of the shipping cost was conducted for each package. These sample observations are given in the file **P16_20.xlsx**.

a. Estimate a simple linear regression model involving shipping cost and package weight. Interpret the slope coefficient of the least squares line as well as the value of $R$-square.

b. Add another explanatory variable—distance shipped—to the regression model in part **a**. Estimate and interpret this expanded model. How does the $R$-square value for this multiple regression model compare to that of the simple regression model estimated in part **a**? Explain any difference between the two $R$-square values. How can you use the adjusted $R$-squares for a comparison of the two models?

21. Suppose that you are interested in predicting the price of a laptop computer based on its various features. The file **P16_21.xlsx** contains observations on the sales price and a number of potentially relevant variables for a randomly chosen sample of laptop computers.

a. Formulate a multiple regression model that includes all potential explanatory variables and estimate it with the given sample data.

b. Interpret the estimated regression equation. Indicate the impact of each attribute on the computer's sales price. For example, what impact does the monitor type have on the average sales price of a laptop computer?

c. How well does the estimated regression model fit the data given in the file?

d. Use the estimated regression equation to predict the price of a laptop computer with the following features: a 60-MHz processor, a battery that holds its charge for 240 minutes, 32 MB of RAM, a DX chip, a color monitor, a mouse, and a 24-hour, toll-free customer service hotline.

# 16.5 OVERVIEW OF TIME SERIES MODELS

To this point, we have discussed regression as a method of forecasting. Because of its flexibility, regression can be used equally well for time series variables and for cross-sectional variables. From here on, however, we focus exclusively on time series variables, and we discuss nonregression approaches to forecasting. All of these approaches fall under the general umbrella of **extrapolation** methods.

With an extrapolation method, we form a time series plot of the variable $Y$ that we want to forecast, we analyze any patterns inherent in this time series plot, and we extrapolate these patterns into the future. We do *not* use any other variables—the $X$'s from regression—to forecast $Y$; we use only past values of $Y$ to forecast future values of $Y$. The idea is that history tends to repeat itself. Therefore, if we can discover the patterns in the historical data, we ought to obtain reasonably good forecasts by projecting these historical patterns into the future.

Before examining specific extrapolation techniques, we discuss the types of patterns we are likely to see in time series data. We also briefly discuss the measures that are typically used to judge how well our methods track the historical data.

## Components of Time Series

A time series variable $Y$ typically contains one or more components. These components are called the *trend* component, the *seasonal* component, the *cyclic* component, and the *random* (or *noise*) component. We provide a brief discussion of these components here.

We start with a very simple time series in which every observation is the same, as shown in Figure 16.20. The graph in this figure shows time $t$ on the horizontal axis and the observation value $Y$ on the vertical axis. We assume that $Y$ is measured at regularly spaced intervals, usually days, weeks, months, quarters, or years. We denote the value of $Y$ in period $t$ as $Y_t$. As indicated in the figure, the individual points are usually joined by straight lines to make any patterns in the time series more apparent. Because all observations in this series are equal, the resulting plot is a horizontal line. We refer to this series as the *base* series. Then we build more interesting times series from this base series.

**Figure 16.20**

The Base Series

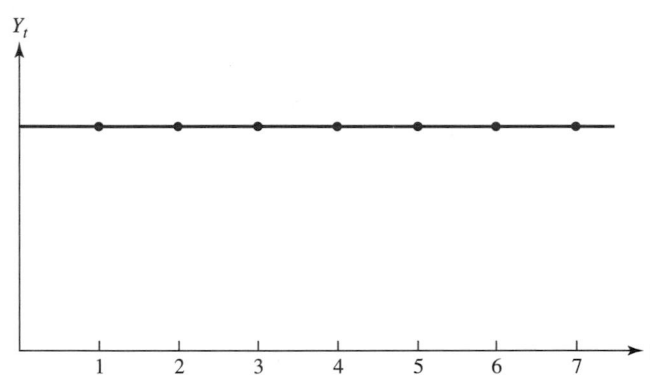

## Trend Component

*A trend implies a consistent upward or downward movement of the series through time.*

If the observations increase or decrease regularly through time, we say that the time series has a **trend.** The graphs in Figure 16.21 illustrate several possible trends. We already discussed the linear trend in Figure 16.21a and the exponential trend in Figure 16.21b in Section 16.3. The curve in Figure 16.21c is an *S-shaped* trend. As an example, this type of trend curve is appropriate for a new product that takes a while to catch on, then exhibits a rapid increase in sales as the public becomes aware of it, and finally tapers off to a fairly constant level. The curves in Figure 16.21 all represent *upward* trends. Of course, we could just as well have *downward* trends of the same types.

**Figure 16.21**   Series with Trends

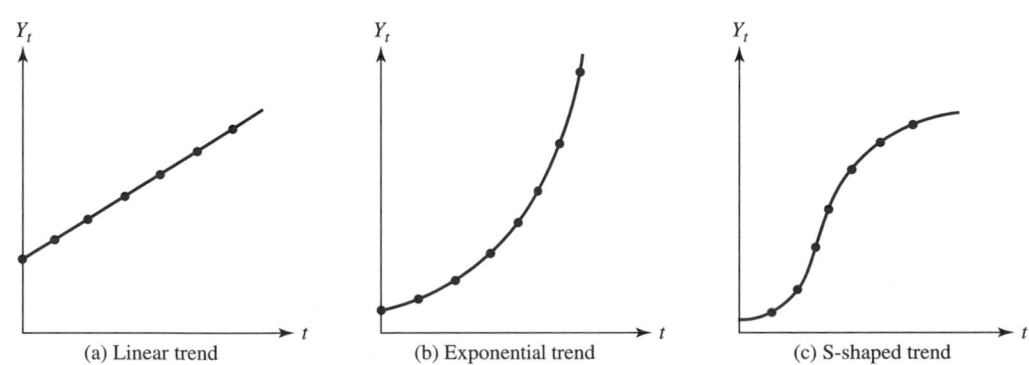

(a) Linear trend    (b) Exponential trend    (c) S-shaped trend

**Excel Tool:** *Creating a Time Series Plot*
*There are (at least) two ways to create a time series plot in Excel. One way is to create a scatterplot of the time series variable versus time, choosing the scatter subtype where the dots are connected. A more flexible way is to create an Excel line chart with one or more series. This allows you, for example, to plot an original series with a series of forecasts superimposed on it. We use this method to create the plots in the next two sections of this chapter.*

## Seasonal Component

*In a seasonal pattern, some seasons are regularly higher than others each year.*

Many time series have a **seasonal** component. For example, a company's sales of swimming pool equipment increase every spring, then stay relatively high during the summer, and then drop off until next spring, at which time the yearly pattern repeats itself. An important aspect of the seasonal component is that it tends to be predictable from one year to the next. That is, the *same* seasonal pattern tends to repeat itself every year.

In Figure 16.22, we show two possible seasonal patterns. Figure 16.22a shows nothing but the seasonal component. That is, if there were no seasonal variation, we would have the base series from Figure 16.20. In Figure 16.22b, we show a seasonal pattern superimposed on an upward-sloping trend line.

**Figure 16.22**

Series with Seasonality

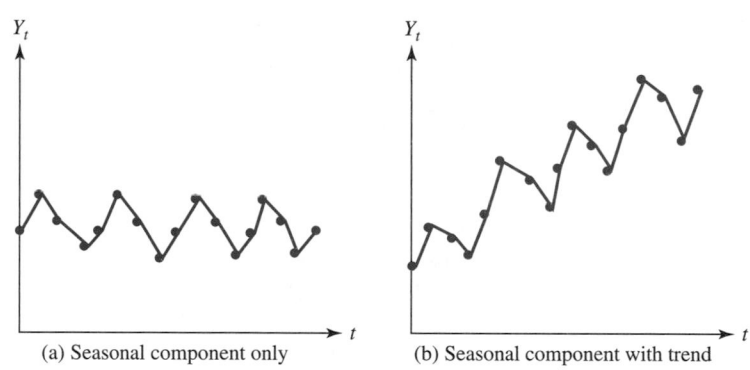

(a) Seasonal component only    (b) Seasonal component with trend

## Cyclic Component

The third component of a time series is the **cyclic** component. By studying past movements of many business and economic variables, it becomes apparent that business cycles affect many variables in similar ways. For example, during a recession, housing starts generally go down, unemployment goes up, stock prices go down, and so on. But when the recession is over, all of these variables tend to move in the opposite direction.

We know that the cyclic component exists for many time series because we are able to see it as periodic swings in the levels of the time series plots. However, the cyclic component is harder to predict than the seasonal component. The reason is that seasonal variation is much more regular. For example, swimming pool supplies sales *always* start to increase during the spring. Cyclic variation, on the other hand, is more irregular because the business cycle does not always have the same length. A further distinction is that the length of a seasonal cycle is generally one year, whereas the length of a business cycle is generally much longer than one year.

The graphs in Figure 16.23 illustrate the cyclic component of a time series. In Figure 16.23a, cyclic variation is superimposed on the base series from Figure 16.20. In

Figure 16.23b, this same cyclic variation is superimposed on the series from Figure 16.22b. The resulting graph has trend, seasonal variation, and cyclic variation.

**Figure 16.23**
Series with Cyclic Component

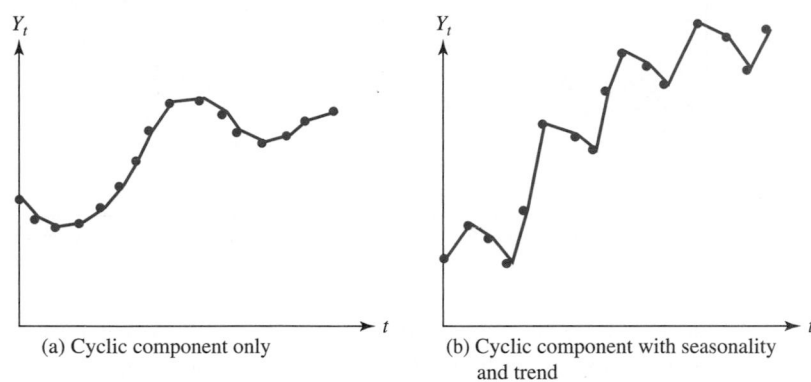

(a) Cyclic component only

(b) Cyclic component with seasonality and trend

## Random (Noise) Component

*By definition, noise is unpredictable. It often makes trends and seasonal patterns more difficult to recognize.*

The final component in a time series is called the **random** component, or simply **noise.** This unpredictable component gives most time series plots their irregular, zigzag appearance. Usually, a time series can be determined only to a certain extent by its trend, seasonal, and cyclic components. Then other factors determine the rest. These other factors might be inherent randomness, unpredictable "shocks" to the system, the unpredictable behavior of human beings who interact with the system, and others.

Figures 16.24 and 16.25 show the affect that noise can have on a time series-graph. The graph on the left of each figure shows the random component only, superimposed on the base series. Then on the right of each figure, the random component is superimposed on the graph of trend with seasonal component from Figure 16.22b. The difference between Figure 16.24 and Figure 16.25 is the relative magnitude of the noise. When it is small, as in Figure 16.24, the other components emerge fairly clearly; they are not disguised by the noise. But if the noise is large in magnitude, as in Figure 16.25, the noise can make it difficult to distinguish the other components.

**Figure 16.24**
Series with Noise

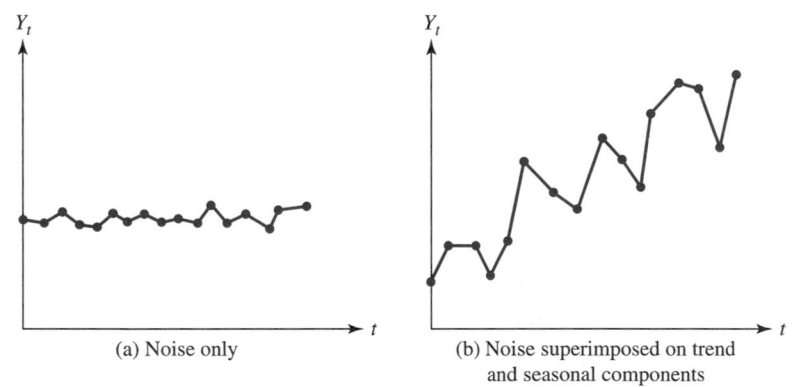

(a) Noise only

(b) Noise superimposed on trend and seasonal components

## Measures of Forecast Error

When we use any extrapolation method, we build a model to track the observed historical data, and then we use this model to forecast future values of the data. The only way we can

**Figure 16.25**

Series with More
Noise

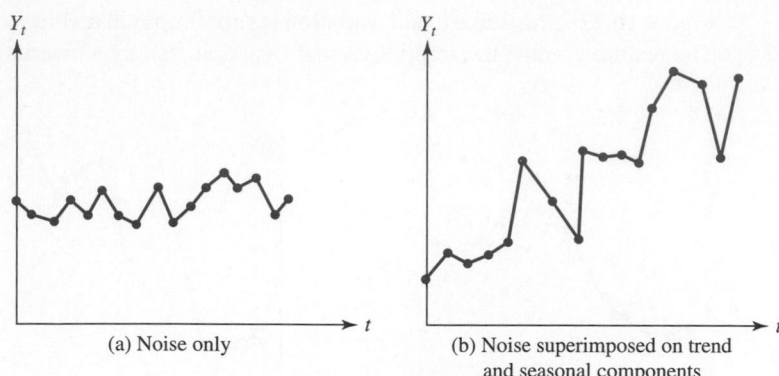

(a) Noise only | (b) Noise superimposed on trend
and seasonal components

judge whether the future forecasts are likely to be any good is to measure how well the model tracks the historical data. Time series analysts typically use several measures. We present three of the most popular measures in this section.

As before, let $Y_t$ be the observed value in time period $t$. Given any forecasting model, let $F_t$ be the "one-period-ahead" forecast of $Y_t$ made at time $t - 1$. For example, for monthly data, if $t$ corresponds to August, then $F_t$ is the forecast of August's value made one month before, in July. Also, let $E_t$ be the corresponding forecast error, $E_t = Y_t - F_t$. If $E_t$ is positive, our forecast is too low, whereas if $E_t$ is negative, our forecast is too high. We want the $E_t$'s to be small, so that our forecasts of the historical data track the actual data closely.

The three measures of forecasting accuracy typically used are MAE (mean absolute error), RMSE (root mean square error), and MAPE (mean absolute percentage error). These are given by the following formulas, where $N$ is the number of historical periods for which our model provides forecasts.

---

***Formula for MAE***

$$\text{MAE} = \frac{\sum_{t=1}^{N} |E_t|}{N} \qquad (16.8)$$

***Formula for RMSE***

$$\text{RMSE} = \sqrt{\frac{\sum_{t=1}^{N} E_t^2}{N}} \qquad (16.9)$$

***Formula for MAPE***

$$\text{MAPE} = \frac{\sum_{t=1}^{N} |E_t/Y_t|}{N} \qquad (16.10)$$

---

RMSE is similar to a standard deviation in that the errors are squared; because of the square root, its units are the same as those of the original variable. MAE is similar to RMSE, except that absolute values of errors are used instead of squared errors. MAPE (the same measure we introduced in Section 16.3) is probably the easiest measure to understand because it does not depend on the units of the original variable; it is always stated as a percentage. For example, the statement that the forecasts are off on average by 2% has a clear meaning, even if you do not know the units of the variable being forecasted.

Depending on the forecasting software package used, one or more of these measures will typically be reported. Fortunately, models that make any one of these measures small

A good forecasting
model typically makes
all three measures of
forecast errors small.

tend to make the others small as well, so that we can choose whichever measure we want to focus on. Also, after we have calculated the $E_t$'s (which follow from the particular forecasting technique being used), we can calculate MAE, RMSE, and MAPE easily from Excel's built-in functions, as we discuss shortly.

One caution is in order, however. We calculate MAE, RMSE, or MAPE to see how well our forecasting model tracks *historical* data. But even if these measures are small, there is no guarantee that *future* forecasts will be accurate. As we stated previously, extrapolation methods all make the implicit assumption that history will repeat itself. However, history does not always repeat itself. When this is the case, a model that closely tracks historical data can yield poor forecasts of the future. In addition, there is a danger of tracking a historical series *too* closely. Tracking every little up and down is pointless if these movements represent random noise that will not repeat in the future.

---

### FUNDAMENTAL INSIGHT

**Limitations of Extrapolation Methods**

All extrapolation forecasting methods, such as the moving averages and exponential smoothing methods discussed next, make the crucial assumption that historical patterns are likely to repeat themselves. If an unexpected "shock" occurs, such as a disruption in oil supplies from the Mid East or a ground-breaking discovery in biotechnology, extrapolation methods can fail miserably in the period after the shock. In addition, extrapolation methods can be *too* finely tuned. If they are optimized to follow all of the ups and downs of a time series, they might just be learning patterns of noise, patterns that are unlikely to continue in the future. This is why smoothed forecasts that follow the basic underlying patterns are often preferred.

---

## 16.6 MOVING AVERAGES MODELS

Perhaps the simplest and one of the most frequently used extrapolation methods is the method of **moving averages.** Very simply, the forecast for any period with this method is the average of the observations from the past few periods. To implement the moving averages method, we first choose a **span,** the number of terms in each moving average. Let's say the data are monthly and we choose a span of six months. Then the forecast of next month's value is the average of the previous six months' values. For example, we average the January to June values to forecast July, we average the February to July values to forecast August, and so on. This is the reason for the term *moving* averages.

> The **span** in the moving averages method is the number of observations in each average.

The larger the span,
the smoother the fore-
cast series will be.

The role of the span is important. If the span is large—say, 12 months—then many observations go into each average, and extreme values have relatively little effect on the averages. The resulting series of forecasts will be much smoother than the original series. (For this reason, the moving average method is called a **smoothing** method.) In contrast, if the span is small—say, 3 months—then extreme observations have a larger effect on the averages, and the forecast series will be much less smooth. In the extreme, if the span is 1, there is no smoothing effect at all. The method simply forecasts next month's value to be the same as this month's value.

What span should we use? This requires some judgment. If we believe the ups and downs in the series are random noise, then we do not want future forecasts to react too quickly to these ups and downs, and we should use a relatively large span. But if we want to track most of the ups and downs—under the belief that these ups and downs are predictable—then we should use a smaller span. We should not be fooled, however, by a plot of the forecast series—that is, a plot of the averages—superimposed on the original series. This graph will almost always look better when a small span is used, because the forecast series will appear to track the original series better. But this does not mean it will provide better future forecasts. Again, tracking random ups and downs closely is pointless if the ups and downs represent unpredictable noise.

The following example illustrates the use of moving averages on a series of weekly sales.

EXAMPLE | **16.5 FORECASTING WEEKLY SALES OF HARDWARE AT LEE'S**

Lee's is a local discount store that sells a variety of merchandise, much like Kmart, Wal-Mart, and Target. In particular, Lee's sells a full line of hardware. The company has kept track of weekly total dollar sales of hardware items for the past 104 weeks. These data appear in the file **Hardware Sales 1.xlsx**. Lee's is planning to use moving averages, with an appropriate span, to forecast future weekly hardware sales. Does this appear to be a good idea?

**Objective**   To judge the effectiveness of the moving averages method, with different spans, to forecast weekly hardware sales at Lee's.

## Solution

A time series plot of weekly sales appears in Figure 16.26. This series appears to meander, with no obvious trend or seasonality. Evidently, sales of hardware at Lee's are relatively constant throughout each year. This type of series is a good candidate for moving averages.

*A series that meanders, with no obvious trend or seasonality, is a good candidate for moving averages.*

**Figure 16.26**
Time Series Plot of Hardware Sales

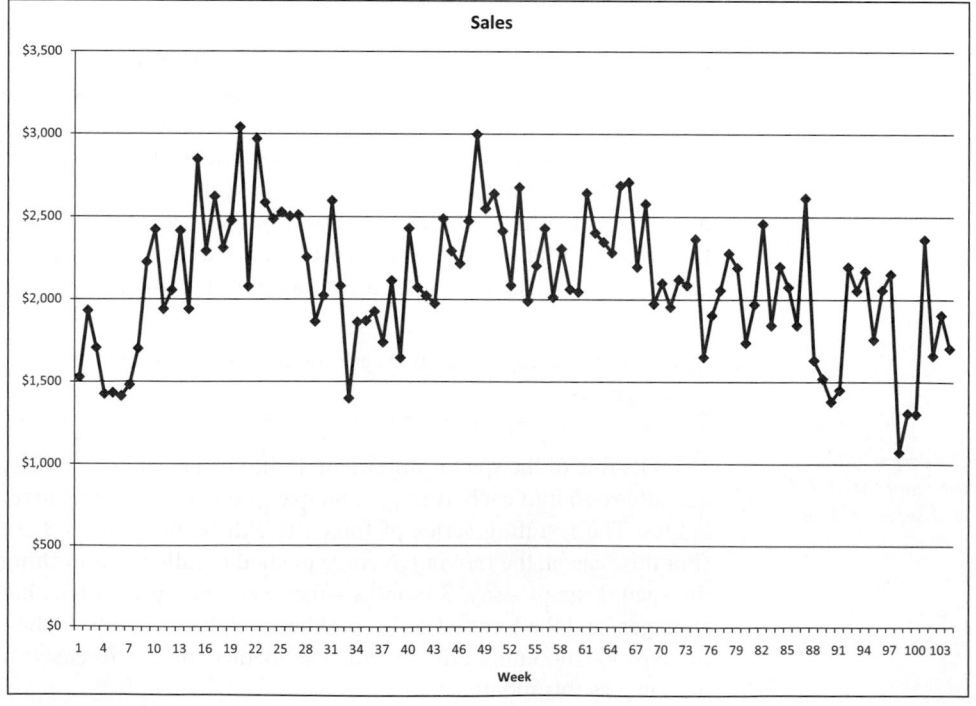

However, it is not clear which span to use. We tried spans of 3, 6, and 12 weeks. Spans of 3 and 6 gave similar results, whereas a span of 12 gave less good results. We illustrate the calculations for a span of 3; you can check the calculations for the other spans in the file **Hardware Sales 1.xlsx**.

### DEVELOPING THE SPREADSHEET MODEL

Using a span of 3, the forecast for week 4 is the average of the observed sales in weeks 1 to 3, the forecast for week 5 is the average of the observed sales in weeks 2 to 4, and so on. The calculations are straightforward in Excel, as shown in Figure 16.27 (with many hidden rows).[5] There are no forecasts for weeks 1 to 3 because we do not have the sales values before week 1 that would be required for the moving averages. Therefore, we start in week 4 with the formula

=AVERAGE(B8:B10)

in cell C11. Then we copy this formula down to cell C112 for the other months.

**Figure 16.27**

Moving Average Forecasts with Span 3

|     | A    | B      | C         | D       | E      | F      |
|-----|------|--------|-----------|---------|--------|--------|
| 7   | Week | Sales  | Forecast_3 | Error_3 | AE_3   | APE_3  |
| 8   | 1    | $1,526 |           |         |        |        |
| 9   | 2    | $1,929 |           |         |        |        |
| 10  | 3    | $1,704 |           |         |        |        |
| 11  | 4    | $1,423 | 1719.7    | -296.7  | 296.7  | 20.8%  |
| 12  | 5    | $1,430 | 1685.3    | -255.3  | 255.3  | 17.9%  |
| 13  | 6    | $1,410 | 1519.0    | -109.0  | 109.0  | 7.7%   |
| 14  | 7    | $1,478 | 1421.0    | 57.0    | 57.0   | 3.9%   |
| 15  | 8    | $1,698 | 1439.3    | 258.7   | 258.7  | 15.2%  |
| 16  | 9    | $2,223 | 1528.7    | 694.3   | 694.3  | 31.2%  |
| 17  | 10   | $2,420 | 1799.7    | 620.3   | 620.3  | 25.6%  |
| 104 | 97   | $2,152 | 1993.7    | 158.3   | 158.3  | 7.4%   |
| 105 | 98   | $1,069 | 1987.7    | -918.7  | 918.7  | 85.9%  |
| 106 | 99   | $1,306 | 1759.0    | -453.0  | 453.0  | 34.7%  |
| 107 | 100  | $1,302 | 1509.0    | -207.0  | 207.0  | 15.9%  |
| 108 | 101  | $2,361 | 1225.7    | 1135.3  | 1135.3 | 48.1%  |
| 109 | 102  | $1,658 | 1656.3    | 1.7     | 1.7    | 0.1%   |
| 110 | 103  | $1,903 | 1773.7    | 129.3   | 129.3  | 6.8%   |
| 111 | 104  | $1,702 | 1974.0    | -272.0  | 272.0  | 16.0%  |
| 112 | 105  |        | 1754.3    |         |        |        |
| 113 | 106  |        | 1786.4    |         |        |        |
| 114 | 107  |        | 1747.6    |         |        |        |
| 115 | 108  |        | 1762.8    |         |        |        |

*To forecast future values with moving averages, use previous forecasts when actual values are not available.*

Note that the forecast in cell C112 is for the *future* week 105, where there is no corresponding sales value. It is a bit trickier to calculate forecasts for weeks further into the future. For example, to forecast sales for week 106, we would like to average sales for weeks 103 to 105, but we have no sales value for week 105. In this case, the convention is to use a *forecast* instead of a sales value whenever a sales value is not available. Therefore, the formula in cell C113 for the week 106 forecast is

=AVERAGE(B110:B111,C112)

The forecasts for weeks 107 and 108 are similar. Each is an average of 3 values, using forecasts instead of sales values when sales values are not available.

After we have the forecasts, we can calculate the forecast errors—for weeks where both sales and forecast values are available—by subtraction. The values in column D are sales values in column B minus forecasts in column C. For later use, we also calculate the absolute errors in column E with the ABS function, and the absolute percentage errors in

---

[5] Analysis ToolPak includes an implementation of the moving averages forecasting method. It calls the span the *interval*. However, its forecasts are (mistakenly, in our opinion) shifted one row up from ours. In any case, the moving averages method is simple enough to implement in Excel without an add-in.

column F. Each value in column F is the absolute error in column E divided by the sales value in column B.

## Discussion of the Results

Two useful graphs are shown in Figures 16.28 and 16.29. The superimposed series of forecasts in Figure 16.28 indicates that the forecasts track the general ups and downs of the sales series fairly well, although the forecast series is smoother than the sales series. This

**Figure 16.28**

Forecasts with Span 3 Superimposed

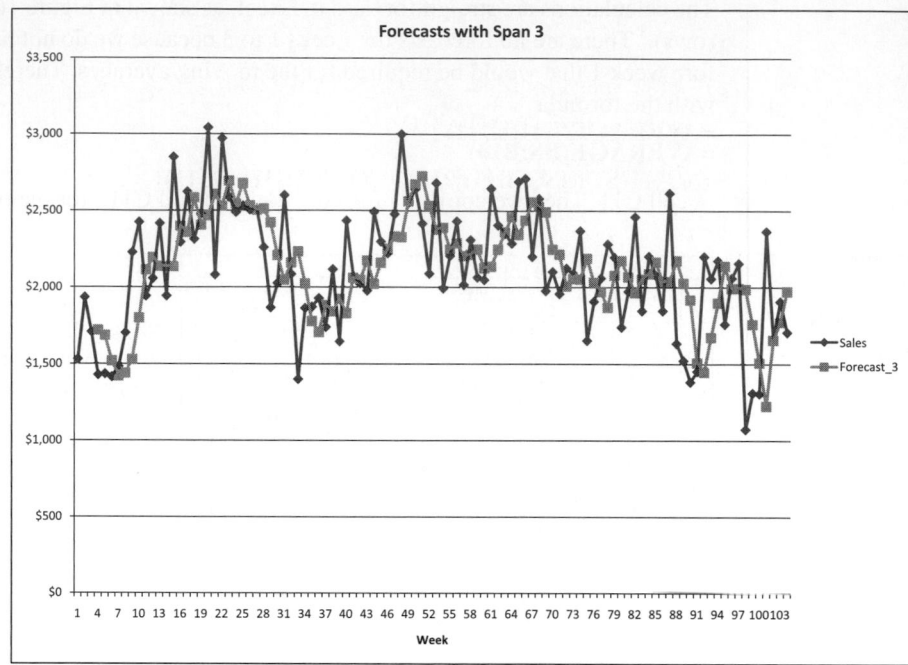

**Figure 16.29**

Forecast Errors with Span 3

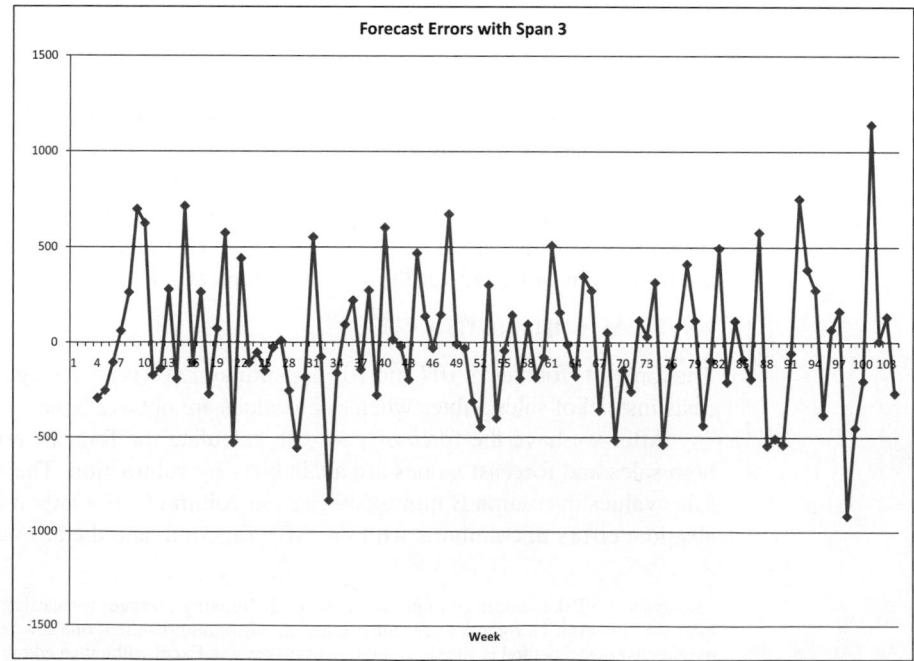

is exactly what we want. The difference between these two series is probably unpredictable noise, which is impossible (and undesirable) to track exactly.

It is also useful to examine the series of forecast errors in Figure 16.29. This series appears to be a random series of ups and downs—again exactly what we want. If the series of forecast errors indicated some sort of pattern, such as an upward trend or a spike every fourth week, then our forecasting method would be missing something, and we would need to try another forecasting method to "pick up" this pattern. The current series of forecast errors shows no such pattern, so our moving averages method is evidently doing about as good a job as possible in tracking the sales series.

To obtain more evidence on how well the moving averages forecasts are doing, we calculate the summary measures MAE, RMSE, and MAPE. These appear in Figure 16.30 for all three spans we tried. The formulas for span 3 in cells B3 to B5 are

**=AVERAGE(E11:E111)**

**=SQRT(SUMSQ(D11:D111)/COUNT(D11:D111))**

and

**=AVERAGE(F11:F111)**

As we see, the forecasts with span 3 are off, on average, by about $278 (from MAE) or about 13.9% (from MAPE), and the errors are only worse with spans of 6 or 12. These errors are fairly sizable, and it isn't clear whether the forecasts will be of much help to Lee's management. However, more accurate forecasts may not be possible because of the high level of noise in the sales series.

**Figure 16.30**

**Summary Measures of Forecast Errors**

|  | A | B | C | D |
|---|---|---|---|---|
| 1 | Summary measures from forecasts below | | | |
| 2 | Span | 3 | 6 | 12 |
| 3 | MAE | 278.1 | 284.4 | 314.8 |
| 4 | RMSE | 358.3 | 360.8 | 387.4 |
| 5 | MAPE | 13.9% | 14.3% | 15.7% |

■

# PROBLEMS

## Skill-Building Problems

**22.** The file **P16_22.xlsx** contains the daily closing prices of American Express stock for a 1-year period.
   **a.** Using a span of 3 days, forecast the price of this stock for the next trading day with the method of moving averages. How well does the moving average method with span 3 forecast the known observations in this data set?
   **b.** Repeat part **a** with a span of 10.
   **c.** Which of these two spans appears to be more appropriate? Explain your choice.

**23.** The closing value of the AMEX Airline Index for each trading day during a 1-year period is given in the file **P16_23.xlsx**.
   **a.** How well does the moving average method track this series when the span is 4 days? When the span is 12 days?
   **b.** Using the more appropriate span, forecast the closing value of this index on the next 15 trading days.

**24.** The closing value of the Dow Jones Industrial Index for each trading day for a 1-year period is provided in the file **P16_24.xlsx**.
   **a.** Using a span of 2 days, forecast this index for the next trading day with the method of moving averages. How well does the moving average method with span 2 forecast the known observations in this data set?
   **b.** Repeat part **a** with a span of 5 days; with a span of 15 days.
   **c.** Which of these three spans appears to be most appropriate? Explain your choice.

**25.** The file **P16_25.xlsx** contains the daily closing prices of Wal-Mart stock during a 1-year period. Use the method of moving averages with a carefully chosen span to forecast this time series for the next 3 trading days. Defend your choice of the span used.

26. Consider the file **P16_26.xlsx**, which contains total monthly U.S. retail sales data. Use the method of moving averages with a carefully chosen span to forecast U.S. retail sales for the following 12 months. What makes this time series more challenging to forecast?

27. The file **P16_27.xlsx** contains quarterly sales of Johnson & Johnson. A time series plot of this series indicates a clear upward trend. Use moving averages to forecast this series, experimenting with the span. What do you conclude about the effectiveness of using moving averages on an upward-trending time series?

# 16.7 EXPONENTIAL SMOOTHING MODELS

*Exponential smoothing forecasts put more weight on recent observations.*

The main criticism of the moving averages method is that it puts equal weight on each value in a typical moving average. Many people would argue that if next month's forecast is to be based on the previous 12 months' observations, say, then more weight ought to be placed on the more recent observations. Exponential smoothing is a method that addresses this criticism. It bases its forecasts on a *weighted* average of past observations, with more weight put on the more recent observations. In addition, most businesspeople can understand exponential smoothing, at least conceptually. Therefore, this method finds widespread use in the business world, particularly when frequent and automatic forecasts of many items are required.

There are several versions of exponential smoothing. The simplest is called, naturally enough, **simple** exponential smoothing. It is relevant when there is no pronounced trend or seasonality in the series. If there is a trend but no seasonality, then **Holt's** method is applicable. If, in addition, there is seasonality, then **Winters'** method can be used. This does not exhaust the list of exponential smoothing models—researchers have invented many other variations—but these are the most common models. We discuss simple exponential smoothing in some detail. Then we provide a brief account of Holt's and Winters' methods.

> **Simple** exponential smoothing is appropriate when there is no trend or seasonality. **Holt's** method is appropriate when there is trend but no seasonality. **Winters'** method is appropriate when there is seasonality (and possibly trend as well).

## Simple Exponential Smoothing

Simple exponential smoothing is appropriate for a series with no obvious trend or seasonal component. An example is the hardware sales data from Example 16.5, earlier in the chapter, which meanders through time but doesn't really have any consistent upward or downward trend. In fact, we reexamine this series in this section.

We first introduce two new terms. Every exponential model has at least one **smoothing constant,** which is always a number between 0 and 1. Simple exponential smoothing has a single smoothing constant denoted by $\alpha$ (alpha). Its role is discussed shortly. The second new term is $L_t$, called the **level** of the series at time $t$. Essentially, the level is where we think the series would be at time $t$ if there were no random noise. $L_t$ is not observable, so it must be estimated.

> The **level** of the series is an estimate of where the series would be if it were not for random noise.

The simple exponential smoothing method is defined by the following equation. It states that the estimated level at time $t$, right after observing $Y_t$, is a weighted average of the current observation $Y_t$ and the *previous* estimated level, $L_{t-1}$. The current observation gets weight $\alpha$ and the previous level gets weight $1 - \alpha$.

> **Formula for simple exponential smoothing**
>
> $$L_t = \alpha Y_t + (1 - \alpha)L_{t-1} \qquad\qquad \textbf{(16.11)}$$

To forecast, we use the most recently calculated level and project it into all future periods. For example, for monthly data, if the most recently observed value is for June, we calculate the level for June from equation (16.11) and then use this level as a forecast for July, August, and so on. In a month, after we have observed July's value, we calculate the level for July, again using equation (16.11), and then use this updated level as a forecast for August, September, and so on. The idea in simple exponential smoothing is that we believe the series is not really going anywhere. So as soon as we estimate where the series ought to be in period *t* (if it were not for random noise), we forecast that this is where it will also be in any future period.

The smoothing constant $\alpha$ is analogous to the span in moving averages. There are two ways to see this. The first way is to rewrite equation (16.11) using the fact that the forecast error, $E_t$, made in forecasting $Y_t$ at time $t - 1$ is $E_t = Y_t - F_t = Y_t - L_{t-1}$. A bit of algebra then gives the following formula:

> **Equivalent formula for simple exponential smoothing**
>
> $$L_t = L_{t-1} + \alpha E_t \qquad\qquad \textbf{(16.12)}$$

Equation (16.12) states that the next estimate of the level is adjusted from the previous estimate by adding a multiple of the most recent forecast error. This makes intuitive sense. If our previous forecast was too high, then $E_t$ is negative, so we adjust the estimate of the level downward. The opposite is true if our previous forecast was too low. However, equation (16.12) says that we do not adjust by the *entire* magnitude of $E_t$, but only by a fraction of it. If $\alpha$ is small, say, $\alpha = 0.1$, then the adjustment is minor; if $\alpha$ is close to 1, the adjustment is large. Therefore, if we want to react quickly to movements in the series, we choose a large $\alpha$; otherwise, we choose a small $\alpha$.

Another way to see the effect of $\alpha$ is to substitute repeatedly into equation (16.11) for $L_t$. After some algebra, it is possible to verify that $L_t$ satisfies the following formula, where the sum in this formula extends back to the first observation at time $t = 1$.

> **Another equivalent formula for simple exponential smoothing**
>
> $$L_t = \alpha Y_t + \alpha(1-\alpha)Y_{t-1} + \alpha(1-\alpha)^2 Y_{t-2} + \alpha(1-\alpha)^3 Y_{t-3} + \cdots \qquad \textbf{(16.13)}$$

Equation (16.13) indicates that the exponentially smoothed forecast is a weighted average of previous observations, just as we promised. Furthermore, because $1 - \alpha$ is less than 1, the weights on the $Y$'s decrease from time *t* backward. Therefore, if $\alpha$ is close to 0, so that $1-\alpha$ is close to 1, the weights decrease very slowly. In this case, observations from the distant past continue to have a large influence on the next forecast. This means that the graph of the forecasts will be relatively smooth, just as with a large span in the moving averages method. But when $\alpha$ is close to 1, the weights decrease rapidly, and only very recent observations have much influence on the next forecast. In this case, forecasts react quickly to sudden changes in the series, and the forecast series isn't much smoother than the original series.

*The smaller the smoothing constant, the smoother the forecast series will be. Typically, a smoothing constant from 0.1 to 0.2 is used.*

Which value of $\alpha$ should you use? Although there is no universally accepted answer to this question, many practitioners recommend a value around 0.1 or 0.2. Others recommend experimenting with different values of $\alpha$ until a measure such as RMSE or MAPE is minimized. Some software packages even have an optimization feature that finds this optimal value of $\alpha$. But as we discussed in general for extrapolation methods, the value of $\alpha$ that tracks the historical series most closely does not necessarily guarantee the most accurate *future* forecasts.

The following example uses the same hardware sales series as in Example 16.5 to see whether simple exponential smoothing can improve on the forecasts made by moving averages.

EXAMPLE | **16.6 FORECASTING HARDWARE SALES AT LEE'S**

In the previous example, we saw that the moving averages method was able to provide only fair forecasts of weekly hardware sales at Lee's. Using the best of three potential spans, its forecasts were still off by about 13.9% on average. The company would now like to try simple exponential smoothing to see whether this method, with an appropriate smoothing constant, can outperform the moving averages method. How should the company proceed?

**Objective** To see whether simple exponential smoothing with an appropriate smoothing constant can provide more accurate forecasts of weekly hardware sales than the moving averages forecasts.

## Solution

We already saw in Example 16.5 that the hardware sales series meanders through time, with no apparent trends or seasonality. Therefore, this series is a good candidate for simple exponential smoothing. This is no guarantee that the method will provide accurate forecasts, but at least we cannot rule it out as a promising forecasting method.

### DEVELOPING THE SPREADSHEET MODEL

To implement simple exponential smoothing, we must use equation (16.11) repeatedly.[6] You can think of this procedure as climbing a ladder. Equation (16.11) shows how to move from one step to the next step (from time period $t - 1$ to time period $t$). However, just as in climbing a ladder, we have to get to the *first* step before we can continue. Note that the equation for $L_1$ requires a value for $L_0$, and no such value is given automatically. Choosing a value for $L_0$ is called *initializing the procedure*. One popular initialization technique is to set $L_0$ equal to $Y_1$, the first observation, so that from equation (16.11), we have

$$L_1 = \alpha Y_1 + (1 - \alpha)Y_1 = Y_1$$

This gets us started, and then equation (16.11) can be used to "climb the rest of the ladder."

The calculations for a smoothing constant of $\alpha = 0.1$ appear in Figure 16.31. (See the file **Hardware Sales 2.xlsx**.) Using our initialization procedure, the first level, $L_1$, is the same as the first observation, so we enter it in cell C8 with the formula =B8. From then on, we calculate each level from equation (16.11). The typical formula, entered in cell C9, is

**=$B$2*B9+(1-$B$2)*C8**

We then copy this formula down to cell C111. Next, because each forecast is the previous level, we enter the formula =C8 in cell D9 and copy it down to cell D112. Finally, the calculations of forecast errors in columns E to G use exactly the same formulas as with moving averages, so we do not repeat these formulas here.

### Discussion of the Results

Note that cell D112 contains the forecast for the first *future* week, week 105. In fact, this same forecast is used for *all* future weeks, at least until week 105's sales value is observed. This accounts for the forecasts in cells D113:D115. However, after week 105's sales value

---

[6] Analysis ToolPak implements simple exponential smoothing, although it refers to a *damping factor*. This damping factor corresponds to our $1 - \alpha$. We believe it is more instructive to implement this method without the help of the add-in.

|     | A | B | C | D | E | F | G |
|-----|---|---|---|---|---|---|---|
| 1 | Summary measures from forecasts below | | | | | | |
| 2 | Smoothing constant | 0.1 | | | | | |
| 3 | MAE | 307.9 | | | | | |
| 4 | RMSE | 381.6 | | | | | |
| 5 | MAPE | 15.4% | | | | | |
| 6 | | | | | | | |
| 7 | Week | Sales | Level | Forecast | Error | AE | APE |
| 8 | 1 | $1,526 | 1526 | | | | |
| 9 | 2 | $1,929 | 1566.3 | 1526 | 403.0 | 403.0 | 20.9% |
| 10 | 3 | $1,704 | 1580.1 | 1566.3 | 137.7 | 137.7 | 8.1% |
| 11 | 4 | $1,423 | 1564.4 | 1580.1 | -157.1 | 157.1 | 11.0% |
| 12 | 5 | $1,430 | 1550.9 | 1564.4 | -134.4 | 134.4 | 9.4% |
| 13 | 6 | $1,410 | 1536.8 | 1550.9 | -140.9 | 140.9 | 10.0% |
| 14 | 7 | $1,478 | 1531.0 | 1536.8 | -58.8 | 58.8 | 4.0% |
| 15 | 8 | $1,698 | 1547.7 | 1531.0 | 167.0 | 167.0 | 9.8% |
| 16 | 9 | $2,223 | 1615.2 | 1547.7 | 675.3 | 675.3 | 30.4% |
| 17 | 10 | $2,420 | 1695.7 | 1615.2 | 804.8 | 804.8 | 33.3% |
| 104 | 97 | $2,152 | 1983.1 | 1964.4 | 187.6 | 187.6 | 8.7% |
| 105 | 98 | $1,069 | 1891.7 | 1983.1 | -914.1 | 914.1 | 85.5% |
| 106 | 99 | $1,306 | 1833.1 | 1891.7 | -585.7 | 585.7 | 44.8% |
| 107 | 100 | $1,302 | 1780.0 | 1833.1 | -531.1 | 531.1 | 40.8% |
| 108 | 101 | $2,361 | 1838.1 | 1780.0 | 581.0 | 581.0 | 24.6% |
| 109 | 102 | $1,658 | 1820.1 | 1838.1 | -180.1 | 180.1 | 10.9% |
| 110 | 103 | $1,903 | 1828.4 | 1820.1 | 82.9 | 82.9 | 4.4% |
| 111 | 104 | $1,702 | 1815.8 | 1828.4 | -126.4 | 126.4 | 7.4% |
| 112 | 105 | | | 1815.8 | | | |
| 113 | 106 | | | 1815.8 | | | |
| 114 | 107 | | | 1815.8 | | | |
| 115 | 108 | | | 1815.8 | | | |

is observed, equation (16.11) will be used once more to estimate the level for week 105, and this value will then be used as a forecast for all future weeks. The procedure continues in this way as future sales values are observed.

*A small smoothing constant $\alpha$ corresponds to a large span in moving averages. Each produces a relatively smooth forecast series.*

As with moving averages, it is useful to create plots of the sales series with the forecast series superimposed. Figure 16.32 shows this plot with $\alpha = 0.1$; Figure 16.33 shows it with $\alpha = 0.3$. As we see, the forecast series is *smoother* with the smaller smoothing constant. In this sense, a small value of $\alpha$ in exponential smoothing corresponds to a large span

**Figure 16.32**

Forecast Series
with Smoothing
Constant 0.1

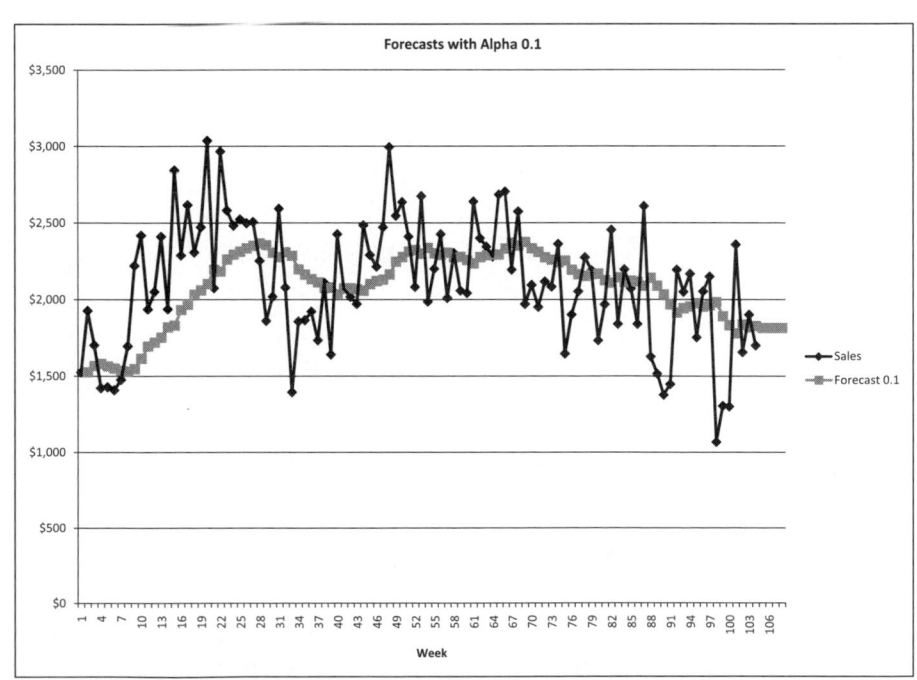

**Figure 16.33**

Forecast Series with
Smoothing
Constant 0.3

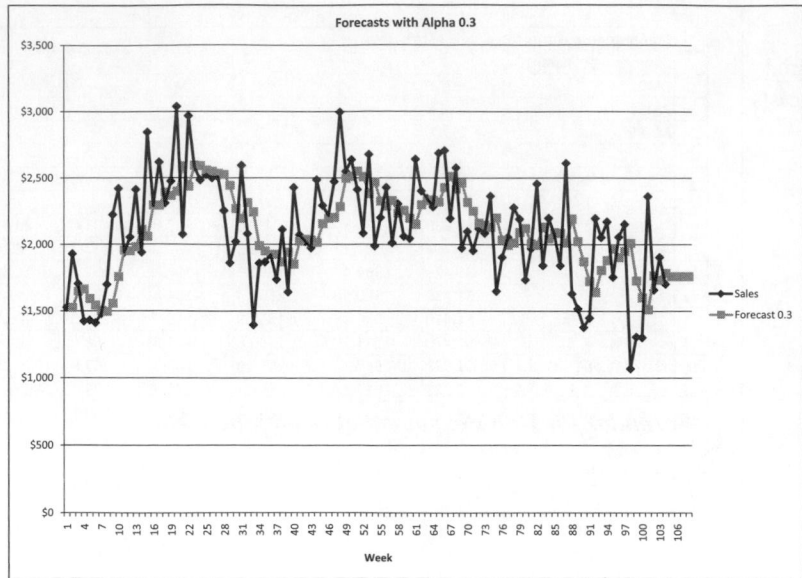

in moving averages. If we want the forecasts to react less to random ups and downs of the series, we choose a smaller value of $\alpha$. This is the reasoning behind the common practice of choosing a small smoothing constant such as 0.1 or 0.2.

We show the summary measures of the forecast errors for potential smoothing constants from 0.1 to 0.9 in Figure 16.34. These are calculated exactly as in the moving averages method for a particular value of alpha. Then we use a data table to find them for various values of alpha. From these summary measures we can make two conclusions. First, the summary measures decrease slightly as the smoothing constant increases, but then they begin to increase. Second, the best of these results is virtually the same as the best moving averages results. The best forecasts with each method have errors in the 13% to 14% range. Again, this is due to the relatively large amount of noise inherent in the sales series. In cases like this, we might be able to track the ups and downs of the historical series more closely with a larger smoothing constant, but this would almost surely not result in better *future* forecasts. The bottom line is that noise, by definition, is not predictable.

**Figure 16.34**

Summary Measures
of Forecast Errors

|    | I | J | K | L |
|----|---|---|---|---|
| 1 | **Data table of summary measures** | | | |
| 2 | Alpha | MAE | RMSE | MAPE |
| 3 |  | 307.9 | 381.6 | 15.4% |
| 4 | 0.1 | 307.9 | 381.6 | 15.4% |
| 5 | 0.2 | 279.3 | 353.5 | 14.1% |
| 6 | 0.3 | 268.4 | 346.3 | 13.5% |
| 7 | 0.4 | 266.7 | 347.6 | 13.3% |
| 8 | 0.5 | 270.9 | 353.4 | 13.5% |
| 9 | 0.6 | 277.1 | 362.2 | 13.7% |
| 10 | 0.7 | 286.4 | 373.4 | 14.1% |
| 11 | 0.8 | 299.1 | 387.0 | 14.7% |
| 12 | 0.9 | 315.8 | 403.1 | 15.5% |

## Holt's Method for Trend

The simple exponential smoothing model generally works well if there is no obvious trend in the series. But if there is a trend, then this method consistently lags behind it. For example, if the series is constantly increasing, simple exponential smoothing forecasts will be consistently low. Holt's method rectifies this by dealing explicitly with trend. In addition to the level of the series $L_t$ and its smoothing constant $\alpha$, Holt's method includes a trend term, $T_t$, and a corresponding smoothing constant $\beta$ (beta). The interpretation of $L_t$ is exactly as before. The interpretation of $T_t$ is that it represents an estimate of the *change* in the series from one period to the next.

After observing all of the data through time period $t$ and calculating the most recent estimates of level and trend, $L_t$ and $T_t$, we then forecast the next value of the series, at time $t + 1$, to be $L_t + T_t$. Similarly, we forecast the value at time $t + 2$ to be $L_t + 2T_t$, the value at $t + 3$ to be $L_t + 3T_t$, and so on. Each future forecast tacks on an additional $T_t$ to the previous forecast.

Holt's method has two defining equations, one for $L_t$ and one for $T_t$. These are similar to equation (16.11) and are as follows:

---

**Formulas for Holt's exponential smoothing method**

$$L_t = \alpha Y_t + (1 - \alpha)(L_{t-1} + T_{t-1}) \qquad \textbf{(16.14)}$$

$$T_t = \beta(L_t - L_{t-1}) + (1 - \beta)T_{t-1} \qquad \textbf{(16.15)}$$

---

Equation (16.14) is reasonable because $L_{t-1} + T_{t-1}$ is where we think the series should be at time $t$, based on information up to period $t - 1$. Similarly, equation (16.15) is reasonable because $L_t - L_{t-1}$ is an estimate of the most recent trend.

Although we could plug into these equations in Excel, the procedure is somewhat tedious. In addition, we have another initialization problem to deal with: how to determine appropriate values of $L_0$ and $T_0$. Unfortunately, Analysis ToolPak does not implement Holt's method. Therefore, we believe this is a good time to rely on another add-in— StatTools—to help us out. (StatTools, developed by Palisade Corporation, is included on the CD-ROM that accompanies this book.) StatTools implements Holt's method and many other statistical procedures in Excel. (In particular, it can be used to implement regression. Try it out!)

### Excel Add-In: *StatTools from Palisade*

*The StatTools add-in implements many statistical procedures. To use StatTools, you must first install it by running the setup program on the CD-ROM that accompanies this book. Then load StatTools by going to the Windows Start button, selecting All Programs, selecting Palisade DecisionTools, and finally selecting StatTools. If Excel is not already running, this will launch Excel.*

The following example briefly describes how StatTools can be used to implement Holt's method on a time series with trend.

---

**EXAMPLE** | **16.7 FORECASTING QUARTERLY SALES AT A PHARMACEUTICAL COMPANY**

The file **Pharmaceutical Sales.xlsx** contains quarterly sales data for a large pharmaceutical company from first quarter 1998 through fourth quarter 2007 (in millions of dollars). The time series plot in Figure 16.35 indicates a fairly consistent upward trend, with a relatively small amount of noise. Can Holt's method be used to provide reasonably accurate forecasts of this series?

**Objective**   To use Holt's exponential smoothing model to track the trend in the pharmaceutical company's quarterly sales data.

Figure 16.35   Quarterly Pharmaceutical Sales

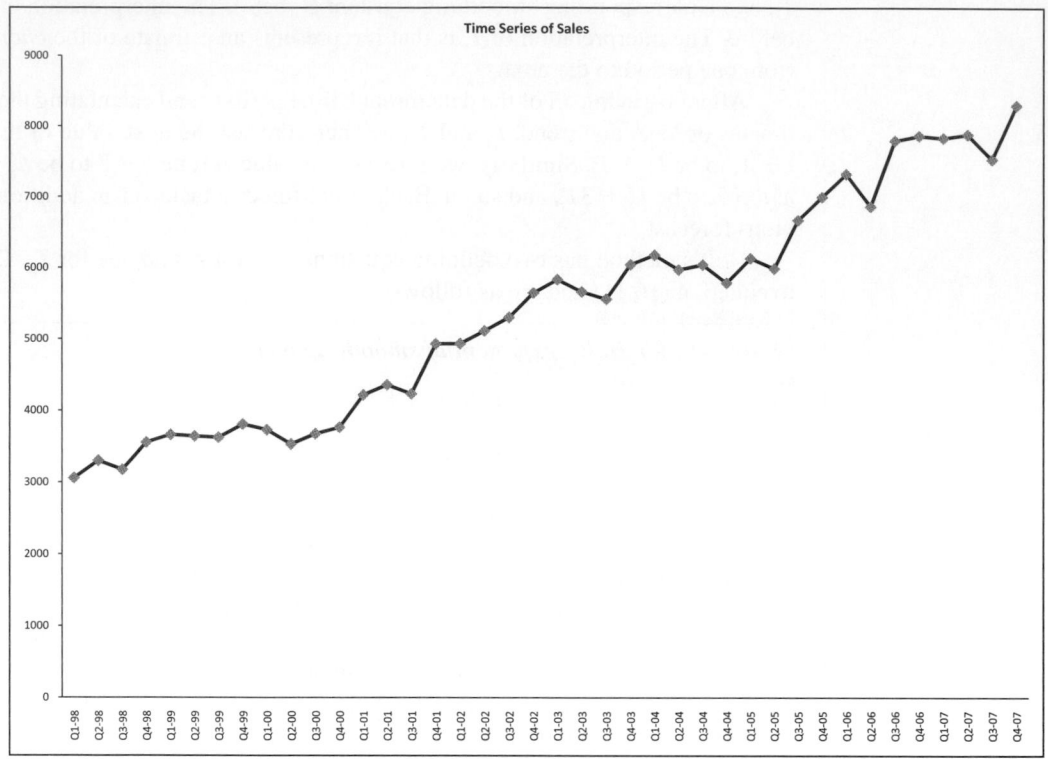

## Solution

We illustrate how StatTools can be used to implement Holt's method on the sales data. This requires two steps: identifying the data set and then doing the forecasting.

### Identifying the Data Set

StatTools works with *data sets,* which you have to specify before performing any statistical analysis. The data in this file, shown in Figure 16.36 (with some hidden rows), are in

**Figure 16.36**

Data Set for Time
Series Data

|   | A | B |
|---|---|---|
| 1 | Quarter | Sales |
| 2 | Q1-98 | 3062 |
| 3 | Q2-98 | 3304 |
| 4 | Q3-98 | 3179 |
| 5 | Q4-98 | 3557 |
| 6 | Q1-99 | 3663 |
| 7 | Q2-99 | 3644 |
| 8 | Q3-99 | 3628 |
| 9 | Q4-99 | 3813 |
| 10 | Q1-00 | 3732 |
| 11 | Q2-00 | 3532 |
| 12 | Q3-00 | 3675 |
| 37 | Q4-06 | 7872 |
| 38 | Q1-07 | 7842 |
| 39 | Q2-07 | 7893 |
| 40 | Q3-07 | 7543 |
| 41 | Q4-07 | 8307 |

the range A1:B41. To specify the data set, select Data Set Manager from the StatTools ribbon, fill out the resulting dialog box as shown in Figure 16.37, and click on OK. Now you are ready to perform a statistical analysis on this data set.

**Figure 16.37**
StatTools Data Set
Manager

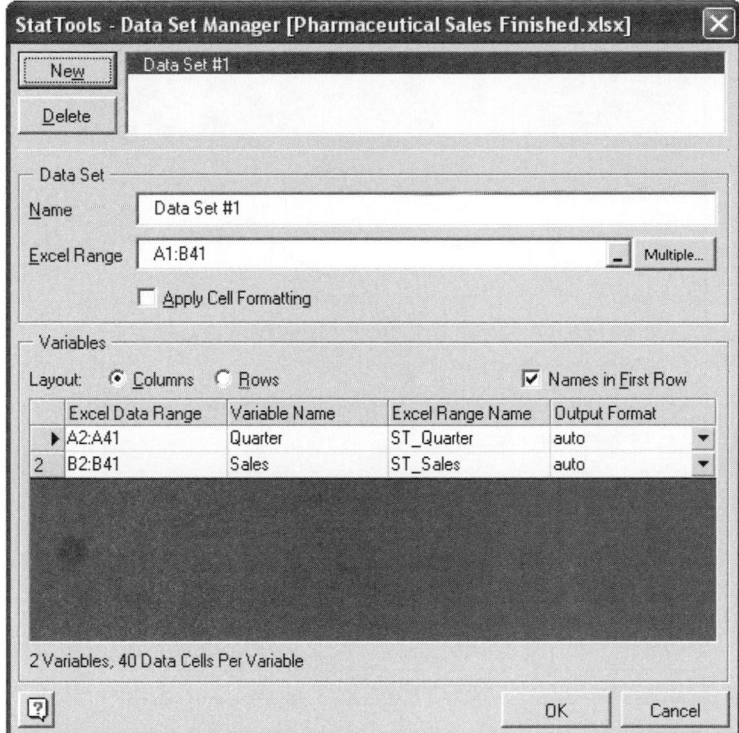

### Applying Holt's Method to Forecast

To apply Holt's method, select Forecast from the Time Series & Forecasting dropdown on the StatTools ribbon. There are three tabs on the resulting dialog box. The most important is the Forecast Settings tab, which you should fill in as shown in Figure 16.38. This indicates that (1) Sales is the time series variable of interest, (2) we want eight quarters of future forecasts, (3) we are using Holt's method, and (4) we want to optimize the smoothing constants (to give the smallest possible RMSE). The other two tabs are straightforward and are not shown here. The Time Scale tab lets you indicate that these are quarterly data, beginning with quarter 1 of 1998, and the Graphs to Display tab lets you choose which of three graphs you want StatTools to create.

### Discussion of the Results

The StatTools output for Holt's method consists of three sections: summary data, detailed data, and charts. The summary data appear in Figure 16.39. They indicate that the best smoothing constants are 0.574 (for level) and 0.0 (for trend). These produce the error measures shown. For example, MAPE is 4.40%. Although the smoothing constants shown here minimize RMSE, you can experiment with other smoothing constants in cells B9 and B10. For example, if you set both smoothing constants equal to 0.2, you will see that RMSE increases to 349.54 and MAPE increases to 5.56%. Clearly, the choice of smoothing constants *does* make a difference.[7]

---

[7] The fact that the optimal smoothing constant for trend is 0 does *not* mean that there is no trend. It means that we never *update* our initial guess of trend, which is 131.13 per quarter.

**Figure 16.38**

StatTools Forecast
Settings

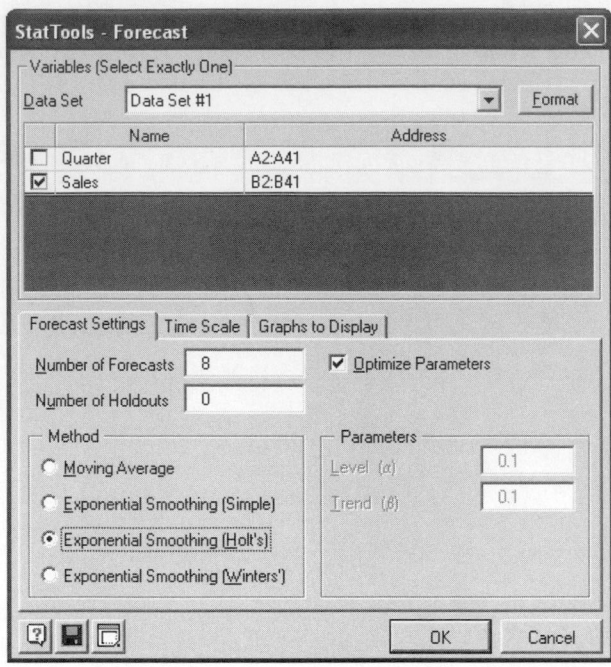

**Figure 16.39**

StatTools Summary
Data

|   | A | B |
|---|---|---|
| 8 | *Forecasting Constants (Optimized)* | |
| 9 | Level (Alpha) | 0.574 |
| 10 | Trend (Beta) | 0.000 |
| 11 | | |
| 12 | | |
| 13 | *Holt's Exponential* | |
| 14 | Mean Abs Err | 237.06 |
| 15 | Root Mean Sq Err | 280.59 |
| 16 | Mean Abs Per% Err | 4.40% |

The detailed data section, shown in Figure 16.40 (with some hidden rows), is where equations (16.14) and (16.15) are implemented. You can look at the formulas in this section to gain a better technical understanding of Holt's method. In particular, note how the future forecasts in rows 103 to 110 project the ending level and trend in row 102 into the future.

Two useful charts produced by StatTools appear in Figures 16.41 and 16.42. The first of these superimposes the forecasts onto the original series. It also shows the projected forecasts at the right. We see that the forecasts track the series well, and the future projections follow the clear upward trend. The chart in Figure 16.42 shows the series of forecast errors. If the forecast method is working well, this chart should be random, with no apparent patterns. The only suspicious pattern evident here is that the zigzags appear to be increasing in magnitude through time. Perhaps a more sophisticated forecasting method could deal with this pattern, but we do not pursue it here. For our purposes, Holt's method seems to be doing very well with this data set. It tracks the historical data closely, and it accurately projects the upward trend.

**Figure 16.40**  Detailed Data from Holt's Method

|     | A | B | C | D | E | F |
|-----|---|---|---|---|---|---|
| 62  | *Forecasting Data* | Sales | Level | Trend | Forecast | Error |
| 63  | Q1-1998 | 3062.0000 | 3062.00 | 131.13 |  |  |
| 64  | Q2-1998 | 3304.0000 | 3256.79 | 131.13 | 3193.13 | 110.88 |
| 65  | Q3-1998 | 3179.0000 | 3267.95 | 131.13 | 3387.92 | -208.92 |
| 66  | Q4-1998 | 3557.0000 | 3489.76 | 131.13 | 3399.08 | 157.92 |
| 67  | Q1-1999 | 3663.0000 | 3645.07 | 131.13 | 3620.88 | 42.12 |
| 68  | Q2-1999 | 3644.0000 | 3700.29 | 131.13 | 3776.19 | -132.19 |
| 69  | Q3-1999 | 3628.0000 | 3714.61 | 131.13 | 3831.41 | -203.41 |
| 70  | Q4-1999 | 3813.0000 | 3826.94 | 131.13 | 3845.73 | -32.73 |
| 71  | Q1-2000 | 3732.0000 | 3828.25 | 131.13 | 3958.06 | -226.06 |
| 72  | Q2-2000 | 3532.0000 | 3713.97 | 131.13 | 3959.38 | -427.38 |
| 98  | Q4-2006 | 7872.0000 | 7786.92 | 131.13 | 7672.18 | 199.82 |
| 99  | Q1-2007 | 7842.0000 | 7874.38 | 131.13 | 7918.05 | -76.05 |
| 100 | Q2-2007 | 7893.0000 | 7940.90 | 131.13 | 8005.50 | -112.50 |
| 101 | Q3-2007 | 7543.0000 | 7768.25 | 131.13 | 8072.03 | -529.03 |
| 102 | Q4-2007 | 8307.0000 | 8133.44 | 131.13 | 7899.37 | 407.63 |
| 103 | Q1-2008 |  |  |  | 8264.57 |  |
| 104 | Q2-2008 |  |  |  | 8395.69 |  |
| 105 | Q3-2008 |  |  |  | 8526.82 |  |
| 106 | Q4-2008 |  |  |  | 8657.94 |  |
| 107 | Q1-2009 |  |  |  | 8789.07 |  |
| 108 | Q2-2009 |  |  |  | 8920.19 |  |
| 109 | Q3-2009 |  |  |  | 9051.32 |  |
| 110 | Q4-2009 |  |  |  | 9182.44 |  |

**Figure 16.41**  Time Series with Forecasts from Holt's Method Superimposed

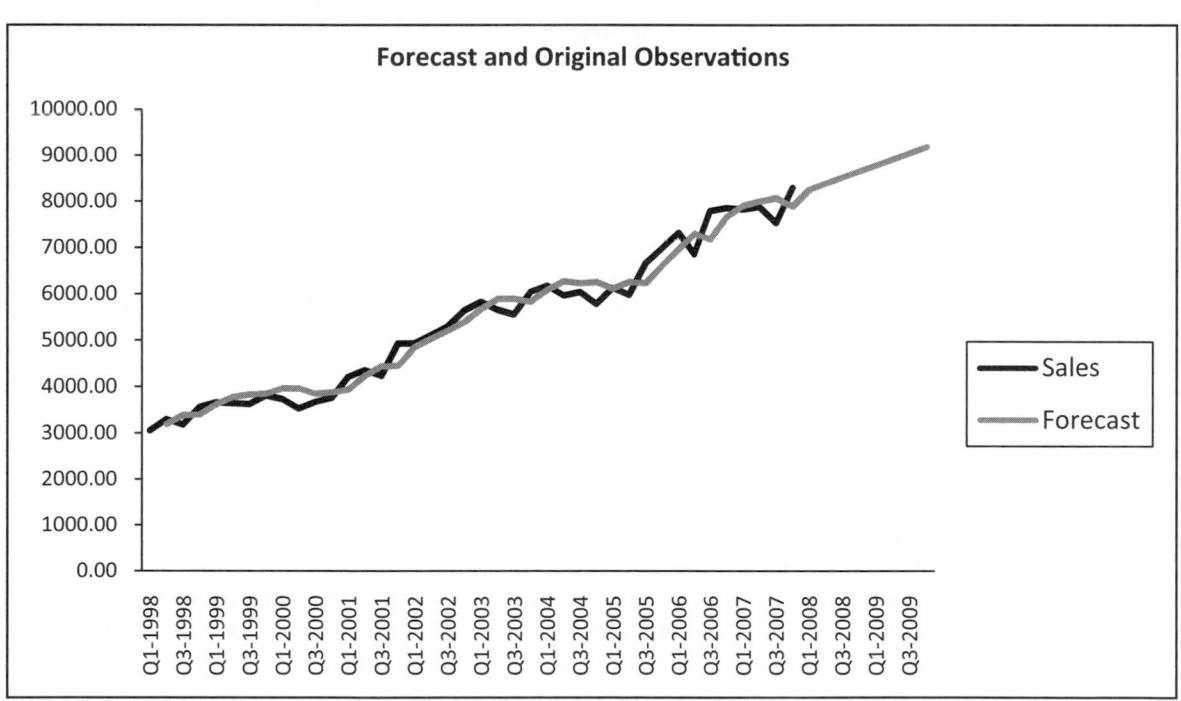

**Figure 16.42** Series of Forecast Errors from Holt's Method

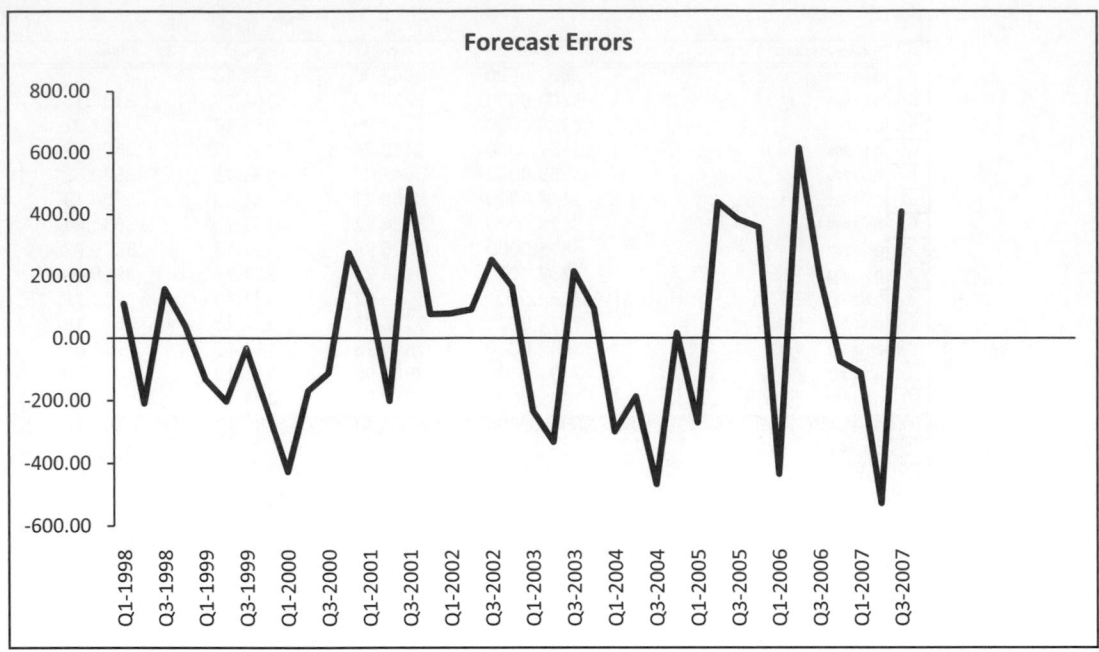

## Winters' Method for Seasonality

When a time series exhibits obvious seasonality, such as swimming pool supply sales that are always higher in the spring and summer than in the rest of the year, none of the extrapolation methods discussed to this point will do a good job. They will all miss the seasonal ups and downs. Various methods have been proposed to deal with seasonality. One possibility is to use regression with dummy variables for the seasons. Another possibility is to *deseasonalize* the series first, then use one of the methods we have discussed to forecast the deseasonalized series, and finally *reseasonalize* the forecasts. We do not discuss these possibilities here, but we do mention that many time series listed in newspapers, magazines, and government reports actually list deseasonalized data—that is, they have already manipulated the data to remove any seasonality, presumably so that we can identify trends more clearly.

Winters' method is a direct extension of Holt's exponential smoothing model. Like Holt's method, Winters' method estimates a level $L_t$ and a trend $T_t$, using smoothing constants $\alpha$ and $\beta$. These have the same interpretation as before. In addition, there is a seasonal factor $S_t$ for each season, where a "season" is usually a month or a quarter. Each seasonal factor represents the percentage by which that season is typically above or below the average for all seasons. For example, if the seasonal factor for June is 1.35, then a typical June value is 35% higher than the average for *all* months. Or if the seasonal factor for February is 0.75, then a typical February value is 25% lower than the average for all months. With

Winters' method, these seasonal factors are continually updated as we observe more values of the time series, using still another smoothing constant $\gamma$ (gamma) and another smoothing equation similar to equations (16.11), (16.14), and (16.15). Due to their complexity, we do not present the smoothing equations for Winters' method here.

To see how forecasting works with Winters' method, suppose we have observed data up through June of some year, and we have used these data to calculate the most recent level $L_t$, the most recent trend $T_t$, and the updated seasonal factors. Then the forecast for July is $(L_t + T_t)S_{\text{July}}$, the forecast for August is $(L_t + 2T_t)S_{\text{August}}$, and so on. In other words, we proceed exactly as with Holt's method, except that we multiply each forecast by the relevant seasonal factor.

Fortunately, we can rely on the StatTools add-in to perform the calculations, as illustrated in the following example.

---

| EXAMPLE | 16.8 FORECASTING QUARTERLY SOFT DRINK SALES |
|---------|---------------------------------------------|

The data in the **Soft Drink Sales.xlsx** file represent quarterly sales (in millions of dollars) for a large soft drink company from quarter 1 of 1992 through quarter 1 of 2007. As we might expect, there has been an upward trend in sales during this period, and there is also a fairly regular seasonal pattern, as shown in Figure 16.43. Sales in the warmer quarters, 2 and 3, are consistently higher than in the colder quarters, 1 and 4. How well can Winters' method track this upward trend and seasonal pattern?

---

**Figure 16.43**  Quarterly Soft Drink Sales

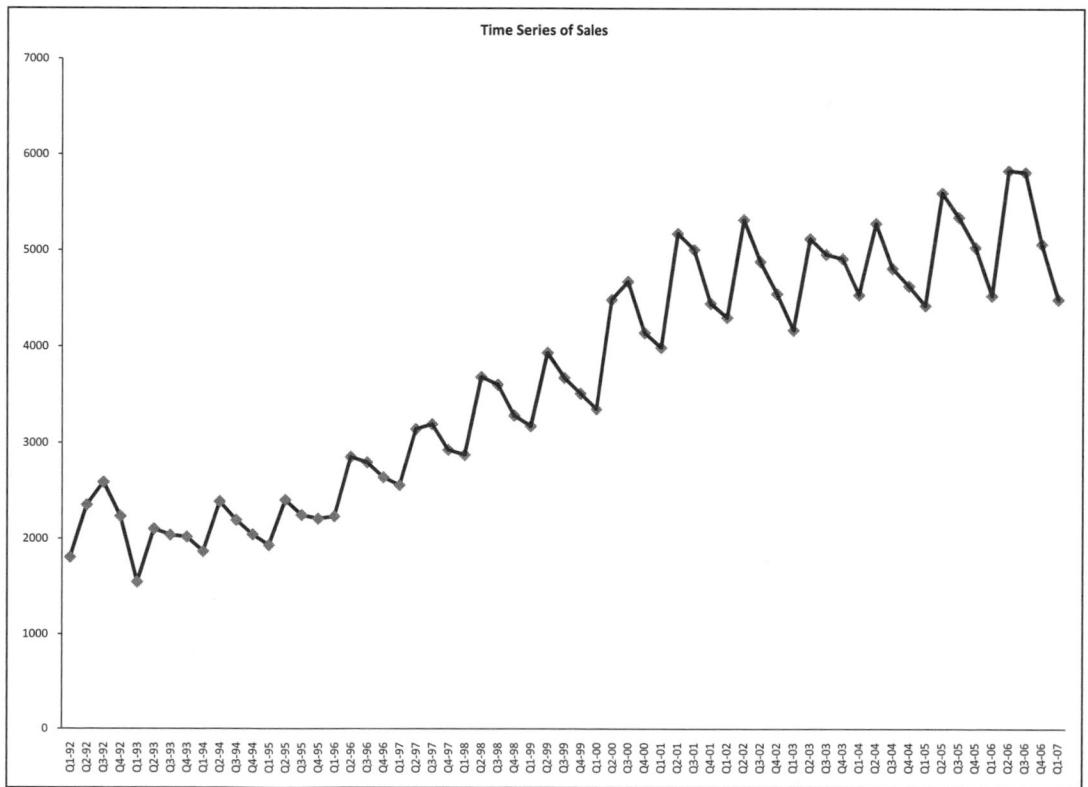

**Objective** To use Winters' exponential smoothing method to track the upward trend and regular seasonal pattern in the company's quarterly soft drink sales.

## Solution

We keep this discussion brief because the procedure required for Winters' method is practically the same as for Holt's method. We again create a data set with StatTools, and then we fill in the dialog box for forecast settings as shown in Figure 16.44. The only difference is that when we check the Winters' option, an extra smoothing constant (for seasonality) appears. For variety, we have chosen not to optimize the smoothing constants and have instead supplied our own.

**Figure 16.44**

StatTools Forecast Settings for Winters' Method

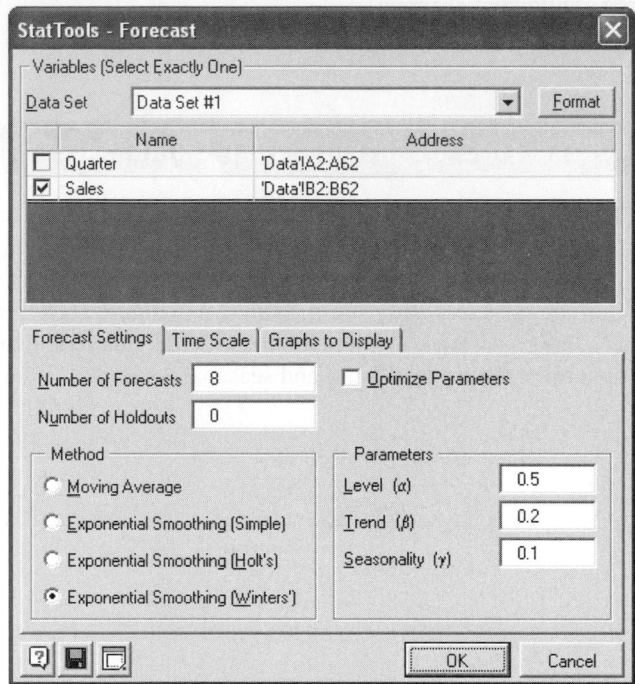

### Discussion of the Results

The StatTools output for Winters' method is very similar to the Holt's method output. The summary section in Figure 16.45 shows the optimal smoothing constants, which produce a

**Figure 16.45**

StatTools Summary Data

|  | A | B |
|---|---|---|
| 8 | *Forecasting Constants* |  |
| 9 | Level (Alpha) | 0.500 |
| 10 | Trend (Beta) | 0.200 |
| 11 | Season (Gamma) | 0.100 |
| 12 |  |  |
| 13 |  |  |
| 14 | *Winters' Exponential* |  |
| 15 | Mean Abs Err | 146.69 |
| 16 | Root Mean Sq Err | 192.17 |
| 17 | Mean Abs Per% Err | 4.41% |

MAPE of 4.41%. Again, you can manually try other smoothing constants in the range B9:B11 to see how sensitive the summary measures are to the smoothing constants.

The detailed data section in Figure 16.46 implements the exponential smoothing equations for Winters' method. Note in particular the seasonality factors in column E. They remain almost constant from year to year and they indicate a clear pattern, where sales in quarters 1 and 4 are always below average, and sales in quarters 2 and 3 are always above average.

---

**Figure 16.46**  Detailed Data from Winters' Method

|  | A | B | C | D | E | F | G |
|---|---|---|---|---|---|---|---|
| 63 | Forecasting Data | Sales | Level | Trend | Season | Forecast | Error |
| 64 | Q1-1992 | 1807.3700 | 2046.27 | 49.93 | 0.88 | | |
| 65 | Q2-1992 | 2355.3200 | 2118.38 | 54.37 | 1.10 | 2306.50 | 48.82 |
| 66 | Q3-1992 | 2591.8300 | 2318.02 | 83.42 | 1.06 | 2286.12 | 305.71 |
| 67 | Q4-1992 | 2236.3900 | 2360.38 | 75.21 | 0.96 | 2315.58 | -79.19 |
| 68 | Q1-1993 | 1549.1400 | 2094.75 | 7.04 | 0.87 | 2151.24 | -602.10 |
| 69 | Q2-1993 | 2105.7900 | 2006.79 | -11.96 | 1.10 | 2315.07 | -209.28 |
| 70 | Q3-1993 | 2041.3200 | 1961.42 | -18.64 | 1.06 | 2112.07 | -70.75 |
| 108 | Q1-2003 | 4176.7900 | 4778.84 | 29.56 | 0.88 | 4282.03 | -105.24 |
| 109 | Q2-2003 | 5125.4000 | 4728.99 | 13.68 | 1.10 | 5300.48 | -175.08 |
| 110 | Q3-2003 | 4962.6500 | 4728.88 | 10.92 | 1.05 | 4991.69 | -29.04 |
| 111 | Q4-2003 | 4917.6300 | 4928.83 | 48.73 | 0.96 | 4554.35 | 363.28 |
| 112 | Q1-2004 | 4542.6000 | 5058.34 | 64.88 | 0.89 | 4399.80 | 142.80 |
| 113 | Q2-2004 | 5284.7100 | 4962.69 | 32.78 | 1.10 | 5638.03 | -353.32 |
| 114 | Q3-2004 | 4817.4300 | 4786.95 | -8.93 | 1.05 | 5256.23 | -438.80 |
| 115 | Q4-2004 | 4634.5000 | 4791.41 | -6.25 | 0.96 | 4608.69 | 25.81 |
| 116 | Q1-2005 | 4431.3600 | 4895.21 | 15.76 | 0.89 | 4236.48 | 194.88 |
| 117 | Q2-2005 | 5602.2100 | 5009.08 | 35.38 | 1.10 | 5386.98 | 215.23 |
| 118 | Q3-2005 | 5349.8500 | 5075.58 | 41.61 | 1.05 | 5284.66 | 65.19 |
| 119 | Q4-2005 | 5036.0000 | 5168.38 | 51.85 | 0.97 | 4937.21 | 98.79 |
| 120 | Q1-2006 | 4534.6100 | 5165.32 | 40.86 | 0.89 | 4632.06 | -97.45 |
| 121 | Q2-2006 | 5836.1700 | 5258.13 | 51.25 | 1.10 | 5721.98 | 114.19 |
| 122 | Q3-2006 | 5818.2800 | 5429.90 | 75.36 | 1.05 | 5565.60 | 252.68 |
| 123 | Q4-2006 | 5070.4200 | 5377.66 | 49.84 | 0.96 | 5316.90 | -246.48 |
| 124 | Q1-2007 | 4497.4700 | 5250.72 | 14.48 | 0.88 | 4810.85 | -313.38 |
| 125 | Q2-2007 | | | | | 5792.56 | |
| 126 | Q3-2007 | | | | | 5546.75 | |
| 127 | Q4-2007 | | | | | 5100.89 | |
| 128 | Q1-2008 | | | | | 4689.66 | |
| 129 | Q2-2008 | | | | | 5856.29 | |
| 130 | Q3-2008 | | | | | 5607.61 | |
| 131 | Q4-2008 | | | | | 5156.70 | |
| 132 | Q1-2009 | | | | | 4740.84 | |

---

The chart in Figure 16.47 indicates how well Winters' method (with these smoothing constants) tracks the sales pattern through time. It even picks up the slight decrease in the upward trend in more recent years and projects this pattern into the future. If we had used Holt's method on this data set, it would have identified the upward trend, but it would have completely missed the seasonal pattern.

**Figure 16.47** Time Series with Forecasts from Winters' Method Superimposed

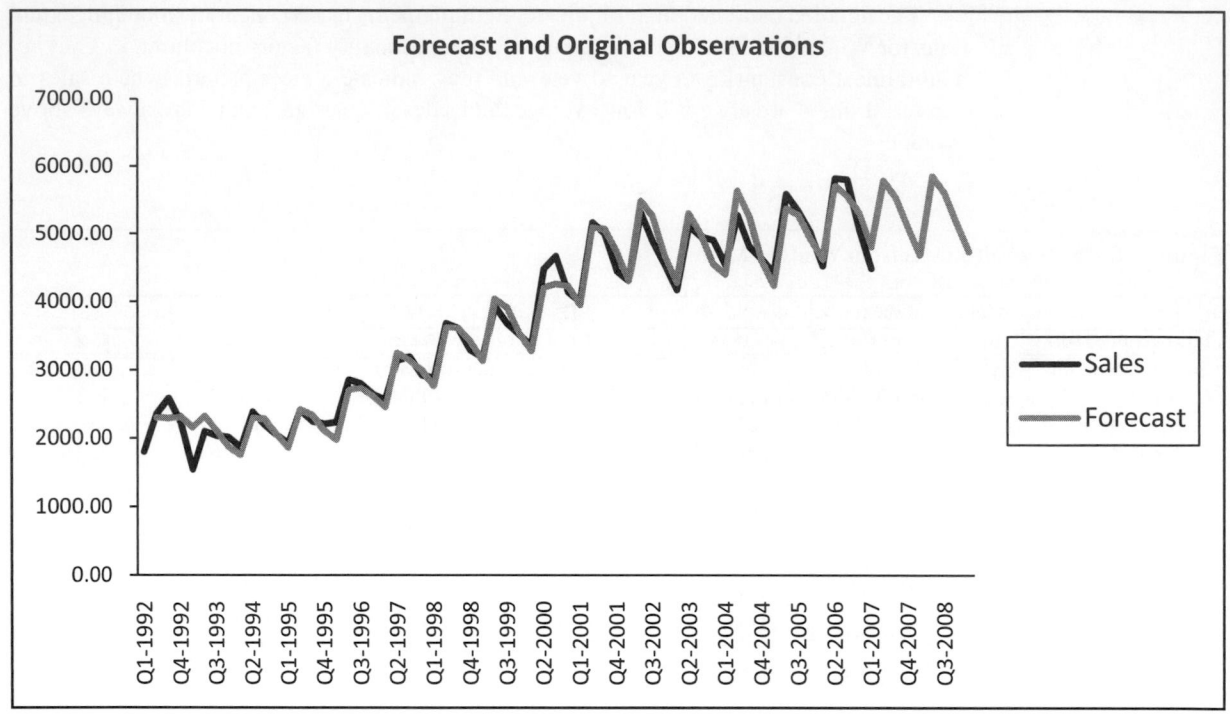

# PROBLEMS

## Skill-Building Problems

**28.** You have been assigned to forecast the number of aircraft engines ordered each month by Commins Engine Company. At the end of February, the forecast is that 100 engines will be ordered during April. During March, 120 engines are ordered. Using $\alpha = 0.3$, determine a forecast (at the end of March) for the number of orders placed during April. Answer the same question for May. Use simple exponential smoothing.

**29.** Simple exponential smoothing with $\alpha = 0.3$ is being used to forecast sales of radios at Lowland Appliance. Forecasts are made on a monthly basis. After August radio sales are observed, the forecast for September is 100 radios.
  **a.** During September, 120 radios are sold. After observing September sales, what do we forecast for October radio sales? For November radio sales?
  **b.** June sales were recorded as 10 radios; however, 100 radios were actually sold in June. After correcting for this error, develop a forecast for October radio sales.

**30.** The file **P16_30.xlsx** contains the quarterly numbers of applications for home mortgage loans at a branch office of Northern Central Bank.
  **a.** Create a time series chart of the data. Based on what you see, which of the exponential smoothing models do you think will provide the best forecasting model? Why?
  **b.** Use simple exponential smoothing to forecast these data, using a smoothing constant of 0.1.
  **c.** Repeat part **b**, but search for the smoothing constant that makes RMSE as small as possible. Does it make much of an improvement over the model in part **b**?

**31.** The file **P16_31.xlsx** contains the monthly number of airline tickets sold by the CareFree Travel Agency.
  **a.** Create a time series chart of the data. Based on what you see, which of the exponential smoothing

models do you think will provide the best forecasting model? Why?

  **b.** Use simple exponential smoothing to forecast these data, using a smoothing constant of 0.1.

  **c.** Repeat part **b**, but search for the smoothing constant that makes RMSE as small as possible. Does it make much of an improvement over the model in part **b**?

32. The file **P16_32.xlsx** contains yearly data on the proportion of Americans under the age of 18 living below the poverty level.

  **a.** Create a time series chart of the data. Based on what you see, which of the exponential smoothing models do you think will provide the best forecasting model? Why?

  **b.** Use simple exponential smoothing to forecast these data, using a smoothing constant of 0.1.

  **c.** Repeat part **b**, but search for the smoothing constant that makes RMSE as small as possible. Create a chart of the series with the forecasts superimposed from this optimal smoothing constant. Does it make much of an improvement over the model in part **b**?

  **d.** Write a short report to summarize your results. Considering the chart in part **c**, would you say the forecasts are "good"?

**33.** The file **P16_33.xlsx** contains weekly data for the S&P 500 stock index from the beginning of 2002 to mid-2003. (It was downloaded from the Yahoo! site. You can follow the hyperlink in the file to obtain more recent data if you like.) In particular, the file lists closing prices in column H, adjusted for dividends and stock splits.

  **a.** Create a time series plot of the adjusted closing prices. Does it look like moving averages and/or simple exponential smoothing will perform well on this series?

  **b.** Run moving averages on the adjusted closing prices, experimenting with the span. Which span appears to work best? Report the MAE, RMSE, and MAPE values, and show a graph of the series with the forecasts superimposed, for the best span.

  **c.** Run simple exponential smoothing on the adjusted closing prices, experimenting with the smoothing constant. Which smoothing constant appears to work best? Report the MAE, RMSE, and MAPE values, and show a graph of the series with the forecasts superimposed, for the best smoothing constant.

34. TOD Chevy is using Holt's method to forecast weekly car sales. Currently, the level of the series is estimated to be 50 cars per week, and the trend is estimated to be 6 cars per week. During the current week, 30 cars are sold. After observing the current week's sales, forecast the number of cars sold 1 week from now; 2 weeks from now; 3 weeks from now. Use $\alpha = \beta = 0.3$.

35. Consider the American Express closing price data from Problem 22 in the file **P16_22.xlsx**.

  **a.** Create a time series chart of the data. Based on what you see, which of the exponential smoothing models do you think will provide the best forecasting model? Why?

  **b.** Use Holt's exponential smoothing to forecast these data, using the smoothing constants $\alpha = \beta = 0.1$.

  **c.** Repeat part **b**, searching for the smoothing constants that make RMSE as small as possible. Does it make much of an improvement over the result in part **b**?

**36.** The University Credit Union is open Monday through Saturday. Winters' method is being used to predict the number of customers entering the bank each day. (The six days of the week are considered the "seasons.") After observing the number of arrivals on Monday, the updated estimates of level and trend of the series are 200 and 1, respectively, and the estimated seasonal factors for Monday through Saturday are 0.90, 0.70, 0.80, 1.10, 1.20, and 1.30. Provide forecasts for Tuesday through Saturday of the current week.

37. The file **P16_37.xlsx** contains monthly retail sales of U.S. liquor stores.

  **a.** Is seasonality present in these data? If so, characterize the seasonality pattern.

  **b.** Use Winters' method to forecast this series with smoothing constants $\alpha = \beta = 0.1$ and $\gamma = 0.3$. Does the forecast series seem to track the seasonal pattern well? What are your forecasts for the next 12 months?

38. The file **P16_38.xlsx** contains monthly time series data for total U.S. retail sales of building materials (which includes retail sales of building materials, hardware and garden supply stores, and mobile home dealers).

  **a.** Is seasonality present in these data? If so, characterize the seasonality pattern.

  **b.** Use Winters' method to forecast this series with smoothing constants $\alpha = \beta = 0.1$ and $\gamma = 0.3$. Does the forecast series seem to track the seasonal pattern well? What are your forecasts for the next 12 months?

## Skill-Extending Problems

39. A version of simple exponential smoothing can be used to predict the outcome of sporting events. To illustrate, consider pro football. We first assume that all games are played on a neutral field. Before each day of play, we assume that each team has a rating. For example, if the rating for the Bears is $+10$ and the rating for the Bengals is $+6$, we would predict the Bears to beat the Bengals by $10 - 6 = 4$ points. Suppose that the Bears play the Bengals and win by 20 points. For this game, we underpredicted the Bears' performance by $20 - 4 = 16$ points. The best $\alpha$ for pro football is

$\alpha = 0.10$. After the game, we therefore increase the Bears' rating by $16(0.1) = 1.6$ and decrease the Bengals' rating by 1.6 points. In a rematch, the Bears would be favored by $(10 + 1.6) - (6 - 1.6) = 7.2$ points.

**a.** How does this approach relate to the equation $L_t = L_{t-1} + \alpha E_t$?

**b.** Suppose that the home field advantage in pro football is 3 points; that is, home teams tend to outscore visiting teams by an average of 3 points a game. How could the home field advantage be incorporated into this system?

**c.** How could we determine the *best* $\alpha$ for pro football?

**d.** How might we determine ratings for each team at the beginning of the season?

**e.** Suppose we try to apply the previous method to predict pro football (16-game schedule), college football (11-game schedule), college basketball (30-game schedule), and pro basketball (82-game schedule). Which sport would probably have the smallest optimal $\alpha$? Which sport would probably have the largest optimal $\alpha$?

**f.** Why would this approach probably yield poor forecasts for Major League Baseball?

**40.** Holt's method assumes an *additive* trend. For example, a trend of 5 means that the level will increase by 5 units per period. Suppose there is actually a *multiplicative* trend. This means that if the current estimate of the level is 50, and the current estimate of the trend is 1.2, we would predict demand to increase by 20% per period. So we would forecast the next period's demand to be $50(1.2)$ and forecast the demand two periods in the future to be $50(1.2)^2$. If we want to use a multiplicative trend in Holt's method, we should use the following equations:

$$L_t = \alpha Y_t + (1-\alpha)U$$
$$T_t = \beta V + (1-\beta)T_{t-1}$$

**a.** What should $U$ and $V$ be to make this a sensible forecasting method.

**b.** Suppose we are working with monthly data and month 12 is December, month 13 is January, and so on. Also suppose that the level and trend, right after observing December's value, are $L_{12} = 100$ and $T_{12} = 1.2$, respectively. Then we observe $Y_{13} = 200$. At the end of month 13, what is the forecast for month 14? For month 15? Assume $\alpha = \beta = 0.2$.

# 16.8 CONCLUSION

We have seen numerous examples in this book where numeric input data for a spreadsheet model is required. In real situations, the data is often obtained through regression or an extrapolation forecasting method. In this chapter, we have discussed regression and some of the more popular extrapolation methods for time series forecasting. These are important tools in any management scientist's tool kit. In fact, they are becoming required tools for just about any business analyst because virtually all business analysts need to relate variables, discover trends and seasonal patterns, and make forecasts. Fortunately, the basic tools we have presented are reasonably easy to understand and use, especially given the built-in capabilities of Excel and the available statistical add-ins for Excel. These tools are extremely widespread, flexible, and powerful. We suspect that most of you will use them at some point in your careers.

# Summary of Key Management Science Terms

| Term | Explanation | Page |
|---|---|---|
| Regression models | Statistical models that estimate an equation to relate one variable to one or more explanatory variables | 905 |
| Extrapolation (time series) models | Statistical models that relate a time series variable to previous values of that same variable | 905 |
| Dependent variable | The variable being explained in a regression model, typically denoted by $Y$ | 906 |
| Explanatory variables | The variables used to explain the dependent variable in a regression model, typically denoted by $X$'s (also called independent or predictor variables) | 906 |
| Simple regression | A regression model with a single explanatory variable | 906 |
| Multiple regression | A regression model with multiple explanatory variables | 906 |
| Least-squares line | The regression line that minimizes the sum of squared residuals; the resulting line from a typical regression analysis | 907 |
| Residual | The difference between an actual $Y$ value and the value predicted by the regression equation | 907 |
| Fitted value | A predicted value of $Y$, as predicted by the regression equation | 907 |
| Standard error of estimate | Essentially, the standard deviation of the residuals; an estimate of the magnitude of prediction errors made from the regression equation | 908 |
| Multiple $R$ | The correlation between the actual $Y$'s and the fitted $Y$'s | 908 |
| $R$-square | The percentage of variation of the $Y$'s explained by the regression | 909 |
| Linear trend | A trend, usually through time, where a variable changes by a constant *amount* each time period | 910 |
| Exponential trend | A trend, usually through time, where a variable changes by a constant *percentage* each time period | 910 |
| Dummy variables | 0–1 variables that are used in regression equations to encode a categorical variable such as Gender or Quarter | 926 |
| Time series components | The items, including trend, seasonality, cyclic behavior, and noise, that produce the patterns observed in most time series variables | 933 |
| MAE, RMSE, MAPE | Three popular measures of forecast errors in time series analysis | 936 |
| Moving averages method | A forecasting method where the forecast for any period is the average of the several most recent periods | 937 |
| Span | The number of terms in each average in moving averages; larger spans produce a smoother forecast series | 937 |
| Exponential smoothing method | A forecasting method where the forecast for any period is a weighted average of previous periods, with more recent periods getting more weight | 942 |
| Smoothing constants | One or more constants, all between 0 and 1, that drive the exponential smoothing equation(s); lower values produce a smoother forecast series | 942 |
| Simple exponential smoothing | Version of exponential smoothing appropriate when there is no obvious trend or seasonality | 942 |
| Holt's method | Version of exponential smoothing appropriate when there is a trend but no obvious seasonality | 942 |
| Winters' method | Version of exponential smoothing appropriate when there is seasonality and possibly a trend | 942 |

## Summary of Key Excel Terms

| Term | Explanation | Excel | Page |
|------|-------------|-------|------|
| Creating scatterplot | Useful for identifying a relationship between two variables | Create a scatter chart from Insert ribbon (can also use StatTools add-in) | 911 |
| Superimposing trendline | Useful for identifying a linear or exponential trend through a scatterplot | Create a scatterplot, then use the Trendline tool | 912 |
| EXP function | Used to raise the special number $e$ to a power; also called the *antilog* function | =EXP(*value*) | 915 |
| SUMSQ function | Used to sum the squares of values in a range | =SUMSQ(*range*) | 918 |
| Analysis ToolPak | A statistical add-in that ships with Excel; useful for regression and several other statistical procedures | Use Data Analysis from Data ribbon | 922 |
| Creating time series plot | Useful for seeing how a time series variable behaves through time | Create a line chart from Insert ribbon (can also use StatTools add-in) | 934 |
| StatTools add-in | A statistical add-in developed by Palisade that is considerably more powerful than Analysis ToolPak | Has its own ribbon | 947 |

# PROBLEMS

## Skill-Building Problems

**41.** The file **P16_41.xlsx** lists sales (in millions of dollars) of Dell Computer during the period from 1987 to 1997 (where year 1 corresponds to 1987).
  **a.** Fit an exponential trendline to these data.
  **b.** Use your part **a** answer to predict 1999 sales for Dell.
  **c.** Use your part **a** answer to describe how the sales of Dell grew from year to year during this period.

**42.** The file **P16_42.xlsx** contains the sales (in millions of dollars) for Sun Microsystems.
  **a.** Use these data to predict the company's sales for the next two years. You need consider only a linear and exponential trend, but you should justify the equation you choose.
  **b.** In words, how do your predictions of sales increase from year to year during this period?

**43.** The file **P16_43.xlsx** contains the sales in (millions of dollars) for Procter and Gamble.
  **a.** Use these data to predict Procter & Gamble sales for the next two years. You need consider only a linear and exponential trend, but you should justify the equation you choose.
  **b.** Use your part **a** answer to explain in words how your predictions of Procter & Gamble sales will increase from year to year.

**44.** Management of a home appliance store in Charlotte wants to understand the growth pattern of the monthly sales of DVD units over the past 2 years. Managers have recorded the relevant data in the file **P16_44.xlsx**. The question is whether the sales of DVD units have been growing *linearly* over the past 24 months.
  **a.** Generate a scatterplot for sales versus time. Comment on the observed behavior of monthly DVD sales at this store.
  **b.** Estimate a simple regression model to explain the variation of monthly DVD sales over the given time period. Interpret the estimated regression coefficients.

**45.** The *beta* of a stock is found by running a regression with the monthly return on a market index as the explanatory variable and the monthly return on the stock as the dependent variable. The beta of the stock is then the slope of this regression equation.
  **a.** Explain why most stocks have a positive beta.
  **b.** Explain why a stock with a beta with absolute value greater than 1 is more volatile than the market, and a stock with a beta with absolute value less than 1 is less volatile than the market.
  **c.** Use the data in the file **P16_45.xlsx** to estimate the beta for Ford Motor Company.

**d.** What percentage of the variation in Ford's return is explained by market variation? What percentage is unexplained by market variation?

**46.** The file **P16_46.xlsx** contains the amount of money spent advertising a product (in thousands of dollars) and the number of units sold (in millions) for eight months.

    **a.** Assume that the only factor influencing monthly sales is advertising. Fit the following two curves to these data: linear ($Y = a + bX$) and power ($Y = aX^b$). Which equation best fits the data?

    **b.** Interpret the best-fitting equation. (See Problem 9 in this chapter.)

    **c.** Using the best-fitting equation, predict sales during a month in which $60,000 is spent on advertising.

**47.** Callaway Golf is trying to determine how the price of a set of clubs affects the demand for clubs. The file **P16_47.xlsx** contains the price of a set of clubs (in dollars) and the monthly sales (in millions of sets sold).

    **a.** Assume the only factor influencing monthly sales is price. Fit the following two curves to these data: linear ($Y = a + bX$) and exponential ($Y = ae^{bX}$). Which equation best fits the data?

    **b.** Interpret your best-fitting equation.

    **c.** Using the best-fitting equation, predict sales during a month in which the price is $470.

**48.** When potential workers apply for a job that requires extensive manual assembly of small intricate parts, they are initially given three different tests to measure their manual dexterity. The ones who are hired are then periodically given a performance rating on a 0 to 100 scale that combines their speed and accuracy in performing the required assembly operations. The file **P16_48.xlsx** lists the test scores and performance ratings for a randomly selected group of employees. It also lists their seniority (months with the company) at the time of the performance rating.

    **a.** Run the regression of JobPerf versus all four explanatory variables. List the equation, the $R$-square value, and the standard error of estimate. Do all of the regression coefficients have the signs you would expect? Briefly explain.

    **b.** Referring to the equation in part **a**, if a worker (outside of the 80 in the sample) has 15 months of seniority and test scores of 57, 71, and 63, give a prediction and an approximate 95% prediction interval for this worker's JobPerf score.

    **c.** Arguably, the three test measures provide overlapping (redundant) information. It might be sensible to regress JobPerf versus only two explanatory variables, Sen and AvgTest, where AvgTest is the average of the three test scores, that is, AvgTest = (Test1 + Test2 + Test3)/3. Run this regression and report the same measures as in part **a**: the equation

itself, $R$-square, and the standard error of estimate. Can you argue that this equation is just as good as the equation in part **a**? Explain briefly.

**49.** The file **P16_49.xlsx** contains quarterly revenues of Toys "R" Us. Discuss the seasonal and trend components of the growth of Toys "R" Us revenues. Also, use any reasonable forecasting method to forecast quarterly revenues for the next year. Explain your choice of forecasting method.

**50.** Let $Y_t$ be the sales during month $t$ (in thousands of dollars) for a photography studio, and let $P_t$ be the price charged for portraits during month $t$. The data are in the file **P16_50.xlsx**.

    **a.** Use regression to fit the following model to these data: $Y_t = a + b_1 P_t + b_2 Y_{t-1}$. This says that current sales are related to current price and sales in the previous month. (*Hint:* You won't be able to use the first month's data because there is no value for the previous month's sales.)

    **b.** If the price of a portrait during month 21 is $10, what would you predict for sales in month 21?

**51.** The file **P16_51.xlsx** contains data on monthly U.S. housing sales (in thousands of houses).

    **a.** Use Winters' method with $\alpha = \beta = 0.1$ and $\gamma = 0.3$ to forecast this series. Ask for 12 months of future forecasts. Then use Winters' method a second time with the values of the smoothing constants that minimize RMSE.

    **b.** Compare the two sets of outputs. How do they track the historical data? How do their future forecasts differ? Which of the two do you believe?

## Skill-Extending Problems

**52.** The auditor of Kiely Manufacturing is concerned about the number and magnitude of year-end adjustments that are made annually when the financial statements of Kiely Manufacturing are prepared. Specifically, the auditor suspects that the management of Kiely Manufacturing is using discretionary write-offs to manipulate the reported net income. To check this, the auditor has collected data from 25 firms that are similar to Kiely Manufacturing in terms of manufacturing facilities and product lines. The cumulative reported third quarter income and the final net income reported are listed in the file **P16_52.xlsx** for each of these 25 firms. If Kiely Manufacturing reported a cumulative third quarter income of $2,500,000 and a preliminary net income of $4,900,000, should the auditor conclude that the relationship between cumulative third quarter income and the annual income for Kiely Manufacturing differs from that of the 25 firms in this sample? Why or why not?

**53.** The file **P16_53.xlsx** contains data on pork sales. Price is in dollars per hundred pounds, quantity sold is in billions of pounds, per capita income is in dollars, U.S. population is in millions, and GNP is in billions of dollars.

a. Use the data on all potential explanatory variables to develop a regression equation that could be used to predict the quantity of pork sold during future periods.

b. Find the correlations between all pairs of variables. (We recommend StatTools.) What evidence do you see of multicollinearity? How could this cause a problem with the regression? Run another regression without potentially redundant variables. How does this new regression compare to the one in part **a**?

c. Suppose that during each of the next two quarters, price is 45, U.S. population is 240, GNP is 2620, and per capita income is 10,000. (These are in the units described previously.) Predict the quantity of pork sold during each of the next two quarters using the equations from parts **a** and **b**. How do they compare?

54. The belief that larger majorities for an incumbent president in a presidential election help the incumbent's party increase its representation in the House and Senate is called the *coattail* effect. The file **P16_54.xlsx** gives the percent by which each president since 1948 won the election and the number of seats in the House and Senate gained (or lost) during each election. Are these data consistent with the idea of presidential coattails? (*Source: Wall Street Journal,* September 10, 1996)

55. The auditor of Kaefer Manufacturing uses regression analysis during the analytical review stage of the firm's annual audit. The regression analysis attempts to uncover relationships that exist between various account balances. Any such relationship is subsequently used as a preliminary test of the reasonableness of the reported account balances. The auditor wants to determine whether a relationship exists between the balance of accounts receivable at the end of the month and that month's sales. The file **P16_55.xlsx** contains data on these two accounts for the last 36 months. It also shows the sales levels 2 months prior to month 1.

a. Is there any statistical evidence to suggest a relationship between the monthly sales level and accounts receivable?

b. Referring to part **a**, would the relationship be described any better by including this month's sales and the previous month's sales (called lagged sales) in the equation for accounts receivable? What about adding the sales from more than a month ago to the equation? For this problem, why might it make accounting sense to include lagged sales variables in the equation? How do you interpret their coefficients?

c. During month 37, which is a fiscal year-end month, sales were $1,800,000. The reported accounts receivable balance was $3,000,000. Does this reported amount seem consistent with past experience? Explain.

56. (Based on an actual court case in Philadelphia.) In the 1994 congressional election, the Republican candidate outpolled the Democratic candidate by 400 votes (excluding absentee ballots). The Democratic candidate outpolled the Republican candidate by 500 absentee votes. The Republican candidate sued (and won), claiming that vote fraud must have played a role in the absentee ballot count. The Republican's lawyer ran a regression to predict (based on past elections) how the absentee ballot margin could be predicted from the votes tabulated on voting machines. Selected results are given in the file **P16_56.xlsx**. Show how this regression could be used by the Republican to support his claim of vote fraud. (*Hint:* Does the 1994 observation fall outside the general pattern? That is, in statistical terms, is it an *outlier*?)

57. The file **P16_57.xlsx** contains data on the price of new and used Taurus sedans. All used prices are from 1995. For example, a new Taurus bought in 1985 cost $11,790, and the wholesale used price of that car in 1995 was $1700. A new Taurus bought in 1994 cost $18,680, and it could be sold used in 1995 for $12,600.

a. You want to predict the resale value (as a percentage of the original price of the vehicle) as a function of the vehicle's age. Find an equation to do this. (You should try at least two different equations and choose the one that fits best.)

b. Suppose all police cars are Ford Tauruses. If you were the business manager for the New York Police Department, what use would you make of your findings from part **a**?

58. Confederate Express is attempting to determine how its monthly shipping costs depend on the number of units shipped during a month. The file **P16_58.xlsx** contains the number of units shipped and total shipping costs for the past 15 months.

a. Use regression to determine a relationship between units shipped and monthly shipping costs.

b. Plot the errors for the predictions in order of time sequence. Is there any unusual pattern?

c. Suppose there was a trucking strike during months 11 to 15, and we believe that this might have influenced shipping costs. How could the answer to part **a** be modified to account for the effects of the strike? After accounting for the effects of the strike, does the unusual pattern in part **b** disappear? (*Hint:* Use a dummy variable.)

59. You are trying to determine the effects of three packaging displays (A, B, and C) on sales of toothpaste.

The file **P16_59.xlsx** contains the number of cases of toothpaste sold for nine consecutive weeks. The type of store (GR = grocery, DI = discount, and DE = department store) and the store location (U = urban, S = suburban, and R = rural) are also listed.

a. Run a multiple regression to determine how the type of store, display, and store location influence sales. Which potential explanatory variables should be included in the equation? Be sure to explain your rationale for including or excluding variables.

b. What type of store, store location, and display appears to maximize sales?

60. Pernavik Dairy produces and sells a wide range of dairy products. Because a government regulatory board sets most of the dairy's costs and prices, most of the competition between the dairy and its competitors takes place through advertising. The controller of Pernavik has developed the sales and advertising levels for the past 52 weeks. These appear in the file **P16_60.xlsx**. Note that the advertising levels for the three weeks prior to week 1 are also listed. The controller wonders whether Pernavik is spending too much money on advertising. He argues that the company's contribution-margin ratio is about 10%. That is, 10% of each sales dollar goes toward covering fixed costs. This means that each advertising dollar has to generate at least $10 of sales or the advertising is not cost-effective. Use regression to determine whether advertising dollars are generating this type of sales response. (*Hint:* The sales value in any week might be affected not only by advertising this week but also by advertising levels in the past one, two, or three weeks. These are called *lagged* values of advertising. Try regression models with lagged values of advertising included, and see whether you get better results.)

61. The file **P16_61.xlsx** contains data on a motel chain's revenue and advertising.

a. Use these data and multiple regression to make predictions of the motel chain's revenues during the next four quarters. Assume that advertising during each of the next four quarters is $50,000. (*Hint:* Try using advertising, lagged by one period, as an explanatory variable. See the previous problem for an explanation of a *lagged* variable. Also, use dummy variables for the quarters to account for possible seasonality.)

b. Use simple exponential smoothing to make predictions for the motel chain's revenues during the next four quarters. Experiment with the smoothing constant.

c. Use Holt's method to make forecasts for the motel chain's revenues during the next four quarters. Experiment with the smoothing constants.

d. Use Winters' method to determine predictions for the motel chain's revenues during the next four quarters. Experiment with the smoothing constants.

e. Which forecasts from parts **a** to **d** would you expect to be the most reliable?

62. The file **P16_62.xlsx** contains five years of monthly data for a company. The first variable is Time (1–60). The second variable, Sales1, has data on sales of a product. Note that Sales1 increases linearly throughout the period, with only a minor amount of noise. (The third variable, Sales2, will be used in the next problem.) For this problem, use the Sales1 variable to see how the following forecasting methods are able to track a linear trend.

a. Forecast this series with the moving averages method with various spans such as 3, 6, and 12. What can you conclude?

b. Forecast this series with simple exponential smoothing with various smoothing constants such as 0.1, 0.3, 0.5, and 0.7. What can you conclude?

c. Repeat part **b** with Holt's method, again for various smoothing constants. Can you do much better than in parts **a** and **b**?

63. The Sales2 variable in the file from the previous problem was created from the Sales1 variable by multiplying by monthly seasonal factors. Basically, the summer months are high and the winter months are low. This might represent the sales of a product that has a linear trend and seasonality.

a. Repeat parts **a** to **c** from the previous problem to see how well these forecasting methods can deal with trend *and* seasonality.

b. Use Winters' method, with various values of the three smoothing constants, to forecast the series. Can you do much better? Which smoothing constants work well?

c. What can you conclude from your findings in parts **a** and **b** about forecasting this type of series?

# 16.1 DEMAND FOR FRENCH BREAD AT HOWIE'S BAKERY

Howie's Bakery is one of the most popular bakeries in town, and the favorite at Howie's is French bread. Each day of the week, Howie's bakes a number of loaves of French bread, more or less according to a daily schedule. To maintain its fine reputation, Howie's gives to charity any loaves not sold on the day they are baked. Although this occurs frequently, it is also common for Howie's to run out of French bread on any given day—more demand than supply. In this case, no extra loaves are baked that day; the customers have to go elsewhere (or come back to Howie's the next day) for their French bread. Although French bread at Howie's is always popular, Howie's stimulates demand by running occasional 10% off sales.

Howie's has collected data for 20 consecutive weeks, 140 days in all. These data are listed in the file

Howies Bakery.xlsx. The variables are Day (Monday–Sunday), Supply (number of loaves baked that day), OnSale (whether French bread is on sale that day), and Demand (loaves actually sold that day). Howie's wants to see whether regression can be used successfully to estimate Demand from the other data in the file. Howie reasons that if these other variables can be used to predict Demand, then he might be able to determine his daily supply (number of loaves to bake) in a more cost-effective way.

How successful is regression with these data? Is Howie correct that regression can help him determine his daily supply? Is any information missing that would be useful? How would you obtain it? How would you use it? Is this extra information *really* necessary? ∎

# 16.2 FORECASTING OVERHEAD AT WAGNER PRINTERS

Wagner Printers performs all types of printing, including custom work, such as advertising displays, and standard work, such as business cards. Market prices exist for standard work, and Wagner Printers must match or better these prices to get the business. The key issue is whether the existing market price covers the cost associated with doing the work. On the other hand, most of the custom work must be priced individually. Because all custom work is done on a job-order basis, Wagner routinely keeps track of all the direct labor and direct materials costs associated with each job. However, the overhead for each job must be estimated. The overhead is applied to each job using a predetermined (normalized) rate based on estimated overhead and labor hours. After the cost of the prospective job is determined, the sales manager develops a bid that reflects both the existing market conditions and the estimated price of completing the job.

In the past, the normalized rate for overhead has been computed by using the historical average of overhead per direct labor hour. Wagner has become increasingly concerned about this practice for two reasons. First, it hasn't produced accurate forecasts of overhead in the past. Second, technology has changed

the printing process, so that the labor content of jobs has been decreasing, and the normalized rate of overhead per direct labor hour has steadily been increasing. The file **Wagner Printers.xlsx** shows the overhead data that Wagner has collected for its shop for the past 52 weeks. The average weekly overhead for the last 52 weeks is $54,208, and the average weekly number of labor hours worked is 716. Therefore, the normalized rate for overhead that will be used in the upcoming week is about $76 (=54,208/716) per direct labor hour.

## Questions

1. Determine whether you can develop a more accurate estimate of overhead costs.

2. Wagner is now preparing a bid for an important order that may involve a considerable amount of repeat business. The estimated requirements for this project are 15 labor hours, 8 machine hours, $150 direct labor cost, and $750 direct material cost. Using the existing approach to cost estimation, Wagner has estimated the cost for this job as $2040 (=150 + 750 + (76 × 15)). Given the existing data, what cost would you estimate for this job? ∎

The Indiana University Credit Union Eastland Plaza branch was having trouble getting the correct staffing levels to match customer arrival patterns. On some days, the number of tellers was too high relative to the customer traffic, so that tellers were often idle. On other days, the opposite occurred; long customer waiting lines formed because the relatively few tellers could not keep up with the number of customers. The credit union manager, James Chilton, knew that there was a problem, but he had little of the quantitative training he believed would be necessary to find a better staffing solution. James figured that the problem could be broken down into three parts. First, he needed a reliable forecast of each day's number of customer arrivals. Second, he needed to translate these forecasts into staffing levels that would make an adequate trade-off between teller idleness and customer waiting. Third, he needed to translate these staffing levels into individual teller work assignments—who should come to work when.

The last two parts of the problem require analysis tools (queueing and scheduling) that we will not pursue here. However, you can help James with the first part—forecasting. The file **Credit Union Arrivals.xlsx** lists the number of customers entering this credit union branch each day of the past year. It also lists other information: the day of the week, whether the day was a staff or faculty payday, and whether the day was the day before or after a holiday. Use this data set to develop one or more forecasting models that James could use to help solve his problem. Based on your model(s), make any recommendations about staffing that appear reasonable. ■

Altschuler, S., D. Batavia, J. Bennett, R. Labe, B. Liao, R. Nigam, and J. Oh. "Pricing Analysis for Merrill Lynch Integrated Choice." *Interfaces* 32, no. 1 (2002): 5–19.

Angel, A., L. Taladriz, and R. Weber. "Soquimich Uses a System Based on Mixed-Integer Linear Programming and Expert Systems to Improve Customer Service." *Interfaces* 33, no. 4 (2003): 41–52.

Apte, A., U. Apte, R. Beatty, I. Sarkar, and J. Semple. "The Impact of Check Sequencing on NSF (Not-Sufficient Funds) Fees." *Interfaces* 34, no. 2 (2004): 97–105.

Armacost, A., C. Barnhart, K. Ware, and A. Wilson. "UPS Optimizes Its Air Network." *Interfaces* 34, no. 1 (2004): 15–25.

Austin, L. "Project EOQ: A Success Story in Implementing Academic Research." *Interfaces* 7, no. 4 (1977): 1–14.

Avriel, M., H. Pri-Zan, R. Meiri, and A. Peretz. "Opti-Money at Bank Hapoalim: A Model-Based Investment Decision-Support System for Individual Customers." *Interfaces* 34, no. 1 (2004): 39–50.

Babich, P. "Customer Satisfaction: How Good Is Good Enough?" *Quality Progress* 25 (Dec. 1992): 65–68.

Bahurmoz, A. "The Analytic Hierarchy Process at Dar Al-Hekma, Saudi Arabia." *Interfaces* 33, no. 4 (2003): 70–78.

Balson, W., J. Welsh, and D. Wilson. "Using Decision Analysis and Risk Analysis to Manage Utility Environmental Risk." *Interfaces* 22, no. 6 (1992): 126–139.

Bangash, A., R. Bollapragada, R. Klein, N. Raman, H. Shulman, and D. Smith. "Inventory Requirements Planning at Lucent Technologies." *Interfaces* 34, no. 5 (2004): 342–352.

Bassett, M., L. L. Gardner, and K. Steele. "Dow AgroSciences Uses Simulation-Based Optimization to Schedule the New-Product Development Process." *Interfaces* 34, no. 6 (2004): 426–437.

Baumol, W. "The Transactions Demand for Cash: An Inventory Theoretic Approach." *Quarterly Journal of Economics* 16 (1952): 545–556.

Bean, J., C. Noon, and G. Salton. "Asset Divestiture at Homart Development Company." *Interfaces* 17, no. 1 (1987): 48–65.

———, S. Ryan, and G. Salton. "Selecting Tenants in a Shopping Mall." *Interfaces* 18, no. 2 (1988): 1–10.

Benninga, S. *Numerical Methods in Finance*. Cambridge, MA: MIT Press, 1989.

Billington, C., G. Callioni, B. Crane, J. Ruark, J. Rapp, T. White, and S. Willems. "Accelerating the Profitability of Hewlett-Packard's Supply Chains." *Interfaces* 34, no. 1 (2004): 59–72.

Black, F., and M. Scholes. "The Pricing of Options and Corporate Liabilities." *Journal of Political Economy* 81 (1973): 637–654.

Blakeley, F., B. Bozkaya, B. Cao, W. Hall, and J. Knolmajer. "Optimizing Periodic Maintenance Operations for Schindler Elevator Corporation." *Interfaces* 33, no. 1 (2003): 67–79.

Borison, A. "Oglethorpe Power Corporation Decides about Investing in a Major Transmission System." *Interfaces* 25, no. 2 (1995): 25–36.

Boykin, R. "Optimizing Chemical Production at Monsanto." *Interfaces* 15, no. 1 (1985): 88–95.

Brahms, S., and A. Taylor. *The Win-Win Solution*. Norton, New York (2000).

Brout, D. "Scientific Management of Inventory on a Hand-Held Calculator." *Interfaces* 11, no. 6 (1981): 57–69.

Brown, G., J. Keegan, B. Vigus, and K. Wood. "The Kellogg Company Optimizes Production, Inventory, and Distribution." *Interfaces* 31, no. 6 (2001): 1–15.

———, R. Dell, and A. Newman. "Optimizing Military Capital Planning." *Interfaces* 34, no. 6 (2004): 415–425.

———, R. Dell, H. Holtz, and A. Newman. "How US Air Force Space Command Optimizes Long-Term Investment in Space Systems." *Interfaces* 33, no. 4 (2003): 1–14.

Brumelle, S. "On the Relation between Customer and Time Averages in Queues." *J. of Applied Probability* 8 (1971): 508–520.

Bukiet, B., H. Rusty, and J. Palacios, "A Markov Chain Model of Baseball," *Operations Research* 45, no. 1 (1997): 14–23.

Butler, J., A. Chebeskov, J. Dyer, T. Edmunds, J. Jia, and V. Oussanov. "The United States and Russia Evaluate Plutonium Disposition Options with Multiattribute Utility Theory." *Interfaces* 35, no. 1 (2005): 88–101.

Callen, J. "DEA: Partial Survey and Applications for Managerial Accounting." *Journal of Management Accounting Research* 3 (1991): 35–56.

Carino, H., and C. Lenoir. "Optimizing Wood Procurement in Cabinet Manufacturing." *Interfaces* 18, no. 2 (1988): 11–19.

Caulkins, J., E. Kaplan, P. Lurie, T. O'Connor, and S. Ahn. "Can Difficult-to-Reuse Syringes Reduce the Spread of HIV Among Injection Drug Users?" *Interfaces* 28, no. 3 (1998): 23–33.

Chalermkraivuth, K. C., S. Bollapragada, M. C. Clark, J. Deaton, L. Kiaer, J. P. Murdzek, W. Neeves, B. J. Scholz, and D. Toledano. "GE Asset Management, Genworth Financial, and GE Insurance Use a Sequential-Linear-Programming Algorithm to Optimize Portfolios." *Interfaces* 35, no. 5 (2005): 370–380.

Charnes, A., and W. W. Cooper. "Generalization of the Warehousing Model." *Operational Research Quarterly* 6 (1955): 131–172.

———, W. W. Cooper, and R. O. Ferguson. "Optimal Estimation of Executive Compensation by Linear Programming." *Management Science* 1, no. 2 (1955): 131–151.

Clemen, R., and R. Kwit. "The Value of Decision Analysis at Eastman Kodak Company, 1990–1999." *Interfaces* 31, no. 5 (2001): 74–92.

Cox, J., S. Ross, and M. Rubinstein. "Option Pricing: A Simplified Approach." *Journal of Financial Economics* 7 (1979): 229–263.

Dantzig, G. "The Diet Problem." *Interfaces* 20, no. 4 (1990): 43–47.

Davis, L. *Handbook of Genetic Algorithms*. Van-Nostrand Reinhold (1991).

de Kok, T., F. Janssen, J. van Doremalen, E. van Wachem, M. Clerkx, and W. Peeters. "Philips Electronics Synchronizes Its Supply Chain to End the Bullwhip Effect." *Interfaces* 35, no. 1 (2005): 37–48.

Dekle, J., M. Lavieri, E. Martin, H. Emir-Farinas, and R. Francis. "A Florida County Locates Disaster Recovery Centers." *Interfaces* 35, no. 2 (2005): 113–139.

Deming, E. *Out of the Crisis*. Cambridge, MA: MIT Center for Advanced Engineering Study, 1986.

Denardo, E., U. Rothblum, and A. Swersey. "Transportation Problem in Which Costs Depend on Order of Arrival." *Management Science* 34 (1988): 774–784.

DeWitt, C., L. Lasdon, A. Waren, D. Brenner, and S. Melhem. "OMEGA: An Improved Gasoline Blending System for Texaco." *Interfaces* 19, no. 1 (1989): 85–101.

Dobson, G., and S. Kalish. "Positioning and Pricing a Product Line." *Marketing Science* 7 (1988): 107–126.

Dolan, R., and H. Simon, *Power Pricing*. The Free Press, New York, 1996.

Duffy, T., M. Hatzakis, W. Hsu, R. Labe, B. Liao, X. Luo, J. Oh, A. Setya, and L. Yang. "Merrill Lynch Improves Liquidity Risk Management for Revolving Credit Lines." *Interfaces* 35, no. 5 (2005): 353–369.

Dunning, D., S. Lockfort, Q. Ross, P. Beccue, and J. Stonebraker. "New York Power Authority Uses Decision Analysis to Schedule Refueling of Its Indian Point 3 Nuclear Power Plant." *Interfaces* 31, no. 5 (2001): 121–135.

Eaton, D., M. Daskin, D. Simmons, B. Bulloch, and G. Jasma. "Determining Emergency Medical Service Vehicle Deployment in Austin, Texas." *Interfaces* 15, no. 1 (1985): 96–108.

Efroymson, M., and T. Ray. "A Branch and Bound Algorithm for Factory Location." *Operations Research* 14 (1966): 361–368.

Evans, J. "The Factored Transportation Problem." *Management Science* 30 (1984): 1021–1024.

Feinstein, C. "Deciding Whether to Test Student Athletes for Drug Use." *Interfaces* 20, no. 3 (1990): 80–87.

Fitzsimmons, J., and L. Allen. "A Warehouse Location Model Helps Texas Comptroller Select Out-of-State Audit Offices." *Interfaces* 13, no. 5 (1983): 40–46.

Fleischmann, M., J. van Nunen, and B. Grave. "Integrating Closed-Loop Supply Chains and Spare-Parts Management at IBM." *Interfaces* 33, no. 6 (2003): 44–56.

Franklin, A., and E. Koenigsberg. "Computer School Assignments in a Large District." *Operations Research* 21 (1973): 413–426.

Franses, P. "Do We Think We Make Better Forecasts Than in the Past? A Survey of Academics." *Interfaces* 34, no. 6 (2004): 466–468.

Friel, B. "Medicare Transactions: A $50 Million Lesson in Project Management." *Government Executive* (April 2000).

Gatalla, A., and W. Oearce. "Telephone Sales Manpower Planning at Qantas." *Interfaces* 9, no. 3 (1979): 1–9.

Gavirneni, S., D. Morrice, and P. Mullarkey. "Simulation Helps Maxager Shorten Its Sales Cycle." *Interfaces* 34, no. 1 (2004): 87–96.

———, L. Clark, and G. Pataki. "Schlumberger Optimizes Receiver Location for Automated Meter Reading." *Interfaces* 34, no. 3 (2004): 208–214.

Gendron, B. "Scheduling Employees in Quebec's Liquor Stores with Integer Programming." *Interfaces* 35, no. 5 (2005): 402–410.

Gido, J., and G. Clements. *Successful Project Management*, 3rd edition. Thomson South-Western (2006).

Glassey, R., and V. Gupta. "A Linear Programming Analysis of Paper Recycling." *Studies in Mathematical Programming*. Ed. H. Salkin and J. Saha. New York: North-Holland, 1978.

Glover, F., and D. Klingman. "Network Applications in Industry and Government." *AIIE Transactions* 9 (1977): 363–376.

Goldberg, D. *Genetic Algorithms in Search Optimization and Machine Learning*. Addison-Wesley (1989).

Golden, B., E. Wasil, and P. Harker. *The Analytic Hierarchy Process*. New York: Springer-Verlag, 1989.

Gorman, M. "Santa Fe Railway Uses an Operating-Plan Model to Improve Its Service Design." *Interfaces* 28, no. 4 (1998): 88–103.

Green, P., A. Krieger, and Y. Wind. "Thirty Years of Conjoint Analysis: Reflections and Prospects." *Interfaces* 31, no. 3 (2): (2001): S56–S73.

Grossman, S., and O. Hart. "An Analysis of the Principal Agent Problem." *Econometrica* 51 (1983): 7–45.

Guide, V. D., L. Muyldermans, and L. van Wassenhove. "Hewlett-Packard Company Unlocks the Value Potential from Time-Sensitive Returns." *Interfaces* 35, no. 4 (2005): 281–293.

Hansen, P., and R. Wendell. "A Note on Airline Commuting." *Interfaces* 11, no. 12 (1982): 85–87.

Heady, E., and A. Egbert. "Regional Planning of Efficient Agricultural Patterns." *Econometrica* 32 (1964): 374–386.

Heyman, D., and S. Stidham. "The Relation between Customer and Time Averages in Queues." *Operations Research* 28 (1980): 983–984.

Hicks, R., R. Madrid, C. Milligan, R. Pruneau, M. Kanaley, Y. Dumas, B. Lacroix, J. Desrosiers, and F. Soumis. "Bombardier Flexjet Significantly Improves Its Fractional Aircraft Ownership Operations." *Interfaces* 35, no. 1 (2005): 49–60.

Holland, J. *Adaptation in Natural and Artificial Systems*. University of Michigan Press (1975).

Hoppensteadt, F., and C. Peskin. *Mathematics in Medicine and the Life Sciences*. New York: Springer-Verlag, 1992.

Howard, R. "Decision Analysis: Practice and Promise." *Management Science* 34, no. 6 (1988): 679–695.

Huerter, J., and W. Swart. "An Integrated Labor-Management System for Taco Bell." *Interfaces* 28, no. 1 (1998): 75–91.

Ignall, E., and P. Kolesar. "Operating Characteristics of a Simple Shuttle under Local Dispatching Rules." *Operations Research* 20 (1972): 1077–1088.

Jacobs, W. "The Caterer Problem." *Naval Logistics Research Quarterly* 1 (1954): 154–165.

Johnson, R., and D. Wichern. *Applied Multivariate Statistical Analysis*, 5th ed. Prentice Hall (2002).

Kahn, J., M. Brandeau, and J. Dunn-Mortimer. "OR Modeling and AIDS Policy: From Theory to Practice." *Interfaces* 28, No. 3 (1998): 3–22.

Kalvaitishi, R., and A. Posgay. "An Application of Mixed Integer Programming in the Direct Mail Industry." *Management Science* 20, no. 5 (1974): 788–792.

Kapuscinski, R., R. Zhang, P. Carbonneau, R. Moore, and B. Reeves. "Inventory Decisions in Dell's Supply Chain." *Interfaces* 34, no. 3 (2004): 191–205.

Keefer, D., and S. Bodily. "Three-Point Approximations for Continuous Random Variables." *Management Science* 29, no. 5 (1983): 595–609.

Keisler, J., W. Buehring, P. McLaughlin, M. Robershotte, and R. Whitfield. "Allocating Vendor Risks in the Hanford Waste Cleanup." *Interfaces* 34, no. 3 (2004): 180–190.

Kekre, S., U. Rao, J. Swaminathan, and J. Zhang. "Reconfiguring a Remanufacturing Line at Visteon, Mexico." *Interfaces* 33, no. 6 (2003): 30–43.

Kelly, J. "A New Interpretation of Information Rate." *Bell System Technical Journal* 35 (1956): 917–926.

Kimbrough, S., and F. Murphy. "A Study of the Philadelphia Knowledge Economy." *Interfaces* 35, no. 3 (2005): 248–259.

Kirkwood, C. "An Overview of Methods for Applied Decision Analysis." *Interfaces* 22, no. 6 (1992): 28–39.

Klastorin, T. *Project Management: Tools and Trade-Offs*. Wiley (2004).

Klinghon, D., and N. Phillips. "Topological and Computations Aspects of Preemptive Multicriteria Military Personnel Assignment Problems." *Management Science* 30, no. 11 (1984): 1362–1375.

Kolesar, P., and E. Blum, "Square Root Laws for Fire Engine Response Distances." *Management Science* 19 (1973): 1368–1378.

———, T. Crabill, K. Rider, and W. Walker. "A Queueing Linear Programming Approach to Scheduling Police Patrol Cars." *Operations Research* 23 (1974): 1045–1062.

Koschat, M., G. Berk, J. Blatt, N. Kunz, M. LePore, and S. Blyakher. "Newsvendors Tackle the Newsvendor Problem." *Interfaces* 33, no. 3 (2003): 72–84.

Lancaster, L. "The Evolution of the Diet Model in Managing Food Systems." *Interfaces* 22, no. 5 (1992): 59–68.

Lanzenauer, C., E. Harbauer, B. Johnston, and D. Shuttleworth. "RRSP Flood: LP to the Rescue." *Interfaces* 17, no. 4 (1987): 27–40.

Laval, C., M. Feyhl, and S. Kakouros. "Hewlett-Packard Combined OR and Expert Knowledge to Design Its Supply Chains." *Interfaces* 35, no. 3 (2005): 238–247.

LeBlanc, L., D. Randels, Jr., and K. Swann. "Heery International's Spreadsheet Optimization Model for Assigning Managers to Construction Projects." *Interfaces* 30, No. 6, (2000): 95–106.

———, J. Hill, G. Greenwell, and A. Czesnat. "Nu-kote's Spreadsheet Linear Programming Models for Optimizing Transportation." *Interfaces* 34, No. 2, (2004): 139–146.

——— and M. Galbreth. "Designing Large-Scale Supply Chain Linear Programs in Spreadsheets." *Communications of the ACM* 50 No. 8, (2007a): 59–64.

——— and M. Galbreth. "Implementing Large-Scale Optimization Models in Excel Using VBA." *Interfaces* 37 No. 4, (2007b): 370–382.

Lee, S., and L. Moore. "Optimizing University Admissions Planning." *Decision Sciences* 5 (1974): 405–414.

Liggett, R. "The Application of an Implicit Enumeration Algorithm to the School Desegregation Problem." *Management Science* 20 (1973): 159–168.

Lin, W., T. Mock, and A. Wright. "The Use of AHP as an Aid in Planning the Nature and Extent of Audit Procedures." *Auditing: A Journal of Practice and Theory* 4, no. 1 (1984): 89–99.

Lindsey, G., "Statistical Data Useful for the Operation of a Baseball Team." *Operations Research* 7, no. 2 (1959): 197–207.

Little, J. D. C. "A Proof for the Queueing Formula $L = \lambda W$." *Operations Research* 9 (1961): 383–387.

Love, R., and J. Hoey. "Management Science Improves Fast-Food Operations." *Interfaces* 20, no. 2 (1990): 21–29.

Luenberger, D. *Investment Science*. Oxford University Press (1997).

Machol, R. "An Application of the Assignment Problem." *Operations Research* 18 (1970): 745–746.

Magoulas, K., and D. Marinos-Kouris. "Gasoline Blending LP." *Oil and Gas Journal* (July 1988): 44–48.

Makuch, W., J. Dodge, J. Ecker, D. Granfors, and G. Hahn. "Managing Consumer Credit Delinquency in the US Economy: A Multi-Billion Dollar Management Science Application." *Interfaces* 22, no. 1 (1992): 90–109.

Marchewka, J. *Information Technology Project Management*, 2nd edition. Wiley (2006).

Marcus, A. "The Magellan Fund and Market Efficiency." *Journal of Portfolio Management* (Fall 1990): 90–109.

Martin, C., D. Jones, and P. Keskinocak. "Optimizing On-Demand Aircraft Schedules for Fractional Aircraft Operators." *Interfaces* 33, no. 5 (2003): 22–35.

McBride, R., and F. Zufryden. "An Integer Programming Approach to the Product Line Selection Problem." *Marketing Science* 7, no. 2 (1988): 126–139.

Meneses, C., Z. Lu, C. Oliveria, and P. Pardalos. "Optimal Solutions for the Closest-String Problem via Integer Programming." *Informs Journal on Computing* 16, no. 4 (2004): 419–429.

Merrick, J., J. R. van Dorp, T. Mazzuchi, J. Harrald, J. Spahn, and M. Grabowski. "The Prince William Sound Risk Assessment." *Interfaces* 32, no. 6 (2002): 25–40.

Miser, H. "Avoiding the Corrupting Lie of a Poorly Stated Problem." *Interfaces* 23, no. 6 (1993): 114–119.

Morrison, D., and R. Wheat. "Pulling the Goalie Revisited." *Interfaces* 16, no. 6 (1984): 28–34.

Moss, S., C. Dale, and G. Brame. "Sequence-Dependent Scheduling at Baxter International." *Interfaces* 30, no. 2 (2000): 70–80.

Muckstadt, J., and R. Wilson. "An Application of Mixed Integer Programming Duality to Scheduling Thermal Generating Systems." *IEEE Transactions on Power Apparatus and Systems* (1968): 1968–1978.

Norton, R. "A New Tool to Help Managers." *Fortune* (May 30, 1994): 135–140.

———— "Which Offices or Stores Perform Best? A New Tool Tells." *Fortune* October 31 (1994).

Owens, D., M. Brandeau, and C. Sox. "Effect of Relapse to High-Risk Behavior on the Costs and Benefits of a Program to Screen Women for Human Immunodeficiency Virus." *Interfaces* 28, no. 3 (1998): 52–74.

Paltiel, A., and K. Freedberg. "The Cost-Effectiveness of Preventing Cytomegalovirus Disease in AIDS Patients." *Interfaces* 28, no. 3 (1998): 34–51.

Patchong, A., T. Lemoine, and G. Kern. "Improving Car Body Production at PSA Peugeot Citroen." *Interfaces* 33, no. 1 (2003): 36–49.

Pfeifer, P., S. Bodily, R. Carraway, D. Clyman, and S. Frey. "Preparing Our Students to be Newsvendors." *Interfaces* 31, no. 6 (2001): 112–122.

Porteus, E. "Investing in Reduced Setups in the EOQ Model." *Management Science* 31, no. 8 (1985): 998–1010.

Quinn, P., B. Andrews, and H. Parsons. "Allocating Telecommunications Resources at L. L. Bean, Inc." *Interfaces* 21, no. 1 (1991): 75–91.

Ramaswami, V., D. Poole, S. Ahn, S. Byers, and A. Kaplan. "Ensuring Access to Emergency Services in the Presence of Long Internet Dial-Up Calls." *Interfaces* 35, no. 5 (2005): 411–422.

Ravindran, A. "On Compact Book Storage in Libraries." *Opsearch* 8 (1971): 245–252.

Reichheld, F. *The Loyalty Effect*. Harvard Business School Press (1996).

Riccio, L., J. Miller, and A. Little. "Polishing the Big Apple." *Interfaces* 16, no. 1 (1986): 83–88.

Robichek, A., D. Teichroew, and M. Jones. "Optimal Short-Term Financing Decisions." *Management Science* 12 (1965): 1–36.

Robinson, P., L. Gao, and S. Muggenborg. "Designing an Integrated Distribution System at DowBrands, Inc." *Interfaces* 23, no. 3 (1993): 107–117.

Rohn, E. "A New LP Approach to Bond Portfolio Management." *Journal of Financial and Quantitative Analysis* 22 (1987): 439–467 Chapter 4 additional application.

Rothstein, M. "Hospital Manpower Shift Scheduling by Mathematical Programming." *Health Services Research* (1973).

Saaty, T. *The Analytic Hierarchy Process*. New York: McGraw-Hill, 1988.

Sartoris, W., and M. Spruill. "Goal Programming and Working Capital Management." *Financial Management* 3 (1974): 67–74.

Schindler, S., and T. Semmel. "Station Staffing at Pan American World Airways." *Interfaces* 23, no. 3 (1993): 91–106.

Schrage, L. *Optimization Modeling Using LINDO*. ITP Publishing (1997).

Schultmann, F., B. Engels, and O. Rentz. "Closed-Loop Supply Chains for Spent Batteries." *Interfaces* 33, no. 6 (2003): 57–71.

Sery, S., V. Presti, and D. E. Shobrys. "Optimization Models for Restructuring BASF North America's Distribution System." *Interfaces* 31, no. 3 (2001): 55–65.

Sherman, H. D., and G. Ladino. "Managing Bank Productivity Using Data Envelopment Analysis (DEA)." *Interfaces* 25, no. 2 (1995): 60–80.

Silver, E., D. Pyke, and R. Peterson. *Inventory Management and Production Planning and Scheduling*, 3rd ed. New York: Wiley, 1998.

Smith, S. "Planning Transistor Production by Linear Programming." *Operations Research* 13 (1965): 132–139.

So, K., C. Tang, and R. Zavala. "Models for Improving Team Productivity at the Federal Reserve Bank." *Interfaces* 33, no. 2 (2003): 25–36.

Sohoni, M., T. G. Bailey, K. Martin, H. Carter, and E. Johnson. "Delta Optimizes Continuing-Qualification-Training Schedules for Pilots." *Interfaces* 33, no. 5 (2003): 57–70.

Sonderman, D., and P. Abrahamson. "Radiotherapy Design Using Mathematical Programming." *Operations Research* 33, no. 4 (1985): 705–725.

Spencer, T., A. Brigandi, D. Dargon, and M. Sheehan. "AT&T's Telemarketing Site Selection System Offers Customer Support." *Interfaces* 20, no. 1 (1990): 83–96.

Spengler, T., and M. Schroter. "Strategic Management of Spare Parts in Closed-Loop Supply Chains—A Sytem Dynamics Approach." *Interfaces* 33, no. 6 (2003): 7–17.

Srinivasan, M., S. Ebbing, and A. Swearingen. "Woodward Aircraft Engine Systems Sets Work-in-Process Levels for High-Variety, Low-Volume Products." *Interfaces* 33, no. 4 (2003): 61–69.

Steuer, R. "Sausage Blending Using Multiple Objective Programming." *Management Science* 30 (1984): 1376–1384.

Stidham, S. "A Last Word on $L = \lambda W$." *Operations Research* 22 (1974): 417–421.

Stonebraker, J. "How Bayer Makes Decisions to Develop New Drugs." *Interfaces* 32, no. 6 (2002): 77–90.

Tanner, M. *Practical Queueing Analysis*. Berkshire, England: McGraw-Hill International (UK) Ltd., 1995.

Tavana, M. "CROSS: A Multicriteria Group-Decision-Making Model for Evaluating and Prioritizing Advanced-Technology Projects at NASA." *Interfaces* 33, no. 3 (2003): 40–56.

Taylor, B., and A. Keown. "Planning Urban Recreational Facilities with Goal Programming." *Journal of Operational Research Society* 29, no. 8 (1984): 751–758.

Thomas, J. "Linear Programming Models for Production Advertising Decisions." *Management Science* 17, no. 8 (1971): B474–B484.

Troyer, L., J. Smith, S. Marshall, E. Yaniv, S. Tayur, M. Barkman, A. Kaya, and Y. Liu. "Improving Asset Management and Order Fulfillment at Deere & Company's C&CE Division." *Interfaces* 35, no. 1 (2005): 76–87.

Tyagi, R., P. Kalish, K. Akbay, and G. Munshaw. "GE Plastics Optimizes the Two-Echelon Global Fulfillment Network at Its High Performance Polymers Division." *Interfaces* 34, no. 5 (2004): 359–366.

van de Klundert, J. J. Kuipers, F. Spieksma, and M. Winkels. "Selecting Telecommunication Carriers to Obtain Volume Discounts." *Interfaces* 35, no. 2 (2005): 124–132.

van den Briel, M., R. Villalobos, G. Hogg. "America West Airlines Develops Efficient Boarding Strategies." *Interfaces* 35, no. 3 (2005): 191–201.

van der Heijden, M., A. van Harten, M. Ebben, Y. Saanen, E. Valentin, and A. Verbraeck. "Using Simulation to Design an Automated Underground System for Transporting Freight Around Schiphol Airport." *Interfaces* 32, no. 4 (2002): 1–19.

Vasko, F., J. Wolfe, and K. Stott. "Optimal Selection of Ingot Sizes via Set Covering." *Operations Research* 35, no. 3 (1987): 346–353.

Volkema, R. "Managing the Process of Formulating the Problem." *Interfaces* 25, no. 3 (1995): 81–87.

Walkenbach, J. *Excel Charts*. Wiley, 2002.

Walker, W. "Using the Set Covering Problem to Assign Fire Companies to Firehouses." *Operations Research* 22 (1974): 275–277.

Weber, S. "A Modified Analytic Hierarchy Process for Automated Manufacturing Decisions." *Interfaces* 23, no. 4 (1993): 75–84.

Welling, P. "A Goal Programming Model for Human Resource Allocation in a CPA Firm." *Accounting, Organizations and Society* 2 (1977): 307–316.

Westerberg, C., B. Bjorklund, and E. Hultman. "An Application of Mixed Integer Programming in a Swedish Steel Mill." *Interfaces* 7, no. 2 (1977): 39–43.

Winston, W. *Decision Making Under Uncertainty with RISKOptimizer*. Palisade Corporation, 1999.

———— *Introduction to Probability Models*, 4th ed. Belmont, CA: Brooks/Cole–Thomson Learning, 2004.

Yu, G., J. Pachon, B. Thengvall, D. Chandler, and A. Wilson. "Optimizing Pilot Planning and Training for Continental Airlines." *Interfaces* 34, no. 4 (2004): 253–264.

————, M. Arguello, G. Song, S. McCowan, and A. White. "A New Era for Crew Recovery at Continental Airlines." *Interfaces* 33, no. 1 (2003): 5–22.

Zahedi, F. "The Analytic Hierarchy Process—A Survey of the Method and Its Applications." *Interfaces* 16, no. 4 (1986): 96–108.

Zangwill, W. "The Limits of Japanese Production Theory." *Interfaces* 22, no. 5 (1992): 14–25.

## A

ABS function, limitations of, 414

Absolute addresses, spreadsheet modeling, 31

Absolute percentage errors (APEs), regression analysis, exponential trend lines, 913–915

Activity duration
  Critical Path Method (CMP) model, 865–872
  resource allocation modeling, crashing the activities, 880–884
  uncertain activity times modeling, 890–895

Activity-on-arc (AOA) networks, Critical Path Method (CMP) model of project management, 865–872

Activity-on-node (AON) networks, Critical Path Method (CMP) model of project management, 865–872
  local area network (LAN) creation, 868–872

Actual value, regression analysis, 908

Additivity, linear modeling, 94–96

Adjusted R-square value, multiple regression analysis, 925

Advertising models
  goal programming scheduling model, 465–471
  linear programming techniques, 133–142
  market share modeling, 706
  multiobjective decision making, exposure trade-offs example, 480–483
  nonlinear response functions, 373–376
  response and selection models, 368–376
  television advertising example, 133–134

After-tax profits
  car development planning model, 674–676
  transportation models, automobile production and shipment, 233–235

Aggregate planning models
  linear programming, 150–160
  worker and production example, 150–160

"Aha" effect, 18

Airline industry
  crew recovery model, 272–273
  network models, 260–273
    crew scheduling, 260–263
    flight scheduling example, 265–273
  on-demand aircraft scheduling model, 272
  pilot training and staffing models, 272
  queueing model example, 793–794
  simulation modeling

online boarding example, 579–580
  real-world applications, 583

Algebraic models
  multiperiod production, 108–117
  product mix model, 100–107
  spreadsheet models vs., 118
  two-variable optimization modeling, 76–85

Algorithms. See also Genetic algorithms
  branch and bound algorithm, optimization programming, 288–289
  Critical Path Method (CMP) model of project management, 866–872
  genetic algorithms, 415–416
  management science models and, 1–2
  nonlinear optimization, pricing models, 355–356
  optimization modeling, 74
  soft Or modeling approach, 2

AllDifferent constraint, traveling salesperson problem, 456–457

Allen-Cunneen approximation, queueing models, nonexponential interarrival/service times, 823–826

Allowable increase/decrease, sensitivity analysis, optimization modeling, 87–93

AMARCO, Inc. case study, linear programming, 207–209

American Office Systems, Inc., linear programming case study, 210–214

Analytical models
  analytic hierarchy process (AHP), 484–493
    consistency checking, 489–492
    consistency index calculation, 491–492
    job selection example, 484–492
    miscellaneous applications, 493
    pairwise comparison matrices, 485–489
  defined, 9
  queueing models as, 795
    short-run behavior approximation, 830–834
    steady-state models, 807–826
      bank queueing model, 812–815, 818–819, 823–826
      basic single-server models, 807–811
      emergency phone service example, 822
      Erlang loss model, 819–820
      fast server/slow servers comparison, 816–817
      fire engine request example, 820–822

multiple-server model, 811–815, 822–826
  nonexponential bank queueing model, 823–826
  postal branch queueing example, 808–811
  traffic intensity effects, 817

Annual costs
  economic order quantity models, setup cost reductions, 752–754
  probabilistic inventory model, (R,Q) ordering policy, 769–771

Approximation techniques
  linear modeling, 95–96
  model development, 11
  portfolio optimization, 347

Arcs and arc capacities
  assignment models, 239
    school bus route example, 237–240
  Critical Path Method (CMP) model of project management, 865–872
  equipment replacement models, 255–258
  flight scheduling network model, 267–271
  geographical shortest path models, 253
  minimum cost network flow models, 241–250
    flow balance, 244–245
    shortest path models, 250
    transportation models, 224–225

Arrivals characteristics. See also Interarrival times, queueing models
  forecasting models of, 965
  queueing models, 796–797
    multiple-server queueing model, 811–815
    processing simulation case study, 847–850
    traffic intensity effects, 818

Asset management
  financial modeling case study, 734–735
  nonlinear optimization modeling, 409–410
  simulation modeling, case studies, 582–583

Assignment models
  basic principles, 235–241
  bus route example, 237–241
  crew scheduling network model, 261–265
  location assignment/fixed cost models, 321–325
  location assignment models, 309–319
  manager assignment example, 240

Assumption validity/nonvalidity
   multiple regression analysis, 929
   nonlinear optimization
         modeling, 350–351
@RISK software
   Asian call options model, 693
   basic features, 19
   customer loyalty modeling, churn reduc-
         tion case study, 702–703
   European call options
         modeling, 686–689
   Latin Hypercube sampling, 619–621
   market share modeling, 705–706
   ordering simulation models, 774–778
   probabilistic inventory model, 761–763
   retirement investment modeling, 681–685
   return on portfolio case study, 690–691
   RISKCORRMAT function, project
         management, 895
   RISKDUNIFORM function, games of
         chance modeling, 709–711
   RISKMEAN function, yield uncertain-
         ties, simulation modeling, 666
   RISKOUTPUT function, simulation
         modeling, 616–621
   RISKPERCENTILE function, yield
         uncertainties, simulation
         modeling, 666
   RISKPERT function, uncertain activity
         times modeling, 892–895
   RISKSIMTABLE function
      government contract bidding
            example, 655–657
      simulation modeling, 624–627,
            633–639
   Simulation Data report, NCAA Basket-
         ball Tournament modeling, 713
   simulation modeling, 615–631
      basic features, 615
      binomial distribution, 597–599
      cash balance model, 679–681
      cumul and general
            distribution, 599–601
      discrete function, 593–594
      flaw of averages, 623–624
      funnel simulation model, 668–671
      limitations, 627
      loading protocols, 616
      normal distribution, 595–596
      probability distribution
            functions, 592–593
      results evaluation, 621–623, 630
      RISKCORRMAT function, 636–639
      RISKSIMTABLE function, 624–627,
            633–639, 721–722
      sensitivity analysis, 630–631
      Server input variables, 627
      single random input variables, 616
      triangular distribution, 596–597
      uniform distribution, 591
      Walton Bookstore case study,
            617–621 628–631

   warranty costs, 657–661
   yield uncertainties, simulation model-
         ing, 661–666
   TOPRANK add-in and, 714–722
Autocorrelation of residuals, multiple
      regression analysis, 930
Automated manufacturing, analytic
      hierarchy process and, 493
Automated meter reading, location assign-
      ment models, 314
Automated teller machines (ATMs), queue-
      ing models
   service evaluation case study, 859–860
   service time distribution
         example, 801–803
Automobile production and shipment
   car development planning
         model, 673–676
   simulated queueing models, car body
         case study, 850
   transportation models
      regional shipments, 223–224
      tax rate variations, 232–235
Average percentage errors (APEs), price-
      demand relationships, 53–56
Average ratings, sports teams ratings
      model, 384–386

**B**
Backlogging
   aggregate planning model, 155–160
   economic order quantity models,
         shortage costs, 749–751
   inventory modeling, shortage/penalty
         costs, 742
   linearization, 157–160
Backorder estimates, probabilistic inven-
      tory model, (R,Q) ordering
      policy, 769–771
Backward pass, Critical Path Method
      (CMP) model of project
      management, 867–872
Balance constraints
   advertising models, goal
         programming, 468–471
   multiperiod production model, 110–111
Balking behavior, queueing models, 797
Banking industry
   arrival times forecasting, 965
   data envelopment analysis case study, 190
   queueing models
      automated teller machine case studies,
            801–803, 859–860
      interarrival and service time
            distributions, 801–803
      multiple-server example, 812–815
      nonexponential interarrival/service
            times, 822–826
      simulated queueing example, 838–842
      traffic intensity effects, 817–818
Base categories, dummy variables, multiple
      regression analysis, 926–930

BASF network modeling example,
      221–222
Batch indexes, simulation modeling, yield
      uncertainties, drug development
      case study, 662–666
Bayes' rule
   decision making uncertainty, 534–538
   drug testing example, 535–538
   multistage decision tree
         drug testing example, 540–541
         marketing example, 545–552
Before-tax profits, car development plan-
      ning model, 674–676
Beginning inventory, ordering simulation
      models, 775–778
Below cost pricing models, 362
Benefit-cost table. *See also* Cost analysis
   economic order quantity models, order
         synchronization, 754–757
   multistage decision tree, 540
   queueing models, multiple-server
         queueing model, 813–815
Best-fitting curves, price-demand
      relationships, 49–51
Best order quantity calculations, simulation
      modeling probability
      distribution, 609–610
   @RISK software, 625–627
Beta stock estimation, modeling
      techniques, 396–401
Bidding process
   decision making uncertainty and,
         513–518
   simulation modeling, 653–657
Binary variables
   capital budget models, 290–297
   fixed-cost models, 297, 299–304, 306
   location assignment models, 319
   optimization modeling, 286–287
Binding constraints, two-variable
      optimization modeling, 85
Binomial distribution, simulation
      modeling, 597–599
Blending models
   linear programming, 160–167
   proportionality, 94–96
Blitzing techniques, market share
      modeling, 703–706
Blocking, simulation queueing
      models, series system
      simulation, 844
Bond investment strategy, investment
      modeling, 733
Bond purchases
   linear programming for, 182–183
   pension fund modeling, 180–183
Bookshelf cost projection model,
      spreadsheet example, 29–33
Bottlenecks, two-variable optimization
      modeling, 85
Bounded probability, simulation modeling,
      587–588

Brainstorming, *soft Or* modeling approach and, 2–3
Branch and bound algorithm
  advertising model, 141–142
  optimization programming, 288–289
Brand dominance, market share modeling and, 703–706
Breakeven analysis
  Cell Comments function and, 36
  Formula Auditing tool and, 39–40
  Goal Seek function and, 38–39
  Great Threads example, 34–35
  limitations, 39
  one-way data tables, 37–38
  range names in, 35–36
  response rates, 36–37
  spreadsheet modeling, 33–41
Budget constraints
  advertising model, 137–138
  advertising models, goal programming scheduling model, 467–471
  capital budget models, 293–294
Buffers, simulation queueing models, 844
  processing example with blocking, 844–850
Business objectives. *See also* Financial modeling
  breakeven analysis, 34
  cost projections, 29–33
  price-demand relationships, 47–56
  quantity discounts and demand uncertainty, 42–46
  time value of money, 58–62

# C

Call options, simulation modeling
  Asian call option, 691–693
  European call options, 686–689
  return on portfolio case study, 690–691
Capacities
  aggregate planning model, 152–153
  combinatorial models, loading products example, 429–432
  fixed-cost models, 299
  location assignment/fixed cost models, 323
  optimization models, strategic planning, 342
  peak-load pricing model, 363–366
  transportation models, 224
    arc capacities, 224–225
    sensitivity analysis, 228–231
Capital asset pricing model
  beta stock estimation, 396–401
  time value of money, 57–62
Capital budget models
  check sequencing on not sufficient funds fees, 295–297
  integer variables, 290–297
Capital costs, inventory modeling, 742
Carrying costs, inventory modeling, 742
Cash balance model, 676–681

Cash flow
  customer loyalty modeling, 697–703
  European call options modeling, 688–689
  financial models, 175–183
  pension fund modeling, 180–183
  return on portfolio case study, 690–691
  time value of money, 60–62
  warranty cost simulation modeling, 659–661
Cash investments, capital budget models, 291
Catalog phone order case study, queueing modeling, 857–858
Categorical variables, multiple regression analysis, 925–930
Causal models, defined, 905
Cell comments
  applications for, 68
  breakeven analysis, 36–41
Certainty equivalents, risk management and, 559–560
Change distributions, market share modeling, 703–706
Changeover costs, combinatorial models, production scheduling example, 433–437
Changing cells
  advertising models
    goal programming, 468–471
    integer constraints, 140
  aggregate planning model, 151–160
  backlogging and, 159–160
  breakeven analysis, 38–41
  data envelopment analysis, 187
  Evolutionary Solver
    genetic algorithms mutations, 418–419
    limits on, 422
  genetic algorithms, 415–416
  optimization modeling, 73–74
  peak-load pricing model, 365–366
  pension fund modeling, 178–183
  product mix model, 101–107
  Solver limitations with, 414
  sports teams ratings model, 384–386
  transportation models, 229–235
    alternative network models, 230–231
  two-variable optimization modeling, 78–85
  workforce scheduling models, 144–149
Chart tools. *See also* Graphical solutions
  cash balance simulation model, 680–681
  cost projection model, 31–33
  Critical Path Method (CMP) model of project management, Gantt Chart, LAN project example, 871–872
  decision analysis
    sensitivity charts, 532–534
    spider chart, 532
    strategy region and tornado charts, 530–531

placement options, 41
product development model, TOPRANK Addin tool, 719–722
queueing models, short-run behavior approximation, 833–834
spreadsheet modeling, 31–33
Check sequencing on NSF fees, capital budget models, 295–297
Chromosomes, genetic algorithms, 415–416
  Evolutionary Solver GAs, 418
Churn/churn rate, customer loyalty modeling, 695–703
  reduction case study, 699–703
Classification matrix, discriminant analysis, 450–453
Closed queueing network (CQN), airline manufacturing example, 793–794
Cluster analysis, Evolutionary software modeling, 444–449
Coefficient of time, regression-based trend models
  exponential trend lines, 913–915
  linear trend lines, 913
College fund investment, simulation modeling, 732
Color coding, spreadsheet modeling, 28
Combinatorial models
  loading products example, 429–432
  optimization of, 428–437
  production scheduling example, 432–437
  traveling salesperson problem, 454–457
Common plant capacity, location assignment/fixed cost models, 325
Communication to management, seven-step modeling process, 9, 12–13
Comparison models, simulation modeling, RISKSIMTABLE function, 634–639
Competition, government contract bidding, simulation modeling, 655–657
Complementary products, pricing models, retailing example, 360–362
Complete backlogging, inventory modeling, 742
Complete enumeration method, optimization programming, branch and bound algorithm, 288–289
Concave function
  nonlinear optimization modeling, 348–349
  risk management, utility function, 555
Conditional formatting tool, price-demand relationships, 53–56
Conditional probability
  decision making uncertainty and, 575
  queueing models, memoryless property, 800–801
Confidence interval, simulation modeling probability distribution, 608–609
Consistency index calculation, analytic hierarchy process (AHP), 491–492

Consistency verification, analytic hierarchy process (AHP), 489–492
Constant elasticity demand, pricing models, 353–356
Constant times, queueing models, processing simulation case study, 848–850
Constraints
  advertising models, 134–142
    integer constraints, 140–142
  aggregate planning model, 151
  airline industry network model, 261
  assignment models, 237–238
  backlogging and, 159–160
  blending models, 161–162, 166–167
  capital budget models, 291
  combinatorial models, loading products example, 430–431
  crew scheduling network model, 261
  cutting stock models, 328
  data envelopment analysis, 185
  efficiency constraints, data envelopment analysis, 187–191
  equipment replacement models, 255
  Evolutionary Solver function, 418–418
  facility location models, 378–381
  financial models, 174, 177–183
  fixed-cost models, 298, 305
  flight scheduling network model, 267
  genetic algorithms, 415–416
  geographical shortest path models, 252
  goal programming, 466
  location assignment/fixed cost models, 321–322
  location assignment models, 315
  minimum cost network flow models, 242
    tomato production and shipping example, 244
  multiperiod production model, 110–117
  nonlinear response functions, advertising models, 373–376
  optimization modeling, 73–74
    sensitivity analysis, 88–93
  peak-load pricing model, 363–366
  pension fund modeling, 178–183
  pricing models, 353
    retailing example, 360–362
  production process models, 168–173
  product mix model, 99–107, 107
  resource allocation modeling, crashing the activities function, 882–884
  set-covering models, 310
  transportation models, 224
    flow balance, 229–235
  traveling salesperson problem, 456–457
  two-variable models, 74–75, 79–85
    dessert example, 88–89
  workforce scheduling models, 143–149
Continental Airlines, network modeling, 272
Contingency plan, multistage decision tree, 544–552
Continuing-qualification-training schedules, network modeling, 272

Continuous probability distribution, simulation modeling, 585–586
Continuous review models, inventory modeling, periodic review vs., 741
Control charts, processing simulation models, 668–671
Convex function, nonlinear optimization modeling, 348–349
Copy capacity
  beta stock estimation, 399
  peak-load pricing model, 364–366
  PrecisionTree® subtree copying, 527
Correlated input variables, simulation modeling, 635–639
Cost analysis
  advertising model, 138–139
  aggregate planning model, 150–160, 160
  combinatorial models, loading products example, 431
  data envelopment analysis, 189–191
  discontinuities and, 414
  economic order quantity models, shortage costs, 749–751
  equipment replacement model, arc costs, 256–258
  inventory management modeling, 741–742
  multiobjective decision making, seasonal production example, 501
  multiple regression analysis
    future cost predictions, 925
    multiple product example, 921–922
  ordering simulation models, 776–778
  product development, project management example, 861–862
  product mix model, 102–107
  queueing models, multiple-server queueing model, 813–815
  regression analysis, single-product cost estimation example, 916–919
  resource monitoring and, 876–880
    crashing the activities models, 883–885
  spreadsheet modeling projections, 29–33
  spreadsheet projections, 29–33
  supply chain inventory models, 782–784
  transportation models, 226
  waiting line optimization model, 6–7
  warranty costs, simulation modeling, 657–661
Counts, multistage decision analysis, Bayes' rule, 536–538
Covariance matrix, portfolio optimization, 392–394
Craps, games of chance modeling, 708–711
Crashing the activities, resource allocation modeling, 880–884
Creaming strategy, model optimization, 15
Crew recovery, network modeling, 272–273
Critical activities
  Critical Path Method (CMP) model of project management, 866–872
  project management, uncertain activity times modeling, 893

Critical fractile, newsvendor inventory model and, 761–763
Critical Path Method (CMP)
  crashing the activities in, 881–884
  project management principles, 863–864
    basic model, 865–872
    uncertain activity times modeling, 892–895
    resource allocation monitoring, 877–880
Crossover, genetic algorithms, 415–416
Cross-sectional data, regression analysis, 906
Cumul distribution, simulation modeling, 599–601
Currency valuations, pricing models, 358–359
Curve fitting. See also Trade-off curve
  optimization modeling, 437–441
  spreadsheet analysis, 47–56
Customer averages, queueing models, 805
Customer demands
  discriminant analysis, 450–453
  economic order quantity models, shortage costs, 749–751
  nonlinear pricing models, 423
  nonlinear response functions, advertising models, 373–376
  queueing models, arrivals characteristics, 796–797
  transportation models, 224
Customer loyalty
  churn reduction model, 699–703
  simulation modeling, 695–703
Cutting stock models, 327–331
Cyclic component
  economic order quantity models, order synchronization, 756
  time series models, 933–937
Cytomegalovirus, treatment modeling for, 24

**D**

Data collection
  advertising models, 134–142
    exposure trade-off example, 480–483
  airline industry network models, 260–261, 266
  analytic hierarchy process, job selection, 484
  capital budget models, 290
  cluster analysis, 445
  combinatorial models
    loading products example, 429
    production scheduling example, 433–437
  crew scheduling network model, 260–261
  Critical Path Method (CMP) of project management, local area network (LAN) creation, 868–872
  cutting stock models, 327–328
  data envelopment analysis, 185

decision making uncertainty
    flaw of averages example, 519
    government contract bidding
        example, 514
discriminant analysis, 451
equipment replacement models, 255
facility location models, 378
financial models, 174
fixed-cost models, 298, 304–305
geographical shortest path
    models, 251–252
goal programming, 465
government contract bidding
    model, 654–657
location assignment/fixed cost
    models, 321
multistage decision tree, 538
    marketing model, 544–552
Pareto optimality and trade-off
    curves, 477
pricing models, 352–356
response and selection advertising
    models, 369
set-covering models, 310
seven-step modeling process, 8, 10–11
simulation modeling, Walton bookstore
    case study, 604–608
S-shaped curve fitting model, 438–441
transportation models, 224
    automobile production and
        shipment, 231–232
    traveling salesperson problem, 454–455
    workforce scheduling models, 143
Data envelopment analysis (DEA), linear
    programming, 184–191
Data sets, exponential smoothing
    models, 948–952
Winter's seasonality method, 954–956
Data tables
    breakeven analysis, 37–41
    quantity discounts and demand
        uncertainty, 44–46
    simulation modeling probability
        distribution, best order quantity
        calculations, 609–612
Decision analysis
    components of, 506–521
    multiobjective decision making
        analytic hierarchy process, 484–493
        goal programming, 465–471
        miscellaneous applications, 493
        NASA project evaluation and prioriti-
            zation case study, 463–464
        optimization strategies, 464
        Pareto optimality and trade-off
            curves, 475–483
    optimization modeling, 15
    seven-step modeling process, 9, 12
    time value of money modeling, 57–62
    uncertainty and
        basic principles, 505–506
        Bayes' rule, 534–538
        decision analysis components, 506–521

drug development case study,
    503–504
examples of, 505–506
flaw of averages, 519–521
government contract bidding
    example, 513–518
multistage decision problems,
    538–552
Precision Tree Addin, 521–534
pricing trends example, 575
risk reduction, 554–560
shoe company case study, 574
technology innovation
    example, 576–577
two-way data table, 45–46
waiting line optimization model, 6–7
Decision support system (DSS)
    investment optimization
        modeling, 395
    linear programming, 118–120
Decision trees
    basic components of, 505
    conventions, 511–512
    folding-back procedures, 512
    government contract bidding
        example, 516–518
    interpretation guidelines, 527–528
    PrecisionTree model, 523–527
        multistage decision tree, 546–552
    risk management and, 557–560
Decision variables
    advertising models, 134–142
    aggregate planning model, 151
    airline industry network model, 261
    analytic hierarchy process (AHP),
        487–488
    assignment models, 237–238
    blending models, 161–162
    breakeven analysis, 36–41
    capital budget models, 291
    cluster analysis, 446–447
    combinatorial models, loading products
        example, 430
    crew scheduling network model, 261
    cutting stock models, 328
    data envelopment analysis, 185
    discriminant analysis, 451
    equipment replacement models, 255
    Evolutionary Solver software, bounds
        on, 420
    facility location models, 378–381
    financial models, 174
    fixed-cost models, 298, 305
    flight scheduling network model, 267
    geographical shortest path models, 252
    goal programming, 466
    location assignment/fixed cost models,
        321–322
    location assignment models, 315
    minimum cost network flow
        models, 242
        tomato production and shipping
            example, 244

multiperiod production model, 110–117
nonlinear pricing models
    optimization modeling, 347
    single price model, 424
    two-part tariff model, 426
nonlinear response functions, advertising
    models, 373–376
optimization modeling, 73–74
peak-load pricing model, 363–366
pension fund modeling, 178–183
pricing models, 353
    retailing example, 360–362
probabilistic inventory model, $(R,Q)$
    ordering policy, 767–771
production process models, 168–173
product mix model, 99–107
quantity discounts case study, 42–46
resource allocation modeling, crashing
    the activities function, 882–884
set-covering models, 310
simulation modeling probability
    distribution, best order quantity
    calculations, 609–610
spreadsheet modeling, 24–25
S-shaped curve fitting model, 439
transportation models, 224
two-variable model, 75–76
    graphical solutions, 77–78
workforce scheduling models, 143–149
Decreasing marginal effect, product mix
    model, 107
Deflators, retirement investment
    modeling, 684
Delinquency movement matrices (DMMs),
    GE Capital case study, 14–16
Dell supply chain inventory model, 737–738
Delta Airlines network modeling
    example, 272
Demand data
    combinatorial models, loading products
        example, 429
    decision making and uncertainty
        and, 574
    economic order quantity models, 743
    forecasting models and, 964
    inventory modeling
        external vs. internal demand, 740
        newsvendor inventory model, 763
    minimum cost network flow
        models, 242–250
    multiperiod production model, 110–117
    nonlinear optimization modeling, 347
        pricing models, 352–356
    optimization models, strategic
        planning, 342
    ordering simulation models, 776–778
    peak-load pricing model, 364–366
    pricing models, retailing
        example, 361–362
    probabilistic inventory model, $(R,Q)$
        ordering policy, 764–771
    probabilistic inventory models,
        newsvendor model, 760–763

Demand data (*Continued*)
quantity discounts and, 42–46
simulation modeling
correlated input effects, 635–639
Walton bookstore case study, 604–608
transportation models, 228–235
Demand-price relationships, spreadsheet
modeling, 47–56
Deming's funnel experiment, simulation
modeling, 667
Demographic data, cluster analysis, 445–449
Density function
continuous probability distribution,
simulation modeling, 585–586
queueing models, exponential
distribution, 799–800
Dependent variables, regression
analysis, 906
Depreciation, car development planning
model, 674–676
Descriptive model
defined, 4
waiting-line example, 4–6
Destination nodes
minimum cost network flow models, 244
transportation models, 223
Deterministic inventory models
defined, 739
probabilistic models *vs.,* 740
Development process
modeling, 8–9, 11
optimization modeling, 73–74
Deviation minimization, goal programming
scheduling model, 468–471
DFI Aeronomics, problem-solving
algorithms, 1–2
Disallowed routes, transportation
models, 230–231
"Disallowed routes," transportation
models, 230–231
Disaster recovery centers, location
assignment models, 314
Discontinuities, Solver limitations with, 414
Discount values
Asian call options, 692–693
customer loyalty modeling, 697–703
defined, 57
European call options modeling, 688–689
quantity discounts and demand uncertainty, 42–46
supply chain inventory models, 781–784
time value of money, 57–62
Discrete variables
decision making uncertainty and, 508–509
simulation modeling probability distribution, 585–586
@RISK function, 593–594
Walton bookstore case study, 606–608
Discriminant analysis, Evolutionary Solver
example, 450–453
Distance calculations
shortest path models, 251–253
traveling salesperson problem, 454–457

Distribution centers (DCs)
BASF network modeling
example, 221–222
fixed cost models and
location of, 307–308
Kellogg Planning System example,
131–132
minimum cost network flow
models, 249
newsvendor inventory model, 763
Divisibility, linear modeling, 94–96
Downtime parameters, airline industry
network models, 263–264
Downward trends, time series
models, 933–934
Drug development case study
decision-making uncertainty
and, 503–504
simulation modeling, yield
uncertainties, 661–666
TOPRANK Addin modeling, 715–722
Drug testing case study
Bayes' rule, 535–538
multistage decision tree, 538–543
Dual-objective optimization model, advertising models, 137–142
Due in later orders, ordering simulation
models, 776–778
Dummy variables, multiple regression
analysis, 926–930
Durations calculations, crashing the
activities models, 883
Dynamic market share estimation, simulation modeling, 703–706

E
Economic analysis
business problem solving and, 2
optimization models, 6–7
queueing models, multiple-server queueing model, 813–815
Economic order quantity models, inventory
management modeling, 743–759
camera ordering example, 744–746
multiple products, 759
order synchronization, 754–757
quantity discounts, 746–748
setup cost reductions, 752–754
shortages models, 749–751
Effective capacities, fixed-cost
models, 299–300
Efficiency constraints
data envelopment analysis, 187–191
portfolio optimization, 393–394
Either-or constraints, fixed-cost
models, 305–306
Elasticity, demand function, pricing
models, 353–356
Emergency orders, ordering simulation
models, 776–778
Emergency phone service, queueing model
applications, 822
Ending cash, financial models, 176–183

Ending inventory
aggregate planning model, 158–160
ordering simulation models, 776–778
Equality, two-variable optimization
models, 83
Equally likely probabilities, supply chain
inventory models, 783–784
Equipment replacement models, 254–258
periodic maintenance example, 258
Erlang loss model, queueing model
applications, 819–822
Errors analysis
beta stock estimation, 399
multiple regression analysis, nonconstant
error variance, 930
multistage decision tree, 542
S-shaped curve fitting model, prediction
errors, 439
time series models, forecasting error
measurement, 935–936
Estimation procedures
beta stock estimation, 396–401
response and selection advertising
models, 370, 372–376
European call options, simulation
modeling, 686–689
Evolutionary Solver software,
413, 416–422
basic properties, 416–417
changing cell limitations, 422
cluster analysis, 444–449
combinatorial models
loading products example, 431–432
production scheduling
example, 432–437
discriminant analysis, 450–453
genetic algorithm applications, 418–419
"incumbent" feature, 421
multiple-project scheduling, 888–889
nonlinear function with local
maxima, 417–418
nonlinear pricing models, 422–428
miscellaneous applications, 427–428
single-pricing model, 423–426
two-part tariff model, 426–427
options dialog box, 419–421
portfolio optimization
modeling, 442–444
random search mechanisms, 420
resource allocation modeling, crashing
the activities function, 883–884
sequence-dependent scheduling, 457
S-shaped curve fitting model, 439–441
student team assignment example, 462
supply chain inventory models, 782–784
traveling salesperson problem, 456–457
Excel software
Add Constraint Dialog Box, 83–85
Add Trendline box, pricing models,
354–356
Analysis ToolPak Add-In
dummy variable creation, 928–930
multiple regression analysis, 922–925

Cell Comments function, 36
cell references, 26–27
ChartTools function, 31–33
Conditional Formatting tool, 53–56
COUNTIF function
    customer loyalty modeling, 698–703
    discriminant analysis, 452
    minimum cost network flow
        models, 246–250
    NCAA Basketball Tournament
        modeling, 713
    portfolio optimization, 443
Ctrl+Enter function
    time value of money model, 60
    workforce scheduling models,
        145–149
EXP function, regression analysis,
    exponential trend lines, 915
features of, 18–19
Formula Auditing tool, 39–41
$f_x$ button, 44
Goal Seek function, 38–41
hard codes, 26
IF function (*See* IF function (Excel))
INDEX function, 54–56
    cluster analysis, 448
    traveling salesperson
        problem, 455–457
intermediate outputs, 27
MATCH function (*See* MATCH function
    (Excel software))
MMULT function, portfolio optimiza-
    tion, 392–394
NORMDIST/NORMSDIST functions,
    probabilistic inventory
    model, 769–771
NPV function, 60
RANDBETWEEN function, games of
    chance modeling, 709–711
RAND function
    customer loyalty modeling, 696–697
    uniform probability
        distribution, 588–591
    yield uncertainties, simulation
        modeling, 664–666
range names in, 27
Recalculation key, simulation modeling,
    probability distribution, 584
Relative and Absolute addresses, cost
    projection model, 31
row and column sum
    calculations, 153
Scenario Manager function, supply chain
    inventory models, 784
simulation modeling tools, 603–613
    best order quantity, 609–610
    confidence intervals, 608–609
    data table applications, 610–612
    demand estimation, 604–613
    freezing options, 610
    histogram creation, 646–648
    results, 607–608
    two-way data table, 612–613

Solver function (*See* Solver function
    (Excel software))
SolverTable Add-In, 89–93
    advertising exposure trade-off
        example, 481–483
    airline industry network
        models, 265–273
    assignment models, 240–241
    combinatorial models, 432
    multiperiod production model, 115–117
    pricing models, 361–362
    production process models, 173
    profit maximization/pollution mini-
        mization trade-off curve, 478–480
    transportation models, 228–235
SolverTolerance setting
    capital budget models, 294–297
    cutting stock models, 330–331
    integer constraints, 147
    optimization programming, 289–290
split screen function, 59
SQRT function, advertising exposure
    trade-off example, 482–483
StatTools add-in, exponential smoothing
    models, 947–956
strengths and limitations of, 17–18
SUMIF function
    airline industry network
        models, 263–264
    assignment models, 239–241
    flight scheduling network
        model, 268–273
    geographical shortest path models, 253
    minimum cost network flow
        models, 245–250
    transportation models, 230–235
SUMPRODUCT function
    advertising exposure trade-off
        example, 481–483
    advertising model, 135–136
    airline industry network models, 264
    Bayes' rule, 537–538
    capital budget models, 291–292
    combinatorial models, 435–437
    cutting stock models, 328–331
    data envelopment analysis, 186
    discriminant analysis, 451
    financial models, 175–183
    fixed-cost models, 299–300
    flaw of averages and decision
        uncertainty, 520–521
    flight scheduling network
        model, 270–273
    goal programming scheduling
        model, 467
    location assignment/fixed cost
        models, 323
    location assignment models, 317
    nonlinear pricing models, 425
    portfolio optimization, 443
    pricing models, 361–362
    product mix model, 100–107
    quantity discount model, 46

set-covering models, hub locations, 311
two-variable optimization
    modeling, 80–85
SUMSQ function, single-product cost
    estimation example, 918–919
SUMXMY2 function, facility location
    models, 379–381
Transpose function, production process
    models, 170–173
Trendline Options function, 49–50
Use Automatic Scaling function, 95–96
VLOOKUP function, 44–46
    cluster analysis, 447–449
    data envelopment analysis, 186
    retirement investment
        modeling, 683–685
    simulation modeling probability
        distribution, 606–608
    sports teams ratings model, 384–386
    traveling salesperson problem,
        455–457
Excess exposures, advertising models,
    137–142
Exchange rates, pricing models, 358–359
Exercise price/exercise date, European call
    options modeling, 686–689
Expected annual return, portfolio
    optimization, 392–394
Expected costs, probabilistic inventory
    model, $(R,Q)$ ordering
    policy, 766–771
Expected monetary value (EMV)
    decision making uncertainty and, 508
        calculation and interpretation, 509–510
        flaw of averages, 520–521
        government contract bidding
            example, 516–518
        PrecisionTree® sensitivity
            analysis, 529–530
        risk profile, 512–513
        sensitivity charts, 532–534
        spider chart, 532
        strategy region and tornado
            charts, 530–531
    decision tree components and, 511–512
    financial simulation modeling, 676
    risk management and, 554–560
    venture capital case study, 557–560
Expected sales revenue, supply chain
    inventory models, 781–784
Expected utility maximizers, risk manage-
    ment and, 554–560
    venture capitalism case study, 560
Expected value of perfect information
    (EVPI), multistage decision
    tree, 543
    marketing case study, 551–552
Expected value of sample information
    (EVSI), multistage decision
    tree, 543
    marketing case study, 551
Expenses, cash balance simulation model,
    679–681

Explanatory variables
   multiple regression analysis, 926–930
   regression analysis, 906, 916
Exponential distribution. *See also*
            Nonexponential interarrival/
            service times
   price-demand relationships, 48–56
   queueing models, 799–804
      bank interarrival and service
            example, 801–803
      memoryless property, 800–803
      miscellaneous models, 818–819
      Poisson process model, 803–804
      processing simulation case
            study, 848–850
      simulation modeling, 835–850
Exponential smoothing models, 942–956
   Holt's trend method, 947–952
   sales forecasting examples, 944–947
   simple smoothing, 942–943
   Winters' seasonality method, 952–956
Exponential trend lines
   limitations of, 915
   regression-based trend models, 913–915
Exposures analysis
   advertising model, 135–136
      nonlinear response functions, advertis-
            ing models, 375–376
   advertising models, goal programming
            scheduling model, 467–471
   dual-objective optimization
            model, 137–138
   response and selection advertising
            models, 371–376
External demand, inventory modeling, 740
Extrapolation methods
   forecasting using, 905
   limitations of, 937
   time series models, 932

**F**
Facility location models, 378–381
Failure times, warranty cost simulation
            modeling, 659–661
False negatives/positives, Bayes' rule, drug
            testing case study, 535–538
"Fast" simplex method, transportation
            models, 231–235
Feasible assignments, airline industry
            network models, 263
Feasible region, optimization modeling, 74
Feasible solutions
   advertising exposure trade-off
            example, 482–483
   combinatorial models, 428
   crew scheduling network model, 263
   goal programming scheduling
            model, 466–471
   optimization modeling, 74
Feedback loops, modeling process, 9–10
Final cash, retirement investment
            modeling, 684

Financial modeling
   asset management example, 734–735
   beta stock estimation, 396–401
   linear programming, 173–183
   nonlinear optimization modeling, 347
   pricing analysis, 366
   product development, TOPRANK Addin
            modeling, 717–722
   simulation modeling
      asset management example, 734–735
      bond investment example, 733
      cash balance models, 676–681
      college fund investments example, 732
      financial planning models, 672–676
      investment models, 681–685
      Merrill Lynch case study, 651–653
      stock prices and options, 685–693
Finish-to-finish relationships, Critical Path
            Method (CMP) model of project
            management, 873
Finish-to-start relationships, Critical Path
            Method (CMP) model of project
            management, 872–873
Fire engine request example, Erlang loss
            model, 820–822
First-come-first-served (FCFS) discipline,
            queueing models, 797
   multiple-server queueing model, 811–815
Fitness function, genetic
            algorithms, 415–416
Fitted values
   multiple regression analysis, 925
   regression analysis, 907–908
Fixed-cost models
   economic order quantity models, setup
            cost reductions, 752–754
   integer variables, 297–309
   location assignment models as, 320–325
   manufacturing example, 304–305
   textile manufacturing example, 298
Flaw of averages
   decision making uncertainty, 519–521
   simulation modeling, @RISK
            software, 623–624
Flow balance constraints
   airline industry network models, 263
   assignment models, school bus route
            example, 239–240
   crew scheduling network
            model, 263–264
   equipment replacement models, 257–258
   flight scheduling network
            model, 268–273
   minimum cost network flow
            models, 242–250
   shortest path models, 250
   transportation models, 224, 229–235
Folding-back process, decision trees, 512
   government contract bidding
            example, 517–518
   PrecisionTree® interpretations in place
            of, 528

Forecasting models. *See also* Regression
            models
   arrival time estimations, 965
   basic principles, 904–905
   combinatorial models, production sched-
            uling deviations, 435
   demand analysis example, 964
   exponential smoothing
            models, 942–956
      Holt's trend method, 947–952
      sales forecasting
            examples, 944–947
      simple smoothing, 942–943
      Winters' seasonality
            method, 952–956
   moving averages models, 937–941
      weekly sales forecast example,
            938–941
   overhead forecasting, 964
   Taco Bell case study, 903–904
   time series models, 932–937
      components, 933
      cyclic component, 934–935
      extrapolation limitations, 937
      forecast error measurements, 935–937
      random (noise) component, 935
      seasonal component, 934
      trend component, 933–934
   workforce scheduling
            models, 143–149
Foreign currency trading, linear program-
            ming case study, 220
Formula Auditing tool, breakeven analysis,
            39–41
Forward pass, Critical Path Method (CMP)
            model of project management,
            867–872
Fractional aircraft ownership programs,
            network modeling, 272
Fractions invested input, portfolio
            optimization, 392
Free slack, project management, 897–898
Freezing techniques, simulation modeling,
            probability distribution
   random numbers, 592
   Walton ordering case study, 610
Funnel experiment, simulation
            modeling, 667
Futures data
   portfolio optimization, Evolutionary
            software, 443–444
   return on portfolio case
            study, 689–691

**G**
Gambling, simulation modeling, 708–713
Games of chance, simulation modeling,
            708–713
   basketball pools, 711–713
   craps, 708–710
Gamma distribution
   simulated queueing model, 837–842

warranty costs, simulation
modeling, 657–661
Gantt chart
Critical Path Method (CMP) model of
project management, LAN example, 871–872
project management, Microsoft Project
applications, 897–898
General distribution, simulation
modeling, 599–601
General Electric Company
Asset Management (GEAM), nonlinear
optimization case study, 345–346
Capital PAYMENT system,
modeling of, 14–16
plastics case study, optimization
modeling, 71–72
Generalized reduced gradient (GRG)
nonlinear algorithm
aggregate planning model, 156–160
Evolutionary Solver and, 418–419
Premium Solver, 413
pricing models, 355–356
Generations of chromosomes, genetic
algorithms, 415–416
Genetic algorithms
basic principles, 415–416
Evolutionary Solver function, nonlinear
model, local maxima, 418
in Premium Solver, 413
strengths and limitations of, 416
Geographical shortest path
models, 251–254
Geometry, two-variable optimization
modeling, 78–85
Global maxima/minima, nonlinear
optimization, 347
Global optima, nonlinear optimization
modeling, 347, 351
Goal programming, multiobjective decision
making, 465–471
advertising scheduling example, 465
Goal Seek function, breakeven
analysis, 38–41
Goodness-of-fit measurement
nonlinear optimization modeling, 347
response and selection advertising
models, 370
regression analysis
basic principles, 908–909
exponential trend lines, 913–915
Government contract bidding
decision making uncertainty
and, 513–518
simulation modeling, 653–657
Gradient options, Evolutionary Solver
software, 420
Graphical solutions
discontinuities and, 414
minimum cost network flow
models, 242–243
moving averages models, 940–941

set-covering models, hub locations, 313
simulation modeling
@RISK software function, 621
correlated inputs, 638–639
input effects, 634–639
S-shaped curve fitting model, 440–441
transportation models, 226–227
two-variable optimization
modeling, 77–85
Greedy analysis, product mix
model, 103–107

H
Hard constraints, advertising models,
goal programming scheduling
model, 467–471
Heuristics
defined, 12
linear programming models, 148
workforce scheduling models, 148–149
High utilization configuration, queueing
models, processing simulation
case study, 847–850
HIM exposures, goal programming scheduling model, 467–471
Histograms
customer loyalty modeling, 698–703
churn reduction case study, 702–703
project management, uncertain activity
times modeling, 894
queueing models, bank interarrival
time/service time distribution
examples, 802–803
simulation modeling
@RISK software function, 620–621
car development example, 675–676
Excel software tools for, 646–648
funnel simulation model, 669–671
government contract bidding
example, 656–657
retirement investment
modeling, 684–685
uniform probability distribution, 590
warranty costs, 660–661
yield uncertainties, simulation
modeling, 665–666
Historical data
customer loyalty modeling, 695–703
regression-based trend models, sales
data, 910–919
retirement investment
modeling, 682–685
HIV/AIDS epidemic, spreadsheet modeling
example, 23–24
HIW exposures, goal programming
scheduling model, 467–471
Hoarding, subway token case study, inventory management and, 792
Holding costs
economic order quantity models, camera
ordering case study, 745–746
inventory modeling, 742

multiperiod production model, 113
supply chain inventory models, 780–784
Holt's trend method, exponential smoothing models, 942, 947–952
Hospital industry, data envelopment analysis case study, 184–191

I
IF function
aggregate planning and backlogging,
155–160
combinatorial models, production
scheduling example, 434–437
discriminant analysis, 452
fixed-cost models, 303–304
limitations of, 414
multiple regression analysis, dummy
variable creation, 927–930
nonlinear pricing models,
422–428, 425–428
portfolio optimization, Evolutionary
software, 443
spreadsheet modeling, 26–27
Illegal solutions, fixed-cost
models, 301, 306
Immediate predecessors/successors, Critical Path Method (CMP) model of
project management, 865–872
Implementation, seven-step modeling
process, 9, 13
Implicit enumeration, optimization programming, branch and bound
algorithm, 288–289
Implied volatility, European call options
modeling, 687–689
Incomes, cash balance simulation
model, 678 681
Incumbent solution, optimization
programming, branch and bound
algorithm, 288–289
Independent variable
probability distribution, simulation
modeling, 589
regression analysis, 906
Index cities, traveling salesperson
problem, 455
Indicator variables, multiple regression
analysis, 926–930
Inequality
fixed-cost models, 299–301
two-variable optimization models, 83
Infeasible solution, optimization
modeling, 74, 96–97
Inflation, equipment replacement
models, 258
Inflow
assignment models, 239
cash balance simulation
modeling, 679–681
minimum cost network flow
models, 241–250
transportation models, 229–235

Information, value of, multistage decision tree, 543, 551–552
Initial conditions, queueing models, short-run *vs.* steady-state behavior, 798–799
Inputs
  advertising models, 135–142
  aggregate planning model, 150–151
  airline industry network models, 263
  analytic hierarchy process (AHP), 491
  Asian call option, 692–693
  assignment models, 239
  blending models, 163
  breakeven analysis and, 36–41
  capital budget models, 291
  combinatorial models
    loading products example, 430
    production scheduling example, 433–437
  cost projections, 29–33
  crew scheduling network model, 261, 263
  Critical Path Method (CMP) model of project management, local area network (LAN) creation, 869–872
  customer loyalty modeling, 696
    churn reduction case study, 701
  cutting stock models, 328
  data envelopment analysis, 186
  decision tree construction, PrecisionTree Add In, 523
  descriptive queueing model, 4–6
  economic order quantity models, order synchronization, 756
  equipment replacement models, 256–258
  European call options modeling, 688–689
  financial models, 175
  fixed-cost models, 299, 305–306
  goal programming scheduling model, 466
  hard codes and cell references, 26–27
  location assignment/fixed cost models, 323
  location assignment models, 317
  market share modeling, 704–706
  minimum cost network flow models, 244
  modeling verification, 11
  multiperiod production model, 112–117
  multistage decision tree
    drug testing example, 540–541
    marketing example, 545
  nonlinear pricing models, single-price model, 424
  nonlinear response functions, advertising models, 374–376
  ordering simulation models, 774–778
  peak-load pricing model, 364–366
  portfolio optimization, 392–394
  pricing models, 355–356
  probabilistic inventory model, *(R,Q)* ordering policy, 767–771

product development model, TOPRANK Addin tool, 718–722
production process models, 169–173
product mix model, 101–107
project management
  multiple-project scheduling, 887
  uncertain activity times modeling, 893
quantity discounts and demand uncertainty, 43–46
queueing models, 796
  processing example with blocking, 844–850
  short-run behavior approximation, 832–834
  simulation modeling, 836–844
resource allocation modeling, crashing the activities function, 883
response and selection advertising models, 371
retirement investment modeling, 682–685
return on portfolio case study, 689–691
set-covering models, 311
simulation modeling
  @RISK software applications, 592–593, 616–621
  binomial distribution, 597–599
  bounded *vs.* unbounded, 587–588
  cash balance model, 677–678
  common probability distribution, 588
  correlated input variables, 635–639
  cumul/general distribution, 599–601
  discrete *vs.* continuous, 585–586
  government contract bidding, 655–657
  multiple random inputs, 628–631
  normal distribution, 595–596
  optimal solution, 633–635
  overview, 581–582
  positive (nonnegative) *vs.* unrestricted, 588
  probability distribution, 583–601
  random number freezing, 592
  shape effects, 632–633
  symmetric *vs.* skewed, 586–587
  triangular distribution, 596–597
  uniform distribution, 588–591
  Walton bookstore case study, 606–608
  yield uncertainties, drug development case study, 662–666
sports teams ratings model, 384–386
spreadsheet modeling, 24–25
  NCAA T-shirt example, 27
S-shaped curve fitting model, 439
supply chain inventory models, 779–780
time value of money, 59–62
transportation models, 224–225
two-variable optimization modeling, 78–85
waiting line example, 4–5
workforce scheduling models, 144–149
Integer constraints/variables
  advertising models, 140–142
  aggregate planning model, 154–160

combinatorial models, production scheduling example, 436–437
Evolutionary Solver software, 421
minimum cost network flow models, 249–250
optimization models
  basic principles, 286–288
  branch and bound algorithm, 288–289
  capital budgeting, 290–297
  cutting stock models, 327–331
  fixed-cost models, 297–309
  set-covering and location assignment models, 309–327
  Solver Tolerance options, 289–290
  strategic planning, 341–342
  U.S. Air Force case study, 285–286
  volume discounts case study, 343
pension fund modeling, 181–183
transportation models, 231–235
workforce scheduling models, 146–149
Integer programming (IP)
  advertising models, 140–142
  optimization modeling, 287
  project management, 862
Interarrival times, queueing models, 796–797
  bank estimation example, 801–803
  nonexponential multiple-server model, 822–826
  Poisson distribution estimation, 803–804
  processing simulation case study, 847–850
Intercepts, regression models, 909–910
Interest rates
  cash balance simulation model, 679–681
  economic order quantity models, setup cost reductions, 752–754
  pension fund modeling, 182–183
*Interfaces* journal, 16
Internal demand, inventory modeling, 740
International Textile Company, Ltd., network modeling example, 280–281
Intuitive calculations, Bayes' rule, 536–538
Inventory management modeling
  aggregate planning model, 153–160
    backlogging and, 157–160
  categories, 739–741
  continuous *vs.* periodic review, 741
  cost categories, 741–742
  Dell supply chain case study, 737–738
  deterministic *vs.* probabilistic, 740
  economic order quantity models, 743–759
    camera ordering example, 744–746
    multiple products, 759
    order synchronization, 754–757
    quantity discounts, 746–748
    setup cost reductions, 752–754
    shortages models, 749–751
  external *vs.* internal demand, 740
  multiperiod production model, 109–117
  ordering simulation models, 773–778
    production models *vs.*, 741

ordering *vs.* production, 741
overview, 739
probabilistic models, 759–771
  deterministic models *vs.*, 740
  newsvendor model, 760–763
  (R,Q) ordering policy, 764–771
simulation modeling, 650
single-product *vs.* multiple-product
    models, 741
subway token hoarding example, 792
supply chain models, 778–784
  Dell supply chain case study, 737–738
Inventory position, ordering simulation
    models, 773–778
Investment models. *See also* Portfolio
    optimization
  asset management example, 409–410
  beta stock estimation, 396–401
  bond investment strategy, 733
  capital budget models, 290–297
  college fund investment example, 732
  decision support for, 395
  Evolutionary Solver software, 442–444
  linear programing, 173–183
  nonlinear optimization modeling, 347
  portfolio optimization, 387–394
  pricing analysis, 366
  simulation modeling, 582–583
    Asian call options, 691–693
    @RISK applications, 691
    European call option, 686–689
    portfolio optimization, 689–691
    retirement example, 681–685
    stock prices and options, 685–686
  stock hedging example, 407–408
Investment weights, retirement investments
    modeling, 681–685

**J**

Job selection, analytic hierarchy process
    example, 484–492
Judgmental methods, forecasting and, 905

**K**

Kellogg Company, production, inventory
    and distribution modeling case
    study, 131–132
Kendall's notation (*M/M/*1), single-server
    queueing model, 807–811

**L**

Labor availability
  aggregate planning model, 151–152
  crew scheduling network model, 261–265
  employee scheduling example, 149
  fixed-cost models, 299
  production process models, 172–173
  product mix model, 106–107
  resource monitoring and, 875–880
  workforce scheduling models, 143–149
Lakefield Corporation Oil Trading Desk,
    linear programming case study,
    215–219

Last-come-first-served (LCFS) discipline,
    queueing models, 797
Layouts, spreadsheet modeling, 28
Lead time
  inventory modeling, ordering *vs.*
    production, 741
  probabilistic inventory model
    random lead times, 771
    (R,Q) ordering policy, 765–771
Least squares estimation
  beta stock estimation, 397–399
  regression analysis, 907–908
  response and selection advertising
    models, 370
Level of the series, exponential smoothing
    models, 942
Lifetimes, warranty cost simulation
    modeling, 659–661
Likelihoods, multistage decision analysis,
    Bayes' rule, 535–538
Limited source queueing model,
    exponential techniques, 818–819
Limited waiting room system, queueing
    models, 797
  exponential effects, 818–819
  simulation modeling, 836
Linear combination of x's, optimization
    modeling, 95
Linear curves, price-demand
    relationships, 48–56
Linear programming (LP) models
  advertising, 133–142
  aggregate planning models, 150–160
  algebraic models, 76
  AMARCO, Inc. case study, 207–209
  American Office Systems, Inc. case
    study, 210–214
  backlogging and, 157–160
  blending models, 160–167
  data envelopment analysis, 184–191
  decision programming systems, 118–120
  financial models, 173–183
  foreign currency trading case study, 220
  goal programming scheduling
    model, 466–471
  integer programming *vs.*, 287–288
  Kellogg Planning System
    example, 131–132
  Lakefield Corporation Oil Trading Desk
    case study, 215–219
  multiperiod production model, 108–117
  network models *vs.*, 222–223
  optimization applications, 72–74, 93–96
  overview, 132–133
  portfolio optimization, 347
  production, inventory and distribution
    case study, 131–132
  production process models, 167–173
  product mix model, 98–107
  resource allocation modeling, crashing
    the activities function, 883–884
  scaling properties, 95–96

sensitivity analysis, 85–93
SUMPRODUCT function and, 80–85
two-variable optimization
    modeling, 76–85
workforce scheduling models, 142–149
Linear trendline, regression-based trend
    models, 911–913
  single-product cost estimation
    example, 918–919
Little's formula, queueing
    models, 805–806
  Erlang loss model, 819–822
Loading products modeling, combinatorial
    models, 429–432
Loan amounts, cash balance simulation
    model, 679–681
Local area network (LAN) creation
  crashing the activities in, 880–884
  Critical Path Method (CMP)
    example, 868–872
  Microsoft Project applications, 896–898
  resource monitoring with, 875–880
  uncertain activity times
    modeling, 891–895
Local maxima/minima, nonlinear
    optimization modeling,
    347, 351
  Evolutionary Solver software, 417–418
Location assignment models, 309–319
  facility location models, 378–381
  fixed-cost models as, 320–325
Logical constraints, location assignment
    models, 319–320
Logic modeling, fixed-cost models, 297
Lognormal model of price changes, stock
    prices and options, 685–686
Long-term value, customer loyalty
    modeling, 695–703
Lookup table, cluster analysis, 447
Lower bound constraints
  combinatorial models, production
    scheduling example, 436–437
  Evolutionary Solver software, 419
    changing cell constraints, 422
  fixed-cost models, 306
  trade-off curve, profit maximization/
    pollution minimization
    example, 477–480
Low utilization configuration, queueing
    models, series simulation with
    blocking, 846–850
Lunchtime rush case study, short-run
    behavior approximation,
    queueing models, 831–834

**M**

Macros, applications for, 68–69
Maintenance costs
  equipment replacement models, 257
  periodic maintenance models, 258
Management communication, seven-step
    modeling process, 9, 12

Management science
　basic principles of, 3
　business problem solving and, 2
　GE Capital case study, 14–16
　*Interfaces* as resource on, 16
　modeling applications in, 14–16
　modeling *vs.* models in, 7–8
　project management principles, 863–864
　seven-step modeling process, 8–14
　strengths and limitations of, 17–18
　traveling salesperson problem, 454–457
Management staffing, assignment model
　　example, 240
Manufacturing operations
　analytic hierarchy process and, 493
　optimization modeling, 71–72
　queueing models, 793–794
Markdown revenue, supply chain inventory
　　models, 781–784
Marketing models
　cluster analysis, 444–449
　discriminant analysis, 450–453
　multistage decision tree, 543–552
　simulation modeling
　　customer loyalty models, 695–703
　　market share models, 703–706
MATCH function (Excel software), 54–56
　cluster analysis, 448
　nonlinear pricing models, 425
Material resources, fixed-cost models, 299
Mathematical models
　defined, 4
　linear models, 93–96
　management science applications, 3
　waiting-line example, 4–7
MAX function, spreadsheet modeling
　genetic algorithms, 416
　limitations of, 414
　nonlinear pricing models, 425–428
Maximax criteria, decision making
　　uncertainty and, 507–508
　risk management and, 554–560
Maximization problems
　economic order quantity models,
　　shortage costs, 749–751
　nonlinear optimization modeling,
　　350–351
　risk management and, 554–560
Maximizing profit
　price-demand relationships, 53–56
　transportation models, 233–235
Maximum capacity, fixed-cost
　　models, 300
Maximum criteria, decision making
　　uncertainty and, 507–508
Maximum Ending Inventory, multiperiod
　　production model, 115–117
Maximum surplus, nonlinear pricing
　　models, 425
Mean absolute error (MAE), time series
　　models, forecasting error
　　measurement, 936–937

Mean absolute percentage error (MAPE)
　price-demand relationships, 51–56
　regression analysis, exponential trend
　　lines, 914–915
　time series models, forecasting error
　　measurement, 936–937
Meandering behavior, moving averages
　　models, 938–941
Mean profits, customer loyalty
　　modeling, 695–703
Means calculations
　cluster analysis, 446–449
　games of chance modeling, 710–711
　queueing models, exponential
　　distribution, 800
　simulation modeling
　　confidence interval, 608–609
　　expected monetary value, 676
　　normal distribution, 595–596
　stock prices and options, 685–686
Medicare prescription plan, decision
　　making uncertainty and, 519–521
Memoryless property, queueing
　　models, 800–801
Merrill Lynch liquidity management
　　case study, simulation
　　modeling, 651–653
Microsoft Project software
　basic components, 896–898
　project management
　　applications, 863–864
MIN function, spreadsheet modeling
　cluster analysis, 448
　genetic algorithms, 416
　limitations of, 414
Minimax criteria
　beta stock estimation, 397
　Pareto optimality and trade-off curves,
　　profit maximization/pollution
　　minimization example, 477–480
Minimization problems
　nonlinear optimization
　　modeling, 350–351
　response and selection advertising
　　models, 371–376
　traveling salesperson
　　problem, 454–457
Minimum cost network flow models,
　　241–250. *See also* Shortest
　　path models
　flight scheduling example, 266–273
　Nu-kote International distribution
　　example, 249
　tomato production and shipment
　　example, 242–243
Model development
　optimization modeling, 73–74
　seven-step modeling process, 8–9, 11
Modeling
　applications for, 14–15
　defined, 7–8
　seven-step process, 8–14

Monetary values
　fixed-cost models, 300
　multistage decision tree assessment, 539
　peak-load pricing model, 365–366
　PrecisionTree® software, 527
　risk management and exponential
　　utility, 556–560
　time value of money, 58
Money allocation, pension fund
　　modeling, 180–183
Monitoring of resources, resource
　　allocation modeling, 874–880
Moving averages models, forecasting
　　applications, 937–941
　weekly sales forecast example, 938–941
Multiattribute utility function, trade-off
　　curves, 483
Multicollinearity, multiple regression
　　analysis, 929–930
Multiobjective decision making
　analytic hierarchy process, 484–493
　goal programming, 465–471
　miscellaneous applications, 493
　NASA project evaluation and
　　prioritization case study, 463–464
　optimization strategies, 464
　Pareto optimality and trade-off
　　curves, 475–483
　resource allocation modeling, 874–885
　seasonal production example, 499–501
Multiperiod production model
　aggregate planning model, 151–160
　optimization techniques, 108–117
　Pigskin Company example, 109–110
　production/inventory planning, 109–110
Multiple optimal solutions, workforce
　　scheduling models, 147
Multiple-product model
　economic order quantity models, order
　　synchronization, 754–757
　inventory modeling, single-product
　　model *vs.,* 741
　multiple regression analysis, cost
　　analysis, 921–922
Multiple products
　economic order quantity models, 759
　minimum cost network flow
　　models, 247–250
Multiple-project scheduling, project
　　management principles, 885–889
Multiple $R$
　basic regression analysis, 908–909
　multiple regression analysis, 924–925
Multiple ranges, two-variable optimization
　　model, 90–93
Multiple regression analysis, 921–930
　assumption limitations, 929
　categorical variables, 925–926
　cost analysis case study, 921–922
　defined, 906
　Excel Analysis ToolPak Add-in,
　　922–925

future cost predictions, 925
multicollinearity, 929–930
nonconstant error variance, 930
nonlinear relationships, 930
production cost estimation example, 926–929
residual autocorrelation, 930
*R*-square adjustment, 925
Multiple-server queueing model
nonexponential interarrival/service times, 822–826
simulated queueing, bank queue example, 838–842
single-server model *vs.*, 816–817
steady-state analysis, 811–815
traffic intensity effects, 817–818
Multistage decision tree
applications, 538–552
Bayes' rule, 534–538
decision tree development, 546–552
drug testing case study, 538–543
product marketing case study, 543–552
sensitivity analysis, 542
value of information parameter, 542–543
Mutation, genetic algorithms, 415–416
Evolutionary Solver changing cells, 418
Myopic solutions, multiperiod production model, 115–117

**N**

Name ranges
data envelopment analysis, 186
multiperiod production model, 112–117
NASA project evaluation and prioritization, multiobjective decision making case study, 463–464
NCAA Basketball Tournament, games of chance modeling, 711–713
Net inflow, minimum cost network flow models, 242–250
Net outflow
geographical shortest path models, 253
minimum cost network flow models, 242–250
Net present value (NPV)
Acron case study, 58–62
capital budget models, 290
sensitivity analysis, 293–294
tolerance settings, 295–297
customer loyalty modeling, 695, 697–703
product development
project management example, 861–862
TOPRANK Addin modeling, 715–722
simulation modeling, 581–582
car development example, 675–676
time value of money, 57–62
warranty cost simulation modeling, 659–661
Network modeling
airline industry example, 260–273
alternative models, 229–235
assignment models, 235–241

BASF North America case study, 221–222
basic principles, 222–223
crew scheduling network model, 260–265
equipment replacement model, 254–258
fractional aircraft ownership, 272
International Textile Co. case study, 280–281
minimum cost network flow models, 241–250
on-demand aircraft scheduling, 272
pilot staffing and training, 272
shortest path models, 250–260
transportation models, 223–235
UPS optimization model, 272
Westvaco optimized motor carrier selection case study, 282–284
Network simplex method, minimum cost network flow models, 249–250
Newsvendor model, probabilistic inventory, 760–763
NFL team rating model, 382–386
95% prediction interval, multiple regression analysis, future cost predictions, 925
Nodes and branches
Critical Path Method (CMP) model of project management, 865–872
decision trees, 511–512
equipment replacement model, 255–258
flight scheduling network model, 267–271
PrecisionTree Add-In, 524–526
end node values, 528
transportation models, 224–225
Noise, time series models, random (noise) component, 935
Nonbinding constraints, two-variable optimization modeling, 85
Nonconstant error variance, multiple regression analysis, 930
Nonconstant returns to scale, nonlinear optimization modeling, 346
Nonexponential interarrival/service times
multiple-server queueing models, 822–826
queueing models, simulation modeling, 835–850
Nonfinancial holding costs, inventory modeling, 742
Nonlinear modeling
advertising models, 141–142
backlogging functions, 155–160
Evolutionary Solver software, local maxima example, 417–418
fixed-cost models, 297
multiple regression analysis, 930
optimization models
advertising response and selection models, 369–376
asset management example, 409–410
basic properties, 346–347
convex and concave functions, 348–349

facility location models, 378–382
General Electric portfolio optimization case study, 345–346
maximization problems, 350
minimization problems, 350
portfolio optimization, 387–395
Solver functions, 350
sports team ratings, 382–386
stock hedging example, 407–408
stock return estimation, 396–401
unverifiable assumptions, 350–351
pricing models
alternative optimization procedures, 422–428
basic optimization models, 351–366
menthos candy example, 422–423
miscellaneous examples, 427–428
proportionality, 94
Solver function limitations with, 413–414
S-shaped curve fitting, 437–441
Nonmonetary cost/benefit analysis, multistage decision tree assessment, 539
Nonnegativity constraints
data envelopment analysis, 187
multiperiod production model, 111–117
optimization modeling, 73–74
simulation modeling, positive probability distribution, 588
two-variable models, 74–75, 79–85
Nonsmooth functions
aggregate planning model, 156–160
combinatorial models, production scheduling example, 434–437
genetic algorithms and, 416
Premium Solver and, 418
Nonstationary systems, queueing models, short-run behavior approximation, 830–834
Nonzero constraints, product mix model, 106–107
Normal distribution
newsvendor inventory model, 762–763
probabilistic inventory model, *(R,Q)* ordering policy, 765–771
simulation modeling, 595–596
input effects, 633–639
Normalized matrices, analytic hierarchy process (AHP), 491–492
Not sufficient funds (NSF) fees, check sequencing, capital budget models, 295–297
No wear-out property, queueing models, 801

**O**

Objective function
analytic hierarchy process, 484–485
nonlinear optimization modeling, assumption validity/nonvalidity, 350–351
optimization modeling, 73–74
sensitivity analysis, 88–93

On-demand aircraft scheduling, network modeling, 272

One-time investment costs, economic order quantity models, setup cost reductions, 752–754

One-way data table
  breakeven analysis, 37–41
  two-variable optimization model, 89–93

One-way sensitivity analysis, decision making uncertainty, 532–534

On-hand inventory, multiperiod production model, 112–117

Operations modeling
  Santa Fe Railway example, 411–412
  simulation modeling, 653–671
    drug development and production example, 661–666
    government contract bidding example, 653–657
    processing example, 666–671
    warranty costs example, 657–661

Operations research, *soft Or* modeling approach and, 2

Optimal order quantity, probabilistic inventory model, 761–763

Optimal solution
  advertising model, 135–142
    exposure trade-off example, 480–483
    goal programming example, 470–471
    nonlinear response functions, advertising models, 375–376
    response and selection advertising models, 369–370
  aggregate planning model, 151–157
  analytic hierarchy process, job selection, 484–492
  assignment model, 237–239
    school bus routes, 240
  backlogging model linearization, 157–159
  beta stock estimation, 398–401
  blending models, 163–164
  breakeven analysis, 34
  cluster analysis, 446–449
  combinatorial models
    loading products example, 429–432
    production scheduling example, 433–437
  data envelopment analysis, 187–189
  decision making uncertainty and, 507
    flaw of averages example, 520–521
    government contract bidding example, 514–518
  defined, 74
  discriminant analysis, 453
  economic order quantity models
    camera ordering case study, 746
    shortage costs, 751
  facility location models, 378–381
  financial models, 176–181
  fixed-cost models, 301–302, 307
  flight scheduling network model, 270–271
  goal programming, 465–471

heuristics and, 12

labor hours availability model, 107–108

linear programming, 73
  multiple optimal solutions, 147

location assignment models, 318–319

minimum cost network flow models, 243–244
  flow analysis, 246–250

multiperiod production model, 113–117

multistage decision tree, 538
  marketing model, 544–552

nonlinear optimization modeling
  local maxima example, 417–418
  pricing models, 352–356, 427

optimization modeling, 74, 83

Pareto optimality and trade-off curves, profit maximization/pollution minimization example, 477–480

peak-load pricing model, 365–366

policy suggestion and risk profile, 528–529

portfolio optimization, 393–394
  Evolutionary Solver software, 442–444

price-demand relationships, 48–56

pricing model, retailing example, 361–362

process for, 79–85

production model, 113–120

production process model, 171–172

product mix model, 103–106

quantity discounts case study, 42–46

response and selection advertising models, 372–376

risk management, 557–560

scheduling model, 143–147

sensitivity analysis, 85–89

set-covering models, 310–311

shortest path model, 250–254

simulation modeling
  input distributions, 633–639
  Walton bookstore case study, 604–608

Solver function and, 19

sports teams ratings model, 383–386

spreadsheet modeling, 78
  NCAA T-shirt example, 26–27

S-shaped curve fitting model, 439–441

time value of money, 58–62

trade-off curve, profit maximization/ pollution minimization example, 479–480

transportation model, 226–228
  tax rate variations, 232–235

traveling salesperson problem, 455–457

two-variable optimization model, 79–85
  dessert models, 86–93

workforce scheduling models, 143–149

Optimal values, product mix model, 102–107

Optimization modeling
  algebraic *vs.* spread sheet modeling, 118
  combinatorial models, 428–437
  decision support system, 118–120
  defined, 4

economic order quantity models, order synchronization, 754–757

forecasting models, Taco Bell forecasting model case study, 904

GE plastics example, 71–72

infeasibility and unboundedness, 96–97

integer variables
  basic principles, 286–288
  branch and bound algorithm, 288–289
  capital budgeting, 290–297
  cutting stock models, 327–331
  fixed-cost models, 297–309
  set-covering and location assignment models, 309–327
  Solver Tolerance options, 289–290
  strategic planning, 341–342
  U.S. Air Force case study, 285–286
  volume discounts case study, 343

linear modeling, 93–96

modeling limitations, 107, 117

multiobjective decision making, 464

multiperiod production model, 108–116

nonlinear models
  advertising response and selection models, 369–376
  asset management example, 409–410
  basic properties, 346–347
  convex and concave functions, 348–349
  facility location models, 378–382
  General Electric portfolio optimization case study, 345–346
  maximization problems, 350
  minimization problems, 350
  portfolio optimization, 387–395
  pricing models, 351–366
  Solver functions, 350
  sports team ratings, 382–386
  stock hedging example, 407–408
  stock return estimation, 396–401
  unverifiable assumptions, 350–351

on-demand aircraft scheduling, 272

overview, 72–74

pilot staffing and training, 272

product mix modeling, 98–107

profit maximization, 56

queueing models, 795–796
  multiple-server queueing model, 814–815

sensitivity analysis, 85–93

seven-step modeling process, 9, 11–12

two-variable model, 74–85

UPS air network example, 272

waiting-line example, 6–7

Options modeling
  Asian call option, 691–693
  European call options, 686–689
  return on portfolio case study, 689–691
  stock prices and options, 685–686

Order cycle, probabilistic inventory model, *(R,Q)* ordering policy, 766–771

Ordering costs
  economic order quantity models,
      camera ordering case study,
      744–746
  inventory modeling
    basic properties, 741
    production models *vs.,* 741
Ordering simulation models
  inventory management, 773–778
  production models *vs.,* 741
  probability distribution
    @RISK software, 629–631
    best order quantity calculations,
      609–610
    Walton bookstore case study,
      606–608
Order synchronization, economic order
      quantity models, 754–757
Origin nodes
  minimum cost network flow
      models, 244
  transportation models, 223
Outcomes
  decision making uncertainty and, 507
    expected monetary value, 508
    government contract bidding example,
      514–518, 515–518
    games of chance modeling, 709–711
Outflow
  assignment models, 239
  cash balance simulation modeling,
      679–681
  minimum cost network flow models,
      241–250
  transportation models, 229–235
Outputs
  Asian call options model, 692–693
  blending models, 163
  cash balance simulation model,
      679–681
  cost projection models, 30–33
  customer loyalty modeling, 697–703
  data envelopment analysis, 186
  descriptive queueing model, 4–6
  European call options modeling,
      688–689
  intermediate, 27
  market share modeling, 705–706
  modeling verification, 11
  multiple regression analysis, future cost
      predictions, 925
  NCAA Basketball Tournament
      modeling, 713
  queueing models, 796
    series simulation with blocking,
      844–850
    short-run behavior approximation,
      833–834
  simulation modeling
    car development example, 676
    government contract bidding
      example, 657

shape effects, 635
  Walton bookstore case study, 607–608
  warranty costs, 660–661
  spreadsheet modeling, 24–25
    NCAA T-shirt example, 27–28
    waiting line example, 4–5
Overhead costs, forecasting models of, 964
Overtime capacity, aggregate planning
      model, 152

# P

Pairwise comparison matrices, analytic
      hierarchy process, 485–492
Palisade software
  basic features, 19
  PrecisionTree® software, 522
  StatTools add-in, exponential smoothing
      models, 947–956
Parallel service characteristics, queueing
      models, 797–798
Pareto optimality, multiobjective decision
      making, 475–483
  profit maximization/pollution
      minimization example, 477–480
Partial backlogging, inventory
      modeling, 742
Patterns, cutting stock models, 328
Payoff tables, decision making uncertainty
      and, 506–508
  EMV calculation and interpretation,
      509–510
  government contract bidding example,
      515–518
  maximax criteria, 507–508
Peak-load pricing model, 363–366
Penalty costs
  combinatorial models, production sched-
      uling example, 435–437
  inventory modeling, 742
  project management, multiple-project
      scheduling, 888
Pension funds, financial models case study,
      178–183
Perfect information envelope, multistage
      decision trees, 543, 551–552
Periodic maintenance model, Schindler
      elevator example, 259
Periodic review model, inventory modeling,
      continuous review *vs.,* 741
Piecewise linear objectives, nonlinear
      pricing models, 422–428
Pilot staffing and training, network
      modeling, 272
Planning models, financial planning,
      672–676
Plant opening decisions, location
      assignment/fixed cost
      models, 323
Plant production costs, transportation
      models, 232–235
Plant shipment data, transportation
      models, 226

Point spreads
  NCAA Basketball Tournament
      modeling, 711–713
  sports teams ratings model, 383–386
Poisson distribution, queueing models
  Erlang loss model, 819–822
  interarrival time estimation, 803–804
  simulation modeling, 836
Policy suggestion
  decision making uncertainty
    multistage decision tree, 547–552
    risk profile and, 528–529
  ordering simulation models, 775–778
Populations, genetic algorithms, 415–416
Portfolio optimization
  asset management example, 409–410
  Evolutionary Solver modeling, 442–444
  matrix functions, 388–390
  nonlinear optimization modeling,
      345–346, 387–394
  selection model, 390–391
  simulation modeling, stocks and stock
      options case study, 689–691
  stock hedging example, 407–408
  weighted sums of random variables,
      387–388
Positive probability distribution, simulation
      modeling, 588
Postal branch queueing model, single-
      service model, 808–811
Posterior probability, multistage decision
      analysis, Bayes' rule, 535–538
Power function, price-demand relationships,
      48–56
Precedence relations, project management,
      Microsoft Project applications,
      897–898
PrecisionTree® software
  allowable entries, 525
  basic features, 19
  decision making uncertainty and, 522–534
  decision tree construction, 523–527
    risk management, 557–560
  end node values, 528
  interpretation guidelines, 527–528
  monetary values in, 527
  multistage decision tree
    drug testing case study, 540–541
    marketing case study, 546–552
    policy suggestion and risk profile,
      528–529
  probability nodes and branches, 525–526
  sensitivity analysis button, 529–530
  strategy region charts, 530–531
  subtree copying, 527
  sum of probabilities function, 527
  tornado chart, 530–531
Predicted demands
  price-demand relationships, 51–56
  S-shaped curve fitting model, 439
Predicted exposures, response and selection
      advertising models, 371–376

Predictions
  beta stock estimation, 399
  multiple regression analysis, future cost
      predictions, 925
  regression analysis, 907–908
    exponential trend lines, 914–915
  sports teams ratings model, 384–386
Predictor variables, regression
      analysis, 906
Premium Solver
  basic properties, 412–413
    GRG nonlinear algorithm, Evolutionary
        Solver and, 418–419
  Multistart Search feature, 418
Present value, time value of money, 57–62
Price-demand relationships
  nonlinear pricing models, 423–428
  sensitivity analysis, Golf Club example,
      47–56
  spreadsheet modeling, 47–56
Pricing models
  Asian call option, 692–693
  below cost pricing, 362
  decision analysis and uncertainty and, 575
  European call options modeling, 686–689
  exchange rate example, 357–359
  nonlinear optimization modeling
    alternative models, 422–428
    basic optimization, 347, 351–366
    manufacturing/retailing case study,
        352–356
    menthos candy example, 422–423
  peak-load utility pricing, 363–366
  retailing example, 359–362
  stock prices and options, 685–686
Prioritization, advertising models, goal
      programming, 467–471
Probabilistic inventory models, 759–771
  defined, 739
  deterministic models vs., 740
  newsvendor model, 760–763
  (R,Q) ordering policy, 764–771
Probability distribution
  breakeven analysis, 39
  decision making uncertainty and, 508–509
    Bayes' rule, 534–538
    pricing trends example, 575
    risk profile, 512–513
  decision tree nodes, 511–512
    monetary values, 527k
    PrecisionTree® construction, 525–527
  games of chance modeling, 708–713
  probabilistic inventory model, (R,Q)
      ordering policy, 765–771
  queueing models
    memoryless property, 800–801
    short-run behavior approximation,
        830–834
  retirement investment modeling, 681–685
  simulation modeling, 583–601
    @RISK software applications for,
        592–593
    binomial distribution, 597–599

bounded vs. unbounded, 587–588
  common probability distribution, 588
  cumul/general distribution, 599–601
  discrete vs. continuous, 585–586
  input distribution effects, 632–639
  normal distribution, 595–596
  positive (nonnegative) vs.
      unrestricted, 588
  random number freezing, 592
  symmetric vs. skewed, 586–587
  triangular distribution, 596–597
  uniform distribution, 588–591
  Walton bookstore case study, 604–608
  yield uncertainties, drug development
      case study, 661–666
supply chain inventory models,
    U-shaped distribution, 783–784
uncertain activity times modeling,
    891–895
Problem definition, seven-step modeling
    process, 8, 10
Problem-solving algorithms, examples
    of, 1–2
Procedure flowchart, seven-step modeling
    process, 9–10
Processing models, simulation modeling,
    667–671
  queueing models, 844–850
Product development
  decision making uncertainty and, 505
  multistage decision tree case study,
      543–552
  project management and, 861–862
  TOPRANK Addin modeling, 715–722
Production data
  aggregate planning model, 150–160
    hiring and firing plan, 151
  combinatorial models, 432–437
  costs data
    multiple regression analysis,
        multiple-plant example, 926–930
    supply chain inventory models,
        780–784
  fixed-cost models, 306
  holding costs
    multiperiod production model, 113–117
    transportation model, tax rate
        variations, 232–235
  inventory modeling, ordering vs., 741
  inventory planning model
    decision support systems, 118–120
    optimization, 108–117
  multiobjective decision making, seasonal
      production example, 499–501
  multiperiod production, 112–117
  process models, linear programming,
      167–173
  quantities, fixed-cost models, 299, 306
  queueing models, car body case study, 850
  regression analysis, single-product cost
      estimation example, 916–919
  shipping operations, minimum cost
      network flow models, 242–245

simulation modeling, 649
supply chain inventory models,
    779–784
Product mix model
  advertising model vs., 134–142
  fixed-cost models, 304–305
  Monet Company example, 98–100
  optimization, 98–107
Profits
  breakeven analysis, one-way data table,
      37–41
  customer loyalty modeling, 695–703
    actual/discounted profits, 697–703
  nonlinear pricing models
    single-price model, 425
    two-part tariff model, 426
  Pareto optimality and trade-off curves,
      477–480
  price-demand relationships, 52–56
  pricing models, 355–356
    retailing example, 361–362
  product mix model, 102–107
  quantity discounts case study, 43–46
  simulation modeling
    @RISK software, 630–631
    average profit vs. order quantity, 610
    car development planning model,
        674–676
    government contract bidding, 656–657
    Walton bookstore case study,
        607–608
  spreadsheet modeling, NCAA T-shirt
      example, 27
  supply chain inventory models, 782–784
  transportation model, after-tax profits,
      233–235
Program Evaluation and Review
    Technique (PERT)
  project management principles, 863–864
  uncertain activity times modeling,
      891–895
Project completion times, Critical Path
    Method (CMP) model of project
    management, 866
  local area network (LAN) example,
      869–872
Project management
  basic principles, 863–864
  critical path method model, 865–872
    office LAN example, 868–872
  Microsoft Project software, 896–898
  multiple project scheduling, 885–889
  new-product development case study,
      861–862
  resource allocation modeling, 874–885
    crashing the activities, 880–884
    resource monitoring, 874–880
  uncertain activity times, 890–895
Proportionality
  advertising exposure trade-offs, 480–483
  fixed-cost models, 298
  linear models, 94–96
  nonlinear optimization modeling, 346

Pseudo-random numbers, simulation
modeling, uniform probability
distribution, 591
Purchase costs
advertising models
goal programming scheduling
model, 466
nonlinear response functions,
advertising models, 374–376
economic order quantity models, 743
quantity discounts model, 747–748
equipment replacement models, 257
nonlinear pricing models, 425
Put options, European call options
modeling, 686–689

## Q

Quality achieved parameters, blending
models, 163–164
Quantitative analysis
business problem solving and, 2
strengths and limitations of, 17–18
Quantity discounts
economic order quantity model,
746–748
economic order quantity models, order
synchronization, 757
spreadsheet modeling, 42–46
Quarter parameters, equipment
replacement models, 257
Queueing models
analytical steady-state models, 807–826
bank queueing model, 812–815,
818–819, 823–826
basic single-server models, 807–811
emergency phone service
example, 822
Erlang loss model, 819–820
fast server/slow servers comparison,
816–817
fire engine request example, 820–822
multiple-server model, 811–815,
822–826
nonexponential bank queueing model,
823–826
postal branch queueing example,
808–811
traffic intensity effects, 817
arrivals characteristics, 796–797
ATM customer example, 859–860
basic principles, 795–796
catalog phone ordering example,
857–858
customer averages, 805
descriptive model, 4–6
exponential distribution models,
799–804
bank interarrival and service example,
801–803
memoryless property, 800–803
miscellaneous models, 818–819
Poisson process model, 803–804
Little's formula, 805–806

optimization model, 6–7
server utilization, 806
service characteristics, 797–798
service discipline, 797
short-run behavior approximation,
830–834
lunchtime rush example, 831–834
short-run vs. steady-state behavior,
798–799
simulation models, 835–850
bank queueing example, 838–842
card body production example, 850
processing systems, 844–850
series system, blocking technique,
844–850
technical support example, 842–844
time averages, 805
workforce scheduling models, 143–149
work-in-process inventory case study,
793–794
Queueing network, defined, 798

## R

Random (noise) component, time series
models, 935
Random number seed, simulated queueing
models, 837
bank queue example, 838–842
Random variables
analytic hierarchy process (AHP),
consistency checking, 489–490
Critical Path Method (CMP) model of
project management, random
durations, 866–872
customer loyalty modeling, churn
reduction case study, 701
decision making uncertainty and,
508–509
Evolutionary Solver genetic
algorithms, 418
probabilistic inventory model, random
lead times, 771
queueing models, exponential
distribution, 799–800
simulation modeling, probability
distribution, 584
@RISK software, 616, 627–631
freezing of, 592
normal distribution, 595–596
uniform probability distribution, 591
Walton bookstore case study,
606–608
Range names
advertising models, 135–142
aggregate planning model, 151
applications for, 68
blending models, 163
breakeven analysis, 35–41
Excel software, 27
financial models, 175
pension fund modeling, 180–183
production process models, 169–173
product mix model, 101–107

quantity discounts and demand
uncertainty, 43–46
time value of money, 59–62
two-variable optimization modeling, 80
workforce scheduling models, 144–149
Ratios
analytic hierarchy process (AHP),
consistency index calculation, 492
data envelopment analysis, 189–191
Raw materials, fixed-cost models, 306
Recalculation mode, simulation modeling
probability distribution, 612
Receivables calculations, transportation
models, 226
Receiver locations, location assignment
models, 314
Reduced costs, sensitivity analysis,
optimization modeling, 87–93
Reference categories, dummy variables,
multiple regression analysis,
926–930
Refund costs, simulation modeling
probability distribution, Walton
bookstore case study, 607–608
Regional economic development, *soft Or*
modeling approach and, 2
Regional shipment data, transportation
models, 223–224, 226, 232–235
Regression coefficients, multiple regression
analysis, 921
Regression models
basic principles, 905–909
explanatory variables, 916–919
goodness-of-fit measures, 908, 913–915
least-squares line, 907
limitations, 930
multiple R and R-square, 908–909
multiple regression, 921–930
assumption limitations, 929
categorical variables, 925–926
cost analysis case study, 921–922
Excel Analysis ToolPak Add-in,
922–925
future cost predictions, 925
multicollinearity, 929–930
nonconstant error variance, 930
nonlinear relationships, 930
production cost estimation example,
926–929
residual autocorrelation, 930
R-square adjustment, 925
optimal solution, 911–913
prediction and fitted values, 907–908
simple models, 909–919
trend models, 910–919
exponential trendline, 913–915
goodness-of-fit measurement,
913–915
linear trendline, 917–919
Relative addresses, spreadsheet
modeling, 31
Relative utility values, risk
management, 555

Reneging behavior, queueing models, 797
Reorder points, probabilistic inventory
  model, *(R,Q)* ordering
  policy, 765–771
Replication functions, simulation modeling
  probability distribution, 609–612
Representations
  assignment models, 235–236
  network models, 224–225
Residuals
  least squares line, regression
    analysis, 907
  multiple regression analysis,
    autocorrelation, 930
Resource allocation modeling, project
    management, 874–885
  crashing the activities, 880–884
  resource monitoring, 874–880
Resource availability
  flight scheduling network
    model, 270–271
  product mix model, 102–107
  project management, 864
Response rates
  breakeven analysis, 36–41
  Goal Seek function and, 38–39
  nonlinear response functions, 373–376
  response and selection advertising
    models, 368–376
  S-shaped curve fitting, 437–441
Retailing, pricing models
  example, 359–362
Retention rate, customer loyalty
    modeling, 695–703
  churn reduction case study, 701
Retirement investments, simulation
    modeling, 681–685
Returns calculations
  beta stock estimation, 398–401
  portfolio optimization, Evolutionary
    software, 443
Revenues
  customer loyalty modeling, churn reduc-
    tion case study, 701–703
  inventory modeling, 742
  location assignment/fixed cost
    models, 323
  nonlinear pricing models, two-part tariff
    model, 426
  product mix model, 102–107
  project management, multiple-project
    scheduling, 887
  quantity discounts and demand
    uncertainty, 43–46
  simulation modeling probability
    distribution, Walton bookstore
    case study, 606–608
  S-shaped curve fitting model, sales
    response estimates, 438–441
  supply chain inventory models, 781–784
Revolving credit lines, simulation model-
    ing case study, 651–653

Risk averseness
  properties of, 554
  venture capital case study, 557–560
Risk management
  attitudes toward, 554–560
  certainty equivalents, 559–560
  decision making uncertainty and, 506
    government contract bidding
      example, 515–518
    policy suggestion and risk
      profile, 528–529
    risk profiles, 512–513
  liquidity risk management case
    study, 651–653
  simulation modeling, 582–583
  utility function and, 554–555
  venture capitalism case
    study, 557–560
RISKOptimizer
  basic features, 20
  newsvendor inventory model and, 760
  retirement investment
    modeling, 681–685
Risk-return charts, portfolio
    optimization, 393–394
Risk tolerance, exponential
    utility and, 555–560
Rolling planning horizon technique
  aggregate planning model, 155
  multiperiod production model, 115–117
Root mean squared error (RMSE)
  response and selection advertising
    models, 371
  time series models, forecasting error
    measurement, 936–937
Roundoff error, product mix model, 105
Route assignment models
  school bus route example, 237–240
  traveling salesperson problem, 455–457
*(R,Q)* ordering policy, probabilistic inven-
    tory model, 764–771
*R*-square value
  multiple regression analysis, 924–925
  regression analysis, 909
Runtime variations, queueing models, sim-
    ulation modeling, 836–837

## S

Safety stock, probabilistic inventory
    model, *(R,Q)* ordering policy,
    765–771, 767–771
Sagarin ratings, NCAA Basketball Tourna-
    ment modeling, 711–713
Sales data
  exponential smoothing models,
    944, 947–956
    Winter's seasonality method, 953–956
  moving averages models, 938–941
  regression-based models
    exponential trend line
      limitations, 915
    trend models, 910–919

simulation modeling, cash balance
    model, 678–681
S-shaped curve fitting model, 437–441
supply chain inventory models, 781–784
Salvage values, equipment replacement
    models, 257
Sample size determination, simulation
    modeling probability distribu-
    tion, confidence intervals, 609
Scaling, linear models, 95–96
Scatterplots
  least squares line, regression
    analysis, 907
  multiple regression analysis, cost
    analysis example, 922
  price-demand relationships, 47–56
  regression-based trend models
    exponential trend lines, 913–915
    sales data, 911–913
    single-product cost estimation
      example, 916–919
Scheduling optimization
  advertising goal programming model,
    465–471
  crew scheduling network model,
    260–265
  flight scheduling network model,
    265–271
  on-demand aircraft scheduling
    model, 272
  project management
    Critical Path Method (CMP) model of
      project management, 866–872
    multiple-project scheduling, 885–889
    resource allocation modeling, crashing
      the activities, 880–884
  sequence-dependent scheduling, 457
  workforce scheduling models, 142–149
Schindler Elevator, periodic maintenance
    case study, 258
School bus transport, data envelopment
    analysis case study, 190
Scope values, project management, 864
Seasonal component
  exponential smoothing models, Winter's
    seasonality method, 952–956
  time series models, 933–937
Selling price
  production process models, 171–173
  transportation model, tax rate variations,
    232–235
Sensitivity analysis
  advertising models, 136–142
    goal programming example, 470–471
    nonlinear response functions, advertis-
      ing models, 376
  aggregate planning model, 154–160
  airline industry network models
    crew scheduling model, 264
    flight scheduling model, 270–271
  assignment models, 240–241
  blending models, 165–167

capital budget model, 293–294
combinatorial models, loading products
    example, 432
customer loyalty modeling, retention
    rates, 698–703
decision making uncertainty, 510–511
    government contract bidding
        example, 518
    sensitivity charts, 532–534
facility location models, 380–381
financial models, 177–183
fixed-cost models, 303–304
linear programming applications, 85–93
    SolverTable add-in, 89–93
location assignment/fixed cost
    models, 324–325
location assignment models, 319
minimum cost network flow
    models, 246–250
model development and, 14
multiperiod production model, 115–117
multistage decision tree
    drug testing example, 542
    marketing example, 548–552
net present value, 61–62
nonlinear optimization modeling, pricing
    models, 356
optimization modeling, 74, 85–93
peak-load pricing model, 366
pension fund modeling, 182–183
portfolio optimization, 393–394
PrecisionTree® software, 529–530
pricing models, 356–359
    retailing example, 361–362
production process models, 171–173
product mix model, 105–107
project management, crashing the
    activities function, 884–885
queueing models, multiple-server
    queueing model, 815
risk management, 559–560
sensitivity charts, TOPRANK Addin
    tool, 719–722
set-covering models, hub
    locations, 313–314
simulation modeling, @RISK
    software, 630–631
transportation models, 227–235
workforce scheduling model, 147–149
Sequence-dependent scheduling
    model, 457
Sequential decision analysis, multistage
    decision tree, 544–552
Series service system, queueing models
    blocking simulation, 844
    defined, 798
    processing example with
        blocking, 844–850
Server utilization, queueing models, 806
    multiple-server example, 813–815
Service centers, location assignment
    models, 314–317

Service characteristics
    inventory modeling, shortage/penalty
        costs, 742
    probabilistic inventory model, $(R,Q)$
        ordering policy, 769–771
    queueing models, 797–798
        arrivals characteristics, 796–797
        Erlang loss model, 820–822
        nonexponential multiple-server
            model, 822–826
        service discipline, 797
        service time distribution, bank exam-
            ple, 801–803
        simulation modeling, 836
Service-in-random-order (SRO) discipline,
    queueing models, 797
Service rates, queueing models
    basic principles, 3–6
    multiple-server queueing
        model, 811–815
    single-service model, 810–811
Set-covering models, 309–319
Setup cost
    economic order quantity models
        order synchronization, 757
        reduction of, 752–754
    inventory modeling
        basic properties, 741
        ordering vs. production, 741
Seven-step modeling process, 8–14
Shadow prices
    product mix model, 107
    sensitivity analysis, optimization
        modeling, 89–93
    transportation models, 228–235
Shape effects, simulation modeling, input
    distribution, 632–633
Shipping costs
    minimum cost network flow
        models, 243–250
    transportation models, 226, 228–231
Shipping plan
    transportation models, 225–226
    warehouse facility location
        models, 380–381
Shortage costs
    aggregate planning model, backlogging
        linearization, 157–160
    combinatorial models
        loading products example, 429–432
        production scheduling example, 435
    economic order quantity models,
        749–751
    inventory modeling, 742
    probabilistic inventory model, $(R,Q)$
        ordering policy, 766–771
Shortest path models, 250–260
    equipment replacement, 254–258
    geographical shortest path models,
        251–254
    traveling salesperson problem,
        454–457

Shortest-processing-time (SPT) discipline,
    queueing models, 797
Short-run behavior, queueing
    models, 798–799
    analytical approximation, 830–834
    lunchtime rush example, 831–834
Shrinkage variables, minimum cost net-
    work flow models, 248–249
Simple exponential smoothing, forecasting
    with, 942–956
Simple regression, defined, 906
Simplex algorithm
    genetic algorithms vs., 416
    optimization modeling, 74
    Premium Solver, 413
    two-variable optimization modeling, 78
Simulation modeling
    airline boarding strategies case
        study, 579–580
    @RISK software tools, 615–631
        basic features, 615
        flaw of averages, 623–624
        limitations, 627
        loading protocols, 616
        results evaluation, 621–623, 630
        RISKSIMTABLE feature, 624–627
        sensitivity analysis, 630–631
        Server input variables, 627
        single random input variables, 616
        TopRank Addin, 714–722
        Walton Bookstore case study,
            617–621, 628–631
    customer loyalty, churn reduction
        model, 700–703
    defined, 9
    Excel software tools, 603–613
        best order quantity, 609–610
        confidence intervals, 608–609
        data table applications, 610–612
        demand estimation, 604–613
        freezing options, 610
        histogram creation, 646–648
        results, 607–608
        two-way data table, 612–613
    financial modeling
        asset management example, 734–735
        bond investment example, 733
        cash balance models, 676–681
        college fund investments example, 732
        financial planning models, 672–676
        investment models, 681–685
        Merrill Lynch case study, 651–653
        stock prices and options, 685–693
    forecasting models, Taco Bell forecast-
        ing model case study, 904
    games of chance
        basketball pools, 711–713
        craps, 708–710
    inventory management example, 650
    marketing models
        customer loyalty models, 695–703
        market share models, 703–706

Simulation modeling (*Continued*)
 operations models, 653–671
  drug development and production
    example, 661–666
  government contract bidding
    example, 653–657
  processing example, 666–671
  warranty costs example, 657–661
 ordering simulation models
  inventory management, 773–778
   production models *vs.*, 741
  probability distribution
   @RISK software, 629–631
   best order quantity
    calculations, 609–610
   Walton bookstore case
    study, 606–608
 overview, 581–582
 probability distribution inputs, 583–601
  @RISK software applications for,
    592–593
  binomial distribution, 597–599
  bounded *vs.* unbounded, 587–588
  common probability distribution, 588
  cumul/general distribution, 599–601
  discrete *vs.* continuous, 585–586
  effects on results, 632–639
  normal distribution, 595–596
  positive (nonnegative) *vs.*
    unrestricted, 588
  random number freezing, 592
  symmetric *vs.* skewed, 586–587
  triangular distribution, 596–597
  uniform distribution, 588–591
 production planning and scheduling
    example, 649
 queueing models, 795, 835–850
  bank queueing example, 838–842
  card body production example, 850
  processing systems, 844–850
  series system, blocking
    technique, 844–850
  technical support example, 842–844
 real applications, 582–583
 uncertain activity times
    modeling, 892–895
Single-price models, nonlinear pricing
    models, 423–428
Single-product models, inventory modeling,
    multiple-product model *vs.*, 741
Single-server (*M/M/1*) queueing
    model, 807–811
 multiple-server model *vs.*, 816–817
 postal branch queueing example, 808–811
 simulated queueing
  bank queue example, 838–842
  basic principles, 835–837
*Six for Success* strategy, 2–3
Skewed distribution
 simulation modeling, 586–587
 warranty costs, simulation
    modeling, 657–658

Skilled labor constraint, product mix
    model, 100–107
Slack difference
 Critical Path Method (CMP) model of
    project management, 867–872
 project management, Microsoft Project
    applications, 897–898
 two-variable optimization modeling, 85
Slope, regression models, 909–910
Smoothing constant, exponential smooth-
    ing models, 942
Smoothing functions
 aggregate planning model, 156–160
 combinatorial models, production sched-
    uling example, 435–437
 exponential smoothing models, 942–956
  Holt's trend method, 947–952
  sales forecasting examples, 944–947
  simple smoothing, 942–943
  Winters' seasonality method, 952–956
 moving averages models, 937–941
 Premium Solver and, 418
 S-shaped curve fitting, 437–441
Soft constraints, advertising models, goal
    programming scheduling
    model, 467–471
*soft Or* modeling approach,
    algorithms and, 2–3
Software for modeling,
    properties of, 18–20
Solver function (Excel software), 19. *See
    also* Premium Solver (Excel);
    Solver function (Excel software)
 advertising models, 136–142
  goal programming scheduling
    model, 467–471
 aggregate planning model, 153–160
 airline industry network models, 264–273
 assignment models, 239–241
 backlogging and, 159–160
 basic properties, 19
 beta stock estimation, 400–401
 blending models, 163–167
 capital budget models, 292–293
 cutting stock models, 329–331
 data envelopment analysis, 187–191
 economic order quantity models
  camera ordering case
    study, 745–746
  order synchronization, 757
  quantity discounts model, 747–748
  setup cost reductions, 754
  shortage costs, 751
 equipment replacement
    models, 257–258
 facility location models, 380–381
 financial models, 176–183
 fixed-cost models, 300–304, 306–307
 int option in, 140
 location assignment/fixed cost
    models, 324–325
 location assignment models, 318

minimum cost network flow
    models, 245–250
multiperiod production model, 113–117
nonlinear models
 optimization modeling, 350
 response functions, advertising
    models, 374–376
 settings, 355–356
nonlinear optimization modeling, 350
nonlinear response functions, advertising
    models, 374–376
nonlinear settings, 355–356
nonsmooth functions, 157
peak-load pricing model, 365–366
pension fund modeling, 181–183
portfolio optimization, 392–394
pricing models, 355–356
probabilistic inventory model, *(R,Q)*
    ordering policy, 769–771
production process models, 170–173
product mix model, 103–107
resource allocation modeling, crashing
    the activities function, 881–884
response and selection advertising
    models, 371–376
sensitivity analysis, 86–93
sensitivity report *vs.* SolverTable, 92–93
set-covering models, hub
    locations, 312–313
sports teams ratings model, 384–386
S-shaped curve fitting model, 439–441
strengths and limitations of, 413–414
Tolerance setting, 147
transportation models, 226–235
two-variable optimization modeling,
    82–85
workforce scheduling models,
    145–149
Space and missile optimization analysis
    (SAMOA) case study, optimiza-
    tion modeling, 285–286
Span, moving averages models, 937–941
Spider chart
 decision analysis, 532
 product development model, TOPRANK
    Addin tool, 719–722
Sports teams ratings, modeling for, 382–386
Spreadsheet modeling
 advertising models, 135–142
  nonlinear response functions,
    advertising models, 374–376
 aggregate planning model, 151–160
 airline industry network models,
    263–273
 algebraic models *vs.*, 118
 analytic hierarchy process (AHP),
    490–492
 assignment models, 236–241
 basic concepts and practices, 24–29
 breakeven analysis, 33–41
 capital budget models, 291–297
 cluster analysis, 446–449

combinatorial models
  loading products example, 429–432
  production scheduling example, 434–437
as communication tool, 12
cost projections, 29–33
Critical Path Method (CMP) model of project management, local area network (LAN) example, 870–872
cutting stock models, 328–331
cytomegalovirus example, 24
data envelopment analysis, 186–191
decision making uncertainty, 510–511
  Bayes' rule, 537–538
descriptive queueing problem, 4–6
development of, 12
discriminant analysis, 451
economic order quantity models
  camera ordering case study, 745–746
  order synchronization, 756–757
  quantity discounts model, 747–748
  setup cost reductions, 753–754
  shortage costs, 750–751
editing/documentation guidelines, 67–69
equipment replacement models, 256–258
exponential smoothing models, 944–956
financial models, 175–183
fixed-cost models, 298–299, 305–306
flight scheduling network model, 267–273
formatting and layout conventions, 34, 67
geographical shortest path models, 252–254
HIV/AIDS virus example, 23–24
layout and documentation, 28
location assignment/fixed cost models, 322–325
location assignment models, 315–316
minimum cost network flow models, 244–250
moving averages, 939–941
multiperiod production, 111–117
NCAA T-shirt example, 25–29
nonlinear optimization modeling, pricing models, 354–356
peak-load pricing model, 363–366
pension funds, 180–183
portfolio optimization, 443–444
price-demand relationship, 47–56
pricing models, retailing example, 360–362
probabilistic inventory model, (R,Q) ordering policy, 767–771
production process models, 169–173
product mix model, 100–107
quantity discounts example, 42–46
queueing models, 3–6
  Erlang loss model, 820–822
  multiple-server example, 812–815
  nonexponential interarrival/service times, 824–826
  simulated queueing, 838–842
  single-service model, 809–811

resource allocation modeling, crashing the activities function, 882–884
response and selection advertising models, 371–376
set-covering models, 310–311
simulation, probability distribution, 584
sports teams ratings model, 384–386
S-shaped curve fitting model, 439–441
supply chain inventory models, 779–784
time value of money, 57–62
transportation models, 225–235
  automobile production and shipment, 233–235
traveling salesperson problem, 455–457
two-variable optimization modeling, 78–85
uncertainty and, 42–46
workforce scheduling models, 144–149
Squared coefficient of variation, queueing models, nonexponential interarrival/service times, 823–826
Squared distances to centers, cluster analysis, 447–448
Square root function
  advertising exposure trade-offs, 480–483
  economic order quantity model, 746
S-shaped curve fitting
  optimization modeling, 437–441
  time series models, trend component, 933–934
Stability, queueing models, 799
  limited waiting room/limited source extensions, 819
  multiple-server queueing model, 811–815
Staffing models
  continuing-qualification-training optimization, 272
  crew recovery model, 272–273
  crew scheduling network model, 260–265
  network modeling, 272
  pilot staffing and training, 272
  set covering models, 313
Standard deviation
  cluster analysis, 446–449
  NCAA Basketball Tournament modeling, 711–713
  portfolio optimization, 392
  queueing models, exponential distribution, 800
  simulation modeling, normal distribution, 595–596
  stock prices and options, 685–686
Standard error of estimate
  multiple regression analysis, 925
  regression analysis, goodness of fit measurement, 908
  simulation modeling probability distribution, confidence interval, 608–609

Start and finish times
  Critical Path Method (CMP) model of project management, 867–872
    local area network (LAN) creation, 869–872
    resource allocation monitoring, 877–880
Start-to-finish relationships, Critical Path Method (CMP) model of project management, 873
Start-to-start relationships, Critical Path Method (CMP) model of project management, 873
StatTools™ software, basic features, 20
Steady-state analysis, queueing models, 798–799, 807–826
  bank queueing model, 812–815, 818–819, 823–826
  emergency phone service example, 822
  Erlang loss model, 819–820
  fast server/slow servers comparison, 816–817
  fire engine request example, 820–822
  limitations, 799
  multiple-server model, 811–815, 822–826
  nonexponential bank queueing model, 823–826
  postal branch queueing example, 808–811
  single-server models, 807–811
  traffic intensity effects, 817
Stock-keeping units (SKUs), 131–132
Stock modeling. *See also* Financial models; Portfolio optimization
  beta stock estimation, 396–401
  Evolutionary Solver software, 442–444
  prices and options simulation modeling, 685–686
  return on portfolio case study, 689–691
  stock hedging example, 407–408
Stockouts, economic order quantity models, 743
Stopping conditions, genetic algorithms, 415–416
Storage data, combinatorial models, loading products example, 430
Strategic planning
  decision making uncertainty and, 506
  optimization with integer variables, 341–342
Strategy region charts
  decision analysis, 530–531
  multistage decision tree, marketing example, 549–552
Student team assignments, Evolutionary Solver software example, 462
Subjective probability, decision making uncertainty and, 508–509
Subscriber/nonsubscriber data
  customer loyalty modeling, churn reduction case study, 701
  discriminant analysis example, 450–453

Summary measures, ordering simulation models, 777
Sum of absolute errors (SAE), beta stock estimation, 397–399
Sum of probabilities, PrecisionTree® software, 527
Sum of squared distances, cluster analysis, 448
Sum of squared errors, beta stock estimation, 397–399
Sum of squared residuals, least squares line, regression analysis, 907
Supplier points, minimum cost network flow models, 242–250
Supply chain inventory models, 778–784
    Dell supply chain case study, 737–738
    production planning example, 779–784
Supply variables, simulation modeling, 629
Surplus value, nonlinear pricing models, 423–428
Symmetric probability distribution, simulation modeling, 586–587
Systematic sensitivity analysis, two-variable optimization model, 93

T

Taco Bell forecasting model case study, 903–904
Tallies, discriminant analysis, 452
Target cell
    cluster analysis, 446–447
    Evolutionary Solver specification, 419
    optimization modeling, 73–74
    two-variable optimization modeling, 78–85
Task relations, project management, Microsoft Project applications, 897–898
Tax rates
    car development planning model, 674–676
    transportation models, 232–235
Technical support case study, simulated queueing model, 842–844
Technological coefficients, product mix model, 99–107
Technology innovation, decision making uncertainty and, 576–577
Television advertising, linear programming models for, 133–142
Text boxes, applications for, 68
Throughput time, simulated queueing models, processing example, 844–850
Time averages
    queueing models, 805
        Little's formula, 805–806
    uncertain activity times modeling, 890–895
Time-series charts, resource allocation monitoring, 878–880

Time series models, 932–937
    components, 933
    cyclic component, 934–935
    exponential smoothing models, 945–956
        Holt's trend method, 951–952
    extrapolation limitations, 937
    forecast error measurements, 935–937
    forecasting using, 905
    random (noise) component, 935
    regression analysis, 906
    regression-based trend models, sales data, 911–919
    sales data example, 938–941
    seasonal component, 934
    trend component, 933–934
Time values
    customer loyalty modeling, churn/churn rates, 696–697
    economic order quantity models, order synchronization, 756–757
    multiperiod production model, 110
    product development, TOPRANK Addin modeling, 716–722
    project management, 864
        Critical Path Method (CMP) model, 865–872
    queueing models
        series simulation with blocking, 846–850
        simulation modeling, 835–836
    simulation modeling
        warranty costs, 659–661
        yield uncertainties, drug development case study, 662–666
    spreadsheet modeling, time value of money, 57–62
Tolerance settings (Excel)
    capital budget models, 294–297
    cutting stock models, 330–331
    optimization programming, 289–290
    workforce scheduling models, 147
TOPRANK Addin tool
    RISKVARY function, 717–718
    simulation modeling with, 714–722
TopRank® software, basic features, 19–20
Tornado charts
    decision analysis, 530–531
    product development model, TOPRANK Addin tool, 719–722
    simulation modeling sensitivity analysis, 630–631
        car development example, 675–676
Total after-tax profits, transportation model, 233–235
Total costs
    advertising models, goal programming scheduling model, 466
    assignment models, school bus routes, 239–240

equipment replacement models, arc costs, 257
nonlinear pricing models
    single-price model, 425
    two-part tariff model, 426
nonlinear response functions, advertising models, 374–376
quantity discounts and demand uncertainty, ordering costs, 43–46
transportation models, shipping costs, 226
Total distance, geographical shortest path models, 253–254
Total slack, project management, 897–898
Total value table, nonlinear pricing models, 424
Trade-off curve
    advertising models, 139–142, 480–483
    multiobjective decision making
        advertising exposure trade-offs example, 480–483
        profit maximization/pollution minimization example, 475–480
        profit maximization/pollution minimization example, 477–480
Traffic intensity, queueing models
    analytical steady-state effects, 817–818
    multiple-server queueing model, 813–815
    single-server queueing model, 808–811
Training sample, discriminant analysis, 450–453
Transient probability distribution, queueing models, short-run behavior approximation, 830–834
Transportation models, 223–235
    alternative models, 229–235
    automobile production and shipment, 232–235
    constraints and limitations, 231–235
    hub location models, 309–310
    input data, 223–224
    regional car shipment example, 223–224
    simplex modeling, 231
Transportation problem, defined, 223
Transshipment points, minimum cost network flow models, 242–250
Traveling salesperson problem, combinatorial modeling, 454–457
Trend component
    exponential smoothing models, Holt's trend method, 946–952
    time series models, 933–937
Trend models, regression-based models, 910–919
    exponential trendline, 913–915
    goodness-of-fit measurement, 913–915
    linear trendline, 917–919
Trial value, quantity discounts and demand uncertainty, 43–46
Triangular distribution, simulation modeling, 596–597
    input effects, 633–639

Two-part tariff pricing, nonlinear
    model, 422, 426–428
Two-period capital budget model, 295–297
Two-variable model
    dessert planning example, 75–85
    minimum cost network flow
        models, 247–250
    optimization, 74–85
Two-way data table
    quantity discounts and demand
        uncertainty, 44–46
    simulation modeling probability
        distribution, 612–613
    two-variable optimization model,
        89–93
Two-way sensitivity chart, decision making
    uncertainty, 532–534

## U

Unboundedness
    optimization modeling, 96–97
    probability distribution, simulation
        modeling, 587–588
Uncertainty
    breakeven analysis, 39–41
    decision making under
        basic principles, 505–506
        Bayes' rule, 534–538
        decision analysis
            components, 506–521
        demand data and, 574
        drug development case
            study, 503–504
        examples of, 505–506
        flaw of averages, 519–521
        government contract bidding
            example, 513–518
        multistage decision
            problems, 538–552
        Precision Tree add-in, 521–534
        risk reduction, 554–560
        technology innovation
            example, 576–577
        two-way data table, 45–46
    demand uncertainty, 42–46
    inventory modeling, newsvendor
        inventory model, 763
    probabilistic inventory model, (R,Q)
        ordering policy, 764–771
    project management, uncertain activity
        times modeling, 890–895
    queueing models, exponential
        distribution, 799–800
    simulation modeling
        Walton bookstore case study, 628–631
        yield uncertainties, drug development
            case study, 661–662
Unconstrained optimization, response
    and selection advertising
    models, 371–376
Uniform probability distribution, simula-
    tion modeling, 588–590

Unit after-tax profits, transportation
    model, 233–235
Unit costs
    cost projection model, 31–33
    data envelopment analysis, 186
    economic order quantity models, 743
    labor costs, cost projection model, 31
    peak-load pricing model, 363–366
    production costs
        aggregate planning model, 150
        inventory modeling, 742
        production process models,
            169–173
        transportation models, 232–235
    purchasing costs, inventory
        modeling, 742
    shipping costs
        minimum cost network flow
            models, 246
        transportation models, 224, 232–235
United Parcel Service (UPS), network
    modeling, 272
Units of measurement
    location assignment models, 317
    two-variable models and, 75
Unit waiting costs, queueing models,
    multiple-server queueing
    model, 815
Unrestricted probability distribution,
    simulation modeling, 588
Upper bound constraints
    assignment models, 240–241
    combinatorial models, production
        scheduling example, 436–437
    Evolutionary Solver software, 419
        changing cell constraints, 422
    fixed-cost models, 300, 306
    minimum cost network flow
        models, 242
    optimization programming, branch and
        bound algorithm, 288–289
    product mix model, 106–107
    trade-off curve, profit maximization/-
        pollution minimization
        example, 477–480
    transportation models, arc
        capacities, 224–225
UPS network optimization model, 272
Upward trends, time series
    models, 933–934
U.S. Air Force, space and missile optimiza-
    tion analysis (SAMOA) case
    study, 285–286
U-shaped probability distribution, supply
    chain inventory models, 783–784
Utilities companies
    decision making uncertainty in, 505
    peak-load pricing model, 363–366
Utility function/utility values, risk manage-
    ment and, 554–555
    exponential utility, 555–560
    venture capitalism case study, 557–560

## V

Value at risk (VAR) percentile, financial
    simulation modeling, 675–676
Value model, decision making uncertainty
    and, government contract bidding
    example, 514–518
Value of information, multistage decision
    tree, 543
Variability, queueing models
    nonexponential interarrival/service
        times, 826
    simulated queueing models, 843–844
Variable cost sensitivity
    inventory modeling, 742
    location assignment/fixed cost
        models, 323
    price-demand relationship, 55–56
Variance parameters, portfolio
    optimization, 392–394
Venture capitalism case study, risk
    management, 557–560
Verification
    discriminant analysis, 452
    seven-step modeling process, 9, 11
Volatility, stock prices and options,
    685–686
Volume discounts, optimization with
    integer variables, 343

## W

Wage rates, aggregate planning
    model, 155
Walton bookstore case study
    newsvendor inventory
        model and, 761–763
    simulation modeling, 604–608
        @RISK software applications, 617–621
        correlated demands, 636–639
        input distributions, 632–633
Warm-up time input, queueing models,
    simulation modeling, 836–837
Warranty costs, simulation
    modeling, 657–661
Weapons disarmament, decision making
    uncertainty and, 505–506
Weighted averages, expected monetary
    value (EMV), calculation and
    interpretation, 509–510
Weighted sum of squared errors, beta stock
    estimation, 397–400
Weights ranges
    analytic hierarchy
        process (AHP), 486–492
    portfolio optimization, 443
    retirement investments
        modeling, 681–685
Westvaco motor carrier selection
    optimization, network modeling
    example, 282–284
What-If questions
    breakeven analysis, 37–41
    one-way data tables, 37–38

What-If questions (*Continued*)
 spreadsheet modeling, 33
 TOPRANK Addin, 714–722
Winter's seasonality method, exponential
  smoothing models, 942, 952–956
Worker/production aggregate planning
  model, 150–160
Worker utilization, project management,
  multiple-project scheduling,
  887–888
Workforce scheduling models
 basic principles, 142–149

postal employee scheduling example,
  142–143
Workforce size, aggregate planning model,
  151–160
Work-in-process inventory (WIP),
  queueing models, 793–794
Wrap-around problem, workforce
  scheduling models, 144–149

**Y**

Yield uncertainties, simulation modeling,
  661–666

**Z**

0-1 variable
 capital budget models, 291
 fixed-cost models, 299–300
 location assignment models, 317
 optimization modeling, 286–287
 set-covering models, hub locations, 311